ELEMENTS OF *Literature*

SIXTH COURSE

Literature of Britain *with* World Classics

ANNOTATED TEACHER'S EDITION

This royal throne of kings,
this scepter'd isle . . .
This blessed plot, this earth,
this realm, this England.

— from *Richard II* by William Shakespeare

HOLT, RINEHART AND WINSTON
Harcourt Brace & Company
Austin • New York • Orlando • Atlanta • San Francisco • Boston • Dallas • Toronto • London

CREDITS

Project Director: Kathleen Daniel
Executive Editor: Mescal Evler
Managing Editor: Robert R. Hoyt
Project Editor: Suzanne Thompson
Editorial Coordinator: Susan Lynch
Grade Level Editors: Laura Cottam, Colleen Hobbs, Kerry Reynolds
Editorial Staff: Joel Bourgeois, Sigman Byrd, Tracy Combs Duncan, Kate Ewing, Kathryn Rogers Johnson, Mary Malone, Michael Neibergall, Kate Unger
Editorial Support Staff: Roni Franki, Ruth A. Hooker, Kelly Keeley, Margaret Sanchez, Pat Stover
Editorial Permissions: Ann Farrar, Janet Harrington

Design, Photo Research, and Production: *Text Designer:* Ruth Riley; *Production and Manufacturing:* Beth Prevelige, *Senior Production Manager;* Simira Davis, *Production Assistant;* Michael Roche, *Manufacturing Coordinator; Electronic Files:* Preface, Inc.; *Cover Designer:* Caroline Abbott, Compendium Design, Inc.; *Cover Senior Art Director:* Pun Nio; *Design and Production Coordination:* Preface, Inc.; *Marketing Design:* Rebecca Bretz

ISBN 0-03-094929-7

3 4 5 6 041 00 99 98 97

PROGRAM AUTHORS

Robert Anderson, John Malcolm Brinnin, and John Leggett established the literary framework of the Elements of Literature *program and developed instructional materials for the elements of drama, poetry, and fiction, respectively. Robert Probst established the pedagogical focus for the 1997 edition, and he developed and evaluated preselection and postselection material. Judith L. Irvin established the conceptual basis for the vocabulary and reading strands in the pupil's editions for grades 6–8 and in the teacher's editions for grades 6–12.*

Robert Probst is Professor of English Education at Georgia State University in Atlanta. For several years he was an English teacher—in both junior and senior high school—in Maryland and Supervisor of English for the Norfolk, Virginia, Public Schools. He is the author of *Response and Analysis: Teaching Literature in Junior and Senior High School*. He has also contributed chapters to such books as *Literature Instruction: A Focus on Student Response; Reader Response in the Classroom: Evoking and Interpreting Meaning in Literature; Handbook of Research on Teaching the English Language Arts; Transactions with Literature: A Fifty-Year Perspective;* and *For Louise M. Rosenblatt.* Dr. Probst has published articles in *English Journal, Journal of Reading, Educational Leadership, Revue des Langues Vivantes, The Clearing House,* and other publications. He is a member of the National Council of Teachers of English and has worked on the Council's Committee on Research, the Commission on Reading, and the Commission on Curriculum. Dr. Probst has also served on the Board of Directors of the Adolescent Literature Assembly. He is a colleague and faculty member of the Creative Education Foundation and a member of the National Conference on Language and Literacy.

Robert Anderson is a playwright, novelist, screenwriter, and teacher. His plays include *Tea and Sympathy; Silent Night, Lonely Night; You Know I Can't Hear You When the Water's Running;* and *I Never Sang for My Father.* His screenplays include *The Nun's Story* and *The Sand Pebbles.* Mr. Anderson has taught at the Writer's Workshop at the University of Iowa, the American Theater Wing Professional Training Program, and the Salzburg Seminar in American Studies. He is a past president of the Dramatists' Guild, vice president of the Authors' League of America, and a member of the Theater Hall of Fame. He lives in Connecticut and New York.

John Malcolm Brinnin, author of six volumes of poetry that have received many prizes and awards, is a member of the American Academy and Institute of Arts and Letters. He is also a critic of poetry and a biographer of poets and was for a number of years director of New York's famous Poetry Center. His teaching career, begun at Vassar College, included long terms at the University of Connecticut and Boston University, where he succeeded Robert Lowell as Professor of Creative Writing and Contemporary Letters. Mr. Brinnin has written *Dylan Thomas in America: An Intimate Journal* and *Sextet: T. S. Eliot & Truman Capote & Others.* His home is in Key West, Florida.

John Leggett is a novelist, a biographer, and a teacher. He went to the Writer's Workshop at the University of Iowa in the spring of 1969, expecting to work there for a single semester. In 1970, he assumed temporary charge of the program, and for the next seventeen years he was its director. Mr. Leggett's novels include *Wilder Stone, The Gloucester Branch, Who Took the Gold Away?, Gulliver House,* and *Making Believe.* He is also the author of the highly acclaimed biography *Ross and Tom: Two American Tragedies* and of the biography of William Saroyan called *A Daring Young Man.* A native New Yorker, Mr. Leggett now lives in California's Napa Valley.

Judith L. Irvin teaches courses in curriculum, middle school education, and educational leadership at Florida State University. Dr. Irvin is Chair of the Research Committee of the National Middle School Association and was the editor of *Research in Middle Level Education* for five years. She taught middle school for eight years before seeking her doctorate in Reading–Language Arts. Dr. Irvin writes a column, "What Research Says to the Middle Level Practitioner," for the *Middle School Journal.* Her many books include *Transforming Middle Level Education: Perspectives and Possibilities* and *Reading and the Middle School Student: Strategies to Enhance Literacy.*

SPECIAL CONTRIBUTORS

The special contributors wrote essays for the various collections of the text. Their essays are signed.

John Algeo is Professor of English at the University of Georgia at Athens. He is coauthor with Thomas Pyles of *The Origins and Development of the English Language.*

Harley Henry is Professor of English at Macalester College in St. Paul, Minnesota. He has also been a senior Fulbright lecturer in Zimbabwe and a Redfield Visiting Professor at the University of Chicago. In addition to the Romantic Period, his teaching specialties include the literature of Zimbabwe, Faulkner, American fiction, 1945–60, and fiction about baseball.

Donald Gray is Professor of English at Indiana University, Bloomington, Indiana. Dr. Gray has written essays on Victorian poetry and culture and has been editor of *College English.*

David Adams Leeming was for many years a Professor of English and Comparative Literature at the University of Connecticut. He is the author of several books on mythology, including *Mythology: The Voyage of the Hero; The World of Myth;* and *Encyclopedia of Creation Myths.* For several years he taught English at Robert College in Istanbul,

Turkey. He also served as secretary and assistant to the writer James Baldwin in New York and Istanbul. In 1994, his biography of Baldwin was published. Leeming now lives in Albuquerque, New Mexico.

C. F. Main was for many years Professor of English at Rutgers University in New Brunswick, New Jersey. He is the editor of *Poems: Wadsworth Handbook and Anthology* and has written reviews and articles on sixteenth-, seventeenth-, and eighteenth-century literature.

William V. Costanza is Professor of English and Film at Westchester Community College, State University of New York. Active within the National Council of Teachers of English, he has chaired the NCTE Commission on Media, the Committee on Film Study, and the Assembly on Media Arts.

Katharina M. Wilson is Professor of Comparative Literature at the University of Georgia and the author of several books on early women writers. She is also the editor of encyclopedias and of diverse anthologies of works by early women.

...red instructional materials for the text under the supervision of Dr. Probst and the editorial staff.

...r
...riter and Editor
.., Florida

..a Dodson
and Creator of Educational Software
..Gatos, California

..ynn Hovland
Former Teacher
Educational Writer and Editor
Berkeley, California

Carole S. Lambert
Educational Writer and Editor
Waterville, Maine

Mary E. McCurnin
Educational Writer and Editor
Tallahassee, Florida

Carroll Moulton
Former Teacher
Educational Writer and Editor
Southampton, New York

Elisabeth H. Piedmont-Marton
Former Teacher
Coordinator of Writing Program
Austin, Texas

Carolyn C. Walter
Teacher and Educational Writer
Oak Park, Illinois

REVIEWERS

The reviewers evaluated collections from the Annotated Teacher's Edition, Sixth Course. For a list of the reviewers for the pupil's edition see p. vii of the Pupil's Edition.

Nancy Bartholomew
Amador Valley High School
Pleasanton, CA

Philip V. Benevento, Jr.
Crosby High School
Waterbury, CT

Joan Carole Boyd
Clinton High School
Clinton, IA

Lillie C. Harris
George Washington High School
Danville, VA

Amy Luce
Fairview High School
Fairview, PA

David L. McDonald
North Allegheny High School
Wexford, PA

Sally P. Pfeifer
Lewis and Clark High School
Spokane, WA

4

ACKNOWLEDGMENTS

For permission to reprint copyrighted material, grateful acknowledgment is made to the following sources:

Blackwell Publishers: From "The Witches" from *Shakespeare's Tragic Frontier* by Willard Farnham. Copyright © 1950 by Blackwell Publishers. **BR Publishing Corporation, a division of D. K. Publishers Distributors (P) Ltd.:** From "Anita Desai" from *Studies in Contemporary Indian-English Short Story,* edited by A. N. Dwivedi. Copyright © 1991 by Amaer Nath Dwivedi. **Cambridge University Press:** From *The Elements of Drama* by J. L. Styan. Copyright © 1960 by Cambridge University Press. **Cambridge University Press:** From "Shakespeare's Imagery in Macbeth" from *Shakespeare's Imagery and What It Tells* by Caroline Spurgeon. Copyright © 1935 by Cambridge University Press. **Chatto and Windus, an imprint of Random House UK Ltd.:** From *Shakespeare and Society* by Terence Eagleton. Copyright © 1967 by Terence Eagleton. **Chelsea House Publishers, a division of Main Line Book Company:** From *Major Literary Characters: Macbeth,* edited and with an introduction by Harold Bloom. Copyright © 1991 by Chelsea House Publishers, a division of Main Line Book Co.; Introduction copyright © 1991 by Harold Bloom. **Jonathan Clowes Limited:** From "On Her Life and Writings" from *A Small Personal Voice* by Doris Lessing. Copyright © 1956, 1957, 1959, 1963, 1966, 1968, 1971, 1972, 1974 by Doris Lessing. **Doubleday, a division of Bantam Doubleday Dell Publishing Group, Inc.:** From Matthew 6:11 and Matthew 18:9 from *The Jerusalem Bible.* Copyright © 1966 by Darton, Longman & Todd, Ltd. and Doubleday, a division of Bantam Doubleday Dell Publishing Group, Inc. **Faber and Faber Limited:** From "Hawk Roosting" from *Lupercal* by Ted Hughes. Copyright © 1960 by Ted Hughes. **Farrar, Straus & Giroux, Inc.:** From *John Milton: A Reader's Guide to His Poetry* by Marjorie Hope Nicolson. Copyright © 1963 by Marjorie Hope Nicolson; copyright renewed © 1991 by Eberhardt E. Le Schin. From "The Virgins" from *Sea Grapes* by Derek Walcott. Copyright © 1976 by Derek Walcott. **Gale Research Inc.:** From "Karen Blixen" from *Contemporary Authors, New Revision Series,* Vol. 22, edited by Deborah A. Straub. Copyright © by Gale Research Inc. **Greenwood Publishing Group, Inc., Westport, CT:** From "The Thickets of Our Separateness" from *Long Drums and Cannons: Nigerian Dramatists and Novelists* by Margaret Laurence. Copyright © 1968 by Margaret Laurence. **Holt, Rinehart and Winston, Inc.:** From *Understanding Poetry: An Anthology for College* by Cleanth Brooks and Robert Penn Warren. Copyright 1938 by Holt, Rinehart and Winston, Inc.; copyright renewed © 1965 by Cleanth Brooks and Robert Penn Warren. **Alfred A. Knopf, Inc.:** From "Frank O'Connor and the *New Yorker*" by William Maxwell from *Michael/Frank: Studies on Frank O'Connor,* edited by Maurice Sheehy. Copyright © 1969 by Harold Macmillan, Honor Tracy, Sean Hendrick, D. A. Binchy, Richard Ellmann, Deborah Averill, Richard Gill, Dermot Foley, Roger McHugh, Eavan Boland, Shevawn Lynam, Wallace Stegner, Brendan Kennelly, Donal Brennan, Maurice Sheehy, Phillip Edwards, David Greene, William Maxwell, Thomas Flanagan. Quotes by Pablo Neruda from *Seven Voices: Seven Latin American Writers Talk to Rita Guibert,* translated by Frances Partridge. Copyright © 1972 by Alfred A. Knopf, Inc. **Arnulfo J. López:** From "A Poem Within a Poem" by Arnulfo J. López from *Heritage,* Vol. 31, Spring 1991. Published by James Madison High School, Vienna, VA. **Macmillan Reference USA, a Division of Simon & Schuster, Inc.:** From *Webster's New World Dictionary,* Third College Edition. Copyright © 1988, 1991, 1994 by Simon & Schuster, Inc. **Methuen & Company:** Quotes by Kenneth Muir from *Macbeth* by William Shakespeare, edited by Kenneth Muir. Editorial Matter copyright © 1962 by Methuen & Co. **New Directions Publishing Corporation:** From "Dulce et Decorum Est" from *The Collected Poems of Wilfred Owen.* Copyright © 1963 by Chatto & Windus, Ltd. From "Not Waving But Drowning" from *Collected Poems of Stevie Smith.* Copyright © 1972 by Stevie Smith. From "Do Not Go Gentle Into That Good Night" and "Fern Hill" from *The Poems of Dylan Thomas.* Copyright © 1952 by Dylan Thomas. **Oxford University Press:** From *A Preface to Paradise Lost* by C. S. Lewis. First published by Oxford University Press, London, 1942. **The Progressive, 409 East Main Street, Madison, WI 53703:** From "Nadine Gordimer: 'I've never left Africa'," an interview by Claudia Dreifus from *The Progressive,* January 1992. Copyright © 1991 by The Progressive, Inc. **Burton Raffel:** From "The Seafarer" from *Poems from the Old English,* translated by Burton Raffel. Copyright © 1960, 1964 by Burton Raffel. **Random House, Inc.:** From "Musée des Beaux Arts" and from "The Unknown Citizen" from *W. H. Auden: Collected Poems,* edited by Edward Mendelson. Copyright © 1940 and renewed © 1968 by W. H. Auden. **Shakespeare Quarterly:** From "*Macbeth*: The Nemesis of the Post-Shakespearian Actor" by Elizabeth Nielsen from *Shakespeare Quarterly,* vol. XVI, no. 2, Spring 1965. Copyright © 1965 by the Shakespeare Association of America, Inc. **Simon & Schuster, Inc.:** From "An Outline of *Gulliver's Travels*" from *Giants and Dwarfs* by Allan Bloom. Copyright © 1990 by Allan Bloom. From "The Second Coming" from *Poems of W. B. Yeats,* edited by Richard J. Finneran. Copyright © 1924 by Macmillan Publishing Company; copyright renewed 1952 by Bertha Georgie Yeats. **W. D. Snodgrass and The Hudson Review:** From "A Rocking-Horse: The Symbol, the Pattern, the Way to Live" by W. D. Snodgrass from *The Hudson Review,* XI, Summer 1958. Copyright © 1958 by The Hudson Review. **Times Newspapers Limited:** From "Mood Indigo" by Victoria Glendinning from *The Times Literary Supplement,* no. 3987, September 1, 1978. Copyright © 1978 by Times Newspapers Ltd. (London). **University of South Carolina Press:** From *Essays on Poetry* by John Stuart Mill, edited by F. Parvin Sharpless. Copyright © 1976 by University of South Carolina Press. **Viking Penguin, a division of Penguin Books USA Inc.:** From "Drama and Life" from *The Critical Writings of James Joyce,* edited by E. Mason and R. Ellmann. Copyright © 1959 by Harriet Weaver and F. Lionel Monro as Administrators for the Estate of James Joyce; copyright renewed © 1987 by F. Lionel Monro. **Yale University Press:** From *The Guest Hall of Eden* by Alvin A. Lee. Copyright © 1972 by Yale University. **Reference:** From *A Dancer to God: Tributes to T. S. Eliot* by Ted Hughes. Copyright © 1992 by Ted Hughes. Published by Faber and Faber Limited.

CONTENTS

The Anglo-Saxons 449–1066

The Middle Ages 1066–1485

COLLECTION *2*

THE ONE STORY WORTH TELLING
COLLECTION PLANNING GUIDE T88A–T88D

The Renaissance 1485–1660

LOVE, DEATH, AND TIME
COLLECTION PLANNING GUIDE **T212A–T212F**

THE POWER OF THE WORD
COLLECTION PLANNING GUIDE T402A–T402D

The Restoration and the Eighteenth Century
1660–1800

The Romantic Period 1798–1832

COLLECTION *8*

THE POWER OF IMAGINATION
COLLECTION PLANNING GUIDE T638A–T638D

The Victorian Period 1832–1901

THE VICTORIAN PERIOD *by* Donald Gray *and*
John Malcolm Brinnin **T782**

TIME LINE **T784**

A CLOSER LOOK
An Age in Need of Heroines: Reform in
Victorian Britain **T788**
The Pre-Raphaelite Brotherhood: Challenging
Artistic Authority **T790**
Victorian Drama: From Relief to Realism **T798**

The Twentieth Century

COLLECTION *12*

THE CENTER CANNOT HOLD
COLLECTION PLANNING GUIDE **T922A–T922D**

COLLECTION 13

THE TRANSFORMING IMAGINATION
COLLECTION PLANNING GUIDE T976A–T976D

COLLECTION 14

OURSELVES AMONG OTHERS
COLLECTION PLANNING GUIDE T1058A–T1058F

CLASHES OF CULTURE
COLLECTION PLANNING GUIDE T1120A–T1120D

RESOURCE CENTER

MAKING CONNECTIONS . . .

The ability to make connections is essential to living and learning. *Elements of Literature* makes the connections between **Literature and Life, Literature and Understanding, Literature and Writing, Literature and Language,** and **Literature Past and Present**.

One fundamental connection has always been at the heart of great literature—the empathetic link that enables a reader to participate fully in another's experience. Now, a new edition of *Elements of Literature* expands on this primary connection between reader and writer, helping students understand the intricate relationships that shape our literature and our lives. Using the world's greatest literature as a springboard, *Elements of Literature* takes students on a journey of discovery to explore the links that bind language and experience.

In this latest edition, the discovery of connections is enhanced by a new, more meaningful organization. The literature is grouped into Collections that help students explore universal themes, experience the treatment of themes in various genres, and understand the factors—both personal and historical—that influence a writer's choices.

Pupil's Edition Organization

LITERARY COLLECTIONS

Literary Collections—each organized around a central theme characteristic of the historical period—form the instructional core of grades 11 and 12. Cross-references throughout each Collection refer students to related content in the *Resource Center*.

RESOURCE CENTER

The *Resource Center* contains material for mini-lessons or for students to refer to independently. The handbooks include helpful information for improving writing, thinking, researching, and studying skills while ensuring concepts are accessible to a wide range of students. The *Resource Center* follows the literary Collections and contains the following sections:

- Handbook of Literary Terms
- Communications Handbook
- Language Handbook
- Glossary

...*with* ELEMENTS OF *Literature.*

Lesson Organization

At every level and in every lesson, ***Elements of Literature*** emphasizes making meaning— clarifying a personal response, shaping an interpretation, and moving beyond the text to make new connections.

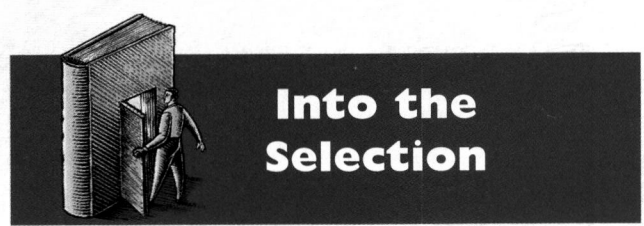

Into the Selection

Author Biography
The **Author Biography** features provide background on the author, including quotations from the author about personal life experiences reflected in the selection. Each feature also explores the author's creative process and suggests other works by the author that may interest students.

Before You Read
Each **Before You Read** page helps students connect events or themes in the selection to their personal experiences and builds historical or literary background.

- **Reading Focus**
  These motivational features have students consider an issue, topic, or situation central to the selection. This early student involvement heightens awareness and makes reading purposeful.

- **Quickwrite**
  Brief writing prompts, often for independent activities, further develop the topic introduced in the *Reading Focus*. Students are asked to return to the *Quickwrite* after reading the selection to validate original impressions or record changes in opinions or feelings.

- **Elements of Literature**
  A key literary element is explained and defined in the context of the upcoming selection.

- **Background**
  Understanding the essential background of a particular selection enhances reading comprehension. *Background* describes historical or cultural contexts, defines key terms, explains critical concepts, or provides additional information about the author.

> **66** Meaning lies in that shared ground where the reader and the text meet— it isn't resident within the text, to be extracted like a nut from its shell. **99**
>
> —Robert Probst
> Author, *Elements of Literature*

> **"We must try, first of all, to respect the nature of literary experience."**
>
> —Robert Probst

Through the Selection

During the "Through" part of the lesson, students have firsthand experiences with the literature. They probe, challenge, and analyze their own and their classmates' responses and perceptions.

A Dialogue with the Text
This frequently occurring activity invites students to use their *Reader's Logs* to record perceptions, predictions, and feelings about the selection as they read.

Words to Own
Words to Own boxes encourage the acquisition of vocabulary by highlighting and defining target vocabulary words for prose selections.

Literature and . . .
These features enhance comprehension by providing additional background information or by making connections to other disciplines such as science, math, social studies, and art.

Connections
A number of selections are followed by a *Connections* feature: an additional work, often in a different genre, that makes a pertinent literary connection to the main selection. Newspaper articles, song lyrics, cartoons, poems, and essays appear as Connections, enabling students to compare and contrast different treatments of a theme and make relevant personal connections.

Making Meanings
Interesting, involving questions follow each selection, moving from personal response to high-level critical thinking.

- First Thoughts
- Reviewing the Text
- Shaping Interpretations
- Connecting with the Text
- Extending the Text
- Challenging the Text

> **"There are various ways of making meaning out of experience, and students should learn to exercise some responsibility in choosing."**
>
> —Robert Probst

Beyond the Selection

Students extend their experiences and knowledge of literature, exploring their reactions through projects and activities.

Choices: Building Your Portfolio
Students follow their interests and develop new ones as they choose activities and projects for their portfolios.

- The *Writer's Notebook: Work in Progress* activities—found on each *Choices* page—help students explore and define topics for writing. These assignments guide students in basic skills that may be used later in the *Writer's Workshop* concluding each historical period.

Other portfolio activities include
- Speaking and Listening • Creative Writing •
- Critical Writing • Research • Art •
- Problem Solving • Cross-Curricular Connections •
- Performance • Cultural Connections •

Elements of Literature
In-depth features on key literary elements, from sonnet form and symbolism to plain style and kennings, reinforce newly encountered literary elements and place them in a broader context.

Language and Style
These activities focus on aspects of literary style and are used in conjunction with the study of the selection.

How to Own a Word
This feature teaches a specific strategy for vocabulary acquisition: semantic mapping, word analogies, and context clues, among others.

...with ELEMENTS OF *Literature*.

Support for All Your Needs
Grades 11 and 12

Teaching Resources A and B

Two booklets per grade level provide Teaching Notes and black-line masters that support instruction in the *Pupil's Edition*.

- *Teaching Notes* introduce literary periods, provide selection summaries and objectives, and identify key literary elements. The notes also rate each selection's level of difficulty as easy, intermediate, or challenging for both vocabulary and concept. They frequently include additional historical/biographical material.
- *Graphic Organizers for Active Reading* are selection-based graphic organizer activities that aid students in one or all stages of the reading process.
- *Language Link* activity worksheets cover a complete scope and sequence of language skills, providing an independent strand of grammar, usage, and mechanics instruction.

- *Words to Own* are selection-based vocabulary activity worksheets that provide practice with and reinforcement of the *Words to Own* identified in the *Pupil's Edition*. Worksheets featuring additional vocabulary words are also provided for the collections containing a majority of poetry selections.
- *Becoming a Strategic Reader* worksheets for each literary period provide instruction and practice in reading strategies.
- *Language Workshop* worksheets reinforce, extend, and provide practice for the *Language Workshop* features in the *Pupil's Edition*.
- *Cross-Curricular Activities* are interdisciplinary, theme-based activities appropriate for team-teaching situations.

Language Development

Language Skills Worksheets offer a complete scope and sequence of language skills instruction and practice.

Assessment Options

Test Booklet
- *Selection Tests*
- *Collection Tests*
- *Literary Period Introduction Tests*
- *The American Language Tests (grade 11)*
- *The English Language Tests (grade 12)*
- *Literary Period Tests*
- *Standardized Test Preparation* worksheets

Integrated Performance Assessment, an independent, holistic assessment program, was developed in cooperation with the Center for Reading and Language Studies at Indiana University, Dr. Roger Farr, Director, and the HB Assessment Group. Each of four assessments consists of a Reading section that provides one or two authentic literary selections with a series of open-ended questions and a Writing section that elicits a specific form of writing.

The **Portfolio Management System** provides support for implementing portfolios in the classroom. It includes forms for self-, peer, and teacher assessment and blackline masters for developing and evaluating the following *Pupil's Edition* activities and projects.

- *Learning for Life* gives you a rubric for evaluating each *Learning for Life* assignment in the *Pupil's Edition.*
- *Writer's Workshop* offers a prewriting worksheet, a self-evaluation form, peer critique prompts and an evaluation rubric for each *Writer's Workshop* activity.
- *Choices: Building Your Portfolio* contains criteria for evaluating each activity that appears in this feature.

Test Generators—available for either Macintosh® or Windows®—enable you to revise, edit, or re-sort existing *Selection Tests* and *Standardized Test Preparation Items.*

Audiovisual Resources

Fine Art Transparencies, organized by Collection, help students make humanities connections with specific themes. Each transparency comes with two blackline masters—specific questions relate the art to a literary selection or to the Collection.

Instructional Transparencies include Literary Element, Reading Strategy, Vocabulary Strategy, and Revision Strategy transparencies.

Audiocassettes with Program Notes provide professional recordings of key selections and reflect a mix of genres, periods, and cultures.

Integrated Technology

Videodisc Programs for each level extend and enrich the literary content of the *Pupil's Edition*. Video segments linked to each Collection offer a variety of interesting connections, such as author biographies or interviews, historical background, cross-curricular content, or dramatic interpretations of literature.

Language Workshop Interactive Multimedia CD-ROM Software provides a comprehensive, interactive course of study in grammar, usage, and mechanics. Functions include automatic scoring of tests and exercises, prescriptions for individualized courses of study, and tracking of student grades. Available for Macintosh® or Windows®.

Writer's Workshop Interactive Multimedia CD-ROM Software provides support in eight challenging, standards-based writing assignments, giving students step-by-step guidance through the writing process. The program includes an on-line thesaurus, dictionary, spell-checker, language handbook, and bibliography-maker (MLA and APA styles). Available for Macintosh® and Windows®.

The **Holistic Scoring Workshop** is easy-to-use software that will introduce you to holistic scoring techniques. You'll practice scoring actual student papers and can compare the scores you would assign with those given by professional scorers.

The **Staff Development Video Package** gives you a comprehensive in-service and training program that provides an overview of **Elements of Literature.** A *User's Guide* is also included.

...MAKING CONNECTIONS
that last a lifetime!

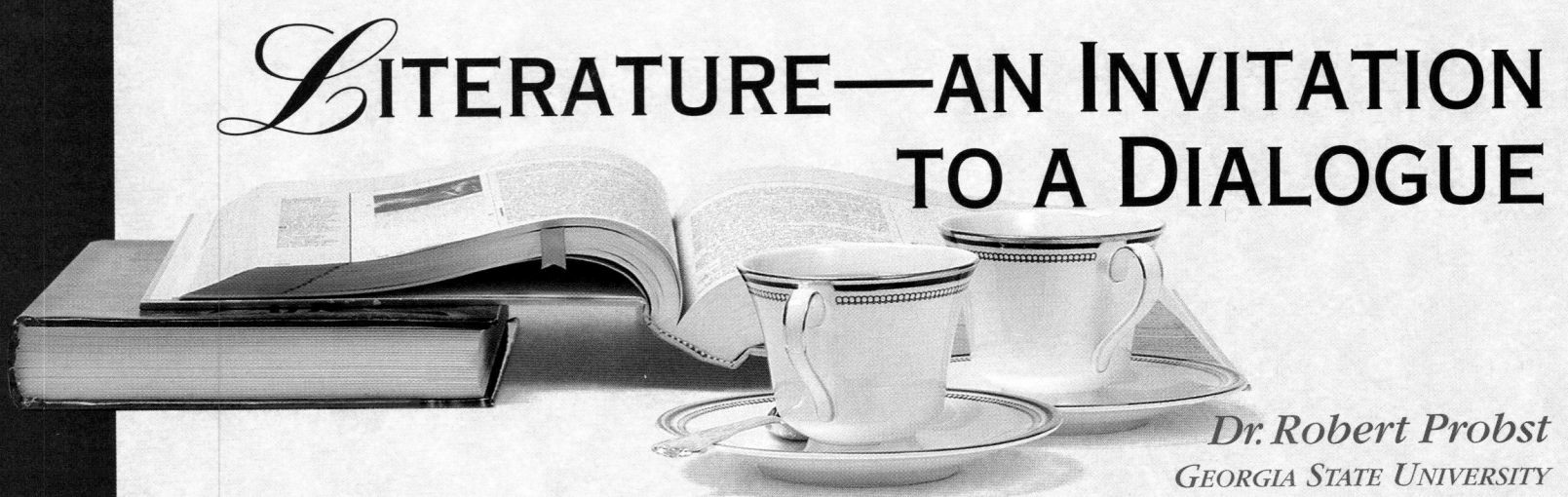

LITERATURE—AN INVITATION TO A DIALOGUE

Dr. Robert Probst
GEORGIA STATE UNIVERSITY

Surely, of all the arts, literature is most immediately implicated with life itself. The very medium through which the author shapes the text—language—is grounded in the shared lives of human beings. Language is the bloodstream of a common culture, a common history. Louise Rosenblatt

Literature and Life

Mathematicians, scientists, and engineers build bridges and send people to the moon, statisticians calculate our insurance premiums and life expectancy, and accountants figure our taxes and amortize our house payments, but the poets, dramatists, novelists, and story-writers have nonetheless remained at the center of life. They bind us together as a society and they define us as individuals within that society.

When we're very young we need stories almost as much as we need food and protection. They entertain us and help us sleep, but they also teach us how to get through the world. They tell us there are pots of gold waiting for us at the end of the rainbow, and they warn us about the trolls hiding under the bridges. They teach us about hope, fear, courage, and all the other elements of our lives. As we grow out of childhood, the great stories, poems, and plays of the world's literature encourage us to reflect on the issues that have intrigued men and women for centuries, inviting us into a continuing dialogue about human experience. When we're older, our own stories represent what we've done, capturing for us what we've made of our lives. Some we'll tell happily, some we'll tell with great pain, and some

we may not tell at all, but they're all important because they are a way of making sense of our lives.

If literature is the ongoing dialogue about what it means to be human, then the language arts classroom is society's invitation to students to join that conversation. The texts we use represent the reflections of the world's cultures on the nature of human experience, and the writings we elicit from our students are their first efforts to join in that reflection. The classroom is the place for students to learn to read and reflect on visions of human possibilities offered them by the great literature and to begin to tell their own.

Literature offers an invitation to reflect, but it doesn't offer formulas to memorize or answers to write dutifully in notes so that

> *Literature offers us access to hidden experiences and perceptions.*

later on, when life presents us with problems, we can pull out our tattered old notebooks and find our path sketched out for us. Literature is an invitation to a dialogue.

That, perhaps more than any other reason, is why it's so important that we teach literature and writing well. It's too easy to avoid the responsible thought demanded by the significant issues, too tempting to

accept someone else's formulation of the truth. "Life imitates art," Richard Peck said in a speech in New Orleans in 1974, "especially bad art." By that he meant, I think, that we may too often give in to tempting laziness and allow our lives to be governed by visions of human possibilities that we take from film, television, or graffiti. The problem for teachers, of course, is to lead students not simply to absorb unthinkingly what art offers, but to reflect on it.

This textbook series tries to support teachers' efforts to lead students to think, to feel, and to take responsibility for themselves. It will have much in common with other textbooks. After all, we'd miss "The Raven" if he didn't land croaking on our window sill one morning just before homeroom, and twelfth grade wouldn't be the same without an evening or two around the hearth with Beowulf. But if this series has much in common with other textbooks, it will also have much that differs—new selections, perhaps by authors we haven't met before, exploring lives and circumstances that previously may not have been well represented in the pages of school texts. And similarly, there will be familiar approaches to teaching—perhaps specific activities—that we've all come to rely upon, but there will be other suggestions that emphasize aspects of literary experience, writing, and discussion that may not have been prominent in other books.

Principles of the Program

First among the principles of the program is that *the subject matter of the language arts* classroom is human experience comprehended and expressed in language. The classroom invites the student into the dialogue about the big issues of human experience. The content of literature is the content of our days and we think and feel about these issues before we enter the classroom and open the text.

When we do finally come to the text, it offers students an opportunity to begin to make sense of experience and to see it captured in the literature.

Implicit in this vision of the language arts is a second principle, *that learning in the English classroom is a creative act,* requiring students to make things with language. Reading literature is a process of engaging the text, weighing it against experience readers bring to it.

Similarly, writing isn't simply a matter of learning and applying the rules of grammar and usage or of memorizing the structure and strategies of narratives, descriptions, and arguments.

The third principle focuses on the encounter between student and content. It doesn't focus exclusively on the information and skills that have at times provided the framework for our instruction.

Nor, on the other hand, is teaching planned with thought *only* for the student's interests, needs, and desires, and thus organized around whatever concerns happen to predominate at the moment. It is, to borrow Rosenblatt's term, transactional.

For this series, *the integration of the several aspects of the English language arts program* is the fourth governing principle. Literature can't be taught effectively without work in composition. Writing, without the inspiration offered by good literature, remains shallow and undeveloped. Oral language has to be acquired in the context of groups working collaboratively. And so, these texts will suggest ways of interrelating instruction in literature, writing, and language.

Goals of the Program

We hope that in a curriculum planned to include these texts students would achieve several goals.

1. *They will learn about themselves, their assumptions and beliefs, through reading, discussing, and writing about literature and their own experience.*

2. *Students will learn about others, including those in their classrooms and communities, but also people of other cultures, other places, other times.*

3. *Students will learn how texts operate, how they shape our thinking and manipulate our emotions.*

4. *Students will learn how context shapes meaning.*

5. *Students will learn that there are many ways of dealing with experience, both literary and otherwise.*

6. *Students should learn the pleasures—aesthetic, intellectual, emotional, and social—of reading and writing, in the hope that these pleasures will capture them as readers and writers for the rest of their lives.*

Education doesn't—or shouldn't—end with the last diploma or degree received. We hope that our students will find some pleasure in learning so they'll continue to learn and think.

Working with the Series

You will find, as you work with selections in this textbook, that students have immediate responses to what they've read. That may be the place to start. The students' responses are very likely to lead you back to the issues you would have wanted to discuss anyway, and so the questions we've suggested might be addressed naturally during the flow of the discussion. Look for the potential in their reactions and their questions even before turning to the questions in the "First Thoughts" section. Then, the questions in the text can extend or expand the discussion.

The same might be said about the writing. The series has been designed so that experiences with literature, with writing, and with group processes will often be interconnected. We

hope that the literature will inspire and shape the students' writing, that their writing will lead back to further reading, and that the discussions and group activities suggested will build a supportive community in which all this work can take place.

The objective in all of this is for students to be able to draw upon their literary heritage and their developing skill with written and spoken language so that, as humane and reasoning people, they may be responsibly engaged with the world around them. If the language arts class helps to achieve that goal, we should be well satisfied with our labors.

Dr. Robert Probst

BECOMING A STRATEGIC READER

Dr. Judith Irvin
FLORIDA STATE UNIVERSITY

Most teachers think that during the elementary grades, students will learn to read and during the middle school years, most will master the process of reading. Unfortunately, many students begin their high school careers without important reading skills. Some may lack the conceptual understanding that most students have acquired developmentally in the lower grades, and this deficit has always kept them behind their peers in literacy abilities. Other students may be impeded by learning disabilities and so must learn alternate reading strategies in order to compensate for these disabilities.

Even though teachers may become frustrated with students who have difficulty reading at the high school level, they can help these students by building on their strengths, by concentrating on their comprehension, and by helping them to develop reading strategies such as skimming and scanning material and connecting texts with prior knowledge.

In the past, reading was viewed as a simple task of decoding words. Educators generally emphasized the strategies of sounding out words, recognizing words out of context by sight, and reproducing content by answering comprehension questions. Research has led to a new conceptualization of the reading process—that reading is a complex learning process. In this new view, readers construct meaning from a text, not simply by decoding words, but by using reading strategies that incorporate and expand their prior knowledge. Prior knowledge includes not only readers' knowledge of the definition of a word, but also their responses to the context of the word—the entire text. Careful reading of a text using strategies like those explained in the following material will allow readers to use their prior knowledge to create meaning and to extend their understanding of a text. As students become more involved in developing and reflecting on their reading and learning processes, meaning may now be defined as "something that is actively created rather than passively received" (Buehl, 1995, p. 8).

As will be explained, the process of constructing meaning is not linear, but recursive and interactive and helps to create a richer, more productive reading experience for the reader.

The Reader

Former models of reading focused on whether students had acquired specific skills. Recent models of reading allow that

> *It is the interaction of what is in readers' minds with what is on the page... that helps them to comprehend what they read.*

students come to a learning context with previous information about particular topics, with definite attitudes about reading, writing, and school in general, and with varying motivations for reading and learning. It is the interaction of what is in readers' minds with what is on the page within a particular context that helps them to comprehend what they read.

Schema Theory

It is impossible for readers to learn anything new without making connections to their prior knowledge or schemata. The schemata are like the components of an elaborate filing system inside every reader's head. If the reader's mind is the filing system, the schemata, then, are the ideas contained in the file folders within the system. For example, you probably have a schema for a computer, a mental picture of what a computer is and what it does. You probably also bring to that basic picture many other associations, ideas, and feelings. If you use computers regularly, your schema may include positive feelings about their limitless applications. If the computer revolution has left you yearning for the days of yellow note pads and typewriters, then you may have feelings of anxiety or frustration as you approach a computer manual. For teachers, it is important to remember that readers encountering new ideas must often be shown how the new material fits into their existing filing system.

The Text

The content, format, and organization of a text are factors that make a text easy or difficult for students to understand. If students' schemata tell them that a particular assignment will be difficult or unrelated to their personal experiences, they will probably be reluctant to read it and will most likely not make much meaning of it. The students know with one look that they will read and respond to a poem differently than they will to a chapter in a science book. A teacher should be prepared to exercise flexibility and sensitivity in presenting the text so as to encourage students to use their schemata to enhance their reading experiences.

The Context

Readers approach texts differently, and they also vary their reading according to their purposes. If they are reading for pleasure, students may skip over a difficult word or read an exciting passage more than once. But if they are reading a text for class, skipping a word might mean not understanding an important concept needed in class the next day. A reader's purpose for reading also dictates how attentive he or she is to details and how much effort will be put into remembering what is read. Similarly, when and where the reading is done affects the reading process. Readers will make less meaning from texts they read on the bus or with thoughts of a sick relative in the backs of their minds than they might make if they had a quiet space and clear thoughts.

Strategic Learning

Suppose that during a racquetball game you hit a straight shot down the right side of the court, and your opponent misses

Becoming a proficient reader and writer is a life-long process.

the ball. The point is yours. This well-placed shot may have been a lucky one, or it may have been the result of a strategy. Before you hit the ball, you may have noticed that your opponent was standing in the middle of the court, and you remembered that she is left-handed with a weak backhand. You hit the ball to exactly the right spot deliberately and strategically. The analogy of planning your shots in a game can be applied to learning.

Strategic learning involves analyzing the reading task, establishing a purpose for reading, and then selecting strategies for making meaning. A strategy is a conscious effort by the reader to attend to comprehension while reading. Weinstein explains that "learning strategies include any thoughts or behaviors that help us to acquire new information in such a way that the new information is integrated with our existing knowledge" (Weinstein, 1987, p. 590). Strategies occur before reading when readers activate prior knowledge by thinking and discussing the title and topic and by identifying a purpose for reading. They also occur during reading as readers use context to figure out unknown words and monitor their understanding, and beyond the reading when readers summarize or evaluate the main ideas of the text.

Metacognition

Reading is often referred to as a cognitive event. It is also a metacognitive event. Cognition refers to a person's using the knowledge and skills he or she possesses; metacognition refers to a person's awareness and understanding of that knowledge and conscious control over those skills. It is, essentially, thinking about one's way of thinking. Metacognition, then, is knowing how and when to use strategies to solve problems in understanding. It develops as a reader matures, usually during adolescence, but it can be taught and strengthened by explicit instruction and practice.

Becoming a proficient reader and writer is a life-long process. Accepting the premise that meaning is constructed in the mind of the learner implies that metacognitive abilities must be operational for learning to occur. The high school years are an ideal time to develop the metacognitive abilities that will serve them throughout life.

Strategic Reading in This Program

Good readers are strategic, and being strategic involves the metacognitive abilities to think, plan, and evaluate their understanding of a text. The following concepts, addressed in the Annotated Teacher's Edition and in Teaching Resources for *Elements of Literature,* help students to focus on their own reading strategies:

- activating schema (prior knowledge) and building background information
- predicting and confirming
- organizing information
- drawing conclusions
- making inferences
- text differences
- retelling/summarizing

Before students read, they are invited to use their prior knowledge by making predictions about the content of a selection, to establish a clear purpose for reading, and to think about reading strategies they might use as they read. During the reading process, students are guided to use context, to connect what they are reading with what they already know, and to continue to monitor and evaluate their comprehension. And, after completing their reading, students have opportunities to review their reading through peer discussion, class discussion, preparing entries in Reader's Logs, and using graphic organizers.

New research and practice in literacy learning reflects a more holistic view of understanding text. The *Elements of Literature* program provides students with opportunities to apply reading strategies to a variety of texts in a meaningful manner.

References

Buehl, D. *Classroom Strategies for Interactive Learning.* Schofield, WI: Wisconsin State Reading Association, 1995.

Weinstein, C. E. "Fostering Learning Autonomy Through the Use of Learning Strategies." *Journal of Reading* 30 (1987) 590–595.

Dr. Judith Irvin

WHAT IS AN INTEGRATED APPROACH?

Dr. Karen Kutiper
HARRIS COUNTY DEPT. OF EDUCATION
HOUSTON, TEXAS

An integrated language arts program focuses on the complementary nature of the literacy processes—reading, writing, listening, and speaking—rather than the teaching of each in isolation from the other. We are very much aware of the strong connections between reading and writing, and in the professional literature and at professional conferences we read and hear about ways to forge those connections. In reality those connections exist among all of the language arts—reading, writing, listening, and speaking. So rather than teaching the processes and their related skills separately, teachers weave them together in instructional contexts. Such an approach avoids the fragmentation of skills, takes advantage of the reciprocal relationship that exists among the literacy processes, and reflects the expanded use of literacy skills in the real world. Initial encounters with a wide range of quality texts often provide the starting points for these integrated classroom experiences.

How does an integrated approach help my students?

When supported by appropriate instruction, the interplay among the linguistic processes can produce greater competence in all areas. As youngsters have opportunities to respond to texts in writing, to share, to defend, and to refine those responses in dialogue with peers or with the teacher, they develop richer understandings of what they have read, leading to greater competence in reading and writing. When students have opportunities to respond both informally and formally to their own reading and writing and to the reading and writing of others, they increase their ability to communicate fluently and flexibly in any setting.

What is the teacher's role in the integrated classroom?

In these classrooms the teacher is a facilitator who guides and focuses the opportunities for response, who assesses student performance in order to plan appropriate supportive instruction, and who ensures that students are writing for a variety of audiences and purposes and

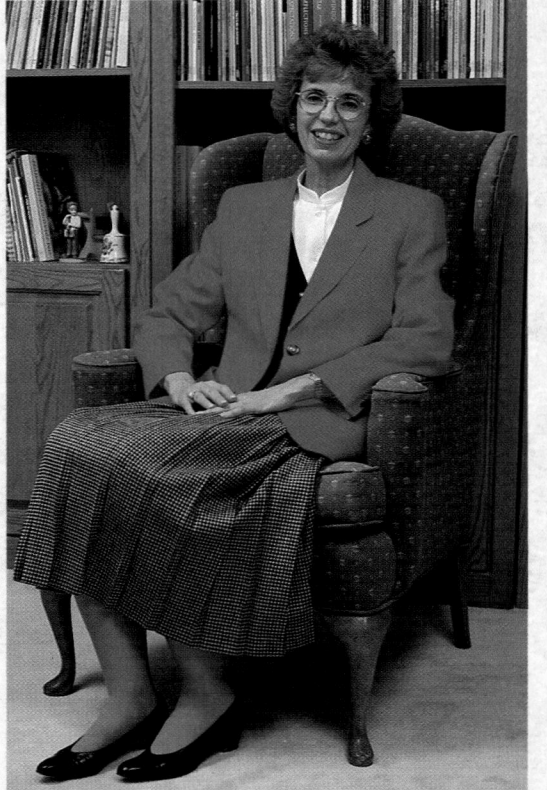

reading widely from a range of texts, both literary and informative. Direct instruction in an integrated classroom takes many forms. Teachers become skilled at teaching mini-strategy lessons at the point of need—brief lessons on language conventions, reading of literature skills. These lessons emerge from a meaningful context for the students and provide real purpose for new learning. Whether a mini-lesson or a more elaborate one, teachers focus on structuring experiences that immerse students in language use and provide meaningful opportunities for reading, writing, listening, and speaking.

What are the key ingredients of the integrated classroom?

Obviously, a wide variety of quality and timely literature forms the foundation of the integrated classroom. The learners need opportunities to read extensively from teacher selected and self-selected materials. The organization of the classroom must facilitate occasions for the informal and formal written and oral responses that emerge from reading. At the heart of this classroom is a teacher who understands that quality instruction builds on students' backgrounds, who provides appropriate instructional scaffolding, and who offers students opportunities to participate in a wide range of literacy activities. Most importantly, this teacher acknowledges the active role students play in developing and refining their own literacy processes and involves them in meaningful and balanced learning experiences in which literacy skills and strategies are interwoven.

THE NEED FOR INCLUSION

Dr. Donna Kearns
UNIVERSITY OF CENTRAL OKLAHOMA

What Is Inclusion?

As the diverse threads of a garment bring beauty and durability to the fabric, so too do the children of today's diverse classrooms bring beauty and sensitivity to our schools and communities. Including all children in schools as we include a variety of threads in a special fabric allows for a fine weave. It becomes a closely knit cloth to provide strength for the community. Inclusion of children with disabilities and diverse needs in our classrooms represents a belief that a class can be made stronger by weaving those students into classrooms where true learning can take place through a variety of different techniques. These techniques are provided in classrooms where all students are included.

The term *inclusion* enjoys no one common definition among today's educators. However, most supporters of inclusion agree that it does provide for six basic principles that are important to the educational rights of all of America's children. Those principles include **zero reject, natural proportions, regular/special education collaboration, home school, age-appropriate,** and **ability awareness.**

The term **zero reject** refers to the fact that no students with disabilities are rejected from the regular education classrooms and schools in which they would participate if they did not have disabilities. We do not reject them in their real classroom placement on the basis of their disability, but rather we find techniques such as those presented in this book to

> *Including all children in schools as we include a variety of threads in a special fabric allows for a fine weave.*

assist them to experience success in the regular classroom in which every other child of their age is placed.

When students with disabilities are placed in the regular education classroom at the rate consistent with the incidence of disabilities, there should be approximately no more than ten percent of students who have disabilities. This **natural proportion** element should ensure and reassure teachers that their classrooms will continue to be a mixture of students, the majority of whom have average or above average learning abilities—including some of those who may have disabilities.

Supporters of inclusion believe that students with disabilities are primarily the responsibility of the classroom teacher— just as every other student in that teacher's room is his or her responsibility. In addition, supporters carry a strong belief that supports must be provided by special education and related services personnel to enable teachers and students to experience success in the regular classroom. This textbook provides techniques for classroom teachers to use as well as some that may be used by those support personnel as they **collaborate** to provide services to students with disabilities who are included in the regular classroom. These support services are not provided in a corner of the room, but rather are intermingled within the same instructional area that is being used for all students in the lessons being presented. A collaborative effort enables the students and the teacher(s) to truly provide successful opportunities. A shared philosophy of inclusion and the rights of all children to learn from the teacher and from each other is essential for inclusion to work.

Children with disabilities have the right to attend the same school as their brothers and sisters as well as their neighborhood friends. The **home school** issue supports students' acceptance within their own community with little if any discrimination. By maintaining daily contact with the same people who live "next door," students with disabilities are viewed as peers and are respected. Classmates and peers begin to have a better awareness of

the abilities of students with disabilities—taking the focus off what they can't do and focusing instead on what they can do!

As students are placed in these general education classrooms, they are given **age-appropriate** placements. Students are not placed based on IQ or label, but rather on where their individual needs can best be met. When placement decisions are made, teachers and parents must work together to ensure that each student's needs are examined independently. Though some students may need to be placed in an educational program with their same-age peers, others may still enjoy opportunities that are considered by some as immature or not age-appropriate. It is important to keep in mind that age-appropriate is a term that differs from same-age.

Why Is Inclusion Important?

In the past, use of the word *inclusion* struck fear in the hearts of many educators. Fortunately, today, more and more educators understand that inclusion itself is not to be feared. It is a term that represents progress toward meeting the diverse needs of students in our changing population. Educational statistics have been presented in a variety of ways, but no matter how we examine the issue, we see that

approximately one third of American children are at risk of school failure. Schools must change to meet the diverse needs of the students in our current population, not the students of even three to five years ago. Cultural groups in this country have changed dramatically over the past ten years. Schools cannot continue to meet the needs of all learners if we continue to educate the way we educated yesterday's students. Not only have cultures changed, but since 1987, one fourth of all preschool children have been living in poverty. Annually about 350,000 infants are born to mothers addicted to cocaine. These infants are entering the public school system in infant and early childhood programs. The "Leave It to Beaver" family exists in only a fraction of the population today. On any given night, approximately 50,000 to 200,000 children are homeless. These factors alone should tell us that we must change the way we educate today's students. These factors alone should tell us that all students need to be accepted and educated with their peers—those same peers who are a part of their community. Including all students in general education classrooms better ensures that all students have had equal opportunities to access the same educational programs and services and that their individual needs have been met—without labeling or discriminating in any manner.

How Can Teachers Use Inclusion Strategies to Help Students?

A strategy is a planned, deliberate activity used to acquire knowledge. It is generally understood that students with disabilities as well as others who are at risk of failure in school have few if any strategies to learn new information. Special educators have most often focused their educational techniques on teaching students strategies to learn new information. Unfortunately, students often misperceived what they were learning because the setting (the special education classroom) was a place they simply "went." It was not considered their classroom or home base. The content was not always developed around the techniques or strategies the teacher was teaching.

On the other hand, in the general

education classroom, many students with disabilities and other special needs had little if any background of experience to draw from and often misperceived the content as it was presented. A merger of the content along with the strategies such as those presented in this text provides the student better information on *how* to learn the information as well as *what* to learn. We must remember that the purpose of education goes beyond learning content. Education is much more accurately described as learning how to learn. Students can enhance their learning by becoming aware of their own skills as they listen, read, write, and experience interactions in school situations. Teachers can promote this learning by assisting students in exploring how they learn while they are learning. Learning to use strategies effectively may encourage students to take responsibility for their learning and to affect positive self-perception as well as motivation. As educators, we must plan strategies to assist students in their learning process—not just in the presentation of the content. A critical element in assisting students in the learning process includes the use of instructional as well as cognitive strategies such as those presented in this text. We must teach students to become aware of their own strategies and to become good trouble-shooters in the learning process. We do this by teaching strategies. It is believed that the use of flexible instructional strategies and the merger of content with cognitive strategies will assist all students to learn concepts presented in class—not just today, but for tomorrow and all the tomorrows to come.

ENGLISH LANGUAGE DEVELOPMENT

Dr. Stephen Krashen
UNIVERSITY OF SOUTHERN CALIFORNIA

The problem of helping the older limited-English-proficient student in a school without special programs, or with partial programs, cannot be totally solved. But the problem and the teacher's burden can be reduced. To see how this can be done, we will first briefly discuss the principles underlying ideal programs, describe an ideal program, and then see how this knowledge can be applied to the less-than-ideal situation.

The principles underlying successful programs for limited-English-proficient students are the same principles underlying successful foreign language programs and language arts programs for first-language and literacy development. There are a few fundamental hypotheses:

1. The Acquisition-Learning Hypothesis

claims that we have two different ways of developing ability in language: Language *acquisition* is a subconscious process, that is, while it is happening, we do not know it is happening. In addition, once an aspect of language is acquired, we are not usually aware of it: The knowledge is stored subconsciously in our brains. A synonym for language acquisition is "picking up" a language.

Language *learning* is a conscious process, and the result of language learning is consciously stored in our brains. When we talk about "rules" and "grammar," we are usually talking about language learning.

2. The Monitor Hypothesis

claims that our ability to use consciously learned language is severely limited. Conscious knowledge of language does not give us our fluency or play much of a role at all in language production or comprehension. It is acquisition, not learning, that is responsible for our ability to communicate. The only significant function of consciously learned knowledge is that it acts as a Monitor, or editor, operating on the output of the acquired system.

To clarify the role of conscious learning, I will first describe what happens in foreign language use. Assume you are trying to speak your intermediate Spanish (or French or German). The sentence you are about to speak pops into your mind. Then just before you produce it, just before you actually say it, you scan the sentence internally, you inspect it, think of the rules you learned in school, and you make corrections using these rules. (Or you blurt the sentence out, realize you made a mistake, and redo it.) This illustrates the use of the Monitor.

The Monitor is also used in the first language. We sometimes "monitor" when our acquired dialect differs from the "standard." I have to monitor, for example, if I want to get the *who/whom* distinction correct, or, in writing, when I need to distinguish *its* and *it's*. In both cases, I think about the rule.

The path to accuracy is not through better monitoring. It is not through developing an industrial-strength Monitor with detailed knowledge of rules and maintaining constant vigilance when we speak and write. The use of the Monitor, even for adults who are interested in the structure of language, is usually limited to the editing stage in writing, where it can make a small contribution. For children it hardly makes any contribution at all. The best way to increase accuracy is through acquisition, as we shall see later.

3. The Input Hypothesis

is the central hypothesis in current language acquisition theory. It claims that we acquire language in only one way, when we understand what people tell us, and when we understand what we read. (I have called the "reading version" of the Input Hypothesis the "Reading Hypothesis.") We acquire language, in other words, when we understand messages, *what* is said or written, not *how* it is said or written. We use the term "comprehensible input" to refer to input that the acquirer understands.

Notice that the input hypothesis states that we acquire language from input (listening and reading), not output (speaking and writing). The ability to produce language, it is claimed, is a result of language acquisition, not a cause.

> *A synonym for language acquisition is "picking up" a language.*

More CI > More Language and Literacy Development

The research supporting the claim that more comprehensible input (CI) results in more language acquisition and literacy development is vast and consistent. This generalization holds in first language and second language, and in informal (outside the classroom) environments and formal (inside the classroom) environments. Studies show, for example, that those who get more comprehensible input outside the classroom acquire more. In addition, those who participate in free reading programs in school, such as sustained silent reading, make better gains in vocabulary and reading than those in traditional classes.

in order to help them establish a reading habit.

The above applications can be termed "direct" application of the principle of comprehensible input: Direct applications present comprehensible input in English. We can also help second language acquirers with methods and techniques that are indirect, but very powerful.

4. The Affective Filter Hypothesis

claims that when language acquirers are in a high anxiety state, a block prevents the input from reaching the "language acquisition device." Thus, anxiety does not affect the process of language acquisition: It prevents input, even when it is comprehensible, from reaching those parts of the brain where language acquisition occurs.

Applications

We begin our discussion of application in the ideal case at the beginning level. Beginners, ideally, would participate in comprehensible-input-based methods such as Natural Approach and TPR for ESL. These methods attempt to fill the classroom time with interesting, comprehensible input, and do not require student production at early stages, nor are errors corrected.

At the intermediate level, limited-English-proficient students participate in sheltered-subject-matter classes, classes that consist only of intermediate-level ESL students and that teach subject matter in a comprehensible way. Research shows that students in these classes acquire a great deal of the second language and learn impressive amounts of subject matter at the same time (Krashen, 1991). They work because they provide a great deal of comprehensible input.

Intermediate students are encouraged to do a great deal of free voluntary reading. One interesting possibility is to combine sheltered-subject-matter teaching and free reading by teaching sheltered popular literature, a class designed to expose second language acquirers to a wide variety of interesting reading in the second language

Making English input more comprehensible using the first language

The first language can be used to supply background knowledge, knowledge of the world, and subject matter knowledge, which can help enormously in making English input more comprehensible.

Consider two limited-English-proficient students entering the fourth grade who are at approximately the same level in English. Child (1), who has been taught in her first language, has had an excellent background in math. Child (2) is very weak in math. In fourth grade, let us presume, math is taught only in English. Obviously child (1) will do much better in math than child (2). Child (1) will not only learn more math, she will also acquire more English, because she will get more comprehensible input. Child (2) will learn neither math nor English.

Developing literacy through the first language

A second indirect means of promoting English language development is the development of literacy through the first language. It is extremely efficient to develop literacy

> *The first language... can help enormously in making English input more comprehensible.*

first in the child's first language. To see this, consider this three-step argument:

(1) We learn to read by reading. There is good evidence that we learn to read by understanding the message on the page, as argued by Smith (1988) and Goodman (1982).

(2) If we learn to read by reading, by making sense of what is on the page, it will be easier to learn to read a language we already understand.

(3) Once we can read, we can read. The ability to read transfers dramatically across languages, even if the writing systems are different. Thus, learning to read any language helps a person learn to read any other.

There is another sense in which literacy transfers across languages: the ability to use language to solve problems. This includes discovering new ideas as the writer moves from draft to draft. It also includes the ability to read selectively for information relevant to a problem one is trying to solve, the ability to use a library, etc. Clearly, once someone has developed this kind of competence in one language, it transfers to any other language: Once we are educated, we are educated.

Principles of successful programs

If the principles presented above are correct, they suggest that successful programs for limited-English-proficient students will have the following characteristics:

1. Comprehensible input in English, in the form of ESL and sheltered classes based on comprehensible input. This provides comprehensible input directly.

2. Subject matter teaching done in the first language, without translation. This indirect help provides background information that helps make the English children read and hear more comprehensible. (Methods that use the first language for concurrent translation are not effective in helping children acquire English [see e.g. Legaretta, 1979]; when a translation is available, the children do not attend to the input in the second language, and teachers do not have to try to make this input comprehensible.)

3. Literacy development in the first language, which transfers to the second language.

Evidence confirming the validity of these principles comes from studies showing that children who participate in programs that have these three characteristics do very well, at least as well as children in all-day English programs, and usually better (Krashen and Biber, 1988).

A fourth very desirable component is the continuation of the development of the primary language. There are good practical reasons (e.g. international business) and cognitive reasons (there is evidence that bilingualism may be beneficial for certain cognitive abilities), and a high level of competence in the first language contributes to a healthy sense of biculturalism, an avoidance of the state of "bicultural ambivalence," shame of the first culture and rejection of the second culture (Cummins, 1981).

Here is one way to set up a program that meets these characteristics. The plan presented here, sometimes referred to as the "Eastman" plan, has three components and several stages. In the beginning stage, all children, limited English proficient and native speakers of English, are mixed for art, music, and physical education. This makes sense for two reasons: It avoids segregation, and much of the English the children will hear will be comprehensible, thanks to the pictures in art and movement in PE. Also, at this stage, children receive high-quality comprehensible-input-based ESL classes and are taught all other subjects in the primary language, subjects that would be difficult to teach in English.

The intermediate-stage child is defined as the child who understands enough English to begin to learn some content through English. We begin with sheltered-subject-matter instruction in those subjects that, at this level, do not demand a great deal of abstract use of language, such as math and science. Subjects such as social studies and language arts remain in the first language.

At the advanced level, limited-English-proficient students join the mainstream, but not all at once: They enter one or two subjects at a time, beginning with math and science. When this occurs, social studies and language arts are taught as sheltered-subject-matter classes. Eventually, students do all subjects in the mainstream and continue first language development in language arts and social studies classes. These continuing first language classes are not all-day programs. Rather, they can take the place of (or supplement) foreign language study. Examine the possible progress of a limited-English-proficient student: She first has math in the primary language, then moves to sheltered math, and then finally to the mainstream. At every stage, instruction is comprehensible, and the sheltered class acts as a bridge from the first language class to the mainstream. This child will be at "grade level" in math when she enters the mainstream and will be familiar with the special kind of English used in math class.

The Less-Than-Ideal Situation

In the less-than-ideal situation, it will not always be possible to supply everything that plans like the Eastman plan provide. We can, however, reduce the problem by attempting to ensure that the principles underlying such plans are satisfied.

A modified Eastman plan can be used in situations in which there are a number of limited-English-proficient children in one school, but they speak different first languages, and/or primary language instruction is not possible for other reasons (staffing, materials).

In these cases, two thirds of the plan can be carried out: the "mainstream" and "ESL/sheltered" components. This kind of program has the advantage of being com-

prehensible all day long, but it lacks the advantages of developing literacy in the first language and using the first language to supply subject matter knowledge. It will be better, however, than ESL "pull-out," simply putting the child in a class that is incomprehensible nearly all day long.

Quite often, however, even the modified Eastman plan is not possible. This occurs when there are a few limited English proficient children in the school and/or when coordination among teachers is not possible. In cases like this, the classroom teacher is faced with great diversity within one classroom.

Before discussing some solutions, some ways of reducing the burden, it needs to be pointed out that teachers today are facing a degree of diversity, of heterogeneity, that has never been seen before in the history of education. It is not usual to see a single class with native and fluent English speakers, students who speak no English at all (and who have a poor background in the primary language), and students who speak a wide variety of first languages. Traditional solutions will not work. Even if paraprofessionals are available, teachers must supervise them and wind up making two, three, or even four lesson plans every period. Bilingual teachers sometimes simply must translate to get through the period, an exhausting procedure that does not result in second language acquisition. And we wonder why teachers burn out so quickly! The real solution is to set up a plan similar to the Eastman plan, with team teaching. But let us consider the situation in which this is not possible. We will return to the principles underlying successful programs and see to what extent we can work toward them for our limited-English-proficient children.

The beginner

We can mimic the Eastman plan to some extent with the beginner. Of course, the art, music, and PE parts of the day will be

> *Clearly, once someone has developed this kind of competence in one language, it transfers to any other language.*

Table 1. The "Eastman" plan

stage	mainstream	ESL/sheltered	first language
beginning	art, music, PE	ESL	all core subjects
intermediate	art, music, PE	ESL, math, science	language arts, social studies
advanced	art, music, PE, development	ESL, social studies, language arts	continuing L1 math, science
mainstream	all subjects		continuing L1 development

Dr. Stephen Krashen

35

the same regardless of whether the Eastman plan can be used or not; the children will be together for this part of the day. Comprehensible-input-based ESL can be of great help, even if it is done on a pull-out basis. The time to pull out the limited English speakers is the time of day when more proficient English speakers are doing

> *When primary language instruction is not possible, there is still a great deal that can be done to get some of the positive effects of bilingual education.*

the subject matter that requires the most abstract use of language and that will be the least comprehensible for the new second language acquirer: language arts and social studies.

When beginners in English are with the other children, we can make life easier on them and us and help their language acquisition by allowing a "silent period" and not forcing language production. When the children do begin to speak, we can help by not insisting on complete sentences and not correcting errors. If the teacher understands some of the child's first language, there is no reason not to utilize the natural approach procedure of allowing the child to respond in the first language. This will greatly facilitate communication.

Home use of the first language When primary language instruction is not possible, there is still a great deal that can be done to get some of the positive effects of bilingual education. First, we can encourage the use of the first language at home. Parents often ask if they should use more English at home, thinking that this will speed up English language development in their children. Unless the parent speaks English extremely well, switching to English has the danger of

disturbing parent-child communication, which cripples both cognitive and emotional development. This view is confirmed by the research. Several studies show that when parents switch to exclusive use of the language of the country, school performance suffers (Cummins, 1981). We would much rather teach a child in kindergarten who does not speak English but who is well-adjusted and ready for school than a child who has picked up some English (from imperfect models) but who has not been communicating very well with his parents.

Helpers Another way we can make use of the first language without a full bilingual program is the judicious use of paraprofessionals and other helpers. If we have a helper who speaks the child's first language, we should use that helper to provide background knowledge and literacy in the child's first language. This help will usually be most effective in those subjects requiring the most use of abstract language: social studies and language arts.

Even when little help is available, it can be very valuable. Consider the case of a class with three Korean-speaking children who know little English. They are progressing fairly well in mathematics, because of their good background in their first language and because math does not require a high level of language ability in early grades. Assume we have a paraprofessional who speaks Korean and is available only one morning per week for one hour. My suggestion is that we inform the helper what will take place the following week in social studies. If it is the Civil War, the helper uses the one hour on Monday to provide the children with background information, in Korean, about the Civil War: who the combatants were, what the issues

were, etc. This will make the history lessons much more comprehensible.

Classmates who speak the limited-English-proficient child's first language can help and sometimes do spontaneously. The first principle to follow is to allow this to occur. It is not a good policy to forbid the use of the first language in school: "English only" rules are not good for English. Peer help should be done the same way we do it in bilingual education programs: as a source of background information and academic knowledge in the first language, not as on-line translation.

There is also nothing wrong with an occasional translation in class: Teachers need not waste time in frustrating pantomime and paraphrase when the meaning of the word resists normal efforts and the teacher or another student knows the word in the child's first language. The problem is when the occasional translation becomes concurrent translation and there is no need to listen to the second language input.

Intermediates

One of the advantages of including sustained silent reading in the school day is that it automatically handles a great deal of heterogeneity. When children select what they want to read themselves, because they do not want to be bored or confused (Smith, 1994), they will select books that are interesting and comprehensible. There is very good evidence, in addition, that children do not simply choose the easiest possible books: Free reading is not always easy reading (Krashen, in press).

We should encourage children to read in their first language, as well as in English, during sustained silent reading. This procedure will help a great deal. First, it builds literacy in the primary language, and as we have argued previously, literacy in the first language transfers to the second language. Second, reading is an excellent source of knowledge. Third, those who read a great deal in their first language probably will read a great deal in the second language.

When our limited-English-proficient students start doing free reading in English, they face a serious problem: the lack of books that are both comprehensible and interesting. Older students will find English books written for children their age too difficult and may find easier books less interesting. There is a solution: comic books. Many (but not all) comics are ideal for the second language acquirer.

There is nothing to fear from comic books. Research shows that children who read comics read as much, and sometimes more, than other children (Krashen, 1993; Ujiie and Krashen, in press). Comics provide a foundation that makes book reading much more comprehensible.

Light reading will not, in itself, produce the highest levels of competence. But it is an important bridge between basic conversational language and more advanced academic language. It is also very likely to be missing from the lives of language minority students, because of financial constraints and, in some cases, because of a view of light reading as unessential and "not serious." It is clear from the research, however, that light reading does not prevent heavier reading and that, in fact, it can act as a conduit to heavier reading.

Free reading is so powerful that it is likely that limited-English-proficient children in schools with a plentiful supply of interesting reading in the first language, plus a minimal bilingual program, will do better than children in a school with a "full" bilingual program but with few books in the first language. This is an easy way to get some of the advantages of bilingual education in cases where full programs are not possible.

What won't work

I have tried to illustrate some ways of helping limited-English proficient students. Let me now devote some time to discussing what won't help.

Create the need

Many people assume that we need to create situations in which children "need" to speak and communicate in English, assuming that language acquisition happens when we are forced to reproduce the language. This happens a great deal in "submersion" programs where no effort is made to make input comprehensible and no silent period is allowed.

But need alone is not enough—comprehensible input must be present. I cannot teach you to speak Russian simply by pointing a gun at your head and insisting you speak Russian. If, however, I speak to you in Russian in a way that is comprehensible, and make the message extremely interesting, you will acquire some Russian, whether you want to or not. Our focus should be on providing comprehensible input, not a highly stressed situation in which children do not understand what is going on.

> We should encourage children to read in their first language, as well as in English, during sustained silent reading.

Time pressure

Politicians commonly propose laws that proclaim that limited-English-proficient students be "at grade level" or transitioned out of bilingual programs in a certain amount of time, usually three years. This estimate is entirely arbitrary. How long a child takes is a matter of the literacy level he or she comes to school with, previous schooling, the print environment of the school, and the quality of the program.

Imposing time limits is based on the premise that LEP students will only acquire English if they are forced to, that they really don't want English. Actually, the opposite is true. LEP students typically have a strong drive for English. They don't need force and time constraints. They need a print-rich environment that provides them with comprehensible input.

Summary

We can utilize the principles underlying successful programs in dealing with cases in which full programs are not possible. Application of these principles in less than ideal situations will not make these situations ideal, but will improve life for both teachers and students. Unlike so many prescriptions given to teachers, the proposals presented here do not increase the teacher's burden. In fact, they reduce it.

Some proposals actually involve doing less:

- Not correcting oral or written errors made by language minority students;
- Not insisting on complete sentences when they speak in class;
- Encouraging free voluntary reading in both the first and second language.

There is no need to mark stacks of papers for grammatical errors, and teachers are given ten minutes (approximately) per day for pleasure reading!

References

Cummins, J. "The Role of Primary Language Development in Promoting Educational Success for Language Minority Students." *Schooling and Language Minority Students.* Sacramento, CA: California Department of Education, 1981. 3–49.

Goodman, K. *Language and Literacy.* London: Routledge and Kegan, 1982.

Krashen, S. "Is Free Reading Always Easy Reading?" *California English.* In Press.

____. *The Power of Reading.* Englewood, CO: Libraries Unlimited, 1993.

____. "Sheltered Subject Matter Teaching" *Cross Currents* 18 (1991): 183–189.

Krashen, S., and D. Biber *On Course: Bilingual Education's Success in California.* Ontario, CA: California Association for Bilingual Education, 1988.

Lagarretta, D. "The Effects of Program Models on Language Acquisition by Spanish Speaking Children." *TESOL Quarterly* 8 (1979): 521-576.

Smith, F. *Understanding Reading.* 5th edition. Hillsdale, NJ: Erbaum, 1994.

Ujiie, J., and S. Krashen. "Comic Book Reading, Reading Enjoyment, and Pleasure Reading Among Middle Class and Chapter I Middle School Students." *Reading Improvement.* In Press.

Dr. Stephen Krashen

POOR SPELLING?

Dr. Rebecca Bowers Sipe
ANCHORAGE SCHOOL DISTRICT,
DEPT. OF CURRICULUM AND INSTRUCTION
ANCHORAGE, ALASKA

Few curricular issues elicit as much concern or cause as much frustration as spelling. While spelling represents a small part of our curricular focus at the secondary level, students who repeatedly demonstrate poor spelling are subject to a host of criticisms.

In a print-intensive society such as ours, inability to spell may place an individual at risk: at risk of appearing uneducated or unconcerned; at risk of being labeled a poor writer and—potentially—at risk of becoming a poor thinker. Society makes few allowances for those who are poor spellers. As classroom teachers, it is imperative that we understand the dilemma confronting poor spellers and that we develop a repertoire of strategies to help struggling writers.

A Nation Obsessed

Despite Benjamin Franklin's suggestion that "an educated man should be able to spell any word at least six ways," today both schools and businesses maintain high expectations for spelling. With such high expectations, one might wonder how widespread spelling problems are in the United States. Dr. Thomas Kelly estimates that between 15 percent and 20 percent of the American population have significant difficulty with routine spelling. He calls these folks "closet bad spellers" (Kelly, 1992). Unfortunately, many poor spellers go through life assuming that their inability to spell condemns them to a lifetime of poor writing.

What does this mean for teachers of English? Certainly, writers need to be understood by readers. The presence of misspelled words in a final draft is a source of distraction and irritation. As teachers, we must help students gain control over spelling while we support them as emerging writers.

Spelling as a Writing Skill

Spelling is a writing skill and gains importance only when we write. Students deserve opportunities to explore the process of writing that works best for them. When students identify the process that works for them, they have a tool for life. Without this tool, each writing experience holds the potential for being a frustrating and mystifying ordeal.

While students need many opportunities to write for a variety of audiences and purposes in order to sense the differences in the requirements of each (Moffett, 1992), spelling gains importance in more formal modes. It is important for young writers to understand that final draft pieces represent them as writers. In such works correctness takes on significance.

Establishing Strategies

Providing poor spellers with appropriate resources is a must. Resources such as dictionaries, spelling checks, and personal spelling lists are valuable tools. Computers provide writers with ease in revision only dreamed of in years past; they allow poor spellers to concentrate on the total process of composing, not just on the spelling. In addition to resources, there are many instructional strategies available to help students who are poor spellers.

These include word study, use of mnemonic devices, and multi-modality approaches. **At the primary level, phonics is a valuable tool for spelling.** Unfortunately, English is an eclectic language; as a student's written vocabulary becomes more sophisticated, phonics becomes a less reliable tool (Gentry, 1981). Poor spellers must go beyond phonics to overcome spelling difficulties.

Studying word families helps students to identify connections and patterns in language. When the word *honor* is studied, students may discuss *honorable, honoring, honored,* and *honorary*.

> *As teachers, we must help students gain control over spelling while we support them as emerging writers.*

From one word base, five new words are added to the written repertoire. Ideally, walls are covered with word webs so that students are literally surrounded with language.

Mnemonic devices often help students with the spelling of difficult words. I looked up the word *accommodate* every time I wrote it for most of my life until someone suggested that I had to remember to accommodate the twins. That's all it took. Now I remember to double both consonants every time. As children, many of us invented phrases to help us with the spelling of words such as arithmetic and geography. Teachers who encourage students to create pictures or jingles for confusing words make spelling less threatening and more fun.

For some learners, strategies must rely on tactile strengths. I have observed children tracing words in the palm of one hand with a finger from the other. These students rely on the feel of a word instead of on the visual image.

Different strategies will work for different learners, thus making a wide variety of instructional strategies necessary for use in the classroom. Tests or tasks that separate learners from the resources they need measure little and may actually hamper the student's progress as a writer.

Classroom Practice

What can we do in the classroom to encourage poor spellers?

- **Recognize that spelling is a writing skill and must be addressed as a part of the writing process.** Adult writers frequently use invented spelling in early drafts to hold the place of a word; young writers may find this a helpful strategy to use in rough drafts. Young writers need to understand that good writing often takes multiple revisions and that spelling really matters in the final draft.
- **Encourage students to maintain and use personal word lists and to analyze their errors**. Students should identify words they routinely use but have difficulty spelling. These words should become part of the student's core words for study. Since

spelling is a developmental skill, not all students will be at the same place at the same time. It is important to recognize that spelling errors are not made at random. Helping students analyze the types of errors they make enables them to recognize their strengths and work on their weaknesses. Error analysis teaches proofreading skills by focusing attention on identification of words spelled correctly and analyzing the reasons why other words are misspelled (Shaughnessy, 1977). Much can be learned about the developmental level of students by studying the patterns of word invention they use. Students should be helped to understand that correct spelling speeds up the writing process. It enables the writer to get words down without having to worry about them. Weber and Henderson refer to this as automaticity, a critical level of development that frees the writer to concentrate on meaning instead of on spelling.

- **Concentrate on high-frequency words that are relevant to student writing.** Lists of such words are easily obtainable and form the basis of most current commercial programs. Dr. Earnest Horn developed one of the earliest lists around 1900. High-frequency words change little over time. As few as one thousand words constitute 90 percent of the words used in everyday writing; five thousand words account for 99.2 percent (Horn, 1926).
- **Make a distinction between vocabulary words and spelling words.** Vocabulary instruction is important, but vocabulary lists are an inappropriate substitute for spelling words. Students may be able to read and use a word long before they are able to spell it correctly. Spelling skill has nothing to do with intelligence. Being a poor speller does not condemn one to being a **poor** writer any more than being a good speller guarantees that one will be a **good** writer. Nonetheless, students must understand that people will make judgments about them based on their writing. Knowing our needs and using appropriate strategies and resources will help students improve their spelling. Fortunately, there are numerous strategies available to learners.

References

Gentry, R. J. "Learning to Spell Developmentally." *The Reading Teacher* January 1981: 378–381.

Horn, E. "A Basic Writing Vocabulary." *University of Iowa Monographs in Education, First Series* April 1926: 4.

Kelly, T.F. "Spelling: Tyranny of the Irrelevant." *The Effective School Report* August 1992: 3.

Moffett, J., and B.J. Wagner. *Student-Centered Language Arts, K-12.* Portsmouth, MA: Boynton/Cook, 1992.

Shaughnessy, M. P. *Spelling: Errors and Expectations.* New York: Oxford University Press, 1979.

Weber, W. R., and E. H. Henderson. "A Computer-Based Program of Word Study: Effects on Reading and Writing." *Reading Psychology* 10 (1989): 157–171.

Dr. Rebecca Bowers Sipe

THE INTEGRATION OF ASSESSMENT AND INSTRUCTION

What could more solidly assure that assessment reflects and measures instructional goals than to make it a part of instruction?

Dr. Roger Farr
INDIANA UNIVERSITY

Assessment of student reading and writing has been important to educators and the public at large since the beginning of this century. Educators have needed some way to determine whether they are meeting their goals and objectives, and the public has wanted some means of making schools accountable for the considerable investment needed to maintain them. The development of large, standardized, very-short-answer tests has been one answer to these demands. They report normed scores that can be compared to a large national sample of students. Similar tests have been developed in most states as criterion-referenced measures that require a student to respond to an arbitrated number of particular educational objectives.

However, at the same time, emerging theory has persuasively described how language abilities actually develop, leading to new emphasis on teaching and measuring language performance as a process—not with the short-answer response typical of most tests used as accountability measures.

Writing tests have been around since 1915 and are now used in at least 35 states. There is new emphasis on writing on college entrance exams. Across all grades reading, writing, and thinking are being integrated in classroom instruction as a combined process.

Teachers have not defensively closed their ears to the critics' and general public's concern for accountability in the schools, however. They have been the primary constructors of city and state criterion-referenced measures attempting to measure and reflect the curricula they also helped structure. Through these tests, they have sought to raise their students' performances and scores on standardized tests and have analyzed the results for their implications for teaching.

Meanwhile, teachers have continued to use a variety of daily classroom assessments to inform their teaching. These include observation and a host of other informal techniques and assessments accompanying the texts they use. Teachers have tended to react to the increased instructional time that testing consumes by making their classroom assessment a valid learning experience for the student and an instructional opportunity. What could more solidly assure that assessment

reflect and measure instructional goals than to make it a part of instruction?

This dynamic trend in school assessment goes far beyond merely using test results as indicators of what needs to be taught or retaught. It assesses student progress on an ongoing basis as youngsters use language to construct meaning by reading, writing, and thinking every day! The teacher assesses both by observing the process and by analyzing the product.

Often this effort involves having their students keep portfolios that include many types of writing. Much of this writing reacts to and applies information from different texts that the students have read. Frequently included, too, in student portfolios are one or more of a variety of journals. These portfolios are of two general types:

- The *working portfolio* contains all the drafts of a particular piece of writing and ideas for future writing and intentions for future reading. It has records (logs) of reading and writing and journal entries or brief descriptions, observations, or sketches that can be expanded or used in other ways. It is like an artist's studio full of works in progress and works finished.
- The *show portfolio* can be designed to serve numerous purposes: It can be a selection of pieces to demonstrate to parents and/or administrators how a student's language use is developing. It can introduce a student to a new teacher or school. It is like a show that an artist mounts from the works kept in his or her studio.

Teachers are learning that there is a host of ways that portfolios and publishing efforts can be analyzed to assess their students' progress as language users. Most of these projects involve rewriting and provide drafts leading to the more finished product, a set that reveals both language product and the process that leads to it.

Language-processing experiences can culminate in some sort of publishing to communicate with peers and other audiences. Classroom newsletters, creative writing magazines, and other publications develop audience awareness and a keen sense of purpose for writing. Frequently, these experiences involve the interaction of students reacting to and editing each other's work as on-going and interactive assessment. Since all this hinges on the belief that the best way to learn to read, write, and think is to do as much of it as possible, just noting the quantity and fluency of student production is highly revealing.

There are many other observations and analyses that teachers can make that systemize this kind of assessment to a degree that supports its use in reporting progress to parents and other educators. Almost all portfolios include logs of what students read. Teachers are now encouraged to set up opportunities for their students to keep such records. These include notes on their reaction to numerous texts, and writing/thinking efforts in which they apply the meaning they have constructed by reading. This basic language/thinking process often involves both synthesis of texts and critical reaction to them. More often than not, it promotes an appreciation of and critical reaction to literature as well as the use of good writing as a model and as the ignition to an original student effort.

Of course, good teachers have long used these kinds of activities. What is new, it appears, is the emphasis on integrating language/thinking processing and on assessing while instructing!

Publishers have come to a similar understanding about language use and assessment. They have developed interactive performance assessments that use text as prompts for student writing. These are usually presented with a prescribed writing task that identifies a believable audience and that is designed to seem highly valid to the student. Most often these prompts present several pieces of writing that may represent several genres. The student's thinking abilities are engaged by a task that

calls for synthesis of and critical reaction to the texts in order to recommend some solution to an authentic problem.

In order to help the teacher analyze the student's performance on these interactive performance assessments, they are accompanied by a rubric that describes several ranks (or scores) for student responses for each of several key factors. For example, a student's response may be ranked from 3 (high) to 1 (low) on its indication (a) of how well the student has comprehended the text or texts, (b) of how well the student has written the response, and (c) of how well comprehension and writing have been integrated to accomplish the assigned task. Each rank for each factor may be described according to several subfactors: in writing, for example, the response may be ranked after considering organization, diction, and mechanics.

A second guide to scoring is even more helpful than the rubric. These assessments are given to a large and varied sample of students at the grade level for which each is created. Then a team of teachers or other

> *Most importantly, portfolios and performance assessment develop the habit of self-assessing so that students go through life interested in personal development as readers, writers, and thinkers.*

specialists selects several sample or anchor papers to demonstrate each score of the ranking system for each factor. These are presented with analytical comments in a booklet with the rubric and are made available to teachers who use the assessment.

Some teachers and groups of teachers are developing these integrated performance assessments on their own. Some of them use published assessments as their models. Although the process is not easy, teachers who have done it remark about how much the experience teaches them about their instructional values and goals.

The ranked results of performance assessments can be reported to parents, administrators, critics of education, and the public at large. The model or anchor papers and rubrics stand as a clear and revealing explication of what the ranks mean if those who would rely on them make the effort to understand the data being used. Thus, integrated performance assessment can serve to inform accountability interests along with scores from standardized and criterion-referenced assessment.

Most importantly, portfolios and performance assessment develop the habit of self-assessing so that students go through life interested in personal development as readers, writers, and thinkers. This awareness can occur only when the student believes that the goals and objectives against which progress is being measured are real, interesting, and empowering.

Portfolios do that in the extreme if the student is allowed to maintain an important degree of control over the collection. Equally important to the success of the portfolio in developing self-assessment is regular student-teacher conferencing to discuss the portfolio contents, analyze progress, and set new goals.

Integrated performance assessments can achieve this if they are built around interesting prompts and if the tasks seem valid. The results of these student efforts, which usually include drafts that can be analyzed for process, can be studied and discussed by the student and the teacher in conference; and their appropriateness for student self-analysis is emphasized when a student is encouraged to include the set in his or her portfolio.

While legislators and educators together struggle with attempts to create assessments that can report on educational progress and accountability, teachers have been demonstrating dynamic new emphases in integrating language and thinking processes while turning assessment into highly effective instruction.

Dr. Roger Farr

The British Isles

LONDON

Dickens's House
British Museum
Gray's Inn
Old Bailey
St. Paul's
The Tower
Tower Bridge
Covent Garden
Piccadilly Circus
Trafalgar Square
Shakespeare Memorial
SOUTHWARK
Thames River
Westminster Bridge
Westminster Abbey
Big Ben and Parliament
Buckingham Palace

SHETLAND ISLANDS

ORKNEY ISLANDS

NORTH

Macduff
Cawdor
Culloden
Inverness
Loch Ness
Dee R.
Birnam Wood
Glamis

HEBRIDES

Iona

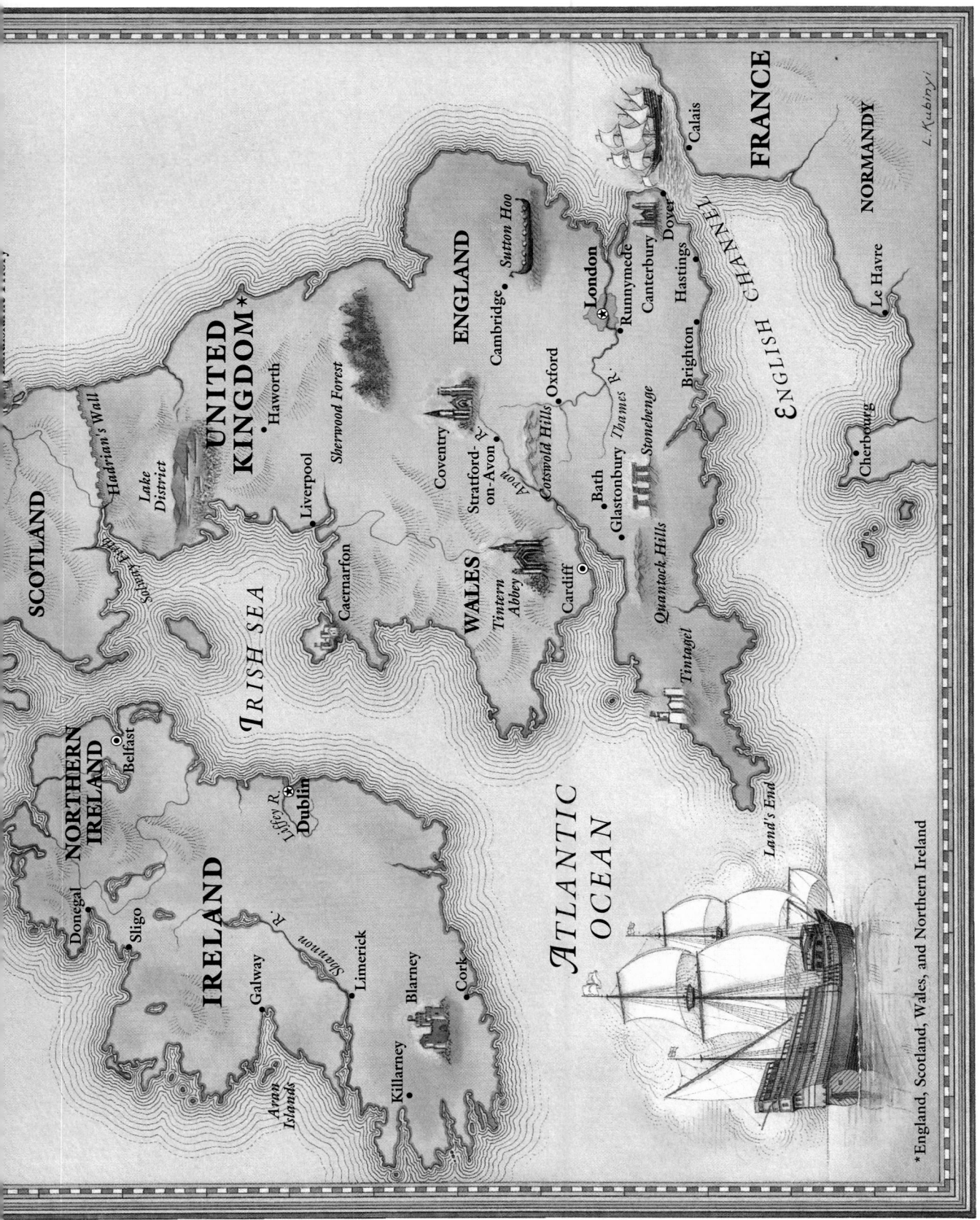

SCOTLAND

Hadrian's Wall

Lake District

Solway Firth

UNITED KINGDOM*

Haworth

Liverpool

Sherwood Forest

Caernarfon

IRISH SEA

WALES

Tintern Abbey

Cardiff

NORTHERN IRELAND

Belfast

Liffey R.

Dublin

IRELAND

Donegal

Sligo

Galway

Shannon R.

Limerick

Killarney

Blarney

Cork

Aran Islands

ENGLAND

Coventry

Stratford-on-Avon

Avon

Cotswold Hills

Oxford

Cambridge

Sutton Hoo

London

Runnymede

Canterbury

Dover

Hastings

Brighton

Bath

Glastonbury Thames R.

Stonehenge

Quantock Hills

Tintagel

Land's End

ATLANTIC OCEAN

ENGLISH CHANNEL

Calais

FRANCE

NORMANDY

Le Havre

Cherbourg

L. Kubinyi

*England, Scotland, Wales, and Northern Ireland

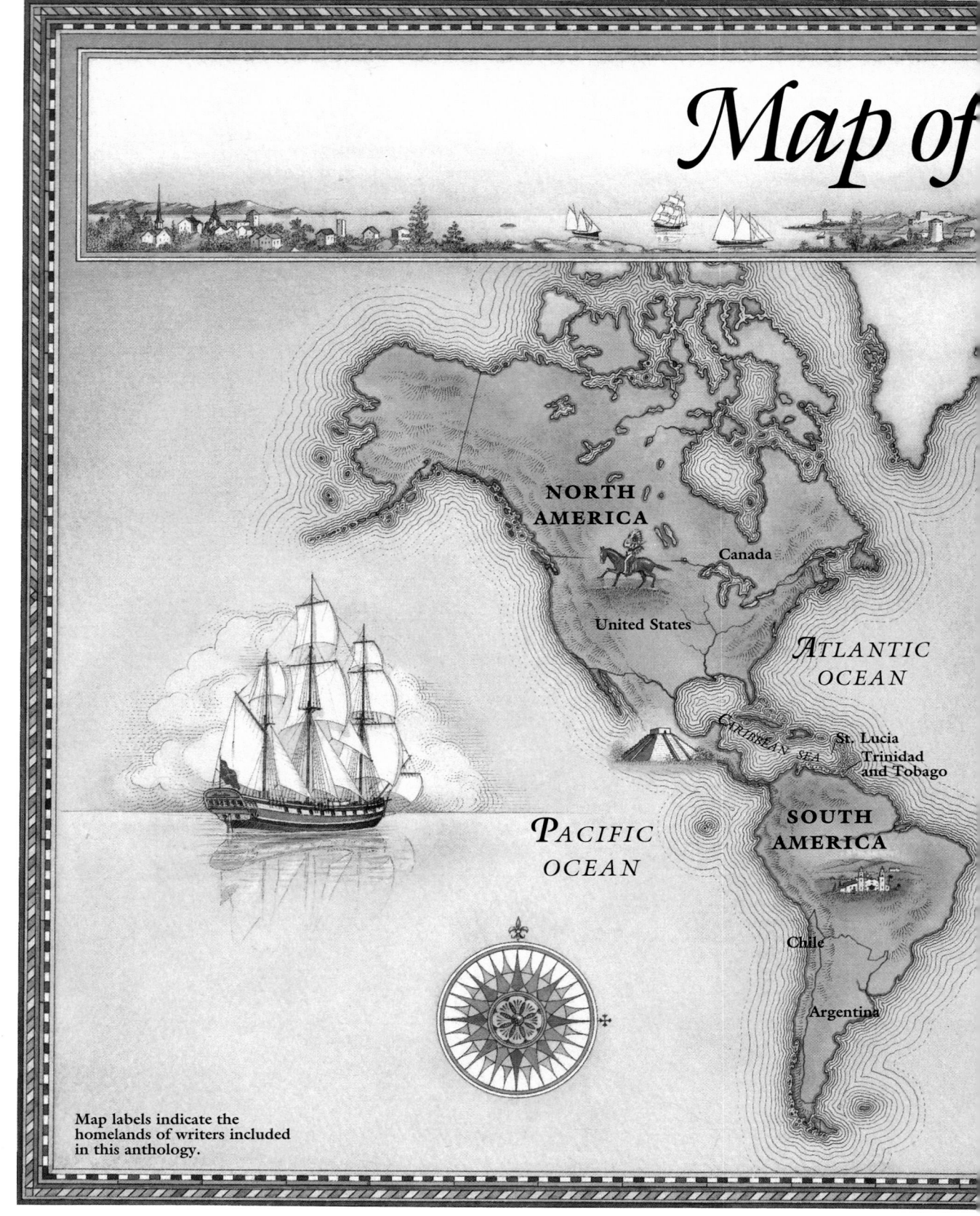

Map of

NORTH AMERICA

Canada

United States

ATLANTIC OCEAN

CARIBBEAN SEA

St. Lucia
Trinidad
and Tobago

SOUTH AMERICA

Chile

Argentina

PACIFIC OCEAN

Map labels indicate the
homelands of writers included
in this anthology.

the World

ARCTIC OCEAN

Russia

United
ngdom
land

Denmark

Germany **EUROPE**
Maginot Line Ukraine

Russia

ASIA

France
Croatia
Italy

Romania

China

Japan

MEDITERRANEAN SEA

*Ancient
Mesopotamia*
Iraq   Iran

Algeria

Egypt

Saudi
Arabia

India

PACIFIC
OCEAN

AFRICA

Liberia   Nigeria

Vietnam

INDIAN
OCEAN

TLANTIC
OCEAN

Zimbabwe

AUSTRALIA

South
Africa

New
Zealand

L. Kubinyi

45

The Anglo-Saxons
449–1066

The Saxon Infantry (in chain mail, visor helmets, and shields) holds off the Norman attack. Detail from the Bayeux Tapestry (11th century).

PROGRAM MANAGER

- **Summative Assessment** See Literary Period Test: The Anglo-Saxons, *Test Booklet,* pp. 12–14 for a test on an additional text from the same historical era.
- **Application** For practice of a reading strategy for this unit, see Becoming a Strategic Reader worksheet, *Teaching Resources A,* pp. 5–6.

- **Performance Assessment** Use Assessment 1 in the *Integrated Performance Assessment, Level G* to evaluate reading and writing skills covered in collections 1–2. For help with evaluation, see *Holistic Scoring Workshop* software.

Responding to the Quotation

 In a society dominated by aggression, what would you expect to find with regard to ethics, family life, role of women, art, literature, and livelihood? [Answers will vary.] After they have read the Unit Introduction, ask students to return to their initial notions to confirm or reject them. Have them use a graphic organizer like the one below.

Anglo-Saxon Life	Before-Reading Ideas	After-Reading Ideas
Ethics	[Do what it takes to win]	[Friendship, loyalty, bravery, generosity]
Family Life		

RESPONDING TO THE PHOTOGRAPH: EXPLORING THE SUBJECT

Built in three stages, Stonehenge is the best known of many such sites in the British Isles. Some archaeologists believe the ring of stones served as a gathering place and ceremonial center. Scholars have shown that the arrangement of the slabs indicated the timing of important astronomical events, but no one is certain who arranged the massive stones or why.

The Anglo-Saxons

by **David Adams Leeming**

Anglo-Saxon England was born of warfare, remained forever a military society, and came to its end in battle.

—*J. R. Lander*

Aerial view of Stonehenge (c. 1800–1400 B.C.), located near Salisbury, England.

2 THE ANGLO-SAXONS

Page from the Book of Kells (8th century).

I solated from the European continent, rain-drenched and often fogged in, but also green and dotted with thatched cottages, quaint stone churches, and mysterious stone ruins, the island of Great Britain seems made for elves, legends, and poets. Yet if this land of mystery, beauty, and melancholy weather has produced Stonehenge, Robin Hood, and Shakespeare, it has also produced the theory of gravity, the Industrial Revolution, radar, penicillin, and the Beatles. We tend to associate the British with their monarchy and their former empire. But we should also remember that while most of the world suffered under various forms of tyranny, the English from the time of the Magna Carta (1215) were gradually creating a political system "by and for the people" that remains today a source of envy and inspiration for many nations. Although Americans rebelled against British rule in 1776, America would not be what it is today without the legacy of English common law—with its emphasis on personal rights and freedom. Nor would America be what it is today without the English parliamentary government, English literature, and the English language.

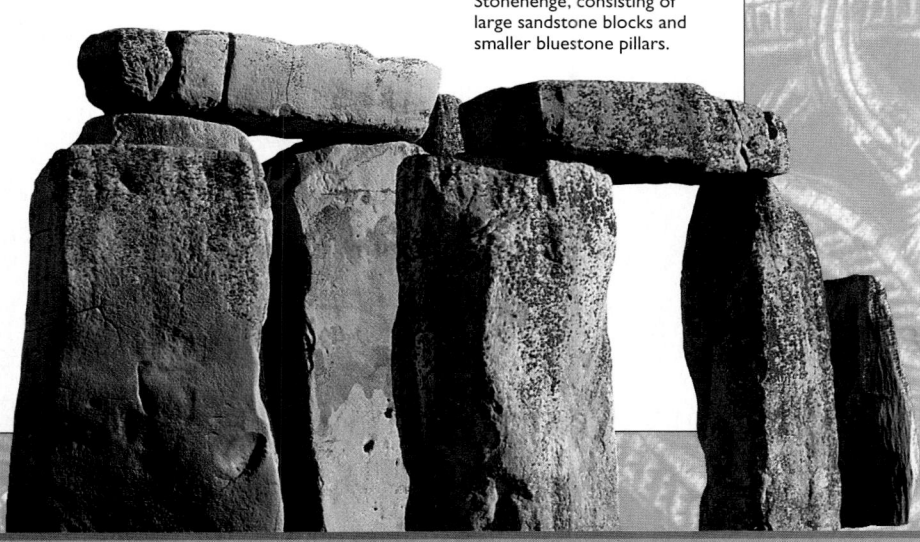

Stonehenge, consisting of large sandstone blocks and smaller bluestone pillars.

A. Humanities Connection

Henry II, believing that justice should be the same for all, set up a system of districts, appointed district judges, and expanded jury functions. However, his son, King John, ignored his father's charter by jailing people without charges or trials and by levying excessive taxes. In response, in 1215, barons and knights met at Runnymede to sign the Magna Carta, or Great Charter. This document, claiming certain liberties for the English aristocracy, further restricted the king with its implication that the king, along with his people, must submit to the rule of law. Later, King Edward I, John's grandson, called the first Parliament—the Great Parliament of 1295—which included representatives from all classes of people from barons to lower clergy. This Parliament is the forerunner of representative bodies like the present U.S. Congress.

PROGRAM MANAGER

- **Planning Instruction** See Teaching Notes, *Teaching Resources A,* p. 1, for additional teaching options about the Anglo-Saxons.
- **Assessment** For assessment of the literary and historical events mentioned in the historical introduction, see Literary Period Introduction Test, *Test Booklet,* pp. 1–2.

Elements of Literature:

Videodisc Use the following bar codes below to locate information about Anglo-Saxon life. For more information, see the Videodisc *Teacher's Manual.*

Videodisc Side A

Begin Play
English Track

Begin Play
Spanish Track

PORTFOLIO ASSESSMENT

Parent/Guardian Involvement For forms that will help a parent or guardian review and respond to a student's portfolio, see *Portfolio Management System,* pp. 62–63.

Time Line

• A.D. 1–399

London grew from two ancient cities, the City of London and the City of Westminster. The Romans established the City of London as a trading center; a thousand years later the City of Westminster, a few miles away, served as the residential area for London's elite around the eleventh century. Present-day London encompasses about 610 square miles along the River Thames.

• 500–599

Shinto, which involves worship of the gods found in nature and of one's ancestors, is the native religion of Japan; however, many who practice Shinto are open to other philosophies as well. In the fifth century, the Japanese began importing technology and ideas, including Confucianism and later Buddhism, which came from China and Korea. Today, approximately 75 percent of the Japanese practice Buddhism, a religion that encourages virtue and wisdom and deemphasizes the importance of material possessions.

The Anglo-Saxons, 449–1066

• Detail from the Book of Kells (8th century). The Board of Trinity College, Dublin. Photograph by The Green Studio Ltd, Dublin.

LITERARY EVENTS

Roman poet Virgil born, 70 B.C.

Alexandria is center of Greek learning; library begun under Ptolemy, 307 B.C.

Throughout Europe, scrolls begin to be replaced by vellum books, c. 360

Roman poet Ovid writes *Metamorphoses*, c. 5

• King Arthur in battle. From a French manuscript.

In China, books printed using carved wooden blocks and ink, 500s

307–1 B.C.	A.D. 1–399	400–499	500–599

CULTURAL/HISTORICAL EVENTS

Celts called "Brythons" live in Britain, 300s B.C.

Julius Caesar invades Britain, 55 B.C.

Cleopatra VII becomes last queen of Egypt, 51 B.C.

Londinium (present-day London) founded by Romans as a supply port, c. 50

Queen Boadicea leads her eastern British tribe in an uprising against the Romans, 61

Christianity proclaimed lawful religion in the Roman Empire, c. 313

• Roman helmet. © British Museum, London.

Roman legions withdraw from Britain, 409

Patrick brings Christianity to Ireland, 432

Angles, Saxons, and Jutes invade Britain, c. 449

Roman Empire falls to Germanic tribes, 476

Semilegendary King Arthur rules Celtic tribe, c. 516

Death of King Arthur at Battle of Camlann, 537

• Dome of the Rock, holy Muslim shrine in Jerusalem.

Widespread plague reaches Britain from Europe, 547

Buddhism introduced to Japan, 552

Saint Augustine converts Anglo-Saxon King Ethelbert and establishes monastery at Canterbury, 597

• Chinese sculpture of a seated Buddha (c. 650) from the T'ang dynasty. The Metropolitan Museum of Art, Rogers Fund, 1919. (19.186). Photograph by Lynton Gardiner.

4 THE ANGLO-SAXONS

USING THE TIME LINE

Have students use an encyclopedia or other reference source to place the following major events in science and the arts on the time line.

- Euclid publishes *The Elements of Geometry*. [c. 300 B.C.]
- Li Po writes poetry during China's "golden age of literature." [c. A.D. 701–762]
- Chang Heng builds the world's first seismograph. [A.D. 132]
- Lady Murasaki writes the world's first significant novel, *The Tale of Genji*. [c. A.D. 970–1050]
- The Greeks build the Pantheon, one of architecture's most influential buildings. [c. A.D. 118–125]

Hymns produced by Caedmon, the earliest English Christian poet, c. 670

At Alexandria, Arabs discover the famous library with 300,000 papyrus scrolls, 640

Lyric poetry of the T'ang period promotes everyday use of Chinese language, 600s

Monks begin the Book of Kells, an illuminated manuscript of Latin Gospels, 760

Compilation of *Manyoshu* ("Collection of Ten Thousand Leaves"), Japanese anthology of about 4,500 poems, c. 759

The Venerable Bede, an English cleric, writes the *Ecclesiastical History of the English People*, 730

Beowulf first recorded, c. 700

• Crown of the Holy Roman Empire (10th century, with later additions).

Anglo-Saxon Chronicle begun, 891

Composition of the Poetic Edda, a famous cycle of Norse mythological poems, c. 850

Japanese court attendant Sei Shōnogan writes diary, *The Pillow Book*, c. 1000

In Japan, Lady Murasaki Shikibu writes the world's first novel, *The Tale of Genji*, c. 1000

The Exeter Book, a collection of English poetry, first copied, c. 975

Beginnings of the Arabian tales, *The Thousand and One Nights*, 900

600–699	700–799	800–899	900–1066

Paulinus is first Roman missionary to arrive in northern England, 601

Golden Age of T'ang dynasty begins in China, 618

Mohammed (b. 570), founder of Islam, begins to dictate the *Koran*, c. 625

Egyptian caliphs introduce the first organized news and postal service, 650

Synod of Whitby unites British Christian Church with Roman Church, 664

Moors invade Spain, 711

Pueblo period begins in southwestern North America, c. 750

Vikings invade Britain, beginning a century of invasions, 793

• Danes attacking an East Anglian town.

In France, Charlemagne crowned Emperor of the West by Pope Leo III, 800

Decline of great Mayan civilization in Central America, c. 800

Incas build fortress-city of Machu Picchu in Peru, c. 800

Algebra devised in Persia, c. 810

School of Astronomy founded at Baghdad, 813

Alfred the Great (849–899) becomes king of England, 871; he forces the Danes from Wessex, 878

Kingdom of Ghana in Africa flourishes, 900s

Norsemen led by Leif Ericson explore northeastern coast of North America (now Nova Scotia), 1000

Normans defeat Saxons; William the Conqueror becomes English king, 1066

• Machu Picchu, Perú, lost city of the Incas.

• Mayan figure holding tortillas.

THE ANGLO-SAXONS 5

• **700–799**
The Moors of northwestern Africa (called the Mauri by the Romans) were a Berber people, many of whom spoke Arabic, in addition to their own language, and became Muslims. Converted to Islam, they conquered Spain with the Arabs in the 700s and ruled there during the Middle Ages, establishing a Moorish civilization. After losing most of their Spanish holdings by the 1200s, the Moors settled primarily in North Africa. Today the term *Moor* refers to all Arabic-speaking Muslims of northwestern Africa or to Muslims of Spanish, Jewish, or Turkish heritage who live in North Africa.

• **900–1066**
An important West African trading center from the fourth through the eleventh centuries A.D., Ghana drew camel caravans from the copper mines in the Sahara and dried produce from North Africa, products sold or traded for slaves, gold, and ivory from areas farther south. Goods from Arabia and Europe were also exchanged for Ghanaian leather items and jewelry.

A. Exploring the Culture

From about 700 B.C., the Celts dominated most of what is now western and central Europe. Skilled craftsmen, they introduced the use of iron to the rest of Europe. They also had a highly developed religion, mythology, and legal system that specified individual rights.

The language of the Celts was dominant in Britain until around the fifth century A.D. Welsh and Gaelic are forms of the Celtic language that may still be heard in Wales, Scotland, and Ireland today.

B. Humanities Connection

Descendants of the Celts still live in Cornwall, the highlands of Scotland, Ireland, Wales, and Brittany. The Welsh refer to themselves as *cymry,* meaning "fellow-countrymen," emphasizing their role as true native Britons. Cymraeg, the language of Wales, shares origins with languages spoken even now from the Hebrides, islands in the Atlantic west of Scotland, to southern Brittany, a region in northwest France.

For centuries the Cambrian mountains of central Wales provided safety for the Britons from the victorious Anglo-Saxons, enabling the Welsh to preserve many Celtic customs along with the language.

C. Exploring the Culture

Using radiocarbon dating methods on charcoal taken from pits within the circle of stones, historians have postulated that Stonehenge was in use around 1848 B.C. The huge stones are a type found only in western Wales, three hundred miles away, and some weigh more than eighty tons; how the stones were moved to the present location and arranged in their original positions is a great mystery.

This relatively small island of Great Britain has been invaded and settled many times: first by ancient people we call the Iberians, then by the Celts (kelts), by the Romans, by the Angles and Saxons, by the Vikings, and by the Normans. Whatever we think of as "English" today owes something to each of these invaders.

A small and isolated country, England is the origin of a legal and political system that many other countries, including America, have since imitated. English traditions and language owe something to each of the island's invaders.

The Celtic Heroes and Heroines: A Magical World

When Greek travelers visited what is now Great Britain in the fourth century B.C., they found an island settled by tall blond warriors who called themselves Celts. Among these island Celts was a group called Brythons (or Britons), who left their permanent stamp in one of the names eventually adopted by the land they settled.

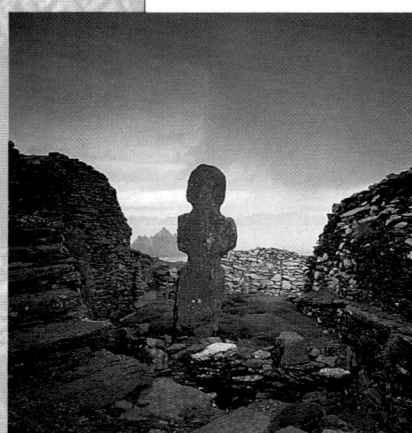

A monk's cell (7th or 8th century) on Skellig Michael, off the coast of Kerry, Ireland.

The religion of the Celts seems to have been a form of **animism,** from the Latin word for "spirit." The Celts saw spirits everywhere—in rivers, trees, stones, ponds, fire, and thunder. These spirits or gods controlled all aspects of existence, and they had to be constantly satisfied. Priests called Druids acted as intermediaries between the gods and the people. Sometimes ritual dances were called for, sometimes even human sacrifice. Some think that Stonehenge—that array of huge stones on Salisbury Plain in Wiltshire—was used by the Druids for religious rites having to do with the lunar and solar cycles.

The mythology of the Celts has influenced English and Irish writers to this day. Sir Thomas Malory in the fifteenth century, having time on his hands in jail, gathered together the Celtic legends about a warrior named Arthur. He mixed these stories generously with chivalric legends from the Continent and produced *Le Morte Darthur,* about the king who ultimately became the very embodiment of English values.

In the twentieth century, William Butler Yeats (page 978) used the Celtic myths in his poetry and plays in an attempt to make the Irish aware of their lost heroic past.

The Celtic stories are very different from the Anglo-Saxon tales that came later (see page 21), although it is the Anglo-Saxon myths that we tend to study in school. Unlike the male-dominated Anglo-Saxon stories, the

All the Britons dye their bodies with woad, which produces a blue color, and this gives them a more terrifying appearance in battle. They wear their hair long, and shave the whole of their bodies except the head and the upper lip.

—Julius Caesar

STRATEGIES FOR INCLUSION

English Language Development
To help students understand the idioms used in the selection, take time to point them out and to explain this nonliteral use of language. Here are some examples from the selection:

- (p. 6) ". . . who *left their permanent stamp* in one of the names. . . ." [influenced]

- (p. 7) ". . . Christianity . . . gradually *took hold.* . . ." [became part of what already existed]
- (p. 10) "Warfare was the *order of the day.*" [typical, expected at a specific time]

Learners Having Difficulty To help students discover the main ideas of this introduction, point out the usefulness of reading the quotations, the subtitles (main ideas), and the spotlighted summaries of each section. Then, have students list facts supporting each main idea. Finally, lead a discussion of the main ideas and the supporting facts, allowing students to add to their notes facts they may have missed originally.

Celtic legends are full of strong women, like the tall and fierce and very beautiful Queen Maeve of Connacht (kân′ôt) in Ireland. Maeve once led her troops in an epic battle over the ownership of a fabulous white herd bull whose back was so broad fifty children could play upon it. Celtic stories, unlike the later, brooding Anglo-Saxon stories, leap into the sunlight (no matter how much blood is spilled). Full of fantastic animals, passionate love affairs, and fabulous adventures, the Celtic myths take you to enchanted lands where magic and the imagination rule.

The first British settlers were the Celts, a people whose daily lives were influenced by their magical religion. Their beliefs survive in Celtic mythology, which has influenced generations of later writers.

The Romans: The Great Administrators

Beginning with an invasion led by Julius Caesar in 55 B.C. and culminating in one organized by the emperor Claudius about a hundred years later, the Britons were finally conquered by the legions of Rome. Using the administrative genius that enabled them to hold dominion over much of the known world, the Romans provided the armies and organization that prevented further serious invasions of Britain for several hundred years. They built a network of roads (some still used today) and a great defensive wall seventy-three miles long. During Roman rule, Christianity, which would later become a unifying force, gradually took hold under the leadership of European missionaries. The old Celtic religion began to vanish.

Ⓓ

Boadicea, queen of a Briton tribe, was flogged by the Romans after they had plundered her dead husband's property. She led the Britons to a fierce retaliation.

Boadicea's tribe, at once the most powerful and hitherto the most submissive, was moved to frenzy against the Roman invaders. They flew to arms. Boadicea found herself at the head of a numerous army, and nearly all the Britons within reach rallied to her standard. There followed an up-rush of hatred from the abyss, which is a measure of the cruelty of the conquest. It was a scream of rage against invincible oppression. . . . Her monument on the Thames Embankment opposite Big Ben reminds us of the harsh cry of liberty or death which has echoed down the ages.

—Winston S. Churchill

D. Expansion
At the height of the Roman Empire, the Roman historian Tacitus (c. A.D. 56–c.120) described the Germanic tribes of the north, including the Angles, as having positive attributes: love of freedom, chaste women, lack of public extravagance.

Hadrian's Wall, the seventy-three-mile defensive barrier built by the emperor Hadrian in about A.D. 122.

INTEGRATING THE LANGUAGE ARTS

Vocabulary To make students more aware of the dependence of modern English on its Anglo-Saxon heritage, have them look up everyday words in *The Oxford English Dictionary* or another dictionary that shows the origin of words. Provide students with a list of common words. Have them look up each word to determine which words are of Anglo-Saxon origin; invite them to list these words on kraft paper or poster board with illustrations to share with the class.

Strategic Reading To organize information about the influences invaders had on England, help the class make a cluster diagram on the chalkboard, showing the different invasions and two or three strong influences brought by each set of invaders. To transfer this activity to an overhead projector, use Transparency 3: Cluster Diagram, available in the Elements of Literature Transparency Package.

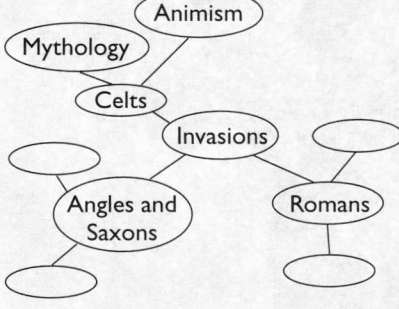

T7

A. Humanities Connection

Students may read more about the heroic Celtic leader King Arthur in Sir Thomas Malory's treatment of the King Arthur legend in *Le Morte Darthur* (c. 1469), in Tennyson's *Idylls of the King* (1859–1885), or in T. H. White's *The Once and Future King* (1958), upon which the musical *Camelot* is based.

B. Expansion

King Alfred may be one king who truly deserves the appellation "the great." Not only did he help save Wessex and other kingdoms in England from the Danes, but he also helped create a cohesive English society from small, fractious kingdoms; restored cities destroyed during the invasions; and revived an interest in learning and in the English language.

A picture stone (8th century) from Gotland showing a Viking ship under sail.
Statens Historiska Museer, Stockholm.

If the Romans had stayed, Londoners today might speak Italian. But the Romans had troubles at home. By A.D. 409, they had evacuated their troops from Britain, leaving roads, walls, villas, and great public baths, but no central government. Without Roman control, Britain was a country of separate clans. The result was weakness, which made the island ripe for a series of successful invasions by non-Christian peoples from the Germanic regions of Continental Europe.

Roman conquerors remained in Britain for more than four hundred years. They built roads and the walls that fended off attacks on Britain for several centuries. When the Romans finished withdrawing in A.D. 409, Britain was left without a centralized government—again susceptible to other invaders.

The Anglo-Saxons Sweep Ashore

This time the attack came from the north. In the middle of the fifth century, the invaders, Angles and Saxons from Germany and Jutes from Denmark, crossed the North Sea. They drove out the old Britons before them and eventually settled the greater part of Britain. The language of the Anglo-Saxons became the dominant language in the land which was to take a new name—Engla land, or England—from the Angles.

But the latest newcomers did not have an easy time of it. The Celts put up a strong resistance before they retreated into Wales in the far west of the country. There, traces of their culture, especially their language, can still be found. One of the heroic Celtic leaders was a Welsh chieftain called Arthur, who developed in legend as Britain's "once and future king."

At first, Anglo-Saxon England was no more politically unified than Celtic Britain had been. The country was divided into several independent principalities, each with its own "king." It was not until King Alfred of Wessex (r. 871–899), also known as Alfred the Great, led the Anglo-Saxons against the invading Danes that England became in any true sense a nation. The Danes were one of the fierce Viking peoples (pirates) who crossed the cold North Sea in their dragon-prowed boats in the eighth and ninth centuries. Plundering and destroying everything in their path, the Danes eventually took over and settled in parts of northeast and central England.

Gold and enamel jewel (9th century) thought to have belonged to King Alfred.
Ashmolean Museum, Oxford.

8 THE ANGLO-SAXONS

It is possible that even King Alfred would have failed to unify the Anglo-Saxons had it not been for the gradual reemergence of Christianity in Britain. Irish and Continental missionaries converted the Anglo-Saxon kings, whose subjects converted also. Christianity provided a common faith and common system of morality and right conduct; it also linked England to Europe. Under Christianity and Alfred, Anglo-Saxons fought to protect their people, their culture, and their church from the ravages of the Danes. Alfred's reign began the shaky dominance of Wessex kings in southern England. Alfred's descendants—Ethelfleda, a brilliant military leader and strategist, and her brother Edward—carried on his battle against the Danes.

The battle continued until both the Anglo-Saxons and the Danes were defeated in 1066 by William, Duke of Normandy, and his invading force of Normans from northwestern France.

The reemergence of Christianity and the role of Alfred the Great combined to unify Anglo-Saxon England. Alfred and his descendants fought the Danish invaders until the Norman Conquest in 1066.

What does "Anglo-Saxon England" mean?

Here are some key features of this age of warriors:

- Anglo-Saxon society developed from kinship groups led by a strong chief.
- The people also farmed, maintained local governments, and created fine crafts, especially metalwork.
- Christianity eventually replaced the old warrior religion, linking England to Continental Europe.
- Monasteries brought learning and literacy and preserved works from the older oral tradition.
- English—not just the Church's Latin—gained respect as a written language.

The coronation of King Harold, from the Bayeux Tapestry (11th century).

Musée de la Tapisserie, Bayeux

THE ANGLO-SAXONS **9**

C. Humanities Connection

In the preface to the *Consolation of Philosophy,* Alfred writes about his authority: "To be brief, I may say that it has always been my wish to live honorably, and after my death to leave to those who come after me my memory in good works." Is Alfred's philosophy of leadership applicable to our lives today? Why? [Answers will vary. Students could cite examples of current or recent political leaders whose leadership does or does not reflect wisdom and honor.]

D. Exploring the Culture

The gradual emergence of Christianity among the Anglo-Saxons was to a great extent due to the work of Irish and Continental missionaries, the most important of whom was probably St. Augustine (the second of that name), who converted King Ethelbert of Kent in A.D. 597, founded the Cathedral of Canterbury, and became the first archbishop of Canterbury, or leader of the Church of England. His mission, however, was not immediately or permanently successful, since the Anglo-Saxon religion persisted.

RESPONDING TO THE ART: ABOUT THE ARTWORK

Seventy scenes with Latin narrative illustrate the Norman Conquest of England on the Bayeux Tapestry. Although a tapestry usually involves the weaving of thread, this "tapestry" is actually an embroidered band of linen, 231 feet long, and $19\frac{1}{2}$ inches wide. Of particular value are the details of battle tactics and equipment.

CROSSING THE CURRICULUM

Geography To give students a clear picture of the geography pertinent to this period, provide on a bulletin board a large outline map of Europe. As students read, have them add names and events to the map as well as labeled arrows showing the invasions. Or if it is available, students may use an atlas program or CD-ROM to locate key areas in Great Britain. Ask students to import these maps to a paintbrush program. Using the draw feature, they can illustrate the raids on England.

TECHNOLOGY

Art Invite students to design an elaborate version of a capital letter on kraft paper or poster board, using colorful pens and glitter or gold dusting powder to imitate the fancy lettering monks used to create illuminated manuscripts.

History Divide the class into groups of three or four students, and have the groups research the Nordic myths that contributed to the naming of the calendar days. Then, ask students to design a special calendar that shows the connection between the myths and the days of the week—for example, why Thursday is named after Thor.

A. Exploring the Culture

An agricultural, seminomadic people, Anglo-Saxons had a two-class society: the earls, who ruled and who were related to the founder of the tribe; and the churls, bondservants whose ancestors had been captured by the tribe. Although they admired their warriors, the Anglo-Saxons insisted on a social organization based on more than courage, a society with strict laws and a sense of obligation to others. An absolute ruler and mighty warrior, the Anglo-Saxon king nevertheless consulted with the *witan* ("wise men"), an assembly of respected earls.

The churls provided the hard labor for this agricultural society and were bound to the earls' service unless they could earn possessions and special royal favor to become freemen (independent landholders). A woman received honor and power only as a queen, as the wife of a powerful earl, or as a churchwoman. Women's duties were chiefly domestic.

WOMEN IN ANGLO-SAXON CULTURE

Anglo-Saxon culture, with its emphasis on warfare, sounds as if it would be an inhospitable place for women. But women had rights in this society that were sharply curtailed after the Norman Conquest in 1066.

Evidence from wills first used during the later Anglo-Saxon period shows that women inherited and held property. Even when married, women still retained control over their own property. In fact, a prospective husband had to offer a woman a substantial gift (called the *morgengifu,* the "morning-gift") of money and land. The woman (not her family or her husband) had personal control over this gift; she could give it away, sell it, or bequeath it as she chose.

Christianity also offered opportunities for women. Women joined religious communities, and some women became powerful abbesses. These abbesses, usually women from noble families, were in charge of large double houses that included both a monastery and a nunnery. Hild (614–680), the abbess of Whitby (in present-day Yorkshire), was one of the most famous of these women. Hild accumulated an immense library and turned Whitby into a center of learning. Vikings sacked Whitby Abbey in the ninth century, but its ruins still stand today, high atop cliffs overlooking the wild, gray North Sea.

Silver figurine (c. 9th–11th century) of Viking woman, from Grödinge, Söndermanland, Sweden. Statens Historiska Museer, Stockholm.

Anglo-Saxon Life: The Warm Hall, the Cold World

As the Sutton Hoo ship treasures of Suffolk show, the Anglo-Saxons were not barbarians, though they are frequently depicted that way. However, they did not lead luxurious lives either, or lives dominated by learning or the arts. Warfare was the order of the day. As *Beowulf* shows, law and order, at least in the early days, was the responsibility of the leader in any given group, whether family, clan, tribe, or kingdom. Fame and success, even survival, were gained only through loyalty to the

A

Silver figurine (c. 9th–11th century) of Viking woman, from Klinta, Öland, Sweden. Statens Historiska Museer, Stockholm.

Rules for Society Ask students to list values they see as most important if they were to develop a workable society. Then, divide the class into groups of four, grouping those who rarely work together. Assign each group to write guidelines for their ideal

society. As a class, compare the guidelines the groups produce with those of Anglo-Saxon society, perhaps by charting the comparisons on an overhead transparency or the chalkboard in the following format. Discuss how various guidelines might affect the quality of life in both Anglo-Saxon society and in the societies students envision.

IDEAL SOCIETY	ANGLO-SAXON SOCIETY
[Individuals vote for leaders]	[Individuals governed by lords]
[All children receive education]	[Few people are literate]

leader, especially during war, and success was measured in gifts from the leader. Beowulf, for instance, makes his name and gains riches by defeating the monsters who try to destroy King Hrothgar.

This pattern of loyal dependency was basic to Anglo-Saxon life. Such loyalty grew out of a need to protect the group from the terrors of an enemy-infested wilderness—a wilderness that became particularly frightening during the long, bone-chilling nights of winter. In most of England, the Anglo-Saxons tended to live close to their animals in single-family homesteads, wooden buildings that surrounded a communal court or a warm, fire-lit chieftain's hall. This cluster of buildings was protected by a wooden stockade fence. The arrangement contributed to a sense of security and to the close relationship between leader and followers. It also encouraged the Anglo-Saxon tendency toward community discussion and rule by consensus.

Anglo-Saxon life was dominated by the need to protect the clan and home against enemies. All groups, from family to kingdom, were organized around a leader who commanded absolute loyalty.

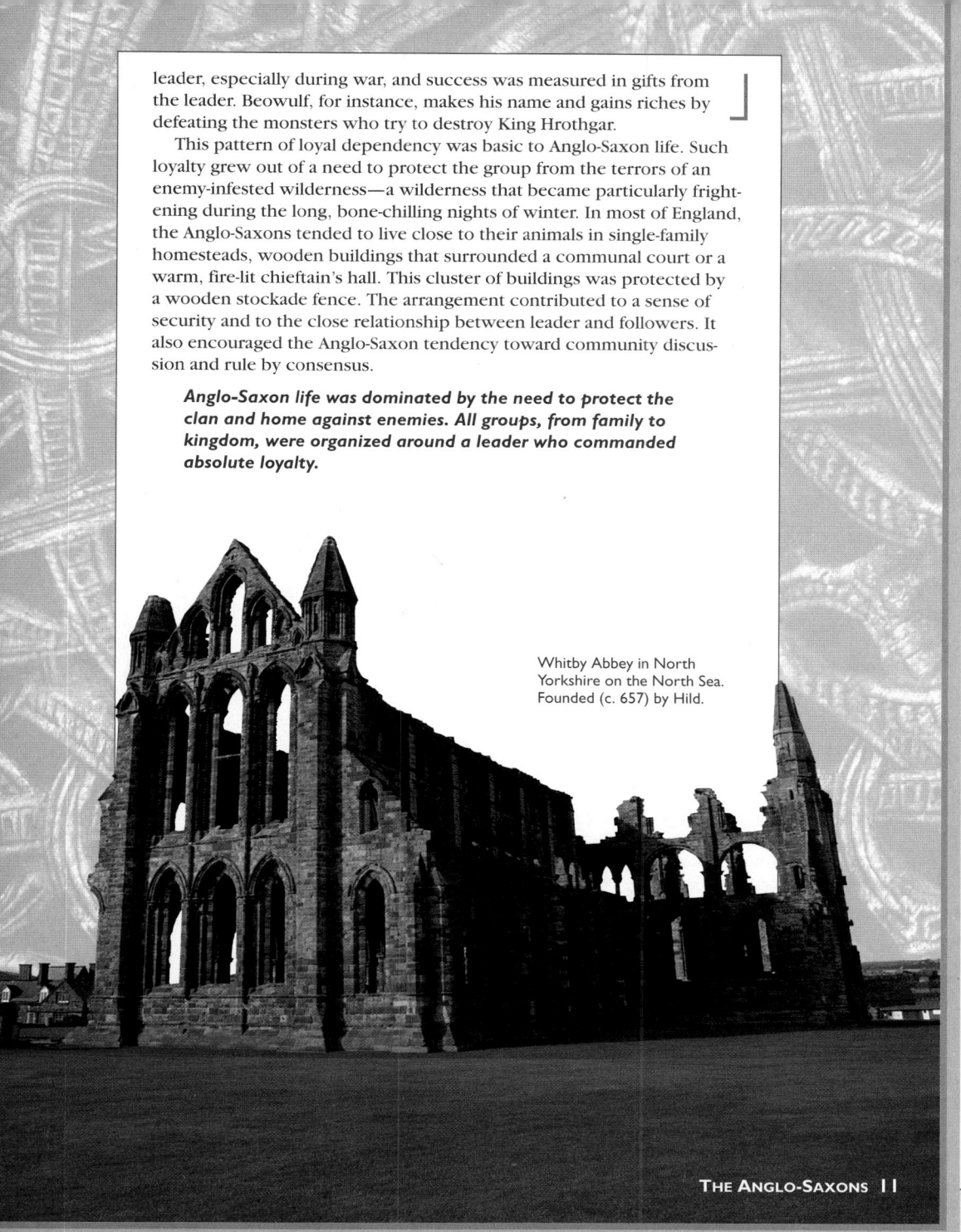

Whitby Abbey in North Yorkshire on the North Sea. Founded (c. 657) by Hild.

PROFESSIONAL NOTES

Cultural Diversity To help students draw a parallel to the way England was influenced by other cultures, discuss how the United States has been influenced by earlier cultures, including legal, governmental, social, and cultural contributions. Discussion might include the influence of the Magna Carta on American democracy, the effect of the early settlers' strong religious background on the development of the country, the effects of enslaving people from Africa, and so on. The students might also notice the multiple origins of holidays celebrated here and of diverse foods now available in the United States. ☞

A. Exploring the Culture

The word *wyrd* was used by the Anglo-Saxons to represent one's fate in life. Since the early Anglo-Saxons did not believe strongly in an afterlife, one lived on or gained immortality through personal fame attained through heroic action.

B. Critical Reading: Making Connections

? Why might Nazi Germany have chosen the swastika for its symbol before World War II? [Possible answer: The swastika denoted thunder and lightning, symbols of power.]

C. Reader's Response: First Thoughts

? What do you associate with the word *dragon*? [Sample responses: It reminds me of fairy tales of damsels in distress or the villainous dragon Smaug in J.R.R. Tolkien's *The Hobbit*.] Explain that since the beginning of recorded history, humans have had strong emotional reactions to serpents. The power of serpents to cause harm could account for the fear and respect they evoke, or it could be that, in a sense, snakes inhabit two worlds: They can live on the earth's surface or below it. In fifteenth-century Europe, a serpent eating its tail symbolized the cyclical, positive nature of life. In China, dragons are benevolent tomb guardians. However, in most Western myths, such as the myth of St. George, the dragon symbolizes evil.

A pendant depicting Thor's hammer.

National Museum, Reykjavik.

The Anglo-Saxon Religion: Gods for Warriors

A Despite the influence of Christianity, the old Anglo-Saxon religion with its warrior gods persisted. A dark, fatalistic religion, it had come with the Anglo-Saxons from Germany and had much in common with what we think of as Norse or Scandinavian mythology.

One of the most important Norse gods was Odin, the god of death, poetry, and magic. The Anglo-Saxon name for Odin was Woden (from which we have *Wednesday*, "Woden's day"). Woden could help humans communicate with spirits, and he was especially associated with burial rites and with ecstatic trances, important for both poetry and religious mysteries. Not surprisingly, this god of both poetry and death played an important role in the lives of people who produced great poetry and who also maintained a somber, brooding outlook on life.

B The Anglo-Saxon deity named Thunor was essentially the same as Thor, the Norse god of thunder and lightning. His sign was the hammer and possibly also the twisted cross we call the swastika, which is found on so many Anglo-Saxon gravestones. (Thunor's name survives in *Thursday*, "Thor's day.")

C Still another significant figure in Anglo-Saxon mythology is the dragon, which seems always, as in *Beowulf*, to be the protector of a treasure. Some scholars suggest that the fiery dragon should be seen as both a personification of "death the devourer" and as the guardian of the grave mound, in which a warrior's ashes and his treasure lay.

On the whole, the religion of the Anglo-Saxons seems to have been more concerned with ethics than with mysticism—with the earthly virtues of bravery, loyalty, generosity, and friendship.

Coifi, the Anglo-Saxon chief priest, advises King Edwin to give up the old gods and accept the new religion of Christianity. Here is his argument.

Your Majesty, when we compare the present life of man on earth with that time of which we have no knowledge, it seems to me like the swift flight of a single sparrow through the banqueting hall where you are sitting at dinner on a winter's day with your thanes and counselors. In the midst there is a comforting fire to warm the hall; outside, the storms of winter rain or snow are raging. This sparrow flies swiftly in through one door of the hall, and out through another. While he is inside, he is safe from the winter storms; but after a few moments of comfort, he vanishes from sight into the wintry world from which he came. Even so, man appears on earth for a little while; but of what went before this life or of what follows, we know nothing. Therefore, if this new teaching has brought any more certain knowledge, it seems only right that we should follow it.

—The Venerable Bede, quoting Coifi in
Ecclesiastical History of the English People

Despite the growth of Christianity, the Anglo-Saxon religion remained strong. Although it drew many of its deities and rites from Scandinavian mythology, the Anglo-Saxon religion was more concerned with ethics than with mysticism.

Critical Comment: Growth of English Language The following quotation from Robert McCrum's *The Story of English* might interest students: "When Julius Caesar landed in Britain nearly two thousand years ago, English did not exist. Five hundred years later, *Englisc,* incomprehensible to modern ears, was probably spoken by about as few people as currently speak Cherokee. . . . Nearly a thousand years later, at the end of the sixteenth century, when William Shakespeare was in his prime, English was the native speech of between five and seven million Englishmen. . . . Between 1600 and the present . . . the speakers of English . . . traveled into every corner of the globe, carrying their language and culture with them. Today, English is used by at least 750 million people. . . . Whatever the total, English at the end of the twentieth century is more widely scattered, more widely spoken and written, than any other language has ever been. It has become *the* language of the planet, the first truly global language."

Three standing figures (Odin, Thor, and Freyr) in tunics, from a Viking tapestry (12th century).

Statens Historiska Museer, Stockholm.

The Bards: Singing of Gods and Heroes

The Anglo-Saxon communal hall, besides offering shelter and a place for holding council meetings, also provided space for storytellers and their audience. As in other parts of the ancient world (notably in Homeric Greece more than one thousand years earlier), skilled storytellers, or bards, sang of gods and heroes. The Anglo-Saxons did not regard these bards (called scops) as inferior to warriors. To the Anglo-Saxons, creating poetry was as important as fighting, hunting, farming, or loving.

ASSESSMENT TOOLS

Check Test: True-False

1. Celtic and Anglo-Saxon stories are so similar that they are often confused. [False]
2. The Roman occupation provided several hundred years of stability for Britain. [True]
3. When the Anglo-Saxons conquered Britain, renaming it England, the Celts retreated to Ireland. [False]
4. *Scop* is another word for "warrior." [False]
5. Before King Alfred, tales and poems in English were not considered great literature. [True]

A. Cultural Connections

The *Angelus* to which Borges refers is the ringing of bells that calls Roman Catholics to devotions in the morning, at noon, and in the evening.

The poets sang to the strumming of a harp. As sources for their improvisational poetry, the storytellers had a rich supply of heroic tales that reflected the concerns of a people constantly under threat of war, disease, or old age. We are told of the king in *Beowulf*:

> . . . sometimes Hrothgar himself, with the harp
> In his lap, stroked its silvery strings
> And told wonderful stories, a brave king
> Reciting unhappy truths about good
> And evil—and sometimes he wove his stories
> On the mournful thread of old age, remembering
> Buried strength and the battles it had won.
> He would weep, the old king.
> —Lines 2107–2114

Anglo-Saxon literature contains many works in this same elegiac strain. Poems such as "The Seafarer" (page 56), for example, stress the transience of a life frequently identified with the cold and darkness of winter. For the non-Christian Anglo-Saxons, whose religion offered them no hope of an afterlife, only fame and its reverberation in poetry could provide a defense against death. Perhaps this is why the Anglo-Saxon bards, uniquely gifted with the skill to preserve fame in the collective memory, were such honored members of their society.

A knight, from a chess set carved from walrus ivory (12th century). British Museum, London.

The Anglo-Saxon bard's ability to recite poetic stories was considered as important a skill as fighting. Fame in the bard's mournful poetry—and a place in the community's memory—was a hero's only consolation against death.

A modern Argentine writer imagines the last Anglo-Saxon:

In a stable which is almost in the shadow of the new stone church, a man with gray eyes and gray beard, lying amidst the odor of the animals, humbly seeks death as one would seek sleep. The day, faithful to vast and secret laws, is shifting and confusing the shadows inside the poor shelter; outside are the plowed fields and a ditch clogged with dead leaves and the tracks of a wolf in the black mud where the forests begin. The man sleeps and dreams, forgotten. He is awakened by the bells tolling the Angelus. In the kingdoms of England the ringing of bells is now one of the customs of the evening, but this man, as a child, has seen the face of Woden, the divine horror and exultation, the crude wooden idol hung with Roman coins and heavy clothing, the sacrificing of horses, dogs, and prisoners. Before dawn he will die and with him will die, and never return, the immediate images of these pagan rites; the world will be a little poorer when this Saxon has died. . . .

—Jorge Luis Borges, *translated by* James E. Irby

OPTIONS FOR TEACHING

ASSESSMENT TOOLS

Performance Assessment Ask students to imagine the life of an Anglo-Saxon and to write a journal entry for a typical day. Remind them to consider information they have learned about Anglo-Saxon society when creating this journal, and use their inclusion of specific presented material as criteria to assess their understanding of the material. The following scale may help to categorize journal entries:

4 Significant number of relevant details; shows mastery of presented material.

3 Details included indicate a clear understanding of presented material.

2 Some details; shows familiarity with certain aspects of presented material.

1 Few details incorporated; lacks application of presented material.

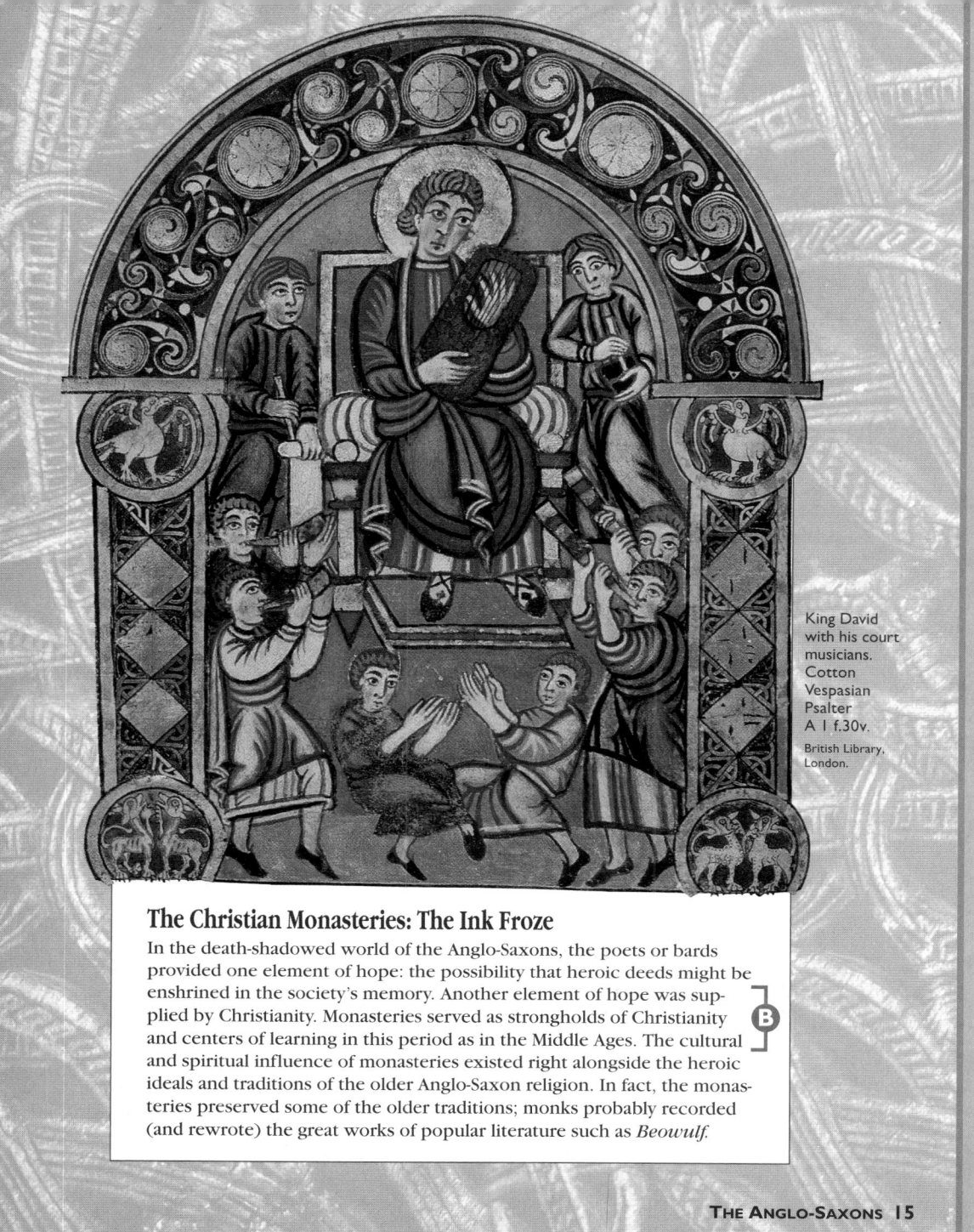

King David with his court musicians. Cotton Vespasian Psalter A I f.30v.

British Library, London.

B. Expansion

Before Henry VIII disbanded the English monasteries in the early sixteenth century, there were twenty-eight abbeys, twenty-six priories, twenty-three convents, thirty friaries, and thirteen cells in Yorkshire alone. All are in ruins today.

The Christian Monasteries: The Ink Froze

In the death-shadowed world of the Anglo-Saxons, the poets or bards provided one element of hope: the possibility that heroic deeds might be enshrined in the society's memory. Another element of hope was supplied by Christianity. Monasteries served as strongholds of Christianity and centers of learning in this period as in the Middle Ages. The cultural and spiritual influence of monasteries existed right alongside the heroic ideals and traditions of the older Anglo-Saxon religion. In fact, the monasteries preserved some of the older traditions; monks probably recorded (and rewrote) the great works of popular literature such as *Beowulf.*

B

A. Exploring the Historical Period

After defeating the Norse, King Alfred maintained political control over southwest England, which was not part of his Wessex domain, by encouraging a common loyalty to England and use of the English language to create a national identity. He used English, not the customary Latin, to educate his people. In his preface to the English translation of Bede's *Historia Ecclesiastica,* King Alfred explains his emphasis on English: "Therefore it seems better to me . . . that we should also translate certain books which are most necessary for all men to know, into the language that we can all understand, and also arrange it . . . so that all the youth of free men now among the English people . . . are able to read English writing as well."

Quickwrite

To help students start their brainstorming, ask them to think back on the information they have read.

Have students create a cluster diagram like the one below to keep track of their ideas.

- reared children
- joined convent
- Women's roles
- sparse shelter
- little education
- harsh climate
- Daily life
- preparing for war
- Life as an Anglo-Saxon
- Community
- controlled by lords
- socialized in community halls
- served their lord
- Men's qualities
- showed strength as soldiers

When the monks recorded the works from the older oral tradition, they wrote in the vernacular, or the language of the people. This was a Germanic tongue that we now classify as Old English. But the principal works of learning in the monasteries were written in Latin, the language of the Church.

Monks assigned to the monastery's scriptorium, or writing room, probably spent almost all their daylight hours copying manuscripts by hand. (Printing was still 800 years away in England.) In Anglo-Saxon England, the scriptorium was actually in a covered walkway (the cloister) open to a court. Makeshift walls of oiled paper or glass helped somewhat, but England in winter is cold: The ink could freeze. Picture a shivering scribe, hunched over sheepskin "paper," pressing painfully with a quill pen, obeying a rule of silence: That's how seriously the Church took learning.

A Latin alone remained the language of "serious" study in England until the time of King Alfred. During his reign, Alfred instituted the *Anglo-Saxon Chronicle,* a lengthy, running history of England that began in the earliest days and continued until 1154. Partly because of King Alfred's efforts, English began to gain respect as a language of culture. Only then did Old English stories and poetry come to be recognized as great works of literature.

Christian monks preserved Anglo-Saxon cultural and literary traditions. These efforts helped English gain respect as a language of culture.

Anglo-Saxon Kings: Caligula. Manuscript (12th century) shows Woden surrounded by founders of royal English lines. Cotton MS A VIII, f.29.

Quickwrite

Life in a small Anglo-Saxon community was obviously very different from life in the United States, wherever you happen to live. Perhaps you can picture a small cluster of huts around the chieftain's central hall, a small fire feebly combating the deep cold of a winter night in old England. Imagining how people lived and thought under such circumstances may be more difficult.

Picture that setting, and consider what you've just read about Anglo-Saxon beliefs and the structure of their society. Now imagine yourself as a young man or woman about to come of age. What do you think your life is like? What choices do you have? What limitations do you face? Jot down your thoughts, and then compare notes with your classmates.

(Opposite) Norse chessmen, carved from walrus ivory, found on Isle of Lewis, Scotland.

The Anglo-Saxons

 Collection *1* | SONGS OF ANCIENT HEROES

Theme: **Heroic Deeds as a Reflection of Personal Glory**
The recounting of heroic deeds is a major feature of Anglo-Saxon literature. These ancient heroes struggle to overcome fear, evil, and danger in the quest for a place in the memory of their people.

Thematic Focus

The heroes in Collection 1 battle internal as well as external forces.

- *from* **Beowulf** In this excerpt from the Anglo-Saxon epic, the hero saves Hrothgar's people from the evil Grendel and from Grendel's mother, and he battles a dragon to protect the Geats.
- **The Head of Humbaba** *from* **Gilgamesh** In this excerpt from the Sumerian epic, the hero Gilgamesh kills Humbaba for threatening his friend. This tale parallels the Anglo-Saxon heroic tradition.
- **The Seafarer** The speaker in this elegiac poem recounts the hardship, fear, and desolation of a life at sea and glorifies the promise of Heaven.

Literary Focus

Literary Element	Selection / Feature
Epic Hero/Alliteration/Kennings	**Beowulf**
Elegy	**The Seafarer**

Writing Focus

The following flowchart shows how the writing assignment for each selection relates to and builds toward the culminating writing assignment presented in the Writer's Workshop at the end of the unit.

Selection	Work-in-Progress Assignment
Beowulf	Freewrite about facing challenges p. 50
The Seafarer	Describe a sense of loss p. 60
Writer's Workshop	Write about an autobiographical incident p. 67

Collection Planner

SELECTION/ FEATURE	Literary Elements / Active Reading	Writing	Speaking and Listening	Language and Vocabulary
from **Beowulf** trans. by Burton Raffel (pp. 18–51) **Connections:** from **Grendel** John Gardner (pp. 36–37) **Connections: Life in 999: A Grim Struggle** Howard G. Chua-Eoan (p. 47) **Student to Student** (p. 48)	• Reader's Log p. 20 • Epic Hero p. 20 • Alliteration and Kennings pp. 48–49	• Critical Writing: Analyze Grendel p. 50 • Creative Writing: Use different point of view p. 50 • Speaking and Listening: Reflect on being bard p. 50	• Speaking and Listening: Retell episode p. 50 • Movies and Television: Compare movies and Beowulf p. 50	• How to Own a Word: Context clues p. 51
World Literature: The Head of Humbaba from **Gilgamesh** retold by Herbert Mason (pp. 52–54)	• Reader's Log p. 52		• Finding Common Ground: Discuss similarities to ancient world p. 54	
The Seafarer trans. by Burton Raffel (pp. 55–61) Primary Sources: The Original Language and the Translator's Task (p. 59) Spotlight On: Anglo-Saxon Riddles trans. by Burton Raffel (p. 61)	• Reader's Log p. 55 • Elegy p. 55	• Critical Writing: Compare ancient and modern poetry p. 60 • Creative Writing: Write "Seafarer" poem p. 60	• Critical Thinking: Debate existence of modern heroes p. 60 • Visual Art: Explain elements in collage p. 60	
The English Language Old English: Where English Came From John Algeo (pp. 63–66)				• Try It Out: Languages p. 66
Writer's Workshop: Autobiograpical Incident (pp. 67–69)		• Writing Process: Auto- biographical incident pp. 67–69		
Language Workshop: Sentence Combining (p. 70)		• Revise Essay p. 70		
Learning for Life: Group Membership (p. 71)			• Talking About Com- munity p. 71	

Collection Resources

Teaching Resources A	Audiovisual Resources Binder	Test Booklet
Cross-Curricular Activity p. 19	Fine Art Transparency 1.1	Collection 1 Test pp. 9–11

 Computer disk or CD-ROM
 Videodisc
 Audiocassette
 Overhead Transparency

PROGRAM RESOURCES

Electronic Media	Teaching Resources with Organizer		Audiovisual Resources Binder
	Teaching Resources A	Other Resources	
• Test Generator • Language Workshop: Parts of speech	• Teaching Notes pp. 1–2 • Reading Organizer p. 7 • Language Link pp. 8–11 • Words to Own pp. 12–13	• Test Booklet: Selection Test pp. 3–4 • Language and Writing Skills Worksheets pp. 11–14 • Portfolio Management System pp. 39, 62–63, 67–68	• Elements of Literature Transparencies 1.2–1.3 • How to Own a Word Transparency 1.5 • Selected Reading Audiocassette 1 Side A
	• Teaching Notes p. 3		
• Test Generator • Language Workshop: Sentence fragments	• Teaching Notes p. 3 • Reading Organizer p. 14 • Language Link pp. 15–16	• Test Booklet: Selection Test pp. 5–6 • Language and Writing Skills Worksheets p. 102 • Portfolio Management System pp. 54–55, 62–63, 69–70	• Elements of Literature Transparency 1.4
• Test Generator • Videodisc, Side A: "English: A Living Language, Part 1"	• Teaching Notes p. 4	• Test Booklet: Selection Test pp. 7–8	
• Writer's Workshop 2: Autobiographical Incident		• Portfolio Management System pp. 71–73	• Revision Transparencies 1.6–1.7
• Language Workshop: Sentence Combining	• Language Workshop pp. 17–18	• Language and Writing Skills Worksheets pp. 111–118	
		• Portfolio Management System p. 74	

Proofreading Warm-ups

You may use the following exercises to help students practice their proofreading skills. Copy a set of incorrect sentences onto the chalkboard, and have students find and correct the spelling, punctuation, usage, and mechanical errors in each sentence. Ask students to share and discuss their responses.

	Sentences with Errors	Sentences Corrected	Skills Covered
1	**a.** the 1st British settlers the Celts were a people influenced by thier magical Religion **b.** the mythology of the Celts have influenced English and Irish Writer's even today	**a.** The first British settlers, the Celts, were a people influenced by their magical religion. **b.** The mythology of the Celts has influenced English and Irish writers even today.	Capitalization, Write out abbreviations, Comma usage, Spelling, Subject-verb agreement, Apostrophe usage, End marks
2	**a.** despite the growth of Christainity the anglo saxon religion remained strong **b.** the anglo saxon religion remains evident in are readings.	**a.** Despite the growth of Christianity, the Anglo-Saxon religion remained strong. **b.** The Anglo-Saxon religion remains evident in our readings.	Capitalization, Spelling, Comma usage, Hyphen usage, End marks
3	**a.** these norse chessman carved of walrus ivory was found on a Scottish island **b.** there arent to many of them left	**a.** These Norse chessmen, carved of walrus ivory, were found on a Scottish island. **b.** There aren't too many of them left.	Capitalization, Plural nouns, Comma usage, Subject-verb agreement, Apostrophe usage, Homonyms, End marks
4	**a.** the epic Beowulf is to England what Homers Iliad is to ancient Greece **b.** Beowulfs name may mean bear but we dont know for sure	**a.** The epic <u>Beowulf</u> is to England what Homer's <u>Iliad</u> is to ancient Greece. **b.** Beowulf's name may mean "bear," but we don't know for sure.	Capitalization, Underlining titles of long works, Apostrophe usage, Spelling, Quotation marks, Comma usage, End marks
5	**a.** Nancy have you read about Humbaba Ms Jones asked **b.** yes that is the story in which gilgamesh is the hero replied Nancy	**a.** "Nancy, have you read about Humbaba?" Ms. Jones asked. **b.** "Yes, that is the story in which Gilgamesh is the hero," replied Nancy.	Quotation marks, Capitalization, Comma usage, Period for abbreviation, End marks
6	**a.** he might of went with them guys but I cant say for sure **b.** are you gonna call over their to see if hes with them	**a.** He might have gone with those guys, but I can't say for sure. **b.** Are you going to call over there to see if he's with them?	Capitalization, Nonstandard usage, Comma usage, Apostrophe usage, Spelling, Homonyms, End marks
7	**a.** a example of a elegy is The Seafarer **b.** could you have wrote a elegy like that	**a.** An example of an elegy is "The Seafarer." **b.** Could you have written an elegy like that?	Capitalization, Nonstandard usage, Quotation marks, Verb error, End marks
8	**a.** were trying to guess the answer's to them riddles **b.** there to hard to figure out	**a.** We're trying to guess the answers to these riddles. **b.** They're too hard to figure out.	Capitalization, Apostrophe usage, Nonstandard usage, Spelling, End marks
9	**a.** did you see them two player's who scored so many points in last weeks game **b.** him and Mike play good cause they practice alot	**a.** Did you see those two players who scored so many points in last week's game? **b.** He and Mike play well because they practice a lot.	Capitalization, Nonstandard usage, Apostrophe usage, Pronoun usage, Spelling, End marks
10	**a.** weve come along way since the anglo saxon times **b.** however our basic vocabulary still come to us from old english	**a.** We've come a long way since the Anglo-Saxon times. **b.** However, our basic vocabulary still comes to us from Old English.	Capitalization, Apostrophe usage, Spelling, Hyphen usage, Comma usage, Subject-verb agreement, End marks

Collection 1

SONGS OF ANCIENT HEROES

from Beowulf
from Gilgamesh
"The Seafarer"

And sometimes a proud old soldier
Who had heard songs of the ancient heroes
And could sing them all through, story after story,
Would weave a net of words for Beowulf's
Victory, tying the knot of his verses
Smoothly, swiftly, into place with a poet's
Quick skill, singing his new song aloud
While he shaped it, and the old songs as well.

—from *Beowulf, translated by* Burton Raffel

Responding to the Quotation

? Why do you think the songs about heroes were popular? [Possible response: They appealed to the listeners' pride and loyalty.] Can you think of any heroes celebrated in other songs or poems? [Possible responses: King Arthur, Joan of Arc, Daniel Boone, Ulysses, Paul Revere, Charlemagne, El Cid, or Kamehameha.]

RESPONDING TO THE ART: VISUAL LITERACY

Have students compare this representation of an ancient warrior to their own ideas of how an ancient hero might have looked and acted. Include in the discussion the qualities an ancient hero might have had, physically and mentally, and whether he would have had to be a warrior.

PROGRAM MANAGER

- **Integrated Assessment** For a summative assessment of the literature and language skills taught in this collection see Collection One Test, *Test Booklet,* pp. 9–11.
- **Instructional Support** See Fine Art Transparency 1.1. Review teacher's notes for transparencies in the *Audiovisual*

Resources Binder for suggestions on how to tie the transparency to specific reading selections.
- **Extending Collection Theme** See Cross-Curricular Activity: Songs of Ancient Heroes, *Teaching Resources A,* p. 19, for an activity in another discipline and for evaluation criteria.

Introduction: Beowulf

Give students the categories below, and as they read, ask them to fill in the information that shows *Beowulf* has epic features. (The first few are filled in.)

Categories	Beowulf
• method of telling	[orally, by minstrels]
• source of story	[dream and legend]
• main characters	[hero, monsters]
• setting	
• conflict	
• length	
• date	

Prow of the Oseberg ship.

University Museum of National Antiquities, Oslo, Norway.

Beowulf

Beowulf is to England what Homer's *Iliad* and *Odyssey* are to ancient Greece: It is the first great work of the English national literature—the mythical and literary record of a formative stage of English civilization. It is also an epic of the heroic sources of English culture. As such, *Beowulf* uses a host of traditional motifs, or recurring elements, associated with heroic literature all over the world.

The epic tells the story of Beowulf (his name may mean "bear"), a Geat from Sweden who crosses the sea to Denmark in a quest to rescue King Hrothgar from the demonic monster Grendel. Like most early heroic literature, *Beowulf* is oral art. It was handed down, with changes and embellishments, from one minstrel to another. The stories of *Beowulf,* like those of all oral epics, are traditional ones, familiar to the audiences who crowded around the harpist-bards in the communal halls at night. The tales in the *Beowulf* epic are the stories of dream and legend, of monsters and of god-fashioned weapons, of descents to the underworld and of fights with dragons, of the hero's quest and of a community threatened by the powers of evil.

By the standards of Homer, whose epics run to nearly 15,000 lines, *Beowulf* is relatively short—approximately 3,200 lines. It was composed in Old English, probably in Northumbria in northeast England, sometime between the years 700 and 750. The world it depicts, however, is much older, that of the early sixth century. Much of the poem's material is based on early folk legends—some Celtic, some Scandinavian. Since the scenery described is the coast of Northumbria, not Scandinavia, it has been assumed that the poet who wrote the version that has come down to us was Northumbrian. Given the Christian elements in the epic, this poet may also have been a monk.

The only manuscript we have of *Beowulf* dates from the year 1000 and is now in the British Museum in London. Burned and stained, it was discovered in the eighteenth century: Somehow it had survived Henry VIII's destruction of the monasteries two hundred years earlier.

Beowulf: People, Monsters, and Places

Beowulf: a Geat, son of Edgetho and nephew of Higlac, king of the Geats. Higlac is both Beowulf's feudal lord and his uncle.

Brecca: chief of the Brondings, a tribe, and Beowulf's friend.

Grendel: man-eating monster who lives at the bottom of a foul mere, or mountain lake. His name might be related to the Old Norse *grindill,* meaning "storm," or *grenja,* "to bellow."

Herot: golden guest-hall built by King Hrothgar, the Danish ruler. It was decorated with the antlers of stags; the name means "hart [stag] hall." Scholars think Herot might have been built near Lejre on the coast of Zealand, in Denmark.

Hrothgar: king of the Danes, builder of Herot. He had once befriended Beowulf's father. His father was called Healfdane (which probably means "half Dane"). Hrothgar's name might mean "glory spear" or "spear of triumph."

Unferth: one of Hrothgar's courtiers, reputed to be a skilled warrior. His sword, called Hrunting, is used by Beowulf in a later battle.

Welthow: Hrothgar's wife, queen of the Danes.

Wiglaf: a Geat warrior, one of Beowulf's select band, and the only one to help him in his final fight with the dragon. Wiglaf might be related to Beowulf.

Viking coin minted in England (10th–11th century). Most such coins consist of precious metals extorted from the English as tribute.
British Museum, London.

A. Expansion
The original, complete *Beowulf* consists of 3,182 lines. An abridged modern English version of 842 lines, divided into seventeen parts, is reprinted here.

Introduction: Beowulf pp. 18–19

Before You Read p. 20

- **Reading Focus:** Students learn about Beowulf as an epic hero.
- **Quickwrite: Prior Knowledge** Analyze contemporary heroes in Reader's Log
- **Elements of Literature: Epic Hero**

Through the Selection

from Beowulf, Sections 1–11 pp. 21–37

Words to Own pp. 22–41

Literature and History pp. 28–29

Connections: A Novel pp. 36–37

from Grendel

Making Meanings p. 38

from Beowulf, Sections 12–17 pp. 39–46

Connections: A Magazine Article p. 47 "Life in 999: A Grim Struggle"

Making Meanings p. 48

Student to Student p. 48

Beyond the Selection

Choices: Building Your Portfolio p. 50

- **Writer's Notebook:** Freewrite for an autobiographical incident
- **Critical Writing:** Write an essay analyzing the character of Grendel
- **Creative Writing:** Retell an episode from another point of view
- **Speaking and Listening:** Retell an episode for an audience
- **Movies and Television:** Report on a comparison of movies and the epic of Beowulf

BEFORE YOU READ

FROM BEOWULF

Reading Focus

The Dragon Slayer

This is a story about a hero from the misty reaches of the English past, a hero who faces violence, horror, and even death to save a people in mortal danger. The epic's events take place many centuries ago, but this story still speaks to people today—perhaps because there are so many people in need of a rescuer, a hero. Beowulf is ancient England's hero. In other times, in other cultures, the hero takes the shape of King Arthur, or Gilgamesh, or Sundiata, or Joan of Arc. In twentieth-century America, the hero may assume the guise of Shane in the Western novel, or perhaps even Superman in the comic strips and movies. This hero-type is the dragon slayer, representing a besieged community facing evil forces that lurk in the cold darkness. And Grendel, the monster lurking in the depths of the lagoon, may represent all those threatening forces.

Quickwrite

In your Reader's Log, list several contemporary fictional heroes from novels, films, or even television. Pick one of them, and briefly analyze him or her using these questions:

- What sort of evil or oppression does he confront?
- Why does she do it? What's her motivation?
- For whom does he do it?

- What virtues does she represent?

Now discuss some of the heroes you and your classmates chose. Do they all seem to qualify as hero-types, or do some of them fall short in one way or another?

Elements of Literature

The Epic Hero

Beowulf, like all epic heroes, has superior physical strength and is supremely ethical. In his quest, he must defeat monsters that embody dark, destructive powers. At the end of the quest, he is glorified by the people he has saved. If you watch current events, particularly about people emerging from years of oppression, you will see this impulse toward glorification still at work. You might also see such glorification in the impressive monuments that are great tourist attractions in Washington, D.C.

Sutton Hoo helmet (7th century). Sutton Hoo ship treasure, Suffolk, England.
British Museum, London.

The **epic hero** is the central figure in a long narrative that reflects the values and heroic ideals of a particular society. An **epic** is a quest story on a grand scale.

For more on the Epic Hero, see the Handbook of Literary Terms.

WORDS TO OWN

The following vocabulary words are defined in the Words to Own at the bottom of the pupil's page.

laments p. 22	taut p. 34
reparation p. 22	sinews p. 34
solace p. 23	murky p. 35
vexed p. 27	pilgrimage p. 35
reprisal p. 30	loathsome p. 41

PROGRAM MANAGER

Application and Reinforcement For reinforcement of the elements of literature introduced in this lesson, see **Transparency 1.2** in the *Audiovisual Resources Binder.*

from Beowulf

translated by **Burton Raffel**

The Monster Grendel

1

    . . . A powerful monster, living down
In the darkness, growled in pain, impatient
As day after day the music rang
Loud in that hall,° the harp's rejoicing
5 Call and the poet's clear songs, sung
Of the ancient beginnings of us all, recalling
The Almighty making the earth, shaping
These beautiful plains marked off by oceans,
Then proudly setting the sun and moon
10 To glow across the land and light it;
The corners of the earth were made lovely with trees
And leaves, made quick with life, with each
Of the nations who now move on its face. And then
As now warriors sang of their pleasure:
15 So Hrothgar's men lived happy in his hall
Till the monster stirred, that demon, that fiend,
Grendel, who haunted the moors, the wild
Marshes, and made his home in a hell
Not hell but earth. He was spawned in that slime,
20 Conceived by a pair of those monsters born
Of Cain, murderous creatures banished
By God, punished forever for the crime
Of Abel's death. The Almighty drove
Those demons out, and their exile was bitter,
25 Shut away from men; they split
Into a thousand forms of evil—spirits
And fiends, goblins, monsters, giants,
A brood forever opposing the Lord's
Will, and again and again defeated.

2

30   Then, when darkness had dropped, Grendel
Went up to Herot, wondering what the warriors
Would do in that hall when their drinking was done.
He found them sprawled in sleep, suspecting
Nothing, their dreams undisturbed. The monster's
35 Thoughts were as quick as his greed or his claws:
He slipped through the door and there in the silence

Lines have been renumbered and do not correspond with the New American Library edition.

4. hall: guest-hall or mead-hall.
(Mead is a fermented drink made
from honey, water, yeast, and malt.)
The hall was a central gathering
place where Anglo-Saxon warriors
could feast, listen to a bard's stories,
and sleep in safety.

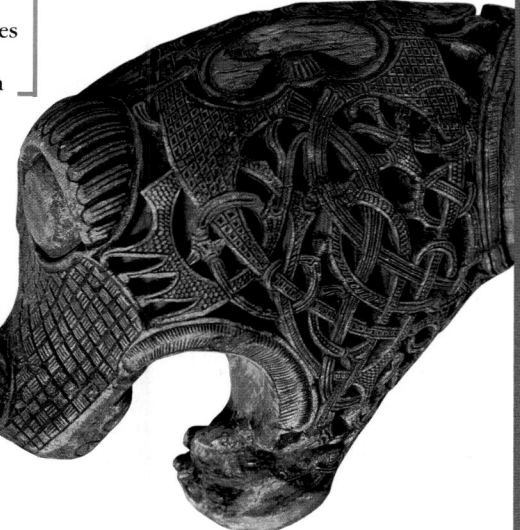

Animal head from Viking ship (c. 800).
University Museum of National Antiquities,
Oslo, Norway. Photo by Eirik Irgens Johnsen.

Into the Selection

Using BEFORE YOU READ p. 20

Reading Focus

Before they read *Beowulf,* let students brainstorm about the attributes of an ideal hero. Be sure students differentiate between heroes and celebrities. Then, ask students to draw pictures of their heroes to display in the classroom.

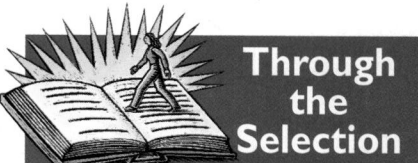

Through the Selection

A. Literary Element: Imagery

? What imagery associated with Grendel hints at his evil nature? [Possible response: Grendel lives in darkness and pain.]

B. Literary Element: Allusion

? What is the poet alluding to in ll. 5–13? [Possible answer: The Biblical story of the Creation. Some critics maintain that Herot represents Creation, the goodness of which is abhorrent to the evil Grendel.] All biblical allusions in Beowulf are from Genesis.

C. Exploring the Culture

Herot means "hart" or "stag." The hart was a symbol of kingship to the Anglo-Saxons.

PROGRAM MANAGER

- **Planning Instruction** See *Teaching Notes, Teaching Resources A,* pp. 1–2 for objectives, and additional information.
- **Instructional Support** See *Graphic Organizer for Active Reading, Teaching Resources A,* p. 7 for a Through the Selection activity.
- **Audiotaped Readings** To help audi-

tory learners, use the *Selected Reading, Audio cassette 1, Side A* in the *Audiovisual Resources Binder.*
- **Assessment** See *Selection Test, Test Booklet,* pp. 3–4.
- **Language Link** For instruction and practice with the parts of speech, see

Language Link, Teaching Resources A, pp. 8–11, and *Language and Writing Skills Worksheets,* pp. 11–14.
- **Reinforcement** Use the *Words to Own* worksheet in *Teaching Resources A,* pp. 12–13.

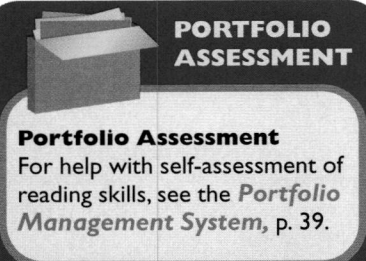

Snatched up thirty men, smashed them
Unknowing in their beds, and ran out with their bodies,
The blood dripping behind him, back
40 To his lair, delighted with his night's slaughter.
    At daybreak, with the sun's first light, they saw
(A) How well he had worked, and in that gray morning
Broke their long feast with tears and <u>laments</u>
For the dead. Hrothgar, their lord, sat joyless
45 In Herot, a mighty prince mourning
The fate of his lost friends and companions,
Knowing by its tracks that some demon had torn
His followers apart. He wept, fearing
The beginning might not be the end. And that night
50 Grendel came again, so set
On murder that no crime could ever be enough,
No savage assault quench his lust
For evil. Then each warrior tried
To escape him, searched for rest in different
(B) 55 Beds, as far from Herot as they could find,
Seeing how Grendel hunted when they slept.
Distance was safety; the only survivors
Were those who fled him. Hate had triumphed.
    So Grendel ruled, fought with the righteous,
60 One against many, and won; so Herot
Stood empty, and stayed deserted for years,
Twelve winters of grief for Hrothgar, king
Of the Danes, sorrow heaped at his door
By hell-forged hands. His misery leaped
65 The seas, was told and sung in all
Men's ears: how Grendel's hatred began,
How the monster relished his savage war
On the Danes, keeping the bloody feud
Alive, seeking no peace, offering
70 No truce, accepting no settlement, no price
In gold or land, and paying the living
For one crime only with another. No one
Waited for <u>reparation</u> from his plundering claws:
That shadow of death hunted in the darkness,
75 Stalked Hrothgar's warriors, old
And young, lying in waiting, hidden
In mist, invisibly following them from the edge
Of the marsh, always there, unseen.
    So mankind's enemy continued his crimes,
80 Killing as often as he could, coming
(C) Alone, bloodthirsty and horrible. Though he lived

Dragonhead from a Viking horse collar (detail) (10th century). Denmark.
National Museum, Copenhagen.

WORDS TO OWN
laments (lə·ments′) *n. pl.:* cries of grief.
reparation (rep′ə·rā′shən) *n.:* payment to compensate for wrongdoing.

In Herot, when the night hid him, he never
Dared to touch king Hrothgar's glorious
Throne, protected by God—God,
85 Whose love Grendel could not know. But Hrothgar's
Heart was bent. The best and most noble
Of his council debated remedies, sat
In secret sessions, talking of terror
And wondering what the bravest of warriors could do.
90 And sometimes they sacrificed to the old stone gods,
Made heathen vows, hoping for Hell's
Support, the Devil's guidance in driving
Their affliction off. That was their way,
And the heathen's only hope, Hell
95 Always in their hearts, knowing neither God
Nor His passing as He walks through our world, the Lord
Of Heaven and earth; their ears could not hear
His praise nor know His glory. Let them
Beware, those who are thrust into danger,
100 Clutched at by trouble, yet can carry no <u>solace</u>
In their hearts, cannot hope to be better! Hail
To those who will rise to God, drop off
Their dead bodies, and seek our Father's peace!

3

So the living sorrow of Healfdane's son°
105 Simmered, bitter and fresh, and no wisdom
Or strength could break it: That agony hung
On king and people alike, harsh
And unending, violent and cruel, and evil.
In his far-off home Beowulf, Higlac's
110 Follower° and the strongest of the Geats—greater
And stronger than anyone anywhere in this world—
Heard how Grendel filled nights with horror
And quickly commanded a boat fitted out,
Proclaiming that he'd go to that famous king,
115 Would sail across the sea to Hrothgar,
Now when help was needed. None
Of the wise ones regretted his going, much
As he was loved by the Geats: The omens were good,
And they urged the adventure on. So Beowulf
120 Chose the mightiest men he could find,
The bravest and best of the Geats, fourteen
In all, and led them down to their boat;
He knew the sea, would point the prow°
Straight to that distant Danish shore. . . .

104. Healfdane's son: Hrothgar.

110. Higlac's follower: Higlac is Beowulf's uncle and feudal lord.

123. prow (prou): front part of a boat.

WORDS TO OWN
solace (säl′is) n.: peace.

Beowulf **T23**

D. Critical Reading: Identifying Main Ides

? What is the purpose of Part 2?
[Possible answer: It establishes the helplessness of Hrothgar and his men, as they try for twelve years to stop Grendel's terrorism.]

E. Critical Reading: Finding Details
Although a pagan scop may have composed and sung the story, the Christian monk transcribing it may have added Christian elements. Ask students to find clues that show this dual authorship. [Possible answer: In ll. 90-94 the pagan elements are intermixed with the generally Christian atmosphere of the poem.]

F. Exploring the Historical Period
The Geats lived in what is today southwestern Sweden. Higlac, king of the Geats and Beowulf's kinsman, was killed in a raid on the Franks in 521. In the complete version, the end of the poem forecasts the Geats' defeat by another tribe, the Swedes.

STRATEGIES FOR INCLUSION

Visual To help them to envision him, invite students to sketch Grendel using information they gather from the text. Have students compare their drawings, discussing the similarities and differences.

Less Proficient Readers Even with the epic translated into modern English, some passages of description and certain complex sentence structures may impose difficulties for some readers. Read these sections aloud, asking students to envision the characters and setting. Audiocassette 1, Side A, should be especially helpful.

RESPONDING
TO THE ART:
VISUAL LITERACY

What do you think is taking place in this scene? Why? [Possible response: Because there are many boats and men close together, the art suggests a feeling of crowding and urgency that may precede a battle.]

Invasion of Danes under Hinguar (Ingvar) and Hubba. From *Life, Passion, and Miracles of St. Edmund* (c. 1130). England.

The Pierpont Morgan Library, New York.

Beowulf arrives in Denmark and is directed to Herot, the mead-hall of King Hrothgar. The king sends Wulfgar, one of his thanes (or feudal lords), to greet the visitors.

The Arrival of the Hero

4

125 . . . Then Wulfgar went to the door and addressed
The waiting seafarers with soldier's words:
    "My lord, the great king of the Danes, commands me
To tell you that he knows of your noble birth
And that having come to him from over the open

24 THE ANGLO-SAXONS

OPTIONS FOR TEACHING

PROFESSIONAL NOTES

Critical Comment: Archetype
Share with students the following material written by the critic Alvin A. Lee: ". . . *Beowulf* is not about an individual as such but about a man of archetypal proportions, whose significance, in the broadest and deepest sense, is social. The poem is an imaginative vision of two kinds of human society, one symbolized by generosity, loyalty, and love, the other by monsters of darkness and bloodshed who prey on the ordered, light-filled world man desires and clings to. . . . *Beowulf* is not about a complex, individual character whose interior mental processes lead plausibly to certain actions and relations with other people. . . . We do not know why, psychologically, Unferth behaves so oddly. . . . [The characters in Beowulf] are all functionaries playing out their roles as long as wyrd (fate) permits, not images of real people but exemplars of human types. . . ."

130 Sea you have come bravely and are welcome.
    Now go to him as you are, in your armor and helmets,
    But leave your battle-shields here, and your spears,
    Let them lie waiting for the promises your words
    May make."
                    Beowulf arose, with his men
135 Around him, ordering a few to remain
    With their weapons, leading the others quickly
    Along under Herot's steep roof into Hrothgar's
    Presence. Standing on that prince's own hearth,
    Helmeted, the silvery metal of his mail shirt°   Ⓐ
140 Gleaming with a smith's° high art, he greeted
    The Danes' great lord:
                    "Hail, Hrothgar!
    Higlac is my cousin° and my king; the days
    Of my youth have been filled with glory. Now Grendel's   Ⓑ
    Name has echoed in our land: Sailors
145 Have brought us stories of Herot, the best
    Of all mead-halls, deserted and useless when the moon
    Hangs in skies the sun had lit,
    Light and life fleeing together.
    My people have said, the wisest, most knowing
150 And best of them, that my duty was to go to the Danes'
    Great king. They have seen my strength for themselves,
    Have watched me rise from the darkness of war,
    Dripping with my enemies' blood. I drove
    Five great giants into chains, chased
155 All of that race from the earth. I swam
    In the blackness of night, hunting monsters   Ⓒ
    Out of the ocean, and killing them one
    By one; death was my errand and the fate
    They had earned. Now Grendel and I are called
160 Together, and I've come. Grant me, then,
    Lord and protector of this noble place,
    A single request! I have come so far,
    Oh shelterer of warriors and your people's loved friend,
    That this one favor you should not refuse me—
165 That I, alone and with the help of my men,
    May purge all evil from this hall. I have heard,
    Too, that the monster's scorn of men
    Is so great that he needs no weapons and fears none.
    Nor will I. My lord Higlac
170 Might think less of me if I let my sword   Ⓓ
    Go where my feet were afraid to, if I hid
    Behind some broad linden shield:° My hands
    Alone shall fight for me, struggle for life
    Against the monster. God must decide
175 Who will be given to death's cold grip.
    Grendel's plan, I think, will be

139. mail shirt: armored garment
made of interlocking metal rings.
140. smith's: metalworker's.

142. cousin: any relative.

172. linden shield: shield made
from wood of the linden tree.

BEOWULF **25**

A. Expansion
This mail shirt would have been composed of as many as twenty thousand
small iron rings riveted or welded shut,
creating a mesh-net effect.

B. Exploring the Culture
❓ Does Beowulf's boasting show
    him to be offensively arrogant?
[Possible responses: Yes, it seems he
is very conceited; or no, he is just
explaining his past successes.] Explain
to students that it would be unfair to
judge him by today's standards of modesty. One *Beowulf* scholar, for example,
notes that while modern readers often
find this boasting offensive, Beowulf
indicates not only his past dedication
to a hero's life but his current desire to
assist. What may appear to be bragging
becomes a promise to help, a way of
presenting credentials. Such boasting is
a tradition of epic poetry.

**C. Reader's Response:
    Connecting with the Text**
❓ In what situations today might
    such boasting be expected?
[Sample responses: Politicians often
use similar tactics to prove their
former achievements and to promise
even greater deeds when elected.
Advertisers also boast.]

**D. Reader's Response: Shaping
    Interpretations**
❓ Why do you think Beowulf
    intends to fight Grendel without a
sword? [Sample responses: Beowulf's
stated reason is his concern for
Higlac's opinion of him. Also, as Grendel carries no weapon, neither Grendel
nor Beowulf will have an unfair advantage. The two battle in hand-to-hand
combat, thus pitting good against evil
on a more elemental level. See Making
Meanings, #7, p. 38.] Later, in ll. 480–
485, readers learn Grendel has put
a spell on all weapons.

PROFESSIONAL NOTES

Cultural Diversity Hrothgar sponsors a feast
for Beowulf upon Beowulf's arrival; breaking
bread in Anglo-Saxon society was an expression
of brotherhood and solidarity as well as a ritual
preparation for battle. The concept is slightly
analogous to a team handshake or to a communal
battle cry in war. Ask students to explain any customs they know from other cultures that express
the same feelings.

Technology Tip Invite students to
look at the original Beowulf manuscript
on-line at **http://portico.bl.uk
/access/beowulf/electronic-beowulf.html**.
At this site, students can view also an article on
the history and location of the manuscript and a
picture of Grendel. *You may want to preview any
Internet activity that you suggest to students. Because*

*these resources are sometimes public
forums, their content can be
unpredictable.*   ☞

A. Reader's Response: Shaping Interpretations

? What do you think is the purpose of Part 4? [Sample responses: To introduce the character of Beowulf, his proposed deeds, and the Anglo-Saxon concept of fate. To include some of the tribe's history in the poem.]

B. Critical Reading: Making Inferences

? Why might Hrothgar find it necessary to remind Beowulf of the time he helped Beowulf's father? [Possible answer: Perhaps to explain to those listening that Hrothgar once, like Beowulf now, was in a position to restore peace to a troubled land. Beowulf now comes to repay his father's debt, to honor the man who enabled his father to return to his country.]

C. Literary Element: Character

? What does Hrothgar's speech tell us about him? [Once a strong king, loyal to his allies, Hrothgar has been broken by Grendel's reign of terror. Hrothgar's great suffering because of the death of his thanes indicates that he is a compassionate ruler.]

What it has been before, to invade this hall
And gorge his belly with our bodies. If he can,
If he can. And I think, if my time will have come,
180   There'll be nothing to mourn over, no corpse to prepare
For its grave: Grendel will carry our bloody
Flesh to the moors, crunch on our bones,
And smear torn scraps of our skin on the walls
Of his den. No, I expect no Danes
185   Will fret about sewing our shrouds,° if he wins.
And if death does take me, send the hammered
Mail of my armor to Higlac, return
The inheritance I had from Hrethel,° and he
From Wayland.° Fate will unwind as it must!"

185. shrouds: cloths used to wrap a body for burial.

188. Hrethel: Beowulf's grandfather, former king of the Geats.
189. Wayland: a smith celebrated for his skill in making swords and mail shirts.

5

190   Hrothgar replied, protector of the Danes:
     "Beowulf, you've come to us in friendship, and because
Of the reception your father found at our court.
Edgetho had begun a bitter feud,
Killing Hathlaf, a Wulfing warrior:°
195   Your father's countrymen were afraid of war,
If he returned to his home, and they turned him away.
Then he traveled across the curving waves
To the land of the Danes. I was new to the throne,
Then, a young man ruling this wide
200   Kingdom and its golden city: Hergar,
My older brother, a far better man
Than I, had died and dying made me,
Second among Healfdane's sons, first
In this nation. I bought the end of Edgetho's
205   Quarrel, sent ancient treasures through the ocean's
Furrows to the Wulfings; your father swore
He'd keep that peace. My tongue grows heavy,
And my heart, when I try to tell you what Grendel
Has brought us, the damage he's done, here
210   In this hall. You see for yourself how much smaller
Our ranks have become, and can guess what we've lost
To his terror. Surely the Lord Almighty
Could stop his madness, smother his lust!
How many times have my men, glowing
215   With courage drawn from too many cups
Of ale, sworn to stay after dark
And stem that horror with a sweep of their swords.
And then, in the morning, this mead-hall glittering
With new light would be drenched with blood, the benches
220   Stained red, the floors, all wet from that fiend's
Savage assault—and my soldiers would be fewer
Still, death taking more and more.
But to table, Beowulf, a banquet in your honor:

194. Wulfing warrior: The Wulfings were a Germanic tribe. Hrothgar's queen might have been a Wulfing.

26 THE ANGLO-SAXONS

Let us toast your victories, and talk of the future."
225   Then Hrothgar's men gave places to the Geats,
Yielded benches to the brave visitors,
And led them to the feast. The keeper of the mead
Came carrying out the carved flasks,
And poured that bright sweetness. A poet
230 Sang, from time to time, in a clear
Pure voice. Danes and visiting Geats
Celebrated as one, drank and rejoiced.

Unferth's Challenge

6

Unferth spoke, Ecglaf's son,
Who sat at Hrothgar's feet, spoke harshly
235 And sharp (vexed by Beowulf's adventure,
By their visitor's courage, and angry that anyone
In Denmark or anywhere on earth had ever
Acquired glory and fame greater
Than his own):

"You're Beowulf, are you—the same
240 Boastful fool who fought a swimming
Match with Brecca, both of you daring
And young and proud, exploring the deepest
Seas, risking your lives for no reason
But the danger? All older and wiser heads warned you
245 Not to, but no one could check such pride.
With Brecca at your side you swam along
The sea-paths, your swift-moving hands pulling you
Over the ocean's face. Then winter
Churned through the water, the waves ran you
250 As they willed, and you struggled seven long nights
To survive. And at the end victory was his,
Not yours. The sea carried him close
To his home, to southern Norway, near
The land of the Brondings, where he ruled and was loved,
255 Where his treasure was piled and his strength protected
His towns and his people. He'd promised to outswim you:
Bonstan's son° made that boast ring true.
You've been lucky in your battles, Beowulf, but I think
Your luck may change if you challenge Grendel,
260 Staying a whole night through in this hall,
Waiting where that fiercest of demons can find you."
Beowulf answered, Edgetho's great son:
"Ah! Unferth, my friend, your face

Anglo-Saxon gold buckle (7th century). Sutton Hoo ship treasure.
British Museum, London.

257. Bonstan's son: Brecca.

WORDS TO OWN
vexed (vekst) *adj.:* highly annoyed.

D. Literary Element: Character

? What is Unferth's motive for challenging Beowulf? [Possibly he is jealous of anyone with greater fame and glory than his own.]

E. Literary Element: Epic Hero
A hero's challenge by a character of inferior status, like Unferth, is a regular motif of heroic poetry, allowing the hero to show not only his self-assertiveness but also his restraint and courtesy.

CROSSING THE CURRICULUM

Architecture After they find descriptions and illustrations from a book or encyclopedia entry about the Middle Ages, have interested students design a model mead hall, construct it, and display it in the class.

Social Studies Have students prepare a presentation about discoveries made during archaeological digs such as Sutton Hoo. Students should

work in a group to research and present their findings to the class, using audiovisual materials as well as a script.

History Have interested students work in groups to research the history behind *Beowulf,* such as Edgetho's battles. Groups may divide the tasks of creating a script, presenting a history lesson to the class, or providing maps, models, and

graphs. Students may want to create a pseudo-epic passage patterned after *Beowulf* as their means of presentation and have a student pretending to be a scop deliver the reading. ☞

A. Critical Reading: Identifying Main Ideas

? What is the purpose of Part 6? [Possible answer: To demonstrate Beowulf's great courage in the swimming match and his compassion in spite of Unferth's challenge.]

B. Language Note: Alliteration

? What examples of alliteration do you find in this passage? [Possible answers: There are many examples, including ll. 272–273, which have both initial consonant and internal vowel sound repetition, and ll. 288–290.]

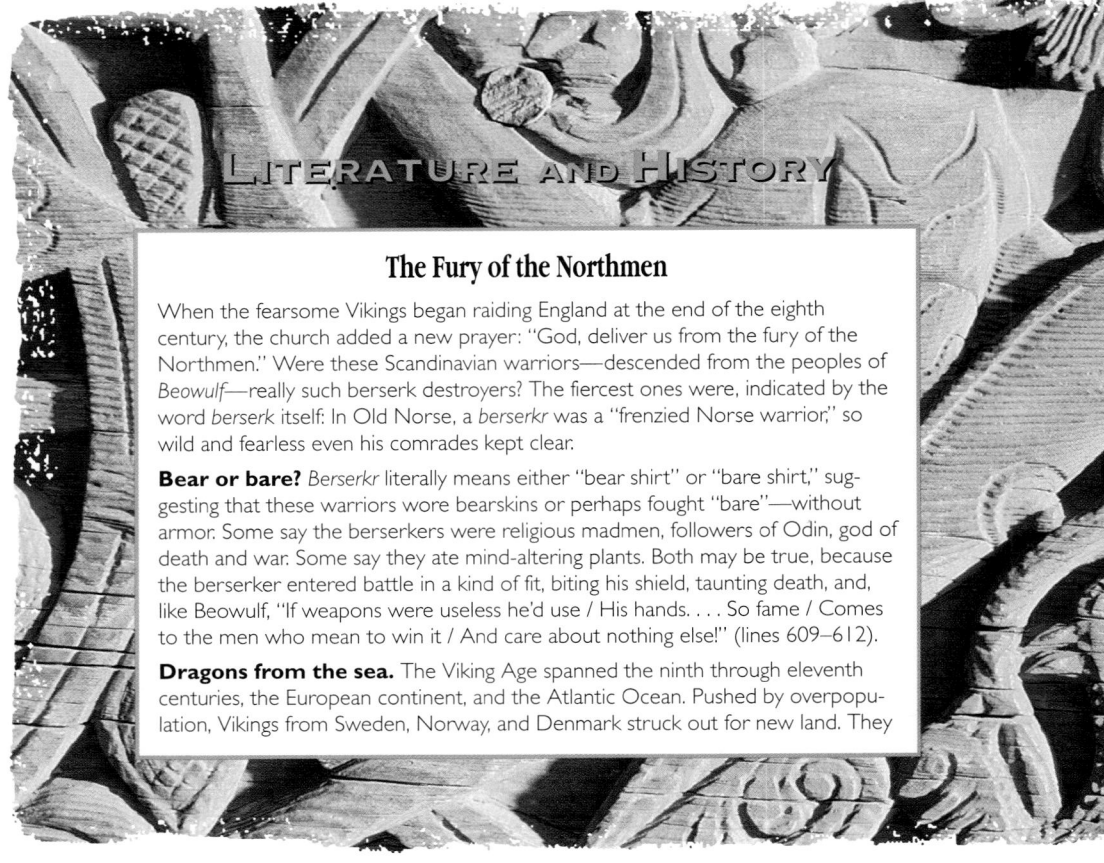

LITERATURE AND HISTORY

The Fury of the Northmen

When the fearsome Vikings began raiding England at the end of the eighth century, the church added a new prayer: "God, deliver us from the fury of the Northmen." Were these Scandinavian warriors—descended from the peoples of *Beowulf*—really such berserk destroyers? The fiercest ones were, indicated by the word *berserk* itself: In Old Norse, a *berserkr* was a "frenzied Norse warrior," so wild and fearless even his comrades kept clear.

Bear or bare? *Berserkr* literally means either "bear shirt" or "bare shirt," suggesting that these warriors wore bearskins or perhaps fought "bare"—without armor. Some say the berserkers were religious madmen, followers of Odin, god of death and war. Some say they ate mind-altering plants. Both may be true, because the berserker entered battle in a kind of fit, biting his shield, taunting death, and, like Beowulf, "If weapons were useless he'd use / His hands. . . . So fame / Comes to the men who mean to win it / And care about nothing else!" (lines 609–612).

Dragons from the sea. The Viking Age spanned the ninth through eleventh centuries, the European continent, and the Atlantic Ocean. Pushed by overpopulation, Vikings from Sweden, Norway, and Denmark struck out for new land. They

Is hot with ale, and your tongue has tried
265 To tell us about Brecca's doings. But the truth
A Is simple: No man swims in the sea
As I can, no strength is a match for mine.
As boys, Brecca and I had boasted—
We were both too young to know better—that we'd risk
270 Our lives far out at sea, and so
We did. Each of us carried a naked
Sword, prepared for whales or the swift
Sharp teeth and beaks of needlefish.
He could never leave me behind, swim faster
B Across the waves than I could, and I
Had chosen to remain close to his side.
I remained near him for five long nights,

28 THE ANGLO-SAXONS

OPTIONS FOR TEACHING

INTEGRATING THE LANGUAGE ARTS

Strategic Reading Have students draw four pictures to summarize a section of *Beowulf*, perhaps in a chart like the one shown here.

Picture 1	Picture 2
Picture 3	Picture 4

Language and Vocabulary Point out the vivid images evoked by the active verbs the poet uses. Then, have pairs of students rewrite the following sentences (on p. T29), using specific verbs to recreate the fierce tone of *Beowulf*. It may be necessary to change other syntax to create smooth sentences. Possible answers are suggested.

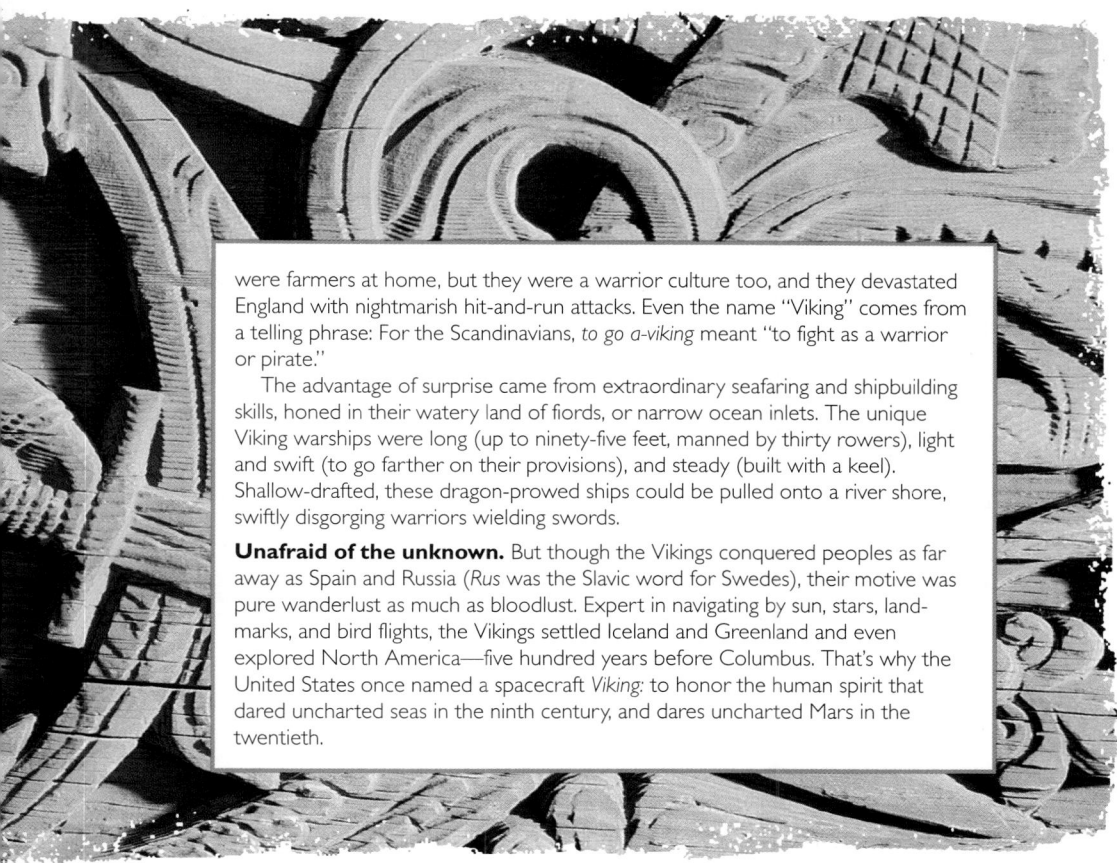

were farmers at home, but they were a warrior culture too, and they devastated England with nightmarish hit-and-run attacks. Even the name "Viking" comes from a telling phrase: For the Scandinavians, *to go a-viking* meant "to fight as a warrior or pirate."

The advantage of surprise came from extraordinary seafaring and shipbuilding skills, honed in their watery land of fiords, or narrow ocean inlets. The unique Viking warships were long (up to ninety-five feet, manned by thirty rowers), light and swift (to go farther on their provisions), and steady (built with a keel). Shallow-drafted, these dragon-prowed ships could be pulled onto a river shore, swiftly disgorging warriors wielding swords.

Unafraid of the unknown. But though the Vikings conquered peoples as far away as Spain and Russia (*Rus* was the Slavic word for Swedes), their motive was pure wanderlust as much as bloodlust. Expert in navigating by sun, stars, landmarks, and bird flights, the Vikings settled Iceland and Greenland and even explored North America—five hundred years before Columbus. That's why the United States once named a spacecraft *Viking:* to honor the human spirit that dared uncharted seas in the ninth century, and dares uncharted Mars in the twentieth.

Universitetets Oldsaksamling, Oslo.

Until a flood swept us apart;
The frozen sea surged around me,
280 It grew dark, the wind turned bitter, blowing
From the north, and the waves were savage. Creatures
Who sleep deep in the sea were stirred
Into life—and the iron hammered links
Of my mail shirt, these shining bits of metal
285 Woven across my breast, saved me
From death. A monster seized me, drew me
Swiftly toward the bottom, swimming with its claws
Tight in my flesh. But fate let me
Find its heart with my sword, hack myself
290 Free; I fought that beast's last battle,
Left it floating lifeless in the sea.

BEOWULF 29

INTEGRATING THE LANGUAGE ARTS

1. The monster waited in the depths of the sea for Gwelf and Gwenter. [The monster lurked in the depths. . . .]
2. The monster raised itself out of the water and took Gwenter by the neck. [The monster leapt out of the water and grabbed Gwenter. . . .]
3. The monster grunted and finished the rest of Gwenter as a warning to Gwelf. [The monster growled and gulped the rest of Gwenter. . . .]

4. Filled with rage and disgust, Gwelf shouted a new challenge to the monster. [Filled with rage and disgust, Gwelf screamed a new challenge at the monster.]

Speaking and Listening Since *Beowulf* was originally oral literature passed on by the storytellers, students may best feel its impact by listening to parts of it read aloud by good readers.

Work with a group of volunteers to prepare parts of the poem to read aloud to the class. Remind speakers to pause and raise or lower their voices when appropriate and to slow down their speech to stress key points. The rest of the class should listen closely and be prepared to write a summary or pose specific questions when the readers finish. ☞

A. Literary Element: Metaphor

? In what ways does Beowulf compare his defeat of the sea monsters to a feast? [He serves them his sword for the feast, but they die at the bottom of the sea from eating the "food" he feeds them.]

B. Critical Reading: Identifying Main Ideas

One theme of *Beowulf* deals with self versus fate (or *wyrd*). Ask students what they think Beowulf believes about fate. [Beowulf says that fate helps those who help themselves.]

C. Literary Element: Foil

In literature a foil is a character who contrasts with another. Ask how Unferth serves as a foil to Beowulf. [Possible answer: Unferth is a spiteful, idle boaster who has committed the unpardonable sin of murdering his kinsmen. Beowulf, on the other hand, has earned glory by defending those more helpless than he.]

D. Expansion

Explain to students that killing one's kindred was considered a heinous act among Anglo-Saxon nobility. *Wergild* ("man-payment"), considered satisfactory recompense to the relatives of the slain man, could not be made to one's own relatives; therefore, one could not make amends for the murder of kin.

Two drinking horns (7th century).
Sutton Hoo ship treasure.
© British Museum, London.

"Other monsters crowded around me,
Continually attacking. I treated them politely,
Offering the edge of my razor-sharp sword.
295 But the feast, I think, did not please them, filled
Their evil bellies with no banquet-rich food,
Thrashing there at the bottom of the sea;
By morning they'd decided to sleep on the shore,
Lying on their backs, their blood spilled out
300 On the sand. Afterwards, sailors could cross
That sea-road and feel no fear; nothing
Would stop their passing. Then God's bright beacon
Appeared in the east, the water lay still,
And at last I could see the land, wind-swept
305 Cliff-walls at the edge of the coast. Fate saves
The living when they drive away death by themselves!
Lucky or not, nine was the number
Of sea-huge monsters I killed. What man,
Anywhere under Heaven's high arch, has fought
310 In such darkness, endured more misery, or been harder
Pressed? Yet I survived the sea, smashed
The monsters' hot jaws, swam home from my journey.
The swift-flowing waters swept me along
And I landed on Finnish soil. I've heard
315 No tales of you, Unferth, telling
Of such clashing terror, such contests in the night!
Brecca's battles were never so bold;
Neither he nor you can match me—and I mean
No boast, have announced no more than I know
320 To be true. And there's more: You murdered your brothers,
Your own close kin. Words and bright wit
Won't help your soul; you'll suffer hell's fires,
Unferth, forever tormented. Ecglaf's
Proud son, if your hands were as hard, your heart
325 As fierce as you think it, no fool would dare
To raid your hall, ruin Herot
And oppress its prince, as Grendel has done.
But he's learned that terror is his alone,
Discovered he can come for your people with no fear
330 Of reprisal; he's found no fighting, here,
But only food, only delight.
He murders as he likes, with no mercy, gorges
And feasts on your flesh, and expects no trouble,
No quarrel from the quiet Danes. Now
335 The Geats will show him courage, soon

WORDS TO OWN
reprisal (ri·pri′zəl) *n.*: punishment in return for an injury.

---

30 THE ANGLO-SAXONS

OPTIONS FOR TEACHING

PROBLEM SOLVING/CRITICAL THINKING

Excavate Links to Modern Language Encourage students to take on the roles of cultural anthropologists on a "dig." Ask them to "mine" *Beowulf* to formulate and list the social mores of the ancient Anglo-Saxon society. Then, challenge students to find proof that links the tale and its characters to the development of the modern English Language, perhaps by hypothesizing how Anglo-Saxon customs may have influenced vocabulary or inspired modern traditions. Invite students to work in groups of four or five to discuss their suggestions and to present their discoveries, using charts, dioramas, panel discussions, or other visual aids.

He can test his strength in battle. And when the sun
Comes up again, opening another
Bright day from the south, anyone in Denmark
May enter this hall: That evil will be gone!"
340   Hrothgar, gray-haired and brave, sat happily
Listening, the famous ring-giver sure,
At last, that Grendel could be killed; he believed
In Beowulf's bold strength and the firmness of his spirit.
    There was the sound of laughter, and the cheerful clanking

E

345 Of cups, and pleasant words. Then Welthow,
Hrothgar's gold-ringed queen, greeted
The warriors; a noble woman who knew
What was right, she raised a flowing cup
To Hrothgar first, holding it high
350 For the lord of the Danes to drink, wishing him
Joy in that feast. The famous king
Drank with pleasure and blessed their banquet.
Then Welthow went from warrior to warrior,
Pouring a portion from the jeweled cup
355 For each, till the bracelet-wearing queen
Had carried the mead-cup among them and it was Beowulf's
Turn to be served. She saluted the Geats'
Great prince, thanked God for answering her prayers,
For allowing her hands the happy duty
360 Of offering mead to a hero who would help
Her afflicted people. He drank what she poured,
Edgetho's brave son, then assured the Danish
Queen that his heart was firm and his hands
Ready:

F

    "When we crossed the sea, my comrades
365 And I, I already knew that all
My purpose was this: to win the good will
Of your people or die in battle, pressed
In Grendel's fierce grip. Let me live in greatness
And courage, or here in this hall welcome
My death!"

G

370   Welthow was pleased with his words,
His bright-tongued boasts; she carried them back
To her lord, walked nobly across to his side.
    The feast went on, laughter and music
And the brave words of warriors celebrating
375 Their delight. Then Hrothgar rose, Healfdane's
Son, heavy with sleep; as soon
As the sun had gone, he knew that Grendel
Would come to Herot, would visit that hall
When night had covered the earth with its net

H

380 And the shapes of darkness moved black and silent
Through the world. Hrothgar's warriors rose with him.
    He went to Beowulf, embraced the Geats'
Brave prince, wished him well, and hoped

E. Reader's Response: Connecting with the Text

? What works can you think of that are based on the basic theme of good versus evil? What are the similarities between the heroes of these works and Beowulf? [Sample responses: Television series and movies about superheroes such as Batman and Superman; science fiction examples like *Star Wars, Star Trek,* or fantasies like Ursula Le Guin's Earthsea books or J.R.R. Tolkien's *The Lord of the Rings,* or Western films like *Shane.* Some of the heroes, like Batman, have superhuman powers, as Beowulf may seem to have when he subdues Grendel. Others are good mortals like Beowulf, facing evil forces.]

F. Exploring the Culture

Welthow exhibits the qualities of Anglo-Saxon women of the time, as they are described in the Exeter Book: beloved, cheerful, generous and gracious. Ask students to consider also how Welthow fits the description in Women in Anglo-Saxon Culture on p. 10.

G. Cultural Connections

For an Anglo-Saxon warrior, life without greatness or courage was death. This concept that winning determines one's worth exists to some extent today in competitions of different sorts, whether they be sports or chess or performance art.

H. Literary Element: Personification

? How is the coming of night personified as the sun sets? [Possible answer: Night, like a fisherman, appears with a net.]

CLASSROOM MANAGEMENT

Managing the Reader's Response Classroom Students may be uncomfortable expressing opinions if the Reader's Response approach is new to them. Be sure to encourage their responses by accepting any that are reasonable and urging students to return to the text for support if the responses are inappropriate.

Working in Pairs Because reading *Beowulf* may be difficult for many students, pair students with different reading abilities. The pairs may sometimes read silently and sometimes aloud. In either case, have students pause to discuss the text after a set number of lines, answer prepared questions, or solve problems.

Block Scheduling Teaching for a longer period of time can be successfully organized with the help of a small spiral notebook. After each class, take a few minutes to record the basics of each lesson. Also, include information regarding absentees, homework assigned, missing homework assignments, problems, solutions, or any other pertinent information. Keeping a notebook will enable the teacher to stay on track if students are not in class every day. ☞

A. Critical Reading: Speculating

? What is the purpose of Hrothgar's promise to Beowulf? [Possible answer: It acts as a contract, summarizing Hrothgar's expectations and Beowulf's intentions, and prepares the reader for the main conflict between Beowulf and Grendel (good and evil).]

That Herot would be his to command. And then
He declared:

385   "No one strange to this land
Has ever been granted what I've given you,
No one in all the years of my rule.
Make this best of all mead-halls yours, and then
Keep it free of evil, fight
390   With glory in your heart! Purge Herot
And your ship will sail home with its treasure-holds full." . . .

The feast ends. Beowulf and his men take the place of Hrothgar's followers and lie down to sleep in Herot. Beowulf, however, is wakeful, eager to meet his enemy.

The Battle with Grendel

8

          Out from the marsh, from the foot of misty
Hills and bogs, bearing God's hatred,
Grendel came, hoping to kill
395   Anyone he could trap on this trip to high Herot.
He moved quickly through the cloudy night,
Up from his swampland, sliding silently
Toward that gold-shining hall. He had visited Hrothgar's
Home before, knew the way—
400   But never, before nor after that night,
Found Herot defended so firmly, his reception
So harsh. He journeyed, forever joyless,
Straight to the door, then snapped it open,
Tore its iron fasteners with a touch,
405   And rushed angrily over the threshold.
He strode quickly across the inlaid
Floor, snarling and fierce: His eyes
Gleamed in the darkness, burned with a gruesome
Light. Then he stopped, seeing the hall
410   Crowded with sleeping warriors, stuffed
With rows of young soldiers resting together.
And his heart laughed, he relished the sight,
Intended to tear the life from those bodies
By morning; the monster's mind was hot
415   With the thought of food and the feasting his belly
Would soon know. But fate, that night, intended
Grendel to gnaw the broken bones
Of his last human supper. Human
Eyes were watching his evil steps,
420   Waiting to see his swift hard claws.

Bronze coin showing a warrior killing a monster.

Statens Historiska Museer, Stockholm.

32 THE ANGLO-SAXONS

OPTIONS FOR TEACHING

ASSESSMENT TOOLS

Check Test: True-False

1. Grendel has been attacking Herot Hall for six months. [False]
2. Beowulf requests that Hrothgar allow him to fight Grendel without his weapons. [True]
3. Beowulf states that no man is his match for strength. [True]

4. Hrothgar gives Beowulf command of Herot, promising him treasures if he succeeds in killing Grendel. [True]
5. Grendel cannot be harmed because he is protected by God. [False]

Informal Assessment To assess understanding at the end of each class period, ask questions orally about what has been read. For the first few days, give students study questions to direct their reading.

Grendel snatched at the first Geat
He came to, ripped him apart, cut
His body to bits with powerful jaws,
Drank the blood from his veins, and bolted
425 Him down, hands and feet; death **B**
And Grendel's great teeth came together,
Snapping life shut. Then he stepped to another
Still body, clutched at Beowulf with his claws,
Grasped at a strong-hearted wakeful sleeper
430 —And was instantly seized himself, claws
Bent back as Beowulf leaned up on one arm.
  That shepherd of evil, guardian of crime, **C**
Knew at once that nowhere on earth
Had he met a man whose hands were harder;
435 His mind was flooded with fear—but nothing
Could take his talons and himself from that tight
Hard grip. Grendel's one thought was to run
From Beowulf, flee back to his marsh and hide there:
This was a different Herot than the hall he had emptied.
440 But Higlac's follower remembered his final
Boast and, standing erect, stopped
The monster's flight, fastened those claws
In his fists till they cracked, clutched Grendel **D**
Closer. The infamous killer fought
445 For his freedom, wanting no flesh but retreat,
Desiring nothing but escape; his claws
Had been caught, he was trapped. That trip to Herot
Was a miserable journey for the writhing monster!
  The high hall rang, its roof boards swayed,
450 And Danes shook with terror. Down
The aisles the battle swept, angry
And wild. Herot trembled, wonderfully
Built to withstand the blows, the struggling
Great bodies beating at its beautiful walls;
455 Shaped and fastened with iron, inside
And out, artfully worked, the building
Stood firm. Its benches rattled, fell
To the floor, gold-covered boards grating **E**
As Grendel and Beowulf battled across them.
460 Hrothgar's wise men had fashioned Herot
To stand forever; only fire,
They had planned, could shatter what such skill had put
Together, swallow in hot flames such splendor
Of ivory and iron and wood. Suddenly
465 The sounds changed, the Danes started
In new terror, cowering in their beds as the terrible
Screams of the Almighty's enemy sang
In the darkness, the horrible shrieks of pain
And defeat, the tears torn out of Grendel's

B. Reader's Response: Shaping Interpretations

? Why do you think Beowulf allows Grendel to slaughter one of the Geats before taking action himself?
[Sample responses: Perhaps Beowulf is taking time to formulate a plan of attack or perhaps Grendel moves too quickly.]

C. Literary Element: Kennings

? What kennings associate Grendel with evil? (See Elements of Literature, pp. 48–49, for more about Kennings.) [Two appear in l. 432.]

D. Language Note: Vivid Verbs

? What specific verbs are used to create a tone of fierceness in Beowulf's confrontation with Grendel?
[Possible responses: *fastened, cracked, clutched, fought.*]

E. Exploring the Historical Period

A burial mound unearthed at Sutton Hoo in East Anglia in 1939 yielded silver dishes, forty-five gold items, and thousands of intricately mounted garnets. The coffin—once an eighty-six-foot warrior's ship—was completely decayed but clearly outlined. A scepter suggests that it was the burial site of a great king. Many scholars believe that the presence of a few Christian artifacts at the otherwise non-Christian burial site point to King Raedwald of East Anglia, who died between A.D. 616 and 627; Raedwald was baptized, but his non-Christian wife kept an altar to the Anglo-Saxon gods. Previous to this find, scholars had doubted that artisans of that era were capable of creating the magnificent treasures described in *Beowulf*. Instead, the golden jewelry at Sutton Hoo is the best example of Germanic work discovered from this period. Since many of the treasures—such as a Coptic bronze bowl from Egypt—were not of Anglo-Saxon origin, they indicate that the Anglo-Saxons carried on a much livelier and more extensive trade than once believed.

The description of Herot in these lines has been confirmed by archaeological finds. The building was apparently built of wood held together with iron bands. The highly gabled roof was overlaid with gold.

B. Literary Element: Symbolism

? What additional evidence is there that the fight between Grendel and Beowulf is symbolic of the war between good and evil? [Line 488 suggests Grendel is doomed to hell. Line 492 indicates Grendel has warred with God. It is also significant that Grendel's power leaves him as he grapples with Beowulf.]

C. Critical Reading: Comparing and Contrasting

Many people think that *Beowulf* may have been sung during three sittings, one for each of the fights. Have students start a three-column chart to compare and contrast Beowulf's battle with Grendel and the two battles that follow.

Battle with Grendel	Battle with Grendel's Mother	Battle with Dragon

470 Taut throat, hell's captive caught in the arms
Of him who of all the men on earth
Was the strongest.

9

That mighty protector of men
Meant to hold the monster till its life
Leaped out, knowing the fiend was no use
475 To anyone in Denmark. All of Beowulf's
Band had jumped from their beds, ancestral
Swords raised and ready, determined
To protect their prince if they could. Their courage
Was great but all wasted: They could hack at Grendel
480 From every side, trying to open
A path for his evil soul, but their points
Could not hurt him, the sharpest and hardest iron
Could not scratch at his skin, for that sin-stained demon
Had bewitched all men's weapons, laid spells
485 That blunted every mortal man's blade.
And yet his time had come, his days
Were over, his death near; down
To hell he would go, swept groaning and helpless
To the waiting hands of still worse fiends.
490 Now he discovered—once the afflictor
Of men, tormentor of their days—what it meant
To feud with Almighty God: Grendel
Saw that his strength was deserting him, his claws
Bound fast, Higlac's brave follower tearing at
495 His hands. The monster's hatred rose higher,
But his power had gone. He twisted in pain,
And the bleeding sinews deep in his shoulder
Snapped, muscle and bone split
And broke. The battle was over, Beowulf
500 Had been granted new glory: Grendel escaped,
But wounded as he was could flee to his den,
His miserable hole at the bottom of the marsh,
Only to die, to wait for the end
Of all his days. And after that bloody
505 Combat the Danes laughed with delight.
He who had come to them from across the sea,
Bold and strong-minded, had driven affliction
Off, purged Herot clean. He was happy,
Now, with that night's fierce work; the Danes
510 Had been served as he'd boasted he'd serve them; Beowulf,

Eagle shield ornament (7th century). Sutton Hoo ship treasure.

British Museum, London.

WORDS TO OWN
taut (tôt) *adj.:* stretched tight.
sinews (sin′yo͞oz) *n. pl.:* tendons or connective tissues.

A prince of the Geats, had killed Grendel,
Ended the grief, the sorrow, the suffering
Forced on Hrothgar's helpless people
By a bloodthirsty fiend. No Dane doubted
515 The victory, for the proof, hanging high
From the rafters where Beowulf had hung it, was the monster's
Arm, claw and shoulder and all.

10

And then, in the morning, crowds surrounded
Herot, warriors coming to that hall
520 From faraway lands, princes and leaders
Of men hurrying to behold the monster's
Great staggering tracks. They gaped with no sense
Of sorrow, felt no regret for his suffering,
Went tracing his bloody footprints, his beaten
525 And lonely flight, to the edge of the lake
Where he'd dragged his corpselike way, doomed
And already weary of his vanishing life.
The water was bloody, steaming and boiling
In horrible pounding waves, heat
530 Sucked from his magic veins; but the swirling
Surf had covered his death, hidden
Deep in murky darkness his miserable
End, as hell opened to receive him.
Then old and young rejoiced, turned back
535 From that happy pilgrimage, mounted their hard-hooved
Horses, high-spirited stallions, and rode them
Slowly toward Herot again, retelling
Beowulf's bravery as they jogged along.
And over and over they swore that nowhere
540 On earth or under the spreading sky
Or between the seas, neither south nor north,
Was there a warrior worthier to rule over men.
(But no one meant Beowulf's praise to belittle
Hrothgar, their kind and gracious king!) . . .

*Grendel's monstrous mother, in grief for her son, next
attacks Herot, and in her dripping claws she carries off one
man—Hrothgar's closest friend. The monster also carries off
Grendel's arm, which Beowulf had hung high from the
rafters. Beowulf is awakened and called for again. In one of*

Detail of picture stone from Larbro, Gotland, Sweden.

WORDS TO OWN
murky (murk′ē) *adj.:* shadowy.
pilgrimage (pil′grim·ij) *n.:* journey made to a place of religious or historical interest.

D. Reader's Response: Shaping Interpretations

? Why do you think Beowulf hangs Grendel's arm from the rafters of Herot? [Sample responses: If Herot, with its shining gold roof, does represent Creation, or good, then this symbol of evil, now made useless, contrasts with the symbol of good. More simply, the torn arm can be seen as a symbol of victory or as a warning to other monsters.]

E. Humanities Connection
Some scholars point out a close parallel between Grendel's mere and the vision of hell in Sermon 17 of the tenth-century *Bickling Homilies,* in which St. Paul visits hell under the protection of St. Michael. The parallel is seen as evidence that the Anglo-Saxons would have equated Grendel's lair with the Christian hell.

A. Reader's Response: Shaping Interpretations

? How do you feel about Grendel as you read Gardner's interpretation? [Sample responses: Grendel seems lonely and sad in the first lines. He seems embittered by his circumstances. He is also sarcastic and seems to relish the evil he does.]

B. Element of Literature: Tone

? What is the tone of this passage? [Possible answer: He seems sarcastic here, using a pleasant word like *greeting* yet describing it as a "cold blast." Readers could also interpret his purported admiration for the Shaper as sarcastic.]

C. Literary Element: Imagery

? What imagery in the description of Grendel's lair associates Grendel with death and darkness? [Possible response: Images of blackness abound, especially in ll. 545–554. When the wind stirs the waves, the waves are dark and black as they splash toward the sky. The deer and stag prefer to die on the shore rather than to attempt to save their lives by jumping into the lair, also associating the lair with death.]

Connections — A NOVEL

Courtesy of Alfred A. Knopf.

In his novel *Grendel* (1971), the contemporary American writer John Gardner (1933–1982) retells part of *Beowulf* from the point of view of the monster. In this excerpt, Grendel tells his own version of one of his raids on Hrothgar's hall.

from Grendel

John Gardner

I sigh, sink into the silence, and cross it like wind. Behind my back, at the world's end, my pale slightly glowing fat mother sleeps on, old, sick at heart, in our dingy underground room. Life-bloated, baffled, long-suffering hag. Guilty, she imagines, of some unremembered, perhaps ancestral crime. (She must have some human in her.) Not that she thinks. Not that she dissects and ponders the dusty mechanical bits of her miserable life's curse. She clutches at me in her sleep as if to crush me. I break away. "Why are we here?" I used to ask her. "Why do we stand this putrid, stinking hole?" She trembles at my words. Her fat lips shake. "Don't ask!" her wiggling claws implore. (She never speaks.) "Don't ask!" It must be some terrible secret, I used to think. I'd give her a crafty squint. She'll tell me, in time, I thought. But she told me nothing. I waited on. That was before the old dragon, calm as winter, unveiled the truth. He was not a friend.

And so I come through trees and towns to the lights of Hrothgar's meadhall. I am no stranger here. A respected guest. Eleven years now and going on twelve I have come up this clean-mown central hill, dark shadow out of the woods below, and have knocked politely on the high oak door, bursting its hinges and sending the shock of my greeting inward like a cold blast out of a cave. "Grendel!" they

the most famous verses in the epic, the old king describes where Grendel and his mother live.

11

545   . . . "They live in secret places, windy
        Cliffs, wolf-dens where water pours
        From the rocks, then runs underground, where mist
        Steams like black clouds, and the groves of trees
        Growing out over their lake are all covered
550   With frozen spray, and wind down snakelike
        Roots that reach as far as the water
        And help keep it dark. At night that lake
        Burns like a torch. No one knows its bottom,
        No wisdom reaches such depths. A deer,

CONNECTING WITH *BEOWULF*

If you accept the interpretation of Grendel that Gardner has written, does it change your perspective on the battle between Grendel and Beowulf? Explain your answer. [Possible answers: Yes, reading about Grendel's feelings makes readers realize that there are two sides to a story—that even evil Grendel may have had a reason for his terrible actions; or no, Grendel was so cavalier about his awful forays into Herot that readers may sympathize even more with Beowulf.]

squeak, and I smile like exploding spring. The old Shaper, a man I cannot help but admire, goes out the back window with his harp at a single bound, though blind as a bat. The drunkest of Hrothgar's thanes come reeling and clanking down from their wall-hung beds, all shouting their meady, outrageous boasts, their heavy swords aswirl like eagles' wings. "Woe, woe, woe!" cries Hrothgar, hoary with winters, peeking in, wide-eyed, from his bedroom in back. His wife, looking in behind him, makes a scene. The thanes in the meadhall blow out the lights and cover the wide stone fireplace with shields. I laugh, crumple over; I can't help myself. In the darkness, I alone see clear as day. While they squeal and screech and bump into each other, I silently sack up my dead and withdraw to the woods. I eat and laugh and eat until I can barely walk, my chest-hair matted with dribbled blood, and then the roosters on the hill crow, and dawn comes over the roofs of the houses, and all at once I am filled with gloom again.

"This is some punishment sent us," I hear them bawling from the hill.

My head aches. Morning nails my eyes.

"Some god is angry," I hear a woman keen.

"The people of Scyld and Herogar and Hrothgar are mired in sin!"

My belly rumbles, sick on their sour meat. I crawl through bloodstained leaves to the eaves of the forest, and there peak out. The dogs fall silent at the edge of my spell, and where the king's hall surmounts the town, the blind old Shaper, harp clutched tight to his fragile chest, stares futilely down, straight at me. Otherwise nothing. Pigs root dully at the posts of a wooden fence. A rumple-horned ox lies chewing in dew and shade. A few men, lean, wearing animal skins, look up at the gables of the king's hall, or at the vultures circling casually beyond. Hrothgar says nothing, hoarfrost-bearded, his features cracked and crazed. Inside, I hear the people praying—whimpering, whining, mumbling, pleading—to their numerous sticks and stones. He doesn't go in. The king has lofty theories of his own.

"Theories," I whisper to the bloodstained ground. So the dragon once spoke. ("They'd map out roads through Hell with their crackpot theories!" I recall his laugh.)

Then the groaning and praying stop, and on the side of the hill the dirge-slow shoveling begins. . . .

555 Hunted through the woods by packs of hounds,
A stag with great horns, though driven through the forest
From faraway places, prefers to die
On those shores, refuses to save its life
In that water. It isn't far, nor is it
560 A pleasant spot! When the wind stirs
And storms, waves splash toward the sky,
As dark as the air, as black as the rain
That the heavens weep. Our only help,
Again, lies with you. Grendel's mother
565 Is hidden in her terrible home, in a place
You've not seen. Seek it, if you dare! Save us,
Once more, and again twisted gold,
Heaped-up ancient treasure, will reward you
For the battle you win!"

Gundestrup cauldron.
National Museum, Copenhagen.

BEOWULF 37

Making Meanings (Parts 1–11)

First Thoughts

1. Responses might include images of Grendel, Herot, Beowulf, the swimming match, or Beowulf's battle with Grendel.

Reviewing the Text

a. Because of Grendel's murderous raids, the warriors of King Hrothgar are afraid to gather in their hall.

b. God protects Hrothgar's throne.

c. Hrothgar's men make sacrifices and vows to the pagan gods. Some have also made ineffective attempts to remain at Herot and ward off the monster.

d. Unferth calls him a boaster and charges that he was bested in the swimming match with Brecca. Beowulf replies that he and Brecca were separated by a storm and that, afterward, Beowulf slew nine sea monsters.

e. After destroying one Geat, Grendel tries to grasp Beowulf. The hero grips the monster and traps him. Beowulf mortally wounds the monster by tearing off his arm, and Grendel flees from the hall.

Shaping Interpretations

2. Herot is a bright hall, a place of drinking, singing, and feasting. Grendel lives in a cold, dark lake that is so forbidding that even hunted deer prefer to die on its shores rather than save their lives by plunging into its waters.

3. Most students will agree that the songs are about creation and that Grendel is associated with destruction. The text of the poem specifically indicates that the bard's songs are about God's creation of the world (see ll. 5–13).

4. The darkness of night is associated with death and destruction—an appropriate time for the evil Grendel to prowl: See especially ll. 1–19, 30, 49–50, 82, 112, 392–396, 547–548, and 562.

5. Herot represents order, light—even godliness. Grendel, God's enemy, would naturally hate such a symbol. Students may suggest that the symbolic meaning is the universal struggle between light and dark, good and evil, life and death.

First Thoughts

1. What **images** came to your mind as you read this part of the epic? Which image was most vivid?

Shaping Interpretations

2. In what specific ways does Herot contrast with the place where Grendel lives?

3. In lines 3–13, the poet describes the bard's songs in Hrothgar's hall. How does the content of the songs contrast with Grendel and his world?

Reviewing the Text

a. Why does Herot remain empty for twelve years?

b. Why doesn't Grendel touch King Hrothgar's throne?

c. What do Hrothgar and his council do to try to save his guest-hall?

d. How is Beowulf taunted by the jealous Unferth? How does Beowulf reply?

e. Describe what happens to Grendel when he raids Herot and finds Beowulf in charge.

4. What significance can you see in the fact that Grendel attacks at night? What **images** describing Grendel might associate him with death or darkness?

5. Why do you think Grendel hates Herot? What **symbolic** meaning might underlie the confrontation between Grendel and Hrothgar?

6. Consider the tale-within-a-tale about Beowulf's swimming match with Brecca. What does this story contribute to your understanding of Beowulf's heroic **character** and of his powers?

7. Why do you think it's important to Beowulf and to his image as an **epic hero** that he meet Grendel without a weapon? What **symbolism** do you see in the uselessness of human weapons against Grendel?

8. What do you think of John Gardner's depiction of Grendel (page 36)? Do you feel any sympathy for Grendel? Why or why not?

Connecting with the Text

9. Review the Reader's Log entry you made before you read this part of *Beowulf*. Does Beowulf remind you of any heroes from history, current events, books, television, or movies? Who? What similarities do you notice among them? Just as important, how are they different?

Silver and gold brooch with amber ornaments (9th century). Roscrea, County Tipperary.

National Museum of Ireland, Dublin.

6. The tale-within-a-tale foreshadows Beowulf's strength and courage in the battles to come. Beowulf's astonishing feats reveal his superiority to the sea and to the sea monsters. This superiority, in turn, foreshadows Beowulf's victory over Grendel, whose habitat is the dark waters of the marshy lake.

7. As an epic hero, Beowulf must show superior physical strength. Because he must also be supremely ethical, he must not take unfair advantage over Grendel. Student responses will vary, but some may suggest that this motif symbolically indicates that the struggle is really on a spiritual level, rather than on a literal, physical level. In other words, the battle against Grendel is really a battle against the forces of evil.

(Answers continue on p. T39.)

Sigurd kills the dragon. Detail of carved portal of Hylestad stave church (12th century).

Universitetets, Oldsaksamling, Oslo.

Carrying the sword Hrunting, Beowulf goes to the lake where Grendel's mother has her underwater lair. Then, fully armed, he makes a heroic dive to the depths of this watery hell.

The Monster's Mother

12

570 . . . He leaped into the lake, would not wait for anyone's
Answer; the heaving water covered him
Over. For hours he sank through the waves;
At last he saw the mud of the bottom.
And all at once the greedy she-wolf
575 Who'd ruled those waters for half a hundred
Years discovered him, saw that a creature

8. Students may sympathize with Grendel or see him as even more evil after reading Gardner's version. If students sympathize, it may be that Gardner helps them see Grendel's perspective; however, the perspective also shows that Grendel laughs about his evil deeds, which students may interpret as mean.

Connecting with the Text

9. Students may think of such heroes as Superman, Abraham Lincoln, Joan of Arc, Colin Powell, or Ulysses. Students may point out that these heroes are strong leaders who stand for a cause. These heroes differ in the ways they show strength and the causes they champion.

RESPONDING TO THE ART: VISUAL LITERACY

Although the design in this Norwegian church portal was carved in the twelfth century and Beowulf was first recorded in 700 A.D., ask students to find any similarities between the portal and the epic. [Possible response: As in Beowulf, here a warrior with a shield battles a dragon.]

OPTIONS FOR TEACHING

STRATEGIES FOR INCLUSION

Advanced Some students may be interested in comparing and contrasting another epic hero—such as Ulysses, Hector, Aeneas, Achilles—to Beowulf. They will need to determine areas of comparison, such as family background, youthful deeds, goals, moral values, relationships with their followers, accomplishments, or deaths. Students could make charts with graphics to display their findings for the class.

Less Proficient Readers Ask pairs of students to write a translation of a section of the poem. To begin each translation, have one student rewrite the first sentence in conversational English. Have the second student evaluate the translation and suggest possible changes. Then, have students switch roles and continue the process until they finish. This process helps the students to see what good readers always do: They make sense of the passage in

their own minds. After you have modeled a few sentences, have each pair involved choose a distinct set of twenty lines to translate. Keep copies to display in the classroom, publish a translation, or use the copies as models for future classes. ☞

A. Literary Element: Character

? When Beowulf fights with Grendel's mother, what characteristics help him remain unbeaten? [Possible answer: A desire for fame and a refusal to give up, even though his sword, Hrunting, is useless. His anger, the strength in his hands, and his persistence bring him victory.]

B. Critical Reading: Finding Details

? What saves Beowulf from being killed by Grendel's mother's dagger? [His chain mail shirt.]

C. Reader's Response: First Thoughts

? Do you feel any sympathy for Grendel's mother? Why? [Sample responses: No, she has an evil nature and murderous ways; or yes, I can sympathize with the way she defends her son.]

From above had come to explore the bottom
Of her wet world. She welcomed him in her claws,
Clutched at him savagely but could not harm him,
580 Tried to work her fingers through the tight
Ring-woven mail on his breast, but tore
And scratched in vain. Then she carried him, armor
And sword and all, to her home; he struggled
To free his weapon, and failed. The fight
585 Brought other monsters swimming to see
Her catch, a host of sea beasts who beat at
His mail shirt, stabbing with tusks and teeth
As they followed along. Then he realized, suddenly,
That she'd brought him into someone's battle-hall,
590 And there the water's heat could not hurt him,
Nor anything in the lake attack him through
The building's high-arching roof. A brilliant
Light burned all around him, the lake
Itself like a fiery flame.
            Then he saw
595 The mighty water witch, and swung his sword,
His ring-marked blade, straight at her head;
The iron sang its fierce song,
Sang Beowulf's strength. But her guest
Discovered that no sword could slice her evil
600 Skin, that Hrunting could not hurt her, was useless
Now when he needed it. They wrestled, she ripped
And tore and clawed at him, bit holes in his helmet,
And that too failed him; for the first time in years
Of being worn to war it would earn no glory;
605 It was the last time anyone would wear it. But Beowulf
Longed only for fame, leaped back
Into battle. He tossed his sword aside,
Angry; the steel-edged blade lay where
He'd dropped it. If weapons were useless he'd use
610 His hands, the strength in his fingers. So fame
Comes to the men who mean to win it
And care about nothing else! He raised
His arms and seized her by the shoulder; anger
Doubled his strength, he threw her to the floor.
615 She fell, Grendel's fierce mother, and the Geats'
Proud prince was ready to leap on her. But she rose
At once and repaid him with her clutching claws,
Wildly tearing at him. He was weary, that best
And strongest of soldiers; his feet stumbled
620 And in an instant she had him down, held helpless.
Squatting with her weight on his stomach, she drew
A dagger, brown with dried blood and prepared
To avenge her only son. But he was stretched
On his back, and her stabbing blade was blunted

Battersea shield.
© British Museum, London.

40 THE ANGLO-SAXONS

Writing: Beowulf's Epitaph
Invite students to write an epitaph for Beowulf, praising his deeds, leadership, or character. They should include at least two lines from the poem in their epitaphs.

Strategic Reading To encourage students to extend each other's thinking, divide the class into pairs to read aloud and exchange interpretations, ideas, and questions. As students read aloud, have them pause to express any thoughts about the content, any problems or dilemmas they encounter and possible ways to resolve them, any connections to actual people or situations, and interpretations they are making.

Language and Style Review participles and participial phrases in the Language Handbook. Then, ask students to find examples of the poem's use of participial phrases to embed information without wasting words. Use the last sentence of Part 17 as an example. Have the class together create another sentence with the same syntax. Then, have students create four of their own sentences modeled after the *Beowulf* syntax.

625 By the woven mail shirt he wore on his chest.
The hammered links held; the point
Could not touch him. He'd have traveled to the bottom of the earth,
Edgetho's son, and died there, if that shining
Woven metal had not helped—and Holy
630 God, who sent him victory, gave judgment
For truth and right, Ruler of the Heavens,
Once Beowulf was back on his feet and fighting.

13

Then he saw, hanging on the wall, a heavy
Sword, hammered by giants, strong
635 And blessed with their magic, the best of all weapons **D**
But so massive that no ordinary man could lift
Its carved and decorated length. He drew it
From its scabbard, broke the chain on its hilt,°
And then, savage, now, angry
640 And desperate, lifted it high over his head
And struck with all the strength he had left,
Caught her in the neck and cut it through,
Broke bones and all. Her body fell
To the floor, lifeless, the sword was wet
645 With her blood, and Beowulf rejoiced at the sight.
The brilliant light shone, suddenly,
As though burning in that hall, and as bright as Heaven's **E**
Own candle, lit in the sky. He looked
At her home, then following along the wall
650 Went walking, his hands tight on the sword,
His heart still angry. He was hunting another
Dead monster, and took his weapon with him
For final revenge against Grendel's vicious
Attacks, his nighttime raids, over
655 And over, coming to Herot when Hrothgar's
Men slept, killing them in their beds,
Eating some on the spot, fifteen
Or more, and running to his loathsome moor
With another such sickening meal waiting
660 In his pouch. But Beowulf repaid him for those visits,
Found him lying dead in his corner,
Armless, exactly as that fierce fighter
Had sent him out from Herot, then struck off
His head with a single swift blow. The body
665 Jerked for the last time, then lay still. . . .

638. scabbard . . . hilt: A scabbard is a case that holds the blade of a sword; a hilt is a sword's handle.

WORDS TO OWN
loathsome (lōth′səm) *adj.:* disgusting.

A. Critical Reading: Drawing Conclusions

? Why does Beowulf not rest on his laurels at this point instead of fighting, as an aged king, a battle whose odds are against him? [Possible answers: Beowulf has always done what needs to be done, regardless of the consequences; he remains the same dedicated, determined defender of good against evil. He cannot give up, no matter what the cost, no matter what the odds.]

B. Humanities Connection

At this point, you might want students to compare Beowulf with Ulysses, as he is portrayed in Lord Tennyson's poem of that name (see p. 822).

C. Literary Element: Character

Ask students to describe Beowulf as he sets out for this final encounter. [Possible answer: Beowulf is firm, calm, determined, almost stoical, as he faces his final enemy. Students should understand that in displaying these characteristics, Beowulf epitomizes the Anglo-Saxon code of valor and courage to the very end.]

D. Reader's Response: Shaping Interpretations

? What do you think Beowulf's motivation is in going after the dragon's treasure hoard? [Sample responses: Collecting treasure through war is seen as a sign of valor on the part of the leader. It is also the leader's responsibility to take care of his followers financially.]

Beowulf carries Grendel's head to King Hrothgar and then returns gift-laden to the land of the Geats, where he succeeds to the throne. After fifty winters pass, Beowulf, now an old man, faces his final task: He must fight a dragon who, angry because a thief had stolen a jeweled cup from the dragon's hoard of gold, is laying waste to the Geats' land. Beowulf and eleven warriors are guided to the dragon's lair by the thief who stole the cup. For Beowulf, the price of this last victory will be great.

The Final Battle

14

. . . Then he said farewell to his followers,
Each in his turn, for the last time:
    "I'd use no sword, no weapon, if this beast
Could be killed without it, crushed to death
670 Like Grendel, gripped in my hands and torn
Limb from limb. But his breath will be burning
Hot, poison will pour from his tongue.
I feel no shame, with shield and sword
And armor, against this monster: When he comes to me
675 I mean to stand, not run from his shooting
Flames, stand till fate decides
Which of us wins. My heart is firm,
My hands calm: I need no hot
Words. Wait for me close by, my friends.
680 We shall see, soon, who will survive
This bloody battle, stand when the fighting
Is done. No one else could do
What I mean to, here, no man but me
Could hope to defeat this monster. No one
685 Could try. And this dragon's treasure, his gold
And everything hidden in that tower, will be mine
Or war will sweep me to a bitter death!"
      Then Beowulf rose, still brave, still strong,
And with his shield at his side, and a mail shirt on his breast,
690 Strode calmly, confidently, toward the tower, under
The rocky cliffs: No coward could have walked there!
And then he who'd endured dozens of desperate
Battles, who'd stood boldly while swords and shields
Clashed, the best of kings, saw
695 Huge stone arches and felt the heat
Of the dragon's breath, flooding down
Through the hidden entrance, too hot for anyone
To stand, a streaming current of fire
And smoke that blocked all passage. And the Geats'
700 Lord and leader, angry, lowered
His sword and roared out a battle cry,

Dragonesque brooch
(2nd century).
Romano-British.

© British Museum, London.

42 THE ANGLO-SAXONS

A call so loud and clear that it reached through
The hoary° rock, hung in the dragon's
Ear. The beast rose, angry,

705 Knowing a man had come—and then nothing
But war could have followed. Its breath came first,
A steaming cloud pouring from the stone,
Then the earth itself shook. Beowulf
Swung his shield into place, held it

710 In front of him, facing the entrance. The dragon
Coiled and uncoiled, its heart urging it
Into battle. Beowulf's ancient sword
Was waiting, unsheathed, his sharp and gleaming
Blade. The beast came closer; both of them

715 Were ready, each set on slaughter. The Geats'
Great prince stood firm, unmoving, prepared
Behind his high shield, waiting in his shining
Armor. The monster came quickly toward him,
Pouring out fire and smoke, hurrying

720 To its fate. Flames beat at the iron
Shield, and for a time it held, protected
Beowulf as he'd planned; then it began to melt,
And for the first time in his life that famous prince
Fought with fate against him, with glory

725 Denied him. He knew it, but he raised his sword
And struck at the dragon's scaly hide.
The ancient blade broke, bit into
The monster's skin, drew blood, but cracked
And failed him before it went deep enough, helped him

730 Less than he needed. The dragon leaped
With pain, thrashed and beat at him, spouting
Murderous flames, spreading them everywhere.
And the Geats' ring-giver did not boast of glorious
Victories in other wars: His weapon

735 Had failed him, deserted him, now when he needed it
Most, that excellent sword. Edgetho's
Famous son stared at death,
Unwilling to leave this world, to exchange it
For a dwelling in some distant place—a journey

740 Into darkness that all men must make, as death
Ends their few brief hours on earth.
          Quickly, the dragon came at him, encouraged
As Beowulf fell back; its breath flared,
And he suffered, wrapped around in swirling

745 Flames—a king, before, but now
A beaten warrior. None of his comrades
Came to him, helped him, his brave and noble
Followers; they ran for their lives, fled
Deep in a wood. And only one of them

750 Remained, stood there, miserable, remembering,
As a good man must, what kinship should mean.

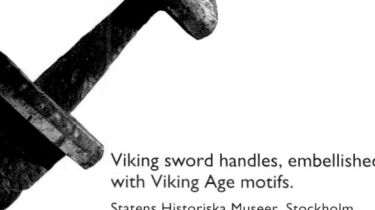

Viking sword handles, embellished
with Viking Age motifs.
Statens Historiska Museer, Stockholm.

BEOWULF 43

A. Reader's Response: Extending the Text

Have students record in their Reader's Logs the words Beowulf might have said to his followers who abandoned him during his fight with the dragon.

Detail of three-ringed gold collar (6th century).
Statens Historiska Museer, Stockholm.

15

His name was Wiglaf, he was Wexstan's son
And a good soldier; his family had been Swedish,
Once. Watching Beowulf, he could see
755 How his king was suffering, burning. Remembering
Everything his lord and cousin had given him,
Armor and gold and the great estates
Wexstan's family enjoyed, Wiglaf's
Mind was made up; he raised his yellow
760 Shield and drew his sword. . . .
        And Wiglaf, his heart heavy, uttered
The kind of words his comrades deserved:
        "I remember how we sat in the mead-hall, drinking
And boasting of how brave we'd be when Beowulf
765 Needed us, he who gave us these swords
And armor: All of us swore to repay him,
When the time came, kindness for kindness
—With our lives, if he needed them. He allowed us to join him,
Chose us from all his great army, thinking
770 Our boasting words had some weight, believing
Our promises, trusting our swords. He took us
For soldiers, for men. He meant to kill
This monster himself, our mighty king,
Fight this battle alone and unaided,
775 As in the days when his strength and daring dazzled
Men's eyes. But those days are over and gone
And now our lord must lean on younger
Arms. And we must go to him, while angry
Flames burn at his flesh, help
780 Our glorious king! By almighty God,
I'd rather burn myself than see
Flames swirling around my lord.
And who are we to carry home
Our shields before we've slain his enemy
785 And ours, to run back to our homes with Beowulf
So hard-pressed here? I swear that nothing
He ever did deserved an end
Like this, dying miserably and alone,
Butchered by this savage beast: We swore
790 That these swords and armor were each for us all!" . . .

44 THE ANGLO-SAXONS

OPTIONS FOR TEACHING

PROFESSIONAL NOTES

Cultural Diversity Divide the class into groups of four to explore the ways different societies regard older people and the process of aging. From their own experiences or from their research, students may share examples of how various cultures treat their elders.

Encourage students also to notice older state, national, and world leaders who have major influence. The groups could then categorize the contributions older family members make to their families and to society as a whole.

Together, Beowulf and the young Wiglaf kill the dragon, but the old king is fatally wounded. Beowulf, thinking of his people, asks to see the monster's treasure. Wiglaf enters the dragon's cave and finds a priceless hoard of jewels and gold.

16

    . . . Then Wiglaf went back, anxious
To return while Beowulf was alive, to bring him
Treasure they'd won together. He ran,
Hoping his wounded king, weak
795 And dying, had not left the world too soon.
Then he brought their treasure to Beowulf, and found
His famous king bloody, gasping
For breath. But Wiglaf sprinkled water
Over his lord, until the words
800 Deep in his breast broke through and were heard.
Beholding the treasure he spoke, haltingly:
    "For this, this gold, these jewels, I thank
Our Father in Heaven, Ruler of the Earth—
For all of this, that His grace has given me,
805 Allowed me to bring to my people while breath **B**
Still came to my lips. I sold my life
For this treasure, and I sold it well. Take
What I leave, Wiglaf, lead my people,
Help them; my time is gone. Have
810 The brave Geats build me a tomb,
When the funeral flames have burned me, and build it
Here, at the water's edge, high
On this spit of land, so sailors can see
This tower, and remember my name, and call it
815 Beowulf's tower, and boats in the darkness
And mist, crossing the sea, will know it."
    Then that brave king gave the golden
Necklace from around his throat to Wiglaf,
Gave him his gold-covered helmet, and his rings,
820 And his mail shirt, and ordered him to use them well:
    "You're the last of all our far-flung family. **C**
Fate has swept our race away,
Taken warriors in their strength and led them
To the death that was waiting. And now I follow them."
825   The old man's mouth was silent, spoke
No more, had said as much as it could;
He would sleep in the fire, soon. His soul **D**
Left his flesh, flew to glory.

Gilded bronze and ivory casket.
National Museum, Copenhagen.

BEOWULF **45**

A. Cultural Connections

? What attitude toward heroes is shown by the Geats? Is our own tradition similar to the Geats'? [Possible answer: The Geats do not dwell on Beowulf's defeat by the dragon but on his life (ll. 832–834). Most Americans pay homage to the founders, to the presidents, and to others who have greatly affected our country.]

Wiglaf berates the faithless warriors who had not gone to the aid of their king. With sorrow, the Geats then cremate the corpse of their greatest king. They place his ashes, along with all of the dragon's treasure, in a huge burial tower by the sea, where it can be seen by voyagers.

17

. . . And then twelve of the bravest Geats
830 Rode their horses around the tower,
Telling their sorrow, telling stories
Of their dead king and his greatness, his glory,
Praising him for heroic deeds, for a life
As noble as his name. So should all men
835 Raise up words for their lords, warm
With love, when their shield and protector leaves
His body behind, sends his soul
On high. And so Beowulf's followers
Rode, mourning their beloved leader,
840 Crying that no better king had ever
Lived, no prince so mild, no man
So open to his people, so deserving of praise.

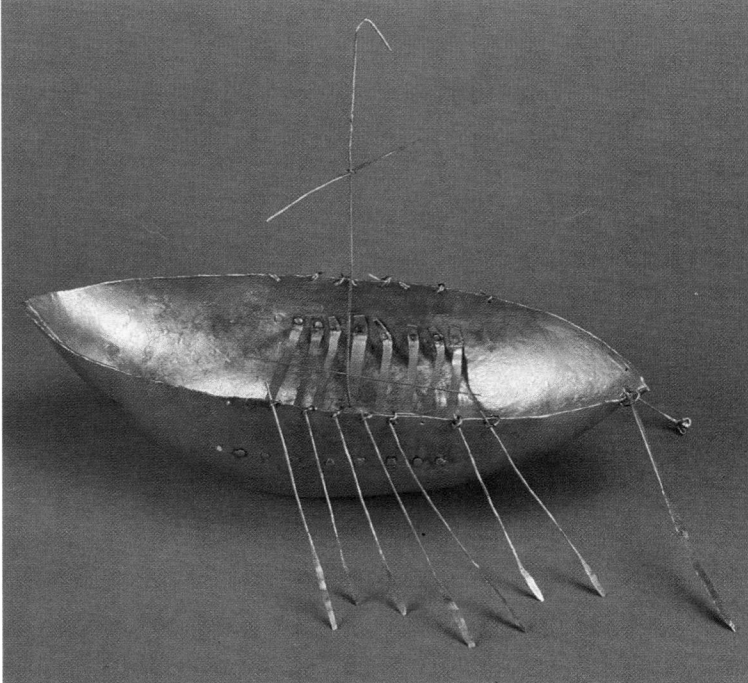

Gold boat (probably 1st century) found at Broighter, County Londonderry, Ireland.

National Museum of Ireland, Dublin.

46 THE ANGLO-SAXONS

OPTIONS FOR TEACHING

ASSESSMENT TOOLS

Check Test: True-False
1. Using his own ancestral sword, Beowulf kills Grendel's mother. [False]
2. Beowulf carries Grendel's head to King Hrothgar and returns home with many fine gifts. [True]
3. Beowulf becomes king of the Geats. [True]
4. After Beowulf's weapons fail him against the dragon, his men rush to help him, but he orders them away. [False]
5. Beowulf names Wiglaf as his successor to the throne. [True]

Ongoing Assessment Allow students to choose a project to show their understanding of the second part of the *Beowulf* excerpts. These projects could include dialectic notes, a cluster diagram, an objective test, or an essay test. You could require one of the tests and one project to be submitted for evaluation.

Life in 999: A Grim Struggle

HOWARD G. CHUA-EOAN

Today's world is measured in light-years and Mach speed and sheathed in silicon and alloy. In the world of 999, on the eve of the first millennium, time moved at the speed of an oxcart or, more often, of a sturdy pair of legs, and the West was built largely on wood. Europe was a collection of untamed forests, countless mile upon mile of trees and brush and brier, dark and inhospitable. Medieval chroniclers used the word *desert* to describe their arboreal world, a place on the cusp of civilization where werewolves and bogeymen still lunged out of the shadows and bandits and marauders maintained their lairs.

Yet the forests, deep and dangerous as they were, also defined existence. Wood kindled forges and kept alive the hearths of the mud-and-thatch huts of the serfs. Peasants fattened their hogs on forest acorns (pork was crucial to basic subsistence in the cold of winter), and wild berries helped supplement the meager diet. In a world without sugar, honey from forest swarms provided the only sweetness for food or drink. The pleasures of the serfs were few and simple: earthy lovemaking and occasional dances and fests.

Feudal lords ruled over western Europe, taking their share of the harvests of primitive agriculture and making the forests their private hunting grounds. Poaching was not simply theft (usually punishable by imprisonment) but a sin against the social order. Without the indulgence of the nobility, the peasants could not even acquire salt, the indispensable ingredient for preserving meat and flavoring a culinary culture that possessed few spices. Though a true money economy did not exist, salt could be bought with poorly circulated coin, which the lord hoarded in his castle and dispensed to the poor only as alms.

It was in the lord's castle too that peasants and their flocks sought refuge from wolf packs and barbarian invaders. In 999, however, castles, like most other buildings in Europe, were made of timber, far from the granite bastions that litter today's imagined Middle Ages. The peasants, meanwhile, were relegated to their simple huts, where everyone—including the animals—slept around the hearth. Straw was scattered on the floors to collect scraps as well as human and animal waste. Housecleaning consisted of sweeping out the straw.

Illness and disease remained in constant residence. Tuberculosis was endemic, and so were scabrous skin diseases of every kind: abscesses, cankers, scrofula, tumors, eczema, and erysipelas. In a throwback to biblical times, lepers constituted a class of pariahs living on the outskirts of villages and cities. Constant famine, rotten flour, and vitamin deficiencies afflicted huge segments of society with blindness, goiter, paralysis, and bone malformations that created hunchbacks and cripples. A man was lucky to survive 30, and 50 was a ripe old age. Most women, many of them succumbing to the ravages of childbirth, lived less than 30 years. There was no time for what is now considered childhood; children of every class had to grow up immediately and be useful as soon as possible. Emperors were leading armies in their teens; John XI became Pope at the age of 21.

While the general population was growing faster than it had in the previous five centuries, there was still a shortage of people to cultivate the fields, clear the woodlands, and work the mills. Local taxes were levied on youths who did not marry upon coming of age. Abortion was considered homicide, and a woman who terminated a pregnancy was expelled from the church.

The nobility spent its waking hours battling foes to preserve its prerogatives, the clergy chanting prayers for the salvation of souls, the serfs laboring to feed and clothe everyone. Night, lit only by burning logs or the rare taper, was always filled with danger and terror. The seasons came and went, punctuated chiefly by the occurrence of plentiful church holidays. The calendar year began at different times for different regions; only later would Europe settle on the Feast of Christ's Circumcision, January 1, as the year's beginning.

Thus there was little panic, not even much interest, as the millennium approached in the final months of 999. For what terrors could the apocalypse hold for a continent that was already shrouded in darkness? Rather Europe—illiterate, diseased, and hungry—seemed grimly resigned to desperation and impoverishment. It was one of the planet's most unpromising corners, the Third World of its age.

—*from Time*

CONNECTING WITH *BEOWULF*

How does the description of Herot compare with the way castles are described in "Life in 999: A Grim Struggle"? [Possible answer: The way Herot's richness and beauty are described in *Beowulf* make it easy to imagine an idyllic castle and fairy tale existence—unless readers stop to think about the realities of that time. This article says that most castles then were made of wood and implies that luxuries were nonexistent.]

B. Critical Reading: Making Inferences

? Why might speed be an important factor in defining an age? [Possible answer: The pace of life affects one's perspective on the world. For example, in today's world, people get impatient in a grocery store line that may take five minutes, whereas obtaining food and preparing a meal or two was an entire day's work in 999.]

C. Reader's Response: Connecting with the Text

? How does this compare with modern expectations for people in their teens or early twenties? [Sample responses: Today, people of that age are considered young. They may be finishing high school or college; they may be starting their first jobs. They are certainly not expected to lead a country or head a church.]

Making Meanings (Parts 12–17)

Questions start on p. 48.

First Thoughts

1. Students will probably express some identity with the themes of loyalty, good versus evil, and courage.

Reviewing the Text

a. Because his sword Hrunting is useless against Grendel's mother, Beowulf fights her with his bare hands. At one point, she pins him to the ground and tries to stab him with a dagger, but Beowulf is protected by his mail shirt and by supernatural aid. He then spies a heavy sword hanging on the wall, and with one stroke he mortally wounds the monster in the neck.

b. The only warrior to come to Beowulf's aid is Wiglaf, who pities Beowulf's suffering and honors his oaths of loyalty.

c. The funeral of Beowulf and the raising of his burial mound conclude the epic.

d. The treasure is buried with Beowulf's body.

A. Critical Reading: Evaluating an Interpretation

? How is the "shrinklet" true to the original? [Students may discuss the battles, major events, and outcomes.]

Answers to First Thoughts and Reviewing the Text appear on p. T47.

Shaping Interpretations

2. This fact might suggest that the dragon, who guards the treasure, is symbolic of death and evil, perhaps even of the devil. Even though Beowulf wants to give the captured treasure to the Geats, it is nevertheless buried with him, symbolically linking Beowulf with death.

3. Details describing the dragon as a serpent, coiled and scaly, occur in ll. 711 and 726. Lines 695–699 and 704–707 also allude to the dragon's fiery breath and the smoke surrounding its lair. The dragon may symbolize death or the devil.

4. In all three battles, Beowulf must fight alone; even his weapons are useless against the enemy. Likewise, in all three battles Beowulf symbolizes goodness fighting against evil. The central conflict might be described as the struggle of good against evil with good ultimately triumphant, but at the price of the hero's death.

5. Given that the structure of Anglo-Saxon society was built on loyalty to a king or protector, the men's failure to help Beowulf is especially ominous. This failure perhaps foreshadows the disintegration of the kingdom after Beowulf's death.

6. Among the words and images students may mention are those in ll. 831, 839, and 840–41. Students may also mention the somber implications of ll. 834–837. Beowulf, who had been the protector, is now dead.

7. Students could mention instances from the epic that reveal the Anglo-Saxon values of courage, loyalty, fighting prowess, and strength (both physical and spiritual). Universal themes are also included: Loyalty and self-sacrifice are admirable traits; good triumphs over evil (but at a painful cost); different members of society have obligations toward one another; and fame can be achieved through good deeds.

Extending the Text

8. **(Synthesis)** Possible responses: The hero story today would probably be told in prose, perhaps in a novel; the setting could be a battleground on earth or in space, or perhaps in a sports arena; the values might include hard work, talent, high monetary rewards, good looks, physical prowess, and power.

9. **(Analysis and Synthesis)** In *Beowulf,* the poet describes the beauty of Herot but neglects to point out the grim circumstances of daily life. Hrothgar's subjects must live in rather unsanitary, brutish conditions without conveniences like regular baths, changes of clothing, or elegant meals. Most are probably poor and uneducated, with little variety in their diets or daily lives.

Challenging the Text

10. **(Evaluation)** Students may point out that most major characters in *Beowulf* are men; only Welthow is described. Encourage students to tie their answers to the text and to information about the role of women in Anglo-Saxon society (p. 10).

A Beowulf Shrinklet

Hrothgar and Grendel could not get along
the populace thought killing was wrong.
Beowulf the hero from o'er the sea,
from monster or dragon he would not flee,
"If treasure I wanteth," the hero thought;
"then I will journey to the great Herot."
Grendel died at the end of the battle
his mother enraged (and all but little);
wanted revenge for her beloved son,
but the great bold hero ended her fun.
For proof he carried the head and the sword,
and traveled back with troops for his reward.
The great Beowulf returned to his home,
over the oceans on seaweed and foam.
His conscience lived happily as the king;
and died at the hands of another thing.

—Calen Wood
Bakersfield High School
Bakersfield, California

MAKING MEANINGS

First Thoughts

1. Beowulf's story is an ancient one, more than one thousand years old. Did its age make it entirely alien to you, or did you find that it deals with issues or themes that seem relevant in our modern society as well? If so, what are they?

Reviewing the Text

a. Describe how Beowulf manages to kill Grendel's mother.

b. Who comes to Beowulf's aid in his final battle with the dragon? Why does he help Beowulf?

c. What sad scene concludes the epic?

d. What happens to the dragon's hoard?

Shaping Interpretations

2. A hoarded treasure in Old English literature usually **symbolizes** spiritual death or damnation. How does this fact add significance to Beowulf's last fight with the dragon?

3. What details describe the dragon? Keeping those details in mind, explain what the dragon might **symbolize** as Beowulf's final foe.

4. Beowulf battles Grendel, Grendel's mother, and the dragon. What do these battles have in common, and what do they suggest Beowulf and his enemies might represent for the Anglo-Saxons?

5. Given what you know about the structure of Anglo-Saxon society, explain what is especially ominous about the behavior of Beowulf's men during the final battle. What does this suggest about the future of the kingdom?

6. The epic closes on a somber, elegiac note—a note of mourning. What words or **images** contribute to this tone?

7. Epic poetry usually embodies the attitudes and ideals of an entire culture. What values of Anglo-Saxon society does *Beowulf* reveal? What universal **themes** does it also reveal?

Extending the Text

8. How would we tell a hero story today? What would the **setting** be, what would the enemy be, and what values would the hero embody?

9. "Life in 999: A Grim Struggle" (page 47) describes daily life in late Anglo-Saxon England. How does this picture of daily life relate to what you've read in *Beowulf*?

Challenging the Text

10. What do you think of the way women are portrayed in (or absent from) *Beowulf*?

ELEMENTS OF LITERATURE

Alliteration and Kennings: Taking the Burden off the Bard

The Anglo-Saxon oral poet was assisted by two poetic devices, alliteration and the kenning.

Alliteration is the repetition of sounds in the beginning of words. In fact, Anglo-Saxon poetry is often called alliterative poetry: Instead of rhyme unifying the poem, the verse line is divided into two halves separated by a rhythmical pause, or **caesura.** In the first half of the line before the caesura, two words alliterate; in the second half, one word alliterates with the two from the first half. Many lines, however, have only two alliterative words, one in each half of the poetic line. Notice the alliterative *g* and the four primary stresses in this Old English line from *Beowulf*:

God mid Geatum Grendles daeda

The **kenning,** a specialized metaphor made of compound words, is a staple of Anglo-Saxon literature that still finds a place in our language today. *Gas guzzler* and *headhunter* are two modern-day kennings you are likely to have heard.

The earliest and simplest kennings are compound words formed of two common nouns: "sky-candle" for *sun,* "battle-dew" for *blood,* and "whale-road" for *sea.* Later, kennings grew more elaborate, and compound adjectives joined the compound nouns. A ship became a "foamy-throated ship," then a "foamy-throated sea-stallion," and finally a "foamy-throated stallion of the whale-road." Once a kenning was coined, it was used by the singer-poets over and over again.

In their original languages, kennings are almost always written as simple compounds, with no hyphens or spaces between the words. When kennings appear in translation, however, they are often written as hyphenated compounds ("sky-candle," "foamy-throated"), as prepositional phrases ("wolf of wounds"), or as possessives ("the sword's tree").

Scholars believe that kennings filled three needs: (1) Old Norse and Anglo-Saxon poetry depended heavily on alliteration, but neither language had a large vocabulary. Poets created the alliterative words they needed by combining existing words. (2) Because the poetry was oral and had to be memorized, bards valued ready-made phrases. Such phrases made finished poetry easier to remember, and they gave bards time to think ahead when they were composing new poetry on the spot during a feast or ceremony. (3) The increasingly complex structure of the kennings must have satisfied the early Norse and Anglo-Saxon people's taste for

elaboration, a taste also apparent in their art and artifacts.

1. Read aloud the account of Beowulf's death (lines 791–828), and listen for the effects of the alliteration. Where are vowels, rather than consonants, repeated?

2. Look back over lines 233–391 from *Beowulf.* Locate at least two examples of kennings written as hyphenated compounds, two examples of kennings written as prepositional phrases, and two examples of kennings written as possessives. What does each kenning refer to?

3. Compile a list of modern-day kennings, such as *headhunter.* Listen for them in everyday conversations, and check advertisements and newspapers for other possibilities.

4. Translators differ dramatically in how they rephrase the Old English to handle alliteration and the kennings. Here is a passage from a translation done many years before the Raffel translation. How does it compare with the corresponding lines (392–398) in Raffel's translation? Which translation sounds more modern? Which do you prefer to listen to?

> Now Grendel came, from his crags of mist
> Across the moor; he was curst of God.
> The murderous prowler meant to surprise
> In the high-built hall his human prey.
> He stalked neath the clouds, till steep before him
> The house of revelry rose in his path,
> The gold-hall of heroes, the gaily adorned.
> —*translated by* J. Duncan Spaeth

Elements of Literature
Mini-Lesson: Alliteration and Kennings

Write a line or two from *Beowulf* on the chalkboard. Identify alliteration and kennings one at a time, demonstrating their use in the examples given. Then, after students have read the lesson for themselves, and discussion indicates they understand, have students work in groups to respond to the assignments and questions.

Possible Answers

1. *"Treasure* they'd won *together"* (l. 793); "Then he *brought* their treasure to *Beowulf,"* (l. 796); "Deep in his *breast broke* through" (l. 800); "For *this, this* gold, *these* jewels," (l. 802); "When the *funeral flames* have burned me" (l. 811); "On this *spit* of land, *so sailors* can *see"* (l. 813). Vowels, rather than consonants, are sometimes repeated within words.

2. Hyphenated compounds—"sea-paths" (l. 247, the sea) and "gold-ringed" (l. 346, wearing rings); kennings written as prepositional phrases—"shapes of darkness" (l. 380, evil) and "fiercest of demons" (l. 261, Grendel). Kennings written as possessives: "beast's last battle" (l. 290, victory over the beast) and "Heaven's high arch" (l. 309, sky).

3. Big bird (airplane), top dog (boss).

4. Spaeth's translation makes the lines even and omits descriptive images, giving mostly narrative facts. The short lines produce an abrupt and unrelenting rhythm. Raffel, on the other hand, retains the power of the verbs and adjectives and lets the line length go as long as necessary for modern English, while maintaining the four-beat line, producing a conversational rhythm, a storyteller's beat. Raffel's translation probably sounds more modern.

PROGRAM MANAGER

Application and Reinforcement
For reinforcement of the elements of literature introduced in this lesson, see **Transparency** 1.3 in the *Audiovisual Resources Binder.*

Beyond the Selection

Choices: Building Your Portfolio

1. **Writer's Notebook** *Remind students to choose a situation they would not mind sharing.* Remind students to save their work. They may use it as prewriting for the Writer's Workshop on p. 67.

2. **Critical Writing** If students complete this activity on a computer, have them do a word count to determine those words most commonly used to describe Grendel; for example, how many times do they use the word *evil* or *scary*? Have students use the thesaurus feature on their word-processing software to discover synonyms they can substitute, such as *nefarious* or *baleful*.

3. **Creative Writing** Have students list the new storyteller's feelings and motives that should be shown in the narration. This activity would be appropriate for either an individual or a group project.

4. **Speaking and Listening** Help students select passages that have a beginning, middle, and end to give their readings the feel of stories. Ask them to work in pairs, sharing comments about ways to dramatize the selection through suspenseful pauses, emphasis of key words, and voice inflections.

5. **Movies and Television** Brainstorm for a few minutes with the whole class for names of movies with heroes who might be compared to Beowulf. Then, form groups to work through the activity for each of the appropriate movies.

PORTFOLIO ASSESSMENT

Choices: Assessment Criteria For help in evaluating these Choices assignments, see the criteria in the *Portfolio Management System,* pp. 67–68.

CHOICES: Building Your Portfolio

Writer's Notebook
1. Collecting Ideas for an Autobiographical Incident

WORK IN PROGRESS

At the end of this collection, you'll write an autobiographical incident (see page 67). To start thinking about possible events to use in your narrative, freewrite for five or ten minutes about a time in your life when you

- faced an intense physical challenge
- were taunted over something you said or did
- overcame fear or dread to achieve a goal

As you describe the incident, be sure to include how you felt at the time. Save your work for later use.

Critical Writing
2. Analyzing a Monster

In a brief essay, analyze the character of Grendel. Look back over the passages in *Beowulf* that describe Grendel, and gather some evidence on how he is described. You might consider some of these questions: How does the storyteller, in describing the creature, also shape our feelings toward him? What accounts for Grendel's evil? What does Grendel seem to represent in the story?

Creative Writing
3. It's All in the Point of View

Just as John Gardner tried imagining this story from Grendel's point of view (page 36), you might try retelling an episode from the perspective of one of the other characters, perhaps Grendel, his mother, the dragon, Hrothgar, or Beowulf's detractor, Unferth.

Speaking and Listening
4. Being a Bard

Retell an episode of *Beowulf* for your classmates, or, if it can be arranged, for a grade-school audience. Be faithful to the plot of the story, but feel free to change or adapt the content to fit your audience and your own storytelling talents. (See, for example, the story of *Beowulf* told in Student to Student on page 48.) Plan an introduction to your story, and try to find ways of involving your listeners. For drama, use gestures, sound effects, and pauses. After your presentation, write a brief reflection about your experience as a bard—what did you learn about *Beowulf* and yourself?

Movies and Television
5. Movies and *Beowulf*

Movies, the cornerstone of American entertainment, often rely on familiar images: Heroes face villains to do battle in all kinds of places—from the ordinary to the strange. How much do these movies have in common with *Beowulf*? Working with a small group, compare *Beowulf* and a movie that has a hero. Use the following questions to guide your comparison:

- Where does each hero come from?
- Who are the hero's trusted aides?
- What role does violence play in the story?
- How does the hero struggle against evil?
- Is the hero an outsider or a part of the community?
- What rewards or glory does the hero receive?

Present your ideas in a brief oral report. You may want to use a visual aid—a chart, for example—for your oral presentation.

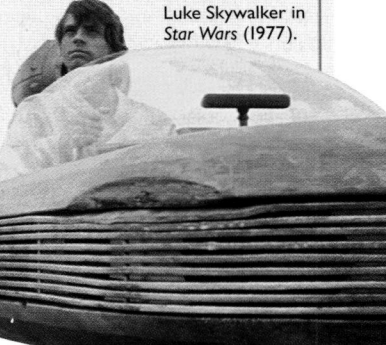

Mark Hamill as Luke Skywalker in *Star Wars* (1977).

STRATEGIES FOR INCLUSION

Spatial To help students collect ideas for activity #1, have them use a cluster diagram, like the one following, rather than freewrite. Model the exercise using Transparency 3: Cluster Diagram, available in the Transparency Package.

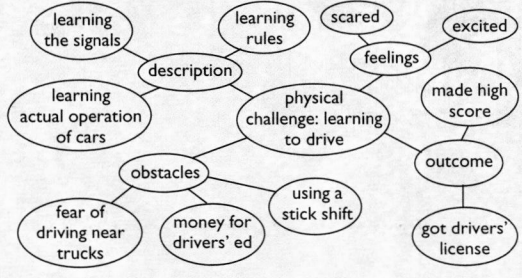

HOW TO OWN A WORD

Using Context Clues to Discover Word Meanings

Sometimes you can determine the meaning of an unfamiliar word by looking for clues in the **context**, the surrounding words, phrases, and sentences. In fact, you've probably learned many words by using context clues. Below are some of the most useful types of context clues:

Restatement: A difficult word might be rephrased in slightly easier language. Restatements may be signaled by specific words or phrases: *that is, or, in other words.* Look at punctuation—dashes and parentheses also serve as signals. Often a restatement will be an appositive set off by commas or an item in a series.

> . . . keeping the bloody feud
> Alive, seeking no peace, offering
> No **truce,** accepting no settlement.
> —*Beowulf,* lines 68–70

A *truce* is something that would end a feud; it's a kind of settlement or a cease-fire.

Comparison: Compare unfamiliar words to familiar words that surround it. Sometimes specific words and phrases may also signal a comparison context clue: *like, as, similar to.*

> . . . but the swirling
> Surf had covered his death, hidden
> Deep in **murky** darkness his miserable
> End.
> —*Beowulf,* lines 531–534

Note all the words that have to do with obscuring from view: *covered, hidden deep, darkness. Murky* means "dark or gloomy, shadowy."

Contrast: An opposition might be set up. Certain key words and phrases signal a contrast context clue: *but, not, although, however, on the other hand.*

> . . . he can come for your people with no fear
> Of **reprisal;** he's found no fighting, here,
> But only food, only delight.
> —*Beowulf,* lines 329–331

Reprisal has to do with resistance, rather than acceptance or encouragement. A *reprisal* is punishment in return for an injury.

A picture stone showing a Viking ship under sail.
Statens Historiska Museer, Stockholm.

Synonym: You might find a word nearby that has the same or nearly the same meaning as the unknown word.

> He murders as he likes, with no mercy, **gorges**
> And feasts on your flesh.
> —*Beowulf,* lines 333–334

Notice the words *feasts on.* To gorge is to glut or to swallow greedily.

Example: Sometimes the text provides an example. Certain words and phrases help you spot example context clues: *such as, including, especially, namely.*

> **Scops,** such as the skilled storytellers who passed down the story of Beowulf, were honored members of Anglo-Saxon society.

Note the key words: *storytellers* and *Anglo-Saxon.* A *scop* is an Old English poet or bard.

Try It Out

Choose any five of the Words to Own from *Beowulf.* For each word, construct a sentence that gives the meaning of the word from its context. Use a different type of context clue for each sentence. To get started, use a chart like the one below. Ask a classmate to find the context clues in your sentences.

Word to Own	Context Clue	Example

How to Own a Word
Mini-Lesson: Context Clues

After the class has read the explanation in the text, list the five kinds of context clues on the chalkboard as you discuss them. In your discussion, give the class the examples from the text that correspond to each type of context clue. Then, lead students slowly through a passage of the poem, perhaps ll. 292–391, asking them to look for the clues that help define more difficult vocabulary.

Try It Out: Possible Answers

- Restatement: They wanted *reparation,* but no payment could really compensate for the man's pain.
- Comparison: The *murky* water, clouded with the shadows of rotting vegetation after the hurricane, revealed nothing about its depths.
- Contrast: He found no *solace,* only repeated accusations and loud demands intruding on his need to be alone.
- Synonym: The rope was *taut,* stretched tight across the chasm.
- Example: She felt as if she were on a *pilgrimage* like one made by a believer of Islam to the holy cities of Mecca and Medina.

PROGRAM MANAGER

Reinforcement To allow students practice and reinforcement of the vocabulary strategy introduced here, see **Transparency 1.5** in the *Audiovisual Resources Binder.*

Learners Having Difficulty If students have trouble identifying context clues, have them create a bulletin board listing the signal words. Associate each type of context clue with a particular color; for example, put the signal words for restatements on pink poster board and the signal words for comparisons on green poster board. Then, have students look through a passage of the text to find five to ten signal words and mark them with the appropriately colored adhesive notes. On each adhesive note, have students write the word that the context clue helps to define.

Identifying Clues Assign groups of three or four students to work together on Try It Out. Ask each group to develop five sentences, using one of the Words to Own in each sentence. Each sentence should give context clues using one of the five techniques modeled in this exercise—such as restatement, comparison, or contrast. Once the sentences are written, have each group exchange their sentences with another group. Then, have each group identify context clues they find.

Mesopotamia

WORLD LITERATURE

BEFORE YOU READ
THE HEAD OF HUMBABA

Background

The men and women who lived four thousand years ago would be astounded by the world we live in, and we, very likely, would be astounded by theirs. Obviously, the world has changed in countless ways. Science and technology have transformed the physical world we inhabit, and social and political evolution have altered the way we live. Nations, empires, religions, and languages have come and gone. People now have different beliefs, different worries, different problems. If, somehow, you could sit down to talk with someone your age from an ancient civilization, you might have a hard time starting the conversation—even if you did have a good translator to help.

So you would expect a story four thousand years old to have little to do with you or anything around you today. Your life is so different from the lives of the storyteller and his characters that you might have nothing in common, no shared experience. *Gilgamesh,* for instance, is such an ancient story—a poem, as all stories were in those days. The story was recorded on clay tablets around 2000 B.C. in Sumer, a part of ancient Mesopotamia.

Gilgamesh is the king of Uruk, an ancient Sumerian city. His great friend is Enkidu. Craving an adventure that will bring fame, Gilgamesh convinces Enkidu to journey with him to the cedar forest. There they confront the forest's guardian, the evil giant Humbaba.

A Dialogue with the Text

READER'S LOG

As you read the scene, ask yourself if you have any feelings in common with Gilgamesh and Enkidu. Record your responses as you read this ancient story of friendship.

Gilgamesh. Relief (8th century B.C.) from Temple of Sargon II. Khorsabad, Iraq.
Louvre, Paris.

(Map) World map by Ptolemy (A.D. 100?–165?). Shaded area indicates general location of Mesopotamia.

PROGRAM MANAGER

Selection Summary
See **Teaching Notes,** *Teaching Resources A,* p. 3, for a summary of this selection.

The Head of Humbaba
from Gilgamesh: A Verse Narrative

retold by **Herbert Mason**

At dawn Gilgamesh raised his ax **A**
And struck at the great cedar.
When Humbaba heard the sound of falling trees,
He hurried down the path that they had seen
5 But only he had traveled. Gilgamesh felt weak
At the sound of Humbaba's footsteps and called to Shamash° **B**
Saying, I have followed you in the way decreed;
Why am I abandoned now? Suddenly the winds
Sprang up. They saw the great head of Humbaba
10 Like a water buffalo's bellowing down the path,
His huge and clumsy legs, his flailing° arms
Thrashing at phantoms in his precious trees.
His single stroke could cut a cedar down
And leave no mark on him. His shoulders,
15 Like a porter's° under building stones,
Were permanently bent by what he bore;
He was the slave who did the work for gods
But whom the gods would never notice.
Monstrous in his contortion, he aroused **C**
20 The two almost to pity.
But pity was the thing that might have killed.
It made them pause just long enough to show
How pitiless he was to them. Gilgamesh in horror saw
Him strike the back of Enkidu and beat him to the ground
25 Until he thought his friend was crushed to death.
He stood still watching as the monster leaned to make
His final strike against his friend, unable
To move to help him, and then Enkidu slid
Along the ground like a ram making its final lunge
30 On wounded knees. Humbaba fell and seemed **D**
To crack the ground itself in two, and Gilgamesh,
As if this fall had snapped him from his daze,
Returned to life

6. **Shamash** (shä′mäsh′): the sun god.

11. **flailing:** swinging.

15. **porter's:** A porter is a person who carries things.

GILGAMESH 53

A. Critical Reading: Drawing Conclusions

? What weakness in Gilgamesh does Humbaba appeal to? [Possible answer: Humbaba appeals to Gilgamesh's love of power.]

B. Critical Reading: Making Inferences

? Why does Gilgamesh kill Humbaba even after Humbaba offers to serve him? [Humbaba has tried to kill Gilgamesh's friend.]

C. Reader's Response: Extending the Text

? What is the poem's statement about friendship? [Sample responses: Friendship is more important than power; friendship brings peace and companionship.]

Finding Common Ground

Remind students to choose a situation that they will not mind sharing with others. To get students started on the Finding Common Ground activity, ask the class to consider how Gilgamesh must have felt as he faced Humbaba. Then, help students to brainstorm about modern situations in which a person might have those same feelings, such as facing the neighbors whose window your team's baseball has just cracked. To prompt additional ideas, list suggestions on the chalkboard.

And stood over Humbaba with his ax
35 Raised high above his head watching the monster plead
In strangled sobs and desperate appeals
A The way the sea contorts under a violent squall.°
I'll serve you as I served the gods, Humbaba said;
I'll build you houses from their sacred trees.
40 Enkidu feared his friend was weakening
And called out: Gilgamesh! Don't trust him!
As if there were some hunger in himself
That Gilgamesh was feeling
That turned him momentarily to yearn
45 For someone who would serve, he paused;
B And then he raised his ax up higher
And swung it in a perfect arc
Into Humbaba's neck. He reached out
To touch the wounded shoulder of his friend,

50 And late that night he reached again
C To see if he was yet asleep, but there was only
Quiet breathing. The stars against the midnight sky
Were sparkling like mica° in a riverbed.
In the slight breeze
55 The head of Humbaba was swinging from a tree.

37. squall: sudden, brief storm.

53. mica (mī′kə): colored, translucent mineral.

FINDING COMMON GROUND

After reading this episode, you probably notice some differences from your experience—you've never been to Sumer, you've never chopped down your neighbor's cedar, and you've never whacked off anyone's head with an ax. Do you notice any similarities, however? Jotting down brief notes, think back over the story, and explain your responses to these prompts:

• Have you ever experienced any of Gilgamesh's feelings?
• Like Gilgamesh, have you ever faced a situation in which you had to summon up your personal courage?

Having something in common, by the way, may not mean you are identical. Think, for instance, about Gilgamesh's hesitation in killing Humbaba. What do you think caused him to hesitate?

After you've taken your notes and reflected on them, discuss with a few of your classmates what you have in common with each other and with Gilgamesh and Enkidu, two people from four thousand years ago.

Stone statues of Mesopotamian god Aby and his wife, from Tell Asmar (2600 B.C.).
Iraq Museum, Baghdad.

54 THE ANGLO-SAXONS

BEFORE YOU READ

THE SEAFARER

Reading Focus

Has the Time of Heroes Passed?

In the PBS television series *The Power of Myth*, the television journalist Bill Moyers and the mythologist Joseph Campbell talk about heroes. At one point, Campbell says that as a child he had two heroes but now he has none. Here's a bit of the conversation that follows Campbell's comment:

Moyers: *We seem to worship celebrities today, not heroes.*
Campbell: *Yes, and that's too bad. A questionnaire was once sent around to one of the high schools in Brooklyn which asked, "What would you like to be?" Two-thirds of the students responded, "A celebrity." They had no notion of having to give of themselves in order to achieve something.*

Quickwrite

Do you think we "worship celebrities today, not heroes"? And if we do, what effect does that have on what we value and whom we present to children as role models? Freewrite for a few moments to focus your thoughts on this question.

Elements of Literature

The Elegy

The dominant mood in Anglo-Saxon poetry is elegiac. As we have seen in *Beowulf*, this sense of sadness over the grimness and transience of earthly life is found in the heroic epic. It is also found in several Old English fragments and poems in which a bard laments the passing of better days and greater glories.

Only a thousand years earlier, the poet who wrote "The Seafarer" addressed the same question: Has the time of heroes passed?

> **A**n **elegy** is a poem that mourns the death of a person or laments something lost.
>
> *For more on the Elegy, see page 606 and the Handbook of Literary Terms.*

Background

"The Seafarer" is from the so-called Exeter Book, a manuscript of miscellaneous Anglo-Saxon poems dating from around A.D. 940, copied in A.D. 975, and now preserved at Exeter Cathedral in England. Though the manuscript survived the raids and fires of the centuries, the Exeter Book had not been well cared for. There are signs that its cover had been used as a chopping board; its pages had been marked by beer stains; and some had been partly burned. But today its "songs"—copied down by monks—are our chief source of Anglo-Saxon poetry.

The Anglo-Saxons were sea voyagers, and the northern seas were then, as now, especially cruel. The speaker in "The Seafarer" is an old sailor who drifted through many winters on ice-cold seas.

THE SEAFARER **55**

Into the Poem

Before You Read p. 55
- **Reading Focus: Set a Purpose** Students read about the differences in celebrities and heroes.
- **Quickwrite: Prior Knowledge** Identify modern role models in Reader's Log
- **Elements of Literature: The Elegy**
- **Background:** Examine the source of "The Seafarer"

Through the Poem

"The Seafarer" pp. 56–58
Primary Sources p. 59
Making Meanings p. 59

Beyond the Poem

Choices: Building Your Portfolio p. 60
- **Writer's Notebook:** Record feelings about an incident
- **Critical Writing:** Write an essay comparing two poems
- **Creative Writing:** Create a poem about hopes
- **Critical Thinking:** Debate an issue
- **Visual Art:** Create a collage representing a speaker's attitude

Spotlight On p. 61

PROGRAM MANAGER

- **Planning Instruction** See *Teaching Notes, Teaching Resources A,* p. 3, for objectives and additional information for this selection.
- **Instructional Support** Before beginning the instructional lesson, see **Graphic Organizer for Active Reading,**

Teaching Resources A, p. 14, for an Into the Poem activity.
- **Assessment** See **Selection Test, Test Booklet,** pp. 5–6.
- **Language Link** For instruction and practice in revising sentence fragments, see **Language Link,** *Teaching*

Resources A, pp. 15–16, and *Language and Writing Skills Worksheet,* p. 102.
- **Reinforcement** For reinforcement of the element of literature introduced in this lesson, see **Transparency** 1.4 in the *Audiovisual Resources Binder.*

Into the Poem

Using BEFORE YOU READ p. 55

Reading Focus

Guide students to realize that being a hero involves sacrificing for the good of others, while being a celebrity means merely that a person is well known. Now students should be ready to discuss the question posed in the focus: Has the time of heroes passed? How would the Seafarer answer this question?

Through the Poem

A. Critical Reading: Metacognition

? How would you know that the Seafarer's life was harsh and lonely even if he had not said so directly in l. 26? [Possible answer: The Seafarer's life of hardship is made clear through his diction. Examples may be found in ll. 10–12 and 16–17.]

B. Reader's Response: Shaping Interpretations

? In this passage, what is the effect of the nature imagery? [Sample responses: It helps readers imagine life at sea. It clarifies how harsh the sailor's life is.]

C. Critical Reading: Finding Cause and Effect

? Why does the Seafarer return to the ocean time after time? [Possible answers: He may feel more at home on the sea than in society. He refers to his excitement at returning to the waves.]

Portfolio Assessment

For help with teacher assessment of reading skills, see the *Portfolio Management System,* pp. 54–55.

The Seafarer
translated by **Burton Raffel**

This tale is true, and mine. It tells
How the sea took me, swept me back
And forth in sorrow and fear and pain,
Showed me suffering in a hundred ships,
5 In a thousand ports, and in me. It tells
Of smashing surf when I sweated in the cold
Of an anxious watch, perched in the bow
As it dashed under cliffs. My feet were cast
In icy bands, bound with frost,
10 With frozen chains, and hardship groaned
Around my heart. Hunger tore
At my sea-weary soul. No man sheltered
On the quiet fairness of earth can feel
How wretched I was, drifting through winter
15 On an ice-cold sea, whirled in sorrow,
Alone in a world blown clear of love,
Hung with icicles. The hailstorms flew.
The only sound was the roaring sea,
The freezing waves. The song of the swan
20 Might serve for pleasure, the cry of the sea-fowl,
The death-noise of birds instead of laughter,
The mewing of gulls instead of mead.
Storms beat on the rocky cliffs and were echoed
By icy-feathered terns° and the eagle's screams;
25 No kinsman could offer comfort there,
To a soul left drowning in desolation.
    And who could believe, knowing but
The passion of cities, swelled proud with wine
And no taste of misfortune, how often, how wearily,
30 I put myself back on the paths of the sea.
Night would blacken; it would snow from the north;
Frost bound the earth and hail would fall,
The coldest seeds. And how my heart
Would begin to beat, knowing once more
35 The salt waves tossing and the towering sea!
The time for journeys would come and my soul
Called me eagerly out, sent me over
The horizon, seeking foreigners' homes.
    But there isn't a man on earth so proud,
40 So born to greatness, so bold with his youth,
Grown so brave, or so graced by God,
That he feels no fear as the sails unfurl,
Wondering what Fate has willed and will do.
No harps ring in his heart, no rewards,

24. **terns:** seabirds related to gulls.

56 THE ANGLO-SAXONS

COOPERATIVE LEARNING

Finding Similarities To show some similarities shared by Anglo-Saxon literature, assign students to work in groups to compare nature imagery in "The Seafarer" and in *Beowulf.* Suggest that they make a chart to keep track of their findings and that they list imagery that describes the weather, the sea, animals, and the land. Have them give oral reports to share their findings.

INTEGRATING THE LANGUAGE ARTS

Speaking and Listening Read aloud a passage of "The Seafarer" to model the way one pauses, emphasizes certain words, and raises or lowers the pitch of the voice to help listeners comprehend. Let students pick their own short passages and practice in pairs to read aloud with proper emphasis and pitch; then, have students present their passages to the class.

45 No passion for women, no worldly pleasures,
   Nothing, only the ocean's heave;
   But longing wraps itself around him.
   Orchards blossom, the towns bloom,
   Fields grow lovely as the world springs fresh,
50 And all these admonish° that willing mind
   Leaping to journeys, always set
   In thoughts traveling on a quickening tide.
   So summer's sentinel, the cuckoo, sings
   In his murmuring voice, and our hearts mourn
55 As he urges. Who could understand,
   In ignorant ease, what we others suffer
   As the paths of exile stretch endlessly on?
              And yet my heart wanders away,
   My soul roams with the sea, the whales'
60 Home, wandering to the widest corners
   Of the world, returning ravenous° with desire,
   Flying solitary, screaming, exciting me
   To the open ocean, breaking oaths
   On the curve of a wave.
                        Thus the joys of God
65 Are fervent° with life, where life itself
   Fades quickly into the earth. The wealth
   Of the world neither reaches to Heaven nor remains.
   No man has ever faced the dawn
   Certain which of Fate's three threats
70 Would fall: illness, or age, or an enemy's
   Sword, snatching the life from his soul.
   The praise the living pour on the dead
   Flowers from reputation: plant
   An earthly life of profit reaped
75 Even from hatred and rancor,° of bravery
   Flung in the devil's face, and death
   Can only bring you earthly praise
   And a song to celebrate a place
   With the angels, life eternally blessed
   In the hosts of Heaven.
80   The days are gone
   When the kingdoms of earth flourished in glory;
   Now there are no rulers, no emperors,
   No givers of gold, as once there were,
   When wonderful things were worked among them
85 And they lived in lordly magnificence.
   Those powers have vanished, those pleasures are dead.

50. admonish: scold mildly.

61. ravenous: very hungry.

65. fervent: passionate.

75. rancor (raŋ'kər): ill will.

THE SEAFARER **57**

D. Literary Element: Theme
Our universal need to experience the world is also an important theme in the *Odyssey* and in Tennyson's "Ulysses," p. 822. Have students who are familiar with the three works compare the various expressions of this theme.

E. Literary Element: Kenning
Have students find the kenning for *sea* in ll. 59–60.

F. Humanities Connection
Compare this passage with Shelley's "Ozymandias," p. 731, an ironic lament on the transience of glory. You might also refer to Tennyson's feelings of loss and bewilderment at the close of the nineteenth century. See "Tears, Idle Tears," p. 804. See also another spokesman for the Victorians, Matthew Arnold, in "Dover Beach," p. 848.

G. Reader's Response: Extending the Text
The kenning in l. 83 refers to the Anglo-Saxon leaders who looked after their followers, even financially. How does this behavior compare to that of our leaders today? [Sample responses: Anglo-Saxon leaders must have been very respected, and people must have depended on them much more than we depend on leaders today. Our leaders do not have to support us financially, although they are responsible for budgeting public funds.]

H. Literary Element: Elegy
? Why might this poem be considered *elegiac*? [It reminds readers of the world's grim realities.]

STRATEGIES FOR INCLUSION

Advanced Have students use lines from the poem to write an essay that will either dispute or support the following statement: "'The Seafarer' has both Christian and non-Christian elements in it."

Learners Having Difficulty Students may have difficulty understanding the poem because the first line leads them to expect a tale. However, the poem is not a story but the speaker's thoughts about life—what he has learned and

what he believes. Before reading the entire poem aloud with students, tell them that there will not be much action to follow. Work with students to look instead for the poet's thoughts and feelings about the lifetime of hardships at sea that he describes so vividly.

Special Needs In ll. 107–115 the poet offers a set of rules to live by that his experiences have presumably taught him. After reading the poem aloud, group students into pairs or small groups

to translate these rules into their own words. Encourage them to restate the passage in two different ways:

• A list of behaviors [Examples: 1. Be humble; 2. Conquer pride; and so on.]

• A short paragraph describing someone who lives successfully. ☞

? How does the Seafarer believe
that people should act? [Possible
answers: They should respect God, live
modestly, and control pride. They
should treat the world fairly and seek
the grace of God.]

B. Expansion

"The Seafarer" has been the subject of
scholarly debate for many years,
because it seems to shift in tone and
subject matter after l. 64. Some critics
believe the poem is a dialogue between
an experienced mariner and a young
man eager to go to sea; others see it as
the conflicting emotions of one man.
Here, in an excerpt from *The Seafarer:
An Interpretation*, the essayist O. S.
Anderson discusses his solution:

". . . The simplest way of uniting the
first part of the poem, which deals with
experiences of sea life whether real or
imagined, firmly with its homiletic second part, so that the poem will form
an intelligible whole, is to assume . . .
that the first part is also in the nature
of a homily, here allegorical. . . . The
cares and sufferings of the poet's
earthly existence, represented by the
lonely and miserable voyage on which
he is embarked, a wintry, cold, and
cheerless passage, make him long for
the joys of heaven with all his soul.
. . . This gives a simple and clear connection between the first part of the
poem and the second: the earthly life
of the poet is full of misery and priva-
tion . . . *therefore* the joys of heaven are
his only real concern. . . ."

Making Meanings

First Thoughts

1. The old sailor has had a hard, lonely
   life. He has traveled in dangerous
   seas and suffered much from cold
   and hunger and exhaustion. He
   does not identify with the modern
   world but believes in God and in an
   eternal home in Heaven.

Shaping Interpretations

2. Lines 27–29 imply that the speaker
   dislikes the false pride of cities.
   Lines 33–38 and 58–64 suggest the
   speaker's love of journeys and
   adventures. No, he is not completely
   satisfied with life at sea.

The weakest survives and the world continues,
Kept spinning by toil. All glory is tarnished.
The world's honor ages and shrinks.
90 Bent like the men who mould it. Their faces
Blanch° as time advances, their beards
Wither and they mourn the memory of friends.
The sons of princes, sown in the dust.
The soul stripped of its flesh knows nothing
95 Of sweetness or sour, feels no pain,
Bends neither its hand nor its brain. A brother
Opens his palms and pours down gold
On his kinsman's grave, strewing his coffin
With treasures intended for Heaven, but nothing
100 Golden shakes the wrath of God
For a soul overflowing with sin, and nothing
Hidden on earth rises to Heaven.
       We all fear God. He turns the earth,
He set it swinging firmly in space,
105 Gave life to the world and light to the sky.
Death leaps at the fools who forget their God.
He who lives humbly has angels from Heaven
 To carry him courage and strength and belief.
A man must conquer pride, not kill it,
110 Be firm with his fellows, chaste for himself,
Treat all the world as the world deserves,
With love or with hate but never with harm,
Though an enemy seek to scorch him in hell,
Or set the flames of a funeral pyre°
115 Under his lord. Fate is stronger
And God mightier than any man's mind.
Our thoughts should turn to where our home is,
Consider the ways of coming there,
Then strive for sure permission for us
120 To rise to that eternal joy,
That life born in the love of God
And the hope of Heaven. Praise the Holy
Grace of Him who honored us,
Eternal, unchanging creator of earth. Amen.

91. blanch: turn pale.

114. funeral pyre: pile (usually of
wood) on which a dead body is
burned.

CROSSING THE CURRICULUM

Art Encourage students to draw the narrator as
they imagine him and to explain which lines of the
poem help them to visualize him.

Mathematics Ask students to research various
types of seagoing vessels and to create a chart to
show how long each vessel would take to travel
between various points. This may help them
understand the long, grueling travels the seafarer
has experienced.

Health To help students see that survival was
difficult, have students research the diet of peasants and sailors in Anglo-Saxon times, and have
them create a poster that compares that diet to
today's Recommended Daily Allowance (RDA) for
vitamins, fats, and minerals.

The Original Language and the Translator's Task

Here are the opening lines of "The Seafarer" in Old English. Following these lines is a translation by Kevin Crossley-Holland. Burton Raffel, whose very different translation is used on page 56, describes the special demands of verse translation: "Verse translation is a minor art, but a unique one. . . . The translator's only hope is to re-create something roughly equivalent in the new language, something that is itself good poetry and that at the same time carries a reasonable measure of the force and flavor of the original. . . ."

MÆg ic be me sylfum soðgied wrecan,
siþas secgan, hu ic geswincdagum
earfoðhwile oft þrowade,
bitre breostceare gebiden hæbbe,
gecunnad in ceole cearselda fela. . . .

I can sing a true song of myself,
Tell of my travels, of many hard times
Toiling day after day; I can describe
How I have harbored bitter sorrow in
   my heart
And often learned that ships are homes
   of sadness.
        —translated by Kevin Crossley-Holland

MAKING MEANINGS

First Thoughts

1. What is your first impression of the speaker in this poem? What is his life like? What does he believe in and hope for?

Shaping Interpretations

2. What passages in the poem explain why the seafarer seeks the rigors of the sea rather than the delights of the land? Does he find what he looked for at sea?

3. Lines 58–63 suggest that the poet is beginning to talk about the glories of adventuring at sea, but then he changes direction. What does he turn his attention to over the next fifteen lines?

4. In line 80, the speaker begins to talk about the present state of the world—what does he think of it? How do these thoughts contribute to the poem's **elegiac** tone?

5. The poem ends with a statement of the poet's beliefs. What are they?

6. This short lyric is full of striking **metaphors**— for example, "frozen chains" in line 10. Select three of these metaphors, and explain what is being compared in each one. What emotional effect does each metaphor create?

7. What do you think the seafarer is searching for?

Connecting with the Text

8. In line 88, the poem's speaker says, "All glory is tarnished." Do you think this idea also applies to today's heroes and to present-day life? Explain your response.

Extending the Text

9. Could the sentiments expressed in this poem be applied to the homeless today? Find passages in the poem to support your answer.

THE SEAFARER **59**

3. To the transience of life on earth. Students may believe the poet suggests that bravery leads to favor in Heaven, or they may interpret this section to mean that bravery is only appreciated in this world, not in Heaven. In either case, students should support their answers with lines from the text.

4. The speaker says that the present is a pale reflection of the past. Humans have grown old and weak, and there is no longer any true glory. These thoughts enhance the poem's elegiac tone as they mourn the loss of the world as the sailor has known it in the past.

5. Student answers may vary, but ask that students support their answers with lines from the text. One possibility is that the poet believes that human beings should live according to the ways of God so they will ultimately find joy in Heaven, as in ll. 117–122.

6. Possible answers: "frozen chains" (l. 10), "drowning in desolation" (l. 26), "summer's sentinel" (l. 53). In the first metaphor, ice is compared to chains, which may help readers sense the imprisonment the Seafarer feels. The second metaphor compares sadness with drowning, which may help readers sense the despair. The third metaphor compares a cuckoo to a sentinel, implying that both stand guard to maintain order.

7. The Seafarer is searching for home —a port where he can settle down or circumstances that will bring peace to his restless spirit.

Connecting with the Text

8. Feelings in the poem that parallel feelings today include praise of the past and unhappiness at the decline of the present. For example, some tend to glorify our country's founders and feel that there are no leaders of that caliber in modern politics.

Extending the Text

9. **(Synthesis and Evaluation)** Some passages which might apply to the homeless today: "No kinsman could offer comfort there, / To a soul left drowning in desolation." (ll. 25–26). "Who could understand, / In ignorant ease, what we others suffer / As the paths of exile stretch endlessly on?" (ll. 55–57).

Goal Setting To help students understand the purpose of reading "The Seafarer," invite them to establish goals and ways to meet them. For example, goal one might be to understand the literal meaning of the poem; the method might be to write a prose version of the poem. Goal two might be to understand all of the figurative language; the method might be to use color-coded, self-adhesive notes to indicate different kinds of figurative language.

Check Test: True-False

1. The narrator claims his tale is true. [True]
2. The narrator states that he never has feared the sea. [False]
3. Fate's three threats are illness, age, and poverty. [False]
4. The narrator states that the days of glory are gone. [True]
5. According to the narrator, man's goal is to get to Heaven. [True]

Beyond the Poem

Choices: Building Your Portfolio

1. **Writer's Notebook** *Remind students to choose a situation they would not mind sharing with others.* Remind students to save their work. They may use it as prewriting for the Writer's Workshop on p. 67.

2. **Critical Writing** Discuss ways to organize this essay. Suggest that students could discuss the poems separately, and then point out likenesses and differences in a concluding section; or they could organize the essay with one section on likenesses and one on differences.

3. **Creative Writing** Give students the option of working alone, in pairs, or in groups for this activity. Encourage students to read their poems aloud to the rest of the class and to exhibit their work on a special bulletin board.

4. **Critical Thinking** To help students prepare for the debate, have them develop a chart of arguments for their position, including a position statement, support for the position, and possible responses.

Position	Support	Possible Responses

5. **Visual Art** To help students get started, brainstorm with the class to find words that represent the speaker's attitude, listing ideas on the chalkboard. Suggest, for example, *powerful sea* or *darkness of life*.

PORTFOLIO ASSESSMENT

Choices: Assessment Criteria For help in evaluating these Choices assignments, see the criteria in the *Portfolio Management System,* pp. 69–70.

CHOICES: Building Your Portfolio

Writer's Notebook
1. Collecting Ideas for an Autobiographical Incident

WORK IN PROGRESS

Earlier in this collection you may have begun collecting ideas for an autobiographical incident (see page 50). Think now of a time when you felt either disillusionment or a sense of loss about something you valued. Perhaps a friend let you down, or you lost faith in a team you played for. Jot down your feelings and memories of the incident. What makes the incident stick in your mind? Save your work for possible use in the Writer's Workshop on page 67.

Critical Writing
2. Comparing Ancient and Modern

Perhaps the most startling aspect of ancient literature is

that it so often deals with emotions and thoughts similar to our own, despite the intervening centuries. Look, for instance, at this short poem by the twentieth-century American poet Robert Frost:

> **Nothing Gold Can Stay**
>
> Nature's first green is gold,
> Her hardest hue to hold.
> Her early leaf's a flower;
> But only so an hour.
> Then leaf subsides to leaf.
> So Eden sank to grief,
> So dawn goes down to day.
> Nothing gold can stay.
>
> —Robert Frost

Write a short essay comparing the thoughts expressed here and in "The Seafarer." What sentiments do they share? How do they differ? How do you feel about the main thrust of each poem?

Creative Writing
3. You Are a "Seafarer"

Create a "Seafarer" poem of your own, opening with the line "This tale is true, and mine." Write about your own or someone else's (old or young) aspirations, hopes, joys, and disillusionments. Try to incorporate alliteration and kennings in your poem, in true Anglo-Saxon style.

Critical Thinking
4. No Heroes? A Debate

"There are no heroes today." Do you agree or disagree with this statement? Refer to your Reader's Log for your responses to the Quickwrite on page 55. Take a position, and then gather evidence to support it—facts, reasons, and examples from life today. Think about what the opposing side might say and how you might respond to their ideas. Hold a debate, with each side allowed three minutes to present its ideas and two minutes to respond to the opposing side's remarks.

Visual Art
5. Depicting a Dilemma

Create a collage that visually represents the speaker's attitudes in "The Seafarer." Working with a partner or a group, put your imaginations to work, and gather images and words from newspapers and magazines. Remember that collages can also contain objects, such as feathers or shells or sand. Be prepared to explain why you included each element in the collage when you present it to your class.

STRATEGIES FOR INCLUSION

Learners Having Difficulty/English Language Development For students needing extra help, break down the work into small, manageable steps. For example, before assigning the essay in activity #2, ask students to (1) list the ideas and emotions in each poem, (2) identify and list ideas and emotions the two poems have in common, (3) identify and list in each poem ideas and emotions that differ. Then, students may use this information to proceed.

Linguistic As prewriting for activity #3, provide students with some prompts to help them create metaphors from which they can build their poems. For example, ask students what kind of food they might associate with the word *joy*. What piece of music? What type of automobile? After they have created ten metaphors in this manner, ask them to start writing their poem, drawing on one metaphor that seems particularly interesting or on several that work together in a pattern.

SPOTLIGHT ON

Everyday Poetry: Anglo-Saxon Riddles

translated by **Burton Raffel**

In the Anglo-Saxon period, riddles were "everyday" poetry and intellectual exercises that entertained by puzzling. Like riddles in most cultures, the Anglo-Saxon riddle can be crude; it usually describes some household or farm object or some aspect of ordinary life. Ninety-five riddles are found in the Exeter Book.

The Anglo-Saxons must have whiled away many a long, dark winter evening by repeating riddles like these and having friends guess the answers. The answer to each riddle is below.

#32

Our world is lovely in different ways,
Hung with beauty and works of hands.
I saw a strange machine, made **A**
For motion, slide against the sand,
5 Shrieking as it went. It walked swiftly
On its only foot, this odd-shaped monster,
Traveled in an open country without
Seeing, without arms, or hands,
With many ribs, and its mouth in its middle.
10 Its work is useful, and welcome, for it loads
Its belly with food, and brings abundance
To men, to poor and to rich, paying
Its tribute year after year. Solve
This riddle, if you can, and unravel its name.

#33

A creature came through the waves, beautiful
And strange, calling to shore, its voice
Loud and deep; its laughter froze
Men's blood; its sides were like sword-blades. It swam
5 Contemptuously along, slow and sluggish,
A bitter warrior and a thief, ripping
Ships apart, and plundering. Like a witch **B**
It wove spells—and knew its own nature,
shouting:
"My mother is the fairest virgin of a race
10 Of noble virgins: She is my daughter
Grown great. All men know her, and me,
And know, everywhere on earth, with what joy
We will come to join them, to live on land!"

#47

A worm ate words. I thought that wonderfully
Strange—a miracle—when they told me a crawling **C**
Insect had swallowed noble songs,
A night-time thief had stolen writing
So famous, so weighty. But the bug was foolish
Still, though its belly was full of thought.

Answers: 32. a ship; 33. an iceberg; 47. a bookworm.

SPOTLIGHT ON 61

A. Language Note: Vocabulary
Use of the word *machine* in this context may give students difficulty if they associate a machine only with something that operates on electricity. Remind students that the word was earlier applied to any apparatus used for doing work.

B. Reader's Response: First Thoughts
? What key words help you solve the riddle, and why? [Sample responses: The word *froze* made me think of ice, and the references to *shore* and *swam* let me know it was in the water.]

C. Critical Reading: Finding Details
? What does the speaker think is strange in Riddle 47? [That a worm could eat words.]

OPTIONS FOR TEACHING

INTEGRATING THE LANGUAGE ARTS

Writing: Riddles Bookworms, icebergs, and ships must have been familiar sights to most Anglo-Saxons. Ask students to choose a familiar object (perhaps a light bulb, a soda can, or a sneaker) and to observe or remember how the object *looks* and how it *functions*. Invite them to write a riddle in prose or verse using metaphors, alliteration, kennings, and personification as clues. Remind them not to give away the identity of the object; then, let them solve one another's riddles.

PROFESSIONAL NOTES

Cultural Diversity Ask students to think of forms of contemporary entertainment that serve the same purpose as Anglo-Saxon riddles. [Possible answers: Crossword puzzles, acrostics, anagrams, and rebuses.]

Critical Comment: Riddles In *A Feast of Creatures: Anglo-Saxon Riddle Songs,* Craig Williamson comments on the metaphoric nature of riddles: "The riddles are primitive flower and lyric seed. To us, they offer a world in which there is an eye (I) in every other, a charged world where as Walt Whitman says, there is 'God in every object.'"

Read On

Portfolio Assessment Options

The following projects can help you evaluate and assess your students' reading accomplishments outside class. Videotapes or photographs of completed projects may be included in students' portfolios.

- **Draw Action Sequences** Invite students to turn the action sequences from a novel they have read into comic-strip sketches. Remind students to return to their novels to find appropriate dialogue to fill the speech or thought balloons of the characters who appear in the sketches. Have students narrate their sketches as they display them for the class.

- **Illustrate the Reading** Have students illustrate one or two of the selections from the anthology *Talk That Talk.* Illustrations should convey some aspect of the written pieces, such as a literal depiction of what is described or images that are evoked in the student's mind. If possible, show examples of traditional African or African American art to provide students with ideas. Remind students to return to the text to find captions or phrases that support or define their illustrations.

- **Write a Movie Script** Some students may find that their reading selection lends itself well to a movie interpretation. Suggest that students choose a section of the reading and rewrite it in script form. They should include stage directions, descriptions, and director's notes about camera angles and lighting. If possible, show students a movie script.

- **Give a Testimonial** Have students create an imaginary award they would like to present to a character in the book they have read. They can then write and give a testimonial speech that explains why the character deserves the award. Before they write, students should consider qualities that they want to celebrate. The testimonial should describe the character as well as incidents from the story that illustrate his or her qualities. If there is time, students might design and create the award.

READ ON

A History Mystery

History and fiction merge in Rosemary Sutcliff's *The Eagle of the Ninth* (Farrar, Straus & Giroux). Travel back in time to Roman Britain, where eighteen-year-old Marcus Flavius Aquila, a centurion in the Roman army, attempts to solve the mystery of his father's disappearance and restore the family's honor.

Great Deeds of Ages Past

An exciting blend of narrative, poetry, and drama, *Sundiata* (Dearborn Trade Publishers) is the best-known African epic. It is the story of Sundiata, son of the king of Mali some eight hundred years ago. Passed down by griots, Africa's oral historians, the epic reflects the rich complexity of the ancient civilization of Mali.

Traveling Talk

Some of the most colorful English spoken today comes from a wide range of sources—American, Irish, Caribbean. How did the English language travel around the globe, and what happened to it during those travels? *The Story of English* (Viking Penguin), by Robert McCrum, et al., traces the continuing evolution of our language.

Beyond the Misty Mountains

Full of mythology, magic, and quiet humor, J.R.R. Tolkien's classic fantasy *The Hobbit* (Ballantine and Fawcett) follows the adventures of a comfort-loving Hobbit named Bilbo Baggins. Baggins is tricked by the wizard Gandalf into going on a hazardous quest to recover stolen treasure from the dragon Smaug. *The Lord of the Rings* trilogy continues the saga of Middle Earth.

The Spoken Word Speaks On

The oral heritage of African Americans, with roots stretching back to Africa, is particularly strong. *Talk That Talk: An Anthology of African-American Storytelling* (Simon and Schuster), edited by Linda Goss and Marian E. Barnes, both celebrates and preserves that tradition.

FOR FURTHER EXPLORATION

Movies
Star Wars (George Lucas, 1977)
Raiders of the Lost Ark (Steven Spielberg, 1981)
The Searchers (John Ford, 1956)

Novels/Epic Fiction
The Epic of Gilgamesh foreword by N. K. Sandars
Jane Eyre by Charlotte Brontë
For Whom the Bell Tolls by Ernest Hemingway
The Earthsea Trilogy by Ursula Le Guin

Poetry
"The Love Song of J. Alfred Prufrock" by T. S. Eliot
"Dulce et Decorum Est" by Wilfred Owen
"On Her Brother" by Al-Khansa

Nonfiction
"Civil Disobedience" by Henry Thoreau
Sojourner Truth: Ain't I a Woman by Patricia and Fredrick McKissack
In Search of the Dark Ages by Michael Woods

The English Language

Old English: Where English Came From   *by John Algeo*

We have biological ancestors, from whom we inherit the tint of our skin, the shape of our skulls, and everything about our bodies. We also have cultural ancestors, from whom we inherit the society in which we live and especially the language we speak. We in the United States have diverse biological ancestors—various types of Caucasian, Mongol, and Negroid peoples from whom we get our genes—but we all share a common cultural ancestry expressed in the language we speak. So in studying English and its history, we learn about our past.

Gold pectoral, or ornamental breastplate (c. 4th–5th century).

Out of the East: The Ancestor of English

Written records of English have been preserved for about 1300 years. Much earlier, however, a people living in the east, near the Caspian Sea, spoke a language that was to become English. We call their language Proto-Indo-European because at the beginning of recorded history varieties of it were spoken from India to Europe. (*Proto—* means the first or earliest form of something.)

The speakers of Proto-Indo-European were a vigorous sort who raised cattle and horses.

They were fighters, farmers, and herders who traveled in large wagons and built fortresses on hilltops. Eventually, they got the urge to travel and began spreading through Turkey, Iran, India, and most of Europe. In various places their language changed into those we now call Persian, Hindi, Armenian, Greek, Russian, Polish, Irish, Italian, French, Spanish, German, English, Dutch, Norwegian, Swedish, and a good many others. Such languages we call Indo-European.

Wanderlust: The Migrations

Speakers of Indo-European languages eventually wandered all over the earth and were the first human beings to travel into space and reach the moon. Some early Indo-Europeans lived in what is now southern Denmark and northern Germany. Called Angles and Saxons, they were part of a large group of Germanic peoples living over much of northern Europe. About the middle of the fifth century (the traditional date is A.D. 449), the Anglo-Saxons migrated across the North Sea to the island of Britain and settled very happily in the green and fruitful land they found there.

The British Isles had already been inhabited by some distant Indo-European cousins of the Anglo-Saxons: the Britons, a Celtic people after whom the island was named. They had been

---

A. **Reader's Response: First Thoughts**

? What events do you already know about that probably influenced the English language? [Sample responses: In this unit students have read about the early Roman occupation of Britain, the invasions of the Angles and Saxons, the conversion of these people to Christianity, and the later invasions of the Vikings. Other influences are the Norman invasion, the colonization of North America, and the waves of immigrants into the United States—any movement of people brings new blood to a language.]

B. **Expansion**
The British judge Sir William Jones and the writer Jakob Grimm were the first to note similarities among Indo-European languages and to trace them back to a common origin.

C. **Exploring the Historical Period**
The text implies that wanderlust urged the Angles and the Saxons to migrate to Britain. However, the Angles were also known to have been particularly barbaric and the availability of plunder also might have been a reason for their move.

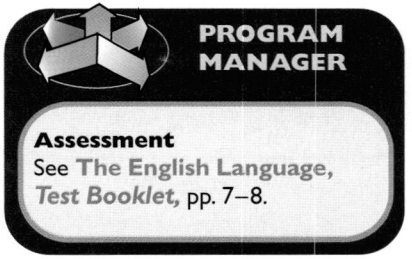

PROGRAM MANAGER

Assessment
See **The English Language, Test Booklet,** pp. 7–8.

A. Exploring the Culture

According to Robert McCrum's *The Story of English*, "There is an old Hindi proverb that 'language changes every eighteen or twenty miles. . . .' Here [in England], depending on which county you are driving through, a donkey can still be called a moke, or a cuddy, or a nirrup, or a pronkus."

B. Expansion

Some language scholars believe that the most significant contribution of the Vikings was the simplification of the system of inflection used in Old English.

Elements of Literature:
Videodisc Use the following bar codes to locate the video segment about the development of the English language from the Anglo-Saxons through the Renaissance. For more information, see the Videodisc *Teacher's Manual.*

Videodisc Side A

Begin Play, English Track

Begin Play, Spanish Track

---

conquered by the Romans, who were Indo-Europeans too, so all this jostling for space in the island was just one branch of the family trying to move in on another, rather like relatives from Chicago moving in with their kin in Florida for the winter.

The Anglo-Saxons got a few words from the Romans in Britain, such as *castra* ("camp"), which can be seen in the names of many English cities (*Chester, Chesterfield, Dorchester, Gloucester, Lancaster, Manchester, Winchester,* and *Worcester*). They also found the cities that the Romans had built, with temples, waterworks, and public baths. They moved into the cities and admired the great buildings, but they never learned to share the Roman passion for bathing.

Meeting the Neighbors

When the Anglo-Saxons first arrived in Britain (which came to be called Engla land, England—the land of the Angles), they had very little to do with the Celts, whom they drove into the west where they still survive today as the Welsh (an Anglo-Saxon word that means "foreigner"). But another group of Celts, the Irish, later sent missionaries to the Angles. About the same time, in A.D. 597, the Roman church also sent St. Augustine

St. Kevin's Monastery (6th century), Glendalough, Ireland.

to do missionary work.

Although there is very little early Celtic influence on the English language—hardly more than a few place names, such as *London* and *Dover*—Latin, the language of the Christian church, was enormously influential. Even while the Anglo-Saxons were still living on the Continent, they had learned some Latin from Roman soldiers and merchants, including words like *mile, street, wall, wine, cheese, butter,* and *dish.* After the Anglo-Saxons settled in England and were converted, they borrowed many other Latin words concerned with religion and learning, such as *school, candle, altar, paper,* and *circle.*

Beginning near the end of the eighth century, other cousins, Northmen or Vikings from Scandinavia, invaded England. They were led by such memorably named worthies as Ivar the Boneless, son of Ragnar Shaggy-britches. It would be a mistake, however, to think of these Vikings as amusingly rough but lovable, like the comic-strip character Hagar the Horrible. They were fierce fighters and very nearly made England into another Scandinavian country. It was the English King Alfred the Great who defeated the Viking invaders

and set about assimilating the Northmen into English life.

The influence of the Vikings' Norse language has been very great. Among the words borrowed are such common ones as *get, give, hit, kick, law, sister, skirt, sky, take, window, they, their,* and *them.*

What Tongue Is This?

Despite all the foreign influences, the language of the early English, which we call Old English or Anglo-Saxon, was clearly a Germanic tongue. An example of this language is the following short piece—a text that most readers of this book will know in a modern form:

> Fæder ūre, þū þe eart on heofonum, sī nama gehālgod. Tōbecume þīn rīce. Gewurðe þīn willa on eorðan swā swā on heofonum. Ūrne gedæghwāmlican hlāf syle ūs tō dæg. And forgyf ūs ūre gyltas, swā wē forgyfað ūrum gylltendum. And ne gelæd þū ūs on costnunge, ac ālȳs ūs of yfele. Sōðlice.

This text is the Lord's Prayer from about the year 1000. It differs from the version we know in many ways. Words are different (*costnunge* instead of the later Latin borrowing *temptation*). Spellings and pronunciations are different (*nama,* pronounced "nah-mah," instead of the present-day *name*). Meanings are different (*hlāf* in the sense of "bread," surviving today

---

OPTIONS FOR TEACHING

CROSSING THE CURRICULUM

Foreign Language Ask students who are fluent in another language or who are studying a foreign language to make a list of words in that language that are similar to words in English. Put these lists around the classroom.

Music Students interested in music may enjoy researching the types of music prevalent in Britain during the time of the Anglo-Saxons, the countries that may have had influence on that music, and the instruments used. Guide students to appropriate sources, and ask them to share their findings in a short oral report.

Geography Maps will help students to visualize how other countries influenced Great Britain. Have interested students post a map of the world, and add information about invasions, alliances, and language as they learn.

as *loaf*). And grammar is different. Note the word order of *Fæder ūre* for *our Father* and the word ending, or case inflection, *–um* in *on heofonum* ("in heaven").

Old English grammar was different from ours in a number of other ways. For example, all nouns were one of three genders—masculine, feminine, or neuter—and the grammatical gender of a noun might have little to do with sex. Thus, of three words for "woman," *hlæfdige* was feminine, *wif* was neuter, and *wifmann* was masculine.

Adjectives had different forms depending on the gender, number, and case of the nouns they modified (*þæt tile wif* but *se tila wifmann,* both meaning "the good woman").

Whereas our verbs have two forms in the present tense (for example, *ride, rides*), Old English verbs had four: *ic ride* ("I ride"), *þū ridest* ("you ride"), *hē rideþ* ("he rides"), and *wē ridon* ("we ride").

Like other Indo-European languages, Old English used end-

> Beginning near the end of the eighth century, other cousins, Northmen or Vikings from Scandinavia, invaded England. They were led by such memorably named worthies as Ivar the Boneless, son of Ragnar Shaggy-britches.

ings on words to show how they relate to one another and how they are used in a sentence. For example, "The boy killed the dragon" was "Se cnapa slōh þone dracan," while "The dragon killed the boy" was "Se draca slōh þone cnapan." The words for "boy" and "dragon" change their forms, according to whether they are the subject or the object of the verb, and the word for "the" is different, depending on the function of the word it modifies. Today word order alone shows the difference in grammar; Old English relied mainly on word form.

Anglo-Saxon scribes wrote in a script they learned from Celtic missionaries. It was a pleasant-looking, rounded style of writing, as the sample below shows.

Occasionally, for special purposes, Old English writers used an altogether different alphabet, called the *futhorc,* composed of letters called runes, which they learned from their Germanic cousins while they still lived on

Detail from the Book of Kells (8th century).
The Board of Trinity College, Dublin. Photograph by The Green Studio Ltd, Dublin.

the Continent. These runes were probably used by the very early pagan English for magic and for monuments. They were straight, angular letters that were used for carving on wood.

Old English was mainly oral. Because writing was important business, it was usually reserved for Latin, the language of church services, books, education, and contact with other nations. To know Latin was to be learned. Not to know Latin was to be illiterate. It is small wonder that Latin came to have a greater and more lasting influence on English than any other language did.

An example of Insular script.

C. Reader's Response: Extending the Text

? Why is it that a common language spoken by two groups of people will change in different ways if those people are separated? [Sample responses: The groups' experiences are likely to be different, and it is these differences that can cause languages to change. When English settlers first came to this country their speech had to incorporate things not found in England; they incorporated into their language American Indian words for food and animals they had not known in England—such as *squash* and *raccoon*.]

D. Humanities Connection

The Book of Kells, an illuminated Latin manuscript of the Gospels, richly and intricately ornamented, is the most remarkable of all the illuminated manuscripts of the Anglo-Saxon period. The chief characteristic of the illuminations is their intricate interlocking patterning of letters and border work. *The Book of Kells,* named for a monastery in Kells, Ireland, was the work of Irish monks and can be seen today in Trinity College, Dublin. A statement made in the twelfth century about an illuminated manuscript, possibly *The Book of Kells* itself, still applies today as we rediscover its beauty: "Examine it carefully, and you will penetrate to the very shrine of art. You will make out intricacies so delicate and subtle, so concise and compact, so full of knots and links, with colors so fresh and vivid, that you might think all this was the work of an angel, not a man."

COOPERATIVE LEARNING

Group Mastery To review, divide the class into groups of three or four. Ask them to create questions about the English language and its history; then, compile these questions for a quiz game to review the unit. Addressing each group in turn, ask a question written by a different group. All group members must agree on the answer before responding to you, and only one designated spokesperson for the group should call out the answer.

INTEGRATING THE LANGUAGE ARTS

Speaking and Listening To acquaint students with the sound of Old English, give them information about the pronunciation of Old English words. Ask them to practice reading a short section of *Beowulf* aloud in Old English, and then have them read their selection to the rest of the class. Have listeners try to determine the meaning of each section read. Remind speakers to pause, raise or lower their voices, or slow their reading to help the audience understand the passage.

Language and Vocabulary Ask students to analyze a piece of writing from their portfolios by looking up the etymology of several words and making observations about word choices. They may notice that few descriptive words derive from Old English.

A. Expansion

Today we often hear a kind of high-tech slang that gives new meaning to old words, a vocabulary derived from ubiquitous computer usage. Here are some examples:

- Give me some *input* on this idea. (Give me <u>your opinion</u> on this idea.)
- The book is really *user friendly*. (The book is <u>easy to understand</u>.)

Try It Out: Answers

1. Possible answers:
- French (France, Ivory Coast, and French Guiana)
- Portuguese (Portugal, Brazil)
- Dutch (Netherlands, Aruba)
2.
- belt: Latin *balteus*
- brother: OE *brōthor*
- filly: Old Norse *fylja*
- horse: OE *hors*
- house: OE *hūs*
- night: OE *niht*
- noon: Latin *nōnus*
- pillow: Latin *pulvinus*
- pipe: Latin *pīpāre*
- rug: Old Norse *rugg*
- skin: Old Norse *skinn*
- until: Old Norse *un + til*
3. Answers will vary. Suggest that students keep their phrases short, and tell them that some letters do not exist in the runic alphabet (q, v, and x), so they will have to use other letters that have similar sounds instead.

Technology Tip

Have students use an on-line encyclopedia or an atlas on CD-ROM to complete Try It Out.

Our Anglo-Saxon Heritage

A We have come a long way since Anglo-Saxon times—in technology, in society, and in language. But much of the Anglo-Saxons' language, Old English, is still evident in our language.

Although today we have borrowed words from most of the world's languages, our basic vocabulary comes to us from Old English. Words like *heart, foot, head, day, year, earth, father, mother, son, daughter, name, east, full, hound, tooth, eat, weave,* and *sew* are survivals of Old English words (*heorte, fōt, hēafod, dæg, gēar, eorþe, fæder, mōdor, sunu, dohtor, nama, ēast, full, hund, tōþ, etan, wefan,* and *siwan*). Indeed, all of those words come to us from Proto-Indo-European; thus, they have been part of our language for thousands of years.

Our noun plural ending *s* and possessive ending *'s* (as in *hounds, hound's*) come to us from Old English (*hundas, hundes*). So do the endings we use to compare adjectives, as in *darker, darkest* (*deorcor, deorcost*). The regular endings for the past tense and past participle of our verbs, as in *healed, has healed,* are from Old English (*hǣlde, hæfþ hǣled*), as are the vowel changes in verbs like *sing, sang, sung* (*singan, sang, sungen*). In many other ways, our English is recognizably the same as the oldest English of which we have any record.

Although we have lost most of the endings that Old English words had and have borrowed far more words from other languages than we have kept from Old English times, the heart of our speech is still the same. The preceding sentence consists entirely of words that have come to us from Old English, and its grammar would have been understood by an English speaker of the year A.D. 700. Despite its many changes, English has remained basically true to itself.

Try It Out

1. On a map of the world, locate the countries where the following Indo-European languages are spoken. Some languages are spoken in more than one country. English and Spanish, for example, are each the national language in many countries.

Detail from the Book of Kells (8th century). The Board of Trinity College, Dublin. Photograph by the Green Studio Ltd, Dublin.

What are at least three other languages that are used in more than one country? (Remember that you can check an encyclopedia to determine where each language is spoken.)

English	Icelandic
Russian	Irish
German	Spanish
Polish	Albanian
Dutch	Portuguese
Czech	Romanian
Danish	French
Serbo-Croatian	Iranian
Swedish	Italian
Bulgarian	Hindi
Norwegian	Greek

2. Four of the following words are native words in Old English, four are Latin words borrowed into English very early (some while English speakers still lived on the Continent), and four are Scandinavian words borrowed as a result of the Norse invasions of England. Which words belong in each group? Check your work by looking at the etymologies in a college or unabridged dictionary.

belt	noon
brother	pillow
filly	pipe
horse	rug
house	skin
night	until

3. The Anglo-Saxons sometimes used an alphabet called *futhorc* or *futhark,* comprised of characters called runes. The first six letters of the runic alphabet—which spell out the word *futhorc*—looked like this:

ᚠᚢᚦᚩᚱᚳ or ᚠᚢᚦᚨᚱᚲ

Look up the entire runic alphabet in an encyclopedia. Working with a small group, write a brief phrase—a personal epitaph, for example—and translate it into the runic alphabet. Compare your "translations" with those created by other groups in the class.

OPTIONS FOR TEACHING

CLASSROOM MANAGEMENT

Exit Slips In the last five minutes of each class period, ask students to write down three things they have learned from this section of the textbook and to turn the papers in to you; or have them answer a specific question to see whether or not they mastered the objective(s) of the lesson. The comments may be used as a quick review in the next class period.

ASSESSMENT TOOLS

Check Test: True-False

1. English originated as a language 1,300 years ago. [False]
2. The Anglo-Saxons migrated to Britain about the middle of the fifth century. [True]
3. The Anglo-Saxons refused to use any words from the Romans. [False]
4. There is a strong Celtic influence on the English language. [False]
5. Latin influenced English more than any other language because the Romans forced all the Anglo-Saxons to learn that language. [False]

Writer's Workshop

The history of the written word is rich a

Page 1

NARRATIVE WRITING

AUTOBIOGRAPHICAL INCIDENT

We all like to recount (and to hear and read about) the pivotal events that fill every life: challenges, triumphs, and sorrows. The **autobiographical incident,** a narrative about an event or experience in a person's life, appears in personal writing—letters, journals, and diaries. But it's also important in other kinds of writing, such as informative or persuasive writing, where narration and anecdote help convey ideas to readers.

Prewriting

1. **Choosing an experience with impact.** You are looking for intense moments in your life. Dramatic physical danger is a possibility, but so are more quiet events. Consider any situation that evokes a strong emotion: fear, pride, a dare, jealousy, success and defeat, honor, revenge, loyalty, friendship, illness, family ties. Brainstorm to trigger brief incidents that have stayed with you. Choose something that occurred in a brief time period, from a few hours to a day. Also, refer to the Writer's Notebook entries (pages 50 and 60) that you may have done earlier in this collection. Be sure, though, that your choice is not an experience too private to share with other readers.

2. **Details: telling versus showing.** To get started

   • In a brief freewrite, set down what happened in the incident. Just go for basic events, but name people and places.

   • Put the freewrite aside. Later, re-read it as if someone else were describing the incident to you. Is anything left out?

   Now comes the heart of the matter in autobiographical writing: details. Your freewrite *tells* what happened, but your essay must *show* readers, so that they experience it too (and keep reading). Along with precise narrative details (who did what, when, where), you'll need descriptive details (words that strike the senses) and sometimes conversational details (dialogue).

   This statement covers an action: *The officer stopped our car and told Brett to get out.* But these details tell a better story: *The officer's arm shot out like a huge blue warning, and Brett braked so roughly my seat belt snapped to attention. "Out of the car, son—slowly," he demanded.* Try the helpful recall strategies given in the box labeled "Strategies for Elaboration" on page 68.

   Once you've recalled details, you can record them in a chart. Using your freewrite, list events and actions, chronologically, on the left. Then fill in details, using any of the memory strategies on page 68.

Technology HELP

See Writer's Workshop 2 CD-ROM. *Assignment: Autobiographical Incident.*

ASSIGNMENT
Write an autobiographical narrative about a significant incident in your life. Use specific details to make the experience live for readers, and to clearly reveal its meaning.

AIM
To tell a story; to express yourself.

AUDIENCE
Your classmates, family, or general readers.

Try It Out
Take each "telling" sentence below, and make it *show* in a paragraph. Invent people, places, and dialogue as needed, and use specific details.
1. I lost my temper.
2. The car was an eyesore.

WW Autobiographical Incident

Prewriting
Choosing an experience with impact **p. 67**
Details: telling versus showing **p. 67**
Stepping back, finding meaning **p. 68**

Drafting
Speaking to your readers **p. 68**
Opening artfully **p. 68**
Framing and pacing **p. 68**
Ending well **p. 69**

Evaluating and Revising
Peer review **p. 69**
Self-evaluation **p. 69**

Proofreading and Publishing p. 69

Reflecting on Your Writing p. 69

PORTFOLIO ASSESSMENT

• **Generating Ideas** To help students in prewriting, use the heuristic in the *Portfolio Management System,* p. 71.
• **Assessment Rubric** For a rubric that can be used to assess students' progress in writing, see the *Portfolio Management System,* p. 73.

Try It Out: Possible Answers
Answers will vary, but make sure that students use specific images and vivid diction to make their paragraphs *show* rather than *tell,* as in the following example: A flush burned my cheeks, and angry tears flooded my eyes.

PROGRAM MANAGER

• **Computer Guided Instruction** For a related autobiographical incident assignment that students may use as additional instruction, see *Writer's Workshop 2.*

• **Modeling or Practicing Revision** To summarize and model the revision process, and to provide student practice, use **Revision Transparencies 1.6–1.7** in the *Audiovisual Resources Binder.*

Motivation

Read aloud a story or an essay that relates an autobiographical incident, and ask students to talk about their reactions to the piece, to identify the meaning they think the author intended to convey, and to pinpoint memorable images from the piece.

Teaching the Lesson

Remind students to choose a situation they would not mind sharing with others.

Prewriting

To facilitate *showing* as opposed to *telling,* present a short, chronological narrative that summarizes an incident. Ask students to use their imaginations to revise the narrative, enhancing it with details and dialogue.

Evaluating and Revising

Divide the class into small groups in which students may read their papers aloud. Have students use the peer review questions and the evaluation criteria on p. 69 to critique each other's papers. Suggest that students frame additional comments as questions, to facilitate more diplomatic criticism.

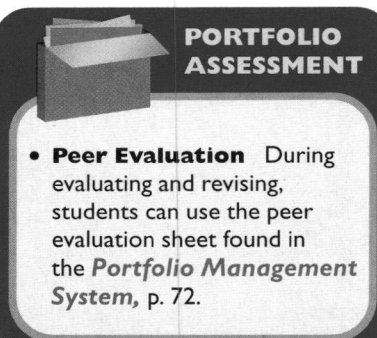

PORTFOLIO ASSESSMENT

- **Peer Evaluation** During evaluating and revising, students can use the peer evaluation sheet found in the *Portfolio Management System,* p. 72.

Model		
Events	Details of people, places, objects, and talk	My feelings
I meet my cousin Gerry outside the house, like he asked: Says he's leaving for Army—a secret.	Dusk, still hot, kids playing like we did, Gerry with one small pack—serious. "I know I can trust you."	Shocked. Flattered but scared—can I promise? Thinking of Uncle G.

Strategies for Elaboration: Prompting Memory

Use the following strategies to recall ideas and details about an incident:

- **Visualizing.** See the scene in your mind's eye.
- **Visiting.** Go back to the place of an event. Note details, giving memories time to emerge.
- **Interviewing.** Talk to other participants.
- **Using objects, sounds, scents.** Find "artifacts" of the incident—a photo, a cap, a song—and let them stir your memory.

3. Stepping back, finding meaning. By the end of your narrative, a reader should not only know what happened, but also know what it meant to you. Again, details can show the importance; you may or may not include a direct statement of meaning (such as *In choosing one loyalty, I betrayed another*).

But for now, review your chart, and write a statement *for yourself.* Consider how you changed or what you learned—about you, others, life.

Drafting

1. **Speaking to your readers.** You'll speak directly to readers in the first person as "I," which means natural, fairly informal language. But your tone, your *attitude* toward your story, can be solemn, comic, suspenseful, nostalgic—whatever fits your feeling about the incident.

2. **Opening artfully.** Remember, you're a storyteller in this essay; you have many elements available for a "hook-them-quickly" opening. You might open with
   - mystery and suspense—a hint of what's to come
   - atmospheric scene-setting
   - arresting dialogue
   - an action in progress

3. **Framing and pacing.** Your focus is one incident out of a full life, so readers may need some background, or context, to understand events. Carefully select background details—about people, relationships, places, prior happenings—that are *necessary* to frame the single incident. This context may occur as an introduction, early in your essay, or as explanatory details throughout the body. But don't bog readers down with background; keep the narrative moving.

   Pacing your story is important. Locate its high point, the moment or scene that glues attention, and keep pulling readers toward it by logically organizing events. Try these ways to create interesting rhythms:

OPTIONS FOR TEACHING

STRATEGIES FOR INCLUSION

Learners Having Difficulty Encourage students to hold individual conferences with you if they face writer's block. Let them talk through what they have written; then, ask questions that will lead them to add main ideas or to furnish details. Have them take notes during the conference to use as they write.

Advanced To help students develop a more sophisticated writing style, model such syntax as introductory participial phrases or items in a series followed by a dash. (Examples: *Knowing that I would probably be in trouble for being so late,* I put on my most confident face to greet my parents waiting inside. *Worry, anger, and relief*—my parents combined all these emotions into bear hugs and the announcement that I was grounded for two weeks.) Encourage students to try these syntactic forms at least once in their papers.

- Alternate long shots and close-ups. For example, narrate an action from a distance, and then zoom in on a person, object, or conversation.
- Use varying sentence patterns and lengths to change the story's tempo and energy.
- Use dialogue for "you-are-there" effects.
- Open with a vivid mid-action scene, and then go back to the beginning, continuing events in chronological order.

4. **Ending well.** You don't have to place your statement of meaning into the last paragraph, but do create a satisfying close. Offer a final reflection, look to the future, echo your opening, or use a quotation or dialogue.

Evaluating and Revising

1. **Peer review.** Here are some good focal points for peer reviewers:
   - Did I *see, hear,* and *feel* this experience? (Where are more or better details needed?)
   - Did events and description steadily pull me in? (Where did interest drop?)
   - What words and phrases did I like best?
   - What did I learn about the writer?

2. **Self-evaluation.** Try to be a stranger to your story, judging it from some distance. Review the four effective writing strategies in "Drafting." Make notes on your rough draft where you used these strategies. Share your best two examples of these strategies, and work with a partner to improve the other two. Also, act on peer-review comments that ring true (and *don't* take helpful criticisms personally).

Proofreading and Publishing

After making all revisions in your narrative's content, structure, and style, do a final polishing with close proofreading. Pay close attention to punctuation in dialogue. Recopy or reprint a final version, and read it slowly for errors.

Besides letting friends and family read your autobiographical story, try an oral reading—for the class or just a few people.

Reflecting on Your Writing

You wrote about an incident that taught you something, but the act of writing itself is another "autobiographical incident." What did the writing process reveal to you? Use these questions for a reflection in your portfolio. Remember to date your reflection and your essay.

1. Was the meaning of the incident clearer (or changed) for you after you wrote? If so, why?
2. Did any memories surprise you? Which memory gave you the most pleasure or pain?
3. What method of memory recall worked best for you?
4. What was the easiest part of writing about yourself and other people in your life? the hardest part? Why do you think so?

Language Workshop HELP

Sentence combining: page 70.

▌ Evaluation Criteria

A good autobiographical incident
1. *speaks directly to readers in informal language, using a consistent tone*
2. *hooks reader with an intriguing beginning*
3. *logically organizes events*
4. *frames a single incident with selected background details about people and setting*
5. *is paced to keep the reader interested and has an obvious ending*
6. *says what the incident means to the writer*

Revision STRATEGIES

Using different colors of pen or pencil, circle each type of detail you've included: narrative, descriptive, and dialogue. Is the balance of details good? Are details sharp? Then add details, or change weak ones. Show a writing partner or peer evaluator the changes you've made.

Language Handbook HELP

Punctuating dialogue: page 1247.

Proofreading and Publishing

Remind students to proofread carefully. One effective technique is to read the paper backward, isolating one sentence at a time, to check for errors in punctuation, spelling, and grammar.

Portfolio

Reflecting On Your Writing

After students have completed their essays and perhaps have heard others read aloud, ask them to answer the questions on student p. 69 on a page attached to their essays. Encourage them to write a few additional comments about what techniques they might be able to apply to other assignments.

Reteaching

Ask students to trade papers with a partner and to circle in each other's stories the parts that are *telling* instead of *showing*. Pairs may work together to revise these sections with vivid details or dialogue.

Closure

Have a Read-Around. Put the desks in a circle and ask volunteers to read their autobiographical essays aloud. Discuss each essay briefly, using the criteria for a good autobiographical incident to evaluate students' work.

Enrichment

Ask students to choose an autobiography to read. Ask them to write a review of this selection, a letter to the author, or dialectical notes on the reading.

PROBLEM SOLVING/CRITICAL THINKING

Accepting Criticism Before groups begin to work together, you may want to talk about the trust that is necessary for them to help each other with their writing. Let them think of ways to give criticism (suggestions) without being offensive and ways to accept suggestions without feeling embarrassed.

ASSESSMENT TOOLS

Grading Scale Give students the grading scale that you will use to evaluate the final drafts of their essays, so they will know what you expect. You might use a scale like the one following.

Possible points	Criteria The essay successfully
20 points	Speaks directly to readers in informal language, using a consistent tone
20 points	Hooks reader with an intriguing beginning, is paced to keep the reader interested, and has a clear ending

Possible points	Criteria The essay successfully
20 points	Logically organizes events
20 points	Frames a single incident with selected background details about people and setting
20 points	Says what the incident means to the writer

Language Workshop

Mini-Lesson: Sentence Combining

Ask students to choose a piece of writing from their portfolios and to highlight the first four words in each sentence. They should check to see whether the subject and verb are in the highlighted section. If they have several sentences in a row with this construction, they can combine them using the strategies listed on this page.

Try It Out: Possible Answers

1. The dragon's flaming breath scorched the shield, melting it at once.
2. Swinging his sword, Beowulf hit the fearsome dragon's impenetrable skin.
3. As the dragon jumped away, flames poured out of its nostrils.
4. Because his sword had failed him, Beowulf knew he faced the monster alone.

PROGRAM MANAGER

- **Extra Practice and Guided Instruction** For more instruction and practice of sentence combining, see *Language Workshop* in *Teaching Resources A,* pp. 17–18.
- **Extra Practice or Guided Instruction** See *Language Workshop:* Sentence combining for more practice or guided instruction in sentence combining.
- **Independent Practice or Reteaching** Use *Language and Writing Skills Worksheets,* pp. 111–118.

Technology HELP

See Language Workshop CD-ROM. *Key word entry: sentence combining.*

Language Handbook HELP

Sentence combining: page 1239.

Try It Out

Combine each pair of sentences below into one sentence.

1. The dragon's flaming breath scorched the shield. The shield melted at once.
2. Beowulf swung his sword at the fearsome dragon. Beowulf hit the dragon's impenetrable skin.
3. Then the dragon jumped away. It jumped with flames pouring out of its nostrils.
4. Beowulf faced the monster alone. Beowulf's sword had failed him.

SENTENCE COMBINING

Read aloud the following sentences. How do they sound?

> Beowulf neared the dragon's cave. He let out a loud battle cry. The dragon rose. The dragon approached Beowulf. It was angry that a man had come to this fearful place. The dragon breathed melting fire and scorching smoke. Beowulf firmly held his sword and shield.

Something holds this scene back, making it stiff: the jerky rhythm of the sentences, which share a basic subject-verb structure. Combining some sentences makes the flow smoother, the action more continuous, and the ideas clearer.

> Beowulf neared the dragon's cave, letting out a loud battle cry. The dragon rose and approached Beowulf, for it was angry that a man had come to this fearful place. While Beowulf firmly held his sword and shield, the dragon breathed melting fire and scorching smoke.

Strategies for Combining Sentences

1. **Insert phrases.** Often you can move phrases (such as *with no warning, shocked by his presence*) from one sentence into another.

   > Beowulf neared the dragon's cave, *letting out a loud battle cry.*

2. **Combine ideas.** When sentences express similar ideas, you may be able to combine subjects, verbs, objects, or entire sentences with conjunctions like *and, but, or, for,* and *yet.*

   > The dragon rose *and* approached Beowulf, *for* it was angry that a man had come to this fearful place.

3. **Subordinate ideas.** When sentences express related ideas, create one sentence with a main clause and a subordinate (dependent) clause. To show the relationship of the clauses, you must add a connecting word (such as *although, because, that, who,* or *while*). Placing the subordinate clause first adds even more variety.

   > *While Beowulf firmly held his sword and shield,* the dragon breathed melting fire and scorching smoke.

Writer's Workshop Follow-Up: Revision

Read aloud the narrative you wrote for the Writer's Workshop on page 67. Do you hear any short, choppy sentences? Does the writing sound monotonous? Use the sentence-combining techniques you've just practiced to create dynamic action sequences, connect thoughts, and break up monotonous sentences. Read aloud your revisions to a peer reviewer: Do your combined sentences sound better? Do they make relationships between ideas clearer?

70 THE ANGLO-SAXONS

✔ QUICK CHECK: Sentence Combining

Have students combine each pair of sentences below into one sentence.

[1] Beowulf must go to the mother's den. He will find Grendel's mother there. [To find Grendel's mother, Beowulf must go to her den.]

[2] Beowulf jumps into the lake. He has all his armor on his back. [Wearing all his armor, Beowulf jumps into the lake.]

[3] He sees Grendel's mother. She is a hideous creature. [He sees Grendel's mother, a hideous creature.]

[4] His sword does not wound her. It cannot cut through her tough skin. [Because it cannot cut through her tough skin, the sword does not wound her.]

[5] Beowulf throws away his useless sword. He wrestles her with his bare hands. [Beowulf throws away his useless sword and wrestles her with his bare hands.]

CREATIVE PROBLEM SOLVING
LEARNING FOR LIFE

Group Membership

Problem

The early Anglo-Saxons found a sense of community in close-knit kinship groups. Where do people turn today to find a sense of community?

Project

Describe the impact that a group you belong to has had on your life. What makes the group more than just a collection of individuals? What do you bring to the group? What do you draw from it?

Preparation

1. From the various groups to which you belong—at home, at school, at work, or through a religious or volunteer organization—choose one that has had a significant effect on you.

2. Analyze what the group members have in common, how they recognize and build on one another's strengths, and how their interrelationships affect the overall functioning of the group.

Procedure

1. The next time the group gets together, observe how the members interact. How do they speak to and listen to one another, what roles do different members assume, and how does the group make decisions and work out compromises?

2. Try not to let your awareness of your role as an observer alter your own behavior. Simply make a conscious effort to observe others more closely than you otherwise might.

3. Jot down your impressions as soon as possible after the meeting. You don't need to use complete sentences—you might even find yourself sketching or doodling. Even fragmentary jottings will help you pull together your conclusions.

Presentation

Use one of the following formats (or another that your teacher approves):

1. **The Group in Motion**
Design and build a mobile that represents the group. Choose sizes, shapes, and textures to capture the makeup of the group, and arrange the pieces so that the motion illustrates the interrelationships between the group members. You must decide, for example, whether the pieces will move all together or separately, and whether they will bump into one another or move on different tracks. Give your mobile a title that expresses your feelings about what the group means to you.

2. **Say It in Pictures**
Create a two-page photo-essay about the group for an illustrated magazine. Select photos that show the cohesiveness of the group (be sure to include yourself in at least one of them), or take new ones if necessary. Write a caption to accompany each of the photos, and include a title that will draw readers into the essay. If you have access to desktop publishing software, use it to produce a camera-ready, or final, version of your photoessay.

3. **Talking About Community**
Get together with three to five other students to present a panel discussion on the various ways in which people fulfill their need for a sense of community in their lives. The panel members should represent a variety of types of groups—for example, a family, a neighborhood group, a sports or academic team, a service club. Meet with the other panel members to phrase a discussion question, prepare a discussion outline, and elect a group leader. Hold the discussion in front of an audience such as the rest of the class or the parent-teacher organization.

Processing

What did you learn from this activity about the importance you and your classmates place on feeling a sense of community? What are some of the various ways people meet that need? Write a brief reflection for your portfolio.

Learning for Life

PORTFOLIO ASSESSMENT

Performance Assessment Rubric So that students may see the evaluation criteria before they begin working on these projects, share the rubric provided in the *Portfolio Management System,* p. 74.

DEVELOPING WORKPLACE COMPETENCIES		
Preparation	**Procedure**	**Presentation**
Processes information Reasons Communicates ideas and information	Acquires data Interprets information Evaluates data	Thinks creatively Makes decisions Designs systems Applies technology to specific tasks

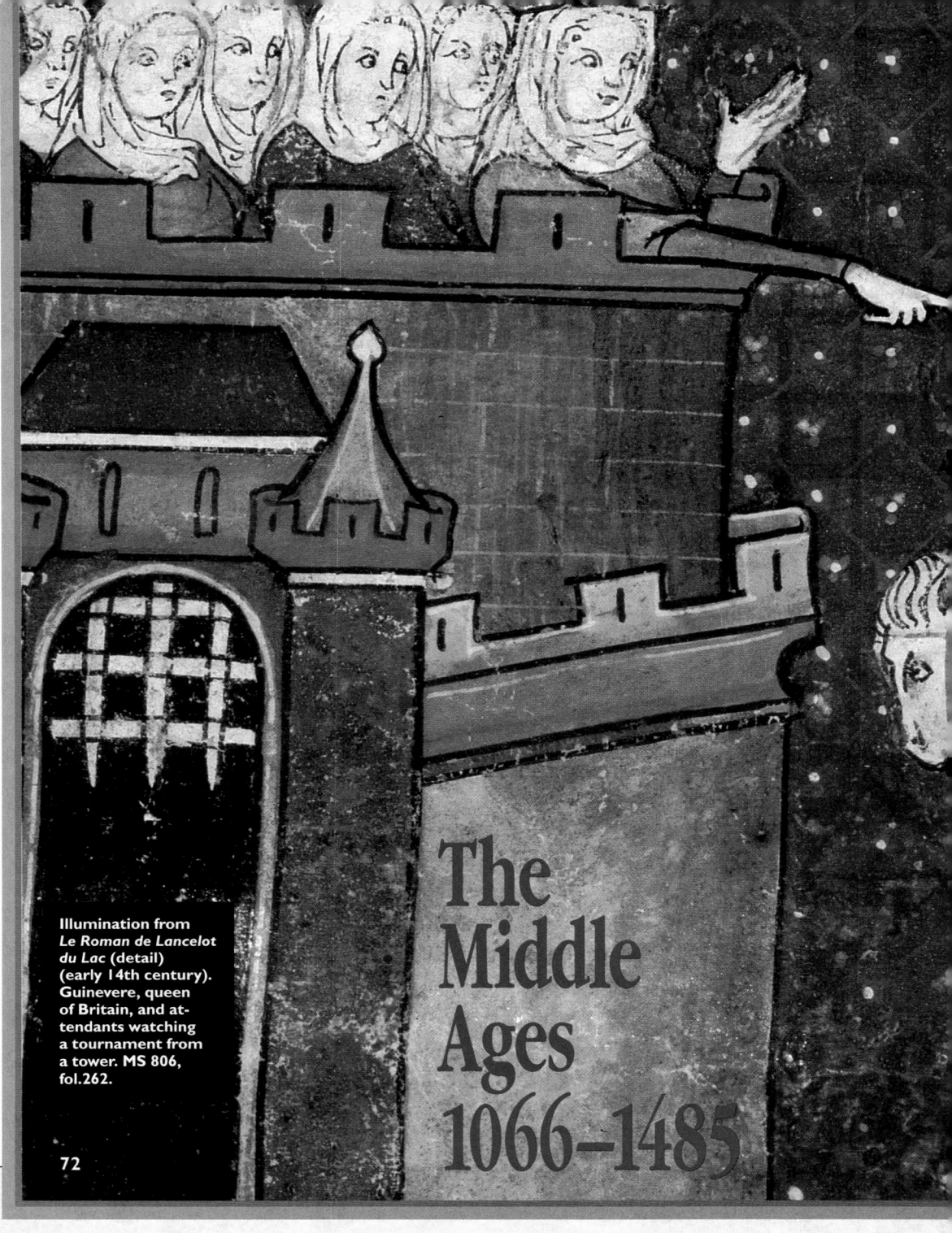

72

The Middle Ages 1066–1485

The Middle Ages

by **David Adams Leeming**

At his most characteristic, medieval man was not a dreamer nor a wanderer. He was an organizer, a codifier, a builder of systems. He wanted "a place for everything and everything in the right place." Distinction, definition, tabulation were his delight. Though full of turbulent activities, he was equally full of the impulse to formalize them. War was (in intention) formalized by the art of heraldry and the rules of chivalry; sexual passion (in intention), by the elaborate code of love. . . . There was nothing which medieval people liked better, or did better, than sorting out and tidying up. Of all our modern inventions I suspect that they would most have admired the card index.
—C. S. Lewis

Illumination from a French manuscript of *Romance of the Rose* (15th century). British Library, London.

In October 1066, a daylong battle near Hastings, England, changed the course of history. There, just ten miles from the channel dividing England from France, Duke William of Normandy, France, defeated and killed King Harold of England, the last of the Anglo-Saxon kings. So began the Norman Conquest, an event that radically affected English history, the English character, and the English language. Unlike the Romans, the Normans never withdrew from England.

Who was this William the Conqueror? He was the illegitimate son of the previous duke of Normandy, who was in turn a cousin of the English king called Edward the Confessor. Edward had died childless earlier in 1066, and Harold, the earl of Wessex, had been crowned the following day. But William claimed that the old king had promised the throne to him. Determined to seize what he considered rightfully his, William sailed the English Channel with an enormous army.

William was an efficient and ruthless soldier, but he wanted to rule the Anglo-Saxons, not eliminate them. Today, as a result, rather than a Norman, French-speaking England (and America), we find a culture and a language that subtly intermingle Norman and Anglo-Saxon elements. To the Anglo-Saxons' more democratic and artistic tendencies, the Normans brought administrative ability, an emphasis on law and order, and cultural unity.

One of William's great administrative feats was an inventory of nearly every piece of property in England—land, cattle, buildings—in the Domesday Book. (The title suggests a comparison between William's judgment of his subjects' financial worth with God's final judgment of their moral worth.) For the first time in European history, people could be taxed based on what they owned.

Although the Normans did not erase Anglo-Saxon culture, they did bring significant changes to England. William and many of his successors remained dukes of Normandy as well as kings of England. The powerful Anglo-Norman entity they molded brought England into mainstream European civilization in a new way. For example, William divided the holdings of the fallen English landowners

A **B**

Norman warriors crossing the Channel in 1066, from a French manuscript (11th century). MS N.a. Lat. 1390, fol. 7.

© cliché Bibliothèque Nationale de France, Paris.

October 14, 1066, was one of the decisive days of history. The battle itself was nip and tuck; the shift only of a few elements here or there, a gift of luck could have given the victory to the Anglo-Saxons. If Harold had won at Hastings and had survived, William would have had no choice but to renounce his adventure. There is little likelihood that anyone would have attempted a serious invasion of England during the next millennium—by water, at least. England would have strengthened its bonds with Scandinavia while remaining distrustful of the western Continent—even more distrustful than it is today. The native Anglo-Saxon culture would have developed in unimaginable ways, and William the Conqueror would be dimly known in history only as William the Bastard.

—Morris Bishop

A. Expansion

Decisions about power during the medieval period were settled by contending rulers and their armies. How would such a power dispute be handled in a democracy? [By a popular election in which the general population would vote for the leader it preferred.]

B. Exploring the Historical Period

William of Malmesbury, one of the greatest of English chroniclers, says of William: "He was of just stature, extraordinary corpulence, fierce countenance: his forehead bare of hair; of such strength of arm that it was often a matter of surprise that no one was able to draw his bow which he himself could bend when his horse was on full gallop: he was majestic whether sitting or standing, although the protuberance of his belly deformed his royal person. . . ."

PROGRAM MANAGER

- **Planning Instruction** See *Teaching Notes, Teaching Resources A,* p. 21, for additional teaching options about the Middle Ages.
- **Assessment** For assessment of the literary and historical events mentioned in the historical introduction, see **Literary Period Introduction Test,** *Test Booklet,* pp. 15–16.

Elements of Literature: **Videodisc** Use the following bar codes to locate the appropriate material on the videodisc. See Videodisc *Teacher's Manual.*

Videodisc Side B
Begin Play
English Track

Begin Play
Spanish Track

Time Line

- **1100–1149**
  Explain to students that the small letter c stands for *circa* and is used before an approximate date. Ask students why more of the dates are marked "circa" in the first half of the time line. [Record keeping and histories became more accurate.]

- **1150–1199**
  Point out that events do not simply occur in history and then disappear forever—their effects may last hundreds of years. For example, during the Crusades, Arabic medicine, with its sophisticated use of drugs derived from plants, was introduced to the West. It was through the Arabs, also, that Europeans first learned the techniques of iron and silk manufacturing that helped to industrialize entire countries. The influences of Gothic architecture, epitomized by the Cathedral of Notre Dame in Paris, are still present. Suggest that students take other events from this time line and trace their effects through history.

The Middle Ages, 1066–1485

• Scene from the *Story of Roland,* from Chartres Cathedral, France (13th century).

LITERARY EVENTS

Death of Omar Khayyám, Persian poet and astronomer, 1131

French heroic poem, *Song of Roland,* written, c. 1100

In France, Chrétien de Troyes writes *Lancelot,* c. 1170s

In Spain, first mass production of paper, c. 1150

Marie de France, first known European woman to write narrative poetry, dies, c. 1216

Persian poet Saadi born, 1213

Beginnings of German epic poem, the *Nibelung-enlied,* c. 1200

1066–1099	1100–1149	1150–1199	1200–1249

CULTURAL/HISTORICAL EVENTS

King Edward the Confessor dies without heir, 1066

Duke of Normandy invades England, 1066

Domesday Book, a record of all land ownership in England, first compiled, 1086

Crusades to conquer and Christianize the Middle East begin, 1095

Knights Templar, a religious order whose mission was to protect pilgrims to the Holy Land, founded, c. 1119

Construction begins on Cathedral of Notre Dame in Paris, 1163

Thomas à Becket murdered, 1170

Minamoto Yoritomo becomes first shogun (military ruler) of Japan, 1192

Mongol leader Genghis Khan invades China, 1211

English barons force King John to sign the Magna Carta, 1215

Pope Gregory IX begins the Inquisition, c. 1232

• Aztec double-headed serpent. Turquoise mosaic (17 ¼" long).

76 THE MIDDLE AGES

USING THE TIME LINE

To help students appreciate the diversity of the events that occurred during this period, play a game of "Time Line Scene-Sketch." Allow students to have their books open to the time line.

After dividing the class into two teams, select someone from each team to draw a picture of one of the events on the chalkboard, and point out an event to the two students who will draw. Their teammates must guess the event and give its

date. The first complete correct answer scores a point for the team. Choose another team member to draw the next sketch, and so on. For a more challenging game, encourage students to memorize the time line, and do the activity with books closed.

• Teotihuacán bird image celebrating growth and fertility.

Thomas Aquinas writes *Summa Theologica*, 1266–1273

Boccaccio writes the *Decameron*, 1349–1351

Geoffrey Chaucer born, c. 1343

Julian of Norwich, one of the first English women of letters, born, c. 1342

Petrarch crowned poet laureate in Italy, 1341

Development of Japanese Nōh plays, 1300s

Dante Alighieri begins writing the *Divine Comedy*, c. 1307?

Chaucer begins *The Canterbury Tales*, c. 1387

Entire Bible translated into English for first time by John Wycliffe, 1380

Oldest written reference to legendary hero Robin Hood appears in *Piers Plowman*, c. 1378

Sir Gawain and the Green Knight written, c. 1375

Margery Kempe, author of first autobiography in English, born, c. 1373

Thomas Malory's *Le Morte Darthur* first printed by Caxton, 1485

William Caxton prints first book in English, c. 1475

First book printed with movable type by Gutenberg, 1455

In France, Christine de Pisan writes famous allegory, *Book of the City of Ladies*, 1405

Chaucer dies, 1400

1250–1299	1300–1349	1350–1399	1400–1485

First commoners allowed in British Parliament, c. 1250

Crusades end, 1270

Marco Polo in Beijing.

Venetian traveler Marco Polo visits court of Kublai Khan in China, 1275

Zimbabwe emerges as major trading empire, 1300s

Aztecs begin to establish empire in Mexico, 1325

Hundred Years' War between England and France begins, 1337

Black Death strikes England, 1348

• Chinese porcelain jar (15th century), Hsuan-te (Xuande) period, Ming dynasty. The Metropolitan Museum of Art, New York. Gift of Robert E. Tod, 1937. (37.191.1).

Ming dynasty begins 300-year rule of China, 1368

Peasants' Revolt in England, 1381

King Richard II deposed, 1399

English language used to open Parliament, 1362

Benin Kingdom in West Africa flourishes, 1400s

In France, Joan of Arc burned at the stake by the English, 1431

Inca Empire established in Peru, c. 1438

Italian inventor and artist Leonardo da Vinci born, 1452

War between the Houses of York and Lancaster (also called the Wars of the Roses), 1455–1485

Birth of Nicolaus Copernicus, European astronomer, 1473

Martin Luther born in Germany, 1483

First Tudor king, Henry VII, is crowned, 1485

• Wooden helmet of an Aztec warrior. © British Museum, London.

THE MIDDLE AGES 77

• **1350–1399**

❓ What two events demonstrate that English was beginning to be accepted in England as the language of learning and politics? [English used to open Parliament (1362) and Bible translated into English (1380).]

Technology Tip

TECHNOLOGY To find pedagogical resources and electronic projects on the Middle Ages, access the Labyrinth: The Medieval Studies Web server maintained by Georgetown University. The URL is **http://www .georgetown.edu/labyrinth**. *You may want to preview any Internet activity that you suggest to students. Because these resources are sometimes public forums, their content can be unpredictable.*

A. Exploring the Historical Period

Oaths of fealty were the backbone of the feudal society. Solemn and unbreakable, these oaths were sworn by a vassal to his chosen lord. The lord, in return, expected faithfulness and service without deception. Often vassals made these pledges over religious relics, or with the vassal's hands between those of his lord, the sacred alliance would be sealed with a kiss. The oath might be similar to this one: "I promise by my faith that from this time forward I will be faithful to Count William and will maintain toward him my homage entirely against every man, in good faith and without any deception."

B. Expansion

The hauberk was made of small metal discs sewn on linen. It was eventually replaced by chain mail, which was composed of interlocking iron rings.

C. Exploring the Historical Period

The tradition of armorial bearings, or coats of arms, was developed to help make clear who the knight was inside the cocoon of armor.

An attack on a fortress, from a French manuscript (detail) (13th–14th century). MS Fr. 1604, fol. 57v.

© cliché Bibliothèque Nationale de France, Paris.

among his own followers. These men and their families brought to England not only a new language—French—but also a new social system—feudalism—which displaced the old Nordic social structure described in *Beowulf*.

The Anglo-Norman entity that resulted from the Norman Conquest brought England into mainstream European civilization, which included feudalism.

Feudalism and Knighthood: Pyramid Power

More than simply a social system, feudalism was also a caste system, a property system, and a military system. Ultimately, it **A** was based on a religious concept of hierarchy, with God as the supreme overlord. In this sense, even a king held land as a vassal

> . . . there was not one hide of land in England that he did not know who owned it, and what it was worth . . .
>
> —from The Anglo-Saxon Chronicle

A CLOSER LOOK

A TERRIBLE WORM IN AN IRON COCOON

If we hear the term "medieval period," we inevitably think of knights and their magnificent suits of armor. During the early Middle Ages, armor consisted of a helmet, a shield, and a rel- **B** atively flexible mail shirt, or hauberk, made of countless riveted or welded iron rings. With the crossbow, however, came the need for more protection, so the knight was forced to compromise flexibility and mobility for self-defense.

Held together by rivets, leather straps, hinges, turning pins, buckles, and pegs, a suit of armor replaced mail as the warrior's chief protection. Knights wore a heavily padded undergarment of leather and a mail shirt under the armor, in addition to plate arm, leg, and foot pieces. Mail covered the neck, elbows, and

other joints, and gauntlets constructed of linked plates covered the hands. Some suits of armor weighed 120 pounds and contained 200 custom-fitted iron plates. The knight also carried a variety of weapons: lance, dagger, sword, battle-ax, and club-headed mace.

The threat of death in battle was bad enough, but the armor itself could also be fatal—causing death from suffocation, heart failure, even drowning. Battle during hot weather was particularly difficult. Since small slits in the helmet allowed only a limited line of vision and little ventilation, heatstroke—often deadly for the knight—was common. One anonymous poem **C** describes the armored knight as "a terrible worm in an iron cocoon."

OPTIONS FOR TEACHING

STRATEGIES FOR INCLUSION

English Language Development Work with students to look up the following words in the dictionary: *caste, hierarchy, vassal,* and *loyalty*. Explain that many organizations in modern society have a hierarchical organization (i.e., government, businesses, schools). As an example, demonstrate the hierarchical organization of your school. Put the job titles in a pyramid form on the chalkboard, and discuss the relevance of the pyramid shape. Have students fill in the names of the people that correspond to each title. Discuss the advantages and disadvantages of such an organization.

Visual Citing the explanation on pp. 78–79, encourage students to work in groups to produce a pyramid chart of feudal vassal-lord relationships. Have them put God at the top, the king under God, and so on. Invite them to use pictures as well as labels.

Learners Having Difficulty To help students relate to the time period, point out that these events took place at the time of the Aztecs in Mexico, in the centuries preceding the arrival of Christopher Columbus in the Americas in 1492. Ask students to jot down in their Reader's Logs what they know of the Middle Ages.

by "divine right." A king as powerful as William the Conqueror could stand firmly at the top of the pyramid. He could appoint certain barons as his immediate vassals, allotting them portions of his land in return for their economic or military allegiance—or both. In turn, the barons could appoint vassals of their own. The system operated all the way down to the landless knights and to the serfs, who were not free to leave the land they tilled.

The feudal system did not always work. Secure in a well-fortified castle, a vassal might choose not to honor his obligations to a weak overlord. The ensuing battles between iron-clad knights around moated castles account for one of the enduring images of the Middle Ages.

Yet the feudal system did carry with it a sense of form and manners that permeated the life, art, and literature of the Middle Ages. This sense of formalism came to life most fully in the institution of knighthood and in the related practice, or code, of chivalry.

We cannot think of the medieval period without thinking of knights. Since the primary duty of males above the serf class was military service to their lords, boys were trained from an early age to become warriors. Often, their training took place in houses other than their own, to be sure that the training was strict. When a boy's training was completed,

> The bond between lord and vassal was affirmed or reaffirmed by the ceremony of homage. The vassal knelt, placed his clasped hands within those of his master, declared, "Lord, I become your man," and took an oath of fealty. The lord raised him to his feet and bestowed on him a ceremonial kiss. The vassal was thenceforth bound by his oath "to love what his lord loved and loathe what he loathed, and never by word or deed do aught that should grieve him."
>
> —Morris Bishop

Only aristocratic knights could afford the huge cost of armor, a war horse, pack-horses, a mount to ride when not in battle, and servants. Because of the armor's weight and the complex fittings required to piece it together, a knight couldn't dress himself for battle. In fact, battles were usually scheduled to allow the warring knights time to be dressed. Servants stood by during battle in case the knight was unhorsed. An armored knight on his back was like an upside-down turtle trying to get on its feet. In this position, the knight was vulnerable to his adversary. If he fell into a shallow body of water, he could drown.

During the fifteenth century, the knight and his horse were considered invulnerable. But this role changed dramatically when the long-bow and later the musket ball came into war-fare. When his armor could no longer protect him in battle, the knight in shining armor became more of a courtier than a combatant. In the last years of their existence, knights participated in exhibitions rather than in warfare.

Chain-mail maker.
Stadtbibliothek, Nürnberg.

THE MIDDLE AGES 79

? Clearly, the lord benefited from the loyalty of the knight, but what did the knight gain from this loyalty?
[Sample responses: Protection from enemies, social status, adventure, wealth.]

CROSSING THE CURRICULUM

Science/Health Have students work in groups to produce posters showing the cycle involved in the spread of bubonic plague. Ask them to include notes about measures that could have been taken to reduce the devastation.

History Invite students to research the new liberties offered by the Magna Carta to the English aristocracy. Have them develop a mock Magna Carta that lists the prominent liberties ensured by the document.

Social Studies Have students work in groups to explore the difference between feudal and democratic power distribution. Ask each group to create a chart like the one that follows, listing qualities of feudalism and qualities of democracy.

	Feudalism	Democracy
Similarities	[loyalty]	[loyalty]
Differences	[leader by birth or by conquest]	[elected leader]

In these examples of art on pp. 80–81, how do the roles of medieval women and men differ? [Possible responses: The women are going to work, or watching the men prepare for battle, fighting, or jousting.] Where do the women appear to be? [Possible responses: The upper-class women appear to stay out of the battle, wishing a knight well or watching from a balcony or some kind of fortress. The peasant woman shares the center of the illustration with her husband.] How do the women react to the action around them? [Possible responses: The ladies seem to be awed, admiring, worried. The peasant woman appears prepared for the day's work.]

A medieval knight in armor. MS 42130, fol. 202v.

By permission of the British Library, London.

he was "dubbed," or ceremonially tapped on his shoulder (originally a hard, testing blow). Once knighted, the youth became a man with the title "sir" and the full rights of the warrior caste.

Knighthood was grounded in the feudal ideal of loyalty, and it entailed a complex system of social codes. Breaking any one of those codes would undermine not only the knight's position but also the very institution of knighthood. Thus, in the story of *Sir Gawain and the Green Knight* (page 161), his code of honor binds Gawain to accept a challenge that he believes will bring him certain death.

Feudalism was a pyramid system based on a religious concept of hierarchy. Expected to serve as warriors, males above the serf class were trained as knights.

Women in Medieval Society: No Voice, No Choice

Since they were not soldiers, women had no political rights in a system that was primarily military. A woman was always subservient to a man, whether husband, father, or brother. Her husband's or father's social

---

OPTIONS FOR TEACHING

INTEGRATING THE LANGUAGE ARTS

Strategic Reading Have students read the boldface summary passages interspersed in the reading material *before* they read the text that precedes these summaries. Have them write down two questions for each summary. Tell them to write answers to these questions after they have read the material.

Speaking and Listening Have students work in groups of four to six to discuss the pros and cons of one of the medieval concerns listed below. Then, have each group present, in a debate format, the pros and cons of the issue. Students should practice in advance to make their statements clear, and they should listen to the opposing side's arguments carefully, so that their responses are relevant.

- Crusades: To go or not to go?
- Feudalism: Blessing or curse?

- Chivalry: Worth keeping or obsolete?
- Magna Carta: Major advance or major mistake?

Writing: Newspapers Have students work in groups of five to produce medieval English newspapers. Require groups to include one article or feature on each of the following topics: the Norman Conquest, feudalism, the bubonic plague, Geoffrey Chaucer, and chivalry; but invite them to add to the list. Remind students to consult the time line for dates. To help ensure equal work by all members, ask each group to include a credit column at the end of its newspaper.

Off for a day of haying, a peasant pushes his wife to work in a wheelbarrow. MS Lat. 1173, fol. 4v.
© cliché Bibliothèque Nationale de France, Paris.

standing determined the degree of respect she commanded. For peasant women, life was a ceaseless round of childbearing, housework, and hard fieldwork. Women of higher station were occupied with childbearing and household supervision. Such women might even manage entire estates while their men were away on business or at war, but the moment the men returned, the women relinquished their temporary powers.

Women in the Middle Ages had no political rights. A woman's social standing depended completely on her husband's or father's status.

A woman is a worthy wight:
She serveth a man both daye and nyght;
Thereto she putteth all her might,
   And yet she hathe but care and woe.

   —Anonymous (fifteenth century)

Chivalry and Courtly Love: Ideal but Unreal

Chivalry was a system of ideals and social codes governing the behavior of knights and gentle- **(A)** women. Among its precepts were adhering to one's oath of loyalty to the overlord and observing certain **(B)** rules of warfare, such as never attacking an unarmed opponent. In addition, adoring a particular lady (not necessarily one's wife) was seen as a means of achieving self-improvement.

Universitätsbibliothek, Heidelberg.

Noblewomen watching a tournament, from a German manuscript (c. 14th century). Cod. Pal. Germ. 848, Codex Manesse, fol. 52v.

A. Expansion
In *The Middle Ages,* Morris Bishop describes how the system of chivalry influences us still: "In time the chivalric code was modified, but it has never died. It set a standard for upper-class behavior, especially in the Victorian era. Our esteem for sentimental love is a medieval relic. 'Women and children first' is a chivalric motto. When the *Titanic* sank and the gentlemen bowed the ladies into the lifeboats, they were 'verray parfit gentil' knights."

B. Cultural Connections
A similar set of ideals and social codes, called *bushido,* developed among the samurai warrior class in medieval Japan. Akira Kurosawa's film *The Seven Samurai* shows the samurai ideals suffering under the development of guns and gunpowder.

COOPERATIVE LEARNING

Medieval Advertisements Have students work in groups to create magazine advertisements for one of the following items. Tell them to direct their "pitch" to a medieval audience.

- Longbows
- Rat poison
- Battle-ax
- Book on writing love poetry
- Maps of the Holy Land
- French phrase book
- Gunpowder

Student-Taught Mini-Lessons Have students work in groups of four to create mini-lessons on one of the distinguishing characteristics of the Middle Ages listed in the box on p. 82. Tell students to try to relate their lesson to a modern concern or event, and require that each lesson include these elements:

- An introduction
- An illustration (diagram, picture, or map)
- An oral review of the content
- A comprehension check (quiz or game)

Each student in the group can take responsibility for one of these requirements. Students will need to use material from the text and perhaps consult outside sources in preparing their lessons.   ☞

A. Expansion

"The Knight's Tale," is derived from Boccaccio's epic poem *Teseida*. Boccaccio's work, twelve cantos written in ottava rima, tells the story of two friends who both fall in love with a woman named Emilia. One finally wins his love in a tournament, but he dies immediately after.

B. Critical Reading: Making Inferences

? To whom is Bishop referring in this quotation? [Movie cowboys.]

A The idea that revering and acting in the name of a lady would make a knight braver and better was central to one aspect of chivalry, courtly love. Courtly love was, in its ideal form, nonsexual. A knight might wear his lady's colors in battle, he might glorify her in words and be inspired by her, but the lady always remained pure and out of reach. She was "set above" her admirer, just as the feudal lord was set above his vassal. Since such a concept flew in the face of human nature, it provided built-in drama for poets and storytellers, as the King Arthur sagas illustrate. When Sir Lancelot and Queen Guinevere, for example, cross the line between courtly and physical love, the whole social system represented by Arthur's Round Table collapses. Camelot crumbles.

Chivalry brought about an idealized attitude toward women, but it did little to improve their actual position. A woman's perceived value remained tied to the value of the lands she brought to a marriage. But chivalry did give rise to a new form of literature, the romance (page 174). The greatest English example of the genre is *Sir Gawain and the Green Knight*. Wandering minstrels told many other romances, but most of them were the equivalents of *dum-de-dum* doggerel verse today.

> *Chivalry led to an idealized attitude toward women and gave rise to a new form of literature, the romance.*

The New City Classes: Out from Under the Overlords

For the most part, medieval society centered around the feudal castle, but as the population grew, an increasing number of people lived in towns and cities. Eventually, those population centers would render the feudal system obsolete.

The development of the city classes—lower, middle, and upper-middle—is evident in the works of Geoffrey Chaucer (page 99). Many of his characters make

---

B We may still see on illumined screens the knight, with a change of clothing and locale. He has gone Western, but still he is the dextrous cavalier, vaulting to his saddle, the mighty fighter for virtue, ill educated but possessed of a salty wisdom, worshipful, faithful, and tongue-tied in the presence of good women.

—Morris Bishop

The Middle Ages: Four Centuries of Change

These characteristics distinguished the Middle Ages:

- The Norman Conquest of England created a powerful Anglo-Norman entity and brought England into the mainstream of European civilization.
- The feudal system centralized military, political, and economic power in the Crown.
- The Catholic Church transcended national boundaries and fostered cultural unity among Europeans.
- The rise of towns and cities freed people to pursue their own commercial and artistic interests.
- The Magna Carta weakened the political power of the Church and laid the groundwork for later English constitutional law.
- Exposure to Eastern civilization as a result of the Crusades broadened Europeans' intellectual horizons.
- The ideals of chivalry improved attitudes toward, but not the rights of, women.
- The rise of the yeoman class paved the way for democracy in England.
- The bubonic plague created a labor shortage that contributed to the end of feudalism and to the passing of the Middle Ages.

OPTIONS FOR TEACHING

CLASSROOM MANAGEMENT

Noise Reduction To prevent excessive noise during the scene-sketch game on p. T76, have groups decide on their answer by quietly conferring. Then, they can write the answer on a slip of paper to give to you.

Cross-Curricular Strategy Ask a colleague in the history department to assist in the creation and evaluation of any of the student projects to help students appreciate the connections between these courses of study.

Managing the Reader's Response Classroom Call attention to comments in the Reader's Log which express an opinion or judgement. Assure students that they are free to verbalize their opinions, but that they should listen willingly to others and return to the text to support their judgements.

their livings outside the feudal system, and their horizons are defined not by any lord's manor but by such cities as London and Canterbury.

More important, the emerging merchant class had its own tastes in the arts and the ability to pay for what it wanted. Consequently, much medieval art is not aristocratic; it is middle class, even "people's art." The people of the cities were free, tied neither to the land nor to knighthood and chivalry. Their point of view was expressed in the ballads sung in alehouses and at firesides (page 91), in the mystery and miracle plays performed outdoors by the new guilds or craft unions, and even in the great cathedrals and municipal buildings that are synonymous with England to so many tourists today.

The new city dwellers' point of view was expressed in ballads, in mystery and miracle plays, and in cathedrals and municipal buildings.

The Great Happenings

Against the backdrop of the feudal system imported from the Continent, several specific events radically influenced the course of English history, as well as English literature.

The Crusades: Ho! for the Holy Land. In Chaucer's *Canterbury Tales*, we meet a knight who has fought in "heathen" places—along the Mediterranean Sea and in North Africa. The knight's adventures in the fourteenth

Scene from *Passages d' Outremer* (detail) (15th century), depicting the Crusaders' attack, in 1153, on Ascalon, a Muslim-held city on the coast of the Holy Land. MS Fr. 5594, fol. 157v.

© cliché Bibliothèque Nationale de France, Paris.

PROBLEM SOLVING/CRITICAL THINKING

A New Suit of Armor Although the suit of armor was necessary for self-protection in battle, its disadvantages were numerous. Ask students to brainstorm a list of modern protective gear, such as helmets, in-line skate pads, shoulder pads, or catcher's masks. Invite students to think of the materials used to make these products and to design a modern suit of armor based upon this technology. Have them present their plans to the class. ☞

A. Exploring the Culture

Baghdad and Damascus had well-established public libraries until the thirteenth century, when they were destroyed. In about 1340, Cairo was a wealthy city of almost half a million people and an important link in the spice trade; London, in contrast, had only fifty thousand inhabitants in the fifteenth century. Arab universities also were established before their European counterparts. Cairo's Al-Azhar University, founded about 970, is one of the oldest operating universities in the world. Oxford, the oldest university in Great Britain, was established in the twelfth century.

B. Exploring the Historical Period

Under Henry II, a system of common law was developed that formed the basis for British common law today. Common law applies to all the people of a country rather than applying only to certain classes of people. The conflict between Henry and Becket developed when Henry attempted to bring the Church under this system. Before this time, Church courts dispensed mild forms of justice for both clergy and for learned men who claimed "benefit of clergy."

century were really an extension of the Crusades (1095–1270), a series of wars waged by European Christians against the Muslims, with Jerusalem and the Holy Land as the prize. Although the Europeans ultimately failed to hold Jerusalem, they benefited enormously from contact with the higher civilization of the Middle East. This contact with Eastern mathematics, astronomy, architecture, and crafts made possible the rich, varied life we find in Chaucer. If the Crusades produced Chaucer's fairly conventional Knight, they were also at least indirectly responsible for his lively Squire and elegant Prioress.

The Crusades exposed Christian Europe to the Middle East's sophisticated civilization.

The martyrdom of Thomas à Becket: Murder in the cathedral. When Chaucer's pilgrims set out for Canterbury, their goal was the shrine of Saint Thomas à Becket (c. 1118–1170). Thomas, a Norman, had risen to great power as chancellor (prime minister) under his friend King Henry II (reigned 1154–1189). At that time, all Christians belonged to the Catholic Church. Even King Henry was a vassal—of the pope, the head of the Church and God's representative. The pope in those days was enormously powerful and controlled most of the crowned heads of Europe. By appointing his trusted friend Thomas as archbishop of Canterbury (head of the Catholic Church in England), Henry hoped to gain the upper hand in disputes with the Church. But the independent and often combative Thomas took the pope's side more than once, infuriating the king. In December 1170, Henry raged, "Will no one rid me of

Martyrdom of Thomas Becket, from an English psalter (detail) (13th century). MS W34, fol. 15v.
The Walters Art Gallery, Baltimore.

84 THE MIDDLE AGES

Cultural Diversity Intellectually, the Middle East led the Middle Ages. The physician Rhazes wrote *Treatise on Smallpox and Measles,* the first accurate study of those infectious diseases. *The Canon of Medicine,* a medical encyclopedia by the physician Avicenna, accurately described many diseases and influenced European medical education for more than 600 years. In the ninth century, the Baghdad teacher al-Khwarizimi wrote an influential mathematics book that was used as a textbook; the word *algebra* is derived from the Arabic title of his work. Arab astronomers also contributed to knowledge of mathematics as they adapted it to their own field; their contributions added to knowledge of trigonometry.

Then the third knight inflicted a terrible wound as he lay, by which the sword was broken against the pavement, and the crown which was large was separated from the head; so that the blood white with the brain and the brain red with blood, dyed the surface of the virgin mother Church with the life and death of the confessor and martyr in the colors of the lily and the rose.

—Thomas Grim, an eyewitness to Becket's death

this turbulent priest?" Taking his words literally, four of Henry's knights murdered Becket—right in his own cathedral. Public outrage at this rash deed led to devotion to St. Thomas the Martyr, and created a backlash against Henry, a significant setback for the monarchy in its power struggles with Rome.

At its worst, this setback led to the kinds of liberties taken by several of the clergymen in *The Canterbury Tales*—corruption that the state was in no position to correct. Thus, Chaucer's Monk lives a life of luxury without regard to the poor, his Friar chases women and money, and his Summoner and his Pardoner blackmail people with threats of eternal damnation.

Yet the medieval Church did have one positive effect: It fostered cultural unity—a system of belief and symbol that transcended the national cultures of Europe. The Church continued to be the center of learning. Its monasteries were the libraries and publishers of the time, and its language, Latin, remained the international language of educated Europeans. Its leader, the pope, was king of all kings—and his "kingdom" had no boundaries.

Public outrage at the political assassination of Thomas à Becket strengthened the power of the Catholic Church. The state became powerless to correct widespread clerical corruption.

The Magna Carta: Power to (some of) the people. The event that most clearly heralded a return to older, democratic tendencies in England was the signing of the Magna Carta (the "Great Charter") by King John in 1215, at Runnymede. The vicious but pragmatic John was strongly backed by the pope, but the English barons forced him to sign the document. The signing was a defeat for central papal power. As aristocrats writing for aristocrats, the barons had no interest in the rights of the common people. But the Magna Carta later became the basis for English constitutional law, in which such rights as trial by jury and legislative taxation were established.

No freeman shall be taken, or imprisoned, or outlawed, or exiled, or in any way harmed, nor will we go upon him nor will we send upon him, except by the legal judgment of his peers or by the law of the land.

To none will we sell, to none deny or delay, right or justice.

—Magna Carta, Clauses 39 and 40

In 1215, English barons forced King John to sign the Magna Carta as an effort to curb the Church's power. The document later became the basis for English constitutional law.

C. Expansion

T. S. Eliot's poetic drama *Murder in the Cathedral* (1935) is a play about the martyrdom of Becket.

D. Critical Reading: Finding Cause and Effect

❓ How did the murder of Thomas à Becket lead to corruption within the Church? [Public outrage caused a backlash against the king; therefore, when there were abuses within the Church, the king, who had lost power in this arena, could not use his influence to correct them.]

Technology Tip

To find supplementary materials, scan the Middle English Collection at the University of Virginia's Electronic Text Center at **http://etext.lib.virginia.edu /mideng.browse.html**. You also may wish to explore the Old English Pages at Georgetown University at **http: //www.georgetown.edu/cball/oe /old_english.html**. *You may want to preview any Internet activity that you suggest to students. Because these resources are sometimes public forums, their content can be unpredictable.*

A. Exploring the Historical Period

Perhaps the best-known figure to come out of the Hundred Years' War is the illiterate French peasant girl known in English as Joan of Arc (1412–1431). Joan persuaded the King of France to allow her to lead the French armies to fight the English. For almost two years she was incredibly successful, until she was captured in Burgundy and sold to the English. Found guilty by an ecclesiastical court for crimes ranging from witchcraft to wearing men's clothes, Joan was burned to death by the English army.

B. Expansion

Shakespeare's play *Henry V* depicts the battle of English yeomen with their longbows against the French armies at Agincourt.

FLEAS, MONEY, AND GUNPOWDER: THE END OF AN ERA

The legendary pageantry, the codes of chivalry, the heroic quests undertaken by valiant knights in honor of fair ladies—these images come to mind at the mention of the Middle Ages. But what happened? Why did this period come to an end? Besides the plague's devastating effects, the development of a monetary system and the introduction of gunpowder contributed to changes in medieval England.

Before the eleventh century, few coins existed in England and western Europe. The English upper classes used gold and silver valued by weight, and foreign coins were usually melted down and transformed into ingots. Feudal lords made their own coins for use only on their property, and serfs used a barter system for purchases within the community. But the Crusades brought an economic change, for crusaders needed money that would be accepted in other lands. Silver was heavy, but gold coins were light and already in use throughout trade routes. The use of gold coins improved the peasants' buying and selling power; instead of the barter system, they were now able to earn gold in exchange for their labor or goods. The minting of coins was essential in the revival of England's economy.

Chivalric codes governed hand-to-hand combat during much of the Middle Ages. But the use of guns and gunpowder (and strategic military planning) changed all that. Discovered by the Chinese, gunpowder was introduced into English warfare around 1325. By 1346, warfare in the western world had changed irreversibly. In

The Hundred Years' War (1337–1453): The arrow is mightier than the armor. What might be called the first national war was waged by England against France. Fought on the Continent, the Hundred Years' War was based on dubious claims to the throne of France by two English kings—Edward III (reigned 1327–1377) and Henry V (reigned 1413–1422).

This protracted war was militarily unsuccessful for the English. But it was an important factor in the gradual development of a British national consciousness. After the war, the English were no longer best represented by the knight in shining armor, an import from the Continent anyway. Instead, they were more accurately represented by the green-clad yeoman (small landowner) with his longbow. These English yeomen had formed the nucleus of the English armies in France. Their yard-long arrows could fly over castle walls and pierce the armor of knights. These small landowners now became a dominant force in the new society that grew out of the ruins of feudalism. The old ideals of chivalry lived on only in stories, such as the King Arthur tales retold by Sir Thomas Malory.

The English lost the Hundred Years' War with France, but in the process they began to think of themselves as British rather than Anglo-Norman. With the advent of the yeoman class, modern, democratic England was born.

Check Test: True-False

1. The Norman Conquest of 1066 radically altered the development of English history, character, and language. [True]
2. Feudalism was a caste system, a property system, a military system, and a system of social behavior. [True]
3. In the feudal system, a woman was considered equal to a man. [False]
4. The Magna Carta, signed in 1215, placed restrictions on democratic tendencies. [False]
5. One long-term result of the Black Death was freedom of the serfs, who were the last support of feudalism. [True]

Observation Assessment Assess whether students have developed a feel for the time period by asking them to use a blank piece of paper to represent their vision of the Middle Ages. They might draw, write words, make symbols, or fold the paper in some way. Probably the best representations will combine several of these techniques.

Assess whether the representations reflect an accurate understanding of the time period with a scale of one to five, five being the highest score.

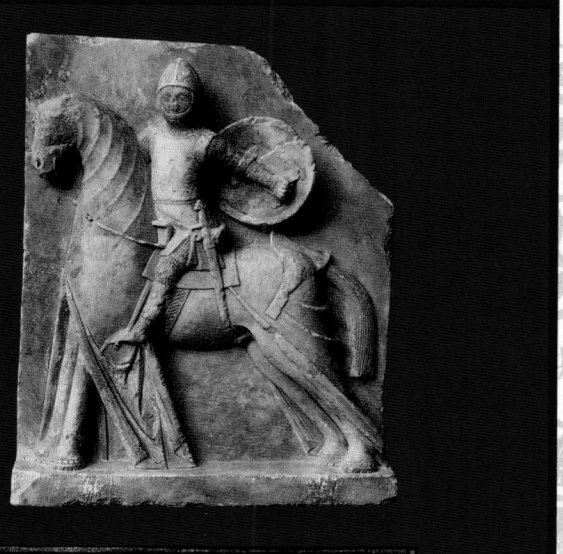

Marble relief (13th century) of mounted knight arrayed in casque and shirt of mail, carrying shield, from the monastery of Poblet, Province of Tarragona, Spain.

The Metropolitan Museum of Art, New York. Dodge Fund. 1913 (13.21).

the landmark battle of Crécy, the French outnumbered the English. The English, aided by the longbow and by explosives, massacred their opponents. Over the next two hundred years, the cannon made the castle—previously impregnable—open to attack.

The rules of war and class had changed. Chivalry was at an end, and feudal obligation became a thing of the past. As a result, a free and prosperous middle class developed, revolutionizing the country's social and economic systems.

Battle of Crécy, from Chroniques de Froissart (detail) (14th century). English longbowmen are depicted overcoming French crossbowmen.

© cliché Bibliothèque Nationale de France, Paris.

RESPONDING TO THE ART: EXPLORING THE SUBJECT

The Battle of Crécy was fought in 1346, the first decade of the Hundred Years' War. In this conflict, the invading forces of Edward III of England withstood sixteen charges from the calvary of Philip VI. The French charge was led by Italian mercenaries, Genoese crossbow men paid to fight in Philip's service. Meeting this attack were English archers who fought with six-foot longbows. Crécy proved the superiority of the longbow, and more than 1,500 French knights and noblemen were killed in the battle. The discipline of English troops—who were paid a regular, fixed wage—played an important role in Edward's victory.

A. Expansion

The United States has had several encounters with the bubonic plague brought into port cities by ships. New York City, San Francisco, New Orleans, and Seattle have been affected, but the quarantines and sanitation measures of the United States Public Health Service have always succeeded in curbing the plague's spread.

B. Reader's Response: Connecting with the Text

A *plague* is defined as "a deadly, infectious epidemic disease." Ask students to discuss modern diseases that could be defined as plagues. [Sample responses: AIDS or the Ebola virus.]

Quickwrite

Point out to students that the loyalty upon which feudalism was based was *required* loyalty; it was not voluntary. Have students consider whether volunteering one's loyalty makes the quality more noble.

Coffin-Making and Burial During the Black Death, from Annales *(14th century) by Giles de Mussis (10¾″ × 8″).*
© Bibliothèque Royale Albert premier, Brussels.

The character of the pestilence was appalling. The disease itself, with its frightful symptoms, the swift onset, the blotches, the hardening of the glands under the armpit or in the groin, these swellings which no poultice could resolve, these tumors which, when lanced, gave no relief, the horde of virulent carbuncles which followed the dread harbingers of death, the delirium, the insanity which attended its triumph, the blank spaces which opened on all sides in human society, stunned and for a time destroyed the life and faith of the world.

—Winston Churchill

The Black Death. The Black Death, or bubonic plague, which struck England in 1348-1349, delivered another blow to feudalism. Highly contagious and spread by fleas from infected rats, the disease reduced the nation's population by a third—causing a labor shortage and inevitably giving the lower classes more leverage than ever before against their overlords. One long-term result was the serfs' freedom, which knocked out feudalism's last support. By the time King Henry VII's 1485 marriage reconciled the warring Houses of York and Lancaster, the Middle Ages were ending in England. Henry, a strong king, began the Tudor line that would lead to Elizabeth I. England's Renaissance was about to begin.

The Black Death caused a labor shortage, leading to the serfs' freedom and to the end of feudalism.

Quickwrite

Loyalty lay at the heart of the feudal system. The landowners extracted loyalty from their serfs, the lords expected loyalty from their knights, and the king demanded loyalty from everyone. Has loyalty remained as important in today's society? To whom, or to what, are you loyal, and why? Your answer might include institutions, like school or church, but does it also include ideas? Whom do you expect to be loyal to you, and in what ways? Jot down your thoughts on the issue to discuss with others in the class.

(Opposite) A master with his pupils, from the *Chronicles of Hainault* (15th century).

88 THE MIDDLE AGES

Collection 2 — THE ONE STORY WORTH TELLING

> ### Theme: A Lesson in a Tale
>
> Each selection teaches a different kind of lesson or provides another view of the variety of human experience. A key feature of each tale is the skillful use of literary elements.

Thematic Focus

All of life, but especially love, is represented in these tales.

- **Lord Randall/Edward, Edward/Get Up and Bar the Door**   Drama and humor are features of these ballads.
- *from* **The Canterbury Tales: The Prologue**   Portraits of the pilgrims represent a cross section of medieval life.
- *from* **The Canterbury Tales: The Pardoner's Tale**   Irony and satire characterize this tale about the love of money.
- *from* **The Canterbury Tales: The Wife of Bath's Tale**   A knight learns what women most desire.
- **World Literature:** *from* the **Decameron: Federigo's Falcon**   After many lessons in hardship, the lover is rewarded by his lady's hand.
- *from* **Sir Gawain and the Green Knight**   Sir Gawain, the model of chivalry, keeps his promise to the Green Knight.

Literary Focus

Literary Element	Selection / Feature
Refrain Characteristics of the Ballad Form	**Lord Randall/ Edward, Edward/ Get Up and Bar the Door**
Characterization Imagery	**The Canterbury Tales: The Prologue**
Couplets	**The Canterbury Tales: The Wife of Bath's Tale**
The Romance	**Sir Gawain and the Green Knight**

Writing Focus

The following flow chart shows how the writing assignment for each selection relates to the writing assignment presented in the Writer's Workshop at the end of the unit.

Selection	Work-in-Progress Assignment
Lord Randall/Edward, Edward/ Get Up and Bar the Door	Freewrite vivid impressions about an individual p. 98
The Canterbury Tales: The Prologue	Collect details for a description of an individual p. 130
The Canterbury Tales: The Pardoner's Tale	Describe individual's physical characteristics p. 139
The Canterbury Tales: The Wife of Bath's Tale	Describe individual using figurative language p. 152
Sir Gawain and the Green Knight	Write a dialogue p. 175
Writer's Workshop	Write an observational essay pp. 185–187

Collection Planner

SELECTION/FEATURE	Literary Elements / Active Reading	Writing	Speaking and Listening	Language and Vocabulary
Ballads: Lord Randall/ Edward, Edward/Get Up and Bar the Door Anonymous (pp. 90–98) **Connections: Frankie and Johnny** Boyd Bunch (p. 96)	• Reader's Log p. 90 • Refrain p. 90 • Characteristics of the Ballad Form p. 97	• Critical Writing: Compare and contrast ballads p. 98 • Creative Writing: Write folk ballad p. 98 • Creative Writing: Retell ballad p. 98 • Research/Critical Writing: Write comparison p. 98	• Creative Writing: Perform TV or radio newscast p. 98 • Music: Sing or play recordings of ballads p. 98	
from **The Canterbury Tales: The Prologue** Geoffrey Chaucer trans. by Nevill Coghill (pp. 99–130) **Connections:** from **The Autobiography of Malcolm X** Malcolm X and Alex Haley (p. 128)	• Reader's Log p. 105 • Characterization p. 105 • Imagery pp. 129–130	• Critical Writing: Write comparison-contrast essay p. 130		
from **The Canterbury Tales: The Pardoner's Tale** (pp. 131–139)			• Drama/Pantomime: Perform Pardoner's Tale p. 139	
from **The Canterbury Tales: The Wife of Bath's Tale** (pp. 140–153) Student to Student (p. 150)	• Couplets p. 151	• Critical Writing: Write character analysis p. 152 • Creative Writing: Write prologue p. 152	• Creative Writing: Perform prologue p. 152 • Dramatization: Present reading p. 152	• How to Own a Word: Word Parts p. 153 • Try It Out: Examine word roots and structure p. 153
from the **Decameron** Giovanni Boccaccio trans. by Mark Musa and Peter Bondanella (pp. 154–159)	• Reader's Log p. 155		• Finding Common Ground: Discuss romantic problems p. 159	
from **Sir Gawain and the Green Knight** trans. by John Gardner (pp. 160–175) **Connections: Holding Out for a Hero** Dean Pitchford and Jim Steinman (p. 173) **Spotlight On: The Weaving of Women's Tales** (pp. 176–179)	• Reader's Log p. 160 • The Romance pp. 160, 174–175	• Critical Writing: Write about modernizing old setting p. 175 • Creative Writing: Write diary entry for wife p. 175	• Critical Thinking/ Speaking: Discuss women's roles p. 175	
The English Language: Middle English John Algeo (pp. 181–184)				• Try It Out: Determine word origins p. 184
Writer's Workshop: Writing an Observational Essay (pp. 185–187)		• Writing Process: Observational essay pp. 185–187		
Language Workshop: Number Agreement (p. 188)		• Revise essay p. 188		• Try It Out: Make sentences agree p. 188
Learning for Life: Emerging Technology (p. 189)		• Write job description p. 189	• Give informal talk p. 189	

Collection Resources

Teaching Resources A
Cross-Curricular Activity p. 54

Audiovisual Resources Binder
Fine Art Transparency 2.1

Test Booklet
Collection 2 Test pp. 29–31

 Computer disk or CD-ROM
 Videodisc
Audiocassette
 Overhead Transparency

PROGRAM RESOURCES

Electronic Media	Teaching Resources with Organizer		Audiovisual Resources Binder
	Teaching Resources A	Other Resources	
• Test Generator • Language Workshop: Subject-Verb Agreement	• Teaching Notes pp. 22–23 • Reading Organizers pp. 31–33 • Language Link pp. 34–35	• Test Booklet: Selection Test pp. 17–18 • Language and Writing Skills Worksheets pp. 25–26 • Portfolio Management System pp. 39, 62–63, 75–76	• Elements of Literature Transparency 2.2 • Selected Reading Audiocassette 1, Side A
• Test Generator • Language Workshop: Subject-Verb Agreement	• Teaching Notes pp. 23–24 • Reading Organizer p. 36 • Language Link pp. 37–38 • Words to Own p. 39	• Test Booklet: Selection Test pp. 19–20 • Language and Writing Skills Worksheets pp. 27–30 • Portfolio Management System pp. 54–55, 77	• Elements of Literature Transparencies 2.3–2.4 • Selected Reading Audiocassette 1, Side A
• Test Generator • Language Workshop: Pronoun-Antecedent Agreement	• Teaching Notes pp. 24–25 • Reading Organizer p. 40 • Language Link pp. 41–42 • Words to Own p. 43	• Test Booklet: Selection Test p. 21–22 • Language and Writing Skills Worksheets pp. 31-32	
• Test Generator	• Teaching Notes pp. 25–26 • Reading Organizer p. 44 • Words to Own p. 45 • Language Link pp. 46–47	• Test Booklet: Selection Test pp. 23–24 • Language and Writing Skills Worksheets pp. 180–181	• Elements of Literature Transparency 2.5 • How to Own a Word Transparency 2.7
	• Teaching Notes p. 27		
• Test Generator • Language Workshop: Pronoun-Antecedent Agreement	• Teaching Notes pp. 27–28 • Reading Organizer p. 48 • Language Link pp. 49–50 • Words to Own p. 51	• Test Booklet: Selection Test pp. 25–26 • Language and Writing Skills Worksheets pp. 31- 32 • Portfolio Management System pp. 48–49, 81–82	• Elements of Literature Transparency 2.6
• Test Generator • Videodisc, Side A: "English, Part 1"	• Teaching Notes p. 28	• Test Booklet: The English Language Test pp. 27–28	
• Writer's Workshop: Observational Writing		• Portfolio Management System pp. 83–85	• Revision Transparencies 2.8–2.9
• Language Workshop: Agreement	• Language Workshop pp. 52–53		
		• Portfolio Management System p. 86	

Proofreading Warm-ups

You may use the following exercises to help students practice their proofreading skills. Copy a set of incorrect sentences onto the chalkboard, and have students find and correct the spelling, punctuation, usage, and mechanical errors in each sentence. Ask students to share and discuss their responses.

	Sentences with Errors	Sentences Corrected	Skills Covered
1	**a.** feudalism a social system replaced the social structure described in beowulf **b.** a women in medieval society was always subservient to a man; weather husband, father, or brother	**a.** Feudalism, a social system, replaced the social structure described in <u>Beowulf</u>. **b.** A woman in medieval society was always subservient to a man, whether husband, father, or brother.	Capitalization, Comma usage, Titles, Spelling, Semicolon usage, Homonyms, End marks
2	**a.** ballads sung in the Applachian mountains were discovered by researchers to be markedly simular to alot of the British ballads **b.** for example the Ballad John Randolph is very much like Lord Randall	**a.** Ballads sung in the Appalachian Mountains were discovered by researchers to be markedly similar to a lot of the British ballads. **b.** For example, the ballad "John Randolph" is very much like "Lord Randall."	Capitalization, Spelling, Nonstandard usage, Comma usage, Quotation marks, End marks
3	**a.** Geoffrey Chaucer often called the founder of english poetry wrote The Canterbury Tales **b.** he was born not to long after the start of the 100 Year's war	**a.** Geoffrey Chaucer, often called the founder of English poetry, wrote <u>The Canterbury Tales</u>. **b.** He was born not too long after the start of the Hundred Years' War.	Comma usage, Capitalization, Titles, Homonyms, Write out numerals, Apostrophe usage, End marks
4	**a.** the greatness of The Canterbury Tales lays partly in Chaucers language **b.** however the sheer strength of Chaucers spirit and personality are also a contributing force	**a.** The greatness of <u>The Canterbury Tales</u> lies partly in Chaucer's language. **b.** However, the sheer strength of Chaucer's spirit and personality is also a contributing factor.	Capitalization, Titles, Verb errors, Apostrophe usage, Comma usage, Subject-verb agreement, End marks
5	**a.** the pilgrim narrater of the General Prologue, meets twenty nine other Pilgrims also bound for Canterbury **b.** "Whan that Aprill with his shoures soote" is a example of middle English Ms Harden said	**a.** The pilgrim narrator of the General Prologue meets twenty-nine other pilgrims also bound for Canterbury. **b.** "'Whan that Aprill with his shoures soote' is an example of Middle English," Ms. Harden said.	Capitalization, Spelling, Comma usage, Hyphen usage, Quotation marks, Non-standard usage, Abbreviations, End marks
6	**a.** do you think that people with the Pardoners ethics and tricks still exist today queried Cheryl **b.** of coarse they do Ive met some personally retorted Alex	**a.** "Do you think that people with the Pardoner's ethics and tricks still exist today?" queried Cheryl. **b.** "Of course they do; I've met some personally," retorted Alex.	Quotation marks, Capitalization, Apostrophe usage, Question mark usage, Homonyms, Semicolon usage, Comma usage, End marks
7	**a.** haveing out-lived 5 husbands the Wife of Bath has strong opinions about men and marriage **b.** alot of her opinions seams quiet bold for the middel ages	**a.** Having outlived five husbands, the Wife of Bath has strong opinions about men and marriage. **b.** Many of her opinions seem quite bold for the Middle Ages.	Capitalization, Spelling, Hyphen usage, Write out numerals, Comma usage, Nonstandard usage, Verb error, End marks
8	**a.** like the Canterbury tales Boccaccios Decameron uses a framing device **b.** in fact Chaucer may of been influenced by Boccaccio's writting during one of his trip's to Italy	**a.** Like <u>The Canterbury Tales</u>, Boccaccio's <u>Decameron</u> uses a framing device. **b.** In fact, Chaucer may have been influenced by Boccaccio's writing during one of his trips to Italy.	Capitalization, Titles, Comma usage, Apostrophe usage, Nonstandard usage, Spelling, End marks
9	**a.** in twelfth century France their was a actual court of love that judged questions of behavior and issues of love **b.** The Art of Courtly Love a document set down the rules' of love	**a.** In twelfth-century France, there was an actual court of love that judged questions of behavior and issues of love. **b.** <u>The Art of Courtly Love</u>, a document, set down the rules of love.	Capitalization, Hyphen usage, Comma usage, Homonyms, Nonstandard usage, Titles, Apostrophe usage, Spelling, End marks
10	**a.** the arthur of Sir Gawain and the Green Knight wrote in an old fashioned style **b.** as the story opens the knights of the round table is feasting	**a.** The author of <u>Sir Gawain and the Green Knight</u> wrote in an old-fashioned style. **b.** As the story opens, the knights of the Round Table are feasting.	Capitalization, Spelling, Titles, Hyphen usage, Comma usage, Subject-verb agreement, End marks

THE ONE STORY WORTH TELLING

Ballads

Chaucer

Boccaccio

from Sir Gawain and the Green Knight

The stories people tell have a way of taking care of them. If stories come to you, care for them. And learn to give them away where they are needed. Sometimes a person needs a story more than food to stay alive. That is why we put these stories in each other's memory. This is how people care for themselves. One day you will be good storytellers. Never forget these obligations.

—Barry Lopez, *from Crow and Weasel*

PROGRAM MANAGER

- **Integrated Assessment** For a summative assessment of the literature and language skills taught in this collection, see **Collection 2 Test,** *Test Booklet,* pp. 29–31.
- **Instructional Support** See **Fine Art Transparency** 2.1. Review teacher's notes for transparencies in the *Audiovisual*

Resources Binder for suggestions on how to tie the transparencies to specific reading selections.
- **Extending Collection Theme** See **Cross-Curricular Activity: The One Story Worth Telling,** *Teaching Resources A,* p. 54, for activities in other disciplines and for evaluation criteria.

PORTFOLIO ASSESSMENT

Parent/Guardian Involvement For forms that will help a parent or guardian review and respond to a student's portfolio, see *Portfolio Management System,* pp. 62–63.

QUICK PLANNING GUIDE

Into the Selections

Before You Read p. 90

- **Reading Focus:** Students learn that ballads explore sensational topics.
- **Quickwrite: Prior Knowledge** Write in Reader's Log on popular music characteristics
- **Elements of Literature: The Refrain**
- **Background:** Ballads, the oral tradition

Through the Selections

"Lord Randall" p. 91

"Edward, Edward" p. 92

Literature and Pop Music p. 93

"Get Up and Bar the Door" pp. 94–95

Connections: A Song p. 96 "Frankie and Johnny"

Making Meanings p. 97

Elements of Literature p. 97

Beyond the Selections

Choices: Building Your Portfolio p. 98

- **Writer's Notebook:** Prewrite for observational essay
- **Critical Writing:** Compare and contrast ballads
- **Creative Writing:** Create original ballad
- **Creative Writing:** Write news story
- **Research/Critical Writing:** Analyze ballad variants
- **Music:** Perform ballads from different cultures

BEFORE YOU READ

BALLADS

Reading Focus

The Sensational

THREE DEAD SONS VISIT MOTHER FOR DINNER . . . SLIGHTED WOMAN SPURNS LOVER'S DEATHBED REQUEST . . . MAIDEN HEADED FOR GALLOWS; FAMILY REFUSES HELP. These aren't the latest tabloid headlines or current soap opera summaries; they're the plots of medieval ballads. In the Middle Ages, just as today, certain forms of popular entertainment tended toward the sensational.

Since ballads were the poetry of the people, just as popular music is today, their subjects were predictably popular—domestic tragedy, false love, true love, the absurdity of husband-wife relationships, and the supernatural. Unlike today's music, the ballads were not copyrighted by a singer, but were passed down orally from singer to singer. Using a strong beat and repetition, the ballads were a gift of story passed from performer to performer, from generation to generation.

Quickwrite

Suppose a historian from the future were to analyze today's popular songs. How would the historian describe the music you and your friends enjoy? What subjects dominate the songs? (Are popular songs sensational the way the ballads are?) What inferences would the historian draw about us and our culture from the analysis of the songs and the stories they tell? Record your thoughts on these pop music questions in a brief entry in your Reader's Log.

Elements of Literature

The Refrain

In concerts today a singer may invite the audience to "join in on the chorus." It's probable that a single singer sang the narrative portions of a ballad while the audience joined in on the **refrain.** The use of the refrain contributed to the song's rhythm and often reinforced its theme, but there was another practical reason for the refrain: It allowed the singer, who sang from memory and often improvised, time to think of the next verse.

A **refrain** is a repeated word, phrase, line, or group of lines.

For more on Refrain, see the Handbook of Literary Terms.

Background

The word *ballad* is originally derived from an Old French word meaning "dancing song." Although the English ballads' connection with dance has been lost, it is clear from their meter and their structure that the original ballads were composed to be sung to music.

The ballads as we know them today probably took their form in the fifteenth century, but they were not printed until three hundred years later when Sir Thomas Percy, Sir Walter Scott, and others traveled around the British Isles and collected them from the people who still sang them.

Illumination from a French manuscript of *Romance of the Rose* (detail) (15th century).

British Library, London.

PORTFOLIO ASSESSMENT

Portfolio Assessment For help with self-assessment of reading skills, see the *Portfolio Management System,* p. 39.

This ballad is sung in different versions in several countries. The basic story of the song varies little, but Randall is variously known as Donald, Randolph, Ramsay, Ransome, and Durango. Sometimes his last meal consists of fish, sometimes snakes. The dialect of this version is Scottish. The ballad is sung entirely as a conversation. Try reading it aloud as a team, so that you have a male and a female voice.

Into the Selections

Using BEFORE YOU READ p. 90

Reading Focus
Draw a cluster centered around "Ballads" with a branch to one side labeled "Subjects." Ask students to identify the subjects of ballads as stated in the text [false love, the supernatural, and so on] as branches. Create a new branch for "Music" and repeat the procedure.

Through the Selections

Lord Randall

"O where hae ye been, Lord Randall, my son?
O where hae ye been, my handsome young man?"
"I hae been to the wild wood; mother, make my bed soon,
For I'm weary wi' hunting, and fain° wald lie down." **A**

5 "Where gat ye your dinner, Lord Randall, my son?
Where gat ye your dinner, my handsome young man?"
"I din'd wi' my true-love; mother, make my bed soon,
For I'm weary wi' hunting, and fain wald lie down."

"What gat ye to your dinner, Lord Randall, my son?
10 What gat ye to your dinner, my handsome young man?"
"I gat eels boil'd in broo;° mother, make my bed soon,
For I'm weary wi' hunting, and fain wald lie down."

"What became of your bloodhounds, Lord Randall, my son?
What became of your bloodhounds, my handsome young man?"
15 "O they swell'd and they died; mother, make my bed soon, **B**
For I'm weary wi' hunting, and fain wald lie down."

"O I fear ye are poison'd, Lord Randall, my son!
O I fear ye are poison'd, my handsome young man!"
"O yes! I am poison'd; mother, make my bed soon,
20 For I'm sick at the heart, and I fain wald lie down." **C**

4. **fain:** gladly.
11. **broo:** broth.

A knight and his lady feeding a falcon, from a German manuscript (detail) (c. 14th century). Cod. Pal. Germ., 848, Codex Manesse, fol. 249v. Universitätsbibliothek, Heidelberg.

A. Literary Element: Ballad
This question-and-answer format is frequently used in ballads. Ask students how this affects their reading. [The question may make students curious to know the answer.] Do you know any songs that are in a question-and-answer format? [Bob Dylan's "A Hard Rain's A-Gonna Fall."]

B. Critical Reading: Speculating
? What is the connection between the death of the dogs and Lord Randall? [He may be dying of whatever killed the dogs.]

C. Literary Element: Refrain
? What is the effect of this repeated element? [It emphasizes that the cause of Lord Randall's weariness is gradually revealed; it provides the poem with a steady rhyme and rhythm.]

PROGRAM MANAGER

- **Planning Instruction** See *Teaching Notes, Teaching Resources A,* pp. 22–23, for objectives, a summary, and a list of literary elements for the selection.
- **Intstructional Support** Before beginning the instructional lesson, see **Graphic Organizers for Active Reading,** *Teaching Resources A,*

pp. 31-33 for Through the Selections activities.
- **Audiotaped Readings** To help less proficient readers or auditory learners through the lesson, use the **Selected Reading, Audiocassette 1, Side A,** in the *Audiovisual Resources Binder.*

- **Assessment** See **Selection Test,** *Test Booklet,* pp. 17–18.
- **Language Link** For instruction and practice in subject-verb agreement, see **Language Link,** *Teaching Resources A,* pp. 34–35, and *Language and Writing Skills Worksheets,* pp. 25–26.

A. Reader's Response: First Thoughts

? Why do you think Edward's sword has blood on it? [Sample responses: He has probably wounded someone in a fight; or perhaps he has killed an animal.]

B. Critical Reading: Summarizing

? Whom has Edward killed? [He has killed his hawk, his horse, and his father.]

C. Critical Reading: Finding Details

? How will Edward show that he is sorry for killing his father? [He will leave home and sail across the sea.]

"Edward, Edward" is an international ballad, one found across northern Europe and brought to England and Scotland by travelers and sailors. Sir Thomas Percy, who compiled many of the popular ballads in the 1760s, found the same character in a Swedish ballad and also noted that another version of this ballad appeared with the title "Son Davie, Son Davie." Another collector changed the hero's name to Edward.

Edward, Edward

A "Why does your brand sae drop wi' blude,°
    Edward, Edward?
Why does your brand sae drop wi' blude,
    And why sae sad gang ye,° O?"—
5 "O I hae kill'd my hawk sae gude,°
    Mither, mither;
O I hae kill'd my hawk sae gude,
    And I had nae mair° but he, O."

B "Your hawk's blude was never sae red,
10   Edward, Edward;
Your hawk's blude was never sae red,
    My dear son, I tell thee, O."—
"O I hae kill'd my red-roan steed,
    Mither, mither;
15 O I hae kill'd my red-roan steed,
    That erst° was sae fair and free, O."

"Your steed was auld,° and ye hae got mair,
    Edward, Edward;
Your steed was auld, and ye hae got mair;
20   Some other dule ye dree,° O."—
"O I hae kill'd my father dear,
    Mither, mither;
O I hae kill'd my father dear,
    Alas, and wae is me, O!"

25 "And whatten penance will ye dree° for that,
    Edward, Edward?
Whatten penance will ye dree for that?
    My dear son, now tell me, O."—
"I'll set my feet in yonder boat,
30   Mither, mither;
C I'll set my feet in yonder boat,
    And I'll fare over the sea, O."

"And what will ye do wi' your tow'rs and your ha',°
    Edward, Edward?
35 And what will ye do wi' your tow'rs and your ha',
    That were sae fair to see, O?"—

1. brand . . . blude: sword so drip with blood.

4. gang ye: go you.
5. gude: good.

8. nae mair: no more.

16. erst: before.

17. auld: old.

20. dule ye dree: grief you suffer.

25. whatten . . . dree: what punishment for sin will you suffer.

33. ha': hall; that is, ancestral home.

OPTIONS FOR TEACHING

STRATEGIES FOR INCLUSION

Kinesthetic Have two students come to the front of the class and role-play Lord Randall and his mother, Edward and his mother, or the good-man and goodwife. Encourage them to read the lines as if they are speaking to each other. Extend this activity by having the performers stop after each stanza. Call on students from the class to interview them about what the characters are thinking.

Visual Help students create a set of icons that represent the ballad characteristics. For example, use a musical note for a refrain, a torn book page for omitted details, and a tapping foot for a strong beat. Then, as students read the ballads, have them note which icons are appropriate to which lines.

Special Needs Be sure that students understand what is happening in the ballad. For example, pause periodically to ask students who Lord Randall dines with and what clues tell his mother he has been poisoned. Help students hypothesize why Lord Randall's beloved might want to poison him.

LITERATURE AND POP MUSIC

American Folk and Country and Western Music

When English, Scottish, Welsh, and Irish people left their homes to settle in America, the old ballads were part of their baggage. Some ballads have changed little since then. When researchers traveled through the southern Appalachian Mountains in the early 1900s to record the songs of the mountain people, they found them singing "John Randolph," a ballad markedly similar to "Lord Randall." On the other hand, "Streets of Laredo," which tells the story of a cowboy dying of a gunshot wound, retains the remnants of its British ancestry only in the line, "Oh beat the drum slowly and play the fife lowly." The fife and drum refer to a British military funeral. Even country and folk ballads written in this century tend to repeat the subjects and themes of the old medieval ballads. Consider:

- **ballads with supernatural elements,** such as the country and western song "Phantom 309" about ghost truck drivers;
- **ballads based on actual tragedies,** such as the country and western song "Ballad of the Green Berets" from the Vietnam War era and the folk songs "Birmingham Sunday" from the civil rights struggle of the sixties and "The Wreck of the Edmund Fitzgerald" about a twentieth-century sea tragedy;
- **ballads about domestic disasters,** such as the country and western song "The Grand Tour," about a singer who tours his home after his wife has left him.

Acoustic guitar.

D. Reader's Response: Shaping Interpretations

? Based on his responses, what sort of person do you think Edward is?
[Sample responses: He is cruel and uncaring; he is not in his right mind; he seems driven.]

LITERATURE AND POP MUSIC

Ask students to research modern ballads in the United States. Suggest that they make a poster of a ballad that they particularly like, incorporating the words from the song, illustrating it, and giving a bit of information about the area where the ballad is popular. If students wish, they may use this research toward completing Choices activity #6 on p. 98.

"I'll let them stand till they doun fa',
    Mither, mither;
I'll let them stand till they doun fa',
40   For here never mair maun° I be, O."

40. maun: must.

"And what will ye leave to your bairns° and your wife,
    Edward, Edward?
And what will ye leave to your bairns and your wife,
    When ye gang owre the sea, O?"—
45 "The warld's room: let them beg through life,
    Mither, mither;
The warld's room: let them beg through life;
    For them never mair will I see, O."

41. bairns: children.

D

"And what will ye leave to your ain° mither dear,
50   Edward, Edward?
And what will ye leave to your ain mither dear,
    My dear son, now tell me, O?"—
"The curse of hell frae me sall ye bear,
    Mither, mither;
55 The curse of hell frae me sall ye bear:
    Sic° counsels ye gave to me, O!"

49. ain: own.

56. sic: such.

BALLADS 93

INTEGRATING THE LANGUAGE ARTS

Strategic Reading Each stanza of "Edward, Edward" begins with a question or statement by the mother and ends with a response by the son. Have students work in pairs to summarize the ballad by writing, in simple, contemporary language, a statement by the mother and a response by the son for each stanza.

Listening Tell students to listen carefully as you read "Lord Randall" or any of the other ballads aloud. Ask them to visualize the details that you describe in order to remember them. After you finish reading the ballad once through, re-read it, but leave out important and vivid details. Have students list the words you leave out. (Students might work in groups of two or three to complete this activity.)

Writing: Story Have students rewrite one of the ballads as a story. Invite them to use all the details in the ballad as well as the dialogue. Students may rewrite the dialogue in contemporary language, adding details and modern allusions. You might review punctuation of dialogue before students begin the assignment. ☞

Saint Martin of Tours (316?–397) is the patron saint of France. He was known for founding churches, healing the sick, and performing miracles. A famous legend tells of his cutting his expensive cloak in half to share it with a freezing beggar. Martin later had a revelation that the beggar was Jesus Christ.

B. Critical Reading: Drawing Conclusions

? What is the agreement between the husband and wife? [They agree that the first person to speak should get up and bar the door.] What does their agreement suggest about their characters? [Possible answers: They are stubborn, shortsighted, and not very talkative.]

C. Expansion
The gentlemen reveal two characteristics of life in the Middle Ages: 1) the times were often lawless, and citizens were at the mercy of bandits and thieves; and 2) the upper classes had many more privileges than the lower class and could treat people like the goodman and goodwife however they pleased.

The story in this ballad exists in many versions in Europe, Asia, and the Middle East—perhaps illustrating the universal theme of the battling married couple. "Goodwife" and "goodman" are terms once applied to married men and women, something like "Mr." and "Mrs." today.

A The story takes place around November 11—Martinmas, or the feast of St. Martin of Tours, which was usually celebrated with a sumptuous meal. As you read, imagine a husband and wife bickering during the preparation of a large meal—perhaps a modern Thanksgiving dinner.

Get Up and Bar the Door

It fell about the Martinmas time,
    And a gay time it was then,
When our goodwife got puddings° to make,
    And she's boild them in the pan.

5 The wind sae cauld blew south and north,
    And blew into the floor;
Quoth our goodman to our goodwife,
    "Gae out and bar the door."

"My hand is in my hussyfskap,°
10   Goodman, as ye may see;
An° it should nae be barrd this hundred year,
    It's no be barrd for me."

B They made a paction tween them twa,
    They made it firm and sure,
15 That the first word whaeer should speak,
    Should rise and bar the door.

C Then by there came two gentlemen,
    At twelve o clock at night,
And they could neither see house nor hall,
20   Nor coal nor candle-light.

"Now whether is this a rich man's house,
    Or whether it is a poor?"
But neer a word ane° o them speak,
    For barring of the door.

25 And first they ate the white puddings,
    And then they ate the black;
Tho muckle° thought the goodwife to hersel,
    Yet neer a word she spake.

3. puddings: sausages, the black ones being made with blood.

9. hussyfskap (hu′zif·skep): household chores.

11. an: if.

23. ane: one.

27. muckle: much.

OPTIONS FOR TEACHING

COOPERATIVE LEARNING

Choral Reading Divide the class into groups of five or six. Assign students the parts required to read "Get Up and Bar the Door" (goodwife, goodman, first gentleman, second gentleman, narrators). Practice reading in groups. Reassemble as a class, and have one or two groups read aloud. Then, have a choral reading: all of the students who are "goodwives" read together, all the "goodmen," and so forth.

PROBLEM SOLVING/CRITICAL THINKING

Compromise Ask students to suggest compromises the characters in "Get Up and Bar the Door" could have made. Students may create and act out a dialogue in which the characters handle the situation better. For example, one could close the door one night and the other could close it the next. Ask students to apply their ideas to a situation they have encountered. *Remind students to choose a situation that they would not mind sharing with others.*

The Chef (15th century).
Woodcut.

Then said the one unto the other,
30   "Here, man, tak ye my knife;
Do ye tak aff the auld man's beard,
    And I'll kiss the goodwife."

"But there's nae water in the house,°
    And what shall we do than?"
35 "What ails ye at the pudding-broo,°
    That boils into the pan?"

O up then started our goodman,
    An angry man was he:
"Will ye kiss my wife before my een,
40   And scad° me wi pudding-bree?"°

Then up and started our goodwife,
    Gied three skips on the floor:
"Goodman, you've spoken the foremost word, ⓓ
    Get up and bar the door."

33. but . . . house: He probably
wants water to soften the husband's
beard.
35. what . . . pudding-broo:
What's wrong with using the
pudding broth?

40. scad: scald. **bree:** broth.

RESPONDING TO THE ART: ABOUT THE ARTWORK

A woodcut is a picture made by pressing on paper an inked block of wood that has been gouged where the white parts of the picture are to be and leaving the parts that are to be black flush with the surface of the block. The woodcut was a popular art form in the Middle Ages because it was inexpensive, it could be colored, and it served the same purpose as a painting. It was one of Germany's most important contributions to late medieval art and it exemplifies two great technological developments of the time: the mechanical printing process and the use of paper.

D. Literary Element: Irony

❓ Why did the door need to be barred? [To provide safety from intruders and to keep out the wind.] What is ironic about the woman's pleasure that her husband lost the agreement? [Intruders have already entered and eaten the food, so one of the reasons for barring the door is now gone.]

BALLADS 95

ASSESSMENT TOOLS

Check Test: Short Answers

1. What two places has Lord Randall visited since he left home? [He has been to the woods to hunt and to his "true-love's" house for dinner.]

2. What has happened to Lord Randall? [He has been poisoned. His dogs have died.]

3. What future does Edward see for himself, his wife and children, and his mother? [He will sail across the sea, his wife and children will become beggars, his mother will be cursed.]

4. What excuse does the wife in "Get Up and Bar the Door" give for not being able to bar the door? [She is busy with her household chores.]

5. What causes the husband in "Get Up and Bar the Door" to speak first? [The husband is enraged at the fact that the visitors are going to kiss his wife and use hot broth to soften his beard and then cut it off.]

A. Language Note: Vocabulary

Students may not know that a transom is a window that can be opened above an interior door. Since the door is closed, Frankie has to stand on the high stool mentioned in the next stanza in order to see Johnny through the transom window.

B. Reader's Response: Shaping Interpretations

? Do you think the ballad portrays Frankie as a sympathetic character? [Sample responses: Yes, the refrain is a constant reminder of Johnny's betrayal of Frankie; no, the ballad ends without really taking sides.] Ask students if they sympathize with Frankie's situation.

C. Critical Reading: Making Connections

? What similarities do you see between the ballad of Frankie and Johnny and the ballad of Edward? [Both involve a murder of a loved one and the punishment of the murderer. Both also involve dialogue, or questions and answers within the ballad. One difference is that Edward lives in exile and Frankie dies in the electric chair.]

Connections A SONG

"Frankie and Johnny" comes out of the Midwest and the Mississippi River region. Like most ballads, it tells of love gone wrong.

Frankie and Johnny

words by **Boyd Bunch**

Frankie and Johnny were lovers
Oh, Lordy, how they could love.
They swore to be true to each other,
True as the stars above.
He was her man, but he was doing her wrong.

Frankie she was a good woman
As everybody knows.
Spent a hundred dollars
Just to buy her man some clothes.
He was her man, but he was doing her wrong.

Frankie went down to the corner
Just for a bucket of beer.
Said: "Mr. Bartender,
Has my loving Johnny been here?
He was my man, but he's a-doing me wrong."

"Now I don't want to tell you no stories,
And I don't want to tell you no lies.
I saw your man about an hour ago
With a gal named Nellie Bligh.
He was your man, but he's a-doing you wrong."

Frankie she went down to the hotel,
Didn't go there for fun.
Underneath her kimono
She carried a forty-four gun.
He was her man, but he was doing her wrong.

A Frankie looked over the transom
To see what she could spy.
There sat Johnny on the sofa
Just loving up Nellie Bligh.
He was her man, but he was doing her wrong.

Frankie got down from that high stool,
She didn't want to see no more.
B Rooty-toot-toot three times she shot
Right through that hardwood door.
He was her man, but he was doing her wrong.

Now the first time that Frankie shot Johnny,
He let out an awful yell.
Second time she shot him
There was a new man's face in hell.
He was her man, but he was doing her wrong.

"Oh, roll me over easy,
Roll me over slow.
Roll me over on the right side,
For the left side hurts me so."
He was her man, but he was doing her wrong.

Sixteen rubber-tired carriages
Sixteen rubber-tired hacks
They take poor Johnny to the graveyard—
They ain't gonna bring him back.
He was her man, but he was doing her wrong.

Frankie looked out of the jailhouse
To see what she could see.
All she could hear was a two-string bow
Crying, "Nearer my God to thee."
He was her man, but he was doing her wrong.

C Frankie she said to the sheriff,
"What do you reckon they'll do?"
Sheriff he said, "Frankie,
It's the electric chair for you."
He was her man, but he was doing her wrong.

This story has no moral.
This story has no end.
This story only goes to show
That there ain't no good in men.
He was her man, but he was doing her wrong.

CONNECTING WITH THE BALLADS

Why are the ballads "Edward, Edward," "Lord Randall," "Get Up and Bar the Door," and the song "Frankie and Johnny" stories worth telling?

[Drama, passion, and humor are always entertaining and universal themes. These all relate timeless stories about life and love.]

MAKING MEANINGS

Lord Randall
Edward, Edward
Get Up and Bar the Door

First Thoughts

1. The appeal of the ballads lies partly in what they don't tell you. What questions does each of these songs leave unanswered for you?

Shaping Interpretations

2. What is the emotional effect of the **refrain's** variation in the fifth stanza of "Lord Randall"?

3. Like many ballads, "Lord Randall" and "Edward, Edward" build up suspense with **incremental repetition**: the repetition of lines with a new element introduced each time to advance the story until a climax is reached. At what point in each of these ballads does the story reach a climax?

4. What could be the implications of Edward's last response to his mother in the final stanza of "Edward, Edward"?

5. How is the possibility of violence combined with ironic humor in "Get Up and Bar the Door"?

Extending the Texts

6. What popular songs or folk ballads do you know that focus on subjects like the ones in these three famous medieval ballads? Refer to your Reader's Log entry (page 90) for possible ideas.

September, calendar page from the Salting Manuscript, *Hours of Margaret de Foix* (c. 1470–1480).
Victoria and Albert Museum, London.

7. People often criticize the media today for glorifying violence. Do you think these ballads (including "Frankie and Johnny" on page 96) glorify violence by singing about it? Why or why not? Is the issue the same? Talk about your responses in a small group.

ELEMENTS OF LITERATURE

Ballads: Popular Poetry

Ballads come from an oral tradition, so there are no strict rules dictating their form. However, a number of characteristics have come to be associated with ballads, and every ballad reflects at least some of them: **supernatural events; sensational, sordid, or tragic subject matter; a refrain;** and the **omission of details.** The ballad singers also used some of the following conventions:

- **incremental repetition,** to build up suspense. A phrase or sentence is repeated with a new element added each time, until the climax is reached.

- **a question-and-answer format,** in which the facts of a story are gleaned little by little from the answers. Again, this device builds up suspense.

- **conventional phrases,** understood by listeners to have meaning beyond their literal ones. "Make my bed soon" in "Lord Randall" is an example. Whenever a character in a ballad asks someone to make his bed, or to make her bed narrow, it means that the speaker is preparing for death.

- **a strong, simple beat,** with verse forms that are relatively uncomplicated. Ballads were sung for a general, rather than an elitist, audience. Only later, in the era of so-called literary ballads (more sophisticated poems that artfully evoked the atmosphere of the originals), did the rhyme scheme (*abcb*) and meter (a quatrain in which lines of four stresses alternate with lines of three stresses) of the ballad stanza become standard.

With a small group, select one of the ballads you've just read, and identify as many of the eight ballad characteristics, printed in boldface type above, as you can. Share your findings with other groups by citing a specific example of each characteristic that you find.

Making Meanings

First Thoughts

1. Possible questions: Why did Lord Randall's true love poison him? Why did Edward kill his father? What "counsels" did his mother give him? What will happen to the goodman and goodwife?

Shaping Interpretations

2. Sadness; he is dying, heartbroken by his true love's treachery.

3. In l. 17, Lord Randall's mother tells him that he has been poisoned. In l. 21, Edward reveals that he has killed his father.

4. Edward blames his mother for the tragedy; she may have counseled him to challenge or kill his father.

5. The gentlemen's threats to kiss the wife and humiliate the husband are menacing and violent. Ironically, the wife is more concerned with the pact of silence than with the threat of violence.

Extending the Texts

6. **(Synthesis)** Start by labeling the subjects of the ballads: betrayal ["Lord Randall"], a tragic mistake ["Edward, Edward"], mindless stubbornness ["Get Up and Bar the Door"]. Students may name popular singers whose songs imitate traditional ballads. Examples include Bob Dylan and Johnny Cash. "Frankie and Johnny" is similar to medieval ballads in subject matter—betrayal, a tragic mistake—and in format, as it has a refrain and familiar rhyme scheme.

7. **(Evaluation)** Discuss whether honestly depicting violence is different from glorifying it.

Elements of Literature

Possible Answers

For "Lord Randall":

- **Supernatural events:** none
- **Tragic:** man poisoned by lover
- **Refrain:** final line each stanza
- **Omitted details:** reason why Randall's lover poisons him
- **Incremental repetition:** first part of third line of each stanza
- **Question and answer:** whole ballad made up of the mother's questions and son's responses
- **Conventional phrases:** "make my bed soon"; "the wild wood"
- **Strong beat:** note that the mother's lines have a stronger beat

---

English Language Development Although these ballads come from a Western European tradition, many cultures have an oral tradition, including ballads, folk tales, and proverbs. Discuss the reasons for an oral tradition and whether the traditions still exist. Ask students to bring examples of ballads or folk tales from their cultures to class. If the piece is short, you might have the student first tell it in his or her own language before telling it in English. Ask the class to notice if the ballad or tale has any of the ballad elements mentioned on this page.

PROGRAM MANAGER

Application and Reinforcement For reinforcement of the elements of literature introduced in this lesson, see *Transparency 2.2* in the *Audiovisual Resources Binder.*

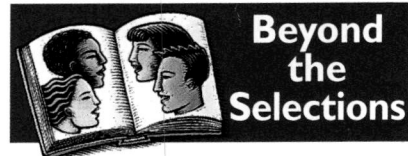

Choices: Building Your Portfolio

1. **Writer's Notebook** Remind students to save their work. They may use it as prewriting for the Writer's Workshop on p. 185.
2. **Critical Writing** Have students make a table with a column for each ballad, and a row for each characteristic. If a ballad lacks a certain characteristic, students should note it. Encourage them to express opinions about which of the ballads uses certain characteristics most effectively.
3. **Creative Writing** Remind students that both "Lord Randall" and "Edward, Edward" record conversations that take place in the wake of tragic incidents. As students prepare to write, ask them to think of conversations that would take place in the aftermath of a tragedy.
6. **Music** Discuss ways for determining whether a certain song is a ballad. To be a ballad, a song must, first of all, tell a story. Point out that many children's songs tell stories, but they are not necessarily ballads. Have students review the list of ballad characteristics before they choose songs to share.

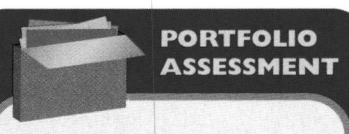

PORTFOLIO ASSESSMENT

Choices: Assessment Criteria For help in evaluating these Choices assignments, see the criteria in the *Portfolio Management System,* pp. 75–76.

CHOICES: Building Your Portfolio

Writer's Notebook
1. Collecting Ideas for an Observational Essay

In the Writer's Workshop on page 185, you'll write an observational essay describing a person. You've just met several characters in the ballads. What interesting people do they remind you of—people you could observe and describe in an essay: neighbors, family members, friends, national celebrities? Brainstorm a list of possibilities. Then select one person to write about. Whom can you observe directly? Who interests you most? Write briefly about this person. Try to capture a few vivid impressions of the individual. Save your notes to use later.

Critical Writing
2. From One Ballad to Another

Write a brief essay in which you compare these three ballads. Refer to the ballad characteristics listed on page 97 to help you explain how the ballads are alike and how they are different. At the end of your essay, tell how you responded to each ballad—the thoughts or feelings each one evoked in you.

Creative Writing
3. The Saddest Story

Try writing a folk ballad in four-line stanzas on a subject of your choice. Look for possible subjects in the newspaper or on television. Your ballad should tell a brief story, perhaps about some domestic or historic tragedy, and should include at least four ballad characteristics. You might imitate "Lord Randall" and "Edward, Edward," and tell your story in dialogue.

Creative Writing
4. Late-Breaking News!

Take one of the basic situations in these ballads, and retell it as a contemporary news story. Be sure to tell *what* happened, *where* and *when* it happened, *whom* it happened to, *why* it happened, and *how* it happened. Present your news story in print form, complete with headlines, or orally as a segment of a simulated television or radio newscast, complete with a lead.

Research/Critical Writing
5. The Many Faces of Lord Randall

"Lord Randall" is supposed to have 103 known variations. Find one or two different versions to compare to the original "Lord Randall." (Or select

A musician, from a German manuscript (c. 14th century). Cod. Pal. Germ. 848, Codex Manesse, fol. 312r.

Universitätsbibliothek, Heidelberg.

another traditional ballad that exists in several versions.) In a short essay, compare the ballad versions, noting similarities and differences. As part of your essay, try speculating on why certain details in the ballad might have been changed by subsequent singers.

Music
6. Bringing the Ballads to Life

If you play a musical instrument or sing, try performing some ballads from another culture for your classmates. Or you may collect recordings of the ballads and play them in class. Discuss the ways these ballads are like or unlike the traditional English ballads. For example, do ballads of other cultures have refrains? Do they emphasize feeling over thought?

STRATEGIES FOR INCLUSION

Logical-Mathematical For activity #4, have students create a bulleted list of events from the plot of the ballad. Ask them to list times accurate to the minute for each significant event in the story. Have them start with an arbitrary time, such as 6 A.M.

Intrapersonal For activity #5, have students record in their Reader's Logs the ways in which different versions of the same story evoke varying emotional responses. Tell them to specifically note which words seem to carry the strongest emotional impact.

Geoffrey Chaucer
(c. 1343–1400)

Geoffrey Chaucer (1400) by an unknown artist.
By Courtesy of the National Portrait Gallery, London.

Geoffrey Chaucer, often called the father of English poetry, made the English language respectable.

Ordinary people in Chaucer's England spoke the Anglo-Norman composite now called Middle English, a language that became the ancestor of Modern English. But in Chaucer's time the languages of literature, science, diplomacy, and religion were still Latin and French. Before Chaucer it was not fashionable for serious poets to write in English. People felt that English couldn't possibly convey all the nuances and complexities of serious literature. There were, it is true, some exceptions: The so-called Gawain poet (page 160) wrote in a northwestern dialect of English, and Chaucer's older contemporary William Langland wrote poems in English, of which the most important is *Piers Plowman*. And, of course, there were the popular ballads.

But the poets who wrote these works lacked the social stature of Chaucer. Chaucer was a well-known government official who served under three kings—Edward III, Richard II, and Henry IV. By composing in the **vernacular**—the everyday language spoken in London and the East Midlands—Chaucer lent respectability to a language that would develop into the medium for one of the world's greatest bodies of literature. In this sense, he was indeed the father of English poetry.

Friends in High Places

Not a great deal is known of Chaucer's life. He was born into a middle-class family in London in the early 1340s, not long after the beginning of the Hundred Years' War. We are told that his father was a wine merchant who had enough money to provide his son with some education. The young Chaucer read a great deal and had some legal training. He became a page to an eminent family from whom he received the finest training in good manners. As he advanced in his government career, he became attached to several noble patrons, especially to Edward III's fourth son, the powerful John of Gaunt, duke of Lancaster, who was made famous by William Shakespeare in his play *Richard II*.

We know, too, that Chaucer was captured in France while serving as a soldier during the Hundred Years' War and that he was important enough to have the king contribute to his ransom. We also know that he married Philippa and had at least two children and that he was on several occasions sent to Europe as the king's ambassador. In 1367, he was awarded the first of several pensions for his services to the Crown. (On April 23, 1374, he was granted the promise of a daily pitcher of wine.) In 1385, he was appointed justice of the peace in the county of Kent, later becoming a member of Parliament. He continued to serve and to enjoy the king's protection even after the death of his great patron, John of Gaunt.

Writing and Holding a Job

It seems clear that Chaucer was a relatively important government servant and that his work took precedence over his writing. (It would be as if a prominent adviser to the United States president were also a highly acclaimed poet.) Yet he wrote a great deal, and sometimes for personal advancement. In about 1369, for example, he composed his first important poem, *The Book of the Duchess*, in memory of John of Gaunt's wife, who had just died of the plague. But Chaucer's writing is just as clearly more than an attempt at political advancement or a passing fancy. Despite his government responsibilities, between 1374 and 1386, Chaucer managed to create several great allegorical poems, including the *House of Fame* and the *Parliament of Fowls*, and his poignant and amusing love story *Troilus and Criseyde*.

The Italian Connection

In 1373 and 1378, Chaucer traveled in Italy, where he was very likely influenced by the poems of Dante and Petrarch and by the stories of Giovanni Boccaccio (page 154). The connection between Boccaccio's collection of tales called the *Decameron* (c. 1348–1353) and Chaucer's *Canterbury Tales* (c. 1387–1400) is evident. Both use a framing device within which the characters tell their tales, and both include tales based on similar old plots. The framing device in the *Decameron* is a group of people who have fled the plague-ridden city of Florence and tell stories to while away their time in the country. Chaucer's frame is a religious pilgrimage during which each traveler is to tell four stories, two going out and two returning.

Chaucer began writing *The Canterbury Tales* in 1387, during a few years of unemployment when his patron was out of the country. Perhaps because he felt that he had lost his ability to find rhymes, he never completed all the stories. But the collection still must be considered one of the very greatest works in the English language. *The Canterbury Tales* alone—perhaps even only the Prologue, where each traveler is described—would be sufficient to place Chaucer in the company of Shakespeare and Milton.

The Force of Personality

What is so great about *The Canterbury Tales*? In part, its greatness lies in Chaucer's language. But its greatness also comes from the sheer strength of Chaucer's spirit and personality. John Gardner, a medieval scholar and one of Chaucer's many biographers, offers a tribute to Chaucer's lasting power:

> In a dark, troubled age, as it seems to us, he was a comfortable optimist, serene, full of faith. For all his delight in irony—and all his poetry has a touch of that—he affirmed this life, to say nothing of the next, from the bottom of his capacious heart. Joy—satisfaction without a trace of sentimental simple-mindedness—is still the effect of Chaucer's poetry and of Chaucer's personality as it emerges from the poems. It is not the simple faith of a credulous man in a credulous age: No poet has ever written better on the baffling complexity of things. But for all the foggy shiftings of the heart and mind, for all the obscurity of God's huge plan, to Chaucer life was a magnificent affair, though sadly transient; and when we read him now, six centuries later, we are instantly persuaded.

The End of the Old Alliterative Anglo-Saxon World

Chaucer used several metrical forms and some prose in *The Canterbury Tales,* but the dominant meter is based on ten syllables, with an unstressed syllable followed by a stressed syllable. We call this meter **iambic pentameter.** It is a rhythm that most closely matches the way English is spoken. You might hear this rhythm if you read aloud this line in Middle English (*swich* means "sweet"):

And bathed every veyne in swich licour

When we read a line such as this, we experience a version of the meter that was to become the most popular metrical line in English. At a stroke, we have abandoned the old, alliterative world of the Anglo-Saxons and have entered the modern world of Shakespeare, Wordsworth, and even America's Robert Frost.

The Father in the Family Vault

Chaucer died on October 25, 1400, if we are to believe the date on his tombstone (which an admirer erected in Westminster Abbey in 1556). Chaucer was the very first of those many famous English writers who would be gathered into what we know as the Poets' Corner in Westminster Abbey—one of the great tourist sights in London today. "The Father of English poetry," notes Nevill Coghill, "lies in his family vault."

The Canterbury Tales: Snapshot of an Age

The Canterbury Tales gives us a collection of good stories and a snapshot, a picture frozen in time, of life in the Middle Ages. To include the complete range of medieval society in the same picture, Chaucer places

Plan of Canterbury by William Smith, from his "Particular Description of England" (c. late 16th century). MS Sloane 2596, fol. 15.

By permission of the British Library, London.

A. Exploring the Historical Period

Almost everyone from every class in Chaucer's day made a pilgrimage. In fact, many people probably had been on more than one. By the time of *The Canterbury Tales,* though, pilgrimages were not just for religious purposes. They were also trips taken for enjoyment. According to one Chaucerian scholar, "In one year alone in the early fifteenth century, more than one hundred thousand persons from all over Europe are said to have made the Canterbury Pilgrimage."

RESPONDING TO THE ILLUSTRATION: EXPLORING THE SUBJECT

Roman soldiers invaded England in the first century A.D., and they renamed the town at the site of Canterbury. Foundations of the Roman town, called Dorovernum Cantiacorum, were identified in 1950, and parts of the Roman wall still remain. Canterbury grew in cultural importance in part because of the cathedral established by St. Augustine in the sixth century. The cathedral was damaged during World War II, but has since been restored.

A. Expansion

Thomas à Becket became a martyr two hundred years before Chaucer's day. In December of the year 1170, the English King Henry II became angry when he heard that Becket, then archbishop, had excommunicated bishops who were supporters of Henry's policies. Becket was killed by four of the king's knights and was named a saint almost immediately. The church believed that his body and blood were sacred and thus had curative powers. People did go to Becket's shrine for other blessings besides healing. For example, Chaucer suggests that the knight is on his pilgrimage to give thanks for a successful campaign. (See pp. 84–85.)

B. Expansion

The pilgrim's way from London to Canterbury was originally a Roman road, known at various times as Cosinge Street and Watling Street. Though one can still travel on the road to Dover, it bears little resemblance to the rural road that passed through hayfields and forests in Chaucer's day. The pilgrims called the road a "slough." It was probably very muddy in April.

C. Exploring the Historical Period

Southwark was the starting point for pilgrimages not just to Canterbury but also to holy places all over England, such as Salisbury, Glastonbury, and Walsingham.

his characters on a pilgrimage, a religious journey made to a shrine or holy place. These pilgrims, like a collection of people on tour today, are from many stations and stages of life. Together they travel on horseback from London to the shrine of the martyr Saint Thomas à Becket at Canterbury Cathedral, about fifty-five miles to the southeast.

The *Tales* begin with a General Prologue, the first lines of which establish that this pilgrimage takes place in the spring, the archetypal time of new life and awakening. Fifty-five miles is a long journey by horseback, especially along muddy tracks that would hardly pass as roads today. An inn was always a welcome oasis, even if it provided few luxuries. The poet-pilgrim narrator, whom many consider to be Chaucer himself, starts out at the Tabard Inn in Southwark, a borough in the south of London, where he meets twenty-nine other pilgrims also bound for Canterbury. It is the host of the Tabard who suggests to the pilgrims, as they sit around the fire after dinner, that they exchange tales to pass the time along the way to Canterbury and back to London. The host's suggestion sets up Chaucer's frame story—the main story of the pilgrimage that includes each pilgrim's story.

As the Prologue progresses and we are introduced to the pilgrims,

Chaucer's brilliant picture of life in late medieval England comes into focus. In translator Nevill Coghill's words, **(D)**

> In all literature there is nothing that touches or resembles the *Prologue*. It is the concise portrait of an entire nation, high and low, old and young, male and female, lay and clerical, learned and ignorant, rogue and righteous, land and sea, town and country, but without extremes. Apart from the stunning clarity, touched with nuance, of the characters presented, the most noticeable thing about them is their normality. They are the perennial progeny of men and women. Sharply individual, together they make a party.

At its most basic level, Chaucer's great work possesses an archetypal unity. As a pilgrimage story, it is one of the world's many quest narratives, and it moves appropriately from images of spring and awakening at the beginning of the Prologue to images of penance, death, and eternal life in the Parson's tale at the end of the work. The storytellers themselves are pilgrims, presumably in search of renewal at the Thomas à Becket shrine. Coming as they do from all walks of life, all social classes, they cannot

Chaucer's Canterbury Pilgrims (1810) by William Blake. Engraving.

By permission of The Huntington Library, San Marino, California.

D. Expansion

Nevill Coghill's translation of *The Canterbury Tales* into modern English won new readers for Chaucer and great critical acclaim for Coghill.

RESPONDING TO THE ART: ABOUT THE ARTWORK

William Blake (see p. 645) painted a fresco of the Canterbury pilgrims as they made their famous journey. In fresco painting, artists apply pigment directly onto wet plaster walls. As the plaster dries, the painting becomes a part of the wall itself. Michelangelo's Sistine Chapel is one famous example of fresco painting. This engraving of Blake's fresco was published in 1810. After students finish the Prologue, ask how many of the pilgrims they can identify. Note that the inn is identified as Henry Bailly's; he was a real innkeeper in Southwark in Chaucer's day.

QUICK PLANNING GUIDE

Into the Selection

Author Biography pp. **99–100**

Introduction pp. **101–104**

Before You Read p. **105**

- **Reading Focus:** Students read about the people who lived in the Middle Ages.
- **Quickwrite: Prior Knowledge** In their Reader's Logs, students describe a person
- **Elements of Literature: Characterization**
- **Background: Scaffolding** The frame story

Through the Selection

from The Canterbury Tales pp. **107–128**

Words to Own pp. **107–126**

Literature and Religion p. **115**

Connections: An Autobiography p. **128**

from The Autobiography of Malcolm X

Making Meanings p. **129**

Elements of Literature p. **129**

Beyond the Selection

Choices: Building Your Portfolio p. **130**

help but represent "everyman," or all of us, on our universal pilgrimage through life.

Chaucer's Middle English is here translated into Modern English by Nevill Coghill. While this version is true to the spirit of Chaucer's original poem, you might attempt at least bits of the *Tales* in the wonderfully musical original.

Brief Pronunciation Guide to Middle English

Vowels

a: *ah*, as in *father.*

ai, ay, ei, ey: a long *a*, as in *pay.*

au, aw: *ow,* as in *house.*

oo: *oh*, as in *oat.*

e: at times, like a long *a*, as in *mate*. When a double *e* is used, it is always long. *Eek* is pronounced āk.

e: at times, like a short *e*, as in *men.*

The final *e* in Middle English is a separate syllable sounded like a final *ah: soote* rhymes with *soda*. But when the final *e* precedes a word that starts with a vowel or an *h*, it is not sounded. In "droghte of March," the final *e* in *droghte* is silent.

Consonants

g: hard *g*, as in *go*, except before *e* or *i* (in words borrowed from French) where it is sounded like *zh*, as in *garage*. *Pilgrimage* rhymes with *garage*.

gh, ch: like the German *ch*, as in *nicht*. (These sounds are usually silent in modern English.) *Knight* is pronounced k·nicht'.

–tion, –cial: The *t* and *c* in such words are not blended with the *i* as they are in modern English (as in the words *condition* and *special*). The *i* is sounded as a separate syllable. *Special* would have three syllables and *condition* four: kon·di·sē·ôn'. (*C* has the sound of *s* when it comes before *i*.)

PROGRAM MANAGER

- **Planning Instruction** See *Teaching Notes, Teaching Resources A,* pp. 23–24, for objectives and a summary for this selection.
- **Instructional Support** Before beginning the instructional lesson, see *Graphic Organizer for Active Reading, Teaching Resources A,* p. 36, for a

Through the Selection activity.

- **Audiotaped Readings** Use the *Selected Reading, Audiocassette 1, Side A,* in the *Audiovisual Resources Binder.*
- **Assessment** See *Selection Test, Test Booklet,* pp. 19–20.

- **Language Link** For instruction and practice in subject-verb agreement, see *Language Link, Teaching Resources A,* pp. 37–38, and *Language and Writing Skills Worksheets,* pp. 27–30.
- **Reinforcement** Use the *Words to Own* worksheet in *Teaching Resources A,* p. 39.

BEFORE YOU READ
FROM THE CANTERBURY TALES

Reading Focus

From Sketch to Portrait

If you went on a tour today, what types of people would you expect to meet? Most of Chaucer's pilgrims are the kinds of people he would have known and perhaps even observed many times riding toward Canterbury on the old pilgrimage road. Here in the *Tales* is a cross section of medieval life: the conservative military man, the talkative and often-married feminist, the lover, the barnyard humorist, the elegant and Frenchified nun, to name a few. Chaucer seems mainly to describe his travelers' appearances in what appear to be mere physical <u>sketches</u>. But a close reading shows that he has cleverly selected details that give us shrewd psychological portraits as well.

Quickwrite

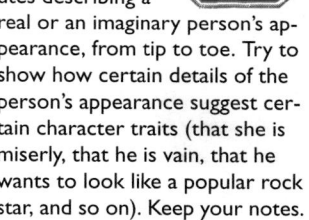

Spend a few minutes describing a real or an imaginary person's appearance, from tip to toe. Try to show how certain details of the person's appearance suggest certain character traits (that she is miserly, that he is vain, that he wants to look like a popular rock star, and so on). Keep your notes.

Elements of Literature

Characterization

To create the portraits of his pilgrim characters—"nine and twenty in a company of sundry folk," Chaucer uses the methods of characterization that writers continue to use to this day. Like his contemporary counterparts, Chaucer reveals his characters

- by telling us directly what the character is like
- by describing how the character looks and dresses
- by presenting the character's words and actions
- by revealing the character's private thoughts and feelings
- by showing how other people respond to the character

> **Characterization** is the process by which the writer reveals the personality of a character.
>
> *For more on Characterization, see the Handbook of Literary Terms.*

Background

When Chaucer chooses to have each of his pilgrims tell a story on the way to Canterbury, he is using a popular literary device, the frame story. A **frame story** is a story that includes any number of different narratives. Chaucer uses the outer story of the pilgrimage to unite his travelers' individual tales, and the tales themselves have thematic unity as well. The hundred tales in Boccaccio's *Decameron* (page 156) and the thousand-and-one tales in *The Arabian Nights* are each set within a single fictional frame as well. The frame story is still used today. If you've read Amy Tan's *The Joy Luck Club,* you've read a modern frame story.

Chaucer reciting his poetry. Ms. 61, fr.

The Master and Fellows of Corpus Christi College, Cambridge.

GEOFFREY CHAUCER 105

Into the Selection

Using BEFORE YOU READ
p. 105

Quickwrite

To get students started, have the class brainstorm to describe a person with whom they are all familiar. Write their suggestions on the chalkboard.

Elements of Literature

Ask students to compare the impact of **direct characterization,** in which an author overtly reveals a character's personality, and **indirect characterization,** in which textual clues show a character's motivation and intent. Have them discuss the kinds of reading strategies that might be useful for following along with each kind of characterization. For further discussion of these terms, see *Handbook of Literary Terms.*

PROGRAM MANAGER

Application and Reinforcement For reinforcement of the elements of literature introduced in this lesson, see *Transparency* 2.3 in the *Audiovisual Resources Binder.*

PORTFOLIO ASSESSMENT

Portfolio Assessment For help with teacher assessment of reading skills, see the *Portfolio Management System,* pp. 54–55.

WORDS TO OWN

The following vocabulary words are defined in the Words to Own at the bottom of the pupil's page.

engendering p. 107	adversity p. 119
stature p. 109	disdainful p. 120
personable p. 112	discreet p. 120
accrue p. 113	obstinate p. 120
statute p. 115	frugal p. 121
benign p. 116	duress p. 123
guile p. 118	deferred p. 126
diligent p. 119	

Geoffrey Chaucer **T105**

A. Language Note: Meter and Rhyme Scheme

Note that the meter of "The Prologue" is iambic pentameter and that the rhyme scheme is in couplets. As students read aloud or follow the reading on the cassette, have them note that the lines are not all end-stopped: To get the sense, you often have to read on to the next line. This means that Chaucer uses "open couplets," a technique that prevents his verse from sounding singsong.

Here bygynneth the Book of the Tales of Caunterbury.

Whan that Aprill with his shoures soote
The droghte of March hath perced to the roote
And bathed every veyne in swich licour
Of which vertu engendred is the flour,
5 Whan Zephirus eek with his sweete breeth
Inspired hath in every holt and heeth
The tendre croppes, and the yonge sonne
Hath in the Ram his half cours y-ronne,
And smale foweles maken melodye
10 That slepen al the nyght with open eye,
So priketh hem Nature in hir corages,
Than longen folk to goon on pilgrymages,
And palmeres for to seken straunge strondes,
To ferne halwes kouthe in sondry londes.
15 And specially, from every shires ende
Of Engelond, to Caunterbury they wende,
The holy, blisful martir for to seke
That hem hath holpen whan that they were seeke
    Bifel that in that sesoun on a day
20 In Southwerk at the Tabard, as I lay
Redy to wenden on my pilgrymage
To Caunterbury with ful devout corage,
At nyght was come into that hostelrye
Wel nyne-and-twenty in a compaignye
25 Of sondry folk by aventure y-falle
In felaweshipe, and pilgrymes were they alle
That toward Caunterbury wolden ryde.
The chambres and the stables weren wyde,
And wel we weren esed atte beste;
30 And shortly, whan the sonne was to reste,
So hadde I spoken with hem everichon
That I was of hir felaweshipe anon;
And made forward erly for to ryse
To take oure wey ther-as I yow devyse.
35   But, nathelees, whil I have tyme and space,
Er that I ferther in this tale pace,
Me thynketh it acordant to resoun
To telle yow al the condicioun
Of ech of hem so as it semed me,
40 And whiche they weren, and of what degree,
And eek in what array that they were inne;
And at a knyght than wol I first bigynne.

Page from *The Canterbury Tales*, from the Ellesmere manuscript (detail) (15th century).
By permission of The Huntington Library, San Marino, California.

OPTIONS FOR TEACHING

STRATEGIES FOR INCLUSION

Less Proficient Readers Pair students with a more proficient reader, and ask pairs to write a brief summarizing description of each of the pilgrims in order of their appearance in the Prologue. For example, after students read about the Knight, they might write:
The Knight—a nobleman, seasoned in battle; brave but not boastful; courteous and sincere.

Auditory Ask for volunteers to read aloud portions of the modern English Prologue to illustrate the rhythm created by the use of iambic pentameter. Then, play the tape of the same sections in the Middle English (see Program Manager) so that students can compare the sounds and rhythms.

from The Canterbury Tales

Geoffrey Chaucer
translated by **Nevill Coghill**

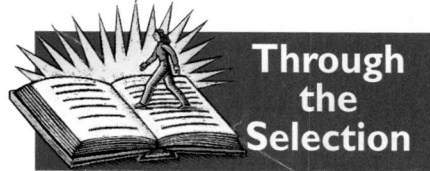
The Prologue

When in April the sweet showers fall
And pierce the drought of March to the root, and all
The veins are bathed in liquor of such power
As brings about the <u>engendering</u> of the flower,   **B**
5 When also Zephyrus° with his sweet breath
Exhales an air in every grove and heath
Upon the tender shoots, and the young sun
His half-course in the sign of the *Ram*° has run,   **C**
And the small fowl are making melody
10 That sleep away the night with open eye
(So nature pricks them and their heart engages)
Then people long to go on pilgrimages
And palmers° long to seek the stranger strands
Of far-off saints, hallowed in sundry lands,
15 And specially, from every shire's end
Of England, down to Canterbury they wend
To seek the holy blissful martyr,° quick   **D**
To give his help to them when they were sick.
    It happened in that season that one day
20 In Southwark, at *The Tabard,* as I lay
Ready to go on pilgrimage and start
For Canterbury, most devout at heart,
At night there came into that hostelry
Some nine and twenty in a company
25 Of sundry folk happening then to fall
In fellowship, and they were pilgrims all
That towards Canterbury meant to ride.
The rooms and stables of the inn were wide:
They made us easy, all was of the best.
30 And, briefly, when the sun had gone to rest,
I'd spoken to them all upon the trip
And was soon one with them in fellowship,
Pledged to rise early and to take the way
To Canterbury, as you heard me say.
35   But none the less, while I have time and space,
Before my story takes a further pace,
It seems a reasonable thing to say

5. Zephyrus (zef′ə·rəs): in Greek mythology, god of the west wind.

8. Ram: the constellation Aries, first sign of the zodiac. The time is mid-April.

13. palmers: people who had visited the Holy Land and wore palm fronds to show it.

17. martyr: Saint Thomas à Becket (c. 1118–1170) was martyred at Canterbury, December 29, 1170.

WORDS TO OWN
engendering (en·jen′dər·iŋ) *v.* used as *n.:* creation; production.

B. Reader's Response: First Thoughts

? Why might people go on pilgrimages at this time of year? [Sample responses: Winter is over. The weather is pleasant. People have been unable to travel during the winter and are eager to be going someplace.]

C. Language Note: Sentence Structure

? Where does the first sentence end? [At the end of l. 18.] Ask students to identify the three pairs of subjects and verbs. [l. 12: people, long; l. 13: palmers, long; l. 16, they, wend.]

D. Language Note: Translation
Compare ll. 17–18 of this translation with the original Middle English lines on p. 106. How has the translator preserved the rhyming couplet? [The modern translations for the Middle English end words do not rhyme exactly (seek/sick), so the translator has reworded the "modern" line.]

STRATEGIES FOR INCLUSION

Spatial Have students work in teams of five or six. Assign each team four pilgrims. Each team first draws and cuts out small sketches of their four pilgrims. Have students decide relative positions of their pilgrims as they ride and something for each of the pilgrims to say to one of the other three (based on, but not necessarily drawn directly from, Chaucer's text). Have them write the pilgrims' comments on comic-book-style balloons. Finally, they should paste or tape these travelers with their comment balloons on a long sheet of paper representing the road to Canterbury. All of the teams should put their pilgrims on the same road. Have each team explain how they decided on riding order and how they decided what their pilgrims would be saying.

Bodily-Kinesthetic Hold a medieval gift exchange, asking students to bring a "gift" of their choice for one of the pilgrims. Request that the choice of gift reflect the intended recipient's personality as described by Chaucer. Gifts may be actual objects or pictures of an imagined present. Invite students to explain the reasoning behind their gifts.

A. Expansion

The Knight's wars covered forty years and fell into three groups: (1) against the Moors at the west end of the Mediterranean, (2) against the Turks at the Mediterranean's east end, and (3) against Lithuanians and Tartars on the Russian border. The Knight's enemies would be considered pagans or infidels—unbelievers in Christ.

Miniature of John Lydgate and the Canterbury pilgrims leaving Canterbury, from a volume of Lydgate's poems (early 16th century). MS Royal 18 D II, fol. 148.

British Library, London.

What their condition was, the full array
Of each of them, as it appeared to me,
40 According to profession and degree,
And what apparel they were riding in;
And at a Knight I therefore will begin.
There was a *Knight,* a most distinguished man,
Who from the day on which he first began
45 To ride abroad had followed chivalry,
Truth, honor, generousness, and courtesy.
He had done nobly in his sovereign's war
And ridden into battle, no man more,
As well in Christian as in heathen places,

108 THE MIDDLE AGES

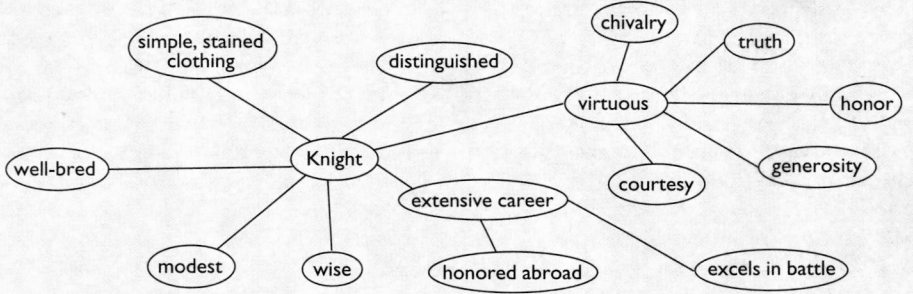

T108 The Middle Ages

50 And ever honored for his noble graces.
　　When we took Alexandria,° he was there.
He often sat at table in the chair
Of honor, above all nations, when in Prussia.
In Lithuania he had ridden, and Russia,
55 No Christian man so often, of his rank.
When, in Granada, Algeciras sank
Under assault, he had been there, and in
North Africa, raiding Benamarin;
In Anatolia he had been as well
60 And fought when Ayas and Attalia fell,
For all along the Mediterranean coast
He had embarked with many a noble host.
In fifteen mortal battles he had been
And jousted for our faith at Tramissene
65 Thrice in the lists, and always killed his man.
This same distinguished knight had led the van
Once with the Bey of Balat, doing work
For him against another heathen Turk;
He was of sovereign value in all eyes.
70 And though so much distinguished, he was wise
And in his bearing modest as a maid.
He never yet a boorish thing had said
In all his life to any, come what might;
He was a true, a perfect gentle-knight.°

B

75 　　Speaking of his equipment, he possessed
Fine horses, but he was not gaily dressed.
He wore a fustian° tunic stained and dark
With smudges where his armor had left mark;
Just home from service, he had joined our ranks

C

80 To do his pilgrimage and render thanks.
　　He had his son with him, a fine young *Squire*,
A lover and cadet,° a lad of fire
With locks as curly as if they had been pressed.
He was some twenty years of age, I guessed.
85 In stature he was of a moderate length,
With wonderful agility and strength.
He'd seen some service with the cavalry
In Flanders and Artois and Picardy
And had done valiantly in little space
90 Of time, in hope to win his lady's grace.
He was embroidered like a meadow bright
And full of freshest flowers, red and white.

D

Singing he was, or fluting all the day;
He was as fresh as is the month of May.

E

95 Short was his gown, the sleeves were long and wide;

WORDS TO OWN
stature (stach′ər) *n.*: height.

---

51. **Alexandria:** city in Egypt captured by the Crusaders in 1365. In the next few lines, Chaucer is indicating the knight's distinguished and extensive career.

The Knight, from the Ellesmere manuscript, fol. 10r.
By permission of The Huntington Library, San Marino, California.

74. **gentle-knight:** In Chaucer's day, *gentle* meant "well bred and considerate."

77. **fustian** (fus′chən): coarse cloth made of linen and cotton.

82. **cadet:** soldier.

The Squire, from the Ellesmere manuscript, fol. 115v.
By permission of The Huntington Library, San Marino, California.

GEOFFREY CHAUCER 109

B. Reader's Response: Connecting with the Text

? What qualities does the Knight possess that are different from what you might expect in a war-hardened soldier? [Sample responses: He is modest. He is considerate and well mannered. He is the ideal of chivalry.]

C. Critical Reading: Analyzing Character

? What does the Knight's clothing reveal about his character? [His clothes are simple and coarse and show signs of his work, suggesting a plain, honest man.]

D. Literary Element: Simile

? What does this simile suggest about the Squire? [He is fresh, pretty, and bright.] How does he compare to his father? [The Squire is more frivolous and lively than his father, but he has his father's honesty and sense of honor and courtesy.]

E. Expansion
According to Chaucerian expert Muriel Bowden, the details of the Squire's clothing stress his youthfulness and frivolity: "Short, embroidered gowns and long, wide sleeves were the marks of the ultrafashionable in the late fourteenth century, and pulpit complaints from the disciplinarians were frequent: short coats were denounced as 'indecent'; embroidery was called unnecessarily expensive (the money so spent should be given to the poor)."

INTEGRATING THE LANGUAGE ARTS

Writing: Obituary Have students imagine that one of the pilgrims dies during the trip, and they are to write the pilgrim's obituary. Suggest that, before students write, they read several obituaries from the newspaper and identify the standard expressions and sequence. Have students share their completed obituaries.

Speaking and Listening Practice with students reading aloud the first sentence of the modern English Prologue. Caution students that, in order to make this sentence understandable to a listener, they must not pause at the end of all lines. Explain that Chaucer uses "open couplets," a technique that prevents his verse from sounding singsong, so punctuation generally dictates pauses. Mark the first sentence on the chalkboard with a single slash (/) for a quick breath and a double slash (//) for a significant pause. Then, ask each student to copy by hand a passage of forty to fifty words and to mark the text for pauses as you have just demonstrated. Ask them to exchange passages with partners and to read the selections as they have been marked. Have students discuss changes based on clarity of meaning for a listener. 👉

A. Literary Element: Irony

? How might this last statement be an example of verbal irony? [The narrator is suddenly calling into question his appraisal of the Yeoman based on the Yeoman's neat and properly attired appearance.]

B. Expansion

A nun was a woman who lived in a convent and took a vow of poverty, chastity, and obedience; a prioress was in charge of the nuns. Have students notice as they read whether the Prioress seems a conventional nun. The Prioress's swearing by St. Loy is ironic because the saint was known for his refusal to swear.

He knew the way to sit a horse and ride.
He could make songs and poems and recite,
Knew how to joust and dance, to draw and write.
He loved so hotly that till dawn grew pale
100 He slept as little as a nightingale.
Courteous he was, lowly and serviceable,
And carved to serve his father at the table.
    There was a *Yeoman* with him at his side,
No other servant; so he chose to ride.
105 This Yeoman wore a coat and hood of green,
And peacock-feathered arrows, bright and keen
And neatly sheathed, hung at his belt the while
—For he could dress his gear in yeoman style,
His arrows never drooped their feathers low—
110 And in his hand he bore a mighty bow.
His head was like a nut, his face was brown.
He knew the whole of woodcraft up and down.
A saucy brace was on his arm to ward
It from the bow-string, and a shield and sword
115 Hung at one side, and at the other slipped
A jaunty dirk,° spear-sharp and well-equipped.
A medal of St. Christopher° he wore
Of shining silver on his breast, and bore
A hunting-horn, well slung and burnished clean,
120 That dangled from a baldrick° of bright green.
(A) He was a proper forester, I guess.
    There also was a *Nun,* a Prioress,
(B) Her way of smiling very simple and coy.
Her greatest oath was only "By St. Loy!"°
125 And she was known as Madam Eglantyne.
And well she sang a service, with a fine
Intoning through her nose, as was most seemly,
And she spoke daintily in French, extremely,
After the school of Stratford-atte-Bowe;°
130 French in the Paris style she did not know.
At meat her manners were well taught withal;
No morsel from her lips did she let fall,
Nor dipped her fingers in the sauce too deep;
But she could carry a morsel up and keep
135 The smallest drop from falling on her breast.
For courtliness she had a special zest,
And she would wipe her upper lip so clean
That not a trace of grease was to be seen
Upon the cup when she had drunk; to eat,
140 She reached a hand sedately for the meat.
She certainly was very entertaining,
Pleasant and friendly in her ways, and straining
To counterfeit a courtly kind of grace,
A stately bearing fitting to her place,

110 THE MIDDLE AGES

The Canon Yeoman, from the Ellesmere manuscript, fol. 194r.
By permission of The Huntington Library, San Marino, California.

116. dirk: long dagger.
117. St. Christopher: patron saint of travelers.

120. baldrick: belt slung over the shoulder and chest to hold a sword.

124. St. Loy: Saint Eligius, known for his perfect manners.

129. Stratford-atte-Bowe: Benedictine convent near London where inferior French was spoken.

The Prioress, from the Ellesmere manuscript, fol. 148v.
By permission of The Huntington Library, San Marino, California.

OPTIONS FOR TEACHING

COOPERATIVE LEARNING

Matchmaking Have students work in pairs to match one of the pilgrims with a well-known personality to whom students will write a letter. In the letter, students will describe the pilgrim and outline the particulars of a planned meeting between the two.

Discuss with students the probable need for persuasive techniques, as the well-known personality will want to know the advantages of such a meeting.

Interviews Have students work in pairs to prepare an interview with the pilgrim of their choice. One student, the interviewer, should attempt to

discover the pilgrim's reason(s) for making the journey to Canterbury and what kind of adventure he or she expects. The other student, the character, should be sure the responses are consistent with the personality of the character as revealed in the Prologue. Encourage students to present their interviews in class.

The Nun's Priest,
from the Ellesmere
manuscript, fol. 179r.

By permission of
The Huntington Library,
San Marino, California.

145 And to seem dignified in all her dealings.
As for her sympathies and tender feelings,
She was so charitably solicitous
She used to weep if she but saw a mouse
Caught in a trap, if it were dead or bleeding.
150 And she had little dogs she would be feeding
With roasted flesh, or milk, or fine white bread.
And bitterly she wept if one were dead
Or someone took a stick and made it smart;
She was all sentiment and tender heart.
155 Her veil was gathered in a seemly way,
Her nose was elegant, her eyes glass-gray;
Her mouth was very small, but soft and red,
Her forehead, certainly, was fair of spread,
Almost a span° across the brows, I own;
160 She was indeed by no means undergrown.
Her cloak, I noticed, had a graceful charm.
She wore a coral trinket on her arm,
A set of beads, the gaudies tricked in green,°
Whence hung a golden brooch of brightest sheen
165 On which there first was graven a crowned A,
And lower, *Amor vincit omnia.*°
   Another *Nun,* the secretary at her cell,°
Was riding with her, and *three Priests* as well.
   A *Monk* there was, one of the finest sort
170 Who rode the country; hunting was his sport.
A manly man, to be an Abbott able;
Many a dainty horse he had in stable.
His bridle, when he rode, a man might hear
Jingling in a whistling wind as clear,
175 Aye, and as loud as does the chapel bell
Where my lord Monk was Prior of the cell.
The Rule of good St. Benet or St. Maur°
As old and strict he tended to ignore;
He let go by the things of yesterday
180 And took the modern world's more spacious way.
He did not rate that text at a plucked hen
Which says that hunters are not holy men
And that a monk uncloistered is a mere
Fish out of water, flapping on the pier,
185 That is to say a monk out of his cloister.
That was a text he held not worth an oyster;
And I agreed and said his views were sound;
Was he to study till his head went round
Poring over books in cloisters? Must he toil
190 As Austin° bade and till the very soil?
Was he to leave the world upon the shelf?
Let Austin have his labor to himself.
   This Monk was therefore a good man to horse;

159. span: nine inches.

163. a set of beads . . . green:
Beads are a rosary, or prayer beads
and a crucifix on a string or chain.
Every eleventh bead is a gaud, a large
bead indicating when the Lord's
Prayer is to be said.
166. *Amor vincit omnia* (ä′môr′
vin′chit ôm′nē·ä′): Latin for "Love
conquers all."
167. cell: a small convent connected to a larger one.

177. St. Benet [Benedict] **or St.
Maur** [Maurice]: Saint Benedict
(c. 480–c. 547) was an Italian monk
who founded numerous monasteries
and wrote a famous code of regulations for monastic life. Saint Maurice
was a follower of Benedict.

190. Austin: Saint Augustine
(354–430), bishop of Hippo in North
Africa. He criticized lazy monks and
suggested they do some hard manual
labor.

GEOFFREY CHAUCER 111

C. Expansion
Nuns were not allowed to keep any
kind of pets. Pets required money that
should have gone to the poor.

D. Literary Element: Imagery
Like his contemporary physiognomists,
Chaucer often used physical characteristics to indicate a character's inner
nature. In this case, the revealing detail
is a high forehead, which was considered a sign of intelligence and good
breeding.

E. Reader's Response: First Thoughts
Coral was considered a defense against
worldly temptation as well as a love
charm. Is coral appropriate for the Prioress to wear? [Sample responses: Yes,
she is both a spiritual leader who is
supposed to deny herself material
goods and, ironically, a lover of worldly
luxuries; or no, she has taken a vow of
chastity and, ironically, wears a love
charm.]

A. Reader's Response: Shaping Interpretations

? Why is the comparison of the glittering of the Monk's eyes to flames beneath a kettle appropriate? [Sample responses: A kettle is used to satisfy an appetite; the Monk seems focused on satisfaction of his appetites. Also, the description makes him sound mischievous.]

B. Critical Reading: Analyzing Detail

A monk is a member of a religious order who has taken vows of poverty, chastity, and obedience. Given this definition, what about the Monk suggests that he is not serious about his vocation? [He rides a fine horse, wears rich clothes and jewelry, and enjoys good food.]

C. Expansion

Unlike monks, who lived in monasteries, friars were supposed to go out into the world to preach. Medieval friars belonged to mendicant religious orders, which meant that they were to live as beggars, relying on the charity of strangers to provide them with food and lodging.

D. Critical Reading: Drawing Conclusions

One of a friar's duties is to hear people's confessions and to absolve or forgive them with a penance or penalty of prayer or doing good works. What is suggested about this particular Friar in these lines? [Chaucer's Friar gives light penances because people pay him. He earns enough by selling forgiveness to make a decent living.]

Greyhounds he had, as swift as birds, to course.°
195 Hunting a hare or riding at a fence
Was all his fun, he spared for no expense.
I saw his sleeves were garnished at the hand
With fine gray fur, the finest in the land,
And on his hood, to fasten it at his chin
200 He had a wrought-gold, cunningly fashioned pin;
Into a lover's knot it seemed to pass.
His head was bald and shone like looking-glass;
So did his face, as if it had been greased.
He was a fat and <u>personable</u> priest;
205 His prominent eyeballs never seemed to settle.
They glittered like the flames beneath a kettle;
Supple his boots, his horse in fine condition.
He was a prelate fit for exhibition,
He was not pale like a tormented soul.
210 He liked a fat swan best, and roasted whole.
His palfrey° was as brown as is a berry.
     There was a *Friar,* a wanton° one and merry,
A Limiter,° a very festive fellow.
In all Four Orders° there was none so mellow,
215 So glib with gallant phrase and well-turned speech.
He'd fixed up many a marriage, giving each
Of his young women what he could afford her.
He was a noble pillar to his Order.
Highly beloved and intimate was he
220 With County folk within his boundary,
And city dames of honor and possessions;
For he was qualified to hear confessions,
Or so he said, with more than priestly scope;
He had a special license from the Pope.
225 Sweetly he heard his penitents at shrift°
With pleasant absolution, for a gift.
He was an easy man in penance-giving
Where he could hope to make a decent living;
It's a sure sign whenever gifts are given
230 To a poor Order that a man's well shriven,°
And should he give enough he knew in verity
The penitent repented in sincerity.
For many a fellow is so hard of heart
He cannot weep, for all his inward smart.
235 Therefore instead of weeping and of prayer
One should give silver for a poor Friar's care.
He kept his tippet° stuffed with pins for curls,
And pocket-knives, to give to pretty girls.

WORDS TO OWN
personable (pur′sən·ə·bəl) *adj.*: attractive in appearance and personality.

---

194. **course:** to cause to chase game.

The Friar, from the Ellesmere
manuscript, fol. 76v.
By permission of The Huntington Library,
San Marino, California.

211. **palfrey:** horse.
212. **wanton:** here, jolly.
213. **Limiter:** a friar having the exclusive right to beg and preach in an assigned (limited) district.
214. **Four Orders:** The four orders of mendicant (beggar) friars are the Franciscans, the Dominicans, the Carmelites, and the Augustinians.

225. **shrift:** confession and absolution.

230. **well shriven:** well confessed and absolved (or forgiven) of sins.

237. **tippet:** hood or long sleeve (of his robe).

**PROBLEM SOLVING/
CRITICAL THINKING**

Making Inferences Explain to students that, if they are to understand fictional characters fully, they must learn to make inferences based on what the writer discloses about the characters' thoughts, actions, words, and appearances. Have students work in groups of three to draw conclusions about each of the pilgrims. Suggest that they add to the following chart.

Information from the Text	Inference Based on the Information
[The Knight's clothes are simple, stained with blood or dirt]	[His deeds speak for him; he has no need for fancy attire.]

CROSSING THE CURRICULUM

Mathematics First have students find the distance to Canterbury from London. [About 55 miles.] Then, have them estimate the pilgrims' pace if they were moving "at a slightly faster pace than walking" (ll. 845–846). [Maybe 4 or 4.5 miles per hour.] Have students allow the pilgrims eight hours of travel each day and two days at the shrine. Ask students to determine how long the trip to Canterbury and back will take.

And certainly his voice was gay and sturdy,
240 For he sang well and played the hurdy-gurdy.°
At sing-songs he was champion of the hour.
His neck was whiter than a lily-flower
But strong enough to butt a bruiser down.
He knew the taverns well in every town
245 And every innkeeper and barmaid too
Better than lepers, beggars and that crew,
For in so eminent a man as he
It was not fitting with the dignity
Of his position, dealing with a scum
250 Of wretched lepers; nothing good can come
Of commerce with such slum-and-gutter dwellers,
But only with the rich and victual-sellers.°
But anywhere a profit might accrue
Courteous he was and lowly of service too.
255 Natural gifts like his were hard to match.
He was the finest beggar of his batch,
And, for his begging-district, paid a rent;
His brethren did no poaching where he went.
For though a widow mightn't have a shoe,
260 So pleasant was his holy how-d'ye-do
He got his farthing° from her just the same
Before he left, and so his income came
To more than he laid out. And how he romped,
Just like a puppy! He was ever prompt
265 To arbitrate disputes on settling days°
(For a small fee) in many helpful ways,
Not then appearing as your cloistered scholar
With threadbare habit hardly worth a dollar,
But much more like a Doctor or a Pope.
270 Of double-worsted was the semi-cope°
Upon his shoulders, and the swelling fold
About him, like a bell about its mould
When it is casting, rounded out his dress.
He lisped a little out of wantonness°
275 To make his English sweet upon his tongue.
When he had played his harp, or having sung,
His eyes would twinkle in his head as bright
As any star upon a frosty night.
This worthy's name was Hubert, it appeared.
280   There was a *Merchant* with a forking beard
And motley° dress; high on his horse he sat,
Upon his head a Flemish beaver hat
And on his feet daintily buckled boots.

240. **hurdy-gurdy:** lutelike instrument played by turning a crank.

252. **victual-sellers:** merchants, especially of food.

261. **farthing:** British coin worth one fourth of a penny but no longer in circulation.

265. **settling days:** days on which disputes could be settled out of court by independent negotiators. Though friars often acted as negotiators (for a fee), they were officially forbidden to do so.
270. **semi-cope:** capelike garment.

274. **wantonness:** here, pretense.

281. **motley:** multicolored.

E. Critical Reading: Analyzing Character

[?] What characteristics might Chaucer want a white neck to represent? Refer students to the table of physical characteristics on p.130. [Possible answers: Perhaps he means, by using the lily, that the friar is cowardly. It could also be a sign of a loose or immoral person.] Make sure students notice that the Friar clearly mocks his religious orders by spending time in taverns rather than with the sick and poor.

F. Reader's Response: Connecting with the Text

[?] Do you know other characters in books or films who are polite and subservient only when they stand to gain from it? The term for this type of person is *sycophant*. [Sample responses: Frank Burns from *M:*A*S*H,* Cassius from *Julius Caesar,* Gaston's sidekick (LeFou) from Disney's *Beauty and the Beast.*]

G. Reader's Response: First Thoughts

[?] What is your impression of the Merchant? [Sample responses: He seems well groomed and appears rich.] What is the flaw that the Merchant keeps hidden? [He is in debt.] Ask students how they evaluate a person they do not know well and if their evaluations are usually right.

WORDS TO OWN
accrue (ə·krōo′) *v.:* increase over time.

Geography Ask students to locate on a detailed map of England as many of the locations listed in the Prologue as possible. Students should also briefly note why each location is mentioned. Canterbury and Southwark are, of course, the destination and point of departure, but there are several more locations included in the descriptions. [Dartmouth, Bath, Norfolk, Baldeswell, Charing Cross, Berwick, Ware.] In addition, this project could be expanded to include all of the non-English locations mentioned.

Cultural Diversity Although Chaucer's collection of pilgrims is not ethnically or religiously heterogeneous, the pilgrims are very dissimilar in other ways. Have students think of heterogeneous groups with which they have worked. Invite them to share with the class which of these groups worked well in spite of differences and which did not. Rather than analyzing why the groups did not

work, students should think about whether the heterogeneous composition of the group was helpful to the group and in what ways. Close the discussion by having students suggest pilgrims that Chaucer might have added to his pilgrimage to provide an even richer diversity.

A. Expansion

In order to enter a medieval university, students had to join a minor religious order of the Church. Once out of school, they were expected to seek secular employment outside of the Church. The Cleric's books would have cost a small fortune because the printing press had not yet been invented, and books were still copied by hand.

B. Critical Reading: Finding Details

? In the description of the Serjeant, what evidence is there of the narrator's disapproval? [To the narrator, the Serjeant only appears to be a man of reverence; he is wealthy from his fame and position; and he seems busier than he really is.]

He told of his opinions and pursuits
285 In solemn tones, he harped on his increase
Of capital; there should be sea-police
(He thought) upon the Harwich–Holland ranges;
He was expert at dabbling in exchanges.
This estimable Merchant so had set
290 His wits to work, none knew he was in debt,
He was so stately in administration,
In loans and bargains and negotiation.
He was an excellent fellow all the same;
To tell the truth I do not know his name.
295   An *Oxford Cleric*, still a student though,
One who had taken logic long ago,
Was there; his horse was thinner than a rake,
And he was not too fat, I undertake,
But had a hollow look, a sober stare;
300 The thread upon his overcoat was bare.
He had found no preferment in the church
And he was too unworldly to make search
For secular employment. By his bed
He preferred having twenty books in red
305 And black, of Aristotle's° philosophy,
Than costly clothes, fiddle, or psaltery.°
Though a philosopher, as I have told,
He had not found the stone for making gold.°
Whatever money from his friends he took
310 He spent on learning or another book
And prayed for them most earnestly, returning
Thanks to them thus for paying for his learning.
His only care was study, and indeed
He never spoke a word more than was need,
315 Formal at that, respectful in the extreme,
Short, to the point, and lofty in his theme.
A tone of moral virtue filled his speech
And gladly would he learn, and gladly teach.
    A *Serjeant at the Law* who paid his calls,
320 Wary and wise, for clients at St. Paul's°
There also was, of noted excellence.
Discreet he was, a man to reverence,
Or so he seemed, his sayings were so wise.
He often had been Justice of Assize
325 By letters patent,° and in full commission.
His fame and learning and his high position
Had won him many a robe and many a fee.
There was no such conveyancer° as he;
All was fee-simple° to his strong digestion,
330 Not one conveyance could be called in question.
Though there was nowhere one so busy as he,
He was less busy than he seemed to be.

The Clerk of Oxford, from the Ellesmere manuscript, fol. 88r.

By permission of The Huntington Library, San Marino, California.

305. Aristotle's (ar′is·tät′′lz): Aristotle (384–322 B.C.) was a Greek philosopher.
306. psaltery (sôl′tər·ē): stringed instrument that is plucked.
308. stone . . . gold: Alchemists at the time were searching for a stone that was supposed to turn ordinary metals into gold.

320. St. Paul's: London cathedral. Lawyers often met outside it to discuss their cases when courts were closed.

325. letters patent: letters from the king permitting people to act as judges at the Assizes, court sessions held periodically.
328. conveyancer: person who draws up a deed.
329. fee-simple: absolute ownership of real property; in other words, either entirely right or entirely wrong.

114 THE MIDDLE AGES

Places of Pilgrimage

Chaucer's pilgrims are hardly alone in their faith that visiting a holy site will have spiritual benefits. Besides Canterbury, many Christians of Chaucer's time made pilgrimages to Rome and to Jerusalem, both sites that the Wife of Bath, something of a professional pilgrim, had visited. Today, Christian pilgrims still travel to Jerusalem and Rome.

In ancient times, the Jews also made pilgrimages to Jerusalem during three major festivals: Pesah (Passover), Shavuot (Pentecost), and Sukkot (Tabernacles). These pilgrimages, associated with festivals that mark the Jews' escape from Egypt and journey to Israel, were expected of Jewish men.

For a follower of Islam, no place is more sacred than Mecca, located near the Red Sea in western Saudi Arabia. Mecca is the site of the Kaaba, a sacred, cube-shaped building made of stone, around which Muslim pilgrims must walk. Mohammed, the founder of Islam, decreed that all Muslims who are physically and financially able to make the trip must journey to Mecca at least once in their lifetime.

Varanasi, a city on the Ganges River in India and site of fifteen hundred temples, is visited by more than a million Hindu pilgrims each year. The Golden Temple, the main Hindu shrine there, is dedicated to the god Shiva. Pilgrims who worship at the Ganges at Varanasi believe they gain special merit in this life, and Hindus who die in Varanasi believe they are guaranteed release from endless rebirths.

The Grand Shrine of Ise, the most sacred site of Japanese Shinto pilgrimages, is located at Ise in Mie Prefecture, Japan. The shrines there are viewed as the dwelling place of two deities, the sun goddess Amaterasu and the agricultural god Toyuke. The history of Ise shrine dates back some two thousand years, but the actual buildings are always fairly new. By tradition, the shrines must be rebuilt in the same style every twenty-one years.

He knew of every judgment, case, and crime
Ever recorded since King William's time.°
335 He could dictate defenses or draft deeds;
No one could pinch a comma from his screeds°
And he knew every statute off by rote.
He wore a homely parti-colored° coat,

334. King William's time: William the Conqueror (c. 1027–1087) was king of England from 1066 to 1087.
336. screeds: tiresome, lengthy writings.
338. parti-colored: multicolored.

WORDS TO OWN
statute (stach′o͞ot) *n.:* law.

GEOFFREY CHAUCER 115

Medieval Britons usually ate only two meals a day—a mid-morning dinner and an early evening supper. The Franklin also eats sop, a mixture of wine, almond milk, ginger, sugar, cinnamon, cloves, and mace poured over good bread.

B. Expansion

Guilds were organizations of tradespeople who taught their kinds of work to their students, or apprentices. The associations were a powerful economic force, controlling the quality and price of the goods they produced.

Girt with a silken belt of pin-stripe stuff;

340 Of his appearance I have said enough.
    There was a *Franklin*° with him, it appeared;
    White as a daisy-petal was his beard.
    A sanguine° man, high-colored and benign,
    He loved a morning sop of cake in wine.
345 He lived for pleasure and had always done,
    For he was Epicurus'° very son,
    In whose opinion sensual delight
    Was the one true felicity in sight.
    As noted as St. Julian° was for bounty
350 He made his household free to all the County.
    His bread, his ale were finest of the fine
    And no one had a better stock of wine.
    His house was never short of bake-meat pies,
    Of fish and flesh, and these in such supplies
355 It positively snowed with meat and drink
    And all the dainties that a man could think.
    According to the seasons of the year
    Changes of dish were ordered to appear.
    He kept fat partridges in coops, beyond,
360 Many a bream and pike were in his pond.
    Woe to the cook unless the sauce was hot
    And sharp, or if he wasn't on the spot!
    And in his hall a table stood arrayed
    And ready all day long, with places laid.
365 As Justice at the Sessions° none stood higher;
    He often had been Member for the Shire.°
    A dagger and a little purse of silk
    Hung at his girdle,° white as morning milk.
    As Sheriff he checked audit, every entry.
370 He was a model among landed gentry.
        A *Haberdasher,*° a *Dyer,* a *Carpenter,*
    A *Weaver,* and a *Carpet-maker* were
    Among our ranks, all in the livery
    Of one impressive guild-fraternity.
375 They were so trim and fresh their gear would pass
    For new. Their knives were not tricked out with brass
    But wrought with purest silver, which avouches
    A like display on girdles and on pouches.
    Each seemed a worthy burgess,° fit to grace
380 A guild-hall with a seat upon the dais.
    Their wisdom would have justified a plan
    To make each one of them an alderman;°
    They had the capital and revenue,
    Besides their wives declared it was their due.

341. Franklin: well-to-do landowner, but not of the nobility.

343. sanguine: ruddy-complexioned. In Chaucer's day this was considered a sign of a cheerful temperament; today the word signifies optimism.
346. Epicurus' (341–270 B.C.): Epicurus, an ancient Greek philosopher, taught that the goal of life is pleasure, which is achieved through virtue and moderation. Most people came to think of Epicureans as pleasure seekers.
349. St. Julian: patron saint of hospitality.

365. Justice at the Sessions: judge at a periodically held court meeting.
366. Member for the Shire: county representative in Parliament.
368. girdle: belt.

371. Haberdasher (hab'ər·dash'ər): seller of men's clothing and accessories.

379. burgess: citizen.

382. alderman: head of a guild and therefore a town council member.

WORDS TO OWN
benign (bi·nīn') *adj.:* kind; gracious.

---

385 And if they did not think so, then they ought;
     To be called *"Madam"* is a glorious thought,
     And so is going to church and being seen
     Having your mantle carried, like a queen.
          They had a *Cook* with them who stood alone
390 For boiling chicken with a marrow-bone,
     Sharp flavoring-powder and a spice for savor.
     He could distinguish London ale by flavor,
     And he could roast and seethe and broil and fry,
     Make good thick soup, and bake a tasty pie.
395 But what a pity—so it seemed to me,
     That he should have an ulcer on his knee.
     As for blancmange,° he made it with the best.
          There was a *Skipper* hailing from far west;
     He came from Dartmouth, so I understood.
400 He rode a farmer's horse as best he could,
     In a woollen gown that reached his knee.
     A dagger on a lanyard° falling free
     Hung from his neck under his arm and down.
     The summer heat had tanned his color brown,
405 And certainly he was an excellent fellow.
     Many a draught of vintage, red and yellow,
     He'd drawn at Bordeaux, while the trader snored.
     The nicer rules of conscience he ignored.
     If, when he fought, the enemy vessel sank,
410 He sent his prisoners home; they walked the plank.
     As for his skill in reckoning his tides,
     Currents, and many another risk besides,
     Moons, harbors, pilots, he had such dispatch
     That none from Hull to Carthage was his match.
415 Hardy he was, prudent in undertaking;
     His beard in many a tempest had its shaking,
     And he knew all the havens as they were
     From Gottland to the Cape of Finisterre,
     And every creek in Brittany and Spain;
420 The barge he owned was called *The Maudelayne.*
          A *Doctor* too emerged as we proceeded;
     No one alive could talk as well as he did
     On points of medicine and of surgery,
     For, being grounded in astronomy,
425 He watched his patient closely for the hours
     When, by his horoscope, he knew the powers
     Of favorable planets, then ascendent,
     Worked on the images for his dependent.
     The cause of every malady you'd got
430 He knew, and whether dry, cold, moist, or hot;°
     He knew their seat, their humor and condition.
     He was a perfect practicing physician.
     These causes being known for what they were,
     He gave the man his medicine then and there.

The Cook, from the Ellesmere manuscript, fol. 47r.

By permission of The Huntington Library, San Marino, California.

397. blancmange (blə·mônzh′): French for "white food." In Chaucer's day this was a sweet dish containing diced chicken, milk, sugar, and almonds.

402. lanyard (lan′yərd): cord.

The Franklin, from the Ellesmere manuscript, fol. 123v.

By permission of The Huntington Library, San Marino, California.

430. dry . . . hot: the four humors or fluids. People of the time believed that one's physical and mental conditions were influenced by the balance of four major fluids in the body—blood (hot), choler (cold), phlegm (wet), and black bile (dry).

GEOFFREY CHAUCER 117

A. Critical Reading: Analyzing Character

? How is Chaucer's depiction of the Doctor satirical? [Although he says the Doctor is a perfect practicing physician, it is clear to Chaucer that the Doctor profits from people's sickness. Although he cares for the ill, his work is motivated by profit instead of good-heartedness.]

B. Readers' Response: Shaping Interpretations

? What is the Wife of Bath concerned about when she goes to church? What does this suggest about her character? [Sample responses: She is concerned that she should be the first into church, and that she should wear the best clothes. She is more concerned about status than spirituality, and she is vain.]

C. Expansion

Jerusalem, Rome, Boulogne (in France), St. James of Compostella (in Spain), and Cologne (in Germany) were all famous pilgrimage centers. Students should be aware that the Wife of Bath's freedom to travel was a luxury not available to many women in her time. Point out to students that a gap between a person's front teeth was thought in the Middle Ages to be a sign that the person would travel far. It also suggested that the person was bold and especially suited for love.

---

435 All his apothecaries in a tribe
Were ready with the drugs he would prescribe
And each made money from the other's _guile_;
They had been friendly for a goodish while.
He was well-versed in Aesculapius° too
440 And what Hippocrates and Rufus knew
And Dioscorides, now dead and gone,
Galen and Rhazes, Hali, Serapion,
Averroes, Avicenna, Constantine,
Scotch Bernard, John of Gaddesden, Gilbertine.
445 In his own diet he observed some measure;
There were no superfluities for pleasure,
Only digestives, nutritives and such.
He did not read the Bible very much.
In blood-red garments, slashed with bluish gray
450 And lined with taffeta, he rode his way;
A Yet he was rather close as to expenses
And kept the gold he won in pestilences.
Gold stimulates the heart, or so we're told.
He therefore had a special love of gold.
455   A worthy _woman_ from beside _Bath_ city
Was with us, somewhat deaf, which was a pity.
In making cloth she showed so great a bent
She bettered those of Ypres and of Ghent.°
In all the parish not a dame dared stir
460 Towards the altar steps in front of her,
And if indeed they did, so wrath was she
B As to be quite put out of charity.
Her kerchiefs were of finely woven ground;°
I dared have sworn they weighed a good ten pound,
465 The ones she wore on Sunday, on her head.
Her hose were of the finest scarlet red
And gartered tight; her shoes were soft and new.
Bold was her face, handsome, and red in hue.
A worthy woman all her life, what's more
470 She'd had five husbands, all at the church door,°
Apart from other company in youth;
No need just now to speak of that, forsooth.
And she had thrice been to Jerusalem,
Seen many strange rivers and passed over them;
475 She'd been to Rome and also to Boulogne,
C St. James of Compostella and Cologne,
And she was skilled in wandering by the way.
She had gap-teeth, set widely, truth to say.
Easily on an ambling horse she sat

439. Aesculapius: This and the names that follow were early Greek, Roman, Middle Eastern, and medieval medical authorities.

The Physician, from the Ellesmere manuscript, fol. 133r.

By permission of The Huntington Library, San Marino, California.

458. Ypres (ē′pr′) **and of Ghent:** Flemish centers of the wool trade.

463. ground: type of cloth.

470. church door: In Chaucer's day the marriage ceremony was performed at the church door.

WORDS TO OWN

guile (gīl) _n._: sly dealings.

---

118 THE MIDDLE AGES

480 Well wimpled° up, and on her head a hat
   As broad as is a buckler or a shield;
   She had a flowing mantle that concealed
   Large hips, her heels spurred sharply under that.
   In company she liked to laugh and chat
485 And knew the remedies for love's mischances,
   An art in which she knew the oldest dances.
      A holy-minded man of good renown
   There was, and poor, the *Parson* to a town,
   Yet he was rich in holy thought and work.
490 He also was a learned man, a clerk,
   Who truly knew Christ's gospel and would preach it
   Devoutly to parishioners, and teach it.
   Benign and wonderfully <u>diligent</u>,
   And patient when <u>adversity</u> was sent
495 (For so he proved in much adversity)
   He hated cursing to extort a fee,
   Nay rather he preferred beyond a doubt
   Giving to poor parishioners round about
   Both from church offerings and his property;
500 He could in little find sufficiency.
   Wide was his parish, with houses far asunder,
   Yet he neglected not in rain or thunder,
   In sickness or in grief, to pay a call
   On the remotest, whether great or small,
505 Upon his feet, and in his hand a stave.°
   This noble example to his sheep he gave
   That first he wrought, and afterward he taught;
   And it was from the Gospel he had caught
   Those words, and he would add this figure too,
510 That if gold rust, what then will iron do?
   For if a priest be foul in whom we trust
   No wonder that a common man should rust;
   And shame it is to see—let priests take stock—
   A shitten shepherd and a snowy flock.
515 The true example that a priest should give
   Is one of cleanness, how the sheep should live.
   He did not set his benefice to hire°
   And leave his sheep encumbered in the mire
   Or run to London to earn easy bread
520 By singing masses for the wealthy dead,
   Or find some Brotherhood and get enrolled.°
   He stayed at home and watched over his fold
   So that no wolf should make the sheep miscarry.

WORDS TO OWN

diligent (dil′ə·jənt) *adj.*: careful and persistent in work.
adversity (ad·vʉr′sə·tē) *n.*: trouble; misfortune.

---

480. **wimpled:** A wimple is a linen covering for the head and neck.

The Parson, from the Ellesmere manuscript, fol. 206v.

By permission of The Huntington Library, San Marino, California.

505. **stave:** staff.

517. **benefice to hire:** He did not hire someone else to perform his duties.

521. **find . . . enrolled:** He did not take a job as a paid chaplain to a guild.

D. Critical Reading: Finding Details

? What words or phrases would you use to describe the Wife of Bath? [Possible answers: Bold, assertive, imposing, earthy, strong, intelligent, frank, snobbish.] Some critics think that the Wife is based on Chaucer's paternal grandmother, who had three husbands.

E. Critical Reading: Predicting

? What sort of tale do you think the Wife of Bath will tell? [Possible answers: A tale involving love and marriage, since she has been married five times; or a story about wealth and beauty as those seem to concern her.] Students can test their predictions when they read her tale.

F. Literary Element: Characterization

Chaucer describes the Parson as poor. From what you know of Chaucer's values so far, do you think he will approve or disapprove of the Parson? Why? [He may approve; poverty is almost always a virtue in Chaucer's characterization, and the Parson is "rich in holy thought and work."]

G. Literary Element: Metaphor

The Biblical metaphor compares the Parson to a shepherd and his parishioners to sheep. The Parson's job is to set an example for and to keep an eye on the spiritual health of the people in his care. The metaphor of gold and iron warns that if gold, a refined, prized metal, may be corroded, then iron, a coarse metal, cannot help but rust. This suggests that if a priest sins, it is unlikely that his parish members will avoid sinning—a prospect the Parson and Chaucer find shameful.

A. Critical Reading: Summarizing

? How does the Parson show that he is a good priest? [He stays with his parish instead of going to the city to make money, and he is kind, soft-spoken, modest, and fair.]

B. Humanities Connection

Chaucer's portrait of the Plowman may refer to the poem *Piers Plowman,* written in the late 1300s by William Langland. In Langland's poem, the plowman is portrayed as an instrument of salvation to his community. Chaucer may be similarly idealizing his Plowman; this is remarkable, as the writings of Chaucer's contemporaries ridiculed peasants.

C. Literary Element: Allusion

This passage is an allusion to Luke 10:27, in which Jesus Christ cites the commandments "Thou shalt love the Lord thy God with all thy heart . . .; and thy neighbor as thyself."

D. Critical Reading: Making Connections

Chaucer praises the Plowman, the Parson, and the Cleric. What qualities do these men share? [Generosity, love of their work, spirituality, and lack of interest in wealth.] In what ways do these men differ? [In education and profession.]

He was a shepherd and no mercenary.
525 Holy and virtuous he was, but then
Never contemptuous of sinful men,
Never <u>disdainful</u>, never too proud or fine,
But was <u>discreet</u> in teaching and benign.
His business was to show a fair behavior
530 And draw men thus to Heaven and their Savior,
Unless indeed a man were <u>obstinate</u>;
And such, whether of high or low estate,
He put to sharp rebuke, to say the least.
I think there never was a better priest.
535 He sought no pomp or glory in his dealings,
No scrupulosity had spiced his feelings.
Christ and His Twelve Apostles and their lore
He taught, but followed it himself before.
        There was a *Plowman* with him there, his brother;
540 Many a load of dung one time or other
He must have carted through the morning dew.
He was an honest worker, good and true,
Living in peace and perfect charity,
And, as the gospel bade him, so did he,
545 Loving God best with all his heart and mind
And then his neighbor as himself, repined
At no misfortune, slacked for no content,
For steadily about his work he went
To thrash his corn, to dig or to manure
550 Or make a ditch; and he would help the poor
For love of Christ and never take a penny
If he could help it, and, as prompt as any,
He paid his tithes in full when they were due
On what he owned, and on his earnings too.
555 He wore a tabard smock° and rode a mare.
        There was a *Reeve,*° also a *Miller,* there,
A College *Manciple*° from the Inns of Court,
A papal *Pardoner*° and, in close consort,
A Church-Court *Summoner,*° riding at a trot,
560 And finally myself—that was the lot.
        The *Miller* was a chap of sixteen stone,°
A great stout fellow big in brawn and bone.
He did well out of them, for he could go
And win the ram at any wrestling show.
565 Broad, knotty, and short-shouldered, he would boast
He could heave any door off hinge and post,
Or take a run and break it with his head.

The Miller, from the Ellesmere manuscript, fol. 34v.

By permission of The Huntington Library, San Marino, California.

555. **tabard** (tab′ərd) **smock:** short jacket.
556. **Reeve:** serf who was the steward of a manor. He saw that the estate's work was done and that everything was accounted for.
557. **Manciple** (man′sə·pəl): minor employee whose principal duty was to purchase provisions for a college or law firm.
558. **Pardoner:** minor member of the Church who bought and sold pardons for sinners.
559. **Summoner:** low-ranking officer who summoned people to appear in church court.
561. **sixteen stone:** 224 pounds.

WORDS TO OWN
disdainful (dis·dān′fəl) *adj.:* scornful.
discreet (di·skrēt′) *adj.:* cautious about one's words and actions.
obstinate (äb′stə·nət) *adj.:* unreasonably stubborn.

His beard, like any sow or fox, was red
And broad as well, as though it were a spade;
570 And, at its very tip, his nose displayed
A wart on which there stood a tuft of hair
Red as the bristles in an old sow's ear.
His nostrils were as black as they were wide.
He had a sword and buckler at his side,
575 His mighty mouth was like a furnace door.
A wrangler and buffoon, he had a store
Of tavern stories, filthy in the main.
His was a master-hand at stealing grain.
He felt it with his thumb and thus he knew
580 Its quality and took three times his due—
A thumb of gold, by God, to gauge an oat!°
He wore a hood of blue and a white coat.
He liked to play his bagpipes up and down
And that was how he brought us out of town.
585   The *Manciple* came from the Inner Temple;°
All caterers might follow his example
In buying victuals; he was never rash
Whether he bought on credit or paid cash.
He used to watch the market most precisely
590 And got in first, and so he did quite nicely.
Now isn't it a marvel of God's grace
That an illiterate fellow can outpace
The wisdom of a heap of learned men?
His masters—he had more than thirty then—
595 All versed in the abstrusest legal knowledge,
Could have produced a dozen from their College
Fit to be stewards in land and rents and game
To any Peer in England you could name,
And show him how to live on what he had
600 Debt-free (unless of course the Peer were mad)
Or be as <u>frugal</u> as he might desire,
And make them fit to help about the Shire
In any legal case there was to try;
And yet this Manciple could wipe their eye.
605   The *Reeve* was old and choleric° and thin;
His beard was shaven closely to the skin,
His shorn hair came abruptly to a stop
Above his ears, and he was docked on top
Just like a priest in front; his legs were lean,
610 Like sticks they were, no calf was to be seen.
He kept his bins and garners° very trim;
No auditor could gain a point on him.

The Manciple, from the Ellesmere manuscript, fol. 203r.
By permission of The Huntington Library, San Marino, California.

581. thumb . . . oat: In other words, he pressed on the scale with his thumb to increase the weight of the grain.

585. Inner Temple: one of the four legal societies in London comprising the Inns of Court. Only the Inns were permitted to license lawyers.

The Reeve, from the Ellesmere manuscript, fol. 42r.

By permission of The Huntington Library San Marino, California.

605. choleric (käl′ər·ik): having too much choler, or yellow bile, and thus (supposedly) bad-tempered.

611. garners: granaries.

E. Literary Element: Simile
? To what objects and animals is the Miller compared? [Sow or fox, spade, sow's ear, a furnace door.] What do the comparisons suggest about the Miller's character? [Roughness, uncouthness, wildness, ordinariness.]

F. Language Note: Idioms
"Could wipe their eye" means that the Manciple could make fools of his masters or could outdo them. Here, *wipe* might mean "to swipe, remove or erase," suggesting that the Manciple could steal their eyes.

G. Expansion
People in Chaucer's time believed that four bodily fluids, called "humors" or "moistures," caused disease and negatively influenced a person's character when their mixture was out of balance. People associated black bile with depression and delusions, and choler, or yellow bile, with unkindness, instability, and pridefulness. Too much phlegm created sloth, obesity, crooked bodies, and hairless skin. Too much blood made a person sensual, or in older people, caused heart attacks.

H. Exploring the Historical Period
The Reeve's hair is cut straight across the forehead, common for priests' hair of the time as a sign of servility.

WORDS TO OWN
frugal (frōō′gəl) *adj.:* thrifty.

GEOFFREY CHAUCER 121

A reeve in the Middle Ages was a manager of an estate whose job it was to inspect everything and to impose fines on the workers if he found anything wrong. Chaucer starts out saying that this reeve does his job well, but ends by implying that he is mean to the workers and has become rich by embezzling from the master.

B. Literary Element: Characterization

People in Chaucer's time would probably have suggested that the Summoner suffers from his severe skin condition because of the strong food and drink he enjoys.

And he could judge by watching drought and rain
The yield he might expect from seed and grain.
615 His master's sheep, his animals and hens,
Pigs, horses, dairies, stores, and cattle-pens
Were wholly trusted to his government.
He had been under contract to present
The accounts, right from his master's earliest years.
620 No one had ever caught him in arrears.
No bailiff, serf, or herdsman dared to kick,
He knew their dodges, knew their every trick;
Feared like the plague he was, by those beneath.
He had a lovely dwelling on a heath,
625 Shadowed in green by trees above the sward.°
A better hand at bargains than his lord,
He had grown rich and had a store of treasure
Well tucked away, yet out it came to pleasure
His lord with subtle loans or gifts of goods,
630 To earn his thanks and even coats and hoods.
When young he'd learnt a useful trade and still
He was a carpenter of first-rate skill.
The stallion-cob he rode at a slow trot
Was dapple-gray and bore the name of Scot.
635 He wore an overcoat of bluish shade
And rather long; he had a rusty blade
Slung at his side. He came, as I heard tell,
From Norfolk, near a place called Baldeswell.
His coat was tucked under his belt and splayed.
640 He rode the hindmost of our cavalcade.
      There was a *Summoner* with us at that Inn,
His face on fire, like a cherubim,°
For he had carbuncles.° His eyes were narrow,
He was as hot and lecherous as a sparrow.
645 Black scabby brows he had, and a thin beard.
Children were afraid when he appeared.
No quicksilver, lead ointment, tartar creams,
No brimstone, no boracic, so it seems,
Could make a salve that had the power to bite,
650 Clean up, or cure his whelks° of knobby white
Or purge the pimples sitting on his cheeks.
Garlic he loved, and onions too, and leeks,
And drinking strong red wine till all was hazy.
Then he would shout and jabber as if crazy,
655 And wouldn't speak a word except in Latin
When he was drunk, such tags as he was pat in;
He only had a few, say two or three,
That he had mugged up out of some decree;
No wonder, for he heard them every day.
660 And, as you know, a man can teach a jay°
To call out "Walter" better than the Pope.

The Summoner, from the Ellesmere manuscript, fol. 81r.

By permission of The Huntington Library, San Marino, California.

625. sward (swôrd): lawn.

642. cherubim: in medieval art, a little angel with a rosy face.
643. carbuncles (kär′bun′kəlz): pus-filled skin inflammations, something like boils.

650. whelks: pus-filled sores.

660. jay: type of bird.

But had you tried to test his wits and grope
For more, you'd have found nothing in the bag.
Then *"Questio quid juris"°* was his tag.
665 He was a noble varlet° and a kind one,
You'd meet none better if you went to find one.
Why, he'd allow—just for a quart of wine—
Any good lad to keep a concubine
A twelvemonth and dispense him altogether!
670 And he had finches of his own to feather:
And if he found some rascal with a maid
He would instruct him not to be afraid
In such a case of the Archdeacon's curse
(Unless the rascal's soul were in his purse)
675 For in his purse the punishment should be.
"Purse is the good Archdeacon's Hell," said he.
But well I know he lied in what he said;
A curse should put a guilty man in dread,
For curses kill, as shriving brings, salvation.
680 We should beware of excommunication.
Thus, as he pleased, the man could bring <u>duress</u>
On any young fellow in the diocese.
He knew their secrets, they did what he said.
He wore a garland set upon his head
685 Large as the holly-bush upon a stake
Outside an ale-house, and he had a cake,
A round one, which it was his joke to wield
As if it were intended for a shield.
    He and a gentle *Pardoner* rode together,
690 A bird from Charing Cross of the same feather,
Just back from visiting the Court of Rome.
He loudly sang *"Come hither, love, come home!"*
The Summoner sang deep seconds° to this song,
No trumpet ever sounded half so strong.
695 This Pardoner had hair as yellow as wax,
Hanging down smoothly like a hank of flax.
In driblets fell his locks behind his head
Down to his shoulders which they overspread;
Thinly they fell, like rat-tails, one by one.
700 He wore no hood upon his head, for fun;
The hood inside his wallet had been stowed,
He aimed at riding in the latest mode;
But for a little cap his head was bare
And he had bulging eye-balls, like a hare.
705 He'd sewed a holy relic on his cap;
His wallet lay before him on his lap,

664. Questio quid juris
(kwest'ē·ō kwid yōō'ris): Latin for "I
ask what point of the law [applies]."
The Summoner uses this phrase to
stall and dodge the issue.
665. varlet (vär'lit): scoundrel.

The Pardoner, from the Ellesmere
manuscript, fol. 138r.

By permission of The Huntington Library,
San Marino, California.

693. deep seconds: harmonies.

WORDS TO OWN

duress (dōō·res') *n.:* pressure.

A. Exploring the Historical Period

Relics were believed to be the remains (bones, hair, garments, fingernails, and so on) of a holy person. Saying a prayer with the relic in hand was thought to bring an indulgence, or limited respite from the pains of purgatory after death. Some relics were fakes—the Pardoner's are made from pig bones—but provided the sellers with income as believers willingly bought their goods.

B. Critical Reading: Making Inferences

? Who is really the author of these tales? Why do you think Chaucer says he is merely recording what other people have said? [Chaucer, of course, invented the characters and their tales, but pretending that he is merely a reporter relieves him of responsibility for the tales' content—which is often bawdy—or any lack of humor perceived by the reader. Also, writing secular poetry was still not a respected profession, and Chaucer, an important government servant and member of the middle class, had a reputation to protect.]

Brimful of pardons° come from Rome, all hot.
He had the same small voice a goat has got.
His chin no beard had harbored, nor would harbor,
710 Smoother than ever chin was left by barber.
I judge he was a gelding, or a mare.
As to his trade, from Berwick down to Ware
There was no pardoner of equal grace,
For in his trunk he had a pillow-case
715 Which he asserted was Our Lady's veil.
He said he had a gobbet° of the sail
Saint Peter had the time when he made bold
To walk the waves, till Jesu Christ took hold.
He had a cross of metal set with stones
720 And, in a glass, a rubble of pigs' bones.
And with these relics, any time he found
Some poor up-country parson to astound,
In one short day, in money down, he drew
More than the parson in a month or two,
725 And by his flatteries and prevarication
Made monkeys of the priest and congregation.
But still to do him justice first and last
In church he was a noble ecclesiast.°
How well he read a lesson or told a story!
730 But best of all he sang an Offertory,°
For well he knew that when that song was sung
He'd have to preach and tune his honey-tongue
And (well he could) win silver from the crowd.
That's why he sang so merrily and loud.
735   Now I have told you shortly, in a clause,
The rank, the array, the number, and the cause
Of our assembly in this company
In Southwark, at that high-class hostelry
Known as *The Tabard,* close beside *The Bell.*
740 And now the time has come for me to tell
How we behaved that evening; I'll begin
After we had alighted at the Inn,
Then I'll report our journey, stage by stage,
All the remainder of our pilgrimage.
745 But first I beg of you, in courtesy,
Not to condemn me as unmannerly
If I speak plainly and with no concealings
And give account of all their words and dealings,
Using their very phrases as they fell.
750 For certainly, as you all know so well,
He who repeats a tale after a man
Is bound to say, as nearly as he can,
Each single word, if he remembers it,
However rudely spoken or unfit,

707. pardons: small strips of parchment with papal seals attached. They were sold as indulgences (pardons for sins), with the proceeds supposedly going to a religious house. Many pardoners were dishonest, and even loyal church members often ridiculed them.

716. gobbet: fragment.

728. ecclesiast (e·klē′zē·ast): practitioner of church ritual.

730. Offertory: hymn sung while offerings are collected in church.

755   Or else the tale he tells will be untrue,
      The things pretended and the phrases new.
      He may not flinch although it were his brother,
      He may as well say one word as another.
      And Christ Himself spoke broad in Holy Writ,
760   Yet there is no scurrility in it,
      And Plato says, for those with power to read,
      "The word should be as cousin to the deed."
      Further I beg you to forgive it me
      If I neglect the order and degree
765   And what is due to rank in what I've planned.
      I'm short of wit as you will understand.
         Our *Host* gave us great welcome; everyone
      Was given a place and supper was begun.
      He served the finest victuals you could think,
770   The wine was strong and we were glad to drink.
      A very striking man our Host withal,
      And fit to be a marshal in a hall.
      His eyes were bright, his girth a little wide;
      There is no finer burgess in Cheapside.°
775   Bold in his speech, yet wise and full of tact,
      There was no manly attribute he lacked,
      What's more he was a merry-hearted man.
      After our meal he jokingly began
      To talk of sport, and, among other things
780   After we'd settled up our reckonings,
      He said as follows: "Truly, gentlemen,
      You're very welcome and I can't think when
      —Upon my word I'm telling you no lie—
      I've seen a gathering here that looked so spry,
785   No, not this year, as in this tavern now.
      I'd think you up some fun if I knew how.
      And, as it happens, a thought has just occurred
      To please you, costing nothing, on my word.
      You're off to Canterbury—well, God speed!

774. Cheapside: district of medieval London.

The Host, from the Ellesmere manuscript, fol. 153v.

? Do you agree or disagree that a writer's or artist's work should be true to life? What arguments can you make for either view? [Sample responses: Disagree, because the truth can be boring or painful; we would have no fiction or fairy tales; or agree, because nonfiction is more serious and more important; the truth should always be told.]

? Why might the pilgrims agree to do as the Host says even before they know what he will propose? [Possible answers: They know the journey will be long. They trust the Host. They know that he is the type of man who will think of something entertaining.]

B. Expansion

If all thirty pilgrims had told two tales on their way to Canterbury and two tales on their way back to London, there would have been 120 tales. At a rate of one per month, it would have taken Chaucer ten years to complete *The Canterbury Tales*. In fact, he wrote only 24 of the tales, so far as we know, in five years.

C. Readers' Response: Extending the Text

The Host's definition of a good story is one that "gives the fullest measure / Of good morality and general pleasure." Do you agree with these criteria? Why or why not? Can you propose other criteria for evaluating good stories? [Sample responses: Yes, these criteria make sense. Or no, morality has nothing to do with a good story. Other criteria might include suspense, elements of surprise, and realistic details.]

---

790 Blessed St. Thomas answer to your need!
        And I don't doubt, before the journey's done
        You mean to while the time in tales and fun.
        Indeed, there's little pleasure for your bones
        Riding along and all as dumb as stones.
795 So let me then propose for your enjoyment,
        Just as I said, a suitable employment.
        And if my notion suits and you agree
        And promise to submit yourselves to me
        Playing your parts exactly as I say
800 Tomorrow as you ride along the way,
        Then by my father's soul (and he is dead)
        If you don't like it you can have my head!
        Hold up your hands, and not another word."
            Well, our opinion was not long deferred,
805 It seemed not worth a serious debate;
        We all agreed to it at any rate
        And bade him issue what commands he would.
        "My lords," he said, "now listen for your good,
        And please don't treat my notion with disdain.
810 This is the point. I'll make it short and plain.
        Each one of you shall help to make things slip
        By telling two stories on the outward trip
        To Canterbury, that's what I intend,
        And, on the homeward way to journey's end
815 Another two, tales from the days of old;
        And then the man whose story is best told,
        That is to say who gives the fullest measure
        Of good morality and general pleasure,
        He shall be given a supper, paid by all,
820 Here in this tavern, in this very hall,
        When we come back again from Canterbury.
        And in the hope to keep you bright and merry
        I'll go along with you myself and ride
        All at my own expense and serve as guide.
825 I'll be the judge, and those who won't obey
        Shall pay for what we spend upon the way.
        Now if you all agree to what you've heard
        Tell me at once without another word,
        And I will make arrangements early for it."
830   Of course we all agreed, in fact we swore it
        Delightedly, and made entreaty too
        That he should act as he proposed to do,
        Become our Governor in short, and be
        Judge of our tales and general referee,
835 And set the supper at a certain price.

WORDS TO OWN
deferred (dē·fʉrd′) *v.*: postponed.

We promised to be ruled by his advice
Come high, come low; unanimously thus
We set him up in judgment over us.
More wine was fetched, the business being done;
840 We drank it off and up went everyone
To bed without a moment of delay.
   Early next morning at the spring of day
Up rose our Host and roused us like a cock,
Gathering us together in a flock,
845 And off we rode at slightly faster pace
Than walking to St. Thomas' watering-place;
And there our Host drew up, began to ease
His horse, and said, "Now, listen if you please,
My lords! Remember what you promised me.
850 If evensong and matins will agree°
Let's see who shall be first to tell a tale.
And as I hope to drink good wine and ale
I'll be your judge. The rebel who disobeys,
However much the journey costs, he pays.
855 Now draw for cut and then we can depart;
The man who draws the shortest cut shall start."

850. if . . . agree: in other words, if you feel the same way in the evening (at evensong, or evening prayers) as you do in the morning (at matins, or morning prayers).

Pigskin binding by Doves Bindery for the Kelmscott *Chaucer* (1896).
Fitzwilliam Museum, University of Cambridge.

RESPONDING TO THE ILLUSTRATION: ABOUT THE ARTWORK

Victorian designer William Morris believed that industrialization had destroyed the beauty of hand-crafted items. He called for the return to ideals of medieval guilds, which valued the work of individual artisans. *The Works of Geoffrey Chaucer*, published by his Kelmscott Press in 1896, illustrated those ideals. The volume featured hand-made paper, elaborately designed borders, and a gothic type that was cut and cast by hand. The care Morris lavished on his edition of Chaucer revolutionized printing and made publishers dissatisfied with unattractive, poorly-made books.

? How does Malcolm X's transportation to Mecca differ from Chaucer's pilgrims' transportation to Canterbury? [Chaucer's pilgrims are on horseback; Malcolm X goes to Mecca by airplane and car.]

B. Expansion
An *ablution* is a washing or cleansing of the body as a religious ceremony of purification.

Making Meanings

First Thoughts

1. Responses will vary. Ask students to explain why they made their choices.

Reviewing the Text

a. April, at the Tabard Inn, to prepare for a pilgrimage.

b. Each pilgrim will tell two tales on the outbound journey, and two on the return journey. The pilgrim with the best tale gets a free dinner at the Tabard, courtesy of the other pilgrims.

c. Feudal system: Knight, Squire, Yeoman, Franklin, Plowman, Reeve, and Miller. Church: Prioress, Nun, Nun's three Priests, Monk, Friar, Cleric, Parson, Pardoner, and Summoner. City: Merchant, Serjeant at the Law, Haberdasher, Dyer, Carpenter, Weaver, Carpetmaker, Cook, Skipper, Doctor, Wife of Bath, and Manciple.

d. He will faithfully report what everyone says, but his readers should not fault him if some stories are ribald or offensive.

Shaping Interpretations

2. For example, the Knight's stained tunic indicates that he is unassuming and cares little for outward show. Other possibilities include the Pardoner, Squire, Monk, and Miller.

3. Students could analyze the satiric descriptions of the Prioress, Monk, Friar, Summoner, and Pardoner. Chaucer presents favorable pictures of the Oxford Cleric and the Parson (among Church representatives.)

4. Merchant: "know-it-all" experts in business; Franklin: the pleasure-loving habits of the lesser nobility; Doctor: the greed of the profession for gold; Miller: people who lack honesty in business dealings.

Connections
AN AUTOBIOGRAPHY

In this passage, Malcolm X describes his first visit to Mecca, the Muslim sacred city.

from The Autobiography of Malcolm X

Malcolm X, with Alex Haley

A Mecca, when we entered, seemed as ancient as time itself. Our car slowed through the winding streets, lined by shops on both sides and with buses, cars, and trucks, and tens of thousands of pilgrims from all over the earth were everywhere.

The car halted briefly at a place where a *Mutawaf*[1] was waiting for me. He wore the white skullcap and long nightshirt garb that I had seen at the airport. He was a short, dark-skinned Arab named Muhammad. He spoke no English whatever.

B We parked near the Great Mosque. We performed our ablution and entered. Pilgrims seemed to be on top of each other, there were so many, lying, sitting, sleeping, praying, walking.

My vocabulary cannot describe the new mosque that was being built around the Kaaba. I was thrilled to realize that it was only one of the tremendous rebuilding tasks under the direction of young Dr. Azzam, who had just been my host. The Great Mosque of Mecca, when it is finished, will surpass the architectural beauty of India's Taj Mahal.

Carrying my sandals, I followed the *Mutawaf.* Then I saw the Kaaba, a huge, black stone house in the middle of the Great Mosque. It was being circumambulated by thousands upon thousands of praying pilgrims, both sexes, and every size, shape, color, and race in the world. I knew the prayer to be uttered when the pilgrim's eyes first perceive the Kaaba. Translated, it is "O God, You are peace, and peace derives from You. So greet us, O Lord,

1. *Mutawaf:* guide for pilgrims visiting Mecca.

with peace." Upon entering the Mosque, the pilgrim should try to kiss the Kaaba if possible, but if the crowds prevent him getting that close, he touches it, and if the crowds prevent that, he raises his hand and cries out "Takbir!" ("God is great!") I could not get within yards. "Takbir!"

My feeling there in the House of God was a numbness. My *Mutawaf* led me in the crowd of praying, chanting pilgrims, moving seven times around the Kaaba. Some were bent and wizened with age; it was a sight that stamped itself on the brain. I saw incapacitated pilgrims being carried by others. Faces were enraptured in their faith. The seventh time around, I prayed two *Rak'a,* prostrating myself, my head on the floor. The first prostration, I prayed the Koran verse "Say He is God, the one and only"; the second prostration: "Say O you who are unbelievers, I worship not that which you worship. . . ."

As I prostrated, the *Mutawaf* fended pilgrims off to keep me from being trampled.

The *Mutawaf* and I next drank water from the well of Zem Zem. Then we ran between the two hills, Safa and Marwa, where Hajar wandered over the same earth searching for water for her child Ishmael.

Three separate times, after that, I visited the Great Mosque and circumambulated the Kaaba. The next day we set out after sunrise toward Mount Arafat, thousands of us, crying in unison: "Labbayka! Labbayka!" and "Allah Akbar!". . . Arriving about noon, we prayed and chanted from noon until sunset, and the *asr* (afternoon) and *Maghrib* (sunset) special prayers were performed.

Finally, we lifted our hands in prayer and thanksgiving, repeating Allah's words: "There is no God but Allah. He has no partner. His are authority and praise. Good emanates from Him, and He has power over all things."

Standing on Mount Arafat had concluded the essential rites of being a pilgrim to Mecca. No one who missed it could consider himself a pilgrim.

CONNECTING WITH *THE CANTERBURY TALES*

Ask the class to compare the pilgrimage Malcolm X describes to the one Chaucer narrates, prompting discussion with the following questions: Are pilgrimages a thing of the past? [No, obviously there are still some taking place.] What other pilgrimages might people make today? [People of many religions go to visit shrines or temples important to their faith; people also make nonreligious pilgrimages, such as visiting historic places or spots of particular beauty.] What is important about these rituals? [A renewal of mind, body, or spirit; perhaps even a chance for a vacation.]

MAKING MEANINGS

First Thoughts

1. If you were the thirty-first pilgrim, which of your fellow travelers would you choose to travel next to? Which would you definitely try to avoid? Whose story would you be most interested in hearing?

Shaping Interpretations

2. Chaucer is a master at using physical details—eyes, hair, complexion, body type, clothing—to reveal **character.** Tell about at least three pilgrims whose inner natures are revealed by their outer appearances.

3. Clearly, Chaucer satirizes the Church of his time. Show how this is true by analyzing two characters connected with the Church. What "good" Church people does Chaucer include to balance his satire?

4. What aspects of society does Chaucer **satirize** in his portrayals of the Merchant? the Franklin? the Doctor? the Miller?

5. Which pilgrims do you think Chaucer idealizes?

6. In describing the pilgrims, what do you think Chaucer as the pilgrim-narrator has revealed about his own personality, biases, and values?

Extending the Text

7. Which of the pilgrims' professions or trades have survived in society today? Which of Chaucer's character types can still be seen in

Reviewing the Text

a. When, where, and for what purposes do the pilgrims gather?

b. What plan, which becomes the basis of the frame story, does the Host propose to the pilgrims?

c. Place each pilgrim within one of these three groups that comprised medieval society: the feudal system (related to the land), the Church, and the city (merchants and professionals).

d. In your own words, explain the pilgrim-narrator's plea in lines 745–762.

airports or pulpits, farms or classrooms, city streets or small towns?

8. When would people from all walks of life today travel together in large groups for a common purpose? How do you think the pilgrimage described in *The Autobiography of Malcolm X* (page 128) is similar to, and different from, the journey that Chaucer's pilgrims undertake?

ELEMENTS OF LITERATURE

Imagery: The Revealing Detail

Chaucer is a master of **imagery,** language that appeals to the senses. Most images are visual, but imagery can also appeal to our senses of hearing, smell, taste, and touch. In a few vivid words, sometimes with a few added figures of speech, Chaucer has created a cast of characters as real to us today as the characters in the latest novel—more real, perhaps, because Chaucer's people exhibit all the essentials of human nature.

With twenty-nine pilgrims to introduce, Chaucer could not develop any character at length. He had to find a few well-chosen details to make immediate impressions. For example, Chaucer devotes only nine lines to the Cook, yet he found just one now-famous image to immortalize the Cook and his unfortunate appearance: The Cook has "an ulcer on his knee," an open sore caused either by a skin disease associated with a bad diet and poor hygiene or by an infectious or communicable disease. With this image in mind, would you be anxious to try the Cook's blancmange, even if it rated "with the best"? How does this detail make you feel about the Cook?

Chaucer also relied upon his readers' knowledge of physiognomy. Based on some of Aristotle's treatises, physiognomy compared varieties of people to animals and asserted that certain physical characteristics revealed one's personality type. Thus, when Chaucer's contemporaries read that the Wife of Bath had "gap-teeth, set widely, truth to say," they knew that the physiognomists believed that a gap between a woman's two front teeth indicated not only that she would travel far but also that she was bold and especially suited for love.

The table on page 130 lists a few physical characteristics and their corresponding physiognomic interpretations. Choose a pilgrim who exhibits each

5. The Parson, the Plowman, the Oxford Cleric, and the Knight.

6. Chaucer reveals himself as worldly, keenly observant of the appearances and motives of others, even-tempered and good-natured, and intensely curious. He values honesty, modesty, simplicity, and genuine piety. He dislikes hypocrisy and corruption.

Extending the Text

7. **(Synthesis)** Surviving occupations include prioress, nun, priest, monk, merchant, lawyer, haberdasher, dyer, carpenter, weaver, carpetmaker, cook, doctor, and miller. In some sense all of Chaucer's character types can still be seen, such as rogues, hypocrites, shrewd businesspeople, good soldiers, and book lovers.

8. **(Synthesis)** A religious or cultural event would most likely bring people together. Like Chaucer's pilgrims, modern pilgrims would vary greatly in occupation, temperament, and appearance. Today's transportation and topics of conversation would differ from those of Chaucer's pilgrims, and today's group would probably contain a racial mix.

Elements of Literature

Mini-Lesson: Imagery

Have students work in groups to find five images from the description of one of the pilgrims in the Prologue (give each group a different pilgrim, avoiding those with very short descriptions) and to identify the sense each of the images appeals to. Ask them to look for at least one image that is not visual. As students share their work, keep track of the senses referred to most often.

OPTIONS FOR TEACHING

STRATEGIES FOR INCLUSION

Special Needs Some students may not understand the difference between an image and a description. To help students make this distinction, ask them to review the following chart and to complete it by adding general descriptions and specific images from the Prologue.

General Description	Specific Image
Guadalupe is pretty.	Her eyes sparkle like diamonds.
Max is strong.	He breaks boards with his hands.

PROGRAM MANAGER

Application and Reinforcement For reinforcement of the elements of literature introduced in this lesson, see **Transparency 2.4** in the *Audiovisual Resources Binder.*

Possible Answers

- Ramlike appearance/strength: Miller is a man capable of powerful physical feats.
- Sowlike appearance/dirtiness: Miller is a man with little regard for social convention.
- Foxlike appearance/slyness: Miller is an expert at stealing grain.
- Goatlike quality/lechery: Pardoner bleats out love songs.
- Thin, fastidious type/bad temper, irritability: Reeve is choleric.
- Flaring or open nostrils/passion: Miller is a wrangler and a boaster.
- Pus-filled sores/lechery and drunkenness: Summoner is a drinker of strong wine.
- High forehead/intelligence, breeding: Prioress is cultured.
- White neck/loose or immoral person: Friar is corrupt.

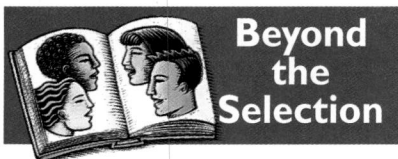

Beyond the Selection

Choices: Building Your Portfolio

1. **Writer's Notebook** Remind students to save their work. They may use it as prewriting for the Writer's Workshop on p. 185.
2. **Critical Writing** Review with students the block method and point-by-point method for organizing information.
3. **Art** Remind students that collages may also include small objects and textiles.

---

characteristic. How does the physiognomic interpretation reinforce what you already know about the character's nature?

Physical Characteristic	Physiognomic Interpretation
ramlike appearance	strength
sowlike appearance	dirtiness
foxlike appearance	slyness
goatlike qualities	lechery
thin, fastidious type	bad temper, irritability
flaring or open nostrils	passion
pus-filled sores	lechery and drunkenness
high forehead	intelligence, breeding
white neck	loose or immoral person

CHOICES: Building Your Portfolio

Writer's Notebook

1. Collecting Ideas for an Observational Essay

Chaucer masterfully chooses details to make his pilgrims come alive. You can do the same. Collect some concrete details about a person you want to describe—the bits of information that, when taken together, create a complete picture. If possible, spend some time observing the person as closely, but unobtrusively, as you can. Look closely at your subject, and try to observe enough detail to distinguish him or her from anyone else. Jot down notes about the person's

- appearance
- speech patterns
- mannerisms
- likes
- memorable words
- profession
- recreational activities
- special interests
- dislikes
- memorable moments

Save your work to use later in the Writer's Workshop on page 185.

Critical Writing
2. Two Memorable Travelers

Chaucer describes only two women at any length in the Prologue: the Wife of Bath and the Prioress. Compare and contrast these two travelers in a brief essay. Use a chart like the following one to gather and organize information for your essay.

Element	Wife of Bath	Prioress
Appearance and clothing		
Manner and personality		
Tastes		
Social position		
Life experiences		

At the end of your essay, tell where the types represented by the Wife of Bath and the Prioress might be found in contemporary life.

Art
3. A Canterbury Gallery

Chaucer uses words to create a picture of each pilgrim. Now it's your turn to go from words to pictures by creating a portrait of a pilgrim. Select one pilgrim, and draw an illustration of him or her. Or, create a collage showing what you find most memorable and important about the pilgrim. You might want to create a class display of your illustrations or collages.

OPTIONS FOR TEACHING

STRATEGIES FOR INCLUSION

English Language Development Before students attempt to write an essay for activity #1, have them practice writing short descriptions based on pictures you give them. First have them brainstorm lists of adjectives for physical appearance and for personality. Students might need help with the structures "He looks like _____." for describing resemblance to other people, and "He looks _____." for personality traits or emotions. Also review "He is _____." (tall, short, fat, thin) versus "He had _____." (brown hair, blue eyes).

Musical Have students choose music to accompany their portraits in activity #3. They might create original compositions or collages of musical clips to express the pilgrim's personality and physical traits using music.

The story in "The Pardoner's Tale" has roots that are old and widespread. Avarice (or greed) as the root of evil is a theme that appears in stories of many lands. Starting from the Latin saying *"Radix malorum est cupiditas,"* or "The love of money is the root of all evil," the Pardoner presents us with an *exemplum,* an anecdote or example inserted into a sermon to teach a moral lesson. As with every tale, Chaucer fits the story to the character of the storyteller.

Chaucer is a master of both **verbal** and **situational irony.** You use both types of irony all the time. You use verbal irony when you say one thing but mean another. For example, when a friend asks how you liked cleaning your room for three hours, you might reply, "It was a blast." Both of you know differently, of course. In situational irony, what actually happens is different from what you expect. You feel situational irony when it rains on the weather forecasters' picnic, or when the police officer's son turns out to be a criminal.

The Pardoner, from the Ellesmere manuscript, fol. 138r.

By permission of The Huntington Library, San Marino, California.

from The Pardoner's Tale

Geoffrey Chaucer

translated by **Nevill Coghill**

The Prologue

"But let me briefly make my purpose plain;
I preach for nothing but for greed of gain
And use the same old text, as bold as brass,
Radix malorum est cupiditas.°
5   And thus I preach against the very vice
I make my living out of—avarice.
And yet however guilty of that sin
Myself, with others I have power to win
Them from it, I can bring them to repent;
10   But that is not my principal intent.
Covetousness is both the root and stuff
Of all I preach. That ought to be enough.
"Well, then I give examples thick and fast
From bygone times, old stories from the past.
15   A yokel mind loves stories from of old,
Being the kind it can repeat and hold.
What! Do you think, as long as I can preach
And get their silver for the things I teach,

4. *Radix malorum est cupiditas* (ra′diks ma·lō′rum est kōō·pi′di·tas): Latin for "The love of money is the root of all evil" (1 Timothy 6:10).

WORDS TO OWN
avarice (av′ə·ris) *n.:* too great a desire for wealth.
covetousness (kuv′ət·əs·nis) *n.:* the quality of craving wealth or possessions.

GEOFFREY CHAUCER **131**

Into the Selection

Headnote: Background p. 131

Through the Selection

from The Pardoner's Tale pp. 131–138
Words to Own pp. 131–138
Making Meanings p. 139

Beyond the Selection

Choices: Building Your Portfolio p. 139

Into the Selection

Using THE HEADNOTE p. 131

Reading Focus
? Why might a story about avarice fit the Pardoner? [Possible answers: Because the Pardoner himself is greedy. Because he wants to persuade his listeners to be more inclined to part with their money.]

PROGRAM MANAGER

- **Planning Instruction** See Teaching Notes, *Teaching Resources A,* pp. 24–25, for information for this selection.
- **Instructional Support** See Graphic Organizer for Active Reading, *Teaching Resources A,* p. 40, for a Through the Selection activity.
- **Assessment** See Selection Test, *Test Booklet,* pp. 21–22.
- **Language Link** See Language Link, *Teaching Resources A,* pp. 41–42, and *Language and Writing Skills Worksheets,* pp. 31–32.
- **Reinforcement** Use the Words to Own worksheet in *Teaching Resources A,* p. 43.

Through the Selection

A. Reader's Response: First Thoughts
? Why might the Pardoner admit so directly that he preaches to make a personal profit? [Sample responses: He feels that all the pilgrims realize this already. He is carried away with his own cleverness in using this tale.]

Geoffrey Chaucer **T131**

A. Expansion

The seven deadly sins would bring spiritual death to the sinner's soul and put him or her in danger of eternal damnation unless the sinner confessed the sin and obtained a pardon from a pardoner. The seven deadly sins were pride, avarice, lust, anger, gluttony, envy, and sloth.

Which of these sins are referred to in the opening twelve lines of the story? [Gluttony, lust, and sloth.]

PORTFOLIO ASSESSMENT

Portfolio Assessment For help with self-assessment of reading skills, see the *Portfolio Management System,* pp. 48–49.

That I will live in poverty, from choice?
20 That's not the counsel of my inner voice!
No! Let me preach and beg from kirk° to kirk
And never do an honest job of work,
No, nor make baskets, like St. Paul, to gain
A livelihood. I do not preach in vain.
25 There's no apostle I would counterfeit;
I mean to have money, wool and cheese and wheat
Though it were given me by the poorest lad
Or poorest village widow, though she had
A string of starving children, all agape.
30 No, let me drink the liquor of the grape
And keep a jolly wench in every town!
   "But listen, gentlemen; to bring things down
To a conclusion, would you like a tale?
Now as I've drunk a draft of corn-ripe ale,
35 By God it stands to reason I can strike
On some good story that you all will like.
For though I am a wholly vicious man
Don't think I can't tell moral tales. I can!
Here's one I often preach when out for winning;
40 Now please be quiet. Here is the beginning."

21. kirk: Scottish for "church."

The Tale

In Flanders once there was a company
Of youngsters haunting vice and ribaldry,°
Riot and gambling, stews and public-houses
Where each with harp, guitar, or lute carouses,
45 Dancing and dicing day and night, and bold
To eat and drink far more than they can hold,
Doing thereby the devil sacrifice
Within that devil's temple of cursed vice,
Abominable in superfluity,
50 With oaths so damnable in blasphemy
That it's a grisly thing to hear them swear.
Our dear Lord's body they will rend and tear.° . . .
It's of three rioters I have to tell
Who, long before the morning service bell,
55 Were sitting in a tavern for a drink.
And as they sat, they heard the hand-bell clink
Before a coffin going to the grave;
One of them called the little tavern-knave
And said "Go and find out at once—look spry!—

42. ribaldry (rib′əl·drē): vulgar language or humor.

52. our . . . tear: Their oaths refer to "God's arms" and "God's blessed bones."

WORDS TO OWN
carouses (kə·rouz′ez) *v.*: drinks and celebrates noisily.
abominable (ə·bäm′ə·nə·bəl) *adj.*: disgusting; hateful.
superfluity (sōō′pər·flōō′ə·tē) *n.*: excess.
blasphemy (blas′fə·mē′) *n.*: mockery of God.

OPTIONS FOR TEACHING

STRATEGIES FOR INCLUSION

Logical-Mathematical Have students construct a flowchart showing the chain of events that lead to the rioters' deaths. Suggest that students fill in the initial box with "Old man sends rioters to tree to look for Death." Encourage students to compare their completed flow charts.

Special Needs Students may find the personification of Death at the beginning of the tale to be

confusing. Before students read, give them some more examples of personification, perhaps from a poem or a short story. Give pairs of students a familiar classroom or household object, and ask them to write a few sentences of personification to describe it. After they read, discuss why it is ironic to personify Death.

60 Whose corpse is in that coffin passing by;
And see you get the name correctly too."
"Sir," said the boy, "no need, I promise you;
Two hours before you came here I was told.
He was a friend of yours in days of old,
65 And suddenly, last night, the man was slain,
Upon his bench, face up, dead drunk again.
There came a privy° thief, they call him Death,
Who kills us all round here, and in a breath
He speared him through the heart, he never stirred.
70 And then Death went his way without a word.
He's killed a thousand in the present plague,
And, sir, it doesn't do to be too vague
If you should meet him; you had best be wary.
Be on your guard with such an adversary,
75 Be primed to meet him everywhere you go,
That's what my mother said. It's all I know."
   The publican° joined in with, "By St. Mary,
What the child says is right; you'd best be wary,
This very year he killed, in a large village
80 A mile away, man, woman, serf at tillage,°
Page in the household, children—all there were.
Yes, I imagine that he lives round there.
It's well to be prepared in these alarms,
He might do you dishonor." "Huh, God's arms!"
85 The rioter said, "Is he so fierce to meet?
I'll search for him, by Jesus, street by street.
God's blessed bones! I'll register a vow!
Here, chaps! The three of us together now,
Hold up your hands, like me, and we'll be brothers
90 In this affair, and each defend the others,
And we will kill this traitor Death, I say!
Away with him as he has made away
With all our friends. God's dignity! Tonight!"
   They made their bargain, swore with appetite,
95 These three, to live and die for one another
As brother-born might swear to his born brother.
And up they started in their drunken rage
And made towards this village which the page
And publican had spoken of before.
100 Many and grisly were the oaths they swore,
Tearing Christ's blessed body to a shred;
"If we can only catch him, Death is dead!"
   When they had gone not fully half a mile,
Just as they were about to cross a stile,°
105 They came upon a very poor old man
Who humbly greeted them and thus began,
"God look to you, my lords, and give you quiet!"
To which the proudest of these men of riot
Gave back the answer, "What, old fool? Give place!

---

67. privy (priv′ē): secretive; furtive.

77. publican: tavern keeper; from *public house,* an inn or tavern.

80. tillage: working the land.

104. stile: steps used for climbing over a wall.

B. Exploring the Historical Period

In the mid-fourteenth century, bubonic plague, called the Black Death, spread across Europe. Why would this be an especially appropriate setting for a story intended to make people repent? [Perhaps the pervasiveness of death in the story reminds listeners of their own deaths and the need to repent before death comes.]

C. Language Note: Oaths

The rioters take God's name in vain through common medieval oaths invoking the parts of Christ's body. As students read, ask them to identify other references to the rioters' profanity. [Examples include ll. 50, 87, 100.]

D. Reader's Response: Shaping Interpretations

? What motivates the rioters to attempt to kill Death? Is it essentially a humane motive or a prideful one? [Sample responses: The motive is humane in that they promise to defend each other against the traitor, Death. The motive is prideful because the first rioter boasts that Death does not seem fierce to him. They want vengeance rather than to prevent more death.]

E. Critical Reading: Drawing Conclusions

The old man has caused much disagreement among critics. A number believe that the old man himself is Death. Others say he is simply an old man looking for Death. Ask students to consider the old man carefully and to draw their own conclusions as to what he might symbolize.

INTEGRATING THE LANGUAGE ARTS

Strategic Reading Ask students to read the story in the following sections and to write a title or headline to summarize each section: Section One (ll. 53–102), Two (ll. 103–161), Three (ll. 162–199), Four (ll. 200–230), Five (ll. 231–274), Six (ll. 275–284).

Grammar To help students realize that verse is constructed with sentences, have students work in groups of three to find sentences of different lengths in "The Pardoner's Tale." For example, ask them to find a complete sentence shorter than a line, one exactly a line long, one that is two lines long, and one that is more than three lines long. Have them write these as prose sentences without division into lines and without capitals to begin the lines.

Writing: Story Have students work in pairs to try writing a story in heroic couplets (five stresses to the line, end rhymes in pairs). Suggest that they rewrite a familiar story: a children's story, a fairy tale, or a story of a personal experience. Have books of fairy tales, children's stories, and rhyming dictionaries available in the classroom.

A. Literary Element: Irony

? What is the situational irony in the attitudes of the rioters and the old man toward Death? [The old man is weary of life and would like to find the ease of death. In contrast, the rioters are so blinded by ease and self-indulgence that they search for death.] The theme of luxurious self-indulgence or riotous behavior in the face of death is also seen in Boccaccio's *Decameron*.

B. Reader's Response: Shaping Interpretations

Death is personified as a mother whose house is surrounded by a gate (the earth). Why might the old man refer to Death as his mother? [Sample responses: Death will be a nurturing relief to his suffering. He will feel comforted as if by a mother.]

C. Literary Element: Foreshadowing

? Do you think the old man adds "—if you should live till then" because he knows something that the rioters do not know? What other explanations for his comment can you think of? [Possible answers: He might be thinking that the rioters are so brash and reckless that they probably will not live long, or he might simply be observing that in this time of plague, people cannot count on living to old age.]

110 Why are you all wrapped up except your face?
Why live so long? Isn't it time to die?"
    The old, old fellow looked him in the eye
And said, "Because I never yet have found,
Though I have walked to India, searching round
115 Village and city on my pilgrimage,
One who would change his youth to have my age.
And so my age is mine and must be still
Upon me, for such time as God may will.
    "Not even Death, alas, will take my life;
120 So, like a wretched prisoner at strife
Within himself, I walk alone and wait
About the earth, which is my mother's gate,
Knock-knocking with my staff from night to noon
And crying, 'Mother, open to me soon!
125 Look at me, mother, won't you let me in?
See how I wither, flesh and blood and skin!
Alas! When will these bones be laid to rest?
Mother, I would exchange—for that were best—
The wardrobe in my chamber, standing there
130 So long, for yours! Aye, for a shirt of hair°
To wrap me in!' She has refused her grace,
Whence comes the <u>pallor</u> of my withered face.
    "But it dishonored you when you began
To speak so roughly, sir, to an old man,
135 Unless he had injured you in word or deed.
It says in holy writ, as you may read,
'Thou shalt rise up before the hoary° head
And honor it.' And therefore be it said,
'Do no more harm to an old man than you,
140 Being now young, would have another do
When you are old'—if you should live till then.
And so may God be with you, gentlemen,
For I must go whither I have to go."
    "By God," the gambler said, "you shan't do so,
145 You don't get off so easy, by St. John!
I heard you mention, just a moment gone,
A certain traitor Death who singles out
And kills the fine young fellows hereabout.
And you're his spy, by God! You wait a bit.
150 Say where he is or you shall pay for it,
By God and by the Holy Sacrament!
I say you've joined together by consent
To kill us younger folk, you thieving swine!"
    "Well, sirs," he said, "if it be your design
155 To find out Death, turn up this crooked way

130. shirt of hair: Coarse shirts of woven horsehair were worn as penance. Here, the old man refers to such a shirt used to wrap his body for burial.

137. hoary: white.

WORDS TO OWN
pallor (pal′ər) *n.:* paleness.

OPTIONS FOR TEACHING

Ranking Evil Have students work in groups of four to define evil and to rank the following actions from "The Pardoner's Tale" from most evil to least evil.

    Rioters drink at the tavern.
    Rioters use profanity.
    Rioters speak rudely to the old man.
    Rioters plan to take the gold that does not belong to them.

COOPERATIVE LEARNING

Two older rioters plan murder of youngest.
Youngest lies to pharmacist.
Youngest puts poison in wine.
Two older rioters stab the youngest.

One member should present the group's definition of evil. A second should defend the choice of the most evil action in relation to the definition. A third should defend the choice of least evil action in relation to the definition. The fourth should read the list and answer questions about the ordering of other actions.

Illustrating a Classic Have students work in six groups that are approximately equal in size. Give each group a section of "The Pardoner's Tale" to illustrate in comic-book fashion: 1: ll. 53–93, 2: 94–132, 3: 133–177, 4: 178–217, 5: 218–263, 6: 264–290. Allow the groups to devise their own designs and to divide duties among members, but require a written summary of each member's contribution to be handed in with the final illustrations. Have each group present its section of the tale to the rest of the class.

Towards that grove, I left him there today
Under a tree, and there you'll find him waiting.
He isn't one to hide for all your prating.
You see that oak? He won't be far to find.
160 And God protect you that redeemed mankind,
Aye, and amend you!" Thus that ancient man.
    At once the three young rioters began
To run, and reached the tree, and there they found
A pile of golden florins° on the ground,
165 New-coined, eight bushels of them as they thought.
No longer was it Death those fellows sought,
For they were all so thrilled to see the sight,
The florins were so beautiful and bright,
That down they sat beside the precious pile.
170 The wickedest spoke first after a while.
"Brothers," he said, "you listen to what I say.
I'm pretty sharp although I joke away.
It's clear that Fortune has bestowed this treasure
To let us live in jollity and pleasure.
175 Light come, light go! We'll spend it as we ought.
God's precious dignity! Who would have thought
This morning was to be our lucky day?
    "If one could only get the gold away,
Back to my house, or else to yours, perhaps—
180 For as you know, the gold is ours, chaps—
We'd all be at the top of fortune, hey?
But certainly it can't be done by day.
People would call us robbers—a strong gang,
So our own property would make us hang.
185 No, we must bring this treasure back by night
Some prudent way, and keep it out of sight.
And so as a solution I propose
We draw for lots and see the way it goes;
The one who draws the longest, lucky man,
190 Shall run to town as quickly as he can
To fetch us bread and wine—but keep things dark—
While two remain in hiding here to mark
Our heap of treasure. If there's no delay,

164. **florins:** coins worth twenty-
four pence. *Pence* is the British
plural of *penny*.

D. Critical Reading: Speculating
? The rioters assume that the gold
has been left by Fortune (another
personification). Is there any other
possible source of this treasure? [Pos-
sible answer: The old man said they
would find Death under the tree;
instead, they find gold. Gold reveals
greed, and greed leads to death.]

The Three Living, The Three Dead, from the
*Psalter and Prayer Book of Bonne of Luxem-
bourg, Duchess of Normandy* (14th century),
fol. 321v–322r. Grisaille, color, gilt, and
brown ink on vellum (4 15/16″ × 3 9/16″).
French, Paris.

The Metropolitan Museum of Art, New York.
The Cloisters Collection. 1969 (69.86).

GEOFFREY CHAUCER 135

**A. Reader's Response:
Connecting with the Text**

? Do you know of any stories where the youngest person is separated from the older ones? [Sample responses: "The Three Feathers" and "The Three Brothers" are examples, as is the Biblical story of Joseph.] In many tales, the younger brother is not respected by the other brothers but turns out to be both kinder and more skilled. What does this lead you to expect of the youngest of the rioters? [Sample responses: He may turn out to be a better person than the other two. He may turn out to be worse.]

B. Critical Reading: Predicting
Ask students to predict what they think will happen next. [Responses will vary. Some might predict that the youngest rioter will disclose their secret in town. Others might say that the remaining rioters will take the gold when the youngest one leaves.]

C. Critical Reading: Making Connections

? All three of the rioters make frequent references to religion, some as if their lives are lived in a religious context. How do their references to religion connect them with the Pardoner? [Both the Pardoner and the rioters live within the context of religion without having their behavior affected positively by religion.]

D. Expansion
Here the Pardoner describes the consequences of sin. The young man has already fallen from grace into sin because of his drunkenness. As a result, God allows the Devil to lure him further. According to this theology, God does not cause evil but allows human beings to be tempted by it.

When night comes down we'll carry it away,
195 All three of us, wherever we have planned."
He gathered lots and hid them in his hand
Bidding them draw for where the luck should fall.
(A) It fell upon the youngest of them all,
And off he ran at once towards the town.
200 As soon as he had gone the first sat down
And thus began a parley with the other:
"You know that you can trust me as a brother;
Now let me tell you where your profit lies;
You know our friend has gone to get supplies
(B) 205 And here's a lot of gold that is to be
Divided equally among us three.
Nevertheless, if I could shape things thus
So that we shared it out—the two of us—
Wouldn't you take it as a friendly act?"
210 "But how?" the other said. "He knows the fact
That all the gold was left with me and you;
What can we tell him? What are we to do?"
"Is it a bargain," said the first, "or no?
For I can tell you in a word or so
215 What's to be done to bring the thing about."
"Trust me," the other said, "you needn't doubt
My word. I won't betray you, I'll be true."
"Well," said his friend, "you see that we are two,
And two are twice as powerful as one.
220 Now look; when he comes back, get up in fun
To have a wrestle; then, as you attack,
I'll up and put my dagger through his back
While you and he are struggling, as in game;
Then draw your dagger too and do the same.
225 Then all this money will be ours to spend,
Divided equally of course, dear friend.
Then we can gratify our lusts and fill
The day with dicing at our own sweet will."
Thus these two miscreants° agreed to slay
230 The third and youngest, as you heard me say.
The youngest, as he ran towards the town,
Kept turning over, rolling up and down
Within his heart the beauty of those bright
New florins, saying, "Lord, to think I might
235 Have all that treasure to myself alone!
(C) Could there be anyone beneath the throne
Of God so happy as I then should be?"
(D) And so the Fiend, our common enemy,
Was given power to put it in his thought
240 That there was always poison to be bought,
And that with poison he could kill his friends.
To men in such a state the Devil sends
Thoughts of this kind, and has a full permission

Death with his spear, from *The Pardoner's Tale*. MS Douce 322, fol. 19v.

The Bodleian Library, Oxford.

229. miscreants (mis′krē·ənts): criminals; literally, "unbelievers."

OPTIONS FOR
TEACHING

**CROSSING THE
CURRICULUM**

Social Studies Have students stage a trial for the youngest murderer as if he recovers from his wounds; he survives but is accused of the murder of his two friends. Select a jury, a defense attorney, a prosecuting attorney, and several witnesses: the old man, the pharmacist, the publican, and the mothers of the older two rioters. Ask students not involved in the performance of the trial to be reporters. Ask them to write news stories about the trial and to read these aloud as a culminating activity.

PROBLEM SOLVING/CRITICAL THINKING

Dealing with a Windfall If the rioters in "The Pardoner's Tale" had found only a little bit of money, they might have stayed friends and stayed alive. Ask students to work in groups of three to decide how much money they could find to share with two friends without problems: problems within each person, problems among the friends, or problems between the friends and the rest of society. Have them decide on an amount, work out how the money would be distributed, and determine how the money could be used.

To lure them on to sorrow and perdition;°
245 For this young man was utterly content
To kill them both and never to repent.
     And on he ran, he had no thought to tarry,
Came to the town, found an apothecary°
And said, "Sell me some poison if you will,
250 I have a lot of rats I want to kill
And there's a polecat too about my yard
That takes my chickens and it hits me hard;
But I'll get even, as is only right,
With vermin that destroy a man by night." **E**
255   The chemist answered, "I've a preparation
Which you shall have, and by my soul's salvation
If any living creature eat or drink
A mouthful, ere° he has the time to think,
Though he took less than makes a grain of wheat,
260 You'll see him fall down dying at your feet;
Yes, die he must, and in so short a while
You'd hardly have the time to walk a mile,
The poison is so strong, you understand."
     This cursed fellow grabbed into his hand
265 The box of poison and away he ran
Into a neighboring street, and found a man
Who lent him three large bottles. He withdrew
And deftly poured the poison into two.
He kept the third one clean, as well he might,
270 For his own drink, meaning to work all night
Stacking the gold and carrying it away.
And when this rioter, this devil's clay, **F**
Had filled his bottles up with wine, all three,
Back to rejoin his comrades sauntered he.
275   Why make a sermon of it? Why waste breath?
Exactly in the way they'd planned his death
They fell on him and slew him, two to one.
Then said the first of them when this was done,
"Now for a drink. Sit down and let's be merry,
280 For later on there'll be the corpse to bury."
And, as it happened, reaching for a sup,
He took a bottle full of poison up
And drank; and his companion, nothing loth,°
Drank from it also, and they perished both.
285   There is, in Avicenna's° long relation
Concerning poison and its operation,
Trust me, no ghastlier section to transcend
What these two wretches suffered at their end.

WORDS TO OWN
sauntered (sôn′tərd) v.: strolled.
transcend (tran·send′) v.: to exceed; surpass.

244. **perdition** (pər·dish′ən): damnation.

248. **apothecary** (ə·päth′ə·ker′ē): druggist. Formerly, apothecaries prescribed drugs.

258. **ere:** before.

283. **loth** (lōth): reluctant; unwilling; alternate spelling of *loath.*

285. **Avicenna's** (av′i·sen′ə): Avicenna (980–1037), a famous Arabic philosopher and doctor, wrote several medical books.

E. Literary Element: Irony
? What is ironic about the reason the young man gives for buying the poison? [He wants it for "vermin that destroy a man by night." Ironically, the "vermin" that he plans to kill are planning to "destroy a man"—him.]

F. Literary Element: Metaphor
? Why does the Pardoner compare the young rioter to clay? What qualities of clay are also applicable to the rioter? [He is compared to clay because he is being molded by the Devil. He is, like clay, changeable, easily manipulated, and without inherent inner form.]

ASSESSMENT TOOLS

Check Test: Questions and Answers
1. What vice does the Pardoner always preach against? [Avarice, greed.]
2. What sin does the Pardoner admit he is guilty of? [Avarice, greed.]
3. For whom are the three rioters looking? [Death.]
4. Why do they want to wait before they take the gold away? [In daylight they might arouse suspicion.]
5. How do they eventually find what they were looking for? [They kill one another in their efforts to get more gold.] ☞

A. Critical Reading: Analyzing Character

? How do these lines add insight into the characters of the Pardoner and the Knight? [Possible responses: The awkward way the Pardoner deals with the Host suggests that he might not be as successful in his sale of pardons as he pretends; the Knight seems to function as a superior who intervenes among his inferiors to invoke order.]

Making Meanings

First Thoughts

1. Although many students will react negatively to the Pardoner, some may find him amusing. Ask students to tie their response to the text.

Reviewing the Text

a. He frankly admits he is corrupt and greedy.

b. They want to kill him.

c. Under a nearby tree; with disrespect and scorn.

d. The rioters decide that the youngest should go to town for food and drink while the other two stay with the treasure until nightfall when they can carry it away. The two rioters left behind decide to murder the youngest; the youngest meanwhile forms a plan to kill the other two with poisoned wine. When the youngest returns, the other two kill him. Then, they drink the poisoned wine and die.

e. The Host refuses to buy a pardon or to kiss the Pardoner's relics. The Knight patches up the quarrel.

Shaping Interpretations

2. The knave calls Death a "privy thief," and the publican says that Death probably lives near the village where many people have died. The rioters are intrigued and decide, ironically, to "kill" Death, indicating their foolishness.

3. He may symbolize death.

4. Ironically, this tale of greed is told by the greedy Pardoner; in the tale, "sworn brothers" should protect, rather than kill, each other. The rioters do find Death under the tree through their greed for gold: their plots backfire and lead to their destruction.

Thus these two murderers received their due,
290 So did the treacherous young poisoner too. . . .

"One thing I should have mentioned in my tale,
Dear people. I've some relics in my bale
And pardons too, as full and fine, I hope,
As any in England, given me by the Pope.
295 If there be one among you that is willing
To have my absolution° for a shilling°
Devoutly given, come! and do not harden
Your hearts but kneel in humbleness for pardon;
Or else, receive my pardon as we go.
300 You can renew it every town or so
Always provided that you still renew
Each time, and in good money, what is due.
It is an honor to you to have found
A pardoner with his credentials sound
305 Who can absolve you as you ply the spur
In any accident that may occur.
For instance—we are all at Fortune's beck°—
Your horse may throw you down and break your neck.
What a security it is to all
310 To have me here among you and at call
With pardon for the lowly and the great
When soul leaves body for the future state!
And I advise our Host here to begin,
The most enveloped of you all in sin.
315 Come forward, Host, you shall be the first to pay,
And kiss my holy relics right away.
Only a groat.° Come on, unbuckle your purse!"
    "No, no," said he, "not I, and may the curse
Of Christ descend upon me if I do! . . ."

320 The Pardoner said nothing, not a word;
He was so angry that he couldn't speak.
"Well," said our Host, "if you're for showing pique,
I'll joke no more, not with an angry man."
    The worthy Knight immediately began,
325 Seeing the fun was getting rather rough,
And said, "No more, we've all had quite enough.
Now, Master Pardoner, perk up, look cheerly!
And you, Sir Host, whom I esteem so dearly,
I beg of you to kiss the Pardoner.
330   "Come, Pardoner, draw nearer, my dear sir.
Let's laugh again and keep the ball in play."
They kissed, and we continued on our way.

296. **shilling:** coin worth twelve pence.

307. **beck:** summons; in other words, subject to Fortune's will.

317. **groat:** silver coin worth four pence.

WORDS TO OWN
absolution (ab′sə·lōō′shən) *n.:* forgiveness.

---

138 THE MIDDLE AGES

OPTIONS FOR TEACHING

Ongoing Assessment Students can enjoy "The Pardoner's Tale" on several levels: (1) as a moral tale warning against greed, (2) as an ironic tale commenting on human nature, (3) as a piece of evidence in understanding the complex personality and worldview of the Pardoner, or as a part of a larger picture of human life constructed by Chaucer. Ask students to write briefly, individually or in groups, about each of these levels. They

ASSESSMENT TOOLS

should answer at each level the question "How does this story work as _____?" Assess each answer on a five-point scale.
1=Exceptional understanding of how the story works on this level
2=Excellent understanding
3=Adequate understanding
4=Limited understanding
5=Minimal understanding

MAKING MEANINGS

First Thoughts

1. How did you respond to the Pardoner's tale? How did you respond to the fact that it was told by a man of the Pardoner's character?

Shaping Interpretations

2. How do the tavern knave and the publican **personify** Death? What does the rioters' response to the description tell you?

3. What do you think the poor, old man may **symbolize**?

4. Irony is a discrepancy between expectations and reality. How many layers of **irony** can you identify in this story?

5. Why is it ironic that the Pardoner preaches a story with this particular moral? How would you account for the psychology of the Pardoner: Is he truly evil, just drunk, or so used to cheating that he does it automatically?

6. What do you think Chaucer is **satirizing** in the Pardoner's tale?

7. What moral does the Pardoner want us to draw from his tale? What moral do you think Chaucer wants you to draw from the Pardoner's tale?

Extending the Text

8. Do people with the Pardoner's ethics and tricks still exist today—in any field of life? Explain.

Reviewing the Text

a. How does the Pardoner describe his own character and morals in his Prologue?

b. According to the Pardoner's tale, why are the three rioters looking for Death?

c. Where does the old man tell the three rioters to look for Death? How do they treat him?

d. Describe the rioters' plan for the gold and how it proves fatal to all three men.

e. Why do the Pardoner and the Host quarrel at the end of the tale? Who patches up their quarrel?

9. How would the Pardoner fill in the following personality profile?

Name: _____
Profession: _____
Last Book I Read: _____
Latest Accomplishment: _____
Why I Do What I Do: _____
Future Goals: _____
Quotation I Like Best: _____

CHOICES:
Building Your Portfolio

Writer's Notebook

WORK IN PROGRESS

1. Collecting Ideas for an Observational Essay

Chaucer creates vivid portraits by using sensory details—for example, describing the Pardoner's locks, or hair, with "Thinly they fell, like rat-tails, one by one." Think about the person you want to describe, and write several short paragraphs describing the person's physical characteristics. (Refer to the notes you took on page 105.) Be specific and descriptive, searching for the words that will help the reader see or hear or even smell the person and feel his or her presence in the room. Then take each observed detail, and make it more precise. For example, perhaps you noted that your subject has "light hair." How could you be more descriptive? You could describe the hair as "blond with brown roots." Save your work to use later in the Writer's Workshop on page 185.

Drama / Pantomime

2. Hamming It Up

Working with a partner or a small group, present a dramatization or a pantomime of "The Pardoner's Tale." To dramatize, write speeches for each character and for a narrator who can fill in the story line. For a pantomime, have one person read Chaucer's text while the others act it out without words.

5. The Pardoner himself points out that he makes his living through avarice, the very sin he preaches against. Any explanation of his behavior should account for the contrast between his frankness before he tells the tale and his deceit afterward.

6. Greed and pride—both of which are embodied in the young men and somewhat in the Pardoner himself. He also satirizes clerics who use their offices to deceive the very people they should serve.

7. Perhaps his moral is that greed can lead to death. The moral of the Pardoner's tale might be that crooks and hypocrites sometimes are disguised as honest, even holy, people.

Extending the Text

8. **(Synthesis)** Students may refer to portrayals of tricksters and con artists in films and literature as well as to real people. Some examples include: Nanabushu from Navajo myth; Loki from Norse myth; the Artful Dodger from Dickens.

9. **(Synthesis)** Refer students to the Prologue for specific details of the Pardoner's personality.

Beyond the Selection

Choices: Building Your Portfolio

1. **Writer's Notebook** Remind students to save their work. They may use it as prewriting for the Writer's Workshop on p. 185.

2. **Drama/Pantomine** Suggest that students review the text closely for clues to the expression characters might have in their voices or on their faces.

PORTFOLIO ASSESSMENT

Choices: Assessment Criteria For help in evaluating these Choices assignments, see the criteria in the *Portfolio Management System*, p. 78.

STRATEGIES FOR INCLUSION

Linguistic Have pairs of students exchange their paragraphs in activity #1. Tell each student to create more specific wording that could replace any general descriptions in their partner's paragraphs. For example, if the partner has the phrase "big smile," the alternatives could be "radiant smile," "enigmatic smile," or "forced smile." After each person has written alternatives for at least five details, have him or her give the alternatives to his or her partner.

Musical For activity #2 have students add music to their dramatizations of "The Pardoner's Tale." Students might select background music appropriate to each section of the story or select songs which could be sung by the characters at emotionally powerful moments in the story.

Into the Selection

Using THE HEADNOTE p. 140

Reading Focus

Ask students what the Wife of Bath might say women want in a marriage.

No one on the road to Canterbury is more real than the Wife of Bath (a married woman from the city of Bath, west of London). She is Chaucer's most vibrant and irrepressible character. Having outlived five husbands (and possibly looking for a sixth on this pilgrimage), she is witty, intelligent, opinionated, and sensual. The tale she tells belongs to the "marriage group," several tales that explore what men and women want and ought to do in marriage.

from The Wife of Bath's Tale

Geoffrey Chaucer
translated by **Nevill Coghill**

The Wife of Bath, from the Ellesmere manuscript, fol. 72r.

By permission of The Huntington Library, San Marino, California.

The Prologue

The Pardoner started up, and thereupon
"Madam," he said, "by God and by St. John,
That's noble preaching no one could surpass!
I was about to take a wife; alas!
5   Am I to buy it on my flesh so dear?
There'll be no marrying for me this year!"

    "You wait," she said, "my story's not begun.
You'll taste another brew before I've done;
You'll find it doesn't taste as good as ale;
10 And when I've finished telling you my tale
Of tribulation in the married life
In which I've been an expert as a wife,
That is to say, myself have been the whip.
So please yourself whether you want to sip
15 At that same cask of marriage I shall broach.
Be cautious before making the approach,
For I'll give instances, and more than ten.
And those who won't be warned by other men,
By other men shall suffer their correction,
20 So Ptolemy° has said, in this connection.
You read his *Almagest;*° you'll find it there."
    "Madam, I put it to you as a prayer,"
The Pardoner said, "go on as you began!
Tell us your tale, spare not for any man.
25 Instruct us younger men in your technique."
"Gladly," she said, "if you will let me speak,
But still I hope the company won't reprove me
Though I should speak as fantasy may move me,
And please don't be offended at my views;
30 They're really only offered to amuse." . . .

20. Ptolemy (täl′ə·mē) (A.D. 100?–165?): ancient geographer, astronomer, and mathematician from Alexandria, Egypt.
21. *Almagest:* word meaning "the greatest"; another title for Ptolemy's major work, *Mathematical Composition,* in which he argued that the earth is the center of the universe, a view held in Europe until 1543.

PROGRAM MANAGER

- **Planning Instruction** See Teaching Notes, *Teaching Resources A,* pp. 25–26, for additional information .
- **Instructional Support** See Graphic Organizer for Active Reading, *Teaching Resources A,* p. 44, for a Through the Selection activity.
- **Assessment** See Selection Test, *Test Booklet,* pp. 23–24.
- **Language Link** See Language Link, *Teaching Resources A,* pp. 46–47, and *Language and Writing Skills Worksheets,* pp. 180–181.
- **Reinforcement** Use the Words to Own worksheet in *Teaching Resources A,* p. 45.

The Tale

When good King Arthur ruled in ancient days
(A king that every Briton loves to praise)
This was a land brim-full of fairy folk.
The Elf-Queen and her courtiers joined and broke
35 Their elfin dance on many a green mead,°
Or so was the opinion once, I read,
Hundreds of years ago, in days of yore.
But no one now sees fairies any more.
For now the saintly charity and prayer
40 Of holy friars seem to have purged the air;
They search the countryside through field and stream
As thick as motes° that speckle a sun-beam,
Blessing the halls, the chambers, kitchens, bowers,
Cities and boroughs, castles, courts and towers,
45 Thorpes,° barns and stables, outhouses and dairies,
And that's the reason why there are no fairies.
Wherever there was wont° to walk an elf
To-day there walks the holy friar himself
As evening falls or when the daylight springs,
50 Saying his matins° and his holy things,
Walking his limit round from town to town.
Women can now go safely up and down
By every bush or under every tree;
There is no other incubus° but he,
55 So there is really no one else to hurt you
And he will do no more than take your virtue.
    Now it so happened, I began to say,
Long, long ago in good King Arthur's day,
There was a knight who was a lusty liver.
60 One day as he came riding from the river
He saw a maiden walking all forlorn
Ahead of him, alone as she was born.
And of that maiden, spite of all she said,
By very force he took her maidenhead.°
65   This act of violence made such a stir,
So much petitioning to the king for her,
That he condemned the knight to lose his head
By course of law. He was as good as dead
(It seems that then the statutes took that view)
70 But that the queen, and other ladies too,
Implored the king to exercise his grace
So ceaselessly, he gave the queen the case
And granted her his life, and she could choose

---

35. **mead:** meadow.

42. **motes:** dust particles.

45. **thorpes:** villages.

47. **wont** (wänt): accustomed.

50. **matins** (mat′′nz): morning prayers.

54. **incubus** (in′kyōō·bəs): evil spirit believed to descend on a sleeping woman and make her pregnant.

64. **maidenhead:** virginity.

WORDS TO OWN
implored (im·plôrd′) v.: begged.

A. Expansion
Students should realize that "The Wife of Bath's Tale" probably precedes "The Pardoner's Tale" in Chaucer's ordering. The Pardoner responds at the beginning of "The Wife of Bath's Tale" to comments made by the Wife of Bath about wanting a husband who is both a debtor and a slave.

B. Literary Element: Metaphor
? Why might the Wife of Bath compare her version of marriage to a drink? [Possible answers: The Pardoner is drinking ale; the Wife of Bath says she will give him something different in her tale; perhaps she is implying that she will give him something to sober him up.]

C. Critical Reading: Drawing Conclusions
? What is the Wife of Bath's opinion of replacing fairies with friars? [Possible answers: She says that women are safer from spirits than they used to be, but she adds that the friars will dishonor women. This is a condemnation of the friars who, even more than other people, are expected to be virtuous.]

D. Expansion
In the chivalric tradition, violence toward women was not tolerated, and perpetrators were dealt with harshly.

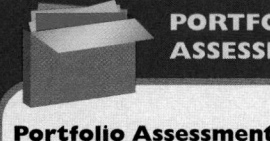

PORTFOLIO ASSESSMENT

Portfolio Assessment For help with self- and teacher assessment of reading skills, see the *Portfolio Management System,* pp. 43, 54–55.

WORDS TO OWN

The following vocabulary words are defined in the Words to Own at the bottom of the pupil's page.

implored p. 141	prowess p. 146
concede p. 142	temporal p. 147
extort p. 142	lineage p. 147
void p. 143	suffices p. 149
bequest p. 146	pestilence p. 149

A. Reader's Response: Connecting with the Text

? What other stories do you know where a character must solve a riddle to save his or her life? [Sample responses: the tale of Rumpelstiltskin; the myth of Oedipus.]

B. Critical Reading: Drawing Conclusions

? Why is the knight unable to find the answer to the riddle even though he asks many women? [Perhaps there is no right answer for women in general because each woman is an individual.]

C. Readers' Response: Shaping Interpretations

Chaucer has the Wife of Bath break off into a long digression at this point. Here Chaucer is interested not in preserving the integrity of the tale but in accurately depicting the way the Wife of Bath's mind works. Why do you think she temporarily loses track of her story at this point? [Sample responses: She is more interested in the things women want than in the story. Or perhaps she wants to create some suspense.]

D. Reader's Response: Connecting with the Text

The Wife of Bath criticizes women by saying they are hypocritical. They want to do as they please but want to appear virtuous. Does her criticism surprise you? Explain. [Sample responses: No, she seems frank and evenhanded in her judgment. Or yes, it is surprising that she acknowledges that women have any shortcomings.]

Whether to show him mercy or refuse.
75   The queen returned him thanks with all her might,
And then she sent a summons to the knight
At her convenience, and expressed her will:
"You stand, for such is the position still,
In no way certain of your life," said she,
80 "Yet you shall live if you can answer me:
What is the thing that women most desire?
Beware the axe and say as I require.

  "If you can't answer on the moment, though,
I will concede you this: You are to go
85 A twelvemonth and a day to seek and learn
Sufficient answer, then you shall return.
I shall take gages° from you to extort
Surrender of your body to the court."
  Sad was the knight and sorrowfully sighed,
90 But there! All other choices were denied,
And in the end he chose to go away
And to return after a year and day
Armed with such answer as there might be sent
To him by God. He took his leave and went.
95   He knocked at every house, searched every place,
Yes, anywhere that offered hope of grace.
What could it be that women wanted most?
But all the same he never touched a coast,
Country, or town in which there seemed to be
100 Any two people willing to agree.
  Some said that women wanted wealth and treasure,
"Honor," said some, some "Jollity and pleasure,"
Some "Gorgeous clothes" and others "Fun in bed,"
"To be oft widowed and remarried," said
105 Others again, and some that what most mattered
Was that we should be cosseted° and flattered.
That's very near the truth, it seems to me;
A man can win us best with flattery.
To dance attendance on us, make a fuss,
110 Ensnares us all, the best and worst of us.
  Some say the things we most desire are these:
Freedom to do exactly as we please,
With no one to reprove our faults and lies,
Rather to have one call us good and wise.
115 Truly there's not a woman in ten score°
Who has a fault, and someone rubs the sore,
But she will kick if what he says is true;

A scene from Virgil's *Aeneid*
(15th century). MS 493, fol. 74v.

Dijon Library, Dijon, France.

87. gages: pledges.

106. cosseted (käs′it·id): pampered.

115. ten score: two hundred. A score is twenty.

WORDS TO OWN
concede (kən·sēd′) *v.:* grant.
extort (eks·tôrt′) *v.:* to get by threats or violence.

---

142 THE MIDDLE AGES

You try it out and you will find so too.
However vicious we may be within
120 We like to be thought wise and void of sin.
Others assert we women find it sweet
When we are thought dependable, discreet
And secret, firm of purpose and controlled,
Never betraying things that we are told.
125 But that's not worth the handle of a rake;
Women conceal a thing? For Heaven's sake!
Remember Midas?° Will you hear the tale?
    Among some other little things, now stale,
Ovid° relates that under his long hair
130 The unhappy Midas grew a splendid pair
Of ass's ears; as subtly as he might,
He kept his foul deformity from sight;
Save for his wife, there was not one that knew.
He loved her best, and trusted in her too.
135 He begged her not to tell a living creature
That he possessed so horrible a feature.
And she—she swore, were all the world to win,
She would not do such villainy and sin
As saddle her husband with so foul a name;
140 Besides to speak would be to share the shame.
Nevertheless she thought she would have died
Keeping this secret bottled up inside;
It seemed to swell her heart and she, no doubt,
Thought it was on the point of bursting out.
145   Fearing to speak of it to woman or man,
Down to a reedy marsh she quickly ran
And reached the sedge.° Her heart was all on fire
And, as a bittern° bumbles in the mire,
She whispered to the water, near the ground,
150 "Betray me not, O water, with thy sound!
To thee alone I tell it: It appears
My husband has a pair of ass's ears!
Ah! My heart's well again, the secret's out!
I could no longer keep it, not a doubt."
155 And so you see, although we may hold fast
A little while, it must come out at last,
We can't keep secrets; as for Midas, well,
Read Ovid for his story;° he will tell.
    This knight that I am telling you about
160 Perceived at last he never would find out
What it could be that women loved the best.
Faint was the soul within his sorrowful breast,

127. Midas: mythical king. Everything he touched turned to gold.

129. Ovid (43 B.C.–c. A.D. 17): Roman poet. Ovid's *Metamorphoses*, a collection of tales, includes one version of the Midas story.

147. sedge: grasslike plant.
148. bittern: type of wading bird.

158. read . . . story: In Ovid's version, it is Midas's barber, not his wife, who tells the secret to a hole in the ground. Reeds grow up in the hole and whisper the secret whenever the wind rustles them.

WORDS TO OWN
void (void) *adj.:* empty.

E. Literary Element: Irony
? What is the rhetorical purpose of the Wife of Bath's story about Midas? [It seems to support her claim that women cannot keep secrets, but as the footnote points out, Ovid's version has a man, not a woman, give up the secret, making the reference ironic.]

F. Cultural Connections
? Why does the knight return to the court when he can only expect to be put to death there? [In the chivalric code, a knight must keep his word even if it means his death.]

INTEGRATING THE LANGUAGE ARTS

Strategic Reading Before they read the old woman's rebuttal to the knight's complaints, have students fill in the second column of the following chart with predictions of her arguments. Ask students to consider what the old woman might say to convince the knight that each of these in turn is not a legitimate reason for rejection. Then, as students read each rebuttal in Chaucer's text, have them summarize in the third column the arguments presented.

Knight's Complaints	My Prediction	Actual Outcome
Old and ugly		
Poor		
Of low birth		

Writing: Letter Have students imagine that they belong to the group of pilgrims on the road to Canterbury, and they have just heard the Wife of Bath's story. In a letter to a friend at home, ask them to record their impressions of the Wife of Bath, of her beliefs, and of her tale.

**A. Reader's Response:
Challenging the Text**

The "four and twenty ladies" never reappear. Does this seem an irrelevant detail? How would the story be different if the knight simply noticed an old woman sitting at the edge of the wood? [Sample responses: The disappearance of the ladies gives us a clue that something magical is happening. The old woman's ugliness is magnified by the contrast with the beautiful vision that disappears.]

B. Critical Reading: Predicting

? What do you think the old woman will ask of the knight?

[Answers will vary. Perhaps she will ask him for something that he least wants to give; since she seems to be a magical character, she might know what this would be.]

C. Language Note: Diction

? Why is the word *crooned* a better choice that *whispered* or *said*?

[Possible answers: *Crooned* implies a certain intimacy and suggests that the crone has romantic interest in the knight.]

As home he went, he dared no longer stay;
His year was up and now it was the day.
165   As he rode home in a dejected mood
Suddenly, at the margin of a wood,
He saw a dance upon the leafy floor
Of four and twenty ladies, nay, and more.
Eagerly he approached, in hope to learn
170   Some words of wisdom ere he should return;
But lo! Before he came to where they were,
Dancers and dance all vanished into air!
There wasn't a living creature to be seen
Save one old woman crouched upon the green.
175   A fouler-looking creature I suppose
Could scarcely be imagined. She arose
And said, "Sir knight, there's no way on from here.
Tell me what you are looking for, my dear,
For peradventure° that were best for you;
180   We old, old women know a thing or two."
       "Dear Mother," said the knight, "alack the day!
I am as good as dead if I can't say
What thing it is that women most desire;
If you could tell me I would pay your hire."
185   "Give me your hand," she said, "and swear to do
Whatever I shall next require of you
—If so to do should lie within your might—
And you shall know the answer before night."
"Upon my honor," he answered, "I agree."
190   "Then," said the crone, "I dare to guarantee
Your life is safe; I shall make good my claim.
Upon my life the queen will say the same.
Show me the very proudest of them all
In costly coverchief or jeweled caul°
195   That dare say no to what I have to teach.
Let us go forward without further speech."
And then she crooned her gospel in his ear
And told him to be glad and not to fear.
       They came to court. This knight, in full array,
200   Stood forth and said, "O Queen, I've kept my day
And kept my word and have my answer ready."
       There sat the noble matrons and the heady
Young girls, and widows too, that have the grace
Of wisdom, all assembled in that place,
205   And there the queen herself was throned to hear
And judge his answer. Then the knight drew near
And silence was commanded through the hall.
       The queen gave order he should tell them all
What thing it was that women wanted most.
210   He stood not silent like a beast or post,
But gave his answer with the ringing word

Medieval knight on horseback.

179. peradventure: perhaps.

194. coverchief . . . caul (kôl): women's headgear. The coverchief covered the entire head; the caul, a small, netted cap, was sometimes ornamented.

OPTIONS FOR TEACHING

COOPERATIVE LEARNING

Creative Teamwork In the story, the knight criticizes his wife's appearance, poverty, and social standing, but the wife manages to make each shortcoming seem either an irrelevant quality or an enhancement. Have students work in groups of three to choose another reason that an individual might reject his or her mate. Possibilities include sloppiness, not being able to cook, lack of education, and poor table manners. (Steer students away from sensitive areas such as height and weight.) Then, have each group compose a refutation in defense of its chosen shortcoming. They might continue with heroic couplets, write a speech or essay, or compose a song. Have groups share their completed products.

Of a man's voice and the assembly heard:
   "My liege° and lady, in general," said he,
   "A woman wants the self-same sovereignty°
215 Over her husband as over her lover,
   And master him; he must not be above her.
   That is your greatest wish, whether you kill
   Or spare me; please yourself. I wait your will."
      In all the court not one that shook her head
220 Or contradicted what the knight had said;
   Maid, wife, and widow cried, "He's saved his life!"
      And on the word up started the old wife,
   The one the knight saw sitting on the green,
   And cried, "Your mercy, sovereign lady queen!
225 Before the court disperses, do me right!
   'Twas I who taught this answer to the knight,
   For which he swore, and pledged his honor to it,
   That the first thing I asked of him he'd do it,
   So far as it should lie within his might.
230 Before this court I ask you then, sir knight,
   To keep your word and take me for your wife;
   For well you know that I have saved your life.
   If this be false, deny it on your sword!"
      "Alas!" he said, "Old lady, by the Lord
235 I know indeed that such was my behest,°
   But for God's love think of a new request,
   Take all my goods, but leave my body free."
   "A curse on us," she said, "if I agree!
   I may be foul, I may be poor and old,
240 Yet will not choose to be, for all the gold
   That's bedded in the earth or lies above,
   Less than your wife, nay, than your very love!"
      "My love?" said he. "By heaven, my damnation!
   Alas that any of my race and station
245 Should ever make so foul a misalliance!"
   Yet in the end his pleading and defiance
   All went for nothing, he was forced to wed.
   He takes his ancient wife and goes to bed.
      Now peradventure some may well suspect
250 A lack of care in me since I neglect
   To tell of the rejoicings and display
   Made at the feast upon their wedding-day.
   I have but a short answer to let fall;
   I say there was no joy or feast at all,
255 Nothing but heaviness of heart and sorrow.
   He married her in private on the morrow
   And all day long stayed hidden like an owl,
   It was such torture that his wife looked foul.
      Great was the anguish churning in his head
260 When he and she were piloted to bed;

213. **liege** (lēj): lord.
214. **sovereignty** (säv′rən·tē): power.

235. **behest:** command; order.

COOPERATIVE LEARNING

Instant Analysis Have students treat the old woman's speech on gentleness, poverty, and age as if it were a presidential address. Ask them to do a TV news "instant analysis" of a part of the speech. Have students work in six groups, each group working on one of the following sections: ll. 285–308, 309–334, 335–352, 353–366, 367–382, 383–392. In each presentation, have one student report the old woman's actual words, another summarize, another give comments on highlights and key phrases, and another give comments on the possible effect on the knight. Although each member has an individual role in the presentation, all should collaborate during the preparation stages.

CLASSROOM MANAGEMENT

Entry-Exit Slips Ask students to turn in half sheets of paper either at the beginning or at the end of each class. The papers should include what the student has learned that day (or the day before), what is unclear, and what new ideas the student is thinking about. You can skim these slips quickly to monitor and adjust your instruction. Besides helping you keep in touch with each student, this activity gives students more responsibility for their own learning.

A. Critical Reading: Analyzing Character

? What does the knight's reaction to the old woman reveal about his character? [Possible answers: He is egotistical and shallow. He places too much emphasis on rank and appearance.]

B. Exploring the Historical Period

The sermon of more than one hundred lines that the crone delivers to her husband on their wedding night begins here and does little to advance the plot. Its inclusion in the tale illustrates how Chaucer was affected by the time and place in which he lived: the concept of "gentleness" was central to fourteenth-century courtly life. Etymologically, *gentle* comes from the Old French word for "noble birth." Current use of the word to describe refined, mild behavior is derived from its use in describing behavior thought to be appropriate to the nobility.

C. Literary Element: Allusion

? What is the purpose of alluding to Dante? [To emphasize and give importance to the point that virtuous conduct—gentleness—is not the product of one's possessions and social rank. Instead, it is a gift from God to those who will nurture it.]

He wallowed° back and forth in desperate style.
His ancient wife lay smiling all the while;
At last she said "Bless us! Is this, my dear,
265 How knights and wives get on together here?
Are these the laws of good King Arthur's house?
Are knights of his all so contemptuous?
I am your own beloved and your wife,
And I am she, indeed, that saved your life;
And certainly I never did you wrong.
270 Then why, this first of nights, so sad a song?
You're carrying on as if you were half-witted
Say, for God's love, what sin have I committed?
I'll put things right if you will tell me how."
      "Put right?" he cried. "That never can be now!
275 Nothing can ever be put right again!
You're old, and so abominably plain,
So poor to start with, so low-bred to follow;
It's little wonder if I twist and wallow!
God, that my heart would burst within my breast!"
280   "Is that," said she, "the cause of your unrest?"
      "Yes, certainly," he said, "and can you wonder?"
      "I could set right what you suppose a blunder,
That's if I cared to, in a day or two,
If I were shown more courtesy by you.
285 Just now," she said, "you spoke of gentle birth,
Such as descends from ancient wealth and worth.
If that's the claim you make for gentlemen
Such arrogance is hardly worth a hen.
Whoever loves to work for virtuous ends,
290 Public and private, and who most intends
To do what deeds of gentleness he can,
Take him to be the greatest gentleman.
Christ wills we take our gentleness from Him,
Not from a wealth of ancestry long dim,
295 Though they bequeath their whole establishment
By which we claim to be of high descent.
Our fathers cannot make us a <u>bequest</u>
Of all those virtues that became them best
And earned for them the name of gentlemen,
300 But bade us follow them as best we can.
      "Thus the wise poet of the Florentines,
Dante° by name, has written in these lines,
For such is the opinion Dante launches:
'Seldom arises by these slender branches
305 <u>Prowess</u> of men, for it is God, no less,

261. **wallowed:** tossed and turned.

Opening page of the *Tale of the Wife of Bath* (c. 1898) from the Kelmscott *Chaucer*.

Spencer Collection. New York Public Library. Astor, Lenox, and Tilden Foundations.

302. **Dante:** Dante Alighieri (dän′tā a′lə·gyer′ē) (1265–1321), Italian poet who wrote *The Divine Comedy*.

WORDS TO OWN

bequest (bē·kwest′) *n.*: gift left by means of a will.
prowess (prou′is) *n.*: outstanding ability.

OPTIONS FOR TEACHING

CROSSING THE CURRICULUM

Social Studies Have students work in groups of four to act as political advisers to the old woman in her run for state senate. Ask them to design a campaign for her based on the ideas in her rebuttal to the knight. The campaign plan should include a short list of reasons why she would be a good state senator, a campaign slogan, an outline of groups to whom she should especially appeal, a list of appearances to make, and a speech in which the duties of a senator are explained and the old woman's qualifications given. (Students might want to choose a name for her to use in the campaign.) Along with each group's completed plan, students should include a written description of each member's contributions.

Drama The wedding of the knight and his bride is not a festive affair, and by the end of the tale, both are changed individuals. Have the class plan a second wedding for the knight after the couple's transformation. Have a group of students make invitations, researching the information required on a wedding invitation and trying to incorporate as many words from Middle English as possible. Ask another group to research possible medieval feast foods and to prepare a menu. Have another group write wedding vows, again using as many Middle English words as can be substituted. Finally, have several students prepare toasts to the couple in heroic couplets.

Wills us to claim of Him our gentleness.'
For of our parents nothing can we claim
Save temporal things, and these may hurt and maim. **D**
    "But everyone knows this as well as I;
310 For if gentility were implanted by
The natural course of lineage down the line,
Public or private, could it cease to shine
In doing the fair work of gentle deed?
No vice or villainy could then bear seed.
315   "Take fire and carry it to the darkest house
Between this kingdom and the Caucasus,°
And shut the doors on it and leave it there,
It will burn on, and it will burn as fair
As if ten thousand men were there to see,
320 For fire will keep its nature and degree,
I can assure you, sir, until it dies.
    "But gentleness, as you will recognize,
Is not annexed in nature to possessions.
Men fail in living up to their professions;°
325 But fire never ceases to be fire.
God knows you'll often find, if you inquire,
Some lording° full of villainy and shame.
If you would be esteemed for the mere name
Of having been by birth a gentleman
330 And stemming from some virtuous, noble clan,
And do not live yourself by gentle deed
Or take your father's noble code and creed,
You are no gentleman, though duke or earl.
Vice and bad manners are what make a churl.°
335   "Gentility is only the renown
For bounty that your fathers handed down,
Quite foreign to your person, not your own;
Gentility must come from God alone.
That we are gentle comes to us by grace
340 And by no means is it bequeathed with place.
    "Reflect how noble (says Valerius)°
Was Tullius surnamed Hostilius,°
Who rose from poverty to nobleness.
And read Boethius,° Seneca° no less,
345 Thus they express themselves and are agreed:
'Gentle is he that does a gentle deed.'
And therefore, my dear husband, I conclude
That even if my ancestors were rude, **G**
Yet God on high—and so I hope He will—
350 Can grant me grace to live in virtue still,

WORDS TO OWN
temporal (tem′pə·rəl) *adj.*: limited to this world; not spiritual.
lineage (lin′ē·ij) *n.*: ancestry.

316. Caucasus (kô′kə·səs): mountain range in southeastern Europe, between the Black Sea and the Caspian Sea; in other words, far away.

324. professions: promises.

327. lording: alternate form of *lord.*

334. churl: ill-mannered person.

341. Valerius (və·lir′ē·əs): first century A.D. Roman writer who compiled historical anecdotes that public speakers could use.
342. Tullius (tul′ē·əs) **surnamed Hostilius** (hos·til′ē·əs): legendary king of Rome who rose from humble origins.
344. Boethius (bō·ē′thē·əs) (c. A.D. 480–c. 524): Roman philosopher. In his *Consolation of Philosophy,* he argues that rank is no guarantee of honorable conduct. **Seneca** (sen′i·kə) (c. 4 B.C.–A.D. 65): Roman philosopher whose works were popular in the Middle Ages.

GEOFFREY CHAUCER 147

D. Critical Reading: Making Inferences

? How could "temporal" things "hurt and maim"? [Possible answer: Too many possessions may spoil a person or distract a person from virtue.]

E. Critical Reading: Drawing Conclusions

? How does the existence of villains in the families of nobility support the argument that gentility and virtue cannot be inherited? [If gentility and virtue could be inherited, the children of genteel parents would always be virtuous.]

F. Critical Reading: Analyzing Details

? To what is the Wife of Bath comparing fire in this passage? [Fire is contrasted to gentleness (gentility) and to men. Fire will burn anywhere; gentility will not grow automatically in men, of noble birth or otherwise. Fire is constant; men are not.]

G. Critical Reading: Analyzing Character

? Applying the old woman's definition of gentility to her own actions, does she qualify as a gentle person? Explain. [Answers will vary. Some students might say that although she tricks the knight into marrying her, she saves his life and frets about his unhappiness.]

CROSSING THE CURRICULUM

Mathematics Have students conduct a survey of at least thirty people on the question "What do women want most?" Have students design a standard questionnaire that asks for gender and age and asks respondents which of the answers the knight collected (ll. 101–124, 214–216) is closest to the truth. As a class, tabulate the results, dividing responses by age groups (ten-year spans) and by gender. Have groups of students report the following results:

1. Bar graph of responses comparing total men and total women.
2. Bar graphs of responses within age groups, ignoring gender differences.
3. Bar graph comparing men under twenty-five with men over twenty-five.
4. Bar graph comparing women under twenty-five with women over twenty-five.

Lead students in an analysis of the differences they discover. ☞

**A. Reader's Response:
Challenging the Text**

? Do you agree with the Wife of
Bath's praise of poverty? Explain.
[Sample responses: Yes, wealth is measured in spirit, not material goods. No,
it is unrealistic; poverty is misery.]

B. Literary Element: Metaphor

? How is poverty "a glass by which
to see one's truest friends"?
[Possible answer: People who have
a great deal of money may have some
doubts about the motives of their
devoted friends.]

**C. Critical Reading: Finding
Cause and Effect**

? What is the cause-and-effect relationship here between "filth and
old age" and "chastity"? [She says filth
(ugliness) and old age cause a woman
to be undesirable to men; undesirabil-
ity causes a wife to have few opportunities to engage in unfaithfulness.]

A gentlewoman only when beginning
To live in virtue and to shrink from sinning.
    "As for my poverty which you reprove,
Almighty God Himself in whom we move,
355 Believe, and have our being, chose a life
Of poverty, and every man or wife
Nay, every child can see our Heavenly King
Would never stoop to choose a shameful thing.
No shame in poverty if the heart is gay,
360 As Seneca and all the learned say.
He who accepts his poverty unhurt
I'd say is rich although he lacked a shirt.
But truly poor are they who whine and fret
And covet what they cannot hope to get.
365 And he that, having nothing, covets not,
Is rich, though you may think he is a sot.°
    "True poverty can find a song to sing.
Juvenal° says a pleasant little thing:
'The poor can dance and sing in the relief
370 Of having nothing that will tempt a thief.'
Though it be hateful, poverty is good,
A great incentive to a livelihood,
And a great help to our capacity
For wisdom, if accepted patiently.
375 Poverty is, though wanting in estate,
A kind of wealth that none calumniate.°
Poverty often, when the heart is lowly,
Brings one to God and teaches what is holy,
Gives knowledge of oneself and even lends
380 A glass by which to see one's truest friends.
And since it's no offense, let me be plain;
Do not rebuke my poverty again.
    "Lastly you taxed me, sir, with being old.
Yet even if you never had been told
385 By ancient books, you gentlemen engage
Yourselves in honor to respect old age.
To call an old man 'father' shows good breeding,
And this could be supported from my reading.
    "You say I'm old and fouler than a fen.°
390 You need not fear to be a cuckold,° then.
Filth and old age, I'm sure you will agree,
Are powerful wardens over chastity.
Nevertheless, well knowing your delights,
I shall fulfill your worldly appetites.
395   "You have two choices; which one will you try?
To have me old and ugly till I die,
But still a loyal, true, and humble wife
That never will displease you all her life,
Or would you rather I were young and pretty

366. sot: fool.

368. Juvenal (jōō′və·n'l)
(c. A.D. 60–c. 140): Roman satirist.

376. calumniate (kə·lum′nē·āt′):
slander.

389. fen: swamp.
390. cuckold (kuk′əld): man
whose wife has been unfaithful
to him.

**OPTIONS FOR
TEACHING**

PROBLEM SOLVING/CRITICAL THINKING

Learning Respect The knight in the
Wife of Bath's story takes a long and
enchanted route to learn respect for
women. Divide the class into groups of
four to create a list of additional ways
to learn respect for other people. Ask

students to discuss how they have learned to
respect others and what they would suggest as
appropriate rehabilitation for those who do not
seem to respect others. Students can use the following chart to analyze specific situations and
solutions.

No-Respect Situation	How to Help Learn Respect	Result

400 And chance your arm what happens in a city
     Where friends will visit you because of me,
     Yes, and in other places too, maybe.
     Which would you have? The choice is all your own."
          The knight thought long, and with a piteous groan
405 At last he said, with all the care in life,
     "My lady and my love, my dearest wife,
     I leave the matter to your wise decision.
     You make the choice yourself, for the provision
     Of what may be agreeable and rich
410 In honor to us both, I don't care which;
     Whatever pleases you <u>suffices</u> me."
          "And have I won the mastery?" said she,
     "Since I'm to choose and rule as I think fit?"
     "Certainly, wife," he answered her, "that's it."
415 "Kiss me," she cried. "No quarrels! On my oath
     And word of honor, you shall find me both,
     That is, both fair and faithful as a wife;
     May I go howling mad and take my life
     Unless I prove to be as good and true
420 As ever wife was since the world was new!
     And if to-morrow when the sun's above
     I seem less fair than any lady-love,
     Than any queen or empress east or west,
     Do with my life and death as you think best.
425 Cast up the curtain, husband. Look at me!"
          And when indeed the knight had looked to see,
     Lo, she was young and lovely, rich in charms.
     In ecstasy he caught her in his arms,
     His heart went bathing in a bath of blisses **E**
430 And melted in a hundred thousand kisses,
     And she responded in the fullest measure
     With all that could delight or give him pleasure.
          So they lived ever after to the end
     In perfect bliss; and may Christ Jesus send
435 Us husbands meek and young and fresh in bed,
     And grace to overbid them when we wed.
     And—Jesu hear my prayer!—cut short the lives
     Of those who won't be governed by their wives; **F**
     And all old, angry niggards of their pence,°
440 God send them soon a very <u>pestilence</u>!

A man on horseback, from *The Devonshire Hunting Tapestries* (detail). Arras 1425–50.

Victoria and Albert Museum, London.

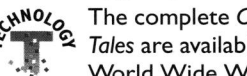
439. niggards (nig'erdz) **of their pence:** stingy persons.

WORDS TO OWN
suffices (sə·fis'iz) *v.*: satisfies.
pestilence (pes'tə·ləns) *n.*: plague.

D. Literary Element: Character

? Why is the knight considered a dynamic character? [In the course of the tale, he has changed from an arrogant, shallow man to a humbler, more considerate man.] What do you think causes the change? [Answers will vary. Perhaps his wife's lecture affected him, or he gains new respect for her with her allusion to her magical powers.]

E. Exploring the Historical Period

? Why might this unusual, and beautiful, metaphor have been even more striking in Chaucer's time? [Given the infrequency of bathing, the idea of taking a bath probably had more connotations of luxury and fewer connotations of routine.]

F. Literary Element: Irony

? What is ironic about this humorous passage? [She is requesting of Jesus rather drastic punishment for husbands who are bossy and stingy.]

Technology Tip

TECHNOLOGY The complete *Canterbury Tales* are available via the World Wide Web at **http://etext.virginia.edu/CT.html**. *You may want to preview any Internet activity that you suggest to students. Because these resources are sometimes public forums, their content can be unpredictable.*

ASSESSMENT TOOLS

Check Test: Questions and Answers
1. Who assigns the knight his task? [The queen.]
2. How long does the knight have to complete his task? [A year and a day.]
3. Why does he leave the road before he sees the old woman? [He sees twenty-four dancing maidens.]
4. When does the old woman tell the knight what she wants from him? [After he has given the answer to the queen.]

5. What physical change does the old woman make at the end of the story? [She becomes young and beautiful.]

Self-Reflection To help students listen critically and to provide feedback, have listeners note, for each presentation, the following information.
- One thing learned from this presentation
- One thing enjoyed about this presentation
- One question about this presentation

A. Literary Element: Simile

? How does this simile function in the poem? [It reinforces the image of green veins, and brings to mind the many lines crossing the hands.]

B. Reader's Response: Shaping Interpretations

? How did the grandmother's hands leave her behind? [Sample responses: Though the grandmother is worn by time, her hands, which appear to embody her spirit, struggle to continue their tasks. Perhaps she has died, but the tasks she has performed with her hands linger as a reminder of her.]

Making Meanings

First Thoughts

1. Responses will vary but should be consistent with the Wife of Bath's character. She would probably say women want power and control over their lives and that men would want the same.

Reviewing the Text:

a. Crime: taking a woman's virginity by force. Original sentence: death. Second sentence: also death, unless he can find out what women most desire.

b. She will tell him the answer to the riddle if he promises to do the next thing she asks.

c. She demands that he marry her. He responds by pleading for her to ask anything else.

d. She gives him the choice of having her ugly and thus being confident of her fidelity or of having her beautiful and taking his chances on her faithfulness. He says that he wants her to decide.

Shaping Interpretations

2. It is ironic that a man whose interactions with women were all based on what *he* wanted should have to save his life by finding out what *they* want.

3. Old and ugly: she says this will guarantee her faithfulness; poor: she says that poverty is a virtue; of low birth: she says that gentility is based on how one acts, not on who one's parents are.

Worn Out

My grandmother's hands
looked like leaves
carved where her veins
stood green.

Her strong fingers were rough.
Her skin gripped her bones,
crinkled and wrinkled,
textured and worn.

Those hands worked.
Ten fingers knitted scarves for the winter cold,
gardened strawberries and snapdragons
and cooked meals on her old stove
while a blue flame swooned
below the burner's glow.
Her hands scrubbed.
Her calloused hands scrubbed
dusty memories off the walls.

Her hands toiled and twisted
the stubborn lid off the jar of homemade
raspberry jam.
Her fingers clenched the stubborn lid
until her face would seize her bones and cling
while the veins in her hands would jump and string,
beneath the worn folds of her skin.

Her bones showed from the inside out
pointing up from beneath, supporting her skin
and revealing the mechanics inside.

Her hands left her behind,
protesting time and clutching will.

—Stephanie Bailey
Taylorsville High School
Salt Lake City, Utah

CONNECTING WITH "THE WIFE OF BATH'S TALE"

How is this poem, "Worn Out," appropriate to read in conjuction with the tale told by the Wife of Bath? [This poem conveys the virtues of an elderly woman and gives the reader a sense of compassion for her; this approach may give readers a new perspective on the virtues of the kind, wise, but withered woman encountered by the knight.]

MAKING MEANINGS

First Thoughts

1. What did you think of the Wife of Bath's opinion about what women want most? If she were asked what men want most, how do you suppose she would respond?

Shaping Interpretations

2. The knight's quest is to find out what women want. What **irony** do you see in this?

3. In lines 276–278, the knight moans about having the old woman for his wife. How does she respond to each objection he raises?

4. How does the knight's response to the choice given him by the old woman show that he's learned his lesson about what women want?

5. What opinions does the Wife of Bath express in the tale? What do all her opinions and her tale itself tell you about her character?

6. Look at the various things the Wife of Bath, in her tale, says people think women want. What do you think of those proposed answers?

Extending the Text

7. What do you think contemporary men and women think about what the other wants most out of life or from a relationship? Do you think they would agree, or do they have different wishes and expectations of one another?

8. How would the Wife of Bath fit into contemporary society? What social trends would she support or reject?

Reviewing the Text

a. What were the knight's crime, his original sentence, and his second sentence?

b. What bargain do the knight and the old woman strike?

c. What payment for her help does the old woman demand, and what is the knight's response?

d. What final choice does the old woman offer the knight at the end of the tale? What is his response?

Challenging the Text

9. Consider the way this story begins and ends. How does the knight get into trouble, and how do things turn out for him? Does the story satisfy or trouble you, and are there any elements that bother you?

ELEMENTS OF LITERATURE

Couplets: Sound and Sense

Chaucer's favorite rhyme scheme in *The Canterbury Tales* was the **couplet,** two consecutive lines of poetry that rhyme: "When good King Arthur ruled in ancient *days* / (A king that every Briton loves to *praise*)." (When he was growing old, Chaucer complained that his faculty of rhyming was leaving him, which may account for the reason he never finished *The Canterbury Tales*.) Nevill Coghill, the translator of the tales used here, followed Chaucer's rhyme scheme, though he did not always use Chaucer's own rhyming words.

1. Read aloud parts of the Prologue to see how the couplets animate the survey of the pilgrims. Find some rhymes that are humorous.

2. Find what you think are these words in the Middle English version of the Prologue (page 106): *flower, breath, eye, courage,* and *condition*. The pronunciation of these words has changed since the Middle Ages. According to the words they're rhymed with in the Prologue, how would each of these words have been pronounced in Chaucer's day?

3. Identify at least two couplets in the Wife's tale that use **half rhymes** (also called **approximate rhymes**), words that share similar but not identical sounds.

4. Compare the couplets Coghill uses in his translation of the first forty-two lines of the Prologue with the couplets Chaucer uses in his original. Then try to translate these original lines of the Prologue yourself, perhaps using more of Chaucer's original couplets.

---

4. He lets her have the power, realizing she must choose for herself who she wants to be.

5. She says that friars are too plentiful (expressed indirectly), women do not like their faults pointed out to them, women cannot keep secrets, the ideal husband is "meek and young," and women should have power in their marriages. Students may say she is assertive, lustful, and self-aware.

6. Responses will vary. Students might list the proposed answers in order of importance.

Extending the Text

7. **(Analysis)** Responses will vary. Many students will probably agree that mutual expectations are common in contemporary relationships.

8. **(Synthesis)** Possible answers: As an assertive woman, she might be active and visible in support of contemporary women's concerns.

Challenging the Text

9. **(Evaluation)** Possible answers: The change in the knight's attitude is too sudden; it should be traced as it changes. Perhaps the old woman should make the knight suffer instead of giving him bliss.

Elements of Literature
Answers

1. Both masculine (stressed final syllable: *bat/sat*) and feminine rhymes (stress on syllable prior to final syllable: *middle/fiddle*) are used in the Prologue. Explain that feminine rhymes are usually more humorous than masculine rhymes.

2. *flower/flour* rhymed with *licour*. *breath/breeth* rhymed with *heeth*. *eye/eye* rhymed with *melodye*. *courage/corage* rhymed with *pilgrymages*. *condition/condicioun* rhymed with *resoun*.

3. Half rhymes in "The Wife of Bath's Tale" include *gentlemen/we can* (ll. 299 and 300), *capacity/patiently* (ll. 373 and 374).

4. Students might try translating the couplets from Chaucer's original without preserving the rhyme. Ask what is gained (more accuracy) and what is lost (music of the verse) with this type of translation.

PROGRAM MANAGER

Application and Reinforcement For reinforcement of the elements of literature introduced in this lesson, see Transparency 2.5 *in the Audiovisual Resources Binder.*

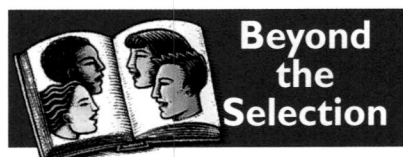

Beyond the Selection

Choices: Building Your Portfolio

1. **Writer's Notebook** Remind students to save their work. They may use it as prewriting for the Writer's Workshop on p. 185.

2. **Critical Writing** Suggest that students create a two-column chart labeled "What sort of person?" on the left and "How do I know?" on the right. In the left column, students should put only *impressions* they have of the character. In the right column, they should cite evidence from the text to support their impressions.

3. **Creative Writing** Tell students they may follow Chaucer's pattern: first, describe the time of year and the characters' reasons for traveling; next, describe the meeting between the other travelers; then, describe each of the travelers.

4. **Visual Art** Good colored pencils or watercolor will give a more authentic look to this project than markers. Students can use the modern versions of illuminated letters.

5. **Dramatization** Allow students to read excerpts or summaries rather than entire tales. Guide students' choices carefully; remember that "The Miller's Tale" and "The Reeve's Tale" are very bawdy and that several other tales, including "The Merchant's Tale" and "The Franklin's Tale," have some sexual content.

6. **Research: Art/Music** Students may find that these artistic interpretations are most valuable when they shed some light on a facet of a pilgrim's character that students might have otherwise overlooked.

CHOICES: Building Your Portfolio

Writer's Notebook

1. Collecting Ideas for an Observational Essay

WORK IN PROGRESS

Metaphoric comparisons suggest a lot in very few words. If you describe someone with the words "he's a pig," your friends will probably have a fairly clear idea of what at least some of his characteristics might be and how you feel about him. Try thinking about the person you're describing metaphorically. What does he remind you of ("He was a dust storm entering the room.")? What do her features call to mind ("Her hairdo was a yard full of autumn leaves, raked up hastily and piled in the gutter.")? Let your imagination spin freely—you can edit later. Try describing your character in figurative language, and save your notes for later use in the Writer's Workshop on page 185.

Critical Writing

2. Characters to Probe

Whom do you find more interesting, the Pardoner or the Wife of Bath? In an essay of several paragraphs, explain your response to one of these pilgrims and then analyze the person's character. Before you write, review the methods of characterization presented on page 105. Use specific details from the text to support your analysis.

Creative Writing

3. Inventing a Frame

Write a prologue to your own frame story. Begin by deciding what kind of journey will bring your characters together. Will they meet in a bus station? at an airport? on a summer visit? Using this frame, list four characters who will travel together on the journey you've outlined. Describe each character from tip to toe, including details of appearance that suggest each character's traits. (Notice how the student writer of "Worn Out" on page 150 describes her grandmother.) Refer to the notes you took for the Quickwrite (page 105) before you started reading the Prologue—in fact, you may even want to include this person in your frame story. In a prologue, introduce your characters. You may either write in prose or try your hand at rhymed couplets like Chaucer's. Devote at least six lines to each character. Share your prologue, either by reading it aloud or by including it in a class collection of story frames.

Visual Art

4. Illuminating Imagery

The illuminated manuscript was a popular art form of the Middle Ages. Its pages contained highly decorated initial letters or words or miniature pictures such as those shown on pages 106 and 167. Select a passage from either "The Wife of Bath's Tale" or "The Pardoner's Tale," and write it out with illuminations.

Dramatization

5. Bringing a Pilgrim to Life

Choose a pilgrim other than the Wife of Bath or the Pardoner. Dress as the character, and present a reading of his or her tale to your classmates. At the end of your reading, explain why you chose this character and why you think the tale was suited to its teller.

Research: Art/Music

6. Re-Seeing Chaucer

Artists William Blake (1757–1827) and William Morris (1834–1896) created their own versions of Chaucer's pilgrims, and Nevill Coghill, a translator of Chaucer, also wrote song lyrics for the musical *Canterbury Tales* (1968). Find copies of these works and evaluate them. Do they adhere to the original *Tales* or offer a new interpretation?

152 THE MIDDLE AGES

STRATEGIES FOR INCLUSION

Special Needs Students may need a modern reference to be able to write the prologue in activity #3. Compare the prologue to the introductory segment at the beginning of the television series *Star Trek*. Remind students that it sets the stage for the journey that the crew will take together. Extend the comparison by asking them to describe, orally, a few of the characters. This gives students a model in addition to Chaucer for their prologues.

PORTFOLIO ASSESSMENT

Choices: Assessment Criteria For help in evaluating these Choices assignments, see the criteria in the *Portfolio Management System*, pp. 79–80.

Analyzing Word Parts

When a word is unfamiliar or difficult to understand, you can often discover its meaning by examining the word's parts. These parts make up the **structure** of the word, which may consist of a **root**, a **prefix**, and a **suffix**.

Roots: Words are built upon a base, or root, which contains the core of the word's meaning. Many words in the English language have Latin or Greek roots. The root *scribe* or *script,* for instance, comes from Latin and means "to write." Notice that the following words contain this root and that all relate to writing: *inscription, manuscript, postscript, prescribe, scribble, scripture.*

Prefixes: Affixes are word parts that can be attached to a root to modify its meaning. A **prefix** is an affix that is placed *before* the root; it can have a general meaning or several meanings. For instance, *a–,* derived from Old English, means "in, on, of, up, to," as in "ashore." The Latin and Latin-French meaning for *a–* is "from, off, away," as in "averse," and the Greek meaning is "lacking, without," as in "amoral." Here are some examples:

Prefixes	Meanings	Examples
a–, ab–, abs–	from, off, away	abide, absolution
be–	around, about	befall, bequest
co–, col–, com–, con–, cor–, syn–	with, together	concede, synchronize
ex–, e–, ef–	away from, out	exhale, extort
en–, em–, in–, super–	in, into, within; over, above, extra	encourage; superfluity, supervisor

By adding a prefix to a root, a new word is formed with the combined meanings of both. Notice that the word *submarine* is composed of the prefix *sub,* meaning "below," and the root *marine,* meaning "water." Prefixes with different spellings but the same meaning often originate in different languages. For example, in the following sentence, the prefixes *quint* (Latin) and *penta* (Greek) both mean "five": The brass *quint*et played in a concert hall that was shaped like a *penta*gon.

Suffixes: A **suffix** is an affix that is placed *after* the root to modify the root's meaning. The plurals of nouns, tenses of verbs, and comparative and superlative forms of adjectives and adverbs are created by suffixes. For example, a present-tense regular verb, such as *saunter,* changes to the past tense by adding *–ed.* A singular noun, such as *stature,* changes to the plural form by adding *–s.* A word's meaning and its part of speech can be changed by other suffixes, sometimes called **derivational suffixes**. The word *glory* is a noun. Notice what happens with the addition of various suffixes: glori-*fication* (noun); glori*fy* (verb); glori*ous* (adjective); glori*ously* (adverb). Here are some examples:

Suffixes	Meanings	Examples
–ous (adjective)	marked by, given to	efficacious, virtuous
–ic (adjective or noun)	dealing with, caused by	classic, choleric
–ence (noun)	act, condition, fact	pestilence, reverence
–ize (verb)	make, cause to be	energize, sterilize

Try It Out

Each of the following words is from *The Canterbury Tales.* Use a dictionary to determine the root and affix(es) of each word, and show how the structure of each word contributes to the word's meaning.

1. diligent
2. obstinate
3. covetousness
4. superfluity
5. transcend

Silver and gold portable sundial (10th century).
Canterbury Cathedral, Kent.

How to Own a Word

Mini-Lesson: Analyzing Word Parts

Point out to the class that the word *inscription* is made up of three parts that contribute to the word's meaning. Write the complete word on the board and then, underneath it, break it down:

inscription

Prefix	Root	Suffix
in–	–scrip–	–tion

Explain that the prefix *in–* (in, into), the root *–scrip–* ("writing, marking, or script"), and the suffix *–tion* (noun: state, act, thing) mean "a message or note written in or on something."

Try It Out: Answers

Answers may vary depending on the dictionary used. Students may have to trace roots back through several words. Remind students that they may look up prefixes and suffixes in a dictionary.

1. **diligent** *di–* (apart) + *legere* (to choose) + *–ent* (adj.: that has, shows, or does) = does apart from choice; that is, doing something because one must—persevering
2. **obstinate** *ob–* (against) + *stare* (to stand) + *–ate* (adj.: characteristic of) = characteristic of standing against; not yielding to reason; stubborn
3. **covetousness** *covet* (long for with envy) + *–ous* (adj.: marked by, given to) + *–ness* (noun: state quality) = greed; avarice (Thus a verb changes to a noun.)
4. **superfluity** *super–* (over) + *fluere* (to flow) + *–ity* (noun: state, quality, condition) = condition of overflowing; excess
5. **transcend** *trans–* (over) + *scandere* (to climb) = to climb over; exceed, surpass

---

Visual Distribute a copy of a chart like the one following to each student in the class. Have them complete it by filling in words from the Try it Out exercise or by filling in words that they choose themselves.

Word	submarine	Meaning	underwater
Root	marine	Meaning	water
Prefix	sub–	Meaning	below
Suffix	[none]	Meaning	

Root and Affix Game Divide the class into groups of five. Begin by reading a root or affix aloud. Give each group two minutes to brainstorm and prepare (without dictionaries) a list of words that contain it. A member from each group should then read its list aloud. Give one point to the group with the shortest list of correct words, two points to the group with the next shortest list, and so on. (Each group earns some points for its efforts.) The group with the longest correct list gets the highest number of points for the round. Continue with different roots and affixes for another four or five rounds. The winning group is the one with the highest overall total.

Italy

Giovanni Boccaccio

(1313–1375)

Giovanni Boccaccio is one of Italy's foremost writers. Raised in Florence, Boccaccio later studied banking in Naples, but he soon transferred his ambitions from banking to literature. In his first prose romance, Boccaccio describes meeting a lovely woman named Fiammetta, with whom he falls immediately in love. Scholars have hotly argued about this woman's real identity—and even whether she existed at all. Fiammetta reappears in many of Boccaccio's later works, which often explore the theme of love. It is Fiammetta who tells the story of Federigo's falcon in the *Decameron*.

The two great subjects of the stories in the *Decameron* are love and the corruption of the clergy. Many of the *Decameron's* stories are adaptations of popular folk tales, fables, anecdotes, and even jokes that Boccaccio might have overheard on the bustling streets of medieval Naples. Boccaccio's stories have served as both a source and a model for many writers who followed him, among them Chaucer, Shakespeare, and Milton.

Boccaccio (15th century) by Andrea del Castagno.
Uffizi, Florence.

(Map) Old map showing the Mediterranean Coast.

BEFORE YOU READ
FEDERIGO'S FALCON

Few experiences are more painful than falling in love with someone who couldn't care less. We get over it—most of us—and it never—well, almost never—does us serious damage. But while we're suffering, we suffer intensely. It's hard to think about anything else; we can't do our work; food, if we bother to eat, is tasteless; we find ourselves staring into space, missing everything going on around us. Worst of all, we're likely to do something, maybe many things, so foolish that we make matters even worse and embarrass ourselves in front of that one person who wouldn't have noticed us at all if we hadn't made ourselves look so ridiculous.

But you never know how it will all turn out. In the most painful moments, when you think that things can't possibly get worse, they very well might. Or they might, surprisingly, turn around. . . .

A Dialogue with the Text

As you read this medieval love story, take notes on the ways the characters are like—and unlike—the characters in love stories today, or even the people you know in actual life. Note the problems facing each character, the mistake each one makes, and his or her values. Could this story happen today—with certain changes in the plot?

Background

"Federigo's Falcon" is part of the *Decameron,* a collection of tales written in fourteenth-century Italy shortly after a devastating plague struck Florence. The stories are grouped loosely within a frame tale about ten wealthy young Florentines who flee to a villa in the country to escape the plague-ravaged city.

To pass the time, the young people decide that for each of ten days (*decameron* is derived from the Greek words for "ten" and "day") they will elect a king or queen, who, in turn, will choose a theme that the others must use to tell a story. "Federigo's Falcon" is the ninth story told on the fifth day, a day devoted to telling stories with happy endings.

Detail from Frederick II's *Treatise on Falconry.* Ms. Pal. Lat. 1071 fol. 5v.

Apostolic Library, Vatican City, Rome.

GIOVANNI BOCCACCIO 155

Background

Ask students in what situations they would tell stories to pass the time. Note that other pastimes, especially watching television, have taken the place of storytelling.

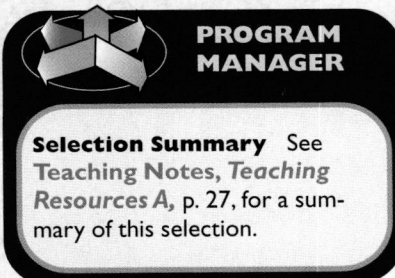

PROGRAM MANAGER

Selection Summary See Teaching Notes, *Teaching Resources A,* p. 27, for a summary of this selection.

A. Language Note: Sentence Structure

Ask students what they notice about the structure of this passage. [It is written as one long sentence.] Explain that long sentences—broken up by commas and semicolons—characterize this story.

B. Critical Reading: Metacognition

? Upon reading that Monna Giovanna is married, did you re-read the beginning of the story to see if perhaps you had missed something? If so, did you find any clues? [Possible answer: Although we are not told she is married, her virtue plays a large part in her refusal to acknowledge Federigo's declarations of love.]

C. Critical Reading: Finding Sequence

List in order the events that lead Monna Giovanna's son to desire Federigo's falcon. [The boy's father dies; Monna Giovanna and her son move to one of their country houses near Federigo's farm; the boy goes hunting with Federigo and admires his falcon.]

Federigo's Falcon
from the Decameron

Giovanni Boccaccio
translated by **Mark Musa and Peter Bondanella**

There was once in Florence a young man named Federigo, the son of Messer[1] Filippo Alberighi, renowned above all other men in Tuscany for his prowess in arms and for his courtliness. As often happens to most gentlemen, he fell in love with a lady named Monna[2] Giovanna, in her day considered to be one of the most beautiful and one of the most charming women that ever there was in Florence; and in order to win her love, he participated in jousts and tournaments, organized and gave feasts, and spent his money without restraint; but she, no less virtuous than beautiful, cared little for these things done on her behalf, nor did she care for him who did them. Now, as Federigo was spending far beyond his means and was taking nothing in, as easily happens he lost his wealth and became poor, with nothing but his little farm to his name (from whose revenues he lived very meagerly) and one falcon which was among the best in the world.

More in love than ever, but knowing that he would never be able to live the way he wished to in the city, he went to live at Campi,[3] where his farm was. There he passed his time hawking whenever he could, asked nothing of anyone, and endured his poverty patiently. Now, during the time that Federigo was reduced to dire need, it happened that the husband of Monna Giovanna fell ill, and realizing death was near, he made his last will. He was very rich, and he made his son, who was growing up, his heir, and, since he had

loved Monna Giovanna very much, he made her his heir should his son die without a legitimate heir; and then he died.

Monna Giovanna was now a widow, and as is the custom among our women, she went to the country with her son to spend a year on one of her possessions very close by to Federigo's farm, and it happened that this young boy became friends with Federigo and began to enjoy birds and hunting dogs; and after he had seen Federigo's falcon fly many times, it pleased him so much that he very much wished it were his own, but he did not dare to ask for it, for he could see how dear it was to Federigo. And during this time, it happened that the young boy took ill, and his mother was much grieved, for he was her only child and she loved him enormously. She would spend the entire day by his side, never ceasing to comfort him, and often asking him if there was anything he desired, begging him to tell her what it might be, for if it were possible to obtain it, she would certainly do everything possible to get it. After the young boy had heard her make this offer many times, he said:

"Mother, if you can arrange for me to have Federigo's falcon, I think I would be well very soon."

When the lady heard this, she was taken aback for a moment, and she began to think what she should do. She knew that Federigo had loved her for a long while, in spite of the fact that he never received a single glance from her, and so, she said to herself:

"How can I send or go and ask for this falcon of his which is, as I have heard tell, the best that ever

---

1. **Messer** (mes′ər): title of address similar to *sir.*
2. **Monna** (mō′nə): In Italian, *Monna* is an abbreviation for *Madonna* (mə·dän′ə), a formal title for a woman, similar to *madam.*
3. **Campi** (käm′pē): small town set in the mountains northwest of Florence. *Campi* literally means "fields."

(Above) From an illuminated manuscript (detail) (14th century). MS Bodl. 264, fol. 123v.
The Bodleian Library, Oxford.

CONNECTING WITH "THE ONE STORY WORTH TELLING"

Ask students to consider how the tale "Federigo's Falcon" is "The One Story Worth Telling." [Answers will vary. Students may find the story a tale of great romance or a moral lesson about generosity of the human spirit.]

flew, and besides this, his only means of support? And how can I be so insensitive as to wish to take away from this gentleman the only pleasure which is left to him?"

And involved in these thoughts, knowing that she was certain to have the bird if she asked for it, but not knowing what to say to her son, she stood there without answering him. Finally the love she bore her son persuaded her that she should make him happy, and no matter what the consequences might be, she would not send for the bird, but rather go herself for it and bring it back to him; so she answered her son:

"My son, take comfort and think only of getting well, for I promise you that the first thing I shall do tomorrow morning is to go for it and bring it back to you."

The child was so happy that he showed some improvement that very day. The following morning, the lady, accompanied by another woman, as if going for a stroll, went to Federigo's modest house and asked for him. Since it was not the season for it, Federigo had not been hawking for some days and was in his orchard, attending to certain tasks. When he heard that Monna Giovanna was asking for him at the door, he was very surprised and happy to run there. As she saw him coming, she greeted him with feminine charm, and once Federigo had welcomed her courteously, she said:

(D)

"Greetings, Federigo!" Then she continued: "I have come to compensate you for the harm you have suffered on my account by loving me more than you needed to; and the compensation is this: I, along with this companion of mine, intend to dine with you—a simple meal—this very day."

To this Federigo humbly replied: "Madonna, I never remember having suffered any harm because of you. On the contrary, so much good have I received from you that if ever I have been worth anything, it has been because of your merit and the love I bore for you; and your generous visit is certainly so dear to me that I would spend all over again that which I spent in the past; but you have come to a poor host."

(E)

And having said this, he received her into his home humbly, and from there he led her into his garden, and since he had no one there to keep her company, he said:

"My lady, since there is no one else, this good woman here, the wife of this workman, will keep you company while I go to set the table."

Though he was very poor, Federigo, until now, had never before realized to what extent he had wasted his wealth; but this morning, the fact that he found nothing with which he could honor the lady for the love of whom he had once entertained countless men in the past gave him cause to reflect. In great anguish, he cursed himself and his fortune and, like a man beside himself, he started running here and there, but could find neither money nor a pawnable[4] object. The hour was late and his desire to honor the gracious lady was great, but not wishing to turn for help to others (not even to his own workman), he set his eyes upon his good falcon, perched in a small room; and since he had nowhere else to turn, he took the bird, and finding it plump, he decided that it would be a worthy food for such a lady. So, without further thought, he wrung its neck and quickly gave it to his servant girl to pluck, prepare, and place on a spit to be roasted with care; and when he had set the table with the whitest of tablecloths (a few of which he still had left), he returned, with a cheerful face, to the lady in his garden, saying that the meal he was able to prepare for her was ready.

(F)

The lady and her companion rose, went to the table together with Federigo, who waited upon them with the greatest devotion, and they ate the good falcon without knowing what it was they were eating. And having left the table and spent some time in pleasant conversation, the lady thought it time now to say what she had come to say, and so she spoke these kind words to Federigo:

(G)

"Federigo, if you recall your past life and my virtue, which you perhaps mistook for harshness and cruelty, I do not doubt at all that you will be amazed by my presumption when you hear what my main reason for coming here is; but if you had children, through whom you might have experienced the power of parental love, it seems certain to me that you would, at least in part, forgive me. But, just as you have no child, I do have one, and I

---

4. **pawnable:** able to be given as security in return for a loan of money or goods.

GIOVANNI BOCCACCIO 157

D. Reader's Response: First Thoughts

? How do you think Monna Giovanna acted as "she greeted him with feminine charm"? [Sample responses: She probably was not flirtatious; she may have smiled shyly, tentative about how she would be received.]

E. Expansion

Although their exchange may seem excessive and exaggerated, it follows the conventions of courtly love.

F. Literary Element: Irony

? What is ironic about Federigo killing his falcon to please Monna Giovanna? [He expects her to be honored with his offering of food at such an enormous cost to himself, but in fact, she is horrified because the live falcon is the thing that she most desires.]

G. Literary Element: Irony

Situational irony occurs when what actually happens is the opposite of what is expected. One example is when Monna Giovanna unexpectedly pays a visit to Federigo after he has lost the means to entertain her. How is this passage an example of situational irony? [Monna Giovanna eats the falcon, even while she expects to receive it from Federigo as a gift for her son.]

OPTIONS FOR TEACHING

COOPERATIVE LEARNING

Presentation and Summary Have students work in small groups to learn more about courtly love during the Middle Ages. Then, ask each group to devise a creative way to present their findings to the class. Options include presenting skits or writing a rule book of courtly love. To ensure equal work by all, ask each group member to write a brief summary of his or her contribution.

CLASSROOM MANAGEMENT

Block Scheduling Encourage students, especially those new to block scheduling, to discuss their impressions of the longer class periods. Students may have concerns which can be addressed quickly. This discussion can accomplish two things: It can allow a short break between activities, and student feedback can be used to plan additional lessons. ☞

Giovanni Boccaccio **T157**

A. Readers' Response: Challenging the Text

? Monna Giovanna just finishes a very long speech at this point. What is gained and/or lost by having her talk for so long without any response from Federigo? [Sample responses: The readers know what Federigo has done, but Monna Giovanna does not. Her lengthy speech allows for suspense and a moment to imagine Federigo's response. On the other hand, it may be unrealistic that Monna Giovanna would not ask her question more quickly.]

B. Cultural Connections

Monna Giovanna does not find it unmanly of Federigo to cry, even when she thinks it is merely for the loss of his falcon. Ask students to consider the questions that follow: In what circumstances do you think it is permissible for a man to cry? Are there times when your culture allows women to cry but not men?

August: Departure for the Hunt with Falcons, from the calendar for the *Très riches heures du duc de Berry* by the Limbourg brothers. MS 65 / 1284, fol. 8v.

Musée Condé, Chantilly, France.

cannot escape the common laws of other mothers; the force of such laws compels me to follow them, against my own will and against good manners and duty, and to ask of you a gift which I know is most precious to you; and it is naturally so, since your extreme condition has left you no other delight, no other pleasure, no other consolation; and this gift is your falcon, which my son is so taken by that if I do not bring it to him, I fear his sickness will grow so much worse that I may

lose him. And therefore I beg you, not because of the love that you bear for me, which does not oblige you in the least, but because of your own nobility, which you have shown to be greater than that of all others in practicing courtliness, that you be pleased to give it to me, so that I may say that I have saved the life of my son by means of this gift, and because of it I have placed him in your debt forever."

When he heard what the lady requested and knew that he could not oblige her since he had given her the falcon to eat, Federigo began to weep in her presence, for he could not utter a word in reply. The lady, at first, thought his tears were caused more by the sorrow of having to part with the good falcon than by anything else, and she was on the verge of telling him she no longer wished it, but she held back and waited for Federigo's reply after he stopped weeping. And he said:

"My lady, ever since it pleased God for me to place my love in you, I have felt that Fortune has been hostile to me in many things, and I have complained of her, but all this is nothing compared to what she has just done to me, and I must never be at peace with her again, thinking about how you have come here to my poor home where, while it was rich, you never deigned to come, and you requested a small gift, and Fortune worked to make it impossible for me to give it to you; and why this is so I shall tell you briefly. When I heard that you, out of your kindness, wished to dine with me, I considered it fitting and right, taking into account your excellence and your worthiness, that I should honor you, according to my possibilities, with a more precious food than that which I usually serve to other people; therefore, remembering the falcon that you requested and its value, I judged it a food worthy of you, and this very day you had it roasted and served to you as best I could; but seeing now that you desired it in another way, my sorrow in not being able to serve you is so great that I shall never be able to console myself again."

158 THE MIDDLE AGES

OPTIONS FOR TEACHING

ASSESSMENT TOOLS

Check Test: Short Answer

1. How did Federigo lose his wealth? [He squandered it in an effort to win the love of Monna Giovanna.]
2. What were the two stipulations Monna Giovanna's husband made before he died? [1. His son would inherit the fortune. 2. If the son died without an heir, Monna Giovanna would inherit the fortune.]
3. Why did Monna Giovanna want the falcon? [To give to her son, who was ill.]
4. Why did Federigo kill the falcon? [To serve as a meal for Monna Giovanna.]
5. Why does Monna Giovanna decide to marry again? [Her brothers insist.]

And after he had said this, he laid the feathers, the feet, and the beak of the bird before her as proof. When the lady heard and saw this, she first reproached him for having killed such a falcon to serve as a meal to a woman; but then to herself she commended the greatness of his spirit, which no poverty was able or would be able to diminish; then, having lost all hope of getting the falcon and, perhaps because of this, of improving the health of her son as well, she thanked Federigo both for the honor paid to her and for his good will, and she left in grief, and returned to her son. To his mother's extreme sorrow, either because of his disappointment that he could not have the falcon, or because his illness must have necessarily led to it, the boy passed from this life only a few days later.

After the period of her mourning and bitterness had passed, the lady was repeatedly urged by her brothers to remarry, since she was very rich and was still young; and although she did not wish to do so, they became so insistent that she remembered the merits of Federigo and his last act of generosity—that is, to have killed

Couple, from an illustrated manuscript of the *Decameron* (c. 14th century).
© cliché Bibliothèque Nationale de France, Paris.

such a falcon to do her honor—and she said to her brothers:

"I would prefer to remain a widow, if that would please you; but if you wish me to take a husband, you may rest assured that I shall take no man but Federigo degli Alberighi."

In answer to this, making fun of her, her brothers replied:

"You foolish woman, what are you saying? How can you want him; he hasn't a penny to his name?"

To this she replied: "My brothers, I am well aware of what you say, but I would rather have a man who needs money than money that needs a man."

Her brothers, seeing that she was determined and knowing Federigo to be of noble birth, no matter how poor he was, accepted her wishes and gave her in marriage to him with all her riches. When he found himself the husband of such a great lady, whom he had loved so much and who was so wealthy besides, he managed his financial affairs with more prudence than in the past and lived with her happily the rest of his days.

C. Critical Reading: Making Connections

? What other stories have you read where a gift intended to please someone turns out to be exactly what they do not need or do not want?
[The most famous of such stories is O. Henry's "The Gift of the Magi." In this story the gift is ironically wrong—combs are given to a woman who has sold her hair, and a watch chain to a man who has sold his watch; but the feeling behind them makes them the best possible gifts.]

D. Critical Reading: Making Connections

? In "The Wife of Bath's Tale" the old woman argues that gentility is not the result of noble birth but of noble actions. Which characters in "Federigo's Falcon" would agree with her, and which characters would disagree? [Monna Giovanna would agree; she is influenced by Federigo's "last act of generosity." However, her brothers judge Federigo by his noble birth and his financial status.]

FINDING COMMON GROUND

Federigo and Monna Giovanna live in fourteenth-century Italy. Their customs and their ways of speaking to one another are different from ours. But we share with them some basic human problems. In your Reader's Log, you may have commented on the lovers' difficulties:

- Federigo loves someone who doesn't love him.
- Giovanna must cope with a dying son's wish.
- Giovanna has to ask a favor of someone she has ignored and rejected.
- Federigo has to deal with the discovery that a noble gesture was actually a terrible mistake.

Try to find some contemporary examples of these lovers' problems. Working with a small group, think about how the lovers in this story might be treated by a contemporary writer or filmmaker. How are the problems faced by Federigo and Monna Giovanna both similar to and different from the problems faced by lovers today? How would their story differ if it were retold—as, say, the story of Joan and Fred—and reset in the late twentieth century? Make a list of the differences and similarities that most intrigue you, and discuss why these differences and similarities exist. Then present your findings to other groups in your class.

GIOVANNI BOCCACCIO 159

QUICK PLANNING GUIDE

Into the Selection

Before You Read p. 160
- **Reading Focus:** Students read about the rules of courtly love.
- **Quickwrite:** Write in Reader's Log on rules of courtly love
- **Elements of Literature:** Romance
- **Background:** The author's attitude

Through the Selection

from Sir Gawain and the Green Knight pp. 161–172

Words to Own pp. 161–171

Literature and Architecture pp. 168–169

Connections: A Song p. 173 "Holding Out for a Hero"

Making Meanings p. 174

Elements of Literature pp. 174–175

Beyond the Selection

Choices: Building Your Portfolio p. 175
- **Writer's Notebook:** Create a dialogue
- **Critical Writing:** Make the story into a movie or TV show
- **Creative Writing:** Write a character diary
- **Critical Thinking/Speaking:** Present a panel discussion

Spotlight On pp. 176–179

BEFORE YOU READ

FROM SIR GAWAIN AND THE GREEN KNIGHT

Reading Focus

The Game of Love

You've heard the expression before: the game of love. You can probably think of some ways in which love might be considered a game: Love requires at least two players who take turns making moves and countermoves, assume various roles, and follow set rules. Love involves tension, strategy, risk, chance, competition, and, for the winners, a prize.

Some medieval historians believe that courtly love, one aspect of chivalry, was primarily a game, an intellectual diversion, in which players assumed certain roles and followed strict rules of behavior. In fact, in twelfth-century France, there was an actual court of love that judged questions of behavior and issues of love.

Quickwrite

One outcome of the court of love was a late-twelfth-century document called *The Art of Courtly Love,* which set down the rules of love, some of which are listed here. As you read each rule, decide whether you agree or disagree with it. Record your reactions, and discuss them with your classmates. Have the rules of love changed or not?

iii No one can be bound by a double love.

xiv The easy attainment of love makes it of little value; difficulty of attainment makes it prized.

xvii A new love puts to flight an old one.

xix If love diminishes, it quickly fails and rarely revives.

Elements of Literature

The Romance

Romances (or at least works with some of the trappings of romances) are still being written today. They take the form of novels, movies, even comic strips. Strictly speaking, a **romance** is a narrative set in a world of pure wish fulfillment, where the ordinary laws of nature are suspended and where idealized and superhuman heroes fight and almost always conquer the forces of evil. The basic narrative pattern of the romance is the quest, in which the hero undertakes a perilous journey in search of something of value.

> **F**rom the thirteenth century onward, **romance** was a term applied to a verse narrative which traced the adventures of a brave knight or other hero who had to overcome danger for love of a noble lady or high ideal.
>
> *For more on the Romance, see page 174 and the Handbook of Literary Terms.*

Background

One of the great works of medieval literature is the verse romance called *Sir Gawain and the Green Knight,* composed in the second half of the fourteenth century, probably around 1375. The unknown author of this work, who wrote in a northwestern dialect of Middle English and in a consciously old-fashioned style, is known simply as the Gawain poet or as the Pearl poet, because many believe he also wrote *Pearl, Patience,* and *Purity,* three poems included with *Sir Gawain* in the same manuscript. Whoever this poet was, he succeeded in transforming popular romance into great art.

When *Sir Gawain* was written, the ideals of knightly conduct—courage, loyalty, and courtesy—were just beginning to erode. As you read the poem, look for clues to the author's attitude toward those ideals. Does he respect them? ridicule them? see them as desirable but unattainable?

As *Sir Gawain and the Green Knight* opens, King Arthur and the knights of the Round Table are feasting. Suddenly an enormous green stranger bursts into the hall. King Arthur greets the Green Knight and asks him to state his business. The Green Knight, after a few scornful words about the manliness of King Arthur's knights, says he only wishes to play a New Year's game. He challenges any knight there to agree to "exchange one blow for another"—he will even give that knight his gisarme (gi·zärm'), his two-bladed ax. The stranger says he will stand for the first blow; the knight must agree to let the Green Knight have *his* turn in a year and a day. Gawain accepts the challenge—no other knight except Arthur himself has dared to.

PORTFOLIO ASSESSMENT

Portfolio Assessment For help with self-assessment of reading skills, see the *Portfolio Management System,* pp. 48–49.

WORDS TO OWN

The following vocabulary words are defined in the Words to Own at the bottom of the pupil's page.

asunder p. 161	efficacious p. 170
subtle p. 163	feinted p. 171
daunted p. 169	

from Sir Gawain and the Green Knight

translated by **John Gardner**

Part One

On the ground, the Green Knight got himself into position,
His head bent forward a little, the bare flesh showing,
His long and lovely locks laid over his crown
So that any man there might note the naked neck.
5 Sir Gawain laid hold of the ax and he hefted it high,
His pivot foot° thrown forward before him on the floor,
And then, swiftly, he slashed at the naked neck;
The sharp of the battleblade shattered <u>asunder</u> the bones
And sank through the shining fat and slit it in two,
10 And the bit of the bright steel buried itself in the ground.
The fair head fell from the neck to the floor of the hall
And the people all kicked it away as it came near their feet.
The blood splashed up from the body and glistened on the green,
But he never faltered or fell for all of that,
15 But swiftly he started forth upon stout shanks
And rushed to reach out, where the King's retainers° stood,
Caught hold of the lovely head, and lifted it up,
And leaped to his steed and snatched up the reins of the bridle,
Stepped into stirrups of steel and, striding aloft,
20 He held his head by the hair, high, in his hand;
And the stranger sat there as steadily in his saddle
As a man entirely unharmed, although he was headless
                    on his steed.
      He turned his trunk about,
25   That baleful° body that bled,
      And many were faint with fright
      When all his say was said.

He held his head in his hand up high before him,
Addressing the face to the dearest of all on the dais;°
30 And the eyelids lifted wide, and the eyes looked out,
And the mouth said just this much, as you may now hear:
"Look that you go, Sir Gawain, as good as your word,
And seek till you find me, as loyally, my friend,
As you've sworn in this hall to do, in the hearing of the knights.
35 Come to the Green Chapel, I charge you, and take
A stroke the same as you've given, for well you deserve
To be readily requited° on New Year's morn.
Many men know me, the Knight of the Green Chapel;

WORDS TO OWN
asunder (ə·sun′dər) *adv.*: apart.

---

6. pivot (piv′ət) **foot:** foot on which he will turn in striking the blow.

16. retainers: attendants.

25. baleful: wretched.

29. dais (dā′is): raised platform.

37. requited (ri·kwīt′ed): repaid.

Into the Selection

Using **BEFORE YOU READ** p. 160

Quickwrite

Before students write, lead a quick brainstorming session. Draw a cluster diagram on the chalkboard, using student suggestions to note what modern rules of love might be.

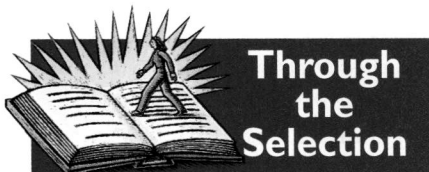

Through the Selection

A. Reader's Response: First Thoughts

? Why do you suppose Gawain accepts this challenge? [Sample responses: He feels he must, to defend his honor. He thinks he can kill the Green Knight and never have to receive a blow himself.]

B. Literary Element: Romance

One of the characteristics of romances is that they often contain supernatural or magical events. Students may wonder why an ordinary mortal like Gawain would accept a challenge, which seems to be trickery, from the clearly superhuman Green Knight. The complete manuscript indicates that although Gawain and Arthur's court might have harbored some suspicions because of the knight's extraordinary size and color, in fact, they took his challenge at face value as a foolhardy but not especially unusual engagement between two gentlemen.

PROGRAM MANAGER

- **Planning Instruction** See **Teaching Notes,** *Teaching Resources A,* pp. 27–28, for objectives, a summary and literary elements for this selection.
- **Instructional Support** Before beginning the instructional lesson, see

Graphic Organizer for Active Reading, *Teaching Resources A,* p. 48, for a Through the Selection activity.
- **Assessment** See **Selection Test,** *Test Booklet,* pp. 25–26.
- **Language Link** For instruction and

practice in pronoun-antecedent agreement, see **Language Link,** *Teaching Resources A,* pp. 49–50, and *Language and Writing Skills Worksheets,* pp. 31–32.

A. Literary Element: Character

? What is the difference between the reactions of Arthur and Gawain and the reactions of the rest of the banqueters? How does this add to your impression of Gawain's character? [To everyone else the spectacle is a marvel and makes them "faint with fright" (l. 26). Arthur and Gawain laugh and grin, which makes Gawain seem fearless.]

B. Expansion

In going out to meet the Green Knight, Gawain is setting out on a quest—a perilous journey for something of value, a journey that will test the knight and result in his exaltation. Many of the tales about Arthur and his knights are about quests to rid the world of evil.

C. Reader's Response: Shaping Interpretations

Why are these consequential activities—courtly love, exchanging blows, now hunting—considered "games"? Why might such games be important to this culture? [Sample responses: Although they have serious consequences, these activities are voluntary rather than necessary. They involve rules and seem to entertain. These arbitrary challenges offer a way to prove oneself. Perhaps the games are a carry-over from times when strength and strategy were crucial for survival.]

Therefore if you seek to find me, you shall not fail.
40   Come or be counted a coward, as is fitting."
     Then with a rough jerk he turned the reins
     And haled° away through the hall-door, his head in his hand,
     And fire of the flint° flew out from the hooves of the foal.
     To what kingdom he was carried no man there knew,
45   No more than they knew what country it was he came from.
                          What then?
             The King and Gawain there
             Laugh at the thing and grin;
             And yet, it was an affair
50   Most marvelous to men.

The next year, just before Christmas, Gawain sets off to honor his pledge. Through moors and forests and mountains he rides, searching for the Green Knight. One day he comes upon the most beautiful castle he has ever seen. The lord of the castle welcomes him and promises to help him find the Green Knight. But he urges Gawain to rest a few days in the castle with him and his lady.

Gawain's host then proposes an unusual "game." He will go hunting each day. Whatever the host wins in the hunt, he will give to Gawain. In turn, Gawain must promise to give the lord whatever he has won that day.

Twice the lord goes hunting, and each time the lord leaves the castle, his wife secretly visits Gawain's room and tries to seduce him. Though Gawain resists the lady and exchanges only innocent kisses with her, he is becoming greatly alarmed. When the host returns from his hunts and gives Gawain what he won that day, Gawain, true to his promises, gives the host the innocent kisses in return.

Now the lord goes out to hunt for the third morning. Gawain is in his room asleep, worried about many things.

From the depths of his mournful sleep Sir Gawain muttered,
A man who was suffering throngs of sorrowful thoughts
Of how Destiny would that day deal him his doom
At the Green Chapel, where he dreamed he was facing the giant
55   Whose blow he must abide without further debate.
     But soon our rosy knight had recovered his wits;
     He struggled up out of his sleep and responded in haste.
     The lovely lady came laughing sweetly,

42. haled: hauled; rushed.
43. fire of the flint: sparks.

Sir Gawain strikes off the head of the Green Knight in King Arthur's presence, from an English manuscript (c. 15th century). MS Cotton Nero A.X., fol. 94v.

162 THE MIDDLE AGES

OPTIONS FOR TEACHING

STRATEGIES FOR INCLUSION

English Language Development
One important aspect of the code of chivalry was a knight's *honor*. Have students work in pairs or small groups to define this term and to give examples. Be sure they include such ideas as keeping one's word, not showing fear, not betraying someone who helps, and not lying. Have students list specific actions Gawain takes that show he is honorable. Have students discuss the

last section of the poem in reference to honor. Why does the Green Knight hurt Gawain a little bit on the third stroke? What is the Green Knight's opinion of Gawain's honor? What is Gawain's opinion of himself? Whom do the students agree with?

Advanced *Don Quixote* by Miguel de Cervantes tells the story of a foolish country gentleman who imagines himself a knight. *A Connecticut Yankee in King Arthur's Court* by Mark Twain tells of a

nineteenth-century American who returns to medieval England. Ask students to read one or both of these books and to write a short report explaining how the books satirize medieval romances or the chivalric ideal.

Linguistic Ask students to work in small groups to summarize, in poetry, the opening, the journey of Gawain to the castle, the first two days in the castle, and the end of the third day in the castle. Suggest that the groups use alliteration for emphasis in the same way it is used in the translation.

Fell over his fair face and fondly kissed him;
60 Sir Gawain welcomed her worthily and with pleasure;
He found her so glorious, so attractively dressed,
So faultless in every feature, her colors so fine
Welling joy rushed up in his heart at once.
Their sweet and <u>subtle</u> smiles swept them upward like wings
65 And all that passed between them was music and bliss
                        and delight.
            How sweet was now their state!
            Their talk, how loving and light!
            But the danger might have been great
70   Had Mary° not watched her knight!

For that priceless princess pressed our poor hero so hard
And drove him so close to the line that she left him no choice
But to take the full pleasure she offered or flatly refuse her;
He feared for his name, lest men call him a common churl,°
75 But he feared even more what evil might follow his fall
If he dared to betray his just duty as guest to his host.
God help me, thought the knight, *I can't let it happen!*
With a loving little laugh he parried her lunges,
Those words of undying love she let fall from her lips.
80 Said the lady then, "It's surely a shameful thing
If you'll lie with a lady like this yet not love her at all—
The woman most brokenhearted in all the wide world!
Is there someone else?—some lady you love still more
To whom you've sworn your faith and so firmly fixed
85 Your heart that you can't break free? I can't believe it!
But tell me if it's so. I beg you—truly—
By all the loves in life, let me know, and hide nothing
                        with guile."
            The knight said, "By St. John,"
90   And smooth was Gawain's smile,
            "I've pledged myself to none,
            Nor will I for awhile."

"Of all the words you might have said," said she,
"That's surely cruelest. But alas, I'm answered.
95 Kiss me kindly, then, and I'll go from you.
I'll mourn through life as one who loved too much."
She bent above him, sighing, and softly kissed him;
Then, drawing back once more, she said as she stood,
"But my love, since we must part, be kind to me:
100 Leave me some little remembrance—if only a glove—
To bring back fond memories sometimes and soften my sorrow."
"Truly," said he, "with all my heart I wish

70. Mary: the Virgin Mary, mother of Jesus. A cult of the Virgin was very strong among the knights.

74. churl (chʉrl): ill-mannered person.

WORDS TO OWN
subtle (sutʹʹl) *adj.:* delicately suggestive; not obvious.

D. Critical Reading: Speculating

? Why do the woman's advances cause such inner turmoil for Gawain? [Possible response: He is struggling with the competing claims of chivalry—that a knight obeys a lady's every command and that a knight has a religious obligation to reject adultery.] Point out the emphasis provided by alliteration in l. 71.

E. Expansion
Gawain has a reputation for being a ladies' man, so his temptation is based on the weakness. If he meets the test, his character will be strengthened; if he fails, he will be doomed.

F. Critical Reading: Drawing Conclusions

? Why does the woman say Gawain's response is the "cruelest" thing he could have said? [His words imply that he will not pledge himself to her. The woman does not seem to see her married status as a justification for Gawain's reluctance.]

INTEGRATING THE LANGUAGE ARTS

Strategic Reading Have students work in pairs to read the selection. Explain that each section of the poem ends with a four-line, rhyming indentation—a total of seventeen sections. Ask pairs to stop after reading each section and to fill in the following chart.

	Main Events	**Comments or Questions**
Sec 1	[Gawain cuts off Green Knight's head.]	[Why doesn't the Green Knight die?]
Sec.2		

Writing: Chapter Titles Have students write chapter titles for *Sir Gawain and the Green Knight* in the style of those found in eighteenth-century novels such as Henry Fielding's *Tom Jones* or *Joseph Andrews*. Although not all of these novels' titles begin in the same way nor are a specified length, require students' titles to start with "In which . . ." and to be at least twenty words long. Share with students these examples from *Tom Jones:*

- In Which a Simile in Mr. Pope's Period of a Mile Introduces as Bloody a Battle as Can Possibly be Fought without the Assistance of Steel or Cold Iron
- In Which the Arrival of a Man-of-War Puts a Final End to Hostilities, and Causes the Conclusion of a Firm and Lasting Peace ☞

Sir Gawain and the Green Knight **T163**

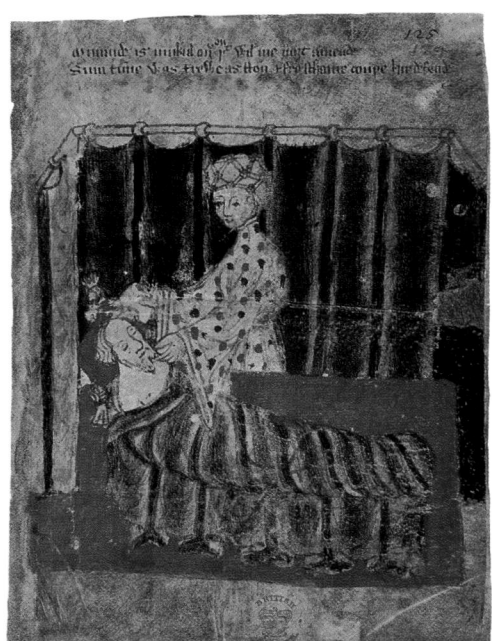
RESPONDING TO THE ART: VISUAL LITERACY

Point out to students that Gawain, a nephew of the legendary King Arthur, appeared as a model of perfection in early Arthurian literature. However, in later literature, he was no longer the ideal knight, unable to seek divine aid and failing in the quest of the Grail. Have students debate the identity of this Gawain among themselves. Is this the heroic, exemplary knight or the weaker, less ideal knight? Ask them to use details from the illustration to support their arguments.

A. Cultural Connections

Cultures have various customs about the giving of gifts, especially gifts brought to hosts and benefactors. Note his quick wit and chivalry, as Gawain says he does not have trunks of treasures from which to choose a gift for the woman. She does not exactly want a formal gift, but it is evidently something that the culture might see as an expectation. Ask students about the gift-giving customs with which they are familiar.

B. Critical Reading: Making Inferences

? Why does Gawain refuse the ring? [Possible responses: He says that he cannot accept it since he has nothing to give back. He would be obligated to give it to the lord at the end of the day. He would be in the lady's debt.]

> I had here with me the handsomest treasure I own,
> For surely you have deserved on so many occasions
> 105 A gift more fine than any gift I could give you;
> But as to my giving some token of trifling value,
> It would hardly suit your great honor to have from your knight
> A glove as a treasured keepsake and gift from Gawain;
> And I've come here on my errand to countries unknown
> 110 Without any attendants with treasures in their trunks;
> It sadly grieves me, for love's sake, that it's so,
> But every man must do what he must and not murmur
>   or pine."
>   "Ah no, my prince of all honors,"
> 115   Said she so fair and fine,
>   "Though I get nothing of yours,
>   You shall have something of mine."
>
> She held toward him a ring of the yellowest gold
> And, standing aloft on the band, a stone like a star
> 120 From which flew splendid beams like the light of the sun;
> And mark you well, it was worth a rich king's ransom.
> But right away he refused it, replying in haste,
> "My lady gay, I can hardly take gifts at the moment;

164 THE MIDDLE AGES

Having nothing to give, I'd be wrong to take gifts in turn." ⌐

125 She implored him again, still more earnestly, but again
    He refused it and swore on his knighthood that he could take nothing.
    Grieved that he still would not take it, she told him then:
    "If taking my ring would be wrong on account of its worth,
    And being so much in my debt would be bothersome to you,
130 I'll give you merely this sash that's of slighter value."
    She swiftly unfastened the sash that encircled her waist,
    Tied around her fair tunic, inside her bright mantle;
    It was made of green silk and was marked of gleaming gold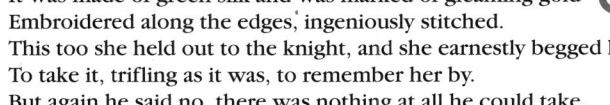
    Embroidered along the edges, ingeniously stitched.
135 This too she held out to the knight, and she earnestly begged him
    To take it, trifling as it was, to remember her by.
    But again he said no, there was nothing at all he could take,
    Neither treasure nor token, until such time as the Lord
    Had granted him some end to his adventure.
140 "And therefore, I pray you, do not be displeased,
    But give up, for I cannot grant it, however fair
                        or right.
            I know your worth and price,   ⌐
            And my debt's by no means slight; |
145   I swear through fire and ice | D
            To be your humble knight."   ⌐

    "Do you lay aside this silk," said the lady then,
    "Because it seems unworthy—as well it may?
    Listen. Little as it is, it seems less in value,
150 But he who knew what charms are woven within it
    Might place a better price on it, perchance.
    For the man who goes to battle in this green lace,
    As long as he keeps it looped around him,
    No man under Heaven can hurt him, whoever may try,
155 For nothing on earth, however uncanny, can kill him."   ⌐
    The knight cast about in distress, and it came to his heart
    This might be a treasure indeed when the time came to take
    The blow he had bargained to suffer beside the Green Chapel.
    If the gift meant remaining alive, it might well be worth it;
160 So he listened in silence and suffered the lady to speak,   E
    And she pressed the sash upon him and begged him to take it,
    And Gawain did, and she gave him the gift with great pleasure
    And begged him, for her sake, to say not a word,
    And to keep it hidden from her lord. And he said he would,
165 That except for themselves, this business would never be known
                        to a man.   ⌐
            He thanked her earnestly,
            And boldly his heart now ran;
            And now a third time she
170   Leaned down and kissed her man.

**C. Literary Element:
Foreshadowing**

? What is the significance of the
scarf? [Its green color indicates
that it will probably play a part in
Gawain's meeting with the Green
Knight.]

D. Expansion
Again, note how Gawain diffuses the
lady's potential anger with chivalry.

**E. Reader's Response: First
Thoughts**

? Does Gawain's acceptance of the
scarf and his pledge to keep it a
secret from his host change your
impressions of Gawain? Are his actions
justified? Explain. [Sample responses:
No, his actions are prudent; or yes, he
gives in and seems to weaken. Even the
most chivalrous knight should take
precautions to save his own life. He
knows that the Green Knight has
magic, and he is afraid that only magic
can save him from death.]

COOPERATIVE LEARNING

Analyze Character Have students work in groups of four or five to assemble a collection of things Sir Gawain could have had in his pockets as he rode back to Camelot from the Green Chapel. Ask each group to divide the poem into sections and to assign one section to each member so that the entire poem is covered. Then, ask each member to identify and produce a number of objects from his or her section. All objects must be of a size and weight that a person could reasonably put in a pocket. For example, they might include several threads from the green sash. Once all objects have been identified and collected or constructed, have the group produce a poster or sculpture of their collection, and ask each group to explain its creation to the class.

Review the Story Have students work in small groups to produce a board game based on the story of Sir Gawain. Give students some ideas about types of game elements that might be included: dice, stacks of direction cards, spinners, trivia questions and a game board with a geographical layout. The games might require students to find details from the text or perform stunts based on actions in the story. Ask each group to write directions for its game. Then, let students play each other's games and evaluate them, using the following questions:
1. Was it fun to play? **2.** Did it relate to the story? **3.** Did it teach or review aspects of the story? **4.** Were the directions clear? ☞

Sir Gawain and the Green Knight **T165**

A. Language Note: Diction

? What imagery suggests eeriness as Gawain searches out the Green Knight? [The water seems to boil, the tree is gnarled, the entrance is overgrown, and the place is deserted.]

When the lord returns from the third hunt, he gives Gawain a fox, and Gawain in return gives him three kisses, but not the lady's sash. The next day is New Year's Day, when Gawain must rendezvous with the Green Knight. Snow and sleet fall that night, and howling winds pile up huge drifts of snow. Before dawn, Gawain dresses in burnished armor and a red velvet cloak, winding the lady's green sash around himself twice. He leaves the castle with a servant to show him the way. The servant urges him not to keep his appointment, for Gawain will surely die, but Gawain insists on going.

Part Two

He put his spurs to Gringolet,° plunged down the path,
Shoved through the heavy thicket grown up by the woods
And rode down the steep slope to the floor of the valley;
He looked around him then—a strange, wild place,
175 And not a sign of a chapel on any side
But only steep, high banks surrounding him,
And great, rough knots of rock and rugged crags
That scraped the passing clouds, as it seemed to him.
He heaved at the heavy reins to hold back his horse
180 And squinted in every direction in search of the Chapel,
And still he saw nothing except—and this was strange—
A small green hill all alone, a sort of barrow,°
A low, smooth bulge on the bank of the brimming creek
That flowed from the foot of a waterfall,
185 And the water in the pool was bubbling as if it were boiling.
Sir Gawain urged Gringolet on till he came to the mound
And lightly dismounted and made the reins secure
On the great, thick limb of a gnarled and ancient tree;
Then he went up to the barrow and walked all around it,
190 Wondering in his wits what on earth it might be.
It had at each end and on either side an entrance,
And patches of grass were growing all over the thing,
And all the inside was hollow—an old, old cave
Or the cleft of some ancient crag, he couldn't tell which
195   it was.
            "Whoo, Lord!" thought the knight,
            "Is *this* the fellow's place?
            Here the Devil might
            Recite his midnight mass.

200 "Dear God," thought Gawain, "the place is deserted enough!
And it's ugly enough, all overgrown with weeds!
Well might it amuse that marvel of green
To do his devotions here, in his devilish way!
In my five senses I fear it's the Fiend himself

171. Gringolet: Gawain's horse.

182. barrow: grave mound.

166 THE MIDDLE AGES

Social Studies Have students research the basics of contract law to find out what goes into a contract, how it is structured, and what makes it legal. Once students know the basic requirements of drawing up a contract, have them work in groups of two or three to prepare a contract that the Green Knight might have signed with Sir Gawain at the beginning of the story. This contract should reflect accurately the terms of the agreement; it should not involve new requirements or consequences.

Art Ask students to design a coat of arms for Sir Gawain or for the Green Knight. Explain that, originally intended as identification in battle, a coat of arms is a group of emblems or figures arranged around or within a shield to symbolize the essence of the wearer.

Music Play for students the beginning of Prokofiev's *Peter and the Wolf*, in which the instruments associated with each of the major characters are introduced. Have students compose a similar introduction to *Sir Gawain and the Green Knight*, associating each character with a specific musical instrument or a certain type of music. Students should make a tape with narration and music or do a live performance for the class.

205 Who's brought me to meet him here to murder me.
May fire and fury befall this fiendish Chapel,
As cursed a kirk° as I ever yet came across!"
With his helmet on his head and his lance in hand
He leaped up onto the roof of the rock-walled room
210 And, high on that hill, he heard, from an echoing rock
Beyond the pool, on the hillside, a horrible noise.
Brrrack! It clattered in the cliffs as if to cleave them,
A sound like a grindstone grinding on a scythe!°
Brrrack! It whirred and rattled like water on a mill wheel!
215 *Brrrrrack!* It rushed and rang till your blood ran cold.
And then: "Oh God," thought Gawain, "it grinds, I think,
For me—a blade prepared for the blow I must take
               as my right!
        God's will be done! But here!
220   He may well get his knight,
        But still, no use in fear;
        I won't fall dead of fright!"

And then Sir Gawain roared in a ringing voice,
"Where is the hero who swore he'd be here to meet me?
225 Sir Gawain the Good is come to the Green Chapel!
If any man would meet me, make it now,
For it's now or never, I've no wish to dawdle here long."
"Stay there!" called someone high above his head,
"I'll pay you promptly all that I promised before."
230 But still he went on with that whetting noise a while,
Turning again to his grinding before he'd come down.
At last, from a hole by a rock he came out into sight,
Came plunging out of his den with a terrible weapon,
A huge new Danish ax to deliver his blow with,
235 With a vicious swine of a bit bent back to the handle,
Filed to a razor's edge and four foot long,
Not one inch less by the length of that gleaming lace.
The great Green Knight was garbed as before,
Face, legs, hair, beard, all as before but for this:
240 That now he walked the world on his own two legs,
The ax handle striking the stone like a walking-stave.°
When the knight came down to the water he would not wade
But vaulted across on his ax, then with awful strides
Came fiercely over the field filled all around
245   with snow.
        Sir Gawain met him there
        And bowed—but none too low!
        Said the other, "I see, sweet sir,
        You go where you say you'll go!

250 "Gawain," the Green Knight said, "may God be your guard!
You're very welcome indeed, sir, here at my place;

207. **kirk:** Scottish for "church."

213. **scythe** (sīth): long-handled cutting tool.

Sir Gawain, from *Le Roman de Lancelot du Lac* (detail) (c. 15th century). MS 805, fol. 48.

The Pierpont Morgan Library, New York.

241. **walking-stave** (stāv): staff.

SIR GAWAIN AND THE GREEN KNIGHT **167**

B. Critical Reading: Analyzing Character

? Why does the Green Knight keep Gawain waiting? [To keep someone else waiting is almost always a way to demonstrate power over the person who must wait. In this case, the Green Knight emphasizes his position of power and incidentally builds the suspense.]

C. Literary Element: Irony

? Is Gawain really "the Good"? Explain. [He is good in that he has resisted the lady's blandishments, but he might more appropriately be called "Sir Gawain Try-To Be-Good" because he has succumbed to the temptation to take the lady's scarf without telling her husband.]

D. Literary Element: Point of View

? What point of view is used in this story? [The point of view is limited third person; however, there are a few violations of strict limitation to Gawain's point of view in the scene at the Green Chapel (the knight's actions are described even when Gawain could not have observed them since his head was down).] Why do we not learn what the ax looks like until this moment? [Possible answer: We learn about the ax at this point because Gawain sees it for the first time. The detailed description of the weapon indicates that Gawain is (understandably) mesmerized by its appearance.]

E. Critical Reading: Analyzing Humor

Ask students to identify the humor in these lines. [Although Gawain bows as a gentleman, he is all too aware of the ax and its potential.]

PROBLEM SOLVING/CRITICAL THINKING

Saying No The Green Knight's wife makes four requests of Sir Gawain: that he love her, that he give her something, that he take her ring, and that he take her sash. Sir Gawain successfully denies three of these requests but gives in to the fourth. Have students use a chart like the one below to identify the ways in which Gawain refuses each request.

Request	Gawain's words of denial	Type of denial	Success of denial

LITERATURE AND ARCHITECTURE

The ranking of people within the castle is a microcosm of medieval hierarchical organization. Where else is this organizational model apparent in medieval life? [Almost all of medieval life involved hierarchy; the feudal system, which spanned kings to serfs; the church, with the Pope at the pinnacle of a vast structure of clergy; the manor, which a lord ruled; the guilds, which ranked craftsmen; and finally the cosmology of the time, the Great Chain of Being, which involved the hierarchical ranking of all things from worms to trees, humans to archangels to God.]

A. Critical Reading: Making Connections

? The actual time span was a year and a day. What other stories do you know in which the span of a year is a crucial deadline? [Students should recall this time span from "The Wife of Bath's Tale."]

The Medieval Castle

Mention the Middle Ages, and romantic images of castles immediately come to mind: fires blazing in huge stone fireplaces, merrymaking at long wooden tables laden with roasted meats and jugs of ale, candles warmly glowing in an immense hall. Are these images at all accurate, or was the medieval castle something other than our idyllic movie image?

In reality, as in our imaginations, medieval castles created an imposing presence. But several design features made living conditions inside a castle communal and somewhat uncomfortable.

The castle's basic living space was the great hall. Although withdrawing rooms were added later for privacy, initially the lord, his family, attendants, and staff *all* ate, slept, and conducted business in the great hall—the first multi-purpose room. For meals, the lord and lady of the castle usually sat on chairs on a dais, or raised floor area, at the hall's end. The castle staff, arranged in descending rank from the dais, sat on benches at trestle tables, which could be taken down. At night the lord might sleep on a feather bed at one end of the

You've timed your travel, my friend, as a true man should.
You recall the terms of the contract drawn up between us:
A At this time a year ago you took your chances,
255 And I'm pledged now, this New Year, to make you my payment.
And here we are in this valley, all alone,
And no man here to part us, proceed as we may;
Heave off your helmet then, and have here your pay;
And debate no more with me than I did then
260 When you severed my head from my neck with a single swipe."
"Never fear," said Gawain, "by God who gave
Me life, I'll raise no complaint at the grimness of it;
But take your single stroke, and I'll stand still
And allow you to work as you like and not oppose
265   you here."
              He bowed toward the ground
              And let his skin show clear;
              However his heart might pound,
              He would not show his fear.

270 Quickly then the man in the green made ready,
Grabbed up his keen-ground ax to strike Sir Gawain;

168 THE MIDDLE AGES

PROFESSIONAL NOTES

Critical Comment: Gawain's Weakness In *The Penguin Short History of English Literature*, Stephen Coote compares Gawain to Adam: "Though [the Green Knight] claims to shrive Gawain, Gawain himself now realizes the depth of his guilt. Despite being the flower of chivalry, he is a 'type' or image of Adam—an ordinary man led to forget his trust in the armour of God by the wiles of a woman. Human excellence is marred by original sin and courtly values alone are no protection. Though Gawain can hope to be excused, the girdle itself remains a perpetual reminder of his weakness." Ask students to argue either for or against the position that the story is essentially about human weakness.

Technology Tip Have your students use computer-assisted design (CAD) software to design a medieval castle. Computer simulation programs also will allow students to re-create a medieval city.

great hall, but everyone else slept either on benches pushed against the wall or on the floor of the great hall itself.

First made with walls of wood and later of stone, castles were full of hard, cold surfaces. Fireplaces, usually in the middle of the floor, provided the only heat. Tapestries, besides decorating the walls, served the more useful function of blocking drafts. Glass was scarce until the very late Middle Ages, so castles were also cold and dark. Windows were fitted with iron bars for protection and closed with wooden shutters. If the shutters were open, cold winds could blow inside; if they were closed, the room was dark.

A hall built at ground level might have a floor composed of beaten earth, stone, or plaster, while the floor of a hall on the second level would be made of wood. Carpets were not introduced to England until the fourteenth century, so before that time floors were strewn with rushes, or grasslike plants, which were periodically swept up and replaced. Herbs were sometimes added to the rushes, but as the medieval philosopher Erasmus observed, often under these rushes lay "an ancient collection of beer, grease, fragments, bones, spittle, excrement of dogs and cats and everything that is nasty."

Page from *Froissart's Chronicles* (detail). MS Fr. 2643, fol. 226v.
© cliché Bibliothèque Nationale de France, Paris.

With all the might in his body he bore it aloft
And sharply brought it down as if to slay him;
Had he made it fall with the force he first intended
275 He would have stretched out the strongest man on earth.
But Sir Gawain cast a side glance at the ax
As it glided down to give him his Kingdom Come,°
And his shoulders jerked away from the iron a little,
And the Green Knight caught the handle, holding it back,
280 And mocked the prince with many a proud reproof:°
"*You* can't be Gawain," he said, "who's thought so good,
A man who's never been <u>daunted</u> on hill or dale!
For look how you flinch for fear before anything's felt!
I never heard tell that Sir Gawain was ever a coward!
285 *I* never moved a muscle when *you* came down;
In Arthur's hall I never so much as winced.
My head fell off at my feet, yet I never flickered;
But you! You tremble at heart before you're touched!
I'm bound to be called a better man than you, then,

277. his Kingdom Come: life after death.

280. reproof: rebuke; scolding.

WORDS TO OWN
daunted (dônt′ed) *adj.*: intimidated.

SIR GAWAIN AND THE GREEN KNIGHT 169

B. Critical Reading: Finding Details

? What conditions made it desirable for many activities to occur in one place? [It would be easier to heat and light one space than many. It was convenient for business and protection. Also, it is easier to exert control if everything and everyone are under one roof.]

C. Critical Reading: Analyzing Character

? What do Gawain's actions indicate about his character? [Possible response: His flinching indicates that perhaps he is not as fearless as he pretends.]

D. Reader's Response: Shaping Interpretations

? How much does the jeering of the Green Knight add to Gawain's punishment? How would it feel to have someone laugh at you like this? [Sample responses: Gawain has indicated that the worst thing would be to be thought a coward. He does not, however, seem particularly upset by the Green Knight's taunts. He swears he will not flinch again.]

A. Critical Reading: Drawing Conclusions

? Why do you think the Green Knight stops the second blow? [Possible answer: He is trying to wear Gawain down. First, he taunts Gawain with his lack of courage; then, he stops the second blow, engaging in a war of nerves with Gawain.]

B. Literary Element: Climax

? Will the next stroke be the final one? Explain. [The emotional intensity of the scene has risen from cordial interchange to vehement shouting. In addition, the number *three* is used in many fairy tales and romantic adventures; this is the third stroke, indicating that we are at an emotional peak in the story.]

C. Critical Reading: Making Inferences

? Why does Gawain react only when he sees blood in the snow rather than when he feels the blade cut his neck? [Readers infer that Gawain does not feel the cut and is sure that the blow has been struck only when he sees the bloody evidence of having been hit. Many students will be able to confirm with stories of wounds to their own bodies the physiological accuracy of this description.]

my lord."
290 Said Gawain, "I shied once:
No more. You have my word.
But if my head falls to the stones
It cannot be restored.

295 "But be brisk, man, by your faith, and come to the point!
Deal out my doom if you can, and do it at once,
For I'll stand for one good stroke, and I'll start no more
Until your ax has hit—and that I swear."
"Here goes, then," said the other, and heaves it aloft
300 And stands there waiting, scowling like a madman;
He swings down sharp, then suddenly stops again,
Holds back the ax with his hand before it can hurt,
And Gawain stands there stirring not even a nerve;
He stood there still as a stone or the stock of a tree
305 That's wedged in rocky ground by a hundred roots.
O, merrily then he spoke, the man in green:
"Good! You've got your heart back! Now I can hit you.
May all that glory the good King Arthur gave you
Prove <u>efficacious</u> now—if it ever can—
310 And save your neck." In rage Sir Gawain shouted,
"*Hit* me, hero! I'm right up to here with your threats!
Is it *you* that's the cringing coward after all?"
"Whoo!" said the man in green, "he's wrathful, too!
No pauses, then; I'll pay up my pledge at once,
315   I vow!"
He takes his stride to strike
And lifts his lip and brow;
It's not a thing Gawain can like,
For nothing can save him now!

320 He raises that ax up lightly and flashes it down,
And that blinding bit bites in at the knight's bare neck—
But hard as he hammered it down, it hurt him no more
Than to nick the nape of his neck, so it split the skin;
The sharp blade slit to the flesh through the shiny hide,
325 And red blood shot to his shoulders and spattered the ground.
And when Gawain saw his blood where it blinked in the snow
He sprang from the man with a leap to the length of a spear;
He snatched up his helmet swiftly and slapped it on,
Shifted his shield into place with a jerk of his shoulders,
330 And snapped his sword out faster than sight; said boldly—
And, mortal born of his mother that he was,
There was never on earth a man so happy by half—

Sir Gawain and the Green Knight (1952) by Dorothy Braby. Golden Cockerel Press.

Rare Books and Manuscripts Division, New York Public Library. Astor, Lenox, and Tilden Foundations.

WORDS TO OWN
efficacious (ef'i·kā'shəs) *adj.*: effective.

"No more strokes, my friend; you've had your swing!
I've stood one swipe of your ax without resistance;

335 If you offer me any more, I'll repay you at once
With all the force and fire I've got—as you
                    will see.
    I take one stroke, that's all,
    For that was the compact we

340   Arranged in Arthur's hall;
    But now, no more for me!"

The Green Knight remained where he stood, relaxing on his ax—
Settled the shaft on the rocks and leaned on the sharp end—
And studied the young man standing there, shoulders hunched,

345 And considered that staunch° and doughty° stance he took, **D**
Undaunted yet, and in his heart he liked it;
And then he said merrily, with a mighty voice—
With a roar like rushing wind he reproved the knight—
"Here, don't be such an ogre on your ground!

350 Nobody here has behaved with bad manners toward you
Or done a thing except as the contract said.
I owed you a stroke, and I've struck; consider yourself
Well paid. And now I release you from all further duties.
If I'd cared to hustle, it may be, perchance, that I might

355 Have hit somewhat harder, and then you might well be cross!
The first time I lifted my ax it was lighthearted sport,
I merely <u>feinted</u> and made no mark, as was right,
For you kept our pact of the first night with honor
And abided by your word and held yourself true to me,

360 Giving me all you owed as a good man should.
I feinted a second time, friend, for the morning
You kissed my pretty wife twice and returned me the kisses;
And so for the first two days, mere feints, nothing more
               severe. **E**

365   A man who's true to his word,
    There's nothing he needs to fear;
    You failed me, though, on the third
    Exchange, so I've tapped you here.

"That sash you wear by your scabbard° belongs to me;

370 My own wife gave it to you, as I ought to know.
I know, too, of your kisses and all your words
And my wife's advances, for I myself arranged them.
It was I who sent her to test you. I'm convinced
You're the finest man that ever walked this earth.

375 As a pearl is of greater price than dry white peas,

---

345. staunch (stônch): steadfast.
doughty (dout'ē): courageous.

369. scabbard (skab'ərd): case that
holds the blade of a sword.

WORDS TO OWN
feinted (fānt'id) _v._: pretended to strike.

? To what do _he_ and _it_ in this line
refer? [The first _he_ refers to
Gawain; the second refers to the
Green Knight; the _it_ refers to Gawain's
"staunch and doughty stance."]

E. Critical Reading: Finding Cause and Effect

? How are the Green Knight's three
strokes a result of Gawain's
actions? [The first two strokes are
feints because Gawain keeps his vow
to give his host anything he wins during
the day. However, on the third day,
Gawain keeps the Green Knight's scarf,
thus breaking his vow. The Green
Knight nicks Sir Gawain on the third
stroke because Gawain only lacks a
little in loyalty and takes the scarf
because he loves his life, not because
he lusts.]

Technology Tip

The complete text of _Sir
Gawain and the Green Knight_
is available via anonymous
FTP at **ota.ox.ac.uk/pub/ota/public
/english/Anon/gawain.1680**. _You
may want to preview any Internet activity
that you suggest to students. Because
these resources are sometimes public
forums, their content can be unpre-
dictable._

A. Reader's Response: Shaping Interpretations

? What do you think is going through Gawain's mind at this point? Recall that in l. 332 he is described as happier than any man on earth. Why is he now miserable and ashamed? [Sample responses: The Green Knight knows about Gawain's failure of honor and courage, and Gawain is ashamed at having been caught. He is ashamed because he has been forced to look at his actions. He is ashamed that even though he has failed, the Green Knight still considers him the finest man on earth.]

B. Literary Element: Symbol

? In what sense is Gawain thinking of the sash itself as he throws it off? In what sense is he thinking of something beyond the physical sash? [Possible Responses: The sash has been an unfair protection against harm, deceptively acquired. Beyond this, it represents to Gawain his lack of faith in his own courage and his failure of honor; therefore, the sash represents his failure to be a perfect knight.]

C. Expansion

In the complete version, Gawain refuses the lady's friendship and speaks out against women in general who have tempted men through the ages. (He mentions Adam tempted by Eve, Solomon by many, and David by Bathsheba.) However, he wears the green sash ever after as a reminder of his failing.

So Gawain indeed stands out above all other knights.
But you lacked a little, sir; you were less than loyal;
But since it was not for the sash itself or for lust
But because you loved your life, I blame you less."
380 Sir Gawain stood in a study° a long, long while,
So miserable with disgrace that he wept within,
And all the blood of his chest went up to his face
And he shrank away in shame from the man's gentle words.
The first words Gawain could find to say were these:
385 "Cursed be cowardice and covetousness both,
Villainy and vice that destroy all virtue!"
He caught at the knots of the girdle° and loosened them
And fiercely flung the sash at the Green Knight.
"There, there's my fault! The foul fiend vex it!
390 Foolish cowardice taught me, from fear of your stroke,
To bargain, covetous, and abandon my kind,
The selflessness and loyalty suitable in knights;
Here I stand, faulty and false, much as I've feared them,
Both of them, untruth and treachery; may they see sorrow
395   and care!
        I can't deny my guilt;
        My works shine none too fair!
        Give me your good will
        And henceforth I'll beware."

400 At that, the Green Knight laughed, saying graciously,
"Whatever harm I've had, I hold it amended
Since now you're confessed so clean, acknowledging sins
And bearing the plain penance of my point;
I consider you polished as white and as perfectly clean
405 As if you had never fallen since first you were born.
And I give you, sir, this gold-embroidered girdle,
For the cloth is as green as my gown. Sir Gawain, think
On this when you go forth among great princes;
Remember our struggle here; recall to your mind
410 This rich token. Remember the Green Chapel.
And now, come on, let's both go back to my castle
And finish the New Year's revels with feasting and joy,
                    not strife,
        I beg you," said the lord,
415   And said, "As for my wife,
        She'll be your friend, no more
        A threat against your life."

380. stood in a study: stood thinking deeply.

387. girdle: sash.

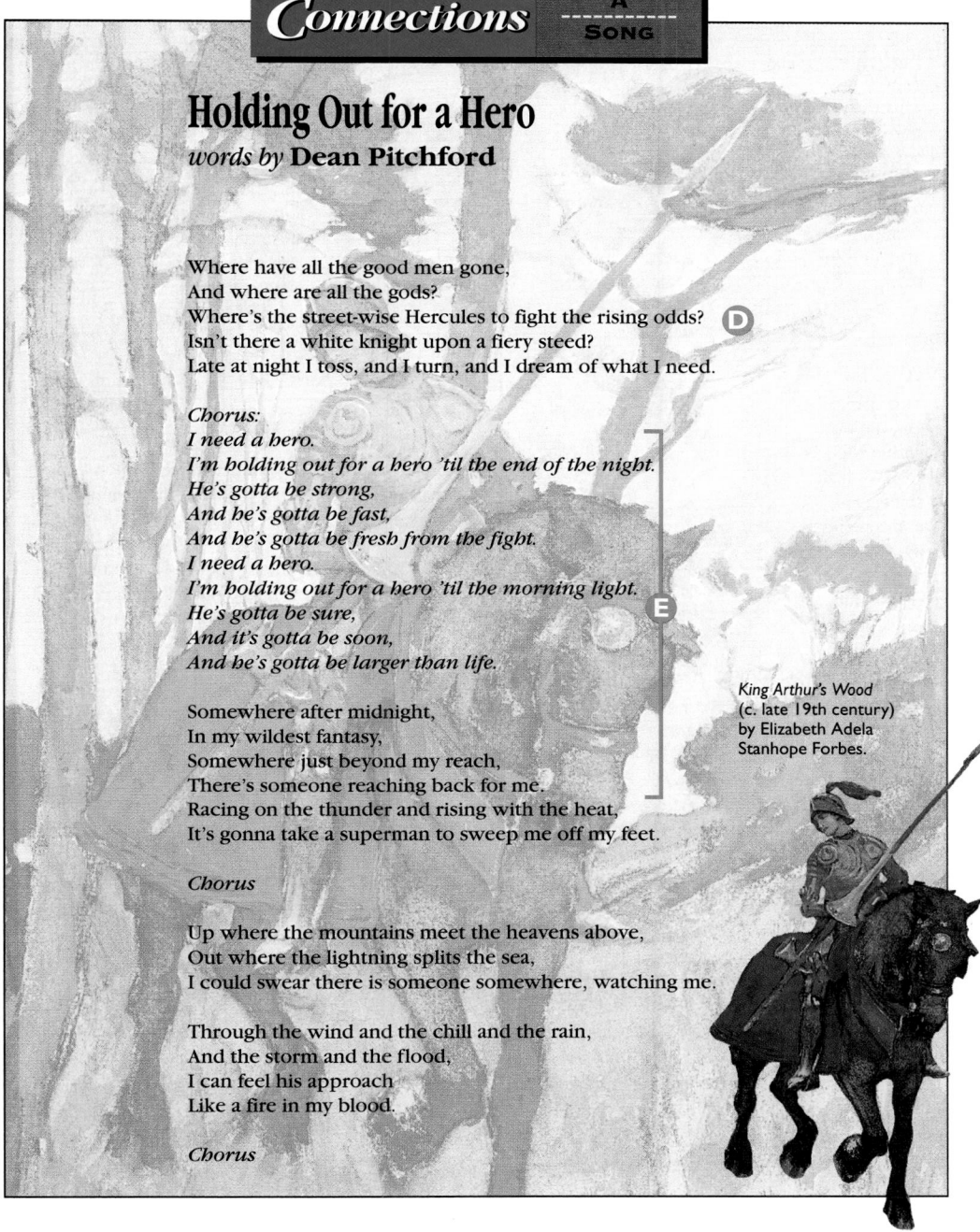

Connections

A SONG

Holding Out for a Hero

words by **Dean Pitchford**

Where have all the good men gone,
And where are all the gods?
Where's the street-wise Hercules to fight the rising odds? **D**
Isn't there a white knight upon a fiery steed?
Late at night I toss, and I turn, and I dream of what I need.

Chorus:
I need a hero.
I'm holding out for a hero 'til the end of the night.
He's gotta be strong,
And he's gotta be fast,
And he's gotta be fresh from the fight.
I need a hero.
I'm holding out for a hero 'til the morning light. **E**
He's gotta be sure,
And it's gotta be soon,
And he's gotta be larger than life.

Somewhere after midnight,
In my wildest fantasy,
Somewhere just beyond my reach,
There's someone reaching back for me.
Racing on the thunder and rising with the heat,
It's gonna take a superman to sweep me off my feet.

Chorus

Up where the mountains meet the heavens above,
Out where the lightning splits the sea,
I could swear there is someone somewhere, watching me.

Through the wind and the chill and the rain,
And the storm and the flood,
I can feel his approach
Like a fire in my blood.

Chorus

King Arthur's Wood
(c. late 19th century)
by Elizabeth Adela
Stanhope Forbes.

SIR GAWAIN AND THE GREEN KNIGHT 173

CONNECTING WITH *SIR GAWAIN AND THE GREEN KNIGHT*

In the terms set out by this song, is Sir Gawain a hero? Explain your answer. [Students may find Gawain a hero because he is a good man, a "street-wise Hercules" in his strength and savvy, "larger than life" and a "superman" in his deeds and honor.]

D. Literary Element: Allusion

? What characteristics would a "street-wise Hercules" have?
[Like the mythological Hercules, this individual would be renowned for strength and courage; in addition, this Hercules would be knowledgeable in dealing with urban street life.

E. Literary Element: Tone

? What is the tone of this song?
[At first the tone is desperation, but hope glimmers at the end.]

Making Meanings

Questions begin on p. 174.

First Thoughts

1. Most students will say the Green Knight because Gawain's short-comings are exposed.

Reviewing the Text:

a. To exchange one blow for another using a two-bladed ax. He will suffer the first blow and the challenger (Gawain) must agree to withstand one blow from the Green Knight one year and one day hence.

b. Conflicts between his desire and his obligation to his host, and between his dedication to chivalry (to be at a woman's command) and his obligation as a knight to reject adultery.

c. He can reassemble detached body parts and can disguise himself as the lord of the castle.

d. He promises to give the host everything he has won during the day, but he is silent about the lady's gift of the magic sash.

e. After two stopped strokes, the Green Knight gives the promised blow with his ax but only nicks Gawain. He then discloses the purpose of his games and forgives Gawain's lapses from the code of chivalry. Gawain is ashamed of his failures.

Answers to Making Meanings begin on p. T173.

Shaping Interpretations

2. Gawain keeps his morality. He loses his fidelity by deceiving the host about the sash. He partially loses his courage by flinching at the first blow.

3. Gawain is superhuman in his determination to act honorably and in his resolution to hide his fear. He displays such human qualities as susceptibility to passion, desire, lying, and fear.

4. Opinions will vary, but he is clearly not presented as totally evil. He might symbolize nature with its renewing qualities.

5. New Year's Day, like the color green, suggests a new beginning or renewal; Sir Gawain renews his knightly vows.

6. The bubbling water and the grave-like mound are the most vivid of the images at the beginning of Part Two that make the setting grim. The setting could suggest that the end of Gawain's present life is near.

7. Gawain seems to struggle hardest against the temptations of sensuality.

8. Possible answer: Renewal and self-knowledge can grow out of sin and weakness.

Extending the Text

9. (Synthesis) The hero in the song and Gawain have many of the same qualities; Gawain is not street wise.

Challenging the Text

10. (Synthesis) Gawain's response is certainly credible. A hero's or heroine's response to sexual temptation would differ from era to era, depending on prevailing mores.

MAKING MEANINGS

First Thoughts

1. Who finally wins the **conflict** between Gawain and the Green Knight? Why do you think so?

Shaping Interpretations

2. The "games" Gawain plays within the castle have high stakes: His courage, fidelity, and sexual morality are at risk. Which of these do you think Gawain "wins" or keeps? Which does he lose?

3. In what ways is Sir Gawain a superhuman **romance hero**? In what ways is he weak or flawed, just as a real person might be?

4. On a "good-evil scale" of 1 to 5 (with 1 as totally evil and 5 as totally good), where would you place the Green Knight, and why would you place him there? What do you think he might **symbolize** in the story?

5. Describe the **symbolic** use of the color green in this story. (Green usually symbolizes hope; it is associated with the appearance of new life in the plant world.) Why do you think the meeting with the Green Knight occurs on New Year's Day?

6. What **images** make the setting of the confrontation seem demonic? Do you think there is any **symbolism** suggested by this setting? Explain.

7. Why might the lord's wife have had such power over Gawain?

8. What do you think is the **theme** of this romance?

Reviewing the Text

a. What is the Green Knight's exact challenge to King Arthur's court? What is his agreement with Sir Gawain?

b. What **conflicts** does Gawain face in the castle?

c. In what ways is the Green Knight a "shape-changer," a typical character of romance?

d. How does Gawain break his promise to his host?

e. What happens when Gawain meets the Green Knight on New Year's Day?

Extending the Text

9. How do you think the **hero** imagined in "Holding Out for a Hero" (page 173) compares to Gawain?

Challenging the Text

10. Compare the romantic triangle in this story—the two men and the woman—with romantic triangles in contemporary fiction or movies. Is Gawain's response believable? Refer to your Reader's Log entry from page 160 as you develop your answer.

ELEMENTS OF LITERATURE

Romances: Wishes Fulfilled

Romances are often too incredible for some modern readers, too lacking in the realistic details of life we have come to expect of literature. Yet in *Sir Gawain and the Green Knight*, we feel the gripping reality of sexual temptation and of life in the medieval castle. This poem is a controlled, unified narrative of great power that speaks to us still.

The **romance** has a simple, inevitable plot: A hero battles an evil enemy and ultimately wins. As part of the story, the hero undertakes a **quest**. The quest usually has three stages: a dangerous journey, a central test or ordeal to determine if the hero truly has the qualities of a hero, and a return to the point from which the journey began.

In *Gawain* we have the model of the chivalric hero whose honor is being tested. This is a serious romance whose purpose is clearly to teach a moral lesson. Yet the hero does not have unlimited powers. Gawain is a human being who, like all of us, is limited in his moral and physical strength.

Elements of Romance
- a near-perfect hero
- an evil enemy
- a quest
- a test of the hero
- supernatural elements
- good vs. evil
- female figures who are usually maidens (in need of rescue), mothers, or crones

Elements of Literature
Possible Answers
- *Sir Gawain:* battle, a three-part quest, including a test, and supernatural elements. Differences from a typical romance: flawed hero, enemy who is not all evil, hero who fails part of the testing.
- *Beowulf:* all-good hero, evil enemy, a quest, no testing prior to battle, supernatural elements, good versus evil.
- "The Wife of Bath's Tale": hero is flawed, enemy is actually good, a quest, supernatural elements, no emphasis on good versus evil, includes maiden, mother, and crone.

Romances are still a popular form found in today's novels, movies, television shows, and comics. The *Back to the Future* and *Indiana Jones* movies are essentially romances, as are these books, which you may have read: C. S. Lewis's *The Chronicles of Narnia,* many of Lloyd Alexander's books, Brian Jacques's *Redwall* series, J.R.R. Tolkien's *The Lord of the Rings,* and L. Frank Baum's *The Wizard of Oz.*

Romances are traditionally set in the past, which is where the Wife of Bath sets her story: "When good King Arthur ruled in ancient days." Today, romances may also be set in the future, as in the *Star Wars* movies. If romances are set in the present, they usually have an "out of time" quality about them, with the hero journeying to remote or isolated settings. Through this journey to a remote time or place, the hero learns something of value.

As part of a small group, discuss the Gawain story as a romance. What elements of a romance does it have? Is the story different from a typical romance in any way? Next, expand your discussion to include other works, using a chart like the one below. Present your ideas to the rest of the class, using specific examples to support your conclusions.

Work	Romance Elements
Sir Gawain	
Beowulf	
The Wife of Bath's Tale	
Current movie or TV show	
Novel	

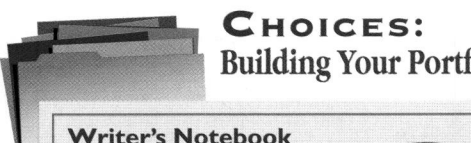

CHOICES: Building Your Portfolio

Writer's Notebook

1. Collecting Ideas for an Observational Essay

WORK IN PROGRESS

Like most characters in stories, Gawain reveals a great deal about himself in conver-sation—especially when he is faced with a momentous decision. Look at the notes you've taken so far about a person you'll describe for the Writer's Workshop on page 185. Try writing a dialogue between that person and someone else. Your aim is to reveal character, so focus on something important in your subject's life—perhaps a decision as crucial as the one faced by Gawain.

Critical Writing

2. Gawain Goes to Hollywood

When the elements of a romance story (or myth) are adapted to a more modern setting, we say that the story has been "displaced." In two or three paragraphs, discuss how *Sir Gawain* might be displaced into a contemporary movie or TV show. Think about the story's **plot, characterization,** and **theme.**

Creative Writing

3. The Wife's Diary

While the lord of the mysterious castle is out hunting, his wife is at home on her own hunt. What might she have to say about the situation? In a diary entry written from the wife's point of view, describe her feelings about entrapping Gawain. How does she feel about Gawain? about her husband? Does she resent or enjoy carrying out her wifely duty?

Critical Thinking / Speaking

4. Roles for Women

In romance literature, women are often represented as (a) maidens, (b) mothers, (c) temptresses, or (d) crones. Is that true in *Sir Gawain*? Do these character roles for women still exist today? Prepare a panel discussion on this issue with four or five other students. Defend your ideas with specific evidence from current fiction and movies, as well as from *Sir Gawain.*

Beyond the Selection

Choices: Building Your Portfolio

1. **Writer's Workshop** Remind students to save their work. They may use it as prewriting for the Writer's Workshop on p. 185.
2. **Critical Writing** For this activity, suggest that students use realistic, contemporary settings. For example, how would the story be displaced if it were a mystery set in a modern large city?

PORTFOLIO ASSESSMENT

Choices: Assessment Criteria For help in evaluating these Choices assignments, see the criteria in the *Portfolio Management System,* pp. 81–82.

STRATEGIES FOR INCLUSION

English Language Development Students may be confused by the use of the word *romance* in the Elements of Literature material. Explain that today the word has a more limited meaning, referring to a love relationship. Before students read these pages, introduce the larger meaning of the term *romantic* by asking them to list activities that they think are romantic versus those which are not. [Example: Walking on the beach versus wind-surfing.] Have students discuss their two lists and brainstorm some general characteristics that make up romance. [Travel, creativity, lack of routine.]

Intrapersonal For activity #3, instead of a diary, invite students to write letters from the wife to her friend (who lives nearby and can receive a letter, by servant, and write back within the course of one day). Then, have students write letters of response back from the friend. Students should write one interchange for each of the three days Gawain spends at the castle.

Advanced For activity #4, have students make a list of all of the notable women they have read

about in this collection. Tell them to think of Lord Randall's true love and Monna Giovanna and the Goodwife and Frankie along with the rest. Have students choose one of the characters and write a short speech for the character in which she discusses how she sees herself in relation to the four categories. The panel discussion can take place among the students in character.

SPOTLIGHT ON

The Weaving of Women's Tales

A By God, if women had but written stories . . .

— Geoffrey Chaucer, *The Wife of Bath's Prologue*

In early Britain, women helped with family and community life, managed estates in their husbands' absence, and pored over books in stone-walled convents. They also composed important works of literature, yet scholars have only recently begun to recognize these women's literary contributions.

The Anglo-Saxon Period: Nameless Voices

Since poems in Anglo-Saxon Britain were composed and transmitted orally, the names of their original authors—whether female or male—have long been obscured. All literary works were generally attrib-uted to the traveling bard (usually male) who recited them. Now, however, many scholars attribute such well-known poems as "The Wife's Lament" and "Wulf and Eadwacer" to women. In these lines from "The Wife's Lament," an anonymous poem, a wife expresses her grief at being banished from her home by her husband (something husbands were permitted to do).

> Our lips had smiled to swear hourly
> That nothing should split us—save dying—
> Nothing else. All that has changed:
> It is now as if it had never been,
> **B** Our friendship. I feel in the wind
> That the man dearest to me detests me.
> I was banished to this knoll knotted by woods
> To live in a den dug beneath an oak.
> Old is this earthen room; it eats at my heart.

—*from* "The Wife's Lament"

No doubt, the names of other women who composed oral works (such as lullabies, elegies, and work songs) were also lost when the works were written down by scribes. One prominent exception to this standard of anonymity was Lioba, a young Wessex nun whose elegant prose was a powerful force in the Church's efforts to convert the Continent.

Anglo-Saxon women also expressed themselves artistically in other (anonymous) ways. Many wove intricate tapestries that recorded the details of their domestic lives amid scenes of men in battle. Others produced beautiful illuminated manuscripts in a few

Timarete painting a portrait, from Giovanni Boccaccio's *De claris mulieribus* (Of famous women), France (2nd half of 15th century). M. 381, fol. 33v.
The Pierpont Morgan Library, New York.

176 THE MIDDLE AGES

The Presentation of an Abbess, written for Raymond Bar, bishop of Metz (early 14th century). Vellum. MS 298, fol. 82v. Fitzwilliam Museum, University of Cambridge.

RESPONDING TO THE ART: EXPLORING THE SUBJECT

What can you surmise about medieval women in the Church from this illustration: [Possible responses: Women were still subservient to men in the Church.]

In medieval times, an abbess was a woman of learning who administered an abbey, or religious community. Her jurisdiction would include not only religious buildings such as churches or chapels, but secular operations such as gardens, hospitals, dining halls, libraries, and book presses. Until Henry VIII abolished Catholic religious houses in the sixteenth century, abbesses could hold secular privileges, for example, belonging to the king's council.

female *scriptoria,* monasteries devoted to copying religious writings. Wealthy women often acted as patrons, commissioning poets and artists to produce works illustrating family history.

The Middle Ages: Court or Cloister

Only two avenues were open to women with literary ambitions in the Middle Ages: the luck to be born into an aristocratic family (girls in such families were sometimes educated alongside their brothers) or service in the Church.

Most women wrote in English rather than in Latin, the formal language used for religious, legal, and political purposes. Women writing in the vernacular wrote mostly about domestic or personal affairs—everyday matters not considered serious or weighty at the time they were written. For both these reasons, few writings by women were preserved in monastery vaults.

For the most part, only in the Church did women have access to the education, economic support, and

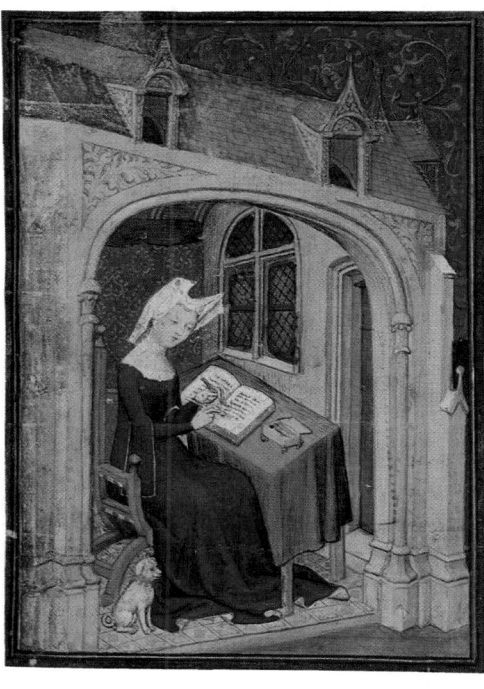

Christine de Pisan, writing, from *The Collected Works of Christine de Pisan* (15th century). French, MS Harley 4431, fol. 4. By permission of the British Library, London.

SPOTLIGHT ON 177

ASSESSMENT TOOLS

Check Test: Short Answer

1. Why don't we know the original authors of poems composed in Anglo-Saxon Britain? [They were transmitted orally.]
2. In what two ways could a woman of the Middle Ages pursue a literary life? [Be born into an aristocratic family or go into the Church.]
3. What qualities of women's writing prevented it from fitting the accepted style of religious writing? [It was personal and subjective.]
4. What was Julian's idea of God? [That God was both Father and Mother.]
5. What unusual obstacle did Margery Kempe overcome in recording her autobiography? [She could probably neither read nor write.]

Describe the facial expression of the woman in the illustration. [Possible responses: Proud, pensive, serious.] How is she different than the women in the illustration on pp. 72–73? [Possible responses: She is engaged in an intellectual activity; she is alone and seems to be involved in her own interests.]

A. Reader's Response: Extending the Text

? Why does it seem that subjective and personal writing has become more accepted as serious literature? [Sample responses: Perhaps we have become more interested in how individual minds see the world than in absolute statements describing it. The people reading have changed. The reading audience is much broader; it was limited almost entirely to the clergy in the twelfth century.]

Writing a letter, from *Les épitres d'Ovide* (detail) (early 16th century). MS Fr. 875, fol. 23v.
© cliché Bibliothèque Nationale de France, Paris.

freedom from family responsibilities necessary for sustained writing. But when women did produce religious writings, they didn't usually fit the accepted mode of orthodox religious works. Women's writings were often more subjective and personal in style. (Today, ironically, we *do* value such personal writing and would probably find the kind of philosophical tract admired in the twelfth century rather dull.)

Julian of Norwich (c. 1342–?)

One of the first English women of letters was a recluse who lived alone in a small cell attached to St. Julian's Church in Norwich. In her only surviving work, *A Book of Showings,* Julian described the sixteen visions of God, or "showings," that she experienced during a critical illness shortly after she turned thirty.

Julian first recorded her revelations in short versions soon after they occurred and in longer

178 THE MIDDLE AGES

versions some twenty years later. Julian's apology to her readers in the short version—"God forbid that you should say or take me for a teacher . . . for I am a woman, ignorant, weak, and frail"— is omitted in the longer version. Perhaps this is a sign that she no longer needed to pretend an inferiority she did not feel.

Julian's visions and reflections revealed a loving, nurturing God. Indeed, the central image in Julian's meditations became "God the Mother."

As truly as God is our Father, so truly is God our Mother, and he revealed that in everything, and especially in these sweet words where he says: I am he; that is to say: I am he, the power and goodness of fatherhood; I am he, the wisdom and the lovingness of motherhood; I am he, the light and the grace which is all blessed love; I am he, the Trinity; I am he, the unity; I am he the supreme goodness of every kind of thing; I am he who makes you to love; I am he who makes you to long; I am he, the endless fulfilling of all true desires. For where the soul is highest, noblest, most honorable, still it is lowest, meekest, and mildest.

—Julian of Norwich, *from A Book of Showings*

Margery Kempe (1373?–?)

The first autobiography in English, *The Book of Margery Kempe,* was dictated by a woman who could probably neither read nor write. Beginning with a religious conversion after the birth of her first child, Margery dictated her lively recollections to two scribes over many years. (The first scribe— thought to be Margery's own son—was nearly illiterate himself, and the work had to be done again with a second.) Although Margery refers to herself almost exclusively as "the creature" rather than "I" (as though to underscore her status as a creation of God), the *Book* projects the voice of a strong-willed, independent personality. In fact, Margery has been compared to Chaucer's vigorous Wife of Bath.

Like Chaucer's pilgrim, Margery was not affiliated with any convent or religious house. At forty, having by this time given birth to fourteen children, Margery made a pact of celibacy with her husband. In the following lines, Margery describes her life of penance.

Observation Assessment After reading this selection, have students work in groups of three to complete in as many different ways as they can the following sentence.

Medieval women writers created stories that were . . .

Informally assess each group's work using the following scales, four being the highest rating:

1. Accuracy: The qualities identified are supported in the text.
   1 2 3 4
2. Quantity: Students are able to think of a variety of things that characterize women's writing.
   1 2 3 4

She gave herself up to great fasting and great watching; she rose at two or three of the clock, and went to church, and was there at her prayers unto the time of noon and also all the afternoon. Then she was slandered and re-proved by many people, because she kept so strict a life. She got a haircloth from a kiln, such as men dry malt on, and laid it in her kirtle as secretly and privily as she might, so that her husband should not espy it. Nor did he, and she lay by him every night in his bed and wore the haircloth every day, and bore children in the time.

—Margery Kempe,
from The Book of Margery Kempe

Dressed entirely in white, Margery traveled ex-tensively in the Holy Land and to shrines in Britain and on the Continent. She made these pilgrimages despite the intolerance and disapproval of her peers. Her plain-spoken declarations of faith and frequent episodes of loud sobbing (she wept daily for fifteen years in sympathy with Christ's suffering) weren't readily understood by others. Indeed, one town even threatened to burn Margery at the stake as a heretic. She also was abandoned—in circum-stances risky for a woman traveling alone—by sev-eral pilgrimage parties.

Margery's manuscript was widely read in the late Middle Ages but then was lost for centuries before resurfacing in an attic of the British Butler-Bowdon family in 1934. We can only wonder how many other women's writings await a similar rediscovery.

Woman Teaching (15th century) from *Le livre des femmes nobles et renommées* by Giovanni Boccaccio. MS. Fr. 598, fol. 71v.
© cliché Bibliothèque Nationale de France, Paris.

A *kirtle* was a dress or skirt. Ask stu-dents why Margery would want to wear the rough and scratchy haircloth next to her skin. [She may have used it as a way to free herself from worldly concerns and pleasures so that she could focus on her spiritual life. Often, a hair shirt was worn as penance.]

C. Exploring the Culture
The medieval period is sometimes considered a time when the culture as a whole valued spiritual life more highly than material existence. What clues from the story of Margery Kempe indicate that expression of spiritual commitment was valued only to a point? [She kept her haircloth a secret from her husband. She was disapproved of and threatened with execution. She was abandoned on several pilgrimages.]

RESPONDING TO THE ART: VISUAL LITERACY
Given what you have already learned about women in the Middle Ages, what can you guess about the woman in the center of this illustra-tion? From what social and eco-nomic class might she come? What can you guess about her family? What kind of education do you think she has had? [Possible responses: She is probably wealthy and a member of the aristocracy; her family may be royalty; she might have brothers since girls were sometimes educated with them; she appears to be teaching, so she can probably read and write.]

READ ON

Read On!

Portfolio Assessment Options

The following projects can help you evaluate and assess your students' reading accomplishments outside of class. Videotapes or photographs of completed projects, or the projects themselves, may be included in students' portfolios.

- **Keep a Three-Column Journal** Have students keep a three-column journal for the stories they read from *The Arabian Nights.* The left-hand column is for a favorite quotation from each of the stories (with story title and page number). The middle column is for an explanation of the quotation and of its relation to the story as a whole. The right-hand column is for a reflection on the connection between the quotation and the reader's experience.

- **Write Postcards** If students choose to read *The Hitchhiker's Guide to the Galaxy,* have them choose fifteen points at which to write postcards home from Arthur Dent to his family and friends. Each postcard should have a message of at least fifty words describing what is happening at that point and what is likely to happen next.

- **Write a Response to History** Have students divide the reading of Arthurian legends such as *The Once and Future King* into sections. Before they start each section, tell them to write down a question in their journals that they would like to have answered or expect to have answered by the end of the section. After they finish the section, they should write two hundred words in response to their question: what they found out, why it wasn't answered, why it turned out to be irrelevant, or what surprise made the question unimportant.

Stories That Save a Life

Perhaps you have been entranced by the story of Sindbad's fantastic voyages—just one of the many tales in *The Arabian Nights,* a framework of stories that dates back to the eighth century (translated by Husain Huddaway, W. W. Norton). Princess Scheherazade, whose husband wants to murder her, saves her own life by telling a dazzling variety of tales (fables, fairy tales, romances, and comic and historical anecdotes), stopping each night at the most suspenseful moment. Since her husband wants to hear what happpens next, he cannot bear to kill his gifted storyteller.

Different Lives in a Different Time

What was a woman's life like in the Middle Ages? The answer depends largely on where she lived and what social class she belonged to. In *Women in the Middle Ages* (Barnes & Noble), Frances and Joseph Gies examine the daily lives of women in the nobility, in religious orders, in the emerging trade classes, and in the peasantry.

Pilgrims in Outer Space

Join earthling Arthur Dent and his trusty sidekick from Betelgeuse, Ford Prefect, on a cosmic (and comic) quest through the galaxy. In *The Hitchhiker's Guide to the Galaxy* (Pocket Books), by Douglas Adams, you may "finally learn once and for all the plain and simple answer to all these nagging little problems of Life, the Universe, and Everything!" (First book of a four-volume series.)

A Lasting Hero

Early manuscripts mention a certain Arthur who led the Britons against the Anglo-Saxon invaders. Enlarged through legend, Arthur was eventually transformed into a romantic hero. Many writers have used the Arthurian legend to explore the grand themes of love, loyalty, and betrayal.

Arthur in our time. The English author T. H. White wrote his version of the Arthurian legend, *The Sword in the Stone* (G. P. Putnam's Sons), before World War II, when England once again needed a hero to shore up its national pride. He later expanded this story into a four-part novel, *The Once and Future King,* that explores the problems of war, justice, and national identity. And though White views Arthur's quest as a tragedy, he balances this somber theme with humorous characters and comic fun.

Magical stories made modern. Since his boyhood, the American writer John Steinbeck had been fascinated with Sir Thomas Malory's *Le Morte Darthur.* Realizing that difficult spelling and archaic words repelled modern readers, Steinbeck rewrote Malory's stories in plain, present-day language. In *The Acts of King Arthur and His Noble Knights* (Farrar, Straus and Giroux), the wonder of the original tales shines on.

180 THE MIDDLE AGES

FOR FURTHER EXPLORATION

Novels
The Mists of Avalon by Marion Zimmer Bradley
Kristin Lavransdatter by Sigrid Undset

Poetry
Fifty Romance Lyric Poems, compiled and translated by Richard Aldington

Nonfiction
The Life and Times of Chaucer by John Gardner
Chaucer and His World by Derek Brewer

A Reader's Guide to Geoffrey Chaucer by Muriel Bowden
Chaucer's World: A Pictorial Companion by Maurice Hussey
English Medieval Romance by W.R.J. Barron

Films
The Lion In Winter
Robin and Marian
Becket

T180 The Middle Ages

The English Language

Middle English: The Language in Transition *by John Algeo*

The history of English is divided into three long periods: Old English (before 1066), Middle English (1066–1485), and Modern English (1485 to the present). To be sure, all English speakers did not go to bed on the night of December 31, 1065, speaking Old English and wake up on the morning of January 1, 1066, saying "Let's talk Middle English now!" Language change is slower and subtler than that. And speakers are seldom aware of changes in their own lifetimes.

Some important changes in pronunciation and grammar happened shortly before 1066, however. Then, in 1066, the Normans conquered England, eventually causing extensive changes in vocabulary. The pre-1066 language looks like a foreign tongue, but by the end of the Middle English period it was quite similar to today's English.

What Happened to the Endings?

In Old English, as in the other Germanic languages, people tended to pronounce words with a strong accent on the first syllable but to rush over the following ones. Unstressed vowels consequently lost their distinctive sounds and were pronounced all alike, as a

The Scriptorium in the Tower of the Monastery of Tavara, from a Spanish manuscript (13th century). M. 429, fol. 183.

The Pierpont Morgan Library, New York.

A. Exploring the Historical Period

? What is the significance of each of these dates? Have students use the time line at the beginning of the unit to find two events in English history for each of these two dates. [Events: King Edward the Confessor dies without heir (1066); Duke of Normandy invades England (1066); Wars of Roses end (1485), First Tudor king, Henry VII, is crowned (1485).]

B. Expansion

Suggest that students look back at the sample of Middle English on p. 106. By comparing this excerpt from *The Canterbury Tales* with its translation on p. 107, students will realize the extent to which Middle English is, indeed, similar to the English we use today. As students will find in examining the rhymes in The General Prologue to *The Canterbury Tales,* speakers of Middle English, unlike speakers of Modern English, usually pronounced a final e as a separate syllable.

Elements of Literature: **Videodisc** Use the following bar codes to locate the video segment about the development of the English language from the Anglo-Saxons to the Renaissance. For more information, see the Videodisc *Teacher's Manual.*

Videodisc Side A

Begin Play, English Track

Begin Play, Spanish Track

Visual Before reading the essay, draw or display a large picture of a door. Ask what it is, and write the word *door* at the bottom of the picture. Then draw the following chart on the chalkboard. Ask students to notice how the word has changed over time.

Old English	Middle English	Modern English
The *duru* opened.	The *doore* opened.	The door opened.
I opened the *dure*.	I opened the *doore*.	I opened the door.
My house has many *dura*.	My house has many *doores*.	My house has many doors.

Auditory Set up an oral reading center, and have a volunteer read aloud the selection to anyone who would like to listen. Alternatively, provide individuals with cassette players, headphones, and the selection on tape so students can replay sections they do not grasp on the first hearing. ☞

By permission of the British Library, London.

Opening of *St. Luke's Gospel*, from the *Lindisfarne Gospels* (7th century). Cotton MS Nero D.IV, fol. 139.

schwa (ə)—the sound in the last syllable of our word *cola.*

The misspellings that began to turn up in manuscripts show that unstressed vowel sounds merged in late Old English. Scribes sat at their desks all day long, tracing out letter shapes on parchment. About the year 1000, scribes had a great deal of trouble in remembering how the endings of words ought to be spelled. They hesitated about writing *stanas* or *stanes* (stones), *comon* or *coman* (they came). Their indecision shows that the scribes had ceased to pronounce the vowels of those endings differently from one another. Eventually, the scribes gave up trying to spell the endings differently and just used the letter *e* to write the unstressed vowel: *stanes, comen.* When that happened, the language became what we call Middle English.

Endings and Order

The change in the pronunciation and spelling of vowels had some far-reaching effects on English grammar. Old English nouns had changed their endings to show various things. For example, the Old English word for "door" as the subject of a sentence was *duru,* but as the direct object, it was *dure.* The plural "doors" was *dura.* After the unstressed vowels had fallen together, all three forms became *dore,* with a schwa sound at the end.

The loss of vowel distinctions meant that English speakers had to find other ways of indicating grammatical meanings, or they had to do without such information.

Effects on gender. For gender, Middle English decided to do without. Today almost no one is sorry that English replaced grammatical with natural gender. Instead of talking about "the door . . . she," "the roof . . . he," and "the wife . . . it," we use *he* for males, *she* for females, and *it* for things without gender.

Effects on plural forms. For number, Middle English came to rely on a few plural endings. Old English had many ways of marking the plural of a noun. A few of these survive in Modern English irregular plurals such as *tooth/teeth, ox/oxen,* and *child/children.* Other Old English plural forms, such as *dura* (doors) from *duru* (door), no longer exist. Middle English used the ending *–es* (from Old English *–as*) for most of its plurals. Thus, Old English *hund/hundas* became Middle English *hound/houndes,* and Old English *dura* was replaced by Middle English *doores.* Today we have only one regular ending, *-s,* as in *hounds* and *doors.*

Effects on case endings. Instead of case endings to show the functions of nouns in a sentence, Middle English came to rely on word order. In Middle English, "The knave slough [killed] the dragon" means something quite different from "The dragon slough the knave"; and that difference is signaled only by the order of the words. The difference from Old English, where word order was much less critical, is profound.

Uninvited Guests

Shortly after the unstressed vowels had come to be pronounced as schwas, a political event occurred that had important consequences for the English language. In 1066, William, duke of Normandy, invaded England with an army of soldiers from France. He defeated the English defenders, led by King Harold, at the Battle of Hastings.

Under William the Conqueror (as he came to be called), French became the language of government, law, education, and upper-class life. English continued to be spoken, of course, by most people: servants, craftsmen, farmers, foresters—the sturdy yeomanry of the land. But

French was the language of the rulers. England—once in danger of becoming an outlying part of Scandinavia—now seemed likely to become a province of France.

The two peoples—Vikings from Scandinavia and Normans from France—were in fact related. The Normans were, as their name suggests, not really French, but Scandinavians from the north who had settled in the western regions of France. They acquired the language of their new home, although they never learned to speak it like the native French people. To elegant Parisians, the Normans always sounded strange, foreign, and provincial.

Thus, the conquerors of Anglo-Saxon England were not at all refined emissaries of a higher civilization who brought culture to primitive England. On the contrary, they were a wild bunch only a few generations removed from their piratical ancestors.

In the long run, however, the Norman Conquest was probably a blessing. English was left to itself, to develop and grow without interference by scholars or government officials. The common folk of the early Middle English period were quite untroubled by traditions of spelling or preconceived notions of what their language ought to be like. So they spoke naturally—letting the vowels fall together and giving up the many gram-

> All English speakers did not go to bed on the night of December 31, 1065, speaking Old English and wake up on the morning of January 1, 1066, saying "Let's talk Middle English now!"

matical endings of Old English, with no sense that they were losing anything of importance. And they were right.

The Battle and the Triumph

For several hundred years, England was a bilingual country. French was spoken by the upper classes among themselves, it was used in law courts and government, and it was used for literature. English was spoken by the lower classes for all the ordinary purposes of daily life—selling grain, buying dishes, scolding children, squabbling with neighbors, and loving the family.

For a time, no one could have said whether French or English would win out as the national language of England. However, several factors tipped the balance to English. Not the least important was the fact that most people spoke English. Also, the Normans in England got into a squabble with France, called the Hundred Years' War. The conflict intensified a feeling of patriotism for things English—especially the English language.

The English language thus gradually reasserted its place in the national life. In the second half of the fourteenth century, about three hundred years after the Conquest, English had again become the primary language in England. This was symbolized by a bill passed in Parliament in 1362 requiring that all law cases be conducted in English instead of in French.

At that time there was no standard English. Instead, people used the English of their native

A. Expansion
To help students understand the extent to which word order signals meaning in our language, you might read aloud the first two stanzas of Lewis Carroll's "Jabberwocky." Let students guess at the meanings of the nonsense words.

'Twas brillig, and the slithy toves
    Did gyre and gimble in the wabe;
All mimsy were the borogoves,
    And the mome raths outgrabe.

"Beware the Jabberwock, my son!
    The jaws that bite, the claws
    that catch!
Beware the Jubjub bird, and shun
    The frumious Bandersnatch!"

B. Expansion
Two hundred years after William's conquest, French was still so often spoken in places of power that Robert of Gloucester writes in the thirteenth century, "I ween that in all the world there is no country that holds not to her own speech, save England alone." Even in the fourteenth century, accounts of the sitting of Parliament were still recorded in French, and many of the prominent poets continued to write in French.

Check Test: Questions and Answers
1. What is a schwa sound? [The "uh" sound used in pronunciation of most unstressed vowels in English.]
2. What letter did eleventh-century scribes use to represent the schwa sound? [The letter e.]
3. How was the difference between subjects and objects indicated in Middle English? [By the order of the words in a sentence, just as in modern English.]
4. What event induced the upper classes to give up speaking French and start speaking English? [The Hundred Years' War against France.]
5. Why did speakers of English at this time borrow many words from French? [Old English had no words for certain ideas and objects, so English speakers simply borrowed the French terms for them.]

? Why do we perceive no difference in the dialect used in the excerpts from *The Canterbury Tales* and *Sir Gawain and the Green Knight* included in this book? [The excerpts in the book have been translated into Modern English.]

Try It Out: Answers

(Answers for dates may vary depending on the dictionary used. All the words in #1 come from the French at some point.)

1. army: fourteenth century
   gentleman: twelfth century
   justice: twelfth century
   royal: fourteenth century
   castle: before twelfth century
   guide: fourteenth century
   master: before twelfth century
   servant: thirteenth century
   chief: fourteenth century
   herb: fourteenth century
   roast: thirteenth century
   soldier: fourteenth century

2. chair (Middle English)
   chaise lounge (Modern English)
   stool (Old English)
   table (Old English)
   tableau (Modern English)
   tablet (Middle English)
   automobile (Modern English)
   (wheel) barrow (Old English)
   car (Middle English)

area. With the reestablishment of English as a language of government, however, the dialect of London (the capital city) quickly became a model to be followed.

In the fourteenth century, literature in English was revitalized. Chaucer, one of our greatest writers, wrote for the English royal court, using the London dialect. The anonymous author of *Sir Gawain and the Green Knight* produced his courtly tale in a northwestern dialect for country gentry. As the language flowered, so did the literature, with the same exuberance and variety.

Both a Borrower and a Lender Be

When English speakers started to use English again to talk about things they had discussed in French for three hundred years, they were literally at a loss for words. They knew no English words for many governmental, legal, military, and artistic things. The simplest thing was to borrow the French terms. And that is just what sensible English speakers did.

Examples of French borrowings are *baron, castle, chancellor, country, duke, government, noble, prince, royal, state; attorney, court, crime, judge, jury, prison; army, captain, corporal, lieutenant, sergeant, soldier; juggler, literature, magic, melody, poetry, sport.* Animals on the hoof looked after by English-speaking workers were, and still are, called by native English names: *cow, hog, sheep, calf, deer.* But when they were slaughtered and served up on the table as food, they were given the French names that the invading nobility used: *beef, pork, mutton, veal, venison.* Thus, our vocabulary continues to echo the English-worker/French-ruler dichotomy of six hundred years ago.

Since the fourteenth century, English has borrowed words from many languages, so English now has one of the richest and most international vocabularies in the world. In turn, English has become a major source of loan-words to other languages. Today there are few languages from which English has not borrowed, and even fewer that have not borrowed from it. That is another benefit of the Norman Conquest that William and his bully boys could not have imagined or understood.

Try It Out

1. Many new words came into English during the Middle English period. Just before the definition of a word, *Merriam-Webster's Collegiate Dictionary,* Tenth Edition, gives the date or century when the word was first recorded in use. Find that date or century for each of these words. What language did each come from?

army	gentleman	justice
royal	castle	guide
master	servant	chief
herb	roast	soldier

2. In each group below, one word was used in Old English, one is a Middle English loan from French, and one is a Modern English loan from French. What origin do you think each word has? Check your guesses in a dictionary.

   a. chair, chaise lounge, stool
   b. table, tableau, tablet
   c. (wheel) barrow, car, automobile

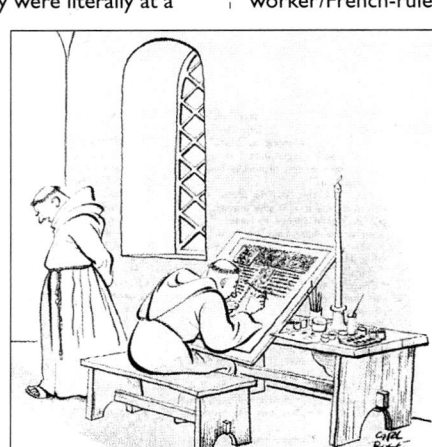

"Period. New paragraph."

Drawing by Carl Rose; ©1950, 1978.
The New Yorker Magazine, Inc.

184 THE MIDDLE AGES

Writer's Workshop

WW Observational Essay

DESCRIPTIVE WRITING

OBSERVATIONAL ESSAY: DESCRIBING A PERSON

If you've ever "people-watched" (and of course you have), you know the enduring fascination of observing others. In an observational essay, you'll describe someone you've observed directly. The techniques of observational writing will help you in other kinds of writing: in reporting events (journalism), in writing about scientific investigations, and in writing about historical events.

Prewriting

1. **Checking your Writer's Notebook.** By doing the Writer's Notebook activities in this collection, you've already begun the prewriting for an observational essay. Check the notes you've taken in your Writer's Notebook. You can use them, but you can also proceed with the prewriting activities that follow.

2. **Selecting a standout subject.** As the portraits in Chaucer's Prologue show, ordinary people can be every bit as interesting as superstars. Choose someone for your essay who has made a strong impression on you. Your subject might be a well-known person, but your subject could also be a family member, best friend, local eccentric, or teacher. Explore both your present and past by thinking through a typical week, noting people you encounter, or by recalling a significant period in your past.

3. **Point of view: adopting a stance.** When you describe a person, you're doing observational writing. In observational writing, you take on the stance of an eyewitness, rather than of a participant. At the same time, you want to choose words carefully to show how you feel about the person you're describing. (Your character sketch won't be fiction, but it's very much an interpretation.) You may write in either the **first** or **third person,** depending on your subject. To describe your grandmother, for example, you might include yourself in the sketch, writing as *I*.

4. **Details: making it specific.** To make readers see and know this person as you do, you must observe the person directly and select revealing **concrete details.** Get started by charting basic information in a Personality Profile like the one on page 186. Then use the Strategies for Elaboration that follow the Personality Profile to build on your observation.

Technology HELP

See Writer's Workshop 2 CD-ROM. *Assignment: Observational Writing.*

ASSIGNMENT
Write a brief observational essay about a real person. Choose someone you can observe, or have observed, directly.

AIM
To inform; to express your point of view.

AUDIENCE
Your classmates, family, or general readers (you decide).

Prewriting
Checking your Writer's Notebook **p. 185**
Selecting a standout subject **p. 185**
Point of view: adopting a stance **p. 185**
Details: making it specific **p. 185**
Language: making it live **p. 186**

Drafting
Beginning and ending **p. 187**
Establish the person's context **p. 187**
Find your design **p. 187**

Evaluating and Revising
Peer review **p. 187**
Self-evaluation **p. 187**

Proofreading and Publishing **p. 187**

Reflecting on Your Writing **p. 187**

PORTFOLIO ASSESSMENT

- **Generating Ideas** To help students in prewriting, use the heuristic in the *Portfolio Management System,* p. 83.
- **Assessment Rubric** For a rubric that can be used to assess students' progress in writing, see the *Portfolio Management System,* p. 85.

OPTIONS FOR TEACHING

STRATEGIES FOR INCLUSION

Auditory Some students might find it helpful to use a tape recorder to make notes for their essays. As they are observing their subjects, they should orally describe what they see. Later, when they work on their drafts, they may replay the tape and listen to the details they noted during their direct observations. Some students might also find it useful to compose their entire essays orally and then play them back to transcribe them.

Kinesthetic Some students might benefit from acting out a mannerism or the posture of the person they are describing. They may videotape themselves in their role-playing and then watch the tape as they prepare notes for their essays. Also, students may videotape their subjects and then refer to the tapes as they write their descriptions. 👉

PROGRAM MANAGER

Computer Guided Instruction For a related observational writing assignment that students may use as additional instruction, see *Writer's Workshop 2.*

Motivation

- Bring a photograph or poster of a person to class, and ask students to look at it for several minutes.
- Ask students to write down one detail from the picture that they think is interesting or unusual and that other people might find interesting or unusual as well.
- Ask volunteers to read their details to the class, and list them on the chalkboard. Discuss with the class why certain details stand out and others do not. Point out that good descriptive writing depends on a sharp eye for detail.

Teaching the Lesson

This lesson includes instructions for each stage of the writing process. You may want to guide students by modeling each stage with your own writing. Tell students that in this Writer's Workshop they will learn about how to make their descriptive writing more lively.

Prewriting

Point out to students that even though the text does not speak of a thesis statement in a descriptive essay, they might find it useful to develop a main idea they want to communicate about the person they are describing. For example, they might decide they want to make the point that Uncle Jerry looks like a person of determination and strong character. Main ideas can help students focus on the language they want to use, the point of view they want to assume, and the kinds of details they want to include.

Try It Out: Possible Answers

1. booming voice, voice like tinkling crystal, explosive laugh, a laugh like an opera singer practicing the scales
2. eyes like twinkling lights, eyes of steel
3. bouncing walk, a walk like a panther
4. volcanic anger, anger like a cornered tiger
5. Answers will vary.

Personality Profile

Name _Rachel Terry_ Age _28_ Occupation _Travel Writer_
Person's setting _San Francisco, CA_
Appearance and voice _Tall, lanky, soft-spoken_
Personality traits _Adventuresome, generous_
Likes _Hiking, watercolor painting_ Dislikes _Loud music, sushi_
Memorable moment _Visit to China on assignment_
Memorable statement _"Standing on the Great Wall with the_
wind in my face — I felt I was part of a great stream of travelers
across time."

Why I chose this person _From the time Rachel used to watch_
me when I was a kid, I've always noticed her determination to meet
her goals.

Strategies for Elaboration: Finding Definitive Details

1. **Actions.** Describe characteristic actions that reveal personality: singing, driving, entertaining lavishly (as Chaucer's Franklin loved to do).
2. **Interactions.** Show your subject in typical encounters with other people (like the Parson with his "flock").
3. **Nonactions.** Describe what a person is like by telling what he or she doesn't do (as the studious Oxford Cleric pays no attention to clothes, food, or fun).
4. **Possessions and places.** Write about the person's flower garden, CD collection, or messy room, for example (remember the Monk's fine horses and greyhounds).

Try It Out

For each item below, create a metaphor or simile to describe a particular person, whether real or imaginary. Share your figures of speech with a group, and then present the group's favorites to the class.

1. voice or laugh
2. eyes
3. walk
4. anger
5. [your choice]

---

5. **Language: making it live.** To make your person come alive, choose descriptive words carefully:

- **Use sensory words.** Chaucer's Prologue is a feast of the senses: sight, hearing, taste, touch, and smell (even garlic breath). From a "blood-red" garment to "black scabby brows" to a "trumpet" voice, Chaucer's sensory words hit the reader full force.

- **Use figurative language.** Striking comparisons create fresh ways of seeing; they can also convey your point of view. A **simile** uses the words *like, as, than,* or *resembles* to state its comparison: The Miller's "mouth was like a furnace door" and the Pardoner's hair "like rat-tails." A **metaphor** doesn't use *like* or other comparison words: The Miller has "a thumb of gold" and the Pardoner a "honey-tongue."

- **Use dialogue.** Speech can reveal character. Chaucer tells us something about the Nun by noting that she even swears gently—she only says "By St. Loy!"

ASSESSMENT TOOLS

Self-Assessment Students can perform a self-assessment of their descriptive essays by applying the following rubric to the Evaluation Criteria on p. 187.

Assessment Criteria

| 1 | 2 | 3 | 4 | 5 | 6 |

Needs Improvement   Superior

INTEGRATING THE LANGUAGE ARTS

Strategic Reading Point out to students that they probably describe people often and that they already know a good bit about writing a description, even if they have never done it before. They can use a KWL chart like the following one to organize their thinking as they read the Writer's Workshop material.

What I Know	What I Want to Know	What I Learned

Drafting

1. **Beginning and ending.** Open with a detail that will catch your reader's attention: a description of the person's clothing, his or her voice, a gesture, a remarkable quality, or a poignant memory. (Chaucer, for example, introduces the Franklin with "White as a daisy-petal was his beard. / A sanguine man, high-colored and benign.") You can also open with a piece of dialogue, a punchy sentence, or a detail of setting. The same attention-getting is true for your ending. Close with a detail—shocking, symbolic, or touching—or with a strong summing-up statement. Just be sure it's a final, finishing stroke.

2. **Establish the person's context.** Be sure to establish time and place, so that the person is anchored in a setting. Also, set up a psychological context when it's appropriate: If the person is important in your life, show why.

3. **Find your design.** Organize your essay in one of these ways: **Spatial order** is useful in physical descriptions: from head to feet, from room to room. Using **order of importance,** you begin with (or end with) the most significant detail. You could use **category order,** and group details by looks, gestures, speech, or actions. **Chronological order** comes into play for narrating an anecdote about your subject or offering glimpses of the person over time. You'll keep the flow interesting, too, if you alternate between **close-ups** and **long shots:** Pull in to describe a scowl; pull back to watch a quarrel.

Evaluating and Revising

1. **Peer review.** When you review your peer's essay, keep the characteristics of a good observational essay in mind. Remember to tell the writer what is effective in his or her piece, noting what needs improvement.

2. **Self-evaluation.** When you evaluate the way a peer reviews your writing, remember that you must take all comments seriously. Notice what reviewers praise, and use that knowledge to strengthen weak areas. You may want to revise content, style, and organization in separate steps.

Proofreading and Publishing

Recopy or reprint your revised essay before the final proofreading. Touch up errors in mechanics and grammar so that nothing distracts from your subject.

If you feel comfortable doing it, show your paper to the person you wrote about. The class could also take turns reading the sketches aloud, as Chaucer's pilgrims took turns telling stories. You might consider grouping your class's sketches by themes, such as Friends, Family, or Mentors.

Reflecting on Your Writing

This paper required a personal point of view—even writing about someone else brings out part of *you.* Here are some questions for reflection.

1. What did you learn about your own powers of observation? Were you already a close observer? Will you be a better one now? Explain.

2. Which of these processes was *most* challenging, and why: choosing details, communicating your stance, or developing sensory and figurative language?

3. Did writing this essay make you see Chaucer's writing differently? How?

▮ *Evaluation Criteria*

A good observational essay
1. *clearly identifies the subject of the essay*
2. *places the subject in a physical and psychological context*
3. *conveys a clear eyewitness point of view about the subject*
4. *uses concrete details, sensory words, figurative language, and dialogue to re-create the subject*
5. *begins and ends by catching the reader's attention*

Revision
STRATEGIES

Examine each detail. Circle any details that seem particularly effective. Underline any details that seem vague or boring. Replace these details with more specific, descriptive ones. Share your changes with a writing partner.

Language Handbook
HELP

Punctuating dialogue: page 1247.

Language Workshop
HELP

Agreement: page 188.

Drafting

Encourage students to write as though they were describing a person orally to someone else. They can later change any expressions that are not to their liking, but the important thing at this stage is to get words down on paper.

Evaluating and Revising

Encourage students to write a statement of the writer's main idea after they have read the writer's essay. The evaluator's main idea should be very close to the one the writer intended to communicate. As students revise their essays, encourage them to refer to the main idea they selected during prewriting.

Reteaching

If students have difficulty finding definitive details for their subjects, suggest they use a chart like the one that follows to organize their thinking. Encourage students to brainstorm additional categories for the chart.

Appearance	Hobbies	Likes	Dislikes

Closure

After students have completed their essays, ask them to write down what they consider the most useful activity performed under each of the following headings: Prewriting; Drafting; Evaluating and Revising; and Proofreading.

Portfolio

Reflecting on Your Writing

Have students use the questions in the text to guide their thinking as they write brief paragraphs reflecting on their writing. Another approach is to have students write answers to these and other questions you pose. In either case, students should attach their reflections to their essays and include both in their portfolios.

PORTFOLIO ASSESSMENT

Peer Evaluation During evaluating and revising, students can use the peer evaluation sheet in the *Portfolio Management System,* p. 84.

PROGRAM MANAGER

Modeling or Practicing Revision
To summarize and model the revision process, and to provide student practice, use **Revision Transparencies 2.8–2.9** in the *Audiovisual Resources Binder.*

Language Workshop
Connecting to Students' Writing

To practice proofreading skills, have students select a piece of their writing from their portfolios. Ask them to draw boxes around all the pronouns and circle all the antecedents. Using a different color of pencil or highlighter, they can repeat the exercises with the subjects and verbs. Students can then verify agreement in compound constructions, between subjects and verbs, and between pronouns and antecedents.

Try It Out: Answers

1. seems; verb agrees with subject closer to it in the case of a compound subject joined by *nor*
2. were; a compound subject joined by *and* usually takes a plural verb, even if one subject is singular
3. was; a singular subject followed by a parenthetical phrase remains singular and takes a singular verb
4. reveal; plural subjects (*sketches*) take plural verbs

PROGRAM MANAGER

- **Extra Practice and Guided Instruction** For more instruction and practice in agreement, see **Language Workshop** in *Teaching Resources A* pp. 52–53.
- **Extra Practice or Guided Instruction** See *Language Workshop:* **Agreement** for more practice or guided instruction in agreement.

Language Workshop

Technology
H E L P

See Language Workshop CD-ROM. *Key word entry: agreement.*

Language Handbook
H E L P

Agreement: page 1223.

Try It Out

Choose the word that creates correct agreement in each sentence.

1. Neither the Squire nor the Doctor (seem, seems) as gallant as the Knight.
2. The Nun's rosary beads and brooch (was, were) brightly polished.
3. We wonder how the Oxford Cleric, as well as his twenty volumes of philosophy, (was, were) carried by a horse "thinner than a rake."
4. If any of the pilgrims' character sketches (reveal, reveals) Chaucer himself, the description of the Host is closest.

188 THE MIDDLE AGES

AGREEMENT: COMMON PROBLEMS

Here's a draft essay about one character from *The Canterbury Tales*.

> The pilgrims who met by chance at the Tabard Inn was an unlikely collection of friends. The Friar, along with the similarly well-fed Nun, were the most outlandish pilgrims. Still, the Miller remains my favorite. His knotty shoulders and wart-tipped nose makes quite a vivid picture. Either his furnace-door mouth or his spadelike, red beard are the detail that best announces the Miller's volatile temper. It's also hard to imagine a man who can break a door with his head playing the mournful-sounding bagpipes, but I guess I've just never seen one.

While the writer uses strong, vivid details, she has trouble with some sticky subject-verb combinations. *All* writers, even professionals, encounter the grammatical problems in this paragraph, but these problems can be mastered.

1. *Subject-verb agreement* means that a singular subject takes a singular verb and plural subjects take plural verbs. A subject's number is **not** changed by a following phrase or clause.

   The **pilgrims** who met by chance at the Tabard Inn **were** an unlikely collection of friends.

2. In formal usage, a singular subject followed by a parenthetical phrase such as *along with . . . , as well as . . . ,* or *in addition to . . .* remains singular.

   The **Friar,** along with the similarly well-fed Nun, **was** the most outlandish **pilgrim.**

3. A *compound subject* is two or more subjects having a single verb. A compound subject joined by *and* usually takes a plural verb, even if one subject is singular.

   His knotty **shoulders and** wart-tipped **nose make** quite a vivid picture.

4. For a compound subject joined by *or* or *nor,* the verb agrees with the subject closer to the verb.

   Either his furnace-door **mouth or** his spadelike, red **beard is** the detail that best announces the Miller's volatile temper.

Writer's Workshop Follow-Up: Proofreading

Re-read the observational essay you wrote for the Writer's Workshop on page 185, checking for agreement problems. Have you maintained subject-verb agreement in each sentence? After you check for agreement in your essay, ask a peer reviewer to look over your paper for agreement problems; then make any necessary corrections.

[handwritten] loves–singular / love –plural

[handwritten] Rule

✓ QUICK CHECK: Agreement

Choose the word that creates correct agreement in each of the following sentences.

[handwritten: 2] **[1]** Our dog, as well as both of our cats, (<u>loves</u>, love) to be held in our laps.
[handwritten: 1] **[2]** A woman who knows how to repair (<u>her</u>, their) own car is less likely to be cheated by garage mechanics than is a man or woman who doesn't know how.
[handwritten: plural subject] *[handwritten: 1]* **[3]** The people who will gather here for the parade next Saturday (knows, <u>know</u>) the best place to be.
[handwritten: 3] **[4]** My sisters, my brothers, and my dad (enjoys, <u>enjoy</u>) watching baseball a lot more than I do.
[handwritten: 4] **[5]** Neither the garden nor the lawn (<u>is</u>, are) in the best shape right now.

CREATIVE PROBLEM SOLVING
LEARNING FOR LIFE

Emerging Technology

Problem

During the Hundred Years' War, the development of armor-piercing arrows made knighthood obsolete. How will advances in technology affect today's occupations?

Project

Investigate how emerging technology is expected to change an occupation that interests you. How will the demand for workers be affected? How will education and training requirements, as well as job tasks, change?

Preparation

1. Choose an occupation that interests you: one you're thinking of pursuing or simply one you're curious about.
2. Use the *5W-How?* questions (*Who? What? When? Where? Why? How?*) to generate questions for gathering information with a focus. The suggestions under "Project," above, will get you started.
3. In addition to library sources, community groups such as trade or professional organizations may be able to provide the information you need.

Procedure

1. To get an overview of the occupation, start with the *Dictionary of Occupational Titles* and the *Occupational Outlook Handbook.* (Both are government publications, and both are available on-line in certain databases; check with your librarian.)
2. In addition to standard sources such as the card catalog and indexes for newspapers, magazines, and databases, consider checking with special-interest newsgroups on the Internet. (Moderated newsgroups are generally more reliable than unmoderated ones.)
3. Keep in mind that the sources you use should be not only reliable but also relevant, recent, and representative. Remember, too, to credit your sources for the facts and figures you use.

Presentation

Use one of the following formats (or another that your teacher approves):

1. **Traveling Exhibit**

   Create a traveling exhibit using hand-drawn or computer-generated graphics to display your findings. For example, you could use bar charts to show current and future job openings or qualifications. Include credit lines that indicate your sources, and give your exhibit a catchy title. Display your exhibit on Career Day at your school or at a local middle school.

2. **Future Expectations**

   Write a job description detailing the tasks and responsibilities an employee in the occupation will be expected to carry out. Use present-tense action verbs (for example, "using an interferometer, a virtual-reality designer measures . . ."), and be as specific as possible. Make your job description accessible to a wider audience by adding a glossary of technical terms arranged in alphabetical order. With classmates who have also chosen this option, compile a booklet of job descriptions, or create a "page" for your school's database system.

3. **Sharing Interests**

   Give an informal talk reporting your findings to a school- or community-based group that shares your interest in the occupation. For example, students in an earth sciences class might enjoy learning how emerging technology is expected to affect the knowledge and skills required of meteorologists. Be sure to adapt your material to suit the interest and ability levels of your listeners—for example, by explaining technical terms or jargon. You may also prepare visuals (charts, graphs, and so on) to augment your presentation.

Processing

Did doing this activity confirm or deflate your interest in the occupation? Did it change your views about the kind of education and training you would need, and if so, how? Write a brief reflection for your portfolio.

Learning for Life

PORTFOLIO ASSESSMENT

Performance Assessment Rubric So that students may see the evaluation criteria before they begin working on these projects, share the rubric provided in the *Portfolio Management System,* p. 86.

DEVELOPING WORKPLACE COMPETENCIES

Preparation	Procedure	Presentation
Identifies general problem	Uses resources well	Processes information
Clarifies problem	Acquires data	Communicates ideas
Generates related ideas	Evaluates data	Teaches others
	Interprets information	

The Renaissance
1485–1660

A Fête at Bermondsey (c.1570) by J. Hoofnagel. Oil on panel.

191

RESPONDING TO THE ART: VISUAL LITERACY

Ask students what they might assume about the people in this painting, based on the activities depicted. How do they occupy their time? [Possible responses: They attend parties and festivals; they play games and have time for leisure.] From what class do you think they come? [Possible responses: Upper class; aristocracy; landed class.] What might the people in this picture value? [Possible responses: Art and culture are important to them. Enjoying life; living for pleasure.]

PROGRAM MANAGER

- **Summative Assessment** See Literary Period Test: Literature of the Renaissance, *Test Booklet,* pp. 85–88, for a test on an additional text from the same historical era.
- **Application** For practice of a reading strategy for this unit, see Becoming a Strategic Reader worksheet, *Teaching Resources A,* pp. 63–64.
- **Performance Assessment** Use Assessment 2 in the *Integrated Performance Assessment,* Level G, to evaluate reading and writing skills covered in collections 3–5. For help with evaluation, see *Holistic Scoring Workshop* software.

Responding to the Quotation

This is part of the chorus at the end of Act I of *Henry V*. King Henry is planning to attack France to claim several dukedoms that are his by right. The chorus praises King Henry and England, and then goes on to warn that three lords are conspiring with the French against Henry.

PROGRAM MANAGER

- **Planning Instruction** See Teaching Notes, *Teaching Resources A,* p. 55, for additional teaching options about the Renaissance.
- **Assessment** For assessment of the literary and historical events mentioned in the historical introduction, see **Literary Period Introduction Test,** *Test Booklet,* pp. 35–36.

The Renaissance

by C. F. Main

O England! model to thy inward greatness,
Like little body with a mighty heart . . .
— *William Shakespeare*

British Library, London.

Tower of London and shipping, with Charles, duke of Orleans, seated in the Tower writing, from the *Poems of Charles Duke of Orleans and Other Works* (c. 1500), Roy 16 F II fol. 73.

Elements of Literature:
Videodisc Use the following bar codes to locate information about Queen Elizabeth I. For more information, see the Videodisc *Teacher's Manual.*

Videodisc Side A
Begin Play
English Track

Begin Play
Spanish Track

What do you think people living a hundred years from now will call the age we live in today? Will they say we lived in the Space Age, the Age of Computers, the Age of Anxiety, the Age of Violence? We might be given a label we can't even imagine.

Just as we don't know what people of the future will think of us, the people of Europe living in the 1400s, 1500s, and 1600s didn't know that they were living in the Renaissance. Historical periods—the Middle Ages, the Renaissance, the Romantic period—are historians' inventions, useful labels for complex phenomena. The Middle Ages in England did not end at 11:59 P.M. on a certain night in 1485, when King Richard III's naked body, trussed up like a turkey, was thrown in an unmarked grave. And the English Renaissance did not begin at 12:01 A.M. when a Tudor nobleman was crowned King Henry VII. The changes in people's values, beliefs, and behavior that marked the emerging Renaissance occurred gradually. Much that could be called "medieval" lingered on long after the period known as the Middle Ages was past. Historical periods cannot be rigidly separated from one another, but they can be distinguished.

Beginning in the late 1400s, the English Renaissance marked changes in people's values, beliefs, and behavior.

Rediscovering Ancient Greece and Rome

The term *renaissance* itself is a French word meaning "rebirth." It refers particularly to renewed interest in classical learning, which means the writings of ancient Greece and Rome. In the long period of the Middle Ages, most European scholars had forgotten the Greek language, and they used a form of Latin that was very different from the Latin of ancient Rome. Very few ordinary people could read. Those who could read were encouraged to concentrate on texts promoting Church doctrine. But in the Renaissance, people discovered the marvels hidden away in old Greek and Latin classics—books that had been tucked away on the cobwebbed shelves of monasteries for hundreds of years. Now people learned to read Greek once more and reformed the Latin that they read, wrote, and spoke.

Some people became more curious about themselves and their world than people in general had been in the Middle Ages, so that gradually there was a renewal of the human spirit—of curiosity and creativity. New energy seemed to be available for creating beautiful things and thinking new, even daring, thoughts. Today we still use the

> Knowledge is power.
> —Francis Bacon, 1597

World map drawn in a fool's head (detail) (1590). Based on *Ortelin's Atlas*, 1570.
© cliché Bibliothèque Nationale de France, Paris.

193

A. Humanities Connection
Historians have come to characterize the changes that began in the time of Charlemagne and continued through the fifteenth or sixteenth century as a series of renaissances.

B. Exploring the Culture
The use of this French term to characterize this historical period began in the nineteenth century.

C. Exploring the Culture
The Greek classics were rediscovered through Byzantine and Arab scholarship.

Time Line

- **1541–1565**
  In 1557, the year before Elizabeth I became queen, a printer named Richard Tottel put out an important collection of poems titled *Songs and Sonnets*. The best poems in this book, which is commonly called *Tottel's Miscellany,* had been written some years earlier by Sir Thomas Wyatt and by Henry Howard, the earl of Surrey. Both Wyatt and Surrey were inspired by the Italian scholar and poet Petrarch and were responsible for introducing Petrarch's work into England.

Technology Tip

TECHNOLOGY Teach your students about Renaissance art by accessing the WebMuseum Web site. The URL for Renaissance information is **http://www.oir.ucf.edu /wm /paint/glo/renaissance**. *You may want to preview any Internet activity that you suggest to students. Because these resources are sometimes public forums, their content can be unpredictable.*

The Renaissance, 1485–1660

LITERARY EVENTS

• Martin Luther's sermon (detail) (16th century) from a triptych by Lucas Cranach.

1485–1515	1516–1540	1541–1565	1566–1590
Niccolò Machiavelli's *The Prince* written, 1513	Book licensing laws introduced in England, 1538 Spanish priest Bernardino de Sahagún begins compiling exhaustive Aztec encyclopedia in Mexico, 1529 Thomas More's *Utopia* published, 1516	**William Shakespeare,** the Bard of Avon, born, 1564 *Tottel's Miscellany* (including poems of Wyatt and Surrey) published, 1557	**Edmund Spenser** publishes first three books of *The Faerie Queene,* 1590 **Christopher Marlowe's** *Doctor Faustus* written, 1588 Okuni, a former priestess, forms first kabuki theater company in Japan (in 1629, Okuni and all other women banned from the kabuki stage), c. 1586 In France, Montaigne begins his *Essais,* 1572

CULTURAL/HISTORICAL EVENTS

1485–1515	1516–1540	1541–1565	1566–1590
Richard III is killed in battle, 1485 John Cabot explores northeast coast of North America, 1497 Vasco da Gama reaches India via Cape of Good Hope, 1498 Leonardo da Vinci paints *Mona Lisa,* c. 1503 Henry VIII crowned king of England, 1509 Balboa crosses Isthmus of Panama and sights Pacific Ocean, 1513	Martin Luther posts his ninety-five theses on church door in Wittenburg, Germany, beginning the Protestant Reformation, 1517 First Africans taken to Americas as slaves, 1517 Magellan leads first expedition to circumnavigate the globe, 1519–1521 Hernando Cortés conquers Mexico, destroying Aztec empire, 1521 In India, Babur conquers Delhi and founds Mogul dynasty, 1526 Henry VIII proclaims himself head of the Church of England, c. 1533	Michelangelo paints *The Last Judgment* on altar wall of the Sistine Chapel, 1534–1541 Polish astronomer Nicolaus Copernicus publishes theory that planets orbit the sun, 1543 Mary Tudor—"Bloody Mary"—reigns, restoring papal authority in England, 1553–1558 Elizabeth I becomes queen of England, 1558	English navy defeats Spanish Armada, 1588

• *Nicolaus Copernicus* (detail) (1575). German School.

• *Mona Lisa* (c. 1503) by Leonardo da Vinci.

• Hernando Cortés (1485–1547), Spanish explorer, meeting Montezuma (c. 1480–1520), Aztec emperor.

USING THE TIME LINE

To enhance their grasp of the innovations and events of this period, ask students to read through the time line and to pick the entry that they find most interesting. Then, have each student identify his or her choice and tell the reason(s) behind it.

Shakespeare's sonnets published (written c. mid-1590s), 1609

Ben Jonson writes *The Masque of Blackness* and *Volpone*, 1605–1606

Shakespeare writes *King Lear* and *Macbeth*, 1605–1606

Cervantes publishes Part I of *Don Quixote* (Part II published in 1615), 1605

Globe Theatre built in London, 1599

In London, outbreak of plague forces theaters to close, 1593–1594

Newspapers first published in London, 1621

Francis Bacon's *Novum Organum* (New Instrument) published, 1620

Aemilia Lanier publishes her book of poetry, *Salve Deus Rex Judaeorum*, 1611

King James Bible published, 1611

John Donne's *Holy Sonnets* written, 1610–1611

• Lithograph showing the arrival of the Pilgrims in Massachusetts Bay (1620).

• English astrolabe (1559), a navigational instrument, made for Queen Elizabeth I by Thomas Gemini.

John Milton begins *Paradise Lost*, 1658

American poet Anne Bradstreet's *The Tenth Muse Lately Sprung Up in America* published in London, 1650

Puritans close all theaters in England, 1642–1660

1591–1610	1611–1640	1641–1660

British East India Company founded for trade with Asia, 1600

Gunpowder Plot, an attempt by Guy Fawkes and others to blow up Parliament and assassinate James I, averted, 1605

First permanent English settlement in North America established at Jamestown, Virginia, 1607

In Italy, Galileo is first to study sky with telescope, 1609

The *Mayflower* lands at Plymouth Rock, Massachusetts, 1620

English physician William Harvey explains the circulation of blood, 1628

Taj Mahal built near Agra, India, c. 1632–c. 1649

Japan expels all Europeans, 1639

• Taj Mahal.

English Civil Wars fought, 1642–1651

Manchus proclaim Ch'ing dynasty in China, 1644

Charles I beheaded, 1649

Dutch establish settlement in South Africa, 1652

Oliver Cromwell rules England as lord protector, 1653–1658

Jews legally readmitted to England (after being expelled in 1290), 1655

Puritan Commonwealth ends; monarchy restored with Charles II, 1660

• The World Map (c. 1540), from the *Portolan Atlas of the World* by Battista Agnese of Venice.

• 1591–1610
Shakespeare described the Globe Theater in the chorus's introduction to Act I of *Henry V*:
". . . But pardon, gentles all,
The flat unraised spirit that hath dar'd
On this unworthy scaffold to bring forth
So great an object: can this cockpit hold
The vasty fields of France? or may we cram
Within this wooden O the very casques
That did affright the air at Agincourt?
O, pardon! since a crooked figure may
Attest in little place a million;
And let us, ciphers to this great acompt,
On your imaginary forces work."

• 1611–1640
Galileo Galilei (1564–1642) made discoveries that challenged the then official teachings of the Roman Catholic Church. Galileo's Copernican view—that the Earth revolved around the Sun, rather than the opposite—was denounced by the Church in 1616 as heresy because it contradicted the Bible and displaced humanity as the center of the universe. Galileo was ordered not to spread his theory. In 1632, however, he published *Dialogue on Two Chief World Systems*. He was again summoned by the Church and this time knelt to recant his views publicly. He is said, however, to have muttered on arising, "Eppur si muove"—"But still it [the earth] moves." He spent the last eight years of his life under house arrest. In 1983, the Church finally rescinded its condemnation of Galileo.

Ladies and Gentlemen Dancing in a Sumptuous Interior by Paulus Vredeman de Vries (1567–c. 1630). Christie's, London.

> God made man and woman at the close of the creation, to know the laws of the universe, to love its beauty, and to admire its greatness. He bound his human creatures to no fixed place, to no prescribed form of work, and by no iron necessity, but gave them freedom to will and to love. "I have set thee," says the Creator, "in the midst of the world, that thou mayst the more easily behold and see all that is therein. I created thee a being neither heavenly nor earthly, neither mortal nor immortal only, that thou mightest be free to shape and to overcome thyself. Thou mayest sink into a beast or be born anew to the divine likeness. To thee alone is given a growth and a development depending on thine own free will."
>
> —Pico della Mirandola (1463–1494), *On the Dignity of Humanity*

term "Renaissance person" for an energetic and productive human being who is interested in science, literature, history, art, and other subjects. (In America, Virginia's Thomas Jefferson, author of the Declaration of Independence, is referred to as a "Renaissance man.")

Fifteenth-century scholars rediscovered the writings of ancient Greece and Rome. At this same time, people became more curious about themselves and their world.

It All Began in Italy: A Flourish of Genius

The new energy and creativity were first observable in Italy, where considerable wealth had been generated by the gold and other riches stolen from the Americas. The Renaissance began in Italy in the fourteenth century and lasted into the sixteenth.

Thinking about just a few of the extraordinary people who flourished in this period—artists such as Leonardo da Vinci and Michelangelo, explorers such as Christopher Columbus, or scientists such as Galileo—reminds us how remarkably rich this period was, and how much we owe to it.

Almost everyone in Europe and Britain at this time was Roman Catholic, in name anyway, so the Church was very rich and powerful, even in political affairs—in ways we would probably object to today. Many of the popes were lavish patrons of artists, architects, and scholars.

OPTIONS FOR TEACHING

INTEGRATING THE LANGUAGE ARTS

Writing: Travel Brochure Have students write a travel brochure for Renaissance/Elizabethan England, mentioning sights and persons of interest that a visitor should see.

Strategic Reading Before students read the historical introduction, ask them to record what

they know and what they want to know on a KWL chart like the one below. After they have finished reading the assignment, have students complete the third column with what they have learned.

Know	Want to Know	Have Learned

Pope Julian II, for example, commissioned the artist Michelangelo to paint gigantic scenes from the Bible on the ceiling of the Sistine Chapel, a small church in the pope's "city" that was called, as it is today, the Vatican. Lying on his back on a scaffold, Michelangelo painted the Creation, the fall of Man and Woman, Noah's flood, and other Biblical and mythological subjects. His bright, heroic figures, which are still admired by thousands of visitors to Rome each year, show individual human beings who are noble and capable of perfection. This optimistic view of human nature was also expressed by many other Renaissance painters and writers.

The Renaissance began in fourteenth-century Italy, where the Catholic Church financed many intellectual and artistic endeavors.

Humanism: Questions About the Good Life

Refreshed by the classics, the new writers and artists were part of an intellectual movement known as **humanism.** The humanists went to the old Latin and Greek classics to discover new answers to such questions as "What is a human being?" "What is a good life?" and "How do I lead a good life?" Of course, Christianity provided complete answers to these questions, answers that the Renaissance humanists accepted as true. Renaissance humanists found no essential conflicts between the teachings of the Church and those of an ancient Roman moralist like Cicero. They sought instead to harmonize these two great sources of wisdom: the Bible and the classics. Their aim was to use the classics to strengthen, not discredit, Christianity.

The Outdoor Concert (detail) (16th century) by the Italian School.

Hotel Lallemand, Bourges, France.

> Some books are to be tasted, others to be swallowed, and some few to be chewed and digested.
> —Francis Bacon, 1625

The humanists' first task was to recover accurate copies of these ancient writings. Their searches through Italian monasteries turned up writers and works whose very existence had been forgotten. Their next task was to share their findings. And so they became teachers, especially of the young men who would become the next generation's rulers—wise and virtuous rulers, they hoped. From the Greek writer Plutarch, for instance, these humanist teachers would learn that the aim of life is to attain virtue, not success or money or fame, because virtue is the best possible human possession and the only source of true happiness.

An intellectual movement known as humanism began to use the Latin and Greek classics, combined with traditional Christian thought, to teach people how to live and how to rule.

C. Expansion

True to the definition of a Renaissance person, Michelangelo excelled in many areas. Not only did he execute the masterwork of the Sistine Chapel, but he created powerful sculptures of monumental proportions that convey human emotion and portray the beauty and force of the human physique. Michelangelo also worked as an architect, becoming chief architect of St. Peter's Basilica in Rome, one of the most important projects of his time. Although he is less famous for it, Michelangelo also wrote poetry, expressing in words the ideas connected to his enormous creative gift.

D. Literary Connections

The aim of humanistic teaching, as Milton summarized it in his essay *Of Education,* was not to produce scholars but to fit students to "perform justly, skillfully, and magnanimously all the offices both private and public, of peace and war."

CROSSING THE CURRICULUM

Architecture Encourage students to choose a single example of Renaissance architecture and to compare it with an example of Gothic architecture. Have students use annotated illustrations to explain the differences. To explore Renaissance architecture, access the collections at the University of Virginia Library's Digital Image Center at **http://www .lib.virginia.edu/dic/colls/ arh102/index .html**. *You may want to preview any Internet activity that you suggest to students. Because these resources* are sometimes public forums, their content can be unpredictable.

Science The Renaissance was a time of increasing scientific knowledge. For example, Leonardo da Vinci is remembered for his inventions and his analysis of the human body. Have students do oral reports on an English Renaissance scientist, such as the physician William Harvey or the botanists John Parkinson or William Turner.

Music Encourage students to choose an English composer such as William Byrd, Thomas Morley, or Thomas Campion, to find a song the composer set to music, and to bring an example to class. Play any recordings they have located, and have students check to see if the lyrics were written by any of the poets in this Collection.

This illustration of a sixteenth-century printing shop was crafted through a process called engraving. In this process a sharp instrument called a burin is used to cut a picture or design into the surface of a copper plate. Applied with a cloth, ink fills the indentations in the plate. After the excess ink is removed, the plate, a piece of paper, and a felt blanket are squeezed between the rollers of a press, a process that forces the ink onto the paper. The print is pulled from the plate, revealing a copy of the design.

A. Expansion
Encourage a discussion, based on students' reading so far, of why Gutenberg chose to print the Bible first rather than some other book. Point out that the Bible remains a best-seller today and that many editions and translations are available.

B. Exploring the Historical Period
Spain, Hungary, and Poland also had their first printing presses between 1474 and 1476; Denmark and Sweden were equipped by 1482–1483. By 1500, forty thousand titles had been printed, constituting a total number of about six million books.

By permission of The Folger Shakespeare Library, Washington, D.C.

Printing Shop (1580s) by Jan van der Straet. Engraving.

The New Technology: A Flood of Print

The computer has radically transformed how we get information today. Similarly, the printing press transformed the way information was exchanged during the Renaissance. Before this, all books were laboriously written out by hand—you can imagine how difficult and expensive this was and how few books were available.

The inventor of printing with movable type was a German named Johannes Gutenberg (1400?–1468). He printed the first complete book, an immense Latin Bible, at Mainz, Germany, around 1455. From there, the art and craft of printing spread to other cities in Germany, in the Low Countries (the Netherlands, Belgium, and Luxembourg), and in northern Italy. By 1500, relatively inexpensive books were available throughout western Europe. In 1476, printing reached England, then regarded as an

Correr Museum, Venice.

RESTAVRATO SOTTO
RATISTA SCHINELLA

Bookbinder (16th century).

Grouping Strategies Team students with various learning styles for group activities. The combination of their strengths should improve the group's dynamics.

Managing the Reader's Response Classroom Create a comfort zone for students by encouraging and praising individuals for their own thoughts. To ensure that students' comments are related to the material, encourage students to return to the text to show the bases of their responses.

Block Scheduling In planning for a longer class period, avoid trying to teach two complete lessons. For some students, too much information can be confusing and exhausting. Instead, add appropriate reteaching or enrichment activities to enhance one lesson.

island remote from the centers of civilization. In that year, William Caxton (1422?–1491), a merchant, diplomat, and writer who had been living in the Low Countries, set up a printing press in Westminster (now part of London). In all, Caxton's press issued about one hundred different titles, initiating a flood of print in English that is still increasing.

> *Gutenberg's printing press helped spread the new knowledge, making more books available to more people than ever before.*

Two Friends—Two Humanists

When you hear people speak of humanism, you may hear the name Erasmus. Desiderius Erasmus (1466?–1536) is today perhaps the best known of all the Renaissance humanists. Erasmus was a Dutch monk, but he lived outside the monastery and loved to travel, visiting many of the countries in Europe, including Italy, France, Germany, and England. He belonged, then, to all Europe. Because he wrote in Latin, he could address his many writings to all the educated people of western Europe.

On his visits to England, Erasmus taught Greek at Cambridge University and became friendly with a number of important people, among them a young lawyer named Thomas More (1477?–1535). More and Erasmus had much in common: They both loved life, laughter, and classical learning, and they both were dedicated churchmen, though they were impatient with some of the Church's corrupt practices at that time.

Like Erasmus, More wrote in Latin—poems, pamphlets, biographies, and his famous treatise on human society, *Utopia* (yōō·tō′pē·ə) (1516). This book became immediately popular, and it has been repeatedly translated into English and many other languages. Hundreds of writers have imitated or parodied it, and it has given us a useful adjective for describing impractical social schemes: *utopian*. More himself was far from impractical; he held a number of important offices, rose to the

Erasmus of Rotterdam (detail) (c. 1523) by Hans Holbein the Younger. Oil on wood (42 cm × 32 cm). Louvre, Paris.

Sir Thomas More (detail) (16th century) by Hans Holbein the Younger. © The Frick Collection, New York.

C. Exploring the Historical Period

Defying custom, More taught Latin to his daughter Meg; few women were given any kind of higher education in Europe at the time.

D. Literary Connections

Book I of More's *Utopia* is a dialogue analyzing the social, economic, penal, and moral problems in England. Book II is a narrative describing Utopia (from Greek *ou*, "not," and *topos*, "place," ironically meaning "nowhere.") In Utopia, poverty, crime, injustice, and other problems do not exist.

COOPERATIVE LEARNING

Brainstorming KWL Have students work in small groups to brainstorm ideas for their KWL charts about Renaissance England (p. T196). Ask each group to produce at least two entries for each column in the chart. Let one member of each group share the group's efforts with the class, making a large list on the chalkboard for everyone to use.

Newscast Ask groups of students to create a modern-day newscast based on newsworthy items from the Renaissance. Students could research and present the events surrounding Marlowe's mysterious death, broadcast "live" from the scene of the defeat of the Armada, report on developments in astronomy, or interview Queen Elizabeth. Be sure each student defines his or her role in the production. ☞

Other English humanists were Sir Thomas Elyot and Roger Ascham. Elyot's *The Book Named the Governor* (1531) argues that England's leaders need a knowledge of ancient literature, history, and philosophy. Ascham's *The Schoolmaster* (1570), according to Samuel Johnson (1709–1784), "contains the best advice that was ever given for the study of languages." Ascham was Queen Elizabeth I's tutor. Both Elyot and Ascham wrote in English, a sign that Latin would cease to be the language of all learned discourse.

B. Exploring the Historical Period

Students should be aware that this was a time of internal reform in the Church, as well as a time of criticism from those who chose to break away. What is known today as the Counter-Reformation had its roots in this internal reform—some of which actually predated the Reformation.

What Was the Renaissance?

Here, reduced to a small list, are the major characteristics of that great era called the Renaissance:

- People expanded their worlds by reading classical Greek and Roman writers rather than only religious writings that promoted Christian doctrine.
- Humanism spread, focusing attention on human life here and now, as well as on eternal life.
- A new technology—printing—made books widely available.
- A growing merchant class, rich with wealth plundered from the Americas, began to challenge the power of the bishops and the pope.
- The spread of scholarly Latin throughout Europe made possible the sharing of ideas.

very top of his profession, was knighted, and, as Lord Chancellor, became one of the king's chief ministers. More continues to fascinate people today. The play *A Man for All Seasons,* by Robert Bolt, later made into a movie (available on videotape), is about More and his tragic stand-off with King Henry VIII over a matter of law (see page 202). You might notice that many lawyers and politicians today hang a picture of Thomas More in their offices (the famous Holbein portrait is shown on page 199).

 Desiderius Erasmus and Thomas More, humanists and close friends, helped shape European thought and history.

The Reformation: Breaking with the Church

While the Renaissance was going on throughout Europe, there occurred in some countries another important series of events called the

> Superstition, idolatry, and hypocrisy have ample wages, but truth goes a-begging.
> —Martin Luther, *Table Talk,* published in 1569

Reformation. In England these two vast movements were closely related, and their forces were felt by all English writers. Although the exact nature of the Reformation varied from country to country, one feature was common to all Reformers: They rejected the authority of the pope and the Italian churchmen. In England, conflicts with the papacy had occurred off and on over the centuries, but adjustments had always been made on both sides. By the 1530s, an open break with the Roman Church could no longer be avoided.

By then, a number of circumstances made such a break possible. Strong feelings of patriotism and national identity made the English people resent the financial burdens imposed on them by the Vatican—the pope, after all, was a foreign power in far-off Italy. Moreover, new religious ideas were coming into England from the Continent, especially from Germany. There, a monk named Martin Luther (1483–1546) had founded a new kind of Christianity, based not on what the pope said, but on a personal understanding of the Bible. Like any institution that has

OPTIONS FOR TEACHING

ASSESSMENT TOOLS

Check Test: True-False

1. The term *Renaissance* refers to a "rebirth" of interest in the writings of classical Greece and Rome. [True]
2. New creativity in the arts first appeared in Italy. [True]
3. Renaissance humanists rejected the Bible. [False]
4. The invention of printing helped make classical texts more readily available. [True]
5. In all countries where the Reformation occurred, a key element was rejection of the authority of the Pope. [True]

been around for a long time and that has ignored corruption within its ranks, the Church needed reform. Right at home in England, humanists like More and Erasmus were ridiculing old superstitions, as well as the ignorance and idleness of monks and the loose living and personal wealth of priests and bishops.

Strong feelings of patriotism and new ideas coming from the Continent encouraged people to question the authority of the Catholic Church and to object to the financial burdens imposed on them by the pope in Rome.

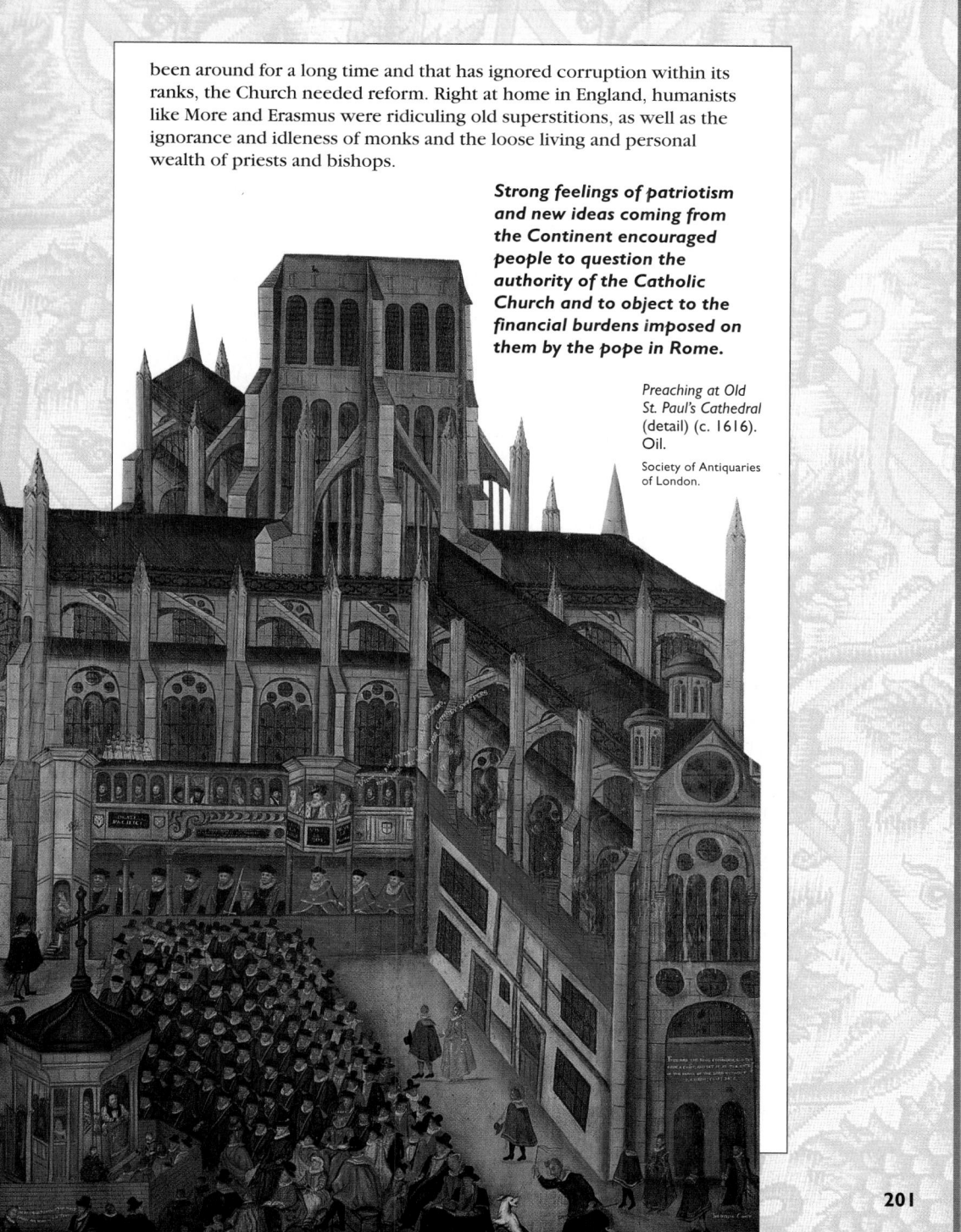

Preaching at Old St. Paul's Cathedral (detail) (c. 1616). Oil.

Society of Antiquaries of London.

201

ASSESSMENT TOOLS

Observation Assessment Complete the following statements for discussion groups by checking the descriptor that applies.

1. Students use their Reader's Log journal entries

___ often   ___ sometimes   ___ seldom

2. Students participate by either speaking or listening

___ often   ___ sometimes   ___ seldom

3. Students move beyond the selection to consider wider issues

___ often   ___ sometimes   ___ seldom

King Versus Pope: All for an Heir

The generations-old conflict between the pope and the king of England came to a climax when Henry VIII wanted to get rid of his wife of twenty-four years. Divorce was not allowed, especially for kings (until recently, that was still true in Britain), so Henry needed a loophole. He asked Pope Clement VII to declare that he, Henry, was not properly married to his Spanish wife, Catherine of Aragon, because she had previously been wedded—for all of five months—to his older brother Arthur, now dead. (It was against Church law to marry a dead sibling's spouse; the Biblical basis for the law is in Leviticus.)

Henry had two motives for wanting to send Catherine back to Spain. First, although she had borne him a princess, she was too old to give him the male heir that he thought

Catherine of Aragon (16th century) by M. Sittou. Kunsthistorisches Museum, Vienna.

he must have. (Catherine had lost five babies.) What is more, another younger woman had won Henry's dangerous affections: The king now wished to marry Anne Boleyn, who had been his "favorite" for several years. (Henry had earlier seduced Anne's sister.) The pope was not able to grant Henry the annulment of his marriage, even if he had wanted to, because the pope was controlled by Queen Catherine's nephew, the emperor of Spain. And so, upon receiving the pope's refusal in 1533, Henry simply declared himself head of the English Church. He then appointed a new archbishop of Canterbury, who obligingly declared Henry's marriage to Catherine invalid.

With Catherine packed away under house arrest—since she refused to accept the annulment of her marriage—Henry closed all of England's monasteries and sold the rich buildings and lands to his subjects. While the vast majority of his subjects agreed with Henry's changes in the Church, some of them did not. The best known of all those who remained loyal to the pope was Sir Thomas More, now the Lord Chancellor of England. More felt he could not legally recognize his friend Henry as head of the Church. For More's stubbornness, Henry ordered that his Lord Chancellor be beheaded. It wasn't the first—or last—time that Henry executed a friend.

B This was the very beginning of Protestantism in England. Many people were dissatisfied with the new church for reasons just the opposite of More's. They felt that it was not reformed enough, that it was merely a copy of Catholicism, as in

> . . . reminding us of a point in astronomy, which is that the longer the days are the farther off is the sun and yet the hotter; so is it with our love, for although by absence we are parted it nevertheless keeps its fervency, at least in my case and hoping the like of yours . . .
> —King Henry VIII, in a letter to Anne Boleyn, 1528

> **A** This hath not offended the king.
> —Sir Thomas More, drawing his beard aside as he placed his head on the block, 1535

some respects it was. These dissidents, known as Puritans, Baptists, Presbyterians, Dissenters, and Nonconformists, wanted to get rid of many things they called "popish," such as the bishops, the prayer book, the priest's vestments, and even the church bells and the stained-glass windows. Some of them said that religion was solely a matter between the individual and God. This idea, which is still the foundation of Protestant churches, is directly traceable to the teachings of those Renaissance humanists who emphasized the freedom of all human beings.

In 1531, refused an annulment by the pope, Henry VIII broke with the Catholic Church in Rome and declared himself head of the English Church. This marked the beginning of the Protestant Reformation in England.

The Great Harry (detail) (1546) from the Anthony Roll manuscript.

Master and Fellows, Magdalene College, Cambridge.

Henry VIII: Renaissance Man and Executioner

The five Tudor rulers of England are easy to remember: They consist of a grandfather, a father, and three children. The grandfather was Henry VII (1457–1509), a Welsh nobleman who seized the throne after England was totally exhausted by the long and bloody struggle called the Wars of the Roses. (Both factions involved used a rose as their emblem, one red, one white.) Henry VII was a shrewd, patient, and stingy man who restored peace and order to the kingdom; without these, there could never have been a cultural Renaissance.

His son Henry VIII (r. 1509–1547) had six wives: After Catherine of Aragon and Anne Boleyn, there were Jane Seymour, Anne of Cleves, Catherine Howard, and Catherine Parr. The fates of these unfortunate women are summarized in a jingle:

> Divorced, beheaded, died,
> Divorced, beheaded, survived.

The sexual intrigues of the court trapped several of Henry's wives: The king could play around, but he couldn't tolerate being suspicious of his wives' fidelity. The price paid by two young wives was heavy. Like Thomas More, Anne Boleyn and Catherine Howard lost their heads on the chopping block.

Despite his messy home life, Henry VIII was a very important figure. He created the Royal Navy, which put a stop to foreign invasions of England and provided the means for this island kingdom to spread its political power, language, and literature all over the globe. If we overlook his use of the sword against his enemies (and friends), Henry VIII himself deserves the title "Renaissance man." He wrote poetry and played many different musical instruments well; he was a champion athlete and a hunter; and he patronized the new humanistic learning. But in his old

C. Exploring the Culture
There is a sixteenth-century saying that "Erasmus laid the egg and Luther hatched it."

D. Exploring the Historical Period
The Wars of the Roses began in 1455 between the rival families of York and Lancaster. By the time the struggle ended in 1485, so many baronial families were extinguished that the hierarchy of succession to the throne in England was permanently altered, allowing Henry VII to become king.

age, Henry was also coarse, dissolute, arrogant, and an unregenerate womanizer. He died without knowing that the child he ignored because she was female would become the greatest ruler England ever had.

Henry VIII's rule was bold and bloody. He increased England's strength and ensured its security by building up the Royal Navy, but those close to the king paid a high price.

An Allegory of the Tudor Succession: The Family of Henry VIII (c. 1589–1595) by the British School, possibly after Lucas de Heere. Oil on panel (45″ × 71¾″).

Yale Center for British Art, Paul Mellon Collection, New Haven.

The Boy King and Bloody Mary

Henry VIII was survived by three children: Mary, daughter of the Spanish princess, Catherine of Aragon; Elizabeth, daughter of Anne Boleyn, a lady-in-waiting at the court; and Edward, son of noblewoman Jane Seymour, who died three days after her son's birth. According to the laws of succession, the son had to be crowned first, and so at age nine the son of Henry and Jane Seymour became Edward VI (r. 1547–1553). An intelligent but sickly boy, he ruled in name only while his relatives wielded the actual power.

When Edward died of tuberculosis, he was followed by his half-Spanish half-sister Mary (r. 1553–1558). Mary was a devout, strong-willed Catholic determined to avenge the wrongs done to her mother. She restored the pope's power in England and ruthlessly hunted down Protestants.

Had she lived longer, and had she exercised better judgment, Mary might have undone all her father's accomplishments. But she made a strategic error when she burned about three hundred of her subjects at the stake. She further lost the support of her people when she married Philip II, king of Spain, a country England was beginning to fear and hate. (Mary was thirty-seven and Philip only twenty-six.) Mary's executions earned her the name "Bloody Mary." When Mary died of a fever, childless, her sister Elizabeth became queen.

> **Mary Tudor succeeded her father Henry VIII. Immediately, she killed Protestants and reversed her father's policies: She restored the pope's power in England.**

Elizabeth: The Virgin Queen

Elizabeth I (r. 1558–1603) was one of the most brilliant and successful monarchs in history. Since she inherited a kingdom torn by fierce religious feuds, her first task was to restore law and order. She reestablished the Church of England and again rejected the pope's authority, and the pope promptly excommunicated her. To keep Spain appeased, she pretended that she just might marry her widowed brother-in-law, King Philip.

Philip was the first of a long procession of noblemen, both foreign and English, who wanted to wed her. But Elizabeth resisted marriage all her life and officially remained "the Virgin Queen" (thereby giving the American colony Virginia its name). She knew that her strength lay in her independence and her ability to play one suitor off against another. "I am your anointed Queen," she told a group from Parliament who urged her to marry. "I will never be by violence constrained to do anything. I thank God I am endued with such qualities that if I were turned out of the realm in my petticoat, I were able to live in any place in Christendom."

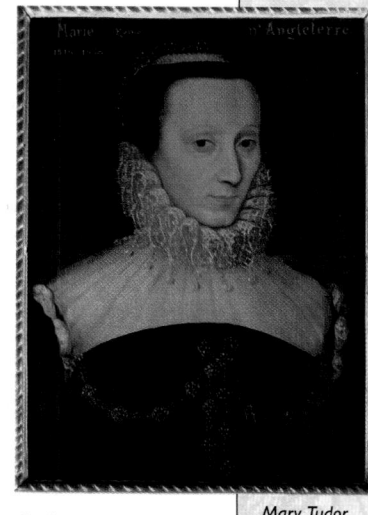

Mary Tudor (16th century) by an unknown artist.
Musée Condé, Chantilly, France.

> Fain would I climb, yet fear I to fall.
> —Sir Walter Raleigh to Elizabeth I, scratched on a windowpane
>
> If thy heart fails thee, climb not at all.
> —Elizabeth's reply, scratched underneath

Portrait of Queen Elizabeth I within the Armada Jewel (16th century) by Nicholas Hilliard.
The Victoria and Albert Museum, London.

A. Responding to the Quotation

? What does Elizabeth's answer mean? [Possible response: If you even wonder whether you have sufficient courage to woo me, then you are certainly not the man for me.]

THE RENAISSANCE **205**

A. Expansion

James I spent an astonishing £36,377 per year on his wardrobe for each of the five years of his reign. Elizabeth I's yearly wardrobe expenses for the last four years of her reign were only £9,535 per year.

B. Humanities Connection

The Puritans strongly condemned what they viewed as excesses and abuses in dress. Phillip Stubbes in *The Anatomie of Abuses* attacks many aspects of culture, including fashions such as ruffs. "No pen is able to well to discribe it, as the eye is to vilify it . . . [The ruffs have] three or foure degrees of minor ruffes, placed by degree, step by step, one beneath the other, and all under the Maister devil ruffe; the skyrts, then, of these great ruffes are long and side every way, pleated and crested ful curiously, God wot. Then last of all they are either clogged with golde, silver, or silk lace of stately price, wrought all over with needle woork, speckled and sparkled here and there with the sonne, the moone, the stares, and many other antiquities straunge to beholde. Some are wrought with . . . purled lace so cloyed, and other gew gawes. . . ."

THE GLASS OF FASHION

They displayed their new costumes from ten to twelve o'clock in the morning, strolling up and down the center aisle of St. Paul's Church. They insisted on rich fabrics: velvet, taffeta, gold brocade, and fur. They wore the finest silk stockings and cork platform shoes. They curled their hair, perfumed their gloves, and (if daring) wore makeup. They showed off favorite jewels—pearls, perhaps—in earrings, bracelets, and designs sewn all over their clothes. The men in the Renaissance were peacocks indeed!

Portrait of Elizabeth Vernon, countess of Southampton (c. 1610) by an unknown artist.
By permission of the Duke of Buccleuch, Kettering, England.

Portrait of a lady said to be Lady Style (detail) (16th century) by the circle of William Larkin.
Christie's, London.

Exquisite excess. Women also dressed flamboyantly in the Renaissance. Elizabeth I herself owned eighty wigs and three thousand gowns at her death.

In the 1580s and 1590s, the Renaissance silhouette was ridiculously exaggerated. Starched linen neck ruffs stretched from shoulder to shoulder. Shoulders themselves were extended with "wings" that make even the most exaggerated of today's shoulder pads look like cotton balls. Hoop skirts (called farthingales) could be four feet wide at the hips, and men's full, thigh-length pants were padded to what critics called "monstrous and outrageous greatness." Women corseted their waists into painful narrowness while men stiffened doublets (an upper garment) with pasteboard and stuffed them with horsehair, rags, or even bran in order to achieve what was called a peascod belly. A man's silhouette was

Portrait of a nobleman said to be the 7th earl of Shrewsbury in garter robes (detail) (16th century) by Paul van Somer.
Christie's, London.

OPTIONS FOR TEACHING

STRATEGIES FOR INCLUSION

Visual Have students draw male and female figures wearing clothing that includes some of the features mentioned above. Then, ask them to label the features. As a comparison, students could also draw figures wearing current fashions; these should be labeled as well.

Kinesthetic Ask students to put on an Elizabethan fashion show, coming as close as they can with common materials to the features of the clothing above. They might also borrow costumes from the drama department.

narrowest at the bottom, where stockings and garters worn above the knee made even shapely legs look better.

Symbols and signals. In the Renaissance, intricate pattern (like poetry's "artificiality") was also a must. Braids, bows, spangles, and lace covered the luxurious fabrics, and slashed sleeves and doublets allowed embroidered underclothes to peek through. Colors were rich and bold—red, gold, black, and white was a favorite combination.

Colors and designs also had symbolic meanings: Green meant love, white and tawny together showed patience in adversity, a pansy represented sadness, a snake flattery, and so on.
Queen Elizabeth often wore white and black together—both colors symbolized chastity. Whole trea-

tises were devoted to color and to defining "emblems" such as rainbows, clouds, worms, and flies.

Reading T-shirts. How will historians of dress read the clothes we wear today? Are bodices embroidered with flies so strange when viewed against the sort of printed T-shirts available by the hundreds in any shopping mall? What messages do our clothes send out to the world, and what will they tell the future?

Lettice Knollys, daughter of Sir Henry Knollys, wife of 4th Lord Paget (detail) (16th century) by the English School.

Manor House, Stanton Harcourt, Oxon, England.

An unknown lady in a masque costume (detail) (c. 1615).
City of Bristol Museum and Art Gallery, Bristol, England.

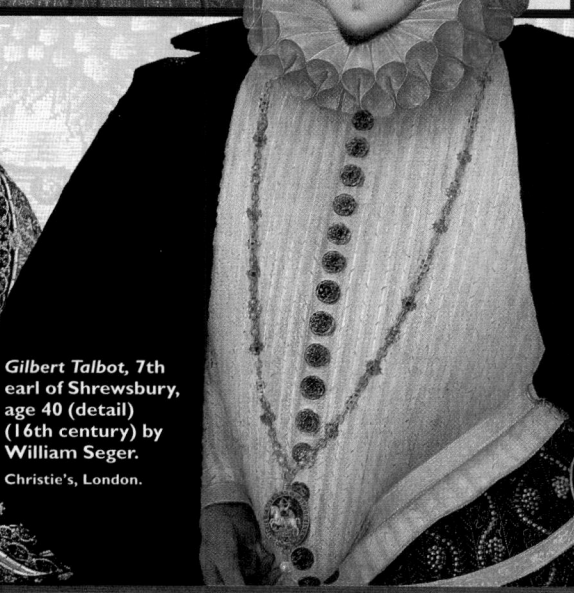

Mary Denton, née Martyn, age 15 in 1573 (detail) (16th century) by the circle of George Gower.
York City Art Gallery, York, England.

Gilbert Talbot, 7th earl of Shrewsbury, age 40 (detail) (16th century) by William Seger.
Christie's, London.

INTEGRATING THE LANGUAGE ARTS

Strategic Reading To help students note how this short essay is organized, ask them to jot down the first few words of each paragraph and to write briefly how these words function to organize the essay. Several paragraphs begin with short titles to signify a main topic. A couple of the paragraphs begin with topic sentences. Finally, the first paragraph begins with a mysterious subject. Who are "they"? This serves to draw the reader in and lends a little surprise at the end of the paragraph.

A. Exploring the Historical Period

Mary Stuart, Queen of Scots (1542–1587), was Elizabeth's cousin. She should not be confused with "Bloody Mary," who was Mary Tudor (1516–1558), Elizabeth's half-sister.

Mary Stuart was the daughter of Henry VIII's nephew, James V. Her mother was French. Married to Francis II of France, Mary returned to Scotland in 1560, after her husband's death, to claim the throne of Scotland, which was still independent from England. Mary Stuart's ties to France and Spain through family and religion made her a powerful threat to Elizabeth's England. She was beheaded at Fotheringay on February 8, 1587.

B. Literary Connections

"The Doubt of Future Foes" is a poem by Queen Elizabeth I in which she expresses her concern about Mary Stuart.

Execution of Mary, Queen of Scots (16th century) by an unknown Dutch artist.

Scottish National Portrait Gallery, Edinburgh.

A A truly heroic person, Elizabeth survived many plots against her life. Several of these plots were initiated by her cousin, another Mary—Mary Stuart, Queen of Scots. As Elizabeth had no children, Mary was heir to England's throne because she, too, was a direct descendant of Henry VII. But Mary, a Catholic, was eventually deposed from her throne in Protestant Scotland. Put under house arrest, she lived as a royal exile in England, carefully watched by her cousin Elizabeth. Elizabeth endured Mary and **B** her plots for twenty years and then, a true daughter of her father, sent her Scottish cousin to the chopping block.

Like her father, Elizabeth quickly and efficiently settled disorder both in her kingdom and in her own household. She once again rejected the pope and reestablished the Church of England. Elizabeth's intelligence and independence made her reign one of the most successful in England's history.

The Spanish Armada Sinks: A Turning Point in History

King Philip of Spain, ever watchful for an excuse to hammer at England, used Mary's execution as an excuse to invade England. He assembled a vast fleet of warships for that purpose: the famous Spanish Armada. In 1588, England's Royal Navy, assisted greatly by nasty weather in the Irish Sea, destroyed the Armada. This victory assured England's and all of northern Europe's

... Then she, lying very still upon the block, one of the executioners holding her slightly with one of his hands, she endured two strokes of the other executioner with an axe, she making very small noise or none at all, and not stirring any part of her from the place where she lay: and so the executioner cut off her head, saving one little gristle, which being cut asunder, he lift up her head to the view of all the assembly and bade God save the Queen. Then, her dress of lawn falling from off her head, it appeared as gray as one of threescore and ten years old, polled very short, her face in a moment being so much altered from the form she had when she was alive, as few could remember her by her dead face. Her lips stirred up and down a quarter of an hour after her head was cut off ...

—Robert Wynkfielde, an eyewitness to the execution of Mary, Queen of Scots, 1587

208 THE RENAISSANCE

(Opposite) *English Ships and the Spanish Armada, August 1588* (detail). English School. Oil.

National Maritime Museum, London.

To be a king and wear a crown is more glorious to them that see it than it is pleasure to them that bear it.

—Elizabeth I, 1601

C

C. Responding to the Quotation

? Why would this be true? [Possible response: People imagine all the glory, honor, and glamour of ruling; but the actual work of being a monarch is not as exciting, glamorous, or easy as it appears.]

RESPONDING TO THE ART: EXPLORING THE SUBJECT

The Spanish Armada, characterized by large battleships meant to carry hundreds of infantry for boarding enemy ships, was perhaps destined for defeat in light of the naval tactics practiced by the British. The slow Spanish ships with heavy, short-range cannon designed for fighting at a short distance met with the low-lying, maneuverable British ships equipped with long-range cannon. Although at first the British narrowly escaped the formidable Spanish ships in tight formation, as the battle unfolded, the wind and the British prevented the Spanish from retreating and forced them to cut anchor and break formation. The Spanish, now disorganized, were vulnerable to British attack.

The names Gloriana, Cynthia, and Faerie Queene come from Edmund Spenser's epic poem *The Faerie Queene*. The name Cynthia was also used by Sir Walter Raleigh in his poem *The Ocean to Cynthia*. Cynthia is another name for Diana, the virgin goddess of the moon.

B. Exploring the Historical Period

James VI was the only son of Mary, Queen of Scots, and her second husband, an English nobleman named Lord Darnly. When James succeeded his mother's cousin Elizabeth as sovereign of England and of Scotland, he was called King James I because he was the first James to rule the newly formed Great Britain. The reign of James is called the Jacobean period. (*Jacobus* is the Latin form of *James*.)

---

independence from the powerful Catholic countries of the Mediterranean. It was a great turning point in history and Elizabeth's finest moment. If Spain had prevailed, history would have been quite different: All of North America, like most of South America, might be speaking Spanish instead of English.

In 1588, the English Royal Navy defeated the Spanish Armada. This stunning sea victory assured England's independence from the powerful Catholic countries of the Mediterranean.

> As for her face, it is and appears to be very aged. It is long and thin and her teeth are very yellow and unequal, compared with what they were formerly, so they say, and on the left side less than on the right. Many of them are missing so that one cannot understand her easily when she speaks quickly. Her figure is fair and tall and graceful in whatever she does; so far as may be she keeps her dignity . . .
>
> —André Hurault, French ambassador, writing about Elizabeth I, 1597

A Flood of Literature

What is the connection between these political events and English literature? With their own religious and national identity firmly established, the English started writing as never before. After the defeat of the Armada, Elizabeth became a beloved symbol of peace, security, and prosperity to her subjects, and she provided inspiration to scores of English authors. They represented her mythologically in poetry, drama, and fiction—as Gloriana, Diana, the Faerie Queene, and Cynthia. Literary works that did not directly represent her were dedicated to her because authors knew she was a connoisseur of literature and a person of remarkably wide learning.

Elizabeth encouraged and inspired many writers. With the era of peace and prosperity that followed the defeat of the Spanish Armada, the English started writing as never before.

Decline of the Renaissance: A Dull Man Succeeds a Witty Woman

Elizabeth died childless, so her second cousin, James VI of Scotland, was her successor. James was the son of Elizabeth's cousin Mary whom Elizabeth had beheaded years before. As James I of England (r. 1603–1625), he lacked Elizabeth's ability to resolve (or postpone) critical issues, especially religious and economic ones. James was a spendthrift where Elizabeth had been thrifty; he was thick-tongued and goggle-eyed where she had been glamorous and witty; he was essentially a foreigner where she had been a complete Englishwoman.

James I tried hard. He wrote learned books in favor of the divine right of kings and against tobacco, he patronized Shakespeare, he sponsored a new translation of the Bible, and he was in many respects an admirable man and a benevolent, peaceful ruler. Yet his relationship with many of his subjects, especially with pious, puritanically minded merchants, went from bad to worse.

The difficulties of James's reign became the impossibilities of his son's. Charles I (r. 1625–1649) turned out to be remote, autocratic, and self-destructive. Some of his most powerful subjects had him beheaded in 1649. For the next eleven years, England was ruled by Parliament and the Puritan dictator Oliver Cromwell, not by an anointed king. When Charles's self-indulgent son returned to power eleven years later, in 1660, England had changed in many important ways.

Of course the Renaissance did not end in 1660 as Charles II returned from exile in France, just as it had not begun at any specific date. Renaissance values, which were primarily moral and religious, gradually eroded, and Renaissance energies gradually gave out. The last great writer of the English Renaissance was John Milton, who lived on into an age in which educated people were becoming more worldly in their outlook. Scientific truths were soon to challenge long-accepted religious beliefs.

The English Renaissance was over.

> All my possessions for a moment of time.
> —Elizabeth I's last words, 1603

The political climate in England began to change after Elizabeth's death. The end of the English Renaissance is usually marked by the return of the exiled king in 1660. By this time, more political and secular values were beginning to challenge the accepted doctrines of religion.

Bird's-eye view of London, from the *Atlas Civitatis Orbis Terrarum* (c. 1574) by Georg Braun. Map L85c #27.

By permission of The Folger Shakespeare Library, Washington, D.C.

C. Exploring the Historical Period

By the time Charles I came to the throne, the Puritans had risen to prominence and their Parliamentary party had gained power. By 1642, England was embroiled in a civil war that pitted the Parliamentary party, led by Oliver Cromwell, against the king's party, or Royalists. Cromwell's followers killed the king, and Cromwell, now considered the foremost military and political strategist of his time, wielded power and asserted England's primacy in world affairs in ways reminiscent of the reign of Elizabeth I.

A. Expansion

Many other restrictions were placed upon Jews. They were not allowed to be high government officials or in any way to exert authority over Christians.

B. Exploring the Historical Period

Jewish people were exiled from France in 1394 and from Spain in 1492.

C. Literary Connections

Menasseh ben Israel, a Jew living in Holland, wrote pamphlets to Oliver Cromwell to encourage the readmission of Jews into England. He suggested that Cromwell strike the laws of the deposed monarchs and welcome Jews to the Commonwealth, allowing them to worship freely and publicly in their synagogues. By identifying religious persecution with the rule of monarchs, ben Israel may have influenced Cromwell's decision.

Quickwrite

Before students begin, ask them to distinguish between the two questions "What is a good life?" and "What is the good life for me?" Encourage them to decide whether both questions should have the same answer and whether either question has different answers for different people.

A CLOSER LOOK

JEWISH LIFE IN ENGLAND: EXPULSION AND RETURN

As you read the literature of Renaissance England, you'll notice that many selections use Christian imagery or are about Christian topics. Certainly, all the writers in these collections were Christian. But what about Jewish life in England?

The most famous Jewish character in Renaissance literature is Shylock, the moneylender in Shakespeare's play *The Merchant of Venice* (c. 1596–1598). Shylock is portrayed as cruel and greedy, a man incapable of mercy. In Shakespeare's play, Shylock is a usurer, which means that he lent money at interest, something commonly done by banks today. But charging interest on borrowed money (called usury) was considered sinful by the Christian church. (Many usurers charged exorbitant interest, and a small loan might ruin a poor widow and her family.) Since Jews were usually not allowed to own land, they became the people who handled money.

With Shylock, Shakespeare presents us with a complicated character who is at once a stereotype and a persecuted individual. Stereotypes like this one of the greedy moneylender were used to justify relentless persecution of the Jews. Without a homeland, Jews had been moving for most of their history. Expelled from many European cities and countries, Jewish refugees streamed into cities that already housed more Jews than their rulers wanted. Some cities, such as Venice (the setting for *The Merchant of Venice*), dealt with Jews by segregating them in ghettos and charging them extra taxes.

There were a few Jews in Shakespeare's England, although English Jews had been banished centuries before by King Edward I in 1290—because of controversy over their purchase of land. (Ownership of land by people considered "outsiders" was alarming then, as it still is in some places.) Some individual Jews probably continued to practice their religion in secret, but it wasn't until the middle of the seventeenth century, under the rule of Oliver Cromwell, that Jews were officially allowed to return to England.

Initial Word-Panel Illumination Showing a Marriage Ceremony, from the *Hamburg Halakhah Miscellany.* Padua (1467–1477). The Hebrew letter means "all." Codex Hebrew 337 (Scrin 132) fol. 75v. Vellum (6" × 4½").

Staats und Universitätsbibliothek, Hamburg.

Quickwrite

The humanists of the Renaissance were concerned with a question that we still ask ourselves today. "What is a good life?" they wondered. How would you answer this same question? What's the good life for you? Will you have a good life if you're rich, or if you're famous, or if you're able to do some good for someone, or if you have power, or if most of your days are simply happy? In your Reader's Log, reflect on the question, difficult as it is, for a few minutes. What's the good life for you? And what do you think has influenced you to see it as you do?

212

Collection Planner

SELECTION / FEATURE	Literary Elements / Active Reading	Writing	Speaking and Listening	Language and Vocabulary
Whoso List to Hunt Sir Thomas Wyatt (pp. 214–216)	• Reader's Log p. 214 • Meter p. 216 • Scansion p. 216	• Creative Writing: Write paragraph p. 216		
from **Amoretti: Sonnets 30** and **75** Edmund Spenser (pp. 217–220) Spotlight On: The Faerie Queene (pp. 221–222)	• Paradox p. 218 • Reader's Log p. 218 • Petrarchan, Spenserian Sonnets pp. 219–220 • Petrarchan conceits p. 220 • Epic p. 221	• Creative Writing: Create imagery p. 220		
Sonnets 29, 73, 116, 130 William Shakespeare (pp. 223–230)	• Shakespearean Sonnets pp. 223–224 • Reader's Log p. 225	• Critical Writing: Write essay p. 230 • Creative Writing: Write sonnet p. 230 • Creative Writing: Write parody p. 230	• Panel Discussion: Evaluate modern messages about love p. 230	
The Passionate Shepherd to His Love Christopher Marlowe, **The Nymph's Reply to the Shepherd** Sir Walter Raleigh (pp. 231–237) **To the Virgins, to Make Much of Time** Robert Herrick, **To His Coy Mistress** Andrew Marvell (pp. 238–243)	• Reader's Log p. 231 • *Carpe Diem* p. 231 • Pastoral p. 233	• Critical Writing: Write essay p. 243 • Critical Writing: Compare poems p. 243 • Creative Writing: Write response p. 243 • Music/Literature: Write song p. 243	• Panel Discussion: Discuss gender traits in modern and Renaissance times p. 243	
Song/A Valediction: Forbidding Mourning/ Meditation 17/ Death Be Not Proud John Donne (pp. 244–255)	• Hyperbole p. 245 • Reader's Log pp. 245, 247, 250, 253 • Metaphysical Poetry p. 246 • Metaphysical Conceits p. 247 • Simile p. 247	• Critical Writing: Write essay p. 255 • Creative Writing: Create hyperbolic statement p. 255 • Creative Writing: Write letter p. 255 • Technology: Create modern conceit p. 255		• Language and Style: Context Clues p. 252
On My First Son/Song: To Celia Ben Jonson, (pp. 256–259) **Connections: Give Us This Day** Joseph Papp and Elizabeth Kirkland (pp. 260–261)	• Reader's Log pp. 257, 258 • Epigram p. 257	• Critical Writing: Write paragraph p. 259 • Creative Writing: Write poem or paragraph p. 259		
Why So Pale and Wan, Fond Lover? Sir John Suckling, **To Lucasta, on Going to the Wars/ To Althea, from Prison** Richard Lovelace (pp. 262–266)	• Reader's Log p. 263 • Tone p. 263	• Critical Writing: Write essay p. 266 • Creative Writing: Write reply p. 266		

Collection Resources

Teaching Resources A	Audiovisual Resources Binder	Test Booklet
Cross-Curricular Activity p. 86	Fine Art Transparency 3.1	Collection 3 Test pp. 53–56

 Computer disk or CD-ROM

Videodisc

Audiocassette

 Overhead Transparency

PROGRAM RESOURCES

Electronic Media	Teaching Resources with Organizer		Audiovisual Resources Binder
	Teaching Resources A	Other Resources	
• Test Generator	• Teaching Notes p. 56 • Reading Organizer p. 65	• Test Booklet: Selection Test pp. 37–38 • Portfolio Management System p. 87	• Elements of Literature Transparency 3.2
• Test Generator	• Teaching Notes p. 56–57 • Reading Organizer p. 66	• Test Booklet: Selection Test pp. 37–38 • Portfolio Management System p. 88	• Elements of Literature Transparency 3.3
• Language Workshop: Verb Tenses • Test Generator	• Teaching Notes pp. 57–58 • Reading Organizer pp. 67–68 • Language Link pp. 69–70	• Test Booklet: Selection Test pp. 39–40 • Portfolio Management System pp. 53, 89–90 • Language and Writing Skills Worksheets pp. 40–42	
• Test Generator	• Teaching Notes pp. 58–59 • Reading Organizer pp. 71–74	• Test Booklet: Selection Test pp. 41–44 • Portfolio Management System pp. 91–92	
• Test Generator	• Teaching Notes pp. 59–61 • Reading Organizer pp. 75–78	• Test Booklet: Selection Test pp. 45–46 • Portfolio Management System pp. 54–55, 93–94	• Elements of Literature Transparency 3.4 • Selected Reading Audiocassette 1, Side A
• Test Generator	• Teaching Notes p. 61 • Reading Organizer p. 79	• Test Booklet: Selection Test pp. 47–48 • Portfolio Management System pp. 43, 95–96	• Selected Reading, Audiocassette 1, Side A
• Test Generator	• Teaching Notes p. 62 • Reading Organizer pp. 80–81 • Words to Own pp. 82–83	• Test Booklet: Selection Test pp. 49–50 • Portfolio Management System p. 97	

Collection Planner *continued*

SELECTION/ FEATURE	Literary Elements / Active Reading	Writing	Speaking and Listening	Language and Vocabulary
World Literature: Sonnets 17 and 79 Pablo Neruda (pp. 267–270)	• Reader's Log p. 268	• Finding Common Ground: Discuss romantic love in today's and in the the poets' terms p. 270		
English Language: The Birth of Modern English John Algeo (pp. 271–274)			• Pronunciation p. 272	• Alternative Spelling p. 274 • Shaw Alphabet: Translation p. 274 • Etymologies p. 273
Writer's Workshop: Interpretive Essay (pp. 275–279)		• Writing process: Interpretive essay pp. 275–279		
Language Workshop: The Literary Present (p. 280)		• Revise essay p. 280		

Collection Resources

Teaching Resources A	Audiovisual Resources Binder	Test Booklet
Cross-Curricular Activity p. 86	Fine Art Transparency 3.1	Collection 3 Test pp. 53–56

 Computer disk or CD-ROM

 Videodisc

 Audiocassette

 Overhead Transparency

PROGRAM RESOURCES

Electronic Media	Teaching Resources with Organizer		Audiovisual Resources Binder
	Teaching Resources A	Other Resources	
• Videodisc, Side A: "English: A Living Language, Part 1"	• Teaching Notes p. 62	• Test Booklet: Selection Test pp. 51–52	
• Writer's Workshop 2: Interpretation		• Portfolio Management System pp. 98–100	• Revision Transparencies 3.5–3.6
• Language Workshop: Verb Tenses	• Language Workshop: Verb Tenses pp. 84–85		

Proofreading Warm-ups

You may use the following exercises to help students practice their proofreading skills. Copy a set of incorrect sentences onto the chalkboard, and have the students find and correct the spelling, punctuation, usage, and mechanical errors in each sentence. Ask students to share and discuss their responses.

	Sentences with Errors	Corrected Sentences	Skills Covered
1	a. The woman Shakespeare wrote about in sonnet 130 must of been real special. b. Most Authors wrote less poems than Shakespeare.	a. The woman about whom Shakespeare wrote in Sonnet 130 must have been very special. b. Most authors wrote fewer poems than Shakespeare wrote.	Capitalization, Usage, Nonstandard usage
2	a. One student which is in our class asked What does this poem mean? b. The meaning of Whoso list to Hunt a sonnet is to transparent.	a. One student who is in our class asked, "What does this poem mean?" b. The meaning of "Whoso List to Hunt," a sonnet, is too transparent.	Nonstandard usage, Commas, Quotation marks, Spelling
3	a. I can't hardly wait to read Shakespeares macbeth b. Marlowes poem isnt anywheres near as clever as Raleighs response.	a. I can hardly wait to read Shakespeare's <u>Macbeth</u>. b. Marlowe's poem isn't nearly as clever as Raleigh's response.	Double negatives, Apostrophes, Titles, End marks, Nonstandard usage
4	a. The cavalier poets work such as To Lucasta on going to the Wars show some of the same ideas we have today. b. Writers of the elizabethan era often wrote about the amount of ships sunk on voyages of discovery.	a. The Cavalier poets' work, such as "To Lucasta, on Going to the Wars," shows some of the same ideas we have today. b. Writers of the Elizabethan era often wrote about the number of ships that were sunk on voyages of discovery.	Capitalization, Apostrophes, Commas, Quotation marks, Subject-verb agreement, Nonstandard usage, Verb tenses
5	a. Many people no longer except the customs and beleifs of the rennaissance b. Because of his subject matter metaphysical conceits and tone John Donne is I believe the best poet of the Renaissance.	a. Many people no longer accept the customs and beliefs of the Renaissance. b. Because of his subject matter, metaphysical conceits, and tone, John Donne is, I believe, the best poet of the Renaissance.	Spelling, Capitalization, Commas, End Marks
6	a. Shakespeares english sonnets lead many people to believe he had discovered a new poetic structure. b. Death be not proud is one of the most known sonnets in english liturture.	a. Shakespeare's English sonnets led many people to believe he had invented a new poetic structure. b. "Death Be Not Proud" is one of the best known sonnets in English literature.	Apostrophes, Capitalization, Spelling, Usage, Verb Tense, Nonstandard usage, Quotation marks
7	a. Many modern readers recognizes the quotation No man is an island, but they don't know that it is a line from Donnes meditation seventeen. b. The Cavalier poets were concerned with honer and were effected by the events in there own time.	a. Many modern readers recognize the quotation "No man is an island," but they don't know that it is a line from Donne's "Meditation 17." b. The Cavalier poets were concerned with honor and were affected by the events of their own time.	Subject-verb agreement, Quotation marks, Apostrophes, Capitalization, Writing numbers, Spelling, Nonstandard usage, Homonyms
8	a. If I forgot the sonnet structure I would have failed the quiz. b. Either Donne or Jonson write in a form called epigrams.	a. If I had forgotten the sonnet structure, I would have failed the quiz. b. Either Donne or Jonson writes in a form called epigrams.	Verb tenses, Commas, Subject-verb agreement
9	a. How come all these pomes was about love death and time. b. Students brought they're poems to class today.	a. Why were all these poems written about love, death, and time? b. Students brought their poems to class today.	Nonstandard usage, Spelling, Verb tenses, Commas, Homonyms, End marks
10	a. Having read carefully these poems make sense to me now. b. Shakespeare could of written about anything, but he often writes about love.	a. Having read carefully, I now can make sense of these poems. b. Shakespeare could have written about anything, but he often wrote about love.	Dangling participles, Nonstandard usage, Verb tenses

Collection _3_

LOVE, DEATH, AND TIME

Wyatt	Raleigh	Jonson
Spenser	Herrick	Suckling
Shakespeare	Marvell	Lovelace
Marlowe	Donne	Neruda

since feeling is first

since feeling is first
who pays any attention
to the syntax of things
will never wholly kiss you;

wholly to be a fool
while Spring is in the world

my blood approves,
and kisses are a better fate
than wisdom
lady i swear by all flowers. Don't cry
—the best gesture of my brain is less than
your eyelid's flutter which says

we are for each other: then
laugh, leaning back in my arms
for life's not a paragraph

And death i think is no parenthesis

—E. E. Cummings

"since feeling is first"
Many of the poems in this Collection express thoughts and feelings about love, death, and time. What is the speaker in this poem saying about these **themes**? [Possible responses: Love is hard to express in words. Grammatical rules and logic do not necessarily apply to love. If people spend a lot of time worrying about rules, then they will have less time to experience love or life. The speaker seems to be saying that we cannot treat life and death as mere paragraphs and punctuation marks. But the poet is using syntax in a very effective way, so the speaker's view is ironic.]

PORTFOLIO ASSESSMENT

Parent/Guardian Involvement For forms that will help a parent or guardian review and respond to a student's portfolio, see _Portfolio Management System,_ pp. 62–63.

PROGRAM MANAGER

- **Integrated Assessment** For a summative assessment of the literature and language skills taught in this collection, see **Collection 3 Test,** _Test Booklet,_ pp. 53–56.
- **Instructional Support** See **Fine**

Art Transparency 3.1. Review teacher's notes for transparencies in the _Audiovisual Resources Binder_ for suggestions on how to tie the transparencies to specific reading selections.

- **Extending Collection Theme** See **Cross-Curricular Activity: Love, Death, and Time,** _Teaching Resources A,_ p. 86, for an activity in another discipline and for evaluation criteria.

Into the Poem

Author Biography p. 214
Before You Read p. 214

Through the Poem

"Whoso List to Hunt" p. 215
Making Meanings p. 215
Elements of Literature p. 216

Beyond the Poem

Choices: Building Your Portfolio p. 216
• **Writer's Notebook:** Make notes about associations
• **Creative Writing:** Write a woman's response

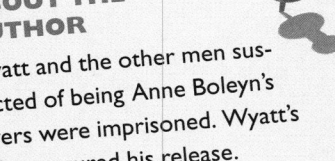

ABOUT THE AUTHOR

Wyatt and the other men suspected of being Anne Boleyn's lovers were imprisoned. Wyatt's father secured his release.

Into the Poem

Using BEFORE YOU READ p. 214

Reading Focus

To help students discuss the extended hunt **metaphor**, make sure they are familiar with hunting terminology, such as *hind,* and hunting conventions: for example, poaching—hunting on someone else's property—is strictly forbidden.

Sir Thomas Wyatt
(1503–1542)

Sir Thomas Wyatt was a courtier of Henry VIII and spent much of his life traveling abroad as an ambassador for the king. The life of anyone who worked for the king could be dangerous as well as glamorous: Twice Henry had Wyatt imprisoned on charges that were probably false, and twice Wyatt managed to regain the king's favor. Besides being a diplomat, Wyatt was also a literary innovator who helped to change the nature of English poetry. Up to Wyatt's time, poetry was still essentially medieval in matter and manner, subject and form. Wyatt greatly admired Italian poetry, and he brought a new kind of poem, the love sonnet, to England from Italy. His English sonnets are actually adaptations of Italian sonnets.

Aside from his sonnets, Wyatt wrote many delightful lyrics modeled on English dance-songs, but he never had any of his works printed and publicly distributed. Wyatt had no ambition to be known as a "clerk," or a learned man of letters, the sort of person who published books. As a courtier he was expected to compose songs and verses, just as he was expected to do battle for his king, joust in tournaments, dance, and carry on intrigues with the ladies. And so Wyatt circulated his poems privately among his friends, in handwritten copies. Not until fifteen years after Wyatt's death did most of his poems appear in print. In 1557, an enterprising printer named Richard Tottel published *Songs and Sonnets,* an anthology containing ninety-seven of Wyatt's poems. This book, now called *Tottel's Miscellany,* has a rather bad reputation today because Tottel "improved" the poems by changing many words so that the poems sounded smoother to his ears. To make certain that we read Wyatt's words, rather than Tottel's, scholars had to search out the handwritten copies of the poems that predated their publication.

Sir Thomas Wyatt (16th century) by an unknown artist. Oil on panel (18½" diameter).

By Courtesy of the National Portrait Gallery, London.

BEFORE YOU READ
WHOSO LIST TO HUNT

Reading Focus

Wounded by Love
The battle of the sexes, Cupid's arrow, the thrill of the chase, conquered by love, a good catch: why do so many metaphors for love suggest a contest between hunter and prey? With your classmates, discuss love as a "hunt." Two questions to consider are these: Who inflicts the wounds in love—the pursuer or the pursued? Who is the one conquered?

A Dialogue with the Text

As you read Wyatt's poem, record your immediate responses or any questions you may have in your Reader's Log.

Background

According to traditional gossip, Wyatt wrote this poem about his longing for Anne Boleyn, a beautiful young woman at court. When he noticed that no less a person than King Henry was also attracted to Anne, he gave up the pursuit to whoever else wanted to "hunt" her. Whether or not the story is true, Anne did become the second of Henry's six queens. Wyatt adapted the poem from an Italian sonnet by Francis Petrarch (1304–1374). He also took from Petrarch's commentators the story about Julius Caesar's tame deer (line 13), whose collars were inscribed *Noli me tangere* (Latin for "touch me not"), warning hunters not to molest Caesar's property.

PROGRAM MANAGER

• **Planning Instruction** See Teaching Notes, *Teaching Resources A,* p. 56, for objectives, a summary, and literary elements for this selection.
• **Instructional Support** Before beginning the instructional lesson, see Graphic Organizer for Active Reading, *Teaching Resources A,* p. 65, for a Through the Poem activity.
• **Assessment** See Selection Test, *Test Booklet,* pp. 37–38.

Whoso List to Hunt

Sir Thomas Wyatt

Whoso list° to hunt, I know where is an hind,°
But as for me, alas, I may no more.
The vain travail° hath wearied me so sore
I am of them that farthest cometh behind.
5 Yet may I, by no means, my wearied mind
Draw from the deer, but as she fleeth afore,
Fainting I follow. I leave off therefore,
Since in a net I seek to hold the wind.

Who list her hunt, I put him out of doubt,°
10 As well as I, may spend his time in vain.
And graven with diamonds in letters plain
There is written, her fair neck round about,
"*Noli me tangere,* for Caesar's I am,
And wild for to hold, though I seem tame."

1. **list:** archaic for "desires." **hind:** female deer (rhymes with *kind*).
3. **travail:** hard work.
9. **put him out of doubt:** assure him (that he).

Anne Boleyn (late 16th century) by an unknown artist. Oil on panel (21⅜″ × 16⅜″).
By Courtesy of the National Portrait Gallery, London.

A. Literary Element: Metaphor

? In Wyatt's extended metaphor, what does the hunter stand for? Who is the hind, or deer? [The hunter is the speaker in the poem, a man in love; the deer is the woman whose affection he seeks.]

B. Literary Element: Irony

? Considering how Anne Boleyn died in 1536, what irony might a reader find in the poem that Wyatt may not have intended? [The reference to Caesar's collar around her neck might be seen as a striking coincidence with her death by beheading at the order of her husband, the king.]

C. Critical Reading: Drawing Conclusions

? Do you think this is a good description of a deer? How might it apply to a woman? [Possible answers: This is a good description because deer do not look wild—they have sad, sweet eyes and look as if they would be gentle, but they are not tame. This might mean that the woman is dangerous to be involved with, either because a great man has claimed her or because she is fickle.]

MAKING MEANINGS

First Thoughts

1. Do you think this poem, specific as it is, describes attitudes and experiences still common in life today? Why or why not? (Check your Reader's Log for ideas, too.)

Shaping Interpretations

2. Given the background information you've just read, who is the hind in this poem and who is Caesar?

3. What warning does the **speaker** give potential hunters of the woman?

4. What **image** does the speaker use to show he's finally decided the chase is hopeless?

5. The **speaker** says the hind may seem tame but is "wild for to hold." Do you think he's referring to the woman herself or to Caesar's claim on her? Explain.

Connecting with the Text

6. If you were King Henry and you came upon this poem, how might you feel about its author? If you were Anne Boleyn, how might you react to the poem?

7. How do you feel about Wyatt's description of love as a hunt or a conquest?

Making Meanings

First Thoughts

1. Possible response: It has expanded—women now may hunt men, too. People still become infatuated with someone who is unattainable and feel what Wyatt describes.

Shaping Interpretations

2. The hind is Anne Boleyn and Caesar is Henry VIII.
3. He gives two warnings: (1) She has already been claimed. (2) Her appearance is deceiving; she seems tame, but she is really wild.

4. Trying to catch the wind in a net.
5. Possible response: The speaker is referring to the woman herself; Caesar's claim has not stopped her innate wildness.

Connecting with the Text

6. Possible responses: King Henry might be glad that he stopped pursuing Anne, or he might want to behead him. Anne Boleyn: might be flattered, or might think he should not quit.
7. Possible responses: Such metaphors are demeaning. Or it's just a poetic technique; it worked for this poem.

Elements of Literature

Mini-Lesson: Poetic Meter

Shakespeare usually writes in iambic pentameter. Write several lines of a Shakespearean sonnet on the chalkboard, and model scansion for students. Have volunteers identify stressed and unstressed syllables. After you have done this, give students a copy of another sonnet for them to mark, and have them write their results one line at a time on the chalkboard. You can also write various polysyllabic words on the chalkboard and ask students to scan them.

Answers

1. a. dactyl
   b. iamb
   c. trochee
   d. anapest
2. Many of the lines are in regular iambic pentameter. The first line has eleven syllables and may be scanned as regular iambic pentameter except for the first foot, which is likely an anapest. Lines that are completely regular are 2, 3, 5, 8, 9, and 10. The others have variations due, in part, to the reader's emphasis and to differences between Elizabethan and modern pronunciation.

Beyond the Poem

Choices: Building Your Portfolio

1. **Writer's Notebook** Remind students to save their work. They may use it as prewriting for the Writer's Workshop on p. 275.
2. **Creative Writing** *Remind students to choose a situation they would not mind sharing with others.* Ask students if love involving the pursuit and capture of a woman as presented in the poem matches anything they have experienced. Have them consider whether they would characterize their own or their friends' concepts of love in the way this poem does.

ELEMENTS OF LITERATURE

Poetic Meter: Giving Form to Feeling

Poetic **meter** is a regular pattern of stressed and unstressed syllables. It is rhythmic "beat"—like the steady pulse that draws you into dance music. Meter's basic unit is the **foot**: A foot consists of one stressed syllable and one or more unstressed syllables (mú·si·cál). The four basic metrical feet are

1. **iamb** (˘ ´), as in *relief*
2. **trochee** (´ ˘), as in *apple*
3. **anapest** (˘ ˘ ´), as in *introduce*
4. **dactyl** (´ ˘ ˘), as in *broccoli*

Poets also use two other metrical devices: the **spondee** (´ ´), or double stress, and the **caesura** (‖), or pause.

The analysis of a poem's meter is called **scansion.** When you scan a poem, you identify the type of foot (or feet) used in each line, and then you count them. (But a poem's meter is seldom strictly regular, and different readers can perceive meter differently.) **Dimeter** means two feet per line; **trimeter,** three; **tetrameter,** four; **pentameter,** five; and **hexameter,** six. This line from Wyatt's poem is **iambic pentameter** (it has five iambs):

˘ ´ ˘ ´ ˘ ´ ˘ ´ ˘ ´
Since in a net I seek to hold the wind.

Few poems are written in a meter that remains exactly regular throughout. The perception of meter may also vary from reader to reader, depending on which parts of phrases or sentences the reader thinks are most heavily stressed. Generally, however, readers can easily identify the dominant metrical pattern used in a poem.

1. Each of the following ordinary phrases uses one type of metrical foot. Identify the metrical foot in each.
   a. Best of all, victory!
   b. I bought a car today.
   c. Look for hidden pitfalls.
   d. in the cool of the night
2. Does Wyatt's "Whoso List to Hunt" show regular iambic pentameter? Scan three or four lines of the poem. What metrical patterns do you identify in these lines? Is the meter irregular in any of these lines? Explain.

216 THE RENAISSANCE

CHOICES:
Building Your Portfolio

Writer's Notebook

1. Collecting Ideas for an Interpretive Essay

When you write an essay about literature, a good starting point can be your own responses. Reflect on "Whoso List to Hunt" for a few minutes, writing freely about any personal connections you can make to the poem—experiences or feelings that you've had, or perhaps that you've witnessed in others. Try to find the one word or phrase from the poem that most strongly affects your feelings. Save your notes for use in the Writer's Workshop on page 275.

Creative Writing

2. A Woman's Place

What does the concept of love in this poem suggest about the position of women in Wyatt's time? How do you respond to the woman's statement "Caesar's I am"? How do you think *she* feels about her situation? Write a paragraph from the point of view of the "hind," and give her response to the situation described in the poem.

Jewel worn by Anne Boleyn, detail from the portrait *Anne Boleyn* (late 16th century) by an unknown artist. Oil on panel (21⅜″ × 16⅜″).

By Courtesy of the National Portrait Gallery, London.

PROGRAM MANAGER

Application and Reinforcement
For reinforcement of the elements of literature introduced in this lesson, see Transparency 3.2 in the *Audio-visual Resources Binder.*

PORTFOLIO ASSESSMENT

Choices: Assessment Criteria For help in evaluating these Choices assignments, see the criteria in the *Portfolio Management System,* p. 87.

Edmund Spenser

(c. 1552–1599)

Edmund Spenser.

The Granger Collection, New York.

Spenser—unlike such gentlemanly writers as Wyatt, Surrey, Sidney, and Raleigh—regarded himself primarily as a poet. Upon graduating from Cambridge University, he served as personal secretary to the earl of Leicester, then the favorite of Queen Elizabeth. In Leicester's household, Spenser became acquainted with several other poets and wrote his first book, *The Shepheardes Calender* (1579), a set of twelve pastoral poems, one for each month. Literary historians recognize 1579 as the date when the great age of Elizabethan literature began.

In 1580, Spenser and his new wife went to Ireland in the service of the English government. Except for two or three visits to England, he was to spend the rest of his life in that war-torn country. English troops had invaded and conquered Ireland, but the Irish did not regard themselves as conquered. They particularly resented people like Spenser, who was given an Irish castle and a vast estate in County Cork. Thirty miles away, Sir Walter Raleigh was the proprietor of an even vaster estate than Spenser's. When Raleigh was in Ireland, the two poets met and discussed their works in progress: Raleigh's *The Ocean to Cynthia* and Spenser's *The Faerie Queene*. Raleigh was so impressed with the latter that he persuaded Spenser to accompany him to London in 1589, and there in the following year Books I–III of *The Faerie Queene* were published.

In 1591, Spenser returned to Ireland, where conditions remained very unsettled and dangerous. But he managed to continue work on *The Faerie Queene* and other poems. When his first wife died, Spenser married Elizabeth Boyle, an Anglo-Irish woman living in Cork. Spenser's sonnet sequence *Amoretti* and his marriage hymn *Epithalamion* (both 1595) can be read autobiographically as records of his intense devotion to his wife. In 1596, Books IV–VI of *The Faerie Queene* appeared, along with another marriage song called *Prothalamion*.

As the century drew to a close, the Irish intensified their efforts to expel the English from their land. During one of their raids, Spenser's castle was burned and his infant son killed. Spenser himself escaped to London, where he died suddenly in 1599. He was given a splendid funeral and burial in the part of Westminster Abbey that has become known as the Poets' Corner. He lies near Chaucer, a poet who provided much of his inspiration.

Chaucer, Spenser, and Milton—these three were long regarded as England's greatest nondramatic poets. Of the three, Spenser is perhaps the least highly regarded today. Our age does not itself produce long poems of very high quality, and Spenser's fame depends mainly on the enormously long *Faerie Queene,* which despite its unfinished state runs about 33,000 lines. This poem is such a characteristic product of the Renaissance that some people find it has little to say to our own time. Moreover, Spenser's language is such a hybrid of Chaucerian and Elizabethan English that even when the work was brand new some purists objected to it. The dramatist and poet Ben Jonson, for instance, said Spenser "writ no language." But Spenser's special language is just right for his subject matter, and all the objections to him are easily overlooked by readers who want to lose themselves in the glorious world of imagination. They will always love Spenser.

EDMUND SPENSER 217

QUICK PLANNING GUIDE

Into the Poems

Author Biography p. 217
Before You Read p. 218
- **Reading Focus:** Students consider the paradox of love.
- **Quickwrite:** Write in Reader's Log images of falling in and out of love
- **Background: Scaffolding** The *Amoretti*

Through the Poems

Sonnet 30 p. 218
Sonnet 75 p. 219
Making Meanings p. 219
Elements of Literature pp. 219–220

Beyond the Poems

Choices: Building Your Portfolio p. 220
- **Writer's Notebook:** Create a dialogue
- **Creative Writing:** Write similes for love

Spotlight On p. 221

ABOUT THE AUTHOR

The headmaster of Spenser's boyhood school taught his top students to act. Every year he presented a play at court, and it is likely that Spenser, while a boy, appeared in such a play before Queen Elizabeth.

PROGRAM MANAGER

- **Planning Instruction** See **Teaching Notes,** *Teaching Resources A,* pp. 56–57, for objectives, a summary, and literary elements for these selections.
- **Instructional Support** Before beginning the instructional lesson, see **Graphic**

Organizer for Active Reading, *Teaching Resources A,* p. 66, for a Through the Poem activity.
- **Assessment** See **Selection Test,** *Test Booklet,* pp. 37–38.

Into the Poems

Using BEFORE YOU READ p. 218

Quickwrite

Have students work in groups to make a chart like the one below to help them brainstorm.

INTENSE DESIRE	LOSS OF INTEREST
Fire	Ice
[Midday sun]	[Waning moon]

Background

Spenser was not the only Elizabethan poet to consider poetry a way of immortalizing what might otherwise be lost to the ravages of death and time. Shakespeare and Jonson also used the eternizing conceit.

Through the Poems

A. Exploring the Culture

Many Renaissance poets wrote sequences of sonnets. These are sometimes taken to be autobiographical in nature, revealing the course of a love affair.

B. Critical Reading: Identifying Main Ideas

? What do you think the first line means? [Possible answer: I am wildly in love, but my loved one is giving me the cold shoulder.]

C. Literary Element: Paradox

Paradox was popular with Renaissance poets, who made statements with internal contradictions for literary effect. Have students restate in their own words the fire-and-ice paradoxes in ll. 2–4, 5–8, and 9–12. [Possible answers: Fire should melt ice, but here the ice is frozen harder by the fire; ice should cool fire, but here the ice makes the fire burn.]

D. Reader's Response: Shaping Interpretations

? How do the last two lines sum up the paradox? [Sample responses: Love is so powerful that it can change natural laws. Someone with a gentle nature can easily be swayed by love.]

T218 The Renaissance

Reading Focus

The Power of Paradox

Anyone who's been in love understands **paradox**: an apparent contradiction that is somehow true. Love makes you blissful and miserable. It's frightening and healing. It's physical and spiritual. It's incredibly fragile and yet so strong it seems deathless. In short, love is a potent puzzle that we never solve.

Quickwrite

Poets search for images to express the complex experience of falling in and out of love. How would you describe these two feelings: intense desire and loss of interest? Try to find a special image that represents each feeling. (Spenser uses fire and ice.)

Background

Spenser's *Amoretti* ("little love poems") is a sequence of eighty-nine sonnets recording a man's yearlong courtship of a woman named Elizabeth (perhaps Spenser's courtship of his bride, Elizabeth Boyle). In Sonnet 30, Spenser uses, in an original way, the convention of the burning man and the icy lady. Sonnet 75 uses another convention, the writer's "eternizing conceit": Submit to my love, and I'll make you famous and even immortal through my writing. But again Spenser gives this old notion a new twist.

218 THE RENAISSANCE

---

from Amoretti

Ⓐ ## Sonnet 30

Edmund Spenser

Ⓑ
My love is like to ice, and I to fire;
How comes it then that this her cold so great
Is not dissolved through my so hot desire,
But harder grows the more I her entreat?
5 Or how comes it that my exceeding heat
Is not delayed° by her heart frozen cold,
But that I burn much more in boiling sweat,
And feel my flames augmented manifold?°
 What more miraculous thing may be told
Ⓒ 10 That fire which all thing melts, should harden ice,
And ice which is congealed° with senseless cold,
Should kindle fire by wonderful device?°
Ⓓ
Such is the power of love in gentle mind,
That it can alter all the course of kind.°

6. **delayed:** tempered.
8. **augmented manifold:** increased in many ways.
11. **congealed:** thickened.
12. **device:** trick.
14. **kind:** nature.

Unknown Man with Flame Background (16th century) by Nicholas Hilliard.
Ham House, Surrey, England.

Sonnet 75

Edmund Spenser

One day I wrote her name upon the strand,°
But came the waves and washèd it away;
Again I wrote it with a second hand,
But came the tide, and made my pains his prey.
5 "Vain man," said she, "that doest in vain assay,°
A mortal thing so to immortalize,
For I myself shall like to this decay,
And eke° my name be wipèd out likewise."
"Not so," quod° I, "let baser things devise°
10 To die in dust, but you shall live by fame:
My verse your virtues rare shall eternize,
And in the heavens write your glorious name.
Where whenas death shall all the world subdue,
Our love shall live, and later life renew."

1. **strand:** beach.
5. **assay:** try.
8. **eke:** archaic for "also."
9. **quod:** quoth; said. **devise:** plan.

Portrait of an Unknown Lady
(16th century) by Nicholas Hilliard.
Victoria and Albert Museum, London.

MAKING MEANINGS

Sonnets 30 and 75

First Thoughts

1. How would you feel if someone in love with you had written these poems? Does your gender affect your response? How?

Shaping Interpretations

2. What **paradoxes** can you find in Sonnet 30? How would you explain them?

3. Fire and ice poems are meant to be clever, but in Sonnet 30, the **speaker** also says something serious about the power of love. What is it?

4. In what sense is the love of the two people in Sonnet 75 still alive today?

5. In Sonnet 75, what **image** does Spenser use for love's impermanence?

Extending the Texts

6. Some attitudes toward love and toward men and women have changed since these sonnets were written. Do you find the speaker's feelings dated or still relevant? Why?

ELEMENTS OF LITERATURE

Petrarchan and Spenserian Sonnets

Renaissance poets wrote with one eye on the past—they made new poems built on older forms and reflecting older themes. Wyatt's sonnets are

EDMUND SPENSER 219

A. Critical Reading: Making Inferences

? What does "second hand" mean?
[He wrote it with his hand a second time.]

B. Literary Element: Metaphor

? To what is the tide compared?
[A hunter; a predator.]

C. Reader's Response: Connecting with the Text

? What from your life would you like to have live on after you die?
[Sample responses: Memories, products, ideas, or children.]

Making Meanings

First Thoughts

1. Possible responses: It would probably depend on how I felt about the person. I do not think gender makes a difference because anyone could be impressed by or make fun of these poems.

Shaping Interpretations

2. The poem has two central paradoxes: ice "kindles" fire, and the fire makes ice colder and harder.
3. Love can change the natural tendencies of things.
4. The sonnet preserves it, and people still read about it.
5. The waves washing away the writing in the sand.

Extending the Texts

6. **(Evaluation)** Possible responses: The sonnets are dated because they show gender bias—the woman is cold, the man hot—or they are dated because of their language, not because of the attitudes expressed.

PROGRAM MANAGER

Application and Reinforcement
For reinforcement of the elements of literature introduced in this lesson, see **Transparency 3.3** in the *Audiovisual Resources Binder.*

Elements of Literature

Mini-Lesson: Petrarchan and Spenserian Sonnets

Have students copy a Petrarchan and a Spenserian sonnet and use different-colored markers to indicate the rhyme schemes. Then, have them draw boxes around the octave and sestet or the quatrains and couplet.

Answers

1. Between octave and sestet. A logical shift: the octave tells other potential hunters about the deer; the sestet warns them off.
2. Conceits will vary. Students' conceits should be creative, and students should be able to explain them if necessary.
3. Sonnet 30: fire/desire; great/entreat/heat/sweat; cold/manifold/told/cold; ice/device; mind/kind
   Sonnet 75: strand/hand; away/prey/assay/decay; immortalize/likewise/devise/eternize; fame/name; subdue/renew

Beyond the Poems

Choices: Building Your Portfolio

1. **Writer's Notebook** Remind students to save their work. They may use it as prewriting for the Writer's Workshop on p. 275.
2. **Creative Writing** Allow students to vary the beginning; for example, "Love feels like _____."

---

adaptations or translations of sonnets written by the Italian Francesco Petrarca (1304–1374), known in English as Francis Petrarch. Petrarch addressed many love poems to a woman identified only as Laura, a proud woman of ideal virtue and beauty who remains totally indifferent to the poet. The poet-lover alternately burns with desire and freezes in Laura's cold disdain.

Sonnets in the Petrarchan manner contain many ingenious comparisons, which in time became known as **Petrarchan conceits**. A **conceit** is a fanciful comparison of two apparently very different things. Love may be compared to a baited hook, for instance, or being in love may be described as plowing water, an obviously futile effort. Petrarchan sonneteers also shape their emotion within a strict structure: fourteen lines of rhymed iambic pentameter, organized in two stanzas, one of eight lines (an **octave**) and one of six lines (a **sestet**). The rhyme in the octave is *abbaabba* and in the sestet usually *cdecde*.

In most Italian sonnets, the octave describes a situation, and the sestet describes a change in the situation. This change is called the **turn**. Sometimes the octave presents a problem and the sestet a solution or even another viewpoint. Sometimes the sestet intensifies the octave's problem with no solution. The possibilities are endless.

Two **English sonnet** forms—the Spenserian and Shakespearean sonnets—originated in the Renaissance. Like the Petrarchan sonnet, both forms use iambic pentameter, but they both differ from the Petrarchan sonnet in having three 4-line stanzas (**quatrains**) and a concluding couplet. The rhyme scheme of the *Amoretti* sonnets is original with Spenser: *abab bcbc cdcd ee*. Since it demands four words for two of the rhymes, only a clever rhymer can manage it.

1. In what line is the turn of Wyatt's "Whoso List to Hunt" (page 215)? Does the turn show a logical or an emotional shift?
2. Make up your own Petrarchan conceit for the experience of love or for a loved one's appearance.
3. Identify the rhyming words in Spenser's Sonnets 30 and 75.

CHOICES:
Building Your Portfolio

Writer's Notebook

1. Collecting Ideas for an Interpretive Essay

If you could talk to Spenser about one of these sonnets (whether to praise, challenge, argue, or just question), which would you focus on? Choose one, and then jot notes as you re-read it carefully. Speak to Spenser directly about his ideas, words, feelings, sounds—anything. Save your dialogue for possible use with the Writer's Workshop assignment on page 275.

Creative Writing

2. Images of Love

In Sonnet 30, what images suggest desire and indifference? In Sonnet 75, what images suggest love's impermanence? Make a love's listing of your own, of the things that love, in all its variations, can be compared to. You could open your lines like this:

Love's passion is like _____ .

Be sure to check the images you jotted down in your Reader's Log before you read Spenser's poems.

Pair of English leather gloves (early 17th century).

Gift of Philip Lehman, "in memory of my wife, Carrie L. Lehman." Courtesy, Museum of Fine Arts, Boston.

PORTFOLIO ASSESSMENT

Choices: Assessment Criteria For help in evaluating these Choices assignments, see the criteria in the *Portfolio Management System,* p. 88.

STRATEGIES FOR INCLUSION

Auditory Have students take turns reading the different sections of the sonnets. One student can read the octave, another the sestet. This will help delineate the distinctions among sonnets and their parts.

Bodily-Kinesthetic Using blocks of color instead of words to indicate octave, sestet, quatrains, and couplet, students can make large posters showing the different types of sonnets. Ask students to write *English* or *Italian* at the top of the poster and to define each block with the number of lines and rhyme scheme.

A. Humanities Connection
Spenser's epic bears more similarities to the epics of the Italians Ariosto and Tasso than to classical epics.

The Faerie Queene:
England Through the Looking Glass

In Spenser's long, complex, and unfinished poem *The Faerie Queene,* the word *faerie* does not mean a wee, airy creature dancing among the flowers. Rather, *faerie* suggests grand, heroic beings whose superhuman powers come from their own virtue and piety. The Faerie Queene herself (who does not even appear in the existing poem) is Gloriana, an idealized portrait of Queen Elizabeth, and her realm is at once the England that Spenser loved and a strange, imaginary country.

The poem is a romantic or chivalric **epic.** Unlike the classical epics of Virgil and Homer, romantic epics have an open form, with multiple characters and multiplying plots spreading out in all directions. The marvels, knights, ladies, battles, tournaments, enchantments, dragons, giants, dwarfs, and demons derive from the medieval romances of chivalry, such as the tales of King Arthur.

But its lively stories are only the surface of *The Faerie Queene.* Spenser's moral purposes are especially evident. In a letter to Raleigh, Spenser said that he intended his work to be an **allegory:** Each leading character in the twelve projected books was to embody one virtue or quality; taken together, they would characterize a truly noble person. The heroes or heroines of the six completed books exemplify holiness, temperance, chastity, friendship, justice, and courtesy.

The poem is a tremendous feat of rhyming: Each nine-line iambic stanza has only three rhymes—*ababbcbcc.* The last line's extra foot makes it hexameter. This line, called an **alexandrine,** often sums up a stanza or finishes it off with a striking image. This verse form, which Spenser created for *The Faerie Queene,* is now called the **Spenserian stanza.**

Trying to experience Spenser's immense poem by reading only a few verses is like trying to experience the ocean by looking at a teacup of sea water. However, the three stanzas that follow, describing the hideous Duessa, show Spenser's delight in heroic violence and the gusto with which he describes ugliness.

The Rainbow Portrait of Queen Elizabeth (16th century) by Federico Zuccaro.
Hatfield House, Hertfordshire, England.

RESPONDING TO THE ART: VISUAL LITERACY

What assumptions can you make about Queen Elizabeth from this portrait, and why? What kind of personality do you think she had? [Possible responses: Commanding, dominating, quiet, quick-tempered, intense; she has a very serious, hard, and authoritative look about her; her posture seems very regal and noble.] **Does her dress reveal anything about her?** [Possible responses: It is very elaborate and looks expensive; it makes her look vain.]

OPTIONS FOR TEACHING

STRATEGIES FOR INCLUSION

Spatial When you cover the material on Spenser and *The Faerie Queene,* give students transparency sheets to place over the poem, and have them highlight groups of rhyming words in each stanza using different highlighter colors for each group of words. Have students write out the rhyme scheme.

Visual Encourage students to create illustrations of Duessa that fit Spenser's description. Let them choose any medium.

Advanced Lead students in listing any symbolic meanings in the description Spenser gives.

Auditory To give students more practice with meter, have them tap or clap the rhythms in *The Faerie Queene* stanzas. Ask them if they can identify the lines that are perfect iambic pentameter.

Spotlight On **T221**

As this part of the story from Canto VIII of Book I opens, a knight has been rescued from the clutches of a foul female creature called Duessa, or Falsehood. The knight is ordered by his traveling companion, Una, or Truth, to disrobe Duessa. (Reading aloud will make Spenser's language easier to understand.)

Ⓐ So as she bad, that witch they disaraid,
    And robd of royall robes, and purple pall,°
    And ornaments that richly were displaid;
    Ne sparèd they to strip her naked all.
5   Then when they had despoild her tire and call,°
    Such as she was, their eyes might her behold,
    That her misshapèd parts did them apall:
Ⓑ A loathly, wrinckled hag, ill favoured, old,
  Whose secret filth good manners biddeth not be told.

10 Her craftie head was altogether bald,
    And as in hate of honorable eld,°
    Was overgrowne with scurfe and filthy scald;°
    Her teeth out of her rotten gummes were feld,°
    And her sowre breath abhominably smeld;
15   Her drièd dugs,° like bladders lacking wind,
    Hong downe, and filthy matter from them weld;°
    Her wrizled° skin as rough, as maple rind,°
  So scabby was, that would have loathd all womankind. . . .

  Which when the knights beheld, amazd they were,
20   And wondred at so fowle deformèd wight.
    "Such then," said Una, "as she seemeth here,
    Such is the face of falsehood, such the sight
    Of fowle Duessa, when her borrowed light
    Is laid away, and counterfesaunce° knowne."
25   Thus when they had the witch disrobèd quight,
    And her filthy feature° open showne,
  They let her goe at will, and wander wayes unknowne.

—Edmund Spenser, *from The Faerie Queene*

2. **pall:** mantle.

5. **tire and call:** attire and headgear.

11. **eld:** old age.
12. **scald:** scabs.
13. **feld:** fallen.

15. **dugs:** breasts.
16. **weld:** ran.
17. **wrizled:** wrinkled. **rind:** bark.

24. **counterfesaunce:** hypocrisy.

26. **feature:** appearance.

OPTIONS FOR TEACHING

INTEGRATING THE LANGUAGE ARTS

Strategic Reading Ask pairs of students to use the following graphic organizer to record main ideas, transitions, and details from paragraphs in the essay on Spenser's *The Faerie Queene*.

| Main Idea/Details |
| Transition |
| Main Idea/Details |
| Transition |
| Main Idea/Details |
| Transition |
| Main Idea/Details |

Ask them to exchange their results with another pair and to compare and edit their charts as a foursome.

Speaking and Listening Present a mini-lesson on reading poetry aloud. Have students in pairs read poems aloud to one another. Then, have students note end stops—where punctuation indicates a pause at the end of a line—and enjambment—where sentence logic requires continuation without pause onto the next line. Inform students that not every poem has every line in perfect iambic pentameter. This will help students to avoid a singsong rendition that ignores meaning.

Shakespeare's Sonnets: The Mysteries of Love

Shakespeare. The name calls to mind characters in the great plays, who have come to life on stages around the world: *Hamlet, Macbeth, Romeo and Juliet, King Lear, Othello.* Yet had Shakespeare written no plays at all, he would still have an immense reputation as a poet for his *Sonnets* (1609). There are 154 sonnets altogether, their speaker is male, and their chief subject is love. Beyond these three points, however, there is little agreement, only questions:

Is the sonnets' speaker a dramatic character invented by Shakespeare, like Romeo, Macbeth, or Hamlet, or is he the poet himself? The speaker does call himself Will a few times, and he does make puns on his name, but is there any evidence that Will is the speaker in all the sonnets? If the sonnets are about the real man Shakespeare, then who are the real people behind the characters the sonnets mention: the rival poet, the beloved young man who may be the subject of many of the first 126 sonnets, or the beautiful and exciting dark-complexioned woman of some later sonnets?

Is the order in which the sonnets were originally published (probably without Shakespeare's consent) the correct or the intended sequence? Could they be arranged to tell a more coherent story? *Should* they be so arranged?

And in the 1609 publication, who is the "Mr. W. H." mentioned as the "only begetter" of the sonnets: the young man? someone else?

These and dozens of other questions about the sonnets have been asked and answered over and over again—but never to everybody's satisfaction. We have hundreds of conflicting theories, but no absolutely convincing answers.

About the individual sonnets, though, if not the whole sequence, agreement is perfect: They are among the supreme utterances in English. They say profound things about important human experiences, and they say them with great art.

Maids and winged hearts (detail) from *Emblèmes et Devises d'Amour* (early 16th century) by Pierre Sala. Stowe 955 fol 12b–13.

British Library, London.

WILLIAM SHAKESPEARE **223**

OPTIONS FOR TEACHING

STRATEGIES FOR INCLUSION

Visual Cut some of Shakespeare's sonnets into individual lines, and give one sonnet to each student. Ask students to put the lines in order and to explain how they figured it out. This will help them with meaning and rhyme scheme.

Learners Having Difficulty Map out the sonnet structure on the chalkboard, reminding students of the set rhyme schemes, pattern of quatrains and couplet, and frequent use of iambic pentameter. Invite them to work in pairs to write a poem that fits the sonnet parameters. 👉

Due to calendar differences when Shakespeare wrote this, May was a summer month, not a spring month, so he can properly refer to a "summer's day" in May.

B. Expansion
This is an example of the eternizing conceit mentioned on p. 218.

PROGRAM MANAGER

- **Planning Instruction** See Teaching Notes, *Teaching Resources A*, pp. 57–58, for objectives, a summary, literary elements, and additional historical information for these selections.
- **Instructional Support** Before beginning the instructional lesson, see **Graphic Organizer for Active Reading**, *Teaching Resources A*, pp. 67–68, for Through the Poem activities.
- **Assessment** See **Selection Test**, *Test Booklet*, pp. 39–40.
- **Language Link** For instruction and practice in verb tenses, see **Language Link**, *Teaching Resources A*, pp. 69–70, and *Language and Writing Skills Worksheets*, pp. 40–42.

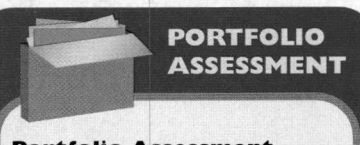

PORTFOLIO ASSESSMENT

Portfolio Assessment
For help with self-assessment of reading skills, see the *Portfolio Management System*, p. 53.

The Sonnets' Form

Each of Shakespeare's sonnets has its formal organization established by the rules of the sonnet form. Each sonnet also has a logical organization of ideas, also established by the sonnet form. Here is how Shakespeare structured Sonnet 18 to make these two organizations cooperate in a way that seems natural, not forced.

Logical organization		Sonnet 18	Formal organization

A question and tentative answers

Shall I compare thee to a summer's day? — a
Thou art more lovely and more temperate. — b } First quatrain
Rough winds do shake the darling buds of May, — a
And summer's lease hath all too short a date. — b

Sometime too hot the eye of heaven shines, — c
And often is his gold complexion dimmed; — d } Second quatrain
And every fair from fair sometime declines, — c
By chance, or nature's changing course untrimmed. — d

The turn

But thy eternal summer shall not fade, — e
Nor lose possession of that fair thou owest, — f } Third quatrain
Nor shall Death brag thou wander'st in his shade — e
When in eternal lines to time thou grow'st. — f

A final answer

So long as men can breathe, or eyes can see, — g } Couplet
So long lives this, and this gives life to thee. — g

In the English sonnet form known as the **Shakespearean sonnet,** the fixed requirements are fourteen iambic pentameter lines divided into three quatrains and a couplet, with the rhyme scheme *ababcdcdefefgg*. (See page 219 for Spenserian and Petrarchan forms.)

The logical organization of ideas, of course, varies from sonnet to sonnet. Here in Sonnet 18, the first line's question is followed by negative answers: The speaker's beloved does have some resemblances to a summer's day, but only superficial ones. The first two quatrains concentrate on the summer day's imperfections rather than on the loved one.

Then comes the **turn,** a shift in focus or thought. Here the speaker turns from the faulty summer's day to the beloved, and by the end of the third quatrain, the speaker has entirely abandoned the opening comparison. Like most literary terms, the word *turn* is a metaphor; the speaker, figuratively speaking, is "turning" from one thing to another.

In an Italian sonnet, divided into an eight-line octave and six-line sestet, the turn usually occurs after the octave. Sonnet 18, with its turn after line 8, follows this pattern, but in an English sonnet, the final couplet is often a second turn of great impact: a final summary or explanation of all that came before. In this sonnet, the couplet says, perhaps with some exaggeration, that by being addressed in this poem, the beloved person has become immortal.

(For Shakespeare's biography, see page 289.)

PROFESSIONAL NOTES

Technology Tip The Internet is host to numerous resources on Shakespeare. Have your students do key word searches to find Web pages, Gopher servers, and FTP sites. *You may want to preview any Internet activity that you suggest to students. Because these resources are sometimes public forums, their content can be unpredictable.*

ASSESSMENT TOOLS

Check Test: True-False
1. Love is the main subject in Shakespeare's sonnets. [True]
2. People know a great deal about the background of the sonnets. [False]
3. Shakespearean sonnets have a rhymed couplet at the end. [True]
4. The "turn" in a sonnet is a shift in focus or thought. [True]
5. Shakespearean sonnets have the same rhyme scheme and structure as Italian sonnets. [False]

BEFORE YOU READ
SONNETS 29, 73, 116, 130

Reading Focus

The Heart of the Matter
Earlier (page 212), we asked the humanist's question, "What is the good life?" A related question may be equally difficult, and that is "What is the happy life?" What is it that makes us happy, that lets us look back over years receding into the past, and ahead to the inevitable conclusion, without sorrow or despair? Wealth hasn't answered the question satisfactorily for many people. Power always seems to dwindle away or be wrenched out of our hands in an instant. Fame evaporates faster than the early morning fog. If there is any answer to this question, for many people it is love. Time passes and death is inescapable, but love, if we are fortunate enough to find it or create it, sustains us through it all.

In these four sonnets, Shakespeare speculates about what love is, and what it does to us and for us.

Quickwrite

READER'S LOG

People warn you not to confuse infatuation with love: Having stars in your eyes makes for a wonderful glow but blurry vision. Eventually, a warm glow comes up against a reality check—and sometimes it doesn't pass. What distinguishes love from infatuation? Write freely for a few minutes trying to identify a few qualities of each, or of the people you've seen enjoying—or suffering from—each.

In this sonnet, the speaker describes how he rids himself of such ugly emotions as envy, self-pity, self-hatred, and the dismal feeling of certainty that everybody else is luckier than he is.

Sonnet 29

William Shakespeare

When, in disgrace° with Fortune and men's eyes, **A**
I all alone beweep my outcast state,
And trouble deaf heaven with my bootless° cries,
And look upon myself and curse my fate,
5 Wishing me like to one more rich in hope,
Featured like him, like him° with friends possessed, **B**
Desiring this man's art,° and that man's scope,°
With what I most enjoy contented least;
Yet in these thoughts myself almost despising,
10 Haply° I think on thee, and then my state, **C**
Like to the lark° at break of day arising
From sullen° earth, sings hymns at heaven's gate;
    For thy sweet love remembered such wealth brings
    That then I scorn to change my state with kings.

1. **disgrace:** out of favor.
3. **bootless:** useless; futile.
6. **one . . . him . . . him:** three different men whom the speaker envies.
7. **art:** literary ability. **scope:** power.
10. **haply:** by chance.
11. **lark:** English skylark, a bird whose song seems to pour down from the sky.
12. **sullen:** gloomy.

Henry Percy, 9th earl of Northumberland.
Rijksmuseum, Amsterdam.

225

Into the Poems

Using BEFORE YOU READ p. 225

Quickwrite

Suggest that students use a two-column chart to list adjectives they associate with infatuation and love.

LOVE	INFATUATION
[peaceful, deep, long-term]	[excited, crazy, short-lived]

Through the Poems

A. Humanities Connection

A complaint is a plaintive poem; many of the sonnets in the major sonnet sequences are complaints, the laments and pleas of unrequited lovers. Shakespeare begins with a complaint, but gives an unexpected ending. At what point does the tone of the poem change? [Line 10.]

B. Critical Reading: Finding Details

? What does the narrator wish for in ll. 5–7? [Possible answers: A hopeful state of mind, good looks, friends, ability, and power.]

C. Language Note: Syntax

Point out that the poem is all one sentence: The first introductory clause in the poem begins with *when* in l. 1 and goes through l. 8; the second introductory clause is in l. 9. The main clause begins at the beginning of l. 10 and is accompanied by the major shift in tone.

STRATEGIES FOR INCLUSION

Visual Have students represent in a drawing the change that occurs in the speaker from the beginning of Sonnet 29 to the end. They might draw two figures: the man of the "bootless cries" and the man "like to the lark," or they might do something more abstract.

Special Needs Have students copy onto 3" × 5" note cards rhyming lines or end rhymes found in any of the sonnets. They may use different colored cards or markers for each rhyme. Depending on the numbers of students, give them appropriate lines or stanzas to copy. Ask students to read the lines of poetry in the correct order and to hold up the matching cards as they read.

A. **Language Note: Syntax**

? What parallel syntax introduces each of the three metaphors? [Words that say, in effect, "You
see in me . . ."]

B. **Reader's Response: First
Thoughts**

? How do you picture the speaker?
[Sample responses: The speaker
is aging or ill, based on lines that refer
to autumn, evening, and dying embers.
The speaker could be someone older
but still passionate.]

C. **Reader's Response: Shaping
Interpretations**

? What do all three metaphors
(ll. 1–12) have in common? Why
are they appropriate for the speaker's
message? [Sample responses: They all
describe the end of something—the
year, the day, a fire. He is talking about
the end of his life.]

D. **Critical Reading: Drawing
Conclusions**

? How has the speaker's advancing
age affected his beloved? [Possible
answer: His beloved seems understanding of the changes caused by age
or illness and continues to love him,
though the end is near.]

In several sonnets, the speaker emphasizes the difference between
his age and his beloved's: He is much older, and so presumably will
die first. In Sonnet 73, the speaker dwells on his advanced years.
This sonnet is rich in striking metaphors, with each quatrain
developing a single metaphor.

Sonnet 73

William Shakespeare

(A) That time of year thou mayst in me behold
When yellow leaves, or none, or few, do hang
(B) Upon those boughs which shake against the cold,
Bare ruined choirs° where late the sweet birds sang.
5 In me thou see'st the twilight of such day
As after sunset fadeth in the west,
Which by and by black night doth take away,
Death's second self, that seals up all in rest.
(C) In me thou see'st the glowing of such fire,
10 That on the ashes of his youth doth lie
As the deathbed whereon it must expire,
Consumed with that which it was nourished by.°
(D) This thou perceivest, which makes thy love more strong,
To love that well which thou must leave ere long.

4. choirs: parts of a church or
cathedral in which services are held.
The landscape of Shakespeare's
England was dotted with church
ruins resulting from Henry VIII's
abolition of monasteries.

12. consumed . . . nourished by:
choked by the ashes of the wood
that once fed its flame.

An October Afterglow (detail) (19th century)
by John Atkinson Grimshaw.
Christie's, London.

**OPTIONS FOR
TEACHING**

STRATEGIES FOR INCLUSION

Intrapersonal After they have read
the four Shakespearean sonnets in this
Collection, ask students to choose the
sonnet that comes closest to expressing their ideas about love. Have students write a paragraph about why
they chose the one they did.

Less Proficient Readers To make Sonnet
116 (p. 228) easier to comprehend, have students
work in pairs to change the negative sentences to
positive constructions. For example, the first sentence might be changed to read: "I want to
encourage the marriage of true minds," and the
second might read: "True love is changeless and
loyal . . ."

Musical Ask students to choose a popular love
song that they know well and to write a parody of
it. (A country or pop song extolling the virtues
of the beloved would probably work well.) Students should use (but should not be limited by)
Shakespeare's technique in Sonnet 130 (p. 229)
of negating the qualities or attributes listed in the
original. Discuss what points the parodies could
make. Students may speak their finished works
or sing them.

MAKING MEANINGS

Sonnets 29 and 73

First Thoughts

1. Obviously, the **speakers** in these two sonnets are in love, but what other emotions do you hear in their voices? Do you hear joy, sorrow, or something else?

Shaping Interpretations

2. Like many of the sonnets, Sonnet 29 is actually a single sentence. In the long introductory clause, what does the speaker say he envies?

3. The main clause of Sonnet 29 begins the **turn.** Where is it? How does the speaker's **tone,** or attitude, change after the turn?

4. In Sonnet 73, what four **metaphors** does the speaker use to describe himself? What contrast is implied between the speaker and his beloved?

5. Find the **turn** of Sonnet 73. What is its logical relationship to what comes before?

6. How do the seasonal and daily **imagery** in Sonnet 73 contribute to the poem's **tone**?

7. In Sonnet 73, the idea of line 12 is somewhat compressed. **Paraphrase** it in your own words, after you have thought about what originally fed ("nourished") the speaker's fires—fires that are now choked ("consumed").

Extending the Texts

8. If you wrote a contemporary version of Sonnet 29 ("When I failed the quiz and left my lunch at home . . ."), what would you replace Shakespeare's complaints with? Look at his list of problems, and see if you can come up with a contemporary version.

9. What people today could you imagine being the speaker in each of these sonnets?

Challenging the Text

10. In Sonnet 29, what do you think is the effect of devoting so many lines to the speaker's mental problems and so few to their cure?

WILLIAM SHAKESPEARE 227

INTEGRATING THE LANGUAGE ARTS

Mechanics The capitalization of the word "Fortune" in Sonnet 29 (p. 225) signals the introduction of an important Renaissance concept. Point out that poets of this period often used capitalization to indicate **personification** in their poetry. Ask how Fortune is personified in this poem. [Fortune holds the speaker in disgrace.]

Writing: Metaphors After students read Sonnet 73 (p. 226), have them compose three

metaphors about themselves. Students should begin by brainstorming their finest qualities, preferably attributes of character rather than appearance. Then, have them work on expressing each quality or aspect as a comparison. They may express their metaphors in poetry or prose. Students may choose to write a single extended metaphor instead of three shorter metaphors. They may also choose to write about someone they know well, rather than themselves. ☞

Making Meanings

First Thoughts

1. Students may say that the mood changes, particularly in Sonnet 29. Possible responses: Reflection, regret, satisfaction.

Shaping Interpretations

2. One who has reason to hope, is handsome, has many friends, and has ability and power.

3. Line 10. From absorbed self-pity to delight in the beloved.

4. Possible response: The metaphors compare the speaker to a bare tree in autumn, ruined choirs, the twilight after sunset, and the glowing embers of a fire. The beloved is young, and the speaker is old.

5. Line 13. In the lines preceding the turn, the speaker says that he is growing old and must die soon. The last lines mean, "Therefore, you love me more because you will soon be without me."

6. They make it poignant and reinforce the sonnet's melancholy tone.

7. Possible response: I think life itself fed the fire (as wood feeds a real fire), so I would say, "I am consumed by the life that I lived— I have used up my time."

Extending the Texts

8. **(Synthesis)** The speaker's complaints in the poem are that he is hopeless and friendless. He lacks artistry and broad knowledge. Students can express these in their own terms.

9. **(Synthesis)** Possible answers: Sonnet 29—a young, lonesome person. Sonnet 73—an older man married to a young woman or vice versa.

Challenging the Text

10. **(Synthesis)** The numerous complaints in ll. 1–8 suggest the sheer weight of the speaker's unhappiness. The power of the cure is emphasized by its unexpectedness and quick effect on the speaker.

A. Literary Element: Alliteration

? How do you think the alliteration of the letter *m* in the first sentence relates to the poem's meaning? [Possible answer: The repeated *m* sound makes the sentence feel connected, possibly emphasizing the strong connection forged by a marriage bond.]

B. Critical Reading: Drawing Conclusions

? Which lines in the poem help define love by telling what it is not? [Possible answers: Lines 2–4, 9, 11.]

C. Critical Reading: Making Inferences

? What is the literal meaning of ll. 5–6? [Possible answer: Love, once set, does not move and is not changed by external events.]

D. Literary Element: Figure of Speech

Synecdoche is a figure of speech in which a part of something represents the whole. What do "rosy lips and cheeks" stand for? Why do you think Shakespeare chooses to mention those particulars? [Possible answers: They stand for youth. He has mentioned attractive features that are subject to the ravages of time.]

E. Critical Reading: Making Connections

Compare the poem's idea of what will last with the ideas expressed in Spenser's Sonnet 75. [Possible answer: Both sonnets note that the body will decay, and both say that love will live on. Sonnet 75 also claims that the speaker's verse will live on—and it has.]

Perhaps the most famous of Shakespeare's sonnets, Sonnet 116 defines true love metaphorically as a "marriage of true minds." Such love is completely firm against all "impediments," a word taken from the priest's remarks to those attending a Church of England wedding: "If any of you know cause or just impediment why these persons should not be joined together . . ."

Sonnet 116

William Shakespeare

(A) Let me not to the marriage of true minds
(B) Admit impediments. Love is not love
Which alters when it alteration finds,
Or bends with the remover to remove.
(C) 5 Oh no! It is an ever-fixèd mark°
That looks on tempests and is never shaken.
It is the star to every wandering bark,°
Whose worth's° unknown, although his height be taken.°
(D) Love's not Time's fool, though rosy lips and cheeks
10 Within his bending sickle's compass° come.
Love alters not with his brief hours and weeks,
(E) But bears it out° even to the edge of doom.°
    If this be error and upon me proved,
    I never writ, nor no man ever loved.

5. **mark:** seamark; a prominent object on shore that serves as a guide to sailors.
7. **bark:** boat.
8. **worth's:** value's.   **height be taken:** altitude measured to determine a ship's position.
10. **compass:** range; reach.

12. **bears it out:** survives.   **doom:** the Last Judgment; the final judgment at the end of the world.

The Bradford Table Carpet, detail of scenes of rural life (late 16th century). Embroidered on linen canvas with colored silks. English.
Victoria and Albert Museum, London.

This sonnet ridicules the fashionable, exaggerated metaphors some of Shakespeare's fellow poets were using to describe the women they loved: Your eyes are suns that set me on fire, your cheeks are roses, your breasts are snowballs. Such metaphors, known as **conceits,** are traceable to Petrarch, but by 1600 they had become, through overuse, tiresome or laughable. (Note that the word *mistress* in this poem simply meant "girlfriend" in the Renaissance.)

Sonnet 130

William Shakespeare

My mistress' eyes are nothing like the sun, (A)
Coral is far more red than her lips' red.
If snow be white, why then her breasts are dun,° (B)
If hairs be wires, black wires grow on her head.
5 I have seen roses damasked,° red and white,
But no such roses see I in her cheeks.
And in some perfumes is there more delight
Than in the breath that from my mistress reeks,°
I love to hear her speak, yet well I know
10 That music hath a far more pleasing sound. (C)
I grant I never saw a goddess go,°
My mistress, when she walks, treads on the ground.
     And yet, by Heaven, I think my love as rare
     As any she belied° with false compare.° (D)

3. **dun:** brown.

5. **damasked:** streaked.

8. **reeks:** is exhaled.

11. **go:** walk.

14. **belied:** misrepresented. **compare:** comparison.

MAKING MEANINGS

Sonnets 116 and 130

First Thoughts

1. Do you agree with Sonnet 116's definition of love? Why or why not?

2. In Sonnet 130, how do you picture the speaker's mistress?

Shaping Interpretations

3. What **metaphors** does Sonnet 116 use to describe the steadiness of love? How is time **personified** in this poem?

4. In Sonnet 116, between which lines does the **turn**—the change in **moods**—occur? How would you speak these lines to convey the change in mood?

5. What does the final **couplet** add to the message of Sonnet 116?

6. Sonnet 130 could have been written by someone who had read too many Petrarchan sonnets. How does the **speaker** poke fun at them?

7. Do you think the speaker's mistress in Sonnet 130 is actually unattractive? Why or why not?

8. Why is the **couplet** in Sonnet 130 absolutely necessary to keep the sonnet from being misunderstood?

9. If you came upon these two sonnets without knowing they were by the same writer, would you infer, from the attitudes expressed, that they were by one writer or two? Why?

Extending the Texts

10. Which of these four Shakespearean sonnets do you think could be read at a wedding? Could any of them be part of a funeral service? Explain.

WILLIAM SHAKESPEARE **229**

Beyond the Poems

Choices: Building Your Portfolio

1. **Writer's Notebook** Remind students to save their work. They may use it as prewriting for the Writer's Workshop on p. 275.

2. **Critical Writing Tone** is the attitude a writer takes toward the reader, a subject, or a character. One choice would be Sonnets 116 and 130.

3. **Critical Writing** Check students' charts before they begin to write the essay. Point out possible thesis statements and organization options based on the information in the chart.

4. **Creative Writing** As an alternative, let students begin their answers in their own way. Students might work in pairs. Boys may imagine what a girl would say were Sonnet 130 written about her.

5. **Creative Writing** Have students volunteer song titles. Write them on the chalkboard. Some examples include "All You Need Is Love," "Love Me Tender," and "Endless Love."

6. **Visual Art** Suggest a variety of mediums such as colored paper, paint, and colored pencils. Students may also wish to use computer graphics.

7. **Panel Discussion** Have students bring in ads clipped from magazines and lists of television commercials, film characters, or entertainment figures to form the basis for discussion. Ask them to identify the messages. For example, "Wear these jeans and you will end up in a Parisian cafe with a good-looking partner." It is also useful to compare messages from different decades.

PORTFOLIO ASSESSMENT

Choices: Assessment Criteria For help in evaluating these Choices assignments, see the criteria in the *Portfolio Management System,* pp. 89–90.

CHOICES: Building Your Portfolio

Writer's Notebook
1. Collecting Ideas for an Interpretive Essay

When you write about literature, repeated readings are a basic step in finding new insights and writing topics. Choose the sonnet that you're most drawn to, and read it again, slowly. Then try reading it aloud, and copy it out on a piece of paper. For each reading, make notes on the words and ideas that affect you most strongly. For each reading, note at least one new detail you didn't see before. (You might want to highlight passages with a different color marker for each reading.) Save your work for possible use with the Writer's Workshop on page 275.

Critical Writing
2. What Makes Tone?

Identify two sonnets in which you detect tones or moods. Compare and contrast the sonnets by focusing on each speaker's tone. Discuss how word choice, figurative language, imagery, and sound effects work together to create a very specific tone for each poem.

Critical Writing
3. From Shakespeare to Cummings

Look back at the modern love poem by the American poet E. E. Cummings (1894–1962) on page 213. Write a brief essay in which you compare that poem with one of Shakespeare's sonnets. Before you write, you might gather the details for your comparison in a chart like the following:

	Poem 1	Poem 2
Message		
Figurative language		
Form		
Tone		

Creative Writing
4. The Mistress Answers Back

Sonnet 130 is written from the male speaker's point of view. But how would his mistress reply? Write your own sonnet (or just a few verses) to a boyfriend, using this as a beginning: "My boyfriend's eyes are . . . "

Creative Writing
5. Mocking Modern Love

Sonnet 130 is a witty parody of love poems popular in Shakespeare's day. Write your own parody of modern love

songs expressed in one style of popular music: country, heavy metal, alternative rock, and so on. Listen to several examples of the style first, paying attention to melody, rhythm, story line, imagery, and tone.

Visual Art
6. Being Moody

Create an emotionally suggestive illustration for each sonnet, using only two colors and one visual image in each illustration. The image may be a real object, such as a lark, or an abstract pattern, such as a heart shape. Combine colors and image creatively to convey the feelings you find in the poem.

Panel Discussion
7. Love in Our Time

In our own time—in art, entertainment, and ads—romantic love is exalted as a pinnacle of human happiness (especially, in the media, love with someone gorgeous, trim, and trendy). But what of people who never find a partner—or a perfect one? Are they losers? Is romantic love essential for happiness? In a panel discussion, critique our culture's messages about love, using examples. Be sure to look back at your Reader's Log entry (page 225) for ideas about what true love is.

STRATEGIES FOR INCLUSION

Special Needs Some students are more successful when they are able to illustrate their knowledge by drawing or doing a tactile activity. For activity #1, give each student a different section of one of the sonnets. Have students draw or use magazine photographs placed on a poster board to illustrate their understanding of the meaning of the section. On the back of the poster they should state in their own words what they think the meaning is.

English Language Development For activity #2, illustrate the meaning of **tone** by saying sentences in different tones of voice. Note that a listener's or reader's emotional response to words will differ depending on the tone used. Point out that word choice affects tone; for example, compare *thrifty* and *stingy*. Work together as a class to develop a list of words that are close in meaning but disparate in tone.

BEFORE YOU READ

THE PASSIONATE SHEPHERD
THE NYMPH'S REPLY
TO THE VIRGINS
TO HIS COY MISTRESS

Reading Focus

Love's Logic

You have heard it before. On the radio or in a music video, a lead singer appeals passionately to a woman to be his love, although the specific lyrics vary. What you may not know is that people have heard this message for centuries. The "invitation to love" is an old poetic tradition. It was especially common in Renaissance England. Along with descriptions of all the delights that await a hesitant young woman, the Renaissance poet pressures her with what may really be the oldest "line" in the world: "We are all going to die, so take your pleasures now."

Quickwrite

What current love songs can you think of—in any popular music style? Look for songs sung by an impatient suitor to a specific lover who hasn't quite committed herself or himself—or not in the way the singer wants. If you can, find the words, or transcribe them. Listen to the songs as closely as you can. How is love treated in popular music today? Note all your reflections in your Reader's Log.

Elements of Literature

Carpe Diem

The poems that follow reflect an ancient theme the Romans called *carpe diem* (kär′pe dē′em), meaning "seize the day." *Carpe diem* is a call to live life to the fullest right now: "Let us eat and drink, for tomorrow we die," as the Roman poet Horace said. *Carpe diem* poems are the literary counterpart of the human skull that was sometimes part of the decor at wild Roman parties— a grisly reminder of the fate none of us can escape.

Carpe diem, literally "seize the day," is a literary theme that urges living in the present moment, especially in pleasurable pursuits.

For more on Carpe Diem, see the Handbook of Literary Terms.

Embroidered picture of a woman, possibly personifying Summer (detail) (late 17th century). Satin embroidered with silk, metal thread, and beads. English.

By Courtesy of the Board of Trustees of the Victoria and Albert Museum, London.

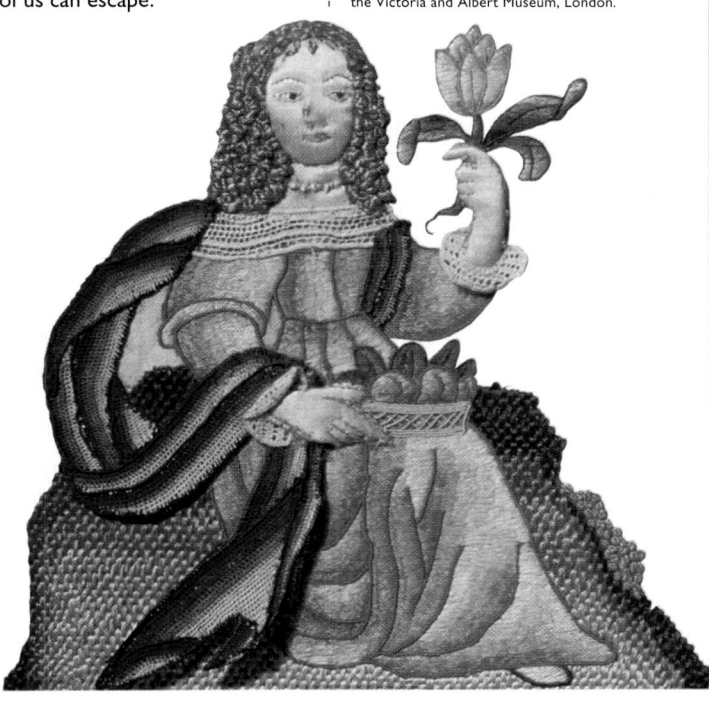

THE PASTORAL POETS **231**

QUICK PLANNING GUIDE

Into the Poems

Before You Read p. 231
Author Biographies: Marlowe p. 232, Raleigh p. 234, Herrick p. 238, Marvell p. 240
- **Reading Focus:** Scaffolding
- **Quickwrite:** Locate *carpe diem* in pop songs
- **Elements of Literature:** Carpe Diem

Through the Poems

"The Passionate Shepherd to His Love" **p. 233**
"The Nymph's Reply to the Shepherd" **p. 235**
Literature and Technology **pp. 236–237**
"To the Virgins, to Make Much of Time" **p. 239**
"To His Coy Mistress" **pp. 241–242**
Making Meanings **p. 236, p. 242**

Beyond the Poems

Choices: Building Your Portfolio pp. 242–243
- **Writer's Notebook:** Analyze elements of a poem for an interpretive essay
- **Critical Writing:** Compare and contrast two *carpe diem* poems
- **Critical Writing:** Respond to Donne's "The Bait"
- **Critical Writing:** Compare a *carpe diem* poem with one by Dorothy Parker
- **Creative Writing:** Respond to the speaker in one of two poems
- **Music/Literature:** Mimic the poets with a *carpe diem* song
- **Art/Literature:** Make a collage illustrating a poem
- **Panel Discussion:** Discuss gender traits in modern and Renaissance times

PROGRAM MANAGER

- **Planning Instruction** See Teaching Notes, *Teaching Resources A,* pp. 58–59, for objectives, a summary, literary elements, and additional information for the selections.
- **Instructional Support** Before beginning the instructional lesson, see Graphic

Organizers for Active Reading, *Teaching Resources A,* pp. 71–74, for Through the Poem activities.
- **Assessment** See Selection Tests, *Test Booklet,* pp. 41–44.

Into the Poems

Using BEFORE YOU READ p. 231

Elements of Literature

Remind students to use situations they would not mind sharing. Ask students for examples of how they might "seize the day." Suggest that "don't put off until tomorrow what you can do today" has a similar message and that *carpe diem* can easily imply that one must make the most of each day.

ABOUT THE AUTHOR

One critic has suggested that Marlowe staged his death by substituting the body of a sailor for his own so that he could escape to Europe. Others have maintained that Marlowe, with his outspoken ways, was dangerous to some of his peers and therefore was silenced by hired killers.

Christopher Marlowe
(1564–1593)

Reputed portrait of Christopher Marlowe (1585). French School. Oil.

The Master and Fellows of Corpus Christi College, Cambridge, England.

Marlowe belonged to the first generation of Elizabethan dramatists. His career ended about the time Shakespeare's began, although he was only two months older than Shakespeare. The son of a shoemaker in Canterbury, Marlowe won scholarships to the King's School in Canterbury and then to Cambridge University. While still a student, he translated some love poems by Ovid, the Roman poet. The poems were declared too erotic by the Bishop of London, who had the books burned.

After completing his studies, Marlowe apparently became a spy. Elizabeth's government maintained an elaborate espionage system to keep track of Roman Catholics, but just what spying Marlowe did for the government remains uncertain. It *is* certain that Marlowe had only six more years to live when, at twenty-three, he came down to London from Cambridge. He also associated with a number of other recent university graduates living near the London theaters and supporting themselves by writing plays and pamphlets. Excitement and danger were part of their lives. Marlowe himself was jailed for his involvement in a street fight that ended with one man murdered.

Another brush with the law came when Marlowe's roommate, a fellow dramatist named Thomas Kyd, accused him of making scandalous, seditious, and atheistic speeches. Marlowe was arrested. A few days before the case was to be heard, he went with some rather shady characters down the Thames to a tavern in Deptford. After supper the men got into a violent fight over the bill; Marlowe was stabbed above the eye and died instantly. The court acquitted his assailant on the grounds of self-defense, though it is very possible that all the testimony in this case was fabricated and that Marlowe was assassinated for reasons not yet discovered. Theories about Marlowe's life and death are abundant; there are even a few people today

who believe, without any evidence, that Marlowe wasn't murdered but lived on to write all of Shakespeare's plays for him.

All of Marlowe's dramatic poems are tragedies: *Dido, Queen of Carthage* (written with Thomas Nashe); *Tamburlaine; The Jew of Malta; The Massacre at Paris; Edward II;* and *Doctor Faustus.* Marlowe's greatest tragic heroes have been called "overreachers": self-driven, power-hungry men who refuse to recognize either their limitations as human beings or their responsibilities to God and their fellow creatures. Tamburlaine seeks power through military conquest; Barabbas, the Jew of Malta, through money; Faustus, through knowledge. They all want to be more than mere men, and only death can put an end to their monstrous ambitions. To express these grandiose themes, Marlowe created wild and soaring poetry, like nothing ever heard before on the stage. Although Marlowe did not write Shakespeare's plays, he showed Shakespeare what was possible in dramatic poetry.

OPTIONS FOR TEACHING

STRATEGIES FOR INCLUSION

English Language Development To make the language of the poems more accessible, point out the change from usual English word order of subject/verb/object in such constructions as "may thee move" or "thy mind may move"(p. 233, ll.19 and 23). Write them on the chalkboard as we would usually say them.

Less Proficient Readers Before students read Marlowe's poem, draw a cluster chart on the chalkboard as students brainstorm what they imagine the shepherd's way of life to be. Have them separate the positive and negative aspects into two lists. [Unpleasant qualities include bad weather, few baths, little company; benefits include peaceful and beautiful surroundings, a slow-paced life, and a lot of time outside.]

Interpersonal Before students begin "The Nymph's Reply," ask them to consider how they would respond to the shepherd. What counter-arguments might they use? Have students work in heterogeneous groups to draft a quick reply. Then, ask them to read Raleigh's poem and to compare their strategies with his. Have students share their work with the class.

This poem is part of two literary traditions. It is part of the *carpe diem* tradition, and it is a **pastoral,** from *pastor,* the Latin word for "shepherd." Pastoral works are set in an idealized countryside, and their characters are often blends of the naive and the sophisticated. The most famous of English pastorals, Marlowe's poem has often been set to music, and several poets have written answers or sequels to it.

The Passionate Shepherd to His Love

Christopher Marlowe

Come live with me, and be my love,
And we will all the pleasures prove°
That valleys, groves, hills, and fields,
Woods, or steepy mountain yields.

5 And we will sit upon the rocks,
Seeing the shepherds feed their flocks
By shallow rivers, to whose falls
Melodious birds sing madrigals.° **Ⓐ**

And I will make thee beds of roses,
10 And a thousand fragrant posies,
A cap of flowers, and a kirtle,°
Embroidered all with leaves of myrtle.

A gown made of the finest wool
Which from our pretty lambs we pull, **Ⓑ**
15 Fair linèd slippers for the cold,
With buckles of the purest gold.

A belt of straw and ivy buds,
With coral clasps and amber studs,
And if these pleasures may thee move, **Ⓒ**
20 Come live with me, and be my love.

The shepherd swains° shall dance and sing
For thy delight each May morning.
If these delights thy mind may move, **Ⓓ**
Then live with me, and be my love.

2. **prove:** experience.

8. **madrigals:** complicated songs for several voices.

11. **kirtle:** dress, gown, or skirt.

21. **swains:** young boys.

Shepherd and Shepherdess with Cupid in Pastoral Landscape (detail) (17th century). Embroidered textile. Colored silk and isinglass on canvas (10 ¼″ × 14″).
The Metropolitan Museum of Art, New York. Gift of Irwin Untermeyer, 1964. (64. 101. 1313).

233

A. Literary Element: Pastoral
A pastoral is a literary work that idealizes the rustic lives of shepherds. What makes this poem a pastoral? [It portrays none of the hardships of the life of rural laborers: work, bad weather, lost or sick sheep, low pay, poor housing, little leisure, and so on.]

B. Critical Reading: Drawing Conclusions
The shepherd promises his beloved a beautiful dress and shoes with gold buckles, among other niceties. Is it likely that he can follow up on his offer? Why or why not? [Possible answers: Unlikely—it is too expensive and suggests the dress of a lady at court, not a peasant.]

C. Literary Element: Refrain
Refrains—short repeated lines—are usually found in songs. What is the effect of l. 1 reappearing as ll. 20 and 24? [Possible answer: It gives the poem a songlike effect and also may suggest the shepherd's repeated attempts to persuade his beloved.]

D. Reader's Response: Challenging the Text
? Would you be persuaded by the shepherd's arguments? Why or why not? [Sample responses: The shepherd tries to convince his beloved by offering her an idealized world, but real life is not like this, so his arguments are unconvincing. If, however, he were capable of giving what he wished he could give, I might be persuaded.]

STRATEGIES FOR INCLUSION

Special Needs In order to demonstrate the poet's use of language that relates to all of the senses, have students make a chart using words from the poem. They can use the chart shown here or the one on Transparency 7: Sensory Details Chart in the Transparency Package.

"The Nymph's Reply to the Shepherd"

HEARING	SIGHT	SMELL/TASTE	TOUCH
[rage of river] [honey tongue (sweet words)]	[gowns] [shoes]	[roses]	[cold rocks]

Learners Having Difficulty Before they read, have students who have difficulty focusing their attention listen with headphones to an audiotape of the poem while highlighting for specific information. For example, students may highlight such pastoral images in "The Passionate Shepherd to His Love" as valleys, groves, hills, fields, birds, and beds of roses. ☞

Raleigh's demeanor at his execution was worthy of note. He checked the ax to see if it was sharp (he originally was condemned to being drawn, hanged, and quartered) and asked those present to pray for him. When asked how he would like to lie on the block, he replied, "So the heart be right, it is no matter which way the head lieth." He forgave the executioner, gave him a sign to proceed, and died after two blows.

Sir Walter Raleigh
(1552?–1618)

R aleigh is one of the most colorful figures of a very colorful age. A handsome, expensively dressed, and probably arrogant man, at the peak of his success he was Queen Elizabeth's confidential secretary and captain of her guard. He fought brilliantly for England in France, Spain, Ireland, and America. He was passionately devoted to the cause of colonizing the Americas, and to advertise its products he became one of the first bold Englishmen to smoke tobacco and grow potatoes.

Sir Walter Raleigh (16th century) by Nicholas Hilliard.
By Courtesy of the National Portrait Gallery, London.

In his rise to power, Raleigh made many enemies, some of whom saw their chance to destroy him when the queen died. They poisoned King James's mind against him, and—on trumped-up evidence—he was convicted of treason. Raleigh was sentenced to death in 1603, though his execution was not carried out until 1618.

Imprisoned in the Tower of London during this long interval, he conducted chemical experiments and wrote a *History of the World* that runs from Adam and Eve to the establishment of the Roman Empire. He also dreamed of another expedition to Guiana, on the northern coast of South America; he had explored Guiana earlier in his life and believed it contained vast hoards of gold and jewels. In 1617, still under a death sentence, he was allowed to undertake his last voyage to Guiana. It turned out to be a disaster. The English obtained no treasure, and the Spanish killed many of Raleigh's men, including his beloved son. Very ill with fever, Raleigh sailed home to face a certain and shameful death. But according to the verdict of history, the shame is King James's, not Raleigh's. Raleigh was sacrificed to satisfy the Spanish, who were clamoring for his death as a condition for maintaining peaceful relations with England. The English, who hated and feared the Spanish, had not forgotten Raleigh when they deposed and beheaded James's son, King Charles I, in 1649.

In his speech on the scaffold, Raleigh described himself as "a seafaring man, a soldier, and a courtier." Although he did publish his *History,* he did not think of himself as a writer. He was carefree with his poems; only about thirty-five of them have survived, and they have been slowly assembled by literary researchers through the past four centuries. His most ambitious poem is *The Ocean to Cynthia,* one of the hundreds of literary works that Queen Elizabeth's subjects wrote to express their love and devotion. It survives only in fragments. This is unfortunate, because Raleigh's poems have considerable merit. They are powerful, outspoken, even blunt, and suffused with the courage of a man who was always ready to accept without self-pity whatever life might bring him. He could have been thinking of himself when he wrote in his *History,* "There is no man so assured of his honor, of his riches, health, or life, but that he may be deprived of either or all, the very next hour or day to come."

INTEGRATING THE LANGUAGE ARTS

Speaking and Listening Have one or more paired sets of male and female speakers read the poems: Marlowe's first, then Raleigh's. Ask the readers to try to imagine themselves as the characters and to ask themselves these two questions: Does the shepherd really think he can convince the nymph with his argument? Does the nymph think that the shepherd believes she would be convinced? The answers should guide them in the tone they use for reading. Ask speakers to practice first, considering where they will pause for suspense, raise or lower their voices, or slow down for emphasis.

Writing: Paragraphs Have students write three words that describe the shepherd's tone on p. 233 [Romantic, idealistic, loving, fervent, optimistic, generous, lying, and so on.] Then, have them write three words describing the nymph's tone in her reply. [Realistic, unsentimental, ironic, bitter, weary, disappointed, betrayed, disgusted and so on.] Have students write one paragraph in each tone. Ask students to exchange papers and to check each other's paragraphs for tone using their lists as guides.

Here is Raleigh's reply to Marlowe's "Passionate Shepherd." Elizabethan London was a small place, and Raleigh's and Marlowe's paths must have crossed more than once. Other poets, including John Donne and Robert Herrick, replied to Marlowe, but Raleigh wrote the best answer. His speaker is identified as a "nymph," which means a young woman. Like her creator, she has a strong character.

The Nymph's Reply to the Shepherd

Sir Walter Raleigh

If all the world and love were young,
And truth in every shepherd's tongue,
These pretty pleasures might me move
To live with thee and be thy love.

5 But Time drives flocks from field to fold,°
When rivers rage and rocks grow cold,
And Philomel° becometh dumb;
The rest complains of cares to come.

The flowers do fade, and wanton° fields
10 To wayward winter reckoning yields;
A honey tongue, a heart of gall°
Is fancy's spring, but sorrow's fall.

Thy gowns, thy shoes, thy beds of roses,
Thy cap, thy kirtle, and thy posies.
15 Soon break, soon wither, soon forgotten,
In folly ripe, in reason rotten.

Thy belt of straw and ivy buds,
Thy coral clasps and amber studs,
All these in me no means can move
20 To come to thee and be thy love.

But could youth last and love still breed,
Had joys no date, nor age no need,
Then these delights my mind might move
To live with thee and be thy love.

5. fold: pen where sheep are kept in winter.

7. Philomel: the nightingale.

9. wanton: luxuriant.

11. gall: a bitter substance.

Embroidered wall hanging of the Morell family, Constanz, East Switzerland (detail) (1601).
Schweizerisches Landesmuseum, Zurich.

SIR WALTER RALEIGH **235**

Making Meanings

First Thoughts

1. Possible responses: Shepherd—4: charming in his infatuation but lacking rational reasoning; or shepherd—10: he is enthusiastic about his love. Nymph—10: logical, realistic, and clever; or nymph—2: too hardhearted.

Shaping Interpretations

2. They will live in a beautiful pastoral setting with no bad or harsh weather and no work. They will have beautiful garments and plenty of entertainment to pass the time.
3. The weather, their amount of free time, and their buying power seem idealized. Lambing, sickness, lost sheep, hunger, and cold are absent.
4. The nymph points out that winter replaces spring, rivers rage, rocks grow cold, birds stop singing, flowers fade, and the pretty dress will rot. She would agree to be his love if youth and joy could last forever.
5. Possible responses: Cynical, realistic, ironic, sarcastic.

Extending the Texts

6. **(Synthesis)** She would laugh at him—being too savvy to take him seriously. Or, she might be swept off her feet by such an unusual approach.
7. **(Synthesis)** Students may have difficulty suggesting examples other than advertisements. Their suggestions may include successful or failed attempts to retreat with the loved one. Students may mention advertisements for cruise ships or vacation and honeymoon spots; the movie *Don Juan de Marco* contains an example of this motif.

First Thoughts

1. Rate the shepherd and the nymph on the persuasiveness of their arguments, using a scale of 0 to 10 (with 10 being most persuasive). Be ready to justify your ratings.

Shaping Interpretations

2. Describe the life that the shepherd envisions with his love. How will they be dressed? How will they spend their time?
3. In **pastoral** writing, the harsh realities of country life do not exist. Which details of the shepherd's description seem distinctly idealistic? What realistic, gritty details of a shepherd's life can you imagine?
4. In her reply, what flaws does the nymph find in the shepherd's idyllic vision? What are her conditions for living with him?
5. What is the **tone** of the nymph's reply?

Extending the Texts

6. How do you think a modern young woman would respond to the shepherd's invitation?
7. Idyllic escape with a loved one still has a strong appeal, whether the retreat is a remote island or a mountaintop hideaway. How is this romantic escape motif used today in literature, television, movies, and advertising?

LITERATURE AND TECHNOLOGY

The Clock Starts Ticking

School bells, alarm clocks, time clocks, schedules: in our time-conscious, time-driven world, life ticks by—even on our wrists. But this sense of time, so natural to us, isn't natural. It began as the medieval age shifted to the first modern age: the Renaissance.

From dawn to dusk. Not until the fourteenth century, with the invention of the mechanical clock, did church towers across Europe and England start ringing out the day's twenty-four hours. While simple clocks and signal bells had been around for many years, such *public* precision was unknown—and simply hadn't been needed. Before the explosion of urban commerce, daily life moved by the natural rhythms of daybreak and nightfall, planting and harvest. People saw their lives as part of an endless continuum; bells pealed only for prayer, gatherings, and disaster.

The beat of life. But to produce more and more goods, people wanted not just to mark time, but to *use* it. That's why the brilliant idea of a

---

OPTIONS FOR TEACHING

CROSSING THE CURRICULUM

Logical-Mathematical Remind students that Raleigh was an archetypal Renaissance man. His poem (p. 235) shows some of his breadth, in that not only is it fashioned after a lyrical love poem that it parodies, but it contains within it a syllogism. Education of this time typically included training in logic, and the well-educated Raleigh puts logic to use in writing the nymph's refusal. The logical proof embedded in the poem is quite simple: If *x* then *y* / not *y* / therefore, not *x*. After writing this on the chalkboard, guide students through the proof. The nymph says she would accept the shepherd's proposal if the world were always young and if shepherds never lied. She uses the imagery of winter to show that the world is not always young (as it is in spring). At the same time, winter proves the shepherd a liar as he promises all roses and sunshine. The nymph further reasons that the progress of time (the world and love getting older) will consume or obliterate all that the shepherd proposes to give her. In the fifth stanza the nymph essentially says that she rejects him on the basis of the arguments she has made. Ask students to write a similar syllogism of their own, with details from their own lives. *Remind students to use material they would not mind sharing.*

mechanical clock filled a new need and changed life forever. Earlier water clocks, which kept time by steadily filling a vessel marked with measuring lines, were technically sophisticated but cumbersome—and in cold winters they froze.

The new clock revolutionized timekeeping by using falling weights to power gears (spoked wheels). The crucial technology, though, was the escapement, a controlling device that alternately caught and released the final wheel's spokes: It produced a steady, regular revolution and an endless, repeating ticktock. The passing of time was now audible.

Do you have the time?   Time became elaborately visible too, and not only because the gears could move hands. In the late Middle Ages, churches, kings, and rich merchants commissioned turret clocks that tracked astronomical and hourly changes with moving figures (automata) depicting, for example, the sun and moon, jousting knights, and the Twelve Apostles.

Then, for the first time, clocks came indoors. Miniaturization allowed "chamber clocks" for the nobility and the merchant classes. Finally, in the fifteenth century, a small, personal, spring-driven clock appeared: the first watch. In Queen Elizabeth's extensive collection of watches, one ring watch came equipped with an alarm: A small prong emerged to scratch her finger.

Keeping time.   By the Renaissance, a whole new concept of time had emerged, mirroring and feeding humanism. Time was personal and finite, and timekeeping meant just that: controlling a precious commodity. *Ticktock*. To us, the pressure of time is often depressing, but not to the new moderns. Renaissance humanists and artists were driven but invigorated. They could be masters of time, seizing the day, reaching for fame's immortality through art.

Works of the first spring-driven clock with fusée (c. 1524) by Joseph Zech.
Society of Antiquaries of London.

CHRISTOPHER MARLOWE AND SIR WALTER RALEIGH 237

Into the Poems

Using BEFORE YOU READ p. 231

Quickwrite

Have students bring in recordings of the songs they have chosen. Play part of the songs and then have the students share their Reader's Log comments.

Robert Herrick

(1591–1674)

We first hear of Herrick as an apprentice to his uncle, a London goldsmith and jeweler; it is pleasant to think that the future poet may have acquired his taste for small, beautiful things in his uncle's workshop. Herrick apparently lacked ambition and drive, since he did not enter the university until he was twenty-two, a very late age in those days, and he did not leave it until he was twenty-nine. For the next few years, he had no regular occupation, but enjoyed himself in London as a member of Ben Jonson's circle of young friends. At some point, he was ordained a priest, but the serious part of Herrick's life did not begin until he was thirty-nine.

Herrick was then called to a parish in Dean Prior, in Devonshire, far from London, in the West Country, which Londoners habitually regarded as wretched and barbaric. According to some of Herrick's poems, this was an intolerable exile; according to others, it was heaven on earth. At any rate, Herrick's stay in Dean Prior came abruptly to an end in 1647 with the arrival of the Parliamentary Army, which deprived him of his parish and substituted in his place a clergyman of a more puritanical stripe. (It would not be easy to find a less puritanical priest than Herrick.) When the king was restored some thirteen years later, so was Herrick, and he lived on at Dean Prior until he died at the age of eighty-three.

While deprived of his parish and living in London, Herrick published a fat little volume containing about 1,400 poems. The book was

Robert Herrick (18th century) by Schiavonetti.

By Courtesy of the National Portrait Gallery, London.

called *Hesperides, or the Works Both Human and Divine of Robert Herrick, Esq.* (1648). Less than a fourth of the poems fit into the "divine" category, and these are mainly witty verses on Biblical characters and events. All the rest of the poems are definitely "human," though the book's last line— "Jocund his Muse was; but his Life was chaste"—shows that Herrick's life was a bit less lively than his poetry. The word *Hesperides* in the title is borrowed from classical mythology; it is the collective name for the nymphs who live in a garden where they watch over a tree that bears golden apples. The title implies that Herrick's book is a garden full of precious things.

Herrick borrowed more than his title from classical antiquity. He was so steeped in Latin poetry that he frequently wrote his poems as if he were an ancient Roman, imposing pagan customs, creeds, and rituals on the English countrypeople and his own household. He imitated the Latin love poets, especially Catullus, when he addressed poems to beautiful women with such classical names as Julia, Corinna, Perilla, Anthea, and Electra.

Herrick also wrote about his small house, his spaniel named Tracy, the royal family in far-off London—whatever came into his mind. Altogether, his poems give us a picture of "Merrie England," which is not so much the England of any particular time or place, but an ideal, pastoral state where sadness is momentary and pleasure innocent.

OPTIONS FOR TEACHING

STRATEGIES FOR INCLUSION

Auditory Have students read Herrick's poem aloud, drawing their attention to the bouncy **rhythm**. Point out that the rhythm is songlike and has a different **meter** than the Elizabethan poetry they have read earlier in the Collection.

Logical-Mathematical After reading Marvell's poem once, point out that this poem is divided into three sections by indentions. Have students write the words that begin each section. These words, "Had we but," "But," and "Now therefore," signal the reasoning and structure of the poem. Have students rephrase each section, maintaining the key words. For example: "If we had all the time in the world, then I would . . ." Write

some of the students' phrases on the chalkboard, grouped by section. Using the students' words, point out that the poem begins with a simple proposition: If A then B. In the second section, the speaker explains why A cannot be so. The final section draws the conclusion: Because A cannot be so, we must waste no time and do C. Have students write a few other if/then phrases that come from their own observation.

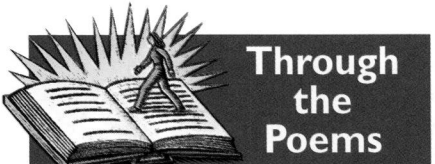

The first line of this little lyric, Herrick's most popular poem, has been a metaphorical part of our language ever since the nineteenth century, when Herrick was "discovered" by people interested in Renaissance literature. Instead of courting one woman, as in most *carpe diem* poems, Herrick addresses all "virgins," or young women. As you read, remember that Herrick was a priest.

To the Virgins, to Make Much of Time

Robert Herrick

Gather ye rosebuds while ye may, (A)
    Old Time is still a-flying;
And this same flower that smiles today,
    Tomorrow will be dying.

5 The glorious lamp of heaven, the sun,
    The higher he's a-getting, (B)
The sooner will his race be run,
    And nearer he's to setting.

That age is best which is the first, (C)
10   When youth and blood are warmer;
But being spent, the worse, and worst (D)
    Times still° succeed the former.

Then be not coy,° but use your time;
    And while ye may, go marry: (E)
15 For having lost but once your prime,
    You may forever tarry.°

12. **still:** always.

13. **coy:** cold; inaccessible; aloof.

16. **tarry:** delay; linger.

Spring (detail) (1595) by Lucas van Valkenborch. Christie's, London.

239

A. Literary Element: Carpe Diem

The Roman poet Catullus (85?–55 B.C.) originated this theme. The actual term *carpe diem,* translated as "reap today," can be found in Horace 1–11: "As we talk, time spites us and runs: reap today: save no hopes for tomorrow." (A Latin dictionary explains that Horace uses *carpe* in a positive sense to mean "enjoy" or "use.") Although *carpe diem* is usually translated as "seize the day," *carpo* in Latin can refer to picking, plucking, or gathering flowers or fruits, an association that fits well with Herrick's imagery.

B. Literary Element: Allusion

? To what characterization of the sun does the poem refer in l. 7? [In Greek mythology, the sun god Helios drove a fiery chariot across the heavens each day.]

C. Reader's Response: Connecting with the Text

? Considering this poem, Shakespeare's Sonnet 73 (p. 226), and "The Passionate Shepherd to His Love" (p. 233), how do the Elizabethans seem to view advanced age? [Sample responses: They do not see it as a time of increased wisdom and knowledge. It's a time of vulnerability and loss of powers. They see youth as a better time.]

D. Critical Reading: Expressing an Opinion

? How are your expectations for growing older similar to or different from the speaker's in this poem? [Students may mention fears about illness and death, as well as the benefits of retirement.]

E. Critical Reading: Making Inferences

? According to the worldview presented by the speaker, what is the most important thing for a young woman to accomplish? [To get married before she gets too much older.]

INTEGRATING THE LANGUAGE ARTS

Strategic Reading Herrick's text has three stanzas of persuasive reasoning with a conclusion in the fourth stanza. Have students identify the reasoning, summarizing each stanza in their own words or with drawings. They can put words or drawings into a flow chart such as the following:

stanza 1 [ ]
+
2 [ ]
+
3 [ ]
↓
4 [ ]

The first edition of *Miscellaneous Poems*(1681) included a certificate from "Mary Marvell" to prove the authenticity of the poems. The document, signed on October 15, 1680, asserted that the poems "are printed according to the exact Copies of my late dear Husband, under his own Hand-Writing...." Some scholars think that if the woman claiming to be his wife had not devised this scheme for her own gain, Marvell's lyrics might never have come to light.

Andrew Marvell
(1621–1678)

Marvell, whose very English name should be accented on its first syllable, like *marvelous,* was the son of a clergyman, who sent him to Cambridge University. There he must have received an excellent education, because the poet John Milton, who was not easily impressed by other men's learning, said that Marvell was "well read in the Greek and Latin classics." After receiving his B.A., he traveled for several years to Holland, France, Italy, and Spain. There is, surprisingly, no record of Marvell's having been involved in the great upheaval of the 1640s. He seems to have survived the Civil Wars without allying himself with either the Royalists or the Parliamentarians. About 1650, he became a tutor to Mary Fairfax, an heiress and a daughter of Sir Thomas Fairfax, who had served as lord general of the Parliamentary armies. The Fairfaxes had several large estates, one of them at a place called Nun Appleton, and there Marvell wrote a remarkable long poem, "Upon Appleton House." But he did not publish this or any of the other poems that are so highly regarded today. In the best Renaissance fashion, he wrote only for his friends' and his own entertainment.

After leaving the Fairfax household, where presumably he wrote his best poems, Marvell became tutor to a ward of Oliver Cromwell, the lord protector and virtual dictator of England in the 1650s. Then, in 1657, he became assistant to John Milton, who needed help in carrying out his duties as Latin secretary to the Council of State because he was blind. Marvell

Andrew Marvell (c. 1655–1660) by an unknown artist. Oil on canvas (23 ½" × 18 ½").
By Courtesy of the National Portrait Gallery, London.

became active in politics, serving as member of Parliament for his native city, Hull, from 1659 until his death. When King Charles II was restored and the Commonwealth government dissolved in 1660, Marvell somehow had enough influence with the Royalists to save Milton's life. At this point in his career, Marvell began to publish verse satires against his political opponents and prose pamphlets on issues of the day. But his lyric poems remained in manuscript until after his death, when his housekeeper, calling herself Mary Marvell and claiming to be his wife, sold them to a publisher, who brought them out.

Marvell's posthumous volume, called *Miscellaneous Poems,* made little impression when it appeared in 1681. Styles in poetry had changed after 1660, so that Marvell's witty, ingenious metaphors must have seemed old-fashioned to readers who admired the lucid, rational poems of the Restoration writers. Today we are in a better position to appreciate Marvell. To many judicious critics, his poems seem to sum up much that is admirable in Renaissance lyric poetry. Like Jonson, he is a master craftsman, always in control of his materials. His poems have the precision, urbanity, and lightness of touch associated with the "sons of Ben." Many of Marvell's poems are also, under their graceful surfaces, deep and thoughtful, like Donne's. No wonder that Marvell is sometimes called the "most major" of the minor poets in English.

OPTIONS FOR TEACHING

CROSSING THE CURRICULUM

Social Studies The concern over not waiting too long to marry may make students wonder about the customary age for marriage in Renaissance society. They may wish to research this, as well as what actually did happen to women who did not marry when very young. Thus, students will discover if the implied threat in the last two lines of the poem is realistic. Have students write a brief letter to a young woman of the time stating the findings of their research.

PROBLEM SOLVING/CRITICAL THINKING

Persuasion Students need to recognize misleading reasoning that people might use to convince them to make bad choices. Divide the class into small groups to discuss the persuasive nature of "To the Virgins, to Make Much of Time." Have students write a response, saying no to the speaker as the nymph did in her reply to the shepherd. They can write in verse, but it is not necessary. Make sure they speak to each part of the argument set forth in the poem. Each student can take one stanza. [Possible answer: Flowers may bloom and die, but only after this stage does the plant bear fruit; I prefer to enjoy the bloom of youth and marry when my character is full and ripe.] Have the groups read and compare their replies.

To His Coy Mistress

Andrew Marvell

Had we but world° enough, and time,
This coyness,° Lady, were no crime.
We would sit down, and think which way
To walk, and pass our long love's day.
5 Thou by the Indian Ganges' side
Shouldst rubies find; I by the tide
Of Humber° would complain.° I would
Love you ten years before the Flood,°
And you should, if you please, refuse
10 Till the conversion of the Jews.°
My vegetable° love should grow
Vaster than empires and more slow;
An hundred years should go to praise
Thine eyes, and on thy forehead gaze;
15 Two hundred to adore each breast,
But thirty thousand to the rest;
An age at least to every part,
And the last age should show your heart.
For, Lady, you deserve this state,°
20 Nor would I love at lower rate.
    But at my back I always hear
Time's wingèd chariot hurrying near;
And yonder all before us lie
Deserts of vast eternity.
25 Thy beauty shall no more be found,
Nor, in thy marble vault, shall sound
My echoing song; then worms shall try
That long-preserved virginity,
And your quaint honor turn to dust,
30 And into ashes all my lust:
The grave's a fine and private place,
But none, I think, do there embrace.
    Now therefore, while the youthful hue
Sits on thy skin like morning dew,
35 And while thy willing soul transpires°
At every pore with instant fires,

1. **world:** geographical space.
2. **coyness:** reluctance to make a commitment.

7. **Humber:** muddy river in Marvell's hometown of Hull; here, ironically compared to the grand Ganges in India. **complain:** utter complaints about not being loved.
8. **Flood:** Noah's flood, described in Genesis.
10. **conversion of the Jews:** Christians once believed that all Jews would be converted to Christianity immediately before the Last Judgment.
11. **vegetable:** plantlike; having the power to grow very large, like oak trees.

19. **state:** ceremony.

Two Lovers (detail) (15th century) from an Italian slipware plate.
© British Museum, London.

35. **transpires:** breathes out.

ANDREW MARVELL 241

A. Literary Element: Imagery

? What is the effect of placing the woman sifting rubies by the Ganges, while the man loafs by the muddy Humber? [Possible answer: The images emphasize that they would have enough time to be apart and that he would be willing to suffer while she enjoyed whatever her romantic fancy desired.]

B. Literary Element: Personification

? How is time personified? How is time a factor in the speaker's argument? [Possible answer: Time is presented as a charioteer chasing the speaker. Time becomes the enemy in this poem. When time overtakes the lovers, it will, through death, negate their love, beauty, and honor.]

C. Language Note: Punctuation

Ask students to identify the punctuation surrounding ll. 31–32. Why does Marvell lead into the couplet with a colon and end with a period? What could this indicate? [Possible answer: With these major stop marks, Marvell separates the couplet from the rest of the poem, creating emphasis. The couplet is a summary statement of the previous lines and of the entire poem. Marvell is underscoring his point about love and death.]

D. Reader's Response: Connecting with the Text

Using your own words to rephrase, explain what tells you this is a *carpe diem* poem. [Sample responses: We cannot spend time sitting around talking. We must act before death takes our youth and beauty. Let's have fun and do our best to outrun time.]

Metacognition How did you decide which phrases fit the definition of *carpe diem*? [Responses will vary. Some students may have started with the definition. Others may have started searching for phrases.]

Making Meanings

First Thoughts

1. Possible response: The speakers in the two poems have quite different purposes and audiences. The speaker in "To His Coy Mistress" is addressing a particular woman. He wants only her and he knows he can do nothing without her agreement. The speaker in "To the Virgins" does not want one particular woman—he is just trying to persuade women in general to be less hesitant. Both speakers talk about the passage of time and the desire to live one's youth to the fullest.

Shaping Interpretations

2. In "To the Virgins" the sun shows the passage of time and emphasizes the speaker's point that one must act before it is too late. Marvell in "To His Coy Mistress" uses the sun in a similar way but makes it more active by making it chase the young lovers. The last two lines say that the lovers cannot stop time but they can make time run after them.

3. In Herrick's poem, time brings death, things get worse with time, and people may not be able to marry once they are past their primes. In Marvell's poem, time brings death, beauty decays, and eventually the worms will eat the body. Marvell compares time to a winged chariot. Students may say they see Helios riding across the sky in his chariot.

4. Herrick's speaker says the women he is addressing should get married while they have the chance because nobody will marry them when they are old. Marvell's speaker does not even mention marriage. He apparently does not think it is necessary to mention it. The mention of marriage would give a solemn note to a poem that is obviously intended to commend freedom and pleasure.

5. The first section displays many examples of hyperbole (ll. 7– 10, 11–12). An example of understatement occurs in ll. 31–32. They add wit and a wry note to the poem.

Now let us sport us while we may,
And now, like amorous birds of prey,
Rather at once our time devour
40 Than languish in his slow-chapped° power.
Let us roll all our strength and all
Our sweetness up into one ball,
And tear our pleasures with rough strife
Through the iron gates of life;
45 Thus, though we cannot make our sun
Stand still, yet we will make him run.

40. slow-chapped: slow-jawed. Time is seen as consuming life.

MAKING MEANINGS

To the Virgins, to Make Much of Time
To His Coy Mistress

First Thoughts

1. Herrick and Marvell have similar objectives but different approaches. How do you react to the two poems and poets? Is one more persuasive than the other? How are their arguments both similar and different?

Shaping Interpretations

2. The sun appears in both "To the Virgins" (line 5) and "To His Coy Mistress" (line 45). How does each poet use the sun? How would you **paraphrase** the last two lines of Marvell's poem to his coy mistress?

3. What does each poet say about time and its effects on youth and beauty? A famous **image** of time appears in couplet form in Marvell's poem, in lines 21–22. What does he compare time to? What does this image make you see?

4. What does the **speaker** in "To the Virgins" say about marriage? How do you think the speaker in Marvell's poem feels about marriage?

5. Marvell's poem contains both **hyperbole** and **understatement.** Find examples of each rhetorical device. What does each device contribute to the poem's effect on the reader?

6. Where in his poem does Marvell seem to be making fun of certain kinds of love poems? Where do you spot echoes of Shakespeare's Sonnet 130 (page 229)?

Extending the Texts

7. Do you think there are echoes of Herrick's poem in contemporary media? Does the **speaker** in this poem hold any values that are shared by modern advertisements, television shows, or popular songs? What are they?

Challenging the Texts

8. What do these two poems imply about the relationship between men and women? Would a modern woman (or man) be likely to challenge any assumptions apparently held by the writer, or by the speaker in each poem? What might they challenge, what might they agree with, and why?

CHOICES:
Building Your Portfolio

Writer's Notebook

WORK IN PROGRESS

1. Collecting Ideas for an Interpretive Essay

Choose a *carpe diem* poem that you would like to write about. Before you start to analyze the poem, read it aloud at least once. Freewrite briefly about your initial reaction to the poem. Then try to state its theme in your own words. Now read it again, this time looking for other elements to focus on—perhaps figures of speech, imagery, or sound effects. Make notes on these elements of the poem, and their effects on you. Save your notes for

---

6. The exaggeration is mockery. Echoes of Shakespeare's sonnet can be found in the speaker's proposal to take hundreds of years to praise various parts of his love's anatomy.

Extending the Texts

7. **(Synthesis)** Some students may perceive values of youth and pleasure expressed both in the poem and in modern popular culture. Others may point out that marriage remains a cultural imperative.

Challenging the Texts

8. **(Synthesis)** Possible responses: Women are only attractive when they are young. Life is worthless without a man. Students might challenge the gender bias found here, but they might also agree with the fear of death and fear of not having a full life.

possible use with the Writer's Workshop on page 275.

Critical Writing
2. Probing Poems

In an essay, compare and contrast at least two of the *carpe diem* poems by Marlowe, Raleigh, Herrick, and Marvell. You might collect your data in a chart like the following one:

Element	Poem 1	Poem 2
Personal reaction Theme Images Figures of speech Sounds Tone		

Critical Writing
3. Donne Answers Back

The poet John Donne (1572–1631) wrote "The Bait," a poem that was clearly inspired by Marlowe's "Passionate Shepherd." Locate Donne's poem (it's commonly found in poetry anthologies). In a brief essay, explain whether this poem is an answer to Marlowe's poem, an imitation of it, or neither. Remember to provide specific references to both poems.

Critical Writing
4. The Moment Passes

In a brief essay, compare the following poem by the American poet Dorothy Parker (1893–1967) to one of the *carpe diem* poems you've just read. How are they alike and different in tone and point of view?

Unfortunate Coincidence

By the time you swear you're his,
　　Shivering and sighing,
And he vows his passion is
　　Infinite, undying—
Lady, make a note of this:
　　One of you is lying.

Creative Writing
5. Silent No More

Write an answer to either (a) the speaker of "To the Virgins," taking the point of view of an older woman, or (b) the speaker of "To His Coy Mistress," beginning your answer with the words "Had we but world enough and time." Your response may be poetry or prose, but give it a title.

Music / Literature
6. Seize the Song

Write your own *carpe diem* song in any musical style. You might write songs that can be paired, as Marlowe's and Raleigh's are. You might try to imitate the melancholic, romantic tone of some of the poems you've read, or you might adopt the more modern style of today's songs, which are sometimes romantic, sometimes plaintive, sometimes humorous. You might also refer to the Reader's Log entry you did on page 231.

Art / Literature
7. Picturing a Poem

Create a collage to illustrate one of the poems you've just read. Find elements for your collage that pick up images in the poem. Be sure to add to your collage the phrase in the poem you think is most important.

Panel Discussion
8. As Time Goes By

Hold a panel discussion in which you exchange views on the gender traits you infer were characteristic of the sixteenth century. Compare these traits with gender traits you find in modern novels, movies, and TV shows. Have things changed in the relations between men and women? Or are these relations in many ways the same? You might also address this question: Are gender traits fixed by genes, or are they learned? Can they be changed?

Beyond the Poems

Choices: Building Your Portfolio

1. **Writer's Notebook** Remind students to save their work. They may use it as prewriting for the Writer's Workshop on p. 275. One example might be the sprightly **rhythm** in Herrick's poem, which contributes to the pleasure-loving approach the speaker takes.

2. **Critical Writing** Show students how they might use the chart by starting one on the chalkboard.

ELEMENT	POEM I MARLOWE	POEM 2 MARVELL
Images	Roses, waterfalls, fields, gold buckles	Marble vault, worms, dust, ashes, morning dew

3. **Critical Writing** Encourage students to draft a basic paraphrase first, keeping the language simple. This should help them compare the two works.

4. **Critical Writing** Ask students to paraphrase Parker's poem, as well as characterize the **tone** and **point of view**, before they begin writing.

5. **Creative Writing** Students may begin by determining the **tone** of their answer. Will it be direct, ironic, parodic? How much of the original will be quoted or transformed? How will it end?

6. **Music/Literature** Tell students that songwriters may start with either the music or the lyrics. Encourage them to decide which they will start with, and then discuss with them what this decision might imply about their process.

7. **Art/Literature** Students can add other words to their collages, perhaps romantic-sounding place names or descriptive adjectives.

8. **Panel Discussion** Before students begin, discuss how, when reading or viewing a work, they can distinguish between (1) a particular man's or woman's traits that may be stereotypical, and (2) gender bias that generalizes certain traits as belonging to an entire gender.

STRATEGIES FOR INCLUSION

Advanced Students may want to compile and publish the class's responses in activity #8, perhaps as part of a Renaissance newspaper.

PORTFOLIO ASSESSMENT

Choices: Assessment Criteria
For help in evaluating these Choices assignments, see the criteria in the *Portfolio Management System,* pp. 91–92.

ABOUT THE AUTHOR

Donne even wrote letters in verse, both to his close friends and to his female patrons, by way of compliment.

John Donne

(1572–1631)

John Donne (c. 1595) by an unknown artist. Private Collection.

Donne (a Welsh name pronounced "dun") wrote learned, passionate, argumentative poetry, most of which he never published, since he was never ambitious to be known publicly as a poet. His first aim in life was to be "courtier"—that is, a member of the queen's government. But he had a serious handicap: He was born into a prominent Roman Catholic family, being descended from no less a person than Sir Thomas More, the Lord Chancellor whom Henry VIII had beheaded in 1535.

When Donne was only eleven years old, he was already studying at Oxford. Catholic boys went to the university very young, to avoid the oath of allegiance to the queen, whom the pope had excommunicated. Barred from taking a degree because of his religion, Donne returned to his native city of London and in his late teens became a law student at Lincoln's Inn, one of the Inns of Court where lawyers were trained. He had no financial worries since his father, a prosperous iron merchant, had died when Donne was four and left him some money. He now became "Jack" Donne, a handsome, well-dressed youth who devoted his mornings to heavy reading in philosophy and foreign literature and his afternoons to circulating in society. A friend described him as being "a great visitor of ladies, a great frequenter of plays, a great writer of conceited verses."

After various adventures, such as taking part in two naval expeditions against Spain, Donne became private secretary to Sir Thomas Egerton, lord keeper of the great seal. This was an important post, the starting point of a brilliant career in government, for by now Donne had abandoned his Catholicism and spent his inheritance. But he blasted all his hopes and ambitions when, in 1601, he secretly married seventeen-year-old Anne More (no relation). Marriage with a minor, without her father's consent, was then a serious crime against both church and state. As soon as Anne's father heard about it, he had Donne arrested, jailed, and dismissed from his position. In jail, Donne wrote his shortest poem:

> John Donne,
> Anne Donne,
> Undone.

Though he was not kept in prison long, Donne never did recover his position, and for years he and Anne had to live off the bounty of friends and relatives. They certainly needed help since they eventually had twelve children, five of whom died in infancy.

In the early 1600s, Donne continued to read voraciously and to write poetry for private circulation and prose for public consumption. He wrote against the Church of Rome so effectively that he became known as an important defender of the Church of England. And so the new king, James I, persuaded Donne to become a clergyman in 1615. His brilliant, theatrical sermons immediately won him advancement in the Church, and he rose to be dean of St. Paul's, the principal cathedral of England, in London.

Thus, Jack Donne became the Reverend Dr. John Donne. He preached outdoors before the cathedral, and he preached at court before the king, always with great effect, for he put into his sermons the same passion and inventiveness that he put into his poems. He died full of years and honors, and a portrait showing how he looked in his death shroud can still be seen in St. Paul's.

PROGRAM MANAGER

- **Planning Instruction** See *Teaching Notes, Teaching Resources A,* pp. 59–61, for objectives, a summary, literary elements, and additional background information for the selections.
- **Instructional Support** Before beginning the instructional lesson, see **Graphic Organizers for Active Reading,** *Teaching Resources A,* pp. 75–78, for

Through the Selection activities.

- **Audiotaped Readings** To help less proficient readers or auditory learners through the lesson, use the **Selected Reading, Audiocassette 1, Side A,** in the *Audiovisual Resources Binder.*
- **Assessment** See **Selection Test,** *Test Booklet,* pp. 45–46.

BEFORE YOU READ

SONG

Reading Focus

Love's Illusions

Unlike the multitude of Renaissance songs idealizing women, the following song satirizes women, using **hyperbole** (hī·pʉr′bə·lē), or extreme exaggeration. Imagine a lover who has fallen hard for the Perfect Woman once too often—and now takes a hard view of perfection.

Quickwrite

Think about songs popular today. Do most of them celebrate faithfulness and joy in a loved one, or do most complain about infidelity and betrayal? Jot down your general impression of today's popular love songs and their lyrics. You might begin by thinking of one or two songs you know fairly well and discussing them with examples.

Background

Donne's love poems are collectively known as his "Songs and Sonnets," but the title is misleading: Most of the poems are too intellectually demanding to be called songs, and none is a sonnet by formal definition. The following poem was indeed a song, however, because one manuscript includes musical accompaniment.

Song

John Donne

Go, and catch a falling star,
    Get with child a mandrake° root,
Tell me, where all past years are,
    Or who cleft° the devil's foot,
5 Teach me to hear mermaids° singing,
    Or to keep off envy's stinging,
            And find
            What wind
Serves to advance an honest mind.

10 If thou be'st born to strange sights,
    Things invisible to see,
Ride ten thousand days and nights,
    Till age snow white hairs on thee,
Thou, when thou return'st, wilt tell me
15 All strange wonders that befell thee,
            And swear
            Nowhere
Lives a woman true, and fair.

If thou find'st one, let me know,
20   Such a pilgrimage were sweet;
Yet do not, I would not go,
    Though at next door we might meet,
Though she were true, when you met her,
And last, till you write your letter,
25   Yet she
            Will be
False, ere I come, to two, or three.

---

2. **mandrake:** plant whose forked root is said to resemble a human being's torso and legs.
4. **cleft:** split.
5. **mermaids:** the sirens of Greek mythology. The song of these sea nymphs lured sailors to crash their ships on rocky shores.

JOHN DONNE **245**

Into the Poem

Using BEFORE YOU READ p. 245

Background

Sonnet, at the time, meant "short poem." It is notable that Donne's love poems consistently use religious **imagery.**

Through the Poem

A. Critical Reading: Making Inferences

? What is similar about all of the activities suggested in the first stanza? What makes each of them impossible? [Possible answer: They are physically impossible (the first two), philosophically impossible (the third), impossible because the subject is unknowable by humans (the fourth) or imaginary (the fifth), or practically impossible (the sixth).]

B. Reader's Response: Extending the Text

? Why might the speaker hold the opinion that a faithful and beautiful woman does not exist? [Sample responses: He was rejected in love; or women have been false to him.]

C. Literary Element: Hyperbole

Everything in this poem is exaggerated: the tasks, the length of the journey, and the generalizations about women's behavior. What outrageous exaggeration is claimed in the last three lines? [Even if a woman had been pure before the messenger met her and stayed faithful long enough for the messenger to inform the speaker, by the time the speaker met her—even if she lived next door to him—she would have betrayed two or even three other men.]

D. Reader's Response: Shaping Interpretations

? Why does Donne exaggerate? [Sample responses: To be funny; to underscore his point.]

PORTFOLIO ASSESSMENT

Portfolio Assessment For help with teacher assessment of reading skills, see the *Portfolio Management System,* pp. 54–55.

INTEGRATING THE LANGUAGE ARTS

Usage Tell students that the poem "Song" is in second person; that is, it is addressed directly to the reader. Ask them to review the poem and to list elements of grammar and usage that indicate this fairly unusual approach. [Imperatives; pronouns *thou, you,* and *your;* verb forms with '*st*.] Have them identify which of these are no longer in current use. [*thou* and the second person singular verb with '*st*.]

John Donne **T245**

Making Meanings

First Thoughts

1. Possible responses: I read it as the overreaction of a man who had love troubles, not as a stereotyping of women, so I found it funny. Or, it is offensive because it generalizes, saying all women are unfaithful.

Shaping Interpretations

2. Possible responses: A friend, the universe. The unhappy ending of a love affair might have occasioned the poem.

3. She does not live anywhere. She does not exist.

4. He will not go see the "true, fair" woman even if his friend finds her because even if she lives next door, she will be false with two or three men before he can walk there.

5. The commands in stanza 1; ten thousand days and nights (l.12); the exaggeration in ll. 25–27.

6. Possible responses: Cynical, dramatic, offensive, not to be taken seriously. Words that reveal a dramatic tone or an attitude that he is not to be taken seriously include "mermaids," "mandrake root," and "ten thousand days." Words that indicate a cynical or offensive tone include "swear / Nowhere / Lives a woman true, and fair." Maybe the speaker is not being serious, but even in jokes there is an implied message.

Connecting with the Text

7. Possible responses: I would respond with outrage; or I would laugh.

Extending the Text

8. (Analysis and Synthesis) Some titles that might help get students started include "Ain't No Mountain High Enough," "How Am I Supposed to Live Without You?," "You're the Top," and "You're My Everything." Students may say that while they may contain hyperbole, love songs are usually more positive.

Challenging the Text

9. (Synthesis) Possible response: Yes. Change all the feminine words and references to masculine.

MAKING MEANINGS

First Thoughts

1. What is your reaction to this poem: Is it offensive to women, funny, both, or something else?

Shaping Interpretations

2. To whom is this **speaker** talking? What do you think might have occasioned the poem?

3. In the second stanza, what does the speaker say his listener will discover about a woman both "true and fair"?

4. In the last stanza, what does the speaker say he will not do? Why?

5. What **hyperbole** does the speaker use to make his points?

6. How would you describe the speaker's **tone**? List at least three words that reveal his attitude. Do you think he is being serious?

Connecting with the Text

7. How would you respond to Donne's challenge in this poem?

Extending the Text

8. What examples of **hyperbole** do you see in love songs, whether modern or from other times? How do the sentiments in Donne's song compare with those in love songs? (Review your Reader's Log for ideas.)

Challenging the Text

9. Could this poem be revised slightly to be about the faithlessness of men? How?

ELEMENTS OF LITERATURE

Metaphysical Poetry

In the nineteenth century, Samuel Coleridge described Donne's inventiveness as a "forge and fireblast" that could twist "iron pokers into true-love knots." In the 1590s, when Donne started writing, this blazing poetic style was truly revolutionary.

Most poets then aimed for sweet, smooth, musical-sounding verse. But Donne would have none of it. "I sing not siren-like, to tempt, for I am harsh," he says in one poem. The new style he forged came to be called, by later critics, metaphysical poetry—a term that reflected its intensity of intellect, its self-conscious invention, and its bold emotion.

For the most part, Donne based the rhythm and sounds of his poems on colloquial—that is, spoken—English. "For God's sake hold your tongue and let me love," he begins one poem. The speaker in his poems frequently sounds blunt and angry, or he broods to himself, or he seems to be thinking out loud. At times the speaker almost seems to be lecturing the woman he is addressing.

Whatever his tone, Donne's speaker is always using his brains and bringing into the poems ideas from books, especially books of philosophy and theology. He also brings in images from everyday activities and trades and from learned disciplines like law, medicine, and science. Reading a metaphysical poem is frequently like figuring out the solution to a riddle—or trying to untangle a complicated knot.

To their critics, metaphysical poets were showoffs. They were accused of writing poems just to display their learning and wit. Dr. Samuel Johnson, who coined the term "metaphysical," even accused Donne and his followers of joining together their odd ideas "by violence."

The seventeenth-century poet and critic John Dryden, who disliked it, said metaphysical poetry "perplexed the minds of the fair sex with nice speculations of philosophy." How do you feel about this kind of intellectual poetry?

Bond of Union (1956) by Maurits Cornelius Escher.

Elements of Literature

Answer

Students may very well agree with Johnson because the conceits are very difficult. However, it is likely that Dryden's view will be seen as antiquated. Students may say that they enjoy philosophical speculation.

PROGRAM MANAGER

Application and Reinforcement
For reinforcement of the elements of literature introduced in this lesson, see **Transparency** 3.4 in the *Audiovisual Resources Binder*.

BEFORE YOU READ

A VALEDICTION: FORBIDDING MOURNING

Reading Focus

Hard Partings

Leaving someone you love for a long time is never easy, but if this poem is autobiographical—as Izaak Walton, Donne's friend and biographer, claimed—Donne was trying to ease a parting of great pain. The poem is typical of Donne's poetry in having a dramatic occasion, a particular situation, on which the poem is spoken. Here, the speaker, a man about to take a long journey, says goodbye ("valediction") to the woman he loves, telling her not to cry or feel sad ("forbidding mourning").

Quickwrite

If you were leaving for a long time, what would you say to someone you love who is left behind? If you were the one left, what would you want to hear? Write your thoughts in your Reader's Log.

Elements of Literature

Metaphysical Conceits

This poem contains the most famous of all **metaphysical conceits.** These are odd and surprising figures of speech in which one thing is compared with another thing that is very much unlike it. The metaphysical poets—as their name suggests—used such conceits for an analytic and psychological investigation of love and life. Here are some examples of these unusual conceits: A lover's tears are newly minted

Mrs. Pemberton (16th century) by Hans Holbein the Younger.
The Victoria and Albert Museum, London.

coins; the king's court is a bowling alley; a man is a world; lovers are holy saints. In this poem, the lovers are said to be the two prongs of a compass, the kind used to draw circles in geometry.

> **M**etaphysical conceits are especially complex and ingenious figures of speech that make surprising connections between two seemingly dissimilar things.
>
> *For more on Metaphysical Conceits, see the Handbook of Literary Terms.*

Background

Walton said Donne wrote the poem for his wife when he left for a diplomatic mission to France. She urged him not to go because she was pregnant and unwell, but he felt obligated to the mission's leader, Sir Robert Drury. Two days after arriving in Paris, Donne had a vision which he described to Sir Robert: "I have seen my dear wife pass twice by me through this room, with her hair hanging about her shoulders, and a dead child in her arms." A messenger sent back to England returned with the news that "Mrs. Donne after a long and dangerous labor . . . had been delivered of a dead child" on the very day Donne had the vision.

In reading the poem, notice that the entire first stanza is a **simile** introduced by *As* and followed by *So.* The dying men in the stanza are not part of the dramatic situation, but only offered as an analogy to the lovers' separation.

JOHN DONNE 247

Using BEFORE YOU READ p. 247

Quickwrite

To help them get started, ask students if they have experienced this kind of parting. *Remind students to use a situation they would not mind sharing.*

A. Reader's Response: First Thoughts

? Can you forbid someone else to mourn? [Sample responses: No, people's feelings are their own; or yes, if you have enough power over someone, and your argument is strong enough.]

B. Critical Reading: Making Inferences

? Why does the speaker consider silence the most fitting way for him and his wife to separate? [Possible answer: Because their love is sacred and their relationship is private. A temporary separation should not be cause for outbursts. Nor do they need to broadcast this event.]

C. Critical Reading: Drawing Conclusions

? What kind of love does the word "refined" suggest? [Superior, spiritual, sensitive, purified, and restrained.]

D. Literary Element: Imagery

? What image does Donne use to express the separation of the lovers' souls? [Possible answer: The souls are a lump of gold beaten thinner than paper. The separation becomes not a division into two, but a golden filament stretched between them.]

E. Literary Element: Metaphysical Conceit

This is the classic metaphysical conceit, a comparison that is more intellectual and complicated than, for example, the hunting metaphor in the sonnets of Petrarch, Wyatt, and Spenser.

Ⓐ A Valediction: Forbidding Mourning

John Donne

As virtuous men pass mildly away,
    And whisper to their souls, to go,
Whilst some of their sad friends do say,
    The breath goes now, and some say, no:

Ⓑ 5 So let us melt, and make no noise,
    No tear-floods, nor sigh-tempests move,
'Twere profanation° of our joys
    To tell the laity° our love.

Moving of th' earth° brings harms and fears,
10   Men reckon what it did and meant,°
But trepidation of the spheres,°
    Though greater far, is innocent.°

Dull sublunary° lovers' love
    (Whose soul° is sense°) cannot admit
15 Absence, because it doth remove
    Those things which elemented° it.

Ⓒ But we by a love, so much refined,
    That ourselves know not what it is,
Interassurèd of the mind,
20   Care less eyes, lips, and hands to miss.

Ⓓ Our two souls therefore, which are one,
    Though I must go, endure not yet
A breach,° but an expansion,
    Like gold to airy thinness beat.

Ⓔ 25 If they be two, they are two so
    As stiff twin compasses are two,
Thy soul the fixed foot, makes no show
    To move, but doth, if th' other do.

And though it in the center sit,
30   Yet when the other far doth roam,
It leans, and hearkens after it,
    And grows erect, as that comes home.

Such wilt thou be to me, who must
    Like th' other foot, obliquely° run;
35 Thy firmness° makes my circle just,°
    And makes me end, where I begun.

7. profanation: lack of reverence.
8. laity: laypersons; here, those unable to understand the "religion" of true love.
9. moving of th' earth: earthquake.
10. meant: "What does it mean?" was a question ordinarily asked of any unusual phenomenon.
11. trepidation of the spheres: irregularities in the movements of remote heavenly bodies.
12. innocent: unobserved and harmless compared to earthquakes.
13. sublunary: under the moon, therefore subject to change.
14. soul: essence. **sense:** the body with its five senses; that is, purely physical rather than spiritual.
16. elemented: comprised; composed.

23. breach: break; split.

34. obliquely: off course.
35. firmness: fidelity. **just:** perfect. A circle symbolizes perfection, hence wedding rings.

OPTIONS FOR TEACHING

STRATEGIES FOR INCLUSION

Spatial Students need to experience the operation of a compass to help them understand the reference in "A Valediction: Forbidding Mourning." Borrow a teacher's chalkboard compass from a geometry teacher, and demonstrate its use, or have students do so. Thus, students will see or feel how the fixed foot and the moving foot are related and how the circle is made.

MAKING MEANINGS

First Thoughts

1. Were your reactions to this poem different in any way from your reactions to the preceding *carpe diem* poems? If so, how, and why?

Shaping Interpretations

2. How would you paraphrase the **simile** in lines 1–8?

3. The **speaker** tells his wife that their love is different from that of other couples. What difference does he see, and how does he express it?

4. Why do you think Donne refers to irregular events on earth and in the spheres in lines 9–12? What kind of event is like the separation of lovers?

5. How would you explain the **conceit** Donne uses in lines 25–36? What does it suggest about the nature of love?

6. Why does the speaker insist that the lovers—obviously two people—are actually one?

7. What impression did you form of the writer as you read and discussed this poem? What sort of man is he?

8. Do you think this poem comforted Mrs. Donne? Why, or why not?

Challenging the Text

9. Samuel Johnson, writing in the eighteenth century, disapproved of metaphysical conceits as "the discovery of occult resemblances in things apparently unlike. . . . The most heterogeneous ideas are yoked by violence together." Do you agree or disagree with Johnson? Do the conceits in this poem work well for you? Why, or why not?

Portrait of a lady with a large ruff, an armillary sphere in the background (16th century), by the English School.

Johnny van Haeften Gallery, London.

JOHN DONNE 249

Making Meanings

First Thoughts

1. Possible response: Yes, this poem about parting brings up different feelings than poems about seizing the opportunity for love. It is an expression of deep love and attachment, and even though it has more serious and obscure language, it is very moving.

Shaping Interpretations

2. Our parting should be like the death of virtuous men who maintain their peaceful dignity and tranquility.

3. Their love is deeper than just the love of the body—they are two souls joined. He contrasts them with ordinary lovers who cannot bear to be parted.

4. These references to earthly upheavals underscore the trauma that "dull sublunary lovers" feel during separation. This separation of the speaker and his wife is like "trepidation of the spheres," movements in the cosmos that have little or no effect on Earth.

5. Compasses are used to draw perfect circles, and the speaker compares himself and his wife to the two legs of a compass. She leans toward him when he moves away, but he always returns to her at her fixed position in the center of his life. The nature of love, as defined by this conceit, is constant even as it allows for movement.

6. To emphasize the sense of union, harmony, and trust that he and his beloved feel.

7. Possible responses: He seems to be ardent, idealistic, and intellectual.

8. Possible response: Because she married him, she may have shared his views, and this would probably have comforted her.

Challenging the Text

9. (Evaluation) Johnson is right; the metaphors are too strained. Or I don't agree with Johnson; Donne makes the conceits work.

Into the Selection

BEFORE YOU READ

MEDITATION 17

Reading Focus

Last Partings

There is one valediction that everyone must make: one parting and passage that time holds in store for all of us, whether we prepare ourselves for the journey or not. In 1624, prompted by a serious illness, Donne wrote a series of meditations. The opening of this one refers to the practice, in Donne's time, of ringing church bells to announce the death of a parish member.

Quickwrite

In the course of a week, newspapers and television tell about many deaths around us. Do you think we are isolated from the deaths of others, or do you think we are tied together—that one person's death affects each of us? Jot down a few notes explaining your answer to this question.

A Wooded Landscape at Evening (detail) (19th century) by Carl Bondel. Bonhams, London.

INTEGRATING THE LANGUAGE ARTS

PROFESSIONAL NOTES

Meditation 17

John Donne

Nunc lento
sonitu dicunt,
Morieris.

Now, this bell tolling softly
for another, says to me,
Thou must die.

Perchance he for whom this bell tolls, may be so ill, as that he knows not it tolls for him; and perchance I may think myself so much better than I am, as that they who are about me, and see my state, may have caused it to toll for me, and I know not that. The Church is catholic, universal, so are all her actions; all that she does belongs to all. When she baptizes a child, that action concerns me; for that child is thereby connected to that Head[1] which is my Head too, and engrafted into that body, whereof I am a member. And when she buries a man, that action concerns me: All mankind is of one Author, and is one volume; when one man dies, one chapter is not torn out of the book, but translated[2] into a better language; and every chapter must be so translated; God employs several translators; some pieces are translated by age, some by sickness, some by war, some by justice; but God's hand is in every translation; and his hand shall bind up all our scattered leaves[3] again, for that Library where every book shall lie open to one another: As therefore the bell that rings to a sermon, calls not upon the preacher only, but upon the congregation to come; so this bell calls us all: but how much more me, who am brought so near the door by this sickness. There was a contention as far as a suit[4] (in which both piety and dignity, religion and estimation,[5] were mingled), which of the religious orders should ring to prayers first in the morning; and it was determined, that they should ring first that rose earliest. If we understand aright the dignity of this bell that tolls for our evening prayer,

we would be glad to make it ours, by rising early, in that application, that it might be ours, as well as his, whose indeed it is. The bell doth toll for him that thinks it doth; and though it intermit[6] again, yet from that minute, that that occasion wrought upon him, he is united to God. Who casts not up his eye to the sun when it rises? but who takes off his eye from a comet when that breaks out?[7] Who bends not his ear to any bell, which upon any occasion rings? but who can remove it from that bell, which is passing a piece of himself out of this world? No man is an island, entire of itself; every man is a piece of the continent, a part of the main;[8] if a clod be washed away by the sea, Europe is the less, as well as if a promontory were, as well as if a manor of thy friends or of thine own were; any man's death diminishes me, because I am involved in mankind; and therefore never send to know for whom the bell tolls; it tolls for thee. Neither can we call this a begging of misery or a borrowing of misery, as though we were not miserable enough of ourselves, but must fetch in more from the next house, in taking upon us the misery of our neighbors. Truly it were an excusable covetousness if we did; for affliction[9] is a treasure, and scarce any man hath enough of it. No man hath affliction enough that is not matured, and ripened by it, and made fit for God by that affliction. If a man carry treasure in bullion, or in a wedge of gold, and have none coined into current monies, his treasure will not defray[10] him as he travels. Tribulation is treasure in the nature of it, but it is not current money in the use of it, except we get nearer and nearer our home, Heaven, by it. Another man may be sick too, and sick to death, and this affliction may lie in his bowels, as gold in a mine, and be of no use to him; but this bell, that tells me of his affliction, digs out, and applies that gold to me; if by this consideration of another's danger I take mine own into contemplation, and so secure myself by making my recourse[11] to my God, who is our only security.

---

1. **Head:** Christ.
2. **translated:** spiritually carried across from one realm to another.
3. **leaves:** pages.
4. **contention . . . suit:** argument that went as far as a lawsuit.
5. **estimation:** self-esteem.

6. **intermit:** cease.
7. **comet . . . out:** Comets were regarded as signs of disaster to come.
8. **main:** mainland.
9. **affliction:** suffering.
10. **defray:** pay for.
11. **making my recourse:** turning for aid.

JOHN DONNE 251

Through the Selection

A. Literary Element: Allusion
The title of Ernest Hemingway's novel *For Whom the Bell Tolls* alludes to this piece by Donne.

B. Cultural Connections
The idea that all Christians are members of the same body to which every one is indispensable can be read in First Corinthians 12:12–27.

C. Literary Element: Metaphor
Explain the literary metaphor Donne uses. [Possible answer: Humanity is a book and God is the author. Each person is a chapter. When a person dies, his or her chapter is translated into a new and better language, the translation being the transition and the new language being the afterlife. God both oversees the translation and rebinds the pages for final opening in the Library, or heaven, where the whole matter of the book will be known to all.]

D. Literary Element: Metaphor
Explain Donne's geographical metaphor. [Possible answer: Humanity is a continent, with all people forming it. If one person dies, the continent is diminished.]

E. Reader's Response: Challenging the Text
? Do you agree with this comparison? Are people really all connected, part of one continent? [Sample responses: Yes, people are all interdependent. What happens in one part of the world eventually affects people everywhere. We cannot ignore injustice or disaster anywhere. Or no, we have to look out for ourselves. We cannot really feel the losses or troubles of people we do not know.]

F. Humanities Connection
This idea is related to the Beatitudes in the Gospels, in which Christ told people that those who mourned with others would be blessed.

G. Literary Element: Theme
? According to Donne, how can people profit from the suffering of others? [By seeing others' suffering as a reminder that suffering and death will come to them as well and by taking the opportunity to turn to God.]

STRATEGIES FOR INCLUSION

Visual After students read "Meditation 17" through once, have them meet in small groups to discuss how any one of Donne's **metaphors** that talk about individuals as part of a larger whole to which all humans belong could be represented in a work of art. Have them make sketches or build models to show their ideas. Discussing the representation and how it would work will encourage them to discuss the fundamental relationship that Donne believes ties all people together.

Less Proficient Readers To help students work through the text of "Meditation 17," divide the class into pairs, and use a Think Aloud Protocol in which they discuss each **metaphor** as they read. This will help bring out the implicit meanings underlying each metaphor before going on to the next.

Making Meanings

First Thoughts

1. Students may find that affliction as treasure is hard to relate to or understand because most people do not welcome affliction.

Shaping Interpretations

2. People are part of the body of which Christ is the head; pages in a book that only God can translate; pieces of the continent. These metaphors imply that society joins everyone irrevocably in important ways.

3. Affliction is a treasure because it helps us to get nearer to our ultimate home, heaven. Tribulation is a secret hoard—if it is left below it is of no use. If it is brought out into the light, it can be useful.

4. He intends to remind readers that everyone must die and that another's death should remind people of their own mortality.

5. Everyone is interconnected; everyone must die; people must not resent affliction, for it helps them get to heaven. Students' opinions will vary.

6. The tone might be described as dignified and optimistic. He holds profound religious values, including belief in the afterlife and in divine protection and mercy.

Extending the Text

7. **(Synthesis)** Possible response: "Any man's death diminishes me, because I am involved in mankind" seems appropriate to the world today; people need to take care of those who are poor and suffering and to seek justice for all.

8. **(Evaluation)** Possible response: A death that has a great effect on others. Other titles might be "No Man Is an Island," "A Wedge of Gold," or "As Gold in a Mine."

Language and Style

Possible Answers

perchance—possibly
Catholic—may refer to the Anglo-Catholic Church or to universality
engrafted—implanted
promontory—headland
aright—correctly
wrought—formed
covetousness—greed
bullion—ingots of gold

MAKING MEANINGS

First Thoughts

1. Are there any ideas in Donne's meditation that you find puzzling or hard to accept or understand? Why?

Shaping Interpretations

2. Several of Donne's **metaphors** suggest something about the relationship of people to one another. Look at those metaphors—what do they imply about society? (As you answer, think about your Reader's Log response on page 250.)

3. Why does the **speaker** feel that affliction is a treasure? In what ways is tribulation like money?

4. How would you explain what Donne means by saying "the bell . . . tolls for thee"?

5. What do you think Donne's **main ideas** are in this meditation? Do you agree with them all?

6. How would you describe the speaker's **tone:** depressed, angry, resigned, or something else? What beliefs and values do you think account for the tone?

Extending the Text

7. Which lines from Meditation 17 do you think are particularly relevant to life today: in your community, in the United States, or in the "global community"?

8. Ernest Hemingway found a title for a novel in Donne's meditation. What would you predict *For Whom the Bell Tolls* (1940) is about? Can you find two or three other phrases in the meditation that would make good titles? Which ones?

LANGUAGE AND STYLE

Context Clues

Context clues can be found in several places: (1) The unfamiliar word might be defined in an appositive; (2) the sentences surrounding the unfamiliar word might give you a clue to its meaning; (3) the structure of the word itself might help you figure out what it means. (See also How to Own a Word on page 51.)

Locate where Donne uses the following words. Use context clues to help you guess at what Donne uses each word to mean. Check all your guesses in a dictionary.

perchance	promontory	covetousness
catholic	aright	bullion
engrafted	wrought	

The Ruins of Holyrood Chapel (c. 1824) by Louis Jacques Mandé Daguerre.

Less Proficient Readers While they work on the Language and Style exercise, have students work in pairs with more proficient students to find context clues. Ask them to discuss the clues they find in each case and to verify in a dictionary the meanings they derive from clues.

Linguistic/Advanced For the exercise above, have students categorize their context clues, listing them as (1), (2), or (3) according to the definition in the text.

Reading Focus

Defeat or Triumph?
Although death is inescapable, it is not, for everyone, an invincible victor. For those who believe in immortality—as Donne firmly did—death is merely an episode in the progress of the soul, the moment of its delivery from the confines of the body to eternal life.

Quickwrite

Use the words *Defeats* and *Triumphs* as two headings in your Reader's Log. Under each head, write down the ways you think some deaths could be seen as triumphs and others as defeats.

Background

In Donne's collected poems, which are grouped by type, "Death Be Not Proud" is one of nineteen "Holy Sonnets" included in the category of "Divine Poems." Because Donne never published the "Holy Sonnets," and because they are arranged in different ways in contemporary manuscripts and in books printed after his death, we do not know the order in which he wanted us to read them.

Into the Poem

Using BEFORE YOU READ p. 253

Reading Focus

Have students brainstorm ways people think they can triumph over death. For example, the Anglo-Saxons believed fame kept one alive, although not literally, after death. The ancient Greeks believed that by embracing one's fate, one could die a good death.

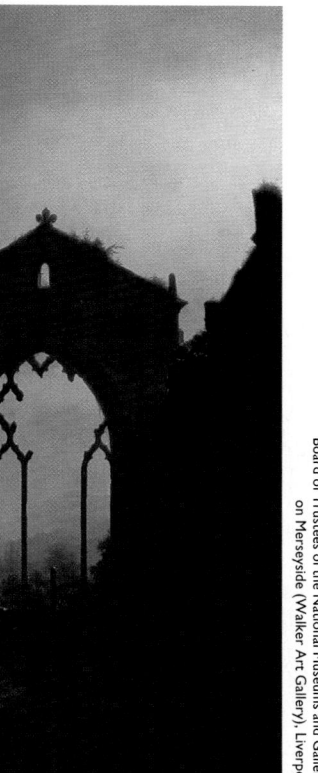

Board of Trustees of the National Museums and Galleries on Merseyside (Walker Art Gallery), Liverpool.

Death Be Not Proud

John Donne

Death be not proud, though some have callèd thee
Mighty and dreadful, for thou art not so, ___ **A**
For those whom thou think'st thou dost overthrow,
Die not, poor Death, nor yet canst thou kill me. ___ **B**
5 From rest and sleep, which but thy pictures° be,
Much pleasure,° then from thee, much more must flow,
And soonest our best men with thee do go,
Rest of their bones, and soul's delivery.°
Thou art slave to fate, chance, kings, and desperate men, **C**
10 And dost with poison, war, and sickness dwell, ___
And poppy,° or charms° can make us sleep as well,
And better than thy stroke; why swell'st° thou then?
One short sleep past, we wake eternally,
And death shall be no more; Death, thou shalt die. **D**

5. **pictures:** images. A sleeping person can resemble a dead person.
6. **much pleasure:** That is, rest and sleep give much pleasure.
8. **rest . . . delivery:** Death gives the body rest and delivers the soul from the bondage of the body.
11. **poppy:** opium. **charms:** magic; hypnotism.
12. **swell'st:** swell with pride.

Through the Poem

A. Literary Element: Apostrophe

An apostrophe is a direct address to an absent or dead person or to an abstract quality or something non-human as if it were present and capable of responding. To whom is this sonnet addressed? [Death.]

B. Critical Reading: Speculating

? Why do the people whom Death thinks it kills not die? [Possible answer: Although Death thinks that it kills people, they do not actually die, but they simply leave their bodies and live on as souls in heaven.]

C. Critical Reading: Making Inferences

? What evidence does the speaker give to prove that Death is not as mighty as it might have thought? [Possible answer: Death itself is subject to other forces: fate, chance, kings, and desperate men, who can call it up at will.]

D. Critical Reading: Analyzing Poetic Structure

? Is this poem a Shakespearean or Petrarchan sonnet? How do you know? [It is a Shakespearean sonnet because of the rhyme scheme and the way the sections are divided, three stanzas of four lines and a concluding couplet.]

COOPERATIVE LEARNING

Cluster Maps Before introducing "Death Be Not Proud," divide the class into groups. Ask each group to create a cluster map that shows the attributes of death. After they have read the poem, have them regroup and draw new cluster maps with the attributes Donne gives death. Have them compare their diagrams. To transfer this activity to an overhead projector, use Transparency 3: Cluster Diagram in the Transparency Package. A sample diagram for Donne's attributes of death follows.

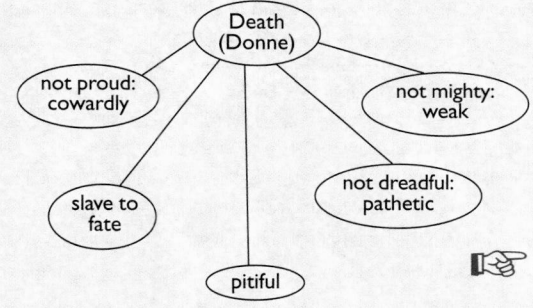

Making Meanings

First Thoughts

1. Students may or may not find any of their own ideas in the poem. Taunts include that death will die and that death is a slave.

Shaping Interpretations

2. Death does not kill anyone. Death serves fate, chance, kings, and desperate people.
3. In rest and sleep the body is immobile, so they look like death.
4. The paradox is resolved if one assumes that there is eternal life.
5. Possible response: Defiant. Words that reveal this include "[you are not] mighty and dreadful" and "Death, thou shalt die."

Connecting with the Text

6. Possible response: It seems brave. I wonder if people could really feel this way when they have lost someone they have loved.

Extending the Text

7. (Synthesis) It suggests that he believes in an afterlife, or that he feels his son triumphed over death.

MAKING MEANINGS

First Thoughts

1. Did you find any of your Reader's Log ideas in Donne's poem? Did any of his taunts to Death seem surprising or highly original to you? If so, which ones?

Shaping Interpretations

2. According to the poem, why shouldn't Death be proud? Whom must Death serve as a slave?
3. Explain how rest and sleep are the "pictures" of Death (line 5).
4. How does the sonnet resolve its **paradoxes,** or seeming contradictions: that those who die do not die and that Death itself will die?

5. What is the speaker's **tone** in this poem—how does he feel toward Death? What words reveal his attitude?

Connecting with the Text

6. How would you respond to Donne's mockery of Death?

Extending the Text

7. John Gunther used this poem's opening words as the title of a book he wrote about the death of his teenage son. What attitude toward this personal tragedy does the father's choice of title suggest?

Still Life—Vanitas (1623) by Pieter Claesz. Oil on wood.
The Metropolitan Museum of Art, New York, Rogers Fund, 1949 (49.107).

254 THE RENAISSANCE

ASSESSMENT TOOLS

Check Test: Multiple Choice

1. The speaker in "Song" (a) is being made fun of because everything he wants is impossible to obtain (b) wants to go on a pilgrimage to worship at the feet of the most beautiful woman in the world (c) believes that finding a woman who is true and fair is as impossible as catching a falling star [c]

2. In "A Valediction: Forbidding Mourning," the speaker says that he and the woman to whom he speaks share a love that (a) makes their two souls one (b) is great because he writes poetry to her (c) makes them travel in circles [a]

3. In "Meditation 17," Donne says that all human lives are interconnected because (a) we are all descendants of the first woman (b) we were all made by God (c) we all live on the same island [b]

4. Donne says in "Meditation 17" that "tribulation is treasure" because (a) it can be hidden (b) we carry it with us (c) it can encourage us to turn to God [c]

5. In "Death Be Not Proud," the speaker argues that (a) death is only mighty and dreadful to those who are not Christians (b) when all have died and awakened in eternal life, death will be no more (c) if we could rid the world of poison, war, sickness, and desperate men, then death would no longer exist [b]

CHOICES: Building Your Portfolio

Writer's Notebook

1. Collecting Ideas for an Interpretive Essay

WORK IN PROGRESS

In questions following Donne's "Song," Meditation 17, and "Death Be Not Proud," you were asked to interpret the speaker's **tone.** Take one of these works, and look for at least three details that support your interpretation of tone. Look for word choice, sound effects, and direct statements. Save your work for possible use in the Writer's Workshop on page 275.

Critical Writing

2. Thinking About Goodbyes

Richard Lovelace's "To Lucasta, on Going to the Wars" (page 264) is also a valediction poem addressed to a beloved woman. Read Lovelace's poem. Then, in an essay, compare and contrast Lovelace's farewell with Donne's "A Valediction: Forbidding Mourning." Focus on the consoling arguments that the speakers use to comfort the one left behind.

Critical Writing

3. Meditating on Metaphors

In a brief essay, take two of the metaphors in Meditation 17, and show how Donne uses them to make his points. Be sure to explain the terms of each metaphor and to show how Donne extends them.

Creative Writing

4. Stretching the Truth

Imitate the first stanza of Donne's "Song" by constructing some hyperbolic statements of your own to show the impossibility of something. You might want to respond to the points Donne raises in "Song."

Creative Writing

5. Just Before Parting

Suppose that you, like Donne, are leaving a loved one behind for a long, possibly dangerous journey. Write your own "valediction" in a brief letter.

Art and Literature

6. Picturing Death

In "Death Be Not Proud," Donne forcefully personifies Death. How do you picture Death from his words and images? Draw or paint an illustration of Death to accompany Donne's poem.

Technology

7. Love in a High-Tech World

If Donne were writing today, he might have chosen a computer and modem, rather than a geometer's compass, as a conceit for the "connectedness" of lovers. Think of a high-tech conceit you could use to express a love relationship. Collaborate with one or two classmates, and express your ideas in a poem, sketch, video, or mixed-media performance. Remember that, to be effective, a conceit must have apt points of comparison.

JOHN DONNE **255**

Choices: Building Your Portfolio

1. **Writer's Notebook** Remind students to save their work. They may use it as prewriting for the Writer's Workshop on p. 275. Suggest that **imagery** can also provide a good basis for interpreting **tone.**
2. **Critical Writing** Before beginning this activity, students could complete Making Meanings items 3, 4, and 5 (p. 266) for Lovelace's poem.
3. **Critical Writing** Have students create a chart for the metaphors that lists, defines the terms of, and identifies the point Donne makes with each metaphor. They could use Transparency 4: Category Chart in the Transparency Package.
4. **Creative Writing** Start students with simple exaggerations, in simile form, then have them elaborate on them to approximate Donne's language.
5. **Creative Writing** Allow students to compose verse letters, as Donne did, if they wish.
6. **Art and Literature** Have students brainstorm a list of images before they begin their artwork.
7. **Technology** For example: Love is like a cellular phone; just when you think you can reach your love any time, he or she drives out of the calling area.

PORTFOLIO ASSESSMENT

Choices: Assessment Criteria For help in evaluating these Choices assignments, see the criteria in the *Portfolio Management System,* pp. 93–94.

STRATEGIES FOR INCLUSION

Learners Having Difficulty Students can use a graphic organizer like the one that follows to order their points for activity #2. Remind them that they can use various logical structures to organize their essay. They can list all the points about one poem and then all the points about the other, or they can move back and forth from one poem to the other for each point they make.

	"Valediction"	"Lucasta"
Tone		
Metaphors		
Separation		
Consolation		

Into the Poems

Author Biography p. 256

Before You Read "On My First Son" p. 257, "Song: To Celia" p. 258

Through the Poems

"On My First Son" p. 257

"Song: To Celia" p. 258

Making Meanings p. 259

Connections: A Book "Give Us This Day Our Daily Bread" pp. 260–261

Beyond the Poems

Choices: Building Your Portfolio p. 259

- **Writer's Notebook:** Write notes on what each poem means to you for an interpretive essay
- **Critical Writing:** Write a paragraph on Jonson's resolution
- **Critical Writing:** Write paragraphs about life in the late 1500s
- **Creative Writing:** Write a poem or paragraph using metaphor
- **Music:** Write a love song

WRITERS ON WRITING

Jonson wrote this about his experience as a writer: "Poetry in this latter Age hath prov'd but a mean Mistress, to such as have wholly addicted themselves to her."

Ben Jonson
(1572?–1637)

Although Jonson was christened Benjamin, he was, and is, always known as Ben. He was probably born in the same year as his friend John Donne, and if his friend William Shakespeare had never existed, Jonson would probably be regarded as the chief dramatist of the age.

Ben's father died before he was born. His stepfather, a bricklayer, intended to make him into a bricklayer too, but while still a boy, Jonson became acquainted with William Camden, scholar and headmaster of the superb Westminster School. Camden enrolled young Ben in his school and educated him at his own expense.

Jonson never attended a university, but he had an immense knowledge of Latin literature and a small acquaintance with Greek. He was no mere pedant or bookish recluse. After leaving Westminster, Ben joined the English army and fought against the Spanish in Flanders. There, while the two massed armies watched, he engaged in single combat with the Spanish champion and killed him. Back in England, he became a playwright and an actor, specializing in loud and roaring parts. He had two brushes with the law: once when he killed a fellow actor in a duel and escaped hanging by demonstrating that he could read, and once when he went to prison for making derogatory remarks about Scotland in a play. In short, Jonson was very much a part of the tough, violent life of the time—a complete Londoner, holding forth at

Benjamin Jonson (early 17th century) after Abraham van Blyenberch. Oil on canvas (18½" × 16½").

By Courtesy of the National Portrait Gallery, London.

the Mermaid Tavern, where his witty combats with Shakespeare and others are mentioned in contemporary writings.

Gradually, Jonson became known as a dramatist. He was particularly good at devising masques (elaborate, expensively mounted productions) for the court of King James. Jonson also wrote tragedies and comedies for the public theaters.

Jonson's attitude toward his writing was different from Donne's and Shakespeare's; Jonson was more like today's writers, who are, for the most part, eager for public notice. In 1616, Jonson astonished the reading public by publishing a number of his plays and poems under the title *Works*, a label traditionally reserved for more intellectual subjects, such as theology and history. But Jonson believed that poems and plays *are* serious works of art, as serious in their own way as history and theology, and as worthy of high regard.

At the height of his career, Jonson was a sort of literary dictator in London—opinionated and crusty but admired by a number of younger writers, who became known as the "tribe of Ben" or the "sons of Ben." They stood by Jonson in his old age, when he was sick and poor and neglected because his blunt and forthright manner had made him many enemies. Jonson was buried near Chaucer in Westminster Abbey, in what later became known as the Poets' Corner. His inscription required only four words: "O rare Ben Jonson."

256 THE RENAISSANCE

PROGRAM MANAGER

- **Planning Instruction** See **Teaching Notes,** *Teaching Resources A,* p. 61, for objectives, a summary, and literary elements for these selections.
- **Instructional Support** Before beginning the instructional lesson, see **Graphic Organizer for Active Reading,** *Teaching Resources A,* p. 79, for a Through

the Poem activity.
- **Audiotaped Readings** To help less proficient readers or auditory learners through the lesson, use the **Selected Reading, Audiocassette 1, Side A,** in the *Audiovisual Resources Binder.*
- **Assessment** See **Selection Test,** *Test Booklet,* pp. 47–48.

BEFORE YOU READ
ON MY FIRST SON

Reading Focus

The Bonds of Love
When you hear the word *love*, do you first think of romantic love? If you do, this is a natural response. But the ties of love also bind us powerfully to family, to friends, even to pets. And one of love's ironies is that a strong bond of love, so strengthening and fulfilling, also opens us to heartache when it is cut.

Quickwrite

What does the word *bond* mean to you? With a few classmates, brainstorm meanings, connotations, and associations (don't

think only of love). You may want to create a cluster diagram to show your ideas. Afterward, look up *bond* in the dictionary, and compare what you find with your brainstormings.

Elements of Literature

The Epigram
Both of Jonson's poems you will read were published in his *Epigrams* (1616), a classical form Jonson favored in contrast to both Elizabethan romanticism and metaphysical complexity. For the ancients, an **epigram** was written to give permanence to an event or observation; it was pointed, polished, and striking—

like engraving on a monument. Jonson's epigrams (which are short poems) often show a two-part structure, the first part establishing the mood or the event, the second making a pithy point.

Background

This poem is about Jonson's son, Benjamin, who died of the plague on his seventh birthday. (Jonson and his wife also lost a daughter, Mary, in infancy.) The name *Benjamin* in Hebrew means "a child of the right hand" and, ironically, connotes "a lucky, clever child."

Into the Poem

Using **BEFORE YOU READ** p. 257

Elements of Literature
Samuel Taylor Coleridge defined an epigram like this: "What is an epigram? A dwarfish whole, / Its body brevity, and wit its soul."

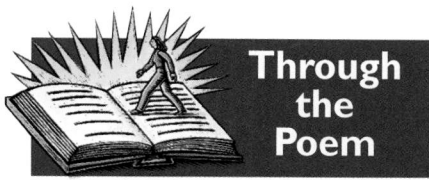

Through the Poem

On My First Son

Ben Jonson

Farewell, thou child of my right hand, and joy; **Ⓐ**
   My sin was too much hope of thee, loved boy:
Seven years thou wert lent to me, and I thee pay,°
   Exacted° by thy fate, on the just° day.
5 Oh, could I lose all father° now! for why
   Will man lament the state he should envy—
To have so soon 'scaped world's and flesh's rage, **Ⓑ**
   And if no other misery, yet age?
Rest in soft peace, and asked, say, "Here doth lie **Ⓒ**
10   Ben Jonson his best piece of poetry;
For whose sake henceforth all his vows be such
   As what he loves may never like too much." **Ⓓ**

3. thee pay: pay thee back.
4. exacted: forced. **just:** exact. Loans were often made for exactly seven years.
5. father: sense of fatherhood; the need to mourn like a father.

Portrait of a boy (16th century) by Robert Peake the Elder.

Christie's, London.

BEN JONSON 257

STRATEGIES FOR INCLUSION

Auditory After they have read "On My First Son," have students write and read to one another epitaphs for Jonson's son.

Kinesthetic While reading "Song: To Celia," have some volunteers act out what the poem describes. You might provide some props: a cup, a wreath. Students might write a script of actions that match Jonson's words. ☞

A. Reader's Response: First Thoughts

? Why do you suppose the speaker calls hope a sin? [Sample responses: Because he lost sight of the fragility of life, and his dashed hopes are now a source of acute pain. Because he may feel that his son's death is a punishment by God to cure Jonson of his too great attachment to the child.]

B. Critical Reading: Making Connections

? How does the view expressed in these lines relate to those expressed in "Death Be Not Proud"? [Possible answers: Donne and Jonson would agree that heaven is the goal of life. Donne's ll. 7–8 in "Death Be Not Proud" suggest that the poets would agree that dying young is not a bad thing.]

C. Critical Reading: Drawing Conclusions

? What do these two lines mean? [Jonson is saying that his son is his greatest creation.]

D. Literary Element: Epigram

? How does this poem fit the definition of an epigram, as given in the Before You Read section? [With this poem, Jonson commemorates the death of his son. The last lines are an epitaph, which is usually engraved in stone, giving it permanence. The language is striking and powerful.]

Into the Poem

Using **BEFORE YOU READ** p. 258

Reading Focus

To help students recognize the song as an expression of love, have students brainstorm titles of contemporary love songs. Possible titles include "Love Letters," "Can't Help Falling in Love with You," and "I Will Always Love You."

Through the Poem

A. Critical Reading: Speculating

The name *Celia* means "heavenly." With what will the speaker compare Celia? [Possible answers: Angels, gods or goddesses, divine things.] After students have read the poem, ask if their speculations are correct. How is Celia heavenly? [The speaker compares Celia's kiss in the cup to the drink of the gods, and attributes to her the ability to breathe life into a dead wreath. Both of these characterizations make her seem like a goddess.]

B. Literary Element: Metaphor

? What is the "thirst that from the soul doth rise"? [The longing for love.]

C. Critical Reading: Drawing Conclusions

? What is a "rosy wreath"? [A little circlet adorned with roses.] Note that "I sent thee late" means "I sent thee recently."

BEFORE YOU READ
SONG: TO CELIA

Reading Focus

Love's Tributes
Part of loving is telling—acting on that burning desire to reveal your heart's devotion. In this short lyric, the speaker addresses Celia, telling her—exuberantly—how much he loves her.

Quickwrite

It isn't easy to find ways to talk about love. How do characters in movies and television shows manage it? Think of one or two characters, and try to recall how each expresses, explains, or describes his or her feelings.

Background

Jonson once said that he always wrote out his poems in prose before turning them into verse, just as his master Camden had taught him to. At times, it must be admitted, the prose that he versified was not his own but someone else's. Jonson crafted this poem out of five different prose passages that he found in the *Epistles* of the Greek philosopher Philostratus (A.D. 170?–245). This poem has a very famous tune that many people still know.

   Throughout his life, Jonson's enemies taunted him for once being a bricklayer. In a sense, he remained a bricklayer all his creative life, a builder whose tiniest construction, like this song, is solid and seamless.

A **Song: To Celia**

Ben Jonson

Drink to me only with thine eyes,
    And I will pledge with mine;
Or leave a kiss but in the cup,
    And I'll not look for wine.
5 The thirst that from the soul doth rise
    Doth ask a drink divine;
But might I of Jove's nectar° sup,
    I would not change° for thine.
C I sent thee late a rosy wreath,
10   Not so much honoring thee
As giving it a hope, that there
    It could not withered be.
But thou thereon didst only breathe,
    And sent'st it back to me;
15 Since when it grows, and smells, I swear,
    Not of itself but thee.

7. Jove's nectar: Jove, more commonly called Jupiter, is the supreme god in Roman mythology. Nectar was the drink that kept the gods immortal.
8. change: exchange.

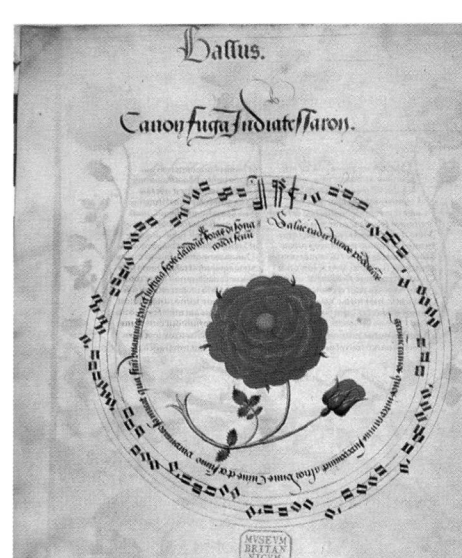

Motets (16th century) by Richard Sampson. Roy 11 E XI fol. 2v Canon, with circular staves and rose at center.

British Library, London.

OPTIONS FOR TEACHING

STRATEGIES FOR INCLUSION

Special Needs Have students who have limited vocabulary retention participate in an activity that will give them practice recalling information. Have students work in pairs or small groups. Give students a list of words from the poetry selections such as *farewell, envy, lament, exacted, doth.* Have students make match-mate cards using 3" × 5" index cards. Each set of cards will be cut in two different parts. On one part, write the vocabulary word and on the other part the meaning. Students exchange cards and practice identifying the correct meaning. They may check their learning by seeing if the parts fit together.

MAKING MEANINGS

On My First Son
Song: To Celia

First Thoughts

1. What to you is the most important single line in each of Ben Jonson's poems? Why? Does your response to each poem relate to what you wrote in your Reader's Log before you read each poem? How?

Shaping Interpretations

2. In "On My First Son," why can the early death of a boy named Benjamin be regarded as ironic?

3. In "On My First Son," what comfort does Jonson suggest is possible in lines 7–8? Do you feel he's comforted?

4. In "To Celia," what do you think it means to "drink" and "pledge" with the eyes?

5. What does "thine" refer to in line 8 of "To Celia"?

6. How would you **paraphrase** lines 9–16 of "To Celia"?

7. These two poems are about two very different situations. Is there, nonetheless, anything that they share—any attitudes or beliefs? If you didn't know they were both by Jonson, would there be any reason to believe that they were written by the same person?

8. Jonson borrowed some of the features from "On My First Son" from Latin works: the direct address to the dead boy in line 9 and the first three words of the **epitaph,** or inscription, "Here doth lie . . . ." But the idea that his son is his best poem is original with Jonson. What do you think of this statement?

Connecting with the Text

9. What seemingly insignificant object—like the wreath returned by the speaker's beloved in "To Celia"—is nevertheless priceless to you because of the associations it evokes? Why is it priceless to you?

CHOICES:
Building Your Portfolio

Writer's Notebook
1. Collecting Ideas for an Interpretive Essay

Your response to "First Thoughts" (opposite) could be the thesis for an interpretive essay. In your Writer's Notebook, gather reasons for your choice of lines. Then make a brief statement of what each poem says to you. Save your work for the Writer's Workshop on page 275.

Critical Writing
2. Rebutting Jonson

In "On My First Son," Jonson resolves never again to love so strongly, because his loss is unbearable. What do you think of Jonson's resolution? What effect could it have on him? Write a paragraph in which you answer these questions.

Critical Writing
3. Everyday Living

In one or two paragraphs, explain how the hard existence described in "Give Us This Day Our Daily Bread" (page 260) corresponds to your previous notion of life in the late 1500s. Conclude by noting some aspects of Renaissance life you'd like to research and know more about.

Creative Writing
4. What Is Love?

In "To Celia," Jonson implicitly defines love as the soul's thirst (line 5). Elaborate on this definition in a paragraph (or a poem, if you like), or create a different definition based on your own metaphor.

Music
5. Crooning About Love

Write a love song of your own that begins with Jonson's first two lines in "To Celia."

BEN JONSON 259

PORTFOLIO ASSESSMENT

Choices: Assessment Criteria
For help in evaluating these Choices assignments, see the criteria in the *Portfolio Management System,* pp. 95–96.

Making Meanings
First Thoughts

1. Possible responses: "Here doth lie Ben Jonson his best piece of poetry." Or the first line of "Song: To Celia." They deliver the poems' emotional impact. Yes, there are connections between what I wrote and what the poems express. There are aspects of love that do not seem to change over time.

Shaping Interpretations

2. Because the name suggests luck.

3. His son, Ben, is free from the cares of the world and the decay of the flesh. Students may feel that the speaker is not really comforted; his last lines seem to suggest the impossible. He liked his son too much to be completely consoled.

4. Traditionally, the meeting of lovers' eyes can convey a world of meaning. Here they pledge their faithfulness.

5. It refers to the lady's nectar, or, by extension, her love.

6. Possible response: I recently sent you a wreath in the hope that it would not die. You sent it back, alive, growing, and with your aroma.

7. Possible response: They both hold love of one kind or another in very high esteem. Yes, the passion in each poem could identify the same author for both poems. The language seems similar, too.

8. Possible answer: It is very moving.

Connecting with the Text

9. Students will probably choose something that reminds them of a happy time. *Be sure they choose something they would not mind sharing with others.*

Beyond the Poems

Choices: Building Your Portfolio

1. **Writer's Notebook** Remind students to save their work. They may use it as prewriting for the Writer's Workshop on p. 275.

2. **Critical Writing** Have students make a quick list of adjectives that might describe a person who lives by such a resolution.

Connections A HISTORY

Three Peasants (detail) (16th or 17th century) by Albrecht Dürer. Oil on panel.
Kunsthistorisches Museum, Vienna.

Had he not crossed paths with the scholar William Camden, Ben Jonson might have spent his life laying brick rather than composing poetry. Most young people of the age—those who didn't come from wealthy families or didn't acquire generous patrons—had difficult, exhausting lives. For them, witty conceits praising adored ladies were as foreign as the moon—and life was consumed with making ends meet.

Give Us This Day Our Daily Bread

Joseph Papp and Elizabeth Kirkland

You are living in England in the late years of the sixteenth century. Like most people, you live with your family in the countryside, eking out a meager existence as best you can. If you're lucky, your father is a yeoman farmer who owns enough land to support his family, or a "husbandman" who has less property but supplements his income by wage earning.

The land you live in is full of contradictions. A woman, Queen Elizabeth, rules the nation, while within the family, men still rule women. A highly educated elite enjoys the fruits of literature, while many people can't even read. The government invests huge sums of money in voyages of exploration and wars with other nations, while science and medicine remain in an appallingly primitive state. In London, the royal court glitters with jewels and finery, while misery reigns in rural hovels. Rich young men wander around Europe for fun, while in England, thousands of homeless people wander from parish to parish, begging and stealing to survive.

The gap between the rich and the poor seems to have widened in the 1570s and 1580s; wealth and power are concentrated in the hands of the few, and many people can't even find a job.

You come from a family of laborers. You don't have much land at all, hardly even a vegetable garden you can call your own, and you are completely dependent on whatever wages you can get by harvesting other people's crops and doing odd jobs around the village. There is no money for such "extras" as education or nice clothes or red meat. In fact, your father's daily income, even when combined with yours, barely covers the cost of feeding you and your brothers and sisters; thank goodness your mother is able to bring in a few extra pennies from her spinning.

Your dependent status as a tenant makes your perch in life still more precarious. To an unjust and unscrupulous landlord, profit is more important than principles, and yours feels no obligation to look out for your best interests. If he decides to "enclose" the land—to stop using it for farming and turn it into grazing pastures for sheep—he has endless means of forcing you out: He might make you give up your lease, or renew it only at great expense, or, most commonly, charge you exorbitant rent.

While your family has been struggling against these odds and worrying about how to make ends meet from day to day, larger forces have been at work that are going to affect you drastically. First, England has been undergoing a huge increase in population. The two-and-a-half million English people who were alive when your grandparents were

CONNECTING WITH JONSON'S POEMS

Papp and Kirkland describe another side of the world into which Ben Jonson was born. Jonson did spend a short time as a workman, but because he was educated, because he lived in the city, and because his stepfather was a tradesman, he did not live with the same threats to his survival as the rural laborers described above. Many of them would not have had the time or the skills to read or contemplate Jonson's poignant verse.

born will practically have doubled by the time your grandchildren die. This unprecedented population growth is already being translated into inflated prices, as too many people chase after scarce resources. It also means that wages stay unacceptably low; with so many laborers on the job market, farmers and other employers can easily find people willing to work for the pathetically low wages they offer if you're not interested.

B Getting and spending have been a constant battle, and staying on the winning side has depended on plentiful harvests, which bring the twofold benefit of jobs and low grain prices. But in recent years the battle has become a losing one: The heavy rains of the last two summers have ruined the harvests, the population has been growing faster than the crops, and famine has begun to cast its long, thin shadow across your life.

Grain—whether you eat the oatmeal cakes of northern England or the coarse wheat bread of the southerners—is a staple of your diet and, if you have no land and have to buy all your grain on the market, your single biggest expense. When prices shoot up, as they do in bad harvest years, it spells disaster for many a citizen; the Carriers in Shakespeare's *Henry IV Part 1* remember a comrade who "never joyed since the price of oats rose. It was the death of him." You try to find cheaper kinds of grain than your usual

wheat, supplementing your diet with stomach-filling peas and beans—but even the prices of these are rising now, and you begin to realize, horrifying though it is, that there aren't many alternatives. Starvation seems inevitable.

You wonder how you and your family are going to cope with the steady advance of such hunger, the hair falling out and the skin turning gray and the bleak prospect of watching your fellow villagers "starving and dying in our streets and in the fields [because] of lack of bread," as a contemporary in the northern town of Newcastle writes. **C**

To make matters worse, there has been an economic recession too, mainly because of a slump in the cloth trade that your mother had been depending on for her livelihood. Many people rely on the cloth and wool trades for their living, and now, "the deadness of that trade and want of money is such that they are for the most part without work, and know not how to live," as an official of one parish reports.

—*from Shakespeare Alive!*

Summer (detail)
(16th century) by
Jorg Breu the Elder.

"Getting and spending" is a phrase from Wordsworth's sonnet, "The World Is Too Much with Us" (see p. 667), in which he laments wasting time on the material aspects of life. Writing about 250 years after the time discussed here, Wordsworth idealized the rural setting that was the site of destitution for many common laborers of the late 1500s.

C. Reader's Response: Connecting with the Text
While we think of Renaissance England as the Golden Age, this article describes another part of life in this period. How does this picture of life compare with that you know of through the literature you have been reading? [Sample responses: Life for the majority of people was much harder than what you understand from the poems, where the problems of love seem to be the focus. Although Jonson and Donne have both encountered death and written about it in effective ways, even the poems about death do not really evoke the hardships of rural life.]

Into the Poems

Author Biographies p. 262

Before You Read p. 263

- **Reading Focus: Scaffolding** Students learn background information on the Cavalier poets.
- **A Dialogue with the Text:** Respond in Reader's Log to the poems
- **Elements of Literature: Tone**

Through the Poems

"Why So Pale and Wan, Fond Lover?" p. 263

"To Lucasta, on Going to the Wars" p. 264

"To Althea, from Prison" p. 265

Making Meanings p. 266

Beyond the Poems

Choices: Building Your Portfolio p. 266

- **Writer's Notebook:** Paraphrase a poem as prewriting for an interpretive essay
- **Critical Writing:** Write an essay about relevance of a seventeenth-century poem to today's world
- **Creative Writing:** Write Lucasta's response to the poem

Sir John Suckling
(1609–1642)

Richard Lovelace
(1618–1657)

Sir John Suckling (detail) (17th century) by an unknown artist. Oil on panel (34.3 cm × 28.6 cm).

By Courtesy of the National Portrait Gallery, London.

It is convenient to consider these two poets together because they were Royalists; that is, they supported King Charles in the Civil Wars of the 1640s. Because of their politics, they are sometimes called Cavalier poets, "Cavalier" being the nickname for a supporter of the king, as "Roundhead" is for a supporter of Parliament. But these poets had more than politics in common; they shared a common literary goal, which was to write poems that sound like elegant conversation. In the next century, Alexander Pope, looking back at the work of the poets of the mid–seventeenth century, referred to them as "the mob of gentlemen who wrote with ease." Pope should have said that they *seemed* to write with ease, because he knew better than most people how hard it is to make any kind of writing, and especially poetry, sound easy and at the same time be technically accomplished.

John Suckling was born rich, but he gambled away his money and spent a lot of it on extravagant clothes. Suckling's military career included service as a gentleman soldier on the Continent and as the commander of a troop of cavalry fighting in Scotland for King Charles. He plotted unsuccessfully to deliver one of the king's chief advisers from the Tower of London; then he fled to France. There, at the age of thirty-three, he died—by suicide or murder (accounts vary). Suckling's poems, which were mostly published after his death, tend to be lighthearted, as was his life. Dryden praised him, saying that he had "the conversation of a gentleman." He is said to be the inventor of cribbage, a card game.

Lovelace (pronounced "love-less"), besides being very handsome, was altogether a more serious person than the playboy Suckling. Like his fellow Cavalier poets, he was very rich, at least at the beginning of his life. He was also a connoisseur of music, painting, and horsemanship. While still a student at Oxford, he made such an impression on King Charles and Queen Henrietta Maria, who were visiting the university, that the royal couple ordered the authorities to confer on him the Master of Arts degree at once. Lovelace became an ardent Royalist, and when the Civil Wars broke out, he fought bravely for King Charles. The Roundheads caught him twice and imprisoned him both times. His last days were sad, his health and fortune ruined in the service of a lost cause.

Richard Lovelace (detail) (17th century) by Wenceslaus Hollar.

By Courtesy of the National Portrait Gallery, London.

262 THE RENAISSANCE

PROGRAM MANAGER

- **Planning Instruction** See *Teaching Notes, Teaching Resources A,* p. 62, for objectives, a summary, and literary elements for the selections.
- **Instructional Support** Before beginning the instructional lesson, see Graphic Organizer for Active Reading, *Teaching Resources A,* pp. 80–81, for Through the Poem activities.
- **Reinforcement** Use the Words to Own worksheet in *Teaching Resources A,* pp. 82–83.
- **Assessment** See Selection Test, *Test Booklet,* pp. 49–50.

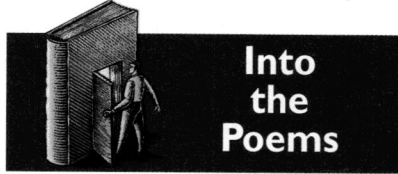

Into the Poems

Reading Focus
Knights Ride Again

Cavalier, cavalry, chivalry: the common root of all three words is the Latin word for "horse," *caballus.* All three also share, in their earliest uses, the dual meanings of "horseman" and "knightly behavior." Thinking about these two ideas gives you a way of understanding the Cavalier poets, who saw themselves as modern-day knights. They adopted the chivalrous code of intense loyalty to a leader, to God, and to one beloved woman. But they were also boisterously masculine, pleasure-loving, worldly, and cynical.

A Dialogue with the Text

READER'S LOG

As you read, write your responses to each poem in your Reader's Log. If you could ask each poet one question, what would it be? What idea would you challenge each poet about?

Elements of Literature
Tone

The Cavalier poets' attitudes toward women, warfare, honor, and the other matters that concerned them shaped the tone of their poetry vividly. In these three poems, you'll hear the tone of voice strongly, and it will let you know how each poet feels about his subject. Try to read these poems as if you were listening to someone speaking aloud.

> **T**one is the attitude a writer takes toward the reader, a subject, or a character.
>
> *For more on Tone, see the Handbook of Literary Terms.*

In Renaissance literature, young men suffer horribly from unrequited love. Part of the convention is that the women whom the men admire show no pity. In fact, they ignore pleas for attention so firmly that the men became "pale and wan"—that is, sickly looking—like the young fellow whom the speaker of this poem is so irritated with.

Why So Pale and Wan, Fond Lover?

Sir John Suckling

Why so pale and wan, fond lover?
  Prithee, why so pale?
Will, when looking well can't move her, **A**
  Looking ill prevail?
5   Prithee, why so pale?

Why so dull and mute, young sinner?
  Prithee, why so mute?
Will, when speaking well can't win her,
  Saying nothing do't? **B**
10   Prithee, why so mute?

Quit, quit, for shame; this will not move,
  This cannot take her.
If of herself she will not love,
  Nothing can make her:
15   The devil take her! **C**

An Unknown Youth Leaning Against a Tree Among Roses (16th century) by Nicholas Hilliard.
Victoria and Albert Museum, London.

SIR JOHN SUCKLING 263

Through the Poems

Using BEFORE YOU READ p. 263
Reading Focus

Ask students to think of some characters who might be modern-day cavaliers. [Steve Martin's character in *Roxanne,* Indiana Jones.]

A. Critical Reading: Drawing Conclusions

? What is supposed to move the lady, according to custom? [Apparently good looks and pleasant words are supposed to be enough to make her love him.]

B. Literary Element: Tone

? What tone do the rhetorical questions in this poem imply? [Mocking and cynical because the speaker expects no answer. The questions tease the person to whom they are addressed.]

C. Critical Reading: Summarizing

? How does the ending create a surprise? [The speaker curses the woman who rejects her suitor.]

OPTIONS FOR TEACHING

STRATEGIES FOR INCLUSION

Advanced Some readers seem to think that the speaker in Suckling's poem is addressing himself. Others believe that he is addressing another. Ask students to re-read the poem, and have them write a paragraph making the case for one interpretation or the other.

English Language Development To clarify the structure of the stanzas in "To Althea, from Prison" on p. 265, show some simple examples of the structure, such as "When I'm with my friends, not even a mother with a new baby could be happier." Have students read the first stanza, and point out that the first six lines describe the situation and the last two lines tell how another compares to it. Explain that these are just longer examples of the structures they just practiced.

☞

A. Reader's Response: First Thoughts

? What is a "quiet mind"? [Sample responses: One that is controlled by the will; one that stays calm; one that belongs to a self-contained person.]

B. Language Note: Pun

? Which word in this line can be read as a pun? [*Arms* can mean a woman's arms or an army's weapons.]

C. Reader's Response: Extending the Text

? What besides honor might someone need to love in order to love another person? [Sample responses: Country, parents, self, God.]

D. Literary Element: Paradox

Paraphrase the paradox of the last two lines. [Possible answer: Contrary to what you would expect me to say—that I love you more than anything—it is only because I love something more than you that I can love you as much as I do.]

The English Civil Wars are the backdrop to this poem. Like John Donne's "A Valediction: Forbidding Mourning" (page 248), the poem takes the form of a lover's goodbye to his beloved. Unlike Donne's, Lovelace's speaker is full of noble sentiments. It is tempting to identify Lovelace himself with this speaker, for the poet was an idealist about king and country, ready to sacrifice his happiness, fortune, and life in their service.

To Lucasta, on Going to the Wars

Richard Lovelace

Tell me not, sweet, I am unkind,
    That from the nunnery°
(A) Of thy chaste breast and quiet mind
    (B) To war and arms I fly.

5 True, a new mistress now I chase,
    The first foe in the field;
And with a stronger faith embrace
    A sword, a horse, a shield.

Yet this inconstancy is such
10   As you too shall adore;
(C) I could not love thee, dear, so much,
    (D) Loved I not honor more.

2. nunnery: metaphor for a pure, safe place.

George Clifford, 3rd earl of Cumberland (16th century) by Nicholas Hilliard.
National Maritime Museum, London.

OPTIONS FOR TEACHING

INTEGRATING THE LANGUAGE ARTS

Strategic Reading After they have read the poems by the Cavalier poets, ask students to create a chart like the one below and jot down characteristics of the poets and their work. This chart will show trends and similarities.

Poet	Characteristics	Features in the poetry
[Lovelace]	[soldier]	[uses military as metaphor]

COOPERATIVE LEARNING

Choral Reading Choral reading may be used as a subtle way of providing support for less able readers by giving them a model to follow. When using choral reading, make sure each group has at least one strong reader who feels confident with the material. Take time to plan pauses and breathing with each group. In reading "To Althea, from Prison," for example, students may plan to breathe after the first four lines of each stanza because in each case there is either a semicolon or period (a longer pause). Remind students that when there is enjambment, they should simply continue on at the end of a line with no pause. Make sure that students have adequate time and a place to practice where they can hear themselves.

Like "To Lucasta, on Going to the Wars," this poem follows the fashion, set by Sir Philip Sidney and Ben Jonson, of giving the women in poems classical names. Whether real women are hidden behind the names Lucasta and Althea, we do not know, nor does it matter, for there is little or no connection between having a love affair and the ability to write a good poem. We do know that Lovelace was imprisoned during the Civil Wars, and it seems likely that a man as attractive as he was would be visited by a female admirer.

To Althea, from Prison

Richard Lovelace

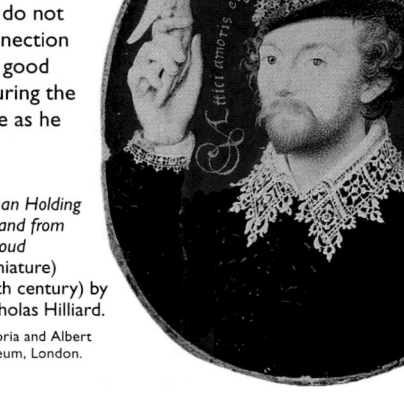

A Man Holding a Hand from a Cloud (miniature) (16th century) by Nicholas Hilliard.
Victoria and Albert Museum, London.

When Love with unconfinèd wings
   Hovers within my gates,
And my divine Althea brings
   To whisper at the grates;
5 When I lie tangled in her hair
   And fettered to her eye,
The gods° that wanton° in the air
   Know no such liberty.

When flowing cups run swiftly round,
10 With no allaying Thames,°
Our careless heads with roses bound,
   Our hearts with loyal flames;
When thirsty grief in wine we steep,
   When healths and drafts go free,
15 Fishes that tipple in the deep
   Know no such liberty.

When, like committed linnets,° I
   With shriller throat shall sing
The sweetness, mercy, majesty,
20 And glories of my King;°
When I shall voice aloud how good
   He is, how great should be,
Enlargèd° winds that curl the flood°
   Know no such liberty.

25 Stone walls do not a prison make,
   Nor iron bars a cage:
Minds innocent and quiet take
   That for an hermitage.°
If I have freedom in my love,
30 And in my soul am free,
Angels alone, that soar above,
   Enjoy such liberty.

7. gods: In many seventeenth-century versions of this poem, "gods" is replaced by "birds." **wanton:** frolic.

10. allaying Thames (temz): That is, the wine is not diluted with water from the Thames River.

17. committed linnets: caged birds.

20. my King: Charles I, king of England from 1625 to 1649.

23. enlargèd: released. **flood:** sea.

28. hermitage: holy refuge.

A. Critical Reading: Finding Details
Find four words in this stanza, two of which refer to freedom and two of which refer to being chained. [*Unconfinèd, liberty; tangled, fettered.*]

B. Literary Element: Paradox
Lovelace uses these words to create the tension of paradox in his poem.

C. Critical Reading: Making Inferences
? What freedoms do fishes have? What do they lack? [Possible answers: They have the freedom to go where they wish. They lack good fellowship and camaraderie.]

D. Critical Reading: Making Inferences
? What freedoms do the winds have? What do they lack? [Possible answers: They, like the fish, go where they wish. They lack the ability to make a commitment.]

E. Critical Reading: Summarizing
? What kinds of activities can walls and bars allow? [Possible answers: Free thought, commitment, love, or friendship. Abstraction, anything that has to do with the mind or heart.]

F. Reader's Response: Extending the Text
? Do you agree with the opinion expressed in the last four lines? Why or why not? [Sample responses: I agree that, among living things on earth, only humans enjoy the freedom to make decisions and to love. Or I don't agree; you can be free in your mind and soul but still be oppressed in your everyday life, making it hard to express the freedom you feel inside.]

Conflicting Duties In "To Lucasta, on Going to the Wars," the speaker resolves a problem by showing that one duty has higher claims on him than another. Students preparing to move away from home may have some concerns in this area. Have students interview someone about a time he or she experienced a conflict between two duties and how the person resolved or dealt with the problem. *You may want to obtain permission from parents or guardians and from the parties students will contact before they begin this activity.*

Check Test: Multiple Choice
1. In "Why So Pale and Wan, Fond Lover?," the speaker chides his friend for (a) continuing interest in a woman whom nothing will move to love (b) paying court in an outdated style (c) shaming him in front of the woman they both love [a]
2. The speaker in "To Lucasta, on Going to the Wars" argues that (a) she should go to a nunnery (b) his new mistress is more beautiful than Lucasta (c) if he did not honor his commitment to serve in the army, he would not be an honorable lover [c]
3. The speaker in "To Althea, from Prison," finds freedom (a) by escaping from prison (b) by imagining he is not confined (c) in his mind even though his body is in a cell [c]

Making Meanings

First Thoughts

1. They might agree that love is worth pursuing but that pride and honor must come before love.

Shaping Interpretations

2. He tells the lover that the woman cannot be made to love him and to forget her. His tone goes from concerned to annoyed to disgusted. In "To Lucasta" the tone is patient, and in "To Althea," peaceful.

3. He uses "mistress" to refer to the army; "chase" to describe his battlefield foe; "embrace" to describe his allegiance to the military; and "inconstancy" to describe his departing from Lucasta for the field of battle. Possible response: It leaves out the ugliness and horror of war.

4. The paradoxes are resolved in the last stanza, ll. 11–12. He is suggesting that a woman cannot expect a man to be loyal to her if he does not honor his other commitments.

5. Most students will point to l. 10, although the reader has only the speaker's words, not Lucasta's.

6. He compares himself to others that seem to have more, but as he states, actually have less liberty. In the last comparison he shows likeness, not difference.

7. The speaker has eyes for Althea alone and is figuratively chained to her glance.

8. Stone walls and iron bars cannot imprison a mind. He feels free because he may still love Althea and praise his king.

9. The poem implies that mental conformity or abandoning one's personal values creates a prison far more confining than a jail. Agree— you cannot be free if you do not stay true to yourself. Or disagree —I cannot imagine anything worse than prison.

Extending the Texts

10. **(Synthesis)** Possible responses: A modern woman would tell Suckling's speaker that he is self-centered. A modern Lucasta would agree that you have to be principled in order to love. A modern Althea would equate the prisoner's situation with that of other political prisoners.

MAKING MEANINGS

Why So Pale and Wan, Fond Lover?
To Lucasta, on Going to the Wars
To Althea, from Prison

First Thoughts

1. Imagine Suckling and Lovelace discussing their conceptions of love. What would they agree and disagree on?

Shaping Interpretations

2. In "Why So Pale and Wan, Fond Lover?" what advice does the **speaker** give the pale lover? What is his **tone,** and how does it differ from Lovelace's in "To Lucasta" and "To Althea"?

3. In "To Lucasta," how does the **speaker** use **metaphors** of love to describe war? What do you think of these romantic ways of talking about war?

4. The speaker in "To Lucasta" implies two **paradoxes:** that his inconstancy (line 9) is really constancy and that to be loyal he must be disloyal. According to the speaker, how could these seemingly contradictory statements be true?

5. What evidence can you find in "To Lucasta" for believing that Lucasta has the same values as the speaker and will therefore not whine or scold him for losing her?

6. In "To Althea," what comparison is made in each stanza's final two-line **refrain**? What is different about the last comparison?

7. How would you explain line 6 in "To Althea"?

8. In "To Althea," what is the famous **paradox** stated in lines 25–26? What makes the jailed speaker free?

9. What does "To Althea" imply about what *does* make a prison? Do you agree or disagree?

Extending the Texts

10. Again, we have three poems either addressed to women or about a woman's treatment of a man. But the women's feelings are unknown. What do you imagine a modern woman's response would be to each speaker?

CHOICES:
Building Your Portfolio

Writer's Notebook

1. Collecting Ideas for an Interpretive Essay

Paraphrasing is a useful technique for preparing to write about any literary work. To paraphrase, you put a literary text into your own words. Paraphrasing helps you to check your own understanding of the work, particularly your understanding of metaphors or paradoxes, and your reading of any unusual syntax. Paraphrasing helps you identify places where your understanding is solid, or places where you need to think more about the text's meaning. Paraphrase any one of the three poems by the Cavalier poets. Save your work for possible use in the Writer's Workshop on page 275.

Critical Writing

2. The Poem Across Time

Does "To Althea, from Prison"—a poem about liberty and bondage—have any relevance to late-twentieth-century life? In a brief essay, give your opinion, referring to actual world conditions or events and citing specific passages from the poem to support your views.

Creative Writing

3. A Modern Lucasta

Write out a modern Lucasta's answer to a man who delivered this poem to her as he set off to war.

Beyond the Poems

Choices: Building Your Portfolio

1. **Writer's Notebook** Remind students to save their work. They may use it as prewriting for the Writer's Workshop on p. 275.

2. **Critical Writing** Discuss political prisoners and others who do not enjoy full rights and freedoms before introducing the topic.

PORTFOLIO ASSESSMENT

Choices: Assessment Criteria For help in evaluating these Choices assignments, see the criteria in the *Portfolio Management System,* p. 97.

Chile

Pablo Neruda campaigning in Chile (1969).

Pablo Neruda
(1904–1973)

I have lived singing and defending them," Pablo Neruda said of the Chilean people. Neruda had two passions in his life: poetry and politics. Neruda was writing poetry seriously by the age of ten. At fourteen, he was literary editor of a newspaper. He published a hugely popular collection of love poems at twenty, and finally, in 1971, he won the Nobel Prize in literature.

Neruda was equally fervent about government service and human rights activism—concerns that often put his life in danger. In 1948, Neruda's anti-censorship writings forced him to cross the Andes and flee his beloved Chile, but by 1952 he returned a hero. Even at the end of his life, Neruda faced possible exile. Just twelve days before Neruda died, Marxist President Salvador Allende—whom Neruda helped elect—was overthrown and possibly murdered in a bloody revolt by right-wing military leaders.

(Map) ©Rand McNally.

PABLO NERUDA 267

CONNECTING WITH "LOVE, DEATH, AND TIME"

Love, death, and time are universal **themes** in poetry and prose, but approaches to them may change from era to era or culture to culture. What aspects of love does Neruda emphasize in his sonnets that are not emphasized by the Elizabethans? [Possible answer: Neruda emphasizes the joining of two lovers so closely that they share everything—even their bodies.]

A Dialogue with the Text

Point out that the poems are presented in Spanish and English. Encourage students to read first whichever poem they are more comfortable with. Students who know Spanish as either a first or a second language can read both and compare their responses to each of them.

BEFORE YOU READ
SONNETS 17 AND 79

Background

Mention the Renaissance poets, and the word *love* comes to mind almost immediately. Their sonnets resonate with the passion born of true love. But the Renaissance does not hold exclusive rights to this often mysterious emotion. Poets in modern times have also explored the experience of love.

The sonnets you are about to read were originally written in Spanish by the famous Chilean poet Pablo Neruda. You may not have had the experience Neruda describes in his sonnets. The speaker and his beloved are mature; they have probably been intimately connected for a long time. Maybe you've known such a deep love, but maybe not.

A Dialogue with the Text

READER'S LOG

As you read these love sonnets, think about the speaker's emotions. Jot down in your Reader's Log what you recognize from your own experience—or from your hopes. If possible, listen to the sonnets read aloud in Spanish to hear their special music.

The Lover's Rock (1963) by David Alfaro Siqueiros.
Mixed media on masonite (80 cm × 60 cm).
Private Collection.

OPTIONS FOR TEACHING

STRATEGIES FOR INCLUSION

Auditory Have a Spanish reader and an English reader alternate readings of Neruda's sonnets. Ask students to compare the sounds and to decide if the Spanish and English versions evoke similar or different feelings.

Visual Ask students to draw a simple box divided into four and to place a sketch for each of the stanzas of Neruda's "Sonnet 17" in each box.

Stanza 1	2
3	4

Intrapersonal Have students choose their favorite poem from the Collection, including Neruda's. Tell them to practice saying the piece with appropriate expression. Then, hold a poetry reading in class. Students can read their choice of selection and answer questions from listeners. If two students choose the same poem, have them each read it, though perhaps not one immediately following the other. They will probably read it differently.

Sonnet 17

Pablo Neruda

translated by **Stephen Tapscott**

I do not love you as if you were salt-rose, or topaz, (A)
or the arrow of carnations the fire shoots off.
I love you as certain dark things are to be loved,
in secret, between the shadow and the soul.

5 I love you as the plant that never blooms
but carries in itself the light of hidden flowers; (B)
thanks to your love a certain solid fragrance,
risen from the earth, lives darkly in my body.

I love you without knowing how, or when, or from where.
10 I love you straightforwardly, without complexities or pride; (C)
so I love you because I know no other way

than this: where *I* does not exist, nor *you*,
so close that your hand on my chest is my hand, (D)
so close that your eyes close as I fall asleep.

Soneto 17

No te amo como si fueras rosa de sal, topacio
o flecha de claveles que propagan el fuego:
te amo como se aman ciertas cosas oscuras,
secretamente, entre la sombra y el alma.

5 Te amo como la planta que no florece y lleva
dentro de sí, escondida, la luz de aquellas flores,
y gracias a tu amor vive oscuro en mi cuerpo
el apretado aroma que ascendió de la tierra.

Te amo sin saber cómo, ni cuándo, ni de dónde,
10 te amo directamente sin problemas ni orgullo:
así te amo porque no sé amar de otra manera,

sino así de este modo en que no soy ni eres,
tan cerca que tu mano sobre mi pecho es mía,
tan cerca que se cierran tus ojos con mi sueño.

A. Critical Reading: Making Inferences

? How would the speaker love a salt-rose or topaz? How would that love be felt and expressed? [Students may talk about loving a possession or a cherished object as opposed to a person. That kind of love might be expressed through looking at, touching, or just thinking about the object.]

B. Reader's Response: First Thoughts

Imagine what this kind of love feels like and looks like. Draw a picture of a person feeling this kind of love.

C. Literary Element: Sonnet

? How is this arrangement, or form, different from the other sonnets you have seen? [The others had either an octave and sestet or three quatrains and a couplet. This, like Petrarch's sonnets, has two quatrains and then, unlike other forms, a divided sestet, or two triplets.]

D. Critical Reading: Identifying Main Ideas

? What is the main idea about love in this poem? [Love has made the speaker's beloved so much a part of him that they share a single body.]

CROSSING THE CURRICULUM

Social Sciences In order to supplement their background material, ask several students to do a little research on Chile, Salvador Allende, or the Nobel Prize and to report orally to the class on their topics. Ask students to write an outline that they may copy so that their classmates may follow their presentation more easily.

ASSESSMENT TOOLS

Check Test: True-False
1. Neruda has nothing in common with the English Renaissance poets. [False]
2. Neruda wrote in Spanish. [True]
3. Neruda won the Nobel Prize in literature. [True]
4. Neruda was Argentinian. [False]
5. Neruda became president of his country. [False]

A. Language Note: Translation

In l. 4 of the translation, the sound and sense match because the consonant blends, the w's, and the heavy stresses give the effect of a thick, wet wall. However, the Spanish version sounds quite different. Ask a native speaker of Spanish to read the Spanish version. Then, ask students to consider whether or not the above comments about l. 4 are important in interpreting the poem. [Answers will vary. Some students will take the striking differences between the original and the translation to mean that such detailed observations are irrelevant. Others may think that it is appropriate to analyze whichever version of a poem is available to you as thoroughly as possible, while recognizing that the translation makes sense in ways different from the original.]

B. Reader's Response: Extending the Text

Surreal means "portraying or interpreting the workings of the unconscious mind as manifested in dreams." Do you think this section of the poem may be surreal? Why or why not? [Sample responses: Some students may feel that they do not have enough information to reach a decision. Some may take the sharp break after the first quatrain to indicate that the speaker has fallen asleep and the disconnected images in the second quatrain are the products of a dream.]

C. Critical Reading: Making Inferences

[?] What is the "constancy that beats in your chest"? [Your heart and faithful love.]

Finding Common Ground

What is romantic love? Have students make a chart like the one below to help them clarify the similarities and differences in the ideas about love expressed in the poem.

The Poems of Neruda	The Poems of Renaissance Poets	Me
[Secret] [Passionate]	[Declared/ not secret] [Passionate, usually]	[Known] [Passionate]

Sonnet 79

Pablo Neruda

translated by **Stephen Tapscott**

By night, Love, tie your heart to mine, and the two
together in their sleep will defeat the darkness
like a double drum in the forest, pounding
against the thick wall of wet leaves.

5   Night travel: black flame of sleep
that snips the threads of the earth's grapes,
punctual as a headlong train that would haul
shadows and cold rocks, endlessly.

Because of this, Love, tie me to a purer motion,
10 to the constancy that beats in your chest
with the wings of a swan underwater,

so that our sleep might answer all the sky's
starry questions with a single key,
with a single door the shadows had closed.

Soneto 79

De noche, amada, amarra tu corazón al mío
y que ellos en el sueño derroten las tinieblas
como un doble tambor combatiendo en el bosque
contra el espeso muro de las hojas mojadas.

5   Nocturna travesía, brasa negra del sueño
interceptando el hilo de las uvas terrestres
con la puntualidad de un tren descabellado
que sombra y piedras frías sin cesar arrastrara.

Por eso, amor, amárrame al movimiento puro,
10 a la tenacidad que en tu pecho golpea
con las alas de un cisne sumergido,

para que a las preguntas estrelladas del cielo
responda nuestro sueño con una sola llave,
con una sola puerta cerrada por la sombra.

FINDING COMMON GROUND

Even if, after listening to the poems' speakers, you did not say, "Those could be *my* words," you may have said "Yes!" to some ideas, moods, feelings, and images. Then again, you may have some arguments to pick with Neruda or his speakers: Your ideas about love may not always mesh with theirs. What is your reaction?

- What do you think Sonnet 17 means about love being dark and secret?
- What do you think of the ideas that love completes people and that it unites them so that they seem as one person? Have you encountered that idea in other poems in this collection? Where?
- Could you relate to the fear of night in Sonnet 79? Do you think love is the answer?
- What was your favorite **image** in each poem?
- Does Neruda use complex **metaphors** that remind you of the metaphysical poets' love of complex and unusual comparisons? Point out one or two examples.
- Do Neruda and the Renaissance poets hold similar notions about love, or are they very different?
- Do you find in Neruda's poems a conviction that love conquers time—as you find in Renaissance poetry?
- Where do your thoughts on love fall—close to Neruda or to the Renaissance poets?

Use your notes to discuss with classmates what you think romantic love is, what it means to people today, and what it has meant in ages past.

The English Language

The Birth of Modern English

*by **John Algeo***

The Modern English period can be dated from 1485, when Henry VII, the first Tudor king of England, came to the throne. The House of Tudor brought peace to the land, introduced the Reformation and Renais-sance to England, helped to promote a pride in things English, and began the spread of our language all over the world. Just ten years before, in 1475, William Caxton had printed the first book in English. That event might also be taken as marking the beginning of the Modern period, for printed books were to help unify and spread English and make the opportunity to read and write readily available to all English-speaking people.

Aerial map and view across the Thames from the South Bank, with St. Paul's and London Bridge (c. 1730) by J. B. Homans.

British Library, London.

A. Exploring the Historical Period

When William Caxton (c. 1422–1491) set up his press at Westminster, he began a great communications revolution. Before 1500, only a total of thirty-five thousand books were printed throughout Europe, mostly in Latin. Between 1500 and 1640, in England alone, more than twenty thousand new items were printed in English. Literacy rose accordingly; by 1600, nearly half the people in towns and cities had minimal literacy.

PROGRAM MANAGER

Planning Instruction See Teaching Notes, *Teaching Resources A*, p.62 for objectives for this selection.
Assessment See The English Language, *Test Booklet*, pp. 51–52.

Elements of Literature:
Videodisc Use the bar codes below to access information about the English language. For more information, see the Videodisc *Teacher's Manual.*

Videodisc Side A
Begin Play
English Track

Begin Play
Spanish Track

A. Language Note: Pronunciation

The change in vowel sounds may look haphazard, but in fact, it is very regular and patterned. Each of the "long" or tense vowels came to be pronounced with the tongue a little higher in the mouth. The two that were originally highest turned into diphthongs (combinations of two vowels pronounced together). The Great Vowel Shift probably began late in the fourteenth century, shortly before Chaucer's death, and was completed during the first years of the Early Modern English period.

B. Language Note: Pronunciation

Read aloud the different pronunciations of the sentence *See the same old moon in the cloudy sky.* Students who have studied modern French, Spanish, or German may notice that the Middle English vowels are like the vowels of these modern European languages.

C. Expansion

The Middle English spelling that Caxton adopted for writing Early Modern English had used the five vowel letters more or less the same way that they are still used in writing Spanish, French, or German. In the post–Great Vowel Shift pronunciation, however, the sounds originally represented by the five vowel letters had become quite different. Because English adopted a pre–Great Vowel Shift spelling for post–Great Vowel Shift sounds, today English speakers use the five vowel letters in a way different from that of other European languages.

The Language Changes That Made Modern English

When William Caxton printed the first books in English, he tried to make them look as much like handwritten manuscripts as he could. The shapes of the letters in his type font, the spellings he used, his choice of words and sentence structures—all suggested the manuscript writing of an earlier time. Because printing was a newfangled invention, Caxton wanted his printed books to look as much as possible like the manuscripts that people were familiar with. Yet, despite his efforts, it is clear that the language of the late 1400s and early 1500s was a new form of English.

English during the first part of the Modern period, when it still resembled Middle English in some ways and had not yet reached the form we recognize as our own, is known as Early Modern English. That term embraces English from about 1485 through the mid-1700s.

Grammatical differences between Middle and Modern English were not very great. Middle English had already lost many of the inflections of Old English. The few it kept and passed on to Early Modern English are mainly ones we still have today: the plural ending *–s* and the possessive ending *–'s* for nouns; the comparative and superlative endings *–er* and *–est* for adjec-

tives; and the verb endings for the past tense (*–ed*), past participle (*–ed* or *–en*), present participle (*–ing*), and the third-person singular of the present tense (*–s*). In place of that *–s,* Early Modern English also had an ending we no longer use, *–eth,* and in addition one for the second-person singular, *–est* (as in "he thinketh" and "thou thinkest").

Shifting Vowels

The greatest change between Middle and Early Modern English was in the pronunciation of the "long" or tense vowels, illustrated by these words (given in their present-day spellings): *bite, feet, cane, mouse, boot, load.* In Middle English times, the vowels of these words had been pronounced as follows: *bite* like "beet," *feet* like "fate," *cane* like "khan" or "con," *mouse* like "moose," *boot* like "boat," and *load* like "laud" or "(out–)lawed."* The sentence *See the same old moon in the cloudy sky* would have sounded in Middle English something like "Say the sahm awld moan in the cloody skee."

If we could go back to Chaucer's London by a time-travel machine, our first impression would be that some language other than English was being spoken. After a while, however, we would probably get used to it and decide that it was English after all, although pronounced very oddly.

No one knows why these changes (called the Great Vowel Shift) happened—many such big changes in language are inexplicable. However, something rather similar is going on in some varieties of English today. In New York City, Philadelphia, and various other places, especially in the middle part of the East Coast and westward from there, words like *bad, cab,* and *fan* sound something like "behd," "kehb," and "fehn." If that kind of change should become general and extend to other words and other parts of the country, two hundred years from now, people may be pronouncing *See the same old moon in the cloudy sky* something like "Sigh the seem oold mown in the clawdy skay." Stranger things have happened in the history of languages, and that change is no more improbable than was the Great Vowel Shift five hundred years ago.

Lagging Spelling

Ever since 1475, when books were first printed in English, we have had a tendency to keep our spelling unchanged, whatever happens to our pronunciation. Therefore, our spelling tends to become further and further out of line with the way we say words. When Caxton started printing books, he used a spelling for English that was already old-fashioned; and we have done little to modernize it since.

Ever since English first began to be printed, people have worried about the failure of our spelling to match our pronuncia-

> Because British explorers, merchants, and settlers had an itch to travel, and scratched it vigorously, the English language has never been the same.

STRATEGIES FOR INCLUSION

Less Proficient Readers Review the endings and the sound changes on p. 272 by recording them on the chalkboard, discussing them, and modeling the sound shifts.

Advanced/Linguistic Encourage students to use *The Oxford English Dictionary* to explore the etymologies of one group of words listed on p. 273. This will familiarize them with word

roots and in some cases show them the changes a word has gone through from the original language to Old or Middle English to modern English.

Logical-Mathematical Encourage students to try to find patterns in Shaw's alphabet on p. 274. For example, it seems the compound sounds have more complicated symbols.

English Language Development Before students read this section, illustrate what is meant by

"long" and "short" vowels. Explain that although English has only five vowel letters, there are many more vowel sounds. Ask students whose native language is not English if this is true in their native language, or if there is only one vowel sound for each vowel letter. Read aloud the list of words with "long" vowel sounds on p. 272 and have students repeat the words. Illustrate the point further by giving students pairs of words to recite, such as *bit/bite* or *fit/feet.*

tion. Many proposals have been made to reform English spelling, ranging from simply omitting silent letters, as in *tho* for *though* and *thru* for *through*, to more thorough reforms: "Wun sistem uv spelling wood seek tu eeliminaet awl iregguelarity." There have been even more radical suggestions, such as abandoning the Latin alphabet altogether and adopting a new one. One example is called the Shaw alphabet, designed for a contest set up by the twentieth-century writer George Bernard Shaw in his will. An example of the Shaw alphabet follows.

> ꙅᏉ ꓲᒫ ꓑᏉꓱᒪᐠꓑ ꓲᒫ Ꝺ ·Ꮯᴢ
> ᴠᏟꓵꓲꓵꓵᴥ, Ꝑ ꓘꓵᒪᴥꓵꓕ Ꝑ ꓑꓵꓵꓑꓵᴄ,
> ᐠ ᴀᒪᴥᴠᴥ ᴄꝐ ꙅʜᴄꓲᒪ ᴄᴥꝺᴄꓵᒪᴄꓲ.

Serious spelling reform has little chance of success. English speakers have been remarkably faithful to the spellings that were decided upon during the Early Modern English period. We seem unlikely to change them now.

O Brave New World: The Spread of English and Foreign Influences

The reign of Queen Elizabeth I saw the beginning of the extension of English to the far corners of the world. The British established colonies in North America—in a land they called Virginia after the Virgin Queen and later in New England and many other places. Exploration, settlement, and commerce all led to the borrowing of words from many other languages.

French contributed *bigot, bombast, duel, explore, jaunty, moustache, shock,* and *vogue.* From Italian came *balcony, cameo, design, duo, fugue, grotto, portico, stanza, trill,* and *violin;* from Spanish or Portuguese, *alligator, apricot, banana, brocade, corral, hammock, renegade,* and *tobacco;* from Indian languages of Central America and the Caribbean, by way of Spanish, *avocado, cannibal, chocolate, maize, potato,* and *tomato;* from Dutch, *cruise, deck, freight, keel, skipper, smuggle, yacht, duffel, spool, knapsack, easel, etch,* and *landscape.*

The adventures of British explorers, merchants, and settlers during the Early Modern English period enriched our vocabulary immensely. Because they had an itch to travel, and scratched it vigorously, the English language has never been the same.

The New Learning: Classical Influences

While English was picking up words from languages abroad, it did not neglect the classical languages, Latin and Greek. The literature, art, philosophy, history, and culture of Rome and Athens were taken as ideals during the Renaissance. Naturally, modern European languages, including English, also borrowed words from Latin and Greek.

Manuscript map of Raleigh's Virginia (c. 1585) by John White.
© British Museum, London.

Among many other words, English borrowed from Latin *abdomen, area, compensate, delirium, editor, gradual, imitate, janitor, medium, orbit, peninsula, quota, series, strict, superintendent, ultimate, urban,* and *urge.* From Greek, usually by way of Latin and sometimes other intermediate languages, came *aristocracy, barbarous, chaos, comedy, cycle, drama, epoch, history, mystery, rhythm, theory, tragedy,* and *zone.*

D. Expansion
This says "One system of spelling would seek to eliminate all irregularity." Note that some words (*eliminate* and *irregularity*) are more complicated when spelled phonetically. Have students suggest other spelling reforms, or have them try to spell their names phonetically.

E. Exploring the Historical Period
Old English was developing into a standard language in the interval between invasions by Norsemen and Normans, but its full development was cut short by the Conquest of 1066. Thereafter, since French was used as the language of government, no variety of English had the opportunity of developing into a standard. During the Early Modern English period, however, such a standard did arise, and has existed ever since.

INTEGRATING THE LANGUAGE ARTS

Strategic Reading To summarize the contents of "The Birth of Modern English," have students enter the headings in the text and the main ideas they find for each heading in a two-column chart like the one below.

HEADING	MAIN IDEAS

Speaking and Listening Play an audio or video recording of the scene in *My Fair Lady* or *Pygmalion* in which Henry Higgins first meets Eliza Doolittle and comments on her language. Ask students to listen for vowel differences and differences in enunciation. Have students make a quick two-column chart, one column marked "Eliza" and the other marked "Henry." They should jot down a vowel, such as "long e," in the appropriate column each time they hear a vowel sound. Discuss how these differences might relate to the contents of the essay. ☞

Try It Out: Answers

1. brooch (brōch, brōōch)
   creek (krēk; *often* krik)
   garage (gə•räzh´, -räj´; *Brit,*
   gar´äzh´, -ij)
   mature (mə•tŏŏr´, -chŏŏr´, -tyŏŏr´)
   roof (rōōf, rŏŏf)
   which (hwich, wich)

2. Some answers will depend on the dictionary a student has. Some dictionaries may provide no answer for particular words.
   adviser/advisor
   cater-cornered/cater-corner
   collectible/collectable
   cozy/cosy
   descendant/descendent
   finicky/finicking
   mama/mamma/momma
   parakeet/parrakeet

3. *balcony*—Italian, *brocade*—Spanish or Portuguese, *canoe*—Spanish, *catastrophe*—Greek, *landscape*—Dutch, *mustache*—French, *scientific*—Latin, *volcano*—Italian

4. Possible answers: Television, films, and radio.

5. "This is printed in the Shaw alphabet, the purpose of which is to reform our spelling completely."

The Rise of Standard English

Languages come in many varieties. A standard language is one that is used widely throughout a country and enjoys the respect of both those who use it and those who do not. It is typically the language of government and education.

The Early Modern English standard language was the result of several influences. The law clerks who recorded the proceedings of courts and who maintained the legal archives of England set a pattern of language usage that others followed. Especially important was the usage of the Court of Chancery, presided over by the Lord High Chancellor of England: Consequently, the widely used and prestigious form of Early Modern English is sometimes called Chancery Standard.

The introduction of the printing press, as already noted, helped to spread the new standard written language throughout England, making it available to all literate English speakers. Literacy was also increasing at this time. English people were reading the Book of Common Prayer (first published during the reign of Queen Elizabeth's brother and predecessor, King Edward VI) and the Authorized Version of the Bible (popularly known as the King James Bible because it was published during the reign of Elizabeth's successor, King James I). The phrases and rhythms of those two books, prayer book and Bible, were powerful influences in shaping the ideal of language to which English speakers looked during the Renaissance and for centuries after.

Try It Out

1. The fact that some words are pronounced in more than one way today is a sign that our language is still in the process of change. What pronunciations do you know for the following words? Look in a dictionary to see whether other pronunciations are listed.

   brooch   garage   roof
   creek   mature   which

2. Although our spelling is more consistent than that of the Renaissance, some words still have more than one possible spelling. What other spellings can the following words have? If you do not know, look in a dictionary.

   adviser   descendant
   cater-cornered   finicky
   collectible   mama
   cozy   parakeet

3. During the Renaissance, English borrowed words from many foreign languages. From what language does each of the following words come? Look up the words in a dictionary that gives etymologies.

   balcony
   brocade
   canoe
   catastrophe
   landscape
   mustache
   scientific
   volcano

4. The standard English of the Renaissance was based on the language used by the government in law courts and was spread by the printing press. What influences affect the way we talk and write today?

5. Using the following key, write the passage in the Shaw alphabet on page 273 in conventional spelling.

THE SHAW ALPHABET READING KEY
The letters are classified as Tall, Deep, Short, and Compound.
Beneath each letter is its full name; its sound is shown in **bold** type.

OPTIONS FOR TEACHING

ASSESSMENT TOOLS

Check Test: True-False

1. The most important change that brought English into the modern period was the Great Vowel Shift. [True]

2. Printers such as William Caxton tried to make printed books look less like handwriting. [False]

3. Some people worry about the failure of English spelling to match the pronunciation. [True]

4. English has borrowed words from only five other languages. [False]

5. Two books with a powerful impact on the English language were the Book of Common Prayer and the King James Bible. [True]

BUILDING YOUR PORTFOLIO
Writer's Workshop

The history of the written word is rich a
Page 1

EXPOSITORY WRITING
INTERPRETIVE ESSAY

One way you can make sense of any experience, including the experience of reading literature, is by **interpreting** it—explaining its meaning in your own words. In this Writer's Workshop, you'll write an interpretive essay about a literary work, aiming to explain the work's meaning and to convince your readers to accept your interpretation.

Prewriting

1. **Check your Writer's Notebook.** By doing the Writer's Notebook activities in this collection, you may have already done much of the prewriting for an interpretive essay. Check back over your Writer's Notebook entries. You can add to or change what you did in your Writer's Notebook, or you can proceed with the prewriting activities that follow.

2. **Act and react.** In a library, bookstore, or video store, find a work that's new to you and that you won't mind reading or viewing more than once. You might instead choose two different works, or two versions of a work (for example, a novel and its movie adaptation) to compare and contrast. Read or view the work.

   Usually, your first reaction to a work is a personal one: delight or dismay, liking or loathing. Take a few minutes to note your response in your Reader's Log, and don't worry about whether your response is "correct": No two people are likely to respond to any work in precisely the same way.

3. **Dig deeper.** To interpret the work for your readers, you need to move beyond personal response to **analysis**—reading (or viewing) the work critically to determine what its parts, or elements, are and how they work together. The charts below show the literary elements to look for in poetry

Elements of Poetry

Elements of Fiction

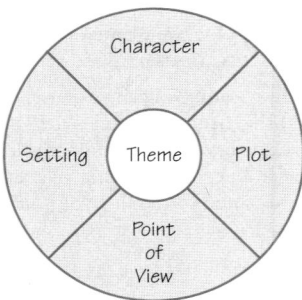

Technology HELP

See Writer's Workshop 2 CD-ROM. *Assignment: Interpretation.*

ASSIGNMENT
Write an interpretive essay of a literary work: a poem, a novel, a short story, or a play.

AIM
To inform; to explain; to persuade.

AUDIENCE
Your classmates or members of reading, literary, or film groups.

Try It Out
Working with a partner or a small group, identify the literary elements used in one of the following:
1. an episode of a TV sitcom or soap opera
2. a popular song

WRITER'S WORKSHOP 275

QUICK PLANNING GUIDE

Interpretive Essay

Prewriting
Check your Writer's Notebook **p. 275**
Act and react **p. 275**
Dig deeper **p. 275**
Strike the right note **p. 276**
Find a focus **p. 276**
Stake your claim **p. 276**
Search for support **p. 277**
Model **p. 277**
Get organized **p. 277**

Drafting
The introduction: setting the stage **p. 278**
The body: building your case **p. 278**
The conclusion: wrapping it up **p. 279**

Evaluating and Revising
Peer review **p. 279**
Self-evaluation **p. 279**

Proofreading and Publishing p. 279

Reflecting on Your Writing p. 279

Try It Out: Possible Answers
1. Students may find motif, climax, hyperbole, foil, protagonist, setting, and suspense among other literary elements.
2. Students may find refrain, tone, symbol, assonance, and alliteration among other literary elements.

PROGRAM MANAGER

Computer Guided Instruction For a related interpretation assignment that students may use as additional instruction, see *Writer's Workshop 2.*

PORTFOLIO ASSESSMENT

- **Generating Ideas** To help students in prewriting, use the heuristic in the *Portfolio Management System,* p. 98.
- **Assessment Rubric** For a rubric that can be used to assess students' progress in writing, see the *Portfolio Management System,* p. 100.

Motivation

Ask students to indicate how often they try to figure out why someone they know did a particular thing or what a person really meant when he or she said something. Point out to students that when they try to understand motives or real meanings, they are engaging in interpretation. Since human nature is central to literature, they can interpret literature in much the same way as they interpret the human behavior they experience every day. The interpretive essay they will write in this Writer's Workshop will help them refine skills that they already have and that they use on a daily basis.

and in fiction. Notice that theme is the central element—it's the key to interpreting any literary work.

Strategies for Elaboration: Analyzing a Work

Use the following strategies to analyze the elements of the work you've chosen.

- Read or view the work again, noting things you missed the first time. New insights may occur to you on a second reading or viewing.
- Interact with the author (or actors, or director). On a sheet of paper, draw two columns, labeling the first one "Note taking" and the second one "Note making." Use the first column to note words, images, and ideas that surprise or puzzle you or that occur more than once. In the second column, jot down your questions and comments about the items in column 1. (If you're working with a video, make liberal use of the pause and rewind buttons on the VCR.)
- Freewrite on the connection you see between the work and its title.
- For a short written work, make a copy for yourself and use different colors of markers to highlight the various literary elements.
- Compare your ideas about the work with the ideas of others who are familiar with it. Their interpretations may differ from yours, but their ideas may help you clarify your own thinking.

---

4. **Strike the right note.** Your purpose is to explain your claims, or major points, about the work's meaning in a way that will convince your readers that your ideas are sound. Knowing who your readers are and how much they already know about the work will help you decide how much background information they'll need and how to shape your argument in a convincing way.

 Usually, the tone of an interpretive essay is relatively formal, to show that the writer takes the work—and the audience—seriously. Avoid using contractions, colloquialisms, sentence fragments, and (unless your teacher suggests otherwise) first-person pronouns such as *I* or *we*.

5. **Find a focus.** In the space of a short essay, it would be difficult to analyze all the elements of a work. To make your interpretation manageable, look back at your personal response and your critical-reading notes. Which elements struck you most? How do those elements help bring out the theme? Choose the ones that seem most significant to you. (More than three may prove unwieldy.) For example, you might focus on how diction and imagery help develop the theme of a poem or on how point of view and character help reveal the theme of a short story.

6. **Stake your claim.** In a sentence or two, state your opinion about the relationship between the elements you've chosen and the work's theme. This preliminary thesis statement will make a useful guide for planning your paper. Keep in mind, though, that you may decide to change it as you gather information to support your opinion and begin drafting your paper.

OPTIONS FOR TEACHING

STRATEGIES FOR INCLUSION

Auditory Some students will find it easier to analyze and interpret shorter literary works if they are able to hear the works read aloud. Make oral readings available to students in several ways: Have students work in small groups on the same literary work, and have the groups read the work aloud; tape-record a reading of the work, or use a commercially prepared audiotape

of the work, and allow students to listen to the reading with headphones; allow students to read the work orally themselves and to tape-record their readings for future reference.

Visual Have students use a chart to organize the information they will use to support their thesis statements. A chart like the following may prove helpful.

Supporting Evidence

Ideas	Quotations	Details from and about the story	Secondary sources

7. **Search for support.** Since your thesis is an opinion, not a cut-and-dried fact, your readers expect you to back it up with reasons and evidence. Your reasons, which serve as the major points or claims of your essay, explain *why* you believe each of the elements you've chosen helps reveal the work's theme. Evidence for each of your reasons consists of ideas, quotations, and details from or about the work. Most evidence comes from the work itself (the *primary source*), but some may come from *secondary sources* such as books and articles about the work or its author.

Communications Handbook
H E L P

Evaluating sources: page 1210; taking notes and documenting sources: page 1211.

Model

Thesis Statement: In Sonnet 30, Edmund Spenser's imagery underscores his theme—that the speaker and his love are in direct opposition to each other.

Major Point: Spenser uses images of fire and ice, of hot and cold.

Evidence to Prove Major Point: In line 1, Spenser says, "My love is like to ice, and I to fire." In lines 5–6, he says, "Or how comes it that my exceeding heat / Is not delayed by her heart frozen cold."

Strategies for Elaboration: Gathering Support

Use the following strategies to gather the information you'll need to support your thesis statement.

• Read the work again with your thesis statement and major points in mind.

• Use note cards or separate sheets of paper to jot down ideas, details, and quotations that support your major points. You don't have to find *every* piece of evidence in the work, but *none* of the evidence in the work should contradict your thesis. (If you do find contradictory evidence, use it to revise your thesis statement.)

• Be sure to copy quotations exactly. For a written work, include the page numbers for quotations from a work of fiction or the line numbers for quotations from a work of poetry.

• If you draw on secondary sources, avoid plagiarism by noting the author, title, and date and place of publication so that you can credit your sources.

• Review your notes to make sure that all your evidence is directly related to your thesis statement.

8. **Get organized.** The easier your ideas are to follow, the more likely your readers will accept them. To organize your material, look again at your thesis statement and your main points. Assessing the kinds of elements you've chosen for your thesis can help you choose a sensible order for your ideas.

Teaching the Lesson

• Remind students as they prepare to write their interpretive essays that re-reading is an important step to uncovering elements that may be crucial to their arguments. They may also verify interpretations they have already made.

• Ask students to make notes before and after they have read or viewed the work a second time.

• This lesson includes instructions for each stage of the writing process. Guide students by modeling each stage with your own writing.

Prewriting

• Ask students to use the Elements of Poetry or the Elements of Fiction pie chart on p. 275 in analyzing the work they have chosen. Ask them to fill in the sections of the chart as they read or view the work for the first time. Remind them to include basic information as well as any unusual or interesting things they notice under each category as they watch or read.

• Ask students to use one of the Strategies for Elaboration on p. 277 as they view or read the work a second time. Have them compare the information they gathered the first time to that they gathered the second time before writing their first drafts.

INTEGRATING THE LANGUAGE ARTS

Strategic Reading As students read the Writer's Workshop text, ask them to summarize the main ideas given for each stage of the writing process. They may use a chart like the following for this purpose.

Writing an Interpretive Essay

Stage of Process	Key Idea	Class Notes

Grammar In quoting the text of the literary work or secondary sources, students may want to leave out some information that is irrelevant to their purposes. Refer them to the section on the use of the ellipsis points in the Language Handbook section of this textbook. Remind students that they must make sure that the information they delete by means of the ellipses does not change the meaning of the quotation in any way.

Usage Students sometimes use *there is* or *there's* with plural nouns, as in "There's often many good reasons for a character to act the way she does." Remind students when they proofread to check every instance of their use of *there is* and *there's* to make sure they are using the terms correctly.

Drafting

- Some students will benefit from seeing a model of an interpretive essay before they begin writing their drafts. Use models from students in other classes, or write an interpretive essay to use as a model. With students' help, highlight the thesis statement, the major points and evidence, and the restatement of the thesis.
- Provide students a sample list of works cited that includes references to books, interviews, magazines, and articles. They may follow these samples in completing their own lists.

Evaluating and Revising

Model for the class the process of evaluating an essay. Make a handout of a sample interpretive essay that needs revising. Have students help to identify in the sample essay the criteria from the Peer Review and Evaluation Criteria sections (p. 279) of the Writer's Workshop. The essay should exclude some of the important criteria, so that students may suggest ways to improve the essay based on the evaluation criteria and questions in the peer review.

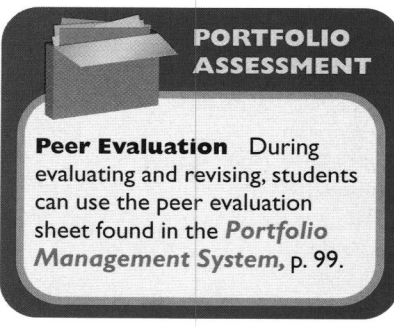

PORTFOLIO ASSESSMENT

Peer Evaluation During evaluating and revising, students can use the peer evaluation sheet found in the *Portfolio Management System,* p. 99.

Language Workshop HELP

Literary present: page 280.

Language Handbook HELP

Quotation marks: page 1247.

Communications Handbook HELP

Parenthetical citation: page 1212; list of Works Cited: page 1213.

- If you're focusing on diction and imagery, you might group related ideas in **logical order,** with points about diction in one group and points about imagery in a second group.
- For a thesis on character, you might arrange examples in **chronological order** to show how a character changes during the story. Or you could use **order of importance,** moving from your most important point to your least important one (or vice versa).
- If you're comparing and contrasting two works, you could treat each of the elements of one work first and then turn to those of the other work, or you could alternate between the works as you discuss each element.

Whichever method you choose, double-check to make sure that it suits the wording of your thesis statement.

Drafting

1. **The introduction: setting the stage.** In your introduction, identify the work's title and author (for a film, the title and either the director or the leading actor or both), and state your thesis. Provide just enough background information about the work so that your readers will be able to follow your ideas, but avoid summarizing the entire work. Remember that your readers are primarily interested in your insights about the work.

2. **The body: building your case.** As you develop the body of your essay, take one or more paragraphs to state each of your major points and to present the evidence that supports it. Use quotations from the work where they help you make a point especially well, but avoid simply stringing together a series of quotes. Instead, combine paraphrases of the author's ideas with your own conclusions about the work.

> ### Documenting Sources
>
> An important part of writing an interpretive essay is giving full credit to your sources. You'll credit your sources in two places in your essay—in parenthetical citations and in the list of Works Cited.
>
> **Parenthetical citations** are source references in parentheses in the body of your paper. Their purpose is to give the reader just enough information to locate the full source information on the Works Cited page at the end of your paper. In many cases, the author's last name and the page numbers are all that are needed. Parenthetical citations are normally placed before the end punctuation mark of the sentence, phrase, or clause you're documenting. For example, an essay on Edmund Spenser's Sonnet 30 might include the following parenthetical citation:
>
> > The speaker of Sonnet 30 is "the victim of his own actions—any increase in passion on his part ensures an increase in her resolve against him" (Gibbs 69).
>
> The list of **Works Cited** contains all the works you cite in your essay. Each listing includes the information readers need to locate the source. For example, the Works Cited entry corresponding to the parenthetical citation given above would be:
>
> > Gibbs, Donna. <u>Spenser's Amoretti: A Critical Study</u>. Brookfield: Gower, 1990.

History Ask students to read a historical document, such as Abraham Lincoln's Gettysburg Address or the Preamble to the U.S. Constitution. Ask them to approach this document as they would a literary work and to write an interpretive essay about the document. Students might find it useful to work together in small groups of three or four to brainstorm ideas for their essays. You may emphasize that literary elements, such as tone, point of view, diction, and figurative language, are as likely to be found in documents of this sort as they are in poetry and prose fiction.

Outside Texts If students are allowed to write about literary works that are not in this textbook, ask them to submit the work when they turn in their papers. Students should also include the work in their portfolios for future reference.

3. **The conclusion: wrapping it up.** Create a satisfying conclusion by stepping back once again to the focused overview you presented in your introduction. Don't just summarize your major points; instead, restate your thesis in a way that echoes the ideas in your introduction.

Evaluating and Revising

1. **Peer review.** As a peer reviewer, comment on these points:

   - **Context:** Does the writer provide enough background information about the work for you to follow the ideas?

   - **Clarity:** Does the thesis statement make clear the writer's focus?

   - **Proof:** Does the writer present enough evidence to convince you to accept the thesis? Are the major points and supporting evidence directly related to the thesis? Are the ideas easy to follow?

   - **Closure:** Does the ending tie the ideas together and reinforce the thesis?

2. **Self-evaluation.** Be open to feedback: Take advantage of comments that will help you make your interpretation clearer and more convincing, but remember that the final decisions are yours. Circle passages in your essay where you have provided context, clarity, proof, and closure. Revise your essay if you can't find a passage to circle for any of these points.

Proofreading and Publishing

Once you've revised your paper to your satisfaction, proofread it carefully—readers will take an error-free paper more seriously. Those readers could be the members of a local reading or literary group as well as your classmates and friends. (Film clubs might enjoy interpretive essays about movies.) Your school or local librarian might help you find other community groups that would enjoy reading, or hearing you read, your interpretation.

Reflecting on Your Writing

For your portfolio, write and date a brief reflection on the experience of writing an interpretive essay. Consider these questions:

1. Did the process of interpreting a literary work or film help you develop new insights into the work? Did it change your ideas about what's involved in creating a literary work or film? Explain your responses.

2. Which was harder for you, developing a thesis or building a convincing case for it? Why?

3. Which part, or parts, of the writing process will you approach differently the next time you write an interpretive essay? Why?

■ *Evaluation Criteria*

An effective interpretive essay

1. *includes an introduction that identifies the title and author (or director) of the work and gives necessary background information about it*

2. *includes a clear and precisely worded thesis statement*

3. *identifies major points that support the thesis*

4. *for each major point, gives ample, specific, and relevant supporting evidence*

5. *is clearly and consistently organized*

6. *has a conclusion that reinforces the thesis of the essay*

Revision
STRATEGIES

Does your conclusion round out your essay smoothly? If not, add a sentence or two using different forms of the key words in your thesis statement. Ask a writing partner to give feedback on your conclusion.

Language Workshop

Connecting to Students' Writing

Ask students to choose a piece of writing from their portfolios. Have them check any quotations they have cited to make sure the verbs are in the same tense the author used. Then, have them check the other verbs in the paper to make sure they are in the literary present. Ask them to exchange papers with another student to check each other's work.

Try It Out: Answers

1. Correct
2. Twice the speaker <u>writes</u> her name in the sand, and twice the waves <u>erase</u> her name.
3. Protesting, the woman <u>points</u> out that she herself "shall like to this decay."
4. The speaker <u>insists</u> that the woman "shall live by fame."

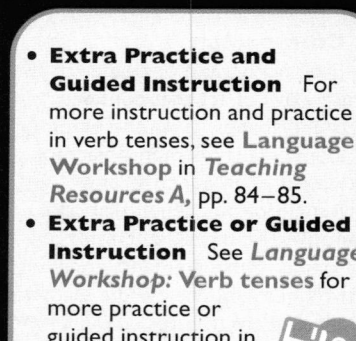

PROGRAM MANAGER

- **Extra Practice and Guided Instruction** For more instruction and practice in verb tenses, see **Language Workshop** in *Teaching Resources A,* pp. 84–85.
- **Extra Practice or Guided Instruction** See *Language Workshop:* **Verb tenses** for more practice or guided instruction in verb tenses.

Language Workshop

Technology HELP

See Language Workshop CD-ROM. *Key word entry: verb tenses.*

Language Handbook HELP

Tenses and their uses: page 1225.

Try It Out

Change the verbs that should be in the literary present in the following sentences.

1. The speaker in Spenser's Sonnet 75 proposes to immortalize his beloved's virtues.
2. Twice the speaker has written her name in the sand, and twice the waves have erased her name.
3. Protesting, the woman pointed out that she herself "shall like to this decay."
4. The speaker has insisted that the woman "shall live by fame."

SENSE THROUGH TENSE: THE LITERARY PRESENT

In English, every verb has six basic tenses to indicate different times when an action or state of being occurs: present, past, future, present perfect, past perfect, and future perfect. When you write, your readers rely on you to use tense forms correctly and consistently to help them understand the order in which things occur.

Each of the six tenses has its own uses. The present tense, for example, is used mainly to express a state of being or action taking place in the present. It also has several especially important uses, one of which is important in writing about literature. Called the **literary present,** this use of the present tense enables writers to summarize or analyze works that outlive their authors, in a sense taking on a life of their own. For example, in discussing one of Edmund Spenser's sonnets in an essay, you might write the following sentence:

> In Sonnet 75, Spenser's speaker **asserts** the eternal nature of his love.

The verb *asserts* is in the literary present.

Here's an important distinction to keep in mind: When you quote directly from a work, use the same tense the author uses, whatever it may be. But when you paraphrase the writer's ideas or draw your own conclusions about the work, use the literary present.

ORIGINAL *(past tense)*	One day I **wrote** her name upon the strand, But **came** the waves and **washèd** it away.
	—Edmund Spenser, Sonnet 75
PARAPHRASE *(literary present)*	The speaker in Edmund Spenser's Sonnet 75 **writes** his beloved's name in the sand, but the waves **erase** it.
CONCLUSION *(literary present)*	In line 5 of Sonnet 75, Spenser **uses** the word *vain* in two different senses: *conceited* and *fruitlessly.*

Writer's Workshop Follow-Up: Proofreading

Look back at the interpretive essay you wrote for the Writer's Workshop beginning on page 275. Have you used the literary present correctly? Check to make sure that in direct quotations you've used the same tense the writer used. Then check again, changing any verbs in your paraphrases of the work and in your own conclusions to the literary present. You might begin by focusing on one or two paragraphs: Circle each verb, and determine whether its tense is correct in that context.

✔ QUICK CHECK: Literary Present

Decide which verbs in the following sentences should be in the literary present tense, and change the ones that should be.

[1] The speaker in Christopher Marlowe's "The Passionate Shepherd to His Love" made promises to his love. [makes]

[2] He offered to make her comfortable with cushions of flowers. [offers]

[3] He also said she will have a beautiful embroidered skirt. [says]

[4] In Sir Walter Raleigh's poem, the young woman replied to Marlowe's shepherd. [replies]

[5] Her answer, based in reality, is a firm refusal. [Correct]

UNDER A HAND ACCURSED

Theme: **The Dark Side of Human Nature**
Two great writers explore the tragedy of evil, a subject which continues to fascinate humankind. Both selections take the reader on an inner journey that descends into the darkest abysses of the human psyche.

Thematic Focus

Many human relationships are marked by intelligence, warmth, and wit. However, when possessed by power, ambition, or greed, normally noble people may perpetuate truly evil acts. This Collection examines how such vices set the stage for a tragic downward spiral into evil—and presents one writer's prediction of the consequences.

- **The Tragedy of Macbeth** Shakespeare examines the motives behind murder and the crime's psychological effects on Macbeth and Lady Macbeth.
- *from* **The Inferno** *of* **The Divine Comedy** The agonies of sin are contemplated on an imaginary journey to Hell.

Literary Focus

Literary Element	Selection / Feature
Tragedy/Soliloquies/Asides/Imagery/ Figurative Language	**The Tragedy of Macbeth**

Writing Focus

The following flowchart shows how the writing assignment for the selection relates to the writing assignment presented in the Writer's Workshop at the end of the unit.

Selection	Work-in-Progress Assignment
The Tragedy of Macbeth	Collect ideas for a cause-effect essay p. 390
Writer's Workshop	Speculate about cause and effect p. 459

COLLECTION OPENER

T280A

Collection Planner

PUPIL'S EDITION

SELECTION/FEATURE	Literary Elements / Active Reading	Writing	Speaking and Listening	Language and Vocabulary
The Tragedy of Macbeth William Shakespeare (pp. 289–391) **Connections:** from **On the Knocking at the Gate in Macbeth** Thomas De Quincey (pp. 330–31) Critical Comment: Macbeth's Porter (p. 332) Critical Comment: The King's Evil (p. 367) Critical Comment: Hecate: Queen of the Night (p. 368) Critical Comment: Soliloquies and Asides (p. 383) Critical Comment: The Mystery of Evil (pp. 384–385) Connections: Macbeth and the Witches Richard Armour (pp. 386–387)	• Reader's Log p. 300 • Tragedy p. 300 • Blank Verse pp. 318, 385 • Soliloquies and Asides p. 383 • Character, Imagery, Poetry pp. 384–85 • Imagery and Figurative Language p. 389	• Critical Writing: Write character analysis p. 390 • Critical Writing: Write speculations about Macbeth p. 390 • Creative Writing: Rewrite banquet scene p. 390	• Oral Interpretation: Perform soliloquy in group p. 390 • Critical Thinking/ Speaking: Stage trial by jury p. 390	• Language and Style: Blank Verse p. 318 • How to Own a Word: Mapping p. 391
World Literature: from **The Inferno** Dante Alighieri Trans. by Robert Pinsky (pp. 392–398)	• Reader's Log p. 393		• Finding Common Ground: Discuss Dante's Hell p. 398	
The English Language: Shakespeare's Language John Algeo (pp. 399–402)				• Try It Out: Find examples p. 402

PROGRAM RESOURCES

Electronic Media	Teaching Resources with Organizer		Audiovisual Resources Binder
	Teaching Resources A	Other Resources	
• Test Generator • Language Work-shop: Active Voice	• Teaching Notes Introduction p. 87 Act I pp. 88–89 Act II p. 89 Act III p. 90 Act IV pp. 90–91 Act V pp. 91–92 The Play As A Whole p. 92 • Reading Organizer Act I p. 93 Act II p. 94 Act III p. 97 Act IV p. 98 Act V p. 99 • Words to Own pp. 95–96 • Language Link pp. 100–102	• Test Booklet: Selection Tests Act I pp. 57–58 Act II pp. 59–60 Act III pp. 61–62 Act IV pp. 63–64 Act V pp. 65–66 • Language and Writing Skills Worksheets pp. 43, 182 • Portfolio Management System pp. 48–49, 62–63, 101–102	• Elements of Literature Transparency 4.2 • How to Own a Word Transparency 4.3 • Selected Reading, Audiocassette 1, Side A
	• Teaching Notes p. 92		
• Test Generator • Videodisc, Side A: "Shakespeare's Tragic Heroes"	• Teaching Notes p. 92	• Test Booklet: Selection Test pp. 67–68	

Proofreading Warm-ups

You may use the following exercises to help students practice their proofreading skills. Copy a set of incorrect sentences onto the chalkboard, and have students find and correct the spelling, punctuation, usage, and mechanical errors in each sentence. Ask students to share and discuss their responses.

	Sentences with Errors	Sentences Corrected	Skills Covered
1	**a.** the english had been performing plays for several centurys before the renaissance **b.** medieval drama as a matter of fact evolved from church ceremonys such as the dialogue songs performed at easter	**a.** The English had been performing plays for several centuries before the Renaissance. **b.** Medieval drama, as a matter of fact, evolved from church ceremonies such as the dialogue songs performed at Easter.	Capitalization, Spelling, Comma usage, End marks
2	**a.** the first public theater, was called appropriately the Theater, it was built in 1576 by James Burbage **b.** the globe the most fameous of the public theaters was owned by Shakespeares company	**a.** The first public theater was called, appropriately, the Theater; it was built in 1576 by James Burbage. **b.** The Globe, the most famous of the public theaters, was owned by Shakespeare's company.	Capitalization, Comma usage, Semicolon usage, Spelling, End marks
3	**a.** the scenery of renaissance plays was kept to a minimum although the costumes was rich elaborate and expencive **b.** in addition to the costumes many props were used beds tents thrones and dragons among other things	**a.** The scenery of Renaissance plays was kept to a minimum, although the costumes were rich, elaborate, and expensive. **b.** In addition to the costumes, many props were used: beds, tents, thrones, and dragons, among other things.	Capitalization, Comma usage, Subject-verb agreement, Spelling, Colon usage, End marks
4	**a.** Shakespeare born in Stratford-on-Avon in 1564 wrote over thirty-six plays **b.** by 1599 Shakespeare was earning money as a playright a actor and a shareholder in a theater	**a.** Shakespeare, born in Stratford-on-Avon in 1564, wrote more than thirty-six plays. **b.** By 1599, Shakespeare was earning money as a playwright, an actor, and a shareholder in a theater.	Comma usage, Nonstandard usage, Capitalization, Spelling, End marks
5	**a.** by 1600, 6 of Shakespeares plays had been given command performances at the court of queen Elizabeth **b.** fortunatly for Shakespeare he prospered even more under Elizabeths successor King James of Scotland	**a.** By 1600, six of Shakespeare's plays had been given command performances at the court of Queen Elizabeth. **b.** Fortunately for Shakespeare, he prospered even more under Elizabeth's successor, King James of Scotland.	Capitalization, Comma usage, Write out numerals, Apostrophe usage, Spelling, End marks
6	**a.** for tomorrow read Act I of "The Tragedy of Macbeth" said Ms. Harden **b.** witch which says When the hurlyburly's done asked Mr. Jaramillo	**a.** "For tomorrow, read Act I of <u>The Tragedy of Macbeth</u>," said Ms. Harden. **b.** "Which witch says 'When the hurlyburly's done'?" asked Mr. Jaramillo.	Quotation marks, Capitalization, Comma usage, Underline play titles, Spelling, Question mark usage, End marks
7	**a.** blank verse or unrhymed iambic pentameter a form of poetry that comes close to imitating the natural rhythm's of english speech **b.** many of Shakespeares plays are written in blank verse	**a.** Blank verse, or unrhymed iambic pentameter, is a form of poetry that comes close to imitating the natural rhythms of English speech. **b.** Many of Shakespeare's plays are written in blank verse.	Capitalization, Comma usage, Sentence fragments, Apostrophe usage, End marks
8	**a.** soliloquies and asides is 2 useful devices for revealing to a audience a characters' innermost thoughts and feelings **b.** Macbeths changeing state's of mind is expressed in soliloquies	**a.** Soliloquies and asides are two useful devices for revealing to an audience a character's innermost thoughts and feelings. **b.** Macbeth's changing states of mind are expressed in soliloquies.	Capitalization, Subject-verb agreement, Write out numerals, Nonstandard usage, Apostrophe usage, Spelling, End marks
9	**a.** Dante Alighieri decided to write The Divine Comedy in Italian rather than Latin thus he became the father of Italian lit. **b.** this complex symbolic poem relates a imaginary journey thru Hell.	**a.** Dante Alighieri decided to write <u>The Divine Comedy</u> in Italian rather than Latin; thus, he became the father of Italian literature. **b.** This complex, symbolic poem relates an imaginary journey through Hell.	Underline long-poem titles, Semicolon usage, Comma usage, Write out abbreviation/Spelling, Nonstandard usage, End marks
10	**a.** shakespeares language is a early form of Modern English **b.** Shakespeares grammer however differ's in numerous ways from our's	**a.** Shakespeare's language is an early form of Modern English. **b.** Shakespeare's grammar, however, differs in numerous ways from ours.	Capitalization, Apostrophe usage, Nonstandard usage, Spelling, Comma usage, End marks

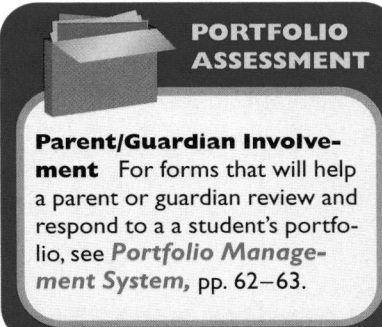

Shakespeare

Dante

Fate has given this man a spirit
Which is always pressing onwards, beyond control,
And whose mad striving overleaps
All joys of the earth between pole and pole.
Him shall I drag through the wilds of life
And through the flats of meaninglessness,
I shall make him flounder and gape and stick
And to tease his insatiableness
Hang meat and drink in the air before his watering lips;
In vain he will pray to slake his inner thirst,
And even had he not sold himself to the devil
He would be equally accursed.

—Johann Wolfgang von Goethe, *from Faust*

(Background) Orson Welles in his film production of *Macbeth* (1948).

Responding to the Quotation

? After reading Goethe's poem, what do you think the theme of this Collection might be? [Possible responses: As it refers to fate's toying with man's spirit, it may suggest there is no way to escape fate. There seems to be a connection between the Collection title and the last line of the poem, talking about someone who is accursed.]

PORTFOLIO ASSESSMENT

Parent/Guardian Involvement For forms that will help a parent or guardian review and respond to a a student's portfolio, see *Portfolio Management System,* pp. 62–63.

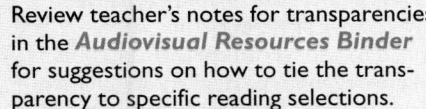

PROGRAM MANAGER

- **Integrated Assessment** For a summative assessment of the literary and language skills taught in this collection, see **Collection 4 Test,** *Test Booklet,* pp. 69–70.
- **Instructional Support** See **Fine Art Transparency** 4.1.

Review teacher's notes for transparencies in the *Audiovisual Resources Binder* for suggestions on how to tie the transparency to specific reading selections.
- **Extending Collection Theme** See **Cross-Curricular Activity: Under a Hand Accursed,** *Teaching Resources A,* p. 103 for an activity in another discipline and for evaluation criteria.
- **Reinforcement** Use the **Words to Own** worksheet in *Teaching Resources A,* pp. 95–96.

PROGRAM MANAGER

Planning Instruction See Teaching Notes, *Teaching Resources A,* p. 87 for additional teaching options to introduce *Macbeth* and Renaissance Theater.

The Renaissance Theater

A Flemish Fair (detail) (late 16th to early 17th century) by David Vinckboons.

282 THE RENAISSANCE

Cheltenham Art Gallery & Museums, Gloucestershire, England.

OPTIONS FOR TEACHING

STRATEGIES FOR INCLUSION

English Language Development To help students establish a context before reading this information, assign them to small groups to discuss any experiences they have had with seeing or participating in live plays. Ask them to describe the theater, the audience, the play itself, the costumes, and the scenery. As they discuss, review the related vocabulary. Ask them to look at pictures of the Globe (pp. 284 and 286) and to compare the pictures with their knowledge of theaters. Work with students to consider the purpose of plays. Are they to inform? To entertain?

Less Proficient Readers Provide students with a study guide that leads them through the feature with questions that follow the order in which the information is presented. Provide one main-idea question for each paragraph.

Drama as Teacher: The Forerunners

Even before the Renaissance, the English had been writing and performing plays for several centuries. Some scholars believe that medieval drama evolved from church ceremonies such as the dialogue songs performed at Easter Eve services. In these tiny playlets, three women would appear at a door representing the tomb of Christ and guarded by an angel. The angel would ask in Latin, "Whom do you seek?" and then he would announce Ⓐ the Resurrection.

From this obscure beginning, drama moved out of the churches and into the marketplaces of towns. There, in the 1300s and 1400s, various workers' guilds cooperated in staging cycles of plays that dramatized the whole history of the human race as then understood: its creation by God, its fall through the wiles of Satan, its life in Old Testament times, its redemption by Christ, and its final judgment at the end of the world. Parts of four cycles of these plays have been preserved, and they are named after the towns where they probably originated: York, Chester, Coventry, and Wakefield. Gradually, the plays became less religious, often relying on *deus ex machina* (an artificial device arbitrarily used to resolve a plot),

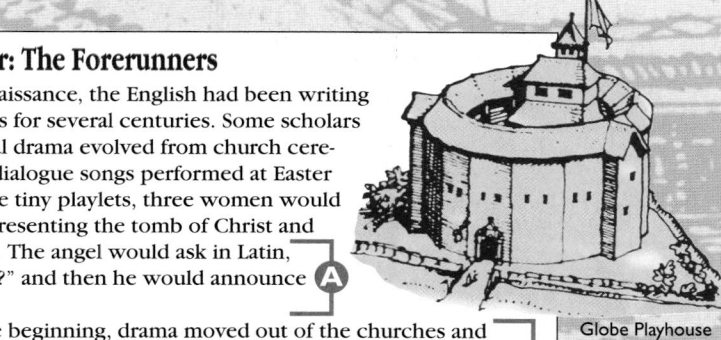

Globe Playhouse (detail) (c. 1599–1613) by C. Walter Hodges.

Representation of a Mystery Play (detail) (1825) by David Jee.
By permission of the British Library, London.

and comedy was incorporated into them. The wife of Noah, for instance, makes a great fuss about entering the ark and is carried kicking and screaming aboard. Comic scenes like this one provide an early example of English skill in mixing the comic with the serious in drama. The most notable play of the period just before the Renaissance is *Everyman,* based on a Dutch original (see page 451).

Several kinds of plays, then, were written and produced before the Renaissance: **miracle** and **mystery plays** that taught people stories from the Bible and saints' legends; **moralities** Ⓒ that taught people how to live and die; and, starting in the early 1500s, a new kind of play called an **interlude.** Interludes were one-act plays, some of them indistinguishable from moralities, others rowdy and farcical. With the interludes the playwrights stopped being anonymous. Even before the new humanist learning came in, there were strong dramatic traditions that the great Ⓓ Renaissance playwrights knew about.

A. Language Note: Vocabulary
"Resurrection" refers to the Christian belief that Christ rose from the dead three days after he was crucified.

B. Exploring the Historical Period
A guild was like a trade union combined with a club. There was one for each trade, and each had its own play to perform in the cycle, which might contain as many as forty-eight plays.

C. Humanities Connection
Examples of mystery plays include *The Second Shepherd's Play* and the York play of *The Crucifixion of Christ; Everyman* is a morality play.

D. Cultural Connections
A humanist was someone who chose to study human things rather than attempting to study the divine. Humanists focused their attention on classical studies and were responsible for reviving interest in the study of Greek. Notable humanists include Petrarch, Erasmus, and Sir Thomas More.

Elements of Literature: Videodisc Use the following bar codes to locate excerpts from Shakespearean plays. For more information, see the Videodisc *Teacher's Manual.*

Videodisc Side A

Begin Play, English Track

Begin Play, Spanish Track

STRATEGIES FOR INCLUSION

Spatial Before students read this section, visit the school auditorium or a local theater that contains a proscenium stage. If possible, also visit a theater in the round. Encourage students to compare and contrast the physical settings of the two and to imagine how the cast might interact differently with the audience in each setting. Assign students to groups of three or four, and have them stage two versions of a scene—one for theater in the round and then another for a proscenium stage.

Special Needs Students with visual impairment may be able to experience the physical characteristics of the theater if they can stand on the stage while a classmate in the audience converses with them and then sit in the audience while a classmate on stage converses with them. This procedure will help them to understand the spatial relationship between the cast and the audience. A guided tour of the stage and the orchestra pit will also help them imagine the size of the facility.

A. Cultural Connections

Theaters built in the suburbs escaped the demands of profit-sharing innkeepers and the rancor of city authorities. The authorities claimed, with some justification, that the boisterous crowds gathered in innyards (especially on Sundays) occasioned a danger not just of "ungodliness" and licentiousness, but also of fire, riot, accident, crime, and the spread of the plague. (Problems with crowds at rock concerts might be a contemporary parallel.)

B. Exploring the Historical Period

Although theater companies were commanded not to perform on Sundays or during the weeks of Lent (the six to seven weeks preceding Easter), these ordinances were frequently ignored, and by 1616, it was possible to obtain an official Lenten Dispensation—for the price of forty-four shillings.

KEY

a Main entrance
b The yard
c Entrance to lowest gallery
d Entrance to staircase and upper galleries
e Corridor serving the different sections of the middle gallery
f Middle gallery ("Twopenny Rooms")
g "Gentlemen's Rooms" or "Lords' Rooms"
h The stage
j The hanging being put up round the stage
k The "hell" under the stage
l The stage trap, leading down to the hell
m Stage doors
n Curtained "place behind the stage"
o Gallery above the stage, used as required sometimes by musicians, sometimes by spectators, and often as part of the play
p Backstage area (the tiring house)
q Tiring-house door
r Dressing rooms
s Wardrobe and storage
t The hut housing the machine for lowering enthroned gods, etc., to the stage
u The "heavens"
w Hoisting the playhouse flag

Old Traditions, New Theaters

By the mid–sixteenth century, the art of drama in England was three centuries old, but the idea of housing it in a permanent building was new. Even after theaters had been built, plays were still regularly performed in improvised spaces when acting companies toured the provinces or presented their plays in the large houses of royalty and nobility.

In 1576, James Burbage, the father of Shakespeare's partner and fellow actor Richard Burbage, built the first public theater and called it, appropriately, the Theater. Shortly thereafter, a second playhouse, called the Curtain, was erected. Both of these were in a northern suburb of London, where they would not offend the staid residents of London proper. Then came the Rose, the Swan, the Fortune, the Globe, the Red Bull, and the Hope— far more public theaters than in any other European capital.

The Globe: "This Wooden O"

The Globe is the most famous of the public theaters because the company that Shakespeare belonged to owned it. Many of his plays received their first performances there. It was built out of timbers salvaged from the Theater, which was demolished in 1599. Unfortunately, the plans for the Globe have not survived, though there still exist old, panoramic drawings of London in which its exterior is pictured. But the most important sources of information about the theater's structure are the plays themselves, with their stage directions and other clues.

Most scholars now accept as accurate the reconstruction of the Globe published by C. Walter Hodges, whose drawing appears on this page. Notice that the theater has three main parts: the building proper, the stage, and the tiring house, or backstage area, with the flag flying from its peak to indicate that there will be a performance that day.

Globe Playhouse (c. 1599–1613) by C. Walter Hodges.

Position of Staircase

OPTIONS FOR TEACHING

INTEGRATING THE LANGUAGE ARTS

Strategic Reading Ask students to scan the article and to record the nine headings. These headings can serve as the main entries for an outline in which students record the article's main ideas as they read.

Writing: Short Play Invite students to work in groups to write scripts for short plays that could be staged at the Globe. Remind students to consider the Globe's special construction and to include clear stage directions in their scripts.

A wooden structure three stories high, the building proper surrounded a spacious inner yard open to the sky. It was probably a sixteen-sided polygon. Any structure with that many sides would appear circular, so it is not surprising that Shakespeare referred to the Globe as "this wooden O" in his play *Henry V.* There were probably only two entrances to the building, one for the public and one for the theater company. But there may have been another public door used as an exit, because when the Globe burned down in 1613, the crowd escaped quickly and safely.

General admission to the theater cost one penny; this entitled a spectator to be a groundling, which meant he or she could stand in the yard. Patrons paid a little more to mount up into the galleries, where there were seats and a better view of the stage. The most expensive seats were chairs set right on the stage along its two sides. People who wanted to be conspicuous rented them, though they must have been a great nuisance to the rest of the audience and the actors. A public theater held a surprisingly large number of spectators—three thousand, according to two contemporary accounts. Since the spectators must have been squeezed together, it is no wonder that the authorities always closed the theaters during plague epidemics.

Up Close and Personal

The stage jutted halfway out into the yard, so that the actors were in much closer contact with the audience than actors are in modern theaters. Thus, every tiny nuance of an actor's performance could affect the audience. The actors were highly trained, and they could sing, dance, declaim, wrestle, fence, clown, roar, weep, and whisper. Large, sensational effects were also plentiful. Spectators loved to see witches or devils emerge through the trapdoor in the stage, which everybody pretended led down to Hell, just as everybody pretended that the ceiling over part of the stage was the Heavens. This ceiling was painted with elaborate suns, moons, and stars, and it contained a trapdoor through which angels, gods, and spirits could be lowered on a wire and even flown over the other actors' heads.

Behind the Scenes

The third part of the theater was the tiring (from *tire,* an archaic form of "attire") house, a tall building that contained machinery and dressing rooms and that provided a two-story back wall for the stage. Hodges's drawing of the Globe shows that this wall contained a gallery above and a curtained space below. The gallery had multiple purposes, depending on what play was being performed: Spectators could sit there, musicians could perform there, or parts of the play could be acted there—as if on balconies, towers, hills, and the like. The curtained area below the gallery was used mainly for "discoveries" of things prepared in advance and hidden from the audience until the proper time. In Shakespeare's *Merchant of Venice,* for example, the curtain is drawn to reveal three small chests, one of which hides the heroine's picture. Apparently, this curtained area

C. Exploring the Historical Period

The fire in the Globe occurred in June 1613 during the first scenes of a new play by Shakespeare, *Henry VIII.* The company lost not just the building, but also costumes, properties, and scripts.

The Globe was rebuilt in 1614 (it stood until pulled down to make room for residences in 1644), but the fire of 1613 marked the close of Shakespeare's London career. (See also pp. 293–294, "The Last Years: Continued Diversity.")

In 1988, the 424th anniversary of Shakespeare's birth, a drive was begun to rebuild the Globe on a site just two hundred yards from the old theater. The only marker indicating the exact location of the original Globe Theater is a plaque on a brewery wall.

D. Expansion

Because of the plague, the London theaters were closed from 1592 to 1594 and again in 1603 and 1609. During these three epidemics, 50,000 of the 200,000 or so residents of London died. This highly infectious disease, caused by *Pasteurella pestis* and transmitted to humans by fleas from infected rats, is characterized by high fever, chills, delirium, and painful, festering enlargements of the lymph glands called "buboes" (hence, "bubonic plague"). Death could come in three or four days. The worst recorded epidemic, in the fourteenth century, is estimated to have killed up to three-fourths of the people in Asia and Europe in less than twenty years.

E. Expansion

The contrast between Renaissance theaters and modern theaters refers specifically to the modern proscenium stage, which is often separated from the audience and elevated.

CROSSING THE CURRICULUM

Social Sciences Students may wish to look up the examples of morality plays and find out what morals were the most popular choices for representation. Ask students to create a pie chart showing their findings or to perform one of the plays as a puppet show.

Architecture Ask students to study different artists' renderings of the Globe Theater and to analyze the artists' accuracy in light of information presented in this article and of their own knowledge of Shakespeare's plays. Encourage students to work in a group to create a model of the Globe.

Music Ask students to research the music for a production of *Macbeth* and to bring some examples to class so everyone can listen. Encourage the class to analyze how the mood of the music fits the play. ☞

Globe Theater at Bankside (detail) (17th century). Watercolor.

© British Museum, London.

was too small, too shallow, and too far out of the sight of some spectators to be used as a performance space. If a performer were "discovered" behind the curtains (as Marlowe's Dr. Faustus is discovered in his study), he would quickly move out onto the stage to be seen **(A)** and heard better. When large properties such as thrones, beds, desks, and so on were pushed through the curtains onto the stage, the audience would know at once that the action was taking place indoors. When the action shifted to the outdoors, the property could be pulled back behind the curtain.

The Power of Make-Believe

Renaissance audiences took for granted that the theater cannot show "reality": Whatever happens on the stage is make-believe. When the people in the audience saw actors carrying lanterns, they knew it was night, even though the sun was shining brightly overhead. Often, instead of seeing a scene, they heard it described, as when Shakespeare has a character exclaim over a sunrise,

> But look, the morn in russet mantle clad
> Walks o'er the dew of yon high eastward hill.
>
> —*Hamlet,* Act I, Scene 1, lines 166–167

When a forest setting was called for, there was no painted scenery imitating real trees, bushes, flowers, and so on. Instead, a few bushes and small trees might be pushed onto the stage, and then the actors spoke lines that evoked images in the spectators' minds. In *As You Like It,* Rosalind simply looks around and announces, "Well, this is the forest of Arden." As the theatrical historian Gerald Bentley put it, Renaissance drama was "a drama of persons, not a drama of places."

286 THE RENAISSANCE

Making Choices Set goals with individual students, clarifying what you expect them to accomplish in reading *Macbeth,* in order to make the purpose of studying such complex material clearer. For some students, it may be an appropriate goal to come away from the play with the basic storyline and an understanding of **themes.** Others may see the study of Renaissance literature in a historical context and hope to make, through this study, a comparison of historical and literary treatments of *Macbeth.* Encourage students to pursue the research most beneficial to the goals you set with them individually.

Block Scheduling Brainstorm with the class for ten to fifteen minutes. Give students three to four topics (one at a time) associated with the Renaissance theater. Using a stopwatch, allow students one minute to generate on paper as many thoughts on the topic as possible. Ask for volunteers to share their ideas after each round. Students may brainstorm independently, in pairs, or in small groups. This activity also may be used as a transition from one activity to another or as closure.

Pomp and Pageantry

The scenery may have been kept to a minimum, but the theaters themselves were ornate. The interiors were painted brightly, with many decorations, and the space at the rear of the stage could be covered with colorful tapestries or hangings. Costumes were rich, elaborate, and expensive. The manager-producer Philip Henslowe once paid twenty pounds (then an enormous sum) for a single cloak for one of his actors to wear. Henslowe's lists of theatrical properties mention chariots, fountains, dragons, beds, tents, thrones, booths, and wayside crosses, among other things.

The audience also enjoyed the processions—religious, royal, military—that occurred in many plays. These would enter the stage from one door, cross the stage, and then exit by the other door. A few quick costume changes as the actors passed through the tiring house could double and triple the apparent number of people in a procession.

Music Most Eloquent

When people went to the London theater, they expected not only to see a tragedy or comedy acted but also to hear music, both vocal and instrumental. Trumpets announced the beginning of the play and important arrivals and departures within the play. High up in the gallery, musicians played between acts and at other appropriate times during the performance. And scattered throughout most of the plays, especially the comedies, were songs.

The songs in Shakespeare's plays are the best of this kind that have come down to us, for Shakespeare excelled in lyric and in dramatic poetry. He included a great variety of songs in his plays: sad, happy, comic, thoughtful songs, each one adapted to the play and scene in which it occurs and to the character who performs it. Some of the songs advance the dramatic action, some help establish the mood of a scene, and some reveal character. Like this invitation to love (from the comedy *Twelfth Night*), all of these songs are fresh and spontaneous, not contrived and artificial.

> O mistress mine, where are you roaming?
> O, stay and hear, your true love's coming,
>   That can sing both high and low.
> Trip no further, pretty sweeting;
> Journeys end in lovers meeting,
>   Every wise man's son doth know . . .
>
> What is love? 'tis not hereafter;
> Present mirth hath present laughter;
>   What's to come is still unsure.
> In delay there lies no plenty;
> Then come kiss me, sweet and twenty;
> Youth's a stuff will not endure.

Lady Masquer (detail) (c. 1610) by Inigo Jones.

B. Expansion
Henslowe's papers are the source of information about the company called Lord Strange's Men and later the Chamberlain's Men. Christopher Marlowe (see p. 232) wrote for Henslowe's troupe.

C. Exploring the Culture
Like Shakespeare's other plays, *Macbeth* demands musical flourishes, trumpets, drums, "alarums" (clamor and martial sounds—clanking swords, galloping hoofs, shouting voices), cannons, and thunder. Available musical instruments included viols and virginals, the recorder (a flutelike instrument), the cornet (a trumpet-sounding cylinder of ivory or wood with finger holes like a recorder), the sackbut (trombone), and a double-reed instrument called the hautboy (hō´boi´), or oboe.

D. Humanities Connection
After the Puritans' temporary closure of the theaters (1642–1660), *Macbeth* was brought back to the stage in a version adapted by William Davenant. A contemporary description by John Downes, who served as the prompter for the Duke's Company, describes it as follows: "The Tragedy of *Macbeth,* alter'd by Sir *William Davenant;* being drest in all it's Finery, as new Cloath's, new Scenes, Machines, as flyings for the Witches; with all the singing and Dancing in it: THE first Compos'd by *Mr. Lock,* the other by *Mr. Channell* and *Mr. Joseph Preist;* it being all Excellently perform'd, being in the nature of an Opera, it Recompenc'd double the Expence; it proves still a lasting Play."

E. Literary Connections
The type of poem called a *carpe diem* (Latin for "seize the day"), of which this is an example, is explained more fully on p. 231.

PROFESSIONAL NOTES

Technology Tip Shakespeare resources on the Internet are boundless. Have your students conduct web and gopher searches for information. (See if they can find the Shakespeare Insult server, a rather interesting way to bring Elizabethan language to life.) Students may also exchange e-mail with Shakespeare scholars on any number of related listservs. *You may want to preview any Internet activity that you suggest to students. Because these resources are sometimes public forums, their content can be unpredictable.*

A. Expansion
Students may be interested to know that Henslowe managed a bear pit as well as a theater company.

B. Exploring the Culture
Richard Burbage (p. 284) earlier had acquired the right to lease Blackfriars Hall (in a former Dominican priory); but moneyed neighbors refused to accept adult actors in their midst, so the hall was leased to a company of boy actors. By 1608, Shakespeare had a coat of arms, and his company had acquired considerable status; the council was happy to turn Blackfriars over to the now respectable adult professionals.

C. Exploring the Culture
In Shakespeare's day, actors formed what we call repertory companies. Instead of signing up to perform a single play for a long run, they were members of an acting company that performed a number of different plays on consecutive days. (Henslowe's company may hold the record, with fifty-five new or recently revised plays performed in one hundred twenty-six weeks.) These companies filled the roles in each play with members of their own group; they employed no outside actors.

The actors shared in the company profits, and boys were apprenticed as they would have been in a guild. Boys acted the women's roles until their voices changed, which accounts for the lack of older women's roles in the plays (the portrayal would have been difficult for boys) and the number of women characters who disguise themselves as men.

Many Shakespearean repertory groups exist today in the United States and other countries. The Shakespearean Festival at Ashland, Oregon, uses a Globe-like theater in its annual summer repertory performances. Also, Minneapolis has the Tyrone Guthrie Theater, designed in the Shakespearean manner but with a closed roof and modern lighting and machinery.

Unfortunately, most of the original music for Shakespeare's songs has been lost. But just as the plays themselves have inspired many composers of music for opera, orchestra, and ballet, so have the songs from the plays been set to music right up to the present.

Varying the Venue
The acting companies performed in two other kinds of spaces: in the great halls of castles and manor houses, and in indoor, fully covered theaters in London.

A — For performances in a great hall, a theater company must have had a portable booth stage, like the one shown here. In these buildings, the usual entertainment was a bear being attacked by dogs. The bear pits were vile places, but their temporary stages could easily accommodate any play except for scenes requiring the use of Heavens overhanging the stage.

B — Something like this booth stage may also have been used in private theaters like the Blackfriars, which Shakespeare's company, the King's Men, acquired in 1608. One great advantage of Blackfriars—a disused monastery that was entirely roofed over—was that the company could perform there in cold weather and, since artificial lighting always had to

C — be used, at night. Thus, the King's Men could put on plays all during the year, increasing profits for the shareholders, among them Shakespeare.

Stage in an amphitheater (detail) (c. 1576) by C. Walter Hodges.

Globe Theater (detail) by G. Shepherd.

British Museum, London.

288 THE RENAISSANCE

OPTIONS FOR TEACHING

ASSESSMENT TOOLS

Check Test: True-False
1. The first public theater was built in the sixteenth century. [True]
2. Many of Shakespeare's plays were performed at the Globe Theater. [True]
3. The scenery in the Renaissance theater was elaborate and detailed, imitating reality precisely. [False]
4. Music was an important part of the performance of a Renaissance play. [True]
5. Blackfriars was a monastery where players went to pray before important performances. [False]

William Shakespeare

(1564–1616)

Every literate person has heard of Shakespeare, the author of more than 36 remarkable plays and more than 150 poems. Over the centuries, these literary works have made such a deep impression on the human race that all sorts of fancies, legends, and theories have been invented about their author. There are even those who say that somebody other than Shakespeare wrote the works that bear his name, although these deluded people cannot agree on who, among a dozen candidates, this other author actually was. Such speculation is based on the misconception that little is known about Shakespeare's life; in fact, Shakespeare's life is better documented than the life of any other dramatist of the time except perhaps for Ben Jonson, a writer who seems almost modern in the way he publicized himself. Jonson was an honest, blunt, and outspoken man who knew Shakespeare well; for a time the two dramatists wrote for the same theatrical company, and Shakespeare even acted in Jonson's plays. Often niggardly in his judgments of other writers, Jonson published a poem praising Shakespeare, asserting that he was superior to all Greek, Roman, and English dramatists, predicting that he would be "not of an age, but for all time." Jonson's judgment is now commonly accepted, and his prophecy has come true.

The Years in Stratford-on-Avon

Shakespeare was born in Stratford-on-Avon, a historic and prosperous market town in Warwickshire, and was christened in the parish church there on April 26, 1564. His father was John Shakespeare, a merchant once active in the town government; his mother—born Mary Arden—came from a prominent family in the county. Presumably, for seven years or so, William attended the Stratford grammar school, where he obtained an excellent education in Latin, the Bible, and English composition. (The students had to translate Latin works into English and then turn them back into Latin.) After leaving school, he may have been apprenticed to a butcher, but because he shows in his plays very detailed knowledge of many different crafts and trades, speculators have proposed a number of different occupations that he could have had. At eighteen, Shakespeare married Anne Hathaway, the twenty-six-year-old daughter of a farmer living near Stratford. They had three children, a daughter named Susanna and twins named Hamnet and Judith.

Flower Portrait of William Shakespeare (detail) by an unknown artist. Oil.

From the Royal Shakespeare Company Collection with the permission of the Governors of the Royal Shakespeare Theater, London.

WRITERS ON WRITING

Beyond his plays and poems, we have nothing else that we can be certain Shakespeare wrote—no letters or essays or commentaries remain. Perhaps, however, we may infer how he felt about reading and writing from this comment, taken from his play *Love's Labor's Lost,* in which Sir Nathaniel excuses Constable Dull's error: "Sir, he hath never fed of the dainties that are bred in a book; he hath not eat paper, as it were; he hath not drunk ink; his intellect is not replenished; he is only an animal, only sensible in the duller parts" (Act IV, Scene 2, ll. 24–27).

RESPONDING TO THE ART: ABOUT THE ARTWORK

The Flower Portrait, so called because Mrs. Charles Flower sold it to the Shakespeare Memorial, bears the inscription "Willm Shakespeare 1609." Some critics believe that it is the only surviving portrait made during Shakespeare's lifetime, but others argue that the painting is an eighteenth-century forgery, copied from an engraving made in 1623—years after Shakespeare's death. The identity of the painter is complicated by the fact that the head and body are disproportionate to each other, suggesting that the head was painted by a master and the imperfect body completed by his student.

Anne Hathaway's cottage in Shottery, a mile outside Stratford.

We don't know how the young Shakespeare supported his family, but according to tradition, he taught school for a few years. The two daughters grew up and married; the son died when he was eleven.

Off to London

How did Shakespeare first become interested in the theater? Presumably, by seeing plays. We know that traveling acting companies frequently visited Stratford, and we assume that he attended their performances and that he also went to the nearby city of Coventry, where a famous cycle of religious plays was put on every year. But to be a dramatist, one had to be in London, where the theater was flourishing in the 1580s. Exactly when Shakespeare left his family and moved to London (there is no evidence that his wife was ever in the city) is uncertain; scholars say that he probably arrived there in 1587. It is certain that he was busy and successful in the London theater by 1592, when a fellow dramatist named Robert Greene attacked him in print and ridiculed a passage in his early play *Henry VI*. Greene, a down-and-out Cambridge graduate, warned other university men then writing plays to beware of this mere actor who was writing plays—an "upstart crow beautified with our feathers." Greene died of dissipation just as his ill-natured attack was being published, but a friend of his named Henry Chettle immediately apologized in print to Shakespeare and commended Shakespeare's acting and writing abilities and his personal honesty.

From 1592 on, there is ample documentation of Shakespeare's life and works. We know where he lived in London, at least approximately when his plays were produced and printed, and even how he spent his money. From 1594 until his retirement in about 1613, he was a member of one company, which also included the great tragic actor Richard Burbage and the popular clown Will Kemp. Although actors and others connected with the theater had a very low status legally, in practice they enjoyed the patronage of noblemen and even royalty. It is a mistake to think of Shakespeare as an obscure actor who somehow wrote great plays; he was well known even as a young man. He first became famous as the author of a best-seller, an erotic narrative poem called *Venus and Adonis* (1593). This poem, as well as the more serious poem *The Rape of Lucrece* (1594), was dedicated to a rich and extravagant young nobleman, the earl of Southampton. The dedication of *Lucrece* suggests that Shakespeare and his wealthy patron were on very friendly terms.

Emma Thompson (left) in Kenneth Branagh's film production of *Much Ado About Nothing* (1993).

Shakespeare's Early Plays: Variety and Prosperity

Among Shakespeare's earliest plays are the following, with the generally but not universally accepted dates of their first performances: *Richard III* (1592–1593), a chronicle or history play about a deformed usurper who became king of England; *The Comedy of Errors* (1592–1593), a rowdy farce about mistaken identity, based on a Latin play; *Titus Andronicus* (1593–1594), a blood-and-thunder tragedy full of rant and atrocities; *The Taming of the Shrew, The Two Gentlemen of Verona,* and *Love's Labor's Lost* (all 1593–1595), three agreeable comedies; and *Romeo and Juliet* (1594–1595), a poetic tragedy about ill-fated lovers—the Shakespeare play still most frequently taught in schools. The extraordinary thing about these plays is not so much their immense variety—each one is quite different from all the others—but the fact that they are all regularly revived and performed on stages all over the world today.

Years of Prosperity

By 1596, Shakespeare was beginning to prosper. He had his father apply to the Heralds' College for a coat of arms that the family could display, signifying that they were "gentlefolk," or people of high social standing. On Shakespeare's family crest is a falcon shaking a spear. To support this claim to gentility, Shakespeare bought New Place, a handsome house and grounds in Stratford, a place so commodious and elegant that the queen of England once stayed there after Shakespeare's daughter Susanna inherited it. Shakespeare also, in 1599, joined with a few other members of his company, now called the Lord Chamberlain's Men, to finance a new theater—the famous

Richard Easton and Hal Holbrook in *King Lear* (1993).

Globe—on the south side of the Thames. The "honey-tongued Shakespeare," as he was called in a book about English literature published in 1598, was now earning money as a playwright, an actor, and a shareholder in a theater. By 1600, Shakespeare was regularly associating with members of the aristocracy, and six of his plays had been given command performances at the court of Queen Elizabeth.

During the last years of Elizabeth I's reign, Shakespeare completed his cycle of plays about England during the Wars of the Roses: *Richard II* (1595–1596), both parts of *Henry IV* (1596–1597), and *Henry V* (1599). Also in this period he wrote the tragedy *Julius Caesar* (1599)—and the comedies that are most frequently performed today: *A Midsummer Night's Dream* (1595–1596), *The Merchant of Venice* (1596–1597), *Much Ado About Nothing* (1598–1599), *As You Like It* (1598–1600), and *Twelfth Night* (1600–1601). And finally at this time he wrote or rewrote *Hamlet* (1600–1601), the tragedy that, of all his tragedies, has provoked the most varied and controversial interpretations from critics, scholars, and actors. Shakespeare indeed prospered under Queen Elizabeth; according to an old tradition, she asked him to write *The Merry Wives of Windsor* (1600–1601) because she

Mel Gibson and Helena Bonham-Carter in Franco Zeffirelli's film production of *Hamlet* (1990).

Christopher Walken (top) and Raul Julia in *Othello,* New York Shakespeare Festival (1991).

wanted to see the merry, fat old knight Sir John Falstaff (of the Henry plays) in love.

Shakespeare prospered even more under Elizabeth's successor, King James of Scotland. Fortunately for Shakespeare's company, as it turned out, James's royal entry into London in 1603 had to be postponed for several months because the plague was raging in the city. While waiting for the epidemic to subside, the royal court stayed in various palaces outside London. Shakespeare's company took advantage of this situation and, since the city theaters were closed, performed several plays for the court and the new king. Shakespeare's plays delighted James, for he loved literature and was starved for pleasure after the grim experience of ruling Scotland for many years. He immediately took the company under his

patronage, renamed them the King's Men, gave them patents to perform anywhere in the realm, provided them with special clothing for state occasions, increased their salaries, and appointed their chief members, including Shakespeare, to be grooms of the royal chamber. All this patronage brought such prosperity to Shakespeare that he was able to make some very profitable real estate investments in Stratford and London.

Shakespeare's "Tragic Period": Beyond Experience

In the early years of the seventeenth century, while his financial affairs were flourishing and everything was apparently going very well for him, Shakespeare wrote his greatest tragedies: *Hamlet* (already mentioned), *Othello* (1601–1602), *King Lear* (1605), *Macbeth* (1605–1606), and *Antony and Cleopatra* (1606–1607). Because these famous plays are so preoccupied with evil, violence, and death, some people feel that Shakespeare must have been unhappy and depressed when he wrote them. Moreover, such people find even the comedies he wrote at this time more sour than sweet: *All's Well That Ends Well* (1602–1603) and *Measure for Measure* (1604). And so, instead of paying tribute to Shakespeare's powerful imagination, which is everywhere evident, these people invent a "tragic period" in Shakespeare's biography, and they search for personal crises in his private life. When they cannot find these agonies, they invent them. To be sure, in 1607, an actor named Edmund Shakespeare, who may well have been William's younger brother, died in London. But by 1607, Shakespeare's alleged "tragic period" was almost over. It is quite wrong to assume a one-to-one

Glenn Close and Alan Bates in Franco Zeffirelli's film production of *Hamlet* (1990).

correspondence between writers' biographies and their works, because writers must be allowed to imagine whatever they can. It is especially wrong in the case of a writer like Shakespeare, who did not write to express himself but to satisfy the patrons of the theater that he and his partners owned. Shakespeare must have repeatedly given the audience just what it wanted; otherwise, he could not have made so much money from the theater. To insist that he had to experience and personally feel everything that he wrote about is absurd. He wrote about King Lear, who cursed his two monstrous daughters for treating him very badly; in contrast, what evidence there is suggests that he got along very well with his own two daughters. And so, instead of "tragic" we should think of the years 1600–1607 as glorious, because in them Shakespeare's productivity was at its peak. It seems very doubtful that a depressed person would write plays like these. In fact, they would likely make their creator feel exhilarated rather than sad.

Denzel Washington in Kenneth Branagh's film production of *Much Ado About Nothing* (1993).

The Last Years: Continued Diversity

In about 1610, Shakespeare decided that, having made a considerable sum from his plays and theatrical enterprises, he would retire to his handsome house in Stratford, a place he had never forgotten, though he seems to have kept his life there rather separate from his life in London. His retirement was not complete, for the records show that after he returned to Stratford he still took part in the management of the King's Men and their two theaters: the Globe, an octagonal building opened in 1599 and used for performances in good weather, and the Blackfriars, acquired in 1608 and used for indoor performances. Shakespeare's works in this period show no signs of diminished creativity, except that in some years he wrote one play instead of the customary two, and they continue to illustrate the great diversity of his genius. Among them are the tragedies *Timon of Athens* (1607–1608) and *Coriolanus* (1607–1608) and five plays that have been variously classified as comedies, romances, or tragicomedies: *Pericles* (1607–1608), *Cymbeline* (1609–1610), *The Winter's Tale* (1610–1611), *The Tempest* (1611–1612), and *The Two Noble Kinsmen* (1612). His last English history play, *Henry VIII* (1613), contained a tribute to Queen Elizabeth—a somewhat tardy tribute, because, unlike most of the other poets of the day, Shakespeare did not praise her in print when she died in 1603. (Some scholars argue, on very little evidence, that he was an admirer of the earl of Essex, a former intimate of Elizabeth whom she had beheaded for rebellion.) During the first performance of *Henry VIII*, in

Kenneth Branagh in his film production of *Henry V* (1989).

June of 1613, the firing of the cannon at the end of Act I set the Globe on fire (it had a thatched roof), and it burned to the ground. Only one casualty is recorded: A bottle of ale had to be poured on a man whose breeches were burning. Fortunately, the company had the Blackfriars in which to perform until the Globe could be rebuilt and reopened in 1614.

Shakespeare's last recorded visit to London was made with his son-in-law Dr. John Hall in November 1614, though he may have gone down to the city afterward because he continued to own property there, including a building very near the Blackfriars Theater. Probably, though, he spent most of the last two years of his life at New Place, with his daughter Susanna Hall (and his granddaughter Elizabeth) living nearby. He died on April 23, 1616, and was buried under the floor of Stratford Church, with this epitaph warning posterity not to dig him up and transfer him to the graveyard outside the church—a common practice in those days to make room for newer corpses:

> Good friend, for Jesus' sake forbear
> To dig the dust enclosèd here!
> Blest be the man that spares these stones,
> And curst be he that moves my bones.

Shakespeare's Genius: Imagination and "Soul"

What sort of man was Shakespeare? This is a very hard question to answer because he left no letters, diaries, or other private writings containing his

Laurence Olivier in his film production of *Henry V* (1944).

personal views; instead, he left us plays, and in a good play the actors do not speak for the dramatist but for the characters they are impersonating. We cannot, then, say that Shakespeare approved of evil because he created murderers or advocated religion because he created clergymen; we cannot say that he believed in fatalism because he created fatalists, or admired flattery

Patrick Stewart and Anjanue Ellis in *The Tempest,* New York Shakespeare Festival (1995).

because he created flatterers. All these would be naive, contradictory reactions to the plays. Shakespeare's characters represent such a vast range of human behavior and attitudes that they must be products of his careful observation and fertile imagination rather than extensions of himself. A critic named Desmond McCarthy once said that trying to identify Shakespeare the man in his plays is like looking at a very dim portrait under glass: The more you peer at it, the more you see only yourself.

A Complete Man of the Theater

One thing is certain: Shakespeare was a complete man of the theater who created works specifically for his own acting company and his own stage. He had, for instance, to provide good parts in every play for the principal performers in the company, including the come-

Mel Gibson in Franco Zeffirelli's film production of *Hamlet* (1990).

Never Out of Print

Although the plays are primarily performance scripts, from earliest times the public has wanted to read them as well as see them staged. In every generation, people have felt that the plays contain so much wisdom, so much knowledge of human nature, so much remarkable poetry that they need to be pondered in private as well as enjoyed in public. Most readers have agreed with what the poet John Dryden said about Shakespeare's "soul": The man who wrote the plays may be elusive, but he was obviously a great genius whose lofty imagination is matched by his sympathy for all

dians acting in tragedies. Since there were no actresses, he had to limit the number of female parts in his plays and create them in such a way that they could readily be taken by boys. For instance, although there are many fathers in the plays, there are very few mothers: While boys could be taught to flirt and play shy, acting maternally would be difficult for them. Several of Shakespeare's young women characters disguise themselves as young men early in Act I— an easy solution to the problem of boys playing girls' parts. Shakespeare also had to provide the words for songs because theatergoers expected singing in every play; furthermore, the songs had to be devised so that they would exhibit the talents of particular actors with good voices. Since many of the plays contain many characters, and since there were a limited number of actors in the company, Shakespeare had to arrange for doubling and even tripling of roles: That is, a single actor would have to perform more than one part. Since, of course, an actor could impersonate only one character at a time, Shakespeare had to plan his scenes carefully, so that nobody would ever have to be on stage in two different roles at the same time. A careful study of the plays shows that Shakespeare handled very masterfully all these technical problems of dramaturgy.

Dear Miss Disdain (Beatrice from *Much Ado About Nothing*) (late 18th to early 19th century) by Louise Jopling.

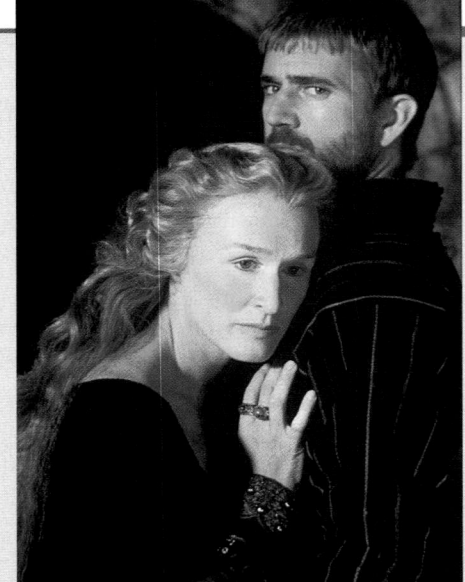

Glenn Close and Mel Gibson in Franco Zeffirelli's film production of *Hamlet* (1990).

kinds of human behavior. Reading the plays, then, is a rewarding experience in itself; it is also an excellent preparation for seeing them performed on stage or on film.

Shakespeare's contemporaries were so eager to read his plays that enterprising publishers did everything possible, including stealing them, to make them available. Of course, the company generally tried to keep the plays unpublished because they did not want them performed by rival companies. Even so, eighteen plays were published in small books called quartos before Shakespeare's partners collected them together and published them after his death. This collection, known as the "first folio" because of its large size, was published in 1623. Surviving copies of this folio are regarded as valuable treasures today. But, of course, the general reader need not consult any of the original texts of Shakespeare because his works never go out of print; they are always available in many different languages and many different formats. The plays that exist in two different versions (one in a quarto and one in the folio) have provided scholars with endless matter for speculation about what Shakespeare actually intended the correct text to be. Indeed, every aspect of Shakespeare has been, and continues to be, thoroughly studied and written about by literary and historical scholars, theater and film people, experts in many fields, and amateurs of every stripe. No wonder that he is mistakenly regarded as a great mystery.

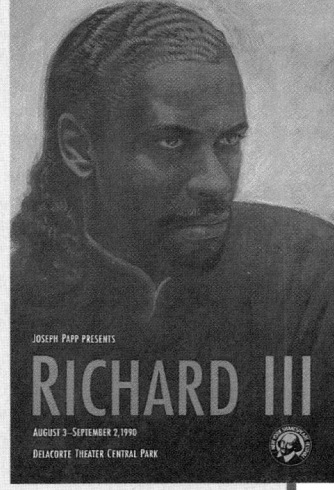

JOSEPH PAPP PRESENTS

RICHARD III

AUGUST 3–SEPTEMBER 2, 1990
DELACORTE THEATER CENTRAL PARK

Poster featuring Denzel Washington in *Richard III* at the New York Shakespeare Festival (1990).

Laurence Olivier and Anna Calder-Marshall in the Mobil Showcase Network production of *King Lear* (1984).

The Tragedy of Macbeth: The Sources of the Play

Orson Welles in his film production of *Macbeth* (1948).

A. Literary Connections

Critics consider additional sources more or less probable, but some are fairly sure that Shakespeare consulted Buchanan's *History of Scotland,* because elements of Macbeth's characterization are more similar to this account than they are to Holinshed's. Other possible sources include Seneca's *Medea* and Aeschylus's *Agamemnon.*

B. Exploring the Historical Period

An account by Nicolo Molin in the *Venetian State Papers* tells how the Gunpowder Plot was discovered: "About two months ago Lord Salisbury received anonymous letters from France, warning him to be on his guard, for a great conspiracy was being hatched by priests and Jesuits. . . . Lord Mounteagle read the letter and, in great astonishment took it to the Earl of Salisbury, who at once carried it to the King. . . . Meantime, the King read the letter and in terrified amaze he said 'I remember that my father died by gunpowder. I see the letter says the blow is to be struck on a sudden. Search the basements of the meeting place.'"

Poster for *Macbeth,* featuring Raul Julia, at the Public Theater, New York (1990).

© 1989 Paul Davis. Courtesy of the artist.

Shakespeare's play *Macbeth* conforms to the general rule of Renaissance tragedies, in which the drama had to be about real people whose deeds are recorded in history. (Renaissance comedies, on the other hand, concerned the imaginary doings of fictitious characters.) Shakespeare took the main events of Macbeth's career as king of Scotland (1040–1057) from Raphael Holinshed's *Chronicles of England, Scotland, and Ireland* (1577), the book that provided Shakespeare with historical material for many of his plays. But there are striking differences between his account of Macbeth and Holinshed's. The historical Macbeth had a much more legitimate claim to King Duncan's throne than Shakespeare's Macbeth did. The historical Macbeth gained the throne with the help of other nobles dissatisfied with King Duncan, and he ruled rather successfully. In contrast, Shakespeare's Macbeth has no supporters except his wife, whose strong and ambitious nature Shakespeare develops from a brief statement in the history. And in the play, the reign of Macbeth and his wife brings nothing but violence and disaster to Scotland.

A witch placing a crown on Macbeth's head in the Faux-Real production of *Htebcam* (1994) ("Macbeth" spelled backward).

One explanation for these changes to Holinshed's story is that Shakespeare wanted to explore—from a safe distance—the events and attitudes of his own time. Contemporary audiences have all but lost sight of the scandal that was a backdrop for the play: the Gunpowder Plot of 1605, in which several Catholic zealots plotted to blow up King James I and his Protestant Parliament. Garry Wills, a professor and political columnist, says that for its Elizabethan audience, *Macbeth* was a thriller. (For Wills, the Gunpowder Plot would compare to a plan to bomb the U.S. Capitol building during a presidential address.) The threat to an anointed king, and the perceived evil behind it, was relived in Macbeth's complete threat to the social order in a Scotland of the distant past.

Shakespeare altered his source text, in ways both small and large, in order to pay homage to his own king and country; his changes were

Ellen Terry as Lady Macbeth (detail) (1888–1889) by John Singer Sargent. Tate Gallery, London.

298 THE RENAISSANCE

The three witches in Roman Polanski's film production of *Macbeth* (1971).

intended for an audience of his *particular* moment in history. If he ever saw it, *Macbeth* must have pleased King James, the patron of Shakespeare's company. Since James had recently survived the Gunpowder Plot, he was especially interested in attacks on kings. James always defended the idea that he ruled by divine right. Moreover, he was a Scot and claimed to be a direct descendant of Banquo, to whom the third witch says, "Thou shalt get kings, though thou be none." For these reasons, scholars have for a long time thought of *Macbeth* as a play written for a command performance at court, though there is absolutely no proof that it was. James refused to sit through long plays, and this royal shortcoming has even been used to explain the fact that *Macbeth* is one of Shakespeare's shortest plays.

We can also say that Shakespeare made many changes in Holinshed's story because he was much more interested in psychological truth than in historical fact. And in this sense, *Macbeth* is also about *real* people, men and women tempted by ambition and power, caught up in a web of wants and needs. In playing out these real feelings and desires, Shakespeare's Macbeth transcends the historical Macbeth and gives us a portrait and a play for all times. As the critic Sylvan Barnet notes, "When one reads or sees *Macbeth,* one cannot help feeling that one is experiencing a re-creation or representation of what a man is, in the present, even in the timeless."

The Banquet (detail) by an unknown artist, from Act III, Scene 4, of *Macbeth* at London's Princess Theatre (1853).

Victoria and Albert Museum, London.

C. Exploring the Historical Period
King James I, for whom Shakespeare may have written this drama, was a writer, and two of his favorite subjects were his own ancestry and witchcraft, both of which are prominent in the play.

QUICK PLANNING GUIDE

Into the Play

Through the Play

Beyond the Play

BEFORE YOU READ
MACBETH

Reading Focus

Crime and Consequence
Have you ever wondered how just one action—whether tremendous or trivial—might affect the entire course of your life? Could one selfish impulse lead to a chain of decisions you will reflect on with the greatest anguish? The seeds of tragedy often lie in the most insignificant or excusable actions. And though Shakespeare's tragic hero Macbeth does not commit petty or insignificant crimes, his great ambition and corrosive guilt compel our understanding.

In *Macbeth*, a brave and intelligent man deliberately murders one of his fellowmen—his friend, his kinsman, his guest, his king—and then he must immediately, as a consequence of his first murder, kill two other innocent men. After that, he cannot turn away from his evil course: It leads him to further appalling crimes and finally to disgrace, alienation, isolation, despair, violent death, and decapitation.

Quickwrite

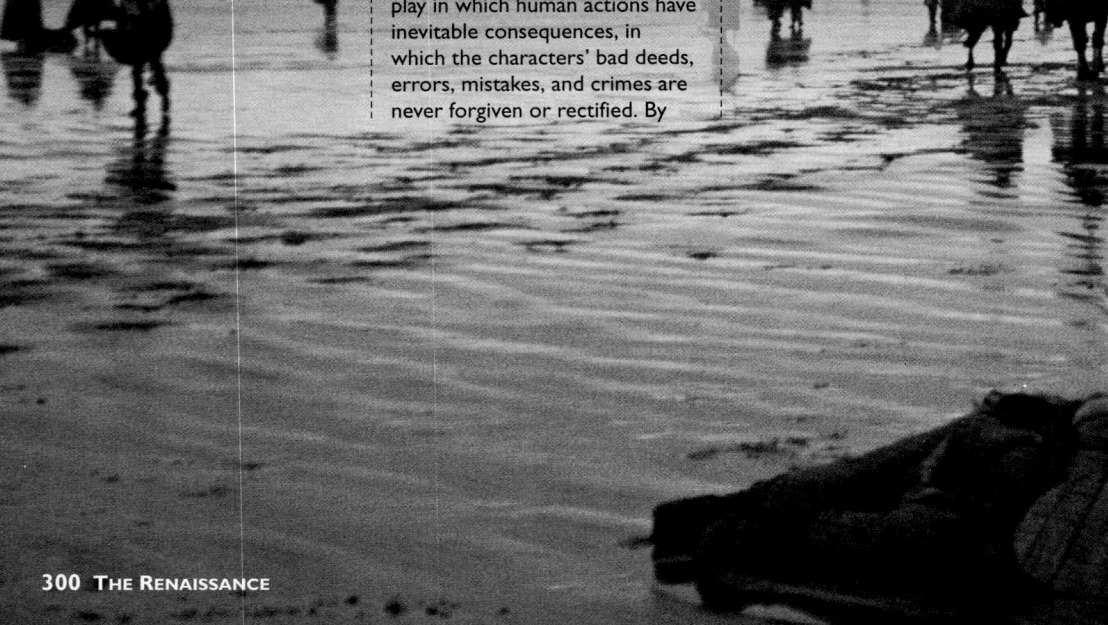

In *Macbeth*, the hero's lust for power brings absolute destruction on himself and his family. Think of people in actual life and in fiction who are obsessed with power. What are the typical consequences of such extravagant ambition? Jot down your thoughts on these questions in your Reader's Log.

Elements of Literature

Tragedy
Macbeth is a **tragedy:** a kind of play in which human actions have inevitable consequences, in which the characters' bad deeds, errors, mistakes, and crimes are never forgiven or rectified. By contrast, the characters in a comedy do not live under this iron law of cause and effect; they can do whatever they please as long as they amuse their audience, and as long as the funny mess they have made is easily cleaned up at the end of the play. But in a tragedy, an ill-judged action will remorselessly lead to a catastrophe, usually but not necessarily a death or multiple deaths.

> **A** **tragedy** is a literary work depicting serious events in which the main character, who is often high-ranking and dignified, comes to an unhappy end.
>
> *For more on Tragedy, see the Handbook of Literary Terms.*

300 THE RENAISSANCE

Portfolio Assessment For help with self-assessment of reading skills, see the *Portfolio Management System,* pp. 48–49.

PORTFOLIO ASSESSMENT

The Tragedy of Macbeth

William Shakespeare

CHARACTERS

Duncan, king of Scotland
Malcolm } his sons
Donalbain
Macbeth A
Banquo
Macduff
Lennox } noblemen of Scotland
Ross
Menteith
Angus
Caithness
Fleance, son to Banquo
Siward, earl of Northumberland, general of the English forces
Young Siward, his son
Seyton, an officer attending on Macbeth

Son to Macduff
An English Doctor
A Scottish Doctor
A Porter
An Old Man
Three Murderers
Lady Macbeth B
Lady Macduff
A Gentlewoman attending on Lady Macbeth
Hecate
Witches
Apparitions
Lords, Officers, Soldiers, Attendants, and Messengers

Setting: Scotland; England

From Roman Polanski's film production of *Macbeth* (1971).

MACBETH 301

Into the Play

Using BEFORE YOU READ p. 300

Reading Focus

Basing his work on Greek drama of the fifth century B.C., Aristotle recorded his observations on the qualities necessary to a tragedy, and these observations influenced the Elizabethan interpretation of tragedy. Aristotle notes that a tragedy centers on a **tragic hero,** generally of high status, who possesses a weakness, or **tragic flaw,** that ultimately causes the character's downfall. The **catastrophe** and its resolution leave the audience with a sense that they have undergone **catharsis,** a cleansing, through the emotions generated by the play.

Ask students to create a double-entry journal. In the left column, ask them to write what they expect of *Macbeth,* knowing it is a tragedy. Have them return to the right-hand column after reading the play to record their thoughts and to compare their responses.

Through the Play

A. Literary Element: Tragedy
True to a tragedy, the leading character Macbeth is the chief of the king's lieutenants, the highest ranking nobleman in Scotland.

B. Expansion
Tell students that the historical Lady Macbeth's first name, as reported in the 1909 British Isles edition of *The Dictionary of National Biography,* was Gruach.

A. Literary Element: Paradox

? How could a battle be both lost and won? [A battle is won by one side and lost by the other; or the winning side may lose something or the losing side actually win in some sense.]

B. Critical Reading: Making Inferences

? What do these statements suggest about the witches? [Possible answers: They seem to know the future. It is unclear whether they determine it or merely predict it.]

C. Reader's Response: First Thoughts

This statement, which is proverbial, sets out one of the major **themes** of the play. What do you think it means? [Sample responses: Values have been reversed. Striking moral divisions have been obscured. Appearances are deceiving.]

D. Expansion

Blood is mentioned more than one hundred times in the play. Ask students to think about its significance as an **image,** and as they read, to think about whether it has different meanings at different points in the story.

Answers to Margin Questions
Line 2. They might use movement (awkward or ritualistic), voice (unnatural pitch and cackling laughs), costumes, and makeup.

Line 7. Possible answer: The captain gasps from weakness but speaks urgently to convey the good news.

ACT I Scene 1. *An open place.*

Thunder and lightning. Enter three WITCHES.

First Witch.
   When shall we three meet again?
   In thunder, lightning, or in rain?
Second Witch.
   When the hurlyburly's done,
   When the battle's lost and won.
Third Witch.
5   That will be ere the set of sun.
First Witch.
   Where the place?
Second Witch.   Upon the heath.
Third Witch.
   There to meet with Macbeth.
First Witch.
   I come, Graymalkin.°
Second Witch.
   Paddock° calls.
Third Witch.   Anon!°
All.
10   Fair is foul, and foul is fair.
   Hover through the fog and filthy air.   [*Exeunt.*]

Scene 2. *A camp.*

Alarum within.° Enter KING DUNCAN, MALCOLM, DONALBAIN, LENNOX, *with* ATTENDANTS, *meeting a bleeding* CAPTAIN.

King.
   What bloody man is that? He can report,
   As seemeth by his plight, of the revolt
   The newest state.
Malcolm.   This is the sergeant
   Who like a good and hardy soldier fought
5   'Gainst my captivity. Hail, brave friend!
   Say to the king the knowledge of the broil°
   As thou didst leave it.
Captain.   Doubtful it stood,
   As two spent swimmers, that do cling together
   And choke their art.° The merciless Macdonwald—
10   Worthy to be a rebel for to that
   The multiplying villainies of nature
   Do swarm upon him—from the Western Isles°
   Of kerns and gallowglasses° is supplied;
   And Fortune, on his damnèd quarrel smiling,
15   Showed like a rebel's whore: but all's too weak:
   For brave Macbeth—well he deserves that name—
   Disdaining Fortune, with his brandished steel,

302 THE RENAISSANCE

? 2. *This scene, played against thunder and lightning, sets the mood of the play. The witches might have made their appearance through the trapdoor on the stage. Thunder would have been produced by rolling cannonballs in the area above the stage. How could these actresses (actors in Shakespeare's day) convey a sense of menace?*

8. Graymalkin: the witches' attendant, a gray cat.

9. Paddock: toad.   **Anon!:** Soon!

Alarum within: trumpets offstage.

6. broil: quarrel.

? 7. *The captain is bloody and could be carried in or supported by others. How would he speak his lines?*

9. choke their art: hinder each other's ability to swim.

12. Western Isles: a region of West Scotland comprising the Outer Hebrides.

13. kerns and gallowglasses: lightly armed Irish soldiers and heavily armed soldiers.

From the Stratford Festival production of *Macbeth* (1983).

"What bloody man is that?"

E. **Literary Element: Metaphor**
Point out that *unseamed* refers to the stitching in a piece of clothing, the first clothing metaphor in the play. Encourage students to look for and keep track of others by using a graphic organizer like the following.

Reference	Image
[Act I, Scene II, l. 22]	[torn apart like ripped clothing]
[Act I, Scene III, ll. 108–109]	[dressed in another's clothes, to act in another's role]

F. **Literary Element: Paradox**
? How does this paradox fit a **theme** already mentioned? [Possible answer: It relates to the "Fair is foul" statement—what appears fair turns out to be foul.]

Answer to Margin Question
Line 23. Macbeth slashed Macdonwald open from navel to jaws, beheaded him, and stuck the head atop the castle wall.

Which smoked with bloody execution,
Like valor's minion° carved out his passage
20 Till he faced the slave;
Which nev'r shook hands, nor bade farewell to him,
Till he unseamed him from the nave to th' chops,° **E**
And fixed his head upon our battlements.
  King.
    O valiant cousin! Worthy gentleman!
  Captain.
25 As whence the sun 'gins his reflection°
Shipwracking storms and direful thunders break,
So from that spring whence comfort seemed to come
Discomfort swells. Mark, King of Scotland, mark: **F**
No sooner justice had, with valor armed,
30 Compelled these skipping kerns to trust their heels
But the Norweyan° lord, surveying vantage,°
With furbished arms and new supplies of men,
Began a fresh assault.
  King.   Dismayed not this
Our captains, Macbeth and Banquo?

19. **minion:** favorite.

22. **unseamed . . . chops:** split him from navel to jaws.

? 23. *Notice how this horrible action is described by a messenger, not shown on stage. What did Macbeth do to the rebellious Macdonwald?*

25. **'gins his reflection:** rises.

31. **Norweyan:** Norwegian. **surveying vantage:** seeing an opportunity.

MACBETH, ACT I, SCENE 2 303

STRATEGIES FOR INCLUSION

Auditory Explain that when reading a play, reading aloud or acting out the scenes is a useful technique, as that will often help students hear the **tone** of the **dialogue.** Read some scenes aloud; then, have students take turns reading selected scenes aloud. Assign reading parts ahead of time so students may practice before reading to the class.

Less Proficient Readers Preview each scene or act with a brief summary of the action, or let students' first encounter with each act be through an audio- or videotape. Covering an act each day may be too quick a pace, so consider dividing the play into smaller portions for study. ☞

A. Reader's Response: First Thoughts

? What are your first impressions of Macbeth? [Sample responses: His disdain of Fortune is unsettling, and the manner in which he kills Macdonwald is barbaric. Or he is a hero and a savior of Scotland.]

B. Critical Reading: Drawing Conclusions

? Why does Duncan give the title of Cawdor to Macbeth? [Possible answer: Macbeth has just taken the lead role in saving the country from internal and external attack. A new title is an appropriate reward.]

C. Critical Reading: Making Connections

? How might this line relate to Act I, Scene I, l. 4? [It shows one way in which something can be both lost and won.]

Answers to Margin Questions

Line 35. Possible responses: Ironically or admiringly.

Line 44. Possible response: Students may come to see Duncan as a man who trusts too easily and is naive at reading character. They may suspect personal weakness as they reflect on his failure to lead his own troops.

Line 67. Possible responses: Robustly; he may be proud to bestow his honor on Macbeth.

   Captain.   Yes;

35   As° sparrows eagles, or the hare the lion.
    If I say sooth,° I must report they were
    As cannons overcharged with double cracks;
    So they doubly redoubled strokes upon the foe.
    Except° they meant to bathe in reeking wounds,
40   Or memorize another Golgotha,°
    I cannot tell—
    But I am faint; my gashes cry for help.
   King.
    So well thy words become thee as thy wounds;
    They smack of honor both. Go get him surgeons.

                    [*Exit* CAPTAIN *attended.*]

   [*Enter* ROSS *and* ANGUS.]

    Who comes here?
45 **Malcolm.**   The worthy Thane° of Ross.
   Lennox.
    What a haste looks through his eyes! So should he look
    That seems to° speak things strange.
   Ross.   God save the king!
   King.
    Whence cam'st thou, worthy thane?
   Ross.   From Fife, great king;
    Where the Norweyan banners flout the sky
50   And fan our people cold.
    Norway himself,° with terrible numbers,
    Assisted by that most disloyal traitor
    The Thane of Cawdor, began a dismal conflict;
    Till that Bellona's bridegroom,° lapped in proof,°
55   Confronted him with self-comparisons,°
    Point against point, rebellious arm 'gainst arm,
    Curbing his lavish° spirit: and, to conclude,
    The victory fell on us.
   King.   Great happiness!
   Ross.   That now
    Sweno, the Norways' king, craves composition;°
60   Nor would we deign him burial of his men
    Till he disbursèd, at Saint Colme's Inch,°
    Ten thousand dollars to our general use.
   King.
    No more that Thane of Cawdor shall deceive
    Our bosom interest:° go pronounce his present° death,
65   And with his former title greet Macbeth.
   Ross.
    I'll see it done.
   King.
    What he hath lost, noble Macbeth hath won.   [*Exeunt.*]

---

35. As: No more than.

? **35.** *This line can be delivered in several ways. How do you imagine the captain speaks it?*

36. sooth: truth.

39. Except: unless.

40. memorize another Golgotha: make the place as memorable as Golgotha, where Christ was crucified.

? **44.** *Duncan can be played in several ways: as a strong but aging king; as a frail old man; as a kind but foolish old man who doesn't understand what's going on. As the play goes on, decide how you interpret Duncan's character.*

45. Thane: Scottish title of nobility.

47. seems to: seems about to.

51. Norway himself: that is, the king of Norway.

54. Bellona's bridegroom: Bellona is the goddess of war. Macbeth, who is a great soldier, is called her mate. **lapped in proof:** clad in armor.

55. self-comparisons: countermovements.

57. lavish: insolent; rude.

59. composition: peace terms.

61. Saint Colme's Inch: island off the coast of Scotland.

64. bosom interest: heart's trust. **present:** immediate.

? **67.** *As you read, notice how later events relate to the king's words. How would you have him say these lines?*

304 THE RENAISSANCE

OPTIONS FOR TEACHING

INTEGRATING THE LANGUAGE ARTS

Strategic Reading Before students begin reading, review the organization of a play (stage directions, listing of **characters, dialogue**) and the format for recording a reference to a particular line, so that they will be able to refer properly to lines and scenes in their discussions and writing. Familiarity with this technique will also allow students to take notes more quickly and easily.

To review how lines are counted, point out that in split lines the number appears only once, even though the line includes the speech of two separate characters. Note that acts are represented by capital Roman numerals, and line numbers are generally written in Arabic numerals. The scene number may be written in either Arabic or lowercase Roman numerals, but the type of numerals should remain consistent for clarity. The act number always appears first, the scene number second, and the line number(s) third.

To practice as a class, read aloud the following list of references. Ask students to write down and locate the reference and to copy the appropriate line.

I.i.10 or I.I.10 ["Fair is foul, and foul is fair."]

I.ii.67 or I.2.67 ["What he hath lost, noble Macbeth hath won."]

I.iii.38 or I.3.38 ["So foul and fair a day I have not seen."]

I.vi.20 or I.6.20 ["We rest your hermits. Where's the Thane of Cawdor?"]

T304 The Renaissance

Scene 3. *A heath.*

Thunder. Enter the three WITCHES.

First Witch.
  Where hast thou been, sister?
Second Witch.
  Killing swine.
Third Witch.
  Sister, where thou?
First Witch.
  A sailor's wife had chestnuts in her lap,
  And mounched, and mounched, and mounched. "Give me,"
5   quoth I.
  "Aroint thee,° witch!" the rump-fed ronyon° cries.
  Her husband's to Aleppo gone, master o' th' *Tiger:*
  But in a sieve° I'll thither sail,
  And, like a rat without a tail,
10 I'll do, I'll do, and I'll do.
Second Witch.
  I'll give thee a wind.
First Witch.
  Th' art kind.
Third Witch.
  And I another.
First Witch.
  I myself have all the other;
15 And the very ports they blow,°
  All the quarters that they know
  I' th' shipman's card.°
  I'll drain him dry as hay:
  Sleep shall neither night nor day
20 Hang upon his penthouse lid;°
  He shall live a man forbid:°
  Weary sev'nights nine times nine
  Shall he dwindle, peak,° and pine:
  Though his bark cannot be lost,
25 Yet it shall be tempest-tossed.
  Look what I have.
Second Witch.
  Show me, show me.
First Witch.
  Here I have a pilot's thumb,
  Wracked as homeward he did come.

  [*Drum within.*]

Third Witch.
30 A drum, a drum!
  Macbeth doth come.

6. Aroint thee: begone.
rump-fed ronyon: fat-rumped, scabby creature.
8. But . . . sieve: Witches were believed to have the power to sail in sieves.

15. ports they blow: harbors they blow into.
17. card: compass.

20. penthouse lid: eyelid.
21. forbid: cursed.

23. peak: grow pale.

D. Exploring the Culture
Women had been executed by James I for acts similar to those described by the witches in this scene.

E. Reader's Response: Connecting with the Text
These lines introduce the **theme** of sleeplessness in the play. What can make people sleepless? [Sample responses: A curse; insufficient exercise; disturbing experiences; guilt; worry.]

F. Literary Element: Characterization
  ? What might these lines suggest about the witches' powers? [Possible answer: They suggest that the witches' powers are limited. Some students may interpret "his bark cannot be lost" to mean that the witches do not have ultimate control over people's lives or that they do not have ultimate control over people's decisions.]

INTEGRATING THE LANGUAGE ARTS

Usage In Act I, Scene 5, l. 28, the noun *tidings* is used with a singular verb *(is)*. Explain that some nouns that are plural in form are sometimes understood as singular in meaning. Some other examples are *checkers, news,* and *whereabouts.* Ask students to look up all four words in the dictionary and to determine the verb form(s) required. [*Tidings*—generally plural; *news*—singular; *checkers*—singular, although plural for individual pieces; *whereabouts*—singular or plural.]

Speaking and Listening Discuss with students the differences between reading a story aloud and reading a play aloud, focusing on characterization through speech. Review elements of speech such as pitch, tone, articulation, accent, and pace. Assign specific passages to students, and have them practice on their own before reading their passages aloud in class. Remind them that you expect them to use the elements of speech mentioned above to dramatize their prepared readings. ☞

A. Critical Reading: Drawing Conclusions

? How is the spectacle of all the witches saying these lines different from that of only one witch saying them? [Possible answer: The unison speaking might suggest a well-established ritual based on common knowledge and power.]

B. Language Note: Etymology

Weird derives from the Old English word *wyrd,* meaning "fate" or "destiny." *The Oxford English Dictionary* notes that one use of the word, in its plural form, refers to "the Fates, three goddesses that determined the course of human life." In addition, it points out that "the evolution of the forms found in Shakspere's *Macbeth* was [apparently] from *weyrd* to *weyard* (retained in Acts III and IV in the First Folio) and *wey-ward* (used in Acts I and II); the latter was no doubt due to association with *wayward,* a word used many times by Shakspere. . . . In several passages the prosody clearly requires the word to be pronounced as two syllables. . . ."

As you look at this passage from *The Oxford English Dictionary,* what conclusions can you gather about spelling and usage at the time *Macbeth* was written? [Possible answers: Spelling was not standardized. Shakespeare does not seem to have been afraid to use words in new ways, and sometimes a word was used to convey various meanings.]

Answers to Margin Questions

Line 38. Remind students that Macbeth has not heard these lines before but is unwittingly echoing the witches' comment in Act I, Scene I, l. 10. Macbeth may consider the day fair because of the victories he achieved. He may refer to bad weather but a wonderful victory, or he may mean that the killing of Macdonwald and defeat of Sweno were foul, but having succeeded has made the day fair.

Line 39. Banquo might step back and reach for his sword or raise his hand to ward them off. He might gasp or sound surprised as he completes his casual question only to be confronted by such a strange trio.

All.
The weird sisters, hand in hand,
Posters° of the sea and land,
Thus do go about, about:
35 Thrice to thine, and thrice to mine,
And thrice again, to make up nine.
Peace! The charm's wound up.

[*Enter* MACBETH *and* BANQUO.]

Macbeth.
So foul and fair a day I have not seen.

Banquo.
How far is't called to Forres?° What are these
40 So withered, and so wild in their attire,
That look not like th' inhabitants o' th' earth,
And yet are on't? Live you, or are you aught
That man may question? You seem to understand me,
By each at once her choppy° finger laying

306 THE RENAISSANCE

33. **Posters:** travelers.

? 38. *What words is Macbeth echoing here? Why, given the weather, does Macbeth think the day is "fair"?*

39. **Forres:** a town in northeast Scotland and site of King Duncan's castle.

? 39. *What should Banquo do as he sees the witches? How should his voice change between the words* Forres *and* What?

44. **choppy:** chapped; sore.

"All hail, Macbeth! Hail to thee, Thane of Glamis!"

From the Stratford Festival production of *Macbeth* (1983).

OPTIONS FOR TEACHING

COOPERATIVE LEARNING

Thematic Awareness Divide the class into four groups, letting each group choose one of the following **themes: 1.** What it means to be a man; **2.** The relationship between humans and nature; **3.** Blood; **4.** Opposites.

Have each group follow their theme through the play, identifying pertinent lines and making notes of the developing patterns they see. Periodically, each group should report its findings to the class.

45 Upon her skinny lips. You should° be women,
And yet your beards forbid me to interpret
That you are so.

Macbeth.   Speak, if you can: what are you?

First Witch.
All hail, Macbeth! Hail to thee, Thane of Glamis!

Second Witch.
All hail, Macbeth! Hail to thee, Thane of Cawdor!

Third Witch.
50 All hail, Macbeth, that shalt be king hereafter!

Banquo.
Good sir, why do you start, and seem to fear
Things that do sound so fair? I' th' name of truth,
Are ye fantastical, or that indeed
Which outwardly ye show? My noble partner
55 You greet with present grace and great prediction
Of noble having and of royal hope,
That he seems rapt withal:° to me you speak not.
If you can look into the seeds of time,
And say which grain will grow and which will not,
60 Speak then to me, who neither beg nor fear
Your favors nor your hate.

First Witch. Hail!

Second Witch. Hail!

Third Witch. Hail!

First Witch.
65 Lesser than Macbeth, and greater.

Second Witch.
Not so happy,° yet much happier.

Third Witch.
Thou shalt get° kings, though thou be none.
So all hail, Macbeth and Banquo!

First Witch.
Banquo and Macbeth, all hail!

Macbeth.
70 Stay, you imperfect° speakers, tell me more:
By Sinel's death I know I am Thane of Glamis;
But how of Cawdor? The Thane of Cawdor lives,
A prosperous gentleman; and to be king
Stands not within the prospect of belief,
75 No more than to be Cawdor. Say from whence
You owe° this strange intelligence?° Or why
Upon this blasted heath you stop our way
With such prophetic greeting? Speak, I charge you.

[WITCHES *vanish*.]

Banquo.
The earth hath bubbles as the water has, **F**
80 And these are of them. Whither are they vanished?

---

45. **should:** must.

51. *Banquo's words give a clue as to how Macbeth reacts to the witches. What is he doing? When Banquo asks, "Are ye fantastical," whom is he addressing?*

57. **rapt withal:** entranced by it.

61. *What does Banquo ask the witches?*

66. **happy:** lucky.

67. **get:** beget.

70. **imperfect:** incomplete.

71. *Sinel is Macbeth's father. What do you think Macbeth's tone is here? Is he overeager? or just casually curious?*

76. **owe:** own; have.
intelligence: information.

Stage direction. *The witches on Shakespeare's stage would have vanished through the trapdoor. Is Banquo, in his next speech, intrigued or disturbed? How does Macbeth feel?*

The first two prophecies are in the present tense, while the third is in the future *(shalt)*. What do you know about the second prophecy that Macbeth does not know? [Duncan has just named him Thane of Cawdor.]

D. Critical Reading: Speculating
Why might Macbeth "start" and "seem to fear"? [Possible answer: Since he is a close kinsman of Duncan's, perhaps he has already had the idea that he will one day be king. And, given the brutal way he treated Macdonwald, perhaps he has secretly thought of killing the king.]

E. Critical Reading: Making Inferences
How could these paradoxes be true? [Possible answers: Banquo could be lesser than Macbeth in public honors but greater in personal honor or achievement; he could be less lucky publicly but luckier in his private affairs; his son could inherit the throne, although Banquo never does.]

F. Literary Element: Imagery
How does this image (perhaps of mineral or sulfur hot springs) contribute to the mood of the scene? [Possible answers: It suggests mysterious forces at work; it may also suggest foulness, as sulfur has a strong, unpleasant odor.]

Answers to Margin Questions
Line 51. Macbeth is startled. He might show fear in different ways, perhaps by the expression on his face or by a gesture of surprise. Banquo addresses the witches.
Line 61. Banquo asks the witches to foretell his future, too, if they can.
Line 71. Macbeth might be puzzled, intrigued, or entranced.
Stage direction. Possible answer: Banquo might be puzzled, disturbed, intrigued. Macbeth is curious to hear more.

CLASSROOM MANAGEMENT

Reading Aloud To involve all students in the process of reading the text aloud, use groups for in-class readings, assigning parts to each student to make sure that everybody gets several chances to read. Each group can simultaneously read aloud the assigned section of text. On the chalkboard, list stopping points at which the group should pause to summarize what has occurred in the passage.

Re-Reading Because much of the thematic content of this play is understood through echoes of previously stated material, re-reading is essential for comprehension. Encourage students to be alert for connections, to take the time to search for lines that are echoed, and to use note cards or self-stick notes to keep track of themes and connections. Encourage them to re-read the whole play at least once after they have studied it piecemeal and to record a journal entry on how this final reading differs from earlier readings. ☞

A. Critical Reading: Comparing and Contrasting

Compare and contrast Banquo's and Macbeth's reactions to the witches.

[Possible answer: Banquo tries to explain their presence, wondering if he and Macbeth were hallucinating. Macbeth refers to them as an accepted authority, but his manner could be either serious or amused.]

B. Exploring the Historical Period

In his book *Daemonologie*, published in 1597, James I asserts that witches are "agents of the devil." Here Banquo echoes James's belief.

C. Literary Element: Metaphor

The clothing metaphor resurfaces here. What does this phrase mean?

[Possible answer: Why are you calling me by someone else's title?]

Macbeth.
  Into the air, and what seemed corporal° melted
  As breath into the wind. Would they had stayed!
Banquo.
  Were such things here as we do speak about?
  Or have we eaten on the insane root°
85 That takes the reason prisoner?
Macbeth.
  Your children shall be kings.
Banquo.   You shall be king.
Macbeth.
  And Thane of Cawdor too. Went it not so?
Banquo.
  To th' selfsame tune and words. Who's here?

[*Enter* ROSS *and* ANGUS.]

Ross.
  The king hath happily received, Macbeth,
90 The news of thy success; and when he reads°
  Thy personal venture in the rebels' fight,
  His wonders and his praises do contend
  Which should be thine or his. Silenced with that,
  In viewing o'er the rest o' th' selfsame day,
95 He finds thee in the stout Norweyan ranks,
  Nothing afeard of what thyself didst make,
  Strange images of death.° As thick as tale
  Came post with post,° and every one did bear
  Thy praises in his kingdom's great defense,
  And poured them down before him.
100 **Angus.**   We are sent
  To give thee, from our royal master, thanks;
  Only to herald thee into his sight,
  Not pay thee.
Ross.
  And for an earnest° of a greater honor,
105 He bade me, from him, call thee Thane of Cawdor;
  In which addition,° hail, most worthy thane!
  For it is thine.
Banquo.   What, can the devil speak true?
Macbeth.
  The Thane of Cawdor lives: why do you dress me
  In borrowed robes?
Angus.   Who was the thane lives yet,
110 But under heavy judgment bears that life
  Which he deserves to lose. Whether he was combined
  With those of Norway, or did line° the rebel
  With hidden help and vantage, or that with both
  He labored in his country's wrack, I know not;
115 But treasons capital,° confessed and proved,
  Have overthrown him.

81. **corporal:** corporeal (bodily, physical).

84. **insane root:** henbane, believed to cause insanity.

90. **reads:** considers.

97. **Nothing . . . death:** killing, and not being afraid of being killed.
98. **post with post:** messenger with a message.

104. **earnest:** pledge.

106. **addition:** title.

112. **line:** support.

115. **capital:** deserving death.

OPTIONS FOR TEACHING

CROSSING THE CURRICULUM

Social Sciences Have students locate Holinshed's work or use *The Arden Shakespeare,* which contains a large portion of Holinshed's version as an appendix. After reading, they can compare Holinshed's account with the play. They may wish to use a Venn diagram or a different graphic organizer to represent the similarities and differences they find.

Art Have students make a mask of one of the character's faces to show what feelings that **character** might convey. Students can use construction paper, plaster of Paris, or other materials. Have them wear their masks to act out scenes appropriate to the characters they have represented.

Architecture Encourage students to research Scottish castles and their locales. Students might be particularly interested to find out whether there is a castle at Inverness and, if so, what it is like. After they research, suggest that they re-read Act I, Scenes 6 and 7, and draw a blueprint of the rooms involved in the scenes.

Macbeth (*aside*).   Glamis, and Thane of Cawdor:
    The greatest is behind. (*To* ROSS *and* ANGUS.) Thanks for
        your pains.
    (*Aside to* BANQUO.) Do you not hope your children shall be
        kings,
    When those that gave the Thane of Cawdor to me
    Promised no less to them?
120 Banquo (*aside to* MACBETH). That, trusted home,°
    Might yet enkindle you unto the crown,°
    Besides the Thane of Cawdor. But 'tis strange:
    And oftentimes, to win us to our harm,
    The instruments of darkness tell us truths,
125 Win us with honest trifles, to betray 's
    In deepest consequence.
    Cousins,° a word, I pray you.
    Macbeth (*aside*).   Two truths are told
    As happy prologues to the swelling act
    Of the imperial theme.—I thank you, gentlemen.—
130 (*Aside.*) This supernatural soliciting
    Cannot be ill, cannot be good. If ill,
    Why hath it given me earnest of success,
    Commencing in a truth? I am Thane of Cawdor:
    If good, why do I yield to that suggestion
135 Whose horrid image doth unfix my hair
    And make my seated heart knock at my ribs,
    Against the use of nature? Present fears
    Are less than horrible imaginings.
    My thought, whose murder yet is but fantastical,
140 Shakes so my single° state of man that function
    Is smothered in surmise, and nothing is
    But what is not.°
    Banquo.   Look, how our partner's rapt.
    Macbeth (*aside*).
    If chance will have me king, why, chance may crown me,
    Without my stir.
    Banquo.   New honors come upon him,
145 Like our strange° garments, cleave not to their mold
    But with the aid of use.
    Macbeth (*aside*).   Come what come may,
    Time and the hour runs through the roughest day.
    Banquo.
    Worthy Macbeth, we stay upon your leisure.
    Macbeth.
    Give me your favor.° My dull brain was wrought
150 With things forgotten. Kind gentlemen, your pains
    Are registered where every day I turn
    The leaf to read them. Let us toward the king.
    (*Aside to* BANQUO.) Think upon what hath chanced, and at
        more time,

D

E

F

MACBETH, ACT I, SCENE 3 309

? **117.** *"Behind" here means "to follow." How should this important aside be spoken? What is Macbeth's mood?*

120. **trusted home:** trusted all the way.
121. **enkindle . . . crown:** arouse in you the ambition to become king.

? **126.** *How does this speech show Banquo as part of the conscience of the play?*
127. **Cousins:** This word is used frequently by Shakespeare to mean "fellows" or "kindred friends" of some sort.
? **Stage direction.** *When a character is delivering an aside, the director or the playwright must arrange for the others on stage to be involved in some way so that it would be natural for them not to notice the character delivering the aside. Where should Macbeth go on stage to deliver this important aside? What do you think he meant by the "swelling act" in line 128? Where are Banquo, Angus, and Ross?*
? **137.** *What do you suppose Macbeth is thinking of that makes his seated (fixed) heart knock at his ribs in an unnatural way?*
140. **single:** unaided; weak.
142. **nothing . . . not:** Nothing is real to me except my imaginings.
? **142.** *What might Macbeth do as Banquo notices him brooding?*
145. **strange:** new.
? **145.** *What does Banquo compare Macbeth and his new honors to? Is Banquo's mood different from Macbeth's?*
149. **favor:** pardon.

D. Literary Element: Aside
Here, the aside functions as a way of letting us know Macbeth's and Banquo's thoughts without the other characters having awareness of them. What might Ross and Angus think if they heard Macbeth and Banquo? [Possible response: Ross and Angus might think Macbeth and Banquo are traitors to the throne.]

E. Critical Reading: Drawing Conclusions
? According to Banquo, what might be the witches' motives? Why does he choose to say this? [Possible answer: Banquo suggests that they may want to create mischief and harm humans. He is warning Macbeth against them.]

F. Critical Reading: Making Inferences
? What are the two different ways Macbeth imagines he could be crowned king? [Macbeth could murder Duncan, or Macbeth could wait to see whether the event follows naturally.]

Answers to Margin Questions
Line 117. He might sound full of craftiness and greed, hopeful and full of wonder, or just very determined. His mood might be impatience, agitation, or awe.
Line 126. He advises Macbeth to temper his ambition with caution—appearances may be deceiving, and the witches may mean him harm.
Stage direction. Macbeth would probably come downstage and face the audience, while the other characters—Banquo, Angus, and Ross—remain grouped in conversation upstage. The "swelling act" may suggest the stately music that heralds a king's coming—perhaps Macbeth sees his new title as a sign of his coming kingship.
Line 137. Macbeth may be imagining that he murders Duncan to become king himself.
Line 142. The power of his imagination, as Macbeth himself says, may be rendering him lost to the world. He may look dazed, absorbed, or brooding.
Line 145. He compares Macbeth's honors to new clothes, not yet broken in. Yes, Banquo seems to have dismissed the witches' comments, while Macbeth has taken their words to heart.

PROBLEM SOLVING/CRITICAL THINKING

Analyzing Reactions In Act I, both Macbeth and Banquo encounter the witches. To Macbeth, this experience is a temptation to evil, but Banquo does not seem to experience it in the same way. Ask students to use a Venn diagram to brainstorm reasons why the two characters might react differently to the same situation. After students complete the diagram, ask them if there are any general conclusions to be drawn about these two characters. To model, use Transparency 5: Venn Diagram in the Transparency Package.

[may want to be king]
[has been a hero—may feel he deserves a reward and may have legitimate claim to throne]
[wants to believe the prophecies]

[curious about the witches]

[seems humble, not as aggressive as Macbeth]
[not in line for throne]
[skeptical of witches and their words]

Macbeth   Banquo

A. Critical Reading: Drawing Conclusions

? What does Duncan's statement mean? [Possible answer: There are no rules for discovering inner disposition by outward expression: Appearances may be either true or deceiving.]

B. Reader's Response: Shaping Interpretations

? What might Macbeth make of these words? [Sample responses: With his imagination so worked up, he might construe this as a promise of the throne. He might appreciate Duncan's deep gratitude.]

Answers to Margin Questions

Line 8. Possible answer: The way he died was the finest, most courageous thing he ever did. This might be taken at face value as showing the courage of his confession and facing death without fear, or it could be construed as an ironic comment about the quality of his life.

Line 12. Duncan has revealed his weak spot—he is too trusting and not a good judge of character. Ironically, even as Duncan is acknowledging his mistake, he is making the same mistake with Macbeth that he made with the previous Thane of Cawdor.

Line 32. Students may hope that seeing the king's trust and acknowledging his praise, Macbeth will change, like the other Thane of Cawdor did; or they may think Macbeth is a phony and Duncan's praise is ironic. The king hugs Banquo, but he gives Macbeth the honor of being Thane of Cawdor and speaks of him with greater admiration and respect. Macbeth might be jealous of Banquo. Macbeth might feel that Duncan is treating him more as an equal and Banquo more as a friend.

The interim having weighed it, let us speak
Our free hearts each to other.

155 **Banquo.**   Very gladly.
Macbeth.
Till then, enough. Come, friends.   [*Exeunt.*]

Scene 4. *Forres. The palace.*

Flourish.° Enter KING DUNCAN, LENNOX, MALCOLM, DONALBAIN, *and* ATTENDANTS.

King.
Is execution done on Cawdor? Are not
Those in commission yet returned?
Malcolm.   My liege,
They are not yet come back. But I have spoke
With one that saw him die, who did report
5   That very frankly he confessed his treasons,
Implored your highness' pardon and set forth
A deep repentance: nothing in his life
Became him like the leaving it. He died
As one that had been studied in his death
10   To throw away the dearest thing he owed°
As 'twere a careless trifle.

King.   There's no art
To find the mind's construction in the face:
He was a gentleman on whom I built
An absolute trust.

[*Enter* MACBETH, BANQUO, ROSS, *and* ANGUS.]

                              O worthiest cousin!
15   The sin of my ingratitude even now
Was heavy on me: thou art so far before,
That swiftest wing of recompense is slow
To overtake thee. Would thou hadst less deserved,
That the proportion° both of thanks and payment
20   Might have been mine! Only I have left to say,
More is thy due than more than all can pay.
Macbeth.
The service and the loyalty I owe,
In doing it, pays itself.° Your highness' part
Is to receive our duties: and our duties
25   Are to your throne and state children and servants;
Which do but what they should, by doing everything
Safe toward° your love and honor.
King.   Welcome hither.
I have begun to plant thee, and will labor
To make thee full of growing. Noble Banquo,
30   That hast no less deserved, nor must be known
No less to have done so, let me enfold thee
And hold thee to my heart.

310 THE RENAISSANCE

? 8. *What does this famous line mean: "nothing in his life / Became him like the leaving it"?*
10. owed: owned.

? 12. *What irony would you feel here? What does Duncan fail to realize about another face?*

19. proportion: greater amount.

23. pays itself: is its own reward.

27. safe toward: safeguarding.

? 32. *You know Macbeth's thoughts. How do you feel about him as the king lavishes praise on him? Is the king's reception of Banquo even warmer? How might Macbeth react here?*

OPTIONS FOR TEACHING

PROFESSIONAL NOTES

Cultural Diversity Point out that Shakespeare was writing about witches for an audience who may have believed in them. Allow students an opportunity to discuss how other writers and film directors have portrayed witches, such as those in fairy tales or in movies like *The Wizard of Oz.*

Critical Comment: Drama Allow students to consider the following comments quoted in J. L. Styan's *The Elements of Drama:* "[The critic] Granville-Barker asks us to envisage the task before the reader: 'He must, so to speak, perform the whole play in his imagination; as he reads, each effect must come home to him; the succession and contrast of scenes, the harmony and clash of the music of the dialogue, the action implied, the mere physical opposition of characters, or the silent figure standing aloof—for that also can be eloquent.' . . . Leave your armchair throne of judgment, says Granville-Barker, submit for the while to be tossed to and fro in the action of the play: drama's first aim is to subdue us."

T310 The Renaissance

"We will establish our estate upon
Our eldest, Malcolm."

From Roman Polanski's film production of *Macbeth* (1971).

Banquo.   There if I grow,
   The harvest is your own.
King.   My plenteous joys,
   Wanton in fullness, seek to hide themselves
35   In drops of sorrow. Sons, kinsmen, thanes,
   And you whose places are the nearest, know,
   We will establish our estate upon
   Our eldest, Malcolm, whom we name hereafter
   The Prince of Cumberland: which honor must
40   Not unaccompanied invest him only,
   But signs of nobleness, like stars, shall shine
   On all deservers. From hence to Inverness,°
   And bind us further to you.
Macbeth.
   The rest is labor, which is not used for you.°
45   I'll be myself the harbinger,° and make joyful
   The hearing of my wife with your approach;
   So, humbly take my leave.
King.   My worthy Cawdor! **E**
Macbeth (*aside*).
   The Prince of Cumberland! That is a step
   On which I must fall down, or else o'erleap,
50   For in my way it lies. Stars, hide your fires;
   Let not light see my black and deep desires:
   The eye wink at the hand;° yet let that be
   Which the eye fears, when it is done, to see.   [*Exit.*]
King.
   True, worthy Banquo; he is full so valiant,
55   And in his commendations° I am fed;
   It is a banquet to me. Let's after him,
   Whose care is gone before to bid us welcome.
   It is a peerless kinsman.   [*Flourish. Exeunt.*]

? **35.** *There's a clue in this line that shows how moved the king is. What is the king doing at the words "drops of sorrow"?*

42. Inverness: Macbeth's castle.
? **43.** *Who is to inherit Duncan's crown?*
44. The rest . . . you: When rest is not used for you, it is labor.
45. harbinger: sign of something to come.

52. wink . . . hand: be blind to the hand's deed.
? **53.** *Where in this speech do we begin to hear Macbeth talk in terms of darkness?*
55. his commendations: praises of him.

MACBETH, ACT I, SCENE 4   **311**

C. Exploring the Historical Period

Apparently this announcement is not as innocent as it seems. Duncan was violating two laws by naming Malcolm his successor: first, a law prohibiting a minor from succeeding to the throne; second, the law of tanistry, in effect from A.D. 843 to 1058 (coinciding with the end of Macbeth's reign) that said no son of a king on the throne could succeed his father directly. Tanistry required that the first ranking adult of the nearest branch of the family be elected to succeed the king, acting as military leader of all the king's forces (as Macbeth does in the play). Then, succession would revert to the original branch of the family, so that the line of succession alternated between the branches of the royal family.

D. Reader's Response: Shaping Interpretations

Just as today the British prince next in line for the throne is named the Prince of Wales, in Macbeth's time the successor to the Scottish throne was named the Prince of Cumberland.

How do you think Macbeth will react to this news? [Sample responses: Macbeth might have expected the title from Duncan, in which case he might be in shock. Macbeth might be angry, thinking he deserves the reward after his performance in battle.]

E. Expansion

Here Duncan first addresses Macbeth by the traitor's name, and in the lines that immediately follow, Macbeth is again plotting murder.

Answers to Margin Questions

Line 35. Duncan is wiping away tears of joy.
Line 43. Duncan promises the crown to his son Malcolm.
Line 53. Macbeth speaks of literal darkness by telling the stars to hide their light and of the darkness in his heart in ll. 50–51.

Check Test: Questions and Answers
1. In Act I, Scene 2, why does King Duncan give Macbeth a new title? [To reward him for bravery.]
2. What do the witches predict for Macbeth and Banquo? [Macbeth will become Thane of Cawdor and king; Banquo will father kings.]
3. When the audience first meets Lady Macbeth, what is she doing? [Reading a letter from Macbeth.]
4. Whom does Duncan name as Prince of Cumberland? [His son Malcolm.]
5. In the final scene of this act, what is the **conflict** between Lady Macbeth and Macbeth? [Whether or not to kill Duncan.] ☞

A. Critical Reading: Drawing Conclusions

? Whom is the letter from? What is the writer's attitude toward the witches' words? [Macbeth; he believes their prophecies.]

B. Critical Reading: Evaluating an Interpretation

? Do you agree with Lady Macbeth's interpretation of Macbeth's character? Why or why not? [Possible answer: Her characterization of him as too kind does not seem fitting to the man who slit in half and beheaded Macdonwald and now plots murder to become king.]

C. Expansion

The great Shakespearean actress Sarah Kemble Siddons, herself tall and strong, was able to project a Lady Macbeth who was fragile and delicate, yet able to dominate Macbeth by her intellect and beauty. Siddons delivered this speech with sudden energy on "shalt be" (l. 13) and a clear association of "my spirits" (l. 24) with the supernatural beings she has read about in her husband's letter.

Answers to Margin Questions

Stage direction. Encourage students to discuss movement, pauses, and reactions. She may be pacing, reading lines with varying emphasis, laughing at some points, or frowning at others.

Line 13. Lady Macbeth may clutch the letter to her breast or tuck it into her dress. She is addressing the absent Macbeth. Students may associate the phrase with caring or sensitive human feelings, possibly associated with the tenderness of a mother nursing her infant.

Scene 5. *Inverness. Macbeth's castle.*

Enter Macbeth's wife, LADY MACBETH, *alone, with a letter.*

Lady Macbeth (*reads*). "They met me in the day of success; and I have learned by the perfect'st report they have more in them than mortal knowledge. When I burned in desire to question them further, they made themselves air, into which they vanished. Whiles I stood rapt in the wonder of it, came
5 missives° from the King, who all-hailed me 'Thane of Cawdor'; by which title, before, these weird sisters saluted me, and referred me to the coming on of time, with 'Hail, king that shalt be!' This have I thought good to deliver thee, my dearest partner of greatness, that thou mightst not lose the
10 dues of rejoicing, by being ignorant of what greatness is promised thee. Lay it to thy heart, and farewell."

Glamis thou art, and Cawdor, and shalt be
What thou art promised. Yet do I fear thy nature;
15 It is too full o' th' milk of human kindness
To catch the nearest way. Thou wouldst be great,
Art not without ambition, but without
The illness° should attend it. What thou wouldst highly,
That wouldst thou holily; wouldst not play false,
20 And yet wouldst wrongly win. Thou'dst have, great Glamis,
That which cries, "Thus thou must do" if thou have it;
And that which rather thou dost fear to do

? **Stage direction.** *As you picture Lady Macbeth reading this letter, try to imagine what she would be doing on stage and what her mood would be, especially at the words "Thane of Cawdor."*

6. **missives:** messengers.

? 13. *What does Lady Macbeth do with the letter? Whom is she addressing here with "thou" and "thy"? How would you explain "th' milk of human kindness"?*

18. **illness:** wickedness; evil nature.

"My dearest love, / Duncan comes here tonight."
From the Stratford Festival production of *Macbeth* (1983).

312 THE RENAISSANCE

OPTIONS FOR TEACHING

Informal Assessment To check that students are using the language of the play to respond to questions and to participate in class discussion, rate students on a scale of one to five (five points being the best) using the following three criteria:

ASSESSMENT TOOLS

1. Students use important words from the play (for example, theme words).
2. Students quote lines from the play when appropriate.
3. Students use citations correctly.

Than wishest should be undone. Hie thee hither,
That I may pour my spirits in thine ear,
25 And chastise with the valor of my tongue
All that impedes thee from the golden round
Which fate and metaphysical° aid doth seem
To have thee crowned withal.

[*Enter* MESSENGER.]

                                    What is your tidings?

Messenger.
    The king comes here tonight.
Lady Macbeth.   Thou'rt mad to say it!
30 Is not thy master with him, who, were't so,
Would have informed for preparation?
Messenger.
    So please you, it is true. Our thane is coming.
One of my fellows had the speed of him,°
Who, almost dead for breath, had scarcely more
Than would make up his message.
35 **Lady Macbeth.**   Give him tending;
He brings great news.   [*Exit* MESSENGER.]
                                    The raven himself is hoarse
That croaks the fatal entrance of Duncan
Under my battlements. Come, you spirits
That tend on mortal° thoughts, unsex me here,
40 And fill me, from the crown to the toe, top-full
Of direst cruelty! Make thick my blood,
Stop up th' access and passage to remorse,
That no compunctious visitings of nature°
Shake my fell° purpose, nor keep peace between
45 Th' effect and it! Come to my woman's breasts,
And take my milk for gall,° you murd'ring ministers,°
Wherever in your sightless° substances
You wait on nature's mischief! Come, thick night,
And pall° thee in the dunnest° smoke of hell,
50 That my keen knife see not the wound it makes,
Nor heaven peep through the blanket of the dark,
To cry "Hold, hold!"

[*Enter* MACBETH.]

                        Great Glamis! Worthy Cawdor!
Greater than both, by the all-hail hereafter!
Thy letters have transported me beyond
55 This ignorant present, and I feel now
The future in the instant.
Macbeth.   My dearest love,
Duncan comes here tonight.
Lady Macbeth.   And when goes hence?
Macbeth.
    Tomorrow, as he purposes.

---

26. *What do you guess the "golden round" is?*

27. metaphysical: supernatural.

33. had . . . him: had more speed than he did.

36. *Who is the raven she refers to as being hoarse? Why does she call him a raven?*

39. mortal: deadly.

43. compunctious . . . nature: natural feelings of compassion.
44. fell: savage.
46. gall: a bitter substance; bile. **murd'ring ministers:** agents of murder.
47. sightless: invisible.
49. pall: cover with a shroud, a burial cloth. **dunnest:** darkest.

52. *How has Lady Macbeth reinforced the witches' statement: "Fair is foul, and foul is fair . . ."?*

57. *Is their passion for each other as great as their passion for power? If you feel it is, how might a director illustrate it here?*

D. Reader's Response: Shaping Interpretations

Why is Lady Macbeth so shocked by this statement? [Sample responses: It seems too good to be true that her idea of catching "the nearest way" should be served by Duncan arriving at her doorstep. This is too near and too quick, and she is afraid that she may not have time to prepare adequately. Or the messenger's mentioning Duncan may seem to echo her thoughts by making her think momentarily that he knows what she is thinking. She has been imagining Macbeth as king and thinks that the messenger is referring to Macbeth as the king.]

E. Reader's Response: First Thoughts

Why does Lady Macbeth ask the spirits to "unsex" her? [Sample responses: She may feel that her feminine nature would not allow her to accomplish what she is set to do. Such a change would make her more like the witches, who have beards, as Banquo describes them in Act I, Scene 3, ll. 45–47.] Ask students to consider how they imagine Lady Macbeth might say these lines.

F. Critical Reading: Drawing Conclusions

Ask students to discuss possible interpretations of these lines. [Macbeth's line could imply that Duncan plans to leave tomorrow but the Macbeths will prevent it—an idea that Lady Macbeth follows with her metaphorical statement that means Duncan will not be alive the following day. Students may also interpret Macbeth's line as innocent, claiming that Lady Macbeth suggests murder.]

Answers to Margin Questions
Line 26. The king's crown.
Line 36. Answers will vary. She may be speaking figuratively of the raven as a symbol of evil, or she may be referring to the messenger as bringing news that bodes ill for Duncan.
Line 52. She has prayed that her finest qualities be turned to foulness.
Line 57. Possible response: Macbeth's greeting suggests real passion. A director might have Macbeth and Lady Macbeth embrace or gaze into each other's eyes.

A. Critical Reading: Making Connections

? How does this line relate to Duncan's statement, "There's no art / To find the mind's construction in the face"(Act I, Scene 4, ll. 11–12)? [Possible answer: It supports Duncan's comment by suggesting that the face can be made to mask the thoughts.]

B. Critical Reading: Speculating

? What does Lady Macbeth think will happen after Duncan's murder? [Possible answer: She assumes Macbeth will be king. Neither Macbeth nor Lady Macbeth has mentioned killing Malcolm, and this fact suggests two things: Malcolm does not have a legitimate claim to the throne, and Macbeth is the lawful successor to be elected as the next king.]

Answers to Margin Questions

Line 69. Possible answers: Impressed by her fervor; eager to pursue the enterprise; desiring assurance that all will be well.

Line 9. Dramatic irony—though readers know evil lurks within (the Macbeths plan to kill Duncan), the visitors remark how pleasant the place is. It is an illustration of the adage that "Fair is foul and foul is fair." Lady Macbeth probably pretends to be pleased and flattered by the royal visit.

Lady Macbeth.   O, never
Shall sun that morrow see!

60 Your face, my thane, is as a book where men
May read strange matters. To beguile the time,°
Look like the time; bear welcome in your eye,
Your hand, your tongue: look like th' innocent flower,
But be the serpent under't. He that's coming

65 Must be provided for: and you shall put
This night's great business into my dispatch;°
Which shall to all our nights and days to come
Give solely sovereign sway and masterdom.

Macbeth.
We will speak further.

Lady Macbeth.   Only look up clear.°
70 To alter favor ever is to fear.°
Leave all the rest to me.   [*Exeunt.*]

Scene 6. *Before Macbeth's castle.*

Hautboys° *and torches. Enter* KING DUNCAN, MALCOLM, DONAL-
BAIN, BANQUO, LENNOX, MACDUFF, ROSS, ANGUS, *and* ATTENDANTS.

King.
This castle hath a pleasant seat;° the air
Nimbly and sweetly recommends itself
Unto our gentle senses.

Banquo.   This guest of summer,
The temple-haunting martlet,° does approve°
5 By his loved mansionry° that the heaven's breath
Smells wooingly here. No jutty,° frieze,
Buttress, nor coign of vantage,° but this bird
Hath made his pendent bed and procreant° cradle.
Where they most breed and haunt, I have observed
The air is delicate.

[*Enter* LADY MACBETH.]

10 **King.**   See, see, our honored hostess!
The love that follows us sometime is our trouble,
Which still we thank as love. Herein I teach you
How you shall bid God 'ield° us for your pains
And thank us for your trouble.

Lady Macbeth.   All our service
15 In every point twice done, and then done double,
Were poor and single business to contend
Against those honors deep and broad wherewith
Your majesty loads our house: for those of old,
And the late dignities heaped up to them,
We rest your hermits.°

20 **King.**   Where's the Thane of Cawdor?
We coursed° him at the heels, and had a purpose

61. beguile the time: deceive people of the day.

66. dispatch: management.

? **69.** *How is Macbeth feeling?*
69. clear: undisturbed.
70. To alter . . . fear: To show an altered face is dangerous.

Hautboys: oboes.

1. seat: situation; setting.

4. martlet: a bird that builds nests in churches.   **approve:** prove.
5. mansionry: nest (dwelling).
6. jutty: projection.
7. coign of vantage: advantageous corner (of the castle).
8. procreant: breeding.
? **9.** *This scene contrasts strongly with the previous one. Again, what irony do you feel as Duncan admires the castle? How do you imagine Lady Macbeth acts as she now enters to greet her guests?*
13. 'ield: reward.

20. We rest your hermits: We'll remain dependents who will pray for you.
21. coursed: chased.

"See, see, our honored hostess!"
From Roman Polanski's film production of *Macbeth* (1971).

C. Literary Element: Character
Ask students to summarize what they know of Duncan's character. [Students may mention positive qualities such as appreciativeness, graciousness, kindness, courtesy, and generosity. They may also include negative traits such as foolishness, gullibility, and manipulation.]

Answers to Margin Questions
Line 31. Perhaps Duncan and Lady Macbeth join hands and move together offstage, or the king may graciously kiss her hand.
Line 1. (1) He is afraid of the consequences of the murder. (2) He has obligations as Duncan's kinsman, subject, and host. (3) He is afraid that Duncan's death might outrage people. (4) He is motivated by ambition, not by hatred of Duncan or disgust with his behavior as king.

To be his purveyor:° but he rides well,
And his great love, sharp as his spur, hath holp° him
To his home before us. Fair and noble hostess,
We are your guest tonight.

25 **Lady Macbeth.**   Your servants ever
Have theirs, themselves, and what is theirs, in compt,°
To make their audit at your highness' pleasure,
Still° to return your own.

King.   Give me your hand.
Conduct me to mine host: we love him highly,
30 And shall continue our graces toward him.
By your leave, hostess.   [*Exeunt.*]

22. purveyor: advance man.
23. holp: helped.

26. in compt: in trust.

28. Still: always.

? **31.** *How do you imagine the scene ends?*

Scene 7. *Macbeth's castle.*

Hautboys. Torches. Enter a SEWER,° *and diverse* SERVANTS *with dishes and service, and pass over the stage. Then enter* MACBETH.

Sewer: butler.

Macbeth.
If it were done when 'tis done, then 'twere well
It were done quickly. If th' assassination
Could trammel up the consequence, and catch,
With his surcease,° success; that but this blow
5 Might be the be-all and the end-all—here,
But here, upon this bank and shoal of time,

? **1.** *This is one of Shakespeare's great soliloquies, in which Macbeth voices his indecision and possibly his conscience. What are his conflicts?*
4. his surcease: Duncan's death.

MACBETH, ACT I, SCENE 7 315

A. Literary Element: Metaphor

? What comparison is Macbeth using here? [Possible answer: He is comparing his intent to a horse that is spurred on by ambition. But his ambition, like an inept rider, often misjudges the horse and leaps so high he vaults to the horse's other side and falls.]

B. Literary Element: Metaphor

Notice the use of clothing metaphors again. How does Lady Macbeth turn the metaphor against Macbeth? [Possible answer: He speaks of being clothed in the golden opinions of others; she turns around and asks him about how he has clothed himself.]

Answer to Margin Question

Line 26. Students may say yes; without ambition there is no reason for Macbeth to kill Duncan; or no, Lady Macbeth provides a spur.

We'd jump° the life to come. But in these cases
We still have judgment here; that we but teach
Bloody instructions, which, being taught, return
10 To plague th' inventor: this even-handed° justice
Commends° th' ingredients of our poisoned chalice
To our own lips. He's here in double trust:
First, as I am his kinsman and his subject,
Strong both against the deed; then, as his host,
15 Who should against his murderer shut the door,
Not bear the knife myself. Besides, this Duncan
Hath borne his faculties° so meek, hath been
So clear° in his great office, that his virtues
Will plead like angels trumpet-tongued against
20 The deep damnation of his taking-off;°
And pity, like a naked newborn babe,
Striding the blast, or heaven's cherubin horsed
Upon the sightless couriers° of the air,
Shall blow the horrid deed in every eye,
25 That° tears shall drown the wind. I have no spur
To prick the sides of my intent, but only
Vaulting ambition, which o'erleaps itself
And falls on th' other——

[*Enter* LADY MACBETH.]

                              How now! What news?
Lady Macbeth.
He has almost supped. Why have you left the chamber?
Macbeth.
Hath he asked for me?
30 **Lady Macbeth.**   Know you not he has?
Macbeth.
We will proceed no further in this business:
He hath honored me of late, and I have bought
Golden opinions from all sorts of people,
Which would be worn now in their newest gloss,
Not cast aside so soon.
35 **Lady Macbeth.**   Was the hope drunk
Wherein you dressed yourself? Hath it slept since?
And wakes it now, to look so green° and pale
At what it did so freely? From this time
Such I account thy love. Art thou afeard
40 To be the same in thine own act and valor
As thou art in desire? Wouldst thou have that
Which thou esteem'st the ornament of life,°
And live a coward in thine own esteem,
Letting "I dare not" wait upon° "I would,"
Like the poor cat i' th' adage?°
45 **Macbeth.**   Prithee, peace!
I dare do all that may become a man;
Who dares do more is none.

7. jump: risk. (Macbeth knows he will be condemned to hell for the sin of murder.)

10. even-handed: impartial.
11. Commends: offers.

17. faculties: powers.
18. clear: clean.

20. taking-off: murder.

23. sightless couriers: winds.

25. That: so that.

? **26.** *Macbeth says he has no spur to prick the sides of his intent. Is that true?*

37. green: sickly.

42. ornament of life: crown.

44. wait upon: follow.

45. poor . . . adage: saying about a cat who wants fish but won't wet its paws.

Lady Macbeth.   What beast was't then
That made you break° this enterprise to me?
When you durst do it, then you were a man;
50   And to be more than what you were, you would
Be so much more the man. Nor time nor place
Did then adhere,° and yet you would make both.
They have made themselves, and that their fitness now
Does unmake you. I have given suck, and know
55   How tender 'tis to love the babe that milks me:
I would, while it was smiling in my face,
Have plucked my nipple from his boneless gums,
And dashed the brains out, had I so sworn as you
Have done to this.
Macbeth.   If we should fail?
Lady Macbeth.   We fail?
60   But° screw your courage to the sticking-place,°
And we'll not fail. When Duncan is asleep—
Whereto the rather shall his day's hard journey
Soundly invite him—his two chamberlains
Will I with wine and wassail° so convince,°
65   That memory, the warder of the brain,
Shall be a fume, and the receipt of reason
A limbeck only:° when in swinish sleep
Their drenchèd natures lie as in a death,
What cannot you and I perform upon
70   Th' unguarded Duncan, what not put upon
His spongy officers, who shall bear the guilt
Of our great quell?
Macbeth.   Bring forth men-children only;
For thy undaunted mettle° should compose
Nothing but males. Will it not be received,
75   When we have marked with blood those sleepy two
Of his own chamber, and used their very daggers,
That they have done't?
Lady Macbeth.   Who dares receive it other,
As we shall make our griefs and clamor roar
Upon his death?
Macbeth.   I am settled, and bend up
80   Each corporal agent to this terrible feat.
Away, and mock the time° with fairest show:
False face must hide what the false heart doth know.

                                        [*Exeunt.*]

---

48. break: disclose; reveal.

52. adhere: suit.

? 54. *How does Lady Macbeth try to intimidate her husband in this speech? Watch what she says about herself in the next lines. There has been some question as to whether "We fail?" (line 59) should be a question. How does the meaning change if the line is spoken as a statement?*

60. But: only. **sticking-place:** the notch in a crossbow.

64. wassail: drinking. **convince:** overcome.

67. the receipt . . . only: The reasoning part of the brain would become like a **limbeck** (or still), distilling only confused thoughts.

? 72. *"Quell" is murder. What are Lady Macbeth's plans?*
73. mettle: spirit.

81. mock the time: deceive the world.
? 81. *Should Macbeth pause here? How should these key words be spoken?*

? 82. *How is this yet another echo of the witches' words in Scene 1?*

C. Exploring the Historical Period
Many people have puzzled over Lady Macbeth's children, especially in light of Macduff's line in Act IV, Scene 3, l. 216, "He has no children," which seems to refer to Macbeth. The critic Elizabeth Nielson says that the historical Lady Macbeth had a son by a former husband who was killed in battle; this might explain why the fictional Lady Macbeth refers to having children although none are mentioned in the play.

D. Expansion
The critic Kenneth Muir gives another interpretation of this line, saying that it refers to the tightening of a viol string.

E. Reader's Response: Shaping Interpretations
? What convinces Macbeth to go ahead with the murder? [Sample responses: Lady Macbeth's practical plan. Perhaps he sees the daggers as a good sign. He really wants to be king.]

F. Critical Reading: Making Connections
Compare Macbeth's words to Lady Macbeth's words in Act I, Scene 5, ll. 61–64. What do you think of the similarity? [Students may say that Macbeth is becoming more evil—he has taken Lady Macbeth's advice so seriously that now he says virtually the same thing as she.]

Answers to Margin Questions
Line 54. Possible answer: She challenges Macbeth's manliness and makes murder sound easy. Students may argue for any choice: The statement could be spoken ironically, unbelievingly, or with ridicule.
Line 72. She plans to get Duncan's chamberlains so drunk that they pass out; she and Macbeth will murder Duncan and frame the servants.
Line 81. A pause and grim voice are one possibility. The tone could also be sadly defiant.
Line 82. The mask of a fair face conceals the foul heart.

Language and Style p. 318: Answers

1. (Model passages in class to help students see the concept.) Students will probably discover that the meter in Macbeth's speeches tends to be less regular than in Lady Macbeth's, which makes his dialogue sound more erratic and hers more calm or logical.

2. No. (Point out that the witches speak in tetrameter.) It separates their speech from that of other, more earthly characters. It emphasizes the incantation-like character of their speech.
3. There is only one: Scene 5, ll. 1–12. It is a quotation from a letter Macbeth had written in prose, so it is appropriate to keep it in prose.

Making Meanings

Act I

First Thoughts

1. Possible responses: She seems cruel, conniving, ambitious, bossy, devilish, evil, and clever. She and Macbeth seem close because of their intimate greetings; she may be the stronger character in this relationship, judging by the way she manipulates him.

Reviewing the Text

a. "Upon the heath"; "to meet with Macbeth"—Act I, Scene 1, ll. 6–7.

b. Macbeth has beaten and beheaded Macdonwald and joined with Banquo to confront Sweno and the Norwegian forces to bring them to terms.

c. Give Cawdor's title to Macbeth; to reward him for saving the nation.

d. They name Macbeth Thane of Glamis and Cawdor and "king hereafter." They tell Banquo that he will be "lesser than Macbeth, and greater"; "Not so happy, yet much happier"; and that he'll "get kings, though [he] be none."

e. Possible answers: Scene 5, l. 39; Scene 5, l. 50; Scene 5, ll. 58–59; Scene 7, ll. 61–72.

Shaping Interpretations

2. This play may be about darkness and evil or about riddles or paradoxes. The weather reflects the stormy passions that will lead to a murderous plot.

3. Possible answer: That the first two prophecies turn out to be true leads Macbeth to contemplate murder to make the third true also (Scene 3, ll. 127–142).

4. The paradox is that the phrase indicates Banquo will be both less than and greater than Macbeth, a seeming contradiction. Students will not know the truth of this until later in the play, but they may guess that it means Banquo will ultimately make greater contributions or receive more honor than Macbeth.

5. While Macbeth "start[s], and seem[s] to fear," Banquo maintains his poise, neither begging nor fearing. Banquo wonders at their vanishing and is skeptical, but Macbeth longs for them to have stayed and commands them to speak. Macbeth seems superstitious and gullible.

MAKING MEANINGS

Act I

First Thoughts

1. What are your impressions of Lady Macbeth at the end of Act I? What is her relationship with Macbeth (beyond being his wife)?

> **Reviewing the Text**
>
> a. In Scene 1, where do the witches plan to meet again, and why?
>
> b. What news about Macbeth does the bloodstained captain bring to the king in Scene 2?
>
> c. What does the king determine to do for Macbeth? Why?
>
> d. What do the witches tell Macbeth and Banquo in Scene 3?
>
> e. In what lines do you discover Lady Macbeth's plans for Duncan when he visits the castle?

Shaping Interpretations

2. In the very first scene of a play, a dramatist must tell the audience what kind of play they are about to see. What does the brief opening scene of *Macbeth* reveal about the rest of the play? How does the weather reflect the human passions revealed in the rest of the act?

3. How does the witches' prophecy of Macbeth's coming greatness act as a temptation for him?

4. Explain the **paradox,** or the apparently contradictory nature, of the witches' greeting to Banquo in Scene 3: "Lesser than Macbeth, and greater." How is this paradox true?

5. How does Banquo's reaction to the witches differ from Macbeth's? What do you think Macbeth's reaction suggests about his **character**?

6. One of the most interesting parts of any serious play is what goes on in the characters' minds. What **conflict** rages in Macbeth after he hears the witches' prophecy? What **resolution** to this conflict does Macbeth express in his aside, in Scene 4, lines 48–53?

318 THE RENAISSANCE

7. Describe the temperamental differences between Macbeth and his wife. Who is more single-minded and logical? Who is more argumentative and sensitive? Which one wins the argument?

8. What **irony** would the audience feel as they watch Duncan enter the castle and hear him praise its peacefulness?

Extending the Text

9. One critic has said that the witches are "in some sense representative of potentialities within" Macbeth. How could that statement be explained? Is there any evidence that Macbeth has wanted to be king before? Explain your answer.

LANGUAGE AND STYLE

Blank Verse

Almost all of *Macbeth* is written in **blank verse,** or unrhymed iambic pentameter, a form of poetry that comes close to imitating the natural rhythms of English speech. An **iamb** is a metrical foot that has one unstressed syllable followed by one stressed syllable. (Each of the following is an iamb: *Macbeth, success, to win.*) **Pentameter** means that each line of verse has five feet, so one line of iambic pentameter has five iambs:

> **Banquo:** Good sír, why dó you start, and seém to feár . . .

Some lines in *Macbeth* are irregular, with fewer feet or with feet that are not iambs. The play even has a few prose passages, indicated by lines that are set full measure.

1. Scan one major speech by Macbeth and one by Lady Macbeth anywhere in Act I. What variations in iambic pentameter do you find? Why do you think these variations exist—how do sound and sense relate to each other?

2. Do the witches speak in blank verse? Why do you suppose Shakespeare wrote their speeches in this way?

3. Find a prose passage in Act I. Why do you think Shakespeare chose to use prose in this passage?

---

6. He weighs his aversion to murdering Duncan against his desire to be king; he wonders whether to see what happens or make the third prophecy come true. When Duncan makes Malcolm his heir, Duncan directly blocks Macbeth's path to the throne, which tips the balance in favor of violence.

7. Possible answers: Lady Macbeth—practical, single-minded, logical, strong. Macbeth—open to persuasion, poetic, sensitive, insecure when not in battle, argumentative, easily impressed. Lady Macbeth wins; Macbeth is persuaded.

8. Dramatic irony: He praises the place where, if his hosts have their way, he will be murdered.

Extending the Text

9. (Synthesis) It could be explained if Macbeth in fact has already wanted or plotted to become king. Possible evidence: Scene 3, l. 51—a guilty conscience might be why he starts; Scene 3, ll. 134–137—he immediately thinks of murder (though the witches say nothing of it and he did not murder to get the first two titles), perhaps because he has already considered murder.

Answers to Language and Style are on p. T317.

ACT II

Scene 1. *Inverness. Court of Macbeth's castle.*

Enter BANQUO, *and* FLEANCE, *with a torch before him (on the way to bed).*

Banquo.
    How goes the night, boy?
Fleance.
    The moon is down; I have not heard the clock.
Banquo.
    And she goes down at twelve.
Fleance.   I take't, 'tis later, sir.
Banquo.
    Hold, take my sword. There's husbandry° in heaven.
5   Their candles are all out. Take thee that too.
    A heavy summons° lies like lead upon me,
    And yet I would not sleep. Merciful powers,
    Restrain in me the cursèd thoughts that nature
    Gives way to in repose!

[*Enter* MACBETH, *and a* SERVANT *with a torch.*]

                Give me my sword!
10   Who's there?
Macbeth.
    A friend.
Banquo.
    What, sir, not yet at rest? The king's a-bed:
    He hath been in unusual pleasure, and
    Sent forth great largess to your offices:°
15   This diamond he greets your wife withal,
    By the name of most kind hostess; and shut up°
    In measureless content.
Macbeth.   Being unprepared,
    Our will became the servant to defect,°
    Which else should free have wrought.
Banquo.   All's well.
20   I dreamt last night of the three weird sisters:
    To you they have showed some truth.
Macbeth.   I think not of them.
    Yet, when we can entreat an hour to serve,
    We would spend it in some words upon that business,
    If you would grant the time.
Banquo.   At your kind'st leisure.
Macbeth.
25   If you shall cleave to my consent, when 'tis,°
    It shall make honor for you.
Banquo.   So° I lose none
    In seeking to augment it, but still keep
    My bosom franchised° and allegiance clear,°
    I shall be counseled.

? **Stage direction.** *Who is Fleance? What would you remember of the witches' prophecy when you see him here? Do we know if Macbeth and his wife have any children?*

4. **husbandry:** economizing.

6. **summons:** call to sleep.

14. **largess to your offices:** gifts to your servants' quarters.

16. **shut up:** concluded.

18. **to defect:** to insufficient preparations.

? 24. *This is the second time Macbeth has suggested he and Banquo talk. Do you think he might want to confide in Banquo? Does he want to get Banquo on his side? How would you characterize his motives?*

25. **cleave . . . 'tis:** join my cause, when the time comes.
26. **So:** provided that.
28. **franchised:** free (from guilt). **clear:** clean.

MACBETH, ACT II, SCENE 1   **319**

A. Exploring the Historical Period

Theaters in Shakespeare's time did not have the elaborate lighting and stage effects that we have today. What indications of the lighting can you find in the dialogue and stage directions? [Possible answers: References to the torch, the moon being down, twelve, "'tis later," candles being out.]

B. Critical Reading: Making Inferences

? Why does Banquo not want to sleep? [Possible answer: Perhaps he is afraid he will dream of evil.]

C. Language Note: Archaic Form

Usually now people say someone is "in bed," not "a-bed." But there are a few forms that are still used with the introductory *a* that means "on" or "in," including *aloft, atop,* and *aboard.*

D. Reader's Response: First Thoughts

? Do you think Macbeth is telling the truth? [Sample responses: Yes, having taken things into his own hands, Macbeth is concentrating less on the prophecy; or no, it is a blatant lie.]

E. Critical Reading: Drawing Conclusions

? What does Banquo's response mean? [Possible answer: Banquo will only support Macbeth's claim to the throne if the succession occurs in the natural order of things. Banquo is also making a pun on the two senses of honor: He does not want to lose his (1) integrity in the attempt to gain a (2) higher office.]

Answers to Margin Questions
Stage direction. Fleance is Banquo's son. Earlier, the witches told Banquo, "Thou shalt get kings, though thou be none" (Act I, Scene 3, l. 67). The play gives no information about the Macbeths' children other than Lady Macbeth's reference to having nursed a baby.
Line 24. He may wish to convince Banquo to side with him or to find out what Banquo is thinking. Because Macbeth uses veiled speech, it is not clear whether he is trying to find out if Banquo would support his claim if Duncan died naturally or if he is trying to make Banquo an accessory to the crime. Students might say his motives are self-serving ones.

PROGRAM MANAGER

- **Planning Instruction** See *Teaching Notes, Teaching Resources A,* p. 89, for objectives and a summary of Act II.
- **Instructional Support** Before beginning the instructional lesson, see **Graphic Organizer for Active Reading,** *Teaching Resources A,* p. 94, for a Through the Selection activity.

- **Assessment** See **Selection Test (Act II),** *Test Booklet,* pp. 59–60.
- **Language Link** For instruction and practice in proofreading and revision, see **Language Link,** *Teaching Resources A,* pp. 100–102 and *Language and Writing Skills Worksheets,* p. 182.

A. Literary Element: Soliloquy

Ask students to identify the conflict in this soliloquy. [Possible answer: Conflict between the senses of sight and touch as to which perceptions are real.] Point out to students that this famous soliloquy extends through l. 64.

Line-by-line analysis or paraphrase (done individually or in groups) will give students insight into Macbeth's complex, tormented character.

B. Critical Reading: Making Connections

[?] How does Macbeth's attitude toward wicked dreams differ from Banquo's in ll. 7–9? [Possible answer: Banquo tries to avoid the temptation of wicked dreams by staying awake. Macbeth accepts them as a matter of course.]

Answers to Margin Questions

Line 32. The bell signals the murder of Duncan.

Line 41. He draws his own dagger to compare it to the imaginary one. Some students may say that an imaginary dagger is more effective, others that an actual dagger would emphasize the power of his imagination.

Macbeth.   Good repose the while!
Banquo.
30   Thanks, sir. The like to you!

                    [*Exit* BANQUO, *with* FLEANCE.]

Macbeth.
        Go bid thy mistress, when my drink is ready,
        She strike upon the bell. Get thee to bed.

                    [*Exit* SERVANT.]

        Is this a dagger which I see before me,
        The handle toward my hand? Come, let me clutch thee.
35   I have thee not, and yet I see thee still.
        Art thou not, fatal vision, sensible°
(A)   To feeling as to sight, or art thou but
        A dagger of the mind, a false creation,
        Proceeding from the heat-oppressèd brain?
40   I see thee yet, in form as palpable°
        As this which now I draw.
        Thou marshal'st me the way that I was going;
        And such an instrument I was to use.
        Mine eyes are made the fools o' th' other senses,
45   Or else worth all the rest. I see thee still;
        And on thy blade and dudgeon° gouts° of blood,
        Which was not so before. There's no such thing.
        It is the bloody business which informs°
        Thus to mine eyes. Now o'er the one half-world
(B) 50 Nature seems dead, and wicked dreams abuse°
        The curtained sleep; witchcraft celebrates

Very important

[?] **32.** *What is to happen upon the ringing of the bell?*

36. sensible: perceptible to the senses.

40. palpable: obvious.

[?] **41.** *What does Macbeth do at this moment? If you were directing the play, would you suspend a dagger in front of Macbeth during this speech? Why or why not?*

46. dudgeon: hilt.   **gouts:** large drops.

48. informs: gives shape.

50. abuse: deceive.

"Is this a dagger which I see before me, The handle toward my hand?"
From the Stratford Festival production of *Macbeth* (1983).

English Language Development Discuss the meaning of *motive,* and help students determine which characters might have a motive to kill Duncan. Lead students to understand, for example, that Malcolm and Donalbain, as Duncan's heirs, may have a

motive. Assign students to re-read, in pairs, the **dialogue** in Scene 3 between Malcolm and Donalbain (starting with l. 129) and to answer these questions: What do these characters think about what has happened? What do they think about their own safety? What is said in Scene 4, ll. 24–29, that confirms their fears?

Intrapersonal Although the play glosses over the murder by placing it offstage, remind students that Macbeth is about to take a human life. Ask students to think about Duncan, who is about to be murdered in his sleep, and to jot down a few notes about the feelings they have about him as a king and as a human being. Ask students to work their ideas into epitaphs and to share them with the class.

Pale Hecate's° offerings; and withered murder,
Alarumed° by his sentinel, the wolf,
Whose howl's his watch, thus with his stealthy pace,
55 With Tarquin's° ravishing strides, towards his design
Moves like a ghost. Thou sure and firm-set earth,
Hear not my steps, which way they walk, for fear
Thy very stones prate of my whereabout,
And take the present horror from the time,
60 Which now suits with it.° Whiles I threat, he lives:
Words to the heat of deeds too cold breath gives.

[*A bell rings.*]

I go, and it is done: the bell invites me.
Hear it not, Duncan, for it is a knell
That summons thee to heaven, or to hell.   [*Exit.*]

Scene 2. *Macbeth's castle.*

Enter LADY MACBETH.

Lady Macbeth.
That which hath made them drunk hath made me bold;
What hath quenched them hath given me fire. Hark! Peace!
It was the owl that shrieked, the fatal bellman,
Which gives the stern'st good-night.° He is about it.
5 The doors are open, and the surfeited grooms
Do mock their charge with snores. I have drugged their
   possets,°
That death and nature do contend about them,
Whether they live or die.
Macbeth (*within*).   Who's there? What, ho?
Lady Macbeth.
Alack, I am afraid they have awaked.
10 And 'tis not done! Th' attempt and not the deed
Confounds° us. Hark! I laid their daggers ready;
He could not miss 'em. Had he not resembled
My father as he slept, I had done't.

[*Enter* MACBETH.]

                    My husband!
Macbeth.
I have done the deed. Didst thou not hear a noise?
Lady Macbeth.
15 I heard the owl scream and the crickets cry.
Did not you speak?
Macbeth.   When?
Lady Macbeth.   Now.
Macbeth.   As I descended?
Lady Macbeth. Ay.

---

52. Hecate's: Hecate (hek'it), goddess of sorcery.

53. Alarumed: called to action.

55. Tarquin's: Tarquin was a Roman tyrant who raped a woman named Lucrece.

60. now suits with it: now seems suitable to it.

? **64.** *Trace in this soliloquy a vision, a call to action, and a leave-taking. What should you be feeling as an audience as Macbeth exits?*

? **3.** *What sound would you hear here? In this soliloquy, who are the "them" and who is "He"?*

4. stern'st good-night: The owl's call is supposed to portend death. The bellman was a person who rang a bell outside a condemned person's cell the night before his execution, to warn him to confess his sins.

6. possets: bedtime drinks.

11. Confounds: ruins.

? **13.** *How should Lady Macbeth say this last line, which reveals why the plans have changed? Do you think she is beginning to show remorse?*

C. Critical Reading: Making Inferences

? What does this mean? [Possible answer: The deed must be done in the heat of the moment: Talking too much dispels the desire to act.]

D. Expansion
Just as he does with the witches' prediction when he claims they are soliciting him (Act I, Scene 3, l. 130), here he says the bell invites him. He is displacing his own desire onto external beings and objects.

E. Critical Reading: Evaluating an Interpretation
One Shakespearean critic, G. Wilson Knight, points out that Shakespeare made *Macbeth* a Christian drama depicting the conflict between grace and evil. If one interprets the play in this way, how does Macbeth, in this soliloquy, reject grace and turn himself over to the powers of evil? [Although he recognizes that there is no such thing as the dagger he imagines, he commits himself to making the imaginary act of killing a real act, thus embracing evil.]

F. Cultural Connections
Ask students how they visualize Lady Macbeth. The English actor and producer William Poel saw Lady Macbeth as about thirty-five years old, with bright red hair. Her head is erect, back straight, and shoulders squared; she moves with a slight swing. Glenda Jackson's aggressive portrayal of Lady Macbeth might have matched Poel's description.

G. Reader's Response: Shaping Interpretations

? Why do you think Shakespeare chooses not to show Duncan's murder? [Sample responses: It might make an audience too sympathetic toward Duncan and unsympathetic toward the Macbeths; it might detract from the suspense that is still unfolding.]

Answers to Margin Questions
Line 64. Vision: ll. 33–47; call to action: l. 62; leave-taking: ll. 63–64. Students may suggest horror, revulsion, or suspense.
Line 3. An owl shrieking. The grooms are "them" and Macbeth is "he."
Line 13. She might speak with tenderness, with surprise at her own inability to overcome her emotions, or with remorse. If she is not feeling remorse, she at least shows a more vulnerable side of her character.

STRATEGIES FOR INCLUSION

Kinesthetic Assign particular scenes to groups of two to four, and ask the groups to perform that scene either as a skit or puppet show. Puppets can be made by backing magazine pictures with poster board and gluing the cut-out figures to wooden sticks.

COOPERATIVE LEARNING

Research Divide the class into groups of three to five to look up and share information about the specific historical references in *Macbeth*. Possible topics are the family trees of Macbeth and Lady Macbeth, showing their relationship to royalty; maps or specific information on the locations mentioned in the text; or the actual chronology of historical events as compared to the events in *Macbeth*. Invite groups to create a presentation that shares their information with the rest of the class.

Macbeth pointing the
dagger at Duncan in
Roman Polanski's film
production of *Macbeth*
(1971).

A. Critical Reading: Making Connections

? How is the deed of killing Duncan different from the deed of killing Macdonwald? Are the acts similar in any way? [Possible answers: On the moral level, killing on the battlefield to defend one's country against a traitor is almost the opposite of the traitorous act of assassinating the head of state. Students may say that the brutal way in which Macdonwald was killed shows a side of Macbeth's nature that comes out even more fully in the murder of Duncan. They may say that Macbeth's ambition is clear in both acts.]

B. Critical Reading: Making Inferences

? What is happening to Macbeth? [Possible answer: He already feels guilt and separation from God. It is ironic that he desires a blessing when he has just killed the king, breaking a religious commandment and murdering the person who supposedly rules by divine right.]

Answer to Margin Question

Line 33. Possible answers: Yes, "must not" and "make us mad" suggest that she is also troubled; or no, she is trying to calm Macbeth.

Macbeth. Hark!
　　Who lies i' th' second chamber?
Lady Macbeth. 　　　　　　　　Donalbain.
20 **Macbeth.** This is a sorry sight.
Lady Macbeth.
　　A foolish thought, to say a sorry sight.
Macbeth.
　　There's one did laugh in 's sleep, and one cried "Murder!"
　　That they did wake each other. I stood and heard them.
　　But they did say their prayers, and addressed them
　　Again to sleep.
25 **Lady Macbeth.** There are two lodged together.
Macbeth.
　　One cried "God bless us!" and "Amen" the other,
Ⓐ　As they had seen me with these hangman's hands:
　　List'ning their fear, I could not say "Amen,"
　　When they did say "God bless us!"
Lady Macbeth. 　　　　　　　Consider it not so deeply.
Macbeth.
30　But wherefore could not I pronounce "Amen"?
Ⓑ　I had most need of blessing, and "Amen"
　　Stuck in my throat.
Lady Macbeth. 　　　These deeds must not be thought
　　After these ways; so, it will make us mad.

? **33.** *Is Lady Macbeth fighting for control here?*

OPTIONS FOR TEACHING

INTEGRATING THE LANGUAGE ARTS

Strategic Reading To help students read more carefully and interpret as they read, encourage them to summarize the tone and meaning of each scene in their Reader's Logs. Invite students to discuss their summaries and to select the best wording to post on a bulletin board as a review of the action, scene by scene.

Writing: Essay Have students write an in-class paper supporting the following thesis statement: Shakespeare's use of nature imagery reinforces Macbeth's unnatural killing of King Duncan. Students must use at least three quotations from Act I or Act II to develop their arguments.

Macbeth.
Methought I heard a voice cry "Sleep no more!
35 Macbeth does murder sleep"—the innocent sleep,
Sleep that knits up the raveled sleave° of care,
The death of each day's life, sore labor's bath,
Balm of hurt minds, great nature's second course,°
Chief nourisher in life's feast——
Lady Macbeth.   What do you mean?
Macbeth.
40 Still it cried "Sleep no more!" to all the house:
"Glamis hath murdered sleep, and therefore Cawdor
Shall sleep no more: Macbeth shall sleep no more."
Lady Macbeth
Who was it that thus cried? Why, worthy thane,
You do unbend your noble strength, to think
45 So brainsickly of things. Go get some water,
And wash this filthy witness from your hand.
Why did you bring these daggers from the place?
They must lie there: go carry them, and smear
The sleepy grooms with blood.
Macbeth.   I'll go no more.
50 I am afraid to think what I have done;
Look on 't again I dare not.
Lady Macbeth.   Infirm of purpose!
Give me the daggers. The sleeping and the dead
Are but as pictures. 'Tis the eye of childhood
That fears a painted devil. If he do bleed,
55 I'll gild the faces of the grooms withal,
For it must seem their guilt.   [*Exit. Knock within.*]
Macbeth.   Whence is that knocking?
How is 't with me, when every noise appalls me?
What hands are here? Ha! They pluck out mine eyes!
Will all great Neptune's ocean wash this blood
60 Clean from my hand? No; this my hand will rather
The multitudinous seas incarnadine,°
Making the green one red.

[*Enter* LADY MACBETH.]

Lady Macbeth.
My hands are of your color, but I shame
To wear a heart so white. (*Knock.*) I hear a knocking
65 At the south entry. Retire we to our chamber.
A little water clears us of this deed:
How easy is it then! Your constancy
Hath left you unattended.° (*Knock.*) Hark! more knocking.
Get on your nightgown, lest occasion call us
70 And show us to be watchers.° Be not lost
So poorly in your thoughts.

---

36. **raveled sleave:** tangled thread.

38. **second course:** sleep (the less substantial first course is food).

? 41. *Who else complained about sleep? In what way has Glamis "murdered sleep"?*

? 46. *What is the "filthy witness"? What actions are the couple engaged in here? In the next line, Lady Macbeth discovers the daggers. Why is she so alarmed at seeing them in her husband's hands? How could Macbeth have been carrying them so they weren't visible before?*

? 55. *What will Lady Macbeth do to the grooms if Duncan bleeds enough?*

61. **incarnadine:** make red.

? 63. *Based on this speech, what does Lady Macbeth look like?*

68. **Your . . . unattended:** Your firmness has deserted you.
70. **watchers:** that is, up late.

? 71. *What is Macbeth acting like?*

C. Literary Element: Metaphor
Identify the metaphors that describe sleep. [A knitter who untangles threads; the coming of night; a bath that soothes a laborer; an ointment that can heal the mind; the body's greatest need after food.]

D. Expansion
The critic Mark Van Doren points out that nothing could be more horrible than that Macbeth has murdered sleep, for in Shakespeare's plays, sleep "is ever the privilege of the good and the reward of the innocent. If it has been put to death, there is no goodness left. One of the witches knows how to torture sailors by keeping sleep from their penthouse lids [Act I, Scene 3, ll. 19–20], but only Macbeth can murder sleep itself."

E. Literary Element: Pun
When one puts gold on (gilds) something, it is then *gilt,* which sounds just like *guilt* when spoken aloud.

F. Expansion
Note that Macbeth's and Lady Macbeth's speeches contrast sharply. Besides the differences in **imagery,** there is a fundamental difference in approach. Lady Macbeth is practical—water washes away blood. Macbeth is speaking on the metaphysical level—his sin will spread through the world.

Answers to Margin Questions
Line 41. Banquo decides not to sleep in order to avoid evil dreams (Act II, Scene 1). Since first imagining Duncan's murder, Macbeth has been stuck in time at the moment of the murder. Now, without sleep to make the transition to a new day, it seems as if he may continue to relive the moment. So the murder of Duncan has put an end to sleep and may have put an end to the passage of time for Macbeth.
Line 46. Duncan's blood. They are cleaning up after the murder. She is probably shocked that Macbeth has removed the murder weapons; being seen with them would implicate him and shows a lack of attention on his part that she may find frightening. Earlier, they might have been in his belt or sleeve.
Line 55. Smear Duncan's blood on their faces.
Line 63. Possible answer: Her hands are bloody from the daggers and from smearing the grooms with blood, but she appears confident.
Line 71. He is lost in thought.

INTEGRATING THE LANGUAGE ARTS

Mechanics Have students study the text to find devices that Shakespeare uses to add or subtract syllables from words to make a ten-syllable line. Invite students to rewrite a fairy tale in lines of ten syllables, using some of the devices Shakespeare does to make the language fit the format. [Devices include contractions, grave accents, and changes in word form.]

Language and Vocabulary As a class, analyze a short passage, identifying individual words that are not in use today or that have different meanings than they did when the play was written. List each word on the chalkboard, and beside each, have students suggest a more modern word. Reread the passage, substituting the modern words, and ask for students' responses to the changed sound of the language.

A. Critical Reading: Drawing Conclusions

? What does this mean? [Possible answer: If I fully acknowledge the horror of my deed, I will be unable to bear knowing I am the person who committed it.]

B. Exploring the Historical Period

This play about the murder of a king would have held great interest for James I and his people, who lived through the discovery of the Gunpowder Plot in November 1605. Some critics believe that the Porter's speech is filled with references to the Jesuit priest Father Henry Garnett, who was implicated in the plot, tried on March 28, 1606, and hanged as a traitor. First, Garnett used the assumed name *Farmer.* Second, Garnett defended the use of equivocation as just.

Answers to Margin Questions

Stage direction. Possible response: He might wish it could awake him from sleep to find that he had not killed Duncan so that he could escape the horror he now feels.

Stage direction. He might stagger, fumble with the gates or keys, pantomime the people he is imagining, put his hands over his ears, pretend to do his own knocking, or forget what he is doing.

"My hands are of your color, but I shame To wear a heart so white."

From the Stratford Festival production of *Macbeth* (1983).

Macbeth.

Ⓐ To know my deed, 'twere best not know myself.

[*Knock.*]

Wake Duncan with thy knocking! I would thou couldst!

[*Exeunt.*]

Scene 3. *Macbeth's castle.*

Enter a PORTER. *Knocking within.*

Porter. Here's a knocking indeed! If a man were porter of hell gate, he should have old° turning the key. (*Knock.*) Knock, knock, knock! Who's there, i' th' name of Beelzebub?° Here's a farmer, that hanged himself on th' expectation of plenty. Come in time! Have napkins enow° about you; here you'll sweat for 't. (*Knock.*) Knock, knock! Who's there, in th' other devil's name? Faith, here's an equivocator,° that could swear in both the scales against either scale; who committed treason enough for God's sake, yet could not equivocate to heaven. O, come in, equivocator. (*Knock.*) Knock, knock, knock! Who's there? Faith, here's an English tailor come hither for stealing out of a French hose:° come in, tailor. Here you may roast your goose.° (*Knock.*) Knock,

5

10

? **Stage direction.** *In the theater, this sharp, loud knocking is frightening. In the next line, what might Macbeth wish the knocking could awake in himself?*

? **Stage direction.** *Note that the porter is drunk. What would he be doing during this long speech while the knocking persists?*

2. have old: grow old.

3. Beelzebub: the Devil.

5. enow: enough.

7. equivocator: The porter means a Jesuit (who allegedly used false arguments in his zeal for souls).

12. French hose: tightfitting stocking.

13. goose: iron used by a tailor for pressing.

OPTIONS FOR TEACHING

CLASSROOM MANAGEMENT

Using Films If you use videos to augment your teaching of *Macbeth,* decide what role you want the film to have. Will you use it to introduce material? To reinforce material? As a culminating experience? Be aware that some students' own images will be overwhelmed by that of the film. Also, it is often worthwhile to present at least portions from more than one film, because one film alone can seem very authoritative to stu-

dents, leading them to believe that it embodies the "correct" interpretation of the play.

Question Slips Give students an opportunity to write down anonymously any questions concerning things they do not understand about the play. This can help you clear up misconceptions that do not surface in class discussion.

knock; never at quiet! What are you? But this place is too
15 cold for hell. I'll devil-porter it no further. I had thought to
have let in some of all professions that go the primrose way
to th' everlasting bonfire. (*Knock.*) Anon, anon! (*Opens an
entrance.*) I pray you, remember the porter.

[*Enter* MACDUFF *and* LENNOX.]

Macduff.
Was it so late, friend, ere you went to bed,
20 That you do lie so late?
Porter. Faith, sir, we were carousing till the second cock:° and
drink, sir, is a great provoker of three things.
Macduff. What three things does drink especially provoke?
Porter. Marry, sir, nose-painting, sleep, and urine. Lechery, sir,
25 it provokes and unprovokes; it provokes the desire, but it
takes away the performance: therefore much drink may be
said to be an equivocator with lechery: it makes him and it
mars him; it sets him on and it takes him off; it persuades
him and disheartens him; makes him stand to and not stand
30 to; in conclusion, equivocates him in a sleep, and giving him
the lie, leaves him.
Macduff. I believe drink gave thee the lie° last night.
Porter. That it did, sir, i' the very throat on me: but I requited
him for his lie, and, I think, being too strong for him, though
35 he took up my legs sometime, yet I make a shift to cast° him.
Macduff. Is thy master stirring?

[*Enter* MACBETH.]

Our knocking has awaked him; here he comes.
Lennox.
Good morrow, noble sir.
Macbeth.   Good morrow, both.
Macduff.
Is the king stirring, worthy thane?
Macbeth.   Not yet.
Macduff.
40 He did command me to call timely° on him:
I have almost slipped the hour.
Macbeth.   I'll bring you to him.
Macduff.
I know this is a joyful trouble to you;
But yet 'tis one.
Macbeth.
The labor we delight in physics° pain.
This is the door.
45 **Macduff.**   I'll make so bold to call,
For 'tis my limited service.°   [*Exit* MACDUFF.]
Lennox.
Goes the king hence today?

21. **second cock:** about 3 A.M.

32. **gave thee the lie:** pun
meaning "called you a liar" and
"stretched you out, lying in bed."

35. **cast:** here, a pun meaning
"to cast in plaster" and "to vomit"
(cast out).

36. *All the time this humorous bantering is going on,
what do we know these king's men
are about to discover?*

40. **timely:** early.

44. **physics:** cures.

46. **limited service:** appointed
duty.

**C. Critical Reading: Finding
Details**

? What explicit details in the Porter's
speech might support the idea
that the castle is hell? ["Porter of hell
gate," "Beelzebub," "here you'll sweat,"
"in th' other devil's name," "this place
is too cold for hell. I'll devil-porter it
no further," and "the primrose way to
th' everlasting bonfire."]

**Answer to Margin Question
Line 36.** The body of Duncan and
the bloodied grooms.

CROSSING THE CURRICULUM

Social Sciences Have students research the
rules for succession to the throne in Scotland and
England. Encourage them to create a chart to
show comparisons between these rules (and the
reasons behind them).

Science Have students brainstorm in groups to
provide natural explanations for the occurrences

mentioned in Act II, Scene 3, ll. 48–55 and Act II,
Scene 4, ll. 1–18. Ask each group to write a brief
report detailing their explanations. [For example,
for the first reference, an earthquake could cause
chimneys to crumble, cries of fear, and shaking
of the earth—perhaps just a coincidence with
Duncan's murder.]   ☞

A. Critical Reading: Comparing and Contrasting

? Why does Macbeth phrase his words this way? [The part before the colon is a lie and the part afterward is true. Perhaps Macbeth does not want to add lying to his other sins, so he corrects his statement.]

B. Literary Element: Pathetic Fallacy

In Lennox's report, we have an instance of nature mirroring events in human society. If students have read Shakespeare's *Julius Caesar,* they may recall the portents that prefigured tragedy for Caesar (Act I, Scene 3).

C. Critical Reading: Making Connections

? What other bird mentioned earlier might line 53 call to mind? [Possible answer: This line suggests the owl Lady Macbeth heard in Act II, Scene 2, ll. 3 and 15.]

D. Exploring the Historical Period

This phrase is a reference to the divine right of kings, James I's pet theory.

E. Critical Reading: Making Connections

Look back at Act II, Scene I, ll. 49–64. How are Macbeth's and Macduff's purposes similar? How is the bell used in each passage? [Both characters are trying to find words that are adequate for the situation—Macbeth to work himself up to commit murder; Macduff to express horror at the evil that has been done. Ironically, the bell signals the time for Macbeth to commit murder in the earlier scene, but here it rings to alert others to that murder.]

Answers to Margin Questions

Line 47. Possible response: Changing his statement as he does makes him seem nervous and unsure of himself.

Line 54. Unnatural winds and voices, screeching owls, and earthquakes parallel the unnatural death of Duncan.

Line 55. The line is ironic because the night was rough for reasons that Macbeth knows but Lennox does not. Macbeth probably tries to sound natural, carrying on his part of the conversation.

Line 63. Macduff speaks of the king as a sacred building that it is a sacrilege to attack. His image suggests the concept of kings as divinely anointed.

(A) **Macbeth.**   He does: he did appoint so.
Lennox.
The night has been unruly. Where we lay,
Our chimneys were blown down, and, as they say,
50   Lamentings heard i' th' air, strange screams of death,
And prophesying with accents terrible
(B) Of dire combustion° and confused events
New hatched to th' woeful time: the obscure bird
(C) Clamored the livelong night. Some say, the earth
Was feverous and did shake.
55   **Macbeth.**   'Twas a rough night.
Lennox.
My young remembrance cannot parallel
A fellow to it.

[*Enter* MACDUFF.]

Macduff.
O horror, horror, horror! Tongue nor heart
Cannot conceive nor name thee.
Macbeth and Lennox.   What's the matter?
Macduff.
60   Confusion now hath made his masterpiece.
Most sacrilegious murder hath broke ope
(D) The Lord's anointed temple,° and stole thence
The life o' th' building.
Macbeth.   What is't you say? The life?
Lennox.
Mean you his majesty?
Macduff.
65   Approach the chamber, and destroy your sight
With a new Gorgon:° do not bid me speak;
See, and then speak yourselves. Awake, awake!

[*Exeunt* MACBETH *and* LENNOX.]

Ring the alarum bell. Murder and treason!
Banquo and Donalbain! Malcolm! Awake!
70   Shake off this downy sleep, death's counterfeit,
And look on death itself! Up, up, and see
The great doom's image! Malcolm! Banquo!
As from your graves rise up, and walk like sprites,
(E) To countenance° this horror. Ring the bell.

[*Bell rings. Enter* LADY MACBETH.]

Lady Macbeth.
75   What's the business,
That such a hideous trumpet calls to parley°
The sleepers of the house? Speak, speak!
Macduff.   O gentle lady,
'Tis not for you to hear what I can speak:

---

47. *How must Macbeth be feeling?*

52. combustion: tumult; uproar.

? **54.** *In Elizabethan times, people often believed that nature mirrored terrible things happening to human beings, especially to kings. How did this weather mirror what was happening to the king in Macbeth's castle?*

? **55.** *A single line, but full of irony. How would Macbeth say it?*

62. Lord's anointed temple: body of the king.

? **63.** *How would you explain Macduff's metaphors?*

66. Gorgon: creature from Greek mythology whose face could turn an onlooker to stone.

74. countenance: be in keeping with.

76. parley: conference of war.

OPTIONS FOR TEACHING

PROBLEM SOLVING/CRITICAL THINKING

Looking for Clues   Explain that, just as police investigators, psychologists, or sociologists must do, literary scholars analyze a **character's** thought process and actions by looking critically for clues. Have students review passages of the text related to Duncan's murder. Based on the evidence so far, have them determine who is responsible for Duncan's murder: Is it the result of Macbeth's choice, the witches' curse, or manipulation by other characters? Students should defend their answers with references from the text in class discussion.

The repetition, in a woman's ear,
Would murder as it fell.

[*Enter* BANQUO.]

80   O Banquo, Banquo!
Our royal master's murdered.
Lady Macbeth.   Woe, alas!
What, in our house?
Banquo.   Too cruel anywhere.
Dear Duff, I prithee, contradict thyself,
And say it is not so.

[*Enter* MACBETH, LENNOX, *and* ROSS.]

Macbeth.

85   Had I but died an hour before this chance,
I had lived a blessèd time; for from this instant
There's nothing serious in mortality:°
All is but toys. Renown and grace is dead,
The wine of life is drawn, and the mere lees°
90   Is left this vault° to brag of.

[*Enter* MALCOLM *and* DONALBAIN.]

Donalbain.
What is amiss?
Macbeth.   You are, and do not know't.
The spring, the head, the fountain of your blood
Is stopped; the very source of it is stopped.
Macduff.
Your royal father's murdered.
Malcolm.   O, by whom?
Lennox.
95   Those of his chamber, as it seemed, had done't:
Their hands and faces were all badged° with blood;
So were their daggers, which unwiped we found
Upon their pillows. They stared, and were distracted.
No man's life was to be trusted with them.
Macbeth.
100   O, yet I do repent me of my fury,
That I did kill them.
Macduff.   Wherefore did you so?
Macbeth.
Who can be wise, amazed, temp'rate and furious,
Loyal and neutral, in a moment? No man.
The expedition° of my violent love
105   Outrun the pauser, reason. Here lay Duncan,
His silver skin laced with his golden blood,
And his gashed stabs looked like a breach in nature
For ruin's wasteful entrance: there, the murderers,
Steeped in the colors of their trade, their daggers

MACBETH, ACT II, SCENE 3   327

? **82.** *The emphasis on Lady Macbeth's gentleness and fairness when we know the foulness underneath might well merit a snicker from the audience. The snicker might be expected to grow into a laugh when she says, "What, in our house?" These are difficult moments to act. How do you think Lady Macbeth should be behaving?*

87. mortality: life.

89. lees: dregs.
90. vault: pun on "wine vault" and the "vault of heaven."

? **94.** *Macbeth and Lady Macbeth might well look at each other at this moment. Does Lennox draw the conclusion they wanted him to draw: that the servants killed Duncan?*
96. badged: marked.

104. expedition: haste.

F. Critical Reading: Analyzing Tone

? How do Macbeth's and Macduff's announcements of Duncan's death to the king's sons differ? [Macbeth speaks in metaphors; Macduff is plain-spoken and matter-of-fact.]

G. Reader's Response: First Thoughts
Macbeth has done something not in the plan. Was this wise? [Sample responses: No, things were fine; there was no reason to complicate things with more murders. Yes, Lennox is already supporting Macbeth's story, a fact that bodes well for the future, and the grooms cannot protest.]

Answers to Margin Questions
Line 82. Possible answer: She must play the part seriously, expressing the surprise and horror that such a deed merits.
Line 94. Some students may say that "as it seemed" suggests that Lennox is not fully convinced. Other students may argue that when Lennox says "No man's life was to be trusted with them," this is as good as an indictment.

PROFESSIONAL NOTES

Thematic Connections: "Under a Hand Accursed" Ask students why this might be an appropriate title for this Collection. [Possible answers: The theme is a specific line from the play (Act III, Scene 6, l. 49), in which Lennox refers to Scotland as suffering under a ruler who has committed murder, so it is appropriate to the Collection centered around Macbeth. Perhaps the phrase refers to the curses of the witches, suggesting that Macbeth's actions were fated. It might be purposefully ambiguous so that readers stop to consider whether events are influenced by choice or fate.] ☞

? Why does Lady Macbeth cry out? [Possible answers: She follows her own suggestion in Act I, Scene 7, l. 78, and makes her "griefs and clamor roar." She is trying to draw attention away from Macbeth's absurd and unnatural speech by pretending to faint; or she is shocked by the murder of the grooms and is beginning to fall apart, and she really faints.]

B. **Critical Reading: Analyzing Character**

? Is Banquo satisfied with the grooms' guilt? [Possible answer: No, he has fears and suspicions and wants to examine the matter further.]

C. **Reader's Response: Shaping Interpretations**

? What does each of the following characters seem to think of the evidence: Lennox, Banquo, Macduff, Lady Macbeth, Macbeth, Malcolm, and Donalbain? [Sample responses: Students may think that Lennox does or does not believe the grooms guilty; Banquo is not sure and may be suspicious of Macbeth because of what he knows from Act I. Lady Macbeth may think that Macbeth reveals too much with the murder of the grooms and his cover-up speech, or, if she thinks Lennox believes it, she may think that her husband is good at deception. Macbeth is starting to act on his own, which may mean that he feels more self-assured. Malcolm and Donalbain do not yet seem to suspect anyone in particular—they just fear for their lives and want to get away.]

D. **Critical Reading: Drawing Conclusions**

? What does Donalbain's parting comment mean? [Those closest to the crown or in line for it are in the most danger of being killed.]

---

110   Unmannerly breeched with gore.° Who could refrain,°
     That had a heart to love, and in that heart
     Courage to make 's love known?

(A) **Lady Macbeth.**   Help me hence, ho!
Macduff.
     Look to the lady.
Malcolm (*aside to* DONALBAIN). Why do we hold our tongues,
     That most may claim this argument for ours?°
Donalbain (*aside to* MALCOLM).
115   What should be spoken here,
     Where our fate, hid in an auger-hole,°
     May rush, and seize us? Let's away:
     Our tears are not yet brewed.
Malcolm (*aside to* DONALBAIN). Nor our strong sorrow
     Upon the foot of motion.°
Banquo.   Look to the lady.

                [LADY MACBETH *is carried out.*]

120   And when we have our naked frailties hid,°
     That suffer in exposure, let us meet
     And question° this most bloody piece of work,
(B)   To know it further. Fears and scruples° shake us.
     In the great hand of God I stand, and thence
125   Against the undivulged pretense° I fight
     Of treasonous malice.
Macduff.   And so do I.
All.   So all.
Macbeth.
     Let's briefly° put on manly readiness,
     And meet i' th' hall together.
All.   Well contented.

        [*Exeunt all but* MALCOLM *and* DONALBAIN.]

(C) **Malcolm.**
     What will you do? Let's not consort with them.
130   To show an unfelt sorrow is an office°
     Which the false man does easy. I'll to England.
Donalbain.
     To Ireland, I; our separated fortune
     Shall keep us both the safer. Where we are
(D)   There's daggers in men's smiles; the near in blood,
     The nearer bloody.
135 **Malcolm.**   This murderous shaft that's shot
     Hath not yet lighted, and our safest way
     Is to avoid the aim. Therefore to horse;
     And let us not be dainty of° leave-taking,
     But shift away. There's warrant° in that theft
140   Which steals itself° when there's no mercy left.

                      [*Exeunt.*]

328 THE RENAISSANCE

---

110. unmannerly breeched with gore: unbecomingly covered with blood, as if wearing red trousers. **refrain:** check oneself.

114. That . . . ours: who are the most concerned with this topic.

116. auger-hole: unsuspected place.

119. Our tears . . . motion: We have not yet had time for tears, nor to express our sorrows in action.

120. naked frailties hid: poor bodies clothed.

122. question: discuss.
123. scruples: suspicions.

125. undivulged pretense: hidden purpose.

127. briefly: quickly.

130. office: function.

138. dainty of: fussy about.
139. warrant: justification.
140. steals itself: steals oneself away.

OPTIONS FOR TEACHING

ASSESSMENT TOOLS

Check Test: Questions and Answers
1. How does Duncan die? [Macbeth stabs him.]
2. Why doesn't Lady Macbeth do it? [The sleeping Duncan reminds her of her father.]
3. What does Lady Macbeth do to make others seem guilty? [She smears blood on the sleeping grooms.]

4. Immediately after Duncan dies, Macbeth hears a voice cry out. What does it say Macbeth has murdered? [Sleep.]
5. Who flees the castle in fear? [Duncan's sons, Malcolm and Donalbain.]

Scene 4. *Outside Macbeth's castle.*

Enter ROSS *with an* OLD MAN.

Old Man.
    Threescore and ten I can remember well:
    Within the volume of which time I have seen
    Hours dreadful and things strange, but this sore° night
    Hath trifled former knowings.°
Ross.   Ha, good father,
5   Thou seest the heavens, as troubled with man's act,
    Threatens his bloody stage. By th' clock 'tis day,
    And yet dark night strangles the traveling lamp:°
    Is't night's predominance,° or the day's shame,
    That darkness does the face of earth entomb,
    When living light should kiss it?
10 **Old Man.**   'Tis unnatural,
    Even like the deed that's done. On Tuesday last
    A falcon, tow'ring in her pride of place,°
    Was by a mousing° owl hawked at and killed.
Ross.
    And Duncan's horses—a thing most strange and certain—
15   Beauteous and swift, the minions° of their race,
    Turned wild in nature, broke their stalls, flung out,°
    Contending 'gainst obedience, as they would make
    War with mankind.
Old Man.   'Tis said they eat° each other.
Ross.
    They did so, to th' amazement of mine eyes,
    That looked upon't.

[*Enter* MACDUFF.]

20   Here comes the good Macduff.
    How goes the world, sir, now?
Macduff.   Why, see you not?
Ross.
    Is't known who did this more than bloody deed?
Macduff.
    Those that Macbeth hath slain.
Ross.   Alas, the day!
    What good could they pretend?°
Macduff.   They were suborned:°
25   Malcolm and Donalbain, the king's two sons,
    Are stol'n away and fled, which puts upon them
    Suspicion of the deed.
Ross.   'Gainst nature still.
    Thriftless° ambition, that will ravin up°
    Thine own life's means!° Then 'tis most like
30   The sovereignty will fall upon Macbeth.

3. **sore:** grievous.
4. **trifled former knowings:** made trifles of former experiences.

7. **traveling lamp:** sun.
8. **predominance:** astrological supremacy.

12. **tow'ring . . . place:** soaring at her summit.
13. **mousing:** normally mouse-eating.
15. **minions:** darlings.
16. **flung out:** lunged wildly.

18. **eat:** ate.

24. **pretend:** hope for. **suborned:** bribed.

28. **Thriftless:** wasteful. **ravin up:** greedily devour.
29. **own life's means:** parent.

MACBETH, ACT II, SCENE 4   329

E. Critical Reading: Making Connections
Ask students to relate the dialogue between the Old Man and Ross to Lennox's speech in Act II, Scene 3, ll. 48–54. [Ross and the Old Man present more evidence that disorders in nature are paralleling the unnatural death of the king.]

F. Literary Element: Metaphor
? How does the horses' behavior parallel Macbeth's actions? [Possible answer: Macbeth, too, has been the minion of his race as the savior of his country. He, too, has turned wild, broken out of his rank, and destroyed one of his own.]

G. Critical Reading: Analyzing Tone
Macduff could appear to be speaking plainly. How would the meaning change if you assume that he is speaking ironically? Why would he not speak clearly about his thoughts? [Possible answer: He could be insinuating that there was a plot. He might not speak clearly if (1) he does not trust Ross yet or (2) he is not absolutely sure he is right.]

H. Literary Element: Irony
? What is ironic about Ross's comment? [He has the motive right but the perpetrator wrong.]

Observation Assessment: Reading As students discuss **themes** revealed in Acts I and II, note whether they are making specific references to echoes and repetitions in the text. The following scale may help you evaluate students.

1 point: General or inaccurate discussion of text
2 points: Speaks generally with some mention of lines or scenes
3 points: Refers to lines or scenes without citing specific references
4 points: Occasionally cites specific references to support discussion
5 points: Frequently cites specific references to support discussion

Macbeth, Act II, Scene 4 **T329**

A. Reader's Response: First Thoughts

? What were your own impressions on reading the section of *Macbeth* that De Quincey refers to? [Sample responses: The knocking did not particularly strike me as I read, but perhaps had I seen the play and heard the knocking, I would have been more impressed. Or it struck me as odd, but when I read of the effect that it had on the Macbeths, I realized the knocking was significant.]

B. Critical Reading: Identifying Main Ideas

Explain De Quincey's point in your own words. [Possible answer: The audience must feel some interest in the murderer and want to understand him, or the play will not mean much.]

C. Exploring the Historical Period

Scottish kings were crowned on the Stone of Destiny—supposedly Jacob's pillow, as mentioned in Genesis 28: 10–13. This stone was stolen and taken to Westminster Abbey by King Edward I in 1296.

D. Reader's Response: Shaping Interpretations

? Why is Macduff not going to Macbeth's coronation? [Sample responses: He is suspicious of circumstances surrounding the murder and does not support Macbeth's assumption of power. His conversation with Ross has indicated that Macduff believes the murder has more sinister implications.]

Metacognition Ask students what evidence supports their theories.

Connections — AN ESSAY

from On the Knocking at the Gate in *Macbeth*

Thomas De Quincey

(A) From my boyish days I had always felt a great perplexity on one point in *Macbeth*. It was this: The knocking at the gate which succeeds to (B) the murder of Duncan produced to my feelings an effect for which I never could account. The effect was that it reflected back upon the murderer a peculiar awfulness and a depth of solemnity; yet, however obstinately I endeavored with my understanding to comprehend this, for many years I never could see *why* it should produce such an effect.

. . . At length I solved it to my own satisfaction; and my solution is this: —Murder, in ordinary cases, where the sympathy is wholly directed to the case of the murdered person, is an incident of coarse and vulgar horror; and for this reason—that it flings the interest exclusively upon the natural but ignoble instinct by which we cleave to life: an instinct which, as being indispensable to the primal law of self-preservation, is the same in kind (though different in degree) amongst all living creatures. This instinct, therefore, because it annihilates all distinctions, and degrades the greatest of men to the level of "the poor beetle that we tread on," exhibits human nature in its most abject and humiliating attitude. Such an attitude would little suit the purposes of the poet. What then must he do? He must throw the interest on the murderer. Our sympathy must be with *him* (of course I mean a sympathy of comprehension, a sympathy by which we enter into his feelings, and are made to understand them—not a sympathy of pity or approbation). In the murdered person, all strife of thought, all flux and reflux of passion and of purpose, are crushed by one overwhelming panic; the fear of instant death smites him "with its petrific mace."[1] But in the murderer, such a murderer as a poet will condescend to, there must be raging some great storm of passion—jealousy, ambition, vengeance, hatred—which will create a hell within him; and into this hell we are to look.

In *Macbeth*, for the sake of gratifying his own enormous and teeming faculty of creation, Shakespeare has introduced two murderers: and, as usual in his hands, they are remarkably discriminated: but—though in Macbeth the strife of mind is greater than in his wife, the tiger spirit not so awake, and his feelings caught chiefly by contagion from her—yet, as both were finally involved in the guilt of murder, the

1. petrific mace: stone club. This is an allusion to Milton's *Paradise Lost* (Book X, line 294), in which Death wields a "mace petrific."

Macduff.
(C) He is already named,° and gone to Scone°
To be invested.°
Ross. Where is Duncan's body?
Macduff.
Carried to Colmekill,°
The sacred storehouse of his predecessors
And guardian of their bones.
35 **Ross.** Will you to Scone?
Macduff.
(D) No, cousin, I'll to Fife.

31. named: elected. **Scone** (sko͞on).
32. invested: installed as king.

33. Colmekill: Iona Island, the ancient burying place of Scottish kings. (It was founded by St. Colm.)

CONNECTING WITH *MACBETH*

Explain that De Quincey presents an argument with proposed solutions, some of which are dismissed based on further evidence. After they read De Quincey's essay and "Macbeth's Porter" (p. 332), have students use the following chart to summarize and evaluate various theories about the inclusion of the knocking, based on the ideas presented by the critics and students' thoughts after they read the scene.

Purpose of the Knocking at the Gate		
Possible Cause for Including the Porter	Reason for Dismissal of Cause	Reason for Acceptance of Cause
[to create a disturbance]	[play loses intensity]	[brings Macbeths back to reality]

murderous mind of necessity is finally to be presumed in both. This was to be expressed; and, on its own account, as well as to make it a more proportionable antagonist to the unoffending nature of their victim, "the gracious Duncan," and adequately to expound "the deep damnation of his taking off," this was to be expressed with peculiar energy. We were to be made to feel that the human nature—i.e., the divine nature of love and mercy, spread through the hearts of all creatures, and seldom utterly withdrawn from man—was gone, vanished, extinct, and that the fiendish nature had taken its place. And, as this effect is marvellously accomplished in the *dialogues* and *soliloquies* themselves, so it is finally consummated by the expedient under consideration; and it is to this that I now solicit the reader's attention. If the reader has ever witnessed a wife, daughter, or sister in a fainting fit, he may chance to have observed that the most affecting moment in such a spectacle is *that* in which a sigh and a stirring announce the recommencement of suspended life.

. . . All action in any direction is best expounded, measured, and made apprehensible, by reaction. Now, applying this to the case in *Macbeth:* Here, as I have said, the retiring of the human heart and the entrance of the fiendish heart was to be expressed and made sensible. Another world has stepped in; and the murderers are taken out of the region of human things,

human purposes, human desires. They are transfigured: Lady Macbeth is "unsexed"; Macbeth has forgot that he was born of woman; both are conformed to the image of devils; and the world of devils is suddenly revealed. But how shall this be conveyed and made palpable? In order that a new world may step in, this world must for a time disappear. The murderers and the murder must be insulated—cut off by an immeasurable gulf from the ordinary tide and succession of human affairs—locked up and sequestered in some deep recess; we must be made sensible that the world of ordinary life is suddenly arrested, laid asleep, tranced, racked into a dread armistice; time must be annihilated, relation to things without abolished; and all must pass self-withdrawn into a deep syncope[2] and suspension of earthly passion. Hence it is that, when the deed is done, when the work of darkness is perfect, then the world of darkness passes away like a pageantry in the clouds: The knocking at the gate is heard, and it makes known audibly that the reaction has commenced; the human has made its reflux upon the fiendish; the pulses of life are beginning to beat again; and the reestablishment of the goings-on of the world in which we live first makes us profoundly sensible of the awful parenthesis that had suspended them.

2. **syncope** (siŋ′kə·pē): unconsciousness.

Ross.   Well, I will thither.
Macduff.
    Well, may you see things well done there. Adieu,
    Lest our old robes sit easier than our new!
Ross.
    Farewell, father.
Old Man.
40   God's benison° go with you, and with those
     That would make good of bad, and friends of foes!
                              [*Exeunt omnes.*]

40. **benison:** blessing.

? What does De Quincey mean by "transfigured"? [Possible answer: The Macbeths have undergone fundamental changes in their personalities and relationships.]

F. Critical Reading: Identifying Main Ideas

? What is De Quincey's main point? [Possible answer: That the knocking represents a return from the devil's world of Duncan's murder to the ordinary, everyday world.]

G. Humanities Connection

Adieu may strike students as a foreign word. It does come from French and means "I commend you to God!" According to *The Oxford English Dictionary,* however, it was used in English as early as Chaucer's time and by Shakespeare in the sense of "formal leave-taking" in *Antony and Cleopatra* and *All's Well That Ends Well,* as well as here.

H. Literary Element: Metaphor

? What warning does Macduff convey using the clothing metaphor? [Possible answer: He hints that with Macbeth as king instead of Duncan, their new positions may not suit them as well as their old ones did.]

I. Reader's Response: Challenging the Text

? Is this line an appropriate end for this bloody act? Explain. [Sample responses: The Old Man's words may foreshadow events or warn that, by attending the coronation, Ross and other Macbeth supporters are hypocritical—trying to "make good of bad, and friends of foes." The line is appropriate not only because the Old Man is disturbed by recent events, but also because it carries on the theme of reversal, of "fair is foul."]

A. Expansion

Sometimes the problem was not to find parts for everyone but to arrange the many roles in the play so that a handful of actors could cover them. Remember, actors were known to play two or even three roles in a single production by changing costumes and appearances.

B. Literary Connections

Not all critics, however, agree with this: One argument for cutting the scene was given by Samuel Taylor Coleridge (see p. 674): "This low soliloquy of the Porter, and his few speeches afterwards, I believe to have been written for the mob by some other hand, perhaps with Shakespeare's consent; and that finding it take, he with the remaining ink of a pen otherwise employed, just interpolated the words 'I'll . . . bonfire' [ll. 15–17]. Of the rest not one syllable has the ever-present being of Shakespeare."

Making Meanings

Act II

First Thoughts

1. Possible responses: It is awful. I wish I knew how the third prophecy could have been fulfilled if Macbeth had decided not to kill Duncan. The murders may be offstage because they are too bloody and upsetting; seeing the murders would take the focus off Macbeth and demand more sympathy for Duncan.

Reviewing the Text

a. He promises Banquo honor if Banquo will stand by him. Banquo agrees to support Macbeth as long as he can maintain his integrity while doing so.

b. Macbeth sees a dagger in the air that becomes coated with blood. This foreshadows the murder of Duncan.

c. Lady Macbeth hears an owl scream and crickets cry. Macbeth hears

---

Critical Comment

Macbeth's Porter

Why does Macbeth's comic porter—speaking a gross, drunken rigmarole—appear just at this point in the play, right after the murder of Duncan? Is this not a monstrous interruption?

One way to account for the scene is to remind ourselves that Shakespeare was writer-in-residence to a company of actors and therefore bound to provide parts for every member in every play—even a part for the chief comedian in a tragedy. But this is not a satisfactory explanation because it was not characteristic of Shakespeare merely to do what was expected of him as a professional writer; he always did something more, almost making a virtue out of theatrical necessity. And so, as a second explanation of the porter's scene, some critics have argued that it is designed to provide comic relief from the tense aftermath of Duncan's murder. But this also is not a convincing reason, because the scene actually increases tension rather than relieves it. As Macbeth and his wife stand whispering about the evil thing they have done, they—and the audience—are startled to hear a loud and totally unexpected knocking on the main gate of the castle. Even a hardened criminal would be startled by the coincidence of these events, and Macbeth and his wife are mere beginners in crime. While they hastily retreat into their bedroom, the porter (a word meaning "door tender") shuffles on stage to answer the knocking at his leisure, thus prolonging the interval between the murder and its discovery and greatly increasing suspense. And, after all, suspense is what makes drama interesting.

Theatergoers in Shakespeare's day were accustomed to comic porters; they were familiar figures in miracle plays, in which they kept the gates of hell. They were expected to be droll and at the same time sinister. "Who's there, i' th' name of Beelzebub?" asks Macbeth's porter, referring to one of the chief devils and implying that the castle is a place the Devil occupies. And indeed it already has become hell, which is as much a state of mind as a particular place. Lady Macbeth has called for the "smoke of hell" in Act I, and Macbeth has been unable to say "Amen" when Duncan's men cried "God bless us!" in Act II. To cut out the porter's scene, as many directors have done (and also many editors of school texts), is to weaken the fabric of the play.

Mervyn Blake as the porter in the Stratford Festival production of *Macbeth* (1983).

Malcolm and Donalbain laugh and cry "Murder" in their sleep and say "God bless us" and "Amen." He also hears a voice cry that he has murdered sleep.

d. The sleeping Duncan resembles her father. She comes up with the plan, lays the daggers ready, returns the daggers, smears the grooms with blood, and plans the cleanup—washing hands and donning nightgowns.

e. He says it will never wash off—it will stain all the waters of the world.

f. That he is the porter to hell.

g. To wake the king as he was requested to do.

h. Love for Duncan.

i. Malcolm goes to England; Donalbain goes to Ireland.

j. Students may find this unclear. Point out that Macduff says, perhaps ironically, that Malcolm and Donalbain are guilty (ll. 24–27), but then he skips Macbeth's coronation, possibly because he suspects Macbeth already.

MAKING MEANINGS

Act II

First Thoughts

1. What was your reaction to the murder of Duncan? Why do you think Shakespeare decided to murder Duncan and his guards offstage?

Reviewing the Text

a. In Scene 1, Macbeth asks Banquo to meet him later for "some words." What incentive does he offer Banquo? How does Banquo reply?

b. Describe the vision that Macbeth has at the end of Scene 1. What details foreshadow the action to come?

c. In Scene 2, as Macbeth kills Duncan, what does Lady Macbeth hear? What does Macbeth hear?

d. Why, according to Lady Macbeth, was she unable to kill Duncan herself? Which tasks related to the murder does she perform?

e. In Scene 2, how does Macbeth respond to Lady Macbeth's suggestion that he go wash the "filthy witness" from his hands?

f. In Scene 3, what is the porter pretending as he goes to open the gate?

g. Why has Macduff come?

h. What reason does Macbeth give for killing Duncan's two guards?

i. Where do Duncan's sons decide to go?

j. In Scene 4, whom does Macduff suspect of Duncan's murder?

Shaping Interpretations

2. Though Macbeth encounters no actual opposition until long after Duncan is murdered, Shakespeare must **foreshadow** some trouble for him and, to build up **suspense,** must start one character edging toward suspicion of Macbeth. Who is this character, and what inkling does he give of his dissatisfaction with Macbeth?

3. In Act I, Scene 7, Lady Macbeth seemed to be planning to murder Duncan herself. But at the last moment, in Act II, Scene 2, she is unable to wield her dagger. Consider the reason she gives, and decide what her actions and explanation reveal about her **character.**

4. In Scene 3, when Duncan's corpse is discovered, Macbeth utters a hypocritical lament beginning, "Had I but died. . . ." But is it really hypocritical? The critic A. C. Bradley argues that, although the speech is meant to be a lie, it actually contains "Macbeth's profoundest feelings." Explain this apparent contradiction. How does Macbeth feel about having murdered Duncan? What clues tell you how he feels?

5. Lady Macbeth's fainting spell, like everything else she has done so far, has a purpose. What message do you think she wants her fainting spell to convey?

6. Macduff becomes an important character in the three remaining acts. Describe how Shakespeare **characterizes** him in Scenes 3 and 4.

7. What would you say is the **mood** of Act II? What **images** and actions help to create this mood? Why might images of blood and water appear in Scene 2? What do they **symbolize**?

Extending the Text

8. A terrible murder is committed in this act. How do various characters respond to the violence? How would people today, say, react to the news that a ruler has been assassinated in cold blood and that a nation is in political chaos?

Challenging the Text

9. In some productions of *Macbeth,* Scene 4 is cut. Why would this be done? Is there any dramatic purpose for keeping it? Why do you think the Old Man is included in the scene?

10. Do you agree with Thomas De Quincey's theories (page 330) on the knocking at the gate? Why or why not?

Extending the Text

8. **(Synthesis)** Possible answers: Macduff is horrified; Malcolm and Donalbain are in shock—they do not really feel grief yet and still feel themselves in too much danger to release their feelings; Lennox seems overwhelmed. Possible answers: Some are horrified, some flee the country; or because people have been desensitized by seeing so much violence in the modern media, some may not be so surprised.

Challenging the Text

9. **(Synthesis)** Possible answers: The Old Man, who does not appear elsewhere, makes the scene seem less connected to the others; or the scene summarizes what is already known. The scene reinforces the sense of building suspicions and indicates that Macduff does not attend the coronation. Perhaps the Old Man represents wisdom or is someone who has come to warn the others about associating with evildoers.

10. **(Evaluation)** Answers will vary. Some students may believe the porter scene is designed to contrast sharply with the deed of the Macbeths and will therefore agree with De Quincey that the author's intent is to set the Macbeths apart and to reacquaint readers with the real world.

Shaping Interpretations

2. Malcolm in Scene 3, ll. 129–131. Also Macduff in Scene 3, l. 101 (questions Macbeth's killing of the grooms); Scene 4, ll. 24–27 (may be ironic); Scene 4, l. 36 (he skips Macbeth's coronation).

3. Perhaps she talks a better game than she plays; she is not as insensitive as she'd like to be.

4. It could be intended as a lie, but it is more likely an equivocation, an ambiguous sentiment. It may be true that Macbeth will never again feel that anything is worthwhile—that he has ruined his own life in taking Duncan's. In this case, the speech would be true, but not as the hearers understand it, as a lament for Duncan. Macbeth is nervous about discovery (Scene 3, l. 47) and feels guilty (Scene 3, l. 55), though not guilty enough to confess.

5. She might want to convey shock and grief.

6. Courteous, dutiful, loyal, sensitive, poetic, thoughtful, discerning, bold, wary, impulsive.

7. Sinister and violent. The mood is set by the dagger vision and what follows (Scene 1, ll. 33–61); the image of Duncan dead (Scene 3, ll. 105–108); the cannibal horses (Scene 4, ll. 14–18). Blood and water might symbolize death and life or guilt and innocence.

A. Critical Reading: Making Inferences

? What does Banquo think of Macbeth now? [Possible answer: He suspects that Macbeth killed Duncan.]

B. Language Note: Pronoun Usage

Here and elsewhere, students may note the use of the pronoun *which* where we would use a form of *who.* How would you say this line in modern English? [Possible answer: "Let your highness, to *whom* my duties are tied forever, command me."]

C. Reader's Response: Shaping Interpretations

? Do you think people would believe in Malcolm and Donalbain's guilt? Why or why not? [Sample responses: People may not believe that the sons killed Duncan, because they must care for their father—or because they have nothing to gain by his death, if a minor cannot inherit the throne.]

Answer to Margin Question
Line 10. Troubled and thoughtful; suspicious that Macbeth has helped the prophecies along; wondering about the prophecies for him and his descendants.

PROGRAM MANAGER

- **Planning Instruction** See **Teaching Notes,** *Teaching Resources A,* p. 90, for objectives and a summary of Act III.
- **Instructional Support** Before beginning the instructional lesson, see **Graphic Organizer for Active Reading,** *Teaching Resources A,* p. 97, for a Through the Selection activity.
- **Assessment** See **Selection Test (Act III),** *Test Booklet,* pp. 61–62.

ACT III   Scene 1. *Forres. The palace.*

Enter BANQUO.

Banquo.
    Thou hast it now: king, Cawdor, Glamis, all,
    As the weird women promised, and I fear
    Thou play'dst most foully for't. Yet it was said
    It should not stand° in thy posterity,
5   But that myself should be the root and father
    Of many kings. If there come truth from them—
    As upon thee, Macbeth, their speeches shine—
    Why, by the verities on thee made good,
    May they not be my oracles as well
10   And set me up in hope? But hush, no more!

[*Sennet*° *sounded. Enter* MACBETH *as king,* LADY MACBETH, LENNOX, ROSS, LORDS, *and* ATTENDANTS.]

Macbeth.
    Here's our chief guest.
Lady Macbeth.   If he had been forgotten,
    It had been as a gap in our great feast,
    And all-thing° unbecoming.
Macbeth.
    Tonight we hold a solemn supper, sir,
    And I'll request your presence.
15 **Banquo.**   Let your highness
    Command upon me, to the which my duties
    Are with a most indissoluble tie
    For ever knit.
Macbeth.
    Ride you this afternoon?
Banquo.   Ay, my good lord.
Macbeth.
20   We should have else desired your good advice
    (Which still° hath been both grave and prosperous°)
    In this day's council; but we'll take tomorrow.
    Is't far you ride?
Banquo.
    As far, my lord, as will fill up the time
25   'Twixt this and supper. Go not my horse the better,°
    I must become a borrower of the night
    For a dark hour or twain.
Macbeth.   Fail not our feast.
Banquo.
    My lord, I will not.
Macbeth.
    We hear our bloody cousins are bestowed°
30   In England and in Ireland, not confessing

334 THE RENAISSANCE

---

4. stand: continue.

? **10.** *What would you say Banquo's mood is? Is he envious or thoughtful and troubled?*
Sennet: trumpet.

13. all-thing: altogether.

21. still: always. **grave and prosperous:** weighty and profitable.

25. Go not my horse the better: unless my horse goes faster than I expect.

29. are bestowed: have taken refuge.

Their cruel parricide, filling their hearers
With strange invention.° But of that tomorrow,
When therewithal we shall have cause of state
Craving us jointly.° Hie you to horse. Adieu,
35 Till you return at night. Goes Fleance with you?
Banquo.
Ay, my good lord: our time does call upon 's.
Macbeth.
I wish your horses swift and sure of foot,
And so I do commend you to their backs.
Farewell.   [*Exit* BANQUO.]
40 Let every man be master of his time
Till seven at night. To make society
The sweeter welcome, we will keep ourself
Till supper-time alone. While° then, God be with you!

[*Exeunt* LORDS *and all but* MACBETH *and a* SERVANT.]

Sirrah, a word with you: attend° those men
45 Our pleasure?
Attendant.
They are, my lord, without the palace gate.
Macbeth.
Bring them before us.   [*Exit* SERVANT.]
To be thus° is nothing, but° to be safely thus—
Our fears in Banquo stick deep,
50 And in his royalty of nature reigns that
Which would be feared. 'Tis much he dares;
And, to° that dauntless temper° of his mind,
He hath a wisdom that doth guide his valor
To act in safety. There is none but he
55 Whose being I do fear: and under him
My genius is rebuked,° as it is said
Mark Antony's was by Caesar. He chid the sisters,
When first they put the name of king upon me,
And bade them speak to him; then prophetlike
60 They hailed him father to a line of kings.
Upon my head they placed a fruitless crown
And put a barren scepter in my gripe,
Thence to be wrenched with an unlineal hand,
No son of mine succeeding. If 't be so,
65 For Banquo's issue have I filed° my mind;
For them the gracious Duncan have I murdered;
Put rancors° in the vessel of my peace
Only for them, and mine eternal jewel°
Given to the common enemy of man,°
70 To make them kings, the seeds of Banquo kings!
Rather than so, come, fate, into the list,°
And champion me to th' utterance!° Who's there?

---

32. invention: lies.

34. us jointly: our joint attention.

35. *Macbeth has asked three important questions in this scene. What are they? How do you think he would ask them?*

42. *Notice that Macbeth uses the "royal we"; that is, he speaks of himself as "we," as a representative of all the people. Why do you think he wants to be alone?*
43. While: until.
44. attend: await.

48. thus: king. **but:** unless.

52. to: added to. **temper:** quality.

56. genius is rebuked: guardian spirit is cowed.

63. *What is an "unlineal hand"? What is a "barren scepter"? What is eating at Macbeth now?*
65. filed: defiled; dirtied.
67. rancors: bitter enmity.
68. eternal jewel: immortal soul.
69. common enemy of man: Satan.
71. list: battle.
72. champion me to th' utterance: fight against me till I give up.
72. *Why exactly is Macbeth so angry? What has he given up in order to make Banquo's sons kings?*

MACBETH, ACT III, SCENE I 335

D. Humanities Connection
In the historical writings of Holinshed, Banquo shares complicity in the murder of Duncan. In the play, has Banquo acquiesced and done nothing, despite his vow to fight against malice (Act II, Scene 3, ll. 120–126)? [Answers will vary. Students may say ll. 1–3 indicate that Banquo knows of Macbeth's guilt but has not acted, and they may conclude that he has broken his vow. Others may suggest Banquo suspects but cannot prove yet—so he seems to be playing along with Macbeth in ll. 15–18. In l. 36, however, his disgust with Macbeth shows in his desire to get quickly away.]

E. Critical Reading: Summarizing
What does Macbeth fear from Banquo? [Macbeth seems to fear that Banquo's honest nature and suspicions might turn him against Macbeth, or that Banquo's valor might give him the courage to face down Macbeth as he faced down the witches. After l. 59, the complaint implies Macbeth's concern that Banquo may take Macbeth's claim to the throne.]

Answers to Margin Questions
Line 35. Macbeth asks if Banquo is going riding, how far, and if Fleance will accompany him. He would probably try to speak casually.
Line 42. He probably wants others to think that he will be alone because it soon becomes obvious he has set up a secret meeting.
Line 63. Both terms refer to the idea of a king without offspring. Macbeth is upset that Banquo's sons will inherit Macbeth's throne.
Line 72. He is angry that he has endangered his own soul with the foul sin of murder so that another man's sons can become kings.

INTEGRATING THE LANGUAGE ARTS

Strategic Reading Assign pairs of students to use Reciprocal Teaching to aid text comprehension. As the students read a passage aloud, one student asks questions that arise during the reading, and the second student answers as many questions as possible. Then they reverse roles after an assigned number of lines. At the end of each scene, both students should summarize what they understand in a short paragraph in their Reader's Logs. Briefly model the process before students begin.

Writing: Psychologist's Report on Macbeth Brainstorm with students about Macbeth's thoughts and motivations in Act III, noting all ideas on the chalkboard. Then, have students write a psychologist's report on Macbeth, answering the following questions: Is he completely in control of his mind? Is he hallucinating from the guilt he feels, or does he really see things that others do not see? Why does he continue to plot additional murders? In their reports, students should cite specific references to support their diagnoses.

Speaking and Listening Have a student read his or her favorite lines from the play. A second student should then volunteer favorite lines and relate them to the lines read by the preceding student. A third student reads and relates to the second student, and so on. Students may identify similarities, differences, changes over time, echoes, and repetitions. ☞

A. Critical Reading: Finding Details

Ask students to examine carefully what Macbeth says to the murderers here and on the next one and a half pages. Note that his speeches reveal his own tyranny and his attempts to deflect blame.

B. Critical Reading: Making Inferences

? What is the point of Macbeth's extended comparison of men and dogs? [Possible answer: He says, in effect, that the word *men* does not distinguish among the different types of men any more than the word *dog* distinguishes among the different breeds of dogs he names. He wants to know if these two are worthy of the job.]

C. Reader's Response: First Thoughts

? What do you think the murderers mean in ll. 108–114? [Sample responses: They are probably poor and out of work—perhaps with families to feed—and are willing to take chances. They are disillusioned and willing to "spite the world."] Do you feel any sympathy for the two murderers? [Sample responses: Yes, they are from the lower class, and Macbeth is just using them; or no, whatever their situation is, committing murder is not acceptable.]

Answers to Margin Questions

Line 74. Answers will vary. After students have read the scene, return to the question. Students might suggest that the murderers may be solid citizens who support Macbeth.

Line 91. Macbeth convinces the murderers that Banquo is to blame for their troubles. He attacks their manhood as Lady Macbeth attacked his.

[*Enter* SERVANT *and two* MURDERERS.]

Now go to the door, and stay there till we call.

[*Exit* SERVANT.]

Was it not yesterday we spoke together?

Murderers.
  It was, so please your highness.

75 **Macbeth.**   Well then, now
  Have you considered of my speeches? Know
  That it was he in the times past, which held you
  So under fortune,° which you thought had been
  Our innocent self: this I made good to you
80 In our last conference; passed in probation° with you,
  How you were borne in hand,° how crossed; the instruments,°
  Who wrought with them, and all things else that might
  To half a soul° and to a notion° crazed
  Say "Thus did Banquo."

First Murderer.   You made it known to us.

Macbeth.
85 I did so; and went further, which is now
  Our point of second meeting. Do you find
  Your patience so predominant in your nature,
  That you can let this go? Are you so gospeled,°
  To pray for this good man and for his issue,
90 Whose heavy hand hath bowed you to the grave
  And beggared yours forever?

First Murderer.   We are men, my liege.

Macbeth.
  Ay, in the catalogue ye go for° men;
  As hounds and greyhounds, mongrels, spaniels, curs,
  Shoughs, water-rugs° and demi-wolves, are clept°
95 All by the name of dogs: the valued file°
  Distinguishes the swift, the slow, the subtle,
  The housekeeper, the hunter, every one
  According to the gift which bounteous nature
  Hath in him closed,° whereby he does receive
100 Particular addition, from the bill°
  That writes them all alike: and so of men.
  Now if you have a station in the file,
  Not i' th' worst rank of manhood, say't,
  And I will put that business in your bosoms
105 Whose execution takes your enemy off,
  Grapples you to the heart and love of us,
  Who wear our health but sickly in his life,°
  Which in his death were perfect.

Second Murderer.   I am one, my liege,
  Whom the vile blows and buffets of the world
110 Hath so incensed that I am reckless what
  I do to spite the world.

336 THE RENAISSANCE

? **74.** *What do you imagine the murderers would be like: the all-too-common "hit men" of contemporary movies? Or could they simply be officers who have a grudge against Banquo? (They have been portrayed in many ways.)*

78. held you / So under fortune: kept you from good fortune.

80. probation: review.

81. borne in hand: deceived. **instruments:** tools.

83. soul: brain. **notion:** mind.

88. gospeled: so meek from reading the Gospel (of Jesus).

? **91.** *What techniques is Macbeth using on the murderers? Does it remind you of the way Lady Macbeth goaded him into killing Duncan?*

92. go for: pass as.

94. Shoughs, water-rugs: shaggy dogs and long-haired water dogs. **clept:** called.

95. valued file: classification by valuable traits.

99. closed: enclosed.

100. bill: list.

107. who wear . . . life: who are "sick" while he (Banquo) still lives.

OPTIONS FOR TEACHING

COOPERATIVE LEARNING

Character Sociograms Have students work in groups of three or four to create Character Sociograms—graphics with symbols and words that show the relationships between characters. Challenge students to include all the characters they have read about in the play so far and to be creative in the kind of symbols they produce to show how each character relates to the others.

From Roman Polanski's film production of *Macbeth* (1971).

"It is concluded: Banquo, thy soul's flight,
If it find heaven, must find it out tonight."

First Murderer.   And I another
     So weary with disasters, tugged with fortune,
     That I would set° my life on any chance,
     To mend it or be rid on't.
Macbeth.   Both of you
     Know Banquo was your enemy.
115 **Both Murderers.**   True, my lord.
Macbeth.
     So is he mine, and in such bloody distance°
     That every minute of his being thrusts
     Against my near'st of life:° and though I could
     With barefaced power sweep him from my sight
120   And bid my will avouch° it, yet I must not,
     For° certain friends that are both his and mine,
     Whose loves I may not drop, but wail his fall
     Who I myself struck down: and thence it is
     That I to your assistance do make love,
125   Masking the business from the common eye
     For sundry weighty reasons.

113. set: risk.

116. distance: quarrel.

118. near'st of life: vital spot.

120. avouch: justify.
121. For: because of.

?   **126.** *How is Macbeth justifying to the murderers the fact that he has to ask them to do the job of killing Banquo?*

MACBETH, ACT III, SCENE 1   **337**

Fielding Questions Put up a large sheet of kraft paper on which students can write questions as they read, leaving room between questions for other students to answer. Periodically check to make sure that misconceptions are cleared up. Leave a few minutes at the beginning or end of class to discuss the posted questions and answers or to allow students to add or answer questions. Once questions are written and answered on kraft paper, keep notes on interpretations that may change as students encounter additional information in the text. Remind them that as new clues to the material surface, readers must rethink or expand their interpretations. (For example, speculation about Lady Macbeth's children must also take into account Act IV, Scene 3, l. 216, which students have not yet read.) ☞

A. Critical Reading: Summarizing

Have students summarize Macbeth's final instructions. [Possible answer: Within the next hour, I will tell you the place and time for killing Banquo. It must be done at some distance from the palace and in such a way that I cannot fall under suspicion. Fleance must be killed also.]

Answer to Margin Question

Line 140. They are waiting for Macbeth to give them the details of carrying out the murder. He is calculating, controlled. Lady Macbeth has no part in the arrangements.

Second Murderer. We shall, my lord,
Perform what you command us.

First Murderer. Though our lives——

Macbeth.
Your spirits shine through you. Within this hour at most
I will advise you where to plant yourselves,
130   Acquaint you with the perfect spy° o' th' time,
The moment on't; for't must be done tonight,
And something° from the palace; always thought°
That I require a clearness:° and with him—

A

To leave no rubs° nor botches in the work—
135   Fleance his son, that keeps him company,
Whose absence is no less material to me
Than is his father's, must embrace the fate
Of that dark hour. Resolve yourselves apart:°
I'll come to you anon.

Murderers. We are resolved, my lord.

Macbeth.
140   I'll call upon you straight. Abide within.

130. perfect spy: exact information.

132. something: some distance.
thought: remembered.

133. clearness: freedom from suspicion.

134. rubs: flaws.

138. apart: alone (make up your minds by yourselves).

140. *What has Macbeth arranged with the murderers? What is his mood here? Does Lady Macbeth have any part in arranging these next murders?*

"Gentle my lord, sleek o'er your rugged looks."

From Roman Polanski's film production of *Macbeth* (1971).

OPTIONS FOR TEACHING

CROSSING THE CURRICULUM

Social Sciences Students may note with uneasiness that as of Act III, Scene 1, l. 10, Banquo has not yet acted on his suspicions. Ask students to research this question: What support should Banquo have for his suspicions before he brings an accusation? Encourage them to consider laws about bringing charges for murder and also the standards of proof required to convict a person of murder. Given these laws, ask them whether Banquo should act now or wait. Have them present an oral investigative report, such as they might hear on a news broadcast, including the pertinent information they find and applying it to the text.

Performing Arts Banquo's ghost presents some interesting staging challenges. Assign students to groups of four or five, and have them stage the scene in which Banquo's ghost appears to Macbeth. Students may find it helpful to learn about the treatment of other famous ghosts in the performing arts, such as the one in *Hamlet*. Remind students that techniques used in film often will not work in live performance; however, the Globe Theater, where Shakespeare's work was often performed, had a trapdoor.

It is concluded: Banquo, thy soul's flight,
If it find heaven, must find it out tonight.   **B**   [*Exeunt.*]

Scene 2. *The palace.*

Enter LADY MACBETH *and a* SERVANT.

Lady Macbeth.
  Is Banquo gone from court?
Servant.
  Ay, madam, but returns again tonight.
Lady Macbeth.
  Say to the king, I would attend his leisure
  For a few words.
Servant.   Madam, I will.   [*Exit.*]
Lady Macbeth.   Nought's had, all's spent,
5 Where our desire is got without content:
  'Tis safer to be that which we destroy
  Than by destruction dwell in doubtful joy.

[*Enter* MACBETH.]

  How now, my lord! Why do you keep alone,
  Of sorriest fancies your companions making,
10 Using those thoughts which should indeed have died
  With them they think on? Things without° all remedy
  Should be without regard: what's done is done.
Macbeth.
  We have scorched° the snake, not killed it:
  She'll close° and be herself, whilst our poor malice°
15 Remains in danger of her former tooth.
  But let the frame of things disjoint,° both the worlds° suffer,
  Ere we will eat our meal in fear, and sleep
  In the affliction of these terrible dreams
  That shake us nightly: better be with the dead,   **C**
20 Whom we, to gain our peace, have sent to peace,
  Than on the torture of the mind to lie
  In restless ecstasy.° Duncan is in his grave;
  After life's fitful fever he sleeps well.
  Treason has done his worst: nor steel, nor poison,
25 Malice domestic,° foreign levy,° nothing,
  Can touch him further.
Lady Macbeth.   Come on.
  Gentle my lord, sleek° o'er your rugged° looks;
  Be bright and jovial among your guests tonight.
Macbeth.
  So shall I, love; and so, I pray, be you:
30 Let your remembrance apply to Banquo;°   **D**
  Present him eminence,° both with eye and tongue:
  Unsafe the while, that we must lave°
  Our honors in these flattering streams

? 7. *What reversal of attitudes is taking place here?*

11. **without:** beyond.

? 12. *This scene can be played in several ways. Is Lady Macbeth hostile to her husband and angry with him? Or can she be shown to have some tenderness in this scene?*

13. **scorched:** slashed.

14. **close:** heal.   **malice:** enmity; hatred.

16. **frame of things disjoint:** universe collapse.   **worlds:** heaven and earth.

22. **ecstasy:** frenzy.

25. **Malice domestic:** domestic war (civil war).   **foreign levy:** exaction of tribute by a foreign country.

? 26. *What do you picture the couple doing in this scene? Are they sitting together? Are they close, or is there a distance between them?*

27. **sleek:** smooth.   **rugged:** furrowed.

30. **Let . . . Banquo:** That is, focus your thoughts on Banquo.

31. **eminence:** honors.

32. **lave:** wash.

MACBETH, ACT III, SCENE 2 **339**

A. Literary Element: Character

? How have Lady Macbeth and Macbeth changed? [Possible answer: In Duncan's murder, she was the planner and leader, but Macbeth murders the grooms on the spur of the moment without consulting her. And now he has planned Banquo's murder without involving her. Some students may think that he has become more evil than she.]

Answer to Margin Question
Line 35. Lady Macbeth speaks with great urgency and fear. She is worried about Macbeth's state of mind.

LITERATURE AND COMPUTERS

The Bard and the Database

In literary circles it's known as the "Authorship Question": Did William Shakespeare, the actor from Stratford-on-Avon, really write the greatest poetry the world has ever known?

This question has been around since the 1700s, and over the years people have proposed as many as fifty-eight various writers as possible authors of Shakespeare's plays and poems, ranging from Sir Francis Bacon to Sir Walter Raleigh to Queen Elizabeth I herself.

Matching Shakespeare. Hoping to apply some twentieth-century computer technology to this seventeenth-century problem, Professor Ward Elliott of Claremont McKenna College near Los Angeles created a database of Renaissance literature, including the King James Bible, all of Shakespeare's poetry, and material from twenty-seven of the most promising candidates, and embarked upon his "Matching Shakespeare" study. Elliott's plan was first to identify Shakespeare's unique style

And make our faces vizards° to our hearts,
Disguising what they are.
35 **Lady Macbeth.**   You must leave this.
Macbeth.
    O, full of scorpions is my mind, dear wife!
    Thou know'st that Banquo, and his Fleance, lives.
Lady Macbeth.
    But in them nature's copy's not eterne.°
Macbeth.
    There's comfort yet; they are assailable.
40   Then be thou jocund. Ere the bat hath flown
    His cloistered flight, ere to black Hecate's summons
    The shard-borne° beetle with his drowsy hums
    Hath rung night's yawning peal, there shall be done
    A deed of dreadful note.
Lady Macbeth.   What's to be done?
(A) Macbeth.
45   Be innocent of the knowledge, dearest chuck,°
    Till thou applaud the deed. Come, seeling° night,
    Scarf up° the tender eye of pitiful day,
    And with thy bloody and invisible hand
    Cancel and tear to pieces that great bond

34. vizards: masks.

? **35.** *With what degree of urgency must Lady Macbeth say this line?*

38. nature's copy's not eterne: That is, they won't live forever.

42. shard-borne: carried on scaly wings.

45. chuck: chick (a term of endearment).
46. seeling: eye-closing; blinding.
47. scarf up: blindfold.

ASSESSMENT TOOLS

Check Test: Questions and Answers
1. Why is Macbeth determined to have Fleance killed? [So Banquo's sons will never rule.]
2. Whom do the murderers kill? [Banquo.]
3. Who escapes? [Fleance.]
4. What does Macbeth see at the banquet? [The ghost of Banquo.]
5. What are Macduff and Malcolm doing in England? [Securing an army to overthrow Macbeth.]

Self-Reflection Ask students to review and to summarize briefly their use of each of the following strategies, using a scale of one through five (five being the best) to indicate students' level of competence in each task: **1.** Visualizing the scenes; **2.** Re-reading for specific references to support their points; **3.** Using the Reader's Log to get questions answered. Hold short conferences with students to discuss their self-assessments.

through computer analysis and then to compare this to the styles of various writers to see if any matched up.

Elliott's "Matching Shakespeare" study applied dozens of different linguistic tests, but five conventional tests and a powerful new one proved most accurate. The conventional tests measured features like the number of relative clauses and hyphenated compound words and length of words and sentences, and the new test used a pattern recognition technique.

And the real Shakespeare is. What have the tests shown? Did Shakespeare write Shakespeare? Based on his studies, Elliott believes that he has been able to eliminate all the principal candidates. Every writer failed at least one of the conventional tests, with some failing four or five. On the other hand, Shakespeare's writings all fell within a consistent profile. Although the study does not definitively prove that it was Shakespeare himself who wrote the works attributed to him, Elliott (along with most reputable scholars) feels that it does demonstrate that one individual *did* write them all.

Why has such a fuss been made about the authorship of Shakespeare's works? In part, it's because people cannot believe that someone who led such a seemingly ordinary life could have been such a genius. Shakespeare still confounds all the scholarly detectives who continue to debate the "Authorship Question."

---

50 Which keeps me pale! Light thickens, and the crow
    Makes wing to th' rooky° wood.
    Good things of day begin to droop and drowse,
    Whiles night's black agents to their preys do rouse.
    Thou marvel'st at my words: but hold thee still; **B**
55 Things bad begun make strong themselves by ill:
    So, prithee, go with me.   [*Exeunt.*]

Scene 3. *Near the palace.*

Enter three MURDERERS.   **C**

First Murderer.
    But who did bid thee join with us?
Third Murderer.   Macbeth.
Second Murderer.
    He needs not our mistrust; since he delivers
    Our offices and what we have to do
    To the direction just.°
First Murderer.   Then stand with us.
5   The west yet glimmers with some streaks of day.
    Now spurs the lated° traveler apace

51. **rooky:** full of rooks, or crows.

? 1. *The identity of the Third Murderer is not made clear. Whom would you name as possible suspects?*

4. **He needs . . . just:** We need not mistrust him (the Third Murderer) since he describes our duties according to our exact directions.

6. **lated:** belated.

MACBETH, ACT III, SCENE 3   341

B. Language Note: Poetry
Notice that Shakespeare ends this scene with two couplets followed by a tag, instead of the usual single couplet. Again, Shakespeare seems to be creating a scene appropriate to a murder, as he does in Act II, Scene 1, when Macbeth prepares to kill Duncan.

C. Expansion
Much has been written about the identity of the third murderer. Although Macbeth is a popular answer, the presence of banquet guests (Scene 4, l. 10) and Macbeth's shock upon hearing that Fleance has escaped (Scene 4, ll. 20–25) serve as evidence that he is not the third murderer. Other explanations suggest that the way Shakespeare's plays were printed may account for an additional character. Perhaps Shakespeare needed to give an actor a part, or perhaps the number of murderers was consistent in some acting scripts of the play, but not in the one used for the First Folio.

Answer to Margin Question
Line 1. Answers will vary. Perhaps he is a messenger sent by Macbeth, Macbeth himself, or one of Macbeth's officers. See annotation C, above.

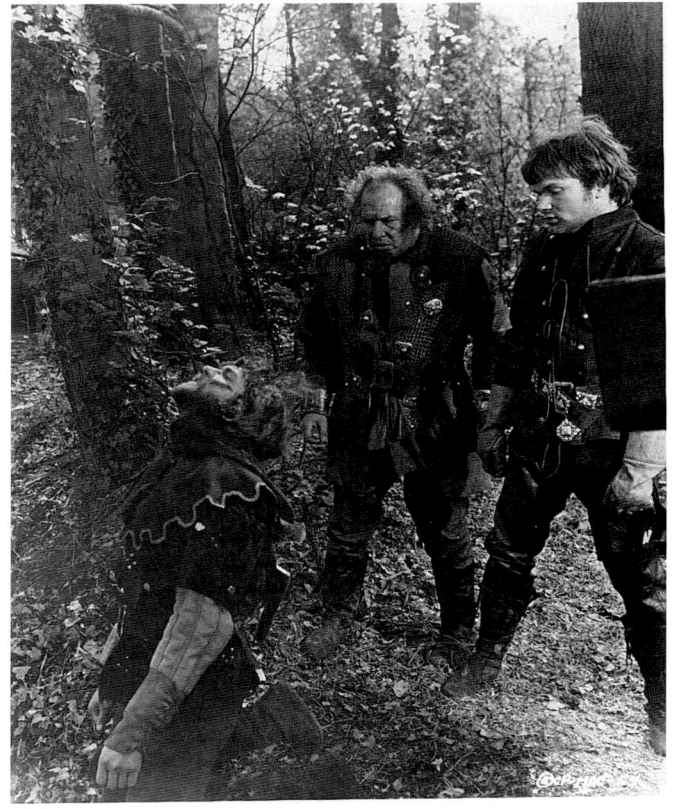

"O, treachery! Fly, good Fleance, fly, fly, fly!"

From Roman Polanski's film production of *Macbeth* (1971).

To gain the timely inn, and near approaches
The subject of our watch.
Third Murderer.   Hark! I hear horses.
Banquo (*within*). Give us a light there, ho!
Second Murderer.   Then 'tis he. The rest
10   That are within the note of expectation°
    Already are i' th' court.
First Murderer.   His horses go about.
Third Murderer.
    Almost a mile: but he does usually—
    So all men do—from hence to th' palace gate
    Make it their walk.

[*Enter* BANQUO *and* FLEANCE, *with a torch.*]

Second Murderer.
    A light, a light!
Third Murderer. 'Tis he.
15 **First Murderer.**   Stand to't.

10. within . . . expectation: on the list of expected guests.

342 THE RENAISSANCE

Banquo.
It will be rain tonight.
First Murderer.   Let it come down.

[*They set upon* BANQUO.] **A**

Banquo.
O, treachery! Fly, good Fleance, fly, fly, fly! **B**

[*Exit* FLEANCE.]

Thou mayst revenge. O slave!   [*Dies.*]
Third Murderer.
Who did strike out the light?
First Murderer.   Was't not the way?°
Third Murderer.
20 There's but one down; the son is fled.
Second Murderer.
We have lost best half of our affair.
First Murderer.
Well, let's away and say how much is done.   [*Exeunt.*]

Scene 4. *The palace.*
Banquet prepared. Enter MACBETH, LADY MACBETH, ROSS, LENNOX,
LORDS, *and* ATTENDANTS.

Macbeth.
You know your own degrees;° sit down:
At first and last, the hearty welcome.
Lords.
Thanks to your majesty.
Macbeth.
Oneself will mingle with society°
5 And play the humble host.
Our hostess keeps her state,° but in best time
We will require° her welcome.
Lady Macbeth.
Pronounce it for me, sir, to all our friends,
For my heart speaks they are welcome.

[*Enter* FIRST MURDERER.]

Macbeth.
10 See, they encounter° thee with their hearts' thanks.
Both sides are even: here I'll sit i' th' midst:
Be large in mirth; anon we'll drink a measure°
The table round. (*Goes to* FIRST MURDERER.) There's blood
    upon thy face.
Murderer.
'Tis Banquo's then.
Macbeth.
15 'Tis better thee without than he within.°
Is he dispatched?

19. *What would the murderers be doing as the light goes out?*
19. way: thing to do.

21. *Disposal of bodies is always a problem for directors of Shakespeare's plays. How would you have Banquo's body carried off? By whom?*

22. *This scene, so necessary to the play, is often called the play's turning point or technical climax. What have been Macbeth's good fortunes so far?*

1. degrees: ranks.

2. *This crucial scene is often called the dramatic climax of the play; it is tremendously exciting when staged well. Notice where Macbeth's subjects become aware of his capacity for irrational behavior.*

4. society: the company.
6. keeps her state: remains seated in her chair of state.
7. require: request.

10. encounter: meet.

12. measure: goblet.

15. thee . . . within: outside you than inside him.

A. Reader's Response: Challenging the Text
The deaths of the traitors (Macdonwald and Cawdor) and the first three murders (Duncan and the two grooms) are all committed offstage. Should this one occur onstage? Why or why not? [Sample responses: The violence of the play would not be as evident if every death were simply reported by the characters but not seen. Seeing the dying Banquo try to save his son makes the audience more sympathetic.]

B. Literary Element: Plot
Why is this a turning point for Macbeth? [Possible answer: Even though we do not know how things will end, Fleance's escape means that the prophecy about Banquo can still come true. Moreover, this is the first time that Macbeth has been openly thwarted, so it may foreshadow a reversal of momentum in the play.]

Answers to Margin Questions
Line 19. As the light goes out, the murderers might be attacking Banquo.
Line 21. Answers will vary. Since Shakespeare's plays were written for theater in the round, one choice would be to have the murderers move the body, since the curtains could not be drawn.
Line 22. He has acquired Cawdor and the throne, and, although he has aroused suspicion, he is apparently without open opposition. Fleance's escape is his first clear failure.
Line 2. The subjects become wary around ll. 48–52.

A. Language Note: Vocabulary

Nonpareil means someone or something that is "without parallel" or "without equal."

B. Reader's Response: Shaping Interpretations

? Do you agree with Macbeth's claim that he would have been "perfect" if only Fleance had been killed? Why or why not? [Sample responses: No, he still wouldn't have a son to inherit the throne; or no, it is the nature of ambition never to be satisfied.]

C. Literary Element: Irony

? Why is this line ironic? [It might sound as if he is asking if Banquo is well, but he is actually asking if Banquo was safely dispatched—that is, murdered.]

D. Literary Element: Metaphor

? Who or what is the snake? [Banquo. Students may recall Act III, Scene 2, l. 13, and connect the two quotations.] Macbeth also points out that Fleance is harmless now but will grow to be a threat.

Answer to Margin Question
Line 20. Surprised, horrified, angry.

"Never shake / Thy gory locks at me."
From the Stratford Festival production of *Macbeth* (1983).

Murderer.   My lord, his throat is cut;
That I did for him.
Macbeth.   Thou are the best o' th' cutthroats.
Yet he's good that did the like for Fleance;
(A) If thou didst it, thou art the nonpareil.
Murderer.
20   Most royal sir, Fleance is 'scaped.
Macbeth (*aside*).
(B) Then comes my fit again: I had else been perfect,
Whole as the marble, founded° as the rock,
As broad and general as the casing air:°
But now I am cabined, cribbed,° confined, bound in
(C) 25 To saucy° doubts and fears.—But Banquo's safe?
Murderer.
Ay, my good lord: safe in a ditch he bides,
With twenty trenchèd° gashes on his head,
The least a death to nature.
Macbeth.   Thanks for that.
(*Aside.*) There the grown serpent lies; the worm° that's fled
(D) 30 Hath nature that in time will venom breed,
No teeth for th' present. Get thee gone. Tomorrow
We'll hear ourselves° again.   [*Exit* FIRST MURDERER.]

? 20. *How would Macbeth react to this line?*

22. **founded:** firmly based.
23. **broad . . . casing air:** unconfined as the surrounding air.
24. **cribbed:** penned up.
25. **saucy:** insolent.

27. **trenchèd:** trenchlike.

29. **worm:** serpent.

32. **hear ourselves:** talk it over.

344 THE RENAISSANCE

Lady Macbeth.   My royal lord,
You do not give the cheer.° The feast is sold
That is not often vouched, while 'tis a-making,
'Tis given with welcome. To feed were best at home;°
35 From thence, the sauce to meat° is ceremony;
Meeting were bare without it. **E**

[*Enter the* GHOST OF BANQUO, *and sits in Macbeth's place.*] **F**

Macbeth.   Sweet remembrancer!°
Now good digestion wait on appetite,
And health on both!
Lennox.   May't please your highness sit.
Macbeth.
40 Here had we now our country's honor roofed,°
Were the graced person of our Banquo present—
Who may I rather challenge for unkindness
Than pity for mischance!°
Ross.   His absence, sir,
Lays blame upon his promise. Please't your highness
45 To grace us with your royal company?
Macbeth.
The table's full.
Lennox.   Here is a place reserved, sir.
Macbeth.
Where?
Lennox.
Here, my good lord. What is't that moves your highness?
Macbeth.
Which of you have done this?
Lords.   What, my good lord?
Macbeth.
50 Thou canst not say I did it. Never shake **G**
Thy gory locks at me.
Ross.
Gentlemen, rise, his highness is not well.
Lady Macbeth.
Sit, worthy friends. My Lord is often thus,
And hath been from his youth. Pray you, keep seat.
55 The fit is momentary; upon a thought°
He will again be well. If much you note him,
You shall offend him and extend his passion.°
Feed, and regard him not.—Are you a man?
Macbeth.
Ay, and a bold one, that dare look on that
Which might appall the devil.
60 **Lady Macbeth.**   O proper stuff!
This is the very painting of your fear.
This is the air-drawn dagger which, you said, **H**
Led you to Duncan. O, these flaws° and starts,
Imposters to° true fear, would well become

---

33. **cheer:** sense of cordiality.

35. **The feast . . . home:** The feast seems sold (not given) when the host fails to welcome the guests. Mere eating is best done at home.

36. **meat:** food.

? 37. *Lady Macbeth has summoned her husband to her area of the stage. What mood is she in?*

? **Stage direction.** *The ghost is crucial to this scene. From what you read here, should the ghost be imagined? Or should it actually appear on stage? How should it look, if so?*

37. **remembrancer:** reminder.
40. **our . . . roofed:** our nobility under one roof.
43. **Who . . . mischance:** whom I hope I may reprove because he is unkind rather than pity because he has encountered an accident.

? 46. *When Macbeth says this line, what does he see?*

? 49. *How should Macbeth ask this question? Whom should he be talking to?*

? 51. *According to Macbeth's speech here, what is the ghost doing? Does anyone else see the ghost? How should the others be acting?*

? 53. *Do you think this is true? Or is Lady Macbeth desperately trying to cover for her husband?*

55. **upon a thought:** as quick as a thought.

57. **extend his passion:** lengthen his fit.

? 58. *Where do you think Lady Macbeth has taken her husband so that she can whisper this intimidating line?*

63. **flaws:** gusts; outbursts.
64. **to:** compared with.

E. Language Note: Pun
Point out the pun on the homophones *meat* and *meet*.

F. Expansion
Banquo's ghost is usually played by the actor who played Banquo.

G. Critical Reading: Finding Details

? In what way is Macbeth's statement true? In what way is it false? [It is true that Macbeth did not strike the blows that killed Banquo. He was, however, the instigator of the crime, and therefore responsible for Banquo's death.]

H. Critical Reading: Making Inferences

? What does Lady Macbeth think is causing Macbeth to cry out? [His imagination.]

Answers to Margin Questions
Line 37. She may be alarmed, concerned, irritated.
Stage direction. Answers will vary. A good case can be made for either an imagined ghost or the actor who plays Banquo. Banquo could appear with gashes on his head or throat.
Line 46. Banquo's ghost occupying Macbeth's seat.
Line 49. He is angry, horrified. He accuses his guests of playing a cruel joke on him.
Line 51. Perhaps shaking its head at him. No one else sees the ghost. The guests would be surprised, embarrassed, alarmed, or frightened by his actions.
Line 53. Even though Macbeth previously imagined a dagger, no specific illness has been mentioned. She is covering for him.
Line 58. She has pulled him away from the guests.

A. Literary Element: Character

Lady Macbeth has resumed her earlier goading role, taunting Macbeth for being womanly. What is her motivation? [Possible answer: She is afraid that either Macbeth will reveal too much and condemn himself or be thought mad. In either case, they will lose their position.]

B. Critical Reading: Evaluating an Interpretation

Other editions put the ghost's entry after the first sentence in l. 91. Why would this change be effective? [Possible answers: The ghost would seem to come when summoned by Macbeth; because Macbeth has already been addressing an invisible ghost, the audience might think that Macbeth is hallucinating.]

Answers to Margin Questions

Line 68. He might stare in a frightening way at Macbeth, shake his head, make threatening gestures.

Line 70. Pointing to the ghost, perhaps turning to Lady Macbeth for confirmation of what he sees. Ideas about tone will vary. Perhaps he speaks in a despairing tone or in a mocking manner.

Line 75. He seems to be talking to himself. He is clearly not talking to the ghost who has exited.

Line 85. Following Lady Macbeth's lead, he has resumed playing the host, with apologies for his behavior. Notice his strength in ll. 84–92 as he, at least momentarily, has dismissed the frightening vision of Banquo's ghost.

Line 93. Banquo's ghost, which stares accusingly at him.

A

65 A woman's story at a winter's fire,
Authorized° by her grandam. Shame itself!
Why do you make such faces? When all's done,
You look but on a stool.
Macbeth.   Prithee, see there!
Behold! Look! Lo! How say you?
70 Why, what care I? If thou canst nod, speak too.
If charnel houses° and our graves must send
Those that we bury back, our monuments
Shall be the maws of kites.°   [*Exit* GHOST.]
Lady Macbeth.   What, quite unmanned in folly?
Macbeth.
If I stand here, I saw him.
Lady Macbeth.   Fie, for shame!
Macbeth.
75 Blood hath been shed ere now, i' th' olden time,
Ere humane statute purged the gentle weal;°
Ay, and since too, murders have been performed
Too terrible for the ear. The time has been
That, when the brains were out, the man would die,
80 And there an end; but now they rise again,
With twenty mortal murders on their crowns,°
And push us from our stools. This is more strange
Than such a murder is.
Lady Macbeth.   My worthy lord,
Your noble friends do lack you.
Macbeth.   I do forget.
85 Do not muse at me, my most worthy friends;
I have a strange infirmity, which is nothing
To those that know me. Come, love and health to all!
Then I'll sit down. Give me some wine, fill full.

B

[*Enter* GHOST.]
I drink to th' general joy o' th' whole table,
90 And to our dear friend Banquo, whom we miss;
Would he were here! To all and him we thirst,°
And all to all.°
Lords.   Our duties, and the pledge.
Macbeth.
Avaunt! and quit my sight! Let the earth hide thee!
Thy bones are marrowless, thy blood is cold;
95 Thou hast no speculation° in those eyes
Which thou dost glare with.
Lady Macbeth.   Think of this, good peers,
But as a thing of custom; 'tis no other.
Only it spoils the pleasure of the time.
Macbeth.
What man dare, I dare.
100 Approach thou like the rugged Russian bear,
The armed rhinoceros, or th' Hyrcan° tiger;

66. Authorized: vouched for.

? 68. *What could the actor playing Banquo do here in mockery of Macbeth?*

? 70. *What action is Macbeth engaged in here? What is his tone?*

71. charnel houses: vaults containing bones.

73. our . . . kites: Our tombs shall be the bellies of rapacious birds.

? 75. *Whom is Macbeth talking to?*

76. purged . . . weal: cleansed the state and made it gentle.

81. mortal . . . crowns: deadly wounds on their heads.

? 85. *What impression is Macbeth trying to create?*

91. thirst: desire to drink.

92. all to all: Let everybody drink to everybody.

? 93. *Whom is Macbeth talking to now? According to this speech, what might the ghost be doing?*

95. speculation: sight.

101. Hyrcan: of Hyrcania (near the Caspian Sea).

Take any shape but that, and my firm nerves°
Shall never tremble. Or be alive again,
And dare me to the desert° with thy sword.

105 If trembling I inhabit then, protest me
The baby of a girl.° Hence, horrible shadow!
Unreal mock'ry, hence!   [*Exit* GHOST.]
                    Why, so: being gone,
I am a man again. Pray you, sit still.

Lady Macbeth.
You have displaced the mirth, broke the good meeting,
With most admired° disorder.

110 **Macbeth.**   Can such things be,
And overcome us° like a summer's cloud,
Without our special wonder? You make me strange
Even to the disposition that I owe,°
When now I think you can behold such sights,

115 And keep the natural ruby of your cheeks,
When mine is blanched with fear.

Ross.   What sights, my lord?

Lady Macbeth.
I pray you, speak not: he grows worse and worse;
Question enrages him: at once, good night.
Stand not upon the order of your going,°
But go at once.

120 **Lennox.**   Good night; and better health
Attend his majesty!

Lady Macbeth.   A kind good night to all!

                    [*Exeunt* LORDS.]

Macbeth.
It will have blood, they say: blood will have blood.
Stones have been known to move and trees to speak;
Augurs and understood relations° have

125 By maggot-pies and choughs and rooks brought forth°
The secret'st man of blood. What is the night?°

Lady Macbeth.
Almost at odds with morning, which is which.

Macbeth.
How say'st thou, that Macduff denies his person
At our great bidding?

Lady Macbeth.   Did you send to him, sir?

Macbeth.
130 I hear it by the way,° but I will send:
There's not a one of them but in his house
I keep a servant fee'd.° I will tomorrow,
And betimes° I will, to the weird sisters:
More shall they speak, for now I am bent° to know

135 By the worst means the worst. For mine own good
All causes° shall give way. I am in blood
Stepped in so far that, should I wade no more,

102. **nerves:** sinews.

104. **desert:** lonely place.

106. **If . . . girl:** If then I tremble, proclaim me a baby girl.

❓ 108. *How "brave" should Macbeth appear to be with all the "brave" talk in these lines? What is his mood when he says "I am a man again"?*

110. **admired:** amazing.

❓ 110. *Lady Macbeth and her husband converse in private again. What would the other guests be doing?*

111. **overcome us:** come over us.

113. **You . . . owe:** You make me wonder what my nature is.

❓ 117. *What clue here would tell the actor playing Macbeth how he is to be behaving?*

119. **Stand . . . going:** Do not insist on departing in your order of rank.

❓ 122. *Read this speech carefully, and decide how Macbeth would deliver it: Slow? Fast? What is his mood?*

124. **Augurs . . . relations:** auguries (omens) and comprehended reports.

125. **By . . . forth:** by magpies, crows, and rooks (telltale birds) revealed.

126. **What . . . night:** What time of night is it?

❓ 127. *Is the old fire still present in Lady Macbeth? Or is she suddenly tired and broken?*

130. **by the way:** incidentally.

132. **fee'd:** that is, paid to spy.

133. **betimes:** quickly.

134. **bent:** determined.

136. **causes:** considerations.

C. Literary Element: Theme
The "overthrow of order" might be called a theme in Macbeth. What other lines might be classified as building on this theme? [Possible answers: Students might cite Act III, Scene 2, l. 16; lines that refer to the "fair is foul" theme as in Act I, Scene 1, l. 10; or Lady Macbeth's speech in Act I, Scene 5, ll. 38–52.]

D. Exploring the Culture
Just as in Act II, Scene 1, ll. 56–58, Macbeth is worried about nature revealing his actions. In Shakespeare's time, many people believed that a victim of a secret murder could identify his murderer. King James in his *Daemonologie* says, "for as in a secret murther, if the dead carkasse bee at any time thereafter handled by the murtherer, it will gush out of bloud, as if the bloud were crying to the heauen for reuenge of the murtherer, God hauing appoynted that secret supernaturall signe, for tryall of that secrete vnnaturall crime."

E. Reader's Response: Shaping Interpretations
❓ What do you think Macbeth thinks of Macduff? [Sample responses: This is the second time that Macduff has refused to attend a ceremony (the first was the coronation) for Macbeth. It must be obvious to Macbeth by now that Macduff suspects him of Duncan's murder. Macbeth may be insulted by Macduff's behavior.]

Answers to Margin Questions
Line 108. He is brave enough to plant his feet firmly on the floor, though he is shaking and terrified. His mood is relief.
Line 110. Speaking in subdued whispers; glancing or gesturing toward Macbeth.
Line 117. "He grows worse and worse": He may be staring goggle-eyed or babbling; he is oblivious to his guests.
Line 122. Answers will vary. The speech is often spoken slowly in a weary, resigned manner.
Line 127. Lady Macbeth is exhausted; her fire is spent.

Line 140. Answers will vary. Students may cite the word *tedious* or the lines in which Lady Macbeth points out that he is exhausted because he lacks sleep. Others may disagree, saying that ll. 139–140 and 143–144 suggest he is ready to move on and immerse himself further in evil.

Line 144. Answers will vary. She may shake her head in sorrow and dismay.

Scene 5. The lines here differ markedly from the blank verse (unrhymed iambic pentameter) of most of the play. It is written, starting at l. 2, in rhymed couplets.

From the Stratford Festival production of *Macbeth* (1983).

"Come, let's make haste; she'll soon be back again."

Returning were as tedious as go o'er.
Strange things I have in head that will to hand,
140   Which must be acted ere they may be scanned.°
Lady Macbeth.
You lack the season of all natures,° sleep.
Macbeth.
Come, we'll to sleep. My strange and self-abuse°
Is the initiate fear that wants hard use.°
We are yet but young in deed.   [*Exeunt.*]

Scene 5. *A witches' haunt.*

Thunder. Enter the three WITCHES, *meeting* HECATE.

First Witch.
Why, how now, Hecate! you look angerly.
Hecate.
Have I not reason, beldams° as you are,
Saucy and overbold? How did you dare
To trade and traffic with Macbeth
5   In riddles and affairs of death;

? **140.** *Does the prospect of a new adventure animate Macbeth? Or is he spent and exhausted?*
140. may be scanned: can be examined.
141. season . . . natures: seasoning (preservative) of all living creatures.
142. self-abuse: delusion.
143. initiate . . . use: beginner's fear that lacks hardening practice.
? **144.** *How might Lady Macbeth react to this last line?*
? **Scene 5.** Macbeth *was published in the first folio in 1623, seven years after Shakespeare had died. Some people think that this scene was written by someone else because the play was short and needed fleshing out. After you read the scene, decide if you think it "sounds" like the rest of the play.*
2. beldams: hags.

348 THE RENAISSANCE

And I, the mistress of your charms,
The close contriver° of all harms,
Was never called to bear my part,
Or show the glory of our art?

10 And, which is worse, all you have done
Hath been but for a wayward son, **(A)**
Spiteful and wrathful; who, as others do,
Loves for his own ends, not for you.
But make amends now: get you gone,

15 And at the pit of Acheron°
Meet me i' th' morning: thither he
Will come to know his destiny.
Your vessels and your spells provide,
Your charms and everything beside.

20 I am for th' air; this night I'll spend
Unto a dismal and a fatal end:
Great business must be wrought ere noon.
Upon the corner of the moon
There hangs a vap'rous drop profound;°

25 I'll catch it ere it come to ground:
And that distilled by magic sleights°
Shall raise such artificial sprites°
As by the strength of their illusion
Shall draw him on to his confusion.°

30 He shall spurn fate, scorn death, and bear
His hopes 'bove wisdom, grace, and fear:
And you all know security°
Is mortal's chiefest enemy.   [*Music and a song.*]
Hark! I am called; my little spirit, see,

35 Sits in a foggy cloud and stays for me.   [*Exit.*]

[*Sing within,* "Come away, come away," *etc.*]

First Witch.
Come, let's make haste; she'll soon be back again.
          [*Exeunt.*]

Scene 6. *The palace.*

Enter LENNOX *and another* LORD.

Lennox.
My former speeches have but hit your thoughts,°
Which can interpret farther. Only I say
Things have been strangely borne.° The gracious Duncan
Was pitied of Macbeth: marry, he was dead.

5 And the right-valiant Banquo walked too late;
Whom, you may say, if't please you, Fleance killed, **(B)**
For Fleance fled. Men must not walk too late.
Who cannot want the thought,° how monstrous
It was for Malcolm and for Donalbain

10 To kill their gracious father? Damnèd fact!°

MACBETH, ACT III, SCENE 6   349

---

7. close contriver: secret inventor.

15. Acheron: river of Hades.

24. profound: heavy.

26. sleights: arts.
27. artificial sprites: spirits created by magic arts.
29. confusion: ruin.

32. security: overconfidence.

1. My . . . thoughts: My recent words have only coincided with what you have in your mind.

3. borne: managed.

8. cannot . . . thought: cannot help but think.

10. fact: evil deed.

A. Critical Reading: Making Inferences

? Why is Macbeth "wayward" in Hecate's eyes? [Possible answer: He is not devoted to the cause of evil but does evil out of self-interest.]

B. Reader's Response: Shaping Interpretations

? What is Lennox's tone here? What does he now think about Duncan's murder? Why? [Sample responses: He seems to be ironic and suspicious—he thinks Macbeth was responsible, perhaps because of the things Macbeth has said and done at the banquet; or he seems perplexed, questioning how these sons —Malcolm, Donalbain, and now Fleance—could be so evil as to kill their fathers.]

A. Critical Reading: Summarizing

? Why did Macduff go to England?
[To raise an army, headed by Siward, to support Malcolm's claim to the throne.]

B. Expansion

In other words, you will regret that you wasted my time by asking that question.

C. Literary Element: Theme

Point out that this line is the source of the Collection theme.

Answers to Margin Questions

Line 24. Lennox has spoken with some irony or doubt in his voice on previous occasions, as in reporting the blood-smeared grooms (p. 327). These lines convey an irony better caught when they are read aloud. Read the speech aloud to the class, or coach a student to read it to express irony.

Line 49. The lords have grown so suspicious about Duncan's death, Macbeth's motive for silencing the grooms, and his placing blame on those who have fled that Malcolm and Macduff are working in England to raise an army against Macbeth.

Making Meanings

Act III

First Thoughts

1. Answers will vary. Possible titles: "Botches in the Work" or "The Bloody Business" (taken from quotations).

Reviewing the Text

a. Banquo suspects that Macbeth murdered Duncan. Although his thoughts are interrupted by Macbeth's arrival, he seems to be waiting to find out whether the rest of the prophecy comes true.

b. Possible answers: He hires two murderers and convinces them that Banquo wronged them. He then sends a third murderer to make sure that they do their job, because Macbeth sees Banquo as a threat. Lady Macbeth is not involved in these plans.

c. Fleance.

d. Macbeth (but no one else) sees Banquo's ghost at Macbeth's chair and speaks to him, refusing to sit. Lady Macbeth tries to cover for

---

How it did grieve Macbeth! Did he not straight,
In pious rage, the two delinquents tear,
That were the slaves of drink and thralls° of sleep?
Was not that nobly done? Ay, and wisely too;
15 For 'twould have angered any heart alive
To hear the men deny't. So that I say
He has borne all things well: and I do think
That, had he Duncan's sons under his key—
As, an 't° please heaven, he shall not—they should find
20 What 'twere to kill a father. So should Fleance.
But, peace! for from broad words,° and 'cause he failed
His presence at the tyrant's feast, I hear,
Macduff lives in disgrace. Sir, can you tell
Where he bestows himself?

Lord.   The son of Duncan,
25 From whom this tyrant holds the due of birth,°
Lives in the English court, and is received
Of the most pious Edward° with such grace
That the malevolence of fortune nothing
Takes from his high respect.° Thither Macduff
30 Is gone to pray the holy king, upon his aid°
To wake Northumberland° and warlike Siward;°
That by the help of these, with Him above
To ratify the work, we may again
Give to our tables meat, sleep to our nights,
35 Free from our feasts and banquets bloody knives,
Do faithful homage and receive free° honors:
All which we pine for now. And this report
Hath so exasperate the king that he
Prepares for some attempt of war.

Lennox.   Sent he to Macduff?
Lord.
40 He did: and with an absolute "Sir, not I,"
The cloudy° messenger turns me his back,
And hums, as who should say "You'll rue the time
That clogs° me with this answer."

Lennox.   And that well might
Advise him to a caution, t' hold what distance
45 His wisdom can provide. Some holy angel
Fly to the court of England and unfold
His message ere he come, that a swift blessing
May soon return to this our suffering country
Under a hand accursed!

Lord.   I'll send my prayers with him.
                                     [*Exeunt.*]

13. thralls: slaves.

19. an 't: if it.

21. for . . . words: because of frank talk.

? **24.** *Lennox is sometimes called the "ironic" character of the play. Do you agree? What tone would he use in this speech?*
25. due of birth: birthright.
27. Edward: Edward the Confessor (reigned 1042–1066).
29. nothing . . . respect: does not diminish the high respect in which he is held.
30. upon his aid: to aid him (Malcolm).
31. To wake Northumberland: that is, to arouse the people in an English county near Scotland. **Siward:** earl of Northumberland.
36. free: freely granted.

41. cloudy: disturbed.

43. clogs: burdens.

? **49.** *This is basically an "information" scene. Can you summarize what it tells you about the plot?*

350 THE RENAISSANCE

Macbeth by saying he customarily has fits; she dismisses the guests.

e. He has gone to the court of Edward, king of England, to ask for an army to help overthrow Macbeth.

f. They believe him guilty of the murders of Duncan and Banquo.

Shaping Interpretations

2. Possible response: Perhaps he wanted to show a change in Macbeth's character—to show him not only growing accustomed to crime but

becoming more devious and arranging matters so he could deny that he did it and his denial would be technically true (an equivocation).

3. Possible answers: Some changes are role reversal—she plans the first murder, and he only goes along because of her plan; but he plans Banquo's murder, arranges to have it done by others, and keeps her out of it. They seem very intimate as they plan and carry out Duncan's murder; now she is not even in his confidence, and he does not share with or depend on her the way he has before. The changes in their relationship are some of the

T350 The Renaissance

MAKING MEANINGS

Act III

First Thoughts

1. What title would you give to Act III?

> **Reviewing the Text**
>
> a. In the short **soliloquy** that opens Scene 1, what does Banquo reveal that he knows about Macbeth? What does he decide to do?
>
> b. How and why does Macbeth arrange Banquo's murder? How is Lady Macbeth involved in the murder?
>
> c. In Scene 3, who escapes the murderers?
>
> d. Describe what happens in Scene 4 when Ross, Lennox, and the other lords invite Macbeth to share their table. What does Macbeth do? What does Lady Macbeth do?
>
> e. Macduff does not appear at all in Act III. Where is he, and why?
>
> f. By Scene 6, what opinion do Lennox and the other lords hold of Macbeth?

Shaping Interpretations

2. Why do you suppose Shakespeare did not have Macbeth kill Banquo with his own hands, as he killed Duncan and his two guards? What can you infer about Macbeth's changing **character** after seeing how he engages in this complex plan involving professional murderers?

3. The relationship between Macbeth and Lady Macbeth has changed in several ways since they became rulers of Scotland. Describe some of these changes. What reasons can you suggest for these changes?

4. In Scene 2, Macbeth describes his surroundings by saying, "Light thickens, and the crow / Makes wing to th' rooky wood." How can these remarks also be seen as a **metaphorical** commentary on the events of the play? What other remarks by Macbeth function in this way?

5. How is Fleance's escape a **turning point** in the play?

6. How does the banquet scene blur the clear-cut and common-sense distinction that most of us make between the real and the imaginary? In what other scenes has this distinction also been blurred?

7. At the beginning of Scene 2, Lady Macbeth quietly tells herself, "Nought's had, all's spent, / Where our desire is got without content." What does she mean? At this point, would her husband agree?

8. Nobody except Macbeth sees Banquo's ghost. In some productions of the play, the ghost does not appear onstage; in others it does. If you were the director, which would you choose? What effect is created by having Banquo appear at the banquet, made up as a ghost? What is gained by having it appear as though no person motivates Macbeth's terrifying behavior?

Extending the Text

9. After his vision of Banquo's ghost in Scene 4, Macbeth finally accepts that "blood will have blood." What does this phrase mean? Is it relevant to today's world? How?

Challenging the Text

10. Shakespeare never reveals the identity of the Third Murderer, introduced in Scene 3. Who do you think the murderer is? Do you think the introduction of this Third Murderer is a flaw in the play? Explain your response.

---

effect also may apply in the witches' scenes and to the descriptions of the natural world's response to Duncan's murder.

7. Students might say she is pointing out that they have committed a terrible crime—in effect, sold their souls—and yet fulfilling their ambitions has not made them happy. Macbeth thinks it is still possible to achieve peace, if only he can kill Banquo and Fleance.

8. Possible answers: Have an actor play the ghost; use technology to project a ghost; use a strong light over the chair to suggest the ghost's presence; or have the ghost be a figment of Macbeth's imagination. Banquo's ghost in the flesh blurs the distinction between the real and the imaginary, and it would show the strong influence murder can have on the mind of the murderer. Showing no ghost on stage would emphasize that Macbeth is hallucinating.

Extending the Text

9. **(Synthesis)** Possible answer: The guilty will be found and pay with their lives. It is relevant in regard to discussion of the death penalty, as society must decide if the murderer should pay with his or her life.

Challenging the Text

10. **(Evaluation)** Possible answers: It may be one of the witches making sure Fleance escapes so the prophecy can come true. Other possibilities are Ross, Seyton, or Macbeth. It is not a flaw—it adds to the creepiness; or it is a flaw because it distracts the audience's attention from other more important issues.

---

effects of committing murder; perhaps they have lost trust in each other as they constantly distrust those around them.

4. Possible answer: Macbeth's words indicate the time in which the scene takes place, probably dusk—a time in which there is a blurring of distinction between light and dark—but in a metaphorical sense, he comments on the blurring between good and evil. Several other remarks can also be taken as both literal and metaphorical: For example, in Scene 4, ll. 126–127 again refer to the blurring of time in the scene and in the motif of reversal. In Scene 4, ll. 78–83 are directed at the ghost,

literally, but could also be taken metaphorically to mean that past misdeeds continue to haunt and "unseat" one.

5. Students might say that it is the first time that Macbeth's plans have definitely gone awry, and it leaves open the possibility that Banquo's descendants will be kings.

6. Possible answer: The scene plays upon the frightening possibility of madness. What seems to be real may not be, as Macbeth can see something no one else at the table can see. Also, if an actor plays the ghost, then a supernatural being is presented as if it had real existence, another blurring of distinction. This

A. Expansion

Students might be upset or angered by some of the ingredients the witches use. While some of the ingredients may reflect biases and beliefs prevalent in Elizabethan England, students should recall that the witches are in league with evil and their disgusting recipe reflects their wickedness.

Answer to Margin Question
Stage direction. Answers will vary. The witches might be gleeful or focused.

PROGRAM MANAGER

- **Planning Instruction** See Teaching Notes, *Teaching Resources A,* pp. 90–91, for objectives and a summary of Act IV.
- **Instructional Support** Before beginning the instructional lesson, see Graphic Organizer for Active Reading, *Teaching Resources A,* p. 98, for a Through the Selection activity.
- **Assessment** See Selection Test (Act IV), *Test Booklet,* pp. 63–64.

ACT IV   Scene 1. *A witches' haunt.*

Thunder. Enter the three WITCHES.

First Witch.
　Thrice the brinded° cat hath mewed.
Second Witch.
　Thrice and once the hedge-pig° whined.
Third Witch.
　Harpier° cries, 'Tis time, 'tis time.
First Witch.
5　Round about the caldron go:
　In the poisoned entrails throw.
　Toad, that under cold stone
　Days and nights has thirty-one
　Swelt'red venom sleeping got,°
　Boil thou first i' th' charmèd pot.
All.
10　Double, double, toil and trouble;
　Fire burn and caldron bubble.
Second Witch.
　Fillet° of a fenny° snake,
　In the caldron boil and bake;
　Eye of newt and toe of frog,
15　Wool of bat and tongue of dog,
　Adder's fork° and blindworm's° sting,
　Lizard's leg and howlet's° wing,
　For a charm of pow'rful trouble,
　Like a hell-broth boil and bubble.
All.
20　Double, double, toil and trouble;
　Fire burn and caldron bubble.

"I conjure you, by that which you profess, Howe'er you come to know it, answer me."
From the Stratford Festival production of *Macbeth* (1983).

Stage direction. *This scene usually begins in darkness. In Shakespeare's day, the caldron might have risen through the trapdoor. How would you have the witches act: gleeful? lamenting?*

1. **brinded:** brindled.
2. **hedge-pig:** hedgehog.
3. **Harpier:** an attendant spirit like Graymalkin and Paddock in Act I, Scene 1.

8. **Swelt'red . . . got:** venom sweated out while sleeping.

12. **Fillet:** slice. **fenny:** from a swamp.

16. **fork:** forked tongue. **blindworm's:** legless lizard's.
17. **howlet's:** owl's.

OPTIONS FOR TEACHING

STRATEGIES FOR INCLUSION

English Language Development
Help students define the word *traitor* by asking the following questions: How might someone be a traitor to his or her country? [Possible answer: By sharing information that would hurt the country.] To one's family? [Possible answer: By refusing to help the family.] Before students read Scene 2, ask them how they think Lady Macduff will feel about her husband's leaving

Scotland. After they have read the scene, discuss whether Macduff is a traitor or if there are other explanations for his behavior.

Bodily-Kinesthetic Divide the class into two teams. Each team should prepare and then pose in five "frozen scenes." If the other team guesses the scene being represented on the first try, the presenting team gets five points. If the others guess it on the second try, the presenting team gets two points, and on the third try, one point. The team

with the most points wins. Remind students to present material the audience sees. They cannot, for example, show Duncan being murdered.

Visual/Auditory If possible, have students work in small groups to create a computer-animated scene with sound. Each group should choose a short portion of a scene from the play. One student might be in charge of getting information on how the technology works, another might do the artwork, another might plan the animation, while another might create the sound.

Third Witch.
Scale of dragon, tooth of wolf,
Witch's mummy,° maw and gulf°
Of the ravined° salt-sea shark,
25 Root of hemlock digged i' th' dark,
Liver of blaspheming Jew,
Gall of goat, and slips of yew
Slivered in the moon's eclipse,
Nose of Turk and Tartar's lips,
30 Finger of birth-strangled babe
Ditch-delivered by a drab,°
Make the gruel thick and slab:°
Add thereto a tiger's chaudron,°
For th' ingredients of our caldron.
All.
35 Double, double, toil and trouble;
Fire burn and caldron bubble.
Second Witch.
Cool it with a baboon's blood,
Then the charm is firm and good.

[*Enter* HECATE *and the other three* WITCHES.]

Hecate.
O, well done! I commend your pains;
40 And every one shall share i' th' gains:
And now about the caldron sing,
Like elves and fairies in a ring,
Enchanting all that you put in.

[*Music and a song:* "Black Spirits," *etc.*]

[*Exeunt* HECATE *and the other three* WITCHES.]

Second Witch.
By the pricking of my thumbs,
45 Something wicked this way comes:
Open, locks,
Whoever knocks!

[*Enter* MACBETH.]

Macbeth.
How now, you secret, black, and midnight hags!
What is't you do?
All.   A deed without a name.
Macbeth.
50 I conjure you, by that which you profess,
Howe'er you come to know it, answer me:
Though you untie the winds and let them fight
Against the churches; though the yesty° waves
Confound° and swallow navigation up;

---

23. Witch's mummy: mummified flesh of a witch. **maw and gulf:** stomach and gullet.
24. ravined: ravenous.

31. drab: harlot.
32. slab: slimy.
33. chaudron: entrails.

? *This exciting scene has five major sections, each with its own intensity. See if you can identify them when you're finished.*

? **48.** *How has Macbeth's attitude toward the witches changed since his earlier encounters with them?*

53. yesty: foamy.
54. Confound: destroy.

· INTEGRATING THE LANGUAGE ARTS

A. Literary Element: Theme

Macbeth's focus has narrowed from his desire to save Scotland, reported at the beginning of the play. What is Macbeth's only interest now? [His own gain.]

Answers to Margin Questions

Line 61. Students who recall Hecate's lines in Act III, Scene 5, may say that Macbeth is not a full participant in evil. Students who focus on Act IV, Scene 1, may say that the witches identify him as an evil person now.

Line 67. Answers will vary. They are tossing ingredients into the caldron and muttering while speaking with Macbeth.

Line 71. Perhaps to warn Macbeth that Macduff could defeat him. The helmet suggests such a defeat might take place in battle.

55   Though bladed corn be lodged° and trees blown down;
Though castles topple on their warders' heads;
Though palaces and pyramids do slope°
Their heads to their foundations; though the treasure
Of nature's germens° tumble all together,
60   Even till destruction sicken,° answer me
To what I ask you.
First Witch.   Speak.
Second Witch.   Demand.
Third Witch.   We'll answer.
First Witch.
Say, if th' hadst rather hear it from our mouths,
Or from our masters?
Macbeth.   Call 'em, let me see 'em.
First Witch.
Pour in sow's blood, that hath eaten
65   Her nine farrow;° grease that's sweaten°
From the murderer's gibbet° throw
Into the flame.
All.   Come, high or low,
Thyself and office° deftly show!

[*Thunder.* FIRST APPARITION: *an Armed Head.*°]

Macbeth.
Tell me, thou unknown power——
First Witch.   He knows thy thought:
70   Hear his speech, but say thou nought.
First Apparition.
Macbeth! Macbeth! Macbeth! Beware Macduff!
Beware the Thane of Fife. Dismiss me: enough.

[*He descends.*]

Macbeth.
Whate'er thou art, for thy good caution thanks:
Thou hast harped° my fear aright. But one word more——
First Witch.
75   He will not be commanded. Here's another,
More potent than the first.

[*Thunder.* SECOND APPARITION: *a Bloody Child.*]

Second Apparition.
Macbeth! Macbeth! Macbeth!
Macbeth.
Had I three ears, I'd hear thee.
Second Apparition.
Be bloody, bold, and resolute! Laugh to scorn
80   The pow'r of man, for none of woman born
Shall harm Macbeth.   [*Descends.*]

354 THE RENAISSANCE

55. bladed . . . lodged: grain in the ear be beaten down.

57. slope: bend.

59. nature's germens: seeds of all life.

60. sicken: sicken at its own work.

? 61. *These exchanges are spoken rapidly. Do the witches now see Macbeth as a participant in evil?*

65. farrow: young pigs.
sweaten: sweated.
66. gibbet: gallows.

? 67. *What are the witches doing all during this scene?*
68. office: function.
Armed Head: helmeted head.

? 71. *Why does the helmeted head deliver this message? How does the form of the apparition support the warning the apparition gives?*

74. harped: hit upon; struck the note of.

OPTIONS FOR TEACHING

COOPERATIVE LEARNING

Creating a Dance Have students work in groups of three or four to create a dance for the song mentioned in the stage directions of Act IV, Scene 1, l. 43. Students should consider mood and atmosphere as they choreograph steps and select accompanying music. Provide an opportunity for the dances to be performed for an audience.

Puzzlers Divide the class into groups of three, and have them analyze the prophecies of the apparitions. Ask them to make notes on what they think each apparition means and why the apparitions take the forms that they do. Have them return to these notes after the final act to compare their thoughts.

Macbeth.
Then live, Macduff: what need I fear of thee?
But yet I'll make assurance double sure,
And take a bond of fate.° Thou shalt not live; **B**
85   That I may tell pale-hearted fear it lies,
And sleep in spite of thunder.

[*Thunder.* THIRD APPARITION: *a Child Crowned, with a tree in his hand.*]

                              What is this,
That rises like the issue° of a king,
And wears upon his baby-brow the round
And top of sovereignty?°
All.   Listen, but speak not to't.
Third Apparition.
90   Be lion-mettled, proud, and take no care
Who chafes, who frets, or where conspirers are:
Macbeth shall never vanquished be until
Great Birnam Wood to high Dunsinane Hill
Shall come against him.   [*Descends.*]
Macbeth.   That will never be.
95   Who can impress° the forest, bid the tree
Unfix his earth-bound root? Sweet bodements,° good! **C**
Rebellious dead, rise never, till the Wood
Of Birnam rise, and our high-placed Macbeth
Shall live the lease of nature,° pay his breath
100   To time and mortal custom.° Yet my heart
Throbs to know one thing. Tell me, if your art
Can tell so much: shall Banquo's issue ever
Reign in this kingdom?
All.   Seek to know no more.
Macbeth.
I will be satisfied.° Deny me this,
105   And an eternal curse fall on you! Let me know.
Why sinks that caldron? And what noise° is this?

[*Hautboys.*]

First Witch. Show!
Second Witch. Show!
Third Witch. Show!
All.
110   Show his eyes, and grieve his heart;
Come like shadows, so depart! **D**

[*A show of eight* KINGS *and* BANQUO, *last* KING *with a glass*° *in his hand.*] **E**

Macbeth.
Thou art too like the spirit of Banquo. Down!
Thy crown does sear mine eyelids. And thy hair,

MACBETH, ACT IV, SCENE 1   355

? 82. *Macbeth takes the child's message to mean he need not fear Macduff. Nonetheless, why should the second apparition's message be approached with caution?*

84. take . . . fate: get a guarantee from fate (that is, he will kill Macduff and thus will compel fate to keep its word).

87. issue: offspring.

89. round . . . sovereignty: that is, crown.

? 93. *What does the third apparition prophesy? What must be Macbeth's mental state at this point?*
95. impress: conscript; draft.
96. bodements: prophecies.

99. lease of nature: natural life span.
100. mortal custom: natural death.
? 102. *What is Macbeth's mood? How might his tone change when he asks about Banquo's issue, or children?*
104. satisfied: that is, fully informed.

106. noise: music.

? Stage direction. *A parade of eight Stuart kings passes before Macbeth. These are the kings of Banquo's line. The last king holds up a mirror (glass) to suggest an infinite number of descendants. Banquo appears last. According to the next speech, how does Banquo act toward Macbeth?*

B. Critical Reading: Drawing Conclusions
? Why will Macbeth kill Macduff despite this prophecy? [So that fate cannot trick him.]

C. Language Note: Poetry
All of a sudden, Macbeth starts speaking entirely in rhymed couplets, whereas previously in the play rhymed couplets are used by him almost always to end a scene. Why might this be? [Possible answer: Macbeth is so influenced by the witches and apparitions that he begins to speak like them.]

D. Critical Reading: Speculating
? Why might the witches initially refuse to answer his question and then give in? [Possible answers: Because it is something he should not know, and they want to make sure that he takes full responsibility for asking for the knowledge. They are just playing with him, tempting him more by refusing.]

E. Expansion
G. Wilson Knight suggests that this scene be played "with deliberation and ceremony." He would have the kings pause as they pass Macbeth and then group themselves around a throne as if posing for a photograph, waiting for Banquo's ghost. Banquo actually seats himself in the throne to illustrate his truly royal spirit, as contrasted with the meanness of Macbeth.

Answers to Margin Questions
Line 82. At first, the message seems to mean no one can harm Macbeth, but the wording is unusual and may be some sort of riddle.
Line 93. Macbeth (in his castle at Dunsinane) will not be defeated until Birnam Wood marches on Dunsinane. He must feel exultant, unbeatable, as the second and third prophecies seem to go against reason.
Line 102. Macbeth is consumed by the desire to know whether Banquo's descendants will inherit his throne. His tone might change from exultation to concern.
Stage direction. He smiles at Macbeth and gestures to indicate that the eight kings are his descendants.

Critic Kenneth Muir says, "The two-fold balls are usually taken to refer to the double coronation of James at Scone and Westminster. . . . The treble scepters are the two used for investment in the English coronation and the one used in the Scottish coronation."

B. Reader's Response: Shaping Interpretations

Review Lennox's speech in Act III, Scene 6. Why is he still attending Macbeth? [Sample responses: He is afraid to leave. He is waiting for more substantial proof. He is a spy in Macbeth's house, just as Macbeth has spies in the thanes' houses.] Some critics believe that Act III, Scene 6, may actually belong after Act IV, Scene 1.

C. Literary Element: Irony

[?] Why are these lines ironic?
[Because Macbeth himself trusts the witches.]

Answers to Margin Questions

Line 124. Banquo still has bloody gashes. Macbeth must be angry and dismayed that, despite the three promising prophecies, Banquo will win in the end.

Line 136. Lennox's return marks the sudden return of everyday reality and sanity, or perhaps his return redirects the audience's attention to the suspense surrounding the thanes' increasing suspicions and Macduff's attempts to raise an army against Macbeth. Lennox tells Macbeth that Macduff has fled to England.

Thou other gold-bound brow, is like the first.
115   A third is like the former. Filthy hags!
Why do you show me this? A fourth! Start,° eyes!
What, will the line stretch out to th' crack of doom?°
Another yet! A seventh! I'll see no more.
And yet the eighth° appears, who bears a glass
120   Which shows me many more; and some I see
That twofold balls and treble scepters° carry:
Horrible sight! Now I see 'tis true;
For the blood-boltered° Banquo smiles upon me,
And points at them for his.° What, is this so?

First Witch.
125   Ay, sir, all this is so. But why
Stands Macbeth thus amazedly?
Come, sisters, cheer we up his sprites,°
And show the best of our delights:
I'll charm the air to give a sound,
130   While you perform your antic round,°
That this great king may kindly say
Our duties did his welcome pay.

[*Music. The* WITCHES *dance, and vanish.*]

Macbeth.
Where are they? Gone? Let this pernicious hour
Stand aye accursèd in the calendar!
Come in, without there!

[*Enter* LENNOX.]

135   **Lennox.**   What's your grace's will?
Macbeth.
Saw you the weird sisters?
Lennox.   No, my lord.
Macbeth.
Came they not by you?
Lennox.   No indeed, my lord.
Macbeth.
Infected by the air whereon they ride,
And damned all those that trust them! I did hear
140   The galloping of horse.° Who was't came by?
Lennox.
'Tis two or three, my lord, that bring you word
Macduff is fled to England.
Macbeth.   Fled to England?
Lennox.
Ay, my good lord.
Macbeth (*aside*).
Time, thou anticipat'st° my dread exploits.
145   The flighty purpose never is o'ertook
Unless the deed go with it.° From this moment

356 THE RENAISSANCE

---

116. Start: that is, from the sockets.

117. crack of doom: blast (of a trumpet) at Doomsday.

119. eighth: King James I of England (the present king).

121. twofold . . . scepters: coronation emblems.

123. blood-boltered: matted with blood.

124. his: his descendants.

[?] **124.** *What does Banquo look like? What must be Macbeth's mental state now?*

127. sprites: spirits.

130. antic round: grotesque, circular dance.

[?] **136.** *How would the mood on stage change as Lennox appears? What crucial information does he give Macbeth?*

140. horse: horses (or horsemen).

144. anticipat'st: foretold.
146. The flighty . . . it: The fleeting plan is never accomplished unless an action accompanies it.

Art Have students work in groups of four to create a piece of scenery for the play. The design of the piece should reflect a thoughtful interpretation of its role in the play. Assign each student a leadership role: an artist (to lead the painting or drawing), a production manager (to oversee the collection of necessary building materials), a director (to compare the details noted in the play to the group's rendering of the scene), and a stage manager (to consider placement and use of the scenery).

Social Sciences Have interested students prepare a debate on whether Macbeth actually sees the apparitions in Act IV. Assign students to two teams to research the subject of parapsychology (a branch of psychology that investigates psychic phenomena) and to plan their strategy in refuting or supporting Macbeth's sightings. At debate time, flip a coin to see which team begins, and alternate between the teams at one-minute intervals until each team member has made a point. Let the class discuss who they believe won the debate and why.

Health Students may be interested in finding out more about the king's "touch" and the disease that it was supposed to cure (scrofula). Encourage them to research both contemporary and current understandings of this phenomenon. Have them present a short oral report to the class on their findings.

The very firstlings of my heart° shall be
The firstlings of my hand. And even now,
To crown my thoughts with acts, be it thought and done:
150 The castle of Macduff I will surprise;°
Seize upon Fife; give to th' edge o' th' sword
His wife, his babes, and all unfortunate souls
That trace him in his line.° No boasting like a fool;
This deed I'll do before this purpose cool:
155 But no more sights!—Where are these gentlemen?
Come, bring me where they are.   [*Exeunt.*]

Scene 2. *Macduff's castle.*

Enter Macduff's wife LADY MACDUFF, *her* SON, *and* ROSS.

Lady Macduff.
What had he done, to make him fly the land?
Ross.
You must have patience, madam.
Lady Macduff.   He had none:
His flight was madness. When our actions do not,
Our fears do make us traitors.
Ross.   You know not
5   Whether it was his wisdom or his fear.
Lady Macduff.
Wisdom! To leave his wife, to leave his babes,
His mansion and his titles,° in a place
From whence himself does fly? He loves us not;
He wants the natural touch:° for the poor wren,
10   The most diminutive of birds, will fight,
Her young ones in her nest, against the owl.
All is the fear and nothing is the love;
As little is the wisdom, where the flight
So runs against all reason.
Ross.   My dearest coz,°
15   I pray you, school° yourself. But, for your husband,
He is noble, wise, judicious, and best knows
The fits o' th' season.° I dare not speak much further:
But cruel are the times, when we are traitors
And do not know ourselves; when we hold rumor
20   From what we fear,° yet know not what we fear,
But float upon a wild and violent sea
Each way and move. I take my leave of you.
Shall not be long but I'll be here again.
Things at the worst will cease,° or else climb upward
25   To what they were before. My pretty cousin,
Blessing upon you!
Lady Macduff.
Fathered he is, and yet he's fatherless.

MACBETH, ACT IV, SCENE 2   357

---

147. **firstlings . . . heart:** that is, first thoughts, impulses.

150. **surprise:** attack suddenly.

153. **trace . . . line:** are of his lineage.

? 156. *By this speech, how does Macbeth show he has fallen ever deeper into evil? How different is Macbeth now from the reluctant murderer of the first part of the play? Why does Macbeth want to murder Macduff's children?*

? **Stage direction.** *In many productions, the mood of this scene contrasts dramatically with the previous scenes of horror. How would you stage this domestic scene to suggest the vulnerability of Lady Macduff and her children?*

7. **titles:** possessions.

9. **wants . . . touch:** that is, lacks natural affection for his wife and children.

14. **coz:** cousin.
15. **school:** control.

17. **fits . . . season:** disorders of the time.
? 17. *How could Ross show his fear in line 17?*
20. **hold . . . fear:** believe rumors because we fear.

24. **cease:** cease worsening.

PROBLEM SOLVING/CRITICAL THINKING

Easing the Blow Being the bearer of bad news can be a very difficult and uncomfortable job. Have students list actions, approaches, or strategies that the speaker can use to lessen the discomfort of the situation. Ask students to consider the following questions: Is a leading statement, such as "I'm really sorry, but I have bad news for you," helpful? Should you ever just blurt out the news? Should you use euphemisms or not? What can or should you do after the message is delivered? Ask the class to share ideas and to determine whether some of their strategies might have helped Ross convey the bad news to Macduff.

☞

A. Humanities Connection

Macduff's son may be referring to Jesus's statement about trusting in God: "Look at the birds in the sky. They neither sow or reap or gather into barns; yet your heavenly Father feeds them. Are you not worth much more than they are?" (Matthew 6:26)

B. Reader's Response: First Thoughts

? How do you feel about Lady Macduff and her son? [Sample responses: It's a relief to find some guiltless characters. I enjoy their witty chatting but worry about their safety.]

C. Literary Element: Plot

? What is the point of having this messenger arrive to warn of danger? [Possible answer: It increases suspense, for the audience hopes the mother and son will escape.]

Answers to Margin Questions

Line 30. He might kiss Lady Macduff's cheek and tousle the boy's hair. Answers about Ross's age will vary.

Line 31. Possible answer: She might act concerned by her husband's absence and by the danger, or she might conceal her fear behind banter with her son.

Ross.
    I am so much a fool, should I stay longer,
    It would be my disgrace° and your discomfort.
    I take my leave at once.   [*Exit* ROSS.]
30 **Lady Macduff.**   Sirrah,° your father's dead:
    And what will you do now? How will you live?
Son.
    As birds do, mother.
 Lady Macduff.   What, with worms and flies?
Son.
    With what I get, I mean; and so do they.
Lady Macduff.
    Poor bird! thou'dst never fear the net nor lime,°
35 The pitfall nor the gin.°
Son.
    Why should I, mother? Poor birds they are not set for.
    My father is not dead, for all your saying.
Lady Macduff.
    Yes, he is dead: how wilt thou do for a father?
Son. Nay, how will you do for a husband?
40 **Lady Macduff.** Why, I can buy me twenty at any market.
Son. Then you'll buy 'em to sell° again.
Lady Macduff.
    Thou speak'st with all thy wit, and yet, i' faith,
    With wit enough for thee.°
Son.
    Was my father a traitor, mother?
45 **Lady Macduff.** Ay, that he was.
Son. What is a traitor?
Lady Macduff. Why, one that swears and lies.°
Son. And be all traitors that do so?
Lady Macduff. Every one that does so is a traitor, and must be
    hanged.
50 **Son.** And must they all be hanged that swear and lie?
Lady Macduff. Every one.
Son. Who must hang them?
Lady Macduff. Why, the honest men.
Son. Then the liars and swearers are fools; for there are liars
55   and swearers enow° to beat the honest men and hang up them.
Lady Macduff. Now, God help thee, poor monkey! But
    how wilt thou do for a father?
Son. If he were dead, you'd weep for him. If you would not, it
    were a good sign that I should quickly have a new father.
60 **Lady Macduff.** Poor prattler, how thou talk'st!

[*Enter a* MESSENGER.]

Messenger.
    Bless you, fair dame! I am not to you known,
    Though in your state of honor I am perfect.°

---

29. It . . . disgrace: That is, I would weep.

? **30.** *In taking his leave, how would Ross show affection for Lady Macduff and her young son? Would you have Ross be younger or older than Lady Macduff?*

30. Sirrah: here, an affectionate address to a child.

? **31.** *How would you have Lady Macduff act in this scene? Frightened? Bitter? Loving? Resigned?*

34. lime: birdlime (smeared on branches to catch birds).

35. gin: trap.

41. sell: betray.

43. for thee: for a child.

47. swears and lies: takes an oath and breaks it.

55. enow: enough.

62. in . . . perfect: That is, I am fully informed of your honorable rank.

Cultural Diversity People suffer from guilt for things they purposely did and knew were wrong, as well as for mistakes and accidents; and they handle guilt in different ways. Some religions account for the need to deal with guilt through penance or confessions or Yom Kippur, the Jewish Day of Atonement.

Other people relieve guilt by discussing their feelings with friends or health professionals.

Thematic Connections: "Under a Hand Accursed" Now that students have learned more about how Macbeth acted after the witches' first predictions, they may feel equipped to discuss the question "What is a curse?" in conjunction

with the title of the Collection. Students might discuss the topics of free will (the belief that actions are the choice of individuals), predestination (fate), and determinism (the concept that everything, even individual choices, results from a series of causes) as shown in this play.

I doubt° some danger does approach you nearly:
If you will take a homely° man's advice,
65 Be not found here; hence, with your little ones.
To fright you thus, methinks I am too savage;
To do worse to you were fell° cruelty,
Which is too nigh your person. Heaven preserve you!
I dare abide no longer.   [*Exit* MESSENGER.]
Lady Macduff.   Whither should I fly?
70 I have done no harm. But I remember now
I am in this earthly world, where to do harm
Is often laudable, to do good sometime
Accounted dangerous folly. Why then, alas,
Do I put up that womanly defense,
75 To say I have done no harm?—What are these faces?

[*Enter* MURDERERS.]

Murderer.
Where is your husband?
Lady Macduff.
I hope, in no place so unsanctified
Where such as thou mayst find him.
Murderer.   He's a traitor.
Son.
Thou li'st, thou shag-eared° villain!
Murderer.   What, you egg!

[*Stabbing him.*]

Young fry° of treachery!
80 **Son.**   He has killed me, mother:
Run away, I pray you!   [*Dies.*] **D**

[*Exit* LADY MACDUFF, *crying* "Murder!"
followed by MURDERERS.]
E

Scene 3. *England. Before the king's palace.*
Enter MALCOLM *and* MACDUFF.

Malcolm.
Let us seek out some desolate shade, and there
Weep our sad bosoms empty.
Macduff.   Let us rather
Hold fast the mortal° sword, and like good men
Bestride our down-fall'n birthdom.° Each new morn
5 New widows howl, new orphans cry, new sorrows
Strike heaven on the face, that° it resounds
As if it felt with Scotland and yelled out
Like syllable of dolor.°
Malcolm.   What I believe, I'll wail;
What know, believe; and what I can redress,

---

63. **doubt:** fear.
64. **homely:** plain.

67. **fell:** fierce.

? 69. *Some readers think that this messenger has been sent by Lady Macbeth. Is there any support for this theory? Would it be within her character? What must Lady Macduff do when she hears this terrible message?*

? 75. *What would Lady Macduff and her son do as they see the murderers enter the room?*

79. **shag-eared:** hairy-eared.

80. **fry:** spawn.

3. **mortal:** deadly.
4. **Bestride . . . birthdom:** protectively stand over our native land.
6. **that:** so that.

8. **Like . . . dolor:** similar sound of grief.

D. Reader's Response: First Thoughts

? How do you feel about this scene?
[Sample responses: I hate it that Macbeth is getting away with this. It is especially touching because just as Banquo cried to Fleance to fly in an attempt to save him, Macduff's son, who is just a little boy, also tries to save his mother with a warning cry, but he fails.]

E. Critical Reading: Evaluating an Interpretation
Read this critical comment by G. Wilson Knight, and ask students to share their reactions: "The murder of Lady Macduff can be best done before simple curtains. Generally it gets laughter. It is, however, not meant to hold any grandeur of action. Macbeth's exploits get less and less dignified and more mad. They are meant to. Duncan's murder was tragically grand; Banquo's melodramatic; and this is almost ludicrous. The producer must bring out its quality of ghoulish horror fearlessly and no one will laugh. He must avoid a lot of screams at the end."

Answers to Margin Questions
Line 69. No, since she does not know of the plans. Lady Macbeth has shown discomfort with Macbeth's mood swings, lack of emotional control, imagination, and distance from her. There has been no evidence that she has initiated any action, so she probably did not send the messenger. Lady Macduff is unbelieving; she panics; she looks for some way to flee, but it is too late.
Line 75. The lines suggest that the boy might try to protect his mother—perhaps he steps in front of her to shield her. Perhaps she tries to shield him. Perhaps they both back away.

MACBETH, ACT IV, SCENE 3 359

ASSESSMENT TOOLS

Check Test: Fill-in-the-Blank
1. When the Second Witch says, "Something wicked this way comes," she is referring to _____. [Macbeth]
2. The Second Apparition says Macbeth cannot be harmed by _____. [anyone born of a woman]
3. The Third Apparition says Macbeth will not be vanquished until Birnam Wood _____. [comes to Dunsinane]
4. Lady Macduff and all her children are murdered by _____. [killers hired by Macbeth]

5. Malcolm tests Macduff's loyalty to Scotland by pretending to _____. [Possible answers: be evil; be lustful, greedy, and bent on destruction; be worse than Macbeth.]

Ongoing Assessment To see whether students are following the **themes** that run through the acts, ask students to write a one-page paper identifying and explaining one of the themes of the play. Students should discuss any **symbols** associated with the theme and refer to dialogue

or scenes that reflect the theme. The following scale may help you score these assignments:
1 Theme is not well defined or supported.
2 Theme is stated; needs clearer support.
3 Theme is defined; support is adequate.
4 Theme is precisely defined; support is thorough.

Macbeth, Act IV, Scene 3 **T359**

A. Critical Reading: Making Inferences

? Why is Malcolm wary? [Macduff was once a good friend of Macbeth and, so far as these two know, has not been injured by him. Malcolm thinks that only someone who can trust Macbeth would dare to leave his wife and children alone and unprotected. Thus, Malcolm is worried lest Macduff, in league with Macbeth, has been sent to trick or kill him.]

Answer to Margin Question

Line 14. Neither Malcolm nor Macduff knows that Macbeth has already had Macduff's family killed.

---

10   As I shall find the time to friend,° I will.
      What you have spoke, it may be so perchance.
      This tyrant, whose sole° name blisters our tongues,
      Was once thought honest:° you have loved him well;
      He hath not touched you yet. I am young; but something
15   You may deserve of him through me;° and wisdom°
      To offer up a weak, poor, innocent lamb
      T' appease an angry god.
Macduff.
      I am not treacherous.
Malcolm.   But Macbeth is.
      A good and virtuous nature may recoil
20   In° an imperial charge. But I shall crave your pardon;
      That which you are, my thoughts cannot transpose:°

10. to friend: to be friendly, favorable.

12. sole: very.

13. honest: good.

? **14.** *What great irony would the audience feel upon hearing this line, given what has just taken place in the previous scene?*

15. deserve . . . me: that is, earn by betraying me to Macbeth. **wisdom:** it may be wise.

20. recoil / In: give way under.
21. transpose: transform.

"He has killed me, mother."
From the Stratford Festival production of *Macbeth* (1983).

360 THE RENAISSANCE

Angels are bright still, though the brightest° fell:
Though all things foul would wear° the brows of grace,
Yet grace must still look so.°

Macduff.   I have lost my hopes.

Malcolm.
25   Perchance even there where I did find my doubts.
Why in that rawness° left you wife and child,
Those precious motives, those strong knots of love,
Without leave-taking? I pray you,
Let not my jealousies° be your dishonors,
30   But mine own safeties. You may be rightly just°
Whatever I shall think.

Macduff.   Bleed, bleed, poor country:
Great tyranny, lay thou thy basis° sure,
For goodness dare not check° thee: wear thou thy wrongs;
The title is affeered.° Fare thee well, lord:
35   I would not be the villain that thou think'st
For the whole space that's in the tyrant's grasp
And the rich East to boot.

Malcolm.   Be not offended:
I speak not as in absolute fear of you.
I think our country sinks beneath the yoke;
40   It weeps, it bleeds, and each new day a gash
Is added to her wounds. I think withal°
There would be hands uplifted in my right;°
And here from gracious England° have I offer
Of goodly thousands: but, for° all this,
45   When I shall tread upon the tyrant's head,
Or wear it on my sword, yet my poor country
Shall have more vices than it had before,
More suffer, and more sundry ways than ever,
By him that shall succeed.

Macduff.   What should he be?

Malcolm.
50   It is myself I mean, in whom I know
All the particulars° of vice so grafted°
That, when they shall be opened,° black Macbeth
Will seem as pure as snow, and the poor state
Esteem him as a lamb, being compared
55   With my confineless harms.°

Macduff.   Not in the legions
Of horrid hell can come a devil more damned
In evils to top Macbeth.

Malcolm.   I grant him bloody,
Luxurious,° avaricious, false, deceitful,
Sudden,° malicious, smacking of every sin
60   That has a name: but there's no bottom, none,
In my voluptuousness:° your wives, your daughters,
Your matrons and your maids, could not fill up

22. the brightest: Lucifer, the angel who led the revolt of the angels and was thrown out of heaven; Satan.

23. would wear: desire to wear.

24. so: like itself.

26. rawness: unprotected condition.

29. jealousies: suspicions.

30. rightly just: perfectly honorable.

32. basis: foundation.

33. check: restrain.

34. affeered: legally confirmed.

? **37.** *This speech might present a problem for the actor playing Macduff because it does not clearly relate to what has gone before it. It seems too grand and philosophical at this point in the play. How would you have the actor deliver this speech?*

41. withal: moreover.

42. in my right: on behalf of my claim.

43. England: the king of England.

44. for: despite.

51. particulars: special kinds. **grafted:** engrafted.

52. opened: in bloom (that is, revealed).

55. confineless harms: unbounded evils.

? **57.** *How has Macduff responded to this speech?*

58. Luxurious: lecherous.

59. Sudden: violent.

61. voluptuousness: lust.

B. Critical Reading: Identifying Main Ideas

? What is Macduff about to do? Why? [He is leaving. He sees that Malcolm does not trust him, so he thinks there is no hope of saving Scotland now. There cannot be an alliance among the thanes who oppose Macbeth and the rightful king (Malcolm), because Malcolm is too nervous to trust anyone.]

C. Exploring the Historical Period

Following Holinshed, Shakespeare has Malcolm charge himself with lust, avarice, and deceit. "Shakespeare is showing the nature of royalty by describing its opposite," says critic Kenneth Muir.

Answers to Margin Questions

Line 37. He may play it as if disheartened, resigned, offended, insulted, and angry.

Line 57. Macduff says that no one, not even a devil from hell, is worse than Macbeth.

A. Critical Reading: Drawing Conclusions

? How does Macduff respond to Malcolm's self-accusation? [He implies that the flaw could be kept secret, preferable to the rule of Macbeth.]

B. Reader's Response: First Thoughts

? Why do you suppose Macduff reacts as he does to Malcolm's "confessions"? [Sample responses: Macduff is a political realist who can tolerate imperfections in a king and does not expect a saint. Here, he rationalizes Malcolm's confessed faults as better than Macbeth's reign.]

C. Reader's Response: First Thoughts

? Why do you think Macduff cannot stomach this statement, although he can deal with the others? [Sample responses: While lust and avarice might exist in men that are otherwise sufficiently moral to rule, Malcolm in his last statement denies that he has any moral virtues and suggests that his rule could cause chaos and strife. This probably sounds, to Macduff, too much like Macbeth.]

Answers to Margin Questions

Line 66. Ask this question after students have read through l. 139. By discussing his imaginary vices, Malcolm can see what Macduff will tolerate. Malcolm seems to be testing to see how sincerely Macduff wants Malcolm to depose Macbeth and determining where Macduff's loyalty lies.

Line 84. Ask this question after students have read through l. 139. Malcolm must convince Macduff, yet let the audience know that all these allegations about himself are false. An ironic delivery would indicate that Malcolm teases and might elicit a jesting tone from Macduff; a serious delivery of the lines might elicit a more concerned response from Macduff.

The cistern of my lust, and my desire
All continent° impediments would o'erbear,
That did oppose my will. Better Macbeth 65
Than such an one to reign.
Macduff.   Boundless intemperance
In nature° is a tyranny; it hath been
Th' untimely emptying of the happy throne,
And fall of many kings. But fear not yet
To take upon you what is yours: you may 70
Convey° your pleasures in a spacious plenty,
And yet seem cold, the time° you may so hoodwink.
We have willing dames enough. There cannot be
That vulture in you, to devour so many
As will to greatness dedicate themselves, 75
Finding it so inclined.
Malcolm.   With this there grows
In my most ill-composed affection° such
A stanchless° avarice that, were I king,
I should cut off the nobles for their lands,
Desire his jewels and this other's house: 80
And my more-having would be as a sauce
To make me hunger more, that I should forge
Quarrels unjust against the good and loyal,
Destroying them for wealth.
Macduff.   This avarice
Sticks deeper, grows with more pernicious root 85
Than summer-seeming° lust, and it hath been
The sword of our slain kings.° Yet do not fear.
Scotland hath foisons to fill up your will
Of your mere own.° All these are portable,°
With other graces weighed. 90
Malcolm.
But I have none: the king-becoming graces,
As justice, verity, temp'rance, stableness,
Bounty, perseverance, mercy, lowliness,
Devotion, patience, courage, fortitude,
I have no relish of° them, but abound 95
In the division of each several crime,°
Acting it many ways. Nay, had I pow'r, I should
Pour the sweet milk of concord into hell,
Uproar° the universal peace, confound
All unity on earth.
Macduff.   O Scotland, Scotland! 100
Malcolm.
If such a one be fit to govern, speak:
I am as I have spoken.
Macduff.   Fit to govern!
No, not to live. O nation miserable!
With an untitled° tyrant bloody-sceptered,

64. **continent:** restraining.

? 66. *Why do you think Malcolm is drawing attention to his vices? What could he hope to accomplish?*
67. **nature:** man's nature.

71. **Convey:** secretly manage.
72. **time:** here, people.

77. **ill-composed affection:** evilly compounded character.
78. **stanchless:** never-ending.

? 84. *How do you imagine Malcolm delivering this speech? How could his delivery affect Macduff's response?*
86. **summer-seeming:** youthful, or transitory.
87. **sword . . . kings:** the cause of death to our kings.
89. **foisons . . . own:** enough abundance of your own to satisfy your covetousness. **portable:** bearable.

95. **relish of:** taste for.
96. **division . . . crime:** variations of each kind of crime.

99. **Uproar:** put into a tumult.

104. **untitled:** having no right to the throne.

362 THE RENAISSANCE

105 When shalt thou see thy wholesome days again,
Since that the truest issue of thy throne
By his own interdiction° stands accursed,
And does blaspheme his breed?° Thy royal father
Was a most sainted king: the queen that bore thee,
110 Oft'ner upon her knees than on her feet,
Died° every day she lived. Fare thee well!
These evils thou repeat'st upon thyself
Hath banished me from Scotland. O my breast,
Thy hope ends here!

Malcolm.   Macduff, this noble passion,
115 Child of integrity, hath from my soul
Wiped the black scruples,° reconciled my thoughts
To thy good truth and honor. Devilish Macbeth
By many of these trains° hath sought to win me
Into his power; and modest wisdom° plucks me
120 From over-credulous haste: but God above
Deal between thee and me! For even now
I put myself to° thy direction, and
Unspeak mine own detraction;° here abjure
The taints and blames I laid upon myself,
125 For° strangers to my nature. I am yet
Unknown to woman, never was forsworn,
Scarcely have coveted what was mine own,
At no time broke my faith, would not betray
The devil to his fellow, and delight
130 No less in truth than life. My first false speaking
Was this upon myself. What I am truly,
Is thine and my poor country's to command:
Whither indeed, before thy here-approach,
Old Siward, with ten thousand warlike men,
135 Already at a point,° was setting forth.
Now we'll together, and the chance of goodness
Be like our warranted quarrel!° Why are you silent?

Macduff.
Such welcome and unwelcome things at once
'Tis hard to reconcile.

[*Enter a* DOCTOR.]

Malcolm.
140 Well, more anon. Comes the king forth, I pray you?

Doctor.
Ay, sir. There are a crew of wretched souls
That stay° his cure: their malady convinces
The great assay of art;° but at his touch,
Such sanctity hath heaven given his hand,
They presently amend.°

145 **Malcolm.**   I thank you, doctor.

[*Exit* DOCTOR.]

---

107. interdiction: curse; exclusion.
108. breed: ancestry.

111. Died: that is, prepared for heaven.

? **114.** *How might the tone change here? How has Macduff proved himself?*

116. scruples: suspicions.

118. trains: plots.
119. modest wisdom: prudence.

122. to: under.
123. detraction: slander.

125. For: as.

135. at a point: prepared.

137. the chance . . . quarrel: May our chance of success equal the justice of our cause.

? **137.** *Where should Malcolm pause in this line? Should he act puzzled, or matter-of-fact?*

142. stay: await.
143. convinces . . . art: defies the efforts of medical science.

145. presently amend: immediately recover.

D. Critical Reading: Analyzing Character

? What differences does this scene show between Malcolm and Duncan? [Possibly Malcolm knows the "art/to find the mind's construction in the face" (Act I, Scene 4, ll. 11–12) and uses it to discern Macduff's true character.]

E. Literary Element: Character
Describe Malcolm's character. [He is chaste, honest, uninterested in possessions, faithful, loyal, and truthful.]

F. Critical Reading: Making Inferences

? What good news has Malcolm been withholding? [Siward and ten thousand men are ready to march on Macbeth.]

G. Expansion
Point out that these lines refer to the special ability Edward the Confessor supposedly possessed. See "The King's Evil," p. 367.

Answers to Margin Questions
Line 114. Malcolm drops his sinful, man-of-the-world air and speaks in his normal, gentle tone. Macduff has shown that he is totally loyal to Scotland and is repulsed by crimes such as those committed by Macbeth.
Line 137. There should be a fairly sharp break before "Why are you silent?" Answers will vary about Malcolm's attitude. Most will feel he is probably matter-of-fact and aware that he has stunned Macduff.

A. Critical Reading: Comparing and Contrasting

Compare this entrance with Ross's first entrance in the play. [In both cases he comes from Fife; in both he recounts wicked acts of the thane of Cawdor; in both cases he reports to the *true* king.]

B. Language Note: Double Meanings

In these lines, Macduff and Ross seem to have a coherent conversation, yet the speech plays upon words that have various meanings. Here, *well* means to Macduff that his family is alive and healthy, while Ross uses *well* to mean that Macduff's family is *at peace* in death, beyond the reach of more evil. Can you find another example in which Shakespeare uses this type of word-play? [Possible answer: It may remind students of Act III, Scene 4, l. 25, "Banquo's safe."]

Answers to Margin Questions

Stage direction. Students may say Ross brings an update on Macbeth, or they may guess he brings the news that Macduff's family has been murdered.
Line 176. He would probably look away, all too aware of the "newest grief" he must report.

Macduff.
What's the disease he means?

Malcolm.   'Tis called the evil:°
A most miraculous work in this good king,
Which often since my here-remain in England
I have seen him do. How he solicits heaven,
150   Himself best knows: but strangely visited° people,
All swoll'n and ulcerous, pitiful to the eye,
The mere° despair of surgery, he cures,
Hanging a golden stamp° about their necks,
Put on with holy prayers: and 'tis spoken,
155   To the succeeding royalty he leaves
The healing benediction. With this strange virtue°
He hath a heavenly gift of prophecy,
And sundry blessings hang about his throne
That speak° him full of grace.

[*Enter* ROSS.]

(A) **Macduff.**   See, who comes here?
Malcolm.
160   My countryman; but yet I know him not.
Macduff.
My ever gentle° cousin, welcome hither.
Malcolm.
I know him now: good God, betimes° remove
The means that makes us strangers!
Ross.   Sir, amen.
Macduff.
Stands Scotland where it did?
Ross.   Alas, poor country!
165   Almost afraid to know itself! It cannot
Be called our mother but our grave, where nothing°
But who knows nothing is once seen to smile;
Where sighs and groans, and shrieks that rent the air,
Are made, not marked;° where violent sorrow seems
170   A modern ecstasy.° The dead man's knell
Is there scarce asked for who, and good men's lives
Expire before the flowers in their caps,
Dying or ere they sicken.
Macduff.   O, relation
Too nice,° and yet too true!
Malcolm.   What's the newest grief?
Ross.
175   That of an hour's age doth hiss the speaker;°
Each minute teems° a new one.
(B) **Macduff.**   How does my wife?
Ross.
Why, well.
Macduff.   And all my children?

146. evil: scrofula, called "the king's evil" because it allegedly could be cured by the king's touch.

150. strangely visited: oddly afflicted.

152. mere: utter.
153. stamp: coin.

156. virtue: power.

159. speak: proclaim.

? **Stage direction.** *Ross is Macduff's countryman. What news do you anticipate he brings with him?*

161. gentle: noble.

162. betimes: quickly.

166. nothing: no one.

169. marked: noticed.
170. modern ecstasy: ordinary emotion.

174. relation / Too nice: tale too accurate.

175. That . . . speaker: The report of the grief of an hour ago is hissed as stale news.
176. teems: gives birth to.
? **176.** *Does Ross look at Macduff on this line, or does he turn away?*

Ross.   Well too.
Macduff.
The tyrant has not battered at their peace?
Ross.
No; they were well at peace when I did leave 'em.
180 **Macduff.**
Be not a niggard of your speech: how goes't?
Ross.
When I came hither to transport the tidings,
Which I have heavily° borne, there ran a rumor
Of many worthy fellows that were out;°
Which was to my belief witnessed° the rather,
185 For that I saw the tyrant's power° afoot.
Now is the time of help. Your eye in Scotland
Would create soldiers, make our women fight,
To doff their dire distresses.
Malcolm.   Be't their comfort
We are coming thither. Gracious England hath
190 Lent us good Siward and ten thousand men;
An older and a better soldier none
That Christendom gives out.°
Ross.   Would I could answer
This comfort with the like! But I have words
That would° be howled out in the desert air,
Where hearing should not latch° them.
195 **Macduff.**   What concern they?
The general cause or is it a fee-grief
Due to some single breast?°
Ross.   No mind that's honest
But in it shares some woe, though the main part
Pertains to you alone.
Macduff.   If it be mine,
200 Keep it not from me, quickly let me have it.
Ross.
Let not your ears despise my tongue forever, Ⓓ
Which shall possess them with the heaviest sound
That ever yet they heard.
Macduff.   Humh! I guess at it.
Ross.
Your castle is surprised;° your wife and babes
205 Savagely slaughtered. To relate the manner,
Were, on the quarry° of these murdered deer,
To add the death of you.
Malcolm.   Merciful heaven!   Ⓔ
What, man! Ne'er pull your hat upon your brows;
Give sorrow words. The grief that does not speak
210 Whispers the o'er-fraught heart,° and bids it break.
Macduff.
My children too?

[?] **179.** *What is the double meaning of this line?*

182. heavily: sadly.
183. out: up in arms.
184. witnessed: attested.
185. power: army.

192. gives out: reports.

194. would: should.
195. latch: catch.

197. fee-grief . . . breast: that is, personal grief belonging to an individual.

[?] **203.** *Macduff's pain becomes visible. How should we see it?*

204. surprised: suddenly attacked.

206. quarry: heap of slaughtered game.

210. Whispers . . . heart: whispers to the overburdened heart.
[?] **211.** *How full, or soft, a voice would you have Macduff use in this line?*

C. Exploring the Culture

Holinshed reports that it was customary for women of Scotland to join men on the battlefield: "In these daies also the women of our countries were of no lesse courage than the men; for all stout maidens and wiues (if they were not with child) marched as well in the field as did the men. . . . When they saw their owne bloud run from them in the fight, they waxed neuer a whit astonished with the matter, but rather doubling their courages with more egernesse they assailed their enimies."

D. Literary Element: Figure of Speech

This is an example of synecdoche—the use of part of something to stand for the whole. What does "your ears" stand for? What does "my tongue" stand for? How could you rephrase this statement in literal language? [Possible answers: You. Me. Please don't hate me for what I am about to tell you.]

E. Reader's Response: Shaping Interpretations

[?] What do you think of the way Ross breaks the news to Macduff? [Sample responses: It reminds me of how Macduff tried gently to break the news of Duncan's death to Lady Macbeth in Act II, except that she not only knew about that but had planned it. Here, Macduff deserves the gentleness that Ross uses. There is no good way to tell someone that his family's been murdered—Ross did the best he could; even though he lied earlier, you can understand why it was hard for him to tell the truth.]

Answers to Margin Questions

Line 179. For Macduff, "peace" means that his family is well. For Ross, it means the peace that comes in death.

Line 203. Probably in his face and tone of voice—he seems to have guessed at least part of the truth from Ross's hedging.

Line 211. Answers will vary. He might whisper or cry out in distress or try to master his feelings and attempt to speak in a controlled, normal tone.

A. Critical Reading: Drawing Conclusions

? To whom is Macduff referring when he says "He"? [Possible answer: Although he could be referring to Malcolm to imply that Malcolm—who presumably does not yet have children—cannot understand the grief Macduff feels, it is more likely that he is referring to Macbeth—either to suggest that Macduff can never take adequate revenge because he cannot kill Macbeth's children, or because Macduff thinks that only a man without children could have committed such actions.]

Answers to Margin Questions

Line 216. If students think Macduff refers to Macbeth, they might think he speaks with pain and scorn. If he speaks of Malcolm, he might seem to be reminding himself that there are reasons for Malcolm's lack of understanding, and his voice and tone might be less harsh, even sad.

Line 220. Malcolm urges Macduff to act on his feelings. Malcolm's desire to grieve his father at the beginning of the scene suggests that he would not criticize Macduff for showing his feelings.

Ross.   Wife, children, servants, all
That could be found.
Macduff.   And I must be from thence!
My wife killed too?
Ross.   I have said.
Malcolm.   Be comforted.
Let's make us med'cines of our great revenge,
215   To cure this deadly grief.
Macduff.
A He has no children. All my pretty ones?
Did you say all? O hell-kite!° All?
What, all my pretty chickens and their dam°
At one fell swoop?
Malcolm.
Dispute° it like a man.
220 **Macduff.**   I shall do so;
But I must also feel it as a man.
I cannot but remember such things were,
That were most precious to me. Did heaven look on,
And would not take their part? Sinful Macduff,

? **216.** *How would Macduff say this line: "He has no children"?*
217. hell-kite: hellish bird of prey.
218. dam: mother.

220. Dispute: counter.
? **220.** *Is Malcolm being critical or encouraging here?*

"Bring thou this fiend of Scotland and myself;
Within my sword's length set him."

From the Stratford Festival production of *Macbeth* (1983).

366 THE RENAISSANCE

225   They were all struck for thee! Naught° that I am,
         Not for their own demerits but for mine
         Fell slaughter on their souls. Heaven rest them now! **B**
     Malcolm.
         Be this the whetstone of your sword. Let grief
         Convert to anger; blunt not the heart, enrage it.
     Macduff.
230   O, I could play the woman with mine eyes,
         And braggart with my tongue! But, gentle heavens,
         Cut short all intermission;° front to front°
         Bring thou this fiend of Scotland and myself;
         Within my sword's length set him. If he 'scape,
         Heaven forgive him too!
235 **Malcolm.**   This time goes manly. **C**
         Come, go we to the king. Our power is ready;
         Our lack is nothing but our leave.° Macbeth
         Is ripe for shaking, and the pow'rs above
         Put on their instruments.° Receive what cheer you may.
240   The night is long that never finds the day. **D**   [*Exeunt.*]

225. Naught: wicked.

232. intermission: interval. **front to front:** forehead to forehead (that is, face to face).

237. Our lack . . . leave: We need only to take our leave.

239. Put . . . instruments: arm themselves.

Critical Comment

The King's Evil

In Act IV, Scene 3, Malcolm and Macduff, ex-iled from Scotland, discuss the characteristics of a good king and praise King Edward, who **E** has given them political asylum in England. Edward, a saintly monarch known to history as "the Confessor," was believed to have the gift of healing any of his subjects who suffered from an ailment known as the king's evil, a kind of scrofula or tuberculosis of the lymphatic glands and primarily a disease of children. Long before Shakespeare's time, the custom of being touched by the king was abandoned, but King James revived the practice and his successors continued it for a century or so. The eighteenth-century writer Samuel Johnson, scrofulous as a child, was one of the last English people to receive the royal touch.

Edward the Confessor (detail of the Wilton Diptych).

The National Gallery, London.

The conversation between Malcolm and Macduff not only compliments King James indirectly, but also implicitly condemns Macbeth, a kingly killer rather than a healer of children. Edward cures evil; Macbeth *is* evil.

MACBETH, ACT IV, SCENE 3   367

B. Exploring the Culture
The critic Kenneth Muir suggests that "Heaven" may have replaced "May God," "Then God," or "God, God" in the original manuscript to sidestep the penalties levied by the Act of Parliament against profanity on the stage. The act read: "For the preventing and avoiding of the great abuse of the holy Name of God, in Stage-plays, Enterludes, May-games, Shews, and such-like . . . if . . . any person do or shall in any Stage-play . . . jestingly or prophanely speak, or use the holy Name of God, or of Jesus Christ, or of the Holy Ghost, or of the Trinity . . . shall forfeit for every such offence . . . ten pounds. . . ." Muir writes, "I suspect that 'God' . . . was what Shakespeare wrote."

C. Expansion
It is disputed by editors whether the word should be *time* or *tune,* but a "manly tune" might be one like a march with a brisk step and military purpose, rather than a dirge, a slow funeral tune. This would fit with Macduff's change of mood.

D. Literary Element: Theme
Malcolm's last line suggests that nature will be restored—possibly Macbeth's reign has seemed like a long night, but morning is coming. How does this fit with all Macbeth's references to night? [Possible answer: Night (darkness) is typically a time for evil, and perhaps this suggests that that period is ending. It may also foreshadow that a natural day and night rhythm will be restored, perhaps ending the nightmares and sleeplessness that have been a theme since Duncan's murder.]

E. Exploring the Historical Period
Edward (1003–1066) ascended the throne of England in 1042 following the death of King Canute, who also ruled Denmark, Norway, and part of Sweden. He is a saint in the Roman Catholic and Anglican Churches, and he is considered the founder of Westminster Abbey.

Because the characterization of Hecate in Middleton's play is so different from that in Shakespeare's, some critics actually think that Middleton is the least likely person to have written the scene.

Making Meanings

Act IV

First Thoughts

1. This is becoming ridiculous; what can Macbeth possibly gain from killing Macduff's family? Most will feel Macbeth has changed from heroic to evil. Macbeth has sunk to the depths of evil—killing grown men is one thing, but innocent children is another.

Reviewing the Text

a. Poisoned entrails, a toad that has been secreting venom through its skin for thirty-one days and was caught when asleep; a slice from a snake that lived in the swamp; eye of newt; toe of frog; wool of bat; tongue of dog; the forked tongue of an adder; a blindworm's sting; a lizard's leg; an owl's wing; dragon's scales; wolf's tooth; witch's mummy; both the gullet and the stomach of a shark; hemlock root dug in the dark; Jew's liver; goat's gall; slips of yew taken during a lunar eclipse; a Turk's nose, a Tartar's lips; fingers of a babe strangled during birth by its umbilical cord and delivered in a ditch by a prostitute; a tiger's entrails; and the blood of a baboon. Perhaps they are putting a spell on Macbeth. Perhaps it is to show how evil the witches are.

b. The witches stop him from voicing his question, but he seems to want to know if he will remain in power (Scene 1, ll. 69–70). He also wants to know if Banquo's issue will ever rule. The witches let the apparitions answer with prophecies and show him a procession of kings (Banquo's descendants).

Critical Comment

Hecate: Queen of the Night

Hecate (here pronounced in two syllables, with the accent on the first: hek´it) is a figure from Greek mythology, a queen of the night and protector of witches and enchanters. This character comes from books, unlike the witches, who were based on older, usually widowed women, whose solitary lives placed them at the margins of Scottish society. Every theatergoer would find the witches believable, and every educated person would know that King James had written an important treatise called *Daemonologie,* asserting that witches "are channels through which the malignity of evil spirits might be visited upon human beings."

Most Shakespearean scholars believe that the scenes involving Hecate (Act III, Scene 5; Act IV, Scene 1) were written by somebody other than Shakespeare and introduced into *Macbeth* at some time before 1623, when the play was first printed. This other writer has never been positively identified, although some people think he was Thomas Middleton (d. 1627), a contemporary of Shakespeare and a fellow writer for the King's Men. Two songs, the first beginning with the words "Come away" (Act III, Scene 5) and the second with "Black Spirits" (Act IV, Scene 1), were also added to the Hecate scenes, and these songs are indeed by Middleton, the complete texts of them occurring in his thriller *The Witch.*

And so the practice of adding things to *Macbeth* began very early, and it has continued throughout most of the play's long stage history. The supernatural elements seem to invite directors to devise spectacles and take liberties, especially with the witches, who have been flown on wires in some productions and whose parts have been played by ballet dancers in others.

Macbeth holding out his hand to the three witches.

From the Stratford Festival production of *Macbeth* (1983).

MAKING MEANINGS

Act IV

First Thoughts

1. What effect did the brutal murders of Lady Macduff and her son have on you? Have your feelings for Macbeth changed from the opening of the play until now? How do you account for your reactions?

Reviewing the Text

a. What ingredients go into the witches' stew? What symbolic purpose does this vile concoction serve?

b. What has Macbeth come to ask the witches, and how do they answer?

c. Describe the three apparitions Macbeth sees when he visits the witches. What does each apparition tell him?

d. Which nobleman does Macbeth plan to murder after talking with the witches? How is his plan foiled?

e. At the end of Scene 1, what does Macbeth vow? How is his vow carried out in Scene 2?

f. According to the conversation between Malcolm and Macduff in Scene 3, what has happened to Scotland during Macbeth's reign?

g. What faults does Malcolm claim to have?

h. How does Macduff respond to each of Malcolm's three "confessions"?

Shaping Interpretations

2. In this act, Macbeth seeks out the witches, just as they initiated the encounter in Act I. How has his situation changed since he last talked with them? How has his moral **character** deteriorated?

3. Do you think the witches have caused any of these changes, directly or indirectly? Explain your reasons for thinking as you do.

4. In Scene 1, the eight kings appear in what was called in Shakespeare's day a **dumb show**— an interpolated brief scene in which nothing is said. What is the point of this particular dumb show?

5. In Scene 2, the lines spoken by Macduff's wife and son illustrate Shakespeare's great skill at **characterization.** Using only a few words, he brings the woman and the child to life. How would you describe Lady Macduff? How would you describe the boy?

6. Both the murderer and Lady Macduff herself call Macduff a traitor. In what sense does each mean it? Do you think Macduff is a traitor, in either sense?

7. In Scene 3, Malcolm deliberately lies to Macduff. What does this behavior, and the reason for it, reveal about Malcolm?

Extending the Text

8. In Scene 3, Malcolm and Macduff decry the chaos that Macbeth's rule has brought to Scotland, as if Macbeth's disorder has become Scotland's. Does that happen today—does the weakness or the evil of a nation's leader become that of a nation itself? Explain your response.

Challenging the Text

9. The murder of Macduff's small son is one of the most pitiful and shocking scenes in Shakespeare. Do you think it might have been better to have it reported after the fact rather than to have shown the carnage on stage? What would be lost and what would be gained by this change?

---

c. First, a helmeted head warns him about Macduff. Second, a bloody child says, "none of woman born / Shall harm Macbeth." Third, a crowned child holding a tree prophesies that Macbeth will never be conquered till Birnam Wood comes to Dunsinane.

d. Macduff; Macduff has fled to England.

e. To kill Macduff's family; those family members found at Fife are murdered.

f. Scotland has fallen into great distress, with many new widows, orphans, and sorrows.

g. He claims to be lustful, greedy, and bent on using power to create chaos.

h. He says that the first two (lust and avarice) can be accommodated, but he denounces Malcolm after his last confession (criminality).

Shaping Interpretations

2. The prophecy has been fulfilled by Macbeth. When they first see him, he is a hero returning from battle, having saved his nation from a traitor. Now he is a murderer and traitor himself—he has betrayed his country and his honor.

3. Possible responses: Yes, I think they are responsible for setting in motion the train of evil. Macbeth resists as best he can, but fate (or the spell of the witches) overcomes him; or no, I think Macbeth chooses to act of his own free will. There is no evidence in the play that he has been forced, and I think he has actually been planning to murder Duncan before ever seeing the witches.

4. It shows Macbeth that not only will Banquo's issue rule, but Banquo's descendants will provide the country with a succession of kings.

5. Possible answers: Lady Macduff: loyal, good, protective, worried, loving. Boy: clever, knows the Bible well, loyal, brave.

6. Lady Macduff calls him a traitor for abandoning his family. The murderers mean that he is a traitor to the king (Macbeth). Students will probably agree that Macduff is not a traitor in either sense.

7. He tests Macduff's loyalty—this shows that he is more savvy than his too-trusting father.

Extending the Text

8. Some students will feel a leader represents the nation's status and collective well-being; others will say one person cannot represent so many individuals.

Challenging the Text

9. **(Evaluation)** Possible answers: No, it is the step that takes Macbeth beyond the pale; it should be seen and acknowledged. Or yes, it should be left to the audience's imagination. Without it, the play might lose the immediacy and audience involvement in wanting Macbeth destroyed. The gain would be that the audience would not feel so distraught.

A. Literary Element: Theme

The connection between nature and unnatural events is one of the themes of the play. Find another quotation from earlier in the play that focuses on this theme. [Possible answers: Act II, Scene 3, ll. 48–55; Act II, Scene 4, ll. 4–18; Act IV, Scene 1, ll. 50–60.]

ACT V   Scene 1.   *Dunsinane. In the castle.*

Enter a DOCTOR *of physic and a waiting* GENTLEWOMAN.

Doctor. I have two nights watched with you, but can perceive no truth in your report. When was it she last walked?

Gentlewoman. Since his majesty went into the field, I have seen her rise from her bed, throw her nightgown upon her,
5   unlock her closet,° take forth paper, fold it, write upon't, read it, afterwards seal it, and again return to bed; yet all this while in a most fast sleep.

Doctor. A great perturbation in nature, to receive at once the benefit of sleep and do the effects of watching!° In this
10   slumb'ry agitation, besides her walking and other actual performances,° what, at any time, have you heard her say?

5. **closet:** chest.

9. **effects of watching:** deeds of one awake.

11. **actual performances:** deeds.

"Out, damned spot! Out, I say!"
From the Stratford Festival production of *Macbeth* (1983).

370   THE RENAISSANCE

Advanced Have interested students compare the historical Macbeth with the Shakespearean character. From their research, have them compose a letter from Shakespeare to his audience, defending the changes he made when writing the play.

STRATEGIES FOR INCLUSION

Intrapersonal As students consider the decision-making process that leads Macbeth to his death, have them complete an Options Tree. Starting with the decision of whether to believe the witches' initial predictions, they should trace the path Macbeth follows through each decision he faces. Ask students to speculate in their Reader's Logs about how different things might have been if, for example, Macbeth had decided not to murder Duncan.

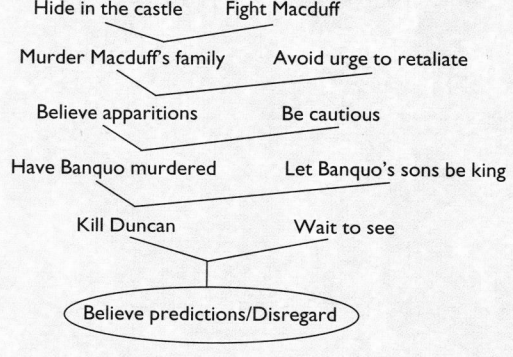

Gentlewoman. That, sir, which I will not report after her.

Doctor. You may to me, and 'tis most meet° you should.

Gentlewoman. Neither to you nor anyone, having no witness
15 to confirm my speech.

[*Enter* LADY MACBETH, *with a taper.*]

Lo you, here she comes! This is her very guise,° and, upon
my life, fast asleep! Observe her; stand close.°

Doctor. How came she by that light?

Gentlewoman. Why, it stood by her. She has light by her con-
20 tinually. 'Tis her command.

Doctor. You see, her eyes are open.

Gentlewoman. Ay, but their sense° are shut.

Doctor. What is it she does now? Look, how she rubs her
hands.

25 **Gentlewoman.** It is an accustomed action with her, to seem
thus washing her hands: I have known her continue in this a
quarter of an hour.

Lady Macbeth. Yet here's a spot.

Doctor. Hark! she speaks. I will set down what comes from
30 her, to satisfy° my remembrance the more strongly.

Lady Macbeth. Out, damned spot! Out, I say! One: two: why,
then 'tis time to do't. Hell is murky. Fie, my lord, fie! A soldier, and afeard? What need we fear who knows it, when
none can call our pow'r to accompt?° Yet who would have
35 thought the old man to have had so much blood in him?

Doctor. Do you mark that?

Lady Macbeth. The Thane of Fife had a wife. Where is she
now? What, will these hands ne'er be clean? No more o'
that, my lord, no more o' that! You mar all with this starting.

40 **Doctor.** Go to,° go to! You have known what you should not.

Gentlewoman. She has spoke what she should not, I am sure
of that. Heaven knows what she has known.

Lady Macbeth. Here's the smell of the blood still. All the perfumes of Arabia will not sweeten this little hand. Oh, oh, oh!

45 **Doctor.** What a sigh is there! The heart is sorely charged.°

Gentlewoman. I would not have such a heart in my bosom for
the dignity° of the whole body.

Doctor. Well, well, well——

Gentlewoman. Pray God it be, sir.

50 **Doctor.** This disease is beyond my practice.° Yet I have known
those which have walked in their sleep who have died holily
in their beds.

Lady Macbeth. Wash your hands; put on your nightgown;
look not so pale! I tell you yet again, Banquo's buried. He
55 cannot come out on 's° grave.

Doctor. Even so?

Lady Macbeth. To bed, to bed! There's knocking at the gate.

---

13. **meet:** suitable.

16. **guise:** custom.
17. **close:** hidden.

20. *Why must Lady Macbeth have light by her continually?*

22. **sense:** powers of sight.

28. *After setting down the taper on a table, what does Lady Macbeth do with her hands?*

30. **satisfy:** confirm.

very important

34. **to accompt:** into account.

35. *What does she think is still on her hands?*

37. *Who is the Thane of Fife?*

40. **Go to:** an exclamation.

43. *What action is suggested by this line?*

45. **charged:** burdened.

47. **dignity:** worth; rank.

50. **practice:** professional skill.

55. **on 's:** of his.

55. *Whom does she think she is speaking to here?*

B. Critical Reading: Finding Cause and Effect

Sleep and sleeplessness are other **themes** of the play. What do you think Lady Macbeth's disturbed sleep represents? [Possible answers: Judging from Macbeth's behavior earlier, disturbed sleep is related to guilt. Lady Macbeth may be suffering from guilt over the murders, or she may be upset by Macbeth's imaginings. Her restlessness may also reflect the idea that Macbeth has murdered sleep.]

C. Critical Reading: Comparing and Contrasting

Re-read Act II, Scene 2, ll. 66–67. How are Lady Macbeth's assumptions in Act II proved incorrect in this passage? [Possible answer: She assumed it would be easy to clean up after the murder because it is physically easy to wash the blood off one's hands. She did not take into account any effects that the murder would have on her emotions.]

D. Critical Reading: Making Inferences

To which events and people does Lady Macbeth refer? What clues let you know? [Duncan—"old man"; Macduff's family—"The Thane of Fife had a wife. Where is she now?"; possibly Banquo— "starting," which may reflect on Macbeth's startled reaction in Act III, Scene 4, l. 63.]

E. Reader's Response: Shaping Interpretations

How do you think the doctor feels as he realizes what Lady Macbeth has just confessed? [Sample responses: He must be shocked and horrified; he must wonder whom to tell or what to do.]

F. Expansion

The gentlewoman plays off the doctor's words, meaning "Pray God that it be well."

Answers to Margin Questions

Line 20. She is afraid of the dark, perhaps associating it with murder or with hell, which she calls *murky,* meaning "dark and gloomy," in l. 32.

Line 28. She checks them and, finding an invisible spot of blood, tries to wash it out.

Line 35. Duncan's blood.

Line 37. Macduff.

Line 43. Lady Macbeth is sniffing at an imaginary spot on one hand.

Line 55. To Macbeth.

STRATEGIES FOR INCLUSION

Less Proficient Readers Pause periodically as the class works through this final act to help students make the connections between the **resolutions** found in Act V and earlier **foreshadowing.** For example, point out the way the prophecies come true, and ask whether students have guessed these riddles. Ask whether, in hindsight, there are any clues in previous acts that Lady Macbeth is disturbed enough to end her own life, or whether Lennox's earlier lines hint that he might turn against Macbeth.

Special Needs Ask students to consider why people still study *Macbeth* today. Guide them with the following questions: Did you learn anything from the downfall of Macbeth? Were there any **characters** you strongly liked or disliked, and why? What was Macbeth's flaw? Can you think of any modern political situations that are similar to this one?

A. Critical Reading: Evaluating an Interpretation

Caroline F. E. Spurgeon writes, "This imaginative picture of a small, ignoble man encumbered and degraded by garments unsuited to him, should be put against the view emphasized by some critics (notably Coleridge and Bradley) of the likeness between Macbeth and Milton's Satan in grandeur and sublimity." Do you think Macbeth is "small and ignoble" or full of "grandeur and sublimity"? Explain your point of view. [Answers will vary. Students should support their responses with phrases from the text from which they determine his character.]

Answers to Margin Questions

Line 59. She thinks she hears knocking at the gate, as in Act II, Scene 2. She leaves the stage in frantic haste.

Line 70. They recognize the truth about Duncan's murder but realize they would endanger their lives by speaking out.

Line 5. The third apparition (Act IV, Scene I, ll. 92–94) said, "Macbeth shall never vanquished be until / Great Birnam Wood to high Dunsinane Hill / Shall come against him."

Come, come, come, come, give me your hand! What's done cannot be undone. To bed, to bed, to bed!

[*Exit* LADY MACBETH.]

60 **Doctor.** Will she go now to bed?

Gentlewoman. Directly.

Doctor.
Foul whisp'rings are abroad. Unnatural deeds
Do breed unnatural troubles. Infected minds
To their deaf pillows will discharge their secrets.
65 More needs she the divine° than the physician.
God, God forgive us all! Look after her;
Remove from her the means of all annoyance,°
And still° keep eyes upon her. So good night.
My mind she has mated° and amazed my sight:
I think, but dare not speak.

70 **Gentlewoman.**   Good night, good doctor.

[*Exeunt.*]

Scene 2. *The country near Dunsinane.*

Drum and colors. Enter MENTEITH, CAITHNESS, ANGUS, LENNOX, SOLDIERS.

Menteith.
The English pow'r° is near, led on by Malcolm,
His uncle Siward and the good Macduff.
Revenges burn in them; for their dear° causes
Would to the bleeding and the grim alarm°
Excite the mortified° man.
5 **Angus.**   Near Birnam Wood
Shall we well meet them; that way are they coming.

Caithness.
Who knows if Donalbain be with his brother?

Lennox.
For certain, sir, he is not. I have a file°
Of all the gentry: there is Siward's son,
10 And many unrough° youths that even now
Protest° their first of manhood.

Menteith.   What does the tyrant?

Caithness.
Great Dunsinane he strongly fortifies.
Some say he's mad; others, that lesser hate him,
Do call it valiant fury: but, for certain,
15 He cannot buckle his distempered° cause
Within the belt of rule.°

Angus.   Now does he feel
His secret murders sticking on his hands;
Now minutely revolts upbraid° his faith-breach.
Those he commands move only in command,
20 Nothing in love. Now does he feel his title

A

372 THE RENAISSANCE

? 59. *Once again there is a sudden dramatic change. What echo from the past brings it about? How do you think Lady Macbeth leaves the stage?*

65. divine: priest.

67. annoyance: injury.
68. still: continuously.
69. mated: baffled.

? 70. *What do the doctor and gentlewoman know? Why won't they speak out?*

1. pow'r: army.

3. dear: heartfelt.
4. alarm: call to arms.
5. mortified: half dead.

? 5. *Where have you heard about Birnam Wood before?*

8. file: list.

10. unrough: beardless.
11. Protest: assert.

15. distempered: swollen with disease.
16. rule: self-control.

18. minutely revolts upbraid: rebellions every minute rebuke.

Hang loose about him, like a giant's robe
Upon a dwarfish thief.

Mentieth.   Who then shall blame
His pestered° senses to recoil and start,
When all that is within him does condemn
Itself for being there?

25 **Caithness.**   Well, march we on,
To give obedience where 'tis truly owed.
Meet we the med'cine° of the sickly weal,°
And with him pour we, in our country's purge,
Each drop of us.°

Lennox.   Or so much as it needs
30   To dew° the sovereign° flower and drown the weeds.
Make we our march towards Birnam.

                    [*Exeunt, marching.*]

Scene 3. *Dunsinane. In the castle.*

Enter MACBETH, DOCTOR, *and* ATTENDANTS.

Macbeth.
Bring me no more reports; let them fly all!
Till Birnam Wood remove to Dunsinane
I cannot taint° with fear. What's the boy Malcolm?
Was he not born of woman? The spirits that know
5   All mortal consequences° have pronounced me thus:
"Fear not, Macbeth; no man that's born of woman
Shall e'er have power upon thee." Then fly, false thanes,
And mingle with the English epicures.
The mind I sway° by and the heart I bear
10   Shall never sag with doubt nor shake with fear.

[*Enter* SERVANT.]

The devil damn thee black, thou cream-faced loon!°
Where got'st thou that goose look?

Servant.
There is ten thousand——

Macbeth.   Geese, villain?

Servant.   Soldiers, sir.

Macbeth.
Go prick thy face and over-red° thy fear,
15   Thou lily-livered boy. What soldiers, patch?°
Death of° thy soul! Those linen° cheeks of thine
Are counselors to fear. What soldiers, whey-face?

Servant.
The English force, so please you.

Macbeth.
Take thy face hence.   [*Exit* SERVANT.]
                    Seyton!—I am sick at heart,
20   When I behold—Seyton, I say!—This push°

---

23. **pestered:** tormented.

27. **med'cine:** that is, Malcolm.
weal: commonwealth.

29. **Each . . . us:** that is, every last
drop of our blood.
30. **dew:** bedew; water (and thus
make grow). **sovereign:** royal;
also, remedial.

31. *The "falling action" of a
Shakespearean play is usually swift. How does this scene
show that the hero's enemies are
now rallying to crush him? What
group is shown in this scene?*

3. **taint:** become infected.

5. **mortal consequences:** future
human events.

9. **sway:** move.

11. **loon:** fool.
12. *Macbeth is in an extreme
state of agitation. Which of
the apparitions' prophecies is he
relying on? How would you stage
his treatment of the servant, which
follows?*

14. **over-red:** cover with red.
15. **patch:** fool.
16. **of:** upon. **linen:** pale.

20. **push:** effort.

MACBETH, ACT V, SCENE 3 373

B. Reader's Response: Shaping Interpretations
Do you think Macbeth senses his impending downfall from power, as these characters imply? [Sample responses: I think he senses the end is near; or I think he is too caught up in his prophesied power to believe he can be beaten.]

C. Literary Element: Tragedy
Is Macbeth's fall that of a **tragic hero,** or is he a villain? [He is a tragic hero in the sense that he starts out as a hero to his country, but he has a character flaw that takes over his personality. Or he is too mean to be a true hero, as he is easily persuaded to kill Duncan and now keeps killing just to maintain his powerful position; he is not noble in any way.]

D. Critical Reading: Making Connections
Macbeth refers here to two of the prophecies brought by the apparitions, but he appears to forget the third. What prophecy does he neglect to mention? ["Beware Macduff!"]

E. Literary Element: Character
How does Macbeth's treatment of his servant reveal his character? [Possible answer: His self-centeredness and condescension are shown by the contempt and rudeness with which he speaks.]

Answers to Margin Questions
Line 31. The thanes of Scotland (those present) are now openly against Macbeth and are marching toward Dunsinane. They report that English forces, along with Malcolm and Macduff, are on the way to join them.
Line 12. He relies on the prophecies that he cannot be defeated until Birnam Wood comes to Dunsinane and that "no man . . . born of woman" can defeat him. He would treat his servant scornfully, standing proud and impatiently finishing the servant's sentences while the servant perhaps cowers in fear of Macbeth.

INTEGRATING THE LANGUAGE ARTS

Language and Vocabulary Have students work in pairs to characterize Lady Macbeth's language in the sleepwalking scene, prompted by the following questions: **1)** How is her language here different from her language elsewhere? **2)** How would you describe the sentence length and construction? **3)** Where in time and space does she think she is?

Speaking and Listening To help students hear the **meter** have them try the following approach:

1) Figure out whether a line is iambic pentameter or tetrameter; **2)** Read the line as if it were absolutely true to the meter, noting where the regular accents on the words come out wrong; **3)** Correct the reading for accents. Students should keep in mind that actors deliver lines differently, varying the tempo, pitch, and pauses. Once they have practiced, let students read their favorite speech to the class. ☞

A. Humanities Connection

Ask students to read Shakespeare's Sonnet 73, on p. 226, and to compare or contrast the poem with this speech of Macbeth's. [Possible answer: The imagery of yellow leaves implies the "fall" of someone's life in both passages; however, in Macbeth's words there is dissatisfaction, while the speaker of the poem seems accepting of death and encouraged by the strong love of someone close to him.]

B. Exploring the Historical Period

According to *Shakespeareana Genealogica*, "The Setons of Touch were (and are still) hereditary armour-bearers to the Kings of Scotland; there is thus a peculiar fitness in the choice of this name."

C. Expansion

The critic Kenneth Muir states, "Cuningham suggests that the doctor should enter at this point. As there is no occasion for his presence until now, and as the names of characters who appear in a scene are sometimes given at the beginning, though they do not appear until later, I agree."

D. Language Note: Punctuation

The dashes in this speech show Macbeth's state of mind. The speech is disjointed and indicates that Macbeth is very agitated.

E. Literary Element: Theme

The health and illness of Scotland is another theme in this play. In this passage, what role does Macbeth seem to be playing in terms of the theme? [He discusses purging the land. It seems as if he is the cause of the country's illness.]

Answers to Margin Questions

Line 22. Answers will vary. Students may be confused by the contradiction between l. 21, in which Macbeth seems to think there is a possibility of success, and l. 22, in which he sounds defeated and resigned.

Line 37. Lady Macbeth.

Line 56. Some possibilities are disgust, irritation, self-pity, concern for the country, and whimsy.

A
Will cheer me ever, or disseat° me now.
I have lived long enough. My way of life
Is fall'n into the sear,° the yellow leaf,
And that which should accompany old age,
25 As honor, love, obedience, troops of friends,
I must not look to have; but, in their stead,
Curses not loud but deep, mouth-honor, breath,
Which the poor heart would fain deny, and dare not.
Seyton!

[*Enter* SEYTON.]

B
Seyton.
What's your gracious pleasure?
30 **Macbeth.** What news more?
Seyton.
All is confirmed, my lord, which was reported.
Macbeth.
I'll fight, till from my bones my flesh be hacked.
Give me my armor.
Seyton. 'Tis not needed yet.
Macbeth.
I'll put it on.
35 Send out moe° horses, skirr° the country round.
Hang those that talk of fear. Give me mine armor.
How does your patient, doctor?
C
Doctor. Not so sick, my lord,
As she is troubled with thick-coming fancies
That keep her from her rest.
Macbeth. Cure her of that.
40 Canst thou not minister to a mind diseased,
Pluck from the memory a rooted sorrow,
Raze out° the written troubles of the brain,
And with some sweet oblivious° antidote
Cleanse the stuffed bosom of that perilous stuff
Which weighs upon the heart?
45 **Doctor.** Therein the patient
Must minister to himself.
Macbeth.
Throw physic° to the dogs, I'll none of it.
Come, put mine armor on. Give me my staff.
Seyton, send out.—Doctor, the thanes fly from me.—
50 Come, sir, dispatch.° If thou couldst, doctor, cast
The water° of my land, find her disease
And purge it to a sound and pristine health,
I would applaud thee to the very echo,
D
E
That should applaud again.—Pull't off, I say.—
55 What rhubarb, senna, or what purgative drug,
Would scour these English hence? Hear'st thou of them?

21. disseat: unthrone (with wordplay on *cheer*, pronounced *chair*).
? 22. *What mood is Macbeth in now?*
23. sear: withered.

35. moe: more. **skirr:** scour.

? 37. *Who is the doctor's patient?*

42. Raze out: erase.
43. oblivious: causing forgetfulness.

47. physic: medical science.

50. dispatch: hurry.
51. cast/The water: literally, analyze the urine.

? 56. *Lines 47–56 contain almost a roller coaster of emotions. Can you cite some?*

OPTIONS FOR TEACHING

COOPERATIVE LEARNING

Sharing Strategies After students have spent a few minutes trying the Strategic Reading activity on p. T372, pause to have students who are guessing successfully share their strategies. Follow up this exercise by giving students a list of what you think are the most important lines, and have students locate these lines in the text to review the play.

Directors for a Day Divide the class into small groups, and have them imagine they are directing a production of *Macbeth*. Ask them to choose one scene and to write directions for characterization, timing, blocking, costuming, and sound effects.

Doctor.
    Ay, my good lord; your royal preparation
    Makes us hear something.
Macbeth.   Bring it° after me.
    I will not be afraid of death and bane°
60   Till Birnam Forest come to Dunsinane.
Doctor (*aside*).
    Were I from Dunsinane away and clear,
    Profit again should hardly draw me here. **F**   [*Exeunt.*]

Scene 4. *Country near Birnam Wood.*

Drum and colors. Enter MALCOLM, SIWARD, MACDUFF, *Siward's son* YOUNG SIWARD, MENTEITH, CAITHNESS, ANGUS, *and* SOLDIERS, *marching.*

Malcolm.
    Cousins, I hope the days are near at hand
    That chambers will be safe.°
Menteith.   We doubt it nothing.°
Siward.
    What wood is this before us?
Menteith.   The Wood of Birnam.
Malcolm.
    Let every soldier hew him down a bough
5   And bear't before him. Thereby shall we shadow **G**
    The numbers of our host, and make discovery°
    Err in report of us.
Soldiers.   It shall be done.
Siward.
    We learn no other but° the confident tyrant
    Keeps still in Dunsinane, and will endure°
    Our setting down before't.
10 **Malcolm.**   'Tis his main hope,
    For where there is advantage to be given°
    Both more and less° have given him the revolt,
    And none serve with him but constrainèd things
    Whose hearts are absent too.
Macduff.   Let our just censures
15   Attend the true event,° and put we on
    Industrious soldiership.
Siward.   The time approaches,
    That will with due decision make us know
    What we shall say we have and what we owe.°
    Thoughts speculative their unsure hopes relate,
20   But certain issue strokes must arbitrate:°
    Towards which advance the war.°   [*Exeunt, marching.*]

58. it: the armor.
59. bane: destruction.
? 60. *Is Macbeth truly courageous here? Or would you suggest that he is merely coasting on a kind of false bravery lent to him by the witches' prophecies?*

2. That . . . safe: that a man will be safe in his bedroom. **nothing:** not at all.

? 5. *Stop and describe what the soldiers are to do here and why.*
6. discovery: Macbeth's scouts.
? 7. *Malcolm seems to have more authority at this point in the play. Can you find specific instances where his new authority could be dramatized?*
8. no other but: nothing but that.
9. endure: allow.
11. advantage . . . given: afforded an opportunity.
12. more and less: high and low.

15. just . . . event: true judgments await the actual outcome.
18. owe: own. The contrast is between "what we shall say we have" and "what we shall really have."
20. certain . . . arbitrate: The definite outcome must be decided by battle.
21. war: army.

F. Critical Reading: Speculating
The doctor does not help Lady Macbeth and does not satisfy Macbeth. What do you think is the purpose of having him appear in the play? [Possible answer: Through him the audience finds out that Lady Macbeth has not remained immune to the emotional consequences of committing murder. The fact that the doctor has been summoned shows that at least Macbeth and the gentlewoman from Scene 1 recognize that Lady Macbeth's illness is serious.]

G. Critical Reading: Making Inferences
? As the camouflaged forces move on Dunsinane, how will they look to an observer on the battlements of the castle? [Birnam Wood will appear to be moving toward Dunsinane.]

Answers to Margin Questions
Line 60. He seems to be shoring himself up with bravado based on the enigmatic words of the apparitions.
Line 5. Each soldier is to cut a leafy branch and carry it in front of him as camouflage.
Line 7. He might lead the troops or give orders; by their manner, others could show that they defer to and protect him.

CROSSING THE CURRICULUM

Health Students may be interested in studying sleepwalking. Have them research the main causes of sleepwalking and current approaches to curing the problem. Ask them to design a poster to share their findings.

Psychology This play is also about a real marriage that is tested and found wanting. After students have read the play, let them act as marriage counselors. Ask them to make references to the miscommunication they see between the Macbeths or to stage directions that describe the Macbeths' relationship. Then, have students work in groups of three, assuming the roles of counselor, Lady Macbeth, and Macbeth, and let them role-play the counseling session. Ask each group to determine whether this marriage can be saved and to defend their answers in class discussion with references from the text.

Social Sciences Some students may wish to focus on the battle strategies in the text and in Holinshed's history. Ask students to write a series of diary entries from a soldier's point of view or to create a diorama showing the battle plans.

A. Critical Reading: Making Connections

 What earlier line does this echo? What strategy is Macbeth planning to use? [Act IV, Scene 1, ll. 79–80, "Laugh to scorn / The pow'r of man." Possible answer: Macbeth is totally allying himself with the witches and their prophecies. He is planning to stay in the castle and let the army besiege it.]

Answer to Margin Question

Line 7. In contrast to Malcolm's calm forcefulness, Macbeth might act bitter and scornful and show false bravery.

"Tomorrow, and tomorrow, and tomorrow Creeps in this petty pace from day to day, To the last syllable of recorded time."
From Orson Welles's film production of *Macbeth* (1948).

Scene 5. *Dunsinane. Within the castle.*

Enter MACBETH, SEYTON, *and* SOLDIERS, *with drum and colors.*

Macbeth.
Hang out our banners on the outward walls.
The cry is still "They come!" Our castle's strength
Will laugh a siege to scorn. Here let them lie
Till famine and the ague° eat them up.
5 Were they not forced° with those that should be ours,
We might have met them dareful,° beard to beard,
And beat them backward home.

[*A cry within of women.*]

         What is that noise?
Seyton.
It is the cry of women, my good lord.   [*Exit.*]
Macbeth.
I have almost forgot the taste of fears:
10 The time has been, my senses would have cooled
To hear a night-shriek, and my fell° of hair
Would at a dismal treatise° rouse and stir
As life were in't. I have supped full with horrors.
Direness, familiar to my slaughterous thoughts,
Cannot once start° me.

4. **ague:** fever.
5. **forced:** reinforced.
6. **met them dareful:** that is, met them on the battlefield boldly.
 7. *Macbeth should contrast with Malcolm now. How should he be acting?*

11. **fell:** pelt.
12. **treatise:** story.

15. **start:** startle.

376 THE RENAISSANCE

[*Enter* SEYTON.]

15   Wherefore was that cry?

Seyton.

The queen, my lord, is dead.

Macbeth.

She should° have died hereafter;

There would have been a time for such a word.°

Tomorrow, and tomorrow, and tomorrow   *Popular soliloquy*

20   Creeps in this petty pace from day to day,

To the last syllable of recorded time;

And all our yesterdays have lighted fools

The way to dusty death. Out, out, brief candle!

Life's but a walking shadow, a poor player

25   That struts and frets his hour upon the stage

And then is heard no more. It is a tale

Told by an idiot, full of sound and fury,

Signifying nothing.

[*Enter a* MESSENGER.]

Thou com'st to use thy tongue; thy story quickly!

Messenger.

30   Gracious my lord,

I should report that which I say I saw,

But know not how to do't.

Macbeth.   Well, say, sir.

Messenger.

As I did stand my watch upon the hill,

I looked toward Birnam, and anon, methought,

The wood began to move.

35 **Macbeth.**   Liar and slave!

Messenger.

Let me endure your wrath, if't be not so.

Within this three mile may you see it coming;

I say a moving grove.

Macbeth.   If thou speak'st false,

Upon the next tree shalt thou hang alive,

40   Till famine cling° thee. If thy speech be sooth,°

I care not if thou dost for me as much.

I pull in resolution,° and begin

To doubt° th' equivocation of the fiend

That lies like truth: "Fear not, till Birnam Wood

45   Do come to Dunsinane!" And now a wood

Comes toward Dunsinane. Arm, arm, and out!

If this which he avouches° does appear,

There is nor flying hence nor tarrying here.

I 'gin to be aweary of the sun,

50   And wish th' estate° o' th' world were now undone.

Ring the alarum bell! Blow wind, come wrack!

At least we'll die with harness° on our back.   [*Exeunt.*]

---

17. **should:** inevitably would.

18. **word:** message.

❓ 28. *A scene that began in defiance changes with the great speech beginning "She should have died hereafter." What is Macbeth's new mood? Does Macbeth speak only for himself here, or for the general human condition?*

❓ 35. *What is Macbeth thinking of now?*

40. **cling:** wither.   **sooth:** truth.

42. **pull in resolution:** restrain confidence.

43. **doubt:** suspect.

47. **avouches:** asserts.

50. **th' estate:** the orderly condition.

52. **harness:** armor.

❓ 52. *Macbeth ends the scene in a state of great emotion. How would you characterize his mental state?*

B. Reader's Response: Shaping Interpretations

The meaning of this line is much debated. Popular interpretations are 1) like all humans, she would inevitably have to die sometime; and 2) at a different time, Macbeth could have given more attention to her death. What do you think Macbeth means, and why? [Sample responses: He feels they have drifted apart, so he accepts her death; or he is so self-absorbed that the emotional impact of her death doesn't register fully.]

C. Critical Reading: Making Connections

❓ Why might Macbeth's speech in Act II, Scene 3, ll. 85–90, come back to haunt him now? [Possible answer: At the time, Macbeth wished he had not killed Duncan but looked forward to the kingship. Now that he has been king for a while, he realizes the pointlessness of his ambition and the insignificance of his struggles.] Point out that the "sound and fury" make the tale appear to have importance when it has none—fitting the theme of false appearances.

D. Humanities Connection

The Southern writer William Faulkner wrote a novel called *The Sound and the Fury,* part of which is told by Benjy, a man of low intelligence who might fit Macbeth's definition of an idiot.

E. Literary Element: Motif

❓ How do these lines reflect the motif of paradox? [Macbeth realizes that the apparition's prophecy is meant to be understood in one sense that would be false, but could, like a riddle, be understood in another way.]

Answers to Margin Questions

Line 28. Possible answer: He shows philosophical resignation to the shortness and meaninglessness of life. Students may not agree with Macbeth but will see that he laments the human condition.

Line 35. He recalls the prophecy about Birnam Wood advancing on Dunsinane.

Line 52. Having seen the duplicity of one prophecy, Macbeth experiences the inner fatigue of final despair. Realizing that it matters little whether he remains in the castle or goes out, he resolves to die fighting.

PROFESSIONAL NOTES

Cultural Diversity   Have students work in pairs to learn how various countries celebrate a government leader's taking office. Assign one country to each pair, and have them find answers to the following questions: What title does the head of state use? Where is the ceremony held? Who attends? Who presides? What promises, if any, does the new officeholder make? Is there a religious element to the ceremony? Students should research the symbolism, costume, and wording used in the ceremonies and report their findings to the class.   ☞

Scene 6. *Dunsinane. Before the castle.*

Drum and colors. Enter MALCOLM, SIWARD, MACDUFF, *and their*
ARMY, *with boughs.*

Malcolm.
  Now near enough. Your leavy° screens throw down,
  And show like those you are. You, worthy uncle,
  Shall, with my cousin, your right noble son,
  Lead our first battle.° Worthy Macduff and we°
5 Shall take upon 's what else remains to do,
  According to our order.°
Siward.   Fare you well.
  Do we° but find the tyrant's power° tonight,
  Let us be beaten, if we cannot fight.
Macduff.
  Make all our trumpets speak; give them all breath,
10 Those clamorous harbingers of blood and death.
                              [*Exeunt. Alarums continued.*]

1. leavy: leafy.

4. battle: battalion. **we:** Malcolm uses the royal "we."

6. order: plan.

7. Do we: if we do. **power:** forces.

"Make all our trumpets speak; give them all breath,
Those clamorous harbingers of blood and death."
From the Stratford Festival production of *Macbeth* (1983).

378 THE RENAISSANCE

PROFESSIONAL NOTES

Critical Comment: The Witches
The critic Willard Farnham discusses the role of the witches: "Before we make up our minds about the guilt of the hero and, finally, the meaning of the tragedy, we must first decide what power these beings [the witches] wield over the actions and fortunes of the hero. They are witches having the forms of repulsive old women, but they are not mortal witches such as the law

might get its hands upon and put to death in the England or Scotland of Shakespeare's day. They are 'weird sisters,' but the word 'weird' as applied to them cannot mean that they have control of Macbeth's destiny and compel him to do all that he does. Macbeth is certainly no mere puppet moving under their manipulation. Nothing is clearer than that Shakespeare writes of Macbeth as of a man who has free will so far, at least, as the choice of good or evil is concerned, and who in choosing evil creates for himself physical

misfortune and a spiritual hell on earth. In what they do the witches show themselves to have a power over Macbeth that is limited, however strong it may be. They are supernatural agents of evil, and in working to make fair into foul they reveal both the capacities and the incapacities that the Christian tradition has attributed to devils. They tempt Macbeth to do evil, and tempt him with great subtlety. They cannot force him to do it."

Scene 7. *Another part of the field.*

Enter MACBETH.

Macbeth.
They have tied me to a stake; I cannot fly,
But bearlike I must fight the course.° What's he
That was not born of woman? Such a one
Am I to fear, or none.

[*Enter* YOUNG SIWARD.]

Young Siward.
What is thy name?

5   **Macbeth.**   Thou'lt be afraid to hear it.
Young Siward.
No; though thou call'st thyself a hotter name
Than any is in hell.
Macbeth.   My name's Macbeth.
Young Siward.
The devil himself could not pronounce a title
More hateful to mine ear.
Macbeth.   No, nor more fearful.
Young Siward.
10   Thou liest, abhorrèd tyrant; with my sword
I'll prove the lie thou speak'st.

[*Fight, and* YOUNG SIWARD *slain.*]

Macbeth.   Thou wast born of woman.
But swords I smile at, weapons laugh to scorn,
Brandished by man that's of a woman born.   [*Exit.*]

[*Alarums. Enter* MACDUFF.]

Macduff.
That way the noise is. Tyrant, show thy face!
15   If thou be'st slain and with no stroke of mine,
My wife and children's ghosts will haunt me still.
I cannot strike at wretched kerns,° whose arms
Are hired to bear their staves.° Either thou, Macbeth,
Or else my sword, with an unbattered edge,
20   I sheathe again undeeded.° There thou shouldst be;
By this great clatter, one of greatest note
Seems bruited.° Let me find him, Fortune!
And more I beg not.   [*Exit. Alarums.*]

[*Enter* MALCOLM *and* SIWARD.]

Siward.
This way, my lord. The castle's gently rend'red:°
25   The tyrant's people on both sides do fight;
The noble thanes do bravely in the war;
The day almost itself professes° yours,

---

2. **course:** bout; round. (He has in mind an attack of dogs or men upon a bear chained to a stake.)

❓ 4. *What is Macbeth desperately clinging to now?*

17. **kerns:** foot soldiers (contemptuous).
18. **staves:** spears.
20. **undeeded:** that is, having done nothing.
22. **bruited:** reported.

24. **gently rend'red:** surrendered without a struggle.

27. **itself professes:** declares itself.

MACBETH, ACT V, SCENE 7   **379**

A. Exploring the Culture

The bear-baiting comparison would have been familiar to Shakespeare's audience. In that bloody sport, the bear, however valiant, had no real chance. What does Macbeth's use of this image reveal about his state of mind? [Possible answer: He feels utterly trapped, like the bear whose chain limits its movements and prevents it from using its strength to advantage.]

B. Critical Reading: Comparing and Contrasting

❓ How does Macduff's motivation contrast with Macbeth's? [Possible answer: Macduff wants to avenge his wrongfully murdered family; Macbeth murders out of selfishness and ambition to gain power.]

Answer to Margin Question
Line 4. The prophecy that he interprets as meaning no living person can harm him, since everyone is born of a woman.

PROFESSIONAL NOTES

Critical Comment: Plot Ask students to discuss this analysis by Terence Eagleton: "*Macbeth* centres around a single action—the murder of Duncan—which . . . is seen as self-defeating. The whole structure of the play makes this clear: Scotland moves from health to sickness and back into health, Malcolm replaces Duncan, and the wheel comes full circle without Macbeth having made any permanent achievement. The energy he expends in trying to secure his position contrasts ironically with this lack of attainment: his actions are canceled out by the circular movement of the play, and he becomes a momentary aberration in Scotland's history, an aberration without lasting consequence: the history rights itself and continues." [Students may agree that Macbeth himself recognized this when he spoke of "a tale told by an idiot, signifying nothing." Or students may say that whatever Malcolm achieves will be partly due to this "aberration"—perhaps Malcolm will be a better king than he might have been had he inherited the throne earlier, without the experiences that made him learn to be wary, unlike his trusting father.] ☞

Macbeth, Act V, Scene 7 **T379**

A. Reader's Response: Shaping Interpretations

? What do you think is Macbeth's motivation in saying "My soul is too much charged / With blood of thine already"? [Sample responses: He really feels guilty about murdering Macduff's family; or he is trying to avoid Macduff because he remembers the prophecy that told him to beware, and he is afraid; or since he does not hesitate to kill young Siward, perhaps Macbeth is remembering that he and Macduff were once friends.]

And little is to do.

Malcolm.   We have met with foes
  That strike beside us.°
Siward.   Enter, sir, the castle.

  [*Exeunt. Alarum.*]

29. **That . . . us:** that is, who deliberately miss us as our comrades.

Scene 8. *Another part of the field.*

Enter MACBETH.

Macbeth.
  Why should I play the Roman fool, and die
  On mine own sword? Whiles I see lives,° the gashes
  Do better upon them.

2. **Whiles . . . lives:** so long as I see living men.

[*Enter* MACDUFF.]

Macduff.   Turn, hell-hound, turn!
Macbeth.
  Of all men else I have avoided thee.
5 But get thee back! My soul is too much charged°
  With blood of thine already.

5. **charged:** burdened.

"I have no words: / My voice is in my sword, thou bloodier villain / Than terms can give thee out!"
From Roman Polanski's film production of *Macbeth* (1971).

OPTIONS FOR TEACHING

ASSESSMENT TOOLS

Check Test: Questions and Answers
1. Name two important actions that Lady Macbeth performs while sleepwalking. [Possible answers: She rubs her hands as if washing; writes a letter; speaks, implicating herself and Macbeth in the murders of Duncan, Banquo, and Lady Macduff.]

2. Macbeth had been planning to let the English besiege his castle, but after the report that Birnam Wood is moving, how do his plans change? [He decides to go out and fight.]
3. What choice does Macduff give Macbeth? [To fight or to yield and be imprisoned and put on display so the public can mock him.]
4. Who becomes the new king of Scotland? [Malcolm.]

Peer Evaluation As students complete group activities, ask them to rate their group's performance on a scale of one to five (five being the best rating) on each of the following criteria:
1. Reads with expression and characterization when quoting the text.
2. Supports ideas with quotations from the text.
3. Makes connections between different parts of the text.

Macduff.   I have no words:
My voice is in my sword, thou bloodier villain
Than terms can give thee out!°   [*Fight. Alarum.*]
Macbeth.   Thou losest labor:
10   As easy mayst thou the intrenchant° air
With thy keen sword impress° as make me bleed:
Let fall thy blade on vulnerable crests;°
I bear a charmèd life, which must not yield
To one of woman born.
Macduff.   Despair° thy charm,
And let the angel° whom thou still hast served
15   Tell thee, Macduff was from his mother's womb
Untimely ripped.
Macbeth.
Accursèd be that tongue that tells me so,
For it hath cowed my better part of man!°   **B**
And be these juggling fiends no more believed,
20   That palter° with us in a double sense;
That keep the word of promise to our ear,
And break it to our hope. I'll not fight with thee.
Macduff.
Then yield thee, coward,
And live to be the show and gaze o' th' time:°
25   We'll have thee, as our rarer monsters° are,
Painted upon a pole,° and underwrit,
"Here may you see the tyrant."
Macbeth.   I will not yield,
To kiss the ground before young Malcolm's feet,
And to be baited° with the rabble's curse.
30   Though Birnam Wood be come to Dunsinane,
And thou opposed, being of no woman born,
Yet I will try the last. Before my body
I throw my warlike shield. Lay on, Macduff;
And damned be him that first cries "Hold, enough!"

[*Exeunt, fighting. Alarums.*] **C**

[*Reenter fighting, and* MACBETH *slain. Exit* MACDUFF,
with MACBETH. *Retreat and flourish.*° *Enter, with drum* **D**
and colors, MALCOLM, SIWARD, ROSS, THANES, *and* SOLDIERS.]
Malcolm.
35   I would the friends we miss were safe arrived.
Siward.
Some must go off;° and yet, by these I see,
So great a day as this is cheaply bought.
Malcolm.
Macduff is missing, and your noble son.
Ross.
Your son, my lord, has paid a soldier's debt:
40   He only lived but till he was a man;   **E**
The which no sooner had his prowess confirmed

8. **terms . . . out:** words can describe you.

9. **intrenchant:** incapable of being cut.

10. **impress:** make an impression on.

11. **vulnerable crests:** heads that can be wounded.

13. **Despair:** despair of.

14. **angel:** that is, fallen angel; fiend.

? 16. *What is the meaning of lines 15–16? How do they relate to the prophecy?*

18. **better . . . man:** manly spirit.

20. **palter:** equivocate.

24. **gaze . . . time:** spectacle of the age.
25. **monsters:** freaks.
26. **Painted . . . pole:** pictured on a banner set by a showman's booth.

29. **baited:** assailed (like a bear by dogs).

Retreat and flourish: trumpet call to withdraw, and fanfare.

36. **go off:** die (theatrical metaphor).

B. Critical Reading: Making Connections

? What support could you offer for the argument that it is fitting for Macbeth to be tricked by "palter[ing] . . . in a double sense"? [Possible answer: Since Macbeth used this technique to escape detection as the murderer of Duncan, it seems right in a way that his own trick be used to trick *him*.]

C. Reader's Response: Connecting with the Text

? Do you think Macbeth's determination to fight it out shows bravery, or does he have other motivations? [Sample responses: No, at this point he has no choice. Maybe he's relieved to be back on the battlefield, where he won his glory and where killing is acceptable. Yes, it's the only respectable trait that remains from his once noble character.]

D. Expansion

The death of Macbeth usually takes place offstage, perhaps to dramatize Macduff's reentry with Macbeth's head. The great Shakespearean actor David Garrick (1717–1779), who had gained a reputation doing death scenes, staged a fight onstage and created a final speech for Macbeth as he was dying.

E. Literary Element: Character

? What role does Ross repeatedly play in the action? Compare and contrast his speech here to Siward with what he says to Macduff in Act IV, Scene 3. What does Ross think it means to be a man? [Possible answers: He is the messenger who brings news of death. Ross had a difficult time earlier because Macduff's innocent family was so heartlessly slain. Also, Ross knew of Macbeth's involvement and probably felt guilty because he had not abandoned Macbeth earlier. Here, in a battle situation where fighters knowingly risk their lives, Ross delivers a brief, but moving, eulogy. Ross seems to think that fighting bravely and being willing to sacrifice for a cause makes a man.]

Answer to Margin Question
Line 16. As the prophecy predicts, Macduff was not "of woman born" in the natural way but was delivered by Caesarean section.

A. Literary Element: Motif

? What earlier event in the play does this mirror? [Possible answer: It mirrors the beheading of Macdonwald by Macbeth (the traitor beheaded by the loyal Scot). Also, the murder of a king (Macbeth) to restore order mirrors the murder of a king (Duncan) that has destroyed order.]

B. Literary Element: Tragedy

Ask students to return to the double-entry journal they created as a Reading Focus, p. T301, and to complete the right-hand column with their thoughts after finishing the play. Given the definitions, ask them if they think Macbeth is a **tragic hero.** [Students may say Macbeth is a tragic hero because at first he is an honorable nobleman, and he encounters a downfall through his tragic flaw, which is ambition; in addition, the audience feels relief when the play is over, which could be considered catharsis. Or they may say although he is recognized as a hero on the battlefield, Macbeth is a brutal person from the start. He has gained recognition by killing, so he continues to murder for ambitious reasons. In that way, he is not typical of a tragic hero—he is just a butcher, as Malcolm calls him.]

Answers to Margin Questions
Line 53. Malcolm exhibits great concern for each missing man and promises some posthumous honor for young Siward. Old Siward, satisfied his son has died bravely, says no further honor is necessary.
Stage direction. Relieved, gracious, moved, jubilant.
Line 75. Answers will vary. Students might suggest that Malcolm should lead the way and that the others should follow in order of rank.

In the unshrinking station° where he fought,
But like a man he died.
Siward.   Then he is dead?
Ross.
  Ay, and brought off the field. Your cause of sorrow
45   Must not be measured by his worth, for then
  It hath no end.
Siward.   Had he his hurts before?
Ross.
  Ay, on the front.
Siward.   Why then, God's soldier be he!
  Had I as many sons as I have hairs,
  I would not wish them to a fairer death:
  And so his knell is knolled.
50 **Malcolm.**   He's worth more sorrow,
  And that I'll spend for him.
Siward.   He's worth no more:
  They say he parted well and paid his score:°
  And so God be with him! Here comes newer comfort.

Ⓐ [*Enter* MACDUFF, *with Macbeth's head.*]

Macduff.
  Hail, king! for so thou art: behold, where stands
55   Th' usurper's cursèd head. The time is free.°
  I see thee compassed° with thy kingdom's pearl,
  That speak my salutation in their minds,
  Whose voices I desire aloud with mine:
  Hail, King of Scotland!
All.   Hail, King of Scotland!

[*Flourish.*]

Malcolm.
60   We shall not spend a large expense of time
  Before we reckon with your several loves,°
  And make us even with you. My thanes and kinsmen,
  Henceforth be earls, the first that ever Scotland
  In such an honor named. What's more to do,
65   Which would be planted newly with the time°—
  As calling home our exiled friends abroad
  That fled the snares of watchful tyranny,
  Producing forth the cruel ministers°
Ⓑ   Of this dead butcher and his fiendlike queen,
70   Who, as 'tis thought, by self and violent hands°
  Took off her life—this, and what needful else
  That calls upon us,° by the grace of Grace
  We will perform in measure, time, and place:°
  So thanks to all at once and to each one,
75   Whom we invite to see us crowned at Scone.
[*Flourish. Exeunt omnes.*]

42. unshrinking station: that is, place at which he stood firmly.

52. parted . . . score: departed well and settled his account.

? 53. *What character traits does Malcolm show in this scene? How is old Siward like a military man to the end?*

? Stage direction. *Macduff enters with Macbeth's head on a pole. A great shout goes up. What is Macduff's tone in the next speech?*

55. The time is free: The world is liberated.

56. compassed: surrounded.

61. reckon . . . loves: reward the devotion of each of you.

65. What's . . . time: What else must be done that should be newly established in this age.

68. ministers: agents.

70. self . . . hands: her own violent hands.

72. calls upon us: demands my attention.

73. in . . . place: fittingly, at the appropriate time and place.

? 75. *Scone is a stone upon which the Scottish kings sat at their coronation. (It is now in Westminster Abbey in London, beneath the coronation chair of the English kings.) Scone is usually pronounced "scoon." How would you have the characters exit? Who would exit last?*

Critical Comment

Soliloquies and Asides

Renaissance playwrights had two useful devices for revealing to an audience or reader a dramatic character's inmost thoughts and feelings: soliloquies and asides.

A **soliloquy** is a meditative kind of speech in which a character, usually alone on stage and pretending that the audience is not present, thinks out loud. Everybody understands that the speaker of a soliloquy tells the truth freely and openly, however discreditable that truth may be. For instance, in his famous soliloquy beginning "To be or not to be," Shakespeare's Hamlet admits to the audience that he is thinking of committing suicide.

Asides are much shorter than soliloquies, but just as truthful. **Asides** are a character's private comments on what is happening at a given moment in a play. They are spoken out of the side of the mouth, so to speak, for the benefit of the audience; the other characters on stage pretend that they do not hear them. For example, Macbeth's asides in Act I, Scene 3, tell us that he cannot put the witches' prophecies out of his mind.

Macbeth's tragic decline can be best traced in his solo speeches—his asides and soliloquies. The most important of these, which are what make the play so interesting psychologically, occur as follows:

Act I, Scene 3, lines 130–142
Act I, Scene 4, lines 48–53
Act I, Scene 7, lines 1–28
Act II, Scene 1, lines 33–64
Act III, Scene 1, lines 48–72
Act IV, Scene 1, lines 144–156
Act V, Scene 3, lines 19–29
Act V, Scene 5, lines 9–15

The early soliloquies show Macbeth's indecision and his fierce inner conflict; then, after he succumbs to evil, they show the terror in his soul and his inability to recover his lost innocence. At times they even show that he is reconciled to his murderous career, especially after the second set of prophecies gives him a false sense of security. But finally the soliloquies show his despair and loss of feeling about, and interest in, life itself. All these changing states of mind are expressed in powerful images that help the audience share Macbeth's suffering. In contrast, we see Lady Macbeth mainly from the outside, though an attentive reader can find speeches in which she also reveals feelings. In *Macbeth,* the inner spiritual catastrophe parallels the outer physical catastrophe.

Nicholas Pennell as Macbeth in the Stratford Festival production of *Macbeth* (1983).

MACBETH, ACT V 383

OPTIONS FOR TEACHING

INTEGRATING THE LANGUAGE ARTS

Strategic Reading After they have read "Soliloquies and Asides," ask students to write a definition for each of the terms defined, to give an example from the play, and to tell what they think the purpose is for each. Have students share with the class their examples and their theories about the specific purposes of the selected soliloquies and asides.

Term	Example	Purpose

A. Reader's Response: Shaping Interpretations

Compare *Macbeth* with other Shakespearean tragedies that you may know (perhaps *Julius Caesar* or *Romeo and Juliet*). Do you agree that Macbeth changes more drastically than the characters in these other works? [Sample responses: No, I think that Brutus and Macbeth are actually quite similar in the changes that they make; both betray—and kill—a former friend. Yes, I think Macbeth makes more drastic changes in himself than even Brutus does; not only does he betray and murder a king, he goes mad in the process.]

B. Exploring the Culture

Students may benefit from analyzing the different words used today to distinguish between different kinds of inflicted death, such as *murder, killing,* and *homicide.* Encourage students to consider the following questions: Do you agree with the implicit distinctions? Is it different to kill a man on the battlefield and in his bed? How? Does evidence in the text suggest that there were similar distinctions during the time of Macbeth?

C. Reader's Response: Challenging the Text

? Do you agree with this critic's analysis of Shakespeare's goals and purposes? Support your opinion with references to the text. [Sample responses: Yes, I think Shakespeare wants us to at least empathize with Macbeth, which is why Shakespeare does not show all the murders onstage and lets us see Macbeth's trepidation over Duncan's murder. Or no, I don't think Shakespeare wants us to think of Macbeth as good, because Shakespeare shows us the utter evil of Macbeth in having him heartlessly order the murder of Macduff's son.]

D. Exploring the Historical Period

If students have become acquainted with a few facts from Holinshed's historical account, they may be able to address these questions in a more sophisticated way.

E. Expansion

Apparently the witches were first played by women in 1888.

Critical Comment

The Mystery of Evil

(A) *Macbeth* fascinates us because it shows, perhaps more clearly than any of Shakespeare's other tragedies, how a character can change as a result of what he does. *Macbeth* also shows that crime does not pay, but that smug cliché is not very relevant to the play: Macbeth is "caught" as soon as he understands the witches' prophecy, and his mental anguish begins before he commits any crimes.

(B) At the start of the play, the mere thought of committing a murder terrifies Macbeth, although he is no novice at carving up men in battle. But it is one thing to fight openly, quite another to kill stealthily. His wife says her great warrior-husband Macbeth is "too full o' th' milk of human kindness." Shakespeare apparently **(C)** wants us to think of Macbeth as a good man and to feel sympathetic toward him even after he becomes a murderer. When Duncan's body is found, Macbeth does not feel excited about becoming king; instead, he mutters to himself, "The wine of life is drawn." He can't enjoy his kingly state; he is too terrified by what he is doing. "Full of scorpions is my mind," he says to his wife. He lives in such constant terror that by the end of the play he is numb to all feeling—even to the death of his beloved wife. A "dead butcher," Malcolm calls him: an automatic killer.

Lady Macbeth's deterioration is different from her husband's but just as dramatic. Legally, she is only an accomplice, never an actual murderer. But she is the first to decide that Duncan must die; Macbeth wavers right up to the last moment. After the first murders, she exerts immense self-control over herself while he surrenders to his nerves. But she does eventually crack under the strain. Malcolm might not have called her a "fiendlike queen" after her death had he known how much she suffered from pangs of conscience. Both Macbeth and his wife are moral beings who excite our pity rather than our contempt or disgust.

(D) But why do they commit their crimes? The customary answer to this question—that they are ambitious—leads only to another question: Why are they so ambitious that they are willing to commit such crimes? Ultimately, these questions are unanswerable, because evil is as mysterious as it is real. Shakespeare makes no attempt to solve the mystery; instead, in *Macbeth,* he uses language to make it even more mysterious. The world of *Macbeth* is filled, from beginning to end, with mysterious and repulsive images of evil.

The Imagery: Darkness, Night, Blood

(E) First of all, there are the witches. The play opens with the three witches performing their sinister rites and chanting, "Fair is foul, and foul is fair," blurring the differences between these opposites. Macbeth's first speech joins the same opposites, as though they were synonyms: "So foul and fair a day I have not seen." Macbeth's speech thus establishes a connection between himself and the witches even before he meets them.

Shakespeare's audience would have immediately recognized the witches as embodiments of evil in league with Satan himself. Several times they refer to themselves as the "weird sisters"—*weird* here meaning maliciously and perversely supernatural, possessing harmful powers given them by evil spirits in the form of nasty pet animals such as old gray tomcats and toads. English and Scottish witches are not to be regarded as the Fates of Greek mythology whose baleful influence could not be resisted. Rather, they are tempters of a kind that Shakespeare's contemporaries believed they should always avoid. One of the witches seems to foretell Macbeth's future by saying, "All hail, Macbeth, that shalt be king hereafter!" After an inner struggle, and under the influence of his wife's goading, Macbeth chooses to make

---

OPTIONS FOR TEACHING

STRATEGIES FOR INCLUSION

English Language Development Be certain that students understand that *character* can mean either a person in a play or story or the moral values a person has. Before they read "The Mystery of Evil," ask students to discuss the moral character of Macbeth and Lady Macbeth and to consider these questions: Do they immediately give in to evil, or do they fight with temptation? Do their moral values change during the course of the play? Then, ask students to read this critic's assessment and to list similarities and differences between the critic's opinion and their own.

"hereafter" happen immediately. Nowhere in the play do the witches *cause* Macbeth to make this wicked decision. Rather, he voluntarily surrenders himself, following a visionary dagger—a manifestation of his decision—that leads him into Duncan's bedroom. Having once given in to evil, Macbeth is thereafter under the control of evil forces stronger than his own moral sense.

Shakespeare expresses these evil forces in images of darkness, night, and blood. He has Banquo call the weird sisters "instruments of darkness," linking them to the thick gloom that pervades the whole play and provides a cover under which evil can do its work. Even in daylight Macbeth and his wife invoke the night: "Come, thick night," Lady Macbeth cries as part of her prayer asking evil spirits to "unsex" her. Macbeth also calls for night to come, to blindfold "the tender eye of pitiful day" so that the killers he has hired can safely murder innocent Banquo and his son.

By setting many of the violent scenes at night and by making the scenes in *Macbeth* "murky," full of "fog and filthy air," and pierced by the cries of owls, Shakespeare suppresses all the pleasant associations night might have, especially as the time for refreshing sleep. Just as he commits his first murder, Macbeth thinks he hears a horrible voice crying, "Macbeth does murder sleep"; thereafter, he becomes an insomniac and his wife a sleepwalker. Darkness, voices, ghosts, hallucinations—these are used to express Macbeth's and his wife's surrender to evil and their subsequent despair.

Evil in *Macbeth* takes the form of violence and bloodshed. Right after the opening scene with the witches, a man covered with gashes appears before King Duncan, who asks, "What bloody man is that?" Between this scene and the final one, in which Macbeth's bleeding and "cursèd" head is displayed on a pike, human blood hardly stops running. Images of blood appeal not only to our sense of sight but also to our sense of touch (Macbeth's bloody and secret murders are "sticking on his hands" in the last act), and even to our sense of smell ("Here's the smell of the blood still," Lady Macbeth moans in Act V as she holds out her "little hand"). Such imagery is designed to make us feel moral revulsion, not just physical disgust: Bloodshed leads only to more bloodshed.

The Poetry: Expressing the Dark Night

All this imagery reminds us that *Macbeth* is a poem as well as a play—a dramatic poem sharing many of the characteristics of lyric poetry. The most obvious of these is **meter,** here the unrhymed iambic pentameter or **blank verse** that Shakespeare's predecessor Christopher Marlowe established as the appropriate medium for tragedy. Poetry is to tragedy as singing is to opera: It elevates and enhances the emotional impact of the experience being communicated. Indeed, without the poetry there could be no tragedy, because without it Shakespeare could not have expressed the dark night into which Macbeth's soul sinks. And a tragic poet is much more concerned with states of mind and feeling than with physical action. Macbeth shares with Shakespeare's other great tragic heroes—Hamlet, Lear, Othello—the ability to express in eloquent, moving language whatever he is feeling. One of the most famous speeches of this kind occurs when, near the end of his bloody career, Macbeth sums up what life means to him:

> Out, out, brief candle!
> Life's but a walking shadow, a poor player
> That struts and frets his hour upon the stage
> And then is heard no more. It is a tale
> Told by an idiot, full of sound and fury,
> Signifying nothing.

—Act V, Scene 5, lines 23–28

The bitter nihilism of these metaphors suggests that Macbeth is already dead in spirit, although his body must undergo a last battle. By murdering Duncan, he has murdered more than sleep: He has destroyed himself.

INTEGRATING THE LANGUAGE ARTS

Strategic Reading Ask students to record main ideas, transitions, and details from paragraphs in "The Mystery of Evil," using a graphic organizer like the one that follows.

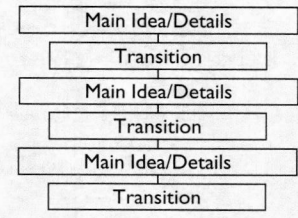

Main Idea/Details
Transition
Main Idea/Details
Transition
Main Idea/Details
Transition

A. Literary Element: Mood

Although the weather described is the same, the mood in Armour's opening paragraph is quite different from the mood of Act I, Scene I, in *Macbeth*. How would you characterize the mood? What content or techniques contribute to this mood? [Possible answers: The mood is humorous or playful. The reference to a picnic (an unexpected juxtaposition) and to the Edinburgh Ugly Contest (a humorous explanation for their strange appearance) contribute.]

B. Literary Element: Pun

Shakespeare uses clever puns to add wit to the conversation in *Macbeth* (for example, in Act III, Scene 4, ll. 36–37). What puns does Armour use? What is the effect? [Possible answer: *Blowing* is used to refer to "forcibly pushing air out of the mouth" and "blowing up with an explosive." The idea of secretly planting bagpipes—a harmless Scottish musical instrument—in the enemy's camp is amusing.]

C. Language Note: Anachronism

Occasionally, writers will make reference to an object or word that was not actually in use at the time in which their story is set, a representation called an anachronism. Armour's use of anachronism is purposeful: What is the effect of his use of anachronism? [Possible answers: Armour creates humor with his references to occupations that did not yet exist.]

D. Critical Reading: Analyzing Humor

Identify techniques that contribute to humor in this paragraph. [Pun on *hail* meaning "greet" and "frozen precipitation"; nonsense words; purposeful confusion of *begetting* and *be getting*.]

E. Language Note: Wordplay

? What misreading of a line in Act I, Scene 3, is this comment based on? ["Stay you imperfect speakers" is purposely misunderstood as a criticism of the witches' enunciation.]

Making Meanings

Act V

First Thoughts

1. Students may pity Macbeth and be repulsed at the violence, or they may feel he deserves such a death.

Nothing is impervious to parody, not even the high seriousness of a play like Shakespeare's *Macbeth*. In the following piece from *Twisted Tales from Shakespeare*, Richard Armour presents another view of the three weird sisters. You and your classmates might want to write a parody of your own.

Macbeth and the Witches

Richard Armour

Three witches, extremely weird sisters, are having a picnic amidst thunder and lightning somewhere in Scotland. Judging from their appearance, they were placed one-two-three in the Edinburgh Ugly Contest.

"When shall we three meet again in thunder, lightning, or in rain?" asks one of them. They hate nice weather and are happiest when they are soaking wet and their hair is all stringy.

"When the hurly-burly's[1] done, when the battle's lost and won," another replies. A battle is going on between the forces of Duncan, the King of Scotland, and some Norwegians, assisted by the rebel Thane of Cawdor. At the moment it's looking good for Duncan, because two of his generals, Macbeth and Banquo, have cunningly put bagpipes into the hands of the enemy, who are blowing their brains out.

The witches hear some dear friend[2] calling and depart. "Fair is foul, and foul is fair," they comment philosophically as they leave. This must have been pretty upsetting to any moralists, semanticists, or baseball umpires who chanced to overhear them.

Shortly afterward, the battle having been won by Macbeth and the weather having turned bad enough to be pleasant, the witches meet again.

"Where hast thou been, Sister?" asks one.

"Killing swine," the second replies. All three of them have been busy doing similar diverting things, and one of them happily shows the others the thumb of a drowned sailor which she is adding to her thumb collection.[3]

---

1. See also hurdy-gurdy, hunky-dory, and okey-dokey.

2. A cat and a toad. Witches have to make friendships where they can.

3. In a comedy, this would be considered tragic relief.

The three witches and Lady Macbeth (in front) from the Faux-Real production of *Htebcam* (1994).

Reviewing the Text

a. Her mind is "infected" with evil; she has a guilty conscience.

b. That he is a tyrant, mad, and a murderer.

c. She dies during Scene 5 when the enemy is approaching.

d. In Scene 5, ll. 2–7, he plans to let them besiege the castle and then drive them home. This is both because the castle is strong and because he has lost troops (they have defected to help Malcolm). In Scene 5, ll. 51–52, he decides to fight because he fears fate is against him yet feels protected by the second apparition's prophecy.

e. He has forgotten what it is like to fear; he is sick of life.

f. Brief, dreary, and meaningless. Life is like a brief candle, a poor actor who plays his part and exits from the stage, a story that an idiot tells—noisy, but without meaning.

g. Macduff kills Macbeth. Macduff was not *born* but was ripped from his mother's womb (removed by surgery, not delivered through the birth canal). Birnam Wood came to Dunsinane, as the army used branches to disguise its advance.

Macbeth and Banquo come by at this point, on their way to inform the King that they have defeated the rebels. They would rather tell him in person than render a report in triplicate.

"Speak, if you can," says Macbeth boldly to the hags. "What are you?" He rather thinks they are witches but would like to hear it from their own skinny lips.

The witches start hailing.[4] They hail Macbeth as Thane of Glamis and Thane of Cawdor and say he will be King Hereafter. Not to leave Banquo out, they hail him as "lesser than Macbeth, and greater." (The witches are masters of gobbledyspook.) He won't be a king, they say, but he'll beget kings, and now they have to begetting along.

Macbeth knows he is Thane of Glamis, but has no idea (or didn't have until now) of becoming Thane of Cawdor or King Hereafter. "Stay, you imperfect speakers, tell me more," he commands. But the witches, perhaps not liking the way he refers to their elocution, vanish into thin air, making it slightly thicker.

While Macbeth is meditating about what the witches have forecast for him, a couple of the King's henchmen, straight from a busy day of henching, ride up. They bring word that Duncan is liquidating the Thane of Cawdor and giving his title to Macbeth, it being an inexpensive gift. (Duncan, as King of Scotland, was Scotcher than anybody.)

"Look how our partner's rapt," remarks Banquo, noticing that Macbeth, stunned with all the good news, acts as if he has been struck on the noggin. But Macbeth is only lost in thought and will find his way out presently. Thus far the witches have been batting 1,000, and Macbeth is beginning to take more than a casual interest in Duncan's health.[5]

4. Until now it has been raining.
5. Henceforth, when he says "How are you?" to the King, it will be a bona fide question.

[These are Richard Armour's footnotes.]

MAKING MEANINGS

Act V

First Thoughts

1. How do you feel about what happens to Macbeth's body after he is dead?

Reviewing the Text

a. Why, according to the doctor, is Lady Macbeth walking in her sleep?

b. In Scene 2, what opinion of Macbeth do the Scottish lords now hold?

c. When does Lady Macbeth die?

d. What is Macbeth's plan for dealing with the attacking troops? Why has he been forced to choose this plan?

e. What changes in his personality does Macbeth describe in Scene 5, lines 9–15?

f. In the speech in Scene 5 that begins "Tomorrow, and tomorrow, and tomorrow . . ." (lines 19–28), how does Macbeth describe life? What metaphors does he use?

g. How are the prophecies proclaimed by the three apparitions in Act IV, Scene 1, fulfilled in Act V?

h. At the end of the play, what has become of Macbeth? Who becomes King?

Shaping Interpretations

2. Theatrically, the spectacle of Lady Macbeth walking in her sleep is one of the most striking scenes in the play. It is entirely Shakespeare's invention, not found or suggested in his source. Why do you suppose Shakespeare has her walk in her sleep? How is this scene related to the remarks that Macbeth makes about sleep in Act II, Scene 2, just after he kills Duncan?

3. In the sleepwalking scene, Lady Macbeth refers to many of her waking experiences. For example, the words "One: two" may refer to the moment in Act II, Scene 1, when she struck the bell

4. Night and day may stand for tyranny and freedom, or evil and good. The remark foreshadows the outcome of the play because it hints that Macbeth will, in the end, be defeated.

5. Possible answers: Macbeth's death is the climax; it is the moment when Macbeth's problems are resolved. Or the climax occurs when Macduff reveals that he was ripped from his mother's womb; since this fulfills the second apparition's prophecy, Macbeth knows that he is doomed.

6. The "Tomorrow, and tomorrow, and tomorrow . . ." soliloquy; it shows his resignation. Or the "I will not yield" speech, before he fights Macduff to the death, shows that he wants to face death bravely.

Connecting with the Text

7. Possible responses: As the play ended, I felt as if nothing we can do in life is permanent or leaves a lasting mark. Or I believe there is much meaning to be found in life, and a person can make a difference in the world.

Challenging the Text

8. (Evaluation) It would make her seem more like Macbeth: She, too, sees ghosts and is vulnerable, and sensitivity would become more of a theme. It might make the other ghost seem more real because Macbeth would not be the only person to see a ghost and treat it as real. It might focus too much attention on Lady Macbeth or it might add to the audience's understanding of her demise. It might seem undignified.

The Play as a Whole

Questions begin on p. 388.

Shaping Interpretations

1. Macbeth also did the country a service by dying after he had become so tyrannical and evil. But Macbeth never begged pardon like Cawdor did, and he did throw away his good name, honor, and integrity. In real life, sometimes convicted murderers repent or at least apologize.

---

h. He has been killed and beheaded by Macduff. All the suffering and guilt have been for nothing; just as Duncan planned, Malcolm takes the throne.

Shaping Interpretations

2. It emphasizes how she has changed—she has been the cool, collected planner, protecting Macbeth from betraying himself. Now she betrays herself and him unawares. Perhaps her sleepwalking represents the sleep disturbance they both endure. It is an effective way to play on the theme of Macbeth murdering sleep.

3. (Some critics think "one: two" is the clock striking and not a reference to Duncan's death.) The washing of hands and donning of nightgown refer to the night of Duncan's murder. The Thane of Fife's wife refers to the murder of Lady Macduff. The burial of Banquo picks up on Macbeth's strange behavior at the banquet. The knocking at the gate refers to the morning after Duncan's murder.

(continued from p. T387)

2. The ending of the play shows the closing of the circle: Malcolm was named Duncan's heir; Malcolm becomes king, and order is restored, so justice triumphs; good overcomes evil. Or since I believe that Macbeth has no choice in his actions, I believe that the play shows evil overcoming good. I think the return of the good king (Malcolm) will be temporary, for he, too, can be corrupted by powers greater than his resistance.

3. Shakespeare makes Macbeth's fall into evil believable, because we can see the mental process by which he begins doing worse and worse deeds. I felt sorry that he gives into murderous impulses, because he has the potential to be good. Or I began losing sympathy once he killed Duncan, who had wished Macbeth well.

4. Macbeth does retain some of his original strengths—such as courage in battle, ambition, imagination— but we see how he turns them to evil use. The courage he shows on the battlefield is what allows him to quickly become used to killing away from the battlefield. His concern about others' opinions is what keeps him noble (Act I, Scene 7, ll. 32–35), but concern about Lady Macbeth's opinion of him makes him give in.

5. Possible responses: One of the grooms awakens in time to avert Macbeth's murder of Duncan; Banquo warns the king of the witches' prophecies and his concern about Macbeth's interest in these predictions so that Duncan is on guard.

6. Internal: ambition versus morality and honesty versus deception, as related to murdering Duncan and Banquo. External: between Macbeth and Banquo, as Macbeth worries that Banquo's descendants will unthrone him, and between Macbeth and Macduff, as Macduff appears to distrust Macbeth. In the end, the Macbeths both suffer the consequences of guilty consciences due to the internal conflicts, and Macduff ultimately kills Macbeth, clearing the way for Banquo's descendants to rule.

Extending the Text

7. **(Synthesis)** Students may mention a variety of modern tyrants and

Lady Macbeth holding a candle in a dark hallway.
From the Stratford Festival production of *Macbeth* (1983).

signaling Macbeth to go kill Duncan. Find traces of other experiences in what she says while sleepwalking.

4. At the end of Act IV, Malcolm says, "The night is long that never finds the day." In what metaphorical sense does he use the terms *night* and *day*? How does his remark **foreshadow** the outcome of the play?

5. The last act of *Macbeth* contains the play's **climax**—the most emotional and suspenseful part of the action—the moment when the characters' conflict is finally resolved. Which part of Act V do you consider the climax? Explain.

6. Shakespeare gave most of his **tragic heroes** an impressive dying speech in which they say something significant about their own life and death. Although he did not write such a speech for Macbeth, which speech of Macbeth's do you think serves in the play as his dying speech? Why do you select this speech rather than some other one?

dictators: Napoleon, Adolf Hitler, Joseph Stalin, Ferdinand Marcos, or Manuel Noriega. Such leaders may be like Macbeth in appearing harsh or having human frailties, but unlike Macbeth in circumstances. Answers will vary; remind students to refer to the definition of a tragic hero.

Challenging the Text

8. **(Synthesis)** Answers will vary. Macbeth's fate is merely foretold by the witches; he is the one who kills Duncan, conspires against Banquo, and sends others to murder Macduff's

Connecting with the Text

7. What are your reactions to the idea expressed by Macbeth that life "is a tale / Told by an idiot, full of sound and fury, / Signifying nothing" (Scene 5, lines 26–28)? Explain your response.

Challenging the Text

8. Sometime shortly after 1660, a playwright named William Davenant (who claimed to be a natural son of Shakespeare) added another sleepwalking scene to *Macbeth:* He had the ghost of Duncan chase Lady Macbeth about the stage. How might this scene change the way audiences perceive Lady Macbeth's character? Might it make the other ghosts in the play seem any more or less real? What might the scene add to the play, and what might it take away?

The Play as a Whole

Shaping Interpretations

1. "Nothing in his life / Became him like the leaving it," says Malcolm in Act I, referring to the traitorous Thane of Cawdor. Malcolm also says that this Thane of Cawdor threw away the dearest thing he owned. How might these two statements also apply to Macbeth? Have you known, or do you know of, other people to whom these lines apply?

2. One of the **themes** of *Macbeth* centers on evil, which Shakespeare saw as a force beyond human understanding. Do you think Shakespeare also saw evil as stronger than the forces of good? Support your answer with events from the play.

3. How does Shakespeare keep his audience from losing all sympathy for and interest in Macbeth in spite of Macbeth's increasing viciousness? Were you in sympathy with Macbeth throughout the play, or was there a point at which you lost sympathy? If so, where?

4. One critic has observed that part of Macbeth's tragedy is the fact that many of his strengths are also his weaknesses. Explain this apparent contradiction. What are Macbeth's strengths? Which ones also work against him?

5. Think of a single event, at any time during the course of the play, that could have averted

family. Or Macbeth is under the spell of the witches; they plant the seeds of murder in his head, create the brew that draws him into their conspiracy, and trick him with the prophecies into believing that he is invincible.

9. **(Evaluation)** Yes, parody is a good reminder not to take ourselves or our literary idols too seriously; or no, writers should not make fun of a well-written piece of literature that teaches worthwhile lessons about human nature.

Macbeth's tragic end. What would this event be? How could it have come about? How would it affect the outcome of the play?

6. **Internal conflicts** rage within Macbeth, as well as **external conflicts** with other characters. Explain some of the play's main conflicts, and trace their resolution.

Extending the Text

7. What modern figure, real or fictional, had a downfall, like Macbeth's, that came after an attempt to gain great power? How is this modern figure like Macbeth, and how different? Would this modern figure make a good **tragic hero**? Refer to your Reader's Log entry on page 300 as you answer this question.

Challenging the Text

8. Think about the quotation from Goethe on page 281. Do you think Macbeth himself has the free will to control his own destiny? Or is he controlled by fate?

9. Do you think people should parody a great tragic play like *Macbeth,* the way Richard Armour does in "Macbeth and the Witches" (page 386)? Why or why not?

ELEMENTS OF LITERATURE

Imagery and Figurative Language

Macbeth's poetry is rich in imagery and figurative language that help to create atmosphere and reveal character and theme.

1. Powerful images in the play contrast the natural and the unnatural, as in Lady Macbeth's speech in Act I, Scene 7, lines 54–59:

. . . I have given suck, and know
How tender 'tis to love the babe that milks me:
I would, while it was smiling in my face,
Have plucked my nipple from his boneless gums,
And dashed the brains out, had I so sworn as you
Have done to this.

Francesca Annis and Jon Finch in Roman Polanski's film production of *Macbeth* (1971).

a. What unnatural sounds and events are reported in Act II, Scenes 2–4? What mood do these images create?

b. Look at the witches' scenes. What would you say is the emotional effect of each scene? Besides the witches themselves, what unnatural images occur in these scenes?

2. We hear about sleep and sleeplessness throughout the play. How is sleep described in these figures of speech?

a. **First Witch**. . . . I'll drain him dry as hay:
Sleep shall neither night nor day
Hang upon his penthouse lid; . . .

—Act I, Scene 3, lines 18–30

b. **Macbeth.** Methought I heard a voice cry "Sleep no more!
Macbeth does murder sleep"—the innocent sleep,
Sleep that knits up the raveled sleave of care,
The death of each day's life, sore labor's bath,
Balm of hurt minds, great nature's second course,
Chief nourisher in life's feast—

—Act II, Scene 2, lines 34–39

3. Choose one of the following images, and find three speeches (from different scenes in the play) in which the image occurs:

blood   darkness   disease   planting

Look back at the context of each speech (what happens just before and after): What is the emotional effect of each one?

Elements of Literature: Possible Answers

1. a. In Scene 2, Macbeth reports that someone cried out "Murder" while asleep and that he heard a voice accusing him of murdering sleep. Scene 3 includes the knocking that unnerves the Macbeths. Lennox's speech (Scene 3, ll. 48–55) chronicles the night's unusual weather and events, as does the dialogue between Ross and the Old Man (Scene 4, ll. 1–20). These images make the mood eerie to reflect the unnatural act of murder.

b. Students might say that the scenes are creepy, disturbing, strange. Unnatural images include the attending toad, the strange comments regarding sailing in a sieve and taking a pilot's thumb, appearances and disappearances into thin air, the horrific ingredients for the brew.

2. a. Sleep is something that weights the eyelid.

b. Sleep is a knitter, bath, balm, and food.

3. Possible answers:
Blood: Act II, Scene 1, ll. 46–47; Act II, Scene 3, ll. 105–110; Act III, Scene 4, ll. 122–126
Darkness: Act I, Scene 5, ll. 48–52; Act II, Scene 4, ll. 5–10; Act III, Scene 2, ll. 46–53
Disease: Act IV, Scene 3, ll. 141–145; Act V, Scene 1, ll. 62–64; Act V, Scene 3, ll. 37–45
Planting: Act I, Scene 4, ll. 28–29; Act IV, Scene 1, ll. 58–61; Act V, Scene 8, ll. 64–69.

Answers regarding the emotional effects of each scene will vary.

Beyond the Play

Choices: Building Your Portfolio

1. **Writer's Notebook** Remind students to save their work. They may use it as prewriting for the Writer's Workshop on p. 459.

2. **Critical Writing** Ask students to cite specific references to or speeches by Lady Macbeth and to discuss why Shakespeare might have included particular wording or actions and what these words or actions suggest.

3. **Critical Writing** Before students begin writing, have them review Macbeth's speeches to look for places in the play in which he uses the same technique as the witches (equivocation, deceit through ambiguity). This will allow students to see the question in a broader perspective.

4. **Oral Interpretation** Suggest that students experiment with various readings to find the most effective pitch, tempo, volume, and pace. Ask them to recopy the speech in large, readable letters and to make notations as to which places require pauses or emphasis.

5. **Critical Thinking/Speaking** Encourage students to consider the witnesses carefully. Possibilities include Banquo's ghost, one of the witches, the gentlewoman who attends Lady Macbeth, the doctor, or Seyton. Suggest that the two teams work together at first so that they will be aware of and able to respond to all the evidence the other side will present.

Writer's Notebook
1. Collecting Ideas for a Cause-Effect Essay

WORK IN PROGRESS

With cause and effect, we often work backward: We are first aware of the effect and then we search for the cause(s). For Thomas De Quincey, the porter scene in *Macbeth* produced a certain effect, "a peculiar awfulness and a depth of solemnity." In his essay (page 330), he explores the cause of this increased tension. What scenes in *Macbeth* had a strong emotional effect on you? Go back to the play and find the words and actions that caused this effect. Save your work for the Writer's Workshop on page 459.

Critical Writing
2. Monster or Not?

Lady Macbeth is sometimes regarded as a monster, ruthlessly ambitious and fiendishly cruel. What clues can you find in the play suggesting that Shakespeare did not want us to judge her so severely? In an essay, analyze her character as it is revealed through her words and actions and her relationship with Macbeth.

Critical Writing
3. Probing Shakespeare's Mind

When Macbeth discovers how Macduff entered the world (Act V, Scene 8), he also discovers that the witches are "juggling fiends" who have given him a false sense of security. Why do you think Shakespeare shows Macbeth taken in by their prophecies? What might Shakespeare be implying about Macbeth's character? about the witches' powers? Write your answer in one or two paragraphs.

Creative Writing
4. Macbeth Today

Rewrite the banquet scene (Act III, Scene 4), when Macbeth sees Banquo's ghost. In your revision, change the setting to a modern time and place, and let the characters speak in today's language. For example, Lady Macbeth might explain to the other banquet guests that Macbeth is suffering from stress or burnout. Describe your setting in your stage directions before you begin writing the scene. If you change characters to make them more modern (the Scottish lords might be cabinet members or board members, for example), provide a list of characters that includes a phrase describing each character.

Oral Interpretation
5. Say the Soliloquy

With a small group, select one of Macbeth's soliloquies and "perform" it in the way a choir interprets a song: Vary voice pitches, volume, tempo, rhythm, meter, and tone. Repeat key lines as a refrain, and use echoing words, vocal sound effects, harmony, and chanting to accentuate and enhance the words.

Critical Thinking / Speaking
6. For the Defense

Imagine that Macbeth, instead of being killed, is brought to trial by a jury of his peers. Plan both a prosecution and a defense, with various class members taking the parts of Macbeth, at least four witnesses (two for each side), and lawyers for both sides. Examine and cross-examine all witnesses, who must remain true to the facts of the play in their responses. Have both sides present closing arguments, and use classmates as jurors.

Art
7. Bringing the Scene to Life

Sketch the set and costumes you would provide for at least one scene of *Macbeth*. In set design, you must indicate placement of furniture and describe lighting. Costume sketches must describe materials and colors.

PORTFOLIO ASSESSMENT

Choices: Assessment Criteria For help in evaluating these Choices assignments, see the criteria in the the *Portfolio Management System,* pp. 101–102.

OPTIONS FOR TEACHING

STRATEGIES FOR INCLUSION

Linguistic/Advanced Some students may want to take activity #3 beyond a one or two paragraph exploration. In addition to suggesting that they study Macbeth's speeches, have students read an account of the trial of the Jesuit priest Henry Garnett for his part in the Gunpowder Plot, focusing on the subject of equivocation. With this background, they will be further able to analyze some of Macbeth's speeches (notably Act II, Scene 3, ll. 85–90, and Act III, Scene 4, ll. 50–51) with greater understanding and come to a better understanding of the porter's speech as well.

HOW TO OWN A WORD

Mapping: Increasing Your Vocabulary

If you draw on your own personal knowledge and experience when learning a new word, the word more readily becomes a part of your working vocabulary. **Mapping** is a vocabulary-building strategy that encourages active participation. Mapping works like this: First, you see a new word used in a sentence. Before you look up the dictionary definition, you guess the word's meaning. After you look the word up in the dictionary, you use the word in a sentence of your own and become familiar with its different forms. Here's an example of mapping:

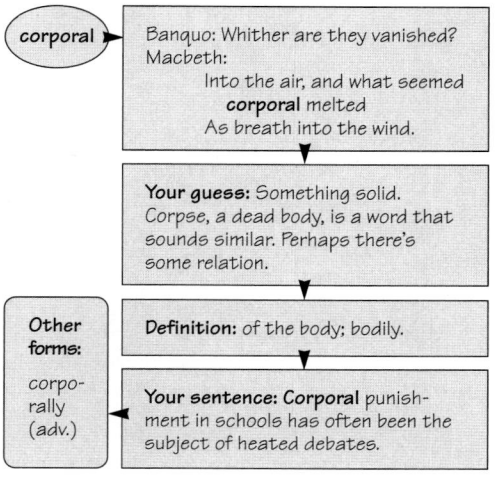

Here are some helpful suggestions for using mapping as one of your vocabulary-building strategies:

1. Scan your memory banks to remember if you've heard the word before. Maybe you've heard a word that sounds similar to it.
2. Are there any clues in the sentence? In the example above, Macbeth seems surprised that something corporal could suddenly vanish into thin air. What does that suggest about the word's meaning?
3. Try substituting your guess for the word. Does it make sense in the context?

4. When you look up the word in the dictionary, make sure you read all the definitions. Select the one that fits best; make sure that it's the right part of speech. *Corporal,* for example, can also refer to an officer in the army. But that definition doesn't work here, and, besides, it's a noun. You're looking for an adjective in this context.
5. Think about the other forms of the word for a few moments. You might also want to use them in some sentences.

Try It Out

In each sentence below, the vocabulary word is given in boldface. Using the mapping example for the word *corporal* as a guide, draw your own map for each of the following words.

1. **Macbeth.** . . . Thou sure and firm-set earth,
   Hear not my steps, which way they walk, for fear
   Thy very stones **prate** of my whereabout,
   And take the present horror from the time,
   Which now suits with it.
   —Act II, Scene 1, lines 56–60

2. **Lady Macbeth. Infirm** of purpose!
   Give me the daggers. The sleeping and the dead
   Are but as pictures. 'Tis the eye of childhood
   That fears a painted devil.
   —Act II, Scene 2, lines 51–54

3. **Macbeth.** . . .Will all great Neptune's ocean wash this blood
   Clean from my hand? No; this my hand will rather
   The **multitudinous** seas incarnadine,
   Making the green one red.
   —Act II, Scene 2, lines 59–62

4. **Macduff.** Confusion now hath made his masterpiece.
   Most **sacrilegious** murder hath broke ope
   The Lord's anointed temple, and stole thence
   The life o' th' building.
   —Act II, Scene 3, lines 60–63

How to Own a Word
Mini-Lesson: Mapping

Begin by having a class discussion about how students know when it is time to look up a word. Encourage students to share their own criteria for stopping the reading process and turning to an outside source for help. Discuss the benefits and problems caused by interrupting reading. Model on the chalkboard the mapping process explained in the text.

Try It Out

As students prepare to do the Try It Out exercises, explain that, when they work with antiquated words, the sentences they create may sound stiff or affected; words like *prate* may not fit smoothly into a modern English sentence. Because these unfamiliar and antiquated words may be difficult for some students to use easily, have students work in pairs so they can concentrate on the concept of mapping. Students may not be able to find other forms for some of the words.

PROGRAM MANAGER

Reinforcement To allow students practice and reinforcement of the vocabulary strategy introduced in this collection, see **Transparency** 4.3 in the *Audiovisual Resources Binder.*

STRATEGIES FOR INCLUSION

Visual Some students may wish to include a pictorial element in their word mapping, associating an image with each word.

Advanced/Linguistic Suggest that some students include other information, such as etymologies, in their maps.

English Language Development Students may benefit by including a translation of the word or a list of related words in their first language.

WORLD LITERATURE

Italy

Dante Alighieri

(1265–1321)

Dante Alighieri (dän'tā a'lə·gyer'ē) decided to write his masterpiece, *The Divine Comedy,* in Italian rather than in Latin, and thus became the father of Italian literature. Dante was born in Florence, but his involvement in the violent politics of his city led to his banishment for life—Dante was warned that he would be burned at the stake if he were ever found in Florence again.

The Divine Comedy, completed during Dante's exile, is the supreme and culminating work of medieval thought. Many people consider this complex, symbolic poem to be the greatest poem ever written in any language. In three sections, Dante tells of an imaginary journey that takes him through Hell, Purgatory, and Heaven. In the course of his journey, Dante gives expression to nearly every major intellectual conception achieved in the Middle Ages.

Dante and His Poems (detail) (1645) by Domenic di Micheloni. Duomo, Florence.

(Map) Old map showing the Mediterranean Coast.

BEFORE YOU READ
FROM THE INFERNO OF DANTE

Background

If you had to name the three most evil people of all time, who would be on your list? The sinner at the pit of Hell in Dante's *Inferno* is Judas Iscariot, who suffers the greatest torment of all because he betrayed Jesus Christ to the Romans. The other two "worst" sinners whom Dante puts in the very jaws of Satan may come as a surprise— although you have probably met them in Shakespeare: Brutus and Cassius, the conspirators of ancient Rome who plotted the assassination of Julius Caesar. Another surprise is Dante's description of the worst part of Hell: Instead of a burning pit of fire and brimstone, the bottom of Hell is a ghastly, windswept lake of ice.

Dante's journey to Hell takes place in the first part of his long epic poem, *The Divine Comedy.* (The epic is a comedy in the sense that it has a happy ending.) Led by the poet Virgil, who, for Dante, symbolized human reason, Dante travels to the Inferno down through a kind of deep funnel that bores into the center of the earth. Around this abysmal cavity run nine ledges, or circles, which grow ever narrower as the cavity bores deeper into the earth. On each circle a certain kind of sin is punished. The sins of the flesh are on the upper circle, where punishment is mildest. Sins of anger are in the middle, and sins against reason are on the lowest circles, where torment is greatest.

Dante in the Valley of Terrors (late 19th to early 20th century) by William Frank Calderon.

From the Inferno, Dante ascends gradually through Purgatory. Then Virgil turns his traveler over to a woman named Beatrice ("blessed") who leads Dante into Paradise, where he is granted a blissful vision of God and salvation. What Dante learns of sin from visiting the agonies of Hell, of renunciation in witnessing the trials in Purgatory, and of joy in sharing the glories of Paradise will turn him from error forever.

As this part of *The Inferno* opens, Dante and his guide approach the last circle of Hell. It is dominated by the gigantic winged figure of Satan, frozen in ice.

Quickwrite

How do you envision Hell? In your Reader's Log, freewrite a description of what you think Hell might be like.

DANTE ALIGHIERI **393**

Background

Dante's concept of various levels or circles of punishment somewhat parallels a theory known as the Great Chain of Being, popular during the Renaissance. This theory espoused, among other things, the idea that the universe was an infinite series of tiers. According to this principle, existence ranges from the basest, or lowest, to the most perfect, which is God.

Quickwrite

Remind students to choose an image they would not mind sharing. Tell students that if they do not believe in Hell, they may create a description based on what they know of others' beliefs or what they imagine a place of punishment would be like. You may wish to allow students to illustrate their descriptions.

A. Expansion

In the complete work from which this selection is taken, Dante explains that the Ninth Circle has several rings. The First Ring contains "Betrayers of Relatives"; the Second Ring, "Betrayers of their Country"; Third Ring, "Betrayers of Guests"; and Fourth Ring, "Betrayers of the Redeemer and Emperor." The Ninth Circle is the place for those who commit "Sins of Fraud which Break Special Obligations." In which ring would you place Macbeth, and why? [Possible responses: Macbeth fits appropriately in all four rings. Macbeth in essence defrauds the country of its rightful ruler and betrays friends in the process.]

B. Critical Reading: Making Connections

? What line in *Macbeth* refers to Satan's beauty before he rebelled against God? According to Dante's model, what did the highest angel become? ["Angels are bright still, though the brightest fell" (Act IV, Scene 3, l. 22). Possible answer: The devil; the source of all evil.]

from The Inferno of Dante

Dante Alighieri
translated by **Robert Pinsky**

Ⓐ Canto 34

"And now, *Vexilla regis prodeunt*
    Inferni°—therefore, look," my master said
    As we continued on the long descent,

"And see if you can make him out, ahead."
5   As though, in the exhalation of heavy mist
    Or while night darkened our hemisphere, one spied

A mill—blades turning in the wind, half-lost
    Off in the distance—some structure of that kind
    I seemed to make out now. But at a gust

10 Of wind, there being no other shelter at hand,
    I drew behind my leader's back again.
    By now (and putting it in verse I find

Fear in myself still) I had journeyed down
    To where the shades were covered wholly by ice,°
15   Showing like straw in glass—some lying prone,

And some erect, some with the head toward us,
    And others with the bottoms of the feet;
    Another like a bow, bent feet to face.

When we had traveled forward to the spot
20   From which it pleased my master to have me see
    Ⓑ That creature° whose beauty once had been so great,

He made me stop, and moved from in front of me.
    "Look: here is Dis," he said, "and here is the place
    Where you must arm yourself with the quality

25 Of fortitude." How chilled and faint I was
    On hearing that, you must not ask me, reader—
    I do not write it; words would not suffice:

I neither died, nor kept alive—consider
    With your own wits what I, alike denuded
30   Of death and life, became as I heard my leader.

2. Vexilla regis prodeunt / Inferni: Latin for "The banners of the king of Hell advance." These words perversely echo a well-known Latin hymn.

14. where . . . ice: This is Judecca (jōō·dek′ə), the final division of Cocytus (kō·sīt′əs) and the innermost part of Hell. Judecca is named for Judas Iscariot, who betrayed Jesus.

21. creature: Satan. Dante also calls him by the names Lucifer, Beelzebub, and Dis. Before Satan rebelled against God and was cast down from Heaven, he was an angel of tremendous beauty.

394 THE RENAISSANCE

CONNECTING WITH "UNDER A HAND ACCURSED"

Ask students to discuss the following question: If you assumed that, as Dante states, Satan is the source of all evil, how would that affect your understanding of Macbeth's actions as "under a hand accursed"? [Possible answers: If Satan can make people be evil, then Macbeth may have had no control over his own choices (no free will) because he was cursed (compelled) to do what he did. Believing in Satan might make the witches seem to play a more significant role in Macbeth's actions.]

The emperor of the realm of grief protruded
    From mid-breast up above the surrounding ice.
    A giant's height, and mine, would have provided

    Closer comparison than would the size
35   Of his arm and a giant. Envision the whole
    That is proportionate to parts like these.

    If he was truly once as beautiful
    As he is ugly now, and raised his brows
    Against his Maker—then all sorrow may well

40   Come out of him. How great a marvel it was
    For me to see three faces° on his head:
    In front there was a red one; joined to this,

    Each over the midpoint of a shoulder, he had
    Two others—all three joining at the crown.
45   That on the right appeared to be a shade

    Of whitish yellow; the third had such a mien
    As those who come from where the Nile descends.
    Two wings spread forth from under each face's chin,

    Strong, and befitting such a bird, immense—
50   I have never seen at sea so broad a sail—
    Unfeathered, batlike, and issuing three winds

    That went forth as he beat them, to freeze the whole
    Realm of Cocytus that surrounded him.
    He wept with all six eyes, and the tears fell

55   Over his three chins mingled with bloody foam.
    The teeth of each mouth held a sinner, kept
    As by a flax rake: thus he held three of them

    In agony. For the one the front mouth gripped,
    The teeth were as nothing to the claws, which sliced
60   And tore the skin until his back was stripped.

    "That soul," my master said, "who suffers most,
    Is Judas Iscariot; head locked inside,
    He flails his legs. Of the other two, who twist

    With their heads down, the black mouth holds the shade
65   Of Brutus: writhing, but not a word will he scream;
    Cassius is the sinewy one on the other side.

41. three faces: grotesque perversion of the Trinity.

Inscription over Hell Gate (late 18th to early 19th century) by William Blake.
Tate Gallery, London.

DANTE ALIGHIERI 395

A. Literary Element: Figure of Speech

? How might Virgil's words apply to more than the task at hand? [Possible answer: He is talking about climbing up the legs of Satan but also about the difficulty of turning away from evil in general.]

RESPONDING TO THE ART: ABOUT THE ARTIST

Pieter Bruegel (1525/30–1569) is considered the greatest Dutch painter of his time. He depicted political and social satire, allegory, and Biblical subjects. His paintings, with titles such as *The Blind Leading the Blind, Avarice,* and *Triumph of Death* (featured here), seem to indicate that Bruegel had a pessimistic and tragic view of humanity. In *Triumph of Death,* covetousness, the root of all other sins, stands out and leaves man, a stupid and cruel beast, to be punished by death.

But night is rising again, and it is time
    That we depart, for we have seen the whole."
    As he requested, I put my arms round him,

70 And waiting until the wings were opened full
    He took advantage of the time and place
    And grasped the shaggy flank, and gripping still,

From tuft to tuft descended through the mass
    Of matted hair and crusts of ice. And then,
75   When we had reached the pivot of the thighs,°

Just where the haunch is at its thickest, with strain
    And effort my master brought around his head
    To where he'd had his legs: and from there on

He grappled the hair as someone climbing would—
80   So I supposed we were heading back to Hell.
    "Cling tight, for it is stairs like these," he sighed

75. pivot of the thighs: This midpoint of Satan's body is also the center of the earth. At this spot Virgil turns himself upside down because henceforth the travelers must journey *up* Satan's legs in order to reach the surface of the Southern Hemisphere.

The Triumph of Death (c. 1562) by Pieter Bruegel the Elder. Oil on panel. Prado, Madrid.

OPTIONS FOR TEACHING

CROSSING THE CURRICULUM

Social Sciences Have students research the Great Chain of Being, the concept of natural hierarchy popular during the Renaissance. Ask students to illustrate a poster showing the levels suggested by this theory compared to the levels in Dante's epic poem. Students should share their posters with the class.

Art Have students create a diorama of the innermost circle of Hell. Ask them to base their artwork on details given in the reading.

Like one who is exhausted, "which we must scale
　　To part from so much evil." Then he came up
　　Through a split stone, and placed me on its sill,

85　And climbed up toward me with his cautious step.
　　I raised my eyes, expecting I would see
　　Lucifer as I left him—and saw his shape

　　Inverted, with his legs held upward. May they
　　Who are too dull to see what point I had passed
90　Judge whether it perplexed me. "Come—the way

　　Is long, the road remaining to be crossed
　　Is hard: rise to your feet," the master said,
　　"The sun is at mid-tierce."° We had come to rest

　　In nothing like a palace hall; instead
95　A kind of natural dungeon enveloped us,
　　With barely any light, the floor ill made.

　　"Before I free myself from the abyss,
　　My master," I said when I was on my feet,
　　"Speak, and dispel my error: where is the ice?

100　And how can he be fixed head-down like that?
　　And in so short a time, how can it be
　　Possible for the sun to make its transit

　　From evening to morning?" He answered me,
　　"You imagine you are still on the other side,
105　Across the center of the earth, where I

　　Grappled the hair on the evil serpent's hide
　　Who pierces the world. And all through my descent,
　　You were on that side; when I turned my head

　　And legs about, you passed the central point
110　To which is drawn, from every side, all weight.
　　Now you are on the opposite continent

　　Beneath the opposite hemisphere to that
　　Which canopies the great dry land therein:
　　Under the zenith of that one is the site

115　Whereon the Man was slain° who without sin
　　Was born and lived; your feet this minute press
　　Upon a little sphere whose rounded skin

93. mid-tierce: Formerly, tierce was the period from 6:00 to 9:00 A.M. (the first third of the day), so mid-tierce is about 7:30 A.M. In Hell, the sun is never consulted in telling time, but now that Dante and Virgil have emerged from Hell, the sun is used for that purpose.

115. Under the zenith . . . slain: Under the zenith, or highest point, of the Northern Hemisphere's sky—a point reached directly through the earth and thus "opposite" where Dante and Virgil now stand—is the city of Jerusalem, the site where Jesus Christ, "the Man," was slain.

DANTE ALIGHIERI 397

B. Critical Reading: Comparing and Contrasting

? How does Virgil characterize each hemisphere for Dante? [Possible answer: One realm is identified with Satan, the source of evil, the other with Jesus Christ, the son of God and source of all good.]

PROFESSIONAL NOTES

Technology Tip You might find useful materials at the ILTweb Digital Dante Project, an on-line multimedia translation of *The Divine Comedy* developed by the Institute for Learning Technologies at Columbia University. The URL is **http://www.ilt.columbia.edu/projects/dante/index.html**. *You may want to preview any internet activity that you suggest to students. Because these resources are sometimes public forums, their content can be unpredictable.*

In Dante's symbolism, souls ascending the mountain of Purgatory were washed free from the memory of sin by Lethe.

Finding Common Ground

- Discuss the situations of Judas, Brutus, and Cassius, and pinpoint their common errors. Ask students what they think Dante means by "sin."
- Ask students to consider the following questions: What type of "sins" does Macbeth commit? How are his "sins" similar to those of Judas and Cassius? How would Dante categorize Macbeth, and what punishment might he allot to Macbeth?
- *Remind students to choose a situation they would not mind sharing.* Ask students to consider how someone feels when he or she is really frightened, and then have them describe those emotions. Point out that often we intend to react a certain way but cannot when actually facing something fearful. Perhaps Dante's description here means he is terrified into inaction—he is conscious but unable to move, think, or act.
- *Remind students to choose a situation they would not mind sharing.* Allow students to work in pairs to brainstorm the "sins" they feel are prevalent today. Require that they explain how they have devised the punishments appropriate to each crime, reminding them to refer to Dante's hierarchy to decide which "sins" are worst.

Forms the Judecca's other, outward face.
    Here it is morning when it is evening there;
120   The one whose hair was like a ladder for us

Is still positioned as he was before.
    On this side he fell down from Heaven; the earth,
    Which till then stood out here, impelled by fear

Veiled itself in the sea and issued forth
125   In our own hemisphere. And possibly,
    What now appears on this side° fled its berth

And rushing upward left a cavity:
    This hollow where we stand." There is below,
    As far from Beelzebub as one can be

130 Within his tomb, a place one cannot know
    By sight, but by the sound a little runnel°
    Makes as it wends the hollow rock its flow

Has worn, descending through its winding channel:
    To get back up to the shining world from there
135   My guide and I went into that hidden tunnel;

And following its path, we took no care
    To rest, but climbed: he first, then I—so far,
    Through a round aperture I saw appear

Some of the beautiful things that Heaven bears,
140 Where we came forth, and once more saw the stars.°

126. What now appears on this side: The island of Mount Purgatory, the pinnacle at which a sinner makes a total renunciation of sin, is apparently formed out of the inner earth displaced by Lucifer's fall. Climbing this peak will be the next leg of Dante's journey.

131. runnel: stream. This rivulet may derive from the river Lethe, the river of forgetfulness in classical mythology.

140. stars: As he does in the *Purgatorio* and *Paradiso,* Dante ends the *Inferno* with the word "stars," which are, for him, symbols of hope toward which the soul constantly moves. The time—just before dawn on Easter morning—is also symbolic of hope.

FINDING COMMON GROUND

Evil has fascinated artists and poets of every age. Certainly, of the three sections of *The Divine Comedy,* Hell is by far the most fascinating place—for readers, that is. Discuss Dante's particular vision of Hell with other students, and see if you can arrive at a consensus on this question: "What acts deserve the worst torments of Hell?" (Review your Reader's Log entry before you begin.)

- What do you think Judas, Brutus, and Cassius may have in common? What sins did all three commit?
- Brutus and Cassius have leading roles in Shakespeare's *Julius Caesar,* but Dante clearly did not regard them as heroes (and neither did Shakespeare). What do you think Dante's attitude would have been toward Shakespeare's Macbeth? Do you think Macbeth would have occupied a

place in Dante's Hell? Cite support from the play to explain your answer.

- In a memorable line, Dante describes his terror in the lowest depths of Hell by saying "I neither died, nor kept alive" (line 28). What do you think he means in this verse? Why would such a fate be especially terrifying?
- Dante carefully classified sin and assigned various levels of Hell to specific sins. The punishments he meted out to the sinners often peculiarly suited their offenses. Suppose Dante were writing today: What categories of "sin" would he find especially prevalent in the modern world? Keep in mind the kinds of sins he felt merited the worst punishment. What kinds of punishments would be especially suitable for the offenders?

398 THE RENAISSANCE

Check Test: True-False

1. The first thing Dante notices about Hell is that it is unbearably hot. [False]
2. Dis is another name for Satan. [True]
3. Brutus and Macbeth were in Satan's mouths. [False]
4. Virgil helps Dante climb up Satan's legs. [True]
5. According to this tale, Lucifer was once an angel. [True]

Self-Reflection: Reading Ask students to rate their reading in each of the following areas.

1. Amount of attention paid while reading.

Great				Little
5	4	3	2	1

2. Effort made to predict events while reading.

Great				Little
5	4	3	2	1

3. Effort made to understand the narrative.

Great				Little
5	4	3	2	1

The English Language

Shakespeare's Language
by John Algeo

Shakespeare's language is an early form of Modern English, basically the same kind of English we speak. But we need glosses, or explanations, for some words and phrases because English has changed during the past four hundred years.

Speaking the Speech: Shakespeare's Pronunciation

The actors who pronounced Shakespeare's lines on the stage of the Globe Theater would not have sounded like modern actors, American or British. We need not be concerned with the details of their pronunciation, but some differences are obvious even from the written text of the plays. For example, Shakespeare's contemporaries, like English speakers today, used a great many contractions. But they contracted words in different ways than we do.

Shakespeare liked to contract the pronouns that begin with vowels (*us* and *it*), as the following examples show:

. . . we / Shall take upon's what else remains to do . . .

. . . To mend it, or be rid on't [of it].

. . . for't must be done to-night.

What is't that moves your Highness?

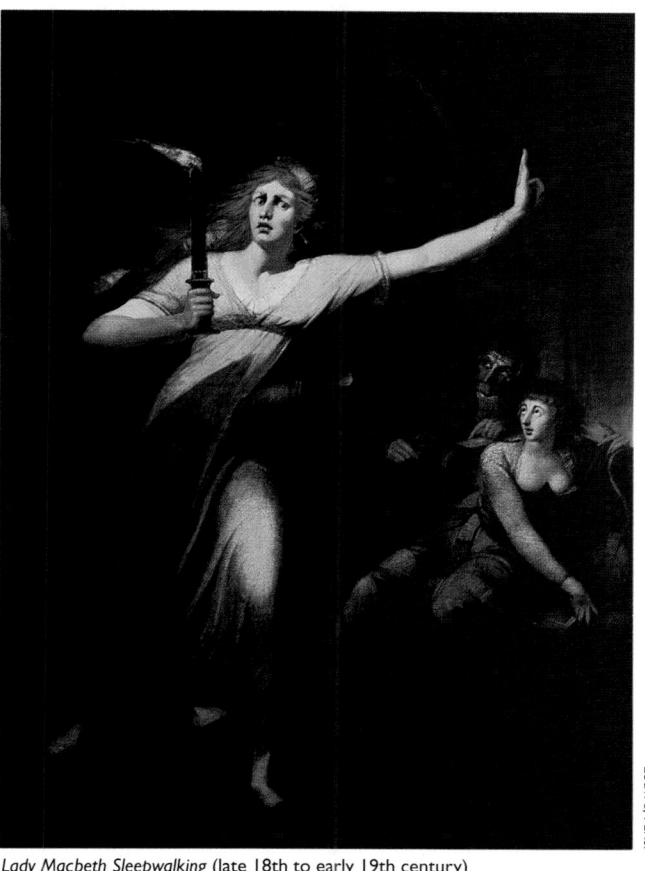

Lady Macbeth Sleepwalking (late 18th to early 19th century) by Henry Fuseli.

Shakespeare also frequently omitted unstressed syllables from the middle of words (as we still do in words like *fam'ly*):

. . . o'er the rest . . .

. . . will these hands ne'er be clean?

. . . my near'st [nearest] of life . . .

Thou marvel'st at my words . . .

Louvre, Paris.

RESPONDING TO THE ART: ABOUT THE ARTIST

Henry Fuseli (1741–1825), a painter born in Zurich, was elected Royal Academician at the Royal Academy of Arts in London in 1790. There, commissioned by the publisher John Boydell, Fuseli painted eight illustrations of various Shakespearean plays for a book of engravings entitled *Shakespeare Gallery*. For *Macbeth,* a play that appealed strongly to Fuseli's imagination, he included this illustration of Lady Macbeth sleepwalking. The forlorn and bewitched expression on her face, the wind mysteriously blowing her hair and her taper, and the unnatural shine on her body contribute to the scene's eeriness.

A. Expansion

Nowadays, we especially favor the contraction of *not* into *n't,* as in "She isn't"; and the contraction of verbs, as in "She's here," "They've gone," and "We'll try," where *'s, 've,* and *'ll* represent *is, have,* and *will,* respectively.

OPTIONS FOR TEACHING

STRATEGIES FOR INCLUSION

Linguistic Although today's English has only one form of the pronoun *you,* invite students to research various languages that do have different forms of *you.* Ask students to share their findings about how and when each form of *you* is used.

Musical Have students find examples of songs we listen to today that employ contractions, accents, or unusual word order to maintain a certain rhythm or emphasis. Ask them to share their findings with the class.

PROGRAM MANAGER

- **Assessment** See The English Language, *Test Booklet,* pp. 67–68.
- **Planning Instruction** See Teaching Resources A, p. 92, for objectives for this selection.

A. Language Note: Pronouns

Students may also have noticed Shakespeare's use of the pronoun *it* for humans, instead of personal pronouns such as *he, she,* or *who.*

B. Humanities Connection

Ask students to give examples from Spanish, French, and other modern languages that still distinguish an intimate *you* from a formal *you.* [Possible responses: *Tu* and *vous* in French or *tú* and *usted* in Spanish.]

Elements of Literature: Videodisc Use these bar codes to locate the video segment about the development of the English language from the Anglo-Saxons to the Renaissance. For more information, see the Videodisc *Teacher's Manual.*

Videodisc Side A

Begin Play, English Track

Begin Play, Spanish Track

A whole syllable could be omitted from the beginning of a word if it was unstressed (as in the use of *'cause* for *because,* an omission we still make today):

> . . . 'cause he fail'd . . .
>
> Point against point, rebellious arm 'gainst arm . . .
>
> . . . 'Twixt this and supper.
>
> . . . if he 'scape . . .
>
> I 'gin to be aweary of the sun . . .

Some of Shakespeare's words are stressed on different syllables from those we would now accent. For example, in "Stop up th' access and passage to remorse," the iambic rhythm of the line shows us that Shakespeare pronounced "acCESS," rather than "ACcess," as we would.

Other words have changed their forms in various ways since Shakespeare's day. In *Macbeth,* we find *murther* for *murder, afeard* for *afraid, aweary* for *weary,* and *alarum* for *alarm.*

Shakespeare's Grammar

Although Shakespeare's grammar is essentially the same as ours, it differs in numerous minor ways.

Shakespeare could use *which* where we use *who* to refer to a person: ". . . the slave / Which ne'er shook hands." He could also use *the which,* especially with broad or unstated antecedents: "He only liv'd but till he was a man; / The which [his manhood] no sooner had his prowess confirm'd, . . . / But like a man he died." Shakespeare could also use the pronoun *who* in an indefinite sense, for which

we use *the one who:* "Who was the thane, lives yet."

In present-day English, we use *mine* as a pronoun and *my* to modify a noun: "It's mine" but "It's my book." Shakespeare used both forms to modify nouns: *mine* before words beginning with a vowel, and *my* before words beginning with a consonant, just as we use *an* and *a* today ("an orange," "a lemon"): "Ha! they pluck out *mine* eyes. / Will all great Neptune's ocean wash this blood / Clean from *my* hand?"

Today, we generally use only a single pronoun for the person or people we talk to: *you* (with its possessives *your* and *yours*). Shakespeare had a choice between *th-* forms (*thou, thee, thy, thine*) and *y-* forms (*ye, you, your, yours*). *Thou* and *ye* were subject forms, like *I; thee* and *you* were object forms, like *me.*

Th- forms were used in talking to one person with whom the speaker was intimate (wife, husband, bosom buddy) or to whom the speaker was socially superior (child, servant, subject). *Y-* forms were used in talking to several persons, or to one person who was a social equal but not an intimate friend, or who was a superior (parent, boss, king). In the singular, *th-* forms showed intimacy or superiority; *y-* forms showed equality or servility.

Shakespeare made careful use of the different connotations of *th-* and *y-* forms. When Macbeth and Banquo meet the weird sisters (Act I, Scene 3), they ad-

dress the witches with *y-* forms because the two soldiers are in awe of these supernatural women; the witches, however, use *th-* forms for Macbeth and Banquo, thereby asserting their superiority over the mere mortals.

Macbeth and Banquo normally address one another with *y-* forms because, though equals, they are not intimates. At the beginning of Act III, however, when Banquo is thinking about the foul deeds that Macbeth has obviously used to come to the throne, he uses *th-* forms for Macbeth, since he regards Macbeth's murderous actions as having made a moral inferior of him. Banquo can think what he wants, but when Macbeth actually appears, Banquo addresses him with *y-* forms again. For Banquo to have called King Macbeth *thou* to his face would have been an insulting breach of etiquette.

The verb in Shakespeare's day had a special ending, *−st,* to go with *thou* as a subject, thus: "thou know'st," "thou didst," and "thou hast." It also had an alternative ending, *−th,* for the third-person singular ending, *−s,* that we still use today. Shakespeare could use "he knows" or "knoweth," "he does" or "doth," and "he has" or "hath." The two forms meant the same thing, although the *−s* ending was more common, and the *−th* probably sounded rather formal or old-fashioned even in Shakespeare's day. Sometimes Shakespeare used the two together—"The

> In some respects, Shakespeare's vocabulary was more complex than ours.

OPTIONS FOR TEACHING

INTEGRATING THE LANGUAGE ARTS

Strategic Reading Before they read this essay by John Algeo, ask students to record their observations about Shakespeare's use of language on a chart like the following. Then, as they read about Early Modern English, have them record in the second column any explanations given in the essay that correspond to their observations:

Observations	Reasons Given
[letter omitted—*th'*]	[to maintain meter]
[*mine* in place of *my*]	[was once proper]

Writing: Eulogy Invite students to write a eulogy for Macbeth in Shakespearean English. Have them work in small groups to develop several lines of blank verse using some of the language devices that this essay explains. They should pay attention to diction, dropped syllables,

contractions, pronoun and verb forms, and helping verb forms. Give volunteers an opportunity to read their poetry to the class.

Speaking and Listening Have students work in pairs, taking turns reading aloud and then rephrasing some of the examples Algeo gives. Have one student select a line in Shakespearean English, and ask the listener to translate the phrase into informal Modern English.

earth hath bubbles, as the water has"—with no apparent difference in meaning.

Shakespeare could omit the helping verb *do* in questions and negative sentences where we must have it: **C**

Live you? [Do you live?]

Ride you this afternoon? [Do you ride this afternoon?]

Fail not our feast. [Don't fail (to be at) our feast.]

He loves us not. [He doesn't love us.]

On the other hand, Shakespeare could use an unstressed *do* where we cannot: **D**

. . . swimmers, that do cling together . . .

. . . such things here as we do speak about . . .

His wonders and his praises do contend . . .

. . . the earth / Was feverous, and did shake.

Shakespeare had a wider choice of past participles than we do in standard English today, although some of Shakespeare's forms have survived even today in nonstandard speech:

I have spoke. [for *spoken*]

And his great love . . . hath holp him. [for *has helped*]

Shakespeare could use forms of *be* instead of *have* to make a perfect tense of verbs indicating motion: "They *are* not yet *come* back."

Where we would say "Come on, *let's go* to the king," Shakespeare has simply "Come, *go we* to the King." Shakespeare's *go we* is an old first-person com-

mand that is more direct than the *let's go* form we now prefer.

In both Shakespeare's English and ours, noun phrases may consist of a determiner (like *the, a, my*), an adjective, and a noun: *the old house*. However, in short expressions used to address a person, Shakespeare could put the adjective first: "Gentle my Lord" [for "My gentle Lord"] and "Gracious my Lord" [for "My gracious Lord"].

Some of what we consider "mistakes" today are also found in Shakespeare. They are actually old ways of using English that have fallen out of favor in standard English; for example:

There's daggers in men's smiles . . . [There *are* daggers]

Who I myself struck down . . . [*Whom* I myself struck down]

. . . ask'd for who . . . [for *whom*]

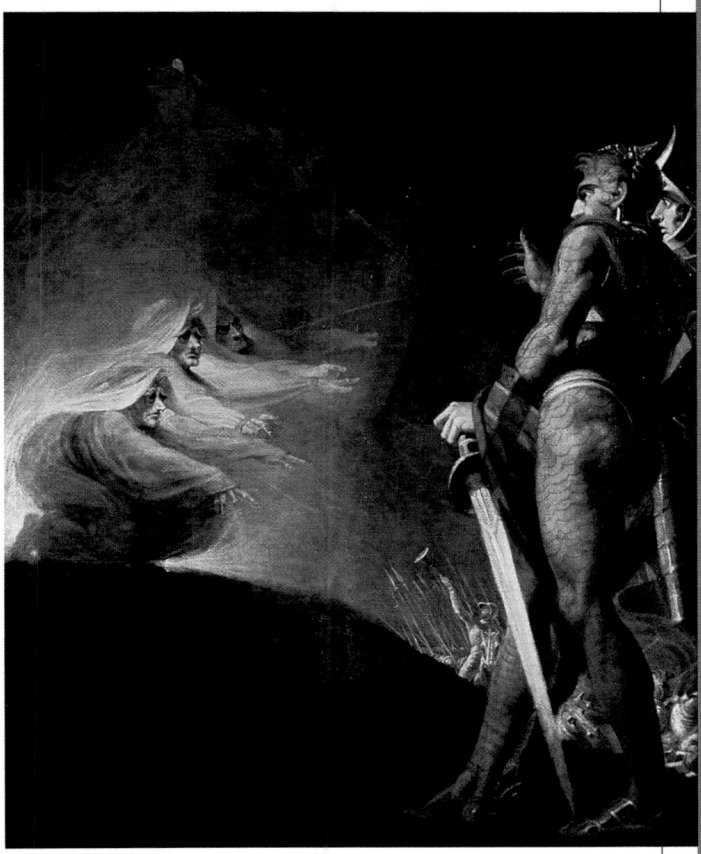

Macbeth and the Witches (late 18th to early 19th century) by Henry Fuseli. Petworth House, Petworth, Sussex, England.

C. Expansion

Today we make a sentence negative by contracting the adverb *not* with the first auxiliary verb, such as in a sentence like "They aren't trying." We make a statement into a question by changing the order of the subject and the first auxiliary verb: "They are trying" to "Are they trying?" If there is no auxiliary verb in the sentence (as in "They try"), we have to add an otherwise meaningless *do* as a filler for negative sentences ("They don't try") and questions ("Do they try?"). Shakespeare did not have to use the filler *do*. He could say "They try not" and "Try they?" which are impossible in our language today when it is spoken formally.

D. Expansion

We cannot use *do* as an auxiliary in unemphatic affirmative statements. We can say "They *do* try" with emphasis on *do* if we want to contradict someone who has suggested that they do not try, but in the United States, it seems stilted to say "They do try" without emphasis on *do*. Shakespeare could and did do this. For him, "They try" and "They do try" (with unstressed *do*) were simply alternative ways of saying the same thing.

A. Expansion

Shakespeare's works contain numerous original phrases familiar today but once fresh from his pen: "It was Greek to me" (*Julius Caesar*); "salad days" (*Anthony and Cleopatra*); "green-ey'd jealousy" (*The Merchant of Venice*); "the crack of doom" (*Macbeth*); and so on. A word like *multitudinous* is a reminder that Shakespeare used one of the largest vocabularies of any English writer—some thirty thousand words. (Estimates vary, but an educated person today probably has a vocabulary of fifteen thousand words.) He was, in his own phrase, "A man of fire-new words." New in the sixteenth century and appearing in his works were *armada, demonstrate, dire, emphasis, prodigious,* and *vast*. Other words that appeared in print for the first time in his First Folio were *accommodation, assassination, dexterously, dislocate, indistinguishable, reliance,* and *submerged*.

Try It Out: Possible Answers

a. Sonnet 73, l. 5, "see'st"
b. Sonnet 116, l. 2, "impediments"; possibly Sonnet 130, l. 5, "damasked"
c. Because this requires judgment calls that students may feel hesitant to make, you may want to answer this question together in class. In Sonnet 116, l. 5, "fixèd" is a certain example because of the accent. Sonnet 73, l. 11, "deathbed," for example, may cause confusion.
d. Sonnet 73, l. 13, "thy"
e. Sonnet 29, l. 10 "thee"; Sonnet 73, l. 14, "thou"
f. Sonnet 73, l. 1, "mayst"; Sonnet 73, l. 13, "perceivest"; Sonnet 73, l. 10, "doth"; Sonnet 73, l. 6, "fadeth"
g. Sonnet 116, l. 11, "Love alters not"
h. Sonnet 73, l. 2, "do hang"
i. Sonnet 116, l. 14, "writ"
j. Sonnet 130, l. 5, "damasked"

Shakespeare's Words

In some respects, Shakespeare's vocabulary was more complex than ours. We commonly use three words for location: *here, there,* and *where*. Shakespeare had nine, because in addition to those three, six others were available that are now rare, if not archaic: *hence, thence, whence* ("from here, from there, from where") and *hither, thither, whither* ("to here, to there, to where"):

> Whence cam'st thou, worthy Thane? [Where did you come from?]

> I will thither. [I will go (to) there.]

> Whither should I fly? [Where should I fly to?]

Shakespeare uses other words that are now rare or obsolete:

> I say sooth . . . [I tell the truth; we still have *sooth* in the form *soothsayer* ("truth teller").]

> This diamond he greets your wife withal [with] . . .

> Send out moe [more] horses. [In Early Modern English, *moe* referred to number, *more* to size.]

In Shakespeare's plays, some of the words that strike us as "fancy" were fancy even when he used them. They were "inkhorn terms"—words borrowed from the classical languages and used for their mouth-filling and impressive sounds, as well as for their subtleties of meaning. Just after he has stabbed King Duncan, Macbeth says that his hand will never be clean again, but will rather

> The multitudinous seas incarnadine . . .

"But the script says, 'Lay on Macduff.'"

He means that the blood on his hands would "make the many seas red," but the word *multitudinous* seems to mean far more than the short word *many*, and the literal meaning of *incarnadine* ("to turn into the blood-red color of raw flesh") is especially appropriate to Macbeth's actions and state of mind. Shakespeare was using fancy words—but for a purpose.

The trickiest words in Shakespeare, however, are those that look familiar but have different meanings than their present-day versions. They are false friends that make us think we understand what the language means, while in fact indicating something different from what we expect. Here are a few examples:

> Sweno, the Norways' king, craves composition [agreement, peace terms] . . . .

> Are ye fantastical [illusory, imaginary], or that indeed / Which outwardly ye show [seem, appear]?

> Say from whence / You owe [own, have] this strange intelligence [information].

Sleep, that knits up [straightens out] the raveled sleave [tangled thread] of care. . . . [The image of reknitting the sleeve of a sweater that has unraveled makes sense, but is wrong.]

Because of differences like these between Shakespeare's English and ours, it takes some effort for us to read his plays and poetry. What we can get from the reading, however, is well worth the effort.

Try It Out

Find an example in Shakespeare's sonnets (pages 225–229) of each of the following:

a. A contraction that we would not use today
b. An "inkhorn term"
c. A word pronounced differently from the way we pronounce it today
d. *Thy* where we would use *your*
e. *Thou, thee,* or *thine* (notice who is talking to whom)
f. The *–th* and *–st* forms of verbs
g. A negative like "They try not" (instead of "They don't try")
h. An unemphatic statement like "They do try" (instead of "They try")
i. An unusual form of a verb (like "I have spoke")
j. A word we no longer have or no longer use with the same meaning

(Opposite) *St. Jerome* (detail) (15th century) by Domenico Ghirlandaio. Chiesa di Ognissanti, Florence.

The Renaissance

Collection 5 THE POWER OF THE WORD

> **Theme:** **Words to Live By**
> In seeking an understanding of the human condition, people have turned to traditional words of wisdom. Whether divinely inspired or not, these words have offered guidance, comfort, and knowledge to readers over hundreds of years.

Thematic Focus

Words can be very effective teachers, providing advice, consolation, or explanation.

- **Of Studies/Axioms** *from the* **Essays**   Sir Francis Bacon offers his observations on various uses of studies.
- *from* **The King James Bible**   These excerpts, offering insights into the nature of humanity, illustrate the eloquence of this version of the Bible.
- **World Literature: Worlds of Wisdom**   These pieces from Africa and Asia suggest how to lead a good life.
- *from* **Paradise Lost**   Satan's choice of evil over good explains the burdens of humanity.

Literary Focus

Literary Element	Selection / Feature
Parallel Structure	**Of Studies**
Imagery	**The King James Bible**
Epic Simile, Syntax, Blank Verse	**Paradise Lost**

Writing Focus

The following flowchart shows how the writing assignment for each selection relates to and builds toward the writing assignment presented in the Writer's Workshop at the end of the unit.

Selection	Work-in-Progress Assignment
Of Studies	Collect ideas on the effects of technology p. 409
The King James Bible	Make notes on the causes and effects of human traits p. 427
Paradise Lost	Make notes on causes of evil p. 450
Writer's Workshop	Write a cause-and-effect essay p. 459

Collection Planner

SELECTION/ FEATURE	Literary Elements / Active Reading	Writing	Speaking and Listening	Language and Vocabulary
Of Studies/Axioms *from the* **Essays** Sir Francis Bacon (pp. 404–409) **Student to Student** (p. 408) Spotlight On: The Example of a Queen: Elizabeth I (pp. 410–412)	• Reader's Log p. 405 • Parallel Structure p. 405	• Critical Writing: Write analysis essay p. 409 • Creative Writing: Write response essay p. 409		
The King James Bible: *from* **Genesis/Psalms 23 and 137/The Parable of the Good Samaritan** (pp. 413–427) **Connections: A Beam of Protons Illuminates Gutenberg's Genius** Malcolm W. Browne (pp. 419–420)	• Reader's Log pp. 415, 422, 423, 425 • Imagery p. 415	• Creative Writing: Write parable p. 427 • Critical Writing: Compare two versions of Psalm 23 p. 427	• Oral Interpretation: Recite psalms p. 427 • Research/Speaking: Present an oral report on Renaissance invention p. 427	
World Literature: Worlds of Wisdom (pp. 428–434)			• Finding Common Ground: Discuss applications of wise insights p. 434	
from **Paradise Lost: The Fall of Satan** John Milton (pp. 435–450) Spotlight On: Allegory: Telling Two Stories at Once (pp. 451–454)	• Reader's Log p. 440 • Epic Simile p. 449 • Blank Verse p. 450	• Critical Writing: Paraphrase excerpt p. 450 • Critical Writing: Write character analysis p. 450 • Creative Writing: Write dramatic dialogue of opening scene p. 450 • Critical Thinking/Art: List images from Milton and Dante p. 450	• Creative Writing: Dramatize opening scene p. 450	• Language and Style: Epic simile, syntax, blank verse pp. 449–450 • How to Own a Word p. 454 • Try It Out: Compare different meanings of the same word p. 454
The English Language: The Growth of Modern English John Algeo (pp. 456–458)				• Try It Out: Compare and modernize language styles p. 458
Writer's Workshop: Speculating About Cause and Effect (pp. 459–463)		• Writing process: Speculating about cause and effect pp. 459–463	• Read essay to class p. 463	
Language Workshop: Effective Transitions (p. 464)		• Revise essay p. 464		
Learning for Life: Modern-Day Renaissance Person (p. 465)		• Write proposal p. 465	• Stage one-person show p. 465	

Collection Resources

Teaching Resources A	Audiovisual Resources Binder	Test Booklet
Cross-Curricular Activity p. 121	Fine Art Transparencies 5.1–5.2	Collection 5 Test pp. 83–84

 Computer disk or CD-ROM

Videodisc

 Audiocassette

 Overhead Transparency

PROGRAM RESOURCES

Electronic Media	Teaching Resources with Organizer		Audiovisual Resources Binder
	Teaching Resources A	Other Resources	
• Test Generator	• Teaching Notes p. 105 • Reading Organizer p. 109	• Test Booklet: Selection Test pp. 71–72 • Portfolio Management System pp. 54–55, 103	
• Test Generator • Language Workshop: Prepositions and Prepositional phrases	• Teaching Notes pp. 106–107 • Reading Organizer pp. 110, 113–115 • Language Link pp. 111–112	• Test Booklet: Selection Tests pp. 73–78 • Language and Writing Skills Worksheets p. 19 • Portfolio Management System pp. 39, 104–105	• Selected Reading, Audiocassette 1, Side B
	• Teaching Notes p. 107		• Selected Reading, Audiocassette 1, Side B
• Test Generator • Language Workshop: Gerunds	• Teaching Notes pp. 107–108 • Reading Organizer p. 116 • Language Link pp. 117–118	• Test Booklet: Selection Test pp. 79–80 • Language and Writing Skills Worksheets p. 74 • Portfolio Management System pp. 43, 106–107	• How to Own a Word Transparency 5.3
• Test Generator • Videodisc, Side A: "English: A Living Language, Part 1"	• Teaching Notes p. 108	• Test Booklet: Selection Test pp. 81–82	
• Writer's Workshop 2: Cause and Effect		• Portfolio Management System pp. 108–110	• Revision Transparencies 5.4–5.5
• Language Workshop: Transitions	• Language Workshop: Transitions pp. 119–120		
		• Portfolio Management System p. 111	

Proofreading Warm-ups

You may use the following exercises to help students practice their proofreading skills. Copy a set of incorrect sentences onto the chalkboard, and have students find and correct the spelling, punctuation, usage, and mechanical errors in each sentence. Ask students to share and discuss their responses.

	Sentences with Errors	Sentences Corrected	Skills Covered
1	**a.** sir francis bacon says that to much studying is lazyness but i disagree **b.** bacons comment is a example of a paradox or seeming contradiction	**a.** Sir Francis Bacon says that too much studying is laziness, but I disagree. **b.** Bacon's comment is an example of a paradox, or seeming contradiction.	Capitalization, Spelling, Comma usage, Apostrophes, Nonstandard usage, End marks
2	**a.** as a young girl Queen Elizabeth's study schedule was quiet rigorous **b.** during her rein Elizabeth was praised by many writer's including Shakespeare for her learning and grace	**a.** As a young girl, Queen Elizabeth had a quite rigorous study schedule. **b.** During her reign, Elizabeth was praised by many writers, including Shakespeare, for her learning and grace.	Capitalization, Comma usage, Dangling modifier, Spelling, Apostrophes, End marks
3	**a.** king Jame's I sponsered a new translation of the bible **b.** the King appointed fifty four clergyman to translate the scriptures	**a.** King James I sponsored a new translation of the Bible. **b.** The king appointed fifty-four clergymen to translate the Scriptures.	Capitalization, Apostrophes, Spelling, Hyphens, Plural nouns, End marks
4	**a.** in english a collection of psalm's are called a psalter **b.** psalm 23 is probably the best known Religious poem in the world	**a.** In English, a collection of psalms is called a psalter. **b.** Psalm 23 is probably the best-known religious poem in the world.	Capitalization, Comma usage, Apostrophes, Subject-verb agreement, Hyphens, End marks
5	**a.** the koran is the holy book of Islam it contains Gods revelation to Mohammed by the angel Gabriel **b.** confucius founder of a chinese philosophicle system left no written works	**a.** The Koran is the holy book of Islam; it contains God's revelation to Mohammed by the angel Gabriel. **b.** Confucius, founder of a Chinese philosophical system, left no written works.	Capitalization, Semicolons, Apostrophes, Comma usage, Spelling, End marks
6	**a.** john miltons famous sonnet On His Blindness was written about his own blindness at fourty-four **b.** milton's daughter's read aloud to him enabling him to continue his study's	**a.** John Milton's famous sonnet "On His Blindness" was written about his own blindness at forty-four. **b.** Milton's daughters read aloud to him, enabling him to continue his studies.	Capitalization, Apostrophes, Quotation marks, Spelling, Comma usage, End marks
7	**a.** to begin a epic a poet does 2 things, invokes the Muse and states the subject of the poem **b.** i find that rather amusing joked Toby with a grin	**a.** To begin an epic, a poet does two things: invokes the Muse and states the subject of the poem. **b.** "I find that rather amusing," joked Toby with a grin.	Capitalization, Nonstandard usage, Comma usage, Write out numbers, Colons, Quotation marks, End marks
8	**a.** miltons Poetic Style included the use of, epic similes **b.** epic smiles allowed Milton to bring alot of material into his epic	**a.** Milton's poetic style included the use of epic similes. **b.** Epic similes allowed Milton to bring a lot of material into his epic.	Capitalization, Apostrophes, Comma usage, Spelling, End marks
9	**a.** a allegory has 2 meanings, a literal meaning and a symbolick one **b.** next to the Bible John Bunyans the Pilgrim's Progress is the most widely read of all english books	**a.** An allegory has two meanings: a literal meaning and a symbolic one. **b.** Next to the Bible, John Bunyan's <u>The Pilgrim's Progress</u> is the most widely read of all English books.	Capitalization, Nonstandard usage, Write out numbers, Colons, Spelling, Comma usage, Apostrophes, Titles, End marks
10	**a.** english speakers of passed centuries was fascinated by grammars of there language intoned Ms. Altizer **b.** us english teachers continue to have that fascination with grammer she added.	**a.** "English speakers of past centuries were fascinated by grammars of their language," intoned Ms. Altizer. **b.** "We English teachers continue to have that fascination with grammar," she added.	Quotation marks, Capitalization, Spelling, Subject-verb agreement, Homonyms, Comma usage, Pronouns, End marks

Collection 5

THE POWER OF THE WORD

Bacon

from The King James Bible

Worlds of Wisdom

Milton

A word is dead
When it is said,
Some say.
I say it just
Begins to live
That day.

—Emily Dickinson

"A word is dead"

? According to Dickinson, what makes a word live and have power? [Possible response: When people use it, speak it, write it, read it, and allow it to move them, the word lives and has the power to shape thought.]

PORTFOLIO ASSESSMENT

Parent/Guardian Involvement For forms that will help a parent or guardian review and respond to a student's portfolio, see the *Portfolio Management System,* pp. 62–63.

PROGRAM MANAGER

- **Integrated Assessment** For a summative assessment of the literature and language skills taught in this collection, see **Collection 5 Test**, *Test Booklet,* pp. 83–84.
- **Instructional Support** See **Fine Art Transparencies** 5.1–5.2. Review teacher's notes for transparencies in the *Audiovisual Resources Binder* for suggestions on how to tie the transparencies to reading selections.
- **Reinforcement** To reinforce the vocabulary strategy introduced in this collection, see **Transparency** 5.3 in the *Audiovisual Resources Binder.*
- **Extending Collection Theme** See **Cross-Curricular Activity: The Power of the Word,** *Teaching Resources A,* p. 121, for an activity in another discipline and for evaluation criteria.

QUICK PLANNING GUIDE

Into the Selections

Author Biography p. 404

Before You Read p. 405

- **Reading Focus: Set a Purpose** Students contrast points of view about the relationship between learning and life.

- **Quickwrite: Prior Knowledge** Write in Reader's Log about why people read

- **Elements of Literature: Parallel Structure**

Through the Selections

"Of Studies" p. 406

"Axioms" p. 407

Student to Student p. 408
"Mind"

Making Meanings p. 409

Beyond the Selections

Choices: Building Your Portfolio p. 409

- **Writer's Notebook:** Collect ideas for an essay on the effects of technology

- **Critical Writing:** Write a short essay about Bacon's view of pretense

- **Creative Writing:** Write an essay agreeing or disagreeing with Bacon

Spotlight On pp. 410–412

Sir Francis Bacon

(1561–1626)

Sir Francis Bacon, Viscount of St. Albans (detail) (late 16th to early 17th century) by Paul van Somer. Oil.
Private Collection.

From his earliest days, Francis Bacon knew that he was an important person. When he was about nine, Queen Elizabeth asked him how old he was, and he is said to have replied, "Two years younger than your Majesty's happy reign." A boy who speaks like this will go far, and Bacon went far. He rose in his chosen profession, the law, until he reached the very top and became Lord Chancellor of England and lord keeper of the great seal, an office that his father, Sir Nicholas Bacon, had also held. He was elevated to the peerage, the British nobility who could govern as members of the House of Lords, and he amassed a large fortune, though he was often in debt because of his extravagant lifestyle. At the height of his political career, he was found guilty of taking bribes and banished to his country estate, where he devoted himself full time to thinking and writing about new ways to discover knowledge.

Bacon once wrote a now-famous letter to his uncle, Lord Burghley, Elizabeth's secretary of state, in which he said, "I have taken all knowledge to be my province." Of course, he did not master all knowledge, but he did make important contributions to many different branches of knowledge: political science, economics, biology, physics, music, architecture, botany, constitutional law, industrial development, philosophy, religious thought, mythology, astronomy, chemistry, landscape gardening, and literature.

But he is most famous for his vision of humanity's future, when knowledge would be based on verifiable experimentation, and science would be separate from theology.

Bacon's best-known literary works, the *Essays,* are intended to help people get ahead in life. Bacon was the first Englishman to use the word *essay* to designate a brief discourse in prose. He took the word from the French writer Montaigne (män·tän′). But, whereas Montaigne's delightful *essais* are mainly about a fascinating person, Montaigne himself, Bacon writes instead about humanity in general.

Bacon had embarked on a new career as a practicing scientist when death overtook him. One wintry day, he descended from his carriage carrying a dead chicken, to freeze it in the snow and thereby test the preservative powers of cold. Today this seems like a painfully obvious thing to do, but nobody had tried it in a systematic way before 1626. Suddenly, in the midst of the experiment, Bacon took a chill. His servants carried him into nearby Highgate, the house of the earl of Arundel. In poor health most of his life, Bacon died there of complications resulting from exposure.

In all his works, Bacon's aim was to make the world better. As the destroyer of old Aristotelian ways of thinking and as the stimulator of "modern" ones, Bacon has no equal.

PROGRAM MANAGER

- **Planning Instruction** See Teaching Notes, *Teaching Resources A,* p. 105, for objectives, a summary, literary elements, and additional biographical information for the selections.

- **Instructional Support** Before beginning the instructional lesson, see Graphic Organizer for Active Reading, *Teaching Resources A,* p. 109, for an Into the Selection activity.

- **Assessment** See Selection Test, *Test Booklet,* pp. 71–72.

BEFORE YOU READ

OF STUDIES

Reading Focus

Why Read?

Two popular sayings present contrasting points of view about the relationship of books and learning to life. According to one axiom, "Knowledge is power." According to the other, more cynical saying, "It's not *what* you know but *whom* you know." Bacon himself coined the first saying, but he would probably have agreed with both views, since he was extremely learned and also very well connected to powerful people. In this famous essay, however, his emphasis lies on the power—and usefulness—of books.

Quickwrite

Bacon's essay is about *his* feelings on reading. Why do *you* read? In your Reader's Log, jot down some notes on the reasons you pick up a book, a magazine, a newspaper, or a CD-ROM for your computer.

A Still Life with Books (detail) (17th century) by Charles E. Bizet d'Annonay.

Musée de l'Ain, Bourg-en-Bresse, France.

Elements of Literature

Parallel Structure

Bacon's sentences have been studied for centuries as models of **parallel structure**—the repetition of words, phrases, or sentences that have the same grammatical structure. Parallelism makes a passage rhythmic and memorable. It can also be used to present contrasting ideas in a provocative way. Used well, parallelism can heighten the emotional impact of a statement. Try an oral reading of the essay to feel the impact of Bacon's famous parallel sentence structures.

Into the Selections

Using BEFORE YOU READ p. 405

Reading Focus

In this information age, perhaps even more than in Bacon's time, knowledge is power. Help students to discuss this by asking them in what ways knowledge translates into power. Give them an idea to get them started. For example, if one knows how to communicate clearly in writing, one can affect others' ideas.

PORTFOLIO ASSESSMENT

Portfolio Assessment For help with teacher assessment of reading skills, see the *Portfolio Management System,* pp. 54–55.

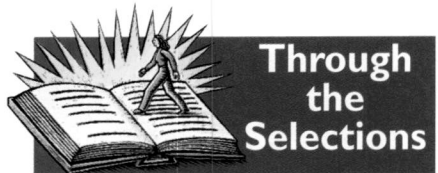
Of Studies

Sir Francis Bacon

A Studies serve for delight, for ornament, and for ability. Their chief use for delight is in privateness and retiring;[1] for ornament, is in discourse; and for ability, is in the judgment and disposition of business. For expert men can execute, and perhaps judge of particulars, one by one; but the general counsels, and the plots and marshalling of affairs, come best from those that are learned. To spend too much time in studies is sloth;[2] to use them too much for ornament is affectation;[3] to make judgment wholly by their rules is the humor[4] of a scholar. They perfect nature **B** and are perfected by experience; for natural abilities are like natural plants that need pruning by study; and studies themselves do give forth directions too much at large, except they be bounded in by experience. Crafty men contemn[5] studies; simple men admire[6] them; and wise men use them: For they teach not their own use; but that is a wisdom without them[7] and above them, won by observation. Read not to contradict and confute;[8] nor to believe and take for granted; nor to find talk and discourse; but to weigh and consider. **C** Some books are to be tasted, others to be swallowed, and some few to be chewed and digested: That is, some books are to be read only in parts; others to be read, but not curiously;[9] and some few to be read wholly, and with diligence and attention. Some books also may be read by deputy, and extracts made of them by others; but that would be only in the less important arguments, and the meaner sort of books; else distilled books are like common distilled waters,[10] flashy[11] things.

1. **privateness and retiring:** privacy and leisure.
2. **sloth:** laziness.
3. **affectation:** artificial behavior designed to impress others.
4. **humor:** whim.
5. **contemn:** despise.
6. **admire:** archaic for "marvel at."
7. **without them:** separate from them; outside them.
8. **confute:** dispute.
9. **curiously:** carefully.
10. **common distilled waters:** homemade concoctions.
11. **flashy:** superficial; vapid.

Reading maketh a full man; conference[12] a ready man; and writing an exact man. And therefore, if a man write little, he had need have a great memory; if he confer little, he had need have a present wit;[13] and if he read little, he had need have much cunning, to seem to know that[14] he doth not. Histories make men wise; poets witty;[15] the mathematics subtle; natural philosophy deep; moral grave; logic and rhetoric able to contend. *Abeunt studia in mores.*[16] **D** Nay, there is no stond[17] or impediment in the wit but may be wrought[18] out by fit studies: like as diseases of the body may have appropriate exercises. Bowling is good for the stone and reins;[19] shooting for the lungs and breast; gentle walking for the stomach; riding for the head; and the like. So if a man's wit be wandering, let him study the mathematics; for in demonstrations, if his wit be called away never so little, he must begin again: If his wit be not apt to distinguish or find differences, let him study the Schoolmen;[20] for they are *cymini sectores:*[21] If he be not apt to beat over[22] matters, and to call one thing to prove and illustrate another, let him study the lawyers' cases; so every defect of the mind may have a special receipt.[23]

12. **conference:** conversation; discussion.
13. **present wit:** ability to think fast.
14. **that:** what.
15. **witty:** imaginative.
16. ***Abeunt . . . mores:*** Latin for "Studies help form character," from Ovid's (43 B.C.–c. A.D. 17) *Heroides.*
17. **stond:** stoppage.
18. **wrought:** worked.
19. **stone and reins:** archaic for "kidney stones and the kidneys."
20. **schoolmen:** medieval philosophers.
21. ***cymini sectores:*** Latin for "hairsplitters"; literally, "dividers of cumin seed."
22. **beat over:** thoroughly discuss.
23. **receipt:** remedy.

Bacon's essays are written in a terse, compressed style that demands a reader's full attention. For the most part, Bacon does not develop his ideas in paragraphs. Instead, he writes a sentence containing one idea, then follows it with a sentence containing another idea. While the sentences are all related to the topic of the essay, they are related in different ways—and they could be rearranged without much damage to the whole. The effect is like a string of beads all the same size.

Many of the sentences contain nuggets of wisdom known as axioms or adages. Like proverbs, axioms do not argue or explain, but merely make positive statements. What do the axioms in this selection suggest about Bacon's values?

Axioms
from the Essays
Sir Francis Bacon

Men fear death as children fear to go in the dark; and as that natural fear in children is increased with tales, so is the other.

—"Of Death"

Revenge is a kind of wild justice, which the more man's nature runs to, the more ought law to weed it out.

—"Of Revenge"

The virtue of prosperity is temperance; the virtue of adversity is fortitude.

—"Of Adversity"

He that hath wife and children hath given **A** hostages to fortune.

—"Of Marriage and Single Life"

There was never proud man thought so absurdly well of himself as the lover doth of the person loved: And therefore it was well said, *That it is impossible to love and to be wise.*

—"Of Love"

They that deny a God destroy man's nobility, for certainly man is of kin to the beasts by his body, and if he be not of kin to God by his spirit, he is a base and ignoble creature.

—"Of Atheism"

A principal fruit of friendship is the ease and discharge of the fullness and swellings of the heart.

—"Of Friendship"

A man's own observation, what he finds good of, and what he finds hurt of, is the best physic [medicine] to preserve health.

—"Of Regiment of Health"

As the baggage is to an army, so is riches to **B** virtue.

—"Of Riches"

No man prospers so suddenly as by others' errors.

—"Of Fortune"

There is no excellent beauty that hath not some strangeness in the proportion.

—"Of Beauty"

God Almighty first planted a garden. And indeed it is the purest of human pleasures.

—"Of Gardens"

Men in great places are thrice servants: servants of the sovereign or state, servants of fame, and **C** servants of business.

—"Of Great Place"

It were better to have no opinion of God at all than such an opinion as is unworthy of him.

—"Of Superstition"

SIR FRANCIS BACON 407

A. Expansion
The complete opening sentence of Bacon's essay adds a comma and the words, "for they are impediments to great enterprises, either of virtue or mischief." Bacon's essay does not reveal that he was, in fact, married, although he did not marry until age forty-five, and he never had children.

Ask students if they think marriage keeps a person from being all he or she can be in life. [Most students will probably agree that a person can have both marriage and success.]

B. Critical Reading: Making Connections
? How does this axiom compare with one from the Bible: "It is easier for a camel to go through the eye of a needle than for a rich man to enter into the Kingdom of God" (Matthew 19:24)? [Possible answers: They are very similar. Baggage slows an army and gets in the way of its work. Those who have lots of money find it more difficult to behave in a virtuous way.]

C. Reader's Response: Extending the Text
? Do you think the president of the United States would agree with this axiom? Would rock stars and movie stars? [Sample responses: Some students may agree that with fame and power comes personal sacrifice. Other students may believe that political leaders and stars sacrifice very little for all that their fame brings.]

INTEGRATING THE LANGUAGE ARTS

Strategic Reading To help students draw together images from all points of "Of Studies," try Random Reading. Ask students to note the words, phrases, or sentences that they find significant or interesting. Have students speak out and read their choices in random order. The same passages may be read by different individuals.

Writing: An Outline Have pairs of students expand on Bacon's thoughts in an outline completing any one of Bacon's axioms. Students should rewrite the axiom in their own words as their thesis statements. The pairs may work together to brainstorm and then organize their points of proof in an outline.

ASSESSMENT TOOLS

Check Test: True-False
1. According to Bacon, you can feel secure if you make judgments based only on what you have studied. [False]
2. Bacon says you do not need to read every book thoroughly. [True]
3. Bacon says if you do not write things down, you need a good memory. [True]
4. Bacon believes that studies are like plants. [False]
5. In study there is a cure for each weakness of the intellect, according to Bacon. [True]

Sir Francis Bacon **T407**

A. Critical Reading: Making Connections

? Would Bacon agree with this statement? [Probably. He says, ". . . there is no . . . impediment to the wit, but it may be wrought out by studies." He believes that natural wit, or the natural mind, must be honed with study: reading, writing, conversation, and so on. So he might add that with training and use, the mind has no limits.]

B. Reader's Response: Shaping Interpretations

? How are thoughts the "last hope of serenity and peace"? [Sample responses: Thoughts can break down the walls of our problems, giving us peace. There is freedom and peace in thinking; you can escape the world for a while.]

C. Critical Reading: Making Connections

? How does this idea relate to the theme of the Collection, "The Power of the Word"? [Possible answer: Words are powerful; they shape our lives. They come from the mind; to be as powerful as they are, their source must be strong, even awe-inspiring.]

Making Meanings

First Thoughts

1. Students might mention classic literature or books about religion or philosophy. Students may say these are books that require reflection and leave a lasting impression.

Reviewing the Text

Students' responses should include the uses and virtues of study.

Shaping Interpretations

2. Bacon means that excessive studying at the expense of the conduct of practical affairs in the world exhibits a lazy nature. Someone who studies too much is probably unwilling or unable to engage in the practical affairs of life. Most students will probably agree with Bacon's thought.

3. Examples include sentences beginning "So if a man's wit be wandering"; "If he be not apt to beat over matters." Students' opinions of Bacon will vary. Some may see him as #3 suggests; some may argue that he is a realist.

Mind

A The mind knows no boundaries,
words no obstacles.
Every problem, a wall
in a maze of society.
And creativity, the rubberband,
leads us out,
but always manages to bring us back
ever so quickly.
Imagination is the tiny cave
in this maze that we hide in
for a moment of rest.
B Thoughts, the last hope
of serenity and peace.
The mind surrounds this society.
It molds this sculpture we call Earth.
Whoever said the pen is mightier than the sword
was correct.
C Writing comes from words,
from thoughts,
from the strongest
thing ever built.
The Mind.

—Andrea D. Marzullo
Bellevue East Senior High School
Bellevue, Nebraska

Untitled (1976) by Jerry Uelsmann.
© 1976 by Jerry Uelsmann.

CONNECTING WITH BACON'S "OF STUDIES"

What are some of the similarities and differences between the student's work and Bacon's? [Possible answers: Similarities—they both discuss the mind and its capabilities; they both express an optimism about humans and their minds. Differences—Bacon writes prose and "Mind" is a poem; Bacon does not address imagination as the student does, but the student does not address memory.]

MAKING MEANINGS

First Thoughts

1. Bacon says that only a few books are to be "chewed and digested." What books would be on your list in this category? Why would you include them?

Reviewing the Text

In no more than three sentences, state what you think is Bacon's main idea in "Of Studies."

Shaping Interpretations

2. Bacon says that too much studying is laziness. Do you agree? Explain how this **paradox,** or seeming contradiction, can be true.

3. Bacon had the reputation of being a hard, ambitious man, and his essays are frequently said to be cynical and lacking in warmth. Find remarks in "Of Studies" that could support this view. How did *you* feel about the person behind this essay?

4. Bacon's fondness for parallel structure and balanced sentences is apparent in "Of Studies." For example: "Some books are to be tasted, others to be swallowed, and some few to be chewed and digested." Find and read aloud other examples of Bacon's **parallelism** and balance.

5. Review the notes you made in your Reader's Log about the reasons you read. Then compare these reasons with Bacon's arguments for reading. How do you feel about the ideas expressed in "Mind" on page 408?

Extending the Text

6. What passages in "Of Studies" do you think could apply especially well to today's arguments about the value of education?

Challenging the Text

7. "Of Studies" was written almost four hundred years ago. Are any of its points dated? Do you disagree with anything Bacon says?

CHOICES:
Building Your Portfolio

Writer's Notebook

1. Collecting Ideas for a Cause-Effect Essay

Bacon's essay upholds the value of books and of reading—but with a seventeenth-century perspective. What effects do you think modern technology has on our use of books and on the reading process itself? Think about CD-ROMs, computer databases, and the video images that constantly engulf us. Do you think people will still read books in the near future? Will they still use books in their studies? Save your notes to use with the Writer's Workshop on page 459.

Critical Writing

2. Having Much Cunning

Bacon maintains that a person who reads little needs to "have much cunning, to seem to know" what he actually doesn't know. Analyze this part of "Of Studies" to determine Bacon's attitude toward such a pretense. Does he speak strongly against it, or does he imply that it is not a serious failing? Explore your findings in a short essay of your own.

Creative Writing

3. Talking Back to Bacon

Write an essay of your own in response to Bacon's reflections on studies. You might focus on the entire essay or on just one statement. Your response to Bacon might be anything—from total disagreement to total approval of all he says, though that's not likely. In your opening statement, tell what the topic of your own essay will be. Be sure to bring in examples and experiences from real life today to support or refute Bacon. Give your essay a title that uses the word "On."

4. Students may mention the sentences beginning: "To spend too much time in studies is sloth"; "Crafty men contemn studies"; and "Reading maketh a full man."

5. Students should demonstrate their knowledge and understanding of Bacon's arguments for reading. Students will probably agree with the ideas expressed in the student poem.

Extending the Text

6. **(Analysis)** Students might mention passages beginning "For expert men can execute"; "Reading maketh a full man"; and "Nay, there is no stond. . . ."

Challenging the Text

7. **(Evaluation)** Most students will agree that Bacon's points are still valid today.

Choices: Building Your Portfolio

1. **Writer's Notebook** Remind students to save their work. They may use it as prewriting for the Writer's Workshop on p. 459.

2. **Critical Writing** Have students think about times they have not prepared for class. Ask them if they had to be crafty or to pretend they knew something they did not. Ask students if they can tell when others do this. Have them consider how they feel about such pretense. Then, have them turn to the essay before they write.

3. **Creative Writing** Have students work in small groups to review their opening statements. Students should read aloud their proposed opening statement and then explain how they intend to support the statement. Students' responses should contain a clear statement of agreement or disagreement with Bacon's views, along with evidence to support their ideas.

OPTIONS FOR TEACHING

STRATEGIES FOR INCLUSION

English Language Development Assist students with activity #2 by first determining if they are familiar with the concept of implied ideas in a text. Explain to students that an author may not directly state an opinion or argument in a text. Have students examine the phrases around the one mentioned here to determine if Bacon's true feelings are clear or implied.

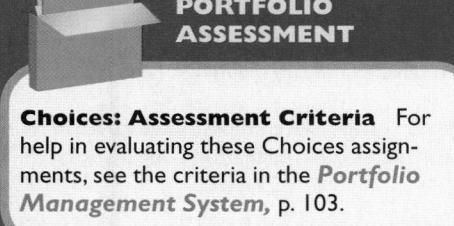

PORTFOLIO ASSESSMENT

Choices: Assessment Criteria For help in evaluating these Choices assignments, see the criteria in the *Portfolio Management System,* p. 103.

SPOTLIGHT ON

The Example of a Queen: Elizabeth I

by **Katharina M. Wilson**

It is your shame (I speak to you all, you young gentlemen of England) that one maid should go beyond you all in excellency of learning and knowledge of diverse tongues.

—Roger Ascham, tutor to the future Queen Elizabeth I

New Opportunities

With the advent of humanism, Renaissance women of upper-class birth enjoyed great opportunities for artistic and intellectual growth. Education, especially classical learning, was no longer restricted to the clergy. Women as well as men of privileged classes were now expected to seek personal fulfillment by studying a wide array of subjects. Sir Thomas More and Desiderius Erasmus—leading humanists of the day—argued that education would make women better wives and mothers (especially since women had traditionally directed the early education of their children), but that their role should remain a private rather than a public one.

Most advocates of women's education also linked its desirability to the growth of moral virtue. Their intent, especially in Protestant countries, was to allow women to participate more fully in religious life. Men *and* women were encouraged to read and understand God's word. Not surprisingly, many English Renaissance works penned by women have a religious or devotional nature.

King Henry VIII, an enlightened monarch who was quite interested in the new philosophy, appointed humanist scholars to tutor both his son Edward and his daughter Elizabeth. Henry's last wife, Catherine Parr, herself a learned woman and an author (she composed a religious treatise, *A Lamentation or Complaint of a Sinner*), encouraged the king's daughter to study and to translate Latin and French texts into English. Many aristocratic families followed the example set by the royal court, taking great pains to employ scholars as tutors for their children.

A Most Extraordinary Pupil

The studious young girl in the royal family eventually became Queen Elizabeth I (1533–1603), the most influential of England's learned women. During her reign, she dazzled the ambassadors at court with her superb literary training, knowledge of the classics, and political and diplomatic skills. Countless poets and dramatists—Shakespeare, Spenser, and Raleigh among them—praised her learning and grace.

Elizabeth Tudor's early childhood was spent happily in the royal household. But following the execution of her mother, Anne Boleyn, in 1536, she was declared illegitimate. Still, her father continued to

Portrait of a Girl (16th century), possibly Queen Elizabeth, by an English School artist.
Victoria and Albert Museum, London.

410 THE RENAISSANCE

A Procession of Queen Elizabeth I (c. 1600) attributed to Robert Peake the Elder.

provide for her education, and her tutors Sir John Cheke and Roger Ascham left us a record of her early training. Her daily schedule was rigorous. Every day she would study Greek (classical authors such as Sophocles and Demosthenes) and Latin (Roman authors like Cicero and Livy, as well as the Scriptures). In studying languages, Elizabeth followed the methods advocated by Renaissance educators: First, she read the Greek or Latin texts; then she translated them into polished English prose; and finally, she retranslated the texts into the original languages, attempting to approximate her source as well as she could.

In addition to Greek and Latin, Elizabeth spoke and read French, Italian, Spanish, Flemish, Welsh, and German. Like most upper-class girls, she also received lessons in riding, music, astronomy, geography, philosophy, mathematics, and needlepoint. In fact, the original manuscript of Elizabeth's translation (done at age eleven, no less) of Queen Marguerite de Navarre's The Mirror of the Sinful Soul is enclosed in an elaborately embroidered silk cover that is most likely her own work. Little wonder, then, that as queen she was highly acclaimed for her learning and talents.

Expressions of Love and Duty

After the death of Elizabeth's staunchly Catholic half-sister, Mary Tudor, Elizabeth herself was crowned queen in 1558. She returned England to Protestantism and ruled with great prudence for the next forty-five years. Often urged to marry, Elizabeth had the political skill to recognize the dangers of such an act. She rejected many proposals of marriage because she had "already joined [her]self in marriage to a husband, namely, the kingdom of England."

This is not to say, however, that Elizabeth didn't entertain the attentions of several suitors who came to woo her. She is thought to once have been deeply in love with Robert Dudley, a member of her court. Later, Elizabeth grew attached to the earl of Essex, an alleged traitor whom she, however regretfully, ordered executed. She wrote the following poem as a going-away gift for still another suitor, the much younger duke of Alençon, whom she affectionately called "Monsieur" and rebuffed because of public hostility to the match. Written in the poetic style practiced by her countrymen Spenser and Wyatt, Elizabeth's poem describes the paradoxes and pangs of love.

D. Exploring the Historical Period

Turmoil between the Catholics and Protestants prevailed in England during this time. When Mary Tudor became queen, she made Catholicism the state religion, thus rescinding the Protestant Church of England founded by her father, Henry VIII. Mary suspected Elizabeth of plotting with the Protestants to gain the throne and had her imprisoned for two months in the Tower of London. There was strong opposition to Elizabeth taking the throne. She was tried on charges of adultery, complicity to rebel, and other charges. Her opponents failed to prove anything against Elizabeth, and when she became queen, Elizabeth took the religious middle ground, restoring the Protestant Church of England but retaining many Catholic features. Throughout her reign, however, many Catholics opposed her, and at the end of her reign, Elizabeth allowed Catholics to be persecuted and executed.

RESPONDING TO THE ART: VISUAL LITERACY

A procession is a parade of people who move forward in an orderly or formal way. What details of this painting suggest order or formality? [Possible responses: The formal, ornate dress of the participants and their elegant postures, the car in which they carry the queen, the quiet and careful manner of the procession.]

Auditory Call on a volunteer to read aloud the excerpt from Elizabeth's "Tilbury Speech" (p. 412). Ask students to jot down adjectives describing Elizabeth's character as they listen to the speech. Have students work in small groups, using their notes and other information from the selection, to discuss a character analysis of the queen. Groups should present their final analyses orally to each other.

Strategic Reading Ask students to use a KWL chart like the following to record what they know and what they want to know about Queen Elizabeth I. After they have finished reading the selection, have them complete the third column.

K	W	L

Writing: A Letter Ask students to write a letter from Elizabeth to the duke of Alençon, paraphrasing the emotions in the poem (on p. 412). The letter should express Elizabeth's feelings about lost love and explain why her royal position dictated her actions when it came to love. ☞

A. Humanities Connection

When Elizabeth came to the throne, England was in need of a strong leader. War and religious conflict had weakened the country, the treasury was depleted, and the rulers of both Spain and France wanted to rule England. By the end of Elizabeth's reign, England was rich and secure. It was enjoying its greatest literary period, English ships ruled the seas, and England had begun to establish itself as a world leader.

B. Exploring the Historical Period

England's ongoing problems with Spain intensified after English privateers began capturing Spanish ships carrying treasure from the American continents. Philip II's decision to invade England came after Elizabeth knighted Francis Drake for sailing around the world and for successfully challenging Spanish dominance in the Americas. Spain's invincible Armada was made up of 130 ships carrying more than 30,000 men. These mighty ships, however, were no match for the speed, maneuverability, and firepower of England's coastal vessels. With the defeat of the Armada, England took its place as master of the world's seas.

C. Literary Connections

During the Elizabethan period, scholarship, translation, literature, exploration, and trade flourished and contributed to the growth of the English language. Although at the beginning of the period it was doubted that English could serve formal writing (replacing Latin), by its end Spenser, Shakespeare, and Jonson had written their masterworks of the English language.

On Monsieur's Departure

I grieve, and dare not show my discontent;
I love, and yet am forced to seem to hate;
I do, yet dare not say I ever meant;
I seem stark mute, but inwardly do prate;
  I am and not; I freeze and yet am burn'd;
  Since from myself, my other self I turn'd;

My care is like my shadow in the sun,
Follows me flying, flies when I pursue it,
Stands and lies by me, doth what I have done;
His too familiar care doth make me rue it:
  No means I find to rid him from my breast
  Till by the end of things it be surpress'd.

Some gentler passions slide into my mind,
For I am soft and made of melting snow;
Or be more cruel, Love, and so be kind—
Let me or float or sink, be high or low,
  Or let me live with some more sweet
    content,
  Or die and so forget what love ere meant.

—Elizabeth I

A Aside from writing poems, letters, prayers, sermons, and translations (not to mention governing the country, conducting foreign policy, fostering the arts, and dedicating herself fervently to the new religion), Queen Elizabeth also wrote masterful speeches and political addresses. One of her best-known orations is the "Tilbury Speech." Given in 1588, before news of the Spanish Armada's destruction had reached England, Elizabeth's speech was meant to rouse her **B** land forces to defend England against Spanish invasion. Here, the English queen powerfully demonstrates her identification with—and pride in—her nation.

My loving people: We have been persuaded by some that are careful of our safety to take heed how we commit ourself to armed multitudes for fear of treachery, but I assure you I do not desire to live to distrust my faithful and loving people. Let tyrants fear. I have always so behaved myself that, under God, I have placed my chiefest strength and safeguard in the loyal hearts and goodwill of my subjects. And therefore I am come amongst you, as you see, at this time, not for my recreation and disport, but being resolved in the midst and heat of the battle to live or die amongst you all, to lay down for my God, and for my kingdom, and for my people, my honor and my blood, even in the dust. I know I have the body but of a weak and feeble woman, but I have the heart and stomach of a king—and of a king of England too—and think foul scorn that Parma, or Spain, or any prince of Europe should dare to invade the borders of my realm. To which, rather than any dishonor shall grow by me, I myself will take up arms, I myself will be your general, judge, and rewarder of every one of your virtues in the field. I know already for your forwardness you have deserved rewards and crowns, and we do assure you, in the word of a prince, they shall be duly paid you.

—Elizabeth I

C And what do we know of those women who were less fortunate than Elizabeth or her aristocratic countrywomen? The literacy rate among them (as among Renaissance men neither nobly born nor affiliated with the Church) is almost impossible to estimate. Many people who could read could not write, and thus could not sign their names to county rolls—one of the standard tools for measuring literacy. Still, judging by the sheer number of books printed and translations produced in this period, we can safely assume that reading for moral improvement and personal pleasure had finally entered the humble home.

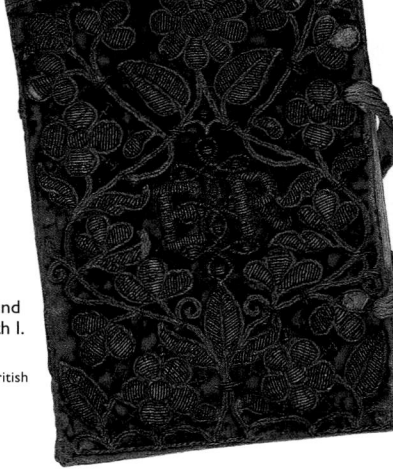

Copy of the New Testament (1603), bearing the initials E. R., probably bound for Queen Elizabeth I. H.D. 37.

By permission of the British Library, London.

INTEGRATING THE LANGUAGE ARTS

Listening Tell students that one aspect of critical listening is being able to distinguish between facts and opinions. A fact can be proven; an opinion is a belief or judgment. Call on a volunteer to read aloud portions of the selection. Have students identify which thoughts are facts and which are opinions.

ASSESSMENT TOOLS

Check Test: True-False

1. Some humanists believed that education would lead women to become better wives and mothers. [True]
2. The type and scope of Elizabeth's education was typical of that received by all young women in Renaissance England. [False]
3. Elizabeth never married because she could not find the right man. [False]
4. Elizabeth resented the fact that any other European country would dare invade England. [True]
5. The masses during Elizabeth's time begin to read for moral instruction and personal pleasure. [True]

The King James Bible (1611): A Masterpiece by a Committee

One of the first acts of James I after he was crowned king of England was to sponsor a new translation of the Bible. There were many translations of the Bible available, but the king, like others, disliked the interpretive comments included in the existing translations. Moreover, Renaissance scholarship had made people more historically minded and sensitive to textual inaccuracies. The new translation would be checked against the most authoritative Hebrew and Greek texts available.

Title page of the Holy Bible (1611).
Printed by Robert Barker, London.

The Pierpont Morgan Library, New York. PML 5460.

To produce the translation, the king appointed a team of fifty-four learned clergymen. They broke up into groups, each with a section of the Scriptures to translate and each with a pair of scholars to check the work. Seven years later, after a committee of bishops gave it a final review, the new translation was published. It has become known variously as the "King James Bible" because James sponsored it; as the "Authorized Version" because the Anglican Church authorized its use; and simply as the "English Bible" because it has been so important to the civilization and literature of all English-speaking countries.

A. Expansion

Students interested in the history of English translations should look up *Bible* in an encyclopedia for an overview. References at the end of the article will suggest more specific materials.

B. Expansion

Many writers contributed to the manuscripts that eventually were translated into the King James Bible. Even though faith was an essential part of their writing, their topics were not always strictly religious ones. In fact, they sometimes wrote about the best use of language and about writing as a craft.

- "My tongue is the pen of a ready writer." (from Psalm 45:1)
- "Death and life are in the power of the tongue, and they that love it shall eat the fruit thereof." (Proverbs 18:21)
- "A word fitly spoken is like apples of gold in pictures of silver." (Proverbs 25:11)
- "Though I speak with the tongues of men and of angels, and have not charity, I am become as sounding brass, or a tinkling cymbal." (I Corinthians 13:1)

The desire to record information in books is also mentioned in the Bible. To King Solomon, David's son, is attributed the statement "Of making many books there is no end" (from Ecclesiastes 12:12); and John, one of Jesus' disciples, concluded his account of Jesus' life by saying, "And there are also many other things which Jesus did, the which, if they should be written every one, I suppose that even the world itself could not contain the books that should be written. Amen." (John 21:25).

PROGRAM MANAGER

- **Planning Instruction** See Teaching Notes, *Teaching Resources A,* pp. 106–107, for objectives, summaries, major literary elements, and additional information for these selections.
- **Instructional Support** Before beginning the instructional lesson, see Graphic Organizer for Active Reading, *Teaching Resources A,* pp. 110, 113–115, for Through the Selection activities.
- **Audiotaped Readings** To help less proficient readers or auditory learners through the lesson, use the Selected Reading, Audiocassette 1, Side B, in the *Audiovisual* Resources Binder.
- **Assessment** See Selection Test, *Test Booklet,* pp. 73–78.
- **Language Link** For instruction and practice in prepositions, see Language Link, *Teaching Resources A,* p. 111–112, and *Language and Writing Skills Worksheets,* p. 19.

A. Literary Connections

The King James Bible has been a major force in stabilizing the English language since the seventeenth century. Part of its effectiveness lies in its limited vocabulary. In contrast to the thirty-thousand-word vocabulary of Shakespeare's First Folio, the King James Bible uses only eight thousand words. Some seventeenth-century religious dissenters even attempted to limit their vocabulary to that of the King James Bible—a program destined to fail, since words were needed for a great many things unheard of in Biblical times, such as *parliament* and the names of North American plants and animals.

B. Expansion

Many students do not know there are reference books for locating Biblical passages. These are Biblical concordances, which are usually shelved in the reference section of a library. A Biblical concordance indexes phrases in the same manner as the index at the back of *Bartlett's Familiar Quotations*. The only difference is that a Bible is needed to look up the quotation in full. Perhaps the most widely used concordances for the King James Bible are *Strong's Exhaustive Concordance of the Bible* and *Young's Analytical Concordance*.

A If English-speaking people living before our time read anything, they read the English Bible. And if they read nothing themselves, they regularly heard the Bible read in Church. For nearly four centuries, most writers in English have been influenced, consciously or unconsciously, by the English Bible. They have quoted it, echoed it, paraphrased it, alluded to it, imitated it, and retold its fascinating stories over and over.

B Everyday English speech is full of words and phrases from the English Bible: "loving kindness," "tender mercy," "long suffering." We "cast pearls before swine" and "wait until the eleventh hour" before acting. We speak of the "wisdom of Solomon" and the "patience of Job." Many Biblical words (such as *scapegoat*) are by now so embedded in our language that we use them without knowing we are using Biblical language.

But even when the King James Bible was first published, its language sounded old-fashioned. The translators had preserved much of the style of William Tyndale, a Bible translator who had been dead for more than seventy years—years in which the language had changed rapidly. In 1611, English people were beginning to address each other as "you," but the new Bible kept the archaic verb forms and the old second-person pronouns *thou, thy, thine,* and *thee.*

Over the years, the language of the King James Bible has become even more distant from ordinary English. For some readers, this remoteness makes it more moving and evokes more sublime feelings than does a Bible in the vernacular. The King James Bible stands with Shakespeare as an exemplar of English when the language was, as many people believe, more flexible and eloquent than at any other time, and more capable of stirring people's hearts and minds.

Title page of the Holy Bible (detail) (1611). Printed by Robert Barker, London.

The Pierpont Morgan Library, New York. PML 5460.

Title page of the Holy Bible (detail) (1611). Printed by Robert Barker, London.

The Pierpont Morgan Library, New York. PML 5460.

BEFORE YOU READ
FROM GENESIS

Reading Focus

How and Why

The first book of the Bible is called Genesis, which means "coming into being." Genesis opens with two accounts of creation: Chapter 1 emphasizes the cosmos or universe; Chapter 2 looks at the earth and humanity. Although Moses is traditionally thought of as the author of Genesis, many Biblical scholars now say that two different writers recorded these two creation accounts, which may well be regarded as complementary. Both narratives are very spare and simple but elevated in style.

Besides telling us how the physical universe we know came into being, the first chapters of Genesis deal with how and why human beings were created, and especially, in Chapter 3, why individual members of the human race must suffer and die, and why the history of the whole race has been so bloody and troubled.

A Dialogue with the Text

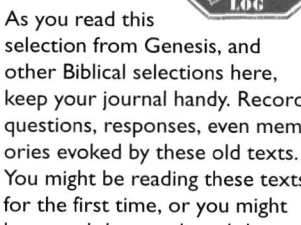

As you read this selection from Genesis, and other Biblical selections here, keep your journal handy. Record questions, responses, even memories evoked by these old texts. You might be reading these texts for the first time, or you might have read them or heard them many times in your childhood. Whatever your past experiences with the Bible, you'll find some of these passages striking strong emotional and intellectual responses.

Elements of Literature

Imagery

The ancient writers of the Bible were addressing an unsophisticated people. To appeal to their audience, they used a pictorial style rich in **imagery** to tell the story of the primordial origins of the whole human race. Through the centuries, many artists have interpreted scenes from Genesis.

Creation of Adam (detail) (1508–1512) by Michelangelo. Fresco.

Sistine Chapel, Vatican Palace, Rome.

THE KING JAMES BIBLE 415

Into the Selection

Using BEFORE YOU READ p. 415

Reading Focus

Ask students what they think are some of the basic questions that people, regardless of time and place, ask about life. Work with the class to brainstorm a list of questions on the chalkboard; then, challenge students to see which questions are addressed, in some fashion, in the Genesis account. Alternatively, encourage students to make these questions personal, for example, "What is my purpose on earth?" Students may record the questions in their Reader's Logs and consider how the Genesis narrative may relate to the answers. *Remind students to choose questions or thoughts they would not mind sharing with others.*

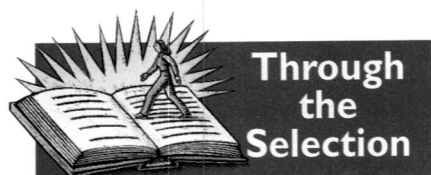

Through the Selection

A. Language Note: Vocabulary
In Hebrew the words used here are *tohu* and *bohu,* "trackless waste" and "emptiness." The images imply the concept of creation *ex nihilo,* or "creation from nothing."

B. Literary Element: Imagery
? What image or images does this description bring to mind? [Possible answers: A snapshotlike sequence of a wide variety of plants that are mature and ready to reproduce; a general image of the earth suddenly turning green and blossoming, as in time-lapse photography.]

C. Reader's Response: Extending the Text
? How would you expect people who believe they were created "in the image of God" to feel about themselves? What would be the advantages and disadvantages to such a view? [Sample responses: People with this belief would feel that they have a special place among God's creations; or they may feel the burden of high expectations. The advantages might be a sense of confidence and an eagerness to live up to what that image implies; the disadvantages might be that some people might be filled with pride and that others might rebel against the idea that they were somehow obligated to God.]

D. Reader's Response: Shaping Interpretations
? When it comes to the use of nature, what do you think that God's directions here allow? [Sample responses: That people may enjoy and take care of the earth, taking what is necessary to meet their needs; or that people rule the earth and may use it in whatever way they see fit.]

from Genesis

A In the beginning God created the heaven and the earth. And the earth was without form, and void; and darkness was upon the face of the deep. And the spirit of God moved upon the face of the waters.[1] And God said, "Let there be light": And there was light. And God saw the light, that it was good: And God divided the light from the darkness. And God called the light Day, and the darkness he called Night. And the evening and the morning were the first day.

And God said, "Let there be a firmament[2] in the midst of the waters, and let it divide the waters from the waters." And God made the firmament, and divided the waters which were under the firmament from the waters which were above the firmament: And it was so. And God called the firmament Heaven. And the evening and the morning were the second day.

And God said, "Let the waters under the heaven be gathered together unto one place, and let the dry land appear": And it was so. And God called the dry land Earth; and the gathering together of the waters called he Seas: And God saw that it was good. And God said, "Let the earth **B** bring forth grass, the herb[3] yielding seed, and the fruit tree yielding fruit after his kind, whose seed is in itself, upon the earth": And it was so. And the earth brought forth grass, and herb yielding seed after his kind,[4] and the tree yielding fruit, whose seed was in itself, after his kind: And God saw that it was good. And the evening and the morning were the third day.

And God said, "Let there be lights in the firmament of the heaven to divide the day from the night; and let them be for signs, and for seasons, and for days, and years: And let them be for lights in the firmament of the heaven to give light upon the earth": And it was so. And God made two great lights; the greater light to rule the day, and the lesser light to rule the night: He made the stars also. And God set them in the firmament of the heaven to give light upon the earth, and to rule over the day and over the night, and to divide the light from the darkness: And God saw that it was good. And the evening and the morning were the fourth day.

And God said, "Let the waters bring forth abundantly the moving creature[5] that hath life, and fowl that may fly above the earth in the open firmament of heaven." And God created great whales, and every living creature that moveth, which the waters brought forth abundantly, after their kind, and every winged fowl after his kind: And God saw that it was good. And God blessed them, saying, "Be fruitful, and multiply, and fill the waters in the seas, and let fowl multiply in the earth." And the evening and the morning were the fifth day.

And God said, "Let the earth bring forth the living creature after his kind, cattle, and creeping thing, and beast of the earth after his kind": And it was so. And God made the beast of the earth after his kind, and cattle after their kind, and everything that creepeth upon the earth after his kind: And God saw that it was good. And God said, "Let us make man in our[6] image, after our likeness: And let them have dominion[7] over the fish of the sea, and over the fowl of the air, and over the cattle, and over all the earth, and over every creeping **C** thing that creepeth upon the earth." So God created man in his own image, in the image of God created he him; male and female created he them. And God blessed them, and God said unto them, "Be fruitful, and multiply, and replenish the earth, and subdue it: And have dominion over the fish of **D** the sea, and over the fowl of the air, and over every living thing that moveth upon the earth." And God said, "Behold, I have given you every herb bearing seed, which is upon the face of all the earth, and every tree, in the which is the fruit of a tree yielding seed; to you it shall be for meat.[8]

---

1. **waters:** Only water existed before the Creation began.
2. **firmament:** sky. Since the sky is blue, it is natural to suppose that there are waters above it. Where, otherwise, would the rain come from?
3. **herb:** vegetation.
4. **his kind:** its nature. *Its* is a word that came into common use late in the seventeenth century.

5. **creature:** created beings; an old plural without the *s.*
6. **our:** my. God refers to himself as "we" to indicate his authority.
7. **dominion:** power to rule.
8. **meat:** food. What we call meat, the Bible calls *flesh.*

416 THE RENAISSANCE

OPTIONS FOR TEACHING

STRATEGIES FOR INCLUSION

Auditory Some students might grasp the power in the language of the King James Bible by hearing the language read aloud. Have students take turns reading orally paragraph by paragraph, breaking longer paragraphs in two. At each break, invite students to comment about the images that the language brings to mind; also, ask whether the language becomes easier to understand after listening to it for a time.

Visual/Spatial To facilitate discussion of this Bible story, have students create a time line on which they chronologically list the events in the selection. They should start with the time the earth was without form and provide as much detail for each day as possible, continuing to the creation of Eve, and including illustrations to capture the images described in the selection.

The Creation of the Animals by a Flemish School artist. Oil.
Navarra Museum, Pamplona, Spain.

And to every beast of the earth, and to every fowl of the air, and to everything that creepeth upon the earth, wherein there is life, I have given every green herb for meat": And it was so. And God saw everything that he had made, and, behold, it was very good. And the evening and the morning were the sixth day.

Thus the heavens and the earth were finished, and all the host[9] of them. And on the seventh day God ended his work which he had made; and he rested on the seventh day from all his work which he had made. And God blessed the seventh day, and sanctified[10] it: because that in it he had rested from all his work which God created and made.

These are the generations of the heavens and of the earth when they were created, in the day that the LORD God made the earth and the heavens, and every plant of the field before it was in the earth, and every herb of the field before it grew: For the LORD God had not caused it to rain upon the earth, and there was not a man to till the ground. But there went up a mist from the earth, and watered the whole face of the ground. And the LORD God formed man of the dust of the

9. **host:** multitude.
10. **sanctified:** made holy.

ground, and breathed into his nostrils the breath of life; and man became a living soul. And the LORD God planted a garden eastward in Eden; and there he put the man whom he had formed. And out of the ground made the LORD God to grow every tree that is pleasant to the sight, and good for food; the tree of life also in the midst of the garden, and the tree of knowledge of good and evil. And a river went out of Eden to water the garden; and from thence it was parted, and became into four heads.[11] The name of the first is Pison:[12] That is it which compasseth the whole land of Havilah, where there is gold; and the gold of that land is good: There is bdellium[13] and the onyx[14] stone. And the name of the second river is Gihon: The same is it that compasseth the whole land of Ethiopia. And the name of the third river is Hiddekel: That is it which goeth toward the east of Assyria. And the fourth river is Euphrates. And the LORD God took the man, and put him into the garden of Eden to dress it and to keep it. And the LORD God commanded the man, saying, "Of every tree of the garden thou mayest freely eat: But of the tree of the knowledge of good and evil, thou shalt not eat of it: For in the day that thou eatest thereof thou shalt surely die."

And the LORD God said, "It is not good that the man should be alone; I will make him an help meet[15] for him." And out of the ground the LORD God formed every beast of the field, and every fowl of the air; and brought them unto Adam to see what he would call them: And whatsoever Adam called every living creature, that was the name thereof. And Adam gave names to all cattle, and to the fowl of the air, and to every beast of the field; but for Adam there was not found an help meet for him. And the LORD God caused a deep sleep to fall upon Adam, and he slept: And he took one of his ribs, and closed up the flesh instead thereof; and the rib, which the LORD God had taken from man, made he a woman, and

11. **heads:** A head is the beginning, or source, of a river.
12. **Pison:** This and the other geographical names (except for Ethiopia, for which modern translations say *Cush*) locate the Garden of Eden in Mesopotamia (modern Iraq).
13. **bdellium** (del' ē·əm): precious substance, either a stone or a resin.
14. **onyx:** gemstone.
15. **help meet:** suitable helper.

E. Cultural Connections
The Sabbath (from the Hebrew *shabbat*, or "rest") is thus of divine origin. Jews count Saturday as the seventh day, the day of rest. Most Christians find a parallel in observing Sunday and Muslims in observing Friday as their weekly day of rest and worship.

F. Critical Reading: Making Connections
? How does the creation of man differ from God's other acts of creation? [Possible answers: God spoke the other things in creation into existence but carefully formed man out of the dust; God also breathed life only into man, making him a living soul.]

G. Literary Element: Allusion
The title of John Steinbeck's novel *East of Eden* refers to this passage.

H. Reader's Response: Shaping Interpretations
? What does the manner of Eve's creation imply about the relationship of Adam and Eve? [Sample responses: God formed Eve from Adam so that they would be of the same bones and flesh, implying a powerful bond; or Eve, being formed of Adam's rib, is a secondary creature.]

INTEGRATING THE LANGUAGE ARTS

Strategic Reading Because this narrative is packed with factual detail—and detail that is presented in a language style with which some students may be unfamiliar—use Reciprocal Teaching with pairs of students. As partners finish each section, have them summarize the reading. Then, have them ask each other two or three questions about anything that they consider important in the section. Have them write the questions and answers down—you may use them for a quiz later.

Language and Style Point out that in the King James Bible's Genesis, nearly every sentence begins with *and*—a poetic way of keeping the narrative flowing. Today, writers use transitional expressions such as these to ensure coherence and to indicate relationships among ideas:
- Adds similar ideas: *and, moreover, in addition, besides*
- Links opposite ideas: *yet, however, on the other hand, in spite of*
- Indicates reasons: *because, since*

- Indicates results: *consequently, then*
- Indicates time: *at once, finally*

Have students work in groups to write a modern telling of an excerpt from Genesis, using appropriate transitional expressions. Encourage groups to share and compare their work.

A. Critical Reading: Analyzing Persuasion

[?] How does the serpent tempt Eve, and why do you think he is effective? [Possible answers: The serpent argues that they will not "surely" die if they eat the fruit but will gain the knowledge of good and evil and will "be as gods." The temptation to be a god, or be like God, proves too much for Eve and perhaps twists her reverence for and obedience to God. She appears to have a common human characteristic—ambition, or striving, for knowledge, wisdom, and power.]

B. Expansion

At no time is the forbidden fruit identified as an apple, the fruit traditionally associated with this story. All that is said is that the fruit is pretty, looks good to eat, and holds a promise of wisdom.

C. Critical Reading: Making Generalizations

[?] What familiar human tendency is presented here? [Possible answer: The tendency to to blame others for our own failings.]

D. Reader's Response: Extending the Text

[?] Think about the destiny that God has just outlined to Adam and Eve. Is withholding the tree of life from them a further punishment? Explain. [Sample responses: It actually may be a blessing, for living forever in a state of pain and frustration would be horrible. Death would be a release from that curse. Or it is a punishment because it involves exile from Eden and prevents people from truly becoming gods, immortal as well as possessing the knowledge of good and evil.]

brought her unto the man. And Adam said, "This is now bone of my bones, and flesh of my flesh: She shall be called Woman, because she was taken out of Man." Therefore shall a man leave his father and his mother, and shall cleave[16] unto his wife: And they shall be one flesh. And they were both naked, the man and his wife, and were not ashamed.

(A) Now the serpent[17] was more subtil[18] than any beast of the field which the LORD God had made. And he said unto the woman, "Yea, hath God said, 'Ye shall not eat of every tree of the garden'?" And the woman said unto the serpent, "We may eat of the fruit of the trees of the garden: But of the fruit of the tree which is in the midst of the garden, God hath said, 'Ye shall not eat of it, neither shall ye touch it, lest ye die.'" And the serpent said unto the woman, "Ye shall not surely die: For God doth know that in the day ye eat thereof, then your eyes shall be opened, and ye shall be as gods, knowing good and evil." And when the woman saw that the tree was good for food, and that it was pleasant to the eyes, and a tree to be desired to make one wise, (B) she took of the fruit thereof, and did eat, and gave also unto her husband with her; and he did eat. And the eyes of them both were opened, and they knew that they were naked; and they sewed fig leaves together, and made themselves aprons. And they heard the voice of the LORD God walking in the garden in the cool of the day: And Adam and his wife hid themselves from the presence of the LORD God amongst the trees of the garden. And the LORD God called unto Adam, and said unto him, "Where art thou?" And he said, "I heard thy voice in the garden, and I was afraid, because I was naked; and I hid myself." And he said, "Who told thee that thou wast naked? Hast thou eaten of the tree, whereof I commanded thee that thou shouldest not eat?" And the man said, "The woman whom (C) thou gavest to be with me, she gave me of the tree, and I did eat." And the LORD God said unto the woman, "What is this that thou hast done?"

16. **cleave:** be faithful.
17. **serpent:** traditionally understood to be the form assumed by Satan to tempt Eve. Satan is also identified with the angel Lucifer, who revolted against God and was expelled from Heaven.
18. **subtil:** subtle.

And the woman said, "The serpent beguiled me, and I did eat." And the LORD God said unto the serpent, "Because thou hast done this, thou art cursed above all cattle,[19] and above every beast of the field; upon thy belly shalt thou go, and dust shalt thou eat all of the days of thy life: And I will put enmity[20] between thee and the woman, and between thy seed and her seed; it shall bruise thy head, and thou shalt bruise his heel." Unto the woman he said, "I will greatly multiply thy sorrow and thy conception;[21] in sorrow thou shalt bring forth children; and thy desire shall be to thy husband, and he shall rule over thee." And unto Adam he said, "Because thou hast hearkened unto[22] the voice of thy wife, and hast eaten of the tree, of which I commanded thee, saying, 'Thou shalt not eat of it': Cursed is the ground for thy sake; in sorrow shalt thou eat of it all the days of thy life; thorns also and thistles shall it bring forth to thee; and thou shalt eat the herb of the field; in the sweat of thy face shalt thou eat bread, till thou return unto the ground; for out of it wast thou taken: For dust thou art, and unto dust shalt thou return." And Adam called his wife's name Eve; because she was the mother of all living. Unto Adam also and to his wife did the LORD God make coats of skins, and clothed them.

(D) And the LORD God said, "Behold, the man[23] is become as one of us, to know good and evil: and now, lest he put forth his hand, and take also of the tree of life,[24] and eat, and live forever": Therefore the LORD God sent him forth from the garden of Eden, to till the ground from whence he was taken. So he drove out the man; and he placed at the east of the garden of Eden cherubims,[25] and a flaming sword which turned every way, to keep the way of[26] the tree of life.

—Genesis 1–3

19. **cattle:** animals.
20. **enmity:** hostility.
21. **conception:** pains in childbearing.
22. **hearkened unto:** listened and obeyed.
23. **man:** both man and woman.
24. **tree of life:** the first indication that the tree granting everlasting life is prohibited to humanity.
25. **cherubims:** large, fierce angels, quite unlike the modern idea of a cherub.
26. **keep the way of:** prevent access to.

Roundtable Divide the class into groups of five to seven students each. Have the groups pass around a sheet of paper, each student writing a question that responds to this statement: "One question that the Genesis account tries to answer is this: _____ ?" Groups' responses can help the class see the rich complexity of the narrative; they also may serve as a study guide.

Cultural Diversity The Genesis account is a key to the beliefs of Jews and Christians, and it has helped to shape the culture of peoples among whom those religions are strong. Other religions have their own creation stories. Encourage students to find (in their own backgrounds or through research) and share such stories; discuss what answers to a culture's questions the stories help to explain.

Thematic Connections: "The Power of the Word" Challenge students to identify various concepts of the Word in this account. [Possible responses: God needed only words to speak most of creation into being (Adam and Eve being the exceptions); the fall of Adam and Eve came from their disobedience to the one word of prohibition declared by God; Genesis is the first book in what often is called the Word of God.]

A Beam of Protons Illuminates Gutenberg's Genius

MALCOLM W. BROWNE

The birth of modern printing four centuries ago is cloaked in obscurity, but with the help of the cyclotron used to develop the atomic bomb, scientists are wresting long-forgotten secrets from Gutenberg Bibles and other antique documents to reconstruct the technology of the Renaissance.

In cooperation with scholars at New York City's Pierpont Morgan Library and elsewhere, a group of researchers at the Davis campus of the University of California has learned that Johann Gutenberg of Mainz, Germany, was an even greater inventor and innovator than historians had known. At Davis, physicists and historians have pioneered a technique capable of probing the atoms making up paper, parchment, and ink, thereby opening a new dimension of history to exploration.

The German invention of movable type around 1450 is one of the farthest-reaching technological achievements in history. Movable type, which could be assembled rapidly and put on a printing press, permitted the mass production of books and documents. Literacy, traditionally reserved to churchmen, scholars, scribes, and aristocrats, spread swiftly to the masses and forever changed the nature of society.

Paradoxically, however, the earliest printers left no written descriptions of their monumental achievement. According to Paul Needham, curator of printed books and bindings at the Morgan Library (which owns three Gutenberg Bibles), no one knows what Gutenberg's printing press looked like.

But Dr. Needham and the cyclotron team at Davis have learned a great deal about how Gutenberg and his associates worked and what materials they used.

Directing the cyclotron analyses of old documents is Thomas A. Cahill, head of the Crocker Nuclear Laboratory at Davis. "One of the most remarkable things we discovered in our five-year study," Dr. Cahill said in an interview, "was that Gutenberg's genius extended to the formulation of inks as well as the development of movable type. Other printers of the late 15th century and printers even today tend to use inks based on oils and carbon black. But for Gutenberg, nothing but the best would do. We found within a few seconds of our first analysis of his ink that it is unusually rich in compounds of lead and copper. Lead and copper were Gutenberg's signature, and their presence in the ink on a document is as convincing a sign of his agency as his own hand would be."

Dr. Cahill believes the high levels of copper and lead in Gutenberg's inks account for the fact that the printing in his books remains as fresh, glossy, and black as it was when it came off his press. Bibliographers regard the Gutenberg Bible, printed between 1454 and 1456, as one of the most perfectly printed books ever, rarely matched in quality even in modern times.

Gutenberg's most famous work is his "forty-two-line Bible," so called because nearly every column of type in its 1,286 pages is forty-two lines long. Some of the forty-two-line Bibles were printed on paper and others on vellum, but experts regard the workmanship in all of them as superb. The left and right margins of each of the two columns on each page are perfectly squared off, and Gutenberg avoided hyphenation by inconspicuously squeezing his type together or spreading it out.

Dr. Cahill and Richard N. Schwab, a history professor at Davis, began applying the cyclotron to historical problems in the early 1980s as an outgrowth of the Crocker Laboratory's work on air pollution. The cyclotron accelerates a narrow beam of protons that pierces a sample, and protons collide with some of the atoms in the sample along the way. When this happens, the atoms emit X-rays, whose varying energies match the specific types of atoms from [which] they were emitted. A detector measures these energies, and with this data a computer can determine the types and quantities of the elements present in the substance being studied.

The analysis of Gutenberg documents required still subtler techniques, Dr. Cahill said. Although the signatures of Gutenberg inks depend on their copper and lead content, the quantities of these and other metals varied appreciably from one batch of ink to another. Gutenberg's workers evidently compounded their inks according to a general recipe but may have been sloppy in their measuring. Similarly, the cyclotron can detect differences among the atomic signatures of various batches of paper (often bearing different watermarks) that Gutenberg used. A single Bible often contains pages from several

A. Critical Reading: Finding Main Ideas

In standard journalistic style, the main points are presented near the beginning of this account. After students have read the article, have them come back to this paragraph and identify its statement of the main idea or ideas. [The main ideas are that Gutenberg was "an even greater inventor and innovator" than had been thought and that the technology used in the study holds great promise for other research projects.]

B. Reader's Response: Connecting with the Text

? How do you think the invention of movable type has affected your life? [Sample responses: It has made possible a wide variety of reading material for both educational and recreational purposes; it has encouraged the education of great numbers of people; almost every aspect of life is made easier because printed materials are readily available.]

C. Expansion

Dr. Cahill appreciates the durability of Gutenberg's lead- and copper-based inks; but both they and the oil- and carbon-based inks of Gutenberg's era are being used less and less on modern presses. Today, printers are increasingly turning to soy-based inks that are more environmentally friendly; however, soy was not grown in western Europe, so Gutenberg had no chance to experiment with it.

D. Critical Reading: Making Inferences

? What does the "workmanship" of which Browne speaks suggest about Gutenberg's character? [Possible answers: That he was a perfectionist; that his respect for the Bible led him to make sure that it came off his press looking beautiful.]

ASSESSMENT TOOLS

Check Test: Questions and Answers

1. What does God do on the first day of creation? On the seventh? [On the first day, God creates light, separates it from darkness, and gives the two the names *Day* and *Night*. On the seventh day, having finished the work of creation, God rests.]

2. Why does God create Eve? [It is "not good" for Adam to be alone.]

3. With what does the serpent tempt Eve? [With the forbidden fruit; with the promise that she and Adam will be as gods.]

4. What punishment does God mete out to Adam and Eve? [Adam is condemned to a life of often unproductive work and to the certainty of death; Eve will experience sorrow and pain in childbirth and will be under Adam's dominion.]

Making Meanings

First Thoughts

1. Students may say that Eden, with its abundance and little hardship, was a great loss. Conversely, they may think that humans thrive on adversity and would have been bored in Paradise.

Shaping Interpretations

2. God's supreme power and authority (omnipotence); God's holiness and justice; God's benevolence; perhaps God's love for diversity.

3. The Sabbath is the day on which God stopped working and rested. That God "blessed" and "sanctified" the Sabbath implies how important it is to have a day without work, a day he established as a period of rest and contemplation for humanity.

4. Humans are formed by God rather than merely spoken into being. This excerpt from Genesis emphasizes the purpose of caring for the earth that has been entrusted to us; it also suggests that part of our original purpose was to enjoy a close personal relationship with the Creator.

5. Adam's creation from dust foreshadows the return of his body to dust after death.

6. It accounts for humanity's existence; it explains why people suffer (in childbirth, in hard and often unproductive work, in self-consciousness) and ultimately die; the narrative also sheds light upon humanity's sense of good and evil and upon its spiritual longings.

7. Some students may feel that the tree had some magical power and that by eating the fruit, Adam and Eve—who existed in a world that had known only goodness—learned about the existence of evil. Other students may feel that the tree symbolizes obedience and that after Adam and Eve ate of the tree, they knew evil by having committed it.

8. Images may correspond to questions that students jot down in their Reader's Logs; most images will relate to the days of creation, the temptation and fall, and the punishment that resulted from that sin.

9. Paradise is pictured as beautiful and abundant, supplying humanity's every need. It also is a place of peace where no animal need fear violence. Students may agree with the images in Genesis; some may add entertainment, technology, or other modern conveniences to their pictures of paradise.

Extending the Text

10. **(Evaluation)** Possible response: Characteristic traits include ambition (a hunger to be like God) and curiosity; these traits remain today. People continue to strive for knowledge and power, and this can be both bad and good, depending on what means people use to achieve their ambitions.

---

different batches of paper that were printed at separate times.

By calculating how various inks and papers were combined in each volume, Dr. Cahill and his associates were able to reconstruct Gutenberg's manufacturing process step by step. "There were times when we could almost hear Gutenberg's press creaking," Dr. Cahill said.

This led to the realization that Gutenberg's workshop was much more sophisticated than many scholars had supposed, he said. The shop evidently employed a team of typesetters, all working simultaneously on separate batches of pages, carefully calculating space and text to make certain the assembled volume would come out exactly right.

These separately composed sections fit together almost seamlessly, but there are a few exceptions. One of the rare visible flaws occurs in the middle of Psalm 79, according to Dr. Needham of the Morgan Library.

"The compositor setting the type up to that point was probably sitting next to the compositor who was setting subsequent pages," he said. "One can see that the planning was not quite perfect, because the first compositor found himself in trouble on his last page, stuck with too much space and too little text. He eliminated abbreviations and stretched out his lines, but even so he came up short, and that page has only forty-one lines."

—*from The New York Times,*
May 12, 1987

Page from Johann Gutenberg's 42-line Latin Bible (1453–1456) printed at Mainz.
The Granger Collection, New York.

MAKING MEANINGS

First Thoughts

1. How do you feel about the world that was lost when Adam and Eve sinned?

Shaping Interpretations

2. What characteristics or qualities of God does the Genesis narrative emphasize? (In your answer, consider the phrases "and it was so" and "it was good.")

3. How does this narrative explain the Sabbath—the day of rest?

4. How does this narrative view God's human creations? According to Genesis, what is our purpose on earth?

5. The name Adam relates to the Hebrew *adamah,* meaning "of the soil." How does Adam's creation from dust **foreshadow** his ultimate fate?

6. What aspects of the human condition does the story of Adam and Eve account for?

7. Scholars have speculated about the meaning of the tree of knowledge of good and evil. Read the text carefully, and decide what you think this tree **symbolizes** and exactly what happened as a result of Adam and Eve's eating of its fruit.

8. What **images** in the Creation and Eden stories do you find most vivid? (Refer to the Reader's Log entry you wrote on page 415.)

9. How does the writer of Genesis picture Paradise? In *your* imagination, what would a paradise be like?

Extending the Text

10. According to Genesis, what traits are characteristic of the human creation? Do you think these traits are still manifested in human life today? Are they totally negative traits, positive traits, or a mixture?

420 THE RENAISSANCE

salms: Worship Through Poetry

The Bible is full of poetry. Every book of it contains poems or fragments of poems inserted into the prose text, and much of the prose itself is highly rhythmical. One book, the Psalms, consists entirely of poems, some of which were set to music and sung during worship services in the ancient temple in Jerusalem. The book of Psalms preserves 150 of these songs, a fraction of the total number that the ancient Hebrews knew and sang. Psalms were used as hymnals and included songs appropriate for many types of worship: thanksgiving, lament, praise, and devotion. Modern scholars now agree that the psalms were written by many authors over many centuries, but seventy-three of the psalms are said to be "for David" or "concerning David," the heroic Hebrew king.

In English, a collection of psalms is called a psalter (the *p* is silent as in the word *psalm* itself). (In Hebrew, the name for the collection is *Tehillim*, or "songs of praise.") There have been dozens of English psalters besides the one in the King James Bible, but none of them has lasted so well and so long. King James's translators did not try to impose rhyme on their versions because there is no rhyme in the originals. Instead, they imitated such Hebrew poetic devices as **repetition** and **parallel structure** (the use of sentences or phrases similar in structure):

> Let the floods clap their hands,
> Let the hills be joyful together.
> —Psalm 98:8

The psalmists were fond of saying essentially the same thing twice, in different words ("thy rod and thy staff" in Psalm 23). The King James Bible uses the numbering of the ancient Hebrew manuscripts; some other Bibles use a different numbering derived from a Greek translation of the Hebrew, and these Bibles have an extra psalm, number 151.

Biblical poetry, then, is much like modern free verse in that it does not have rhyme and meter but it does have other patterns of repetition, balance, antithesis, and parallelism. Metaphors and similes abound, and so do images drawn from nature and everyday experience:

> My God, in him will I trust.
> Surely he shall deliver thee from the snare of the fowler,
> And from the noisome pestilence.
> He shall cover thee with his feathers,
> And under his wings shalt thou trust:
> His truth shall be thy shield and buckler.
> Thou shalt not be afraid for the terror by night;
> Nor for the arrow that flieth by day;
> Nor for the pestilence that walketh in darkness;
> Nor for the destruction that wasteth at noonday.
> —Psalm 91:2–6

(Above left) Illuminated "P" (detail) (c. 1500) from a Flemish Bible.
Victoria and Albert Museum, London.

421

A. Expansion
Poems appear even in books of the Bible that are essentially prose (such as David's lament for Saul and Jonathan in 2 Samuel 1:19–27, Mary's "Magnificat" in Luke 1:46–55). Much of the wisdom literature (Job, Proverbs, the Song of Solomon, and Ecclesiastes) and prophetic literature (Isaiah, Jeremiah) of the Bible is also lyrical.

B. Language Note: Etymology
Explain to students that the English word *psalms* comes from Latin *psalmi,* coming in turn from Greek *psalmoi,* "sacred songs chanted with accompaniment."

C. Literary Connections
John Calvin praised Psalms as "the mirror of man." Historically, the Gospels and Psalms have been the books of the Bible most often published as separate volumes. *The Bay Psalm Book* (1640) was the first book published in America.

Into the Selection

Using BEFORE YOU READ p. 422

Reading Focus
Some students will have read or heard some version of Psalm 23. They also may be aware of some of its key expressions; ask them if they have heard the following phrases: "The Lord is my shepherd," "the valley of the shadow of death," and "my cup runneth over." Ask them to jot down in their Reader's Logs in what context they have heard them and to consider why these expressions have passed into common usage. Ask for volunteers to share their responses.

English Language Development To help students who may have difficulty with the archaic language used to create Psalm 23, have students as a class activity rewrite the psalm in the language of today. Divide the class into small study groups, making sure to combine English-language learners with English-proficient peers. Assign each group two or three lines. Have each group decide how

its section would be spoken or sung today. Put each group's creation on the chalkboard or on a transparency for all students to copy into their Reader's Logs.

Less Proficient Readers Some comparisons might help students access the images of shepherding and of captivity. For Psalm 23, ask students

to think of the person they trust most; students may write notes in their Reader's Logs about why that person inspires trust. You might relate Psalm 137 to the experience of oppressed peoples, and have students discuss comparisons that strike them as they read.

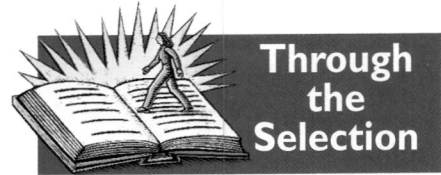

Through the Selection

A. Reader's Response: First Thoughts

Encourage responses to the images of "green pastures" and "still waters." Students might freewrite in their Reader's Logs about these images or sketch a scene that these images suggest. [Sample responses: The scene is very peaceful. This is a place anyone would want to be. The pool has perfect reflections in it.]

B. Critical Reading: Identifying Main Ideas

After students have read Psalm 23 in its entirety, have them come back to this line. Ask how the idea in this sentence surfaces again and again in the psalm's details. [Possible answer: At first, the psalmist's soul is restored because he can trust God to supply his needs and to deal kindly with him. Then his soul is restored because it inhabits "the paths of righteousness." It need not fear danger, for the shepherd is there. It can rejoice over its enemies and in its shepherd's hospitality. Its restoration comes in the promise of "goodness and mercy" throughout life and in a certain place "in the house of the Lord forever."]

C. Reader's Response: Connecting with the Text

[?] What kinds of experiences do you think people would describe as "walk[ing] through the valley of the shadow of death"? [Sample responses: Dealing with life-threatening illness; living with depression or another emotional problem; being attacked physically or verbally.]

Reading Focus

The Lord Is . . .
This song of trust, affirming the speaker's faith and confidence in God, is probably the best-known religious poem in the Western world. The opening verses, comparing God to a shepherd, use the kind of pastoral imagery found throughout the Bible. Then the metaphors in the psalm change, and the Lord becomes a host providing a banquet for the speaker, whose enemies watch him enviously as he eats, not daring to harm him. Among the rich and varied images of the poem, there is also a suggestion of the speaker as a pilgrim traveling through a dangerous world.

Quickwrite

READER'S LOG

This song was sung by a pastoral people, so the comparison of the Lord to a shepherd is appropriate. The world is very different for most people today. What metaphors would you use to describe the comforting presence of God?

Bas-relief of shepherds.
Lintel over west portal.
Cathedral, Chartres, France.

Psalm 23

The LORD is my shepherd; I shall not want.
He maketh me to lie down in green pastures:
He leadeth me beside the still waters.
He restoreth my soul:
5 He leadeth me in the paths of righteousness for his name's sake.°
Yea, though I walk through the valley of the shadow of death,
I will fear no evil: For thou art with me;
Thy rod and thy staff they comfort me.
Thou preparest a table before me in the presence of mine enemies:
10 Thou anointest my head with oil; my cup runneth over.
Surely goodness and mercy shall follow me all the days of my life:
And I will dwell in the house of the LORD forever.

5. his name's sake: That is, he will live up to his name as shepherd.

422 THE RENAISSANCE

OPTIONS FOR TEACHING

Strategic Reading Students may have strong responses to these psalms, especially if the Bible dominates their ethnic or spiritual background. As small groups meet for Collaborative Talk about these psalms, remind students of the value of considering various responses and the importance of mutual respect.

INTEGRATING THE LANGUAGE ARTS

Grammar Challenge students to use these psalms to explore characteristics of the grammar in the King James Bible. Have them consider the following questions: In Psalm 23, why is it "*my* shepherd" but "*mine* enemies"? [*My* modifies singular nouns; *mine*, plurals.] In Psalm 137, how are *thee* and *thou* used? [*Thee* is the direct object; *thou* is the subject.] When are the –*eth* and –*est* endings appropriate for a verb? [The suffix –*eth* is used for the third person; –*est* for the second person.]

CLASSROOM MANAGEMENT

Managing the Reader's Response Classroom After students have expressed their own reactions, encourage them to expand the possibilities. Invite them to consider the possible responses of people with various backgrounds and experiences.

Reading Focus

Captivities

This is a song of entreaty on the occasion of a national catastrophe: The Jewish people are being held captive in Babylon.

Quickwrite

What other experiences in the history of the world might have inspired people to beg for release from captivity or even to seek vengeance on their captors?

Background

In the sixth century B.C., Nebuchadnezzar, king of Babylonia, conquered Jerusalem and deported the Hebrews to Babylon, a great ancient city that is now a ruin near Baghdad on the Euphrates River. The speaker of Psalm 137 is a captive Hebrew, bitterly lamenting his people's exile. The Babylonians have asked their captives to sing to entertain them, but what do the captives have to sing about?

Into the Selection

Using BEFORE YOU READ p. 423

Reading Focus

Write the word *captive* in a circle on the chalkboard. Then, work with the class to create a word web, branching from the circle to jot down feelings and images that students associate with captivity. When students have completed their suggestions, ask them which items they think someone would want to sing about.

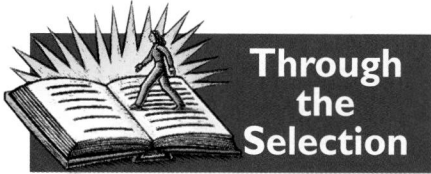

Through the Selection

Psalm 137

By the rivers of Babylon, there we sat down, yea, we wept,
When we remembered Zion.°
We hanged our harps
Upon the willows in the midst thereof.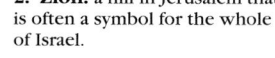
5 For there they that carried us away captive required of us a song;
And they that wasted us required of us mirth,
Saying, "Sing us one of the songs of Zion."
How shall we sing the LORD's song
In a strange land?
10 If I forget thee, O Jerusalem,
Let my right hand forget her cunning.
If I do not remember thee,
Let my tongue cleave° to the roof of my mouth;
If I prefer not Jerusalem above my chief joy.
15 Remember, O LORD, the children of Edom° in the day of Jerusalem;
Who said, "Raze it,° raze it, even to the foundation thereof."
O daughter of Babylon,° who art to be destroyed;
Happy shall he be, that rewardeth thee
As thou hast served us.
20 Happy shall he be, that taketh
And dasheth thy little ones against the stones. **B**

2. Zion: a hill in Jerusalem that is often a symbol for the whole of Israel.

13. cleave: adhere; stick.

15. children of Edom: The Edomites, neighbors of the Hebrews, rejoiced when the Hebrews were conquered and deported.
16. Raze it: Level it to the ground.
17. daughter of Babylon: the Babylonian people.

THE KING JAMES BIBLE 423

A. Literary Element: Imagery

? What kind of feelings do you think are being expressed in the unusual image of "harps / Upon the willows"? How do those feelings relate to the singer's situation? [Possible answers: A feeling of displacement, or not belonging, because the singer is a displaced person in Babylon; depression and a sense of uselessness, because the speaker longs for his homeland.]

B. Critical Reading: Making Inferences

Read this line so that *thy* is emphasized. Does the emphasis help you to understand the singer any better? Explain.
[Possible answer: Yes; it suggests that the singer has seen his or her own babies dashed to death by the captors. It also better illustrates ll. 18–19, which indicate that the form of Babylon's judgment will be similar to the form of the wrongs that it has dealt the captive Hebrews.]

CROSSING THE CURRICULUM

Music Psalm 23 and Psalm 137 express markedly different feelings. How might these psalms have sounded when sung? Pairs or groups of students may begin to explore the question by finding one or more pieces of music that they feel capture the essence of each psalm. As they play their selections for the class, have them explain their choices.

Social Studies Offer these activities to interested students:
- For Psalm 23: Find out more about shepherding. Try to discover what characteristics would make some shepherds more valuable than others.
- For Psalm 137: Do some research to learn why the city of Jerusalem is so important to the singer's past and to his present thoughts.

Students may present their findings in a format of their own choosing.

Technology Tip

The complete King James version of the Bible is available on CD-ROM. Also, a cross-referenced, hypertext version is available from the Web site of Jubilee Christian Center at **http://www.jubilee.org/bible/index.html**. *You may want to preview any Internet activity that you suggest to students. Because these resources are sometimes public forums, their content can be unpredictable.*

Making Meanings

First Thoughts

1. Psalm 23 might remind the singer of Psalm 137 that God, the Shepherd, could guide the Hebrews through their captivity—a "valley of the shadow of death"—and bring them again to the lush fields and clear lakes of their own land. Psalm 23 also stresses God's provision for all needs, even those of a captive, with the hint of a promise that the singer's enemies would see this and be amazed.

Shaping Interpretations

2. The speaker describes the metaphorical "green pastures" and "still waters" to which God will lead him (sheep will not drink from rapidly moving water); he speaks of the comforting presence of the Shepherd's rod and staff.
3. The speaker describes the Host's graciousness in preparing a table for him and in providing a cup that overflows.
4. Homesickness is conveyed strongly in ll. 1–2 and 10–14, as is revenge in ll. 15–21. Reactions to the final line will vary, but could include horror, fear, or understanding.

Connecting with the Text

5. In general, the psalm might reassure the survivors of God's care for them; specifically, its images of "walk[ing] through the valley of the shadow of death" and "dwell[ing] in the house of the Lord forever" are easily applied to death and to the hope that the departed has been welcomed into heaven.

Jeremiah Lamenting over Jerusalem.

MAKING MEANINGS

Psalms 23 and 137

First Thoughts

1. How do you think Psalm 23 could be used to provide solace to the singer of Psalm 137?

Shaping Interpretations

2. In Psalm 23, how does the singer extend the **metaphor** comparing God to a shepherd?
3. The second metaphor in Psalm 23 compares God to a generous host. (In the ancient Middle East, it was a sign of hospitality to anoint a guest's head and dusty feet with oil.) How does the speaker extend this metaphor of God as a gracious host and the singer as his guest?

4. The speaker in Psalm 137 is both homesick and vengeful. Which lines convey these emotions most vividly to you? How did you react to the final line?

Connecting with the Text

5. Psalm 23 is often read at funerals or memorial services. Why do you think people find it consoling? (Refer to your Reader's Log entry for page 422.)
6. Both psalms are full of vivid **imagery.** What pictures does each song put in your mind?

Extending the Text

7. On what occasion might Psalm 137 be sung? What relevance does this lament have for people today? (You might want to refer to your Reader's Log entry for page 423.)

6. Possible responses: Psalm 23 creates pictures of green fields and pools of water, a dark, frightening valley, and a welcoming table. The vastly different imagery in Psalm 137 creates visions of people weeping by a river and sorrowfully hanging their harps on the willows; of faltering hands and people unable to speak; of burning cities and children brutally killed.

Extending the Text

7. **(Analysis)** Psalm 137 would have meaning for any group facing literal or figurative captivity; it also might be appropriate for times of warfare. What keeps the psalm universally relevant, despite its historical context, is the emotion expressed by the singer—love for homeland, a lament at being away from it, and a desire to see wrongs avenged.

Reading Focus

Profound Truths

A **parable** is a very short anecdote that teaches a moral or religious lesson. In the Christian Bible, instead of speaking abstractly and philosophically, Jesus often taught his followers by means of parables. On the surface, parables seem to be simple stories. Looked at closely, they concern the profound truths and moral laws on which human happiness depends.

Quickwrite

READER'S LOG

To test your Biblical knowledge, write down quickly what you think a Good Samaritan is.

Background

To understand this parable, you have to know that it is set in a totally Jewish context. According to Jewish law, the priest and the Levite (a member of the priestly tribe) would be considered legally unclean if they touched a dead person. Samaritans were people from Samaria who had a mixed ancestry and a mixed religion. They used the Torah of the Hebrew Bible as their scriptures, but the Hebrews to the south frowned on the Samaritans' mixed religious practices. The lawyer is questioning Jesus.

The Parable of the Good Samaritan

And, behold, a certain lawyer stood up, and tempted him, saying, "Master, what shall I do to inherit eternal life?" He said unto him, "What is written in the law? how readest thou?" And he answering said, "Thou shalt love the Lord thy God with all thy heart, and with all thy soul, and with all thy strength, and with all thy mind; and thy neighbor as thyself." And he said unto him, "Thou hast answered right: This do, and thou shalt live." But he, willing to justify himself, said unto Jesus, "And who is my neighbor?" And Jesus answering said, "A certain man went down from Jerusalem to Jericho, and fell among thieves, which stripped him of his raiment,[1] and wounded him, and departed, leaving him half dead. And by chance there came down a certain priest that way: And when he saw him, he passed by on the other side. And likewise a Levite, when he was at the place, came and looked on him, and passed by on the other side. But a certain Samaritan, as he journeyed, came where he was: And when he saw him, he had compassion on him, and went to him, and bound up his wounds, pouring in oil and wine,[2] and set him on his own beast, and brought him to an inn, and took care of him. And on the morrow when he departed, he took out two pence, and gave them to the host, and said unto him, 'Take care of him; and whatsoever thou spendest more, when I come again, I will repay thee.' Which now of these three, thinkest thou, was neighbor unto him that fell among the thieves?" And he said, "He that showed mercy on him." Then said Jesus unto him, "Go, and do thou likewise."

—Luke 10:25–37

1. **raiment:** clothing.
2. **oil and wine:** ancient medicine.

Into the Selection

Using BEFORE YOU READ p. 425

Background

Given the poor relationship between Jews and Samaritans, Jesus' choice of a Samaritan for the hero of the parable is probably surprising. But Jesus, who often thwarted people's expectations, did not look down on Samaritans. Most of John 4 is set in Samaria where Jesus had a long religious discussion with a woman who was amazed at this teacher's lack of prejudice.

Through the Selection

A. Exploring the Historical Period

A lawyer was an expert in the Mosaic law, not an attorney in the modern sense. The word *tempted* here means *tested,* and it identifies the lawyer as one of those critics who often challenged the authority of Jesus by setting a trap of difficult questions.

B. Critical Reading: Finding Sequence

? What importance do you attach to the order in which passersby encounter the victim? [Possible response: Jesus first names a priest whose ethics and calling would make him the most likely rescuer. Then comes a Levite—not quite as important as a priest but still (as a person whose life is dedicated to service in the Temple) someone whom one would expect to help. Last of all is the Samaritan—not only is he not a Jewish religious leader, but he follows "mixed religious practices" and is, to some extent, the victim's enemy. The sequence emphasizes the teaching that anyone can be one's neighbor, even those one might least expect.]

STRATEGIES FOR INCLUSION

Auditory Because the parable is so short, students can easily read it aloud. You can have them read the parable only, or to emphasize the story within a story, break up the reading so that one student reads the parable and another reads the introductory and closing material.

INTEGRATING THE LANGUAGE ARTS

Language and Style Although this parable was intended to teach rather than to entertain, it shows that Jesus knew how to hold an audience with a story. Invite students to examine the language, style, and narrative elements in the parable by drawing five boxes to represent the five sentences in the parable. In the boxes, have them record in their own words what each sentence accomplishes in the parable. This activity will emphasize how compact the parable is. ☞

Making Meanings

First Thoughts

1. Anyone could be a neighbor. A neighbor is actually someone who lives next door or nearby.

Shaping Interpretations

2. The law says that in order to achieve eternal life, one must love God with all the strength of one's being and love others as one loves oneself.

3. The lawyer wants to prove that he has a good reason for questioning Jesus, and he may want to test Jesus further.

4. The traveler was attacked by thieves, who robbed and beat him, and then left him half dead along the road.

5. The audience would have expected the priest and the Levite to be sensitive to the higher demands of charity, even if it meant defiling themselves. But the Samaritan, who is not only an outsider but a heretic (living outside of obedience to the law), is the one who has compassion for the victim.

Extending the Text

6. **(Evaluation)** Students might name a famous person, such as Mother Teresa or someone they know personally. The closest parallel to the Good Samaritan would be a person who willingly inconveniences himself or herself without thought of reward to help a stranger.

Challenging the Text

7. **(Analysis and Synthesis)** Possible response: The idea of the thieves' attack might not need modifying; but the identities of the first two passersby might change from priest and Levite to broader and better-known professions (perhaps minister and social worker).

8. **(Evaluation)** Some students may believe life in the late twentieth century is much more complex; more prejudice exists, and people have many more excuses to avoid the inconvenience that the Good Samaritan accepted. Other students may suggest that the point of the parable is more relevant today than ever.

The Good Samaritan (1633) by Rembrandt van Rijn.

©Rijksmuseum-Stichting, Amsterdam.

MAKING MEANINGS

First Thoughts

1. According to the **parable,** how are you supposed to answer the question "Who is my neighbor?" In actuality, how would you answer the question?

Shaping Interpretations

2. Jesus asks the lawyer at the beginning what the law says about eternal life. What does the law say?

3. Why does the lawyer press on and ask another question: Who is my neighbor?

4. According to the parable, what happened to the man who journeyed from Jerusalem to Jericho?

5. Why is it **ironic** that the priest and the Levite ignore the wounded man, but the Samaritan helps him?

Extending the Text

6. What Good Samaritans do you know of in the world today? How does your response compare with your Reader's Log entry for page 425?

Challenging the Text

7. If you were writing an updated version of this parable, which details would you change to make it relevant to life in our society today?

8. Do you think this parable makes a point that is still important today? Talk about its relevance at the end of the twentieth century.

426 THE RENAISSANCE

PROFESSIONAL NOTES

Cultural Diversity Jesus makes the amazing statement that an enemy who comes to your rescue in a time of need is your neighbor. The context he refers to is the clash between Hebrews and Samaritans. Have students name other clashes of peoples (from history or from their knowledge of world cultures) and figures within those clashes to which Jesus' parable could apply. [Students may suggest clashes based on politics, religion, or race.

For example, in Hitler's Germany, Oskar Schindler could be considered a Samaritan figure; in the racial clashes of the 1960s in the United States, Martin Luther King, Jr. would fit the Samaritan role in that he preached for the good of all people. Mother Teresa is certainly a good Samaritan, for though she is a Catholic nun, she helps people of various faiths.]

CHOICES: Building Your Portfolio

Writer's Notebook

1. Collecting Ideas for a Cause-Effect Essay

The effects of disobedience are the focus of the opening chapters of Genesis. This tendency to disobedience is one of many characteristics fundamental to human nature. Jot down some notes about another human trait, such as loyalty or ambition. You could ask yourself why: Why are some people loyal or ambitious? Or you could ask yourself what if: What if all competition were removed from society so that ambition was stifled? Save your notes to use in the Writer's Workshop on page 459.

Creative Writing

2. A Parable for Today

Try writing your own parable to illustrate a practical lesson about life today. First, identify the moral or spiritual truth you want to illustrate. Then, think of an everyday event that happened to you or someone you know that could illustrate this lesson. The parables in the Christian Bible find lessons in a poor woman who loses a coin, a dishonest employee who cheats his boss, bridesmaids who are asleep when the wedding party arrives, and a father who welcomes back a son who has been so wasteful he becomes the Biblical equivalent of a homeless person.

Critical Writing

3. Same Psalm, Different Words

The version of Psalm 23 below appeared in a psalter translated by the Massachusetts Puritans and published in the *Bay Psalm Book* (1640). Write an essay comparing it to the version in the King James Bible. Tell which version you prefer and why.

Oral Interpretation

4. Making a Psalm Sing

Prepare a group of the psalms for oral recitation. As you prepare for your presentation, pay particular attention to the way the psalms use **repetition** and **parallel structure** to create rhythm. How many speakers will you assign to each psalm? The psalms were originally sung to the accompaniment of a harp. Will you provide any background music to dramatize your interpretations?

Research/Speaking

5. The Inventive Renaissance

In "A Beam of Protons Illuminates Gutenberg's Genius" (page 419), you read about Gutenberg's innovations. What other remarkable inventions or technological innovations date from the Renaissance? Who are the people behind these creations? Select one person or invention to write about, and present your findings in a brief oral report.

Psalm 23

The Lord to me a shepherd is; want therefore shall not I.
He in the folds of tender grass doth cause me down to lie.
To waters calm me gently leads, restore my soul doth he;
He doth in paths of righteousness for his name's sake lead me.
5 Yea, though in valley of death's shade I walk, none ill I'll fear,
Because thou art with me; thy rod and staff my comfort are.
For me a table thou hast spread in presence of my foes;
Thou dost anoint my head with oil; my cup it overflows.
Goodness and mercy surely shall all my days follow me.
10 And in the Lord's house I shall dwell so long as days shall be.

STRATEGIES FOR INCLUSION

Kinesthetic For activity #5, some students might want to create a model of one of the Renaissance inventions and show how it works, in addition to explaining the theory behind it. Not all the inventions need to be things that succeeded. A report on Leonardo da Vinci's flying machine and his theories surrounding it, for example, would be interesting.

PORTFOLIO ASSESSMENT

Choices: Assessment Criteria For help in evaluating these Choices assignments, see the criteria in the *Portfolio Management System,* pp. 104–105.

Beyond the Selections

Choices: Building Your Portfolio

1. **Writer's Notebook** Remind students to save their work. They may use it as prewriting for the Writer's Workshop on p. 459.
2. **Creative Writing** Invite students to gain experience as oral historians by interviewing people and asking them to share experiences from which they learned something. Students may change their subjects' names and other details in the parables but should keep the narratives simple. As students share their efforts, if two or more parables teach a similar lesson, have the class discuss how the stories that present the lesson differ.
3. **Critical Writing** Encourage students to use a two-column response journal for their evaluation. As they compare the two versions verse by verse, have them make one note about each version in the appropriate column. When they have finished, students will find enough common positive and negative comments to lead them to an overall evaluation.
4. **Oral Interpretation** Since the text provides only two psalms, you might add others to create a group. For variety, you might include Psalm 51 (a confession of sin), Psalm 136 (a recounting of the Hebrews' early history, unusual for its use of refrain), or Psalm 150 (a call to joyful praise). Background music, if used, should reflect the general tone of the psalm. Encourage students to experiment with recitation techniques, including
(1) working with not only chorus and soloists but with duets and trios of readers;
(2) splitting a group to reflect parallel expressions of thought;
(3) repeating key words for echo effect (as with the last word of Psalm 23).
If possible, videotape the presentation for students' evaluation and enjoyment.

Background

One of the most powerful political philosophies in history was based on the teachings of Confucius (c. 551–c. 479 B.C.). Used by the rulers of the Chinese empire to maintain obedience and social harmony, Confucianism taught that a prosperous and cohesive society must be structured with roles for all members and with mutual obligation among them.

A Dialogue with the Text

Have students work in small groups to create mobiles of those prophecies, fables, parables, anecdotes, and proverbs they find most meaningful to them.

WORLD LITERATURE

Worlds of Wisdom

BEFORE YOU READ

Background

From age to age, from culture to culture, human beings have wrestled with the same problems and questions: How should we live? How can we be happy? What is justice?

Although the pieces of world wisdom that follow come from a wide variety of sources in Africa and Asia, they have two features in common. First, the forms represented here—prophecy, fable, parable, anecdote, and proverb—all spring from the oral tradition. Second, just as with the wisdom literature in the Hebrew Bible, many of these pieces have religious contexts.

The Koran, the holy book of Islam, contains God's revelation to Mohammed by the angel Gabriel. The text was first written down in Arabic in the middle of the seventh century.

The text of *The Panchatantra,* the most famous Sanskrit collection of fables from ancient India, probably dates from 100 B.C. to around A.D. 400.

According to tradition, this anthology was created as a practical manual in statecraft for young princes.

The parables illustrating the insights of Zen Buddhism are drawn from a philosophical and religious tradition within Buddhism that originated in China and then flowered in Japan starting in the twelfth century.

The poet Saadi, whose real name was Musharrif Od-Din Muslih Od-Din, lived in thirteenth-century Persia (now Iran). As a follower of Sufism, a mystical sect of Islam, he believed in the holiness of all creation. His witty, practical sayings and lush lyrics made him one of Persia's best-loved poets.

Taoism (dou′iz′əm), another Eastern tradition of religion and philosophy, developed in China shortly after the time that Buddhism first began in India, during the last centuries B.C.

Confucius, the founder of yet another Chinese philosophical system, left no written works. After his death in around 479 B.C., his disciples gathered his sayings in a collection known as the *Analects.*

For many centuries, the Jabo people of Liberia in West Africa have relied on proverbs in many key aspects of their social life and legal proceedings.

A Dialogue with the Text

READER'S LOG

As you read the pieces that follow, jot down notes on the ones that strike a chord in you. (You might also copy down quotes that you especially like.) What do these pieces say about how to lead a good and happy life?

428 THE RENAISSANCE

(Map) The world, from Mercator's *Atlas* (c. 1595).

PROGRAM MANAGER

- **Selection Summary** See Teaching Notes, *Teaching Resources A,* p. 107, for a summary of this selection.
- **Audiotaped Readings** To help less proficient readers or auditory learners through the lesson, use the Selected Reading, Audiocassette 1, Side B, in the *Audiovisual Resources Binder.*

Night

from the Koran

translated by **N. J. Dawood**

In the Name of Allah, the Compassionate, the Merciful

By the night, when she lets fall her darkness, and by the radiant day! By Him that created the male and the female, your endeavors have different ends!

For him that gives in charity and guards himself against evil and believes in goodness, We shall smooth the path of salvation; but for him that neither gives nor takes and disbelieves in goodness, We shall smooth the path of affliction. When he breathes his last, his riches will not avail him.

It is for Us to give guidance. Ours is the life of this world, Ours the life to come. I warn you, then, of the blazing fire, in which none shall burn save the hardened sinner, who denies the truth and gives no heed. But the good man who purifies himself by almsgiving[1] shall keep away from it: and so shall he that does good works for the sake of the Most High only, not in recompense[2] for a favor. Such men shall be content.

1. **almsgiving:** performing deeds of charity.
2. **recompense:** repayment.

Leaf from a Koran (11th century) in Kufic calligraphy. Iranian. Ink, colors, gold on paper.
The Metropolitan Museum of Art, New York. Rogers Fund, 1940 (40.164.2a).

A. Critical Reading: Drawing Conclusions

? According to the text, what kind of life should a person live? What will happen to those who live otherwise? [Possible responses: A person should live a good, charitable life. Those who do not will be punished, and no amount of money will save them.]

CONNECTING WITH "THE POWER OF THE WORD"

"In the beginning was the Word. . . ." (John 1:1) This striking statement about the power of the word comes from the New Testament. Its message resonates in this World Literature selection because these words from many cultures are beginnings. They are the foundation of societies; they embody people's definitions of themselves. These powerful words teach people not only how to behave, but who they are at the core of their moral being.

A. Literary Element: Foreshadowing

Here the storyteller inserts an air of suspense and warning. What do you think is going to happen? [Possible response: The turtle will probably not follow his own plan.]

B. Literary Element: Irony

? Why is it ironic that people chattering caused the turtle to lose his grip on the stick? [Possible response: He himself had taken a vow of silence; it was his inability to keep quiet that caused his downfall.]

C. Critical Reading: Making Generalizations

? If this fable were written to give advice to young Indian princes, what message would the storyteller be giving them? [Possible response: When a trusted friend gives you good advice, follow it.]

Shell-Neck, Slim, and Grim
from The Panchatantra

translated by **Arthur W. Ryder**

A Pair of Wild Fowls (detail) (1600–1625) attributed to Mansūr, Imperial Mughal.
Collection Navin Kumar, New York.

In a certain lake lived a turtle named Shell-Neck. He had as friends two ganders whose names were Slim and Grim. Now in the vicissitudes[1] of time there came a twelve-year drought, which begot ideas of this nature in the two ganders: "This lake has gone dry. Let us seek another body of water. However, we must first say farewell to Shell-Neck, our dear and long-proved friend."

When they did so, the turtle said: "Why do you bid me farewell? I am a water dweller, and here I should perish very quickly from the scant supply of water and from grief at loss of you. Therefore, if you feel any affection for me, please rescue me from the jaws of this death. Besides, as the water dries in this lake, you two suffer nothing beyond a restricted diet, while to me it means immediate

death. Consider which is more serious, loss of food or loss of life."

But they replied: "We are unable to take you with us since you are a water creature without wings." Yet the turtle continued: "There is a possible device. Bring a stick of wood." This they did, whereupon the turtle gripped the middle of the stick between his teeth, and said: "Now take firm hold with your bills, one on each side, fly up, and travel with even flight through the sky, until we discover another desirable body of water."

A But they objected: "There is a hitch in this fine plan. If you happen to indulge in the smallest conversation, then you will lose your hold on the stick, will fall from a great height, and will be dashed to bits."

"Oh," said the turtle, "from this moment I take a vow of silence, to last as long as we are in heaven." So they carried out the plan, but while the two ganders were painfully carrying the turtle over a neighboring city, the people below noticed the spectacle, and there arose a confused buzz of talk as they asked: "What is this cartlike object that two birds are carrying through the atmosphere?"

B Hearing this, the doomed turtle was heedless enough to ask: "What are these people chattering about?" The moment he spoke, the poor simpleton lost his grip and fell to the ground. And persons who wanted meat cut him to bits in a moment with sharp knives.

C "And that is why I say:
  To take advice from kindly friends
  Be ever satisfied:
The stupid turtle lost his grip
  Upon the stick, and died."

1. **vicissitudes:** unpredictable changes.

430 THE RENAISSANCE

OPTIONS FOR TEACHING

STRATEGIES FOR INCLUSION

Intrapersonal Have students write, then read aloud, advice column letters about real or imagined problems in society today. Call on volunteers to reply to the problem by citing appropriate quotations from Worlds of Wisdom.

Visual Have students draw cartoons depicting any one of the moral or life lessons gained from the wisdom literature. Students may want to include captions.

INTEGRATING THE LANGUAGE ARTS

Strategic Reading As students read the World Literature selection, have them use a graphic organizer like the following to chart the main points and to add class notes.

Worlds of Wisdom

Literature	Background	Class Notes

Zen Parables

compiled by **Paul Reps**

The Moon Cannot Be Stolen

Ryokan, a Zen master, lived the simplest kind of life in a little hut at the foot of a mountain. One evening a thief visited the hut only to discover there was nothing in it to steal.

Ryokan returned and caught him. "You may have come a long way to visit me," he told the prowler, "and you should not return empty-handed. Please take my clothes as a gift."

The thief was bewildered. He took the clothes and slunk away.

Ryokan sat naked, watching the moon. "Poor fellow," he mused, "I wish I could give him this beautiful moon."

Temper

A Zen student came to Bankei and complained: "Master, I have an ungovernable temper. How can I cure it?"

"You have something very strange," replied Bankei. "Let me see what you have."

"Just now I cannot show it to you," replied the other.

"When can you show it to me?" asked Bankei.

"It arises unexpectedly," replied the student.

"Then," concluded Bankei, "it must not be your own true nature. If it were, you could show it to me at any time. When you were born, you did not have it, and your parents did not give it to you. Think that over."

The Gates of Paradise

A soldier named Nobushige came to Hakuin, and asked: "Is there really a paradise and a hell?"

"Who are you?" inquired Hakuin.

"I am a samurai," the warrior replied.

"You, a soldier!" exclaimed Hakuin. "What kind of ruler would have you as his guard? Your face looks like that of a beggar."

Nobushige became so angry that he began to draw his sword, but Hakuin continued: "So you have a sword! Your weapon is probably much too dull to cut off my head."

As Nobushige drew his sword, Hakuin remarked: "Here open the gates of hell!"

At these words the samurai, perceiving the master's discipline, sheathed his sword and bowed.

"Here open the gates of paradise," said Hakuin.

Square dish (Edo period, early 18th century) by Ogata Kenzan and Ogata Korin. Stoneware with underglaze and enamel decoration.

The First Principle

When one goes to Obaku temple in Kyoto, he sees carved over the gate the words "The First Principle." The letters are unusually large, and those who appreciate calligraphy[1] always admire them as being a masterpiece. They were drawn by Kosen two hundred years ago.

When the master drew them he did so on paper, from which workmen made the larger carving in wood. As Kosen sketched the letters, a bold pupil was with him who had made several gallons of ink for the calligraphy and who never failed to criticize his master's work.

"That is not good," he told Kosen after the first effort.

"How is that one?"

"Poor. Worse than before," pronounced the pupil.

Kosen patiently wrote one sheet after another until eighty-four First Principles had accumulated, still without the approval of the pupil.

Then, when the young man stepped outside for a few moments, Kosen thought: "Now is my chance to escape his keen eye," and he wrote hurriedly, with a mind free from distraction: "The First Principle."

"A masterpiece," pronounced the pupil.

1. **calligraphy:** the art of beautiful handwriting.

A. Critical Reading: Analyzing Vocabulary

? What does the word *slunk* express about the thief's behavior? [Possible response: It indicates that he knew what he was doing was wrong, but he did it anyway.]

B. Reader's Response: Shaping Interpretations

? What does the master mean by his remark in this passage? [Sample responses: The moon is beyond the control of humans; it cannot be given or stolen. It has more meaning than material possessions.]

C. Reader's Response: Extending the Text

? What life message do you get from this parable? Do you agree with it? [Sample responses: A temper is not part of your true nature. Attitudes and actions, like a temper, are learned, not part of one's true nature, and can be controlled. Genetic qualities, chemical imbalances, and parental behavior may at least partially influence a person's nature.]

D. Critical Reading: Drawing Conclusions

? What is Hakuin telling the samurai? [Possible responses: Anger and assault are hell. A peaceful, disciplined life is paradise.]

E. Reader's Response: Extending the Text

? What message do you receive from this parable? [Sample responses: Use your natural talent and be yourself; don't try so hard to please others. You do your best work when you are calm and not afraid of scrutiny.]

Sayings of Saadi

translated by **Idries Shah**

Portrait of a dervish (early 17th century), Turkish. Colors on paper (8⅝″ × 4³/₁₆″).

The Metropolitan Museum of Art, New York. The Cora Timken Burnett Collection of Persian Miniatures and Other Persian Art Objects. Bequest of Cora Timken Burnett. (57.51.30).

The Unfed Dervish

When I see the poor dervish[1] unfed
My own food is pain and poison to me.

Information and Knowledge

A | However much you study, you cannot know
      without action.
   A donkey laden with books is neither an
      intellectual nor a wise man.
   Empty of essence, what learning has he—
   Whether upon him is firewood or book?

The Elephant Keeper

Make no friendship with an elephant keeper
If you have no room to entertain an elephant.

Safety and Riches

B | Deep in the sea are riches beyond compare.
   But if you seek safety, it is on the shore.

The Fox and the Camels

A fox was seen running away in terror. Someone asked what was troubling it. The fox answered: "They are taking camels for forced labor." "Fool!" he was told, "the fate of camels has nothing to do with you, who do not even look like one." "Silence!" said the fox, "for if an intriguer were to state that I was a camel, *who* would work for my release?"

1. **dervish:** Muslim monk dedicated to a life of poverty.

Taoist Anecdotes

translated and edited by **Moss Roberts**

Laozi (detail) from *Homage to the First Principle,* a Yüan dynasty wall painting.
Courtesy of the Royal Ontario Museum, Toronto.

Gold, Gold

Many, many years ago there was a man of the land of Ch'i who had a great passion for gold. One day at the crack of dawn he went to the market—straight to the gold dealers' stalls, where he snatched some gold and ran. The market guards soon caught him. "With so many people around, how did you expect to get away with it?" a guard asked.

"When I took it," he replied, "I saw only the gold, not the people."

—Lieh Tzu

A Clever Judge

In the days when Ch'en Shu-ku was a magistrate in Chienchou, there was a man who had lost an article of some value. A number of people were arrested, but no one could discover exactly who the thief was. So Shu-ku laid a trap for the suspects. "I know of a temple," he told them, "whose bell can tell a thief from an honest man. It has great spiritual powers."

The magistrate had the bell fetched and reverently enshrined in a rear chamber. Then he had the suspects brought before the bell to stand and testify to their guilt or innocence. He explained to them that if an innocent man touched the bell it would remain silent, but that if the man was guilty it would ring out.

Then the magistrate led his staff in solemn worship to the bell. The sacrifices concluded, he had the bell placed behind a curtain, while one of his assistants secretly smeared it with ink. After a time he took the suspects to the bell and had each one in turn extend his hands through the curtain and touch the bell. As each man withdrew his hands, Shu-ku examined them. Everyone's hands were stained except for those of one man, who confessed to the theft under questioning. He had not dared touch the bell for fear it would ring.

—Chang Shih-nan

from The Analects of Confucius

translated and annotated by **Arthur Waley**

The Master said, "Yu, shall I teach you what knowledge is? When you know a thing, to recognize that you know it, and when you do not know a thing, to recognize that you do not know it. That is knowledge."

The Master said, "Even when walking in a party of no more than three I can always be certain of learning from those I am with. There will be good qualities that I can select for imitation and bad ones that will teach me what requires correction in myself."

Tzu-kung asked saying, "Is there any single saying that one can act upon all day and every day?" The Master said, "Perhaps the saying about consideration: 'Never do to others what you would not like them to do to you.'"

Portrait of Confucius based on ancient traditions. Relief from the stele in the Pei Lin de Siganfou.

WORLDS OF WISDOM 433

A. Critical Reading: Analyzing Theme

? What do you think is the lesson learned in this anecdote? [Possible response: The thief's narrow vision of what he wanted led to a failure to see the consequences of his actions.]

B. Critical Reading: Speculating

? Why does the magistrate have the suspects testify in front of the bell? [Possible response: He hopes the presence of the bell will intimidate the thief.]

C. Reader's Response: Extending the Text

? What would you say is the moral of this story? Explain. [Sample responses: The guilty will betray themselves eventually. The clever man triumphs. Whether or not the bell has spiritual powers, the fact that the thief believes that it does is all that matters.]

D. Reader's Response: Shaping Interpretations

Ask students to paraphrase Confucius's thoughts about knowledge. [Sample responses: Knowledge is knowing one's self. Or knowledge is knowing what you don't know.]

E. Critical Reading: Making Inferences

? Do you think Confucius would agree with the saying, "You can't teach an old dog new tricks"? [Possible response: No, he believed that you can always learn something valuable from others.]

F. Cultural Connections

Confucius's thought is similar to the Golden Rule, the precept stated by Jesus in the Sermon on the Mount: "Always treat others as you would like them to treat you." In addition to Confucius, this ethical principle has been espoused by Jewish writers, Aristotle, Plato, and Seneca.

ASSESSMENT TOOLS

Check Test: Questions and Answers

1. According to the Koran, what must people do to avoid "the blazing fire"? [Give alms (money, food, clothing) without expecting anything in return.]

2. What happens to Shell-Neck in the fable from the Panchatantra and why? [The turtle dies because he forgot his friends' advice.]

3. What is the message in the Zen story of the samurai? [Embracing violence opens the gates of hell.]

4. In the Taoist story of the magic bell, how does the judge discover the thief? [By putting ink on the bell and having suspects touch it. The thief is afraid to touch it because he thinks it might ring.]

5. Would it be accurate to say that Confucius taught honesty, humility, and consideration for others? [Yes.]

A. Literary Element: Metaphor

Ask students to explain this metaphor. [Possible response: Words have great influence.]

B. Critical Reading: Identifying Main Ideas

Ask students to rephrase these proverbs in their own words or to relate them to modern sayings they know. [Possible responses: Timing is everything; talk is cheap.]

Finding Common Ground

To help students better grasp the literal meanings of the works, have them work in pairs to use Think Aloud Protocol. Students should freely express any thoughts about the content, any problems or dilemmas to be resolved, any connections to real-life characters or situations, and any interpretations or judgments they are making. *Remind students to choose situations they would not mind sharing.*

Grebo face mask from the Ivory Coast. Wood, paint (27 ½″ high).

The Metropolitan Museum of Art, New York. The Nelson A. Rockefeller Collection.

Jabo Proverbs

translated by **George Herzog**

 As the sky extends over all, so do words that have been spoken.

One doesn't throw the stick after the snake has gone.

 Daring talk is not strength.

It is not the person who looks at you with sparkling eyes when you speak who understands your words; but the one who bends his head down, he is the one who really understands.

FINDING COMMON GROUND

You probably recognized some ways you could apply these insights to life today. Looking over your Reader's Log notes and thinking back over the selections, jot down some responses to the following questions, or talk about them with a small group.

- How could these insights be applied to life today? Are any of them hopelessly outdated? Why?
- Wisdom literature often uses **metaphor** and conveys its moral or message indirectly. Did you understand what all these bits of wisdom mean? Talk about the advice that you found difficult or obscure.
- These selections cover a wide range of topics, including good works, greed, foolishness, self-discipline, anger, guilt, prudence, true knowledge, friendship, and practical foresight. Did you disagree with any of this worldly wisdom? Why?

John Milton

(1608–1674)

Early in his life, John Milton resolved to be a great poet. His teachers and his parents encouraged him in this ambition because they believed, as Milton said later in his life, that he "might perhaps leave something so written to aftertimes as they should not willingly let it die." Time has confirmed his parents' and his teachers' confidence in him: Milton's *Paradise Lost*, his major epic, is one of the most brilliant achievements in English poetry and perhaps the richest and most intricately beautiful poem in the world. Posterity has not let *Paradise Lost* die.

Milton was fortunate in his parents. His father, a musician and prosperous businessman, had Milton educated at St. Paul's School (which he loved) and Cambridge University (which he hated). Indulged in every way by his parents, Milton spent the next eight years after college (1632–1640) continuing his education by himself, since he firmly believed that a poet must be a person of learning, familiar with ancient and contemporary philosophy, history, languages, and literatures. He made a leisurely tour of Italy, whose language and culture he had long admired, and there he visited many interesting people, including the astronomer Galileo. Throughout this period, he wrote poems in English, Latin, Greek, and Italian. Some of these he collected and published in 1645. It has become customary to refer to them as Milton's "Minor Poems," but they would not be minor if anyone else had written them.

An Early, Brilliant Career

The two outstanding poems of Milton's early career are known today by their short titles: *Comus* and *Lycidas*. *Comus* is a masque, an elaborate pageant of the sort that Ben Jonson

John Milton (c. 1650) by Robert Streater. Oil on canvas (27 1/4″ × 21 1/2″).

The Metropolitan Museum of Art, New York. Gift of Mrs. Wheeler Smith, 1908. (08.237.1).

was famous for writing. *Comus* was presented at Ludlow Castle in 1634, for and by the earl of Bridgewater's family. It opens with two brothers and a sister—played by the earl's children—lost in a forest. The sister, separated from her brothers, is invited by a flashy magician named Comus to join his troupe and live a life of pleasure. But the girl is able to resist all his seductions because her heart is pure. *Comus* gave Milton an early opportunity to dramatize an idea he firmly believed in: Human beings have been given the ability and freedom to choose between good and evil, and so long as they choose the good they will remain strong and free.

Just as *Comus* surpasses all other Renaissance masques by the beauty of its language and the depth of its thought, so does *Lycidas* surpass all other pastoral elegies written in English. An **elegy** celebrates the memory of a dead person; this poem remembers Edward King, a fellow student of Milton's who was shipwrecked and drowned in the Irish Sea in 1637. The elegy is called pastoral because it imitates some ancient elegies by using imagery of shepherds and their flocks. Milton and Edward King (renamed Lycidas), both of whom had been preparing for careers in the Church, are the young shepherds feeding their flock. Milton changed his mind about the Church, and King—a most promising youth—was killed. To lament this loss, Milton harmonizes the classical and Christian views of death, in a way characteristic of Christian humanists. But the poem is more about life than death because it celebrates a human being's capacity to create something significant, even in a short lifetime.

ABOUT THE AUTHOR

Milton has been described as a noble but difficult man who was least admirable in his personal relationships. In June 1642, he married Mary Powell, a young girl who left him within six weeks and did not return until 1645. After bearing him three daughters and a son who died in infancy, Mary Powell died in 1652. In 1656, Milton married Katherine Woodcock, who died in childbirth in 1658. In 1663, Milton—now blind, impoverished, and discredited, married his third wife, Elizabeth Minshul, who survived him by many years.

Milton's Political Activity: Intelligent Devotion

In the 1640s, an ongoing struggle between King Charles and his Parliament came to a head. Milton, believing that a poet must be active in the life of his time, entered the paper warfare that accompanied the conflict and started publishing prose works—some of them very elaborate and a few of them very insulting—in support of the Parliamentary Party. For this reason, some people have referred to Milton as a Puritan, but this is a label that has only limited application to a person of Milton's stature. If he shared some of the Puritans' ideas and attitudes, such as their extreme dislike of kings and bishops, he also differed greatly from them in other important ways. For instance, he advocated divorce for incompatible married couples, and he argued that the press should be free from government censorship and interference. Although we take these freedoms for granted, most people in the seventeenth century, particularly most Puritans, considered them dangerously radical.

During part of this period, Milton served in the government of England under Oliver Cromwell, who, with the title of lord protector, ruled England after the Parliamentary Party had won the Civil Wars and executed King Charles.

As Latin secretary to the Council of State, Milton was responsible for all correspondence with foreign countries, Latin then being the language of diplomacy.

But Milton's eyesight was gradually failing. By 1652, he could only distinguish day from night; otherwise, by the age of forty-four, before he had finished his life's work, Milton was totally blind. Among the few poems he wrote during this time is the following sonnet about the calamity of his middle age:

On His Blindness

When I consider how my light is spent
　Ere half my days in this dark world and wide,
　And that one talent which is death to hide
　Lodged with me useless, though my soul more bent
To serve there with my Maker, and present
　My true account, lest He returning chide,
　"Doth God exact day-labor, light denied?"
I fondly ask. But Patience, to prevent
That murmur, soon replies, "God doth not need
　Either man's work or His own gifts. Who best
　Bear His mild yoke, they serve Him best. His state
Is kingly: Thousands at His bidding speed,
　And post o'er land and ocean without rest;
　They also serve who only stand and wait."

The Blind Milton Dictating Paradise Lost *to His Daughters* (19th century) by Michaly von Munkacsy. Oil.

Collection of the New York Public Library, New York. Astor, Lenox, and Tilden Foundations.

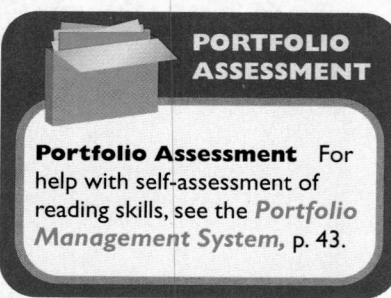

PORTFOLIO ASSESSMENT

Portfolio Assessment For help with self-assessment of reading skills, see the *Portfolio Management System,* p. 43.

All for Nothing

To Milton, the ideal government was a republic in which the most capable, intelligent, and virtuous men would serve as leaders. To establish and maintain such a government in England, he had devoted most of his intelligence and energy for twenty years. Then suddenly, in 1660, the cause for which he had worked so hard became totally discredited; the English recalled their dead king's son from exile and crowned him as King Charles II. Overnight, Milton found himself stripped of his possessions and under arrest as a traitor. Fortunately, influential friends, including the poet Andrew Marvell, intervened, and Milton was allowed to go into retirement rather than to the scaffold. From then on, he lived in seclusion with his three daughters and his third wife, his first two wives and only son having died. By reading aloud to him, in foreign languages as well as in English, his daughters enabled him to carry on the studies he thought necessary for a poet.

Milton's Great Epic: *Paradise Lost*

Being a poet, in Milton's view, was not a matter of writing short lyrics that expressed his private feelings and insights; being a poet meant emulating the great writers of antiquity, the epic poets Homer and Virgil and the Greek dramatists Aeschylus, Sophocles, and Euripides. Because they each chose subjects drawn from their own nation's history, Milton first pondered various English subjects for his works, especially King Arthur and the knights of the Round Table. But finally, after years of thinking and reading, Milton decided that King Arthur's exploits were mainly fictitious, and so he settled on subjects drawn from the Bible. Milton thought the Bible alone contained everything people needed to know for the practice of true religion; he rejected not only the Roman Catholic Church and the Church of England, but also the immense number of sects—Puritan or otherwise—that had proliferated in England in the century since the Reformation began. While the Christian religion was the most important matter in his life, to Milton it was a matter involving only God, God's Word (the Bible), and each individual human being.

Milton published *Paradise Lost* twice: first in a ten-book version in 1667 and then in twelve books in 1674, the year of his death. It's no exaggeration to say that Milton in one way or another worked on this epic all his life. He made many different plans and even once thought of it as a tragedy with Satan, the fallen archangel transformed into the chief devil, as its protagonist. In the finished poem, Satan is still very conspicuous. The first two books are devoted mainly to him, he appears frequently in Books III through X, and Milton lavishes on him some of his most glorious writing. It's not surprising, then, that many readers have regarded Satan as the secret hero of the poem, especially since he receives no such grand treatment in the Bible. Milton was "of the Devil's party without knowing it," asserted the poet and artist William Blake. But this argument is convincing only to those who concentrate on certain parts of the poem and ignore the rest of it. Moreover, in literary works, evil frequently seems more interesting than good, and if any part of *Paradise Lost* fails from a literary point of view, it is Milton's portrayal of God.

In *Paradise Lost,* Milton took relatively few verses from the Bible, mainly from Genesis, and developed them into a 10,565-line poem. He used the conventions and devices of the classical epic to make the poem a work of art; he used his great learning and wide experience of human affairs to make the poem profound. Although the poem ranges back and forth between Hell and Heaven, the most important action takes place on Earth, where the first human beings, Adam and Eve, are given the choice of obeying or disobeying God. They choose, as everybody knows, to disobey, and having done so, they accept their punishment and make the best of the life that is left to them. They are the heroes of Milton's epic, and they represent us all.

Technology Tip

To find links to Milton-related sites, access The Milton-L Home Page at **http://www.urich.edu/~creamer /milton.html**. *You may want to preview any Internet activity that you suggest to students. Because these resources are sometimes public forums, their content can be unpredictable.*

A. Expansion

In *Areopagitica,* Milton wrote of the power of books. He said that books "are not absolutely dead things, but do contain a potency of life in them to be as active as that soul was whose progeny they are; nay, they do preserve as in a vial the purest efficacy and extraction of that living intellect that bred them." Therefore, he concluded, "who kills a man kills a reasonable creature, God's image; but he who destroys a good book kills reason itself, kills the image of God, as it were, in the eye."

B. Literary Connections

Homer's *Iliad* begins, "Sing, goddess, the anger of Peleus's son Achilleus. . . ." the *Odyssey* begins, "Sing in me, Muse, and through me tell the story. . . ."

C. Literary Element: Iambic Pentameter

Have students scan the first few lines of "The Fall of Satan." Except for l. 1, with the five-syllable word *disobedience* in the middle, the first five lines are regular iambic pentameter. This is a good opportunity to review the rules of meter students learned in Collection 3, pp. 215–216.

Paradise Lost: Milton's Epic

A At the very beginning of *Paradise Lost,* Milton describes the content of his epic as "things unattempted yet in prose or rhyme" (line 16). His allusions to Homer, Virgil, Dante, and a host of lesser epic poets leave no doubt that Milton wanted *Paradise Lost* to sum up and also surpass all previous epics. The quality that would set Milton's epic apart, of course, was that it dealt with great deeds on a cosmic scale at the dawn of Creation—rather than with earthly matters.

B There is a formal, set way to begin an epic. At the outset, an epic poet does two things: The speaker invokes the Muse (one of the nine Greek goddesses who inspire poets and other practitioners of the arts and sciences) to speak or sing through the poet; and the speaker states the subject of the poem. Milton does both these things in the first, complicated sentence (lines 1–16) of *Paradise Lost.* Grammatically, this sentence begins in line 6 with the command "Sing, Heavenly Muse." "Sing," says Milton, and now we move back to line 1, "Of man's first disobedience," which is Adam and Eve's first act of disobedience against God, who has forbidden them to eat the fruit of a particular tree in Eden (see the selection from Genesis, page 416). The result, or "fruit," of their disobedience is expulsion from and loss of Paradise, another name for the Garden of Eden. Yet all is not lost, because a "greater Man" (line 4), Jesus Christ, has restored the possibility of Paradise to the human race.

Milton calls this argument "great" (line 24), for he is attempting to resolve a dilemma that has puzzled many people throughout the ages. On the one hand, we are told that through his Eternal Providence (line 25) God takes loving care of creation; on the other hand, we know that there are many very bad things in the world, such as war, crime, poverty, disease, oppression, and injustice. In *Paradise Lost,* Milton asserts that God is not responsible for these evils; instead, Adam and Eve's disobedience to God "Brought death into the world, and all our woe" (line 3). God gave Adam and Eve the freedom to choose between good and evil, and the strength to resist evil; yet they chose evil, and their offspring—all of us—have suffered the effects of their choice ever since.

This explanation is not original to Milton; many Christians have accepted it for centuries. Yet a reader need not accept this traditional explanation of the evil in the world in order to enjoy and admire the poem. (Indeed, some readers have found evidence in the poem that Milton himself did not really believe it.) The poem is rich enough to provide support for many different interpretations.

Reading *Paradise Lost*

C Milton decided to write his epic in his native language and in Shakespeare's meter, which is **blank verse,** or unrhymed iambic pentameter. Though blank verse was the usual meter in dramatic poetry, it was not used at all for nondramatic poems in Milton's day and for long after. Most of Milton's sentences are long, and many of them are not in normal word order (subject-verb-object). Also, his vocabulary includes words not used in ordinary prose today. (Unfamiliar proper nouns are explained in the notes, but they still have to be understood in their context.)

In Milton's heroic, optimistic view of life, goodness was not goodness unless it resulted from a struggle to overcome evil. God purposely let Satan escape from Hell and establish himself on Earth, not only so that Satan's deeds would damn him further but also so that human beings would have something to fight against—and with God's help triumph over. In one of his prose tracts, *Areopagitica* (1644), Milton describes life as a race in which good must compete with bad. Virtue, he says, is not virtue unless it is won in the "dust and heat" of the conflict with evil. And so, when Adam and Eve lose Paradise, they also gain something: the opportunity to prove themselves in the real world. The Archangel Michael, who comes to dispossess them of their perfect garden, tells them how to live in the new, imperfect world. Practice good deeds, he says, and patience, temperance, faith, and love, and

> then wilt thou be not loath
> To leave this Paradise, but shalt possess
> A Paradise within thee, happier far.

—*Paradise Lost,* Book XII, lines 585–587

The Fallen Angels Entering Pandemonium, from *Paradise Lost,* Book I (exhibited 1841).

Tate Gallery, London

JOHN MILTON 439

QUICK PLANNING GUIDE

Into the Poem

Author Biography pp. 435–437
Introduction pp. 438–439
Before You Read p. 440

- **Reading Focus: Prior Knowledge** Students think about the existence of evil.
- **Quickwrite: Set a Purpose** Write in Reader's Logs on why God allows evil to exist

Through the Poem

"The Fall of Satan" p. 441
Literature and Society p. 444–445
Making Meanings p. 449
Language and Style p. 449–450

Beyond the Poem

Choices p. 450

- **Writer's Notebook** Make notes for an essay about causes of evil
- **Critical Writing:** Paraphrase a speech
- **Critical Writing:** Write an essay on the characterization of Satan
- **Creative Writing:** Write a dramatic dialogue
- **Critical Thinking/Art:** Compare Milton's and Dante's Satan with lists and drawings

Spotlight On pp. 451–453

How to Own a Word p. 454

BEFORE YOU READ
THE FALL OF SATAN

Reading Focus

Evil on an Epic Scale
Why does evil exist? What is the source of its power to fascinate? The struggle of good versus evil is central to *Paradise Lost*—in this case, the conflict exists on a truly epic scale, as Satan first rebels (in Book I) against God and then (in Book IX) ensnares Adam and Eve to do likewise. In Milton's epic, and in the Bible, this original choice of evil over good explains the burdens of humanity and our fateful tendency to misuse our reason and freedom to let pride override fear of God.

Quickwrite

Milton's purpose in *Paradise Lost* is to "justify the ways of God to man." Before you read the epic, freewrite on this idea: Why does a just and good God allow evil to exist?

The Angel of Divine Presence
(late 18th to early 19th century)
by William Blake. Watercolor.

Fitzwilliam Museum, University of Cambridge.

PROGRAM MANAGER

- **Planning Instruction** See Teaching Notes, Teaching Resources A, pp. 107–108, for objectives, a summary, literary elements, and additional biographical information for this selection.
- **Instructional Support** Before

beginning the instructional lesson, see Graphic Organizer for Active Reading, *Teaching Resources A,* p. 116, for a Through the Poem activity.

- **Assessment** See Selection Test, *Test Booklet,* pp. 79–80.

- **Language Link** For instruction and practice in identifying gerunds, see Language Link, *Teaching Resources A,* pp. 117–118, and *Language and Writing Skills Worksheets,* p. 74.

The Fall of Satan
from Paradise Lost
John Milton

Of man's first disobedience, and the fruit
Of that forbidden tree, whose mortal taste
Brought death into the world, and all our woe,
With loss of Eden, till one greater Man°

5 Restore us, and regain the blissful seat,
Sing, Heavenly Muse,° that on the secret top
Of Oreb, or of Sinai,° didst inspire
That shepherd,° who first taught the chosen seed°
In the beginning how the Heavens and Earth

10 Rose out of Chaos; or if Sion hill°
Delight thee more, and Siloa's brook° that flowed
Fast by the oracle of God, I thence
Invoke thy aid to my adventurous song,
That with no middle flight intends to soar

15 Above the Aonian mount,° while it pursues
Things unattempted yet in prose or rhyme.
And chiefly thou, O Spirit,° that dost prefer
Before all temples the upright heart and pure,
Instruct me, for thou know'st; thou from the first

20 Wast present, and with mighty wings outspread
Dove-like sat'st brooding on the vast abyss
And mad'st it pregnant: what in me is dark
Illumine, what is low raise and support;
That to the height of this great argument

25 I may assert Eternal Providence,°
And justify the ways of God to men.
    Say first, for Heaven hides nothing from thy view,
Nor the deep tract of Hell, say first what cause
Moved our grand parents° in that happy state,

30 Favored of Heaven so highly, to fall off
From their Creator, and transgress his will
For one restraint,° lords of the world besides?°
Who first seduced them to that foul revolt?
The infernal Serpent;° he it was, whose guile,

35 Stirred up with envy and revenge, deceived
The mother of mankind, what time his pride
Had cast him out from Heaven, with all his host
Of rebel angels, by whose aid aspiring
To set himself in glory above his peers,°

40 He trusted to have equaled the Most High,
If he opposed; and with ambitious aim
Against the throne and monarchy of God,
Raised impious war in Heaven and battle proud

4. one greater Man: Christ.

6. Heavenly Muse: Urania, the muse of astronomy and sacred poetry. Milton hopes to be inspired by Urania, just as Moses was divinely inspired to receive and interpret the word of God for the Jews.
7. Oreb . . . Sinai: alternate names for the mountain where Moses received heavenly inspiration.
8. shepherd: Moses. **chosen seed:** the Jews.
10. Sion hill: Zion, a hill near Jerusalem on which the Temple was built.
11. Siloa's brook: stream that flowed past the Temple, "the oracle of God," on Sion hill.
15. Aonian mount: in Greek mythology, Mount Helicon, the home of the Muses. Milton intends to write an epic greater than those of the classical Greek poets Homer (c. eighth century B.C.) and Virgil (70–19 B.C.).
17. Spirit: the Holy Spirit; divine inspiration.
25. Providence: God's benevolent guidance.

29. grand parents: first parents; that is, Adam and Eve.

32. one restraint: the command not to eat of the fruit of the tree of knowledge. **besides:** in every other way.
34. Serpent: Milton anticipates Satan's final form.

39. peers: his equals; the other archangels.

JOHN MILTON 441

Into the Poem

Using BEFORE YOU READ p. 440

Quickwrite
Students may have wondered about this question without ever trying to answer it. Provide this more personal alternative: Which would be better—to have the freedom to choose to be good (which implies the freedom to choose evil), or to have no freedom to choose at all? In any case, encourage students to consider the issue of free will both now and as they read about the fall of Satan.

Through the Poem

A. Language Note: Syntax
The first sentence of Milton's epic does not follow the standard subject-verb-object word order. Note that the subject *(you)* is understood, that the verb is *sing,* and that the opening prepositional phrase, "Of man's first disobedience," precedes the verb. Have students try to rewrite this part of the sentence in conventional word order. ["Heavenly Muse, sing of man's first disobedience. . . ."]

B. Critical Reading: Metacognition
If you read the account from Genesis on pp. 416–418, how did you find it helpful to your understanding of Milton's invocation? [Possible answer: I realized that Genesis contains the plot of Milton's work, and I noticed that Milton echoes the Genesis account in referring to the void/abyss, to making light of darkness, and to the spirit of God.]

C. Literary Element: Plot
With the words "what time (meaning "when") his pride / Had cast him out from Heaven," Milton's narrative begins. The words also suggest that to understand what happened in the Garden of Eden, readers first must understand the earlier fall of Satan.

A. Literary Element: Alliteration

? How does alliteration make this statement vivid to the reader? [Possible answer: The repeated *h* sound—*Him, Hurled headlong, hideous*—strengthens the statement, presenting the event as if it were a single explosive action.]

B. Reader's Response: Extending the Text

? What kind of talk might you expect from people who respond to loss with "obdurate pride and steadfast hate"? [Sample responses: Self-justification and a turning of every subject of conversation to one's own sense of injury; threats; a failure to listen to reason; a broad use of synonyms to continue complaints about the circumstances that caused the loss.] Have students look for those characteristics in the words of Satan (beginning on l. 84).

C. Literary Element: Allusion

This description echoes the inscription over the entrance of Hell in Dante's *Inferno*: "All hope abandon ye who enter here."

D. Expansion

Beelzebub is described in Matthew's gospel as "the prince of the devils," but the literal translation of his name is "lord of the flies" or "lord of filth" (specifically, dung).

E. Critical Reading: Analyzing Imagery

Beelzebub's glory, now lost, must have been something to see. How does Satan quickly build image upon image in these few lines to help you see it? [Possible answer: He says that Heaven was a realm of light and that Beelzebub was one of the brightest of all the creatures who lived there.]

With vain attempt. Him the Almighty Power
45 Hurled headlong flaming from the ethereal sky
With hideous ruin and combustion down
To bottomless perdition,° there to dwell
In adamantine° chains and penal° fire,
Who durst° defy the Omnipotent to arms.
50 Nine times the space that measures day and night
To mortal men, he with his horrid crew
Lay vanquished, rolling in the fiery gulf,
Confounded though immortal. But his doom
Reserved him to more wrath; for now the thought
55 Both of lost happiness and lasting pain
Torments him; round he throws his baleful eyes,
That witnessed huge affliction and dismay
Mixed with obdurate° pride and steadfast hate.
At once as far as angels ken° he views
60 The dismal situation waste and wild:
A dungeon horrible on all sides round
As one great furnace flamed, yet from those flames
No light, but rather darkness visible
Served only to discover sights of woe,
65 Regions of sorrow, doleful shades, where peace
And rest can never dwell, hope never comes
That comes to all; but torture without end
Still urges,° and a fiery deluge, fed
With ever-burning sulfur unconsumed:
70 Such place Eternal Justice had prepared
For those rebellious, here their prison ordained
In utter darkness, and their portion set
As far removed from God and light of Heaven
As from the center thrice to the utmost pole.°
75 O how unlike the place from whence they fell!
There the companions of his fall, o'erwhelmed
With floods and whirlwinds of tempestuous fire,
He soon discerns, and weltering° by his side
One next himself in power, and next in crime,
80 Long after known in Palestine, and named
Beelzebub.° To whom the Arch-Enemy,
And then in Heaven called Satan,° with bold words
Breaking the horrid silence thus began:
    "If thou beest he—but O how fallen! how changed
85 From him, who in the happy realms of light
Clothed with transcendent brightness didst outshine
Myriads though bright—if he whom mutual league,
United thoughts and counsels, equal hope
And hazard in the glorious enterprise,
90 Joined with me once, now misery hath joined
In equal ruin: into what pit thou seest
From what height fallen! so much the stronger proved
He with his thunder;° and till then who knew

47. perdition: damnation.
48. adamantine (ad′ə·man′tin): unbreakable.   **penal:** punishing.
49. durst: dared.

58. obdurate: stubborn; unrepentant.
59. ken: can see.

68. still urges: always afflicts.

74. center . . . pole: three times the distance from the Earth, or "center," to the outermost point in the universe. In Milton's cosmos, the Earth is the center of ten concentric spheres.
78. weltering: rolling about.

81. Beelzebub (bē·el′zə·bub′): next in power to Satan; described as prince of the devils in Matthew 12:24.
82. Satan: Hebrew for "adversary" or "opposer."

93. He . . . thunder: God.

442 THE RENAISSANCE

The force of those dire arms? Yet not for those,
95   Nor what the potent Victor in his rage
Can else inflict, do I repent or change,
Though changed in outward luster, that fixed mind
And high disdain, from sense of injured merit,
That with the Mightiest raised me to contend,
100 And to the fierce contention brought along
Innumerable force of spirits armed
That durst dislike his reign, and, me preferring,
His utmost power with adverse power opposed
In dubious battle on the plains of Heaven,
105 And shook his throne. What though the field be lost?
All is not lost; the unconquerable will,
And study° of revenge, immortal hate,
And courage never to submit or yield:
And what is else not to be overcome?
110 That glory never shall his wrath or might
Extort from me. To bow and sue for grace
With suppliant knee, and deify his power
Who from the terror of this arm so late
Doubted° his empire, that were low indeed,
115 That were an ignominy° and shame beneath
This downfall; since by fate the strength of gods
And this empyreal substance° cannot fail,
Since through experience of this great event,
In arms not worse, in foresight much advanced,
120 We may with more successful hope resolve
To wage by force or guile eternal war
Irreconcilable to our grand Foe,
Who now triumphs, and in the excess of joy
Sole reigning holds the tyranny of Heaven."
125   So spake the apostate° Angel, though in pain,
Vaunting° aloud, but racked with deep despair;
And him thus answered soon his bold compeer:°
  "O Prince, O Chief of many thronèd Powers,
That led the embattled Seraphim° to war
130 Under thy conduct, and in dreadful deeds
Fearless, endangered Heaven's perpetual King,
And put to proof his high supremacy,
Whether upheld by strength, or chance, or fate;
Too well I see and rue the dire event,°
135 That with sad overthrow and foul defeat
Hath lost us Heaven, and all this mighty host
In horrible destruction laid thus low,
As far as gods and heavenly essences
Can perish: for the mind and spirit remains
140 Invincible, and vigor soon returns,
Though all our glory extinct, and happy state
Here swallowed up in endless misery.
But what if he our Conqueror (whom I now

Illustration from *Paradise Lost* (17th century). Engraving.

Rare Books and Manuscript Division. The New York Public Library, New York.

107. **study:** pursuit.
114. **doubted:** archaic for "feared for."
115. **ignominy** (ig′nə·min′ē): dishonor.
117. **empyreal** (em·pir′ē·əl) **substance:** heavenly—and therefore indestructible—substance of which all angels (including Satan) are made.

125. **apostate:** guilty of abandoning one's beliefs.
126. **vaunting:** boasting.
127. **compeer:** companion; equal.

129. **Seraphim:** highest order of angels.

134. **event:** archaic for "outcome."

JOHN MILTON 443

F. Critical Reading: Analyzing Character

? How did Satan begin this speech? [By expressing sympathy for Beelzebub.] What is he talking about now? [Himself and his determination not to "repent or change."] What does this rapid change suggest about Satan's personality? [Possible answers: That he really cares only for himself; that he is obsessed with anger.]

G. Critical Reading: Evaluating an Interpretation

Commenting on Satan's "sense of injured merit," the author and critic C. S. Lewis notes: "No one had in fact done anything to Satan. . . . In the midst of a world of light and love, of song and feast and dance, he could find nothing to think of more interesting than his own prestige." Lewis bases his comment, in part, upon Satan's fall later in the poem; ask students whether Lewis's view seems justified at this point in the poem. [Possible answer: Satan has not fully manifested himself as Lewis describes, but Satan's self-serving declarations foreshadow this possibility.]

H. Literary Element: Theme

Satan introduces "the unconquerable will," a theme that will color his speeches in the rest of this excerpt (and elsewhere in the poem). Students might keep a list of what Satan says about the power of the will, using these words as a starting point. Ask students what Satan suggests about God's will compared to his own.
[Possible response: It is not as strong as Satan's, for God was shaken (Satan believes) and doubted the outcome of the battle in Heaven (a claim that Satan makes again in l. 114).]

Censorship has been the rule rather than the exception, existing in periods throughout history, including fifth-century Athens, thirteenth-century Spain, Russia both before and after the Communist revolution, twentieth-century Europe and United States. Currently, according to a study by Freedom House, about two billion people live in countries where the strictest forms of censorship govern their daily lives. Roughly the same number of people live in countries where free speech and a free press form the cornerstone of their civil liberties.

LITERATURE AND SOCIETY

Censoring the Word

Most of us tend to associate censorship with either foreign dictatorships or the issue of obscenity. For the authorities of seventeenth-century England, however, the power of the word was great—potentially so great that freedom of speech and freedom of the press were unknown. Newspapers, books, and pamphlets were all subject to strict censorship.

Keeping a wary eye. Even in Elizabethan times, the government had kept a wary eye on literary activity, especially on drama. Plays and players had to be licensed, and playwrights were careful to avoid offending the powerful. For example, in his play *Henry IV*, Shakespeare changed the name Sir John Oldcastle to Sir John Falstaff to avoid offending the Oldcastle family, friends of Queen Elizabeth.

Government control of the press had its origins in the rise of newspapers and journalism early in the seventeenth century. Oliver Cromwell, a Puritan and the lord protector of England, banned all unofficial periodicals in 1655. After the Restoration of King Charles II in 1660, so-called licensing laws were regularly enacted by Parliament. The laws forbade publishing any material contrary to the doctrine of the Church of England or scandalous to the government. Penalties were stiff: fines, imprisonment, and sentencing to the pillory, where the offender was fastened to a wooden board with holes for the head and hands.

A censor's who's who. The list of writers who ran afoul of the licensing laws reads like a "who's who" of seventeenth-century literature.

In 1605, Ben Jonson was arrested and in danger of having his nose and ears slit for his coauthorship of *Eastward Hoe*. The play contained disrespectful remarks

```
       Of force° believe almighty, since no less
145  Than such could have o'erpowered such force as ours)
       Have left us this our spirit and strength entire
       Strongly to suffer and support our pains,
       That we may so suffice° his vengeful ire,
       Or do him mightier service as his thralls°
150  By right of war, whate'er his business be,
       Here in the heart of Hell to work in fire,
       Or do his errands in the gloomy deep?
       What can it then avail,° though yet we feel
       Strength undiminished, or eternal being
155  To undergo eternal punishment?"
            Whereto with speedy words the Arch-Fiend replied:
```

144. of force: of necessity.

148. suffice: archaic for "satisfy."
149. thralls: slaves.

153. avail: be of help or advantage.

444 THE RENAISSANCE

OPTIONS FOR TEACHING

CLASSROOM MANAGEMENT

Cooperative Learning Cooperative learning can arise from the way in which a completed assignment is shared. Try having two students who completed the same independent activity for this selection compare their responses. Have them report (to you or to the class) on what they learned from seeing another person's understanding or interpretation of the

same material. Alternatively, have two independent workers collaborate on a format for sharing their work.

Budgeting Time If time constraints make it difficult to cover this excerpt from *Paradise Lost* entirely through in-class reading, cover through l. 49 (p. 442). Offer the following questions to guide students as they complete the reading independently.

- How did Milton want his readers to view Beelzebub as opposed to Satan?
- What will Satan and other fallen angels say about the "impious war" that they instigated in Heaven?
- How will Satan's pride be evident as the story continues?
- This section focuses on Satan. In what ways does it "justify the ways of God to men"?

A. Critical Reading: Predicting

? How do you suppose Satan will "disturb / His inmost counsels from their destined aim," or inflict havoc on God's designs? [Possible answers: He will introduce evil into the world. He will tempt Adam and Eve.] Note that in the council of demons that follows this excerpt, God's plan to create a world—a plan that was spoken of in Heaven before the rebellion—is brought up. The demons quickly agree that the best revenge is to ruin that creation. Students may check their predictions against ll. 215–220.

about the Scots that were offensive to King James I. John Milton was arrested and fined for his support, in print, of the Commonwealth. John Bunyan spent twelve years in prison for preaching without a license, and Daniel Defoe was put in the pillory for his pamphlet *The Shortest Way with the Dissenters*. (Defoe fought back while in prison by composing a mock ode called *Hymn to the Pillory*, a best-seller.)

Andrew Marvell, the poet, helped rescue Milton from imprisonment and possible execution. Marvell had considerable influence with several governments, but even he wasn't immune from the long arm of censorship. In 1678, the official *London Gazette* advertised a reward for information about the author of a certain satirical pamphlet entitled *An Account of the Growth of Popery and Arbitrary Government in England*. Marvell, ever prudent, had published it anonymously the year before.

Defenders of free speech. There were two especially eloquent spokesmen against censorship. The first was John Milton, who published a pamphlet in 1644 titled *Areopagitica*, arguing for freedom of the press. Milton contended that licensing was unworthy of the government and would hamper the growth of learning.

The second strenuous defender of free speech and a free press was John Locke, the political philosopher whose ideas on government influenced the framers of the United States Constitution in the late 1700s. In 1694, Locke prepared the case against the renewal of the Licensing Act in Parliament, and the law was allowed to lapse. Other measures and authorities were invoked to continue censorship for some time, however. As late as 1810, the journalist William Cobbett was fined a thousand pounds and served two years in prison for publishing an attack on the British army's practice of flogging soldiers.

"Fallen Cherub, to be weak is miserable,
Doing or suffering:° But of this be sure,
To do aught° good never will be our task,
160 But ever to do ill our sole delight,
As being the contrary to his high will
Whom we resist. If then his providence
Out of our evil seek to bring forth good,
Our labor must be to pervert that end,
165 And out of good still° to find means of evil;
Which ofttimes may succeed, so as perhaps
Shall grieve him, if I fail not, and disturb
His inmost counsels from their destined aim.
But see the angry Victor° hath recalled

158. doing or suffering: whether active or passive.
159. aught: anything whatever.

165. still: always.

169. angry Victor: God.

JOHN MILTON 445

Architecture Book I closes with the building of Pandæmonium ("the place of all demons"), a citadel to serve as the capitol of Hell. Have students sketch a design for this building, keeping in mind Satan's lust for God's glory and stated goal to "reign in Hell." If possible, locate a copy of the entire poem, and read Milton's own description in ll. 678–768 so that students may compare their designs with Milton's ideas.

Music In this early part of Milton's epic, Satan presents himself as king of Hell. Ask pairs of students to bring in an instrumental recording that would seem to fit Satan's character. Some of the more sinister pieces in the soundtracks of John Williams's *The Empire Strikes Back* and *Raiders of the Lost Ark* would be good starting places. Have one partner play the recording while the other reads an appropriate excerpt from the text.

Science Line 74 of this selection offers a clue to Milton's view of the cosmos. Challenge students to find out about the views of astronomy that had developed by this time (c. 1650). Invite them to share their findings with the class by making posters or presenting orally with chalkboard drawings; together, discuss how Milton's comment reflects or contrasts with the thinking of his day.

A. Critical Reading: Finding Details

[?] What does Satan's description indicate about the way in which his troops left Heaven? [Possible answer: They were driven over the edge of Heaven and fell to Hell, chased by "sulfurous hail" and "thunder / Winged with red lightning."] Now that the moment has passed, what does Satan seem to believe about the power that God displayed? [Possible answer: That God has stopped showing his rage and power because He has worn Himself out.]

RESPONDING TO THE ART: ABOUT THE ARTWORK

William Blake rejected not only the neoclassical literary style of the eighteenth century but also defied contemporary conventions in the visual arts, materially and philosophically. He refused to paint in oil, believing that oils lacked precision, instead choosing to use watercolors and, sometimes, tempera, a process of painting that results in a dull finish. He hated academic rules of painting, stressed imagination over reason, and constructed his ideal forms from inner visions, not from natural observations.

170 His ministers of vengeance and pursuit
     Back to the gates of Heaven; the sulfurous hail
     Shot after us in storm, o'erblown hath laid
     The fiery surge, that from the precipice
     Of Heaven received us falling, and the thunder,
175 Winged with red lightning and impetuous rage,
     Perhaps hath spent his shafts, and ceases now
     To bellow through the vast and boundless deep.
     Let us not slip° the occasion, whether scorn
     Or satiate° fury yield it from our Foe.
180 Seest thou yon dreary plain, forlorn and wild,
     The seat of desolation, void of light,
     Save what the glimmering of these livid flames
     Casts pale and dreadful? Thither let us tend
     From off the tossing of these fiery waves,
185 There rest, if any rest can harbor there,
     And reassembling our afflicted powers,
     Consult how we may henceforth most offend
     Our Enemy, our own loss how repair,
     How overcome this dire calamity,

178. **slip:** lose.
179. **satiate:** satisfied.

Satan in His Original Glory
(late 18th to early 19th century)
by William Blake.

Tate Gallery, London.

PROFESSIONAL NOTES

Critical Comment: Great, Not Admirable Introducing Milton's Satan, Marjorie Nicholson, in *A Reader's Guide to John Milton,* says, "The character of Satan is one of the greatest creations in any language. The greatness lies not only—indeed, not primarily—in the depiction of the majestic character of Books I and II, but in the slow and steady degeneration of an angel who once stood next to God Himself in Heaven. As we read *Paradise Lost* we watch the subtlety of Milton's art as the character gradually diminishes from grandeur and magnificence to baseness and final degradation, so that we are inevitably alienated from admiration." Ask students what comments from or about Satan in Book I suggest that he may have further to fall.

Critical Comment: Satan and Futility
In *Paradise Lost and the Modern Reader,* Thomas Wheeler notes, "Our final impression of Satan is that he is above all futile. It is no small trick to have . . . brought Sin and Death into the world. But to do so with no hope of ever regaining what was lost, in the knowledge that a full and satisfying revenge is forever denied—this is indeed to chew the bitter ashes of defeat. While Milton may not have succeeded in showing that obedience to God's will brings joy and fulfillment, he has given us in Satan a powerful demonstration of how futile disobedience is." Students can observe how Wheeler's comment is reflected in Book I.

190 What reinforcement we may gain from hope,
 If not, what resolution from despair."
  Thus Satan talking to his nearest mate
 With head uplift above the wave, and eyes
 That sparkling blazed; his other parts besides,
195 Prone on the flood, extended long and large,
 Lay floating many a rood,° in bulk as huge
 As whom the fables name of monstrous size,
 Titanian or Earth-born, that warred on Jove,
 Briareos or Typhon,° whom the den
200 By ancient Tarsus held, or that sea-beast
 Leviathan,° which God of all his works
 Created hugest that swim the ocean stream:
 Him haply slumbering on the Norway foam,
 The pilot of some small night-foundered° skiff,
205 Deeming some island, oft, as seamen tell,
 With fixèd anchor in his scaly rind
 Moors by his side under the lee, while night
 Invests° the sea, and wishèd morn delays:
 So stretched out huge in length the Arch-Fiend lay
210 Chained on the burning lake; nor ever thence
 Had risen or heaved his head, but that the will
 And high permission of all-ruling Heaven
 Left him at large to his own dark designs,
 That with reiterated crimes he might
215 Heap on himself damnation, while he sought
 Evil to others, and enraged might see
 How all his malice served but to bring forth
 Infinite goodness, grace, and mercy shown
 On man by him seduced, but on himself
220 Treble confusion, wrath, and vengeance poured.
  Forthwith upright he rears from off the pool
 His mighty stature; on each hand the flames
 Driven backward slope their pointing spires, and rolled
 In billows, leave in the midst a horrid vale.
225 Then with expanded wings he steers his flight
 Aloft, incumbent° on the dusky air
 That felt unusual weight, till on dry land
 He lights, if it were land that ever burned
 With solid, as the lake with liquid fire;
230 And such appeared in hue, as when the force
 Of subterranean wind transports a hill
 Torn from Pelorus,° or the shattered side
 Of thundering Etna,° whose combustible
 And fueled entrails thence conceiving fire,
235 Sublimed° with mineral fury, aid the winds,
 And leave a singèd bottom all involved°
 With stench and smoke: such resting found the sole
 Of unblest feet. Him followed his next mate,
 Both glorying to have scaped the Stygian° flood

196. rood: an old unit of measure varying locally from about six to eight yards.

199. Titanian . . . Typhon: Milton compares Satan to the Titans and Giants of Greek mythology. Briareos, a hundred-handed Giant, helped Zeus (Jove) battle the Titans. Typhon, a hundred-headed serpent-monster from Cilicia (near Tarsus), attacked heaven and was imprisoned by Zeus.
201. Leviathan: Biblical sea monster, either a reptile or a whale.
204. night-foundered: overtaken by night.
208. invests: covers.

226. incumbent: lying.

232. Pelorus: headland in Sicily, Italy; now called Cape Faro.
233. Etna: volcano in Sicily, Italy.

235. sublimed: vaporized.
236. involved: enveloped.
239. Stygian (stĭj′ē·ən): of or like the river Styx; infernal, hellish. In Greek mythology, the river Styx encircles the underworld.

JOHN MILTON 447

PROFESSIONAL NOTES

Critical Comment: Satan—So Easily Drawn
C. S. Lewis, in *A Preface to Paradise Lost,* explains why of all Milton's characters, Satan "is incomparably the easiest to draw. Set a hundred poets to tell the same story and in ninety of the resulting poems Satan will be the best character." Test Lewis's assertion by investigating *The Screwtape Letters,* his wry portrait of an apprentice learning the art of capturing souls.

Cultural Diversity The Bible's narrative is not the only tale among world cultures to include gods or demigods who challenge the Almighty. Have students find examples in classical mythology (as in the story of Prometheus) and Norse mythology (as in the character of Loki); then, invite them to look for similar characters in other myths and folktales and to write a brief summary of the story involved. Students may present the stories orally and then discuss what purpose or purposes the characters might serve. ☞

A. Reader's Response: First Thoughts

Ask students to record in their Reader's Logs their reactions to Satan's declarations. If necessary, prompt them with questions: Why does Satan seem so proud to possess the "infernal world"? [Sample responses: Satan is bluffing for the sake of Beelzebub. Satan is embracing his role because he has no other choice. Satan believes himself to be God's equal in reason and is happy to set up an opposing kingdom.] Note that "Be it so" echoes the "And it was so" refrain in Genesis; Milton twists the phrase; by putting it in Satan's mouth, Milton makes it a declaration of rebellion.

B. Critical Reading: Expressing an Opinion

Satan is implying that Hell is so miserable that God would not want it back; thus, it is Satan's to do with as he pleases. What do you think of Satan's logic? [Students may agree that Satan is self-deluded but may feel that he has no choice. Some students may point out that Satan accepts Hell only until he can regain Heaven.]

C. Reader's Response: Connecting with the Text

[?] How does the proverb "misery loves company" apply here? [Sample responses: Satan is eager to rally his forces so that they may "share with us their part / In this unhappy mansion." He needs support to seek revenge against God; but he also may feel that sharing the torment with others will alleviate his own pain.]

---

240 As gods, and by their own recovered strength,
     Not by the sufferance° of supernal° power.
         "Is this the region, this the soil, the clime,"
     Said then the lost Archangel, "this the seat
     That we must change for Heaven, this mournful gloom
245 For that celestial light? Be it so, since he
     Who now is sovereign can dispose and bid
     What shall be right: farthest from him is best,
     Whom reason hath equaled, force hath made supreme
     Above his equals. Farewell, happy fields,
250 Where joy forever dwells! Hail, horrors! hail,
     Infernal world! and thou, profoundest° Hell,
     Receive thy new possessor; one who brings
     A mind not to be changed by place or time.
     The mind is its own place, and in itself
255 Can make a Heaven of Hell, a Hell of Heaven.
     What matter where, if I be still the same,
     And what I should be, all but less than he
     Whom thunder hath made greater? Here at least
     We shall be free; the Almighty hath not built
260 Here for his envy, will not drive us hence:
     Here we may reign secure, and in my choice
     To reign is worth ambition, though in Hell:
     Better to reign in Hell than serve in Heaven.
     But wherefore let we then our faithful friends,
265 The associates and copartners of our loss,
     Lie thus astonished° on the oblivious° pool,
     And call them not to share with us their part
     In this unhappy mansion, or once more
     With rallied arms to try what may be yet
270 Regained in Heaven, or what more lost in Hell?"

241. sufferance: permission.
supernal: heavenly.

251. profoundest: lowest; deepest.

266. astonished: dazed.
oblivious: causing forgetfulness.

The Fall of Satan (1825) (detail)
by William Blake.
Illustration for *The Book of Job.*
Tate Gallery, London.

ASSESSMENT TOOLS

Observation Assessment Note students' responses in class discussion, group work, and Reader's Logs. Rate their reading performance with the following statements.

1 = Rarely   2 = Sometimes   3 = Never

____ 1. Makes connections between this selection and others
____ 2. Shows knowledge of poetic devices
____ 3. Considers multiple levels of meaning
____ 4. Makes personal connections
____ 5. Challenges the text

Check Test: True-False

1. The Heavenly Muse sings about "man's first disobedience," the story of Satan's, and then Adam and Eve's fall from grace. [True]
2. Satan had been one of God's favored angels. [True]
3. Satan plans to launch battleships on the fiery lake. [False]
4. When Satan says, "[F]arthest from him is best" he means that the rebels can do as they please when away from God. [True]
5. Satan rebels because God made him a slave. [False]

MAKING MEANINGS

First Thoughts

1. How did you react to Milton's portrait of Satan? What images describing Satan or words spoken by Satan made the greatest impression on you?

Shaping Interpretations

2. According to Milton, how is the rebellion of Satan and the angels against God connected with "man's first disobedience" and the origin of evil in the world? How do your comments in your Reader's Log entry (page 440) compare with Milton's ideas?

3. Re-read Milton's first description of Hell (lines 53–74). How is hell both a psychological state and a physical place? What do you make of the poet's use of **paradox** in the phrase "darkness visible" (line 63)?

4. In his opening speech, Satan vows never to "repent or change" (line 96). Nevertheless, do you catch any hint of longing in this speech for the angels' former state? How might this yearning be related to Milton's mention of "the thought . . . of lost happiness" in lines 54–55?

5. Beelzebub reminds Satan that even in Hell the evil angels may be unwittingly serving God's

---

> ### Reviewing the Text
>
> a. Whom does Milton call upon at the outset (lines 1–16)? What question does he ask about Adam and Eve (lines 27–33)?
>
> b. What is Milton's purpose in writing this epic story?
>
> c. Why was Satan cast out of Heaven?
>
> d. In his first speech, what does Satan tell Beelzebub that he will never do? What course does he favor instead?
>
> e. According to Milton in lines 210–220, who allows Satan the freedom to pursue his evil intentions?
>
> f. In his last speech, what does Satan claim are the advantages of life in Hell?

---

purposes. How does Satan reply to this objection in lines 157–168?

6. In lines 210–220, Milton offers a solemn assurance that despite all Satan's power and grandeur, the devil is still subject to God's purposes. How do these lines contribute a level of **dramatic irony** to Satan's ringing assertion of freedom in his final speech (lines 242–270)?

7. Discuss why some people see Milton's Satan as a heroic figure. How do you feel about this heroic depiction of Satan?

8. What **images** in the story helped you to see and smell Hell?

Connecting with the Text

9. Perhaps the most famous verses of this passage are in Satan's last speech (lines 254–255):

> The mind is its own place, and in itself
> Can make a Heaven of Hell, a Hell of
>   Heaven.

In your experience, is this an accurate description of what the mind can do?

Extending the Text

10. Do people today use the arguments and rationalizations used by Satan and his old crony Beelzebub in their dialogue (lines 143–168)? If so, how?

LANGUAGE AND STYLE

Milton's Poetic Style

Epic Simile

The word *as* in Milton's epic tells us that a simile is coming, an elaborate **epic simile,** in which something in the poem is compared to something quite outside the poem—often an animal, sometimes a human being or human action. These epic similes allowed Milton to bring into his epic a variety of non-Biblical material.

1. What epic similes are used to describe Satan's bulk in lines 196–208?

2. What epic simile describes Satan's landing on dry land in lines 230–237?

JOHN MILTON **449**

---

3. Physical torment is found in Hell, but "lost happiness" (l. 55) and "dismay" (l. 57) also suggest psychological pain. "Darkness visible" suggests a state where the impossible can come true. Physical laws do not apply in Hell, so flames do not give off light, yet the darkness is visible.

4. Satan's tone is mournful as he laments Beelzebub's lost glory. His greatest sorrow, however, is losing his status in Heaven and losing the battle in Heaven. His "lost happiness" drives Satan to revenge rather than repentance.

5. Satan rejects the possibility as weak, declaring it a source of misery. He says that his angels will devote themselves to subverting any of God's plans for good.

6. Satan's assertions about ability to rule his own mind contrast sharply with Milton's statement that his actions are allowed by "high permission of all-ruling Heaven." Lines 214–215 suggest that Satan increases his torment by opposing God.

7. Satan's intensity, persuasion, and rebellion strike many people as heroic. Students may suggest that heroic doesn't necessarily mean good, and that Satan's heroism may degenerate as the epic progresses.

8. Possible responses: "fiery gulf" (l. 52), "great furnace" (l. 62), "floods and whirlwinds of tempestuous fire" (l. 77), "ever-burning sulfur" (l. 69).

Connecting with the Text

9. Students may feel that a positive attitude helps overcome adversity, but that Satan's idea is extreme and unrealistic.

Extending the Text

10. **(Evaluation)** Satan's comment that he will adopt his enemy's tactics when they next meet seems quite modern. His list of Hell's advantages resembles the rationalizations that many people apply to their failures.

Making Meanings

First Thoughts

1. Possible response: Satan is evil, but his audacity and persuasiveness are charismatic. Compelling images include his blazing eyes and his immense size (ll. 193–202).

Reviewing the Text

a. The Heavenly Muse, Urania; why Adam and Eve violated God's one restriction.

b. To affirm God's benevolence and to explain God's treatment of humanity (ll. 25–26).

c. He led a rebellion of angels (l. 43).

d. He will never "repent or change" (l. 96). He seeks revenge by thwarting God's plans and mounting another attack against Heaven.

e. "All-ruling Heaven," or God.

f. He and his angels are assured control there.

Shaping Interpretations

2. Satan (ll. 157–168) plans to corrupt God's creation of humanity. Reader's Log entries may note that free will makes possible the rebellion of Satan, Adam, and Eve.

John Milton **T449**

Language and Style

Answers

Epic Simile

1. The giants Briareos and Typhon of Greek mythology and the huge Biblical sea creature Leviathan.
2. The coming to earth of a hill or a volcano moved from its original site and carried by the wind.

Syntax

1. *He*/*discerns*/*companions*. To clarify, repeat the verb or supply a synonym. ("He discerns his companions and sees Beelzebub weltering by his side.")
2. Possible answer: "Fallen Cherub, weakness is miserable. Let us be strong in avoiding good; let us delight in acting contrary to God."

Blank Verse

1. Infernal world! and thou, profoundest Hell,/ Receive thy new possessor, one who brings/ A mind not to be changed by place or time. (Note variance in l. 253.)
2. Milton varies meter, putting a preposition or relative pronoun in a stressed position. For example, ll. 27–29, "Say first, for Heaven hides nothing from thy view,/ Nor the deep tract of Hell, say first what cause / Moved our grand parents in that happy state,"

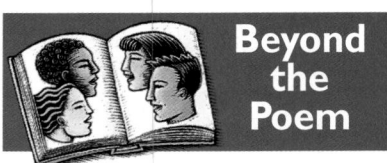

Beyond the Poem

Choices

1. **Writer's Notebook** Remind students to save their work. They may use it as prewriting for the Writer's Workshop on p. 459.

PORTFOLIO ASSESSMENT

Choices: Assessment Criteria For help in evaluating these Choices assignments, see the criteria in the *Portfolio Management System*, pp. 106–107.

Syntax

To accommodate the demands of his meter, Milton often uses irregular syntax in which the sentences do not follow the normal subject-verb-complement order. In addition, Milton's sentences are long, and often words are omitted which have to be supplied by the reader.

1. In lines 76–78, what are the subject, the verb, and the direct object? What additional words should be supplied in lines 78–81 to make sense of the rest of this sentence?
2. Using normal English syntax, how would you rephrase lines 157–162?

Blank Verse

Milton uses **blank verse,** or unrhymed iambic pentameter, to give his epic an exalted tone. Iambic pentameter means that each line of the poem has ten syllables, with five strong stresses alternating with five weaker stresses (the lines begin with an unstressed syllable and end with a stressed one). An **iamb** is an unstressed syllable followed by a stressed one, as in the word refér.

1. Scan lines 251–253 to show that they are written in iambic pentameter.
2. Choose a passage to read aloud so that you can hear the beat of the iambs. Where does Milton vary the meter to give his verse variety and to prevent a singsong rhythm?

CHOICES:
Building Your Portfolio

Writer's Notebook

1. Collecting Ideas for a Cause-Effect Essay

WORK IN PROGRESS

In *Paradise Lost*, Milton argues that God is not responsible for the evils of our world. Rather, Adam and Eve's disobedience, their misuse of reason and freedom, caused these evils. What do you think is one of the biggest evils that exists in the world today? What are its causes? What are its effects? As you note your ideas, draw from your own experience, but also consider other sources, such as historical evidence, newspapers, and newsmagazines. Save your work to use in the Writer's Workshop on page 459.

Critical Writing

2. Paraphrasing Milton

Choose one of the long speeches in this excerpt from *Paradise Lost*: for example, lines 84–124 (Satan), 128–155 (Beelzebub), 157–191 (Satan), or 242–270 (Satan). Write a prose paraphrase of the speech you select. You'll have to supply words that Milton omits and use normal English syntax.

Critical Writing

3. Analyzing the Arch-Fiend

In a brief essay, discuss Milton's characterization of Satan. Examine Satan's appearance, his actions, his words, and his effect on others. Where does Milton directly characterize Satan? Open with a general statement summing up the character of the Arch-Fiend.

Creative Writing

4. A Fallen Angel Dialogue

Milton originally planned *Paradise Lost* as a drama. Working with a small group, try recreating the opening scene of the poem as a dramatic dialogue between Satan and Beelzebub. Start by compressing the two characters' speeches. How will you incorporate Milton's background narration and descriptive details into your dialogue?

Critical Thinking / Art

5. Two Hells

Another famous description of Hell and its overlord appears in the selection from *The Inferno of Dante* on page 394. Prepare two lists, one for Milton and one for Dante, and compare their images of Satan and his infernal domain. If you wish, draw the two underworlds—they are dramatically visual.

✔ **Quick Check: Milton's Poetic Style**

Indicate whether the example illustrates epic simile, inverted syntax, or blank verse.

[1] "A dungeon horrible . . . / As one great furnace flamed" (ll. 61–62) [Epic simile]
[2] "But wherefore let we then our faithful friends . . . Lie thus astonished" (ll. 264, 266) [Inverted syntax]
[3] "Invoke thy aid to my adventurous song, / That with no middle flight intends to soar" (ll. 13–14) [Blank verse]
[4] "So spake the apostate Angel" (l. 125) [Inverted syntax]
[5] "Their portion set / As far removed from God and light of Heaven / As from the center thrice to the utmost pole" (ll. 72–74) [Epic simile]

Allegory: Telling Two Stories at Once

Modern photographers sometimes create striking effects by superimposing one image on another to produce a double exposure. In the same way, writers sometimes use the literary form known as **allegory** to tell two stories at once. Allegories are usually used for teaching. In an allegory, characters, settings, and events stand for abstract ideas. Allegories thus have two meanings: a literal meaning and a symbolic one.

Allegories were especially popular during the Middle Ages. Around 1509, an enduringly relevant play called *Everyman* used the techniques of allegory to teach people the value of good deeds. Everyman (who stands for exactly what his name indicates) is summoned by Death to give an account of his life. Everyman asks his friends, who have allegorical names such as Fellowship, Beauty, and Strength, to go with him, but only Good Deeds stays with him to the end. *Everyman* is periodically dusted off and revived for the stage today. It still gets good reviews.

The Renaissance produced two masterly allegories. Edmund Spenser's *The Faerie Queene* is a long, rich allegory about the adventures of characters who embody such things as holiness, chastity, truth, falsehood, hypocrisy, and despair. (See page 221.) John Bunyan's allegorical novel *The Pilgrim's Progress from This World to That Which Is to Come* (1678), commonly called *The Pilgrim's Progress,* was such a success that, like many filmmakers today, he produced a second part.

The Perils of Piety

The narrator of *The Pilgrim's Progress* is a dreamer. Asleep, he dreams about a man called Christian who lives with his family in a city called Destruction. Besides living in a city with this appalling name, Christian has another problem: On his back he bears an immense burden that he cannot get rid of. It is like a part of himself. And so he decides to leave home and go on a "progress," or journey, to a wonderful place that he has heard of called the Celestial City. On this trip, described through most of the book, he has a few pleasant experiences, such as his visit to House Beautiful and the Delectable Mountains, but most of his adventures are unpleasant and even dangerous. He falls into the Slough (a mudhole; rhymes with "cow") of Despond, he climbs the Hill Difficulty, he fights a dragon-like monster called Apollyon, and he is arrested and unjustly punished in a place called Vanity Fair. His most insidious encounters are with characters who try to distract him from his progress: Mr. Worldly Wiseman, Talkative, Little-Faith, and Ignorance. Finally, all these obstacles overcome, Christian enters the Celestial City, where he will dwell eternally in bliss and where he is eventually joined by his wife

©The Frick Collection, New York.

Christian Reading in His Book
(late 18th or early 19th century)
by William Blake.

A. Literary Element: Allegory

The word *allegory* comes from two Greek words: *allos,* or "other," and *agoreuein,* "to speak in assembly." Even as the word has close ties with the *agora,* or "marketplace," so an allegory is meant for public sharing—either with an immediate viewing audience (as in the case of *Everyman*) or with a reading audience that may extend around the world and across centuries (as in the case of *The Pilgrim's Progress*).

B. Expansion

Born near Bedford, John Bunyan (1628–1688) served in the Parliamentary army from 1644 to 1646. Some time after his marriage in 1649, Bunyan turned to religious matters, undergoing a great spiritual struggle. He came through it with a dedication to views that were not in line with those of the Church of England, as well as a membership in the Baptist congregation at Bedford.

Bunyan became a lay preacher at a time when nonconformist preaching was banned; as a result, he was arrested for preaching without a license and imprisoned from 1660 to 1672. From the Bedford jail he wrote nine books.

Released from prison and licensed to preach, Bunyan became the pastor of the Baptist congregation that he had joined years before. He remained at that post for the rest of his life. In 1675, however, he saw a second but brief imprisonment; and it was during this time that he completed the first part of *The Pilgrim's Progress*.

OPTIONS FOR TEACHING

STRATEGIES FOR INCLUSION

Less Proficient Readers To determine students' comprehension of the twofold nature of allegories, literal and symbolic, ask them to discuss the character of Hopeful in the story. First, check students' understanding of the word *hopeful.* Next, have students review the text and provide evidence which supports the literal and symbolic role of this character. Have students find passages that suggest a truly symbolic function for this person, and read aloud the pertinent information.

INTEGRATING THE LANGUAGE ARTS

Strategic Reading Have students team up with partners to work through the introduction to and excerpt from *The Pilgrim's Progress.* Encourage a Think Aloud Approach, in which students freely question each other and share ideas as they read. Afterward, ask partners to form an interpretative or evaluative conclusion about Bunyan's work and share it with the class. ☞

A. Expansion

Note that the travelers' imprisonment is partly their own fault; for Christian, finding the road rough and discouraging, persuaded Hopeful to take an easier path, not knowing that it crossed Giant Despair's property. Self-recrimination colors Christian's attitude in this excerpt.

B. Literary Connections

Most students will recognize this reference to Psalm 23 (page 422). They may surmise from the comparison that Christian survived the Valley of the Shadow of Death by finding his protection in God.

Title page of *The Pilgrim's Progress* by John Bunyan.

Christiana and their children. Bunyan describes their journey in the second part of *The Pilgrim's Progress*.

In the following excerpt, Christian and his companion, Hopeful, have been imprisoned in the dungeon of Giant Despair's Doubting Castle. Goaded by his wife, Diffidence, the giant has starved them, beaten them mercilessly, and urged them to kill themselves. Christian and Hopeful talk about what to do.

Christian: "Brother," said Christian, "what shall we do? The life that we now live is miserable. For my part I know not whether it is best to live thus, or to die out of hand. 'My soul chooseth strangling rather than life,'[1] and the grave is more easy for me than this dungeon. Shall we be ruled by the Giant?"

Hopeful: "Indeed our present condition is dreadful, and death would be far more welcome to me than thus forever to abide; but yet let us consider, the Lord of the country to which we are going hath said, 'Thou shalt do no murder': no, not to another man's person; much more then are we forbidden to take his counsel to kill ourselves. Besides, he that kills another can but commit murder upon his body; but for one to kill himself is to kill body and soul at once. And moreover, my brother, thou talkest of ease in the grave; but hast thou forgotten the hell whither for certain the murderers go? For 'no murderer hath eternal life,'[2]

1. **My soul . . . life:** quotation from Job 7:15.
2. **no murderer . . . life:** quotation from 1 John 3:15.

452 THE RENAISSANCE

etc. And let us consider again that all the law is not in the hand of Giant Despair. Others, so far as I can understand, have been taken by him, as well as we; and yet have escaped out of his hand. Who knows but that God that made the world may cause that Giant Despair may die? Or that at some time or other he may forget to lock us in? Or but he may in short time have another of his fits before us, and may lose the use of his limbs? And if ever that should come to pass again, for my part, I am resolved to pluck up the heart of a man,[3] and to try my utmost to get from under his hand. I was a fool that I did not try to do it before; but however, my brother, let's be patient, and endure a while. The time may come that may give us a happy release; but let us not be our own murderers." With these words Hopeful at present did moderate the mind of his brother; so they continued together (in the dark) that day, in their sad and doleful condition.

Well, toward evening the Giant goes down into the dungeon again, to see if his prisoners had taken his counsel; but when he came there he found them alive; and truly, alive was all; for now, what for want of bread and water, and by reason of the wounds they received when he beat them, they could do little but breathe. But, I say, he found them alive, at which he fell into a grievous rage, and told them that, seeing they had disobeyed his counsel, it should be worse with them than if they had never been born.

At this they trembled greatly, and I think that Christian fell into a swoon; but coming a little to himself again, they renewed their discourse about the Giant's counsel; and whether yet they had best to take it or no. Now Christian again seemed to be for doing it, but Hopeful made his second reply as followeth:

Hopeful: "My brother," said he, "rememberest thou not how valiant thou hast been heretofore? Apollyon could not crush thee, nor could all that thou didst hear, or see, or feel, in the Valley of the Shadow of Death. What hardship, terror, and amazement hast thou already gone through, and art thou now nothing but

3. **pluck . . . man:** be brave.

OPTIONS FOR TEACHING

INTEGRATING THE LANGUAGE ARTS

Language and Style John Bunyan and John Milton were contemporaries, and both wrote about religious faith; but there is a world of difference in their writing styles. Have students compare this excerpt from *The Pilgrim's Progress* to the excerpt from Book I of *Paradise Lost* (pp. 441–448) and identify at least three stylistic differences, supporting their statements with examples from the texts. Students may use a chart similar to the one here to organize and present their material.

Style Differences

	Bunyan	Milton
vocabulary	simple	heightened
syntax	plain	irregular
literary elements	allegory	epic simile

fear? Thou seest that I am in the dungeon with thee, a far weaker man by nature than thou art; also this Giant has wounded me as well as thee, and hath also cut off the bread and water from my mouth; and with thee I mourn without the light. But let us exercise a little more patience; remember how thou playedst the man[4] at Vanity Fair, and wast neither afraid of the chain, nor cage, nor yet of bloody death. Wherefore let us (at least to avoid the shame that becomes not a Christian to be found in) bear up with patience as well as we can."

Now night being come again, and the Giant and his wife being in bed, she asked him concerning the prisoners, and if they had taken his counsel. To which he replied, "They are sturdy rogues, they choose rather to bear all hardship than to make away themselves." Then said she, "Take them into the castle yard tomorrow, and show them the bones and skulls of those that thou hast already dispatched, and make them believe, ere a week come to an end, thou also wilt tear them in pieces, as thou hast done their fellows before them."

So when the morning was come, the Giant goes to them again, and takes them into the castle yard, and shows them, as his wife had bidden him. "These," said he, "were pilgrims as you are once, and they trespassed in my grounds, as you have done; and when I thought fit, I tore them in pieces, and so within ten days I will do you. Go, get you down to your den again"; and with that he beat them all the way thither. They lay therefore all day on Saturday in a lamentable case, as before. Now when night was come, and when Mrs. Diffidence and her husband the Giant were got to bed, they began to renew their discourse of their prisoners; and withal the old Giant wondered that he could neither by his blows nor his counsel bring them to an end. And with that his wife replied, "I fear," said she, "that they live in hope that some will come to relieve them, or that they have picklocks about them, by the means of which they hope to escape." "And sayest thou so, my dear?" said the Giant; "I will therefore search them in the morning."

4. **thou playedst the man:** you were brave.

Well, on Saturday about midnight they began to pray, and continued in prayer till almost break of day.

Now a little before it was day, good Christian, as one half-amazed, brake out in this passionate speech: "What a fool (quoth he) am I, thus to lie in a stinking dungeon, when I may as well walk at liberty! I have a key in my bosom called Promise, that will (I am persuaded) open any lock in Doubting Castle." Then said Hopeful, "That is good news, good brother; pluck it out of thy bosom and try." Then Christian pulled it out of his bosom, and began to try at the dungeon door, whose bolt (as he turned the key) gave back, and the door flew open with ease, and Christian and Hopeful both came out. Then he went to the outward door that leads into the castle yard, and with his key opened that door also. After, he went to the iron gate, for that must be opened, too; but that lock went damnable hard, yet the key did open it. Then they thrust open the gate to make their escape with speed, but that gate, as it opened, made such a creaking that it waked Giant Despair, who, hastily rising to pursue his prisoners, felt his limbs to fail, for his fits took him again, so that he could by no means go after them. Then they went on and came to the King's highway, and so were safe because they were out of his jurisdiction. . . .

—John Bunyan, *from The Pilgrim's Progress*

Next to the Bible, *The Pilgrim's Progress* is the most widely read of all English books. What accounts for Bunyan's enormous appeal? He wrote for people who believed that every human being is engaged in a continuous battle against forces of evil that, while powerful, are not as powerful as God. And so Bunyan told his readers what they most wanted to hear: how, with God's help, they could defeat evil and attain eternal life. He expressed his message in language familiar to his readers, drawn from their daily experiences and from the Bible, folk tales, and popular literature. In Bunyan's literary double exposure, his readers recognized their own lives made surprising and interesting.

C. Expansion

In the events at Vanity Fair, Hopeful was not yet Christian's companion. There, Christian suffered with his friend Faithful, who ultimately was executed for his faith. Hopeful, a citizen of that town, was converted through the power of their example and took Faithful's place on the journey.

D. Expansion

It is no accident that the travelers' escape from prison comes on a Sunday morning—the day and time when, as Christians believe, Jesus arose from the prison of the grave. A hope in what the resurrection represents may be the essence of the "Promise" that provides the key to the captives' release, but Bunyan is not specific. He also may mean to include all of the Bible's promises of protection and deliverance for the faithful.

E. Humanities Connection

The Pilgrim's Progress was one of the first books brought by the Puritans to America.

ASSESSMENT TOOLS

Ongoing Assessment One way to make a rough evaluation of students' grasp of the material is to take a yes/no vote on the following statements, following up with small-group discussions.

1. Allegory is intended primarily to appeal to an unsophisticated audience.
2. If an allegorical figure has a clear symbolic value, it need not also be entertaining.
3. In the excerpt from *The Pilgrim's Progress,* Giant Despair is meant to represent the forces that

tempt Christians to turn their backs on their beliefs.
4. Readers are intended to see in the allegorical character Hopeful the importance of remembering the power of God.

Remind students that arguments can be made on each side. After the small groups have discussed and determined their rationales, have them report to the class.

How to Own a Word

Mini-Lesson: Multiple Meanings of Words

Have students compare and contrast a printed dictionary or thesaurus with a computerized dictionary, thesaurus, or spelling checker. They may easily chart the advantages or disadvantages of one or the other.

Try It Out: Possible Answers

1. (a) light: noun (Greek, *leukos*—white; Latin, *lux* and *lumen*—"light") As the evening waned, Eva turned on the light. (b) light: adjective (Greek, *elaphros;* Latin, *levis*—"having little weight") Imagine such a small, light fruit carrying the weight of humanity's first sin.

2. (a) mind: noun (Greek, *menos*—spirit; Latin, *mens* —"mind") Satan will not change his mind.
(b) "mind": transitive and intransitive verbs have the same origin as the noun. (intransitive) The unruly children refused to mind their parents. (transitive) He did not mind the heat.

3. (a) bear: transitive verb (Latin, *ferre;* Greek, *pherein;* Sanskrit, *bharati*—"to carry," "bring") Adam and Eve bear the responsibility for their exile from Eden. Eve would bear children with pain. (b) bear: noun (Old English, *bera;* Indo-European, *bheros*—"brown animal") Adam named all the animals, including the bear.

4. (a) arm: noun (Old English, *earm;* Latin, *armus;* Old High German, *arm*) Their arms were linked as they walked down the path. (b) arm: noun or transitive/intransitive verb (Old French, *armes*/Latin, *arma*—"implements," "weapons") Satan armed himself with his wits.

5. (a) fast: adjective (Old English, *faest,* akin to German *fest*—"firm," "stable") The Good Samaritan held fast to his principles. (b) fast: intransitive verb (Middle English *fasten,* akin to German *fasten*—"hold fast") Some people fast on the Sabbath.

HOW TO OWN A WORD

Multiple Meanings of Words

Many words have, over time, accumulated more than one meaning. This helps to expand our language, and it makes writing more interesting and reading more of a challenge. One word that has developed more than one meaning is *humor*:

> To spend too much time in studies is sloth . . . to make judgment wholly by their rules is the **humor** of a scholar.
>
> —Sir Francis Bacon, *from "Of Studies"*

Bacon uses the word *humor* to mean a person's general disposition or temperament. But if we say "My sister has a great sense of humor," we are referring to her ability to appreciate what is funny or amusing. These two definitions are related, however; they share the same origin and so are found under the same entry in the dictionary.

Arrangements of definitions may vary from dictionary to dictionary. In some dictionaries, the most frequently encountered meaning appears as the first definition, specialized senses follow, and rare, archaic, and obsolete senses are listed at the end. In other dictionaries, definitions are arranged in order from the oldest sense to the most recent.

Some words not only have different meanings but also have different origins. The fact that such words are spelled identically is an accident. Take the word *mean,* for example:

> Some books also may be read by deputy, and extracts made of them by others; but that would be only in the less important arguments, and the **meaner** sort of books . . .
>
> —Sir Francis Bacon, *from "Of Studies"*

Here, *meaner* means "inferior." A look at the word's etymology reveals that it originated from the Old English word for "plentiful" or "common." (This makes sense—the more plentiful something is, the less value it usually has.) If people are bad-tempered or disagreeable, we also call them mean. This is a different definition of the word, but it shares the same origin and is found under the same entry. But *mean* can also refer to what is halfway between extremes, what is medium or average: "What is the mean amount of television that you watch each

night?" This definition has a different origin, and so it has a separate entry in the dictionary. It is derived from the Latin word for "middle." There is a third entry for *mean* in the dictionary, too: "to have in mind, to intend." This meaning originated from an Old English word that meant relatively the same thing—"to mean, tell, or complain."

Word	Origin	Present Meanings
1. mean	Old English *mænan:* to mean, tell, complain	to have in mind; intend; propose
2. mean	Old English *(ge)mæne:* plentiful, common	low in value; poor; inferior; stingy; miserly; bad-tempered
3. mean	Latin *medius:* middle	halfway between extremes; medium; average

Sometimes a writer intends that only one precise meaning of a word be used. But sometimes two meanings of the word can be used with different, but equally strong and relevant effects:

> . . . the thought
> Both of lost happiness and lasting pain
> Torments him; round he throws his **baleful** eyes,
> That witnessed huge affliction and dismay
> Mixed with obdurate pride and steadfast hate.
>
> —John Milton, *Paradise Lost,* Book I, lines 54–58

Baleful can mean "wretched," as well as "evil." Since the subject of these lines is Satan, both of these meanings work well here. Milton uses the multi-faceted nature of language to complicate our image of Satan, making it more interesting. All writers, especially poets, revel in this rich complexity.

Try It Out

Using a dictionary, look up the origin and different meanings of each word listed below. Then use each word in two sentences to illustrate two of the word's different meanings.

1. light **2.** mind **3.** bear **4.** arm **5.** fast

STRATEGIES FOR INCLUSION

Less Proficient Readers To emphasize the difference between slang and traditional usage, ask volunteers to write on the chalkboard a list of slang words they commonly use, for example, *chill* or *lame.* Have students use the word in a sentence. Then, have them give examples of sentences that use the same word with its regular definition. If necessary, students should refer to a dictionary for the more traditional meanings.

Special Needs To develop students' competence with the vocabulary words presented in the Try It Out activity, have students attempt to use each of the words in a paragraph or short poem they create. Place students in pairs, matching students with different abilities. In the pairs, students should try to capture one or two meanings of the words in their writing. Afterward, have students share their work with the rest of the class.

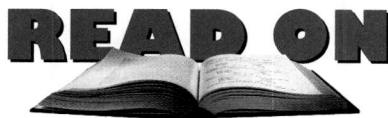

Love and War

The filmmaker Kenneth Branagh has brought a lively new perspective to some of Shakespeare's plays. *Henry V* (1989), about the warrior-king who led the attack on Agincourt in the early fifteenth century, is packed with action and adventure. The confused lovers in *Much Ado About Nothing* (1993), played by Branagh and Emma Thompson, spar and spark against a sunny Italian landscape. Both films are available on video.

Motorcycle Meditations

Part travelogue, part meditation, part rambling discourse, Robert Pirsig's *Zen and the Art of Motorcycle Maintenance* (Bantam Books) is above all an inquiry into human values. While taking an extended motorcycle trip, Pirsig pursues the same questions that intrigued Francis Bacon, John Milton, and the writer(s) of Genesis: What is the nature of the universe, and what is our place in it? How should we conduct our lives?

The Bard's Background and Playground

People flocked to Renaissance London in droves, where the theater was a major attraction. Shakespeare was an integral part of this world, but there's been a tendency to divorce the man from his background. *Shakespeare of London* (Penguin) by Marchette Chute and *Shakespeare Alive!* (Bantam Books) by Joseph Papp and Elizabeth Kirkland help bring the legend back to life, placing Shakespeare in the theatrical and social context where he thrived.

A Crisis of Conscience

Scholar, ambassador, Lord Chancellor, family man—Sir Thomas More had it all. But then King Henry VIII changed everything by deciding to divorce his wife, which meant breaking with the pope—an action More opposed. More's decision to follow his personal beliefs rather than his political interests serves as the basis for Robert Bolt's play, *A Man for All Seasons* (Vintage/Random House), also a 1966 film starring Paul Scofield and Orson Welles, as well as a 1988 made-for-television movie with Charlton Heston, John Gielgud, and Vanessa Redgrave. (Both versions are available on videotape.)

Love Is . . .

In *The Love Poems of Robert Herrick and John Donne* (Barnes & Noble), the works of two of the most well-known Renaissance poets come gloriously together. Even though both poets write about love, their ideas and style differ. The editor, Louis Untermeyer, notes that "Donne plunges the reader into emotion with nervous desperation," while Herrick "is all delicacy and delight." Donne's metaphysical passion and Herrick's spirited banter make this collection a complete exploration of the power of love.

FOR FURTHER EXPLORATION

Poetry
John Milton: Complete Poems and Major Prose edited by Merritt Y. Hughes
Emelia Lanier's long poem, *Salve Deus Rex Judaeorum (1611)* appears as *The Poems of Shakespeare's Dark Lady* edited by A. L. Rowse
The Gulistan by Saadi

Fiction
Anne of the Thousand Days: A Novel by Edward Fenton
Orlando by Virginia Woolf

Nonfiction
Essays on Shakespeare by William Empson
Queen Elizabeth I by J. E. Neale
Michelangelo by Howard Hibbard
Essays by Francis Bacon
John Donne: A Literary Life by George Parfit

Read On
Portfolio Assessment Options

The following projects can help you evaluate and assess your students' reading accomplishments outside of class. Videotapes or audiotapes of completed projects may be included in students' portfolios.

- **Hold a Talk-Show Discussion** Have students act out a talk show in which one or more of the characters they have read about are the guests. The show should include videotape or overhead projector photos that depict scenes from the book. One student should serve as the host of the show, two should role-play the guests, and class members should serve as the audience, asking questions that relate to actions and thoughts in the book.

- **Create a Museum Exhibit** Have students set up a museum exhibit depicting the life and times of Shakespeare or More. Students should use mechanical arts skills (perhaps showing the Globe Theater), as well as photographic and art representations to present a clear picture of the man and the times.

- **Act Out a Scene** Have students act out a scene from *A Man for All Seasons*. Students should act out the scene in front of the class, with props, music, and costumes. A narrator might be used to set up the scene. Students may enjoy having their performance videotaped.

- **Create an Anthology** Have students create a book of their favorite poems, speeches, or passages from the book they have read, adding captions that reflect their own feelings or thoughts about each selection. Students may also add drawings as well as an original cover for their book.

- **Write a Review** Have students write a film review of Branagh's renderings of Shakespeare. They might even write a comparison with a stage version they have seen or with Lawrence Olivier's *Henry V.*

A. Humanities Connection

The Greek tradition of language study, which included grammar, logic, and rhetoric, informs grammar study today. Greek scholars in Alexandria developed the formal system we know as grammar. In *The Art of Letters,* c.100 B.C., Dionysus Thrax writes on sentences, words, syllables, and letters, and on how they coalesce to express thought in recognizable patterns.

B. Expansion

In 1623, Henry Cockeram published his *English Dictionarie,* the first dictionary to be given that name. In 1656, Thomas Blount published *Glossographia,* which had some nine thousand words, fuller definitions, and etymologies, although he, too, included only "hard" words.

C. Humanities Connection

The *Webster's Third New International Dictionary,* considered the most comprehensive English-language dictionary currently published in the United States, is a descendent of Noah Webster's *An American Dictionary of the English Language,* which was first published in 1828. When the 1961 edition was published, it was not without controversy. Critics regarded its "permissiveness" as an abdication of the dictionary's responsibility to foster good English. Among other things, the dictionary was criticized for including words such as "ain't" and other words outside the educated usage.

D. Humanities Connection

This unrest resulted in the publication of more than twenty thousand books and pamphlets on political and religious issues.

The English Language

The Growth of Modern English

by John Algeo

During the seventeenth century, interest in the English language grew rapidly. English scholars vigorously studied the grammar, vocabulary, and style of written English.

The First Grammars and Dictionaries

The first grammars of English appeared shortly before the end of the sixteenth century. These small books imitated widely used Latin grammars and were intended to help English-speaking students learn Latin and foreigners learn English. The first such grammar was William Bullokar's *Pamphlet for Grammar* (1586). Although it would not compare well with the best grammars of our language written today, four hundred years later, it was no small achievement for its day. To write a grammar of a language for which there were no other grammar books was an accomplishment.

By the end of the seventeenth century, a great many grammar books had been written, and more continued to appear through the eighteenth and nineteenth centuries. Difficult as it may be for some of us to understand today, English speakers were fascinated by grammars of their language. Popular as grammar books were, however, readers and writers of English were even more interested in dictionaries.

The first English dictionary appeared at the beginning of the seventeenth century. In 1604, Robert Cawdrey published *A Table Alphabeticall . . . of Hard Usuall English Wordes.* As that title suggests, the earliest dictionaries made no effort to list all the words in the English language. Rather they were simply lists of "hard" words—learned, often borrowed words—that a reader might come across but that would be difficult for the ordinary person to understand.

The first dictionaries gave only a familiar synonym for each hard word. Gradually, dictionaries began to expand the number of words they listed and the kinds of information they included about each word. Definitions increased from single-word synonyms to fuller descriptions of meaning. In the eighteenth century, efforts were made to include all the words of the language and to define all their uses. New sorts of information added to the entry for a word included its etymology (origin and history), its part of speech, quotations illustrating its use, and its pronunciation.

As English dictionaries increased the number of words they included and the information they gave about each word, they became better and better. Today, English has the best dictionaries of any language on earth. The greatest of English dictionaries is the *Oxford English Dictionary* in twenty large volumes. It attempts to trace the history of all English words from their first appearance in the language until today. The biggest dictionary a high school student is likely to need is one like the *Webster's Third New International Dictionary,* and for most ordinary uses, smaller desk dictionaries serve very well.

The Battle of Styles: Ornate vs. Plain

The seventeenth century was an age of social unrest. In England, the Cavaliers, who supported the king and the established Anglican church, were opposed by the Puritans, who supported Parliament and a congregational form of church. The Cavaliers dressed elegantly, ate with gusto, attended the theater, and generally lived a high life. Puritans, on the other hand, dressed and ate plainly, thought the theater was wicked, and generally lived sober, God-fearing, dull lives. There was bound to be trouble between them. And so there was, with

- **Planning Instruction** See Teaching Notes, *Teaching Resources A,* p. 108, for objectives for this feature.
- **Assessment** See The English Language, *Test Booklet,* pp. 81–82.

OPTIONS FOR TEACHING

STRATEGIES FOR INCLUSION

Learners Having Difficulty Model one of the words in Try It Out #1 by showing students an enlarged copy of a dictionary entry. Reproduce the same on an overhead projector. As you explain, have students take note of each kind of information in the entry.

Spatial Have students design posters that state the message and reflect the meaning of the expressions in Try It Out #2.

Auditory Call on volunteers to read aloud sentences and passages in *Paradise Lost* or "Of Studies" that they consider to be written in ornate style. Have other students restate the passage using plain-style English.

the Puritans eventually gaining control of Parliament, executing the king, closing the theaters, and establishing a military and church dictatorship in England.

The difference in lifestyles between the Cavaliers and the Puritans was echoed in a difference in language styles: an ornate style versus a plain style. However, there was by no means a simple equivalence between Cavaliers and ornate style on the one hand and Puritans and plain style on the other. Indeed, in some cases, it was the other way around.

The ornate style used many words borrowed from foreign languages and learned words, thus creating what were scornfully called "inkhorn terms." An inkhorn was a container made from the horn of an animal and was used to hold ink for writing with a quill pen. **Inkhorn terms** were words that scholars might use in writing, but that seemed out of place in ordinary conversation. It was such inkhorn terms that were listed in the dictionaries of "hard" words.

Another aspect of the ornate style was called **euphuism** (after Euphues, a character in two books by John Lyly, who used alliteration, balanced expressions, antitheses, fantastic similes, mythological allusions, and other verbal tricks to create an artificial elegance of language). An example is the following sentence, in which Euphues cites some proverbs

> Popular as grammar books were, readers and writers of English were even more interested in dictionaries.

against rash and excessive action: "The vine watered with wine is soon withered, the blossom in the fattest ground is quickly blasted, the goat the fatter she is the less fertile she is; yea, man the more witty he is the less happy he is."

Still another aspect of the ornate style was the **metaphysical conceit,** an extended and exaggerated metaphor, such as that in Donne's poem "A Valediction: Forbidding Mourning."

Plain style, on the other hand, valued simplicity and clarity. It came to be favored especially by those with scientific interests, something that is natural enough. If you are going to describe a scientific experiment or observation, you are less interested in having people admire your cleverness with language than in having them understand what you did or saw. Scientists try not to intrude personally into the object of study. Their work and their language are supposed to be impersonal and public.

In the metaphysical or euphuistic ideal, on the other hand, the reader sees the world through the highly personal eyes of the writer. The aim is to surprise the reader by revealing the world in a fresh way. Thus, the two styles, contrasting sharply in their aims, contrast also in their techniques.

The plain style was promoted especially through the work of the Royal Society. Founded in

the second half of the seventeenth century, the Royal Society is one of the oldest organizations in Europe for "improving natural knowledge," that is, promoting scientific study. Members of the Society did much to combat the excesses of ornate style. As a result of their work and example, today the plain style is the unchallenged ideal for good prose.

What Is Style?

Although a plain style is our ideal today, we still find other kinds of style in use. What makes a style?

When we talk or write, we have a choice of ways to express our meaning. For example, if we want to mention our male parent, we can call him father, dad, papa, sire, pater, pop, my old man, or various other names. Obviously, those words, although they all mean the same thing in that they can all refer to the same person, are very different from one another in how they are used. If you are filling out an employment questionnaire, you are not going to be asked, "What is your daddy's name?" If you are telling a friend why you can't use the family car tonight, you are probably not going to say, "My sire is using it."

The options we take in talking or writing determine the style of our language. **Style** is the choice we make among alternative ways of saying the same thing. Among the elements that make up a style are options like these:

1. **Short and simple versus long and complex**

E. Literary Connections
Inkhorn terms were referred to as far back as 1553 when Thomas Wilson observed in *Art of Rhetorique:* "Among all other lessons this should first be learned, that wee never affect any straunge ynkehorne termes, but to speake as is commonly received. . . ." Among his examples of inkhornisms are: *revoluting; ingent affabilitie; ingenious capacity; magnifical dexteritie; dominicall superioritie;* and *splendidious.*

F. Expansion
Founding members of the Royal Society included architect Christopher Wren, chemist Robert Boyle, and Bishop John Wilkins. Isaac Newton would later serve as president of the society. In the beginning, it was largely a Puritan venture whose purpose was to discuss scientific matters in the spirit of Francis Bacon. The journal *Philosophical Transactions of the Royal Society,* begun in 1665, was one of the world's earliest periodicals.

Elements of Literature: **Videodisc** Use the bar codes below to access information about the English language. For more information, see the Videodisc *Teacher's Manual.*

Videodisc Side A

Begin Play, English Track

Begin Play, Spanish Track

Strategic Reading To help students grasp the differences between plain and ornate styles, have them use this three-column graphic organizer to take notes.

Plain and Ornate Styles

key words	notes	summary points

Writing: Research Report Have students research government publications and political speeches to find examples of wordy, puffed-up language. Students should then write a brief report identifying a specific document, its purpose, and examples of poor writing. Students may discuss whether they believe the language is an intentional attempt to fool or mislead the public.

A. Exploring the Culture

Today's supporters of a plainer English advocate avoiding any usage that confuses and misleads readers or listeners. Failure to use plain English is sometimes referred to as *doublespeak* and *psychobabble*.

B. Literary Connections

In *The Elements of Style,* Strunk and White advise: "Rich, ornate prose is hard to digest, generally unwholesome, and sometimes nauseating. If the sickly-sweet word, the overblown phrase are a writer's natural form of expression, as is sometimes the case, he will have to compensate for it by a show of vigor and by writing something as meritorious as Solomon's Song of Songs."

Try it Out: Answers

1. Students might include etymology, specific and general definitions, cross-references, parts of speech, variation of word use.
2. Possible answers:
   a. responsible for another's welfare
   b. someone who is in an unaccustomed situation
   c. a place that offers one all that is needed to live
   d. excessive self-love often causes a defeat or loss
   e. prepare oneself for the inevitable, such as death
   f. have a close call; survive in spite of all odds
   g. the humble, pious people will survive the wicked and unjust
   h. show kindness without expecting a reward
   i. forsake war and idolatry and adopt the ways of peace
   j. character flaw
3. Most students will agree that "A Valediction: Forbidding Mourning" uses an ornate style involving complex figures of speech and involved and indirect statements; "Song to Celia" has a plain style, using short and simple statements. Milton's *Paradise Lost* is written in ornate style, using long sentences and many adjectives and adverbs; the King James version is a plain style written with ordinary words and short sentences.

---

sentences. A sequence of short, simple sentences is likely to seem childish or simple-minded, but many long, complex ones are likely to seem confused.

2. **Active versus passive verbs,** as in "The Puritans chopped off King Charles's head" (active) versus "King Charles's head was chopped off" (passive). Passive verbs are especially useful for telling that something happened without telling who did it. They are favorites of scientific and bureaucratic writers, but many other people find them mealy-mouthed.

3. **Direct versus qualified statements.** Direct statements tell the facts just as they are. Qualified statements add words like *perhaps, possibly, it seems, it would appear, it is likely that, generally, make an effort to,* and so on. Writers may think that using qualifications will get them off the hook if they say something wrong. But readers find the result wishy-washy.

4. **Noun- versus verb-centeredness.** We can *agree* on something, or *reach an agreement* about it. We can *wash* the car, or *give* it a *wash.* We can *decide* to go, or *come to a decision* to do so. We can *promise* our friends something, or *make a promise* to them *about* it. When we put the main meaning into the verb, we have a more direct and forceful sentence, but

putting the main meaning into a noun after the verb lets us emphasize it.

5. **Plain versus fancy words.** Plain words like *newspaper, home, watery,* and *to run* are more comfortable than fancy words like *periodical, domicile, aqueous,* and *to course.* There are times, to be sure, when we want our language to be fancy. The danger in using fancy words, however, is that we will use them not quite right, and the result will be, not fancy, but unintentionally funny.

Try It Out

1. The English dictionary began its development during the seventeenth century with lists of "hard" words and their meanings. Look at the entry for a word in a modern desk dictionary. You may choose any word you like, but the following are suggestions:

   atom   dwarf   hopefully
   map   sphinx   learn

   What different kinds of information does the entry give you about the word? To start off, you will find the spelling and pronunciation of the word. What else? (You will find somewhat different kinds of information in the entries for various words and for the same word in various dictionaries.)

2. The language of the King James Bible and of the Book of Common Prayer has influenced the way we use English. What do the following

expressions mean? Find the passage in which each expression was originally used (it is indicated in parentheses).
   a. My brother's keeper (Genesis 4:9)
   b. A stranger in a strange land (Exodus 2:22)
   c. A land flowing with milk and honey (Exodus 3:8)
   d. Pride goes before a fall. (Proverbs 16:18)
   e. Put one's house in order (2 Kings 20:1; Isaiah 38:1)
   f. Escape by the skin of one's teeth (Job 19:20)
   g. The meek shall inherit the earth. (Psalm 37:11)
   h. Cast your bread upon the waters (Ecclesiastes 11:1)
   i. Beat swords into plowshares (Isaiah 2:4)
   j. Feet of clay (Daniel 2:33)

3. Compare the style either of John Donne's "A Valediction: Forbidding Mourning" (page 248) and Ben Jonson's "Song: To Celia" (page 258), or of the King James account of the temptation and fall of Adam and Eve (page 416) and Milton's account of the fall of Satan in *Paradise Lost* (page 441). Note differences in vocabulary, length and complexity of sentences, repeated versus varied patterns of language, simple and direct statements versus involved and indirect ones, and the use of descriptive adjectives and adverbs (few versus many). Which work is in plain style, and which is in ornate style?

ASSESSMENT TOOLS

Check Test: Multiple Choice

1. English grammar books first appeared shortly before the end of the (a) fifteenth century, (b) sixteenth century, (c) seventeenth century, (d) eighteenth century. [b]
2. English dictionaries appeared at the beginning of the (a) fifteenth century, (b) sixteenth century, (c) seventeenth century, (d) eighteenth century. [c]
3. The plain style is most likely to include (a) inkhorn terms, (b) clear terms, (c) euphemisms, (d) metaphysical conceit. [b]
4. Members of the Royal Society favored (a) plain style, (b) Latin-based language, (c) ornate style, (d) combination of plain and ornate style. [a]
5. Style can best be defined as (a) ability to write a good story, (b) command of the English language, (c) use of figurative language, (d) the characteristic use of words. [d]

BUILDING YOUR PORTFOLIO
Writer's Workshop

EXPOSITORY WRITING

SPECULATION ABOUT CAUSES AND EFFECTS

Thomas De Quincey wondered for years why the knocking at the gate after Duncan's murder had such a solemnly awful effect, and playgoers debate to this day what drove Macbeth and Lady Macbeth to such bloody abandon. Speculation about **causes** and **effects** in both literature and life is never ending. We do it to explain our world. Speculating about causes and effects involves narrating brief anecdotes and observing and gathering data, and is also useful in reflective writing.

Prewriting

1. **Checking your Writer's Notebook.** By doing the Writer's Notebook activities on pages 390, 409, 427, and 450, you may have already completed the prewriting for an essay that speculates about causes and effects. Check back over your Writer's Notebook entries. You can repeat any activity to add to or improve what you've already done, or you can proceed with the prewriting activities that follow.

2. **What invites speculation?** Speculating about causes and effects involves conjecture, so your first task is to find a topic that invites speculation—that is, one whose causes or effects aren't absolutely certain. For example, "why water freezes" is not an appropriate topic, because its explanation is a report of facts. The two questions that cause-and-effect writing answers are *Why?* and *What's the result?* You do not have to answer both in your essay, though you may—for example, as De Quincey explains why Shakespeare "invented" the knocking at the gate and also describes its emotional and theatrical effect (page 330). To find a topic to write about, consider

   - **events:** occurrences, such as Macduff's leaving his family in *Macbeth*

   - **situations,** or **phenomena:** ongoing conditions, such as increasing vandalism in a community

   - **trends:** changes over time, such as the availability of CD-ROM technology

3. **A topic from literature or life?** Like De Quincey, you may want to explain something that intrigues (or irritates or moves) you in a poem or play: *Why does Macduff leave his family? What are the effects of this event, in the play or on the audience?* You may also pose a "What if?" question and predict

Technology HELP

See Writer's Workshop 2 CD-ROM. *Assignment: Cause and Effect.*

ASSIGNMENT
Write an essay speculating about the causes and/or effects of an event, situation, or trend.

AIM
To explain causes, effects, or both; to persuade your readers.

AUDIENCE
Your classmates or people affected by the subject.

WRITER'S WORKSHOP 459

QUICK PLANNING GUIDE

WW | **Speculation About Causes and Effects**

Prewriting
Checking your Writer's Notebook **p. 459**
What invites speculation? **p. 459**
A topic from literature or life? **p. 459**
Mapping the possibilities **p. 460**
Identifying a thesis **p. 460**
The evidence, please **p. 461**
Being believable **p. 461**

Drafting
The introduction **p. 462**
The body **p. 462**
The conclusion **p. 462**

Evaluating and Revising
Peer review **p. 462**
Self-evaluation **p. 462**

Proofreading and Publishing p. 463

Reflecting on Your Writing p. 463

PORTFOLIO ASSESSMENT

- **Generating Ideas** To help students in prewriting, use the heuristic in the *Portfolio Management System,* p. 108.
- **Assessment Rubric** For a rubric that can be used to assess students' progress in writing, see the *Portfolio Management System,* p. 110.

PROGRAM MANAGER

Computer Guided Instruction For a related cause-and-effect assignment that students may use as additional instruction, see *Writer's Workshop 2.*

Writer's Workshop **T459**

Motivation

Ask for two volunteers to role-play a discussion between a parent and a child about why the child came home late last night. Have the volunteers leave the room for five minutes to organize. Tell the other students that they should notice during the role-playing the causes and effects each volunteer uses to make his or her point. Conclude the activity by discussing the causes and effects after the performance and by explaining that students will use this kind of cause-effect thinking in this Writer's Workshop.

Teaching the Lesson

This lesson includes instructions for each stage of the writing process. Guide students by modeling each stage with your own writing.

Prewriting

- To help students arrive at topics, compile a list of questions about literary works or general topics that the class generates during a brainstorming session. Make a poster or handout with these questions on it to serve as a source of possible topics for this assignment.
- As students work on their causes-effects maps, encourage them to include citation information in their drafts. For example, if they are writing about a literary work such as *Macbeth,* they should write down act, scene, and line numbers for any quotations that support the causes and effects that they will include in their drafts. This will save them time and frustration when they write the final versions of their essays.

plausible results: *What if Lady Macbeth had not gone mad?* Or you might extend a literary work: *How will Banquo's son react when Malcolm is crowned?*

For a real-life topic, you'll write best about something that concerns you or stirs your curiosity: *Why are daytime talk shows so popular? What will happen when your TV is also a computer? Why is your advanced math class three-fourths male?*

Notice that your topic may have a broad or a personal focus. Also consider more abstract speculation. For example, *Macbeth* brings up the traits of ambition, leadership, and dominance, suggesting topics such as *What creates a good leader? What are the effects of friendship with a bold, dominant person?*

4. **Mapping the possibilities.** A visual map of ideas can open your mind to many perspectives. One technique is to begin by writing and circling a statement of your topic (the event, situation, or trend). Analyze it. What produced it? What happened (or might happen) because of it? Then write down *any* possibilities, showing the connections with arrows. You might discover a chain of causes and effects: *A causes B, B causes C,* and so on. Stimulate your thinking with the Strategies for Elaboration that follow the diagram.

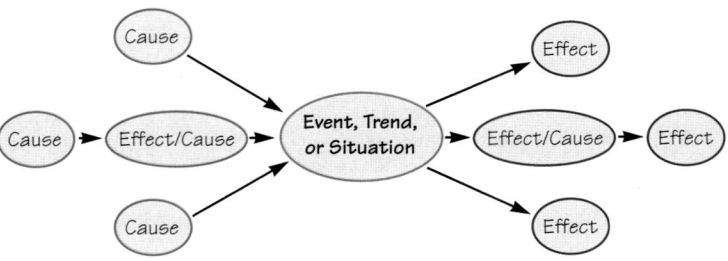

Strategies for Elaboration: Probing Causes and Effects

- **Begin with obvious causes and effects.** A simple start lays the foundation for more ideas.
- **Look for hidden causes and effects.** Always probe beyond the obvious, using both reason and imagination.
- **Consider both immediate and distant causes and effects.** Don't stop at the times just before and just after the event.
- **Be open to alternative explanations.** Record plausible causes and effects *even if you finally reject them.* They may prove useful in your paper.

5. **Identifying a thesis.** After generating ideas, assess them. First, have you mapped out the situation or event to your satisfaction? If not, you need more ideas or another topic. Next, decide on a thesis for your essay: a statement of your topic that clearly indicates if you'll discuss causes, effects, or both.

STRATEGIES FOR INCLUSION

Visual The body of a cause-effect essay can be arranged in several different ways. Some students may benefit from seeing different arrangements illustrated in charts. You might put the following examples on the chalkboard or on a poster.

BODY: Situation, cause, cause, cause, effect, effect, effect.

BODY: Situation, effect, effect, effect, cause.

BODY: Situation, cause, effect, cause, effect, cause, effect.

Kinesthetic Suggest that students write each cause and effect on a separate index card. Remind them to include supporting facts or evidence on each card. Then, students can lay the index cards on their desks and rearrange the cards until they find the most effective order.

6. **The evidence, please.** In this paper, you are conjecturing, or advancing an explanation. You must convince your readers that the causes or effects you propose are *plausible and likely*—and that means providing solid evidence or support. Stating your opinion isn't enough.

Strategies for Elaboration: Piling Up Proof

For some topics, support will come from outside sources, not just your logic and experience. Recognize your many options for sufficient and accurate evidence:

- Facts, data, historical evidence
- Similar situations (analogies)
- Literary quotations, imagery, and paraphrases
- Expert opinions
- Anecdotes
- Eyewitness accounts
- Personal experience
- Responses to opponents

Note the last item about responses to opponents. To be really persuasive, you must think like a skeptical reader! Keep your audience in mind, imagine good objections to (or questions about) your explanation, and provide **counterarguments.**

To compile your evidence, you might use a two-column chart. On the left, write the causes or effects you've chosen from your map. To the right of each one, write all your ideas for evidence, as well as objections and counterarguments.

Model

Topic: Why do Donalbain and Malcolm keep silent and flee in fear right after their father's murder?

Causes	Supporting Evidence
shock	They feel "strong sorrow" but tears aren't "brewed" yet—too soon. **Objection?** They're thinking pretty well for being in shock. **Counterargument:** Yes, but shock suspends horror; people function "normally," and then they collapse.
suspicion	Macduff raised the question of why Macbeth killed the guards. Malcolm: Fake grief is easy if there's a motive.

7. **Being believable.** Choosing evidence also means considering who's reading it. What support will your audience find compelling, thought-provoking, or in line with its interests? And no matter who your readers are, you must

Communications Handbook HELP

Taking notes and documenting sources: page 1211.

Try It Out

With a small group, brainstorm at least three causes and three effects for the topics below. Then, suggest possible evidence (or where to find it) for each cause and each effect.

1. high salaries of professional athletes or rock stars
2. Banquo's murder
3. computer technology for home use

Try It Out: Possible Answers

1. **Causes:** Importance of entertainment to Americans; value of sports as a rallying point for people; desire to obtain the very best players possible; willingness of people to spend money on tapes and CDs.
   Effects: Sports figures and entertainers are held up as models; sports figures and entertainers have greater status than they might deserve; sports figures and entertainers lose touch with the people they entertain.
2. **Causes:** Macbeth is jealous of him; Macbeth fears Banquo will father more children, thus increasing the likelihood that the witches' prophecy will come true; Macbeth is psychologically disturbed and out of control.
   Effects: The thanes begin to mistrust Macbeth more than they already did; Macbeth's guilt increases; Macbeth adds to the chaos in Scotland.
3. **Causes:** Relatively inexpensive; people see its value for work and entertainment; people want to keep up with the modern world.
   Effects: Technological literacy among children; more efficient work at home; increased sources of information in the home.

INTEGRATING THE LANGUAGE ARTS

Speaking and Listening Arrange students in groups of four, and ask them to consider the following scenario. "The principal has just announced that a rich graduate has donated five million dollars to the school. The only restriction is that the money must be used to improve students' learning." Ask students to brainstorm a list of possible causes of the donor's generosity and the effects a gift of this sort would have on their school. Have a spokesperson from each group present the group's ideas to the class.

Grammar Students may benefit from a review of the punctuation rules associated with conjunctive adverbs such as *therefore* and *however.* Refer them to the relevant section in the Language Handbook, or conduct a brief review lesson on the chalkboard. Use the following sentences as examples.

1. My new car has to last many years; therefore, I take good care of it.
2. The leaders of the two nations saw no hope for a settlement; however, they were willing to meet again.

Drafting

Ask students to work with a partner after they have written their first drafts. Partners should read the opening paragraphs to make sure that there is a thesis statement, that the opening is interesting and makes readers want to continue, and that the situation is defined clearly with enough background information for readers to understand the rest of the essay. Ask partners to offer constructive criticism and ideas for improvements.

Evaluating and Revising

In addition to cautioning students about oversimplification and the *post hoc* fallacy, warn those who are writing about real-life topics to avoid using hypothetical effects. Sometimes writers, in an effort to make their cases stronger, create dire hypothetical effects that are not based in reality and tend to weaken arguments. Another practice to warn students about is the use of made-up research. The signs of this problem are expressions such as "Studies show . . .," "Research proves . . .," and "The evidence indicates . . .," which are not backed up with a citation to any source. As students evaluate their papers and the papers of others, they should question any claim that is put forth as fact and demand documentation.

Proofreading and Publishing

- Encourage students to wait a day or two between finishing the final version and proofreading it. A waiting period often helps writers see errors that they may miss if they proofread as soon as they have finished writing the paper.
- Encourage students to explore the Internet as a means of publishing their papers. Some of the Usenet newsgroups may be appropriate audiences for essays, especially essays on real-life topics of general interest. *You may want to preview any Internet activity that you suggest to students. Because these resources are sometimes public forums, their content can be unpredictable.*

Language Workshop HELP

Effective transitions: page 464.

■ *Evaluation Criteria*

An effective essay that speculates on causes and effects
1. *clearly describes the event, situation, or trend*
2. *clearly focuses on causes and/or effects and discusses them thoroughly*
3. *presents convincing arguments and refutes counterarguments*
4. *presents causes or effects in an effective order*
5. *presents sufficient and accurate evidence*
6. *uses an authoritative tone*
7. *opens engagingly and concludes decisively*

Revision STRATEGIES

To improve your opening and closing, read them together. (Skip everything else.) Could you link them in some way? Is one stronger or clearer than the other? Why? If necessary, add or cut details.

462 THE RENAISSANCE

come across as reasonable and trustworthy. You don't have to be stiffly serious; you might even be funny about the effects of forbidding off-campus lunches, for example. Your **tone,** however, must convey assurance and conviction.

Drafting

1. **The introduction.** Your essay should open in a way that will capture your readers' attention, while also quickly getting to what you're explaining. Always describe or define the situation clearly, in as much detail as your readers need. Classmates will need minimal scene setting for Malcolm and Donalbain's escape in *Macbeth*, but if your topic is the potential effects of televising court proceedings, readers will need sufficient data and information to see and understand current and past court situations. Also include your thesis statement.

2. **The body.** Redraw your cause-effect map to use as a good guide for writing. Take the causes or effects you've settled on, determine their order, number them, and redraw the map with numbers included. Refer to this map as you write your draft. Here are some general rules and tips for organizing the body of your essay:
   - Discuss causes before effects.
   - Use chronological order for cause-effect chains and for some topics spread out over time.
   - Otherwise, choose an arrangement that's easy to follow and persuasive: least/most important, least/most familiar, personal/social concerns, concrete/abstract explanations.
   - Answer objections to a cause or effect along with the cause or effect.
   - Bring up alternative explanations either before or after your own. ("Before" gets them out of the way; "after" lets you refer to your better ideas.)

3. **The conclusion.** Write a conclusion that sums up your explanation of causes and/or effects. You might also refer to your introduction.

Evaluating and Revising

1. **Peer review.** Read like a skeptic, someone who's tough to convince and itching to find a legitimate flaw. (But when the explanation's good, admit it and point out why.) Look for sound logic. Beware of
   - **oversimplification:** having too few causes or effects to explain the situation, or mistaking a contributing cause for a necessary one
   - **the *post hoc, ergo propter hoc* fallacy ("after this, therefore because of this"):** assuming that if A preceded B, then A must have caused B

2. **Self-evaluation.** If you do get objections from reviewers, answer them calmly. Put a check mark on your paper by each spot where you include one of the features given in the Evaluation Criteria to the left. Then go back and revise your paper to include any of the features you didn't find.

CROSSING THE CURRICULUM

Science Ask students who are taking science to develop a demonstration experiment for the class that illustrates cause and effect. Let them put on the demonstration without explaining the cause-effect relationships, and ask the rest of the class to observe carefully to determine the causes and effects. Ask the class to write a paragraph outlining their observations, and let volunteers share their paragraphs with the class.

PORTFOLIO ASSESSMENT

Peer Evaluation During evaluating and revising, students can use the peer evaluation sheet found in the *Portfolio Management System,* p. 109.

Proofreading and Publishing

As you proofread a clean copy of your final revision, check your sentence structures. Cause-effect writing always involves some complexity of thought, and you want to be sure your sentences clearly convey the relationships among ideas.

Since you've tried to convince someone that your explanation makes sense, let your topic lead you to readers. For real-life topics, send your essay to the newspaper's Op-Ed pages, to the newsletter of a group or club, or to legislators (you can even e-mail the president). More personal essays may go to good friends, family, or teen magazines. And for literary topics, read your essay aloud in class to see if others challenge or applaud your insights.

Reflecting on Your Writing

Speculating about causes and effects presents unique challenges to a writer. Here are some suggestions for reflections about this type of writing to add to your portfolio. (Be sure to date your responses.)

1. What was hardest for you: finding a topic, generating the causes and effects, finding enough sound support, checking your own reasoning, or not sounding boring? Why?

2. How do you like speculating, in general? Did you feel timid about it? Explain your response.

3. Did you like delving into something undefined? Did you see too many possibilities but no "answer" for your topic? Explain your response.

Language Handbook
H E L P

Sentence combining: page 1239.

Portfolio

Reflecting on Your Writing

Instead of having students write their reflections or write answers to the questions in the text, consider having them role-play news interviews in which a reporter asks them how they felt about writing their cause-effect essays. The interviews can be videotaped, and the videotapes can be included in the students' portfolios.

Closure

Write the words *Introduction, Body,* and *Conclusion* horizontally on the chalkboard. Then, ask volunteers to come up to the chalkboard and to write under one of the words an element that section of a cause-effect essay should contain. For example, under *Introduction,* students may write "attention grabber," "statement that establishes the situation," and "thesis." Under *Body,* they may write "cause no. 1" or "effect no. 1" and "evidence." Under *Conclusion,* they may write "summary of main points," "reference to introduction," and "thought-provoking comment."

Enrichment

Science Connection

Ask students to view a videotape of a nature program from TV or a film on some aspect of science. As they watch the videotape or film, ask them to outline the cause-and-effect structure used to present information visually. Check with a science teacher for suggestions of visual presentations that would be appropriate.

As students work together checking the transitions in their cause-effect essays, suggest they read their essays aloud to their partners. As they read, their partners should listen carefully for any sentence or paragraph that does not flow smoothly to the next sentence or paragraph. The partners should make notes of these spots so students can add needed transitions. As an alternative, you can have students tape-record oral readings of their papers and listen to them with their partners.

Try It Out: Possible Answers

For three years now the Panthers have made it all the way to the state championships, and every year they have lost in the first round. As this record shows, the Panthers have obviously been good, but why do they keep losing in the first round? One explanation leaps out when you study the Panthers' stats. In each first-round game, three or four players fouled out in the first half. When this happens, the best players are on the bench, not on the floor. First, that fact is simply demoralizing for other players. Second, it means the opposing team gets more free shots.

PROGRAM MANAGER

- **Extra Practice and Guided Instruction** For more instruction and practice of transitions, see **Language Workshop** in *Teaching Resources A,* pp. 119–120.
- **Extra Practice or Guided Instruction** See *Language Workshop: Transitions* for more practice or guided instruction in transitions.

Technology HELP

See Language Workshop CD-ROM. *Key word entry: transitions.*

Try It Out

Turn these sentences into a clear paragraph by inserting logical, effective transitions. You may combine sentences, add words and phrases, and replace words and phrases with better ones.

For three years now the Panthers have made it all the way to state championships. And they have lost in the first round. The Panthers have obviously been good. Why do they keep losing here? One explanation leaps out when you study the stats. In each game either three or four fouled out in the first half. The best are on the bench, not on the floor. First, that's simply demoralizing for others. The opposing team gets more free shots.

EFFECTIVE TRANSITIONS: CONNECTING IDEAS

An essay that speculates about causes and effects delves into relationships. When you write, you're leading readers not just to see the facts or events *X, Y, Z,* but exactly how *X, Y,* and *Z* are connected. If readers must labor to understand the links, you won't be very convincing. That's why **transitions,** ways to connect ideas, are so important in cause-effect writing. Notice how the boldface words in the following paragraph make it easy to follow; they create coherence both by connecting words and thoughts and by stating relationships.

> Immediately after their father's murder, Malcolm and Donalbain don't even cry. **The two brothers** speak to no one and hastily leave Scotland in fear—**even though** the obvious murderers are dead. Are **they two** cold, uncaring **children**? Or are there good reasons for **this behavior**? Yes, and one **reason** is simple: shock. Malcolm himself asks, "Why do we hold our tongues . . . ?" **so that** we know he is not just **upset and confused.**

Techniques for Creating Effective Transitions

1. Use a pronoun, noun, or synonym to refer to a word or phrase used earlier. Notice how "the two brothers" and "children" refer to Malcolm and Donalbain, and how "this behavior" and "upset and confused" are related.

2. Repeat a word used earlier. For example, "they two" refers back to "the two brothers," and "reason" refers to "good reasons."

3. Use transitional expressions that express relationship. In the paragraph above, the phrases "even though" and "so that" link ideas. Here are some other examples of transitional expressions:
   - cause / effect: *as a result, because, consequently, since, therefore*
   - time: *after, eventually, finally, immediately, meanwhile, next, then*
   - importance: *first, last, mainly, most important, primarily*

Writer's Workshop Follow-Up: Revision

Take another look at the cause-effect essay you wrote on page 459. Have you implied a link that you need to state directly? Have you signaled to the reader what is important or in what sequence events occurred? Have you used pronouns and nouns to add variety and to refer back to previous words and ideas? Working with a writing partner, underscore the transitions you've used. Then, go back and add transitions to make your sentences and paragraphs flow as clearly and smoothly as possible.

✔ QUICK CHECK: Effective Transitions

Underline the transitional words in the following paragraph. [Answers are underlined.]

Shakespeare wrote historical plays, tragedies, comedies, and sonnets. His tragic works include *Julius Caesar, Romeo and Juliet, Hamlet,* and *Macbeth.* When *Hamlet* was published, Shakespeare had already produced *Romeo and Juliet* and *Julius Caesar.* Even though the latter was created before *Macbeth,* both plays appeared for the first time in the posthumously published First Folio in 1623. Shakespeare never saw the first collection of his plays; nevertheless, he had a very full life in the theater, producing his works at the Globe theater and before royalty.

CREATIVE PROBLEM SOLVING
LEARNING FOR LIFE

Education for a Modern-day Renaissance Person

Problem

The term *Renaissance person* is still used to describe someone who is skilled and knowledgeable in many areas. What would a person need to *know* and be able to *do* to be considered a Renaissance person today? How should we educate children to be "Renaissance people"?

Project

Identify a real person, or create an imaginary one, who exemplifies the characteristics of a modern-day Renaissance person. Suggest educational innovations to produce "Renaissance people."

Preparation

1. Working with a small group, brainstorm to generate a list of the areas in which a person of the twenty-first century should be skilled and knowledgeable. To get started, you might consider the areas at which Leonardo da Vinci, the model Renaissance person, excelled in the fifteenth century—among them art, architecture, engineering, music, and science. Then, move on to other areas of knowledge.

2. Taking each area in turn, work together to establish the criteria necessary to qualify as a new Renaissance person. Be as specific as you can. If one area is languages,

for example, should the person be able to speak, read, and write more than one language? Are two languages sufficient, or are three (or more) required? Make it a group decision.

3. Review the curricula in all major subject areas in your school. Form a committee to study them, and make recommendations.

Procedure

1. Decide whether you'll develop your presentation around a real person or create an imaginary character. If you decide on a real person, someone may come to mind immediately, or you may need to do some research. To create an imaginary character, you can draw on the methods of direct and indirect characterization you've studied in this book, and in your composition text.

2. Think, too, about whether you'll approach this activity straightforwardly or handle it with humor. Deciding now which mode of presentation you'll use (see below) can help you choose the approach you prefer.

Presentation

Use one of the following formats (or another that your teacher approves):

1. **Write a Proposal**

   Focus on your study of the school's curricula, and write a proposal for revised curricula

for all major areas. Open with an overview or your proposal and a summation of your recommendations. Describe in your introduction the kind of learning a Renaissance person of the twenty-first century will require.

2. **Coming to Life**

   Stage a one-person show depicting the Renaissance person you've chosen or created. Your production can be as simple or elaborate as you like, with or without scenery, costumes, props, and special lighting or sound effects. Present your show live, or arrange to have a friend videotape it for showing, at a schoolwide assembly or a meeting of the school board.

3. **Images and Essences**

   Create a collage that conveys the multifaceted characteristics of a Renaissance person of our own time. Combine various objects and materials such as photographs, scraps of material, and string—anything you find meaningful—using shapes, colors, and textures to capture the essence of the person.

Processing

Did doing this activity change your ideas about what should be taught in the schools? Did it make you want to be a modern-day Renaissance person yourself? Write a brief reflection for your portfolio.

Learning for Life

PORTFOLIO ASSESSMENT

Portfolio Assessment Rubric So that students may see the evaluation criteria before they begin working on these projects, share the rubric provided in the *Portfolio Management System,* p. 111.

DEVELOPING WORKPLACE COMPETENCIES		
Preparation	**Procedure**	**Presentation**
Works on teams	Thinks creatively	Communicates information and ideas
Generates ideas	Processes information	Draws conclusions
Makes inference	Interprets information	Exhibits self-esteem
Ranks alternatives	Acquires data	Uses self-management skills

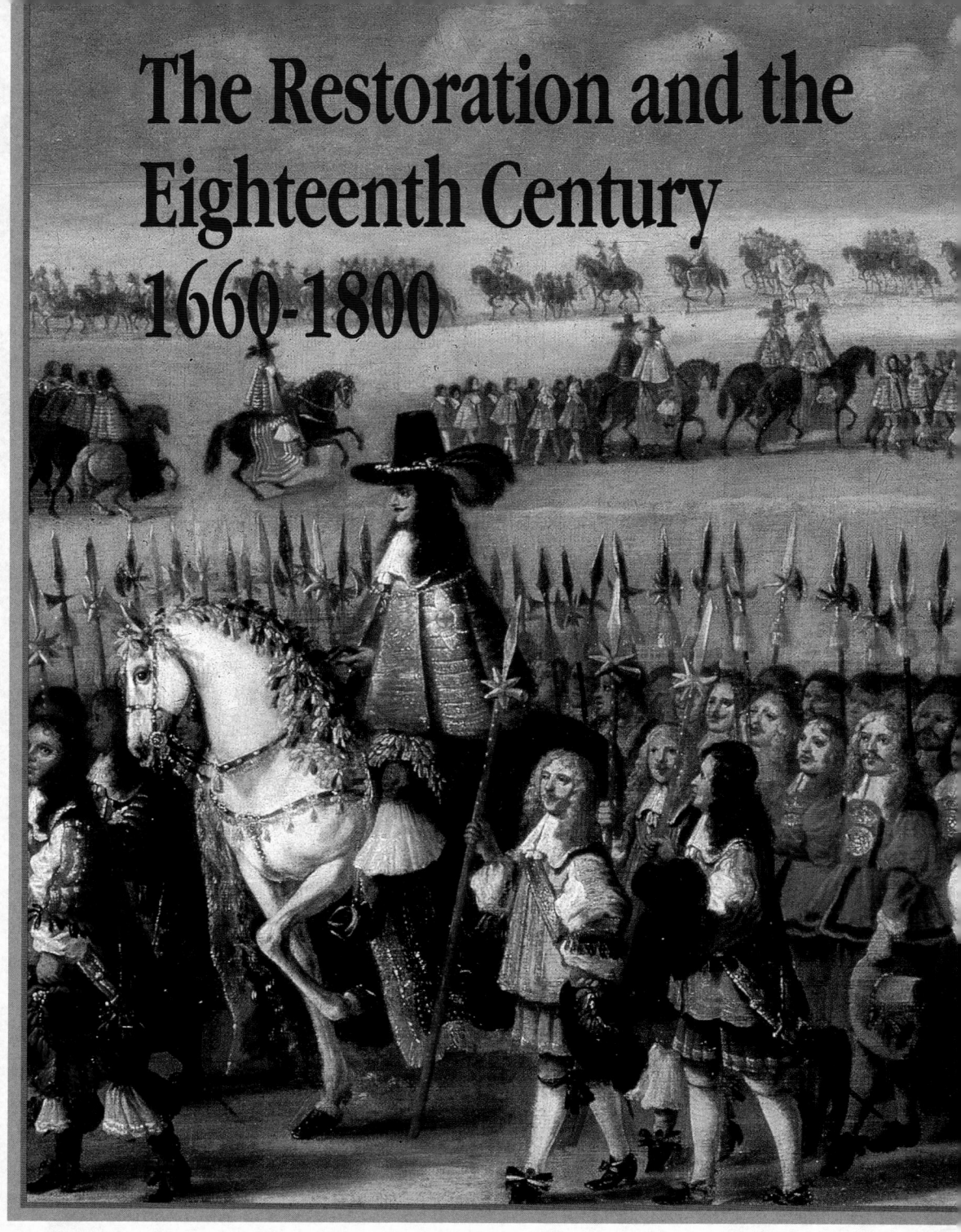

The Restoration and the Eighteenth Century
1660-1800

Coronation Procession of Charles II to Westminster from the Tower of London (detail) (1661) by Dirck Stoop. Museum of London.

467

PROGRAM MANAGER

- **Summative Assessment** See **Literary Period Test: The Restoration and the Eighteenth Century,** *Test Booklet,* pp. 120–122 for a test on an additional text from the same historical era.

- **Application** For practice of a reading strategy for this unit, see **Becoming a Strategic Reader** worksheet, *Teaching Resources A,* pp. 129–130.

Responding to the Quotation

? How does modern society in the United States compare to Defoe's description of English society? [Possible responses: The descriptions are still accurate; or money still plays a part in class distinction.]

The Restoration and the Eighteenth Century

by C. F. Main

There are seven groups in English society
1. *The Great, who live profusely.*
2. *The Rich, who live very plentifully.*
3. *The Middle Sort, who live well.*
4. *The Working Trades, who labor hard, but feel no want.*
5. *The Country People, Farmers, etc., who fare indifferently.*
6. *The Poor, that fare hard.*
7. *The Miserable, that really pinch and suffer want.*

—*Daniel Defoe*

Southwark Fair (18th century) by William Hogarth.

Tate Gallery, London.

From 1660 to 1800, people from England and Europe were pouring into North America. These eager voyagers not only sought freedom from religious and political persecution; they also saw money to be made in the American continent's rich lands and forests—in furs, tobacco, and logs for British sailing ships. They also began transporting Africans for use as slave labor in the Americas. In 1775, these Colonies rebelled against British rule and eventually won their freedom. The United States was a raw, vigorous, brand-new nation. Across the Atlantic, things were very different.

In 1660, England was utterly exhausted by nearly twenty years of civil war. By 1700, it had lived through a devastating plague and a fire that left more than two thirds of Londoners homeless. By the middle of the eighteenth century, however, England had settled into a period of calm and order, at least among the upper classes. Despite the loss of the American Colonies, the reinvigorated British military forces established new settlements around the globe. And though life for many was wretched, the middle class grew. Throughout this long period in a very old nation with tastes much more refined than raw, British men and women also produced many brilliant works of philosophy, art, and literature.

This long period of time in England—from 1660 to 1800—has been given several labels: the Augustan Age, the Neoclassical Period, the Enlightenment, and the Age of Reason. But labels are more convenient than accurate; each of these labels applies to some characteristics of these 140 years, but none applies to all.

In contrast to the vital Colonies of North America, England was exhausted by war and disease in 1660. But by the end of the eighteenth century, England had transformed itself.

Augustan and Neoclassical: Comparisons with Rome

Many people liked to find similarities between England in this period and ancient Rome, especially during the reign of the emperor Octavian (63 B.C.–A.D. 14). When he became emperor, Octavian was given the high-sounding name *Augustus,* meaning "the exalted one." Augustus restored peace and order to Rome after Julius Caesar's assassination. Similarly, the Stuart monarchs of England restored peace and order to England after the civil wars that led up to the execution of King Charles I in 1649, and that continued even after the king was dead.

> I would have been glad to have lived under my woodside, and to have kept a flock of sheep, rather than to have undertaken this government.
>
> —Oliver Cromwell,
> speaking to
> Parliament, 1658

Lady Playing a Keyboard Instrument (18th century) by Tomkins.
Victoria and Albert Museum, London.

The Execution of King Charles I at Whitehall, London, January 30, 1649. Woodcut.
The Granger Collection, New York.

THE RESTORATION AND THE EIGHTEENTH CENTURY **469**

A. Expansion
In 1607, the Jamestown colonists numbered 100; by 1753, the total Colonial population had reached 1,328,000. There were 3,125,000 people living in the new United States of America at the end of the American Revolution in 1783. By the end of this literary era being studied, the U.S. population had climbed to nine million (9,358,000 in 1819).

B. Expansion
Africans brought to the American continent by slave traders comprised approximately twenty percent of the population in the colonial United States.

C. Humanities Connection
The balanced, elegant qualities of the music of the Neoclassical Period—for example, compositions by Henry Purcell (1659–1695) and George Frideric Handel (1685–1759)—are thoroughly consistent with the style of the period's literature and philosophy. Both Purcell and Handel turned to classical motifs for inspiration. Examples are Purcell's opera *Dido and Aeneas* and Handel's *Julius Caesar* and *Xerxes.*

D. Expansion
Octavian, the great-nephew and adopted son of Julius Caesar, later joined with Mark Antony to pursue Brutus and Cassius, who had conspired to murder Caesar. Antony married Octavian's sister, whom he later deserted for Cleopatra, queen of Egypt. When Antony bequeathed Roman provinces to his children by Cleopatra, whom the Romans hated, Octavian went to war against the famous lovers. Agrippa defeated Antony's and Cleopatra's fleets at Actium.

The Senate granted Octavian the name *Augustus* and gave him power over the Roman Empire's religious, civil, and military affairs. Augustus reigned during the golden age of Roman literature and architecture, and he boasted that he had "found Rome brick and left it marble." After his death, the Romans worshiped him as a god.

Time Line

- **1660–1669**
  France was becoming the cultural center of Europe. Molière's plays, such as *The Misanthrope,* satirized the upper class and the new rich, setting the standard for European comedies: Witty, urbane, fast-paced plays that depicted relationships between men and women.

- **1670–1689**
  The Test Acts passed by Parliament in 1673 and 1678 restricted activities of people who were not members of the Church of England. The law required that all people holding civilian or military positions swear allegiance to the English Crown and take communion in the Church of England. A series of laws passed between 1828 and 1871 finally repealed the Test Acts.

- **1690–1709**
  For an example of the social significance of coffee, see Alexander Pope's *The Rape of the Lock,* Canto III, ll. 33–48 (pp. 528–529).

The Restoration and the Eighteenth Century, 1660–1800

LITERARY EVENTS

1660–1669	1670–1689	1690–1709	1710–1739
In France, Jean-Baptiste Molière's *The Misanthrope* first performed, 1666	Aphra Behn publishes *Oroonoko,* an early anti-slavery novel, 1688	First issue of **Addison** and **Steele**'s *The Tatler* printed (*The Spectator* is begun in 1711), 1709	**Jonathan Swift** publishes *Gulliver's Travels,* 1726
London theaters re-open; actresses appear on stage for the first time in England, 1660s	Poems of Bashō help popularize haiku poetry in Japan, 1680s	In Mexico, Sor Juana Inés de la Cruz publishes *Respuesta a Sor Filotea* (Reply to Sister Philotea), a defense of women's intellectual rights, 1691	**Daniel Defoe** publishes *Robinson Crusoe,* 1719
Samuel Pepys begins his diary, 1660	John Dryden's *All for Love, or The World Well Lost* first produced, 1678		**Alexander Pope** writes *The Rape of the Lock,* 1712
	John Bunyan publishes *The Pilgrim's Progress,* Part 1 (Part 2 appears in 1684), 1678		

CULTURAL/HISTORICAL EVENTS

1660–1669	1670–1689	1690–1709	1710–1739
Charles II proclaimed king of England (crowned in 1661), 1660	Ashanti empire formed in Africa, c. 1670s	John Locke publishes *An Essay Concerning Human Understanding,* 1690	In England, Lady Mary Wortley Montagu introduces Turkish practice of inoculation against smallpox, 1718
In Massachusetts, John Eliot translates the Bible into Algonquian, 1661	English Test Act bans Roman Catholics from public office, 1673	Coffee first planted in Brazil for export to Europe, 1700s	Manchus rule in Tibet, 1720
Plague claims more than 68,000 people in London, 1665	English Royal Observatory established at Greenwich, 1675	England, Wales, and Scotland politically unified as Great Britain, 1707	
Great Fire destroys much of London, 1666	Newton publishes *Philosophiae Naturalis Principia Mathematica* (Mathematical Principles of Natural Philosophy), 1687		
	"Glorious Revolution": James II succeeded by Protestant rulers William and Mary, 1688		

• **Turtle-shaped Ashanti emblem** (17th or 18th century) from Ghana. Gold.

• **Newton's reflecting telescope (1688).** Royal Society, London.

• **The Great Fire of London** (1666) by an unknown artist.

USING THE TIME LINE

During the 140 years that this Collection spans, many events took place on all the inhabited continents. To help students visualize how human events and achievements mesh across physical and cultural boundaries, make a large time line on kraft paper. Assign each student an item from the time line to research, and have students each write a paragraph or two of explanation about the items on the kraft paper. Encourage creativity; for example, students might add a photo or a drawing to their entry, or they might play representative musical recordings. Students may want to connect ideas and events with colored string; for example, green string might be used to connect revolutionary philosophers, figures, ideas, and events (Voltaire, Rousseau, Locke, events of the American Revolution and the French Revolution).

• Frontispiece of Phillis Wheatley's *Poems on Various Subjects, Religious and Moral* (1773).

Voltaire publishes *Candide*, 1759

Samuel Johnson publishes his *Dictionary of the English Language*, 1755

Thomas Gray publishes "Elegy Written in a Country Churchyard," 1751

Samuel Richardson publishes *Pamela, or Virtue Rewarded*, 1740

American poet Phillis Wheatley's *Poems on Various Subjects, Religious and Moral* published in London, 1773

Oliver Goldsmith publishes *The Vicar of Wakefield*, 1766

Wordsworth and **Coleridge** publish *Lyrical Ballads*, 1798

Mary Wollstonecraft publishes *A Vindication of the Rights of Woman*, 1792

James Boswell's *The Life of Samuel Johnson* published, 1791

Olaudah Equiano, a former slave in Colonial America, publishes his autobiography in Britain, 1789

Jean-Jacques Rousseau's *Confessions* published, 1781

1740–1764	1765–1779	1780–1800

In France, Denis Diderot begins work on the *Encyclopédie*, 1751

Benjamin Franklin invents the lightning rod, 1752

Britain fights the Seven Years' War, 1756–1763

Catherine II ("Catherine the Great") becomes czarina of Russia, 1762

• *Catherine the Great (1762–1769)* by Vigilius Erichsen.

British Parliament passes Stamp Act for taxing American Colonies, 1765

Mozart writes *Symphony No. 1* at age nine, 1765

• Teapot reading "Stamp Act Repeal'd" (English, 1766).

Boston Tea Party protests tax on tea, 1773

American Revolution begins, 1775

James Watt invents the steam engine, 1780s

• French Revolution button (c. 1789–1793) translating to "Liberty or Death." Brass with miniatures painted on ivory.

French Revolution begins with storming of the Bastille, 1789

First electric battery invented by Alessandro Volta in Italy, 1790s

Rosetta stone (key to deciphering Egyptian hieroglyphics) found in Egypt, 1799

Napoleon becomes head of revolutionary government in France, 1799

- **1740–1764**
  The Seven Years' War actually began in 1754 in North America, where it is commonly called the French and Indian War, which was a fight between the British and the French over territory in North America. The war expanded to include Europe, where Britain's ally Prussia did most of the fighting against France and its allies Austria and Russia. Meanwhile Great Britain carried on the war in North America and India. In defeat, France turned over all its territory in India and North America, where the British took almost all French territory in Canada and all French possessions east of the Mississippi River except New Orleans.

- **1740–1764**
  Catherine II (1729–1796), a German princess who became empress of Russia when she overthrew her husband Peter (who was later found murdered), became interested in the liberal ideas of the Age of Reason and promoted European culture in Russia. Although extravagant, she also spent money building schools and hospitals. Though teachers, scientists, writers, artists, and actors enjoyed freedoms and a golden age, Catherine brutally suppressed peasant revolts.

- **1780–1800**
  William Wordsworth (1770–1850) and Samuel Taylor Coleridge (1772–1834) collaborated on *Lyrical Ballads*, which is now thought to be the foundation for English Romantic poetry. They announced that in *Lyrical Ballads* they were attempting to eschew the specialized, formal language of eighteenth-century poetry for language Wordsworth said was "really used by men."

- **1780–1800**
  Rousseau (1712–1778) is considered an important writer of the Age of Reason, and many of his ideas fostered the political events leading to the French Revolution: Government by common consent; a legal system that expresses the general will of the people; and the idea that humans in their natural state are good and kindly but become evil because they must live in society, which brings out aggression and selfishness.

A. Literary Connections

Remind students that Shakespeare was heavily influenced by the Latin classics, especially works by Terence, Ovid, and Seneca.

B. Language Note: Pathetic Fallacy

When used as a literary technique, this view of unusual events as portentous is called the pathetic fallacy.

King Charles II of England (c. 1675) by (school of) Nicholas Dixon. Vellum.

Fitzwilliam Museum, University of Cambridge, England.

The people of both Rome and England were weary of war, suspicious of revolutionaries and radicals, and ready to settle down, make money, and enjoy life. The Roman Senate had hailed Augustus as the second founder of Rome; in 1660, the English people brought back the son of Charles I from his exile in France, crowned him as King Charles II, and hailed him as their savior. As a warning to revolutionaries, they dug up the corpse of Oliver Cromwell, who had ruled England between Charles I and Charles II, and cut off its head. The monarchy was restored without shedding a drop of blood.

In this age, many English writers consciously modeled their works on the old Latin classics, which they had studied in school and university. These writings that imitate Latin works were called neoclassical—"new classical." The classics, it was generally agreed, were valuable because they represented what was permanent and universal in human experience. All educated people knew the Latin classics better than they knew their own English literature.

With the restoration of the king, England likened itself to Augustan Rome: Both had entered a period of calm and order after an era of political turmoil.

Reason and Enlightenment: Asking "How?"

Labels like the "Age of Reason" and the "Enlightenment" reveal how people were gradually changing their view of themselves and the world. For instance, Shakespeare, the greatest writer of the Renaissance, expressed a commonly held view when he described the unusual events that preceded the assassination of Julius Caesar—"a tempest dropping fire" and "blue lightning." These unnatural events, says a character in the play *Julius Caesar,* are "instruments of fear and warning." For centuries people had believed that before a great public disaster

A CLOSER LOOK

LIFE AMONG THE "HAVES" . . .

According to the law, all men were equal. But some were more equal than others, especially England's wealthy, during the Restoration and the eighteenth century. Famous for its excesses, this artificial age offered extreme luxuries to those known as "quality" or "polite" society—the rich.

Greatly influenced by the French in manners, dress, furniture, gardens, and recreation, the elite gathered regularly at London's fashionable coffeehouses—numbering three thousand by the early eighteenth century. These centers of news, gossip, and gambling were places to see and to be seen in. Another venue, the city's formal gardens, offered illuminated groves, dining, and fireworks.

Whatever their haunt, both men and women devoted themselves to colorful and extravagant fashion. Men carried snuffboxes and wore velvet or satin coats, lace ruffles, silk knee breeches, high-heeled shoes with gold or silver buckles, and broad-brimmed hats decorated with feathers. Women wore low-cut silk dresses with hoops made from whalebones. Their elaborate petticoats were fashioned from colorful silk, velvet, or chintz, often quilted or trimmed with silver.

472 THE RESTORATION AND THE EIGHTEENTH CENTURY

OPTIONS FOR TEACHING

STRATEGIES FOR INCLUSION

Auditory Students can stage a classroom debate between the "haves" and the "have-nots" of the era. Remind students that they will need to research the social and economic issues and class divisions of the time to represent their viewpoints. Students might even choose to dress the part for their debates, donning typical garb associated with their chosen socioeconomic groups.

Logical-Mathematical Using the population information provided in annotation A on p. T469, have students figure the growth rates of the period. Groups should then work cooperatively to make a chart or graph depicting the rates and explain them to the class. Students also should report on how such growth affects a culture. [Possible answer: Such rapid growth can strain infrastructure such as housing and roads.]

like the assassination of a ruler, the earth and sky gave warnings. People believed that unusual events such as earthquakes, comets, and even babies born with malformations had some kind of meaning, and that they were sent as punishment for past misdoings or as warning of future troubles. People did not ask, "*How* did this unusual event take place?" but "*Why* did this unusual event take place, and what does it *mean*?"

Gradually, during the Enlightenment, people stopped asking "Why?" questions and started asking "How?" questions, and the answers to those questions—about everything from the workings of the human body to the laws of the universe—became much less frightening and superstitious.

A Scene from "The Beggar's Opera" (c. 1728) by William Hogarth. Oil.

Collection of Paul Mellon, National Gallery, Washington.

By 1664, wigs and makeup were the rage for men and women. Powdered and stuffed with horsehair, women's headdresses grew to enormous proportions. Jewels, flowers, ribbons, plumage, and even fruit decorated these monstrous structures—reaching two to three feet in height. Men also wore their hair in pigtails—tied with a bow and powdered. In 1795, a tax was created to generate income from the rich—a guinea on every powdered head. Cosmetics were made from ingredients such as borax, vinegar, bread, eggs, and pigeon wings. Black patches, or fake beauty marks, were an important fashion accessory.

The wealthy divided the year between London, country estates, and health resorts. A whirlwind of masked balls, dances, and formal dinner parties, known as the London season, ended by the first week in June. Summers were often spent in seaside towns and at freshwater springs. Daniel Defoe described one trendy health resort: "[The attendants] present you with a little floating dish like a basin, in which the lady puts her handkerchief and a nosegay, of late the snuffbox is added, and some patches; through the bath occasioning a little perspiration, the patches do not stick as kindly as they should."

It was a careless, hedonistic time centered on dancing, dining, drinking, theatergoing, card playing, and gambling. As is always the case with fashion, change was inevitable. By the end of the eighteenth century, the lifestyle of the wealthy leaned toward simplicity and sobriety.

Embroidered casket (c. 1665).

Lady Lever Art Gallery, Port Sunlight, England.

THE RESTORATION AND THE EIGHTEENTH CENTURY 473

INTEGRATING THE LANGUAGE ARTS

Strategic Reading Have students analyze how the quotes in the introduction's margins illuminate or complicate the text itself. Students can jot down in their Reader's Logs how each quote further explains a passage. The following graphic organizer might help students organize their thoughts as they re-read the material.

Quote Notes

Quote	Main Points in Passage	How Quote Relates

Conclude with a class discussion on students' notes. Be sure students tie the quotes to the introductory information and make judgments regarding the appropriateness of the quotes in light of the respective passages. ☞

A. Expansion

Among the early, prominent members of the Royal Society were the Irish scientist Robert Boyle (considered the founder of modern chemistry), the architect Christopher Wren (who designed much of London, including St. Paul's Cathedral, after the Great Fire), and the poet and playwright John Dryden.

B. Critical Reading: Summarizing

? How would you summarize the characteristics of modern English prose? [Straightforward; precise; efficient; simple rather than elaborate; accessible; concise.]

C. Expansion

Deism, a product of the Age of Enlightenment, was a religion based on reason and the observation of nature. The philosophers Jean Jacques Rousseau and Voltaire of France and Germany's Immanuel Kant embraced Deism, which also appears in the U.S. Declaration of Independence and in the Preamble to the Constitution ("we are endowed by the Creator with certain inalienable rights"). The contents of these documents were influenced by leading Colonial Deists, including Benjamin Franklin, Thomas Jefferson, and Thomas Paine.

> The truth is, the science of Nature has been already too long made only a work of the brain and the fancy: It is now high time that it should return to the plainness and soundness of observations on material and obvious things.
>
> —Robert Hooke

For instance, the astronomer Edmond Halley (1656–1742) took the terror out of celestial phenomena by calculating when they were going to occur. He computed, with "immense labor," he said, the orbit of the comet that still bears his name. He predicted it would appear in 1758, 1834, 1910, and 1986—and it did. And how did he know it would reappear at seventy-six-year intervals? Because that was the time it took to complete its orbit. Such a reasonable, mathematical explanation made no connection at all between the comet and human affairs.

Natural phenomena were increasingly explained by scientific observation as people began to ask how things happened in the natural world.

The Birth of Modern English Prose: Stripping Down

A In 1662, to answer questions about the universe, King Charles II chartered a group of philosophers: the Royal Society of London for the Promotion of Natural Knowledge. **B** Among other things, its members called for a kind of writing that was precise, exact, and not decorated with the elaborate metaphors or odd allusions of their predecessors. Above all, these new scientists wanted to shorten the endless sentences of their predecessors. And so in this age is born what we think of as modern English prose.

While the Royal Society affected the course of English prose, the "founder and first true master" of modern English prose was John Dryden (1631–1700), an all-around man of letters. Because of his influence, the era in which Dryden lived is often referred to as the "age of Dryden." In the *Essay of Dramatic Poesy* (1668), a major critical work, Dryden sought to "vindicate the honor of our English writers." He also wrote comedies, as well as the best tragedy of the day, *All for Love* (1677), a neoclassical version of Shakespeare's *Antony and Cleopatra*. Among Dryden's achievements in poetry were perfecting the technique of English poetry, regularizing meter, and making diction precise. He was a master of explaining ideas, of reasoning in verse. Dryden set the standards that most of the poets of the next century aspired to.

Under the influence of the Royal Society and John Dryden, English prose became more precise, exact, and plain.

Changes in Religion: More Questions

The new scientific and rational explanations of phenomena gradually began to affect some people's religious views. If comets were not sent by God to warn people, perhaps God didn't interfere at all in human affairs. **C** Perhaps the universe was like an immense piece of clockwork, set in motion by a Creator who more or less withdrew from this perfect mechanism and let it run by itself. Such a view, part of a complex of ideas known as Deism, could make people feel self-satisfied and complacent,

474 THE RESTORATION AND THE EIGHTEENTH CENTURY

INTEGRATING THE LANGUAGE ARTS

Writing: Oral History *You may want to obtain permission from parents or guardians and from the parties students will contact before they begin work on this activity.* Just as British people said farewell to the eighteenth century's age of elegance, have students record goodbyes to the twentieth century. Encourage students to interview people of different ages and backgrounds to get their observations on the significance of the century's end. What changes have people seen during this period? What invention or advancement do they believe has been the most important? Ask students to edit their interviews and to present excerpts of their oral histories to the class. Encourage them to summarize the conversations they have had and to characterize the century, comparing its qualities to the eighteenth century's Age of Reason.

Speaking and Listening To illustrate the perspectives of the age, you might have students write and perform interviews with famous or ordinary people of the age. Students might want to represent a particular social class, or they might focus on prominent people of this time period. You might videotape their interviews to achieve a television-like effect instead of using a standard classroom presentation format.

T474 The Restoration and the Eighteenth Century

Interior of Henry VII's Chapel, Westminster Abbey (c. 1750) by Canaletto.

Museum of London.

- Rationalism emphasizes the authority of human reason. In the seventeenth century, *philosophical rationalism* held that reason is more powerful than sensory experience and that, through reason, humans can understand the nature of reality. In the eighteenth century, *cultural rationalism* emphasized reason over faith in explaining human destiny. Thomas Paine, the author of *The Age of Reason* (1793), was a prominent figure in this movement.
- Materialism holds that everything is a state of matter. Even human consciousness, this theory argues, is caused by chemical reactions. Materialism can be traced to the fifth century B.C., when the Greek philosophers Leucippus and Democritus developed *atomism,* the notion that invisible particles (atoms) make up everything that exists. Because of the spread of Christianity and its emphasis on spirituality, interest in materialism waned for several centuries. However, the rise of modern science during the 1600s renewed discussion of materialism among philosophers.

especially if they believed, as Alexander Pope noted in his long poem *Essay on Man* (page 524), that "Whatever is, is right." Some philosophers even argued that "In this best of all possible worlds, . . . all is for the best"—a view that the French writer Voltaire ridiculed in his novel *Candide* (1759). (See page 538.) But, other than a tiny minority of "enlightened" rationalists and materialists, most people, including great philosophers and scientists like Sir Isaac Newton (1642–1727) and John Locke (1632–1704), remained religious. Christianity in its various forms continued to exercise an undiminished power over almost all Europeans in this period, just as it had in the Middle Ages and the Renaissance.

> Nature and Nature's laws lay hid in night:
> God said, Let Newton be! and all was light.
>
> —Alexander Pope, epitaph
> intended for Sir Isaac Newton

The new science influenced religion: A movement called Deism viewed the universe as a perfect mechanism, which God had built and left to run on its own.

CROSSING THE CURRICULUM

Architecture St. Paul's Cathedral is considered the quintessential combination of neoclassical and baroque architecture. Have a volunteer show photos, slides, drawings, or models of Wren's masterpiece. Be sure the student can identify specific features characteristic of these two major architectural styles.

Music To introduce students to the music of the time, have a group of students set up a radio station using this music, complete with a playlist, disc jockeys, commercials, and interviews with musicians. Then, have the radio show audiotaped and played for the class. You might want to set a time limit for the final version of the radio show so

students will select excerpts from long musical works; this will keep the radio show varied and interesting. Encourage students to find examples of folk or popular music of the time as well as classical pieces.

A. Exploring the Historical Period

The outlawing of these various religious groups was largely a reaction to the revolutionary fervor of Oliver Cromwell and his followers.

B. Expansion

One infamous act that inspired such rumors was the Gunpowder Plot of 1605, in which the Catholic Guy Fawkes was convicted of attempting to blow up the Houses of Parliament when King James I and government officials were scheduled to be there. The plot was discovered, the assassination averted, and the conspirators killed, but anti-Catholic hostility remained strong for more than a century. Today, English people still hold a festival on the anniversary of the event (November 5) and burn Guy Fawkes in effigy. To commemorate the plot, the vaults beneath the Houses of Parliament are searched before a new session begins.

Covent Garden with St. Paul's Church (detail) (18th century) by Balthasar Nebot.
Guildhall Art Gallery, London.

Religion and Politics: Repression of Minority Sects

Religion determined people's politics in this period. Charles II reestablished the Anglican Church as the official church of the country, which it continues to be in England to this day. (In the United States, this denomination is called the Episcopal Church.) With the approval of Parliament, the king attempted to outlaw all the various Puritan and Independent sects—dozens of them, all happily disagreeing among themselves—that had caused so much uproar during the preceding thirty years. Persecution of these various sects continued throughout the eighteenth century.

> **When Charles II reestablished the Anglican Church as the official church of the country, other sects were outlawed and persecuted.**

> A brave world, sir, full of religion, knavery, and change: We shall shortly see better days.
> —Aphra Behn

The Bloodless Revolution: Protestants from Now On

Charles II had a number of illegitimate children, but no legal heir. When he died in 1685, he was succeeded by his brother James II, a practicing Roman Catholic. Most English people were utterly opposed to James. After all, it was widely believed that Roman Catholics had not only set fire to London and caused other disasters, but were actively plotting to hand the country over to the pope. When James's queen produced a little boy—a Catholic heir—pressure on the royal family became so great that, in 1688, they suddenly fled to France. Thus, the so-called Glorious (bloodless) Revolution (1688) was accomplished. James II was succeeded by his Protestant daughter, Mary, and her Dutch husband,

476 THE RESTORATION AND THE EIGHTEENTH CENTURY

OPTIONS FOR TEACHING

COOPERATIVE LEARNING

Interview Pairs Have students form pairs to write and present their interviews in the Speaking and Listening activity on p. T474. Remind them that they will need to research their subjects to develop realistic representations. They also will need to carefully consider the interviewer's style. They can use the format of a modern journalist, of a writer working for *The Spectator* or *The Tatler,* or of one famous writer of the period interviewing another. You can pair students with complementary needs and talents: For example, a student who enjoys writing could work with a student who enjoys acting.

William of Orange. Ever since, the rulers of England have been, at least nominally, Anglicans.

During the "Glorious Revolution," Charles's Roman Catholic successor was forced into exile, and Protestant rule resumed with the ascension of William of Orange and Mary to the throne.

Addicted to the Theater

For more than twenty years, while the Puritans held power, the theaters in England were closed. During the exile of the royal court in France, Charles had become addicted to theatergoing, so one of the first things he did after regaining his throne was to repeal the ban on play performances, imposed in 1642.

The Restoration and the Eighteenth Century

After the reestablishment of the monarchy, these major events occurred in the arts and sciences:

- With King Charles II's return to the throne and a period of increased stability, writers drew on the "new classical" style of Roman, Greek, and Latin models.
- Thinkers in this Age of Reason emphasized logic, scientific observation, and factual explanation, with these rational explanations affecting some people's religious views.
- Literary tastes turned to wit and satire to expose excesses and moral corruption.
- In journalism, the periodical essay developed, commenting on public manners and values.
- To satisfy the reading tastes of a developing middle class, writers began to experiment with long fictional narratives called novels.
- Theaters closed by the Puritans reopened, and female actors were now included on the stage; drama during the Restoration was witty, bawdy, and cynical.
- By the end of the period, the excesses of the rich and the onset of industrialization turned people's taste to an appreciation of nature and simplicity.

C. Exploring the Culture
Queen Elizabeth II is still the titular head of the Church of England.

RESPONDING TO THE ILLUSTRATION: ABOUT THE ARTIST

Artist William Capon (1757–1827) practiced his talents in a variety of genres. He learned portrait painting from his father, but he later became a scene painter for the Italian Opera and the Drury Lane Theater. He also worked as an architect, building a theater in County Kildare, Ireland, in 1794; later, he was appointed draftsman to the Duke of York. He produced numerous watercolor paintings of London scenes.

The First Opera House in the Haymarket (18th century) by William Capon.
Guildhall Library. Corporation of London.

477

CLASSROOM MANAGEMENT

Team Building Have students form groups of eight to stage their debates for the Auditory activity on p. T472. Together, they can choose a resolution to address—for example, "Resolved: The English class structure of the eighteenth century served the upper class at the expense of the lower classes," or "Resolved: The rise of the middle class provided opportunity for class mobility." Students might choose to debate two sides with four to a team, or they might opt to represent more than two socioeconomic groups in their debates. Encourage students to divide the research responsibilities and then meet to share their findings. ☞

A. Expansion

Among these writers was John Bunyan. Bunyan's life and religious works such as *The Pilgrim's Progress* strongly contrast with the frivolity associated with the age.

B. Expansion

Remind students that until the work of Louis Pasteur in the mid-1800s, germs were not known to cause disease.

Charles and his brother James patronized companies of actors. Boys and men no longer acted the female roles. The new theater had real actresses, like the famous Nell Gwyn, and the new plays emphasized the sexual relations of men and women in very unsentimental and unromantic ways. The great, witty comedies produced during this period (such as William Wycherly's *The Country Wife* and William Congreve's *The Way of the World*) reflected the life of the rich and leisured people of that time—the Frenchified, pleasure-loving upper classes—and their servants and hangers-on. In addition to dramatists, a large number of prose and verse writers, many of them Dissenters, did not cater to the tastes of sophisticated people but wrote solely for ordinary readers.

Upon his return from France, Charles II reopened the London theaters. For the first time, female actors acted in the witty, urbane comedies written by Restoration dramatists.

A CLOSER LOOK

. . . AND LIFE AMONG THE "HAVE-NOTS"

For the poor, life is always hard, but during the Restoration and the eighteenth century, the poor lived in deplorable conditions, without the aid of doctors or police, and beyond the reach of education, religion, and charity. As if that were not enough, the poor also lived under the threat of debtors' prisons where torture was common.

Overcrowding in London's tenements and workhouses reached an all-time high during the period. Entire families lived together in one-room garrets or cellars infested with rats, lice, snails, and bedbugs. Unhealthy conditions worsened with the institution of a window tax in 1696. In order to avoid the tax, many blocked up their windows, creating stagnant air and cutting off light. Space and air seemed luxuries that only the rich could afford. Adding to the filth and discomfort, household garbage and human waste were thrown out into the streets. Butcher shops and slaughterhouses matter-of-factly tossed bloody remnants into open drains that intersected with streets and walkways.

Although medical science had begun to develop, superstition still marked the treatment of the sick in the early part of the eighteenth century. For example, smallpox was commonly treated with a black powder made by burning thirty to forty live toads. Bleeding served as a

Night (18th century) by William Hogarth.

remedy for most ailments. As odd as it might seem today, the connection between dirt and disease hadn't been made by the medical profession. And since physicians practiced medicine almost

478 THE RESTORATION AND THE EIGHTEENTH CENTURY

OPTIONS FOR TEACHING

ASSESSMENT TOOLS

Peer Assessment To give students feedback about the persuasiveness of their arguments for the Auditory activity on p. T472, have the class determine the winners of the debate. You might use the following format for student feedback.
I agree with _____ team because:
(Check all that apply.)

____ 1. Arguments supported the position.
____ 2. Arguments were grounded in fact.
____ 3. The weight of the evidence supported this team's conclusions.
____ 4. The presentation was convincing.
____ 5. The presentation was interesting.

The Age of Satire: Attacks on Immorality and Bad Taste

Today, Alexander Pope and Jonathan Swift are regarded as the most accomplished literary artists of the early eighteenth century. And though their era became known as the "age of Pope," both men had a profound influence on succeeding writers. During their own lifetimes, however, Pope and Swift were frequently out of harmony with the values of the age, and both often criticized it severely.

Although Pope addressed his works exclusively to the educated and leisured classes, he also attacked the members of these classes for their immorality and their bad taste, two failings that were usually associated in Pope's mind. Pope loved order, discipline, and craftsmanship; both he and Swift were appalled by the squalor and shoddiness—in art, manners, and morals—that underlay the polished surfaces of Augustan life. This violent and filthy underside of eighteenth-century life is illustrated in the

exclusively with the upper classes, they knew little of the ailments of the poor. Personal hygiene, or the lack of it, certainly contributed to the general state of health. One observer described a pauper woman's petticoats as "standing alone with dirt."

During the first part of the eighteenth century, the overall death rate surpassed the birthrate. In the worst years, more than 74 percent of London's children died before the age of five. Many of those children who did survive were forced to work for a living as soon as physically able, and sometimes sooner. Often, they suffered abuse by their guardians, supervisors, or employers.

It's no wonder that many sought comfort and warmth in inexpensive alcohol. Starting in 1720 and for the next thirty years, cheap gin was readily available in the capital. The poor were especially susceptible to the disastrous effects of gin—high crime and death rates throughout most of the century. In fact, during a two-year period, 12,000 people out of London's population of 800,000 were convicted of illegally selling gin. Not until the Act of 1751, when spirits were highly taxed, did the death rate fall dramatically.

Eventually, improvements in agriculture created a demand for manure, and a use for street filth was found. That, coupled with the Paving Acts of 1762, did much to clean up London's streets. In 1769, a dispensary movement

provided free advice and medicine for the underprivileged. Only then was the belief dispelled that the London poor owed their maladies to vice and foolishness.

The Old Fleet Prison (closed 1844) by an unknown artist.

? How does this treatment of children compare to the way we treat them today? [Most students will say that while health care and life expectancy have improved, abuse and exploitation remain.] The graphic below can help students organize their thoughts.

Treatment of Children: Eighteenth and Twentieth Centuries

Item	18th Century	20th Century
mortality rate		
child labor		
abuse		

The Laughing Audience (1733) by William Hogarth.

> Neither is it true that this fineness of raillery is offensive. A witty man is tickled when he is hurt in this manner, and a fool feels it not. . . . There is still a vast difference betwixt the slovenly butchering of a man, and the fineness of a stroke that separates the head from the body, and leaves it standing in its place.
>
> —John Dryden, *from An Essay of Dramatic Poesy*

paintings and engravings of William Hogarth (1697–1764). Swift shared many of Pope's attitudes and ideals, and in his exposure of the mean and sordid in human behavior, Swift's works resemble Hogarth's art. Neither Swift nor Pope felt smug or satisfied with the world, as many English people did. Both writers deplored the corrupt politics of the time and the growing commercialism and materialism of the English people.

Pope and Swift both used satire to expose the moral corruption and crass commercialism of eighteenth-century England.

Journalism: A New Profession

Ⓐ In contrast with Swift and Pope and their aristocratic values, a writer named Daniel Defoe (1660–1731) stood for values that we think of as being middle class: thrift, prudence, industry, and respectability. Defoe had no interest in polished manners and social poise. Swift and Pope looked down their noses at him. "Defoe has written a vast many things," Pope once said, "and none bad, though none excellent."

> The newspapers! Sir, they are the most villainous—licentious—abominable—infernal—Not that I ever read them—no—I make it a rule never to look into a newspaper.
>
> —Richard Sheridan, *from The Critic*

Defoe, like the essayists Joseph Addison and Sir Richard Steele, followed a new profession: journalism. Eighteenth-century journalists did not merely describe contemporary **Ⓑ** political and social matters; they also saw themselves as reformers of public manners and morals. Journalists today—using both print and video—still see themselves in reformer roles.

As the middle class grew, journalists—and the reforms they advocated—became increasingly important.

Public Poetry: Conceived in Wit

Today when we think of great poetry, we think of great lyrics: the sonnets of Shakespeare, Keats, and Wordsworth, the religious poems of Donne and Eliot, the private poems of Emily Dickinson, and the lyrics of such twentieth-century poets as William Butler Yeats, Robert Frost, and Elizabeth Bishop. These poets reveal in their poems their innermost thoughts and feelings, their honest and original responses to life. "Genuine poetry," said Matthew Arnold, a nineteenth-century poet and critic, "is conceived and composed in the soul."

Later critics like Matthew Arnold put down the poetry of people such as Alexander Pope because, he said, it was conceived and composed in their "wits"—that is, in their minds, not their souls. But these so-called Augustan poets did not define poetry in Arnold's way and so should not be judged by his standards. They had no desire to expose their souls; they thought of poetry as having a public rather than a private function.

Augustan poets would write not merely a poem, but a particular kind of poem. They would decide in advance the kind of poem, much as a carpenter decides on the kind of chair to make. The best Augustan poems are like things artfully made for a particular purpose, usually a public purpose. Many of the popular kinds of poetry were inherited from classical antiquity.

If, for instance, a grand person such as a general or a titled lady died, the poets would celebrate that dead person in **elegies,** the appropriate kind of poem for the occasion. Augustan elegies did not tell the truth about a dead person, even if the truth could be determined; rather, they said the very best things that the poet could think of saying.

At the opposite extreme, a poet might decide that a certain type of behavior, or even a certain conspicuous person, should be exposed to public ridicule. The poet would then write a **satire,** a kind of writing that does not make a just and balanced judgment of people and their behavior but rather says the worst things about them that the poet can think of saying.

Mr. and Mrs. William Chase (18th century) by Joseph Wright of Derby. Agnew & Sons, London.

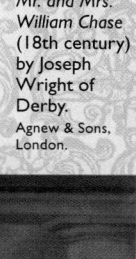

Another important kind of poem was the **ode**—an ambitious, often pompous poetic utterance expressing a public emotion, like the jubilation felt after a great naval victory.

Regardless of its kind, every poem had to be carefully and artificially constructed; every poem had to be dressed in exact meter and rhyme. Poems were not to sound like spontaneous and impromptu utterances, just as people were not to appear in public except in fancy dress. Those who could afford it adorned themselves with vast wigs, ribboned and jeweled clothing, and red shoes with high heels. People's movements were dignified and stately in public. Nothing was what we would today call natural—neither dress nor manners nor poetry.

Poetry of the period was not private, intimate, or spontaneous; rather, it was highly artificial and carefully crafted for public occasions.

The First English Novels

By the mid–eighteenth century, people were writing—and others, including women, were eagerly buying (or borrowing)—long fictional narratives called **novels** ("something new"). These novels, which were a development of the middle class, were often broad and comical—the adventures, for example, of a handsome ne'er-do-well or lower-class beauty, frequently recounted in endless episodes or through a series of letters. Authorities disagree as to whether *Robinson Crusoe* and Defoe's other fictional narratives are true novels, but many agree that the novel began either with Defoe or with the writers of the next generation.

Robinson Crusoe leaving his island.

Tom Jones Refused Admittance by the Nobleman's Porter (18th century) by Thomas Rowlandson.

The novels of one of the most prominent eighteenth-century novelists, Henry Fielding (1707–1754), are literally crammed with rough and rowdy incidents, and though Fielding does manage to make his characters seem good, they are never soft or sentimental. Fielding's rollicking novel *Tom Jones* has even been made into an Oscar-winning movie, proof that his high-spirited characters are still fresh and funny today. Samuel Richardson (1689–1761) was perhaps the first novelist to explore in great detail the emotional life of his characters, especially his heroines (in *Pamela* and *Clarissa*). The novels of Laurence Sterne (1713–1768) are experimental and whimsical—and still unique despite the efforts of many imitators to copy them. All these novels tell us something of what life at this time was like. They also help us understand the humor and disappointments of human experience in all ages.

> *Novels, so named because they were "new," became very popular during the mid eighteenth century, in part because they were both realistic and funny.*

The Commanding Figure of Johnson

Along with all the other labels given to parts of this long period in English history, some people refer to the last part of the eighteenth century as the "age of Johnson." Even today, Samuel Johnson remains a commanding figure who speaks with authority about many of the things that matter to men and women. Johnson's views of humanity were conservative and traditional. He combated such tendencies of his time as the belief in progress (the belief that things are inevitably getting better) and the

---

C. Language Note: Style and Structure

Point out that Richardson's works illustrate the genre of the *epistolary* novel, a story composed as a collection of serialized letters. Letters provide an intimate, immediate account of a character's emotions and activities; those are just the qualities Fielding ruthlessly mocks in his fictional parodies of Richardson's works, *Shamela* and *Joseph Andrews*.

D. Exploring the Historical Period

Because the Industrial Revolution began in Great Britain, its people were the first to experience the disruptive changes of rapid urbanization and environmental pollution. Workers whose jobs were eliminated by industrial improvements often rioted and wrecked the equipment in protest. In 1769, Parliament made the destruction of some machinery a capital crime.

A. Expansion

The phrases "age of Johnson" or "age of sensibility" are used to describe the transitional period in which aesthetic tastes turned away from the wit and technical brilliance of Neoclassicism. The age of Romanticism ushered in an interest in the Middle Ages, a love of gothic horror, and a delight in primitive art and architecture antithetical to Augustan ideals.

Quickwrite

Help students to identify examples of major cultural changes they have witnessed and to connect with this literary period by having them devise time lines of their own lives. They might include items from the mentioned subject areas (religion, science, fashion, art, and politics) or they might add some of their own. Encourage them to incorporate visual as well as verbal entries into their time lines. For example, they might choose to use photographs or drawings to show the changes they have observed. They might also compile an auditory time line to exemplify changing musical or spoken-language trends, or an audiovisual time line revealing changes in television programming (for instance, examples of children's educational programs over time). Students may enjoy sharing their results with the class.

---

assumption that men and women are naturally good (that is, the notion that if society is reformed, people will automatically do what is right).

> **The commanding figure at the end of the eighteenth century was Dr. Samuel Johnson, a man of conservative and traditional beliefs. His wariness of progress epitomized the era.**

> Johnson's conversation was by much too strong for a person accustomed to obsequiousness and flattery; it was *mustard in a young child's mouth!*
>
> —Hester Lynch Thrale Piozzi, Johnson's friend

Searching for a Simpler Life

By the time of Johnson's death in 1784, the world was changing in disturbing and profound ways. The Industrial Revolution was turning English cities and towns into appalling, smoky slums. Across the English Channel, the French were about to murder a king and set their whole society on a different political course. The century was closing, and—just as now, at the end of the twentieth century, people sense a new era about to begin—people in England at the close of the eighteenth century knew the age of elegance, taste, philosophy, and reason was gone.

As a reflection of all this change, writers were developing new interests. Appalled at the industrial blight, they were turning to external nature and writing about the effect of the natural landscape on the human psyche. Disgusted with the excessive focus on the upper classes and "good taste," they were looking back at the past and searching out the simple poems and songs composed by nameless, uneducated folk poets. They were even becoming interested in the literary possibilities of the humble life and were trying to enter into the consciousness of the poor and simple. Nothing could be less Augustan than these tendencies. In short, a new literary age was already beginning during the lifetime of the last great representative of the older age.

> **At the end of the century, as industrialization mushroomed, English writers rejected their Augustan predecessors and returned to nature and folk themes for inspiration.**

Quickwrite

During the eighteenth century, there was a great shift in the way most people thought about the world. Natural phenomena were more and more being explained by the new method of rational, scientific observation. The Renaissance love of the pastoral was abandoned, in favor of eighteenth-century tastes in fashion and art that ran to the artificial and highly formal. What are the prevailing philosophies and tastes in your world? What changes in people's thinking—about religion, science, fashion, art, politics, the environment, or anything else—have you seen during your lifetime?

(Opposite) *"Well-a-day! Is this my son Tom!"* (detail) (18th century) by Samuel Hieronymous Grimm.

British Library, London.

THE STING OF SATIRE

Theme: **Satire as a Corrective Force**
Although sometimes called the Age of Reason, the period from 1660 to 1800 offered the antithesis of a reasonable and just society. Several writers of conscience turned to satire to remind readers of moral and social concerns.

Thematic Focus

These selections offer a cross section of the foibles and failings of English society.

- *from* **Gulliver's Travels** Spoofing the popular genre of travel literature, Swift pokes fun at the inflated view the English have of themselves.
- **A Modest Proposal** Swift's outrageous solution to the problems of the poor in Ireland underscores the callous attitudes of the English toward the Irish.
- **Heroic Couplets** These bits of wisdom culled from several of Pope's works offer examples of his satirical techniques.
- *from* **An Essay on Man** This philosophical poem uses antithesis to portray a paradoxical view of humanity.
- *from* **The Rape of the Lock** This mock epic trivializes the petty concerns of the leisure class, whose problems are minor compared to those of the poor.
- *from* **Candide** Voltaire's satire lampoons the overly optimistic philosophy that everything happens for the best.

Literary Focus

Literary Element	Selection / Feature
Irony/Satire	**Gulliver's Travels/A Modest Proposal**
Antithesis/Heroic Couplet/ Mock Epic/Wit	**Heroic Couplets/An Essay on Man/ The Rape of the Lock**

Writing Focus

The following flowchart shows how the writing assignment for each selection relates to and builds toward the culminating writing assignment presented in the Writer's Workshop at the end of the unit.

Selection	Work-in-Progress Assignment
Gulliver's Travels/ A Modest Proposal	Jot down ideas about a contemporary issue p. 514
Heroic Couplets/An Essay on Man/ The Rape of the Lock	Collect ideas about social issues and values p. 535
Writer's Workshop	Write a persuasive essay pp. 612–617

Collection Planner

SELECTION/ FEATURE	Literary Elements / Active Reading	Writing	Speaking and Listening	Language and Vocabulary
from **Gulliver's Travels/ A Modest Proposal** Jonathan Swift (pp. 486–515) Critical Comment: Under the Guise of Lilliput (p. 495) **Connections: Top of the Food Chain** T. Coraghessan Boyle (pp. 509–512) Spotlight On: Women Writers of the Restoration and the Eighteenth Century (pp. 516–519)	• Reader's Log p. 487 • Irony p. 487 • Satire pp. 500–501	• Critical Writing: Compare satires p. 514 • Creative Writing: Write "modest proposal" p. 514 • Creative Writing: Write first-person fantasy narrative p. 514 • Creative Writing: Reply to Swift p. 514	• Art/Speaking: Present research on artist William Hogarth p. 514	• Language and Style: Examine Swift's diction p. 513 • How to Own a Word: Shades of meaning p. 515
Heroic Couplets/ from **An Essay on Man/** from **The Rape of the Lock** Alexander Pope (pp. 520–535)	• Reader's Log pp. 521, 526 • Antithesis p. 521 • Heroic Couplet p. 522 • Epigram p. 525 • Mock Epic p. 526 • Wit pp. 533–534	• Critical Writing: Write essay about targets of Pope's satire p. 535 • Critical Writing: Compare Pope's mock epic with serious one p. 535 • Creative Writing: Write mock epic about contemporary life p. 535 • Creative Writing: Write prose description using inflated language p. 535	• Language and Style: Read Pope's poetry to class p. 525 • Speaking and Listening: Present rebuttal of one of Pope's sayings p. 535	• Language and Style: Experiment with readings of Pope's poetry p. 525
World Literature: from **Candide** Voltaire (pp. 536–540)	• Reader's Log p. 537		• Finding Common Ground: Discuss satiric intent of Candide with classmates p. 540	

Collection Resources

Teaching Resources A	Audiovisual Resources Binder	Test Booklet
Cross-Curricular Activity p. 143	Fine Art Transparencies 6.1–6.2	Collection 6 Test pp. 101–103

 Computer disk or CD-ROM

 Audiocassette

 Overhead Transparency

PROGRAM RESOURCES

Electronic Media	Teaching Resources with Organizer		Audiovisual Resources Binder
	Teaching Resources A	Other Resources	
• Test Generator • Language Workshop: Participles and Participial phrases	• Teaching Notes pp. 124–126 • Reading Organizers pp. 131, 136 • Language Link pp. 132–133 • Words to Own pp. 134, 135, 137	• Test Booklet: Selection Tests pp. 91–92, 93–94, 95–96 • Language and Writing Skills Worksheet p. 73 • Portfolio Management System pp. 39, 62–63, 112–113	• Elements of Literature Transparency 6.3 • Selected Reading Audiocassette 1, Side B
• Test Generator • Language Workshop: Infinitives and Infinitive phrases	• Teaching Notes pp. 126–128 • Reading Organizers pp. 138–140 • Language Link pp. 141–142	• Test Booklet: Selection Tests pp. 97–98, 99–100 • Language and Writing Skills Worksheet p. 75 • Portfolio Management System pp. 39, 62–63, 114–115	• Elements of Literature Transparencies 6.4 and 6.5 • Selected Reading Audiocassette 1, Side B
	• Teaching Notes p. 128		

Proofreading Warm-ups

You may use the following exercises to help students practice their proofreading skills. Copy a set of incorrect sentences onto the chalkboard, and have students find and correct the spelling, punctuation, usage, and mechanical errors in each sentence. Ask students to share and discuss their responses.

	Sentences with Errors	Sentences Corrected	Skills Covered
1	**a.** the period from 1660 to 1800 was given several lables in England; the Augustan age, the Neoclassical Period, the Enlightenment, and the Age Of Reason **b.** british men and woman produced many brilliant works of Philosophy, Art, and Literature during this time	**a.** The period from 1660 to 1800 was given several labels in England: the Augustan Age, the Neoclassical Period, the Enlightenment, and the Age of Reason. **b.** British men and women produced many brilliant works of philosophy, art, and literature during this time.	Capitalization, Spelling, Colon usage, End marks
2	**a.** many types of litrature was produced during the enlightenment **b.** novels a new type of literature became popular in the mid eighteenth century	**a.** Many types of literature were produced during the Enlightenment. **b.** Novels, a new type of literature, became popular in the mid-eighteenth century.	Capitalization, Spelling, Subject-verb agreement, Comma usage, Hyphen usage, End marks
3	**a.** other literary development's, of the Age of Reason, included the appearence of the periodical essay **b.** writer's, Joseph Addison and Sir Richard Steele, were essayists who saw their-selves in reformer roles	**a.** Other literary developments of the Age of Reason included the appearance of the periodical essay. **b.** Writers Joseph Addison and Sir Richard Steele were essayists who saw themselves in reformer roles.	Capitalization, Apostrophe usage, Comma usage, Spelling, Nonstandard usage, End marks
4	**a.** because of the morale corruption of society writers Alexander Pope and Jonathan Swift turned to satire **b.** satire is any piece of writing, that is intended to make it's readers feel critical of themselfs, others, or society	**a.** Because of the moral corruption of society, writers Alexander Pope and Jonathan Swift turned to satire. **b.** Satire is any piece of writing that is intended to make its readers feel critical of themselves, others, or society.	Capitalization, Spelling, Comma usage, Apostrophe usage, Nonstandard usage, End marks
5	**a.** jonathan swift like many satirists uses irony to sharpen the sting of his' satire **b.** their are 3 types of irony verbal, situational, and dramatic	**a.** Jonathan Swift, like many satirists, uses irony to sharpen the sting of his satire. **b.** There are three types of irony: verbal, situational, and dramatic.	Capitalization, Comma usage, Apostrophe usage, Spelling, Write out numerals, Colon usage, End marks
6	**a.** swift urges reform of Politics and Religion in his satire "Gulliver's Travels" **b.** swift's pamphlet A Modest Proposal offers a solution to poverty	**a.** Swift urges reform of politics and religion in his satire <u>Gulliver's Travels</u>. **b.** Swift's pamphlet <u>A Modest Proposal</u> offers a solution to poverty.	Capitalization, Underline book/pamphlet titles, End marks
7	**a.** popular fiction that was written by woman were flooding the bookstalls by the late 18th century **b.** ann radcliffe the most famous writer of eighteenth century Gothic novels	**a.** Popular fiction that was written by women was flooding the bookstalls by the late eighteenth century. **b.** Ann Radcliffe was the most famous writer of eighteenth-century Gothic novels.	Capitalization, Spelling, Subject-verb agreement, Write out abbreviations, Fragments, Hyphen usage, End marks
8	**a.** the most important poet of the early eighteenth-century Alexander Pope was a child prodigy **b.** he began his career writting pastorals poems describeing the countryside	**a.** The most important poet of the early eighteenth century, Alexander Pope, was a child prodigy. **b.** He began his career writing pastorals, poems describing the countryside.	Capitalization, Hyphen usage, Comma usage, Spelling, End marks
9	**a.** pope used parallell structures for a balanced contrast a technic called antithesis **b.** a example of antithesis is Patrick Henrys famous speech: "Give me liberty, or give me death	**a.** Pope used parallel structures for a balanced contrast, a technique called antithesis. **b.** An example of antithesis is Patrick Henry's famous speech: "Give me liberty, or give me death!"	Capitalization, Comma usage, Spelling, Nonstandard usage, Apostrophe usage, Quotation marks, End marks
10	**a.** popes mock epic The Rape of the Lock uses epic devises in a comic way **b.** pope trivializes a incident that actually took place a lock of hair was cut w/out the owners permission	**a.** Pope's mock epic <u>The Rape of the Lock</u> uses epic devices in a comic way. **b.** Pope trivializes an incident that actually took place: a lock of hair was cut without the owner's permission.	Capitalization, Apostrophe usage, Underline epic poem titles, Spelling, Nonstandard usage, Colon usage/Semicolon usage, Write out abbreviations, End marks

THE STING OF SATIRE

Collection 6

Swift

Pope

Voltaire

> **S**atire is a sort of glass, wherein beholders do generally discover everybody's face but their own.
>
> —Jonathan Swift,
> Preface to *The Battle of the Books*

RESPONDING TO THE ART: ABOUT THE ARTIST

Samuel Hieronymus Grimm (1733–94) was known for his illustrations of William Shakespeare's work and for his caricatures. He was a skilled topological draftsman, and his landscape drawings included illustrations for Gilbert White's famous observation of nature and wild life, *The Natural History and Antiquities of Selbourne* (1789). Describing Grimm's technique, White said, "He first of all sketches his scapes with a lead-pencil; then he pens them all over, as he calls it, with Indian ink, rubbing out the superfluous pencil-strokes; then he gives a charming shading with a brush dipped in Indian ink; and last he throws a light tinge of water-colours over the whole."

Responding to the Quotation

Ask students to name a modern satirical piece from literature, movies, television programs, magazine articles, comic books, and so on, and to identify its target(s). Students should discuss whom the "beholders" recognize in the mirror of satire.

PORTFOLIO ASSESSMENT

Portfolio Assessment Parent/Guardian Involvement For forms that will help a parent or guardian review and respond to a student's portfolio, see *Portfolio Management System*, pp. 62–63.

PROGRAM MANAGER

- **Integrated Assessment** For a summative assessment of the literature and language skills taught in this collection, see **Collection 6 Test**, *Test Booklet*, pp. 101–103.
- **Instructional Support** See **Fine Art Transparencies** 6.1–6.2. Review teacher's notes for transparencies in the *Audiovisual*

Resources Binder for suggestions on how to tie the transparencies to specific reading selections.
- **Extending Collection Theme** See **Cross-Curricular Activity: The Sting of Satire**, *Teaching Resources A*, p. 143 for an activity in other disciplines and for evaluation criteria.

Jonathan Swift

(1667–1745)

Jonathan Swift (c. 1718) by Charles Jervas.
Oil on canvas (48 ½″ × 38 ¼″).

By Courtesy of the National Portrait Gallery, London.

Jonathan Swift is the principal prose writer of the early eighteenth century and England's greatest satirist. He was an Anglo-Irishman, a label applied to people who live in Ireland but who regard themselves as more English than Irish. Swift was born in Dublin of English parents, seven months after the death of his father, a lawyer. His mother returned to England when Swift was three years old, and the boy was looked after by his uncle Godwin.

Although Swift was poor, his prosperous uncle paid for his education. Hoping to advance himself, Swift went to England and became secretary to Sir William Temple, a distant relative—a writer, a wealthy country gentleman, and a statesman. The job gave Swift the opportunity to mingle with public figures, read, and look about for a more important and permanent position. Unfortunately, nothing came of Temple's patronage. After several years of disappointment, Swift took his life into his own hands, obtained a master's degree from Oxford University, and was ordained a priest in the Church of Ireland, a counterpart to the Church of England.

Swift seemed fated to live in Ireland, although he desperately wanted a career in England. Now, as a priest, he was assigned to remote parishes in the Irish countryside. To Swift, Ireland seemed a cultural desert, inhabited mainly by Roman Catholic natives and Scottish Presbyterian immigrants—people whom Swift neither admired nor respected. And so he escaped to England whenever possible. Swift hoped to be made an English bishop, but his political friends fell from power, and the only appointment he could obtain was back in Ireland, as the dean of St. Patrick's Cathedral in Dublin. Swift returned to his native city, was installed as dean, and held that office for the remaining thirty years of his life.

Swift did not write for fame or money; most of his books and pamphlets were published anonymously. Nor did he write simply to divert or entertain, though most of his works are marked by his powerful imagination and many of them are amusing. Swift's aim in writing was to improve human conduct, to make people more decent and humane. His first important book, *A Tale of a Tub* (1704), is a lively, outspoken exposure of "gross corruptions in religion and learning," to quote Swift's own words. It scandalized many respectable readers when they discovered that a clergyman had written it, because it seemed to treat sacred matters irreverently. *Gulliver's Travels* (1726) attacks many different varieties of human misbehavior, vice, and folly. Swift even became an Irish patriot in his pamphlets, defending the Irish against the oppressive policies of their English rulers. The most famous of his pamphlets is *A Modest Proposal* (1729). In a letter to Pope, Swift justified these pro-Irish writings: "What I do is owing to perfect rage and resentment, and the mortifying sight of slavery, folly, and baseness about me, among which I am forced to live."

As the years passed, Swift made fewer and fewer visits to London, though he continued to correspond with Alexander Pope and with many other friends. His last days were sad: He suffered from a disease of the inner ear which made him dizzy, deaf, and disoriented. He was buried in his cathedral in Dublin, where troops of tourists now pause every day of the year to read his epitaph, which ends: "Go, traveler, and imitate, if you can, one who strove with all his strength to champion liberty."

PROGRAM MANAGER

- **Planning Instruction** See Teaching Notes, *Teaching Resources A,* pp. 124–126, for objectives and additional historical and biographical information.
- **Instructional Support** See Graphic Organizer for Active Reading, *Teaching Resources A,* pp. 131 and 136, for Through the Selection activities.

- **Audiotaped Readings** To help auditory learners, use the Selected Reading, Audiocassette 1, Side B, in the *Audiovisual Resources Binder.*
- **Assessment** See Selection Tests, *Test Booklet,* pp. 91– 96.
- **Language Link** For instruction and

practice in using participles and participle phrases, see Language Link, *Teaching Resources A,* pp. 132–133 and *Language and Writing Skills Worksheets,* p. 73.
- **Reinforcement** Use the Words to Own worksheets in *Teaching Resources A,* pp. 134–135 and 137.

BEFORE YOU READ

FROM GULLIVER'S TRAVELS
A MODEST PROPOSAL

Reading Focus

Reforming the World

When some people look around, they do not see the glass of life half full; they see it as half empty. Human society, as well as social institutions, is riddled with vices, follies, foibles, absurdities, and quirks. The way some people see it, the world stands in urgent and constant need of reform. Some would-be reformers write editorials or preach sermons. Others use a different weapon to stress the need for change: the stinging criticism of satire.

Quickwrite

Many of the faults that Swift attacked in people and institutions are still targets for satirical criticism today. Think, for example, of political cartoonists who poke fun at greed or corruption. In your Reader's Log, jot down notes on some current examples of satire that display an urge to reform human beings or aspects of society. Remember that satire can appear in a variety of forms, including essays, novels, cartoons, bumper sticker slogans, TV comedy routines, monologues, and songs.

Elements of Literature

Irony

Swift, like all satirists, assumes he will make his readers recognize the gap between things as they are and things as they ought to be. To force them to feel this contrast, Swift constantly resorts to the use of **irony** to sharpen the sting of his satire.

> **I**rony is a pointed contrast between reality and expectations. There are three types of irony: **Verbal irony** is a contrast between what is said and what is actually meant; **situational irony** is a contrast between what is expected to happen and what actually does happen; and **dramatic irony** is a contrast between what a character knows and what the reader or audience knows.
>
> *For more on Irony, see page 994 and the Handbook of Literary Terms.*

Lilliputians examining the man-mountain's possessions, illustration from *Gulliver's Travels* (1726).

JONATHAN SWIFT 487

PORTFOLIO ASSESSMENT

Portfolio Assessment For help with self-assessment of reading skills, see the *Portfolio Management System,* p. 39.

WORDS TO OWN

The following vocabulary words are defined in the Words to Own at the bottom of the pupil's page.

conjectured p. 488	copious p. 497
diminutive p. 491	prevailed p. 497
alleged p. 493	odious p. 498
edict p. 494	viscous p. 499
quelled p. 494	pernicious p. 499

Using BEFORE YOU READ p. 487

Elements of Literature

For practice in distinguishing among the three types of **irony,** have students keep a running tally of which types they notice as they are reading (see sample format below).

Types of Irony in *Gulliver's Travels*

Page #	Verbal	Situational	Dramatic

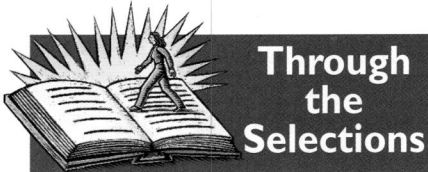

Through the Selections

A. Reader's Response: First Thoughts

? What do you think is Gulliver's probable frame of mind in this opening passage? [Sample responses: Confusion, surprise, fear, curiosity.] Jot down your impressions in your Reader's Log.

B. Critical Reading: Making Generalizations

? What does the made-up language contribute to the narrator's report? [Possible answers: Authenticity; a parody of any language—English in this case; humor.]

The full title that Swift gave his most famous book is *Travels into Several Remote Nations of the World. In Four Parts. By Lemuel Gulliver, First a Surgeon, and then a Captain of Several Ships.* Immediately upon publication, it was a sensational success. It seemed so convincing that some readers went about claiming that they had heard of, or even met, its author. But Gulliver is, of course, a figment of Swift's imagination.

The book seems to be a true account of actual adventures because Swift includes many realistic-sounding details and even maps of the places Gulliver visits. The first part, describing the visit to Lilliput, opens with a very circumstantial account of Gulliver's early life: his birth, parentage, and schooling. After studying medicine, Gulliver becomes a ship's doctor and embarks on a long voyage; when the ship breaks up in a storm, he manages to swim ashore and, exhausted, falls into a deep sleep. What could be more convincing?

from Gulliver's Travels
from Part 1: A Voyage to Lilliput

Jonathan Swift

I lay down on the grass, which was very short and soft, where I slept sounder than ever I remember to have done in my life, and, as I reckoned, above nine hours; for when I awaked, it was just daylight. I attempted to rise, but was not able to stir: For as I happened to lie on my back, I found my arms and legs were strongly fastened on each side to the ground; and my hair, which was long and thick, tied down in the same manner. I likewise felt several slender ligatures[1] across my body, from my armpits to my thighs. I could only look upward; the sun began to grow hot, and the light offended my eyes. I heard a confused noise about me, but in the posture I lay, could see nothing except the sky.

In a little time I felt something alive moving on my left leg, which advancing gently forward over my breast, came almost up to my chin; when bending my eyes downward as much as I could, I perceived it to be a human creature not six inches high, with a bow and arrow in his hands, and a quiver at his back. In the meantime, I felt at least forty more of the same kind (as I conjectured) following the first. I was in the utmost astonishment, and roared so loud, that they all ran back in a fright; and some of them, as I was afterward told, were hurt with the falls they got by leaping from my sides upon the ground. However, they soon returned, and one of them, who ventured so far as to get a full sight of my face, lifting up his hands and eyes by way of admiration, cried out in a shrill, but distinct voice, *Hekinah degul:*[2] The others repeated the same words several times, but then I knew not what they meant. I lay all this while, as the reader may believe, in great uneasiness: At length, struggling to get loose, I had the fortune to break the strings, and wrench out the pegs that fastened my left arm to the ground; for, by lifting it up to my face, I discovered the methods they had taken to bind me, and at the same time with a violent pull, which gave me excessive pain, I a little loosened the strings that tied down my hair on the left side, so that I was just able to turn my head about two inches. But the creatures

2. *Hekinah degul:* This and other examples of the Lilliputian (lil'ə·pyoo͞'shən) tongue are mainly nonsense words. Swift was very fond of puns, pig Latin, and other kinds of word games.

WORDS TO OWN
conjectured (kən·jek'chərd) *v.:* reasoned; guessed.

1. ligatures: ties or bonds.

OPTIONS FOR TEACHING

STRATEGIES FOR INCLUSION

English Language Development Students may benefit from translating Swift's highly visual language into a series of sketches or cartoon panels of the following scenes described in the selection: Gulliver tied down with Lilliputians moving over him; Lilliputians giving him food and drink; Lilliputian boys and girls playing hide and seek in Gulliver's hair. Have students read the selection carefully to find as many details as possible to include in their drawings.

Interpersonal Ask students who take particular interest in political or interpersonal relationships to identify the personalities and groups in Lilliput and their interrelationships through an Influence Tree (a chart showing position and power in a society), which they present to the entire class.

Gulliver awakens in Lilliput (c. 1880), illustration by an unknown artist.

some of them attempted with spears to stick me in the sides; but, by good luck, I had on me a buff jerkin,[3] which they could not pierce. I thought it the most prudent method to lie still, and my design was to continue so till night, when, my left hand being already loose, I could easily free myself: And as for the inhabitants, I had reason to believe I might be a match for the greatest armies they could bring against me, if they were all of the same size with him that I saw. But fortune disposed otherwise of me.

When the people observed I was quiet, they discharged no more arrows; but, by the noise increasing, I knew their numbers were greater; and about four yards from me, over against my right ear, I heard a knocking for above an hour, like that of people at work; when turning my head that way, as well as the pegs and

ran off a second time, before I could seize them; whereupon there was a great shout in a very shrill accent, and after it ceased, I heard one of them cry aloud, *Tolgo phonac;* when in an instant I felt above an hundred arrows discharged on my left hand, which pricked me like so many needles; and besides, they shot another flight into the air, as we do bombs in Europe, whereof many, I suppose, fell on my body (though I felt them not), and some on my face, which I immediately covered with my left hand. When this shower of arrows was over, I fell a-groaning with grief and pain, and then striving again to get loose, they discharged another volley larger than the first, and

C

strings would permit me, I saw a stage erected, about a foot and a half from the ground, capable of holding four of the inhabitants, with two or three ladders to mount it: From whence one of them, who seemed to be a person of quality, made me a long speech, whereof I understood not one syllable. But I should have mentioned, that before the principal person began his oration, he cried out three times, *Langro dehul san* (these words and the former were afterward repeated and explained to me). Whereupon

D

3. **buff jerkin:** short, closefitting leather jacket, often without sleeves.

C. Literary Element: Simile
Here Swift compares the flurry of random arrows to bombs. How might this be a significant comparison? [Possible answers: He makes light of the wars in Europe by comparing the bombs to tiny arrows that feel like pinpricks. It draws a parallel between this make-believe society and his own, and indicates that his amusing story may have more serious undertones.]

D. Critical Reading: Finding Details
? What details lead Gulliver to conclude this character is the "principal person"? What type of leader might Swift be spoofing? [Possible answers: He speaks from a stage and gives a long speech; the Lilliputians respond to his directions by cutting some of the strings; he is taller than his attendants; one attendant carries his train. This leader could represent a monarch, an absolute ruler, or a leader with finery and the trappings of power.] Remind students to think of the target of Swift's satire at every opportunity.

CROSSING THE CURRICULUM

Geography/Art Explain that detailed maps lend authenticity to Swift's original edition of *Gulliver's Travels*. If possible, bring in a facsimile of an original edition so students can look at the maps. Otherwise, invite students to draw their own maps of Lilliput and to explain what parts of the text influence the way they imagine the place.

Science *Gulliver's Travels* is an example of the science fiction of Swift's day, combining the technology and scientific understanding of the era with extrapolation. In order to see how Swift incorporates science in this selection, students should identify the ways Gulliver's sojourn in Lilliput fits into the science fiction genre and to illustrate on poster board some of the technology Swift describes.

Social Sciences Because fashion often represents time periods in the popular culture, ask students to research the costumes of Swift's era and to write an editorial commenting on the interdependence of dress, action, and thought. ☞

A. Critical Reading: Making Inferences

? How does one act "every part of an orator"? [Possible answers: With a pompous air, broad gestures, loud voice, or announcing tone.]

B. Reader's Response: Challenging the Text

? Do you find Gulliver's ability to communicate through sign language and gestures convincing? Why or why not? [Sample responses: Communicating hunger is convincing because Gulliver receives what he needs; certain gestures are shared by Gulliver and the Lilliputians such as those representing "more" and throwing an object down; expressing ideas such as swearing sincerity might fail to cross cultural boundaries.]

immediately about fifty of the inhabitants came and cut the strings that fastened the left side of my head, which gave me the liberty of turning it to the right, and of observing the person and gesture of him who was to speak. He appeared to be of a middle age, and taller than any of the other three who attended him, whereof one was a page who held up his train, and seemed to be somewhat longer than my middle finger; the other two stood one on each side to support him. **A** He acted every part of an orator, and I could observe many periods of threatenings, and others of promises, pity, and kindness.

I answered in a few words, but in the most submissive manner, lifting up my left hand, and both my eyes to the sun, as calling him for a witness; and being almost famished with hunger, having not eaten a morsel for some hours before I left the ship. I found the demands of nature so strong upon me, that I could not forbear showing my impatience (perhaps against the strict rules of decency) by putting my finger frequently on my mouth, **B** to signify that I wanted food. The *Hurgo*[4] (for so they call a great lord, as I afterward learnt) understood me very well. He descended from the stage, and commanded that several ladders should be applied to my sides, on which above an hundred of the inhabitants mounted and walked toward my mouth, laden with baskets full of meat,[5] which had been provided and sent thither by the King's orders, upon the first intelligence[6] he received of me. I observed there was the flesh[7] of several animals, but

Gulliver in Lilliput, illustration by Gennady Spirin.

could not distinguish them by the taste. There were shoulders, legs, and loins, shaped like those of mutton, and very well dressed, but smaller than the wings of a lark. I ate them by two or three at a mouthful, and took three loaves at a time, about the bigness of musket bullets. They supplied me as fast as they could, showing a thousand marks of wonder and astonishment at my bulk and appetite.

I then made another sign that I wanted drink. They found by my eating, that a small quantity would not suffice me; and being a most ingenious

4. **Hurgo:** This Lilliputian word is perhaps a partial anagram (a word formed by rearranging the letters of another word) of the English word *rogue.* It would be characteristic of Swift to call a "great lord" a rogue.
5. **meat:** archaic for "food."
6. **intelligence:** news.
7. **flesh:** meat.

OPTIONS FOR TEACHING

INTEGRATING THE LANGUAGE ARTS

Strategic Reading Ask students to jot down how they think Gulliver will handle a particular situation. Then, they can compare their thoughts to the events of the story as it unfolds, using a chart like the following.

My Prediction	Actual Outcome
[Gulliver will try to break free.]	[Gulliver waits to communicate with the Lilliputians.]

Writing: Story Much of the **imagery** of this selection revolves around perspective. Invite students to work with partners to switch the perspective and to write a short story describing what they might see and sense from the **point of view** of a small creature held captive in a land of large creatures. Have students include descriptions of the emotions they might feel in such a situation.

Speaking and Listening Assign sections of the selection to students so that the entire story is covered. Then, assign students to pairs and have them read their assigned sections to their partners. Have each listener provide feedback (using words like *needs work, adequate,* or *outstanding*) in the following presentation areas: pronunciation, speed of delivery, nonverbal communication, intonation, and expression. Once students have practiced, have the class read the complete selection aloud.

Reprinted by permission of Philomel Books from *Gulliver's Travels in Lilliput,* retold by Ann Keay Beneduce, illustrations ©1993 by Gennady Spirin.

people, they slung up with great dexterity one of their largest hogsheads,[8] then rolled it toward my hand, and beat out the top; I drank it off at a draft, which I might well do, for it hardly held half a pint, and tasted like a small wine of Burgundy, but much more delicious. They brought me a second hogshead, which I drank in the same manner, and made signs for more, but they had none to give me. When I had performed these wonders, they shouted for joy, and danced upon my breast, repeating several times as they did at first, *Hekinah degul.* They made me a sign that I should throw down the two hogsheads, but first warned the people below to stand out of the way, crying aloud, *Borach mivola,* and when they saw the vessels in the air, there was an universal shout of *Hekinah degul.* I confess I was often tempted, while they were passing backward and forward on my body, to seize forty or fifty of the first that came in my reach, and dash them against the ground. But the remembrance of what I had felt, which probably might not be the worst they could do, and the promise of honor I made them, for so I interpreted my submissive behavior, soon drove out those imaginations. Besides, I now considered myself as bound by the laws of hospitality to a people who had treated me with so much expense and magnificence. However, in my thoughts, I could not sufficiently wonder at the intrepidity of these <u>diminutive</u> mortals, who durst venture to mount and walk on my body, while one of my hands was at liberty, without trembling at the very sight of so prodigious a creature as I must appear to them.

After some time, when they observed that I made no more demands for meat, there appeared before me a person of high rank from his Imperial Majesty. His Excellency, having mounted on the small of my right leg, advanced forward up to my face, with about a dozen of his retinue. And producing his credentials under the Signet Royal,[9] which he applied close to my eyes, spoke about ten minutes, without any signs of anger, but with a kind of determinate resolution; often pointing forward, which, as I afterward found, was toward the capital city, about half a mile distant, whither

it was agreed by his Majesty in council that I must be conveyed. I answered in few words, but to no purpose, and made a sign with my hand that was loose, putting it to the other (but over his Excellency's head for fear of hurting him or his train) and then to my own head and body, to signify that I desired my liberty. It appeared that he understood me well enough, for he shook his head by way of disapprobation, and held his hand in a posture to show that I must be carried as a prisoner. However, he made other signs to let me understand that I should have meat and drink enough, and very good treatment. Whereupon I once more thought of attempting to break my bonds; but again, when I felt the smart of their arrows, upon my face and hands, which were all in blisters, and many of the darts still sticking in them, and observing likewise that the number of my enemies increased, I gave tokens[10] to let them know that they might do with me what they pleased. Upon this, the *Hurgo* and his train withdrew, with much civility and cheerful countenances.

Soon after I heard a general shout, with frequent repetitions of the words, *Peplom selan,* and I felt great numbers of people on my left side relaxing the cords to such a degree, that I was able to turn upon my right, and to ease myself with making water; which I very plentifully did, to the great astonishment of the people, who conjecturing by my motions what I was going to do, immediately opened to the right and left on that side, to avoid the torrent which fell with such noise and violence from me. But before this, they had daubed my face and both my hands with a sort of ointment very pleasant to the smell, which in a few minutes removed all the smart of their arrows. These circumstances, added to the refreshment I had received by their victuals and drink, which were very nourishing, disposed me to sleep. I slept about eight hours, as I was afterward assured; and it was no wonder, for the physicians, by the Emperor's order, had mingled a sleeping potion in the hogshead of wine. . . .

10. **gave tokens:** signaled.

WORDS TO OWN

diminutive (də·min′yo͞o·tiv) *adj.:* very small.

----

8. **hogsheads** (hôgz′hedz′): barrels.
9. **Signet Royal:** royal seal; the seal used as a signature to mark documents as official.

JONATHAN SWIFT 491

COOPERATIVE LEARNING

Explore Alternatives Have students suppose that Gulliver devises an escape plan and that their mission is to assist him. Assign groups of five to brainstorm, gather information from the text, and invent a way for Gulliver to leave Lilliput gracefully. Encourage students to be as specific about their schemes as possible. For example, picking up on text clues about Lilliputian etiquette, students could detail techniques Gulliver might use to win

the confidence of his captors and thus regain his freedom. Have students share their escape plans with the class.

Modernize the Text Have students form teams of five to identify language forms that sound outmoded or confusing to the modern reader. Each member of a team should find one passage of approximately three sentences and modernize

the language. Then, let each team try to stump the other teams by reading the modern versions and having the other teams identify the original passage. The first team to name the correct passage wins ten points. Since each team has five members, hold five rounds. ☞

A. Language Note: Humor

? What humorous details enliven this description of the Lilliputians? What is the effect of this humor? [Possible answers: Dancing on Gulliver's hand; playing hide and seek in his hair; playing children's games. These details show Gulliver as kind and playful rather than as a dangerous giant, show the playfulness of the Lilliputians, and show the trust Gulliver has built with the Lilliputians.]

B. Literary Element: Satire

? What might Swift be satirizing in the rope-dancing ritual? [Possible answers: Courtly behavior; the English court of his time; the irrelevance of the test to the position; the ridiculousness of office politics and favoritism.]

C. Literary Element: Pun

The word *fall* can be read as an actual fall or as a fall from favor.

D. Literary Element: Satire

? What seems to be Swift's satirical point in describing the "diversion" with the blue, red, and green threads? [Possible answers: He seems to be poking fun at the courtiers' "agility" in sidestepping responsibility.]

My gentleness and good behavior had gained so far on the Emperor and his court, and indeed upon the army and people in general, that I began to conceive hopes of getting my liberty in a short time. I took all possible methods to cultivate this favorable disposition. The natives came by degrees to be less apprehensive of any danger from me. I would sometimes lie down, and let five or six of them dance on my hand. And at last the boys and girls would venture to come and play at hide-and-seek in my hair. I had now made a good progress in understanding and speaking their language. The Emperor had a mind one day to entertain me with several of the country shows, wherein they exceed all nations I have known, both for dexterity and magnificence. I was diverted with none so much as that of the rope dancers,[11] performed upon a slender white thread, extended about two foot, and twelve inches from the ground. Upon which I shall desire liberty, with the reader's patience, to enlarge a little.

This diversion is only practiced by those persons who are candidates for great employments, and high favor, at court. They are trained in this art from their youth, and are not always of noble birth, or liberal education. When a great office is vacant, either by death or disgrace (which often happens), five or six of those candidates petition the Emperor to entertain his Majesty and the court with a dance on the rope, and whoever jumps the highest without falling, succeeds in the office. Very often the chief ministers themselves are commanded to show their skill, and to convince the Emperor that they have not lost their faculty. Flimnap, the Treasurer, is allowed to cut a caper on the straight rope, at least an inch higher than any other lord in the whole empire. I have seen him do the summerset[12] several times together upon a trencher[13] fixed on the rope, which is no thicker than a common packthread[14] in England. My friend Reldresal, principal Secretary for Private Affairs, is, in my opinion, if I am not partial, the second after the Treasurer; the rest of the great officers are much upon a par.

These diversions are often attended with fatal accidents, whereof great numbers are on record. I

11. **rope dancers:** tightrope dancers.
12. **summerset:** somersault.
13. **trencher:** wooden platter usually used for serving food.
14. **packthread:** twine.

myself have seen two or three candidates break a limb. But the danger is much greater when the ministers themselves are commanded to show their dexterity; for, by contending to excel themselves and their fellows, they strain so far, that there is hardly one of them who hath not received a fall, and some of them two or three. I was assured that a year or two before my arrival, Flimnap would have infallibly broke his neck, if one of the King's cushions, that accidentally lay on the ground, had not weakened the force of his fall.

There is likewise another diversion, which is only shown before the Emperor and Empress, and first minister, upon particular occasions. The Emperor lays on the table three fine silken threads of six inches long. One is blue, the other red, and the third green. These threads are proposed as prizes for those persons whom the Emperor hath a mind to distinguish by a peculiar mark of his favor. The ceremony is performed in his Majesty's great chamber of state, where the candidates are to undergo a trial of dexterity very different from the former, and such as I have not observed the least resemblance of in any other country of the Old or the New World. The Emperor holds a stick in his hands, both ends parallel to the horizon, while the candidates advancing one by one, sometimes leap over the stick, sometimes creep under it backward and forward several times, according as the stick is advanced or depressed. Sometimes the Emperor holds one end of the stick, and his first minister the other; sometimes the minister has it entirely to himself. Whoever performs his part with most agility, and holds out the longest in leaping and creeping, is rewarded with the blue-colored silk; the red is given to the next, and the green to the third, which they all wear girt[15] twice round about the middle; and you see few great persons about this court, who are not adorned with one of these girdles. . . .

One morning, about a fortnight after I had obtained my liberty, Reldresal, principal Secretary (as they style him) of Private Affairs, came to my house attended only by one servant. He ordered his coach to wait at a distance, and desired I would give him an hour's audience; which I readily consented to, on account of his quality and personal

15. **girt:** encircled.

492 THE RESTORATION AND THE EIGHTEENTH CENTURY

OPTIONS FOR TEACHING

CLASSROOM MANAGEMENT

Performance Pairs Consider keeping the students assigned to the same pairs throughout a Collection or a grading period in order to develop relationships between partners that foster sharing, learning, and cooperation to achieve goals.

Block Scheduling Continual reassessment of curriculum is important to successful teaching

during a longer class period. Focus on quality, not quantity. Ask yourself the following evaluative questions: Am I covering this concept thoroughly? Am I rushing to complete the same things I always have? This reassessment can lead to more productive teaching techniques and teaching concepts in a more in-depth manner.

Gulliver is measured by the tailors (c. late 19th to early 20th century), illustration by Arthur Rackham.

merits, as well as of the many good offices he had done me during my solicitations at court. I offered to lie down, that he might the more conveniently reach my ear; but he chose rather to let me hold him in my hand during our conversation. He began with compliments on my liberty, said he might pretend to some merit in it; but, however, added, that if it had not been for the present situation of things at court, perhaps I might not have obtained it so soon. "For," said he, "as flourishing a condition as we appear to be in to foreigners, we labor under two mighty evils: a violent faction at home, and the danger of an invasion

by a most potent enemy from abroad. As to the first, you are to understand, that for about seventy moons past there have been two struggling parties in this empire, under the names of *Trameck-san* and *Slamecksan,* from the high and low heels on their shoes, by which they distinguish themselves. It is <u>alleged</u> indeed, that the high heels are most agreeable to our ancient constitution: But however this be, his Majesty hath determined to make use of only low heels in the administration of the government, and all offices in the gift of the Crown, as you cannot but observe; and particularly, that his Majesty's Imperial heels are lower at least by a *drurr* than any of his court; (*drurr* is a measure about the fourteenth part of an inch). The animosities between these two parties run so high, that they will neither eat nor drink, nor talk with each other. We compute the *Trameck-san,* or High-Heels, to exceed us in number; but the power is wholly on our side. We apprehend his Imperial Highness, the Heir to the Crown, to have some tendency toward the High-Heels; at least we can plainly discover one of his heels higher than the other, which gives him a hobble in his gait. Now, in the midst of these intestine[16] disquiets, we are threatened with an invasion from the island of Blefuscu, which is the other great empire of the universe, almost as large and powerful as this of his Majesty. For as to what we have heard you affirm, that there are other kingdoms and states in the world inhabited by human creatures as large as yourself, our philosophers are in much doubt, and would rather conjecture that you dropped from the moon, or one of the stars; because it is certain, that an hundred mortals of your bulk would, in a short time, destroy all the fruits and cattle of his Majesty's dominions. Besides, our histories of six thousand moons make no mention of any other regions, than the two great empires of Lilliput and Blefuscu. Which two mighty powers have, as I was going to tell you, been engaged in a most obstinate war for six and thirty moons past. It began upon the following

---

16. **intestine:** internal.

WORDS TO OWN

alleged (ə·lejd′) *v.*: declared or asserted, often without proof.

Point out to students that, from the Anglican perspective, the two mighty evils are the domestic threat of Roman Catholicism and the international threat of France, England's traditional enemy.

F. Critical Reading: Analyzing Satire

[?] How does Swift diminish the philosophical division between the two factions in England? [Possible answers: He parodies the factions, using two nearly identical but nonsensical names; he indicates that their violent differences are based on something as insignificant as the height of the heels of their shoes.]

G. Exploring the Historical Period

Given the historical context, Swift might be satirizing the Anglicans and the Roman Catholics, the nobility and the common people, the nobility and the bureaucrats, the Royalists and the Parliamentarians, or the Whigs and the Tories. Swift's reference to "seventy moons," which may translate as seventy months (or about six years), could refer to the English Civil Wars which began in 1642 or to Oliver Cromwell's brief rule (1653–1658).

H. Literary Element: Satire

[?] Why does the heir walk with "a hobble"? [Possible answers: Literally—he is wearing shoes of two different heights; figuratively—he cannot make up his mind, so he is hobbled by indecision.]

I. Critical Reading: Making Inferences

[?] What does Swift satirize in these lines? [Possible answer: Narrow-mindedness—when events or people do not fit into preconceived notions of the way the world works.]

J. Reader's Response: First Thoughts

[?] Are you amused by this description of the egg-breaking conflict? Explain. [Sample responses: Yes, it is funny to think of anyone getting upset about the way an egg is broken; or no, I don't see the humor.]

Metacognition How do you decide if something is funny or not? [Possible answers: If it creates a humorous image in my mind; or if it reminds me of a similar experience that made me laugh.]

PROBLEM SOLVING/CRITICAL THINKING

Nonverbal Communication Lead a class discussion to identify the various nonverbal methods Gulliver uses to inform the Lilliputians of his needs and to interpret the actions of others; list on the chalkboard each cue and its meaning. Remind students that Gulliver's reliance on nonverbal cues reinforces the importance of such universal communication. Then, group students into the following teams: art, clothing, and gestures.

Challenge each group to produce and present several examples of nonverbal communication within their assigned category. For example, the clothing group might develop costumes that indicate an individual's status or mood. Ask the other students to guess the content of each group's messages. The accuracy and response time of the guesses will measure the effectiveness of the groups' examples. 👉

A. Critical Reading: Analyzing Parody

? What does this passage parody? [Possible answers: Making narrow-minded appeals to Scripture to justify prejudice; using obscure Biblical references that are difficult to refute; arguing fine points that cannot be settled.]

B. Critical Reading: Finding Details

? What additional alternative does the speaker offer in the egg-breaking debate? [Possible answer: The choice is a matter of individual conscience.]

C. Critical Reading: Making Inferences

? How is Gulliver's decision satirical? [Possible answer: Although he first states that he will not interfere, Gulliver quickly rationalizes his decision to do the expedient thing—fight for Lilliput.]

occasion. It is allowed on all hands, that the primitive way of breaking eggs[17] before we eat them, was upon the larger end: But his present Majesty's grandfather, while he was a boy, going to eat an egg, and breaking it according to the ancient practice, happened to cut one of his fingers. Whereupon the Emperor his father published an <u>edict</u>, commanding all his subjects, upon great penalties, to break the smaller end of their eggs. The people so highly resented this law, that our histories tell us there have been six rebellions raised on that account; wherein one Emperor lost his life, and another his crown. These civil commotions were constantly fomented by the monarchs of Blefuscu; and when they were <u>quelled</u>, the exiles always fled for refuge to that empire. It is computed, that eleven thousand persons have, at several times, suffered death, rather than submit to break their eggs at the smaller end. Many hundred large volumes have been published upon this controversy: But the books of the Big-Endians have been long forbidden, and the whole party rendered incapable by law of holding employments. During the course of these troubles, the emperors of Blefuscu

17. way of breaking eggs: The English eat a boiled egg by standing it up in an egg cup, cutting off one end with a knife, and scooping out the contents with a spoon.

Lilliput (19th century), illustration by Grandville.

did frequently expostulate by their ambassadors, accusing us of making a schism[18] in religion, by offending against a fundamental doctrine of our great prophet Lustrog, in the fifty-fourth chapter of the Brundrecal (which is their Alcoran).[19] This, however, is thought to be a mere strain upon the text, for the words are these: *That all true believers shall break their eggs at the convenient end;* and which is the convenient end, seems, in my humble opinion, to be left to every man's conscience, or at least in the power of the chief magistrate to determine. Now the Big-Endian exiles have found so much credit in the Emperor of Blefuscu's court, and so much private assistance and encouragement from their party here at home, that a bloody war has been carried on between the two empires for six and thirty moons with various success; during which time we have lost forty capital ships, and a much greater number of smaller vessels, together with thirty thousand of our best seamen and soldiers; and the damage received by the enemy is reckoned to be somewhat greater than ours. However, they have now equipped a numerous fleet, and are just preparing to make a descent upon us; and his Imperial Majesty, placing great confidence in your valor and strength, has commanded me to lay this account of his affairs before you."

I desired the Secretary to present my humble duty to the Emperor, and to let him know, that I thought it would not become me, who was a foreigner, to interfere with parties; but I was ready, with the hazard of my life, to defend his person and state against all invaders.

18. schism: division.
19. Alcoran: archaic English name for the Koran, Islam's sacred book.

WORDS TO OWN
edict (ē′dikt′) *n.:* official order.
quelled (kweld) *v.:* subdued.

OPTIONS FOR TEACHING

PROFESSIONAL NOTES

Thematic Connections: "The Sting of Satire" Who is stung, and why? Explain to students that without a specific target, satire loses its punch. Using a graphic organizer like the following, record on the chalkboard student responses regarding the target(s) of this selection's satire. Be sure students link their answers

to the text's page, paragraph, and sentence whenever possible.

Text Reference	Who	Why

Critical Comment

Under the Guise of Lilliput

Swift's contemporaries immediately understood that Swift was doing two things in this part of *Gulliver's Travels.* Under the pretense of describing politics in Lilliput, he was indirectly referring to politicians and political events in his own country. Swift's first readers were quick to identify the actual statesmen lurking behind such made-up names as Reldresal and Flimnap, and they saw parallels between events in Lilliput and events in England.

While it is interesting to know something about the real political background of *Gulliver's Travels,* it is much more important to understand that Swift is **satirizing** certain characteristics to be found in the political struggles of all countries at all times in history. For instance, in the imaginary Lilliput there are two major parties, distinguished by a trivial detail: the height of the heels on the shoes they wear. Similarly, in many actual countries there are also two major parties that struggle for power. Swift wants us to think about what distinguishes such real political parties from each other. Are the issues important or minor?

Later in this section, Gulliver discovers another characteristic that distinguishes the two parties: the way they eat their eggs. The Big-Endians always cut open the big end of the boiled egg, and the Little-Endians always cut open the little end. These parties have had a long and bitter history: One emperor has lost his life, another his throne, and many Lilliputians have had to go live in another country, Blefuscu. All these details suggest that Swift was thinking of specific events in English history, and these events determined what he said about Lilliput. It is even possible to identify the parallels between Swift's fictions and historical facts. Lilliput, for example, represents England; and Blefuscu represents France, where some English Catholics lived in exile.

The Big-Endians are people loyal to Catholicism, England's old religion, and the Little-Endians are those loyal to Anglicanism, England's new religion. The emperor who lost his life can be identified with Charles I; the one who lost his throne is James II.

Any narrative incorporating parallels of this kind is called an **allegory** (see page 451). But again, knowing how to interpret the allegory in a particular way is much less important than understanding the general meaning of the satire, which is directed against follies and excesses wherever they are found.

George III, as the King of Brobdingnag, inspects Napoleon, as Gulliver (c. 1803) by James Gillray.

JONATHAN SWIFT **495**

A. Literary Element: Satire
The satire of Swift's story may surprise some modern readers, since *Gulliver's Travels* is often associated with children's literature. The criticism of Swift's remarks becomes more evident when the tale is read in its context. Critic Robert Adams finds that *Gulliver's Travels* is "a cruel and cutting book indeed, strong medicine for most adults."

B. Exploring the Historical Period
Part of the political conflict reflected in Swift's story is the opposition of the Whig and Tory parties. Tories were associated with the country gentry, and they sought the return of the Catholic Stuart heirs to the British throne, James the Old Pretender and his son Charles. Whigs, whose interests were those of the wealthy middle classes, supported the limited constitutional monarchy of Protestant rulers.

ASSESSMENT TOOLS

Check Test: True-False
1. Gulliver's captors provide him with both food and drink. [True]
2. Gulliver eventually learns that his captors have put a sleeping potion in his drink. [True]
3. Gulliver says government offices are filled by rope dancers. [True]
4. The principal Secretary for Private Affairs says there are no opposing parties in the kingdom. [False]

5. He also says some citizens did not abide by a new law regarding the breaking of eggs. [True]

Informal Assessment: Writing Remind students that you will judge their creative writing by certain standards, using a scale of one to five, five being the highest, to rate each of the following areas:
- Descriptive language
- Vivid imagery
- Originality
- Grammar, Usage, and Mechanics

Making Meanings

First Thoughts

1. Some students may think the image of Gulliver tied down with tiny ropes is funny. The serious points might include mockery of corruption, political parties, court life, and bureaucracy. Students may conclude that satire usually makes a serious point.

Reviewing the Text

a. Lilliputians are less than six inches high. Gulliver is restrained by fear that the Lilliputians may renew their attack, social obligation after the Lilliputians have fed him, desire for good treatment, and admiration for the Lilliputians' courage.

b. Gulliver calls the test *rope dancing,* or tightrope walking. Flimnap almost breaks his neck when he tumbles from the rope, but one of the king's cushions breaks his fall.

c. Reldresal identifies the evils that threaten Lilliput as a violent domestic faction and the danger of an invasion by a powerful enemy.

d. The Lilliputians decreed that all eggs must be broken at the small end, but certain rebels continued to break their eggs at the big end. The kingdom of Blefuscu alienated Lilliput by giving sanctuary to the Big-Endians.

Shaping Interpretations

2. Swift parodies travel books with fantastic lies: a large man staked to the ground by tiny people; the Lilliputians' remarkable social order, politics, and court life; and the Lilliputian language. Swift includes trivial details about eating, drinking, sleeping, body positions, and attempts at communication.

3. These officials are expected to nimbly rope-dance; they also must leap over or creep under a stick that is held by the king or the first minister. These activities satirize some absurdities required of those holding office. Some students may note that the Lilliputians think they are important (big), although they are actually small, and that their values are petty and meaningless.

4. Students may agree that the smallness of the Lilliputians also suggests their pettiness.

MAKING MEANINGS

First Thoughts

1. What do you think is the funniest part of Gulliver's adventures in Lilliput? What serious point, if any, do you see beneath the surface of the humor?

> ### Reviewing the Text
>
> a. How large are the Lilliputians? Why doesn't Gulliver seize and harm the Lilliputians who come close to his free hand?
>
> b. What test do the candidates for high office in Lilliput have to undergo? What disaster almost happened to Flimnap?
>
> c. Describe the two evils that threaten Lilliput, according to Reldresal.
>
> d. Explain how the war between Lilliput and Blefuscu began.

Shaping Interpretations

2. The travel books of Swift's time were famous for containing two types of details: fantastic lies about exotic places, as well as trivial details about the traveler's daily life there. How does this selection **parody,** or imitate and make fun of, these travel books?

3. Swift also uses the travel book as a medium for **satire.** He expects his readers to find similarities between what happens in Lilliput and what goes on at home. What qualifications are the officials of Lilliput expected to have in order to hold high office? How does Swift use **irony** in his description of the Lilliputian officials?

4. Is there any relationship between the physical size of the Lilliputians and the way Swift wants us to evaluate their behavior? Does their size **symbolize** some other kind of "smallness"? Explain.

5. Compare the way Swift **characterizes** the Lilliputians with the way Chaucer characterizes the pilgrims in the Prologue to *The Canterbury Tales* (page 107). How does each writer **satirize** the moral failings of his characters?

6. The institutions for which Swift urges reform here include politics and religion. What does he think of the differences that divide people into factions and sects? What other aspects of Lilliputian (and by implication English) life does Swift suggest are ripe for reform?

7. Because of the bitterness of his satire, some readers have concluded that Swift despaired of true reform and was really a confirmed misanthrope, or hater of humanity. Do you think someone as bitter as Swift is about life has to be a misanthrope? Explain your answer.

Extending the Text

8. The Critical Comment on page 495 explains how Lilliputian politics paralleled British politics of Swift's time. What parallels can you detect between Lilliput and what you know of modern politics, either in this country or some other one?

Gulliver's Travels drawing (c. 1800) by R. Corbould, embellished under the direction of C. Cooke, from *Cooke's Pocket Edition of Select Novels.*

---

5. Swift's satire plays with the idea that size indicates moral character. Chaucer examines the deception of appearances, emphasizing that his pilgrims' true characters do not match the images they project.

6. This selection suggests that Swift thinks these differences often are overstated. He suggests, for example, the need to reform hiring practices (basing government position and service on merit rather than politics), the need to eliminate ceremony surrounding the monarchy, and the need to reevaluate the importance of philosophical differences.

7. Students may say that Swift is bitter or may perceive that his tone combines humor and bitterness. Some may believe that such biting satire indicates a strong dislike of humanity, while others may perceive that Swift hopes for change.

Extending the Text

8. (Synthesis) Parallels drawn may relate to two-party systems, religious schisms, feuding, and awarding of government positions for reasons other than merit.

On his second voyage, Gulliver finds himself marooned in Brobdingnag. Here everything—people, animals, buildings—is twelve times larger than in England or anywhere else in the known world. The situation in Part I is now completely reversed, and Gulliver discovers what it is like to be an insignificant, timid midget among giants. He also learns that nothing is either big or little except by comparison. All sorts of humiliating accidents happen to him: A baby picks him up and tries to suck on his head; a monkey stuffs him with food and carries him up onto a roof; he is almost drowned in a bowl of cream; a farmer exhibits him for money, as though he were a trained flea. Finally he goes to live at court, where he tries to impress the king and queen with his importance, and especially with the importance of England and its civilization, which nobody in Brobdingnag has ever heard of.

Although its inhabitants look like immense and ugly brutes, Brobdingnag is a kind of utopia, a model civilization with an enlightened and benevolent king. Notice how the king treats Gulliver in spite of his opinion of Gulliver's size and civilization.

from Part 2: A Voyage to Brobdingnag
Jonathan Swift

It is the custom that every Wednesday (which, as I have before observed, was their Sabbath) the King and Queen, with the royal issue of both sexes, dine together in the apartment of his Majesty, to whom I was now become a favorite; and at these times my little chair and table were placed at his left hand, before one of the salt-cellars.[1] This prince took a pleasure in conversing with me, inquiring into the manners, religion, laws, government, and learning of Europe; wherein I gave him the best account I was able. His apprehension was so clear, and his judgment so exact, that he made very wise reflections and observations upon all I said. But, I confess, that after I had been a little too copious in talking of my own beloved country, of our trade, and wars by sea and land, of our schisms in religion, and parties in the state; the prejudices of his education prevailed so far, that he could not forbear taking me up in his right hand, and stroking me gently with the other, after an hearty fit of laughing, asked me, whether I were a Whig or a Tory.[2] Then turning to his first minister, who waited behind him with a white staff, near as tall as the mainmast of the *Royal Sovereign,*[3] he observed how contemptible a thing was human grandeur, which could be mimicked by such diminutive insects as I. "And yet," said he, "I dare engage, those creatures have their titles and distinctions of honor, they contrive little nests and burrows, that they call houses and cities; they make a figure in dress and equipage;[4] they love, they fight, they dispute, they cheat, they betray." And thus he continued on, while my color came and went several times, with indignation to hear our noble country, the mistress of arts and arms, the scourge of France, the arbitress of Europe, the seat of virtue, piety, honor, and truth, the pride and envy of the world, so contemptuously treated.

But as I was not in a condition to resent injuries, so, upon mature thoughts, I began to doubt whether I were injured or no. For, after having

---

3. ***Royal Sovereign:*** one of the largest British warships of Swift's age. A white staff is the symbol of the office of the British treasurer.
4. **equipage** (ek′wi·pij′): carriage and horses with attendant servants.

WORDS TO OWN
copious (kō′pē·əs) *adj.*: wordy; profuse.
prevailed (prē·vāld′) *v.*: predominated; held sway.

---

1. **saltcellars:** dishes of salt.
2. **Whig . . . Tory:** the two chief political parties of eighteenth-century Great Britain.

A. Reader's Response: First Thoughts

[?] Why does the King of Brobdingnag take an interest in Gulliver? [Sample responses: The king is fascinated by the customs, beliefs, and government of Gulliver's country. Gulliver's size renders him novel to the king.]

B. Critical Reading: Finding Details

[?] How does the king belittle England? [He remarks upon the ridiculousness of self-importance and intrigue in such a small, insignificant land.]

C. Literary Element: Irony

[?] What is ironic about Gulliver's reference to his "noble country"? [Possible answers: He loves a country filled with wars, schisms, and party politics; he does see how petty it must seem from the perspective of the king (twelve times larger), who views England as tiny and unimportant.]

D. Reader's Response: Extending the Text

[?] How does this passage affect your opinion of Gulliver and his reliability as a narrator? [Sample responses: Although he is defensive at first, he tries to be reasonable and then considers that all things are relative. Because he is willing to consider differing perspectives, the reader can believe him.]

OPTIONS FOR TEACHING

STRATEGIES FOR INCLUSION

Learners Having Difficulty Before students read this selection from Part 2 of *Gulliver's Travels,* tell them this part presents an opposite situation for Gulliver from the previous one: Here he is in a land of giants. Give students some specific contrasts between Lilliput and Brobdingnag to look for: (1) at least one specific example of the size of things in each place in relation to Gulliver, (2) how Gulliver feels about himself in each place, and (3) how Gulliver feels about his country and its people in each place.

INTEGRATING THE LANGUAGE ARTS

Strategic Reading Have students take notes in a three-column format. The middle column is for taking notes, the left for key words arising from the notes, and the right for a summary.

Key Words	Notes	Summary
[flies]	[Flies attack Gulliver after king ridicules insect-sized English society—an apt reinforcement of the point.]	[Gulliver is attacked by flies and admired for his skills in fending them off.]

A. Reader's Response: Challenging the Text

? Why does Swift include the passage about the enormous flies?

[Sample responses: To show the relativity of size to bravery; to emphasize Gulliver's small size and vulnerability; to describe scientific detail on a near-microscopic level; to entertain.] **Do you think the imagery is effective?**

[Sample responses: Yes, it is memorable; or no, it is disgusting.]

Gulliver Exhibited to the Brobdingnag Farmer (19th century) by Richard Redgrave.

been accustomed several months to the sight and converse of this people, and observed every object upon which I cast my eyes, to be of proportionable magnitude, the horror I had first conceived from their bulk and aspect was so far worn off, that if I had then beheld a company of English lords and ladies in their finery and birthday clothes,[5] acting their several parts in the most courtly manner, of strutting, and bowing, and prating;[6] to say the truth, I should have been strongly tempted to laugh as much at them as this King and his grandees[7] did at me. Neither indeed could I forbear smiling at myself, when the Queen used to place me upon her hand toward a looking glass, by which both our persons appeared before me in full view together; and there could

be nothing more ridiculous than the comparison; so that I really began to imagine myself dwindled many degrees below my usual size. . . .

I was frequently rallied[8] by the Queen upon account of my fearfulness, and she used to ask me whether the people of my country were as great cowards as myself. The occasion was this: The kingdom is much pestered with flies in summer; and these odious insects, each of them as big as a Dunstable lark, hardly gave me any rest while I sat at dinner, with their continual humming and buzzing about my ears. They would sometimes alight upon my victuals, and leave their loathsome excrement or spawn behind, which to me was very visible, though not to the natives of that country, whose large optics were not so acute as

5. **birthday clothes:** new outfits worn on a royal's birthday.
6. **prating:** talking pompously.
7. **grandees** (gran·dēz′): important persons; from *grande,* Spanish and Portuguese for "a nobleman of the highest rank."

8. **rallied:** teased.

WORDS TO OWN
odious (ō′dē·əs) *adj.:* hateful; offensive.

498 THE RESTORATION AND THE EIGHTEENTH CENTURY

OPTIONS FOR TEACHING

INTEGRATING THE LANGUAGE ARTS

Language and Vocabulary To show contrasting **points of view** and resulting differences in **diction,** have the class list Gulliver's words describing his society and then record the king of Brobdingnag's vocabulary for Gulliver's society. Have the class compare and contrast the two lists, matching the synonyms and antonyms in the lists and then drawing conclusions about the effect word choice has on communication. Organize information using a chart like the following.

Gulliver's Words	The King's Words

Writing: Handbook Swift used Gulliver's situation to expose his society's shortcomings and idiosyncrasies. Ask students to imagine explaining their world to a being from another planet; then, have them write a handbook on understanding and surviving in their own culture, group, organization, or society. Ask them to consider as they write what someone unfamiliar with that group or society might find unusual or difficult to understand.

T498 The Restoration and the Eighteenth Century

mine in viewing smaller objects. Sometimes they would fix upon my nose or forehead, where they stung me to the quick, smelling very offensively, and I could easily trace that <u>viscous</u> matter, which our naturalists tell us enables those creatures to walk with their feet upward upon a ceiling. I had much ado to defend myself against these detestable animals, and could not forbear starting when they came on my face. It was the common practice of the dwarf to catch a number of these insects in his hand, as schoolboys do among us, and let them out suddenly under my nose, on purpose to frighten me, and divert the Queen. My remedy was to cut them in pieces with my knife as they flew in the air, wherein my dexterity was much admired. . . .

He [the King] was perfectly astonished with the historical account I gave him of our affairs during the last century, protesting it was only an heap of conspiracies, rebellions, murders, massacres, revolutions, banishments; the very worst effects that avarice, faction, hypocrisy, perfidiousness, cruelty, rage, madness, hatred, envy, lust, malice, and ambition, could produce.

His Majesty, in another audience, was at the pains to recapitulate the sum of all I had spoken; compared the questions he made with the answers I had given; then taking me into his hands, and stroking me gently, delivered himself in these words, which I shall never forget, nor the manner he spoke them in. "My little friend Grildrig,[9] you have made a most admirable panegyric upon your country. You have clearly proved that ignorance, idleness, and vice, are the proper ingredients for qualifying a legislator: that laws are best explained, interpreted, and applied by those whose interest and abilities lie in perverting, confounding, and eluding them. I observe among you some lines of an institution, which in its original might have been tolerable, but these half erased, and the rest wholly blurred and blotted by corruptions. It doth not appear from all you have said, how any one perfection[10] is required toward the procurement of any one station among you; much less that men are ennobled on account of their virtue, that priests are advanced for their piety or learning, soldiers for their conduct or valor, judges for

9. **Grildrig:** the Brobdingnagians' name for Gulliver.
10. **perfection:** virtue.

their integrity, senators for the love of their country, or counselors for their wisdom. As for yourself (continued the King), who have spent the greatest part of your life in traveling, I am well disposed to hope you may hitherto have escaped many vices of your country. But by what I have gathered from your own relation, and the answers I have with much pains wringed and extorted from you, I cannot but conclude the bulk of your natives to be the most <u>pernicious</u> race of little odious vermin that nature ever suffered to crawl upon the surface of the earth."

Gulliver in Brobdingnag (c. late 19th to early 20th century). Original watercolor illustration by Arthur Rackham for *Gulliver's Travels.*

Private Collection.

WORDS TO OWN
viscous (vis′kəs) *adj.*: having the form of a sticky fluid.
pernicious (pər·nish′·əs) *adj.*: wicked; extremely harmful.

JONATHAN SWIFT 499

B. Literary Element: Satire
? What clues indicate that the king's words are lambasting English society? [Possible answers: His manner of delivery; his heavy sarcasm in noting that "proper" qualifications for leaders include "ignorance, idleness, and vice"; his insinuation that those who should govern with justice are actually deceitful.]

C. Reader's Response: Connecting with the Text
? Do you think the criticism of England applies as well to other societies? [Sample responses: Yes, many societies fall prey to vice, corruption, or hypocrisy; or no, the king assumes the worst about the English due to Gulliver's account, so the king's criticisms are not well founded.]

PROFESSIONAL NOTES

Critical Comment: Swift's Genius Allan Bloom calls Swift's travelogue "an amazing rhetorical achievement. It is the classic children's story and it is a rather obscene tale. Swift was able to charm innocence and amuse corruption, and this is a measure of his talent. . . . Swift had not only the judgment with which to arrive at a reasoned view of the world, but the fancy by means of which he could recreate that world in a form which teaches where argument fails and which satisfies all while misleading none." Ask students how the travelogue "teaches where argument fails." [Possible answers: Swift shows rather than tells; his symbolic use of size implies that power is relative; conversations, rather than lectures, lead readers to Swift's conclusions.]

ASSESSMENT TOOLS

Check Test: True-False
1. Gulliver is never invited to dine with the king and queen. [False]
2. Gulliver and the king have many conversations about manners, religion, government, and other matters. [True]
3. The queen holds Gulliver in her hand to compare their sizes in a mirror. [True]
4. Gulliver is disturbed by the flies in the kingdom. [True]
5. The king decides Gulliver's countrymen are admirable people. [False]

Making Meanings

First Thoughts

1. Many students will see the royal family as benevolent, while some might see the king and queen as condescending and patronizing. They might be thought condescending, arrogant, cruel in their humor, and judgmental. Some possible virtues are kindness, sympathy, encouragement, inquisitiveness, and cleverness.

Reviewing the Text

a. An insect.
b. According to Gulliver, English people think of themselves as noble, creative, powerful, virtuous, and honorable.
c. He uses his knife to kill in midair huge flies that annoy him.
d. According to the king, the qualifications for English legislators are ignorance, idleness, and vice.

Shaping Interpretations

2. The king implies that he finds the distinction between the political factions silly, although British society finds it important.
3. Possible response: He sees himself next to the queen in the mirror; and the flies, to him, are as large as larks.
4. The king's speeches to Gulliver indicate that he is intelligent and perceptive, perhaps even cynical. The king's gentle treatment of Gulliver may mean he is kind, or it may also imply condescension.
5. One example is Gulliver's indignation that the king sullies England's reputation, although the king is going by Gulliver's account. Another instance of verbal irony occurs when the king says that "ignorance, idleness, and vice" are the qualifications for officials in England.
6. Gulliver is sickened by the flies, and the king is disgusted by Gulliver's people.
7. In Part 2, the king points out the shortcomings of English society *directly,* although Gulliver has already alluded to the same issues with the Lilliputians.

MAKING MEANINGS

First Thoughts

1. What do you think of the Brobdingnagian royal family? What faults and virtues do you see in them?

Shaping Interpretations

2. Explain why the king roars with laughter when he asks Gulliver whether he is a Whig or a Tory.
3. Why does Gulliver begin to think of himself as small?
4. How does Swift **characterize** the king of Brobdingnag? Which actions show the king's personality traits?
5. Where does Swift use **verbal irony** to make his points?
6. What connections can you make between Gulliver's experience with the Brobdingnagian flies and the king's dismissal of humanity as "little odious vermin"?
7. In comparison to the **satire** in Part 1 of the *Travels,* how does the satire in Part 2 increase the urgency of Swift's case for the reformation of vice and folly?
8. What evidence can you find in the text to suggest that Gulliver is learning little or nothing from his experiences in Brobdingnag?

Extending the Text

9. Find at least one passage in the Brobdingnag episode that could apply to politics in the United States today.

> ## Reviewing the Text
>
> a. To what form of life does the king first compare Gulliver?
> b. In comparison, what do English people think of themselves, according to Gulliver?
> c. What feat of dexterity can Gulliver perform that impresses the Brobdingnagians?
> d. From Gulliver's defense of England, the king evaluates English officials and institutions. According to the king, what are the qualifications for English legislators?

8. Gulliver reacts indignantly to the king's comparison of human beings with insects. After his experiences in Lilliput, he should understand the relationship of perspective to individual interpretation of reality. Students might also bring up Gulliver's naive defense of England.

ELEMENTS OF LITERATURE

Satire: Bitter Laughter

A **satire** is any piece of writing designed to make its readers feel critical—of themselves, of their fellow human beings, of their society. Some satires are intended to make us laugh at human follies and weaknesses; others make us angry and indignant at human vices and crimes. In *The Rape of the Lock* (page 527), Alexander Pope provides many examples of the good-natured, laughable kind of satire. Like Pope's, Swift's satire also provokes laughter, but often laughter of a bitter kind.

While satire is usually directed at humanity in general, or at stereotyped groups of people such as clumsy surgeons or greedy lawyers, it can also be aimed at a particular person. In *Gulliver's Travels,* for instance, Swift satirizes the prime minister Sir Robert Walpole, whom he believed to be corrupt, calling him "Flimnap."

Satirists are dissatisfied with things as they are, and they want to make them better. Instead of giving constructive advice, though, they emphasize what is wrong with the world and its inhabitants. They don't say "Be good!" "Obey the Golden Rule!" "Put others before yourself." Instead, they make fun of vicious, selfish, mean-spirited people in the hope that we will see ourselves in such people and mend our ways. Satirists perform an important function in society when they expose errors and absurdities that we no longer notice because custom and familiarity have blinded us to them.

One of the devices that satirists use to make folly and vice appear ridiculous, and therefore unattractive, is **exaggeration.** We must not expect satirists to be objective, to give both sides of a question, to show the good as well as the bad traits of a character. Instead, satirists are likely to exaggerate by picturing all politicians as corrupt, all members of the clergy as hypocritical, all teachers as pedantic, all young adults as irresponsible. They realize that such generalizations cannot be 100 percent accurate, but for satirical purposes exceptions do not count. Wildly extravagant exaggeration, or **hyperbole,** is conspicuous in popular magazines such as *Mad*—though *Mad*'s satire lacks the moral purposes and subtlety of Swift's and Pope's satire.

Extending the Text

9. **(Analysis and Evaluation)** One point is political corruption: "'They love, they fight, they dispute, they cheat, they betray.'"

The great satirists expect their readers to be alert and intelligent enough to detect the presence of satire even when there is no exaggeration. For instance, Swift once wrote, without any explanation at all, "Last week I saw a woman flayed, and you will hardly believe how much it altered her appearance for the worst." Since to "flay" a person is to peel off the skin (a common form of capital punishment in those days), Swift's remark is a complete **understatement**—the opposite of an exaggeration. By making the statement sound shockingly casual and offhanded, Swift implies that such cruelty is common but that people do not become upset by it and instead pretend to have no concern at all.

Understatement is a form of **irony,** the device of saying one thing and meaning just the opposite. When irony is particularly cruel or cutting, it can come close to **sarcasm.** "Great!" we say sarcastically, when we actually mean "Terrible!" In literature, irony is extended far beyond mere sarcasm. In his *Directions for Servants,* for instance, Swift, under the pretense of telling servants how to behave, actually tells them how to misbehave—and in great detail. Here is how he advises servants to respond to a request for a drink.

> When you carry a glass of liquor to any person who hath called for it, do not bob him on the shoulder, or cry, "Sir, or madam, here's the glass!" That would be unmannerly, as if you had a mind to force it down one's throat. But stand at the person's left shoulder and wait his time; and if he strikes it down with his elbow by forgetfulness, that was his fault and not yours.

Ironic advice of this sort is more amusing and much more memorable than straightforward, sincere advice.

A writer who habitually uses irony runs the risk of being misunderstood, especially by people who are mentally inert. As an ironist, Swift earned a reputation for being scandalous, irresponsible, and even irreligious. Yet he claimed he never wrote anything "without a moral view."

COOKE'S POCKET EDITION SELECT NOVELS.

Brobdingnag (c. 1800) drawn by R. Corbould, engraved by C. Warren, from *Cooke's Pocket Edition of Select Novels.*

1. According to Swift, what is basically wrong with the world and its inhabitants? How do you feel about the moral standards he implies we should follow in public and private life?
2. Where do you see the techniques of Swiftian satire put to use today? What are some of the specific targets of contemporary satire?
3. Swift's novel is highly visual, and many artists have illustrated Gulliver and his travels. If you like to draw, you might try to illustrate one of Gulliver's adventures. Try to make the satire obvious by visual exaggeration.

Elements of Literature

Mini-Lesson: Satire

Ask students to summarize their responses to Swift's satire. [Responses include: Laughter, disgust, enlightenment, curiosity, judgment, inspiration, or action.] Map their various reactions on the chalkboard, using a cluster diagram with **satire** in the center circle, including also the reasons behind students' responses. Point out that satire often elicits different interpretations.

Continue by reviewing **exaggeration** and **understatement, irony** and **sarcasm.** Show students their similarities by asking students to make a point using first exaggeration and then rephrasing the point using understatement. Demonstrate also that understatement is a form of irony, and that irony and sarcasm overlap.

Answers

1. Two main ideas pervade these selections from *Gulliver's Travels:* Corruption and pettiness. Some students will feel Swift is too strict and unrealistic in his expectations of moral behavior, while others will support his implied standards of honesty, integrity, and reluctance to enter into conflict.
2. Students will most likely mention examples from electronic media, particularly comedy skits, sitcoms, animated cartoons, or movies. Others cited might be magazine features, novels, comic strips, or editorial cartoons. There are many popular targets, including politicians, celebrities, and social behavior.
3. Encourage students to use visual exaggeration, perhaps through caricature, size, or incongruous activity.

Considering this was written more
than two centuries ago, there are striking similarities to modern society.
What details in this paragraph relate
to contemporary social issues? [Sam-
ple responses: Hunger, homelessness,
or poverty.]

B. Critical Reading: Identifying
Main Ideas

? What does Swift claim as his purpose in writing this essay? [Possi-
ble answers: To discover a fair, cheap,
and easy method for turning the street
urchins into productive members of
society; to propose solutions for the
panhandling problem; to receive praise
for halting the cycle of poverty.]

This is the best and most famous pamphlet that Swift wrote describing the desperate conditions in Ireland and protesting the English treatment of the Irish. For three
years before Swift published this pamphlet in 1729, the Irish harvests had been so
poor that little remained for the farmers, after selling their crops, to pay the rents
demanded by their English landlords. Beggars and starving children were everywhere. Money was in short supply. Swift argued that most of the money was
shipped off to England, where the landlords lived, and little remained in Ireland
to be spent on Irish goods. English policies kept the Irish poor and hungry.

In *A Modest Proposal,* Swift offers an outrageous solution to these problems of
human misery—perhaps the most outrageous solution ever offered. But there is
nothing outrageous about Swift's manner. In this pamphlet, he assumes the role of
a "practical" economic planner, pretending to be knowledgeable and objective,
reasonable and fair, and full of common sense and even benevolence. It is this
difference between its straightforward style and its appalling content that gives
the pamphlet its force.

Ultimately, Swift is protesting against a purely statistical view of humanity—a
view that would reduce people to breeders and babies to meat. Swift risks appearing as a monster himself in order to expose the monstrous behavior of others. As
you read, notice where in the essay you first realize what Swift's modest proposal is.

A Modest Proposal

Jonathan Swift

It is a melancholy object to those, who walk through this great town,[1] or travel in the country, when they see the streets, the roads, and
cabin doors, crowded with beggars of the female
sex, followed by three, four, or six children, all in
rags, and importuning every passenger for an
alms.[2] These mothers instead of being able to
work for their honest livelihood, are forced to employ all their time in strolling, to beg sustenance
for their helpless infants, who, as they grow up
either turn thieves for want[3] of work, or leave their
dear native country to fight for the Pretender[4] in
Spain, or sell themselves to the Barbadoes.[5]

I think it is agreed by all parties, that this prodigious number of children, in the arms, or on the

backs, or at the heels of their mothers, and
frequently of their fathers, is in the present deplorable state of the kingdom, a very great additional grievance; and therefore whoever could
find out a fair, cheap, and easy method of making
these children sound and useful members of the
commonwealth would deserve so well of the public, as to have his statue set up for a preserver of
the nation.

But my intention is very far from being confined to provide only for the children of professed
beggars; it is of a much greater extent, and shall
take in the whole number of infants at a certain
age, who are born of parents in effect as little able
to support them, as those who demand our charity in the streets.

As to my own part, having turned my thoughts,
for many years, upon this important subject, and

1. **town:** Dublin.
2. **importuning . . . alms:** asking passersby for a handout.
3. **want:** lack; need.
4. **the Pretender:** James Edward (1688–1766), son of
England's last Catholic king, the deposed James II
(1633–1701); James Edward made several attempts to gain
the English throne.
5. **sell . . . Barbadoes:** go to the West Indies and work as
indentured servants to pay their passage.

502 THE RESTORATION AND THE EIGHTEENTH CENTURY

OPTIONS FOR TEACHING

STRATEGIES FOR INCLUSION

Special Needs To help students distinguish
between literal and nonliteral interpretations,
remind them that both understatement (in the
title) and exaggeration (in the selection itself)
are techniques used for calling attention to a
problem and for making a point.

Less Proficient Readers Assign students to
pairs, and have one partner read aloud the first
sentence in a designated passage; have the other
translate the phrase into modern English. Then,
have the partners exchange roles for the next
sentence and continue until they finish the
passage.

maturely weighed the several schemes of other projectors,[6] I have always found them grossly mistaken in their computation. It is true a child, just dropped from its dam,[7] may be supported by her milk, for a solar year[8] with little other nourishment, at most not above the value of two shillings, which the mother may certainly get, or the value in scraps, by her lawful occupation of begging, and it is exactly at one year old that I propose to provide for them, in such a manner, as, instead of being a charge upon their parents, or the parish, or wanting food and raiment[9] for the rest of their lives, they shall, on the contrary, contribute to the feeding and partly to the clothing of many thousands.

There is likewise another great advantage in my scheme, that it will prevent those voluntary abortions, and that horrid practice of women murdering their bastard children, alas! too frequent among us, sacrificing the poor innocent babes, I doubt,[10] more to avoid the expense, than the shame, which would move tears and pity in the most savage and inhuman breast.

The number of souls[11] in Ireland being usually reckoned one million and a half, of these I calculate there may be about two hundred thousand couples whose wives are breeders, from which number I subtract thirty thousand couples, who are able to maintain their own children, although I apprehend there cannot be so many under the present distresses of the kingdom, but this being granted, there will remain an hundred and seventy thousand breeders. I again subtract fifty thousand for those women who miscarry, or whose children die by accident, or disease within the year. There only remain an hundred and twenty thousand children of poor parents annually born: The question therefore is, how this number shall be reared, and provided for, which, as I have already said, under the present situation of affairs, is utterly impossible by all the methods hitherto proposed, for we can neither employ them in handicraft,[12] or agriculture; we neither build houses (I mean in the country) nor cultivate land: They can very seldom pick up a livelihood by stealing until they arrive at six years old, except where they are of towardly parts,[13] although, I confess they learn the rudiments much earlier, during which time, they can however be properly looked upon only as probationers,[14] as I have been informed by a principal gentleman in the county of Cavan,[15] who protested to me, that he never knew above one or two instances under the age of six, even in a part of the kingdom so renowned for the quickest proficiency in that art.[16]

I am assured by our merchants, that a boy or girl, before twelve years old, is no saleable commodity, and even when they come to this age, they will not yield above three pounds, or three pounds and half a crown at most on the exchange, which cannot turn to account[17] either to the parents or the kingdom, the charge of nutriment and rags having been at least four times that value.

I shall now therefore humbly propose my own thoughts, which I hope will not be liable to the least objection.

I have been assured by a very knowing American[18] of my acquaintance in London, that a young healthy child well nursed is at a year old a most delicious, nourishing, and wholesome food, whether stewed, roasted, baked, or boiled, and I make no doubt that it will equally serve in a fricassee,[19] or ragout.[20]

I do therefore humbly offer it to public consideration, that of the hundred and twenty thousand children, already computed, twenty thousand may be reserved for breed, whereof only one-fourth part to be males, which is more than we allow to sheep, black cattle, or swine, and my reason is that these children are seldom the fruits of marriage, a circumstance not much regarded by our savages; therefore one male will be sufficient to serve four females. That the remaining hundred thousand

13. **of towardly parts:** exceptionally advanced or mature for their age.
14. **probationers:** apprentices.
15. **Cavan:** inland county in Ireland that is remote from Dublin.
16. **art:** stealing.
17. **turn to account:** be profitable.
18. **American:** To Swift's readers, this label would suggest a barbaric person.
19. **fricassee** (frĭk′ə·sē′): stew with a light gravy.
20. **ragout** (ra·gōō′): highly flavored stew.

6. **projectors:** speculators; schemers.
7. **dam:** mother (ordinarily used only of animals).
8. **solar year:** from the first day of spring in one year to the last day of winter in the next.
9. **raiment** (rā′mənt): clothing.
10. **doubt:** suspect.
11. **souls:** people.
12. **handicraft:** manufacturing.

C. Language Note: Diction

? Up to this point, what words seem particularly derogatory, and why? What do you think Swift's purpose is in selecting these words? [Answers will vary. "Breeders" seems particularly demeaning to women; "strolling" implies that some are begging at leisure instead of in desperation. Swift may have selected these words to mimic the attitude of people who have no sympathy for the population he describes; the words make the tone of the essay seem coldhearted, calculating, and efficient.]

D. Critical Reading: Making Inferences

? How are these remarks about stealing **ironic**? [Possible answers: Generally people want children to grow up and get good jobs, so it is ironic to train them to steal. The remarks mock the English stereotype of the Irish as dishonest.] Are these ideas reflected in modern stereotypes? [Possible answers: Often people with more money are suspicious of those who have less; some groups distrust others whom they believe are less honorable.]

E. Literary Element: Satire

? What methods of satire are used in this passage about the market value of children? [Answers may include understatement (the idea of pricing a child); verbal irony (society's most valuable human resource, a child, is worthless); situational irony (the author's suggestion is not "modest," but instead outrageous); exaggeration (presenting the ridiculous as real); and parody (mimicking a scientific method).]

F. Exploring the Historical Period

? What does this comment reveal about attitudes of the time? How is it **ironic**? [Possible answers: Swift plays on the attitude that the people he calls "Americans" are uncivilized and inferior to Europeans; he even insinuates that they are cannibals. However, the comment is hypocritical: Cannibalism is exactly what Swift proposes.]

G. Critical Reading: Identifying Main Ideas

? What does Swift propose to do with the children? [Answers include: Eat them; cook them; harvest them; or sell them.] Point out that many readers took Swift literally and accused him of promoting cannibalism.

STRATEGIES FOR INCLUSION

Logical-Mathematical Have students work through the formulas Swift presents, determining whether his calculations are accurate and whether he has accounted for appropriate variables.

Advanced Ask students to research the various political parties in the British Isles and their interactions at the time Swift published *A Modest Proposal* (1729). Also ask them to find out how this essay was received once it was published. Have them share their findings in class discussion.

INTEGRATING THE LANGUAGE ARTS

Strategic Reading As they are reading the essay, have students record the textual references that lead them to guess the proposal. Then, have them compare results after they finish reading the essay: What is the first inkling or hint recorded by the students? Do some disagree? Why? ☞

A. Literary Element: Pun

? How does Swift play on the meanings of *devoured*? [Possible answer: Not only does it refer to eating, it refers to the idea that the rich have already consumed the resources of the parents.]

B. Critical Reading: Identifying Main Ideas

? According to the speaker, what is another positive outcome of this proposal? [There would be fewer Roman Catholics, as their children would be eaten.] Note Swift's allusion to Lent. *Prolific* refers to the alleged capacity of fish to enhance fertility. Catholics observing Lenten practices would abstain from meat and eat more fish.

Dudley Street, Seven Dials, London.

may at a year old be offered in sale to the persons of quality, and fortune, through the kingdom, always advising the mother to let them suck plentifully in the last month, so as to render them plump, and fat for a good table. A child will make two dishes at an entertainment for friends, and when the family dines alone, the fore or hind quarter will make a reasonable dish, and seasoned with a little pepper or salt will be very good boiled on the fourth day, especially in winter.

I have reckoned upon a medium, that a child just born will weigh twelve pounds, and in a solar year if tolerably nursed increaseth to twenty-eight pounds.

I grant this food will be somewhat dear,[21] and therefore very proper for landlords, who, as they have already devoured[22] most of the parents, seem to have the best title to the children.

21. **dear:** expensive.
22. **devoured:** made poor by charging high rents.

Infant's flesh will be in season throughout the year, but more plentiful in March, and a little before and after, for we are told by a grave author,[23] an eminent French physician, that fish being a prolific diet, there are more children born in Roman Catholic countries about nine months after Lent, than at any other season, therefore reckoning a year after Lent, the markets will be more glutted than usual, because the number of popish[24] infants, is at least three to one in this kingdom, and therefore it will have one other collateral advantage by lessening the number of papists among us.

23. **author:** François Rabelais (frän·swȧ′ rab′ə·lā′) (c. 1483–1553), French satirist; his work is comic, not "grave."
24. **popish:** Roman Catholic; a derogatory term.

WORDS TO OWN
glutted (glut′id) *v.*: overfilled.

504 THE RESTORATION AND THE EIGHTEENTH CENTURY

INTEGRATING THE LANGUAGE ARTS

Language and Vocabulary To see why many readers took Swift's proposal seriously, students might study Swift's word choice and style. Have students work in pairs to search the text for words and phrases that may be taken either literally or satirically. A sample graphic organizer follows.

Phrase	Literal Meaning	Satiric Meaning
["I profess in the sincerity of my heart that I have not the least personal interest in endeavoring to promote this necessary work"]	[He does not have a personal motive—implies he puts the good of others first.]	[Ironically, he really does not want to promote this plan; he wants people to see its absurdity.]

Writing: Satire Have students write **satires** about a school or community issue of their choice. Encourage the use of logical language and reason, as well as the devices of satire: exaggeration, understatement, irony, and sarcasm. Remind students of the value of humor in making a point, poking fun at a ridiculous situation, or offering a "reasonable" solution to a problem.

I have already computed the charge of nursing a beggar's child (in which list I reckon all cottagers,[25] laborers, and four-fifths of the farmers) to be about two shillings per annum,[26] rags included, and I believe no gentleman would repine to give ten shillings for the carcass of a good fat child, which, as I have said will make four dishes of excellent nutritive meat, when he hath only some particular friend, or his own family to dine with him. Thus the squire will learn to be a good landlord, and grow popular among his tenants, the mother will have eight shillings net profit, and be fit for work until she produceth another child.

Those who are more thrifty (as I must confess the times require) may flay[27] the carcass; the skin of which, artificially[28] dressed, will make admirable gloves for ladies, and summer boots for fine gentlemen.

As to our city of Dublin, shambles[29] may be appointed for this purpose, in the most convenient parts of it, and butchers we may be assured will not be wanting, although I rather recommend buying the children alive, and dressing them hot from the knife, as we do roasting pigs.

A very worthy person, a true lover of his country, and whose virtues I highly esteem, was lately pleased, in discoursing on this matter, to offer a refinement upon my scheme. He said, that many gentlemen of this kingdom, having of late destroyed their deer, he conceived that the want of venison might be well supplied by the bodies of young lads and maidens, not exceeding fourteen years of age, nor under twelve, so great a number of both sexes in every country being now ready to starve, for want of work and service:[30] and these to be disposed of by their parents if alive, or otherwise by their nearest relations. But with due deference to so excellent a friend, and so deserving a patriot, I cannot be altogether in his sentiments, for as to the males, my American acquaintance assured me from frequent experience, that their flesh was generally tough and lean, like that of our schoolboys, by continual exercise, and their taste disagreeable, and to fatten them would not

25. **cottagers:** tenant farmers.
26. **per annum:** Latin for "by the year"; annually.
27. **flay:** remove the skin of.
28. **artificially:** with great artifice; that is, skillfully.
29. **shambles:** slaughterhouses.
30. **service:** employment as servants.

answer the charge. Then as to the females, it would, I think with humble submission,[31] be a loss to the public, because they soon would become breeders themselves: And besides it is not improbable that some scrupulous people might be apt to censure such a practice (although indeed very unjustly) as a little bordering upon cruelty, which, I confess, hath always been with me the strongest objection against any project, how well soever intended.

But in order to justify my friend, he confessed that this expedient was put into his head by the famous Sallmanaazor,[32] a native of the island Formosa, who came from thence to London, above twenty years ago, and in conversation told my friend, that in his country when any young person happened to be put to death, the executioner sold the carcass to persons of quality, as a prime dainty, and that, in his time, the body of a plump girl of fifteen, who was crucified for an attempt to poison the emperor, was sold to his imperial majesty's prime minister of state, and other great mandarins[33] of the court, in joints[34] from the gibbet,[35] at four hundred crowns. Neither indeed can I deny, that if the same use were made of several plump young girls in this town, who, without one single groat to their fortunes, cannot stir abroad without a chair,[36] and appear at the playhouse, and assemblies in foreign fineries, which they never will pay for; the kingdom would not be the worse.

31. **with humble submission:** with all due respect to those who hold such opinions.
32. **Sallmanaazor:** George Psalmanazar (c. 1679–1763), a Frenchman who pretended to be from Formosa, an old Portuguese name for Taiwan; his writings were eventually exposed as fraudulent.
33. **mandarins** (man′də·rinz): officials. The term comes from *mandarim*, the Portuguese word for high-ranking officials in the Chinese empire, with which the Portuguese traded.
34. **joints:** pieces of meat.
35. **gibbet** (jib′it): gallows.
36. **chair:** sedan chair; a covered seat carried by servants.

- -

WORDS TO OWN
deference (def′ər·əns) *n.*: respect.
scrupulous (skrōō′pyə·ləs) *adj.*: extremely careful and precise in deciding what is right or wrong.
censure (sen′shər) *v.*: to condemn.
expedient (ek·spē′dē·ənt) *n.*: convenient means to an end.

- -

JONATHAN SWIFT **505**

C. Critical Reading: Making Generalizations

? How do the mathematical and statistical references enhance the **irony** of the essay? [Possible answers: The writer seems precise and scientific while proposing a shocking solution; the references lend authenticity to a facetious proposal.]

D. Reader's Response: Shaping Interpretations

? What is your reaction to this comment? How do comments like this seem to further Swift's purpose? [Sample responses: It is ironic that he pretends to object to cruelty, just after a discussion of flaying people. He seems critical of "scrupulous people" yet pretends himself to be scrupulous, which makes me distrust his words even more. Swift probably intended to appall readers. This sarcasm indicates that the essay is not to be taken seriously.]

CROSSING THE CURRICULUM

Geography Have students research relationships among the European nations during the eighteenth century. Distribute outline maps of Europe so that students can color-code the various alliances that grew from the animosity between Ireland and England.

Social Sciences Since the shortage of food is addressed in this selection, have students research the nineteenth-century potato famine in Ireland.

Ask them to write a newspaper-style article about the causes, effects, and results.

Mathematics Have students figure the current population, the number of childbirths per year, the number of marriages per year, and the average number of children per family for their community, town, or state. Ask them to graph these figures and to calculate the population for that microcosm in ten years, assuming that no one moves away.

CLASSROOM MANAGEMENT

Rewards Humorous or small rewards work well: a copy of a cartoon or caricature of the time; a copy of a contemporaneous map of the British Isles, Ireland, or Dublin; a chapbook of *A Modest Proposal;* a bookmark; a book plate; a shamrock plant; special pens or pencils; extra time in the library or at the computer; or extra credit. ☞

A Some persons of a desponding spirit are in great concern about that vast number of poor people, who are aged, diseased, or maimed, and I have been desired to employ my thoughts what course may be taken, to ease the nation of so grievous an encumbrance. But I am not in the least pain upon that matter, because it is very well known, that they are every day dying, and rotting, by cold, and famine, and filth, and vermin,[37] as fast as can be reasonably expected. And as to the younger laborers they are now in almost as hopeful[38] a condition. They cannot get work, and consequently pine away for want of nourishment, to a degree, that if at any time they are accidentally hired to common labor, they have not strength to perform it, and thus the country and themselves are in a fair way[39] of being soon delivered from the evils to come.

I have too long digressed, and therefore shall return to my subject. I think the advantages by the proposal which I have made are obvious and many as well as of the highest importance.

For first, as I have already observed, it would greatly lessen the number of papists, with whom we are yearly overrun, being the principal breeders of the nation, as well as our most dangerous enemies, and who stay at home on purpose with a design to deliver the kingdom to the Pretender, hoping to take their advantage by the absence of so many good Protestants,[40] who have chosen rather to leave their country, than stay at home, and pay tithes[41] against their conscience, to an idolatrous Episcopal curate.

B **C** Secondly, the poorer tenants will have something valuable of their own, which by law may be made liable to distress,[42] and help to pay their landlord's rent, their corn and cattle being already seized, and money a thing unknown.

D Thirdly, whereas the maintenance of an hundred thousand children, from two years old, and upwards, cannot be computed at less than ten shillings apiece per annum, the nation's stock will be thereby increased fifty thousand pounds per annum, besides the profit of a new dish, introduced to the tables of all gentlemen of fortune in the kingdom, who have any refinement in taste, and the money will circulate among ourselves, the goods being entirely of our own growth and manufacture.[43]

Fourthly, the constant breeders, besides the gain of eight shillings sterling per annum, by the sale of their children, will be rid of the charge of maintaining them after the first year.

Fifthly, this food would likewise bring great custom to taverns, where the vintners[44] will certainly be so prudent as to procure the best receipts[45] for dressing it to perfection, and consequently have their houses frequented by all the fine gentlemen, who justly value themselves upon their knowledge in good eating, and a skillful cook, who understands how to oblige his guests will contrive to make it as expensive as they please.

Sixthly, this would be a great inducement to marriage, which all wise nations have either encouraged by rewards, or enforced by laws and penalties. It would increase the care and tenderness of mothers toward their children, when they were sure of a settlement for life to the poor babes, provided in some sort by the public to their annual profit instead of expense, we should soon see an honest emulation[46] among the married women, which of them could bring the fattest child to the market, men would become as fond of their wives, during the time of their pregnancy, as they are now of their mares in foal, their cows in calf, or sows when they are ready to farrow,[47] nor offer to beat or kick them (as is too frequent a practice) for fear of a miscarriage.

Many other advantages might be enumerated. For instance, the addition of some thousand car-

---

37. vermin: pests such as lice, fleas, and bedbugs.
38. hopeful: actually, hopeless. Swift is using the word with intentional irony.
39. are in a fair way: have a good chance.
40. good Protestants: that is, in Swift's view, bad Protestants, because they object to the Church of Ireland's bishops and regard them as "idolatrous."
41. tithes (tīthz): monetary gifts to the church equivalent to one tenth of each donor's income.
42. liable to distress: That is, the money from the sale of their children may be seized by their landlords.

43. own growth and manufacture: home-grown, edible children, not imported ones.
44. vintners (vint′nərz): wine merchants.
45. receipts: old-fashioned for "recipes."
46. emulation (em′yoō·lā′·shən): competition.
47. farrow (far′ō): produce piglets.

WORDS TO OWN

digressed (di·grest′) v.: wandered off the subject.
procure (prō·kyoor′) v.: to obtain; get.

---

casses in our exportation of barreled beef. The propagation of swine's flesh, and improvement in the art of making good bacon, so much wanted among us by the great destruction of pigs, too frequent at our tables, which are no way comparable in taste, or magnificence to a well-grown, fat yearling child, which roasted whole will make a considerable figure at a Lord Mayor's feast, or any other public entertainment. But this, and many others I omit being studious of _brevity_.

Supposing that one thousand families in this city, would be constant customers for infants' flesh, besides others who might have it at merry meetings, particularly weddings and christenings, I compute that Dublin would take off annually about twenty thousand carcasses, and the rest of the kingdom (where probably they will be sold somewhat cheaper) the remaining eighty thousand.

I can think of no one objection, that will possibly be raised against this proposal, unless it should be urged that the number of people will be thereby much lessened in the kingdom. This I freely own, and it was indeed one principal design in offering it to the world. I desire the reader will observe, that I calculate my remedy for this one individual kingdom of Ireland, and for no other that ever was, is, or, I think, ever can be upon earth. Therefore let no man talk to me of other expedients:[48] *Of taxing our absentees[49] at five shillings a pound; of using neither clothes, nor household furniture, except what is of our own growth and manufacture; of utterly rejecting the materials and instruments that promote foreign luxury; of curing the expensiveness of pride, vanity, idleness, and gaming[50] in our women; of introducing a vein of parsimony,[51] prudence, and temperance; of learning to love our country, wherein we differ even from Laplanders, and the inhabitants of Topinamboo;[52]*

London beggars (1692). Engraving.

of quitting our <u>animosities</u>, and factions,[53] nor act any longer like the Jews, who were murdering one another at the very moment their city[54] was taken; of being a little cautious not to sell our country and consciences for nothing; of teaching landlords to have at least one degree of mercy toward their tenants. Lastly of putting a spirit of honesty, industry, and skill into our

48. other expedients: At one time or another, Swift had advocated all these measures for the relief of Ireland, but they were all ignored by the government. This section was italicized in all editions printed during Swift's lifetime to indicate that Swift made these proposals sincerely rather than ironically.
49. absentees: English people who refused to live on their Irish property.
50. gaming: gambling.
51. parsimony (pär′sə·mō′nē): thriftiness; economy.
52. Topinamboo: Swift is referring to a region of Brazil in which reside various native peoples collectively called the Tupinambá. Here, Swift suggests that if Brazilian

peoples and Laplanders can love their seemingly inhospitable lands, the Irish should love Ireland.
53. factions: political groups that work against the interests of other such groups or against the main body of government.
54. city: Jerusalem, which the Roman emperor Titus (A.D. 39–81) destroyed in A.D. 70, while Jewish factions fought one another.

WORDS TO OWN
brevity (brev′ə·tē) *n.:* being brief.
animosities (an′ə·mäs′ə·tēz) *n. pl.:* hostilities; violent hatreds or resentments.

E. Critical Reading: Drawing Conclusions

? Are the other "expedients" listed here constructive suggestions? Why does Swift dismiss them? [Possible answers: Many of the solutions here are quite reasonable; Swift dismisses these suggestions to emphasize that they have been previously rejected.] This passage reveals some biases of the eighteenth century: Note the cynical references to Laplanders and Brazilians (regarded by the eighteenth-century British as barbarians) and Jews.

PROFESSIONAL NOTES

Cultural Diversity Have students observe television news programs (daily news, features, news magazines) for examples of responses to or treatment of poverty. Have them record the program date, the example of poverty, the location, and the responses to or treatment of the issue. Wrap up by discussing these notes and drawing conclusions about the various ways people react to poverty and help the poor. ☞

A. Critical Reading: Making Connections

? What clues tell readers Swift's true feelings? What are those feelings? [Possible answers: His reference to "visionary" thoughts hints that he favors the solutions suggested previously. Swift seems to believe that society lacks the unity and determination to improve the lives of the poor and common, and he seems weary and frustrated by this.]

B. Critical Reading: Summarizing

From information in the essay, describe the cycle of poverty in Ireland at this time. [Possible answers: The system of oppression by landlords ensures that the working people, unable to make any money to pay rent, will have a chronic lack of shelter and clothing and will pass on the cycle to the next generation.]

C. Reader's Response: Challenging the Text

? What is the purpose behind Swift's concluding paragraph? [Sample responses: To adopt the pose of an unbiased, benevolent advocate; to disclaim any self-interest regarding the implementation of his proposal; to sound rational while proposing the irrational. It also shows hypocrisy, in that the speaker's family would not be affected by the practice he appears to advocate.]

shopkeepers, who, if a resolution could now be taken to buy only our native goods, would immediately unite to cheat and exact[55] upon us in the price, the measure, and the goodness, nor could ever yet be brought to make one fair proposal of just dealing, though often and earnestly invited to it.

Therefore I repeat, let no man talk to me of these and the like expedients, till he hath at least a glimpse of hope, that there will ever be some hearty and sincere attempt to put them in practice.

A But as to myself, having been wearied out for many years with offering vain, idle, visionary thoughts, and at length utterly despairing of success, I fortunately fell upon this proposal, which as it is wholly new, so it hath something solid and real, of no expense and little trouble, full in our own power, and whereby we can incur no danger in disobliging[56] England. For this kind of commodity will not bear exportation, the flesh being of too tender a consistence, to admit a long continuance in salt, although perhaps I could name a country,[57] which would be glad to eat up our whole nation without it.

After all I am not so violently bent upon my own opinion, as to reject any offer, proposed by wise men, which shall be found equally innocent, cheap, easy, and effectual. But before something of that kind shall be advanced in contradiction to my scheme, and offering a better, I desire the author, or authors will be pleased maturely to consider two points. First, as things now stand, how they will be able to find food and raiment for a hundred thousand useless mouths and backs. And **B** secondly, there being a round million of creatures in human figure, throughout this kingdom, whose whole subsistence[58] put into a common stock would leave them in debt two millions of pounds sterling, adding those who are beggars by profession to the bulk of farmers, cottagers, and laborers, with their wives and children, who are beggars in effect; I desire those politicians, who dislike my overture, and may perhaps be so bold to attempt an answer, that they will first ask the parents of these mortals, whether they would not

55. **exact:** force payment.
56. **disobliging:** offending.
57. **country:** England.
58. **whole subsistence:** all their possessions.

Orange Court, Drury Lane (19th century) by Gustave Doré.

at this day think it a great happiness to have been sold for food at a year old, in the manner I prescribe, and thereby have avoided such a perpetual scene of misfortunes, as they have since gone through, by the oppression of landlords, the impossibility of paying rent without money or trade, **B** the want of common sustenance, with neither house nor clothes to cover them from inclemencies of weather, and the most inevitable prospect of entailing[59] the like, or great miseries, upon their breed forever.

I profess in the sincerity of my heart that I have not the least personal interest in endeavoring to promote this necessary work, having no other motive than the public good of my country, by ad- **C** vancing our trade, providing for infants, relieving the poor, and giving some pleasure to the rich. I have no children, by which I can propose to get a single penny; the youngest being nine years old, and my wife past childbearing.

59. **entailing:** passing on to the next generation.

OPTIONS FOR TEACHING

ASSESSMENT TOOLS

Check Test: True-False

1. Swift's proposal takes into account only the children of beggars. [False]
2. Swift says the children born to poor parents in Ireland could become useful, productive citizens if they were well fed. [False]
3. The majority of male children would be saved for breeding purposes. [False]
4. Swift points out that one advantage of the proposal would be an increase in marriages. [True]
5. Swift recommends against exporting the new commodity. [True]

Peer Assessment Assign pairs of students to read and evaluate each others' satires from the Writing activity on p. T504 by answering these questions:
- Is the language of the solution logical, even if the concept is farfetched?

- How does the essay use **satire**?
- What is the **tone** of the essay: Is it humorous? Does it provoke anger? Does it move the reader to action?
- What is the essay's strongest point? weakest point?
- Is it an effective essay overall?

Top of the Food Chain

T. Coraghessan Boyle

The thing was, we had a little problem with the insect vector[1] there, and believe me, your tamer stuff, your Malathion and pyrethrum and the rest of the so-called environmentally safe products,[2] didn't begin to make a dent in it, not a dent, I mean it was utterly useless—we might as well have been spraying Chanel No. 5 for all the good it did. And you've got to realize these people were literally covered with insects day and night—and the fact that they hardly wore any clothes just compounded the problem. Picture if you can, gentlemen, a naked little two-year-old boy so black with flies and mosquitoes it looks like he's wearing long johns, or the young mother so racked with the malarial shakes she can't even lift a Diet Coke to her lips—it was pathetic, just pathetic, like something out of the Dark Ages . . . Well, anyway, the decision was made to go with DDT.[3] In the short term. Just to get the situation under control, you understand.

Yes, that's right, Senator, *DDT*: Dichlorodiphenyltrichloroethane.

Yes, I'm well aware of that fact, sir. But just because *we* banned it domestically, under pressure from the bird-watching contingent and the hopheads down at the EPA, it doesn't necessarily follow that the rest of the world—especially the developing world—was about to jump on the bandwagon. And that's the key

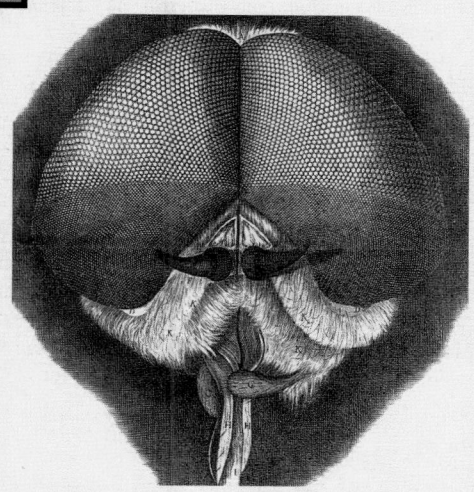

Eye of a Fly (1665) by Robert Hooke, from *Micrographia* (The Royal Society, London, 1665).

Rare Books and Manuscripts Division. The New York Public Library. Astor, Lenox and Tilden Foundations.

word here, Senator: developing. You've got to realize this is Borneo we're talking about here, not Port Townsend or Enumclaw. These people don't know from square one about sanitation, disease control, pest eradication. It rains a hundred and twenty inches a year, minimum.[4] They dig up roots in the jungle. They've still got headhunters along the Rajang River, for god's sake.

And please don't forget they *asked* us to come in there, practically begged us—and not only the World Health Organization but the Sultan of Brunei and the government in Sarawak too. We did what we could to accommodate them and reach our objective in the shortest period of time and by the most direct and effective means. We went to the air. Obviously. And no one could have foreseen the consequences, no one, not even if we'd gone

---

1. **vector:** bearer or carrier of disease.
2. **Malathion** (mal′ə·thī′än′) **and pyrethrum** (pī·reth′rəm) **. . . safe products:** Malathion and pyrethrum are insecticides made from organic substances. Though they are less toxic than synthetic, or human-made, insecticides, their safety is still debated.
3. **DDT:** a synthetic compound first discovered to be an insecticide in 1939. Widely used during World War II, DDT was later found to cause such toxic effects in other animal populations that its use was severely restricted in the United States in 1972.
4. **hundred and twenty inches . . . minimum:** In comparison, the average yearly rainfall in most of the United States is less than half this figure.

A. Critical Reading: Predicting

? What images brought to mind by this reference to the Dark Ages do you predict will appear later in this story? Jot answers in your Reader's Log. [Possible answers: The plague, rats, disease, suffering, ignorance, or helplessness.]

B. Critical Reading: Making Inferences

? What process or event is Boyle parodying or imitating in this story? [Possible answers: A Senate committee investigation; a governmental hearing.] What is the effect of reading only one side of this investigation, rather than also hearing any questions the speaker is asked? [Possible answers: Readers put the story in context through their own knowledge of historical situations; the style puts the narrator on the defensive.]

C. Reader's Response: First Thoughts

? What does the speaker's use of the word *developing* imply? [Sample responses: He thinks the country is uncivilized; he thinks scientific advances can only help the country.]

D. Literary Element: Foreshadowing

? What is the purpose of this passage? [To foreshadow negative consequences; to heighten suspense; to connect the consequences with the environment.]

CONNECTING WITH "A MODEST PROPOSAL"

What devices do both Boyle and Swift use to create their satires? [Outrageous solutions; exaggeration; biting barbs that condemn those the authors believe to be at fault; understatement.] Which satire do you find more effective and why?

[Boyle's satire of modern bureaucracy is more immediate, and so more humorous; or Swift's outrageous solution shows more of satire's range and power.]

A. Reader's Response: Shaping Interpretations

? What is the purpose of the reference to running shorts? [Sample responses: To emphasize the contrast between what the people wear and their traditional lifestyles; to show that manifestations of a more commercial society have appeared in Borneo; to make the people appear ridiculous.]

B. Language Note: Diction

? What does the use of the verb *shrug* reveal about the narrator's attitude? [Possible answers: He is acting cool and cavalier; he is indifferent.]

C. Critical Reading: Predicting

? What do you think might cause the collapse of palm-leaf roofs? [Possible answers: Insects; an imbalance in nature; the rain.]

Metacognition What textual clues support your explanation of the cause? [Possible answers: Foreshadowing of problems; caterpillars; pesticide spraying; disappearance of mosquitoes; the concern of the headman.] As students continue to read, have them note the accuracy of their prediction(s).

D. Critical Reading: Drawing Conclusions

? What attitude is shown by the narrator? [Possible answers: Patronizing; defensive; dismissive of valid complaints.]

out and generated a hundred environmental impact statements—it was just one of those things, a freak occurrence, and there's no defense against that. Not that I know of, anyway . . .

Caterpillars? Yes, Senator, that's correct. That was the first sign: caterpillars.

But let me backtrack a minute here. You see, out in the bush they have these roofs made of thatched palm leaves—you'll see them in the towns too, even in Bintulu or Brunei—and they're really pretty effective, you'd be surprised. A hundred and twenty inches of rain, they've got to figure a way to keep it out of the hut, and for centuries, this was it. Palm leaves. Well, it was about a month after we sprayed for the final time and I'm sitting at my desk in the trailer thinking about the drainage project at

Blue Fly (1665) by Robert Hooke, from *Micrographia* (The Royal Society, London, 1665).

Rare Books and Manuscripts Division. The New York Public Library. Astor, Lenox and Tilden Foundations.

Kuching, enjoying the fact that for the first time in maybe a year I'm not smearing mosquitoes all over the back of my neck, when there's a knock at the door. It's this elderly gentleman, tattooed from head to toe, dressed only in a pair of running shorts—they love those shorts, by the way, the shiny material and the tight machine stitching, the whole country, men and women both, they can't get enough of them. . . . Anyway, he's the headman of the local village and he's very excited, something about the roofs—*atap,* they call them. That's all he can say, *atap, atap,* over and over again.

It's raining, of course. It's always raining. So I shrug into my rain slicker, start up the 4 × 4, and go have a look. Sure enough, all the *atap* roofs are collapsing, not only in his village but

throughout the target area. The people are all huddled there in their running shorts, looking pretty miserable, and one after another the roofs keep falling in, it's bewildering, and gradually I realize the headman's diatribe has begun to feature a new term I was unfamiliar with at the time—the word for caterpillar, as it turns out, in the Iban dialect. But who was to make the connection between three passes with the crop duster and all these staved-in roofs?

Our people finally sorted it out a couple weeks later. The chemical, which, by the way, cut down the number of mosquitoes exponentially, had the unfortunate side effect of killing off this little wasp—I've got the scientific name for it somewhere in my report here, if you're interested—that preyed on a type of caterpillar that in turn ate palm leaves. Well, with the wasps gone, the caterpillars hatched out with nothing to keep them in check and chewed the roofs to pieces, which was unfortunate, we admit it, and we had a real cost overrun on replacing those roofs with tin . . . but the people were happier, I think, in the long run, because, let's face it, no matter how tightly you weave those palm leaves, they're just not going to keep the water out like tin. Of course, nothing's perfect, and we had a lot of complaints about the rain drumming on the panels, people unable to sleep, and what-have-you . . .

Yes, sir, that's correct—the flies were next.

Well, you've got to understand the magnitude of the fly problem in Borneo, there's nothing like it here to compare it with, except maybe a garbage strike in New York. Every minute of every day you've got flies everywhere, up your nose, in your mouth, your ears, your eyes, flies in your rice, your Coke, your Singapore sling, and your gin rickey. It's enough to drive you to distraction, not to mention the diseases these things carry, from dysentery to typhoid to cholera and back round the loop again. And once the mosquito population was down, the flies seemed to breed up to fill in the gap—Borneo wouldn't be Borneo without some damned insect blackening the air.

Of course, this was before our people had tracked down the problem with the caterpillars and the wasps and all of that, and so we figured we'd had a big success with the mosquitoes, why not a series of ground sweeps, mount a fogger in the back of a Suzuki Brat, and sanitize the huts, not to mention the open sewers, which as you know are nothing but a breeding ground for flies, chiggers, and biting insects of every sort. At least it was an error of commission rather than omission. At least we were trying.

I watched the flies go down myself. One day they were so thick in the trailer I couldn't even *find* my paperwork, let alone attempt to get through it, and the next they were collecting on the windows, bumbling around like they were drunk. A day later they were gone. Just like that. From a million flies in the trailer to none . . .

Well, no one could have foreseen that, Senator.

The geckos ate the flies, yes. You're all familiar with geckos, I assume, gentlemen? These are the lizards you've seen during your trips to Hawaii, very colorful, patrolling the houses for roaches and flies, almost like pets, but of course they're wild animals, never lose sight of that, and just about as unsanitary as anything I can think of, except maybe flies.

Yes, well don't forget, sir, we're viewing this with twenty-twenty hindsight, but at the time no one gave a thought to geckos or what they ate—

they were just another fact of life in the tropics. Mosquitoes, lizards, scorpions, leeches—you name it, they've got it.

When the flies began piling up on the windowsills like drift, naturally the geckos feasted on them, stuffing themselves till they looked like sausages crawling up the walls. Where before they moved so fast you could never be sure you'd seen them, now they waddled across the floor, laid around in the corners, clung to the air vents like magnets—and even then no one paid much attention to them till they started turning belly-up in the streets. Believe me, we confirmed a lot of things there about the buildup of these products[5] as you move up the food chain and the efficacy—or lack thereof—of certain methods, no doubt about that . . .

The cats? That's where it got sticky, really sticky. You see, nobody really lost any sleep over a pile of dead lizards—though we did tests routinely and the tests confirmed what we'd expected, that is, the product had been concentrated in the geckos because of the number of contaminated flies they consumed. But lizards are one thing and cats are another. These people really have an affection for their cats—no house, no hut, no matter how primitive, is without at least a couple of them. Mangy-looking things, long-legged and scrawny, maybe, not at all the sort of animal you'd see here, but there it was: They loved their cats. Because the cats were functional, you understand—without them, the place would have been swimming in rodents inside of a week.

You're right there, Senator, yes—that's exactly what happened.

You see, the cats had a field day with these feeble geckos—you can imagine, if any of you have ever owned a cat, the kind of joy these animals must have experienced to see their nemesis, this ultra-quick lizard, and it's just barely creeping across the floor like a bug.

5. **these products:** insecticides.

E. Literary Element: Satire
? Why is the reference to Hawaiian trips satirical? [The narrator suggests that the senators experience the same lizards found in Borneo in Hawaii, a popular tourist destination—implying that while the countries they are supposedly helping suffer, the senators have been vacationing.]

A. Critical Reading: Making Connections

Point out to students that this passage is similar to descriptions of the medieval plagues. Have students refer to their Reader's Logs to see how many predictions made about medieval images came true.

B. Reader's Response: Shaping Interpretations

? How would you describe the narrator? [Sample responses: He's afraid to take responsibility, so he's hiding behind his job. He's cavalier and insensitive.] What shapes your interpretation of him? [Sample responses: He implies that he was trying to fix the problem, yet he shirks responsibility. He uses flippant phrases that imply that Borneo's traditions are unsophisticated and that the lives of its inhabitants are not worth much.]

C. Reader's Response: Challenging the Text

? What do you think might have been the author's intent in writing this piece? [Sample responses: To criticize bungled government missions in other countries; to encourage readers to think about the interrelations between the environment and human actions.] Is the piece effective? [Sample responses: No, the piece is disturbing, but I'm not sure what to do about the problem it dramatizes. Or yes, it shows clearly that one society does not necessarily know what is best for another.]

Making Meanings

First Thoughts

1. Students might believe that any response to injustice, no matter how extreme, is justified; or they might feel Swift's proposal is too graphic and that his irony might be lost on some readers.

Reviewing the Text

a. The narrator says that the landlords should have the first claim on the flesh of the children, since they have already figuratively devoured the parents.

b. The narrator says males are too tough and their taste is disagreeable. Females would be a loss to the breeding population. Also, some people think the practice borders on cruelty.

A Well, to make a long story short, the cats ate up every dead and dying gecko in the country, from snout to tail, and then the cats began to die . . . which to my mind would have been no great loss if it wasn't for the rats. Suddenly there were rats everywhere—you couldn't drive down the street without running over half-a-dozen of them at a time. They fouled the grain supplies, fell in the wells and died, bit infants as they slept in their cradles. But that wasn't the worst, not by a long shot. No, things really went down the tube after that. Within the month we were getting scattered reports of bubonic plague, and of course we tracked them all down and made sure the people got a round of treatment with antibiotics, but still we lost a few and the rats kept coming . . .

B It was my plan, yes. I was brainstorming one night, rats scuttling all over the trailer like something out of a cheap horror film, the villagers in a panic over the threat of the plague and the stream of nonstop hysterical reports from the interior—people were turning black, swelling up and bursting, that sort of thing—well, as I say, I came up with a plan, a stopgap, not perfect, not cheap, but at this juncture, I'm sure you'll agree, something had to be implemented.

We wound up going as far as Australia for some of the cats, cleaning out the SPCA facilities and what-have-you, though we rounded most of them up in Indonesia and Singapore—approximately fourteen thousand in all. And yes, it cost us—cost us upfront purchase money and aircraft fuel and pilots' overtime and all the rest of it—but we really felt there was no alternative. It was like all nature had turned against us.

And yet still, all things considered, we made a lot of friends for the U.S.A. the day we dropped those cats, and you should have seen them, gentlemen, the little parachutes and harnesses we'd tricked up, fourteen thousand of them, cats in every color of the rainbow, cats with one ear, no ears, half a tail, three-legged cats, cats that could have taken pride of show in Springfield, Massachusetts, and all of them twirling down out of the sky like great big oversized snowflakes . . .

It was something. It was really something.

Of course, you've all seen the reports. There were other factors we hadn't counted on, adverse conditions in the paddies and manioc fields[6]—we don't to this day know what predatory species were inadvertently killed off by the initial sprayings, it's just a mystery—but the weevils[7] and whatnot took a pretty heavy toll on the crops that year, and by the time we dropped the cats, well—the people were pretty hungry, and I suppose it was inevitable that we lost a good proportion of them right then and there. But we've got a CARE program going there now and something hit the rat population—we still don't know what, a virus, we think—and the geckos, they tell me, are making a comeback.

C So what I'm saying is it could be worse, and to every cloud a silver lining, wouldn't you agree, gentlemen?

6. paddies and manioc fields: Paddies, or rice paddies, are small, flooded fields used to grow rice in eastern and southern Asia. Manioc, also called cassava, is a kind of tuber cultivated in tropical areas.
7. weevils: snouted beetles extremely destructive to rice and grain crops.

---

c. He says that they are dying off quickly enough in the natural course of events, due to cold, famine, filth, and vermin.

d. According to the narrator, his plan: (1) Reduces number of Catholics; (2) gives the poor a tangible asset; (3) aids the economy and introduces a new food; (4) decreases the time "breeders" have to raise children; (5) improves tavern business; (6) encourages marriage.

e. The narrator anticipates the objection that the proposal, if carried out, would diminish the population.

Shaping Interpretations

2. Both the expression of the hope and the description of the proposal as "modest" are ironic, given the outlandish character of the proposal. Without the irony, readers might take the proposal seriously.

3. Some sentences revealing the narrator's professed virtues are paragraph 4, sentence 1; paragraph 8, sentence 1; last paragraph, sentence 1.

MAKING MEANINGS

First Thoughts

1. Do you think Swift goes too far in his essay? Why or why not?

Shaping Interpretations

2. Why do you think the narrator expresses the hope that his plan "will not be liable to the least objection" just before he introduces it? Why does he call his proposal "modest"?

3. Find sentences in which the speaker **characterizes** himself favorably and claims to possess certain virtues that—considering the nature of his proposal—he could not possibly have.

4. How would you state the **purpose** of this essay? Whom or what is Swift trying to reform?

5. Describe the narrator's real meaning when he asserts that England will not mind if Ireland kills and eats its babies. What element of **satire** is evident here?

6. Near the end of the pamphlet, the speaker lists "other expedients" that might help lessen the present distress in Ireland. Some of these options are very constructive. Why, then, does the narrator brush these ideas for reform aside?

Reviewing the Text

a. Why does the narrator think the food he proposes is "very proper for landlords"?

b. Why does the narrator reject the idea of selling and eating the twelve- to fourteen-year-olds?

c. Why is the narrator unconcerned about old people suffering from sickness, poverty, and neglect?

d. About midway in the pamphlet, the narrator lists the advantages of his proposal. What are the six principal advantages?

e. Describe the one objection that the narrator anticipates to his proposal.

Extending the Text

7. What other human disasters resulting from bureaucratic incompetence around the world could be targets for another "modest proposal"?

LANGUAGE AND STYLE

Diction and Connotations

Diction, or word choice, is especially important in persuasive writing. Swift is particularly skillful in choosing words with strong **connotations**—that is, words loaded with strong feelings, associations, or even judgments. Here are some of Swift's loaded words:

savages	beggars	filth
male and female	rags	idolatrous
popish infants	breeders	carcasses

In each instance, another word or term could have been chosen to create a different, less harsh effect. For example, *male* and *female*—as opposed to *man* and *woman*—make us think of animals, not human beings, which is Swift's intention.

1. Find the places in the text where the words listed above are used. What is the emotional effect of each word choice?

2. What other tamer or more positive words could have been used to create different emotional effects?

4. Swift is attempting to draw attention to the predicament of the Irish by recommending extreme and ridiculous solutions. Swift hopes to reform English landlords, ineffective political leadership, and "rational" social planners.

5. One interpretation is that the narrator is criticizing the cruelty and insensitivity of the English. He purposely overstates the case, using exaggeration to call attention to hardships in Ireland.

6. By mentioning reasonable solutions, Swift emphasizes Britain's failure to design and implement constructive programs to improve the miserable conditions in Ireland.

Extending the Text

7. **(Analysis and Evaluation)** Refer students to the daily newspaper for situations in which incompetence causes hardship or disaster.

Language and Style

Possible Answers

1. Pity; sympathy; empathy; outrage; a desire to take action; hatred; aversion to overgeneralizing; fear; superiority.

2. Instead of *savages*—the Irish; *beggars*—the poor, the downtrodden; *filth*—dirt, lack of proper facilities, unsanitary environment; *male* and *female*—man and woman, people; *rags*—clothing, tattered clothes, hand-me-downs; *idolatrous*—of another religion, Catholic; *popish infants*—Catholic children, children raised in the Catholic church; *breeders*—mothers; *carcasses*—bodies, corpses.

✔ QUICK CHECK: Diction and Connotations

In the following sentences, find synonyms for the underlined words that would alter the reader's perceptions of the statement.

[1] The mayor threw rose petals to her constituents along the parade route. [Politician, leader; fans, electorate, voters.]

[2] Due to increasing traffic, the state decided to monitor car emissions. [Exhaust, pollution.]

[3] The disappointed pitcher watched the rain fall on game day. [Pouty, disgruntled, sad; pour, drizzle.]

[4] The attorney encouraged the witness. [Prodded, badgered, coaxed.]

[5] Someone purchased the well-worn sofa at the garage sale. [Acquired, bargained for; depreciated, shabby, threadbare.]

Beyond the Selections

Choices: Building Your Portfolio

1. **Writer's Notebook** Remind students to save their work. They may use it as prewriting for the Writer's Workshop on p. 612.

2. **Critical Writing** Suggest that students work together to compare the two authors' works. Individual students can gather examples from Swift's or Boyle's text. Then the pairs can share their examples and examine the points that the authors make through satire.

3. **Creative Writing** Have students review their answers for Making Meanings #7 and the discussion of **diction** in Language and Style. Then, ask students to use columns as shown to list specific problems that their outrageous solutions solve.

Problem	Exaggerated Solution

4. **Creative Writing** To prompt brainstorming, list a few possible scenarios on the chalkboard, and invite students to quickwrite in their Reader's Logs. For example:
   - Imagine being transported through time and waking in one hundred years.
   - Describe awakening on another planet.

5. **Creative Writing** Reproduce several recent examples of editorials on overhead transparencies. Lead a discussion of each editorial, marking structural and linguistic aspects as they appear. Point out that a good editorial clearly states a purpose, a point of view, and a related action or solution, if applicable.

6. **Visual Art** To assist students in identifying targets and applying the size motif, have them use a graphic organizer like the following. For each target, have students consider what is physically or psychologically huge and what is tiny.

Target	Huge	Tiny
[Congress]	[budget, staff]	[minds, consciences, hearts, results]

7. **Art/Speaking** Display posters or photographs of some Hogarth paintings. Invite the class to list the techniques used for satiric effect. Students will probably observe exaggeration and quality of light. Some students will consider composition and medium.

CHOICES: Building Your Portfolio

Writer's Notebook

1. Collecting Ideas for a Persuasive Essay

A Modest Proposal is an outrageous satire, not a sincere proposition, but the passion that drove Swift is the right starting point for persuasion. To write a good persuasive essay, you have to *care*. Think about the contemporary issues raised in your Reader's Log (page 487) and Extending the Text answers (pages 496, 500, and 513). If some fire your passion, quickly jot down what you feel about them, and *why*. If none does, find your "hot-button" issue by freewriting to these phrases: *What really makes me angry is _____*, or *If I had the power, I would change _____*. Save your notes for the Writer's Workshop on page 612.

Critical Writing

2. From One Satirist to Another

What similarities do you notice between Swift's satire in *A Modest Proposal* and Boyle's in "Top of the Food Chain" (page 509)? In a brief essay, explore how each writer uses satirical devices. Are the targets of each satire similar?

Creative Writing

3. A New Modest Proposal

Attack an evil you see in society today by writing an ironic "modest proposal" for its solution—so outrageously horrifying that readers will see at once the tragedy of the situation. Remember: As Swift was, you might be attacked for insensitivity. Your moral outrage must be made clear by gross exaggeration.

Creative Writing

4. Slumberers Awake

Many characters in literature awaken from a deep sleep to find themselves in strange, new circumstances. Rip Van Winkle, for example, wakes to find he's been sleeping for twenty years and that his country is no longer a British colony. The hero of Franz Kafka's *The Metamorphosis* wakes to find he has become a horrible bug. Imagine that overnight some fantastic change happens to you. Write a first-person narrative of at least two pages describing what happened, where and when it happened, and why it happened.

Creative Writing

5. A Blast at Swift

Imagine that you do not understand the irony of *A Modest Proposal*, but read the pamphlet as a straightforward plan for solving social and economic problems. Write a reply to Swift in the form of a modern newspaper editorial. Focus on details that seem particularly cruel and horrible to you, and attack Swift for his complete lack of humanity. You might give your reply a long, informative subtitle (Swift often did this). Your editorial essay should be at least three paragraphs long.

Visual Art

6. A Matter of Perspective

Working with a small group, review the kinds of satire and their targets that you see around you today. (Review your Reader's Log notes from page 487.) Choose one of those targets, and create a cartoon about the topic. Use the motif of size, either huge or tiny, to make your satirical point.

Art / Speaking

7. Artistic Barbs

Research the paintings of William Hogarth (1697–1764), an English artist who, like Swift, powerfully criticized the problems of eighteenth-century English life. Then present your findings to your class. What techniques do artists use to satirize something? Also include your opinion on this question: Do artists (and cartoonists) today use their art to criticize society as Hogarth did?

PORTFOLIO ASSESSMENT

Choices: Assessment Criteria For help in evaluating these Choices assignments, see the criteria in the *Portfolio Management System*, pp. 112–113.

HOW TO OWN A WORD

Identifying Shades of Meaning

Our language is rich and varied, in part because many words communicate various shades of meaning. Even words that have very similar definitions have subtly different meanings, emotional overtones, and associations, including associations with their opposite meanings.

Denotation and connotation: The dictionary definition or explicit meaning of a word is called its **denotation.** The denotation of *odious* as it is used in the following quotation from *Gulliver's Travels* is "causing or deserving loathing or disgust."

> But by what I have gathered from your own relation, and the answers I have with much pains wringed and extorted from you, I cannot but conclude the bulk of your natives to be the most pernicious race of little **odious** vermin that nature ever suffered to crawl upon the surface of the earth.

However, words can communicate more than ideas; they can also convey attitudes and emotions. These associated attitudes and emotional overtones that are communicated by words are called **connotations.** For example, while both *odious* and *hateful* mean "causing or deserving loathing," most people associate different emotions with each word. *Odious* is associated with a particular, loathsome quality in a thing or person that causes feelings of disgust. On the other hand, *hateful* is associated with a more general unpleasantness of character that causes feelings of strong dislike and aversion.

Synonyms and antonyms: Words that have similar meanings are called **synonyms.** *Odious* and *hateful* are synonyms. Dictionaries usually give one or more synonyms for each word and, in some cases, give synonym articles, which are brief explanations of how the word's synonyms differ in denotation and connotation. You can also find synonyms in a thesaurus, a dictionary of synonyms.

When choosing a synonym or figuring out the meaning of a word from a synonym, you need to be sure its meaning suits the context. For example, *hateful* is a synonym for *odious* when it means "causing or deserving loathing." However, it is not a synonym for *odious* when it means "showing or feeling hate."

1. Everyone at court disliked and avoided the **hateful** young queen.
2. His long illness had made the old king so **hateful** that he could not even love his own children anymore.

Words that have opposite or almost opposite meanings are called **antonyms.** *Odious* and *lovable* are antonyms. *Attractive* and *appealing* are also antonyms for *odious*. Dictionaries sometimes list antonyms at the end of the entry for a word.

Try It Out

On your own paper, draw a chart like the following one, excluding the example *odious*. In the appropriate column beside each of the other five Words to Own from *Gulliver's Travels,* write the denotation as it is used in the selection, the connotations, a synonym, and an antonym. Use a dictionary and a thesaurus as necessary.

Word to Own	Denotation	Connotations	Synonym	Antonym
odious	causing loathing	loathsome quality, disgust	hateful	lovable
diminutive				
quelled				
copious				
prevailed				
pernicious				

Mini-Lesson: Identifying Shades of Meaning

The study of denotations, connotations, synonyms, and antonyms involves using a thesaurus. Review the traditional thesaurus, newer dictionary format, and computerized version.

If possible, demonstrate to students the ways to access a computerized thesaurus, using either a computer or a transparency of a screen printout that shows appropriate entries.

Try It Out: Possible Answers

Word: diminutive
Denotation: small
Connotation: derision, condescension
Synonym: tiny
Antonym: huge

Word: quelled
Denotation: put an end to
Connotation: superiority
Synonym: stopped
Antonym: encouraged

Word: copious
Denotation: plentiful amount
Connotation: generous
Synonym: abundant
Antonym: lack

Word: prevailed
Denotation: triumphed over
Connotation: win, subdue
Synonym: succeeded
Antonym: failed

Word: pernicious
Denotation: causing injury
Connotation: evil, wicked
Synonym: destructive
Antonym: harmless

STRATEGIES FOR INCLUSION

Linguistic Have students research and report on the etymologies of words from this Collection. Help students with their research by showing them how the dictionary presents this information. The most thorough source is *The Oxford English Dictionary.* When students present their etymologies to the class, have them include examples of usage so the other students can experience the words in context.

PROGRAM MANAGER

Reinforcement To allow students practice and reinforcement of the vocabulary strategies introduced here, see **Transparency 6.6** in the *Audiovisual Resources Binder.*

A. Exploring the Culture
Several factors contributed to the increasing numbers of women who wrote: the rise of the middle class, which meant more money in the hands of more people; more leisure time; more education, and thus more interest in literature. These factors fueled the publishing business, and publishers needed more material to print that would appeal to their readers, so they turned to women writers as well as men.

B. Expansion
Point out that a novel in which the characters are thinly disguised society people or celebrities is called a *roman à clef* ("novel with a key"), which figuratively refers to the key(s) that unlock, or reveal, the true identities of the characters.

C. Humanities Connection
Gothic architecture, a product of the Middle Ages, is characterized by immense edifices that reach to the sky with flamboyant (literally "flamelike") patterns. Many of these edifices are decorated with frightening, supernatural statuary such as gargoyles. The complex and sometimes grotesque ornamentation of Gothic buildings is echoed in the complex **plot** structures of Gothic novels, which twist and turn and reveal dark secrets.

SPOTLIGHT ON

Women Writers of the Restoration and the Eighteenth Century

by **C. F. Main**

For now that Aphra Behn had done it, girls could go to their parents and say, You need not give me an allowance; I can make money by my pen.

—Virginia Woolf, *from A Room of One's Own*

Living by the Pen

Samuel Johnson once said that a woman who issued her opinions to the public was something like a dog walking on its hind legs. "It is not done well; but you are surprised to find it done at all," he quipped. Had he looked around, Johnson might have been surprised indeed. During his lifetime the number of women writers in England increased enormously. Of course, there had always been many women who wrote letters, kept journals and diaries, and recorded in notebooks their recipes, prayers, poems, and private thoughts. But eighteenth-century women—fortuitously aided by the explosion of the middle class and emergence of a literary marketplace—were increasingly able to have their work published, even able to earn a living by writing. They no longer needed a well-to-do family or patron, as Renaissance women writers had; in this new era, if a woman's work was likely to appeal to readers, a printer was bound to print it.

The variety of these women's writings is astonishing. In the mid-1600s, Katherine Philips—who called herself Orinda, and whom admirers took to calling "the Matchless Orinda"—became England's first famous woman writer. Her rather traditional poems, mostly on the theme of friendship, were addressed to a circle of confidants, mainly but not entirely women, to whom she gave such fancy names as Lucasia, Rosania, Cratander, and Silvander.

Illustration (detail) from an 1803 edition of Ann Radcliffe's Gothic romance *The Mysteries of Udolpho.*

By the late eighteenth century, the Minerva Press was flooding the bookstalls with popular fiction written mostly by women. Scandalous romances and satirical novels, with characters who were often thinly disguised society folk, became a staple. Also popular were the new Gothic novels, in which frightening and apparently supernatural events took place in remote castles. In fact, the best-selling novels of Ann Radcliffe (1764–1823), the most famous writer of eighteenth-century Gothics, are recognizable ancestors of today's horror fiction.

516 THE RESTORATION AND THE EIGHTEENTH CENTURY

OPTIONS FOR TEACHING

STRATEGIES FOR INCLUSION

Spatial/Visual Encourage students to think of different ways to organize the information given in the article into a graphic. Students may want to make a flowchart that plots the progression of ideas or a chart that compares descriptions of the authors. Emphasize that students' graphics should reinforce the main ideas of the article—students should be able to use the graphics as a study aid.

Interpersonal/Auditory Students may benefit from reading the article aloud with partners. Encourage partners to pause occasionally in their reading to comment on interesting points in the article or to give their own opinions or descriptions of experiences. Have partners take notes on their consultations, which they can later share in class discussion.

Women also publicly commented—as journalists, advocates, and critics—on the most important and controversial issues of the day. Early feminists like Mary Astell (1666–1731) and Lady Mary Chudleigh (1656–1710) wrote that marriage laws enslaved women, making them little more than their husbands' property. (In contrast, Margaret Cavendish [1623–1674], duchess of Newcastle, took it for granted that marriage was an arrangement ordained by God, and published a huge biography of her husband the duke, whom she presented as a paragon.) Hannah More (1745–1833), an early British voice for the abolition of slavery, produced many widely circulated tracts about the moral education of women and the poor.

Aphra Behn (1640–1689)

Aphra Behn, born Aphra Johnson to working-class parents in Kent, was the first English woman to earn her living by writing. She was a free spirit, the sort of woman who used to be called an adventuress, and she had the luck to write in the era when women were at last permitted to work in the theater as actors, playwrights, and producers. In her lifetime, she and her writings were both very well known, but during the two hundred years after her death, her works and her life came to be regarded as outrageous and were forgotten.

Consequently, at this late date it is impossible to recover many details of her biography. She perhaps spent most of her early years in Guiana, she married a Mr. Behn (usually pronounced "bane") who may have died in the Great Plague of 1664–1665, and she was a spy for her country during a war against the Dutch. Beyond these bare facts lies much interesting speculation. What is certain is that she left an impressive literary legacy. For nearly ten years in a row, her plays, comedies for the most part, were successively produced in London. In *The Rover* (1677–1681), her best-known play, three young Spanish women, who are curious about sex, encounter three young traveling Englishmen during carnival time in Spain.

Behn also published several collections of translations and poems, as well as a dozen short novels, one of which is her masterpiece *Oroonoko* (1688). Its hero is an African prince, a powerful man with a noble mind and body, who has been tricked into slavery and transported to the island of Surinam.

D

E

F

Aphra Behn.

Behn's genius makes him seem very real to the reader, who is bound to be moved by his suffering.

In the following speech, Oroonoko, who has been renamed Caesar by his slave master, exhorts his fellow slaves to fight the unjust rule of the English.

"And why," said he, "my dear friends and fellow sufferers, should we be slaves to an unknown people? Have they vanquished us nobly in fight? Have they won us in honorable battle? And are we, by the chance of war, become their slaves? This would not anger a noble heart, this would not animate a soldier's soul. No, but we are bought and sold like apes, or monkeys, to be the sport of women, fools, and cowards, and the support of rogues, renegades that have abandoned their own countries for raping, murders, thefts, and villainies. Do you not hear every day how they upbraid each other with infamy of life, below the wildest savages, and shall we render obedience to such a degenerate race, who have no one human virtue left to distinguish them from the vilest creatures? Will you, I say, suffer the lash from such hands?" They all replied with one accord, "No, no, no; Caesar has spoke like a great captain, like a great king."

—Aphra Behn, *from Oroonoko*

D. Expansion

Behn sought favor at Charles II's court and worked as a secret agent in the Netherlands during the Second Dutch War (1665–1667). Her code name, Astraea, became her nickname among her literary colleagues. However, because she was not paid for spying, she served a term in debtors' prison when she returned to England.

E. Expansion

Filled with wit, Behn's plays were as ribald as those of any male writer during the Restoration, a literary era known for its bawdiness.

F. Expansion

This novel about a slave revolt led by an African prince influenced the development of prose fiction in England and presaged some of the work of Daniel Defoe. Behn's work was hugely popular during her lifetime, and her lasting contributions to English literature and culture were later recognized when she was buried in Westminster Abbey.

Technology Tip

Aphra Behn's *The Rover* is available at **http://ernie. bgsu.edu/~smorgan/ publick/behn.html**. *You may want to preview any Internet activity that you suggest to students. Because these resources are sometimes public forums, their content can be unpredictable.*

INTEGRATING THE LANGUAGE ARTS

Strategic Reading Students can learn to sort out cause and effect by paying attention to textual clues. Have students use a chart like the following to identify and to link causes and effects in the passage about Fanny Burney's panic (p. 519). Have students use the same method to identify three other pairings of cause and effect in the essay.

Causes	Effects
[reading of Evelina, speculation about its author]	[panic that relatives would recognize her writing]

? What does this passage reveal about the behavior of many society women in Montagu's day? [Students may say that the women were impolite, conformist, judgmental, hierarchical, and obsessed with fashion.]

Lady Mary Wortley Montagu (1689–1762)

Though she had a more privileged upbringing than Aphra Behn, Lady Mary Wortley Montagu also educated herself, spending much of her childhood buried among the books in her father's vast library. From an early age, she was known as clever and daring. At twenty-three, she eloped on horseback with Edward Wortley Montagu, flouting her family's wish that she marry for money. After a serious bout with smallpox, she championed smallpox inoculations in Britain. Later, she dared to refuse the romantic attentions of her one-time good friend, Alexander Pope, who then tried, unsuccessfully, to destroy her in his satires.

Although she was herself a talented poet, her fame now rests on her letters, which were published in four volumes immediately after her death. They are still a valuable source of information about eighteenth-century life in England, France, and even Turkey, where she lived for a time while her husband was the English ambassador to Constantinople.

In the following passage, taken from a letter written to a friend in 1717, Lady Montagu describes a trip to the women's public baths in the Turkish city of Sofia.

> I was in my traveling habit, which is a riding dress, and certainly appeared very extraordinary to them, yet there was not one of 'em that showed the least surprise or impertinent curiosity, but received me with all the obliging civility possible. I know no European court where the ladies would have behaved themselves in so polite a manner to a stranger. I believe in the whole there were two hundred women and yet none of those disdainful smiles or satiric whispers that never fail in our assemblies when anybody appears that is not dressed exactly in fashion. They repeated over and over to me, "Uzelle, pek uzelle," which is nothing but, "Charming, very charming." The first sofas were covered with cushions and rich carpets, on which sat the ladies, and on the second their slaves behind 'em, but without any distinction of rank by their dress, all being in the state of nature, that is, in plain English, stark naked. . . .
>
> The lady that seemed the most considerable amongst them entreated me to sit by her and would fain have undressed me for the bath. I excused myself with some difficulty, they all being so earnest in persuading me. I was at last forced to open my skirt and show them my stays, which satisfied 'em very well, for I saw they believed I was so locked up in that machine that it was not in my own power to open it, which contrivance they attributed to my husband.
>
> —Lady Mary Wortley Montagu

Montagu spent the last twenty years of her life living alone in a villa in Italy. The letters to her daughter that survive from this period provide a record of Montagu's continuing curiosity about the world; her pride in her granddaughter's scholarly bent, which she encourages her daughter to nourish; and her own deep sense of self-reliance.

Fanny Burney (1752–1840)

Fictionalized letters, as funny and reflective as those of the prolific Lady Montagu, soon found their way into print as epistolary novels, or novels composed of letters.

One of the first and most important epistolary novels is *Evelina* (1778), by Frances "Fanny" Burney, the daughter of well-known musicologist Charles Burney. The heroine of this novel, Burney's first, is a beautiful, intelligent girl who must overcome many obstacles in order to win the man she loves, a good man whose wealth and social position are well beyond her own. Due to a misunderstanding, her father has abandoned her, and most of her other relatives are eccentric and socially awkward.

Frances d'Arblay Burney (1785) by Edward Francis Burney.

By Courtesy of the National Portrait Gallery, London.

Speaking and Listening To broaden their understanding of gender differences in the eighteenth century, have students participate in an informal mock debate in which they cite quotations from various authors they have read and from the authors treated in this feature. Start by reading an opinion on women writers that is clearly on one side of the issue, and ask a student to refute the view you have read by citing another author or an example from the feature. Continue, letting each student have a turn to respond to the prior speaker's citation or example. Emphasize that students should respond not with their own opinion but with a point of view expressed in this Collection.

Writing: Historical Diary Entry Have students write a diary entry from the point of view of a woman writer during the Restoration. Encourage students to address the importance of women's writing and the forms that their writing took. Students should also mention briefly any fears of discovery or other problems one might encounter as a female author. Students can use Burney's entry as a model for their own writing and should draw additional material from the text.

But they are also quite funny. Burney had a real gift for comedy, which is a distinguishing feature of the English novel. The plot twists in *Evelina* and the odd behavior of the characters hold the reader's attention right up to the inevitable happy ending.

Burney had a keen eye and ear for the hypocrisy—and humor—of social relations in her day. Her work was praised by such notables as Samuel Johnson and David Garrick, and she was accepted into the Bluestocking Circle, a group of prominent women who shared literary and scholarly interests. Burney was also appointed to a position in the queen's household (which she found dreadfully boring and only escaped when she became quite ill).

This praise and prominence implies Burney had a brilliant education. However, like Behn and Montagu before her, she was largely self-taught. She also had qualms about the propriety of a writing career. At fifteen, thinking that her already voluminous work was inconsequential, Burney made a great bonfire of the pages, including the beginnings of *Caroline Evelyn*, a novel that she later rewrote as *Evelina*. Indeed, Burney was so insecure about her writing that she published *Evelina* anonymously at first; its great success finally encouraged her to put her name on the title page.

In the following passage from her diary, Burney announces the publication of *Evelina* with an endearing mock grandeur.

> This year was ushered in by a grand and most important event! At the latter end of January, the literary world was favored with the first publication of the ingenious, learned, and most profound Fanny Burney! I doubt not but this memorable affair will, in future times, mark the period whence chronologers will date the zenith of the polite arts in this island! . . .
>
> My little book, I am told, is now at all the circulating libraries. I have an exceeding odd sensation when I consider that it is now in the power of *any* and *every* body to read what I so carefully hoarded even from my best friends, till this last month or two; and that a work which was so lately lodged, in all privacy, in my bureau, may now be seen by every baker and butcher, cobbler and tinker, throughout the three kingdoms, for the small tribute of threepence.
>
> —Fanny Burney

Yet the thought that she might be identified as *Evelina*'s author (a fact known by few but her sisters Susanna and Charlotte) sends Burney into a panic.

> My aunt and Miss Humphries being settled at this time at Brompton, I was going thither with Susan to tea, when Charlotte acquainted me that they were then employed in reading *Evelina* to the invalid, my cousin Richard.
>
> This intelligence gave me the utmost uneasiness—I foresaw a thousand dangers of a discovery—I dreaded the indiscreet warmth of all my confidants. In truth, I was quite sick with apprehension, and was too uncomfortable to go to Brompton, and Susan carried my excuses.
>
> Upon her return, I was somewhat tranquilized, for she assured me that there was not the smallest suspicion of the author, and that they had concluded it to be the work of a *man*!
>
> —Fanny Burney

Despite the assumption of Burney's relatives, and the reading public in general, that most published works were authored by men, eighteenth-century Britain was relatively open to women writers. In fact, for a brief period, women writers were in the ascendancy, and some male writers resorted to using female pseudonyms to get their work into print. Yet this freedom didn't last. By the mid-1800s, when a woman's sphere had again narrowed to home and hearth, women with literary aspirations once more faced enormous obstacles.

Mr. B. Finds Pamela Writing (18th century), illustration by Joseph Highmore from Samuel Richardson's *Pamela*.
Victoria and Albert Museum, London.

B. Expansion
David Garrick, one of Samuel Johnson's pupils, became the greatest actor and theatrical entrepreneur of the age.

C. Exploring the Historical Period
A "golden age" of libraries occurred during the seventeenth and eighteenth centuries, during which time the first state-supported libraries were opened and many private libraries that are still in existence today were founded.

COOPERATIVE LEARNING

Book Jackets Arrange students in groups of four and have each group create a book jacket for one of the works mentioned in this feature. Group members should divide among themselves the tasks of creating cover art, biography, synopsis, and layout. For the cover art and synopsis, students should be able to name some of the primary **themes, settings, characters,** and the work's significance. Ask the groups to present their book jackets to the class.

ASSESSMENT TOOLS

Peer Assessment Have students edit with a partner their diary entries from the Writing activity on p. T518. Each student can use the questions given below to assess his or her partner's first draft. Students may then exchange their papers and assessments and use their partners' comments to complete final drafts of their entries.

1. Is the **first-person point of view** convincing? Why or why not?
2. Does the entry refer to specific arguments or examples?
3. What is the strongest part of the entry? What is its weakest point?
4. What suggestions do you have for its revision?

QUICK PLANNING GUIDE

Into the Poems

Author Biography p. 520
Before You Read p. 521, p. 526

Through the Poems

Heroic Couplets pp. 522–523
from An Essay on Man p. 524
from The Rape of the Lock
pp. 527–531
Making Meanings p. 523, p. 525, p. 533
Language and Style p. 525
Literature and the Arts p. 532
Elements of Literature p. 533–534

Beyond the Poems

Choices: Building Your Portfolio p. 535
- **Writer's Notebook:** Gather notes on celebrities to prepare for a persuasive essay
- **Critical Writing:** In an essay, analyze Pope's satirical targets
- **Critical Writing:** Compare two epics
- **Creative Writing:** Write a mock epic about a contemporary issue
- **Creative Writing:** Describe a common event in elevated language
- **Speaking/Listening:** Construct a rebuttal to Pope's arguments

Alexander Pope

(1688–1744)

Alexander Pope, the most important poet of the early eighteenth century, was a child prodigy. As a very little boy, he later admitted, he "lisped in numbers." That is, he could speak in meter even before he could pronounce English properly. Such a talented youth would ordinarily be educated at Cambridge or Oxford. But Pope's family was Roman Catholic and therefore prohibited from attending these universities, as well as from voting, from holding public office, and even from practicing their religion.

Pope's father, a retired linen merchant, could afford to educate his son at home, which was perhaps the best place for Pope since his health was very delicate. Early in life he contracted a kind of tuberculosis that stunted his growth and disfigured his body, so that eventually his servants had to lace him into a canvas brace before he could sit upright. Since he continually suffered pains in his head, bones, and joints, it is no wonder he spoke of his life as "this long disease."

In spite of all of this, Pope led a remarkably busy and productive life. When he was sixteen, he began his poetic career, as the Roman poet Virgil did, by writing **pastorals**—poems describing the countryside. When he was twenty-three, he published An Essay on Criticism, a poem inspired in part by the Latin poet Horace's Art of Poetry. At twenty-four, he published a miniature classical epic, The Rape of the Lock. And before he was thirty, he had translated into English two enormous Greek epics, Homer's Iliad and, with the help of two assistants, Homer's Odyssey. In these works, Pope was not at all limited by his classical models, but used them to make works that were fresh and original. For

Alexander Pope and Dog Bounce (detail) (c. 1718) attributed to Jonathan Richardson.
Hagley Hall, Worcestershire, England.

this reason, he is sometimes referred to as a neoclassical (that is, new classical) poet.

Pope's early, brilliant successes inspired envy in lesser writers, who lampooned and ridiculed him. To defend himself he turned to satire, a kind of writing highly congenial to his temperament. The great satires of Pope's maturity include The Dunciad (1728, enlarged and revised in 1742), which attacks dull, uninteresting writers of all kinds and shows the forces of stupidity, ignorance, and folly taking over the world, and the Moral Essays (1731–1735), which pass judgment on certain immoral men and women as well as on very rich people who lack common sense and good taste. Finally, An Epistle to Dr. Arbuthnot (1735) contains both a defense of Pope's career as a writer and attacks on his literary enemies.

As a man Pope was, and still is, both loved and hated. In his lifetime and long after, he had a reputation for cruelty, malice, and ill nature. It now seems clear that he had none of these bad qualities but could appear to have them when provoked—as a caged tiger would have them when poked with a stick. We now realize that he was often goaded into writing satire, but that does not necessarily prove that Pope himself was peevish and mean. On the contrary, Pope had a large circle of friends, men and women, including some of the best writers of the day, who found him good-natured, generous, and brilliant in conversation. His agreeable manners, his large expressive eyes, and his way of dressing elegantly in bright colors charmed his friends. At his beautiful estate on the river Thames below London, he entertained important writers, artists, and political figures of the day. Pope became rich and famous; as for the people who raged against him, most of them are remembered today only because they disliked Alexander Pope.

PROGRAM MANAGER

- **Planning Instruction** See *Teaching Notes, Teaching Resources A,* pp. 126–128, for objectives, a summary, a list of literary elements, and additional information for this selection.
- **Instructional Support** Before beginning the instructional lesson, see *Graphic Organizer for Active Reading,*

Teaching Resources A, pp. 138–140, for Through the Poem activities.
- **Audiotaped Readings** To help less proficient readers or auditory learners through the lesson, use the *Selected Reading,* Audiocassette 1, Side B, in the *Audiovisual Resources Binder.*

- **Assessment** See *Selection Tests, Test Booklet,* pp. 97–100.
- **Language Link** For instruction and practice in identifying and using infinitives and infinitive phrases, see *Language Link, Teaching Resources A,* pp. 141–142, and *Language and Writing Skills Worksheets,* p. 75.

BEFORE YOU READ
HEROIC COUPLETS
FROM AN ESSAY ON MAN

Reading Focus

Quotable Wisdom

For the writers of Pope's time, the purpose of poetry was to combine the pleasing with the useful. The clarity, elegance, and compression of Pope's own style ensured that his works would more than fulfill this ideal. With the exception of Shakespeare, Pope is the most widely quoted writer in all of English literature, perhaps because he often wrote in heroic couplets, in which a memorable thought is expressed in a pair of rhyming lines.

A Dialogue with the Text

As you read Pope's couplets and his lines from *An Essay on Man,* keep your Reader's Log handy. You might record your responses in the form of a double-entry journal: a quote that catches your attention on the left and your response to it on the right.

Pope Quote	My Response

Elements of Literature

Antithesis

Pope habitually expresses himself in antitheses (an·tith'ə·sēz'). An **antithesis** uses parallel structures to present a balanced contrast: "Give me liberty, or give me death." ("Give me liberty, or kill me" fails as an antithesis because it isn't parallel or balanced.) By compressing elements of similarity and difference, antithesis helps to make a statement more forceful and (often) more memorable.

> **A**ntithesis is a contrast of ideas expressed in a grammatically balanced statement.
>
> *For more on Antithesis, see the Handbook of Literary Terms.*

Title page of Pope's *An Essay on Man,* designed by Pope.

ALEXANDER POPE 521

Using **BEFORE YOU READ** p. 521

Reading Focus

To help students make a connection between *heroic couplets* and classical epic poems, point out characters' *heroic* qualities: They demonstrate bravery and cunning, fight for noble causes, and appear larger than life through words and deeds.

Elements of Literature

To help students identify **antithesis,** have them keep a log in the format shown below as they read Pope's poetry. Students may each compare findings with a partner.

Citation (antithesis)	How is it parallel?	How does it contrast?
["To err is human, to forgive, divine."]	[Similar sentence structure, wording; related situation.]	[Human imperfection versus divine goodness.]

ABOUT THE AUTHOR

Alexander Pope's translation of the *Iliad,* Homer's Greek epic poem, made him at once very popular and successful. With his profits, Pope purchased a five-acre estate at Twickenham, where he continued to write and also to entertain his friends, the cultured elite of that era. He was extremely sensitive about his appearance—he had a hunched posture as a result of contracting a tubercular spinal infection at age twelve—but that never prevented him from socializing, and it certainly never stopped him from joining the cultural debates that raged during his time.

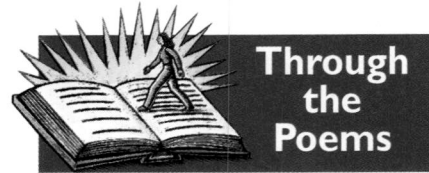

Through the Poems

A. Literary Element: Allusion

This allusion to the Pierian spring, said in antiquity to have inspired the nine Muses, is typical of Pope's style. Remind students that Pope (unlike Defoe) wrote for a highly educated, upper-class audience. His readers considered such classical allusions elegant.

B. Critical Reading: Finding Details

? What type of **figurative language** is used here? [Simile.] To what is the ability to write easily compared? [To dancing.] What aspects of writing lend themselves to this comparison? [Students may say that both are difficult artistic performances that require talent and work, and that both rely on the use of rhythm.]

Making Meanings

First Thoughts

1. Students might think the advice is old-fashioned due to the language and complex sentence structure, or they may feel that, despite the language, the messages are timeless. Encourage students to explain and support their opinions.

Shaping Interpretations

2. **a.** Couplet 3; **b.** Verse 1; **c.** Couplet 7; **d.** Couplet 3 might be construed as doing so; **e.** Couplet 8; **f.** Couplet 6; **g.** Couplet 4.
3. Possible responses: Someone who knows a little bit about medicine decides on a self-treatment plan but does not cure the problem; an amateur chemist may try to figure out the right mixture but combine the wrong chemicals.
4. He suggests that *art* is purposeful and carefully practiced, while *chance,* or luck, merely relies on fortune.
5. Possible paraphrase for Couplet 5: Praise merit when you recognize it; your praise is meaningless or empty if you wait until it is the popular

Pope is the greatest master of the *heroic couplet,* so-called because both he and his predecessor John Dryden used this form in their translations of the epic poems of antiquity. Each heroic couplet consists of two rhymed lines of iambic pentameter. (For variety, Pope occasionally introduces a *triplet.*) Many express a thought in a complete sentence: Such a couplet is called *closed:*

> Trust not yourself; but your defects to know,
> Make use of every friend—and every foe.

Although this couplet from *An Essay on Criticism* is part of a long and carefully organized explanation, it still makes good sense when it is plucked out of its context and allowed to stand by itself. Yet removing couplets from the poems in which they are embedded is dangerous, because it may lead us to think of the poems as strings of beads that can be easily broken apart. In reality, Pope's couplets are so carefully arranged into verse paragraphs that they are more like the forged links of an iron chain than separable units.

Heroic Couplets
Alexander Pope

1 Music resembles poetry: in each
Are nameless graces[1] which no methods[2] teach,
And which a master hand alone can reach.
    —*An Essay on Criticism,* lines 143–145

A 2 A little learning is a dangerous thing;
Drink deep, or taste not the Pierian[3] spring.
    —*An Essay on Criticism,* lines 215–216

3 Be not the first by whom the new are tried,
Nor yet the last to lay the old aside.
    —*An Essay on Criticism,* lines 335–336

B 4 True ease in writing comes from art, not chance,
As those move easiest who have learned to dance.
    —*An Essay on Criticism,* lines 362–363

1. **nameless graces:** pleasing passages that cannot be explained.
2. **methods:** instruction books showing how to write poems.
3. **Pierian** (pī·ir′ē·ən): an allusion to the Muses, Greek goddesses of the arts and literature. The Muses were said to live in a district of Greece called Pieria.

thing to do. Most students will agree that Pope gains concise phrasing and still makes his point memorable. Many of the couplets might even qualify as epigrams.

6. Have students find examples with parallel structures and contrasting ideas. Possibilities are: Verse 1: "which no methods teach, / And which a master hand alone can reach"; and Couplet 6: "To err is human, to forgive, divine."

5 Be thou the first true merit to befriend;
His praise is lost, who stays till all commend.

—*An Essay on Criticism*, lines 474–475

6 Good nature and good sense must ever join;
To err is human, to forgive, divine.

—*An Essay on Criticism*, lines 524–525

7 Hope springs eternal in the human breast:
Man never is, but always to be blest.

—*An Essay on Man*, Epistle I, lines 95–96

8 'Tis education forms the common mind,
Just as the twig is bent, the tree's inclined.

—*Moral Essays*, Epistle I, lines 149–150

9 But when to mischief mortals bend their will,
How soon they find fit instruments of ill!

—*The Rape of the Lock*, Canto III, lines 125–126

10 Satire's my weapon, but I'm too discreet
To run amuck, and tilt[4] at all I meet.

—*Imitations of Horace*, Satire I, Book II,
lines 69–70

4. **tilt:** charge at or thrust a weapon toward an opponent.

View Across Greenwich Park Towards London (detail) (18th century) by Jean Rigaud.
Roy Miles Gallery, London.

MAKING MEANINGS

First Thoughts

1. Share the responses to the couplets you recorded in your Reader's Log. Do you find the advice in the couplets useful, or does it seem out-of-date? Why?

Shaping Interpretations

2. Tell in which of the couplets Pope does each of the following:
   a. Advocates a mean between two extremes.
   b. Suggests that geniuses are born, not made.
   c. Explains why people are never satisfied with what they have.
   d. Compares writing to putting on clothes.
   e. Shows how important education is for the young.
   f. Advises critics to be generous.
   g. Suggests that good writing results from practice and skill, not luck or accident.

3. Give some examples showing how a little learning can be dangerous (Couplet 2).

4. Read the couplet on true ease in writing, and explain the difference between what is suggested by the words *art* and *chance*.

5. Pope compresses a large amount of meaning into the twenty or so syllables of each of his couplets. Try paraphrasing, or expressing in your own words, the idea expressed in any couplet that you find hard to understand. What does Pope gain by compressing his meaning?

6. Pope habitually uses **antithesis** to focus and clarify his meaning. List all the antitheses you can find in these couplets.

Extending the Text

7. Does any couplet particularly connect with life today—in politics, education, or the arts? Explain the connection you see.

Challenging the Text

8. Do you take issue with any of these pronouncements? How would you rephrase any of them to get at a different point altogether?

ALEXANDER POPE 523

C. Literary Element: Antithesis

The technique of antithesis contrasts opposing ideas but presents them through a similar structure. For example, in the second line of the couplet, Pope repeats the infinitive structure "to err" and "to forgive." This parallel structure juxtaposes the concepts of human frailty and divine compassion.

D. Language Note: Style

Point out that the pause indicated by the comma can be seen as corresponding to the idea of suspended hope, and that the pause may emphasize the difference between the ideal and the real.

E. Humanities Connection

Mention that a common literary theme explores the ability humans have for using their talents in negative ways. Shakespeare's *A Midsummer Night's Dream* is a light-hearted yet satiric treatment of mischief and the resulting mayhem. Remind students that Shakespeare predated Pope by a century.

F. Reader's Response: First Thoughts

In the first line, Pope uses a **metaphor** to compare satire to a weapon. Is the comparison effective? Why or why not? [Sample responses: Yes, it's a memorable comparison, because words can be sharp, and I can imagine satire cutting people down; or no, satire softens the message and is less damaging than a weapon.]

Extending the Text

7. **(Analysis)** Responses will vary. For example, Couplet 6 might apply to those who continually criticize a public figure for past mistakes rather than judging the person's capacity to learn and lead. The variety of responses should show students that each couplet may be interpreted in several ways; have students back up their opinions with specific references to the text.

Challenging the Text

8. **(Evaluation and Synthesis)** Students may disagree with some of the advice in the couplets. Possible rephrasing of Couplet 9: "When to goodness mortals bend their mind, / How soon they find fit reasons to be kind."

INTEGRATING THE LANGUAGE ARTS

Strategic Reading Ask students to use a chart like the one below to identify the targets of satire in the couplets. The second couplet can be used as an example.

Reference	Who Is Stung?	Why?
[Couplet 2]	[People with just a little learning]	[Superficiality, thinking they know more than they do]

An Essay on Man is Pope's long (1,304 lines) philosophical poem, published when he was forty-five. A lifetime of reading, in both English and foreign languages, contributed to its composition. The poem is concerned not only with "man," by which Pope means the whole human race, but with the entire universe as well. It's important to know that the ideas in the poem are not merely the private notions of Pope and his friends, but that they come from many authors, including Plato, Aristotle, St. Thomas Aquinas, Dante, Erasmus, Shakespeare, Bacon, and Milton.

In the following lines from the *Essay,* Pope generalizes about the human race. Pope's "man" is all of us. Do you agree that everyone has the characteristics Pope describes?

from An Essay on Man

Alexander Pope

Know then thyself,° presume not God to scan;°
The proper study of mankind is man.
Placed on this isthmus of a middle state,°
A being darkly wise, and rudely great:
5 With too much knowledge for the skeptic° side,
With too much weakness for the Stoic's pride,°
He hangs between; in doubt to act, or rest;
In doubt to deem himself a god, or beast;
In doubt his mind or body to prefer;
10 Born but to die, and reasoning but to err;
Alike in ignorance, his reason such,
Whether he thinks too little, or too much:
Chaos of thought and passion, all confused;
Still° by himself abused, or disabused;°
15 Created half to rise, and half to fall;
Great lord of all things, yet a prey to all;
Sole judge of truth, in endless error hurled:
The glory, jest, and riddle of the world!

1. Know . . . thyself: a moral precept of Socrates and other ethical philosophers. **scan:** pry into; speculate about.
3. middle state: that is, having the rational intellect of angels and the physical body of beasts.
5. skeptic: The ancient Skeptics doubted that humans can gain accurate knowledge of anything. They emphasized the limitations of human knowledge.
6. Stoic's pride: The ancient Stoics' ideal was a calm acceptance of life and an indifference to both pain and pleasure. Stoics are called proud because they refused to recognize human limitations.
14. still: always; continually. **disabused:** undeceived.

Alexander Pope (18th century). Self-portrait. Oil.
Bryn Mawr College, Bryn Mawr, Pennsylvania.

524

MAKING MEANINGS

First Thoughts

1. What one word would you use to summarize the human condition as Pope describes it? Why do you choose this word?

Shaping Interpretations

2. In almost every sentence of this passage, Pope says something flattering about the human race, only to follow it with something insulting. What characteristics does he think we should be proud of? What characteristics should we be ashamed of?

3. How many sentences are in this verse?

4. In what ways do you think human beings could be seen as the "glory" of this world? as its "jest"? as its "riddle"?

5. How does the wording of lines 5–6 and lines 15–16 exhibit **antithesis**? Try paraphrasing each of these couplets in your own words.

6. These couplets from the *Essay* are like variations on a single theme, in that each one expands on a paradoxical view of humanity. Which couplet do you think is the most interesting and true? Explain your choice.

Challenging the Text

7. Discuss your opinion of Pope's opening couplet.

8. How does Pope's view of humanity compare with the view expressed by William Shakespeare's Hamlet in the following lines: "What a piece of work is a man! how noble in reason! how infinite in faculties! in form and moving how express and admirable! in action how like an angel! in apprehension how like a god! the beauty of the world, the paragon of animals!" (*Hamlet*, II, 2). Whose view do you accept?

LANGUAGE AND STYLE

Pope's Poetics

Metrical pattern. Although heroic couplets follow a rigid metrical pattern, Pope takes pains to keep them from being monotonous. For instance, he varies the location of the main pause within a line, as in this quotation from "Elegy to an Unfortunate Lady" (note the position of the commas).

> Poets themselves must fall, like those they sung;
> Deaf the praised ear, and mute the tuneful tongue;
> Even he, whose soul now melts in mournful lays,
> Shall shortly want the generous tear he pays.

Some lines move fast, and some are slow—as these lines from "Windsor-Forest" show.

> See the bold youth strain up the threatening steep,
> Rush through the thickets, down the valleys sweep,
> Hang o'er their coursers' heads with eager speed,
> And earth rolls back beneath the flying steed.

In the first line of this passage, Pope uses language that imitates the effort of riding a horse uphill; in the second, the speed of riding downhill. For variety, Pope occasionally introduces **triplets**—three rhymed lines instead of two.

Present "Two Minutes of Pope" to the class. Read a selection of couplets aloud to feel the effect of pauses, rhymes, **assonance,** and **alliteration.** Be sure to experiment with alternate readings before you make your presentation.

Epigrams. Pope had a dog named Bounce, one of whose puppies he gave to his friend Frederick, Prince of Wales, who lived in Kew. Pope had an epigram engraved on the puppy's collar. An **epigram** is a short poem, often satirical, that ends in a witticism or clever turn of thought. To whom do you think the epigram is addressed? (Don't say, "the prince," because surely the prince knows his own dog.)

> **Epigram Engraved on the Collar of a Dog**
> I am his Highness' dog at Kew;
> Pray tell me, sir, whose dog are you?

✔ QUICK CHECK: Pope's Poetics

The following questions refer to the Heroic Couplets on pp. 522–523.

[1] Find examples of pauses in different places within the lines of the Heroic Couplets. [Verse 1, l. 1; Couplet 2, l. 2; Couplet 4, l. 1; Couplet 5, l. 2; Couplet 6, l. 2]

[2] Find an example of a rhymed triplet. [Verse 1.]

[3] Find an example in the Heroic Couplets of a line that moves along quickly. What words create the effect? [Couplet 3, ll. 1–2: One-syllable words and alliteration speed the rhythm. Couplet 9, l. 2: Assonance—the repetition of the short i sound—speeds this line.]

[4] Where does alliteration lend emphasis in the excerpt from An Essay on Man? [l.1, "then thyself"; l. 2, "mankind is man"; l. 5, "skeptic side"; l.8 "doubt to deem"; l.12 "too ... too"; l.15 "half ... half";]

Making Meanings

First Thoughts

1. Possible responses: Ambiguous or paradoxical. Have students connect their descriptions to examples from the text.

Shaping Interpretations

2. Positive qualities include wisdom, knowledge, and judgment. Detrimental traits include weakness, doubt, error, ignorance, arrogance, passion, confusion.

3. Pope writes only two sentences, one of which is only two lines long. The second sentence comprises the remainder of the poem (16 lines).

4. Possible responses: "glory"—human accomplishments, such as knowledge and fine arts; "jest"—human foibles, such as aggression, greed; for "riddle"—the ambiguity of human behavior (for example, our ability to help and hurt others, to gain knowledge and choose ignorance).

5. The wording is parallel, yet the sentences contrast nearly opposite human qualities. Possible paraphrases: People have proved that they can push the limits of knowledge, yet they are limited by their physicality (ll. 5–6). Humans are in control of their world yet vulnerable to all its perils (ll. 15–16).

6. Students may like ll. 15–16 because they say human beings are both vulnerable and glorious.

Challenging the Text

7. **(Synthesis)** Students may agree that humans should know themselves; however, many will take exception to the notion that people should not also explore spiritual issues.

8. **(Synthesis and Evaluation)** Students will probably agree that, taken out of context, Hamlet's view of mankind is more generous than Pope's. Be sure students support their opinions with examples.

Language and Style

Possible Answer

The epigram may be addressed to other dogs, to anyone who might find the prince's dog should it get lost, or to status-conscious people in general.

Into the Poem

Using BEFORE YOU READ p. 526

Reading Focus

Ask students why they think so many readers find celebrities' trivial problems and petty quarrels fascinating. [Responses might include curiosity, jealousy, a desire to see the high and mighty fall, to see that celebrities are like the rest of us, or to live vicariously.]

Elements of Literature

Have students tie their knowledge or experience to the situations Pope has satirized by identifying seemingly small complaints that have become major battles. Examples might be global or local in nature; possibilities might be a boundary dispute, a perceived slight, or a simple misunderstanding.

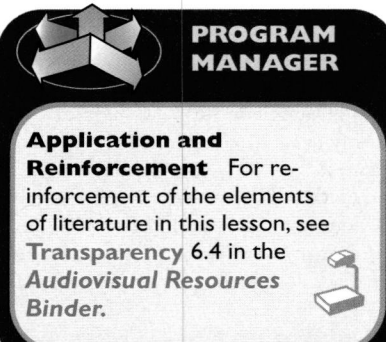

PROGRAM MANAGER

Application and Reinforcement For reinforcement of the elements of literature in this lesson, see **Transparency 6.4** in the *Audiovisual Resources Binder.*

Reading Focus

A Tempest in a Teapot

If you notice the newspapers and magazines at a supermarket checkout counter, you'll probably agree that ordinary Americans like to read about rich and famous people—those in politics, sports, show business, and society. Many readers find it especially interesting to learn about the trivial problems or petty quarrels of prominent people. *The Rape of the Lock* tells the story of a petty quarrel among the eighteenth-century English nobility. After you've read the first part of the poem, see if you don't agree that some tastes in reading haven't changed very much since Pope's day.

Quickwrite

Scan some recent magazines and newspapers, focusing on the gossip columns or on feature articles about the rich and famous. In your Reader's Log, jot down some notes about episodes or incidents that might offer a present-day writer material for a lighthearted, ironic spoof in the spirit of Pope.

Elements of Literature

Mock Epic

A poem like *The Rape of the Lock* is called a **mock epic.** The comedy of a mock epic arises from the discrepancy between a subject and its treatment: The subject is trivial, while its treatment is grandiose. In mock epics, fleas become elephants, and cracked teacups become major catastrophes. Pope used the traditional epic devices in a comic way, and his educated contemporaries had the pleasure of recognizing many similarities between *The Rape of the Lock* and serious epics like Homer's *Iliad,* Virgil's *Aeneid, Beowulf,* and Milton's *Paradise Lost.* For instance, the classical epics all have gods and goddesses who intervene in human affairs, and Milton uses several kinds of angels as his superhuman agents. Following these models, Pope includes some tiny, airy spirits called sylphs, who try in vain to prevent the "rape" from taking place. Readers would also recognize the epic device of the warning dream: Such a dream comes to Belinda from a supernatural being. Since epics always include battles, Pope includes a card game in his poem as well as a screaming match after Belinda loses her curl. In the complete poem of 794 lines (158 of which appear here), there are many such parallels to serious epics.

> **A** **mock epic** is a comic narrative poem that parodies the epic by treating a trivial subject in a lofty, grand manner. A mock epic uses dignified language, elaborate figures of speech, and supernatural intervention.
>
> *For more on the Mock Epic, see the Handbook of Literary Terms.*

Background

When Pope wrote about people, he wrote mainly about the rich, perhaps because the general public found it more interesting to read about the rich than about the poor. The chief characters in *The Rape of the Lock* all belong to the leisure classes, and they spend their time amusing themselves rather than working for a living.

The title of Pope's comic masterpiece means "the violent theft of a lock of hair." The poem is based on a real incident. The lock in question belonged to a certain rich and fashionable young lady named Arabella Fermor. The theft in question was committed by a certain rich and fashionable young man named Robert, Lord Petre. When Robert snipped a curl from Arabella's hairdo, he set off a quarrel between the Fermor and the Petre families. Had the two families been less sensible, their row might have escalated into bitter hatred. As it turned out, the feud subsided into laughter—thanks to Alexander Pope.

At the suggestion of a friend of the two families and patron of Pope's, Pope composed *The Rape of the Lock,* changing the name of Arabella to Belinda and calling Robert "the Baron." To make the warring families realize how trivial the "rape" actually was, Pope treated it very, very seriously. He dressed his poem in all the trappings of heroic poetry, as though he were Homer or Virgil writing an epic of the fall of Troy.

OPTIONS FOR TEACHING

STRATEGIES FOR INCLUSION

Linguistic Students may take special interest in the poem's many **puns.** Encourage students to keep a list of the poem's puns as they read. In columns beside their lists, students should explain how each pun relates to the context and how it is successfully humorous. Have students work in small groups to compare their lists after they have read the poem.

Visual Encourage students to illustrate scenes from the poem to better appreciate the work's **tone** and techniques of **mock epic.** Emphasize to students that they should pay attention to how the scene or scenes they choose to illustrate are described in the poem. They should attempt to reflect the same perspective in their drawings. Students can present their drawings to the class with a brief discussion of the scene. Display students' work around the room.

Spatial Students may better understand the relationships between the **characters** in the poem if they use a cluster diagram to record the characters' interactions. Students should include each character in their diagrams. Encourage them to record any data, impressions, or observations they deem important—the diagrams will help students follow the **plot** of the poem. Model this exercise on the overhead projector, using Transparency 3: Cluster Diagram from the Transparency Package.

Pope's poem is divided into five sections called cantos. Canto I begins like a proper epic, with a statement of the subject and an invocation to the Muse—a female deity who was supposed to inspire poets and other artists. Pope, however, clearly signals his comic intentions in the very first couplet:

> What dire offense from amorous causes springs,
> What mighty contests rise from trivial things,
> I sing—

In Canto II, Belinda and her friends take a boat up the river Thames to a party. All who see her admire the two beautiful curled locks that hang down her back. And despite the small army of sprites (spirits) assigned to protect Belinda's beautiful hair, the Baron resolves to possess these locks.

from The Rape of the Lock
Alexander Pope

Canto III

    Close by those meads, forever crowned with flowers,
Where Thames with pride surveys his rising towers,
There stands a structure° of majestic frame,
Which from the neighboring Hampton takes its name.
5 Here Britain's statesmen oft the fall foredoom
Of foreign tyrants, and of nymphs° at home;
Here thou, great Anna!° whom three realms obey,
Dost sometimes counsel take—and sometimes tea.
    Hither the heroes and the nymphs resort,
10 To taste awhile the pleasures of a court;
In various talk th' instructive hours they passed,
Who gave the ball, or paid the visit last;
One speaks the glory of the British queen,
And one describes a charming Indian screen;
15 A third interprets motions, looks, and eyes;
At every word a reputation dies.
Snuff,° or the fan,° supply each pause of chat,
With singing, laughing, ogling, and all that.
    Meanwhile, declining from the noon of day,
20 The sun obliquely shoots his burning ray;
The hungry judges soon the sentence sign,
And wretches hang that jurymen may dine. . . .
Belinda now, whom thirst of fame invites,
Burns to encounter two adventurous knights,
25 At omber° singly to decide their doom;
And swells her breast with conquests yet to come. . . .
The nymph exulting fills with shouts the sky;
The walls, the woods, and long canals reply.
    Oh thoughtless mortals! ever blind to fate,
30 Too soon dejected and too soon elate.

3. structure: Hampton Court, a royal residence on the river Thames, upstream from London.

6. nymphs: young ladies.
7. Anna: Queen Anne (1665–1714), who ruled England, Ireland, and Scotland.

17. snuff: powdered tobacco product sniffed or rubbed on the teeth and gums. **fan:** standard equipment for a lady.

25. omber: a card game for three players, popular in the eighteenth century.

ALEXANDER POPE 527

Through the Poem

A. Literary Element: Diction

? What is the double meaning of the verb *take*, as it is used in this line? [It means both to accept (advice) and to drink (tea).] Explain that this figure of speech is called *zeugma* (zyōōg′mə), from Greek for "yoke." *Zeugma* occurs when a verb has two subjects or objects, or an adjective modifies two nouns, yet the two contexts have significantly different connotations; one example would be the phrase "to open one's wallet and one's heart." In l. 8, *take* has two sharply different objects, *counsel* and *tea*.

B. Literary Element: Mock Epic

? How is the epic form mocked in ll. 11–16? [Students may say that the way the mundane is elevated (small talk and gossip become instructive) mocks the epic form, or that the irony of "instructive" rumormongering satirizes the upper class, usually heroes of epics.]

C. Critical Reading: Making Inferences

? What does the narrator's interjection in ll. 29–32 seem to foreshadow? [Possible answers: The interjection implies that Belinda exults prematurely and will come to grief; or those who celebrate too soon will see their honors disappear.] What is the tone of the narrator's comment? [Possible answers: Comic; satirical; or serious, in that it regards observations about the human condition and fate.] Are there any earlier hints at gloom? [Possible responses: Lines 21–22 are shockingly serious in light of the conversation; l. 25 suggests that a card game may send the players to their doom.]

INTEGRATING THE LANGUAGE ARTS

Strategic Reading Many modern readers have problems understanding eighteenth-century English usage. One strategy for attacking difficult passages is *explication*, a careful study word by word, line by line, for the purpose of explaining, resolving, and untangling challenging language structures or styles. Have students read the poem in pairs, and ask them to clarify by explication any lines they find confusing or difficult to read. After students have finished reading the poem, ask each pair to share with the class one or two lines that they explicated. Students can compare the strategies they used to clarify the passages.

Writing: Character Letter Ask students to work in pairs to write a letter from Belinda to the Baron or vice versa. Encourage students to mimic the elevated language used in Pope's mock epic. Have students read their letters aloud to the class.

☞

Sudden, these honors shall be snatched away,
And cursed forever this victorious day.
    For lo! the board with cups and spoons is crowned,
The berries° crackle, and the mill° turns round;
35 On shining altars of Japan° they raise
The silver lamp; the fiery spirits blaze:
From silver spouts the grateful liquors glide,
While China's earth° receives the smoking tide.°
At once they gratify their scent and taste,
40 And frequent cups prolong the rich repast.
Straight hover round the fair her airy band;
Some, as she sipped, the fuming liquor fanned,

34. berries: coffee beans.   **mill:** coffee grinder.
35. altars of Japan: small lacquered tables.

38. China's earth: china cups, made of earthenware.   **smoking tide:** coffee.

Sir Plume Demands the Restoration of the Lock (1854) by C. R. Leslie. Oil.
Private Collection.

528 The Restoration and the Eighteenth Century

Some o'er her lap their careful plumes displayed,
Trembling, and conscious of the rich brocade.
45 Coffee (which makes the politician wise,
And see through all things with his half-shut eyes)
Sent up in vapors to the Baron's brain
New stratagems, the radiant lock to gain.
Ah, cease, rash youth! desist ere 'tis too late,
50 Fear the just gods, and think of Scylla's fate!° ┐
Changed to a bird, and sent to flit in air,   │ **B**
She dearly pays for Nisus' injured hair!   ┘
    But when to mischief mortals bend their will, ┐ **C**
How soon they find fit instruments of ill!   ┘
55 Just then, Clarissa drew with tempting grace
A two-edged weapon from her shining case:
So ladies in romance assist their knight,
Present the spear, and arm him for the fight.
He takes the gift with reverence, and extends
60 The little engine° on his fingers' ends;
This just behind Belinda's neck he spread,
As o'er the fragrant steams she bends her head.
Swift to the lock a thousand sprites repair,
A thousand wings, by turns, blow back the hair;
65 And thrice they twitched the diamond in her ear;
Thrice she looked back, and thrice the foe drew near.
Just in that instant, anxious Ariel° sought
The close recesses of the virgin's thought;
As on the nosegay in her breast reclined,
70 He watched th' ideas rising in her mind,
Sudden he viewed, in spite of all her art,
An earthly lover lurking at her heart.°
Amazed, confused, he found his power expired,
Resigned to fate, and with a sigh retired.
75   The peer now spreads the glittering *forfex*° wide, ┐ **D**
T' enclose the lock; now joins it, to divide.   ┘
Even then, before the fatal engine closed,
A wretched sylph too fondly interposed;
Fate urged the shears, and cut the sylph in twain,
80 (But airy substance soon unites again).
The meeting points the sacred hair dissever
From the fair head, forever, and forever!
    Then flashed the living lightning from her eyes,
And screams of horror rend th' affrighted skies.
85 Not louder shrieks to pitying Heaven are cast,
When husbands, or when lapdogs breathe their last;
Or when rich china vessels fallen from high,
In glittering dust, and painted fragments lie!
    "Let wreaths of triumph° now my temples twine,"
90 The victor cried, "the glorious prize is mine!
While fish in streams, or birds delight in air,
Or in a coach and six the British fair, **E**

50. Scylla's fate: In Greek mythology, Scylla is turned into a seabird by the gods after she betrays her father Nisus by cutting off his purple lock of hair, on which his life and kingdom depend.

60. engine: instrument.

67. Ariel: chief of the heavenly sprites sent to protect Belinda.

72. earthly lover . . . heart: If in her heart Belinda wants the Baron to succeed, the sprites cannot protect her.

75. *forfex:* Latin for "scissors."

89. wreaths of triumph: like the ones worn by athletic and military heroes in ancient times.

B. Literary Element: Allusion

? What is the allusion here, and how is the allusion appropriate?

[Possible answers: The allusion is one that Pope's upper-class readers would have been familiar with—the story of Scylla Nisus in Ovid's *Metamorphoses*. The allusion parodies the epic, using a classical reference to heighten the comic effect by comparing Nisus's lock of hair (on which his life depended) and Belinda's (which is a bit of vanity).]

C. Critical Reading: Making Connections

Point out that these lines appear among Pope's Heroic Couplets on p. 523.

D. Literary Element: Antithesis

? In ll. 75–76, what is particularly clever about the use of antithesis in the description of the scissors? [The Baron spreads the scissors to enclose the lock; he joins the scissors to divide the lock from Belinda's head—the verbs name contradictory actions but work together to produce a unified description.]

E. Critical Reading: Drawing Conclusions

? How long will the Baron's reputation last? [Students may read the lines literally and respond that the Baron's reputation will live forever, as long as fish and birds live; other students may view the lines as satirical and say his reputation will be short-lived, because no one now reads the novel *Atalantis,* few people pay visits on solemn days, few people use candles in large numbers, and few people believe in nymphs.]

COOPERATIVE LEARNING

Character Talk Show Have students play a part in a round-table discussion of the plot of the poem, from the viewpoints of the characters of Belinda, the Baron, Clarissa, Ariel, and Belinda's friend (the "virago" of Canto V, l. 1). A sixth student should interview the five characters at various times during the story. Encourage students to consider how their real-life analogues during Pope's day would react to seeing themselves so represented in Pope's mock epic. Give each group a time limit for their discussions, and suggest they prepare at least five questions beforehand.

PROBLEM SOLVING/CRITICAL THINKING

Mediation The plot of *The Rape of the Lock* hinges on a comic dispute, but people involved in disputes generally are serious. Use the poem to help students hone their conflict-resolution skills. Have student groups resolve the dispute in the poem, considering every character's point of view. Encourage groups to use the following graphic organizer in devising their resolution. For additional practice, suggest a modern scenario. Detail for the class your imaginary situation, and ask the groups to work toward a resolution, again using the graphic organizer.

Brief Overview of Conflict	Poem	Modern Scenario
Viewpoints of Parties Involved		
Ideas for Possible Peaceable Settlement		
Best Idea for Resolution (and Why)		

Alexander Pope **T529**

Describe Belinda's immediate acts of revenge on the Baron. [She throws snuff in his face to make him sneeze; she embarrasses him, threatens him with a bodkin.] **What is anticlimactic about it?** [The revenge proves to be trivial; in an epic, the reader expects a brave fight with impressive weaponry, not a scuffle fought with snuff.]

Technology Tip

Selected poetry by Alexander Pope is available from the University of Toronto English Library's Web site at **http://library.utoronto.ca/www /utel/rp/authors/pope.html**. *You may want to preview any Internet activity that you suggest to students. Because these resources are sometimes public forums, their content can be unpredictable.*

As long as *Atalantis*° shall be read,
Or the small pillow grace a lady's bed,
95 While visits shall be paid on solemn days,
When numerous wax lights in bright order blaze,
While nymphs take treats, or assignations give,
So long my honor, name, and praise shall live!
What time would spare, from steel receives its date,°
100 And monuments, like men, submit to fate!". . .

93. Atalantis: *The New Atalantis* (1709), a fashionable novel by Mrs. Delarivière Manley (1663–1724), which thinly disguised some contemporary scandals.

99. date: destruction.

In Canto IV, Pope describes an incident that occurs in all proper epics: a descent into the underworld. Just as Virgil had Aeneas travel down to Hades, Pope has Umbriel, a "melancholy sprite," fly down to a dismal, imaginary place called the Cave of Spleen. (Spleen was the eighteenth century's name for what we call depression; rich, idle people were particularly subject to spleen in Pope's day.) In the cave, Umbriel obtains a vial of "soft sobs, melting griefs, and flowing tears," as well as an immense bag full of "sighs, sobs, and passions," which somewhat resembles the bag of unfavorable winds in Homer's Odyssey, *given to Odysseus to keep tightly closed so his ship won't be blown off course. Umbriel then returns to the earth's surface and empties the contents of the bag and vial over Belinda and her girlfriend, who is even angrier than Belinda. The canto ends with Belinda lamenting to the Baron:*

> "O, hadst thou, cruel! been content to seize
> Hairs less in sight, or any hairs but these!"

The others in Belinda's tea-party audience shed tears of pity, but the Baron ignores her pleas: "Fate and Jove had stopped the Baron's ears."

"Belinda still her downy pillow prest . . ."

Canto V

"To arms, to arms!" the fierce virago° cries,
And swift as lightning to the combat flies.
All side in parties, and begin th' attack;
Fans clap, silks rustle, and tough whalebones° crack;
5 Heroes' and heroines' shouts confus'dly rise,
And bass and treble voices strike the skies.
No common weapons in their hands are found,
Like gods they fight, nor dread a mortal wound.° . . .
    See, fierce Belinda on the Baron flies,
10 With more than usual lightning in her eyes:
Nor feared the chief th' unequal fight to try,
Who sought no more than on his foe to die.
But this bold lord with manly strength endued,

1. virago: ferocious woman; here, Belinda's girlfriend, who leads the attack on the Baron and his friends.

4. whalebones: used to shape and stiffen women's clothing.

8. like gods . . . mortal wound: Like gods, who are immortal and have no fear of physical wounds, these fighters do not fear the wounds inflicted by words.

Cultural Diversity Read aloud a passage from Robert Fitzgerald's translation of the *Iliad*—for example, the first few stanzas of Book Four—to familiarize students with a traditional epic. Point out the lofty language and phrasing, and ask students to listen for similarities to *The Rape of the Lock* (such as intercession by supernatural beings). Remind students that Pope also translated the *Iliad* and was familiar with this and other epics.

Critical Comment: Pope Pope writes in a letter to Arabella Fermor, "As to the following cantos, all the passages of them are as fabulous as the vision at the beginning, or the transformation at the end (except the loss of your hair, which I always mention with reverence). The human persons are as fictitious as the airy ones; and the character of Belinda, as it is now managed, resembles you in nothing but in beauty." What do you think is Pope's purpose in writing this letter? **What is his tone?** [Students may say he is trying to keep her from being upset that he has written about her. Some students may think this letter sounds insincere in its flattery. Others may find it simply an explanation of his work.]

She with one finger and a thumb subdued:
15 Just where the breath of life his nostrils drew,
A charge of snuff the wily virgin threw;
The gnomes direct, to every atom just,
The pungent grains of titillating dust.
Sudden with starting tears each eye o'erflows,
20 And the high dome re-echoes to his nose.
    "Now meet thy fate," incensed Belinda cried,
And drew a deadly bodkin° from her side. . . .
    "Boast not my fall," he cried, "insulting foe!
Thou by some other shalt be laid as low.
25 Nor think, to die dejects my lofty mind:
All that I dread is leaving you behind! **(B)**
Rather than so, ah, let me still survive,
And burn in Cupid's flames—but burn alive."
    "Restore the lock!" she cries; and all around
30 "Restore the lock!" the vaulted roofs rebound.
Not fierce Othello° in so loud a strain
Roared for the handkerchief that caused his pain.
But see how oft ambitious aims are crossed,
And chiefs contend till all the prize is lost!
35 The lock, obtained with guilt, and kept with pain,
In every place is sought, but sought in vain:
With such a prize no mortal must be blessed,
So Heaven decrees! with Heaven who can contest?
    Some thought it mounted to the lunar sphere,
40 Since all things lost on earth are treasured there.
There heroes' wits are kept in ponderous vases, **(C)**
And beaux'° in snuffboxes and tweezer cases.
There broken vows and deathbed alms are found,
And lovers' hearts with ends of riband bound. . . .
45   But trust the Muse—she saw it upward rise,
Though marked by none but quick, poetic eyes: . . .
A sudden star, it shot through liquid air,
And drew behind a radiant trail of hair.° . . . **(D)**
    Then cease, bright nymph! to mourn thy ravished hair,
50 Which adds new glory to the shining sphere!
Not all the tresses that fair head can boast,
Shall draw such envy as the lock you lost.
For, after all the murders° of your eye,
When, after millions slain, yourself shall die;
55 When those fair suns shall set, as set they must,
And all those tresses shall be laid in dust,
This lock, the Muse shall consecrate to fame, **(E)**
And midst the stars inscribe Belinda's name.

22. bodkin: long, ornamental hair-pin, shaped like a dagger.

31. Othello: Shakespeare's tragic hero Othello gave his wife a handkerchief, which his enemy stole and then used as evidence of the wife's unfaithfulness.

42. beaux': fashionable gentlemen's.

48. trail of hair: the word *comet* derives from a Greek word for "long-haired."

53. murders: Just as Belinda's eyes are said to "eclipse the day" (Canto I, line 14), here they are said to murder the young men who admire her. Both compliments are ancient and trite in love poetry.

B. Critical Reading: Making Inferences

? What are the Baron's feelings toward Belinda? [He loves her, and death means nothing to him other than leaving her behind.]

C. Reader's Response: Shaping Interpretations

? What do you think Pope is saying about the intelligence of beaux in ll. 41–42? [Sample responses: Pope implies the gentlemen are unintelligent—they have small minds (since their wits fit into such small boxes); or, the society that develops such elaborate cases must be vain and frivolous.]

D. Literary Element: Parody

? In ll. 45–50, what happens to Belinda's lock? [The lock flies through the air and becomes a comet.] Point out to students that Pope's conclusion is a parody of the conclusion to Ovid's *Metamorphoses,* in which the recently assassinated Julius Caesar is transformed into a comet.

E. Literary Element: Mock Epic

? What does Pope describe in ll. 55–58? [Old age and death.] What characteristics of the mock epic are used? [Possible answers: Exaggeration, humor, and elaborate figures of speech.]

PROFESSIONAL NOTES

Thematic Connections: "The Sting of Satire" Ask students to review the poem and to identify elements of satire in Pope's work. Students can fill out a chart such as the following to record the example of satire, its target, and the techniques by which it strikes its intended target. Direct students to find at least five examples of satire.

Example of Satire	Target of Satire	Technique
[coffee ritual]	[those who drink coffee socially]	[elevated prose to describe a daily activity]

ASSESSMENT TOOLS

Check Test: True-False
1. The Baron is determined to have one of Belinda's locks. [True]
2. After the Baron cuts off one of Belinda's locks, she faints. [False]
3. A sprite named Umbriel pours a bag of sobs, grief, and tears over Belinda and her friend. [True]
4. Belinda tells the Baron she would have given him the lock if he had asked her for it. [False]
5. The poet concludes by telling Belinda to stop mourning the loss of her lock of hair. [True]

Bring the Baroque period to life by exposing students to representative art, architecture, and music. Present, or ask students to research and present, examples from the period, particularly those mentioned here (the artists Rubens, Van Dyck, and Hogarth; the architect Wren; and the composer Purcell, particularly *Dido and Aeneas*).

Making Meanings

First Thoughts

1. Although some students may see the Baron as victorious because he acquires the lock, most will agree that the narrator implies that Belinda wins because she will have undying fame.

Reviewing the Text

Students should mention at least the following events in chronological order:

- The socialites gossip.
- The group has coffee, and the Baron gets the idea of gaining the lock.
- Clarissa gives the Baron a pair of scissors.
- He cuts the lock and gloats.
- Belinda throws snuff at him to make him sneeze.
- Belinda and the Baron trade words, and a melee ensues.
- The lock is lost, and the narrator contends it has become a comet.

Shaping Interpretations

2. Most students will agree that Pope is tolerantly amused. His humor is especially evident in the juxtaposition of important and utterly trivial elements in many of the couplets (for example, in ll. 5–6, the mention of the fall of "foreign tyrants" and the fall of "nymphs at home," or the mention of counsel and tea in l. 8). A scornful tone might reveal itself through harsher words, a more direct approach, and serious consequences to the fight at the end of the poem.

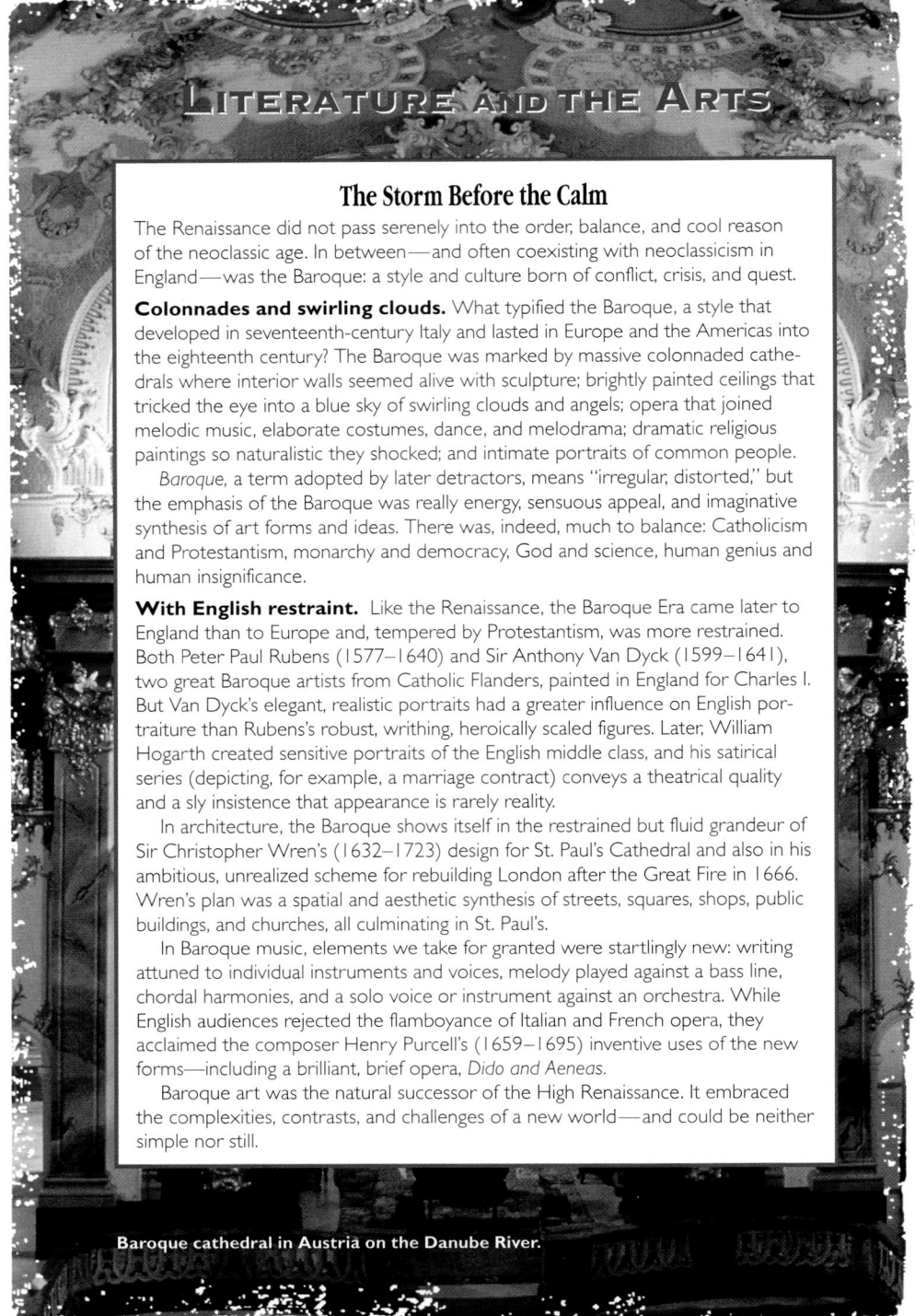

The Storm Before the Calm

The Renaissance did not pass serenely into the order, balance, and cool reason of the neoclassic age. In between—and often coexisting with neoclassicism in England—was the Baroque: a style and culture born of conflict, crisis, and quest.

Colonnades and swirling clouds. What typified the Baroque, a style that developed in seventeenth-century Italy and lasted in Europe and the Americas into the eighteenth century? The Baroque was marked by massive colonnaded cathedrals where interior walls seemed alive with sculpture; brightly painted ceilings that tricked the eye into a blue sky of swirling clouds and angels; opera that joined melodic music, elaborate costumes, dance, and melodrama; dramatic religious paintings so naturalistic they shocked; and intimate portraits of common people.

Baroque, a term adopted by later detractors, means "irregular, distorted," but the emphasis of the Baroque was really energy, sensuous appeal, and imaginative synthesis of art forms and ideas. There was, indeed, much to balance: Catholicism and Protestantism, monarchy and democracy, God and science, human genius and human insignificance.

With English restraint. Like the Renaissance, the Baroque Era came later to England than to Europe and, tempered by Protestantism, was more restrained. Both Peter Paul Rubens (1577–1640) and Sir Anthony Van Dyck (1599–1641), two great Baroque artists from Catholic Flanders, painted in England for Charles I. But Van Dyck's elegant, realistic portraits had a greater influence on English portraiture than Rubens's robust, writhing, heroically scaled figures. Later, William Hogarth created sensitive portraits of the English middle class, and his satirical series (depicting, for example, a marriage contract) conveys a theatrical quality and a sly insistence that appearance is rarely reality.

In architecture, the Baroque shows itself in the restrained but fluid grandeur of Sir Christopher Wren's (1632–1723) design for St. Paul's Cathedral and also in his ambitious, unrealized scheme for rebuilding London after the Great Fire in 1666. Wren's plan was a spatial and aesthetic synthesis of streets, squares, shops, public buildings, and churches, all culminating in St. Paul's.

In Baroque music, elements we take for granted were startlingly new: writing attuned to individual instruments and voices, melody played against a bass line, chordal harmonies, and a solo voice or instrument against an orchestra. While English audiences rejected the flamboyance of Italian and French opera, they acclaimed the composer Henry Purcell's (1659–1695) inventive uses of the new forms—including a brilliant, brief opera, *Dido and Aeneas.*

Baroque art was the natural successor of the High Renaissance. It embraced the complexities, contrasts, and challenges of a new world—and could be neither simple nor still.

Baroque cathedral in Austria on the Danube River.

3. The effect of the juxtaposition in this line is humorous: Husbands and lapdogs appear to have the same significance, belittling the husbands or elevating the status of lapdogs. Other juxtapositions students may name are the mention of counsel and tea (Canto III, l. 8), the British queen and an Indian screen (Canto III, ll. 13–14), and hungry judges and jurymen's dinners (Canto III, ll. 21–22).

MAKING MEANINGS

First Thoughts

1. Who, if anyone, do you think is victorious by the end of the action? Cite examples to support your response.

Shaping Interpretations

2. In the satirical passage that opens Canto III (lines 1–18), what seems to be Pope's **tone**—his attitude toward the queen and her courtiers? Is he scornful or tolerantly amused? How can you tell?

3. In Canto III, line 86, Pope juxtaposes—that is, places side by side—dying husbands and dying lapdogs. What is the effect of this juxtaposition? Find other juxtapositions of this kind in the poem.

4. A mock epic amusingly parodies the style and conventions of the epic. Since Homer, one epic hallmark has been the elaborate **epic simile,** or extended comparison between two unlike things. Explain how the extended similes in Canto III (lines 57–58 and 85–88) and Canto V (lines 31–32) contribute to Pope's mock-heroic style in the poem.

5. In the complete poem, Pope frequently makes **satirical** remarks about the world outside the privileged ranks to which Belinda and her friends belong. Two examples of such remarks occur in Canto III, lines 21–22 and lines 45–46. Who or what are Pope's targets in these couplets?

6. The world outside the poem and the world inside it come together in Canto III, lines 7–8. What is the effect of the three words after the dash?

7. Belinda's victory at cards (Canto III, lines 23–28) and her cries of triumph are ironic because her happiness is so momentary; it's about to be shat-

---

Reviewing the Text

Get together with two or three classmates, and devise a story map that shows all the important events in the poem in the order in which they occur. Compare your story outlines in class to see if you all agree on the main events that lead up to and follow the "rape."

---

tered by the rape of her lock. **Irony** always involves a discrepancy of some kind. Explain why Belinda's victory over the Baron (Canto V, lines 13–22) also might be considered ironic.

8. Based on the extracts you have read, how would you state Pope's **theme** in this mock epic?

Extending the Text

9. Do you think Pope's poem applies to any aspects of contemporary life? If so, how? As you review the notes you made in your Reader's Log about possibilities for modern-day spoofs, can you find passages from Pope that could serve as satiric commentaries on people's behavior in the late twentieth century?

ELEMENTS OF LITERATURE

Wit: Ne'er So Well Expressed

Pope and his contemporaries admired a quality they called **wit.** Writers and other people who possessed wit were intellectually brilliant. Their ability to detect resemblances enabled them to write in images, similes, metaphors, and other figures of speech. Their language was polished and exact; their manner, cool and controlled.

The opposite of wit was dullness. Pope ridiculed the dull writers of his day, calling them dunces, in a long, brilliant, and insulting poem called the *Dunciad.* The chief dunce of the first version of the *Dunciad* (1728) was Lewis Theobald (pronounced "tibbald"), an editor of Shakespeare whom Pope called "piddling" because he was so concerned with the minute details of Shakespeare's texts. In 1742, when Pope reissued the *Dunciad,* Theobald was replaced as chief dunce by Colley Cibber, an actor and playwright who promoted his own career by publishing an egotistical biography. Theobald and Cibber lacked wit; Pope and such friends of his as Jonathan Swift and John Gay had wit.

Wit, then, meant cleverness. But it also meant something more serious:

> True wit is Nature to advantage dressed:
> What oft was thought, but ne'er so well
>   expressed.

---

4. Pope's mock epic employs the same techniques as the epic but uses them to gently criticize his targets. In Canto III, ll. 57–58, Pope compares the frivolous characters of the poem with ladies and their knights preparing for battle. In Canto III, ll. 85–88, Pope sets up a contrast between true tragedy (mourning a mate's death) and mock tragedy (lamenting the breakage of a household item). Again, in Canto V, ll. 31–32, Pope alludes to a classic tragedy (betrayal and murder) with Othello's handkerchief, but the effect is humorous because the "death" of the lock (it cannot be restored) is insignificant compared to Othello's betrayal.

5. In the first case (Canto III, ll. 21–22), students might see a criticism of judges or a judicial system so corrupt it rushes people to sentencing so the jury can eat on schedule. In the second example (Canto III, ll. 45–46), they may interpret the target as leaders who think they see the whole situation when they only see what they want.

6. Most students will see that the effect is to deflate the solemnity of royal councils with the mention of an everyday activity—drinking tea. Others may think the lines humanize a powerful monarch.

7. The major discrepancy is between Belinda's desire to have the lock restored and the fact that it cannot be found. Another irony is Pope's use of elevated language to describe a silly fight, which consists of throwing snuff (the weapon) and the Baron's resulting sneeze (the wound).

8. Although students will see a variety of secondary themes (such as criticism of the English judicial systems), most will agree that Pope's major theme throughout the excerpts comments on the petty disputes that can preoccupy people.

Extending the Text

9. **(Analysis and Evaluation)** Students will note similarities between Pope's poem and contemporary life, such as ridiculous feuds, cagey politicians, and a questionable judicial system. Have students cite specific lines to support their comparisons.

Elements of Literature

Mini-Lesson: Wit

Reinforce the ideas in the feature by drawing diagrams like the following on the chalkboard. Working with the class, write words that Pope associates with witty and dull people in the area between the inner and middle circles on the appropriate circle diagrams. In the outer rings, record Pope's examples of witty and dull literature or sayings about wit.

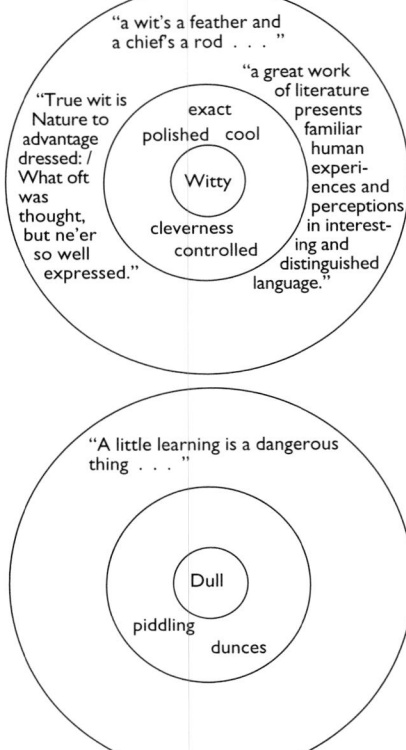

Possible Answers

1. The cleverness of the play on "take" (l. 8), or the glorified details of ceremonial coffee-drinking (ll. 34–38) in *The Rape of the Lock,* Canto III, or witty couplets like Couplet 10.
2. Human truths are found in Couplets 2, 4, or 6 or in lines from *An Essay on Man.*
3. Wit is expressed through satiric television comedies, popular songs, editorials, comedy acts, or cartoons that lampoon politics and human nature. Students might mention cartoonists Gary Larson (*The Far Side*) or Scott Adams (*Dilbert*), columnist Dave Barry, or comedian Damon Wayans.

In this couplet from *An Essay on Criticism* (lines 97–98), Pope describes something he calls "true wit." The nearest modern equivalent of true wit is what we think of as great literature, or the classics. According to Pope, these great works express ideas that people have always accepted as true ("what oft was thought"). In great works, these familiar thoughts are not expressed in dull language, but are "to advantage dressed." The term *Nature* in this couplet refers not only to what we now think of as nature—the great outdoors with its birds, beasts, trees, plants, oceans, deserts—but also to human nature and the experiences of human beings.

The couplet on true wit might be summarized as follows: "A great work of literature presents familiar human experiences and perceptions in interesting and distinguished language. A great work reminds us, in an exciting and memorable way, of what we already know about the universe and its inhabitants."

But Pope did not regard wit as the most important quality a person can have:

A wit's a feather and a chief's a rod;
An honest man's the noblest work of God.

In this couplet, from Pope's *An Essay on Man* (Epistle IV, lines 247–248), the word *wit* is used as the name of a person, a writer. The writer is compared with a chief (a great leader, such as a general, king, or president) and with an honest man. Of the three, Pope gives first place to the honest man, God's noblest work. In comparison with this virtuous person, a wit is a mere "feather"—a light and flighty decoration—and a great man of action is a mere "rod"—a defender and corrector of society. Pope came to believe that virtue and morality are more important than intellectual brilliance (though he always was inclined to feel that second-rate writing was a kind of immorality, because a bad writer defrauds the reading public). Pope spoke his final words on morality while lying on his deathbed, when he said to the attending priest, "There is nothing that is meritorious but virtue and friendship, and indeed friendship itself is only part of virtue."

To summarize, Pope thought of wit as the power enabling a writer to represent the familiar world in language that is correct, interesting, and memorable. Though he thought it important to be a wit, he thought it more important to be a virtuous person.

1. Find at least two examples from *The Rape of the Lock* that illustrate wit in the sense of "cleverness." What do you especially admire about Pope's use of language in each example?

2. Now find an example of Pope's wit in its deeper sense: the elegant expression of a truth about human nature.

3. How would you define "wit" in today's world? Is there anyone on the contemporary scene whom you admire as an exponent of wit?

Pope's Villa, Twickenham by Samuel Scott.
Ackermann and Johnson Ltd., London.

OPTIONS FOR TEACHING

STRATEGIES FOR INCLUSION

Advanced Challenge students to search for quotations on the subject of wit or examples of wit and to present their examples to the class. They might use photos or drawings to enhance their presentations.

Visual/Spatial Ask students to depict in words or sketches the contents of the minds of a witty person and a dull person, according to Pope's definitions. You may also want students to create collages or mobiles depicting the trappings or objects they associate with Pope's ideas of wit and dullness. Display students' work in the classroom, with examples of wit on one side and those of dullness on the other.

CHOICES: Building Your Portfolio

Writer's Notebook

1. Collecting Ideas for a Persuasive Essay

Why not, like Pope, use the rich, the famous, and even the trivial to find serious social issues and values to write about in a persuasive essay? A focus on entertainment or sports superstars may yield surprising results. Vigilantly scan TV programs about celebrities, print and TV ads in which celebrities endorse products or causes, and newspaper photos and stories about athletes and stars. Jot down brief descriptions (who, what, and why). Then react imaginatively. Brainstorm *issues*—perhaps of censorship, privacy, health, sexism, elitism, or wealth. Save your ideas for the Writer's Workshop on page 612.

Critical Writing

2. Targeting Pope's Targets

In an essay, identify the targets of Pope's satire in *The Rape of the Lock,* and describe the devices Pope uses to ridicule these targets. Consider what Pope says about social role-playing and about the foolishness of human behavior in general.

Critical Writing

3. From *Beowulf* to Pope

Compare Pope's mock epic with a serious epic: *Beowulf,* or, if you know them well, Homer's *Iliad* or *Odyssey.* Consider these elements of the epic in your discussion: invocations to the Muse, statement of subject, intervention of gods and goddesses, epic battles, a hero or heroine who reflects the values of a particular society, and use of elevated language.

Creative Writing

4. Mocking Modern Life

Write a mock epic about some event in contemporary life that's blown out of proportion: two teenage girls wearing the same dress at a school dance, two teenage boys who show up for a date with the same girl at the same time, a school mascot that gets lost, and so on. Be sure to include these devices: an invocation to the Muse, intervention by the gods, an epic battle, and a warning dream.

Creative Writing

5. Your Mock-Heroic Style

In Canto III of *The Rape of the Lock,* Pope describes making and drinking coffee in rich, elevated, and roundabout language (lines 33–40). This mock-heroic writing style breaks the elementary rule which says that writers must try to use simple, direct language when describing simple activities. As an exercise in mock-heroic writing, write a prose description of a common activity (such as riding a bicycle or cooking and eating a hamburger), using inflated language and rich images. Do not strain for comic effects; instead, try to be elegant. Study the way Pope uses these two words: *instructive* (Canto III, line 11) and *ravished* (Canto V, line 49). Try to use one of your words in this way.

Speaking / Listening

6. Talking Back to Pope

Which one of Pope's sayings about human nature do you disagree with? Prepare for oral delivery a lighthearted rebuttal of the poet's position, starting with a sentence such as the following: "Resolved: That Alexander Pope erred when he claimed that . . . " Support your rebuttal with specific examples and incidents.

ALEXANDER POPE 535

STRATEGIES FOR INCLUSION

Visual Invite students to draw a scene to help them focus on activities #4, #5, or #6. Encourage them to review their drawings as inspiration for rich description in their writing. Students may include their artwork in presentations or as illustrations with their writing.

PORTFOLIO ASSESSMENT

Choices: Assessment Criteria For help in evaluating these Choices assignments, see the criteria in the *Portfolio Management System,* pp. 114–115.

Beyond the Poems

Choices: Building Your Portfolio

1. **Writer's Notebook** Remind students to save their work. They may use it as prewriting for the Writer's Workshop on p. 612.
2. **Critical Writing** To help students notice the targets and devices in *The Rape of the Lock,* encourage them to log references as they re-read the poem.
3. **Critical Writing** Students can use a checklist like the following to compare the epic form with Pope's mock epic. Ask students to include a brief description of each element.

Elements	True Epic	Mock Epic
Invocation to the muse	_____	_____
Statement of subject	_____	_____
Serious subject	_____	_____
Superhuman intervention	_____	_____
Battles	_____	_____
Representative hero/heroine	_____	_____
Elevated language	_____	_____
Wordplay	_____	_____
Satiric devices	_____	_____
Target(s) of criticism	_____	_____

4. **Creative Writing** Have students work in groups to enact a modern mock epic. Invite group members to write their own parts and then work together to stage the production. Videotape the performances if possible, so students can analyze them afterward.
5. **Creative Writing** Suggest that students keep logs as they carefully observe common activities. Emphasize that they should find details that can provide vivid imagery and targets for their satire.
6. **Speaking/Listening** Have students work with partners to review Pope's statements. The partners should invite each other to react to specific statements that seem controversial or daring. Students should work individually on their rebuttals.

Alexander Pope **T535**

WORLD LITERATURE — France

Voltaire
(1694–1778)

François-Marie Arouet (ár·we), better known by his pen name Voltaire, is remembered chiefly for his lifelong fight against injustice. Throughout his life, he implored his fellow philosophers to "Crush the infamous," by which he meant all things inhumane and oppressive. As a satirist, philosopher, historian, dramatist, and poet, Voltaire continually criticized the wastefulness of war, the intolerance of organized religion, and the plight of the poor.

Born in Paris to middle-class parents, Voltaire studied law for a time but soon gave it up to become a writer. His early reputation was based on his classical tragedies and his lampoons of the government. Yet Voltaire's celebrity did not prevent his being brutally beaten at the hands of an offended nobleman, imprisoned in the Bastille, and exiled to England in 1726.

Voltaire (1833) engraved by James Mollison from an original by Nicolas de Largillière.

In London, Voltaire met Jonathan Swift and Alexander Pope and was deeply influenced by the works of Bacon, Newton, and Locke, which emphasized the experimental method in science. When he returned to Paris, Voltaire wrote philosophical essays and historical studies that reflected this influence—he avoided the abstract in favor of a concrete focus on the way people actually lived and worked according to their beliefs. Many of these writings, collected under the title *Philosophical Letters,* were considered heretical and burned by the French parliament in 1734. Voltaire lived much of his later life near the Swiss border with France. He died during a rare visit to Paris, taken at age eighty-three to see his last play produced. Initially refused a Christian burial, Voltaire's remains were interred in Paris with great ceremony thirteen years later, following the revolution so greatly influenced by his ideas for reform.

(Map) Europe in 1721.
©Rand McNally.

536 THE RESTORATION AND THE EIGHTEENTH CENTURY

OPTIONS FOR TEACHING

STRATEGIES FOR INCLUSION

Intrapersonal Ask students to keep notes as they read, paying particular attention to the characters' names and the layers of meaning those names might impart. Alert students that each name may have an allegorical significance that indicates the character represents a specific group or human trait.

Linguistic Ask students to use a dictionary to analyze the name of Pangloss's brand of philosophy: metaphysico-theologo-cosmolonigology. Have students share their ideas about the sense and nonsense of the word with the class. Challenge students to relate the label to Pangloss's practice.

BEFORE YOU READ

FROM **CANDIDE**

Background

In the tumultuous social climate of eighteenth-century Europe, writers, scientists, and philosophers questioned the "settled truths" of society as they never had before. Yet direct challenges to authority can be dangerous, in the eighteenth century or in any age. Satire—with its indirect criticism and deflating humor—thus became the weapon of choice for many eighteenth-century thinkers.

Voltaire used the device of the travel book, as Jonathan Swift did in *Gulliver's Travels,* to satirize everything—the Church, the State, and the mindless optimism of some eighteenth-century philosophers. Voltaire's hero Candide is an innocent who has been schooled by the repellent Doctor Pangloss to believe that everything that happens in the world happens for the best. The convictions of sweet-tempered Candide are severely tested in a series of outrageous and hilarious adventures. And, just as Swift's use of the name "Gulliver" may suggest the adjective "gullible," Voltaire's choice of "Candide"—punning on "candor,

King Frederick II Comes to See Voltaire (c. 1750) drawn by Mousiau, engraving by P. Baquoy.

candid"—points to the qualities of childlike honesty, trust, and naïveté.

In the opening chapters of the novel, Voltaire singles out for his wicked satire some of the most important social institutions of eighteenth-century Europe. When Candide presumes to court the Baron's daughter, he is tossed out of the castle in short order. No sooner does he become the hero of the Bulgarians than he is thrown into chains and flogged. (Master of the humorous overstatement, Voltaire has his

hero thrashed a ridiculous four thousand times.) Candide's experiences, however funny, reveal that the worlds of both the castle and the army are deeply flawed by snobbery, hypocrisy, and brutality.

Another target for the author's stinging criticism is the complacency of the philosopher Doctor Pangloss, whose name means "all tongue." Throughout the increasingly wretched events of *Candide,* Pangloss blithely mouths the theories of the German philosopher Gottfried Leibniz, who believed that an utterly rational God made a rational world in which everything, including evil, has a place and a purpose. Like Leibniz, Doctor Pangloss's perpetual slogan is "In this best of all possible worlds, . . . all is for the best."

A Dialogue with the Text

As you read these chapters, think about how Voltaire's satire might apply to aspects of today's world. Jot down notes in your Reader's Log.

Background

To connect their experiences and perspectives to the selection, students might tell about a travel experience of their own in a satirical way. The travel need not be exotic; a trip to the library or a walk to a bus stop qualifies as a journey. Remind students that, like Candide, their heroes (in this case, the students themselves) must be tested in the process.

A Dialogue with the Text

Students might use a chart like the following to organize their notes, identifying Voltaire's issues and targets and relating them to modern society. After students have finished reading the story, have them compare their findings in small groups.

Voltaire's Times	Modern Times	Differences? Observations?
[military impressment]	[military draft]	[today one must register to be drafted]

Ask students to explain how Voltaire's *Candide* expands on the satires already studied in this Collection. [Students may say that the story is more openly philosophical than the other selections or that it more blatantly ridicules human folly than the others because of its allegorical nature.]

PROGRAM MANAGER

Selection Summary See **Teaching Notes, *Teaching Resources A,*** p. 128, for a summary of this selection.

A. Reader's Response: First Thoughts

? What type of person do you think the Baron is, given his name?

[Sample responses: He is probably loud, larger than life, like thunder. He is strict and Germanic.]

B. Critical Reading: Finding Details

? Why is the Baron one of the most powerful lords in Westphalia?

[Because his castle has a door and windows, and because his Great Hall boasts a single tapestry.] What image of Westphalia does this elicit? [Students may say that it reveals the land to be poverty-stricken (if a person wields power because his or her castle has a door and windows and only one tapestry, the others must not have these simple "luxuries"), materialistic, lacking in aesthetics, and barbaric.]

C. Critical Reading: Identifying Main Ideas

Ask students to summarize Pangloss's philosophy. [Possible answers: There is no effect without cause; there are no accidents; everything has a purpose to serve human needs; all is for the best.]

D. Literary Element: Parody

Voltaire parodies the attempts of his age to apply reason in all situations, including matters of the heart; he parodies objectivity and the scientific method.

---

from Candide

Voltaire
translated by **Richard Aldington**

Chapter I

How Candide was brought up in a noble castle and how he was expelled from the same

(A) In the castle of Baron Thunder-ten-tronckh in Westphalia[1] there lived a youth, endowed by Nature with the most gentle character. His face was the expression of his soul. His judgment was quite honest and he was extremely simple-minded; and this was the reason, I think, that he was named Candide. Old servants in the house suspected that he was the son of the Baron's sister and a decent honest gentleman of the neighborhood, whom this young lady would never marry because he could only prove seventy-one quarterings,[2] and the rest of his genealogical tree was lost, owing to the injuries of time. **(B)** The Baron was one of the most powerful lords in Westphalia, for his castle possessed a door and windows. His Great Hall was even decorated with a piece of tapestry. The dogs in his stableyards formed a pack of hounds when necessary; his grooms were his huntsmen; the village curate was his Grand Almoner.[3] They all called him "My Lord," and laughed heartily at his stories. The Baroness weighed about three hundred and fifty pounds, was therefore greatly respected, and did the honors of the house with a dignity which rendered her still more respectable. Her daughter Cunegonde,[4] aged seventeen, was rosy-cheeked, fresh, plump, and tempting. The Baron's son appeared in every respect worthy of his father. The tutor Pangloss[5] was the oracle of the house, and little

Le Baron....voyant cette cause & cet effet, chassa Candide du Château à grands coups de pied dans le derriere;
Candide Chap.1er

"The Baron . . . observing this cause and effect, expelled Candide from the castle by kicking him in the backside frequently and hard."

Candide followed his lessons with all the candor of his age and character. **(C)** Pangloss taught metaphysico-theologo-cosmolonigology.[6] He proved admirably that there is no effect without a cause and that in this best of all possible worlds, My Lord the Baron's castle was the best of castles and his wife the best of all possible Baronesses. **(D)** "'Tis demonstrated," said he, "that things cannot be otherwise; for, since everything is made for an end, everything is necessarily for the best end. Observe that noses were made to wear spectacles; and so we have spectacles. Legs were visibly instituted to be breeched, and we have breeches.

1. **Westphalia** (west·fā'lē·ə): region in western Germany, noted for its excellent ham. In a letter to his niece, Voltaire described Westphalia as "vast, sad, sterile, detestable."
2. **quarterings:** divisions on a coat of arms or family tree. Seventy-one is an absurdly high number, tracing a person's genealogy back over 2,000 years.
3. **Grand Almoner:** member of a noble household responsible for allotting charity to the poor.
4. **Cunegonde** (kyōo'nā·gônd').
5. **Pangloss:** Greek for "all tongue."
6. **metaphysico-theologo-cosmolonigology:** This nonsense term is a satirical poke at the philosopher Leibniz and his followers, especially the embedded syllable *-nig-*, a shortened form of *nigaud*, which is French for "simpleton."

OPTIONS FOR TEACHING

INTEGRATING THE LANGUAGE ARTS

Strategic Reading Before you discuss the selection as a class, assign each student a passage of the selection to study. Ask students to write in their Reader's Logs any information they learn from their assigned passage that is not explicit; for example, in learning that the Baron is powerful because his castle has windows and a door, readers can infer that Westphalia must be

relatively poor. Later, as the class discusses the selection, have students share their insights.

Speaking and Listening To help students identify the **tone** of the piece, ask them to work in pairs, reading aloud excerpts to one another; have the partners try out different tones and inflections until they feel they have determined how each line is best spoken. Reconvene the class, and have several students read aloud the

sentences in tones they feel are appropriate. Most likely students will find the sentences ironic or ridiculous, yet phrased in a sophisticated manner—therefore humorous in tone.

Writing: Letter Ask students to write a letter to Candide. Encourage them to give Candide advice and perhaps explain their own philosophies for getting along in the world.

Stones were formed to be quarried and to build castles; and My Lord has a very noble castle; the greatest Baron in the province should have the best house; and as pigs were made to be eaten, we eat pork all the year round; consequently, those who have asserted that all is well talk nonsense; they ought to have said that all is for the best." Candide listened attentively and believed innocently; for he thought Mademoiselle Cunegonde extremely beautiful, although he was never bold enough to tell her so. He decided that after the happiness of being born Baron of Thunder-ten-tronckh, the second degree of happiness was to be Mademoiselle Cunegonde; the third, to see her every day; and the fourth to listen to Doctor Pangloss, the greatest philosopher of the province and therefore of the whole world. One day when Cunegonde was walking near the castle, in a little wood which was called The Park, she observed Doctor Pangloss in the bushes, giving a lesson in experimental physics to her mother's waiting-maid, a very pretty and docile brunette. Mademoiselle Cunegonde had a great inclination for science and watched breathlessly the reiterated experiments she witnessed; she observed clearly the Doctor's sufficient reason, the effects and the causes, and returned home very much excited, pensive, filled with the desire of learning, reflecting that she might be the sufficient reason of young Candide and that he might be hers. On her way back to the castle she met Candide and blushed; Candide also blushed. She bade him good morning in a hesitating voice; Candide replied without knowing what he was saying. Next day, when they left the table after dinner, Cunegonde and Candide found themselves behind a screen; Cunegonde dropped her handkerchief, Candide picked it up; she innocently held his hand; the young man innocently kissed the young lady's hand with remarkable vivacity, tenderness, and grace; their lips met, their eyes sparkled, their knees trembled, their hands wandered. Baron Thunder-ten-tronckh passed near the screen, and, observing this cause and effect, expelled Candide from the castle by kicking him in the backside frequently and hard. Cunegonde swooned; when she recovered her senses, the Baroness slapped her in the face; and all was in consternation in the noblest and most agreeable of all possible castles.

Chapter II

What happened to Candide among the Bulgarians

Candide, expelled from the earthly paradise, wandered for a long time without knowing where he was going, turning up his eyes to Heaven, gazing back frequently at the noblest of castles which held the most beautiful of young Baronesses; he lay down to sleep supperless between two furrows in the open fields: It snowed heavily in large flakes. The next morning the shivering Candide, penniless, dying of cold and exhaustion, dragged himself toward the neighboring town, which was called Waldberghoff-trarbk-dikdorff. He halted sadly at the door of an inn. Two men dressed in blue noticed him. "Comrade," said one, "there's a well-built young man of the right height."[7] They went up to Candide and very civilly invited him to dinner. "Gentlemen," said Candide with charming modesty, "you do me a great honor, but I have no money to pay my share." "Ah, sir," said one of the men in blue, "persons of your figure and merit never pay anything; are you not five feet five tall?" "Yes, gentlemen," said he, bowing, "that is my height." "Ah, sir, come to table; we will not only pay your expenses, we will never allow a man like you to be short of money; men were only made to help each other." "You are in the right," said Candide, "that is what Doctor Pangloss was always telling me, and I see that everything is for the best." They begged him to accept a few crowns,[8] he took them and wished to give them an IOU, they refused to take it, and all sat down to table. "Do you not love tenderly . . ." "Oh, yes," said he. "I love Mademoiselle Cunegonde tenderly." "No," said one of the gentlemen. "We were asking if you do not tenderly love the King of the Bulgarians." "Not a bit," said he, "for I have never seen him." "What! He is the most charming of kings, and you must drink his health." "Oh, gladly, gentlemen." And he drank. "That is sufficient," he was told. "You are now the support, the aid, the defender, the hero of the Bulgarians, your fortune is made, and your glory assured." They immediately put

7. **height:** Voltaire is making fun of the recruiting practices of the "King of the Bulgarians"—Voltaire's satiric name for King Frederick the Great of Prussia—who chose and organized soldiers according to their height.
8. **crowns:** units of money.

E. Literary Element: Allusion

? What is Voltaire alluding to? [The expulsion of Adam and Eve from the Garden of Eden in the Bible.]

F. Reader's Response: First Thoughts

? What is your first reaction when you read the soldier's comment "men were only made to help each other"? [Sample responses: The comment makes me suspicious of the man's motives. The line is admirable, but things are never so good.] What might this passage **foreshadow**? [Sample responses: It foreshadows the opposite of men helping each other—brutality and trouble for Candide. It foreshadows a change in Candide's luck.]

Technology Tip

TECHNOLOGY The complete *Candide* is available in English from the Voltaire Foundation at Oxford University at **http://www .voltaire.ox.ac.uk/tx/Candide /candide00.html**. *You may want to preview any Internet activity that you suggest to students. Because these resources are sometimes public forums, their content can be unpredictable.*

Critical Comment: Voltaire Ben Ray Redman, editor of *The Portable Voltaire,* writes, "[Voltaire] was, obviously, not a great creative writer. . . . He created no characters, he filled no scenes with bustling life, he explored no depths of human nature, he exposed and manipulated no psychological subtleties. In other words, he was not a great modern novelist, for the good and sufficient reason that in his day the modern novel had not yet been born; and he was no originator,

no pioneer in literature. *Candide* is, indeed, a masterpiece, the origins and elements of which have been traced to *The Thousand and One Nights* [and] *Gulliver's Travels*. It is, in short, the tale at its highest level. But, even at its highest, this form is not one which is capable of bearing burdens that other literary forms can bear; not one in which the experience of life can find its fullest, most profound, and most affecting expression." Ask students whether they agree or not with this

evaluation. Allow students to debate the evaluation's specific points: Is Candide a character or a caricature? What experiences stand out from the others? Does *Candide* have emotional content? What literary traditions does Voltaire incorporate in *Candide*?

A. Literary Element: Satire

Ask students to describe the types of satire employed and to identify examples. [Students may point to faulty logic—Candide's choice is called liberty; irony—the contrast between liberty and the gauntlet; and exaggeration—for example, his punishment (running the gauntlet thirty-six times), the size of the regiment that formed the gauntlet (two thousand men), and the number of strokes Candide survived (four thousand).]

B. Reader's Response: Shaping Interpretations

? Why do you think Voltaire uses the phrase *vast genius* to describe the King of the Bulgarians? [Sample responses: He's a genius because he lets Candide go. Or, Voltaire is being facetious. His genius is not vast, because he is credited with perception but knows only what he is told, and he is lacking in judgment because he pardons a metaphysician (a stab at metaphysicians of the day).]

Finding Common Ground

So students might easily refer to their notes when answering the questions, suggest that they use graphic organizers like the following to record their thoughts. For the third set of questions, encourage students to brainstorm as a class for elements of the popular romance or adventure narrative.

Modern "Candide"

What he would be taught today	
Modern attitudes	
Modern corruptions	
Platitudes tested	

Modern "Panglosses"

In education	
In politics	
In religion	
Other	

Modern Entertainment

Qualities of popular entertainment	Parodied in Candide?

---

irons on his legs and took him to a regiment. He was made to turn to the right and left, to raise the ramrod and return the ramrod, to take aim, to fire, to march double time, and he was given thirty strokes with a stick; the next day he drilled not quite so badly, and received only twenty strokes; the day after, he only had ten and was looked on as a prodigy by his comrades. Candide was completely mystified and could not make out how he was a hero. One fine spring day he thought he would take a walk, going straight ahead, in the belief that to use his legs as he pleased was a privilege of the human species as well as of animals. He had not gone two leagues[9] when four other heroes, each six feet tall, fell upon him, bound him, and dragged him back to a cell. He was asked by his judges whether he would rather be thrashed thirty-six times by the whole regiment or receive a dozen lead bullets at once in his brain. **A** Although he protested that men's wills are free and that he wanted neither one nor the other, he had to make a choice; by virtue of that gift of God which is called *liberty,* he determined to run the gauntlet[10] thirty-six times and actually did so

9. **leagues:** A league is a unit of distance equal to about three miles.
10. **run the gauntlet:** run between two rows of soldiers who strike the victim with clubs or other weapons.

twice. There were two thousand men in the regiment. That made four thousand strokes which laid bare the muscles and nerves from his neck to his backside. As they were about to proceed to a third turn, Candide, utterly exhausted, begged as a favor that they would be so kind as to smash his head; he obtained this favor; they bound his eyes and he was made to kneel down. At that moment the King of the Bulgarians came by and inquired the victim's crime, and as this King was possessed of a vast genius, he perceived from what he **B** learned about Candide that he was a young metaphysician[11] very ignorant in worldly matters, and therefore pardoned him with a clemency which will be praised in all newspapers and all ages. An honest surgeon healed Candide in three weeks with the ointments recommended by Dioscorides.[12] He had already regained a little skin and could walk when the King of the Bulgarians went to war with the King of the Abares.[13]

11. **metaphysician** (met′ə·fə·zish′ən): philosopher who studies the nature of reality and the origin and structure of the universe.
12. **Dioscorides** (dī′əs·kôr·ə·dēz′): Greek army physician who wrote a treatise on medicine in the first century A.D. Even in Voltaire's day, Dioscorides' work was out-of-date.
13. **Abares** (a·bär′): that is, the French, who fought against the "Bulgarians," or Prussians, in the Seven Years' War (1756–1763).

FINDING COMMON GROUND

The disasters that befall the innocent Candide—including expulsion from the Baron's castle and impressment into a foreign army—are presented with such deft wit that readers often laugh out loud. Yet Voltaire's humor never obscures his deeper point, that humanity and social institutions are in need of reform. The need for reform, as well as admonitions couched in satire, may continue to be found in our world.

Thinking back over the story, jot down some brief notes in response to the following questions:

• If a "Candide" were created today, what would he be taught? What attitudes and corruptions in society would a modern Candide face, testing all those platitudes he'd learned about life?

• Are there "Panglosses" in the world today—in education, politics, or religion? Where and why

do you still hear people saying things like "It's all for the best"?

• Is *Candide* a parody of the popular adventures or romances on today's best-seller lists or in the movies? Why do the kind of romances *Candide* makes fun of continue to have such an appeal for audiences?

Take a moment to reflect on your responses and the notes you've already made in your Reader's Log; then get together with a few classmates for a discussion of *Candide* and its satiric intent. Be sure your agenda includes discussion of whether or not Voltaire's underlying message against intolerance, cruelty, and smugness still has some timely applications in today's world. After your group has finished its discussion, share your findings with the class.

(Opposite) *Astronomy, 1750* by Richard Houston.
Museum of the History of Science, Oxford.

CROSSING THE CURRICULUM

Geography Have students locate Westphalia, Bulgaria, and Prussia on a map, preferably a map from Voltaire's time. Some editions of *Candide* contain maps of actual places as well as Voltaire's imaginary locales. Invite students to share their findings by bringing books, maps, or photographs of the locations to display in the classroom.

ASSESSMENT TOOLS

Check Test: True-False
1. Candide is a deceptive person. [False]
2. The Baron is a powerful person. [True]
3. Candide loves the Baroness. [False]
4. Candide volunteers for the Bulgarian army. [False]
5. Candide survives four thousand strokes from the gauntlet. [True]

The Restoration and the Eighteenth Century

 Collection 7

AN APPETITE FOR EXPERIENCE

> ***Theme:*** **This Great, Wide World**
> The Restoration and the eighteenth century were times of great intellectual and artistic achievement. Several genres flourished during this period, reflecting the great appetite for life that marked the lives of their writers.

Thematic Focus

Each selection offers a look at the wide-ranging interests, experiences, and activities that were a part of this age.

- *from* **The Diary of Samuel Pepys** This detailed diary contains firsthand accounts of some of the great public events of seventeenth–century England.
- *from* **A Journal of the Plague Year** Defoe's semifictional reconstruction of the bubonic plague that ravaged London in 1665 still fascinates readers.
- *from* **A Dictionary of the English Language/Letter to Lord Chesterfield** Johnson's dictionary and his letter provide pointed examples of eighteenth-century wit.
- *from* **The Life of Samuel Johnson** Boswell's biography successfully captures not only the details of Johnson's life, but of the age as well.
- *from* **Faust** A quest for experience leads to a bargain with the devil.
- **Elegy Written in a Country Churchyard** Gray's immensely popular poem immortalizes the lives of humble, ordinary people.

Literary Focus

Literary Element	Selection / Feature
Diary	**The Diary of Samuel Pepys**
Journal	**A Journal of the Plague Year**
Style	**A Dictionary of the English Language/Letter to Lord Chesterfield**
Biography	**The Life of Samuel Johnson**
Elegy	**Elegy Written in a Country Churchyard**

Writing Focus

The following flowchart shows how the writing assignment for each selection relates to the writing assignment presented in the Writer's Workshop at the end of the unit.

Selection	Work-in-Progress Assignment
The Diary of Samuel Pepys	Test validity of opinions for a persuasive essay p. 555
A Journal of the Plague Year	Chart ideas and support for a persuasive essay p. 566
A Dictionary of the English Language/Letter to Lord Chesterfield	Create persuasive arguments p. 579
The Life of Samuel Johnson	Generate opposing ideas p. 589
Elegy Written in a Country Churchyard	Write thesis statements p. 607
Writer's Workshop	Write a persuasive essay pp. 612–617

Collection Planner

SELECTION/ FEATURE	Literary Elements / Active Reading	Writing	Speaking and Listening	Language and Vocabulary
from **The Diary of Samuel Pepys** Samuel Pepys (pp. 542–555) **Connections: On Keeping a Notebook** Joan Didion (pp. 552–553)	• Reader's Log p. 543 • Diary p. 543	• Critical Writing: Write about Pepys's character p. 555 • Creative Writing: Make plans for diary p. 555		• Language and Style: Compare seventeenth-century usage to modern usage p. 554
from **A Journal of the Plague Year** Daniel Defoe (pp. 556–569) Spotlight On: Joseph Addison and Sir Richard Steele (pp. 567–569)	• Reader's Log p. 557 • Journal p. 557	• Critical Writing: Write comparison essay p. 566– • Critical Writing: Write opinion essay p. 566 • Creative Writing: Describe natural disaster p. 566		
from **A Dictionary of the English Language/ Letter to Lord Chesterfield** Samuel Johnson (pp. 570–581) Spotlight On: In Support of Shakespeare (pp. 580–581)	• Reader's Log p. 575 • Style pp. 578–579	• Critical Writing: Describe Johnson's character p. 579 • Critical Writing: Write about satire p. 579 • Creative Writing: Reply to Johnson's letter p. 579 • Creative Writing: Create dictionary p. 579 • Creative Writing: Modernize Johnson's letter p. 579		• Style: Find examples of Johnson's individual style pp. 578–579
from **The Life of Samuel Johnson** James Boswell (pp. 582–589)	• Reader's Log p. 583 • Biography p. 583	• Critical Writing: Write essay p. 589 • Creative Writing: Write biographical sketch p. 589 • Social Studies: Research Literary Club p. 589		
from **Faust** Johann Wolfgang von Goethe (pp. 590–598)	• Reader's Log p. 591		• Discuss character type p. 598	
Elegy Written in a Country Churchyard Thomas Gray (pp. 599–607) **Student to Student** (p. 605)	• Reader's Log p. 600 • Elegy p. 606	• Critical Writing: Compare elegies p. 607 • Creative Writing: Write epitaph p. 607 • Creative Writing: Write brief meditation p. 607		• Language and Style: List Gray's use of poetic words and inversions/Paraphrase pp. 606–607
The English Language: Decorum and Order John Algeo (pp. 609–611)				• Try It Out: Compare definitions p. 611
Writer's Workshop: Persuasive Essay (pp. 612–617)		• Writing process: Persuasive essay pp. 612–617		
Language Workshop: Effective Sentences (p. 618)		• Revise essay p. 618		
Learning for Life: Employment Services (p. 619)		• Design brochure p. 619 • Write public service announcement p. 619	• Broadcast public service announcement p. 619	

Collection Resources

Teaching Resources A	Audiovisual Resources Binder	Test Booklet
Cross-Curricular Activity p. 166	Fine Art Transparency 7.1	Collection 7 Test pp. 117–119

 Computer disk or CD-ROM

 Videodisc

 Overhead Transparency

PROGRAM RESOURCES

Electronic Media	Teaching Resources with Organizer		Audiovisual Resources Binder
	Teaching Resources A	Other Resources	
• Test Generator • Language Workshop: Appositives	• Teaching Notes p. 145 • Reading Organizer p. 150 • Language Link pp. 151–152 • Words to Own p. 153	• Test Booklet: Selection Test pp. 105–106 • Language and Writing Skills Worksheets pp. 54, 76 • Portfolio Management System pp. 39, 116	
• Test Generator • Language Workshop: Clauses	• Teaching Notes p. 146 • Reading Organizer p. 154 • Language Link pp. 155–156 • Words to Own p. 157	• Test Booklet: Selection Test pp. 107–108 • Language and Writing Skills Worksheets pp. 79–83 and 115 • Portfolio Management System pp. 53, 62–63, 117	
• Test Generator	• Teaching Notes pp. 146–147 • Reading Organizers p. 158–159 • Words to Own p. 160	• Test Booklet: Selection Test pp. 109–110 • Portfolio Management System pp. 54–55, 62–63, 118–119	• Elements of Literature Transparency 7.2
• Test Generator	• Teaching Notes pp. 147–148 • Reading Organizer p. 161 • Words to Own p. 162	• Test Booklet: Selection Test pp. 111–112 • Portfolio Management System pp. 62–63, 120	
	• Teaching Notes p. 148		
• Test Generator	• Teaching Notes pp. 148–149 • Reading Organizer p. 163	• Test Booklet: Selection Test pp. 113–114 • Portfolio Management System pp. 48–49, 121	
• Test Generator • Videodisc, Side A: "English: A Living Language, Part 2"	• Teaching Notes p. 149	• Test Booklet: Selection Test pp. 115–116	
• Writer's Workshop 2: Controversial Issue		• Portfolio Management System pp. 122–124	• Revision Transparencies 7.3–7.4
• Language Workshop: Parallel structure	• Language Workshop pp. 164–165		
		• Portfolio Management System p. 125	

COLLECTION PLANNER

Proofreading Warm-ups

You may use the following exercises to help students practice their proofreading skills. Copy a set of incorrect sentences onto the chalkboard, and have students find and correct the spelling, punctuation, usage, and mechanical errors in each sentence. Ask students to share and discuss their responses.

	Sentences with Errors	Sentences Corrected	Skills Covered
1	**a.** did you know that many people kept detailed diarys in the seventeenth century asked Ms. Lanford **b.** and she continued a surprisingly large amount of these diaries has survived	**a.** "Did you know that many people kept detailed diaries in the seventeenth century?" asked Ms. Lanford. **b.** "And," she continued, "a surprisingly large number of these diaries have survived."	Quotation marks, Capitalization, Spelling, Question marks, Comma usage, Standard usage, Subject-verb agreement, End marks
2	**a.** historians find "The Diary of Samuel Pepys" useful **b.** pepys not only witnessed such public events as the Great Fire of London but he also recorded trivial personnel one's	**a.** Historians find <u>The Diary of Samuel Pepys</u> useful. **b.** Pepys not only witnessed such public events as the Great Fire of London, but he also recorded trivial personal ones.	Capitalization, Underline book titles, Comma usage, Spelling, Apostrophe usage, End marks
3	**a.** some of the words in Pepyss work sound wrong today said Ms. Scott **b.** "however if you would of used them in the seventeenth century it would of been considered correct," she added	**a.** "Some of the words in Pepys's work sound wrong today," said Ms. Scott. **b.** "However, if you had used them in the seventeenth century, it would have been considered correct," she added.	Quotation marks, Apostrophes, Capitalization, Comma usage, Nonstandard usage, Verb error, End marks
4	**a.** journals are records of events that are kept on a regular bases by someone whom is a eyewitness or a participant **b.** do you, keep a journal	**a.** Journals are records of events that are kept on a regular basis by someone who is an eyewitness or a participant. **b.** Do you keep a journal?	Capitalization, Spelling, Who/Whom usage, Nonstandard usage, Comma usage, End marks
5	**a.** i have read the writing's of both Johnson and Boswell proclaimed Pat **b.** "who did you find the more interesting of the two," asked Janine?	**a.** "I have read the writings of both Johnson and Boswell," proclaimed Pat. **b.** "Whom did you find the more interesting of the two?" asked Janine.	Quotation marks, Capitalization, Apostrophe usage, Comma usage, Who/Whom usage, Question marks, End marks
6	**a.** one popular eighteenth century periodical, was The Tatler **b.** written by Addison and Steele the periodical reported on Current Event's as well as entertainment	**a.** One popular eighteenth-century periodical was <u>The Tatler</u>. **b.** Written by Addison and Steele, the periodical reported on current events as well as entertainment.	Capitalization, Hyphens, Underline titles, Comma usage, Apostrophe usage, End marks
7	**a.** is The Life of Samuel Johnson a biography or a autobiography **b.** its a biography because it was not wrote by Sam himself	**a.** Is <u>The Life of Samuel Johnson</u> a biography or an autobiography? **b.** It's a biography because it was not written by Johnson himself.	Capitalization, Underline book titles, Nonstandard usage, Question marks, Apostrophe usage, Verb errors, Formal usage (Sam), End marks
8	**a.** goethes literary work Faust is based on a legend about a man who sold his soul to the devil **b.** goethes Faust character is unique among the many versions of this legend cause he is granted salvation	**a.** Goethe's literary work <u>Faust</u> is based on a legend about a man who sold his soul to the devil. **b.** Goethe's Faust character is unique among the many versions of this legend because he is granted salvation.	Capitalization, Apostrophe usage, Underline play titles, Formal usage (cause), End marks
9	**a.** thomas gray arthur of the poem Elegy Written in a Country Churchyard was a shy man **b.** gray who's poem was popular wrote about the lifes of ordinary people	**a.** Thomas Gray, author of the poem "Elegy Written in a Country Churchyard," was a shy man. **b.** Gray, whose poem was popular, wrote about the lives of ordinary people.	Capitalization, Comma usage, Spelling, Quotation marks, Who's/Whose usage, Nonstandard usage, End marks
10	**a.** the nature of Languages are to change which is not necessarily a bad thing **b.** the english language has changed alot, Chaucer's Middle English is one example	**a.** The nature of languages is to change, which is not necessarily a bad thing. **b.** The English language has changed a lot; Chaucer's Middle English is one example.	Capitalization, Subject-verb agreement, Comma usage, Spelling, Semicolon usage, End marks

AN APPETITE FOR EXPERIENCE

Pepys   Johnson   Goethe

Defoe   Boswell   Gray

He who neglects to drink of the spring of experience is likely to die of thirst in the desert of ignorance.

—Ling Po

Responding to the Quotation

? How is experience, like water, something that a person needs?

[Possible responses: One learns from experience what one needs for one's life; or experience is something that the human mind craves as the body needs water.]

RESPONDING TO THE ART: EXPLORING THE SUBJECT

Galileo used a telescope to explore the sky in the early 1600s; Isaac Newton wrote about the law of gravity in the late 1600s and by the early 1700s, most scientists agreed that the sun was the center of the universe. In 1755, Immanuel Kant, a German philosopher, suggested that the planets and the sun were formed in the same way. It was the Age of Reason, a time of great intellectual achievement. In this eighteenth-century etching by Richard Houston (1721–1775), young scientists inspired by the quest for knowledge, study the universe by means of telescopes, globes, and other instruments.

PROGRAM MANAGER

- **Integrated Assessment** For a summative assessment of the literature and language skills taught in this collection, see **Collection 7 Test**, *Test Booklet*, pp. 117–119.
- **Instructional Support** See **Fine Art Transparency** 7.1. Review teacher's notes for transparencies in the **Audiovisual Resources Binder**

for suggestions on how to tie the transparencies to specific reading selections.

- **Extending Collection Theme** See **Cross-Curricular Activity: An Appetite for Experience**, *Teaching Resources A,* p. 166, for activities in other disciplines and for evaluation criteria.

PORTFOLIO ASSESSMENT

Parent/Guardian Involvement For forms that will help a parent or guardian review and respond to a student's portfolio, see the *Portfolio Management System,* pp. 62–63.

QUICK PLANNING GUIDE

Into the Selection

Author Biography p. 542

Before You Read p. 543

- **Reading Focus: Set a Purpose** Students note details of seventeenth-century diaries.
- **Quickwrite:** Write in Reader's Log about today's coverage of disasters
- **Elements of Literature: Diary**
- **Background: Scaffolding** A life in volumes

Through the Selection

from The Diary of Samuel Pepys pp. 544–554

Words to Own pp. 545–553

Literature and Science pp. 546–547

Connections: An Essay pp. 552–553 "On Keeping a Notebook"

Making Meanings p. 554

Language and Style p. 554

Beyond the Selection

Choices: Building Your Portfolio p. 555

- **Writer's Notebook:** Test validity of opinions for a persuasive essay
- **Critical Writing:** In an essay evaluate Pepys's character
- **Creative Writing:** Write paragraphs describing a plan for a diary

Samuel Pepys
(1633–1703)

Samuel Pepys (1670) by a follower of Peter Lely. Oil.

The Master and Fellows, Magdalene College, Cambridge.

For nine years—1660 to 1669—Samuel Pepys, whose name is pronounced "peeps," kept a secret diary which, when published long after his death, made him very famous. Pepys was not a writer but an official in the government office that maintained the Royal Navy and provided it with ships and supplies. Although a cousin helped Pepys obtain his first appointment in the Navy Office, it was Pepys's own diligence and skill that accounted for his rapid advancement. He did much to increase the honesty and efficiency of naval supply and maintenance.

Along with his public career, Pepys's private affairs also prospered. Starting humbly in life as the son of a tailor who managed to send him to Cambridge University, Pepys became so rich that when he was forced to retire in 1688 for political reasons, he could live the rest of his life like a gentleman, in leisure, comfort, and elegance.

Pepys had an insatiable appetite for experience, a vast capacity for pleasure, and an immense desire for learning—languages, literature, science, and everything connected with his naval occupation. Small things delighted him. When he heard "a fellow whistle like a bird exceeding well," he resolved to take lessons in bird whistling. Of a new watch he said, "I could not forbear carrying it in my hand and seeing what o'clock it was a hundred times." His house was full of creatures: cats, two dogs, a whistling blackbird, canaries, even for a time an eagle. He owned many books, carpenters' tools, maps and charts, a telescope, and several musical instruments that he could play—a flageolet, a lute, a flute, and a small harpsichord (which he never mastered). He composed a few songs

that are still regarded as singable, he was proud of his dancing, and he liked expensive clothes and oil paintings. In everything he sought pleasure, and he usually found it. Whenever his head ached from business or his wife was angry at him for flirting with other women, he took refuge in the theater. He saw so many plays and recorded his impressions of them so accurately that the *Diary* is now regarded as an important document for theater history.

Historians of all kinds find the *Diary* useful because Pepys was a firsthand observer of public events and contemporary life. In 1660, he was one of the Englishmen who went to bring exiled King Charles II back to England. He witnessed joyous occasions like Charles's coronation in 1661 and national disasters like the Plague of 1665 and the Great Fire of 1666. These important public happenings he recorded in his *Diary* along with trivial personal ones. For instance, on one occasion he records something that happened at the theater:

I went to Mr. Crew's house and thence to the theater, where I saw again *The Lost Lady,* which doth now please me better than before. And here, I sitting behind in a dark place, a lady spat backward upon me by a mistake, not seeing me. But after seeing her to be a very pretty lady, I was not troubled at all.

According to the *Diary,* Pepys's life was full of unexpected little events like this one. Reading the *Diary* over Pepys's shoulder, we see the lively panorama of Restoration London—and in many of his observations, we also see ourselves.

PROGRAM MANAGER

- **Planning Instruction** See *Teaching Notes, Teaching Resources A,* p. 145, for objectives, a summary, literary elements, and additional biographical information for this selection.
- **Instructional Support** Before beginning the instructional lesson, see

Graphic Organizer for Active Reading, *Teaching Resources A,* p. 150, for a Through the Selection activity.

- **Assessment** See **Selection Test,** *Test Booklet,* pp. 105–106.
- **Language Link** For instruction and practice in appositives and appositive

phrases, see **Language Link,** *Teaching Resources A,* pp. 151–152, and *Language and Writing Skills Worksheets,* pp. 54 and 76.

- **Reinforcement** Use the **Words to Own** worksheet in *Teaching Resources A,* p. 153.

BEFORE YOU READ

FROM THE DIARY OF SAMUEL PEPYS

Reading Focus

Capturing the Moment

Many people kept detailed diaries in the seventeenth century, and a surprisingly large number of these diaries have survived, most of them concerned with religion. The pious people we now call Puritans used their diaries to analyze their moral behavior and record their spiritual progress. In contrast, Pepys in his *Diary* pays little attention to the state of his soul or to his personal relationship with God, though he almost always mentions going to church on Sunday, often with disparaging comments ("a sorry, silly sermon"), and he sometimes mentions family prayers. But Pepys was not an introspective or contemplative person; his *Diary* is interesting because it tells us what he saw and heard and said and did.

Quickwrite

The Great Fire of 1666 was one of the worst disasters in London's history. Drawing on your knowledge of newspaper and TV reports about disasters in today's world, freewrite in your Reader's Log about the kinds of information and details that you might expect Pepys to have recorded in his *Diary* during the four days that the fire lasted. What kinds of information do we expect today when disasters on this scale occur?

Elements of Literature

Diary

Pepys's *Diary* is so detailed, wide-ranging, and frank that it has become a byword for this form of writing. Each page of this vivid chronicle reveals Pepys's curious eye, candid opinions, and clear relish for life in the great city.

> **A** **diary** is a daily, personal account of feelings, impressions, and events. Unlike journals, which are usually less personal records of events often written with another reader in mind, most diaries are quite intimate, and written only for the owner's private reference and pleasure.
>
> *For more on the Diary, see the Handbook of Literary Terms.*

Background

Pepys's diary was truly a secret one. He wrote it only for his own use and in a kind of shorthand that had recently been invented. He doubly safeguarded the most intimate details of his life by recording them in a private foreign language that appears to mix together Latin, French, and Spanish words. Yet, since he did not destroy the *Diary* at the end of his life but bequeathed it along with his other books to Cambridge University, he must have recognized its value as literature and history. He must, in other words, have imagined people reading it. But not until the 1970s was it possible to read everything in the *Diary*, because earlier editors could not bring themselves to transcribe and print the more personal entries. And though it covers only nine years, the *Diary* is immense; in the 1970s and 1980s it was published—along with notes, commentaries, and indexes—in eleven fat volumes.

When he began the *Diary,* in 1660, Pepys was twenty-seven, married to twenty-year-old Elizabeth St. Michel, and in the service of Edward Montagu. Until recently, he and his wife had been living in a turret room in Whitehall Palace, without servants or proper facilities for washing and cooking. Nine years later, when he stopped keeping the *Diary* because of eye trouble, Pepys and his family had their own handsome townhouse, one of a complex of buildings that comprised the Navy Office. Their household was not much like most modern ones because they had several live-in servants who did most of their work: three housemaids, a waiting woman for Elizabeth, a footboy for Samuel, and a coachman to drive and look after their coach and horses. Although Pepys and his wife had no children, their house was always full of people.

SAMUEL PEPYS 543

Using **BEFORE YOU READ** p. 543

Background

Emphasize the size of Pepys's diary. Ask students to think of interesting things that they would put in their own diaries—what can they find that is remarkable about even the most ordinary day? For example, they may eat something different, receive something interesting in the mail, or meet a new student. Ask them to imagine how they might fill eleven volumes with details from their lives.

ABOUT THE AUTHOR

In 1667, the Royal Society (see p. 547) recommended that its members avoid in their writing any "swellings of style" and instead reflect "a close, naked, natural way of speaking." Samuel Pepys had at the time been a member of the Society for two years, but he needed no such advice—his writing style is from the beginning of the *Diary* plain and frank, more descriptive than expressive. Though he was a passionate bibliophile, his comments on the books he purchased are more often about their cost or maintenance than about their literary value. His reputation has been made only by the *Diary,* in which his style is that of the consummate observer.

PORTFOLIO ASSESSMENT

Portfolio Assessment For help with self-assessment of reading skills, see the *Portfolio Management System,* p. 39.

WORDS TO OWN

The following words are defined in the Words to Own at the bottom of the pupil's page.

cavalcade p. 545	malicious p. 552
proffered p. 546	discoursing p. 553
civility p. 546	

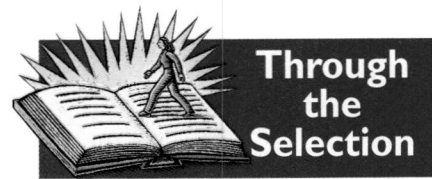

Through the Selection

A. Expansion

Hanging, drawing, and quartering was a common form of execution in Pepys's day. The victim was hanged and eviscerated (drawn) and the body cut into four parts (quartered). Quartering also occasionally meant that the four limbs were tied, usually to four horses, and the body was pulled apart. Have students discuss their reactions to the fact that executions were witnessed by the public.

B. Reader's Response: First Thoughts

? What impression do you have of Pepys after reading the first paragraph? [Sample responses: He has a strong stomach; he's witty and observant; he's not given to emotional outbursts.]

C. Critical Reading: Analyzing Details

? What is Pepys's point in this passage? [He saw both the execution of King Charles I in 1649 during the English Civil War and the execution of those who plotted to kill the king. Pepys seems aware of the momentous events he is witnessing.]

D. Expansion

Pepys married Elizabeth St. Michel, a Frenchwoman, in 1655. Although Pepys often complained about his wife in his diary, he commemorated her after her death by placing a sculpture of her in the church where he worshipped.

---

from The Diary of Samuel Pepys

Samuel Pepys

October 13, 1660
A Public Execution, A Private Explosion

To my Lord's[1] in the morning, where I met with Captain Cuttance. But my Lord not being up, I went out to Charing Cross to see Major General Harrison[2] hanged, drawn, and quartered—which was done there—he looking as cheerfully as any man could do in that condition. He was presently cut down and his head and his heart shown to the people, at which there was great shouts of joy. It is said that he said that he was sure to come shortly at the right hand of Christ to judge them that now have judged him. And that his wife doth expect his coming again.[3]

Thus it was my chance to see the King beheaded at Whitehall and to see the first blood shed in revenge for the blood of the King at Charing Cross. From thence to my Lord's and took Captain Cuttance and Mr. Sheply to the Sun tavern and did give them some oysters. After that I went by water home, where I was angry with my wife for her things lying about, and in my passion kicked the little fine basket which I bought her in Holland and broke it, which troubled me after I had done it.

Within all the afternoon, setting up shelves in my study. At night to bed.

April 23, 1661
The Coronation of Charles II

. . . About four in the morning I rose. And got to the Abbey,[4] where I followed Sir J. Denham the surveyor with some company that he was leading in. And with much ado, by the favor of Mr.

Cooper his man, did get up into a great scaffold across the north end of the Abbey—where with a great deal of patience I sat from past four till eleven before the King came in. And a pleasure it was to see the Abbey raised in the middle, all covered with red and a throne (that is a chair) and footstool on the top of it. And all the officers of all kinds, so much as the very fiddlers, in red vests.

At last comes in the Dean and Prebends[5] of Westminster with the Bishops (many of them in cloth-of-gold copes[6]); and after them the nobility all in their Parliament robes, which was a most magnificent sight. Then the Duke[7] and the King with a scepter (carried by my Lord of Sandwich) and sword and mond[8] before him, and the crown too.

The King in his robes, bareheaded, which was very fine. And after all had placed themselves—there was a sermon and the service. And then in the choir at the high altar he passed all the ceremonies of the coronation—which, to my very great grief, I and most in the Abbey could not see. The crown being put upon his head, a great shout begun. And he came forth to the throne and there passed more ceremonies: as, taking the oath and having things read to him by the Bishop,[9] and his Lords (who put on their caps as soon as the King put on his crown) and Bishops came and kneeled before him.

And three times the King-at-arms went to the three open places on the scaffold and proclaimed that if anyone could show any reason why Ch. Steward [Charles Stuart] should not be King of England, that now he should come and speak.

And a general pardon also was read by the Lord Chancellor; and medals flung up and down by my

---

1. **my Lord's:** Edward Montagu (1625–1672), earl of Sandwich; he was a cousin of Pepys and his superior at the Naval Office.
2. **Harrison:** Thomas Harrison (1606–1660), one of the people responsible for the execution of King Charles I in 1649.
3. **coming again:** with Christ, on Christ's return to earth.
4. **Abbey:** Westminster Abbey, the church in London where all monarchs of England are crowned and where many of them are buried.

5. **Prebends** (prĕ′bəndz): prebendaries; clergy who receive a prebend, or salary paid from the church's revenues.
6. **copes:** ceremonial robes.
7. **Duke:** James II (1633–1701), duke of York and the king's brother.
8. **mond:** golden globe and cross; a symbol of royal power.
9. **Bishop:** bishop of London. (The archbishop of Canterbury, who ordinarily would have officiated, was too ill to do so.)

544 THE RESTORATION AND THE EIGHTEENTH CENTURY

OPTIONS FOR TEACHING

STRATEGIES FOR INCLUSION

Advanced/Linguistic Pepys wrote his observations of and reactions to what happened around him; sometimes those events were significant, and sometimes they were mundane. But because he recorded and preserved them, his commentary has outlived him and given us a glimpse into his times. Just as Pepys chronicled the coronation of Charles II or the London fire, students might select significant events

they actually witnessed and write diary entries for that day. Remind students that an event does not have to be globally or nationally important; the goal is to select an event or a memory that stands out and to express the experience as accurately and as vividly as possible.

Spatial/Visual Several famous structures appear in Pepys's diary. To enhance students' visualizations, have them draw views of these public buildings.

- One student (or a group of students) might choose church architecture and identify the various parts, including the choir and explaining the reference to the abbey being "raised in the middle."
- Another option is to research and draw Westminster Abbey.
- A third building mentioned is the Tower of London, which provides plenty of historical intrigue as well as architectural detail to research.

Lord Cornwallis—of silver;[10] but I could not come by any.

But so great a noise, that I could make but little of the music; and indeed, it was lost to everybody. But I had so great a list to piss, that I went out a little while before the King had done all his ceremonies and went round the Abbey to Westminster Hall, all the way within rails, and 10,000 people, with the ground covered with blue cloth —and scaffolds all the way. Into the hall I got—where it was very fine with hangings and scaffolds,

Charles II's entry into London at his restoration, 1660. Engraving.

one upon another, full of brave ladies. And my wife in one little one on the right hand.

Here I stayed walking up and down; and at last, upon one of the side stalls, I stood and saw the King come in with all the persons (but the soldiers) that were yesterday in the cavalcade; and a most pleasant sight it was to see them in their several robes. And the King came in with his crown on and his scepter in his hand—under a canopy borne up by six silver staves, carried by Barons of the Cinque Ports—and little bells at every end.

And after a long time he got up to the farther end, and all set themselves down at their several tables—and that was also a rare sight. And the King's first course carried up by the Knights of the Bath. And many fine ceremonies there was of the heralds leading up people before him and bowing; and my Lord of Albemarles going to the kitchen and eat a bit of the first dish that was to go to the King's table.

But above all was these three Lords, Northumberland and Suffolk and the Duke of Ormond, coming before the courses on horseback and

10. **medals . . . of silver:** coronation badges.

staying so all dinnertime; and at last, to bring up Dymock, the King's Champion, all in armor on horseback, with his speare and target carried before him. And a herald proclaim that if any dare deny Ch. Steward to be lawful King of England, here was a champion that would fight with him; and with those words the champion flings down his gauntlet;[11] and all this he doth three times in his going up toward the King's table. At last, when he is come, the King drinks to him and then sends him the cup, which is of gold; and he drinks it off and then rides back again with the cup in his hand.

I went from table to table to see the Bishops and all others at their dinner, and was infinite pleased with it. And at the Lords' table I met with Wll. Howe and he spoke to my Lord for me and he did give him four rabbits and a pullet; and so I got it, and Mr. Creed[12] and I got Mr. Michell to give us some bread and so we at a stall eat it, as everybody else did what they could get.

I took a great deal of pleasure to go up and down and look upon the ladies—and to hear the music of all sorts; but above all, the twenty-four violins.

About six at night they had dined; and I went up to my wife and there met with a pretty lady

11. **gauntlet:** leather glove covered with metal plates to protect the hand during combat.
12. **Howe . . . Creed:** Pepys's fellow workers in the Navy Office.

WORDS TO OWN
cavalcade (kav′əl·kād′) *n.:* parade of horses and carriages.

A. Critical Reading: Analyzing Character

? What does the passage show about Pepys's character? [Possible answers: He is skeptical of attributing too much to God; he thinks it is foolish to think natural phenomena are signs from God.]

LITERATURE AND SCIENCE

Mad for Science

Whether in computers, audio equipment, laser surgery, or virtual reality, dizzying scientific change greets us daily. *New!* shifts to *Obsolete!* at warp speed, so our age seems more scientifically turbulent than any before. Yet today's innovations, in many ways, are a small blip on the screen compared to the scientific revolution taking off in the seventeenth and eighteenth centuries.

From alchemy to method. This new science was a defiant break with the past, with "science" that was really metaphysical philosophy or magical alchemy. Instead, the Enlightenment's "natural philosophy" (physical science) insisted on observation, hypothesis, testing, and mathematical analysis—in short, the scientific method you learn in lab class today.

Geniuses, experiments, and arguments. Dominated by the genius of Isaac Newton (1642–1727), seventeenth-century England was truly ablaze with brilliant scientific minds, avid amateur experimenting, and passionate public quarrels (which Newton's nasty temper inflamed). Robert Boyle (1627–1691) founded modern chemistry. Edmond Halley (1656–1742) accurately predicted a comet's appearance centuries in the future. William Harvey (1578–1657) outlined our blood's circulation. Robert Hooke (1635–1703), a typical encyclopedist, coined the word *cell,* invented a watch spring, built a calculator, and first posed Kepler's planetary-motion laws in mechanical terms.

(Mrs. Frankelyn, a doctor's wife, a friend of Mr. Bowyers) and kissed them both—and by and by took them down to Mr. Bowyers's. And strange it is, to think that these two days have held up fair till now that all is done and the King gone out of the hall; and then it fell a-raining and thundering **A** and lightning as I have not seen it do some years—which people did take great notice of God's blessing of the work of these two days— which is a foolery, to take too much notice of such things. . . .

At Mr. Bowyers's, a great deal of company; some I knew, others I did not. Here we stayed upon the leads[13] and below till it was late, expecting to see the fireworks; but they were not

13. **leads:** rooftop; from the sheets of lead used to cover a roof.

performed tonight. Only, the City had a light like a glory round about it, with bonfires.

At last I went to King Street; and there sent Crockford[14] to my father's and my house to tell them I could not come home tonight, because of the dirt and a coach could not be had.

And so after drinking a pot of ale alone at Mrs. Harper's, I returned to Mr. Bowyers's; and after a little stay more, I took my wife and Mrs. Frankelyn (who I <u>proffered</u> the <u>civility</u> of lying with my wife at Mrs. Hunt's tonight) to Axe Yard. In which, at

14. **Crockford:** apparently a servant.

WORDS TO OWN
proffered (präf′ərd) *v.:* offered; proposed.
civility (sə·vil′ə·tē) *n.:* courtesy.

546 THE RESTORATION AND THE EIGHTEENTH CENTURY

OPTIONS FOR TEACHING

INTEGRATING THE LANGUAGE ARTS

Language and Vocabulary For the purpose of practicing and later analyzing their writing, have students write accounts of both an actual and an imaginary event. Ask them to draw conclusions about which event, actual or imaginary, produced the more vivid description, the better use of vocabulary, the more figurative language, the more intriguing plot structure, the more objective rendition, the more

emotional response, or other characteristics. To help them analyze their writing, they could use a chart like the one following.

Characteristic	Actual Event	Imaginary Event

Strategic Reading Before reading Pepys's diary entries, students should scan the text, focusing on

the subtitles of the sections. Have them use a chart like the one below to list events they predict will occur in the diary. After reading the selection, students should return to their predictions and record the actual events.

Subtitle Hint	Prediction	Actual Event

T546 The Restoration and the Eighteenth Century

Newton (awing even Queen Anne, who knighted him) explained the world's mysteries as never before—partly because he invented a tool to do it: calculus. Among Newton's other stunning achievements were discovering that white light contains all colors, formulating the three laws of motion (every physicist's bedrock), and defining universal gravitation. Newton realized, as no one else had, that gravitational pull accounts both for orbiting planets and for falling apples.

Promoting natural knowledge. But even without Newton's genius, there were so many new ideas and inventions—the vacuum pump, barometer, compound microscope—that a group of Londoners created the "Invisible College," essentially a science club that evolved into the Royal Society of London for the Promotion of Natural Knowledge. While never a government body (its brash motto was *Nullius verba,* "at the dictation of no one"), the Royal Society was chartered by Charles II in 1662. Dedicated both to hands-on experimenting and to publishing journal articles, it was a prototype information highway, giving scientists across Europe new knowledge—faster than ever before.

Newton served as Royal Society president, but so did the nonscientist Samuel Pepys, showing the age's fascination with natural curiosities and cutting-edge thought. While some of the Society's experiments were crackpot and cruel to animals—as satirized by both Joseph Addison and Jonathan Swift—the Society was, and still is centuries later, one of the world's most prestigious and influential scientific groups.

Gunter's scale, globe, dividers, cross staff, sandglass (detail) (all pre-1700).
National Maritime Museum, London.

LITERATURE AND SCIENCE

Encourage students to discuss the directions the development of technology is taking and the changes they have witnessed in their own lives. You might give examples from your own life to get them started. What sorts of scientific laws and inventions will future generations take for granted as we now take the Newtonian laws of physics? (For example, quark theory, microchips, and interfaces of telephone and television.) You may also wish to emphasize that the lines between scientists and nonscientists were not as rigid in Pepys's time as they are today.

the further end, there was three great bonfires and a great many great gallants,[15] men and women; and they laid hold of us and would have us drink the King's health upon our knee, kneeling upon a fagot;[16] which we all did, they drinking to us one after another—which we thought a strange frolic. But these gallants continued thus a great while, and I wondered to see how the ladies did tipple.

At last I sent my wife and her bedfellow to bed, and Mr. Hunt and I went in with Mr. Thornbury (who did give the company all their wines, he being yeoman of the wine cellar to the King) to his house; and there, with his wife and two of his sisters and some gallant sparks that were there, we drank the King's health and nothing else, till one of the gentlemen fell down stark drunk and there lay spewing. And I went to my Lord's pretty well. But no sooner a-bed with Mr. Sheply but my head begun to turn and I to vomit, and if ever I was foxed it was now—which I cannot say yet, because I fell asleep and sleep till morning—only, when I waked I found myself wet with my spewing. Thus did the day end, with joy everywhere; and blessed be God, I have not heard of any mischance to anybody through it all, but only to Serjeant Glynne,[17] whose horse fell upon him

15. **gallants:** merrymakers.
16. **fagot:** bundle of twigs or sticks used to make a bonfire. The toast of loyalty was often drunk while kneeling.

17. **Serjeant Glynne:** The title is legal rather than military. Sir John Glynne and Sir John Maynard were unpopular because they had been prominent judges during the Commonwealth period.

CROSSING THE CURRICULUM

Geography Because an understanding of the locations of various places mentioned in the text will help students visualize the country, the city, and the progress of the fire, have volunteers interested in geography locate some of the places mentioned. Have students point out London, Northumberland, and Suffolk on a map of England. Encourage students to find a map of London from Pepys's time (the map on p. 271 might be helpful) and to use it as a model to sketch one of their own. Then, students can see how much of the path of the Great Fire they can trace. Be sure they identify as many of the landmarks Pepys mentions as possible.

Social Sciences Have students work in groups to learn about the history and culture of Pepys's time. After they have completed their research, set up panels to present the findings as at a scholarly conference. Sample topics include
- the abbey system
- the Barons of the Cinque Ports, the Knights of the Bath, and other orders of nobility
- Whitehall
- the English monarch's royal treasures mentioned in the text: scepter, sword, mond, and crown
- chocolate and the social practice of chocolate drinking
- the coinage and money of the time
- the Great Fire of London
- London Bridge

A. Reader's Response: Shaping Interpretations

Pepys states that he will never bother to see another state event because nothing can compare to the coronation. Would you have reached the same conclusion if you had witnessed the events Pepys describes? Why or why not? [Sample responses: Yes, the splendor and ceremony of the occasion are impressive, and any other event would seem dull by comparison. No, you shouldn't miss other events just because one is so grand.]

B. Language Note: Vocabulary

[?] What is a *theorbo*? [A lute.] How do you know? [From a context clue.]

C. Critical Reading: Finding Details

[?] What everyday functions does Pepys perform on October 28? [Possible answer: Works in the office, picks up his repaired lute, and buys a belt.]

D. Literary Element: Diary

[?] What is the effect of the description of mundane activities in a diary? [Possible answers: It makes Pepys seem real; shows the universality of human experience; demonstrates how little times have changed.]

E. Language Note: Vocabulary

Wenches is archaic for "female servants."

yesterday and is like to kill him; which people do please themselves with, to see how just God is to punish that rogue at such a time as this—he being now one of the King's Serjeants and rode in the cavalcade with Maynard, to whom people wished the same fortune.

There was also this night, in King Street, [a woman] had her eye put out by a boy's flinging of a firebrand into the coach.

(A) Now after all this, I can say that besides the pleasure of the sight of these glorious things, I may now shut my eyes against any other objects, or for the future [not] trouble myself to see things of state and show, as being sure never to see the like again in this world.

Waked in the morning with my head in a sad taking through the last night's drink, which I am very sorry for. So rise and went out with Mr. Creed to drink our morning draft, which he did give me in chocolate to settle my stomach. And after that to my wife, who lay with Mrs. Frankelyn at the next door to Mrs. Hunt's.

And they were ready, and so I took them up in a coach and carried the lady to Paul's and there set her down; and so my wife and I home—and I to the office.

October 28–29, 1661
Two Ordinary Days

(B) At the office all the morning, and dined[18] at home; and so to Paul's churchyard to Hunt's,[19] and there find my theorbo done. Which pleases me very well, and costs me 26s to the altering—but now (C) he tells me it is as good a lute as any is in England, and is worth well 10£. Hither I sent for Captain Ferrers to me, who comes with a friend of his and they and I to the theater and there saw *Argalus* (D) *and Parthenia;*[20] where a woman acted Parthenia and came afterward on the stage in man's clothes, and had the best legs that I ever saw; and I was very well pleased with it. Thence to the Ringo alehouse, and thither sent for a belt maker

18. **dined:** Dinner was eaten at midday.
19. **Hunt's:** Hunt, a musical instrument maker, repaired and altered Pepys's theorbo, or lute.
20. ***Argalus and Parthenia:*** an old play by Henry Glapthorne (c. 1610–c. 1643). In the revival Pepys saw, female actors played the women's roles rather than boy actors, as had been customary.

and bought of him a handsome belt for second mourning,[21] which cost me 24s and is very neat. So home and to bed.

This day I put on my half-cloth black stockings and my new coat of the fashion, which pleases me well; and with my beaver[22] I was (after office was done) ready to go to my Lord Mayor's feast,[23] as we are all invited; but the Sir Wms.[24] were both loath to go because of the crowd, and so none of us went; and I stayed and dined with them, and so home; and in the evening, by consent, we met at the Dolphin, where other company came to us and would have been merry; but their wine was so naught[25] and all other things out of order, that we were not so; but stayed long at night and so home and to bed. My mind not pleased with the spending of this day, because I had proposed a great deal of pleasure to myself this day at Guildhall.

This Lord Mayor, it seems, brings up again the custom[26] of Lord Mayors going the day of their installment to Paul's,[27] and walking round about the cross and offering something at the altar.

July 11, 1664
A Bad Night

. . . Home, weary; and not being very well, I betimes[28] to bed.

And there fell into a most mighty sweat in the night, about eleven o'clock; and there, knowing what money[29] I have in the house and hearing a noise, I begin to sweat worse and worse, till I (E) melted almost to water. I rung, and could not in half an hour make either of the wenches hear me; and this made me fear the more, lest they might be gagged; and then I begin to think that there

21. **second mourning:** period of less solemn mourning following the deep mourning Pepys had been observing for his uncle Robert, who had died three months earlier.
22. **beaver:** hat made of beaver fur.
23. **Lord Mayor's feast:** an annual event held at the Guildhall.
24. **Sir Wms.:** Sir William Penn (1621–1670) and Sir William Batten (?–1667), both officials in the Navy Office.
25. **naught:** worthless.
26. **custom:** These ceremonies had not been observed during the Commonwealth period.
27. **Paul's:** St. Paul's Cathedral. A huge cross stood in the square before the cathedral.
28. **betimes:** archaic for "early."
29. **money:** about £1,000—a very large sum.

OPTIONS FOR TEACHING

PROBLEM SOLVING/CRITICAL THINKING

Setting Priorities During the Great Fire, Pepys observed numerous goods floating in the river, as well as lighters (open barges) packed with belongings. Ask students to imagine they are fleeing the fire and to set their own priorities for loading their barges. Small groups should rank and discuss the items from the list below that they would load on the barge, those they would leave behind, and their reasons.

Rank	List of Goods	Rank	List of Goods
____	book collection	____	crate of food
____	family mementos	____	clothes trunk
____	harpsichord	____	riding horse
____	sterling silverware	____	box of important papers
____	oil paintings	____	favorite dog

Suggest to students that they try a process of elimination:

(1) Select the two or three most important items; (2) select the two or three least important items; (3) rank the top two or three in order of significance; (4) rank the bottom two or three in order of significance. This process leads students to determine those items (and the values they represent) that are most important and least important and how to make decisions about those items that fall between. Have students compare their rankings by writing a chart on the chalkboard, and ask students to discuss their rationales.

was some design in a stone being flung at the window over our stairs this evening, by which the thieves meant to try what looking there would [be] after them and know our company. These thoughts and fears I had, and do hence apprehend the fears of all rich men that are covetous and have much money by them. At last Jane[30] rose and then I understand it was only the dog wants a lodging and so made a noise. So to bed, but hardly slept; at last did, and so till morning.

September 2, 1666
The First Day of the Great Fire of London

Lord's Day. Some of our maids sitting up late last night to get things ready against our feast today, Jane called us up, about three in the morning, to

30. Jane: Jane Birch, the Pepyses' servant.

tell us of a great fire they saw in the City.[31] So I rose, and slipped on my nightgown and went to her window, and thought it to be on the backside of Mark Lane at the furthest; but being unused to such fires as followed, I thought it far enough off, and so went to bed again and to sleep. About seven rose again to dress myself, and there looked out at the window and saw the fire not so much as it was, and further off. So to my closet[32] to set things to rights after yesterday's cleaning. By and by Jane comes and tells me that she hears that above three hundred houses have been burned down tonight by the fire we saw, and that it was

31. City: London. The Great Fire started in a bakery, raged for four days and four nights, and destroyed some 13,000 residences. It leveled four fifths of the City and left about 100,000 people homeless.
32. closet: private room.

F. Critical Reading: Making Inferences

? What generalization does Pepys make in conjunction with this description of a bad night? [He reflects that rich people are prone to fear of having their goods stolen.]

RESPONDING TO THE ART: EXPLORING THE SUBJECT

Four-fifths of the city burned from September 2 to September 5. The Great Fire destroyed most of London's civic buildings, old St. Paul's Cathedral, 87 parish churches, and about 13,000 houses. Notice how the widespread destruction of the fire is represented by swirling flames that consume almost the entire skyline and reach high into the sky. A sense of panic and chaos is conveyed by the traffic of boats on the Thames River, some of them also on fire.

The Great Fire of London (17th century).

Inform students that there is evidence that this story about the origin of the fire is true, but at the time religious acrimony was so great that many Londoners believed that Catholics had set the fire.

B. Critical Reading: Analyzing Character

? What does this passage reveal about Pepys? [Possible answers: He has a high position; he is an advisor to the king and the Lord Mayor; he is trusted; his opinion is valued.]

Technology Tip

TECHNOLOGY Have students note the picture of the pages of Pepys's *Diary,* and ask them to think about the difference between the physical act of writing with a pen and keying in words on a computer. Will keyboarding skills replace the art of handwriting? How might Pepys's diary have been different had he kept it on diskette? [Possible answers: People will always learn to write. Keyboarding will be replaced by voice activated computers. Pepys's diary might have been shorter, or more reflective, if he had kept it on disk and edited it from time to time.]

Opening pages of Pepys's *Diary* (1659–1660).
The Master and Fellows, Magdalene College, Cambridge.

now burning down all Fish Street by London Bridge. So I made myself ready presently, and walked to the Tower[33] and there got up upon one of the high places, Sir J. Robinson's little son going up with me; and there I did see the houses[34] at that end of the bridge all on fire, and an infinite great fire on this and the other side the end of the bridge—which, among other people, did trouble me for poor little Michell and our Sarah[35] on the bridge. So down, with my heart full of trouble, to the Lieutenant of the Tower, who tells me that it begun this morning in the King's baker's house in Pudding Lane, and that it hath burned down St. Magnes Church and most part of Fish Street already. So I down to the waterside and there got a boat and through bridge, and there saw a lamentable fire. Poor Michell's house, as far

as the Old Swan,[36] already burned that way and the fire running further, that in a very little time it got as far as the Steelyard while I was there. Everybody endeavoring to remove their goods, and flinging into the river or bringing them into lighters[37] that lay off. Poor people staying in their houses as long as till the very fire touched them, and then running into boats or clambering from one pair of stair by the waterside to another. And among other things, the poor pigeons I perceive were loath to leave their houses, but hovered about the windows and balconies till they were some of them burned, their wings, and fell down.

Having stayed, and in an hour's time seen the fire rage every way, and nobody to my sight endeavoring to quench it, but to remove their goods and leave all to the fire; and having seen it get as far as the Steelyard, and the wind mighty high and driving it into the City, and everything, after so long a drought, proving combustible, even the very stones of churches, and among other things, the poor steeple by which pretty Mrs. —— lives, and whereof my old schoolfellow Elborough is parson, taken fire in the very top and there burned till it fall down—I to Whitehall with a gentleman with me who desired to go off from the Tower to see the fire in my boat—to Whitehall, and there up to the King's closet in the chapel, where people came about me and I did give them an account dismayed them all; and word was carried in to the King, so I was called for and did tell the King and Duke of York what I saw, and that unless his Majesty did command houses to be pulled down, nothing could stop the fire. They seemed much troubled, and the King commanded me to go to my Lord Mayor from him and

33. **Tower:** Tower of London, a short walk from Pepys's house.
34. **houses:** Shops and dwellings were built on London Bridge.
35. **Sarah:** maid whom Mrs. Pepys discharged on December 5, 1662. Pepys wrote: "The wench cried, and I was ready to cry too."

36. **Michell's house . . . Old Swan:** Betty Michell, a former sweetheart of Pepys, lost her house in the fire. The Old Swan was a tavern on Thames Street, near London Bridge.
37. **lighters:** large, open barges.

550 THE RESTORATION AND THE EIGHTEENTH CENTURY

OPTIONS FOR TEACHING

PROFESSIONAL NOTES

Thematic Connections: "An Appetite for Experience" What Pepys experienced for nine years comprised his diary, and those experiences became a part of history. Have students write in their Reader's Logs about how diaries provide insight into the daily experiences as well as the momentous experiences of the past.

Cultural Diversity Many of Pepys's experiences were motivated by his appetites, including that for food. Students interested in the history of cultural practices related to food and food preparation might enjoy researching the foods mentioned in Pepys's diary; they might expand their research to include other foods of Pepys's time. Then, have them report their findings, which might include written menus, paintings of banquets

or other meals representative of the historical period, or even samples of actual dishes. (Have students check with local health regulations; photographs or drawings and verbal descriptions might have to suffice.)

command him to spare no houses but to pull down before the fire every way. The Duke of York bid me tell him that if he would have any more soldiers, he shall; and so did my Lord Arlington afterward, as a great secret. Here meeting with Captain Cocke, I in his coach, which he lent me, and Creed with me, to Paul's; and there walked along Watling Street as well as I could, every creature coming away loaden with goods to save—and here and there sick people carried away in beds. Extraordinary good goods carried in carts and on backs. At last met my Lord Mayor in Canning Street, like a man spent, with a hankercher about his neck. To the King's message, he cried like a fainting woman, "Lord, what can I do? I am spent. People will not obey me. I have been pull[ing] down houses. But the fire overtakes us faster than we can do it." That he needed no more soldiers; and that for himself, he must go and refresh himself, having been up all night. So he left me, and I him, and walked home—seeing people all almost distracted and no manner of means used to quench the fire. The houses too, so very thick thereabouts, and full of matter for burning, as pitch and tar, in Thames Street—and warehouses of oil and wines and brandy and other things. Here I saw Mr. Isaacke Houblon,[38] that handsome man—prettily dressed and dirty at his door at Dowgate, receiving some of his brothers' things whose houses were on fire; and as he says, have been removed twice already, and he doubts (as it soon proved) that they must be in a little time removed from his house also—which was a sad consideration. And to see the churches all filling with goods, by people who themselves should have been quietly there at this time.

By this time it was about twelve o'clock, and so home and there find my guests, which was Mr. Wood and his wife, Barbary Shelden, and also Mr. Moone—she mighty fine, and her husband, for aught I see, a likely man. But Mr. Moone's design and mine, which was to look over my closet and please him with the sight thereof, which he hath long desired, was wholly disappointed, for we were in great trouble and disturbance at this fire, not knowing what to think of it. However, we had

an extraordinary good dinner, and as merry as at this time we could be.

While at dinner, Mrs. Batelier came to inquire after Mr. Woolfe and Stanes (who it seems are related to them), whose houses in Fish Street are all burned, and they in a sad condition. She would not stay in the fright.

As soon as dined, I and Moone away and walked through the City, the streets full of nothing but people and horses and carts loaden with goods, ready to run over one another, and removing goods from one burned house to another—they now removing out of Canning Street (which received goods in the morning) into Lumbard Street and further; and among others, I now saw my little goldsmith Stokes receiving some friend's goods, whose house itself was burned the day after. We parted at Paul's, he home and I to Paul's Wharf, where I had appointed a boat to attend me; and took in Mr. Carcasse and his brother, whom I met in the street, and carried them below and above bridge, to and again, to see the fire, which was now got further, both below and above, and no likelihood of stopping it. Met with the King and Duke of York in their barge, and with them to Queenhithe[39] and there called Sir Rd. Browne to them. Their order was only to pull down houses apace, and so below bridge at the waterside; but little was or could be done, the fire coming upon them so fast. Good hopes there was of stopping it at the Three Cranes[40] above, and at Buttolph's Wharf below bridge, if care be used; but the wind carries it into the City, so as we know not by the waterside what it doth there. River full of lighter[s] and boats taking in goods, and good goods swimming in the water; and only, I observed that hardly one lighter or boat in three that had the goods of a house in, but there was a pair of virginals[41] in it. Having seen as much as I could now, I away to Whitehall by appointment, and there walked to St. James's Park, and there met my wife and Creed and Wood and his wife and walked to my boat, and there upon the water again, and to the fire up and down, it still

---

38. **Houblon:** Houblon and others mentioned in the following paragraphs were prominent Londoners, all friends or acquaintances of Pepys.

39. **Queenhithe** (kwēn·hĭth'): harbor off Thames Street. *Hithe* is archaic for "port" or "haven."
40. **Three Cranes:** name for a set of stairs that led down to the river.
41. **virginals:** small, sixteenth-century stringed instruments; harpsichords.

C. Exploring the Historical Period

Point out that the Lord Mayor, a wine merchant by the name of Sir Thomas Bludworth, was a member of the business or middle class. What does this reveal about politics of the time? [Possible answers: A person did not have to be a member of the aristocracy to assume a high-ranking position; money helped people of the middle class achieve positions of political power; it hints at the beginning of the democratization of the English political system.]

D. Reader's Response: Shaping Interpretations

? What does the juxtaposition of fear and anxiety with the enjoyment of "an extraordinary good dinner" reveal about Pepys? [Sample responses: He is insensitive because he dines while the city burns; he is human because he carries on in the midst of a catastrophe.]

E. Expansion

Tell students that the fire reached Lumbard Street late on the second day (Tuesday); the fire burned for four days and was finally stopped by using gunpowder to blow up buildings to create a firebreak.

ASSESSMENT TOOLS

Check Test: True-False

1. Pepys witnesses the hanging of a man involved in the execution of King Charles I. [True]
2. According to Pepys, women were not allowed to attend the coronation. [False]
3. Pepys advises the king to stop the fire in London by pulling down houses. [True]
4. Pepys, distressed about all the destruction he has seen during the Great Fire, cannot eat. [False]

5. Pepys states that he is lucky he does not have to move any of his goods or money out of the house. [False]

Self-Evaluation Have students complete the following statements to assess their writing skills. *Remind them that these answers, like their diaries, should include situations they would not mind sharing.*

1. The easiest type of diary entry to write was . . .
2. The most difficult thing to write about was . . .
3. As I re-read my entries, I found the most compelling one to be . . .
4. It was the most effective entry because . . .

A. Critical Reading: Drawing Conclusions

? Based on this passage, what do you think Didion would say about Pepys's diary? [Possible answers: That his is the very kind of diary she could not write. That he was more successful at recording the day's events in a meaningful way than she is.]

B. Language Note: Diction

? Why might Pepys use three consecutive adjectives ("horrid malicious bloody flame") to describe the fire? [Possible answers: To emphasize the horror of the scene; to show the fury of the fire; to stress the destructiveness of the fire.]

C. Critical Reading: Finding Details

Describe Pepys's feelings and reactions to the calamity he observes. [Possible answers: He weeps; he is afraid; he is anxious; he helps an acquaintance; he is generous; he secures his money and valuables in his cellar; he prepares his gold and valuable papers for a quick escape.]

Connections

AN ESSAY

The American writer Joan Didion (1934–   ) explains her reasons for keeping a notebook in this excerpt from her collection of essays *Slouching Towards Bethlehem* (1968). While not secret like Pepys's diaries, Didion's notebooks nonetheless serve as a storehouse of her experiences.

On Keeping a Notebook

Joan Didion

. . . So the point of my keeping a notebook has never been, nor is it now, to have an accurate factual record of what I have been doing or thinking. That would be a different impulse entirely, an instinct for reality which I sometimes envy but do not possess. At no point have I ever been able successfully to keep a diary; my approach to daily life ranges from the grossly negligent to the merely absent, and on those few occasions when I have tried dutifully to record a day's events, boredom has so overcome me that the results are mysterious at best. What is this business about "shopping, typing piece, dinner with E, depressed"? Shopping for what? Typing what piece? Who is E? Was this "E" depressed, or was I depressed? Who cares?

In fact I have abandoned altogether that kind of pointless entry; instead I tell what some would call lies. "That's simply not true," the members of my family frequently tell me when they come up against my memory of a shared event. "The party was *not* for you, the spider was *not* a black widow, *it wasn't that way at all.*" Very likely they are right, for not only have I always had trouble distinguishing between what happened and what merely might have happened, but I remain unconvinced that the distinction, for my purposes, matters. The cracked crab that I recall having for lunch the day my father came home from Detroit in 1945 must certainly be embroidery, worked into the day's pattern to lend verisimilitude; I was ten years old and would not now remember the cracked crab. The day's events did not turn on cracked crab. And yet it is precisely that fictitious crab that makes me see the afternoon all over again, a home movie run all too often, the father bearing gifts, the child weeping, an exercise in family love and guilt. Or that is what it was to me. Similarly, perhaps it never did snow that August in Vermont; perhaps there never were flurries in the night wind, and maybe no one else felt the ground hardening and summer already dead even as we pretended to bask in it, but that was how it

increasing and the wind great. So near the fire as we could for smoke; and all over the Thames, with one's face in the wind you were almost burned with a shower of firedrops—this is very true—so as houses were burned by these drops and flakes of fire, three or four, nay five or six houses, one from another. When we could endure no more upon the water, we to a little alehouse on the bankside over against the Three Cranes, and there stayed till it was dark almost and saw the fire grow; and as it grew darker, appeared more and more, and in corners and upon steeples and between churches and houses, as far as we could see up the hill of the City, in a most horrid malicious bloody flame, not like the fine flame of an ordinary fire. Barbary and her husband away before us. We stayed till, it being darkish, we saw the fire as only one entire arch of fire from this to the other side the bridge, and in a bow up the hill, for an arch of above a mile long. It made me weep to see it. The churches, houses, and all on fire and

WORDS TO OWN

malicious (mə·lish′əs) *adj.*: intentionally mischievous or harmful; spiteful.

CONNECTING WITH *THE DIARY OF SAMUEL PEPYS*

Ask students to discuss the differences and similarities between Didion's notebooks and Pepys's diary. [Possible answers: Pepys's work is a daily account of events—it is more like record keeping, whereas Didion's work consists of anecdotal material and depends on what she finds interesting; it may include memories as well as incidents that occurred on a given day. The notebook and diary are similar in that the writers write them for themselves. Didion will publish some of the work in some form perhaps, but her notebook is not for publication. Pepys never intended his volumes to be published.]

felt to me, and it might as well have snowed, could have snowed, did snow.

How it felt to me: that is getting closer to the truth about a notebook. I sometimes delude myself about why I keep a notebook, imagine that some thrifty virtue derives from preserving everything observed. See enough and write it down, I tell myself, and then some morning when the world seems drained of wonder, some day when I am only going through the motions of doing what I am supposed to do, which is write—on that bankrupt morning I will simply open my notebook and there it will all be, a forgotten account with accumulated interest, paid passage back to the world out there: dialogue overheard in hotels and elevators and at the hatcheck counter in Pavillon (one middle-aged man shows his hat check to another and says, "That's my old football number"); impressions of Bettina Aptheker and Benjamin Sonnenberg and Teddy ("Mr. Acapulco") Stauffer; careful *aperçus* about tennis bums and failed fashion models and Greek shipping heiresses, one of whom taught me a significant lesson (a lesson I could have learned from F. Scott Fitzgerald, but perhaps we all must meet the very rich for ourselves) by asking, when I arrived to interview her in her orchid-filled sitting room on the second

day of a paralyzing New York blizzard, whether it was snowing outside.

I imagine, in other words, that the notebook is about other people. But of course it is not. I have no real business with what one stranger said to another at the hatcheck counter in Pavillon; in fact I suspect that the line "That's my old football number" touched not my own imagination at all, but merely some memory of something once read, probably "The Eighty-Yard Run." Nor is my concern with a woman in a dirty crepe de Chine wrapper in a Wilmington bar. My stake is always, of course, in the unmentioned girl in the plaid silk dress. *Remember what it was to be me:* That is always the point. . . .

Joan Didion.

flaming at once, and a horrid noise the flames made, and the cracking of houses at their ruin. So home with a sad heart, and there find everybody discoursing and lamenting the fire; and poor Tom Hater came with some few of his goods saved out of his house, which is burned upon Fish Street Hill. I invited him to lie at my house, and did receive his goods: but was deceived in his lying there, the noise coming every moment of the growth of the fire, so as we were forced to begin to pack up our own goods and prepare for their removal. And did by moonshine (it being brave, dry, and moonshine and warm weather) carry

much of my goods into the garden, and Mr. Hater and I did remove my money and iron chests into my cellar—as thinking that the safest place. And got my bags of gold into my office ready to carry away, and my chief papers of accounts also there, and my tallies into a box by themselves. So great was our fear, as Sir W. Batten had carts come out of the country to fetch away his goods this night. We did put Mr. Hater, poor man, to bed a little; but

---

WORDS TO OWN
discoursing (dis·kôrs′iŋ) v. used as *adj.*: talking.

Making Meanings

First Thoughts

1. Students may say that they are surprised that Pepys writes unflatteringly about himself and that they would not be as frank. Or they may think that a diary is the best place to put your most honest assessments of yourself.

Reviewing the Text

Students' responses should include the execution, the coronation, and the Great Fire.

Shaping Interpretations

2. Possible responses: Pepys probably does not want to dwell morbidly on the execution; at the time, much must have been written and said about it, so perhaps he did not feel the need to record it in his diary.

3. Both occasions are elaborately ceremonial, witnessed by large crowds, and are cause for parties, fireworks, and so on. Both the president and the king take oaths. However, the inauguration of a president is usually held in front of the Capitol, rather than in a cathedral, and the president, naturally, is not crowned.

4. Pepys's account of the fire would be of great use as a primary source because it is a detailed eyewitness account that notes the extent of the fire, its probable source, and its effect on the inhabitants of London. Note that Pepys himself is involved in the official efforts to contain the fire.

5. Pepys's rare and quickly passing remarks about his wife seem to indicate that their relationship is not a particularly close or devoted one.

Extending the Text

6. **(Synthesis)** Students will probably say that their lives are similar to Pepys's in the attention he gives to friends and good times and in his worries about money but that their lives differ in many material ways, such as in manners of transportation.

7. **(Evaluation)** Pepys's account gives details along with personal experiences and remarks of authorities, but it is not as succinct as present-day reporting. Also, Pepys concentrates more on his own experience than that of others, which is not usually acceptable in reporting today.

---

he got but very little rest, so much noise being in my house, taking down of goods.

About four o'clock in the morning, my Lady Batten sent me a cart to carry away all my money and plate[42] and best things to Sir W. Rider's at Bednall Green; which I did, riding myself in my nightgown in the cart; and Lord, to see how the streets and the highways are crowded with people, running and riding and getting of carts at any rate to fetch away thing[s]. I find Sir W. Rider tired with being called up all night and receiving things from several friends. His house full of goods—and much of Sir W. Batten and Sir W. Penn's. I am eased at my heart to have my treasure so well secured. Then home with much ado to find a way. Nor any sleep all this night to me nor my poor wife.

42. **plate:** gold- or silver-plated dishes, eating utensils, and the like.

MAKING MEANINGS

First Thoughts

1. What do you think of the entries in which Pepys records that he behaved less than admirably? If you were keeping a **diary,** would you be equally frank about your own shortcomings? Explain.

> **Reviewing the Text**
>
> Trace, day by day, the major events covered in these diary entries. You might record the events in the form of a time line.

Shaping Interpretations

2. Pepys gives very few details in the *Diary* about the execution that he witnessed. Why do you suppose he doesn't devote much space to it?

3. How is the inauguration of a U.S. president both like and unlike the king's coronation?

4. Of what use would Pepys's account of the Great Fire be as a **primary source** for a later historian?

5. From Pepys's references to his wife Elizabeth, what can you conclude about their relationship?

Extending the Text

6. How is Pepys's life in any way like your own? How is it different? Do you think that the attitudes and values of seventeenth-century life, as Pepys describes it, are similar to those of your own time, or different? Explain your answer.

7. Today, reporting like Pepys's description of the fire would be done by newspapers or television. How does Pepys's account compare with present-day reporting? You may wish to look back at your Reader's Log for ideas.

8. Which style of keeping a diary—Pepys's detailed method or Joan Didion's impressionistic approach (page 552)—appeals to you? Why?

LANGUAGE AND STYLE

Seventeenth-Century Usage

These extracts from Pepys's *Diary* have been modernized for ease of reading. That is, the archaic spellings have been brought up to date. For example, in the first entry, the words *abbey, followed, surveyor, chair, footstool,* and *fiddlers* are spelled *abby, fallowed, surveyour, chaire, footstoole,* and *fidlers* by Pepys. Capitalization has also been modernized; Pepys tended to capitalize indiscriminately, especially nouns.

1. Here are some other words from these entries (including a surname), spelled as Pepys spelled them. How would each word be spelled today? From these and other archaic spellings, what inferences can you make about how some words might have been pronounced in Pepys's day?

bonefyres	turne	alter
musique	themselfs	noyse
frolique	shewe	loaden
tiple	Frankelyn	ruine

2. Look over the diary entries, and find examples of archaic syntax—sentence structures that would not be used in formal English today.

3. Find examples of verb forms that are different from standard verb forms used today.

---

8. **(Synthesis)** Students may express preference for Pepys's method because it is simple and more direct, or for Didion's because it seems more artistic.

> ✔ **QUICK CHECK: Spelling**
>
> Change the following archaic spellings to the modern ones.
> **[1]** oyle [oil]
> **[2]** shelfes [shelves]
> **[3]** custome [custom]
> **[4]** enquire [inquire]
> **[5]** fallowed [followed]

CHOICES: Building Your Portfolio

Writer's Notebook

1. Collecting Ideas for a Persuasive Essay

Personal records can suggest many controversial issues. Embedded in Pepys's *Diary*, for example, are questions about capital punishment and civil disaster planning. But beware: In using your journal, take care not to argue an opinion or preference that's wholly personal—for instance, that public executions are "healthy" (someone who is horrified will never agree). Review any of your Reader's Log entries, and develop two strong opinions about suggested issues. Then test each: Is it supportable with evidence, or is it a personal preference? Save your notes for the Writer's Workshop on page 612.

Critical Writing

2. Pepys: What Manner of Man?

Using the *Diary* excerpts as evidence, evaluate Pepys's character: What kind of man does he seem to be—socially, politically, religiously, and personally? Present your conclusions in an essay, using citations from the *Diary* to support your statements. Be sure to open your character study with a thesis statement.

Creative Writing

3. Dear Diary

If you were to keep a **diary,** what sort of material would you put in it? What would you omit? Write two or more paragraphs describing the plan for your diary, explaining why you would make a record of some matters (the weather, disasters) but not others (mistakes you make, moments of self-satisfaction). Explain whether you would include public events or only private occurrences, and whether you would keep track of routine work as well as leisure activities. Would you need to safeguard the privacy of your diary? If not, why not? Think about what you might want to read twenty-five years from now about your life at the present time.

Leather bucket and helmet used in the Great Fire of London (17th century).
London Museum, London.

SAMUEL PEPYS 555

Language and Style

Answers

1. *Bonfires, music, frolic, tipple, turn, themselves, show, Franklin, altar, noise, laden, ruin.* Remind students that, since there was no dictionary during this time, people probably wrote words exactly as they pronounced them. Students' inferences of the words' pronunciation will differ, but many of the words probably have long vowels where modern versions have short, or they might have an extra syllable.

2. Some examples include: "Here I stayed walking up and down"; "It fell a-raining and thundering and a light-ening"; "his wife doth expect his coming again." Another example: "And all the officers of all kinds . . . in red vests." Unlike this example, today we avoid beginning a sentence with *and* and do not consider a sentence complete without a verb.

3. Some examples are *doth* and *hath* instead of *does* and *has,* and *he is come* instead of *has come.*

Beyond the Selection

Choices: Building Your Portfolio

1. **Writer's Notebook** Remind students to save their work. They may use it as prewriting for the Writer's Workshop on p. 612.

PORTFOLIO ASSESSMENT

Choices: Assessment Criteria For help in evaluating these Choices assignments, see the criteria in the *Portfolio Management System,* p. 116.

OPTIONS FOR TEACHING

STRATEGIES FOR INCLUSION

Less Proficient Readers To prepare students for activity #2, provide a model of a graphic organizer for students to copy and complete on their own. On the chalkboard or on a transparency, create a table with headings for the different aspects of Pepys's character: social, political, religious, and personal. Have students review the text, and list phrases in the appropriate columns.

Logical-Mathematical For activity #3, suggest to students that they first formulate a purpose for their diaries. Ask them what they want their diaries to cover and for whom they are writing. Then, students may write in an outline a list of elements that will fulfill their stated purpose.

Into the Selection

Author Biography p. 556

Before You Read p. 557

- **Reading Focus:** Students learn the horrors of the plague.
- **Quickwrite: Prior Knowledge** Write in Reader's Log about morbid curiosity
- **Elements of Literature:** Journal
- **Background: Scaffolding** The journal's sources

Through the Selection

from A Journal of the Plague Year pp. 558–564

Words to Own pp. 558–564

Making Meanings p. 565

Beyond the Selection

Choices: Building Your Portfolio p. 566
- **Writer's Notebook:** Chart ideas and support for a persuasive essay
- **Critical Writing:** In an essay, compare and contrast Pepys's and Defoe's accounts
- **Critical Writing:** Write an essay taking a stand on the value of remembering depressing events
- **Creative Writing:** Write an account of a natural disaster

Spotlight On pp. 567–569

Daniel Defoe

(1660–1731)

Daniel Foe—he added the aristocratic prefix *De* to his name when he was about thirty-five—attended an excellent academy where he studied history, law, economics, geography, and natural science. Defoe's family were Dissenters, Protestants who did not approve of the Church of England, and so he was barred from attending either Oxford or Cambridge. When he was around twenty, he set himself up as a merchant, trading in haberdashery, brandy, wool, real estate, and eventually civet cats. He married when he was twenty-four. Meanwhile, he began publishing books and pamphlets.

Throughout his long life, Defoe was a very busy person, sometimes successful in business, sometimes bankrupt and hiding from his creditors. He often traveled about the country as a spy, even performing such services for his favorite monarch, King William III. And he constantly wrote and wrote and wrote—altogether over five hundred different works, in prose and verse, including a news pamphlet, *The Review,* which he put out three times a week for over seven years. He touched on every conceivable subject: the choice of a wife, the history of the Devil, the manufacture of glass.

Defoe's innumerable writings might be roughly classified into four groups. A large number are concerned with political and religious controversies. His pamphlet *The Shortest Way with the Dissenters* (1702) called for the punishment of the Dissenters—Defoe's own party—and confiscation of their property. When the Church of England party discovered, to their anger, that the pamphlet was ironic, Defoe was arrested, exposed in the pillory three times, and indefinitely jailed. He was released on the condition that he become a spy and a writer for the very government that had locked him up because of his satire.

Daniel Defoe (detail) (17th century). Engraving. London Library.

A second, didactic group of writings advises people on how to become virtuous as well as rich: *The Family Instructor* (1715–1718), for example, and *The Complete English Tradesman* (1726). A third group is made up of journalistic accounts of sensational events, such as "A True Relation of the Apparition of one Mrs. Veal" (1706), a remarkable ghost story based on the alleged reappearance of a real Mrs. Veal who had died, and *A Journal of the Plague Year* (1722). The fourth group contains Defoe's fiction, including the novels *Robinson Crusoe* (1719) and *Moll Flanders* (1722).

The story of Robinson Crusoe is well known in a general way: A sailor is shipwrecked on a tropical island and for many years manages to lead a more or less civilized life there, without human companionship, until he meets a young native of the island whom he saves from certain death at the hands of "cannibals" and names Friday. This classic book has an almost universal appeal because it portrays a single, strong individual who, all alone, triumphs over his desolate, hostile surroundings. Readers of the book are bound to ask themselves, "Could I survive if I were cast away on an island by myself?"

Many people believe that Defoe modeled Robinson Crusoe on an actual person, a Scottish sailor named Alexander Selkirk, who had written a memoir of his experiences as a castaway. But it was only the *idea* of a marooned man that Defoe used. Though he presents Crusoe's experiences as true autobiography, they are entirely Defoe's own invention; the episodes in the book have nothing to do with Selkirk or with anyone else. It is a tribute to Defoe's skill that many readers have assumed the tale to be true. An irony of literary history becomes apparent when one realizes that, in spite of his voluminous contributions to literature, Defoe is usually remembered as the author of only this one book.

556 THE RESTORATION AND THE EIGHTEENTH CENTURY

PROGRAM MANAGER

- **Planning Instruction** See Teaching Notes, *Teaching Resources A,* p. 146, for objectives, a summary, literary elements, and additional biographical information for this selection.
- **Instructional Support** Before beginning the instructional lesson, see

Graphic Organizer for Active Reading, *Teaching Resources A,* p. 154, for Through the Selection activity.
- **Assessment** See Selection Test, *Test Booklet,* pp. 107–108.
- **Language Link** For instruction and practice in clauses, see Language Link,

Teaching Resources A, pp. 155–156, and *Language and Writing Skills Worksheets,* pp. 79–83 and 115.
- **Reinforcement** Use the Words to Own worksheet in *Teaching Resources A,* p. 157.

BEFORE YOU READ

FROM A JOURNAL OF THE PLAGUE YEAR

Reading Focus

The Contagion of Fear
The events were grim indeed. When the London plague was raging at its worst, in August and September of 1665, it may have killed as many as ten thousand people every week—an enormous toll in a city whose total population was less than half a million. During the plague, people who could afford to leave London did so, in large numbers. Wherever they went, to outlying villages and towns, they terrified the local inhabitants, who believed that they could become infected from any city dweller, sick or well. Inside London, if any family member came down with the plague, the whole family was confined by law to its dwelling.

Quarantines of this kind were totally ineffective. Although everybody in those days assumed that the plague could be caught from another person, modern medical research now tells us that it is primarily a disease of rats, transmitted from rat to rat and from rat to person by fleas. Fleas prefer to bite rats, but when rats become scarce (because they die of plague), the fleas bite people. When the last rat has died of plague, then people stop dying. Since Defoe and his contemporaries did not understand how the plague was communicated, the disease seemed not only horrible, but also mysterious and irrational, as though an angry God were punishing them for their wrongdoings. And since the disease was almost always fatal, its

victims suffered in their minds as well as in their bodies. Many people became mad when the very painful and discolored buboes (swellings) first appeared on them, for they knew they were to die very soon.

Quickwrite

Daniel Defoe knew his audience would be infinitely—even morbidly—interested in the details of his sensational account. What do we mean by the expression "morbid curiosity"? Where does this kind of curiosity appear in contemporary life, and how do you account for it? Freewrite some notes about these questions in your Reader's Log.

Elements of Literature

Journal
Defoe was a practical man, and he realized that the materials of history might be a source of profit. Thus, *A Journal of the Plague Year* illustrates the form of the **journal**—but at one remove from an actual eyewitness account. This work is, in effect, a semifictional reconstruction of an authentic, contemporaneous record, ingeniously written to make readers feel that the narrator was really an eyewitness to the events—when, in fact, he wasn't.

By blending a nonfiction form with made-up details, Defoe became one of the first writers to fuel a debate that continues into our own time. How far can **journalists** (note the formation of the word from **journal**) go in

stretching the literal truth in order to re-create a real event?

> **A journal** is a record of events, kept daily or on a regular basis, by a person who is an eyewitness or a participant. A journal is usually less personal and intimate than a diary.
>
> *For more information on the Journal, see the Handbook of Literary Terms.*

Background

This work, which Defoe published in 1722, pretends to be a firsthand account of an epidemic of bubonic plague that had ravaged London fifty-seven years before, in 1665, when Defoe was five years old. To tell the story, Defoe invented a narrator called "H. F.," who may be Henry Foe, an uncle of Defoe's who may have lived in London during the epidemic and who may have told Defoe about it. "H. F." is said to be a saddler, one who manufactures, repairs, or sells horses' saddles—in other words, an ordinary citizen.

Altogether, Defoe had four kinds of materials to aid his powerful imagination: his own childhood memories; the reminiscences of his uncle Henry and other older people; city records; and printed matter such as pamphlets, books, and sermons about the plague. He worked these materials into a convincing narrative that seems to be related by somebody who is actually experiencing, from day to day, the grim events that he describes.

DANIEL DEFOE 557

Into the Selection

Using **BEFORE YOU READ** p. 557

Background

Have students make a list of the sources they would expect to be able to use to write an account of a disaster that happened in their area. Does it match Defoe's? Ask them what form their account would take—a novel, a journal, or a newspaper article, and why they would choose one over the other.

WRITERS ON WRITING

Daniel Defoe said that he had a gift for "lying like the truth" that served him well. Given a character or plot familiar to the public or the journalistic crowd, he could construct a tale at once plausible and unexpected at every turn, usually, he claimed, in the service of a moral. In his own words, he wrote to recommend to his readers an "invincible patience under the worst of misery; indefatigable application and undaunted resolution under the greatest and most discouraging circumstances." Given the hardships and struggle he himself faced in his career, the words are wisdom born of experience.

PORTFOLIO ASSESSMENT

Portfolio Assessment For help with self-assessment of reading skills, see the *Portfolio Management System,* p. 53.

WORDS TO OWN

The following words are defined in the Words to Own at the bottom of the pupil's page.

mortal p. 558	promiscuously p. 562
inimitable p. 558	prodigious p. 562
garret p. 558	diverted p. 563
lunacy p. 559	abated p. 564
importuning p. 562	calamitous p. 564

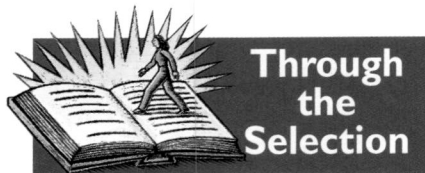
A. Reader's Response: First Thoughts

? What emotions would you have experienced in this situation?
[Sample responses: Fear; anxiety; paranoia; will for self-preservation.]

B. Language Note: Vocabulary

A *visitation* is a disaster or severe trial seen as an instance of divine wrath.

C. Literary Element: Point of View

? What point of view does Defoe use? [First person; or first person but with a degree of omniscience.]
What is the effect of using this point of view? [Possible answers: The account seems authentic; it seems as though it is really happening at the moment. It also personalizes the story, making it sound less objective.]

D. Critical Reading: Drawing Conclusions

? Why does Defoe protect the identity of the merchant? [Possible answer: Because the man kills himself, which at the time of Defoe's writing is considered both sinful and shameful.]
Remind students that suicide was considered a sin in both the Roman Catholic and Anglican churches. Known suicide victims were generally denied burial in hallowed ground, so many people conspired to keep suicides secret.

from A Journal of the Plague Year
Daniel Defoe

1. The Infection Spreads

A Here the opinion of the physicians agreed with my observation afterward, namely, that the danger was spreading insensibly, for the sick could infect none but those that came within reach of the sick person; but that one man who may have really received the infection and knows it not, but goes abroad and about as a sound person, may give the plague to a thousand people, and they to greater numbers in proportion, and neither the person giving the infection or the persons receiving it know anything of it, and perhaps not feel the effects of it for several days after.

B For example, many persons in the time of this visitation never perceived that they were infected till they found to their unspeakable surprise, the tokens come out upon them; after which they seldom lived six hours; for those spots they called the tokens were really gangrene spots, or mortified flesh[1] in small knobs as broad as a little silver penny, and hard as a piece of callus or horn; so that, when the disease was come up to that length, there was nothing could follow but cer-

C tain death; and yet, as I said, they knew nothing of their being infected, nor found themselves so much as out of order, till those mortal marks were upon them. But everybody must allow that they were infected in a high degree before, and must have been so some time, and consequently their breath, their sweat, their very clothes, were contagious for many days before. . . .

2. Dismal Scenes

I had some little obligations, indeed, upon me to go to my brother's house, which was in Coleman Street[2] parish and which he had left to my care, and I went at first every day, but afterward only once or twice a week.

---

1. **gangrene . . . flesh:** decay of soft tissues from a blockage of blood flow.
2. **Coleman Street:** This place and other places Defoe names are all within the old City of London, unless otherwise noted.

In these walks I had many dismal scenes before my eyes, as particularly of persons falling dead in the streets, terrible shrieks and screechings of women, who, in their agonies, would throw open their chamber windows and cry out in a dismal, surprising manner. It is impossible to describe the variety of postures in which the passions of the poor people would express themselves.

Passing through Tokenhouse Yard, in Lothbury, of a sudden a casement[3] violently opened just over my head, and a woman gave three frightful screeches, and then cried, "Oh! death, death, death!" in a most inimitable tone, and which struck me with horror and a chillness in my very blood. There was nobody to be seen in the whole street, neither did any other window open, for people had no curiosity now in any case, nor could anybody help one another, so I went on to pass into Bell Alley.

D Just in Bell Alley, on the right hand of the passage, there was a more terrible cry than that, though it was not so directed out at the window; but the whole family was in a terrible fright, and I could hear women and children run screaming about the rooms like distracted, when a garret window opened and somebody from a window on the other side the alley called and asked, "What is the matter?" upon which, from the first window, it was answered, "Oh Lord, my old master has hanged himself!" The other asked again, "Is he quite dead?" and the first answered, "Ay, ay, quite dead; quite dead and cold!" This person was a merchant and a deputy alderman, and very rich. I care not to mention the name, though I knew his name too, but that would be an hardship to the family, which is now flourishing again.

---

3. **casement:** hinged window.

WORDS TO OWN

mortal (môr'təl) *adj.:* fatal.
inimitable (in·im'i·tə·bəl) *adj.:* difficult or impossible to imitate.
garret (gar'it) *n.:* attic.

Logical-Mathematical So students can grasp the immense impact of this epidemic, have them figure the mortality rate from the bubonic plague in London, the British Isles, other European countries, and in Europe as a whole. They may present statistics to the class in visual form, such as graphs, charts, or maps.

Kinesthetic/Auditory Give students six large note cards, one for each anecdote. Have them list the main plot and main interpretive points on the cards. In pairs, students may then use the cards to quiz each other, selecting one point from a card and asking their partners to identify the section of the story where the point can be found.

Less Proficient Readers To help students' comprehension of the journal, have them locate the discussions in the text in which physical symptoms are described. Students should synthesize these details in order to create a unified account of how the plague attacked the human body. Have students write a brief description based on the sections they have re-read.

Lord, have mercy on London. Woodcut.

But this is but one; it is scarce credible what dreadful cases happened in particular families every day. People in the rage of the distemper, or in the torment of their swellings, which was indeed intolerable, running out of their own government,[4] raving and distracted, and oftentimes laying violent hands upon themselves, throwing themselves out at their windows, shooting themselves, etc.; mothers murdering their own children in their lunacy, some dying of mere grief as a passion, some of mere fright and surprise without any infection at all, others frighted into idiotism and foolish distractions, some into despair and lunacy, others into melancholy madness.

The pain of the swelling was in particular very violent, and to some intolerable; the physicians and surgeons may be said to have tortured many poor creatures even to death. The swellings in some grew hard, and they applied violent drawing

4. **out of their own government:** unable to control themselves.

plasters or poultices[5] to break them, and if these did not do they cut and scarified[6] them in a terrible manner. In some those swellings were made hard partly by the force of the distemper and partly by their being too violently drawn, and were so hard that no instrument could cut them, and then they burnt them with caustics,[7] so that many died raving mad with the torment, and some in the very operation. In these distresses, some, for want of help to hold them down in their beds, or to look to them, laid hands upon

5. **drawing plasters or poultices** (pōl'tis·iz): hot packs used to soften sores and draw infection to the skin's surface.
6. **scarified:** punctured.
7. **caustics:** chemicals that can burn or eat away flesh.

WORDS TO OWN
lunacy (lōō'nə·sē) *n.*: madness. This word is derived from *luna,* Latin for "moon." People once believed that the phases of the moon could affect the human mind.

DANIEL DEFOE 559

RESPONDING TO THE ART: VISUAL LITERACY

This woodcut was made during the Plague of London. Ask students to interpret what it depicts. [Possible response: It shows the physical and emotional effects of the plague on its victims. In the center of the woodcut stands a skeleton astride coffins, representing death. To his left are Londoners attempting to flee the destruction of the plague, but they seem trapped by the armed men at the right of the picture.]

E. Critical Reading: Speculating
? What sources is Defoe likely to have used for this description of the plague's physical effects? [Possible answers: City records during the plague; others' writings; memories of people who lived through the plague; his own childhood memories; his imagination.]

INTEGRATING THE LANGUAGE ARTS

Grammar "A Violent Cure," part 6 (p. 563), consists of only one long, complex sentence. For the purpose of deciphering this sentence, have students form pairs to divide it into shorter, simpler sentences. If some pairs seem stuck, suggest they use punctuation (first, the semicolons) as their clues to separating the complex sentence into its major components. Identifying independent clauses will help students get a handle on meaning; linking dependent clauses to their respective independent clauses will help them

untangle the sentence. Allow students to edit freely, as long as they maintain the essential details of the anecdote. Conclude by having the pairs share their results with the rest of the class. This would also be a good time to discuss run-on sentences.

Strategic Reading Have students use the KWL system to help them work through the text. Students should record in their Reader's Logs a list of what they already know (K) about the

plague in the left column, what they want (W) to know in the center, and what they actually learned (L) in the right column.

K	W	L

☞

themselves as above. Some broke out into the streets, perhaps naked, and would run directly down to the river if they were not stopped by the watchman or other officers, and plunge themselves into the water wherever they found it.

It often pierced my very soul to hear the groans and cries of those who were thus tormented, but of the two this was counted the most promising particular in the whole infection, for if these swellings could be brought to a head, and to break and run, or, as the surgeons call it, to digest, the patient generally recovered; whereas those who, like the gentlewoman's daughter, were struck with death at the beginning, and had the tokens come out upon them, often went about indifferent easy till a little before they died, and some till the moment they dropped down, as in apoplexies[8] and epilepsies is often the case. Such would be taken suddenly very sick, and would run to a bench or bulk,[9] or any convenient place that offered itself, or to their own houses if possible, as I mentioned before, and there sit down, grow faint, and die. This kind of dying was much the same as it was with those who die of common mortifications,[10] who die swooning, and, as it were, go away in a dream. Such as died thus had very little notice of their being infected at all till the gangrene was spread through their whole body; nor could physicians themselves know certainly how it was with them till they opened their breasts or other parts of their body and saw the tokens.

8. **apoplexies** (ap′ə·plek′sēz): strokes.
9. **bulk:** low stall projecting from a wall or storefront.
10. **mortifications:** early term for gangrene.

3. Escape from Quarantine

I remember one citizen who, having thus broken out of his house in Aldersgate Street or thereabout, went along the road to Islington;[11] he attempted to have gone in at the Angel Inn, and after that the White Horse, two inns known still by the same signs, but was refused; after which he came to the Pied Bull, an inn also still continuing the same sign. He asked them for lodging for one night only, pretending to be going into Lincolnshire,[12] and assuring them of his being very sound and free from the infection, which also at that time had not reached much that way.

They told him they had no lodging that they could spare but one bed up in the garret, and that they could spare that bed for one night, some drovers being expected the next day with cattle; so, if he would accept of that lodging, he might have it, which he did. So a servant was sent up with a candle with him to show him the room. He was very well dressed, and looked like a person not used to lie in a garret; and when he came to the room he fetched a deep sigh, and said to the servant, "I have seldom lain in such a lodging as this." However, the servant assuring him again that they had no better, "Well," says he, "I must make shift; this is a dreadful time; but it is but for one night." So he sat down upon the bedside, and bade the maid, I think it was, fetch him up a pint of warm ale. Accordingly the servant went for the ale, but some hurry in the house, which perhaps

11. **Islington:** suburb north of London.
12. **Lincolnshire:** county on the east coast of England.

Londoners fleeing into the countryside to escape the plague. Woodcut.
The Granger Collection, New York.

employed her other ways, put it out of her head, and she went up no more to him.

The next morning, seeing no appearance of the gentleman, somebody in the house asked the servant that had showed him upstairs what was become of him. She started. "Alas!" says she, "I never thought more of him. He bade me carry him some warm ale, but I forgot." Upon which, not the maid, but some other person was sent up to see after him, who, coming into the room, found him stark dead and almost cold, stretched out across the bed. His clothes were pulled off, his jaw fallen, his eyes open in a most frightful posture, the rug of the bed being grasped hard in one of his hands, so that it was plain he died soon after the maid left him; and 'tis probable, had she gone up with the ale, she had found him dead in a few minutes after he sat down upon the bed. The alarm was great in the house, as anyone may suppose, they having been free from the distemper till that disaster, which, bringing the infection to the house, spread it immediately to other houses round about it. . . .

4. Burial Pits and Dead-Carts

There was a strict order to prevent people coming to those pits, and that was only to prevent infection. But after some time that order was more necessary, for people that were infected and near their end, and delirious also, would run to those pits, wrapped in blankets or rugs, and throw themselves in, and, as they said, bury themselves. . . .

This may serve a little to describe the dreadful condition of that day, though it is impossible to say anything that is able to give a true idea of it to those who did not see it, other than this, that it was indeed very, very, very dreadful, and such as no tongue can express.

I got admittance into the churchyard[13] by being acquainted with the sexton who attended; who, though he did not refuse me at all, yet earnestly persuaded me not to go, telling me very seriously (for he was a good, religious, and sensible man) that it was indeed their business and duty to venture, and to run all hazards, and that in it[14] they might hope to be preserved; but that I had no

apparent call to it but my own curiosity, which, he said, he believed I would not pretend was sufficient to justify my running that hazard. I told him I had been pressed in my mind to go, and that perhaps it might be an instructing sight, that might not be without its uses. "Nay," says the good man, "if you will venture upon that score, name of God go in; for, depend upon it, 'twill be a sermon to you, it may be, the best that ever you heard in your life. 'Tis a speaking sight," says he, "and has a voice with it, and a loud one, to call us all to repentance," and with that he opened the door and said, "Go, if you will."

His discourse had shocked my resolution a little, and I stood wavering for a good while, but just at that interval I saw two links[15] come over from the end of the Minories, and heard the bellman,[16] and then appeared a dead-cart, as they called it, coming over the streets; so I could no longer resist my desire of seeing it, and went in. There was nobody, as I could perceive at first, in the churchyard, or going into it, but the buriers and the fellow that drove the cart, or rather led the horse and cart; but when they came up to the pit they saw a man go to and again, muffled up in a brown cloak, and making motions with his hands under his cloak, as if he was in great agony, and the buriers immediately gathered about him, supposing he was one of those poor delirious or desperate creatures that used to pretend, as I have said, to bury themselves. He said nothing as he walked about, but two or three times groaned very deeply and loud, and sighed as he would break his heart.

When the buriers came up to him they soon found he was neither a person infected and desperate, as I have observed above, or a person distempered in mind, but one oppressed with a dreadful weight of grief indeed, having his wife and several of his children all in the cart that was just come in with him, and he followed in an agony and excess of sorrow. He mourned heartily, as it was easy to see, but with a kind of masculine grief that could not give itself vent by tears; and calmly defying the buriers to let him alone, said he would only see the bodies thrown in and go

---

13. **churchyard:** location of the cemeteries.
14. **in it:** in doing it (going up to the rim of the pits).

15. **links:** torches.
16. **bellman:** bell ringer who accompanied the dead-cart.

DANIEL DEFOE **561**

CROSSING THE CURRICULUM

Health/Science Because this selection focuses on a public health phenomenon, have students research and report on bubonic plague. They might include causes, symptoms, and treatments as they were understood in the seventeenth and eighteenth centuries; they might add what we know about this communicable disease today. Ask students to create a simple chart to help with their presentation.

Art Have students illustrate Defoe's anecdotes. You may want them to express the tone of the story with the style of drawing; for example, the story of the piper could be done in a comic-book style. They may also wish to explore engravings and lithographs of the time and to copy that style.

A. Critical Reading: Finding Cause and Effect

? Does the episode, in fact, have a sermonlike effect on the narrator, as the sexton has predicted? [Possible answers: Despite the sexton's prediction, the narrator does not seem to feel repentant; he does, however, feel sympathy for the dead and is sobered by the reminder of human mortality.]

B. Critical Reading: Analyzing Narrative Technique

Note how Defoe introduces a first-hand account here, increasing the impression of accuracy.

away, so they left <u>importuning</u> him. But no sooner was the cart turned round and the bodies shot into the pit <u>promiscuously</u>, which was a surprise to him, for he at least expected they would have been decently laid in, though indeed he was afterward convinced that was impracticable; I say, no sooner did he see the sight but he cried out aloud, unable to contain himself. I could not hear what he said, but he went backward two or three steps and fell down in a swoon. The buriers ran to him and took him up, and in a little while he came to himself, and they led him away to the Pie Tavern over against the end of Houndsditch, where, it seems, the man was known, and where they took care of him. He looked into the pit again as he went away, but the buriers had covered the bodies so immediately with throwing in earth, that though there was light enough, for there were lanterns, and candles in them, placed all night round the sides of the pit, upon heaps of earth, seven or eight, or perhaps more, yet nothing could be seen.

This was a mournful scene indeed, and affected me almost as much as the rest; but the other was awful and full of terror. The cart had in it sixteen or seventeen bodies; some were wrapped up in linen sheets, some in rags, some little other than naked, or so loose that what covering they had fell from them in the shooting out of the cart, and they fell quite naked among the rest; but the matter was not much to them, or the indecency much to any one else, seeing they were all dead, and were to be huddled together into the common grave of mankind, as we may call it, for here was no difference made, but poor and rich went together; there was no other way of burials, neither was it possible there should, for coffins were not to be had for the <u>prodigious</u> numbers that fell in such a calamity as this.

5. A Poor Piper

. . . John Hayward . . . was at that time undersexton of the parish of St. Stephen, Coleman Street. By undersexton was understood at that time gravedigger and bearer of the dead. This man carried, or assisted to carry, all the dead to their graves which were buried in that large parish, and

Plague of London (1665). Woodcut.

Master and Fellows, Magdalene College, Cambridge.

who were carried in form;[17] and after that form of burying was stopped, went with the dead-cart and the bell to fetch the dead bodies from the houses where they lay. . . .

It was under this John Hayward's care, and within his bounds, that the story of the piper,[18] with which people have made themselves so merry, happened, and he assured me that it was true. It is said that it was a blind piper; but, as John told me, the fellow was not blind, but an ignorant, weak, poor man, and usually walked his

17. **in form:** according to the customary burial rites.
18. **piper:** bagpiper.

WORDS TO OWN

importuning (im′pôr·tōōn′iŋ) v. used as n.: making repeated demands of.
promiscuously (prə·mis′kyōō·əs·lē) adv.: casually.
prodigious (prō·dij′əs) adj.: huge.

OPTIONS FOR TEACHING

PROFESSIONAL NOTES

Thematic Connections: "An Appetite for Experience" Defoe puts himself into the scene of the plague as he writes *A Journal of the Plague Year*. To begin a classroom discussion, ask students if they ever imagine themselves in other places at other times. What kind of experiences would they choose? Can they imagine themselves in Pepys's time or in London of 1665? Perhaps they wish they were living in the time of the American Revolutionary War or simply in a different part of the country or world. Remind students that if they decide to take a step back, they can be observers of their own lives.

rounds about ten o'clock at night and went piping along from door to door, and the people usually took him in at public houses[19] where they knew him, and would give him drink and victuals, and sometimes farthings;[20] and he in return would pipe and sing and talk simply, which <u>diverted</u> the people; and thus he lived. It was but a very bad time for this diversion while things were as I have told, yet the poor fellow went about as usual, but was almost starved; and when anybody asked how he did he would answer, the dead-cart had not taken him yet, but that they had promised to call for him next week.

It happened one night that this poor fellow, whether somebody had given him too much to drink or no—John Hayward said he had not drink in his house, but that they had given him a little more victuals than ordinary at a public house in Coleman Street—and the poor fellow, having not usually had a bellyful for perhaps not a good while, was laid all along upon the top of a bulk or stall, and fast asleep, at a door in the street near London Wall, towards Cripplegate; and that upon the same bulk or stall the people of some house, in the alley of which the house was a corner, hearing a bell which they always rang before the cart came, had laid a body really dead of the plague just by him, thinking, too, that this poor fellow had been a dead body, as the other was, and laid there by some of the neighbors.

Accordingly, when John Hayward with his bell and the cart came along, finding two dead bodies lie upon the stall, they took them up with the instrument they used and threw them into the cart, and all this while the piper slept soundly.

From hence they passed along and took in other dead bodies, till, as honest John Hayward told me, they almost buried him alive in the cart; yet all this while he slept soundly. At length the cart came to the place where the bodies were to be thrown into the ground, which, as I do remember, was at Mount Mill; and as the cart usually stopped some time before they were ready to shoot out the melancholy load they had in it, as soon as the cart stopped the fellow awaked and struggled a little to get his head out from among

19. **public houses:** taverns.
20. **farthings:** small British coins (no longer in use) worth one quarter of a penny.

the dead bodies, when, raising himself up in the cart, he called out, "Hey! where am I?" This frighted the fellow that attended about the work; but after some pause John Hayward, recovering himself, said, "Lord, bless us! There's somebody in the cart not quite dead!" So another called to him and said, "Who are you?" The fellow answered, "I am the poor piper. Where am I?" "Where are you?" says Hayward. "Why, you are in the dead-cart, and we are going to bury you." "But I an't dead though, am I?" says the piper, which made them laugh a little—though, as John said, they were heartily frighted at first; so they helped the poor fellow down, and he went about his business.

I know the story goes he set up his pipes in the cart and frighted the bearers and others so that they ran away; but John Hayward did not tell the story so, nor say anything of his piping at all; but that he was a poor piper, and that he was carried away as above I am fully satisfied of the truth of. . . .

6. A Violent Cure

I heard of one infected creature who, running out of his bed in his shirt in the anguish and agony of his swellings, of which he had three upon him, got his shoes on and went to put on his coat; but the nurse resisting, and snatching the coat from him, he threw her down, ran over her, ran downstairs and into the street, directly to the Thames in his shirt, the nurse running after him, and calling to the watch to stop him; but the watchman, frighted at the man, and afraid to touch him, let him go on; upon which he ran down to the Stillyard stairs, threw away his shirt, and plunged into the Thames, and, being a good swimmer, swam quite over the river; and the tide being coming in, as they call it (that is, running westward) he reached the land not till he came about the Falcon stairs, where landing, and finding no people there, it being in the night, he ran about the streets there, naked as he was, for a good while, when, it being by that time high water,[21] he takes the river again, and swam back to the Stillyard,

21. **high water:** high tide.

- -

WORDS TO OWN
diverted (də·vʉrt′id) v.: amused.

- -

C. Critical Reading: Drawing Conclusions

? Why does Defoe include this poor fellow in his anecdotes about the plague? [To show how the plague affects people.] What is the effect of the piper's comment about the dead-cart at the end of the passage? [It shows humor; the piper entertains people and has not stopped. This statement also sets a tone for the story: it will have humor in it.]

D. Reader's Response: Shaping Interpretations

? How would you describe the story of the piper? [Sample responses: Ironic; grotesque; funny; pathetic.]

ASSESSMENT TOOLS

Check Test: True-False
1. The effects of the plague showed up immediately on an infected person. [False]
2. If tokens (buboes) were opened and drained, people often recovered from the disease. [True]
3. People were allowed to go to the burial pits, since the plague could not be spread by corpses. [False]
4. One man was cured of the plague after an arduous swim in the Thames River. [True]

5. Even after the plague had diminished, people were afraid to touch or even talk to each other. [False]

Ongoing Assessment For group presentations an assessment chart similar to the one that follows will help students know what you expect from them. Let them see a copy, informing them that three is high, and then use it to assess their presentations.

Group: _____

Content/Information:			
Amount	1	2	3
Accuracy	1	2	3
Presentation:			
Organization	1	2	3
Originality	1	2	3

landed, ran up the streets again to his own house, knocking at the door, went up the stairs and into his bed again; and that this terrible experiment cured him of the plague, that is to say, that the violent motion of his arms and legs stretched the parts where the swellings he had upon him were, that is to say, under his arms and his groin, and caused them to ripen and break; and that the cold of the water abated the fever in his blood. . . .

7. The Plague Diminishes

A . . . The contagion despised all medicine; death raged in every corner; and had it gone on as it did then, a few weeks more would have cleared the town of all, and everything that had a soul. Men everywhere began to despair; every heart failed them for fear; people were made desperate through the anguish of their souls, and the terrors of death sat in the very faces and countenances of the people.

B In that very moment when we might very well say, "Vain was the help of man,"—I say, in that very moment it pleased God, with a most agreeable surprise, to cause the fury of it to abate, even of itself; and the malignity declining, as I have said, though infinite numbers were sick, yet fewer died, and the very first weeks' bill[22] decreased 1,843; a vast number indeed!

C It is impossible to express the change that appeared in the very countenances of the people that Thursday morning when the weekly bill came out. It might have been perceived in their countenances that a secret surprise and smile of joy sat on everybody's face. They shook one another by the hands in the streets, who would hardly go on the same side of the way with one another before. Where the streets were not too broad they would open their windows and call from one house to another, and ask how they did, and if they had heard the good news that the plague was abated. Some would return, when they said good news, and ask, "What good news?" and when they answered that the plague was abated and the bills decreased almost two thousand, they would cry out, "God be praised!" and would weep aloud for joy, telling them they had heard nothing of it; and such was the joy of the

22. **bill:** count of the dead that was published every week so long as the plague raged.

Title page of *A Collection of All the Bills of Mortality* (1665).

people that it was, as it were, life to them from the grave. I could almost set down as many extravagant things done in the excess of their joy as of their grief; but that would be to lessen the value of it. . . .

8. I'm Alive!

. . . I shall conclude the account of this calamitous year . . . with a coarse but sincere stanza of my own, which I placed at the end of my ordinary memorandums the same year they were written:

D A dreadful plague in London was
   In the year sixty-five,
Which swept an hundred thousand souls
   Away; yet I alive!

H. F.

- -

WORDS TO OWN
abated (ə·bāt′id) v.: lessened.
calamitous (kə·lam′ə·təs) adj.: bringing great trouble.

- -

Making Meanings
First Thoughts
1. Students' choice of image will vary. Some may identify the screaming woman, some the corpse gripping the blanket, some the man lamenting the loss of his family.

Reviewing the Text
a. Defoe refers to the time of the plague in the past tense in the first section, when he speaks of "the time of this visitation." In the third section, he introduces an episode by saying, "I remember . . ." At the end, he refers to his "ordinary memorandums" from the time, which suggests that this account is a more literary rendering of the narrator's original journal.

MAKING MEANINGS

First Thoughts

1. What did you feel was the strongest image in this account of an urban epidemic? Why?

Shaping Interpretations

2. What seems to be the **tone** of the *Journal*—the attitude of the writer toward the events he is recounting? Do you think the tone would have been different if the *Journal* really had been written during the plague?

3. What techniques does Defoe use to make his journal seem authentic?

4. Why does Defoe, or his narrator, say that the manner of burial makes no difference to a dead person? To whom do you think the manner of burial *does* make a difference?

5. Why would the story of the piper be improved if it contained the bit about his playing the pipes while he was in the dead-cart? Why, then, does the narrator refuse to include this bit?

6. Review what you wrote in your Reader's Log about morbid curiosity. In which of the incidents recounted here does the narrator appear to be morbidly curious? Do you think his appetite for facts and experience is justified?

7. Why does H. F. call his little poem "coarse"?

Connecting with the Text

8. How do you think experiencing a plague of this sort would change a person's attitude toward life and death?

Reviewing the Text

a. Where does Defoe let the reader know his *Journal* is being written long after the plague took place? How does he explain this change in form?

b. Who are the four characters whom the narrator features? How does each of their situations differ?

c. What were the symptoms of the disease?

d. What attempts were made to cure people?

Extending the Text

9. Few words in English have the shock value of "plague." Can you think of anything in your own world that is described as a plague? How does the plague Defoe describes compare to the "plagues" of today?

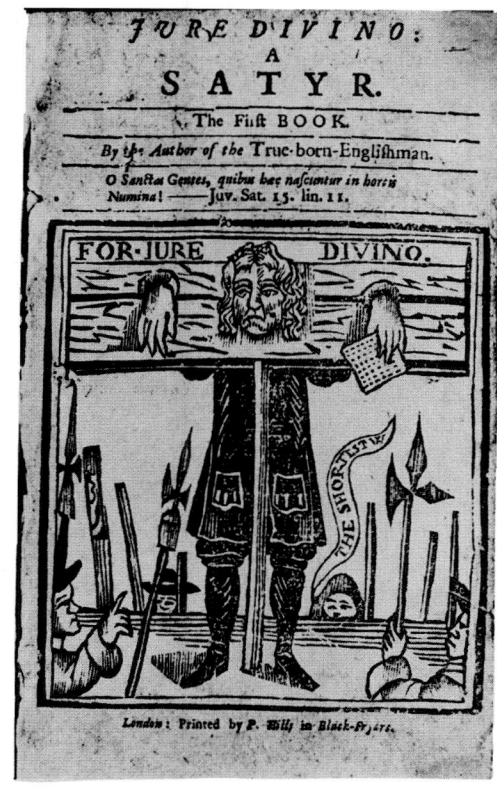

Defoe in the Pillory (detail) (17th century), from a chapbook edition of *Jure Divino*.
By permission of the British Library, London.

DANIEL DEFOE **565**

Shaping Interpretations

2. The tone is sober; the tone of a journal written during the plague could have been more fearful and panicked.

3. The techniques include eyewitness accounts, direct quotations of plague victims, and the citation of statistics.

4. The narrator's statement shows his practical, sober point of view; the dead person can no longer care about his or her burial, but how a plague victim is buried does matter to the living relatives or friends.

5. The addition would add ironic humor. The narrator refuses to include it because he insists on accuracy—the omission makes the journal seem more genuine.

6. The narrator seems to be morbidly curious in the fourth section when he persuades the sexton to allow him to watch the burials at the churchyard. Students' opinions about the narrator's appetite for experience will vary: Some may argue that this information makes his story better; others may believe that the information is unnecessary and his interest is morbid.

7. He calls his poem "coarse" because it is unpolished in its expression of self-centered relief at remaining alive.

Connecting with the Text

8. Possible responses: The experience might make people enjoy life more because they have witnessed the inevitability of death. Or they might take a darker view of life after seeing the horrors of the plague.

Extending the Text

9. **(Synthesis)** Students may name horrible scenes of destruction that are referred to as "plagues": bloody wars, natural disasters, or scenes of environmental devastation. They may also think of modern diseases for which there are no cures. Defoe describes a plague that cannot be understood or stopped; today's plagues may be easier to understand but are probably just as hard to fight.

b. The four characters are the citizen who tries to escape from the quarantine, the bereaved husband in the brown cloak, the poor piper, and the man who swims across the Thames and is cured. Each situation is different. The first character lies about his condition and is later found dead, the second is shocked at the burial of his wife and children in a common grave, the third wakes up in the dead-cart and wonders if he is dead, and the fourth is cured by his strenuous exercise.

c. The symptoms included gangrenous swellings or boils, fever, pains, debility.

d. Doctors tried to draw or burn the infection out of patients.

Beyond the Selection

Choices: Building Your Portfolio

1. **Writer's Notebook** Remind students to save their work. They may use it as prewriting for the Writer's Workshop on p. 612.

2. **Critical Writing** To help students arrive at a conclusion about Defoe's success at imitating a **journal**, ask them if Defoe's account of the plague is as believable—if it sounds as authentic—as Pepys's account of the Great Fire and why or why not. Suggest that it may be possible that Defoe's fiction seems more authentic than Pepys's eyewitness account. Ask students to give reasons why they agree or disagree with this possibility.

3. **Critical Writing** Encourage students to consider a few disasters that happened in the recent past before they write. Ask students if any lessons are learned by remembering the horrible events. Then, have students apply their opinions about recent calamities to Defoe's description of the plague.

4. **Creative Writing** Have students begin to organize their details for their narratives with a *5W–How?* chart. Have students list the facts of *what, who, where, when, why,* and *how* that relate to their topic. They may check their graphic organizers for details as they write.

CHOICES: Building Your Portfolio

Writer's Notebook

1. Collecting Ideas for a Persuasive Essay

Defoe uses officials (the sexton, for example) to make his journal account more convincing—a strategy also important in persuasion. If you are arguing that children's inoculations should be government-funded, strong evidence may come from a health-department doctor. Make a three-column chart headed *Public Disasters, Issues,* and *Experts.* Then, for each column, brainstorm ideas for persuasive essays (TV and newspaper stories can help). Save your notes for the Writer's Workshop on page 612.

Critical Writing

2. Charting Pepys and Defoe

In an essay, compare and contrast Defoe's *A Journal of the Plague Year* and Pepys's diary entry about the Great Fire of London (page 549). (Remember that Pepys's *Diary* is a nonfiction account, unlike Defoe's

	Pepys's Diary	Defoe's Journal
Tone		
Point of view		
Use of details		

Journal.) Gather information for your essay by filling out a chart like the one above. Conclude your essay by deciding how good (or bad) a job Defoe does of imitating a personal journal.

Critical Writing

3. Forgetting or Confronting?

Some people argue that life itself is often very disagreeable—so why should we have to read about dreadful, depressing events in books like Defoe's? Wouldn't it be better just to forget calamities, atrocities, and disasters, and remember only the pleasant things that have happened? How do you feel about this point of view? Using the events in the *Journal* as support, write an essay in which you either defend or attack this position.

Creative Writing

4. You Are There!

Examine several accounts (from newspapers, magazines, or television or radio) of a recent natural disaster in which lives were lost. Then, write a narrative of the event as though you were an observer or a participant. Use either the format of a newspaper article or that of a TV news documentary. Be as creative as you wish, but make sure you include the details that will make your story believable: names, dates, places, times, causes, effects, motives, and so on.

PORTFOLIO ASSESSMENT

Choices: Assessment Criteria For help in evaluating these Choices assignments, see the criteria in the *Portfolio Management System,* p. 117.

OPTIONS FOR TEACHING

Interpersonal Have partners debate the two sides in activity #3 before they begin to write. Debating the topic privately with a partner will allow students to consider both points of view before they write their own judgment in the matter. Make sure students take notes. If partners want to take the same side, have them decide between them who will take the other side by flipping a coin.

STRATEGIES FOR INCLUSION

Visual Have students concentrate on pictures and maps they find of the disaster they will write about in activity #4. Students may study the pictures and then imagine themselves at the scene. Encourage students to make a list of what they would notice using all five senses. They may organize their ideas in a graphic similar to the one on Transparency 7: Sensory Details Chart in the Transparency Package.

Joseph Addison and Sir Richard Steele

Wit, morality, and coffeehouse gossip. In the early eighteenth century, London's thriving coffeehouse scene provided politicians, actors, and aristocrats a place to meet, to read newspapers, and to gossip. Coffeehouse conversations reflected the nation's commercial, cultural, and political life to such an extent that they were called "the penny universities" because one could receive a complete education there for the price of a newspaper.

Ⓐ

Sir Richard Steele and Joseph Addison's contribution to this intellectual scene was the periodical essay, a forerunner of modern newspapers and magazines. This publication consisted of a single printed sheet, issued at least once a week and usually containing a single piece of writing. Steele and Addison are often paired because of their work on

Joseph Addison (detail) (before 1717) by Sir Godfrey Kneller. Oil on canvas (36″ × 28″).

By Courtesy of the National Portrait Gallery, London.

two enormously popular periodicals, *The Tatler,* which appeared three times a week from April 1709 to January 1711, and *The Spectator,* which appeared daily except Sunday from March 1, 1711, to December 6, 1712. Both publications elevated the periodical essay to an art form.

Ⓑ

Two very different talents. Sir Richard Steele (1672–1729), born of English parents in Dublin and orphaned early, was educated in London at a privately endowed school, the Charterhouse. There he met his future collaborator Joseph Addison, a brilliant student who was the son of an English clergyman. Steele followed him to Oxford two years later but left the university before graduating and

Sir Richard Steele (1711) by Sir Godfrey Kneller. Oil on canvas (36″ × 28″).

By Courtesy of the National Portrait Gallery, London.

SPOTLIGHT ON 567

A. Exploring the Culture
The first recorded coffeehouse in England was located in Oxford in 1650. By 1730, there were five hundred coffeehouses in London. Some of the most popular ones were Garraway's, Slaughter's, and White's. Those who shared certain professions would meet at certain houses. Writers, for example, usually met at Will's.

B. Expansion
The Spectator enjoyed a strong circulation of three thousand copies a day. Historians estimate that each copy was shared by as many as ten readers.

Technology Tip

TECHNOLOGY A collection of axioms from Joseph Addison is available from Columbia University's Project Bartleby, at **http://www.columbia.edu/acis/bartleby/bartlett/216.html**. *You may want to preview any internet activity that you suggest to students. Because these resources are sometimes public forums, their content can be unpredictable.*

STRATEGIES FOR INCLUSION

Visual Students may use a Venn diagram to compare the two authors. First, ask students what the writers have in common, then have students concentrate on differences between the two. Students may use a graphic similar to the one on Transparency 5: Venn Diagram in the Transparency Package.

Advanced Challenge students to place these writers in the bigger picture of the age in which they live. After students review the historical introduction on pp. 466–484, ask them to consider how Addison and Steele's work reflects the spirit of the times. They can then share their theories and observations with the rest of the class in an oral presentation.

Auditory So that students may hear the differences between the two writers, ask students to read aloud the excerpts from Addison and Steele's writing and to focus on the distinctiveness of the voice, or style, of the writing.

A. Humanities Connection

When Steele found favor after the accession of George I, one of his interesting posts was as supervisor of the Drury Lane Theatre, the renowned playhouse where David Garrick later in the century made his reputation as an actor.

B. Literary Connections

Samuel Johnson praised Joseph Addison in his *Lives of the Poets* (1781), saying that "Whoever wishes to attain an English style . . . must give his days and nights to the volumes of Addison."

C. Literary Connections

After Addison's death, Pope condemned him indirectly in the character of Atticus in his *An Epistle to Dr. Arbuthnot* (1735). Atticus, Pope said, was cold and cautious, the sort of critic who would

> Damn with faint praise, assent with civil leer,
> And without sneering, teach the rest to sneer;
> Willing to wound, and yet afraid to strike,
> Just hint at fault, and hesitate dislike;
> Alike reserved to blame or to commend,
> A timorous foe and a suspicious friend.

returned to London, where he became an officer in the Life Guards, the royal escort unit, and a young man about town. After serving in the army at home and abroad, Steele devoted himself to politics, journalism, and managing a theater. He even became a member of Parliament, and for a time edited the *London Gazette,* the government's official newspaper. A warmhearted, jovial, impulsive man, and a devoted husband, Steele was often short of money. Being knighted by George I in 1715 did not make him any richer. In debt and suffering from a stroke, he was thoroughly miserable during the last years of his life.

Joseph Addison (1672–1719) was a different sort of man, with a reputation for being cold and haughty. After receiving bachelor's and master's degrees from Oxford, he wrote poems and dedicated them to various statesmen in hopes of advancing his career in government. Eventually his talents were noticed, and he was elected to Parliament, finally becoming secretary of state. Both Steele and Addison wrote plays, but Steele's, characteristically, were comedies. Addison's most successful play, *Cato*—an immensely successful tragedy first performed in 1713—was a history of Rome that referred to contemporary politics. In politics and literature Addison was successful, but his final years were as troubled as Steele's. Addison quarreled with, and died without being reconciled to, his partner Steele and his good friends Jonathan Swift and Alexander Pope.

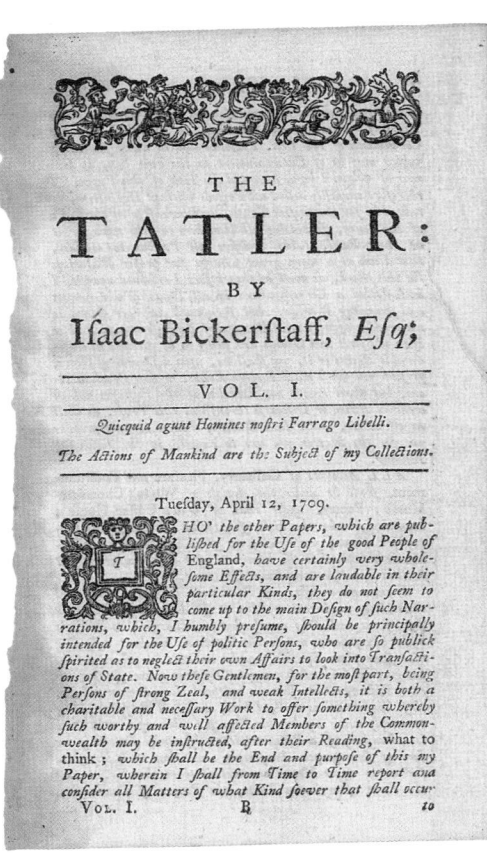

Opening page of *The Tatler,* volume 1 (1709).

A brief but remarkable partnership. Addison and Steele wrote more than nine hundred essays during their partnership; these essays remain the pair's most enduring work. The first issue of *The Tatler* promised current reports from reliable sources. For example, they claimed that new poetry would come straight from Will's Coffeehouse; St. James's Coffeehouse would provide current events; accounts of "gallantry, pleasure, and entertainment" would be obtained from White's Chocolate House. In other words, the paper promised the city's best gossip in a single printed sheet. In the first issue of *The Tatler,* Steele said, "The general purpose of this paper is to expose the false arts of life, to pull off the disguises of cunning, vanity, and affectation, and to recommend a general simplicity in our dress, our discourse, and our behavior." And in issue Number 10 of *The Spectator,* Addison said, "I shall endeavor to enliven morality with wit and temper wit with morality."

Addison and Steele were both ardent Whigs, a political party that supported reforms opposed by the conservative Tories. However, their periodicals practiced moderation when commenting on public affairs. Their essays sought to educate the new reading public of upper-class women and prosperous merchants on matters of taste, style, and politics. In Addison's words, *The Spectator*'s goal was to bring "philosophy out of the closets and libraries, schools and colleges, to dwell in clubs and assemblies, at tea tables and in coffeehouses."

One way Addison made philosophy more accessible was by critiquing entertainment. He reviewed popular stage productions, asking why "the

Strategic Reading Before students read the Spotlight On section, ask them to think of what they know about the time period—the style of writing, people's concerns, and so on. Have them record this information in the first of three columns drawn on a sheet of paper. In the second column, have students write questions they would like answered by the section, for example, questions they have about the successful partnership between two writers. After they have read the section, have them list in the third column of their organizers what they have learned about Addison and Steele.

Writing: Short Essay Have students write a one-page essay that seeks to instruct the reader on a specific topic by using humor and common sense. If students have trouble deciding on a topic, encourage them to think of a piece of advice on ways people could change their behavior to make the world a better place. They may use essays by Addison and Steele as models, or they may want to examine a few editorials from a local newspaper. After students have finished, have them edit their papers with a partner.

ordinary method of making a hero is to clap a huge plume of feathers upon his head." "One would believe," reasons *The Spectator,* "that we thought a great man and a tall man the same thing." The essay urged readers to look beyond scenery and costume and to explore the power of their own imagination:

> A good poet will give the reader a more lively idea of an army or a battle in a description, than if he actually saw them drawn up in squadrons and battalions, or engaged in the confusion of a fight. Our minds should be opened to great conceptions and inflamed with glorious sentiments by what the actor speaks, more than by what he appears. Can all the trappings or equipage of a king or hero give Brutus half that pomp and majesty which he receives from a few lines in Shakespeare?
>
> —from *The Spectator*

Addison and Steele's original combination of satire and sentiment resulted in playful essays such as *The Tatler's* Number 217. This essay comments on marital relations with a clever "translation" of Milton's *Paradise Lost:* In Addison and Steele's version, Adam upbraids Eve by complaining:

> Madam, if my advices had been of any authority with you when that strange desire of gadding possessed you this morning, we had still been happy: But your cursed vanity and opinion of your own conduct . . . has ruined both yourself, and me who trusted you.
>
> —from *The Tatler*

Eve's rebuttal protests:

> Was I to have been always at your side, I might as well have continued there, and been but your rib still: But if I was so weak a creature as you thought me, why did you not interpose your sage authority more absolutely? . . . Had you not been too easy, neither you or I had now transgressed.
>
> —from *The Tatler*

The editors gently, wryly show their readers the folly of domestic strife while advising a moderate path that will avoid "conjugal enmity." Their essays could ridicule bad puns or ponder the nature of true literary "genius." The only constant in their coverage was an intolerance for vanity and excess.

Steele and Addison's collaboration in *The Tatler* and *The Spectator* expanded the genre of the periodical essay with a blend of humor and instruction. In addition, the partnership left a detailed literary record of eighteenth-century society and thought. Their essays are models of insight, wit, and common sense that compel readers of any age.

Stockjobbers Extraordinary (18th century), satirical sketch by Robert Dighton.
Guildhall Library. Corporation of London.

D. Literary Connections

One of the partners' vehicles of entertainment was casting the essays in the form of conversations between members of a fictitious club. These gentlemen included Sir Andrew Freeport (representing the rich trading class), Sir Roger de Coverly (representing the conservative landed gentry), and Captain Sentry (representing the army).

RESPONDING TO THE ART: ABOUT THE ARTIST

Robert Dighton (1752–1814) was an English painter, caricaturist, and writer who became well-known for a series of caricatures of famous people of the eighteenth century, mostly politicians, actors and officers. In his sketch, *Stockjobbers Extraordinary,* Dighton pokes fun at stockjobbers (British slang for stockbrokers), portraying them as portly, stodgy characters. Dighton's shrewd caricature exaggerates the facial features of the stockjobbers and distorts their expressions and bodies, leaving a less than favorable impression of this profession.

INTEGRATING THE LANGUAGE ARTS

Language and Style Have students review the excerpts from Addison and Steele's writing with the writers' purpose in mind. Ask students how the writers' purpose is reflected in their style. What methods do the writers use to make their moral instruction entertaining, inoffensive, and persuasive? Help students begin by giving them the following example: "One would believe that we thought a great man and a tall man the same thing." [The sentence is entertaining because it is humorous, inoffensive because it does not point a finger at a specific person, and persuasive because it appeals to common sense: Just because a man is tall, he is not necessarily great. The sentence thus has a moral (the measure of greatness is not simple) without moralizing.] **Have students find their own examples.**

ASSESSMENT TOOLS

Check Test: Questions and Answers
1. What form did Addison and Steele's writing take? [Essays.]
2. Where was their work published? [In periodicals, *The Tatler* and *The Spectator.*]
3. How did the characters of the two men differ? [Steele was warmhearted but usually broke; Addison was colder and more successful.]
4. About how many essays did the two collaborate on? [About nine hundred.]
5. What was their stated purpose? [To educate and instruct in an entertaining fashion.]

QUICK PLANNING GUIDE

Into the Selections

Author Biography p. 570
Before You Read p. 571, p. 575

Through the Selections

from A Dictionary of the English Language pp. 572–574
Letter to Lord Chesterfield pp. 576–577
Words to Own pp. 576–577
Making Meanings p. 574, p. 578
Elements of Literature pp. 578–579

Beyond the Selections

Choices: Building Your Portfolio p. 579
• **Writer's Notebook:** Write ideas for an essay about stopping injustice
• **Critical Writing:** Analyze Johnson's character in a paragraph
• **Critical Writing:** Write a short essay to explain Johnson's use of satire
• **Creative Writing:** Write a reply to Johnson's letter
• **Creative Writing:** Make a twenty-word dictionary
• **Creative Writing:** Rewrite Johnson's letter in a more contemporary style

Spotlight On pp. 580–581

Samuel Johnson
(1709–1784)

Samuel Johnson (detail) (1756)
by an unknown artist.
Private Collection.

Samuel Johnson was the dominant literary figure in England during the latter part of the eighteenth century. Johnson is famous not for one or two masterpieces, but for a great variety of writings and for three large projects: *A Dictionary of the English Language* (1755); an edition of Shakespeare's plays (1765) with an important critical preface and useful notes; and *The Lives of the Poets* (1779–1781) in ten volumes, a series of biographical-critical introductions. A wise man, a moralist, a talker, an eminent writer and critic, a beloved friend of people rich, poor, young, and old, Johnson became in his own day an English institution. Even today, his personality is vivid because so many of his contemporaries recorded their impressions of him. We think of him as a large, imposing person of untidy appearance and odd mannerisms, very fond of drinking tea and of discoursing with his friends on just about every subject that concerns human beings.

Of course, he was not always like that. Johnson's beginnings were humble and unpromising. The son of an unsuccessful bookseller in the small city of Lichfield, he was a puny, weak infant who suffered from the effects of smallpox and scrofula, an infection of the lymph glands of the neck, which made him blind in one eye and deaf in one ear.

Despite his early weaknesses, Johnson grew into a sturdy youth, gradually exhibiting the qualities that characterized him as an adult: vigor, courage, pride, bossiness, and dedication to learning. He had to leave Oxford after only one year because he lacked money to continue; after that, he was spectacularly unsuccessful as a teacher in a private school. In 1737, Johnson moved to London with his wife Elizabeth Porter, a widow twenty years his senior, whom he called Tetty and loved passionately.

To support himself and his wife, Johnson wrote a tragedy, *Irene* (1736), which was moderately successful. For many years he did hack work for periodicals, especially the *Gentleman's Magazine,* often called the first magazine. In these years, while Johnson was struggling for recognition, he became addicted to the city life in London and began to disparage life in the countryside and provincial cities. "There is in London," he once said, "all that life can afford"; and "When a man is tired of London, he is tired of life."

But gradually Johnson's days of poverty and obscurity came to an end. In 1750, a series of essays called *The Rambler* made him famous as "a teacher of moral and religious wisdom," to quote his biographer, James Boswell. Meanwhile, his remarkable *Dictionary* had been published. And in 1762, in recognition of his services to literature, Johnson received a life pension from King George III—an English monarch that most Americans have heard of.

Johnson shared his prosperity with others, for he was always a devout man and his religion required him to be charitable. He also could not stand to be alone, with no one to talk to. He numbered among his intimates the painter Sir Joshua Reynolds, the statesman Edmund Burke, the historian Edward Gibbon, the musicologist Dr. Charles Burney, and his fellow writer Oliver Goldsmith.

Unlike most habitual talkers, Johnson attracted people because he talked so well. He also liked to be asked questions, so that his talk was never a monologue. His words came out in beautifully rounded sentences, just as though he were writing. Many people offered him their hospitality, especially Henry and Hester Thrale, a rich brewer and his wife. After Johnson's death, Mrs. Thrale published her *Anecdotes* about him, in which she said "No man loved laughing better."

PORTFOLIO ASSESSMENT

Portfolio Assessment For help with teacher assessment of reading skills, see the *Portfolio Management System,* pp. 54–55.

PROGRAM MANAGER

• **Planning Instruction** See *Teaching Notes, Teaching Resources A,* pp. 146–147, for objectives, summaries, literary elements, and additional biographical information for these selections.
• **Instructional Support** Before beginning the instructional lesson see *Graphic Organizer for Active Reading, Teaching Resources A,* pp. 158–159, for Through the Selection activities.
• **Assessment** See *Selection Test, Test Booklet,* pp. 109–110.
• **Reinforcement** Use the *Words to Own* worksheet in *Teaching Resources A,* p. 160.

BEFORE YOU READ
FROM **A DICTIONARY**

Background

Johnson's *Dictionary*—the first comprehensive and authoritative one in English—contains about 40,000 words and many, many definitions. The verb *to take,* for instance, has one hundred thirteen different meanings, and *to set,* sixty-six. Most of these definitions Johnson wrote himself; those he took from the word-books of his predecessors he is careful to identify. Before Johnson's time, academies of scholars in France and in Italy had produced large dictionaries of French and Italian, but there was no such academy in England. Therefore, Johnson took on the job himself; England must have its own dictionary, and Johnson was the man to write it!

How did he do it? First, he read an enormous number of literary, religious, philosophical, scientific, and technical books, most of them borrowed from friends. As he read, he marked passages and underlined a key word in each passage; this was the word he intended to define.

Next, his copyists—he had six of them, all Scotsmen except one—copied out the marked passages on slips of paper and filed each slip alphabetically according to the key word. The slips were pasted into eighty large note-books. Finally, using the passages, Johnson wrote definitions of the key words. There were originally about 240,000 passages—too many to be printed. When the *Dictionary* was finally put out in 1755 by a combination of five publishing firms, it contained about 114,000 illustrative passages.

Johnson's *Dictionary* was, and is, a prodigious accomplishment. Forty members of the French Academy worked for forty years on the French dictionary; Johnson and his six copyists worked for about nine years on the English one. The *Dictionary* made Johnson's name familiar to every literate person in England and the American Colonies. It was the basis of all subsequent English dictionaries, including those of the American Noah Webster

(1758–1843), who did little else in his lifetime except compile dictionaries that contained thousands of definitions and illustrative quotations taken without acknowledgment from Johnson. Johnson's *Dictionary* was not completely superseded until 1928, when the last of the ten volumes of *A New English Dictionary* was published. This work, revised in thirteen volumes, is now called *The Oxford English Dictionary* (*OED*).

Although more comprehensive dictionaries have since been produced, Johnson's *Dictionary* lives on because it reflects its author's interesting character and sense of humor. None of the selections given here is a complete entry; there are no etymologies or origins of the words, no definitions reflecting the various shades of meaning, and few illustrative quotations. For an example of a complete definition, here is the entry for the words *giggle* and *giggler:*

To GI′GGLE. *v. n.* [*gichgelen,* Dutch.] To laugh idly ; to titter ; to grin with merry levity. It is retained in Scotland.

GI′GGLER. *n. ſ.* [from *giggle.*] A laugher ; a titterer ; one idly and fooliſhly merry.

A ſad wiſe valour is the brave complexion,
That leads the van, and ſwallows up the cities:
The *giggler* is a milk-maid, whom infection,
Or the fir'd beacon, frighteth from his ditties.   *Herbert.*
We ſhew our preſent, joking, *giggling* race ;
True joy conſiſts in gravity and grace.   *Garrick's Epilogue.*

SAMUEL JOHNSON 571

Into the Selection

Using BEFORE YOU READ p. 571

Background

Point out to students that even if Johnson had worked every day of the nine years on the *Dictionary,* he would have had to produce more than 70 of the original 240,000 passages *per day.* Ask students what they think the statistic says about Johnson's character and drive, and what it says about the number of books he must have read when compiling passages for the *Dictionary.*

WRITERS ON WRITING

Johnson once remarked that "The only end of writing is to enable the readers better to enjoy life, or better to endure it." He was known to say that every man who writes thinks he can amuse or inform people, and they must be the best judges of his pretensions. As to the method of writing itself, the main thing was hard work. One of his best-known sayings is "What is written without effort is in general read without pleasure." And if you are going to go to so much trouble, make sure you are rewarded for it. "No man but a blockhead ever wrote," he would say, "except for money."

OPTIONS FOR TEACHING

PROFESSIONAL NOTES

Technology Tip The Samuel Johnson Web site includes electronic texts by and about Johnson as well as quotations and information by related writers. The URL is **http://www.english.upenn.edu/~jlynch/Johnson**. *You may want to preview any internet activity that you suggest to students. Because these resources are sometimes public forums, their content can be unpredictable.*

Technology Tip Technology changes rapidly as does its lexicon. Language today is peppered with words and phrases that develop alongside technological advances. Ask your students to research these changes in the language and create a Johnson-like dictionary of computer jargon. ☞

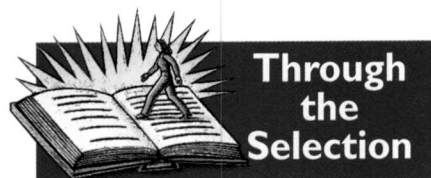
A. Reader's Response: First Thoughts

Point out that alligators and crocodiles are distinct species. How might such a mistake happen? [Sample responses: They were thought to be the same at the time because they looked similar; Johnson was misinformed; Johnson was emphasizing the similarities between the African and American animals.]

B. Critical Reading: Making Generalizations

According to Johnson, to *budge* is a "low word," or slang. Is it considered slang today? [Possible answer: No, not usually.] What does this indicate about language? [Possible answers: Language changes; what was once inappropriate frequently becomes accepted; linguistic standards are relative to time and place.]

C. Language Note: Word Changes

Because students may be confused by *catsup* being defined as a "pickle," tell them that the word *pickle* as used in the British Isles often refers to any pungent sauce used to flavor meat.

D. Exploring the Culture

? What do you suppose Johnson means by "a woman's word"? [Possible answers: What women usually say; feminine; a man would not use it.] What does such a distinction reveal about Johnson's culture? [Possible answers: The differences between men and women were emphasized; speech mirrored gender; the culture had rigid rules regarding social behavior.]

---

from A Dictionary of the English Language

Samuel Johnson

alligator. The crocodile. This name is chiefly used for the crocodile of America, between which, and that of Africa, naturalists have laid down this difference, that one moves the upper, and the other the lower jaw; but this is now known to be chimerical,[1] the lower jaw being equally moved by both.

to apricate. To bask in the sun.

athletick. Strong of body; vigorous; lusty; robust.

> Science distinguishes a man of honor from one of those *athletick* brutes, whom undeservedly we call heroes.
>
> —Dryden.

autopsy. Ocular demonstration; seeing a thing oneself.

balderdash. Anything jumbled together without judgment; rude mixture; a confused discourse.

bedpresser. A heavy lazy fellow.

> This sanguine coward, this *bedpresser,* this horseback-breaker, this huge hill of flesh.
>
> —Shakespeare, *Henry IV,* Part 1.

to blab. To tell what ought to be kept secret.

board. A piece of wood of more length and breadth than thickness.

to budge. To stir; to move off the place: a low word.

catsup. A kind of pickle, made from mushrooms.

companion. A familiar term of contempt; a fellow.

> I scorn you, scurvy *companion*! What? you poor, base, rascally, cheating, lack-linen mate: Away, you moldy rogue, away.
>
> —Shakespeare, *Henry IV,* Part 2.

cough. A convulsion of the lungs, vellicated by some sharp serosity. It is pronounced *coff.*

dedication. A servile address to a patron.

den. A cavern or hollow running horizontally, or with a small obliquity, underground; distinct from a hole, which runs down perpendicularly.

dull. Not exhilarating; not delightful; as, *to make dictionaries is* dull *work.*

eel. A serpentine, slimy fish that lurks in mud.

essay. A loose sally of the mind; an irregular indigested piece; not a regular and orderly composition.

excise. A hateful tax levied upon commodities, and adjudged not by the common judges of property, but wretches hired by those to whom excise is paid.

favorite. One chosen as a companion by his superior; a mean wretch whose whole business is by any means to please.

fillip. A jerk of the finger let go from the thumb.

frightfully. Disagreeably; not beautifully. A woman's word.

fun. (A low cant[2] word.) Sport; high merriment; frolicsome delight.

gambler. (A cant word, I suppose, for *game* or *gamester.*) A knave whose practice it is to invite the unwary to game and cheat them.

goose. A large waterfowl proverbially noted, I know not why, for foolishness.

gravy. The serous juice that runs from flesh not much dried by the fire.

> They usually boil and roast their meat until it falls almost off from the bones; but we love it half raw, with the blood trickling down from it, delicately terming it the *gravy,* which in truth looks more like an ichorous or raw bloody matter.
>
> —Harvey, *On Consumptions.*

to hiss. To utter a noise like that of a serpent and some other animals. It is remarkable, that this word cannot be pronounced without making the noise which it signifies.

---

2. **cant:** a word Johnson uses to describe language he disapproves of because he perceives it to be of base origins.

1. **chimerical** (kī·mer′i·kəl): fanciful.

OPTIONS FOR TEACHING

STRATEGIES FOR INCLUSION

Linguistic To give students an idea of Johnson's erudition and creativity, divide the class into small groups, and choose some of Johnson's words for each group. Have the groups define their words as best they can, and then have groups take turns reading their definitions aloud as the rest of the class writes down words that match the definitions.

Intrapersonal To emphasize the connection between analysis and its basis in the text, have students compile lists of the comments Johnson makes about himself within the context of the *Dictionary.* Then, ask them to jot down what the comments reveal about Johnson and to use the comments in writing a brief character description of Johnson. Students may share their character descriptions and their quotations.

English Language Development The definitions written by Samuel Johnson provide an excellent opportunity for students to practice with modern dictionaries. Divide the class into small groups, and assign each group several words from Johnson's dictionary. Students should use a modern version to check how these words may have changed over time. Students should then use each word in a sentence, placing it in a context that demonstrates the students' comprehension.

immaterial. (1) Incorporeal; void of matter. (2) Unimportant; without weight; impertinent; without relation. This sense has crept into the conversation and writings of barbarians; but ought to be utterly rejected.

jogger. One who moves heavily and dully.

lexicographer. A writer of dictionaries; a harmless drudge, that busies himself in tracing the original, and detailing the signification of words.

to lift. To rob; to plunder.

lingo. Language; tongue; speech. A low cant word.

lunch, luncheon. As much food as one's hand can hold.

merrythought. A forked bone on the body of fowls; so called because boys and girls pull in play at the two sides, the longest part broken off betokening priority of marriage.

mouth. (1) The aperture in the head of any animal at which the food is received. (4) A speaker; a rhetorician; the principal orator. In burlesque language.

> Every coffeehouse has some particular statesman belonging to it, who is the *mouth* of the street where he lives.
>
> —Addison.

mushroom. An upstart; a wretch risen from the dunghill; a director of a company.

network. Anything reticulated or decussated, at equal distances, with interstices between the intersections.

osprey. The sea-eagle, of which it is reported, that when he hovers in the air, all the fish in the water turn up their bellies, and lie still for him to seize which he pleases.

parody. A kind of writing, in which the words of an author or his thoughts are taken, and by a slight change adapted to some new purpose.

pastern. The knee of a horse.

pat. Fit; convenient; exactly suitable either as to time or place. This is a low word, and should not be used but in burlesque writings.

Dr. Samuel Johnson's house, City of London. The house was designed by Johnson in the 18th century.

patron. One who countenances, supports, or protects. Commonly a wretch who supports with insolence, and is paid with flattery.

pension. An allowance made to anyone without an equivalent. In England it is generally understood to mean pay given to a state hireling for treason to his country.

to period. To put an end to. A bad[3] word.

pompous. Splendid; magnificent; grand.

rhinoceros. A vast beast in the East Indies armed with a horn in his front.

river. A land current of water bigger than a brook.

romance. A tale of wild adventures in war and love.

3. **bad:** low; vulgar.

E. Language Note: Echoic Words/Onomatopoeia

Hiss is an example of what lexicographers today call an echoic word. Poets use such words for onomatopoeia.

F. Critical Reading: Making Connections

? How is this word used today? [Possible answers: A runner; a healthy person; a slender person; the opposite of Johnson's definition.]

G. Language Note: Vocabulary

? What are some other modern meanings of the word *pat*? [Possible answers: Tap; small, molded mass (pat of butter); apt.]

CROSSING THE CURRICULUM

Social Sciences Times have changed since Johnson's day, when lunch was "[a]s much food as one's hand can hold." This image perhaps seems crude, as the reader visualizes Johnson, great literary figure, grabbing as much food as his hand can hold and stuffing it into his mouth. But how did the people of this era actually eat?

- Have students research and write a paragraph on lunch as defined by Johnson.
- Have students search for works of art depicting eating habits of the day for presentation to the class.

CLASSROOM MANAGEMENT

Group Work As members are inspired by others' contributions, the number of ideas generated increases. The larger the group, the more interaction. However, groups of four to six tend to produce just as many ideas but with better quality and less silliness. Assure accountability by having each person fill out and turn in the assignment, and always wrap up by discussing the ideas gathered by all of the groups.

INTEGRATING THE LANGUAGE ARTS

Strategic Reading Have students scan the text for words that interest them. Before they read the definition, have them jot down a quick prediction of what the definition will be. Have students volunteer to read their definitions and then to read Johnson's definition.

Making Meanings

First Thoughts

1. Possible responses: *Catsup* is surprising because it is so different from our definition; *lexicographer* is interesting and amusing because Johnson refers to himself as a drudge in his own reference work, which is supposed to be objective.

Shaping Interpretations

2. Possibilities include *alligator* and *rhinoceros.*
3. Johnson does not value or respect slang terms.
4. Many of Johnson's definitions are idiosyncratic or eccentric. His sense of humor comes through in the definitions for *hiss, lunch,* and *osprey.* His political and religious preferences are shown in the definitions for *excise, oats,* and *whig.*
5. Possible response: Language changes with use. The changes in language allow it to remain living. Words enter the dictionary as slang and many eventually become accepted forms of expression. For example, *fun,* which Johnson calls a low word, is now perfectly acceptable. However, some words have not changed all that much: *traipse* is still considered colloquial. You may want to mention that Johnson was opposed to the idea that language is a fossilized, unchanging thing that should be preserved pure and inviolate.

---

to romp. To play rudely, noisily, and boisterously.

> A stool is the first weapon taken up in a general *romping* or skirmish.
>
> —Swift, *Rules to Servants.*

smoke. The visible effluvium, or sooty exhalation from anything burning.

to sneeze. To emit wind audibly by the nose.

sonnet. A short poem consisting of fourteen lines, of which the rhymes are adjusted by a particular rule. It is not very suitable to the English language, and has not been used by any man of eminence since Milton.

soup. Strong decoction[4] of flesh for the table.

Ⓐ **stammel.** Of this word I know not the meaning.

suds. A lixivium[5] of soap and water.

tiny. Little; small; puny. A burlesque word.

tittletattle. Idle talk; prattle; empty gabble.

4. **decoction** (dē·käk′shən): extract made by boiling a substance down to its essence.
5. **lixivium** (liks·iv′ē·əm): mixture; solution.

---

torpedo. A fish which while alive, if touched even with a long stick, benumbs the hand that so touches it, but when dead is eaten safely.

tory. (A cant term, derived, I suppose, from an Irish word signifying a savage.) One who adheres to the ancient constitution of the state, and the apostolical hierarchy of the Church of England, opposed to a whig.

to traipse. (A low word, I believe, without any etymology.) To walk in a careless or sluttish manner.

tree. A large vegetable rising, with one woody stem, to a considerable height.

unkindly. Unnatural; contrary to nature.

vivacious. Long-lived.

whale. The largest of fish.

whig. The name of a faction.

to worm. To deprive a dog of something, nobody knows what, under his tongue, which is said to prevent him, nobody knows why, from running mad.

zed. The name of the letter *z.*

OATS. *n. ʃ.* [aꞇen, Saxon.] A grain, which in England is generally given to horſes, but in Scotland ſupports the people.

MAKING MEANINGS

First Thoughts

1. Which definition surprised or interested you the most? Explain your answer.

Shaping Interpretations

2. Which definitions contain what we would regard as errors of fact?
3. What is Johnson's attitude toward slang, which he calls "low words" or "cant"?
4. How does Johnson's personality come through in the voice of the *Dictionary*? Which definitions show the writer's sense of humor? Which show his political and religious preferences?

5. Based on your own experiences and the answers you gave to the preceding questions, what inferences can you make about language, especially about the way it changes?

Connecting with the Text

6. How do these entries compare with entries for the same words in your current dictionary?

Challenging the Text

7. Who, in your opinion, should decide what a word means and how it is pronounced?

Check Test: True-False

1. Johnson's *Dictionary* was the first comprehensive dictionary in English. [True]
2. Johnson derived most of his dictionary definitions from the work of his predecessors. [False]
3. Johnson chose the words for his *Dictionary* by asking friends what words they had the most difficulty with. [False]

4. Because of the *Dictionary,* Johnson's name became familiar to every literate person in England and the American colonies. [True]
5. Johnson's dictionary was the basis of all subsequent English dictionaries, except those of American Noah Webster. [False]

Peer Assessment After groups have finished their work, ask each group member to fill out the following evaluation.

1. My group used the following strategies to generate ideas: _____.
2. The method that generated the most ideas was _____.
3. My group used the following procedures for making decisions: _____.
4. The best procedure for making decisions was _____.
5. The best way to achieve full participation is _____.

BEFORE YOU READ
LETTER TO LORD CHESTERFIELD

Reading Focus

Pride and Protest

Long before Johnson completed work on his dictionary, he put out a pamphlet titled *Plan of a Dictionary of the English Language* (1747). The pamphlet was dedicated, at his publisher's suggestion, to Philip Dormer Stanhope, fourth earl of Chesterfield—an accomplished, rich, elegant, and learned nobleman. The publisher, Robert Dodsley, wanted Chesterfield's patronage, or financial support, of Johnson's *Dictionary,* a very expensive venture. But nothing came of the attempt to capture the great man's interest. Johnson even called on Chesterfield a few times, but he was denied entrance at least once. He received only a token contribution from Chesterfield: ten pounds.

Quickwrite

Suppose you found out that someone else had taken credit for one of your accomplishments, such as a piece of writing, a contribution to a team victory, or a community project. Freewrite for a few minutes in your Reader's Log about how you would feel and what action you would take.

Dr. Johnson in the Anteroom of Lord Chesterfield Waiting for an Audience (1748) by Edward Matthew Ward.

Tate Gallery, London.

Background

In 1755, just before the finished dictionary actually appeared, Dodsley again approached Chesterfield, who by this time had probably forgotten all about the *Plan* and its dedication to him. After all, Chesterfield was a very busy and important man. This time he did respond, though not by giving money. Without ever having seen the dictionary, Chesterfield published two letters praising it in a weekly newspaper.

Johnson, not knowing that Dodsley had again approached Chesterfield, read the two generous letters with surprise and indignation. They could easily be misconstrued; the public might conclude that Chesterfield had given what today would be called a "grant" to Johnson. The letters put Johnson in an embarrassing position because he had asserted in the preface to the *Dictionary* that he had received no "patronage of the great." And so he wrote Chesterfield a letter that has since become famous. The letter's language is very formal; how would you describe its tone?

SAMUEL JOHNSON **575**

Connecting with the Text

6. Many entries, including *autopsy, companion, essay, favorite, jogger,* and *vivacious,* have changed drastically.

Challenging the Text

7. **(Synthesis)** Students' responses will vary but should demonstrate an understanding that language changes and is maintained not by a single person but by an entire society. New editions of dictionaries are years in the making and require large numbers of contributors.

Into the Selection

Using BEFORE YOU READ p. 575

Reading Focus

Twenty years before the *Dictionary,* Johnson wrote his first work, a translation of a book from the French. The fee for the job was five guineas, an amount that is a little over half of Lord Chesterfield's contribution to the *Dictionary.* Ask students how the amount of the earl's offering, as well as his timing of his praise of the work, may be seen as insulting.

Background

Tell students that Johnson was quickly sobered by the effort of producing the *Dictionary.* He later described the enthusiasm with which he began as "the dreams of a poet doomed at last to wake a lexicographer." Ask students to look for images of waking in their examination of the letter's tone. Encourage students to see how Johnson's use of irony and polished indignation reflects the idea of waking to a sad reality from a beautiful dream.

WORDS TO OWN

The following vocabulary words are defined in the Words to Own at the bottom of the pupil's page.

contending p. 576	impart p. 577
repulsed p. 576	cynical p. 577
encumbers p. 577	

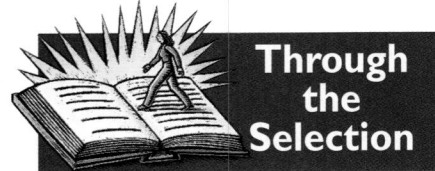
A. Expansion
Chesterfield (1694–1773) achieved considerable literary distinction for his *Letters* to his son, which commented on gentlemanly manners and deportment.

B. Reader's Response: First Thoughts
? Judging from your prior knowledge of Johnson and from his tone, how does Johnson receive Chesterfield's recommendation? [Sample responses: As an insult; with anger and disdain.]

C. Literary Element: Irony
? How does Johnson use the word *patron*? [Possible answers: Ironically; to make fun of Chesterfield; to make Chesterfield feel guilty.]

D. Literary Element: Allusion
? What reasons might Johnson have for including a classical allusion? [Possible answers: To show his education and intelligence; to establish his superior intellect; to either flatter or humiliate Chesterfield, depending on Chesterfield's knowledge of the allusion; to make a complex comparison quickly.]

Letter to Lord Chesterfield
Samuel Johnson

A To the Right Honorable the Earl of Chesterfield
February 7, 1755

My Lord:

I have been lately informed by the proprietor of the World,[1] that two papers, in which my Dictionary is recommended to the public, were written by your Lordship. To be so distinguished is an honor which, being very little accustomed to favors from the great, I know not well how to receive, or in what terms to acknowledge.

When, upon some slight encouragement, I first visited your Lordship, I was overpowered, like the rest of mankind, by the enchantment of your address;[2] and could not forbear to wish that I might boast myself le vainqueur du vainqueur de la terre;[3] that I might obtain that regard for which I saw the world contending; but I found my attendance so little encouraged that neither pride nor modesty would suffer me to continue it. When I had once addressed your Lordship in public, I had exhausted all the art of pleasing which a retired and uncourtly scholar can possess. I had done all that I could; and no man is well pleased to have his all neglected, be it ever so little.

Seven years, my Lord, have now passed since I waited in your outward rooms, or was repulsed from your door, during which time I have been pushing on my work through difficulties of which it is useless to complain, and have brought it, at last, to the verge of publication without one act of assistance, one word of encouragement, or one smile of favor. Such treatment **C** I did not expect, for I never had a patron before.

D The shepherd in Virgil[4] grew at last acquainted with Love, and found him a native of the rocks.

1. **World:** name of the newspaper in which Chesterfield (1694–1773) published his letters praising Johnson's *Dictionary*.

2. **address:** conversational manner or skill.

3. **le vainqueur . . . terre:** French for "the conqueror of the conqueror of the world." Chesterfield would have recognized that Johnson is quoting a famous line of a poem by the French poet Nicolas Boileau (1636–1711).

4. **the shepherd in Virgil:** In a pastoral poem by the Roman poet Virgil (70–19 B.C.), a shepherd discovers that love is unkind; Johnson similarly discovered that patrons are unkind.

WORDS TO OWN
contending (kən·tend′iŋ) v. used as *adj.*: competing; struggling.
repulsed (ri·pulst′) v.: driven away.

576 THE RESTORATION AND THE EIGHTEENTH CENTURY

Is not a patron, my Lord, one who looks with unconcern on a man struggling for life in the water, and, when he has reached ground, encumbers him with help? The notice which you have been pleased to take of my labors, had it been early, had been kind; but it has been delayed till I am indifferent, and cannot enjoy it; till I am solitary,[5] and cannot impart it; till I am known, and do not want[6] it. I hope it is no very cynical asperity[7] not to confess obligations where no benefit has been received, or to be unwilling that the public should consider me as owing that to a patron, which Providence has enabled me to do for myself.

Having carried on my work thus far with so little obligation to any favorer of learning, I shall not be disappointed though I should conclude it, if less be possible, with less; for I have been long wakened from that dream of hope, in which I once boasted myself with so much exultation, my Lord,

Your Lordship's most humble,
most obedient servant,

Sam. Johnson

Dr. Johnson, Mrs. Johnson, Mr. Garrick, and others assembled for a play performed by Samuel Richardson (1748) at The Pantiles, Tunbridge Wells. Engraving by Thomas Loggan.

5. **solitary:** Johnson's wife had been dead for three years.
6. **want:** need.
7. **asperity:** bitterness.

WORDS TO OWN
encumbers (en·kum′bərz) v.: burdens or hinders.
impart (im·pärt′) v.: share; tell.
cynical (sin′i·kəl) adj.: mistrustful.

E. Critical Reading: Making Inferences

? What is the definition Johnson gives for *patron* in his rhetorical question here? [Possible answers: One who is not interested when someone is really suffering; one who saves a person as he is about to save himself; one who gets in the way; an unnecessary and unhelpful person.] How is this an example of an ironic statement? [Johnson defines the word with its exaggerated opposite.]

F. Critical Reading: Summarizing

? How would you paraphrase Johnson's conclusion? [Possible answers: Do not rely on patrons; depend on yourself; he would rather achieve less than owe too much.]

PROBLEM SOLVING/CRITICAL THINKING

Pair Processing On enough small pieces of paper to provide one for each pair, write the names of powerful, important, or famous people (one per slip of paper). Then, do the same for requests students can make of these people. One member of each pair draws the name of a person, and the other member draws a request. Working together, students determine how to present the request to the person. They must examine desired outcomes, explore alternative approaches, decide on one, and execute it. The actual approach could be a letter, an exposé, a conversation, a lawsuit, and so on. Conclude by having pairs present their respective requests, alternatives, and chosen approaches.

CROSSING THE CURRICULUM

Social Sciences Who is the earl of Chesterfield? How and why does he wield so much power? Have students research and give a brief oral report on Philip Dormer Stanhope, fourth earl of Chesterfield, and his holdings.

Making Meanings

First Thoughts

1. Students will probably say that writing such a letter would have made them feel independent, assertive, worthy of respect.

Reviewing the Text

a. He stopped because he received no encouragement or aid from the earl.

b. He ironically defines a patron as someone who looks with indifference on a drowning man and then when the man has reached ground "encumbers" him with help.

c. Johnson recognizes Providence as enabling him to complete the task by himself.

d. He says that in this situation hope was a dream.

Shaping Interpretations

2. Johnson's purpose was primarily to set the record straight.

3. Johnson uses irony in describing the "honor" that Chesterfield has paid him and in defining *patron*. The tone is one of dignified reproach.

4. Modesty, honesty, simplicity, self-reliance. Such a person has no important or politically influential connections.

5. Some students may suggest that Chesterfield, as a cultivated man, knew he had been in the wrong and displayed the letter to admit to his error. Others may say that he left the letter on display because Johnson was by now a famous man, and Chesterfield may have valued the well-written letter even though it took him to task.

Connecting with the Text

6. Students' responses will vary but should be accompanied by well-reasoned explanations of their chosen methods of protest. They might choose picketing or boycotting.

Elements of Literature

Possible Answers

1. From the definition of *network*: *reticulated* and *decussated.*

2. From the letter: "The notice which you have been pleased to take of my labors, had it been early, had been kind; but it has been delayed till I am

---

MAKING MEANINGS

First Thoughts

1. If you had been in Johnson's position, what kind of satisfaction would writing this letter have given you?

Shaping Interpretations

2. What, apparently, was Johnson's purpose in writing the letter? To set the record straight? To annoy Chesterfield? To rebuke him? To gloat over him?

3. Where in the letter does Johnson use **irony?** How would you describe the letter's **tone?**

4. Johnson refers to himself as an "uncourtly scholar." What traits does such a person typically possess?

5. Chesterfield did not take offense at the letter, but kept it lying on a table in his office where any visitor might read it. Why do you suppose he didn't become angry?

Connecting with the Text

6. Review the notes you made in your Reader's Log. What kind of complaint would you make to someone who had stolen credit from you or had otherwise failed to treat you with the respect you deserve? Would you write a letter, as Johnson did, or would your protest take another form? Explain your answer.

Reviewing the Text

a. Johnson says that he had asked the earl for help, but then stopped. Why did he stop?

b. How does Johnson define a patron?

c. To whom does Johnson give credit for his accomplishment?

d. What does Johnson say about hope at the letter's end?

ELEMENTS OF LITERATURE

Style: A Personal Mark

Like most important writers, Johnson developed an individual style, a way of writing and speaking like

578 THE RESTORATION AND THE EIGHTEENTH CENTURY

---

nobody else's. Johnson's style is more complicated than the plain, simple style of Swift. Johnson ordinarily wrote long but carefully constructed sentences, like this one from the preface to his *Dictionary:*

> Such is the exuberance of signification which many words have obtained, that it was scarcely possible to collect all their senses; sometimes the meaning of derivatives must be sought in the mother term, and sometimes deficient explanations of the primitive may be supplied in the train of derivation.

This sentence illustrates Johnson's fondness for

1. longish words of Latin derivation: *exuberance, signification, derivatives, deficient, explanations.*

2. parallel structure: the two clauses beginning *sometimes.*

3. exact expression: The words *exuberance of signification* may sound strange, but they say exactly what Johnson means.

Like Sir Francis Bacon in the Renaissance, Johnson could also sum up an idea in a very few words so that it has the sound of an adage or proverb:

> If you are idle, be not solitary; if you are solitary, be not idle.

Notice how the first part of this sentence is both balanced against and contrasted with the second. Here are two more sentences by Johnson in which the contrasts are held in balance:

> Let me smile with the wise, and feed with the rich.
> Marriage has many pains, but celibacy has no pleasures.

But at times Johnson could be pompous and wordy. Instead of saying "Charity begins at home," he would say, "A man should first relieve those who are nearly connected to him, by whatever tie; and

---

indifferent, and cannot enjoy it; till I am solitary, and cannot impart it; till I am known, and do not want it."

3. From the letter: *cynical asperity.*

4. From the *Dictionary:* "**romance.** A tale of wild adventures in war and love."

5. From the letter: "Is not a patron, my Lord, one who looks with unconcern on a man struggling for life in the water, and, when he has reached ground, encumbers him with help?"

PROGRAM MANAGER

Application and Reinforcement
For reinforcement of the elements of literature introduced in this lesson, see Transparency 7.2 in the *Audiovisual Resources Binder.*

then, if he has anything to spare, may extend his bounty to a wider circle."

And finally, like all great writers, Johnson is a master inventor of metaphors. During a conversation about Shakespeare and a forgotten minor writer, for instance, Johnson remarked, "We must not compare the noise made by your teakettle here with the roaring of the ocean."

Look at the *Dictionary* and the "Letter to Chesterfield." Find at least one example of Johnson's use of

1. long, Latin-based words
2. parallel structure and balance in sentences
3. unusual, but exact, expressions
4. concise statements of ideas
5. strong metaphors

CHOICES: Building Your Portfolio

Writer's Notebook

1. Collecting Ideas for a Persuasive Essay

Johnson's protest against Lord Chesterfield might have developed into a public stand—urging sincere patrons, for instance, to have writers formally "apply" for aid, not beg for favors. What stand could you develop from your complaint in Connecting with the Text on page 578? If the issue is plagiarism, for example, you might argue for more serious punishment. Freewrite ideas about how to prevent or react to the injustice. Save your ideas for the Writer's Workshop on page 612.

Critical Writing

2. The Man Behind the Pen

Study Johnson's definitions and his letter to Lord Chesterfield, and write a long paragraph in which you describe the character of the man who wrote them. Consider these questions: What is he interested in? What are his likes and dislikes and biases? Is he proud? Is he capable of laughing at himself? Is he ever modest? Cite parts of the *Dictionary* excerpts and the letter to illustrate your points.

Critical Writing

3. Applying Satire's Sting

What elements of **satire** do you find in Johnson's letter to Lord Chesterfield? In a short essay, explain how Johnson uses satire. Use quotations from the letter to illustrate your points.

Creative Writing

4. Getting the Last Word

Imagine that you are Lord Chesterfield. Write a reply to Johnson explaining why you did not support his efforts and why you later wrote the letters to the newspapers. Write in formal language, as befits an earl.

Creative Writing

5. Imitating Johnson

Make your own dictionary of twenty words. In each entry, first give the part of speech; second, give at least one common definition; last, write a complete sentence that illustrates how the word is used. The only rule for this activity is that you can't look in a dictionary until after your definitions are finished. You might include these in your list of twenty: *apple, door, growl, nose, song, turtle.*

Creative Writing

6. Modernizing the Master

Johnson was a master of both written and oral language, and this letter illustrates his formal writing style. Use a less formal, more contemporary style to rewrite Johnson's letter, retaining all of his meaning. You may restructure his sentences, but try to make your letter flow smoothly and sound pleasant to the ear.

SAMUEL JOHNSON **579**

Beyond the Selections

Choices: Building Your Portfolio

1. **Writer's Notebook** Remind students to save their work. They may use it as prewriting for the Writer's Workshop on p. 612.
2. **Critical Writing** Have students make a list of their answers to the questions posed here. Then, send students back to the texts to find quotations that support their answers.
3. **Critical Writing** Ask students to look up the definition of the word *satire* in a dictionary and to use the definition to break down the genre into techniques. Ask them what methods satirists use. Encourage students to study Johnson's letter and the excerpts from the *Dictionary* to expand their lists of satirical techniques before they begin writing.
4. **Creative Writing** To help students make their letters as polished as possible, have them include two steps at the beginning and end of the writing process. Before they begin writing, encourage them to outline their letters, placing at the top of the page the goal or purpose of the letter. Then, after they have finished writing, have them make a special pass over the letter to concentrate only on revising the style, especially the diction and syntax.
5. **Creative Writing** Have students use a graphic organizer when choosing their entries, with four columns that contain the word, its part of speech, its definition, and a sentence demonstrating its use.
6. **Creative Writing** Before students rewrite Johnson's letter, they may need to summarize it to clarify the meaning of every passage. After they have finished, have them compare and discuss their modern versions of the letter.

STRATEGIES FOR INCLUSION

Learners Having Difficulty Before students begin activity #4, direct them to make a list of Johnson's points in his letter. Next to each of the points students may write an answer from Lord Chesterfield's point of view. The list may then be reordered for use as an outline for the student's reply.

PORTFOLIO ASSESSMENT

Choices: Assessment Criteria
For help in evaluating these Choices assignments, see the criteria in the *Portfolio Management System*, pp. 118–119.

A. Literary Connections

The pettiness of some of Shakespeare's critics is epitomized by Thomas Rymer (1641–1713) in *A Short View of Tragedy* (1693). Rymer criticized Othello's jealousy as improperly motivated and remarked that the lesson provided by the episode with Desdemona's handkerchief in the play *Othello* was that "ladies should look to their linen." Johnson referred to such censures as "the petty cavils of petty minds."

B. Exploring the Historical Period

Many scholars refer to the last years of the seventeenth century as the "Age of Dryden" because of the writer's domination of the literary scene of that time. He was appointed poet laureate in 1668, and when he died, he was buried in the Poet's Corner in Westminster Abbey beside Geoffrey Chaucer.

RESPONDING TO THE ART: ABOUT THE ARTIST

William Hogarth (1697–1764) was an engraver and art critic as well as a painter. He was well-known and, because of his engravings, well-off. Although he was a student of Italian, French and Dutch painting, Hogarth often turned to his British contemporaries for subject matter. He painted both portraits and scenes from everyday life.

SPOTLIGHT ON

In Support of Shakespeare

A Literature, like certain styles of clothing and music, moves in and out of fashion, and no less a writer than William Shakespeare fell victim to the trend toward neoclassical standards of order and taste. But two key writers of the age, John Dryden and Samuel Johnson, saw beyond contemporary fashion and helped reestablish Shakespeare's reputation with influential critical essays.

B **Dryden's case for Shakespeare.** John Dryden (1631–1700)—poet, dramatist, critic, and translator of foreign works into English—was an all-around "man of letters," perhaps the first Englishman to deserve that title. Samuel Johnson himself called Dryden "the father of English criticism." Dryden's literary career spanned the last forty years of the seventeenth century, and he cast a long shadow into the eighteenth.

Dryden's lasting reputation is based on his critical writings, and the centerpiece of these is *Of Dramatic Poesy: An Essay* (1668), a work that includes his comments on Shakespeare. (The word *poesy* means "literature.") In order to appreciate Dryden's observations, remember that Shakespeare had been dead only fifty years when Dryden wrote this piece. Shakespeare's plays were not being studied in nearly every English-speaking school, read in translation all over the world, and constantly performed by profes-

David Garrick as Richard III (1745) by William Hogarth.
Board of Trustees of the National Museum and Galleries on Merseyside. Walker Art Gallery, Liverpool, England.

OPTIONS FOR TEACHING

STRATEGIES FOR INCLUSION

Advanced Challenge students to determine what the supporters of Shakespeare value in his writing, given their comments. What is their standard of a great writer? Encourage students to write a list of the qualities of a great writer, drawn from Dryden's and Johnson's assessments of Shakespeare.

Learners Having Difficulty Too often students do not realize that the authors they study from a past era were not the only people writing then, and that they may not have been appreciated by their contemporaries. Emphasize to students the role of the critic in making an author's reputation. You might liken the critic's role to that of the modern film critic, and ask students how many films they have gone to see or not gone to see because of the recommendations and warnings of other people.

Special Needs Students will benefit from a pre-reading activity for *In Support of Shakespeare* that focuses their attention on its topic and links it to their lives. Ask each student to name a book, artist, movie, television show, public or historical figure, political leader, band, or activity that she or he thinks is underrated and to give three reasons it should be rated, or valued, more highly. This activity will also provide students with possible topics for their persuasive essays.

T580

sionals and amateurs everywhere—as they are today. Shakespeare was then only one of the many dramatists of the preceding age and far from the most popular one. When Dryden praised Shakespeare highly, he was not echoing a commonly held opinion; he was advancing a new idea—that Shakespeare's genius is his ability to represent nature as it really is. (*Nature* here includes human nature as well as the natural universe.) In his trademark lucid prose, Dryden makes the case for Shakespeare in the passage below.

> To begin, then, with Shakespeare: He was the man who, of all modern and perhaps ancient poets, had the largest and most comprehensive soul. All the images of nature were still [always] present to him, and he drew them not laboriously, but luckily; when he describes anything, you more than see it, you feel it too. Those who accuse him to have wanted [lacked] learning give him the greater commendation: He was naturally learned; he needed not the spectacles of books to read nature; he looked inwards, and found her there.
>
> —John Dryden, *from Of Dramatic Poesy: An Essay*

Johnson: defending the Bard. Nearly a century after Dryden argued for Shakespeare's universal appeal, Samuel Johnson published his now-famous *Preface to Shakespeare* in 1765. Following Dryden, Johnson also praises Shakespeare for his ability to render nature truthfully:

> Shakespeare is, above all writers, at least above all modern writers, the poet of nature; the poet that holds up to his readers a faithful mirror of manners and of life. His characters are not modified by . . . the accidents of transient fashions or temporary opinions: They are the genuine progeny of common humanity, such as the world will always supply and observation will always find. His persons act and speak by the influence of those general passions and principles by which all minds are agitated and the whole system of life is continued in motion. In the writings of other poets a character is too often an individual: In those of Shakespeare it is commonly a species.
>
> —Samuel Johnson, *from Preface to Shakespeare*

David Garrick in four of his principal tragic roles: Lear, Macbeth, Richard III, and Hamlet (detail) by an unknown artist.
Victoria and Albert Museum, London.

Convinced of Shakespeare's preeminence as a dramatic poet, Johnson also refutes charges that Shakespeare took too many liberties with the three dramatic unities. These unofficial rules limited dramatists to representing only those events that occur in a single day at a single location, and forbade them to combine elements of tragedy and comedy in a single play. Because he believed so strongly in the value of common sense and experience, Johnson contends that the "unities are not essential to a just drama," and that, especially in Shakespeare's case, "they are always to be sacrificed to the nobler beauties of variety and instruction."

Both Dryden and Johnson left considerable legacies to English literature. Perhaps, though, they are best remembered not just as writers but as eloquent speakers for an entire community of readers.

SPOTLIGHT ON **581**

Into the Selection

Author Biography p. 582

Before You Read p. 583

- **Reading Focus:** Students consider recorded events.
- **Quickwrite: Prior Knowledge** Record in Reader's Log the details of a day
- **Elements of Literature: Biography**
- **Background: Scaffolding** The many aspects of a biography

Through the Selection

from The Life of Samuel Johnson pp. 584–588

Words to Own pp. 585–587

Making Meanings p. 588

Beyond the Selection

Choices: Building Your Portfolio p. 589

- **Writer's Notebook:** Write opposing ideas for a position paper
- **Critical Writing:** Write an explanation of whether Johnson would have been a good friend
- **Creative Writing:** Write a biographical sketch using dialogue
- **Social Studies:** Make a biographical sketch of three members of Johnson's club

James Boswell (1740–1795)

James Boswell was a Scotlander, the heir to a large fortune, and eldest son of Lord Auchinleck (pronounced aff-leck), a strait-laced judge who expected his son to settle down in Scotland and carry on the family profession of law. Young Boswell had other plans. While studying law and classics at Glasgow and Edinburgh, he yearned to travel, to write, to visit great cities, to know famous people and become famous himself, to frequent taverns, and to pursue beautiful women. Boswell's father was totally unsympathetic to these desires, but finally, in 1762, he capitulated and allowed his twenty-two-year-old son to escape to London.

There, a year later, Boswell met Samuel Johnson, then age fifty-three and famous for his *Dictionary*. Gradually Boswell discovered a serious purpose for his life: He would become familiar with Johnson, study his character and personality, record his ideas and opinions, and eventually write his biography—one of the greatest biographies in English—*The Life of Samuel Johnson* (1791). Boswell published only two other books: *An Account of Corsica* (1768) and *Journal of a Tour to the Hebrides* (1785).

Johnson advised Boswell not only to read in the literal sense of the word, but also to "read diligently the great book of mankind." This Boswell did, not only in Scotland and England and while studying law in Holland, but also on a leisurely tour of Germany, Switzerland, France, and Italy. Wherever he went, Boswell kept a written record of his own and other people's behavior and conversation. To avoid taking notes in public, he trained his memory to recall the exact details of an event and the exact words of a conversation. These he later wrote down in private. During his lifetime he accumulated an immense number of journals, memoranda to himself, and letters—thousands of pages of personal writing.

Although he used some of this material in his three books, he died with most of it unpublished. For about 125 years, Boswell's papers

James Boswell (1765) by George Willison. Oil.

Scottish National Portrait Gallery, Edinburgh.

were stored in such places as an old croquet box and the loft over a stable until—between 1920 and 1949—they were purchased from Boswell's heirs and deposited in the Yale University Library. Now that many of them have been published, we perhaps have available more firsthand written information on Boswell than on any other person, living or dead. The youthful journals, *Boswell's London Journal* and *Boswell on the Grand Tour*, are particularly frank and interesting reading.

"Good Heaven! What is Boswell?" he once asked in a letter to a friend. The journals show that he was a person full of contradictions and contrasts, as all people are to some degree. Eventually he became a family man and followed his father's legal profession in Edinburgh and, later, in London. But after an evening of highly moral conversation, he would prowl for the rest of the night in the more disreputable parts of the city, often behaving in a loud and brash manner. Once, before the beginning of a play, he entertained a theater audience by mooing like a cow. Often he could not restrain himself from "effusions of ludicrous nonsense and intemperate mirth." No wonder to some of his contemporaries he seemed to be an uncouth buffoon. We know better.

PROGRAM MANAGER

- **Planning Instruction** See *Teaching Notes, Teaching Resources A,* pp. 147–148, for objectives, a summary, a list of literary elements, and additional information for this selection.
- **Instructional Support** Before beginning the instructional lesson see *Graphic Organizer for Active Reading, Teaching Resources A,* p. 161, for a Through the Selection activity.
- **Assessment** See *Selection Test, Test Booklet,* pp. 111–112.
- **Reinforcement** Use the *Words to Own* worksheet in *Teaching Resources A,* p. 162.

Reading Focus

Looking Back

When James Boswell sat down to write his great biography of Johnson in 1785, his subject was already dead. Yet Boswell didn't have to rely on his memory alone. He had a wealth of material to work from: voluminous letters and notes, every scrap of information Johnson's friends could provide, and—most important—his own vivid and detailed journals. Countless other writers have also followed Boswell's method, re-reading and transforming their own journal entries into polished pieces of biography, journalism, even fiction. What do you think is gained, and lost, in looking back at notes recorded days or decades ago?

Quickwrite

Try recording the activities of a day in your own life. With an eye to a time when you might read this entry again, include details about people and places, anecdotes, conversations, and your own unique perceptions.

Elements of Literature

Biography

In his *Life of Samuel Johnson,* Boswell was not only a recorder of facts, but also a master storyteller with an eye for the rich details that make an incident interesting. Boswell brings to life the whole Johnson household: the wretched Dr. Levett, whom Johnson supported; the blind Miss Williams, who made her home with Johnson and who, when she poured tea, put her finger in the cup to tell when it was full; the black servant Francis Barber, who was Johnson's friend and heir—even the cat Hodge, who loved oysters. Thanks to Boswell, we know of Johnson's deep attachments to women: first to his wife and then, after her death, to others, especially Hester Thrale, who disappointed him so bitterly by marrying a music teacher.

Throughout the biography, we often see Boswell provoking Johnson to speak out on a topic, or manipulating the conversation for dramatic effect, in much the same way a playwright manages the dialogue of his or her characters. Perhaps the most brilliant parts of the *Life* are the civilized conversations it records.

It is precisely this detail—the large number of actual conversations he reports—that sets Boswell's *Life* apart from other biographies. We have more of Johnson's ordinary talk than that of any other person who lived before the invention of tape recorders. Of course, Johnson's talk was never "ordinary"; it was original, forthright, vigorous, astonishing, and well worth preserving.

> **A biography** is an account of a person's life written or told by another person.
> *For more on Biography, see the Handbook of Literary Terms.*

Background

To call Boswell a successful biographer is to say that he possessed several literary talents. He was, first of all, an accurate historian. *The Life of Samuel Johnson* was based on a great mass of journals, records, letters, notes, and memoranda, and condensed to produce a reliable account not only of Johnson but of the whole age as well. Johnson had circles of friends from all walks of life, but Boswell emphasized his relations with people whose names are still well known: among many others, the painter Joshua Reynolds, the actor David Garrick, the statesman Edmund Burke, the musicologist Charles Burney, and the novelist and dramatist Oliver Goldsmith. All study of the artistic and intellectual life of the times begins with Boswell's biography.

Boswell also aimed to show his subject "more completely than any man who has ever yet lived." To do so, he had to be a "psychologist" in the popular sense of that word, a person who listens to, understands, and feels deep sympathy for other people. Boswell appreciated Johnson's sudden outbursts of anger, his fits of depression, his morbid fear of madness and death, just as he appreciated Johnson's cheerfulness, cleverness, and fatherly feelings toward himself. What is more important, Boswell's literary talent enabled him to capture in words all the inconsistency and astonishing humanity of Samuel Johnson.

JAMES BOSWELL 583

Using BEFORE YOU READ p. 583

Quickwrite

Give students a tighter focus for their writing so that they can concentrate more on recording a detailed account. Encourage them to select one conversation or event from a day and write only about that event. Suggest that their audience could be themselves decades from now.

Background

Challenge students to think of a person who through his or her influence and connections has come to represent modern times to the extent that Johnson represented his own age. Encourage students to debate their opinions. Then, have students compare their "Person of the Modern Age" with Johnson.

WRITERS ON WRITING

James Boswell was a tireless diarist, continually analyzing his life in his writing and re-reading his journal entries at regular intervals. In one entry, he writes that "Mr. Johnson said I should read my Journal about every three years." Keeping a journal allowed him to practice writing, gave him discipline, made him consider and judge his behavior, and gave him much entertainment. All of these reasons he recognized himself. About the only reason for keeping a journal he did not name is the reason his writing has survived: the entertainment and instruction it provides for readers other than himself.

WORDS TO OWN

The following vocabulary words are defined in the Words to Own at the bottom of the pupil's page.

deterred p. 585	aversion p. 586
slovenly p. 585	candor p. 587
noxious p. 586	

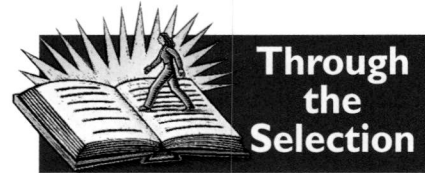
A. Reader's Response: First Thoughts

? What might Boswell's opening sentence show about his personality? [Sample responses: He is self-effacing; he is humble; he admires his subject; he can praise another without jealousy.]

B. Expansion

Johnson's prejudices, including his aversions to Scotland and the United States, were well known among his contemporaries. It is unclear whether he was really prejudiced or whether he fostered these dislikes simply for the sake of witty remarks or *bon mots*. For example, when Johnson was asked which of the French philosophers he favored, Voltaire or Rousseau, he replied, "It is difficult to decide the proportion of iniquity between them."

C. Expansion

Garrick, later to become one of the most famous actors of his day, had been one of Johnson's school pupils.

from The Life of Samuel Johnson

James Boswell

Boswell's First Meeting with Johnson, 1763

A This is to me a memorable year; for in it I had the happiness to obtain the acquaintance of that extraordinary man whose memoirs I am now writing; an acquaintance which I shall ever esteem as one of the most fortunate circumstances in my life. Though then but two-and-twenty, I had for several years read his works with delight and instruction, and had the highest reverence for their author, which had grown up in my fancy into a kind of mysterious veneration, by figuring to myself a state of solemn elevated abstraction, in which I supposed him to live in the immense metropolis of London. . . .

Mr. Thomas Davies the actor, who then kept a bookseller's shop in Russel Street, Covent Garden, told me that Johnson was very much his friend, and came frequently to his house, where he more than once invited me to meet him; but by some unlucky accident or other he was prevented from coming to us. . . .

At last, on Monday the 16th of May, when I was sitting in Mr. Davies's back parlor, after having drunk tea with him and Mrs. Davies, Johnson unexpectedly came into the shop; and Mr. Davies having perceived him through the glass door in the room in which we were sitting, advancing toward us—he announced his awful[1] approach to me, somewhat in the manner of an actor in the part of Horatio, when he addresses Hamlet on the appearance of his father's ghost, "Look, my Lord, it comes." I found that I had a very perfect idea of Johnson's figure, from the portrait of him painted by Sir Joshua Reynolds soon after he had published his *Dictionary,* in the

Samuel Johnson (18th century) by an unknown artist. From *The Life of Samuel Johnson* by James Boswell.

attitude of sitting in his easy chair in deep meditation, which was the first picture his friend did for him, which Sir Joshua very kindly presented to me, and from which an engraving has been made for this work. Mr. Davies mentioned my name, **B** and respectfully introduced me to him. I was much agitated; and recollecting his prejudice against the Scotch, of which I had heard much, I said to Davies, "Don't tell where I come from."—"From Scotland," cried Davies roguishly. "Mr. Johnson (said I), I do indeed come from Scotland, but I cannot help it." I am willing to flatter myself that I meant this as light pleasantry to soothe and conciliate him, and not as an humiliating abasement at the expense of my country. But however that might be, this speech was somewhat unlucky; for with that quickness of wit for which he was so remarkable, he seized the expression "come from Scotland," which I used in the sense of being of that country, and, as if I had said that I had come away from it, or left it, retorted, "That, Sir, I find, is what a very great many of your countrymen cannot help." This stroke stunned me a good deal; and when we had sat down, I felt myself not a little embarrassed, and apprehensive of what might come next. He then addressed himself to Davies. "What do you think of Garrick?[2] He has refused me an order for the play for Miss Williams, because he knows the house will be full, and that an order would be worth three shillings." Eager to take any opening to get into conversation with him, I ventured to say, "O, Sir, I cannot think Mr. Garrick would grudge such a trifle to you." "Sir (said he, with a **C** stern look), I have known David Garrick longer than you have done: and I know no right you have

---

1. **awful:** producing awe; now more commonly "awesome."

2. **Garrick:** the English actor David Garrick (1717–1779), a former pupil of Johnson.

OPTIONS FOR TEACHING

STRATEGIES FOR INCLUSION

Auditory/Bodily-Kinesthetic Have students do a dramatic reading of the exchanges Johnson has with Boswell, Thrale, or Burney. Encourage the person playing Johnson to include some of the mannerisms Boswell describes. Help students to adopt the attitude of these learned conversationalists. A student playing Boswell may narrate the scenes as well.

Visual Boswell provides many physical descriptions of Samuel Johnson in his biography. To help students synthesize this information, have them create an artistic portrait of this imposing figure. Students should scan the text for details and use these to create a sketch which could serve as an illustration or cover for Boswell's work.

Interpersonal Have students select a well-known, perhaps eccentric, person they wish to interview. Students should compile a list of questions they might ask, including questions that are specific to the person. Students may need to do a little research on their subject to give focus to their list of interview questions.

to talk to me on the subject." Perhaps I deserved this check; for it was rather presumptuous in me, an entire stranger, to express any doubt of the justice of his animadversion[3] upon his old acquaintance and pupil. I now felt myself much mortified, and began to think that the hope which I had long indulged of obtaining his acquaintance was blasted. And, in truth, had not my ardor been uncommonly strong, and my resolution uncommonly persevering, so rough a reception might have deterred me forever from making any further attempts. Fortunately, however, I remained upon the field not wholly discomfited. . . .

I was highly pleased with the extraordinary vigor of his conversation, and regretted that I was drawn away from it by an engagement at another place. I had, for a part of the evening, been left alone with him, and had ventured to make an observation now and then, which he received very civilly; so that I was satisfied that though there was a roughness in his manner, there was no ill nature in his disposition. Davies followed me to the door, and when I complained to him a little of the hard blows which the great man had given me, he kindly took upon him to console me by saying, "Don't be uneasy. I can see he likes you very well."

Boswell's First Visit to Johnson

A few days afterward I called on Davies, and asked him if he thought I might take the liberty of waiting on Mr. Johnson at his Chambers in the Temple.[4] He said I certainly might, and that Mr. Johnson would take it as a compliment. So upon Tuesday the 24th of May, . . . I boldly repaired to Johnson. His Chambers were on the first floor of No. 1, Inner-Temple-lane, and I entered them with an impression given me by the Reverend Dr. Blair,[5] of Edinburgh, who had been introduced to him not long before, and described his having "found the Giant in his den," an expression, which, when I came to be pretty well acquainted with Johnson, I repeated to him, and he was diverted at this picturesque account of himself. . . .

He received me very courteously; but, it must be confessed, that his apartment, and furniture, and morning dress, were sufficiently uncouth. His brown suit of clothes looked very rusty; he had on a little old shriveled unpowdered wig, which was too small for his head; his shirtneck and knees of his breeches were loose; his black worsted stockings ill drawn up; and he had a pair of unbuckled shoes by way of slippers. But all these slovenly particularities were forgotten the moment that he began to talk. Some gentlemen, whom I do not recollect, were sitting with him; and when they went away, I also rose; but he said to me, "Nay, don't go." "Sir (said I), I am afraid that I intrude upon you. It is benevolent to allow me to sit and hear you." He seemed pleased with this compliment, which I sincerely paid him, and answered, "Sir, I am obliged to any man who visits me." I have preserved the following short minute[6] of what passed this day:

"Madness frequently discovers itself merely by unnecessary deviation from the usual modes of the world. My poor friend Smart[7] showed the disturbance of his mind, by falling upon his knees, and saying his prayers in the street, or in any other unusual place. Now although, rationally speaking, it is greater madness not to pray at all, than to pray as Smart did, I am afraid there are so many who do not pray, that their understanding is not called in question."

Concerning this unfortunate poet, Christopher Smart, who was confined in a madhouse, he had, at another time, the following conversation with Dr. Burney:[8] BURNEY. "How does poor Smart do, Sir; is he likely to recover?" JOHNSON. "It seems as if his mind had ceased to struggle with the disease; for he grows fat upon it." BURNEY. "Perhaps, Sir, that may be from want of exercise." JOHNSON. "No, sir; he has partly as much exercise as he used to have, for he digs in the garden. Indeed, before

---

6. **minute:** note; memo.
7. **Smart:** Christopher Smart (1722–1771), a poet.
8. **Dr. Burney:** Charles Burney (1726–1814), a musicologist and father of the novelist Fanny Burney (1752–1840).

WORDS TO OWN
deterred (dē·turd') v.: prevented.
slovenly (sluv'ən·lē) adj.: untidy.

---

3. **animadversion** (an'i·məd·vur'zhən): critical comment.
4. **Temple:** area in London where lawyers and other professional people lived and worked.
5. **Blair:** Hugh Blair (1718–1800), a Presbyterian clergyman and writer.

D. Critical Reading: Analyzing Character
Based on this passage, have students list the character traits they associate with Johnson in their Reader's Logs, and then have them add to the list as they read this selection.

E. Expansion
Although apparently prejudiced in some matters, Johnson exhibited remarkable tolerance (for the age) in others. He himself suffered from a lifelong fear of madness, and this might explain his empathy with Christopher Smart.

M + S

STRATEGIES FOR INCLUSION

Less Proficient Readers Students may think the conversations portrayed in the selection are dull. To help students relate to the conversations, ask them to offer examples of popular topics in their own conversations. Make a list of these topics on the chalkboard, and accompany it with a list of topics from the selection. Conclude by having students evaluate their own conversations; ask them how their conversations are different from those of Johnson's friends and colleagues.

INTEGRATING THE LANGUAGE ARTS

Strategic Reading Students might find this selection overwhelming because there are many incidents strung together in a somewhat plotless structure. As a class, map the selection on the chalkboard or an overhead projector, using a box for each major experience and identifying the transitions between experiences. This way students can see the structure in operation. Encourage them to enter this scheme in their Reader's Logs so they can quickly review the major points of this selection.

A. Critical Reading: Identifying Main Ideas

? How would you paraphrase Johnson's comment on humans? [Possible answers: Humanity is anti-intellectual; humans view intellectual endeavor as hard work; humans are so lazy intellectually that they believe ignorance is bliss.]

B. Critical Reading: Analyzing Style

? What kind of exchange is taking place in this passage? [Possible answers: An interview or an interrogation.] This episode illustrates the remarkable talent Boswell has for drawing Johnson out, even on extremely hypothetical or trivial issues. Although Boswell occasionally looks foolish, it is clear that both men enjoy each other's conversation and that Boswell himself is an accomplished conversationalist.

C. Reader's Response: Connecting with the Text

? Do you know of anyone in literature or public life whom you consider eccentric? [Sample responses: Kramer from *Seinfeld,* Elton John, Dickens' Miss Havisham.]

D. Reader's Response: Shaping Interpretations

? Are the eccentricities as Boswell describes them really that eccentric? [Sample responses: No, many people talk to themselves and are superstitious; yes, he wastes time over such nonsense; yes, because he prided himself on being an intellectual, and superstition seems anti-intellectual.]

Oliver Goldsmith, James Boswell, and Samuel Johnson (left to right).

his confinement, he used for exercise to walk to the alehouse; but he was *carried* back again. I did not think he ought to be shut up. His infirmities were not <u>noxious</u> to society. He insisted on people praying with him; and I'd as lief[9] pray with Kit Smart as anyone else. Another charge was, that he did not love clean linen; and I have no passion for it." Johnson continued. "Mankind have a great <u>aversion</u> to intellectual labor; but even supposing knowledge to be easily attainable, more people would be content to be ignorant than would take even a little trouble to acquire it.". . .

Boswell Quizzes Johnson

I know not how so whimsical a thought came into my mind, but I asked, "If, Sir, you were shut up in a castle, and a newborn child with you, what would you do?" JOHNSON. "Why, Sir, I should not much like my company." BOSWELL. "But would you take the trouble of rearing it?" He seemed, as may well be supposed, unwilling to pursue the subject: but upon my persevering in my question, replied, "Why yes, Sir, I would; but I must have all conveniences. If I had no garden, I would make a shed on the roof, and take it there for fresh air. I should feed it, and wash it much, and with warm water to please it, not with cold water to give it pain." BOSWELL. "But, Sir, does not heat relax?" JOHNSON. "Sir, you are not to imagine the water is to be very hot. I would not *coddle*[10] the child. No,

9. **lief** (lēf): willingly.
10. **coddle:** cook in hot water. Johnson is having fun with the two distinct meanings of the word, the other being "treat tenderly."

Sir, the hardy method of treating children does no good. I'll take you five children from London, who shall cuff[11] five Highland children. Sir, a man bred in London will carry a burden, or run, or wrestle, as well as a man brought up in the hardiest manner in the country." BOSWELL. "Good living, I suppose, makes the Londoners strong." JOHNSON. "Why, Sir, I don't know that it does. Our chairmen[12] from Ireland, who are as strong men as any, have been brought up upon potatoes. Quantity makes up for quality." BOSWELL. "Would you teach this child that I have furnished you with, anything?" JOHNSON. "No, I should not be apt to teach it." BOSWELL. "Would not you have a pleasure in teaching it?" JOHNSON. "No, Sir, I should *not* have a pleasure in teaching it." BOSWELL. "Have you not a pleasure in teaching men? *There* I have you. You have the same pleasure in teaching men, that I should have in teaching children." JOHNSON. "Why, something about that.". . .

Johnson's Eccentricities

. . . Talking to himself was, indeed, one of his singularities ever since I knew him. I was certain that he was frequently uttering pious ejaculations; for fragments of the Lord's Prayer have been distinctly overheard. His friend Mr. Thomas Davies, of whom Churchill[13] says, "That Davies hath a very pretty wife," when Dr. Johnson muttered "lead us not into temptation," used with waggish and gallant humor to whisper [to] Mrs. Davies, "You, my dear, are the cause of this."

He had another particularity, of which none of his friends ever ventured to ask an explanation. It appeared to me some superstitious habit, which he had contracted early, and from which he had never called upon his reason to disentangle him. This was his anxious care to go out or in at a door or passage by a certain number of steps from a

11. **cuff:** win a fight or a scuffle with.
12. **chairmen:** porters who transported people through the London streets in sedan chairs (covered seats).
13. **Churchill:** Charles Churchill (1731–1764), author of satirical and comic poems.

- -

WORDS TO OWN

noxious (näk′shəs) *adj.*: harmful.
aversion (ə·vʉr′zhən) *n.*: dislike.

- -

586 THE RESTORATION AND THE EIGHTEENTH CENTURY

certain point, or at least so as that either his right or his left foot (I am not certain which) should constantly make the first actual movement when he came close to the door or passage. Thus I conjecture: For I have, upon innumerable occasions, observed him suddenly stop, and then seem to count his steps with a deep earnestness; and when he had neglected or gone wrong in this sort of magical movement, I have seen him go back again, put himself in a proper posture to begin the ceremony, and, having gone through it, break from his abstraction, walk briskly on, and join his companion. A strange instance of something of this nature, even when on horseback, happened when he was in the Isle of Skye.[14] Sir Joshua Reynolds has observed him to go a good way about rather than cross a particular alley in Leicesterfields;[15] but this Sir Joshua imputed to his having had some disagreeable recollection associated with it.

That the most minute singularities which belonged to him, and made very observable parts of his appearance and manner, may not be omitted, it is requisite to mention, that while talking or even musing as he sat in his chair, he commonly held his head to one side toward his right shoulder, and shook it in a tremulous manner, moving his body backward and forward, and rubbing his left knee in the same direction, with the palm of his hand. In the intervals of articulating he made various sounds with his mouth, sometimes as if ruminating, or what is called chewing the cud, sometimes giving a half whistle, sometimes making his tongue play backward from the roof of his mouth, as if clucking like a hen, and sometimes protruding it against his upper gums in front, as if pronouncing quickly under his breath, *too, too, too:* all this accompanied sometimes with a thoughtful look, but more frequently with a smile. Generally when he had concluded a period, in the course of a dispute, by which time he was a good deal exhausted by violence and vociferation, he used to blow out his breath like a whale. This I supposed was a relief to his lungs; and seemed in him to be a contemptuous mode of expression, as if he had made the arguments of his opponent fly like chaff before the wind.

I am fully aware how very obvious an occasion I here give for the sneering jocularity of such as have no relish of an exact likeness; which to render complete, he who draws it must not disdain the slightest strokes. But if witlings[16] should be inclined to attack this account, let them have the candor to quote what I have offered in my defense. . . .

---

16. **witlings:** people who think they're witty.

WORDS TO OWN
candor (kan′dər) *n.*: honesty.

---

14. **Isle of Skye:** largest of the Inner Hebrides, a group of islands off the west coast of Scotland.
15. **Leicesterfields** (les′tər·fēldz): square in London.

An Early London Coffeehouse (detail) (c. 1705) signed A. S.
British Museum, London.

JAMES BOSWELL 587

Making Meanings

First Thoughts

1. Possible responses: His greatest strength was his intellect; his greatest weakness was his arrogance.

Reviewing the Text

a. He felt awe-struck and apprehensive.

b. Johnson's clothes were rumpled and disorderly, and his wig was too small for his head.

c. He had a habit of passing through a doorway or passage with a particular number of steps.

d. He held his head toward his right shoulder and spoke in a tremulous manner; he moved his body backward and forward and rubbed his left knee; and he made various unusual sounds and movements with his tongue. When he had ended what he had to say, he blew out his breath like a whale.

e. According to Boswell, Johnson did this to exercise and display his ingenuity.

Shaping Interpretations

2. When Boswell finally met Johnson, he found him to be down-to-earth, rather slovenly, and far less awe-inspiring than he had expected.

3. Students' log entries will vary. Johnson's friends may have found his eccentricities refreshing, and they were probably afraid to risk his anger by trying to persuade him to act more conventionally.

4. Boswell's treatment of Johnson is mostly informal, for example, Boswell describes how they laughed over the description of Johnson as "the Giant in his den."

5. Boswell says that he is only being accurate, which most students will probably appreciate as an adequate defense.

6. Most students will agree that Johnson was less impolite than just eccentric.

7. Possible responses: Boswell's comments on himself explain the point of view from which the biography was written and add entertaining detail to his descriptions and remembrances. Or Boswell should leave himself out of the book so it will seem more objective and focus entirely on Johnson.

Johnson's Love of Argument

. . . I mentioned a new gaming club,[17] of which Mr. Beauclerk[18] had given me an account, where the members played to a desperate extent. JOHNSON. "Depend upon it, Sir, this is mere talk. *Who* is ruined by gaming? You will not find six instances in an age. There is a strange rout made about deep play: Whereas you have many more people ruined by adventurous trade,[19] and yet we do not hear such an outcry against it." THRALE. "There may be few people absolutely ruined by deep play; but very many are much hurt in their circumstances by it." JOHNSON. "Yes, Sir, and so are very many by other kinds of expense." I had heard him talk once before in the same manner; and at Oxford he said, "he wished he had learnt to play at cards." The truth, however, is, that he loved to display his ingenuity in argument; and therefore would sometimes in conversation maintain opinions which he was sensible were wrong, but in supporting which, his reasoning and wit would be most conspicuous. He would begin thus: "Why, Sir, as to the good or evil of card playing—" "Now (said Garrick), he is thinking which side he shall take." He appeared to have a pleasure in contradiction, especially when any opinion whatever was delivered with an air of confidence; so that there was hardly any topic, if not one of the great truths of religion and morality, that he might not have been incited to argue, either for or against. . . .

17. **gaming club:** gambling club.
18. **Beauclerk:** Topham Beauclerk (1739–1780), a fashionable gentleman descended from King Charles II.
19. **trade:** business.

MAKING MEANINGS

First Thoughts

1. Judging from these accounts, what do you think was Johnson's greatest strength as a person? What was his greatest fault?

Shaping Interpretations

2. Before meeting Johnson, Boswell thought that he lived in "a state of solemn elevated abstraction." Explain how the actual experience of meeting and talking with Johnson differed from Boswell's expectations.

3. Look back at your Reader's Log, and see if you've recorded any behavior that you consider unconventional. Would others agree with you?

Reviewing the Text

a. How did Boswell feel as he was about to meet Johnson?

b. How was Johnson dressed when Boswell first visited him in his study?

c. What superstitious habit did Johnson have?

d. Describe the peculiar mannerisms Johnson exhibited when he was talking.

e. Why, according to Boswell, did Johnson sometimes express opinions that he did not really believe?

Why didn't Boswell ask Johnson about his eccentricities or attempt to make him more conventional?

4. By the time of their first meeting, Johnson was already a very famous man. Does Boswell show him as conscious of his own greatness, or is Boswell's picture refreshingly informal on the whole? Discuss your opinions.

5. What defense does Boswell offer for describing Johnson's eccentricities in the *Life*? Do you think the defense is valid?

6. Was Johnson an impolite person, or did he only seem rude? Explain your answer.

7. In this **biography,** Boswell often mentions himself—his own feelings, impressions, and conclusions about Johnson. Do you think these references contribute significantly to Boswell's work, or should he have been more detached and objective in your view? Explain your answer.

8. What do we mean when we call someone "eccentric"? How is *eccentricity* different from *insanity*?

Extending the Text

9. Do you think Johnson would have been more or less interesting had his behavior been more conventional? Why is eccentricity of behavior important to society? How is eccentricity regarded in our society today?

OPTIONS FOR TEACHING

STRATEGIES FOR INCLUSION

Visual Students may test the vividness of their sketches for activity #4 by attempting to visualize the person described. Have students ask themselves if they could draw a picture from their sketches. If they cannot, they should revise their work to make it more descriptive.

Special Needs Purpose and audience are extremely important to effective writing, especially for students to whom writing does not come easily. Before students begin work on any of their Choices activities, briefly discuss purposes for writing and possible audiences. Have students write their purpose on one 3" × 5" note card and describe their audience on another. They may then keep these cards visible as they write.

CHOICES: Building Your Portfolio

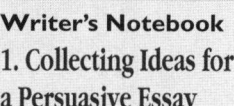

Writer's Notebook

1. Collecting Ideas for a Persuasive Essay

Johnson's enjoyment in arguing "either for or against" a position is a good lesson for persuasive writers. To make your position convincing, you must foresee *counterarguments:* opposing points. Which of these subjects in Boswell's remembrance most intrigues you—gambling, childrearing, mental illness, national prejudice? Think of any issue, and state a position you could support ("Our state lottery should be abolished"). Quickly write two possible supporting points. Then disagree with yourself, and write one opposing point. Save your notes for the Writer's Workshop on page 612.

Critical Writing

2. Friends Across Centuries

Write an explanation of whether you would, or would not, have liked to have been a friend of Samuel Johnson's, had you lived in the eighteenth century. Consider Johnson's own writings as well as Boswell's biographical reports.

Creative Writing

3. Sketching a Friend

Write a two- or three-page **biographical sketch** of someone you know well. Include an account of your first meeting and any other interesting anecdotes that will help a reader to know the person you are writing about. As Boswell does, record some of your subject's words, and incorporate them into your sketch as **dialogue**. (See the Writer's Workshop on the observational essay on page 185.)

Social Studies

4. Johnson and His Cronies

Together with a number of his friends, Johnson founded a social group called the Literary Club in 1764. The club met at a tavern called the Turk's Head in the London neighborhood of Soho. Research the membership of the club. See if you can come up with thumbnail biographical sketches as well as pictures of at least three of its famous members besides Boswell, who was elected to membership in 1773.

Samuel Johnson with James Boswell (18th century).

JAMES BOSWELL 589

8. The word *eccentric* usually is used to describe someone who departs in an amusing or unusual way from conventional behavior. *Insanity* denotes an unconscious break with reality.

Extending the Text

9. **(Evaluation)** Most students will agree that Johnson would have been less interesting had his behavior been conventional. Eccentricity is usually tolerated because people appreciate variety and respect a person's individuality. Eccentricity marks the borders of permissible behavior and may even bring about change within society.

Beyond the Selection

Choices: Building Your Portfolio

1. **Writer's Notebook** Remind students to save their work. They may use it as prewriting for the Writer's Workshop on p. 612.
2. **Critical Writing** Encourage students to begin with a simple pro-and-con graphic organizer in two columns on a sheet of paper. In their explanations of whether or not they would have liked to have been Johnson's friend, challenge students to mention situations in which Johnson's behavior would have been difficult for them to tolerate.
3. **Creative Writing** Direct students to begin by freewriting adjectives that characterize the friend they will describe. When they have drawn up a list of adjectives, students may rank the words by their accuracy and vividness. Students may then focus on the top five or six descriptive words while they write, picking anecdotes and details that fit the descriptions.
4. **Social Studies** Students may research the membership of the Literary Club by consulting an encyclopedia or by skimming Boswell's *Life of Samuel Johnson* for notes on the members. Instruct students to put their thumbnail sketches in a context, perhaps a meeting between the three members at the Turk's Head.

Germany

WORLD LITERATURE

Johann Wolfgang von Goethe (1749–1832)

Johann Wolfgang von Goethe (gö'tə), born in Frankfurt, Germany, is one of the towering giants in world literature. Goethe had a huge intellectual appetite and was accomplished in several fields. Indeed, when Napoleon met Goethe in 1808, he exclaimed "Voilà un homme!" ("There is a man!"). During his long and prolific career (his published works run to 133 volumes), Goethe made significant contributions to politics, science, and philosophy. As a writer, he is mentioned in the same breath with Shakespeare, Dante, Homer, and Virgil.

Early in Goethe's career he became a leader of the *Sturm und Drang* (Storm and Stress) movement. This movement, which opposed the Enlightenment's emphasis on cool reason and promoted use of the imagination and spontaneous expression, heralded the start of German Romanticism. In

Goethe in the Countryside (late 18th to early 19th century) by Johann Heinrich Tischbein.

Staedelsches Kunstinstitut, Frankfurt.

1774, publication of his romantic novel *The Sorrows of Young Werther,* the story of a sensitive young man engaged in an unhappy love affair, gave Goethe international recognition. One year later and for the next decade, he was prime minister at the court of Saxe-Weimar, the cultural center of Germany.

Like many of his characters, Goethe was inspired from youth to old age by a series of love affairs. Bettina von Arnim-Brentano, perhaps the most influential woman in Goethe's life, also loved Ludwig van Beethoven.

Goethe was also an accomplished musician. "I can always work better after I have been listening to music," he wrote. But he was so extremely sensitive to noise that the sound of a barking dog or an orchestra's kettledrums was torture to him.

590

(Map) Europe in 1810, at the height of Napoleon's power.
©Rand McNally.

PROGRAM MANAGER

Selection Summary See **Teaching Notes,** *Teaching Resources A,* p. 148, for a summary of this selection.

BEFORE YOU READ

FROM FAUST

Background

The selection you are about to read is based on the life of an actual sixteenth-century magician, Georg Faust. Legend has it that this magician sold his soul to the Devil in return for comprehensive knowledge about magic. Tales of Faust's exploits circulated widely in the late 1500s. These tales, though crudely narrated and full of clodhopping humor, inspired the English playwright and poet Christopher Marlowe to write his own version, *The Tragical History of Doctor Faustus* (1604). Marlowe invests Faust with a tragic dignity not seen in the earlier folk tales. Centuries later, the German novelist Thomas Mann

(1875–1955) created in *Doktor Faustus* a modern composer who sells his soul in exchange for musical genius. The French composer Charles Gounod (1783–1852) also used the legend in his famous opera *Faust.*

Presented as a Romantic hero, Goethe's Faust is unique among all versions of the tragic story. At the end of his long sufferings, he is granted salvation as others are dragged off to Hell.

As this excerpt from Goethe's play opens, Faust is overwhelmed with despair. He feels he doesn't understand the meaning of existence. Scholarship is not enough for him; he wants to *experience* life fully. Distracted from his suicidal thoughts by the sound of

church bells, Faust sets out on a walk through the countryside. He is soon soothed by the beauty of spring and concludes that he might be able to accept his own limitations and simply enjoy living. But when he returns to his study, Mephistopheles, a demon, plays the Devil's advocate.

Quickwrite

To what lengths would you go to get something that you are passionate about? Write down what you would sacrifice or trade in return for your quest. Then write down your limits— what you would *not* sacrifice or trade for any amount of money or fame.

Faust and Marguerite watched by Mephistopheles.

JOHANN WOLFGANG VON GOETHE **591**

Background

Ask students to consider the story of Adam and Eve in Genesis in the Bible, and other stories from books, films, or TV shows in which knowledge is a dangerous thing. Encourage the class to relate the theme to modern-day science and to think of examples in which science has had a disastrous effect. Ask if students think there are elements that humans should not tamper with, if there are questions best not answered.

Quickwrite

Remind students to choose a situation they would not mind sharing, as you point out that the line between what they would and would not do to fulfill their quests is determined by their own values about life. After students have finished writing in their Reader's Logs, ask them to discuss what is important to them, what they would not give up for any price. Encourage students to find common elements in their lists.

CONNECTING WITH "AN APPETITE FOR EXPERIENCE"

What happens when one's appetite for experience is out of control? Faust's appetite for experience is so extreme that it provokes his pact with the devil; he loses his reason; he desires to explore things better left alone. Goethe uses Faust to critique the Enlightenment hunger for knowledge and to make the Romantic argument for an appreciation of beauty and an acceptance of things mysterious and sublime in life.

A. **Language Note: Persuasion**

? How does Mephistopheles attempt to gain Faust's confidence? [Possible answer: He encourages him not to wallow in his grief and offers to be his partner and servant.]

B. **Critical Reading: Analyzing Details**

? What does Faust know about the devil? [Possible answers: The devil is self-centered; he does nothing without expecting something in return; he is dishonest; he is dangerous.] Even though he knows these things, why might Faust be willing to listen to Mephistopheles' proposal? [Possible answers: He is weak; he is self-centered; he is desperate.]

C. **Reader's Response: Extending the Text**

Faust seems unmoved at the thought of serving Mephistopheles on the "other side." How do you think others might feel in his situation? [Sample responses: Scared, uneasy, disturbed, ambivalent, apprehensive, intrigued.]

D. **Critical Reading: Drawing Conclusions**

? What is Faust's philosophical approach in this passage? [Possible answers: He is more concerned with the world in which he exists than a world to come—about which he knows nothing.]

from Faust, Part I

Johann Wolfgang von Goethe

translated by **Louis MacNeice**

Mephistopheles.
　Stop playing with your grief which battens°
　Like a vulture on your life, your mind!
　The worst of company would make you feel
　That you are a man among mankind.
5　Not that it's really my proposition
　To shove you among the common men;
　Though I'm not one of the Upper Ten,°
　If you would like a coalition
　With me for your career through life,
10　I am quite ready to fit in,
　I'm yours before you can say knife.
　I am your comrade;
　If you so crave,
　I am your servant, I am your slave.

Faust.
15　And what have I to undertake in return?

Mephistopheles.
　Oh it's early days to discuss what that is.

Faust.
　No, no, the devil is an egoist
　And ready to do nothing gratis°
　Which is to benefit a stranger.
20　Tell me your terms and don't prevaricate!
　A servant like you in the house is a danger.

Mephistopheles.
　I will bind myself to your service in this world,
　To be at your beck and never rest nor slack;
　When we meet again on the other side,
25　In the same coin you shall pay me back.

Faust.
　The other side gives me little trouble;
　First batter this present world to rubble,
　Then the other may rise—if that's the plan.
　This earth is where my springs of joy have started,
30　And this sun shines on me when broken-hearted;
　If I can first from them be parted,
　Then let happen what will and can!
　I wish to hear no more about it—
　Whether there too men hate and love
35　Or whether in those spheres too, in the future,
　There is a Below or an Above.

1. **battens:** grows fat.

7. **Upper Ten:** aristocracy; upper ranks. The phrase is short for "upper ten thousand."

18. **gratis** (grat′is): for free.

OPTIONS FOR TEACHING

STRATEGIES FOR INCLUSION

English Language Development Faust and Mephistopheles discuss their agreement in this excerpt. To monitor students' comprehension of the plot, have students work together to create in today's language a written contract which directly states the terms of their agreement. Encourage students to provide as much detail as possible.

Interpersonal In pairs, have students use a Venn diagram to map the characteristics of Faust and Mephistopheles. Ask students to comment on the meaning of any overlap. [Responses include: No one is all good or all evil; humans are a combination, so Faust will share some of the devil's traits; the areas of overlap are vulnerable to Mephistopheles' temptations.]

Auditory Have students choose one of the longer speeches to memorize and speak in front of the class. Or have pairs of students memorize an important exchange between the characters and present this to the class.

Faust and Mephistopheles
(1826–1827)
by Eugène Delacroix.
Wallace Collection, London.

E. Reader's Response: Shaping Interpretations

? How might Mephistopheles' statement be interpreted? [Sample responses: As humor—Mephistopheles treats a very grave matter in an offhanded way. As encouragement—Mephistopheles reasons that because Faust questions everything in his search for knowledge, he can take this opportunity to learn more.]

RESPONDING TO THE ART: ABOUT THE ARTIST

French painter Eugene Delacroix (1798–1863), often drew his subject matter from literature. His attraction to the works of Shakespeare and Byron formed the basis of his painting of literary themes, and in 1825, inspired by Goethe's *Faust*, he endeavored to complete 17 lithographs, prints made from a specially prepared stone or metal plate, for a French edition of the play. He chose to depict moments of high drama by setting light against dark with the deep black of his lithograph crayon. Goethe himself felt that the Faust he had envisioned had been truly captured by Delacroix.

Mephistopheles.
    With such an outlook you can risk it. **E**
    Sign on the line! In these next days you will get
    Ravishing samples of my arts;
40   I am giving you what never man saw yet.
  Faust.
    Poor devil, can *you* give anything ever?
    Was a human spirit in its high endeavour
    Even once understood by one of your breed?
    Have you got food which fails to feed?
45   Or red gold which, never at rest,
    Like mercury runs away through the hand?
    A game at which one never wins?
    A girl who, even when on my breast,
    Pledges herself to my neighbour with her eyes?
50   The divine and lovely delight of honour
    Which falls like a falling star and dies?

JOHANN WOLFGANG VON GOETHE **593**

INTEGRATING THE LANGUAGE ARTS

Writing: Modern Aphorisms Have students work with partners to search Goethe's writing for aphorisms or adages, such as "Time is short, art is long." Have students record all of the maxims they find, locations in the poem (for example, line numbers), responses and attempts to rewrite (either correcting the aphorism or making it more understandable or accessible to modern readers), using a graphic like the one following.

Aphorism	Text Reference	Response	Rewrite

Conclude by having students share their results with the class.

Strategic Reading It does not take much to convince Faust to enter into the contract with

Mephistopheles. As they read, have students work with partners to outline the conversation between the characters, paying special attention to what is important to Faust versus what is important to Mephistopheles. They may use a two-column chart or a series of boxes to record the characters' desires and main points. ☞

A. Critical Reading: Identifying Details

? What is Faust's wager? [Possible answers: That he will die when he rests from his quest for experience, when he is satisfied with himself, when he prefers pleasure to striving.]

B. Critical Reading: Analyzing Purpose

? What is the purpose of this line? [Possible answers: To foreshadow trouble; to emphasize Faust's promise; to warn Faust.]

C. Critical Reading: Analyzing Character

? What does Faust think of written contracts? [Possible answers: That they are dead promises; that they are only paper and not the promises themselves.] What does this speech reveal about Faust's character? [That he believes he is a man of his word, a man of honor for whom written contracts are unnecessary.]

Show me the fruits which, before they are plucked, decay
And the trees which day after day renew their green!

Mephistopheles.
    Such a commission° doesn't alarm me,
55   I have such treasures to purvey.
    But, my good friend, the time draws on when we
    Should be glad to feast at our ease on something good.

Faust.
    If ever I stretch myself on a bed of ease,
    Then I am finished! Is that understood?
60   If ever your flatteries can coax me
    To be pleased with myself, if ever you cast
    A spell of pleasure that can hoax me—
    Then let *that* day be my last!
    That's my wager!

Mephistopheles.
          Done!

Faust.
        Let's shake!
65   If ever I say to the passing moment
    'Linger a while! Thou art so fair!'
    Then you may cast me into fetters,
    I will gladly perish then and there!
    Then you may set the death-bell tolling,
70   Then from my service you are free,
    The clock may stop, its hand may fall,
    And that be the end of time for me!

Mephistopheles.
    Think what you're saying, we shall not forget it.

Faust.
    And you are fully within your rights;
75   I have made no mad or outrageous claim.
    If I stay as I am, I am a slave—
    Whether yours or another's, it's all the same.

Mephistopheles.
    I shall this very day at the College Banquet°
    Enter your service with no more ado,
80   But just one point—As a life-and-death insurance
    I must trouble you for a line or two.

Faust.
    So you, you pedant,° you too like things in writing?
    Have you never known a man? Or a man's word? Never?
    Is it not enough that my word of mouth
85   Puts all my days in bond for ever?
    Does not the world rage on in all its streams
    And shall a promise hamper *me*?
    Yet this illusion reigns within our hearts
    And from it who would be gladly free?
90   Happy the man who can inwardly keep his word;
    Whatever the cost, he will not be loath to pay!

54. commission: authorization to perform duties.

78. College Banquet: dinner given by a successful candidate for the Ph.D. degree.

82. pedant (ped′′nt): overly precise scholar.

Frontispiece of Christopher Marlowe's *Dr. Faustus* (1636).

OPTIONS FOR TEACHING

CROSSING THE CURRICULUM

Art Have students draw their interpretations of images in *Faust.* Students might depict an actual scene in the poem or an image mentioned by one of the speakers, such as the beast being driven in circles.

Music Bring a recording of Charles Gounod's opera *Faust.* Listen to excerpts, following the libretto. Ask students to compare the characters of Faust and Mephistopholes in the opera with the same characters they have read about here.

Social Sciences Have students research German Romanticism or Goethe's life and historical era, and prepare a brief oral report to the class. Encourage students to write and organize note cards in preparation for their presentation. They should focus on main ideas and events, since the topics are wide ranging and complex.

But a parchment, duly inscribed and sealed,
Is a bogey° from which all wince away.
The word dies on the tip of the pen
95 And wax and leather lord it then.
What do you, evil spirit, require?
Bronze, marble, parchment, paper?
Quill or chisel or pencil of slate?
You may choose whichever you desire.

Mephistopheles.
100 How can you so exaggerate
With such a hectic rhetoric?
Any little snippet is quite good—
And you sign it with one little drop of blood.

Faust.
If that is enough and is some use,
105 One may as well pander to your fad.°

Mephistopheles.
Blood is a very special juice. **E**

Faust.
Only do not fear that I shall break this contract.
What I promise is nothing more
Than what all my powers are striving for.
110 I have puffed myself up too much, it is only
Your sort that really fits my case.
The great Earth Spirit has despised me
And Nature shuts the door in my face.
The thread of thought is snapped asunder,
115 I have long loathed knowledge in all its fashions.
In the depths of sensuality
Let us now quench our glowing passions!
And at once make ready every wonder
Of unpenetrated sorcery!
120 Let us cast ourselves into the torrent of time,
Into the whirl of eventfulness,
Where disappointment and success,
Pleasure and pain may chop and change
As chop and change they will and can;
125 It is restless action makes the man.

Mephistopheles.
No limit is fixed for you, no bound;
If you'd like to nibble at everything
Or to seize upon something flying round—
Well, may you have a run for your money!
130 But seize your chance and don't be funny!

Faust.
I've told you, it is no question of happiness.
The most painful joy, enamoured hate, enlivening
Disgust—I devote myself to all excess.
My breast, now cured of its appetite for knowledge,
135 From now is open to all and every smart,

93. **bogey:** evil spirit.

105. **pander to your fad:** go along with your frivolous request.

JOHANN WOLFGANG VON GOETHE **595**

A. Literary Element: Symbolism

? What does Mephistopheles imply about humanity when he says "your sole portion is day and night"? [Possible answers: That humans are both good and evil; that humans exist in both God's light and the devil's darkness; that man is conflicted about being good or evil.]

B. Critical Reading: Making Inferences

? What does this line mean? [Art lasts longer than a human's life; mortality keeps humans from perfection, whereas art can be made perfect and endures.]

C. Cultural Connections

Point out that in these lines Mephistopheles uses associations to communicate vividly. The problem is that the reader must share or at least understand the connotations. Explore the associations we have with "Fire of Italy" [Possible answers: Love of life; hotblooded; exciting; zesty.] and "Northern tenacity." [Possible answers: Perseverant; sober; ruthless.] Do these stereotypes still exist? [Possible answers: Yes, we think of southerners as more hot-blooded and northerners as cool and calm; yes, we think of northerners as being industrious and tenacious; yes, ethnic stereotyping exists. Or no, whether people are industrious or not does not depend on where they live, people no longer use most ethnic stereotypes.]

D. Humanities Connection

Mephistopheles recommends a little artistic advice from a poet. What do these lines say a poet can do? [Possible answer: With the creative powers of the imagination the poet can create the impossible, the ideal—Mephistopheles' example: a heart that is both crafty and noble.]

And what is allotted to the whole of mankind
That will I sample in my inmost heart,
Grasping the highest and lowest with my spirit,
Piling men's weal and woe upon my neck,
140 To extend myself to embrace all human selves
And to founder in the end, like them, a wreck.

Mephistopheles.
O believe *me,* who have been chewing
These iron rations many a thousand year,
No human being can digest
145 This stuff, from the cradle to the bier.°
This universe—believe a devil—
Was made for no one but a god!

(A) *He* exists in eternal light
But *us* he has brought into the darkness
150 While *your* sole portion is day and night.

Faust.
I will all the same!

Mephistopheles.
                                    That's very nice.
There's only one thing I find wrong;
(B) Time is short, art is long.
You could do with a little artistic advice.
155 Confederate with one of the poets
And let him flog his imagination
To heap all virtues on your head,
A head with such a reputation:
(C) Lion's bravery,
160 Stag's velocity,
Fire of Italy,
Northern tenacity.
(D) Let *him* find out the secret art
Of combining craft with a noble heart
165 And of being in love like a young man,
Hotly, but working to a plan.
Such a person—*I'd* like to meet him;
'Mr. Microcosm'° is how I'd greet him.

Faust.
What am I then if fate must bar
170 My efforts to reach that crown of humanity
After which all my senses strive?

Mephistopheles.
(E) You are in the end . . . what you are.
You can put on full-bottomed wigs° with a million locks,
You can put on stilts instead of your socks,
175 You remain for ever what you are.

Faust.
(F) I feel my endeavours have not been worth a pin
When I raked together the treasures of the human mind,
If at the end I but sit down to find

145. bier (bir): platform on which a coffin or corpse is placed.

168. Mr. Microcosm (mī′krō·kä′zəm): that is, representing the microcosm, or essence, of the world.

173. full-bottomed wigs: wigs that cover the back and shoulders. Popular among men and women in seventeenth-century Europe, such wigs were considered signs of upper-class status.

596 THE RESTORATION AND THE EIGHTEENTH CENTURY

No new force welling up within.

180 I have not a hair's breadth more of height,
I am no nearer the Infinite.

Mephistopheles.

My very good sir, you look at things
Just in the way that people do;
We must be cleverer than that

185 Or the joys of life will escape from you.
Hell! You have surely hands and feet,
Also a head and you-know-what;
The pleasures I gather on the wing,
Are they less mine? Of course they're not!

190 Suppose I can afford six stallions,
I can add that horse-power to my score
And dash along and be a proper man
As if my legs were twenty-four.
So good-bye to thinking! On your toes!

Mephistopheles
appearing to Faust,
by Alexander Mayer.

JOHANN WOLFGANG VON GOETHE 597

**E. Reader's Response:
Extending the Text**

? What does Mephistopheles say in
answer to Faust's "What am I"
question? [Sample responses: That we
are what we are; that we can't hide
who we are; that identity comes from
oneself and not from another source.]
**Do you agree with Mephistopheles'
observation? Explain.** [Sample
responses: Yes, you are what you are;
your identity comes from within.
Or no, you can change who you are
to some extent.]

**F. Critical Reading:
Summarizing**

? What does this passage tell you
about the kind of man Faust is?
[Faust is deeply dissatisfied. He feels he
has worked hard to find nothing, to
end up devoid of the "new force" he
seeks. He is an empty man, adrift without meaning in his life. He is a desperate man who will do anything to find
the meaning, the force, that he lacks.]

A. Critical Reading: Drawing Conclusions

? How can Mephistopheles own a person body and soul? [Possible answers: When that person devalues knowledge and rational thought and substitutes magical thinking for them; when humans abandon reason, they are doomed to superstition and magic and ultimately the death of the soul.]

B. Critical Reading: Making Connections

? How does the Mephistopheles in this speech compare to the presentation of himself he gives in the opening lines of the selection? Does he sound as though he will be the partner and slave that he promised he would be to Faust? [No, in these lines he reveals his true intentions: to tempt and torture and destroy Faust.]

Metacognition How did you answer this question? [Students may say that they went back and looked at the first speech and compared it to Mephistopheles' parting speech. Or they may have remembered his initial approach to Faust.]

C. Reader's Response: Shaping Interpretations

? In ll. 217–218, why does Mephistopheles call Faust "equally accursed" whether he sells himself to the devil or not? [Sample responses: Faust will be cursed if he deals with the devil, but even if he doesn't, he will be cursed with his unrealizable quest. Faust is a doomed man by his very nature—he is what he is; his fate is to be insatiable to the point of madness.]

195   The world's before us. Quick! Here goes!
       I tell you, a chap who's intellectual
       Is like a beast on a blasted heath
       Driven in circles by a demon
       While a fine green meadow lies round beneath.
       Faust.
         How do we start?
       Mephistopheles.
200   We just say go—and skip.
       But please get ready for this pleasure trip.
                                    [*Exit Faust.*]

       Only look down on knowledge and reason,
       The highest gifts that men can prize,
       Only allow the spirit of lies
205   To confirm you in magic and illusion,
       And then I have you body and soul.
       Fate has given this man a spirit
       Which is always pressing onwards, beyond control,
       And whose mad striving overleaps
210   All joys of the earth between pole and pole.
       Him shall I drag though the wilds of life
       And through the flats of meaninglessness,
       I shall make him flounder and gape and stick
       And to tease his insatiableness
215   Hang meat and drink in the air before his watering lips;
       In vain he will pray to slake his inner thirst,
       And even had he not sold himself to the devil
       He would be equally accursed.

Faust's covenant with Mephistopheles (detail) by Franz Strassen.

FINDING COMMON GROUND

Working with a small group, discuss other plays, movies, novels, or television shows in which a character has wanted—passionately—what he or she could not have. (Also think about your own Reader's Log entry.) As you discuss these other characters, consider the following questions:

- Do these characters have any qualities in common? If so, what are they?
- How do the people around these characters regard them—fearfully? respectfully? dispassionately? Why do other people have the reactions they do?
- Are some characters, like Shakespeare's Macbeth, *entitled* to push beyond all limitations, even if it alters the lives of others and eventually makes them unhappy? Why do you think so?

Finding Common Ground

Arrange students in groups as large as four or five so that they are sure to think of a number of characters. Direct the groups to edit their lists and place their examples in a graphic organizer like the one that follows. A similar grid may be used to keep track of how the characters are viewed by others. For the last question, challenge students to think of characteristics that would make it all right for a person to be entitled to push beyond all limitations.

	[Lady Macbeth]	[Lancelot]	[Napoleon]
[ambitious]	[✓]		[✓]
[charismatic]	[✓]	[✓]	[✓]
[honorable]		[✓]	
etc.			

Thomas Gray
(1716–1771)

Thomas Gray is perhaps the best lyric poet of the mid–eighteenth century, an age that is not known for its great lyric poets. The son of a London merchant, he spent nine years at one of the great English "public" schools, Eton College, which is neither public nor a college. (It is the equivalent of a prep school for boys who expect to go to Cambridge or Oxford.) At eighteen, Gray entered Cambridge University, where he lived for the remaining thirty-seven years of his life, reading literature in a variety of languages; studying archaeology, law, history, botany, and zoology; painting landscapes; playing the harpsichord; and growing geraniums in his window boxes. In a quiet, inconspicuous way, he became very learned. These years were interrupted only briefly by a grand tour of France, Switzerland, and Italy with Horace Walpole, a friend from Eton and son of England's prime minister, who paid the expenses.

The great crisis of Gray's life came when Richard West, his best friend from Eton, died of tuberculosis at the age of twenty-four. Gray sought consolation in writing poetry. He was always reluctant to publish his verses; although he carefully and fastidiously revised and re-wrote them, they never seemed to him to be quite finished. Moreover, he was painfully shy and, unlike most writers, he really did not want the world's applause. Imagine his distress when his "Elegy Written in a Country Churchyard" made him famous. Gray's other poems—only thirteen of which he published during his lifetime—were also widely admired. Most of them are elegant, gloomy, and artificial: exactly what midcentury taste demanded. Few of these other poems are of much interest today except to historians of English poetry, who find that in several ways Gray anticipated the Romantic age to come.

Gray led a quiet, frugal, low-key existence. Unlike everybody else in his century, he was never on the back of a horse. Although he was made a professor of history at Cambridge, he never delivered any lectures, which is all that a professor did in those days. He spent his vacations in London, reading in the British Museum (now the British Library), or in the Lake District (a picturesque part of northern England made famous by the poets of the next age), or in Stoke Poges, a village where his mother and aunt lived. There he is buried, beside his mother, in the cemetery that he immortalized in his "Elegy."

Thomas Gray (1747–1748) by John Giles Eccardt. Oil on canvas (15⅞″ × 12⅞″).

By Courtesy of the National Portrait Gallery, London.

WRITERS ON WRITING

"As to matter of stile (sic)," Gray once wrote, "I have this to say: The language of the age is never the language of poetry. . . . Our [English] poetry . . . has a language peculiar to itself; to which almost everyone that has written, has added something by enriching it with foreign idioms and derivatives." Gray particularly admired Shakespeare's creative language. "Every word in him is a picture," he once observed. As to his own style and the effect of criticism on him, Gray is more humble: "I am a sort of spider; and have little else to do but spin [my web] over again, or creep to some other place and spin there."

PROGRAM MANAGER

- **Planning Instruction** See **Teaching Notes,** *Teaching Resources A,* pp. 148–149, for objectives, a summary, a list of major literary elements, and additional information for this selection.
- **Instructional Support** Before beginning the instructional lesson, see **Graphic** **Organizer for Active Reading,** *Teaching Resources A,* p. 163, for a Through the Poem activity.
- **Assessment** See **Selection Test,** *Test Booklet,* pp. 113–114.

Into the Poem

Author Biography p. 599

Before You Read p. 600

- **Reading Focus:** Students consider the lives of ordinary people.
- **Quickwrite: Prior Knowledge** Analyze lines from the poem in Reader's Logs
- **Background:** Gray's wishes concerning the poem's publication

Through the Poem

Elegy Written in a Country Churchyard pp. 601–604

Student to Student p. 605 "Searching for a Future in the Dusk"

Making Meanings pp. 605–606

Elements of Literature p. 606

Language and Style pp. 606–607

Beyond the Poem

Choices: Building Your Portfolio p. 607

- **Writer's Notebook:** Write trial thesis statements for a persuasive essay
- **Critical Writing:** In an essay, compare two elegies
- **Creative Writing:** Write an epitaph for one of the villagers
- **Creative Writing:** Write a meditation about a graveyard experience

BEFORE YOU READ
ELEGY WRITTEN IN A COUNTRY CHURCHYARD

Reading Focus

Ordinary People

Have you ever wondered about the hidden lives of ordinary people—or about the dashed hopes and lost dreams that lie behind the anonymity of a name on a roadside mailbox or on a cemetery tombstone? If fate had been slightly different, could one of those names have been that of a great artist or writer, president of the United States, or maybe the scientist who discovered the cure for cancer? Gray was one of the first writers in English to believe that the lives of ordinary people were suitable subjects for serious poetry.

Quickwrite

In lines 55–56, Gray writes, "Full many a flower is born to blush unseen, / And waste its sweetness on the desert air." Just working from your own instincts, what do you think these lines mean? Jot down some ideas in your Reader's Log.

Haycarting
(18th century)
by George Stubbs.
Board of Trustees of the National Museums and Galleries on Merseyside (Lady Lever Art Gallery, Port Sunlight, England).

Background

Gray had this poem published anonymously in 1751—only because a copy of it had fallen into the hands of an unscrupulous magazine editor who threatened to print it with Gray's name on it. The poem immediately became a great favorite of readers, a position it still maintains because it sounds so beautiful and because what it says about death is so true. Everybody dies: The famous people of the earth are no different from the rest of us in that respect. We all eventually come to the same dusty end. Painfully obvious truths of this kind are called *truisms*, and a poet can be forgiven his truisms only if he utters them memorably. Gray's "Elegy" exemplifies Pope's definition of true wit: "What oft was thought but ne'er so well expressed."

Gray wanted this poem printed without any spaces between stanzas "because the sense is in some places continued beyond them." The fact that it is almost never printed in this way perhaps justifies Gray's misgivings about publishers and makes the reading of lines 61–73 a bit more difficult than it should be.

600 THE RESTORATION AND THE EIGHTEENTH CENTURY

PORTFOLIO ASSESSMENT

Portfolio Assessment For help with self assessment of reading skills, see the *Portfolio Management System,* pp. 48–49.

Elegy Written in a Country Churchyard

Thomas Gray

The curfew tolls the knell of parting day,
The lowing herd wind slowly o'er the lea,°
The plowman homeward plods his weary way,
And leaves the world to darkness, and to me.

5 Now fades the glimmering landscape on the sight,
And all the air a solemn stillness holds;
Save where the beetle wheels his droning flight,
And drowsy tinklings lull the distant folds.

Save that from yonder ivy-mantled tower
10 The moping owl does to the moon complain
Of such, as wand'ring near her secret bower,
Molest her ancient solitary reign.

Beneath those rugged elms, that yew tree's shade,
Where heaves the turf in many a mold'ring heap,
15 Each in his narrow cell forever laid,
The rude° forefathers of the hamlet sleep.

The breezy call of incense-breathing morn,
The swallow twitt'ring from the straw-built shed,°
The cock's shrill clarion, or the echoing horn,°
20 No more shall rouse them from their lowly bed.

For them no more the blazing hearth shall burn,
Or busy housewife ply her evening care:
No children run to lisp their sire's return,
Or climb his knees the envied kiss to share.

25 Oft did the harvest to their sickle yield,
Their furrow oft the stubborn glebe° has broke;
How jocund did they drive their team afield!
How bowed the woods beneath their sturdy stroke!

Let not Ambition mock their useful toil,
30 Their homely joys and destiny obscure;
Nor Grandeur hear with a disdainful smile,
The short and simple annals of the poor.

The boast of heraldry,° the pomp of power,
And all that beauty, all that wealth e'er gave,
35 Awaits alike th' inevitable hour.
The paths of glory lead but to the grave.

2. lea: meadow.

16. rude: uneducated; unpolished.

18. shed: nest.
19. horn: hunting horn.

26. glebe: soil.

33. boast of heraldry: pride in one's ancestry. Heraldry is the study of family coats of arms.

THOMAS GRAY 601

Into the Poem

Using BEFORE YOU READ p. 600

Quickwrite

Encourage students to reword or paraphrase the quotation several different ways before writing. Ask students to share with the class their own poetic restatements of the truism.

Through the Poem

A. Literary Element: Tone

? What tone is immediately established in the first stanza? [Possible answers: Sober; somber; melancholy; sad; pensive; peaceful.] What details create the tone? [Possible answers: The rhythm of the poem; the sounds slow down the poem; the images—the tolling bell at sunset, the herd ambling across the dusky meadow, the tired farmer making his way home, the darkness.]

B. Literary Element: Meter and Rhyme

? What is the predominant meter of the poem? [iambic pentameter.] What is the rhyme scheme? [abab; every other line rhymes in each stanza.]

C. Critical Reading: Analyzing Imagery

? Why might Gray include the images he does in these stanzas, and what kind of people do the images portray? [Possible answers: To emphasize the contrast between the dead and the living or the life they led; to express everyday life in poetic terms. The people are ordinary, common people; farm families.]

D. Reader's Response: First Thoughts

This is one of the often-quoted lines from the elegy. Do you agree that the stories of the poor are "short and simple"? Explain. [Sample responses: Yes, the poor live simple lives with a simple plot line—the struggle to survive. No, the struggle is different for each individual; rich or poor, human life is complex.]

OPTIONS FOR TEACHING

INTEGRATING THE LANGUAGE ARTS

Writing: Descriptive Stanzas Using a literary work as a model for student writing is an excellent way for students to develop their writing skills and their understanding of the author's techniques. Have students write their own stanzas after reading the following lines:

- lines 1–8 (descriptions of a scene at dusk)
- lines 17–20 (descriptions of a scene at dawn)
- lines 21–28 (descriptions of ordinary life)

Ask volunteers to share their stanzas. ☞

Ode to a Country Churchyard (Gray's Elegy) (1883) by Jasper F. Cropsey. Oil on canvas (13 ½″ × 25 ⅕″).
The Newington-Cropsey Foundation, Hastings-on-Hudson, New York.

A. Reader's Response: Shaping Interpretations

? What does Gray lament in this stanza? [Sample responses: The wasted talent of the poor; what they might have been or done had they not been poor.]

B. Critical Reading: Finding Cause and Effect

? To what does Gray attribute the lost ambitions of the previous stanza? [Possible answers: Poverty and lack of knowledge and education are the reasons these people did not influence empires and express themselves.]

C. Critical Reading: Identifying Main Ideas

This stanza sums up one of the poet's central themes. What is that theme? [Possible answers: Many beautiful creations are wasted because they are not seen; the beautiful in life is often obscured by the harshness. The potential and the individually important moments of the humble people most often go unnoticed.]

Nor you, ye proud, impute to these the fault,
If Mem'ry o'er their tomb no trophies° raise,
Where through the long-drawn aisle and fretted vault°
40 The pealing anthem swells the note of praise.

Can storied urn° or animated° bust
Back to its mansion call the fleeting breath?
Can Honor's voice provoke° the silent dust,
Or Flatt'ry soothe the dull cold ear of Death?

A
45 Perhaps in this neglected spot is laid
Some heart once pregnant with celestial fire,
Hands that the rod of empire might have swayed,
Or waked to ecstasy the living lyre.

B
But Knowledge to their eyes her ample page
50 Rich with the spoils of time did ne'er unroll;
Chill Penury° repressed their noble rage,°
And froze the genial current° of the soul.

C
Full many a gem of purest ray serene,
The dark unfathomed caves of ocean bear:
55 Full many a flower is born to blush unseen,
And waste its sweetness on the desert air.

38. trophies: monuments.
39. fretted vault: elaborately ornamented church ceiling.

41. storied urn: an urn with an in-scription on it. **animated:** lifelike.

43. provoke: evoke; call forth.

51. penury: poverty. **rage:** emo-tion; feeling.
52. genial current: warm impulses.

602 THE RESTORATION AND THE EIGHTEENTH CENTURY

Some village Hampden° that with dauntless breast
The little tyrant of his fields withstood;
Some mute inglorious Milton here may rest,
60 Some Cromwell° guiltless of his country's blood.

Th' applause of list'ning senates to command,
The threats of pain and ruin to despise,
To scatter plenty o'er a smiling land,
And read their hist'ry in a nation's eyes

65 Their lot forbade: nor circumscribed alone
Their growing virtues, but their crimes confined;
Forbade to wade through slaughter to a throne,
And shut the gates of mercy on mankind,

The struggling pangs of conscious° truth to hide,
70 To quench the blushes of ingenuous° shame,
Or heap the shrine of Luxury and Pride
With incense, kindled at the Muse's flame.°

Far from the madding° crowd's ignoble strife,
Their sober wishes never learned to stray;
75 Along the cool sequestered vale of life
They kept the noiseless tenor° of their way.

Yet ev'n these bones from insult to protect
Some frail memorial° still erected nigh,
With uncouth° rhymes and shapeless sculpture decked,
80 Implores the passing tribute of a sigh.

Their name, their years, spelt by th' unlettered muse,°
The place of fame and elegy supply:
And many a holy text around she strews,
That teach the rustic moralist to die.

85 For who to dumb Forgetfulness a prey,
This pleasing anxious being e'er resigned,
Left the warm precincts of the cheerful day,
Nor cast one longing ling'ring look behind?

On some fond breast the parting soul relies,
90 Some pious drops° the closing eye requires;
Ev'n from the tomb the voice of Nature cries,
Ev'n in our ashes live their wonted fires.

For thee,° who mindful of th' unhonored dead
Dost in these lines their artless tale relate;
95 If chance, by lonely Contemplation led,
Some kindred spirit shall inquire thy fate,

57. village Hampden: an obscure person who, with opportunity, might have been famous like John Hampden (1594–1643), an English statesman who defied the king over unjust taxation shortly before the English Civil Wars.
60. Cromwell: Lord Protector Oliver Cromwell, who ruled England from 1653 to 1658.

69. conscious: guiltily aware; conscientious.
70. ingenuous: naively innnocent.

72. incense . . . flame: tributes paid to them by poets.

73. madding: frenzied.

76. tenor: course.

78. frail memorial: modest tombstone, in contrast to the elaborate tombs inside the church.
79. uncouth: unsophisticated; artless.
81. unlettered muse: humble engraver of the tombstone.

90. drops: mourners' tears.

93. thee: Gray himself.

D. Literary Element: Allusion
Note the historical allusions in ll. 57–60. What is a "mute" Milton? [Possible answers: A person unable to use language or speak; a person without the ability or opportunity to write; a writer unsuccessful at getting published.] Why does the poet allude to Milton and Cromwell? [Those buried in the courtyard might have achieved the stature of Milton and Cromwell.]

E. Expansion
Gray's elegy has been repeatedly quoted, memorized by generations of schoolchildren, and alluded to by countless other writers. Thomas Hardy, for example, took the title of his first popularly successful novel—*Far from the Madding Crowd* (1874)—from l. 73.

F. Critical Reading: Drawing Conclusions
? What is the significance of the rhetorical question in ll. 85–88? [Possible answer: It emphasizes that love of life and fear of death are common to rich and poor alike.]

G. Critical Reading: Analyzing Details
? Whom does the poet or speaker address in this stanza? [Himself.] Note this change as well as the one in the following stanza where he begins to quote a swain speaking about him. Why does Gray make these changes? [To give a variety of voices in the poem.]

CROSSING THE CURRICULUM

Music Have students search out music they think might be appropriate for Gray's poem. Encourage them to look for instrumental music, dirges, and requiems. Have a tape or CD player available for their choices, and play the music as students read the elegy.

Social Sciences Every culture has its own way of dealing with death. Gray copes with his grief and disillusionment in this selection; others choose different ways. Have students research and report on famous burial places and practices around the world. Remind students that their reports will benefit from photographs, drawings, or models.

PROFESSIONAL NOTES

Thematic Connections: "An Appetite for Experience"
Although many readers and critics consider the eighteenth century one that venerated reason, this historical period also heralded the hunger for raw experience and emotion, which characterized the Romantic period. Gray's famous elegy may seem rational and based on a reasonable reaction to death, but many of the most vivid and lasting images, as opposed to thoughts and advice, emerge from experience.

A. Literary Element: Alliteration

? What words alliterate here, and what sound do they imitate? [Possible answers: *brook* and *babble*, the *b*'s suggest the sound of the brook. Note the possible pun of the words *pore/pour*. *Pore* has a rarely used meaning—to gaze intently, steadily.]

B. Critical Reading: Making Inferences

? Whose epitaph concludes the poem? [The speaker's, the poet's —the person who cared to think about those who rested in the cemetery where he himself is now laid.]

Making Meanings

First Thoughts

1. Possible responses: "Drowsy tin-klings lull the distant folds," evokes the time of day especially well; the far-off sound evokes a peacefulness, a time of settling down. In "For them, no more the blazing hearth shall burn," the warmth of the fire contrasts with cold graves of death. This is the first of several references to fire and the life it represents.

Reviewing the Text

a. The speaker is in a country church-yard at dusk. He hears the tinkling of bells from the sheepfolds and the hooting complaint of the owl.

b. Among the things the people will never again experience are the twit-tering of the swallow, the crowing of the cock, the sound of the hunt-ing horn, the sight of a blazing hearth, the sight of the housewife, the greetings of their children, the experience of driving their team across the fields, and the labor of planting and harvesting.

c. The speaker imagines that one might have become an emperor, another a poet, and another a sol-dier. The details of the neglected gems and flowers show that excel-lence and virtue often go unrecog-nized or are unfulfilled. They are symbols of the potential of the dead that was never brought to fruition when they were alive.

Haply° some hoary-headed swain° may say,
"Oft have we seen him at the peep of dawn
Brushing with hasty steps the dews away
100 To meet the sun upon the upland lawn.

"There at the foot of yonder nodding beech
That wreathes its old fantastic roots so high,
His listless length at noontide would he stretch,
A And pore upon the brook that babbles by.

105 "Hard° by yon wood, now smiling as in scorn,
Mutt'ring his wayward fancies he would rove,
Now drooping, woeful wan, like one forlorn,
Or crazed with care, or crossed in hopeless love.

"One morn I missed him on the customed hill,
110 Along the heath, and near his fav'rite tree;
Another came; nor yet beside the rill,°
Nor up the lawn, nor at the wood was he.

"The next with dirges due in sad array
Slow through the churchway path we saw him borne.
115 Approach and read (for thou canst read)° the lay,
Graved on the stone beneath yon aged thorn."°

The Epitaph

*Here rests his head upon the lap of Earth
A youth to Fortune and to Fame unknown:
Fair Science frowned not on his humble birth,°*
B
120 *And Melancholy marked him for her own.*

*Large was his bounty, and his soul sincere,
Heaven did a recompense as largely send:
He gave to Mis'ry all he had, a tear:
He gained from Heaven ('twas all he wished) a friend.*

125 *No farther seek his merits to disclose,
Or draw his frailties from their dread abode,
(There they alike in trembling Hope repose)
The bosom of his Father and his God.*

97. haply: perhaps. **hoary-headed swain:** white-haired countryman.

105. hard: close.

111. rill: brook.

115. thou canst read: The "swain" who is speaking is apparently illiterate.
116. thorn: hawthorn bush.

119. fair . . . birth: He was educated—*science* meant learning in general—despite his modest beginnings.

604 THE RESTORATION AND THE EIGHTEENTH CENTURY

OPTIONS FOR TEACHING

ASSESSMENT TOOLS

Check Test: True-False
1. Gray describes the lives of the poor. [True]
2. Gray envies the lives the dead have led. [False]

3. Gray mourns the loss of the potential contri-butions to humankind. [True]
4. The epitaph at the end of the poem is written for an aristocrat. [False]
5. Gray draws on both thought and experience to create this poem. [True]

Searching for a Future in the Dusk

In the dusk of a soft summer's eve,
Crushing the cool, prickly lawn,
I lie stretched out
And gaze at the dome sky
like the tip of an enormous egg
Polished to a shiny blue. **A**

I can feel myself soaring
Up, up,
Until I reach out
And touch the thin shell
Of my prison.

The light fades
And my wall drains of color,
Like finger paints in the rain,
Until I can see through it
To the universe beyond;
The purple sea
With a thousand lighthouses
Sprinkling its surface like glitter. **B**

I imagine then,
If I broke the shell,
How far I would tumble
Into my future,
Where I could ride the fireflies
Of possibility
Into the heavens
Of the me to come.

And I wonder,
If I might glance back,
For a moment,
To the shadowing past,
And long
For the prickle of a lawn
At dusk. **C**

—Melynn Minson
Hillcrest High School
Midvale, Utah

First Thoughts

1. What did you feel was the strongest **image** in this poem? Why?

Reviewing the Text

a. Where is the speaker, and what time of day is it? What, according to the **images** in stanzas 2 and 3, does he hear?

b. In the fourth through eighth stanzas, the speaker describes the ordinary people in the churchyard. Name the various things they will never again experience.

c. What does the speaker imagine these humble people might have become if they'd had the chance (lines 45–60)? What do the details in lines 53–56 have to do with this idea?

d. What did their "lot" or place in life forbid the poor people to experience, according to lines 61–72?

e. What does the speaker imagine an old man (the "hoary-headed swain") might say of him one day (lines 98–116)?

Shaping Interpretations

2. The poet **personifies** ambition and grandeur in lines 29 and 31. What does he warn them not to do? What other examples of **personification** can you find in the poem?

3. According to lines 77–92, what evidence on their gravestones shows that humble, ordinary people also wish to be remembered?

4. Many readers of the "Elegy" have assumed that Gray himself is the poet whose epitaph is given in the final lines. Is it necessary to make this assumption to understand the poem? Why does the assumption seem attractive?

5. Suppose that Gray is being autobiographical. What defense does he give of his life? Would *you* be happy with such an epitaph—or would you wish to be remembered differently?

6. From Gray's time almost to the present, many people have thought of poets as possessing the

THOMAS GRAY 605

A. Critical Reading: Finding Details

? Where is the speaker, both literally and figuratively? [Possible answers: Lying on a lawn, looking up at the sky. Inside an eggshell.]

B. Literary Element: Metaphor

? What is the poet describing with this metaphor? [The night sky.]

C. Reader's Response: Shaping Interpretations

? What is the speaker expressing about the future and the past? [Sample responses: A yearning for the future but with some apprehension— maybe it would be better just to stay on the lawn, to enjoy the moment. Though we dream about the future, when it becomes the present, we may feel nostalgic for the past.]

d. Their station in life forbade them to experience high political office and commemoration in their nation's history. Their lot also limited their virtues and crimes; none of them, at least, became tyrants, murderers, or worshippers of luxury and pride.

e. He imagines that the swain may remember him after his death as a humble and good man, just as he is now remembering the other dead who are buried in the churchyard.

Shaping Interpretations

2. The poet warns Ambition not to mock the people's toil or their homely joys and obscure destiny; he warns Grandeur not to smile disdainfully at these people's short and simple history. Other examples of personification include Honor (l. 43), Flattery (l. 44), Knowledge (l. 49), Penury (l. 51), Luxury and Pride (l. 71), Forgetfulness (l. 85), Nature (l. 91), Earth (l. 117), Science (l. 119), Melancholy (l. 120), Misery (l. 123).

3. The epitaphs are evidence the people wish to be remembered; the poet reflects that such a wish is universal among humanity.

4. Most students will agree that the assumption is not necessary in order to understand the poem. It is attractive, however, because it would provide an elegant structural parallel between Gray's own situation and the situation he is describing in the poem.

5. He offers that he was generous, sincere, and pious.

CONNECTING WITH "ELEGY WRITTEN IN A COUNTRY CHURCHYARD"

Ask students to review the elements of literature (pastoral, Gothic, generalizations) detailed on p. 606. Does "Searching for the Future in the Dusk" have the same elements as those present in "Elegy Written in a Country Churchyard"? Explain. [Possible answers: Yes, the poem is pastoral in its setting; because the speaker can see the stars so vividly, the setting must be outside a city. The reference to prison and to the "shadowing past" might be seen as Gothic, but the general tone of the poem is not gloomy. The poem steers clear of the generalizations that distinguish Gray's poem.]

6. Most students will answer that the stereotype of the poet as a dreamy, melancholic, and intensely reflective person hardly fits the facts of all poets' lives.

7. The quotations underscore the themes of life's transience and the fact that excellence may go without being recognized or fulfilled.

8. Gray straddles the two definitions. The poem concentrates on central ideas about the human condition, but emotional effect is clearly important to Gray as well.

Extending the Text

9. (Synthesis) Students may imagine various responses; many may comment on the similarities in setting and theme.

Elements of Literature
Possible Answers

1. The "lowing herd," the plowman, the "lea," the "glimmering landscape," and the "ivy-mantled tower"

2. The "rugged elms," the "shade" of the yew tree, "moldering" turf, and the mention of the grave as a "narrow cell"

3. Line 32: "The short and simple annals of the poor"; ll. 55–56: "Full many a flower is born to blush unseen, / And waste its sweetness on the desert air"; ll. 73–74: "Far from the madding crowd's ignoble strife, / Their sober wishes never learned to stray."

Language and Style
Possible Answers

1. "O'er" (l. 63), "thee" (l. 93), "yon" (l. 105); *over, you,* and *that* or *yonder.*

2. Students will probably say the words give the poem a formal air.

3. "The moping owl does to the moon complain" (l. 10).

4. Students may say that the inverted word order is more poetic, or simply that inverting the words allowed Gray to construct a certain rhythm without using awkward words.

5. Possible paraphrase: The poor people's lot forbade them to command respect or to take pride in their history. Their lot forbade them to hide from the struggle, pain, and shame of poverty.

---

characteristics described in lines 98–112. Gray established here a **stereotype** that the public long accepted as genuine. Does this stereotype fit any of the poets you have studied so far in this book? (Think particularly of Chaucer, Shakespeare, Donne, Milton, Pope, and Swift.)

7. The poem contains at least two statements that are still frequently quoted:

   a. "The paths of glory lead but to the grave." (line 36)

   b. "Full many a flower is born to blush unseen, And waste its sweetness on the desert air." (lines 55–56)

   How do these lines relate to the poem's **theme**? (Look back at your Reader's Log for your initial interpretation of lines 55–56.)

8. In one sense, most neoclassical writers thought the purpose of literature was to convey ideas. Most Romantic writers, by contrast, thought the purpose of literature was to convey emotions. Judging by his "Elegy," in which group do you think Gray seems to fit?

Extending the Text

9. What do you imagine Thomas Gray might say to the student writer of the poem on page 605?

ELEMENTS OF LITERATURE

The Elegy

The term **elegy** originally referred to a poem written in a particular meter; in Roman literature, elegies are frivolous and sensual. By Gray's time the term *elegy* was applied to longish, serious poems reflecting on death—either death in general or the death of a particular person. Gray ends his "Elegy" with an epitaph—a poem short enough to be inscribed on a particular person's tombstone.

Gray's "Elegy" combines elements from several literary traditions. First of all, it is a **pastoral** elegy. Like Milton's famous elegy *Lycidas,* its setting is outdoors in a beautiful summery landscape. The poet keeps a certain distance from the dirt and bad smells of actual country life. His rural people are not individuals but types: the weary plowman, the

---

busy housewife, the hoary-headed swain. These figures are idealized; oafs and boors do not appear. Rural life in a pastoral is always placid and civilized.

Another element in the "Elegy" is the **Gothic,** which supplies the "moping" owl, the graveyard, and the general gloominess. But unlike most Gothic writers, Gray isn't interested in giving his readers shivers and thrills; he is trying instead to create an atmosphere.

Finally, like many other writers of his time, Gray decorates his poem with polished **generalizations** about life and death: "The paths of glory lead but to the grave." These generalizations give the elegy the solidity of classical architecture.

1. What are five details of **setting** that Gray uses to idealize the **pastoral** landscape in the poem?

2. What are the **Gothic** details that contribute to the atmosphere in lines 13–16?

3. Find at least three additional examples of Gray's use of polished **generalizations.**

LANGUAGE AND STYLE

A Poetic Style

Many words in this poem were regarded—until the twentieth century—as particularly "poetic." Examples of such words are *oft* (line 25), *e'er* (line 34), and *ye* (line 37).

1. List three other "poetic" words you find in the elegy. What words would be used in their place today?

2. What effect do such words have on you as you read this poem?

In many of Gray's sentences, the normal word order of English (subject-predicate-complement) is violated. Gray writes "The air a solemn stillness holds" instead of "The air holds a solemn stillness."

3. Find one other example of inverted word order in the poem.

4. Can you propose reasons why Gray took such liberties with idiomatic English?

Perhaps the most difficult lines to sort out syntactically are lines 61–72. The following outline might help to clarify the syntax of these lines:

✔ QUICK CHECK: Poetic Style

Have students paraphrase ll. 97–100 (p. 604) in a manner similar to that which they have just used in the Language and Style exercises.

[Possible paraphrase: Maybe some white-haired farmer will say, "Often we have seen him at dawn walking quickly in the dew, so that he can reach the field just as the sunlight hits it."]

"Their lot forbade" them
　"to command" "the applause of list'ning
　　senates"
　"to despise" "the threats of pain and ruin"
　"to scatter plenty o'er a smiling land,
　　And read their hist'ry in a nation's eyes."

"Nor" has their lot ever
　"circumscribed alone
　　Their growing virtues, but their crimes
　　confined."

Their lot also forbade them
　"To hide" "the struggling pangs of conscious
　　truth"
　"To quench the blushes of ingenuous shame,
　Or heap the shrine of Luxury and Pride
　With incense, kindled at the Muse's flame."

5. Try now to **paraphrase** lines 61–72 using conventional syntax and as many sentences as you need.

CHOICES: Building Your Portfolio

Writer's Notebook
1. Collecting Ideas for a Persuasive Essay

When Thomas Gray writes "the paths of glory lead but to the grave," you have a clear idea of his stance: Despite fame, one inevitable destination awaits us all. Effective persuasive writing also relies on a clear stance—a thesis statement that conveys the writer's position on an issue. Review the issues you've explored in your Reader's Log entries. Which issues grab your interest? Select two issues; then write a thesis statement that conveys your position on each issue. Working with a partner, discuss your thesis statements. How can you make your stance clearer or stronger? Save your work for the Writer's Workshop on page 612.

Critical Writing
2. Elegies Across the Centuries

In a brief essay, discuss the similarities and differences between Gray's "Elegy" and another famous elegy, "The Seafarer," on page 56. Consider the elements of **speaker, theme,** and **tone.**

Creative Writing
3. Talking Back to the Poet

Suppose one of the villagers was allowed to speak his or her epitaph. Write out what he or she might say to the poet. You might consider these characters: the busy housewife; the children's sire; the person once full of "celestial fire"; the person who might have ruled an empire; the person who might have "waked" the lyre; the village Hampden; the mute inglorious Milton; the Cromwell; the hoary-headed swain.

Creative Writing
4. Graveyard Meditations

Suppose you were standing in a graveyard today. Write a brief meditation about the experience, including a description of the place, of the imagined lives of the people buried there, and of your feelings about death. Be sure to describe the time of day, the weather, and the sounds you hear. (If you don't want to use yourself as the speaker, make up a speaker.)

THOMAS GRAY 607

Choices: Building Your Portfolio

1. **Writer's Notebook** Remind students to save their work. They may use it as prewriting for the Writer's Workshop on p. 612.
2. **Critical Writing** Direct students to use a Venn diagram to organize their notes on the two elegies before they begin writing. In the central area covered by both circles, students may list the characteristics of speaker, theme, and tone that the poems have in common. In the areas of each circle not held in common, students may list the elements that are unique to each poem.
3. **Creative Writing** Challenge students to make their responses poetic as well. The epitaphs need not be composed of poetic language, but they may use rhyme, meter, or other poetic devices to reflect the person's character. Students who write from the same point of view may gather in small groups to compare their versions of the characters' speech.
4. **Creative Writing** Have students start by constructing a *5 W-How?* graphic organizer that lists the when, where, why, who, what and how of their meditations. Then, tell students to expand on these facts by listing sensory details describing the setting as well as ideas about the lives of the people buried in the graveyard.

STRATEGIES FOR INCLUSION

Learners Having Difficulty For activity #2, students might prepare an outline before they begin writing. Making an outline will ensure that students consider both similarities and differences between the two poems. The outline will also help them to remember all the points they want to make while writing.

Spatial/Kinesthetic Before they write in activity #4, allow students to go for a brief walk, or direct them to take notes while walking in a park or even a graveyard, if one is nearby. Tell students to consider what they would think about if they were in the speaker's position of walking through a rural graveyard and reflecting on those buried there. Students may use their observations in writing their "Graveyard Meditations."

PORTFOLIO ASSESSMENT

Choices: Assessment Criteria For help in evaluating these Choices assignments, see the criteria in the *Portfolio Management System,* p. 121.

Read On

Portfolio Assessment Options

The following projects can help you evaluate and assess your students' reading outside of class. Videotapes or audiotapes of completed projects may be included in students' portfolios.

- **Write a Diary Commentary** Ask students to pretend they are Boswell to Ivan Denisovich, King George III, or Isaac Newton. They must write a Boswellian account of at least one anecdote from the person's life. Remind them that in this case it is all right to use the first person, as students must make it seem as though they were there conversing with the character.

- **Perform Interviews** Have students work with a partner to perform an interview with a character from one of the books or the movie on this page. One of the students may be the character; the other is the interviewer. The partners may perform their interviews for the class, with the pair taking turns playing the roles of the interviewer and interviewee.

- **Propose an Experiment** Have students think of experiments they would like to perform, and then create a proposal to submit to the Royal Academy. Encourage students to follow their curiosity—what questions would they want answered? Students may write their proposals from the perspective of a seventeenth-century scientist, perhaps writing to enlist Newton's aid or citing Newton as a model for their own pursuits.

- **Write a Screenplay** Students must extract a pivotal or particularly moving scene from their books and transform it into a script for a movie. Ask them to include descriptions of settings, costumes, types for characters, and film shots, as well as dialogue with notes on intonation and emphasis. Have students write a brief explanation of why they chose this scene, what it represents, and why it is central to their book. If possible, they may realize their production and film it with a video camera.

READ ON

Diary of a Castaway

Since its publication in 1719, Daniel Defoe's *Robinson Crusoe* has spawned countless imitations, adaptations, and even a TV sitcom (*Gilligan's Island,* which remains popular decades after its debut in the 1960s). Perhaps the story contained in Crusoe's fictional autobiography has endured because it poses an age-old question: How might *we* react if plucked from our ordinary lives and set on a barren island? Could we face the physical hardships and mental isolation of such an extraordinary new life?

An "Ordinary" Day

As it did in Daniel Defoe's *A Journal of the Plague Year,* the raw material of life serves as a basis for fiction in *One Day in the Life of Ivan Denisovich* (Penguin). Aleksandr Solzhenitsyn took firsthand materials—his own eight years in a Stalinist labor camp—and reworked these personal experiences into a narrative related by an everyman character dubbed Ivan (Russian for "John").

Down on the Farm

Like Pope and Swift, George Orwell uses satire to reveal the absurdities of human nature. In his 1945 novel *Animal Farm* (Harcourt Brace & Company), Orwell satirizes the problems of a supposedly equal society. The animals of Manor Farm revolt against their incompetent owner and install the "Seven Commandments of Animalism," which the sheep simply remember as "four legs good, two legs bad." But when the pigs Napoleon and Snowball disagree about the future of the farm, a rivalry for power ensues.

The Mad Monarch

King George III (r. 1760–1820) lost the American Colonies for good, and his mind for a brief spell. His suffering transforms him from a distant, public figure in control of others to a person of flesh and blood, at the mercy of nature and those around him. Nigel Hawthorne stars in *The Madness of King George,* a 1995 film directed by Nicholas Hytner and based on Alan Bennett's play, *The Madness of George III.*

A Scientific Star

Scientific activity flourished in the second half of the seventeenth century, with London as an important center. Isaac Newton was the first notable hero of modern science, the man who brought the heavenly bodies down to earth with his theory of gravitation. But did an apple *really* fall on his head? Find out in *Physics: From Newton to the Big Bang* (Franklin Watts), Albert and Eve Stwertka's interesting history of modern physics.

608 THE RESTORATION AND THE EIGHTEENTH CENTURY

FOR FURTHER EXPLORATION

Poetry
The Dunciad by Alexander Pope

Nonfiction
The Diary of a Young Girl by Anne Frank
Lives of the English Poets by Samuel Johnson
Of Dramatic Poesy: An Essay by John Dryden

Novels
Oroonoko, or The History of the Royal Slave
  by Aphra Behn
Gulliver's Travels by Jonathan Swift
The History of Tom Jones, a Foundling
  by Henry Fielding
The Plague by Albert Camus

The English Language

Decorum and Order

*by **John Algeo***

In the eighteenth century, some English speakers believed that the English language had become as good as it could be. Therefore, they should try to prevent any more changes, which could only lead to the degeneration of the language. It was a foolish opinion, but some people today still hold it. Only, they think that English has reached perfection in *our* time, so any change from the way *we* talk and write will lead to the death of our language.

Change, Degeneration, and Growth

A language does not die or degenerate simply because it changes. A language dies only when nobody speaks it. The oft-predicted death of English is like that of Mark Twain, who read his own obituary in an American newspaper while he was in England. He cabled the newspaper: "The reports of my death are greatly exaggerated." So are reports of the "death" of English.

Throughout its history, English has grown in the number of its speakers and the uses it is put to. Today, English is the most widely distributed language in the world and is used for more purposes—scientific, technical, commercial, and personal—than any other language. Far from being in danger of degenerating or dying, English is among the most vital of all human languages.

Change in language is natural. It is, moreover, a good thing, for without change a language would indeed die. Change in language has many causes. When English speakers first settled North America, they found animals, plants, land formations, and other things for which they had no names. To talk about these unfamiliar things, they had to adapt old words, coin new words, or borrow words from other languages.

Americans have done all three things. English sailors had used the word *bluff* as an adjective to mean "broad and flat"; Americans adapted it as a noun to mean "cliff," of which they encountered a good many. To name the action of reorganizing an election district for the unfair advantage of one party, Americans coined the word *gerrymander* (from Elbridge *Gerry,* a nineteenth-century

> Change in language, far from being a sign of degeneracy, is the way language adapts to new conditions. It is the way language stays alive.

governor of Massachusetts, who helped carve out an election district that looked like a *salamander*). In the Southwest, English-speaking cowboys learned from their Spanish-speaking counterparts how to catch horses and cattle with a long rope that had a loop with a slipknot at one end. They borrowed the Spanish name for the rope: *lasso.*

Another cause of change is a natural drift in the way we use language. As each new generation learns English, it introduces little changes. And so over the generations, a language gradually changes, until one day we realize that some very big and important changes have happened over a thousand years, although none of the thirty generations who lived during that time was aware of using language very differently from those who came before or after them.

Change in language, far from being a sign of degeneracy, is the way language adapts to new conditions. It is the way language stays alive. Change is not degeneration; it is growth.

A. Expansion

English is the language used for international aviation. In addition, English, along with Arabic, Chinese, French, Russian, and Spanish, is one of the official languages of the United Nations.

B. Exploring the Culture

Among the words borrowed from Native American languages are *succotash* (a dish consisting of lima beans and corn), *toboggan* (a long, narrow sled without runners), and *skunk*.

PROGRAM MANAGER

- **Planning Instruction** See Teaching Notes, *Teaching Resources A,* p. 149 for objectives for this feature.
- **Assessment** See The English Language, *Test Booklet,* pp. 115–116.

Elements of Literature: Videodisc Use the bar codes below to access information about the English Language, Restoration to the Twentieth Century. For more information, see the Videodisc *Teacher's Manual.*

Videodisc Side A

Begin Play, English Track

Begin Play, Spanish Track

OPTIONS FOR TEACHING

STRATEGIES FOR INCLUSION

Auditory Have students take turns reading aloud the examples of different pronunciations, and the examples of good and bad English. Reading the pronunciations aloud will help students recognize the differences between the pronunciations and should help them understand the errors in the examples of bad English.

Intrapersonal/Interpersonal Before students read the section on the English language, have them take a few minutes to freewrite about why they think people may resist change in language. Challenge them to think of contemporary examples. After students have finished reading, arrange them in groups to compare their original notes and the observations they had during the reading.

Linguistic Encourage students to come up with their own examples of good and bad English. Write an example of bad English on the chalkboard, and ask for ways to make the sentence better. Ask students to think of many ways to improve each example.

A. Expansion

In spite of a similar fear French speakers have for their own language, American words such as *hamburger* and *weekend* continue to make their way into spoken French.

B. Exploring the Culture

In 1604, Robert Cawdrey, a schoolteacher, prepared the first English dictionary, which he called *The Table Alphabeticall of Hard Words*. This book defined approximately 3,000 difficult English words that had been taken from other languages. Later in the 1600s, larger dictionaries that offered more information were published. In 1721, in an attempt to include all English words rather than only hard ones, Nathan Bailey produced a dictionary containing approximately 60,000 words.

C. Expansion

Homophones are not to be confused with homographs, which are words that are spelled the same but that have different meanings and different origins. An example of a homographic pair is *bluff*, meaning "a steep bank or cliff," and *bluff*, meaning "to fool or mislead." The first word is derived from the Dutch *blaf*, meaning "flat, broad." The second word is derived from the Dutch *bluffen* or *verbluffen*, meaning "to baffle, mislead."

All living things must grow through change. Languages are no exception.

Correcting, Improving, and Ascertaining English

(A) Some English speakers today are obsessed with the fear that the changes they notice in English mean the language is about to slip into incoherence and to disintegrate, unless we do something about it—and fast. That obsession first became a large-scale concern of English speakers during the eighteenth century.

Jonathan Swift was one of the writers of this period who was concerned about the well-being of English and the dangers he saw for it. He especially disliked the idea that a language should be "perpetually changing." So Swift wrote *A Proposal for Correcting, Improving, and Ascertaining the English Tongue* (1712), in which he suggested that a group of persons should take on themselves the responsibility of overseeing the language, improving it, unifying it, and above all stabilizing it so that it would stop changing. A number of other countries in Europe had established or were to develop such groups, usually called "academies": Italy, France, and Spain are examples.

The idea of an English Academy never caught on, however. One reason for its failure was the individualism of many English speakers, who were loath to let anybody else tell them how they ought to talk. **(B)** Another reason was the rapid development of English dictionaries, which became "authorities" for English speakers who were insecure about their own language and wanted advice about what to say and write.

The Dictionary

The tradition of making English dictionaries reached a high point with Samuel Johnson, who in 1755 published his two-volume *Dictionary of the English Language*. In the United States, Noah Webster produced a dictionary that came to fill the place in U.S. life that Johnson's dictionary filled in Great Britain. Webster wanted to produce a dictionary that would record the English of the United States, not just that of the mother country.

Webster's dictionary was so successful that today many dictionaries use *Webster* in their titles, but none of them preserve anything from old Noah's book. *Webster* in a dictionary's title is no guarantee of anything—it is only an advertising technique to take advantage of the fact that people associate Webster with dictionaries. With dictionaries, you can't always tell a book by its cover.

In the nineteenth century, a group of English scholars began to work on a dictionary to replace Johnson's, which had become very outdated. Their work eventually developed into the greatest dictionary in the world: *The Oxford English Dictionary*. Recently this dictionary has been expanded to twenty volumes and also put into electronic form as a compact disc.

Samuel Johnson wrote his dictionary single-handedly and by candlelight. Today, teams of lexicographers cooperate in producing dictionaries using the latest computer techniques. As the language changes, so do the ways we keep up with it.

Change All Around Us

Jonathan Swift was not able to stop English from changing, however much he wanted to. Nor can anyone else. The nature of languages is to change, and we can see change going on around us today.

Pronunciation is constantly changing. Not long ago, many Americans pronounced the words *horse* and *hoarse* or *morning* and *mourning* differently from each other; now most pronounce them alike. Today most Americans still pronounce the words *cot* and *caught* or *pond* and *pawned* differently, but increasingly many of us are pronouncing them alike. In a hundred years or so, it is likely that **(C)** such pairs will be **homophones** (words that sound the same, but are different in meaning and spelling) for the majority of our fellow citizens. *Forehead* used to be generally pronounced to rhyme with *horrid;* today, it usually rhymes with *more bread*.

The very words we use are also changing. We make up new words out of elements already in English, like *to eyeball, feedback,* and *minibike*. We borrow others from foreign languages, like *karate* from Japanese, *klutz* from Yiddish, and *macho* from Spanish. Words also change their meaning, or disappear altogether

---

OPTIONS FOR TEACHING

INTEGRATING THE LANGUAGE ARTS

Strategic Reading Before they read the essay, have students skim it and scan for signal words. Signal words comprise section headings, boldfaced words, highlighted excerpts, and words that show order or conclusion, such as *then* and *thus*. Ask students to predict what the essay will be about in a class discussion. After students have read the essay, have them list the main ideas and details from each section along with the transitions that connect the sections. Students may display this information in a graphic organizer that shows the box containing each section's main ideas and details linked by way of a transition with the next box.

Language and Style Point out to students that the essay uses a very efficient style to inform the reader in an interesting manner. Have students locate examples of the different elements of this style. Use the first section to demonstrate that the author uses precise diction ("degeneration") and vivid imagery ("death"), straightforward syntax ("In the eighteenth century, some English speakers believed . . ."), and that he draws a parallel between the eighteenth century and modern times (". . . but some people today still hold it."). Have students find other examples of these elements in the other sections of the essay.

if we stop using them, often because the things they name have changed or disappeared. For example, people used to preserve food by keeping it in a chest with blocks of ice; such a chest was called an *icebox*. When gas and electric refrigerators were invented, some people continued to use the old word for them, thus changing the meaning of *icebox*. But gradually the word has been disappearing; it is rare today and soon will probably drop out of the language altogether.

We also change our grammar. For example, the older past tense of the verb *dive* is *dived*. But today we use a new past form, *dove*, invented by analogy with irregular verbs like *drive*, whose past tense is *drove*.

The words we use, the way we use them, and the way we say them are all changing constantly. Often, when a change begins, many people do not like it. It sounds odd, sloppy, or mistaken. And new uses do often begin as mistakes. But whether the new use has been deliberately introduced or has slipped into the language as an error, if many people adopt it, it becomes part of the language—just one more option we have for saying things. When a change is new or has not yet been widely accepted, we need to be careful about using it, because some people will be so distracted by the way we are talking that they will fail to hear what we are saying.

What Is Good English?

Good English is English that communicates the ideas and

effects we want to get across. Bad English is language that does not communicate successfully. Bad English may be ambiguous: "Mike lost his textbook, but somebody found it and put it in his locker." Whose locker did the book go in, Mike's or somebody's? Bad English may actually be clear, but distracting: "Everybody should have his own textbook." Is everybody male? Aren't there any females around? If we say, "Everybody should have their own textbook," someone will object that *everybody* is singular, whereas *their* is plural, so the two don't go together. If we say, "Everybody should have his or her own textbook," someone else will object that the statement sounds too legalistic.

Each of the choices above is likely to distract someone who hears or reads it. All of them may interfere with communication, and therefore all of them are, to that extent, bad English. The best English in such cases avoids the problem by rewording the statement: "Everybody should have a textbook" or "All students should have their own textbooks." Good English does not get in the way; it does not call attention to itself and away from the message. Good English communicates just what we want to communicate and nothing else.

Try It Out

1. Compare the sample entry for the word *giggle* in Johnson's *Dictionary* (page 571) with the entry for that word in a modern dictionary.

What kinds of information does the modern dictionary give that Johnson's does not? How do the meanings Johnson gives compare with those in the modern dictionary?

2. Choose any one of the sample definitions from Johnson's *Dictionary* (page 572), and compare it with the most similar definition of the same word in a modern dictionary. Tell how the two definitions differ.

3. The following words and expressions are all relatively new to the English language. How many of them are familiar to you? Which of them are listed in the dictionary you use?

Catch-22
ego trip
laptop
schlepp
in-line skates
CD-ROM
play hardball
ten-speed

4. The following are words about whose correct use people disagree. Do you know what the disagreement is? Look up these words in at least two dictionaries to see what is said about them.

impact (verb)
hopefully
data
irregardless

5. Why is it impossible to stop the language we use from changing?

D. Expansion

Often, distinctions between good and bad English depend on the mode of communication used. For example, what might be considered "bad English" is more likely to be heard in speech; what might be considered "good English" is more likely to be written.

Try It Out: Answers

1. A modern dictionary specifies the type of verb (for example, intransitive), gives a phonetic spelling, the different forms of the verb, and sometimes a date for the word's origins. The modern dictionary gives a neutral, factually descriptive definition and does not mention Scotland.

2. Students' findings will vary but should follow the example of *giggle*.

3. Students answers will vary, and their findings will depend on the dictionary used. A good, recent dictionary should list most of the words.

4. *impact* (verb): many hold that the word cannot be used as a verb; *data:* some say the singular form is *datum; hopefully:* some do not accept its use in the sense "it is hoped"; *irregardless:* regarded by many as nonstandard

5. Students' answers will vary but should reflect the ideas that people constantly borrow words from other languages and that people invent words for new things. As the world changes, so does the language to express it.

Check Test: Short Answers

1. When does a language die? [When nobody speaks it anymore.]

2. What are some strategies Americans used to name new things? [Borrowing words from other languages, coining new words, and adapting old words.]

3. How does the author characterize change in language? [As growth, vital to a language's survival.]

4. What purpose does a dictionary fulfill? [It provides an authority for definitions, pronunciations, and derivations.]

5. What is good English? [English that communicates clearly.]

Persuasive Essay

BUILDING YOUR PORTFOLIO
Writer's Workshop

**Technology
HELP**

See Writer's Workshop 2
CD-ROM. *Assignment:
Controversial Issue.*

ASSIGNMENT
**Write a persuasive
essay on a controver-
sial issue.**

AIM
**To persuade; to in-
form and explain.**

AUDIENCE
**People who disagree
on the issue or are
undecided.**

PERSUASIVE WRITING
PERSUASIVE ESSAY

Both Jonathan Swift and Alexander Pope were attuned to the **controversial
issues** of their day, and they didn't shy away from addressing those issues and
trying to win others to their way of thinking. When you care deeply about
a controversial issue, it's only natural to take a stand on it and to defend
your position against objections. That's the essence of writing a persuasive
essay. Persuasive writing will force you to draw on a wide range of writing
skills: speculating about causes and effects, recounting autobiographical incidents, reporting information, and evaluating points for refuting objections to
your arguments.

Prewriting

1. **Checking your Writer's Notebook.** By completing the
Writer's Notebook activities in Collections 6 and 7, you
may have already completed some of the prewriting for a
persuasive essay. Check your entries for usable material, and
then proceed with the prewriting activities that follow.

2. **Exploring possible issues.** Today, no less than in Swift's and Pope's time,
our society is confronted with controversial social and political issues that
thinking people feel compelled to sort out for themselves. To find an issue
that intrigues you, try the Strategies for Elaboration that follow.

Strategies for Elaboration: Exploring Issues

- Watch or listen to TV or radio news programs and talk shows.
  They'll give you ideas about current controversies.
- Look through recent newspapers and magazines, noting the issues
  raised in articles, editorials, editorial cartoons, and news photos.
- Read through your writer's journal for entries dealing with your
  beliefs and values.
- Brainstorm with friends, classmates, and family members about
  possible controversial issues.
- Draw up a series of "Should . . . ?" questions. One example:
  "Should failing students be allowed to participate in school-
  sponsored extracurricular activities?"

**PROGRAM
MANAGER**

Computer Guided Instruction For a
related controversial issue assignment that
students may use as additional
instruction, see *Writer's
Workshop 2.*

**PORTFOLIO
ASSESSMENT**

- **Generating Ideas** To help students in
  prewriting, use the heuristic in the *Portfolio Management System,* p. 122.
- **Assessment Rubric** For a rubric
  that can be used to assess students'
  progress in writing, see the *Portfolio
  Management System,* p. 124.

The history of the written word is rich and...
Once upon a tim...

3. **Choosing an issue.** After you've explored possible issues, you'll have to select one for your essay. To choose one issue to write about, use these guidelines:

- Do you really care? You'll write more convincingly about an issue that you feel strongly about.

- Is the issue arguable? Make sure the issue is one that reasonable people may disagree on. For instance, you'd have a hard time finding anyone to argue that citizens *shouldn't* vote.

- Is it truly a controversial issue, not merely a matter of taste? You may believe that Broadway musicals are the ultimate American musical form, but you won't convince jazz buffs that jazz is inferior. It's a personal preference.

4. **Taking a stand.** Begin your exploration of the issue by spending a few minutes freewriting about it. Then state your opinion on the issue in one or two sentences. Even if your mind's not completely made up yet, writing this preliminary **thesis statement**—also known as a **proposition** or **position statement**—now will guide you as you gather information. Remember that you can always change the wording of your proposition once you've reached a final conclusion.

5. **Targeting your audience.** Even more than other types of writing, persuasive writing is audience-centered. To convince readers that your opinion has merit (even if they don't agree with it), you need to know and understand their views and values. Adopting a formal, serious tone will help you create a favorable impression and make readers inclined to take your ideas seriously, as will approaching them with appeals tailored to their needs and interests.

- **Tap into their feelings. Emotional appeals** stir readers' feelings. Used sparingly, such appeals can help personalize the issue for readers. If you're advocating the use of "signers" to translate sports events for students with hearing disabilities, try to let your audience know how it *feels* to be unable to participate fully in school activities. Words with strong **connotations** (ones with powerful positive *or* negative overtones) can be particularly effective in tapping into people's emotions.

- **Reason with them. Logical appeals** engage your readers' reasoning skills, their ability to think clearly. Readers expect you to offer sound reasons for your position (statements that explain *why* you hold your opinion

WRITER'S WORKSHOP 613

Motivation

Pass out copies of back issues of a national news magazine and ask students to find the advertisement that they think is the most persuasive. Ask volunteers to explain why they chose the ads they did. Encourage students to think about what the regular readers of the magazine are probably like. Point out that to be effective, persuasive writing needs to target a particular audience. Also, point out to students that even though they might not produce persuasive writing on a regular basis, they are the targets of persuasion every day. By learning about the methods of persuasion that this Writer's Workshop highlights, they are learning to be critically aware of persuasion.

Teaching the Lesson

Remind students that if the purpose of their writing is to persuade, they must consider their audience as well as their arguments. This lesson includes instructions for each stage of the writing process. You may want to guide students by modeling each stage with your own writing.

Prewriting

When students are selecting topics, you might want to encourage them to select issues about which they have some firsthand knowledge. Suggest that they consider topics related to an issue at your school or in your community. Also, some students may be tempted to select topics that are apparently controversial but that few people disagree with intellectually. For example, few people disagree that something should be done about violence in schools, although they may disagree about what should be done. Further, students should avoid abstract topics like "parents and teenagers should communicate more with one another." These topics tend not to be controversial, and they tend to produce hypothetical examples that are rarely persuasive.

Try It Out: Answers

1. Circular reasoning; "Sixteen-year-olds are mature enough to vote and should be allowed to do so."
2. Circular reasoning; "A dress code might be the solution to our problems."
3. Either-Or reasoning; "The crime rate may decline if we build more prisons."

Try It Out

Identify the logical fallacy in each of the following sentences. Then revise the fallacy to make the statement logical.

1. The voting age should be lowered to sixteen because sixteen-year-olds are mature enough to vote.
2. Our school needs a dress code because a dress code is the solution to our problems.
3. Unless the state builds more prisons, the crime rate will continue to rise.

---

on the issue) and to back up your reasons with solid evidence, or proof. Appropriate factual evidence may consist of statistics, examples, and anecdotes (brief stories based on personal experience)—all of which can be verified by testing, by drawing on personal observations, or by consulting reliable sources. Expert testimony (statements by recognized authorities on the issue) also qualifies as evidence.

Strategies for Elaboration: Avoiding Fallacies

In listing reasons for your position, take care to avoid these **fallacies,** or mistakes in logic.

- **Hasty generalization**—basing a conclusion on insufficient evidence or overlooking exceptions: *No local merchants will suffer if the proposed chain store is approved.*
- **Attacking the person** (in Latin, *ad hominem,* meaning "to the person"; informally, "name-calling")—attacking people who support the issue: *Hunters just enjoy killing animals.*
- **False authority**—quoting an expert in one field as an authority in an unrelated field: *According to former state Supreme Court Justice Eldon Bates, the state's annual vehicle inspections are a waste of taxpayers' time and money.*
- **Circular reasoning**—offering as a reason a statement that's actually a restatement of an opinion: *The City Council should build more bike paths because our community needs bike paths.*
- **Either-or reasoning**—assuming that an issue has only two possible sides: *Either we abolish the welfare system or we foster perpetual dependence on government handouts.*
- **Non sequitur** (Latin for "It does not follow")—presenting unrelated ideas as though one were the logical consequence of the other: *Our city's rapid population growth demands an easing of land-use restrictions.*

- **Earn their trust. Ethical appeals** invoke your readers' sense of fair play, establishing your credibility and character. Demonstrating that you're knowledgeable, reasonable, sincere, and trustworthy helps win respect for you and, in turn, for your ideas.

  One way to establish your trustworthiness is to consider different sides of an issue, to acknowledge the most significant **counterarguments** (opposing points). By **conceding,** or accommodating, opposing points that do have merit, you establish common ground without sacrificing your principles. Then you can concentrate on **refuting,** or providing conclusive evidence against, those counterarguments that you consider invalid.

6. **Coping with counterarguments.** Once you've listed possible reasons in support of your position, get together with a partner or a small group to brainstorm for likely counterarguments. Think about the kinds of evidence that will convince your particular audience to rethink their counterarguments. You may find it helpful to chart the most significant counterarguments and possible refutations for them, as in the following example.

614 THE RESTORATION AND THE EIGHTEENTH CENTURY

OPTIONS FOR TEACHING

INTEGRATING THE LANGUAGE ARTS

Grammar Review with students the concepts of the simple, the compound, the complex, and the compound-complex sentence structures. You can use the following examples for this review:
Simple: It rained on Saturday. We had to stay home.
Compound: It rained on Saturday, and we had to stay home.

Complex: Because it rained on Saturday, we had to stay home.
Compound-Complex: We had made plans for Saturday, but, because it rained, we had to stay home.
Encourage students to vary the sentence structures they use in their essays by combining sentences and by using subordination.

Proposition: The City Council should approve the construction of a sports stadium proposed for the city's south side.

Counterarguments	Refutations
• Taxpayer dollars should not be directed to building this facility.	• Tax revenues generated by the new facility will balance out any expenditures.
• Property taxes will increase city-wide to pay for construction.	• Construction of the new facility will be paid for by a bond issue and by funds from the professional sports teams that will use the facility.
• The new facility will disturb residents in the area.	• Traffic and sound pollution control measures are a fundamental part of construction plans.

7. **Marshaling your forces.** As you begin to organize your material, decide whether you'll present your argument **deductively** (moving from your proposition to your reasons and evidence) or **inductively** (moving from your reasons and evidence to your proposition). These two different approaches can be thought of as a pair of pyramids, one upside-down and the other right-side up.

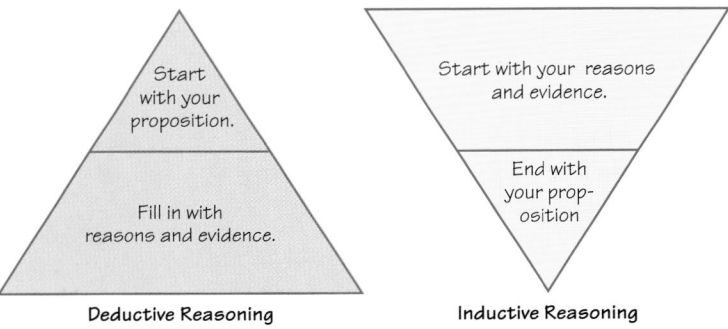

Deductive Reasoning   Inductive Reasoning

Think, too, about how you'll work in the counterarguments you've chosen to concede or refute—before, after, or along with your own argument. Three basic types of organizational patterns can work well for a persuasive essay:

- **Order of importance**—beginning or ending with the appeal likely to have the strongest impact on your audience.
- **Chronological order**—proposing (or attacking) a course of action in the order events occurred or would occur.

Drafting

Some students may have difficulty writing the introductions to their essays. One activity that might help is to have them each write a brief statement on the background of the issues they are writing about. Encourage them to use these statements as the basis of their introductory paragraphs. They can use one of the techniques mentioned in the text to catch readers' attention in the first sentence and then add their thesis statements to the ends of their background statements to form basic introductions.

INTEGRATING THE LANGUAGE ARTS

Vocabulary Ask students to review persuasive essays they find in newspaper editorials, letters to the editor, and political speeches to identify transitional words and expressions that are useful in persuasive writing. Ask individual students to make lists of these words and then have a committee of students design a poster or handout with all of the words that individual students have identified. If students are unsure of the kinds of words they should be looking for, you can offer the following examples to guide their searches:

although	nevertheless
admittedly	nonetheless
even though	however

Strategic Reading As students read the material in this Writer's Workshop, encourage them to predict what they might learn. Ask them to create a KWL chart and use it to help define and refine their knowledge of persuasive writing.

Evaluating and Revising

- As students evaluate and revise their essays, encourage them to imagine a fictional character who is speaking each essay. What is this character's personality like? Do all of the words and sentences sound like something this character would say? Is the character's voice consistent throughout the essay? Do the character's attitudes come across clearly? If students find inconsistencies or are unable to "hear" a clear voice, encourage them to make changes to their essays to create a character's presence.
- Have students refer to the Evaluation Criteria on p. 617 and use highlighters to mark each element as it appears in their peers' papers.

Proofreading and Publishing

- Remind students that errors in grammar, usage, and mechanics will affect the clarity of their writing. If students are going to be successful in convincing people of their positions on controversial issues, their readers are going to have to be able to understand their points easily. Students can suggest possible vehicles of publication other than the ones mentioned in the text, including uploading their papers to selected sites on the Internet.
- Strong writing is important in a persuasive essay. Encourage students to look for strong, parallel phrasing and to edit sentences for use of parallel structure. The Language Workshop on p. 618 includes models and practice in parallel sentence structure.

Communications Handbook HELP

Taking notes and documenting sources: page 1211.

Language Workshop HELP

Parallel structure: page 618.

Language Handbook HELP

Sentence structure: page 1233; sentence style: page 1236.

- **Logical order**—comparing and contrasting opposing positions and your refutations, either by grouping all objections and following them with all your refutations or by alternating opposing positions and refutations.

Drafting

1. **The introduction: defining the issue.** Before readers can begin to follow your line of reasoning, they need to know precisely what the issue is. Get them involved immediately with a vivid image, a startling statistic, an engaging anecdote, or a rhetorical question (one asked merely for effect, with no answer expected). Define the issue clearly, provide any background your readers will need, and (if you've organized your argument deductively) state your proposition succinctly.

2. **The body: developing your argument.** As you present each of your reasons, buttress it with evidence drawn from your investigation of the issue. Emphasize your most compelling reason by devoting the most space to it. In arguing your case and accommodating or refuting counterarguments, remember to keep your tone reasonable and confident.

Strategies for Elaboration: Drafting Persuasively

Focus on the following strategies to develop your persuasive essay:

- **Repetition.** Focus attention on key terms and core ideas by arranging them in parallel structure.
- **Rhythm.** Create a rhythmic flow of sound by using words or syllables with similar vowel or consonant sounds, by varying the length and structure of sentences, and by beginning some sentences with a phrase, a clause, or a one-word modifier instead of with the subject.
- **Language.** Formal needn't be forbidding, nor must serious language be stuffy. In fact, using familiar, everyday language is a subtle but effective way of establishing common ground with your readers. A persuasive essay isn't the place for using slang and sentence fragments, but it *is* the place for speaking your mind directly, forcefully, and self-confidently.

3. **The conclusion: driving the message home.** To bring your essay to an effective end, restate your opinion forcefully, summarize your reasons, or issue a call to action. If you've organized your paper inductively, try to present your proposition in such a way that it seems the natural outgrowth of everything that has led up to it.

Evaluating and Revising

1. **Peer review.** As you read your classmate's draft, evaluate these four characteristics:
   - **Issue.** Is the issue clearly defined? Is it arguable? Is enough background information on the issue provided?
   - **Position.** Is the writer's proposition clearly stated? Is its placement effective?

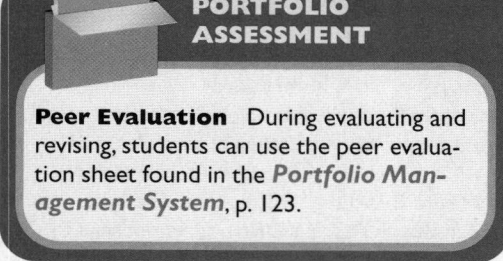

PROGRAM MANAGER

Modeling or Practicing Revision To summarize and model the revision process, and to provide student practice, use **Revision Transparencies 7.3–7.4** in the *Audiovisual Resources Binder.*

PORTFOLIO ASSESSMENT

Peer Evaluation During evaluating and revising, students can use the peer evaluation sheet found in the *Portfolio Management System*, p. 123.

CROSSING THE CURRICULUM

Debate Have students debate with a partner the controversial issues they choose to write about. The first partner should present his or her arguments in favor of the position he or she wants to write about, and the second student should offer objections and counterarguments. The partners should then switch roles. Students can take notes during the debates to use later in addressing counterarguments in their essays.

- **Support.** Are the writer's reasons and evidence relevant and convincing? Are significant counterarguments accommodated or refuted? Is enough evidence provided to make the writer's argument convincing?
- **Tone.** Is the writer's tone knowledgeable, reasonable, and sincere? Is it appropriate for the issue and the audience?

2. **Self-evaluation.** Think of your reviewer's evaluation as a kind of road test, one that gives you the opportunity to fine-tune your paper. Focus on your reviewer's comments about issue, position, support, and tone. Are any of these items particularly strong in your essay? What makes them effective? Do any of these items need improvement? Why? As you evaluate and revise your essay, make the changes you think are needed to convert a confusing or weak argument into a convincing one.

Proofreading and Publishing

Add to the ethical appeal of your paper by proofreading it carefully, correcting mistakes that could detract from your credibility. You might also ask a classmate to check your final paper. Then find an audience for your ideas: Submit your essay to a newspaper or magazine, or make arrangements to read it to a local organization whose members share your interest in (if not your opinion on) the issue.

Reflecting on Your Writing

As you've seen, writing about a controversial issue requires varied writing skills. For your portfolio, write a brief reflection on your writing experience. Consider these questions:

1. How was writing a persuasive essay different from the other kinds of writing you've done this year?
2. Which gave you more difficulty, constructing your own argument or conceding and refuting counterarguments?
3. Which persuasive appeals did you find easiest to develop (logical, emotional, or ethical appeals)? Which ones did you find most difficult? Why?
4. What did you learn about the power of language as you shaped your argument to your audience?
5. What have you learned about the persuasive appeals you see in television and magazine advertisements?

▌ *Evaluation Criteria*

An effective persuasive essay
1. *focuses on a controversial issue*
2. *defines the issue clearly for readers*
3. *provides sufficient background information on the issue*
4. *includes a clearly worded proposition or position statement*
5. *supports the writer's position with relevant and convincing reasons and evidence*
6. *concedes or refutes counterarguments*
7. *conveys a reasonable, knowledgeable, and sincere tone*
8. *concludes by underscoring the writer's position on the issue*

Revision
STRATEGIES

Is your tone assertive rather than arrogant, reasonable rather than derisive? Working with a partner, circle any words in your draft that seem arrogant or derisive. Then replace these inappropriate words with more suitable ones.

Portfolio

Reflecting on Your Writing

You can have students answer the questions in the text, attach these answers to their essays, and file the essays in their portfolios. As an alternative, you can ask students to write letters to younger students or to the editors of your school newspaper to share with them information about persuasive writing. Students can base their letters on what they learned while working on their persuasive essays.

Reteaching

If students have trouble coming up with counterarguments, ask them to consider carefully whether their issues are really controversial. Sometimes counterarguments to changes in the status quo are more implicit than explicit. Ask students to discuss with others how people might react to their suggestions and to consider the reasons for negative reactions as counterarguments they should address in their essays.

Closure

After students have evaluated and revised their essays, ask them to name one strength and one weakness they discovered in reading their own or other students' essays. Ask students to suggest ways to correct the weaknesses they identify. Make a list of the strengths and weaknesses on the chalkboard or write them on a piece of poster board to display in the classroom.

Enrichment

Political Science Connection
Many political speeches are intended to be persuasive. Ask students to read some of the major political speeches from history, such as speeches by President Lincoln or President Kennedy, and to analyze the persuasive devices they contain. You might even have students suggest ways in which the speeches could be modified to suit particular audiences, such as modern high school students.

ASSESSMENT TOOLS

Self-Assessment Students can use the following checklist and a scale of one (needs improvement) to four (superior) for self-assessment.
1. My essay focuses on an arguable issue.
2. My essay defines the issue clearly for readers.
3. My essay provides sufficient background information on the issue.

4. My essay includes a clearly worded proposition or position statement.
5. My essay supports my position with relevant and convincing reasons and evidence.
6. My essay concedes or refutes counterarguments.
7. My essay conveys a reasonable, knowledgeable, and sincere tone.
8. My essay concludes by underscoring the writer's position on the issue.

Language Workshop
Connecting to Students' Writing

Ask students each to choose a piece of writing from their portfolios and identify examples of parallelism. Students can underline or highlight the parallel structures. This exercise should help them to discover places where their writing is not parallel and to correct it.

Try It Out: Possible Answers

1. The narrator of *A Modest Proposal* considers his solution fair, cheap, and easy.
2. He refutes the suggestion of selling and eating twelve- to fourteen-year-olds, arguing that the males' flesh would be too tough and the females would be lost as breeders.
3. His ideas are horrifying, not only because they are vulgar, but also because they are cruel.

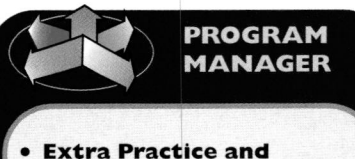

PROGRAM MANAGER

- **Extra Practice and Guided Instruction** For more instruction and practice in parallelism, see Language Workshop in *Teaching Resources A,* pp. 164–165.
- **Extra Practice or Guided Instruction** See *Language Workshop: Parallel Structure* for more practice or guided instruction in parallelism.

The history of the written word is rich and

Page 1

Technology HELP

See Language Workshop CD-ROM. *Key word entry: parallel structure.*

Language Handbook HELP

Parallel structure: page 1237.

Try It Out

Correct the faulty parallelism in each of the following sentences.

1. The narrator of *A Modest Proposal* considers his solution fair, cheap, and being easy.
2. He refutes the suggestion of selling and eating twelve- to fourteen-year-olds, arguing that the males' flesh would be too tough and the females to be lost as breeders.
3. His ideas are horrifying, not only because they are vulgar, but also for their cruelty.

EFFECTIVE SENTENCES: THE POWER OF PARALLELISM

One way to create a sense of urgency about a persuasive issue is to focus attention on key terms and core ideas by using **parallel structure.**

Parallel structure is the use of matching *forms* for sentence elements that have the same *function.* Pairing adjectives with adjectives, prepositional phrases with prepositional phrases, noun clauses with noun clauses (and so on) emphasizes the relationship between the elements. You can use parallel structure to link coordinate ideas, to compare or contrast ideas, and to link ideas with correlative conjunctions *(both . . . and, either . . . or).*

Compare the awkwardness of these examples of faulty parallelism with the clarity of Jonathan Swift's phrasing in *A Modest Proposal:*

FAULTY   **To tax** our absentees at five shillings a pound; **of using** neither clothes, nor household furniture, except what is of our own growth and manufacture. . . . [infinitive paired with prepositional phrase]

PARALLEL   **Of taxing** our absentees at five shillings a pound; **of using** neither clothes, nor household furniture, except what is of our own growth and manufacture. . . . [prepositional phrase paired with prepositional phrase]

—from A Modest Proposal

FAULTY   . . . I rather recommend **buying the children alive,** and **to dress them hot from the knife**. . . . [gerund phrase paired with infinitive phrase]

PARALLEL   . . . I rather recommend **buying the children alive,** and **dressing them hot from the knife**. . . . [gerund phrase paired with gerund phrase]

—from A Modest Proposal

Writer's Workshop Follow-up: Proofreading

Look at the persuasive essay you wrote for the Writer's Workshop on page 612. What key terms or ideas do you want to emphasize? Where could you use parallel structure to stress your ideas? Working with a writing partner, put a check mark next to any sentences where the use of parallel structure would strengthen your essay. Then revise these sentences to incorporate parallel structures. Also, look for sentences where you have not used parallel structure correctly, and revise these sentences so the grammatical elements are parallel.

618 THE RESTORATION AND THE EIGHTEENTH CENTURY

✔ QUICK CHECK: Parallel Structure

Correct the faulty parallelism in each of the following sentences. [Possible answers in brackets.]

[1] When my younger brother, Jerry, was a little boy, his favorite activities were singing for his friends and to pretend to play the piano. [When my younger brother, Jerry, was a little boy, his favorite activities were singing for his friends and pretending to play the piano.]

[2] Our parents decided to buy a piano and were hiring a music teacher. [Our parents decided to buy a piano and to hire a music teacher.]

[3] Jerry was more interested in playing by ear than to take lessons. [Jerry was more interested in playing by ear than in taking lessons.]

[4] Jerry went on to become as successful at writing music as he was as a performer. [Jerry went on to become as successful at writing music as he was at performing.]

CREATIVE PROBLEM SOLVING
LEARNING FOR LIFE

Employment Resources

Problem

Poet Laureate John Dryden was one of many people put out of work as a result of the political upheavals that took place between 1660 and 1800. What resources exist today for people in your community who lose their jobs through downsizing or layoffs?

Project

Investigate what services are available locally through federal, state, and city or county offices for dislocated workers in need of job-search and placement assistance or retraining. Who is eligible to receive the services, and how does a person go about obtaining them?

Preparation

1. Use brainstorming or clustering to determine what you already know about the topic. Have you seen or heard advertisements about such services? Has anyone you know used one of the services?

2. Plan your strategy for conducting research. What print and nonprint sources will you check for information? Use the library, but don't overlook such possible sources as the telephone book and the student services offices of the local community college, university, or vocational-technical center. Your school's guidance counselor may also be able to direct you to people you can interview for further information.

Procedure

1. As you identify the various services and gather information on them, keep a record of your findings and their sources. If you interview someone, for example, take careful notes, or ask permission to tape-record the interview for later review.

2. Look for ways to personalize the information for your intended audience—those who have lost their jobs through no fault of their own. Facts and figures are important, but an anecdote about someone who found a new job through one of the services might go even further to motivate unemployed workers to use the services available.

Presentation

Use one of the following formats (or another that your teacher approves):

1. **Modern-day Pamphleteering**

   Design a brochure that details the services available and eligibility requirements and that lists addresses, telephone numbers, and hours of operation. If you have access to desktop publishing software, use it to produce and publish your brochure. Obtain permission to place copies of the brochure where many people will see it—for example, at the public library or at a supermarket, shopping mall, or neighborhood center.

2. **Poster Promotion**

   Design a poster that promotes the services and that motivates people to take advantage of them. Briefly highlight all necessary information (services offered, eligibility requirements, addresses, telephone numbers, and hours of operation), and consider including tear-off strips that people can take with them for later reference. Obtain permission to display the poster at one of the sites suggested under the first item above, or at another site where many people will see it.

3. **Going on the Radio**

   Prepare a thirty-second public service announcement (PSA) promoting one of the services for broadcast by a local radio station. To ensure that your PSA is in keeping with the station's format, consider the kind of programming it features (news, sports, music, or a mixture) and the demographics (age, sex, income, and so on) of its intended audience. Ask the station manager to schedule air time for your PSA.

Processing

What is your opinion about the number and variety of services available to dislocated workers? Write a brief reflection for your portfolio.

Learning For Life

PORTFOLIO ASSESSMENT

Performance Assessment Rubric So that students may see the evaluation criteria before they begin working on these projects, share the rubric provided in the *Portfolio Management System,* p. 125.

DEVELOPING WORKPLACE COMPETENCIES

Preparation	Procedure	Presentation
Uses self-management skills	Organizes and maintains files for data	Synthesizes information
Determines relevant information	Compares similarities and differences	Communicates information and ideas
Makes inferences	Interprets information	Demonstrates individual responsibility
Locates resources	Recognizes relationships	Exhibits self-esteem

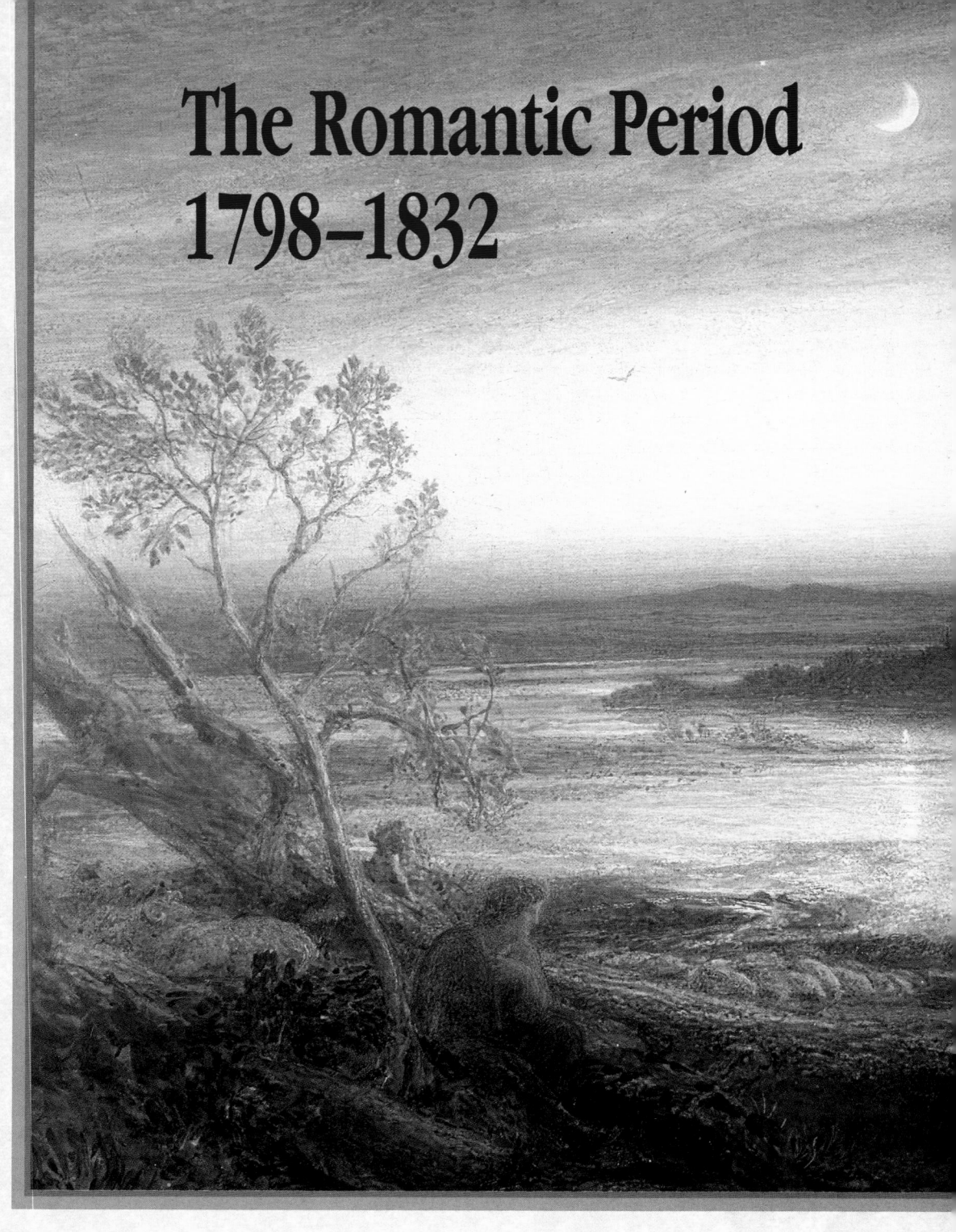

The Romantic Period
1798–1832

The Curfew (detail) (19th century)
by Samuel Palmer.

621

RESPONDING TO THE ART: VISUAL LITERACY

Curfew in the Middle Ages was the time at which a bell was rung to signal the people of the town to extinguish candles and fires for the evening, and, by the nineteenth century, referred to the bell itself. In Samuel Palmer's *The Curfew,* the sun is setting and the landscape is obscured by shadows and foliage. Everything seems to come to a kind of rest or peace for the night. What mood does this scene convey? How might the images here help you predict the essence of Romantic literature? [The scene is tranquil. The lighting, trees, and calm water might indicate that the Romantics focused on the peace found in natural surroundings.]

PROGRAM MANAGER

- **Summative Assessment** See Literary Period Test: The Romantic Period, *Test Booklet,* pp. 159–162, for a test on an additional text from the same historical era.

- **Application** For practice of a reading strategy for this unit, see **Becoming a Strategic Reader** worksheet, *Teaching Resources B,* pp. 10–11.

- **Performance Assessment** Use Assessment 3 in the *Integrated Performance Assessment Level G* to evaluate reading and writing skills covered in collections 8–9. For help with evaluation, see *Holistic Scoring Workshop* software.

Responding to the Quotation

The quotation is from a letter Blake wrote. Do you agree that the imagination forms the "real world"? What is the "vegetable universe"? [Some students may agree that imagination can be richer and more "real" than reality, but other students will probably regard the statement as exaggerated. The "vegetable universe" may be observable nature.]

The Romantic Period

by **Harley Henry**

The divine arts of imagination: imagination, the real & eternal world of which this vegetable universe is but a faint shadow.

—William Blake

Worcester (19th century) by Sir John Gilbert.
Guildhall Art Gallery, Corporation of London.

During the spring of 1798, two young English poets, aged 27 and 25, sold some of their poems to raise money for a trip to Germany. Each had published books of poetry, but a new joint work was to be anonymous. As Samuel Taylor Coleridge, the younger of the pair, told the printer: "Wordsworth's name is nothing . . . mine *stinks*."

Soon after they left England, their book, *Lyrical Ballads, with a Few Other Poems,* appeared. Among the "few other poems" was Coleridge's long narrative *The Rime of the Ancient Mariner* (page 684) and a last-minute addition, Wordsworth's "Lines Composed a Few Miles Above Tintern Abbey" (page 658). Both of these works are now among the most important poems in English literature.

So began what is now called the "Romantic period" in England. Literary historians have found other momentous events to mark its beginning and end, but we should remember the casual, modest appearance of *Lyrical Ballads* as we consider the Romantic period and the writers associated with it.

> *The publication of a collection of poems called* Lyrical Ballads, *a collaboration between William Wordsworth and Samuel Taylor Coleridge, began the Romantic period in England.*

Frontispiece of *America, a Prophecy* (1793) by William Blake.

The Pierpont Morgan Library, New York. PML 16134 copy A.

Turbulent Times, Bitter Realities

Another way to date the Romantic period is to say that it started with the French Revolution in 1789 and ended with the Parliamentary reforms of 1832 that laid the political foundations for modern Britain. The era was dominated by six poets: Three (William Blake, William Wordsworth, and Samuel Taylor Coleridge) were born before the period began and lived through most or all of it, while three others (the "second generation" of Percy Bysshe Shelley, John Keats, and George Gordon, Lord Byron) began their short careers in the second decade of the new century but died before 1825. It was a turbulent, revolutionary age, one in which England changed from an agricultural society to an industrial nation with a large and restless working class concentrated in the teeming mill towns.

We think about this era in terms of some important historical events. Beginning in America in 1776, an age of revolution swept across

> It was the best of times, it was the worst of times, it was the age of wisdom, it was the age of foolishness, it was the epoch of belief, it was the epoch of incredulity, it was the season of Light, it was the season of Darkness, it was the spring of hope, it was the winter of despair, we had everything before us, we had nothing before us, we were all going direct to Heaven, we were all going direct the other way. . . .
>
> —Charles Dickens,
> *from A Tale of Two Cities*

A. Expansion
Coleridge said his name "stinks" because he was a radical in a time when Britain feared radical ideas and influences from the French Revolution. The penniless, already-married Coleridge had been about to become a Unitarian minister, a post he did not anticipate with enthusiasm, when he received a grant from the wealthy Wedgwood family, giving him a life income of 150 pounds a year to explore his talents. This surprising windfall enabled Coleridge to make the journey to Germany and to devote his life to literature.

Elements of Literature: Videodisc Use the bar codes below to locate the appropriate material on the videodisc. See the Videodisc *Teacher's Manual.*

Videodisc Side B

PROGRAM MANAGER

- **Planning Instruction** See Teaching Notes, *Teaching Resources B,* p. 1, for additional teaching options about the Romantic Period.

- **Assessment** For assessment of the literary and historical events mentioned in the historical introduction, see Literary Period Introduction Test, *Test Booklet,* pp. 123–124.

Time Line

- **1794–1801**

Napoleon Bonaparte (1769–1821) rose to power in France in an astonishingly short period of time, through the combination of a brilliant military career and ruthless opportunism. In 1785, the young Napoleon was a new army officer; in 1799, a coup made him the military dictator of France. He had himself crowned emperor, and by 1810, he had consolidated most of Europe under his rule. After France's defeat at Waterloo, he was exiled to the island of St. Helena, where he died.

- **1809–1813**

Jacob Ludwig Carl Grimm and Wilhelm Carl Grimm (1785–1863; 1786–1859) were German brothers whose collections of folk songs and folk tales led almost single-handedly to the birth of folklore as a science. Realists in a Romantic era, they gave up plans for legal careers to pursue scholarly research, and the work of Jacob especially has had a lasting and significant impact on philology and etymology. The brothers' final project was a huge German dictionary that has only recently been completed, after the work of generations of scholars; Jacob survived his brother to see the project as far as the letter *F*. Their works are still studied and celebrated today.

- **1809–1813**

The Luddites, named after the probably mythical Ned Ludd, were a group of handicraftsmen who protested the machinery that was taking over their jobs. They opposed violence to people but rioted to destroy the textile machinery. In 1812, many Luddites were shot down under orders of a machinery owner, and the movement dissolved after the hanging of many members in York in 1813. The word *Luddite* survives today to denote someone who opposes the development and encroachment of new technology.

The Romantic Period, 1798–1832

LITERARY EVENTS

1786–1793	1794–1801	1802–1808	1809–1813
Mary Wollstonecraft critiques female educational restrictions in *A Vindication of the Rights of Woman*, 1792	Maria Edgeworth's *Castle Rackrent*, the first historical novel in English, satirizes absentee landowners in Ireland, 1800		Jane Austen publishes *Pride and Prejudice*, 1813
William Blake publishes *Songs of Innocence*, 1789	**William Wordsworth** and **Samuel Taylor Coleridge** publish *Lyrical Ballads*, 1798	Johann Wolfgang von Goethe publishes Part I of *Faust*, 1808	Brothers Grimm begin to publish *Grimm's Fairy Tales*, 1812
Robert Burns publishes *Poems, Chiefly in the Scottish Dialect*, 1786	Ann Radcliffe's *The Mysteries of Udolpho* popularizes the Gothic novel, 1794	Charles and Mary Lamb publish *Tales from Shakespeare*, 1807	Charles Dickens born, 1812
			Lord Byron publishes first two cantos of *Childe Harold's Pilgrimage*, 1812

CULTURAL/HISTORICAL EVENTS

- **Drawing (late 18th century) by Jacques-Louis David of Marie Antoinette, queen of France, being led to execution.**

1786–1793	1794–1801	1802–1808	1809–1813
French Revolution begins with storming of Bastille, 1789	Thomas Jefferson elected U.S. president, 1800	Workday of pauper children limited to 12 hours in England, 1802	Simón Bolívar begins series of South American rebellions against Spain, 1810
King Louis XVI of France beheaded, 1793	Napoleon conquers Italy, 1800	United States purchases Louisiana Territory from France, 1803	Venezuela declares independence from Spain, 1811
France declares war on England, 1793	Act of Union creates United Kingdom of Great Britain and Ireland, 1801	Napoleon crowns himself emperor in France, 1804	English artisans called Luddites riot and destroy textile machines, fearing that industrialism threatens their livelihoods, 1811
		Egypt gains independence from Ottoman Turks, 1805	Napoleon invades Russia, 1812
		Lord Nelson defeats Napoleon's navy at Battle of Trafalgar, 1805	United States declares war on Great Britain, 1812
		Construction begins on Arc de Triomphe in Paris, 1806	Mexico declares its independence from Spain, 1813
		United States bans importation of slaves from Africa, 1808	

- *Napoleon I in Royal Garb* (1806) by Jean Auguste Dominique Ingres. Musée de l'Armée, Paris.

624 THE ROMANTIC PERIOD

USING THE TIME LINE

Ask students to choose five familiar events or publications from the time line. Have students combine what they know about the events or publications to look for connections between them and to determine what the items reveal about the era. Encourage students to speculate about the spirit of the times: How would they have felt if they had lived in the Romantic era? Students can use a chart like the following to organize their observations and ideas.

Event or Publication	What I Know	Its Relation to Others	Spirit of the Time?
[Children's workday limited to 12 hrs.]	[Eventually child labor became illegal.]	[Dickens wrote about this.]	[People began to see that child labor was harsh.]

• Natty Bumppo, from James Fenimore Cooper's *The Last of the Mohicans.*

Mary Shelley, daughter of Mary Wollstonecraft, publishes *Frankenstein,* 1818

Noted actor Edmund Kean debuts as Shylock in Shakespeare's *The Merchant of Venice,* 1814

Sir Walter Scott publishes *Ivanhoe,* 1819

John Keats writes his greatest poems between January and September, 1819

Noah Webster publishes *An American Dictionary of the English Language,* 1828

John James Audubon begins publishing *The Birds of America,* 1827

James Fenimore Cooper publishes *The Last of the Mohicans,* 1826

Alexander Pushkin begins his novel in verse, *Eugene Onegin,* 1823

• *Scarlet Ibis* (1837) by John James Audubon.

Victor Hugo publishes *The Hunchback of Notre Dame,* 1831

Emily Dickinson born in Amherst, Massachusetts, 1830

1814–1818	1819–1821	1822–1828	1829–1833

British forces burn Washington, D.C., 1814

Allied British, Dutch, and German forces defeat Napoleon at Waterloo, 1815

German confederation created to replace Holy Roman Empire, 1815

First in series of ineffective Factory Acts prohibits employment of all children under 9 years of age, 1819

First steamship, the *Savannah,* crosses the Atlantic in 29 days, 1819

Antarctica sighted by Russian, British, and American sealing ships, 1820

George III, mentally unstable since 1810, dies, 1820

Cherokee system of writing created by Sequoyah, 1821

Liberia founded as home for former U.S. slaves, 1822

Rosetta stone deciphered, allowing Egyptian hieroglyphics to be read, 1822

In the U.S., Monroe Doctrine closes the Americas to further European colonization, 1823

First labor unions permitted in Great Britain, 1824

Catholic Emancipation Act allows British Roman Catholics to hold public office, 1829

Charles Darwin serves as naturalist on HMS *Beagle* during expedition along coast of South America, 1831

• *Horrid Massacre in Virginia* (detail) (early 1830s). Virginia Historical Society, Richmond.

Nat Turner leads slave rebellion in Virginia, 1831

Reform Act extends voting rights in Britain to upper-middle-class men, 1832

Slavery abolished in British Empire, 1833

• *Se-Quo-Yah* (19th century) printed by Lehman and Duval after a painting by Charles Bird King. Lithograph (11″ × 8½″).

• *Rosetta stone* (detail) (196 B.C.), Egypt.

THE ROMANTIC PERIOD 625

• **1822–1828**
Liberia is a republic on the western coast of Africa covering an area of 38,250 square miles. Freed slaves emigrated to the country in the years 1820–1865, and many African Americans have emigrated to the country since then, but immigrants still account for a small percentage of the population. The official language is English. In recent years, the country has been plagued by civil war.

• **1829–1833**
Charles Darwin (1809–1882) spent five years as a naturalist aboard HMS *Beagle* on its voyage along the west coast of South America and to some Pacific islands. On his return to England, it took him another twenty years to assimilate all that he had observed and recorded and to explore and develop his theories before he published his account of evolution in the work *On the Origin of Species by Means of Natural Selection* (1859). The work has had a vitally important impact on nearly every area of Western thought.

A. Exploring the Culture

? Why did the English ruling class fear democracy? [They feared that the masses of uneducated poor would overthrow the government, take away their wealth, and threaten their lives, as had happened in France.]

B. Literary Connections

The words are from *The Prelude,* Book XI. Wordsworth follows them with "France standing on the top of golden hours / and human nature seeming born again."

Storming of the Bastille (18th century) by an unknown artist.

western Europe, releasing political, economic, and social forces that produced, during the next century, some of the most radical changes ever experienced in human life.

The American Revolution had lost for England her thirteen colonies. This was a great economic loss, but it was also a loss of prestige and of confidence. The more radical revolution in France, which started with the storming of the prison called the Bastille on July 14, 1789, had far more serious repercussions. For the ruling classes in England, the French Ⓐ Revolution came to represent their worst fears: the overthrow of an anointed king by a democratic "rabble." To English conservatives, the French Revolution meant the triumph of radical principles, and they feared that the revolutionary fever would spread across the Channel.

> The Executioners, desperate lest themselves be murdered . . . seize the hapless Louis: six of them desperate, him singly desperate, struggling there; and bind him to their plank. Abbé Edgeworth, stooping, bespeaks him: "Son of Saint Louis, ascend to Heaven." The Axe clanks down; a King's Life is shorn away.
>
> —Thomas Carlyle, describing the execution of Louis XVI on January 21, 1793 Ⓑ

But democratic idealists and liberals like Wordsworth felt exhilarated by the events in France. During the revolution's early years, they even made trips to France to view the "new regime" at first hand, as if it were a tourist attraction like the Acropolis in Greece. Wordsworth later wrote, "Bliss

626 THE ROMANTIC PERIOD

OPTIONS FOR TEACHING

STRATEGIES FOR INCLUSION

Spatial Ask students to make their own short time lines as they read the introduction. Students should note on their time lines events that seem to them to be of particular importance. Students may also benefit from comparing the developments and pace of change during the Romantic period with those of modern times. Students may do this by making a parallel line that covers recent years of the same span of time, with a number of points marking important events (for example, the moon landing).

Linguistic Work with students to choose five or six uses of the word *romantic* in the introduction and to consider the connotations of each usage. Are they all the same? Have students compare their findings with a partner.

Auditory After students have read the introduction, have them close their books. Then, read aloud to the class the boldfaced portions of the introduction. Ask students to respond to the ideas. Challenge students also to cite examples from the introduction that support the assertions you read aloud. After you have covered each item, students may then open their books and review the introduction.

T626 The Romantic Period

C. Humanities Connection
The historical event left its mark on language. What does the expression "to meet your Waterloo" mean?
[It means to be completely, finally defeated.]

Fin Tragique de Louis XVI (Tragic End of Louis XVI) (18th century) by an unknown artist.

Musée Carnavalet, Paris.

was it in that dawn to be alive, / But to be young was very heaven!"

Even Wordsworth became disillusioned, however, when in 1792 the "September massacre" took place in France. Hundreds of French aristocrats—some with only the slightest ties to the regime of King Louis XVI—had their heads severed from their bodies by a grisly new invention, the guillotine.

And that wasn't the end of it. In the midst of the blood and turmoil and calls from France for worldwide revolution, control of the government changed hands again. Napoleon Bonaparte, an officer in the French army, emerged first as dictator and then, in 1804, as emperor of France. In the end, Napoleon—whose very name today suggests a tyrant—became as ruthless as the executed king himself.

All of these bewildering changes in western Europe made conservatives in England more rigid than ever. England instituted severe repressive measures: They outlawed collective bargaining and kept suspected spies or agitators in prison without a trial. In 1805, England began a long war against Napoleon. English guns first defeated Napoleon's navy at the Battle of Trafalgar and, finally, in 1815, with the help of allies, sent his army packing at Waterloo, Belgium.

The conservatives in England felt they had saved their country from a despot and from chaos; the early supporters of the revolution, like Wordsworth, felt betrayed. For them, Waterloo was simply the defeat of one despot by another.

Napoleon at the St. Bernard Pass (detail) (1800) by Jacques-Louis David.

Kunsthistorisches Museum, Vienna.

Political upheaval in France and the United States touched England as well. Conservative economic and political measures and a lengthy war against Napoleon radically affected English life.

627

INTEGRATING THE LANGUAGE ARTS

Strategic Reading As students read the introduction, ask them to stop after each section to take note of the section's main ideas. Students may list their summaries as a cluster diagram, with five circles, one for each of the introduction's sections, surrounding a blank central circle. After they have finished reading, have students review

their notes to determine the main ideas: What does the introduction say about literature during the Romantic era? How does it support these generalizations? Ask students to record their summaries of the introduction's central ideas in the central circle. Then, have students compare their diagrams in small groups.

Speaking and Listening Have partners take turns reading to each other the excerpts from poems and the quotations of poets in the introduction. Students should give an expressive reading of each. Partners may critique each other's performances and discuss the "voice" of the Romantics (if there is one) that is revealed by the excerpts.

The Tyranny of Laissez Faire

At the same time, the Industrial Revolution was bringing about other changes in English life. Previously, goods had been made by hand, at home. Now, production switched to factories, where machines worked many times faster than human beings could work by hand. Since factories were in cities, the city populations increased, along with housing conditions that would appall even the most hardened social worker today.

In addition, the communal land once shared by small farmers was taken over by private owners. Some of these rich owners transformed the fields into vast private parks, generously stocked with deer for private Christmas hunts. Others divided the land neatly into privately held fields. Whatever happened to the land, it was no longer communally owned. This resulted in large numbers of landless people. Just as some unemployed and homeless do today, these landless people migrated to cities in search of factory work. Or they went on the dole.

> Every man, as long as he does not violate the laws of justice, is left perfectly free to pursue his own interest his own way, and to bring both his industry and capital into competition with those of any other man or order of men.
>
> —Adam Smith,
> *from The Wealth of Nations*

The economic philosophy that kept all this misery going was a policy called laissez faire (les′ā fer′), "let people do as they please." According to this policy, economic laws should be allowed to operate freely without government interference. The result of

A Surrey Cornfield (19th century) by George Vicat Cole.

628 THE ROMANTIC PERIOD

OPTIONS FOR TEACHING

CROSSING THE CURRICULUM

Social Sciences Have each student research one event mentioned in the introduction. Ask students to expand on the introduction's treatment of the event by finding more details and by making new connections with other events of the time. Students may present their findings to the class in a brief oral report.

Art Ask students to find photographs and reproductions of art from the Romantic period. Would they describe each particular work as Romantic? Why or why not? Have students make a copy of the work they critique and include with it their evaluations, which should be no longer than one or two pages.

Science Challenge students to find out more about technological advances of the Romantic period. For example, students might research the subject of the new mills. What did the mills look like? What did they do? How did they do it? Ask students to present their information in the form of a letter to the editor, either supporting or decrying the new advances.

OPTIONS FOR TEACHING — **CROSSING THE CURRICULUM**

Social Sciences Have each student research one event mentioned in the introduction. Ask students to expand on the introduction's treatment of the event by finding more details and by making new connections with other events of the time. Students may present their findings to the class in a brief oral report.

Art Ask students to find photographs and reproductions of art from the Romantic period. Would they describe each particular work as Romantic? Why or why not? Have students make a copy of the work they critique and include with it their evaluations, which should be no longer than one or two pages.

Science Challenge students to find out more about technological advances of the Romantic period. For example, students might research the subject of the new mills. What did the mills look like? What did they do? How did they do it? Ask students to present their information in the form of a letter to the editor, either supporting or decrying the new advances.

T628 The Romantic Period

laissez faire was that the rich grew richer, and the poor suffered even more. The system, of course, had its most tragic effects on the helpless, especially the children. Small children of the poor were often used like beasts of burden. In the coal pits, for example, very small children were even harnessed to carts for dragging coal, just as if they had been small donkeys.

Frustrated by England's resistance to political and social change that would improve conditions, the Romantic poets turned from the formal, public verse of the eighteenth-century Augustans to a more private, spontaneous, lyric poetry. These lyrics expressed the Romantics' belief that imagination, rather than mere reason, was the best response to the forces of change. Wordsworth spoke of imagination this way:

> . . . spiritual love acts not nor can exist
> Without imagination, which, in truth,
> Is but another name for absolute power
> And clearest insight, amplitude of mind,
> And Reason in her most exalted mood.
>
> —*from The Prelude*

The poets of the Romantic period responded to social and economic changes caused by rapid industrialization and to governmental policies that ignored the problems of the poor.

Children pushing a coal cart through a mine shaft (1842).

Bedlam Furnace, Madeley Dale, Shropshire (1803) by Paul Sandby Munn.
Private Collection.

A. Literary Connections

[?] How do Wordsworth's ideas compare with Blake's from the quotation (p. 622) that opened the introduction? [The two poets seem to agree that real power lies in the imagination.]

THE ROMANTIC PERIOD 629

CLASSROOM MANAGEMENT

Block Scheduling Devote a portion of each department or team meeting to discussion of the block. Communicate with colleagues about problems, issues, successes, failures, concerns, or advantages of the longer class period. Making this a regular feature of meetings will help reduce teacher anxiety as well as provide additional ideas and support.

Managing the Reader's Response Classroom To encourage students to see that there is more than one way to look at material, allow several students to express their opinions on each topic. Offer students the opportunity to amend their responses after they have considered other input. ☞

Romance comes from the Old French word *romanz (escrire),* which refers to the act of writing in Roman, the vernacular, or common language of the people, of the time.

The Sleeping Princess (19th century) by Sir Edward Burne-Jones.

What Does "Romantic" Mean?

The word *romantic* comes from the term *romance,* one of the most popular genres of medieval literature. (See page 174.) Later, Romantic writers self-consciously used the elements of romance in an attempt to go back beyond the refinements of neoclassical literature to older types of writing that they saw as more "genuine." The romance genre also allowed writers to explore new, more psychological and mysterious aspects of human experience.

Today, the word *romantic* is often a derogatory label used to describe sentimental writing, particularly those best-selling paperback "romances" about love—a subject that many people mistakenly think the Romantic poets popularized. As a historical term, however, *romantic* has at least three useful meanings, all of them relevant to the Romantic poets.

First, the term *romantic* signifies a fascination with youth and innocence, with "growing up" by exploring and learning to trust our emotions and our sense of will and identity. Second, the term *romantic* is applied to a stage in the cyclical development of societies: This is the stage when people

What Was Romanticism?

Romanticism is characterized by these general features:

- Romanticism turned away from the eighteenth-century emphasis on reason and artifice. Instead, the Romantics embraced imagination and naturalness.
- Romantic-era poets rejected the public, formal, and witty works of the previous century. They preferred poetry that spoke of personal experiences and emotions, often in simple, unadorned language.
- The Romantics each used the lyric as the form best suited to expressions of feeling, self-revelation, and the imagination.
- Wordsworth urged poets to adopt a democratic attitude toward their audiences; though endowed with a special sensibility, the poet was always "a man speaking to men."
- Many Romantics turned to a past or an inner dream world that they felt was more picturesque and magical than the ugly industrial age they lived in.
- Most Romantics believed in individual liberty and sympathized with those who rebelled against tyranny.
- The Romantics thought of nature as transformative; they were fascinated by the ways nature and the human mind "mirrored" the other's creative properties.

Cultural Diversity The position of poet laureate is that of a salaried member of the British royal household. The office was created in 1616, when James I provided a pension and the title for Ben Jonson, and it still exists today, the current holder being Ted Hughes. William Wordsworth was appointed to the post by Queen Victoria in 1843, long after the decline of his poetic powers but at the height of popular appreciation. Many critics continued to view Wordsworth, as Byron and Shelley had renounced him, as a traitor to the Romantic cause because of his waning imagination and his increasingly conservative political views. He was mocked as a sentimental "Daddy Wordsworth," but he still exerted some influence. Twenty years before Tennyson took the post of poet laureate in 1850, Wordsworth heralded the emerging power of his eventual successor, remarking to a friend, "We have also a respectable show of blossom in poetry, two brothers of the name of Tennyson, in particular one not a little promising."

need to question tradition and authority in order to imagine better—that is, happier, fairer, and healthier—ways to live. Romantic in this sense is associated with idealism. (The 1966–1975 period in the United States might be called a "romantic" era.) And third, in the so-called Romantic period of the first half of the nineteenth century (up to the Civil War in America), Western societies reached the conditions necessary for industrialization. This demanded that people acquire a stronger and stronger awareness of change and that they try to find ways to adapt to it. In this sense, we still live with the legacy of the Romantic period.

> *The term romantic relates to being fascinated with youth and innocence, to questioning authority and tradition for idealistic purposes, and to developing an awareness of adapting to change.*

Poetry, Nature, and the Imagination

Lyrical Ballads did not remain unnoticed or anonymous for long. In 1800, with Coleridge looking over his shoulder, Wordsworth composed a Preface for the expanded collection. In it he declared that he was writing a new kind of poetry that he hoped would be "well adapted to interest mankind permanently. . . ." The subject matter would be different from that of earlier giants of poetry—like Dryden and Pope—who used

Private Collection.

Autumn Leaves (20th century) by Daniel Sherrin.

Check Test: Short Answer

1. The publication of which book started the Romantic era in England? [*Lyrical Ballads, with a Few Other Poems,* by William Wordsworth and Samuel Taylor Coleridge.]

2. What economic transformation was England undergoing during the Romantic period? [It was changing from an agricultural society to an industrial nation.]

3. What does *laissez faire* mean, and what was it in the context of this time period? [It means "let people do as they please"; it was an economic philosophy.]

4. What did the Romantics emphasize about human experience? [They emphasized imagination, emotions, the common bonds between people, and humanity's relationship with nature.]

A. Literary Connections

The first edition of Wordsworth and Coleridge's *Lyrical Ballads* had as its introduction a shorter version of the Preface, entitled an "Advertisement." Wordsworth called the poems in it "experiments" to see "how far the language of conversation in the middle and lower classes of society is adapted to the purposes of poetic pleasure."

> Not the poem we have *read,* but that to which we *return,* with the greatest pleasure, possesses the genuine power, and claims the name of *essential poetry.*
>
> —Samuel Taylor Coleridge

A poetry to satirize, or to persuade the reader with argumentative techniques. For Wordsworth, good poetry was "the spontaneous overflow of powerful feelings." And such poetry should use simple, unadorned language to deal with commonplace subjects for a particular purpose. The form is often a lyric that lends itself to spontaneity, immediacy, a quick burst of emotion, and self-revelation. Furthermore, Wordsworth focused on rural life instead of city life, because in the country "the passions of men are incorporated with the beautiful and permanent forms of Nature." Wordsworth found hope in "certain inherent and indestructible qualities of the human mind, and likewise . . . certain powers in the great and permanent objects that act upon it, which are equally inherent and indestructible." In other words, there is nature, and there are human beings to experience nature.

A CLOSER LOOK

AN IRRESISTIBLE BAD BOY: THE BYRONIC HERO

"Mad, bad, and dangerous to know."

—Lady Caroline Lamb, speaking of George Gordon, Lord Byron

"A man proud, moody, cynical, with defiance on his brow, and misery in his heart, a scorner of his kind, implacable in revenge, yet capable of deep and strong affection." This model of reckless, wounded manhood described by Thomas Babington Macaulay (1800–1859) became known as the Byronic hero. Both in his life and in his poetry, George Gordon, Lord Byron (1788–1824) gave his name to a type of hero who was devastatingly attractive yet fatally flawed.

Byron's personal charms and poetic talents offset a physical disability (a clubfoot), which embarrassed him terribly, and the complicated romantic entanglements that made him a social outcast. His heroes, whom he often invited his readers to identify with himself, were also passionate yet flawed individualists: intellectually searching, incapable of compromise, forever brooding over some mysterious past sin, painfully yet defiantly alone.

Heroes for an unheroic age. The immense popularity of the Byronic hero and the Romantic-age celebration of his prototypes—Cain, Faust, Prometheus, and Napoleon—wasn't hard to understand. These were rash rebels, hailed or resurrected in reaction to a neoclassical world in which order and restraint ruled the day. Most of these daring figures, whose ambitions were doomed from the start, also embodied the deep pessimism of early nineteenth-century life. The failure of the French Revolution had dampened idealism throughout Europe. And the

Byron, 6th Baron (detail) (1835) by Thomas Phillips.
By Courtesy of the National Portrait Gallery, London.

The Romantics are often called nature poets. This description is misleading if it suggests that their poetry is full of charming scenes of forests, mountains, and streams—like the scenic overlooks on highways or the pictures on travel brochures.

The Romantics prized experiences of the beauty and majesty of nature. They did not think of nature as hostile, but they had a strong sense of its mysterious forces, and they were intrigued by the ways that nature and the human mind act upon each other. In the Preface, Wordsworth says that the poet "considers man and nature as essentially adapted to each other, and the mind of man as naturally a mirror of the fairest and most interesting properties of nature."

Each of the Romantic poets had his own special view of the creative power of the imagination and of the ways in which the human mind is

> I think Poetry should surprise by a fine excess and not by Singularity—it should strike the Reader as a wording of his own highest thoughts, and appear almost a Remembrance.
>
> —John Keats, in a letter written February 27, 1818

labyrinthine restrictions of state, church, and society allowed no suitable outlets for the outsized energy of creative young men like Byron and his fictional heroes.

Marlon Brando in Laslo Benedek's film *The Wild One* (1954).

The American heirs. The model of a sensitive rebel continues to be an engaging one for popular heroes of recent time: In post–World War II America, for example, as society had settled into a bland conformity, several searching, sensitive malcontents arrested the attention of moviegoers everywhere.

One version of the Byronic bad boy was played by Marlon Brando, who popularized motorcycles, leather jackets, and a sullen demeanor in his 1954 film *The Wild One*. The leader of a motorcycle gang, Brando is asked, "What are you rebelling against?" His response: "What have you got?" The actor James Dean personified youthful rebellion in both his brief film career and his tragically short life. In *Rebel Without a Cause*

B

(1955), Dean's portrayal of Jim Stark, an alienated character searching for the meaning of manhood, made him a cult hero.

Like all Byronic heroes, these modern characters beckon us to explore personal freedoms and to reject confining conventions. Because this freedom is achieved only by questioning accepted social behavior, these heroes are invariably lonely and misunderstood. And because this freedom often compels them to perform dangerous acts, the lives of these heroes can be much too short. Lord Byron died of a fever at age thirty-six, while fighting for Greek independence. James Dean died in an automobile accident at age twenty-four.

C

James Dean in Nicholas Ray's film *Rebel Without a Cause* (1955).

B. Expansion
Rebel Without a Cause made James Dean a star, and the movie received an Academy Award nomination for original story by the director, Nicholas Ray. Dean received an Academy Award nomination for his role in *Giant*. The film follows two generations of characters on a Texas cattle ranch.

C. Humanities Connection
Another example of the Romantic hero can be found in history, in the person of T. E. Lawrence (1888–1935), also known as "Lawrence of Arabia" for his legendary efforts in fighting the Turks on the Arabian Peninsula during World War I. Lawrence was unconventional, sometimes shocking his superiors and the society in which he lived. Never fully comfortable with his fame and never able to shake the sense of despair that haunted him throughout his life, he died at the young age of forty-six, after a motorcycle accident.

THE ROMANTIC PERIOD 633

RESPONDING TO THE ART: ABOUT THE ARTWORK

Romanticism, "the age of sensibility," preached feeling and sympathy over reason and the formalities of courtly society. In the art world, Romanticism was a reaction against Rococo, its lavish, decorative, and extravagant predecessor. Sentimental and emotional subjects were the focus in paintings such as *Das Schweigen (Silence)* by Henri Fuseli, in which a woman sits on the floor cradling herself as if overcome by sleep or strong emotion. Here, Fuseli omits the excesses of ornamentation of previous art movements and presents emotion as it is felt by the subject.

adapted to nature. You will notice that the poems usually present imaginative experiences as very powerful or moving. This suggests that, in addition to being a special faculty of the mind, the imagination is also a kind of desire, a motive that drives the mind to learn and to know things it cannot learn by rational and logical thinking. So, although the mind is naturally a "mirror" of nature, as Wordsworth thought, the imagination actually moves the mind in mysterious ways to imitate (without being sacrilegious) the powers of its Maker. The purpose of this imitation is to create new realities in the mind and (as a result) in poetry.

In the Romantic period, poetry was no longer used to make complex arguments in a witty, polished style. Romantic poets used unadorned language to explore the significance of commonplace subjects, the beauty of nature, and the power of the human imagination.

Das Schweigen (Silence) (detail) (1799–1801) by Johann Heinrich Füssli. Oil on canvas (63.5 cm × 51.5 cm).

Kunsthaus, Zurich.

The Idea of the Poet

In 1802, in order to clarify his remarks about poetry, Wordsworth added to his Preface a long section on the question, *What is a poet?* His answer began: "He is a man speaking to men."

If this seems strange, consider what happens in a good many of the poems in the following collections. There is a person in the poem—we will call him the "speaker" to distinguish him from the poet—who is "speaking to" someone or something else: a young Highland girl, a baby asleep in a cottage, a skylark, even a Greek vase or a season of the year.

Each poem of this type not only asks us to imagine (pretend) that the "speaking" is taking place, but also makes us consider what *kind* of speaking is taking place. Is the speaker praising or confessing or complaining or worshipping or expressing envy? That is, what is the speaker doing by "speaking"?

> I will not Reason & Compare: my business is to Create.
>
> —William Blake

The speaking in lyric poetry is not the Augustan reasoning in verse. It **A** is a more emotional, passionate speaking from the heart. It has been said that we do not *hear* lyric poetry so much as *overhear* it—as if (using our imagination again) we are eavesdropping on a private conversation or on someone talking to himself or herself out loud. The Romantic lyric, then, speaks in what has been called the true voice of feeling or the language of the heart. In writing this way, the Romantics created a kind of poetry that poets today continue to use.

For lyric poetry to be successful, the speaker and the speaking must be convincing. Thus, the poet must create an artful illusion of the voice of the speaker that conveys certain truths or ideas. Though they did not reason in verse like the Neoclassic poets, the Romantics were deeply concerned with the truths of the heart and the imagination—with truth, **B** as Wordsworth said, "carried alive into the heart by passion." Or, as Keats once wrote to a friend, "What the imagination seizes as beauty must be truth whether it existed before or not."

Wordsworth's deceptively simple definition of the poet as "a man speaking to men" was thus a revolutionary concept in a number of ways. If we think of the speaker (not the poet) as an ordinary person, then it is a very democratic definition. Poetry is to be about human experience, about the fundamental relationship between the mind (including the heart and the imagination) and other people and other things. The speaking should be convincing so that it can seem a genuine and sincere account of that experience, no matter how special or extravagant the experience may appear to be.

The speakers in Romantic poetry speak in the language of feelings, or of the heart. This exploration of the emotional experiences of ordinary people was revolutionary.

A. Exploring the Culture

Remind students that the Augustan poets wrote in a time of order restored to a society badly in need of it, and thus they celebrated order and happy rule. The Romantics, on the other hand, lived in a society badly in need of social changes, in a time of revolution.

B. Literary Connections

The context of Wordsworth's comment is this: "[Men] talk of poetry as of a matter of amusement and idle pleasure; who will converse with us as gravely about a taste for poetry, as they express it, as if it were a thing as indifferent as a taste for rope-dancing, or Frontiniac or sherry. Aristotle, I have been told, hath said, that poetry is the most philosophic of all writing: it is so: its object is truth, not individual and local, but general, and operative; not standing upon external testimony, but carried alive into the heart by passion; truth which is its own testimony, which gives strength and divinity to the tribunal to which it appeals, and receives them from the same tribunal. Poetry is the image of man and nature."

A. Expansion

Other highlights of the Gothic romance include Ann Radcliffe's *Italian* (1797), Matthew Gregory Lewis's *The Monk* (1796), William Beckford's *Vathek* (1786), and Charles Robert Maturin's Irish version of the Faust legend, *Melmoth the Wanderer* (1820).

B. Literary Connections

Modern practitioners of the Gothic include Stephen King, Clive Barker, Ira Levin, Whitley Strieber, Anne Rice, William Peter Blatty, and Dean Koontz.

C. Expansion

Ann Radcliffe never visited the countries where her stories took place, yet *The Mysteries of Udolpho* made her the most popular novelist in England at the time. The novel is set in the eerie atmosphere of a haunted castle high in the Apennines in Italy. The main character, Emily St. Aubert, is imprisoned by her evil guardians until freed by her lover. Among Radcliffe's admirers were Christina Rossetti, Samuel Taylor Coleridge, and Lord Byron.

The Romantic Poet

In saying that the poet is "a man speaking to men," Wordsworth did not mean that the poet is just a man. In the Preface, it is clear that the poet is a special person, "endowed with more lively sensibility, more enthusiasm and tenderness . . . a greater knowledge of human nature, and a more comprehensive soul, than are supposed to be common among mankind." Though the word *supposed* (meaning *thought*) may suggest that Wordsworth thought his fellow citizens had too low an estimate of much of humankind, all of the Romantic poets described the poet in such lofty terms.

> . . . what we have loved,
> Others will love, and we will teach them how;
> Instruct them how the mind of man becomes
> A thousand times more beautiful than the earth
> On which he dwells, above this frame of things
> (Which, 'mid all revolution in the hopes
> And fears of men, doth still remain unchanged)
> In beauty exalted, as it is itself
> Of quality and fabric more divine.
>
> —William Wordsworth,
> from The Prelude

A CLOSER LOOK

THE LURE OF THE GOTHIC

Literature of the Romantic period is filled with examples of the eerie and supernatural: Samuel Coleridge's haunted *The Rime of the Ancient Mariner* and Mary Shelley's famously horrible *Frankenstein*. The Romantics' taste for terror grew from a sensibility called "Gothic" that set stories in gloomy medieval castles. The intention of the Gothic? To make readers' blood run cold.

A "little gothick Castel." Much credit for the popularity of the Gothic style must go to a dramatically unorthodox construction project. In 1747, Horace Walpole (1717–1797) began building what he called a "little gothick Castel." A more conventional choice by the son of wealthy, powerful Prime Minister Robert Walpole (1676–1745) would have been a mansion in the popular neoclassical style. Neoclassical architecture—like the White House in the United States—is inspired by ancient Roman and Greek models and emphasizes balance and symmetry. In stark contrast, the Gothic revels in rustic irregularity: quirky battlements (medieval-style fortifications with openings for defenders) or overgrown landscaping. Walpole's home, named Strawberry Hill, was designed to be gloriously imperfect; when its odd, medieval battlements collapsed, the ruin only enhanced its charm and intensified its melancholy atmosphere.

Making monsters. Walpole had constructed a Gothic ruin; in 1764, he filled it with monsters. His novel *The Castle of Otranto* uses ghosts, living statues, and an eerie forest cave to illustrate a royal family's collapse. With this terrifying, imaginative story, Walpole created the first Gothic novel, a genre of horror tales that we recognize today.

The effects of Walpole's creations were far-reaching. The model of his crumbling house and of stories that provoked violent emotions helped begin the Romantic period's love affair with all things Gothic. Contemporary tastes thought that Gothic architecture reflected the wild, unpredictable aspects of nature; its ruins reflected human aspirations and failures. A melancholy painting or a desolate landscape could enhance spiritual awareness. Ann Radcliffe (1764–1823), one of the best-known Gothic novelists, describes this ideal awareness in *The Mysteries of Udolpho* (1794). In twilight gloom, a character finds "that delicious melancholy which no person, who had felt it once, would resign for the gayest pleasures. They awaken our best and purest feelings; disposing us to benevolence, pity, and friendship."

Exploring unseen "evils." The turn from rational enlightenment to Gothic sensationalism indicated

For William Blake, for example, the poet was the bard, an inspired revealer and teacher. The poet, wrote Coleridge, "brings the whole soul of man into activity" by employing "that synthetic and magical power . . . the imagination." Shelley called poets "the unacknowledged legislators of the world." Keats wrote that a poet is a "physician" to all humanity and "pours out a balm upon the world." Nothing, wrote Wordsworth in *The Recluse*,

> . . . can breed such fear and awe
> As fall upon us often when we look
> Into our Minds, into the Mind of Man—
> My haunt, and the main region of my song.

The poet, in sum, is someone human beings cannot do without.

The Romantic poets found a way through the imagination to fulfill the poet's traditional role as "prophet, priest, and king" in a time of change.

more than just a fad for terrifying tales and quirky architecture. The Gothic was one way in which people of the age expressed a sense of helplessness about forces beyond their control: frightening revolutions in Europe and industrialization's unsettling economic changes. The familiar, sensational trappings of the Gothic novel that we know today were less important than its ability to let readers, if only for a moment, share their fears about the age's suffering, injustice, and other unseen "evils."

Two Men Contemplating the Moon (1819) by Casper David Friedrich.

Staatliche Kunstsammlungen Dresden, Gemäldegalerie Neue Meister.

Europe, a Prophecy: Famine (detail) (1794) by William Blake. Relief etching with white line engraving, watercolor.
Private Collection.

Quickwrite The Romantic poets used simple language to explore commonplace subjects, the beauty of nature, and the power of the imagination. Do you think contemporary writers, songwriters, and filmmakers show that we still live with the legacy of the Romantic period? Take some notes on how you think the Romantics' revolutionary tradition is carried on in society today.

(Opposite) *Donati's Comet over Balliol College* (19th century) by William of Oxford (circle of).
The Maas Gallery, London.

THE POWER OF IMAGINATION

Theme: **Finding Insight in the Ordinary**

Beginning with the publication of *Lyrical Ballads,* the Romantic poets turned from formal public verse to a more spontaneous lyric poetry. These lyrics expressed the Romantics' belief that imagination, rather than mere reason, was the best response to forces of change. For the Romantics, imagination encompassed fantasy as well as insight found in nature.

Thematic Focus

Each selection in Collection 8 illustrates one of the common features of the Romantic period.

- **To a Mouse** The choice of fearing or embracing the unknown arises when a plow destroys the nest of a mouse.
- **The Tyger/The Lamb/The Chimney Sweeper/A Poison Tree** Blake examines contraries in these poems.
- **Lines Composed a Few Miles Above Tintern Abbey/She Dwelt Among the Untrodden Ways/Composed upon Westminster Bridge/The World Is Too Much with Us** Wordsworth highlights the way nature transforms its viewers.
- **I Have Visited Again** A revisited landscape speaks to Pushkin.
- **Kubla Khan/This Lime-Tree Bower My Prison/The Rime of the Ancient Mariner** Coleridge explores how imagination shapes perception.

Literary Focus

Literary Element	Selection / Feature
Dialect	**To A Mouse**
Parallelism	**The Tyger/The Lamb/The Chimney Sweeper/ A Poison Tree**
Blank Verse	**Lines Composed a Few Miles Above Tintern Abbey**
Personification	**Composed upon Westminster Bridge**
Literary Ballad/Folk Ballad/ Meter/Rhyme Scheme/ Internal Rhyme	**The Rime of the Ancient Mariner**

Writing Focus

The following chart shows how the writing assignment for each selection relates to and builds toward the culminating writing assignment presented in the Writer's Workshop at the end of the unit.

Selection	Work-in-Progress Assignment
To a Mouse	Remember emotions an animal stirred p. 644
The Tyger ...	Recall a touching song or film p. 655
Tintern Abbey ...	Explore a significant moment p. 669
Kubla Khan ...	Write about wonder p. 708
Writer's Workshop	Write a reflective essay pp. 773–777

Collection Planner

SELECTION/ FEATURE	Literary Elements / Active Reading	Writing	Speaking and Listening	Language and Vocabulary
To a Mouse Robert Burns (pp. 640–644)	• Reader's Log p. 641 • Dialect p. 641	• Critical Writing: Write response p. 644 • Creative Writing: Address creature p. 644	• Oral interpretation p. 641	
The Tyger/The Lamb/ The Chimney Sweeper/ A Poison Tree William Blake (pp. 645–655)	• Reader's Log pp. 647, 650, 652, 654 • Parallelism p. 655	• Critical Writing: Write comparative essay p. 655 • Critical Writing: Write analysis p. 655 • Creative Writing: Write prose narrative p. 655		• Language and Style: Parallelism p. 655
Lines Composed a Few Miles Above Tintern Abbey/She Dwelt Among the Untrodden Ways/Composed Upon Westminster Bridge/ The World Is Too Much with Us William Wordsworth (pp. 656–669)	• Reader's Log pp. 657, 663, 665, 667 • Blank verse p. 657 • Personification p. 665 • Forms of poetry p. 668 • Apostrophe p. 668	• Critical Writing: Write about progression of thought p. 669 • Critical Writing: Write about themes and imagery p. 669 • Creative Writing: Rewrite poem p. 669 • Creative Writing: Write prose description p. 669	• Oral interpretation p. 662 • Technology and Literature: Create talk show p. 669	
World Literature: I Have Visited Again Alexander Pushkin (pp. 670–673)	• Setting p. 673		• Finding Common Ground: Discuss settings p. 673	
Kubla Khan/This Lime-Tree Bower My Prison/ The Rime of the Ancient Mariner Samuel Taylor Coleridge (pp. 674–708)	• Reader's Log pp. 675, 679, 683 • Rhyme Scheme p. 683 • Meter p. 683 • Literary Ballad p. 683	• Critical Writing: Write analysis of theme p. 708 • Critical Writing: Compare two poems p. 708 • Critical Writing: Analyze poem p. 708 • Critical Writing: Write about allegory p. 708 • Creative Writing: Summarize ending p. 708 • Creative Writing: Write narrative p. 708		• Language and Style: Archaic Words p. 707

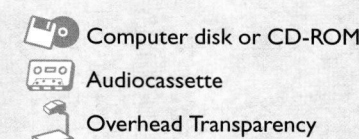

Collection Resources

Teaching Resources B	Audiovisual Resources Binder	Test Booklet
Cross-Curricular Activity p. 29	Fine Art Transparency 8.1	Collection 8 Test pp. 139–140

- Computer disk or CD-ROM
- Audiocassette
- Overhead Transparency

PROGRAM RESOURCES

Electronic Media	Teaching Resources with Organizer		Audiovisual Resources Binder
	Teaching Resources B	Other Resources	
• Test Generator	• Teaching Notes pp. 1–2 • Reading Organizer p. 12 • Words to Own pp. 27–28	• Test Booklet: Selection Test p. 125 • Portfolio Management System pp. 43, 62–63, 126	• Selected Reading Audiocassette 1, Side B
• Test Generator	• Teaching Notes pp. 2–4 • Reading Organizers pp. 13–16 • Words to Own pp. 27–28	• Test Booklet: Selection Tests pp. 126–129 • Portfolio Management System pp. 48–49, 62–63, 127–128	• Selected Reading, Audiocassette 1, Side B
• Test Generator • Language Workshop: Parallel structure	• Teaching Notes pp. 4–6 • Reading Organizers pp. 17, 20–22 • Language Link pp. 18–19 • Words to Own pp. 27–28	• Test Booklet: Selection Tests pp. 130–134 • Language and Writing Skills Worksheets p. 101 • Portfolio Management System pp. 54–55, 62–63, 129–130	• Selected Reading Audiocassette 1, Side B • Elements of Literature Transparencies 8.2 and 8.3
	• Teaching Notes p. 6		
• Test Generator	• Teaching Notes pp. 6–9 • Reading Organizers pp. 23–25 • Language Link p. 26 • Words to Own pp. 27–28	• Test Booklet: Selection Tests pp. 135–138 • Portfolio Management System pp. 61, 62–63, 131–132	• Selected Reading Audiocassette 2, Side A

Proofreading Warm-ups

You may use the following exercises to help students practice their proofreading skills. Copy a set of incorrect sentences onto the chalkboard, and have students find and correct the spelling, punctuation, usage, and mechanical errors in each sentence. Ask students to share and discuss their responses.

	Sentences with Errors	Sentences Corrected	Skills Covered
1	**a.** In 1786, a scottish farmer joined the scottish and english literary world. **b.** writing in dilect made Burns famus.	**a.** In 1786, a Scottish farmer joined the Scottish and English literary worlds. **b.** Writing in dialect made Burns famous.	Capitalization, Plurals, Spelling
2	**a.** As an engraver, William Blake was trained before he became a writer. **b.** The teacher asked us what colors were in the poem the Tiger.	**a.** William Blake was trained as an engraver before he became a writer. **b.** The teacher asked us what colors are in the poem "The Tyger."	Misplaced modifiers, Verb errors, Quotation marks for titles of short poems, Spelling
3	**a.** if you would of looked at the timeline then you would know that William Wordsworth and Samuel Taylor Coleridge published Lyrical Ballads in 1798. **b.** Wordsworth and Dorothy his sister went on a walking tour in Whales.	**a.** If you had looked at the time line, then you would know that William Wordsworth and Samuel Taylor Coleridge published <u>Lyrical Ballads</u> in 1798. **b.** Wordsworth and his sister Dorothy went on a walking tour in Wales.	Capitalization, Nonstandard usage, Underlining book titles, Spelling
4	**a.** After meeting each other, a book of poems called Lyrical Ballads was published by Wordsworth and Coleridge. **b.** Whom was the author of The Rhyme of the Ancient Mariner?	**a.** After Coleridge and Wordsworth met each other, they published a book of poems called <u>Lyrical Ballads</u>. **b.** Who was the author of <u>The Rime of the Ancient Mariner</u>?	Misplaced modifiers, Pronouns, Underlining titles of books and long poems, Spelling
5	**a.** We followed a route that Wordsworth took on vacation last year. **b.** Coleridge was a poet who the critics praised.	**a.** On vacation last year, we followed a route that Wordsworth took. **b.** Coleridge was a poet whom the critics praised.	Misplaced modifiers, Pronouns
6	**a.** He is the one about who we were talking. **b.** Pushkin and Wordsworth both wrote about places they have revisited.	**a.** He is the one about whom we were talking. **b.** Pushkin and Wordsworth both wrote about places they had revisited.	Pronouns, Verbs
7	**a.** Wordsworth and Coleridge was also known as the lake poets. **b.** Because of the bird in Coleridges The Rime of the Ancient Mariner the albatross has become a metaphor for a toublesome burden.	**a.** Wordsworth and Coleridge were also known as the Lake Poets. **b.** Because of the bird in Coleridge's <u>The Rime of the Ancient Mariner</u>, the albatross has become a metaphor for a troublesome burden.	Subject-verb agreement, Capitalization, Apostrophes, Underlining titles of long poems, Comma usage, Spelling
8	**a.** I can't hardly imagine what the garden looks like in Kubla Khan. **b.** I would of liked to visit Xanadu.	**a.** I can hardly imagine what the garden in "Kubla Khan" looks like. **b.** I would have liked to visit Xanadu.	Double negatives, Quotation marks for titles of short poems, Usage
9	**a.** wordsworth saw ruins walking on tour. **b.** i think the lake poets were nature lovers.	**a.** Walking on tour, Wordsworth saw ruins. **b.** The Lake Poets were nature lovers.	Capitalization, Misplaced modifiers, Style
10	**a.** i wouldn't of wanted to be sold as a chimney sweep in london. **b.** The romantic poets didn't hardly right love pomes.	**a.** I would not have wanted to be sold as a chimney sweep in London. **b.** The Romantic poets wrote relatively few love poems.	Capitalization, Usage, Double negatives, Spelling, Style

THE POWER OF IMAGINATION

Burns
Blake
Wordsworth
Pushkin
Coleridge

The poet's eye, in a fine frenzy rolling,
Doth glance from heaven to earth, from earth to heaven;
And, as imagination bodies forth
The forms of things unknown, the poet's pen
Turns them to shapes, and gives to airy nothing
A local habitation and a name.

—William Shakespeare, *from A Midsummer Night's Dream*

Responding to the Quotation

? What does the quotation suggest about the power of the imagination? [Students will probably say that the quotation suggests a poet can create anything by way of the imagination and can even make the unknown familiar enough to have a name.]

PORTFOLIO ASSESSMENT

Parent/Guardian Involvement For forms that will help a parent or guardian review and respond to a student's portfolio, see *Portfolio Management System,* pp. 62–63.

PROGRAM MANAGER

- **Integrated Assessment** For a summative assessment of the literature and language skills taught in this collection, see Collection 8 Test, *Test Booklet,* pp. 139–140.
- **Instructional Support** See Fine Art Transparency 8.1. Review teacher's

notes for transparencies in the *Audiovisual Resources Binder* for suggestions on how to tie the transparencies to specific reading selections.
- **Extending Collection Theme** See Cross-Curricular Activity: The Power

of Imagination, *Teaching Resources B,* p. 29, for activities in other disciplines and for evaluation criteria.
- **Reinforcement** Use the Words to Own worksheet in *Teaching Resources B,* pp. 27–28.

Robert Burns

(1759–1796)

In 1786, a Scottish farmer thrust himself into the Scottish and English literary worlds. The farmer was Robert (Robby) Burns, and the book that catapulted him out of the barnyard was *Poems, Chiefly in the Scottish Dialect.*

Within a year, Burns had left his native Ayrshire (in southwestern Scotland) for the first time and become the toast of Edinburgh. He seized the moment to issue a new edition of his poems (1787) with an Edinburgh publisher. In a new preface to this edition, he proclaimed, "The poetic genius of my country found me . . . at the plow; and threw her inspiring mantle over me. . . . I tuned my wild, artless notes, as she inspired."

Burns was certainly eager to cultivate an audience among the literati of Edinburgh, but he also consciously reinforced his image as an untutored rustic inspired by Scotland itself. He was fully aware that his fame would probably be temporary, and it was. After this auspicious beginning, Burns's stature declined. He actually wrote relatively little poetry afterward. Instead, he devoted himself to collecting, editing, rewriting, and creating over three hundred Scottish folk songs; most of the lyrics he wrote he set to traditional airs. This is the work that established Burns's most enduring reputation. Scottish immigrants to North America and elsewhere took his song collections with them, and they sang Burns's words to remember their homeland. Even now, many people mark the New Year by singing "Auld Lang Syne," one of Burns's lyrics.

Only ten years after his first success, Burns died of heart disease. Though his reputation includes credible legends of heavy drinking, it is clear that poor nutrition and the long-term physical hardships of farming led to his early death.

By the early nineteenth century, Burns was well on the way to becoming the single most important symbol of Scottish literature. Burns was an extraordinary poet in part because

Robert Burns (c. 1792) by Alexander Nasmyth. Oil on canvas (12½" × 9½").
By Courtesy of the National Portrait Gallery, London.

Scottish culture, both popular and refined, seems to have spoken through him. He grew up in the folk culture of small isolated Scottish villages and farms, where the few pleasures were all the more precious. Much of what Wordsworth noted as the "presence of human life" in Burns's work comes from his immersion in the lives of ordinary human beings. The pleasure we take from his poetry comes in part from our recognition of things common and enduring in human experience.

At the same time, Burns himself was quite aware of the tradition of Scottish literature, which was undergoing a studied revival in the eighteenth century. Burns had the benefit of some excellent (though short-lived) formal education before he was needed full time for farm labor, and he was well read in English authors. The apparent artlessness of what he wrote and the simple pose he adopted as a humble plowman mask a mastery of literary forms. Burns, in fact, could write perfectly well in the literary English of his time as well as in a range of Scottish, from heavy dialect to a beautiful blending of folk idioms and literary language.

THE POWER OF IMAGINATION

Burns
Blake
Wordsworth
Pushkin
Coleridge

> The poet's eye, in a fine frenzy rolling,
> Doth glance from heaven to earth, from earth to heaven;
> And, as imagination bodies forth
> The forms of things unknown, the poet's pen
> Turns them to shapes, and gives to airy nothing
> A local habitation and a name.
>
> —William Shakespeare, *from A Midsummer Night's Dream*

Responding to the Quotation

? What does the quotation suggest about the power of the imagination? [Students will probably say that the quotation suggests a poet can create anything by way of the imagination and can even make the unknown familiar enough to have a name.]

PORTFOLIO ASSESSMENT

Parent/Guardian Involvement For forms that will help a parent or guardian review and respond to a student's portfolio, see *Portfolio Management System,* pp. 62–63.

PROGRAM MANAGER

- **Integrated Assessment** For a summative assessment of the literature and language skills taught in this collection, see **Collection 8 Test,** *Test Booklet,* pp. 139–140.
- **Instructional Support** See **Fine Art Transparency** 8.1. Review teacher's notes for transparencies in the *Audiovisual Resources Binder* for suggestions on how to tie the transparencies to specific reading selections.
- **Extending Collection Theme** See **Cross-Curricular Activity: The Power** of Imagination, *Teaching Resources B,* p. 29, for activities in other disciplines and for evaluation criteria.
- **Reinforcement** Use the **Words to Own** worksheet in *Teaching Resources B,* pp. 27–28.

Robert Burns

(1759–1796)

Robert Burns (c. 1792) by Alexander Nasmyth. Oil on canvas (12½″ × 9½″).
By Courtesy of the National Portrait Gallery, London.

In 1786, a Scottish farmer thrust himself into the Scottish and English literary worlds. The farmer was Robert (Robby) Burns, and the book that catapulted him out of the barnyard was *Poems, Chiefly in the Scottish Dialect.*

Within a year, Burns had left his native Ayrshire (in southwestern Scotland) for the first time and become the toast of Edinburgh. He seized the moment to issue a new edition of his poems (1787) with an Edinburgh publisher. In a new preface to this edition, he proclaimed, "The poetic genius of my country found me . . . at the plow; and threw her inspiring mantle over me. . . . I tuned my wild, artless notes, as she inspired."

Burns was certainly eager to cultivate an audience among the literati of Edinburgh, but he also consciously reinforced his image as an untutored rustic inspired by Scotland itself. He was fully aware that his fame would probably be temporary, and it was. After this auspicious beginning, Burns's stature declined. He actually wrote relatively little poetry afterward. Instead, he devoted himself to collecting, editing, rewriting, and creating over three hundred Scottish folk songs; most of the lyrics he wrote he set to traditional airs. This is the work that established Burns's most enduring reputation. Scottish immigrants to North America and elsewhere took his song collections with them, and they sang Burns's words to remember their homeland. Even now, many people mark the New Year by singing "Auld Lang Syne," one of Burns's lyrics.

Only ten years after his first success, Burns died of heart disease. Though his reputation includes credible legends of heavy drinking, it is clear that poor nutrition and the long-term physical hardships of farming led to his early death.

By the early nineteenth century, Burns was well on the way to becoming the single most important symbol of Scottish literature. Burns was an extraordinary poet in part because Scottish culture, both popular and refined, seems to have spoken through him. He grew up in the folk culture of small isolated Scottish villages and farms, where the few pleasures were all the more precious. Much of what Wordsworth noted as the "presence of human life" in Burns's work comes from his immersion in the lives of ordinary human beings. The pleasure we take from his poetry comes in part from our recognition of things common and enduring in human experience.

At the same time, Burns himself was quite aware of the tradition of Scottish literature, which was undergoing a studied revival in the eighteenth century. Burns had the benefit of some excellent (though short-lived) formal education before he was needed full time for farm labor, and he was well read in English authors. The apparent artlessness of what he wrote and the simple pose he adopted as a humble plowman mask a mastery of literary forms. Burns, in fact, could write perfectly well in the literary English of his time as well as in a range of Scottish, from heavy dialect to a beautiful blending of folk idioms and literary language.

PROGRAM MANAGER

- **Planning Instruction** See Teaching Notes, *Teaching Resources B,* pp. 1–2, for objectives, a summary, literary elements, and additional historical and biographical information for this poem.
- **Instructional Support** Before beginning the instructional lesson, see Graphic Organizer for Active Reading, *Teaching Resources B,* p. 12, for a Through the Poem activity.
- **Audiotaped Readings** To help auditory learners through the lesson, use the Selected Reading, Audiocassette 1, Side B in the *Audiovisual Resources Binder.*
- **Assessment** See Selection Test, *Test Booklet,* p. 125.

Reading Focus

The Persistence of the Unforeseen

Here a plowman speaks to a mouse whose nest he has overturned—a seemingly insignificant event. But the speaker also recognizes his own human dilemma in the sudden disruption of the mouse's shelter, carefully constructed against the cruel winter—what the British writer Thomas Hardy was to call "the persistence of the unforeseen."

Quickwrite

What do you think of Hardy's notion of the persistence of the unforeseen? Do you fear the future or see it as a place of promise? In your Reader's Log, jot down your responses to these questions.

Elements of Literature

Dialect

When used as thickly and consistently as Robert Burns uses it here, Scottish dialect sounds like a foreign language. Yet, while the poems seem to call for translation, they also contain some easy-to-read passages that will help you understand others that are not easy to grasp. The meanings of some words can be figured out by their sounds or their context in a phrase or line. Others are so deeply rooted in their Scottish origins that a dictionary will be essential.

Dialect is speech native to particular geographical areas. Many people born and brought up in these places know no other kind of speech, and need no other—even though the transactions of government, law, and educated society are conducted in an official language. In the case of Scotland, that official language is English.

> **D**ialect is speech characteristic of a particular region or group.
> *For more on Dialect, see the Handbook of Literary Terms.*

Background

As an educated and well-read man, Burns had the option of using either Scottish dialect or the King's English. Depending on the subject or occasion of a poem, he proceeded to use both. But there is little question that, if it were not for his poems in dialect, he would figure in literary history as no more than a pleasant poet who accepted the genteel conventions of his time and its sentimental distortions of "the simple life."

The difficulties of poems in dialect have caused some people to attempt to translate them into contemporary language. They make the verses palatable by adding touches of modern slang. But attempts to render dialect poetry into plain English often fail. This is simply because the logic of a poem is only part of what it means to convey. When sound is divorced from sense, the qualities of rhythm, music, and color are diminished, and meaning becomes prosaic.

To enjoy and relish the music, rhythm, and color in "To a Mouse," listen to it read aloud in its own lilting Scottish dialect. Do you recognize in these lines the title of a novel by John Steinbeck?

Robert Burns's Birthplace (19th century) by George Washington Brownlow.

ROBERT BURNS 641

QUICK PLANNING GUIDE

Into the Poem

Author Biography p. 640
Before You Read p. 641
- **Reading Focus: Set a Purpose** Students discuss the unknown.
- **Quickwrite: Prior Knowledge** Write about the future
- **Elements of Literature:** Dialect
- **Background:** Defining dialect

Through the Poem

"To a Mouse" pp. 642–643
Making Meanings p. 644

Beyond the Poem

Choices: Building Your Portfolio p. 644
- **Writer's Notebook:** Gather ideas for a reflective essay
- **Critical Writing:** In an essay, respond to the poem
- **Creative Writing:** Address an animal

STRATEGIES FOR INCLUSION

Special Needs Students who are hearing impaired but retain residual hearing can often recognize rhythms and other sound patterns, such as rhyme. To help hearing-impaired students recognize the rhythm of a poem, provide visual cues while the poem is being read aloud. For example, pat the rhythm on a table top as you read.

Auditory The phonetic spelling of dialect in Burns's "To a Mouse" may be difficult for some students to read. Give students the option of listening to the poem (Audiocassette 1, Side B in the *Audiovisual Resources Binder*) in addition to reading it. Discuss with students their responses to hearing the appropriate accent. Encourage students to share their impressions of particular details with the class. ☞

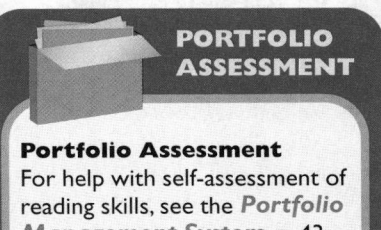

PORTFOLIO ASSESSMENT

Portfolio Assessment For help with self-assessment of reading skills, see the *Portfolio Management System*, p. 43.

Into the Poem

Using BEFORE YOU READ p. 641

Quickwrite

Students can focus on the future by making predictions about how the world may change in the next few decades. Ask students whether they think things will become better or worse. Have students support their answers with specific examples.

Through the Poem

A. Reader's Response: First Thoughts

? How would the poem be different if the adjectives from the Scots dialect were replaced with conventional English? [Sample responses: It would be easier to read; the poem would lose its individuality and spoken quality.]

B. Literary Element: Point of View

? What do ll. 5–6 tell the reader about the speaker? [He is sympathetic to the little animal and dislikes violence.]

C. Critical Reading: Making Connections

? How do ll. 7–8 display a typical Romantic concern? [Possible answers: The speaker worries that humanity and nature are at odds and that humanity is destroying nature.]

D. Critical Reading: Finding Cause and Effect

? Why can't the mouse build another house, a problem the speaker recognizes in l. 21? [It is winter, and there is no vegetation for the mouse to build another nest.]

Highland Landscape, Scotland (late 19th or early 20th century) by Charles Stuart. Private Collection.

To a Mouse

Robert Burns

On Turning Her Up in Her Nest, with the Plow, November, 1785.

A Wee, sleeket,° cowran, tim'rous beastie,
O, what a panic's in thy breastie!
Thou need na start awa sae hasty,
        Wi' bickering brattle!°
B 5 I wad be laith° to rin an' chase thee,
        Wi' murd'ring pattle!°

C I'm truly sorry man's dominion
Has broken Nature's social union,
An' justifies that ill opinion,
10   Which makes thee startle
At me, thy poor, earth-born companion,
        An' fellow mortal!

    I doubt na, whyles,° but thou may thieve;
What then? poor beastie, thou maun° live!
15 A daimen-icker in a thrave°
        'S a sma request:
I'll get a blessin wi' the lave,°
        An' never miss 't!

    Thy wee-bit housie, too, in ruin!
20 It's silly wa's° the win's are strewin!
An' naething, now, to big° a new ane,
D   O' foggage° green!
An' bleak December's winds ensuin,
        Baith snell° an' keen!

1. **sleeket:** sleek.

4. **bickering brattle:** skirmishing, rattling sounds.
5. **laith:** loath; unwilling.
6. **pattle:** plow staff.

13. **whyles:** sometimes.
14. **maun:** must.
15. **daimen-icker in a thrave:** occasional ear of grain out of a bundle.
17. **lave:** remainder.

20. **silly wa's:** feeble walls.
21. **big:** build.
22. **foggage:** moss.

24. **snell:** bitter.

OPTIONS FOR TEACHING

INTEGRATING THE LANGUAGE ARTS

Strategic Reading Have pairs of students rewrite each line of the poem in their own words as they read to make sure they understand the meaning of the work.

Speaking and Listening After students have listened carefully to the professional recording of the poem (Audiocassette 1, Side B), give them

an opportunity to mimic some of the speaking techniques. Have them pay particular attention to which syllables are accented and where the speaker's voice rises and falls. Ask students to use Echo Reading to read the poem aloud in pairs. It may be effective to play one or two stanzas of the recording at a time, and have students practice each short section.

25   Thou saw the fields laid bare an' wast,
      An' weary winter comin fast,
      An' cozie here, beneath the blast,
           Thou thought to dwell,
      Till crash! the cruel coulter° past
30   Out thro' thy cell.

      That wee-bit heap o' leaves an' stibble,
      Has cost thee monie a weary nibble!
      Now thou's turn'd out, for a' thy trouble,
          But° house or hald,°
35   To thole° the winter's sleety dribble,
          An' cranreuch° cauld!

      But Mousie, thou art no thy-lane,°
      In proving foresight may be vain:
      The best laid schemes o' mice an' men
40   Gang aft agley,°
      An' lea'e us nought but grief an' pain,
          For promis'd joy!

      Still, thou art blest, compar'd wi' me!
      The present only toucheth thee:
45 But och! I backward cast my e'e,
          On prospects drear!
      An' forward, tho' I canna see,
          I guess an' fear!

29. coulter: plow blade.

34. but: without. **hald:** land.
35. thole: endure.
36. cranreuch: hoarfrost.

37. no thy-lane: not alone.

40. gang aft agley: go often amiss.

Ploughing (detail) (late 19th or early 20th century) by Aldin Cecil.

ROBERT BURNS 643

E. Literary Element: Dialect

[?] What is the effect of the repetition of "wee" and "wee-bit," as in ll. 1, 19, and 31? [The repetition emphasizes the difference in size between the mouse and man. *Wee* is also a word that connotes "endearing" and "small," so the word colors readers' perceptions of the speaker and the mouse.]

F. Critical Reading: Identifying Main Ideas

[?] What is the moral of the poem as expressed by the poet in ll. 39–42? [The poet declares that even the best plans are unreliable and that humans and mice are equally dependent on chance.] Point out that John Steinbeck's novel *Of Mice and Men* may have been titled after this famous line.

G. Reader's Response: Extending the Text

[?] Do you agree with the speaker's comparison of himself to the mouse in ll. 43–48? Why or why not? [Sample responses: I agree with the speaker that the mouse seems to have a much more carefree existence. Or I disagree with the speaker; it is hard sometimes to worry about the future, but ignorance isn't really bliss either.]

PROFESSIONAL NOTES

Cultural Diversity Every January 25, Scots around the world gather to celebrate Robert Burns's birthday and Scottish culture. The evening includes traditional food such as haggis, the recitation of a number of Burns's poems, and perhaps the singing of a few of Burns's songs. Robert Burns is more than just a favorite son of Scotland; he is a national symbol. In Burns's time, Scotland was struggling to maintain its national identity. The Act of Union in 1707 brought Scotland under direct

British rule, and in 1745, the attempts by Scottish Jacobites to overthrow the English government was crushed. The English punished Scotland by charging tariffs and by outlawing tartan cloth and bagpipes. The revival of Scotland's literature, of which Burns was a central figure, provided a way for Scots to regain their individuality and national pride. Other poets wrote in the Lowlands Scottish, called "Lallan," that Burns used, but his attention to the techniques of English poetry and the

traditions of the Scottish folk song made him a success at home and abroad. The result was that as Burns's fame grew, so did Scotland's glory; these Burns Suppers celebrate therefore not only the birth of a man but the rebirth of a culture. 👉

Making Meanings

First Thoughts

1. The speaker's mood is contemplative, playful, sympathetic, compassionate, and then melancholy. Students will probably say that they have had similar feelings in situations in which they have witnessed a small tragedy.

Shaping Interpretations

2. The tone changes by l. 37, becoming more philosophical. The past is dreary, and he can only guess at the future and fear it.

3. *Dominion* may refer to human rule over the earth; *union* may refer to the fact that humans and animals are fellow creatures united on the earth. The words imply that humans are part of nature, but their need for dominion ruins the union. The speaker regrets that he has destroyed the mouse's home; he understands why the mouse is afraid of him, and he is sorry.

4. For both mice and people, plans do not always turn out as intended. The mouse, the speaker feels, is fortunate because it deals only with the present, while humans worry about failure and the future.

5. Comical sound effects include "bickering brattle" in l. 4 and end rhymes in the fourth and sixth stanzas.

Connecting with the Text

6. Students may say that humans do not have total control of their lives. Students may share experiences of plans that had to be changed.

Extending the Text

7. **(Synthesis)** Students may say that dialects are prevalent in drama, songs, and fiction today. Dialect adds to a work's realism.

Beyond the Poem

Choices: Building Your Portfolio

1. **Writer's Notebook** Remind students to save their work. They may use it as prewriting for the Writer's Workshop on p. 773.

First Thoughts

1. How would you describe the **speaker's** mood? Do you ever feel the same? When?

Shaping Interpretations

2. Where does the speaker's **tone** change? What does the speaker imply in the last stanza about his own past and his prospects for the future?

3. When you paraphrase the second stanza, what are the meanings of the words *dominion* and *union* here, in your view? What attitude about people and nature does the use of these words imply?

4. What comparisons between the mouse and himself does the speaker make in the last two stanzas?

5. Read aloud some uses of **alliteration** in the poem. Are any of the poem's sound effects comical?

Connecting with the Text

6. How do you feel about the philosophy of the future expressed in lines 39–40 (the best-known lines of the poem)? How does your own experience reflect or contradict these lines? Look in your Reader's Log for ideas.

Extending the Text

7. Burns's use of **dialect** was a great departure from the elegant language of most eighteenth-century poets. What dialects are used in drama, songs, films, and fiction today? How do you feel about the use of dialect for realism?

Writer's Notebook

1. Collecting Ideas for a Reflective Essay

Have you ever felt fear, joy, wonder, or grief because of an animal? To remember incidents, create a time line of family pets since you were young. Photo albums may spark memories, too. To recall other animal encounters, cluster associations from the words *circus, outdoors,* or *camping.* And don't forget lowly animals like bugs and mice: *any* experience that raises lingering feelings or questions is a good topic. Save your notes for the Writer's Workshop on page 773.

Critical Writing

2. Frankly Speaking

Write an essay explaining your response to this poem, including its use of dialect. Be as frank as you want to be, but support your response with specific reasons and quotations from the poem.

Creative Writing

3. Creature Connections

Have another speaker address another creature—fly, cockroach, spider, moth. Imitate Burns, and imagine what the creature is thinking of the encounter. What connection does the speaker see between the creature and himself or herself?

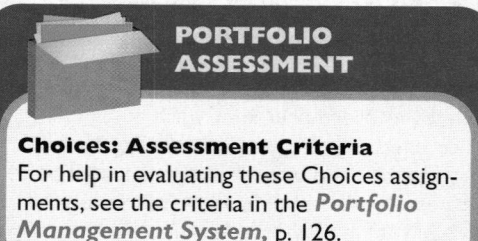

PORTFOLIO ASSESSMENT

Choices: Assessment Criteria
For help in evaluating these Choices assignments, see the criteria in the *Portfolio Management System,* p. 126.

STRATEGIES FOR INCLUSION

English Language Development Allow students to explore the informal language spoken today in the United States as they complete activity #2. Since students are to have a speaker address another creature, point out that they can have the speaker use any dialect they choose. English-language learners should work with a partner to encourage accuracy.

William Blake

(1757–1827)

By Courtesy of the National Portrait Gallery, London.

William Blake's life is not as "romantic" or "poetic" as the lives of Coleridge, Shelley, and Keats were. By all accounts, he was somewhat happily married to the same woman for much of his life. He never traveled, and he lived outside London for only three years (1800–1803). He began his artistic training at ten, when his

William Blake (detail) (1807) by Thomas Phillips. Oil on canvas (35¼″ × 17¼″).

father, a London shopkeeper, sent him to one of the best drawing schools. Apprenticed to an engraver at fourteen, Blake worked steadily at his craft as an engraver and as a professional artist throughout a long life, in good times and bad.

During his lifetime, Blake's work received very little attention, and a great deal of his poetry was never published in the sense of being "public." When his work was noticed, readers and viewers too often decided that it, and therefore Blake himself, was weird, confused, or mad. What we really know of Blake—from the enormous energy and variety of his poetry, paintings, drawings, and engravings—is that he was quite simply a great artist in the fullest sense.

A woman at a gathering is said to have asked Blake *where* he had come upon the scene he had just vividly described to her. "*Here, madam,*" he said, pointing his finger at his forehead. To paraphrase Blake, if we see with imagination, we see all things in the infinite. But if we see only with reason, we see only ourselves. "I know that this world is a world of imagination & vision," he wrote.

> I see everything I paint in this world, but everybody does not see alike. To the eyes of a miser, a guinea [a coin] is more beautiful than the sun, & a bag worn with the use of money has more beautiful proportions than a vine filled with grapes. . . . But to the eyes

of the man of imagination nature is imagination itself. As a man is, so he sees. . . . To me this world is all one continued vision of fancy or imagination.

One of the purposes of Blake's art was to change the way people "see" and thus to open up new worlds to them—"one continued vision" of what had once been ordinary and commonplace, but would become "imagination itself." One of Blake's most famous statements about his art (in the prophetic poem *Jerusalem*) is "I must create a system or be enslaved by another man's." But in creating the "system" for his own works, Blake was also aware that he himself could be trapped by it. The line that follows the one above is "I will not Reason & Compare: my business is to Create."

The history of Blake the poet cannot really be separated from that of Blake the visual artist. Not only did he provide illustrations for most of his poems, but he also printed much of his poetry himself (and sometimes only for himself), using engraving methods he himself had created. According to Blake's nineteenth-century biographer Alexander Gilchrist, "the poet and his wife did everything in making the book [*Songs of Innocence* (1789)]—writing, designing, printing, engraving—everything except manufacturing the paper; the very ink, or color rather, they did make. Never before surely was a man so literally the author of his own book."

A good deal of what Blake wrote other than his poems is cryptic and needs illumination from his art. But one characteristic of the man himself shines through clearly—the optimism sustained by his continuous joy in the "one continued vision" of his art. As one acquaintance described Blake, "He was a man without a mask; his aim single, his path straightforward, and his wants few; so he was free, noble, and happy."

WRITERS ON WRITING

In William Blake's copy of a volume of poetry by William Wordsworth, Wordsworth's explanation of the poetic process begins "The powers requisite for the production of poetry are, first, those of observation and description . . . 2dly, Sensibility." The marginal note in Blake's handwriting reads "One Power alone makes a Poet: Imagination, The Divine Vision." Blake's poetry is certainly visionary, and he makes no apologies for locating its source in the divine. "I am not ashamed, afraid, or averse to tell you what Ought to be Told," he writes in one letter, "That I am under the direction of Messengers from Heaven, Daily & Nightly."

PORTFOLIO ASSESSMENT

Portfolio Assessment
For help with self-assessment of reading skills, see the *Portfolio Management System,* pp. 48–49.

Into the Poems

Through the Poems

Beyond the Poems

Choices p. 655

- **Writer's Notebook:** Collect ideas for a reflective essay
- **Critical Writing:** Compare the final version of "The Tyger" to a draft
- **Critical Writing:** In an essay, analyze two poems
- **Creative Writing:** Write the opening or closing of a narrative from a child's viewpoint
- **Music:** Create background music for "A Poison Tree"
- **Art:** Illustrate a poem

Blake's Poems: Exploring Contraries

William Blake first published the *Songs of Innocence* in 1789. In 1794, these songs and the *Songs of Experience* were issued together in one volume, the title page promising a demonstration of "the two Contrary States of the Human Soul."

Blake conceived the first of these states, "Innocence," as a state of genuine love and naive trust toward all humankind, accompanied by unquestioned belief in Christian doctrine. Though a firm believer in Christianity, Blake thought that its doctrines were being used by the English Church and other institutions as a form of social control: to encourage among the people passive obedience and acceptance of oppression, poverty, and inequality. Recognition of this marks what Blake called the state of "Experience," a profound disillusionment with human nature and society. One entering the state of "Experience" sees cruelty and hypocrisy only too clearly but is unable to imagine a way out. Blake also conceived of a third, higher state of consciousness he called "Organized Innocence," which is expressed in his later works. In this state, one's sense of the divinity of humanity coexists with oppression and injustice, though involving continued recognition of and active opposition to them.

When reading the *Songs of Innocence* and, to a lesser extent, the *Songs of Experience,* it is important to remember that Blake intended them not as simple expressions of religious faith. The poems are demonstrations of viewpoints that are necessarily limited or distorted by each narrator's or speaker's state of consciousness.

The Ghost of Samuel Appearing to Saul (1800) by William Blake. Pen and ink with watercolor over graphite (12 9/16″ × 13 1/2″).

Rosenwald Collection, © Board of Trustees, National Gallery of Art, Washington, D.C.

646 THE ROMANTIC PERIOD

PROGRAM MANAGER

- **Planning Instruction** See Teaching Notes, *Teaching Resources B,* pp. 2–4, for objectives, summaries, and additional historical and biographical information for these poems.
- **Instructional Support** Before beginning the instructional lesson, see Graphic Organizers for Active Reading, *Teaching Resources B,* pp. 13–16, for Through the Poem activities.
- **Audiotaped Readings** To help less proficient readers or auditory learners through the lesson, use the Selected Reading, Audiocassette 1, Side B, in the *Audiovisual Resources Binder.*
- **Assessment** See Selection Test, *Test Booklet,* pp. 126–129.

Reading Focus

More Than Meets the Eye
While almost everyone agrees that "The Tyger" is one of the most powerful of Blake's *Songs of Experience,* there has been much disagreement about the meaning of the poem's central **symbol,** the tiger itself. One possibility is that the tiger represents a strong revolutionary energy that can enlighten and transform society—a positive but dangerous force Blake believed was operating in the French Revolution. The poem's speaker, at any rate, cannot comprehend such a startling energy, and can only wonder whether it is demonic or godlike.

The Tyger

William Blake

Tyger! Tyger! burning bright
In the forests of the night,
What immortal hand or eye
Could frame thy fearful symmetry?

5 In what distant deeps or skies
Burnt the fire of thine eyes?
On what wings dare he aspire?
What the hand dare seize the fire?

And what shoulder, and what art,
10 Could twist the sinews of thy heart?
And when thy heart began to beat,
What dread hand? and what dread feet?

What the hammer? what the chain?
In what furnace was thy brain?
15 What the anvil? what dread grasp
Dare its deadly terrors clasp?

When the stars threw down their spears,°
And watered heaven with their tears,
Did he smile his work to see?
20 Did he who made the Lamb make thee?

Tyger! Tyger! burning bright
In the forests of the night,
What immortal hand or eye,
Dare frame thy fearful symmetry?

17. stars . . . spears: a reference to the angels who fell with Satan and threw down their spears after losing the war in Heaven.

Quickwrite

READER'S LOG

What will the tiger in Blake's poem mean to you? Spend two minutes freewriting whatever comes into your mind when you think about the word *tiger.*

Background

To William Blake, who saw visions and devoted his life to worshiping God with his poetry and art, the world was filled with symbols. He believed that every object and event on earth had a mystical or spiritual meaning. He gave each symbol a rich assortment of meanings that even his contemporaries could not fully understand.

The Tyger (1793) by William Blake from his book *Songs of Innocence.* Hand-colored etching.
Library of Congress, Washington, D.C.

Into the Poem

Using BEFORE YOU READ p. 647

Reading Focus

Ask students to consider a natural phenomenon or feature they have experienced, such as a storm or a waterfall, that startled them with its energy and power. Then, encourage students to describe how the same vital energy may be seen in an animal.

Through the Poem

A. Reader's Response: First Thoughts

? What does the image of the tiger's "burning" in the first line suggest? [Sample responses: The images of fire in the poem hint at the animal's ferocity, power, or mystery.]

B. Literary Element: Apostrophe

? What is the effect of the speaker's addressing the animal directly in l. 4? [The use of **apostrophe** produces the illusion of facing a tiger, making the poem more immediate.]

C. Reader's Response: Shaping Interpretations

? Why does Blake allude to the war in heaven? [Sample responses: The allusion makes the animal seem to be a symbol of something; it adds greater meaning and drama to the poem.]

Making Meanings

First Thoughts

1. Students may say that the tiger's "burning" appeals to them the most, as it is a powerful theme. The wording conjures up a tiger's pattern of orange on black, along with its bright eyes.

Shaping Interpretations

2. The speaker repeatedly asks the tiger who created it; the implication is that the creator is even more daring and powerful—and perhaps even more dangerous—than the tiger.

3. God as creator is suggested in ll. 3 and 19–20. A demonic creator is implied in ll. 5–12. The fourth stanza suggests a blacksmith.

4. Enlightenment is suggested by the images of "deeps" and skies, the construction of the tiger, and mention of the angels. Violence is suggested by the tiger's burning and association with "dread" and "deadly terrors."

5. The phrase could describe the animal's markings, its graceful movement, or the balance of its physical appearance.

6. The word *could* is changed to *dare.* The word *dare* suggests something dangerous or forbidden.

7. The increasingly specific questions indicate that the speaker is in awe of the tiger's power yet fearful of its destructive capability.

8. Students will probably say that their understanding of the central symbol is deeper and that the tiger represents a powerful natural force that is both creative and destructive.

Connecting with the Text

9. Students may suggest lions, volcanoes, or sharks, which also embody fierce but beautiful power.

Extending the Text

10. **(Evaluation)** The poem's simple meter and rhyme and its vivid descriptions appeal to younger readers. To a young child, a tiger might be exciting and scary.

MAKING MEANINGS

First Thoughts

1. Which of the poem's images appeals most strongly to you? Why do you think it does?

Shaping Interpretations

2. What question does the poem's **speaker** ask the tiger over and over? What answer is implied?

3. Where in the poem does the speaker wonder if the tiger may have been created by God? What **imagery** tells us that the speaker also suspects that the tiger could be a demonic creation? What images suggest a human creator—like a blacksmith or a goldsmith?

4. What **imagery** suggests that the tiger could be a force of enlightenment? of violence?

5. What do you think is meant by the tiger's "fearful symmetry"?

6. The last stanza of the poem virtually repeats the first. In your view, what is the significance of the one word that is changed in the last stanza?

7. How does the poem testify to the simultaneous attraction to and repulsion from evil?

8. Review the Reader's Log entry you made before you read the poem. What do you think is the meaning of the poem's central **symbol,** the tiger?

Connecting with the Text

9. If you had to choose your own **symbol** for all the things represented by Blake's tiger, what would your symbol be? Why?

Extending the Text

10. Why do you think this poem has always appealed to children as well as to adults? What qualities might the word *tiger* connote to a young child?

Elohim Creating Adam
(1795–1805) by William Blake.

PRIMARY
Sources
A LETTER

Charles Lamb (1775–1834), perhaps the most accomplished Romantic essayist, uses a letter to sing his praises of William Blake.

"Blake is a real name . . ."

To Bernard Barton

Blake is a real name, I assure you, and a most extraordinary man, if he be still living. He is the Robert [William] Blake, whose wild designs accompany a splendid folio edition of the *Night Thoughts,* which you may have seen, in one of which he pictures the parting of soul and body by a solid mass of human form floating off, God knows how, from a lumpish mass (facsimile to itself) left behind on the dying bed. He paints in watercolors marvelous strange pictures, visions of his brain, which he asserts that he has seen. They have great merit. He has *seen* the old Welsh bards on Snowden—he has seen the beautifulest, the strongest, and the ugliest man, left alone from the massacre of the Britons by the Romans, and has painted them from memory (I have

Tate Gallery, London.

INTEGRATING THE LANGUAGE ARTS

Strategic Reading For students' first experience of either poem, have them try Guided Imagery. Read a poem by Blake aloud to the class as students listen with their eyes closed. Encourage students to use their five senses to imagine the scenes in the poem. After this first reading, have students share their sensory observations and then read the poem by themselves.

Speaking and Listening Concentrating on the tone of the speaker's voice will help students understand a particular poem's meaning. Invite students to read one of Blake's poems aloud in groups of three or four and to mimic the tone they find in the poem's language and style. As they take turns reading, have listeners write their reactions to the tone of each reading. Then, groups may discuss which tone seems particularly effective and why.

The Agony in the Garden (c. 1799–1800) by William Blake.
Tate Gallery, London.

seen his paintings), and asserts them to be as good as the figures of Raphael and Angelo, but not better, as they had precisely the same retrovisions and prophetic visions with himself. The painters in oil (which he will have it that neither of them practiced) he affirms to have been the ruin of art, and affirms that all the while he was engaged in his water paintings, Titian was disturbing him, Titian the III Genius of Oil Painting. His pictures—one in particular, the Canterbury Pilgrims (far above Stothard's)—have great merit, but hard, dry, yet with grace. He has written a catalogue of them with a most spirited criticism on Chaucer, but mystical and full of vision.

His poems have been sold hitherto only in manuscript. I never read them; but a friend at my desire procured the Sweep Song. There is one to a tiger, which I have heard recited, beginning:

> Tiger, Tiger, burning bright,
> Thro' the desarts of the night,

which is glorious. But, alas! I have not the book; for the man is flown, whither I know not, to Hades or a madhouse—But I must look on him as one of the most extraordinary persons of the age.

—Charles Lamb

Into the Poem

Using BEFORE YOU READ p. 650

Quickwrite
Tell students to try to recall stories that include lambs as characters or symbols. Students can use the stories to focus their thoughts about a lamb's characteristics. Have students compare their stories about lambs.

Through the Poem

A. Literary Element: Tone
? How do the first two lines differ in tone from those of "The Tyger"? [The tone of "The Lamb" is immediately gentle, simple, caring, and child-like; the question that begins "The Tyger" is fevered and clever, perhaps even fearful.]

B. Reader's Response: First Thoughts
? Whom do you imagine as the speaker in the poem, and whom does the speaker address? [Sample responses: Perhaps a child is speaking to a lamb; or perhaps a parent is talking with a young child about a lamb.]

C. Expansion
Lambs are associated with several important religious rituals. Just before the exodus from Egypt, the Israelites smeared the blood of a lamb on their doorposts so the angel of God "passed over" their homes and did not slay their firstborn sons (Exodus 12). This event is commemorated during the Hebrew tradition of Passover with a meal that includes the paschal lamb. In the Christian tradition, Jesus is sometimes identified with the paschal lamb.

BEFORE YOU READ
THE LAMB

Reading Focus
The Balance of Contraries
William Blake's poetry and art reflect his fascination with the Bible and his struggles to find answers to questions that profoundly disturbed him: Why do human beings do evil? Why do evil people sometimes prosper? Why does God allow innocent children to suffer?

One of Blake's early conclusions about the problem of good and evil is his idea that "Without contraries is no progression." "The Lamb" and "The Tyger" reflect what Blake termed "two contrary states of the human soul," both of which are as essential to humanity as joy and sadness, innocence and experience.

Quickwrite
If *tiger* connotes fierceness, mystery, and awe, what qualities does *lamb* suggest? Jot down some words and images that come to mind when you visualize a lamb.

Background
One of the *Songs of Innocence,* this poem has often been read as a statement of Christian faith. However, we know that Blake's other writings show Christ as an active fighter against injustice, not the "meek" and "mild" lamb—a common symbol for Christ—with which this innocent speaker identifies. The speaker's viewpoint is thus an incomplete representation of Blake's beliefs.

The Lamb
William Blake

A
Little Lamb, who made thee?
Dost thou know who made thee?
Gave thee life, and bid thee feed
By the stream and o'er the mead,°
5 Gave thee clothing of delight,
Softest clothing, wooly, bright;
Gave thee such a tender voice,
Making all the vales° rejoice?
Little Lamb, who made thee?
10 Dost thou know who made thee?

B
Little Lamb, I'll tell thee,
Little Lamb, I'll tell thee:

C
He° is called by thy name,
For He calls himself a Lamb.
15 He is meek, and he is mild;
He became a little child.
I a child, and thou a lamb,
We are called by his name.
Little Lamb, God bless thee!
20 Little Lamb, God bless thee!

4. **mead:** meadow.
8. **vales:** valleys.
13. **He:** Christ.

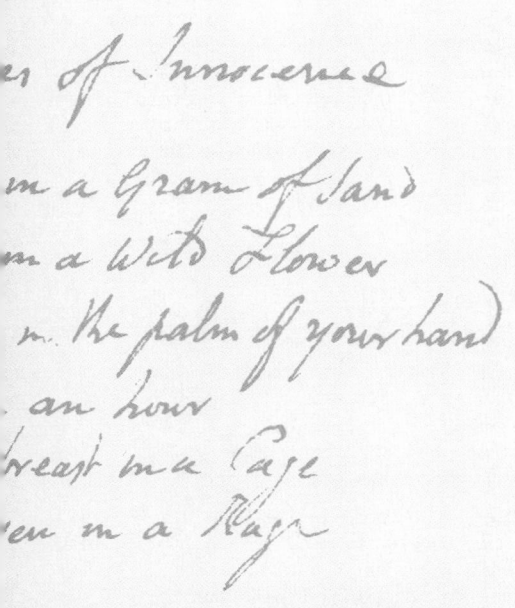

"Auguries of Innocence" by William Blake (transcribed c. 1807) from the Pickering or Ballads Manuscript.

The Pierpont Morgan Library, New York. MA 2879.

The Lamb (c. 1789–1794) by William Blake from his book Songs of Innocence and of Experience. Relief etching finished in pen and watercolor.

Fitzwilliam Museum, University of Cambridge, England.

MAKING MEANINGS

First Thoughts

1. Look back at your Reader's Log entry. How does the poem fit with your associations with the word *lamb*?

Shaping Interpretations

2. What did its creator do for the lamb in the first stanza?
3. How does the second stanza respond to the question posed in the first?
4. What do you know about the **speaker** of the poem?
5. How is the lamb both a literal object and a **symbol** in this poem?
6. Christ called himself a lamb because, like the Passover lamb slain to save the people of Israel, he sacrificed himself for the people. What might this imply about the fate of the young **speaker** in this poem?
7. How do you think the voice of the speaker in "The Lamb" is different from the voice of the speaker in "The Tyger"? Why do you think the questions in "The Lamb" get answers?

Connecting with the Text

8. How would you represent innocence? How would you represent experience? Why?

Challenging the Text

9. Blake wrote a two-line poem called "An Answer to the Parson" in which the parson (or preacher) asks, "Why of the sheep do you not learn peace?" The **narrator** replies, "Because I don't want you to shear my fleece." How would the narrator of this poem disagree with the narrator of "The Lamb"?

Making Meanings

First Thoughts

1. Students will probably say that the poem fulfilled their expectations by portraying a lamb as a sweet, meek creature.

Shaping Interpretations

2. The creator gave the lamb life, food, clothing (its fleece), and a gentle voice.
3. The speaker answers the questions raised in the first stanza.
4. The speaker of the poem is a child.
5. It is a lamb in the literal sense, but it is also a symbol of meekness, purity, and innocence.
6. The young speaker may have to make sacrifices.
7. The speaker in "The Lamb" is more sentimental, more childlike. Possibly the questions in the poem get answers because it is a poem of innocence, so answers seem easy to find, although they may be oversimplified.

Connecting with the Text

8. Students may suggest that babies or children, dolls or teddy bears, or flowers represent innocence. Experience might be represented by eyeglasses, beards, or graying hair.

Challenging the Text

9. **(Synthesis)** The narrator of "An Answer to the Parson" would object to this poem's simplicity and would probably say the narrator of "The Lamb" is naive and inexperienced in the real world.

PROFESSIONAL NOTES

Cultural Diversity William Blake has long been known as much for his painting as for his poetry, and many regard him as one of the greatest artists England has produced. He showed much artistic promise as a child, so he was apprenticed to an engraver. He was to earn his living for the rest of his life as an engraver, and it influenced his painting, which is characteristically bold in outline and vigorous in its modeling. Blake created his own engraving technique. Although experts still disagree about the particular methods of the techniques, it is known that Blake claimed the technique was revealed to him by his dead brother in a dream. His style of painting was also highly original, and it influenced a number of contemporary painters. The Swiss painter Henry Fuseli, a friend of Blake's, once remarked that Blake was a source of inspiration. Yet despite, or maybe because of, the originality of his genius, Blake and his wife often existed at a near-poverty level. That Blake had the time at all to produce some of his finest painting and poetry is due to the generosity and dedication of a handful of friends, patrons, and art collectors.

Into the Poem

Using BEFORE YOU READ p. 652

Background
Ask students to compare conditions in Blake's time with present conditions and to discuss whether society's attitudes and actions about poverty and homelessness have changed since the end of the eighteenth century.

Through the Poem

A. Exploring the Historical Period
During William Blake's lifetime, the population and the cost of living in England doubled while the average wage only increased by one-half. In this new age, the wife and children often earned the larger part of the family's poverty-level income. As for the job of sweeping chimneys, some of the dangerous horizontal flues the chimney sweeps cleaned were no larger than seven inches high and wide—the smaller the child, and therefore the younger, the better.

B. Literary Element: Symbolism
? What do the "coffins of black" in l. 12 suggest, besides literal death? [The dark confines of the chimney.]

C. Critical Reading: Analyzing Tone
? What is the tone of the last line? [Possible response: The last line is ironic; the best the boy has to look forward to, if he does his duty, is death.]

Metacognition What are some strategies for determining if something is ironic or not? [Exaggeration, contradiction, and a lack of unity between tone and subject matter are all good signs of irony.]

BEFORE YOU READ
THE CHIMNEY SWEEPER

Reading Focus
Heaven's Comforts
In Blake's London, buildings were heated by coal- or wood-burning fireplaces, so every house had at least one chimney that had to be cleaned regularly. Children were often employed as chimney sweepers because they could more easily fit into narrow chimneys. Some poor parents—as the second line of this poem indicates—sold their children to "masters" who managed crews of young chimney sweepers. The work was dirty and dangerous, and the children, poorly fed and badly clothed by masters concerned only with profits, were social outcasts. Blake's chimney sweeper, like the other speakers of the *Songs of Innocence,* is able to take comfort for the time being in his belief in a heaven that he has been taught awaits him after death.

Quickwrite

If you could cry out against an evil of our day—and get people to listen—which social problem would you choose? Why would you choose it?

Background
In the late 1700s, prices for food and housing increased sharply, and work became as scarce as food. William Blake saw starving people rooting through garbage, homeless families sleeping in doorways, and children begging on the streets or working at backbreaking jobs. Most members of the upper class believed that they deserved their worldly success, and that the poor must be innately evil, deserving the hunger and appalling conditions that they suffered.

Blake was said to be mad, not only because he saw visions, but also because his poems cry out against the social problems he saw all around him: the growing division between classes, the wretched working conditions, and child labor. No one should go hungry, he said, in a land as green and wealthy as England.

The Chimney Sweeper
William Blake

A When my mother died I was very young,
And my father sold me while yet my tongue
Could scarcely cry "'weep! 'weep! 'weep! 'weep!"°
So your chimneys I sweep, and in soot I sleep.

5   There's little Tom Dacre, who cried when his head,
That curled like a lamb's back, was shaved: so I said
"Hush, Tom! never mind it, for when your head's bare
You know that the soot cannot spoil your white hair."

And so he was quiet, and that very night,
10 As Tom was a-sleeping, he had such a sight!—
B That thousands of sweepers, Dick, Joe, Ned, and Jack,
Were all of them locked up in coffins of black.

And by came an Angel who had a bright key,
And he opened the coffins and set them all free;
15 Then down a green plain leaping, laughing, they run,
And wash in a river, and shine in the Sun.

Then naked and white, all their bags left behind,
They rise upon clouds and sport in the wind;
And the Angel told Tom, if he'd be a good boy,
20 He'd have God for his father, and never want° joy.

And so Tom awoke; and we rose in the dark,
And got with our bags and our brushes to work.
Though the morning was cold, Tom was happy and warm;
C So if all do their duty they need not fear harm.

3. 'weep . . . 'weep: the child's attempt at the chimney sweeper's cry of "Sweep! Sweep!"
20. want: lack.

OPTIONS FOR TEACHING

CROSSING THE CURRICULUM

History To help students understand the context of "The Chimney Sweeper," have them research working conditions at the time of the poem's writing. Discuss possible subjects (child-labor laws, labor uprisings, the rise of industrialization, or methods of manufacture) with the class, and then have students form small groups according to interest. Ask each group to prepare a brief presentation on its findings, and encourage a class discussion of the state of labor at the time.

Social Sciences Have students research some of the various aspects of culture during the Romantic period, including business practices, philosophy, society, and fashion. Invite students to create a time capsule that includes various items representative of the era.

THE LONDON SWEEP.

[*From a Daguerreotype by* BEARD.]

The London Sweep from a daguerreotype by Beard.

MAKING MEANINGS

First Thoughts

1. How does the last line of the poem affect you? Why does it have this effect?

Shaping Interpretations

2. What do you learn about the **speaker** in the first stanza? How does he try to reassure Tom Dacre in the second stanza?

3. How does the angel reassure Tom in his dream? What moral lesson does the speaker draw from Tom's dream?

4. How does Tom's dream of heaven contrast with the actual condition of his daily life?

5. Why would the angel's promise that Tom (and presumably any "good" boy) can "have God for his father" be especially significant for the speaker?

6. Re-read line 3 carefully. How is the child's mis-pronunciation of the chimney sweeper's cry at once poignant and **ironic**? Is it possible, in your view, that the irony here establishes a certain **tone** for the entire poem? What is that tone?

7. Where in the poem does the speaker try to make the best of a degrading situation? Does his reasoning convince you?

Challenging the Text

8. Think about your Reader's Log entry. What do you think was Blake's goal in writing this poem? Do you think the last stanza of the poem is effective in meeting Blake's purpose, or could it be strengthened? Why?

WILLIAM BLAKE 653

Making Meanings

First Thoughts

1. Students will probably say the bitter irony of the last line has a chilling effect; it may shock, anger, incite, or sadden students.

Shaping Interpretations

2. The speaker's mother died when he was young, and his father sold him off as a chimney sweeper. The speaker tries to comfort Tom by saying that Tom will be spared the discomfort and ugliness of sooty blond hair.

3. The angel promises Tom that if he is good, he will have God as his father and will always be happy. The speaker draws the lesson that if he performs his duties, he will be rewarded eventually.

4. In the dream, Tom is clean and care-free. In reality, he lives in filthy, depressing, and difficult conditions.

5. The speaker needs a father because his own sold him off.

6. The speaker means to say "sweep," but he says "'weep," ironic because it conveys his miserable condition. This irony establishes a tone that pervades the poem: In trying to describe his comforts and hopes, the speaker unknowingly reveals a clear picture of his suffering.

7. In the second and the last stanzas, the speaker tries to rationalize the misery of the situation, but his arguments are hardly convincing.

Challenging the Text

8. **(Evaluation)** Blake's purpose was to expose the degrading conditions and despair of innocent children in the practice of chimney sweeping. The last stanza of the poem may be subtle, but the irony of its trusting naiveté effectively outrages the reader.

PROBLEM SOLVING/CRITICAL THINKING

Constructive Use of Anger In "A Poison Tree" (p. 654), Blake examines the problem of letting anger fester. Have students work in small groups to produce a list of positive ways to release or express angry energy. On the chalkboard, jot a few ideas to start the process, including such suggestions as running laps or writing letters.

Into the Poem

Using **BEFORE YOU READ** p. 654

Reading Focus

Ask students to define the word *grudge* and to share their opinions on what the outcome usually is when someone holds a grudge. Students may provide examples from other literature, films, or TV shows.

Through the Poem

A. Literary Element: Parallelism

? What is the effect of the series of sentences all beginning with "I"? [The sentences seem emphatic and perhaps childish in their repetition and simplicity.] Are there other examples of parallel sentence structure later in the poem? [Sentences starting with "And."]

B. Reader's Response: First Thoughts

? Do you agree with the poet's remark in l. 4 about the danger of hidden anger? Why or why not? [Sample responses: Yes, the only way to get rid of one's anger is to express it. Or no, sometimes it hurts someone's feelings to express anger, so it may be better to wait until the anger is diffused.]

Making Meanings

First Thoughts

1. Students may say they would emphasize the last line, because it brings the poem to a conclusion and contains an important twist.

Shaping Interpretations

2. The two methods are expressing anger or suppressing it, thus letting it grow. The speaker's foe dies in the last stanza.
3. The poison tree is the symbol of the speaker's growing anger.

BEFORE YOU READ
A POISON TREE

Reading Focus
The Fruits of Anger
What happens to anger that is allowed to grow and fester, anger that is nurtured with our own deceit? In this poem, one of Blake's *Songs of Experience,* the speaker describes what happens when anger is left unresolved. As you read, think about how anger is symbolized in the poem—and about other ways it's portrayed.

Quickwrite

In your Reader's Log, describe the ways anger can be destructive, not only to the object of the anger, but also to the person feeling it.

A Poison Tree

William Blake

> I was angry with my friend:
> I told my wrath, my wrath did end.
> I was angry with my foe:
> I told it not, my wrath did grow.
>
> 5 And I watered it in fears,
> Night and morning with my tears;
> And I sunned it with smiles,
> And with soft deceitful wiles.°
>
> And it grew both day and night,
> 10 Till it bore an apple bright;
> And my foe beheld it shine,
> And he knew that it was mine,
>
> And into my garden stole
> When the night had veiled the pole:
> 15 In the morning glad I see
> My foe outstretched beneath the tree.
>
> **8. wiles:** cunning tricks.

A Poison Tree (1794) by William Blake from his book *Songs of Experience.* Relief etching with watercolor and pen additions.

Private Collection.

MAKING MEANINGS

First Thoughts
1. If you were reading this poem aloud, which part of the last stanza would you emphasize? Why?

Shaping Interpretations
2. What two ways of handling anger are mentioned in the poem? What actually happens to the speaker's foe in the last stanza?

3. What is the "poison tree"?
4. Who are the victims in the poem?
5. How is the speaker both good and evil?
6. What is the **theme** of the poem?
7. What do you make of Blake's allusion to forbidden fruit in the third stanza?

OPTIONS FOR TEACHING

ASSESSMENT TOOL

Check Test: Short Answer
1. How does the speaker describe the tiger? [Burning eyes, symmetrical, fearful.]
2. Who are the lambs in "The Lamb"? [A lamb, a child, Christ.]
3. How does the tone of "The Tyger" differ from that of the tone of "The Lamb"? [The tone of "The Tyger" is intense, awed, fearful, excited; the tone of "The Lamb" is quiet, gentle, childlike, and strangely ironic.]
4. Who is the speaker in "The Chimney Sweeper"? [A child working as a chimney sweeper.]
5. What makes the tree grow in "A Poison Tree"? [Fears, tears, smiles, and wiles.]

Connecting with the Text

8. Does the poem describe ways that anger can be destructive that are similar to the ways you wrote about in your Reader's Log? Explain your response.

LANGUAGE AND STYLE

Parallelism

When words are arranged in balanced, similar structures, they are said to be **parallel.** Blake was especially fond of parallelism, and the use of this device contributes to the childlike simplicity on the surface of his poems.

For example, much of "The Tyger" consists of questions that start with the word *what*. Sometimes the questions occupy one or two full verses; occasionally, Blake varies them so that one verse is split into two or three questions.

1. What examples of parallelism can you find in "The Lamb"?

2. How does Blake use parallelism in "The Chimney Sweeper"?

3. How does "A Poison Tree" use parallelism to link ideas from stanza to stanza?

CHOICES: Building Your Portfolio

Writer's Notebook

1. Collecting Ideas for a Reflective Essay

The occasion for a reflective essay may be a work of literature, or even a passage from some work of literature. Did any of Blake's poems give you food for thought? Do you feel strongly about something he wrote? Check your Reader's Log notes as well: Did you note anything in your log that might give you an occasion to write about? Pick an "occasion" and freewrite for five minutes on the topic. Save your notes for the Writer's Workshop on page 773.

Critical Writing

2. Second-Guessing Blake

In an early draft of "The Tyger," Blake inserted the following lines after the third stanza:

> Could fetch it from the furnace deep
> And in thy horrid ribs dare steep
> In the well of sanguine wee
> In what clay and in what mold
> Were thy eyes of fury rolled

This early version also lacked the fifth stanza of the final version. In a brief essay, compare and contrast the early draft and the final version of "The Tyger," commenting on why you think Blake made the changes he did.

Critical Writing

3. Below the Surface

In a brief essay, explain how both "The Tyger" and "The Lamb," although they seem to be simple lyrics, are concerned with very profound questions of religion. Comment on the **structure** and **imagery** of the two poems.

Creative Writing

4. Down the Chimney

Based on details in "The Chimney Sweeper," write the opening or closing paragraphs of a prose narrative (fiction or autobiography) that tells about the childhood of a chimney sweeper in Blake's London.

Music

5. To Read By

Working with a small group, create original music or find a piece of classical or popular music that would serve as background for a reading of "A Poison Tree."

Art

6. Be Like Blake

Part of Blake's genius is the illustrations he created for his poems. Be like Blake: Create an illustration for any one of Blake's poems you've read.

PORTFOLIO ASSESSMENT

Choices: Assessment Criteria
For help in evaluating these Choices assignments, see the criteria in the *Portfolio Management System,* pp. 127–128.

---

4. The speaker's foe is the victim, although the speaker can also be seen as a victim of anger allowed to fester and possess him.

5. The speaker is good in expressing anger to the friend but evil in allowing the anger for the foe to grow.

6. The **theme** of the poem is that unexpressed anger builds up and releases itself destructively.

7. The tree may be similar to the tree in the Garden of Eden.

Connecting with the Text

8. Students will probably have described in their logs how built-up anger can lead to tragedy.

Language and Style
Possible Answers

1. The use of couplets and two stanzas as a call-and-response, the repetition of questions (ll. 1–2, 9–10) and answers (ll. 11–12, 19–20), the identification between the speaker and lamb and creator are all examples of parallelism in "The Lamb."

2. In "The Chimney Sweeper," parallelisms include the use of couplets, the inclusion of two contrasting settings, and the division of lines at their midpoints grammatically or typographically (ll. 1–3, 5–7, 9–11, 13–24).

3. The ideas in "A Poison Tree" are linked between stanzas by the balance of logical constructions: expansion on a theme (stanzas 1 and 2), and cause and effect (stanzas 2 and 3, 3 and 4).

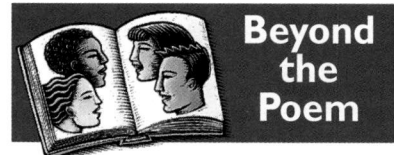

Beyond the Poem

Choices: Building Your Portfolio

1. **Writer's Notebook** Remind students to save their work. They may use it as prewriting for the Writer's Workshop on p. 773.

2. **Critical Writing** Write on an overhead transparency the early version of the poem as described so students can compare both poems before beginning this assignment.

William Wordsworth

(1770–1850)

William Wordsworth
(detail) (1842)
by Benjamin Robert Haydon.
Oil on canvas (49″ × 39″).
By Courtesy of the National Portrait Gallery, London.

Surveying Wordsworth's life can be like walking around a large statue, awed by its presence and puzzled by its apparent importance. Sometimes Wordsworth must have felt the same way. As he thought about his early life and re-created it in his autobiographical poem *The Prelude,* Wordsworth said he felt as if he were "two consciousnesses"—one remembering, the other one remembered.

When Wordsworth's mother died in 1778, he and his three brothers were sent to school at Hawkshead in the Lake District. His sister Dorothy, aged seven, had to live with relatives. When their father died in 1783, the children were placed under the guardianship of two uncles. William managed to get a degree from Cambridge in 1791, but had little interest in the few careers open to him—the main one being the Church—as an educated young man with no title, wealth, or head for business. In late 1791, he went to France to learn the language and, as it turned out, the bliss of being young in that time of birth and rebirth known as the French Revolution. Thus began a decade of painful growth, as he searched for and eventually found his vocation as a poet.

After he returned from France in 1792, Wordsworth was sickened by the war between France and England that began in 1793 and gradually became deeply disillusioned about his hopes for change. Late that year he went on a long walking tour. This experience—and the collapse of his radical hope of perfecting society—drove him back to poetry. Luckily, he was reunited with his sister Dorothy, who became a constant companion and inspiration.

In 1795, his fortunes began to change. He inherited some money from a friend, he and Dorothy took up residence in a rent-free cottage, and the poet Samuel Taylor Coleridge suddenly burst upon their lives. By June 1797, when he and Dorothy moved to a country house four miles from the village where Coleridge lived, Wordsworth had produced a good deal of new poetry, none yet published, including a play and some stark narratives. Coleridge and Wordsworth quickly became powerful influences on each other's work. *Lyrical Ballads* (1798) was the fruit of their friendship and mutual influence. During the following decade, Wordsworth wrote most of his best poetry.

But sometime after 1805, Wordsworth's poetic powers began to decline. By the time he was in his forties, his life was centered on his family; on his duties as a minor government official in the land of his boyhood, the Lake District, where he settled for good in 1799; and on his unflagging diligence as a poet. As his writing lost its energy and his political opinions grew more conservative, he became a kind of literary monument.

By the Victorian era, Wordsworth was the poet laureate (1843), a cartoon image of an old gentleman delighting in daffodils and butterflies while wandering about the Lake District. This image endured in part because the family suppressed the fact that in 1792 Wordsworth had fathered a child in France with a young woman he never married.

The distinguishing quality of Wordsworth's best lyric poetry comes from his simple delight in the nature of experience itself and in the mind's capacity to shape everyday experience into something lasting and poetic. Poetry, he wrote in the preface to *Lyrical Ballads,* is the "spontaneous overflow of powerful feelings"; but, he added, poems of lasting value are produced only by someone who has "thought long and deeply." The marriage of feeling and thought, as Coleridge recognized, made Wordsworth "the best poet of the age."

BEFORE YOU READ
LINES COMPOSED A FEW MILES ABOVE TINTERN ABBEY

Reading Focus

Nature's Power

William Wordsworth loved nature in all of its forms, especially the hills, lakes, trees, and waterfalls of his native England, and believed that nature made him a better person. Loving nature, he writes in this poem, quiets his mind, lightens his mood, guides him to kind acts, and brings him closer to God—all ideas Wordsworth expresses as though exploring his thoughts with a friend.

Quickwrite

Think of a scene in nature that you remember well and perhaps even daydream about because it brings back happy memories. Jot down a brief description of the place. How does this particular place make you feel?

Elements of Literature

Blank Verse

Wordsworth composed poetry in his head while he walked, "his jaws working the whoal time," recalled a country person who observed him. He spoke the words aloud to memorize them and to get the rhythm right. When Wordsworth was a child, under the direction of his father, he had memorized and recited long passages in **blank verse** from the works of Shakespeare and Milton. In "Tintern Abbey," Wordsworth uses for the first time a less formal, "conversa-

tional" blank verse that he had learned from Coleridge. The words and phrases he repeats give his poetry the flowing rhythm of natural speech.

> **B**lank verse is poetry written in unrhymed iambic pentameter. Each line contains five iambs; each iamb, or metrical foot, is an unstressed syllable followed by a stressed syllable.
>
> *For more on Blank Verse, see the Handbook of Literary Terms.*

Background

"Tintern Abbey" (which refers to the ruined abbey mentioned only in the title) is one of the most important short lyric works in English literature. A major step forward in Wordsworth's writing and a definitive statement of some of the Romantics' ideas, it has inspired and guided many poets since. The ease with which Wordsworth wrote it is therefore even more astonishing.

In July 1798, Wordsworth and his sister Dorothy went on a vigorous walking tour in southern Wales. Shortly after leaving the Wye River valley, Wordsworth, by his own account, began to compose this poem about revisiting the valley, concluding it "just as I was entering Bristol in the evening after a ramble of four or five

days. . . . Not a line of it was altered, and not any part of it written down till I reached Bristol. It was published almost immediately after."

Wordsworth had previously written two long descriptive poems and a few other descriptive lyrics, but nothing quite like this. He had been hard at work on the narrative ballads that make up *Lyrical Ballads* when he went on his tour. But he had learned something important from two poems by Coleridge, "This Lime-Tree Bower My Prison" and "Frost at Midnight": the use of a flowing blank verse and the easy maneuvering of the meditative poem.

This style was explored and refined in the many poems Coleridge and Wordsworth termed "conversation poems." First perfected by Coleridge, the conversation poem is usually a deeply personal meditation, seemingly spoken to a silent listener or to a loved one who is absent or asleep.

The apparent ease of its composition hides the art of "Tintern Abbey," evident even in the title, which asks us to imagine that these lines were poured out at the time the speaker returned to the Wye valley after five years' absence. The many days of composition on the way back to Bristol were spent creating a poem in which we seem to hear the easy, immediate utterance of what is going on in the heart and mind of the speaker.

PORTFOLIO ASSESSMENT

Portfolio Assessment For help with teacher assessment of reading skills, see the *Portfolio Management System,* pp. 54–55.

QUICK PLANNING GUIDE

Into the Poems

Author Biography p. 656
Before You Read p. 657, p. 663, p. 665, p. 667

Through the Poems

Beyond the Poems

Choices: Building Your Portfolio p. 669
- **Writer's Notebook:** Write about a significant moment
- **Critical Writing:** In an essay, analyze the progression of thought in a poem
- **Critical Writing:** In an essay, identify the Romantic in Wordsworth's poetry
- **Creative Writing:** Rewrite a poem, changing the gender of the speaker
- **Creative Writing:** Describe a city from afar
- **Technology and Literature:** Create a talk show where Wordsworth is interviewed.

Into the Poem

Using BEFORE YOU READ p. 657

Elements of Literature

Work with students to review as an example of **blank verse** the quotation that begins the Collection. Have students concentrate on the rhythm of the third line, and ask whether they can imagine blank verse that may be described as conversational.

Through the Poem

A. Language Note: Diction

? What words suggest the sounds the speaker hears? [*Rolling, soft, murmur*—all describing the sound of water.]

B. Literary Element: Imagery

? What images does Wordsworth use to "paint" the rural scene? [Dark sycamore trees, plots around cottages, green orchards, hedges, green farms, smoke wreaths.]

C. Critical Reading: Making Inferences

? How has the landscape not been like one in a "blind man's eye" in the speaker's absence (l. 24)? [Possible answer: The speaker has carried the memory with him and returned to it often in his imagination.]

D. Reader's Response: First Thoughts

? What scenes or remembrances bring you peace of mind? [Sample responses: A morning watching the waves of the ocean; watching the sun set over the mountains.]

Lines Composed a Few Miles Above Tintern Abbey

On Revisiting the Banks of the Wye During a Tour. July 13, 1798

William Wordsworth

Five years have past; five summers, with the length
Of five long winters! and again I hear
A These waters, rolling from their mountain springs
With a soft inland murmur.—Once again
5 Do I behold these steep and lofty cliffs,
That on a wild secluded scene impress
Thoughts of more deep seclusion; and connect
The landscape with the quiet of the sky.
The day is come when I again repose
10 Here, under this dark sycamore, and view
These plots of cottage ground, these orchard tufts,
Which at this season, with their unripe fruits,
Are clad in one green hue, and lose themselves
B 'Mid groves and copses.° Once again I see
15 These hedgerows,° hardly hedgerows, little lines
Of sportive wood run wild: these pastoral farms,
Green to the very door; and wreaths of smoke
Sent up, in silence, from among the trees!
With some uncertain notice, as might seem
20 Of vagrant dwellers in the houseless woods,
Or of some Hermit's cave, where by his fire
The Hermit sits alone.
                              These beauteous forms,
C Through a long absence, have not been to me
As is a landscape to a blind man's eye:
25 But oft, in lonely rooms, and 'mid the din
Of towns and cities, I have owed to them
In hours of weariness, sensations sweet,
Felt in the blood, and felt along the heart;
D And passing even into my purer mind,
30 With tranquil restoration:—feelings too
Of unremembered pleasure: such, perhaps,
As have no slight or trivial influence
On that best portion of a good man's life,
His little, nameless, unremembered acts
35 Of kindness and of love. Nor less, I trust,
To them I may have owed another gift,
Of aspect more sublime; that blessed mood,
In which the burden of the mystery,

14. copses: areas densely covered with shrubs and small trees.
15. hedgerows: rows of bushes, shrubs, and small trees that serve as fences.

Tintern Abbey (1834) by J.M.W. Turner.
British Museum, London.

658

OPTIONS FOR TEACHING

STRATEGIES FOR INCLUSION

Spatial Encourage students to draw the scene the poet describes in "Tintern Abbey," using text references to support the choices in their artwork. Have students compare and discuss differences in their drawings.

Less Proficient Readers Have students prepare to read "Composed upon Westminster Bridge" and "The World Is Too Much with Us" by imagining a city scene at two different times: at dawn on a weekend and in the middle of the afternoon rush hour on a weekday. Ask students to record their impressions of each scene on different halves of a piece of paper. Students can use their notes to better understand the contrast between the two poems.

In which the heavy and the weary weight
40 Of all this unintelligible world,
Is lightened:—that serene and blessed mood,
In which the affections° gently lead us on,—
Until, the breath of this corporeal° frame
And even the motion of our human blood
45 Almost suspended, we are laid asleep
In body, and become a living soul:
While with an eye made quiet by the power **E**
Of harmony, and the deep power of joy,
We see into the life of things.
                   If this
50 Be but a vain belief, yet, oh! how oft—
In darkness and amid the many shapes
Of joyless daylight; when the fretful stir
Unprofitable, and the fever of the world,
Have hung upon the beatings of my heart—
55 How oft, in spirit, have I turned to thee,
O sylvan° Wye! thou wanderer through the woods, **F**
How often has my spirit turned to thee!
   And now, with gleams of half-extinguished thought,
With many recognitions dim and faint,
60 And somewhat of a sad perplexity,
The picture of the mind° revives again:
While here I stand, not only with the sense
Of present pleasure, but with pleasing thoughts
That in this moment there is life and food
65 For future years. And so I dare to hope,
Though changed, no doubt, from what I was when first
I came among these hills; when like a roe°
I bounded o'er the mountains, by the sides
Of the deep rivers, and the lonely streams, **G**
70 Wherever nature led: more like a man
Flying from something that he dreads, than one
Who sought the thing he loved. For nature then
(The coarser pleasures of my boyish days,
And their glad animal movements all gone by)
75 To me was all in all.—I cannot paint
What then I was. The sounding cataract°
Haunted me like a passion: the tall rock,
The mountain, and the deep and gloomy wood,
Their colors and their forms, were then to me
80 An appetite; a feeling and a love, **H**
That had no need of a remoter charm,°
By thought supplied, nor any interest
Unborrowed from the eye.—That time is past,
And all its aching joys are now no more.
85 And all its dizzy raptures. Not for this
Faint° I, nor mourn nor murmur; other gifts

42. affections: feelings.
43. corporeal: bodily.

56. sylvan: associated with the forest or woodlands.

61. picture of the mind: primarily the picture in the mind, but also the picture the individual mind has of itself.

67. roe: deer.

76. cataract: waterfall.

81. remoter charm: appeal other than the scene itself.

86. faint: become weak; lose heart.

WILLIAM WORDSWORTH 659

E. Critical Reading: Identifying Main Ideas

? How do ll. 45–49 express one of the main ideas of the poem?
[Possible answer: The lines explain the transcendental feeling that nature brings the speaker, the feeling the poem explores.]

F. Literary Element: Personification

? What personification implies that the river and the speaker share similar habits? [They both are wanderers in the forest.]

G. Critical Reading: Finding Details

? How does the speaker describe his past relationship with the landscape? [The speaker believes he once was more like a man fleeing something he dreads than a man who came to find the things he loves.]

H. Literary Element: Blank Verse

Remind students to listen for the downbeats, remembering that Wordsworth associated poetic rhythm with his footsteps.

Technology Tip

The Complete Poetical Works of William Wordsworth is available on the World Wide Web as part of Columbia University's Project Bartleby. The URL is **http://www.cc.columbia.edu/acis/bartleby/wordsworth/**. *You may want to preview any Internet activity that you suggest to students. Because these resources are sometimes public forums, their content can be unpredictable.*

STRATEGIES FOR INCLUSION

Interpersonal Have students in pairs try to describe to one another the most beautiful scene they have ever beheld. After they exchange descriptions, ask students to discuss the difficulties they encountered in relating the significance of their scene to someone who had not experienced it. Invite partners to make a list of strategies they would use if they had such a task again. Have the class re-read "Tintern Abbey" or "Composed upon Westminster Bridge" to see if the poet uses any of the techniques students have listed. ☞

? What is the change in the speaker's attitude toward nature that is described in ll. 88–93? [He no longer feels as recklessly passionate about nature, but in exchange he has found a deeper understanding of both nature and humanity.] Tell students that l. 91 is often quoted.

B. Reader's Response: Shaping Interpretations

? How would you describe the speaker's attitude toward nature now? [Sample responses: He appreciates nature and feels it nurtures him. His attitude is calm and peaceful.]

C. Critical Reading: Analyzing Character

? Why does the speaker's sister remind him of himself in ll. 115–121? [She is seeing the scene for the first time with great joy and "wild eyes" that echo his former passion for nature.]

D. Literary Element: Tone

? What is the subtle shift in tone in the middle of l. 134? [The speaker shifts from recalling the role of nature in his own life to blessing his sister.]

Have followed; for such loss, I would believe,
Abundant recompense.° For I have learned
To look on nature, not as in the hour
90 Of thoughtless youth; but hearing oftentimes
The still, sad music of humanity,
Nor harsh nor grating, though of ample power
To chasten and subdue. And I have felt
A presence that disturbs me with the joy
95 Of elevated thoughts; a sense sublime
Of something far more deeply interfused,
Whose dwelling is the light of setting suns,
And the round ocean and the living air,
And the blue sky, and in the mind of man:
100 A motion and a spirit, that impels
All thinking things, all objects of all thought,
And rolls through all things. Therefore am I still
A lover of the meadows and the woods,
And mountains; and of all that we behold
105 From this green earth; of all the mighty world
Of eye, and ear—both what they half create,
And what perceive; well pleased to recognize
In nature and the language of the sense
The anchor of my purest thoughts, the nurse,
110 The guide, the guardian of my heart, and soul
Of all my moral being.
                              Nor perchance,
If I were not thus taught, should I the more
Suffer° my genial° spirits to decay:
For thou art with me here upon the banks
115 Of this fair river; thou my dearest Friend,°
My dear, dear Friend; and in thy voice I catch
The language of my former heart, and read
My former pleasures in the shooting lights
Of thy wild eyes. Oh! yet a little while
120 May I behold in thee what I was once,
My dear, dear Sister! and this prayer I make,
Knowing that Nature never did betray
The heart that loved her; 'tis her privilege,
Through all the years of this our life, to lead
125 From joy to joy: for she can so inform
The mind that is within us, so impress
With quietness and beauty, and so feed
With lofty thoughts, that neither evil tongues,
Rash judgments, nor the sneers of selfish men,
130 Nor greetings where no kindness is, nor all
The dreary intercourse° of daily life,
Shall e'er prevail against us, or disturb
Our cheerful faith, that all which we behold
Is full of blessings. Therefore let the moon

88. **recompense:** repayment.

113. **suffer:** allow.
genial: creative.

115. **my dearest Friend:** Wordsworth's sister Dorothy.

131. **intercourse:** dealings; social contacts.

(Opposite) *Landscape* (detail) (19th century) by Patrick Nasr

Roy Miles Gallery, London.

OPTIONS FOR TEACHING

INTEGRATING THE LANGUAGE ARTS

Strategic Reading Have students read one of Wordsworth's poems in small groups of three or four. Ask each student in a group to read the poem once aloud and then share with the group what he or she finds meaningful and interesting in the work. Students in each group should take notes on their fellow members' comments and then discuss their findings with the class.

Language and Style Have students examine the ways that Wordsworth organizes the broad themes and rolling descriptions of "Tintern Abbey" into structures like paragraphs, with breaks in between. Challenge students to find key words that unify each "paragraph" and the main idea, if there is one, of each. For example, the first section of the poem is held together by the repetition of words such as *again* (ll. 4, 9, 14), and the main idea of the section is the idea of return after many years.

Writing: Poems Challenge students to write their own poems on the importance of a single moment in the past, using as a model a passage of "Tintern Abbey" or "Composed upon Westminster Bridge." Suggest that students use blank verse to compose a poem of twelve to twenty lines in a conversational tone, or challenge students to write their description as a sonnet.

135   Shine on thee in thy solitary walk;
     And let the misty mountain winds be free
     To blow against thee: and, in after years,
     When these wild ecstasies shall be matured
     Into a sober pleasure; when thy mind
140   Shall be a mansion for all lovely forms,
     Thy memory be as a dwelling place
     For all sweet sounds and harmonies; oh! then,
     If solitude, or fear, or pain, or grief,
     Should be thy portion, with what healing thoughts
145   Of tender joy wilt thou remember me,
     And these my exhortations!° Nor, perchance—
     If I should be where I no more can hear
     Thy voice, nor catch from thy wild eyes these gleams
     Of past existence—wilt thou then forget
150   That on the banks of this delightful stream
     We stood together; and that I, so long
     A worshipper of Nature, hither came
     Unwearied in that service: rather say
     With warmer love—oh! with far deeper zeal
155   Of holier love. Nor wilt thou then forget
     That after many wanderings, many years
     Of absence, these steep woods and lofty cliffs,
     And this green pastoral° landscape, were to me
     More dear, both for themselves and for thy sake!

E

146. exhortations: strong advice.

F

158. pastoral: relating to herds or flocks, pasture land, and country life.

CROSSING THE CURRICULUM

Architecture To help students imagine the scene in "Tintern Abbey," have them research an abbey or castle ruins in Great Britain. Encourage students to choose different structures in different areas of the country and to present their observations, with a picture or drawing, to the class. Ask students to focus on the atmosphere of the site and its effect on a viewer.

Industrial Arts To expand on the themes of "Composed upon Westminster Bridge" (p. 665) and "The World Is Too Much with Us" (p. 667), ask students to research the topic of urban design by comparing two cities: one that seems well designed and one that has had difficulty adjusting to growth or combating urban decay. If they wish, students may also investigate the history of a city's

design; Washington, D.C., would be an interesting subject. Encourage students to use their research to develop suggestions for future city planners.

Making Meanings

First Thoughts

1. Students' responses will vary but may include a picture of the young poet's enthusiasm, his current meditative view of the landscape, or his evaluation of his sister's excitement.

Reviewing the Text

a. He hears the murmur of the river and sees steep cliffs, a quiet sky, a sycamore tree, orchard thickets, and hedgerows that mark the boundaries of small farms.

b. Unlike a blind man, the speaker has seen the landscape firsthand and has been able to experience it emotionally and reorganize it through memory.

c. He has lost the purity and innocence of his youth. He is older and responds to nature meditatively rather than spontaneously.

d. He sees passion in the "shooting lights / Of thy wild eyes" (ll. 118–119)—her spontaneous joy in nature.

e. The meter is unrhymed **iambic pentameter,** or **blank verse.** Instances of run-on lines include ll. 3, 9, 17, 34, 39, 45, 47.

Shaping Interpretations

2. The reference is to the mystery of an "unintelligible world."

3. The speaker describes his boyhood days, his later youth, and his present maturity.

4. The gifts are understanding and maturity. He continues to perceive nature with joy but not with the rapture of the past.

5. The speaker sees in his sister a picture of his own past. The sister's role of intermediary between speaker and nature may seem contrived to some students who see the poem as essentially a personal reverie; those who accept the circumstances in the speaker's return to the scene will see the sister's presence as natural.

6. The speaker recollects a more passionate time in the tranquillity of the present moment.

7. The speaker looks back on his past with a mixture of awe and regret, on his present with a meditation on his losses and gains, and on his future with hope.

8. The speaker realizes that the scene means even more to him now, because of his deeper appreciation

---

MAKING MEANINGS

First Thoughts

1. What single **image,** feeling, or idea in this poem do you think you will remember longest? Why?

Shaping Interpretations

2. What do you think is meant by "the burden of the mystery" (line 38)?

3. What three stages of his growing up does Wordsworth describe (lines 73–111)?

4. What "gifts" (line 86) and "abundant recompense" (line 88) does the **speaker** believe he has received for his "loss" (line 87)?

5. What role does the speaker's sister play in this poem? Does Dorothy's presence here seem contrived or natural? Why?

6. How is this poem an example of Wordsworth's idea that poetry "takes its origin from emotion recollected in tranquility"?

7. What would you say is Wordsworth's attitude toward his past, his present, and his future?

> ### Reviewing the Text
>
> a. What does the speaker hear and see in the first verse paragraph (lines 1–22)?
>
> b. Why are these "beauteous forms" not, for the speaker, "As is a landscape to a blind man's eye" (line 24)?
>
> c. What has the speaker lost since he first "came among these hills" (line 67)?
>
> d. What does the speaker see in his "dear Sister" that makes him more aware of what he "was once" (line 120)?
>
> e. Scan the **meter** of the poem. Find three examples of **run-on lines** that keep the poem from sounding mechanical and singsong.

8. Summarize and comment on the significance of the speaker's conclusion, beginning with line 102. Have you ever been in a situation where you had to come to terms with losing part of your past? How did you resign yourself to its loss?

9. Notice the stanza structure in "Tintern Abbey." Why do you think Wordsworth ends one stanza and begins a new one, often even in the middle of a line?

Connecting with the Text

10. Imagine that you were away for five years from the place you described in your Reader's Log, just as Wordsworth was away from Tintern Abbey. How do you think you might have changed in that time?

LANGUAGE AND STYLE

Reading Aloud: Verse Paragraphs

Wordsworth's **blank verse** is best read aloud in the long, rolling movements of his verse paragraphs, or groups of lines that develop a main idea. These verse paragraphs mark five major transitions of thought in "Tintern Abbey."

In the first paragraph (lines 1–22), the poet unifies his long clauses by repeating the word *again* in lines 4, 9, and 14. The function of the paragraph is to establish the time interval between the speaker's visits to the Wye (five years) and to describe the scene. In the second paragraph (lines 22–49), Wordsworth makes his thought easier to follow by repeating a phrase ("blessed mood," lines 37 and 41).

Slowly and carefully read aloud another verse paragraph of "Tintern Abbey," observing the punctuation and **run-on lines.** Then, write a few sentences stating whether or not you think that the verse paragraph you have chosen is unified by one main idea. If so, state the main idea.

---

and the presence of his sister, and he hopes she will also remember. Students may share departures or losses and means of coping such as letter-writing or reminiscing. *Remind students to choose a situation they would not mind sharing with others.*

9. With each new idea, the stanza changes, so that one main idea unifies each stanza.

Connecting with the Text

10. Students may agree with Wordsworth that they would be more sober and calmly appreciative of their return.

Language and Style

Possible Answers

Main ideas: The second verse paragraph describes the value of the speaker's memories. The third verse paragraph reiterates this importance, even if the memories are not as significant as the speaker believes. The fourth gives the speaker's history of dealings with nature. The fifth paragraph returns to the presence of the speaker's sister and the landscape as experienced through her.

Reading Focus

Lucy—Love and Loss
This graceful lyric, written during Wordsworth's stay in Germany in 1799, is one of five poems called the "Lucy poems" that were published together in 1800 in the expanded *Lyrical Ballads*. As in other "literary mysteries" where we suspect a hidden connection between the writer's life and his work, there has been much speculation about who "Lucy" was. "She lived unknown," but because Wordsworth had immortalized her in his poems, Lucy became famous throughout nineteenth-century England as an enduring symbol of the universal experience of love and loss. Still, in reading this poem it is much more important to stress the workings of the speaker's imagination than it is to think about Lucy's identity. What does the speaker make of Lucy, and how does he reveal his feelings?

Quickwrite

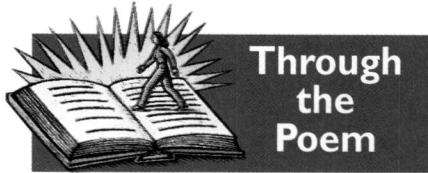

Alfred, Lord Tennyson, who was Wordsworth's contemporary, wrote that it is ". . . better to have loved and lost / Than never to have loved at all." What do you think? Write a brief response to Tennyson's words.

(Opposite) *The Shadowy Stream* (detail) (19th century) by Samuel Palmer.
Victoria and Albert Museum, London.

Profile (late 19th or early 20th century) by Odilon Redon.

Christie's, London.

She Dwelt Among the Untrodden Ways

William Wordsworth

She dwelt among the untrodden ways
   Beside the springs of Dove,°
A Maid whom there were none to praise **A**
   And very few to love:

5 A violet by a mossy stone
   Half hidden from the eye!
—Fair as a star, when only one **B**
   Is shining in the sky.

She lived unknown, and few could know
10   When Lucy ceased to be; **C**
But she is in her grave, and, oh,
   The difference to me!

2. Dove: river in central England.

WILLIAM WORDSWORTH 663

Into the Poem

Using **BEFORE YOU READ** p. 663

Reading Focus

Challenge students to think of other examples of "literary mysteries," such as the person addressed in some of Shakespeare's sonnets. Then, ask students to discuss whether the air of mystery distracts the reader or merely adds another level of possible meaning to a great work.

Through the Poem

A. Reader's Response: First Thoughts

? What does this phrase suggest? [Sample responses: For some reason, she was not striking or admired; or perhaps there were not many people around to appreciate her, as the place she lived was "untrodden."]

B. Literary Element: Figures of Speech

? What do the comparisons in ll. 5–8 suggest about the woman who is the subject of the poem? [The violet metaphor suggests that the woman is unaffected and shy, and the star simile suggests that she has a rare beauty and lives alone. The huge difference in scale between the two hints at a strong emotion.]

C. Critical Reading: Expressing an Opinion

? Does the information in ll. 10–11 come as a surprise? [Most readers will probably say that the past tense and mournful tone of the poem prepared them for the news of the woman's death.]

OPTIONS FOR TEACHING

STRATEGIES FOR INCLUSION

Learners Having Difficulty Present students with a rearranged version of "She Dwelt Among the Untrodden Ways," which they must assemble into its original form. On the chalkboard or on a transparency, write the lines of the poem in random order. Work with students to reconstruct the text based on their understanding of the poem.

Invite students to further research the Lake District. Ask students to find maps, pictures, and travel descriptions of the area, as well as poetry inspired by its natural beauty. Challenge students to think of an area in the United States that has inspired so many writers. [Students might mention the mountains of New York that attracted early settlers, areas of Massachusetts as described by Thoreau and Emerson, or the California of both the Beats and naturalists.]

Making Meanings

First Thoughts

1. Students will probably ask who Lucy is. They can answer the question by making a hypothesis about Wordsworth's life (such as Lucy is Dorothy) or by understanding the character as existing only in the poem.

Shaping Interpretations

2. The word *difference* means that Lucy's death matters to the speaker; the speaker is sad.
3. He uses a metaphor of a violet and a simile of a star. The woman may have qualities of both, such as beauty, or the speaker may see differing facets to her personality.
4. The speaker loves Lucy. She lives alone, is not known, is little loved, but she is beautiful and pure. The information is enough to justify the speaker's concern.

Extending the Text

5. **(Synthesis)** Responses will vary, but students should mention a beautiful, pure, but solitary woman.

Challenging the Text

6. **(Synthesis)** Students' responses depend on their log entries, but they should recognize that the speaker would probably agree with Tennyson's evaluation of love and loss.

LITERATURE AND GEOGRAPHY

The "Frightful" Lake District

The novelist Daniel Defoe described the mountainous northwestern corner of his country as "the wildest, most barren and frightful in England." Most of his contemporaries shared his opinion of the Lake District, an area carved by Ice Age glaciers and transformed by volcanoes. The area was set apart even by its place names, which reflect the language of Norsemen who colonized the region: *thwaite* (meadow), *how* (hill), *tarn* (mountain lake), *beck* (stream) and *force* (waterfall). In the late eighteenth century, the haunting beauty of this area began to inspire writers and painters who embraced the Romantic ideal of wild, gothic landscapes. Writers were so drawn to the area's beauty (William Wordsworth wrote thirty-five poems on the Duddon Valley alone) that the literary group including Wordsworth, Samuel Taylor Coleridge, and Robert Southey became known as the Lake Poets.

Situated just below the southern border of Scotland, the Lake District is about thirty miles long and twenty-five miles wide, a small area to contain such geographic diversity. Here sits England's tallest mountain, Scafell Pike, towering over the countryside's lonely moorlands and bracken-covered slopes. The dramatic blue of the Irish Sea, Morecambe Bay, and the district's sixteen lakes contrasts with the intense greens of meadows and forests. Coleridge is credited with popularizing the pastime of "fell walking," which rewards walkers who brave the rocky, barren hills, or "fells," with scenic views of the countryside.

In 1802, Wordsworth's sister Dorothy could enjoy the peacefulness of "the gentle flowing of the stream, the glittering lively lake, [and] green fields without a living creature to be seen on them." Today, ironically, hordes of tourists flock to the region searching for the solitude of England's remotest corner.

Keswick in the Lake District, England.

MAKING MEANINGS

First Thoughts

1. What question immediately comes to your mind when you finish reading this poem? How would you answer the question?

Shaping Interpretations

2. What does "difference" in the last line of the poem refer to?
3. What two contrasting **figures of speech** does the speaker use to describe Lucy? How could one person be both of these very different things?

4. Why do you suppose Lucy is special to the speaker? What do you learn about Lucy? Is this information enough on its own to justify the speaker's concern for her?

Extending the Text

5. Does any popular song or film or television drama remind you of the woman in this poem? Why do you see this connection?

Challenging the Text

6. Review the Reader's Log entry you made before reading the poem. How do you think the speaker in the poem would respond to what you wrote?

CLASSROOM MANAGEMENT

Managing the Reader's Response Classroom Because students are often called on to form a response rather quickly, try posing Reader's Response possibilities before students have read a selection. Have them record an immediate reaction in their Reader's Logs, and encourage them to make alterations as they read but before they share their thoughts with the class.

CROSSING THE CURRICULUM

Geography To help students envision the cityscape in conjunction with the study of "Composed upon Westminster Bridge" (p. 665), invite students to research travel magazines, books, and travel guides in order to design a tour of London. Students should prepare an itinerary of places they believe visitors should go, perhaps supplemented by photos or illustrations, and write an accompanying script that shares interesting historical or cultural facts relevant to the proposed tour.

Reading Focus

The Effect of Imagination
Wordsworth chose to spend most of his time in the English countryside, especially in the beautiful Lake District where, he believed, Nature had made him a poet. First published in 1807, this sonnet shows that Wordsworth, the nature lover, could be moved not only by mountains and water-falls, but also by the majesty of a sleeping city, in this case London. But this is clearly a different London from the one where Blake's chimney sweeper lived and from the city known as the "great wen [boil]" that shocked many of Wordsworth's contemporaries because of its filth and poverty. It is London seen from a distance, and by a man happily journeying to see his daughter in France. Here, London's filth and poverty are disguised and transfigured by the poet's imagination.

Quickwrite

What are your impressions of a city at the start of the day? Freewrite on your ideas about a wakening cityscape.

Elements of Literature

Personification
Wordsworth breathes life into his sonnet by using **personification,** a kind of metaphor in which a nonhuman thing is talked about as if it were human. Look for details that personify the city, the sun, the river, even the houses of London.

Composed upon Westminster Bridge
September 3, 1802

William Wordsworth

Earth has not anything to show more fair:
Dull would he be of soul who could pass by
A sight so touching in its majesty:
This City now doth, like a garment, wear
5 The beauty of the morning; silent, bare,
Ships, towers, domes, theaters, and temples lie
Open unto the fields, and to the sky;
All bright and glittering in the smokeless air.
Never did sun more beautifully steep
10 In his first splendor, valley, rock, or hill;
Ne'er saw I, never felt, a calm so deep!
The river glideth at his own sweet will:
Dear God! the very houses seem asleep;
And all that mighty heart is lying still!

Westminster Bridge, London (detail)
(late 19th or early 20th century)
by Louis H. Grimshaw.

Into the Poem

Using BEFORE YOU READ p. 665

Elements of Literature

Ask students to evaluate the use of **personification.** How would it affect a poet's description of something? What kind of freedom does this figure of speech give the poet? [Students may say that personification allows the poet to react to an object with the same attention and sympathy the poet would give a person. Personification frees the poet's imagination from a mundane objectivity.]

Through the Poem

A. Reader's Response: First Thoughts

How do you envision a city clothed in morning yet "bare"? [Sample responses: Perhaps the sunlight makes the bare buildings look as if they wear a new garment; or perhaps the image is ethereal—the city is wearing the sheer cloak of a morning haze.]

B. Literary Element: Personification

What is "that mighty heart"? [Possible answers: The pulse, the activity of the city.]

C. Literary Element: Sonnet

Identify the type of sonnet and the rhyme scheme of this poem. [Italian or Petrarchan sonnet; *abba abba cdc dcd*.]

PROFESSIONAL NOTES

Cultural Diversity Students may work in small groups to explore various cultures' relationships with nature. Ask students to examine how cultures use special natural features like a certain mountain, river, or forest. Assign groups to research specific topics such as the River Ganges, Mount Fuji, and the Black Forest. Have students discuss their findings.

Critical Comment: *Lyrical Ballads* The critical reception of *Lyrical Ballads* was lukewarm at best. In 1799, the Reverend Charles Burney wrote that "Tintern Abbey" was "... poetical, beautiful, and philosophical: but somewhat tinctured with gloomy, narrow, and unsociable ideas of seclusion from the commerce of the world: as if men were born to live in woods and wilds, unconnected with each other."

Making Meanings

First Thoughts

1. Students may say that the city's "glittering" or "calm" most appeals to them; perhaps the images they mention will be particularly vivid to them. Students should describe specifically how the feature compares with their descriptions of a city.

Shaping Interpretations

2. The speaker notices ships, towers, domes, theaters, temples, smokeless air, the river, silence.
3. The city wears beauty "like a garment"; the houses sleep; the city's heart is still.
4. A heart cannot be alive and still.
5. The city's majesty and calm move the speaker most.

Connecting with the Text

6. Students' comparisons will vary but should refer to specific details, such as the city's beauty, its quiet, and its features.

MAKING MEANINGS

First Thoughts

1. What one feature of the city described in the poem appeals most to you? Why? How does this feature compare to the impressions you described in your Reader's Log entry?

Shaping Interpretations

2. What details and features of the city are noticed by the speaker?

3. What details **personify** the city?
4. What **paradox** do you find in the poem's last line?
5. What quality or characteristic of the scene seems to move the **speaker** most?

Connecting with the Text

6. Using a particular place or scene, compare the city that you know best, either from personal experience or from reading, to the London described in this poem.

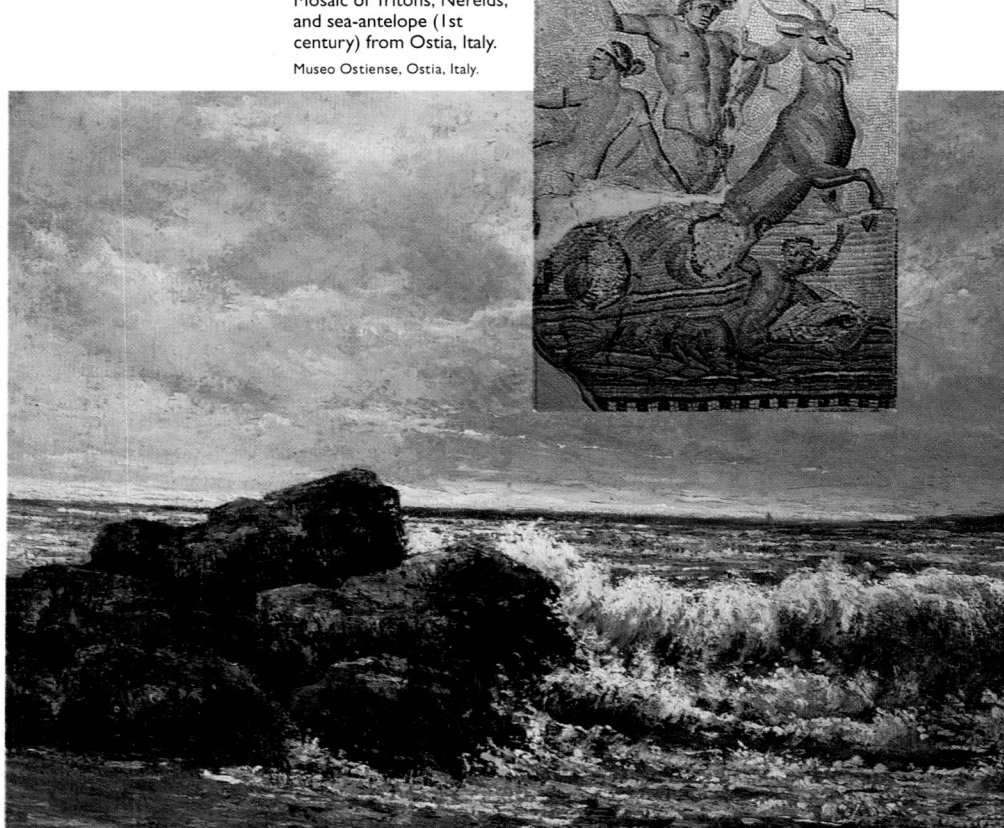

Mosaic of Tritons, Nereids, and sea-antelope (1st century) from Ostia, Italy.
Museo Ostiense, Ostia, Italy.

The Wave (detail) (19th century) by Gustave Courbet.

Pushkin Museum, Moscow.

666 THE ROMANTIC PERIOD

PROBLEM SOLVING/CRITICAL THINKING

Real-Life Romantic Applications
Encourage students to make a connection between Romantic concerns and environmental awareness by having students consider ways their town or city could improve its relationship with nature. Divide the class into groups of five, and encourage each group to imagine what the speaker of "The World Is Too Much with Us" (p. 667) would say about the area where they live. Then, have each group develop a plan that would put their neighborhood in closer touch with nature. Groups may present their proposals to the class and explain how their suggestions would work to make their area a prettier and healthier place. Suggestions could include anything from beautification projects to recycling programs. Each student should present part of the proposal and participate in the group's summary.

Reading Focus

Out of Tune

The "world" is usually thought of as the world of material objects—the world of money and status symbols, the world of power, competition, and ambition. In seeking out the pleasures of this material world, what could a person lose?

Quickwrite

Do you ever feel "out of tune" with the world you live in? In your Reader's Log, freewrite for a few minutes about times when you have felt that modern life was taking you away from something you cherished or toward something you felt was wrong.

Background

Wordsworth wrote this sonnet in 1807 at a time when he realized that his imaginative powers were beginning to fail. Although he continued to compose new works and to edit *The Prelude,* a long poem published after his death, he knew he was no longer responding to nature with the youthful passion that had inspired his earlier poems.

This sonnet also counterattacks the ferocious criticism that Wordsworth was receiving from conservative reviewers, especially from Francis Jeffrey in the *Edinburgh Review.* Jeffrey accused Wordsworth of using unpoetic language, but, even more, of conspiring against society, brooding needlessly over problems "instead of contemplating the wonders and pleasures which civilization has created for mankind." Many critics considered Wordsworth an enemy of progress because of his "idle discontent with the existing institutions of society" and his yearning for an earlier, less civilized time when people lived in harmony with nature.

Into the Poem

Using BEFORE YOU READ p. 667

Quickwrite

Remind students to choose a situation they would not mind sharing with others. Start students off by asking them to think of ways the world frustrates them or ways they disagree with the status quo.

Through the Poem

The World Is Too Much with Us

William Wordsworth

The world is too much with us; late and soon, **(A)**
Getting and spending, we lay waste our powers:
Little we see in Nature that is ours;
We have given our hearts away, a sordid boon!°
5   This Sea that bares her bosom to the moon;
The winds that will be howling at all hours,
And are upgathered now like sleeping flowers;
For this, for everything, we are out of tune; **(B)**
It moves us not.—Great God! I'd rather be
10   A Pagan suckled in a creed outworn;
So might I, standing on this pleasant lea,°
Have glimpses that would make me less forlorn;
Have sight of Proteus° rising from the sea;
Or hear old Triton° blow his wreathèd horn. **(C)**

4. sordid boon: foul gift. That is, the act of giving our hearts away is shameful.

11. lea: meadow.
13. Proteus (prō′tē·əs): in Greek mythology, a sea god who can change shape at will.
14. Triton (trī′tən): in Greek mythology, a sea god who controls the waves by blowing a conch shell.

A. Reader's Response: First Thoughts

? What do you think the first phrase means? [Sample responses: There are too many pressing problems, or we pay too much attention to material things.]

B. Critical Reading: Finding Cause and Effect

? What is the cause of people being "out of tune"? [Modern society's embracing materialism has diminished its ability to value nature.]

C. Reader's Response: Connecting with the Text

? How does the speaker's preferred vision of nature in ll. 13–14 relate to images in other poems you have read? [Sample responses: In Gray's "Elegy" (p. 601), the speaker also finds in nature meaningful, dramatic emblems; it is a recurring Romantic device.]

ASSESSMENT TOOLS

Self-Reflection Ask students to assess their involvement in group work by completing the following prompts:
I helped the group by _____.
One thing I would do differently next time is _____.
I would grade my participation as _____, because _____.

Check Test: Short Answer
1. In "Tintern Abbey," how have the speaker's attitudes toward nature changed since his youth? [He is calmer and not as passionate.]
2. Who is with the speaker in "Tintern Abbey"? [His sister.]
3. To what does the speaker compare the woman in "She Dwelt Among Untrodden Ways"? [A violet and a star.]

4. What is the attitude of the speaker toward the city in "Composed upon Westminster Bridge"? [The speaker praises the city's beauty.]
5. What is the "world" in "The World Is Too Much with Us"? [Commerce, industry, urban living.]

Making Meanings

First Thoughts

1. Students may answer that one of ll. 1–4 or 8 is the most important, since these lines contain direct statements of the main ideas.

Shaping Interpretations

2. By "world," the speaker means the material, commercial world. He thinks people have given up too much for material things; by "hearts," he means the most important things in our lives, such as nature. Students may or may not agree with the speaker, but they should support their answers with specific references to the poem's arguments.

3. The speaker believes that the pagan world at least understood the significance of nature in people's lives, as evidenced by their worship of gods of nature.

4. The sonnet is divided in half by the dash in the middle of the ninth line. The first part is stately, restrained, illustrative; the second half is angry, exasperated, demonstrative.

5. Possible response: Humanity has given up its most important gift, nature, in return for the so-called progress of civilization, although even the ancient pagans knew how important nature was to humanity.

Connecting with the Text

6. Students' responses will vary. If they disagree with Wordsworth, they should refer to the specific lines where they feel his argument fails; for example, they may take issue with l. 4. If they agree with Wordsworth, they should outline why nature is so important in making people happier and less materialistic; for example, they may point out how rejuvenating it is simply to watch the ocean.

Extending the Text

7. **(Evaluation)** Students may identify with the speaker in the poem, having related in their Reader's Logs how materialism and progress have affected them adversely.

First Thoughts

1. What do you think is the most important line in this poem? Explain your choice.

Shaping Interpretations

2. What does the speaker mean by the "world"? What do you think the speaker means when he says "We have given our hearts away" (line 4)? Do you agree with the speaker?

3. Why does the speaker think he might prefer to live in the days of the pagans?

4. What are the two parts of this sonnet? How is the **tone** of the second part different from the tone of the first part?

5. Write one sentence that, in your opinion, states the **theme** of the poem.

Connecting with the Text

6. What is your first reaction to the speaker's attack on modern life? Do you agree with Wordsworth that if people were "in tune" with Nature they would be happier and less materialistic? Why or why not?

Extending the Text

7. How are the ideas about materialism and progress expressed in this poem relevant to today's world? (Think about your Reader's Log entry.)

ELEMENTS OF LITERATURE

Romantic Lyrics

The poems in this section represent a number of lyric forms—from variations of traditional sonnet schemes and experiments with the ode to the distinctive Romantic lyric form, the "meditative poem."

The **sonnet** was popular in Romantic poetry as a traditional type of occasional poem written on an important subject, public or private. Milton, for example, had used the sonnet in this way. But for the Romantics the sonnet was also used for experimen-

tation. Coleridge's early sonnets, called "effusions" to excuse their looseness, helped him create the meditative poem. Keats's sonnets shaped the stanza forms for his odes. The main sonnet form was the **Italian,** or **Petrarchan,** sonnet, composed of an octave (eight lines) and a sestet (six lines). But the Romantics also used the **Shakespearean** sonnet of three quatrains and a couplet.

The Romantic **ode** was a self-conscious use of a classical form that had been brought into English literature in the seventeenth and eighteenth centuries by the writers John Dryden and Thomas Gray. The structure of the Romantic ode was certainly influenced by the Romantic meditative poem. Sometimes a poem in the manner of an ode was called a "hymn." An ode has two distinctive features: (1) It uses heightened, impassioned language, and (2) it addresses some object. The ode may speak to, or **apostrophize,** objects (an urn), creatures (a skylark, a nightingale), and presences or powers (intellectual beauty, autumn, the west wind). The speaker first invokes the object and then creates a relationship with it, either through praise or through prayer.

The Romantics developed the **meditative poem** and passed it on to later generations of poets. It is the best example of the "artful illusion" of the lyric in which we are to imagine a person speaking. The prototypes of the form—Coleridge's "This Lime-Tree Bower My Prison" and Wordsworth's "Tintern Abbey"—are in a flowing **blank verse** in which the stanzas are the equivalent of paragraphs, beginning and ending where sense, rather than strict form, dictates. The tone of these lyrics is much easier and more colloquial than the tone of the odes. Coleridge called one of his meditative lyrics a "conversation poem."

1. As you read these lyric poems, think about their various speakers: the bard or prophet who speaks about matters of great concern; the wanderer who happens upon something that turns out to be revealing; the traveler who returns from far-off lands with his tale to tell; and the aesthete or lover of poetic experiences who finds beauty in all the details of life. Which of the speakers do you see in each of Wordsworth's poems?

2. What are examples of a colloquial tone in "Tintern Abbey"?

Elements of Literature

Possible Answers

1. Speakers in Wordsworth's poetry include each type mentioned.

2. Examples of a colloquial **tone** in "Tintern Abbey" include conversational words such as "perhaps" (l. 31) and "I trust" (l. 35), the speaker's honest, self-critical attitude, and run-on lines such as ll. 3, 9, and 34.

PROGRAM MANAGER

Application and Reinforcement
For reinforcement of the elements of literature introduced in this lesson, see **Transparency 8.3** in the *Audio-visual Resources Binder.*

CHOICES: Building Your Portfolio

Writer's Notebook

1. Collecting Ideas for a Reflective Essay

In your Reader's Log entries for "Tintern Abbey" and "The World Is Too Much with Us," you've already uncovered significant moments in your life. Now explore one incident more fully by interviewing yourself with these questions: *Where and when did the event take place? Who was with you? Exactly what happened?* (Even if you sat still, describe it.) *How would you express what you learned about life?* Save your work for the Writer's Workshop on page 773.

Critical Writing

2. Following the Thought

In a brief essay, trace and comment on the progression of thought in "Tintern Abbey." Be sure to analyze the significance of the poem's division into verse paragraphs.

Critical Writing

3. Typecasting Wordsworth

In an essay, identify the themes and images of Wordsworth's poems that you would classify as typically Romantic. Use at least one example from each of the poems you have read.

Creative Writing

4. Changing the Gender

Rewrite "She Dwelt Among the Untrodden Ways" with a woman as the speaker, writing about a man she has loved and lost. Keep the meter and tone of the poem, and some of the original words if you like. What title will you give your poem?

Creative Writing

5. A City as a Person

Write a prose description of a city or town that a speaker is seeing from afar. Use personification to characterize your city or town. You might open with Wordsworth's first line: "Earth has not anything to show more fair."

Technology and Literature

6. Wordsworth Live!

Imagine that Wordsworth, through the miracle of time travel, is a talk show guest in our century. With others, create a radio talk program in which one student plays the part of Wordsworth, answering questions about humanity's relationship to nature called in by the audience. Have other students in the class act as the show's audience.

Composed upon Westminster Bridge (1802) by William Wordsworth. Ms. 47864, fol. 30v. Printer's copy of the 1802 sonnet, wrongly dated 1803 by Wordsworth.

By permission of the British Library, London.

WILLIAM WORDSWORTH 669

PORTFOLIO ASSESSMENT

Choices: Assessment Criteria For help in evaluating these Choices assignments, see the criteria in the *Portfolio Management System,* pp. 129–130.

Beyond the Poems

Choices: Building Your Portfolio

1. **Writer's Notebook** Remind students to save their work. They may use it as prewriting for the Writer's Workshop on p. 773.

2. **Critical Writing** Encourage students to paraphrase the separate verse paragraphs as a guide for their essays. Have students think of how the poem would read if it were not arranged in paragraphs.

3. **Critical Writing** Have students organize their notes in a cluster. In the center, students may write a brief definition of *Romantic.* (If they have difficulty beginning, tell them to free-associate words that describe the poets they have read so far in this Collection.) Then, radiating from the central definition, students should place examples of Wordsworth's poetry that fit the definition. Remind students to include at least one example from each poem.

4. **Creative Writing** Ask groups to begin by brainstorming qualities that a female Romantic poet would praise in a man. Group members may then compare those qualities with the ones Wordsworth emphasizes about Lucy and consider how the poem would change if the new qualities were substituted. Group members may rewrite the poem individually after adequate discussion and then rejoin their groups to compare their efforts.

6. **Technology and Literature** Have students prepare their talk programs beforehand, meeting in groups of four or five to decide on questions and answers for their "guest." Each group should choose one member to act the role of Wordsworth and one member to play the host of the talk program. The other members of the group may join the audience and "call in" their questions to Wordsworth when the host gives them their cue.

Russia

Alexander Pushkin

(1799–1837)

The Russians revere, re-read, and quote Pushkin as the English do Shakespeare. A master of verse, drama, and fiction, Pushkin is usually called the father of modern Russian literature. Even in his early works, influenced in style by the Russian Romantics and French neoclassicists, he focused on Russian settings and folk tales. As his genius matured, he developed a new realism in characterization and a vigorous, simple, and natural language unlike any in Russian literature. Born into an old aristocratic (though not wealthy) family in Moscow, Pushkin also had an African great-grandfather—Abram Hannibal, a general under Peter the Great—whose ancestry he cherished.

Through both his father's extensive library and his beloved nurse's old tales, Pushkin steeped himself in imaginative literature. He gained fame early and took a government post, but his radical political verse and wild living resulted in years of exile from St. Petersburg—and the beginning of his masterwork *Eugene Onegin,* a verse novel. Pushkin, like one of his own Romantic characters, was fatally wounded in a duel over his wife's honor, fought under

Alexander Pushkin (19th century) by W. Troponin.

circumstances that remain partly mysterious today. While his wife was a great flirt, the evidence against her came in anonymous letters that some thought were motivated by a political vendetta against Pushkin.

(Map) Europe in 1815, after the Treaty of Vienna.
©Rand McNally.

BEFORE YOU READ
I HAVE VISITED AGAIN

Background

Though Alexander Pushkin was only in his mid-thirties when he wrote this poem, he had already led a tumultuous, often disappointing, yet brilliant life in nineteenth-century Russia. Like Wordsworth revisiting Tintern Abbey, Pushkin is returning to a dearly remembered place: his ancestral home near Pskov. Some dark memories hover too, however, for his previous visit was enforced—a two-year exile from St. Petersburg because of his revolutionary sympathies. Partly because Pushkin was a literary hero, Czar Nicholas I ended the exile—but not the close surveillance and censorship of Pushkin. As Pushkin writes this poem, he is again a "free" man working in the government in St. Petersburg, but now he hates court social life (which his young wife loves). He wants only to live in the country and write, but his repeated requests to leave have been denied.

Quickwrite

Project yourself ten years into the future, living in another place. What one setting from your life now, or from your childhood, would you be drawn to revisit? Describe it briefly, and explain why it has meaning for you.

An Autumn Lane (detail) (late 19th or early 20th century) by Edward Wilkins Waite.

By Courtesy of Burlington Paintings, London.

ALEXANDER PUSHKIN 671

Background

Ask students to consider how being exiled would change their views of the places in which they live. Would they attach more or less importance to a place? How would they feel about their home?

Quickwrite

Remind students to choose a situation they would not mind sharing with others. Encourage students to brainstorm a list of meaningful settings. Once they have narrowed this list, remind them to describe their choice with a variety of sensory details.

PROGRAM MANAGER

Selection Summary See **Teaching Notes,** *Teaching Resources B,* p. 6, for a summary of this selection.

A. Critical Reading: Making Inferences

? What does the phrase "obedient to life's law" reveal about the speaker's changes since he was last at this place? [Students will probably say the phrase describes the maturity and physical changes that have come with age, perhaps along with a decline in energy or a rebellious nature.]

I Have Visited Again

Alexander Pushkin

translated by **D. M. Thomas**

> . . . I have visited again
> That corner of the earth where I spent two
> Unnoticed, exiled years. Ten years have passed
> Since then, and many things have changed for me,
> **A** 5 And I have changed too, obedient to life's law—
> But now that I am here again, the past
> Has flown out eagerly to embrace me, claim me,
> And it seems that only yesterday I wandered
> Within these groves.
>
> 10   Here is the cottage, sadly
> Declined now, where I lived with my poor old nurse.
> She is no more. No more behind the wall
> Do I hear her heavy footsteps as she moved
> Slowly, painstakingly about her tasks.
>
> 15   Here are the wooded slopes where often I
> Sat motionless, and looked down at the lake,
> Recalling other shores and other waves . . .
> It gleams between golden cornfields and green meadows,
> A wide expanse; across its fathomless waters
> 20 A fisherman passes, dragging an ancient net.

Birch Trees (late 19th or early 20th century) by Kuinji Arkhip.
Tretyakov Gallery, Moscow.

672 THE ROMANTIC PERIOD

CONNECTING WITH "THE POWER OF THE IMAGINATION"

? How does "I Have Visited Again" allude to the power of the poet's imagination? [Lines 15–17 indicate that the place lets him imagine other places. The speaker imagines that the trees welcome him with human friendliness and have families. The poem is so descriptive that it allows readers to imagine the place easily.]

Along the shelving banks, hamlets are scattered
—Behind them the mill, so crooked it can scarcely
Make its sails turn in the wind . . .

                    On the bounds
25 Of my ancestral acres, at the spot
    Where a road, scarred by many rainfalls, climbs
    The hill, three pine trees stand—one by itself,
    The others close together. When I rode
    On horseback past them in the moonlit night,
30 The friendly rustling murmur of their crowns
    Would welcome me. Now, I have ridden out
    Upon that road, and seen those trees again.
    They have remained the same, make the same murmur—
    But round their aging roots, where all before
35 Was barren, naked, a thicket of young pines
    Has sprouted; like green children round the shadows
    Of the two neighboring pines. But in the distance
    Their solitary comrade stands, morose,
    Like some old bachelor, and round its roots
40 All is barren as before.

                    I greet you, young
    And unknown tribe of pine trees! I'll not see
    Your mighty upward thrust of years to come
    When you will overtop these friends of mine
45 And shield their ancient summits from the gaze
    Of passersby. But may my grandson hear
    Your welcome murmur when, returning home
    From lively company, and filled with gay
    And pleasant thoughts, he passes you in the night,
50 And thinks perhaps of me . . .

B

C

FINDING COMMON GROUND

Only one speaker appears in Pushkin's poem, but the lovely landscape he describes becomes practically a second character. The narrator greets new pine trees, recalls past encounters with wooded hills, and imagines his own grandchild engaging in the same conversations with nature. Working with a small group, and referring to your Reader's Logs, respond to Pushkin's description of his particular "corner of the earth." Here are some ideas you might focus on.

• Can an urban landscape evoke the kinds of feelings that Pushkin describes? Why or why not?

• In the Romantic period, many writers looked to nature to explain complex feelings about themselves or their culture. Have people in your group summarize the responses to nature in Percy Bysshe Shelley's "Ode to the West Wind" (page 734), John Keats's "Ode to a Nightingale" (page 755), or William Wordsworth's "Tintern Abbey" (page 658). How does Pushkin's relationship with nature compare with these?

B. Literary Element: Personification

? What does the speaker personify in these lines? [The speaker personifies the pine trees by speaking of the "murmur of their crowns" that would "welcome" him.] How do the characters of the trees differ? [The pair of trees are like a couple, with little saplings like children around their roots. The solitary tree is a "bachelor," and the ground around its roots is bare.]

C. Reader's Response: Challenging the Text

? Does the wish that ends the poem bring a fitting end to the poem— that is, does it somehow complete the thoughts of the speaker on a certain theme? [Sample responses: The speaker meditates on the effect of time on beauty, personality, and a remembered place; completing the poem with the wish that the beauty of the special place might remind someone of the speaker is a fitting end to such meditations. Then again, the poem ends without a sense of finality, leaving readers to wonder how things actually end.]

Finding Common Ground

Arrange students in groups of three or four so that the members have an opportunity to share their own views on the subject. Have the groups brainstorm answers for each question. Students should record their own thoughts as well as those of their fellow members. After students have brainstormed, they may then review the questions to discuss them in greater depth. Then, students may write their responses individually.

STRATEGIES FOR INCLUSION

INTEGRATING THE LANGUAGE ARTS

Musical Invite students to find music that expresses the same emotions they believe Pushkin is trying to express in "I Have Visited Again." Ask students to explain their choices as they share their musical selections with the class.

Writing: Diary Entry Challenge students to recast Pushkin's poem into a diary entry of his visit to the place he has written about. Encourage students to return to the text of the poem for details to include in the diary, such as the emotions Pushkin expresses and particular landmarks.

Coleridge always strove for a unity in his poetry and criticism, a unity that took many different forms. At the time he composed "Kubla Khan," Coleridge was enthusiastically searching through works of comparative religion and mythology for hints of a universal consciousness that manifested itself in all of humankind's higher thought. It was a search that continued through the *Biographia Literaria,* perhaps his greatest prose work. In this book, he expressed his opinion that poetry integrates contraries, such as the universal and specific, by uniting emotion and thought in imagination. His poetry is a beautiful record of putting his ideas to the test.

About his writing of "Kubla Khan," Coleridge explains: "In consequence of a slight indisposition, an anodyne had been prescribed, from the effect of which he fell asleep in his chair at the moment that he was reading the following sentence . . . 'Here the Khan Kubla commanded a palace to be built, and a stately garden thereunto: and thus ten miles of fertile ground were inclosed with a wall.' The author continued for about three hours in a profound sleep . . . during which time he has the most vivid confidence that he could not have composed less than from two to three hundred lines. . . . On awakening he appeared to himself to have a distinct recollection of the whole, and taking his pen, ink, and paper, instantly and eagerly wrote down the lines that are here preserved."

By Courtesy of the
National Portrait Gallery, London.

Samuel Taylor Coleridge

(1772–1834)

He was "the most wonderful man that I have ever known," said Wordsworth. The three poems that follow are only sketches in comparison to the full portrait of Coleridge, a man who was unquestionably a genius—poet, critic, journalist, essayist, and philosopher.

Samuel Taylor Coleridge (1792) by Peter Vandyke. Oil on canvas (21½" × 17½").

The youngest child of a village parson in southwestern England, Coleridge began his classical education at home and later continued it in London. When he arrived at Cambridge University in 1792, he already had a reputation for insatiable curiosity and wide reading, especially "out-of-the-way" books.

He left the university in 1794 without a degree, but with a commitment to a utopian colony in America. The experiment never materialized, but Coleridge gave radical lectures and married one of the prospective utopians. In 1796, he moved to a village in Somerset, with one book of poetry published but no prospects of a career. The next twenty months, which ended when he and Wordsworth went to Germany to study, were a time of miracles.

By June 1797, Coleridge had persuaded Wordsworth to live nearby. They became catalysts for each other, and the friendship helped Coleridge write most of his best poems. But, convinced that Wordsworth was "the best poet of the age," the poet in Coleridge hid in the "giant's" shadow ever after. After the year in Germany, Wordsworth returned in late 1799 to his native Lake District in northwestern England. Coleridge abandoned his own roots and followed (as he told a friend) "a great, a true poet—I am only a kind of metaphysician."

Despite this characteristic self-disparagement, Coleridge was, if only in brief periods, a "true poet" and, moreover, a profound philosopher. The middle period of his life, from 1800 to 1818, produced great achievements, most notably his lectures on Shakespeare and the *Biographia Literaria,* a work on philosophy and criticism disguised as his literary life and opinions. These works laid the foundations of twentieth-century literary theory.

But for Coleridge this period was also a time of pain and despair, memorialized in "Dejection: An Ode" (1802) and played out in the collapse of his marriage, his increasing addiction to opium, and his inability to discipline his wonderful mind.

Coleridge was a formidable figure, the "Sage of Highgate" as he came to be known after 1816, when he began to live in a rural suburb north of London with a kindly physician, Dr. James Gillman. Through his extraordinary conversation at his "Thursday evenings," he made a lasting impression as a genius on a stream of visitors, including the young American writer Ralph Waldo Emerson.

Genius means a "guiding spirit." Like the spirit of the South Pole in his *Rime of the Ancient Mariner,* Coleridge's guiding spirit was powerful in its effect on himself and others, but the man himself was lonely. The loneliness came from a lifelong need for the affection and support of others—a need that made the isolation of the writer's life often unbearable for him. His addiction to laudanum (a mixture of alcohol and opium), which began before he was thirty, was not controlled until his residence with the Gillmans.

As a thinker and as a writer, Coleridge was truly magnanimous, generous of his intellect and spirit, and devoted to the good of his fellow human beings as only a youthful utopian and son of a parson can be. The pity is that we must be content with sketches. The full portrait—and the breadth of the man's learning and interests—is too great for anyone to master. Anyone, that is, except someone like Coleridge himself.

674 THE ROMANTIC PERIOD

PORTFOLIO ASSESSMENT

Portfolio Assessment For help with teacher assessment of reading skills, see the *Portfolio Management System,* p. 61.

Reading Focus

Dream World

The poem you are about to read may challenge the limits of your imagination. Fantastical and strange, it is like a vivid yet incomprehensible dream. Coleridge, in fact, suggested that the poem came to him in a dream. And like a dream, the poem contains allusions to the deepest human desires—for pleasure, order, beauty, awe, even chaos and war. It also holds within it the moment when—upon awaking—the vividness and logic of the dream are suddenly, perhaps forever, lost to the dreamer. As you read, think about how dreams work and how the poem may imitate or reproduce that process.

A Dialogue with the Text

Take notes as someone reads this poem aloud to you. After the reading is over, describe at least one image that remains vividly in your mind. Jot down at least one question you'd like to ask the poet.

Background

An enchanting poem, "Kubla Khan" has a lyrical tone and manner that resembles a meditative ode. Full of mystery and dread, "Kubla Khan" was composed at about the same time (late 1797 or early 1798) as *The Rime of the Ancient Mariner*.

"Kubla Khan" has always intrigued readers, including Byron, who, after reading it in manuscript, apparently prevailed on Coleridge to publish it in 1816. At the time, Coleridge added a prose introduction that offered a rational account of the poem's origins. He claimed it was written in a reverie brought on by opium taken after he read a provocative passage in a seventeenth-century travel book. Coleridge contended that he woke from his dream and was interrupted by a visitor while composing the poem. Only a fragment of his original vision could be reproduced, he claimed.

Kubla Khan (1216–1294) was the grandson of Genghis Khan and was the Mongol conqueror of China.

Kublai Khan (Yüan Dynasty, China).

National Palace Museum, Taipei, Taiwan, Republic of China.

SAMUEL TAYLOR COLERIDGE 675

PROGRAM MANAGER

- **Planning Instruction** See Teaching Notes, *Teaching Resources B,* pp. 6–9, for additional historical and biographical information for these poems.
- **Instructional Support** Before beginning the instructional lesson, see

- Graphic Organizers for Active Reading, *Teaching Resources B,* pp. 23–25, for Through the Poem activities.
- **Audiotaped Readings** To help less proficient readers or auditory learners

through the lesson, use the Selected Reading, Audiocassette 2, Side A in the *Audiovisual Resources Binder*.

- **Assessment** See Selection Tests, *Test Booklet,* pp. 135–138.

Into the Poem

Using BEFORE YOU READ p. 675

Reading Focus

Discuss the subject of dreams with students. Ask them how dreams differ from reality, and write their ideas on the chalkboard. Then, have students consider what people mean when they speak of *dreams* as a word for "ambition," "absent-mindedness," or "foolish projects." Encourage students to examine a variety of different uses and connotations of the word *dream*.

Through the Poem

A. Cultural Connections

Kubla Khan was the emperor of China for more than thirty years. *Khan* is from a Turkic word meaning "prince" or "ruler."

B. Reader's Response: First Thoughts

? Do the measurements given in l. 6 make the poem's setting a realistic place? Why or why not? [Sample responses: The measurements do not alter the fantastical picture created by details such as "sacred river," "caverns measureless to man," and "sunless sea." Or the speaker seems to be telling the truth, if he can give specific measurements.]

C. Literary Element: Tone

? How does the tone change suddenly in ll. 14–16? [The land becomes demonic in addition to being exotic; the new tone is more sinister or haunting.]

Kubla Khan

Samuel Taylor Coleridge

(A) In Xanadu did Kubla Khan
A stately pleasure-dome decree:
Where Alph,° the sacred river, ran
Through caverns measureless to man
5   Down to a sunless sea.
(B) So twice five miles of fertile ground
With walls and towers were girdled round:
And there were gardens bright with sinuous rills,°
Where blossomed many an incense-bearing tree;
10 And here were forests ancient as the hills,
Enfolding sunny spots of greenery.

But oh! that deep romantic chasm which slanted
Down the green hill athwart a cedarn cover!°
A savage place! as holy and enchanted
(C) 15 As e'er beneath a waning moon was haunted
By woman wailing for her demon-lover!

3. Alph: probably a reference to the Greek river Alpheus, which flows into the Ionian Sea, and whose waters are fabled to rise up again in Sicily.

8. sinuous (sin′yo͞o·əs) **rills:** winding streams.

13. athwart a cedarn cover: crossing diagonally under a covering growth of cedar trees.

Palace of Kublai Khan at Peking (detail) (14th century).
Miniature from the *Livre des Merveilles*. Ms. Fr. 2810, fol. 37.
© cliché Bibliothèque Nationale de France, Paris.

676 THE ROMANTIC PERIOD

OPTIONS FOR TEACHING

INTEGRATING THE LANGUAGE ARTS

Strategic Reading Encourage students to work in pairs to paraphrase each sentence of the poem in language they understand. Have each pair of students read their paraphrased versions of the poem and discuss with the class any differences in interpretation. Remind them to return to the text for support when clarification is needed.

And from this chasm, with ceaseless turmoil seething,
As if this earth in fast thick pants were breathing,
A mighty fountain momently° was forced:
20 Amid whose swift half-intermitted burst
Huge fragments vaulted like rebounding hail,
Or chaffy grain beneath the thresher's flail:°
And 'mid these dancing rocks at once and ever
It flung up momently the sacred river.
25 Five miles meandering with a mazy° motion
Through wood and dale the sacred river ran,
Then reached the caverns measureless to man,
And sank in tumult to a lifeless ocean:
And 'mid this tumult Kubla heard from far
30 Ancestral voices prophesying war!
     The shadow of the dome of pleasure
     Floated midway on the waves;
     Where was heard the mingled measure°
     From the fountain and the caves.
35 It was a miracle of rare device,
A sunny pleasure-dome with caves of ice!

     A damsel with a dulcimer°
     In a vision once I saw:
     It was an Abyssinian° maid,
40   And on her dulcimer she played,
     Singing of Mount Abora.°
     Could I revive within me
     Her symphony and song,
     To such a deep delight 'twould win me,
45 That with music loud and long,
I would build that dome in air,
That sunny dome! those caves of ice!
And all who heard should see them there,
And all should cry, Beware! Beware!
50 His flashing eyes, his floating hair!
Weave a circle round him thrice,
And close your eyes with holy dread,
For he on honeydew hath fed,
And drunk the milk of Paradise.

19. momently: at each moment.

22. thresher's flail: heavy, whiplike tool used to thresh, or beat, grain in order to separate the kernels from their chaff, or husks.
25. mazy: like a maze; having many turns.

33. measure: rhythmic sound.

37. dulcimer: musical instrument that is often played by striking the strings with small hammers.
39. Abyssinian: Ethiopian. Ethiopia is in northeast Africa.
41. Mount Abora: probably a reference to John Milton's (1608–1674) *Paradise Lost,* in which Mount Amara, in Ethiopia, is a mythical, earthly paradise.

D. Literary Element: Simile
? What image of the earth do the similes in ll. 18 and 22 give the reader? [The comparisons to panting breath and "grain beneath the thresher's flail" show the earth in violent turmoil.]

E. Critical Reading: Finding Details
An inexplicable conflict arises that is reflected in words with contrary connotations, such as *pleasure* and *war* in ll. 30–31. What are some other contrary words? [Students will probably identify on one side terms such as *stately, sacred, bright,* and *holy* and on the other side words such as *sunless, savage, enchanted,* and *haunted.*]

Metacognition Do you find the vague conflict in the symbolism to be confusing? [Students may say it is not confusing if readers understand it as a dream, but it is confusing if a reader is trying to picture the place.]

F. Literary Element: Point of View
? What is the sudden change in point of view in ll. 37–38? [The speaker stops relating the story of Kubla Khan and starts to describe a personal vision.]

G. Reader's Response: Connecting with the Text
? In ll. 45–46, how is the speaker's desire to build the dome by means of music like the poet's creation of the poem? [Sample responses: The poet similarly creates a magical land with the music of poetry, but the poem seems incomplete, just as the dome seems impossible. Both dreams and music are tangible yet intangible—they have an ethereal quality.]

SAMUEL TAYLOR COLERIDGE **677**

Primary Sources

Challenge students to take five minutes to freewrite a description of a close friend or family member and to make the description as accurate as possible. Then, ask students if they had any problems in their descriptions capturing their subject's likeness. [Students will probably answer yes.] Why does a physical description so often fail to evoke a person? [The way a person appears depends on more than just looks but also gestures, body language, and the effect the person has on the observer.] Encourage students to discuss Dorothy Wordsworth's description with these ideas in mind. Students can imagine how Coleridge might appear to them, given the description in the letter.

Making Meanings

First Thoughts

1. Responses will vary. Striking images may include the sacred river, the floating dome, the damsel with a dulcimer, or the speaker's flashing eyes.

Shaping Interpretations

2. Within the chasm, turmoil seethes, and a fountain spews from the earth. In l. 30, ancestral voices warn of war.

3. He sees a damsel with a dulcimer. He imagines himself re-creating the pleasure dome in air.

4. The rhyme scheme in the first stanza is *abaabccdbdb;* it varies in the later stanzas. The meter is iambic with varying numbers of feet in each line. Lines 19, 27, and 50 provide a few examples of the poem's rich alliteration.

5. The speaker is an artist who wants to create beauty, just as Kubla Khan created the pleasure dome. The damsel is important to the speaker because she represents imagination, the power or "song" by which the speaker may rebuild the dome.

6. The speaker can rebuild the dome in the "air"—out of words and imagination. The dome represents some mysterious, miraculous creation.

7. Examples occur in ll. 14, 26, 47. The contrast is still unresolved in line 47, but the tone changes to a celebration of the opposites instead of a conflict between them.

Dorothy Wordsworth, William Wordsworth's sister, wrote this letter to Mary Hutchinson, the woman who would later become William's wife and Dorothy's closest and lifelong friend. Coleridge, by the way, returned Dorothy's admiration.

Dorothy Wordsworth Describes Coleridge

Racedown, June, 1797

. . . You had a great loss in not seeing Coleridge. He is a wonderful man. His conversation teems with soul, mind, and spirit. Then he is so benevolent, so good tempered and cheerful, and, like William, interests himself so much about every little trifle. At first I thought him very plain, that is, for about three minutes: he is pale and thin, has a wide mouth, thick lips, and not very good teeth, longish loose-growing half-curling rough black hair. But if you hear him speak for five minutes you think no more of them. His eye is large and full, not dark but gray, such an eye as would receive from a heavy soul the dullest expression; but it speaks every emotion of his animated mind; it has more of the "poet's eye in a fine frenzy rolling" than I ever witnessed. He has fine dark eyebrows, and an overhanging forehead. . . .

MAKING MEANINGS

First Thoughts

1. What **image** in the poem do you remember most vividly? (Check your Reader's Log notes.)

Shaping Interpretations

2. Why is the "deep romantic chasm" of line 12 called a "savage place"? What ominous note is introduced in the second stanza?

3. What does the **speaker** see in a vision in the third stanza? How does the speaker imagine himself in this stanza?

4. Describe the **rhyme scheme** and **meter** of the poem. What examples of **alliteration** add to the poem's music?

5. Who is the **speaker** of the poem? Compare him with Kubla Khan. Why is the "damsel with a dulcimer" important to the speaker?

6. How could the **speaker** "build that dome in air"? What do you think the dome **symbolizes**?

7. Where does the poet use contrasting **images**? In your view, does he offer any synthesis of these images in the concluding stanza?

8. Many ancient cultures regarded poets as seers who had a special relationship with the gods and thus were to be treated with special reverence. How may Coleridge be alluding to such beliefs in the closing lines of the last stanza?

Challenging the Text

9. Does the poem seem to you to bear out Coleridge's own description of it as a fragment? Or do you think that these lines were all the poet really intended to write? Why?

---

8. The people protect themselves against the sight of the prophetic poet by means of magic ritual (l. 51) and regard the poet with fear and awe, because he has "drunk the milk of Paradise."

Challenging the Text

9. **(Evaluation)** Students may believe the poem is a dream fragment, as it seems surreal and unfinished. However, they may be skeptical of the poet's explanation; the "fragment" has an intensity that would be difficult to sustain in a longer work.

BEFORE YOU READ

THIS LIME-TREE BOWER MY PRISON

Reading Focus

The Pleasures of Solitude

In a preface attached to this poem, Coleridge matter-of-factly notes the events that occasioned it: Shortly after the arrival of some friends at his rural cottage, Coleridge was accidentally scalded and could not walk during the rest of their stay. One evening, when his friends embarked on a long walk on the heath, Coleridge had to stay behind, resting in the garden.

We may imagine that Coleridge's poem was born out of his loneliness in the green enclosure while his friends enjoyed the spectacular countryside and each other's company. Yet, in the end, this is not a bitter poem. If *you* were in these circumstances, how would you console yourself? In what way might this time spent alone actually be valuable to you?

Quickwrite

Think about a time when you've been alone for a while, just thinking about the people who are important to you. How did your immediate surroundings affect your thinking? What kinds of places in today's world are especially suited to meditation? Jot down some of your ideas.

Background

It is curious that this poem, written in the summer of 1797, was not included in *Lyrical Ballads*. Quite likely, Coleridge's philosophic, religious side worried over the precision and orthodoxy of the revelation imagined in lines 37–43. Nevertheless, this is the first great Romantic-era meditative poem, a development from some similar but less successful poems that Coleridge had written in the preceding two years.

The "bower" was located between Coleridge's cottage in Nether Stowey, Somerset, a village at the foot of the Quantock Hills in southwestern England, and the home of Thomas Poole, a local tanner and Coleridge's loyal supporter. The "wide landscape" depicted in the poem can be seen today from the north side of the Quantocks looking out over the Bristol Channel, which separates England from southern Wales. The two tiny islands are still there, but the "fair bark" would probably be a motorboat today.

The "friends" referred to in the poem are William and Dorothy Wordsworth, who had recently taken up residence in the neighborhood, and the essayist Charles Lamb (1775–1834), a friend from Coleridge's London school days. Lamb's "strange calamity" refers obliquely to a horrible event that took place in September 1796 when Lamb's sister, Mary, in a temporary fit of insanity, killed their mother. Lamb made a long-wished-for visit to Coleridge's rural retreat in July 1797. It is to him that Coleridge dedicated this poem.

Study of Sky and Trees (1821) by John Constable.
By Courtesy of the Board of Trustees of the Victoria and Albert Museum, London.

SAMUEL TAYLOR COLERIDGE 679

Using **BEFORE YOU READ** p. 679

Quickwrite

Remind students to choose situations they would not mind sharing with others. Encourage students to imagine several scenarios to see how the setting affects their thinking. Ask them, for example, if a sunny day produces different thoughts than a cloudy afternoon or if the season sets the tone for their moods.

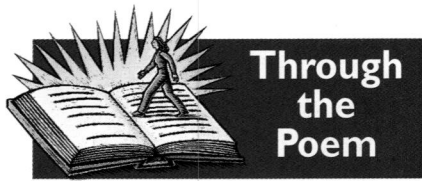

Through the Poem

A. Critical Reading: Finding Details

? What does the speaker feel he has lost? ["Beauties and feelings."] Point out to students that this motif is repeated throughout the poem, as the speaker recounts these beauties and feelings by remembering and imagining them.

B. Reader's Response: First Thoughts

? Why might the speaker never meet his friends again in this place? [Sample responses: Perhaps he is waxing philosophical, sensing his own mortality or theirs. Maybe something has changed dramatically—an upcoming move or a falling-out that affects the friendship.]

C. Reader's Response: Shaping Interpretations

? What is the effect of the exclamation marks in ll. 32–37? [Sample responses: He seems to command nature to perform for his friend. He seems excited by the workings of nature.]

This Lime-Tree Bower My Prison

Samuel Taylor Coleridge

Well, they are gone, and here must I remain,
This lime-tree bower my prison! I have lost
A Beauties and feelings, such as would have been
Most sweet to my remembrance even when age
5 Had dimmed mine eyes to blindness! They, meanwhile,
B Friends, whom I never more may meet again,
On springy heath,° along the hilltop edge,
Wander in gladness, and wind down, perchance,
To that still roaring dell,° of which I told;
10 The roaring dell, o'erwooded, narrow, deep,
And only speckled by the midday sun;
Where its slim trunk the ash from rock to rock
Flings arching like a bridge—that branchless ash,
Unsunned and damp, whose few poor yellow leaves
15 Ne'er tremble in the gale, yet tremble still,
Fanned by the waterfall! and there my friends
Behold the dark green file° of long lank weeds,
That all at once (a most fantastic sight!)
Still nod and drip beneath the dripping edge
Of the blue clay-stone.

20   Now, my friends emerge
Beneath the wide wide heaven—and view again
The many-steepled tract° magnificent
Of hilly fields and meadows, and the sea,
With some fair bark,° perhaps, whose sails light up
25 The slip° of smooth clear blue betwixt two isles
Of purple shadow!° Yes! they wander on
In gladness all; but thou, methinks, most glad,
My gentle-hearted Charles! for thou hast pined
And hungered after Nature, many a year,
30 In the great city pent,° winning thy way
With sad yet patient soul, through evil and pain
And strange calamity! Ah! slowly sink
Behind the western ridge, thou glorious Sun!
C Shine in the slant beams of the sinking orb,
35 Ye purple heath-flowers! richlier burn, ye clouds!
Live in the yellow light, ye distant groves!
And kindle, thou blue Ocean! So my friend
Struck with deep joy may stand, as I have stood,
Silent with swimming sense;° yea, gazing round
40 On the wide landscape, gaze till all doth seem

7. heath: open, uncultivated land covered with low vegetation.

9. dell: small, deep valley. (In the locale in which this poem was written, these dells are usually overgrown and therefore only speckled with sunlight.)

17. file: row.

22. tract: expanse. It is "many-steepled" because of the churches in the small villages that dot the landscape.
24. bark: small boat.
25. slip: strip.
26. purple shadow: two islands seen dimly in the distance.

30. pent: imprisoned. In Milton's *Paradise Lost,* Book IX, Satan leaves Hell and enters Eden, enjoying it "As one who long in populous city pent" enjoys the country.

39. swimming sense: blurred sight, presumably because of the different types of light playing on the landscape.

680 THE ROMANTIC PERIOD

OPTIONS FOR TEACHING

English Language Development
Encourage students to write down words or phrases they find difficult to imagine. Then, assign students to groups of three or four to work through and understand the phrases each member has noted.

STRATEGIES FOR INCLUSION

Visual Have students sketch the scene they imagine, using details from the poem to develop the drawing.

Advanced Coleridge's criticism and philosophy have been just as influential as his poetry. Have students read excerpts of Coleridge's literary criticism, such as his original reevaluation of Shakespeare. Ask students to write an evaluation addressing how such work might have been valuable.

INTEGRATING THE LANGUAGE ARTS

Strategic Reading Before beginning the poem, ask students to create a two-column page in their Reader's Logs. Invite students to write in the left-hand column the images they associate with the phrases "lime-tree bower" and "my prison." Ask them to write the images they associate with those same phrases in the right-hand column after reading the poem. Discuss as a class the differences.

Less gross than bodily;° and of such hues
As veil the Almighty Spirit, when yet he makes
Spirits perceive his presence.

                     A delight
Comes sudden on my heart, and I am glad
45 As I myself were there! Nor in this bower,
This little lime-tree bower, have I not marked
Much that has soothed me. Pale beneath the blaze
Hung the transparent foliage; and I watched
Some broad and sunny leaf, and loved to see
50 The shadow of the leaf and stem above
Dappling its sunshine! And that walnut tree
Was richly tinged, and a deep radiance lay
Full on the ancient ivy, which usurps
Those fronting elms, and now, with blackest mass
55 Makes their dark branches gleam a lighter hue
Through the late twilight: and though now the bat
Wheels silent by, and not a swallow twitters,
Yet still the solitary humblebee
Sings in the bean-flower! Henceforth I shall know
60 That Nature ne'er deserts the wise and pure;
No plot so narrow, be but Nature there,
No waste° so vacant, but may well employ
Each faculty of sense, and keep the heart
Awake to Love and Beauty! and sometimes
65 'Tis well to be bereft° of promised good,
That we may lift the soul, and contemplate
With lively joy the joys we cannot share.
My gentle-hearted Charles! when the last rook°
Beat its straight path along the dusky air
70 Homeward, I blest it! deeming its black wing
(Now a dim speck, now vanishing in light)
Had crossed the mighty orb's° dilated glory,
While thou stood'st gazing; or, when all was still,
Flew creeking° o'er thy head, and had a charm
75 For thee, my gentle-hearted Charles, to whom
No sound is dissonant which tells of Life.

41. less gross than bodily: less solid than a physical object. Here, Coleridge is trying to be philosophically precise.

62. waste: wasteland.

65. bereft (bē·reft′): deprived.

68. rook: crow.

72. orb's: sun's.

74. creeking: squawking.

D. Critical Reading: Making Inferences

? What might be the purpose of this change and the speaker's focus on the details of this setting? [Possible answer: The switch brings readers back to the starting point of the poem; the effect is that of enthralling listeners in a tale but then bumping them back into the present. The speaker points out that this spot, which he earlier calls a prison, holds much beauty.]

E. Critical Reading: Identifying Main Ideas

? Which lines seem to summarize the poem's theme? [Possible answer: Lines 60–64 summarize some of the poem's main ideas.]

F. Expansion

Charles Lamb, also an essayist in the Romantic era, was known for his wit and practical jokes. To his close friend Coleridge, whom he had known since boyhood, Lamb complained: "Don't make me ridiculous any more by terming me gentle-hearted in print, or do it in better verses. Substitute drunken dog, ragged-head, self-shaven, odd-eyed, stuttering, or any other epithet which truly and properly belongs to the gentleman in question." Coleridge addresses "my gentle-hearted Charles" three times in this poem.

PROFESSIONAL NOTES

Critical Comment: Coleridge Ask students to comment on the following excerpt from Coleridge's lecture "On Prose Style," delivered in 1818:

"In order to form a good style, the primary rule and condition is, not to attempt to express ourselves in language before we thoroughly know our own meaning: —when a man perfectly understands himself, appropriate diction will generally be at his command either in writing or speaking. . . . The source of bad writing is the desire to be something more than a man of sense, —the straining to be thought a genius. . . . If men would only say what they have to say in plain terms, how much more eloquent they would be!" 👉

First Thoughts

1. Responses will vary. Students may imagine fields or wilderness or the acreage around a country house.

Reviewing the Text

a. The speaker is sitting in a lime-tree bower while his friends have gone for a walk. They will see fields, villages, the sea, and two islands.
b. It is sunset. The passage of time is from daylight to nightfall.
c. He sees light playing on leaves, branches, and trees.
d. Charles Lamb.

Shaping Interpretations

2. The speaker feels trapped there while his friends walk. Other prisons are age (ll. 4–5) and the city (l. 30). Escape comes from awareness of love and beauty.
3. Lines 1–9 are mournful; ll. 32–43 are joyful; ll. 59–67 are contemplative; ll. 68–76 are comforting.
4. Because Charles has seen its beauty. Its squawking reminds one of the vigor of being alive.
5. Some sounds are harsh or sad (*tolls* suggests funereal bells), yet l. 76 implies paradoxically that all are harmonious reminders of life.
6. Nature frees and comforts those who open themselves to her beauty.
7. He suggests it nurtures the soul; in ll. 32–37, the speaker treats nature as if it could purposefully respond to his commands.

Connecting with the Text

8. Students may say nature is an escape, a solace; however, their experience with nature probably differs from that of Coleridge. They may be inspired by the beauty of cities or mountains.

Extending the Text

9. **(Synthesis)** Some students may disagree, thinking that not every natural spot is pretty; others, imagining vacant lots turned into gardens, may agree.

MAKING MEANINGS

First Thoughts

1. Describe what you saw as you read this poem. You may want to compare your mental images with those of classmates. Did the poem affect different readers in different ways?

Shaping Interpretations

2. In what sense is the bower a prison? What other prisons, literal or **figurative,** are alluded to in the poem? How does the poem suggest that one can escape from them?
3. How does the speaker's **tone** change in different sections of the poem? Look again at these four sections: lines 1–9, 32–43, 59–67, and 68–76.
4. Why does the speaker bless the "last rook" (lines 68–70)? What consolation does he suggest the rook brings?
5. How does the wording of the final line, especially the verb *tells,* suggest a **paradox,** or apparent contradiction?
6. Paraphrase what the speaker seems to have learned from his own experience. Look carefully at the statement beginning "Henceforth I shall know . . ." (line 59).
7. What qualities does the speaker attribute to nature in the poem? How is nature **personified**?

> **Reviewing the Text**
>
> a. What is the situation at the beginning of the poem? Describe the scene the speaker imagines his friends will see when they "emerge / Beneath the wide wide heaven" (lines 20–21).
> b. What time of day is it in lines 32–37? Can you tell approximately how much time passes in lines 43–59?
> c. Describe in your own words the scene the speaker sees from his bower in lines 43–59.
> d. Whom does the speaker address by name in the poem?

Connecting with the Text

8. What does nature mean to you? Does your idea of nature resemble the speaker's, or do you find comforting or awe-inspiring qualities in completely different surroundings? Look back at the notes you made in your Reader's Log.

Extending the Text

9. Think about the following lines from the poem:
   "No plot so narrow, be but Nature there,
   No waste so vacant, but may well employ
   Each faculty of sense, and keep the heart
   Awake to Love and Beauty!" (lines 61–64)
   Could you say this about the modern world? Why or why not?

Challenging the Text

10. Do you agree with the following statements from the poem?
    "Nature ne'er deserts the wise and pure." (line 60)
    "No sound is dissonant which tells of Life." (line 76)
    Explain your response for each line. Is it possible to agree with one and not the other?

ELEMENTS OF LITERATURE

Personification

In this poem Coleridge uses **personification,** a kind of figure of speech in which an abstract quality or nonhuman thing is endowed with human characteristics. But he doesn't describe the physical "dress" of his surroundings, as Wordsworth does in "Composed upon Westminster Bridge" (page 665). Instead, Coleridge's autobiographical "I" speaks of his environment as emotionally receptive, as filled with a human compassion. His use of **apostrophe,** or the direct address of nonhuman objects, contributes to this personification: The Sun, Ocean, and Nature itself form a community of benevolent souls able to comfort both the speaker and his friends walking on the heath.

Challenging the Text

10. **(Evaluation)** Students may agree with l. 60 that those who appreciate nature are comforted by it. Of l. 76, students may agree that life is beautiful or disagree, pointing out that there is much sadness in the world, too. Students may find the two statements fairly interdependent.

BEFORE YOU READ
THE RIME OF THE ANCIENT MARINER

Into the Poem

Reading Focus
Crime and Confession
Have you ever done something on impulse, knowing even in the act of doing it that you will regret it forever? The Ancient Mariner's strange tale turns on just such an action. And the dreadful consequences of this impulsive decision are as hypnotizing to us as they are to the Mariner's spellbound listener. As you read, try to chart your responses to the Mariner's story. When do you feel sympathy for the Mariner— or sorrow or horror or fear? When do you feel his story is true, and when is it hopelessly distorted by his own guilt?

Quickwrite
Jot down a few ideas about what confession means to you. What purpose does confession have for the teller and the listener? Is a listener even necessary? Why do you think the act of confession plays such an important part in law and religion?

Elements of Literature
The Literary Ballad
Coleridge's **literary ballad** imitates the traditional **folk ballad** in both subject matter and form. Like the old folk ballads, his sensational narrative blends real with supernatural events. Coleridge was a skilled poet, and, to avoid monotony, he often varies his **meter** and **rhyme scheme**. He also uses sophisticated sound devices like **internal rhyme** ("The guests are *met*, the feast is

set") and **assonance** ("'Tis sweeter far to *me*"). To give his ballad an archaic sound, he uses language that was even old-fashioned in his own time.

> **A** **literary ballad,** a songlike poem that tells a story, is written in imitation of the folk ballad, which springs from a genuine oral tradition.
>
> *For more on the Literary Ballad, see the Handbook of Literary Terms.*

Background
Coleridge wrote *The Rime of the Ancient Mariner* as part of the collaboration with Wordsworth in 1797–1798 that culminated in *Lyrical Ballads.* Twenty years later, in the *Biographia Literaria,* Coleridge recalled that he and Wordsworth had made a poetic division of labor based on their interest in the two powers of poetry: (1) to represent ordinary events and objects in an unfamiliar way so as to make them fresh and interesting and (2) to make believable the unfamiliar and strange.

Coleridge's task was to write about "persons and characters supernatural, or at least romantic; yet so far as to transfer from our inward nature a human interest and semblance of truth sufficient to procure for these shadows of imagination that willing suspension of disbelief for the moment, which constitutes

poetic faith." "With this view," he said, "I wrote the *Ancient Mariner.*" The poem was the first item in the 1798 edition of *Lyrical Ballads.* But partly because of Wordsworth's discomfort with the incongruity between it and the rest of the poems in the volume, Coleridge modernized many of the deliberately old-fashioned words he had used to give the poem the flavor of an ancient and previously undiscovered ballad. The marginal notes were added in 1817, and need to be viewed as "modern" and rational comments on the Mariner's tale.

Coleridge's poem no doubt reflects his avid reading of travelers' accounts of strange lands. It was apparently Wordsworth who suggested the use of the albatross. It is helpful in reading this hypnotic narrative to keep in mind three things. First, there is no explanation for the killing of the albatross. The results of the act, rather than the act itself, are important. Second, the moral of the story, pronounced by the Mariner at the end, is, as Coleridge later observed, too much and too little; that is, it is too obtrusive and yet not adequate. Finally, the poem must be seen in the light of Coleridge's own more settled religious convictions, which contrast with the spiritual despair of the Mariner:

> Alone on a wide wide sea:
> So lonely 'twas, that God himself
> Scarce seemed there to be.

Elements of Literature
Have students reflect on the folk tradition Coleridge draws on in his ballad. Challenge students to consider a variety of folk material: traditional stories, events, songs, legends, and art. If students do not think they know any folk traditions, ask them what they did with a tooth that had fallen out when they were children.

Through the Poem

A. Critical Reading: Making Inferences

? What purpose do you think the introductory summary has? [Students may say that it indicates that plot will be less important than other elements in the poem or that the poem starts out so abruptly that it needs an introduction.]

The Rime of the Ancient Mariner

Samuel Taylor Coleridge

Argument

A How a Ship having passed the Line was driven by storms to the cold Country toward the South Pole; and how from thence she made her course to the tropical Latitude of the Great Pacific Ocean; and of the strange things that befell; and in what manner the Ancient Mariner came back to his own Country.

"It is an ancient Mariner, / And he stoppeth one of three."

OPTIONS FOR TEACHING

STRATEGIES FOR INCLUSION

English Language Development To aid students in identifying their responses to the Mariner's story, have them create a time line on which they will list the most important events in the poem as they read. Students should concentrate on significant details and events so that they are able to track their own responses to the consequences of the Mariner's actions.

Less Proficient Readers Help students read Coleridge's long poem *The Rime of the Ancient Mariner* by giving them a very specific purpose for reading. Give students blank transparency sheets on which to mark striking images as they read.

You could have students mark visual images with one color marker, auditory images with another, and tactile images with still another. After each page, have students share the images they marked and tell what type of image each is and why they marked it.

Part I

It is an ancient Mariner,
And he stoppeth one of three.
"By thy long gray beard and glittering eye,
Now wherefore stopp'st thou me?

5 The Bridegroom's doors are opened wide,
And I am next of kin;
The guests are met, the feast is set:
May'st hear the merry din."

He holds him with his skinny hand,
10 "There was a ship," quoth he.
"Hold off! unhand me, gray-beard loon!"
Eftsoons° his hand dropt he.

He holds him with his glittering eye—
The Wedding Guest stood still,
15 And listens like a three years' child:
The Mariner hath his will.

The Wedding Guest sat on a stone:
He cannot choose but hear;
And thus spake on that ancient man,
20 The bright-eyed Mariner.

"The ship was cheered, the harbor cleared,
Merrily did we drop
Below the kirk,° below the hill,
Below the lighthouse top.

25 The Sun came up upon the left,
Out of the sea came he!
And he shone bright, and on the right
Went down into the sea.

Higher and higher every day,
30 Till over the mast at noon°—"
The Wedding Guest here beat his breast,
For he heard the loud bassoon.

The bride hath paced into the hall,
Red as a rose is she;
35 Nodding their heads before her goes
The merry minstrelsy.°

The Wedding Guest he beat his breast,
Yet he cannot choose but hear;
And thus spake on that ancient man,
40 The bright-eyed Mariner.

An ancient Mariner meeteth three Gallants bidden to a wedding feast, and detaineth one.

12. eftsoons: archaic for "at once."

The Wedding Guest is spellbound by the eye of the old seafaring man, and constrained to hear his tale.

23. kirk: church.

The Mariner tells how the ship sailed southward with a good wind and fair weather, till it reached the Line.

30. over . . . noon: The ship has reached the equator, here called the Line.

The Wedding Guest heareth the bridal music; but the Mariner continueth his tale.

36. minstrelsy (min′strəl·sē): group of musicians.

SAMUEL TAYLOR COLERIDGE 685

B. Reader's Response: First Thoughts

? What is the effect of the contrast between the Mariner's appearance and the feast that is described in ll. 7–8? [Sample responses: The contrast makes the sailor seem even more out of place; it also increases the tension in the poem.]

C. Critical Reading: Analyzing Character

? How do the two characters compare in ll. 9–16? [The Mariner is much older and stronger of will; the Wedding Guest is easily swayed and conventional.] Point out that *loon*, in l. 11, means an "ill-bred, awkward person." It is also interesting to note that Wordsworth wrote ll. 15–16.

D. Language Note: Imagery

? What does the imagery of ll. 22–24 describe? [The ship's departure; the ship seems to "drop" below the structures because of the curvature of the earth's surface.] The Scottish word *kirk* suggests the voyage originated in Scotland.

E. Critical Reading: Finding Details

? In what direction does the information in ll. 25–28 tell you the ship is traveling? [South; the sun rises in the east, which is on the ship's left side.]

F. Reader's Response: Shaping Interpretations

? What is the effect of the interruption and return to the wedding feast scene in ll. 31–36? [Sample responses: The interruption creates suspense; the joy of the celebration contrasts with the somber tone of the Mariner's tale.]

STRATEGIES FOR INCLUSION

Special Needs Question #9 in the Making Meanings section (p. 706) asks students to identify examples of sound devices, such as **alliteration, assonance,** and **internal rhyme.** Adapt the question for students who have a hearing impairment by having them give examples of **repetition** (for example, in ll. 58–60, *ice* is repeated four times) and vivid **imagery** (such as "All in a hot and copper sky, / The bloody sun . . .").

Visual Before students begin reading the poem, have them look up *albatross* in an encyclopedia.

To further help them visualize the context of the tale, encourage students to examine paintings of the sea or the engravings that illustrate the poem.

☞

A. Language Note: Structure

? Why do you think the basic stanza form changes in ll. 45–50? [The extra lines prolong the suspense of the ship's flight before the storm.]

B. Exploring the Historical Period

At the time Coleridge wrote *The Rime of the Ancient Mariner*, sailors were still subjected to barely edible food, exhausting labor, pitiful living conditions, and countless dangers. Among the more mundane dangers were disease and shipwreck, but other dangers readily lent themselves to tales of the supernatural. The threat of cannibalism, though exaggerated, was real—if not from the natives of exotic lands then from one's own shipmates if the ship wrecked or food ran out.

C. Expansion

Coleridge had never been to sea when he wrote this poem. The descriptions and images have been traced back to travel books he had read about the Antarctic regions.

D. Language Note: Connotation

? Why might the poet use the word *vespers* instead of *evenings* or *nights* in l. 76? [*Vespers* has a religious connotation that adds an ominous weight and significance to the bird's presence.]

"And now the STORM-BLAST came, and he
Was tyrannous and strong:
He struck with his o'ertaking wings,
And chased us south along.

The ship driven by a storm toward the South Pole.

45 With sloping masts and dipping prow,
As who° pursued with yell and blow
Still° treads the shadow of his foe,
And forward bends his head,
The ship drove fast, loud roared the blast,
50 And southward aye° we fled.

46. who: one.
47. still: archaic for "always."

50. aye: archaic for "continually."

And now there came both mist and snow,
And it grew wondrous cold:
And ice, mast-high, came floating by,
As green as emerald.

55 And through the drifts° the snowy cliffs°
Did send a dismal sheen:
Nor shapes of men nor beasts we ken°—
The ice was all between.

The land of ice, and of fearful sounds where no living thing was to be seen.
55. drifts: windblown snow and fog.
cliffs: icebergs.
57. ken: archaic for "saw."

The ice was here, the ice was there,
60 The ice was all around:
It cracked and growled, and roared and howled,
Like noises in a swound!°

62. swound: swoon.

At length did cross an Albatross,
Thorough the fog it came;
65 As if it had been a Christian soul,
We hailed it in God's name.

Till a great seabird, called the Albatross, came through the snow fog, and was received with great joy and hospitality.

It ate the food it ne'er had eat,
And round and round it flew.
The ice did split with a thunder fit;
70 The helmsman steered us through!

And a good south wind sprung up behind;
The Albatross did follow,
And every day, for food or play,
Came to the mariners' hello!

And lo! the Albatross proveth a bird of good omen, and followeth the ship as it returned northward through fog and floating ice.

75 In mist or cloud, on mast or shroud,°
It perched for vespers° nine;
Whiles all the night, through fog-smoke white,
Glimmered the white Moonshine."

75. shroud: support rope that stretches from the top of the mast to the side of the ship.
76. vespers: evenings; also, evening prayers.

OPTIONS FOR TEACHING

INTEGRATING THE LANGUAGE ARTS

Strategic Reading Have students make predictions as they read the poem. The subject of their predictions can be the main idea of the next lines, the development of certain imagery, or a possible ending for the poem. Have them keep track of their predictions on a sheet of paper divided into three columns marked "Prediction," "Confirmation," and "Comprehension." They can make predictions before each stanza and then use their organizer to confirm their predictions and see how the prediction helped their comprehension while they read the stanza.

Speaking and Listening Have students memorize a passage of four to twelve lines from one of the poems in the Collection. Allow students to practice inflection, pronunciation, and pacing in pairs, so they may receive constructive feedback from a partner. Then, ask each student to recite the prepared passage for the rest of the class, and encourage listeners to comment on what they find beautiful or meaningful about each polished recitation.

Writing: Ship's Log Invite students to rewrite the events in the poem in the form of a ship's log kept by the Ancient Mariner. Remind them to be true to the chronology and events of the poem, but encourage creativity in the wording and additional observations noted in the log.

"God save thee, ancient Mariner!
80 From the fiends, that plague thee thus!—
Why look'st thou so?"—With my crossbow
I shot the ALBATROSS.

E

The ancient Mariner inhospitably killeth the pious bird of good omen.

Part II

The Sun now rose upon the right:
Out of the sea came he,
85 Still hid in mist, and on the left
Went down into the sea.

F

And the good south wind still blew behind,
But no sweet bird did follow,
Nor any day for food or play
90 Came to the mariners' hello!

And I had done a hellish thing,
And it would work 'em woe:
For all averred,° I had killed the bird
That made the breeze to blow.
95 Ah wretch! said they, the bird to slay,
That made the breeze to blow!

His shipmates cry out against the ancient Mariner for killing the bird of good luck.
93. averred (ə·vʉrd´): asserted; claimed.

G

Nor dim nor red, like God's own head,
The glorious Sun uprist:°
Then all averred, I had killed the bird
100 That brought the fog and mist.
'Twas right, said they, such birds to slay,
That bring the fog and mist.

But when the fog cleared off, they justify the same, and thus make themselves accomplices in the crime.
98. uprist: archaic for "rose."

The fair breeze blew, the white foam flew,
The furrow° followed free;
105 We were the first that ever burst
Into that silent sea.

H

The fair breeze continues; the ship enters the Pacific Ocean, and sails northward, even till it reaches the Line.
104. furrow: ship's wake.

Down dropt the breeze, the sails dropt down,
'Twas sad as sad could be;
And we did speak only to break
110 The silence of the sea!

The ship hath been suddenly becalmed.

All in a hot and copper sky,
The bloody Sun, at noon,
Right up above the mast did stand,
No bigger than the Moon.

I

115 Day after day, day after day,
We stuck, nor breath nor motion;
As idle as a painted ship
Upon a painted ocean.

SAMUEL TAYLOR COLERIDGE **687**

E. Reader's Response: Shaping Interpretations

? Why do you think the Mariner shoots the albatross? [Sample responses: He is annoyed by the bird's presence; "the fiends" cause him to do it; or his lack of motive adds mystery to the poem.]

F. Literary Element: Setting

The ship has probably rounded Cape Horn, the most southerly part of South America, and is now sailing north.

G. Critical Reading: Analyzing Plot

? Why does the shipmates' opinion of the Mariner change in ll. 93–102? [They see the bird's death as the cause of the calm, so they are mad the Mariner has killed the bird; but during the fog, they are glad he killed the albatross because they think the bird caused the mist.]

H. Literary Element: Alliteration

? What is the effect of the alliteration and internal rhyme in these lines? [The alliteration and internal rhyme speeds up the rhythm of the poem to mirror the increase in speed of the ship.]

I. Critical Reading: Finding Details

? Where does this stanza suggest the ship is becalmed? [The equator; the tropics.]

A. Expansion

This is one of the most frequently quoted stanzas from the poem. Suggest some of these verses for memorization.

B. Literary Element: Mood

? What is the mood created by the description in ll. 123–130? [The mood of the poem turns even more fantastical with the Mariner's seeming hallucinations of "slimy things" and "death-fires."]

C. Expansion

In reality, the albatross is too large a bird to be hung around a person's neck. However, this phrase is often used in contemporary English to indicate that someone has some type of burden to bear.

D. Language Note: Imagery

? What illusion of movement is created by the imagery in ll. 149– 152? [The growing size of the spotted object indicates it is moving toward the ship.]

Water, water, everywhere,
120 And all the boards did shrink;
Water, water, everywhere,
Nor any drop to drink.

The very deep did rot: O Christ!
That ever this should be!
125 Yea, slimy things did crawl with legs
Upon the slimy sea.

About, about, in reel and rout°
The death-fires° danced at night;
The water, like a witch's oils,
130 Burnt green, and blue and white.

And some in dreams assured were
Of the Spirit that plagued us so;
Nine fathom deep he had followed us
From the land of mist and snow.

135 And every tongue, through utter drought,
Was withered at the root;
We could not speak, no more than if
We had been choked with soot.

Ah! welladay!° what evil looks
140 Had I from old and young!
Instead of the cross, the Albatross
About my neck was hung.

Part III

There passed a weary time. Each throat
Was parched, and glazed each eye.
145 A weary time! a weary time!
How glazed each weary eye,
When looking westward, I beheld
A something in the sky.

At first it seemed a little speck,
150 And then it seemed a mist;
It moved and moved, and took at last
A certain shape, I wist.°

A speck, a mist, a shape, I wist!
And still it neared and neared:
155 As if it dodged a water sprite,
It plunged and tacked and veered.°

688 THE ROMANTIC PERIOD

A Spirit had followed them; one of the invisible inhabitants of this planet, neither departed souls nor angels; concerning whom the learned Jew, Josephus, and the Platonic Constantinopolitan, Michael Psellus, may be consulted. They are very numerous, and there is no climate or element without one or more.
127. reel and rout: violent, whirling movement.
128. death-fires: a firelike, luminous glow that is said to be seen over dead bodies.

The shipmates, in their sore distress, would fain throw the whole guilt on the ancient Mariner: in sign whereof they hang the dead seabird round his neck.
139. welladay: archaic for "alas," an exclamation of sorrow.

The ancient Mariner beholdeth a sign in the element afar off.

152. wist: archaic for "knew."

156. tacked and veered: turned toward and then away from the wind.

OPTIONS FOR TEACHING

CROSSING THE CURRICULUM

Social Sciences Ask students to research the topic of British sailing at the time of the poem's composition. Have students note in particular the type of life sailors had at sea: their duties, hardships, adventures, provisions, discoveries, and tall tales. Encourage students to investigate one aspect of sailors' lives and to present a brief talk to the class. Students may use visual aids in their presentations, but each talk should last no longer than a few minutes.

Geography Have students draw a map of the British empire around the year 1800. Ask students to include the names of important colonies and provinces and to designate shipping routes and areas of exploration to see the routes that the Ancient Mariner might have traversed. Display students' maps in the classroom while covering this time period.

Art Have students pick one scene from the poem and draw a picture of it. Students should include a caption of the lines depicted in their work. Encourage students to be creative and Romantic in their renderings.

"Through utter drought all dumb we stood!"

E. **Reader's Response: Shaping Interpretations**

? What might the shape's position in ll. 175–176 foreshadow? [Sample responses: The shape's eclipse of the sun suggests that it will bring the sailors' doom; the "eclipse" could be a bad omen.]

With throats unslaked,° with black lips baked,
We could not laugh nor wail;
Through utter drought all dumb we stood!
160 I bit my arm, I sucked the blood,
And cried, A sail! a sail!

With throats unslaked, with black lips baked,
Agape° they heard me call:
Gramercy!° they for joy did grin,
165 And all at once their breath drew in,
As they were drinking all.

See! see! (I cried) she tacks no more!
Hither to work us weal;°
Without a breeze, without a tide,
170 She steadies with upright keel!

The western wave was all aflame.
The day was well-nigh done!
Almost upon the western wave
Rested the broad bright Sun;
175 When that strange shape drove suddenly **E**
Betwixt us and the Sun.

At its nearer approach, it seemeth him to be a ship; and at a dear ransom, he freeth his speech from the bonds of thirst.
157. unslaked: unrelieved of thirst.

163. agape: with mouths wide open in wonder or fear.
A flash of joy.
164. gramercy (grə·mʉr′sē): from Middle French *grand merci*, an exclamation of great thanks.

And horror follows. For can it be a ship that comes onward without wind or tide?
168. work us weal: do us good.

COOPERATIVE LEARNING

Panel Discussion Arrange students in groups of five for panel discussions. Have each group member create a question about the poem's structure, meaning, or technical strategies. Then, the groups should discuss possible answers to each question in preparation for their panel discussion in front of the class. After each panel, ask for comments from the audience before another group takes its turn.

Group Storytelling Discuss with the class the purpose of framework stories, reminding students that the Ancient Mariner purportedly tells his tale to the Wedding Guest. Assign groups of four students to devise their own story within a story. Suggest that the groups brainstorm situations where it might seem natural for someone to be telling a tale—around a campfire, on a long car trip—and determine what lesson they want the story to convey. Once the setting is invented,

group members can contribute to the story that is told. Have each group read their finished tale within a tale to the class. Afterward, ask students to comment on the merits and drawbacks of framing a tale. Alert students that other famous framework stories include *The Canterbury Tales, Heart of Darkness, The Arabian Nights,* and *Frankenstein.* ☞

? What is suggested by the gossamer sails and ribs? [The ship is a skeleton of a ship.] In what ways does this poem imitate the traditional folk ballad? [The tale combines realistic and supernatural events, and it is a tale told in rhyme.]

B. Critical Reading: Predicting

? What do you think the woman's words and actions in ll. 197–198 indicate will happen to the Mariner? [They suggest that the Mariner is spared death but will endure "Life-in-Death."]

And straight the Sun was flecked with bars,
(Heaven's Mother send us grace!)
As if through a dungeon grate he peered
180 With broad and burning face.

Alas! (thought I, and my heart beat loud)
How fast she nears and nears!
Are those *her* sails that glance in the Sun,
Like restless gossameres?°

A

185 Are those *her* ribs through which the Sun
Did peer, as through a grate?
And is that Woman all her crew?
Is that a DEATH? and are there two?
Is DEATH that woman's mate?

190 *Her* lips were red, *her* looks were free,
Her locks were yellow as gold:
Her skin was as white as leprosy,
The Nightmare LIFE-IN-DEATH was she,
Who thicks man's blood with cold.

B

195 The naked hulk alongside came,
And the twain were casting dice;
"The game is done! I've won! I've won!"
Quoth she, and whistles thrice.

The Sun's rim dips; the stars rush out:
200 At one stride comes the dark;
With far-heard whisper, o'er the sea,
Off shot the specter bark.°

We listened and looked sideways up!
Fear at my heart, as at a cup,
205 My lifeblood seemed to sip!
The stars were dim, and thick the night,
The steersman's face by his lamp gleamed white;
From the sails the dew did drip—
Till clomb° above the eastern bar
210 The hornèd° Moon, with one bright star
Within the nether tip.°

One after one, by the star-dogged Moon,
Too quick for groan or sigh,
Each turned his face with a ghastly pang,
215 And cursed me with his eye.

Four times fifty living men,
(And I heard nor sigh nor groan)
With heavy thump, a lifeless lump,
They dropped down one by one.

It seemeth him but the skeleton of a ship.

And its ribs are seen as bars on the face of the setting Sun.

184. gossameres: filmy cobwebs.

The Specter Woman and her Death-mate, and no other onboard the skeleton ship.

Like vessel, like crew!

Death and Life-in-Death have diced for the ship's crew, and she (the latter) winneth the ancient Mariner.

No twilight within the courts of the Sun.

202. specter bark: ghost ship.

At the rising of the Moon,

209. clomb (klōm): archaic for "climbed."
210. hornèd: crescent.
210–211. star . . . tip: A star dogging, or following, the moon is believed by sailors to be an evil omen.
One after another,

His shipmates drop down dead.

PROBLEM SOLVING/ CRITICAL THINKING

Trying the Mariner Have students hold a mock trial for the Ancient Mariner. Imagine that he is being held accountable for the deaths of the others on board his ship. Divide the class into two groups, asking one to look for text that supports the Mariner's innocence and the other to look for proof that the Mariner's misdeed brought about the crew's destruction. Each team should present their evidence with visual aids and specific text references. After both teams have made their presentations, ask the whole class to determine which side has a stronger case.

PROFESSIONAL NOTES

Critical Comments: Readings There are many possible readings of the poem's symbolism. Four important perspectives are listed below.
1. **Death and Rebirth** The critic Maud Bodkin sees the poem as an archetypal story—that is, a narrative that is found in all cultures. She believes its theme has to do with death and rebirth. There are many powerful images in the poem of death and rebirth: sleep and waking, winter and spring, night and day, the waxing and waning of the moon.
(continued next page)

220 The souls did from their bodies fly,—
   They fled to bliss or woe!
   And every soul, it passed me by,
   Like the whizz of my crossbow!

But Life-in-Death begins her work on the ancient Mariner.

Part IV

   "I fear thee, ancient Mariner!
225 I fear thy skinny hand!
   And thou art long, and lank, and brown,
   As is the ribbed sea sand.

The Wedding Guest feareth that a Spirit is talking to him;

   I fear thee and thy glittering eye,
   And thy skinny hand, so brown."—
230 Fear not, fear not, thou Wedding Guest!
   This body dropt not down.

   Alone, alone, all, all alone,
   Alone on a wide wide sea!
   And never a saint took pity on
235 My soul in agony.

But the ancient Mariner assureth him of his bodily life, and proceedeth to relate his horrible penance.

   The many men, so beautiful!
   And they all dead did lie:
   And a thousand thousand slimy things
   Lived on; and so did I.

He despiseth the creatures of the calm,

240 I looked upon the rotting sea,
   And drew my eyes away;
   I looked upon the rotting deck,
   And there the dead men lay.

And envieth that they should live, and so many lie dead.

   I looked to heaven, and tried to pray;
245 But or° ever a prayer had gusht,
   A wicked whisper came, and made
   My heart as dry as dust.

245. or: before.

   I closed my lids, and kept them close,
   And the balls like pulses beat;
250 For the sky and the sea, and the sea and the sky
   Lay like a load on my weary eye,
   And the dead were at my feet.

   The cold sweat melted from their limbs,
   Nor rot nor reek did they:
255 The look with which they looked on me
   Had never passed away.

But the curse liveth for him in the eye of the dead men.

SAMUEL TAYLOR COLERIDGE **691**

C. Critical Reading: Speculating

? Do the Wedding Guest's suspicions in ll. 224–231 seem reasonable? [After such a tale, the idea that the Mariner is a ghost is not farfetched.]

D. Language Note: Repetition

? What is the effect of the **alliteration** and **assonance** in the repeated words in lines 232–233? [The repetition underscores the desolation of the Mariner's loneliness.]

PROFESSIONAL NOTES

Continued from p. T690

2. Crime and Punishment In his book *The Romantic Imagination*, Cecil M. Bowra suggests that readers might ask why there is "all this 'pother about a bird." Bowra goes on to say, "The poem is a myth of a guilty soul and marks in clear stages the passage from crime through punishment to such redemption as is possible in this world." Some critics suggest the Mariner's crime represents original sin.

3. Suffering In *Coleridge's Poetic Intelligence*, John Beer links the Ancient Mariner's desolation and fear to the oft-quoted lines from a contemporary play by Wordsworth: "Suffering is permanent, obscure and dark / and shares the nature of infinity" (*The Borderers*, ll. 1543–4). Beer suggests that, in the poem, Coleridge meant to explore ideas the two poets had been sharing about the relationships of persecution, life, and death and to examine how suffering might awaken "sleeping faculties."

4. The Creative Imagination American poet and novelist Robert Penn Warren believes that the death of the albatross represents the poet's "crime against his imagination," which leaves the poet unable to write.

Ask students to write in the Reader's Logs their own interpretation of the poem. ☞

Samuel Taylor Coleridge **T691**

An orphan's curse would drag to hell
A spirit from on high;
But oh! more horrible than that
260 Is the curse in a dead man's eye!
Seven days, seven nights, I saw that curse,
And yet I could not die.

The moving Moon went up the sky,
And nowhere did abide:
265 Softly she was going up,
And a star or two beside—

Her beams bemocked the sultry main,°
Like April hoarfrost° spread;
But where the ship's huge shadow lay,
270 The charmèd water burnt alway°
A still and awful red.

Beyond the shadow of the ship,
I watched the water snakes:
They moved in tracks of shining white,
275 And when they reared, the elfish light
Fell off in hoary° flakes.

Within the shadow of the ship
I watched their rich attire:
Blue, glossy green, and velvet black,
280 They coiled and swam; and every track
Was a flash of golden fire.

O happy living things! no tongue
Their beauty might declare:
A spring of love gushed from my heart,
285 And I blessed them unaware:
Sure my kind saint took pity on me,
And I blessed them unaware.

The selfsame moment I could pray;
And from my neck so free
290 The Albatross fell off, and sank
Like lead into the sea.

Part V

Oh sleep! it is a gentle thing,
Beloved from pole to pole!
To Mary Queen the praise be given!
295 She sent the gentle sleep from Heaven,
That slid into my soul.

In his loneliness and fixedness he yearneth toward the journeying Moon, and the stars that still sojourn, yet still move onward; and everywhere the blue sky belongs to them, and is their appointed rest, and their native country and their own natural homes, which they enter unannounced, as lords that are certainly expected and yet there is a silent joy at their arrival.

267. main: archaic for "open sea."
268. hoarfrost: crystalline deposits from freezing dew; frost.

270. alway: archaic for "always."

By the light of the Moon he beholdeth God's creatures of the great calm.

276. hoary: white or gray.

Their beauty and their happiness.

He blesseth them in his heart.

The spell begins to break.

692 THE ROMANTIC PERIOD

The silly° buckets on the deck,
That had so long remained,
I dreamt that they were filled with dew;
300 And when I awoke, it rained.

My lips were wet, my throat was cold,
My garments all were dank;
Sure I had drunken in my dreams,
And still my body drank.

305 I moved, and could not feel my limbs:
I was so light—almost
I thought that I had died in sleep,
And was a blessèd ghost.

And soon I heard a roaring wind:
310 It did not come anear;
But with its sound it shook the sails,
That were so thin and sere.°

The upper air burst into life!
And a hundred fire flags sheen,
315 To and fro they were hurried about!
And to and fro, and in and out,
The wan stars danced between.°

And the coming wind did roar more loud,
And the sails did sigh like sedge;°
320 And the rain poured down from one black cloud;
The Moon was at its edge.

The thick black cloud was cleft,° and still
The Moon was at its side:
Like waters shot from some high crag,
325 The lightning fell with never a jag,
A river steep and wide.

D

By grace of the holy Mother, the ancient Mariner is refreshed with rain.
297. silly: simple; plain.

He heareth sounds and seeth strange sights and commotions in the sky and the element.

312. sere: archaic for "worn."

313–317. The upper . . . danced between: apparently describes the shifting lights of an aurora, which sometimes resemble waving, luminous folds of fabric.

319. sedge: reedy plants.

322. cleft: split.

D. Literary Element: Simile

? What is the effect of the simile in ll. 324–326? [The simile unites the image of the waterfall with the sight of the lightning, producing an especially vivid picture of a violent storm.]

"I dreamt that they were filled with dew;
And when I awoke, it rained."

ASSESSMENT TOOLS

Observation Assessment Use the following checklist to assess students' comprehension and communication as they discuss the story.

1 = Rarely   2 = Sometimes   3 = Often

___ Takes part in discussion
___ Demonstrates independent reasoning
___ Processes others' remarks and ideas
___ Relates the text to personal experience
___ Makes connections between ideas
___ Challenges the text

Check Test: Short Answer

1. Who is the narrator of the story? To whom does he tell his story? [The Ancient Mariner; the Wedding Guest.]

2. What act of the Mariner's seems to cause the complications for the crew? [He kills the albatross.]

3. Who "wins" the Mariner at dice? [Life-in-Death, the woman on the skeleton ship.]

4. What is the effect of the story on the Wedding Guest? [He is saddened, feels wiser.]

A. Expansion

Wordsworth claimed credit for the idea of having the ship manned by dead sailors. Tales of ships with dead crews were common at this time among sailors.

B. Critical Reading: Analyzing Plot

The Wedding Guest interrupts the tale again. How does the Mariner console him? [The Mariner consoles him by explaining that the bodies were animated by angelic spirits.]

The loud wind never reached the ship,
Yet now the ship moved on!
Beneath the lightning and the Moon
330 The dead men gave a groan.

The bodies of the ship's crew are inspired and the ship moves on.

A They groaned, they stirred, they all uprose,
Nor spake, nor moved their eyes;
It had been strange, even in a dream,
To have seen those dead men rise.

335 The helmsman steered, the ship moved on;
Yet never a breeze up-blew;
The mariners all 'gan work the ropes,
Where they were wont° to do;
They raised their limbs like lifeless tools—
340 We were a ghastly crew.

338. wont (wänt): accustomed.

The body of my brother's son
Stood by me, knee to knee:
The body and I pulled at one rope,
But he said nought to me.

345 "I fear thee, ancient Mariner!"
B Be calm, thou Wedding Guest!
'Twas not those souls that fled in pain,
Which to their corses° came again,
But a troop of spirits blest:

But not by the souls of the men, nor by demons of earth or middle air, but by a blessed troop of angelic spirits, sent down by the invocation of the guardian saint.
348. corses: archaic for "corpses."

350 For when it dawned—they dropt their arms,
And clustered round the mast;
Sweet sounds rose slowly through their mouths,
And from their bodies passed.

Around, around, flew each sweet sound,
355 Then darted to the Sun;
Slowly the sounds came back again,
Now mixed, now one by one.

Sometimes a-dropping from the sky
I heard the skylark sing;
360 Sometimes all little birds that are,
How they seemed to fill the sea and air
With their sweet jargoning!°

362. jargoning: archaic for "twittering."

And now 'twas like all instruments,
Now like a lonely flute;
365 And now it is an angel's song,
That makes the heavens be mute.

694 THE ROMANTIC PERIOD

It ceased; yet still the sails made on
A pleasant noise till noon,
A noise like of a hidden brook
370 In the leafy month of June,
That to the sleeping woods all night
Singeth a quiet tune.

Till noon we quietly sailed on,
Yet never a breeze did breathe:
375 Slowly and smoothly went the ship,
Moved onward from beneath.

Under the keel nine fathom deep,
From the land of mist and snow,
The spirit slid: and it was he
380 That made the ship to go.
The sails at noon left off their tune,
And the ship stood still also.

The Sun, right up above the mast,
Had fixed her° to the ocean:
385 But in a minute she 'gan stir,
With a short uneasy motion—
Backwards and forwards half her length
With a short uneasy motion.

Then like a pawing horse let go,
390 She made a sudden bound:
It flung the blood into my head,
And I fell down in a swound.

How long in that same fit I lay,
I have not to declare;
395 But ere my living life returned,
I heard and in my soul discerned
Two voices in the air.

"Is it he?" quoth one, "Is this the man?
By him who died on cross, **D**
400 With his cruel bow he laid full low
The harmless Albatross.

The spirit who bideth by himself
In the land of mist and snow,
He loved the bird that loved the man
405 Who shot him with his bow."

The other was a softer voice,
As soft as honeydew:
Quoth he, "The man hath penance done,
And penance more will do." **E**

The lonesome Spirit from the South Pole carries on the ship as far as the Line, in obedience to the angelic troop, but still requireth vengeance.

384. fixed her: seemed to hold the ship motionless.

The Polar Spirit's fellow demons, the invisible inhabitants of the element, take part in his wrong; and two of them relate, one to the other, that penance long and heavy for the ancient Mariner hath been accorded to the Polar Spirit, who returneth southward.

SAMUEL TAYLOR COLERIDGE 695

A. Critical Reading: Analyzing Speaker

? Whose voices begin Part VI? Why is this change of speaker necessary? [The voices are not those of the two spirits that spoke in ll. 398–409. They are describing the ship's progress while the Mariner lies in his "swound."]

B. Literary Element: Personification

? How are the moon and ocean personified in ll. 414–421? [The ocean looks to the moon for guidance—perhaps a reference to the relationship of moon and tide, as the sea is personified as slave to the moon.]

C. Literary Element: Allusion

The swift, magical movement of the ship while the Mariner is in a trance (ll. 426–429) parallels Odysseus' homeward journey in Homer's *Odyssey* (Book 13), in which the gods put Odysseus in a trance while they speed his ship home. What is the effect of this allusion? [It gives the poem a classical flavor and adds to the Mariner's characterization.]

Ⓐ Part VI

FIRST VOICE

410 "But tell me, tell me! speak again,
     Thy soft response renewing—
     What makes that ship drive on so fast?
     What is the ocean doing?"

SECOND VOICE

     "Still as a slave before his lord,
415 The ocean hath no blast;°
     His great bright eye most silently
     Up to the Moon is cast—

     If he may know which way to go;
     For she guides him smooth or grim.
420 See, brother, see! how graciously
     She looketh down on him."

FIRST VOICE

     "But why drives on that ship so fast,
     Without or wave or wind?"°

SECOND VOICE

     "The air is cut away before,
425 And closes from behind.

     Fly, brother, fly! more high, more high!
     Or we shall be belated:
     For slow and slow that ship will go,
     When the Mariner's trance is abated."°

430 I woke, and we were sailing on
     As in a gentle weather:
     'Twas night, calm night, the Moon was high;
     The dead men stood together.

     All stood together on the deck,
435 For a charnel dungeon° fitter:
     All fixed on me their stony eyes,
     That in the Moon did glitter.

     The pang, the curse, with which they died,
     Had never passed away:
440 I could not draw my eyes from theirs,
     Nor turn them up to pray.

415. **blast:** wind.

The Mariner hath been cast into a trance; for the angelic power causeth the vessel to drive northward faster than human life could endure.
423. **without . . . wind:** with neither wave nor wind.

429. **abated:** lessened.

The supernatural motion is retarded; the Mariner awakes, and his penance begins anew.

435. **charnel** (chär′nəl) **dungeon:** burial vault.

And now this spell was snapt: once more
I viewed the ocean green,
And looked far forth, yet little saw
445 Of what had else° been seen—

Like one, that on a lonesome road
Doth walk in fear and dread,
And having once turned round walks on,
And turns no more his head;
450 Because he knows, a frightful fiend
Doth close behind him tread.

But soon there breathed a wind on me,
Nor sound nor motion made:
Its path was not upon the sea,
455 In ripple or in shade.

It raised my hair, it fanned my cheek
Like a meadow gale of spring—
It mingled strangely with my fears,
Yet it felt like a welcoming.

460 Swiftly, swiftly flew the ship,
Yet she sailed softly too:
Sweetly, sweetly blew the breeze—
On me alone it blew.

Oh! dream of joy! is this indeed
465 The lighthouse top I see?
Is this the hill? is this the kirk?
Is this mine own countree?

We drifted o'er the harbor bar,
And I with sobs did pray—
470 O let me be awake, my God!
Or let me sleep alway.

The harbor bay was clear as glass,
So smoothly it was strewn!°
And on the bay the moonlight lay,
475 And the shadow of the Moon.

The rock shone bright, the kirk no less,
That stands above the rock:
The moonlight steeped in silentness
The steady weathercock.°

The curse is finally expiated [removed, after penance is done].

445. had else: would have otherwise.

"And on the bay the moonlight lay,
And the shadow of the Moon."

And the ancient Mariner beholdeth his native country.

473. strewn: stretched out; calmed.

479. weathercock: rooster-shaped weather vane.

SAMUEL TAYLOR COLERIDGE 697

D. Reader's Response: Connecting with the Text

? How does the Mariner's interpretation of his journey make you feel about his experience? [Sample responses: It helps readers understand the eerie feeling the Mariner describes; the comparison adds to the suspense of the poem.]

E. Language Note: Alliteration

? What is the effect of the alliteration and assonance in ll. 460–463? [The devices suggest the swiftness and gentleness of the ship's passage; the hissing of the s sounds may also suggest the blowing of the wind.]

F. Critical Reading: Making Connections

? How do the welcome sights in ll. 464–467 compare to the Mariner's departure in ll. 23–24? [The landmarks are mentioned in reverse order, because the ship is "climbing" instead of "dropping."]

How is the possibly gruesome sight of corpses and angels in ll. 490–495 made into a positive, beautiful picture? [The scene is described with repeated references to light and with words such as *lovely* and *heavenly*; the gesture of the angels, too, is a gentle wave.]

RESPONDING TO THE ART: VISUAL LITERACY

Have students discuss the etching in the context of the Romantic period. Ask them what aspects of the subject matter and the style are particularly appropriate to this period in art and literature and whether the etching seems appropriate to Coleridge's poem. [Students may want to discuss the fantastic nature of the angels emerging from the shadows and how this embodies the Romantic fixation with the mysterious and supernatural. Others may note details such as the lonely crescent moon and the eerie beating of the angels' wings that express the gothic imagination of the artist.]

480 And the bay was white with silent light,
Till rising from the same,
Full many shapes, that shadows were,
In crimson colors came.

A little distance from the prow
485 Those crimson shadows were:
I turned my eyes upon the deck—
Oh, Christ! what saw I there!

Each corse lay flat, lifeless and flat,
And, by the holy rood!°
490 A man all light, a seraph man,°
On every corse there stood.

This seraph band, each waved his hand:
It was a heavenly sight!
They stood as signals to the land,
495 Each one a lovely light;

This seraph band, each waved his hand,
No voice did they impart—
No voice; but oh! the silence sank
Like music on my heart.

500 But soon I heard the dash of oars,
I heard the Pilot's cheer;
My head was turned perforce away
And I saw a boat appear.

The Pilot and the Pilot's boy,
505 I heard them coming fast:
Dear Lord in Heaven! it was a joy
The dead men could not blast.

The angelic spirits leave the dead bodies,

And appear in their own forms of light.

489. rood: crucifix.
490. seraph man: angel of the highest rank.

"Full many shapes, that shadows were,
In crimson colors came."

698 THE ROMANTIC PERIOD

I saw a third—I heard his voice:
It is the Hermit good!
510 He singeth loud his godly hymns
That he makes in the wood.
He'll shrieve° my soul, he'll wash away **B**
The Albatross's blood.

Part VII

This Hermit good lives in that wood
515 Which slopes down to the sea.
How loudly his sweet voice he rears!
He loves to talk with marineres
That come from a far countree. **C**

He kneels at morn, and noon, and eve—
520 He hath a cushion plump:
It is the moss that wholly hides
The rotted old oak stump.

The skiff boat° neared: I heard them talk,
"Why, this is strange, I trow!"°
525 Where are those lights so many and fair,
That signal made but now?"

"Strange, by my faith!" the Hermit said—
"And they answered not our cheer!
The planks looked warped! and see those sails,
530 How thin they are and sere!
I never saw aught° like to them,
Unless perchance it were

Brown skeletons of leaves that lag°
My forest brook along;
535 When the ivy tod° is heavy with snow, **D**
And the owlet whoops to the wolf below,
That eats the she-wolf's young."

"Dear Lord! it hath a fiendish look—
(The Pilot made reply)
540 I am afeared"—"Push on, push on!" **E**
Said the Hermit cheerily.

The boat came closer to the ship,
But I nor spake nor stirred;
The boat came close beneath the ship,
545 And straight° a sound was heard.

512. shrieve (shrēv): archaic for "after hearing confession, release from guilt."

The Hermit of the Wood,

523. skiff boat: rowboat.
524. trow: archaic for "believe."

Approacheth the ship with wonder.

531. aught: anything.

533. lag: drift; move more slowly than the current.

535. ivy tod: clump of ivy.

545. straight: straightaway; at once.

SAMUEL TAYLOR COLERIDGE 699

B. Critical Reading: Making Inferences

? What is the Mariner's hope in ll. 512–513? [He hopes that the Hermit can, like a holy man, absolve him of the crime of shooting the albatross.]

C. Reader's Response: Challenging the Text

? Do you think the shift in focus to the Hermit is effective? Why or why not? [Sample responses: Yes, the Hermit might represent all that the Mariner should be: pious, wholesome, joyful. Or no, the Hermit seems unrelated to the story, an added distraction.]

D. Literary Element: Mood

? What is the effect of the simile in ll. 533–537 on the mood of the poem? [The simile is eerie, because the ship's sails are compared to a deathly image of the "skeletons of leaves," and the allusion to the owl eating the wolf's young adds a further savage note.]

E. Literary Element: Irony

? What is the result in ll. 538–541 of the characters' rushing to see what the reader already knows? [The result is dramatic irony, and the reader expects them to react in horror as soon as they arrive at the ship.]

❓ What do the characters' reactions to the Mariner in ll. 560–569 tell you about their personalities? [The Pilot's faint suggests he is easily frightened and perhaps superstitious; the Hermit's prayer shows the strength of his faith; and the boy's crazed laughter and comment hint at an ironic wit.]

Under the water it rumbled on,
Still louder and more dread:
It reached the ship, it split the bay;
The ship went down like lead.

The ship suddenly sinketh.

550 Stunned by that loud and dreadful sound,
Which sky and ocean smote,°
Like one that hath been seven days drowned
My body lay afloat;
But swift as dreams, myself I found
555 Within the Pilot's boat.

The ancient Mariner is saved in the Pilot's boat.
551. smote: struck.

Upon the whirl, where sank the ship,
The boat spun round and round;
And all was still, save that the hill
Was telling of the sound.

A

560 I moved my lips—the Pilot shrieked
And fell down in a fit;
The holy Hermit raised his eyes,
And prayed where he did sit.

I took the oars: the Pilot's boy,
565 Who now doth crazy go,
Laughed loud and long, and all the while
His eyes went to and fro.
"Ha! ha!" quoth he, "full plain I see,
The Devil knows how to row."

570 And now, all in my own countree,
I stood on the firm land!
The Hermit stepped forth from the boat,
And scarcely he could stand.

"It reached the ship, it split the bay;
The ship went down like lead."

"O shrieve me, shrieve me, holy man!"
575 The Hermit crossed° his brow.
"Say quick," quoth he, "I bid thee say—
What manner of man art thou?"

Forthwith° this frame of mine was wrenched
With a woeful agony,
580 Which forced me to begin my tale;
And then it left me free. **B**

Since then, at an uncertain hour,
That agony returns:
And till my ghastly tale is told, **C**
585 This heart within me burns.

The ancient Mariner earnestly en-
treateth the Hermit to shrieve him;
and the penance of life falls on him.
575. crossed: made the sign of the
cross.

578. forthwith: at once.

And ever and anon throughout his
future life an agony constraineth
him to travel from land to land;

B. Literary Element: Climax

? How is the Mariner's discovery in
l. 581 a climax to the tale? [He
realizes that telling the tale brings him
some peace.]

C. Critical Reading: Making
Inferences

? Do the Mariner's comments in
ll. 584–585 explain why he has
forced the Wedding Guest to hear his
story? [The Mariner's "agony" has
probably returned, so to rid himself of
his pain, he has to tell his story, and by
chance he meets the Wedding Guest.]

"Upon the whirl, where sank the ship,
The boat spun round and round."

"'Ha! ha!' quoth he, 'full plain I see,
The Devil knows how to row.'"

SAMUEL TAYLOR COLERIDGE 701

A. Literary Element: Setting

? What is the effect of the setting switching once again to the feast scene in ll. 591–596? [It creates a sharp, dramatic contrast in mood as the narrative returns to the story that frames the poem.]

B. Critical Reading: Drawing Conclusions

? Why would walking to the church be a "sweeter" experience to the Mariner than joining the feast? [He might be able to tell his tale to the "goodly company" on the way; perhaps at the church, the Mariner can again gain some peace by asking forgiveness for his crime.]

C. Reader's Response: Extending the Text

? Is the message of ll. 612–617 a moral that will benefit readers? Why or why not? [Sample responses: No, the moral is unsatisfying because it doesn't explain why shooting the albatross was such a crime. Or yes, the moral is a lesson that humanity must learn over and over—that we must be kind to all creatures.]

D. Reader's Response: Challenging the Text

This narrative is framed within another story: That is, readers learn of the Mariner's tale as he tells it to a guest at a wedding. Do you think this is an effective way to relate a story? Why or why not? [Sample responses: Yes, because the two stories act as significant contrasts; for example, at a celebration where others are merry and seemingly carefree, a guest gets a grim reminder of the importance of loving all creatures. Or no, the tale could be told just as effectively without the extra distraction of the wedding in progress.]

I pass, like night, from land to land;
I have strange power of speech;
That moment that his face I see,
I know the man that must hear me:
590   To him my tale I teach.

A   What loud uproar bursts from that door!
The wedding guests are there:
But in the garden bower the bride
And bridemaids singing are:
595   And hark the little vesper bell,
Which biddeth me to prayer!

O Wedding Guest! this soul hath been
Alone on a wide wide sea:
So lonely 'twas, that God himself
600   Scarce seemed there to be.

B   O sweeter than the marriage feast,
'Tis sweeter far to me,
To walk together to the kirk
With a goodly company!—

605   To walk together to the kirk,
And all together pray,
While each to his great Father bends,
Old men, and babes, and loving friends
And youths and maidens gay!

610   Farewell, farewell! but this I tell
To thee, thou Wedding Guest!
He prayeth well, who loveth well
Both man and bird and beast.

C   He prayeth best, who loveth best
615   All things both great and small;
For the dear God who loveth us,
He made and loveth all.

D   The Mariner, whose eye is bright,
Whose beard with age is hoar,
620   Is gone: and now the Wedding Guest
Turned from the bridegroom's door.

He went like one that hath been stunned,
And is of sense forlorn:°
A sadder and a wiser man,
625   He rose the morrow morn.

"The Mariner, whose eye is bright,
Whose beard with age is hoar,
Is gone."

And to teach, by his own example, love and reverence to all things that God made and loveth.

623. forlorn: deprived.

Joseph Cottle was a close friend of the poet and the first publisher of *Lyrical Ballads*.

Coleridge Describes His Addiction

TO JOSEPH COTTLE

April 26, 1814

You have poured oil in the raw and festering wound of an old friend's conscience, Cottle! but it is *oil of vitriol*! I but barely glanced at the middle of the first page of your letter, and have seen no more of it—not from resentment, God forbid! but from the state of my bodily and mental sufferings, that scarcely permitted human fortitude to let in a new visitor of affliction.

The object of my present reply is to state the case just as it is—first, that for ten years the anguish of my spirit has been indescribable, the sense of my danger staring, but the conscience of my GUILT worse, far worse than all! I have prayed with drops of agony on my brow, trembling not only before the justice of my Maker, but even before the mercy of my Redeemer. "I gave thee so many talents. What hast thou done with them?" Secondly, overwhelmed as I am with the sense of my direful infirmity, I have never attempted to disguise or conceal the cause. On the contrary, not only to friends have I stated the whole case with tears, and the very bitterness of shame; but in two instances, I have warned young men, mere acquaintances, who had spoken of having taken laudanum, of the direful consequences, by an ample exposition of its tremendous effects on myself.

Thirdly, though before God I cannot lift up my eyelids, and only do not despair of his mercy, because to despair would be adding crime to crime, yet to my fellow men I may say, that I was seduced into the ACCURSED habit ignorantly. I had been almost bedridden for many months with swelling in the knees. In a medical journal I unhappily met with an account of a cure performed in a similar case, or what appeared to me so, by rubbing in of laudanum, at the same time taking a given dose internally. It acted like a charm, like a miracle! I recovered the use of my limbs, of my appetite, of my spirits, and this continued for near a fortnight. At length, the unusual stimulus subsided, the complaint returned—the supposed remedy was recurred to—but I cannot go through the dreary history. Suffice it to say, that effects were produced, which acted on me by terror and cowardice of PAIN and sudden death, not (so help me God!) by any temptation of pleasure, or expectation, or desire of exciting pleasurable sensations. On the very contrary, Mrs. Morgan and her sister will bear witness so far, as to say that the longer I abstained, the higher my spirits were, the keener my enjoyments—till the moment, the direful moment arrived, when my pulse began to fluctuate, my heart to palpitate, and such a dreadful falling abroad, as it were, of my whole frame, such intolerable restlessness and incipient bewilderment, that in the last of my several attempts to abandon the dire poison, I exclaimed in agony, what I now repeat in seriousness and solemnity, "I am too poor to hazard this!" Had I but a few hundred pounds, but £200, half to send to Mrs. Coleridge, and half to place myself in a private madhouse, where I could procure nothing but what a physician thought proper, and where a medical attendant could be constantly with me for two or three months (in less than that time, life or death would be determined) then there might be hope. Now there is none! O God! how willing would I place myself under Dr. Fox in his establishment; for my case is a species of madness, only that it is a derangement, an utter impotence of the volition, and not of the intellectual faculties. You bid me rouse myself: go, bid a man paralytic in both arms to rub them briskly together, and that will cure him. "Alas," he would reply, "that I cannot move my arms is my complaint and my misery."

Your affectionate, but most afflicted,

S. T. Coleridge

Primary Sources

Ask students to remember a time when they were very ill with a fever. How did their illness affect the way they saw things? [Students will probably say that their thoughts were unfocused, that they couldn't concentrate, that they were depressed or just frustrated by the illness.] Point out to students that an addiction is like a disease in the way it affects one's perception and outlook. Have students then discuss the letter as coming from someone afflicted with a disease. Start the discussion by asking students what effect Coleridge's addiction probably had on his health and his ability to work. [Students will probably recognize that Coleridge might have produced other great works if he had not become addicted.]

OPTIONS FOR TEACHING

STRATEGIES FOR INCLUSION

Visual Have students draw a picture of Coleridge based on the description in the letter above. Have students make a sketch from Coleridge's famous "portrait" of himself in his letter to John Thelwall dated November 19, 1796. Have students compare their pictures.

INTEGRATING THE LANGUAGE ARTS

Strategic Reading Ask students how the picture Coleridge gives of himself above differs from the description Dorothy Wordsworth gives of him (p. 678). Encourage students to make a chart like the one following to compare how he looks, speaks, and acts in the two versions.

	Looks	Speaks	Acts
According to S. Coleridge			
According to D. Wordsworth			

A. Expansion

The Strait of Magellan is a narrow passageway of water between the southernmost mainland of South America and the islands of Tierra del Fuego. Before the opening of the Panama Canal, this waterway was part of the shortest route between the Atlantic and Pacific Oceans. The strait was named for the Portuguese explorer, Ferdinand Magellan, who led the first European expedition through the passage in his quest to sail around the world in 1520.

B. Exploring the Historical Period

Only in recent centuries have developments in navigational techniques allowed ships to determine accurately the position of known islands. At one time, even if a sailing ship sighted land, it might wait three weeks for favorable winds and then not be able to find suitable anchorage.

Connections

In this passage from his classic travel book, the writer Bruce Chatwin (1940–1989) tells a chilling story. Before this extract opens, Chatwin has said: "Albatrosses and penguins are the last birds I'd want to murder." He had been describing the penguin colony in Patagonia, on the south coast of Argentina. Now he flashes back to 1593.

from In Patagonia

Bruce Chatwin

On October 30, 1593, the ship *Desire,* of 120 tons, limping home to England, dropped anchor in the river at Port Desire, this being her fourth visit since Thomas Cavendish named the place in her, his flagship's, honor, seven years before.

The captain was now John Davis, a Devon man, the most skilled navigator of his generation. Behind him were three Arctic voyages in search of the Northwest Passage. Before him were two books of seamanship and six fatal cuts of a Japanese pirate's sword.

Davis had sailed on Cavendish's Second Voyage "intended for the South Sea." The fleet left Plymouth on August 26, 1591, the Captain-General in the galleon *Leicester;* the other ships were the *Roebuck,* the *Desire,* the *Daintie,* and the *Black Pinnace.* . . .

Cavendish was puffed up with early success, hating his officers and crew. On the coast of Brazil, he stopped to sack the town of Santos. A gale scattered the ships off the Patagonian coast, but they met up, as arranged, at Port Desire.

The fleet entered the Magellan Strait with the southern winter already begun. A sailor's frostbitten nose fell off when he blew it. Beyond Cape Froward, they ran into northwesterly gales and sheltered in a tight cove with the wind howling over their mastheads. Reluctantly, Cavendish agreed to revictual in Brazil and return the following spring.

On the night of May 20, off Port Desire, the Captain-General changed tack without warning. At dawn, the *Desire* and the *Black Pinnace* were alone on the sea. Davis made for port, thinking his commander would join him as before, but Cavendish set course for Brazil and thence to St. Helena. One day he lay down in his cabin and died, perhaps of apoplexy, cursing Davis for desertion: "This villain that hath been the death of me."

Davis disliked the man but was no traitor. The worst of the winter over, he went south again to look for the Captain-General. Gales blew the two ships in among some undiscovered islands, now known as the Falklands.

This time, they passed the Strait and out into the Pacific. In a storm off Cape Pilar, the *Desire* lost the *Pinnace,* which went down with all hands. Davis was alone at the helm, praying for a speedy end, when the sun broke through the clouds. He took bearings, fixed his position, and so regained the calmer water of the Strait.

He sailed back to Port Desire, the crew scurvied and mutinous and lice lying in their flesh, "clusters of lice as big as peason, yea, and some as big as beans." He repaired the ship as best he could. The men lived off eggs, gulls, baby seals, scurvy grass, and the fish called *pejerrey.* On this diet they were restored to health.

Ten miles down the coast, there was an island, the original Penguin Island, where the sailors clubbed twenty thousand birds to death. They had no natural enemies and were unafraid of their murderers. John Davis ordered the penguins dried and salted and stowed fourteen thousand in the hold. . . .

As they came up to the Equator, the penguins took their revenge. In them bred a "loathsome worme" about an inch long. The

---

CONNECTING WITH *THE RIME OF THE ANCIENT MARINER*

Encourage students to create a Venn diagram comparing the events in this narrative to *The Rime of the Ancient Mariner.* Then, ask students to write a short, persuasive essay supporting or refuting the idea that Coleridge may have based the Ancient Mariner's tale on the voyage of John Davis. Remind students to cite specific examples from the text to support their points.

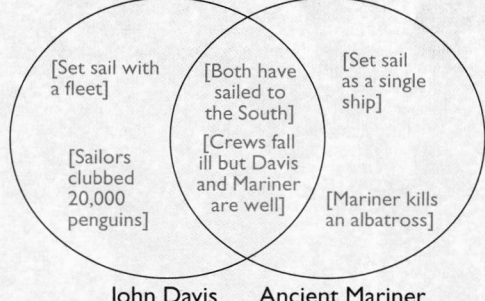

John Davis   Ancient Mariner

worms ate everything, iron only excepted—clothes, bedding, boots, hats, leather lashings, and live human flesh. The worms gnawed through the ship's side and threatened to sink her. The more worms the men killed, the more they multiplied.

Around the Tropic of Cancer, the crew came down with scurvy. Their ankles swelled and their chests, and their parts swelled so horribly that "they could neither stand nor lie nor go."

The Captain could scarcely speak for sorrow. Again he prayed for a speedy end. He asked the men to be patient; to give thanks to God and accept his chastisement. But the men were raging mad, and the ship howled with the groans and curses of the dying. Only Davis and a ship's boy were in health, of the seventy-six who left Plymouth. By the end there were five men who could move and work the ship.

And so, lost and wandering on the sea, with topsails and spritsails torn, the rotten hulk drifted, rather than sailed, into the harbor of Berehaven on Bantry Bay on June 11, 1593. The smell disgusted the people of that quiet fishing village. . . .

"The Southern Voyage of John Davis" appeared in Hakluyt's edition of 1600. Two centuries passed and another Devon man, Samuel Taylor Coleridge, set down the 625 controversial lines of *The Ancient Mariner,* with its hammering repetitions and story of crime, wandering, and expiation.

John Davis and the Mariner have these in common: a voyage to the Black South, the murder of a bird or birds, the nemesis which follows, the drift through the tropics, the rotting ship, the curses of dying men. Lines 236–239 are particularly resonant of the Elizabethan voyage:

The many men, so beautiful!
And they all dead did lie:
And a thousand thousand slimy things
Lived on; and so did I.

In *The Road to Xanadu,* the American scholar John Livingston Lowes traced the Mariner's victim to a "disconsolate Black Albitross" shot by one Hatley, the mate of Captain George Shelvocke's privateer in the eighteenth century. Wordsworth had a copy of this voyage and showed it to Coleridge when the two men tried to write the poem together. . . .

Lowes demonstrated how the voyages in Hakluyt and Purchas fueled Coleridge's imagination. "The mighty great roaring of ice" that John Davis witnessed on an earlier voyage off Greenland reappears in line 61: "It cracked and growled, and roared and howled." But he did not, apparently, consider the likelihood that Davis's voyage to the Strait gave Coleridge the backbone for his poem.

Engraving (1875) by Gustave Doré for Coleridge's *The Rime of the Ancient Mariner.*

C. Expansion
The Rime of the Ancient Mariner was published in *Lyrical Ballads* in 1798.

Making Meanings

Questions begin on p. 706.

First Thoughts

1. Students may say the poem suggests that compassion and feeling for one's fellow creatures are qualities that every human being should have.

Reviewing the Text

a. The poem begins with an omniscient narrator, but from l. 41 on, the narrator is the Ancient Mariner. He tells his story to the Wedding Guest. The Mariner kills an albatross—the embodiment of love and good fortune. Because of his act of irrational destruction, the Mariner is punished with a life of permanent alienation. The crew dies but continues to sail the ship, and the Mariner's journey continues as he does penance for his sin. Eventually, he returns home, but he is fated always to travel and retell his story, thereby reliving his horrors and shame.

b. The ship is becalmed; the Mariner and crew suffer heat and thirst.

c. A woman (Life-in-Death) and Death are the occupants. The crewmen die, leaving the Mariner the last living person on the ship.

d. A "wicked whisper" makes his heart "as dry as dust." When he turns his attention away from himself and his circumstances, he blesses the water snakes, then he is able to pray.

e. The Mariner says he is destined to travel from land to land, telling his tale as penance. His lesson is to have reverence for all living things.

Answers begin on p.T705.

Shaping Interpretations

2. The wedding is mentioned at the beginning, in the middle (11.345-346), and at the end of the poem. The joy of the wedding party (a celebration of love) contrasts with the Mariner's grim tale (a lack of love).

3. The Mariner begins by seeing himself as cursed and his surroundings as ugly. When he recognizes the beauty of the water snakes and blesses them, he begins to love, and the albatross falls from his neck. The changes are believable, because in his isolation he can recognize his need for other living beings. Focusing only on himself—his regret and shame and guilt—is deadly. Shifting his focus to others offers him life, symbolized by his ability to pray.

4. Shame focuses on the self; it is the concern that one has lost respect. Guilt focuses on the victims of one's actions; it is a feeling of self-reproach for having done something unethical. The Mariner experiences shame after he kills the albatross. He feels guilt when he acknowledges the great harm he caused to the bird.

5. The Mariner's immediate penance is to suffer alone on the ship. His lifetime penance is to be an outcast, wandering and telling his story to relieve his agony. Students may say that, literally, the penance makes little sense, for the Mariner only shot a bird; allegorically, however, the penance is fitting, for the albatross is a symbol of all living creatures.

6. The Mariner's moral is basically that one who loves generously and completely will live happily and therefore well. To the Mariner, this moral is sufficient, but students may have various suggestions for enhancing the ending.

7. The guest is sad because he has heard a tragic story and wiser because he has learned the importance of loving others. Kubla Khan hears ancestral voices prophesying war.

8. The side notes are helpful in summarizing the plot. Reading them does not alter the meaning of the poem, but it does add a critical or scholarly voice to the poem. Students may feel the notes are part of the poem and should be consulted in a careful reading, or they may feel the original poem should stand alone; in either case, their views should be supported.

MAKING MEANINGS

First Thoughts

1. Do you think that this poem tells us something significant about human conduct? Why or why not? If so, would it apply to most people?

Shaping Interpretations

2. Where in the poem is the wedding mentioned? How does this context for the ballad affect your response to it?

3. Describe in detail the changing states of the Mariner in Part IV. Given the circumstances, are these changes believable?

4. After he shoots the albatross, the Mariner experiences both shame and guilt. What is the difference between these two emotions? Where in the poem does he experience each emotion?

5. What is the Mariner's "penance" (line 408)? What penance does he have left to do? Does it seem fair to you that he should have to do any sort of penance? Why? (Refer to your Reader's Log notes for ideas.)

Reviewing the Text

a. Who is presented as the **narrator** of the ballad? To whom is he telling his story? In a time line, summarize the main events of the Mariner's story.

b. According to Part II, what consequences follow the Mariner's killing of the albatross?

c. Who are the occupants of the strange ship that appears in Part III? What results from their appearance?

d. In Part IV, why is the Mariner unable to pray? What happens that enables him to pray?

e. At the end of the ballad, how does the Mariner describe his current life? What lesson does he draw for the Wedding Guest from this tale?

6. Explain in your own terms the Mariner's **moral** (lines 612–617). Does the story indicate that he ought to have added something to his moral conclusion? Explain.

7. Why is the Wedding Guest sadder but wiser after hearing the Mariner's tale? What other figures in Coleridge's poems in this collection are also listening to a speaker?

8. What do you think of Coleridge's side notes to the poem? Do you think reading them alters the meaning of the poem? Should they be consulted in a careful reading of the poem? Why or why not?

9. This ballad is famous for its use of vivid **figurative language** and memorable sound devices. What do you think are several especially effective examples of **simile, metaphor, personification, alliteration, assonance,** and **internal rhyme**?

10. For the most part, the form of the poem is the regular **ballad stanza.** Occasionally, however, Coleridge varies the **meter** of the lines and the length of the stanzas. Read aloud several examples of such variations.

11. What differences do you notice between Coleridge's tale of the ancient Mariner and the story described in Bruce Chatwin's *In Patagonia* (page 704)?

Extending the Text

12. There was a time in American history when almost every schoolchild could recite parts of *The Rime of the Ancient Mariner.* Find some stanzas that strike you as particularly quotable. What situations in contemporary life could you apply the lines to?

Challenging the Text

13. Coleridge once said that he would have preferred to write *The Rime of the Ancient Mariner* as a work of "pure imagination." He believed that it had "too much" of a moral, and that the moral was stated too openly. Do you agree or disagree with Coleridge about the message in his poem? Why?

706 THE ROMANTIC PERIOD

9. In ll. 33–34, a simile likens the bride's beauty to that of a rose. In ll. 195–199, a metaphor describes Death and Life-in-Death casting dice for the Mariner's life. Lines 41–44 contain personification that shows the power of the storm. In ll. 171–173, the repetition of *w* sounds speed up the poem's rhythm and suggest the absent breeze. Assonance occurs in ll. 521–522 to emphasize the stump and to enhance the lyrical quality of the stanza. Internal rhyme of "noon" and "tune" slows l. 381 to reflect the sudden stopping of the ship.

10. Lines 45–50, 91–102, and 586–596 exemplify the breaks in the pattern. These shifts call attention to the events described. The varied stanzas also help to avoid a singsong quality that could lull the readers into a daze.

11. Possible response: In Coleridge's version, the bird is a single albatross, rather than thousands of penguins, and there is no mention made of other boats, as exist in Chatwin's story.

T706 The Romantic Period

LANGUAGE AND STYLE

Archaic Words

To give his ballad an antique flavor, Coleridge used many words that were archaic even at the time of his writing, and which, of course, are even more archaic today.

1. Here is a list of some of the archaic words in the poem. Note what each one means, and then substitute a modern synonym in the poem for each one. How does the flavor of the ballad change?

   a. *eftsoons* (line 12)

   b. *uprist* (line 98)

   c. *wist* (line 152)

   d. *Gramercy* (line 164)

   e. *clomb* (line 209)

   f. *wont* (line 338)

   g. *corses* (line 348)

   h. *rood* (line 489)

   i. *shrieve* (line 512)

   j. *trow* (line 524)

2. Are any forms of those words still in use today? Which ones?

3. Sometimes the archaic meaning of a word gives us a clue to the history of a word in current use. Look at the use of the word *jargoning* in line 362. What does the word *jargon* mean today? How is contemporary "jargon" like a bird twittering? (Check the derivation of the word in a dictionary.)

"With my crossbow / I shot the ALBATROSS."

Language and Style
Possible Answers

1. a. at once—quickly, rapidly
   b. rose up—came up, emerged
   c. knew—understood, thought
   d. an expression of great thanks—thank goodness
   e. climbed—went up, rose, ascended
   f. accustomed—used to, habituated to
   g. corpses—bodies
   h. crucifix—cross
   i. release from guilt—forgive, absolve
   j. believe—think, say

   Replacing the archaic word with a modern equivalent diminishes some of the antique flavor and mystery of the ballad.

2. Forms of the words still in use are risen *(uprist)*, mercy *(Gramercy)*, climb *(clomb)*, wont *(wont)*, corpses *(corses)*, and shrive *(shrieve)*.

3. The word *jargon* today can denote an unintelligible language or a language that is specific to a certain professional group. Contemporary jargon is like bird twittering in that to anyone who is not part of the group, jargon is meaningless, simply noise.

Extending the Text

12. **(Evaluation and Synthesis)** Students' responses will vary but may include ll. 115–118 for the way they express the hopelessness of being all alone and ll. 285–291, which express the relief of overcoming a terrible burden and rediscovering happiness.

Challenging the Text

13. **(Evaluation)** Students may agree that the moral is unsuited for the tale or seems out of place stated so baldly, but some may say that if the poem were a work of "pure imagination," it would be impossible to understand and frustrating to read. Have students support their answers.

Beyond the Poems

Choices: Building Your Portfolio

1. **Writer's Notebook** Remind students to save their work. They may use it as prewriting for the Writer's Workshop on p. 773.
2. **Critical Writing** Direct students to focus on a few meaningful symbols in the poem. Students may use a cluster diagram to organize their thoughts by listing around each specific symbol their ideas about its significance.
4. **Critical Writing** After students have thought of their own questions about the plot of the poem, ask them to imagine the poem with the answers to their questions included. How would the poem differ? Would it be better or worse? Have students focus on two or three examples in their papers.
5. **Critical Writing** To help students determine the elements of the allegory, direct them to write down the events that illustrate the moral of the tale. Then, have students name the symbolic purpose of the **characters, setting,** and **plot** as they relate to these significant events.
6. **Creative Writing** Have students begin the activity by listing questions they have that were left unanswered by the poem. Students can then think of answers for their own questions and use the answers as a guide for their prose summaries.
7. **Creative Writing** Encourage students to link the Mariner's peace to the method by which he gains this temporary respite: confession. Students should review their narrative to make sure their solutions do not contradict the poem's allegory.
8. **Art** Students may create their art using a computer-drawing software package.

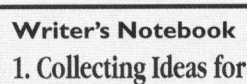

Writer's Notebook
1. Collecting Ideas for a Reflective Essay

Coleridge's ancient Mariner tells a story that prompts the Wedding Guest to wonder at life's meaning—leaving him, at the poem's end, a "sadder and a wiser man." What causes you to wonder? To discover significant experiences to write about, freewrite using one of these sentence starters: *I wonder why I become so angry (embarrassed, ecstatic, and so on) when . . .* or *I wonder about the power of words (friendships, determination, and so on) when . . .* Save your work for the Writer's Workshop on page 773.

Critical Writing
2. Probing the Imagination

There is general agreement that one of the major themes of "Kubla Khan" concerns the power of imagination. In a brief essay, analyze how Coleridge develops this theme in the poem. What symbolic hints does he provide about the powers, dangers, and limits of the human imagination? Also, discuss whether you agree or disagree with Coleridge's views.

Critical Writing
3. *Do Great Minds Think Alike?*

In a brief essay, compare and contrast Coleridge's "This Lime-Tree Bower My Prison" (page 680) with Wordsworth's meditative lyric "Lines Composed a Few Miles Above Tintern Abbey" (page 658).

Critical Writing
4. Moving the Plot Along

Although Coleridge keeps the plot moving along briskly in *The Rime of the Ancient Mariner,* he ignores characters' motives that other writers might have explained. For example, how could the Mariner tell that the Wedding Guest was a fit audience for his tale? Why did the Mariner shoot the albatross? How can the Mariner's punishment be regarded as fitting his crime? In a brief essay, analyze these or other questions that you think are unsatisfactorily resolved by the ballad. Does Coleridge succeed in distracting our attention from these issues so that they do not interfere with our enjoyment of his poem?

Critical Writing
5. A Symbolizing Tale

An **allegory** is a prose or verse tale in which the characters, actions, and settings are **symbolic;** that is, they have both a literal and a figurative meaning. Could Coleridge's ballad be regarded as an allegory? If so, what do the various elements in the ballad symbolize? How may the tale as a whole be interpreted on an allegorical level? In a brief essay, explain your answers.

Creative Writing
6. Finishing Out the Khan

Suppose that we take Coleridge at his word and assume that "Kubla Khan" is really an unfinished fragment. Basing your idea on the existing lines, write a summary in prose of how the poem might be completed. Specify what you imagine the story line might be.

Creative Writing
7. Finding Peace

The Ancient Mariner has much in common with other legendary figures, such as the Flying Dutchman, who are condemned to wander the world in a quest for atonement or redemption. Imagine that the Mariner ultimately finds peace. Describe in a brief narrative how this might occur.

Art
8. Dreaming, Drawing, Remembering

Suppose that Coleridge kept a dream journal, and that he drew pictures in it to remind him of what he had seen in the dream that resulted in "Kubla Khan." Sketch three or four drawings that he might have used to help him recall the images he saw in his dream.

STRATEGIES FOR INCLUSION

Special Needs Students' difficulties with multistage assignments are often related to problems with understanding directions. In activity #4, modify directions by limiting their number and length and by providing both oral and written directions. Encourage students to ask questions and request clarification when they do not understand. To verify comprehension, ask students who have a particularly hard time with directions to paraphrase.

PORTFOLIO ASSESSMENT

Choices: Assessment Criteria For help in evaluating these Choices assignments, see the criteria in the *Portfolio Management System,* pp. 131–132.

Collection 9 · THE QUEST FOR BEAUTY

> ### *Theme:* Ah, the Beauty of Life!
> Beauty manifests itself in many forms, including the search for wisdom and meaning. The Romantic poets embraced all aspects of existence—the sublime and ordinary, the passionate and the detached, the transitory and the permanent—in their quest for beauty.

Thematic Focus

The speaker in each selection acknowledges, contemplates, or seeks beauty in its myriad forms.

- **She Walks in Beauty/The Destruction of Sennacherib/** *from* **Don Juan, Canto II/** *from* **Childe Harold's Pilgrimage, Canto IV**   Byron's poems celebrate and explore beauty while satirizing elements of Romanticism.
- **Ozymandias/Ode to the West Wind/To a Skylark**   Shelley contemplates images evoked by an Egyptian monument, the wind, and a bird.
- **World Literature: Jade Flower Palace**   The crumbled ruins of a great palace fill the beholder with pathos.
- **On First Looking into Chapman's Homer/When I Have Fears/La Belle Dame sans Merci/Ode to a Nightingale/Ode on a Grecian Urn**   Keats's poems illustrate the excitement of discovery and the wistful yearning of pain and loss.
- **World Literature: Question and Answer Among the Mountains/Word-Pattern/To Tan Ch'iu**   The poet turns to nature for spiritual and poetic renewal.

Literary Focus

Literary Element	Selection / Feature
Anapestic Rhythm/Ottava Rima	**Poems of Byron**
Apostrophe/Symbol	**Poems of Shelley**
Sonnet/Ballad	**Poems of Keats**

Writing Focus

The following flowchart shows how the writing assignment for each selection relates to and builds toward the writing assignment presented in the Writer's Workshop at the end of the unit.

Selection	Work-in-Progress Assignment
She Walks in Beauty/The Destruction of Sennacherib/Don Juan/Childe Harold's Pilgrimage	Note sense impressions about a natural scene p. 725
Ozymandias/Ode to the West Wind/To a Skylark	Reflect on a poem p. 742
On First Looking into Chapman's Homer/When I Have Fears/La Belle Dame sans Merci/Ode to a Nightingale/Ode on a Grecian Urn	Freewrite about a personal experience p. 764
Writer's Workshop	Write a reflective essay pp. 773–777

Collection Planner

PUPIL'S EDITION

SELECTION/ FEATURE	Literary Elements / Active Reading	Writing	Speaking and Listening	Language and Vocabulary
She Walks in Beauty/ The Destruction of Sennacherib/from **Don Juan**/from **Childe Harold's Pilgrimage** George Gordon, Lord Byron (pp. 710–723) Primary Sources: Byron Writes to Shelley (p. 724) Spotlight On: Women Writers in the Romantic Period (pp. 726–728)	• Reader's Log pp. 711, 712, 714, 721 • Anapestic Rhythm p. 712 • Ottava Rima p. 714	• Critical Writing: Analyze similes p. 725 • Critical Writing: Compare and contrast Byron and Pope p. 725 • Critical Writing: Describe verse form p. 725 • Creative Writing: Write sequel to *Don Juan* p. 725 • Creative Writing: Write prose apostrophe p. 725		
Ozymandias/Ode to the West Wind/To a Skylark Percy Bysshe Shelley (pp. 729–742) Critical Comment (p. 737)	• Reader's Log pp. 730, 734, 739 • Apostrophe p. 738 • Symbol p. 739	• Critical Writing: Examine Shelley's sound effects p. 742 • Critical Writing: Compare "Ozymandias" to Renaissance sonnet p. 742 • Creative Writing: Write parody p. 742		• Language and Style: Terza Rima and the Sonnet p. 738
World Literature: Jade Flower Palace Tu Fu (pp. 743–744)	• Reader's Log p. 744	• Finding Common Ground: Write poem p. 744	• Finding Common Ground: Discuss Tu Fu's theme p. 744	
On First Looking into Chapman's Homer/ When I Have Fears/La Belle Dame sans Merci/ Ode to a Nightingale/ Ode on a Grecian Urn John Keats (pp. 745–765) Primary Sources: Keats's Last Letter (p. 749) **Student to Student** (p. 753) **Connections: O sweet spontaneous** E. E. Cummings (p. 758) Critical Comment (pp. 759, 763)	• Reader's Log p. 746, 748, 750, 754, 760 • Ballad p. 750 • Language and Style: Imagery p. 759	• Critical Writing: Analyze Keats sonnet p. 764 • Critical Writing: Compare odes p. 764 • Critical Writing: Compare bird poems p. 764 • Critical Writing: Analyze poem p. 764 • Creative Writing: Write extended simile p. 764 • Creative Writing: Write letter p. 764 • Creative Writing: Explain character p. 764 • Creative Writing: Address painting p. 764	• Music: Write/perform melody for "La Belle Dame sans Merci" p. 764	• Language and Style: Imagery p. 759 • How to Own a Word: Homonyms, Homophones, and Homographs p. 765
World Literature: Question and Answer Among the Mountains/ Word-Pattern/To Tan-Ch'iu Li Po (pp. 766–768)	• Reader's Log p. 767	• Finding Common Ground: Write poem imitative of one of Li Po's p. 768	• Finding Common Ground: Discuss how nature affects each member of group p. 768	
The English Language: Variety in Language John Algeo (pp. 770–772)				• Try It Out: Examine regional dialects p. 772
Writer's Workshop: Reflective Essay (pp. 773—777)		• Writing process: Reflective essay pp. 773–777		
Language Workshop: Style, Voice, Tone (p. 778)		• Revise essay p. 778		• Try It Out: Formal and informal words p. 778
Learning for Life: Population Trends (p. 779)		• Write editorial p. 779	• Present speech p. 779	

Collection Resources

Teaching Resources B	Audiovisual Resources Binder	Test Booklet
Cross-Curricular Activity p. 60	Fine Art Transparency 9.1	Collection 9 Test pp. 156–158

- Computer disk or CD-ROM
- Videodisc
- Audiocassette
- Overhead Transparency

PROGRAM RESOURCES

Electronic Media	Teaching Resources with Organizer		Audiovisual Resources Binder
	Teaching Resources B	Other Resources	
• Test Generators • Language Workshop: Adverb Clauses	• Teaching Notes pp. 31–33 • Reading Organizers pp. 40–42, 45 • Language Link pp. 43–44 • Words to Own pp. 56–57	• Test Booklet: Selection Tests pp. 141–145 • Portfolio Management System pp. 62–63, 133–134 • Language and Writing Skills Worksheets p. 82	• Selected Reading, Audiocassette 2, Side A
• Test Generators	• Teaching Notes pp. 33–35 • Reading Organizers pp. 46–48 • Words to Own pp. 56–57	• Test Booklet: Selection Tests pp. 146–148 • Portfolio Management System pp. 54–55, 62–63, 135	• Elements of Literature Transparency 9.2 • Selected Reading, Audiocassette 1, Side B
	• Teaching Notes p. 35		• Selected Reading, Audiocassette 1, Side B
• Test Generators • Language Workshop: Adjective Clauses	• Teaching Notes pp. 36–39 • Reading Organizers pp. 49–52, 55 • Language Link pp. 53–54 • Words to Own pp. 56–57	• Test Booklet: Selection Tests pp. 149–153 • Portfolio Management System pp. 48–49, 62–63, 136–138 • Language and Writing Skills Worksheets p. 80	• Selected Reading, Audiocassette 1, Side B • How To Own a Word Transparency 9.3
	• Teaching Notes p. 39		
• Test Generator • Videodisc, Side A: "English: A Living Language, Part 2"	• Teaching Notes p. 39	• Test Booklet: The English Language pp. 154–155	
• Writer's Workshop 2: Reflective Essay		• Portfolio Management System pp. 139–141	• Revision Transparencies 9.4–9.5
• Language Workshop: Voice and Tone	• Language Workshop: Style, Voice, Tone, and Diction pp. 58–59		
		• Portfolio Management System p. 142	

Proofreading Warm-ups

You may use the following exercises to help students practice their proofreading skills. Copy a set of incorrect sentences onto the chalkboard, and have students find and correct the spelling, punctuation, usage, and mechanical errors in each sentence. Ask students to share and discuss their responses.

	Sentences with Errors	Sentences Corrected	Skills Covered
1	**a.** byron used the ottava rima an old verse form in the long poem Don Juan **b.** byrons premature death reinforced the perception that he was a romantic writer	**a.** Byron used the ottava rima, an old verse form, in the long poem <u>Don Juan</u>. **b.** Byron's premature death reinforced the perception that he was a Romantic writer.	Capitalization, Comma usage, Underline titles of long poems, Apostrophes, End marks
2	**a.** byron uses Anapestic Rhythm in the destruction of sennacherib **b.** childe harold the pilgrim of the poem "Childe Harold's Pilgrimage," became the prototype for the byronic hero	**a.** Byron uses anapestic rhythm in "The Destruction of Sennacherib." **b.** Childe Harold, the pilgrim of the poem <u>Childe Harold's Pilgrimage</u>, became the prototype for the Byronic hero.	Capitalization, Quotation marks for poem titles, Comma usage, Underline titles of long poems, End marks
3	**a.** jane austen published all her novels anonymous because being known as a female novelist was more a stigma than a honor **b.** austen satirized the social, and educational status quo by using irony, and humor	**a.** Jane Austen published all her novels anonymously because being known as a female novelist was more a stigma than an honor. **b.** Austen satirized the social and educational status quo by using irony and humor.	Capitalization, Nonstandard usage, Comma usage, End marks
4	**a.** mary wollstonecraft godwin eloped with the poet Percy Bysshe Shelley they had 4 children **b.** mary shelley is the author of the novel Frankenstein which she began when she was just nine-teen	**a.** Mary Wollstonecraft Godwin eloped with the poet Percy Bysshe Shelley; they had four children. **b.** Mary Shelley is the author of the novel <u>Frankenstein</u>, which she began when she was just nineteen.	Capitalization, Semicolon usage, Write out numerals, Underline book titles, Comma usage, Hyphen usage, End marks
5	**a.** a apostrophe has two uses its not only a punctuation mark but also a literary device **b.** when a writer addresses a person (usually absent) or a abstract idea he or she is using an apostrophe	**a.** An apostrophe has two uses; it's not only a punctuation mark but also a literary device. **b.** When a writer addresses a person (usually absent) or an abstract idea, he or she is using an apostrophe.	Capitalization, Nonstandard usage, Semicolon usage, Apostrophe usage, Spelling, Comma usage, End marks
6	**a.** shelley uses a extended apostrophe, in his ode to the west wind **b.** that everything human is transitory, is a theme of Shelleys sonnet Ozymandias	**a.** Shelley uses an extended apostrophe in his "Ode to the West Wind." **b.** That everything human is transitory is a theme of Shelley's sonnet "Ozymandias."	Capitalization, Nonstandard usage, Comma usage, Quotation marks for poem titles, Apostrophe usage, End marks
7	**a.** keats poem "On First Looking into Chapman's Homer" was wrote after reading Chapman's translation of Homers Iliad **b.** when i have fears is one of my favorite sonnets said Ms. Thompson	**a.** Keats's poem "On First Looking into Chapman's Homer" was written after reading Chapman's translation of Homer's <u>Iliad</u>. **b.** "'When I Have Fears' is one of my favorite sonnets," said Ms. Thompson.	Capitalization, Apostrophe usage, Past participles, Underline long poem titles, Quotation marks (double and single), Comma usage, End marks
8	**a.** the title of the poem La Belle Dame sans Merci is french **b.** translated the title mean's "The Beautiful Woman w/out Pity"	**a.** The title of the poem "La Belle Dame sans Merci" is French. **b.** Translated, the title means "The Beautiful Woman Without Pity."	Capitalization, Quotation marks for poem titles, Comma usage, Apostrophe usage, Write out abbreviations, End marks
9	**a.** some modern american poets experimented with poetrys form. **b.** the poem O sweet spontaneous praise's nature's mystery	**a.** Some modern American poets experimented with poetry's form. **b.** The poem "O sweet spontaneous" praises nature's mystery.	Capitalization, Apostrophe usage, Quotation marks for poem titles, End marks
10	**a.** dialects variations in a language is shaped by several facters **b.** their are regional, ethnic, class, sex, educational, and age group dialect's	**a.** Dialects, variations in a language, are shaped by several factors. **b.** There are regional, ethnic, class, sex, educational, and age-group dialects.	Capitalization, Comma usage, Subject-verb agreement, Spelling, Homonyms, Hyphen usage, Apostrophe usage, End marks

THE QUEST FOR BEAUTY

Collection 9

Byron   Keats
Shelley   Li Po
Tu Fu

A thing of beauty is a joy forever:
Its loveliness increases; it will never
Pass into nothingness.
—John Keats, *from Endymion*

Night (detail) (late 19th or early 20th century) by Edward Robert Hughes.

Responding to the Quotation

? Do you agree with this statement? Why or why not? [Students may agree that a work of art could survive over millennia, but they may argue that Keats exaggerates when he writes that it will "never / Pass into nothingness."]

RESPONDING TO THE ART: ABOUT THE ARTWORK

Neoclassicism, the dominant style of eighteenth-century art, required artists to suppress feelings in the expression of aesthetic ideals. Nineteenth-century painters, frustrated with these strictures, desired a different interpretation of humans as free, vital beings. Artists, such as Edward Robert Hughes (1851–1914), began to approach their works subjectively, creating art that reflected their passions and emotions.

Technology Tip

When beginning this Collection, you may want to browse Columbia University's Project Bartleby, a resource of on-line literary texts. This Web site features works by Romantic poets and can be found at **http://www.cc.columbia.edu/acis/bartleby**. *You may want to preview any Internet activity that you suggest to students. Because these resources are sometimes public forums, their content can be unpredictable.*

PROGRAM MANAGER

- **Integrated Assessment** For a summative assessment of the literature and language skills taught in this collection, see **Collection 9 Test,** *Test Booklet,* pp. 156–158.
- **Instructional Support** See **Fine Art Transparency** 9.1. Review teacher's notes for transparencies in the *Audiovisual Resources Binder* for suggestions on how to tie the transparency to specific reading selections.
- **Extending Collection Theme** See **Cross-Curricular Activity: The Quest for Beauty,** *Teaching Resources B,* p. 60, for an activity in another discipline and for evaluation criteria.

PORTFOLIO ASSESSMENT

Parent/Guardian Involvement For forms that will help a parent or guardian review and respond to a student's portfolio, see *Portfolio Management System,* pp. 62–63.

QUICK PLANNING GUIDE

Into the Poems

Author Biography p. 710
Before You Read p. 711, p. 712, p. 714, p. 721

Through the Poems

"She Walks in Beauty" p. 711
"The Destruction of Sennacherib" p. 713
from Don Juan, Canto II pp. 715–720
from Childe Harold's Pilgrimage, Canto IV pp. 722–723
Making Meanings p. 711, p. 713, p. 720, p. 725
Primary Sources p. 724

Beyond the Poems

Choices: Building Your Portfolio p. 725
- **Writer's Notebook:** Collect notes for a reflective essay
- **Critical Writing:** In an essay, analyze a poem's similes
- **Critical Writing:** In an essay, compare and contrast two satirical works
- **Critical Writing:** Analyze a poem's form
- **Creative Writing:** Write a sequel for a poem
- **Creative Writing:** Apostrophize part of nature

Spotlight On pp. 726–728

George Gordon, Lord Byron
(1788–1824)

Until one fateful day in 1794, George Gordon Byron seemed destined to grow up confined by the harsh Calvinism of Scotland. On that day, Byron's cousin was killed in battle and young George became first in line to be the sixth Baron Byron of Rochdale. Byron assumed the title when he was ten years old.

Byron's literary elevation came no less suddenly. In 1812, the midpoint of the Romantic period, Byron became a celebrity with the publication of the first two cantos of a poem called *Childe Harold's Pilgrimage,* based on his recent travels to Europe and Asia Minor. Byron "awoke one morning," as he later said, "and found myself famous."

Byron seems to have had an obsessive determination to prove himself in every way. Extraordinarily handsome, he was born with a clubfoot, and in compensation he learned swimming, boxing, and horse riding. His lifestyle aggravated a glandular problem and a tendency toward obesity, so he would go on brutal binge diets.

The shocking aspects of Byron's private life have become legendary as a result of his literary fame, not the reverse. But they are shocking, nevertheless—and sometimes rather sad. Scandal concerning his affairs (including a relationship with his half sister Augusta), his scandalous separation from his wife, and his radical, pro-French political views made life in England uncomfortable. Byron left for the Continent in 1816, never to return.

Byron's literary career had begun modestly in 1807 with a small collection of short lyric pieces that was harshly reviewed by the *Edinburgh Review.* In response, Byron wrote the satire *English Bards and Scotch Reviewers* (1809), which reveals the vein of wit that helped cast Byron as a rebellious mocker of established conventions. His target in this satire was not

Byron, 6th Baron (late 18th to early 19th century) by Richard Westall.

only the *Edinburgh Review;* he also took on such Romantic icons as Wordsworth and Coleridge.

When Byron left England in 1816, he was drawn into contact with Percy Shelley and his wife Mary in Switzerland. Because of the association with Shelley, Byron's writing life now began in earnest. It intensified when he moved to Italy. The Byron we glimpse in these years, despite the debauchery and the circuslike menagerie he kept about him in Venice, is a man who works very hard at his writing. His wildness and aristocratic ease obscure what was, in fact, a period of great literary productivity.

As a poet, Byron was not a "Romantic" in style. His masters, in fact, were the neoclassical writers whose wit and precision he admired. Yet throughout the nineteenth century he was regarded as the incarnation of "Romantic." His premature death seemed to reinforce this image. Byron set sail for Greece in July 1823 to support the Greek nationalists in their struggle for independence from Turkey. In a marshy town in Greece called Missolonghi, he came down with fevers that took his life only a few months after his thirty-sixth birthday.

PROGRAM MANAGER

- **Planning Instruction** See **Teaching Notes,** *Teaching Resources B,* pp. 31–33, for objectives, summaries, literary elements, and additional biographical information for these selections.
- **Instructional Support** Before beginning the instructional lesson, see **Graphic Organizer for Active Reading,**
Teaching Resources B, pp. 40–42 and 45, for Through the Poems activities.
- **Audiotaped Readings** To help less proficient readers or auditory learners through the lesson, use the **Selected Reading, Audiocassette 2, Side A,** in the *Audiovisual Resources Binder.*
- **Assessment** See **Selection Tests, Test Booklet,** pp. 141, 142, 143–144, and 145.
- **Language Link** For instruction and practice in adverb clauses, see **Language Link,** *Teaching Resources B,* pp. 43–44, and *Language and Writing Skills Worksheets,* p. 82.

BEFORE YOU READ
SHE WALKS IN BEAUTY

Reading Focus

The Eye of the Beholder
No matter how often we hear that beauty is only skin deep, we all know the mysterious attraction of a beautiful person. Beauty moves us. We want to believe that outer appearances express inner qualities.

Quickwrite

If a man compares a woman's beauty to night, what qualities do you expect he sees in her? Write down what you think.

Background

"She Walks in Beauty," one of Byron's most famous poems, was supposedly inspired by Lady Wilmot Horton, a beautiful woman whom Byron saw at a ball, perhaps in the spring of 1814. Lady Horton was in mourning and, in the fashion of the times, was wearing a black dress decorated with glittering spangles.

She Walks in Beauty

George Gordon, Lord Byron

She walks in beauty, like the night
   Of cloudless climes° and starry skies;
And all that's best of dark and bright
   Meet in her aspect° and her eyes:
5 Thus mellowed to that tender light
   Which heaven to gaudy day denies.

One shade the more, one ray the less,
   Had half impaired the nameless grace
Which waves in every raven tress,
10   Or softly lightens o'er her face;
Where thoughts serenely sweet express
   How pure, how dear their dwelling place.

And on that cheek, and o'er that brow,
   So soft, so calm, yet eloquent,
15 The smiles that win, the tints that glow,
   But tell of days in goodness spent,
A mind at peace with all below,
   A heart whose love is innocent!

2. **climes:** atmospheres; climates.
4. **aspect:** face; look.

MAKING MEANINGS

First Thoughts

1. How does Byron respond to this "dark" beauty? (Compare his response with your Reader's Log notes.)

Shaping Interpretations

2. What in the woman's appearance does the speaker praise? What conclusions does he draw about her character and personality?

3. What does the speaker imply about day when he calls it "gaudy"?

4. "Dark and bright" (line 3) suggests a balance of opposites. How is this idea developed?

5. What do you think the speaker means by "below" in line 17?

Challenging the Text

6. This poem has been criticized as sentimental and dependent on clichés. Tell whether or not you agree and why.

7. Do you think that inward nature can be revealed by outward appearances? Explain.

GEORGE GORDON, LORD BYRON 711

Making Meanings
First Thoughts

1. Byron responds passionately; he seems to be in awe. Students may note that "dark" beauty evokes mystery.

Into the Poem

Using **BEFORE YOU READ** p. 711

Reading Focus

Have students compare pictures of historical fashions and then discuss beauty's timeless elements. You may want to list students' ideas on the chalkboard to compare with the poem.

Through the Poem

A. Literary Element: Imagery
? What is the focus of the imagery? [The contrast between dark and light.]

B. Critical Reading: Finding Details
? How does the description in ll. 11–12 relate the woman's attractiveness to an inner beauty? [The woman's face reveals her beautiful thoughts.]

Shaping Interpretations

2. The speaker praises the meeting of darkness and light in the woman's appearance. The balance suggests her peacefulness and goodness.

3. Daylight is garish compared to the soft light of night.

4. The pairing occurs again in ll. 7 and 9–10. See also ll. 13–14.

5. Possible response: "Below" could refer to earthly concerns. The woman's innocence gives her peace amid earthly strife.

Challenging the Text

6. **(Evaluation)** Students may say that the poet's praise is a cliché, but that the poem's startling images overcome mere sentiment.

7. **(Analysis)** Agree—a person's facial expression and body language can give clues to their nature. Disagree—beauty does not mean a person is happy or good as Byron implies.

Into the Poem

Using BEFORE YOU READ p. 712

A Dialogue with the Text

Direct students to list the details in the transformation of the picture the poem creates. Their notes tracking the change should record the changes in the few essential elements as well as personal impressions and reactions to the changes.

Elements of Literature

Encourage students to create a line of poetry using anapestic rhythm. Then, have them share their creations. What are their impressions of the rhythm? Does it display certain characteristics, or have certain effects? [Students may say that the rhythm is too dramatic, exaggerated, or comical in its effect.]

Through the Poem

A. Literary Element: Anapestic Rhythm

? What does the rhythm of ll. 1–2 suggest? [Students may say Byron's anapestic rhythm mimics the sound of pounding horses' hooves. Others may find that the steady third beat of the meter suggests steady drumbeat or heartbeat.]

B. Critical Reading: Summarizing

? How do ll. 5–8 visually summarize the poem's events? [The Assyrians begin their attack in full strength and with much color, like summer leaves. When they die, they are like withered, scattered autumn leaves.]

BEFORE YOU READ
THE DESTRUCTION OF SENNACHERIB

Reading Focus
Old Tales of Miracles
The Romantics loved old stories, old ballads, tales of heroism and fantasy—like this Biblical story of the miraculous deliverance of the Israelites from the Assyrian army. Watch for the images that romanticize the conflict—that glorify the victor and demonize the enemy.

A Dialogue with the Text

Be sure to read this poem aloud. After the first stanza, jot down a few notes about the picture Byron is creating. Then, as you continue to read, make notes on how the picture changes.

Elements of Literature
Anapestic Rhythm
Byron skillfully uses the bouncy **anapestic rhythm** (˘ ˘ ´), which was quite popular in the nineteenth century but has seldom been used by serious poets since.

Background
In both Kings and Chronicles, the Bible tells the story of the Assyrian king Sennacherib's (sə·nak′ər·ib) attempt to capture and enslave Jerusalem. With his mighty army about to descend on the city, "the Angel of Death"—in the form of a sudden pestilence or plague—killed man and beast alike, yet spared the king. Sennacherib's failure so disgraced "Ashur" (Assyria) that his own sons murdered him on his return. This poem and "She Walks in Beauty" are from a collection called *Hebrew Melodies,* lyrics that were to be set to music.

Cavalryman Fording a Stream. Fragment of a wall relief (8th–7th century B.C.) from the palace of Sennacherib at Nineveh, Assyria.

The Metropolitan Museum of Art, New York. Gift of John D. Rockefeller, Jr., 1932. (32.143.8)

OPTIONS FOR TEACHING

STRATEGIES FOR INCLUSION

Advanced Students might like to read the Biblical description of the battle in II Kings 18–19 before they read the poem. They can compare the poet's account with the Biblical description.

English Language Development Before students read the poem, ask them to imagine a city that has succumbed to a plague. What does it look like? If you were to walk around that city, what do you think you would see, hear, or smell? Ask students to write down their responses and then to share them with a partner. Have them record their thoughts in their Reader's Logs so that they can compare their images with the poet's after they have read the poem.

The Destruction of Sennacherib

George Gordon, Lord Byron

The Assyrian came down like the wolf on the fold, **(A)**
And his cohorts were gleaming in purple and gold;
And the sheen of their spears was like stars on the sea,
When the blue wave rolls nightly on deep Galilee.°

5 Like the leaves of the forest when summer is green, **(B)**
That host° with their banners at sunset were seen:
Like the leaves of the forest when autumn hath blown,
That host on the morrow lay withered and strown.

For the Angel of Death spread his wings on the blast,
10 And breathed in the face of the foe as he passed;
And the eyes of the sleepers waxed deadly and chill,
And their hearts but once heaved, and forever grew still!

And there lay the steed with his nostril all wide, **(C)**
But through it there rolled not the breath of his pride;
15 And the foam of his gasping lay white on the turf,
And cold as the spray of the rock-beating surf.

And there lay the rider distorted and pale, **(D)**
With the dew on his brow, and the rust on his mail:°
And the tents were all silent, the banners alone,
20 The lances unlifted, the trumpet unblown.

And the widows of Ashur are loud in their wail,
And the idols are broke in the temple of Baal;°
And the might of the Gentile,° unsmote° by the sword, **(E)**
Hath melted like snow in the glance of the Lord!

4. sea . . . Galilee: lake north of Jerusalem.

6. host: the army; also, a great number.

18. mail: kind of body armor made of linked metal rings.

22. Baal (bā′əl): the Assyrian god.
23. Gentile: Sennacherib and the Assyrians (non-Hebrews).
unsmote: not destroyed.

MAKING MEANINGS

First Thoughts

1. After reading the poem, what **image** do you remember most vividly? Compare your visual memories in class.

Shaping Interpretations

2. What are the Assyrians doing in the first stanza, and what has happened in the second? What **similes** describe the changing scenes? (Look at your Reader's Log notes for ideas.)

3. How is the army's defeat **personified**?

4. What **images** and **similes** in the last three stanzas help you see the aftermath of the plague?

5. Identify the poem's **meter,** and describe how it helps reinforce the poem's action. How do you think this meter would suit a modern battle poem?

6. What do you feel Byron wanted to accomplish in writing this poem?

Challenging the Text

7. Does the poem still have appeal for you today? Why or why not? What does it say to modern readers?

GEORGE GORDON, LORD BYRON 713

C. Critical Reading: Expressing an Opinion

? Why is the idea of breathing repeatedly mentioned in ll. 13–16? [Students may say that the repetition emphasizes the stillness of the dead.]

Metacognition How would you read ll. 13–16 differently if you were painting the scene? [Students may say they would pay more attention to details than to mood or symbolism.]

D. Language Note: Diction

? What words in ll. 17–20 emphasize the scene's stillness? ["Lay" and "dew" suggest a gentle settling; "unlifted" and "unblown" emphasize actions that cannot be done.]

E. Reader's Response: Shaping Interpretations

? What do ll. 22–24 tell you about the Lord's might? [Sample responses: It is like the sun's rays. Or it is powerful and capable of destruction.]

Making Meanings

First Thoughts

1. Students may appreciate particularly vivid imagery, such as the Assyrians' charge or the Angel of Death.

Shaping Interpretations

2. The Assyrians attack in the first stanza; in the second, they lie dead. The leaf simile unites the two events.

3. Sleepers die when the Angel of Death breathes on their faces.

4. The dead horse, the dead rider, and the wails of the Assyrian women show the plague's effects.

5. The anapestic tetrameter evokes the charging hoof beats of the horses; this meter might not fit a description of a modern battle.

6. Students may say that Byron sought to illustrate how the divine may decisively influence the lives of human beings.

Challenging the Text

7. **(Evaluation)** Students may say that the harsh realities of modern war make it difficult to appreciate the poem's enthusiasm for war's glory.

Into the Poem

Reading Focus

Ask students what they know about the Don Juan legend, and ask them what they expect from Byron's changes in the theme. [Students may say they expect humorous situations and satirical commentary rather than a serious discussion of passion and conquests.] You may also want to have students discuss how the quest of Don Juan (both the Spanish legend and Byron's character) compares with other adventures they have seen or read.

Background

Byron acted on the liberty and independence he celebrated in his poetry when he made his ill-fated expedition to aid the Greek rebellion against the Turks. His death in the Greek cause focused attention on the struggle for freedom of oppressed people throughout Europe. Sir Herbert Grierson remarked that "when he went to Greece it was not only a man and an English peer who went but a Power in Europe." Throughout the nineteenth century Byron remained a symbol of a new spirit in European culture and politics.

BEFORE YOU READ
FROM DON JUAN

Reading Focus
Chasing a Dream

The legendary Don Juan (in Spanish, hwän) is a notorious seducer of women, the greatest lover in history, a man whose passion for women drove him from one to another—with narrow escapes in between. But Byron's Don Juan (jōō'ən) is different from other versions. His hero is an innocent who becomes involved in many amorous adventures simply because he is, like Byron, so handsome and irresistible. However, the narrator (also like Byron) is not innocent, and that makes for lively satire. As women chase the innocent beauty of Don Juan around the world, the narrator shows us another fruitless quest: for pure beauty and love in a hypocritical world.

A Dialogue with the Text

Some things in this excerpt are sure to catch you off guard. Label a column in your Reader's Log "Surprises." Every time Byron or his lively speaker catches you with something unexpected—a joke, sarcasm, a funny rhyme, an odd detail, a "modern" idea—make a quick note, with line numbers.

Elements of Literature
Ottava Rima

The eight-line stanza form of *Don Juan* is based on the Italian ottava rima (ō·tä'və rē'mə). While Byron adheres strictly to the demands of the form, his tone is loosely conversational, colloquial, and continually punctuated by digressions. One of the poem's charms is that it moves at a pace appropriate to the narrator's quick shifts of attention. He is confident that the reader will stay with him when, every now and then, he slows down and dawdles over something he sees from the corner of his eye.

> **O**ttava rima, in its English form, is eight lines of iambic pentameter, rhyming *ababab cc.*
>
> *For more on Ottava Rima, see the Handbook of Literary Terms.*

Background

Don Juan is the longest satirical poem in English literature. Left unfinished at Byron's death, it comprises sixteen long divisions (cantos) and part of a seventeenth. The form the poem would take came to Byron late in his comparatively brief life. But once Byron mastered it, he found it accommodated everything he wanted to say about the world he knew. The result was a poem of enormous popularity and scandalous interest, since Byron's own erotic exploits lay behind it. In contrast with the solemn lyricism of his contemporaries, Byron hearkened back to poets like Alexander Pope, with their penchant for wit as both social grace and weapon against folly. This extract comes from the early part of *Don Juan,* where the hero finds himself shipwrecked on a Greek island. Haidee, the daughter of a pirate, falls in love with Don Juan. To enjoy the fun, read the poem aloud.

Sunset on the Yorkshire Coast (c. 1885) by Richard Weatherill.

Chris Beetles Ltd., London.

from Don Juan, Canto II

George Gordon, Lord Byron

It was a wild and breaker-beaten coast,
  With cliffs above, and a broad sandy shore,
Guarded by shoals and rocks as by an host,°
  With here and there a creek, whose aspect wore
5 A better welcome to the tempest tost;°
  And rarely ceased the haughty billow's roar,
Save on the dead long summer days, which make
The outstretched ocean glitter like a lake.

· · · · · · · · · · · · · · · · 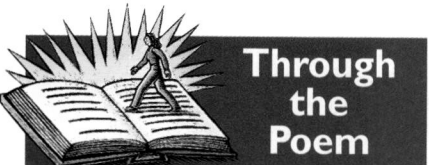 A

The coast—I think it was the coast that I
10 Was just describing—Yes, it *was* the coast— B
Lay at this period quiet as the sky,
  The sands untumbled, the blue waves untost, C
And all was stillness, save the seabird's cry,
  And dolphin's leap, and little billow crost
15 By some low rock or shelf, that made it fret
Against the boundary it scarcely wet.

And forth they° wandered, her sire being gone,
  As I have said, upon an expedition;
And mother, brother, guardian, she had none,
20 Save Zoe, who, although with due precision
She waited on her lady with the sun,
  Thought daily service was her only mission,
Bringing warm water, wreathing her long tresses,
And asking now and then for castoff dresses. D

25 It was the cooling hour, just when the rounded ⌐
  Red sun sinks down behind the azure° hill,
Which then seems as if the whole earth it bounded,
  Circling all nature, hushed, and dim, and still,
With the far mountain crescent half surrounded E
30 On one side, and the deep sea calm and chill
Upon the other, and the rosy sky,
With one star sparkling through it like an eye. ⌊

And thus they wandered forth, and hand in hand, ⌐
  Over the shining pebbles and the shells,
35 Glided along the smooth and hardened sand,
  And in the worn and wild receptacles F
Worked by the storms, yet worked as it were planned,
  In hollow halls, with sparry° roofs and cells,
They turned to rest; and, each clasped by an arm,
40 Yielded to the deep twilight's purple charm. ⌊

3. **host:** army.

5. **tempest tost:** storm tossed.

17. **they:** Haidee and Don Juan.

26. **azure:** sky-blue.

38. **sparry:** made of shiny rock.

GEORGE GORDON, LORD BYRON **715**

Through the Poem

A. Expansion
This dotted line indicates text not printed here in which Byron digresses.

B. Critical Reading: Analyzing Tone
? What do you think is the purpose of this comment on the narrator's wandering attention? [The effect is a comic contrast with the serious narration.]

C. Language Note: Diction
? What is the common link between the adjectives in l. 12?
[They both begin with the prefix *un–*, a fact that emphasizes the scene's stillness.]

D. Literary Element: Point of View
? What is the narrator's perspective in l. 24? [The narrator's view of servants is aristocratic and satiric.]

E. Literary Element: Tone
? How does the tone in ll. 25–32 contrast with the preceding stanza? [The tone shifts from a satiric, informal social commentary to a highly poetic appreciation of nature.]

F. Literary Element: Ottava Rima
Ask students to mark the stanza's-*abababcc* rhyme scheme. Ask them to discuss how this format affects the poem. [Students may say rhyming words such as *hand*, *sand*, and *planned* help carry the reader through the stanza. They also may say that the final couplet (*arm*, *charm*) helps mark the stanza's ending.]

OPTIONS FOR TEACHING

STRATEGIES FOR INCLUSION

Auditory Encourage students to notice the stanzas' witty endings. Have volunteers read the stanzas aloud, allowing students to note how rhythm and rhyme contribute to the humor of each. Students can share their notes after they have finished reading the poem.

Advanced Challenge students to look for changes in **tone** and **point of view** as they read the poem. Ask students to keep track of such changes and to try to discern the purpose behind them. Students may use their notes in a discussion of Byron's place among the Romantics. ☞

George Gordon, Lord Byron **T715**

A. Critical Reading: Analyzing Metaphor

? Is the metaphor in ll. 63–64 apt or is it somewhat strained? [Strained.] Do you think that the strain is intentional? [The poem explodes some Romantic conventions, and it is openly satirical, so students may say the metaphor's strain is intentional; its absurdity also reflects the inexpressible quality of the characters' love for each other.]

B. Literary Element: Satire

? What is the subject of the narrator's satire in ll. 81–84? [The narrator indirectly mocks women's demands for constancy from their lovers and men's reputation for infidelity.]

They looked up to the sky, whose floating glow
    Spread like a rosy ocean, vast and bright;
They gazed upon the glittering sea below,
    Whence the broad moon rose circling into sight;
45 They heard the wave's splash, and the wind so low,
    And saw each other's dark eyes darting light
Into each other—and, beholding this,
Their lips drew near, and clung into a kiss;

A long, long kiss, a kiss of youth and love,
50   And beauty, all concentrating like rays
Into one focus, kindled from above;
    Such kisses as belong to early days,
Where heart, and soul, and sense, in concert° move,
    And the blood's lava, and the pulse a blaze,
55 Each kiss a heart quake—for a kiss's strength,
I think, it must be reckoned by its length.

By length I mean duration; theirs endured
    Heaven knows how long—no doubt they never reckoned;
And if they had, they could not have secured
60   The sum of their sensations to a second:
They had not spoken; but they felt allured,
    As if their souls and lips each other beckoned,
Which, being joined, like swarming bees they clung—
Their hearts the flowers from whence the honey sprung.

65 They were alone, but not alone as they
    Who shut in chambers think it loneliness;
The silent ocean, and the starlight bay,
    The twilight glow, which momently° grew less,
The voiceless sands, and dropping° caves, that lay
70   Around them, made them to each other press,
As if there were no life beneath the sky
Save theirs; and that their life could never die.

They feared no eyes nor ears on that lone beach,
    They felt no terrors from the night, they were
75 All in all to each other: Though their speech
    Was broken words, they *thought* a language there—
And all the burning tongues the passions teach
    Found in one sigh the best interpreter
Of nature's oracle°—first love—that all
80 Which Eve has left her daughters since her fall.

Haidee spoke not of scruples, asked no vows,
    Nor offered any; she had never heard
Of plight° and promises to be a spouse,
    Or perils by a loving maid incurred;
85 She was all which pure ignorance allows,
    And flew to her young mate like a young bird;
And, never having dreamt of falsehood, she
Had not one word to say of constancy.

53. **in concert:** together.

68. **momently:** at each moment.
69. **dropping:** dripping.

79. **oracle:** revelation.

83. **plight:** promise of marriage.

(Background) *Norfolk Coast* (detail) (late 19th or early 20th century) by Albert Goodwin.
Bonhams, London.

716 THE ROMANTIC PERIOD

OPTIONS FOR TEACHING

STRATEGIES FOR INCLUSION

Less Proficient Readers Students may have difficulty with the poem's wandering **point of view.** Ask them to note the main idea of each stanza as they read. They can reflect on the poem's themes and organization before re-reading it to improve their comprehension.

Special Needs This excerpt from *Don Juan* is quite long and contains language that might prove daunting to students with reading disabilities. Read the poem aloud as students follow along in their texts. Pause frequently to make observations and ask questions that relate the poem to students' lives. For example, after the speaker's provocative statement in ll. 153–154, "for man, to man so oft unjust, / Is always so to women," pause and ask students to paraphrase the lines. Then, ask them if they agree, and why or why not.

Night and Sleep (1888)
by Simeon Solomon.
Pencil and chalk (349 mm × 286 mm).

Birmingham Museums & Art Gallery,
Birmingham, England.

C. Literary Element: Point of View

? How does the perspective change in ll. 97–104? [The nostalgic narrator initially praises the lovers' passion, but he ends with a jaded view of the pain lovers bring each other.]

D. Reader's Response: Connecting with the Text

? Is the allusion to Adam and Eve in l. 107, "our first parents," typically Romantic? [Sample responses: Romantics alluded often to Greek and Roman myth and to the Bible, so the allusion itself is typical; or its irreverent use is atypical of Romantic poetry.]

She loved, and was beloved—she adored,
90   And she was worshipped; after nature's fashion,
Their intense souls, into each other poured,
     If souls could die, had perished in that passion,—
But by degrees their senses were restored,
     Again to be o'ercome, again to dash on;
95 And, beating 'gainst *his* bosom, Haidee's heart
Felt as if never more to beat apart.

Alas! they were so young, so beautiful,
     So lonely, loving, helpless, and the hour
Was that in which the heart is always full,
100   And, having o'er itself no further power, **C**
Prompts deeds eternity can not annul,°
     But pays off moments in an endless shower
Of hellfire—all prepared for people giving
Pleasure or pain to one another living.

105 Alas! for Juan and Haidee! they were
     So loving and so lovely—till then never,
Excepting our first parents, such a pair **D**
     Had run the risk of being damned forever;
And Haidee, being devout as well as fair,

101. annul: cancel.

GEORGE GORDON, LORD BYRON 717

INTEGRATING THE LANGUAGE ARTS

Strategic Reading Have students take turns reading parts of the poem aloud to the class. Ask one student to read the first stanza aloud and then to pick another student to read the next stanza. Students should continue until they have finished the poem.

CROSSING THE CURRICULUM

Journalism Have students look for examples of gossip, satire, and opinions on current events in a newspaper. Ask each student to share an example with the class and to draw a parallel between the item and an example in the poem by writing a brief paragraph. You may want to provide issues of local and national newspapers for students to use as resources.

Music Play a selection or a few selections from Mozart's *Don Giovanni*. Encourage the class to discuss how the opera differs from the poem. Students should refer to specific musical passages in their comments. ☞

A. Language Note: Repetition

? What is the effect of the repetition of comparisons in ll. 121–128? [The repetition creates suspense and emphasizes the bounty of the lovers' joy.]

110   Had, doubtless, heard about the Stygian river,°
       And hell and purgatory—but forgot
       Just in the very crisis she should not.

       .   .   .   .

       And when those deep and burning moments passed,
           And Juan sunk to sleep within her arms,
115   She slept not, but all tenderly, though fast,°
           Sustained his head upon her bosom's charms;
       And now and then her eye to heaven is cast,
           And then on the pale cheek her breast now warms,
       Pillowed on her o'erflowing heart, which pants
120   With all it granted, and with all it grants.

       An infant when it gazes on a light,
           A child the moment when it drains the breast,
       A devotee when soars the Host° in sight,
           An Arab with a stranger for a guest,
125   A sailor when the prize has struck in fight,°
           A miser filling his most hoarded chest,
       Feel rapture; but not such true joy are reaping
       As they who watch o'er what they love while sleeping.

110. Stygian river: the river Styx. In Greek mythology, the Styx encircles Hades (hā′dēz′), the underworld.

115. fast: firmly.

123. Host: the Eucharistic wafer that is lifted up during the Anglican or Catholic Mass. Devout church members believe it is the Body of Christ.
125. prize . . . fight: captured enemy ship that has lowered its flag in surrender.

Miranda (1878) by Sir Frank Dicksee.
The Maas Gallery, London.

718 THE ROMANTIC PERIOD

For there it lies so tranquil, so beloved,
130   All that it hath of life with us is living;
So gentle, stirless, helpless, and unmoved,
          And all unconscious of the joy 'tis giving;
All it hath felt, inflicted, passed, and proved,
          Hushed into depths beyond the watcher's diving;
135   There lies the thing we love with all its errors
And all its charms, like death without its terrors. **B**

The lady watched her lover—and that hour
          Of Love's, and Night's, and Ocean's solitude,
O'erflowed her soul with their united power;
140   Amidst the barren sand and rocks so rude°
She and her wave-worn love had made their bower,°
          Where nought upon their passion could intrude,
And all the stars that crowded the blue space
Saw nothing happier than her glowing face.

145   Alas! the love of women! it is known
          To be a lovely and a fearful thing;
For all of theirs upon that die° is thrown,
          And if 'tis lost, life hath no more to bring
To them but mockeries of the past alone,
150   And their revenge is as the tiger's spring, **C**
Deadly, and quick, and crushing; yet, as real
Torture is theirs, what they inflict they feel.

They are right; for man, to man so oft unjust,
          Is always so to women; one sole bond
155   Awaits them, treachery is all their trust;°
          Taught to conceal, their bursting hearts despond°
Over their idol, till some wealthier lust **D**
          Buys them in marriage—and what rests beyond?
A thankless husband, next a faithless lover,
160   Then dressing, nursing, praying, and all's over.

Some take a lover, some take drams° or prayers,
          Some mind their household, others dissipation,°
Some run away, and but exchange their cares,
          Losing the advantage of a virtuous station;
165   Few changes e'er can better their affairs,
          Theirs being an unnatural situation,
From the dull palace to the dirty hovel:°
Some play the devil, and then write a novel. **E**

Haidee was Nature's bride, and knew not this;
170   Haidee was Passion's child, born where the sun
Showers triple light, and scorches even the kiss
          Of his gazelle-eyed daughters; she was one
Made but to love, to feel that she was his
          Who was her chosen: What was said or done
175   Elsewhere was nothing—She had nought to fear,
Hope, care, nor love beyond, her heart beat *here*.

140. **rude:** rough.
141. **bower:** rustic dwelling place.

147. **die:** one of a pair of dice.

155. **treachery . . . trust:** Treachery is the only thing women can count on getting from men.
156. **despond:** despair.

161. **drams:** shots of liquor.
162. **dissipation:** riotous, wild living.

167. **hovel:** open shed or hut; miserable dwelling.

GEORGE GORDON, LORD BYRON   719

B. Reader's Response: Challenging the Text

? Does the poet's comparison of the object of one's love to "death without its terrors" (l. 136) make sense to you? Explain. [Sample responses: Don Juan is asleep, which is like a death that is not frightening; or it is hard to imagine death as a positive thing.]

C. Literary Element: Satire

? What is the narrator's attitude toward women in ll. 145–152? [He satirizes them as depending entirely on love, causing their lovers to grow bored, and quickly seeking revenge.]

D. Literary Element: Tone

? What is the tone of the narrator's comments on marriage in ll. 153–160? [Cynical and hopeless.]

E. Expansion

In 1816, Lady Caroline Lamb published a novel, *Glenarvon,* that was based on her scandalous affair with Byron. The novel included a letter that Byron wrote to break off the relationship.

A. Literary Element: Climax

Lines 177–184 bring a climax to the lovers' relationship that results in their marriage in the next stanza. What is the effect of this climactic stanza? [Ironically, the climax is deflated by humor in l. 184.]

Making Meanings

First Thoughts

1. Students may say the poem's scandal seems unremarkable today, or they may say that themes of sexuality may still be controversial.

Reviewing the Text

a. The setting is a rocky coast with cliffs and a sandy shore.

b. Haidee's maid Zoe; her father is on an expedition.

c. Haidee cannot imagine falsehood. She does not ask for promises because she does not see the need for them.

d. Women seek revenge. Some take lovers, drink, or pray; some run away. They want revenge because without love, life becomes meaningless to them.

e. The priest was solitude, the nuptial torches were stars, the witness was the ocean, and their bed was the cave.

Shaping Interpretations

2. Haidee does not know of falsehood so is "ignorant" of evil.

3. The two lovers are alone in paradise. Byron compares their innocence and impending downfall to Adam and Eve's in l. 107.

4. Examples include the star "eye" in l. 32, "blood's lava" in l. 54, and the comparison of the lovers to "swarming bees" in l. 63. Exaggeration balances the idyllic scenes with humor.

5. Humorous final couplets include ll. 23–24, 167–168, and 183–184.

6. It is satirical and exaggerated, yet indulgent and sentimental.

7. Some of Byron's targets are Lady Caroline Lamb, Castlereagh, conventional morality, and religion. The poem satirizes the exaggerated sincerity and sentimentality of Romantic tradition.

And oh! that quickening of the heart, that beat!
　　How much it costs us! yet each rising throb
Is in its cause as its effect so sweet,
180　　That Wisdom, ever on the watch to rob
Joy of its alchemy,° and to repeat
　　Fine truths, even Conscience, too, has a tough job
To make us understand each good old maxim,
So good—I wonder Castlereagh° don't tax 'em.

185 And now 'twas done—on the lone shore were plighted
　　Their hearts; the stars, their nuptial torches, shed
Beauty upon the beautiful they lighted:
　　Ocean their witness, and the cave their bed,
By their own feelings hallowed° and united,
190　　Their priest was Solitude, and they were wed:
And they were happy, for to their young eyes
Each was an angel, and earth paradise.

181. alchemy (al′kə·mē): chemistry (here, miraculous power to change things).

184. Castlereagh: British foreign secretary from 1812 to 1822, much disliked by radicals, including Byron and Shelley.

189. hallowed: made holy.

MAKING MEANINGS

First Thoughts

1. Though Byron insisted it was a moral poem, *Don Juan* was the focus of scandalous interest when it was published. How would readers today respond to the supposed "scandalous" passages?

Shaping Interpretations

2. What do you think the speaker means by linking Haidee with "pure ignorance" (line 85)?

3. In what way could this story be analogous to the story of Adam and Eve (page 416)? Where does Byron suggest the association directly?

4. Find at least three exaggerated **figures of speech,** and discuss Byron's intended effects.

5. Where does Byron use the final couplet in the **ottava rima** for comic effect?

6. What is the speaker's **tone** when he describes Don Juan and Haidee falling in love?

7. If *Don Juan* is in part witty **satire,** who or what are Byron's targets? Where do you find some barbs directed at the whole Romantic tradition, as exemplified by Wordsworth and Coleridge?

Reviewing the Text

a. What is the **setting**?

b. Who is Haidee's only companion (besides Don Juan), and why?

c. In what ways is Haidee, lines 81–88, described as totally innocent? Why doesn't she ask her lover for a vow of constancy?

d. According to lines 145–168, what do women do when they lose love? Why?

e. Describe the nuptials that Haidee and Juan celebrate in lines 185–190.

Connecting with the Text

8. Check your Reader's Log. What was your favorite or biggest "surprise" in the poem? Why?

9. What do you think of Byron's attitude toward women?

720 THE ROMANTIC PERIOD

Connecting with the Text

8. Students may be surprised at the political commentary inserted in the climactic description of the couple's love in l. 184.

9. Students may find that both Byron's condemnation of typical women and his idealization of the innocent, ignorant, natural woman Haidee are outdated.

ASSESSMENT TOOLS

Check Test: Questions and Answers

1. Who are the lovers in the poem? [Haidee and Don Juan.]

2. Why is Haidee alone with Don Juan? [Her father is on an expedition.]

3. What is the speaker's attitude toward the lovers? [By turns idealizing and mocking, sometimes cynical.]

4. How are the two characters married? [By expressing their love to each other.]

BEFORE YOU READ
FROM CHILDE HAROLD'S PILGRIMAGE

Reading Focus

The Journey Out—and In
A quest may have a goal, but if the journey is long enough, the traveler may discover that in the quest itself lies the prize. What is explored, all alone on a journey, is the lonely self. That may be true even when the pilgrim, like Byron's Childe Harold, cuts a spirited path through exotic lands. And it is especially true when the pilgrim is alone in vast, glorious, but heartless nature.

Quickwrite

Briefly freewrite about your strongest memory or mental image of the ocean. How do you feel about the sea?

Background

This long poem—which made Byron suddenly famous—appeared in sections (cantos) from 1812 to 1818. It is a thinly disguised autobiographical account of Byron's own journeys. Its pilgrim, Childe Harold, became the prototype for the moody, dashingly handsome character type who would eventually be dubbed the "Byronic hero." (In medieval times, *child* likely meant a young noble awaiting knighthood; Byron uses it as a title, like Lord or Sir, for a youth of "gentle" birth.) In this excerpt from the final canto, the speaker addresses the ocean. The last two verses are Byron's personal conclusion to the whole poem. By this time, Byron said, he had ceased trying to separate himself from the figure of Childe Harold.

The Wanderer over the Sea of Clouds (1818) by Casper David Friedrich.
Hamburger Kunsthalle, Hamburg, Germany.

GEORGE GORDON, LORD BYRON 721

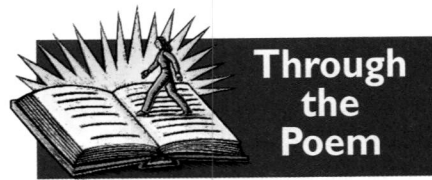

Through the Poem

A. Literary Element: Apostrophe

? How does the apostrophe in l. 10 add to the descriptive imagery of the ocean? [The speaker urges the sea to "roll on," which both depicts the sea's action and suggests the strength of its motion.]

B. Language Note: Repetition

? Do the adjectives in l. 18 display a common technique in Byron's poetry? Explain. [Yes; Byron frequently repeats sounds, and the adjectives all begin with the prefix *un–*.]

C. Literary Element: Alliteration

? What is the effect of the repetition of *b* sounds in ll. 20–22? [Students may say the repetition has a playful sound and lightens the tone.]

Metacognition Recognizing the effects of rhythm, rhyme, sound, and imagery is important for understanding a poem. What is a good strategy for recognizing important elements of a poem? [Students may suggest reading the poem aloud, reading it more than once, or consulting other people or books about the poem. Have students discuss their ideas.]

D. Critical Reading: Drawing Conclusions

? How does the speaker describe himself in ll. 33–36? [The speaker says his visions and energy, and perhaps also his inspiration, have waned.]

---

from Childe Harold's Pilgrimage, Canto IV
George Gordon, Lord Byron

1

There is a pleasure in the pathless woods,
There is a rapture on the lonely shore,
There is society, where none intrudes,
By the deep sea, and music in its roar:
5 I love not man the less, but Nature more,
From these our interviews, in which I steal°
From all I may be, or have been before,
To mingle with the Universe, and feel
What I can ne'er express, yet cannot all conceal.

6. **steal:** remove myself.

2

(A) 10 Roll on, thou deep and dark blue Ocean—roll!
Ten thousand fleets sweep over thee in vain;
Man marks the earth with ruin—his control
Stops with the shore; upon the watery plain
The wrecks are all thy deed, nor doth remain
15 A shadow of man's ravage, save his own,
When, for a moment, like a drop of rain,
He sinks into thy depths with bubbling groan,
(B) Without a grave, unknelled,° uncoffined, and unknown.

18. **unknelled** (un·neld′): without the traditional ringing of a church bell to announce his death.

3

And I have loved thee, Ocean! and my joy
20 Of youthful sports was on thy breast to be
Borne, like thy bubbles, onward: From a boy
(C) I wantoned° with thy breakers—they to me
Were a delight; and if the freshening° sea
Made them a terror—'twas a pleasing fear,
25 For I was as it were a child of thee,
And trusted to thy billows far and near,
And laid my hand upon thy mane—as I do here.

22. **wantoned:** frolicked; played happily.
23. **freshening:** becoming rough as the wind comes up.

4

My task is done, my song hath ceased, my theme
Has died into an echo; it is fit
30 The spell should break of this protracted dream.
The torch shall be extinguished which hath lit
My midnight lamp—and what is writ, is writ;
(D) Would it were worthier! but I am not now

CROSSING THE CURRICULUM

Art Have each student find a picture reflecting a lonely or meditative quality about nature. Encourage students to browse art books or to look up other works by artists whose illustrations and paintings have accompanied the material in the textbook. Students may share their findings with each other in an informal discussion.

CLASSROOM MANAGEMENT

Theme Day Plan a theme day on which students view art, listen to music, and read aloud pieces of writing all related to Romanticism. Students could listen to music by Liszt, Schubert, Mendelssohn, or Chopin; read selections from Goethe; or view art by Blake, Fuseli, and others. You also could encourage students to set up stations for the theme day themselves by finding contemporary examples of Romanticism.

That which I have been—and my visions flit
35 Less palpably° before me—and the glow
Which in my spirit dwelt is fluttering, faint, and low.

35. **palpably:** clearly.

5

Farewell! a word that must be, and hath been—
A sound which makes us linger;—yet—farewell!
Ye! who have traced the Pilgrim to the scene
40 Which is his last, if in your memories dwell
A thought which once was his, if on ye swell
A single recollection, not in vain
He wore his sandal shoon and scallop shell;°
Farewell! with *him* alone may rest the pain,
45 If such there were—with *you*, the moral of his strain.°

43. **sandal shoon . . . shell:** *Shoon* is archaic for "shoes." Sandals and a scallop shell worn on a hat were traditional emblems of pilgrims. The scallop shell is a symbol of St. James, whose shrine in Spain was a great attraction to pilgrims.

45. **strain:** passage of poetry or song.

Wreckers off the Brittany Coast (1911) by Georges P. C. Maroniez.
Bonhams, London.

GEORGE GORDON, LORD BYRON 723

Primary Sources

Byron's letter refers to the poets Alexander Pope and John Keats. Unlike his contemporaries, Byron admired the neoclassical poets' technical brilliance. He claimed the innovations of Romantics such as Wordsworth, Coleridge, and Keats were "all in the wrong, one as much as another . . . we are upon a wrong revolutionary poetical system." Shelley's elegy for Keats, *Adonais* (1821), mistakenly attributed Keats's illness to a scathing review of *Endymion*. In fact, Keats died from tuberculosis, which he contracted while nursing his brother Tom.

The poet John Keats had died in Rome on February 23, 1821. Here is Byron's response to the news. (The child mentioned in the first sentence is Allegra, the daughter Byron had with Claire Clairmont, Mary Shelley's stepsister. Allegra would not live long.)

Byron Writes to Shelley

Ravenna, April 26, 1821

The child continues doing well, and the accounts are regular and favorable. It is gratifying to me that you and Mrs. Shelley do not disapprove of the step which I have taken, which is merely temporary.

I am very sorry to hear what you say of Keats—is it *actually* true? I did not think criticism had been so killing. Though I differ from you essentially in your estimate of his performances, I so much abhor all unnecessary pain, that I would rather he had been seated on the highest peak of Parnassus than have perished in such a manner. Poor fellow! though with such inordinate self-love he would probably have not been very happy. I read the review of *Endymion* in the *Quarterly*. It was severe—but surely not so severe as many reviews in that and other journals upon others.

. . . I have published a pamphlet on the Pope controversy, which you will not like. Had I known Keats was dead—or that he was alive and so sensitive—I should have omitted some remarks upon his poetry, to which I was provoked by his *attack* upon *Pope,* and my disapprobation of *his own* style of writing.

You want me to undertake a great poem—I have not the inclination nor the power. As I grow older, the indifference—*not* to life, for we love it by instinct—but to stimuli of life, increases. Besides, this late failure of the Italians has latterly disappointed me for many reasons—some public, some personal. My respects to Mrs. S.

Yours ever,
B.

P. S.—Could not you and I contrive to meet this summer? Could not you take a run here *alone*?

Byron Among the Ancient Ruins (early 19th century). Steel engraving.
The Granger Collection, New York.

STRATEGIES FOR INCLUSION

Interpersonal Arrange students in groups of four or five, and have them consider this line from Byron's letter above: "As I grow older, the indifference—*not* to life, for we love it by instinct—but to stimuli of life, increases." What is the difference between "life" and its "stimuli"? Ask each group to use Byron's work and the letter to form an answer, and then have the groups share their conclusions.

Logical-Mathematical Ask students to divide the letter above into sections by topic. They can then list Byron's aim in writing the letter. Challenge them to identify any points in the letter in which his purpose wavers. [Students may say that Byron's response to Keats's death reveals a mixture of pity and defensiveness.]

MAKING MEANINGS

First Thoughts

1. Think about your Reader's Log entry. How do your memories and feelings about the sea compare with the speaker's?

Shaping Interpretations

2. In stanza 2, what does the speaker say man does to earth? What can man do to the sea—or the sea do to him?

3. In stanza 3, what **figure of speech** describes the sea as a horse?

4. What single aspect of the ocean does the speaker repeatedly emphasize?

5. In spite of the ocean's destructive aspects, the speaker professes that he loves it passionately. What does this tell you about his personality?

6. What link does the speaker imply between the pilgrim and himself in the final two stanzas?

7. From this brief excerpt, what would you guess the pilgrim was searching for?

Extending the Text

8. How can the fierce identification and rapture experienced by this speaker in the presence of nature be felt today? Which of the poem's lines strike you as being particularly **ironic,** from the vantage point of the twentieth century? Why?

CHOICES: Building Your Portfolio

Writer's Notebook

1. Collecting Ideas for a Reflective Essay

Reflective essays are often inspired by the writer's thoughts on some natural scene—perhaps on a memory or a strong image that persists in the mind. Refer to your Quickwrite notes to see if they might give you the occasion for a reflective essay. Jot down notes on what you see when you place yourself in that natural scene or in another one that means a great deal to you. Record what you smell, hear, taste, and touch. Save your notes for the Writer's Workshop on page 773.

Critical Writing

2. The Force of Words

In a brief essay, analyze all of the **similes** in "The Destruction of Sennacherib." How do they affect the visual impact of the poem?

Critical Writing

3. Wit Across the Centuries

In an essay, compare and contrast Byron's *Don Juan* and Alexander Pope's *The Rape of the Lock* (page 527). Consider each work's narrative and at least two of these elements: **verse form, tone, satirical targets,** and use of **irony.**

Critical Writing

4. From Spenser to Byron

Byron's verse form in *Childe Harold's Pilgrimage* is the **Spenserian stanza** (page 221). Describe the technical requirements of the form, and discuss its use by Byron.

Creative Writing

5. Don Juan Lives On

Using Byron's hints in the selection, write a brief sequel, in poetry or prose, about Don Juan and Haidee's future. How will he treat her, and she him? You might also include some satirical jabs at popular romance novels that top the best-seller lists today.

Creative Writing

6. Speaking to Nature

In stanzas 2 and 3 of *Childe Harold,* the speaker uses an **apostrophe** (see page 738) to address the sea. Write a prose apostrophe, or address, to some element of nature—sea, wind, fire, snow, rain. Use stanzas 2 and 3 as a model.

PORTFOLIO ASSESSMENT

Choices: Assessment Criteria

For help in evaluating these Choices assignments, see the criteria in the *Portfolio Management System,* pp. 133–134.

Making Meanings

First Thoughts

1. Students may have similar recollections of the surf; they may associate the ocean with ideas much like the speaker's.

Shaping Interpretations

2. Man destroys the earth but cannot destroy the sea, which can cause shipwrecks and loss of life.

3. Metaphor: A horse's mane.

4. The ocean's boundlessness.

5. It reveals the speaker's love of nature, a central characteristic of the Romantic spirit.

6. The two are about to embark on the final journey toward death.

7. The pilgrim may seek self-knowledge or meaning and beauty in life.

Extending the Text

8. **(Synthesis)** Students may say that natural wonders would provoke a similar reaction today. Lines 12–13 are ironic because oceans are now polluted.

Beyond the Poems

Choices: Building Your Portfolio

1. **Writer's Notebook** Remind students to save their work. They may use it as prewriting for the Writer's Workshop on p. 773.

2. **Critical Writing** Direct students to list the similes in the poem. Encourage them to find connections between the images.

3. **Critical Writing** Students may use a graphic organizer like the one below to outline their essays, numbering the elements in the order they will appear in their essays.

	Don Juan	*The Rape of the Lock*	Similarity or Difference
Verse Form			
Tone			
Satirical Target			
Irony			

A. Expansion

For many years, Mary Wollstonecraft worked for the London publisher James Johnson, who later published *A Vindication of the Rights of Woman*. She left England for Paris in 1792 and witnessed the French Revolution. When she returned in 1795, she joined the intellectual circle that gathered at William Godwin's home, a group including Thomas Paine, William Blake, and William Wordsworth. She married Godwin in 1797.

B. Literary Connections

Horace Walpole was a writer and collector who helped launch the English Gothic style in literature and architecture. His medieval horror story *The Castle of Otranto* (1765) had many admirers and emulators, as did the house he built on Strawberry Hill that sported turrets and battlements. Among his many friends was Thomas Gray, whose *Odes of 1757* Walpole printed on his private printing press.

C. Literary Connections

William Godwin's social philosophy advanced the ideas of anarchism, atheism, and personal freedom, and was thus a tremendous influence on the Romantic movement. His most famous work is *An Enquiry Concerning Political Justice, and Its Influence on General Virtue and Happiness* (1793).

D. Expansion

Jane Austen's mother was well known for her wit and easy improvisation of stories and verses. One of the family's favorite diversions was acting.

SPOTLIGHT ON

Women Writers in the Romantic Period

Critics and historians may continue to quibble over the dates and definitions of Romanticism, but all agree that the period 1798–1832 in England was characterized by profound social change and unprecedented literary productivity. These phenomena altered the position that women occupied in society and brought about new opportunities and new problems for women writers. As the major male Romantic writers (the so-called Big Six) solidified their claim to poetry as the genre that represented the highest literary achievement, women writers turned to the novel. Two of these writers, Mary Shelley and Jane Austen, can be said to be Romantics; however, their social position as women writers prevented them from simply adopting their male contemporaries' philosophies and literary styles.

Mary Wollstonecraft (late 18th century) by John Opie.

Romantic writers embraced certain elements of Enlightenment philosophy; for example, they applauded Enlightenment philosophers' idealism and faith in the perfectibility of human beings. However, these writers deplored the insistence on reason over emotion, and an emphasis on science that discounted the spiritual and supernatural. As a result, male writers increasingly incorporated qualities associated with women—such as extreme emotional sensitivity—into their own work. Inspired by Mary Wollstonecraft's *A Vindication of the Rights of Woman* (1792), literary women, on the other hand, countered the prevailing Romantic trends by writing books that portrayed women as rational as well as sensitive creatures, possessing both sense *and* sensibility, to borrow the title of one of Jane Austen's novels.

As encouraging as Wollstonecraft's *Vindication* must have been to some women of the day, it produced quite the opposite reaction in most male, and many female, members of society: The novelist Horace Walpole (1717–1797) called her "a hyena in petticoats." The resulting backlash, which had been simmering since the publication of *Vindication* in 1792, reached full boil when William Godwin published *Memoirs of the Author of a "A Vindication of the Rights of Woman"* (1798), a tribute to his late wife that scandalized the public with its accounts of her illicit love affairs. In this climate, women who challenged the conventional views of marriage and women's roles were ridiculed. Those who spoke their minds in print risked being publicly renounced and having their work rejected by publishers.

Jane Austen (1775–1817)

Jane Austen was already practicing her craft when Mary Shelley was born. The daughter of an Anglican minister, Austen grew up in a respectable family with social status but little money. What few resources they had were spread thin among two

---

STRATEGIES FOR INCLUSION

Advanced As they read the feature above, ask students to take notes that compare the women writers treated in the essay to the "Big Six." Students should think of as many points of comparison as possible: for example, genre, tone, or subject matter. Ask for volunteers to share their notes with the class, and ask for other students to share their own insights in response.

Interpersonal Arrange students in small groups to read the feature above. They should take turns reading and stop periodically to discuss what they find interesting about the essay. You may want to suggest that groups stop for discussion at the end of every section. Encourage students to share their own knowledge of the topics covered in the feature and their opinions on the subject.

Bodily-Kinesthetic Ask students to give a dramatic reading of the excerpts from the women's writing in the feature above. Ask for volunteers to play the roles of narrator and speakers for the Austen excerpt, and for a narrator and actors to perform the vision in Mary Shelley's description. Each excerpt will involve three performers.

Jane Austen (late 18th or early 19th century). Engraving.
New York Public Library. Miriam and Ira D. Wallach Division of Art,
Prints, and Photographs. Astor, Lenox and Tilden Foundations.

daughters and five sons, with the largest expenses being devoted, as was common practice, to the formal education of the boys. Jane and her sister received an education typical for girls of the gentry: two years at a boarding school and lessons at home in the female accomplishments of drawing, music, and needlework. Jane also must have made good use of her father's library.

In an era when being known as a lady novelist was often more a stigma than an honor, it is not surprising that Austen published all her novels anonymously, despite the fact that critics generally agreed her stories would not harm young female readers' moral development. Careful readers, however, could see Austen's subtle but fierce satire of the social and educational status quo. Austen's novels about the social habits, marriage conventions, and manners of the English gentry quietly insist that women are rational creatures, much the same assertion that brought so much scorn upon the writer of *A Vindication of the Rights of Woman.* Furthermore, Austen's exquisitely rendered descriptions of her characters are often cloaked in an irony detectable only to those sympathetic to her critique of society's constraints on women. The opening sentences of her most famous novel, *Pride and Prejudice,* illustrate her trademark irony and humor:

It is a truth universally acknowledged that a single man in possession of a good fortune must be in want of a wife.

However little known the feelings or views of such a man may be on his first entering a neighborhood, this truth is so well fixed in the minds of the surrounding families that he is considered as the rightful property of some one or other of their daughters.

"My dear Mr. Bennet," said his lady to him one day, "have you heard that Netherfield Park is let at last?"

Mr. Bennet replied that he had not.

"But it is," returned she; "for Mrs. Long has just been here, and she told me all about it."

Mr. Bennet made no answer.

"Do not you want to know who has taken it?" cried his wife impatiently.

"*You* want to tell me, and I have no objection to hearing it."

This was invitation enough.

"Why, my dear, you must know, Mrs. Long says that Netherfield is taken by a young man of large fortune from the north of England. . . ."

"Is he married or single?"

"Oh! single, my dear, to be sure! A single man of large fortune . . . What a fine thing for our girls!"

"How so? how can it affect them?"

"My dear Mr. Bennet," replied his wife, "how can you be so tiresome! You must know that I am thinking of his marrying one of them."

"Is that his design in settling here?"

"Design! nonsense, how can you talk so! But it is very likely that he *may* fall in love with one of them, and therefore you must visit him as soon as he comes."

—Jane Austen, *from Pride and Prejudice*

The Austen family remained so protective of their daughter's reputation (and presumably their own as well) that when Jane Austen died at the age of forty-one, the headstone made for her grave made no mention of the six novels that, to this day, have never been out of print. Instead, it praised "the benevolence of her heart, the sweetness of her temper, and the extraordinary endowments of her mind."

E. Exploring the Historical Period

One of Austen's earliest fans was the prince regent, later George IV. Austen's novel *Emma* was dedicated to him at his request.

Technology Tip

In studying women writers of the Romantic period, you may wish to have students examine the Jane Austen Information Page on the World Wide Web. Much of Austen's work has been included in hypertext format. The address is **http ://uts.cc.utexas.edu/~churchh /janeinfo.html**. *You may want to preview any Internet activity that you suggest to students. Because these resources are sometimes public forums, their content can be unpredictable.*

SPOTLIGHT ON 727

INTEGRATING THE LANGUAGE ARTS

Strategic Reading As students look at the title of this Spotlight On, have them record their thoughts and expectations on the subject. What do they know about women writers during this time period? Ask students to write their observations in the first column of a KWL chart like the one that follows. As students work through the selection, have them complete the second and third columns. Discuss their questions and findings.

What I Know	What I Want to Know	What I Have Learned

The young couple eloped after declaring their love for each other at the graveside of Mary Wollstonecraft, Mary Shelley's mother.

B. Literary Connections

Mary Wollstonecraft Shelley's first published work, entitled *History of a Six Weeks' Tour* (1817), was a record of her tour of Europe with Percy Bysshe Shelley after their elopement.

Mary Wollstonecraft Shelley (1797–1851)

Mary Wollstonecraft Shelley, child of two of the most influential writers of the period, grew up in an unconventional and intellectual household frequented by leading artists and writers of the day. Her famous mother had died a few days after giving birth, and William Godwin remarried a woman who was everything Mary Wollstonecraft was not: dull and conventional. Because her stepmother tried to force her into domesticity, the young girl escaped by reading in her father's library and engaging in stimulating adult conversation with the artists and intellectuals who considered themselves students of William Godwin's philosophy. One of these guests was a brilliant young poet named Percy Bysshe Shelley, with whom Mary went on to share a brief eight years of passion, intellectual partnership, adventure, and tragedy.

In 1814, a teenage Mary Wollstonecraft Godwin eloped with Shelley (who was married at the time), and in 1816 she married him after the death of his legal wife. The couple endured the deaths of three of their four children, and in 1822, Shelley drowned in a boating accident in Italy. Mary Shelley never remarried, and when she died at age fifty-three she was survived by her son, Percy Florence Shelley, and by a literary legacy of six novels, volumes of essays, poems, travel narratives, and a comprehensive journal. Whatever her other accomplishments, however, the reputation of Mary Shelley is forever linked to her first novel, *Frankenstein,* which she began when she was just nineteen.

Mary Shelley (detail) (1840)
by Richard Rothwell. Oil on canvas (29″ × 24″).

By Courtesy of the National Portrait Gallery, London.

728 THE ROMANTIC PERIOD

The Author's Introduction to the 1831 edition explains the origins of this most famous book. The Shelleys spent the summer of 1816 at Lake Geneva with Mary Shelley's stepsister Claire and Lord Byron. Since the weather had been cold and rainy, the group decided that for amusement and an exercise in composition, each one of them would make up a ghost story. Frustrated during the daylight hours by her lack of inspiration, Mary Shelley was visited in her dreams by a vision that would become the subject of the most enduring ghost story in English literature.

> I saw—with shut eyes, but acute mental vision—I saw the pale student of unhallowed arts kneeling beside the thing he had put together. I saw the hideous phantasm of a man stretched out, and then, on the working of some powerful engine, show signs of life and stir with an uneasy, half-vital motion. . . . He would hope that, left to itself, the slight spark of life which he had communicated would fade, that this thing which had received such imperfect animation would subside into dead matter, and he might sleep in the belief that the silence of the grave would quench forever the transient existence of the hideous corpse which he had looked upon as the cradle of life. He sleeps; but he is awakened; he opens his eyes; behold, the horrid thing stands at his bedside, opening his curtains and looking on him with yellow, watery, but speculative eyes.
>
> —Mary Wollstonecraft Shelley, *from Frankenstein*

With the story of Victor Frankenstein's monstrous, motherless creation, Mary Shelley could examine her own fears of motherhood and her own orphaned condition; in addition, she could vent an anger and violence considered especially unfeminine in her day.

For twentieth-century readers, poetry dominates the literary landscape of the Romantic period; however, novelists such as Mary Shelley and Jane Austen remind us of women's participation in a flourishing genre. In the fantasies of Gothic novels, in the privacy of letters and journals, or in very public and forceful essays, women writers recorded their perspectives on the events of a turbulent age.

OPTIONS FOR TEACHING

INTEGRATING THE LANGUAGE ARTS

Language and Style   Point out that Jane Austen's combination of wit and social commentary is her hallmark. Ask students to look for humor in the excerpt from *Pride and Prejudice* and to examine how it attacks a target. Students may record their findings in a graphic organizer like the following.

Instance of humor	Why is it funny?	What is its target?	How does it attack?

ASSESSMENT TOOLS

Check Test: Questions and Answers
1. Who wrote *A Vindication of the Rights of Woman?* [Mary Wollstonecraft.]
2. Jane Austen influenced the direction of what genre of writing? [The novel.]
3. Who were Mary Shelley's parents? [Mary Wollstonecraft and William Godwin.]
4. Where was Mary Shelley inspired to write *Frankenstein?* [At Lake Geneva with her stepsister, husband, and Lord Byron.]
5. What is "unfeminine" about *Frankenstein?* [It is angry and violent.]

Percy Bysshe Shelley

(1792–1822)

When young Percy Shelley arrived at Oxford in 1810, his father introduced him to that bookish town's most important bookseller: "My son here," he said, "has a literary turn; he's already an author . . . do pray indulge him in his printing freaks." By spring, one of those "freaks"— an unsigned pamphlet on atheism—got Percy expelled and started a lifelong quarrel with his father. It was the first of many upheavals in the short, ill-fated life of an author who followed his "literary turn" wherever it led. In his own time, though, Shelley was better known for his shocking domestic life and opinions than for his impressive body of writing.

Shelley was convinced that human thought and expression had the power to change life for the better. And neither the upheavals of his personal life nor the strenuous reaching of his imagination toward a cosmic vision ever subverted his energies or optimism.

At nineteen, already estranged from his family, Shelley embarked on a career of courting the unconventional. To "rescue" her from a tyrannical father, he eloped with sixteen-year-old Harriet Westbrook, a classmate of his sisters. Three years later, he ran away with seventeen-year-old Mary Godwin, daughter of two of the most important radicals of the 1790s, Mary Wollstonecraft and William Godwin. Godwin was a rationalist who had been Percy's intellectual idol before he became his father-in-law. Percy's alliance with Mary also involved responsibility for Mary's fifteen-year-old stepsister Jane (soon changed to Claire)

Shelley Composing Prometheus Unbound (detail) (1845) by Joseph Severn.

Keats-Shelley Memorial House, Rome.

Clairmont, who accompanied the pair on their elopement to Switzerland. Claire's brief affair with Byron brought Shelley and Byron together in Switzerland in 1816 in one of the age's most important literary relationships.

Shortly after their return to England after a second trip to Switzerland, Mary's older half sister, Fanny, committed suicide. Then Harriet, only twenty-one, drowned herself in a pond in London's Hyde Park. Percy was now free to wed Mary, but was denied custody of his two children with Harriet.

Shelley and Mary now fled their debts and notoriety in England and returned to the Continent. The next four years were Shelley's most productive, with one inspired work following another. The year 1821 saw the publication of his great elegy on the death of Keats, *Adonais.*

In 1822, when he was not yet even thirty, Shelley and a companion, Edward Williams, drowned when their sailing boat, the *Ariel,* sank in a storm off the northwestern coast of Italy. Almost two weeks later, Shelley's body washed ashore, a copy of Sophocles in one pocket and of Keats in the other. The body was burned in a pyre on the beach while friends (including Byron) stood by, and Shelley's ashes were buried in the Protestant cemetery in Rome. The epitaph on Shelley's gravestone, composed by his friend and fellow poet Leigh Hunt, read *Cor Cordium,* Latin for "heart of hearts."

Shelley's literary career, though obscured by the soap-opera character of his life, is all the more remarkable because of it. His literary productivity was, with but a few slow periods, unceasing. As his father recognized, Shelley was certainly an "author."

It is said that the Italian sailors who encountered Shelley's boat in the storm on July 8, 1822, offered in vain to take Shelley and Williams on board. When this offer was refused, the sailors pleaded with the Englishmen to furl their sails lest they be lost. As Williams tried to do so, Shelley seized his arm and stopped him. We must certainly regret Shelley's untimely death, but at the same time, we can't help but wonder at his power to capture, and be captured by, the great dark forces that so fascinated him.

WRITERS ON WRITING

Shelley once remarked to Keats, "In poetry I have sought to avoid system and mannerism." Shelley emphasizes spontaneity in writing, and his essay "A Defence of Poetry" describes how poetry is created by a divine, imaginative spirit. "Poetry is not like reasoning," he argues, "a power to be exerted according to the determination of the will. A man cannot say, 'I will compose poetry.' The greatest poet even cannot say it; for the mind in creation is as a fading coal, which some invisible influence, like an inconstant wind, awakens to transitory brightness."

PROGRAM MANAGER

- **Planning Instruction** See *Teaching Notes, Teaching Resources B,* pp. 33–35, for objectives, summaries, literary elements, and additional biographical information for these selections.
- **Instructional Support** Before beginning the instructional lesson, see *Graphic Organizer for Active Reading, Teaching*

Resources B, pp. 46–48, for Through the Poems activities.
- **Audiotaped Readings** Use the *Selected Reading, Audiocassette 1, Side B,* in the *Audiovisual Resources Binder.*
- **Assessment** See *Selection Test, Test Booklet,* pp. 146–148.

Into the Poem

Using BEFORE YOU READ p. 730

Reading Focus

Have students list human constructions that have endured, comparing them in a class discussion. Encourage them to look for patterns among the ancient items. What kind of human work has lasted the longest?

Background

Ask students what the brief introduction tells them about Ozymandias. What do they think the ruler was like? What kind of monument would they expect him to have built? Write students' ideas on the chalkboard, and have students review them after reading the poem.

PORTFOLIO ASSESSMENT

Portfolio Assessment
For help with teacher assessment of reading skills, see the *Portfolio Management System,* pp. 54–55.

BEFORE YOU READ
OZYMANDIAS

Reading Focus
The Test of Time
All human beings, and all human beauty, must perish. But can't great works—of art, of life—survive beyond the individual? We leave, but isn't what we leave behind proof that the passage matters? Like the poets of another restless age, the Renaissance, the Romantic poets posed these questions. See how Shelley answers here.

Quickwrite

READER'S LOG

Suppose you're a creator. Among architecture, sculpture, music, and literature, which do you think offers you the most promise of an enduring monument? Explain your answer.

Background
Shelley wrote relatively few sonnets, and this is certainly one of his best. It is all the more interesting because it was written as part of a friendly and informal poetry competition with Keats in 1817. Their poetic topic was Egypt: Some extraordinary fragments from the empires of several Egyptian kings named Ramses had recently been put on display at the British Museum in London. Ozymandias is the Greek name for Ramses II (ruled c. 1290–1224 B.C.), who left monuments all over Egypt, including the temples of Karnak and Luxor. This Ramses is thought to be the pharaoh who contended with Moses at the time of the Hebrews' exodus from Egypt.

INTEGRATING THE LANGUAGE ARTS

Strategic Reading Ask students to read the poem in groups of three or four. Each member of a group should take a turn reading the poem aloud and then sharing what he or she finds interesting or significant about the poem. Challenge students to strive for a number of different interpretations

of the poem. They may share their ideas afterward in a class discussion.

Writing: Epitaph Ask students to write an epitaph for a public figure (living or dead) in the style of the one found on the tomb of the pharaoh Ozymandias. Their epitaph may be written in a few sentences, such as those in Shelley's work, or

it may be a poem or epigram. When students have completed their epitaphs, ask them to write a short paragraph explaining what qualities about the public figure they wanted to convey—for example, the person's pride, integrity, or compassion.

Ozymandias

Percy Bysshe Shelley

I met a traveler from an antique land
Who said: Two vast and trunkless legs° of stone
Stand in the desert . . . Near them, on the sand,
Half sunk, a shattered visage° lies, whose frown,
5 And wrinkled lip, and sneer of cold command,
Tell that its sculptor well those passions read
Which yet survive, stamped on these lifeless things,
The hand that mocked them, and the heart° that fed:
And on the pedestal these words appear:
10 "My name is Ozymandias, king of kings:
Look on my works, ye Mighty, and despair!"
Nothing beside remains. Round the decay
Of that colossal wreck, boundless and bare
The lone and level sands stretch far away.

2. trunkless legs: that is, the legs without the rest of the body.

4. visage: face.

8. hand . . . heart: the hand of the sculptor who, with his art, derided the passions to which Ozymandias gave himself wholeheartedly.

Fallen colossus, Ramesseum, Thebes, Egypt. Photograph (1857) by Francis Frith.
Private Collection.

Through the Poem

A. Reader's Response: Connecting with the Text

? Why do you think the storyteller, like Coleridge's Ancient Mariner, is given no introduction? [Sample responses: An introduction would be irrelevant to the poem's message; or in both instances, the mystery surrounding the storyteller adds to the poem's drama.]

Metacognition Ask students whether they find it easy or difficult to compare elements of different works. Encourage them to explore methods of connecting the poems.

B. Critical Reading: Analyzing Details

? How has the sculptor "mocked" Ozymandias? [The sculptor accurately portrayed the ruler's arrogance, and the result is unflattering.]

C. Expansion

Shelley's inscription revises that recorded by an ancient Greek historian: "I am Ozymandias, king of kings; if anyone wishes to know what I am and where I lie, let him surpass me in some of my exploits."

D. Literary Element: Setting

? How does the setting add to the poem's meaning? [The setting reinforces the irony that the king's great works have disappeared and only barren sands remain.]

CROSSING THE CURRICULUM

Architecture Ask students to research a monument and write a few paragraphs about it. Ask students to concentrate on the quality that makes it monumental and to decide if the monument is appropriate for its purpose. Encourage students to choose monuments from around the world. If students want to design a monument, have them write a proposal explaining their intent and include a sketch of the structure.

History Napoleon Bonaparte's invasion of Egypt in 1798 created a renewed interest in ancient Egyptian culture. However, it was not until the discovery of King Tutankhamen's tomb in 1922 that an enormous exhibit of artifacts from one tomb was possible. Invite students to work in pairs to research Napoleon's conquest of Egypt or the discovery of King Tutankhamen's tomb and the treasures that were uncovered there. ☞

Making Meanings

First Thoughts

1. The ruler's passions may include greed, self-aggrandizement, and contempt for others.

Shaping Interpretations

2. Speakers are a narrator, a traveler, and Ozymandias.
3. The king boasted of his might, but his monument is now in ruins.
4. The speaker shows that pride is foolhardy, yet validates artists' pride by showing that their skills remain evident even in monument's ruins.

Extending the Text

5. **(Synthesis and Evaluation)** Students will probably point to politicians whose reputations have suffered or have fallen in the public's estimation through revelations of their hypocrisy or greed. Ask students to describe the figures' irony.

MAKING MEANINGS

First Thoughts

1. What do you think are the passions that the sculptor captured in Ozymandias's "visage"?

Shaping Interpretations

2. Even in the brief space of a sonnet, Shelley suggests a number of narrative frames: How many **speakers** do you hear in this poem?
3. **Irony** is a discrepancy between expectations and reality. Explain the fundamental irony in the sonnet.
4. Discuss what you think is the speaker's **message** about pride—and whether it also applies to artists. (Is your Reader's Log entry relevant?)

Extending the Text

5. Could this poem apply to any contemporary figures who wield political power? Explain.

Manuscript pages from "Ozymandias" by Percy Bysshe Shelley. MS. Shelley e. 4, fol. 85 recto and verso.
The Bodleian Library, Oxford.

A Glimpse of an Antique Land

In 1807, the poet Robert Southey complained about a new British fad. "Everything now must be Egyptian," he said. "The ladies wear crocodile ornaments and you sit on a sphinx in a room hung round with mummies." General Napoleon Bonaparte, later emperor of France, started this craze when he invaded Egypt in 1798. Bonaparte's campaign was unusual because his troops were accompanied by a small army of geographers, astronomers, geologists, meteorologists, and artists. The general wanted information about his new territory, and scholars' pictures and reports on Egyptian culture fascinated Western audiences. In England, the people who decorated their homes in Egyptian style wanted more information on the vanished culture of ancient Egypt, with its immense wealth and knowledge. The carefully preserved bodies of ancient pharaohs, a religion that stressed a belief in the afterlife, the tales of fantastic temples buried in desert sand—all these fed Romantic appetites for the occult, the exotic, and the mysterious.

Looking for loot. When Napoleon returned to France, he took his wife, Josephine, seven small antiquities. That tiny collection began a plundering of Egypt's art that eventually filled museums around the world. Soon collectors were producing a steady stream of antiquities: immense appendages—arms, feet, heads—that had been broken from larger statues; elaborate stone tombs called sarcophagi; and tapered pillars, called obelisks, that represented the holy rays of the sun and guarded the tombs of kings. These, in turn, were incorporated into the Romantic imagination as they were painted by artists and described by poets—for example, the "two vast and trunkless legs of stone" in Percy Bysshe Shelley's "Ozymandias."

Poster (19th century) advertising Professor Pepper at Egyptian Hall.
The Hulton Deutsch Collection.

Art collecting or grave robbing? One of the best-known collectors was the Italian adventurer Giovanni Battista Belzoni (1778–1823). Many of his findings were sold to the British Museum. In 1815, he described a bust of Ramses II as lying on the sand "apparently smiling at me, at the thought of being taken to England." The success of collectors like Belzoni, however, ensures that today many Egyptian treasures can be seen only in museums in London, Paris, and New York. Before the discovery of King Tutankhamen's tomb in 1922, explorers were thought to be the rightful owners of Egypt's historical artifacts. In the controversy surrounding that excavation, a member of the British Parliament questioned the fairness of this policy when he asked the prime minister "if he has received any request from Egyptian citizens for permission to ransack the tombs of British kings and queens in Westminster Abbey." Governments and archeologists now have a heightened awareness of the importance of a nation's treasures, and removing such important artifacts would be impossible today. King Tut's body remains in its grave, and most of the magnificent artifacts from his tomb are housed in the Egyptian Museum, in Cairo.

Edfu Temple, Egypt.

PERCY BYSSHE SHELLEY 733

Ramses II was a successful warrior who ruled from c. 1304–c. 1273 B.C. To mark his victories, he inscribed numerous monuments with his name and likeness, many of which survive today. One of Ramses' best-known works is found at Abu Simbel, a temple cut into a sandstone cliff that includes four sixty-seven-foot figures of the pharaoh. When the Egyptian government built the Aswan High Dam in the 1960s, Ramses' temple was threatened with submersion by the Nile's waters. From 1964 to 1966, a team of engineers worked to disassemble the site and cut it away from the cliff. The temple Ramses dedicated to the gods of the sun is now safely reconstructed two hundred feet from the river.

PROFESSIONAL NOTES

Critical Comment: Art Aquisition In 1816, the historical painter Benjamin Robert Haydon expressed a common sentiment when he announced: "This year the Elgin Marbles were bought and produced an Aera in public feeling." He refers to the sensation created by the British Museum's acquisition of ancient Greek sculpture from Lord Elgin, who brought the sculptures to London from Athens some years before. At the time, Elgin had been the British ambassador to Turkey, which then ruled Greece. The Acropolis in Athens, the original site of the marble sculptures, was then being used as a Turkish garrison. In 1645, gunpowder kept at the fortress exploded, damaging much of the art there, and priceless sculpture still littered the ground during Elgin's ambassadorship. The French ambassador convinced the Turkish authorities to allow him to collect antiquities, and Elgin quickly followed his example. The works were received in London with amazed enthusiasm by artists and public alike, as the sculptures were assessed to be among the finest, if not the finest, works of classical art in existence. Some of the admirers, including Lord Byron, mocked the manner of the sculptures' acquisition, calling them "Lord Elgin's robberies." The debate still continues over whether the sculptures should be returned to Greece.

Into the Poem

Using BEFORE YOU READ p. 734

Reading Focus

Have students compare the experience of witnessing the terrifying power of nature to viewing a horror film. Why do people like to be frightened? [Students may say that being scared is exhilarating.] Ask students to keep their ideas in mind as they read the poem.

Through the Poem

A. Literary Element: Apostrophe
Throughout the poem, Shelley personifies the wind and addresses it directly.

B. Literary Element: Personification
[?] How are the wind and seeds personified in ll. 6–7? [The wind drives a chariot, taking the seeds to their bed.]

BEFORE YOU READ
ODE TO THE WEST WIND

Reading Focus

Swept Away
The faces of nature range from pacifying to terrifying, all of which the Romantics explored. Yet what so often attracted them in nature was the aspect philosophers call the sublime: the wildness, immensity, terror, and awesome grandeur of natural phenomena like the Alps or violent storms. To suddenly grasp nature's power—whether just by seeing Niagara Falls or by living through a hurricane—is, while terrible, also exhilarating, even transporting. When you read this poem, consider why people find such power (and fear) thrilling. What moves Shelley so? Why would he shout to the wind, "Be thou me . . . !"?

Quickwrite

Have you ever experienced the sublime aspect of nature? When? Briefly freewrite about the scene and your emotions.

Background

This major lyric, written in late October 1819, was provoked by Shelley's watching an oncoming storm near Florence, Italy, where he was living. It marks, in his creative life, a temporary note of exaltation after a period of intense grief over the death of his three-year-old son, William. The ode demands to be read aloud.

Ode to the West Wind

Percy Bysshe Shelley

I

(A) O wild West Wind, thou breath of Autumn's being,
Thou, from whose unseen presence the leaves dead
Are driven, like ghosts from an enchanter fleeing,

Yellow, and black, and pale, and hectic° red,
5 Pestilence-stricken multitudes: O thou,
(B) Who chariotest to their dark wintry bed

The winged seeds, where they lie cold and low,
Each like a corpse within its grave, until
Thine azure° sister of the Spring shall blow

10 Her clarion° o'er the dreaming earth, and fill
(Driving sweet buds like flocks to feed in air)
With living hues and odors plain and hill:

Wild Spirit, which art moving everywhere;
Destroyer and preserver; hear, oh, hear!

4. hectic: relating to the feverish flush caused by wasting diseases such as tuberculosis.

9. azure: sky-blue.

10. clarion: type of trumpet.

(Opposite) *The Bard* (1817) by John Martin.
Laing Art Gallery, Newcastle-upon-Tyne, England (Tyne & Wear Museums).

OPTIONS FOR TEACHING

Visual As students read the poem, have them stop occasionally to imagine each scene the poem describes. Then, have them sketch the scene quickly or jot down their impressions of the scene.

STRATEGIES FOR INCLUSION

Interpersonal Have students discuss whether the poem's extended apostrophe becomes a silent dialogue. Does the wind give the speaker any answers or ideas? Does the wind "reply" to the speaker at all? Tell students to refer to the poem for support of their answers.

Less Proficient Readers Ask students to close their eyes and imagine the scene described in the poem. Then, ask them how the wind connects the elements of the scene with its wanderings. Thinking of the wind's movement over the poem's varied settings should help students better follow the speaker's wandering thoughts.

STRATEGIES FOR INCLUSION

English Language Development The inspiration for this poem came from an approaching storm. Imagine that you are home alone and that you have just heard, on either TV or radio, that an extremely dangerous storm with winds of over seventy-five miles per hour is heading directly toward you. With this in mind, create a journal entry that describes the change in the weather. Include where you are, what your thoughts and feelings are, and what you see and hear as the storm approaches.

INTEGRATING THE LANGUAGE ARTS

Language and Style Work with students to analyze the poem's use of the terza rima form, which contains three lines of interlocking rhyme. Encourage students to identify the rhyme scheme in each section, to look for variations, and to notice that each section is a sonnet. Challenge students to locate a turn in thought in each section. ☞

A. Reader's Response: Shaping Interpretations

In ll. 23–24, the poet calls the wind a "dirge." Do you find that the poem's overall tone is sad or funereal? Explain. [Sample responses: It is gloomy that the wind brings a kind of death during autumn; or the poem's imagery is so rich and active that it evokes hope.]

B. Critical Reading: Making Inferences

? What desire does the speaker express in ll. 14 and 28? [He wants the wind to "hear" his words because he wants to make a request.]

C. Expansion

Baiae, now known as Baia, is an ancient city west of Naples, Italy. In 1500, the city was abandoned because of malaria.

D. Critical Reading: Making Connections

? How do ll. 43–45 summarize the first three sections of the poem? [Each line reintroduces the imagery from a previous section.]

Metacognition Ask students whether they are more comfortable analyzing or imagining the images. Encourage them to explore their reading strengths and to think of ways to improve both skills.

II

15 Thou on whose stream, mid the steep sky's commotion,
Loose clouds like earth's decaying leaves are shed,
Shook from the tangled boughs of Heaven and Ocean,

Angels of rain and lightning: there are spread
On the blue surface of thine aery° surge,
20 Like the bright hair uplifted from the head

Of some fierce Maenad,° even from the dim verge
Of the horizon to the zenith's height,
The locks of the approaching storm. Thou dirge°

Of the dying year, to which this closing night
25 Will be the dome of a vast sepulcher,
Vaulted with all thy congregated might

Of vapors, from whose solid atmosphere
Black rain, and fire, and hail will burst: oh, hear!

III

Thou who didst waken from his summer dreams
30 The blue Mediterranean, where he lay,
Lulled by the coil of his crystalline streams,

Beside a pumice° isle in Baiae's bay,°
And saw in sleep old palaces and towers
Quivering within the wave's intenser day,

35 All overgrown with azure moss and flowers
So sweet, the sense faints picturing them! Thou
For whose path the Atlantic's level powers

Cleave° themselves into chasms, while far below
The sea-blooms and the oozy woods which wear
40 The sapless foliage of the ocean, know

Thy voice, and suddenly grow gray with fear,
And tremble and despoil° themselves: oh, hear!

IV

If I were a dead leaf thou mightest bear;
If I were a swift cloud to fly with thee;
45 A wave to pant beneath thy power, and share

The impulse of thy strength, only less free
Than thou, O uncontrollable! If even
I were as in my boyhood, and could be

The comrade of thy wanderings over Heaven,
50 As then, when to outstrip thy skiey° speed
Scarce seemed a vision; I would ne'er have striven

19. aery: archaic for "airy"; unsubstantial; seen only in the mind.

21. Maenad (mē′nad′): in Greek mythology, a woman who performs frenzied dances in the worship of Dionysus, the Greek god of wine and crops.
23. dirge: slow, solemn poem or song that expresses grief or mourning.

32. pumice: light, porous volcanic stone. **isle . . . bay:** in the Bay of Naples where pumice is found. These islands were once summer resorts for Roman nobility and, in Shelley's time, were notable for their ruins of ancient villas and monumental baths.

38. cleave: divide.

42. despoil: strip.

50. skiey: like the sky; also, coming from the sky.

CROSSING THE CURRICULUM

Social Studies Have students research Greek and Roman mythology to find the names of figures mentioned in the poems they have read. Encourage each student to find a story or interesting fact about either mythology. Students may share their findings in an informal discussion.

CLASSROOM MANAGEMENT

Discussion Shake-Up One way to keep an air of discovery in the classroom is to vary the location of the class discussions; take the class outside or to the library or any other location. In the classroom itself, change students' seating arrangement to create a feeling of newness.

Managing the Reader's Response Classroom Because students are often called on to form a response rather quickly, try posing Reader's Response possibilities before students have read a selection. Have them record an immediate reaction in their Reader's Logs and make alterations as they read but before they share with the class.

As thus with thee in prayer in my sore need.
Oh, lift me as a wave, a leaf, a cloud!
I fall upon the thorns of life! I bleed! (E)

55 A heavy weight of hours has chained and bowed
One too like thee: tameless, and swift, and proud.

V

Make me thy lyre,° even as the forest is:
What if my leaves are falling like its own!
The tumult of thy mighty harmonies

60 Will take from both a deep, autumnal tone,
Sweet though in sadness. Be thou, Spirit fierce, (F)
My spirit! Be thou me, impetuous° one!

Drive my dead thoughts over the universe
Like withered leaves to quicken a new birth!
65 And, by the incantation of this verse,

Scatter, as from an unextinguished hearth°
Ashes and sparks, my words among mankind!
Be through my lips to unawakened earth

The trumpet of a prophecy! O, Wind, (G)
70 If Winter comes, can Spring be far behind?

57. lyre: the Aeolian (ē·ō′lē·ən) harp, a stringed instrument that emits sound when the wind blows across its strings.

62. impetuous: forceful; rushing.

66. unextinguished hearth: from "A Defense of Poetry": "The mind in creation is as a fading coal, which some invisible influence, like an inconstant wind, awakens to transitory brightness. . . ."

*C*ritical *C*omment

Shelley and the Ode

This ode is both an expression of Shelley's sense of purpose as a public poet, and a personal meditation on the role. In what a biographer calls a moment of both "triumph and defiance," Shelley copied a Greek phrase from the dramatist Euripides in his notebook after finishing the poem: "By virtuous power, I, a mortal, vanquish thee, a mighty god." (H)

A genuine **ode** in its overall style and arrangement, the form of this poem is special. It consists of five sonnets in **terza rima,** with each section ending, as a Shakespearean **sonnet** does, with a couplet. Each group of three lines picks up the rhyme of the second line of the preceding three lines.

Shelley's admirers have been a little embarrassed by the exaggerated self-dramatization of "I fall upon the thorns of life! I bleed!" (line 54). But the poem is full of such heightened effects. They are consistent with the manner of the ode, with its large scale—the earth, the air, and the sea—with its imagery, and with the situation of the speaker, who is striving in "sore need" in prayer with a higher power.

"Ode to the West Wind" expresses Shelley's fascination with power and with those forces—both destroyers and preservers—that inspire the same powers within the poet.

E. Reader's Response: Challenging the Text
Line 54 is often quoted either to defend Shelley as the most Romantic of the Romantic poets or to caricature him as ridiculously self-absorbed. How do you analyze the line? [Sample responses: The line shows the strain of being overly dramatic; or since the line fits the impassioned tone of the poem, there is no reason to mock it.]

F. Critical Reading: Making Inferences
? How does the speaker's description of himself change? [The speaker moves from thinking of himself as a passive object of the wind, as in section 4, to a powerful view of himself as a lyre for the universe.]

G. Critical Reading: Drawing Conclusions
? What is the "prophecy" of l.69? [Humanity, like the earth, is renewed in the spring.]

H. Literary Connections
Euripides (*c.* 480–406 B.C.) was the last of ancient Greece's three great tragedians, after Aeschylus and Sophocles. He took no part in the city's public affairs, preferring instead to sit in a cave and look out at the sea. His behavior earned him the reputation of an unsociable eccentric. His plays, of which nineteen survive, are famous for their psychological insight and moral exploration.

INTEGRATING THE LANGUAGE ARTS

Strategic Reading Before students read the Critical Comment, have them make predictions about how the ode might be assessed, according to its strengths, weaknesses, theme, and form. Students may record their predictions in a graphic organizer like the one below. After they have read the section, have them fill out the "Confirmations" column, explaining how their predictions differed from the article and why.

Predictions	Confirmations

PROFESSIONAL NOTES

Critical Comment: Shelley's Imagery John Stuart Mill compared Shelley's imagery to Wordsworth's, finding that "Never did a fancy so teem with sensuous imagery as Shelley's. Wordsworth economizes an image, and detains it until he had distilled all the poetry out of it, and it will not yield a drop more: Shelley lavishes his with a profusion which is unconscious because it is inexhaustible. [The one, like a thrifty housewife, uses all his materials and wastes none: the other scatters them with a reckless prodigality of wealth of which there is perhaps no similar instance.]" Ask students to comment on Mill's assessment, referring to specific examples in their answers.

☞

Making Meanings

First Thoughts

1. Students may be moved by the images of nature's power, and they may be struck by the final lines' message of hope.

Shaping Interpretations

2. The images are blowing leaves, fleeting clouds, and the sea.
3. In the final sections, the speaker asks for the wind's power, rather than describing its effects.
4. The wind scatters leaves (l. 2), but it also drops seeds to the earth (ll. 6–7).
5. He sees himself as "swift, and proud" (l. 56) as the wind, and he longs to be as free as it is.
6. It calls to and asks something of the wind.
7. A smoldering hearth contains both dead ashes and living sparks. Words can contain the weariness of death and the prophecy of life.
8. The speaker asks the wind to give him the voice of prophecy and power of expression. In winter dormancy (grief, silence), he asks whether spring (poetry, rebirth) will follow.

Connecting with the Text

9. Students may suggest images of power, such as the wind's force.

Challenging the Text

10. **(Evaluation)** The speaker identifies his creative powers with the might of a natural force.

Elements of Literature

Mini-Lesson: Apostrophe

Outline on the chalkboard the three types of apostrophe mentioned in the selection, and have students name examples. Encourage students to think of situations in which they address an absent person or an object. The class could research titles or first lines of Romantic poems to discover the topics poets often address in apostrophes.

Answers

1. Shelley addresses the wind in ll. 1–2, 5, 9, 13–14, 15, 19, 23, 26, 28, 29, 36, 41–42, 43–57, 59, and 61–70.
2. Possible subjects include seeds, clouds, rain, lightning, and seasons.

MAKING MEANINGS

First Thoughts

1. Which lines of this poem do you think are most important or have the most beautiful sounds?

Shaping Interpretations

2. What is the central **image** of each of the first three sections?
3. How are sections four and five different in approach and emphasis from the first three?
4. How is the wind both a "destroyer and preserver" (line 14)? Cite lines to support your ideas.
5. Why do you think the speaker identifies with the wind so intensely?
6. Why would the speaker call his verse an "incantation" (line 65)?
7. How do you explain the **paradox** that words are like "ashes and sparks" (line 67)?
8. What do you think lines 68–70 mean?

Connecting with the Text

9. What aspect of nature would you choose to represent the sublime? Refer to your Reader's Log entry for ideas.

Challenging the Text

10. To some, this ode argues that poetry is created only when the poet is inspired by an outside, greater force. Explain whether you agree.

ELEMENTS OF LITERATURE

Apostrophe: Throwing Words to the Wind

An **apostrophe** is a figure of speech in which a writer directly addresses a person (usually absent), a personified inanimate object, or an abstract idea. Shelley's opening invocation "O wild West Wind" is an apostrophe, with the device recurring repeatedly. In fact, this poem, like several of Shelley's, might be called an **extended apostrophe.**

Perhaps the origins of the apostrophe lie in the repeated invocations of prayer, when the faithful call upon God to hear them. Indeed, not only is the apostrophe a favorite Romantic device, but many Romantic poems are also titled or described as "hymns."

The apostrophe also has an interesting relation to Romantic "empathy," or deep sympathy or identification with a person or object. Shelley, for example, closes "Ode to the West Wind" with an ecstatic prayer to *be* or *become* what he apostrophizes.

1. In what lines of "Ode to the West Wind" does Shelley directly address the wind?
2. Many natural elements are depicted in Shelley's poem. Choose one (not the wind), and write an apostrophe to it within the poem's context.

LANGUAGE AND STYLE

Terza Rima and the Sonnet

In "Ode to the West Wind," Shelley adapts a rhyme scheme called **terza rima** to the sonnet form. Terza rima consists of sequences of three lines of interlocking rhyme. As a technician, Shelley adjusts sound to sense in passages of chiming, onomatopoeic beauty; as a thinker, he dramatizes cycles of death and rebirth.

1. Identify Shelley's **rhyme scheme** in each fourteen-line section. Are the schemes all the same?
2. Each section is also a **sonnet.** Review sonnet forms (pages 219 and 223), and tell how Shelley has adapted them. Explain whether Shelley's sonnets have **turns.**
3. Working in groups, prepare each section of the ode for choral reading. When you prepare your scripts, be sure to note passages that use **onomatopoeia** and **alliteration.**

Language and Style

Answers

1. Yes; *ababcbcdcdedee.*
2. Shelley has no octave or sestet, using only terza rima for the first twelve lines of each section. Final couplets are in sonnet form. Shelley varies his subject, tone, and manner of address, but there are no turns that answer questions.
3. Examples of **alliteration** and **onomatopoeia** include ll. 1, 7, 9, 31 and ll. 39, 60.

PROGRAM MANAGER

Application and Reinforcement

For reinforcement of the elements of literature introduced in this lesson, see **Transparency** 9.2 in the *Audio-visual Resources Binder.*

Into the Poem

Reading Focus
Sky-Drunk, Earthbound
The singing bird is a favorite romantic comparison or *analogue* for the poet: The human singer yearns to capture the ethereal beauty of the bird's song but often must face, as Shelley does here, the fact that human life can never produce pure song. (See also John Keats's "Ode to a Nightingale," page 755.)

While the Romantic poets loved nature, they were not interested in making exact and detailed observations of natural phenomena. To them, nature often represented a higher realm of being, harmony, and even divinity. Shelley composed this poem in June 1820 at his summer residence on the northwestern coast of Italy.

Quickwrite
What qualities of a bird do you think a poet might envy? Brainstorm some answers to this question.

Elements of Literature
Symbol
Shelley's skylark is used in the poem as a **symbol**—it is a skylark, but at the same time, it stands for something much larger than itself. As you read, think about what the skylark symbolizes to the poet, and then consider how appropriate the comparison is. The lark is a small bird resembling a sparrow. It seldom lights in trees or shrubs but soars high above the ground, singing. Often the skylark soars so high it cannot be seen—only its song can be heard. There are no skylarks in the United States.

The Skylark (c. 1792–1797) by Thomas Bewick.

Iain Bain Collection, Hertfordshire, England.

To a Skylark

Percy Bysshe Shelley

Hail to thee, blithe° Spirit!
  Bird thou never wert,
That from Heaven, or near it,
  Pourest thy full heart
5 In profuse° strains of unpremeditated° art. **Ⓐ**

Higher still and higher
  From the earth thou springest
Like a cloud of fire;
  The blue deep thou wingest,
10 And singing still dost soar, and soaring ever singest.

In the golden lightning
  Of the sunken sun,
O'er which clouds are bright'ning,
  Thou dost float and run;
15 Like an unbodied joy whose race is just begun. **Ⓑ**

1. **blithe:** joyful; carefree.

5. **profuse:** abundant. **unpremeditated:** unplanned; done without forethought.

Reading Focus
Ask students to concentrate on the metaphor of the poet-as-bird by comparing the "songs" of both poet and bird. Students may use a Venn diagram to describe each song's appeal to a reader or listener.

Through the Poem

A. Literary Element: Symbol
? How does the poet explain in ll. 2–5 his assertion that the skylark is not a bird? [He claims it is a heavenly spirit.] Why would the poet make such an assertion? [Possible responses: The skylark has come to symbolize art and beauty to the poet; or, the bird's beautiful song is inspiring to the poet and its "art" transcends any material form.]

B. Reader's Response: Extending the Text
? What is your impression of the speaker's insistence on the bird's ephemeral quality as an "unbodied joy"? [Sample responses: The repeated idea makes the skylark seem more amazing and wonderful; or it reflects the fact that the speaker focuses on the bird's song, not its appearance.]

Intrapersonal Have students concentrate for a few minutes on the image of a singing bird. Challenge students to think of what the bird might be saying or what they would sing if they were a bird. Students may make notes of their ideas.

English Language Development Ask students to form small groups to portray the poem through images. The entire poem may be condensed, or students may illustrate a theme or character. The group should use sketches or illustrations to represent the poem and then add captions to the images. The captions may be quotations from the poem, invented titles, or brief descriptions. After the groups share their sketches, ask the students to work individually to write a paragraph explaining how they made their decisions. ☞

A. Critical Reading: Making Generalizations

[?] How is this question addressed to the reader as well as to the speaker? [The speaker is asking the reader to imagine similes for the sky-lark; the question also prepares the speaker to create the similes.]

B. Language Note: Structure

[?] How does this line's unusual length and stilted structure affect its meaning? [The line describes a faint-ness that arises from the scent of flowers on wind, and it meanders over the thought almost drunkenly.]

The pale purple even°
   Melts around thy flight;
Like a star of Heaven,
   In the broad daylight
20 Thou art unseen, but yet I hear thy shrill delight,

Keen as are the arrows
   Of that silver sphere,°
Whose intense lamp narrows
   In the white dawn clear
25 Until we hardly see—we feel that it is there.

All the earth and air
   With thy voice is loud,
As, when night is bare,
   From one lonely cloud
30 The moon rains out her beams, and Heaven is overflowed.

(A) What thou art we know not;
   What is most like thee?
From rainbow clouds there flow not
   Drops so bright to see
35 As from thy presence showers a rain of melody.

Like a Poet hidden
   In the light of thought,
Singing hymns unbidden,
   Till the world is wrought
40 To sympathy with hopes and fears it heeded not:

Like a high-born maiden
   In a palace-tower,
Soothing her love-laden
   Soul in secret hour
45 With music sweet as love, which overflows her bower:°

Like a glow-worm golden
   In a dell° of dew,
Scattering unbeholden
   Its aereal hue
50 Among the flowers and grass, which screen it from the view!

Like a rose embowered°
   In its own green leaves,
By warm winds deflowered,
   Till the scent it gives
(B) 55 Makes faint with too much sweet those heavy-winged thieves:

Sound of vernal° showers
   On the twinkling grass,
Rain-awakened flowers,
   All that ever was
60 Joyous, and clear, and fresh, thy music doth surpass:

16. even: archaic for "evening."

22. silver sphere: "a star of Heaven" (line 18).

45. bower: archaic for "boudoir," a woman's bedroom, dressing room, or private sitting room.
47. dell: small valley.

51. embowered: enclosed; sheltered.

56. vernal: occurring in the spring.

OPTIONS FOR TEACHING

INTEGRATING THE LANGUAGE ARTS

Strategic Reading Have students read the ode aloud with a partner, alternating readers after each stanza. After completing a stanza, students should paraphrase the action or emotions described by the poet.

Speaking and Listening Ask students to select their favorite passage from the poem and to read it aloud to the class. Students should tell what they find remarkable about the passage and then compare their opinion to the preceding student's. Start the activity by sharing your favorite lines and then calling on the next reader.

Teach us, Sprite or Bird,
    What sweet thoughts are thine:
I have never heard
    Praise of love or wine
65 That panted forth a flood of rapture so divine.

Chorus Hymeneal,°
    Or triumphal chant,
Matched with thine would be all
    But an empty vaunt,°
70 A thing wherein we feel there is some hidden want.

What objects are the fountains
    Of thy happy strain?°
What fields, or waves, or mountains?
    What shapes of sky or plain?
75 What love of thine own kind? what ignorance of pain?

With thy clear keen joyance°
    Languor° cannot be:
Shadow of annoyance
    Never came near thee:
80 Thou lovest—but ne'er knew love's sad satiety.°

Waking or asleep,
    Thou of death must deem
Things more true and deep
    Than we mortals dream,
85 Or how could thy notes flow in such a crystal stream?

We look before and after,
    And pine for what is not:
Our sincerest laughter
    With some pain is fraught;
90 Our sweetest songs are those that tell of saddest thought.

Yet if we could scorn
    Hate, and pride, and fear;
If we were things born
    Not to shed a tear,
95 I know not how thy joy we ever should come near.

Better than all measures
    Of delightful sound,
Better than all treasures
    That in books are found,
100 Thy skill to poet were, thou scorner of the ground!

Teach me half the gladness
    That thy brain must know,
Such harmonious madness
    From my lips would flow
105 The world should listen then—as I am listening now. **G**

66. chorus Hymeneal: wedding song. *Hymeneal* is derived from Hymen, the Greek god of marriage.

69. vaunt: boast.

72. strain: melody.

76. joyance: archaic for "rejoicing."
77. languor: indifference; lack of spirit or interest.

80. satiety: feeling of weariness due to overfulfillment of appetite or desire.

Nature's Glory (c. 1860s) by John Wainwright.
Courtesy Christopher Cole, Beaconsfield, England.

PERCY BYSSHE SHELLEY 741

C. Reader's Response: Shaping Interpretations

? Why would the speaker compare his praise of the skylark to "praise of love or wine"? [Sample responses: Love and wine are traditional subjects of odes; or the superior qualities of love and wine are explored in poetry.]

D. Critical Reading: Identifying Main Ideas

? What does the speaker want to learn from the skylark? [The source of its joy.]

E. Language Note: Rhetorical Question

? What is the purpose of this repeated questioning? [The speaker is grasping for possible answers.]

F. Reader's Response: Extending the Text

? Do you agree with the speaker's assertion that pleasure is always accompanied by pain? [Sample responses: Yes, because even a completely pleasurable experience will not last; or no, sorrow does not tinge every positive experience.]

G. Critical Reading: Making Inferences

? How has the world come to listen, as the speaker desires? [People are reading his poem, which reflects some of the beauty and wonder of the skylark's song.]

CROSSING THE CURRICULUM

Science Challenge students to find other animals that can represent Romantic qualities. They might research an animal in an encyclopedia or other resource and write a brief factual description or a Romantic appreciation of the animal. Students may enjoy comparing in a class discussion the two ways of viewing the subject.

CLASSROOM MANAGEMENT

Constructive Peer Feedback Encourage students to develop an atmosphere of trust and cooperation in the classroom. At every available opportunity, have students meet in small groups, varying the members each time. In these groups, students can provide constructive feedback on a project or assignment that is still being revised. As students become used to remarks from their peers, they will be better able to collaborate in group efforts and discussions.

Making Meanings

First Thoughts

1. Students may say the poet envies the song's infectious joy. Their predictions should observe that the speaker's desires reflect Romantic elements.

Shaping Interpretations

2. The speaker asks the bird the objects of its song (ll. 71–75) and how it sings so purely (ll. 81–85). He asks the bird to teach him its thoughts (ll. 61–62) and its gladness (ll. 101–105).

3. Responses should refer to the bird's effusive song (ll. 4–5), its soaring (l. 10), its immateriality (ll. 1, 15). Sound effects include its "shrill delight" (l. 20).

4. The speaker compares the skylark to a poet, a maiden in a tower, a glow-worm, and a rose. With each simile, the speaker grows more contemplative.

5. The speaker would have to be free from hate, pride, fear, and sorrow.

6. Students may point to ll. 63–65 or 76–77 to say that the bird represents joy or artistic beauty.

7. Passages include ll. 1–5, 36–40, 46–50, and 61–65.

8. The phrases reinforce the idea that the skylark is unreachable.

Connecting with the Text

9. Students should note that much Romantic poetry centers on loss, and some will probably recognize the theme; they may also point to themes of heartbreak and alienation in popular music.

Beyond the Poems

Choices: Building Your Portfolio

1. **Writer's Notebook** Remind students to save their work. They may use it as a prewriting for the Writer's Workshop on p. 773.

MAKING MEANINGS

First Thoughts

1. What, in your opinion, does the speaker most envy about a skylark? (What did you predict in your Reader's Log?)

Shaping Interpretations

2. What questions does the speaker ask the bird, and what does he ask the bird to teach him?

3. What **images** and **sound effects** do you think suggest the special quality of the skylark's music?

4. How are the four **similes** in lines 36–55 related, and what do you think they show about the skylark and about the speaker?

5. What, according to lines 91–95, would be necessary for "harmonious madness" to flow from the speaker of the poem?

6. In your opinion, what does this skylark **symbolize** to the speaker? What lines support your interpretation?

7. What passages in the poem seem to reflect the Romantics' esteem for spontaneity in poetry?

8. How do you interpret these phrases: "unbodied joy" (line 15), "ignorance of pain" (line 75), "ne'er knew love's sad satiety" (line 80), "scorner of the ground" (line 100), "harmonious madness" (line 103)?

Connecting with the Text

9. Lines 86–90 are among the most quoted in English poetry. Do you see these lines reflected in your life? If so, how?

CHOICES: Building Your Portfolio

Writer's Notebook

1. Collecting Ideas for a Reflective Essay

WORK IN PROGRESS

A reflective essay begins with an occasion—an event or an object or a scene that gets the speaker thinking. An "occasion" for a reflective essay can also come from a text, from a passage or character or message that you'd like to write about. See if a passage from "Ozymandias" could give you an occasion for a reflective essay. Or, the poem might remind you of a situation you've experienced that you'd like to reflect on. Save your notes for the Writer's Workshop on page 773.

Critical Writing

2. Turning Words into Music

Shelley's poetry is marked by sound effects (**alliteration, onomatopoeia, assonance,** and **rhyme**) that create a musical quality. In a brief essay, cite outstanding examples of these sound effects in "Ode to the West Wind" and "To a Skylark." Conclude your essay with a statement of your response to Shelley's style.

Critical Writing

3. Shelley's Renaissance Ancestors

Compare and contrast the **structure, subject, theme,** and **tone** of "Ozymandias" with those of any Renaissance sonnet you read in Collection 3.

Creative Writing

4. I Bleed! I Swoon! I Parody!

The Romantics, like all great writers, have been objects of parody. Parody is an amusing imitation of a work's style or subject matter. Try your hand at a parody of one of Shelley's great poems. You might get a start by using one of Shelley's first lines. If you're artistic, try a cartoon sequence parodying one of the poems.

---

2. **Critical Writing** Ask students to review the poems and list the musical qualities of each type. Students may organize these notes in a graphic organizer like the one shown below, dividing their essay into paragraphs that examine each type of sound effect separately.

Example	Location of example	Type of sound effect	Effect in context

PORTFOLIO ASSESSMENT

Choices: Assessment Criteria For help in evaluating these Choices assignments, see the criteria in the *Portfolio Management System,* p. 135.

China

Tu Fu

(712–770)

Portrait of Tu Fu (Ch'ing dynasty) from *Travels of a Chinese Poet* by Florence Ayscough (London: Jonathan Cape, 1934).

New York Public Library, General Research Division. Astor, Lenox and Tilden Foundations.

In a poem, Tu Fu (doo foo) wrote, "I shall not die in peace until I have found words that will startle the readers." At once an unequaled innovator and a master of exacting *lü-shih* (lyoo'shi), or "regulated verse," Tu Fu indeed changed Chinese poetry forever. Unlike earlier poets, he did not restrict a poem to a single subject, setting, or mood; he mixed private and public concerns; and he wrote honestly—even bitterly and blackly—about current events. Yet he could see humor even in his own poverty, and his striking images show how nature nourished him. Tu Fu's difficult life began when he failed the imperial writing exams. Thereafter, he took minor government positions (he eventually passed a special exam), constantly moving throughout China to support a large family he cherished.

In 759, he bravely left official service without any financial support. Though Tu Fu barely eked out a living from patrons, he wrote nearly 80 percent of his elegant, objective poetry in his last years. Along with his friend Li Po (page 766), Tu Fu was one of the most brilliant poets of the High T'ang. During his life, Tu Fu's reputation never matched Li Po's, but now Tu Fu is often called China's greatest poet.

(Map) Mongolia showing Japan and China (c. 1680) by Frederick de Wit.

PROGRAM MANAGER

- **Selection Summary** See Teaching Notes, *Teaching Resources B,* p. 35, for a summary of this selection.
- **Audiotaped Readings** To help less proficient readers or auditory learners through the lesson, use the Selected Reading, Audiocassette 1, Side B in the *Audiovisual Resources Binder.*

CONNECTING WITH "THE QUEST FOR BEAUTY"

Have students discuss how Tu Fu's solitary reflection fits with the Collection's themes. [The poem examines the ephemeral quality of beauty and, like Keats's "Ode to a Nightingale," yearns for a beauty that will endure. The poem examines humankind's relation to nature, a central Romantic tenet.]

A. Critical Reading: Finding Details

? How do ll. 3–5 juxtapose two different scenes in the same setting? [The speaker of the poem stands where the ancient prince built his palace, imagining the glory that is now in ruins.]

B. Literary Element: Tone

? What is the speaker's attitude toward his subject? [He is weary of ruins and overcome by the waste and destruction.] What is implied about the speaker's attitude toward his writing? [He doubts his ability to express the feelings that the place evokes in him.]

C. Reader's Response: Challenging the Text

? Does the final question expand on the poem's content to make it a fitting question with which to leave the reader? [Sample responses: The question is slightly shocking, because it implies continued human destruction; or the question expands the poem from a contemplation of the past to a meditation on time itself.]

Finding Common Ground

Challenge students to think of contemporary examples of the abuse of power that do not relate to government leaders such as Ozymandias. Specifically, direct students to think of examples of humanity's hubris in making decisions based on short-term gains rather than long-term ramifications. Students can use these thoughts as an introduction to the discussion topics. Instruct them to discuss the topics in groups and to choose a specific topic on Tu Fu's theme. Students can write their poems individually and then rejoin their groups to help edit each other's work.

BEFORE YOU READ
JADE FLOWER PALACE

Background

Two intense quests informed Tu Fu's troubled life: to write poetry and to obtain a high government position. The combination could have been glorious, for Tu Fu lived during the eighth century, part of China's T'ang era: a peak of cultural and artistic achievement. Although Tu Fu showed great brilliance, in 736 (at twenty-four) he failed the imperial examinations and lost all chance at an exalted office. For a Confucian who saw service to the emperor as life's greatest good, the blow cut deeply. An even sharper and sadder blow—but one that produced great poetry—was Tu Fu's disillusionment with imperial wisdom and power. In a 755 rebellion that Tu Fu witnessed, 36 million of China's 53 million people were killed or driven from their homes. His own son died of starvation. During this period, Tu Fu wrote "Jade Flower Palace."

Quickwrite

Write your associations to the poem's title: jade flower palace.

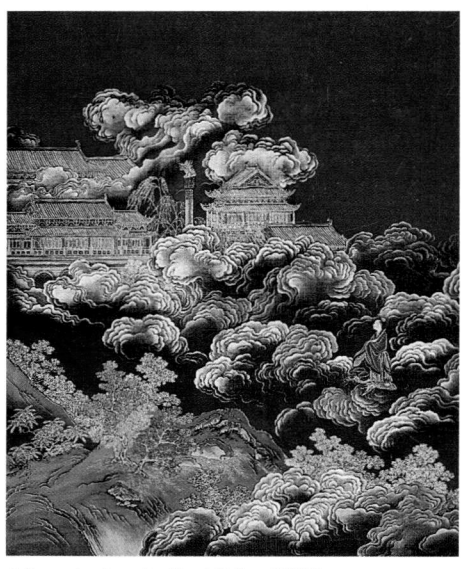

A Keepsake from the Cloud Gallery (1750). Chinese ADD Ms. 22689.

By permission of the British Library, London.

Jade Flower Palace
Tu Fu

translated by **Kenneth Rexroth**

> The stream swirls. The wind moans in
> The pines. Gray rats scurry over
> Broken tiles. What prince, long ago,
> Built this palace, standing in
> 5 Ruins beside the cliffs? There are
> Green ghost fires in the black rooms.
> The shattered pavements are all
> Washed away. Ten thousand organ
> Pipes whistle and roar. The storm
> 10 Scatters the red autumn leaves.
> His dancing girls are yellow dust.
> Their painted cheeks have crumbled
> Away. His gold chariots
> And courtiers are gone. Only
> 15 A stone horse is left of his
> Glory. I sit on the grass and
> Start a poem, but the pathos of
> It overcomes me. The future
> Slips imperceptibly away.
> 20 Who can say what the years will bring?

A (ll. 1–16)
B (ll. 16–19)
C (l. 20)

FINDING COMMON GROUND

The similarities between this poem and Shelley's "Ozymandias" (page 731) are striking. Like these eighth- and eighteenth-century observers, you can also ponder the ruins of power.

• How do the associations in your Reader's Log entry relate to Tu Fu's theme?

• Working with a partner or small group, explore the differences and similarities between "Jade Flower Palace" and "Ozymandias."

• To write a poem on the same theme today, what physical site would you choose? (It might be an abandoned site, not necessarily a destroyed one.) What objects would you focus on? Work with a partner or a small group to write a poem on Tu Fu's theme.

John Keats

(1795–1821)

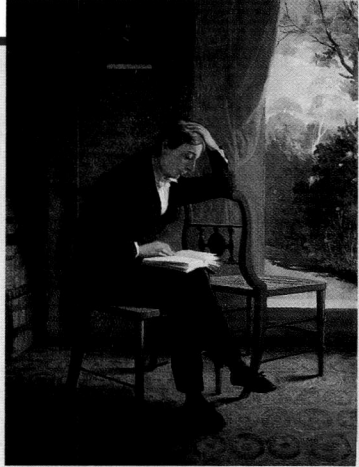

John Keats at Wentworth Place (1821–1823) by Joseph Severn. Oil on canvas (22 ¼″ × 16 ½″).
By Courtesy of the National Portrait Gallery, London.

It is surprising that Keats became a poet at all, and surely a wonder that, when he died at the age of twenty-five, he had accomplished enough to become one of our major poets.

John Keats's short life was plagued with troubles, and he lacked most of the advantages a poet often needs to get started. His father, who ran a London livery stable, died when Keats was eight. His mother died of tuberculosis when he was fourteen, leaving the family finances tied up and inaccessible to the Keats children. After four years in a school where his literary interests were encouraged, he was apprenticed at the age of fifteen to learn medicine. Keats saw something of his own country as a young man, but his only foreign travel was a desperate trip to Italy when he was dying, enduring what he called a "posthumous existence." He had friends and supporters who recognized his poetic genius, but he never enjoyed a close collaborative relationship with another poet. A man of small stature (he was barely over five feet tall), he lived in close acquaintance with death and the fragile nature of human life.

In 1816, not yet twenty-one, Keats completed his medical studies at Guy's Hospital in London. Before he could be legally licensed as a surgeon, he made the momentous decision to become a poet. Some harsh reviews of his first book of poetry (1817) stung him and added to the periodic doubts that made his dedication to poetry sometimes seem an awful burden. Now much of Keats's time was spent nursing his brother Tom, who was dying of tuberculosis.

After Tom's death in December 1818, Keats had a little more than two years to make what he could of his determination to lead a "literary life." Great passages and nearly perfect poems poured from him in that miraculous time. Already in failing health, he never knew the great-

ness of his achievements, which might have given him at least the consolation of literary success. He had fallen in love—her name was Fanny Brawne—but his poor health and money problems kept him from marrying. "I am three and twenty," he wrote despairingly in March 1819, "with little knowledge and middling intellect. It is true that in the height of enthusiasm I have been cheated into some fine passages, but that is not the thing."

In the next six months, he wrote some of his most glorious poems. Yet, he lamented in a November letter to his brother George (who had emigrated to Kentucky in 1817), "Nothing could have in all circumstances fallen out worse for me than the last year has done, or could be more damping to my poetical talent." Three months later he coughed up blood. His medical training and the nursing of Tom made the truth obvious: "That drop of blood is my death warrant." His only chance, a slim one, was to live in a warmer climate.

After declining an invitation from Percy Bysshe and Mary Shelley to join them in Pisa, Italy, Keats and a companion settled in Rome in late 1820. There he died in February 1821 and was buried in the Protestant cemetery—that "camp of death," as Shelley called it in *Adonais,* his powerful elegy for Keats.

The stark sadness of Keats's life heightens our awareness of the qualities of his poems—not bleak, subdued, or heavy with resignation, but rich in sensuous detail and exciting representations of intense emotional experiences, full of courageous hope for what the imagination can seize and enjoy in life. Above all, they show us what Keats was able to wrest from his troubled life by singlemindedly working at the art of poetry.

PROGRAM MANAGER

- **Planning Instruction** See **Teaching Notes,** *Teaching Resources B,* pp. 36–39, for objectives, summaries, and background for these selections.
- **Instructional Support** Before beginning the instructional lesson, see **Graphic Organizer for Active Reading,** *Teaching Resources B,* pp. 49–52 and 55, for

Through the Poems activities.
- **Assessment** See **Selection Test,** *Test Booklet,* pp. 149–153.
- **Language Link** For instruction and practice in adjective clauses, see **Language Link,** *Teaching Resources B,* pp. 53–54, and *Language and Writing Skills Worksheets,* p. 80.

Into the Poems

Using BEFORE YOU READ p. 746

Reading Focus

Have students reflect on the excitement of a new experience. Ask them to imagine how they would feel if they were an explorer discovering lands new to them or a painter exploring a bold, new style.

ABOUT THE AUTHOR

Keats was confidently defiant of conventions and always ready for a literary confrontation. In Keats's discussions with friends over the hostile tone of his preface for *Endymion*, his first published poem, he remarked: "I never wrote one single Line of Poetry with the least Shadow of public thought." What Keats did listen to, in his own words, was "the eternal Being, the Principle of Beauty,—and the Memory of great Men."

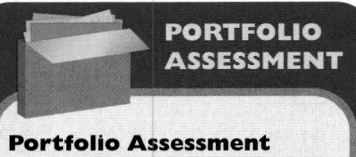

PORTFOLIO ASSESSMENT

Portfolio Assessment
For help with self-assessment of reading skills, see the *Portfolio Management System,* pp. 48–49.

BEFORE YOU READ
ON FIRST LOOKING INTO CHAPMAN'S HOMER

Reading Focus

The Wonders of Words
For all the Romantics, poetry was the true adventure. Imagination opened whole worlds; the best poetry opened thrilling vistas of absolute newness—as Keats says here.

Quickwrite

What work of imagination, in any form (painting, movie, novel, poem, video), has made you see the world in a new way? Why?

Elements of Literature

The Sonnet
Sonnets usually have two parts, no matter what the stanzaic structure is. The first part may present a problem, question, or idea that the second part resolves, answers, or emphasizes. The **turn** begins the second part.

Background

In 1816—just before his twenty-first birthday—Keats wrote this poem, his first mature work, in a few hours. Keats once said that "if poetry comes not as naturally as the leaves to a tree, it had better not come at all."

This poem was connected with an exciting literary experience. Keats's favorite teacher, Charles Cowden Clarke, had invited him to spend an evening reading a translation of Homer's *Iliad* by George Chapman, a contemporary of Shakespeare. They stayed up all night. Keats went home at dawn and by ten that morning sent Clarke this sonnet.

The Chariot of Apollo (late 19th or early 20th century) by Odilon Redon.
Louvre, Paris.

STRATEGIES FOR INCLUSION

Spatial For Keats's first sonnet, have students study the organization of the poem, and ask them why some lines are indented and some are not. [The indentation follows the rhyme scheme.]

Learners Having Difficulty Ask students to recall an experience in which they re-read a story or saw a film they had seen before and suddenly discovered new meaning and emotion that had totally escaped them before. Have them share these experiences with one another, and then tell them that Keats's poem describes a similar discovery.

INTEGRATING THE LANGUAGE ARTS

Strategic Reading Have students read the poem with a partner. Each student should take a turn reading the poem aloud and sharing his or her thoughts about the poem. When both students have taken a turn, have them compare their notes of each other's thoughts. Then, encourage the pairs to re-read the poem without pause.

On First Looking into Chapman's Homer

John Keats

Much have I traveled in the realms of gold,
   And many goodly states and kingdoms seen;
   Round many western islands have I been
Which bards in fealty to Apollo° hold.
5 Oft of one wide expanse had I been told
   That deep-browed Homer ruled as his demesne;°
   Yet did I never breathe its pure serene°
Till I heard Chapman speak out loud and bold:
Then felt I like some watcher of the skies
10   When a new planet swims into his ken;°
Or like stout Cortez° when with eagle eyes
   He stared at the Pacific—and all his men
Looked at each other with a wild surmise—
   Silent, upon a peak in Darien.

4. bards in fealty to Apollo: poets in loyal service (as feudal tenants to their lord) to Apollo, the Greek god of poetry.
6. demesne (di·mān'): domain.
7. serene: archaic for "clear air."
10. ken: range of vision.
11. Cortez: sixteenth-century Spanish explorer. In this now famous mistake, Keats confuses Cortez with Balboa, another Spanish explorer. Balboa was actually the first European to see the eastern shore of the Pacific Ocean from the heights of Darien in Panama.

MAKING MEANINGS

First Thoughts

1. Which **image** from the poem can you still see?

Shaping Interpretations

2. What does the speaker say he had already experienced before he read Homer? How does he say he felt on reading Homer?

3. What could "realms of gold" (line 1) be?

4. Look at the two famous **similes** in lines 9–14. What is Keats telling you about how he felt on reading Homer? By implication, what is he comparing the experience of reading poetry to?

5. What would you say are the two parts of this sonnet?

Extending the Text

6. Keats could not have dreamed of film, computers, and virtual reality. What do you imagine he would think of their powers, as compared to those of poetry? How do *you* feel about that issue? (Check your Reader's Log entry.)

Painted fan (mid–19th century). English.
Victoria and Albert Museum, London.

JOHN KEATS 747

Making Meanings

First Thoughts

1. Possible responses: "Deep-browed Homer," the astronomer, or perhaps the final image of the men silent on the mountain peak.

Shaping Interpretations

2. He has already read many great poets, but when he reads Homer, he feels like the discoverer of a new planet.

3. They are imaginary lands.

A. Reader's Response: Shaping Interpretations

❓ What are all the lands the speaker has visited (ll. 1–4)?
[Sample responses: Places described in poetry; perhaps imaginary lands.]

B. Critical Reading: Making Inferences

❓ What does the epithet "deep-browed" tell you about Homer's character? [It suggests that Homer is serious, distinguished, and possesses a powerful mind.]

C. Literary Element: Sonnet

❓ Where does the **turn** occur in this sonnet? [Between ll. 8 and 9.]

D. Expansion

Line 10 may refer to the then relatively recent discovery of Uranus by William Herschel in 1781.

E. Language Note: Diction

❓ What do the words "wild surmise" in l. 13 suggest about the actions and expressions of Cortez's men? [The word illustrates men silenced with amazement, barely daring to guess that they have reached a new sea.]

4. Keats's similes describe the shock of discovery. The comparison implies that poetry can reveal new truths to readers.

5. Part I, ll. 1–8 recounts the speaker's past literary experience and sets up the second part, ll. 9–14, which describes his awe upon reading Chapman.

Extending the Text

6. **(Synthesis)** Students may say that he would be as impressed as he was when reading Homer; they may also point out that while film, computers, and virtual reality effectively present information, they do not seem to tap the imagination as well as the written word.

Into the Poem

Using BEFORE YOU READ p. 748

Reading Focus

Ask students to imagine Keats's situation, given what they know about him. What would Keats fear? How do students think he would express these fears? Write students' ideas on the chalkboard so that they may review them after reading the poem.

Through the Poem

A. Literary Element: Imagery

? How are harvest images appropriate to a poem about death? [The harvest signals the coming of winter; death is called "the grim reaper."]

B. Literary Element: Turn

? Why do you think the speaker's thoughts on death should change his attitude toward love and fame? [Possible answers: Thinking of death puts things into perspective; it makes one realize what is important.] Note that the attitude change is reflected in the poem's change, or turn.

Reading Focus

The End in Sight

An intense creative mission may be both a blessing and a burden: It focuses life but increases time's pressure. In Keats's case, the fears of this poem become even more poignant because we know his early death at age twenty-five confirmed them. His aspirations to love as well as to fame would both be frustrated. John Keats would "cease to be" within three years of writing this sonnet.

Quickwrite

If you knew your time was short, what would you most regret not being able to do or experience?

Background

By 1820, shortly before he died, Keats had published his new poems in "one of the richest volumes in the history of English poetry." He also hoped to nurture his "little dramatic skill" by writing a few more narrative poems to "nerve me up to the writing of a few fine plays—my greatest ambition." He longed to follow Shakespeare into "the fierce dispute / Betwixt damnation and impassioned clay."

When I Have Fears

John Keats

When I have fears that I may cease to be
   Before my pen has gleaned my teeming brain,
Before high-pilèd books, in charact'ry,°
   Hold like rich garners the full-ripened grain;
5 When I behold, upon the night's starred face,
   Huge cloudy symbols of a high romance,
And think that I may never live to trace
   Their shadows, with the magic hand of chance;
And when I feel, fair creature of an hour,
10   That I shall never look upon thee more,
Never have relish in the fairy° power
   Of unreflecting love!—then on the shore
Of the wide world I stand alone, and think
Till Love and Fame to nothingness do sink.

3. charact'ry: the characters of the alphabet.
11. fairy: supernatural; unearthly.

The Poet's Theme (19th century) by John Callcott Horsley.

OPTIONS FOR TEACHING

INTEGRATING THE LANGUAGE ARTS

Strategic Reading As students read the poem, have them think of how they would answer the speaker's fears. Encourage them to imagine the poem as part of a conversation they are having with Keats himself. Ask students to write their responses and then compare their ideas with a partner.

Writing: Requiem Keats rightly feared that his life would be a short one. Ask students to reflect on the emotions and experiences his poem predicts will be cut short. Then, have students write a requiem that addresses these ideas. Taking the form of a chant, song, or poem, the requiem can explore both Keats's thoughts on human mortality and aspiration, and the reader's own knowledge of Keats as a well-known poet.

Keats's Last Letter

Rome, 30 November 1820

My dear Brown,

'Tis the most difficult thing in the world to me to write a letter. My stomach continues so bad, that I feel it worse on opening any book, yet I am much better than I was in quarantine. Then I am afraid to encounter the pro-ing and con-ing of anything interesting to me in England. I have an habitual feeling of my real life having passed, and that I am leading a posthumous existence. God knows how it would have been—but it appears to me—however, I will not speak of that subject. I must have been at Bedhampton nearly at the time you were writing to me from Chichester—how unfortunate—and to pass on the river too! There was my star predominant! I cannot answer anything in your letter, which followed me from Naples to Rome, because I am afraid to look it over again. I am so weak (in mind) that I cannot bear the sight of any handwriting of a friend I love so much as I do you. Yet I ride the little horse, and, at my worst, even in quarantine, summoned up more puns, in a sort of desperation, in one week than in any year of my life. There is one thought enough to kill me; I have been well, healthy, alert, etc., walking with her, and now—the knowledge of contrast, feeling for light and shade, all that information (primitive sense) necessary for a poem, are great enemies to the recovery of the stomach. There, you rogue, I put you to the torture; but you must bring your philosophy to bear, as I do mine, really, or how should I be able to live? Dr. Clark is very attentive to me; he says, there is very little the matter with my lungs, but my stomach, he says, is very bad. I am well disappointed in hearing good news from George, for it runs in my head we shall all die young. I have not written to Reynolds yet, which he must think very neglectful; being anxious to send him a good account of my health, I have delayed it from week to week. If I recover, I will do all in my power to correct the mistakes made during sickness; and if I should not, all my faults shall be forgiven. Severn is very well, though he leads so dull a life with me. Remember me to all friends, and tell Haslam I should not have left London without taking leave of him, but from being so low in body and mind. Write to George as soon you receive this, and tell him how I am, as far as you can guess; and also a note to my sister—who walks about my imagination like a ghost—she is so like Tom. I can scarcely bid you goodbye, even in a letter. I always made an awkward bow.

God bless you!
John Keats

MAKING MEANINGS

First Thoughts

1. How do the feelings you recorded in your Reader's Log entry compare to the ones Keats expresses in this poem?

Shaping Interpretations

2. What **simile** describes the books the speaker hopes to write?

3. Whom does the speaker address, and what line tells you?

4. Where is this sonnet's **turn**?

5. Describe the speaker's **tone**. Do you think it is constant or does it change? Explain.

Connecting with the Text

6. What do you think the last line means? How does it make you feel about the speaker and what is soon to happen to him?

JOHN KEATS 749

Primary Sources

Remind students to choose a situation they would not mind sharing with others. Ask students to imagine they are writing what they think may be the last letter they will be able to write to their best friend. What would they want to tell their friend? What images, ideas, and feelings would they like to survive them in a letter? Have students freewrite on the theme for a few minutes, and then ask them to volunteer ideas. After the discussion, turn their attention to Keats's last letter: What do they think it says? Ask students to write down a few ideas and compare them with their ideas for their own last letters.

Making Meanings

First Thoughts

1. Like Keats, students will probably have considered lost love and lost opportunity among their regrets.

Shaping Interpretations

2. The simile of the harvest describes the act of writing poetry.
3. The speaker is addressing his lover; this is revealed in ll. 9–10.
4. In the middle of l. 12, the poem shifts from a consideration of regrets to the effects of that meditation.
5. The tone is anxious, melancholy, regretful. The end of the poem becomes more calm and sad.

Connecting with the Text

6. The last line tells how in the face of death, love and fame no longer matter. Students may say the line reveals the speaker's despair and creates empathy for the speaker.

STRATEGIES FOR INCLUSION

Visual As students read Keats's letter in the Primary Sources, they should take note of pairs of complementary or contradictory words, images, and ideas and organize the pairs into two thematic columns on a sheet of paper. Ask students to compare their groupings and discuss what the pairs suggest about the author's state of mind.

Advanced Point out to students that the letter in the Primary Sources evokes a sense of a continuing conversation between the two correspondents. Challenge students to use specific details from the letter to make inferences about Brown's personality and the relationship between him and Keats. Students may share their findings with the class. ☞

Into the Poem

Using BEFORE YOU READ p. 750

Reading Focus

Discuss with students how such a character as the temptress might appeal to Keats, given what they know about his life and poetry. Have students record their ideas on one half of a sheet of paper. After they have read the poem, direct students to fill the other half of the sheet with reasons why the character of the knight is attracted to the temptress. Students can then compare both sets of notes.

Background

Ask students to reflect on Romantic borrowings of old techniques and forms. Why might the title have appealed to Keats enough for him to take it as the title of his poem? [That it is in French recalls the courtly ballads of the troubadours, so that the title evokes another place and time, which adds to the mystery of the poem.]

BEFORE YOU READ
LA BELLE DAME SANS MERCI

Reading Focus
Under Beauty's Spell
The figure of woman as temptress—irresistibly beautiful, but emotionally cold—is ancient. Indifferent to the fate of those who come under her spell, she vanishes as swiftly and mysteriously as she arrives, leaving her victim spiritless, deprived of his manhood—and forever obsessed with the unobtainable. Let your reading of this poem move on two levels: How does the woman so captivate the speaker? What is it about the tale that so captivates Keats, the Romantic poet?

Quickwrite

From music, books, movies, or television, brainstorm some examples of heartless, beautiful women who bend men to their will. Why are they so captivating?

Elements of Literature
Ballad
Like many of Wordsworth's ballads, this songlike **ballad** has a seemingly direct simplicity. Like Coleridge's story of the Ancient Mariner, it re-creates the medieval ballad's air of mystery and enchantment. The poem looks back to older literature, but the story it tells is still heard in today's folk music repertoire.

Background
"La Belle Dame sans Merci" (The Beautiful Woman Without Pity) repeats the title of a poem by the fifteenth-century French poet Alain Chartier. Keats, who was fascinated with the self-destroying experiences of intense passion, wrote his poem in the spring of 1819.

La Belle Dame sans Merci (late 19th or early 20th century) by Sir Frank Dicksee.

City of Bristol Museum and Art Gallery, Bristol, England.

750 THE ROMANTIC PERIOD

La Belle Dame sans Merci

John Keats

O, what can ail thee, knight-at-arms,
    Alone and palely loitering?
The sedge° has withered from the lake,
    And no birds sing.

5   O, what can ail thee, knight-at-arms, **A**
    So haggard and so woebegone?
The squirrel's granary° is full,
    And the harvest's done.

I see a lily on thy brow,
10 With anguish moist and fever dew,
And on thy cheeks a fading rose **B**
    Fast withereth too.

I met a lady in the meads,° **C**
    Full beautiful—a fairy's child,
15 Her hair was long, her foot was light,
    And her eyes were wild.

I made a garland for her head,
    And bracelets too, and fragrant zone;°
She looked at me as she did love, **D**
20   And made sweet moan.

I set her on my pacing steed,
    And nothing else saw all day long,
For sidelong would she bend and sing
    A fairy's song. **E**

25 She found me roots of relish sweet,
    And honey wild, and manna dew,°
And sure in language strange she said
    "I love thee true."

She took me to her elfin grot,°
30   And there she wept and sighed full sore,
And there I shut her wild wild eyes
    With kisses four.

And there she lulled me asleep,
    And there I dreamed—Ah! woe betide!
35 The latest° dream I ever dreamed
    On the cold hill side.

I saw pale kings and princes too,
    Pale warriors, death-pale were they all;
They cried, "La Belle Dame sans Merci **F**
40   Hath thee in thrall!"°

3. sedge: reedy plants.

7. granary: place for storing grain.

13. meads: archaic for "meadow-lands."

18. zone: archaic for "belt" or "girdle."

26. manna dew: the sweet juice exuded by the European ash tree and by certain other plants. Also, in Exodus 16:13–36, manna is the food God miraculously provides for the Israelites.
29. grot: archaic for "cave" or "grotto."

35. latest: archaic for "last."

40. in thrall: archaic for "enslaved."

JOHN KEATS 751

Through the Poem

A. Literary Element: Ballad
What is the effect of repeating the first line of the poem in l. 5? [The repetition is characteristic of ballads, and it gives the poem a songlike quality.]

B. Literary Element: Metaphor
What do the "lily" and "fading rose" of ll. 9 and 11 describe? [The knight's paleness; they are ghostly images.]

C. Literary Element: Point of View
What is the change in point of view beginning with l. 13? [The knight begins to tell his tale.]

D. Language Note: Dual Meaning
How does the meaning of l. 19 change if the word *as* is read as *as if* instead of *while*? [The reader would be more uncertain of the lady's honesty. The lady might take on a sinister quality.]

E. Literary Element: Rhythm
What is the effect of the shorter length and different rhythm of l. 24, compared to the other lines in the stanza? [The variation makes it stand out and gives the lady's "fairy song" a mysterious sound.]

F. Critical Reading: Analyzing Details
What do the details in ll. 37–42 suggest about the men's appearance? [They resemble skeletons, ghosts, or images of death.]

INTEGRATING THE LANGUAGE ARTS

Strategic Reading Before students read the poem, ask them to look over the title and the form of the poem and to recall past reading that had a similar theme and form. Tell students to write in one column on a sheet of paper what they know of the ballad form and what they would expect from the poem given its title. In a second column, ask them to write questions they would like answered in the poem—questions about form, plot, character, or any other element. After they have finished reading the poem, have students list in a third column what they have learned in answer to their questions and also what has surprised them or fascinated them about the poem. ☞

PROGRAM MANAGER

- **Audiotaped Readings** To help less proficient readers or auditory learners through the lesson, use the **Selected Reading, Audiocassette 1, Side B**, in the *Audiovisual Resources Binder*.

A. Reader's Response: Shaping Interpretations

? What does the knight realize has happened to him when he awakes?

[Sample responses: The knight has died; or has been brought close to death; or has been robbed by the lady of his youth and power.]

I saw their starved lips in the gloam,°
    With horrid warning gaped wide,
And I awoke, and found me here,
    On the cold hill's side.

45 And this is why I sojourn° here,
    Alone and palely loitering,
Though the sedge is withered from the lake,
    And no birds sing.

41. gloam: archaic for "twilight."

45. sojourn: visit.

La Belle Dame Sans Merci (1926) by Frank Cadogan Cowper. Private Collection.

CROSSING THE CURRICULUM

Social Studies Keats's poem draws on many elements of folklore. Ask students to research and find their own pieces of folklore. Students might ask family and friends for scary stories or for stories that are plausible but difficult to believe. Or encourage students to look up old folk tales or fairy tales in the library. During one class period, students may trade their folk tales.

Music Have students research the traditions of the French troubadours in medieval and Renaissance times. Ask each student to find a song or a description of a type of song they would sing. Also, challenge students to find a modern parallel to the troubadour.

CLASSROOM MANAGEMENT

Reading Notebook Have students keep in a special notebook the notes that they take while reading. Students may review the notes periodically to remember the impressions a work made on them, to find helpful strategies they have used, or to see how their reading has improved over time. Telling students that the notebook will be checked for completion—not graded—may encourage them to be more free with their thoughts as they read.

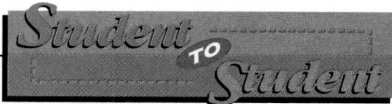

Student to Student

A Poem Within a Poem

Once I was pensive, very pensive
watching a mysterious, melancholic poet
writing a poem

All that he was writing
was just a poem within a poem: **A**

A dark night of bitterness,
the song of a bird,
the solitude of the Aurora,
the smell of a rose
make a poem within a poem

Take this poem to a poet
who remembers a beloved who does not come—
Take it to a disconsolate poet who wants to reach Diana
Take it to a singer who wants the moon to fall in love
To a man who feels the sadness of being alone
To Neruda who once wrote the sad verses of the night
To the passionate poet
who writes what comes from his heart.

—Arnulfo J. López
James Madison High School
Vienna, Virginia

MAKING MEANINGS

First Thoughts

1. What to you is the most important word in the descriptions of the woman, and why?

Shaping Interpretations

2. Who are the poem's two **speakers,** and where does one stop speaking and the other begin?

3. How do the poem's **images** help you visualize the knight and the time of year?

4. How do you interpret the dream in stanza 10?

5. Where does Keats vary each stanza's **meter,** and what is the effect of the rhythmic change?

6. How does the student poem above relate to the poems by Keats and the other Romantic poets?

7. How does this literary **ballad** compare with the old folk ballads on pages 91–95?

Connecting with the Text

8. Look closely at the poem's descriptions of the enchantress and her actions, and compare these to the "belles dames" of your Reader's Log entry. What idea is being expressed about the relationship between men and women? How do you feel about it?

JOHN KEATS 753

CONNECTING WITH "LA BELLE DAME SANS MERCI"

Ask students to work in pairs to compare the theme of "A Poem Within a Poem" with the theme of "La Belle Dame sans Merci." Encourage students to look for connections with other Romantic ideals as well.

	"A Poem"	"La Belle Dame"
Poem's Tone		
Type of Language		
Poet's Desire		
Objects Praised or Admired		

☞

A. Reader's Response: First Thoughts

? What do you think is a "poem within a poem?" [Sample responses: The author may mean that a thing of beauty is a poem itself; or he may mean that the lives of the Romantic poets were poetical works themselves, thus their poems existed within the poetry of their lives.]

Making Meanings

First Thoughts

1. Students may point out the word *wild,* as it is repeated often in describing the woman. The word suggests that the woman is not quite human but is some mysterious natural force.

Shaping Interpretations

2. The first speaker (stanzas 1–3) is the narrator. The second speaker (stanzas 4–12) is a knight. The shift occurs when the knight responds to the narrator's questions.

3. The images of the knight's loneliness, pallor, aimlessness, fatigue, and feverishness help the reader see the man's sickness and loss. The withered sedge and harvest indicate the season is late fall.

4. The knight's dream tells him that the woman is more than she appears, perhaps some sort of demon—the destructive power of her enchantment horrifies him.

5. The meter varies in the last line of each stanza. The change arrests the reader's progress, and breaks the flow of the first three lines.

6. The student poem mentions several themes common to Romantic poets: melancholy, passion, and loss.

7. This ballad contains the question and answer format, supernatural events, and tragic subject matter, among other elements of traditional ballads.

Connecting with the Text

8. Students may say that the theme expressed by the "belles dames" is that women somehow entrap and endanger men with their beauty. Students may find this a sexist idea; they might also see how the relation between the sexes is often a struggle, so that the theme may be a metaphorical description of the male perspective of the struggle.

Into the Poem

Using BEFORE YOU READ p. 754

Reading Focus

Have students consider the role of the imagination in the fear and fascination people have for dreams and darkness. Ask students to discuss and compare their ideas, and then direct students to think of how going out into darkness or into dreams can be an adventure of the mind. They may keep these ideas in mind as they read the poem.

A Dialogue with the Text

After students have read the poem, ask them to return to their Reader's Log lists of the speaker's mood in each stanza. Students may review the poem and list next to the descriptions of the speaker's mood details that support their analyses. Have them compare their lists and supporting details with a partner.

Background

Point out that the poem was written in the morning. Why then would its **setting** be dark? [Students may say that the darkness reflects the speaker's imaginative, melancholy mood or his dream state.]

BEFORE YOU READ
ODE TO A NIGHTINGALE

Reading Focus
Dark Mysteries
From the first lines of this poem, you know the speaker is passing into an altered state, a reverie not wholly of the waking world. It is an intense poem of extremes, a searching flight of the mind at once joyful and despairing, spiritual and startlingly concrete. If you let yourself take this journey with Keats (as unfamiliar as it may at first seem), you will find yourself in a daring poem. Keats is not afraid of the dark.

A Dialogue with the Text

READER'S LOG

Chart the speaker's mood as you read. After each stanza, quickly write one phrase describing his mood.

Background
When Keats was twenty-three, he spent a few months at the Hampstead home of his friend Charles Brown, who remembered: "In the spring of 1819 a nightingale had built her nest near my house. Keats felt a tranquil and continual joy in her song, and one morning he took his chair from the breakfast table to the grass plot under a plum tree, where he sat for two or three hours. When he came into the house, I perceived he had some scraps of paper in his hand, and these he was quietly thrusting behind the books. On inquiry, I found those scraps, four or five in number, contained his poetic feeling on the song of our nightingale." There are no nightingales in North America. Their unearthly, sad, sweet song can only be heard in the British Isles and in Central and Western Europe.

The Nightingale, published in *Harper's Monthly* (1866). Woodcut.

OPTIONS FOR TEACHING

STRATEGIES FOR INCLUSION

Less Proficient Readers For this reading activity, you may need to emphasize to students that they should not try to read the poem quickly. Encouraging students to read slowly will help less proficient readers feel more comfortable as they take their turns reading aloud and as they read along with the speaker.

Special Needs Students will benefit from active interaction with what they are reading. Place a blank transparency over "Ode to a Nightingale," and have students use colored markers to highlight or underline images they find beautiful or striking. Remind students that imagery is language that appeals to any sense or combination of senses. This activity will help students to stay on task, learn to analyze imagery, and answer the Making Meanings questions that follow.

Ode to a Nightingale

John Keats

1

My heart aches, and a drowsy numbness pains
   My sense, as though of hemlock° I had drunk, **(A)**
Or emptied some dull opiate to the drains°
   One minute past, and Lethewards° had sunk:
5 'Tis not through envy of thy happy lot,
   But being too happy in thine happiness—
      That thou, light-wingèd Dryad° of the trees,
        In some melodious plot
Of beechen° green, and shadows numberless,
10   Singest of summer in full-throated ease.

2

O, for a draft of vintage!° that hath been
   Cooled a long age in the deep-delvèd earth,
Tasting of Flora° and the country green,
   Dance, and Provençal° song, and sunburnt mirth!
15 O for a beaker full of the warm South, **(B)**
   Full of the true, the blushful Hippocrene,°
      With beaded bubbles winking at the brim,
        And purple-stainèd mouth;
That I might drink, and leave the world unseen, **(C)**
20   And with thee fade away into the forest dim:

3

Fade far away, dissolve, and quite forget
   What thou among the leaves hast never known, **(D)**
The weariness, the fever, and the fret
   Here, where men sit and hear each other groan;
25 Where palsy° shakes a few, sad, last gray hairs,
   Where youth grows pale, and specter-thin, and dies; **(E)**
      Where but to think is to be full of sorrow
        And leaden-eyed despairs,
   Where Beauty cannot keep her lustrous eyes,
30   Or new Love pine at them beyond tomorrow.

4

Away! away! for I will fly to thee,
   Not charioted by Bacchus and his pards,° **(F)**
But on the viewless wings of Poesy,°
   Though the dull brain perplexes and retards:
35 Already with thee! tender is the night,

---

2. hemlock: poison made from the hemlock plant.
3. drains: dregs.
4. Lethewards (lē′thē·wərds): toward Lethe. In Greek and Roman mythology, Lethe is the river of forgetfulness that flows through the underworld.
7. Dryad (drī′ad′): in Greek mythology, nature goddess associated with trees.
9. beechen: archaic for "pertaining to beech trees."

11. vintage: wine.

13. Flora: the richness of flowers. Flora is the Roman goddess of flowers.
14. Provençal (prō′vän·säl′): from Provence, a region in southern France known in the Middle Ages for its troubadors singing love songs.
16. blushful Hippocrene (hip′ō·krēn′): wine, which he would drink for inspiration. In Greek mythology, Hippocrene is the Muses' fountain, whose waters inspire the poets who drink from it.

25. palsy: a disease of the nervous system that causes partial paralysis and involuntary shaking.

32. not . . . pards: not by getting drunk. Bacchus, the Roman god of wine, was sometimes pictured in a chariot pulled by leopards, shortened here to "pards."
33. on . . . Poesy: on the invisible wings of poetry; that is, by using his poetic imagination.

JOHN KEATS 755

A. Literary Element: Mood

? How does the speaker feel in the opening lines of the poem?
[Melancholic, heartbroken, and numb, as if drugged.]

B. Critical Reading: Making Inferences

? What does this line mean? [The speaker wants a glass of wine that reminds him of the warm southern place where the grapes were grown.]

C. Critical Reading: Finding Cause and Effect

? What does the speaker hope will be the effect of drinking the wine?
[He hopes it will allow him to escape his cares and to withdraw.]

D. Literary Element: Alliteration

? What sounds are repeated in these lines and to what effect?
[Keats chooses to repeat *f*, *n*, and *w* sounds, giving the lines a muffled sound that underscores the desire to retreat into a softer world.]

E. Expansion

Keats's younger brother Tom had died of tuberculosis several months before Keats wrote this poem. It could be that the poet was thinking of him when writing l. 26.

F. Literary Element: Tone

? How does the tone of the poem change in ll. 31–33? [The speaker begins to have hope and courage to escape his pain, not with wine but with poetry.]

INTEGRATING THE LANGUAGE ARTS

Writing: Advice Column Ask students to address Keats's wistful ode in the style of an advice column. They may write a short paragraph that answers his yearning address to the nightingale with modern answers to his observations and contemporary responses to his heartache. Tell students that their responses may be either thoughtful or humorous. Students may read their columns aloud to the class to see the range of suggestions that Keats's poem elicits. ☞

And haply the Queen-Moon is on her throne,
   Clustered around by all her starry Fays;°
    But here there is no light,
Save what from heaven is with the breezes blown
40   Through verdurous° glooms and winding mossy ways.

37. Fays: fairies.

40. verdurous (vʉr′jər·əs): full of green foliage.

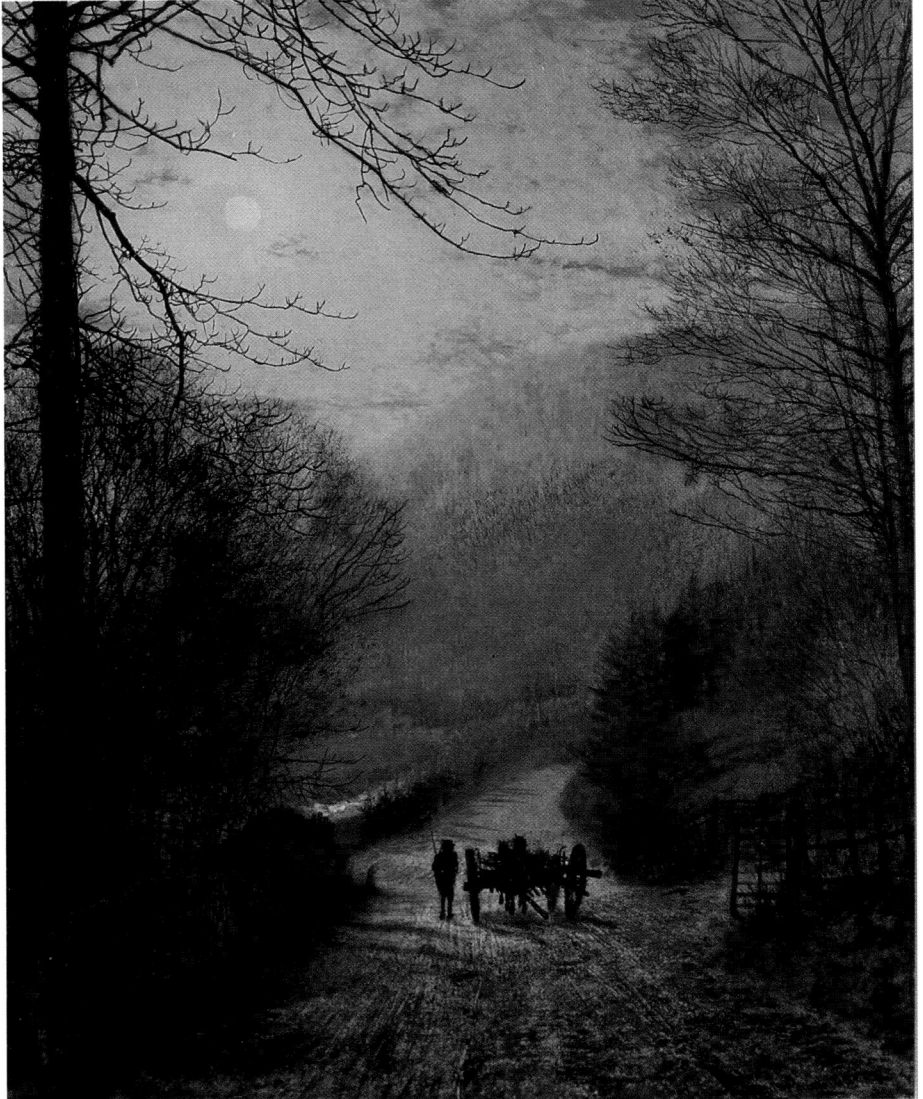

Christopher Wood Gallery, London.

Forge Valley, Scarborough (19th century) by John Atkinson Grimshaw.

OPTIONS FOR TEACHING

INTEGRATING THE LANGUAGE ARTS

Language and Style Keats's "Ode to a Nightingale" is famous for its lush imagery. Ask students to review the poem and pick out an especially vivid image. Then, have students describe how the image successfully works together with its context and the theme of the poem to paint a picture for the reader. You may also want to challenge students to find examples of **synaesthesia**, which is discussed on p. 759. Have students share their findings with the class.

Strategic Reading Ask students to hypothesize about Keats's intent in writing this ode. Is his poem primarily a tribute to the beauty of the nightingale's song? Or is it more an exploration of his own thoughts about transcending human limitations? Have a volunteer read the poem aloud one stanza at a time, pausing for discussion of vocabulary and interpretation.

5

I cannot see what flowers are at my feet,
    Nor what soft incense hangs upon the boughs,
But, in embalmèd° darkness, guess each sweet **(A)**
    Wherewith the seasonable month endows
45 The grass, the thicket, and the fruit tree wild;
    White hawthorn, and the pastoral eglantine;°
      Fast fading violets covered up in leaves;
        And mid-May's eldest child,
    The coming° musk rose, full of dewy wine,
50   The murmurous haunt of flies on summer eves.

43. embalmèd: perfumed.

46. eglantine (eg'lən·tīn'): kind of rose.

49. coming: soon to bloom.

6

Darkling° I listen; and, for many a time
    I have been half in love with easeful Death,
Called him soft names in many a musèd rhyme,
    To take into the air my quiet breath;
55 Now more than ever seems it rich to die, **(B)**
    To cease upon the midnight with no pain,
      While thou art pouring forth thy soul abroad
        In such an ecstasy!
    Still wouldst thou sing, and I have ears in vain—
60   To thy high requiem° become a sod.°

51. darkling: archaic for "in the dark."

60. requiem (rek'wē·əm): Mass or song for the dead. **sod:** piece of topsoil held together by the matted roots of living grasses.

7

Thou wast not born for death, immortal Bird! **(C)**
    No hungry generations tread thee down;
The voice I hear this passing night was heard
    In ancient days by emperor and clown:
65 Perhaps the selfsame song that found a path
    Through the sad heart of Ruth,° when, sick for home, **(D)**
      She stood in tears amid the alien corn;°
        The same that ofttimes hath
    Charmed magic casements,° opening on the foam
70   Of perilous seas, in fairy lands forlorn.

66. Ruth: in the Bible, a young widow who left her own people to go with her mother-in-law to a strange land.
67. corn: British generic term for grain.
69. casements: windows. Images of open windows intrigued Keats.

8

Forlorn! the very word is like a bell **(E)**
    To toll me back from thee to my sole self!
Adieu! the fancy° cannot cheat so well
    As she is famed to do, deceiving elf.
75 Adieu! adieu! thy plaintive° anthem fades
    Past the near meadows, over the still stream,
      Up the hillside; and now 'tis buried deep
        In the next valley glades:
    Was it a vision, or a waking dream?
80   Fled is that music:—Do I wake or sleep?

73. fancy: imagination.

75. plaintive: sad; mournful.

JOHN KEATS 757

A. Literary Element: Imagery
? How do the descriptions of the vegetation in ll. 41–45 evoke smells without describing their sources? [The speaker uses words such as *incense, embalmèd,* and *sweet,* as well as giving suggestive details such as the presence of fruit trees.]

B. Reader's Response: Shaping Interpretations
? What does this passage convey about the speaker's state of mind? [Sample responses: The speaker is so desperate for escape that he clearly wishes for death, thinking it all the more appealing to die while the nightingale sings. He is confused but then realizes that he will hear the nightingale no more if he should die.]

C. Critical Reading: Drawing Conclusions
? How can the bird be immortal? [The nightingale's song has been heard through the ages.]

D. Literary Element: Allusion
? What is the effect of the Biblical allusion in ll. 66–67? [The allusion suggests how timeless and inspirational the bird's song is.]

E. Language Note: Transition
? What key word links the last stanza of the poem to the stanza that precedes it? [*Forlorn.*] Note how the repetition gives the sound of the tolling bell Keats mentions.

CROSSING THE CURRICULUM

Music Have students compare the effect of a particular song on themselves to the effect of the nightingale's song on the poem's speaker. Ask students to consider specific elements of the song that appeal to them or move them. Have them concentrate on the tune, not the lyrics. Challenge students to put into words how the music affects them so strongly.

CLASSROOM MANAGEMENT

Library Research When assigning them research to complete in the library, pair students even if they do not share a common topic. The partners could help each other find the information each seeks, and in the event that one becomes frustrated with his or her search, the other can help brainstorm for new ideas. ☞

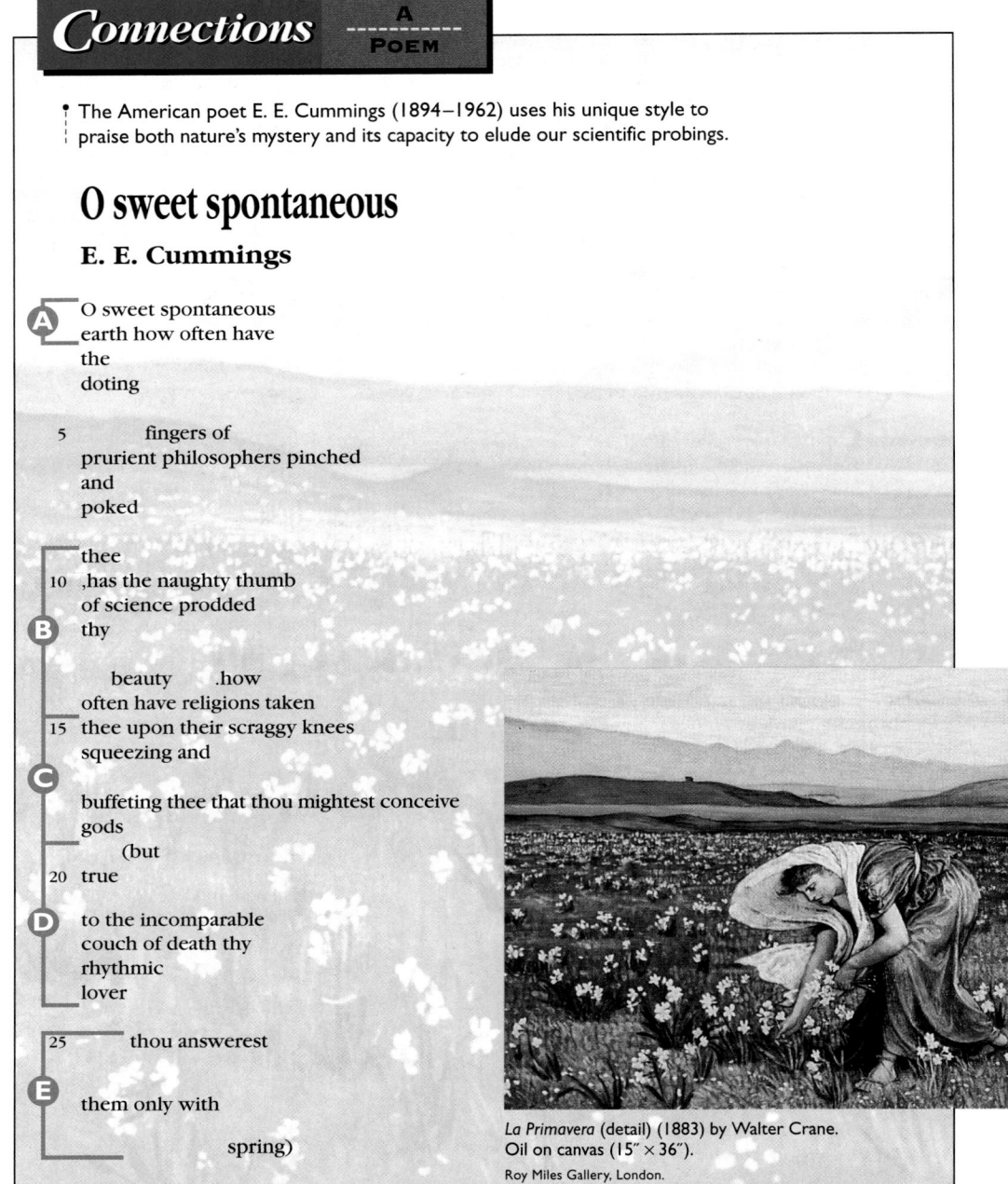

Connections — A POEM

The American poet E. E. Cummings (1894–1962) uses his unique style to praise both nature's mystery and its capacity to elude our scientific probings.

O sweet spontaneous

E. E. Cummings

A O sweet spontaneous
earth how often have
the
doting

5   fingers of
prurient philosophers pinched
and
poked

B thee
10 ,has the naughty thumb
of science prodded
thy

beauty   .how
often have religions taken
15 thee upon their scraggy knees
squeezing and

C buffeting thee that thou mightest conceive
gods
    (but
20 true

D to the incomparable
couch of death thy
rhythmic
lover

E 25   thou answerest

them only with

                spring)

La Primavera (detail) (1883) by Walter Crane.
Oil on canvas (15″ × 36″).
Roy Miles Gallery, London.

OPTIONS FOR TEACHING

PROFESSIONAL NOTES

Critical Comment: Analysis of the Poem The critics Cleanth Brooks and Robert Penn Warren offer the following reading of "Ode to a Nightingale": "This poem is essentially a reverie induced by the poet's listening to the song of the nightingale. In the first stanza the poet is just sinking into the reverie; in the last stanza, he comes out of the reverie and back to a consciousness of the actual world in which he and all other human beings live. The first lines of the poem and the last, therefore, constitute a sort of frame for the reverie proper. . . .

"The poet has chosen to present his reverie largely in terms of imagery—imagery drawn from nature, the flowers and leaves, etc., actually associated with the bird physically, and imagery drawn from myth and literature. . . . The images are elaborate and decorative and the poet dwells upon them lovingly and leisurely, developing them in some detail as pictures. . . . The loving elaboration and slowed movement resembles the slowed movement of meditative trance, or dream, and therefore is appropriate to the general tone of this poem." Ask students to comment on the critics' analysis.

Critical Comment

Dialogue with the Soul

Keats's completed poem is not "about" or "on" the nightingale but, as the title tells us, "to" the nightingale. The speaker seems, as the poem opens, to have already passed beyond the limit of ordinary experience and become "too" happy in the experience conveyed in the nightingale's song. The poem consists of a series of propositions, each containing its own rejection as to how the speaker might imitate the "ease" of the song he hears—wine, poetry, even death are considered. Each time, the speaker in his humanness is drawn back to his "sole self," to a preference for poetry as a celebration, not of "summer" but of human life as a process of soul making.

MAKING MEANINGS

First Thoughts

1. When you finish Keats's poem, what **image** is strongest in your mind?

Shaping Interpretations

2. Describe the **setting** of the poem—its time and place.

3. Why do you think the speaker wants to capture the nightingale's "ease," and why is he "too happy in [its] happiness" (stanza 1)?

4. Describe the changing desires and ideas that the speaker passes through in stanzas 2–3, 4–5, and 6–7. How does he resolve each one?

5. What differences are emphasized between the realm (or experience) of the nightingale and that of the speaker?

6. What do you think the speaker realizes by the end of the poem?

7. Review your Reader's Log, and explain whether you feel the speaker's **mood** is more, or less, exalted at the poem's end than at its beginning.

Connecting with the Text

8. How would you answer the speaker's final question? Explain your response.

9. Do you see any similarity between Keats's response to nature and Cummings's? Explain.

10. Can you think of any experience a person today might have that compares with Keats's—say, a city person? Explain your response.

LANGUAGE AND STYLE

Imagery: Poets' Conjurings

This poem is famous for its lush imagery. Several of its images, in fact, have been used by other writers as titles. (The American novelist F. Scott Fitzgerald called one of his tragic love stories *Tender Is the Night*.)

1. What concrete **images** in the poem conjure up quite different historical or mythological periods?

2. In the poetic device called **synaesthesia,** one sense experience (such as smell) is described in terms of another (such as touch): "soft incense" (line 42). Find other examples of **synaesthesia** in Keats's ode.

First Thoughts

1. Possible responses: The images of a pale, dying youth or of a peaceful summer evening.

Shaping Interpretations

2. The setting is a garden in summer.

3. The speaker wants the bird's "ease" for his worldly troubles. He is "too happy" because his ties to the bird are illusory.

4. In the second stanza, the speaker wants to join the bird by drinking; in the third stanza, he thinks of death. In the fourth stanza, he connects with the bird through poetry. His mood calms in the fifth stanza as he hears the song. In the sixth and seventh stanzas, the speaker contemplates death but gains strength from the song.

5. The speaker's realm is that of time and decay; the nightingale's is a realm of eternity.

6. The speaker realizes that the song offers hope of transcending human pain but that, ultimately, there is no escape. However, he does achieve a heightened awareness through the encounter with the nightingale.

7. Because of the vision provoked by the nightingale, the speaker's mood is more exalted, if just barely, at the poem's end.

Connecting with the Text

8. Students may reply that the reverie combined reality and dreams. They should support their answers with specific passages.

9. Both poems acknowledge the inevitability of death and celebrate nature's inspiration.

10. A person today might experience a bird's song or the glow of city lights which could cause the same questioning and bring the same conclusions about the human condition.

Language and Style

Answers

1. The poet refers to the Biblical character of Ruth and to the classical Roman deities such as Bacchus.

2. The image "leaden-eyed" (l. 28) combines sight and touch; "embalmèd darkness" (l. 43) combines smell and sight.

Strategic Reading Ask students to summarize the main ideas of the Critical Comment above. Challenge students to make their summaries as concise and precise as possible. Also, have students consider the following questions as they edit their summaries: Have I included each main idea of the article? Is my summary easy to read? Are there any unnecessary words or irrelevant ideas?

Advanced Extend the Language and Style activity by having students look for examples of synaesthesia and evocative images in Keats's other poems. Ask for volunteers to share their ideas on how these other examples compare with those in "Ode to a Nightingale."

Into the Poem

Using BEFORE YOU READ p. 760

A Dialogue with the Text

Students may want to compare sketches with a partner or collaborate on a sketch with another student. Have students read the poem once through uninterrupted before they make their sketches.

Background

Have students study the decoration of ancient Greek vases from photographs. Ask them to discuss how the decoration relates to the function of the urns. Ask them also what stories they find presented in the decorations. They may compare their readings of the urns with that of Keats.

BEFORE YOU READ
ODE ON A GRECIAN URN

Reading Focus
Unheard Melodies
This poem is a work of art about the contemplation of a work of art—a Grecian urn, or jar. That means the ode is both concrete (descriptive) and contemplative (philosophical). It moves from rich images to abstract ideas about art/life, permanence/change, and body/spirit.

A Dialogue with the Text

READER'S LOG

Stop after reading stanzas 1–3, and then after stanza 4, and record the urn's pictures as you see them. Make sketches if you like.

Background
Antique Greek vases are usually black with reddish painting, often depicting mythological subjects. They show gods, goddesses, heroes, and the mortals entangled in their adventures. Traditionally, urns have been used for planting and for burial. No one knows exactly what urn Keats had in mind when he wrote this ode. Probably it is an imaginative combination of several vases he had seen, including two in the British Museum.

Youth singing and playing the kithara, attributed to the Berlin Painter. Terra-cotta amphora (c. 490), said to be from Nola.
The Metropolitan Museum of Art, New York. Fletcher Fund, 1956. (56.171.38)

760 THE ROMANTIC PERIOD

Advanced Before students begin to read "Ode on a Grecian Urn," have them reflect on the technique of **apostrophe**. On a sheet of paper, have them list the technique's benefits and limitations. Ask students to use these notes after they have read the poem to write a short essay on how effective the apostrophe is in this poem.

Learners Having Difficulty Often, students' difficulty with poetry comes not from its level of vocabulary but from its elliptical use of language. Work with students to do a step-by-step close reading of "Ode on a Grecian Urn." Write on the chalkboard its famous ending, including the lines, "Beauty is truth, truth beauty." Have students expand this well-known epigram to explore both its connotative and its denotative meanings.

Ode on a Grecian Urn

John Keats

1

Thou still unravished bride of quietness,
   Thou foster child of silence and slow time,
Sylvan° historian, who canst thus express
   A flowery tale more sweetly than our rhyme:
5 What leaf-fringed legend haunts about thy shape
   Of deities or mortals, or of both,
     In Tempe or the dales of Arcady?°
   What men or gods are these? What maidens loath?°
What mad pursuit? What struggle to escape?
10   What pipes and timbrels?° What wild ecstasy?

3. sylvan: of the forest. (The urn is decorated with a rural scene.)

7. Tempe (tem′pē) **. . . Arcady** (är′kə·dē): valleys in ancient Greece; ideal types of rural beauty.
8. loath: reluctant.
10. timbrels: tambourines.

2

Heard melodies are sweet, but those unheard
   Are sweeter; therefore, ye soft pipes, play on;
Not to the sensual ear, but, more endeared,
   Pipe to the spirit ditties° of no tone:
15 Fair youth, beneath the trees, thou canst not leave
   Thy song, nor ever can those trees be bare;
     Bold Lover, never, never canst thou kiss,
   Though winning near the goal—yet, do not grieve;
     She cannot fade, though thou hast not thy bliss,
20   Forever wilt thou love, and she be fair!

14. ditties: short, simple songs.

3

Ah, happy, happy boughs! that cannot shed
   Your leaves, nor ever bid the Spring adieu;°
And, happy melodist, unwearied,
   Forever piping songs forever new;
25 More happy love! more happy, happy love!
   Forever warm and still to be enjoyed,
     Forever panting, and forever young;
All breathing human passion far above,
   That leaves a heart high-sorrowful and cloyed,°
30   A burning forehead, and a parching tongue.

22. adieu (á·dyö′): French for "goodbye."

29. cloyed (kloid): satiated; wearied with excess.

4

Who are these coming to the sacrifice?
   To what green altar, O mysterious priest,
Lead'st thou that heifer lowing° at the skies,
   And all her silken flanks° with garlands dressed?

33. lowing: mooing.
34. flanks: sides between the ribs and the hips.

JOHN KEATS **761**

Through the Poem

A. Critical Reading: Drawing Conclusions

? What is the meaning of each of the metaphors in the first three lines? [They describe the urn as not ruined by time, lasting for centuries, and preserving history.]

B. Critical Reading: Summarizing

? What is the scene depicted on the urn as described in ll. 5–10? [Men and gods are chasing maidens, there is a struggle, and musicians are playing.]

C. Reader's Response: Extending the Text

? Do you agree with the speaker's assertion that "unheard" melodies, imagined experiences, are "sweeter" than real ones? [Sample responses: As Keats argues, "unheard" music, music that one imagines when inspired, is music of the spirit and therefore is sweeter. Imagination can often conjure something better, "sweeter," than what one experiences in reality.]

D. Critical Reading: Identifying Main Ideas

? How does l. 20 sum up a main idea in the poem? [The line refers to the enduring scene on the urn; the youth and girl will always remain as they are; art can preserve beauty, love, and youth forever.] Note that the next stanza continues this theme.

E. Critical Reading: Finding Details

The speaker is now looking at another side of the urn. What does he see? [People going to present a sacrifice. The speaker imagines a town, still and empty. This is a more solemn and even mournful side of life.]

CROSSING THE CURRICULUM

Social Studies Ask students to consider what a person in the future would think upon finding a relic from modern times, such as a halogen lamp or a car. Have students write a paragraph that shows the person's response to the artifact. Encourage students to be creative in their responses; they could write an ode or may prefer to analyze the object.

History The Romantic poets traveled to Europe and were interested in the political and social events that took place there. Have students create a time line of events in Europe—perhaps focusing on France, Greece, and Italy—from 1789 to 1825. Students may also want to read more about the French Revolution and its ideals, as well as the Napoleonic era, to have a better sense of the ideological framework against which the poets wrote. ☞

A. Critical Reading: Making Inferences

? What is the effect of viewing the urn as described in ll. 44–45?

[Possible answers: Because the urn has lasted so long, it seems immortal, and viewing it is like contemplating eternity; the result is that the speaker is saddened by thinking of the passage of time and of his own brief life.]

B. Expansion

Two years before writing "Ode on a Grecian Urn," Keats wrote the following lines to a friend: "I am certain of nothing but of the holiness of the Heart's affections, and the truth of the imagination. What the Imagination seizes as Beauty must be truth— whether it existed before or not—for I have the same idea of all our passions as of love: They are all in their sublimity, creative of essential beauty."

C. Cultural Connections

Discuss with students how the idea of beauty is relative to a culture and time period. Taking the quotation above into account, ask students what kind of universal absolutes the poet could have meant in ll. 49–50.

35 What little town by river or seashore,
　　Or mountain-built with peaceful citadel,°
　　　Is emptied of this folk, this pious morn?
　And, little town, thy streets forevermore
　　Will silent be; and not a soul to tell
40　　　Why thou art desolate, can e'er return.

5

　O Attic° shape! Fair attitude!° with brede°
　　Of marble men and maidens overwrought,°
　With forest branches and the trodden weed;
　　　Thou, silent form, dost tease us out of thought
45　As doth eternity: Cold Pastoral!°
　　　When old age shall this generation waste,
　　　Thou shalt remain, in midst of other woe
　　　Than ours, a friend to man, to whom thou say'st,
　"Beauty is truth, truth beauty,"—that is all
50　　Ye know on earth, and all ye need to know.

36. citadel (sit′ə·del′): fortress.

41. Attic: Athenian; classically elegant. **attitude:** disposition or feeling conveyed by the postures of the figures on the urn. **brede:** interwoven design.
42. overwrought: decorated to excess; also, in reference to the men and maidens, overexcited.
45. pastoral: artwork depicting idealized rural life.

Attic vase painting showing transport of amphoras.
Louvre, Paris.

762 THE ROMANTIC PERIOD

Check Test: Questions and Answers

1. In "On First Looking into Chapman's Homer," who is Chapman? [A translator of Homer's *Iliad*.]

2. What exciting feeling does the poet describe in "On First Looking into Chapman's Homer"? [The feeling of discovery.]

3. What is the speaker's central fear in "When I Have Fears"? [That he will soon die.]

4. What is the final scene the speaker imagines in "When I Have Fears"? [Himself "on the shore / Of the wide world," alone.]

5. In "La Belle Dame sans Merci," what does the knight dream? [He dreams of dead men who warn him about the lady.]

Critical Comment

The Arc of Experience

This poem depicts a beautiful curve of emotion and engagement that begins and ends with detachment. At its center, it abandons all restraints, including those of art itself, to live in that world which is "happy" and "forever." By itself, the third stanza seems "overwrought" (a word used in the more detached fifth stanza)—so much so that we feel that all controls have been lost. But this is precisely the nature of the speaker's experience. Bit by bit, a miniature world of human passions comes alive, only to remind us that it is as dead as the clay on which it is represented. Keats has shown us that in the midst of change, art seems to provide the only truth. Yet this is a truth that depends not on sensory experience, but on the human imagination.

MAKING MEANINGS

First Thoughts

1. What passages in this poem do you think are most important, and why?

Shaping Interpretations

2. Discuss your understanding of the three **metaphors** for the urn in lines 1–3.

3. Expand on your Reader's Log entry to describe the details and actions "frozen" on the vase.

4. How do you interpret lines 28–30?

5. Why do you think "unheard" melodies (line 11) are "sweeter" to the speaker? How would you relate this idea to Romanticism?

6. If the urn could "tease us out of thought" (line 44), what state would we be in, and would it be better than thinking? Explain.

7. What do lines 46–50 mean to you?

8. According to stanza 5, what will happen to the urn when the speaker is dead? What message does the urn give to people?

Challenging the Text

9. Some critics complain that stanza 3 is badly written because Keats used "happy" and "forever" too many times. How would you respond to this criticism? Explain.

10. A famous textual difficulty surrounds the poem's last two lines. Based on the manuscript, some scholars enclose the entire couplet with quotation marks. Explain how this could change the meaning.

Making Meanings

First Thoughts

1. Students may say that the most important passages are the first four and last two lines.

Shaping Interpretations

2. "Still unravished bride of quietness" describes the urn's intact survival; "foster child of silence and slow time" indicates that the urn has survived by being hidden; and "sylvan historian" relates how the decorations on the urn tell a pastoral story.

3. The frozen actions are men or gods chasing young women, and youths making music under the trees. A procession to a sacrifice is also portrayed.

4. Possible response: The lines describe the results of the emotional excess described in the lines preceding it.

5. The "unheard" melodies appeal to imagination rather than to the ear and transcend time. Romantic elements include the tension between timelessness in an ideal world and change in the actual world, and the suggestion that imagination may overcome time.

6. "Out of thought" would be a state of lifeless limbo—the opposite of the vivacity the speaker sees in the urn. The state is not better than thought because it is cold, death-like, and lacking passion.

7. Students may say that the speaker asserts that beauty is an ideal that never fades; it is truth in the sense that it cannot be questioned or changed.

8. The urn will survive the speaker, reminding future generations that "beauty is truth."

Challenging the Text

9. **(Evaluation)** Students may agree with the complaints—"happy" is repeated six times; "forever," five times. The repetition does indicate the moment of the speaker's unbridled enthusiasm for the urn's beauty and the passion it represents.

10. **(Synthesis)** If the entire couplet is enclosed in quotation marks, the urn speaks for itself; if only the phrase is quoted, the conclusion is the speaker's.

Beyond the Poems

Choices: Building Your Portfolio

1. **Writer's Notebook** Remind students to save their work. They may use it as prewriting for the Writer's Workshop on p. 773.

2. **Critical Writing** Direct students to identify the rhyme scheme and meter of the Shakespearean sonnet and then relate its form to its meaning by evaluating the sonnet's turn. Tell students then to apply their notes to a Keats sonnet.

3. **Critical Writing** Students may begin their comparisons by paraphrasing the poets' statements on inspiration. They should then review each poem and look for how the poems show different perspectives. They might use the two sets of notes as they write their comparisons.

4. **Critical Writing** Ask students to consider separately each of the elements they are examining. For subject, encourage students to characterize the bird as well as the setting of the poem. Have them examine the symbolism of the bird's song. For tone and theme, students should think about the author's situation and emotions, focusing on his message to the reader.

CHOICES: Building Your Portfolio

Writer's Notebook
1. Collecting Ideas for a Reflective Essay

Death and love, the combined subjects of both "When I Have Fears" and "La Belle Dame sans Merci," urge most of us to soul-searching thought. Often, too, sharing our thoughts with someone— even to say "I'm confused"—helps us define and refine them. Choose an experience of death or love (an experience not too private to share), and freewrite about it. Save your notes for the Writer's Workshop on page 773.

WORK IN PROGRESS

Critical Writing
2. Taking a Turn

Choose one of Keats's **sonnets** (pages 747 and 748), and show how it follows the structure of the Shakespearean sonnet. Be sure to identify where the shift in focus or attention, the **turn,** occurs.

Critical Writing
3. Poets on Poets

Both Keats's "Ode to a Nightingale" and Shelley's "Ode to the West Wind" (page 734) are concerned, at least partially, with the subject of poetic inspiration. In a brief essay, write a comparison of these two odes. Focus on how each poem treats the subject.

Critical Writing
4. Poets on Birds

Like Keats, Shelley addresses a poem to a bird—a skylark. In an essay, compare and contrast Shelley's "To a Skylark" (page 739) with Keats's "Ode to a Nightingale." Consider **subject, symbolism** of the bird, **theme,** and **tone.**

Critical Writing
5. What? Me Worry?

Many of Keats's odes portray the speaker in a state of tension or ambiguity that is explored and then tentatively resolved. In a brief essay, trace this structure in "Ode on a Grecian Urn." What positive and negative aspects of human art does Keats explore in this ode?

Creative Writing
6. Astronomers, Explorers, and . . .

Review the astronomer and explorer similes in "On First Looking into Chapman's Homer," and create another **extended simile** to capture the same experience.

Creative Writing
7. If You Have Fears . . .

From your perspective— nearly two hundred years after this sonnet was written— write a personal letter to the speaker of "When I Have Fears," and respond to his fears.

Creative Writing
8. The Knight Talks Back

Are you satisfied with the knight's explanation of his problem in "La Belle Dame sans Merci"? Create your own explanation of what "ails" the knight in Keats's poem.

Creative Writing
9. Copying Keats

Select a painting in this book, and, like Keats in "Ode on a Grecian Urn," directly address it. In a paragraph, tell what is happening in the painting, pose questions about what will never happen, and describe your feelings.

Music
10. Being a Balladeer

Try to improvise a musical setting for "La Belle Dame sans Merci." Write a melody for the poem, and perform your song.

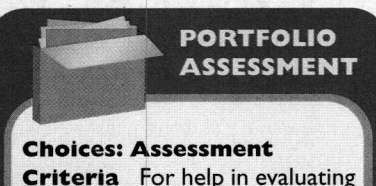

PORTFOLIO ASSESSMENT

Choices: Assessment Criteria For help in evaluating these Choices assignments, see the criteria in the *Portfolio Management System,* pp. 136–138.

STRATEGIES FOR INCLUSION

Interpersonal Activities #7 and #8 can be made into dialogues by pairs of students and read to the class. Direct the pairs of students to divide between them the opposing points of view for each (for #7, reader and speaker of the poem; for #8, knight and person giving the diagnosis). Students may use a question-and-answer format for each activity. Also, give partners a time limit of about five minutes for their performances.

Bodily-Kinesthetic For activity #9, encourage students to pick, as Keats has done, a work of art in which humans are performing actions. Students may then perform the actions themselves, mimic the motions, or remember a time when they performed the same or a similar action. Tell students to concentrate on determining the physical, mental, and emotional states involved in performing the action.

Words Often Confused: Homonyms, Homophones, and Homographs

Some words cause reading, spelling, and pronunciation problems because they are either spelled or sound like other words, or they are both spelled and sound like other words. These homonymous words have different origins and different meanings. Therefore, they have separate entries in the dictionary. As a group, homonymous words are sometimes simply called homonyms. However, this may seem somewhat confusing because one of the three specific classes of words in this group is also called **homonyms.** The other two kinds are classified as **homophones** and **homographs.**

Homonyms. Two or more individual words that have the same spelling and the same pronunciation are called **homonyms.** Notice how Wordsworth uses the word *roe* in the following excerpt.

> when like a **roe**
> I bounded o'er the mountains, by the sides
> Of the deep rivers, and the lonely streams,
> Wherever nature led. . . .
>
> —William Wordsworth, *from*
> "Lines Composed a Few Miles
> Above Tintern Abbey"

Roe, as Wordsworth uses it, means a deer. However, *roe,* meaning the eggs of a fish, has the same pronunciation as well as the same spelling. Thus, *roe* and *roe* are homonyms.

Homophones. You are probably most familiar with this category. **Homophones** are two or more words that sound alike but have different spellings, such as *soar* and *sore.* In the following passages, *soar* means to fly upward, while *sore* means extreme.

> The blue deep thou wingest,
> And singing still dost **soar,** and soaring ever singest.
>
> —Percy Bysshe Shelley, *from* "To a Skylark"

> I would ne'er have striven
> As thus with thee in prayer in my **sore** need.
>
> —Percy Bysshe Shelley, *from* "Ode to the West Wind"

Homographs. Two or more words that have the same spelling but are pronounced differently are **homographs.** In the following lines, Shelley uses the word *desert* (dez'ərt), meaning an arid geographical region.

> I met a traveler from an antique land,
> Who said: Two vast and trunkless legs of stone
> Stand in the **desert** . . .
>
> —Percy Bysshe Shelley, *from* "Ozymandias"

The meaning of the word *desert* (dez'ərt), as Shelley uses it, may be the one you most often associate with the word's spelling. However, *desert* (di·zurt') means deserved punishment or reward. For example, a criminal who receives punishment for his crime is said to receive his just *deserts* (di·zurts'). A second homograph for *desert* (dez'ərt) is the verb *desert* (di·zurt'), which has the same etymology as the noun *desert* but means to abandon or forsake.

Classification	Homonymous Word	Meaning
Homonyms	host	an army
	host	one who entertains a guest
	host	the Eucharist wafer
Homophones	holy	sacred
	wholly	completely
Homographs	wind (wind)	air movement
	wind (wīnd)	to coil

Try It Out

Using a dictionary, find a homonym, homophone, or homograph for each of the words listed below. Remember that the words you look up will be separate dictionary entries. On your own paper, write each word, and indicate whether it is a homonym, homophone, or homograph. Then, use each homonym, homophone, or homograph in a sentence.

1. slay
2. bark
3. fair
4. bow
5. bare

How to Own A Word

Mini-Lesson: Homonyms, Homophones, and Homographs

Remind students that puns are one type of homophone. Ask students for examples of puns, or discuss the glossary entry for *pun* in the Handbook of Literary Terms. Discuss what makes a pun successful. [A pun relies on the confusion between same-sounding words or phrases.]

Try It Out: Possible Answers

1. Homophone: Sleigh; We rode the sleigh through the snow. Did David slay Goliath?
2. Homonym: Bark; The chihuahua's bark is worse than its bite. The bark on this tree feels rough.
3. Homonyms: Fair (celebration; beautiful; not stormy; honest; according to the rules).
   Homophone: Fare; We paid the fare for the bus. We would have walked if the weather were fair.
4. Homograph: Rhymes with *go* or *prow*; I like the bow in your hair. After the dance, he made a bow.
   Homonyms: Bow (a curve or arch; an instrument that propels arrows; a decorative knot; a device used in playing a stringed instrument).
5. Homonyms: Bare (naked or unadorned; to make open to view). The table was clean and bare. I bared my arm for the doctor to give me a shot.
   Homophone: Bear; The circus bear wore a vest, but his head was bare.

Linguistic Direct students to look up the roots of words they commonly confuse. Students may make a list from memory to look up in a dictionary, or they might keep a running list as they read.

Learners Having Difficulty Students may not fully understand the differences between the words in the charts. Tell students to use each of the words in a sentence and to compare their sentences. Also, relate the terms *homonym, homophone,* and *homograph* to easy words they know: the ending *–nym* is similar to *name,* so *homonyms* are spelled and pronounced the same; a *phone* makes a sound, so *homophones* only sound alike; and a *graph* is something written, so *homographs* are only written alike.

PROGRAM MANAGER

Reinforcement To allow students practice and reinforcement of the vocabulary strategy introduced here, see **Transparency 9.3** in the *Audiovisual Resources Binder.*

Background

Discuss with students what they know of Li Po from the notes about his life. What do they think he would be like? Would he have fit in with the English Romantics if they had lived in the same place and time? Also, encourage students to discuss what they expect from the poem they are about to read.

China

WORLD LITERATURE

Li Po

(701–762)

A wandering, pleasure-loving poet, Li Po embodies for many the creative spirit of the T'ang dynasty (618–906) at its peak. Unlike the age's other great poet, Tu Fu (page 743), Li Po had no desire for government service or advancement. Reared in a wealthy family in Szechwan province, he chose life as a hermit-poet, drifting where his spirit took him. Walking, writing, marrying (four times), and socializing with poets, peasants, and leaders, Li Po became famous and was eventually invited to the emperor's court.

With his unconventional behavior, he was dismissed after only three years.

While an excellent poetic technician, Li Po favored looser folk forms, which he adapted for his original, bold, and sometimes ecstatic language. In a legend appropriate to a nature mystic, Li Po supposedly drowned while trying to embrace the moon's reflection in water. In fact, he may have died from mercury poisoning. Like other Taoists, he took alchemical potions believed to guarantee immortality.

Li Po Chanting in Stroll (southern Sung dynasty, 13th century) by Liang Kai.
Tokyo National Museum.

(Map) Mongolia showing Japan and China (c. 1680) by Frederick de Wit.

CONNECTING WITH "THE QUEST FOR BEAUTY"

Have students analyze how Li Po's poems show some of the same elements that are found in the poetry in the Romantic period. For their comparison, students may use a chart similar to the one following.

Romantic Characteristics	Elements in Li Po's Poetry
nature	wind and moon in autumn
emotions	loneliness of absent lover

[In the poems, the speaker tries to find a beauty that transcends time and place and the common concerns of the bustle of humanity. This quest for beauty is very similar to that of the Romantics.]

Background

Li Po believed in the Taoist philosophy and religion, in which nature—spontaneous, creative, uncomplicated by will—shows life's essence. The conventional human world, on the other hand, debased and deformed by ambition and materialism, is not true reality. Li Po was a social man who had many friends, but for spiritual and poetic renewal, he retreated reclusively to nature.

Quickwrite

READER'S LOG

Would your ideal life include frequent solitary retreats into nature? Why or why not?

Fragment of Chinese wallpaper (18th century).

Victoria and Albert Museum, London.

Question and Answer Among the Mountains

Li Po

translated by **Robert Kotewell** *and* **Norman L. Smith**

You ask me why I dwell in the green mountain;
I smile and make no reply for my heart is free of care.
As the peach-blossom flows down stream and is gone into **(A)**
    the unknown,
I have a world apart that is not among men. **(B)**

Word-Pattern

Li Po

translated by **Florence Ayscough** *and* **Amy Lowell**

The Autumn wind is fresh and clear;
The Autumn moon is bright.
Fallen leaves whirl together and scatter.
The jackdaws, who have gone to roost, are startled again.
We are thinking of each other, but when shall we see each other? **(C)**
Now, tonight, I suffer, because of my passion. **(D)**

To Tan-Ch'iu

Li Po

translated by **Arthur Waley**

My friend is lodging high in the Eastern Range,
Dearly loving the beauty of valleys and hills.
At green Spring he lies in the empty woods,
And is still asleep when the sun shines on high.
A pine-tree wind dusts his sleeves and coat; **(E)**
A pebbly stream cleans his heart and ears.
I envy you, who far from strife and talk
Are high-propped on a pillow of blue cloud. **(F)**

LI PO 767

A. Literary Element: Symbolism

? What does the blossom following the stream's current symbolize? [The blossom mirrors the speaker's own aimless wandering in nature.]

B. Reader's Response: Shaping Interpretations

? What does the speaker suggest is "a world apart"? [Sample responses: The speaker suggests that nature is beyond man's control. Nature is a deeper, more meaningful reality than the affairs of humankind.]

C. Critical Reading: Analyzing Focus

? How does this line mark a shift in the attentions of the speaker? [The speaker stops contemplating nature around him and begins to think of someone he misses and wishes he could see again.]

D. Reader's Response: Challenging the Text

? Does the speaker's conclusion adequately complete the picture he is creating of his situation, or does it seem too sudden and out of place? [Sample responses: The conclusion fits in with the rest of the poem, because the other images in the poem are lonely and sad as well. It does seem to break from the rest of the poem; it's abrupt.]

E. Critical Reading: Making Inferences

? Why does the poet describe the wind as a "pine-tree wind"? What is the phrase's effect? [The phrase makes efficient use of words to show how the wind "looks" in the scene around him.]

F. Literary Element: Imagery

? How is the speaker's friend on a cloud "pillow"? [Students' ideas will vary, but the phrase suggests that the friend's eyes are on the sky; his spirit is lifted by the sky's beauty and is resting in comfort.]

Finding Common Ground

Brainstorm with the class on how the poems students have just read may be considered Romantic. Encourage students to consider in their comparisons the poet's techniques, tone, subject matter, and language. Write students' ideas on the chalkboard. [Students may point out elements such as the poet's use of common language and heightened emotion, the concentration of observations about nature, the inclusion of figurative language, and the focus on being alone in a natural setting.]

When students experiment with Li Po's verse by changing specific words and images, direct them also to pay attention to the subtle changes in connotation, mood, and tone. Students may make a list of the original words and images in Li Po's verse, and in a second and third column, keep track of their changes and the consequences both in literal meanings and in the feel of the poem. Students can more easily compare findings if they all use the same format.

The Emperor Ming Huang Traveling in Shu (T'ang dynasty, A.D. 618–906) by an unknown artist.
Collection of the National Palace Museum, Taipei, Taiwan, Republic of China.

FINDING COMMON GROUND

These terse poems may seem very different from those of the English Romantics. And yet, in Li Po's poems, the same profound communion with nature is present. Their subject is not just nature, but what nature means to human life.

- How does nature affect you? In a small group, try to pinpoint a significant personal experience (not necessarily dramatic or earth-shattering) linked to a natural setting. (Also, check your Reader's Log.)
- Now turn that experience into a poem imitating one of Li Po's. Focus on Li Po's poems with these questions: What do you think the last line of

"Question and Answer Among the Mountains" means? What does the image in the third line suggest to you? Try changing any sensory word in "Word-Pattern" to another, and notice the effect. What is changed or lost? Which images in "To Tan-Ch'iu" evoke the qualities of remoteness, pleasure, and peace?

- If you were planning a poetry anthology, which of Li Po's poems would you pair with Keats's "Ode to a Nightingale"? Why? Discuss in your group the similarities and differences you see in the two poets. Which one do most readers prefer?

ASSESSMENT TOOLS

Response to the Literature Use the following criteria to assess students' written or oral responses to literature.

Key: A = Always   S = Sometimes
      R = Rarely   N = Never

Characteristic	Date	Rating
shows enjoyment/ involvement of/with literature		
makes personal and universal connections to the literature		
gets beyond "I like/dislike the literature"		
interprets the literature, giving evidence of multiple meanings		
discusses author's control of elements in creating the literature		

Revolutionary Fever

The revolution that occurred in France at the end of the eighteenth century had enormous repercussions on the other side of the English Channel. People recognized that the revolution was the consequence of oppression, but the violence of the mobs disillusioned and frightened them. *A Tale of Two Cities,* one of Charles Dickens's most popular (and shortest) novels, examines the period that "was the spring of hope" as well as "the winter of despair."

Share in the Terror

Mary Shelley said of *Frankenstein* (Penguin) that she wanted to write a story that "would speak to the mysterious fears of our nature and awaken thrilling horror." She succeeded, writing what many consider to be the first science fiction novel as well as a vivid version of the Romantic mythology of the self. The 1931 film, which made Boris Karloff a star, is the best of the film versions.

The Evil That Men Do

In his classic novel *The Strange Case of Dr. Jekyll and Mr. Hyde,* Robert Louis Stevenson advances the genre Mary Shelley began. This is the horrifying account of Dr. Henry Jekyll's attempt to scientifically separate his own goodness and evil based on his belief that "man is not truly one, but truly two." While Victor Frankenstein questions the creation of humanity, Dr. Jekyll ponders its very essence. When his self-imposed experiments succeed and the utterly evil Mr. Hyde emerges, Dr. Jekyll's problems begin—and multiply. (Also available on videotape in several classic film versions.)

Tinkering with Nature

Like the Romantic poets, Annie Dillard turns to nature for inspiration and reflection. In *Pilgrim at Tinker Creek* (Harper's Magazine Press), her collection of essays, Dillard muses about her past, her present, and her environment while describing the interplay among the plants and animals of Virginia's Tinker Creek. For Dillard, life at the creek reflects "the intricacy of beauty, the pressure of fecundity, the elusiveness of the free, and the flawed nature of perfection."

Love and Marriage

Originally published in 1813, Jane Austen's novel *Pride and Prejudice* (Norton) is about five husband-hunting sisters in nineteenth-century England and the delicate tangles of love and courtship they ensnare themselves in. What struck people then, and strikes us now, is Austen's ability to make commonplace people and events interesting. The superficially trivial content is deceptive; it masks a deeper irony that exposes the manners and mores of the period.

Read On
Portfolio Assessment Options

The following projects can help you evaluate your students' reading outside class. Consider recording projects for students' portfolios.

- **Create a Newspaper** Have students work in groups to create a newspaper of reports related to events in one of the books, including editorials, headline stories, and even advertisements and cartoons. Display the finished products.
- **Write a Poem** Students may write a poem reflecting the themes they have encountered in the book they have read. Ask them to imitate the style of one of the poets in this Collection. Decide whether you will accept something as short as a sonnet or would prefer the length of a ballad or ode.
- **Be a Dramaturge** Have students present a theatrical presentation of one of the books. They may design sets, write soliloquies, or do preproduction work for a drama. They should be able to discuss the ideas behind their creations and how they relate to the themes of the book.
- **Illustrate a Dream World** Ask students to draw, paint, or represent a dream world from one of the books they have read. Students may accompany their art with a description, or they may write a poem or brief narrative that takes place in the world they create. Ask students to display their art and give a reading.

FOR FURTHER EXPLORATION

Nonfiction
"Defence of Poetry," Percy Bysshe Shelley
Preface to *Lyrical Ballads,* William Wordsworth
Biographia Literaria, Samuel Taylor Coleridge
Black Elk Speaks, as told to John G. Neihardt
Walden, or Life in the Woods, Henry David Thoreau
Charles Lamb's letter to Wordsworth on the *Lyrical Ballads,* dated January 30, 1801

A Vindication of the Rights of Woman, Mary Wollstonecraft
History of the French Revolution, Thomas Carlyle

Novels
Northanger Abbey, Jane Austen
The Sorrows of Young Werther, Johann Wolfgang von Goethe
Dracula, Bram Stoker

Wide Sargasso Sea, Jean Rhys
The Italian, Ann Radcliffe

Movies
Persuasion (1995)
Impromptu (1991)
Amadeus (1984)

A. Literary Connections
Robert Burns's best-known and best-appreciated poems are all in the Scottish dialect. William and Dorothy Wordsworth were both interested in the dialect of the people of the Scottish Highlands (see, for example, William Wordsworth's "The Solitary Reaper").

B. Expansion
You may want to emphasize this point. Standard English is considered proper not because it is intrinsically better than another dialect, but because a common ground is needed to make communication easier and more reliable.

Elements of Literature: Videodisc Use the following bar codes to locate the video segment about the development of the English language. For more information, see the Videodisc *Teacher's Manual.*

Videodisc Side A

Begin Play, English Track

Begin Play, Spanish Track

The English Language

Variety in Language
by **John Algeo**

William Wordsworth wrote a preface to *Lyrical Ballads,* in which he talked about the kind of poetry he and Samuel Taylor Coleridge tried to produce, especially about its subjects and its language. He said that their subject matter was to be "incidents and situations from common life" and that their language was to be that "really used" by ordinary people. One aspect of the Romantic movement was its fascination with common, especially rural, life and customs; with earthiness; and with simple people and their language.

The study of dialect was encouraged by a Romantic conviction that the simple country life was better than the complex city life. As a result, we often think of dialect as a form of language spoken by uneducated rural people. But, in fact, it is far more than that.

What Are Dialects?
We have already seen that language has many ways of saying the same thing. How we talk depends partly on where we come from, what ethnic or social group we belong to, whether we are male or female, what education we have had, and how old we are. Such kinds of variation are called *dialects:*

regional, ethnic, class, sex, educational, and age-group dialects. Dialects are the various forms in which a language exists, not some peculiar or quaint versions of it.

A language is like ice cream; it comes in various flavors. If you want ice cream, you ask for chocolate, vanilla, butter pecan, peppermint, or a lot of other flavors. But it would make no sense to say, "I just want plain ice cream—none of those flavors, just the real stuff." Ice cream only comes in flavors; apart from its flavors, no ice cream exists. In the same way, a language only comes in dialects; apart from its dialects, no language exists.

Many of us think that the way we talk is real English, whereas the way others talk is some odd dialect. However, we all talk dialects, none intrinsically odder (or better) than any of the others.

How Odd That You Should Say That
Dialects differ among themselves in the words that are

> Many of us think that the way we talk is real English, whereas the way others talk is some odd dialect. However, we all talk dialects, none intrinsically odder (or better) than any of the others.

used, the way words are pronounced, and the way words are put together.

Depending on where you come from, a *porch* may be a *gallery, piazza, stoop,* or *veranda.* A *dragonfly* may be a *darning needle, mosquito hawk, snake doctor,* or *snake feeder.* Pancakes may be *batter cakes, flannel cakes, fritters, griddlecakes,* or *hot cakes.*

In most parts of the United States, *rubber band* is the term for an elastic loop that holds things together; but if you are from the Minneapolis–St. Paul area, you may call it a *rubber binder. Soft drink* is what most of us call a flavored carbonated beverage, though it may also be *soda, pop,* or *soda pop;* an old-fashioned term is *phosphate.* If you are from New England, you may call it *tonic,* which means something more specific (quinine water) in the rest of the country.

Most Americans pronounce *fog, hog,* and *log* as "fawg," "hawg," and "lawg," with the same vowel they use in *law, paw,* and *raw.* But they use a different vowel sound in *lock, pot,* and *top.* In parts of New York and the north central states, however,

---

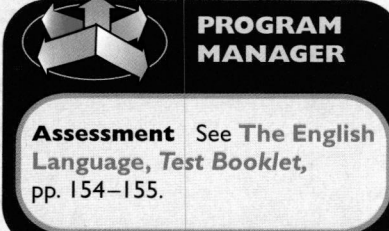

PROGRAM MANAGER

Assessment See **The English Language,** *Test Booklet,* pp. 154–155.

OPTIONS FOR TEACHING

STRATEGIES FOR INCLUSION

Auditory While they are reading the feature, encourage students to take the time to pronounce aloud each dialect word as it is mentioned in the text. Reading aloud will help students listen to examples carefully and form a picture in their mind of a word's speaker.

Learners Having Difficulty Ask students to note the characteristics of their own dialect. Have students work in pairs to list examples of words or phrases that are particular to their peers, their family, or people in their geographic region. When students have completed their lists, have the class discuss what qualities make their speech patterns or sounds unique.

fog, hog, and log have the same vowel as lock, pot, and top, whereas law, paw, and raw have a different sound. In eastern New England and in western Pennsylvania and some places westward from there, including most of the Far West, all of those words may be pronounced with the same vowel (either an "aw"-like or an "ah"-like sound).

Those who come from the southern United States tend to pronounce greasy as "greazy," whereas those from the northern states tend to make it sound like "greassy." TV ads for dishwasher detergents generally use the northern pronunciation, which seems to be gaining ground. Some people, having heard both pronunciations, use them both, but may develop special meanings for the two ways of saying the word. They may think that "greassy" means literally "coated with grease," while using "greazy" as a metaphor meaning "untrustworthy, disagreeable." In this way, two pronunciations of the same word may eventually turn into different words, as happened long ago with shade and shadow, of and off, and flour and flower.

Prepositions are especially subject to dialect variation. Whether you are sick to, at, in, or on your stomach depends mainly on where you learned to talk. So also does how you tell time—whether you say a quarter of, till, or to the hour. In most of the United States, people stand in line, but in New York City, they stand on line. Most Americans, when they are not away, are at home, but some are to home.

For a long time, English has had a problem with the second person pronoun you. We make one word do double duty—for both the singular and the plural, for talking to one person and for talking to many. Some dialects, however, have tried to distinguish between the singular and plural forms. In certain parts of the North, especially in cities, some people say youse or yuzz for the plural; in the Appalachian Mountain region, some people say you'uns. But neither of those forms has ever made much headway in educated use. Throughout the South, however, the plural form y'all is widely used by the best-educated speakers, only, however, when referring to more than one person. Another new plural form that is gaining ground, especially among younger people and for informal use, is you guys.

American Regional Dialects

The first English settlers in America brought with them the dialects that they spoke in the British Isles. As soon as they settled into their new country, however, they began to develop new dialects.

Today, regional dialect boundaries are clearest along the eastern coast of the United States, where English speakers first settled. There are three main dialect areas: Northern, Midand, and Southern.

Nowadays, some of the traditional differences among these regions are disappearing as our lifestyles change and become more uniform. What used to be called a skillet in the South and a spider in parts of the North is now almost everywhere a frying pan or a frypan. When horses pulled wagons, the horizontal wooden bar by which the wagon was attached to the animals' harness was called a singletree or swingletree in the South and a whippletree or whiffletree in the North. But now the object is foreign to the experience of most of us, so we have no name whatever for it.

New dialect terms, however, will doubtless come into existence. For example, we might

ROTHCO

"A host? You call that a host! Why, back in the States . . ."

Cartoon by Mike Williams. © Punch. Courtesy Rothco.

C. Expansion
Point out that many languages (including English at one time) have a way to differentiate between a common and polite you. Remind students of the difference between Shakespeare's use of you and of thou.

STRATEGIES FOR INCLUSION

Interpersonal Arrange students in small groups to discuss dialects before they work on the Try It Out activities. Direct them to characterize the way they speak in contrast to the speech of other people they have encountered who are from other geographical areas. Encourage students not to use words such as normal or ordinary.

Advanced Challenge students to come up with equivalent dialect terms for the examples given in the text. Write students' suggestions on the chalkboard, and have them provide a definition and a description of use for each word.

INTEGRATING THE LANGUAGE ARTS

Strategic Reading Ask students to complete for each section of the selection an explanation of its main ideas and a list of supporting details. Students may record their findings in a graphic organizer in which every section is represented by a box. Students should make notes of the transitions between sections by filling out a "connection" between each of the boxes. Have students compare their work with a partner.

| main idea | connection | main idea | connection | main idea |

A. Expansion

Ask students for their terms for each of the definitions. [Possible answers include, respectively, *freeways, rest stops, islands, bodega,* and *sandal.*]

Try It Out: Answers

1. If students' answers differ, encourage them to compare the histories of the places where they have lived in the United States. Possible additions to the lists: *tennis shoe, sneaker, village, town.*

2. *acknowledge the corn:* a chiefly Midwestern phrase meaning "to admit to being drunk" (the word *corn* is short for "corn liquor") or "to admit to any mistake."
Adam's off-ox: Midwest, South, and Southwest; meaning "a person or thing one does not know and cannot identify" or "a person that is especially slow, poor, or stubborn. "
all in: chiefly Northern, old-fashioned, meaning "exhausted" or "uncomfortable."
bayou: around Louisiana, meaning "a creek or small river with a sluggish current"; in the West, meaning "a dry watercourse," "a body of still water," or "a small lake or pond."
bismarck: upper Midwest, meaning "a deep-fried cake."
blinky: chiefly Plains States, meaning "sour," especially in regard to milk.
chill bumps: South, the equivalent of "gooseflesh" or "goose bumps."

3. The way people speak reflects the changes around them, so interest in both dialects and change in life is not unusual. In contemporary life, the connection may be used to trace peoples' concerns and attitudes in a fast-changing world.

Ⓐ expect dialect variation in the terms we use for limited-access highways, for the rest areas along them, and for the center barrier that divides the two directions of traffic. In addition, there will be varied terms for a small neighborhood store that is open early and late hours, or for an informal kind of open shoe that has a strap between the big toe and the other toes. Such objects have many names.

American Ethnic Dialects

Another important kind of dialect is ethnic speech. People who share a common cultural heritage tend to talk alike. Almost every immigrant group has its own ethnic dialect. Among the larger are Yiddish English, spoken by many Jews; Hispanic English of several kinds, spoken by Latinos, Cuban Americans, and Puerto Ricans; and black English, a mixture of African influences, Southern dialect, and features that developed in the African American community.

Among the features of black English (which are, however, by no means found in the speech of all African Americans) are the following: In pronunciation, final clusters of consonants are simplified, usually by dropping all except the first consonant: *most* becomes "mose," and *find* becomes "fine." *Nice* and *mine* become something like "nahs" and "mahn." The article *a* is used instead of *an* before words beginning with a vowel: *a orange, a apple.* These features are typical of the Southern dialect too.

Other features, although often found in Southern speech, are much more common in black English. The ending *–s* is frequently omitted from verbs, possessive nouns, and plural nouns that have a number before them: "He work hard," "my brother car," "four ticket." The verb *be* is either omitted altogether or used in the unchanged form of *be,* rather than *am, is, are.* These two uses, however, mean different things: "She here" means "She is here right now," while "She be here" means "She is usually or regularly here."

Black English also has distinctive words, some of which have become a part of general English vocabulary: *chigger* (sand flea), *goober* (Southern and Midland for peanut), *gumbo, jazz, juke (box), nitty-gritty,* and *zombie.* Other uses are known outside the black-English-speaking community as slang, such as *bad* pronounced with a long, drawn-out vowel ("baaaad") meaning "very good."

As new influences come to bear on the life and language of the nation, new dialects are likely to arise. Language changes continually, but in different ways among different groups—and that is why dialects exist.

Try It Out

1. Which of the following groups contains words that seem most familiar to you?

   a. pail, quarter of, angle-worm, mud wasp, fuss-budget, brook

   b. bucket, quarter till, fishing worm, mud dauber, fuss-button, run

   c. bucket, quarter to, wiggler, dirt dauber, fuss-box, branch

   The first group is of predominantly Northern words, the second of Midland words, and the third of Southern words. Name at least two other words that are part of your regional dialect, and then locate their equivalents in at least one other regional dialect. (Classmates or neighbors from different parts of the country might be good resources.)

2. Here are some terms with special meanings in dialect use. Look up these words in the *Dictionary of American Regional English* (or some other dialect dictionary) to find out where they are used and what they mean.

   acknowledge the corn

   Adam's off-ox

   all in

   bayou

   bismarck

   blinky

   chill bumps

3. The Romantics were concerned with change in life and society. Some of them were also concerned with varieties of dialects. How are these two concerns connected? How could these concerns also be important in contemporary life?

THE ROMANTIC PERIOD

OPTIONS FOR TEACHING

INTEGRATING THE LANGUAGE ARTS

Speaking and Listening Play for the class a recording of a story read in a distinctive dialect, such as a selection from *Adventures of Huckleberry Finn* by Mark Twain or "Tam O' Shanter" by Robert Burns. Ask students to listen to the story and then to share their impressions after the story is completed. Have students concentrate on such questions as the following: How does the dialect affect the telling of the story? What does the dialect tell about the speaker and the story? How would the story be different if it were in standard English?

ASSESSMENT TOOLS

Check Test: Questions and Answers

1. With what kind of language were the Romantics fascinated? [Common, everyday language.]

2. What is a dialect? [The manner of a person's speech depending on where the person is from, what social or ethnic groups the person belongs to, and the person's education, sex, and age.]

3. How do dialects differ? [In the words that are used, pronunciation, and the way words are put together.]

4. Which pronoun differs greatly among American dialects of English? [The second-person pronoun *you.*]

5. Where are American regional dialects clearest? [On the Atlantic coast.]

Writer's Workshop

EXPOSITORY WRITING
REFLECTIVE ESSAY

At one time or another, we've all stopped to reflect on something, to explore what an experience or an event really means to us. Reflecting literally means "thinking back on," and though reflective writing may never provide one definite, or "right," answer, it usually leads the writer (and reader) through a process that extends and deepens the meaning of an experience. The Romantic poets often reflected on incidents or observations and from them drew conclusions about their own behavior and about human nature in general. In "Lines Composed a Few Miles Above Tintern Abbey" (page 658), William Wordsworth's visit to the Wye valley prompts reflection on his other boyhood visits, on the cycle of human life, and, finally, on the power of nature to renew the human spirit. Whether the occasion for reflection is momentous or trivial, reflective writing always moves out from its center—a specific context or an incident in the writer's own life—to larger ideas about the world and human life, from the personal to the universal. For both writer and reader, what could be more important?

Prewriting

1. **Checking your Writer's Notebook.** By doing the Writer's Notebook activities in Collections 8 and 9, you may already have a topic—or the germ of a topic—for a reflective essay. Look back over your Writer's Notebook entries, and see if there's an idea or experience you wish to explore further. Then you can also proceed with the prewriting activities that follow.

2. **Finding a point of departure.** Reflective writing always begins with a stimulus, a specific occasion or experience that prompts deeper thinking. This jumping-off point may be something that's happened to you, something that you've observed others doing, or something you've observed in nature. You may even begin with a series of such experiences rather than just one. Use the following strategies to explore possible experiences to write about:

   • Freewrite for a few minutes, beginning with one of the following statements: *I began to think about the power of words when . . .* or *I wonder why I become so angry when . . .* or *I was struck by the power of peer pressure when . . .* or *I wonder why I become so embarrassed when . . .*

   • Move from a more detached beginning point—an observation, a quotation or idea from a story or poem, or a concept, like justice or compassion—to a more personal connection. (That personal connection may

---

Technology HELP

See Writer's Workshop 2 CD-ROM. *Assignment: Reflective Essay.*

ASSIGNMENT
Write an essay about an experience you have had or a situation you have observed that caused you to think about life and human behavior more broadly.

AIM
To explore the meaning of an experience; to express yourself.

AUDIENCE
Your classmates.

WRITER'S WORKSHOP 773

PORTFOLIO ASSESSMENT

• **Generating Ideas** To help students in prewriting, use the heuristic in the *Portfolio Management System,* p. 139.

• **Assessment Rubric** For a rubric that can be used to assess students' progress in writing, see the *Portfolio Management System,* p. 141.

OPTIONS FOR TEACHING

STRATEGIES FOR INCLUSION

Auditory While students are evaluating and revising their essays, they may benefit from recording a reading of their work. They can listen to the taped reading and note any awkward elements that break the tone they are trying to establish. As an alternative, allow students to work in pairs. One can read the other's paper aloud while the listener notes areas needing revision.

Visual Some students might find it helpful to create a modified time line as a visual representation of the major points in their essays. Using a horizontal line as the basis of the time line, they should draw vertical lines to indicate major aspects of the incident they are describing. Then, they should briefly describe the aspects above each of these lines and use the time line to help draft their essays.

PROGRAM MANAGER

Computer Guided Instruction For a related reflective assignment that students may use as additional instruction, see *Writer's Workshop 2.*

Motivation

The day before you begin this assignment in class, ask students to pay attention to conversations during the next twenty-four hours and to note times when people recall incidents. In class, ask students to share some of these incidents. Then, ask the class to share any conclusions about human nature they drew from their incidents. Point out that people often learn important lessons about life by reflecting on events. Tell students that they will practice this important skill in this Writer's Workshop.

even point you to a general theme.) You may want to make a chart like the one that follows and insert your own examples.

Model

Occasion for Reflection	Personal Connection	Theme
My friend Mary's outrageous wardrobe	My own embarrassment/awkwardness when I wore my new sequined skirt to school. But why?	It's hard to be different?
"Getting and spending, we lay waste our powers." —Wm. Wordsworth	My preoccupation with my allowance	Security? Competition?
Dignity	Experience of watching older man take his seat on the bus	How do stereotypes develop?

- Brainstorm with a small group of classmates about common human experiences and what they may mean. Take notes, re-read them privately, and then choose a thread or idea that you can test against your own experience or observation.

  You will probably generate several suitable experiences to explore, so be sure that the one you choose for your essay is genuinely interesting to you, something that you want to think about carefully, and something that you'll feel comfortable sharing with others.

3. **Fleshing it out, making it real.** Now you have an experience to anchor your essay. How will you enable your reader to share this experience? In some reflective essays, the experience or observation is treated only briefly before the writer begins the process of reflection; in other essays, a description of the experience itself assumes more importance. In either case, you'll need concrete details to set the stage for your reflections. Details make a situation real and vivid for the reader, and they help to communicate the mood or atmosphere of a situation as you first experienced it.

Strategies for Elaboration: Showing Details

Use the following strategies to "show" details to your reader:
- Rather than simply naming an emotion such as sadness, *show* an expression of that emotion. For example, to show sadness a writer might mention the lump in her throat or the tears he tried to fight back.
- Help the reader see what you saw. Instead of merely saying that a garden was beautiful, describe the yellow roses, the green vines curling along the fence, the slant of the sunlight, and the sweet fragrance of the lilac bushes.
- Make yourself and other people you're writing about come alive for the reader by using **dialogue.** For instance, instead of just naming the topic of conversation, repeat some of what was said.

- **Narrative details** tell specifically about actions and events: *Mary clomped into English class.* Or, *The ball bounced off the wall and whizzed by my head.*
- **Descriptive details** describe people, places, and objects: *Mrs. Wood's eyes danced with amusement.* Or, *Mary's flouncy white dress created quite a contrast with her red high-tops.*

774 THE ROMANTIC PERIOD

- **Thoughts and feelings** you include give more depth to the events you're narrating.
- **Examples** from other experiences or people help illustrate your reflections in this essay.
- **Anecdotes** about other people extend and explain your own experience.

  Spend a few moments jotting down all the factual and sensory details you can recall. You might start with a basic sketch of the event (answering such questions as who was involved, where and when the event took place, and so on) and then proceed to a more finely detailed description. When you've finished recording all the details you can recall, review your list, and note which ones will help you strike the right mood and create a vivid scene.

4. **But what does it *mean*?** After settling on a specific experience and recalling it in some detail, explore its wider meanings through **analysis.** Analyzing an experience is a bit like studying the ripples made when a stone is thrown into a pond: The widening circles of water are like your thoughtful reflections, moving away from the incident itself to your feelings about it, and then to larger speculations about human nature. Use the following questions to guide an analysis of the meaning of the particular experience you've chosen to write about:

- What does the experience mean to me?
- What does the experience reveal about what I believe, the way I act, what I think is important?
- What ideas about people or life in general do my own reactions to the experience lead to?
- What other related experiences show the same ideas? That is, what **analogies** can I draw to my own experience?

  The answers to these questions will provide, in rough form, the components of your essay—all are circles of meaning, one moving out to the next. Here's one writer's process of discovering meaning.

Communications
Handbook
H E L P

Taking notes and documenting sources: page 1211.

Model

Experience: Observing my friend Mary in the outrageous outfits she wears to school
1. Sometimes I admire her bravery; other times I feel embarrassed for her (even though she never shows the slightest embarrassment!).
2. Clothes are important to me—I like to feel accepted but wonder why I think dressing in a certain way will make people like me.
3. Some ideas about people: dressing a certain way often allows people to fit in or defines them as part of a particular group; it's unnerving to appear different; it's safe and easy to be part of a crowd.
4. Related experiences: watching my friend Sarah change outfits three times before school; being afraid to take tae kwon do lessons because none of my girlfriends do; knowing that my requests for new clothes put a financial burden on my parents; wondering how often I misjudge others, and they misjudge me, according to our interpretation of surface things (like clothes).

Teaching the Lesson
Encourage students to make connections between the incidents they describe and the conclusions they reach about human nature. This lesson includes instructions for each stage of the writing process. Guide students by modeling each stage with your own writing.

Prewriting
If students have difficulty thinking of an incident on which to reflect, suggest they review events of the previous day. Have students start with waking up and getting ready for school and end with going to bed. Point out that the event does not have to be of enormous importance and that the insight about themselves or human nature does not have to be profound. The incident can include reading or watching a movie, as long as it enables students to draw some conclusion about people.

COOPERATIVE LEARNING

Brainstorming Conclusions Engaging in group reflection might help students learn to draw conclusions about human nature from incidents. Form students into groups of three or four, and ask them to consider a news event. Have the groups brainstorm a list of possible conclusions about individuals or human nature in general based on these events. It might be helpful to furnish groups with a newspaper account of the events. Let each group share its conclusions with the class.

CROSSING THE CURRICULUM

Journalism Ask students to write an advice column or an editorial that describes an incident and then draws some conclusion, about the individuals involved or about people in general, based on the incident. If time permits, have students create a mock newspaper. The news articles can describe incidents, and the editorials, letters to the editor. Other parts of the newspaper can elaborate on conclusions drawn from the news articles. ☞

Drafting

Drafting this essay is probably the most serious reflection that students will engage in during this assignment. For this reason, the discovery students make about human behavior may evolve during the drafting stage. Encourage students to be willing to make changes in their original plans. Some students might find it helpful to write the body of their essays before the introduction, since writing is likely to produce ideas they may use to open their essays.

Try it Out: Answers

Responses will vary. Here are some examples.
1. A waste of time.
2. There was a time of year we called "rainbow days" because brief showers in one part of the valley would create rainbows in another almost every day.
3. It is harder to come so close than to lose decisively.
4. Sometimes I like having no direction, but sometimes I feel lost.
5. Courage is quiet; recklessness noisy.

Try It Out

If each of the following subjects were the starting point for a reflective essay, what reflections might it prompt in *you*?
1. TV talk shows
2. A rainbow
3. Losing a game by one point
4. "There is a pleasure in the pathless woods."
    —Lord Byron
5. Courage vs. recklessness

Language Workshop
H E L P

Aspects of a writer's style: page 778.

Language Handbook
H E L P

Quotation marks: page 1247.

5. **Taking a leap in thought.** Although reflective thinking can easily trail off into a series of unanswerable questions, a reflective essay should end with an insight or understanding about life or people in general. In describing your experience and analyzing it, you may have already hit on just such an insight, or epiphany. More often, this moment of insight does not appear in a flash—like the comic book image of a light bulb snapping on—but comes about through persistent thinking.

    Consider the thinking you've done so far. What insight or generalization about human life might cap your reflections? Think in terms of *maybe* or *perhaps* or *what if* instead of *should* or *should not*. Human behavior is complicated. Here is your opportunity to speculate on some of its complexities. Try to identify the largest idea, or theme, revealed by your reflections so far. Making such a generalization will provide a possible end point for your essay.

6. **Creating order.** The most brilliant details, ideas, and insights will be lost if they aren't organized clearly for your audience. In a reflective essay, you might use *chronological order, spatial order, order of importance,* or *logical order* as the organizing pattern of your essay—or even a combination of these patterns.

    For instance, if you want the first part of your essay to reveal your experience to the reader, you may choose chronological order, only hinting at your thoughts and feelings as the events unfold. Then, to help your reader understand why this experience stimulated you to think more deeply, you may present your thoughts on the experience in the order of their importance, saving what you feel is your most important observation or insight for last. Or you may wish to weave together two organizational patterns, reflecting on each part of an experience while you describe it.

Drafting

1. **Finding a voice.** This essay is a reflection of you, so you should use the voice that best represents you—your natural conversational voice. Because you are sharing personal experiences and insights with your classmates, an informal, warm, and friendly tone is most appropriate. In addition, if your essay explores some of the more absurd aspects of human behavior, you may want to let your sense of humor show. Your style should be open, natural, and personal.

2. **The introduction: intriguing your reader.** Like other essays, your reflective essay should have a beginning that makes the reader want to read more. You might begin with a question—a technique that William Blake often uses in his reflective poetry. Or you might begin by establishing the time frame of an event you plan to recount, as Wordsworth does when he considers the meaning of his experiences at Tintern Abbey. You might describe a scene or a person or begin with an interesting quotation. The important thing is to intrigue your readers so that they will want to continue reading.

3. **The body: orchestrating with style.** Managing all the elements of a reflective essay is a bit like conducting an orchestra: When should narration be balanced by reflection? When should dialogue give way to description? Try to interweave all the elements in your essay in an engaging way but without losing the overall pattern—the body of your essay should be coherent, not confusing. Your reflections should also include a steadily expanding

---

CLASSROOM MANAGEMENT

Focus To help students stay focused during group activities, set time limits. For example, if students are brainstorming, tell the class ahead of time how long they will have to complete the task. You might set a minimum number of items that the brainstorming list must contain, and you can have students initial the items they contribute to the lists to ensure participation of all members.

ASSESSMENT TOOLS

Self-Assessment Students can perform a self-assessment of their reflective essays by applying the following rubric to the Evaluation Criteria on p. 777.

Assessment Criteria

1	2	3	4	5	6
Needs Improvement					Superior

circle of interest, from self to world, personal to universal. (Think about those ripples in a pond.)

4. **The conclusion: rounding it out.** To communicate a sense of completeness in your conclusion, you may want to look again at your opening experience, this time from a slightly different angle. Or you may choose to explain how you expect your behavior or attitudes to change in the future as a result of reflecting on your experience. Remember, the conclusion of a reflective essay calls for an insight rather than a judgment, a deeper awareness of how things are rather than a prescription about how they *should be*.

Evaluating and Revising

1. **Peer review.** After you read your classmate's essay, get together to discuss what stands out most in the essay—descriptions, pieces of narration and dialogue, or an insight that strikes a responsive chord. Be prepared to discuss the essay's beginning: Does it grab your attention? If not, what could the writer add to make it more engaging? Also, think about the writer's language. What tone is conveyed in the essay? Is it appropriate to the topic?

2. **Self-evaluation.** Consider your peer reviewer's comments carefully, and decide which suggestions might improve your work. Also, look back at your essay, and circle one place where you think you used details effectively. Then, circle one place where you used dialogue to bring your experience to life. Finally, circle at least three words or phrases that help establish the essay's tone. If you can't find a passage to circle, you may need to add details or dialogue, or you may need to adjust the language of your essay.

Proofreading and Publishing

Once you have finished revising your essay, recopy or reprint your new version, and proofread it carefully. A clean, correct, and attractively presented paper encourages readers to consider you a writer worth reading.

You may wish to share your essay with friends and family. You and your classmates might also compile your reflective essays into an anthology of reflections. You might send your essay to one of the national magazines published for teenage audiences, or it may fit the criteria for the essay part of a college admission application.

Reflecting on Your Writing

This assignment has required you to reflect on personal experience and human nature. Now it is time for you to reflect again—this time on what completing the assignment has meant to you. Here are some questions to guide you. For your portfolio, date both your responses and your essay.

1. What is the most important discovery you made while writing this essay?

2. What did you learn about the way you think?

3. Which of the following processes was most challenging: deciding on an experience to explore, re-creating the experience for a reader, or extending the meanings of the experience to a wider context? Why?

4. Do you think reflective writing is valuable to the writer? Why or why not?

An effective reflective essay

1. *makes the writer's main concern clear from the beginning*
2. *centers on a topic that grows out of real-life experiences*
3. *portrays events, people, and places realistically and vividly*
4. *is organized in a way that makes sense to the reader*
5. *has a conversational and thoughtful tone*
6. *includes the writer's comment on the possible universal significance of the experience*
7. *comes to a satisfactory conclusion*

Revision
S T R A T E G I E S

Do your reflections move outward from an experience to its larger meanings? Mark with pencil the stages of reflection in your essay. Re-order your reflections if the progression is not logical; add to your thoughts if broad levels of reflection are absent.

Evaluating and Revising

As students evaluate and revise their essays, encourage them to look for details that do not contribute to their main point. Students should eliminate this extra material to make their essays more direct.

Proofreading and Publishing

As they proofread, encourage students to review the grammar and mechanics topics emphasized in class. Students can publish their essays by sharing them with the people involved in the incident described.

Portfolio

Reflecting on Your Writing

Students may answer questions in the text and attach these to essays in their portfolios. They may also write memoranda on what they learned in the assignment. If students are keeping a list of do's and don't's based on their writing, they can add to it from experiences with this assignment.

Reteaching

As students evaluate and revise their essays, suggest that they read them aloud in the tone they wish to project. As they read, they should note any phrases inconsistent with their tone.

Closure

Have students outline their writing experience, and ask volunteers to share their information. You can list their comments on the chalkboard and discuss any that offer insight into the writing process.

Enrichment

History Connection

Learning from history involves reflection like that in which students engaged to write their essays. Ask students to think of events they have studied that taught lessons. Have students share the lessons they learned with the class. Some possible events include the Vietnam War or U. S. Prohibition.

PORTFOLIO ASSESSMENT

Peer Evaluation During evaluating and revising, students can use the peer evaluation sheet found in the *Portfolio Management System,* p. 140.

Language Workshop

Try It Out: Answers

Possible answers, ranking from most formal to least formal:
1. Rationalization, excuse, alibi, cop-out.
2. Percuss, strike, hit, wallop.
3. Erudition, knowledge, learning, know-how.
4. Alluvium, earth, soil, dirt.

PROGRAM MANAGER

- **Extra Practice and Guided Instruction** For more instruction and practice of style, voice, tone, and diction, see Language Workshop in *Teaching Resources B,* pp. 58–59.
- **Extra Practice or Guided Instruction** See *Language Workshop: Voice and tone* for more practice or guided instruction in agreement.

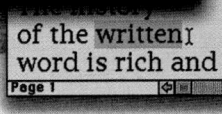

Language Workshop

The history of the written word is rich and

Page 1

Technology HELP

See Language Workshop CD-ROM. *Key word entry: voice.*

ASPECTS OF A WRITER'S STYLE

The Romantic poets drew upon the expressive power of ordinary speech. As a result, the **style** of Romantic poetry is different from that of eighteenth-century poetry. Romantic poets rejoiced in the uniqueness of each poet's **voice.** However, style and voice are sometimes difficult concepts to separate. Along with **tone** and **diction,** they form a unique fabric, one thread reliant on the others. Nevertheless, each term has a different technical definition.

- **Style** is the way a writer uses and adapts language to express ideas. Writers adapt their language to the writing situation much as people adapt their dress to the occasion—formal for formal occasions, casual for casual occasions, and a whole range of choices in between. Style is a matter of making many choices about sentence structure, punctuation, and diction.

- **Voice** is the unique sound and rhythm of the writer's language—the writer's personal way of communicating. In other words, the writer sounds like himself or herself, no matter what the situation, just as the writer would be recognizable in formal wear or in jogging clothes.

- **Tone** is the attitude the writer takes toward his or her subject. A writer's voice is capable of more than one tone. For instance, a writer may sound both angry and sarcastic or both sad and sentimental.

- **Diction,** the writer's choice of words, is an element of style and helps to establish both voice and tone.

Sentences that are formal in style can become informal with a few changes.

> **EXAMPLE** Earth has not anything to show more fair . . .
> —William Wordsworth, *from* "Composed upon Westminster Bridge"
>
> Nothing on Earth is more beautiful.

Tone can be changed by substituting synonyms with other connotations.

> **EXAMPLE** It is an ancient Mariner . . .
> —Samuel Taylor Coleridge, *from* "The Rime of the Ancient Mariner"
>
> It is a doddering old sailor.

Try It Out

Rank the words in each group below, identifying them as most formal, formal, somewhat formal, or least formal. Then discuss your choices with some classmates.
1. rationalization, excuse, alibi, cop-out
2. hit, strike, percuss, wallop
3. knowledge, erudition, know-how, learning
4. soil, earth, dirt, alluvium

Writer's Workshop Follow-Up: Revision

Re-read the reflective essay you wrote for the Writer's Workshop on page 773. Is the overall style informal, but not too casual? Does it communicate your true attitude toward your subject? Examine the diction. Replace words that seem too formal with simpler, more conversational words. Cut or replace slang and other words that are too casual. For words that have misleading emotional overtones, substitute synonyms that convey your true attitude.

778 THE ROMANTIC PERIOD

✔ QUICK CHECK: Style

Identify the most formal word in the groups of words below.
[1] teacher, guide, mentor [mentor]
[2] draft, configuration, outline [configuration]
[3] select, choose, decide [select]
[4] rough, bumpy, irregular [irregular]
[5] accelerate, hurry, rush [accelerate]

LEARNING FOR LIFE

Population Trends

Problem

During the Romantic period, as the Industrial Revolution began, cities grew up around factories. How is the current change from an industrial base to a service economy affecting where people live and work?

Project

Research current and projected population trends in the United States. What factors account for the growth of some areas and the decline of others? Where will the jobs of the future be?

Preparation

1. Working with a partner or a small group, use brainstorming or the *5W-How?* questions (*Who? What? When? Where? Why? How?*) to develop questions to guide your research.

2. Exchange ideas about the kinds of information that will help you answer your research questions and about possible sources. You'll need facts and figures, naturally, but keep in mind that examples, anecdotes, and quotations can help you interpret the data as well as add interest to your presentation.

Procedure

1. One way to gain an overview of your topic is to read several newspaper or magazine articles written for a general audience. (Check your library's indexes to newspapers, essays, and articles.) Such articles may mention other sources as well as authors who are experts in the field.

2. Two good secondary sources for data on population distribution are *The World Almanac and Book of Facts* and the *Statistical Abstract of the United States.* The Census Bureau also issues numerous publications, such as *Current Population Reports* (available on microfiche in some libraries.)

3. As you review the facts, opinions, and theories you find, draw your own conclusions about the relationship between the nation's transformation to a service economy and the distribution of population.

Presentation

Use one of the following formats (or another that your teacher approves):

1. **Communicating Graphically**

   Communicate your findings in a graphic display combining two or more types of illustrations such as maps, charts, and graphs. Include only essential information, so that the finished product will be legible and uncluttered, and use color, pattern, or both to make the display not only accurate but also attractive. Ask one of your high school's American history or economics teachers to "field-test" the display with his or her students at a suitable point in the course.

2. **Being Persuasive**

   Write an editorial summarizing your findings and expressing your views on why students should use the information in planning their careers. Convince your audience to take your ideas seriously by using a formal, serious tone and by tailoring your persuasive appeals to their needs and interests. Submit your editorial to the school newspaper or to a local newspaper.

3. **Speaking Out**

   Prepare a speech explaining what your research suggests about your community's future. Since your investigation focused on national trends, you'll need to extrapolate from your findings—that is, to speculate on the basis of what you discovered. Present your speech to a meeting of a civic or social group such as the Rotary Club or the American Business Women's Association.

Processing

Did doing this activity make you rethink your career plans? Did it change your ideas about where you're likely to find work in your chosen field? Write a brief reflection for your portfolio.

DEVELOPING WORKPLACE COMPETENCIES

Preparation	Procedure	Presentation
Generates related ideas	Uses resources well	Interprets information
Makes inferences	Works well on teams	Communicates ideas
Recognizes relationships	Acquires data	Teaches others
Predicts consequences	Processes information	Demonstrates responsibility
	Evaluates data	and self-esteem

The Victorian Period
1832–1901

The Railway Station
(detail) (19th century)
by William Powell Frith.

781

PROGRAM MANAGER

- **Summative Assessment** See **Literary Period Test: The Victorian Period**, *Test Booklet*, pp. 195–197 for a test on an additional text from the same historical era.

- **Application** For practice of a reading strategy for this unit, see **Becoming a Strategic Reader** worksheet, *Teaching Resources B*, pp. 68–69.

The Victorian Period

by **Donald Gray** and **John Malcolm Brinnin**

So many worlds, so much to do,
So little done, such things to be . . .

—*Alfred, Lord Tennyson*

(Inset) Pot lid depicting Crystal Palace, Dale Hall, Longport, Staffordshire (1851), by T. J. and J. Mayer.
Fitzwilliam Museum, University of Cambridge.

Transept of the Crystal Palace by G. Hawkins (19th century). Published by Day and Son and Ackerman and Co.
Stapleton Collection, London.

Many Victorians thought of themselves as living in a time of great change. They were right. But the changes during Queen Victoria's long reign (1837–1901) occurred in a period of relative political and social stability, and many were the result of conditions that began before Victoria and most of her subjects were born.

Peace and Economic Growth: Britannia Rules

After Napoleon's defeat at Waterloo in 1815, Britain was not involved in a major European war until World War I began in 1914. The empire that had begun in the seventeenth and eighteenth centuries with British interests in India and North America grew steadily, until by 1900, Victoria was queen-empress of more than two hundred million people living outside Great Britain.

At the same time, the Industrial Revolution of the eighteenth century greatly expanded. It moved through booms and depressions, but over the course of the century it steadily created new towns, new goods, new wealth, and new jobs for tens of thousands of people climbing through the complicated levels of the middle class. These social and economic changes were expressed in gradual political reforms. Piece by piece, middle-class and ultimately working-class politicians and voters achieved political power while leaving the monarchy and aristocracy in place.

(A)

The Victorian era was a time of relative peace and economic growth. The British Empire grew steadily, the Industrial Revolution expanded, and political power was extended to the middle and working classes.

Cotton handkerchief probably produced for Queen Victoria's Golden Jubilee in 1887 (66 cm × 74 cm).
Museum of London.

The Idea of Progress: "An Acre in Middlesex"

The English historian Thomas Babington Macaulay eloquently voiced the middle-class Victorian attitude toward government, history, and civilization. For Macaulay, history meant progress, and progress largely meant material improvement that could be seen and touched, counted and measured. "An acre in Middlesex is better than a principality in Utopia," he once

(B)

> The history of England is emphatically the history of progress.
>
> —Thomas Babington Macaulay

- **1832–1846**
  Oliver Twist depicts the poverty and the criminal underground that existed in Victorian England. Dickens believed that poverty leads to crime.

  Dickens may have drawn from his own memories when he wrote about Oliver's impoverished childhood. When his father was thrown into debtors' prison, young Dickens was forced to leave school and work in a factory. Hurtful images of those days would later find their way into many of Dickens's novels.

- **1847–1859**
  A feminist and abolitionist, Sojourner Truth delivered her famous "Ain't I a Woman" speech at a women's rights convention in Akron, Ohio, in 1851. "Look at me! Look at my arm! I could work as much and eat as much as a man—when I could get it—and bear the lash as well! And ain't I a woman?"

  Born into slavery as Isabella Baumfree (c. 1797–1883), this woman was an inspiring speaker, although she could neither read nor write. She worked throughout her life for the suffrage of African Americans. After slavery was abolished, she helped former slaves find homes and jobs.

  Sojourner Truth may or may not have known that women in faraway Victorian England were making the same demands at the same time. It would not be until the twentieth century, however, that women in both countries would gain the right to vote.

The Victorian Period, 1832–1901

LITERARY EVENTS

Elizabeth Barrett and **Robert Browning** elope; during their courtship, she writes poems included in *Sonnets from the Portuguese,* 1846

William Wordsworth becomes poet laureate, 1843

Nikolai Gogol draws attention to the plight of Russian serfs with his comic epic *Dead Souls,* 1842

Margaret Fuller helps found *The Dial,* a U.S. Transcendentalist journal that publishes Henry David Thoreau and Ralph Waldo Emerson, 1840

Edgar Allan Poe publishes "The Fall of the House of Usher," 1839

Charles Dickens publishes *Oliver Twist* in periodical form, 1837–1838

Charles Darwin publishes *On the Origin of Species by Means of Natural Selection,* 1859

Mary Ann Evans publishes stories in *Blackwood's Magazine,* using her pen name, George Eliot, 1857

Sojourner Truth delivers her "Ain't I a Woman?" speech in Akron, Ohio, 1851

Nathaniel Hawthorne publishes *The Scarlet Letter,* 1850

Alfred, Lord Tennyson becomes poet laureate, 1850

Karl Marx and Friedrich Engels publish *The Communist Manifesto,* 1848

Charlotte Brontë publishes *Jane Eyre;* Emily Brontë publishes *Wuthering Heights,* 1847

1832–1846	**1847–1859**

CULTURAL/HISTORICAL EVENTS

First Reform Bill extends vote to men who own property worth £10 or more, 1832

Mexican army defeats Texans at the Alamo, 1836

Victoria becomes queen of England, 1837

Reforms included in Custody Act allow divorced women legal access to their children, 1839

First of what China terms "unequal treaties" makes Hong Kong a British colony, 1842

In the U.S., Samuel F. B. Morse sends first telegraph message, 1844

Potato famine begins in Ireland; close to one million people die from starvation or famine-related diseases, 1845

Ten Hours Act limits the number of hours that women and children can work in factories, 1847

Seneca Falls, New York, women's rights convention is led by Elizabeth Cady Stanton and Lucretia Mott, 1848

Social and political revolutions in France, Germany, and the Austrian Empire mostly fail, 1848

Japan opens trade to West, 1854

Change in laws allows Lionel de Rothschild to become first Jewish member of Parliament, 1858

Medical Education Act closes loophole that briefly allowed women to become physicians in Great Britain, 1858

- Imperial State Crown (1837) made for Victoria's coronation.

- Front page of *The Lily* (August 1852).

784 THE VICTORIAN PERIOD

USING THE TIME LINE

One way to use the time line is to discuss or debate what are the most important contributions listed on the chart as judged from a present-day vantage point.

Ask students which events cited on the chart still affect the present day. [Students might mention the invention of the telegraph, the Irish famine, the publication of *The Communist Manifesto,* Darwin's theory of evolution, the emancipation of American slaves, the birth of Gandhi, the invention of the electric light, or the discovery of radium.]

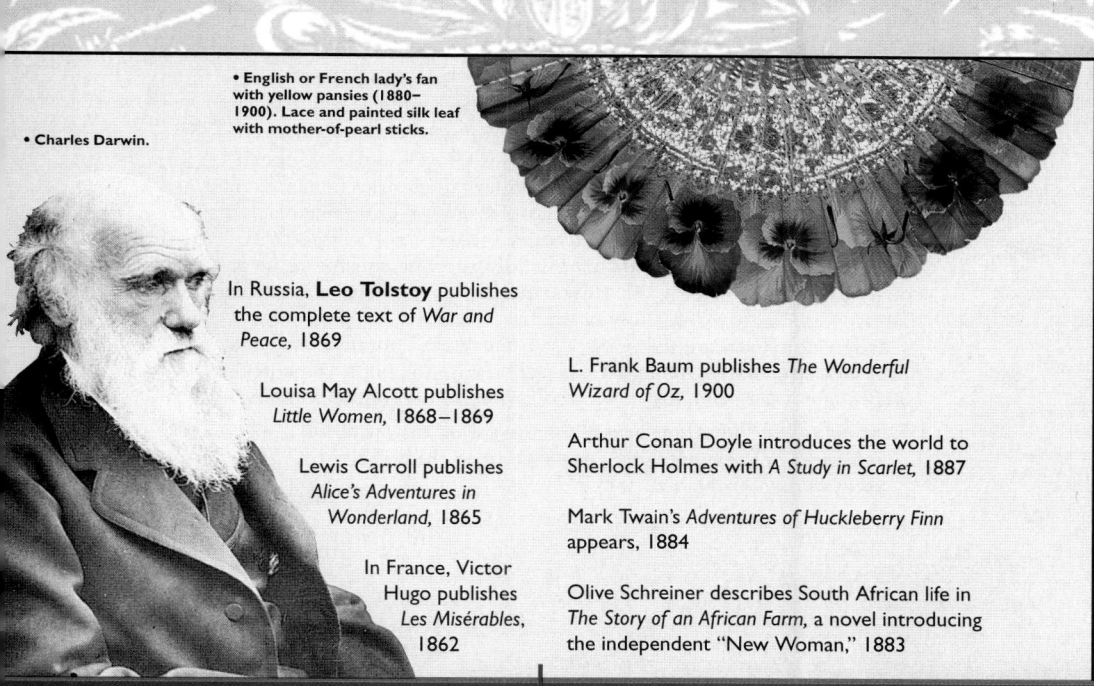

- English or French lady's fan with yellow pansies (1880–1900). Lace and painted silk leaf with mother-of-pearl sticks.

- Charles Darwin.

In Russia, **Leo Tolstoy** publishes the complete text of *War and Peace*, 1869

Louisa May Alcott publishes *Little Women*, 1868–1869

Lewis Carroll publishes *Alice's Adventures in Wonderland*, 1865

In France, Victor Hugo publishes *Les Misérables*, 1862

L. Frank Baum publishes *The Wonderful Wizard of Oz*, 1900

Arthur Conan Doyle introduces the world to Sherlock Holmes with *A Study in Scarlet*, 1887

Mark Twain's *Adventures of Huckleberry Finn* appears, 1884

Olive Schreiner describes South African life in *The Story of an African Farm*, a novel introducing the independent "New Woman," 1883

1860–1869

U.S. Civil War begins, 1861

Russian serfs are emancipated, 1861

Abraham Lincoln's Emancipation Proclamation declares slavery illegal in the U.S., 1863

Last Japanese shogun resigns; power returns to emperor, 1867

Second Reform Act gives vote to most male industrial workers, doubling the number of voters, 1867

Britain ends eighty-year practice of sending convicts to Australia, 1868

Debtors' prisons are abolished in England, 1869

Suez Canal opens, 1869

Gandhi born in India, 1869

1870–1901

Zulu War against British in South Africa begins, 1879

Thomas Edison invents an incandescent lamp, 1879

Married Women's Property Act allows wives possession of property held before and after marriage, 1882

Indian National Congress is formed; begins agitating for Indian self-rule, 1885

German engineer Karl Benz makes first successful test of gasoline engine automobile, 1885

Emmeline Pankhurst forms Women's Franchise League, arguing for British women's suffrage, 1889

More than 140 Sioux villagers are killed by U.S. soldiers at Wounded Knee Creek, South Dakota, 1890

French scientists Pierre and Marie Curie discover radium, 1898

Queen Victoria dies, 1901

- **1860–1869**

The tens of thousands of convicts sent to Australia from England made up a large part of the population in Australia for over fifty years. Today, Australia maintains strong ties with Great Britain; the two countries share a common language, are close trading partners, and have similar legislative systems.

During the Victorian period, the English people enjoyed books that told them more about Australia and what they might find there. Two such books were Charles Rowcroft's *Tales of the Colonies* (1843) and Henry Kingsley's *Geoffrey Hamlyn* (1859). Convicts themselves, such as James Vaux, published memoirs and books that told the story of the convicts in Australia.

wrote. Macaulay admired cleanliness and order. He wanted the London streets free of garbage, drained and paved, lighted at night, and patrolled by a sober police force. He wanted the city planned so that residents of respectable neighborhoods did not live next to hovels and were not annoyed by beggars and peddlers. He would have the houses numbered and a population literate enough to read signs. He did not claim that his own time had entirely met these standards of material comfort and security, but his cool, almost amazed regard of the disorder and squalor of the past conveyed his sense of progress: How could those people have lived like that? How different we are; how far we have come.

Many Victorians regretted or disputed Macaulay's confident tone and materialistic standards. But in his satisfaction with the improvements time had brought to England, his views were typical of his contemporaries.

Middle-class Victorians prided themselves on the material advances of the nineteenth century and on their ability to solve human problems.

Boys waiting to go to work in the coal mines in the Alfreton pit in Derbyshire, England (19th century).
Royal Holloway and Bedford New College, Surrey, England.

The "Hungry Forties"

Whatever its advances, the first decade of Victoria's reign was full of troubles—the period came to be known as the "Hungry Forties." Victoria came to the throne in the first year of a depression that by 1842 had put a million and a half unemployed workers and their families (in a population of sixteen million in England and Wales) on some form of poor relief. Government commissions investigating working conditions learned of children mangled when they fell asleep at machines at the end of a twelve-hour working day. They discovered young girls and boys hauling sledges of coal through narrow mine tunnels, working shifts so long that in winter they saw the sun only on Sunday.

OPTIONS FOR TEACHING

STRATEGIES FOR INCLUSION

Visual To review the section "The 'Hungry Forties'" or "The Movement for Reform: Food, Factories, and Optimism," have students find editorial cartoons depicting a social or political issue discussed in these sections. Call on volunteers to explain to the class the meaning and social or political significance of their cartoons.

Interpersonal Have students work in groups of four or five to create a time capsule of the Victorian period. Students should include drawings, photographs, or replicas of Victorian items. Ask students to consider dress, literature, and innovations in science and technology.

London Street Scene (1835) by J. O. Parry.

Alfred Dunhill Collection.

A. **Exploring the Culture**
Cities were important in Victorian society—a result of the rise of industry and increasing wealth. Remind students that Liverpool and Manchester are still industrial centers today. Some novelists, notably Charles Dickens, dealt memorably with life in urban settings. Others, such as George Eliot and Thomas Hardy, continued to turn to village and country life for the sources of their fiction.

In Ireland, the potato blight (1845–1849) caused a famine that killed perhaps a million people and forced two million others—nearly 20 percent of Ireland's population—to emigrate. Some went to English cities, where they lived ten or twelve to a room in slums that had two toilets for every 250 people.

The rapid growth of cities often made them filthy and disorderly. Nearly two million people lived in London during the 1840s, and commercial and industrial cities such as Manchester and Liverpool expanded rapidly. In Manchester in the 1840s, 40 percent of the streets were still unpaved. The Thames River in London was polluted by sewage, industrial waste, and the drainage from graveyards where bodies were buried in layers six or eight deep. In the 1850s, Parliament had sometimes to adjourn from its new riverside building because of the stench from the Thames.

Serious problems surfaced during the early years of Victoria's reign: economic depression, widespread unemployment, famine in Ireland, and deplorable living and working conditions brought on by rapid urbanization and a lack of measures safeguarding young workers.

> From the butchers' and greengrocers' shops the gaslights flared and flickered, wild and ghastly, over haggard groups of slipshod dirty women, bargaining for scraps of stale meat and frostbitten vegetables, wrangling about short weight and bad quality. Fish stalls and fruit stalls lined the edge of the greasy pavement, sending up odors as foul as the language of sellers and buyers. Blood and sewer water crawled from under doors and out of spouts, and reeked down the gutters among offal, animal and vegetable, in every stage of putrefaction.
>
> —Charles Kingsley

INTEGRATING THE LANGUAGE ARTS

Writing: Newspaper Article Have students suppose they are Victorian newspaper editors assigned to write articles assessing the state of society. As they compose their pieces, remind them to consider whom they would write about and what issues they think are on the minds of Victorians.

Strategic Reading To help students relate what they know to what they have learned about the Victorian period, have them record their thoughts on a KWL chart like the one that follows. Before they read the text, have students fill in the first and second columns. After they finish reading the text, ask them to complete the third column. Follow up by asking students what more they would like to know about the Victorian period and by brainstorming possible resources with students.

Know	Want to Know	Have Learned

A. Critical Reading: Making Connections

? Does this type of conservation still occur? Have you ever visited a historic site that has been preserved? [Most students will recognize modern efforts to revitalize downtown areas or restore important historical buildings. Answers will vary.]

B. Expansion

Nightingale was a meticulous statistician, and as such collected convincing data about the health benefits of sanitary conditions. In her *Notes on Matters Affecting the Health, Efficiency and Hospital Administration of the British Army* and a later document written under the auspices of the Royal Sanitary Commission on the Health of the Army, she explains in a clear and convincing manner that inadequate food, clothing, and conditions—more than wounds from the fighting—contributed to the disastrous mortality rate among soldiers of the Crimean War and in the barracks. Her efforts won favor with the Queen, who backed Nightingale in presenting her research to the Secretary of State for War.

AN AGE IN NEED OF HEROINES: REFORM IN VICTORIAN BRITAIN

Be good, sweet maid, and let who will be clever;
Do noble things, not dream them, all day long.

—Charles Kingsley

Great Britain was the world's first industrialized nation, and its smoky cities illustrated the dangers of "progress": Unsanitary housing and rampant disease were unremarkably common. There were legal remedies for abuses, but Victorian social reform was not only a parliamentary process. It was also a passionate struggle to change public opinion through hard work and education.

"Do noble things." Following the Reverend Charles Kingsley's urging to "Do noble things, not dream them," many women approached social reform as a moral and religious duty. The social worker Octavia Hill (1838–1912) believed that adequate housing could "make individual life noble, homes happy, and family life good," and she became an authority on housing reform. She was also a conservationist, founding the National Trust to protect historic buildings and scenic spots from industrial development. Because of Hill's efforts, the public can visit sites such as the Runnymede meadow. Thanks to the National Trust, it looks much as it did when King John accepted the Magna Carta there in 1215.

Spoiling the "brutes." Perhaps the best-known Victorian reformer is Florence Nightingale (1820–1910), who transformed the public's perception of modern nursing during the Crimean War. Two unlikely inventions—the camera and the war correspondent—made her career possible. Newspaper reports revealed that bureaucratic bungling had cost thousands of lives in the army's hospitals in Scutari, Turkey. Public indignation gave Nightingale the unprecedented opportunity to become an army nurse. In Turkey, she saw scores of wounded soldiers dying from diseases caused by poor hygiene, lack of medical supplies, and sheer neglect. The ordinary British soldier was thought to be, in the words of the duke of Wellington, "the scum of the earth." When Nightingale asked medical authorities for clean bedding or warm clothing, she was told: "You will spoil the brutes."

Nightingale believed British soldiers were "murdered" by incompetence, and she vowed to avenge them. With gritty tenacity, she became an authority on public health, observing that sanitation could save lives. Queen Victoria read her meticulous reports and said, "I wish we had her at the War Office." Nightingale's efforts fundamentally changed hospital management and made nursing a respected career.

The Movement for Reform: Food, Factories, and Optimism

Violence broke out at massive political rallies called in the 1840s to protest government policies that kept the price of bread and other food high and deprived most working men (and all women) of the vote and representation in Parliament. In 1848, a year of revolution in Europe, nervous British politicians got the army ready and armed the staffs of museums and government offices when working-class political reformers organized what they called a "monster rally" in London to petition Parliament and the queen.

Still, most middle-class Victorians believed that things were better than in the past and that they were going to be better yet in the future. Their opinion was in part founded on a steady improvement throughout the Victorian era in the material condition of people in all social classes. The

788 THE VICTORIAN PERIOD

Science Have students work in groups of three or four to report on a significant technological or scientific advancement made during the Victorian period. Students should provide a replica, schematic drawing, or other physical representation of the invention or innovation. The project should also include some form of background information, such as a bulletin board, a videotaped presentation, or other method of explaining the scientific or technological significance of the subject. Have the groups present their findings to the class.

Geography Prompted by the time line entries, students might research a subject in another part of the world that occurred during the Victorian period. Ask each student to prepare a brief presentation using visuals to show how the selected event relates to other events in Victorian England.

Florence Nightingale tending the wounded during the Crimean War (19th century).

"We make no compromise." Reformers such as Nightingale and Hill devoted themselves to aiding the victims of Victorian "progress," agitating for better conditions and for improved educational opportunities. In the name of charity, they often stepped outside the bounds of "ladylike" behavior. Josephine Butler (1828–1906) exposed the exploitation of women and girls, working to repeal acts that deprived poor women of their constitutional rights.

In the name of reform, she declared that "we make no compromise; and we are ready to meet all the powers of earth and hell combined."

These reformers redefined the idea of "women's work"; in the process, they set public policies that curbed many abuses and saved countless lives. As we enter the twenty-first century, we continue to benefit from their efforts to improve the Victorian quality of life.

price of food dropped after midcentury, largely because of trade with other countries and the growing empire. Diet improved as meat, fruit, and margarine (a Victorian invention) began to appear regularly in working-class households. Factories and railroads made postage, newspapers, clothing, furniture, travel, and other goods and services cheap.

A series of political reforms gave the vote to almost all adult males by the last decades of the century. In 1832, the First Reform Bill extended the vote to all men who owned property worth ten pounds or more in yearly rent. Continued pressure led to the Second

> The principle which regulates the existing social relations between the two sexes—the legal subordination of one sex to the other—is wrong in itself, and now one of the chief hindrances to human improvement.
>
> —John Stuart Mill,
> *from The Subjection of Women*

PROBLEM SOLVING/CRITICAL THINKING

Have students work in groups to devise a list of modern American values. Then, ask students to create a chart like the one that follows, comparing modern values to the ones in fashion in Victorian England. Reconvene as a class to discuss the groups' findings and to answer the question: Who defines the values of a society?

Modern Values in the United States	Values of Victorian England
[individuality]	[social order]

☞

A. Expansion

It was not until 1971 that eighteen-year-olds could vote in all states, a change made by the 26th Amendment. Previously, all but ten states required voters to be twenty-one.

B. Literary Connections

Refer to Blake's poem "The Chimney Sweeper," on p. 652, which discusses child labor.

Reform Act in 1867, which gave the right to vote to all working-class men except for agricultural workers. Decades of agitation by Victorian women for suffrage succeeded only in the next century. Strengthened by their **A** domestic contributions during the Great War, women age thirty and over won the vote in 1918. Universal adult suffrage in 1928 extended the vote to women at age twenty-one.

B A series of Factory Acts limited child labor and reduced the usual working day to ten hours, with a half-holiday on Saturday. State-supported schools were established in 1870, made compulsory in 1880, and made

---

A CLOSER LOOK

THE PRE-RAPHAELITE BROTHERHOOD: CHALLENGING ARTISTIC AUTHORITY

The Times called it "plainly revolting." The *Literary Gazette* found it "a nameless atrocity." Charles Dickens thought its central character "a hideous, wry-necked, blubbering, red-haired boy in a nightgown." The painting that elicited such scathing abuse was *Christ in the House of His Parents* (1850) by John Everett Millais (1829–1896). Millais shocked the art world with his innovative techniques and the treatment of his subject—he portrayed the Holy Family as ordinary people in a shavings-strewn carpentry shop.

Millais belonged to the Pre-Raphaelite Brotherhood (PRB), a group that embraced the ordinary while rejecting "conventionalities and feeble reminiscences from the Old Masters." Dissatisfied with Victorian complacency, a group of seven young men modeled their work after medieval painters—those *before* the Renaissance painter Raphael—that they believed had a more natural vision. Founded in 1848, the PRB never shared a unifying style or principle. But they were united in their sense, as the artist Sir Edward Burne-Jones (1833–1898) said, that "the time is out of joint."

Christ in the House of His Parents (1850) by Sir John Everett Millais.
Tate Gallery, London.

790 THE VICTORIAN PERIOD

OPTIONS FOR TEACHING

CLASSROOM MANAGEMENT

Block Scheduling At the end of the unit, show a movie related to the Victorian era—perhaps *Middlemarch* or *Wuthering Heights*. With the longer class period, most videos can be viewed in one to two blocks. There is also enough time for an in-depth discussion or for an appropriate follow-up writing assignment.

Managing the Reader's Response Classroom Make sure to emphasize diplomacy in peer review of ideas or assignments. Request that students phrase comments as questions directed to the speaker or writer, and offer students an opportunity to assess the peer review process and the helpfulness of criticism received.

free in 1891. In 1859, 40 percent of the couples getting married could not write their names on their marriage certificates. By 1900, using that simple definition of literacy, more than 90 percent of the population was literate.

As the nineteenth century progressed, living conditions gradually improved. Food and other commodities became more readily available, most adult males won the right to vote, laws regulated the use of child labor, and compulsory education brought about widespread literacy.

C. Critical Reading: Identifying Main Ideas
Ask students to summarize this statement according to information in the article. [Possible answer: The ordinary can be beautiful and the natural, as opposed to the conventional, deserves attention.]

Artistic "treason." The PRB is widely known for Dante Gabriel Rossetti's sensuous portraits. A favorite model was Jane Morris, and her long neck and abundant, wavy hair in works such as *Proserpine* (1874) are a PRB trademark.

To members of the Royal Academy of Art, however, PRB members were artistic outlaws. Their shading techniques violated the academy's guidelines that one "principal light" should focus a painting's main elements. Their minute rendering of details seemed busy and bewildering, "a strange disorder of the mind or the eyes." PRB member William Holman Hunt (1827–1910) prided himself on botanical and geologic accuracy, laboring over his paintings' individual rocks and flowers. "Our talk is the deepest treason against our betters," Hunt said.

Art and cultural values. The PRB disbanded in 1853, but it attracted followers, drawn by the PRB's medieval models, who had turned away from industrial Britain's materialism. The art critic John Ruskin (1819–1900) asserted that art and artists suffered from mechanization: He argued that the way art was produced could shape a culture's values.

The artist William Morris (1834–1896) applied these theories in a decorating firm that revived traditional methods of producing furniture, tapestries, and stained glass. His Kelmscott Press crafted fine books with the painstaking detail of hand-printed engravings and hand-sewn bindings. Morris, Ruskin, and former PRB members taught artisans these skills

Proserpine (1874) by Dante Gabriel Rossetti.
Tate Gallery, London.

and principles at the Working Men's College, an educational experiment begun in London in 1854.

Modern viewers delight in the PRB's exuberant excess of elaborate designs and glorious medieval trappings. Yet the Pre-Raphaelites' work also made a social statement. The tensions of the Industrial Revolution bonded the Brotherhood, and their rebellious movement raised difficult questions about the place of art and artists in a rapidly changing society.

ASSESSMENT TOOLS

Check Test: Multiple Choice
1. The Victorian era was a time of _____. [c]
   a. increased hardships for all classes
   b. civil wars at home
   c. peace and economic growth
2. Victorian decorum supported strong ideas about _____. [c]
   a. sex
   b. authority and the place of women
   c. both of the above

3. Most Victorians believed that history meant _____. [b]
   a. regression
   b. progress
   c. hardship
4. It can be said that Dickens believed that things usually work out well for _____. [a]
   a. decent people
   b. rich people
   c. the aristocracy

5. Victorian literature indicated that rapid industrialization included _____. [c]
   a. many dangers
   b. many benefits
   c. both dangers and benefits

A. Exploring the Culture
Ask students if they think contemporary attitudes about censorship are significantly different from Victorian attitudes. You might remind students of movie ratings and of books that are kept out of classrooms.

B. Literary Connections
Direct students to the biography of Elizabeth Barrett Browning on p. 837. An example of an autocratic father in fiction is Mr. Murdstone of Charles Dickens's *David Copperfield*.

The Drawing Room (late 19th or early 20th century) by Paul Gustav Fischer.

Decorum and Authority

Many Victorians thought of themselves as progressing morally and intellectually, as well as materially. In fact, the powerful, mostly middle-class obsession with gentility or decorum has made *prudery* almost a synonym for *Victorianism*. Book publishers and magazine editors deleted or altered words and episodes that might, in the phrase of the day, bring a blush to the cheek of a young person. In art and popular fiction, sex, birth, and death were softened by sentimental conventions into tender courtships, joyous motherhoods, and deathbed scenes in which old people became saints and babies became angels. In the real world, people were arrested for distributing information about sexually transmitted diseases. Victorian society regarded seduced or adulterous women (but not their male partners) as "fallen" and pushed them to the margins of respectability.

Victorian decorum also supported powerful ideas about authority. Many Victorians were uneasy about giving strong authority to a central government (although it is revealing of the fundamental decorum of British society that its version of the 1848 European revolutions was a meeting to petition Parliament). In Victorian private lives, however, the autocratic father of middle-class households is a vivid figure in both fact (Elizabeth Barrett Browning's father, for example) and fiction.

> I still cling fondly to the hope that some system of female instruction will be discovered, by which the young women of England may be sent from school to the homes of their parents, habituated to be on the watch for every opportunity of doing good to others; making it the first and the last inquiry of every day, "What can I do to make my parents, my brothers, or my sisters, more happy? . . . I hope to pursue the plan to which I have been accustomed, of seeking my own happiness only in the happiness of others."
>
> —Sarah Stickney Ellis, essayist who argued that women's education should cultivate "the heart," not the mind

Women in particular were subject to male authority. Middle-class women especially were expected to marry and make their homes a comfortable refuge for their husbands from the male domains of business, politics, and the professions. Women who did not marry had few occupations open to them. Working-class women could find jobs as servants in affluent households, while unmarried middle-class ladies could become governesses or teachers. Many middle-class women remained unmarried because men often postponed marriage until they achieved financial security. The problem of these unmarried, "redundant women," as they were called, was painful, although in literature, especially literature written by men, the figure of the middle-aged maiden was often played for comedy.

The excesses, cruelties, and hypocrisies of all these repressions were obvious to many Victorians. But the codes and barriers of decorum changed slowly because they were part of the ideology of progress. Prudery and social order were intended to control the licentiousness that Victorians associated with the political revolutions of the eighteenth century and the social corruption of the Regency of George IV (1811–1820).

> When the views advanced by me in this volume . . . are generally admitted, we can dimly foresee that there will be a considerable revolution in natural history.
>
> —Charles Darwin, *from On the Origin of Species*

The Victorian emphasis on decorum grew from the conviction that life would be improved if it steadily became more refined, more rationally organized, better policed, and therefore safer.

Intellectual Progress: The March of Mind

The intellectual advances of the Victorian period were dramatically evident to those living in it. Humans began to understand the earth, its creatures, and its natural laws. Geologists worked out the history written in rocks and fossils. From countless

C. Literary Connections
As an indication of the growing role of women in English literature, review the women writers cited in the table of contents of this anthology.

Awaiting Admission to the Casual Ward (1874) by Luke Fildes. Oil on canvas.

Royal Holloway and Bedford New College, Surrey, England.

observations, Charles Darwin and other biologists theorized about the evolution of species. The industrialization of England depended on and supported science and technology, especially chemistry (in the iron and textile industries) and engineering.

Those who made and used scientific and technological knowledge had a confidence of their own. Thomas Huxley, a variously accomplished scientist who wrote and lectured frequently on the necessity of scientific education, imagined science as an exhilarating, high-stakes chess game with the physical universe.

> The chessboard is the world, the pieces are the phenomena of the universe, the rules of the game are what we call the laws of Nature. The player on the other side is hidden from us. We know that his play is always fair, just, and patient. But also we know, to our cost, that he never overlooks a mistake, or makes the smallest allowance for ignorance. To the man who plays well, the highest stakes are paid, with that sort of overflowing generosity with which the strong shows delight in strength. And one who plays ill is checkmated—without haste, but without remorse.
>
> —Thomas Huxley, *from A Liberal Education*

Huxley resembles those confident Victorians who built railways and sewers, organized markets and schools, and pushed through electoral reforms and laws regulating the conditions of work. These reformers believed that the world offered a challenging set of problems that could be understood by human intelligence and solved by science, government, and other human institutions. Huxley made the game exciting by warning that humans could lose. But so long as the game is played in the material world, Huxley and others like him saw no reason that they would not win.

Charles Dickens (1859) by William Powell Frith. Victoria and Albert Museum, London.

Advances in science and technology convinced nineteenth-century intellectuals and reformers that human efforts could overcome all material problems.

Questions and Doubts

The Victorian period, and especially its literature, was filled with voices asking questions and raising doubts. Speaking for many of their contemporaries, and speaking to others they thought shallow and complacent, Victorian writers asked whether material comfort fully satisfied human needs and wishes. They questioned the cost of exploiting the

794 THE VICTORIAN PERIOD

earth and human beings to achieve such comfort. They protested or mocked codes of decorum and authority.

In the first half of the period, some writers complained that materialist ideas of reality completely overlooked the spirit or soul that made life beautiful and just. Later in the century, writers like Thomas Hardy and A. E. Housman thought that Macaulay's and Huxley's ideas of history and nature presupposed a coherence and generosity that did not really exist.

Literature in Victorian culture often reassured its readers that, rightly perceived, the universe made sense. But some writers unsettled their readers by telling them that they were not rightly perceiving the universe, or by asking them to consider whether human life and the natural world made as much sense as they had once hoped.

Charles Dickens, the most popular and most important figure in Victorian literature, is a case in point. The son of an improvident clerk, Dickens lived out one of the favorite plots of Victorian progress by rising through his own enormous talents and energy to become a wealthy and famous man. His was a peculiarly Victorian success, made possible by the increasing affluence and literacy that gave him a large reading public and by improved printing and distribution that made book publishing a big business.

The conventional happy endings of Dickens's novels satisfied his readers', and probably his own, conviction that things usually work out well for decent people. But from the beginning of his career in the 1830s to the publication of his last complete novel in 1865, many of Dickens's most memorable scenes showed decent people

Who Were the Victorians?

Here are some of the social and material changes that marked the long reign of Queen Victoria.

- Industrialism made England the workshop of the world, with a mechanized factory system and extensive railways.

- Much of the British population moved from rural areas to rapidly growing cities.

- Expanded educational opportunities increased literacy; flourishing lending libraries and cheap periodicals created a mass reading public.

- Continued advances in science and technology gave Victorians hope that all social problems—disease, poverty, even immorality—could be resolved by the era's "progress."

- The human cost of industrialization was heavy: abuses of child labor, unsafe conditions in factories, and widespread disease from contaminated air and water.

- By the end of the century, the disruption and materialism of the era made people question changes brought on by rapid industrialization and reevaluate their definitions of progress.

neglected, abused, and exploited. The hungry Oliver Twist asks for more gruel in the workhouse; the crippled Tiny Tim in *A Christmas Carol* cheerfully hobbles toward his possible early death; and David Copperfield is beaten and exiled by the cold, dark Mr. Murdstone.

In his later novels, Dickens also created characters and scenes to show that even the winners in the competition for material gain had reason to be as desperate and unhappy as the losers. In *Our Mutual Friend*, his last novel, he describes a dinner party at the home of a family called the Veneerings, a name that emphasizes the family's superficial qualities. They are "bran-new people in a bran-new house in a bran-new quarter of London":

> The great looking-glass above the sideboard reflects the table and the company. Reflects the new Veneering crest, in gold and eke in silver, frosted and also thawed, a camel of all work. The Herald's College found out a Crusading ancestor for Veneering who bore a camel on his shield (or might have done it if he had thought of it), and a caravan of camels take charge of the fruits and flowers and candles, and kneel down to be loaded with the salt. Reflects Veneering; forty, wavy-haired, dark, tending to corpulence, sly, mysterious, filmy. . . . Reflects Mrs. Veneering; fair, aquiline-nosed and fingered, not so much light hair as she might have, gorgeous in raiment and jewels. . . . Reflects Podsnap; prosperously feeding, two little light-colored wiry wings, one on either side of his else bald head, looking as like his hairbrushes as his hair. . . . Reflects Mrs. Podsnap; . . . quantity of bone, neck, and nostrils like a rocking horse, hard

Many Happy Returns of the Day (19th century) by William Powell Frith.

Harrogate Museums and Art Gallery, North Yorkshire, England.

features, majestic headdress in which Podsnap has hung golden offerings. . . . Reflects . . . mature young gentleman; with too much nose in his face, too much ginger in his whiskers, too much sparkle in his studs, his eyes, his buttons, his talk, and his teeth.

Attacks like Dickens's on the hollowness, glitter, superficiality, and excesses of Victorian affluence were common in Victorian literature, for example, in Robert Browning's portrayal of the murderously possessive duke in "My Last Duchess." Dickens also raised questions about the costs of progress in his descriptions of the huddle and waste of cities and the smoke and fire of industrial landscapes. In 1871, the art historian and social critic John Ruskin noted a new phenomenon that we call smog; he called it the plague wind, or "the storm-cloud of the nineteenth century," and concluded, chillingly, ". . . [M]ere smoke would not blow to and fro in that wild way. It looks more to me as if it were made of dead men's souls."

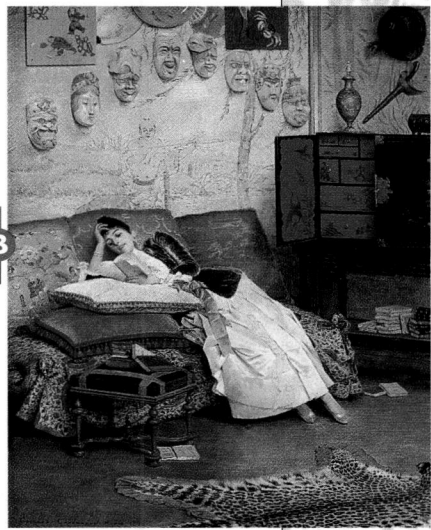

La Liseuse (19th century) by Georges Croegaert.

> **The materialism, secularism, vulgarity, and sheer waste that accompanied Victorian progress led some writers to wonder if their culture was really advancing by any measure.**

From Trust to Skepticism and Denial

Trust in a transcendental power was characteristic of the early Victorian writers. They were the immediate heirs of the Romantic idea of a finite natural world surrounded by and interfused with an infinite, ideal transcendental reality. The highest purpose of a poet, of any writer, was to make readers aware of the connection between earth and heaven, body and soul, material and ideal. Fundamentally, as Thomas Carlyle wrote in his essay "The Hero as Poet," reality is spiritual, a divine idea. "All Appearances, from the starry sky to the grass of the field, but especially the Appearance of Man and his work, is but *vesture*, the embodiment that renders it [the divine idea] possible." The poet penetrates to the divine idea and makes it palpable in language and story to those of lesser power and vision. "That is always his message; he is to reveal that to us— that sacred mystery which he more than others lives ever present with."

With some exceptions—Gerard Manley Hopkins is one and Christina Rossetti another—writers younger than Alfred Tennyson and Ruskin found it increasingly difficult to believe in an infinite power and order that

> If we had a keen vision of all that is ordinary in human life, it would be like hearing the grass grow or the squirrel's heart beat, and we should die of that roar which is the other side of silence.
>
> —George Eliot, *from Middlemarch*

B. Expansion

Ask whether students are surprised to learn that smog existed in the Victorian age. Point out that John Ruskin (1819–1900) wrote on social, political, and artistic topics. His proposals for social improvement were less grand and aggressive than those of that other critic of society, Thomas Carlyle (1795–1881). Carlyle admired strong national leaders such as Cromwell and Frederick the Great, but Ruskin urged individual actions, such as boycotting the products of industrial and economic systems that demeaned human labor.

A. Responding to the Quotation

? What is your response to this quotation by Arnold? [Sample responses: It has an empty, lonely feel and makes me think about how tiny our planet is in the universe. It is clear that he, like other Victorian writers, did not believe God was caring for the people of the world.]

B. Expansion

The real name of George Eliot (1819–1880) was Mary Ann Evans. Her use of a pseudonym was one of a series of self-defining acts. After her father's death, she left her family's strongly religious household and went to London to edit an important magazine of liberal intellectual opinion. Eliot became one of the most accomplished Victorian novelists. Her fiction is based on her close knowledge of the small worlds of families and provincial towns. Her novels include *Adam Bede* (1859), *The Mill on the Floss* (1860), *Silas Marner* (1861), and *Middlemarch* (1872).

Cass in *Silas Marner* is a squire who seduces and abandons a young woman. Their child is found and reared by a miser, Silas Marner. The novel tells of Silas's redemption through love.

---

made sense of material and human existence. Some simply thought it unnecessary. Algernon Charles Swinburne and Rudyard Kipling, in their different ways, celebrated a relation between humans and the natural world that could be joyous and even redemptive.

Other writers at midcentury, sometimes reacting to explanations of the world that excluded the spiritual, were saddened by what seemed to them to be the withdrawal of the divine from the world. The dominant note of much mid-Victorian writing was struck by Matthew Arnold in his poem "Dover Beach": "The Sea of Faith," Arnold wrote, had ebbed. There was no certainty; or if there was, what was certain was that existence was not governed by a benevolent intelligence that cared for its creatures.

By the end of the century, this skepticism and denial had become pervasive in the works of Hardy, Housman, and others. Early- and mid-Victorian novelists such as Dickens and George Eliot had dramatized a human ideal achieved through sympathy and unselfishness. They made sad or frightening examples of people like the Murdstones in *David Copperfield* and Godfrey Cass in *Silas Marner*—all hard surface and no

> **A** Yes! in the sea of life enisled,
> With echoing straits between us thrown,
> Dotting the shoreless watery wild,
> We mortal millions live *alone.*
>
> —Matthew Arnold, *from* "To Marguerite—Continued"

A CLOSER LOOK

VICTORIAN DRAMA: FROM RELIEF TO REALISM

Interior of Drury Lane Theater, 1808 (19th century) by Thomas Rowlandson and A. Pugin.

Though Queen Victoria, who came to the throne in 1837, loved the theater, it was she who once remarked, "We are not amused." And certainly the theater of the early part of her reign provided little to amuse anyone. Comedy must have license to explore, to expose, to look under the bed, and to ridicule, but Victoria's England was marked by prudery, good taste, repression of natural feelings, high-mindedness, and official censorship.

Irreverent ridicule. The operettas that William S. Gilbert wrote to Arthur Sullivan's music, beginning with *Trial by Jury* (1875), provided some delightful comic relief. Though today we think of these operettas (such as *The Pirates of Penzance* and *H.M.S. Pinafore*) merely as charming, tuneful, witty entertainments, in their period they irreverently ridiculed the law, the navy, the world of aesthetes, and the aristocracy.

soul. Their heroes and heroines learned to find happiness in nurturing marriages and in small communities of family and friends. But there were few such marriages and communities in the fiction and poetry of Hardy and Housman. These late-Victorian writers told stories of lovers and friends bereft and betrayed by unfaithfulness, war, and the other troubles that humans add to the natural troubles of mortal life.

> *Over the century, the trust in a transcendental power inherited from the Romantics eroded, giving way to uncertainty and spiritual doubt. Late-Victorian writers turned to a pessimistic exploration of the human struggle against indifferent natural forces.*

Revealing Reality, Creating Coherence

Victorian writers had purposes as various as the ideas of reality they believed in. Some writers wanted to scare or shame readers into effective moral and political actions that they optimistically believed were possible. Some wanted to show readers what it is like to live in a pleasurable moment of intense feeling like that caught in a lyric or in the interesting perspectives of a character in a dramatic monologue or novel. Victorian literature entertained, informed, warned, and reassured.

Program cover for October 17, 1881, Savoy Theatre production of *Patience* by Sir W. S. Gilbert and Sir Arthur Sullivan.

Victoria and Albert Museum, London.

Intrinsic to Gilbert and Sullivan operettas was a world-turned-on-its-head view of life that would influence both Oscar Wilde and Bernard Shaw. In Gilbert and Sullivan, "Things are seldom what they seem. / Skim milk masquerades as cream."

Moving toward realism. Coming into the era of Oscar Wilde and Bernard Shaw, drama was moving toward realism, which has been the dominant dramatic mode for the last hundred years. In England and in Europe, fiction writers were dealing with the social realities of the time—Charles Dickens among others in England, Émile Zola in France. From Scandinavia came the revolutionary voices of Henrik Ibsen in plays such as *An Enemy of the People* (1882) and of August Strindberg in *Miss Julie* (1888).

While some playwrights were assimilating new points of view and style, the theaters were also undergoing changes to accommodate the new plays. For years, London had been dominated by two huge

theaters, Covent Garden and Drury Lane, each seating well over three thousand people—large theaters not congenial to intimate realistic drama.

In the early part of the nineteenth century, new, smaller theaters were built. The forestage, or apron, was removed, and gaslight (and soon electricity) took the place of candles once used to illuminate the stage. These changes cleared the way for the staging of smaller-scale realistic dramas, which an audience might view as though through an invisible "fourth wall," allowing the audience to eavesdrop on the action. In smaller theaters, on such a stage with new lighting, playwrights could now achieve an illusion of reality.

C

C. Critical Reading: Making Connections
Encourage students to compare this information about stages to what they learned from "The Renaissance Theater" (pp. 282–288).

Quickwrite

Some students may argue that progress should not be measured only in improvements in material comfort and security, but that progress must also be measured in humanistic growth and concern both for the earth and for each individual.

Even the playfulness of Lewis Carroll and Oscar Wilde shows the two most important and consistent purposes or effects of Victorian literature. The first was to make readers hope or wonder if reality was really like that—really as whole and satisfying as in Tennyson's *In Memoriam,* as briskly coherent as in a poem by Browning or an essay by Macaulay. The second principal purpose or effect was to demonstrate that, however bleak and chaotic reality seemed to be, the writer and reader could make a pleasing order in it. Even when a story or poem said that the world was ugly or made no sense, the story or the poem could seem beautiful and make sense to its audience. In every successful act of writing and reading literature, one more satisfyingly coherent thing in the world is created or discovered.

Finally, it is important to remember that these purposes and effects happened first to readers who were living Victorian lives. Victorian literature did not exist above or outside the comfortable and often confident lives of its readers. Many of the people who read Dickens settled down with his books after dining in rooms as garishly decorated as the Veneerings'. Most of the young men and women who thrilled to Dante Gabriel Rossetti's sensualism and to Housman's tender gloom probably moved on to make proper and modestly happy marriages and to find worthy occupations. People who were making a lot of money listened to Carlyle and Ruskin telling them that they were foolish and damned. People who were disturbed by how much money was being made listened to Macaulay reminding them that a century or so before they might not have been able to afford, or even to read, his book.

> We are all in the gutter, but some of us are looking at the stars.
>
> —Oscar Wilde, *from Lady Windermere's Fan*

Victorian literature needs to be read not just as a comment on the complexity of its culture, but also as an important part of that culture. Its writers sent their words to work in the world to alter, to reinforce, to challenge, to enlarge, or to temper the ideas and feelings with which their contemporaries managed their lives.

Victorian writing reflects the dangers and benefits of rapid industrialization, while encouraging readers to examine closely their own understanding of the era's progress.

Quickwrite

What do you think of the Victorian idea of progress? Do you agree that tangible improvements in material comfort and security constitute human progress? Or do you think there's more to it than that? Why? Jot down your thoughts about what progress means to you. If you'd like to, ask a classmate to respond to your written ideas.

(Opposite) *The Daydream* (detail) (19th century) by Dante Gabriel Rossetti.
Victoria and Albert Museum, London.

Collection 10

LOVE AND LOSS

> ### *Theme:* The Human Condition
> The Victorian era was known for its wide-ranging scientific inquiry as well as for its rigid societal structure. A questioning of traditional beliefs sometimes led to new ways of seeing the world. However, the time-honored paths of love, nature, and God were the means used to explore the human condition.

Thematic Focus

The age-old themes of love and loss are explored through the contemplation of God, nature, and the human heart.

- **Tears, Idle Tears/The Eagle: A Fragment/Flower in the Crannied Wall/The Lady of Shalott/***from* **In Memoriam A.H.H./Ulysses/Crossing the Bar** Tennyson plumbs the depths of human emotion.
- **My Last Duchess/Porphyria's Lover** Robert Browning explores a sinister side of love.
- **Sonnet 43** *from* **Sonnets from the Portuguese** An expression of a joyful, transforming love, this sonnet is also tempered with maturity.
- **Spring and Fall: To a Young Child/Pied Beauty** Hopkins encourages readers to take a second look.

Literary Focus

Literary Element	Selection / Feature
Tercet/Meter/Rhyme/Alliteration/Assonance	**Tears, Idle Tears/The Eagle/Flower in the Crannied Wall/The Lady of Shalott/In Memoriam/Ulysses/Crossing the Bar**
Dramatic Monologue	**My Last Duchess/Porphyria's Lover**
Petrarchan sonnet/Turn	**Sonnet 43**
Assonance/Imagery/Sprung rhythm	**Spring and Fall: To a Young Child/Pied Beauty**

Writing Focus

The following flowchart shows how the writing assignment for each selection relates to and builds toward the culminating writing assignment presented in the Writer's Workshop at the end of the unit.

Selection	Work-in-Progress Assignment
Tears, Idle Tears/The Eagle/Flower in the Crannied Wall/The Lady of Shalott/In Memoriam/Ulysses/Crossing the Bar	Evaluate a poem p. 825
My Last Duchess/Porphyria's Lover	List criteria for a dramatic poem p. 836
Sonnet 43	Compare two sonnets p. 839
Spring and Fall: To a Young Child/Pied Beauty	Evaluate Hopkins's diction p. 844
Writer's Workshop	Write an evaluation p. 899

Collection Planner

SELECTION/ FEATURE	Literary Elements / Active Reading	Writing	Speaking and Listening	Language and Vocabulary
Tears, Idle Tears/ The Eagle/Flower in the Crannied Wall/ The Lady of Shalott/ In Memoriam/Ulysses/ Crossing the Bar Alfred, Lord Tennyson (pp. 802–825) Critical Comment: Escaping a World of Shadows (p. 813) Spotlight On: The Enduring Arthurian Legend (pp. 826–827)	• Reader's Log pp. 803, 805, 807, 814, 821, 824 • Tercet p. 805 • Meter, Rhyme, Alliteration, Assonance p. 807	• Critical Writing: Respond to criticism of Tennyson's poems p. 825 • Critical Writing: Compare and contrast Tennyson's and Homer's heroes p. 825 • Creative Writing: Write Telemachus's reply to Ulysses' speech p. 825 • Literature and Film: Sketch storyboard with captions for "The Lady of Shalott" p. 825		
My Last Duchess/ Porphyria's Lover Robert Browning (pp. 828–836) **Connections: Scenes from a Modern Marriage** Julia Markus (p. 832)	• Reader's Log pp. 829, 833 • Dramatic monologue p. 829	• Critical Writing: Write comparison essay on themes in Browning's poems p. 836 • Creative Writing: Write dramatic monologue using voice of duchess p. 836	• Improvisational Theater: Reconstruct relationship between Porphyria and her lover/ Improvise scene for the class p. 836	
Sonnet 43 from **Sonnets from the Portuguese** Elizabeth Barrett Browning (pp. 837–839) **Student to Student** (p. 839)	• Reader's Log p. 838 • Petrarchan sonnet p. 838 • Turn p. 838	• Creative Writing: Write love poem p. 839	• Performance: Select and perform series of love poems p. 839	
Spring and Fall: To a Young Child/Pied Beauty Gerard Manley Hopkins (pp. 840–844)	• Reader's Log pp. 841, 843 • Sprung rhythm p. 840 • Assonance p. 841 • Imagery p. 843	• Critical Writing: Rewrite "Spring and Fall" in prose paraphrase p. 844 • Creative Writing: Make personal list of things that are "original, spare, strange" p. 844 • Research: Research usage and definitions of unusual terms in "Pied Beauty" p. 844		• Research usage and definitions of unusual terms in "Pied Beauty" p. 844

Collection Resources

Teaching Resources B	Audiovisual Resources Binder	Test Booklet
Cross-Curricular Activity p. 86	Fine Art Transparencies 10.1–10.2	Collection 10 Test pp. 179–180

 Computer disk or CD-ROM

 Audiocassette

 Overhead Transparency

PROGRAM RESOURCES

Electronic Media	Teaching Resources with Organizer		Audiovisual Resources Binder
	Teaching Resources B	Other Resources	
• Test Generator • Language Workshop: Noun clauses	• Teaching Notes pp. 62–64 • Reading Organizers pp. 70–72, 75–77 • Language Link pp. 73–74 • Words to Own pp. 84–85	• Language and Writing Skills Worksheet p. 81 • Test Booklet: Selection Tests pp. 165–173 • Portfolio Management System pp. 54–55, 62–63, 143–144	• Selected Readings Audiocassette 1, Side B • Elements of Literature Transparency 10.3
• Test Generator	• Teaching Notes pp. 64–65 • Reading Organizers pp. 78–79 • Language Link p. 80 • Words to Own pp. 84–85	• Test Booklet: Selection Tests pp. 174–175 • Portfolio Management System pp. 53, 62–63, 145	• Selected Reading Audiocassette 2, Side B
• Test Generator	• Teaching Notes p. 66 • Reading Organizer p. 81	• Test Booklet: Selection Test p. 176 • Portfolio Management System pp. 48–49, 62–63, 146	• Selected Reading Audiocassette 1, Side B
• Test Generator	• Teaching Notes pp. 66–67 • Reading Organizers pp. 82–83 • Words to Own pp. 84–85	• Test Booklet: Selection Tests pp. 177–178 • Portfolio Management System pp. 54–55, 62–63, 147	

Proofreading Warm-ups

You may use the following exercises to help students practice their proofreading skills. Copy a set of incorrect sentences onto the chalkboard, and have students find and correct the spelling, punctuation, usage, and mechanical errors in each sentence. Ask students to share and discuss their responses.

	Sentences with Errors	Sentences Corrected	Skills Covered
1	**a.** tennyson published In Memoriam in 1850 it is an Elegy to his closest friend who dyed young **b.** that same year Tennyson was named poet laureate and he finaly married after a fourteen year engagement	**a.** Tennyson published <u>In Memoriam</u> in 1850; it is an elegy to his closest friend, who died young. **b.** That same year, Tennyson was named poet laureate, and he finally married after a fourteen-year engagement.	Capitalization, Underline title of long poem, Semicolon usage, Spelling, Comma usage, Hyphen usage, End marks
2	**a.** tennyson had wrote alot of poetry before the gov't. granted him an annual pension **b.** altho his pension of two hundred pounds is'nt much by today's standards it was a fair am't. of money back then	**a.** Tennyson had written a lot of poetry before the government granted him an annual pension. **b.** Although his pension of two hundred pounds isn't much by today's standards, it was a fair amount of money back then.	Capitalization, Verb error, Spelling, Write out abbreviations, Apostrophe usage, Comma usage, End marks
3	**a.** queen victoria who reined from 1837–1901 morned for fourty years after Prince Albert died **b.** she took consolation in Tennysons poetic tribute to his friend, In Memoriam	**a.** Queen Victoria, who reigned from 1837 to 1901, mourned for forty years after Prince Albert died. **b.** She took consolation in Tennyson's poetic tribute to his friend, <u>In Memoriam</u>.	Capitalization, Comma usage, Spelling, Apostrophe usage, Underline title of long poem, End marks
4	**a.** ulysses was a greek leader who fought in the ten year Trojan war **b.** the poem Ulysses is about this heroe	**a.** Ulysses was a Greek leader who fought in the ten-year Trojan War. **b.** The poem "Ulysses" is about this hero.	Capitalization, Hyphen usage, Quotation marks for poem titles, Spelling, End marks
5	**a.** a poem in which the speaker address a listener is called a dramatic monologue **b.** my last duchess is a dramatic mono-logue	**a.** A poem in which the speaker addresses a listener is called a dramatic monologue. **b.** "My Last Duchess" is a dramatic mono-logue.	Capitalization, Subject-verb agreement, Quotation marks for poem titles, End marks
6	**a.** like Edgar Allan Poe an american con-temporary of his Robert Browning was fascinated w/ morbid psychology **b.** brownings poem Porphyria's Lover explore's the complexity of humane emotions	**a.** Like Edgar Allan Poe, an American con-temporary of his, Robert Browning was fascinated with morbid psychology. **b.** Browning's poem "Porphyria's Lover" explores the complexity of human emotions.	Capitalization, Comma usage, Write out abbreviation, Apostrophe usage, Quota-tion marks for poem titles, Spelling, End marks
7	**a.** elizabeth barrett who was 6 yrs. older then Robert Browning eloped with him **b.** her father forbade his 9 adult children to marry all of them lived to home	**a.** Elizabeth Barrett, who was six years older than Robert Browning, eloped with him. **b.** Her father forbade his nine adult children to marry; all of them lived at home.	Capitalization, Comma usage, Write out abbreviation and numerals, Usage, Semi-colon usage, Nonstandard usage, End marks
8	**a.** after Elizabeth Barrett eloped with Robert Browning they lived in italy **b.** her father did not never forgive Eliza-beth for her marriage and he never seen her again	**a.** After Elizabeth Barrett eloped with Robert Browning, they lived in Italy. **b.** Her father did not ever forgive Elizabeth for her marriage, and he never saw her again.	Capitalization, Comma usage, Double negatives, Verb error, End marks
9	**a.** Elizabeth Barrett Browning wrote more than fourty sonnets **b.** there all written in the traditional petrarchan or italian sonnet form	**a.** Elizabeth Barrett Browning wrote more than forty sonnets. **b.** They're all written in the traditional Petrarchan, or Italian, sonnet form.	Capitalization, Spelling, Usage, Comma usage, End marks
10	**a.** many of gerard manley hopkins poem's are characterized by something he called sprung rhythm **b.** sprung rhythm is found in Spring and Fall: To a Young Child	**a.** Many of Gerard Manley Hopkins's poems are characterized by something he called "sprung rhythm." **b.** "Sprung rhythm" is found in "Spring and Fall: To a Young Child."	Capitalization, Apostrophe usage, Quotation marks, End marks

LOVE AND LOSS

Tennyson

Browning

Barrett Browning

Hopkins

I cannot say what loves have come and gone;
I only know that summer sang in me
A little while, that in me sings no more.

—Edna St. Vincent Millay,
from "What Lips My Lips Have Kissed"

Responding to the Quotation

? What one word would you use to describe this speaker's feelings about lost love? [Possible responses: Sadness, regret, melancholy, longing, or wistfulness.]

RESPONDING TO THE ART: ABOUT THE ARTIST

Although a contemporary of the Realists Courbet and Manet, the English painter and poet Dante Gabriel Rossetti (brother of writer Christina Rossetti) disdained the trend toward authentic color and light and preferred to idealize his subjects. He disliked the material-ism and starkness of the industrial-izing world, appreciating instead the romance of the Middle Ages and Early Renaissance.

PORTFOLIO ASSESSMENT

Parent/Guardian Involve-ment For forms that will help a parent or guardian review and respond to a student's portfolio, see the *Portfolio Manage-ment System,* pp. 62–63.

PROGRAM MANAGER

- **Integrated Assessment** For a sum-mative assessment of the literature and language skills taught in this collection, see **Collection 10 Test,** *Test Booklet,* pp. 179–180.
- **Instructional Support** See **Fine Art Transparencies** 10.1–10.2. Review

teacher's notes for transparencies in the *Audiovisual Resources Binder* for suggestions on how to tie the transparencies to specific reading selections.
- **Extending Collection Theme** See **Cross-Curricular Activity: Love and**

Loss, *Teaching Resources B,* p. 86 for an activity in another discipline and for evaluation criteria.
- **Reinforcement** Use the **Words to Own** worksheet in *Teaching Resources B,* pp. 84–85.

Into the Poems

Author Biography p. 802
Before You Read p. 803, p. 805, p. 807, p. 814, p. 821, p. 824

Through the Poems

Beyond the Poems

• **Writer's Notebook:** Write a review of one of Tennyson's poems
• **Critical Writing:** Respond to a characterization of Tennyson's poems
• **Critical Writing:** Compare two poem endings
• **Critical Writing:** Research and write a comparison/contrast essay
• **Creative Writing:** Write a reply from Telemachus, using dialogue
• **Literature and Film:** Sketch a storyboard

Alfred, Lord Tennyson

(1809–1892)

When Alfred Tennyson learned that Lord Byron had died while helping Greek nationalist rebels, he went to the woods and carved on a piece of sandstone, "Byron is dead." Tennyson was fourteen years old. He felt sure that he would be a poet, and he was already practicing the dramatic gestures of the Romantic poets he admired.

Tennyson's father was a clergyman of good family but little money, who encouraged young Alfred's interest in poetry. At Cambridge University Alfred joined a group of young intellectuals, called the Apostles, who believed that their friend was destined to become the greatest poet of their generation.

In 1831, when his father died, lack of funds forced Tennyson to leave Cambridge, and he entered a troubled period. In 1832, he published his first significant book of poems, which some reviewers derided for its melancholy themes and weak imitations of Keats's language. The next year Tennyson was devastated by the death of his closest friend, Arthur Henry Hallam. He became engaged to marry in 1836, but the marriage was postponed for fourteen years because of his uncertain financial prospects. In 1843, he invested in a woodcarving machine and lost what little remained of his family's money.

During this difficult period, when both his physical and mental health suffered, Tennyson apparently never considered any career but poetry. He polished his style to develop the melodious line and rich imagery of poems like "The Lady of Shalott." Tennyson published almost nothing in his "ten years' silence" from 1832 to 1842, but the friends to whom he read his poems remained convinced of his promise.

Gradually, Tennyson began to make his way. The two-volume *Poems* (1842) was favorably reviewed, and in 1845 the government granted him an annual pension of two hundred pounds. In 1850, he published *In Memoriam,* an elegy to

Caricature of Alfred, Lord Tennyson (1872) by Frederick Waddy.

The Granger Collection, New York.

Hallam that was immediately successful. It tells the story of his own recovery of faith in the immortality of the soul and of the harmony of creation—despite the new, unsettling discoveries of science and his deep sense of the unfairness of Hallam's death. That year, he was named poet laureate (after Wordsworth's death), and he finally married. Now Tennyson settled into the long, successful career that had been expected of him, and for the rest of his life he was considered the greatest living English poet.

In the forty years before his death in 1892, Tennyson published nearly a dozen volumes of poems. These include *The Idylls of the King,* which makes the rise, fall, and possible return of King Arthur into a kind of parable about the moral qualities of good political leaders and of their betrayal by the rest of us. His books sold like best-selling novels and made him rich. In 1884, he was made a peer of the realm and became Alfred, Lord Tennyson.

Tennyson never lost the melancholy and sense of chaos that friends and reviewers found in his early poems. He was immensely popular with his contemporaries because he spoke in a beautiful, measured language of their sense of the precariousness and sadness of life. And he also assured his readers that his own experience of sadness and disorder had taught him that everything was part of a benevolent plan in which eventually all losses would be made good.

PORTFOLIO ASSESSMENT

Portfolio Assessment For help with teacher assessment of reading skills, see the *Portfolio Management System,* pp. 54–55.

BEFORE YOU READ
TEARS, IDLE TEARS

Reading Focus

Shadows of the Past

Remembering the past: do you find it sad or satisfying to look backward? You're probably thinking, "Obviously, that depends on what's being remembered— happy or sad times." But is that the only view? Is there a way in which memory itself—the very *fact* of the past—always shadows life in the present?

Quickwrite

READER'S LOG

How can tears be "idle"—can you cry without knowing why? Write a quick response.

Background

This poem is the most famous of eleven lyric songs that are interspersed in *The Princess,* a long narrative poem about women's education and emancipation. Tennyson wrote the lyric while visiting Tintern Abbey in the autumn, the same site Wordsworth contemplated in his famous meditation (page 658).

Disappointed Love (1821) by Francis Danby.
By Courtesy of The Board of Trustees of the Victoria and Albert Museum, London.

ALFRED, LORD TENNYSON **803**

Into the Poem

Using BEFORE YOU READ p. 803

Quickwrite

Remind students to choose a situation they would not mind sharing. Ask the class for circumstances that might prompt melancholy feelings—a dreary day; slow, sad music; ceremonies like graduation—and ask students why these circumstances might bring on idle tears.

ABOUT THE AUTHOR

During his lifetime, Tennyson enjoyed the type of popularity that is given today to rock and movie stars and top athletes. In the biography *Tennyson: Aspects of His Life, Character and Poetry,* Harold Nicolson says that Tennyson's birthdays took on the gravity of a national celebration; his compatriots sent honey, garden chairs, and rolls of tweed. Lakes, cliffs, and roses were named in his honor. Tennyson's actions, his clothes, and his tobacco were chronicled in the journals.

PROGRAM MANAGER

- **Planning Instruction** See **Teaching Notes,** *Teaching Resources B,* pp. 62–64, for additional historical and biographical information for these poems.
- **Instructional Support** Before beginning the instructional lesson, see **Graphic Organizers for Active Reading,** *Teaching Resources B,*

pp. 70–72 and 75–77, for Through the Poem activities.
- **Audiotaped Readings** To help auditory learners, use the **Selected Reading, Audiocassette 1, Side B,** in the *Audiovisual Resources Binder.*

- **Assessment** See **Selection Tests,** *Test Booklet,* pp. 165–173.
- **Language Link** For instruction and practice in noun clauses, see **Language Link,** *Teaching Resources B,* pp. 73–74, and *Language and Writing Skills Worksheets,* p. 81.

A. Critical Reading: Drawing Conclusions

? Why might you expect the speaker of this poem to be an older person? [Talk of the "good old days" is associated with the elderly; the "autumn fields" might symbolize a speaker in the "autumn" of life.] In fact, Tennyson said that in this poem he was attempting to capture "the yearning that young people occasionally experience for that which seems to have passed away from them for ever."

B. Reader's Response: Shaping Interpretations

? Why do you think Tennyson appeals to so many senses? [Sample responses: He is trying to make an abstract idea easy to understand; he wants to show that the feeling of loss has affected every aspect of the speaker's life.]

Making Meanings

First Thoughts

1. Remind students to refer to their Reader's Logs responses.

Shaping Interpretations

2. The poem begins with a statement of an emotion (ll. 1–3) and then analyzes the cause of that emotion in the scenes that follow. Scenes include fields in autumn, sunrise and sunset, a summer dawn, and remembered kisses after a loved one has died. The scenes seem somewhat chronological.

3. Most students will agree that the poem's sequence of images creates an increasingly dark tone. The poem moves from simple images of autumn fields, to images of boats carrying the dead, to images of birds singing to dying ears, to intimate images of a dead loved one.

4. Students may agree that *divine despair* refers to the Biblical fall; human beings are destined to struggle, to experience sorrow, and to die.

Tears, Idle Tears

Alfred, Lord Tennyson

> **A** Tears, idle tears, I know not what they mean,
> Tears from the depth of some divine despair
> Rise in the heart, and gather to the eyes,
> In looking on the happy autumn fields,
> 5 And thinking of the days that are no more.
>
> Fresh as the first beam glittering on a sail,
> That brings our friends up from the underworld,
> Sad as the last which reddens over one
> That sinks with all we love below the verge;
> 10 So sad, so fresh, the days that are no more.
>
> **B** Ah, sad and strange as in dark summer dawns
> The earliest pipe of half-awakened birds
> To dying ears, when unto dying eyes
> The casement slowly grows a glimmering square;
> 15 So sad, so strange, the days that are no more.
>
> Dear as remembered kisses after death,
> And sweet as those by hopeless fancy feigned
> On lips that are for others; deep as love,
> Deep as first love, and wild with all regret;
> 20 O Death in Life, the days that are no more!

The Offer by Thomas Faed (1866).

MAKING MEANINGS

First Thoughts

1. After reading this poem, would you change what you wrote about "idle tears" in your Reader's Log entry? Why or why not?

Shaping Interpretations

2. What is the scene of each stanza of "Tears, Idle Tears"? Why do you think Tennyson orders the stanzas as he does?

3. Do you think the poem's sequence of images creates an increasingly dark **tone**? Explain.

4. What do you think the "divine despair" is in line 2? Could you relate it to Adam and Eve's fall in Genesis (page 416)—would that story explain the speaker's existential sadness? Explain.

5. Stanzas 2–4 present a series of comparisons that attempt to make concrete the abstract memory of "the days that are no more." What are these comparisons?

Connecting with the Text

6. Does the contradiction in the phrase "Death in Life" (line 20) make sense to you? Explain. What is your response to this line? Have you ever felt this way?

5. In stanza 2, the days past are as fresh as the first beam of the rising sun and as sad as the last sunbeam. In stanza 3, they are as sad as the morning sound of birds to dying ears, as sad as the morning light to dying eyes. In stanza 4, they are as dear as kisses remembered after death, as sweet as imagined kisses, and as deep as first love.

Connecting with the Text

6. Responses will vary. Some students may say that the phrase suggests that thinking of the past is like experiencing death in the midst of life. *Remind students to choose a situation they would not mind sharing with others.*

Reading Focus

Lessons Large and Small
The poet, the scientist, and the religious believer don't necessarily have conflicting ideas about the phrase *mysteries of nature*. And yet to some nineteenth-century artists and believers, modern science's scrutiny of nature was a threat—a fearful one. Would a microscope reveal the secrets of matter, but at the expense of our traditional concepts of beauty and faith?

Part of Tennyson's immense popularity was that he addressed these philosophical issues and, for many, offered ways of resolving them.

A Dialogue with the Text

Stop after reading each poem, and jot down what quality of nature you think each poem evokes.

Elements of Literature

Tercet
Although Tennyson called "The Eagle" a fragment, its verse form and organization give it a feeling of completeness. Each stanza is a **tercet:** three lines with one rhyme. The eagle and the world are at rest in the first stanza and are moving in the second.

The Eagle: A Fragment

Alfred, Lord Tennyson

He clasps the crag with crooked hands; **A**
Close to the sun in lonely lands,
Ringed with the azure world, he stands.

The wrinkled sea beneath him crawls; **B**
He watches from his mountain walls,
And like a thunderbolt he falls. **C**

ALFRED, LORD TENNYSON **805**

Into the Poem

Using BEFORE YOU READ p. 805

A Dialogue with the Text

After students have read the poem once, invite them to create a cluster diagram in their Reader's Logs. At the center, ask them to write the quality of nature they believe the poem evokes and to cluster words or phrases from the text that support their choice.

Through the Poem

A. Reader's Response: First Thoughts

? What would you expect an eagle to use for clasping? [Sample responses: Claws, talons.] Why, then, do you think Tennyson chose the word *hands?* [Sample responses: The language suggests that there is a kinship between the eagle and the speaker or reader; perhaps humans and eagles have similar characteristics.]

B. Critical Reading: Finding Details

Challenge students to identify words and phrases that create an image of the eagle as a lordly but solitary creature. [Sample responses: Lordliness is suggested by the eagle's position above the everyday world, while the sea "crawls" beneath his presence. His solitude is suggested by Tennyson's choice to associate him with inanimate aspects of nature rather than with other living creatures.]

C. Literary Element: Tercet

Encourage students to identify the **rhymes** in the poems and to consider as they read how these rhymes affect the **tone** of each poem.

OPTIONS FOR TEACHING

STRATEGIES FOR INCLUSION

Less Proficient Readers/Visual To give students a context for "Tears, Idle Tears," display one picture for each scene—autumn fields, a sunset, the world at dawn, and a remembered kiss. Encourage students to focus on the emotion each scene evokes. Then, ask students to determine how each scene represents memories of the past.

Advanced Invite interested students to compare "The Eagle: A Fragment" to Ted Hughes's "Hawk Roosting" (p. 965) or Gerard Manley Hopkins's "The Windhover." Have students present their findings to the class in a short oral report. ☞

A. Reader's Response: First Thoughts

? What do you think it is about this flower that sparks the speaker's eagerness to understand? [Sample responses: The flower's delicate beauty; its ability to survive in the cranny of a wall.]

B. Literary Element: Rhyme

? What is the rhyme scheme of this short poem? [abccab] What type of rhyme falls in ll. 2 and 6, and why might those lines be different? [The rhyme is slant rhyme; the idea is more important than the exactness of the rhyme.]

Making Meanings

First Thoughts

1. Students may say that the speaker admires delicate beauty .

Shaping Interpretations

2. The eagle perches on a high mountaintop, surrounded by blue sky, watching the sea below. The waves make the sea look wrinkled from the high perch. The comparison to thunder suggests power in the eagle's sudden flight.

3. From up high, the waves probably look like wrinkles. Like the thunderbolt, the eagle is quick and powerful.

4. Responses will vary. "All in all" may refer not to just the flower, but to everything that life and nature represent. If the speaker could understand the creation of a flower, he would better understand the relationship between God and all living things.

5. The beauty and strength of nature or the isolation of the individual.

Challenging the Text

6. **(Analysis)** Students may agree that the flower represents isolation, majesty, or tenacity and inspires the speaker. A scientist might analyze the parts or purpose of the flower and be impressed by its perfect adaptation to its environment.

Flower in the Crannied Wall

Alfred, Lord Tennyson

Flower in the crannied wall,
I pluck you out of the crannies,
I hold you here, root and all, in my hand,
Little flower—but *if* I could understand
What you are, root and all, and all in all,
I should know what God and man is.

MAKING MEANINGS

The Eagle: A Fragment
Flower in the Crannied Wall

First Thoughts

1. What contrasting qualities of nature do you think Tennyson captures in these lyrics? (Check your Reader's Log.)

Shaping Interpretations

2. How does Tennyson use the **tercet** form to describe what is happening in "The Eagle"?

3. How could the sea, in "The Eagle," be "wrinkled"? What is suggested about the eagle's power in the last **simile**?

4. What do you think "all in all" (line 5) means in "Flower in the Crannied Wall"? What does the speaker seek to learn from the flower?

5. Suppose the eagle and the flower are used as **symbols.** What would you say they symbolize to Tennyson?

Challenging the Text

6. Do you agree with what Tennyson says a flower could tell us? How would a scientist regard the same flower?

Strategic Reading As they study Tennyson's poems, have students keep a double-entry chart in their Reader's Logs. In the left column, they should note words and phrases that catch their attention. In the right column, they may offer comments or interpretations as they read.

Speaking and Listening Have students meet in groups of three and work through "The Eagle: A Fragment" and "Flower in the Crannied Wall" in Read-Around fashion, changing readers with each line. Students who have come to "own" certain lines by reading them aloud should comment on those lines in class discussion.

Reading Focus

Shattering Glass

One of the main symbols in this dreamlike ballad is a mirror that the Lady uses with her weaving. Watch for how the mirror with its reflected images is in opposition to the "real" world. This is only one opposition, or tension, in the world of the Lady of Shalott, of whom Tennyson said: "The newborn love for something, for someone in the wide world from which she had been so long secluded, takes her out of the region of shadows into that of realities."

A Dialogue with the Text

As you read, be alert to oppositions—in setting, actions, or imagery—and record the first example you notice. Then, when Sir Lancelot appears in Part III, jot down at least one other contrast that he introduces.

Elements of Literature

Word Music

Be sure to read this poem aloud to hear the famous music of Tennyson's language. That music is created by the expert use of *meter* and by the dazzling use of **rhymes, alliteration,** and **assonance.** For many years schoolchildren in both England and the United States could recite the mysterious story of the Lady of Shalott from memory. You might try it.

Using **BEFORE YOU READ** p. 807

Reading Focus

Ask students to decide, as they read, the purpose of the mirror in this poem. Invite them to think of other tales that involve mirrors ["Snow White," *Alice in Wonderland.*] and to compare or contrast the purposes of mirrors in these different stories.

PROGRAM MANAGER

Application and Reinforcement For reinforcement of the elements of literature introduced in this lesson, see **Transparency 10.3** in the *Audiovisual Resources Binder.*

The Lady of Shalott (1888) by John William Waterhouse.

Tate Gallery, London.

ALFRED, LORD TENNYSON 807

STRATEGIES FOR INCLUSION

Visual/Spatial As the narrator of "The Lady of Shalott" speaks of the Lady and her relationship to Camelot, sketch on the chalkboard (or have students sketch on paper) a rough map of the location: the river and its island, the barley and rye fields, the rolling hills, the highway, and Camelot itself. Students might then re-read the poem and discuss how having a map aids their understanding.

English Language Development So that English-language learners can more easily negotiate the meaning of this poem, have them write a short summary of each of the parts. When they reach the end of a section, have them write in their Reader's Logs one or two sentences that capture the main idea of that part. You may want to have these students work with English-proficient peers so that they have a consultant for the more difficult and archaic language forms.

Bodily-Kinesthetic Have volunteers re-create the scene in the tower to show how the Lady would have been weaving, using the mirror and its reflection of the outside world.

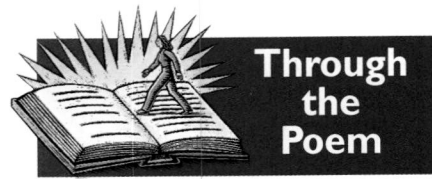
A. Reader's Response: First Thoughts

? What images come to mind when you hear of "many-towered Camelot"? [Sample responses: A beautiful castle; knights in armor; a bygone world of fantasy.]

B. Critical Reading: Analyzing Setting

? How do the details set up a contrast within this stanza? [Possible answer: The details in ll. 10–14 suggest a setting of color and movement; the details in ll. 15–18 suggest drabness and silence.]

C. Literary Element: Word Music

The short, rhythmic lines, the consecutive rhyming words, and the repetition of *Camelot*, *Shalott*, and later *Lancelot* contribute to the poem's music.

The Lady of Shalott

Alfred, Lord Tennyson

Part I

On either side the river lie
Long fields of barley and of rye,
That clothe the wold° and meet the sky;
And through the field the road runs by
5   To many-towered Camelot;°
And up and down the people go,
Gazing where the lilies blow°
Round an island there below,
     The island of Shalott.

10 Willows whiten,° aspens quiver,
Little breezes dusk and shiver
Through the wave that runs forever
By the island in the river
     Flowing down to Camelot.
15 Four gray walls, and four gray towers,
Overlook a space of flowers,
And the silent isle imbowers°
     The Lady of Shalott.

By the margin, willow-veiled,
20 Slide the heavy barges trailed
By slow horses; and unhailed
The shallop° flitteth silken-sailed
     Skimming down to Camelot:
But who hath seen her wave her hand?
25 Or at the casement seen her stand?
Or is she known in all the land,
     The Lady of Shalott?

Only reapers, reaping early
In among the bearded barley,
30 Hear a song that echoes cheerly°
From the river winding clearly,
     Down to towered Camelot;
And by the moon the reaper weary,
Piling sheaves in uplands airy,
35 Listening, whispers "'Tis the fairy
     Lady of Shalott."

3. wold: rolling plain.

5. Camelot: legendary city, site of King Arthur's court and Round Table.

7. blow: blossom.

10. whiten: show the white undersides of their leaves when blown by the wind.

17. imbowers: shelters with trees, gardens, and flowers.

22. shallop: small, open boat.

30. cheerly: archaic for "cheerily."

OPTIONS FOR TEACHING

INTEGRATING THE LANGUAGE ARTS

Strategic Reading As students work through "The Lady of Shalott," have them note in their Reader's Logs anything that creates a strong mental image or that moves them. Then, consolidate images that provide an overall tone for the poem by keeping notes on the chalkboard as students share their notes with the class.

Writing: News Feature Assign groups of three or four to produce a news feature about the mysterious death of the Lady of Shalott. Encourage students to "interview" the reapers who heard her song and the residents of Camelot, to reenact the preparation of the boat, to show closing comments made at her grave, and so on. Students may report "live" or go "on location" with videotape. Encourage the class to comment on the content and presentation of each report.

The Lady of Shalott (c. 1886–1905)
by William Holman Hunt. Oil.

©Manchester City Art Galleries, England.

Part II

There she weaves by night and day
A magic web with colors gay.
She has heard a whisper say,
40   A curse is on her if she stay
        To look down to Camelot.
She knows not what the curse may be,
And so she weaveth steadily,
And little other care hath she,
45   The Lady of Shalott.

And moving through a mirror clear°
That hangs before her all the year,
Shadows of the world appear.
There she sees the highway near
50   Winding down to Camelot;
There the river eddy whirls,
And there the surly village churls,°
And the red cloaks of market girls,
        Pass onward from Shalott.

46. mirror clear: Weavers worked
on the back of the tapestry so that
they could easily knot their yarns.
To see the front of their designs,
weavers looked in a mirror that
reflected the front of the tapestry.

52. churls: peasants; country folk.

ALFRED, LORD TENNYSON 809

CROSSING THE CURRICULUM

Fine Arts Challenge students to gather information about tapestries (for example, *The Hunt of the Unicorn* series that is displayed in New York City's museum of medieval art, The Cloisters). Then, have students sketch or paint what they think the Lady is creating on her loom. Note that, according to l. 65, she depicts "the mirror's magic sights." Work with students to create a display of the finished "tapestries."

Music Have pairs or groups of students attempt a musical interpretation of part or all of "The Lady of Shalott," either creating melodies or using established musical works. Set aside some class time for students to share their music.

A. Literary Element: Theme

Ask students how ll. 62–63 reinforce the sense of the Lady's isolation. [These lines contrast sharply with the people described in ll. 52–61—the damsels, the knights, all on their way to Camelot—and show that the Lady is conscious of the fact that she has no companion or connection to society.]

B. Critical Reading: Predicting

Tennyson himself said these two lines are a key to the poem (Critical Comment, p. 813). If the Lady means what she says, what do you think she will do? [Possible answers: She might leave her island and go to Camelot, despite the curse, or she might attempt to thwart the curse by bringing people from Camelot to Shalott.]

C. Expansion

In Arthurian legend, Lancelot is something of an enigma—he is the most noble of the knights of the Round Table, yet he seduces the queen and plays a key role in Camelot's demise. (In chasing after Lancelot and Guinevere, Arthur loses his unguarded throne to Mordred and, in the resulting fight for the kingship, is killed.) Point out that the arrival of Sir Lancelot in the poem is so momentous that Tennyson chooses to rhyme *Lancelot* (l. 77) with *Shalott* (l. 81)—the only place in the poem where *Camelot* is not the rhyming word.

D. Literary Element: Alliteration

Note the effects created by the alliterative *g* and *b* sounds in ll. 84–85 and 87. Encourage students to whisper these lines to themselves to get a feel for the alliteration.

E. Critical Reading: Speculating

Meteors, shooting stars, comets—all have been regarded as harbingers of misfortune, even catastrophe. Note that Lancelot's gleaming armor makes him seem like a "bearded meteor" above Shalott, pointed toward Camelot. Ask students whether they think the simile suggests disaster. [In retrospect, students should note that Lancelot's arrival results in the Lady's death. They also may remember that Lancelot eventually plays a part in the demise of Camelot.]

---

55 Sometimes a troop of damsels glad,
       An abbot on an ambling pad,°
       Sometimes a curly shepherd lad,
       Or long-haired page in crimson clad,
              Goes by to towered Camelot;
60 And sometimes through the mirror blue
       The knights come riding two and two:
       She hath no loyal knight and true,
              The Lady of Shalott.

A But in her web she still delights
65 To weave the mirror's magic sights,
       For often through the silent nights
       A funeral, with plumes and lights
              And music, went to Camelot;
       Or when the moon was overhead,
70 Came two young lovers lately wed:
       "I am half sick of shadows," said
B   The Lady of Shalott.

Part III

       A bowshot from her bower eaves,
       He rode between the barley sheaves,
75 The sun came dazzling through the leaves,
       And flamed upon the brazen greaves°
C   Of bold Sir Lancelot.
       A red-cross knight° forever kneeled
       To a lady in his shield,
80 That sparkled on the yellow field,
              Beside remote Shalott.

       The gemmy° bridle glittered free,
       Like to some branch of stars we see
       Hung in the golden Galaxy.°
85 The bridle bells rang merrily
              As he rode down to Camelot;
D And from his blazoned baldric° slung
       A mighty silver bugle hung,
       And as he rode his armor rung,
90   Beside remote Shalott.

       All in the blue unclouded weather
       Thick-jeweled shone the saddle leather,
       The helmet and the helmet feather
       Burned like one burning flame together,
95   As he rode down to Camelot;
E As often through the purple night,
       Below the starry clusters bright,
       Some bearded meteor, trailing light,
              Moves over still Shalott.

810 THE VICTORIAN PERIOD

---

56. pad: easy-gaited horse.

76. greaves: armor for the lower legs.

78. red-cross knight: The red cross is the emblem of St. George, England's patron saint.

82. gemmy: set with jewels.

84. Galaxy: Milky Way.

87. blazoned baldric: richly decorated sash worn across the chest diagonally.

₁₀₀ His broad clear brow in sunlight glowed;
On burnished° hooves his war horse trode;
From underneath his helmet flowed
His coal-black curls as on he rode,
    As he rode down to Camelot.
₁₀₅ From the bank and from the river
He flashed into the crystal mirror,
"Tirra lirra," by the river
    Sang Sir Lancelot.

She left the web, she left the loom,
₁₁₀ She made three paces through the room,
She saw the waterlily bloom,
She saw the helmet and the plume,
    She looked down to Camelot.
Out flew the web and floated wide;
₁₁₅ The mirror cracked from side to side;
"The curse is come upon me," cried
    The Lady of Shalott.

Part IV

In the stormy east wind straining,
The pale yellow woods were waning,
₁₂₀ The broad stream in his banks complaining,
Heavily the low sky raining
    Over towered Camelot;
Down she came and found a boat
Beneath a willow left afloat,
₁₂₅ And round about the prow° she wrote
    The Lady of Shalott.

And down the river's dim expanse
Like some bold seër° in a trance,
Seeing all his own mischance—
₁₃₀ With a glassy countenance
    Did she look to Camelot.
And at the closing of the day
She loosed the chain, and down she lay;
The broad stream bore her far away,
₁₃₅   The Lady of Shalott.

Lying, robed in snowy white
That loosely flew to left and right—
The leaves upon her falling light—
Through the noises of the night
₁₄₀   She floated down to Camelot;
And as the boat head wound along
The willowy hills and fields among,
They heard her singing her last song,
    The Lady of Shalott.

101. burnished: polished.

125. prow: front part of a boat.

128. seër: prophet.

ALFRED, LORD TENNYSON 811

F. Literary Element: Climax

? How does Lancelot's arrival bring the narrative to its point of greatest tension? [The Lady's desire for a better look at Lancelot causes her to defy the curse. Somewhere between that first glance and that final step to the window, she had to weigh the threat of the curse against the fulfilling of her heart's desire.] Point out the irony that Lancelot continues on to Camelot, never realizing the effect that he has had upon the Lady.

G. Literary Element: Pathetic Fallacy

A pathetic fallacy occurs when a writer uses nature to reflect human emotions and moods. How does this stanza qualify as a pathetic fallacy? [Possible answer: The Lady of Shalott knows that she is doomed. The roughness of the wind and the river may symbolize her doom (or may be nature's protest against it); the sky is raining over Camelot.]

H. Reader's Response: First Thoughts

? Why do you think the Lady feels it important to write her title around the prow of her boat? [Sample responses: It probably will provide the only identification of the corpse of this isolated woman; perhaps it is part of her final artistic expression.]

I. Critical Reading: Making Inferences

? What is the significance of the Lady's dressing in white? [Possible answers: Perhaps it represents the purity of the isolated, artistic life she is leaving behind; if she is traveling to Camelot out of devotion to Lancelot, she may imagine herself as a bride.]

? What **tone** does Lancelot's prayer establish at the conclusion of this narrative? Explain. [The prayer is ironic, for it is only at her death that the Lady of Shalott wins the attention of Lancelot, the object of her desire and the indirect cause of her death.]

Making Meanings

First Thoughts

1. The Lady must die if she leaves her weaving and her isolated existence for the outside world. Lines 39–45 first indicate there may be some sort of curse. When she finally decides to look out the window and leave her room, the Lady acts as if she knows she is doomed and the mirror cracks so that she no longer sees her art or her view of the world.

Shaping Interpretations

2. The plot involves the lonely existence of the Lady of Shalott, who lives in the castle and spends her days weaving. A curse warns the Lady not to look at the world outside. The climax is when a song entices her to look out the window and she is compelled to leave her secluded world.

3. The poem is written chiefly in iambic tetrameter. (The last line of each stanza is iambic trimeter.) For emphasis, many lines are trochaic and open with a stressed syllable (ll. 7–8, 10–17). The rhyme scheme is *aaaabcccb*. The poem's lilt comes from alliteration such as "Willows whiten" (l. 10) or "silken-sailed" (l. 22) and assonance such as "Listening, whispers" (l. 35).

145   Heard a carol, mournful, holy,
      Chanted loudly, chanted lowly,
      Till her blood was frozen slowly,
      And her eyes were darkened wholly,
           Turned to towered Camelot.
150   For ere she reached upon the tide
      The first house by the waterside,
      Singing in her song she died,
           The Lady of Shalott.

      Under tower and balcony,
155   By garden wall and gallery,
      A gleaming shape she floated by,
      Dead-pale between the houses high,
           Silent into Camelot.
      Out upon the wharfs they came,
160   Knight and burgher,° lord and dame,
      And round the prow they read her name,
           The Lady of Shalott.

      Who is this? and what is here?
      And in the lighted palace near
165   Died the sound of royal cheer;
      And they crossed themselves for fear,
           All the knights at Camelot:
      But Lancelot mused a little space;
      He said, "She has a lovely face;
170   God in his mercy lend her grace,
           The Lady of Shalott."

160. **burgher:** townsperson.

The Lady of Shalott (19th century) by John William Waterhouse.

812 THE VICTORIAN PERIOD

Thematic Connections: "Love and Loss"
Point out that the Lady of Shalott's decisions—first to go to the window and then to travel to Camelot—are not easy for her to make. Ask students what conflicts relating to the ideas of love

and loss the Lady of Shalott faces. [She is attracted to society and possibly to romance, but she also loves her art. By literally turning her back on her loom, she will lose not only her art but her life as well.]

Critical Comment

Escaping a World of Shadows

Readers may differ in regard to the meaning or moral of the simple story this richly ornamented and carefully wrought poem tells. As you learned before you read the poem, no one should disregard the clue offered by Tennyson himself: "The newborn love for something," he said of the Lady of Shalott, "for someone in the wide world from which she had been so long secluded, takes her out of the region of shadows into that of realities." He is referring particularly to the last lines of Part II when, having watched a young bride and groom in the moonlight, the Lady declares that she is "half sick of shadows."

Like the weaving that perpetually occupies the heroine—"A magic web with colors gay" —

the narrative moves from scene to scene with a tapestried grace that quietly captures the romantic heart of the Age of Chivalry. The Lady is appropriately beautiful, wan, sequestered, and mysterious. Sir Lancelot, panoplied to the hilt with every object in the book of heraldry, is less a man than a vision of a man. And Camelot itself, "many-towered," exists like a little city afloat in time.

The "mirror clear" in line 46 is crucial to both the poem's narrative line and to its meaning. In the custom of weavers, the Lady has placed this mirror in a spot facing the loom from which she is able to see at a glance how her work is going. But, for the purposes of the story, the more important function of the mirror is to allow the Lady glimpses or "shadows" of the world in which she takes no part.

MAKING MEANINGS

First Thoughts

1. What do you think the Lady's "curse" is? Why do you think so?

Shaping Interpretations

2. Summarize the main events in the **plot** of this narrative poem. What moment marks its climax?

3. Scan the poem to find its metrical form. What is its **rhyme scheme**? What examples of **alliteration** and **assonance** help create the haunting music?

4. Point out **images** of dazzling light associated with Sir Lancelot in Part III. Find contrasting images associated with the Lady. What do you think is the meaning of this contrast? (Refer to your Reader's Log notes.)

5. Explain why lines 66–72 could **foreshadow** Lancelot's arrival and the Lady's actions in the

second half of the poem. What yearning do you think the Lady expresses when she exclaims, "I am half sick of shadows" (line 71)?

6. How does Tennyson contrast the Lady's life with the lives of the villagers and court in Camelot? Do you think that Tennyson indicates a preference for any of these ways of life?

7. This poem was written during Tennyson's ten years of silence. Can you see any connection between the poem and his own life? Explain.

Challenging the Text

8. Think of the "magic web" the Lady weaves and the conditions under which she creates her art. What commentary do you think Tennyson is making on the role and life of an artist? How do you feel about his ideas? When would artistic seclusion be necessary, and when might it be undesirable?

4. The sun flames on his "brazen greaves"; his shield sparkles; his bridle glitters like a branch of stars. Lancelot contrasts with the Lady's world of shadows. Even her castle is gray. The contrast sums up the gloom of Shalott.

5. The Lady notices two young lovers and is envious of them. These feelings could foreshadow her falling in love with Lancelot and her decision to leave the tower. When she says she is "half sick of shadows," she means she is tired of living her life apart from the world and wants to experience life firsthand.

6. The Lady lives alone in a world of shadows, seeing the world only as a reflection in a mirror while villagers and the court go down the road to Camelot. The Lady's remark, "I am half sick of shadows," might indicate the poet believes any participation in life is preferable to nonparticipation.

7. Tennyson may have seen himself as isolated by his art, poetry; just as the lady must weave in her tower, he may have felt he had to write alone.

Challenging the Text

8. **(Evaluation)** Tennyson seems to be making a statement about the private versus the public roles of an artist. In this poem, the artist finds that isolation is unsatisfying, but public participation destroys both the art and the artist. Students may see his point, or they may say that artists must associate with the rest of the world if their art is to be relevant. An artist who turns from art to the ordinary world may find that his or her art is affected.

ASSESSMENT TOOLS

Into the Poem

Using BEFORE YOU READ p. 814

Quickwrite

Remind students to choose a situation they would not mind sharing. Ask students to consider how, in modern times, a person may be remembered in the world after death. Students might suggest contributions to society such as art, literature, a family, a business or product, or political change.

BEFORE YOU READ
FROM IN MEMORIAM A.H.H.

Reading Focus

Surviving Grief

Why? That is often the first question an early or terrible death wrings from us. Tragic loss can make life seem arbitrary or ruthless; grief can even cause us to question our personal beliefs.

Quickwrite

Think of someone (perhaps a public figure) you have admired but who has died. What questions did that death raise for you?

Background

In Memoriam (Latin for "in memory of") is Tennyson's elegy for Arthur Henry Hallam, his closest friend at Cambridge and his sister's fiancé. Hallam, who died of a sudden brain seizure, was thought to be an extraordinarily promising young man, and his death shook the poet deeply.

Tennyson struggled to survive not only his grief but also the religious doubt that Hallam's death bred. In the 132 separate lyrics of his elegy, which was written over seventeen years, Tennyson asks and gradually answers profound questions about life and death, religion and science, and the immortality of the soul.

Autumn Morning (19th century) by John Atkinson Grimshaw.

Christopher Wood Gallery, London.

from In Memoriam A.H.H.

Alfred, Lord Tennyson

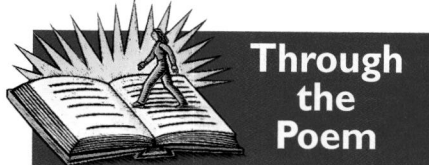

55

    The wish, that of the living whole Ⓐ
       No life may fail beyond the grave,
       Derives it not from what we have
    The likest God within the soul?

5 Are God and Nature then at strife, Ⓑ
       That Nature lends such evil dreams?
       So careful of the type° she seems,
    So careless of the single life,

    That I, considering everywhere
10   Her secret meaning in her deeds,
       And finding that of fifty seeds
    She often brings but one to bear,

    I falter where I firmly trod,
       And falling with my weight of cares
15   Upon the great world's altar stairs
    That slope through darkness up to God,

    I stretch lame hands of faith, and grope,
       And gather dust and chaff, and call Ⓒ
       To what I feel is Lord of all,
20 And faintly trust the larger hope.°

7. type: species.

56

    "So careful of the type?" but no.
       From scarpèd° cliff and quarried stone
       She° cries, "A thousand types are gone;
    I care for nothing, all shall go.

5 "Thou makest thine appeal to me:
       I bring to life, I bring to death;
       The spirit does but mean the breath: Ⓓ
    I know no more." And he, shall he,

    Man, her last work, who seemed so fair,
10   Such splendid purpose in his eyes,
       Who rolled the psalm to wintry skies,
    Who built him fanes° of fruitless prayer, Ⓔ

    Who trusted God was love indeed Ⓕ
       And love Creation's final law—
15   Though Nature, red in tooth and claw°
    With ravine, shrieked against his creed—

20. larger hope: Tennyson explains this phrase in his *Memoirs:* "that the whole human race would through, perhaps, ages of suffering, be at length purified and saved."

2. scarpèd: eroded to a steep slope.
3. She: Nature.

12. fanes: temples.

15. red . . . claw: The phrase refers to the view of all life as a ruthless struggle for survival.

ALFRED, LORD TENNYSON 815

A. Critical Reading: Identifying Main Ideas

Ask students to rephrase this wish. [Possible answers: That life would not end at death, that there is an afterlife of some sort.]

B. Expansion

As the speaker tries to make sense of his loss, he turns to what his culture sees as the two great controlling forces of existence. The expanded scientific inquiry of the Victorian age often challenged views of God and Nature. On the basis of that fact, Tennyson can be said to be writing not only for himself but for his era.

C. Reader's Response: Shaping Interpretations

❓ Why can the speaker grasp only "dust and chaff" (the husks of grain, which are discarded in the winnowing process)? [Sample responses: His hands are too weak to hold anything more substantial; the answers to existence that his era has offered him fail to satisfy him.]

D. Critical Reading: Finding Details

❓ How does the poem say that Nature feels about human beings? [Nature brings everything to life and to death but does not particularly worry about the fate of humans.]

E. Language Note: Syntax

Be sure students understand that the question in l. 8 beginning "And he, shall he" is interrupted by several lines and does not continue until l. 19, "Be blown about the desert dust."

F. Exploring the Historical Period

Remind students that, especially during the earlier part of the era, the British took pride in material, intellectual, and moral progress.

OPTIONS FOR TEACHING

STRATEGIES FOR INCLUSION

Learners Having Difficulty To help students break the poem into manageable parts, give them clear transparency sheets to place over the poem in their text. Also, give them two different colors of highlighters. Ask students to read the poem and to highlight the pairs of rhyming lines in each stanza with the same color (ll. 1 and 4 with one color and 2 and 3 with the other color). Then, have students work in small groups to paraphrase each stanza.

Spatial To clarify the speaker's changes of heart and mind in the poem, ask students to draw chronological story boxes to show the progression of the speaker's thoughts.

Picture 1	Picture 2	Picture 3	Picture 4

☞

A. Reader's Response: Shaping Interpretations

? What might this sentence mean? [Sample responses: The dragons fighting each other are mellow in comparison to a God who will let humans simply die and turn to dust. Or it may mean that humans without a soul are out of step with the world, discordant, and more horrible than raging dragons.]

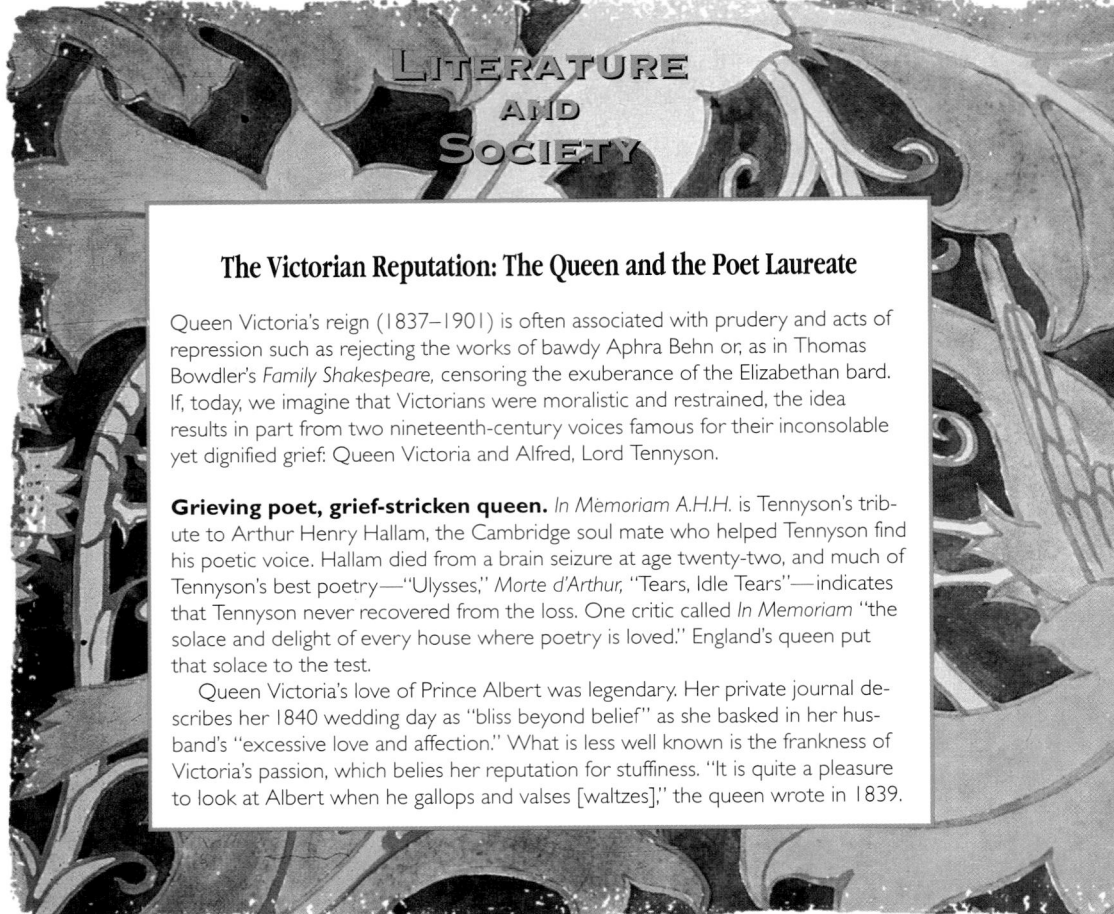

LITERATURE AND SOCIETY

The Victorian Reputation: The Queen and the Poet Laureate

Queen Victoria's reign (1837–1901) is often associated with prudery and acts of repression such as rejecting the works of bawdy Aphra Behn or, as in Thomas Bowdler's *Family Shakespeare,* censoring the exuberance of the Elizabethan bard. If, today, we imagine that Victorians were moralistic and restrained, the idea results in part from two nineteenth-century voices famous for their inconsolable yet dignified grief: Queen Victoria and Alfred, Lord Tennyson.

Grieving poet, grief-stricken queen. *In Mèmoriam A.H.H.* is Tennyson's tribute to Arthur Henry Hallam, the Cambridge soul mate who helped Tennyson find his poetic voice. Hallam died from a brain seizure at age twenty-two, and much of Tennyson's best poetry—"Ulysses," *Morte d'Arthur,* "Tears, Idle Tears"—indicates that Tennyson never recovered from the loss. One critic called *In Memoriam* "the solace and delight of every house where poetry is loved." England's queen put that solace to the test.

Queen Victoria's love of Prince Albert was legendary. Her private journal describes her 1840 wedding day as "bliss beyond belief" as she basked in her husband's "excessive love and affection." What is less well known is the frankness of Victoria's passion, which belies her reputation for stuffiness. "It is quite a pleasure to look at Albert when he gallops and valses [waltzes]," the queen wrote in 1839.

Who loved, who suffered countless ills,
 Who battled for the True, the Just,
 Be blown about the desert dust,
20 Or sealed within the iron hills?°

No more? A monster then, a dream,
 A discord. Dragons of the prime,
 That tare° each other in their slime,
Were mellow music matched with him.

25 O life as futile, then, as frail!
 O for thy° voice to soothe and bless!
 What hope of answer, or redress?
 Behind the veil, behind the veil.°

20. sealed . . . hills: preserved like fossils in rock.

23. tare: archaic for "tore."

26. thy: Hallam's.

28. veil: the veil of death.

816 THE VICTORIAN PERIOD

OPTIONS FOR TEACHING

INTEGRATING THE LANGUAGE ARTS

Strategic Reading As students reach the end of each section of *In Memoriam,* encourage them to write a one- or two-sentence summary of the main thoughts in that section and to jot down a short personal response to Tennyson's words. Then, have students provide a title for each section. These titles and notes might facilitate class discussion or serve as a study outline for later review.

Language and Vocabulary Words such as *kine, empyreal,* and *freshlier* from *In Memoriam* are not likely to be part of students' everyday vocabulary. Encourage students to keep a written log of unfamiliar words and their meanings and then to use any words that seem appropriate in their own writing.

"He does it so beautifully, and holds himself so well with that beautiful figure of his." Victoria was inconsolable when the prince consort died of typhoid in 1861.

Poetic comfort. Victoria took comfort from *In Memoriam;* even the descriptions of Hallam's blue eyes reminded her of Albert. Because of this poem, the queen interrupted her mourning to entertain the poet laureate. Tennyson recalled that the solemn widow compared herself to "Mariana," the poem's heroine, who weeps for an absent lover. She greeted him, saying, "I am like your Mariana now." Tennyson dedicated the 1862 edition of *Idylls of the King* to Prince Albert, offering a public consolation to his widow: "Break not, O woman's-heart, but still endure; / Break not, for thou art royal, but endure."

Setting a new standard. Victoria formally mourned her husband for forty years—until her death in 1901. At Windsor Castle, she ordered that Albert's clothes continue to be laid out each night and that his basin be filled with water each morning. If the queen's grief was extreme, it also was dignified, and dignity was a quality that the British monarchy sorely lacked before Victoria's reign. Her "wicked uncles" had given the House of Hanover a reputation for rakish carousing, and in her widowhood, Victoria continued the task, begun with Albert, of restoring popularity and respectability to a badly tarnished crown. Her sense of duty won her subjects' heartfelt admiration, and the poet who shared her grief comforted her by saying, "The love of all thy people comfort thee, / Till God's love set thee at his side again!"

95

By night we lingered on the lawn,
   For underfoot the herb was dry; **B**
   And genial warmth; and o'er the sky
The silvery haze of summer drawn;

5 And calm that let the tapers° burn
   Unwavering: Not a cricket chirred;
   The brook alone far off was heard, **C**
and on the board the fluttering urn.°

And bats went round in fragrant skies,
10 And wheeled or lit the filmy shapes°
   That haunt the dusk, with ermine capes
And woolly breasts and beaded eyes;

Design for printed linen (detail) (1893) by Charles Francis Annesley Voysey, printed by G. O. and J. Baker.
Victoria and Albert Museum, London.

5. tapers: candles.

8. fluttering urn: teapot or coffee urn heated by a candle.

10. filmy shapes: moths.

ALFRED, LORD TENNYSON 817

**A. Reader's Response:
Connecting with the Text**

? Remember a time when you saved a letter and re-read it much later; how did time change your perspective? [Sample responses: Time added a layer of memories of all that had passed since then; some old concerns didn't matter but things we hadn't even thought of then were now very important.]

B. Literary Element: Oxymoron

Silent-speaking words is a compact verbal paradox, or oxymoron. Challenge students to find another oxymoron in this stanza ["love's dumb cry"] and to comment on the effect of these expressions. [Oxymorons give a sense of things not being what they seem, of a world in which anything can happen.]

**C. Critical Reading: Analyzing
Imagery**

Note that the speaker's vision, especially his sense of the "deep pulsations of the world" and of "Aeonian music" are what one might expect of a Romantic writer. Ask students how they think these images relate to other things that the speaker has said about cosmic forces. [Possible answers: At this point, he may see Nature as a more kindly force; he may find solace in a belief that God is working behind the scenes of Nature.]

**D. Reader's Response:
Extending the Text**

Many other people who have had unusual experiences may identify with the speaker here. Why might it be difficult for the speaker to share what has happened? [Sample responses: It is hard to find the words that will capture the experience adequately; or life in the real world makes extraordinary experiences seem dubious.]

While now we sang old songs that pealed
    From knoll to knoll, where, couched at ease,
15   The white kine° glimmered, and the trees
Laid their dark arms about the field.

But when those others, one by one,
    Withdrew themselves from me and night,
    And in the house light after light
20 Went out, and I was all alone,

A A hunger seized my heart; I read
    Of that glad year which once had been,
    In those fallen leaves which kept their green,
The noble letters of the dead.

25 And strangely on the silence broke
B   The silent-speaking words, and strange
    Was love's dumb cry defying change
To test his worth; and strangely spoke

The faith, the vigor, bold to dwell
30   On doubts that drive the coward back,
    And keen through wordy snares to track
Suggestion to her inmost cell.

So word by word, and line by line,
    The dead man touched me from the past,
35   And all at once it seemed at last
The living soul° was flashed on mine,

C And mine in this was wound, and whirled
    About empyreal° heights of thought,
    And came on that which is, and caught
40 The deep pulsations of the world,

Aeonian° music measuring out
    The steps of Time—the shocks of Chance—
    The blows of Death. At length my trance
Was canceled, stricken through with doubt.

45 Vague words! but ah, how hard to frame
    In matter-molded forms of speech,
    Or even for intellect to reach
D Through memory that which I became;

Till now the doubtful dusk revealed
50   The knolls once more where, couched at ease,
    The white kine glimmered, and the trees
Laid their dark arms about the field;

And sucked from out the distant gloom
    A breeze began to tremble o'er
55   The large leaves of the sycamore,
And fluctuate all the still perfume,

818 THE VICTORIAN PERIOD

---

15. kine: archaic for "cattle."

36. the living soul: Originally, the phrase read "his living soul." Tennyson said he changed it because he wanted the soul to be not Hallam's but the soul of "the Deity, maybe."
38. empyreal (em·pir′ē·əl): heavenly.

41. aeonian (ē·ō′nē·ən): eternal.

PROFESSIONAL NOTES

Critical Comment: The "Arranging Impulse" According to critic Timothy Peltason, "*In Memoriam* is a poem about many things, but especially about the arranging impulse in human consciousness, about the conditions under which we find ourselves pressed into making new sense of experience. . . . For the poet, the impulse to arrange his life into some meaningful order is simultaneously the impulse to identify his own life with all other lives and with the course of human history. And so he finds his loss of Hallam analogous to the fall of man and looks forward to reunion with Hallam as he does to the 'far-off divine event' that is the goal of the race. Or he finds his history of trials and sufferings analogous to the geological history of the planet or the evolution of the species. Or he finds the model for his own expression of grief and renewal in the forms of pastoral and romantic elegy. In this variety of ways, the poet experiences and interprets and calls into question the gathering up of his life into some larger order. . . ." Work with students to analyze Peltason's comments, and ask students to decide whether or not they agree with his perspective.

And gathering freshlier overhead
　　Rocked the full-foliaged elms, and swung
　　The heavy-folded rose, and flung
60　The lilies to and fro, and said,

"The dawn, the dawn," and died away;
　　And East and West, without a breath,
　　Mixed their dim lights, like life and death,
To broaden into boundless day.

View on the Coast of Cornwall
(19th century) by Frank Goodwin.
Maidstone Museum and Art Gallery,
Kent, England.

A. Literary Element: Theme

❓ How has Tennyson's speaker resolved the conflict between God and Nature, which earlier caused him such anguish? [By concluding that his departed friend not only is with God but remains a part of the physical world that the speaker inhabits.]

B. Critical Reading: Finding Cause and Effect

❓ How have the speaker's experiences changed his attitude toward his departed friend? [He finds that his love is greater than ever before and feels his friend is still with him.]

Making Meanings

First Thoughts

1. Hopeful; blessed; renewed by nature. The speaker feels a renewed sense of faith and believes he is reunited with his lost friend.

Shaping Interpretations

2. The speaker wishes to believe in life after death but finds no evidence of it in Nature. Nature has no regard for individual lives.

3. Nature claims she does not care. She brings life and death to all.

4. The setting is the lawn of a country house on a summer night, where people gather and sing. At the poem's end, the speaker is alone in the same or a similar setting but at dawn.

5. In the earlier lyrics, Nature is portrayed as a cold, unfeeling force that cares nothing about an individual soul. In Lyric 130, Nature is seen as a positive force no longer in conflict with God. The speaker senses his friend Hallam's soul diffused throughout Nature; images of the air, water, sunrise, sunset, star, and flower are positive.

6. Lyrics 55 and 56 express the speaker's doubt and despair as interpreted through Nature, and Lyric 130 expresses his joyful celebration of faith in life and death as interpreted through Nature. In this change of heart, as well as that of Lyric 95, the speaker returns to the original scene—but with a new perspective.

7. The rhyme scheme is *abba*. Students may think the short lines and stanzas and regular rhyme sustain readers' interest and allow readers to hear the poem's music.

130

Thy° voice is on the rolling air;
   I hear thee where the waters run;
   Thou standest in the rising sun,
And in the setting thou art fair.

5 What art thou then? I cannot guess;
   But though I seem in star and flower
   To feel thee some diffusive power,
I do not therefore love thee less.

My love involves the love before;
10   My love is vaster passion now;
   Though mixed with God and Nature thou,
I seem to love thee more and more.

Far off thou art, but ever nigh;
   I have thee still, and I rejoice;
15   I prosper, circled with thy voice;
I shall not lose thee though I die.

1. **Thy:** Hallam's.

MAKING MEANINGS

First Thoughts

1. What word or phrase would you use to describe the speaker's final emotional state? Why?

Shaping Interpretations

2. In Lyric 55, why does the speaker envision the possibility that God and Nature may be "at strife" (line 5)? What complaint does the speaker voice against Nature in this poem?

3. How does Nature answer this complaint in Lyric 56?

4. Describe the **setting** at the beginning of Lyric 95. How does this setting contrast with the setting at the end of the poem?

5. What is the difference between the aspects of Nature described in Lyrics 55 and 56 and those in Lyric 130?

6. Lyric 95 moves from a local scene to "empyreal heights of thought" to the original scene. How is this movement related to the speaker's mood in Lyrics 55 and 56 as well as in Lyric 130?

7. Describe the **rhyme scheme** of these lyrics. How do you think the poem's short lines and stanzas and the rhyme scheme affect the reader?

8. Did Tennyson address the issues you raised in your Reader's Log entry? Were any of his questions, worries, or doubts surprising to you? Why or why not?

Challenging the Text

9. This poem was popular because it satisfied readers who believed poetry should deal with serious subjects, such as grieving. Do you agree or disagree with such expectations for poetry? What do you think are the proper functions of poetry?

---

8. Students should indicate a connection between the issues they raised in their Reader's Logs and the issues Tennyson addressed.

Challenging the Text

9. **(Evaluation and Synthesis)** Students may agree that poetry should address serious philosophical issues, or they may suggest that the purpose of poetry is to delight the senses, to amuse the intellect, to expand the imagination, or to stir the emotions.

Reading Focus

Acting Your Age

An old adage says that youth is wasted on the young—that only older people have the experience and perspective to appreciate the joys of youthful health and exuberance. Stereotypes of "proper" activities for older adults may not take into account the skills and talents honed in a lifetime of living. Tennyson's adventure-seeking Ulysses may appear to be pursuing a young man's dream, but how can he abandon the passions of a lifetime, merely because of his age?

Quickwrite

READER'S LOG

Famous singers, dancers, athletes: some continue their careers long after their skills have peaked. What (besides money) do you think motivates them, and would you do the same in their place?

Background

Ulysses (*Odysseus* in Greek) is one of the Greek leaders who fought in the ten-year Trojan War. Homer's epic poem *The Odyssey* tells of his equally long journey home from Troy to Ithaca. In Tennyson's poem, Ulysses, an old king, is at home with his wife and son, Telemachus (tə·lem′ə·kəs). After a tumultuous life of both marvels and horrors, the old king might finally rest—either thankfully or regretfully. But here Ulysses wants to leave home again for a final journey. He knows lost youth cannot be regained, but he seeks something else.

Tennyson said of this poem, "'Ulysses' was written soon after Arthur Hallam's death, and gave my feeling about the need of going forward, and braving the struggle of life perhaps more simply than anything in *In Memoriam*."

Ulysses Deriding Polyphemus (19th century) by J.M.W. Turner.

The National Gallery, London.

ALFRED, LORD TENNYSON 821

Into the Poem

Using **BEFORE YOU READ** p. 821

Background

Ask students to think of other literature they have read in which an old king returns to the battlefield. [*Beowulf*.] Ask them to keep track in their Reader's Logs of any similarities to *Beowulf* they come across as they read "Ulysses."

RESPONDING TO THE ART: ABOUT THE ARTIST

J.M.W. Turner continued in the tradition of the Romantic painters by expressing human emotions and experiences through depictions of nature, more particularly through his influential landscape paintings. Preferring to expose the terror and grandeur of nature over its peacefulness, his work represented reality in a new way. The intensity of the environment often dissolves the outlines and structures of his subjects, like the ships of *Ulysses Deriding Polyphemus*, into near liquid impressions. The drama and romance of his watercolors and oils are achieved through the warm, brilliant colors and consuming atmospheres.

OPTIONS FOR TEACHING

STRATEGIES FOR INCLUSION

Advanced/Linguistic Have interested students relate "Ulysses" to "Do Not Go Gentle into That Good Night" (p. 1039), written by Dylan Thomas a century later. Encourage students to apply Thomas's line "Old age should burn and rave at close of day" to Ulysses' situation. Have students discuss how Ulysses fits into Thomas's classification of different kinds of people who "rage against the dying of the light."

CROSSING THE CURRICULUM

Geography/Social Sciences If Ulysses sails away to find adventure, where might he go? Ask interested students to examine atlases, to plot a potential route for Ulysses, and then to find out about the cultures of those areas at that time (c. 1200 B.C.). Which European peoples might Ulysses have met? Which peoples of the Americas? Encourage students to present their findings in a format of their own choosing.

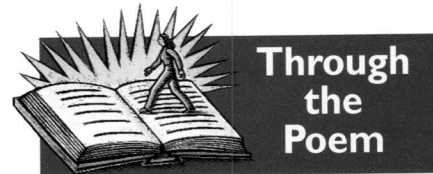

Through the Poem

A. Critical Reading: Summarizing

? In your own words, what is Ulysses' complaint? [Possible answers: He is tired of life at home, where all he does is see his wife and attempt to rule unruly people. He wants to live life to the fullest.]

B. Reader's Response: Shaping Interpretations

If students do not guess the meaning of *lees* from the context, explain that *lees* are the bitter sediment left in a glass of wine, synonymous with *dregs*. Ask students why they think Tennyson chose *lees*. [Sample responses: Matching *lees* with *life* creates an alliteration. Perhaps he uses this metaphor to show that Ulysses most wants the intensity of an experience, whether happy or bitter.]

C. Exploring the Historical Period

A time of intellectual fervor, the Victorian era was marked by a spirit of inquiry. Perhaps Ulysses speaks not only for himself in these lines but for many of Tennyson's contemporaries.

D. Reader's Response: Extending the Text

? Do you think someone like Telemachus would make a good ruler? Why or why not? [Sample responses: Yes, it sounds like he has respect for convention and the ability to do what is expected of him. Or no, he may not perform well in a crisis, when quick thinking—and sometimes a defiance of tradition—is needed.]

Ulysses

Alfred, Lord Tennyson

A
It little profits that an idle king,
By this still hearth, among these barren crags,
Matched with an aged wife, I mete and dole°
Unequal laws unto a savage race,
5 That hoard, and sleep, and feed, and know not me.
B
I cannot rest from travel; I will drink
Life to the lees.° All times I have enjoyed
Greatly, have suffered greatly, both with those
That loved me, and alone; on shore, and when
10 Through scudding drifts the rainy Hyades°
Vexed the dim sea. I am become a name;
C
For always roaming with a hungry heart
Much have I seen and known,—cities of men
And manners, climates, councils, governments,
15 Myself not least, but honored of them all,—
And drunk delight of battle with my peers,
Far on the ringing plains of windy Troy.
I am a part of all that I have met;
Yet all experience is an arch wherethrough
20 Gleams that untraveled world whose margin fades
Forever and forever when I move.
How dull it is to pause, to make an end,
To rust unburnished, not to shine in use!
As though to breathe were life! Life piled on life
25 Were all too little, and of one to me
Little remains; but every hour is saved
From that eternal silence, something more,
A bringer of new things; and vile it were
For some three suns to store and hoard myself,
30 And this gray spirit yearning in desire
To follow knowledge like a sinking star,
Beyond the utmost bound of human thought.
    This is my son, mine own Telemachus,
To whom I leave the scepter and the isle,°—
35 Well-loved of me, discerning to fulfill
This labor, by slow prudence to make mild
A rugged people, and through soft degrees
D
Subdue them to the useful and the good.
Most blameless is he, centered in the sphere
40 Of common duties, decent not to fail
In offices of tenderness, and pay
Meet° adoration to my household gods,
When I am gone. He works his work, I mine.

3. mete and dole: measure and give out.

7. lees: dregs or sediment.

10. Hyades (hī′ə·dēz′): stars that were thought to indicate rainy weather.

34. isle: Ithaca, Ulysses' island kingdom off the west coast of Greece.

42. meet: proper.

822 THE VICTORIAN PERIOD

OPTIONS FOR TEACHING

COOPERATIVE LEARNING

Silent Dialogue Encourage groups of three to respond to "Ulysses" by assuming the characters of Ulysses, his wife, and his son Telemachus. Have students, in character, create a silent dialogue by passing a paper back and forth and "conversing" about this question: Why cannot Ulysses be content with the adventures of his past?

Encourage students to think of logical arguments the wife and son might use to persuade Ulysses to stay.

Prototyping Ulysses Have students working in groups of four or five imagine that they are a marketing committee charged with developing an action figure of Ulysses. Students should consider the following questions: Will they portray Homer's

or Tennyson's Ulysses? What will their figure look like, and why? What message do they want to get across? What products will they develop? How will they advertise the figure? What age group will they target? Students should sell their ideas to corporate executives (the class). They should include sketches or a model of the figure in their presentations.

There lies the port; the vessel puffs her sail;
45 There gloom the dark, broad seas. My mariners,
Souls that have toiled, and wrought, and thought with me,—
That ever with a frolic welcome took
The thunder and the sunshine, and opposed
Free hearts, free foreheads,—you and I are old;
50 Old age hath yet his honor and his toil.
Death closes all; but something ere the end,
Some work of noble note, may yet be done,
Not unbecoming men that strove with Gods.
The lights begin to twinkle from the rocks;
55 The long day wanes; the slow moon climbs; the deep
Moans round with many voices. Come, my friends,
'Tis not too late to seek a newer world.
Push off, and sitting well in order smite
The sounding furrows;° for my purpose holds
60 To sail beyond the sunset, and the baths
Of all the western stars, until I die.
It may be that the gulfs will wash us down;
It may be we shall touch the Happy Isles,°
And see the great Achilles,° whom we knew.
65 Though much is taken, much abides; and though
We are not now that strength which in old days
Moved earth and heaven, that which we are, we are,—
One equal temper of heroic hearts,
Made weak by time and fate, but strong in will
70 To strive, to seek, to find, and not to yield.

E

F

59. **smite . . . furrows:** row against the waves.

63. **Happy Isles:** in Greek mythology, Elysium (ē·liz'ē·əm), where dead heroes lived for eternity.
64. **Achilles** (ə·kil'ēz'): Greek warrior and leader in the Trojan War.

MAKING MEANINGS

First Thoughts

1. "Ulysses" is about a brave, or foolish, response to the securities and comforts of an orderly life very like that of middle-class mid-Victorian England. What do you think of Ulysses' decision? (Refer to your Reader's Log.)

Shaping Interpretations

2. How does Ulysses contrast his past and present lives? From this comparison, what conclusions can you draw about his values?

3. In lines 19–21, what does Ulysses claim about "all experience"?

4. Whom does Ulysses address in the second half of the poem? In the concluding lines of the poem, what qualities does he say that he shares with his mariners?

5. Where does Tennyson emphasize Ulysses' great endurance and insatiable curiosity? How would you **characterize** Ulysses?

6. Find Ulysses' references to his wife and son, and tell what you think his words reveal about his underlying feelings toward them. Then, explain whether you accept Ulysses' point of view.

7. What do you think Ulysses is determined not to "yield" to (line 70)?

Connecting with the Text

8. What lines in this poem do you think would encourage someone who needed to go forward despite the temptation to give up the struggle?

Challenging the Text

9. Ulysses knows that his journey is like pursuing the horizon. Do you think he is foolish for setting out on a journey he cannot complete? Explain.

ALFRED, LORD TENNYSON 823

Making Meanings
First Thoughts

1. Students may find him admirable in his courage and determination; selfish in leaving his family and kingdom to satisfy his desire for adventure; or foolish in thinking that he can replicate his youthful success in battle.

Shaping Interpretations

2. His present life is boring and unfulfilling compared with his past. Students may say Ulysses values conquest or adventure.
3. Experience is an arch through which he sees a boundless, untraveled world.

E. Critical Reading: Making Generalizations

? How does Ulysses' attitude toward his companions contrast with his attitude toward his son? [Possible answer: Ulysses feels he and his son differ, but he seems to feel camaraderie among his fellow seafarers.]

Metacognition Name two clues that helped shape your answer. ["He works his work, I mine" (l. 43) shows how Ulysses differs from Telemachus. "My mariners,/Souls that have toiled, and wrought, and thought with me" (ll. 45–46) shows he feels close to his comrades.]

F. Humanities Connections
Achilles was the greatest of the Greek warriors who fought against Troy; his death caused great mourning among his comrades. Achilles may represent Tennyson's friend Arthur Hallam, the subject of *In Memoriam* (pp. 815–820).

4. He addresses his loyal sailors from past adventures. They share heroic hearts and wills.
5. Lines 6–7, 12, 30–32, 45–48, 51–52, 56–65, and 70. Students may see him as selfish; others may view him as living life fully.
6. In l. 3, he calls his wife "aged." He seems to have ambivalent feelings toward her. He says he loves Telemachus but seems to feel that Telemachus is not adventurous, which may disappoint Ulysses. Students may agree with Ulysses, as the poem is from his perspective, or they may step back and find fault with his reasoning.
7. To old age or to a slower pace.

Connecting with the Text
8. Students may suggest ll. 56–57 or ll. 65–70.

Challenging the Text
9. (Synthesis) Many students will feel Ulysses is foolish because he cannot achieve what he wants to do; others may admire his taking the chance to fulfill his dreams.

Alfred, Lord Tennyson **T823**

Into the Poem

Using **BEFORE YOU READ** p. 824

Quickwrite
Encourage students to jot down the meanings the images of a harbor, a sandbar, and the sea have for them. Then, invite students to translate these ideas into the larger context: What might these images mean to Victorian society? To society today?

Through the Poem

A. Literary Element: Extended Metaphor
The first stanza establishes the two controlling metaphors of the poem: Crossing the bar represents dying, and the sea represents whatever mystery comes after death. Ask students to comment on the auditory image in this stanza of the "moaning of the bar."
[Possible answers: It may refer to the cries of people who will mourn the speaker's death; perhaps—more literally—it is the sound of waves or the hull of a boat grating across the bar.]

B. Literary Element: Rhythm
? What do you think Tennyson was trying to accomplish by alternating long and short lines? [Possible answers: He was imitating the ebb and flow of the tides; he varied the line length to hold his readers' interest.]

C. Reader's Response: Shaping Interpretations
? How would you characterize the speaker's attitude toward death?
[Sample responses: Awed by the mysteries of death and the afterlife but determined to meet both with dignity; at peace with the natural cycle of life and death.]

BEFORE YOU READ
CROSSING THE BAR

Reading Focus
Riding the Tide
In the last forty years of his life, Tennyson lived in the country like an affluent gentleman. Occasionally, he went to London to walk about in his black cloak and broad-brimmed hat and to meet with distinguished writers, scientists, churchmen, politicians, and sometimes the queen. Tourists hung around his country house on the Isle of Wight and climbed trees to get a glimpse of him. People sent him mountains of poetry; he once estimated that he had received a verse for every three minutes of his life. How would you expect such a person to face death?

Quickwrite
READER'S LOG
What do you predict the images of harbor, sandbar, and sea in this poem will stand for?

Background
Tennyson wrote this poem in 1889, at the age of eighty, while crossing the channel that separates England from the Isle of Wight. Before his death in 1892, he directed that the poem be printed at the end of all editions of his collected verse.

Sunset on Wet Sand (1845) by J.M.W. Turner. Watercolor over pencil.
The Whitworth Art Gallery, University of Manchester, England.

Crossing the Bar

Alfred, Lord Tennyson

> Sunset and evening star,
>   And one clear call for me!
> And may there be no moaning of the bar,
>   When I put out to sea,
>
> 5 But such a tide as moving seems asleep,
>   Too full for sound and foam,
> When that° which drew from out the boundless deep
>   Turns again home.
>
> Twilight and evening bell,
> 10   And after that the dark!
> And may there be no sadness of farewell,
>   When I embark;
>
> For though from out our bourne° of Time and Place
>   The flood may bear me far,
> 15 I hope to see my Pilot° face to face
>   When I have crossed the bar.

7. that: the soul.
13. bourne (bōrn): archaic for "boundary."
15. Pilot: person who knows the local waters and guides a ship as it enters or leaves a harbor.

OPTIONS FOR TEACHING

STRATEGIES FOR INCLUSION

Auditory Consider setting the tone for "Crossing the Bar," which expresses a fairly traditional Christian faith, by playing a traditional hymn (or excerpts from a few hymns) from that era. ("Rock of Ages, Cleft for Me," "My Faith Looks Up to Thee," and "Jesus, Savior, Pilot Me," still sung today, relate well to Tennyson's **theme** and **imagery**.) Ask students to consider how "Crossing the Bar" might be a natural progression of thought for someone who might have sung such songs.

MAKING MEANINGS

First Thoughts

1. Do you find this poem personally comforting, or do you feel some other emotion? Explain.

Shaping Interpretations

2. Explain the extended **metaphor** of the sea voyage. How well did your Reader's Log entry predict Tennyson's development of it?

3. Who might the "Pilot" be in line 15?

4. Paraphrase each of the speaker's wishes and hopes, and explain what you think they show about the feelings of an older person. Is the speaker accepting, afraid, or both?

5. What mental image does Tennyson's poem create for you? Describe it.

CHOICES: Building Your Portfolio

Writer's Notebook

1. Collecting Ideas for an Evaluation

Suppose you're a critic, assigned to review one of Tennyson's poems. Your review can be high praise, harsh criticism, or some judgment in between. Which poem could you sink your teeth into? State whether you'll give the poem a positive or negative evaluation, and write the quality or element of the poem that influences your initial reaction. Save your work for the Writer's Workshop on page 899.

Critical Writing

2. An Overview

Tennyson's poems are about how to respond to the losses and disorders of love, death, old age, the passing of leaders, and challenges to old standards of political and moral authority.

In an essay, respond to this characterization of Tennyson's poems. Take your evidence from the poems in this collection.

Critical Writing

3. New Ending, New Meaning

When Tennyson published the first version of "The Lady of Shalott" in 1832, the last stanza ended thus:

> "The web was woven curiously
> The charm is broken utterly
> Draw near and fear not—this is I,
>   The Lady of Shalott."

In an essay, compare this scenario to what occurs in the last stanza on page 812. What do you think of Tennyson's revision? Which ending do you think is more moving? Explain.

Critical Writing

4. Ulysses Across Time

Research the plot of Homer's *Odyssey*, and read portions of the epic, especially from Books 8, 13, and 19. In an essay, compare and contrast Homer's and Tennyson's hero figures. Also, draw conclusions about what Tennyson's alterations to Homer's text show about Tennyson and his times.

Creative Writing

5. Man to Man

Write Telemachus's reply (poetry or prose) to his father's speech in "Ulysses." How does Telemachus feel about his father's leaving him and his mother for more adventures?

Literature and Film

6. Visualizing the Enchantment

"The Lady of Shalott" is vividly descriptive. Sketch a storyboard of shot-by-shot illustrations for a filmed version of the story. Show Tennyson's sparse dialogue (including the "whispers" of the curse) in captions.

Making Meanings
First Thoughts

1. Students may sense the comfort the speaker feels; some may find the talk of death depressing.

Shaping Interpretations

2. The voyage is a metaphor for leaving the harbor of life for death and perhaps an afterlife. Students should review their Reader's Log entries to compare their predictions to the poet's use of the images of harbor, sandbar, and sea.

3. The "Pilot" is probably God.

4. The speaker hopes that there will be no moaning of the bar when he puts out to sea; he wants no sadness when it is time for him to go; he hopes to see his Pilot when he crosses the bar. Student responses about an older person's feelings will vary; many will agree that the speaker accepts death, but faith has made him hopeful of life after death.

5. Responses will vary. Remind students to refer to the text to support their images.

Beyond the Poems

Choices: Building Your Portfolio

1. **Writer's Notebook** Remind students to save their work. They may use it as prewriting for the Writer's Workshop on p. 899.

4. **Critical Writing** Before they begin writing, suggest that students work in pairs to create a Venn diagram of the similarities and differences between the heroes.

Interpersonal For activity #2, allow students to work in groups to discuss and review the themes of Tennyson's poems. Ask students to keep notes on their group's comments, but encourage them to decide on their own exactly how they would evaluate the characterization of Tennyson's poems.

PORTFOLIO ASSESSMENT

Choices: Assessment Criteria For help in evaluating these Choices assignments, see the criteria in the *Portfolio Management System,* pp. 143–144.

A. Literary Connections

Sir Walter Scott (1771–1832) is known for his novels such as *Waverley, Old Mortality, Rob Roy,* and *Ivanhoe.*

B. Expansion

From the French word *chevalier,* or "horseman," medieval knights took the name for their code of ethical conduct. Medieval feudalism, with its emphasis on loyalty to one's liege lord, contributed to this system of values that combined Christian virtues with military skills. Chivalry called for the battlefield prowess, but also for courtesy and generosity toward those in need.

C. Expansion

The title of Arthur's story allegedly came from "The French book"; therefore, the title is sometimes spelled *Le Morte D'Arthur.* "Gododdin," a Welsh poem from the seventh century, first mentions the legendary king. In the ninth century, the Welsh writer Nennius collected notes on a historical king named Arthur. Nennius's *Historia Britonum* draws on numerous sources to describe twelve battles in which Arthur led the Britons against the Saxons.

SPOTLIGHT ON

The Enduring Arthurian Legend

Chivalry rediscovered. Blame King George IV, who remodeled Windsor Castle with the feudal embellishments of arms and chivalric heraldry. Or perhaps blame the immensely popular Sir Walter Scott, whose novels were packed full of jousting tournaments and knights errant. With the help of these influential figures and many more, the ideals of King Arthur's royal city, Camelot, flourished in the nineteenth century. The model of chivalry had seemed barbarous in the elegant, classical eighteenth century; however, as scholars looked back on English history, they rediscovered fascinating rituals and antiquities. Historians republished medieval ballads, printed illustrations of medieval architecture, and, in the process, piqued public interest in the Middle Ages. Tennyson's "The Lady of Shalott" (page 808) is just one example of the nineteenth century's medieval mania, an obsession that reintroduced images of "many-towered Camelot" and lovely, secluded ladies into popular culture.

Hope, honor, and nobility. Chivalry's message was, in part, one of hope. Kenelm Henry Digby's 1844 manual on chivalry asserts that "the noble fellowship of the Round Table cannot be broken forever; but fresh aspirants will again appear to . . . keep ahead of the degraded world." In describing the renewal of "noble fellowship," Digby provides a Victorian interpretation of an enduring English legend. The myth of King Arthur combines Christian morals with ancient pagan fertility rites to form a fascinating story of romance, magic, and betrayal. Arthur, king of the Britons, may actually have lived in the sixth century and resisted the Anglo-Saxon invasions of Britain. More important for an understanding of the Round Table and its code of chivalry is the work of Sir Thomas Malory (c. 1405?–1471). Malory borrowed from French tales of the King Arthur legend to create *Le Morte Darthur* (The Death of Arthur), which is the first real masterpiece of English prose.

Glory and deceit. Malory's story centers around King Arthur, who as a child gained a kingdom when he magically pulled a sword named Excalibur from a stone. Arthur is guided by the magician Merlin as he fights to free his kingdom. To create order in his lawless land, Arthur brings together a group of noble knights whose mission, as stated by

The Beguiling of Merlin (1874) by Sir Edward Burne-Jones. Oil on canvas (73″ × 43½″).

826 THE VICTORIAN PERIOD

STRATEGIES FOR INCLUSION

Learners Having Difficulty Ask students to imagine they are rulers needing new knights. Taking into consideration the information they have read about Victorian values, students should create scrolls calling for new knights, indicating the traits and experience a knight recruit should offer.

Auditory/Visual If possible, show students *Knights of the Round Table,* available on VHS videocassette by MGM/UA and other classroom media providers. Have students discuss why the Arthurian legend lives on.

INTEGRATING THE LANGUAGE ARTS

Strategic Reading Have students use a KWL chart to record what they know, what they want to know, and what they have learned about the Arthurian legend. Before they read, ask them to fill in the first two columns. After they finish reading, have them complete the third column. Follow up by asking students what more they would like to learn about the Arthurian legend. Discuss books they might enjoy reading on the subject.

La Mort d'Arthur (1860) by Jones Archer. Oil on millboard (17″ × 20″).

D. Humanities Connection
The presidency of John F. Kennedy (1960–63) is often referred to as "Camelot." Many people in the United States were thrilled with the idea of a leader who was a handsome, vigorous, youthful war hero and who brought new ideas and a new image to the White House.

E. Expansion
Malory's work is considered the chief source of the Arthurian legend. In more modern times, T. H. White's *The Once and Future King* served as the basis for the musical *Camelot* (1960) and the animated film *The Sword in the Stone* (1963).

Tennyson, is to "live pure, speak true, right wrong, [and] follow the king." Of this group, Sir Lancelot becomes the ideal of chivalrous behavior. At his death, Sir Ector describes Lancelot as "the courteoust knight that ever bore shield! And . . . the kindest man that ever struck with sword."

Beguiling contradictions. The story of Camelot is a bundle of contradictions. Lancelot, the perfect flower of knighthood, betrays his king by falling in love with Queen Guinevere. The revelation of their affair plunges the court into a war in which Arthur is killed. Arthur encourages his knights to undertake religious quests, yet he himself is not without sin: His illegitimate son seals his own downfall. The darker side of chivalry, it seems, is bound up inextricably with compelling ideals of bravery and honesty. The novelist John Steinbeck describes how these contradictions captured his attention the moment he read the tales of Camelot. "In that scene were all the vices that ever were—and courage and sadness and frustration, but particularly gallantry. . . . I was not frightened to find that there were evil knights, as well as noble ones. . . . Children are violent and cruel—and good—and I was all of these—and all of these were in the secret book."

In an age of industrial change, Victorians were drawn to images of simple feudal loyalties. They romanticized an age when disputes could be settled by the king's champion, a knight on horseback who threw down his gauntlet to anyone challenging royal authority. Similarly, modern readers are drawn to the magic of Camelot, nostalgically hoping for goodness and nobility to succeed in the face of overwhelming odds. Or, as the youthful King Arthur is taught in T. H. White's *The Once and Future King* (1958), "right" *can* prevail over "might." Malory tells us that "King Arthur is not dead" but "shall come again, and he shall win the Holy Cross." For five hundred years, readers have believed.

SPOTLIGHT ON 827

Robert Browning
(1812–1889)

Robert Browning wrote of his first published book, a long poem about the spiritual development of a poet, that it was part of a "foolish plan." He intended, he said, to write in many forms and under different names. Browning eventually gave up this idea, but he held on to his ambition of dazzling the world with his range and variety.

Browning's education allowed him to indulge his wide-ranging interests in music, art, the history of medicine, drama, literature, entomology, and other oddly assorted topics. Browning attended boarding school briefly but was mainly educated at home in a London suburb by tutors and by his omnivorous reading in his banker father's extensive library. As a teenager, Browning was brilliant, undisciplined, and determined to be a poet like his idol, Percy Bysshe Shelley. After a term at the University of London, he published (at his family's expense) several poems, plays, and pamphlets, but not until he began writing the short dramatic monologues of the 1840s—poems like "My Last Duchess" and "Porphyria's Lover"—did Browning find his proper form. While Browning struggled to gain recognition for his writing, he lived comfortably at home, supported by his parents, until he married at thirty-four.

In 1845, Browning wrote to Elizabeth Barrett, already an established poet: "I do . . . love these books with all my heart—and I love you too." Barrett was then a semi-invalid in her father's London house, where she submitted to his sternly protective care. Four months after the two poets began their correspondence, they met and fell in love. They secretly married in 1846, and a week later eloped to Italy. Mr. Barrett estranged himself from his famous daughter for the rest of his life.

Browning's happy marriage confirmed his belief that only by acting boldly can one wrest

Robert Browning (1858) by Michele Gordigiani. Oil on canvas (29″ × 23″). By Courtesy of the National Portrait Gallery, London.

what is good from an imperfect world. "I was ever a fighter," he wrote in "Prospice." He liked to see himself in strenuous but joyous contests with difficulties. In his dramatic poems, he also liked to emphasize the error, weakness, and even the viciousness of his characters. His standing as a poet grew slowly in the 1840s and 1850s, for readers did not know how to react to speakers like the Duke in "My Last Duchess" and the lover in "Porphyria's Lover," who act boldly but for selfish and perverse motives. It was also hard for readers used to Tennyson's melodic lyrics to hear the music in Browning's quick, rough sounds.

Browning lived in Italy until Elizabeth's death in 1861, when he returned to England with their twelve-year-old son. During the 1860s, his fame began to grow. His first immediate success came with *The Ring and the Book* (1868–1869), a long poem spoken by characters involved in a seventeenth-century murder in Rome. Gradually, readers understood that by asking them to figure out and judge wicked men like the Duke in "My Last Duchess," Browning was really challenging them to discover what is virtuous and healthy, when love nourishes, and when and why it kills. Browning believed that human beings must act by a moral standard, just as he believed that those who love constantly and act bravely will be rewarded.

During the 1880s, admirers all over England and the United States founded Browning Societies and met to read and discuss his work and philosophy. By the time of his death in 1889, Browning had won a place next to Tennyson as the other great Victorian poet. Like Tennyson, he was read as a kind of sage who assured his contemporaries that "This world's no blot for us, / Nor blank; it means intensely, and means good" ("Fra Lippo Lippi").

BEFORE YOU READ
MY LAST DUCHESS

Reading Focus
A Portrait of a Marriage
The speaker in this poem begins by describing a painting of a woman, and by the speech's end he has revealed an entire relationship. Yet nothing in this poem may be quite what it seems.

A Dialogue with the Text

As you read, jot down the names—and brief descriptions—of all the characters that Browning manages to introduce in this short narrative.

Elements of Literature
Dramatic Monologue
"My Last Duchess" is one of Browning's earliest and most popular **dramatic monologues,** poems in which a speaker, who is not the poet, addresses a listener who doesn't speak. Instead of commenting directly on the speaker, Browning provides us with clues and expects us to make inferences. We are required to think about the character of the speaker, to reconstruct the situation in which he or she speaks, and to guess at the speaker's motives.

Background
The speaker in this poem is the Duke of Ferrara, a powerful Italian nobleman of the Renaissance. In the poem, the Duke negotiates to marry his second wife, the niece of a count. He addresses the count's representative.

A Lady with a Gold Chain and Earrings (1861)
by Robert Braithwaite Martineau.
Oil on panel (14″ × 10″).

© Manchester City Art Galleries, England.

ROBERT BROWNING 829

QUICK PLANNING GUIDE

Into the Poems

Author Biography p. 828
Before You Read p. 829, p. 833

Through the Poems

"My Last Duchess" pp. 830–831
Connections: A Newspaper Article p. 832
"Scenes from a Modern Marriage"
"Porphyria's Lover" pp. 834–835
Making Meanings p. 831, p. 836

Beyond the Poems

Choices: Building Your Portfolio p. 836
- **Writer's Notebook:** Collect ideas for an evaluation
- **Critical Writing:** Write an essay comparing themes and techniques
- **Creative Writing:** Write a dramatic monologue
- **Improvisational Theater:** Improvise a scene

Into the Poem

Using BEFORE YOU READ p. 829

Elements of Literature
Ask students to think of contemporary examples of dramatic monologue, making sure that their examples embody all the characteristics mentioned in the definition. [One literary example would be "Top of the Food Chain," p. 509.]

OPTIONS FOR TEACHING

INTEGRATING THE LANGUAGE ARTS

Strategic Reading Have students keep a double-entry journal, noting in the left column the phrases or lines that strike them and in the right column their reactions to those lines. In discussion, encourage students to refer to these notes as they prepare to comment.

Writing: Companion Stories Invite pairs or groups of students to write a companion story to "My Last Duchess." Some students may try a prequel, expanding on the painting of the portrait and the events leading up to the day that "all smiles stopped together." Other students might attempt a sequel, focusing on the Duke's next marriage. Choose two stories to share with the class, or display the stories for students to read. ☞

A. Expansion

The research that led Browning to learn about Alfonso II, the fifth Duke of Ferrara, probably included the information that the Duke's first wife (of three wives in all) was a fourteen-year-old girl whom the Duke, after marrying, left for two years. She died about a year after his return. It is believed that she was poisoned.

B. Reader's Response: First Thoughts

? Do you like the way the poem begins in midconversation, or would you prefer it start where the conversation itself started? Explain. [Sample responses: I prefer the full conversation; or starting the poem in the middle of the conversation makes it more interesting. This technique requires the reader to be a detective, looking for clues about what has gone on before.]

C. Critical Reading: Making Inferences

? What do these lines suggest about the Duchess? [That she was unfaithful.]

Metacognition Is this statement enough to convict her? Explain. [Possible answer: No; the Duke will have to provide more evidence, for this is just his judgment about her.] **Point out that the Duke offers no evidence that she was unfaithful; rather, her downfall was that she did not pay her husband as much attention as he felt he deserved.**

My Last Duchess

Robert Browning

A That's my last Duchess painted on the wall,
Looking as if she were alive. I call
That piece a wonder, now; Frà Pandolf's° hands
Worked busily a day, and there she stands.
B 5 Will 't please you sit and look at her? I said
"Frà Pandolf" by design, for never read
Strangers like you that pictured countenance,
The depth and passion of its earnest glance,
But to myself they turned (since none puts by
10 the curtain I have drawn for you, but I)
And seemed as they would ask me, if they durst,
How such a glance came there; so, not the first
C Are you to turn and ask thus. Sir, 'twas not
Her husband's presence only, called that spot
15 Of joy into the Duchess' cheek; perhaps
Frà Pandolf chanced to say, "Her mantle° laps
Over my lady's wrist too much," or, "Paint
Must never hope to reproduce the faint
Half flush that dies along her throat." Such stuff
20 Was courtesy, she thought, and cause enough
For calling up that spot of joy. She had
A heart—how shall I say?—too soon made glad,
Too easily impressed; she liked whate'er
She looked on, and her looks went everywhere.
25 Sir, 'twas all one! My favor° at her breast,
The dropping of the daylight in the West,

3. Frà Pandolf's: Brother Pandolf, a fictitious painter and monk.

16. mantle: cloak.

25. favor: gift; token of love.

Man with Glove (16th century) by Titian (Tiziano Vecellio).
Louvre, Paris.

The bough of cherries some officious fool
Broke in the orchard for her, the white mule
She rode with round the terrace—all and each
30 Would draw from her alike the approving speech,
Or blush, at least. She thanked men—good! but thanked
Somehow—I know not how—as if she ranked
My gift of a nine-hundred-years-old name
With anybody's gift. Who'd stoop to blame
35 This sort of trifling? Even had you skill
In speech—(which I have not)—to make your will
Quite clear to such an one, and say, "Just this
Or that in you disgusts me; here you miss,
Or there exceed the mark"—and if she let
40 Herself be lessoned so, nor plainly set
Her wits to yours, forsooth,° and made excuse,
—E'en then would be some stooping; and I choose
Never to stoop. Oh sir, she smiled, no doubt,
Whene'er I passed her; but who passed without
45 Much the same smile? This grew; I gave commands;
Then all smiles stopped together. There she stands **D**
As if alive. Will 't please you rise? We'll meet
The company below, then. I repeat,
The Count your master's known munificence
50 Is ample warrant° that no just pretense
Of mine for dowry will be disallowed;
Though his fair daughter's self, as I avowed
At starting, is my object. Nay, we'll go
Together down, sir. Notice Neptune,° though, **E**
55 Taming a seahorse, thought a rarity,
Which Claus of Innsbruck° cast in bronze for me!

41. **forsooth:** archaic for "in truth."

50. **warrant:** guarantee.

54. **Neptune:** in Roman mythology, god of the sea.
56. **Claus of Innsbruck:** an imaginary sculptor.

MAKING MEANINGS

First Thoughts

1. What do you think happened to the Duchess? Why do you think so?

Shaping Interpretations

2. According to the Duke, what happened to the last Duchess?
3. Describe the poem's **rhyme** and **meter**. Read aloud two passages that strike you as examples of natural, colloquial speech.
4. What impression of himself do you think the Duke intends to create in his remarks to the Count's emissary? Why would he choose to present himself in this way?
5. What kind of man do you think the Duke really

is? What lines reveal his true **character**? (Check your Reader's Log entry.)

6. Why do you think Browning had the Duke's monologue begin and end by referring to art?
7. How is the marriage portrayed in the poem like or different from the Brownings' own marriage, described in the article on page 832?
8. What do you think of the Duke's description of his last Duchess? Do you question his assessments? Why or why not?

Extending the Text

9. Can you imagine the situation implied in this poem taking place today? Explain.

ROBERT BROWNING 831

Connections — A NEWSPAPER ARTICLE

Scenes from a Modern Marriage

BY JULIA MARKUS

The letter that began the most famous courtship of the 19th century opened, "I love your verses with all my heart, dear Miss Barrett." The writer, Robert Browning, a thirty-three-year-old poet respected in literary circles, was writing to a woman six years his senior, an invalid and a poet of national and international fame. Elizabeth Barrett had not long before recognized his own genius in a poem, "Lady Geraldine's Courtship," likening his poetic heart to a pomegranate "blood-tinctured" with "a veined humanity."

Cloistered in the airless bed-sitting room she never left, Elizabeth Barrett was a famous yet mysterious poet. Little could Robert know that her household on Wimpole Street was one of enforced celibacy. Her father, scion of Jamaican wealth, forbade any of his nine adult children, male or female, to marry; all were still living at home. Elizabeth's allowing Robert to visit for the first time was in its own way a dangerous act, a rebellion.

The courtship that followed—daily letters for more than twenty months, secret weekly visits while Papa Barrett was at work—is one of the most romantic and obsessively documented love stories in our tradition.

They met 150 years ago, but their successful marriage has something to say to us today as we race toward the millennium wondering if we have learned anything at all about the art of love.

Not that any marriage is easy. Robert was disturbed by his wife's lifelong use of morphine, which she believed kept her alive, and he was skeptical of her attraction to spiritualism and furious at some of the mediums she befriended. Elizabeth also suffered four miscarriages, giving birth at the age of forty-three to one healthy son. But the birth of Pen Browning came on the day Robert's mother died in England, and his despondency drew him away from his son.

Desperate to help, Elizabeth told Robert she had once secretly written poems about him, during the courtship. She hesitantly handed him the *Sonnets from the Portuguese* as if to say, Look how love led me from despair; can I now lead you from it? "How I see the gesture, and hear the tones," he remembered years after her death, "and, for the matter of that, see the window at which I was standing, with the tall mimosa in front, and the little church court to the right."

The careers of these two poets were on different levels, which could have led to the kind of troubled celebrity marriage we read about today in the tabloids. Though they both wrote their best poetry during their marriage, Robert Browning's greatest collection, "Men and Women"—still in print—was hacked to death by the critics and sold fewer than two hundred copies. This failure added to his money worries—and, since the interest on her money supported them through most of their marriage, to his grave discomfort.

She in the meantime had written a daring novel in verse, "Aurora Leigh," which exposed the abuses against women in Victorian society and suggested, among other things, that what a female artist needed was not a husband but enough money for a garret of her own.

Elizabeth defied conventions only to find her book a best-seller that quickly went through five editions and was read and discussed everywhere. Yet while he was bitter about the critics who destroyed his hopes of critical and commercial success, "golden-hearted" Robert was thrilled by her success. He could talk of nothing else, and he always considered her the superior artist. To her sister Arabel she wrote, when people "write & talk of the 'jealousy' of authors & husbands, let them look at him!"

If this all seems too good to be true, let it be known the couple quarreled. They had very different ideas about child rearing, for one thing. Elizabeth, coming from a home in which her father's "thunder" dictated obedience and having been a child prodigy, wished for her son happy, carefree, unstructured days. Robert, who was doted on by his parents, wanted Pen to take his piano lessons seriously and learn to count. She kept Pen in long curls and velvet frocks; he wanted him to look like a real boy.

But both believed that arguments were important to the marriage. "You know I do think for myself (if the thought is right or wrong) and I do speak the truth (as I am capable of apprehending it) to my husband always," Elizabeth wrote to Arabel. "What you used to call 'our quarreling' is an element of our loving one another, & a very important element too."

—*from The New York Times,* February 14, 1995

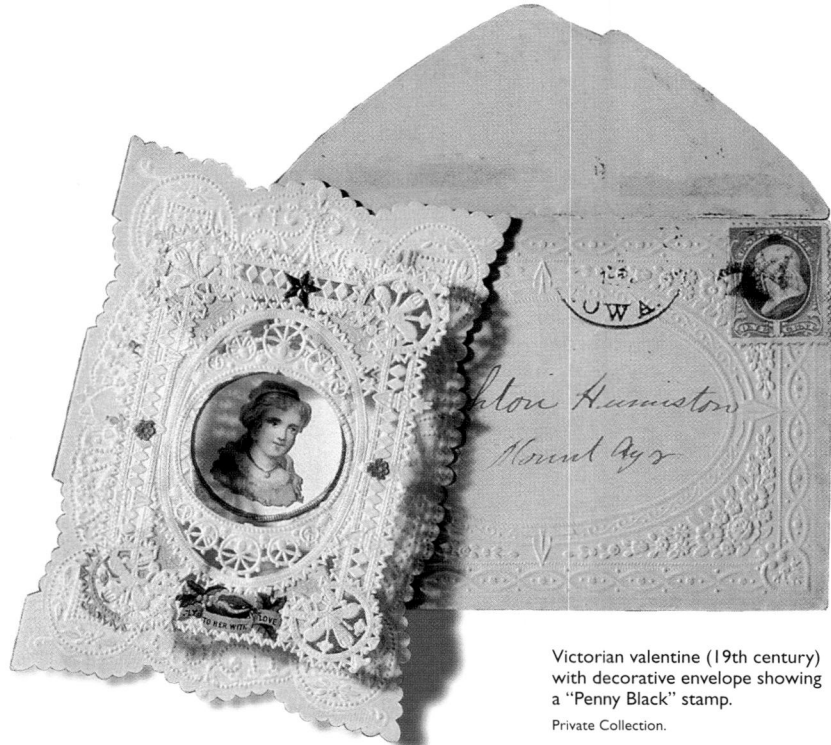

Victorian valentine (19th century) with decorative envelope showing a "Penny Black" stamp.
Private Collection.

BEFORE YOU READ

PORPHYRIA'S LOVER

Reading Focus

Mad for Love

Readers might expect a poem titled "Porphyria's Lover" to be a romance. The speaker in the poem is a man whose character and identity we can deduce only by what he says. However, one thing is clear: He is a man of intense emotion. Impressed by his direct speech and unruffled manner, we then shudder at what we learn late in the poem. Yet we continue to hear the man out—fascinated, however uneasy—and are eventually led to ask, "Is he lovesick or genuinely disturbed?"

Quickwrite

Someone has said that the opposite of love is not hate but control. Think about some examples from history or fiction. What is your reaction to this idea?

Background

Like his American contemporary Edgar Allan Poe, Browning had a taste for morbid psychology; he once accused his wife, Elizabeth Barrett Browning, of lacking "a scientific interest in evil." In poems such as "Porphyria's Lover," he pursues that interest, exploring the complexity of human motivations. Browning is different from other nineteenth-century authors. This psychological poet seems more modern to us than his Victorian contemporaries.

ROBERT BROWNING 833

Using **BEFORE YOU READ** p. 833

Quickwrite

Remind students to choose situations they would not mind sharing. King Henry VIII's mistreatment of his successive wives might be an example. Suggest students first think of their definition of true *love;* then, ask them if the idea of *control* fits into that definition.

OPTIONS FOR TEACHING

STRATEGIES FOR INCLUSION

English Language Development Monitor English-language learners' comprehension of the poem by having them create a time line on which they list, chronologically, the events of the poem. Then, as a class activity, have students name one at a time the events which lead up to the dramatic conclusion.

Intrapersonal The speaker in "Porphyria's Lover" offers the reader many clues to his isolated nature. Have students examine his monologue for evidence that suggests ways in which the speaker currently is or has been a loner. ☞

Robert Browning **T833**

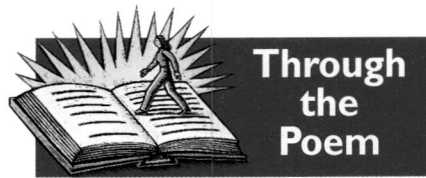

Through the Poem

A. Reader's Response: First Thoughts

? What kind of **mood** do you think this **setting** is meant to evoke? Explain. [Sample responses: The violence of the weather may reflect a frightful violence in the characters or events of the poem; the darkness suggests mystery or dark deeds; the lake and trees, which indicate an isolated locale, may evoke a sense of foreboding—a sense that whatever takes place will do so out of sight of witnesses.]

B. Critical Reading: Drawing Conclusions

? What seems to be the complication in this relationship? [Possible answers: Porphyria is not strong enough to break the ties of a relationship to which she already is committed; perhaps a previous marriage or the disapproval of her family prevents her formal commitment to the speaker.]

C. Reader's Response: Connecting with the Text

Ask students to contrast the speakers in "My Last Duchess" and in this **dramatic monologue.** [Sample responses: The speaker here is sure that Porphyria worships him. On the other hand, the speaker in "My Last Duchess" is not sure that his Duchess did worship him; he believes that she had a roving eye and was flirtatious. The speakers are similar in that each is obsessed with a woman. When the Duke felt his Duchess was beyond changing, he ensured his mastery, probably by killing her; if this speaker comes to a similar conclusion about Porphyria, perhaps he, too, is capable of murder.]

D. Reader's Response: First Thoughts

? What is your reaction as you read these lines? [Sample responses: Surprise, shock, disbelief, revulsion.]

Porphyria's Lover

Robert Browning

A The rain set early in tonight,
    The sullen wind was soon awake,
It tore the elm tops down for spite,
    And did its worst to vex the lake:
5   I listened with heart fit to break.
When glided in Porphyria; straight
    She shut the cold out and the storm,
And kneeled and made the cheerless grate
    Blaze up, and all the cottage warm;
10 Which done, she rose, and from her form
Withdrew the dripping cloak and shawl,
    And laid her soiled gloves by, untied
Her hat and let the damp hair fall,
    And, last, she sat down by my side
15 And called me. When no voice replied,
She put my arm about her waist,
    And made her smooth white shoulder bare,
And all her yellow hair displaced,
    And, stooping, made my cheek lie there,
20 And spread, o'er all, her yellow hair,
B Murmuring how she loved me—she
    Too weak, for all her heart's endeavor,
To set its struggling passion free
    From pride, and vainer ties dissever,°
25 And give herself to me forever.
But passion sometimes would prevail,
    Nor could tonight's gay feast restrain
A sudden thought of one so pale
    For love of her, and all in vain:
30 So, she was come through wind and rain.
Be sure I looked up at her eyes
    Happy and proud; at last I knew
C Porphyria worshiped me: Surprise
    Made my heart swell, and still it grew
35 While I debated what to do.
That moment she was mine, mine, fair,
    Perfectly pure and good: I found
D A thing to do, and all her hair
    In one long yellow string I wound
40 Three times her little throat around,
And strangled her. No pain felt she;
    I am quite sure she felt no pain.
As a shut bud that holds a bee,
    I warily oped° her lids; again
45 Laughed the blue eyes without a stain.

24. **dissever:** separate.

44. **oped:** archaic for "opened."

834 THE VICTORIAN PERIOD

And I untightened next the tress
    About her neck; her cheek once more
Blushed bright beneath my burning kiss:
    I propped her head up as before,
50   Only, this time my shoulder bore
Her head, which droops upon it still;
    The smiling rosy little head,
So glad it has its utmost will,
    That all it scorned at once is fled,
55   And I, its love, am gained instead!
Porphyria's love: She guessed not how
    Her darling one wish would be heard.
And thus we sit together now,
    And all night long we have not stirred,
60   And yet God has not said a word!

April Love (1856)
by Arthur Hughes.
Tate Gallery, London.

E. Literary Element: Characterization

? What do the speaker's comments suggest about him? [These lines strongly suggest that he is deranged. His obsession with Porphyria is so strong that he is content to cuddle her corpse and thinks her happy to be dead.]

F. Reader's Response: Challenging the Text

? Do you think the ending is effective? Explain. [Sample responses: Yes, it leaves a reader with a dreadful understanding of how deranged the speaker is, that he might even think God approves; or no, the last line seems out of place with the rest of the poem and leaves a reader wondering how to interpret the tone.]

CROSSING THE CURRICULUM

Health Although Porphyria's murderer speaks quite coherently and rationally, his words reveal a mental or emotional disorder. Have interested students imagine themselves as court psychiatrists studying this person's condition. Encourage them to find and to share information that would lead them to conclude whether or not the speaker is sane, thus competent to stand trial.

PROFESSIONAL NOTES

Thematic Connections: "Love and Loss" Referring to "Porphyria's Lover" and "My Last Duchess," ask students what macabre twist Browning puts upon the theme of this Collection. [Possible answer: He suggests in both poems that too much love (an obsession) can result in great loss (literally, the murder of the beloved).]

ASSESSMENT TOOLS

Informal Assessment Conduct a brief, informal assessment of students' comprehension of "Porphyria's Lover" or "My Last Duchess" by asking each student to list five words or phrases that characterize the speaker. Collect responses and read anonymous answers randomly, discussing each with the class to summarize the lesson.

Making Meanings

First Thoughts

1. Most students will point to ll. 37–42 because the murder is shocking.

Shaping Interpretations

2. In the beginning, he is sad and irritable, although Porphyria's devotion cheers him; in the end, he is calm and satisfied.

3. He wants to preserve forever the moment when she is totally his. He complains (ll. 21–25) that she is too weak to commit herself to him forever. Students should relate his reasons to the Quickwrite answers in their Reader's Logs.

4. His own delusions: He thinks that after she is dead, her blue eyes laugh (ll. 44–45) and her cheek blushes (ll. 47–48). Most students will agree these reactions are proof of the violent conditions under which she dies.

5. The speaker's action is less surprising if readers already associate him with a madhouse. Students may think the poem is set in a cabin or country house.

6. The speaker seems to recognize the awfulness of his deed and perhaps is surprised that he has not been condemned by God—or perhaps he is so deranged he interprets God's silence as approval. The line implies the speaker's concern about the consequences of his actions.

7. Responses will vary. Browning definitely links the crime with insanity, so perhaps he would approve of such a plea.

Connecting with the Text

8. Students may say the speaker must be insane to do what he did and should not be held accountable; others will say he has committed a willful act and is guilty whether he is insane or not, depending on their interpretation of the tone and language.

MAKING MEANINGS

First Thoughts

1. What, to you, is the most disturbing passage in the poem? Why?

Shaping Interpretations

2. What are the speaker's different moods in the poem?

3. What reasons does the speaker give for strangling Porphyria? Do any of his reasons relate to what you jotted in your Reader's Log entry?

4. What leads the speaker to assert that Porphyria "felt no pain"? What do you think of this claim?

5. Browning first published this poem, with another, under the general title *Madhouse Cells.* How does a knowledge of that **setting** affect your response to and interpretation of the poem? Where did you think the poem was set before you knew about Browning's original title?

6. "And yet God has not said a word!" Why do you think the speaker expects God to say something? What does the line tell you about the speaker's **character** and his awareness of what he has done?

7. From this poem, what do you think Browning's views might be on the legal plea "not guilty by reason of insanity"? What in the poem makes you think so?

Connecting with the Text

8. If you were serving on a jury for a trial of Porphyria's lover, would you find him not guilty by reason of insanity? Why or why not?

CHOICES: Building Your Portfolio

Writer's Notebook

1. Collecting Ideas for an Evaluation

An evaluation doesn't depend on personal taste. Your dislike of westerns, for instance, doesn't mean there are *no* good westerns. In evaluation, you use criteria, or standards of judgment, specific to the type of work, whether western film or dramatic monologue. Use the Before You Read information (pages 829 and 833) and the Making Meanings questions (pages 831 and 836) to list criteria for a strong dramatic poem—for example, realistic dialogue. Save your work for the Writer's Workshop on page 899.

Critical Writing

2. Love Stories?

In a brief essay, compare the themes of "My Last Duchess" and "Porphyria's Lover." Explain which poem you consider the more effective monologue.

Creative Writing

3. The Duchess Talks Back

Write a **dramatic monologue**, in prose, using the voice of the wife in "My Last Duchess." Base your monologue on an imaginary incident, and take into account the personality portraits of both the Duchess and the Duke in Browning's poem.

Improvisational Theater

4. Prelude to a Crime

Working with other students, imaginatively reconstruct the relationship between Porphyria and her lover before Porphyria's last visit. Look for clues in the poem that help you set up the speaker's state of mind, time, place, and basic circumstances of a next-to-last meeting, and improvise the scene for the class.

Beyond the Poems

Choices: Building Your Portfolio

1. **Writer's Notebook** Remind students to save their work. They may use it as prewriting for the Writer's Workshop on p. 899.

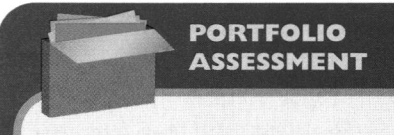

PORTFOLIO ASSESSMENT

Choices: Assessment Criteria For help in evaluating these Choices assignments, see the criteria in the *Portfolio Management System,* p. 145.

Elizabeth Barrett Browning

(1806–1861)

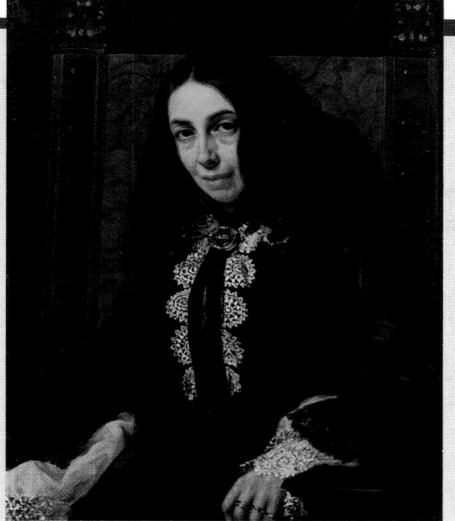

Elizabeth Barrett Browning (1858) by Michele Gordigiani. Oil on canvas (73.7 cm × 58.4 cm).

By Courtesy of the National Portrait Gallery, London.

Elizabeth Barrett Browning was one of the most famous poets of her day—more successful during her lifetime than her husband Robert Browning. She is remembered today for her *Sonnets from the Portuguese,* of which "How Do I Love Thee?" is the best known.

During her lifetime, Barrett Browning was well known as an audacious, versatile poet who frequently wrote on intellectual, religious, and political matters. As a girl, she had studied Greek, Latin, French, Italian, history, and philosophy—an uncommon education for a woman in nineteenth-century England. She published long narratives, a novel in verse, translations of Greek plays, and poems that dealt with the abolition of slavery, the exploitation of children in factories, religious belief, and Italian nationalism.

Through the first half of her busy literary career, Elizabeth Barrett was a semi-invalid. Her illnesses have been variously diagnosed, but it is certain that their effect was enlarged by the sometimes bullying protectiveness of her father and perhaps by the drugs routinely prescribed in those days for a "nervous collapse." She wrote to Robert Browning during their courtship, "Papa says sometimes when he comes into this room unexpectedly and convicts me of having dry toast for dinner, . . . that obstinacy and dry toast have brought me to my present condition, and if I *pleased* to have porter and beefsteaks instead, I should be as well as ever I was, in a month!"

In 1845, she met Robert Browning, and the next year they married secretly and eloped to the Continent. Her father never forgave her for the marriage (he had forbidden all his children to marry), nor did he ever see her again. Barrett Browning flourished in Italy and bore a son when she was forty-three years old: her own "young Florentine" with "brave blue English eyes."

The Browning Readers
(late 19th or early 20th century)
by Sir William Rothenstein.

Bradford Galleries and Museums, London.

837

QUICK PLANNING GUIDE

Into the Poem

Author Biography p. 837
Before You Read p. 838

Through the Poem

Sonnet 43 p. 838
Student to Student p. 839
"Tu B'shvat"
Making Meanings p. 839

Beyond the Poem

Choices: Building Your Portfolio p. 839
- **Writer's Notebook:** Collecting ideas for an evaluation
- **Creative Writing:** Write a short love poem
- **Performance:** Present a series of love poems

PORTFOLIO ASSESSMENT

Portfolio Assessment
For help with self-assessment of reading skills, see the *Portfolio Management System,* pp. 48–49.

PROGRAM MANAGER

- **Planning Instruction** See Teaching Notes, *Teaching Resources B,* p. 66, for objectives, a summary, and literary elements for this selection.
- **Instructional Support** Before beginning the instructional lesson, see

- Graphic Organizer for Active Reading, *Teaching Resources B,* p. 81, for a Through the Poem activity.
- **Audiotaped Readings** To help auditory learners, use the Selected Reading, Audiocassette 1, Side B, in the *Audiovisual Resources Binder.*
- **Assessment** See Selection Test, *Test Booklet,* p. 176.

Into the Poem

Using BEFORE YOU READ p. 838

Background

Students may find it interesting that Robert Browning often called Barrett Browning "my little Portuguese" because of her dark complexion.

Through the Poem

A. Critical Reading: Making Inferences

Ask students to discuss their interpretations of these lines. [Possible answer: The speaker says that her love is as great as the urge she feels to reach for ideals ("the ends of Being and ideal Grace") that are beyond her grasp.]

B. Literary Element: Petrarchan Sonnet

? Why might Barrett Browning decide to use the formal limitations of sonnet form to express such a sweeping passion? [Possible answers: The form juxtaposes passion with the gentility and quaintness of a rhyming, regularly metered poem. The form contains the passion, preventing the poem from being overly sentimental.]

BEFORE YOU READ
SONNET 43

Reading Focus

Love Without Limits

This poem expresses an ardent, joyful love—a truly transforming love. And yet, it is not a blind, infatuated love. Amid the fervor, you may find hints that love must weather more than joy.

Quickwrite

Expressions of love are often exaggerated. Robert Burns wrote a love poem in which the speaker vows to love until the seas go dry. Think of some exaggerations you could use to say "I love you."

READER'S LOG

Elements of Literature

Petrarchan Sonnet

All forty-four poems in *Sonnets from the Portuguese* are written in traditional **Petrarchan,** or Italian, **sonnet** form: an octave (eight lines) and sestet (six lines) in iambic pentameter, rhyming *abbaabba cdcdcd.* Sonnet 43 does not have the usual **turn,** or break in thought, at the sestet. Rather, the poem is broken into short units of thought.

Background

Barrett Browning wrote her sonnets before her marriage, but did not show them to her husband until three years later. Reluctant to publish the poems because they were so autobiographical, she deliberately gave them a title that suggested that they were a translation into English from an original Portuguese source.

Sonnet 43

Elizabeth Barrett Browning

How do I love thee? Let me count the ways.
I love thee to the depth and breadth and height
My soul can reach, when feeling out of sight
For the ends of Being and ideal Grace.
5 I love thee to the level of everyday's
Most quiet need, by sun and candlelight.
I love thee freely, as men strive for Right;
I love thee purely, as they turn from Praise.
I love thee with the passion put to use
10 In my old griefs, and with my childhood's faith.
I love thee with a love I seemed to lose
With my lost saints°—I love thee with the breath,
Smiles, tears, of all my life!—and, if God choose,
I shall but love thee better after death.

12. **lost saints:** childhood faith.

Love Among the Ruins (1894) by Sir Edward Burne-Jones.
Wightwick Manor/National Trust Photographic Library, London.

English Language Development
To check that English-language learners have understood the poem as it is presented, have them reconstruct it line by line. On the chalkboard or on a transparency, rewrite the lines of the poem in random order. Students must then draw upon their comprehension of the poem as well as their knowledge of the sonnet's rhyme scheme to arrange the lines in their original order.

Visual Selected poems by Elizabeth Barrett Browning can be found on the University of Maryland's electronic information server, accessible via Gopher at **gopher.inform.umd.edu:70/11/EdRes/Topic /WomensStudies/ReadingRoom/Poetry /BarrettBrowning**. *You may want to preview any Internet activity that you suggest to students. Because these resources are sometimes public forums, their content can be unpredictable.*

TECHNOLOGY

Less Proficient Readers This sonnet is so brief, and so lacking in concrete detail, that students may be challenged to follow the speaker's thoughts. Take a cue from Barrett Browning's "Let me count the ways," and work with students (or have students work with partners) to complete a numbered list of "I love thee . . ." statements that outline the poem.

Student to Student

Tu B'shvat
(A Jewish holiday that celebrates trees)

When I turn to look for you
the door swings back and forth
chilling the air
and smoke wavers in the empty doorway.
I become a tree
capable of nothing
but to stand here
and watch you go
hoping one of my branches
will snag
on your mulberry silk skirt
and bring you back.

      —Michelle Dorrien
      Clarkstown High School North
      New City, New York

MAKING MEANINGS

First Thoughts

1. If someone sent Sonnet 43 to you, how would you feel?

Shaping Interpretations

2. How many distinct ways does the speaker say that she loves her beloved?
3. What do you think the poem expresses about the speaker's religious faith?
4. How are the pauses in the last three lines different in **rhythm** from those in the rest of the poem? What do you think is the effect of this change in rhythm?

Challenging the Text

5. In your opinion, has Barrett Browning described all of the important aspects and emotions of love? Explain your response. (Refer to your Reader's Log entry for ideas.)

CHOICES:
Building Your Portfolio

Writer's Notebook

1. Collecting Ideas for an Evaluation

WORK IN PROGRESS

In an evaluation of a literary work, you can find evidence for your position by comparing the work to another of the same type. What do you think is the best love sonnet you've read in this book? (Review your Reader's Log entries.) Re-read it and Sonnet 43, and then create a dialectical journal entry comparing the two. On the left, write a positive statement about the earlier poem; on the right, freewrite a response about Sonnet 43. Save your work for the Writer's Workshop on page 899.

Creative Writing

2. Counting the Ways

Write a short love poem that answers the question: How do I love you? You might even try to write your poem in **sonnet** form. Before you begin, examine the ways that Barrett Browning and the student writer of "Tu B'shvat" (left column) use **metaphor** in their love poems.

Performance

3. How Do You Say Love?

Select some other love sonnets from this book, and present an hour of "love talk." You might be able to arrange your sonnets as a series of statements and responses. Which sonnets should be spoken by men? Which by women? If you are interested in adding a modern woman's voice, read Millay's "What Lips My Lips Have Kissed" (lines from the poem are quoted on page 801).

ELIZABETH BARRETT BROWNING 839

A. Reader's Response: First Thoughts

? What do you think has happened? [Sample responses: Someone has left the room; perhaps this is a metaphor for a bigger leave-taking, such as a breakup or a parent leaving children.]

B. Critical Reading: Speculating

? Do you think the speaker will wait for love to return? What in the poem makes you think so? [Possible answers: The speaker is compared to a tree that will stand fast; the speaker will wait because he or she feels capable only of watching. The hope that a branch will snag the leave-taker's skirt seems to indicate that the speaker feels at the mercy of the leave-taker's whims.]

Making Meanings
First Thoughts

1. Most students will agree that this poem would move them because of its simple yet heartfelt words and tone.

Shaping Interpretations

2. Seven, plus the expectation of love after death.
3. The speaker expresses religious faith in ll. 9–12 and 13–14.
4. The pauses through l. 11 indicate the end of a thought or a natural pause. The pauses in ll. 12–13 indicate an emotional interruption. These lines contrast with the earlier, more measured declarations.

Challenging the Text

5. **(Evaluation)** Responses will vary. Students may add at least two or three items, such as the importance of similar values and interests or of physical attraction. Students should expand on their Reader's Log responses.

Beyond the Poem

Choices: Building Your Portfolio

1. **Writer's Notebook** Remind students to save their work. They may use it as prewriting for the Writer's Workshop on p. 899.

Gerard Manley Hopkins
(1844–1889)

Hopkins was the eldest son of highly educated parents who were devoted to the Church of England. His father, British consul-general of the Hawaiian Islands, sent the young Hopkins to Highgate, a London boarding school, where he won a poetry prize and later a scholarship to study classics at Oxford University. Hopkins intended to prepare himself for the Anglican ministry, but after much soul-searching, converted to Roman Catholicism in 1866—a radical and shocking thing to do at the time.

In 1868, when he entered the Jesuit order, Hopkins burned almost all his poetry (a few poems remain) and "resolved to write no more, as not belonging to my profession, unless it were by the wish of my superiors." He wrote no poetry for seven years, but in 1875, he was asked to write an ode in memory of five Franciscan nuns who had drowned at sea. He sent "The Wreck of the *Deutschland*" to a Jesuit periodical, whose editors "dared not print it."

Hopkins, an unusually conscientious man, was ordained as a Jesuit priest in 1877 and devoted himself to the immediate demands of the priesthood. He served in parishes in poor sections of English and Scottish cities, writing sermons and ministering to the sick. As a teacher of classics at a Jesuit seminary and later as a professor of Greek at the Roman Catholic university in Dublin, Hopkins worked hard at lecturing, grading papers, and planning a series of scholarly papers. In 1889, at the age of forty-four, he died of typhoid fever in Dublin.

Hopkins published one of his poems in 1863, the year he entered college, but after that only a few insignificant poems appeared during his lifetime. He composed a small but very powerful body of poetry that he sent to his friends with careful instructions about how to understand them. In his letters, he elaborated on his ideas about using the stock of native English words for the diction of his verse. Hopkins's poems are also characterized by what he called **sprung rhythm,** and by **assonance, alliteration,** and **internal rhyme.** Robert Bridges, a friend and fellow poet, published the first edition of Hopkins's poems after his death.

Hopkins attempted in his sprung rhythm to imitate the sound of natural speech. He explained: "It consists in scanning by accents or stresses alone, . . . so that a foot may be but one strong syllable or it may be many light and one strong." In conventional metrics, a foot consists of a prescribed number of stressed and unstressed syllables (an *iamb,* for example, is an unstressed syllable followed by a stressed syllable). Sprung rhythm is not concerned with using only one kind of foot in a poem; in Hopkins's poems, a line may consist of many kinds of feet: iambs, trochees, dactyls, spondees, and so on.

For a while, literary critics regarded Hopkins as a twentieth-century poet—rather than a Victorian poet—because of his strongly individual language, compression of meaning, unconventional forms, and singular sound. But Hopkins is unmistakably rooted in the nineteenth century. In his almost ecstatic love of nature, his passionate conviction of a transcendental power, and his striving for individuality, Hopkins resembled the Romantic poets. In the "terrible sonnets" of his last four years, Hopkins expressed the doubts and spiritual anguish of many late-nineteenth-century writers.

Gerard Manley Hopkins (1880). Photograph by Forshaw and Coles.
By Courtesy of the National Portrait Gallery, London.

PROGRAM MANAGER

- **Planning Instruction** See **Teaching Notes,** *Teaching Resources B,* pp. 66–67, for additional historical and biographical information for this selection.
- **Instructional Support** Before beginning the instructional lesson, see **Graphic**

Organizers for Active Reading, *Teaching Resources B,* pp. 82–83, for Through the Poem activities.
- **Assessment** See **Selection Tests,** *Test Booklet,* pp. 177–178.

BEFORE YOU READ
SPRING AND FALL

Reading Focus

A Change of Seasons
Human life is often compared to the year's seasons, and in that **metaphor**, youth is springtime. In this deceptively simple lyric, Hopkins combines autumn, a child, and an adult speaker for a layered, poignant effect. From the girl's sorrow and sense of loss over falling leaves, the speaker moves to a much deeper grief.

A Dialogue with the Text

As you first read, be alert to words with multiple meanings. Then, read again, and jot down those words that could have more than one meaning.

Elements of Literature

Assonance
In words placed close together, **assonance** is the repetition of similar vowel sounds followed by different consonants. *Hate* and *pale* create assonance. *Hate* and *fate* are exact rhymes.

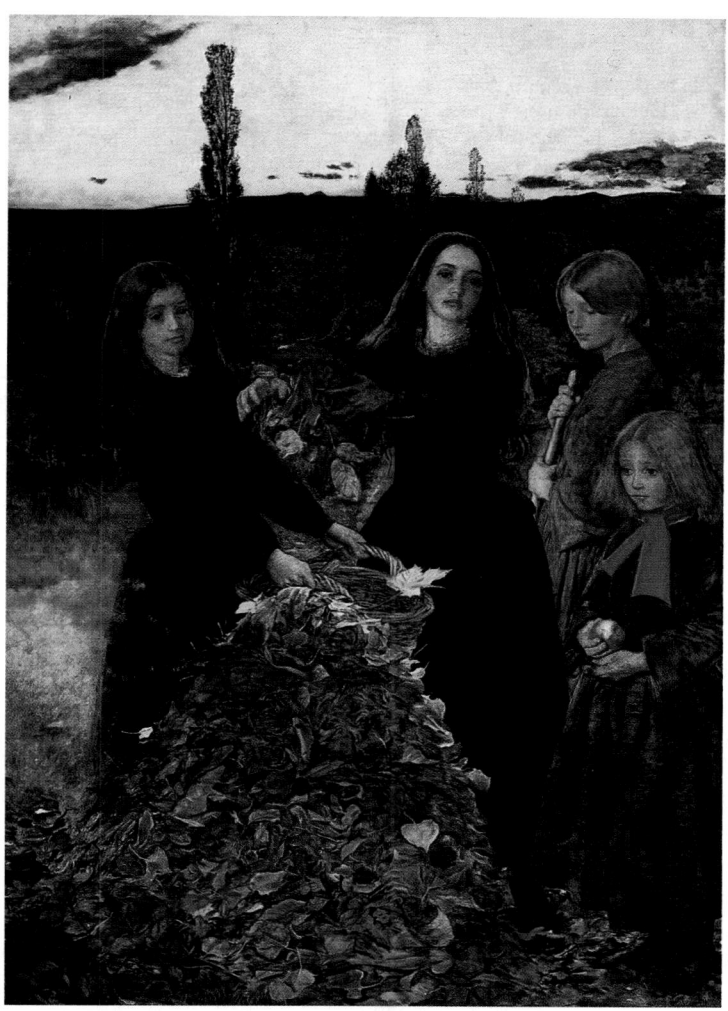

Autumn Leaves (1856) by Sir John Everett Millais. Oil on canvas (41 1/16″ × 57 1/16″).
© Manchester City Art Galleries, England.

GERARD MANLEY HOPKINS 841

QUICK PLANNING GUIDE

Into the Poems

Author Biography **p. 840**
Before You Read **p. 841, p. 843**

Through the Poems

"Spring and Fall" **p. 842**
"Pied Beauty" **p. 843**
Making Meanings **p. 842, p. 844**

Beyond the Poems

Choices: Building Your Portfolio p. 844
- **Writer's Notebook:** Evaluate Hopkins's intended effects
- **Critical Writing:** Rewrite poem into prose
- **Creative Writing:** List things that are "original, spare, strange"
- **Research:** Research unusual terms

Into the Poem

Using BEFORE YOU READ **p. 841**

A Dialogue with the Text
Ask students to create cluster diagrams in their Reader's Logs that show the possible meanings for each word that has various connotations.

OPTIONS FOR TEACHING

STRATEGIES FOR INCLUSION

English Language Development This poem was written in a style that more closely resembles natural speech than many other poems from this era. To demonstrate this, perform a choral reading with the class in which you read the poem aloud together. Then, look back to another poem from this period and read it aloud as well. Invite students to share their impressions of the sound of each poem. Does "Spring and Fall" sound more natural to them? Ask students to share why this is true or not.

CROSSING THE CURRICULUM

Science Invite interested students to do some research into the scientific aspect of trees losing their leaves in autumn: What causes the leaves' change of color? What variety of colors can be found in your area? Allow students to report their information, illustrating it with maps, slides, and other visuals and referring to Hopkins's poem when appropriate.

A. Literary Element: Assonance and Alliteration

Why might Hopkins have chosen to use assonance and alliteration? [Sample responses: They draw attention to certain words; they make the poem sound singsongy, reflecting the notion that the poem addresses a child.]

B. Reader's Response: First Thoughts

? How might the term *Sórrow's springs* be a play on words? [Sample responses: Margaret is sorrowful because of fall, but the speaker tells her that sorrow also is connected with spring; perhaps Margaret's tears are like a spring of water that wells up from the sorrow in her soul.] Point out that *spring* and *fall* may also reflect Hopkins's belief that humanity's sorrow springs from the fall of its first parents.

Making Meanings

First Thoughts

1. Students may wonder if Margaret is really crying for the reasons the speaker suggests or if she is sad about the leaves.

Shaping Interpretations

2. For the autumn leaves fallen from the trees. The speaker says she is really mourning her own mortality.

3. That she will grow "colder" and not care about fallen leaves.

4. Line 11: All sorrows have the same source (probably original sin). Line 14 refers to the Biblical fall: All human beings are destined to experience sorrow and to die.

5. Lines 1–8 suggest Margaret will outgrow her sensitivity, but in ll. 10–12 the speaker shifts to say Margaret's sadness is about a larger grief. The speaker says Margaret grieves for her future losses.

6. Alliteration: ll. 1–2, *grieving/Goldengrove*; l. 6, *such/sights*; l. 8, *worlds/wanwood*; l. 11, *Sórrow's/springs/same*. Assonance: l. 5, *grows/older*; ll. 7–9, *by/by/sigh/lie/why*; ll. 8–9, *leafmeal/weep*; and l. 13, *heart/heard*.

Spring and Fall:
To a Young Child

Gerard Manley Hopkins

Márgarét, áre you gríeving
Over Goldengrove unleaving?°
Leáves, líke the things of man, you
With your fresh thoughts care for, can you?
5 Áh! ás the heart grows older
It will come to such sights colder
By and by, nor spare a sigh
Though worlds of wanwood° leafmeal° lie;
And yet you *will* weep and know why.
10 Now no matter, child, the name:
Sórrow's springs áre the same.
Nor° mouth had, no nor mind, expressed
What heart heard of, ghost° guessed:
It ís the blight man was born for,
15 It is Margaret you mourn for.

2. Goldengrove unleaving: grove of trees whose autumn leaves are falling.

8. wanwood: pale wood. **leafmeal:** reduced to decaying leaves (a pun on "piecemeal").

12. nor: neither.
13. ghost: spirit.

MAKING MEANINGS

First Thoughts

1. What questions do you have after reading this poem twice?

Shaping Interpretations

2. What is Margaret grieving for at the opening? Whom does the speaker say she is really grieving for?

3. What does the speaker predict about Margaret's feelings when her "heart grows older"?

4. What do you think the speaker means by saying "sorrow's springs are the same" (line 11)? Think back to the account of Adam and Eve in Genesis

842 THE VICTORIAN PERIOD

(page 416), and explain the "blight man was born for" (line 14).

5. How does the speaker's attitude toward Margaret and her grief shift in the course of the poem? How would you interpret the poem's last line?

6. Read the poem aloud. Identify at least four examples of **alliteration** and **assonance**.

7. Discuss the multiple meanings of *spring, fall,* and *leaves* in the poem. (Refer to your Reader's Log entry.)

Extending the Text

8. How does the source of grief in this poem compare with the "divine despair" in Tennyson's "Tears, Idle Tears" (page 804)?

7. Spring and fall refer to the seasons. *Springs* (l. 11) refers to the source of water or of sorrow. The fall of man is suggested in l. 14. *Leáves* (l. 3) refers to the leaves of trees as well as to the verb *leaves* ("goes away").

Extending the Text

8. **(Synthesis)** Students will probably say that both poems focus on sadness that arises from a subconscious source.

Reading Focus

In Praise of Imperfection
This poem, perhaps not surprising from a poet as unconventional as Hopkins, is his song of praise to God for all things that are *pied*: covered with different-colored spots. As you read, think of the poem as being like a psalm—a praise song.

Quickwrite

What examples of spotted things do you think Hopkins will offer? Give two guesses, and tell why you do or don't find them beautiful.

Elements of Literature

Imagery
Imagery is language that appeals to the senses. In this poem, Hopkins's images follow one another with the instantaneous clarity of a movie's quick cuts. Most of his images are visual, but a few tap other senses, too.

Pied Beauty

Gerard Manley Hopkins

Glory be to God for dappled things—
    For skies of couple-color as a brinded° cow;
        For rose-moles all in stipple° upon trout that swim;
Fresh-firecoal chestnut-falls;° finches' wings;
5   Landscape plotted and pieced°—fold, fallow, and plow;
        And áll trádes, their gear and tackle and trim.
All things counter, original, spare, strange;
    Whatever is fickle, freckled (who knows how?)
        With swift, slow; sweet, sour; adazzle, dim;
10 He fathers-forth° whose beauty is past change:
                Praise him.

2. **brinded:** archaic for "brindled"; streaked with a darker color.
3. **stipple:** random dots or spots.
4. **fresh-firecoal chestnut-falls:** freshly roasted chestnuts.
5. **pieced:** parceled into fields.
10. **fathers-forth:** creates.

Evening Shadows (late 19th or early 20th century)
by Viggo Christien Frederik Wilhelm Pedersen.

GERARD MANLEY HOPKINS 843

Into the Poem

Using BEFORE YOU READ p. 843

Quickwrite

After students have had a few minutes to jot down their ideas in their Reader's Logs, let volunteers share their ideas with the class.

Through the Poem

A. Reader's Response: First Thoughts

What overall impression of the world does this list give you? [Sample responses: The world is wonderfully varied; Nature delights in complexity.]

B. Critical Reading: Making Generalizations

Re-read the adjectives in these lines and explain what they have in common. [Possible answer: All express the speaker's fascination with unconventional things, the things that run counter to typical expectations. In ll. 7–8, that idea is expressed in single-word adjectives; in l. 9, it comes through pairings of opposites.]

C. Literary Element: Imagery

Ask students to discuss what images each of these adjectives call to mind. Point out that Hopkins is able to create pictures with careful but concise diction.

OPTIONS FOR TEACHING

STRATEGIES FOR INCLUSION

Less Proficient Readers The overall picture that Hopkins presents in "Pied Beauty" is complex, but he has structured the poem so that it can be explored one line at a time. Invite students to gather for a line-by-line study of "Pied Beauty." The group leader can guide discussion of each line and decide when the group should move on.

INTEGRATING THE LANGUAGE ARTS

Language and Vocabulary "Pied Beauty" has many synonyms and antonyms that create images and establish rhythm. Invite students to look for instances of each. [The synonyms in ll. 7–8; words throughout the poem that are synonymous with *dappled* (l. 1); the antonyms in l. 9.] Ask students to describe how the use of these words enriches the poem and affects the reader.

Making Meanings

First Thoughts

1. Some students may say the poet is filled with wonder and faith. Most students will share the poet's sense of wonder at nature's intricate beauty.

Shaping Interpretations

2. A multicolored sky, a brindled cow, rose-colored spots on trout, roasted chestnuts, finches' wings, and a patchwork landscape.
3. All things unlike the norm.
4. The line has three pairs of words with opposite meanings. Two pairs repeat s and sw sounds; one pair repeats the d sound.
5. He praises God as the creator of all beauty.
6. The beauty of the physical world is transitory; God's beauty is eternal.
7. Its abruptness creates emphasis.

Extending the Text

8. **(Analysis)** Both praise God's creations.

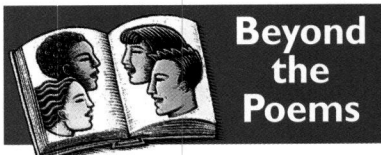

Choices: Building Your Portfolio

1. **Writer's Notebook** Remind students to save their work. They may use it as prewriting for the Writer's Workshop on p. 899.
2. **Critical Writing** Review with the class the figurative language in the poem, such as in ll. 12–13, to make sure students understand the poet's meaning.
3. **Creative Writing** Encourage students to look through natural history magazines or collections of nature photography to find examples of dappled things. Students' suggestions should fit Hopkins's own criteria for "pied beauty," as expressed in ll. 7–9.

MAKING MEANINGS

First Thoughts

1. How would you describe the speaker's emotional state, and did this poem make you share it?

Shaping Interpretations

2. What specific examples of pied beauty does the poet mention in lines 2–6?
3. What do you think the poet means by saying "all things counter" (line 7)?
4. How does the poet combine **alliteration** with **antithesis** (opposites) in line 9?
5. According to the last two lines, why does the poet offer glory and praise to God?
6. In line 10, what contrast does the poet suggest between the beauty of the physical world and the beauty of God the creator?
7. How does the **rhythm** of the last line make it especially effective?

Extending the Text

8. How is this poem, like Psalm 23 (page 422), a "praise song"?

CHOICES: Building Your Portfolio

Writer's Notebook
1. Collecting Ideas for an Evaluation

A highly original and unconventional text is always a challenge to evaluate. Is the newness a breakthrough we should learn to admire, or is it merely odd (as it first seems)? In Hopkins's case, what is your judgment? Review both poems and find three examples of inverted word order, of unusual compounds, and of invented words. For each example, write what you feel is Hopkins's intended effect and your judgment of its success. Save your work for the Writer's Workshop on page 899.

Critical Writing
2. Literal Meanings

Rewrite "Spring and Fall" in a prose paraphrase, using normal syntax and changing figurative language. Be sure to include all the poem's major ideas in your version.

Creative Writing
3. Another Look at Loveliness

Hopkins names a number of "dappled" things whose beauty he celebrates. Starting from your Reader's Log, make your own list of things that are "original, spare, strange" in Hopkins's sense.

Research
4. Pied Lexicon

Hopkins's poem contains a number of unusual words, such as "brinded" or "stipple." The poet also coins some compound words, such as "couple-color" and "fresh-firecoal." Use a dictionary to help you define at least six unusual terms from the poem. If illustrations will help, provide them.

(Opposite) *The Astrologer* (detail) (19th century) by Sir Edward Burne-Jones.
Agnew and Sons, London.

PORTFOLIO ASSESSMENT

Choices: Assessment Criteria For help in evaluating these Choices assignments, see the criteria in the *Portfolio Management System,* p. 147.

STRATEGIES FOR INCLUSION

Interpersonal As brainstorming for activity #2, ask students to list the points the poem makes. Then, as they write, invite them to imagine writing a letter to Margaret. After they have completed their work, have students discuss whether or not a young child would be able to really understand the speaker's thoughts in "Spring and Fall."

The Victorian Period

Collection *11*

THE PARADOX OF PROGRESS

Theme: **Loss and Gain**

In an age when great advances were made in science, people often questioned the validity of this so-called progress. For each gain, a price was paid and a loss was borne. The literature of this era mirrors the personal and social turmoil that can accompany progress.

Thematic Focus

Each selection reflects on loss and gain in a particular way.

- **Dover Beach** Love is a kind of faith to cleave to in a world where science has eclipsed religion.
- **The Darkling Thrush/Channel Firing/Ah, Are You Digging on My Grave?** Hardy chronicles the hopes and despairs of the end of a century.
- **When I Was One-and-Twenty/To an Athlete Dying Young/Is My Team Ploughing** In these poems by A. E. Housman, age, experience, and death diminish youth, glory, and innocence.
- **The Mark of the Beast** In the struggle for dominance, the winner does not always emerge victorious.
- **How Much Land Does a Man Need?** According to Tolstoy, the perils of greed include the seeds of our own destruction.

Literary Focus

Literary Element	Selection / Feature
Mood/Atmosphere	**Dover Beach**
Anticlimax	**Ah, Are You Digging on My Grave?**
Allusion	**The Mark of the Beast**

Writing Focus

The following flow chart shows how the writing assignment for each selection relates to and builds toward the writing assignment presented in the Writer's Workshop at the end of the unit.

Selection	Work-in-Progress Assignment
Dover Beach	Consider poem's message p. 850
The Darkling Thrush/Channel Firing/ Ah, Are You Digging on My Grave?	Cite quotations in support of evaluations p. 858
When I Was One-and-Twenty/To An Athlete Dying Young/Is My Team Ploughing?	Compare poems p. 869
The Mark of the Beast	Determine principles of a good short story p. 881
Writer's Workshop	Write an evaluation essay pp. 899–903

COLLECTION OPENER

T844A

Collection Planner

SELECTION/ FEATURE	Literary Elements / Active Reading	Writing	Speaking and Listening	Language and Vocabulary
Dover Beach Matthew Arnold (pp. 846–851) Critical Comment (p. 849)	• Reader's Log p. 847 • Mood/Atmosphere p. 847	• Critical Writing: Write contrast essay p. 850 • Creative Writing: Write dialogue between newly-weds p. 850		• How to Own a Word: Context Clues in Similes and Metaphors p. 851
The Darkling Thrush/ Channel Firing/ Ah, Are You Digging on My Grave? Thomas Hardy (pp. 852–861) Spotlight On: Victorian Novelists (pp. 859–861)	• Reader's Log pp. 853, 855, 857 • Anticlimax p. 857	• Critical Writing: Compare bird imagery in two poems p. 858 • Creative Writing: Sum up your views of past and future p. 858 • Creative Writing: Write editorial about war p. 858 • Creative Writing: Write character sketch p. 858	• Oral interpretation: Present dramatic reading of Hardy poem in small group p. 858	
When I Was One-and- Twenty/To an Athlete Dying Young/Is My Team Ploughing A. E. Housman (pp. 862–869) **Connections: Death and Other Grave Matters** Daniel Pool (p. 868)	• Reader's Log pp. 863, 865, 867	• Critical Writing: Compare Housman's three poems p. 869 • Creative Writing: Write diary entries based on poems p. 869 • Creative Writing: Write newspaper article p. 869	• Music and Literature: Select background music and present dramatic reading of Housman poem p. 869 • Current Events/ Speaking: Compare tones p. 869	
The Mark of the Beast Rudyard Kipling (pp. 870–881)	• Reader's Log p. 871 • Allusion p. 871	• Creative Writing: Create an outline to continue story p. 881	• Historical Research: Present report on British civil servants p. 881 • Research/Speaking: Compare werewolf stories p. 881	
World Literature: How Much Land Does a Man Need? Leo Tolstoy (pp. 882–894)	• Reader's Log p. 883		• Finding Common Ground: Discuss contrast between modern attitudes and those of ancient cultures p. 894	
The English Language: One Language—Many Nations John Algeo (pp. 896–898)			• Pronunciation pp. 897–898	• Try It Out: American and British English p. 898
Writer's Workshop: Evaluation (pp. 889–903)		• Writing process: Evaluation pp. 899–903		
Language Workshop: Sentence Style (p. 904)		• Revise essay p. 904		
Learning for Life: A Livable Community (p. 905)		• Freewrite p. 905 • Write brochure p. 905	• Plan and stage debate p. 905	

Collection Resources

Teaching Resources B	Audiovisual Resources Binder	Test Booklet
Cross-Curricular Activity p. 107	Fine Art Transparency 11.1	Collection 11 Test pp. 192–194

 Computer disk or CD-ROM

 Videodisc

 Audiocassette

 Overhead Transparency

PROGRAM RESOURCES

Electronic Media	Teaching Resources with Organizer		Audiovisual Resources Binder
	Teaching Resources B	Other Resources	
• Test Generator	• Teaching Notes p. 87 • Reading Organizer p. 92	• Test Booklet: Selection Test p. 181 • Portfolio Management System pp. 39, 148	• How to Own a Word Transparency 11.2
• Test Generators • Language Workshop: Wordy phrases	• Teaching Notes pp. 88–89 • Reading Organizers pp. 93–95 • Language Link pp. 96–97	• Test Booklet: Selection Tests pp. 182–184 • Language and Writing Skills Worksheets p. 107 • Portfolio Management System pp. 43, 149–150	• Selected Reading, Audiocassette 2, Side B
• Test Generators	• Teaching Notes pp. 89–90 • Reading Organizers pp. 98–100	• Test Booklet: Selection Tests pp. 185–187 • Portfolio Management System pp. 151–152	
• Test Generator • Language Workshop: Wordy sentences	• Teaching Notes pp. 90–91 • Reading Organizer p. 101 • Language Link pp. 102–103 • Words to Own p. 104	• Test Booklet: Selection Test pp. 188–189 • Language and Writing Skills Worksheets p. 107 • Portfolio Management System pp. 48–49, 153	
	• Teaching Notes p. 91	• Portfolio Management System pp. 54–55	
• Test Generator • Videodisc, Side A : "English: A Living Language, Part 2"	• Teaching Notes p. 91	• Test Booklet: Selection Test pp. 190–191	
• Writer's Workshop 2: Evaluation		• Portfolio Management System pp. 154–156	• Revision Transparencies 11.3 and 11.4
• Language Workshop: Sentence style	• Language Workshop pp. 105–106		
		• Portfolio Management System p. 157	

Proofreading Warm-ups

You may use the following exercises to help students practice their proofreading skills. Copy a set of incorrect sentences onto the chalkboard, and have students find and correct the spelling, punctuation, usage, and mechanical errors in each sentence. Ask students to share and discuss their responses.

	Sentences with Errors	Sentences Corrected	Skills Covered
1	a. matthew arnold a major Victorian Writer acheived fame as both a poet and a critic b. essays in criticism arnolds 1st work on literary topics were published in 1865	a. Matthew Arnold, a major Victorian writer, achieved fame as both a poet and a critic. b. <u>Essays in Criticism</u>, Arnold's first work on literary topics, was published in 1865.	Capitalization, Comma usage, Spelling, Underline book title, Apostrophe usage, Write out abbreviations, Subject-verb agreement, End marks
2	a. have you read the poem's of Thomas Hardy yet Mrs McQuiston asked John and Micah b. yes him and me read them poems said John	a. "Have you read the poems of Thomas Hardy yet?" Mrs. McQuiston asked John and Micah. b. "Yes, he and I read those poems," said John.	Quotation marks, Capitalization, Apostrophe usage, Question marks, Period for abbreviations, Comma usage, Pronoun usage, Nonstandard usage, End marks
3	a. thomas hardy begun and ended his literary career as a poet but he was also a major novelist b. however the bleakness pessimism and irony of Hardys novels was upsetting to many of his readers	a. Thomas Hardy began and ended his literary career as a poet, but he was also a major novelist. b. However, the bleakness, pessimism, and irony of Hardy's novels were upsetting to many of his readers.	Capitalization, Verb errors, Comma usage, Apostrophe usage, Subject-verb agreement, End marks
4	a. even though queen Victorias reign produced notable poetry the period is best known for it's novels b. novels published in 3 volume editions were called 3 deckers	a. Even though Queen Victoria's reign produced notable poetry, the period is best known for its novels. b. Novels published in three-volume editions were called three-deckers.	Capitalization, Apostrophe usage, Comma usage, Write out numbers, Hyphen usage, End marks
5	a. novels became a medium for instruction, they was considered a legitimate way to learn history, and etiquette b. charles dickens addressed social problems; in his novel's	a. Novels became a medium for instruction; they were considered a legitimate way to learn history and etiquette. b. Charles Dickens addressed social problems in his novels.	Capitalization, Semicolon usage, Subject-verb agreement, Comma usage, Apostrophe usage, End marks
6	a. a e housmans collection of poems titled A Shropshire Lad were quiet popular b. soldiers during world war I saw theirselfs in the homesick lad from Shropshire	a. A. E. Housman's collection of poems titled <u>A Shropshire Lad</u> was quite popular. b. Soldiers during World War I saw themselves in the homesick lad from Shropshire.	Capitalization, Periods for abbreviations, Apostrophe usage, Underline book titles, Subject-verb agreement, Spelling, Nonstandard usage, End marks
7	a. rudyard kipling born in Bombay India to English parents was the first British writer to win the nobel prize in literature b. the title of the short story The Mark of the Beast is a illusion to Revelation in the new testament	a. Rudyard Kipling, born in Bombay, India, to English parents, was the first British writer to win the Nobel Prize in literature. b. The title of the short story "The Mark of the Beast" is an allusion to Revelation in the New Testament.	Capitalization, Comma usage, Quotation marks for short-story titles, Nonstandard usage, Spelling, End marks
8	a. leo tolstoy russian writer who wrote the novel War and Peace b. that novel along with another one called Anna Karenina was a masterpeace of realistic fiction	a. Leo Tolstoy was a Russian writer who wrote the novel <u>War and Peace</u>. b. That novel, along with another one called <u>Anna Karenina</u>, was a masterpiece of realistic fiction.	Capitalization, Fragments, Underline book titles, Comma usage, Spelling, End marks
9	a. english became a World Language durring the victorian age b. the establishment of the british empire helped english to become either the 1st or 2nd language in many countrys	a. English became a world language during the Victorian Age. b. The establishment of the British Empire helped English to become either the first or second language in many countries.	Capitalization, Spelling, Write out numbers, End marks
10	a. did you no that english is used more widely and for more purposes as a second language then any other language b. its the language of international aviation to name a example	a. Did you know that English is used more widely and for more purposes as a second language than any other language? b. It's the language of international aviation, to name an example.	Capitalization, Spelling, Question mark, Apostrophe usage, Comma usage, Nonstandard usage, End marks

Collection 11

THE PARADOX OF PROGRESS

Arnold
Hardy
Housman
Kipling
Tolstoy

Wandering between two worlds, one dead,
The other powerless to be born . . .

—Matthew Arnold, *from Stanzas
from the Grande Chartreuse*

Responding to the Quotation

? What is a *paradox*? [A statement that seems to contradict itself yet also is true.] As the British made progress in technology and in international influence, they faced new questions about the faith and the values in which they long had trusted. They also realized that humanity, despite its outward progress, had changed little inwardly. In light of this, what world referred to in the quotation might be "dead," and why might the other one be "powerless to be born"? [Possible response: The "dead" world might be the simpler past—a world in which life might have been harder but in which more people felt confident in their worldview. The "powerless" world could be the future, or just a way to make sense of the present; in both cases, some source of strength is needed.]

 PROGRAM MANAGER

- **Integrated Assessment** For a summative assessment of the literature and language skills taught in this collection, see Collection 11 Test, *Test Booklet*, pp. 192–194.
- **Extending Collection Theme** See Cross-Curricular Activity: The Paradox of Progress, *Teaching Resources B*, p. 107,

for an activity in other disciplines and for evaluation criteria.

- **Instructional Support** See Fine Art Transparency 11.1. Review teacher's notes for transparencies in the *Audiovisual Resources Binder* for suggestions on how to tie the transparency to specific reading selections.

 PORTFOLIO ASSESSMENT

Parent/Guardian Involvement For forms that will help a parent or guardian review and respond to a student's portfolio, see the *Portfolio Management System*, pp. 62–63.

QUICK PLANNING GUIDE

Into the Poem

Author Biography p. 846

Before You Read p. 847

- **Reading Focus: Set a Purpose**
  Students think about how to cope
  with problems.
- **Quickwrite: Prior Knowledge**
  List valued people and things
- **Elements of Literature: Mood**
- **Background:** Arnold's first draft
  of the poem

Through the Poem

"Dover Beach" p. 848

Critical Comment p. 849

Making Meanings p. 850

Beyond the Poem

Choices: Building Your Portfolio p. 850
- **Writer's Notebook:** Evaluate the
  message of the poem
- **Critical Writing:** Write a brief contrast essay
- **Creative Writing:** Write a dialogue
  between newlyweds

How to Own a Word p. 851

Matthew Arnold

(1822–1888)

U nlike the other major
Victorian poets,
Matthew Arnold achieved
fame as both a poet and a
critic. He is as famous today
for his essays of literary and
social criticism as he is for
his poetry. His poems stand
with the achievements of
Tennyson and Browning,
their quiet tones and carefully shaped figures
of speech expressing his reflections on what
Victorian society was like, what it would become, and what it had cost.

Arnold had difficulty in his youth living up
to the expectations of his famous father, Dr.
Thomas Arnold, one of the leading thinkers of
the Victorian era and headmaster of Rugby
School. An uneven student at Rugby, Arnold
nevertheless won a scholarship to Oxford
University in 1841. Although he was less than
enthusiastic as a student, he seemed to thoroughly enjoy playing the role of a dandy. His
performance at Oxford was a failure by Rugby
standards, and he graduated without knowing
clearly what he wanted to do. In 1847, he
became private secretary to Lord Lansdowne,
head of the Council of Education.

Arnold had won prizes for his poetry at
both Rugby and Oxford. In 1849, he published
his first book of poetry, *The Strayed Reveller,* to
mixed reviews. Two more volumes of poetry
followed in 1852 and 1853, and as a result
Arnold was elected an Oxford professor of
poetry in 1857.

After his marriage in 1851, Arnold became
a government inspector of schools for poor
children, a job he held for thirty-five years.
His work was exhausting, requiring him to
travel all over England and write daily reports.
Though he continued to write poetry in his
free time, he found it increasingly difficult. In
1853, he told a friend, "I am past thirty, and

Portrait of Matthew Arnold (1880)
by George Frederic Watts.
By Courtesy of the
National Portrait Gallery, London.

three parts iced over—
and my pen, it seems to
me, is even stiffer and more
cramped than my feeling."

After 1860, Arnold
almost completely stopped
writing poetry and began a
second career as a critic.
His travels and his work
had given him firsthand
knowledge of pressing social problems, and he
became an energetic essayist and lecturer on
literary, political, social, and religious questions. *Essays in Criticism,* his first work on literary topics, was published in 1865; a second
series appeared after his death in 1888. During the 1870s, Arnold's essays addressed religion and education. In *Culture and Anarchy*
(1869) and in his essays on literature and
religion, Arnold urged his readers to acquire
a knowledge of history and to study "the best
that has been thought and known in the
world"—the Greeks, Dante, and Shakespeare—in order to judge ideas and personal
conduct. Without the steadying influence of
what he called culture, Arnold warned, the
nineteenth century's technological and political changes would accelerate into a grossly
materialistic democracy. He feared also an
intellectual anarchy in which every opinion
was seen to be as good as any other.

All through his life, Arnold was capable
of knowing both the excitement of trying to
change the temper of his age and the loneliness of not being comfortable in his own time.
Lionel Trilling, the twentieth-century literary
critic, writes that as both poet and critic,
Arnold remains fresh and relevant for modern
readers: "As a poet he reaches us not more
powerfully but, we sometimes feel, more
intimately than any other. As a critic he
provided us with the essential terms for our
debate in matters of taste and judgment."

PROGRAM MANAGER

- **Planning Instruction** See *Teaching
  Notes, Teaching Resources B,* p. 87, for
  objectives, a summary, literary elements, and
  additional historical and biographical information for this selection.
- **Instructional Support** Before beginning the instructional lesson, see Graphic

Organizer for Active Reading, *Teaching
Resources B,* p. 92, for a Through the Poem
activity.
- **Assessment** See Selection Test, *Test
  Booklet,* p. 181.

BEFORE YOU READ
DOVER BEACH

Reading Focus

On a Darkling Plain

Where do people look for answers in times of crisis? Do they look to science? to religion? to government? Enormous problems may seem to call for sweeping solutions. Instead of thinking big, however, what if we thought *small*? Arnold reminds people that they also can look to personal relationships to find the hope, love, and integrity that can make sense of the world.

Quickwrite

What do you think people cling to in troubled times? Write down a short list of people, places, or things you value the most when times are tough.

Elements of Literature

Mood

Arnold creates a **mood** that shifts at certain points in the poem like the ebb and flow of the tide he describes. **Mood** is the feeling, or **atmosphere,** in a work created by the writer's choice of descriptive details, images, and sounds.

Background

Arnold's first draft of "Dover Beach" dates from 1851, when he and his wife spent a night at Dover during their honeymoon trip on the English coast.

At the Gallery (late 19th or early 20th century) by Paul Gustav Fischer.

Into the Poem

Using BEFORE YOU READ p. 847

Elements of Literature

Rapture, grief, outrage, amusement, awe—these are but a few kinds of **mood** that often appear in literature. Invite students to choose one of these examples or one of their own, and then to suggest details, images, and sounds that they might find in writing with that mood.

WRITERS ON WRITING

It should come as no surprise that Arnold, a literary critic, wrote about the craft of writing. Share the following comments, and encourage students to apply them to "Dover Beach" or to their own writing.

- "Poetry is nothing less than the most perfect speech of man, that in which he comes nearest to being able to utter the truth."
- "More and more mankind will discover that we have to turn to poetry to interpret life for us, to console us, to sustain us. Without poetry, our science will appear incomplete; and most of what now passes with us for religion and philosophy will be replaced by poetry."

PORTFOLIO ASSESSMENT

Portfolio Assessment For help with self-assessment of reading skills, see the *Portfolio Management System,* p. 39.

Through the Poem

A. Literary Element: Mood

? If the first six lines establish one mood and setting in the poem, what do the words "Only" and "Listen!" in ll. 7 and 9 create in the poem? [Possible answers: "Only" creates an opposition to the peaceful setting that begins the poem. "Listen!" is a strong interjection, which also breaks the calm mood.]

B. Literary Element: Metaphor

The sea functions as a controlling metaphor in the poem. To help students appreciate the metaphor, ask them what power or powers the speaker attributes to the sea in these lines. [Possible answer: The sea has the power to change its world (in that it can "draw back and fling" the pebbles) and to reach into eternity (bringing an "eternal note of sadness" into the world).] Encourage students to note that in the third stanza these powers are also traditional characteristics of faith—a faith that the speaker sees in retreat.

C. Exploring the Culture

Despite their zest for progress, the Victorians were, in many ways, plagued by doubts. One of their greatest challenges was to reconcile faith with the new discoveries of science. The speaker here sounds like many of his day, who felt that if new theories, with all their implications, were accepted, faith could not stand. Thus, Arnold (like Tennyson in *In Memoriam*) can be said to speak not merely for himself but for his era.

Dover Beach

Matthew Arnold

The sea is calm tonight.
The tide is full, the moon lies fair
Upon the straits°—on the French coast the light
Gleams and is gone; the cliffs of England stand,
5 Glimmering and vast, out in the tranquil bay.
Come to the window, sweet is the night air!
Only, from the long line of spray
Where the sea meets the moon-blanched land,
Listen! you hear the grating roar
10 Of pebbles which the waves draw back, and fling,
At their return, up the high strand,°
Begin, and cease, and then again begin,
With tremulous cadence slow, and bring
The eternal note of sadness in.

15 Sophocles° long ago
Heard it on the Aegean,° and it brought
Into his mind the turbid ebb and flow
Of human misery; we
Find also in the sound a thought,
20 Hearing it by this distant northern sea.

The Sea of Faith
Was once, too, at the full, and round earth's shore
Lay like the folds of a bright girdle° furled.
But now I only hear
25 Its melancholy, long, withdrawing roar,
Retreating, to the breath
Of the night wind, down the vast edges drear
And naked shingles° of the world.

Ah, love, let us be true
30 To one another! for the world, which seems
To lie before us like a land of dreams,
So various, so beautiful, so new,
Hath really neither joy, nor love, nor light,
Nor certitude, nor peace, nor help for pain;
35 And we are here as on a darkling plain
Swept with confused alarms of struggle and flight,
Where ignorant armies clash by night.

3. straits: Strait of Dover, a body of water separating southeastern England and northwestern France.

11. strand: shore.

15. Sophocles (säf′ə·klēz′) (c. 496–406 B.C.): one of the principal writers of ancient Greek tragedies.
16. Aegean (ē·jē′ən): sea between Greece and Turkey.

23. girdle: belt.

28. shingles: beaches covered with pebbles.

848 THE VICTORIAN PERIOD

OPTIONS FOR TEACHING

STRATEGIES FOR INCLUSION

Auditory To help set the scene for reading, play a recording of the sound of surf. Have students comment on the images and thoughts that come to mind as they listen. Briefly relate the recording to "Dover Beach," explaining that the sea is an important image in the poem; then, if the noise is not distracting, play the recording softly as students read independently.

English Language Development Each stanza of this poem builds upon the previous one to convey Arnold's sentiment. To help students assemble this message, have them focus on each stanza to come up with a main idea for that set of lines. Have students write in their Reader's Logs a sentence each that captures the most important idea for each stanza. Then, have them compare their interpretations in a class discussion.

Interpersonal Arnold's speaker concludes that in a world that at best offers only images of comfort, people need to "be true / To one another!" Invite students each to work with a partner and to focus on this last stanza, commenting in particular upon the speaker's answer to his world and to the closing image. Have each pair write a paraphrase and an example that represent the last stanza.

T848 The Victorian Period

Pegwell Bay, Kent—A Recollection of October 5, 1858 (1859–1860) by William Dyce.
Tate Gallery, London.

*C*ritical *C*omment

Love Is Itself a Faith

More than any other poem written in the nineteenth century, "Dover Beach" continues to echo through the consciousness of every generation of the twentieth century. To say why involves matters of both technique and meaning.

Compared with the characteristic product of the Romantic or Victorian poets, "Dover Beach" is low-keyed. The speaker's tone is largely that of quiet conversation in which iambs and anapests are congenially mixed. For all its conversational tone, however, the poem is remarkably ambitious in its claim to render a universal condition.

Unlike his predecessors and contemporaries, Arnold neither reaches for the sublime nor dwells on the sentimental in this poem. Instead, he writes a love poem that, incidentally, expresses the crisis of conscience brought about by the dwindling of religion—"the Sea of Faith"—and the rise of science. Science has transformed human life through industrialism and through the mass warfare that scientific inventions made possible. Against these bewildering developments, Arnold poses the notion that love is itself a faith to cling to and, by implication, that individual integrity and a humanistic vision broad enough to include the tragic conclusions of Sophocles are the only defenses against a world moving toward anarchy.

E

INTEGRATING THE LANGUAGE ARTS

Strategic Reading Ensure students' understanding of "Dover Beach"—considered to be a key poetic statement of the doubts felt by many Victorians—by using Reciprocal Teaching with pairs of students. As partners finish each stanza, have them summarize the reading. Then, have them ask each other questions (perhaps two per student) about anything that they consider important in the stanza.

COOPERATIVE LEARNING

Roundtable After dividing the class into groups, ask students to complete this sentence: "The most significant part of this poem is _____ ." Give the groups five minutes to pass around a sheet of paper, each student writing an answer. As groups share their answers, note on the chalkboard the answers that appear most frequently, as well as the answers that show special insight.

Making Meanings

First Thoughts

1. Although responses will vary, most students probably will have the strongest emotional response either to the first stanza, whose vivid images evoke a quiet melancholy, or to the final stanza, in which the speaker cries out for a loving commitment that will provide strength to face the world.

Shaping Interpretations

2. It is night in a room in Dover, England, overlooking the moonlit sea. The speaker is a person addressing a loved one.

3. The mood in ll. 1–6 is calm, peaceful, perhaps even joyful. In l. 7 "Only" suggests an upcoming contrast. The "grating roar" and the sea flinging pebbles change the mood.

4. Referring to the "tremulous cadence" of the sea, which brings in the "eternal note of sadness," the speaker says that the same sound was heard centuries ago by Sophocles.

5. The "Sea of Faith" (a metaphor for religious belief) once surrounded the earth, encompassing it like the folds of a bright belt (a simile) that supported and decorated the earth. The speaker's faith has weakened; it has withdrawn, leaving the speaker as barren as the beaches he describes.

6. The speaker urges that the couple be true to one another because life, which is filled with chaos, is difficult and painful. Students probably will have similar comforts on their lists.

Extending the Text

7. **(Evaluation)** The speaker sees the world as a chaotic, painful place without joy or peace. Students may suggest that the view remains relevant because the political struggles of established nations and emerging countries often erupt into wars, which constantly threaten to spread.

MAKING MEANINGS

First Thoughts

1. Which lines of the poem do you respond to most strongly? Why?

Shaping Interpretations

2. What is the **setting** of the first stanza? Who is the speaker, and whom is he addressing?

3. What **mood** do the first six lines evoke for you? What images in the second half of the first stanza begin to change this mood?

4. Where does the poem begin to move from a personal experience to a timeless and universal theme? What does the speaker imagine Sophocles also heard long ago?

5. Explain the **figures of speech** used to describe faith in lines 21–23. What do you think has happened to the speaker's faith, according to lines 24–28?

6. What does the speaker urge in the last stanza, and why? How does the speaker's resolution compare to the comforting things you cited in your Reader's Log entry?

Extending the Text

7. What is the speaker's view of his world as it is presented in the last stanza? Do you think this view is relevant to today's world? Explain why or why not.

CHOICES:
Building Your Portfolio

Writer's Notebook

1. Collecting Ideas for an Evaluation

In evaluating a poem, one of the things you will most likely focus on is **meaning**. The reader of any poem asks: What is the poet telling me, and how do I feel about that "message"? Ask yourself these questions about "Dover Beach." Save your notes about the poem's meaning and your response to it for the Writer's Workshop on page 899.

Critical Writing

2. A Changing Picture of the World

Arnold starts his poem with a moonlit sea and ends with a dark plain. Write a brief essay focusing on the contrasts in "Dover Beach." Discuss the importance of these contrasts in developing the universal theme of the poem.

Creative Writing

3. Newlywed Dialogue

Working with another student, write the dialogue between newlywed Arnold and his wife Fanny Lucy (Arnold called her "Flu") that might have inspired this poem. Be sure to express the feelings of both characters.

Matthew Arnold (1871), published in Vanity Fair.

PORTFOLIO ASSESSMENT

Choices: Assessment Criteria For help in evaluating these Choices assignments, see the criteria in the *Portfolio Management System,* p. 148.

HOW TO OWN A WORD

Context Clues in Similes and Metaphors

You can sometimes figure out the meaning of a new word—or a familiar word used in a new way—by using **context clues.** These are hints that are found in the surrounding words, phrases, and sentences.

Similes and **metaphors** often provide excellent context clues. In both types of figure of speech, writers associate and compare two apparently dissimilar things or ideas to vividly communicate images and emotions. In a **simile,** words such as *like, as, than,* or *resemble* are used to compare one thing to another, as in "an inquisitive child is like a blossoming flower." In a **metaphor,** one thing is referred to as if it were something else, either directly, as in "an inquisitive child is a blossoming flower," or indirectly, as in "an inquisitive child grows and blossoms."

Because each of the two equivalent parts of the comparison describes the other, each part provides clues to the meanings of words in the other part. For example, if you read "an inquisitive child is like a blossoming flower" and do not know what *inquisitive* means, you can probably at least figure out that it is a desirable and pleasant quality because you know that in the equivalent part of the comparison the descriptive word, *blossoming,* signifies a desirable and pleasant quality.

Simile. In Robert Browning's poem "Porphyria's Lover" (page 834), the lover uses a simile to describe how he opens Porphyria's eyes after strangling her to death.

> As a shut bud that holds a bee,
>   I warily oped her lids.

In this simile, the word *as* is used to compare the two similar actions. The lover warily opens the dead woman's eyes, as he would open a bud that holds a bee. The following diagram shows the almost equivalent relationship of the two parts.

open a bud that holds a bee	as ≈	warily open the dead woman's eyes

If *warily* is an unfamiliar word, knowing that it describes an action similar to opening a bud that

holds a bee gives you a clue. You might guess that it means "cautiously."

Metaphor. In the following passage from "Ulysses" by Alfred, Lord Tennyson (page 822), Ulysses, who had been a warrior and world traveler, uses a metaphor that equates his "pause"—his current, inactive retirement—to an unused sword.

> How dull it is to pause, to make an end,
> To rust unburnished, not to shine in use!

This metaphor includes what might be an unfamiliar word—*unburnished.* However, like many metaphors, this one is rich with context clues. It contains three clues. First, the metaphoric comparison implies that an inactive warrior is an unburnished sword. The following diagram shows the equivalent relationship of the two parts.

inactive warrior	=	unburnished sword

The equivalent descriptive word for *unburnished,* then, is *inactive,* meaning "idle, retired, dull, sluggish." Second, the sword is rusting, and third, it does not "shine in use." From these clues, you may not yet know that *unburnished* means "unpolished," but you can probably guess that it does have something to do with a neglected condition in which the blade is not brilliantly shiny.

Try It Out

On your own paper, identify the first of the two figures of speech in the following passage from "Dover Beach" by Matthew Arnold as either a metaphor or a simile. Then, draw two boxes as in the preceding diagrams. For a metaphor, use = (equals) between the two boxes; for a simile, use ≈ (almost equals). Write one of the things being compared in each box. Repeat this procedure for the second figure of speech. Finally, write your guess at the meaning of the italicized word, *furled.* Check your guess by looking up the italicized word in a dictionary.

> The Sea of Faith
> Was once, too, at the full, and round earth's shore
> Lay like the folds of a bright girdle *furled.*

Choices: Building Your Portfolio

1. **Writer's Notebook** Remind students to save their work. They may use it as prewriting for the Writer's Workshop on p. 899.
2. **Critical Writing** Point out that the contrasts need not all lie in specific details; for example, students already may have noted the contrast in mood between the poem's beginning and its end. Have students organize their ideas in a graphic similar to Transparency 6: Comparison and Contrast Chart in the Transparency Package.
3. **Creative Writing** Have the class brainstorm ideas about a situation that might have prompted the dialogue. Challenge writers to see if there are any phrases or statements in "Dover Beach" that they might incorporate into the dialogue (ultimately giving the impression that these words showed up in the poem because they had come up in the earlier dialogue).

How to Own a Word
Try It Out: Answers

Diagrams for the two figures of speech should be similar to these:

Sea	=	Faith

sea at the shore	≈	folds of a girdle

Students probably will guess from context clues that *furled* has something to do with a folded or rolled-up piece of cloth; they also may know its antonym, *unfurled,* from associations with flags. Students should be able to verify in a dictionary that *furled* means "curled or rolled up."

Learners Having Difficulty To help them grasp the metaphors for the exercise on this page, have students draw the sea and the shore, making the waves look like a folded sash. Have a volunteer put his or her drawing on the chalkboard. Ask students to draw an island with such a sea all around it and then to label the sea "Faith." Thus, the sea may be seen as the protective force of Arnold's poem, whose receding waves no longer embrace the shore, but leave it barren.

 PROGRAM MANAGER

Reinforcement To allow students practice and reinforcement of the vocabulary strategy introduced here, see **Transparency 11.2** in the *Audio-visual Resources Binder.*

Into the Poems

Author Biography p. 852
Before You Read: p. 853, p. 855, p. 857

Through the Poems

"The Darkling Thrush" p. 853
"Channel Firing" p. 855
"Ah, Are You Digging on My Grave?"
p. 857
Making Meanings: p. 854, p. 856, p. 858

Beyond the Poems

Choices: Building Your Portfolio p. 858
- **Writer's Notebook:** Find support for evaluations of literary elements
- **Critical Writing:** In an essay, compare two poems that use bird imagery
- **Creative Writing:** Write a short essay or poem about the past and future
- **Creative Writing:** Write a persuasive editorial about war
- **Creative Writing:** Create a character sketch
- **Oral Interpretation:** Present a dramatic reading

Spotlight On pp. 859–861

Thomas Hardy

(1840–1928)

Thomas Hardy (1894).

Thomas Hardy was one of the principal novelists of late-Victorian Britain, but he began and ended his literary career as a poet. The oldest of four children, Hardy was born in a small village in Dorsetshire in southwestern England, the setting (under its ancient name of Wessex) of many of his novels and poems. His father was a stonemason and carpenter who loved music and taught Hardy to play the violin. Hardy went to the village school until he was sixteen, when he became an apprentice to an architect. He read widely on his own for the next six years, "reading the *Iliad,* the *Aeneid,* or the Greek Testament from six to eight in the morning, would work at Gothic architecture all day, and then in the evening rush off with his fiddle under his arm . . . to play country dances, reels, and hornpipes at an agriculturist's wedding." In 1861, Hardy began working as an architect in London, writing poems and stories in his free time. He tried unsuccessfully to publish his poems, but by the time he returned to Dorset in 1867 as an architect specializing in church restoration, he had started to publish fiction.

Hardy's fourth novel, *Far from the Madding Crowd* (1874), was enough of a popular success to enable him to stop working as an architect. During the next twenty years, he published ten novels and three collections of stories. The plots and themes of Hardy's fiction, like those of his poetry, express his belief in a world governed by chance and natural laws that are not hostile, but simply indifferent, to what humans want and deserve. Chance gives us pain when we try for gladness or glory; sometimes in his novels the entire course of lives is determined by coincidence. Hardy liked to play the big scenes of his novels against the backdrop of powerful natural forces that take no account of human life, such as the vast heath of *The Return of the Native* (1878). To chance and the indifference of nature, humans add the folly of war, the cruelty of ingratitude and neglect, and the irrationality of laws and customs that frustrate talent and desire. Finally, the central characters' own weaknesses—Henshard in *The Mayor of Casterbridge* (1886), Jude in *Jude the Obscure* (1895), even Tess in *Tess of the D'Urbervilles* (1891)—make them vulnerable to the destructive powers of nature and society.

The bleakness, pessimism, and irony of Hardy's novels disturbed many of his readers. In 1892, after reading an unfavorable review of *Tess of the D'Urbervilles,* he wrote, "Well, if this sort of thing continues no more novel-writing for me. A man must be a fool to deliberately stand up to be shot at." In 1895, when *Jude the Obscure* was severely denounced by readers and critics (some called it "Jude the Obscene"), Hardy decided to have his say thereafter in poetry: "Perhaps I can express more fully in verse ideas and emotions which run counter to the inert crystallized opinion—hard as a rock—which the vast body of men have vested interests in supporting."

He began collecting old, new, and revised poems in a series of volumes. He published the first in 1898 and was putting together an eighth collection thirty years later, the year of his death. "My poetry was revolutionary," he wrote, "in the sense that I meant to avoid the jeweled line." Twentieth-century critics have praised Hardy's poems for their simple, compressed forms and their sad, ironic tone.

- **Planning Instruction** See *Teaching Notes, Teaching Resources B,* pp. 88–89, for objectives, summaries, and literary elements for these selections.
- **Instructional Support** Before beginning the instructional lesson, see *Graphic Organizer for Active Reading, Teaching Resources B,* pp. 93–95, for Through the Poem activities.
- **Audiotaped Readings** To help less proficient readers or auditory learners through the lesson, use the *Selected Reading, Audiocassette 2, Side B,* in the *Audiovisual Resources Binder.*

- **Assessment** See *Selection Tests,* *Test Booklet,* pp. 182–184.
- **Language Link** For instruction and practice in identifying weak words and clichés, see *Language Link, Teaching Resources B,* pp. 96–97, and *Language and Writing Skills Worksheets,* p. 107.

Reading Focus

Difficult Transitions

A stark winter scene can emphasize physical and emotional desolation. Yet the gloom of winter also precedes the promise of springtime renewal. Gloomy though it may appear at the time, the midwinter death of an old year marks the birth of a new one, and with it the hope for a new beginning.

Quickwrite

READER'S LOG

Imagine that it's the last day of the twentieth century. What details would you want to remember on such a historical occasion? Write down your ideas.

Background

Hardy wrote this poem on December 31, 1900, the last day of both the year and the century. As night falls, the speaker in the poem hears a thrush (a bird) singing joyfully. His thrush, like the century, is worn out and diminished—but still singing.

The Darkling Thrush (A)

Thomas Hardy

I leant upon a coppice° gate
    When Frost was specter-gray,
And Winter's dregs made desolate
    The weakening eye of day.
5 The tangled bine-stems° scored the sky
    Like strings of broken lyres,
And all mankind that haunted nigh
    Had sought their household fires.

The land's sharp features seemed to be
10   The Century's corpse outleant,°
His crypt the cloudy canopy,
    The wind his death-lament.
The ancient pulse of germ° and birth
    Was shrunken hard and dry,
15 And every spirit upon earth
    Seemed fervorless as I.

At once a voice arose among
    The bleak twigs overhead
In a fullhearted evensong
20   Of joy illimited;
An aged thrush, frail, gaunt, and small, (B)
    In blast-beruffled plume,
Had chosen thus to fling his soul
    Upon the growing gloom.

25 So little cause for carolings
    Of such ecstatic sound
Was written on terrestrial things
    Afar or nigh around,
That I could think there trembled through
30   His happy good-night air
Some blessed Hope, whereof he knew
    And I was unaware.

1. coppice: thicket of small trees or shrubs.
5. bine-stems: climbing plants.
10. outleant: leaning out. Here, the word refers to leaning out of the crypt.
13. germ: seed or bud.

Into the Poem

Using BEFORE YOU READ p. 853

Reading Focus

Especially if your community does not experience severe winters, point out that winters are not all snowball fights and New Year's Eve parties: they also can include gray skies, barren trees, bone-chilling cold, puddles of slush, and the flu. Encourage students to share personal experiences with the less-desirable elements of winter.

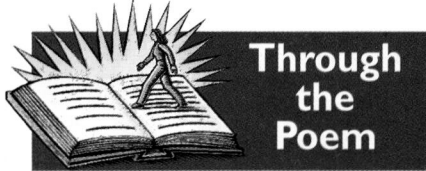

Through the Poem

A. Language Note: Vocabulary
Have students briefly discuss the word *darkling* in the title. You also might refer them to the uses of this word in Keats's "Ode to a Nightingale" (p. 757, l. 51) and in Arnold's "Dover Beach" (p. 848, l. 35).

B. Reader's Response: Shaping Interpretations

? Why do you think Hardy chooses a thrush and makes it "aged . . . frail, gaunt, and small" rather than a young, robust, and perhaps more exotic songbird? [Sample responses: The thrush is common enough that anyone might feel kinship with it. Its age may reflect the fact that it is singing on the last day of the nineteenth century. The details make the bird seem as old as the century and underscore the point that no matter how old or small, creatures can still sing hopeful songs.]

PORTFOLIO ASSESSMENT

Portfolio Assessment For help with self-assessment of reading skills, see the *Portfolio Management System,* p. 43.

STRATEGIES FOR INCLUSION

Intrapersonal Students will note that the speaker of "The Darkling Thrush" thinks of himself as alone in a dying world—until he hears the thrush's song. In their Reader's Logs, students might relate the speaker's experiences to their own, especially noting any occasion when they were challenged to take a larger view of life. *Remind students to write about something about which they feel comfortable.*

Making Meanings

First Thoughts

1. Responses will vary, but students may have noted some gloomy details that would fit the mood of the first two stanzas of "The Darkling Thrush" or may have noted some reasons for hope, as do the poem's final two stanzas.

Shaping Interpretations

2. "Coppice gate" (l. 1), "Frost" (l. 2), "Winter's dregs" (l. 3), "weakening eye of day" (l. 4). Students will probably see a gray, snowy, bleak scene.
3. The thrush is introduced in the third stanza, when the speaker hears its joyful song.
4. Most students will feel that the thrush's song gives the speaker hope; others may feel that his hopeless mood remains.
5. The speaker suggests that the thrush knows of "some blessed Hope" (l. 31).
6. Darkling means "in the dark"; it suggests emotional gloom as well as physical darkness. Interpretations of the thrush's song will vary; encourage students to support their positions with details from the poem.

Connecting with the Text

7. Students may mention a beautiful sunset or the first flower of spring.

Extending the Texts

8. (**Evaluation**) Possible response: The poems are insightful and prophetic; they also show how the horror of war and uncertainty about the future exist in all centuries.

MAKING MEANINGS

First Thoughts

1. Compare the speaker's observations about the end of the century with what you described in your Reader's Log. What observations, if any, do you and the speaker share?

Shaping Interpretations

2. What details in the first stanza establish the **setting** for the poem? Describe what you see.
3. At what point in the poem is the thrush introduced? How does the bird first come to the attention of the speaker?
4. Does the speaker's **mood** change significantly in the course of the poem? If so, how?

5. What does the speaker say about the thrush's air, or melody, in the last stanza?
6. What do you think is the significance of the word *darkling* in the title? Do you think the thrush's song seems hopeful or hopeless? Explain.

Connecting with the Text

7. Has something in nature ever given you hope, or cheered you? If so, describe your experience.

Extending the Texts

8. Both Arnold (page 846) and Hardy wrote their poems many, many years ago—well before two global wars shattered the world. Do you think the poems are prophetic—do they pertain to the history of the twentieth century in a particular way? Explain.

Winter Work (late 19th or early 20th century) by Sir George Clausen.

Reading Focus

Wake-up Call

In an age of almost miraculous technological advances, humanity sometimes stops to ask itself: When will we be too advanced, or too civilized, or too sane to wage war? Hardy's poem brings a different perspective to that question, imagining what the dead would say if they were awakened by violence in the land of the living.

Quickwrite

READER'S LOG

If they could speak, what do you think the dead would say to the living? Briefly write down your ideas.

Background

The subject of "Channel Firing" is the testing of guns at sea and on the shores of the English Channel. Hardy wrote this poem in April 1914, when a naval rivalry was growing between Great Britain and Germany. Four months later, World War I began.

The word "chancel" (line 3) refers to the part of a church nearest the altar; a "glebe" (line 9) is a plot of land attached to a church or its rectory. In the poem's last stanza, the sound of guns reaches three sites famous in British history: Alfred's Tower, near Stourton, which honors King Alfred's defeat of a Danish invasion in 879; Camelot, the legendary site of King Arthur's court; and Stonehenge, the prehistoric arrangement of huge stones on the Salisbury Plain.

Channel Firing

Thomas Hardy

That night your great guns, unawares,
Shook all our coffins as we lay,
And broke the chancel window-squares,
We thought it was the Judgment Day

5 And sat upright. While drearisome
Arose the howl of wakened hounds:
The mouse let fall the altar-crumb,
The worms drew back into the mounds,

The glebe cow drooled. Till God called, "No;
10 It's gunnery practice out at sea
Just as before you went below;
The world is as it used to be:

"All nations striving strong to make
Red war yet redder. Mad as hatters
15 They do no more for Christés sake
Than you who are helpless in such matters.

"That this is not the judgment hour
For some of them's a blessed thing,
For if it were they'd have to scour
20 Hell's floor for so much threatening. . . .

"Ha, ha. It will be warmer when
I blow the trumpet (if indeed
I ever do; for you are men,
And rest eternal sorely need)."

25 So down we lay again. "I wonder,
Will the world ever saner be,"
Said one, "than when He sent us under
In our indifferent century!"

And many a skeleton shook his head.
30 "Instead of preaching forty year,"
My neighbor Parson Thirdly said,
"I wish I had stuck to pipes and beer."

Again the guns disturbed the hour,
Roaring their readiness to avenge,
35 As far inland as Stourton Tower,
And Camelot, and starlit Stonehenge.

THOMAS HARDY 855

Into the Poem

Using **BEFORE YOU READ** p. 855

Background

By 1914, Europe was divided into two powerful camps. Tension was high between the Triple Alliance, which included Germany, Austria-Hungary, and Italy, and the Triple Entente, which included France, Great Britain, and Russia. A seemingly small event ignited the conflict that became World War I: on June 28, 1914, Archduke Franz Ferdinand of Austria-Hungary and his wife were assassinated in Sarajevo by a Serbian nationalist. Despite attempts to settle the matter diplomatically, Austria-Hungary declared war on Serbia on July 28. When Russia, which had promised to protect the Serbs, started to mobilize, Germany declared war on Russia on August 1. Two days later, Germany declared war on France and invaded neutral Belgium, resulting in Britain's entrance into the war.

Through the Poem

A. Reader's Response: Connecting with the Text

? Are nations still "striving strong to make / Red war yet redder"? Explain. [Sample responses: War remains a part of life on this planet, and weapons continue to proliferate. On the other hand, countries often try to use the United Nations and other means to resolve conflicts.]

B. Critical Reading: Making Connections

Divine laughter at this moment may be a reference by Hardy to the Second Psalm, which describes God's sovereignty over the nations. According to that psalm, when God sees the raging of the nations, then "He that sitteth in the heavens shall laugh: the Lord shall have them in derision" (verse four).

STRATEGIES FOR INCLUSION

Auditory To highlight the fact that Hardy puts many sounds into this poem but leaves much open to interpretation, have students list the noises they would notice (not just the guns, for example, but the scurrying of mice in the church, or the occasional lowing of the cow) if they were a part of this **setting.** Then, encourage an interpretive reading with sound effects. Ask students to be sure their interpretations speak to what God's voice might sound like and to what they make of God's laughter and the trumpet of judgment.

Learners Having Difficulty Extend the situation in the poem to have students reflect on what their ancestors would think of the world's situation today. To develop the discussion, have students work in small groups to create conversations their great-grandparents might have if they could see the world today from their graves. Students should address issues similar to those in the poem. Invite the groups to share their results with the class.

Making Meanings

First Thoughts

1. Students may voice surprise over God's laughter, and although they might expect a dead wicked person to regret his or her misdeeds in life, they have in this poem a good person who regrets his life of upright living since the world was left no better off by it.

Shaping Interpretations

2. The speaker is one of the dead (the *we* in l. 4), buried in a churchyard near the English Channel.

3. In God's eyes, the firing is a pointless activity that accomplishes no more than do the actions of the dead.

4. Examples include the fact that the guns disturb the dead but not the living; that Parson Thirdly wishes he had stuck to pipes and beer; and that the threatening sound of the guns reaches inland, shaking what it is meant to protect.

5. God declares that it is a good thing that it is not Judgment Day for some of the living, who would be doomed to scour the floors of Hell for their violence.

6. Some students may prefer to express their responses in private writing. Students are likely to connect with Hardy's distaste for war, saying that it is foolish and unjustifiable, though some students might acknowledge the possibility of a just war.

Challenging the Text

7. **(Evaluation)** Students may suggest that the roughness of Hardy's language befits the roughness of his subject. The diction roots the poem in reality.

L'Enfer (Hell) (early 20th century) by Georges Paul Leroux.

MAKING MEANINGS

First Thoughts

1. Does anything in the poem surprise or even shock you? Explain why or why not. (Be sure to check your Reader's Log.)

Shaping Interpretations

2. Who is the **speaker** in the poem? Who are "we" in line 4?

3. What do you make of God's irritation at those who fire the guns?

4. Point out at least three examples of **irony** in the poem.

5. What does God say about Judgment Day in the fifth stanza?

6. What do you think this poem says about war? Explain whether you agree or disagree with the **themes** of the poem.

Challenging the Text

7. In his own time, Hardy was criticized for his deliberate use of "unpoetic" language (such as "drooled" in line 9 and "mad as hatters" in line 14). What is your response to Hardy's critics? How does his **diction** affect his point about war?

OPTIONS FOR TEACHING

INTEGRATING THE LANGUAGE ARTS

Strategic Reading Have students respond in their Reader's Logs to each stanza with a sentence or two. As they read the stanzas, they should write a summary, a thought about the meaning, or a question for discussion. When class discussion takes place, have students refer to and read some of their notes. Using student ideas, create an outline of the poem on the chalkboard.

Reading Focus

Do You Miss Me?

It's comforting to know that people miss us when we're gone. What if we could come back from the dead and find out how *much* they miss us? We all have expectations of how loved ones would respond to our absence, but we might be surprised at what they say about us when we're not around.

Quickwrite

Cemeteries can be perceived either as solemn sites or as places to remember loved ones joyously. Briefly describe a cemetery you have seen, or imagine the kind of atmosphere you think a cemetery would have.

Elements of Literature

Anticlimax

The power of this poem in part depends on Hardy's use of **anticlimax**, the arrangement of narrative details so that something unimportant appears where we expect something significant. In this poem, Hardy challenges our conventional beliefs about death and grieving by creating a narrator who has only limited information about her situation—she therefore receives some very unexpected answers to her repeated question.

Ah, Are You Digging on My Grave?

Thomas Hardy

"Ah, are you digging on my grave,
    My loved one?—planting rue?"°
—"No: Yesterday he went to wed
One of the brightest wealth has bred.
5 'It cannot hurt her now,' he said,
    'That I should not be true.'"

"Then who is digging on my grave?
    My nearest dearest kin?"
—"Ah, no: They sit and think, 'What use!
10 What good will planting flowers produce?
No tendance of her mound can loose
    Her spirit from Death's gin.'"°

"But some one digs upon my grave?
    My enemy?—prodding sly?"
15 —"Nay: When she heard you had passed the Gate
That shuts on all flesh soon or late,
She thought you no more worth her hate,
    And cares not where you lie."

"Then, who is digging on my grave?
20   Say—since I have not guessed!"
—"O it is I, my mistress dear,
Your little dog, who still lives near,
And much I hope my movements here
    Have not disturbed your rest?"

25 "Ah, yes! *You* dig upon my grave . . .
    Why flashed it not on me
That one true heart was left behind!
What feeling do we ever find
To equal among human kind
30   A dog's fidelity!"

"Mistress, I dug upon your grave
    To bury a bone, in case
I should be hungry near this spot
When passing on my daily trot.
35 I am sorry, but I quite forgot
    It was your resting place."

2. **rue:** yellow-flowered herb associated with grief.
12. **gin:** trap.

THOMAS HARDY 857

Into the Poem

Using **BEFORE YOU READ** p. 857

Reading Focus

Ask students to apply the proverb "Out of sight, out of mind" to a relationship that is stretched by time or distance. Have them think about how quickly people resume a "normal" life, retaining thoughts of an absent person only as occasional memories.

Through the Poem

A. Critical Reading: Drawing Conclusions

? Why might the "loved one" have been concerned about hurting the speaker? [Possible answers: If she were still alive, she would have been hurt to learn that the man had rejected her in favor of someone with more wealth and more "flash"; perhaps the man wonders whether he has spent enough time in mourning before marrying this other woman.]

B. Reader's Response: Extending the Text

Many people would agree with the "nearest dearest kin" that tending the grave will do nothing to restore the person in it. Why, then, do you think that people often spend thousands of dollars on elaborate funerals, ornate headstones, and perpetual care of beautiful gravesites? [Sample responses: Out of love or respect for the one who has died; out of the need (or pressure) to make a public show of their grief; out of tradition (and a hope that their survivors will be as caring).]

C. Literary Element: Anticlimax

In the poem Hardy has raised the speaker's hopes, only to let them down. What does the use of anticlimax elicit in a reader? [Possible answers: Feel sympathy for the dead woman; wonder how well anyone is remembered after death.]

STRATEGIES FOR INCLUSION

Logical-Mathematical Ask students to come up with a graphic representation or outline of "Ah, Are You Digging on My Grave?" Their responses should show not only how each response differs from the one before it, but also how Hardy, through the responses, builds tension until he reveals the visitor's identity and reason for visiting.

INTEGRATING THE LANGUAGE ARTS

Mechanics If students need a refresher in the use of quotation marks in dialogue, this poem provides several examples of the rules at work. The first two stanzas even offer examples of direct quotations within quotations. For practice, you might have students rewrite the poem as if it were prose, using capitalization and punctuation correctly and beginning new paragraphs where necessary.

Making Meanings

First Thoughts

1. Students probably will conclude that Hardy either mocks sentiment about death or finds it misguided. If the situation in this poem is accurate, then a person who dies is gone and forgotten.

Shaping Interpretations

2. From the woman's guesses about her visitors' identities, one can assume that she had a husband or fiancé and a family and that there was a woman with whom she had a conflict. The dog's answers reveal that her family is no longer grieving, that her enemy (like the dog itself) has forgotten her, and that her beloved has just married someone else.

3. Animal traits include such behavior as routine surveillance of territory and burying bones. At the same time, more human traits lie in the dog's having forgotten the woman's gravesite and in its addressing the woman.

4. For each speculation that the woman makes about how the possible visitor is behaving, it is revealed that none of those mentioned are devoting themselves to grief.

5. Students should agree that the tone is wry, ironic, perhaps even bitter. These probably are not among the responses that students described earlier in their Reader's Logs.

Challenging the Text

6. **(Analysis and Evaluation)** Most students probably will agree that Hardy's use of irony of situation is quite effective. Even if students initially find the responses to the woman's questions somewhat comical, upon reflection they should recognize the sadness of her situation. Students may suggest that Hardy's irony is effective because her repeated guesses and repeated ironic disappointments become pathetic.

MAKING MEANINGS

First Thoughts

1. After reading this poem, how do you think Hardy feels about sentimental attitudes toward death?

Shaping Interpretations

2. In the first three stanzas, what information about the dead woman's life do you get from her guesses and from the dog's answers?

3. In the last stanza, how does the dog's answer combine animal traits with qualities we consider human?

4. **Anticlimax,** or **bathos,** is the deflating effect we feel when our lofty expectations are let down. How does Hardy employ the device of bathos in each of the first three stanzas?

5. How would you characterize the **tone** of this poem? How does it compare with your description of cemeteries in your Reader's Log?

Challenging the Text

6. In **irony of situation,** there is a sharp discrepancy between what is expected and what actually happens. Do you think that Hardy's use of irony is effective in this instance? Why or why not?

CHOICES:
Building Your Portfolio

Writer's Notebook

1. Collecting Ideas for an Evaluation

On page 856, questions 6 and 7 asked you to evaluate the elements of theme and diction in "Channel Firing." Whatever your evaluations were, you need concrete evidence from the poem to support them in an essay. Cite two quotations from the poem to support each

of your responses to questions 6 and 7. Save your notes for the Writer's Workshop on page 899.

Critical Writing
2. Bird Sightings

In a brief essay, compare "The Darkling Thrush" to any poem in this book in which the poet uses the conventional Romantic images of bird and song—for example, Keats's "Ode to a Nightingale" (page 755) or Shelley's "To a Skylark" (page 739).

Creative Writing
3. Passages and Reflections

Imagine that you are in a creative mood on the final evening of the twentieth century. Write a short essay or poem summing up your view of the past and your hopes or fears for the future.

Creative Writing
4. What's Your Opinion?

Hardy's "Channel Firing" indirectly makes a point about war through the use of fantasy, dialogue, and irony. Write a persuasive editorial that expresses your ideas about war.

Creative Writing
5. The Rest of the Story

Write a short character sketch of the woman who speaks in "Ah, Are You Digging on My Grave?" (For help, see the Writer's Workshop on page 185.)

Oral Interpretation
6. Acting the Part

In a small group, present a dramatic reading of "Channel Firing" or "Ah, Are You Digging on My Grave?" Decide who will speak each line, and rehearse your interpretation. Include music, costumes, and sound effects to make your presentation more dramatic.

Beyond the Poems

1. **Writer's Notebook** Remind students to save their work. They may use it as prewriting for the Writer's Workshop on p. 899.

PORTFOLIO ASSESSMENT

Choices: Assessment Criteria For help in evaluating these Choices assignments, see the criteria in the *Portfolio Management System,* pp. 149–150.

SPOTLIGHT ON

Victorian Novelists

I am neither a man nor a woman but an author.
—Charlotte Brontë, 1849

Victorian tastes seem remarkable today for the excesses of abundant hoop skirts and living rooms crowded with knickknacks. Literary fashions of the period were no different.

Magnificent Storytelling, Huge Books

The most remarkable product of Victorian literature was the novel—hefty volumes regularly published in three-volume editions called three-deckers. The lucrative phenomenon of magazine serialization encouraged authors to write long texts sometimes criticized as "loose, baggy monsters"; in this wealth of pages, however, novelists of the period perfected the art of storytelling. Victoria's reign produced notable poetry, but the period is best known for the passion, scope, and originality of its novels.

A nineteenth-century audience recognized categories of novels including historical fiction, suspenseful detective stories, and "Newgate" or criminal novels with tales taken directly from prison records. Novels became a medium for instruction and were considered a legitimate way to learn history and etiquette. Writers also could address the social problems caused by the nineteenth century's rapid industrialization. For example, Charles Dickens lampoons the abuses of the court system in *Bleak House* (1852–1853) and exposes the horrors of workhouses in *Oliver Twist* (1837–1838). These books reached an increasingly large audience through lending libraries, periodicals, and affordable "cheap editions," ensuring a diverse Victorian readership that included a growing middle class and increasing numbers of female readers.

"Lady Novelists"

In the nineteenth century, the novel was a relatively new genre that was still developing its own traditions. The originality of this format, combined with the increase in literacy and the explosion of nineteenth-century publishing, presented large numbers of average, middle-class women with unprecedented opportunities to showcase their talents. Women no longer had to have exceptional wealth or education in order to write, and, though their work was often slighted by the literary men of the period, female novelists were no longer in danger of being branded "outrageous" or "unladylike" merely because they wrote. The success of "lady novelists" is reflected in the American writer Nathaniel Hawthorne's complaint about "the d——d mob of scribbling women" whom he saw as competition. William Thackeray, a well-known novelist, could grumble at the success of Frances Trollope's *The Vicar of Wrexhill* (1837) by saying that the author "had much better remained at home, pudding making or stocking mending." The complaints of such established writers only confirm the success of female novelists. Prohibited from entering many lucrative professions, the "lady novelists" produced profitable books that often addressed the difficulties faced by talented, literary women.

George Eliot (1819–1880)

The author Mary Ann Evans adopted the pen name George Eliot to keep her identity secret at a time when serious literature by women could receive

A. Critical Reading: Drawing Conclusions

? What do you think that Brontë means by this comment? [Possible answer: I do not want to be judged by my gender but by the quality of my writing.]

B. Humanities Connection

Perhaps the best contemporary parallel to magazine serialization is daytime drama (soap operas). Like magazine serializations, "the soaps" have long, convoluted story lines and a style that could be described as "loose" and "baggy"; further, the audience of either form enjoys the anticipation of the stories' end or next installment.

C. Exploring the Culture

The fact that Dickens found "an increasingly large audience" is illustrated by the public response to *The Pickwick Papers,* which was printed in monthly installments. In *The Life of Charles Dickens,* author John Forster notes that it "sprang into a popularity that each part carried higher and higher, until people at this time talked of nothing else, tradesmen recommended their goods by using its name, and its sale, outstripping at a bound that of all the most famous books of the century, had reached to an almost fabulous number. Of part one, the binder prepared four hundred; and of part fifteen, his order was for more than forty thousand."

D. Cultural Connections

? Why was writing considered an "unladylike" activity? [Possible answers: By writing and being published, women were entering an area that men had dominated for centuries; by writing novels, women were showing that they knew things about the world that perhaps men did not want to believe they knew.]

E. Expansion

Adam Bede (1859), Eliot's first novel, established her as a leading writer. *Silas Marner* and *The Mill on the Floss,* mentioned in the text, are still widely read today, as is *Middlemarch* (1871–1872), which is considered one of the finest Victorian novels.

OPTIONS FOR TEACHING

STRATEGIES FOR INCLUSION

Less Proficient Readers To help them remember what they have read in this feature, pair students; have each pair create a list of five to ten words or phrases that they think capture the essence of the Victorian novel. Items on their lists can include names of authors and titles of works, Victorian subjects and themes, and other details that help them distinguish the topic. Have pairs share their lists; work with students to compile a master list.

English Language Development Each of the five sections of this reading contributes to the overall picture of novelists of this era. To determine students' comprehension of the text, have them complete an outline enumerating the points presented. On the chalkboard or on a transparency, write the frame of the outline. Students should identify the main points and supporting details in short phrases. Have students copy the outline into their Reader's Logs for future reference.

A. Critical Reading: Drawing Conclusions

? Why is Maggie cutting her hair? [Possible answer: It is an act of defiance, a declaration of independence, through which Maggie hopes to get her family to see her differently.]

What do you think of her plan? [Possible answer: Undoubtedly she will get the attention that she wants, but it may not produce the result she had in mind. Even in the middle of her action, she seems to be having second thoughts about her method.]

B. Cultural Connections

? When and why do people today take pseudonyms? [Possible answers: A writer might choose a pseudonym to protect his or her privacy; an actor might change his or her name because an agent has recommended a name with more "star appeal"; a well-known artist or musician might produce a work under another name, hoping (as the Brontës did) that it will be judged on its own merit.]

C. Critical Reading: Making Inferences

? According to Woolf, what made the Brontës inventive writers? [They constantly felt that they were struggling against tradition and convention.]

---

biased criticism—like Thackeray's. Known for her ability to capture rural village life in novels such as *Silas Marner* (1861), Eliot created talented heroines limited by circumstance and social propriety. For example, the young protagonist of *The Mill on the Floss* (1860) tires of her troublesome long hair and asks for her brother Tom's aid. In the process, Maggie Tulliver calls our attention to the Victorians' emphasis on "proper" feminine appearance.

> Tom followed Maggie upstairs into her mother's room, and saw her go at once to a drawer, from which she took out a large pair of scissors.
> "What are they for, Maggie?" said Tom, feeling his curiosity awakened.
> Maggie answered by seizing her front locks and cutting them straight across the middle of her forehead.
> "Oh, my buttons, Maggie, you'll catch it!" exclaimed Tom; "you'd better not cut any more off."
> Snip! went the great scissors again while Tom was speaking; and he couldn't help feeling it was rather good fun: Maggie would look so queer. . . .

A > Maggie felt an unexpected pang. She had thought beforehand chiefly of her own deliverance from her teasing hair and teasing remarks about it, and something also of the triumph she should have over her mother and her aunts by this very decided course of action: she didn't want her hair to look pretty— that was out of the question—she only wanted people to think her a clever little girl, and not to find fault with her.

—George Eliot, *from A Mill on the Floss*

Eliot's novels show that a clever little girl's problems only increase when she grows into a clever young woman. Unlike Dickens, who provides his audience with miraculous happy endings, George Eliot looks unflinchingly at heroines whose intelligence and talent have no place in their culture. Her perspective indicates the limitations of Victorian progress and prosperity.

860 THE VICTORIAN PERIOD

George Eliot (1849), age 30. Engraving by G. J. Stodart from a painting by M. D'Albert-Durand.

The Sisters Brontë: Charlotte (1816–1855) and Emily (1818–1848)

The Brontë sisters offer a striking example of the novel's success because they produced two of the most perpetually popular novels, *Jane Eyre* and *Wuthering Heights,* while living in the same Yorkshire household. Minister's daughters, Charlotte and Emily determined that they could support themselves as novelists, and they wrote passion-

B ately of the isolated moor country they loved. Like George Eliot, they adopted men's names, Currer Bell and Ellis Bell, in the hopes of receiving fair, unbiased responses to their work. Describing the sisters, the writer Virginia Woolf said that "There is in them some untamed ferocity perpetually at war

C with the accepted order of things which makes them desire to create instantly rather than to observe patiently."

We can see this "ferocity" in Emily's *Wuthering Heights* (1847), a disturbing love story that draws on the Gothic themes of the Romantic poets she loved. Brontë attributes to her characters Catherine Earnshaw and Heathcliff a love that transcends even death, with Cathy haunting her soul mate from the grave. Heathcliff recalls these events from the day of her funeral:

"Being alone, and conscious two yards of loose earth was the sole barrier between us, I said to myself—

"'I'll have her in my arms again! If she be cold, I'll think it is this north wind that chills *me;* and if she be motionless, it is sleep.'

"I got a spade from the toolhouse, and began to delve with all my might—it scraped the coffin; I fell to work with my hands, the wood commenced crackling about the screws, I was on the point of attaining my object, when it seemed that I heard a sigh from some one above, close at the edge of the grave, and bending down.—'If I can only get this off,' I muttered, 'I wish they may shovel in the earth over us both!' and I wrenched at it more desperately still. There was another sigh, close at my ear. I appeared to feel the warm breath of it displacing the sleet-laden wind. I knew no living thing in flesh and blood was by—but as certainly as you perceive the approach to some substantial body in the dark, though it cannot be discerned, so certainly I felt that Cathy was there, not under me, but on the earth. . . ."

—Emily Brontë, *from Wuthering Heights*

Emily's novel shocked Victorian audiences by bringing Gothic evil, violence, and horror into a seemingly safe domestic setting. Charlotte's *Jane Eyre* (1847) was no less shocking in its rejection of

The Brontë Sisters (1834) by Patrick Branwell Brontë.

By Courtesy of the National Portrait Gallery, London.

docile, sentimental heroines. The popular novelist Margaret Oliphant wrote in 1855, "Ten years ago we professed an orthodox system of novel making. Our lovers were humble and devoted, when suddenly, without warning, *Jane Eyre* stole upon the scene." Charlotte constructs a love story containing a scandalous secret marriage and a mad woman hidden in the attic of a country mansion. Just as daring, though, is the independence of Jane Eyre, the self-possessed governess who refuses to accept the limitations of her social station or her sex:

Nobody knows how many rebellions besides political rebellions ferment in the masses of life which people earth. Women are supposed to be very calm generally: but women feel just as men feel; they need exercise for their faculties, and a field for their efforts as much as their brothers do; they suffer from too rigid a restraint, too absolute a stagnation, precisely as men would suffer; and it is narrow-minded in their more privileged fellow creatures to say that they ought to confine themselves to making puddings and knitting stockings, to playing on the piano and embroidering bags. It is thoughtless to condemn them, or laugh at them, if they seek to do more or learn more than custom has pronounced necessary for their sex.

—Charlotte Brontë, *from Jane Eyre*

Three-Deckers and Victorian Values

Novels offered Victorian audiences opportunities to discuss, explore, and explain the rapid changes in the nineteenth-century social fabric. Female authors often described the friction between the period's social constraints and their own need for autonomy. In the twentieth century, many modern authors reject the idea that stories can—or should—convey lessons in morality, just as they reject the notion that simple remedies exist for difficult social problems. Yet in Victoria's reign, with its proud, growing empire, Britons could still harbor bright hopes for social and scientific progress. The novels of the era could capture audiences with three-deckers that examined conflicts in fascinating detail; their hope, whether stated or not, was that solutions could be found.

SPOTLIGHT ON 861

D. Reader's Response: Connecting with the Text

Margaret Oliphant wrote that *Jane Eyre* made novelists rethink the "orthodox," or traditional, aspects of their stories. Can you think of a story that made you look at something in a new way? [Sample responses: The novel *Beloved* by Toni Morrison made me see freedom from a new perspective. The movie *Unforgiven* gave me a different view of the western.]

E. Exploring the Culture

Jane Eyre was widely praised for its narrative power, and the moral values it presents are in many ways traditional. Nevertheless, the novel at first was considered to be unacceptable reading. Negative comments came from some of Brontë's peers; Matthew Arnold, for example, wrote that her mind contained "nothing but hunger, rebellion and rage."

F. Reader's Response: First Thoughts

Ask students to make some notes in their Reader's Logs about ways in which they think "women feel just as men feel." Allow volunteers to share responses in small-group settings; also encourage students to refer to these notes when they are looking for ideas for original writing.

QUICK PLANNING GUIDE

Into the Poems

Author Biography p. 862
Before You Read: p. 863, p. 865, p. 867

Through the Poems

"When I Was One-and-Twenty"
p. 863
"To an Athlete Dying Young" p. 865
"Is My Team Ploughing" p. 867
Connections: A Book p. 868
"Death and Other Grave Matters"
Making Meanings: p. 864, p. 866, p. 869

Beyond the Poems

Choices: Building Your Portfolio p. 869
• **Writer's Notebook:** Compare two poems using a chart
• **Critical Writing:** In an essay compare Housman's three poems
• **Creative Writing:** Write diary entries based on the poems
• **Creative Writing:** Write a newspaper article about the young athlete in the poem
• **Music and Literature:** Present a dramatic reading to music
• **Current Events/Speaking:** Compare the tones used regarding Housman's athlete and an athlete who died young recently

A. E. Housman
(1859–1936)

Alfred Edward Housman (1926) by Francis Dodd.
Pencil drawing (14¾" × 10¾").
By Courtesy of the National Portrait Gallery, London.

Housman said that he was careful not to think of poetry while he was shaving, for "if a line of poetry strays into my memory, my skin bristles so that the razor ceases to act." For Housman, poetry was all feeling. The feelings produced physical effects (shivers along the spine, tears, the sensation of being pierced by a spear) that came from what Housman said was the source of his own poems, "the pit of the stomach."

Housman's poetry is more restrained than his comments suggest. His poems evoke a narrow range of subdued feelings that are controlled by simple, tight verse forms and clear language and syntax. Although he uses simple words, his diction is precise and carefully polished: Each word is the right word in the right place.

Alfred Edward Housman was born in Worcestershire in western England, the oldest of seven children. He was close to his mother, who died on his twelfth birthday. His father, a lawyer, allowed his practice, money, and talent to dwindle away in despondency and drink. At sixteen, Housman won a scholarship to Oxford, where he prepared for a career as a scholar and teacher of classical literature. But he attended classes irregularly, preferring to study on his own, and failed his final examinations.

In 1882, Housman entered the civil service as a clerk in the patent office, determined to prove himself as a classical scholar despite his failure at Oxford. For the next ten years, he set himself a rigorous program: writing and publishing papers on Greek and Latin literature while working as a patent clerk. In 1892, his series of scholarly papers won him an appointment as professor of Latin at London University. He stayed until 1911, when he moved to Cambridge University as professor of Latin and fellow at Trinity College. Housman spent the rest of his life as a formal and rather aloof teacher, a reserved participant in the small world of his college, and an authority in the yet smaller world of classical scholarship.

During his lifetime, Housman published only two books of poems containing a little more than one hundred poems. His first collection, *A Shropshire Lad* (1896), became popular because its graceful recollection of youthful pleasures and their transience fit a late-century mood of disillusionment in a world that has "much good, but much less good than ill." In "Terence, This Is Stupid Stuff," Housman acknowledged that his poems could be dismissed as self-indulgent bellyaching. The test of poetry, he believed, is not what is said but how it is said. In the refined elegance of his poems, he expressed his pessimism about the cold emptiness of the world. Unlike the major Romantic and Victorian poets who preceded him, Housman saw no hope of improvement or change, but only the possibility of enduring and making bearable the conditions of human experience.

862 THE VICTORIAN PERIOD

PROGRAM MANAGER

• **Planning Instruction** See Teaching Notes, *Teaching Resources B,* pp. 89–90, for objectives, summaries, literary elements and additional information.
• **Instructional Support** Before beginning the instructional lesson, see Graphic Organizer for Active Reading, *Teaching Resources B,* pp. 98–100, for Through the Poems activities.
• **Assessment** See Selection Tests, *Test Booklet,* pp. 185–187.

Reading Focus

Advice to the Lovelorn
Thousands of poems have been written about the experience of falling in love, and not all of the stories end happily. The tale told in "When I Was One-and-Twenty" is an ancient one, and it reaches a conclusion observed many times before.

Quickwrite

What is "first love" like? How do people feel about love as they grow older? Jot down your thoughts about these questions.

Background

The tone of Housman's poetry is often nostalgic and bittersweet. This brief lyric from *A Shropshire Lad* is a good example. In fact, its lesson may have come from events in the poet's own life. At age twenty-two, Housman fell in love and was rejected. He became severely depressed and failed his Oxford examinations.

Using **BEFORE YOU READ** p. 863

Background

A Shropshire Lad, published in 1896 and set in the English countryside, made Housman a famous poet. Other poems of his were published later, but all of them were written at approximately the same time as the poems in *A Shropshire Lad*.

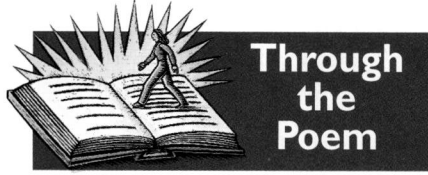

When I Was One-and-Twenty

A. E. Housman

When I was one-and-twenty
    I heard a wise man say,
"Give crowns and pounds and guineas°
    But not your heart away;
5 Give pearls away and rubies
    But keep your fancy free."
But I was one-and-twenty,
    No use to talk to me.

When I was one-and-twenty
10   I heard him say again,
"The heart out of the bosom
    Was never given in vain;
'Tis paid with sighs a plenty
    And sold for endless rue."°
15 And I am two-and-twenty,
    And oh, 'tis true, 'tis true.

3. crowns and pounds and guineas: units of money in Great Britain.

14. rue: sorrow; regret.

A. E. HOUSMAN 863

A. Critical Reading: Summarizing
Have students rephrase the wise man's advice in these lines. [Possible answer: "Spend a little money or spend a lot, but hold onto your heart."]

B. Critical Reading: Evaluating an Interpretation
Housman is often described as one of the late Victorian writers who held a grim view of life. Do you see that view at work in this poem? Explain. [Possible answer: The view is rather grim. In these lines, the wise man's words (with which the speaker comes to agree) express a belief that love is always painful.]

Metacognition How might you arrive at the conclusion that a grim view of love leads to a negative outlook on life? [Possible answer: Love is perhaps the most noble of human emotions. If love is doomed, then life cannot hold much promise.]

Making Meanings

First Thoughts

1. Some students may feel that there are not enough specific details to establish a personal connection. Other students (perhaps students who are romantic by nature or who already have had a relationship fail) may sympathize with the speaker.

Shaping Interpretations

2. A year (or part of a year). Possible response: The speaker has learned the truth in what the wise man said.

3. The repetition of "'tis true" emphasizes the speaker's agreement, suggests the pain of the experience that he has had without giving any information about that experience, and brings the poem to an emphatic close. Students may also note the repetition of whole lines (1 and 9), similar lines (2 and 10), and syntax in the two stanzas.

4. Students may suggest themes such as "Falling in love is foolishness," "Young love is doomed," or "Love does not last." Most students would agree that Housman's attitude is one of ironic humor.

Connecting with the Text

5. Some students might agree with the wise man, believing that the pain and disillusionment of a failed relationship should be avoided; others may be more optimistic, feeling that the experience of being in love is worth the risk of pain.

The Sonnet (1839) by William Mulready.
Victoria and Albert Museum, London.

MAKING MEANINGS

First Thoughts

1. Did the speaker's story move you? Why or why not?

Shaping Interpretations

2. How much time has passed between the first and second stanzas? In your opinion, what has the speaker learned in this time?

3. What is the effect of Housman's use of **repetition** in the last line of the poem? What other kinds of repetition do you find in the poem?

4. What do you think is the poem's **theme,** or message? Do you think Housman is being serious or humorous in his attitude toward falling in love?

Connecting with the Text

5. If the wise man advised you that it is better to give away money than to give away your heart, what would you say in reply? Refer to your Reader's Log notes, and explain your response.

864 THE VICTORIAN PERIOD

Strategic Reading "When I Was One-and-Twenty" explores the conflict that young people face when trying both to learn from their elders and to find their own answers. Have students chart the course of the poem with summary sentences in boxes: box #1, summary of the advice; box #2, action the youth takes; box #3, result of action; box #4, conclusion. Point out to students that some of the story is left unwritten in the poem, but that it is easy to infer what has happened from the speaker's comments.

Writing: Character Dialogue Encourage pairs of students to respond to "When I Was One-and-Twenty" by assuming the "characters" of Housman's speaker—one as the twenty-one-year-old, the other as the twenty-two-year-old. Have them, in character, create a silent dialogue by passing a paper back and forth and "conversing" about this question: How much can a person's world change in just a year's time, and why?

Reading Focus

The Prime of Life

The strong, healthy athletes who earn fame and fortune seem to live charmed lives. But what happens when the cheering stops? When an athlete dies in the prime of life and at the peak of fame, faithful supporters discover a very sobering truth: Even these special young men and women are not invincible.

Quickwrite

At what age do you think you might be in the prime of your life—in top physical and mental condition? Jot down your thoughts about when you hope to achieve your peak, and what you hope to be doing then.

Background

In 1896, Housman himself paid to have the first edition of *A Shropshire Lad* published. He scarcely made a profit from his book of sixty-three verses, which often told their stories in the voice of a young soldier or farm boy. However, Housman lived to see his poems become enormously popular during World War I. Soldiers saw themselves in the homesick lad from Shropshire and heard in his voice the echo of their own melancholy.

To an Athlete Dying Young

A. E. Housman

The time you won your town the race
We chaired you through the marketplace;
Man and boy stood cheering by,
And home we brought you shoulder-high.

5 Today, the road all runners come,
Shoulder-high we bring you home,
And set you at your threshold down,
Townsman of a stiller town.

Smart lad, to slip betimes° away
10 From fields where glory does not stay
And early though the laurel° grows
It withers quicker than the rose.

Eyes the shady night has shut
Cannot see the record cut,
15 And silence sounds no worse than cheers
After earth has stopped the ears:

Now you will not swell the rout
Of lads that wore their honors out,
Runners whom renown outran
20 And the name died before the man.

So set, before its echoes fade,
The fleet foot on the sill of shade,
And hold to the low lintel° up
The still-defended challenge cup.

25 And round that early-laureled head
Will flock to gaze the strengthless dead,
And find unwithered on its curls
The garland briefer than a girl's.

9. betimes: archaic for "early."
11. laurel: classical symbol of victory. Victorious Greek and Roman athletes were crowned with laurel wreaths.
23. lintel: top of a doorframe.

Young man, from *Penelope and Her Suitors* (detail) (1912) by John William Waterhouse.
City of Aberdeen Art Gallery and Museums Collection, Scotland.

Into the Poem

Using **BEFORE YOU READ** p. 865

Quickwrite

Through this activity, students can extend the Quickwrite for "When I Was One-and-Twenty" (p. 863), adding personal notes that define *the prime of life* and further develop a written self-portrait.

Through the Poem

A. Critical Reading: Drawing Conclusions

Suppose you did not know the title of this poem. What clues in this stanza help you to conclude that this is a funeral procession? [Possible answers: The road is described as one along which "all runners come," for all people die; "shoulder-high" suggests the carrying of a coffin; "a stiller town" could refer to a graveyard or to the realm of the dead in general.]

B. Literary Element: Tone

How would you describe the speaker's tone, or attitude, regarding the death of the young athlete? [Possible answer: The tone seems ironic, but in a kindly or sympathetic way. Instead of mourning the athlete, the speaker praises him for being wise enough to leave this life while he was still in his prime.]

STRATEGIES FOR INCLUSION

Learners Having Difficulty Two of Housman's poems in this Collection focus on the remembrance of people who have died. Ask students to write monologues or to make home video recordings of themselves expressing the qualities, characteristics, and accomplishments for which they would most want to be remembered. Encourage them to include memorabilia in their oral presentations. They may wish to include a musical background and variety of settings as well. Following the same basic guidelines, students for whom oral presentations are difficult may choose to create paintings, drawings, or collages to illustrate the things for which they would most like to be remembered.

Visual Have students draw an image for each stanza. As you read and discuss the poem, have students in small groups share their drawings, comparing the details they chose to represent. Then, ask each group to come to a consensus about which drawings express the poem best. All the drawings chosen do not have to be by the same student. Each group should share its drawings with the class. ☞

Making Meanings

First Thoughts

1. Some students would hope for more obvious words of praise, such as a review of playing records, and would want the poem to avoid mention that the career would have ended eventually anyway. Other students may appreciate the poem's more realistic words about athletic careers.

Shaping Interpretations

2. Both stanzas mention being brought home "shoulder-high" by a crowd. In the first stanza, such treatment is an act of adulation, but in the second stanza, it is an act of mourning (carrying a coffin "shoulder-high"). The repetition emphasizes the parallel.

3. The speaker suggests that, although the athlete probably did not anticipate an early death, his departing while at the prime of life is better—"smarter"—than lingering on after glory has passed. Especially if they have sensed the disillusionment in "When I Was One-and-Twenty," students may conclude that the speaker's words are tinged with irony but are nonetheless sincere.

4. Possible response: The scene involves the young man about to enter the afterworld as the shades of the dead gather to meet him and gaze upon him.

5. Students whose Reader's Log entries suggest an early peak might see merit in Housman's idea; other students might argue that no matter what one predicts his or her peak to be, it is always possible that new and unforeseen goals may appear in the future.

Challenging the Text

6. **(Evaluation)** Possible response: There is something poignant about a young person's death, but aging has its poignancy, too.

MAKING MEANINGS

First Thoughts

1. How would you react to this poem if it were written about you?

Shaping Interpretations

2. What parallel events are described in the first and second stanzas? What is the significance of repeating "shoulder-high"?

3. In line 9, why does the speaker call the athlete "smart"? Do you think the speaker means what he says in lines 9–20? Explain.

By Unfrequented Ways (late 19th or early 20th century) by William Henry Gore.

4. What scene do you *see* in the last two stanzas of the poem? (Where is the athlete now?)

5. The speaker suggests that it's best to die at one's peak, before glory begins to fade. After thinking about your Reader's Log entry, describe your response to this idea.

Challenging the Text

6. Housman's poem movingly describes a young athlete's death. If he had written a similar poem about an aging athlete, could the poem be as powerful? Explain your answer.

INTEGRATING THE LANGUAGE ARTS

Speaking and Listening If "To an Athlete Dying Young" were referring to events taking place today, it might well be presented as a televised commentary at the end of an evening news program or weekly sports review. Encourage an interested student to present it as such; invite the rest of the class to evaluate the presentation.

COOPERATIVE LEARNING

Grouping Strategy As student groups meet to discuss the poem or to work on activities related to it, note students who play in school sports or who are sports enthusiasts. Make sure that each group has the chance to hear comments from one of these students; alternatively, have several of these students meet in their own group. In either case, encourage the class as a whole to consider the insights from students who have this perspective.

Reading Focus

Remember Me?

When friends tell you they missed you while you were gone, it confirms that you're an important part of their lives. If people we love move away or die, we expect to change and to gradually grow accustomed to their loss. The paradox is that we also hope to keep their memories alive and to not forget our loved ones too quickly.

Quickwrite

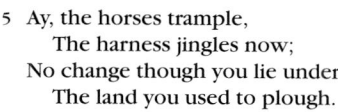

Imagine you have moved away from your friends. What kinds of questions would you ask them after a long absence? Briefly record your response.

Elements of Literature

Literary Ballads

Housman once claimed that his inspiration came from "Shake-speare's songs, [and] the Scottish Border ballads." To describe the country life of a "Shropshire lad," Housman borrows from the simple style of traditional folk ballads, featuring a question-and-answer format in a conversation. In **literary ballads,** such as this one by Housman, poets adapt the structure and spirit of traditional ballads to modern uses.

Is My Team Ploughing

A. E. Housman

"Is my team ploughing,
    That I was used to drive
And hear the harness jingle
    When I was man alive?" **A**

5 Ay, the horses trample,
    The harness jingles now;
No change though you lie under
    The land you used to plough.

"Is football playing
10   Along the river shore,
With lads to chase the leather,
    Now I stand up no more?"

Ay, the ball is flying,
    The lads play heart and soul; **B**
15 The goal stands up, the keeper
    Stands up to keep the goal.

"Is my girl happy,
    That I thought hard to leave,
And has she tired of weeping
20   As she lies down at eve?"

Ay, she lies down lightly,
    She lies not down to weep:
Your girl is well contented.
    Be still, my lad, and sleep.

25 "Is my friend hearty,
    Now I am thin and pine,
And has he found to sleep in
    A better bed than mine?"

Yes, lad, I lie easy,
30   I lie as lads would choose;
I cheer a dead man's sweetheart, **C**
    Never ask me whose.

A. E. HOUSMAN 867

Into the Poem

Using BEFORE YOU READ **p. 867**

Reading Focus

Most students have experienced the death of a relative or neighbor; many also know what it is like to have a good friend move away. Invite volunteers to draw upon those experiences as they share thoughts about how one might become accustomed to life without that person and yet hope to keep the memories alive. *Remind students to include circumstances they would not mind sharing.*

Through the Poem

A. Literary Element: Literary Ballad

Remind students of the ballads they read in Collection 2, pp. 90–96. In this poem, what is reminiscent of the ballad form? [The questions and answers create a ballad pattern. The "yes" answers form a refrain of sorts.]

B. Reader's Response: Shaping Interpretations

Compare this reply to the reply in the second stanza. How might this new reply create tension in the poem? [Sample responses: The first reply was fairly matter of fact. Here, however, more emotion is involved. The primary speaker is reminded of a world where people "play heart and soul," but it is a world that he no longer can touch.]

C. Literary Element: Tone

? With what sort of tone does this poem conclude? Explain. [Possible answer: It is bittersweet, a mix of irony and sympathy (much as in "To an Athlete Dying Young"). There is irony in the fact that the secondary speaker has taken his friend's place in the girl's heart; yet the secondary speaker seems to be genuinely concerned that his dead friend not be hurt by the truth.]

STRATEGIES FOR INCLUSION

Advanced If students have read the poems by Thomas Hardy in this Collection, ask them to compare (orally or in writing) "Is My Team Ploughing" with "Ah, Are You Digging on My Grave?" (p. 857) Have them use the questions in each poem to consider what things each speaker considers important and whether the answers to those questions suggest similar or differing views of humanity.

INTEGRATING THE LANGUAGE ARTS

Strategic Reading After dividing the class into small groups, have each group create a diagram that represents the relationship that the primary speaker had, when alive, with each subject about which he asks:

his work	his beloved
his teammates	his best friend

Students can use the resulting diagrams to analyze the changes that have taken place since the speaker's death.

A. Critical Reading: Analyzing Details

Think about hearing the sound of the "passing bell" echoing across town. In what sense would this be a sound of respect? of rejoicing? of warning? [Possible answer: The "passing bell" and its toll of the years of the person's life offer a tribute; they signify that the town should realize that one of its own is dying or has died and that the person's life mattered. It could be a sound of rejoicing, especially in a Christian community, that a fellow citizen is entering heaven. It could be a warning, as if to say, "This person has died. Will you be next?"]

Metacognition Ask students which meaning occurred to them first when they thought about the sound of the bell.

B. Critical Reading: Making Connections

George Eliot addresses this point in *The Mill on the Floss,* where she writes: "Funerals were always conducted with peculiar propriety in the Dodson family. The hatbands were never of a blue shade, the gloves never split at the thumb, everybody was a mourner who ought to be, and there were always scarfs for the bearers."

C. Reader's Response: Challenging the Text

? Do these "rules" about what people could and could not wear and how long people were supposed to mourn make sense to you? Why or why not? [Sample responses: They make sense in that they provide some structure for mourners, who may feel emotionally lost; they do not make much sense in our culture today, where we generally are encouraged to put our grief behind us as quickly as possible.]

Connections

A — HISTORY

Housman's poems somberly explore death. In the following excerpt, Daniel Pool explains the rituals the Victorians developed to respond to death.

Death and Other Grave Matters

Daniel Pool

Death—early death—was no stranger to the nineteenth-century English family, and perhaps that is why they loved to weep over the lingering demises of Dickens's small heroes and heroines. Certainly, they made a big production out of it in every other respect.

In some rural communities the ritual began even before one died, with the ringing of a "passing bell" in the parish church to signal that a member of the community lay on his or her deathbed. Characteristically, the bell tolled six times to indicate the passing of a woman, nine (the famous "nine tailors") to indicate the passing of a man, followed by a peal for each year of the dying person's life.

When a person died, a large funeral was held with everyone dressed in black (unless the deceased were a child or a young, unmarried girl, when the costume was white); mourners received black gloves and black scarfs. . . .

In most communities, funerals were an important social event, and propriety and due regard for the family's social standing necessitated that they be done right. . . . Characteristically, the undertaker would provide professional mourners, or "mutes," dressed in black to stand about and lend dignity to the affair. "There's an expression of melancholy in his face, my dear," says Mr. Sowerberry, the undertaker, to his wife when he takes on Oliver Twist as an apprentice, "which is very interesting. He would make a delightful mute, my love . . . I don't mean a regular mute to attend grown-up people, my dear, but only for children's practice. It would be very new to have a mute in proportion." When the body was actually brought to the gravesite for burial, there was often an additional tolling of the bells—the death knell—to let the parish know of the final laying to rest of the deceased. . . .

The departed were always to be mourned for specifically prescribed periods of time, which, in practice, affected mostly the clothes the survivors were permitted to wear and whether they could have fun or not. Men had it easy; they needed only to wear black armbands, a custom adopted from the military in the early years of the century. Women, however, were supposed to dress all in black. "My dear Celia," says Lady Catherine Chettam of Dorothea Casaubon [in George Eliot's novel *Middlemarch*] after her husband's death, "a widow must wear mourning at least a year." This meant an all-black wardrobe (the so-called widow's weeds), frequently of bombazine, a material especially favored because it did not gleam in light, and no jewelry or ornaments except for beads made of jet, a kind of coal. . . . A widow was expected to mourn her husband for two years, but she could moderate her funereal clothing a bit after a while to "half mourning," which consisted of pinstripe black. Parents and children were to be mourned for a year, a brother, sister, or grandparent for six months, an uncle or aunt for three months, and a first cousin got six weeks. (In-laws were mourned too, but for lesser periods of time.) Some women remained in their mourning garb for the rest of their lives. . . .

Of course, the lead in this fashionable mourning was set in part by the queen. After the death of her beloved Albert in 1861 until her own death in 1901, portraits generally show Victoria in the somber black and white attire suitable for honoring the memory of a late departed.

—from What Jane Austen Ate and Charles Dickens Knew

CONNECTING WITH HOUSMAN'S POEMS

What is it about Housman's poetry that convinces you that Daniel Pool has chosen his subject well? [Possible answers: Both Housman's and Hardy's poetry indicate that death and loss were on the minds of the Victorians as the new century approached. Though they may not suggest a preoccupation with death, the poems do imply a familiarity with death and certain attitudes that were part of the Victorian culture and are worthy of study.]

MAKING MEANINGS

First Thoughts

1. Why do you think the speaker has been forgotten so quickly? Is this cruel, or is it just normal?

Shaping Interpretations

2. Housman's dialogue format doesn't explain the speakers' identities. Who are the two **speakers**?

3. What significance do you find in the order of the four questions asked in the poem? How do these questions compare with the ones you asked in your Reader's Log entry?

4. How would you describe the speaker's attitude in the last stanza? Was he a true friend to his dead companion? Why or why not?

Extending the Text

5. People complain that the modern world moves too fast, quickly forgetting people like the plowman. Do you think Housman's story reflects the tension of modern times, or is this predicament timeless?

6. To cope with death, why do you think people write poetry and practice rituals like the ones Daniel Pool describes in "Death and Other Grave Matters" (page 868)? What are some of the ways we deal with death today?

CHOICES:
Building Your Portfolio

Writer's Notebook

1. Collecting Ideas for an Evaluation

Housman's "Is My Team Ploughing" and Hardy's "Ah, Are You Digging on My Grave?" (page 857) have many similarities. Re-read both poems now, and decide quickly which you think is more effective. Then make a chart comparing specific elements in the two poems (you *may* change your judgment).

You could focus on such elements as theme, imagery, emotional content, and music. Save your notes for the Writer's Workshop on page 899.

Critical Writing
2. Heartaches

In a brief essay, compare Housman's treatment of death and loss in these three poems. What is his attitude toward suffering and pain?

Creative Writing
3. In Your Own Voice

Imagine that you are the speaker, the Shropshire lad, in all three poems by Housman. (In "Is My Team Ploughing," assume that you are the speaker who answers.) Write three diary entries that tell about the events suggested in each poem.

Creative Writing
4. Read All About It

Write the front-page newspaper article that describes the career Housman's young athlete had before his or her death. Invent any details needed to describe why the athlete was so loved and why he or she will be missed.

Music and Literature
5. Housman's Soundtrack

Suggest a musical background for one of Housman's poems. Present a dramatic reading of the poem with the music you selected. Tape your presentation, or present it live.

Current Events / Speaking
6. Mourning Young Athletes

Even today, athletes often die young. Research a library's newspaper files for information on a young athlete who died or retired early. How does the tone of the newspaper accounts compare with the tone of Housman's poem? Present your findings in a brief oral report to your class.

Making Meanings
First Thoughts

1. Students may note that "forgetting" is a normal part of putting aside grief—not that the survivors consider the dead person unimportant, but that they, of necessity, focus on going on with their own lives.

Shaping Interpretations

2. The first speaker is a dead farmer, a man who enjoyed playing football and who had a girlfriend or wife ("my girl"). The other speaker seems to be a friend of the dead man.

3. The questions move from objective to more personal and more emotional. Housman establishes an order of importance in which each succeeding question draws in the reader a little more, making the reader as vulnerable to the answers—especially the final answer—as is the dead man.

4. The attitude seems kindly but evasive. Students may differ over whether he is a true friend (for taking care of someone that the dead man no longer could help) or a traitor (for loving the woman the deceased loved).

Extending the Text

5. **(Evaluation)** Possible responses: The situation is timeless. Housman avoids fixing a specific time for the poem; however, the plowman was certainly a doomed breed, as modern machinery replaced him and his horses. Thus, this could be construed as a modern lament for times past.

6. **(Analysis)** Possible responses: When people are grieving, ritual can provide distraction and help them get through a difficult time. Poetry gives expression to grief people might not otherwise communicate. Many people still use ritual to deal with death.

Beyond the Poems

1. **Writer's Notebook** Remind students to save their work. They may use it as prewriting for the Writer's Workshop on p. 899.

2. **Critical Writing** Remind students that Housman urges readers to view death from the perspective of both the living and the dead, and have students brainstorm a list of "losses" to examine.

PORTFOLIO ASSESSMENT

Choices: Assessment Criteria For help in evaluating these Choices assignments, see the criteria in the *Portfolio Management System,* pp. 151–152.

Into the Story

Author Biography p. 870

Before You Read p. 871

- **Reading Focus: Set a Purpose** Students think about the blurred lines of conflict.
- **A Dialogue with the Text:** List questions
- **Elements of Literature: Allusion**
- **Background: Scaffolding** Kipling's allusion to the Bible

Through the Story

"The Mark of the Beast" pp. 872–880

Words to Own pp. 872–880

Literature and History pp. 876–877

Making Meanings p. 881

Beyond the Story

Choices: Building Your Portfolio p. 881

- **Writer's Notebook:** Make and support evaluations
- **Creative Writing:** Create an outline to continue the story
- **Research/Speaking:** Compare were-wolf stories
- **Historical Research:** Report on the Anglo-Indian world of the late nineteenth century

Rudyard Kipling
(1865–1936)

Rudyard Kipling was born in Bombay, India, where his father was a professor at the University of Bombay. Since it was customary for English citizens living in India (Anglo-Indians) to send their children home for their education, the six-year-old Kipling and his sister were left in the care of foster parents in England. Kipling recalled some of the unhappiness and rebelliousness of his school years in a novel called *Stalky & Co.* (1899).

At seventeen, Kipling returned to India to work as a journalist on a newspaper in Lahore. He quickly became popular for his stories, sketches, and poems that were published in newspapers and then collected in cheap editions sold at Indian railroad stations. His books were distributed in England as well, preparing the way for his return to England as a writer in 1889. *Barrack-Room Ballads* (1892), his first collection of poems published in England, went into three editions in its first year, and fifty more editions over the next thirty years. By the end of Queen Victoria's reign, Kipling had become the most popular British poet since Tennyson, and the most popular prose writer since Dickens. Kipling's popularity and public influence

Rudyard Kipling (detail) (1899) by Philip Burne-Jones. Oil on canvas (29½" × 24½").

By Courtesy of the National Portrait Gallery, London.

can be attributed in part to his strong endorsement of the British Empire.

But Kipling's ideas about "empire" were not simple. He was fascinated by the contrast and conflict of European civilization with the ancient cultures of the places into which it intruded. This conflict is the theme of many of his Indian stories, beginning with *Plain Tales from the Hills* (1888) and continuing in *Kim* (1901), his novel about a British boy submerged in the mystery of India. Kipling did not always see European culture as superior (though he nearly always presented it as such), and he knew that empires do fall. He urged readers not to trust in guns to justify their dominion over large parts of the earth. The purpose of the British Empire, he argued, was not to make the imperial nation rich, but rather to extend British efficiency, decency, and comfort throughout the world. Today, however, many readers—even as they admire Kipling's craft—view his argument as a rationalization of the often brutal practices of British Imperialism.

In 1907, Kipling became the first British writer to win the Nobel Prize in literature.

PROGRAM MANAGER

- **Planning Instruction** See *Teaching Notes, Teaching Resources B,* pp. 90–91, for objectives, a summary, and literary elements for this selection.
- **Instructional Support** Before beginning the instructional lesson, see **Graphic Organizer for Active**

Reading, *Teaching Resources B,* p. 101, for a Through the Story activity.
- **Assessment** See Selection Test, *Test Booklet,* pp. 188–189.
- **Language Link** For instruction and practice in identifying wordiness, see **Language Link,** *Teaching Resources*

B, pp. 102–103 and *Language and Writing Skills Worksheets,* p. 107.
- **Reinforcement** Use the **Words to Own** worksheet in *Teaching Resources B,* p. 104.

BEFORE YOU READ
THE MARK OF THE BEAST

Reading Focus
When Gods and Worlds Collide

The battles in this story will be obvious as you watch cultures clash. The victor may also seem obvious—at first. Beware of seeing a clear-cut contest between good and evil, the spiritual and the bestial, or progress and the primitive. When the hideous battle scene is over, you have seen a defeat. But of whom—or what?

Elephants and pilgrims,
Sonepur Fair in Binhar, India (1988).

A Dialogue with the Text

Record your responses as you read this mysterious story. What questions does Kipling plant in your mind?

Elements of Literature
Allusion

An **allusion** is an indirect, or passing, reference to a person, event, place, quotation, or work of art the reader might be expected to know. Through allusion, a reader's knowledge can supply enriching details and relevance, without the writer explicitly providing them.

Background

Kipling's early childhood in India, followed by lonely school years in England, resulted in a respect for the religions of India. Still, Kipling knew the Bible well and alluded to it often in his writings. The title of this story comes from the prophetic Book of Revelation in the New Testament. According to Chapter 13 of that book, there will be a future time of great evil in the world. The ruler of the world will be a horrible beast that is like a leopard. All the beast's followers will be branded with his mark on the right hand or forehead.

RUDYARD KIPLING 871

PORTFOLIO ASSESSMENT

Portfolio Assessment For help with self-assessment of reading skills, see the *Portfolio Management System,* pp. 48–49.

Into the Story

Using BEFORE YOU READ p. 871

Background

Read aloud Revelation 13:16–17: "And he causeth all, both small and great, rich and poor, free and bond, to receive a mark in their right hand, or in their foreheads: And that no man might buy or sell, save he that had the mark, or the name of the beast, or the number of his name." Note that what makes this mark so horrible is that it comes from a creature who is evil personified. Then, as students read Kipling's tale, have them look for the recurrence of the "mark of the beast." Challenge them to consider who the "beast" of the story really is.

WRITERS ON WRITING

Kipling was his own strictest editor, trimming his drafts again and again until he was satisfied with them. Here is Kipling's explanation of what he calls "Higher Editing": "Take of well-ground Indian ink as much as suffices and a camel-hair brush proportionate to the interspaces of your lines. In an auspicious hour, read your final draft and consider faithfully every paragraph, sentence and word, blacking out where requisite. Let it lie by to drain as long as possible. At the end of that time, re-read it aloud alone and at leisure. Maybe a shade more brushwork will then indicate or impose itself. If not, praise Allah and let it go, and 'when thou hast done, repent not.' . . . I have had tales by me for three or four years which shortened themselves almost yearly. The magic lies in the Brush and the Ink."

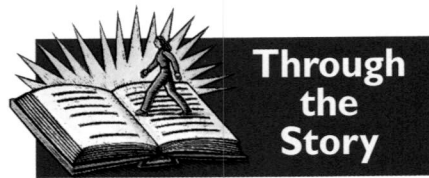

Through the Story

A. Literary Element: Allusion
The story's title is an allusion to the book of Revelation in the Bible. Ask students if, even without knowledge of the allusion, the title is ominous or indicative of evil.

B. Reader's Response: First Thoughts

? How does this epigraph set a **tone** for the story to come or suggest the general content of that story? [Sample responses: The tone could be ominous, or it could be open-ended, suggesting that anything could happen. Some sort of battle is going to take place between religions or cultures. Things may happen beyond the knowledge or power of mortals.]

C. Critical Reading: Predicting

? What do the narrator's comments regarding Strickland and Dumoise suggest about the story that he is preparing to tell? [Possible answer: That it will seem mysterious and even unbelievable; that it is not a fantasy, for witnesses were present; that it somehow will involve the native culture of colonial India.]

The Mark of the Beast

Rudyard Kipling

Your Gods and my Gods—do you or I know which are the stronger?
—*Indian Proverb*

East of Suez, some hold, the direct control of Providence ceases; Man being there handed over to the power of the Gods and Devils of Asia, and the Church of England Providence only exercising an occasional and modified supervision in the case of Englishmen.

This theory accounts for some of the more unnecessary horrors of life in India; it may be stretched to explain my story.

My friend Strickland of the Police, who knows as much of natives of India as is good for any man, can bear witness to the facts of the case. Dumoise, our doctor, also saw what Strickland and I saw. The inference which he drew from the evidence was entirely incorrect. He is dead now; he died in a rather curious manner, which has been elsewhere described.

When Fleete came to India he owned a little money and some land in the Himalayas, near a place called Dharmsala. Both properties had been left him by an uncle, and he came out to finance them. He was a big, heavy, genial, and inoffensive man. His knowledge of natives was, of course, limited, and he complained of the difficulties of the language.

He rode in from his place in the hills to spend New Year in the station, and he stayed with Strickland. On New Year's Eve there was a big dinner at the club, and the night was excusably wet.[1] When men foregather from the uttermost ends of the Empire they have a right to be riotous. The Frontier had sent down a contingent o' Catch-'em-Alive-O's[2] who had not seen twenty white faces for a year, and were used to ride fifteen miles to dinner at the next Fort at the risk of a Khyberee[3] bullet where their drinks should lie. They profited by their new security, for they tried to play pool with a curled-up hedgehog found in the garden, and one of them carried the marker round the room in his teeth. Half a dozen planters had come in from the south and were talking "horse" to the Biggest Liar in Asia, who was trying to cap all their stories at once. Everybody was there, and there was a general closing up of ranks and taking stock of our losses in dead or disabled that had fallen during the past year. It was a very wet night, and I remember that we sang "Auld Lang Syne" with our feet in the Polo Championship Cup, and our heads among the stars, and swore that we were all dear friends. Then some of us went away and annexed Burma, and some tried to open up the Sudan and were opened up by Fuzzies[4] in that cruel scrub outside Suakim,[5] and some found stars and medals, and some were married, which was bad, and some did other things which were worse, and the others of us stayed in our chains and strove to make money on insufficient experiences.

Fleete began the night with sherry and bitters, drank champagne steadily up to dessert, then raw, rasping Capri with all the strength of whiskey, took benedictine with his coffee, four or five whiskeys and sodas to improve his pool strokes, beer and bones[6] at half-past two, winding up with old brandy. Consequently, when he came out, at half-past three in the morning, into fourteen degrees of frost, he was very angry with his horse for coughing, and tried to leapfrog into the saddle. The horse broke away and went to his stables;

---

1. **the night was excusably wet:** In other words, they drank a lot.

2. **Catch-'em-Alive-O's:** men who were forced into service as soldiers.
3. **Khyberee:** reference to the people of Kyber (kī'bər), a region now part of Pakistan and Afghanistan.
4. **Fuzzies:** Sudanese natives. British soldiers gave them this name because of their long, frizzy hair. In the poem "Fuzzy-Wuzzy" (1890), Kipling calls the Sudanese soldier "a first-class fightin' man."
5. **Suakim:** Suakin (swä'kən), Sudan; city on the Red Sea.
6. **bones:** dice.

WORDS TO OWN
genial (jēn'yəl) *adj.:* mild-mannered; friendly.

STRATEGIES FOR INCLUSION

Advanced As students read and discuss "The Mark of the Beast," have them chart details that support any or all of these statements:
• The Indian religion is stronger than the British religion.
• The British religion is stronger than the Indian religion.

• Fleete's curse merely magnifies the worst of his characteristics.
• Although the narrator voices respect for native traditions, he still considers them inferior.
When students have finished reading, have them organize a debate, using their evidence to argue whether the statements are true or false.

Visual Have students draw representations of several pivotal moments in the story. This may help them to sort out, for example, the scene at the temple, or the scene in which Strickland and the narrator encounter the beast. Post the illustrations in chronological order around the classroom, and ask students to comment on them in terms of content and effectiveness in displaying some crucial point in the story.

Shrine to the Monkey-god in Chamundi Hill Temple, Mysore, India.

so Strickland and I formed a Guard of Dishonor to take Fleete home.

Our road lay through the bazaar, close to a little temple of Hanuman, the Monkey-god, who is a leading <u>divinity</u> worthy of respect. All gods have good points, just as have all priests. Personally, I attach much importance to Hanuman, and am kind to his people—the great gray apes of the hills. One never knows when one may want a friend.

There was a light in the temple, and as we passed we could hear voices of men chanting hymns. In a native temple the priests rise at all hours of the night to do honor to their god. Before we would stop him, Fleete dashed up the steps, patted two priests on the back, and was gravely grinding the ashes of his cigar butt in to the forehead of the red stone image of Hanuman. Strickland tried to drag him out, but he sat down and said solemnly:

"Shee that? Mark of the B—beasht! *I* made it. Ishn't it fine?"

In half a minute the temple was alive and noisy, and Strickland, who knew what came of polluting gods, said that things might occur. He, by virtue of his official position, long residence in the country, and weakness for going among the natives, was known to the priests and he felt unhappy. Fleete sat on the ground and refused to move. He said that "good old Hanuman" made a very soft pillow.

Then, without any warning, a Silver Man came out of a <u>recess</u> behind the image of the god. He was perfectly naked in that bitter, bitter cold, and his body shone like frosted silver, for he was what the Bible calls "a leper as white as snow." Also he had no face, because he was a leper of some years' standing, and his disease was heavy upon him. We two stooped to haul Fleete up, and the temple was filling and filling with folk who seemed to spring from the earth, when the Silver Man ran in under our arms, making a noise exactly like the mewing of an otter, caught Fleete round the body and dropped his head on Fleete's breast before we could wrench him away. Then he retired to a corner and sat mewing while the crowd blocked all the doors.

The priests were very angry until the Silver Man touched Fleete. That nuzzling seemed to sober them.

At the end of a few minutes' silence one of the priests came to Strickland and said, in perfect English, "Take your friend away. He has done with Hanuman but Hanuman has not done with him." The crowd gave room and we carried Fleete into the road.

Strickland was very angry. He said that we might all three have been knifed, and that Fleete should thank his stars that he had escaped without injury.

Fleete thanked no one. He said that he wanted to go to bed. He was gorgeously drunk.

We moved on, Strickland silent and wrathful, until Fleete was taken with violent shivering fits and sweating. He said that the smells of the bazaar were overpowering, and he wondered why

---

WORDS TO OWN
divinity (də·vin′ə·tē) *n.:* god; sacred being.
recess (rē′ses) *n.:* indentation.

D. Cultural Connections
In Hindu writings, Hanuman, chief of the monkeys, is described as being perfect in learning. He is a hero of the *Ramayana,* one of India's sacred epic poems, for he plays a key role in reuniting Rama (one of the human incarnations of the god Vishnu) with Sita, his kidnapped wife. Hanuman sometimes is called Mahavira—"The Great Hero." He also is seen as a fertility god and as a general helper of humans.

E. Critical Reading: Analyzing Allusion
Here Kipling directly employs the title allusion to Revelation. Ask students how the allusion relates to the story at this point. [Possible answer: It suggests, ironically, that Fleete is the "Beast," who has set his mark upon the forehead of a pagan god.]

F. Critical Reading: Speculating
[?] What do you think Strickland "knew" about "what came of polluting gods"? [Possible answer: He knew that Fleete's action could cause a riot and that the trio could be hurt or even killed by Hanuman's followers.]

G. Cultural Connections
In times past, lepers were forced to live in isolation from most people, out of fear of contagion. Today, leprosy can be treated (although a universal, permanent cure has not yet been found); in Kipling's day, however, the thought of leprosy was horrifying.

INTEGRATING THE LANGUAGE ARTS

Speaking and Listening One of this story's most notable characteristics is the narrator's editorial tone. Invite students to read aloud relevant sections, such as his first description of Hanuman (p. 873) and his comments that "Strickland hates being mystified by natives" (p. 874). To extend this activity, have a group of interested students present part or all of this story as a radio drama, complete with sound effects and background music.

Writing: Two Views Help students make a personal connection by having them write two paragraphs on the topic "The Age of Empire." The first time, they should each adopt the persona of a European official thinking about colonies; the second time, the persona of a colonial national thinking about Europe. How do the results affect one's view of "foreign culture"? How do they shed light upon the Collection's theme, "The Paradox of Progress?"

T874 The Victorian Period

A. Reader's Response: Challenging the Text

To make these comments, Kipling must stop the action of his story. Of what value are the comments? If you were trying to tell this story, would you have stopped to make these comments? [Sample responses: Yes, the comments help with the characterization of Strickland and perhaps inject a note of humor after a tense scene. No, the comments do not advance the action of the story.]

B. Critical Reading: Making Connections

? What connections has the narrator made, leaving him "cold, depressed, and unhappy"? [Possible answer: The narrator's gloom probably stems from worry that the Silver Man has somehow infected Fleete or from general concern about the mystery of it all and the upset at the temple.]

C. Literary Element: Symbol

? Is this "the mark of the beast"? What do you think it represents? [Many students will agree that it is the mark spoken of in the title, but interpretations will vary. Students may suggest that it represents the animal kingdom, which Fleete could have offended when he defiled Hanuman's temple.]

---

slaughterhouses were permitted so near English residences. "Can't you smell the blood?" said Fleete.

We put him to bed at last, just as the dawn was breaking, and Strickland invited me to have another whiskey and soda. While we were drinking he talked of the trouble in the temple, and admitted that it baffled him completely. Strickland hates being mystified by natives, because his business in life is to overmatch them with their own weapons. He has not yet succeeded in doing this, but in fifteen or twenty years he will have made some small progress.

"They should have mauled us," he said, "instead of mewing at us. I wonder what they meant. I don't like it one little bit."

I said that the Managing Committee of the temple would in all probability bring a criminal action against us for insulting their religion. There was a section of the Indian Penal Code which exactly met Fleete's offense. Strickland said he only hoped and prayed that they would do this. Before I left I looked into Fleete's room, and saw him lying on his right side, scratching his left breast. Then I went to bed cold, depressed, and unhappy, at seven o'clock in the morning.

At one o'clock I rode over to Strickland's house to inquire after Fleete's head. I imagined that it would be a sore one. Fleete was breakfasting and seemed unwell. His temper was gone, for he was abusing the cook for not supplying him with an underdone chop. A man who can eat raw meat after a wet night is a curiosity. I told Fleete this and he laughed.

"You breed queer mosquitoes in these parts," he said. "I've been bitten to pieces, but only in one place."

"Let's have a look at the bite," said Strickland. "It may have gone down since this morning."

While the chops were being cooked, Fleete opened his shirt and showed us, just over his left breast, a mark, the perfect double of the black rosettes—the five or six irregular blotches arranged in a circle—on a leopard's hide. Strickland looked and said, "It was only pink this morning. It's grown black now."

Fleete ran to a glass.

"By Jove!" he said, "this is nasty. What is it?"

We could not answer. Here the chops came in, all red and juicy, and Fleete bolted three in a most offensive manner. He ate on his right grinders only, and threw his head over his right shoulder as he snapped the meat. When he had finished, it struck him that he had been behaving strangely, for he said apologetically, "I don't think I ever felt so hungry in my life. I've bolted like an ostrich."

After breakfast Strickland said to me, "Don't go. Stay here, and stay for the night."

Seeing that my house was not three miles from Strickland's, this request was absurd. But Strickland insisted, and was going to say something, when Fleete interrupted him by declaring in a shamefaced way that he felt hungry again. Strickland sent a man to my house to fetch over my bedding and a horse, and we three went down to Strickland's stables to pass the hours until it was time to go out for a ride. The man who has a weakness for horses never wearies of inspecting them; and when two men are killing time in this way they gather knowledge and lies the one from the other.

There were five horses in the stables, and I shall never forget the scene as we tried to look them over. They seemed to have gone mad. They reared and screamed and nearly tore up their pickets;[7] they sweated and shivered and lathered and were <u>distraught</u> with fear. Strickland's horses used to know him as well as his dogs; which made the matter more curious. We left the stable for fear of the brutes throwing themselves in their panic. Then Strickland turned back and called me. The horses were still frightened, but they let us "gentle" and make much of them, and put their heads in our bosoms.

"They aren't afraid of *us,*" said Strickland. "D'you know, I'd give three months' pay if *Outrage* here could talk."

But *Outrage* was dumb, and could only cuddle up to his master and blow out his nostrils, as is the custom of horses when they wish to explain things but can't. Fleete came up when we were in the stalls, and as soon as the horses saw him, their

---

7. pickets: hitching posts.

WORDS TO OWN
distraught (di·strôt′) *adj.:* agitated.

OPTIONS FOR TEACHING

CLASSROOM MANAGEMENT

Budget Time If you cannot cover "The Mark of the Beast" entirely through in-class reading, work with students through the paragraph that ends, "The crowd gave room and we carried Fleete into the road" (p. 873). Offer the following questions to guide students as they complete the story.

- How will the priest's prophecy—"Hanuman has not done with him"—come true? Will it have something to do with the narrator's comments in the first paragraph?
- What importance will the Silver Man have as the story continues?

- Will Strickland and the narrator continue to be friends with each other? with Fleete?
- At the end, the narrator will say that this has been "a rather unpleasant story." What will he mean?

fright broke out afresh. It was all that we could do to escape from the place unkicked. Strickland said, "They don't seem to love you, Fleete."

"Nonsense," said Fleete; "my mare will follow me like a dog." He went to her; she was in a loose box;[8] but as he slipped the bars she plunged, knocked him down, and broke away into the garden. I laughed, but Strickland was not amused. He took his moustache in both fists and pulled at it till it nearly came out. Fleete, instead of going off to chase his property, yawned, saying that he felt sleepy. He went to the house to lie down, which was a foolish way of spending New Year's Day.

Strickland sat with me in the stables and asked if I had noticed anything peculiar in Fleete's manner. I said that he ate his food like a beast; but that this might have been the result of living alone in the hills out of the reach of society as refined and elevating as ours for instance. Strickland was not amused. I do not think that he listened to me, for his next sentence referred to the mark on Fleete's breast, and I said that it might have been caused by blister flies, or that it was possibly a birthmark newly born and now visible for the first time. We both agreed that it was unpleasant to look at, and Strickland found occasion to say that I was a fool.

"I can't tell you what I think now," said he, "because you would call me a madman; but you must stay with me for the next few days, if you can. I want you to watch Fleete, but don't tell me what you think till I have made up my mind."

"But I am dining out tonight," I said.

"So am I," said Strickland, "and so is Fleete. At least if he doesn't change his mind."

We walked about the garden smoking, but saying nothing—because we were friends, and talking spoils good tobacco—till our pipes were out. Then we went to wake up Fleete. He was wide awake and fidgeting about his room.

"I say, I want some more chops," he said. "Can I get them?"

We laughed and said, "Go and change. The ponies will be round in a minute."

"All right," said Fleete. "I'll go when I get the chops—underdone ones, mind."

He seemed to be quite in earnest. It was four

o'clock, and we had had breakfast at one; still, for a long time, he demanded those underdone chops. Then he changed into riding clothes and went out into the veranda. His pony—the mare had not been caught—would not let him come near. All three horses were unmanageable—mad with fear—and finally Fleete said that he would stay at home and get something to eat. Strickland and I rode out wondering. As we passed the Temple of Hanuman the Silver Man came out and mewed at us.

"He is not one of the regular priests of the temple," said Strickland. "I think I should peculiarly like to lay my hands on him."

There was no spring in our gallop on the racecourse that evening. The horses were stale, and moved as though they had been ridden out.

"The fright after breakfast has been too much for them," said Strickland.

That was the only remark he made through the remainder of the ride. Once or twice, I think, he swore to himself; but that did not count.

We came back in the dark at seven o'clock, and saw that there was no lights in the bungalow. "Careless ruffians my servants are!" said Strickland.

My horse reared at something on the carriage drive, and Fleete stood up under its nose.

"What are you doing, groveling about the garden?" said Strickland.

But both horses bolted and nearly threw us. We dismounted by the stables and returned to Fleete, who was on his hands and knees under the orange bushes.

"What the devil's wrong with you?" said Strickland.

"Nothing, nothing in the world," said Fleete, speaking very quickly and thickly. "I've been gardening—botanizing, you know. The smell of the earth is delightful. I think I'm going for a walk—a long walk—all night."

Then I saw that there was something excessively out of order somewhere, and I said to Strickland, "I am not dining out."

Words to Own

ruffians (ruf′ē·ənz) *n. pl.*: hoodlums; lawless persons.
groveling (gräv′əl·iŋ) *v.*: crawling with the face close to the ground.

---

8. **loose box:** stall in which the horse is free to move about.

A. Reader's Response: Connecting with the Text

? Do the narrator's description and Strickland's comment remind you of any stories that you have seen on television or at the movies? Explain. [Sample responses: The scene seems familiar; it is like something out of a classic horror movie. It is like a werewolf movie.]

The Age of Empire

A breakfast table during the time of Queen Victoria's reign held many of the same items that we expect to find today: Indian tea, Kenyan coffee (more popular in the United States and Germany), perhaps Brazilian cocoa—all sweetened with Caribbean sugar.

Victorians were keenly aware that traders circled the globe to provide their morning beverages. Their knowledge came in part from writers such as Rudyard Kipling and Olive Schreiner (1855–1920), who so carefully documented the experience of Europeans abroad. (Schreiner wrote of South Africa.) Kipling's descriptions of the British presence in India capture the controversies of a period known as the Age of Empire. The nineteenth century provided European scholars with opportunities to study ancient civilizations, but the emphasis on indigenous peoples was eclipsed by the lucrative market for raw tropical materials: rubber, oil, cotton. The relationship between Europe and its colonies is summarized by the remark of an administrator, who observed in 1862 that "the traffic with half-civilized peoples has risks of its own, which are generally compensated by more than ordinary profits."

European powers were in such keen competition for colonies that, between 1876 and 1914, about a quarter of the globe's land surface was distributed as colonies among a half-dozen countries. In Victoria's reign, the British prided themselves on the fact that the sun never set on their far-flung empire.

"Bless you!" said Strickland. "Here, Fleete, get up. You'll catch fever there. Come in to dinner and let's have the lamps lit. We'll dine at home."

Fleete stood up unwillingly, and said, "No lamps—no lamps. It's much nicer here. Let's dine outside and have some more chops—lots of 'em and underdone—bloody ones with gristle."

Now a December evening in Northern India is bitterly cold, and Fleete's suggestion was that of a maniac.

"Come in," said Strickland sternly. "Come in at once."

Fleete came, and when the lamps were brought, we saw that he was literally plastered with dirt from head to foot. He must have been rolling in the garden. He shrank from the light and went to his room. His eyes were horrible to look at. There was a green light behind them, not in them, if you understand, and the man's lower lip hung down.

Strickland said, "There is going to be trouble—big trouble—tonight. Don't you change your riding things."

We waited and waited for Fleete's reappearance, and ordered dinner in the meantime. We could hear him moving about his own room, but there was no light there. Presently from the room came the long-drawn howl of a wolf.

People write and talk lightly of blood running cold and hair standing up, and things of that kind. Both sensations are too horrible to be <u>trifled</u> with.

WORDS TO OWN
trifled (trī′fəld) v.: mocked; treated lightly.

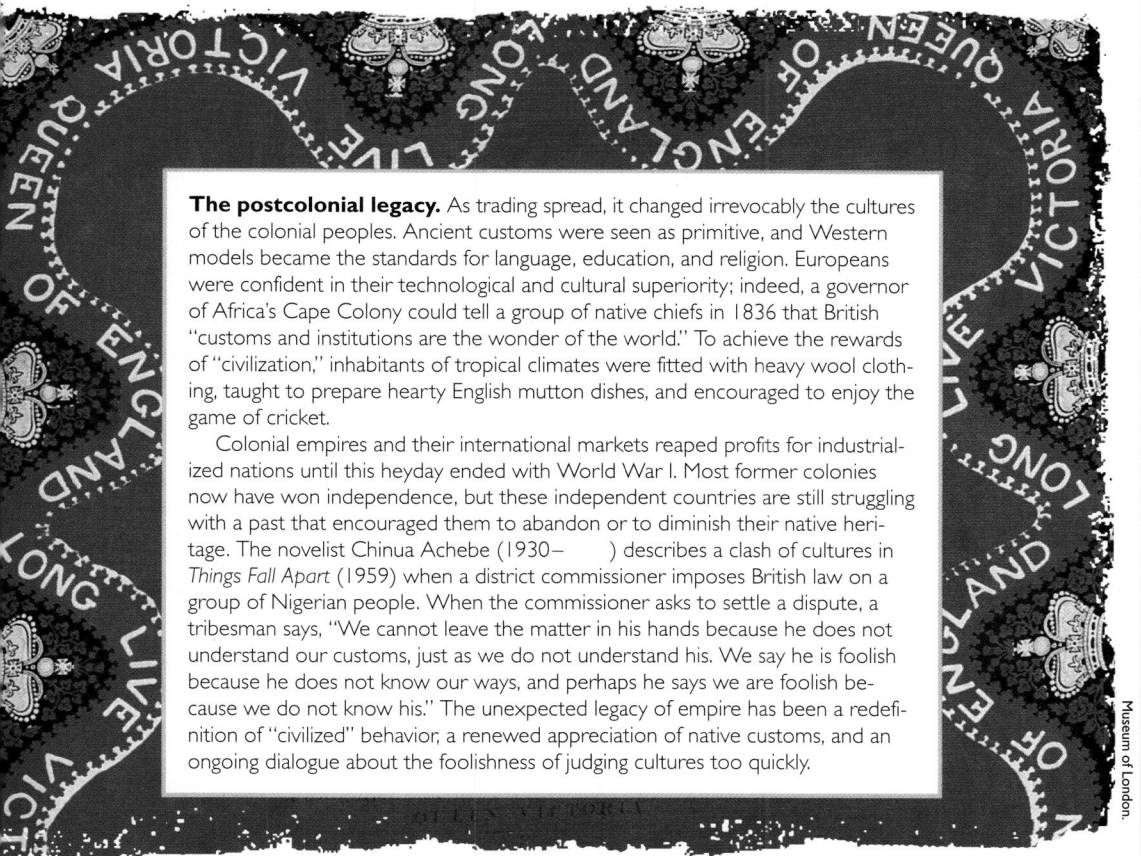

The postcolonial legacy. As trading spread, it changed irrevocably the cultures of the colonial peoples. Ancient customs were seen as primitive, and Western models became the standards for language, education, and religion. Europeans were confident in their technological and cultural superiority; indeed, a governor of Africa's Cape Colony could tell a group of native chiefs in 1836 that British "customs and institutions are the wonder of the world." To achieve the rewards of "civilization," inhabitants of tropical climates were fitted with heavy wool clothing, taught to prepare hearty English mutton dishes, and encouraged to enjoy the game of cricket.

Colonial empires and their international markets reaped profits for industrialized nations until this heyday ended with World War I. Most former colonies now have won independence, but these independent countries are still struggling with a past that encouraged them to abandon or to diminish their native heritage. The novelist Chinua Achebe (1930–   ) describes a clash of cultures in *Things Fall Apart* (1959) when a district commissioner imposes British law on a group of Nigerian people. When the commissioner asks to settle a dispute, a tribesman says, "We cannot leave the matter in his hands because he does not understand our customs, just as we do not understand his. We say he is foolish because he does not know our ways, and perhaps he says we are foolish because we do not know his." The unexpected legacy of empire has been a redefinition of "civilized" behavior, a renewed appreciation of native customs, and an ongoing dialogue about the foolishness of judging cultures too quickly.

Museum of London.

Silk handkerchief commemorating the coronation of Queen Victoria in 1837.

My heart stopped as though a knife had been driven through it, and Strickland turned as white as the tablecloth.

The howl was repeated, and was answered by another howl far across the fields.

That set the gilded roof on the horror. Strickland dashed into Fleete's room. I followed, and we saw Fleete getting out of the window. He made beast noises in the back of his throat. He could not answer us when we shouted at him. He spat.

I don't quite remember what followed, but I think that Strickland must have stunned him with the long bootjack,[9] or else I should never have been able to sit on his chest. Fleete could not speak, he could only snarl, and his snarls were those of a wolf, not of a man. The human spirit must have been giving way all day and have died out with the twilight. We were dealing with a beast that had once been Fleete.

The affair was beyond any human and rational experience. I tried to say "hydrophobia,"[10] but the word wouldn't come, because I knew that I was lying.

We bound this beast with leather thongs of the punkah[11] rope, and tied its thumbs and big toes together, and gagged it with a shoehorn, which makes a very efficient gag if you know how to

9. **bootjack:** device for pulling off boots, often made of cast iron.

10. **hydrophobia:** rabies. One of the effects of rabies is an inability to swallow water.
11. **punkah** (puŋ'kə): swinging fan suspended from the ceiling. It is operated by pulling an attached cord or rope.

RUDYARD KIPLING 877

A. Critical Reading: Making Inferences

? What would the doctor give as the cause of Fleete's death? [Rabies, or hydrophobia.] What is the "reality" that Strickland and the narrator seem unwilling to admit aloud? [That Fleete is suffering from a curse placed upon him by the Silver Man.]

B. Reader's Response: Shaping Interpretations

Notice the items that Strickland brings into Fleete's room. How do you think these items relate to Strickland's character, to his muttered statement to the narrator, and to the overall **plot** of the story? [Sample responses: The items can be used for violence, possibly torture, and Strickland already has suggested a desire to do violence to the Silver Man. He may use those items for just that purpose, in hopes of keeping the Silver Man from killing Fleete.]

C. Critical Reading: Evaluating an Interpretation

- In *Rudyard Kipling: Realist and Fabulist,* Bonamy Dobrée says of the "deliberate cruelty" that begins at this point in the story: "Kipling, we see, could understand cruelty; possibly he could be aware of tendencies towards it in himself, as he seems to confess: but the man or woman who can honestly say that he has not at some time or other felt this when sufficiently provoked by some horror must be rare indeed."

- As students read from here to the end of the section, ask them to comment upon Dobrée's interpretation. [Students may point to "sufficiently provoked" as the key to Dobrée's comment, agreeing unknowingly with Dobrée's conclusion that the action is justified when its "purpose is the saving of a human soul."]

---

arrange it. Then we carried it into the dining room, and sent a man to Dumoise, the doctor, telling him to come over at once. After we had dispatched the messenger and were drawing breath, Strickland said, "It's no good. This isn't any doctor's work." I, also, knew that he spoke the truth.

The beast's head was free, and it threw it about from side to side. Anyone entering the room would have believed that we were curing a wolf's pelt. That was the most loathsome accessory of all.

Strickland sat with his chin in the heel of his fist, watching the beast as it wriggled on the ground, but saying nothing. The shirt had been torn open in the scuffle and showed the black rosette mark on the left breast. It stood out like a blister.

In the silence of the watching we heard something without mewing like a she-otter. We both rose to our feet, and, I answer for myself, not Strickland, felt sick—actually and physically sick. We told each other, as did the men in *Pinafore*,[12] that it was the cat.

(A) Dumoise arrived, and I never saw a little man so unprofessionally shocked. He said that it was a heart-rending case of hydrophobia, and that nothing could be done. At least any palliative measures would only prolong the agony. The beast was foaming at the mouth. Fleete, as we told Dumoise, had been bitten by dogs once or twice. Any man who keeps half a dozen terriers must expect a nip now and again. Dumoise could offer no help. He could only certify that Fleete was dying of hydrophobia. The beast was then howling, for it had managed to spit out the shoehorn. Dumoise said that he would be ready to certify to the cause of death, and that the end was certain. He was a good little man, and he offered to remain with us; but Strickland refused the kindness. He did not wish to poison Dumoise's New Year. He would only ask him not to give the real cause of Fleete's death to the public.

So Dumoise left, deeply agitated; and as soon as the noise of the cart wheels had died away, Strickland told me, in a whisper, his suspicions. They

---

12. *Pinafore:* *H.M.S. Pinafore* (1878), a comic operetta by W. S. Gilbert and Arthur Sullivan. Lovers in the play attempt to elope. When they are discovered, the cast sings, "Why, what was that? . . . It was—it was the cat!"

were so wildly improbable that he dared not say them out aloud; and I, who entertained all Strickland's beliefs, was so ashamed of owning to them that I pretended to disbelieve.

"Even if the Silver Man had bewitched Fleete for polluting the image of Hanuman, the punishment could not have fallen so quickly."

As I was whispering this the cry outside the house rose again, and the beast fell into a fresh paroxysm of struggling till we were afraid that the thongs that held it would give way.

"Watch!" said Strickland. "If this happens six times I shall take the law into my own hands. I order you to help me."

(B) He went into his room and came out in a few minutes with the barrels of an old shotgun, a piece of fishing line, some thick cord, and his heavy wooden bedstead. I reported that the convulsions had followed the cry by two seconds in each case, and the beast seemed perceptibly weaker.

Strickland muttered, "But he can't take away the life! He can't take away the life!"

I said, though I knew that I was arguing against myself, "It may be a cat. It must be a cat. If the Silver Man is responsible, why does he dare to come here?"

(C) Strickland arranged the wood on the hearth, put the gun barrels into the glow of the fire, spread the twine on the table, and broke a walking stick in two. There was one yard of fishing line, gut lapped with wire, such as is used for *mahseer*[13] fishing, and he tied the two ends together in a loop.

Then he said, "How can we catch him? He must be taken alive and unhurt."

I said that we must trust in Providence, and go out softly with polo sticks into the shrubbery at the front of the house. The man or animal that made the cry was evidently moving round the house as regularly as a night watchman. We could wait in the bushes till he came by and knock him over.

Strickland accepted this suggestion, and we slipped out from a bathroom window into the front veranda and then across the carriage drive into the bushes.

---

13. mahseer (mä′sir): large Indian freshwater fish of the carp family.

CROSSING THE CURRICULUM

Architecture/Fine Arts Challenge students to research and report on some of the architectural and artistic treasures of India. Examples might include the Taj Mahal, in Agra; the ancient Buddhist monasteries and shrines at Ajanta, and the frescoes that they contain; and miniature paintings of scenes from Hindu mythology. Students should report their findings, using visuals wherever possible.

Health Students might research three medical conditions related to this story: (1) leprosy (the cause of the Silver Man's appearance); (2) hydrophobia, or rabies (the "official" cause of Fleete's condition); and (3) lycanthropy, a mental disorder in which a person believes that he or she is a wolf (related to the "werewolf" idea of the story). Students may share their research in a format of their own choosing but should relate their findings to Kipling's story.

Music Have students suggest music that they would use to create a soundtrack for "The Mark of the Beast." They might choose a particular theme song for each character and use music to set the moods of different scenes. As time permits, have volunteers play and explain their suggestions.

In the moonlight we could see the leper coming round the corner of the house. He was perfectly naked, and from time to time he mewed and stopped to dance with his shadow. It was an unattractive sight, and thinking of poor Fleete, brought to such degradation by so foul a creature, I put away all my doubts and resolved to help Strickland from the heated gun barrels to the loop of twine—from the loins to the head and back again—with all tortures that might be needful.

The leper halted in the front porch for a moment and we jumped out on him with the sticks. He was wonderfully strong, and we were afraid that he might escape or be fatally injured before we caught him. We

English officer attended by his Indian servant (1870s).
Albumen print by Willoughby Wallace Hooper and George Western.

By permission of the British Library, London.

had an idea that lepers were frail creatures, but this proved to be incorrect. Strickland knocked his legs from under him and I put my foot on his neck. He mewed hideously, and even through my riding boots I could feel that his flesh was not the flesh of a clean man.

He struck at us with his hand- and feet-stumps. We looped the lash of a dog-whip round him under the armpits, and dragged him backward into the hall and so into the dining room where the beast lay. There we tied him with trunk straps. He made no attempt to escape, but mewed.

When we confronted him with the beast the scene was beyond description. The beast doubled backward into a bow as though he had been poisoned with strychnine, and moaned in the most pitiable fashion. Several other things happened also, but they cannot be put down here. **D**

"I think I was right," said Strickland. "Now we will ask him to cure this case."

But the leper only mewed. Strickland wrapped a towel round his hand and took the gun barrels out of the fire. I put the half of the broken walking stick through the loop of fishing line and **E** buckled the leper comfortably to Strickland's

bedstead. I understood then how men and women and little children can endure to see a witch burnt alive; for the beast was moaning on the floor, and though the Silver Man had no face, you could see horrible feelings passing through the slab that took its place, exactly as waves of heat play across red-hot iron—gun barrels, for instance.

Strickland shaded his eyes with his hands for a moment and we got to work. This part is not to be printed.

The dawn was beginning to break when the leper spoke. His mewings had not been satisfactory up to that point. The beast had fainted from exhaustion and the house was very still. We unstrapped the leper and told him to take away the evil spirit. He crawled to the beast and laid his hand upon the left breast. That was all. Then he fell face down and whined, drawing in his breath as he did so.

We watched the face of the beast, and saw the **F** soul of Fleete coming back into the eyes. Then a sweat broke out on the forehead and the eyes—they were human eyes—closed. We waited for an hour, but Fleete still slept. We carried him to his

---

D. Reader's Response: Challenging the Text

Here and at the end of the section, the narrator refuses to supply details. Do you consider this a weakness in Kipling's story? Explain. [Sample responses: While one may feel cheated out of a scene that one might like to see, it is possible that Kipling was trying to spare readers of a more sensitive era. The acts are so horrible that they are unspeakable; it adds to the mystery of the story.]

E. Literary Element: Tone

Notice the calm, matter-of-fact way in which the narrator provides these details, even referring to buckling the leper "comfortably." How do you explain this tone? [Possible answer: The narrator is filled with grim determination and cannot allow himself any sympathy for the Silver Man; the word *comfortably* is offered with bitter humor.]

F. Literary Elements: Climax and Resolution

The climax of the story's action—the torture of the Silver Man—is left to the reader's imagination, but the immediate resolution is quickly apparent. Ask students to find a phrase or sentence that seems to signal the resolution. [Possible answer: "We . . . saw the soul of Fleete coming back into his eyes."]

ASSESSMENT TOOLS

Check Test: Questions and Answers

1. How does Fleete get drunk, and what crime does he commit while in that state? [He drinks nonstop at a British New Year's Eve party; then, on the way home, he defiles a temple of Hanuman.]

2. Why do the temple priests let the British intruders go in peace? [The Silver Man, a leper, embraces Fleete—a sign, according to the priests, that Hanuman will avenge himself.]

3. What are the first signs that something strange is happening to Fleete? [Fleete demands bloody meat to eat, and the place on his chest where the Silver Man touched him has darkened into something that resembles the rosette on a leopard's hide.]

4. What does Dumoise believe has happened to Fleete? [He thinks that Fleete is suffering from hydrophobia, or rabies.]

5. How do Strickland and the narrator restore Fleete to his former self? [They trap the Silver Man and torture him until he removes the curse.]

A. Reader's Response: Shaping Interpretations

Fleete awakens with no memory of what has happened; thus, he learns nothing from his experience. How do you think that this realization is meant to affect the reader? [Sample responses: Even if Fleete has learned nothing, the narrator has, and he shares that lesson with the reader. It is disappointing that Fleete is no better than when he started, but the ending as it is leaves the reader with unknowns and a less-than-clear resolution, which is more realistic.]

Making Meanings

First Thoughts

1. Possible responses: Kipling's story is less scary because it is harder to visualize; Kipling's use of suspense and the unknown makes the story at least as scary.

Reviewing the Text

Possible responses, in an unmapped format, appear below.

Main conflict: West *vs.* East; or the ways of the English *vs.* the traditions of Indians.

Important events: After getting drunk, Fleete pollutes a temple; a leper, the Silver Man, touches him; where the leper has touched him, Fleete develops a mark; Fleete develops a taste for bloody meat, and his favorite horse reacts to him in terror; when Fleete howls like a wolf and no longer acts remotely human, Strickland and the narrator tie him up; they call in a doctor, who declares it a case of rabies; they capture the Silver Man and torture him; the Silver Man finally cures Fleete; Fleete has no memory of what has happened; for years afterward, Strickland and the narrator try to make sense out of the incident.

Points of keen suspense: The Silver Man's first embrace of Fleete; the discovery of Fleete groveling in the dirt; the green light in his eyes; his wolflike howl; Strickland's whispered suggestion that this is a curse from Hanuman; the implied torture of the Silver Man; the wait to see if the curse upon Fleete has, in fact, been lifted.

Climax: Strickland and the narrator capture the Silver Man and torture him into curing Fleete.

---

room and bade the leper go, giving him the bedstead, and the sheet on the bedstead to cover his nakedness, the gloves and the towels with which we had touched him, and the whip that had been hooked round his body. He put the sheet about him and went out into the early morning without speaking or mewing.

Strickland wiped his face and sat down. A night gong, far away in the city, made seven o'clock.

"Exactly four-and-twenty hours!" said Strickland. "And I've done enough to ensure my dismissal from the service, besides permanent quarters in a lunatic asylum. Do you believe that we are awake?"

The red-hot gun barrel had fallen on the floor and was singeing the carpet. The smell was entirely real.

That morning at eleven we two together went to wake up Fleete. We looked and saw that the black leopard rosette on his chest had disappeared. He was very drowsy and tired, but as soon as he saw us, he said, "Oh! Confound you fellows. Happy New Year to you. Never mix your liquors. I'm nearly dead."

"Thanks for your kindness, but you're over time," said Strickland. "Today is the morning of the second. You've slept the clock round with a vengeance."

The door opened, and little Dumoise put his head in. He had come on foot, and fancied that we were laying out Fleete.

"I've brought a nurse," said Dumoise. "I suppose that she can come in for . . . what is necessary."

"By all means," said Fleete cheerily, sitting up in bed. "Bring on your nurses."

Dumoise was dumb. Strickland led him out and explained that there must have been a mistake in the diagnosis. Dumoise remained dumb and left the house hastily. He considered that his professional reputation had been injured, and was inclined to make a personal matter of the recovery. Strickland went out too. When he came back, he said that he had been to call on the Temple of Hanuman to offer redress for the pollution of the god, and had been solemnly assured that no white man had ever touched the idol, and that he was an incarnation of all the virtues laboring under a delusion. "What do you think?" said Strickland.

I said, "'There are more things . . .'"[14]

But Strickland hates that quotation. He says that I have worn it threadbare.

One other curious thing happened which frightened me as much as anything in all the night's work. When Fleete was dressed he came into the dining room and sniffed. He had a quaint trick of moving his nose when he sniffed. "Horrid doggy smell, here," said he. "You should really keep those terriers of yours in better order. Try sulfur, Strick."

But Strickland did not answer. He caught hold of the back of a chair, and, without warning, went into an amazing fit of hysterics. It is terrible to see a strong man overtaken with hysteria. Then it struck me that we had fought for Fleete's soul with the Silver Man in that room, and had disgraced ourselves as Englishmen forever, and I laughed and gasped and gurgled just as shamefully as Strickland, while Fleete thought that we had both gone mad. We never told him what we had done.

Some years later, when Strickland had married and was a churchgoing member of society for his wife's sake, we reviewed the incident dispassionately, and Strickland suggested that I should put it before the public.

I cannot myself see that this step is likely to clear up the mystery; because, in the first place, no one will believe a rather unpleasant story, and, in the second, it is well known to every right-minded man that the gods of the heathen are stone and brass, and any attempt to deal with them otherwise is justly condemned.

---

14. **"There are more things":** a reference to William Shakespeare's *Hamlet*, Act I, scene 5, lines 166–167: "There are more things in heaven and earth, Horatio, than are dreamt of in your philosophy."

WORDS TO OWN
redress (rē′dres′) *n.:* compensation for wrong.
delusion (di·loō′zhən) *n.:* false belief.
dispassionately (dis·pash′ə·nət·lē) *adv.:* without emotion; impartially.

Outcome: Fleete returns to normal; those at Hanuman's temple deny any involvement, and Strickland and the narrator are left to wonder about what has happened.

Shaping Interpretations

2. The first conflict is an overall one, and one that the narrator suggests: "Providence" and "the Church of England" *vs.* "the Gods and Devils of Asia." The first conflict to arise directly from the action of the story comes when the drunken Fleete grinds his cigar into the statue of Hanuman, offending the worshipers and perhaps the god himself. Both conflicts arise from a clash of cultures. An external conflict arises between Fleete and his friends as the curse takes hold; Strickland and the narrator also struggle to make sense of the situation in the light of their English culture.

MAKING MEANINGS

First Thoughts

1. Is Kipling's story as scary as other werewolf stories or movies you know? Why or why not?

Reviewing the Text
Working with others, use your Reader's Logs to map the main conflict, important events, points of keen suspense, climax, and outcome in the story.

Shaping Interpretations

2. Describe the story's opening **conflict** and as many others, internal or external, as you can find. What tensions specifically arise from cultural misunderstandings?

3. Compare the **characterizations** of Fleete, Strickland, and the narrator. How does **point of view** affect what you know about each character?

4. Who or what is the Silver Man? What details in the story support your interpretation?

5. What does this story reveal about the British presence in India?

6. What **allusions** to the Book of Revelation in the Bible are used in this story? Consider these allusions, and tell what you think the story's **theme** is.

7. Do you think this story has a valuable message despite—or even because of—its racist elements? Cite details from the story to support your answer.

Challenging the Text

8. Critics have called this story "nasty," "poisonous," and even "sadistic." Explain why you agree or disagree with these assessments.

CHOICES: Building Your Portfolio

Writer's Notebook

1. Collecting Ideas for an Evaluation

How do you rate Kipling's story? Is it a well-told, suspenseful horror story? Is it a racist story? Are its characters stereotypes? Is it offensive or problematic in other aspects? Make three general statements evaluating Kipling's story. Then list at least two details from the text to support each evaluation. Keep your notes for the Writer's Workshop on page 899.

Creative Writing

2. A Silver Man Sequel

The Silver Man survives, and the temple priests deny the whole incident. Use these facts to create a story outline for "The Mark of the Beast II."

Research / Speaking

3. The Evolution of a Myth

Werewolfism, or lycanthropy, is an ancient, enduring myth, but its significance can change. In Kipling's 1890 story and in the 1985 American film *Teen Wolf*, the werewolf has different characteristics. Prepare a multimedia report about werewolf stories in different periods and cultures, showing both the universal and specific social concerns they reflect.

Historical Research

4. The Jewel in the Crown

India was part of the British Empire until 1947; Victoria referred to it as the jewel in her crown. Explore the Anglo-Indian connection by researching the kind of lifestyle a British civil servant like Kipling might have had in late-nineteenth-century India. As a contrast, describe the lifestyles of most Indians. Present your findings in an informal report.

---

5. Among other things, the story reveals that the British tried to make their contacts with the native population as British as possible; that they sometimes never even tried to understand Indian ways; and that even an Englishman with some respect for Indians would abuse an Indian to accomplish his goals.

6. The mark on Fleete and the story's title refer to the Book of Revelations. Students may suggest themes such as "culture clash" or "logic vs. the supernatural."

7. Most students will agree that Kipling's story has a valuable message about respect for other cultures. They may argue that because racism—in the form of Fleete's disrespect for Hanuman's temple—drives the plot, it is an essential element of the story.

Challenging the Text

8. **(Evaluation)** Some students might agree, pointing especially to the Silver Man's treatment. Others, while noting that it is a sinister tale, may feel that adjectives such as *nasty, poisonous,* and *sadistic* are too strong.

Beyond the Story

Choices: Building Your Portfolio

1. **Writer's Notebook** Remind students to save their work. They may use it as prewriting for the Writer's Workshop on p. 899.

PORTFOLIO ASSESSMENT

Choices: Assessment Criteria For help in evaluating these Choices assignments, see the criteria in the *Portfolio Management System,* p. 153.

---

3. Fleete is characterized as boorish, with little interest in India and its people. Strickland seems to have a greater understanding of India, but he is intense and nervous throughout. The narrator seems more easygoing, following Strickland's lead. Readers know no more about Fleete or Strickland than the facts and opinions that the narrator provides.

4. The Silver Man is a leper, but there is also something mysterious about him. He may be under the special protection of Hanuman's temple; Strickland suggests that Fleete's transformation is the result of the Silver Man's having "bewitched Fleete for polluting the image of Hanuman."

Tolstoy's final flight from his home attracted a great deal of publicity. As he traveled, Tolstoy followed the newspapers. "Everything is known already," he complained when he saw headlines like "LEO TOLSTOY LEAVES YASNAYA POLYANA." The newspapers followed him, too, with journalists continually telegramming their editors and trying to get close enough for a scoop. Wherever he went, he was recognized. As he was dying at Astopovo, press bulletins about his condition were released, and reporters jammed the railway telephone lines.

Russia

Portrait of Leo Tolstoy (1873) by Ivan Nikolayevich Kramskoy.

Leo Tolstoy

(1828–1910)

Ironically, Tolstoy, whose story provides a surprising answer to the title question, was born into wealthy, landed aristocracy. Count Leo Nikolayevich Tolstoy was orphaned at nine; at age nineteen, he took possession of a huge rural estate. There he wrote *War and Peace* and *Anna Karenina,* masterpieces of realistic fiction that capped his already immense reputation.

But by age fifty, Tolstoy reached a moral and spiritual crisis. Wanting to be and to do good, he found his best models in Russia's self-sufficient, Christian peasants. His writings became fervent attacks on the government, church, and private ownership (because he felt all three operated by threat of force). Instead, Tolstoy celebrated communal, utopian ideals of pure love and honest labor.

Because he was already a famous writer, educational reformer, and war hero, the repressive Russian government left him alone as pilgrims worldwide journeyed to his home. Tolstoy tried to live the simple life he preached, but he was a man with many children and a wife who did not share his extreme views. With much bitter quarreling, she obtained Tolstoy's substantial royalties to support the family. Finally, as an old man of eighty-two, Tolstoy decided to lead a poor, reclusive life. He fled his home in secret, at night, with his doctor and youngest daughter. At a tiny, remote railroad station, the fugitives got off the train, and Tolstoy, ill with a high fever, was taken to the stationmaster's house. There, amid a mob scene of reporters and family who had eventually tracked him down, Tolstoy died of pneumonia.

(Map) Europe in 1914.
©Rand McNally.

PORTFOLIO ASSESSMENT

Portfolio Assessment For help with teacher assessment of reading skills, see the *Portfolio Management System,* pp. 54–55.

PROGRAM MANAGER

Selection Summary See *Teaching Notes, Teaching Resources B,* p. 91, for a summary of this selection.

Background

You will have no trouble seeing why this story is included under the theme "The Paradox of Progress." Very early, one character proclaims, "Loss and gain are brothers twain." Yet the historical setting makes the paradox much deeper. The nineteenth-century Russia that Leo Tolstoy is describing had just abandoned feudalism—a way of life dead in England since the Middle Ages.

Until Czar Alexander II ordered an emancipation in 1861, Russian peasants, called serfs, were slaves of landowners and aristocrats: They could be bought or sold, and they owned no property. When Tolstoy wrote this story, serfs had had twenty-five years of freedom and rights. No one, certainly not the reformer Tolstoy, would wish them slaves again. Yet in this parable he could wonder—with sharp humor—whether the peasants' "progress" brought losses they would regret.

Quickwrite

Answer these questions as honestly as you can. First, in your ideal life, how much property (a home and land) do you wish for? Then, how much property do you think a person really needs?

How Much Land Does a Man Need?

Leo Tolstoy
translated by **Louise** *and* **Aylmer Maude**

An elder sister came to visit her younger sister in the country. The elder was married to a tradesman in town, the younger to a peasant in the village. As the sisters sat over their tea talking, the elder began to boast of the advantages of town life: saying how comfortably they lived there, how well they dressed, what fine clothes her children wore, what good things they ate and drank, and how she went to the theater, promenades, and entertainments.

The younger sister was piqued, and in turn disparaged the life of a tradesman, and stood up for that of a peasant.

"I would not change my way of life for yours," said she. "We may live roughly, but at least we are free from anxiety. You live in better style than we do, but though you often earn more than you need, you are very likely to lose all you have. You know the proverb, 'Loss and gain are brothers twain.' It often happens that people who are wealthy one day are begging their bread the next. Our way is safer. Though a peasant's life is not a fat one, it is a long one. We shall never grow rich, but we shall always have enough to eat."

The elder sister said sneeringly:

"Enough? Yes, if you like to share with the pigs and the calves! What do you know of elegance or manners! However much your goodman may slave, you will die as you are living—on a dung heap—and your children the same."

"Well, what of that?" replied the younger. "Of course our work is rough and coarse. But, on the other hand, it is sure, and we need not bow to anyone. But you, in your towns, are surrounded

LEO TOLSTOY 883

Quickwrite

Point out that this activity requires a shift in thinking. To answer the first question, students can let their imaginations wander, and their responses will be fantasies. For the second question, however, they must be more practical. Urge students to think of themselves as the person whose actual needs they must consider. Since the activity asks for candor, make sharing of responses voluntary.

A. Literary Elements: Conflict and Theme

Tolstoy's story begins by presenting a conflict between sisters with very different ways of life. What do the sisters argue about? [Possible answer: Whose way of life is better.] The elder sister is about to drop out of the story, and the younger will have a very minor role. How does their quarrel help establish the theme of the story? [Possible answer: Even if they have little to do with the story to come, their quarrel raises the main issue—what it takes to be satisfied with one's way of life. That issue will be carried along by one or more other characters.]

B. Reader's Response: First Thoughts

Give students a few minutes to freewrite about their initial reactions to the younger sister's argument. Do her reasons seem valid to you? Why or why not? [Sample responses: Her reasons seem valid; she and her husband are not risk-takers. They would rather live simply and not risk losing everything. Or the younger sister is just making excuses for her poverty.]

C. Literary Element: Foreshadowing

? From the younger sister's warning, what do you think will happen to her or her family? Explain. [Possible answer: Because of her talk about the Devil and temptation, it would be ironic if she or someone in her family were tempted, "and all [would] go to ruin." The younger sister's warning seems to foreshadow some kind of temptation for her or her family.]

A. Cultural Connections

Remind students of the account in Genesis of the fall of Adam and Eve (pp. 416–418). Even as the text there shows Eve leading Adam into temptation, so folk tales, fairy tales, and great works of literature from around the world often present wives or lovers as temptresses. As Tolstoy will show, however, the woman's husband, after overhearing this argument, is quite capable of getting into trouble on his own, without his wife's prompting.

B. Reader's Response: Challenging the Text

? Do you think it necessary to include the Devil as a character in this story? Defend your answer. [Sample responses: Having the Devil introduce the temptation makes the story less real, less believable; or the inclusion of the Devil makes the story more like a folk tale or fable, and thus more universal, more like a moral lesson.]

C. Critical Reading: Making Generalizations

? What advantage would there have been in group ownership of the land? [Possible answers: There might have been no more fines and taxes (or if there had been, they might have been agreed upon by the group); all of the farmers would have had a personal stake in making the venture succeed.] Why, then, were they unable to come to an agreement? [The narrator says that the Devil caused them to argue; perhaps they could not agree on how to use the land.]

Metacognition Ask students if in answering the last question they relied on the details in the text that imply that the Devil was responsible for the disagreement or if they concluded from prior knowledge that joint ownership is difficult and that so many owners would surely disagree.

---

by temptations; today all may be right, but tomorrow the Evil One may tempt your husband with cards, wine, or women, and all will go to ruin. Don't such things happen often enough?"

Pahom, the master of the house, was lying on the top of the stove[1] and he listened to the women's chatter.

"It is perfectly true," thought he. "Busy as we are from childhood tilling mother earth, we peasants have no time to let any nonsense settle in our heads. Our only trouble is that we haven't land enough. If I had plenty of land, I shouldn't fear the Devil himself!"

The women finished their tea, chatted a while about dress, and then cleared away the tea things and lay down to sleep.

(A) But the Devil had been sitting behind the stove, and had heard all that was said. He was pleased that the peasant's wife had led her husband into boasting, and that he had said that if he had plenty of land he would not fear the Devil himself.

(B) "All right," thought the Devil. "We will have a tussle. I'll give you land enough; and by means of that land I will get you into my power."

Close to the village there lived a lady, a small landowner who had an estate of about three hundred acres. She had always lived on good terms with the peasants until she engaged as her steward an old soldier, who took to burdening the people with fines. However careful Pahom tried to be, it happened again and again that now a horse of his got among the lady's oats, now a cow strayed into her garden, now his calves found their way into her meadows—and he always had to pay a fine.

Pahom paid up, but grumbled and, going home in a temper, was rough with his family. All through that summer, Pahom had much trouble because of this steward, and he was even glad when winter came and the cattle had to be stabled. Though he grudged the fodder when they could no longer graze on the pastureland, at least he was free from anxiety about them.

In the winter the news got about that the lady was going to sell her land and that the keeper of

---

1. **lying . . . stove:** Pahom's house is lacking in luxury if the family's oven, made of brick or tile, is used as an item of furniture.

---

the inn on the high road was bargaining for it. When the peasants heard this they were very much alarmed.

"Well," thought they, "if the innkeeper gets the land, he will worry us with fines worse than the lady's steward. We all depend on that estate."

So the peasants went on behalf of their Commune,[2] and asked the lady not to sell the land to the innkeeper, offering her a better price for it themselves. The lady agreed to let them have it.

(C) Then the peasants tried to arrange for the Commune to buy the whole estate, so that it might be held by them all in common. They met twice to discuss it, but could not settle the matter; the Evil One sowed discord among them and they could not agree. So they decided to buy the land individually, each according to his means; and the lady agreed to this plan as she had to the other.

Presently Pahom heard that a neighbor of his was buying fifty acres, and that the lady had consented to accept one half in cash and to wait a year for the other half. Pahom felt envious.

"Look at that," thought he, "the land is all being sold, and I shall get none of it." So he spoke to his wife.

"Other people are buying," said he, "and we must also buy twenty acres or so. Life is becoming impossible. That steward is simply crushing us with his fines."

So they put their heads together and considered how they could manage to buy it. They had one hundred rubles laid by. They sold a colt and one half of their bees, hired out one of their sons as a laborer, and took his wages in advance; borrowed the rest from a brother-in-law, and so scraped together half the purchase money.

Having done this, Pahom chose out a farm of forty acres, some of it wooded, and went to the lady to bargain for it. They came to an agreement, and he shook hands with her upon it and paid her a deposit in advance. Then they went to town and signed the deeds, he paying half the price down, and undertaking to pay the remainder within two years.

So now Pahom had land of his own. He borrowed seed, and sowed it on the land he had bought. The harvest was a good one, and within a year he had managed to pay off his debts both

---

2. **Commune:** village council.

OPTIONS FOR TEACHING

STRATEGIES FOR INCLUSION

Less Proficient Readers The sequence of events in this story provides an opportunity for students to practice the reading strategy of making predictions. Each time Pahom is preparing to obtain more land, have students stop and reflect on what they think will happen next. Students should jot down one or two sentences apiece in their Reader's Logs. Have students compare their predictions once they have completed the story.

Auditory Though this story is in translation, we can probably assume that Tolstoy's Russian has a similar tone and style. Read aloud a paragraph or two of Tolstoy's story and the same from Kipling's (pp. 872–880). Ask students if they can hear a difference in the styles in which the stories are written. How does Tolstoy make his story sound more like a folk tale? What is it about the sound of Kipling's story that adds to the feeling of a gap between the two cultures represented?

to the lady and to his brother-in-law. So he became a landowner, plowing and sowing his own land, making hay on his own land, cutting his own trees, and feeding his cattle on his own pasture. When he went out to plow his fields, or to look at his growing corn,[3] or at his grass

3. **corn:** any plants producing grain, such as wheat, rye, or oats.

meadows, his heart would fill with joy. The grass that grew and the flowers that bloomed there seemed to him unlike any that grew elsewhere. Formerly, when he had passed by that land, it had appeared the same as any other land, but now it seemed quite different.

So Pahom was well contented, and everything would have been right if the neighboring peasants would only not have trespassed on his cornfields

The Gleaners (1885–1886) by Isidore Verheyden. Oil on canvas (92 cm × 69 cm).
Collection Crédit Communal, Brussels, Belgium.

LEO TOLSTOY 885

D. Reader's Response: Shaping Interpretations

? Why does the land now appear more wonderful than and different from any other land? [Sample responses: It now belongs to Pahom. When it wasn't his own, it was just part of his life of toil.]

E. Literary Element: Conflict

? What conflict arises from Pahom's new situation? [Possible answer: He becomes very protective of his land and sees his neighbors as trespassers.]

RESPONDING TO THE ART: ABOUT THE ARTWORK

Painting with only visual sensation as inspiration, the Impressionists sustained a movement in art that celebrated light, color, atmosphere, and landscape. In order to examine their subjects directly, this revolutionary generation of artists boldly moved the canvas from the inner world of the imagination to, quite literally, the outdoors. Isisdore Verheyden's *The Gleaners* gives the impression that the artist deliberately chose to work on his painting in the presence of his subject—here, two women gathering grain—and to capture the very quality of light and color that is displayed at a specific time of day in that very field, and not rely on his memory or imagination.

STRATEGIES FOR INCLUSION

Visual/Spatial To Pahom, each chance to buy land is like an open door to a better life. Students might map out the story by drawing a series of "open door" diagrams. For each diagram, they should note the circumstances that provide the "door" and, inside, how Pahom's life changes when he takes advantage of the opportunity. Here is an example:

Cause: Effect:

[buys first plot of land]

[takes new pride in land]

Special Needs Students should have access to reference materials at or near their ability levels. Easy-to-read reference books on Russia that include many drawings or photographs may help students better appreciate the setting and the people described by Tolstoy. One such reference is *Tolstoy—The Making of a Novelist* which includes many photographs of Tolstoy and the people

about whom he wrote. Also included are paintings and drawings for many of his stories. Of particular interest is a large drawing on p. 189 of a Bashkir on horseback, in costume and wearing the sort of hat Tolstoy refers to in "How Much Land Does A Man Need?"

A. Literary Element: Character

? How do you see Pahom's personality changing in just these few sentences? [He goes from sympathy (an understanding that it was "no evil intent on their part, that caused the trouble") to a desire to help them mend their ways (a wish to teach them a lesson) to more aggressive retaliation (using the District Court to give them "one lesson, and then another," until the neighbors turn against him).] **What changes his personality?** [Being a land-owner.]

B. Critical Reading: Finding Cause and Effect

? What is the result of Pahom's feud with his neighbors? [There is so much resentment against him that he loses standing in the Commune, despite his land ownership.]

C. Literary Element: Theme

Relate Pahom's "As it is, I am still too cramped to be comfortable" to the title of this story. Ask students how much land Pahom thinks he needs at this point. [Possible answer: Enough to put a greater distance between himself and the other villagers, allowing him the "comfort" of not always worrying about trespassers.]

D. Critical Reading: Identifying Main Ideas

? How does Pahom's comment here underscore a main idea of this story? [Having made some progress through buying a bit of land, he has become increasingly dissatisfied; whenever he considers the possibility of gaining more land, he cannot be happy until he has it.]

---

and meadows. He appealed to them most civilly, but they still went on: Now the Communal herdsmen would let the village cows stray into his meadows, then horses from the night pasture would get among his corn. Pahom turned them out again and again, and forgave their owners, and for a long time he forbore to prosecute anyone. But at last he lost patience and complained to the District Court. He knew it was the peasants' want of land, and no evil intent on their part, that caused the trouble, but he thought:

"I cannot go on overlooking it or they will destroy all I have. They must be taught a lesson."

So he had them up, gave them one lesson, and then another, and two or three of the peasants were fined. After a time Pahom's neighbors began to bear him a grudge for this, and would now and then let their cattle on to his land on purpose. One peasant even got into Pahom's wood at night and cut down five young lime trees[4] for their bark. Pahom passing through the wood one day noticed something white. He came nearer and saw the stripped trunks lying on the ground, and close by stood the stumps where the trees had been. Pahom was furious.

"If he had only cut one here and there it would have been bad enough," thought Pahom, "but the rascal has actually cut down a whole clump. If I could only find out who did this, I would pay him out."

He racked his brain as to who it could be. Finally he decided: "It must be Simon—no one else could have done it." So he went to Simon's homestead to have a look round, but he found nothing, and only had an angry scene. However, he now felt more certain than ever that Simon had done it, and he lodged a complaint. Simon was summoned. The case was tried, and retried, and at the end of it all Simon was acquitted, there being no evidence against him. Pahom felt still more aggrieved, and let his anger loose upon the Elder and the Judges.

"You let thieves grease your palms," said he. "If you were honest folk yourselves you would not let a thief go free."

So Pahom quarreled with the Judges and with his neighbors. Threats to burn his building

began to be uttered. So though Pahom had more land, his place in the Commune was much worse than before.

About this time a rumor got about that many people were moving to new parts.

"There's no need for me to leave my land," thought Pahom. "But some of the others might leave our village and then there would be more room for us. I would take over their land myself and make my estate a bit bigger. I could then live more at ease. As it is, I am still too cramped to be comfortable."

One day Pahom was sitting at home when a peasant, passing through the village, happened to call in. He was allowed to stay the night, and supper was given him. Pahom had a talk with this peasant and asked him where he came from. The stranger answered that he came from beyond the Volga,[5] where he had been working. One word led to another, and the man went on to say that many people were settling in those parts. He told how some people from his village had settled there. They had joined the Commune, and had had twenty-five acres per man granted them. The land was so good, he said, that the rye sown on it grew as high as a horse, and so thick that five cuts of a sickle made a sheaf. One peasant, he said, had brought nothing with him but his bare hands, and now he had six horses and two cows of his own.

Pahom's heart kindled with desire. He thought:

"Why should I suffer in this narrow hole, if one can live so well elsewhere? I will sell my land and my homestead here, and with the money I will start afresh over there and get everything new. In this crowded place one is always having trouble. But I must first go and find out all about it myself."

Toward summer he got ready and started. He went down the Volga on a steamer to Samara,[6] then walked another three hundred miles on foot, and at last reached the place. It was just as the stranger had said. The peasants had plenty of land: Every man had twenty-five acres of Communal land given him for his use, and anyone who had money could buy, besides, at a ruble an acre as much good freehold land as he wanted.

---

4. **lime trees:** linden trees.

5. **Volga:** river in western Russia flowing into the Caspian Sea.

6. **Samara** (su·mä′rə): city on the Volga River in southwestern Russia.

886 THE VICTORIAN PERIOD

OPTIONS FOR TEACHING

INTEGRATING THE LANGUAGE ARTS

Strategic Reading Students can show that they have been affected by some of the story's powerful images and poignant moments by presenting them as part of a Random Reading. As students work through the story, have them note in their Reader's Logs any

thing that creates a strong mental image or that otherwise moves them. Then invite them to read aloud what they have noted—randomly, when they are ready to share. Allow more than one student to share the same part. Do not analyze the material shared; the purpose is to gather images that provide an overall "feel" for the work.

Writing: A Poem Invite students to react to Pahom by writing a brief impressionistic poem—perhaps a haiku. Poems can mourn Pahom's death, comment upon the attitudes that brought him to it, or offer the reader a warning based upon Pahom's fate. Encourage students to present a single feeling in their poems. Work with students to prepare a display for the finished poems.

T886 The Victorian Period

Having found out all he wished to know, Pahom returned home as autumn came on, and began selling off his belongings. He sold his land at a profit, sold his homestead and all his cattle, and withdrew from membership in the Commune. He only waited till the spring, and then started with his family for the new settlement.

As soon as Pahom and his family reached their new abode, he applied for admission into the Commune of a large village. He stood treat to the Elders[7] and obtained the necessary documents. Five shares of Communal land were given him for his own and his sons' use: that is to say—125 acres (not all together, but in different fields) besides the use of the Communal pasture. Pahom put up the buildings he needed, and bought cattle. Of the Communal land alone he had three times as much as at his former home, and the land was good corn land. He was ten times better off than he had been. He had plenty of arable land and pasturage, and could keep as many head of cattle as he liked.

At first, in the bustle of building and settling down, Pahom was pleased with it all, but when he got used to it he began to think that even here he had not enough land. The first year, he sowed wheat on his share of the Communal land and had a good crop. He wanted to go on sowing wheat, but had not enough Communal land for the purpose, and what he had already used was not available; for in those parts wheat is only sown on virgin soil or on fallow land. It is sown for one or two years, and then the land lies fallow till it is again overgrown with prairie grass. There were many who wanted such land and there was not enough for all; so that people quarreled about it. Those who were better off wanted it for growing wheat, and those who were poor wanted it to let to dealers, so that they might raise money to pay their taxes. Pahom wanted to sow more wheat, so he rented land from a dealer for a year. He sowed much wheat and had a fine crop, but the land was too far from the village—the wheat had to be carted more than ten miles. After a time Pahom noticed that some peasant dealers were living on separate farms and were growing wealthy; and he thought:

"If I were to buy some freehold land and have a homestead on it, it would be a different thing altogether. Then it would all be nice and compact."

The question of buying freehold land recurred to him again and again.

He went on in the same way for three years, renting land and sowing wheat. The seasons turned out well and the crops were good, so that he began to lay money by. He might have gone on living contentedly, but he grew tired of having to rent other people's land every year, and having to scramble for it. Wherever there was good land to be had, the peasants would rush for it and it was taken up at once, so that unless you were sharp about it you got none. It happened in the third year that he and a dealer together rented a piece of pastureland from some peasants; and they had already plowed it up, when there was some dispute and the peasants went to law about it, and things fell out so that the labor was all lost.

"If it were my own land," thought Pahom, "I should be independent, and there would not be all this unpleasantness."

So Pahom began looking out for land which he could buy; and he came across a peasant who had bought thirteen hundred acres, but having got into difficulties was willing to sell again cheap. Pahom bargained and haggled with him, and at last they settled the price at 1,500 rubles,[8] part in cash and part to be paid later. They had all but clinched the matter when a passing dealer happened to stop at Pahom's one day to get a feed for his horses. He drank tea with Pahom and they had a talk. The dealer said that he was just returning from the land of the Bashkirs,[9] far away, where he had bought thirteen thousand acres of land, all for 1,000 rubles. Pahom questioned him further, and the tradesman said:

"All one need do is to make friends with the chiefs. I gave away about one hundred rubles' worth of silk robes and carpets, besides a case of tea, and I gave wine to those who would drink it; and I got the land for less than a penny an acre." And he showed Pahom the title deeds, saying:

"The land lies near a river, and the whole prairie is virgin soil."

8. **rubles:** units of money in Russia, Ukraine, and other countries.
9. **Bashkirs** (bash·kirz'): Turkish-speaking peoples who live on the Russian steppes, or plains.

7. **stood treat to the Elders:** provided the Elders with a meal.

LEO TOLSTOY **887**

INTEGRATING THE LANGUAGE ARTS

Speaking and Listening Call on pairs of volunteers to present dialogues based on this story. Each dialogue should be a spontaneous conversation between two characters in the narrative, such as the characters in the following examples:
- Pahom and his wife
- Pahom and Simon
- Pahom and the tradesman

- Pahom and his servant
- Bashkirs who are watching Pahom run
- the Bashkir chief and Pahom's servant

These characters may have differing (even conflicting) attitudes about materialism. After each dialogue, have the class discuss which character seems to reflect Tolstoy's ideas more accurately, and why. ☞

RESPONDING TO THE ART: VISUAL LITERACY

How does this painting illustrate the story? [Possible responses: The story takes place in a landscape much like this one. The road could signify the road Pahom traces to find his new land, or in a more metaphorical sense, the road he takes to ruin.]

A. Reader's Response: First Thoughts

? How do you feel when you first read this description of the Bashkirs? [Sample responses: Disappointed that any people would be described as being "as simple as sheep"; frustrated that Pahom once again will find a reason to attempt to satisfy his greed; wary for Pahom, whose greed seems too easily fulfilled.]

Road in the Woods (detail) (late 19th century) by Fiodor Vasilyev.

Pahom plied him with questions, and the tradesman said:

A "There is more land there than you could cover if you walked a year, and it all belongs to the Bashkirs. They are as simple as sheep, and land can be got almost for nothing."

"There now," thought Pahom, "with my one thousand rubles, why should I get only thirteen hundred acres, and saddle myself with a debt besides? If I take it out there, I can get more than ten times as much for the money."

Pahom inquired how to get to the place, and as

888 THE VICTORIAN PERIOD

OPTIONS FOR TEACHING

CROSSING THE CURRICULUM

Geography Although Tolstoy's story has universal application, it is tied to a specific locale. As students read "How Much Land Does a Man Need?" have available a map that features Russia. Ask volunteers to point out the steppes, the Volga River, and Bashkiriya (Bashkortostan).

Social Sciences Invite interested students to learn more about the Russian feudal system that was abolished by Czar Alexander II, the land-use system that replaced it, and the management of land under Communist rule. How did each system challenge those who dreamed of owning their own land? Under which system did the average Russian have the greatest chance to own land? Have students share their information with the class using outlines and diagrams they can post on the bulletin boards.

Mathematics Have students compute how fast Pahom would have to walk to cover the perimeter of an area 35 miles square in a day. They may wish to determine certain givens, such as the number of hours of daylight and the number and length of rest stops or stops for digging. Students who have hiked may wish to offer comparisons of what it is like to hike a given distance, such as 10 miles—how long it took them, under what conditions, and so on.

Tretyakov Gallery, Moscow.

On and on they went until they had gone more than three hundred miles, and on the seventh day they came to a place where the Bashkirs had pitched their tents. It was all just as the tradesman had said. The people lived on the steppes, by a river, in felt-covered tents. They neither tilled the ground, nor ate bread. Their cattle and horses grazed in herds on the steppe. The colts were tethered behind the tents, and the mares were driven to them twice a day. The mares were milked, and from the milk kumiss[10] was made. It was the women who prepared kumiss, and they also made cheese. As far as the men were concerned, drinking kumiss and tea, eating mutton, and playing on their pipes, was all they cared about. They were all stout and merry, and all the summer long they never thought of doing any work. They were quite ignorant, and knew no Russian, but were good natured enough.

As soon as they saw Pahom, they came out of their tents and gathered round their visitor. An interpreter was found, and Pahom told them he had come about some land. The Bashkirs seemed very glad; they took Pahom and led him into one of the best tents, where they made him sit on some down cushions placed on a carpet, while they sat round him. They gave him some tea and kumiss, and had a sheep killed, and gave him mutton to eat. Pahom took presents out of his cart and distributed them among the Bashkirs, and divided the tea amongst them. The Bashkirs were delighted. They talked a great deal among themselves, and then told the interpreter to translate.

"They wish to tell you," said the interpreter, "that they like you, and that it is our custom to do all we can to please a guest and to repay him for his gifts. You have given us presents, now tell us which of the things we possess please you best, that we may present them to you."

"What pleases me best here," answered Pahom, "is your land. Our land is crowded and the soil is exhausted; but you have plenty of land and it is good land. I never saw the like of it."

The interpreter translated. The Bashkirs talked among themselves for a while. Pahom could not understand what they were saying, but saw that they were much amused and that they shouted and

soon as the tradesman had left him, he prepared to go there himself. He left his wife to look after the homestead, and started on his journey taking his man with him. They stopped at a town on their way and bought a case of tea, some wine, and other presents, as the tradesman had advised.

10. **kumiss** (ko͞o′mis): fermented drink made from mare's milk.

LEO TOLSTOY 889

B. Cultural Connections

- Descended primarily from the Turks, the Bashkirs once were nomads, and Tolstoy's description of their way of life is accurate. Most Bashkirs are Muslims, although there is an Eastern Orthodox minority.

- Sadly, it is because of people like Pahom that the Bashkirs' traditional way of life ended. Portions of the Bashkirs' land were constantly being bought up, and by the middle of the nineteenth century they found it impossible to continue as pastoral nomads. Most turned to agriculture and to village life. Today, the Bashkirs are a minority in the land that they used to roam.

C. Critical Reading: Making Inferences

? Why do you think Pahom describes his situation in this way? Do you think that he is being honest? [Possible answers: He is trying to flatter his hosts, hoping that they will be more willing to sell him land. He may be honest in his evaluation of the Bashkirs' land, but he was recently quite happy with the land that he now describes as overcrowded and "exhausted."]

D. Critical Reading: Predicting

? Based on the Bashkirs' response, what do you think will happen to Pahom? [Their laughter, which Pahom seems to interpret as pleasure with the offer he has made, appears to be a form of ridicule. Perhaps they know that they will get the better of and humiliate this stranger.]

CLASSROOM MANAGEMENT

Sharing Responses Cooperative learning need not be limited to a method of completing an assignment; at times it can arise from the way in which a completed assignment is shared. You might try having two students who completed the same activity for this story compare their responses. Have them report (to you or to the class) on what they learned from seeing another person's ideas about the same material.

Block Scheduling Use part of the block for a lecture presenting general information, such as material about Victorian novelists, and then use the balance of the period for small group discussion or activities that reteach or reinforce the material you have just presented. This way students experience the traditional teaching method they will encounter to a large degree on college campuses, but they also will have other tools with which to grasp the material. ☞

A. Critical Reading: Analyzing Persuasion

? What are the main points of Pahom's appeal? [Possible answer: I want just a small part of your land; to guarantee that it remains mine, I need to have the proper papers drawn up; you are good people; God oversees all.] How does the statement "Life and death are in God's hands" strengthen Pahom's case? [The statement makes him seem pious and thus less likely to deceive them.]

B. Critical Reading: Finding Details

? How much money does Pahom have to bargain with? [When he earlier considered the stranger's words, he thought about his own one thousand rubles.] In essence, what is the price of the land? [Everything Pahom has.]

C. Reader's Response: Shaping Interpretations

? Do you think that this arrangement is fair? Why or why not? [Sample responses: The condition seems odd but fair. Anyone could gain some land under this arrangement, but it does present a real temptation to go after more than one can cover.]

D. Reader's Response: Extending the Text

? How wise do you think it is for Pahom to be making all these plans? [Sample responses: Pahom cannot help dreaming a bit; or a circuit of thirty-five miles may be too optimistic, and Pahom perhaps should set his sights a bit lower.]

---

laughed. Then they were silent and looked at Pahom while the interpreter said:

"They wish me to tell you that in return for your presents they will gladly give you as much land as you want. You have only to point it out with your hand and it is yours."

The Bashkirs talked again for a while and began to dispute. Pahom asked what they were disputing about, and the interpreter told him that some of them thought they ought to ask their chief about the land and not act in his absence, while others thought there was no need to wait for his return.

While the Bashkirs were disputing, a man in a large fox-fur cap appeared on the scene. They all became silent and rose to their feet. The interpreter said, "This is our chief himself."

Pahom immediately fetched the best dressing gown and five pounds of tea, and offered these to the chief. The chief accepted them, and seated himself in the place of honor. The Bashkirs at once began telling him something. The chief listened for a while, then made a sign with his head for them to be silent, and addressing himself to Pahom, said in Russian:

"Well, let it be so. Choose whatever piece of land you like; we have plenty of it."

"How can I take as much as I like?" thought Pahom. "I must get a deed to make it secure, or else they may say, 'It is yours,' and afterward may take it away again."

"Thank you for your kind words," he said aloud. "You have much land, and I only want a little. But I should like to be sure which bit is mine. Could it not be measured and made over to me? Life and death are in God's hands. You good people give it to me, but your children might wish to take it away again."

"You are quite right," said the chief. "We will make it over to you."

"I heard that a dealer had been here," continued Pahom, "and that you gave him a little land, too, and signed title deeds to that effect. I should like to have it done in the same way."

The chief understood.

"Yes," replied he, "that can be done quite easily. We have a scribe, and we will go to town with you and have the deed properly sealed."

"And what will be the price?" asked Pahom.

"Our price is always the same: one thousand rubles a day."

Pahom did not understand.

"A day? What measure is that? How many acres would that be?"

"We do not know how to reckon it out," said the chief. "We sell it by the day. As much as you can go round on your feet in a day is yours, and the price is one thousand rubles a day."

Pahom was surprised.

"But in a day you can get round a large tract of land," he said.

The chief laughed.

"It will all be yours!" said he. "But there is one condition: If you don't return on the same day to the spot whence you started, your money is lost."

"But how am I to mark the way that I have gone?"

"Why, we shall go to any spot you like, and stay there. You must start from that spot and make your round, taking a spade with you. Wherever you think necessary, make a mark. At every turning, dig a hole and pile up the turf; then afterward we will go round with a plow from hole to hole. You may make as large a circuit as you please, but before the sun sets you must return to the place you started from. All the land you cover will be yours."

Pahom was delighted. It was decided to start early next morning. They talked a while, and after drinking some more kumiss and eating some more mutton, they had tea again, and then the night came on. They gave Pahom a featherbed to sleep on, and the Bashkirs dispersed for the night, promising to assemble the next morning at daybreak and ride out before sunrise to the appointed spot.

Pahom lay on the featherbed, but could not sleep. He kept thinking about the land.

"What a large tract I will mark off!" thought he. "I can easily do thirty-five miles in a day. The days are long now, and within a circuit of thirty-five miles what a lot of land there will be! I will sell the poorer land, or let it to peasants, but I'll pick out the best and farm it. I will buy two ox teams, and hire two more laborers. About a hundred and fifty acres shall be plow land, and I will pasture cattle on the rest."

Pahom lay awake all night, and dozed off only just before dawn. Hardly were his eyes closed

890 THE VICTORIAN PERIOD

PROFESSIONAL NOTES

Critical Comment: Tolstoy's Standing
Matthew Arnold wrote, "Whatever else we have or have not in Count Tolstoi, we have at least a great soul and a great writer. . . . [W]hatever he may do in the future, the work which he has already done . . . is more than sufficient to signalise him as one of the most marking, interesting, and sympathy-inspiring men of our time. . . ." Have students interpret and discuss this evaluation.

Cultural Diversity Use Tolstoy's story to discuss the concept of land ownership in various cultures. Ask students to draw from their own backgrounds and their knowledge of world cultures to explore reasons for owning land and ways in which land may be seen as a great treasure. To extend discussion, note that many people in the United States today rent property instead of owning it; ask what these people lose or gain by not having land of their own.

when he had a dream. He thought he was lying in that same tent and heard somebody chuckling outside. He wondered who it could be, and rose and went out, and he saw the Bashkir chief sitting in front of the tent holding his sides and rolling about with laughter. Going nearer to the chief, Pahom asked: "What are you laughing at?" But he saw that it was no longer the chief, but the dealer who had recently stopped at his house and had told him about the land. Just as Pahom was going to ask, "Have you been here long?" he saw that it was not the dealer, but the peasant who had come up from the Volga, long ago, to Pahom's old home. Then he saw that it was not the peasant either, but the Devil himself with hoofs and horns, sitting there and chuckling, and before him lay a man barefoot, prostrate on the ground, with only trousers and a shirt on. And Pahom dreamt that he

looked more attentively to see what sort of a man it was that was lying there, and he saw that the man was dead, and that it was himself! He awoke horror-struck.

"What things one does dream," thought he.

Looking round he saw through the open door that the dawn was breaking.

"It's time to wake them up," thought he. "We ought to be starting."

He got up, roused his man (who was sleeping in his cart), bade him harness, and went to call the Bashkirs.

"It's time to go to the steppe to measure the land," he said.

The Bashkirs rose and assembled, and the chief came too. Then they began drinking kumiss again, and offered Pahom some tea, but he would not wait.

E

The Rainbow by Kuinji Arkhip.

Russian State Museum, St. Petersburg.

LEO TOLSTOY 891

A. Literary Element: Rising Action

With the chief's words and Tolstoy's vivid description, Pahom cannot turn back. Such land is a temptation too great to pass up, as is the offer of owning all the land he can cover in a day. These few sentences push the action into high gear; from here on out, the element of suspense will rise as Pahom tries to outpace the sun.

B. Critical Reading: Drawing Conclusions

? What obstacle stands between Pahom and his goal? [Himself—specifically, his own physical inability to complete the circuit that he has in mind.]

Metacognition Which details from this passage helped you reach this conclusion? [Possible answers: His pace, which he quickens very early into his trek; the rapidity with which the temperature goes from what Pahom feels is "cool" to "quite warm"; his need to stop for breakfast.]

C. Literary Element: Theme

? How do Pahom's thoughts relate to the theme of this story? [Possible answer: His comment "The further one goes, the better the land seems" seems an apt metaphor for what has been happening to Pahom throughout this story: the further he progresses in his quest for self-sufficiency and wealth, the better the next step seems.]

D. Literary Element: Character

? Is this action consistent with what you know of Pahom's character? Explain. [Most students will agree that it is quite consistent, for it shows that even at this critical moment he can be swayed by the chance to obtain just a little bit more than he had before.]

"If we are to go, let us go. It is high time," said he.

The Bashkirs got ready and they all started: some mounted on horses, and some in carts. Pahom drove in his own small cart with his servant and took a spade with him. When they reached the steppe, the morning red was beginning to kindle. They ascended a hillock (called by the Bashkirs a *shikhan*) and dismounting from their carts and their horses, gathered in one spot. The chief came up to Pahom and stretching out his arm toward the plain:

(A) "See," said he, "all this, as far as your eye can reach, is ours. You may have any part of it you like."

Pahom's eyes glistened: It was all virgin soil, as flat as the palm of your hand, as black as the seed of a poppy, and in the hollows different kinds of grasses grew breast high.

The chief took off his fox-fur cap, placed it on the ground, and said:

"This will be the mark. Start from here, and return here again. All the land you go round shall be yours."

Pahom took out his money and put it on the cap. Then he took off his outer coat, remaining in his sleeveless undercoat. He unfastened his girdle and tied it tight below his stomach, put a little bag of bread into the breast of his coat, and tying a flask of water to his girdle, he drew up the tops of his boots, took the spade from his man, and stood ready to start. He considered for some moments which way he had better go—it was tempting everywhere.

"No matter," he concluded, "I will go toward the rising sun."

He turned his face to the east, stretched himself, and waited for the sun to appear above the rim.

(B) "I must lose no time," he thought, "and it is easier walking while it is still cool."

The sun's rays had hardly flashed above the horizon, before Pahom, carrying the spade over his shoulder, went down into the steppe.

Pahom started walking neither slowly nor quickly. After having gone a thousand yards he stopped, dug a hole, and placed pieces of turf one on another to make it more visible. Then he went on; and now that he had walked off his stiffness he quickened his pace. After a while he dug another hole.

Pahom looked back. The hillock could be distinctly seen in the sunlight, with the people on it,

and the glittering tires of the cart wheels. At a rough guess Pahom concluded that he had walked three miles. It was growing warmer; he took off his undercoat, flung it across his shoulder, and went on again. It had grown quite warm now; he looked at the sun, it was time to think of breakfast.

"The first shift is done, but there are four in a day, and it is too soon yet to turn. But I will just take off my boots," said he to himself.

He sat down, took off his boots, stuck them into his girdle, and went on. It was easy walking now.

(C) "I will go on for another three miles," thought he, "and then turn to the left. This spot is so fine, that it would be a pity to lose it. The further one goes, the better the land seems."

He went straight on for a while, and when he looked round, the hillock was scarcely visible and the people on it looked like black ants, and he could just see something glistening there in the sun.

"Ah," thought Pahom, "I have gone far enough in this direction, it is time to turn. Besides I am in a regular sweat, and very thirsty."

He stopped, dug a large hole, and heaped up pieces of turf. Next he untied his flask, had a drink, and then turned sharply to the left. He went on and on; the grass was high, and it was very hot.

Pahom began to grow tired: He looked at the sun and saw that it was noon.

"Well," he thought, "I must have a rest."

He sat down, and ate some bread and drank some water; but he did not lie down, thinking that if he did he might fall asleep. After sitting a little while, he went on again. At first he walked easily: The food had strengthened him; but it had become terribly hot and he felt sleepy, still he went on, thinking: "An hour to suffer, a lifetime to live."

(D) He went a long way in this direction also, and was about to turn to the left again, when he perceived a damp hollow: "It would be a pity to leave that out," he thought. "Flax would do well there." So he went on past the hollow, and dug a hole on the other side of it before he turned the corner. Pahom looked toward the hillock. The heat made the air hazy: It seemed to be quivering, and through the haze the people on the hillock could scarcely be seen.

"Ah!" thought Pahom, "I have made the sides too long; I must make this one shorter." And he went

OPTIONS FOR TEACHING

ASSESSMENT TOOLS

Peer Assessment Groups of five to seven students can gather for Grand Conversations. Each group's leader initiates discussion by asking, "What did you think of Tolstoy's story and why is it in this Collection?" The secretary records the main ideas discussed. After leaders share their

ideas, ask each group to assign a holistic score to the other groups based upon their ability to relate the story to the Collection's theme and upon the thoughtfulness of their comments. You might use a simple three-point rating scale: 1 = excellent; 2 = satisfactory; 3 = unsatisfactory.

The Sower (1888) by Vincent van Gogh.

RESPONDING TO
THE ART: ABOUT
THE ARTIST

Emerging from Impressionism (see p. T885), the Post-Impressionists were influenced by their predecessors' use of light and color, but distinguished themselves as a new generation through systematic painting as opposed to the Impressionists' radical, free-form style. Vincent Van Gogh (1853–1890) developed his own style, applying violent strokes of bright, intense colors to the canvas, evoking a sense of vitality and action in his paintings not seen in Impressionist paintings. Obvious, harsh brushstrokes create tension between colors in his paintings. In *The Sower*, bands of orange grain and the green and blue of a man sowing seeds, emphasize two atmospheres in the painting, that of the sky and the earth.

---

along the third side, stepping faster. He looked at the sun: It was nearly halfway to the horizon, and he had not yet done two miles of the third side of the square. He was still ten miles from the goal.

"No," he thought, "though it will make my land lopsided, I must hurry back in a straight line now. I might go too far, and as it is I have a great deal of land."

So Pahom hurriedly dug a hole, and turned straight toward the hillock.

Pahom went straight toward the hillock, but he now walked with difficulty. He was done up with the heat, his bare feet were cut and bruised, and his legs began to fail. He longed to rest, but it was impossible if he meant to get back before sunset. The sun waits for no man, and it was sinking lower and lower.

"Oh dear," he thought, "if only I have not blun-dered trying for too much! What if I am too late?"

He looked toward the hillock and at the sun. He was still far from his goal, and the sun was already near the rim.

Pahom walked on and on; it was very hard walking but he went quicker and quicker. He pressed on, but was still far from the place. He began running, threw away his coat, his boots, his flask, and his cap, and kept only the spade which he used as a support.

"What shall I do," he thought again. "I have grasped too much and ruined the whole affair. I can't get there before the sun sets."

And this fear made him still more breathless. Pahom went on running, his soaking shirt and trousers stuck to him, and his mouth was parched. His breast was working like a blacksmith's bellows, his heart was beating like a hammer, and his legs

LEO TOLSTOY 893

E. Reader's Response: Challenging the Text

? Do you think that you are meant to feel sympathy for Pahom? Why or why not? [Sample responses: Yes, even though Pahom has brought this situation upon himself, and even though he can free himself from it (at the cost of one thousand rubles), it is hard not to feel some sympathy for his suffering—especially the sense of being trapped that he must feel. No, it is his own greed that brought him to this state.]

F. Literary Element: Symbolism
Notice what Pahom tosses aside and what he keeps. What do you think these items represent? [Possible answer: His discarded coat, boots, flask, and cap are clothing and sustenance—those things of life that are considered essential; the spade, which he keeps, represents his continued obsession with land ownership, which he does not need to survive.]

A. Critical Reading: Finding Cause and Effect

Tolstoy clearly shows Pahom's terror that he will not survive the run. Why, then, does he continue to run? Give a reason of your own; then, find Tolstoy's explanation. [According to Tolstoy, Pahom keeps running so that the Bashkirs will not consider him a fool. He also is running because he wants the land and feels trapped into completing what he started that sunrise.]

B. Critical Reading: Evaluating an Interpretation

? Is the Bashkir chief the Devil? Defend your interpretation. [Students who support this interpretation may point to the vividness of Pahom's "last chance" dream; students who disagree may suggest that Pahom's greed makes the appearance of the Devil unnecessary. Both interpretations may note that the chief is just one of several characters who enable Pahom's greed to surface.]

C. Literary Element: Climax

The action of the story here reaches its highest point, as Pahom's heart is strained to its limits; it then suddenly stops, and Pahom's life ends.

D. Literary Element: Irony

? What irony or ironies do you find in this conclusion? [Possible answers: It turns out that the only land Pahom needs is a burial plot. In addition, Pahom's own spade—the one thing he refused to give up during his run—is used to dig his grave. Furthermore, the Bashkirs seem to express pity over Pahom's death, but by now one suspects that they knew the outcome of their offer.]

Finding Common Ground

After students have read "How Much Land Does a Man Need?" ask them to review their responses to the Quickwrite activity on p. 883. As they consider the case of Pahom, invite comments about ways in which their original assessments have changed or have been confirmed. Ask small groups to discuss the questions and then to share responses in class discussion.

---

were giving way as if they did not belong to him. Pahom was seized with terror lest he should die of the strain.

Though afraid of death, he could not stop. "After having run all that way they will call me a fool if I stop now," thought he. And he ran on and on, and drew near and heard the Bashkirs yelling and shouting to him, and their cries inflamed his heart still more. He gathered his last strength and ran on.

The sun was close to the rim, and cloaked in mist looked large, and red as blood. Now, yes now, it was about to set! The sun was quite low, but he was also quite near his aim. Pahom could already see the people on the hillock waving their arms to hurry him up. He could see the fox-fur cap on the ground and the money on it, and the chief sitting on the ground holding his sides. And Pahom remembered his dream.

"There is plenty of land," thought he, "but will God let me live on it? I have lost my life, I have lost my life! I shall never reach that spot!"

Pahom looked at the sun, which had reached the earth: One side of it had already disappeared. With all his remaining strength he rushed on, bending his body forward so that his legs could hardly follow fast enough to keep him from falling. Just as he reached the hillock it suddenly grew dark. He looked up—the sun had already set! He gave a cry: "All my labor has been in vain," thought he, and was about to stop, but he heard the Bashkirs still shouting, and remembered that though to him, from below, the sun seemed to have set, they on the hillock could still see it. He took a long breath and ran up the hillock. It was still light there. He reached the top and saw the cap. Before it sat the chief laughing and holding his sides. Again Pahom remembered his dream, and he uttered a cry: His legs gave way beneath him, he fell forward and reached the cap with his hands.

"Ah, that's a fine fellow!" exclaimed the chief. "He has gained much land!"

Pahom's servant came running up and tried to raise him, but he saw that blood was flowing from his mouth. Pahom was dead!

The Bashkirs clicked their tongues to show their pity.

His servant picked up the spade and dug a grave long enough for Pahom to lie in, and buried him in it. Six feet from his head to his heels was all he needed.

FINDING COMMON GROUND

Tolstoy's story of a Russian farmer's land acquisition illustrates the perils of greed. In describing his disillusionment with private land ownership, Tolstoy provides twentieth-century readers with a parable about the "progress" of materialism. In small groups, talk about the contrast the story presents between modern attitudes and those of ancient cultures that are said to be "simple as sheep."

• Find examples in the text that reveal the Bashkir culture's attitudes about property and values. How would you compare them to the beliefs of the North American Plains Indians, or to those of another culture you know well?

• The nomadic Bashkirs come into contact with outsiders who buy their land for a token sum.

How is this clash of cultures similar to or different from the one depicted in Kipling's "The Mark of the Beast" (page 872)?

• You have seen British writers questioning the progress of nineteenth-century industrialization and modernization. Does this questioning change in a Russian setting? In what ways does Tolstoy share or extend the debate about progress?

• Pahom's dreams of wealth are mocked in the story's ironic last line. Think of the stark contrast between what he wanted and "all he needed." What parallels do you find with our culture today? How and why do people's wants differ from their actual needs?

READ ON

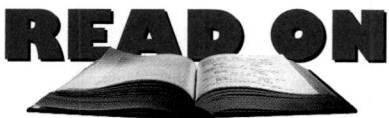

Dark Shadows

Although there have been numerous movie (and stage) versions in the twentieth century, Bram Stoker's *Dracula* (Putnam) is rooted firmly in the Victorian psyche. Written in 1897, this Gothic masterpiece is not only a supreme story of horror and suspense, but also a reflection of the dark underside of an extremely moralistic age. The progressive values of high Victorian culture are pitted against—and ultimately triumph over—the deep-rooted desires and dreads of the subconscious.

Romantic Rebellion

"If there's one thing Papa will never, *never* permit, it's a marriage in the family." Rudolf Besier's play *The Barretts of Wimpole Street* (Little, Brown) is based on the relationship between Elizabeth Barrett and Robert Browning, which developed under less than auspicious circumstances: Elizabeth's father forbade any of his nine adult children to marry. But in spite of Mr. Barrett's extraordinary attitude, his whole house is literally seething with romance and rebellion.

A Peek at Victorian Private Lives

Welcome to nineteenth-century England! In *What Jane Austen Ate and Charles Dickens Knew* (Simon and Schuster), Daniel Pool gives new life to the daily life of the last century. Both the nitty-gritty details (How did they keep clean?) and the posh etiquette (How did one address a duke?) of the time are covered. Find out what the Victorians ate, what they wore, how they traveled, and whom they married.

Found in a Handbag

Much of the satire in Oscar Wilde's play *The Importance of Being Earnest* (Penguin) is targeted at the British class system. Wilde openly flouted Victorian ideas of respectability and presented his own philosophy as an alternative. The seemingly contradictory logic of the play is part of this philosophy: "The truth is rarely pure and never simple." The play is also available as a film, made in England in 1952, with Michael Redgrave.

Pastoral Problems

Thomas Hardy's *Far from the Madding Crowd* (Oxford University Press) is about one very beautiful woman and the profound effect she has on three very different men. Opening on a note of almost lighthearted comedy, the novel gradually evolves into a starker tale of thoughtlessness, abandonment, death, and derangement. The 1967 British film version of the novel, directed by John Schlesinger, with Julie Christie, Peter Finch, and Alan Bates, is available on videotape.

READ ON 895

FOR FURTHER EXPLORATION

Poetry
Collected Poems by A. E. Housman
Dover Beach and Other Poems by Matthew Arnold
Sonnets from the Portuguese by Elizabeth Barrett Browning

Novels
Jane Eyre by Charlotte Brontë
Kim by Rudyard Kipling

Oliver Twist by Charles Dickens
The Return of the Native by Thomas Hardy
Silas Marner by George Eliot
Wuthering Heights by Emily Brontë

Nonfiction
Imperialism and Popular Culture ed. by John M. MacKenzie
Victorian People by Asa Briggs

Read On
Portfolio Assessment Options

The following projects can help you evaluate and assess your students' reading outside of class. Videotapes or audiotapes of completed projects may be included in students' portfolios.

- **Create a Silent Dialogue** Encourage pairs of students to respond to their reading by assuming the identities of two characters—from the same book or from different books. Have them, in character, create a silent dialogue by passing a paper back and forth and "conversing" about these questions: What obstacles did I have to face to achieve my goals? How did I deal with them? Was I successful?

- **Join the "Proper Patrol"** Ask a group of students representing several or all of the recommended books to plan and present a panel discussion on the topic of "propriety" in the books that they read. If they so choose, all of the students in a group may assume the personae of characters in the books. As they discuss their books, encourage them to focus on what the books set forth as "proper" behavior and what they suggest are the results of "impropriety."

- **Invent a Game** Have interested students create a board game adapted from the book that they have read. Work with students to come up with a premise for each game; encourage them to include dead ends on the course as well as several locations at which a card must be drawn and its directions followed. Have students present the game and invite classmates to play.

- **Advertise a Miniseries** Ask students to imagine that the book they read is being produced as a television miniseries. Have them decide how many episodes they would need; then, have them write (1) a summary of each segment, to be printed in a television program guide, and (2) promotional copy (perhaps with a slogan) for each segment. Writers and artists together might plan an advertising campaign to present to the class.

A. Expansion

As the Victorian Age saw English become a world language, it also saw the establishment of the notion of "the Queen's English"—the spoken standard to which all classes could aspire.

B. Cultural Connections

There are three main regional dialects in American English: Northern, Midland, and Southern. Within those regions, there may be subtypes; for example, a Bostonian and a New Yorker will not sound exactly the same, and someone from Charleston may have slight speech differences from someone from New Orleans. Still, the language remains relatively uniform. One of the very few exceptions is Gullah, spoken on some islands off the southeastern United States coast. In Great Britain, on the other hand, a large number of speech variations can be found in a small geographical area.

C. Exploring the Culture

In many parts of the world (Japan and Saudi Arabia, for example), students choose which type of English to learn: British or American.

Elements of Literature: Videodisc Use the following bar codes to locate the video segment about the development of the English language from the Restoration to the Twentieth Century. For more information, see the Videodisc *Teacher's Manual.*

Videodisc Side A

Begin Play, English Track

Begin Play, Spanish Track

The English Language

One Language—Many Nations

by John Algeo

A Although the spread of English outside the British Isles began in the early seventeenth century, it was during the Victorian Age and the establishment of the British Empire that English became a world language. Primarily because of the empire, English became either the first or an important second language in the British Isles, the United States, Canada, and also in Jamaica, Trinidad and Tobago, Australia, New Zealand, Malaysia, Myanmar, India, Sri Lanka, Pakistan, Israel, Ghana, Sierra Leone, Nigeria, Sudan, Kenya, Tanzania, Malawi, Zambia, Zimbabwe, Swaziland, and South Africa. American expansion, although modest by comparison, extended English to the Philippines, Liberia, and a few other places.

English as an International Language

English first spread around the world as a result of political and commercial activities, empire building, and colonization. In addition, scientific and technological advances, movies and television programs, popular music, and fashions of clothing have all served to reinforce the prestige of English as an international language. Today, English is used more widely and for more purposes as a second language than any other human tongue.

To take only one example: English is the language of international aviation. If a Swedish pilot is landing an airplane in Greece, he or she uses English to converse with the controller on the ground. Having a single language for international aviation is obviously sensible. It would not do for a pilot who spoke only Swedish to ask for landing instructions from ground controllers who spoke only Greek. A common language is needed as a safety measure for international flights, and English was chosen because of the prominence of English-speaking people in making and flying airplanes. It is for such reasons that English has become the most widely used international language.

Dialects of English

Today, there are dialects of English all over the world. Each place where it is spoken has its own variety of the language, and **B** old countries like England or large ones like the United States have many regional dialects. However, standard English—the English found in books, magazines, and large newspapers—is relatively uniform. That uniformity also helps to make English useful as an international language. Differences exist, to be sure, but they are minor fluctuations in what is obviously a single language.

Each country in which English is the main language of communication has its own national standard that differs in small, but recognizable, ways from the standards of other English-speaking lands. Among these national standards are those of Australia, Canada, the United Kingdom (England, Scotland, Wales, and Northern Ireland), Jamaica, New Zealand, the Republic of Ireland, and the United States.

Two Close Cousins: British and American English

C The two most important national standards are those of the United Kingdom and of the United States: British and American English. The differences between them can be illustrated by a few expressions:

American	British
baby stroller	push-chair
baked potato	jacket potato
barrette	hair slide
coffee with cream	coffee white
daylight saving time	summer time

PROGRAM MANAGER

- **Planning Instruction** See Teaching Notes, *Teaching Resources B,* p. 91, for objectives for this selection.
- **Assessment** See The English Language, *Test Booklet,* pp. 190–191.

divided highway	dual carriage way
hood (of a car)	bonnet
Main Street	High Street
pharmacist	dispensing chemist
public restroom	convenience
savings and loan association	building society
subway	underground or tube
traffic circle	roundabout
trunk (of a car)	boot
wastepaper basket	bin
Watch your step.	Mind your step.
whole-wheat bread	brown bread
yield (highway sign)	give way

The differences tend to occur especially in technical areas like automotive terms, in domestic matters like food names, and in specialized commercial terms like names for kinds of businesses. The specialized terminologies of American and British English differ considerably, but the words of the ordinary language—the everyday nouns and most verbs, adverbs, adjectives, and grammatical words like prepositions and conjunctions—are very much alike in the two national standards.

Each national standard also has words for which there is no exact equivalent in the other. **D** For example, in England a *bap* is a soft roll that may be used to make a sandwich; a *crumpet* is a kind of muffin; a *gateau* is a kind of cake; a *scone* is a type of biscuit; a *free house* is a pub or

Entrance to the underground station at Piccadilly Circus, London.

bar where more than one brand of beer is sold; and a *purveyor* is a company that sells or deals in some product.

Each country has influenced the language of the other. In America, people who drive British cars may begin to use British automotive terms because they appear in the cars' operating manuals. The expression "Not to worry" is a Briticism that has become popular here. On the other hand, American expressions like "nitty-gritty" turn up in England, as do many **E** technical terms.

Strange combinations of the two national standards sometimes emerge. American clothing, food, and television programs, like *Dallas,* are very popular in England. A store in the Chelsea area of London announces itself as the "Texas Lone Star Saloon, Purveyors of the Best Chili, Tacos, Nachos." Everything about the store's sign is pure American—except the word *purveyors,* which is as British as crumpets and scones.

Pronunciation, Spelling, and Grammar

British and American English obviously differ in pronunciation. The British pronounce words like *bath, class,* and *can't* with the vowel sound of *father,* rather than with the vowel sound of *cat.* Like people from eastern New England, New York City, and the coastal South, but unlike most other Americans, the British drop r sounds unless they have a vowel after them, so that *poppa* and *popper* sound alike. American English tends to have more stresses on its words than does British English; so we pronounce *secretary* **F** as sek′rə·ter′ē, whereas the British say it as sek′rə·trē. Perhaps the most striking difference between the two national standards, however, is in intonation, the "tune" of the sentence. To British ears, American speech sounds flat and dull—it has a more uniform, lower pitch and **G** minimizes the difference between high and low notes. To

D. Exploring the Culture
While British and American English are closely related, there are in fact so many differences between the two that the American news agency the Associated Press and the British news agency Reuters have to translate English into English.

E. Expansion
The expression *nitty-gritty* (meaning "the basic facts or elements of a situation") became part of American slang in the 1960s. It is thought originally to have referred to nits, the gritlike eggs or larvae of head lice, which can be very hard to get rid of.

F. Language Note: Vocabulary
In its transition from British to American English, the word *missile* lost the emphasis and long ī sound that British speakers pronounce on the final syllable. It is pronounced in America like *missal.*

G. Expansion
In addition, British and American English differ in the speed with which they are spoken. Britons speak more quickly than Americans do.

THE ENGLISH LANGUAGE 897

INTEGRATING THE LANGUAGE ARTS

Writing: Humorous Skit Invite groups of interested students to choose some of the differences between British and American pronunciation, spelling, and grammar discussed in the article and to use them to write a humorous piece (a skit, for example, or perhaps an exchange of letters). After they share their writing, ask them to comment on what they learned about the differences (or about their own use of English) through this activity.

Strategic Reading Before students read Algeo's article, ask them to create a KWL chart. In the first column of the chart, have them record two or three things that they now know about the use of English outside the United States; in the second, they should write two or three questions about the topic that they would like to have answered. As or after they read the article, they can fill in the third column with answers to those questions or clues about how to find answers for the questions that remain unanswered.

Vocabulary Students who enjoyed considering the differences between British and American terminology may be interested in finding more examples. Encourage them to do so, perhaps giving them the British terms *caravan, lorry, perambulator (pram), public school,* and *treacle* to begin with. Allow them to present their findings in formats of their own choosing.

The English Language **T897**

A. Literary Connections

It is to Noah Webster (1758–1843) that we credit these changes. Webster, a schoolteacher from Connecticut, published his first spelling book in 1783 and the first edition of his masterful dictionary in 1806. His 1828 edition had perhaps the greatest influence of all: It included several Americanisms and the American meanings of some older British terms, and it set forth for many words a spelling and pronunciation that differed from the British standard.

B. Expansion

Linguists believe that the languages of approximately one third of the human race come from an Indo-European common source. Some of the languages that derive from this source are the European descendants of Latin (including French, Spanish, Italian, and Portuguese); Russian; the Celtic languages (Irish and Scottish Gaelic); and various offshoots of German, with Dutch and English among them.

Folklorist Jakob Grimm established that the German word *vater* (the English word *father*) has the same root as the Sanskrit/Latin *pitar/pater*. This breakthrough, known as Grimm's Law, supports the thesis of Indo-European as a common source.

Try It Out: Answers

1. accumulator = car battery; banger = sausage; flog = sell (especially illegally); nous = savvy or intelligence; queue = line (of people, cars, and so on); rates = property taxes; scoff = gobble up; lift = elevator; toffee-nosed = stuck-up; wellies = high rubber boots

2. **a.** What do you want to do this afternoon?
   b. She says that she tried to phone us, but that can't be true.
   c. It looks as if the vote will be close.
   d. After long discussions, they agreed on the plan.
   e. I carry two pencils in case one gets lost.

3. ageing = aging; analyse = analyze; centre = center; labour = labor; marvelled = marveled

4. boomerang = a curved stick, used as a weapon, that returns to the point from which it is thrown (Australia); boondocks = any remote rural region (Philippines); thug = a hoodlum, robber, murderer, or other tough criminal (India); trek = a journey (South Africa); walkabout = a walking tour (Australia)

American ears, British speech sounds fluting, high-pitched, quavering, and slightly hysterical—British speech has a more varied, higher pitch and exaggerates the difference between high and low notes.

Ⓐ Spelling also differs slightly in the two countries. British English uses –*our* in words like *colour* and *honour*, where American English uses –*or*. British uses –*re* in words like *centre* and *metre*, where American uses –*er*. British doubles the *l* at the end of unstressed syllables before adding a suffix beginning with a vowel in words like *travelling*, for which American usage typically keeps a single *l, traveling*. There are also a few miscellaneous differences: British *pyjamas* versus American *pajamas*. The differences are all trivial, although the British often insist that American books published in England be reset using British spelling. Americans seldom notice the difference.

Grammatical differences between the two countries are also few and unimportant. The British sometimes omit the definite article where we would use it: "in hospital" (British) versus "in the hospital" (American). They use a plural verb with some collective nouns (the word *government* and names of sports teams) for which we use a singular verb: "The government *have* decided . . ." "Nebraska *are* winning the bowl game." They treat *have* as a special verb that does not require an auxiliary in questions: "Have you the answer?" versus "Do you have the answer?" The British use only the past participle *got*, whereas we use both *got* and *gotten*, in different ways: "I've got it" versus American "I've got it" (meaning "I have it") and "I've gotten it" (meaning "I've obtained it"). Other British and American grammatical differences are equally minor.

Ⓑ Actually, the differences between British and American English have often been exaggerated, as they were by Oscar Wilde, who said that the English "have really everything in common with America nowadays, except, of course, language." In fact, not only these two countries, but all the nations of the English-speaking world share a common linguistic heritage that goes back to the Anglo-Saxons and before them to Proto-Indo-European tribes wandering from Asia across Europe. Today, despite the linguistic differences that divide us— the small distinctions of grammar, spelling, and pronunciation, and the greater but still not insuperable ones of terminology— English is a unified language. The core of English—our basic words and how we use them— is one.

> Oscar Wilde said that the English "have really everything in common with America nowadays, except, of course, language."

Try It Out

1. What are the American counterparts of the British English terms listed below? Look up the British words in a dictionary to determine their American equivalents.

accumulator	queue
banger	rates
flog	scoff
lift	toffee-nosed
nous	wellies

2. The following sentences in British English have grammatical constructions that differ from American use. What part of each sentence seems unusual to you? Rewrite each sentence as you would say it.
   a. What had you in mind to do this afternoon?
   b. She says she tried to ring us, but she can't have done.
   c. It looks like being a close vote.
   d. After long discussions, they agreed the plan.
   e. I carry two pencils in case one goes missing.

3. The following words are spelled in British fashion. Write the corresponding American spellings.

ageing	labour
analyse	marvelled
centre	

4. The following words come from several different national varieties of English. Look up the words in a dictionary to see what they mean and where they originated.

boomerang	trek
boondocks	walkabout
thug	

ASSESSMENT TOOLS

Check Test: True-False

1. English became the first language, or a major second language, in many parts of the world as a result of British trade and imperialism. [True]
2. Two other factors that have helped to establish English as an international language are its general superiority as a language and the fact that it is easy to learn. [False]
3. Dialects of English are spoken only in countries other than England. [False]
4. Speakers of British English use a more varied intonation than do speakers of American English. [True]
5. English is spoken in Canada, New Zealand, and the Republic of Ireland. [True]

BUILDING YOUR PORTFOLIO
Writer's Workshop

The history of the written word is rich a
Page 1

PERSUASIVE WRITING
EVALUATION

"I love it!" "I hate it!" "It's boring." "It's great!" Every day of our lives we make a range of judgments. Some are based on personal preference or whim, but others are careful, reasoned evaluations. Many Victorian writers considered it a *duty* to evaluate the changes taking place around them: Hardy, Arnold, and Dickens each made judgments, carefully measuring the benefits of industrial growth against the misery of working-class Britishers. Often our own judgments concern smaller things than what makes an ideal society, but they are still vital—our lives would be chaos if we never truly evaluated which classes to take, which job offers to accept, which candidates to vote for, and which products to buy. Evaluation, or judging something against a definite standard, is one of the most basic forms of writing—and thinking.

Prewriting

1. **Checking your Writer's Notebook.** By doing the Writer's Notebook activities in Collections 10 and 11, you may already have done some of the prewriting necessary for an evaluation. Look back through your entries for usable ideas, and then proceed with the prewriting activities that follow.

2. **Exploring the possibilities: art or life?** What will you evaluate? Because you've studied literature for several years, you're probably prepared to make some judgments about poetry, drama, or fiction—perhaps one of the selections you've recently read. Other possible subjects related to literature and the arts include movies, television shows, music, and dance or theater performances. You should also consider subjects from the "real world": candidates for local or national office, sports equipment, or ideas about the formation of "black holes" in space. For a few minutes, freewrite a list of things that pique your interest or that you remember well—stories, shows, theories you've read or heard about, consumer goods. Then circle the one or two that you have strong feelings about. (It doesn't matter whether these feelings are positive or negative. The important thing is that you choose something to write about that prompts definite feelings in you.)

3. **How much do you already know?** Writing an evaluation has persuasive elements, including convincing an audience to accept your judgment. To do so, you'll have to appear knowledgeable about the topic. At this early stage, take a few moments to examine what you know about the subject you've chosen. First, describe your subject in a few sentences. Then, state your initial judgment of it. Now, freewrite for several minutes, exploring your prior knowledge of your topic. Use these questions to guide your writing:

Technology HELP

See Writer's Workshop 2 CD-ROM. *Assignment: Evaluation.*

ASSIGNMENT
Write an evaluation, based on appropriate criteria and supported by reasons and evidence.

AIM
To persuade your readers to accept your informed judgment.

AUDIENCE
Your classmates, or a specialized audience within your school— a literary society, a film club, or the student council, for example.

WRITER'S WORKSHOP 899

PROGRAM MANAGER

Computer Guided Instruction For a related evaluation assignment that students may use as additional instruction, see *Writer's Workshop 2.*

PORTFOLIO ASSESSMENT

- **Generating Ideas** To help students in prewriting, use the heuristic in the *Portfolio Management System,* p. 154.
- **Assessment Rubric** For a rubric that can be used to assess students' progress in writing, see the *Portfolio Management System,* p. 156.

Motivation

Bring to class enough copies of a national news magazine so that every student in the class has one to work with. Ask students to look through the magazine and to count the number of evaluation articles it contains. Then, ask students to share the number of articles they find. Point out that evaluation essays, usually in the form of reviews, are an important part of journalism. Tell students that by learning how to write an evaluation essay about a work of literature, they are also learning how to become better readers of evaluation essays. This improved reading skill will help them to be better-informed consumers of a variety of goods and services.

Teaching the Lesson

Mention to students that evaluation is an expression of personal opinion, but people will only take others' opinions seriously if they are based on sensible reasons. The evaluation criteria students will develop in writing this essay, and the evidence they cite for each criterion, are those reasons.

Try It Out: Possible Answers

1. Vision, achievements, integrity, service, personal style.
2. Quality of food/food preparation, ambiance, service, location.
3. Effectiveness, ease of use, efficiency, simplicity.
4. Expense, usefulness, durability, taste (food product), quality.
5. Information, quality of writing, readability, illustrations.

> ### Try It Out
> What criteria would you apply to evaluate the following subjects?
> 1. An extraordinary person (a politician, an artist, an athlete, or some other noteworthy figure)
> 2. A local restaurant
> 3. A new way of doing things (such as a medical advancement or a governmental policy)
> 4. A product (such as a car or a brand of cereal)
> 5. A magazine or newspaper

- Do I like (or dislike) everything about my subject, or only particular parts?
- What other objects or ideas should I consider—other movies, cars, or theories, for example? (Comparison with other similar things can be a vital part of an evaluation.)
- Will I need to do any research? Are research materials readily available?

Now review your notes. Think carefully about whether you have enough information (or whether you can gather enough information) to describe your subject and to provide evidence to support your evaluation. If you can't be authoritative about your subject, you may want to consider choosing another subject to write about.

4. **How do I judge thee?** With a firm subject to evaluate, you can now determine the criteria for your evaluation. **Criteria** are the characteristics a particular thing must have to be judged as an excellent example of its type or kind—that is, as an excellent lyric poem, mystery story, sports car, action movie, economic theory, and so on. You need to look beyond your subject to the particular type, or genre, it belongs to. For example, if you're going to evaluate a poem, is the poem a sonnet, or a lyric? Ask yourself: *What makes this a lyric poem?* or *What makes this poem a sonnet?* You can't evaluate a sonnet with the same criteria you'd use to evaluate a lyric any more than you would evaluate a four-wheel-drive utility vehicle with the same criteria you'd use to evaluate a luxury car.

   What criteria apply to the category your subject falls into? List as many as you can think of. For example, criteria for movies often include direction, theme, characterization, and cinematography. But the more specific criteria for an action-adventure movie (car chases and special effects) will differ from criteria selected for a comedy (pacing and physical humor). Then, because some criteria are more important than others when you make a judgment, rank the criteria on your list in order of importance.

5. **Making a judgment, backing it up.** Establishing criteria is an important step in evaluating something, but it's just one step on the way. You also have to measure your subject against the criteria you've developed, *and* you have to convince your audience that the judgments you develop are sound. To be convincing, you need to supply reasons and evidence for your judgments. **Reasons** tell why a judgment should be accepted; **evidence** provides proof for each reason: quotations, examples, facts, details, or expert opinions. Generating reasons and evidence will build a convincing argument—the informed judgment that makes your evaluation worth reading (and accepting).

   One way to develop your case is to create a three-column chart. In the first column, list each of your criteria for judging your subject, starting with your most important criterion. In the second column, list each **reason** for judging your particular subject successful or unsuccessful, worthy or unworthy. In the third column, supply specific **evidence** for the judgments you've made in the second column. The following chart lists criteria, reasons, and evidence for evaluating *Sense and Sensibility,* a 1995 film adaptation of Jane Austen's 1811 novel.

900 THE VICTORIAN PERIOD

Auditory Some students might benefit from using an audiotape recorder to "talk-write" their essays. After they have completed prewriting activities, allow students to compose their drafts orally. When they have finished composing, they may listen to the tape and transcribe it. When they evaluate and revise their drafts, they may listen to the tape again as they follow the text to note any places that need revision.

Visual One way to help some students notice details that could serve as evidence to support their evaluations is to have them illustrate the literary work. They may draw pictures of individual characters and scenes, or they may create a mural that includes details from the entire work. The illustrations may be posted in the classroom, or they may be attached to the essays for inclusion in the students' portfolios.

Criteria	Reasons	Evidence
Well-developed characters	Characters complex enough to seem real; flaws and strengths both shown.	Sisters reveal different facets with family, with suitors, and alone; Elinor's humor tempers her moral highhandedness.
Theme	Without preaching, story reveals a truth about the real world.	By end, Marianne realizes what Elinor already knows—that ordinary pleasures of real love outweigh any grand passion.

This writer draws evidence from the movie itself. Other kinds of evidence often used in evaluations include

- personal anecdotes (This consists of your own experience with the subject, particularly incidents that your readers might have shared.)

- illustrations (quotations, descriptive details, paraphrases)

- statistics (For example, published data may indicate that the car you're evaluating gets 35 miles per gallon, while similar ones get 25.)

- testimony (what others, especially those with personal experience or authoritative knowledge, have said about your topic)

6. **Whittling away.** Winnow your list down to the most compelling criteria, reasons, and evidence you have. The less convincing material you've thought about can be eliminated, or only briefly described in your essay. If you think your audience will expect you to deal with aspects of your subject for which you don't have a strong case, think about how you will discuss them without weakening your overall argument.

   This involves analyzing your **audience.** Are they beginners or experts? The members of your school's film club will probably have more knowledge about filmmaking than a general audience, so you'll want to address some fine points of direction and cinematography in a movie review. If your subject is personal computers, and you're writing for your classmates, think about how you will explain the more technical points to the computer novices among them.

7. **Shaping your argument.** The sequence of points in your evaluation should have some logical order. You may decide to proceed from most obvious to least obvious, from most general to most complicated, from least important to most important, or the reverse. Whatever pattern you choose, your reader should be able to easily follow your argument. At this point, try to outline your evaluation, at least in rough form. This can guide you as you begin drafting.

WRITER'S WORKSHOP 901

Prewriting

Consider limiting students to two or three choices of literary works to use for their essays. If you do limit choices, allow students who wish to write about the same literary work to get together in small groups to discuss criteria. If students decide to evaluate a film, they may find the criteria listed in the model helpful. However, you might want students to have the experience of developing criteria of their own.

INTEGRATING THE LANGUAGE ARTS

Mechanics Students will want to quote the text of the literary work they are evaluating, and you might want to spend some time reviewing how quotations are punctuated. In addition to the use of quotation marks, you may review the use of ellipses in quotations. Also, refresh students' memories on the use of square brackets to indicate changes to the text of the literary work by the writer of the essay.

Strategic Reading: Summarizing Main Ideas As part of their reading of the Writer's Workshop material, have students use a chart like the following one to summarize the main ideas related to each stage of the writing process. They may refer to the chart as they work on their essays and keep it on file in their notebooks for future reference.

Evaluating a Literary Work

Stage of process	Key ideas	Notes

Drafting

- Ask students to include explicit statements of each criterion and how their subject meets this criterion. This will help them to build a strong case.
- Encourage students to keep a journal as they draft, noting such things as approaches that are proving effective and trouble spots for which they might seek advice from you or a classmate.

Evaluating and Revising

As students evaluate their essays and those of others, encourage them to look carefully at evidence given to support judgment with respect to each criterion. Students should ask themselves if the detail cited really relates to the particular criterion it is used to support (accuracy) and whether the evidence is strong enough to justify the writer's conclusion (sufficiency). If students do not feel that the evidence is both accurate and sufficient, they should call it to the writer's attention. The writer, in turn, should revise his or her judgment to fit the available evidence. Evaluators should also point out any repetitious paragraph patterns for writers to revise.

Proofreading and Publishing

Remind students that careful proofreading is one way they have of showing respect for their readers and of helping to have their work taken seriously. Encourage students to publish their writing over the Internet. If your school or school district sponsors a home page on the World Wide Web, have students investigate posting their essays there.

Strategies for Elaboration: Avoiding Pitfalls

As you evaluate and refine your points and shape your argument, make sure you've avoided the following pitfalls:

- **Avoid using criteria based merely on personal tastes.** Make sure that your praise for a television show doesn't rely on the fact that the main character reminds you of your nice neighbor Hank.
- **Avoid using irrelevant criteria.** Are your criteria appropriately connected to the subject of your essay? Don't fault a certain model of bicycle because you don't like the salesperson's shoes.
- **Avoid making hasty generalizations.** Don't praise something because you have overvalued a certain part of it. A play is not worthy of praise just because you've always liked the leading actor's work; a novel is not good just because the novelist's other novels are considered classics.
- **Avoid making one-sided comparisons.** No one will believe your subject is absolute perfection (or thoroughly horrible) when compared with other things like it. To appear thoughtful and convincing, you must mention weaknesses in the things you praise and strengths in the things you criticize.
- **Avoid including straw-man arguments.** If there are closer comparisons to be made, don't compare the subject of your essay with something clearly inferior (or clearly superior). Your audience will suspect you have unfairly rigged your argument in favor of your judgment. (A "straw man" is something easily knocked down or dismissed.)
- **Don't avoid accepting the burden of proof.** Make sure that you can supply concrete evidence for all the judgments you make in your essay. It's up to you to show why your judgment is sound.

Communications Handbook HELP

Taking notes and documenting sources: page 1211.

Drafting

1. **Reflecting on purpose and audience: the message and the messenger.** Before you begin drafting, think again about what you want your readers to think after reading your evaluation. Who are your readers? Will they need extensive description or definitions of unfamiliar terms before you move into the meat of your evaluation?

    Your **tone** should be authoritative and convincing but also engaging. It also should be consistent throughout your essay. Think about what kind of tone will suit your subject *and* your audience: formal or casual, dramatic and serious, or full of humor?

2. **The introduction: finding a hook.** How will you capture your readers' attention right from the start? You might begin with an anecdote, a startling image, or a quote from an authority. Or you could just throw down the gauntlet and begin by announcing your judgment (of course, you'll still need to justify it later on). You've already thought quite a bit about your readers, so you know how much knowledge they have about your subject and whether you'll need to begin with a thorough description before moving into your evaluation.

3. **The body: building your case.** Your judgment of your subject is the controlling idea, or thesis, of your evaluation. Now you must construct the case to support your judgment, brick by brick. Before you begin writing, consult the outline you formulated in prewriting. Do you still think the order of reasons and evidence you established is the most effective? If not, reorder them. (And remember that even this order isn't engraved in stone—many logical patterns emerge as you're writing). Make sure that each reason for your judgment is adequately reinforced with evidence, and explain any criteria you think your readers will question or mistrust. Also, try to achieve balance, giving proper emphasis to description, reasons, and evidence without overexplaining or scrimping on any of them.

902 THE VICTORIAN PERIOD

---

4. The ending: driving it home. Here's your chance to leave your readers thoroughly convinced that your evaluation is solid. You might end with a summary of the reasons you've presented or a restatement of your judgment, or you might refer back to the beginning of the essay. In any event, leave your readers with something memorable—some ideas to turn over in their minds. (Any essay that just "ends" leaves readers feeling as though they were engaged in conversation with someone who abruptly walked away.)

Evaluating and Revising

1. Peer review. One of the most helpful ways to respond to someone else's writing is to ask questions. As you read, pause where you have a question, and write it either in the margin or on a separate sheet of paper. Then discuss your questions with the writer of the evaluation.

2. Self-evaluation. Using your peer reviewer's comments as a map, go through your essay again. Address any concerns about your criteria and evidence first. Put a check mark next to each criterion; then underscore the evidence that supports it. Remember that you should include evidence for all the criteria you present in your evaluation. If your reviewer has raised any counterarguments to your case, think about how to defuse them. Finally, check to see if you should vary your sentence style.

Proofreading and Publishing

Carefully proofread your essay, checking for mistakes in mechanics, grammar, and usage. Then, make your clean, final copy.

In daily life, evaluations appear in many different places—as editorials, as informative articles in consumer magazines, or in the feature section of the newspaper. They also play a role in politics—in campaign materials, for example. Consider submitting your evaluation to your school or local newspaper.

If you've evaluated a novel or piece of music, you might submit your review to a local arts periodical. You and your classmates could also compile your evaluations into an informal journal (*The Journal of Victorian Literature,* for example) and circulate it among students in other classes.

Reflecting on Your Writing

As you reflect on this assignment, consider the following questions. Be sure to date your responses and your evaluation for your portfolio.

1. Which step in the writing process was most difficult for you? Why?

2. What changes did you make between draft and revision? Why?

3. What do you like best about your essay? What still needs improvement?

4. Did writing an evaluation affect your perception of the evaluations you see in the mass media—such as movie reviews, commentaries on athletic teams, or recommendations for consumer products? Explain your response.

▌ *Evaluation Criteria*

An effective evaluation

1. *orients the reader to the subject being evaluated*
2. *includes a clear statement of the writer's judgment*
3. *includes criteria that are appropriate, clear, and, if necessary, explained by the writer*
4. *includes relevant, convincing, and logically ordered reasons for the writer's judgment*
5. *includes sufficient evidence to support each reason*
6. *has a tone that is authoritative, consistent throughout, and appropriate for the intended audience*
7. *has an engaging beginning and an ending that restates the judgment in a satisfying way*

Revision
STRATEGIES

Consider your readers one last time. Do you need to explain anything more clearly? Or have you overexplained anything they probably know already? Working with a writing partner, mark any explanations that need further clarification or some that need cutting. Revise, and then consult with your writing partner again to discuss your revisions.

Language Workshop
HELP

Sentence style: page 904.

Portfolio

Reflecting on Your Writing

Before students write their reflections or write answers to the questions in the text, consider having them discuss the questions with a partner. This may lead them to consider views they did not have before.

Reteaching

If students have difficulty developing or applying criteria, work with them using a review of a currently popular movie or TV show. Ask students to read the review and apply the Evaluation Criteria in the checklist. Ask them to use different colors to highlight each of the major components of the Evaluation Criteria. Then, lead the class in a discussion of how the author structures the review to create a convincing evaluation of the work. Encourage students to use the review as a model for their own essays.

Closure

After students have completed their essays, lead the class in a discussion of the steps they followed in writing them. Have a student volunteer write the comments on the chalkboard, and then have students refer to the text of the Writer's Workshop to make sure that they did not omit any of the steps and that they got the steps in the correct order. Have students copy the material in their notebooks or onto a chart for posting in the classroom.

Enrichment

History Connection
Find a short document, other than a literary work, that was written during the Victorian age and show it to students. Ask them to work in small groups to establish evaluation criteria according to their own standards of good writing and to apply these criteria to the document. Have one member of each group report on the group's criteria and another member report on the group's overall evaluation of the document.

PORTFOLIO ASSESSMENT

Peer Evaluation During evaluating and revising, students can use the peer evaluation sheet found in the *Portfolio Management System,* p. 155.

PROGRAM MANAGER

Modeling or Practicing Revision
To summarize and model the revision process, and to provide student practice, use **Revision Transparencies 11.3–11.4** in the *Audiovisual Resources Binder.*

Connecting to Students' Writing

Divide the class into groups of five or six, and have them read each other's essays for sentence style. Each member of the group may read for one of the elements indicated in the questions on p. 904. Thus, one student would analyze all the papers for sentence length, one for structure, one for word order, and so on. Each reader should write a comment on the stylistic effect of the element he or she analyzes. When the writer receives the comments, he or she should decide whether to revise or to retain the wording for stylistic reasons.

Try It Out: Possible Answers

By running the list of the various things the friends have done into one long sentence, Kipling diminishes the importance of the individual achievements or events. The word order is normal; the phrases are simple, making the events that have marked the lives of these men seem commonplace. The repetition of *some of us* and *some* adds to the matter-of-fact and even somewhat world-weary tone. The repetition of the word *open(ed)*, which takes on two different meanings, lends an element of dark humor or cynicism to the passage. Students may use diction that breaks the sentence up, that suggests a different tone, or that relies on more inflated vocabulary.

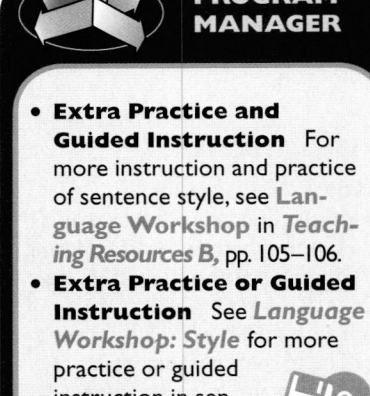

PROGRAM MANAGER

- **Extra Practice and Guided Instruction** For more instruction and practice of sentence style, see *Language Workshop* in *Teaching Resources B,* pp. 105–106.
- **Extra Practice or Guided Instruction** See *Language Workshop: Style* for more practice or guided instruction in sentence style.

Technology HELP

See Language Workshop CD-ROM. *Key word entry: sentence style.*

Language Handbook HELP

Sentence style: page 1236.

Try It Out

How does Kipling's style affect the impact of the passage below? Rewrite the passage in other "styles": Is the impact changed?

[We] swore that we were all dear friends. Then some of us went away and annexed Burma, and some of us tried to open up the Sudan and were opened up by the Fuzzies in that cruel scrub outside Suakim, and some found stars and medals, and some were married, which was bad, and some did other things which were worse, and others of us stayed in our chains.

—Rudyard Kipling, from "The Mark of the Beast"

SENTENCE STYLE: WAYS OF STRENGTHENING MEANING

Most writers tend to have an identifiable general style that distinguishes their writing. For example, Matthew Arnold's poetic style differs from that of Gerard Manley Hopkins. **Style** is the way a writer uses language to express ideas and adapts language to suit the occasion. Style involves both the kinds of words a writer chooses (or **diction,** which you studied in the Language Workshop on page 778) and the way that writer joins those words to form sentences. In all good writing, the **sentence style** reflects the substance, or content, of the work. The beginning of Charles Dickens's *A Tale of Two Cities* contains one famous example of meaning reinforced by style. Notice how the use of **parallelism** contributes to the paradoxical nature of the passage—each statement is weighed against another, and both appear equally true:

> It was the best of times, it was the worst of times, it was the age of wisdom, it was the age of foolishness, it was the epoch of belief, it was the epoch of incredulity, it was the season of Light, it was the season of Darkness, it was the spring of hope, it was the winter of despair. . . .
> —Charles Dickens, *from A Tale of Two Cities*

Strategies for Analyzing Sentence Style

The following questions are useful in analyzing a writer's style. When answering each question, make notes about how each characteristic affects the meaning and overall impact of the writing.

- Are the sentences long, short, or varied?
- Are the sentences primarily declarative, interrogative, or imperative?
- Are the sentences simple, compound, complex, compound-complex, or varied in structure?
- Are the sentences primarily in the active or passive voice?
- Do the sentences follow the normal word order of English, or is the syntax inverted or varied in some way?
- Do the sentences use stylistic devices such as repetition or parallelism?

Writer's Workshop Follow-Up: Revision

Look back at the evaluation you wrote for the Writer's Workshop on page 899. Use the questions given above to analyze the sentence style of your evaluation. Working with a writing partner, identify at least three sentences you can revise to reinforce their meaning; then, share your revisions with your partner.

904 THE VICTORIAN PERIOD

✔ QUICK CHECK: Sentence Style

Review the following passage from Matthew Arnold's essay "Wordsworth" for elements of sentence style using the questions in "Strategies for Analyzing Sentence Style" (p. 904). "Wordsworth has been in his grave for some thirty years, and certainly his lovers and admirers cannot flatter themselves that this great and steady light of glory as yet shines over him. He is not fully recognized at home; he is not recognized at all abroad. Yet I firmly believe that the poetical performance of Wordsworth is, after that of Shakespeare and Milton, of which all the world now recognizes the worth, undoubtedly the most considerable in our language from the Elizabethan age to present time." [Possible answer: Arnold's lengthy, compound-complex sentences, mostly in the active voice, give an air of dignity and almost majesty to his opening argument about the greatness of Wordsworth.]

CREATIVE PROBLEM SOLVING
LEARNING FOR LIFE

A Livable Community

Problem

Rapid growth made some cities in Victorian England practically unlivable. What makes a community a good place in which to live and work?

Project

Identify the qualities you consider essential in a livable community. Are job opportunities an absolute prerequisite? What about size, location, climate, and other physical and nonphysical characteristics?

Preparation

1. Use brainstorming or freewriting to generate an initial list of essential qualities.

2. Pool your ideas with those of three or four other students. Even ideas phrased negatively can suggest usable items; for example, the suggestion "no slums" can lead to "ample affordable housing."

Procedure

1. From the group's master list, select the three or four items you consider most important, keeping in mind that this winnowing process will involve a series of trade-offs: Would you be willing to give up recreational facilities for cultural ones (or vice versa)? Then, rank the items in order of their importance to you.

2. Develop reasons to support your opinions by using freewriting to explore why you consider each item essential.

3. From your own experience and the experience of others (such as experts in city planning and sociology), gather evidence—facts, statistics, examples, or anecdotes—to support each of your reasons.

Presentation

Use one of the following formats (or another that your teacher approves):

1. **Agreeing to Disagree**

   With a classmate whose list of essential qualities differs significantly from yours, plan a debate. (Check page 1217 of the Communications Handbook for details about debate formats.) First, agree on two or three judges for the debate. Next, develop a proposition in the form of a values resolution—for example: *Resolved,* that cultural facilities are more important in a community than recreational ones. Finally, decide which one of you will take the affirmative position. After you've each prepared a debate brief, stage the debate in front of the judges.

2. **Down to Scale**

   Design and build a scale model of a community that incorporates your list of essential qualities. Before you begin construction, think about how you'll allocate space for residential, commercial, and industrial areas and how you'll lay out the streets. Think, too, about what materials you'll use and whether you'll include human figures and vehicles. (Your list of essential qualities will suggest other considerations.) With other students who have chosen this option, display your model at the public library along with comment cards for viewers' responses.

3. **Appealing to Residents**

   Create a promotional brochure for a planned community built to embody your list of essential qualities. Give your community an inviting name, and use logical, emotional, and ethical appeals (page 613) to convince potential residents that it's a good place in which to live and work. If you'd like, illustrate your brochure with line drawings or clip art. If you have access to desktop publishing, prepare a camera-ready copy of your brochure. With other students who have chosen this option, invite members of the city council to respond to the ideas in your brochure.

Processing

Did doing this activity change your feelings about your own community? Did it make you want to find ways to improve your hometown? Why? Write a reflection for your portfolio.

Learning for Life

PORTFOLIO ASSESSMENT

Performance Assessment Rubric So that students may see the evaluation criteria before they begin working on these projects, share the rubric provided in the *Portfolio Management System,* p. 157.

DEVELOPING WORKPLACE COMPETENCIES		
Preparation	**Procedure**	**Presentation**
Works on teams	Processes information	Communicates information and ideas
Evaluates data	Interprets information	Thinks creatively
Ranks alternatives	Designs systems	Draws conclusions
Makes decisions	Evaluates arguments	Demonstrates integrity

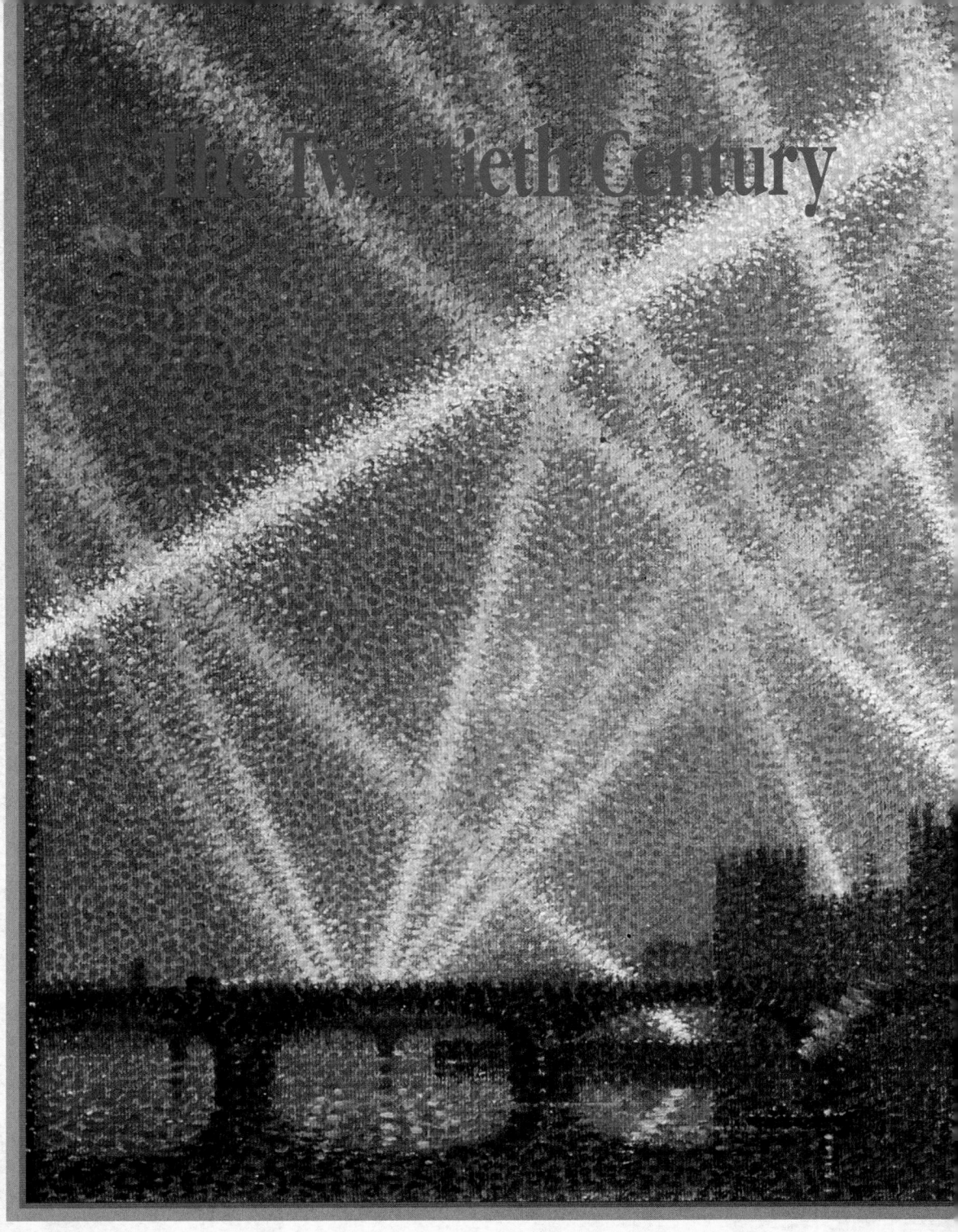

The Twentieth Century

Searchlights illuminated the sky over London during Battle of Britain, the first battle fought to control the air. On July 16, 1940, Adolph Hitler ordered planes to invade Great Britain, and on August 8, the German Luftwaffe began nightly bombing missions. The nation relied on the Royal Air Force for its defense; although outnumbered, the RAF pilots benefited from the warning provided by radar stations along the coast and from the technology of the Spitfire, one of the most advanced fighter planes of the war. By May 1941, Germany abandoned its air attacks; Prime Minister Winston Churchill praised the efforts of the RAF, saying that "Never in the field of human conflict was so much owed by so many to so few."

The Houses of Parliament—A Wartime Nocturne 1941 (detail) by Sir Claude Francis Barry.

907

PROGRAM MANAGER

- **Summative Assessment** See *Literary Period Test: Literature of The Twentieth Century, Test Booklet,* pp. 258–260, for a test on an additional text from the same historical era.
- **Application** For practice of a reading strategy for this unit, see *Becoming a Strategic Reader* worksheet, *Teaching Resources B,* pp. 114–115.
- **Performance Assessment** Use *Assessment 4* in the *Integrated Performance Assessment, Level G,* to evaluate reading and writing skills covered in collections 12–15. For help with evaluation, see *Holistic Scoring Workshop* software.

The Twentieth Century

by **John Leggett**

. . . England will still be England, an everlasting animal stretching into the future and the past, and, like all living things, having the power to change out of recognition and yet remain the same.

—*George Orwell*

The Tube Train (c. 1934) by Cyril E. Power.

© British Museum, London.

A View of
Fleet Street
(20th century)
by Christian
Snijders.

hat a story of change, of the erosion of a proud, complacent, well-ordered society, is told by the early years of the twentieth century in Great Britain!

If we had lived in the era of Victoria, which ended with the great queen's death in 1901, or during the ten-year reign of her son, Edward VII, we would have believed that Britain, with its moral and economic dominance of the world, would sail on majestically forever. But of course that is the misconception of every stable age and society—that life will go on just as it always has.

Even during this long, fairly stable period in Great Britain, though, profound changes were taking place, both externally and internally. Although the British imperial policy remained much the same throughout the Victorian era, several major colonies—Australia, South Africa, and New Zealand—gained their independence in the first decade of the twentieth century. Internally, Britain was experiencing social reforms that were to have far-reaching consequences. The rise in literacy, the growing power and influence of the Labour party, the widespread interest in socialist ideology—all were to dramatically change Great Britain and the world.

Political and social events during the early twentieth century would alter Great Britain's preeminent position as a world power and would dramatically change its society.

The Arrival (1923–1924)
by Christopher R. W. Nevinson.
Tate Gallery, London.

909

A. Exploring the Historical Period

Australia gained its independence on January 1, 1901, when it proclaimed itself the Commonwealth of Australia. Since then, its ties to Britain have weakened, and it has aligned itself more closely with the United States. New Zealand loosened its ties to Britain much more reluctantly: the country was given dominion in 1907 and autonomy in 1931, but it did not formally accept the latter until 1947.

Time Line

- **1911–1916**
  The Czech-born German writer Franz Kafka (1883–1924) is best known for his exploration of humanity's alienation in the twentieth century. The story *The Metamorphosis* describes a man who wakes up to find himself inexplicably changed into a hideous insect. Other works by Kafka include the novels *The Trial* (1925) and *The Castle* (1926).

- **1911–1916**
  World War I developed from many complex and subtle circumstances: old rivalries, allegiances, treaties, grudges, and fears about the balance of power in Europe. The event that triggered conflict, however, was the assassination of Archduke Francis Ferdinand of Austria by a Serbian nationalist in Sarajevo on June 28, 1914.

- **1911–1916**
  Albert Einstein (1879–1955) published four research papers in the same year he obtained his doctorate at the Polytechnic Academy in Zurich, and each paper contained an important discovery in physics. One of Einstein's theories, that of relativity, brought him international fame when it was verified in 1919. Two years later he was awarded the Nobel Prize in Physics. Einstein became a U.S. citizen in 1940 and alerted the U.S. government that nuclear energy might be used to fuel weapons.

The Twentieth Century

• Sir Winston Churchill.

LITERARY EVENTS

1900–1910	1911–1916	1917–1926	1927–1939
Swedish writer Selma Lagerlöf is first woman awarded the Nobel Prize in literature, 1909	**James Joyce** publishes *A Portrait of the Artist as a Young Man*, 1916	African American writer Langston Hughes publishes first book of verse, *The Weary Blues*, 1926	Spanish writer Federico García Lorca's play *Blood Wedding* produced, 1933
Dublin's Abbey Theatre founded by **W. B. Yeats** and Lady Gregory to produce plays by and about the Irish, 1904	Czech writer Franz Kafka's *The Metamorphosis* published, 1915	E. M. Forster's *A Passage to India* published, 1924	**W. H. Auden**'s *Poems* published; Noel Coward's play *Private Lives* produced, 1930
Joseph Conrad's *Heart of Darkness* published, 1902	G. B. Shaw's *Pygmalion* first produced; **D. H. Lawrence**'s *Sons and Lovers* published, 1913	**W. B. Yeats** receives the Nobel Prize in literature, 1923	**Virginia Woolf** publishes *To the Lighthouse*, 1927
		Publication of **Joyce**'s *Ulysses* and **T. S. Eliot**'s *The Waste Land*, 1922	

CULTURAL/HISTORICAL EVENTS

1900–1910	1911–1916	1917–1926	1927–1939
Queen Victoria dies and is succeeded by her son, Edward VII, 1901	In New York City, the Armory Show introduces postimpressionism and cubism in art; in Paris, the first performance of Stravinsky's *Rite of Spring* causes a riot among bewildered spectators, 1913	U.S. enters the war in Europe; Russian Revolution begins, 1917	U.S. stock market crashes, triggering worldwide depression, 1929
Sigmund Freud visits U.S. to lecture on psychoanalysis, 1909	World War I begins with the assassination of Archduke Francis Ferdinand, 1914	World War I ends with nearly 10 million dead; voting rights in England extended to women over 30, 1918	Adolf Hitler appointed chancellor in Germany; Germans build first concentration camp, at Dachau, 1933
South Africa gains independence from Britain, 1910	Albert Einstein announces his general theory of relativity, 1915		In Russia, Stalinist purges force over 10 million people into labor camps, 1934–1938
	Easter Rebellion in Dublin; uprising leaders executed by British, 1916	Britain refuses to grant Ireland republic status; civil war begins in Ireland, 1922	Spanish Civil War fought, 1936–1939
			Pablo Picasso paints *Guernica*, protesting German firebombing of the Spanish city, 1937
			Germany invades Poland; World War II begins, 1939

• Food coupon issued by the Ministry of Food during World War I.

• Suffragist medal (c. 1908) featuring Emmeline Goulden Pankhurst.

• Formerly unemployed men go to work selling apples.

910 THE TWENTIETH CENTURY

USING THE TIME LINE

As the class studies the time line, encourage each student to choose a different item and to research its significance. Then, ask students to present briefly what they know about the items they have researched. Invite listeners to add observations, allowing the discussion to give a fuller sense of the forces, events, and ideas that shaped the period.

• *Guernica* (1937) by Pablo Picasso. Centro de Arte Reina Sofia, Madrid. © 1997 Artists Rights Society (ARS), New York / SPADEM, Paris.

Irish writer **Seamus Heaney** receives Nobel Prize in literature, 1995

Japanese writer Kenzaburo Oe awarded Nobel Prize in literature, 1994

Winston Churchill receives Nobel Prize in literature; Samuel Beckett's play *Waiting for Godot* first produced in Paris, 1953

George Orwell's *Animal Farm* published; Chilean poet Gabriela Mistral awarded Nobel Prize in literature, 1945

Colombian writer Gabriel García Márquez publishes *One Hundred Years of Solitude,* 1967

Nigerian writer **Chinua Achebe**'s *Things Fall Apart* published, 1958

St. Lucian writer **Derek Walcott** publishes *Omeros,* a long poem inspired by Homer's *Odyssey,* 1990

Egyptian writer **Naguib Mahfouz** awarded Nobel Prize in literature, 1988

1940–1954	1955–1974	1975–1995

In the Battle of Britain, British Royal Air Force prevents German invasion of England, 1940

U.S. declares war on Italy, Germany, and Japan, 1941

Germany surrenders; U.S. drops atom bombs over Hiroshima and Nagasaki, ending World War II, 1945

Development of ENIAC at the University of Pennsylvania marks first generation of modern computers, 1946

India gains independence from Britain, 1947; Mohandas Gandhi assassinated, 1948

State of Israel created, 1948

Twenty-six counties in Ireland win independence from Britain, and remaining six form British-controlled Northern Ireland, 1949

Martin Luther King, Jr., leads boycott of buses in Montgomery, Alabama, 1955

Nigeria wins independence from Britain, 1960

British singing group the Beatles revolutionizes popular music, 1960s

Apollo 11 astronauts are first people to walk on the moon, as 600 million people watch live telecast, 1969

• **The Beatles** (1964).

Fall of Saigon marks end of Vietnam War, 1975

Core meltdown causes nuclear disaster at Chernobyl plant in the Ukraine, 1986

Berlin Wall is dismantled; Chinese army cracks down on pro-democracy students in Tiananmen Square, 1989

Soviet Union is dissolved, 1991

Conflict in Bosnia begins, 1992

Nelson Mandela elected president of South Africa, 1994

• **Mushroom cloud (August 9, 1945)** from the atomic bomb dropped on Nagasaki, Japan, during World War II.

• **Astronaut Edwin E. Aldrin, Jr., lunar module pilot (1969).**

911

- **1941–1954**
  The atomic bomb dropped on Hiroshima on August 6, 1945, immediately killed about 66,000 of the city's inhabitants. The atomic bomb dropped on Nagasaki on August 9, 1945, had the force of 21,000 tons of TNT and killed about 39,000 people instantly.

- **1955–1974**
  Martin Luther King, Jr. (1929–1968), the central leader of the civil rights movement in the United States, was awarded the Nobel Peace Prize in 1964. He was assassinated in 1968. The U.S. Congress voted to establish a national holiday in his honor, and in 1986, the third Monday in January was declared Martin Luther King, Jr., Day.

- **1975–1995**
  Even the official close of the Vietnam War did not end the controversy or speculation surrounding U. S. involvement in that conflict. From 1946 to 1954, France battled the Vietnam Independence League, or Viet Minh, in order to maintain French influence in Indochina. When the French forces were badly defeated in a key battle, peace was negotiated and the country was separated into the Communist North and the French-controlled South. War broke out again shortly afterward. The United States feared a unified Communist Vietnam and became involved, taking over the French role in the conflict. By 1973, when the United States withdrew from the war, approximately 58,000 U. S. troops had been killed in the fighting. Vietnamese casualties on both sides totaled approximately 2,000,000.

A. Responding to the Quotation

? What makes the call a rousing or persuasive one? [It declares dramatically that the proletarians have nothing to lose and everything to win.]

B. Exploring the Culture

Marx and his friend and close collaborator, Friedrich Engels (1820–1895), coauthored the *Communist Manifesto* (1848), which sought to address many of the persistent problems in European industrialized society. Later in 1848, both participated in the German revolution that attempted to replace an authoritarian government with a representative one; when it failed, they both moved to England. There they finished the three volumes of *Das Kapital,* with Engels revising Marx's notes for the last two volumes, which were published after Marx's death in 1883.

C. Expansion

Sigmund Freud (1856–1939) founded the field of psychoanalysis, and a great many of his ideas have entered into common parlance and become part of the theory and practice of other fields and sciences. Freud himself applied his theories to the areas of anthropology, mythology, and religion, with such works as *Totem and Taboo* (1913) and *Civilization and Its Discontents* (1930). His name has become an adjective for an illumination or action of the unconscious, as in the phrase "Freudian slip."

D. Responding to the Quotation

? What is the unconscious discovered by the poets and philosophers made of—that is, how do the writers represent the unconscious? [Students may suggest that poets express an idea of the unconscious through their creativity and their imagination and that philosophers describe it in their examinations of the contradictions and conflicts of human nature.]

Darwin, Marx, and Freud: Undermining Victorian Ideas

Many of the social and intellectual changes that were taking place had their roots in the nineteenth-century work of three men: Charles Darwin (1809–1882), Karl Marx (1818–1883), and Sigmund Freud (1856–1939).

Darwin's *Origin of Species* (1859) propounded a theory of the evolution of animal species based on natural selection—those species that successfully adapted to their environments survived, those that did not became extinct. This theory, which seemed to contradict the Biblical account of the special creation of each species, fueled a debate between science and religion that has continued from Victorian times to the present. Social Darwinism, the notion that in society, as in nature, only the fittest should survive and flourish, became a controversial aspect of political, social, and economic thought.

B In *Das Kapital* (1867), Karl Marx, a German philosopher and political economist who spent the last twenty years of his life in London, advocated the abolition of private property. Marx traced economic injustices to the capitalist system of ownership and argued that workers should own the means of production. His theories of social and economic justice revolutionized political thought and eventually led to sweeping changes in many governments and economic systems, including those of Britain.

C The psychological theories of Sigmund Freud, a doctor from Vienna, were equally revolutionary and far-reaching in their effects. In *The Interpretation of Dreams* (1900) and later works, Freud found the motives for human behavior not in our rational, conscious minds, but in the irrational and sexually driven realm of the unconscious, which is visible to us only in our dreams. Conservative Victorians were outraged by Freud's claims that sex influenced their behavior, but artists and writers found the notion of the unconscious and its mysterious, illogical workings fascinating.

> **A** The proletarians have nothing to lose but their chains. They have a world to win. Working men of all countries, unite!
>
> —Karl Marx and Friedrich Engels

> **D** The poets and philosophers before me discovered the unconscious; what I discovered was the scientific method by which the unconscious can be studied.
>
> —Sigmund Freud

Karl Marx.

Charles Darwin.

Sigmund Freud.

OPTIONS FOR TEACHING

CROSSING THE CURRICULUM

Visual Invite students to make collages of the time period covered in the Collection. Encourage them to represent the radical changes in science, philosophy, political boundaries, and lifestyles, using photocopies of old newspapers or magazines from the library.

Logical-Mathematical Challenge students to look for cause-and-effect relationships between the ideas and the events of the period. Ask students to isolate one or two important events or ideas from each section of the introduction and to analyze the causes and effects of the event(s). Model the exercise using Transparency 8: Cause or Effects Organizer in the Transparency Package.

The work of these thinkers helped to undermine the political, religious, and psychological ideas that had served as the foundation of British society and the British Empire for generations. With the calamity of the Great War and the events that followed, that foundation was largely swept away.

The writings of Charles Darwin, Karl Marx, and Sigmund Freud caused people to question many of the social, religious, and economic beliefs of the Victorian period.

The Great War: "A War to End All Wars"

The truly great disaster of the first half of the century was the breakdown of the European balance of power. In 1914, Britain, France, and Russia, bound by treaties, were locked in opposition to Germany and Austria-Hungary. The confrontation plunged the whole of Europe into World War I, or what was first known as the Great War.

The Victorian writer Rudyard Kipling celebrated the British character as essentially patriotic, and he was right. When war broke out, a young Englishman felt that to be called on to defend his nation was likely to be the most exalted experience of his life. For centuries, in all sorts of wars and skirmishes, the most ordinary youth of England had donned smart uniforms and marched off to faraway battlefields, just as

Return to the Front, 1917 by Richard Jack.

York City Art Gallery, York, England.

they might to major sports events. There they would perform heroic acts. For the most part, these soldiers returned to be honored and to add their tales to the romantic lore of their regiments.

When Britain declared war on Germany in 1914, young Britons crowded to the recruiting stations to enlist. Six months later, hordes of them lay slaughtered in the miserable, rain-soaked, vermin-infested trenches of France. Sixty thousand young British men were killed or wounded on the first day of the Battle of the Somme alone. Three hundred thousand were killed, wounded, or frozen to death at the Battle of Ypres. The generals would not stop the terrible—and in the end futile—carnage, and over the

> You are ordered abroad as a soldier of the king to help our French comrades against the invasion of a common enemy. . . . Do your duty bravely. Fear God. Honor the king.
>
> —Lord Kitchener to the British Expeditionary Force, 1914

E

F

E. Responding to the Quotation

? What impresses you about the tone of the command? [Some students may be impressed by the lofty ideals of the statement, especially in the last three sentences; others may be surprised at the curt expectation of obedience that informs the letter.]

F. Expansion

Ypres is a city in northwestern Belgium, near the French border.

INTEGRATING THE LANGUAGE ARTS

Strategic Reading Have students take notes on the main ideas of each section as they read the introduction to the time period. Students should record the main ideas and then list the transitions between the sections—the events, ideas, or topics that connect one section to the next. Have students use a graphic organizer like the one that follows to organize the main ideas and transitions. Students may review their findings in small groups.

main idea	transition		

A. Exploring the Historical Period

Henry VIII's (r. 1509–1547) marital problems and his need for a male heir led to the creation of the Church of England as a separate entity from the Roman Catholic Church. His wives were, in order, Catherine of Aragon (mother of future queen Mary I), Anne Boleyn (mother of future queen Elizabeth I), Jane Seymour (mother of Henry's successor, Edward VI), Anne of Cleves, Catherine Howard, and Catherine Parr.

> To be in the trenches was to experience an unreal, unforgettable enclosure and constraint, as well as a sense of being unoriented and lost. One saw two things only: the walls of an unlocalized, undifferentiated earth and the sky above. . . . It was the sight of the sky, almost alone, that had the power to persuade a man that he was not already lost in a common grave.
>
> —Paul Fussell

course of four years an entire generation of young Englishmen was fed to the insatiable furnace of the war.

With the armistice in 1918, a new cynicism arose. The old values of national honor and glory had endorsed a war whose results were gradually recognized as a weakened economy, a tottering colonial empire, and a loss of life equal to that caused by many plagues. Out of disillusionment came a pessimism about the state and the individual's relation to society. A new realism swept in, an antidote to the "romantic nonsense" of the past and in particular to the propaganda machine that had led a whole people into war.

After the Great War, in which nearly one million British soldiers died, many people in Great Britain developed a cynical attitude toward government and such values as national honor and glory.

A CLOSER LOOK

ROYAL TRADITION AND SCANDAL

In its thousand-year history, England's monarchy has seen turbulent times. The fates of Henry VIII's wives (divorced, beheaded, died, divorced, beheaded, survived) provide a notorious example. Britons pride themselves on their love of ritual and tradition, but their liege lords often appear to be awkward anachronisms. When the extravagant and hugely unpopular George IV died in 1830, the London *Times* reflected, "There never was an individual less regretted by his fellow creatures."

The House of Windsor. As the British monarchy enters the twenty-first century, the House of Windsor rules a kingdom in transition from its colonial past. Today, the crown's functions are mostly ceremonial. Royals serve at official functions and charitable affairs, and the family's joking reference to itself as "the firm" indicates they take their business seriously.

Yet, with the business of ceremony comes the pressure of public scrutiny.

Queen Elizabeth with her family (June 17, 1995), London.

914 THE TWENTIETH CENTURY

OPTIONS FOR TEACHING

CROSSING THE CURRICULUM

Writing: News Report Have students choose a specific event from the introduction—a single important date, for example. Ask students to research the event and to prepare a news report of one to two minutes that might have run on the newsreels or TV newscasts of the time. Students may read their news reports to the class.

Social Sciences Have students find and read an excerpt from the works of Marx, Freud, or Darwin. Direct students to take notes on how the excerpt augments the description of the thinker given in the introduction. Students may use their notes to present a brief oral report to the class.

Geography Ask students to draw two contrasting maps of the British Empire. One map should show the empire's territories before World War I, and the other should show the empire after World War II. Keep the maps on display in the classroom as students work through the unit.

Experimentation in the Arts: Shocking in Form and Content

The decade before the war had seen the beginnings of a transformation in all the arts, especially on the Continent. In Paris, Henri Matisse and other new painters exhibiting in 1905 were called *les fauves* (the wild beasts) by critics for their bold, new use of line and color. Pablo Picasso's first cubist painting, *Les Demoiselles d'Avignon,* was finished in 1907, the same year that John Millington Synge's play *The Playboy of the Western World* caused a riot at its première at Dublin's Abbey Theatre. (The audience was outraged by the suggestion that the Irish would make a hero out of a boy who would murder his father.) In 1913, Igor Stravinsky's revolutionary ballet, *The Rite of Spring,* which was marked by strong, primitive (read sexual) rhythms and dissonant harmonies, caused a riot at *its* première in Paris. The year after that, James Joyce's *Dubliners,* containing stories written up to a decade before, finally found an Irish publisher brave enough to publish it. All these works challenged traditional values of beauty and order and opened new avenues of expression.

> Never trust the artist. Trust the tale.
> —D. H. Lawrence

Queen Elizabeth II called 1992 the *annus horribilis,* or "horrible year," because during that time three of her children separated from their spouses and several were caught in scandals highly publicized by the British tabloids. The year also saw another disaster: Ancient Windsor Castle caught fire. Because of the royal children's marital scandals and undignified antics, the public balked at paying for the restoration of Elizabeth's family home.

Royal retrenching. Responding to public opinion—Britons were clearly mortified by the royals' indiscretions—Queen Elizabeth instituted a number of reforms. The richest woman in Great Britain because of her extensive family estates, the queen in 1992 voluntarily agreed to pay income taxes on her fortune. She agreed to publish an annual accounting of spending on royal palaces. And she reduced the number of family members paid by the state for their official duties. (The gener-ous stipends of a number of minor royals are now paid by the queen herself.)

Institution or anachronism? Still, the larger question remains: What is the monarchy's role in postcolonial Britain? Prince Philip, the queen's husband, has said that if "people feel it has no further part to play, then for goodness' sake let's end the thing on amicable terms without having a row about it." Ending the monarchy might be economical, but such a pragmatic solution would end a thousand years of tradition. The monarchy has endured not only because it provides historical continuity, but also because it captures the public imagination and, in an unromantic age, feeds the public appetite for pageantry and for a need to escape. As Prince Charles observed, "Something as curious as the monarchy won't survive unless you take account of people's attitudes. . . . After all, if people don't want it, they won't have it."

B. Exploring the Culture
Both D. H. Lawrence and James Joyce had lifelong problems with censorship of their work, and both reacted in much the same way: leaving their home countries and seeking independent publication of their work. James Joyce left Ireland and, except for a brief period back in Dublin, lived the rest of his life in Paris, Trieste, and Zurich. Lawrence left England shortly after the banning of his novel *The Rainbow* in 1915 and spent his remaining years writing and wandering in Italy, Australia, Mexico, and southern France.

C. Exploring the Culture
Point out to students Queen Elizabeth II's use of Latin in nicknaming the year. Where are Roman numerals used for dates, and why? [Students will probably say that Roman numerals are used to date films, books, some TV shows, and some works of art. Opinions will vary, but students will probably say that the separate system seems more formal or official, and adds a gravity that Arabic numerals, because of their common usage, do not convey.]

D. Expansion
The British monarchy traces its roots back to Egbert, of the house of Wessex, king from 802 to 825. The House of Windsor, formerly known as Saxe-Coburg-Gotha, has been in power since 1917. Royal powers are mostly honorific now; the United Kingdom is a constitutional monarchy and a parliamentary democracy.

A. Exploring the Culture

On December 6, 1933, Judge Woolsey lifted the United States's ban of *Ulysses*, eleven years after the book first appeared.

The Sadness of the King (1952) by Henri Matisse. Gouache cutout pasted on canvas (292 cm × 386 cm).

Musée Nationale d'Art Moderne, Paris. © 1997 Succession H. Matisse, Paris / Artists Rights Society (ARS), New York.

The twentieth century's vision of the future might well be summed up in the final line of Joseph Conrad's *Heart of Darkness* (1902): "The offing was barred by a black bank of clouds, and the tranquil waterway leading to the uttermost ends of the earth flowed somber under an overcast sky—seemed to lead into the heart of an immense darkness."

The novelists that followed Conrad were moving from a concern with society to a focus on introspection. Virginia Woolf was even rejecting traditional chronological order in storytelling. Experimenting with novelistic structure and with a shifting point of view, Woolf probed with the delicacy of a surgeon the human mind to examine all its shifts of moods and impressions.

In his novels, D. H. Lawrence was writing out his own strong resentment against British society with its class system, industrialism, militarism, and prudery. Lawrence shocked the British with his glorification of the senses and his heated descriptions of relations between the sexes. His novel *Lady Chatterley's Lover* (1928), about an affair between an upper-class woman and her gamekeeper, was explicitly sexual, and its full publication was banned in England until 1960.

A Most influential of all was the Irish poet and novelist James Joyce, whose novel *Ulysses* appeared to a storm of controversy in 1922. *Ulysses,* based on Homer's *Odyssey,* narrates the events of a single day in the

Les Demoiselles d'Avignon. Paris (June–July 1907), by Pablo Picasso. Oil on canvas 8′ × 7′8″ (243.9 x 233.7 cm).

The Museum of Modern Art, New York. Acquired through the Lillie P. Bliss Bequest. Photograph © 1997 The Museum of Modern Art, New York. © 1997 Estate of Pablo Picasso / Artists Rights Society (ARS), New York.

ASSESSMENT TOOLS

Check Test: Short Answers

1. Which three nineteenth-century thinkers had an enormous impact on twentieth-century developments? [Charles Darwin, Karl Marx, and Sigmund Freud.]
2. What common political developments occurred in Italy, Germany, and Russia before World War II? [In each country, dictators rose to power.]
3. What quality characterized the important works of art of the twentieth century before World War II? [Experimentation.]
4. What quality characterized most works of British literature just after World War II? [Pessimism.]
5. What are some of the reasons for contemporary British literature's amazing diversity? [The influence of different social and philosophical movements, the influx of literature from Britain's former colonies, innovations in technology and communication, and the effects of various political concerns.]

> Signatures of all things I am here to read, sea-spawn and seawrack, the nearing tide, that rusty boot. Snotgreen, bluesilver, rust: coloured signs.
>
> —James Joyce

lives of a Jewish Dubliner named Leopold Bloom and a young man named Stephen Dedalus, as they unwittingly recapitulate the actions of Homer's Odysseus and his son Telemachus. Joyce drew, in a wholly revolutionary way, on myth and symbol, on Freudian explorations of sexuality, and on new conceptions of time and the workings of human consciousness.

> *In literature, novelists such as Joseph Conrad, Virginia Woolf, D. H. Lawrence, and James Joyce began experimenting with both form and content to challenge the conventions and limits of the novel.*

The Rise of Dictatorships: Origins of World War II

The Great War, which had been called "a war to end all wars," ironically led to another war. The League of Nations, the idealistic dream of the U.S. president, Woodrow Wilson, had no sooner been created than it was abandoned by a newly isolationist U.S. government. A worldwide economic depression that began in 1929 encouraged the rise of dictators in Germany, Italy, and Russia.

In Italy and Germany, the form of totalitarianism that developed was Fascism, a type of government that relies on the rule of a single dictator whose power is absolute and backed by force. Benito Mussolini, who came to power in Italy in 1922, held control through brutality and manipulation. Adolf Hitler and the Nazi party capitalized on Germany's economic woes to convince many Germans that their problems were caused by Jews, Communists, and immigrants.

> You cannot make a revolution with silk gloves.
>
> —attributed to Joseph Stalin

B

Russia's totalitarian government, based on the political theories of the economist Karl Marx, was Communist. Its founder, Nikolai Lenin, had sought in the 1920s to create a society without a class system, one in which the state would distribute the country's wealth equally among the people. But, in reality, the new government became as repressive as the rule of the czars had been. After Lenin's death in 1924, Joseph Stalin took power. In 1941, he became premier and continued to rule with an iron fist. Under Stalin's rule, as many as 15 million people were sent to the Gulag, or system of forced labor and detention camps.

The Twentieth Century

The following ideas and events distinguish the twentieth century:

- Radically new thinking in science, psychology, and economics replaced many ideas of the Victorian period.
- With the huge British losses suffered in the Great War, conventional patriotism and romantic notions of bravery were swept away.
- Disillusioned by the war, British and European artists radically experimented with, even rejected, traditional notions of beauty and order.
- After a worldwide economic depression, Fascist dictatorships arose in Germany and Italy, along with an equally brutal Communist regime in Russia.
- By the end of World War II, the Nazis had murdered millions of Jews in what is now known as the Holocaust. The Nazis also killed millions of other people.
- Its postwar economy in shambles, Britain could not hold on to the territories that had constituted its empire; one after another, most of Britain's colonies won their independence.
- Since the 1960s, British writing has been marked primarily by its diversity, and many of the most extraordinary writers in English have come from Britain's former colonies.

C

B. Responding to the Quotation

? Do you find the statement disturbing? Why or why not? [Possible response: The statement understates a ruthless efficiency and cruelty, because it suggests that nothing is immoral in a revolution. Students familiar with Stalin will probably find the comment chilling.]

C. Exploring the Historical Period

Germany and Italy announced their "Axis" coalition on October 25, 1936, and then included Japan in an agreement on November 25, 1936. The three countries solidified their forces and intentions with the Tripartite Pact, signed on September 27, 1940.

Walter Hussey Bequest, Pallant House, Chichester, England. © The Henry Moore Foundation.

Two Apprehensive Shelterers (1942) by Henry Moore.

By 1939, the Nazis were sweeping through Europe with their motorized army and crack air force. Hitler's plan for the systematic destruction of the Jews and other minorities, scapegoats on whom he blamed Germany's economic woes, resulted in the deaths of millions of innocent men, women, and children—including the 6 million Jews who were killed in the Holocaust. Only twenty years after the "war to end all wars," the world had again plunged into a bloody, brutal conflict. In 1940, Germany defeated France and then prepared to invade Britain by launching devastating air attacks against London and other cities. Prime Minister Winston Churchill declared: "We shall go on to the end." The British *did* persevere, but only after the Soviet Union and the United States entered the war did Germany's defeat become inevitable. In Japan, the war ended in the ultimate horror. On August 6, 1945, the entire city of Hiroshima was wiped out by a single atomic bomb dropped from an American plane. Small wonder, then, that the literature following the Second World War has often been dark and pessimistic.

A We shall not flag or fail. We shall go on to the end, we shall fight in France, we shall fight on the seas and oceans, we shall fight with growing confidence and growing strength in the air, we shall defend our island, whatever the cost may be, we shall fight on the beaches, we shall fight on the landing grounds, we shall fight in the fields and in the streets, we shall fight in the hills; we shall never surrender.

—Sir Winston Churchill, June 4, 1940

The worldwide depression of the 1930s gave rise to dictatorships in Europe and led to the horrors of World War II.

Britain After World War II: The Sun Sets on the Empire

After the war ended in Europe, Winston Churchill and his Conservative party were defeated by the Labour party, and Britain was transformed into a welfare state. The government assumed responsibility for providing medical care and other basic benefits for its citizens. While recovering from the war and rebuilding its own economy, Great Britain could not hold on to its many colonies. Most of them became independent nations, and the sun now sank nightly over the British Empire.

Up until 1994, when an agreement with the radical Sinn Fein political group in Northern Ireland seemed to promise an end to violence, Britain's most vexing political and social problem had been its uneasy dealings with the Irish question. Turmoil caused by the Irish Republican Army (IRA) and by the equally violent Ulster Voluntary Force has resulted in the deaths of thousands of soldiers and civilians in the seemingly endless controversy over British rule in Northern Ireland.

> *After World War II, most of Great Britain's colonies became independent nations, and Britain's role in world affairs decreased.*

> In the end it may well be that Britain will be honored by the historians more for the way she disposed of an empire than for the way in which she acquired it.
> —David Ormsby Gore

British Writing Today: A Remarkable Diversity

Two of the most conspicuous literary figures in England before World War II were the poets W. H. Auden and Stephen Spender (see "Twentieth-Century British Poetry," pages 932–934). They shared a common intellectual background and a left-wing, anti-Fascist political point of view. But after the war, a group of younger novelists and playwrights emerged who disliked the values of the Auden group. These writers, who became known as the Angry Young Men, criticized the pretensions of intellectuals and the bland lives of the newly prosperous middle class. One of the major works of the period was Kingsley Amis's novel *Lucky Jim* (1953), a scathing satire of British university life.

The period since the 1960s has been marked by great diversity, though it is still satire that the British excel at. Landmark novels published in Britain from the 1960s on include the sharp and witty novels of Muriel Spark (*The Prime of Miss Jean Brodie,* 1961); the moral and linguistic experiments of Anthony Burgess (*A Clockwork Orange,* 1963); the feminist novels of Margaret Drabble (*Gates of Ivory,* 1991); and the exuberant novels of Roddy Doyle about Dublin working-class life (*Paddy Clarke Ha Ha Ha,* 1993).

B. Expansion
Sir Winston Churchill (1874–1965) served again as prime minister after the war, from 1951 to 1955, when he resigned. He was awarded the Nobel Prize in Literature in 1953 for his many writings, especially *The Second World War,* which comprises six volumes.

A. Responding to the Quotation

? What is odd or amusing about the comment? [Students will probably recognize that the statement is contradictory in that it asserts the English are serious only about humor; it suggests the dry wit (the understatement and irony) of the English.]

B. Expansion

Monty Python's Flying Circus is a nonsensical, meaningless name taken by six performers: John Cleese, Graham Chapman, Eric Idle, Terry Gilliam, Terry Jones, and Michael Palin. The troupe's BBC TV shows (forty-five episodes, each a half-hour long) began airing in the United States in 1974 in syndication on public television.

DRY, DELICIOUS PARODY

A *Humor is practically the only thing about which the English are utterly serious.*

—*Malcolm Muggeridge*

In "London Homesick Blues," the unamused American songwriter Gary P. Nunn offers to "substantiate the rumor that the English sense of humor is drier than the Texas sand." British humor is a source of national pride, although uncomprehending foreigners may not get the joke. Their comedy is notable for its ability to parody the national reputation for stiff-upper-lip reserve. For example, the novelist Sir P. G. Wodehouse mocks the notoriously poor traveling skills of British tourists, describing his character's "look of furtive shame, the shifty hangdog look which announces that an Englishman is about to talk French."

"Fabulous" silliness. British comedy revels in the ridiculous, and the television series *Absolutely Fabulous* brings that absurdity to its spoof of the fashion industry. American audiences clamored to see the ruthless fashion sitcom, even acquiring bootleg tapes of *AbFab* when no American network bought the series.

Bubble: I've booked every model in the world. . . .
Edina: I know, darling, but what about the party?
Bubble: That is all completely under control. We've moved Stonehenge to a tent in Hyde Park.
Edina: Did you get permission for that, darling?
Bubble: They were very happy for us to use it, as long as it's back for the summer solstice. They realize how important the fashion industry is to this country.

When they recognized the program's devoted American followers, television officials aired *AbFab* in the United States. Yet, despite its success, one American public television official explained that his station does not buy British comedies because "most . . . are quite silly."

B **Pythons and dead parrots.** The comedy troupe Monty Python's Flying Circus made silliness its specialty. In a scene well known to Python followers, a customer complains to a pet shop proprietor that he has been sold a dead parrot. As the store owner ignores the obvious

An important development in the years since the war is the growing eminence of writers from Britain's former dependencies. One result of Great Britain's empire was the spread of English around the world. We are now reaping the benefits of that linguistic dominance, with works written in English from the Caribbean (V. S. Naipaul, Derek Walcott), Africa (Doris Lessing, Wole Soyinka, Nadine Gordimer, Chinua Achebe, Ben Okri), and India (R. K. Narayan, Ruth Prawer Jhabvala, Salman Rushdie, Anita Desai).

Contemporary British literature is marked by great diversity. Satire is a dominant mode.

World Literature: Writing from Afar Near at Hand

Though our world isn't really a global village, innovations in technology and transportation have linked us in ways our ancestors couldn't have imagined. Ideas travel as fast as myriad channels can carry them, and one writer may profoundly influence another living continents away. Today, evidence, the exasperated customer finds increasingly imaginative ways to describe the dead bird.

> It's not pining. It's passed on. This parrot is no more. It has ceased to be. It's expired and gone to meet its maker. This is a late parrot. It's a stiff. Bereft of life, it rests in peace. If you hadn't nailed it to its perch, it would be pushing up the daisies. It's rung down the curtain and joined the choir invisible. This is an ex-parrot.

The Pythons began their career by horrifying audiences with their bawdy, outrageous performances. Yet the parrot speech became so celebrated that the former prime minister Margaret Thatcher mentioned it in a political speech—which just goes to show that British humor is an acquired taste.

Terry Jones and John Cleese in *Monty Python's The Meaning of Life* (1983).

C. Expansion

The Pythons' humor is laden with allusions. Here, the phrase "choir invisible" refers to a poem by Victorian author George Eliot. The poem reads, in part:

"O may I join the choir invisible
Of those immortal dead who live again
In minds made better by their presence."

when important British, Asian, European, or Latin American authors write in their native languages, enterprising publishers have the work promptly translated for eager book buyers around the world. Thus, readers of English can go to bookstores or libraries and find translations of works by Naguib Mahfouz (Egyptian), Julio Cortázar (Argentine), Pablo Neruda (Chilean), Aleksandr Solzhenitsyn (Russian), and hundreds of others.

Political concerns appear more often in current world literature than they have appeared in past British literature. The Nobel Prize–winner Aleksandr Solzhenitsyn, for example, has written much about human suffering and loss of freedom under the totalitarian government of the Soviet Union. Literally hundreds of writers from former British colonies explore the problems of personal identity and the effects of cultural domination and racism.

> All paths lead to the same goal: to convey to others what we are. And we must pass through solitude and difficulty, isolation and silence, in order to reach forth to the enchanted place where we can dance our clumsy dance and sing our sorrowful song.
>
> —Pablo Neruda, on receiving the Nobel Prize in literature, 1971

Tea Time (20th century) by Penelope Beaton.

Photograph by kind permission of Waterman Fine Art Ltd., St. James, London.

And many writers in developing nations, to whom the niceties of Western living are foreign, document their raw struggle for existence. Such a variety of writing can only broaden and deepen our understanding of the human condition. As Solzhenitsyn said in his Nobel Prize acceptance speech, "The only substitute for what we ourselves have not experienced is art and literature. They have the marvelous capacity of transmitting from one nation to another—despite differences in language, customs, and social structure—practical experience, the harsh national experience of many decades never tasted by the other nation."

> **Twentieth-century technology has made an extraordinary amount of world literature available to readers around the world.**

Quickwrite

Throughout the first half of this century, artistic expression mirrored the general disillusionment of the times. Many works portrayed a civilization in ruins, human beliefs and morals challenged. What do you think the artistic expression of our day—from television to painting, music to comic books—reveals about our own society? List a few examples; then jot down some ideas about how these works of art reflect a sense of where we are today.

THE CENTER CANNOT HOLD

Theme: **Things Fall Apart**
In the first half of the twentieth century, it seemed that anarchy had unleashed itself upon the world. Two world wars had devasted not only the landscape but many people's psyches as well. The literature of the period mirrors the sense of loss, chaos, and despair many felt.

Thematic Focus

These selections depict the aftermath of war and its emotional impact.

- **The Rear-Guard/Dulce et Decorum Est** These poems illustrate the horrors of war and express disillusion with patriotic sentimentalism.
- **Thoughts of Hanoi** A yearning for news of old places, since changed by war, pervades this poem.
- *from* **Night** Humanity's cruelty is shown from the victim's point of view.
- **The Destructors** The physical destruction of war is mirrored in the moral dissolution of society, especially among the young.
- **Hawk Roosting** This poem suggests that there are ruthless, destructive forces in creation.
- **Freedom to Breathe/The Ants and the Bonfire** These prose poems evoke strong images of the preciousness of freedom and home.
- **In the Shadow of War** War is seen through the eyes of a child who has a limited understanding of the events he witnesses.

Literary Focus

Literary Element	Selection / Feature
Oxymoron	**The Rear-Guard/Dulce et Decorum Est**
Setting	**The Destructors**
Personification	**Hawk Roosting**
Limited Third-Person Point of View	**In the Shadow of War**

Writing Focus

The following flowchart shows how the writing assignment for each selection relates to and builds toward the writing assignment presented in the Writer's Workshop at the end of the Unit.

Selection	Work-in-Progress Assignment
The Rear-Guard/ Dulce et Decorum Est	Brainstorm topics about Trench Poets for an informative report p. 931
The Destructors	Jot down research ideas p. 963
Hawk Roosting	Record questions about poem p. 966
In the Shadow of War	Record questions about story p. 976
Writer's Workshop	Write an informative essay p. 1053

Collection Planner

PUPIL'S EDITION

SELECTION/ FEATURE	Literary Elements / Active Reading	Writing	Speaking and Listening	Language and Vocabulary
The Rear-Guard Siegfried Sassoon **Dulce et Decorum Est** Wilfred Owen (pp. 924–931) Spotlight On: Twentieth-Century British Poetry (pp. 932–934)	• Reader's Log p. 924 • Oxymoron p. 924	• Critical Writing: Compare and contrast imagery, structure, and sound devices p. 931 • Critical Writing: Write essay on patriotism p. 931 • Critical Writing: Write comparison-contrast essay on two works p. 931		
World Literature: Thoughts of Hanoi Nguyen Thi Vinh (pp. 935–937) Spotlight On: T. S. Eliot (pp. 938–943)	• Reader's Log p. 936	• Finding Common Ground: Write poem about a time or place you miss p. 937	• Finding Common Ground: Create a dialogue between the two brothers p. 937	
World Literature: from **Night** Elie Wiesel (pp. 944–949)	• Reader's Log p. 945		• Finding Common Ground: Discuss reactions to Wiesel's account p. 949	
The Destructors Graham Greene (pp. 950–963)	• Reader's Log p. 951 • Setting p. 951	• Critical Writing: Write essay on imagery p. 963 • Creative Writing: Write letter in voice of Mr. Thomas p. 963	• Critical Thinking/ Role-Playing: Stage a trial p. 963	• Language and Style: Explain slang used in Greene's story p. 963
Hawk Roosting Ted Hughes (pp. 964–966)	• Reader's Log p. 964 • Personification p. 964	• Critical Writing: Write about main theme of poem p. 966 • Critical Writing: Compare views of three poems p. 966 • Creative Writing: Select an animal and let it explain its "philosophy" p. 966		
World Literature: Freedom to Breathe/ The Bonfire and the Ants Aleksandr Solzhenitsyn (pp. 967–969)	• Reader's Log p. 968		• Finding Common Ground: Discuss perceptions of these prose poems and challenge or query author p. 969	
In the Shadow of War Ben Okri (pp. 970–976) **Connections: Zagreb: A Letter to My Daughter** Slavenka Drakulíc (pp. 974–975)	• Reader's Log p. 970 • Limited Third-Person Point of View p. 970	• Critical Writing: Explain symbol p. 976 • Critical Writing: Write about connections among poem, story, and letter p. 976		

Collection Resources

Teaching Resources B Cross-Curricular Activity p. 128	**Audiovisual Resources Binder** Fine Art Transparency 12.1	**Test Booklet** Collection 12 Test pp. 208–210

 Computer disk or CD-ROM

 Audiocassette

 Overhead Transparency

PROGRAM RESOURCES

Electronic Media	Teaching Resources with Organizer		Audiovisual Resources Binder
	Teaching Resources B	Other Resources	
• Test Generator	• Teaching Notes pp. 109–111 • Reading Organizer p. 116 • Language Link pp. 117–118	• Test Booklet: Selection Tests pp. 201–202 • Portfolio Management System pp. 39, 62–63, 158–159	• Selected Reading, Audiocassette 2, Side B
	• Teaching Notes p. 111		
	• Teaching Notes p. 111		
• Test Generator • Language Workshop: Punctuation	• Teaching Notes pp. 111–112 • Reading Organizer p. 119 • Language Link pp. 120–121 • Words to Own p. 122	• Test Booklet: Selection Test pp. 203–204 • Language and Writing Skills Worksheets p. 129 • Portfolio Management System pp. 43, 160	• Elements of Literature Transparency 12.2
• Test Generator	• Teaching Notes p. 112 • Reading Organizer p. 123	• Test Booklet: Selection Test p. 205 • Portfolio Management System pp. 54–55, 161	
	• Teaching Notes p. 113		
• Test Generator • Language Workshop: Modifiers	• Teaching Notes p. 113 • Reading Organizer p. 124 • Language Link pp. 125–126 • Words to Own p. 127	• Test Booklet: Selection Test pp. 206–207 • Language and Writing Skills Worksheets pp. 66–67 • Portfolio Management System p. 162	• Selected Reading, Audiocassette 2, Side B

Proofreading Warm-ups

You may use the following exercises to help students practice their proofreading skills. Copy a set of incorrect sentences onto the chalkboard, and have students find and correct the spelling, punctuation, usage, and mechanical errors in each sentence. Ask students to share and discuss their responses.

	Sentences with Errors	Sentences Corrected	Skills Covered
1	**a.** whom do you think wrote the poem The Second Coming asked Mrs. San Miguel **b.** i do not know, but me and Jessie liked it replied Paul	**a.** "Who do you think wrote the poem 'The Second Coming'?" asked Mrs. San Miguel. **b.** "I do not know, but Jessie and I liked it," replied Paul.	Quotation marks (single and double), Capitalization, Who/Whom usage, Question marks, Pronoun usage, Comma usage, End marks
2	**a.** no mans land is the few hundred yards separating one armys lines from anothers **b.** the Trench Poets world war i writers felt that war itself was a kind of dehumanizing no mans land	**a.** "No man's land" is the few hundred yards separating one army's lines from another's. **b.** The Trench Poets, World War I writers, felt that war itself was a kind of dehumanizing no man's land.	Quotation marks, Capitalization, Apostrophe usage, Spelling, Comma usage, End marks
3	**a.** a oxymoron is, a figure of speech that combine's apparently contradictory idea's **b.** the word bittersweet is a example of a oxymoron	**a.** An oxymoron is a figure of speech that combines apparently contradictory ideas. **b.** The word <u>bittersweet</u> is an example of an oxymoron.	Capitalization, Nonstandard usage, Comma usage, Apostrophe usage, Underscoring words, End marks
4	**a.** t s eliot who was born in St Louis Missouri had a vast influence as a poet **b.** he dominated english lit. in a way not seen sence the days of Dr Johnson	**a.** T. S. Eliot, who was born in St. Louis, Missouri, had a vast influence as a poet. **b.** He dominated English literature in a way not seen since the days of Dr. Johnson.	Capitalization, Abbreviations, Comma usage, Writing out abbreviations, Spelling, End marks
5	**a.** elie wiesel a romanian jew survived german concentration camps during w w ii **b.** his parent's and a sister, however died	**a.** Elie Wiesel, a Romanian Jew, survived German concentration camps during World War II. **b.** His parents and a sister, however, died.	Capitalization, Comma usage, Writing out abbreviations, Apostrophe usage, End marks
6	**a.** the black and white american movies of the 1940s and 50s known as film noir **b.** film noir, is french for "black film	**a.** The black-and-white American movies of the 1940s and '50s were known as film noir. **b.** Film noir is French for "black film."	Capitalization, Hyphen usage, Apostrophe usage, Fragments, Comma usage, Quotation marks, End marks
7	**a.** ted hughes poem Hawk Roosting, uses personification **b.** which is the giveing of humane characteristics to something nonhuman	**a.** Ted Hughes's poem "Hawk Roosting" uses personification, which is the giving of human characteristics to something nonhuman. **b.** NOTE: This sentence was combined with the preceding one to fix the fragment.	Capitalization, Apostrophe usage, Quotation marks for poem titles, Comma usage, Fragments, Spelling, End marks
8	**a.** early twentieth century british poets was quiet conventional **b.** even when they was responding to the violent experiance of War	**a.** Early twentieth-century British poets were quite conventional, even when they were responding to the violent experience of war. **b.** NOTE: This sentence was combined with the preceding one to fix the fragment.	Capitalization, Hyphen usage, Subject-verb agreement, Spelling, Fragments, End marks
9	**a.** aleksandr solzhenitsyns novel The Gulag Archipelago is a factual account of soviet labor camps **b.** as a result of writing that novel solzhenitsyn was arrested and exiled	**a.** Aleksandr Solzhenitsyn's novel <u>The Gulag Archipelago</u> is a factual account of Soviet labor camps. **b.** As a result of writing that novel, Solzhenitsyn was arrested and exiled.	Capitalization, Apostrophe usage, Underscoring book titles, Comma usage, End marks
10	**a.** ben okri grew up in nigeria but he latter moved to london **b.** he wrote about the nigerian civil war (1967-1970) which is often called the biafran war	**a.** Ben Okri grew up in Nigeria, but he later moved to London. **b.** He wrote about the Nigerian Civil War (1967–1970), which is often called the Biafran War.	Capitalization, Comma usage, Spelling, End marks

THE CENTER CANNOT HOLD

Sassoon
Owen
Nguyen
Eliot
Wiesel

Greene
Hughes
Solzhenitsyn
Okri

The Second Coming

Turning and turning in the widening gyre
The falcon cannot hear the falconer;
Things fall apart; the center cannot hold;
Mere anarchy is loosed upon the world,
The blood-dimmed tide is loosed, and everywhere
The ceremony of innocence is drowned;
The best lack all conviction, while the worst
Are full of passionate intensity.

Surely some revelation is at hand;
Surely the Second Coming is at hand.
The Second Coming! Hardly are those words out
When a vast image out of *Spiritus Mundi*
Troubles my sight: somewhere in sands of the desert
A shape with lion body and the head of a man,
A gaze blank and pitiless as the sun,
Is moving its slow thighs, while all about it
Reel shadows of the indignant desert birds.
The darkness drops again; but now I know
That twenty centuries of stony sleep
Were vexed to nightmare by a rocking cradle,
And what rough beast, its hour come round at last,
Slouches towards Bethlehem to be born?

—William Butler Yeats

"The Second Coming"

 What does "the center cannot hold" mean in the context of the poem? [It suggests that things cannot stay as they are or that balance cannot be maintained.] What might the poem say about the age in which it is written? [The poem anticipates an apocalypse; everything seems to be falling apart.] Why might it be chosen as the theme of this Collection? [Perhaps the selections are about troubled times or tough issues in which it is hard to strike a balance.]

 PROGRAM MANAGER

- **Integrated Assessment** For a summative assessment of the literature and language skills taught in this collection, see Collection 12 Test, *Test Booklet*, pp. 208–210.
- **Instructional Support** See Fine Art Transparency 12.1. Review teacher's notes for transparencies in

the *Audiovisual Resources Binder* for suggestions on how to tie the transparencies to specific reading selections.
- **Extending Collection Theme** See Cross-Curricular Activity: The Center Cannot Hold, *Teaching Resources B*, p. 128, for an activity in another discipline and for evaluation criteria.

PORTFOLIO ASSESSMENT

Parent/Guardian Involvement For forms that will help a parent or guardian review and respond to a student's portfolio, see the *Portfolio Management System*, pp. 62–63.

Into the Poems

Author Biographies p. 925, p. 928

Before You Read p. 924

- **Reading Focus: Prior Knowledge** Students learn about Trench Poets.
- **Quickwrite** Record war images in Reader's Log
- **Elements of Literature: Oxymoron**

Through the Poems

"The Rear-Guard" p. 926

"Dulce et Decorum Est" p. 929

Making Meanings pp. 927, 930

Beyond the Poems

Choices: Building Your Portfolio p. 931

- **Writer's Notebook:** Jot down research ideas suggested by poems
- **Critical Writing:** In an essay, compare and contrast the literary devices in two poems
- **Critical Writing:** In an essay, relate Owen's poem to the concept of patriotism
- **Critical Writing:** In an essay, compare two poems
- **Interviewing/Researching:** Make an oral report on an interview

Spotlight On pp. 932–934

BEFORE YOU READ
THE REAR-GUARD
DULCE ET DECORUM EST

Reading Focus

No Man's Land

In war, *no man's land* is the few hundred yards that separate one army's lines from another's. But for the group of writers who became known as the Trench Poets, war itself became a no man's land: a dehumanizing, horrific experience that made a mockery of civilization. Each of the Trench Poets either died in the muddy trenches of World War I (as Wilfred Owen did) or survived as a bitter but articulate ghost trapped by memories from which there was no escape (see page 932).

Quickwrite

For many English people during World War I, poetry brought home war's full brutality for the first time. Today, even though you've never been in battle, you've probably seen images of war in movies and newspapers or on TV.

What is your most vivid mental image of war's horror? Recall impressions you've absorbed from film, war photographs, the nightly news, what war veterans have told you, literary works, or other sources. Close your eyes, think "war," and then record, in words, in your Reader's Log what you saw in your mind.

Elements of Literature

The Oxymoron

Have you ever had a bittersweet moment, a moment when you felt happy and sad at the same time? The word *bittersweet* is an example of an **oxymoron,** a figure of speech that combines apparently contradictory ideas to create a strong emphasis. Other oxymorons common in ordinary speech are *cold comfort, honest thief,* and *tough love.* In literature, "darkness visible" is a famous example from Milton. The Trench Poets found oxymorons useful in describing the unimaginable slaughter of trench warfare.

> **A**n **oxymoron** is a figure of speech that combines apparently contradictory ideas.
>
> For more on Oxymorons, see the Handbook of Literary Terms.

The Menin Road, 1919 by Paul Nash.

Imperial War Museum, London.

PROGRAM MANAGER

- **Planning Instruction** See Teaching Notes, *Teaching Resources B,* pp. 109–111, for objectives, a summary, literary elements, and additional biographical information for these poems.
- **Instructional Support** Before beginning the instructional lesson, see Graphic Organizer for Active

Reading, *Teaching Resources B,* p. 116, for a Through the Poems activity.
- **Audiotaped Readings** To help less proficient readers or auditory learners through the lesson, use the Selected Reading, Audiocassette 2, Side B, in the

Audiovisual Resources Binder.
- **Assessment** See Selection Tests, *Test Booklet,* pp. 201–202.
- **Language Link** For instruction and practice in diction, see Language Link, *Teaching Resources B,* pp. 117–118.

Siegfried Sassoon

(1886–1967)

Siegfried Sassoon (1915). Photograph by Beresford.

Siegfried Sassoon was born into that high level of English society at which lifelong privilege is sustained by income from landed estates and assured inheritances. Educated at Cambridge University, and under no pressure to adopt a profession, he lived the life of a country gentleman until the outbreak of World War I. Along with the pursuit of leisure—which he would later write about in a famous book called *Memoirs of a Fox-Hunting Man* (1928)—Sassoon also wrote poetry. He had sufficient skill to win a place in the anthologies of the Georgian movement, in which the value of all things English was celebrated—from scones and honey at teatime to the bells of Winchester Cathedral.

The war would change all that. For Sassoon, it would also lead to a career entirely at odds with his earlier expectations. Enlisting in the army as a patriot and an idealist determined to put an end to "Teutonic barbarism," he distinguished himself as an officer and was awarded a prestigious medal for bravery under fire. But, within two years of his enlistment, Sassoon's attitude toward the war underwent a change amounting to a total reversal of his earlier commitment. His new attitude was expressed in stark, almost savage poems detailing the brutality and debasement of trench warfare. The publication of these bitter testaments sent a shock wave of doubt through the minds of

the English (among them, Winston Churchill, then minister of munitions, whose secretary, Edward Marsh, was the leader of the comforting Georgian poets and their most outspoken publicist).

Dissatisfied even with the depth of response his poems evoked, Sassoon wrote to the war department to protest a war he now believed was "being deliberately prolonged by those who have the power to end it." In a statement handed to his commanding officer, which Sassoon himself regarded as "an act of willful defiance," he spelled out his disillusionment: "I believe that this war, upon which I entered as a war of defense and liberation, has now become a war of aggression and conquest."

Expecting court-martial, and entirely prepared to sacrifice himself for his own cause, Sassoon was thwarted by the unsolicited and unwanted kindness of some of his friends, notably the poet Robert Graves, who shunted him toward a medical board of examiners. Diagnosed as shellshocked, Sassoon was committed to a military hospital in Scotland. There he met fellow patient Wilfred Owen, and the two began one of the most famous and mutually beneficial relationships in modern literature.

Disgust controlled by irony gives Sassoon's war poems their indelible imprint; the poems stand by themselves in an otherwise pedestrian career marked by one great parenthesis—the Great War itself.

Using BEFORE YOU READ p. 924

Reading Focus

Ask students to consider the role of poetry in society. Do they think of poetry as offering protest or warning as well as solace or beauty? Challenge students to name poems they have read that include both messages. Write students' ideas on the chalkboard, and have students try to characterize the types of subjects poetry addresses.

Elements of Literature

Ask students why they think **oxymorons** would be useful for describing trench warfare. [Perhaps oxymorons would capture the contradictions and complexities.]

WRITERS ON WRITING

Remarking on the lightheartedness and success of a fellow poet, Siegfried Sassoon once wrote in his diary: "For him literature is a glorious game. For me it is a struggle against disillusionment and disgust." Sassoon's greatest struggle, of course, was against the war, and he was aware that his pen was his best weapon. To Wilfred Owen he gave his best advice on writing: "Sweat your guts out writing poetry! Sweat your guts out, I say!" Owen was understandably impressed, not only by the man (whose "general expression," he noted, was "one of boredom") but by the poet, about whose work Owen remarked: "There is nothing better this century can offer. . . ."

PORTFOLIO ASSESSMENT

Portfolio Assessment For help with self-assessment of reading skills, see the *Portfolio Management System,* p. 39.

STRATEGIES FOR INCLUSION

Bodily-Kinesthetic Stage the poem as a small one-act drama. Assign one student to act as narrator/reader and two others to perform the roles of officer and soldier in pantomime. If there is time, assign two students to provide some props to furnish the tunnel as Sassoon describes it. Ask the class to concentrate on the officer—on the poem's description of him and his actions—as they watch the play. Discussion should focus on what the dramatization might add to students' understanding of the poem and of the officer in particular.

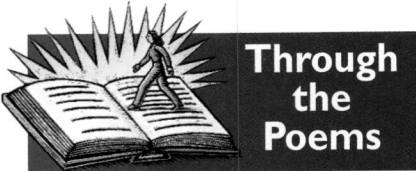

A. Reader's Response: First Thoughts

? What might the title of the poem suggest? [Sample responses: A rear guard is a detachment of troops that protects the rear of a military force; maybe the poem will be about a battle or about brave soldiers guarding their comrades in a war.]

B. Literary Element: Oxymoron

? What kind of effect does the phrase "rosy gloom" have? [Possible answers: The word *rosy* is usually cheerful, but it is contradicted by the word *gloom;* the phrase is a disturbing way to describe how explosions light up the sky.]

C. Critical Reading: Drawing Conclusions

? Why does the soldier respond as he does to the "sleeper"? [He is tired from lack of sleep, lost and disoriented in the dark tunnel, and frightened; he is obviously used to giving orders.]

D. Literary Element: Imagery

? What does *livid* mean? What other descriptive words or images are used to describe the soldier's body? [*Livid* sometimes is taken to mean "grayish" or "pale"; other images include "terribly glaring" and "agony dying hard."]

E. Literary Element: Irony

? What does the officer feel as he climbs up out of the tunnel? How is this ironic? [He feels relief that he is "unloading hell behind him." The irony of this sense of relief is that he is emerging into the thick of battle.]

In the battlefield trenches of World War I, enlisted men lived for weeks, sometimes years, in interconnected underground caverns infested by rats, with no drainage, poor ventilation, and only occasional dim shafts of natural light. In this poem, the "he" who recalls a grisly trench episode is the officer-poet, Siegfried Sassoon himself.

Ⓐ The Rear-Guard

Siegfried Sassoon

(Hindenburg Line,° April 1917.)

Groping along the tunnel, step by step,
He winked his prying torch° with patching glare
From side to side, and sniffed the unwholesome air.

Tins, boxes, bottles, shapes too vague to know,
5   A mirror smashed, the mattress from a bed;
And he, exploring fifty feet below
Ⓑ   The rosy gloom of battle overhead.

Tripping, he grabbed the wall; saw someone lie
Humped at his feet, half-hidden by a rug,
10   And stooped to give the sleeper's arm a tug.
"I'm looking for headquarters." No reply.
Ⓒ   "God blast your neck!" (For days he'd had no sleep.)

"Get up and guide me through this stinking place."
Savage, he kicked a soft, unanswering heap,
15   And flashed his beam across the livid face
Terribly glaring up, whose eyes yet wore
Agony dying hard ten days before;
Ⓓ   And fists of fingers clutched a blackening wound.

Alone he staggered on until he found
20   Dawn's ghost that filtered down a shafted stair
To the dazed, muttering creatures underground
Who hear the boom of shells in muffled sound.
At last, with sweat of horror in his hair,
He climbed through darkness to the twilight air,
Ⓔ 25   Unloading hell behind him step by step.

Hindenburg Line: German defensive barricade running across northern France. It was made of massive barbed-wire entanglements and deep trenches.
2. **torch:** flashlight.

OPTIONS FOR TEACHING

STRATEGIES FOR INCLUSION

English Language Development The images that Sassoon relates in his dark poem are similar to those that would be reported by a journalist in a different manner. To help students comprehend the text, have them work in pairs to recount the events as if writing for a news agency, creating a short article that paraphrases Sassoon's ideas. Point out that students should try to answer the central questions of who, what, when, where, why, and how.

INTEGRATING THE LANGUAGE ARTS

Speaking and Listening Remind students to read poetry sentence by sentence rather than line by line to avoid a stilted, singsong quality that could be produced by this poem's regular **rhythm** and **rhyme scheme** (*abb cdcd effeg hghiij,* and so on). Read the poem aloud twice for the class—once with a forced emphasis on the rhythm and rhyme, and once for the sense of the sentences and clauses. Then, ask selected students to read, focusing on the story Sassoon is telling. **Rhythm** and **rhyme** become something heard in the background. Give as many students as possible the chance to read aloud and experience the sound of the lines.

Oppy Wood, 1917 by John Northcote Nash.

Imperial War Museum, London.

MAKING MEANINGS

First Thoughts

1. What did you feel when you finished this poem? What do you think the poet *wanted* you to feel?

Shaping Interpretations

2. Why is the man in the tunnel, and what happens there? How is the man's behavior simultaneously brutal and pathetic?

3. Where does **onomatopoeia** help you hear the sounds in the tunnel? What **oxymoron** does the poet use to describe the battle overhead?

4. The poet uses many strong present and past participles, such as *groping, prying, smashed,* and *humped.* What do these words help you *see?*

5. Explain the **irony** of what the speaker says in line 13.

6. How do you interpret the phrase "unloading hell" in line 25?

Connecting with the Text

7. How do the images in "The Rear-Guard" compare with your own mental pictures of war? (Recall what you recorded in your Reader's Log on page 924.) Are visual depictions of war more or less powerful than verbal descriptions—like the ones in Sassoon's poem?

Making Meanings

First Thoughts

1. Students will probably be appalled, shocked, disgusted, or saddened by the poem, which is the poet's intent.

Shaping Interpretations

2. The man is looking for headquarters, and when he asks a sleeping man to wake up and give him directions, he discovers the sleeper is actually dead. His behavior is brutal (he curses and kicks the "sleeper"), yet his horror and his aloneness are pathetic.

3. In l. 22, the tunnel echoes with the "boom" of war overhead. The battle is described by the oxymoron "rosy gloom" in l. 7.

4. The words lend the poem a sense of immediacy, and they hint at the officer's powerlessness.

5. The officer is asking a dead man to be his guide.

6. By ascending the stair and leaving the grisly scene, the officer leaves the "hell" of war's grisly aftermath behind him and probably feels lighter because of his relief in getting away.

Connecting with the Text

7. Students may say that the images in the poem are similar in tone to their ideas of war but that the poem is a detailed and personal account. Students may say that a visual depiction of war more efficiently expresses war's horrors, yet words or phrases may echo in a reader's memory.

INTEGRATING THE LANGUAGE ARTS

Writing: Character Journal Immediately after the poem is read and acted in the Strategies for Inclusion activity on p. T925, have students write a page the officer might have written in his journal, describing the experience from his point of view. Prompt students with questions like these: "What type of person is the officer?" "What does he feel as he walks through the tunnel?" Ask students to tie their impressions to specific words and images in the poem and to details in the performance. Have several students read what they have written to the class. There may be some disagreement in their feelings about this officer, which is an excellent spur to class discussion.

CROSSING THE CURRICULUM

Social Sciences Have a group of students research the Hindenburg Line, encouraging them to find information and photographs of World War I fortifications and trenches. Students also may draw a map showing the geographic location of the line. The group may present its research in a report to the class, or group members may contribute informally to class discussion.

Wilfred Owen

(1893–1918)

Wilfred Owen is one of the most poignant figures in modern literature. "The Poetry is in the pity," he said, and this famous remark could serve as his epitaph. Within the few adult years granted to him, Owen pursued a course of development that went from strength to strength. His interest in experimental techniques led him to master the use of half rhyme; this would become his most easily recognizable poetic signature. He also had a gift for lyricism that was bitterly tempered by "the truth untold, / The pity of war, the pity war distilled." The result was a series of elegies and metrical statements as terse and stark as those carved on tombstones.

Like an apprentice determined to master his art, Owen immersed himself in the long history of English poetry. He chose for his model and mentor the poet John Keats, whose astonishing life's work had ended with his death at twenty-five (about the same age Shakespeare was when he had only begun to write his plays). As a tutor in France for two years, Owen studied the French poets who were producing the tradition-shattering art that would become known as modernist. But all these literary influences were to become secondary to the devastating impact of a war Owen witnessed firsthand.

World War I broke out when Owen was twenty-one; he joined the British army, and the course of his life was determined. His progress in poetry was not made in the arcades of an ancient university or in the pastoral retreats where his literary forerunners were privileged to pursue their careers. His progress took place in the muddy purgatory of trench warfare and in the twilight existence of military hospitals.

In one of those hospitals, Craiglockhart, in Edinburgh, the young Owen met Siegfried

Wilfred Owen.

Sassoon, a fellow officer and poet who had already distinguished himself for bravery in battle. Ironically, Sassoon was also the author of some of the most biting antiwar verses ever written. Temperamentally, the two men were far apart. Owen was an idealistic youth thwarted by circumstance; Sassoon was an aristocrat appalled by the wartime complacency of his own class. Even so, they became friends and artistic colleagues at once. After Owen's death, Sassoon became the first important British writer to herald the younger man's genius and to call attention to what he had accomplished under the most appalling conditions. By that time, events had told the sad story.

In 1918, Owen was listed among those killed in action—a mere seven days before the war ended with a joyous ringing of bells and dancing in the streets.

This poem's title is taken from the Latin statement *Dulce et decorum est pro patria mori,* meaning "It is sweet and honorable to die for one's country." The statement originally appeared in an ode by the ancient Roman poet Horace and has been used for centuries as a morale builder—and an epitaph—for soldiers. Here the motto is given a bitter twist by a soldier-poet who cannot reconcile the thought it expresses with the reality he has experienced.

After the introduction of poison gas as a battlefield weapon during World War I, every man in the trenches was equipped with a gas mask: lifesaving armor, if donned in time. This poem describes the horrible consequences of not getting the mask on promptly.

Dulce et Decorum Est

Wilfred Owen

Bent double, like old beggars under sacks,   **Ⓐ**
Knock-kneed, coughing like hags, we cursed through sludge,
Till on the haunting flares we turned our backs
And toward our distant rest began to trudge.
5 Men marched asleep. Many had lost their boots   **Ⓑ**
But limped on, blood-shod. All went lame; all blind;
Drunk with fatigue; deaf even to the hoots
Of tired, outstripped Five-Nines° that dropped behind.

Gas! GAS! Quick, boys!—An ecstasy of fumbling,   **Ⓒ**
10 Fitting the clumsy helmets just in time;
But someone still was yelling out and stumbling
And flound'ring like a man in fire or lime . . .
Dim, through the misty panes and thick green light,   **Ⓓ**
As under a green sea, I saw him drowning.

15 In all my dreams, before my helpless sight,   **Ⓔ**
He plunges at me, guttering, choking, drowning.

If in some smothering dreams you too could pace
Behind the wagon that we flung him in,
And watch the white eyes writhing in his face,
20 His hanging face, like a devil's sick of sin;
If you could hear, at every jolt, the blood
Come gargling from the froth-corrupted lungs,
Obscene as cancer, bitter as the cud
Of vile, incurable sores on innocent tongues,—
25 My friend, you would not tell with such high zest   **Ⓕ**
To children ardent for some desperate glory,
The old Lie: *Dulce et decorum est*   **Ⓖ**
Pro patria mori.

8. **Five-Nines:** gas shells measuring 5.9 inches each.

WILFRED OWEN 929

A. Literary Element: Simile
In the first two lines, find two similes that Owen uses to describe the soldiers. ["Like old beggars," "like hags."]

B. Literary Element: Hyperbole
? What examples of hyperbole, or exaggeration, can you find in ll. 5–6? ["Men marched asleep," "All went lame; all blind."]

C. Exploring the Historical Period
World War I was the first time poison gas had been used as a battlefield weapon, and gas masks were issued to all soldiers as standard equipment.

D. Reader's Response: First Thoughts
? Why do you think Owen compares the gassed soldier to a drowning man? [Sample responses: It is an image more people can identify with; it shows how gas affects the soldier.]

E. Critical Reading: Making Inferences
? What can you infer from ll. 15–16 about the character of the speaker in the poem? [Possible answer: He is sensitive and is deeply affected by the events he witnesses, even to the point of nightmares long after.]

F. Reader's Response: Shaping Interpretations
? Who are the "children" the poet is talking about in l. 26? [Sample responses: Young men eager to go off to war; young people eager to prove their worth and independence.] Why does he choose the word *children* to describe them? [Sample responses: They are innocent, enthusiastic; they haven't seen the harsher realities of life or war.]

G. Reader's Response: Challenging the Text
? Is it effective for Owen to end this poem about World War I (1914–1918) with a Latin quotation from the Roman poet Horace? Explain your opinion. [Sample responses: Yes, because after this poem, the line is heavily ironic; or no, most people aren't familiar with the phrase and may miss the point.]

Making Meanings

First Thoughts

1. Students may say that, even though circumstances may differ in modern warfare, the poem is relevant because every method of destruction has the same dehumanizing, horrific nature.

Shaping Interpretations

2. The "misty panes" are the visor in the gas mask the speaker wears.
3. The oxymorons "an ecstasy of fumbling" and "desperate glory" describe the complex emotions of fear and desire involved in getting the gas mask on in time and the enthusiasm and confusion with which youth wants to be successful.
4. The rhyme scheme is *ababcdcd effegh gh ijijklklmnmn.* One half rhyme is "glory"/"mori" (ll. 26 and 28).
5. Those who preach a simplistic patriotism.
6. The similes compare the tainted blood that pours forth from the gassed soldier to cancer and to a cud of sores. These graphic images imply that war is a disease of humanity, and, by associating the soldier indirectly with a cow chewing cud, show the soldier as dehumanized and powerless.
7. The tone is tormented and angry, brutally realistic. The tone of modern accounts varies but may be sarcastic or ironic, as in the TV series *M*A*S*H* or the film *Gallipoli,* or dramatic and suspenseful, as in *The Hunt for Red October* or *The Great Escape.*

Extending the Text

8. **(Synthesis)** Each slogan appeals to one's pride and sense of adventure and glory.

Paths of Glory, 1917 by Christopher R. W. Nevinson.

Imperial War Museum, London.

MAKING MEANINGS

First Thoughts

1. Do you think a poem like this has any relevance to wars as they are fought today? Why or why not?

Shaping Interpretations

2. What are the "misty panes" in line 13 through which the speaker glimpses the dying man?
3. What **oxymorons** can you find in the poem's second and last stanzas? Why is a figure of speech that expresses contradiction appropriate for the speaker's purposes?
4. What is the poem's **rhyme scheme**? Can you find any **half rhymes**?

5. Who is the "you" addressed in the final stanza?
6. Explain the **similes** in lines 23–24. How do they relate to the **theme** of the poem?
7. How would you describe the speaker's **tone**? How does it compare to the tone of today's war stories or war movies? (Cite some examples in your answer.)

Extending the Text

8. In recent years, the U.S. Army has recruited with the slogan "Be all that you can be," referring to educational and job opportunities in the military. Compare this slogan with the one mentioned in the poem. What does each slogan appeal to?

OPTIONS FOR TEACHING

CROSSING THE CURRICULUM

Social Sciences Have students work in groups of two or three to prepare reports on World War I, providing basic facts about dates, countries, major battles, casualties, new weapons, and the outcome of the war. The presentation to the class should include a report of the facts, a discussion that ties the facts to Owen's poem, a display of World War I photographs, and perhaps a map of battles.

Music Students can learn about the Great War by listening to popular music of the era. Find recordings of songs such as "Over There" or "Hello, Central! Give Me No Man's Land," and ask students to discuss what these songs reveal about the attitudes of the period. Have students compare the songs of World War I to those of other conflicts—for example, the protest songs of the Vietnam War.

CHOICES: Building Your Portfolio

Writer's Notebook

1. Collecting Ideas for an Informative Report

Reading can give you ideas for informative reports. In fact, reading often leads us to want to know more about a subject—that is exactly what you'll be doing when you do research for an informative report. Think back on the introduction to these two Trench Poets and to what the poems themselves suggest about the experience of World War I. Brainstorm for a few minutes, and jot down topics suggested by the poems that you might want to learn more about. It's possible that you might focus on details in the lives of the two young poets themselves. Save your notes for the Writer's Workshop on page 1053.

WORK IN PROGRESS

Critical Writing

2. Side-by-Side Poems

In an essay, compare and contrast the imagery, structure, and sound devices of "The Rear-Guard" and "Dulce et Decorum Est."

Critical Writing

3. It's Your Turn

In the last lines of his poem, Owen refers to an honorable death for one's country as "the old Lie." Do you agree that patriotism's high-minded idealism is a lie? Or is Owen perhaps stacking the deck by including so many gruesome battle details? Or do you think the poem presents a valid but insoluble conflict? In a brief essay, relate Owen's poem to your own concept of patriotism.

Critical Writing

4. Another View

In an essay, point out the similarities and differences between Owen's "Dulce et Decorum Est" and the poem below by Rupert Brooke. (Brooke served in World War I but did not experience trench warfare; he died of blood poisoning en route to Europe.) Consider how each poet uses at least three of these elements: imagery, theme and sentiments about war, tone, sound devices, and figurative language.

Interviewing/Researching

5. Through Other Eyes

Interview a veteran about his or her memories of war. Or read the memoirs or published letters of someone who experienced war firsthand (some libraries even have collections of wartime oral histories on tape or film). Then prepare a brief oral report in which you compare your research findings with the poems of the Trench Poets.

The Soldier

If I should die, think only this of me;
   That there's some corner of a foreign field
That is forever England. There shall be
   In that rich earth a richer dust concealed;
A dust whom England bore, shaped, made aware,
   Gave, once, her flowers to love, her ways to roam,
A body of England's breathing English air,
   Washed by the rivers, blest by suns of home.

And think, this heart, all evil shed away,
   A pulse in the eternal mind, no less
   Gives somewhere back the thoughts by England given;
Her sights and sounds; dreams happy as her day;
   And laughter, learnt of friends; and gentleness,
   In hearts at peace, under an English heaven.

—Rupert Brooke (1887–1915)

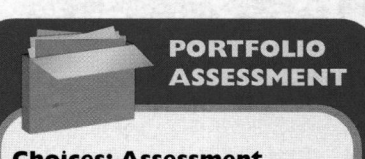

Beyond the Poems

Choices: Building Your Portfolio

1. **Writer's Notebook** Remind students to save their work. They may use it as prewriting for the Writer's Workshop on p. 1053.
2. **Critical Writing** Before students begin their comparisons, have them prepare a checklist of items they will study in each poem. Each student's checklist should include imagery; details of structure, such as rhyme scheme, meter, and form; and specific sound devices, such as onomatopoeia and dialogue.
3. **Critical Writing** Have students freewrite first on the topic of patriotism. Encourage students to think of images, stories, or other words that define patriotism for them. Then, students may compare their ideas of patriotism to Owen's.
4. **Critical Writing** Have students use a graphic organizer like the one below to keep track of literary elements in the poems. Students may complete the chart by comparing or contrasting the two poets.

	Imagery/theme	Tone	Sound devices	Figurative languages
Owen				
Brooke				
Comparison				

5. **Interviewing/Researching** *You may want to obtain permission from parents or guardians and from the parties students will contact before assigning this activity.*

STRATEGIES FOR INCLUSION

Auditory Pair students for activity #2; partners may take turns reading the poems aloud. The listening partner should take notes on the imagery, structure, and sound devices brought out by the reading. Students may compare their notes before writing their essays.

Visual Encourage students to visualize images of patriotism for activity #3. Students may sketch the images and then use the drawings to gauge their reactions to Owen's criticism.

Learners Having Difficulty For activity #4, have students transcribe the poems side by side on a single sheet of paper to more easily compare them. Direct students to make notes of their ideas and observations on these handwritten copies and then to organize their thoughts into an outline.

PORTFOLIO ASSESSMENT

Choices: Assessment Criteria For help in evaluating these Choices assignments, see the criteria in the *Portfolio Management System,* pp. 158–159.

A. Expansion
The libretto is the text or the words
of a musical work.

SPOTLIGHT ON

Twentieth-Century British Poetry

by John Malcolm Brinnin

B ritish poets in the early twentieth century were not experimenters. They did not make the daring adaptations that their American cousins were quick to try out. Instead, the main concern of British poets in the twentieth century has been to express themselves in very conventional forms— even when they are responding to the most violent of experiences.

The Trench Poets: Poetry and Pity

You will see this use of traditional forms in a group of poets who wrote about the first great war of our war-torn century: the Trench Poets. What these poets wrote was categorized as "war poetry." Yet the poets themselves hoped their works would stand as testaments beyond the usual reach of poetic art—and as warnings.

As Wilfred Owen wrote, "The Poetry is in the pity," meaning that the shame of war overwhelms every attempt to make sense of it, in verse or by any other means. Intimately acquainted with miseries and horrors inconceivable to civilians, the Trench Poets stripped war of its glory. They positioned themselves against the Romantic rhetoric of their immediate predecessor, Rupert Brooke (himself a casualty of the Great War), who put into rhyme the expected patriotic response.

In contrast, the Trench Poets dwelt on the degradation of body and soul caused by trench warfare, and the humiliation that the trenches represented. In their view, the war that began as an assertion of righteousness and a test of national will became an exercise in slaughter. To them, the war demeaned the very idea of civilization and turned history itself into a "no man's land"—the few hundred yards of dead terrain that divided German trenches from British trenches, a terrain that bore

all the features of Hell. Killed in action, or crippled, blinded, gassed, and shellshocked, the Trench Poets, dead and alive, spoke to and for the youth of generations to come.

The two poets among them who most clearly showed signs of genius were the young soldiers Wilfred Owen and Isaac Rosenberg. On April 1, 1918, Rosenberg was killed in action. Owen, whose poems later formed the libretto for Benjamin Britten's *War Requiem,* met the same fate six months later.

The English Group: A Political Agenda

One of the most exciting developments of the early 1930s was the emergence of four poets popularly known in America as "the English Group." The group consisted of the British writers W. H. Auden (page 1091) and Stephen Spender and the Irish-born writers Cecil Day-Lewis and Louis MacNeice. The audience for these poets was a generation that blamed the failure of capitalism for the devastation of World War I. This failure, they felt, was made even more apparent in the social unrest of the 1920s and in the economic collapse of 1929 that led to the Great Depression. The English Group's audience was also the generation that began to look toward socialism as an alternative to Great Britain's capitalist class system, and to the unequal distribution of wealth which perpetuated that system.

The most important concern in these poets' political thinking, however, was the rise of Fascism. Fascism was the dictatorial, militaristic system that swept Germany, Italy, and Spain—it would eventually unite the democracies of the world in opposition to it and lead to World War II.

Without quite being aware of the fact, poetry, like everything else, was becoming politicized:

932 THE TWENTIETH CENTURY

OPTIONS FOR TEACHING

STRATEGIES FOR INCLUSION

Linguistic Challenge students to think of reasons behind the name of each school of poetry. Ask students for their impressions of each school's name. How are the names accurate and useful? How could they be misleading?

Spatial Students may want to organize the information given in the article into a time line. Time lines should be marked by years and labeled with the names of schools and authors. Have students compare their finished efforts.

Logical-Mathematical Tell students that often the creation of a school comes as a reaction to another, preexisting school. Have students make a flowchart in which they trace the stances and reactions of the various movements in poetry in chronological order. Ask students to present their flowcharts to the class.

The qualities which distinguished us from the writers of the previous decade lay not in ourselves, but in the events to which we reacted. These were unemployment, economic crisis, . . . fascism, approaching war. . . . The older writers were reacting . . . to the exhaustion and hopelessness of a Europe in which the old regimes were falling to pieces. We were a "new generation," but it took me some time to appreciate the meaning of this phrase . . . that we had begun . . . in circumstances strikingly different from those of our immediate predecessors and that a consciousness of this was shown in our writing. . . . We were the 1930s.

—Stephen Spender, *from World Within World*

Already entrenched in Italy and Germany, Fascism threatened to spread to Spain when General Francisco Franco overthrew the elected Spanish Republican government in 1936. Franco's move was supported by Benito Mussolini, dictator of Italy, and Adolf Hitler. More than any other event of the decade, the events in Spain unified the artists and intellectuals of a generation in support of Spanish democracy. The Spanish Civil War became *their* war. Some, unwilling to remain bystanders, enlisted as volunteers in the Republican Army and were counted among its casualties. As in World War I, some of the most brilliant poets of an era were silenced by the Spanish Civil War before they could fulfill their promise.

Dylan Thomas: A Return to Romanticism

When Auden, whose poetry surpassed that of others in the English Group, became an American citizen and established residence in New York City, it was the opinion of at least one critic that British poetry was "up the creek," but not "without a paddle." The paddle that he thought might rescue British poetry was Dylan Thomas (page 1032). This young man from Wales effectively ended one phase of poetic history and set the stage for another.

Never a part of any group, Thomas established his own poetic goals as a very young man. On the evidence of the remarkable notebooks he left behind, he pursued these goals throughout the brief course of his adult life. Yet, in the minds of critics

who are more comfortable with poetry when it comes as the product of a "school" or a movement than from an individual of genius, Thomas was associated with certain writers more or less his own age. As time would tell, these other writers were more gifted as theorists than as poets.

Ambitious and bold, they called themselves "the New Apocalypse." In their opinion, it was time to halt the tendency of British poets to be concerned with politics and psychology—a concern that had turned poetry into a form of intellectual debate. They wanted a return to poetry as incandescent language—the language of the great English Romantics. They wanted to render individual experience in sacramental imagery—such as that found in the Psalms and in the high rhetoric of the King James Bible, in the visionary world of William Blake, and in the compacted wordplay and religious wit of Gerard Manley Hopkins. The young poets also admired the dream imagery of the subconscious, which had been dredged up and used by the spectacular new painters who called themselves Surrealists.

These poets of the New Apocalypse believed that a new wave of Romanticism was about to break, bringing with it a heightening of verbal music and a delight in language for its own sake. They believed that this kind of poetry had been curbed by other kinds of poetry that emulated public speech and demanded clarity, logic, and a message. True to

Expansion of the Lyric (1913) by Leonardo Dudreville.
Richard Miller Collection, New York.

INTEGRATING THE LANGUAGE ARTS

Language and Style Point out to students that the author of the article makes good use of citations and examples to support the points he makes about twentieth-century poetry. Ask students to review the article and to extract four examples of the author's use of supporting facts and quotations. For example, in the first section, the quotation of Owen typifies the group of poets under discussion, and the facts about Owen's and

Rosenberg's deaths in action link the pity of their poetry to that of their lives. Have students compare their findings in class discussion.

Speaking and Listening Have students work in pairs to practice reading aloud Philip Larkin's poem "The Mower." Prompt them by asking for their impressions: Is the poem, as the author of the article maintains, "quiet, low-keyed," balanced

between "disgust and disdain" and between "heartbreak and despairing humor"? [Students will probably agree with the description. Ask them to support their opinions.] Have students practice reading the poem, using pitch, emphasis, and pace to convey their impressions of the poem. Ask volunteers to read their versions aloud.

A. Expansion

Eliot became a British citizen in 1927, after some of his most famous work was behind him. "The Love Song of J. Alfred Prufrock" had appeared in 1915 and *The Waste Land* in 1922. Eliot's major works concluded in 1943 with the completion of "Four Quartets."

the name they chose, they saw themselves as apocalyptic: They regarded poems not as arguments or conclusions but as revelations, not as commentaries upon experience but, literally, as re-creations of experience still in the process of becoming intelligible.

The poets of the New Apocalypse got their message across, but they did not have the talent to give it substance. As they faded from the scene, Dylan Thomas alone was left to carry on their ideas. His famous career brought a new dimension to British poetry, reminding readers that poetry could be both as sensually exciting as music and as philosophically profound as Greek tragedy.

The Contemporary Scene

But Dylan Thomas died at the age of thirty-nine, and British poetry again entered a conservative and technically unadventurous phase. Then, out of this fallow period, two exceptional poetic personalities arose. Each in his own way showed that individual talent can make a mark and still have nothing to do with groups or movements. Each poet also rejected the nineteenth-century belief that—like sermons or editorials—poetry should be morally uplifting, or, at least, addressed to public issues.

These two poets were Ted Hughes (page 964), who is now poet laureate of England, and Philip Larkin (1922–1985). Philip Larkin was the most widely admired poet in the generation succeeding that of Dylan Thomas. In their quiet, low-keyed way, his poems reflect all the great themes of contemporary experience. In his handling of these themes, Larkin keeps to an intimately human scale, in which the balance lies somewhere between disgust and disdain on the one hand, and heartbreak and despairing humor on the other.

The Mower

The mower stalled, twice; kneeling, I found
A hedgehog jammed up against the blades,
Killed. It had been in the long grass.

I had seen it before, and even fed it, once.
Now I had mauled its unobtrusive world
Unmendably. Burial was no help:

Next morning I got up and it did not.
The first day after a death, the new absence
Is always the same; we should be careful

Of each other, we should be kind
While there is still time.

—Philip Larkin

Today, British poetry is closer to its twentieth-century beginnings than it has been for many years. British poetry was never modern in the energetically experimental ways that produced the extraordinary succession of American poets that includes Ezra Pound, T. S. Eliot, Hart Crane, Wallace Stevens, William Carlos Williams, Elizabeth Bishop, Robert Lowell, and James Merrill. But now that the age of poetic schools, movements, and other kinds of labeled association seems to have run its course, certain older British poets who followed no program but their own have begun to shine more brightly than ever. Chief among these are Thomas Hardy and D. H. Lawrence. As it comes full circle, British poetry may have surrendered some of its vitality, but none of its character. The individual voice is still the one to listen for, and the measure of English poets today is still the degree to which they make our common language sound like their own.

Diurnal Rhythm (20th century) by Maurice Cockrill.

Richard Miller Collection, New York.

934

Check Test: Questions and Answers

1. Wilfred Owen and Isaac Rosenberg are grouped in what school of poetry? [The Trench Poets.]
2. Name two members of the English Group. [The group includes W. H. Auden, Stephen Spender, Cecil Day Lewis, and Louis MacNeice.]
3. Dylan Thomas's poetry marked a return to what movement in poetry? [The Romantic movement.]
4. Who is England's poet laureate? [Ted Hughes.]

Vietnam

WORLD LITERATURE

(Map) ©Rand McNally.

Nguyen Thi Vinh
(1924–   )

Nguyen Thi Vinh (noo'yin ti vin'), while never a soldier, drew on her own experience for "Thoughts of Hanoi." Born in North Vietnam, she fled south to Saigon, the capital of newly created South Vietnam, in the 1950s to escape Communist rule. She quickly gained acclaim as a fiction writer with *Two Sisters* (1953), beginning a distinguished and successful literary career.

Her work constantly probed the pain, loss, and dislocation of a civil war that transformed friends into foes. When the Communists gained control of all of Vietnam in 1975, Nguyen stayed, despite the danger that made millions in the South flee.

Finally, however, in 1983, she followed others in her family to Norway. Her exile seems particularly wrenching since Nguyen's ancestors, for centuries, were members of one of Vietnam's two ruling families.

NGUYEN THI VINH **935**

Technology Tip

TECHNOLOGY

After students have read "Thoughts of Hanoi," they can access Vietnam Veterans Memorials Around the World, a Web site with information on a large number of such memorials. The URL is **http://grunt.space.swri.edu /vietmems.htm**. *You may want to preview any Internet activity that you suggest to students. Because these resources are sometimes public forums, their content can be unpredictable.*

PROGRAM MANAGER

Selection Summary See **Teaching Notes,** *Teaching Resources B,* p. 111, for a summary of this selection.

Ask students, before they begin writing, to think of stories they have heard about the American Civil War. How were families and friends divided in that conflict? Also, have students consider how long the grudges and resentment between the Northern and Southern states lasted, and how much effort it took for the wounds to heal.

A. Language Note: Repetition

? What is the effect of the repetition in ll. 10 and 11 of the words "still I . . ."? [The repetition emphasizes the recurring nature of the two emotions and the length of time the speaker has endured away from home.]

B. Literary Element: Apostrophe

In l. 14, the speaker addresses the "brother" directly. Explain that addressing an absent person as if that person were present is a figure of speech known as apostrophe. Do you think the speaker is addressing an actual brother or someone else? Why is this term effective, regardless of the relationship? [Possible responses: The speaker may be addressing a real brother, but possibly he is addressing a childhood friend. The term shows how close these two people were; the allusion to a family tie emphasizes the extent of the damage done by the political division of the country.]

C. Language Note: Structure

? What does the structure in the lines describing the girls suggest? [The list of characteristics and actions suggests a busy confusion of activity; the lines are less formal, more light-hearted.]

BEFORE YOU READ
THOUGHTS OF HANOI

Background

If you've ever been caught up in a feud, or observed one from the sidelines, you know how senseless the consequences sometimes are. Often entire communities are divided—sometimes for generations—over a simple misunderstanding or a perceived slight.

Other feuds, of course, aren't trivial. They start over important and painful issues. And people can find themselves drawn into dangerous conflicts with those they love. In the poem you're about to read, that's the case. The "feud" is the devastating civil war between North and South Vietnam, which lasted from 1957 to 1975. The speaker, a Southern soldier who grew up in the North, is addressing his "brother." His longing for his old way of life and the people from his past is heartfelt. The stakes are the ultimate: life itself.

Quickwrite

READER'S LOG

Imagine that you are forced to become a soldier in a civil war. On the other side are people with whom you grew up. In your Reader's Log, jot down some notes about how you think this situation would make you feel.

Perfume River, Hue, Vietnam.

936

Thoughts of Hanoi

Nguyen Thi Vinh

translated by **Nguyen Ngoc Bich**

The night is deep and chill
as in early autumn. Pitchblack,
it thickens after each lightning flash.
I dream of Hanoi:
5 Co-ngu° Road
ten years of separation
the way back sliced by a frontier of hatred.
I want to bury the past
to burn the future
A 10 still I yearn
still I fear
those endless nights
waiting for dawn.

B Brother,
15 how is Hang Dao° now?
How is Ngoc Son° temple?
Do the trains still run
each day from Hanoi
to the neighboring towns?
20 To Bac-ninh,° Cam-giang,° Yen-bai,°
the small villages, islands
of brown thatch in a lush green sea?

The girls
bright eyes
25 ruddy cheeks
four-piece dresses
C raven-bill scarves°
sowing harvesting
spinning weaving
30 all year round,
the boys
ploughing
transplanting
in the fields
35 in their shops
running across
the meadow at evening
to fly kites
and sing alternating songs.°

5. Co-ngu (kō′noo′).

15. Hang Dao (häng′ dou′).
16. Ngoc Son (nŏk′ sŏn′).

20. Bac-ninh (bäk′nin′), **Cam-giang** (käm′gyäng′), **Yen-bai** (yen′bī′): towns near Hanoi.

27. raven-bill scarves: head scarves folded into straight-edged triangular forms, like the bill or beak of a raven.

39. alternating songs: songs sung in rounds, with participants beginning at staggered intervals.

CONNECTING WITH "THE CENTER CANNOT HOLD"

Ask students how ll. 6–7 echo the theme of the Yeats poem and the Collection? [Possible answers: "Ten years of separation" repeats the idea of things falling apart, the center not holding; the frontier of hatred reminds readers of anarchy and the "blood-dimmed tide." Students may say that the idea of brothers fighting against each other shows that something is seriously wrong with the culture.]

40 Stainless blue sky,
    jubilant voices of children
  stumbling through the alphabet,
    village graybeards strolling to the temple,
  grandmothers basking in twilight sun,
45   chewing betel leaves°
  while the children run—

  Brother,
  how is all that now?
  Or is it obsolete?
50 Are you like me,
  reliving the past,
  imagining the future?
  Do you count me as a friend
  or am I the enemy in your eyes?
55 Brother, I am afraid
  that one day I'll be with the March-North Army°
  meeting you on your way to the South.
  I might be the one to shoot you then
  or you me
60 but please
  not with hatred.

  For don't you remember how it was,
  you and I in school together,
  plotting our lives together?
65 Those roots go deep!

  Brother, we are men,
  conscious of more
  than material needs.
  How can this happen to us
70 my friend
  my foe?

45. betel (bēt′'l) **leaves:** leaves of the betel pepper. These and the nuts of the betel palm are mild stimulants, often chewed like chewing gum in Southeast Asia.

56. March-North Army: that is, the South Vietnamese army marching into North Vietnam.

FINDING COMMON GROUND

Besides anguish at the irrationality of civil war, this poem also expresses a great homesickness and yearning. The speaker's memory is startlingly sharp, producing scenes that are like vivid snapshots. Isn't that one of the hardest parts of an unresolved conflict: looking back on experiences, sights, and sounds you may never recapture?

Explore your responses to this kind of loss in one or both of these ways:

• Write a personal "Thoughts of X," a short poem or description about a time or place that you miss. In your "snapshots," don't forget sounds, smells, and sensations—in addition to sights—that have stayed with you.

• Working with others, write the dialogue that might occur between the two "brothers" in "Thoughts of Hanoi" if they met during or after the war. Draw on the poem's details as well as on what you yourself might say and feel in such a situation. (Refer to the notes you recorded in your Reader's Log.)

NGUYEN THI VINH **937**

A. Expansion

Other influential American expatriate writers included Ezra Pound, Ernest Hemingway, F. Scott Fitzgerald, Archibald MacLeish, Sinclair Lewis, and Gertrude Stein. Stein coined the phrase "lost generation" to describe these exiles.

B. Exploring the Historical Period

On what would have been T. S. Eliot's ninety-eighth birthday, a plaque was placed outside the London apartment where the poet lived from 1957 until his death in 1965. The British poet laureate Ted Hughes unveiled the plaque and gave a speech. Hughes praised Eliot as the poet regularly regarded by even other great poets as "*the* poet of our times." "Eliot was the prophet of a new world," Hughes said. "It is the world which has already, in its soul, and throughout all its peoples, suffered the global holocaust, and must now, somehow, find in its own ashes the spiritual strength to resurrect itself. And it was Eliot's humility to know, with what seemed like knowledge inborn, that nothing matters now but to search for this strength, and to find it." Eliot's genius, Hughes pointed out, lies in his "attempts to deal with his sense of inner devastation" and the way his search broadened to encompass the "general spiritual catastrophe" around him, so that his poetry speaks not only to "Western man, [but] perhaps, even, simply spiritual man."

T. S. Eliot: The Voice of an Age

by **John Malcolm Brinnin**

Unlike poets whose long, outstanding careers eventually turn them into cultural monuments, T. S. Eliot was a monument who later became known as a man. Internationally famous at an early age, he was the product of an aristocratic New England family. The Eliots valued privacy and regarded self-exploitation and public exposure—even fame itself—as a form of vulgarity. Consequently, millions of readers knew T. S. Eliot less as a real personality than as a presence. Eliot was remote, austere, and self-possessed, a man whose sparse output was nevertheless the most celebrated and influential poetry written in English over a span of three decades.

T. S. Eliot was born in 1888 in St. Louis, Missouri, where his grandfather had established Washington University. In spite of this geographical displacement, the Eliots remained New Englanders. They could trace their ancestry back to the first Puritan settlements in North America. Young Tom Eliot was educated at Harvard College, after which he did graduate studies at the Sorbonne in Paris. Like many other young American writers of his generation, he found life abroad so stimulating that he decided not to return home. Settling in London before World War I, he worked in a bank, married an Englishwoman, and became an editor and a publisher. He made his expatriation complete by becoming a British citizen in 1927. In 1948, he was awarded the Nobel Prize. Not long before his death in 1965, on one of his several visits to the United States, so many people wanted to see and hear Eliot read his poetry that a football stadium had to be taken over to hold the audience.

Eliot had a vast influence as a poet. His techniques, along with those of his friend and fellow American, Ezra Pound, became the hallmarks of modern poetry. For over thirty years, in classrooms and in critical studies, his was *the* voice that expressed the dislocation and despair of the twentieth century. Eliot's world-weariness, his grave, restrained, and impersonal cadences, so much like the voices he heard in New England pulpits, were widely imitated and instantly recognized. Eliot dominated English literature in a way not seen since the days of Dr. Johnson.

Eliot's critical studies were also far-reaching. He argued against the commonly held view that

T. S. Eliot (1907) during his first year at Harvard, age 19.

By permission of the Houghton Library, Harvard University, Cambridge, Massachusetts.

OPTIONS FOR TEACHING

STRATEGIES FOR INCLUSION

Advanced Ask students to comment on the allusions they recognize in the poem "The Hollow Men" (p. 942). Encourage the class to make a chart showing how the borrowed lines or forms add layers of meaning to the poem.

Visual Have students illustrate scenes from one of Eliot's poems. Students may compile their drawings to make a visual map of the poem. Ask students to comment on how the visual map

version of the poem compares with their own individual understanding of the work.

Logical-Mathematical Challenge students to think of how the symbolism and allusions in "The Hollow Men" (p. 942) fit the theme. Have students do this by first writing the theme of the poem at the top of a sheet of paper. Then, they may list supporting details. Ask students what kind of argument the poem makes.

poets were romantics who had superior powers of observation and expression. Eliot regarded poets as craftspeople who used traditional literary materials not for personal revelations but for the creation of better-made poems. The poet, according to these theories, was like those anonymous master artisans who made individual contributions to the great medieval cathedrals but who remained personally unknown. Like these humble artisans, the poet is just part of the background. What is important is the poem (or the cathedral), not the worker who made it. This point of view deplored the notion that a search through the poet's life would give clues to the meaning of the work. The work, all important, stood apart from its creator. Submitting to Eliot's instruction, poets, students, and critics for generations studied a poem not for its messages or meaning, but for its method and structure—for its architecture.

In 1950, when I was director of New York's Poetry Center, Eliot made a visit to the United States. I recalled the event in a book called *Sextet:*

"This late in his life (he was sixty-one) Eliot had given less than a handful of readings in the United States and had read only once before in New York. The response to our announcement of the event suggested that many people thought his reading at the Poetry Center might well be his last. On the morning after we had named his date in *The New York Times,* fifteen or twenty requests were made for every seat available. Pursued and badgered to use my influence to produce tickets, I found that people who'd never read a sonnet since the seventh grade were suddenly lovers of poetry whose devotion I was implored not to dismiss."

A Vision of the Street

In music, *preludes* are brief works, usually free in form, that introduce larger and more formal compositions. When Eliot chose a musical title, he no doubt meant to suggest that these short poems introduced the mood and method of longer works written in the same period.

The images in "Preludes" are all drawn from city life. Horse-drawn carriages had not yet been replaced by automobiles, nor gas lamps by electricity, but nevertheless the dehumanizing aspects of a growing metropolis like Eliot's Boston were already sadly in evidence. Eliot saw multitudes of workers

every day moving to and fro like debris washed in and out by the tides. He saw massive slums that blocked out forever the gentle rural landscapes of a preindustrial age.

"Preludes" are the observations of a wanderer through city streets. The speaker attempts to come to some conclusion about the meaning of the life around him, yet he finally gives up. Still, in the process, he gives us "a vision of the street," a scene for which he feels compassion but which, finally, he considers beyond redemption. Eliot wrote these poems when he was in his twenties. How many images suggest life as a wasteland? How do these descriptions of city life relate to urban landscapes today? (Note: In line 2, "steaks" refers to cheap cuts of meat.)

Preludes

T. S. Eliot

I

The winter evening settles down
With smell of steaks in passageways.
Six o'clock.
The burnt-out ends of smoky days. **D**
5 And now a gusty shower wraps
The grimy scraps
Of withered leaves about your feet
And newspapers from vacant lots;
The showers beat
10 On broken blinds and chimney-pots,
And at the corner of the street
A lonely cab-horse steams and stamps.
And then the lighting of the lamps.

II

The morning comes to consciousness
15 Of faint stale smells of beer
From the sawdust-trampled street
With all its muddy feet that press
To early coffee-stands.
With the other masquerades
20 That time resumes,
One thinks of all the hands
That are raising dingy shades
In a thousand furnished rooms.

A. Language Note: Connotation

Sordid is just one of the poem's many adjectives with negative connotations. Have students identify other such adjectives from earlier in the poem. [Almost all the adjectives have negative connotations. Students may note in particular ll. 4, 6, 16, or 22.]

B. Reader's Response: Shaping Interpretations

? Who do these details suggest the *you* might be? [Sample responses: A woman who has disappointed the speaker or who is disappointed in herself. Or perhaps it refers to the reader, anyone who might have shared these feelings.]

C. Critical Reading: Comparing and Contrasting

? How is the final stanza related to the four lines that precede it? [The preceding lines express a hope for humanity—a hope that the final stanza refutes.]

III

You tossed a blanket from the bed,
25 You lay upon your back, and waited;
    You dozed, and watched the night revealing
 A The thousand sordid images
    Of which your soul was constituted;
    They flickered against the ceiling.
30 And when all the world came back
    And the light crept up between the shutters
    And you heard the sparrows in the gutters,
    You had such a vision of the street
 B As the street hardly understands;
35 Sitting along the bed's edge, where
    You curled the papers from your hair,
    Or clasped the yellow soles of feet
    In the palms of both soiled hands.

IV

His soul stretched tight across the skies
40 That fade behind a city block,
    Or trampled by insistent feet
    At four and five and six o'clock;
    And short square fingers stuffing pipes,
    And evening newspapers, and eyes
45 Assured of certain certainties,
    The conscience of a blackened street
    Impatient to assume the world.

    I am moved by fancies that are curled
    Around these images, and cling:
50 The notion of some infinitely gentle
    Infinitely suffering thing.

 C   Wipe your hand across your mouth, and laugh;
    The worlds revolve like ancient women
    Gathering fuel in vacant lots.

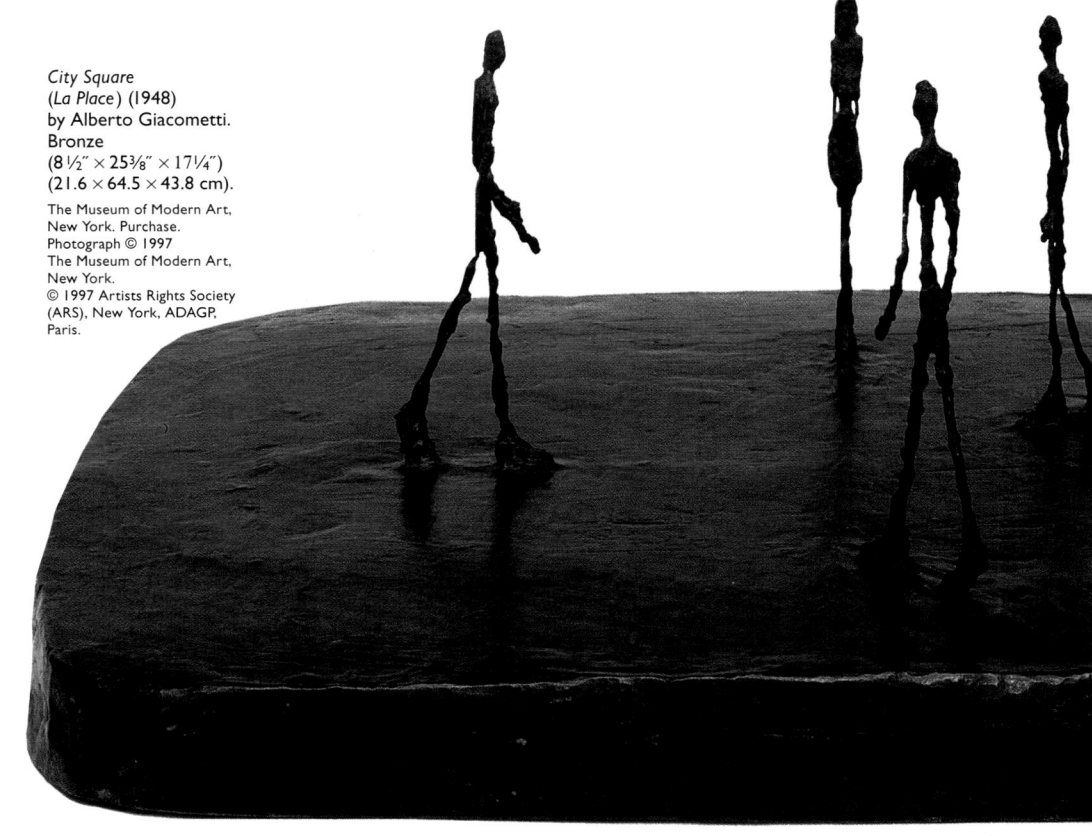

City Square
(*La Place*) (1948)
by Alberto Giacometti.
Bronze
(8½″ × 25⅜″ × 17¼″)
(21.6 × 64.5 × 43.8 cm).

The Museum of Modern Art, New York. Purchase. Photograph © 1997 The Museum of Modern Art, New York. © 1997 Artists Rights Society (ARS), New York, ADAGP, Paris.

OPTIONS FOR TEACHING

INTEGRATING THE LANGUAGE ARTS

Strategic Reading Before students read the feature on T. S. Eliot, ask them to make a list of things they know about T. S. Eliot and the poet's historic period. Students may write their lists in the left column of a sheet of paper divided into three columns. Direct students to list in the middle column things they would want to know about an important, influential poet from this time period and also what they would want or expect from the poet's work. After students read the feature and the poems, they may return to their graphic organizers and fill in the third column with the answers to their questions and the elements that surprised them.

Listening For students' first experience of the poem, read "Preludes" aloud to the class. After the reading, ask students to respond to the poem. What ideas did they find interesting? How would they characterize the poem? After each student has shared his or her thoughts, ask students to read the poem to themselves.

A Lament for the Weary

There are many references to religion in Eliot's poem "The Hollow Men," which follows. You may, for instance, recognize a line from the Lord's Prayer on sight (see lines 77 and 91–94). But Eliot's main concern here is not to affirm his Christianity, but to give us a picture of a world of godless despair, a world without religion or the promise of salvation.

Taken from Joseph Conrad's famous story *Heart of Darkness,* the first line after the title is significant in two ways. First, it calls attention to the story of a man named Kurtz, who journeys to the center of Africa and falls into degradation. Kurtz is redeemed by self-awareness, only to find that this painful knowledge is not liberating but useless. Second, the line strikes the note of futility heard throughout the poem.

The next line—"A penny for the Old Guy"— refers to one of the most notorious incidents in British history, the Gunpowder Plot. On November 5, 1605, a band of conspirators made plans to kill King James I by planting barrels of gunpowder in the underground vaults of Parliament. The man chosen to light the fuse that would result in a fatal explosion was a soldier named Guy Fawkes. But before the plot could be carried out, the conspirators were discovered. Guy Fawkes was arrested and, in the cruel custom of the day, first hanged, then drawn and quartered.

To commemorate this grisly event, every year on November 5, huge bonfires are set all over England. When these fires are lit, straw-filled effigies of Fawkes—the "stuffed men" of the poem—that look like scarecrows go up in flames, lighting up the skies. Children join in the fun by becoming beggars who ask passersby to give them "a penny for the guy."

The last four lines of this poem are among the most famous in modern poetry. What is the difference between ending with a "bang" and ending with only a "whimper"?

Writing: Character Sketch Have students write a character sketch of the speaker in one of Eliot's poems. Students should imagine the speaker in as much detail as possible. How old is he? What kind of house does he live in? What job does he have? Allow students to imagine their speaker as someone living today, someone perhaps their grandparents' age. Read aloud in class as many of these sketches as possible. *Remind students to choose a situation they would not mind sharing with others.*

Technology Tip For further discussion of T. S. Eliot's poetry, students can access the Eliot page on the World Wide Web. The URL is **http:/www.next.com/~bong/eliot/index .html**. *You may want to preview any Internet activity that you suggest to students. Because these resources are sometimes public forums, their content can be unpredictable.*

A. Language Note: Diction

Read this stanza aloud two or three times in succession, emphasizing in your reading both the repetition of the word *dry* and the use of sibilants (speech sounds that mimic hissing). Point out the use of alliteration and repetition and their effectiveness in communicating the stanza's main image of speakers whose voices and lives are empty and meaningless.

B. Critical Reading: Analyzing Speaker

? Who is the speaker in this poem? [Possible answers: People of the modern age or Eliot's contemporaries, aware of the emptiness of their lives.]

C. Language Note: Pronoun

? What is the effect of the change in Part II from the plural pronoun to the singular one? [It makes the poem more personal, singles out *one* of the subjects with whom readers can identify.]

D. Reader's Response: Shaping Interpretations

? To what do you think the speaker wants to be no closer? What is he avoiding with his disguises? [Sample responses: The final judgment of death; in the previous stanza, perhaps the eyes represent things he doesn't want to see about his life.]

RESPONDING TO THE ART: ABOUT THE ARTIST

Painter Maksim Kantor's social criticism rejects the art style called Socialist Realism, which emphasizes the benefits of Soviet socialism. Because of his perspective, Kantor has been accused of *mrak dushi*, having a gloomy soul. The subjects of Kantor's paintings are often victims of political oppression, for example, inmates in a Soviet concentration camp. One critic observes a recurring type in Kantor's "scenes of suffering and cruelty: large-eared, shaven-headed, vulnerable, ugly."

The Hollow Men

T. S. Eliot

Mistah Kurtz—he dead.

A penny for the Old Guy

I

We are the hollow men
We are the stuffed men
Leaning together
Headpiece filled with straw. Alas!
5 Our dried voices, when
We whisper together
Are quiet and meaningless
As wind in dry grass
Or rats' feet over broken glass
10 In our dry cellar.

Shape without form, shade without color,
Paralyzed force, gesture without motion;

Those who have crossed
With direct eyes, to death's other Kingdom°
15 Remember us—if at all—not as lost
Violent souls, but only
As the hollow men
The stuffed men.

II

Eyes I dare not meet in dreams
20 In death's dream kingdom
These do not appear:
There, the eyes are
Sunlight on a broken column
There, is a tree swinging
25 And voices are
In the wind's singing
More distant and more solemn
Than a fading star.

13–14. Those . . . Kingdom: Those with "direct eyes" have crossed from the hollow men's haunts into Paradise. The allusion is to Dante's *Paradiso*.

Let me be no nearer
30 In death's dream kingdom
Let me also wear
Such deliberate disguises
Rat's coat, crowskin, crossed staves°
In a field
35 Behaving as the wind behaves
No nearer—

Not that final meeting
In the twilight kingdom

33. staves: rods or staffs; "crossed staves / in a field" form a scarecrow.

People in Desolation (1987) by Maksim Kantor.
Galerie Nannen, Emden, Germany.

942 THE TWENTIETH CENTURY

CLASSROOM MANAGEMENT

Organizing Choral Reading Tell students to try for a stereo effect by having them read from different parts of the room. A class of thirty students could be separated into fifteen pairs, placed as far away from each other as classroom space allows. Each pair could read one of the fifteen stanzas in "The Hollow Men."

CROSSING THE CURRICULUM

Fine Arts Bring to class pictures that reflect the harsh landscape of Eliot's poems. Post these pictures on the bulletin board at the beginning of the discussion, and ask students to add to the collection for a week. Keep this collection visible and point to it occasionally when an image in the poetry corresponds to one of the photographs students have brought.

III

This is the dead land
40 This is cactus land
Here the stone images
Are raised, here they receive
The supplication of a dead man's hand
Under the twinkle of a fading star.

45   Is it like this
In death's other kingdom
Waking alone
At the hour when we are
Trembling with tenderness
50 Lips that would kiss
Form prayers to broken stone.

IV

The eyes are not here
There are no eyes here
In this valley of dying stars
55 In this hollow valley
This broken jaw of our lost kingdoms

    In this last of meeting places
We grope together
And avoid speech
60 Gathered on this beach of the tumid river°

    Sightless, unless
The eyes reappear
As the perpetual star
Multifoliate rose°
65 Of death's twilight kingdom
The hope only
Of empty men.

V

Here we go round the prickly pear°
Prickly pear prickly pear
70 Here we go round the prickly pear
At five o'clock in the morning.

    Between the idea
And the reality
Between the motion
75 And the act°
Falls the Shadow

                    For Thine is the Kingdom°

    Between the conception
And the creation
80 Between the emotion
And the response
Falls the Shadow

                     Life is very long

    Between the desire
85 And the spasm
Between the potency
And the existence
Between the essence
And the descent
90 Falls the Shadow

                     For Thine is the Kingdom

    For Thine is
Life is
For Thine is the

95   *This is the way the world ends*
This is the way the world ends
This is the way the world ends
Not with a bang but a whimper.

---

60. tumid river: Hell's swollen river, the Acheron (ak′ər·än′), in Dante's *Inferno.* The damned must cross this river to enter the land of the dead.
64. multifoliate rose: Dante describes Paradise as a rose of many leaves (*Paradiso,* Canto 32).

68. prickly pear: cactus.
74–75. Between . . . act: a reference to Shakespeare's *Julius Caesar:* "Between the acting of a dreadful thing / And the first motion, all the interim is / Like a phantasma or a hideous dream" (II. 1. 63–65).
77. For . . . Kingdom: closing lines of the Lord's Prayer: "For thine is the kingdom, and the power, and the glory, forever and ever."

E. Critical Reading: Finding Details

? What specific images does Eliot use to describe the landscape?
[The images of a dead land with statues worshipped by a corpse in the light of one fading star.]

F. Literary Element: Allusion

Eliot alludes to Dante in his reference to the river that mortals cross to enter the land of the dead.

G. Literary Element: Allusion

? What are the words of the nursery rhyme that Eliot adapted? What does his revision suggest?
[Possible answers: "Here we go round the mulberry bush"; readers would associate the prickly pear with a harsh landscape like the scene Eliot depicts.]

H. Reader's Response: Connecting with the Text

? What purpose is served by quoting this fragment of the Lord's Prayer?
[Sample responses: It conveys the fragmented nature of the lives of the hollow men; it makes the prayer seem desperate.]

I. Language Note: Style

? What idea is conveyed by the choice of the word *whimper*? [It supports the theme that the hollow men's lives have no meaning or importance.]

For the past thirty-five years, Elie Wiesel has written about Nazi death camps, but he still fears that the effort may be beyond anyone's abilities. "You must speak," he recently told an interviewer, "but how can you, when the full story is beyond language?" Egil Aarvik, chairman of the Norwegian Nobel Committee, summed up Wiesel's writing as having crucial significance for the entire world: "Wiesel is a messenger to mankind. . . . His message is one of peace, atonement and human dignity. His belief that the forces fighting evil in the world can be victorious is a hard-won belief . . . repeated and deepened through the works of a great author."

Technology Tip

For more ideas, access Teaching the Holocaust Web page at **http://pages .prodigy.com/NC/bbvk86b/hcaust .html**. *You may want to preview any Internet activity that you suggest to students. Because these resources are sometimes public forums, their content can be unpredictable.*

WORLD LITERATURE

Romania

Elie Wiesel.

Elie Wiesel

(1928–   )

Elie Wiesel (el′ē- wi·zel′) boarded the cattle cars in 1944, along with fifteen thousand other arrested Jews from his remote Romanian town, Sighet. When his family disembarked at Auschwitz, he and his father were immediately separated from his mother and sisters. By April 1945, when Wiesel was liberated from another concentration camp at Buchenwald, Germany, where he and his father had been sent as slave laborers, both his parents and a sister were dead.

Wiesel could not write of the horror of the Holocaust for a decade after the experience because as he says, "I was afraid that words might betray it." But when he did, he became a lifelong witness against evil. He has written over thirty works of fiction, memory, journalism, drama, and religious studies; given hundreds of lectures; and headed important humanitarian commissions and councils. In 1986, he was awarded the Nobel Peace Prize for his work.

Educated at the Sorbonne in Paris, Wiesel began his career as a journalist in France and still writes mainly in French. He came to the United States in 1956 to cover the United Nations as a reporter, became a citizen in 1963, and is now a distinguished professor of humanities at Boston University.

(Map) ©Rand McNally.

Background

World War II forced modern people to face not only the atrocities of the battlefield, but also the evils of the human heart. In the Holocaust—which Elie Wiesel lived through as a teenager—the Nazis killed 6 million Jews. (In all, more than 11 million people were executed by the Nazis—Gypsies, homosexuals, political opponents, and captured Resistance fighters among them.)

This was an appalling evil: the systematic torture, starvation, and murder of other human beings—without even the pretense that they posed a physical threat, as on the battlefield. But it happened.

This section of Wiesel's memoir occurs en route to a concentration camp, with Romanian Jews crowded into the cattle car of a train. At this point, the passengers are ignorant of both their destination and their destiny. In fact, the focus here is on the victims' behavior, and Wiesel doesn't sanitize it.

You probably haven't had this experience (though some of your relatives may have), but it may suggest some situations that you can identify with. For example, what does *deep* fear feel like? How does it change you? Do you sometimes do things in a group that you wouldn't do if you were alone?

These questions hint at an awful dread the Holocaust won't let us evade: What horrors are all of us, as humans, capable of?

Quickwrite

Choose one of the questions posed above, and freewrite your thoughts.

READER'S LOG

from Night

Elie Wiesel

translated by Stella Rodway

The train stopped at Kaschau, a little town on the Czechoslovak frontier. We realized then that we were not going to stay in Hungary. Our eyes were opened, but too late.

The door of the car slid open. A German officer, accompanied by a Hungarian lieutenant-interpreter, came up and introduced himself.

"From this moment, you come under the authority of the German army. Those of you who still have gold, silver, or watches in your possession must give them up now. Anyone who is later found to have kept anything will be shot on the spot. Secondly, anyone who feels ill may go to the hospital car. That's all."

The Hungarian lieutenant went among us with a basket and collected the last possessions from those who no longer wished to taste the bitterness of terror.

"There are eighty of you in the wagon," added the German officer. "If anyone is missing, you'll all be shot, like dogs. . . ."

They disappeared. The doors were closed. We were caught in a trap, right up to our necks. The doors were nailed up; the way back was finally cut off. The world was a cattle wagon hermetically sealed.[1]

We had a woman with us named Madame Schächter.[2] She was about fifty; her ten-year-old son was with her, crouched in a corner. Her husband and two eldest sons had been deported with the first transport by mistake. The separation had completely broken her.

---

1. **hermetically sealed:** completely sealed off from any route of escape. Literally, this phrase means "airtight."
2. **Schächter** (shekh′tər).

ELIE WIESEL **945**

Background

Discuss with students what they know of the Holocaust from film, literature, and television shows. Also, talk with students about how the names of Nazi death camps have come to stand for indescribable horror. For example, ask students to free-associate words, given the name *Auschwitz*.

Quickwrite

Remind students to choose a situation they would not mind sharing with others. Direct students to provide examples that support their answers, no matter which question they choose. Encourage them to consider counterarguments or another person's perspective as they write.

A. Exploring the Historical Period

Point out the three countries mentioned here—Czechoslovakia, Hungary, and Germany. Use a map to quickly locate these countries, and tell the class that at this time Hitler was moving into the countries of Eastern Europe.

CONNECTING WITH "THE CENTER CANNOT HOLD"

Have students discuss how the essay shows that "the center cannot hold." [The story focuses on one of the most horrifying events of human brutality in the twentieth century—the Holocaust, an event that epitomized an extreme lack of balance in society.]

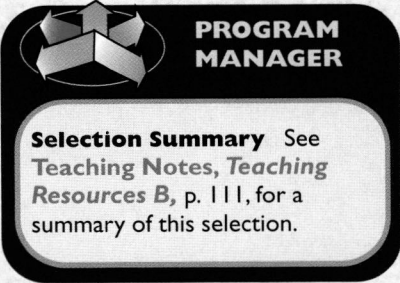

PROGRAM MANAGER

Selection Summary See Teaching Notes, *Teaching Resources B,* p. 111, for a summary of this selection.

A. Reader's Response: First Thoughts

? What does the description "tense, burning eyes" tell you about how the woman was before she came to be on the train? [Sample responses: The phrase suggests she is nervous; or she is different from the others.]

B. Critical Reading: Identifying Cause and Effect

? How does the screaming intensify the people's fear? [Possible answers: It makes them panic; it shocks them out of their sleep; it seems eerie and foreboding.] Point out that what happens to Madame Schächter is an example of the dehumanizing effects of war and violence. The intense, hardworking wife of a scholarly, religious husband, she has lost everything, has gone insane, and is reduced to moaning and screaming.

Arriving at Auschwitz from Hungary (spring 1944).

A I knew her well. A quiet woman with tense, burning eyes, she had often been to our house. Her husband, who was a pious man, spent his days and nights in study, and it was she who worked to support the family.

Madame Schächter had gone out of her mind. On the first day of the journey she had already begun to moan and to keep asking why she had been separated from her family. As time went on, her cries grew hysterical.

On the third night, while we slept, some of us sitting one against the other and some standing, a piercing cry split the silence:

"Fire! I can see a fire! I can see a fire!"

There was a moment's panic. Who was it who **B** had cried out? It was Madame Schächter. Standing in the middle of the wagon, in the pale light from the windows, she looked like a withered tree in a cornfield. She pointed her arm toward the window, screaming:

"Look! Look at it! Fire! A terrible fire! Mercy! *Oh, that fire!*"

Some of the men pressed up against the bars. There was nothing there; only the darkness.

The shock of this terrible awakening stayed with us for a long time. We still trembled from it. With every groan of the wheels on the rail, we felt that an abyss was about to open beneath our bodies. Powerless to still our own anguish, we tried to console ourselves:

"She's mad, poor soul. . . ."

Someone had put a damp cloth on her brow, to calm her, but still her screams went on:

"Fire! Fire!"

Her little boy was crying, hanging onto her skirt, trying to take hold of her hands. "It's all

946 THE TWENTIETH CENTURY

STRATEGIES FOR INCLUSION

Interpersonal As students discuss the given topics, make sure that everyone has a turn to express ideas. Ask students to make notes of others' points and to ask themselves if they agree or disagree with the person. Have students also note whether the person's comment sparks any associations or ideas for them.

Advanced Assign a small group of students to research and map the progress of the German army through Eastern Europe, with emphasis on Czechoslovakia and Hungary. Include some visual learners in the group, and have them draw a map, large enough to display in the classroom, which plots the army's progress and locates Auschwitz.

right, Mummy! There's nothing there. . . . Sit down. . . ." This shook me even more than his mother's screams had done.

Some women tried to calm her. "You'll find your husband and your sons again . . . in a few days. . . ."

She continued to scream, breathless, her voice broken by sobs, "Jews, listen to me! I can see a fire! There are huge flames! It is a furnace!"

It was as though she were possessed by an evil spirit which spoke from the depths of her being.

We tried to explain it away, more to calm ourselves and to recover our own breath than to comfort her. "She must be very thirsty, poor thing! That's why she keeps talking about a fire devouring her."

But it was in vain. Our terror was about to burst the sides of the train. Our nerves were at breaking point. Our flesh was creeping. It was as though madness were taking possession of us all. We could stand it no longer. Some of the young men forced her to sit down, tied her up, and put a gag in her mouth.

Silence again. The little boy sat down by his mother, crying. I had begun to breathe normally again. We could hear the wheels churning out that monotonous rhythm of a train traveling through the night. We could begin to doze, to rest, to dream. . . .

An hour or two went by like this. Then another scream took our breath away. The woman had broken loose from her bonds and was crying out more loudly than ever:

"Look at the fire! Flames, flames everywhere. . . ."

Once more the young men tied her up and gagged her. They even struck her. People encouraged them:

"Make her be quiet! She's mad! Shut her up! She's not the only one. She can keep her mouth shut. . . ."

They struck her several times on the head—blows that might have killed her. Her little boy clung to her; he did not cry out; he did not say a word. He was not even weeping now.

An endless night. Toward dawn, Madame Schächter calmed down. Crouched in her corner, her bewildered gaze scouring the emptiness, she could no longer see us.

She stayed like that all through the day, dumb, absent, isolated among us. As soon as night fell, she began to scream: "There's a fire over there!" She would point at a spot in space, always the same one. They were tired of hitting her. The heat, the thirst, the pestilential stench, the suffocating lack of air—these were as nothing compared with these screams which tore us to shreds. A few days more and we should all have started to scream too.

But we had reached a station. Those who were next to the windows told us its name:

"Auschwitz."

No one had ever heard that name.

The train did not start up again. The afternoon passed slowly. Then the wagon doors slid open. Two men were allowed to get down to fetch water.

When they came back, they told us that, in exchange for a gold watch, they had discovered that this was the last stop. We would be getting out here. There was a labor camp. Conditions were good. Families would not be split up. Only the young people would go to work in the factories. The old men and invalids would be kept occupied in the fields.

The barometer of confidence soared. Here was a sudden release from the terrors of the previous nights. We gave thanks to God.

Madame Schächter stayed in her corner, wilted, dumb, indifferent to the general confidence. Her little boy stroked her hand.

As dusk fell, darkness gathered inside the wagon. We started to eat our last provisions. At ten in the evening, everyone was looking for a convenient position in which to sleep for a while, and soon we were all asleep. Suddenly:

"The fire! The furnace! Look, over there! . . ."

Waking with a start, we rushed to the window. Yet again we had believed her, even if only for a moment. But there was nothing outside save the darkness of night. With shame in our souls, we went back to our places, gnawed by fear, in spite of ourselves. As she continued to scream, they began to hit her again, and it was with the greatest difficulty that they silenced her.

The man in charge of our wagon called a German officer who was walking about on the platform, and asked him if Madame Schächter could be taken to the hospital car.

"You must be patient," the German replied. "She'll be taken there soon."

ELIE WIESEL **947**

C. Reader's Response: Shaping Interpretations

? Why would the image of the boy calming his mother disturb the narrator more than the woman's screams? [Sample responses: The image is a role reversal, indicating the chaotic nature of the situation. The child is as lost and terror-stricken as his mother (symbolic of the plight of all the people in the car) but tries pathetically to comfort her.]

D. Critical Reading: Analyzing Dialogue

? Who is speaking these lines? [One of the prisoners; the line's anonymity suggests that the prisoners have offered many theories to explain the woman's screaming.]

E. Language Note: Structure

? What is the effect of the repeated infinitives in this sentence? [The repetition mirrors the people's exhaustion and the train's rhythm.]

F. Literary Element: Irony

? What is ironic about the way the young men in the train are treating Madame Schächter? [They are acting just like the violent German soldiers of whom they are so afraid; they have become like their oppressors.]

G. Reader's Response: Shaping Interpretations

? What has happened to the boy that he does not even cry anymore? [Sample responses: He is so shocked by the experience he cannot do or say anything; he is resigned, helpless.]

H. Literary Element: Diction

? What does the word *scouring* suggest about the woman's gaze? [Her searching eyes have an abrasive effect on anyone that may see her.]

I. Literary Element: Irony

? What is so ironic about this line? [The prisoners have not heard of Auschwitz and are hopeful this will be the stop that gets them off the train, but readers recognize the name of the infamous concentration camp.]

OPTIONS FOR TEACHING

INTEGRATING THE LANGUAGE ARTS

Strategic Reading Have students make predictions about Madame Schächter's vision and compare their predictions with the outcome of Wiesel's account. They may write their predictions in the first column of the chart that follows. After studying the selection, ask students to read their predictions and complete the second column. Encourage volunteers to read their entries to the class.

My Prediction	Actual Outcome

A. Language Note: Imagery

? What does the image of the fire in the black sky suggest to you?

[Students may say it is a picture of hell or that it signals disaster.]

Toward eleven o'clock, the train began to move. We pressed against the windows. The convoy was moving slowly. A quarter of an hour later, it slowed down again. Through the windows we could see barbed wire; we realized that this must be the camp.

We had forgotten the existence of Madame Schächter. Suddenly, we heard terrible screams:

"Jews, look! Look through the window! Flames! Look!"

 And as the train stopped, we saw this time that flames were gushing out of a tall chimney into the black sky.

Madame Schächter was silent herself. Once more she had become dumb, indifferent, absent, and had gone back to her corner.

1943 A.D. (c. 1943) by Ben Shahn.

Courtesy of the Syracuse University Art Collection, New York. © 1997 Estate of Ben Shahn / Licensed by VAGA, New York, New York.

CROSSING THE CURRICULUM

History   Arrange students in small groups, and have each group research a different aspect of the Holocaust. Encourage students to consult an encyclopedia for possible topics. Students in a group should collaborate to write a factual, objective treatment of the topic to present to the class. Group papers should be no longer than four or five pages. Possible topics include the Holocaust Museum, specific camps, or eyewitness accounts by survivors or liberating soldiers.

We looked at the flames in the darkness. There was an abominable odor floating in the air. Suddenly, our doors opened. Some odd-looking characters, dressed in striped shirts and black trousers, leapt into the wagon. They held electric torches[3] and truncheons.[4] They began to strike out to right and left, shouting:

"Everybody get out! Everyone out of the wagon! Quickly!"

We jumped out. I threw a last glance toward Madame Schächter. Her little boy was holding her hand. **B**

In front of us flames. In the air that smell of burning flesh. It must have been about midnight. We had arrived—at Birkenau, reception center for Auschwitz. **C**

3. **electric torches:** flashlights.
4. **truncheons** (trun'chənz): short sticks or clubs.

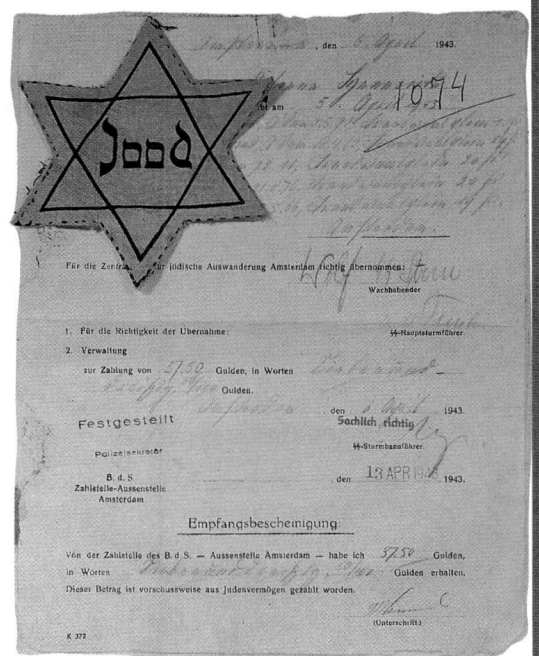

Jewish identification card from World War II with Star of David attached.
Private Collection.

FINDING COMMON GROUND

You may have seen movies like *The Hiding Place,* read Anne Frank's diary, or heard family memories of the concentration camps—or maybe this is the first time you've been taken *inside* the experience of the Holocaust. What thoughts and feelings did Wiesel's memoir trigger in you? What possible relevance can it have to your life now? Look back at your Reader's Log notes, and then gather with some classmates to discuss Wiesel's story. Here are some questions to spark discussion.

- You've no doubt seen disaster movies (about plane hijackings, shipwrecks, earthquakes) in which people are marooned together in life-threatening situations. What usually happens in such movies? Do you see a pattern? Are the depictions of disaster victims realistic?

- How would you define *evil*?
- Why are tales like Wiesel's—firsthand accounts of even the most shocking events of human history—so important to us? How do we use them in our own lives?
- When Wiesel accepted the Nobel Peace Prize in 1986, he said that if humanity ever forgets the Holocaust, "we are guilty, we are accomplices." What do you think Wiesel meant? Do you agree?
- After his experiences at Auschwitz and Buchen-wald, Wiesel vowed never to be silent in the face of human suffering. Who speaks out against human misery today, and what forms do such protests take?

? What is the last impression made on the reader by the image of the mother and son? [Possible answer: The detail is starkly terrifying and sad, as it seems inevitable that the two will be separated and probably die.]

C. Literary Element: Irony
We are told early in the story that Madame Schächter has lost her mind; point out the irony of the fact that this "crazy" woman is the only character who perceives the truth in their situation.

Finding Common Ground

Divide the class into four groups, and have each group focus on one of the topics. Direct each group to discuss its topic and to outline a panel discussion they can enact for the rest of the class. Each panel discussion should cover each question related to the topic, as well as provide illustrative examples that support the points. Encourage groups to anticipate criticisms that could be made of their points and to consider these in their discussions. Their talks may be led by one of the group members in the role of moderator, or the talks may be freeflowing, but emphasize that each student should play a part in his or her group's panel discussion. Set a time limit, such as ten minutes, on each presentation. Have the audience discuss the group's efforts afterward.

ASSESSMENT TOOLS

Check Test: Questions and Answers
1. What is the setting of the story? [A train car bound for a Nazi concentration camp.]
2. What does Madame Schächter see? [A fire.]
3. Who is with the woman? [Her ten-year-old boy.]
4. How do the people quiet the woman? [They bind and gag her and then strike her.]
5. With what imagery does the narrator end the excerpt? [With the sight of fire and the smell of burning flesh.]

Into the Story

Author Biography p. 950

Before You Read p. 951

- **Reading Focus: Scaffolding**
  Students read about the setting of the story.
- **A Dialogue with the Text**
  Analyze in Reader's Log the main character
- **Elements of Literature: Setting**

Through the Story

"The Destructors" pp. 951–962

Words to Own pp. 951–958

Literature and the Movies p. 960

Making Meanings pp. 962–963

Language and Style p. 963

Beyond the Story

Choices: Building Your Portfolio p. 963

- **Writer's Notebook:** Take notes on community vandalism
- **Critical Writing:** In an essay, analyze symbolic images
- **Creative Writing:** Write a personal letter from a character in the story
- **Critical Thinking/Role-Playing:** Stage a trial for the main character

Graham Greene
(1904–1991)

Graham Greene (1957).

For his serious idealistic novels dealing with contemporary moral dilemmas and for his light "entertainments" and thrillers, Graham Greene has won a rare combination of popular and critical admiration. His intention in his writing was always to tell the truth, which he saw as a primary duty of the artist, and, as you will see, Greene often wrote about life's losers—at least those whom we conventionally think of as losers.

Henry Graham Greene was born to a comfortable family in Berkhamsted, Hertfordshire. His father was the headmaster of Berkhamsted School, which Greene attended as a child. For reasons that are not clear, as Greene grew into adolescence, he became increasingly depressed and unhappy at school, which he described as his first impression of hell. After he tried to run away, he was sent to London to undergo psychoanalysis. He would later recall those six months in London as among the happiest of his life.

While he was still at Berkhamsted, Greene had a story published by a local newspaper, and he recalled feeling a sense of true literary triumph "for the first and last time." The experience convinced him to become a professional writer. He attended Oxford University, wrote a novel that failed to find a publisher, and published a book of poems in 1925, the year he graduated. As an apprenticeship, he went to work as a reporter for the Nottingham *Journal*.

In 1926, Greene became engaged to a Roman Catholic woman, Vivien Dayrell-Browning, and agreed to take instruction in her faith. Although he had been a confirmed atheist, he became convinced of "the probable existence of something we call God." His Catholic faith would turn out to be an important factor in his writing.

Greene took a job with the London *Times* and worked there until his first novel, *The Man Within,* was published in 1929. His next books were adventure stories, but they received little attention. Greene began to come into his own with the thriller *Stamboul Train* (1932; also published under the title *Orient Express*). This story of a train journey to Istanbul was the first of Greene's works that were made into movies.

Greene brought his religious concerns into his fiction with the novel *Brighton Rock* (1938), in which he explored the nature of good and evil and the inexplicable workings of divine grace. Pursuing the theme further in *The Power and the Glory* (1940), Greene revealed an unorthodox kind of Catholicism in which naturally sinful men and women, living in a fallen world, are often given a last-minute chance at redemption. As one critic notes, Greene's characters live "on the border between love and hate, good and evil, heaven and hell."

During World War II, Greene worked for the British Foreign Office, and afterward he became a director for a publishing house. During the 1950s, he was a celebrated foreign correspondent assigned to Malaysia, Indochina, Africa, and Cuba. His experiences as a journalist were reflected in novels such as *The Quiet American* (1955), which prophetically dealt with the implications of American involvement in Vietnam.

Greene's novels came out steadily, among them *The Heart of the Matter* (1948), *The End of the Affair* (1951), and *A Burnt-Out Case* (1961). Many of his books have been made into films, including *The Third Man* (1950) and *Our Man in Havana* (1958). He also published several plays, as well as a number of travel books describing his journeys.

In the first volume of his autobiography, *A Sort of Life* (1971), Greene revealed his motives for writing fiction as "a desire to reduce the chaos of experience to some sort of order, and a hungry curiosity. We cannot love others, so the theologians teach, unless in some degree we can love ourselves, and curiosity too begins at home."

PROGRAM MANAGER

- **Planning Instruction** See Teaching Notes, *Teaching Resources B,* pp. 111–112, for objectives, a summary, and literary elements for this selection.
- **Instructional Support** Before beginning the instructional lesson, see Graphic Organizer for Active Reading, *Teaching Resources B,* p. 119, for

a Through the Story activity.
- **Assessment** See Selection Test, *Test Booklet,* pp. 203–204.
- **Language Link** For instruction and practice in end punctuation, see Language Link, *Teaching Resources B,* pp. 120–121, and *Language and Writing Skills Worksheets,* p. 129.

- **Reinforcement** Use the Words to Own worksheet in *Teaching Resources B,* p. 122.
- **Application and Reinforcement** For reinforcement of the elements of literature introduced in this lesson, see Transparency 12.2 in the *Audiovisual Resources Binder.*

Reading Focus

Man the Destroyer

This story is set in 1954, about nine years after the end of World War II. During the war, the city of London had been regularly "blitzed" by German planes dropping firebombs, which destroyed many buildings in the city. Years after the war, the people of London still walked along bomb-blasted streets. More troubling than this physical destruction, though, was what many people saw as the moral destruction of society, the collapse of goodness and hope,

especially among gangs of young people. Before you read, think about your own knowledge of or experience with vandalism. What motivates some people to want to destroy beautiful things?

A Dialogue with the Text

Each section of this story gives you a bit more insight into the enigmatic main character, T. After each section, jot down how you see him, and note details of his words and actions that you find revealing. What do you think motivates him to commit the acts he does?

Elements of Literature

Setting

At one point in this story, the word *beautiful* appears several times. As readers, we are struck by the word's incongruity. We recognize, as do certain characters in the story, that the word somehow doesn't belong here. Until this scene and in all the scenes that follow, we are immersed in the seediness of Greene's **setting**. Greene's characteristic use of coarse imagery and language has created a world full of drabness and shabby violence.

The Destructors

Graham Greene

1

It was on the eve of August Bank Holiday that the latest recruit became the leader of the Wormsley Common gang. No one was surprised except Mike, but Mike at the age of nine was surprised by everything. "If you don't shut your mouth," somebody once said to him, "you'll get a frog down it." After that Mike had kept his teeth tightly clamped except when the surprise was too great.

The new recruit had been with the gang since the beginning of the summer holidays, and there were possibilities about his brooding silence that all recognized. He never wasted a word even to tell his name until that was required of him by the rules. When he said "Trevor" it was a statement of fact, not as it would have been with the others a statement of shame or defiance. Nor did anyone laugh except Mike, who finding himself without

support and meeting the dark gaze of the newcomer opened his mouth and was quiet again. There was every reason why T., as he was afterward referred to, should have been an object of mockery—there was his name (and they substituted the initial because otherwise they had no excuse not to laugh at it), the fact that his father, a former architect and present clerk, had "come down in the world" and that his mother considered herself better than the neighbors. What but an odd quality of danger, of the unpredictable, established him in the gang without any <u>ignoble</u> ceremony of initiation?

WORDS TO OWN

ignoble (ig·nō′bəl) *adj.:* shameful; degrading.

GRAHAM GREENE 951

PORTFOLIO ASSESSMENT

Portfolio Assessment For help with self-assessment of reading skills, see the *Portfolio Management System,* p. 43.

Into the Story

Using **BEFORE YOU READ** p. 951

Reading Focus

Remind students to choose a situation they would not mind sharing with others. Ask students for examples of destructive behavior, such as writing graffiti and creating pollution, and write their suggestions on the chalkboard. Prompt discussion with the following questions: Is there a common motivation? If so, what is it and how should it be handled?

Through the Story

A. Reader's Response: First Thoughts

? What are your first impressions of the Wormsley Common gang? [Sample responses: The gang members are young boys (Mike is nine); they talk tough like kids, threatening Mike that they will put a frog in his mouth.]

B. Critical Reading: Analyzing Character

? What about Trevor impresses the gang? [Possible answer: Trevor, the new recruit, seems quieter, slightly mysterious—uncommon qualities in their adolescent group.]

C. Literary Element: Irony

? In contrast to T.'s impressive demeanor, what elements of his background and person might invite ridicule from the other boys? [His family, which has "come down in the world"; his mother, who gives herself airs; and his rather upper-class name.]

A. Literary Element: Setting
Point out that the Blitz took place in 1940–1941 and, assuming that Blackie is around fourteen or fifteen, the story is probably set in 1954 or 1955. Help students visualize the setting more clearly by displaying a photograph of a London neighborhood after the Blitz. Ask students to consider ways in which this setting affects the story.

B. Literary Element: Character
? What does T.'s comment about the architect Christopher Wren suggest about his character and, in this exchange with Blackie, what do we see as another difference between T. and the gang? [T.'s knowledge of the famous architect and his appreciation of the house suggest that he is better educated and more sensitive than the other boys.]

C. Critical Reading: Speculating
? What in the description of Old Misery connects him to Trevor?
[Possible answer: Old Misery, like Trevor's father, was a builder and has now fallen on hard times.]

Juvenile Counsel: Boys on a Doorstep (20th century) by Henry Lamb.

Private Collection.

The gang met every morning in an impromptu car-park, the site of the last bomb of the first blitz. The leader, who was known as Blackie, claimed to have heard it fall, and no one was precise enough in his dates to point out that he would have been one year old and fast asleep on the down platform of Wormsley Common Underground Station. On one side of the car-park leaned the first occupied house, number 3, of the shattered Northwood Terrace—literally leaned, for it had suffered from the blast of the bomb and the side walls were supported on wooden struts. A smaller bomb and some incendiaries had fallen beyond, so that the house stuck up like a jagged tooth and carried on the further wall relics of its neighbor, a dado,[1] the remains of a fireplace. T., whose words were almost confined to voting "Yes" or "No" to the plan of operations proposed each day by Blackie, once startled the whole gang by saying broodingly, "Wren[2] built that house, father says."

"Who's Wren?"

"The man who built St. Paul's."[3]

"Who cares?" Blackie said. "It's only Old Misery's."

Old Misery—whose real name was Thomas—had once been a builder and decorator. He lived alone in the crippled house, doing for himself: Once a week you could see him coming back across the common with bread and vegetables, and once as the boys played in the car-park he put his head over the smashed wall of his garden and looked at them.

---

1. **dado** (dā′dō): wood paneling along the lower part of the walls of a room.

2. **Wren:** Sir Christopher Wren (1632–1723), a celebrated English architect.
3. **St. Paul's:** cathedral in London.

WORDS TO OWN
impromptu (im·prämp′tōō′) *adj.*: unplanned.

952 **THE TWENTIETH CENTURY**

OPTIONS FOR TEACHING

STRATEGIES FOR INCLUSION

Less Proficient Readers Divide the class into small reading groups to read aloud the first numbered section of the story; all students should read at least once. The groups should discuss what they have read, summarize the action in this section, and try to predict what will happen next. The groups should discuss their passages, with one member taking notes, prompted by the following questions: (1) What happened in this section? (2) What characters are introduced and described? What do you think of them? (3) What are the main ideas or themes? (4) What images, language, and literary devices can you identify? (5) What details seem to foreshadow events to come? All responses should be firmly tied to specifics in the text. The groups should appoint one or two spokespersons to report to the class.

English Language Development Ask students to construct a time line listing the most important events in the story. Keeping their Reader's Logs handy, students should jot down actions as the story unfolds. As a class activity, have students name important events in order as you list their ideas on the chalkboard.

"Been to the loo,"[4] one of the boys said, for it was common knowledge that since the bombs fell something had gone wrong with the pipes of the house and Old Misery was too mean to spend money on the property. He could do the redecorating himself at cost price, but he had never learned plumbing. The loo was a wooden shed at the bottom of the narrow garden with a star-shaped hole in the door: It had escaped the blast which had smashed the house next door and sucked out the window frames of number 3.

The next time the gang became aware of Mr. Thomas was more surprising. Blackie, Mike, and a thin yellow boy, who for some reason was called by his <u>surname</u> Summers, met him on the common coming back from the market. Mr. Thomas stopped them. He said glumly, "You belong to the lot that play in the car-park?"

Mike was about to answer when Blackie stopped him. As the leader he had responsibilities. "Suppose we are?" he said ambiguously.

"I got some chocolates," Mr. Thomas said. "Don't like 'em myself. Here you are. Not enough to go round, I don't suppose. There never is," he added with somber conviction. He handed over three packets of Smarties.

The gang were puzzled and perturbed by this action and tried to explain it away. "Bet someone dropped them and he picked 'em up," somebody suggested.

"Pinched 'em and then got in a bleeding funk," another thought aloud.

"It's a bribe," Summers said. "He wants us to stop bouncing balls on his wall."

"We'll show him we don't take bribes," Blackie said, and they sacrificed the whole morning to the game of bouncing that only Mike was young enough to enjoy. There was no sign from Mr. Thomas.

Next day T. astonished them all. He was late at the rendezvous, and the voting for that day's exploit took place without him. At Blackie's suggestion the gang was to disperse in pairs, take buses at random, and see how many free rides could be snatched from unwary conductors (the operation was to be carried out in pairs to avoid cheating).

---

4. **loo:** British slang for "bathroom." *Loo* comes from the French word *lieux,* short for *les lieux d'aisances* (lä lyö də·zäns'), which means "places of convenience."

They were drawing lots for their companions when T. arrived.

"Where you been, T.?" Blackie asked. "You can't vote now. You know the rules."

"I've been *there,*" T. said. He looked at the ground, as though he had thoughts to hide.

"Where?"

"At Old Misery's." Mike's mouth opened and then hurriedly closed again with a click. He had remembered the frog.

"At Old Misery's?" Blackie said. There was nothing in the rules against it, but he had a sensation that T. was treading on dangerous ground. He asked hopefully, "Did you break in?"

"No. I rang the bell."

"And what did you say?"

"I said I wanted to see his house."

"What did he do?"

"He showed it me."

"Pinch anything?"

"No."

"What did you do it for then?"

The gang had gathered round: It was as though an impromptu court were about to form and to try some case of deviation. T. said, "It's a beautiful house," and still watching the ground, meeting no one's eyes, he licked his lips first one way, then the other.

"What do you mean, a beautiful house?" Blackie asked with scorn.

"It's got a staircase two hundred years old like a corkscrew. Nothing holds it up."

"What do you mean, nothing holds it up. Does it float?"

"It's to do with opposite forces, Old Misery said."

"What else?"

"There's paneling."

"Like in the Blue Boar?"

"Two hundred years old."

"Is Old Misery two hundred years old?"

Mike laughed suddenly and then was quiet again. The meeting was in a serious mood. For the first time since T. had strolled into the car-park on the first day of the holidays his position was in danger. It only needed a single use of his real name and the gang would be at his heels.

WORDS TO OWN
surname (sur'nām') *n.*: last name.

INTEGRATING THE LANGUAGE ARTS

Strategic Reading Have students work in small groups to explore Trevor's character. Each group should focus on a specific passage and take notes while reading. Then, the group should discuss how the section reveals character. Give groups a chance to report their findings and to compare their ideas in discussion.

Speaking and Listening Several scenes in this story consist primarily of dialogue. Assigning one student as narrator and others as characters, have small groups stand and do a dramatic reading of some of these scenes. Ask them to imagine themselves in the roles and to read with as much drama and energy as possible. Suggested scenes include the conversation between T. and the gang after T. has seen Old Misery's house (p. 952); the short scene between Blackie and T. (p. 957); and the scene between a boy and Mr. Thomas (p. 958). Encourage the audience to discuss presentation techniques that are particularly effective. ☞

"What did you do it for?" Blackie asked. He was just, he had no jealousy, he was anxious to retain T. in the gang if he could. It was the word "beautiful" that worried him—that belonged to a class world that you could still see parodied at the Wormsley Common Empire by a man wearing a top hat and a monocle, with a haw-haw accent. He was tempted to say, "My dear Trevor, old chap," and unleash his hell hounds. "If you'd broken in," he said sadly—that indeed would have been an exploit worthy of the gang.

"This was better," T. said. "I found out things." He continued to stare at his feet, not meeting anybody's eye, as though he were absorbed in some dream he was unwilling—or ashamed—to share.

"What things?"

"Old Misery's going to be away all tomorrow and Bank Holiday."

Blackie said with relief, "You mean we could break in?"

"And pinch things?" somebody asked.

Blackie said, "Nobody's going to pinch things. Breaking in—that's good enough, isn't it? We don't want any court stuff."

"I don't want to pinch anything," T. said. "I've got a better idea."

"What is it?"

T. raised eyes, as gray and disturbed as the drab August day. "We'll pull it down," he said. "We'll destroy it."

Blackie gave a single hoot of laughter and then, like Mike, fell quiet, daunted by the serious implacable gaze. "What'd the police be doing all the time?" he said.

"They'd never know. We'd do it from inside. I've found a way in." He said with a sort of intensity, "We'd be like worms, don't you see, in an apple. When we came out again there'd be nothing there, no staircase, no panels, nothing but just walls, and then we'd make the walls fall down—somehow."

"We'd go to jug," Blackie said.

"Who's to prove? And anyway we wouldn't have pinched anything." He added without the smallest flicker of glee, "There wouldn't be anything to pinch after we'd finished."

"I've never heard of going to prison for breaking things," Summers said.

"There wouldn't be time," Blackie said. "I've seen housebreakers at work."

"There are twelve of us," T. said. "We'd organize."

"None of us know how—"

"I know," T. said. He looked across at Blackie. "Have you got a better plan?"

"Today," Mike said tactlessly, "we're pinching free rides—"

"Free rides," T. said. "You can stand down, Blackie, if you'd rather. . . ."

"The gang's got to vote."

"Put it up then."

Blackie said uneasily, "It's proposed that tomorrow and Monday we destroy Old Misery's house."

"Here, here," said a fat boy called Joe.

"Who's in favor?"

T. said, "It's carried."

"How do we start?" Summers asked.

"He'll tell you," Blackie said. It was the end of his leadership. He went away to the back of the car-park and began to kick a stone, dribbling it this way and that. There was only one old Morris[5] in the park, for few cars were left there except lorries:[6] Without an attendant there was no safety. He took a flying kick at the car and scraped a little paint off the rear mudguard. Beyond, paying no more attention to him than to a stranger, the gang had gathered round T.; Blackie was dimly aware of the fickleness of favor. He thought of going home, of never returning, of letting them all discover the hollowness of T.'s leadership, but suppose after all what T. proposed was possible—nothing like it had ever been done before. The fame of the Wormsley Common car-park gang would surely reach around London. There would be headlines in the papers. Even the grown-up gangs who ran the betting at the all-in wrestling and the barrow-boys[7] would hear with respect of how Old Misery's house had been destroyed. Driven by the pure,

---

5. **Morris:** car made by the Morris firm, a British automaker.
6. **lorries:** British for "trucks."
7. **barrow-boys:** boys who sold fruit or vegetables from a barrow, or cart.

WORDS TO OWN
implacable (im·plā′kə·bəl) *adj.:* inflexible; relentless; obstinate.

---

simple, and altruistic ambition of fame for the gang, Blackie came back to where T. stood in the shadow of Misery's wall.

T. was giving his orders with decision: It was as though this plan had been with him all his life, pondered through the seasons, now in his fifteenth year crystallized with the pain of puberty. "You," he said to Mike, "bring some big nails, the biggest you can find, and a hammer. Anyone else who can better bring a hammer and a screwdriver. We'll need plenty of them. Chisels too. We can't have too many chisels. Can anybody bring a saw?"

"I can," Mike said.

"Not a child's saw," T. said. "A real saw."

Blackie realized he had raised his hand like any ordinary member of the gang.

"Right, you bring one, Blackie. But now there's a difficulty. We want a hacksaw."

"What's a hacksaw?" someone asked.

"You can get 'em at Woolworth's," Summers said.

The fat boy called Joe said gloomily, "I knew it would end in a collection."

"I'll get one myself," T. said. "I don't want your money. But I can't buy a sledgehammer."

Blackie said, "They are working on number fifteen. I know where they'll leave their stuff for Bank Holiday."

"Then that's all," T. said. "We meet here at nine sharp."

"I've got to go to church," Mike said.

"Come over the wall and whistle. We'll let you in."

2

On Sunday morning all were punctual except Blackie, even Mike. Mike had had a stroke of luck. His mother felt ill, his father was tired after Saturday night, and he was told to go to church alone with many warnings of what would happen if he strayed. Blackie had had difficulty in smuggling out the saw, and then in finding the sledgehammer at the back of number 15. He approached the house from a lane at the rear of the garden, for fear of the policeman's beat along the main road. The tired evergreens kept off a stormy sun: Another wet Bank Holiday was being prepared over the Atlantic, beginning in swirls of dust under the trees. Blackie climbed the wall into Misery's garden.

There was no sign of anybody anywhere. The loo stood like a tomb in a neglected graveyard. The curtains were drawn. The house slept. Blackie lumbered nearer with the saw and the sledgehammer. Perhaps after all nobody had turned up: The plan had been a wild invention: They had woken wiser. But when he came close to the back door he could hear a confusion of sound, hardly louder than a hive in swarm: a clickety-clack, a bang bang bang, a scraping, a creaking, a sudden painful crack. He thought, It's true, and whistled.

They opened the back door to him and he came in. He had at once the impression of organization, very different from the old happy-go-lucky ways under his leadership. For a while he wandered up and down stairs looking for T. Nobody addressed him: He had a sense of great urgency, and already he could begin to see the plan. The interior of the house was being carefully demolished without touching the outer walls. Summers with hammer and chisel was ripping out the skirting-boards[8] in the ground floor dining room: He had already smashed the panels of the door. In the same room Joe was heaving up the parquet[9] blocks, exposing the soft wood floorboards over the cellar. Coils of wire came out of the damaged skirting and Mike sat happily on the floor, clipping the wires.

On the curved stairs two of the gang were working hard with an inadequate child's saw on the banisters—when they saw Blackie's big saw they signaled for it wordlessly. When he next saw them a quarter of the banisters had been dropped into the hall. He found T. at last in the bathroom—he sat moodily in the least cared-for room in the house, listening to the sounds coming up from below.

"You've really done it," Blackie said with awe. "What's going to happen?"

8. **skirting-boards:** baseboards; boards placed along the base of the walls of a room.
9. **parquet** (pär·kā′): fancy wood floor made of boards arranged in geometric patterns.

WORDS TO OWN
altruistic (al′trōō·is′tik) *adj.:* unselfish.

D. Critical Reading: Analyzing Character
[?] What qualities does Trevor exhibit as the work of destruction begins? [He is completely focused and committed to the project; he is efficient, skilled, and knowledgeable about the tools they'll need; he has good organizational skills.]

E. Literary Element: Imagery
Point out the images of sleeping and death with which Greene describes Blackie's view of the grounds and the exterior of the house, and contrast these images with the sounds of activity from inside.

F. Reader's Response: Shaping Interpretations
[?] Why do you think that, ironically, the gang is putting so much creative skill and organization into this wanton and complete destruction of a beautiful, historical house? [Sample responses: Maybe T. and the gang just want to achieve the notoriety such a task would bring them. Perhaps they are so used to destruction, they are caught up in the thrill of it; or they are mimicking the destruction of war seen all around them.]

G. Critical Reading: Making Inferences
We are told that Mike "sat happily . . . clipping the wires," while Trevor "sat moodily . . . listening." What can you infer about their respective reactions to what is going on? [Mike, the youngest member of the gang, is busy, excited, and impressed with the importance and danger of what they are doing; Trevor is unmoved emotionally, seeing only what is left to be done, methodically destroying for the sake of destroying.]

CROSSING THE CURRICULUM

Social Sciences The social phenomenon of youth gangs described in this story is not limited to London in the 1950s. Assign students to do some research on current street gangs in the United States and to discuss with the class the similarities and the differences between the Wormsley Common gang and gangs today. The best source for this kind of research may be news periodicals. Have students write a short comparison paper that describes their findings.

COOPERATIVE LEARNING

Practicing the Law Have students take the Wormsley Common gang to court, assuming that Mr. Thomas has pressed charges. Assign two students to be the prosecution and defense attorneys; assign other students the roles of Blackie, Mike, Trevor, and other gang members. Let one student be the judge and the rest of the class serve as jury. Take some open class time at the beginning of this project to brainstorm the specifics of the case: Exactly what are the boys charged with? Who are the primary defendants? What are the likely arguments on both sides of the case? Then, allow students class time to rehearse. Following the staged courtroom scene, the class should vote for acquittal or conviction.

A. Critical Reading: Identifying Main Ideas

This is a succinct statement of the main irony of the story, that Trevor's considerable creative talents and knowledge are being used to completely destroy a beautiful house. How does this reversal express the Collection theme of worldly chaos? [Possible answers: The center is, literally, not holding in Mr. Thomas's house; a gang of children is destroying a house that withstood bombs; or a bright, promising, young boy is using all his skills for destruction.]

B. Critical Reading: Summarizing

? What specifically do the boys do in the house the first day? [They rip off all the baseboards and doors; smash furniture, china, and glass; tear up papers; rip mattresses and pillows; empty drawers and destroy the contents; break the bathtub and sink; and pry up floors.]

C. Critical Reading: Making Inferences

? Why do you think Trevor chooses Old Misery's money as the "something special" he wants to destroy himself? [Possible answers: Old Misery is a miser, and Trevor knows the hoard of money is important to him; or the money represents what Trevor and his family have lost.]

D. Reader's Response: Connecting with the Text

? What do you think of Trevor's speech about hate and love? [Sample responses: Trevor is completely cold with no feelings; Trevor has no loyalties but is just a sort of destroying machine; or Trevor is covering up terrible anger, shame, and sorrow about his own family and their humiliation and poverty.]

"We've only just begun," T. said. He looked at the sledgehammer and gave his instructions. "You stay here and break the bath and the washbasin. Don't bother about the pipes. They come later."

Mike appeared at the door. "I've finished the wire, T.," he said.

"Good. You've just got to go wandering round now. The kitchen's in the basement. Smash all the china and glass and bottles you can lay hold of. Don't turn on the taps—we don't want a flood—yet. Then go into all the rooms and turn out drawers. If they are locked get one of the others to break them open. Tear up any papers you find and smash all the ornaments. Better take a carving knife with you from the kitchen. The bedroom's opposite here. Open the pillows and tear up the sheets. That's enough for the moment. And you, Blackie, when you've finished in here crack the plaster in the passage up with your sledgehammer."

"What are you going to do?" Blackie asked.

"I'm looking for something special," T. said.

It was nearly lunchtime before Blackie had finished and went in search of T. Chaos had advanced. The kitchen was a shambles of broken glass and china. The dining room was stripped of parquet, the skirting was up, the door had been taken off its hinges, and the destroyers had moved up a floor. Streaks of light came in through the closed shutters where they worked with the seriousness of creators—and destruction after all is a form of creation. A kind of imagination had seen this house as it had now become.

Mike said, "I've got to go home for dinner."

"Who else?" T. asked, but all the others on one excuse or another had brought provisions with them.

They squatted in the ruins of the room and swapped unwanted sandwiches. Half an hour for lunch and they were at work again. By the time Mike returned, they were on the top floor, and by six the superficial damage was completed. The doors were all off, all the skirtings raised, the furniture pillaged and ripped and smashed—no one could have slept in the house except on a bed of broken plaster. T. gave his orders—eight o'clock next morning—and to escape notice they climbed singly over the garden wall, into the car-park. Only Blackie and T. were left; the light had nearly gone, and when they touched a switch, nothing worked—Mike had done his job thoroughly.

"Did you find anything special?" Blackie asked.

T. nodded. "Come over here," he said, "and look." Out of both pockets he drew bundles of pound notes. "Old Misery's savings," he said. "Mike ripped out the mattress, but he missed them."

"What are you going to do? Share them?"

"We aren't thieves," T. said. "Nobody's going to steal anything from this house. I kept these for you and me—a celebration." He knelt down on the floor and counted them out—there were seventy in all. "We'll burn them," he said, "one by one," and taking it in turns they held a note upward and lit the top corner, so that the flame burnt slowly toward their fingers. The gray ash floated above them and fell on their heads like age. "I'd like to see Old Misery's face when we are through," T. said.

"You hate him a lot?" Blackie asked.

"Of course I don't hate him," T. said. "There'd be no fun if I hated him." The last burning note illuminated his brooding face. "All this hate and love," he said, "it's soft, it's hooey. There's only things, Blackie," and he looked round the room crowded with the unfamiliar shadows of half things, broken things, former things. "I'll race you home, Blackie," he said.

3

Next morning the serious destruction started. Two were missing—Mike and another boy, whose parents were off to Southend and Brighton in spite of the slow warm drops that had begun to fall and the rumble of thunder in the estuary like the first guns of the old blitz. "We've got to hurry," T. said.

Summers was restive. "Haven't we done enough?" he said. "I've been given a bob for slot machines. This is like work."

"We've hardly started," T. said. "Why, there's all the floors left, and the stairs. We haven't taken

---

WORDS TO OWN

shambles (shamʹbəlz) n.: scene of great disorder. Derived from *schamel*, a Middle English name for a bench used to display raw meat for sale, the word came to mean a butcher shop or slaughterhouse and, by extension, any great mess.

restive (resʹtiv) adj.: impatient; nervous.

---

out a single window. You voted like the others. We are going to *destroy* this house. There won't be anything left when we've finished."

They began again on the first floor picking up the top floorboards next the outer wall, leaving the joists exposed. Then they sawed through the joists and retreated into the hall, as what was left of the floor heeled and sank. They had learned with practice, and the second floor collapsed more easily. By the evening an odd exhilaration seized them as they looked down the great hollow of the house. They ran risks and made mistakes: When they thought of the windows it was too late to reach them. "Cor,"[10] Joe said, and dropped a penny down into the dry rubble-filled well. It cracked and span among the broken glass.

"Why did we start this?" Summers asked with astonishment; T. was already on the ground, digging at the rubble, clearing a space along the outer wall. "Turn on the taps," he said. "It's too dark for anyone to see now, and in the morning it won't matter." The water overtook them on the stairs and fell through the floorless rooms.

It was then they heard Mike's whistle at the back. "Something's wrong," Blackie said. They could hear his urgent breathing as they unlocked the door.

"The bogies?"[11] Summers asked.

"Old Misery," Mike said. "He's on his way." He put his head between his knees and retched. "Ran all the way," he said with pride.

"But why?" T. said. "He told me. . . ." He protested with the fury of the child he had never been, "It isn't fair."

"He was down at Southend," Mike said, "and he was on the train coming back. Said it was too cold and wet." He paused and gazed at the water. "My, you've had a storm here. Is the roof leaking?"

"How long will he be?"

"Five minutes. I gave Ma the slip and ran."

"We better clear," Summers said. "We've done enough, anyway."

"Oh, no, we haven't. Anybody could do this—" "This" was the shattered hollowed house with nothing left but the walls. Yet walls could be pre-

---

10. **cor:** British exclamation of strong surprise or irritation. *Cor* is from *Gor,* or *Gord,* an earlier regional dialect pronunciation of "God."
11. **bogies** (bō′gēz): slang for "police."

---

served. Façades were valuable. They could build inside again more beautifully than before. This could again be a home. He said angrily, "We've got to finish. Don't move. Let me think."

"There's no time," a boy said.

"There's got to be a way," T. said. "We couldn't have got thus far . . ."

"We've done a lot," Blackie said.

"No. No, we haven't. Somebody watch the front."

"We can't do any more."

"He may come in at the back."

"Watch the back too." T. began to plead. "Just give me a minute and I'll fix it. I swear I'll fix it." But his authority had gone with his ambiguity. He was only one of the gang. "Please," he said.

"Please," Summers mimicked him, and then suddenly struck home with the fatal name. "Run along home, Trevor."

T. stood with his back to the rubble like a boxer knocked groggy against the ropes. He had no words as his dreams shook and slid. Then Blackie acted before the gang had time to laugh, pushing Summers backward. "I'll watch the front, T.," he said, and cautiously he opened the shutters of the hall. The gray wet common stretched ahead, and the lamps gleamed in the puddles. "Someone's coming, T. No, it's not him. What's your plan, T.?"

"Tell Mike to go out to the loo and hide close beside it. When he hears me whistle he's got to count ten and start to shout."

"Shout what?"

"Oh, 'Help,' anything."

"You hear, Mike," Blackie said. He was the leader again. He took a quick look between the shutters. "He's coming, T."

"Quick, Mike. The loo. Stay here, Blackie, all of you till I yell."

"Where are you going, T.?"

"Don't worry. I'll see to this. I said I would, didn't I?"

GRAHAM GREENE 957

E. Reader's Response: First Thoughts

Describe how you think the boys are feeling at this moment. [Sample responses: They are punchy with fatigue, excited, awed by the extent of the destruction, scared, out of their usual range of experience.]

F. Critical Reading: Analyzing Plot

This point marks a climax in the story—Trevor's icy calm breaks for the first time when he sees that his plans to completely destroy the house might be thwarted. Ask students to be on the lookout from here on for shifts in the balance of power in the gang.

G. Critical Reading: Analyzing Character

? What does Blackie do? Why?
[Possible answers: Blackie comes to Trevor's defense; or Blackie reclaims leadership of the gang. He acts out of loyalty to the gang, out of a desire for success, out of a genuine sensitivity to T.'s predicament and weakness, and out of respect for T.'s ideas and leadership.]

PROFESSIONAL NOTES

Cultural Diversity Ask students to go through the story and to make notes about the different values held by Trevor, the rest of the gang, and Mr. Thomas, using a chart like the one that follows. Ask students to decide: What does each think is important? What does each think is right or wrong? What are Trevor's values? How are Trevor's values like either the gang's or Mr. Thomas's? The gang, under Blackie's leadership, represents the blue collar/labor class in England;

Mr. Thomas and Trevor's father represent the educated professional class. Have students extrapolate from the story some qualities of those two social groups.

Trevor's Values	Gang's Values	Mr. Thomas's Values

☞

A. Literary Element: Irony

[?] What is the irony in Old Misery carefully scraping his shoes before entering his house? [A little dirt can hardly hurt the house, which is by now completely demolished inside.]

B. Reader's Response: First Thoughts

[?] Are you surprised at T.'s gentleness with Mr. Thomas? Why or why not? [Sample responses: Yes, because T. has seemed so ruthless and uncaring up to this point in the story, it is hard to believe he would suddenly be nice to Mr. Thomas; or no, we have seen that T. can behave like a gentleman and that he does not hate or want to hurt Mr. Thomas, only his "things." He may also want to be sure Mr. Thomas does not get hurt because he wants him to witness the house's destruction.]

C. Literary Element: Irony

Identify the irony of Mr. Thomas's horoscope. [He is certainly about to experience a "crash."]

D. Literary Element: Suspense

Point out the suspense in the story: The crisis is past; Mr. Thomas has resigned himself to just sitting and waiting, powerless; readers do not yet know what is going to happen as this section ends and the next begins.

Old Misery came limping off the common. He had mud on his shoes and he stopped to scrape them on the pavement's edge. He didn't want to soil his house, which stood jagged and dark between the bomb sites, saved so narrowly, as he believed, from destruction. Even the fanlight had been left unbroken by the bomb's blast. Somewhere somebody whistled. Old Misery looked sharply round. He didn't trust whistles. A child was shouting: It seemed to come from his own garden. Then a boy ran into the road from the car-park. "Mr. Thomas," he called, "Mr. Thomas."

"What is it?"

"I'm terribly sorry, Mr. Thomas. One of us got taken short, and we thought you wouldn't mind, and now he can't get out."

"What do you mean, boy?"

"He's got stuck in your loo."

"He'd no business—Haven't I seen you before?"

"You showed me your house."

"So I did. So I did. That doesn't give you the right to—"

"Do hurry, Mr. Thomas. He'll suffocate."

"Nonsense. He can't suffocate. Wait till I put my bag in."

"I'll carry your bag."

"Oh, no, you don't. I carry my own."

"This way, Mr. Thomas."

"I can't get in the garden that way. I've got to go through the house."

"But you *can* get in the garden this way, Mr. Thomas. We often do."

"You often do?" He followed the boy with a scandalized fascination. "When? What right . . ."

"Do you see . . . ? The wall's low."

"I'm not going to climb walls into my own garden. It's absurd."

"This is how we do it. One foot here, one foot there, and over." The boy's face peered down, an arm shot out, and Mr. Thomas found his bag taken and deposited on the other side of the wall.

"Give me back my bag," Mr. Thomas said. From the loo a boy yelled and yelled. "I'll call the police."

"Your bag's all right, Mr. Thomas. Look. One foot there. On your right. Now just above. To your left." Mr. Thomas climbed over his own garden wall. "Here's your bag, Mr. Thomas."

"I'll have the wall built up," Mr. Thomas said. "I'll not have you boys coming over here, using my loo." He stumbled on the path, but the boy

caught his elbow and supported him. "Thank you, thank you, my boy," he murmured automatically. Somebody shouted again through the dark. "I'm coming, I'm coming," Mr. Thomas called. He said to the boy beside him, "I'm not unreasonable. Been a boy myself. As long as things are done regular. I don't mind you playing round the place Saturday mornings. Sometimes I like company. Only it's got to be regular. One of you asks leave and I say Yes. Sometimes I'll say No. Won't feel like it. And you come in at the front door and out at the back. No garden walls."

"Do get him out, Mr. Thomas."

"He won't come to any harm in my loo," Mr. Thomas said, stumbling slowly down the garden. "Oh, my rheumatics," he said. "Always get 'em on Bank Holiday. I've got to go careful. There's loose stones here. Give me your hand. Do you know what my horoscope said yesterday? '<u>Abstain</u> from any dealings in first half of week. Danger of serious crash.' That might be on this path," Mr. Thomas said. "They speak in parables and double meanings." He paused at the door of the loo. "What's the matter in there?" he called. There was no reply.

"Perhaps he's fainted," the boy said.

"Not in my loo. Here, you, come out," Mr. Thomas said, and giving a great jerk at the door he nearly fell on his back when it swung easily open. A hand first supported him and then pushed him hard. His head hit the opposite wall and he sat heavily down. His bag hit his feet. A hand whipped the key out of the lock and the door slammed. "Let me out," he called, and heard the key turn in the lock. "A serious crash," he thought, and felt dithery and confused and old.

A voice spoke to him softly through the star-shaped hole in the door. "Don't worry, Mr. Thomas," it said, "we won't hurt you, not if you stay quiet."

Mr. Thomas put his head between his hands and pondered. He had noticed that there was only one lorry in the car-park, and he felt certain that the driver would not come for it before the morning. Nobody could hear him from the road in

---

WORDS TO OWN

abstain (ab·stān′) *v.*: refrain from; hold oneself back from.

Critical Comment: Greene's Reading In the autobiographical essay "The Lost Childhood," Graham Greene describes the amazement with which he found "a key turned in a lock": He could read. The books he read during his childhood were to have a lasting effect on him. The memory of a scene from one book grew into a scene in one of his own novels; the magic of another work kept him going when working later in life in "a little stuffy office in Freetown, Sierra Leone."

The ideal characters of the fantastical tales he read early on failed to keep ringing true, however, and his reading expanded until he came to a startling truth. As Greene describes it, "Goodness has only once found a perfect incarnation in a human body and never will again, but evil can always find a home there. Human nature is not black and white but black and gray." His writing is a lifelong study of the finer shadings.

After the Blitz, 7th September 1940 by Lawrence Stephen Lowry.

Courtesy of Mrs. Carol Ann Danes.

RESPONDING TO THE ART: EXPLORING THE SUBJECT

From August 24 to August 29, 1940, the Royal Air Force bombed the city of Berlin. In retaliation, the German Luftwaffe ceased its bombing of military bases and turned to major British cities as targets. For fifty-seven nights, an average of 160 bombers attacked London in raids that journalists called "the Blitz." For a time during the Blitz, almost one person in seven was sleeping in a railway arch, a subway or "tube" station, or other municipal shelter for protection.

front, and the lane at the back was seldom used. Anyone who passed there would be hurrying home and would not pause for what they would certainly take to be drunken cries. And if he did call "Help," who, on a lonely Bank Holiday evening, would have the courage to investigate? Mr. Thomas sat on the loo and pondered with the wisdom of age.

After a while it seemed to him that there were sounds in the silence—they were faint and came from the direction of his house. He stood up and peered through the ventilation-hole—between the cracks in one of the shutters he saw a light, not the light of a lamp, but the wavering light that a candle might give. Then he thought he heard the sound of hammering and scraping and chipping. He thought of burglars—perhaps they had employed the boy as a scout, but why should

GRAHAM GREENE 959

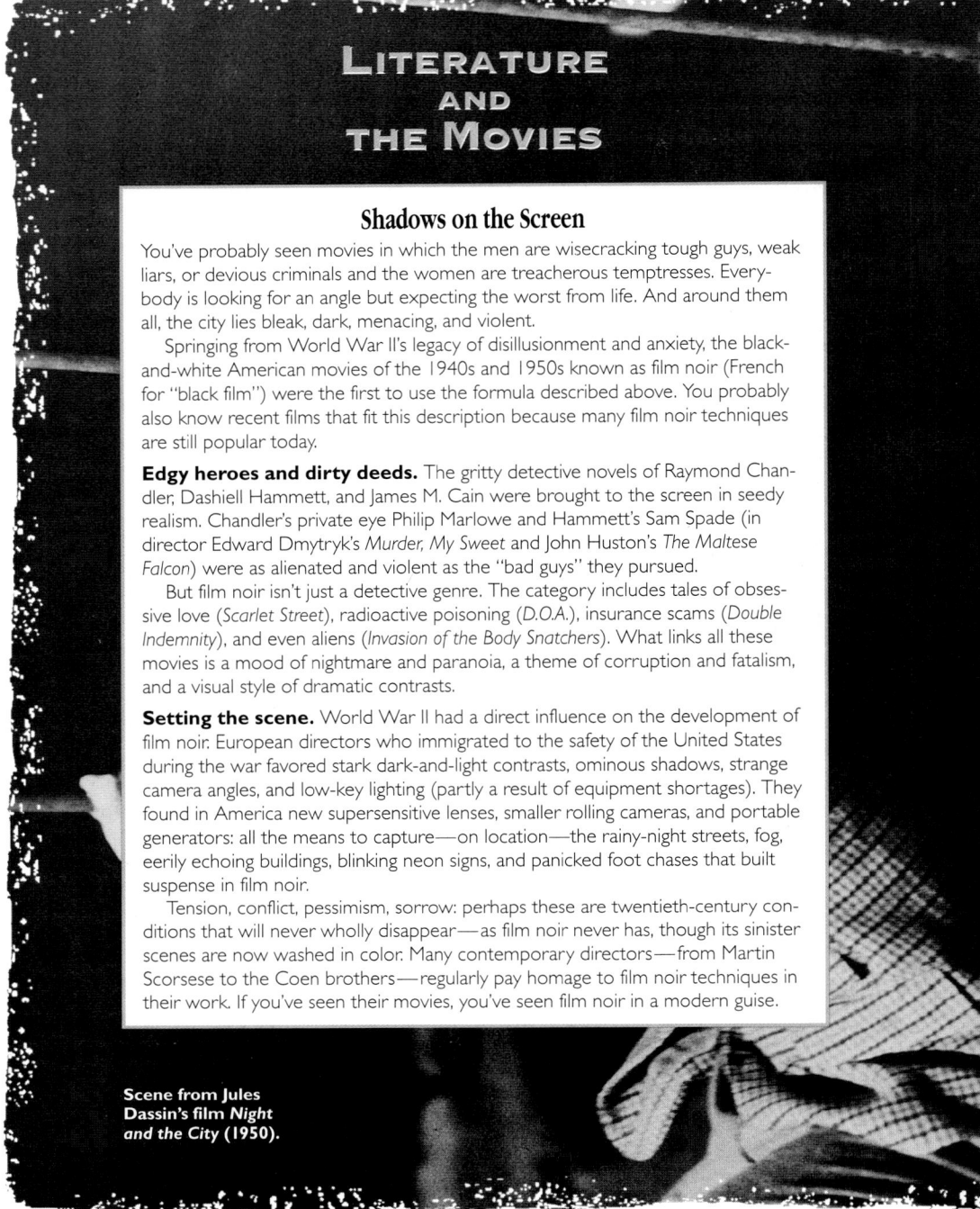

LITERATURE AND THE MOVIES

Shadows on the Screen

You've probably seen movies in which the men are wisecracking tough guys, weak liars, or devious criminals and the women are treacherous temptresses. Everybody is looking for an angle but expecting the worst from life. And around them all, the city lies bleak, dark, menacing, and violent.

Springing from World War II's legacy of disillusionment and anxiety, the black-and-white American movies of the 1940s and 1950s known as film noir (French for "black film") were the first to use the formula described above. You probably also know recent films that fit this description because many film noir techniques are still popular today.

Edgy heroes and dirty deeds. The gritty detective novels of Raymond Chandler, Dashiell Hammett, and James M. Cain were brought to the screen in seedy realism. Chandler's private eye Philip Marlowe and Hammett's Sam Spade (in director Edward Dmytryk's *Murder, My Sweet* and John Huston's *The Maltese Falcon*) were as alienated and violent as the "bad guys" they pursued.

But film noir isn't just a detective genre. The category includes tales of obsessive love (*Scarlet Street*), radioactive poisoning (*D.O.A.*), insurance scams (*Double Indemnity*), and even aliens (*Invasion of the Body Snatchers*). What links all these movies is a mood of nightmare and paranoia, a theme of corruption and fatalism, and a visual style of dramatic contrasts.

Setting the scene. World War II had a direct influence on the development of film noir. European directors who immigrated to the safety of the United States during the war favored stark dark-and-light contrasts, ominous shadows, strange camera angles, and low-key lighting (partly a result of equipment shortages). They found in America new supersensitive lenses, smaller rolling cameras, and portable generators: all the means to capture—on location—the rainy-night streets, fog, eerily echoing buildings, blinking neon signs, and panicked foot chases that built suspense in film noir.

Tension, conflict, pessimism, sorrow: perhaps these are twentieth-century conditions that will never wholly disappear—as film noir never has, though its sinister scenes are now washed in color. Many contemporary directors—from Martin Scorsese to the Coen brothers—regularly pay homage to film noir techniques in their work. If you've seen their movies, you've seen film noir in a modern guise.

Scene from Jules
Dassin's film *Night
and the City* (1950).

960 THE TWENTIETH CENTURY

ASSESSMENT TOOLS

Ongoing Assessment In order to assess the general success of the discussion of this story, ask the class to write responses to the following questions and to assign a number value of one to five (five being the most positive) to each of the following criteria.

1. Small group presentations
   a. Was your own small group organized and did everyone do his or her job?
   b. How generally effective were other small-group presentations?

2. Analysis and comprehension
   a. Did the discussion help you understand the story's basic themes?
   b. Did general discussion and presentations help you see how elements of the story contributed to those themes?
   c. Do you see how the story connects with the theme of the Collection?

burglars engage in what sounded more and more like a stealthy form of carpentry? Mr. Thomas let out an experimental yell, but nobody answered. The noise could not even have reached his enemies.

4

Mike had gone home to bed, but the rest stayed. The question of leadership no longer concerned the gang. With nails, chisels, screwdrivers, anything that was sharp and penetrating they moved around the inner walls worrying at the mortar between the bricks. They started too high, and it was Blackie who hit on the damp course[12] and realized the work could be halved if they weakened the joints immediately above. It was a long, tiring, unamusing job, but at last it was finished. The gutted house stood there balanced on a few inches of mortar between the damp course and the bricks.

There remained the most dangerous task of all, out in the open at the edge of the bomb site. Summers was sent to watch the road for passers by, and Mr. Thomas, sitting on the loo, heard clearly now the sound of sawing. It no longer came from his house, and that a little reassured him. He felt less concerned. Perhaps the other noises too had no significance.

A voice spoke to him through the hole. "Mr. Thomas."

"Let me out," Mr. Thomas said sternly.

"Here's a blanket," the voice said, and a long gray sausage was worked through the hole and fell in swathes over Mr. Thomas's head.

"There's nothing personal," the voice said. "We want you to be comfortable tonight."

"Tonight," Mr. Thomas repeated incredulously.

"Catch," the voice said. "Penny buns—we've buttered them, and sausage-rolls. We don't want you to starve, Mr. Thomas."

Mr. Thomas pleaded desperately. "A joke's a joke, boy. Let me out and I won't say a thing. I've got rheumatics. I got to sleep comfortable."

"You wouldn't be comfortable, not in your house, you wouldn't. Not now."

"What do you mean, boy?" but the footsteps receded. There was only the silence of night: no

12. **damp course:** layer of waterproof material placed between two layers of brick in a house's foundation to keep moisture from rising up through the walls.

GRAHAM GREENE 961

A. Reader's Response: Shaping Interpretations

? Why is the gang no longer concerned with who the leader is? [Sample responses: Both Blackie and Trevor have taken control, in turn, and are now cooperatively running the show; the obsession with pulling the house down has overtaken them.]

B. Reader's Response: Shaping Interpretations

? Does the fact that the boys give Mr. Thomas a blanket and food make them seem more humane? Why or why not? [Sample responses: It reinforces the fact that they do not want to hurt him physically; or in destroying his house, they have done about as much damage as possible to this man. They are not humane by most standards.]

ASSESSMENT TOOLS

Check Test: Questions and Answers
1. What plan does T. propose? [That they destroy Mr. Thomas's house.]
2. What is the "something special" that T. finds to destroy? [Old Misery's money.]
3. What does T. say when Blackie asks him if he hates Mr. Thomas? [He says if he hated Mr. Thomas, the destruction would not be fun.]
4. How do the boys prevent Mr. Thomas from finding them before they have finished their task? [They trap him in the loo.]

Making Meanings

First Thoughts

1. Students may respond that the story reminds them of harmful graffiti, vandalism, and similar destructive acts.

Reviewing the Text

a. Blackie is the gang's first leader, but leadership passes to T. when T. proposes destroying Old Misery's house.

b. His father is a former architect, and his mother is haughty.

c. It was built by a renowned architect.

d. First, the gang destroys the inside. On the second day, they start destroying the structure itself. Finally, they tie a wooden support to the lorry, which pulls down the house.

Shaping Interpretations

2. The boys are not trying to harm the man. Since they burn the money, they are not interested in material gain.

3. Students may suggest that T. perversely admires destruction of beauty; clues might be his emphasis on the words *beautiful* and *destroy*.

4. T.'s special talents for destruction are ironic because such leadership is usually constructive; his father's former occupation as an architect is ironic; that the house survives the bombing but not the boys' gang is ironic; and Old Misery's horoscope ironically predicts a "serious crash."

5. The gang values sensation and ready cash. They find pleasure in cruelty. The group's antisocial stance probably springs from the conflict between old and new values. England's orderly society is being eroded, just as Old Misery's house is pulled down.

6. The image of Wormsley Common, described as a grimy, shattered place bombed in the war. This adds to the atmosphere of corruption.

7. Students may say the theme is that creative imagination is now focused on destruction.

8. Students may respond that T. prefers the irrational spite that motivates his destructiveness. Having a reason would diminish the scandal of the act.

---

sound of sawing. Mr. Thomas tried one more yell, but he was daunted and rebuked by the silence—a long way off an owl hooted and made away again on its muffled flight through the soundless world.

At seven next morning the driver came to fetch his lorry. He climbed into the seat and tried to start the engine. He was vaguely aware of a voice shouting, but it didn't concern him. At last the engine responded and he backed the lorry until it touched the great wooden shore[13] that supported Mr. Thomas's house. That way he could drive right out and down the street without reversing. The lorry moved forward, was momentarily checked as though something were pulling it from behind, and then went on to the sound of a long rumbling crash. The driver was astonished to see bricks bouncing ahead of him, while stones hit the roof of his cab. He put on his brakes. When he climbed out the whole landscape had suddenly altered. There was no house beside the car-park, only a hill of rubble. He went round and examined the back of his car for damage, and found a rope tied there that was still twisted at the other end round part of a wooden strut.

The driver again became aware of somebody shouting. It came from the wooden erection which was the nearest thing to a house in that desolation of broken brick. The driver climbed the smashed wall and unlocked the door. Mr. Thomas came out of the loo. He was wearing a gray blanket to which flakes of pastry adhered. He gave a sobbing cry. "My house," he said. "Where's my house?"

"Search me," the driver said. His eye lit on the remains of a bath and what had once been a dresser and he began to laugh. There wasn't anything left anywhere.

"How dare you laugh," Mr. Thomas said. "It was my house. My house."

"I'm sorry," the driver said, making heroic efforts, but when he remembered the sudden check to his lorry, the crash of bricks falling, he became convulsed again. One moment the house had stood there with such dignity between the bomb sites like a man in a top hat, and then, bang, crash, there wasn't anything left—not anything. He said, "I'm sorry. I can't help it, Mr. Thomas. There's nothing personal, but you got to admit it's funny."

13. **shore:** beam.

962 THE TWENTIETH CENTURY

MAKING MEANINGS

First Thoughts

1. What acts of vandalism and destruction in our culture does this story remind you of?

Reviewing the Text

a. Who is the gang's leader at first? Who takes over? Why?

b. What is T.'s family background?

c. Why is Mr. Thomas's house valuable?

d. Describe how the house is destroyed.

Shaping Interpretations

2. T.'s **motives** for destroying Old Misery's house are important. What motives can you *eliminate* based on how the boys treat Old Misery and on what they do with the money? What motives from your Reader's Log notes can you also rule out?

3. What *are* T.'s motives? Support your answer with details from the story. (Your Reader's Log will help.)

4. How are these elements of the story **ironic**: (a) T.'s special talents, (b) T.'s father's former profession, (c) the history of the house, (d) Old Misery's horoscope?

5. A gang is an entity with a set of values. What are this gang's values, and where do you think they spring from?

6. What images are used to describe the setting of the Wormsley Common car-park and its surroundings? How does the **setting** contribute to the story's emotional atmosphere?

7. Consider the following excerpt from the story:

"... they worked with the seriousness of creators—and destruction after all is a form of creation. A kind of imagination had seen this house as it had now become."

Do you think it expresses the story's **theme**? Explain.

8. When Blackie asks T. whether he hates Mr. Thomas, T. answers, "Of course I don't . . . . There'd be no fun if I hated him." How would you explain T.'s answer?

Extending the Text

9. **(Analysis)** Students may suggest that people need to be more appreciative of beauty or that society needs to stop praising destructive, individualistic acts and to focus on constructive, communal acts. People usually do not destroy what they see as their own.

Challenging the Text

10. **(Evaluation)** Students will probably say that the story is more powerful as is. As written, the focus is on Mr. Thomas's pain, which may be a stronger message than a moralistic punishment scene.

Extending the Text

9. What "cure," if any, do you think might put an end to vandalism?

Challenging the Text

10. Some people feel the story should have continued to show the boys' punishment. Do you agree, or is the story more powerful as it is? Explain.

LANGUAGE AND STYLE

Slang

Greene's dialogue uses a good deal of British slang. Use a dictionary to explain the meanings of these expressions:

1. "**Pinched** 'em and then got in a **bleeding funk**. . . ."
2. ". . . a man . . . with a **haw-haw** accent"
3. "We'd go to **jug**."
4. "I've been given a **bob** for slot machines."

Can you rewrite each expression above using American slang?

Devastation City, Twisted Girders
(20th century) by Graham Sutherland.

Ferens Art Gallery, Hull, England. © 1997 Artists Rights Society (ARS), New York / Pro Litteris, Zurich.

CHOICES: Building Your Portfolio

Writer's Notebook

1. Collecting Ideas for an Informative Report

Even though "The Destructors" takes place half a century ago in London, the problem it examines is a timeless one. Explore what you know about the prevalence of random violence and vandalism in your own community using the *5W-How?* questions (*Who? What? When? Where? Why? How?*). Then jot down your ideas about what library and community resources you might use to gather additional details for an informative paper. Save your work for the Writer's Workshop on page 1053.

Critical Writing

2. Rotten to the Core?

Images of hollowness—of rotting from within—pervade the story. In the first part of an essay, cite these images, and discuss how they apply to the house, to Wormsley Common, and even to the story's characters. In the second part of the essay, discuss the ways "The Destructors" connects with images in W. B. Yeats's "The Second Coming" (page 923) and in T. S. Eliot's "The Hollow Men" (page 942).

Creative Writing

3. The Other Side of the Story

Imagine you are Mr. Thomas. In a letter, tell a friend what happened to your house. Include your feelings about the gang and its motives.

Critical Thinking / Role-Playing

4. The Destructor Trial

Is T. a vicious criminal who should be punished or a disturbed victim of society who deserves understanding? Stage a trial for T., with students taking the parts of T., prosecutor, defense attorney, witnesses, judge, and jury.

GRAHAM GREENE 963

Language and Style

Mini-Lesson: Slang

Ask students to recall other literary uses of slang. How does slang affect the narrative? [Students may say that the slang adds a quality of reality to a narrative, and it helps distinguish the characters in their speech mannerisms.] Does Greene's use of slang have the same effect? [Although the slang may be unfamiliar to students, they will probably say that the slang does add realism and individuality to the dialogue.]

Possible Answers

1. "'*Lifted* them and then *got all worked up about it.* . . .'"
2. ". . . with a *backwoods* accent."
3. "'We'd go to *the slammer*.'"
4. "'I've been given a *buck* for slot machines.'"

Beyond the Story

Choices: Building Your Portfolio

1. **Writer's Notebook** Remind students to save their work. They may use it as prewriting for the Writer's Workshop on p. 1053.
2. **Critical Writing** Have students brainstorm for the first part of the essay, using a three-column chart like the following.

Image of Hollowness	Application to House	Character

3. **Creative Writing** Before students begin their letters, ask them to review what they know of Mr. Thomas and to carefully note his personality. Challenge students to take on the character's persona as they write.

Into the Poem

Author Biography p. 964
Before You Read p. 964

Through the Poem

"Hawk Roosting" p. 965
Making Meanings p. 966

Beyond the Poem

Choices: Building Your Portfolio p. 966
- **Writer's Notebook:** Jot down questions about hawks
- **Critical Writing:** Find and respond to the poem's theme
- **Critical Writing:** Compare the view of nature in two poems
- **Creative Writing:** In a poem or paragraph, express an animal's "philosophy"

Into the Poem

Using **BEFORE YOU READ** p. 964

Elements of Literature

Ask students to freewrite for a few minutes on how they would personify a hawk. They may expand on their Quickwrite entries for the exercise. Have them discuss their ideas.

PORTFOLIO ASSESSMENT

Portfolio Assessment
For help with teacher assessment of reading skills, see the *Portfolio Management System,* pp. 54–55.

Ted Hughes

(1930–   )

Ted Hughes (1959).
© Rollie McKenna.

Ted Hughes, who often uses violent nature imagery to symbolize the human condition, has been called "a twentieth-century Aesop whose fables lack an explicit moral." Hughes was born in West Yorkshire, where his father was a carpenter. After serving two years in the Royal Air Force, he studied archaeology and anthropology at Cambridge. In 1956, he married the now-legendary American poet Sylvia Plath. In 1963, after the couple had been separated, Plath, ill and depressed, took her own life in an unheated flat during one of the worst winters in London history.

The titles of Hughes's books of poetry reveal his recurring subjects: *The Hawk in the Rain* (1957), *Animal Poems* (1967), *A Few Crows* (1970), and *Cave Birds* (1975). Although Hughes writes of nature, he has nothing in common with the Romantics, who saw in nature a reflection of divine providence and primeval innocence. In Hughes's poems, nature represents the darkest impulses of the human heart; violence is not only an accepted fact of life, but also the impulse that links all creatures on earth. Hughes is known as an intensely private writer. In 1984, he was named poet laureate of England, succeeding Sir John Betjeman.

BEFORE YOU READ
HAWK ROOSTING

Reading Focus

Deadly Instincts

Is violence really part of the natural order of things in the world? And what about the human capacity for murder and war? Is it *natural,* too? This poem—or rather its unusual speaker, a hawk—makes us face these troubling questions.

The ruthless, feathered killing machine of this poem presents us with a frightening message:

There are forces in creation that pay no attention to moral discriminations.

Quickwrite

Quickly write down whatever comes to mind when you hear the word *hawk:* characteristics, images, behavior, your emotional response.

Elements of Literature

Personification

We're so accustomed to discussing our pets' "personalities"—a haughty cat, a mischievous puppy—that we don't think of these descriptions as a form of **personification,** but in reality they are. When Ted Hughes tries to imagine what it's like to be a hawk, he gives the creature characteristics of human consciousness, desire, and will. His entire poem is a personification.

964 THE TWENTIETH CENTURY

PROGRAM MANAGER

- **Planning Instruction** See *Teaching Notes, Teaching Resources B,* p. 112, for objectives, a summary, literary elements, and additional biographical information for this selection.
- **Instructional Support** Before beginning the instructional lesson, see *Graphic Organizer for Active Reading, Teaching Resources B,* p. 123, for a Through the Poem activity.
- **Assessment** See *Selection Test, Test Booklet,* p. 205.

Hawk Roosting

Ted Hughes

I sit in the top of the wood, my eyes closed.
Inaction, no falsifying dream
Between my hooked head and hooked feet:
Or in sleep rehearse perfect kills and eat.

5 The convenience of the high trees!
The air's buoyancy and the sun's ray
Are of advantage to me;
And the earth's face upward for my inspection.

My feet are locked upon the rough bark.
10 It took the whole of Creation
To produce my foot, my each feather:
Now I hold Creation in my foot **B**

Or fly up, and revolve it all slowly—
I kill where I please because it is all mine.
15 There is no sophistry° in my body:
My manners are tearing off heads—

The allotment of death.
For the one path of my flight is direct
Through the bones of the living.
20 No arguments assert my right:

The sun is behind me.
Nothing has changed since I began.
My eye has permitted no change.
I am going to keep things like this.

15. sophistry: clever but unsound reasoning.

Making Meanings

First Thoughts

1. Students may say that the hawk's way of thinking is cold, selfish, cruel, conceited, and deadly.

Shaping Interpretations

2. The hawk thinks as a person and also talks of arguments and manners. Students may say they did not see the hawk as calculating but as instinctive in its actions.

3. The hawk has the entire world at its mercy, and its statement expresses a cruel sense of power. The notion that God holds the world in his hands suggests power used for good instead of selfish impulses.

4. The only manners I need are knowing the best way to tear off heads. My power is death; it is inevitable, and I, like death, need no argument to explain my existence.

5. The hawk attacks from its prey's blind side, where the sun is; and also that the sun supports the hawk's existence.

Extending the Text

6. **(Synthesis)** Students may say that the hawk's philosophy is too cruel to be human; but they might note that people can be destructive and self-centered like the hawk.

Beyond the Poem

Choices: Building Your Portfolio

1. **Writer's Notebook** Remind students to save their work. They may use it as prewriting for the Writer's Workshop on p. 1053.

2. **Critical Writing** Have students freewrite about possible main ideas. Students may focus on a central theme by eliminating possibilities not supported by the poem's details.

4. **Creative Writing** Ask students to brainstorm about the common behaviors of the animal they choose and to record this information in freewriting or in a graphic organizer. Suggest that students use questions such as "How would the animal describe its purpose in life?" and "What are its morals?"

MAKING MEANINGS

First Thoughts

1. How did you react to the hawk's personality and way of looking at the world?

Shaping Interpretations

2. What human qualities does the poet give the hawk in this **personification**? How do these qualities compare with your Reader's Log associations?

3. What does the hawk mean by saying it holds Creation in its foot? How is this different from the idea that God has "the whole world in His hands"?

4. How would you **paraphrase** lines 16–20?

5. What two meanings can you propose for the line "The sun is behind me"?

Extending the Text

6. In what ways is the hawk's philosophy inhuman? In what ways is it like the attitude of some people?

CHOICES:
Building Your Portfolio

Writer's Notebook

1. Collecting Ideas for an Informative Report

Hughes's aim in "Hawk Roosting" is neither to inform nor to explain, yet he manages to distill a great deal of information about hawks into these few lines. To explore how you might approach the same subject in an informative paper, re-read the poem slowly, jotting down questions it raises about the hawk's natural history and place in the food chain. Save your work for the Writer's Workshop on page 1053.

Critical Writing

2. What's It All About?

In a paragraph, state and discuss what you take to be the main theme of the poem. In a second paragraph, present your response to the theme.

Critical Writing

3. Birds of a Feather?

In a brief essay, compare the view of nature expressed in "Hawk Roosting"—and Hughes's bird itself—with those of Shelley's "To a Skylark" (page 739) and Keats's "Ode to a Nightingale" (page 755). Be sure to discuss how the poems differ and how they are alike.

Creative Writing

4. Creature Feature

Select some other animal, and, in a short paragraph or poem, let it explain its "philosophy."

PORTFOLIO ASSESSMENT

Choices: Assessment Criteria For help in evaluating these Choices assignments, see the criteria in the *Portfolio Management System,* p. 161.

Russia

Arctic Ocean

SOVIET UNION

EUROPE

MONGOLIA

Aleksandr Solzhenitsyn

(1918–)

If to Aleksandr Solzhenitsyn (sōl′zhə·nēt′sin) his Soviet homeland was the burning log of "The Bonfire and the Ants," you could say he was swept from the fire in 1974. That's when he was arrested and exiled—for writing *The Gulag Archipelago,* a factual account of Soviet labor camps. Yet twenty years later, in May 1994, his apparently unquenchable love for his country drew him back to live again, as a free citizen, in Moscow.

Solzhenitsyn's troubled relationship with his homeland began much earlier. After becoming a decorated front-line officer in World War II, he was suddenly arrested in 1945 and served eight years in prison and labor camps for criticizing the premier Joseph Stalin in a letter to a friend.

Later, under the anti-Stalinist premier Nikita Khrushchev, Solzhenitsyn was able to publish his famous prison novel, *One Day in the Life of Ivan Denisovich* (1962). But during the 1960s and 1970s, the Soviet government continually harassed him, attempting to silence his criticisms of political realities. On winning the Nobel Prize in 1970, Solzhenitsyn did not travel to Sweden for the ceremonies, because he feared the Soviet regime would bar his return.

In 1974, the Soviet government revoked Solzhenitsyn's citizenship. Solzhenitsyn was deported and, for most of his twenty-year exile, lived quietly and wrote prolifically in Cavendish, Vermont. Now on Russian soil again, he is a world-famous symbol of both the former Soviet Union's repression and its more recent *glasnost* (openness).

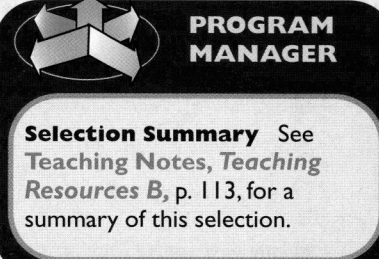

Aleksandr Solzhenitsyn (1994).

(Map) ©Rand McNally.

ALEKSANDR SOLZHENITSYN 967

CONNECTING WITH "THE CENTER CANNOT HOLD"

"Freedom to Breathe" and "The Bonfire and the Ants" seem on first reading to have differing messages. What do these pieces have in common, and how do they tie to the theme of the Collection? [Possible answers: Both pieces show the power of certain intangible needs—whether that means personal freedoms or attachment to one's home. The center cannot always hold; things do not always make sense. Breathing may not seem like something one would miss; it seems odd that ants would return to perish in their burning home.]

Encourage students to look at the description of the ants' behavior as a metaphor for the behavior of human beings. Ask students to write briefly and then to share with the class their thoughts about that comparison. [Possible answer: The ants have a strong sense of home and belonging and a firm commitment to what they want to do and where they are going, unlike the people in Yeats's poem; however, they lack a clear instinct for survival and are committed to a doomed and foolish course of action.]

Quickwrite

Suggest that students expand the boundaries of "home" by thinking of places where they feel comfortable. Have students consider their real homes, of course, but also less obvious places—a grandparent's home; a school; a friend's house; perhaps even some places that are not geographical, for example, wherever a friend is. *Remind students to choose a situation they would not mind sharing with others.*

A. Language Note: Repetition

? What is the effect of the repetition in these lines? [The repetition of the phrase "I breathe" has a lulling effect that parallels the speaker's relaxed mood.]

B. Reader's Response: First Thoughts

? What does the word "steeped" suggest to you? [Sample responses: The word emphasizes the saturation of the air with the scent of the flowers; it suggests that the air, like steeping tea, is soaked through with the scent, that it is infused with it.]

Metacognition Ask students what process they used in thinking about the connotations of the word.

C. Literary Element: Setting

? What effect does this belated description of the setting have? [Students may say the effect is surprise or irony that so exquisite an experience of nature can happen in a grimy urban setting.]

BEFORE YOU READ
FREEDOM TO BREATHE
THE BONFIRE AND THE ANTS

Background

"There's no place like home." Usually those words are spoken fondly, but—whether you love your home, loathe it, or just take it for granted—there's still a certain truth to the saying.

Take a minute to brainstorm images of the place that you think of as home. Don't stop with your physical dwelling, though. Include the neighborhood, the section of the city or countryside, the whole city or county—whatever flavors the physical sense of place and people that defines your life.

Once you've done your brainstorming, consider how you feel about home. Are you dying to get away, or do you hope you never have to leave?

Whatever your answer, your feelings would probably be different, or sharper, if you were forced out of your homeland and locked up somewhere far away. They would almost certainly be affected if danger suddenly loomed—perhaps gunfire or a raging flood—and common sense said, "Leave *now!*"

Quickwrite

The two prose poems you are about to read were written by a Russian who had to contemplate his homeland from a prison cell and, later, from a twenty-year exile. Keeping in mind the powerful emotions and images that make up your idea of "home," jot down in your Reader's Log how you think you might feel if you were suddenly forced to leave.

Freedom to Breathe

Aleksandr Solzhenitsyn
translated by **Michael Glenny**

A shower fell in the night and now dark clouds drift across the sky, occasionally sprinkling a fine film of rain.

A I stand under an apple tree in blossom and I breathe. Not only the apple tree but the grass round it glistens with moisture; words cannot describe the sweet fragrance that pervades the air. I inhale as deeply as I can, and the aroma invades my whole being; I breathe with my eyes open, I breathe with my eyes closed—I cannot say which gives me the greater pleasure.

B This, I believe, is the single most precious freedom that prison takes away from us: the freedom to breathe freely, as I now can. No food on earth, no wine, not even a woman's kiss is sweeter to me than this air steeped in the fragrance of flowers, of moisture and freshness.

C No matter that this is only a tiny garden, hemmed in by five-story houses like cages in a zoo. I cease to hear the motorcycles backfiring, radios whining, the burble of loudspeakers. As long as there is fresh air to breathe under an apple tree after a shower, we may survive a little longer.

STRATEGIES FOR INCLUSION

Bodily-Kinesthetic If time and weather allow, take the class outside so they may experience firsthand breathing deeply and consciously, looking at the trees or grass, feeling the air on their skin, and smelling whatever there is to smell. Read the first prose poem aloud while they stand, eyes closed and eyes open, and do what Solzhenitsyn describes himself doing. If you cannot get outside, then have students keep their eyes closed and imagine themselves outside while they do the exercise in the classroom. Before discussing this experience, have students jot down what they noticed while they were doing this exercise.

Linguistic To help students see "The Bonfire and the Ants" in a broader sense, ask them to read Lewis Thomas's essay on ants, "Antaeus in Manhattan," in *The Lives of a Cell,* and to select some passages to read aloud to the class. They should preface each selection with a brief statement about their reasons for choosing it and should make comparisons with the prose poem.

The Bonfire and the Ants

Aleksandr Solzhenitsyn

translated by **Michael Glenny**

I threw a rotten log onto the fire without noticing that it was alive with ants.

The log began to crackle, the ants came tumbling out and scurried around in desperation. They ran along the top and writhed as they were scorched by the flames. I gripped the log and rolled it to one side. Many of the ants then managed to escape onto the sand or the pine needles.

But, strangely enough, they did not run away from the fire.

They had no sooner overcome their terror than they turned, circled, and some kind of force drew them back to their forsaken homeland. There were many who climbed back onto the burning log, ran about on it, and perished there.

A. Reader's Response: First Thoughts

? How would you describe the poem's style, given the first sentence? [Sample responses: Terse, dense, matter-of-fact, meditative.]

B. Critical Reading: Making Inferences

? What does the use of the word *homeland* suggest to you about the purpose of the poem? [Possible answer: The word may indicate that the prose poem is an allegory for the speaker's homeland.]

C. Critical Reading: Finding Main Ideas

? What is the main idea of the allegory? [Possible answer: Ties to one's home are so hard to break that sometimes one destroys oneself rather than leave.]

FINDING COMMON GROUND

Reading these two thought sketches isn't really like following an arrow-straight path. For a while, you may have *thought* you understood the speaker every step of the way, but by the end, he probably managed to surprise you with a sudden twist of thought. What was your reading experience like? Did it resemble other people's? Discuss with classmates how and why, in each sketch, your perceptions of the prose poem changed as you read further.

Once you've absorbed Solzhenitsyn's surprises, though, here's the question: What do these writings mean to *you*? For your Reader's Log, you were invited to think of your own home and how you might respond to being exiled from it—a fertile field for discussion. Another way of "finding common ground," of connecting with Solzhenitsyn or any writer, is by digging into the differences between your perspective and the writer's—just as a discussion of differences can sometimes bring friends into a closer relationship with one another. You aren't necessarily expected to understand or agree with everything a writer says.

For each prose poem, challenge or query Solzhenitsyn about something, whether an idea, an experience, an image, or something else. Here are examples of two challenges:

- Isn't it possible to have "fresh air to breathe" and not be free?

- Isn't an allegory that equates people with ants already manipulating readers? Would all humans drawn back to a homeland just "run about" and perish pointlessly?

ALEKSANDR SOLZHENITSYN 969

Finding Common Ground

Ask volunteers to share their impressions of the prose poems and their experiences with interpreting these works. Challenge students to make reading maps of the poems that list their impressions and ideas at each stage of the poem's organization. Have students compare their work.

Arrange students in groups of four or five to answer the questions posed in the Finding Common Ground exercise. Ask them to imagine discussing the questions with the author himself and to imagine how Solzhenitsyn would answer their questions.

Into the Story

Author Biography p. 970

Before You Read p. 970

- **Reading Focus: Scaffolding** Students read about siege mentality.
- **Quickwrite: Prior Knowledge** Freewrite about children of war
- **Elements of Literature: Point of View**

Through the Story

"In the Shadow of War" pp. 971–973

Words to Own pp. 971–973

Connections: A Letter pp. 974–975 "Zagreb: A Letter to My Daughter"

Making Meanings p. 976

Beyond the Story

Choices: Building Your Portfolio p. 976

- **Writer's Notebook:** Note questions about story and Nigerian civil war
- **Critical Writing:** Write an essay explaining the significance of a symbol
- **Critical Writing:** Write an essay connecting Yeats' poem to prose selections

Ben Okri
(1959–   )

Ben Okri.

Ben Okri grew up in the delta area of southern Nigeria. Although he later moved to London, his stories are set in Nigeria. Okri seems especially haunted by remembrances of the Nigerian Civil War (1967–1970), often called the Biafran War. This war began when the Ibo (ē′bō) peoples tried to secede from Nigeria and form their own state, called the Republic of Biafra. Thousands of people were killed in the civil war that ensued, and many more died of starvation. In fact, the very word *Biafra* today suggests images of swollen-bellied children holding up bowls and begging for food. The image of the starving child in Okri's story is a stark reminder of the horror of this war.

Okri first gained recognition in England with the publication of two novels, *Flowers and Shadows* (1980) and *The Landscapes Within* (1981), and a collection of short stories, *Incidents at the Shrine* (1986). The short story that follows, "In the Shadow of War," is from *Stars of the New Curfew* (1988), Okri's first book to be published in the United States.

Okri's awards include the Commonwealth Writers' Prize for Africa and the *Paris Review* Aga Khan Prize for fiction. His 1991 novel, *The Famished Road,* received England's Booker Prize. *Songs of Enchantment,* a sequel to *The Famished Road,* appeared in 1993 and *Astonishing the Gods,* in 1995.

BEFORE YOU READ
IN THE SHADOW OF WAR

Reading Focus

Siege Mentality

The United States has not known war on its own soil since 1865. But in some parts of the world, a state of war is almost constant, especially in places where ethnic and religious strife runs high. In such places the tension of war weighs constantly on people's minds and spirits, even while life's routines go on.

This story is set in a village in the heart of Nigeria during the Nigerian Civil War. Right outside the village is a dense forest where magical transformations seem possible—adding to the mysteries of this unsettling story.

Quickwrite

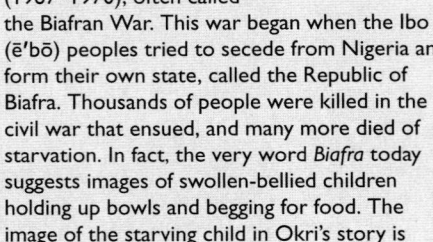

How might children who grow up amid war be different from other children? Freewrite your ideas.

Elements of Literature

Point of View

Ben Okri was only eight years old when the Nigerian Civil War broke out, so it's not surprising that his main character, Omovo, is a child. Okri uses the **limited third-person point of view** to tell the story through Omovo's eyes and childlike understanding. War is a frightening, confusing time for children, but a civil war, when neighbor fights neighbor, is especially so. Are the soldiers in this story good-hearted or evil? Is the veiled woman a supernatural being or a mere mortal? And if she is a mortal, is she an innocent or a spy? Because Omovo has a limited understanding of what is happening, the limited third-person point of view deepens all these enigmas.

970 THE TWENTIETH CENTURY

- **Planning Instruction** See *Teaching Notes, Teaching Resources B,* p. 113, for additional information for this selection.
- **Instructional Support** See *Graphic Organizer for Active Reading, Teaching Resources B,* p. 124, for a Through the Story activity.

- **Audiotaped Readings** To help auditory learners through the lesson, use the *Selected Reading, Audiocassette 2, Side B,* in the *Audiovisual Resources Binder.*
- **Assessment** See *Selection Test, Test Booklet,* pp. 206–207.
- **Language Link** For instruction and

practice in identifying dangling and misplaced modifiers, see *Language Link, Teaching Resources B,* pp. 125–126, and *Language and Writing Skills Worksheets,* pp. 66–67.
- **Reinforcement** Use the *Words to Own* worksheet in *Teaching Resources B,* p. 127.

In the Shadow of War

Ben Okri

That afternoon three soldiers came to the village. They scattered the goats and chickens. They went to the palm-frond bar and ordered a calabash[1] of palm wine. They drank amidst the flies.

Omovo watched them from the window as he waited for his father to go out. They both listened to the radio. His father had bought the old Grundig[2] cheaply from a family that had to escape the city when the war broke out. He had covered the radio with a white cloth and made it look like a household fetish.[3] They listened to the news of bombings and air raids in the interior of the country. His father combed his hair, parted it carefully, and slapped some after-shave on his unshaven face. Then he struggled into the shabby coat that he had long outgrown.

Omovo stared out of the window, irritated with his father. At that hour, for the past seven days, a strange woman with a black veil over her head had been going past the house. She went up the village paths, crossed the Express road, and disappeared into the forest. Omovo waited for her to appear.

The main news was over. The radio announcer said an eclipse of the moon was expected that night. Omovo's father wiped the sweat off his face with his palm and said, with some bitterness:

"As if an eclipse will stop this war."

"What is an eclipse?" Omovo asked.

"That's when the world goes dark and strange things happen."

"Like what?"

His father lit a cigarette.

"The dead start to walk about and sing. So don't stay out late, eh."

Omovo nodded.

"Heclipses hate children. They eat them."

Omovo didn't believe him. His father smiled, gave Omovo his ten kobo[4] allowance, and said:

1. **calabash** (kal′ə·bash′): cup made from a calabash, a type of gourd.
2. **Grundig:** German brand of radio.
3. **fetish** (fet′ish): object believed to have magical powers.
4. **kobo** (käb′ō): Nigerian monetary unit.

"Turn off the radio. It's bad for a child to listen to news of war."

Omovo turned if off. His father poured a libation[5] at the doorway and then prayed to his ancestors. When he had finished he picked up his briefcase and strutted out briskly. Omovo watched him as he threaded his way up the path to the bus stop at the main road. When a danfo bus[6] came, and his father went with it, Omovo turned the radio back on. He sat on the windowsill and waited for the woman. The last time he saw her she had glided past with agitated flutters of her yellow smock. The children stopped what they were doing and stared at her. They had said that she had no shadow. They had said that her feet never touched the ground. As she went past, the children began to throw things at her. She didn't flinch, didn't quicken her pace, and didn't look back.

The heat was <u>stupefying</u>. Noises dimmed and lost their edges. The villagers stumbled about their various tasks as if they were sleepwalking. The three soldiers drank palm wine and played draughts[7] beneath the sun's <u>oppressive</u> glare. Omovo noticed that whenever children went past the bar the soldiers called them, talked to them, and gave them some money. Omovo ran down the stairs and slowly walked past the bar. The soldiers stared at him. On his way back one of them called him.

"What's your name?" he asked.

Omovo hesitated, smiled mischievously, and said:

"Heclipse."

The soldier laughed, spraying Omovo's face with spit. He had a face crowded with veins. His companions seemed uninterested. They swiped flies and concentrated on their game. Their guns

5. **libation** (lī·bā′shən): liquid poured onto the ground as a sacrifice to the gods.
6. **danfo bus:** small bus. In the region surrounding Lagos, *danfo* means "in disrepair."
7. **draughts** (drafts): British game of checkers.

WORDS TO OWN

stupefying (stoo′pə·fī′in) *v.* used as *adj.:* dulling the mind and senses; bringing on a state of lethargy.
oppressive (ə·pres′iv) *adj.:* hard to bear.

Into the Story

Using **BEFORE YOU READ** p. 970

Quickwrite
Before they write, direct students to review their ideas of how day-to-day life in a war zone might differ from life during peacetime.

Through the Story

A. Reader's Response: First Thoughts
❓ What are your impressions of the soldiers and the village? [Sample responses: The soldiers seem disruptive and bored. The village is small and placid.]

B. Critical Reading: Analyzing Character
❓ What kind of man is Omovo's father? [Possible answers: The father is frugal and cautious. He is staying informed about the war. Earlier in the passage, he is meticulous about his appearance, even in an air raid. There is a contrast between this reticent man and the war around him.]

C. Critical Reading: Analyzing Setting
Beginning with the introduction of the "strange woman," find details that create an atmosphere of confusion and unreality—the rumor that the woman has no shadow, the eclipse, and "sleepwalking" villagers.

WORDS TO OWN
The following vocabulary words are defined in the Words to Own at the bottom of the pupil's page.

stupefying p. 971	ostentatious p. 972
oppressive p. 971	dementedly p. 973
succumbed p. 972	

STRATEGIES FOR INCLUSION

Strategic Reading Have several students read aloud one passage of the text—for example, the section that describes the woman, as Omovo and the soldiers follow her. Have everyone record their impressions of the woman. This should just be a list of words and phrases that occur to them without thought or analysis (the woman is "injured," "mysterious"). In group discussion, students should identify the specific words or phrases in the story that give those impressions.

INTEGRATING THE LANGUAGE ARTS

Visual Have students draw a flowchart representing the events in the story. Wherever they think it is appropriate, they should draw a representation of an interruption in the flow, where things do not follow, do not make sense.

A. Critical Reading: Analyzing Character

Despite his initial interest in the soldiers' money, Omovo refuses it. What does this refusal suggest about his character? [Possible answers: He has principles, even though he lies to the soldiers; he may not understand the political situation, but he resents being bribed to spy on the woman.]

B. Language Note: Word Choice

? What kinds of **imagery** does the author use to describe the soldiers? Why? How is it different from the imagery he has used previously to describe the woman? [The soldiers are coarse and sensual—one is so large he is nearly splitting his clothes—and they stumble in the heat; the woman is dressed in faded gray wrappers and a veil that covers her face, and she seems to float and leave no shadow.]

C. Critical Reading: Finding Details

? What details reveal that there is a war going on? [In this paragraph, dilapidated signs and fences, a deserted factory that may indicate that people have fled the village, and the ominous skeleton may be cited. Earlier details include mention of the bombing, air raids, news of the war, and soldiers in the village bar.] Discuss with the class things that they envision about wartime from reading and watching television newscasts or movies about war.

D. Literary Element: Point of View

? What is the point of view from which this story is written? [Third-person limited point of view.] We see what Omovo sees without an adult understanding or analysis of what it might mean. Have students discuss possible implications of the unfinished estates, empty cement factory, deserted workers' sheds. What is going on here that the boy can observe but is not mature enough to interpret? [These details depict the devastating effect of war on the landscape and suggest that people may have fled the violence.]

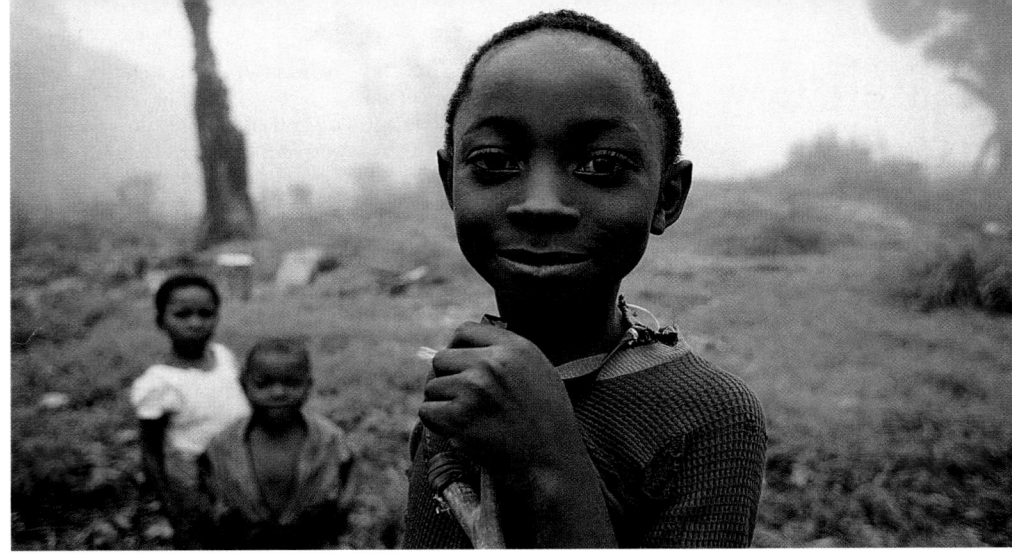

At Obudu Cattle Ranch on Sonkwala Mountain, Nigeria (May 1989).

were on the table. Omovo noticed that they had numbers on them. The man said:

"Did your father give you that name because you have big lips?"

His companions looked at Omovo and laughed. Omovo nodded.

"You are a good boy," the man said. He paused. Then he asked, in a different voice:

"Have you seen that woman who covers her face with a black cloth?"

"No."

The man gave Omovo ten kobo and said:

"She is a spy. She helps our enemies. If you see her, come and tell us at once, you hear?"

Omovo refused the money and went back upstairs. He repositioned himself on the windowsill. The soldiers occasionally looked at him. The heat got to him and soon he fell asleep in a sitting position. The cocks, crowing dispiritedly, woke him up. He could feel the afternoon softening into evening. The soldiers dozed in the bar. The hourly news came on. Omovo listened without comprehension to the day's casualties. The announcer succumbed to the stupor, yawned, apologized, and gave further details of the fighting.

Omovo looked up and saw that the woman had already gone past. The men had left the bar. He saw them weaving between the eaves of the thatch houses, stumbling through the heat-mists.

972 THE TWENTIETH CENTURY

The woman was further up the path. Omovo ran downstairs and followed the men. One of them had taken off his uniform top. The soldier behind had buttocks so big they had begun to split his pants. Omovo followed them across the Express road. When they got into the forest the men stopped following the woman, and took a different route. They seemed to know what they were doing. Omovo hurried to keep the woman in view.

He followed her through the dense vegetation. She wore faded wrappers and a gray shawl, with the black veil covering her face. She had a red basket on her head. He completely forgot to determine if she had a shadow, or whether her feet touched the ground.

He passed unfinished estates, with their flaking, ostentatious signboards and their collapsing fences. He passed an empty cement factory: Blocks lay crumbled in heaps and the workers' sheds were deserted. He passed a baobab[8] tree,

---

8. baobab (bā′ō·bab′): thick-trunked African tree; often called "upside-down tree" because its branches look like roots.

WORDS TO OWN
succumbed (sə·kumd′) v.: yielded; gave way to.
ostentatious (äs′tən·tā′shəs) adj.: showy.

---

under which was the intact skeleton of a large animal. A snake dropped from a branch and slithered through the undergrowth. In the distance, over the cliff edge, he heard loud music and people singing war slogans above the noise.

He followed the woman till they came to a rough camp on the plain below. Shadowy figures moved about in the half-light of the cave. The woman went to them. The figures surrounded her and touched her and led her into the cave. He heard their weary voices thanking her. When the woman reappeared she was without the basket. Children with kwashiorkor[9] stomachs and women wearing rags led her halfway up the hill. Then, reluctantly, touching her as if they might not see her again, they went back.

He followed her till they came to a muddied river. She moved as if an invisible force were trying to blow her away. Omovo saw capsized canoes and trailing, waterlogged clothes on the dark water. He saw floating items of sacrifice: loaves of bread in polythene[10] wrappings, gourds of food, Coca-Cola cans. When he looked at the canoes again they had changed into the shapes of swollen dead animals. He saw outdated currencies on the riverbank. He noticed the terrible smell in the air. Then he heard the sound of heavy breathing from behind him, then someone coughing and spitting. He recognized the voice of one of the soldiers urging the others to move faster. Omovo crouched in the shadow of a tree. The soldiers strode past. Not long afterward he heard a scream. The men had caught up with the woman. They crowded round her.

"Where are the others?" shouted one of them.

The woman was silent.

"You dis witch! You want to die, eh? Where are they?"

She stayed silent. Her head was bowed. One of the soldiers coughed and spat toward the river.

"Talk! Talk!" he said, slapping her.

The fat soldier tore off her veil and threw it to the ground. She bent down to pick it up and stopped in the attitude of kneeling, her head still bowed. Her head was bald, and disfigured with a deep corrugation.[11] There was a livid gash along the side of her face. The bare-chested soldier pushed her. She fell on her face and lay still. The lights changed over the forest and for the first time Omovo saw that the dead animals on the river were in fact the corpses of grown men. Their bodies were tangled with riverweed and their eyes were bloated. Before he could react, he heard another scream. The woman was getting up, with the veil in her hand. She turned to the fat soldier, drew herself to her fullest height, and spat in his face. Waving the veil in the air, she began to howl dementedly. The two other soldiers backed away. The fat soldier wiped his face and lifted the gun to the level of her stomach. A moment before Omovo heard the shot a violent beating of wings just above him scared him from his hiding place. He ran through the forest screaming. The soldiers tramped after him. He ran through a mist which seemed to have risen from the rocks. As he ran he saw an owl staring at him from a canopy of leaves. He tripped over the roots of a tree and blacked out when his head hit the ground.

When he woke up it was very dark. He waved his fingers in front of his face and saw nothing. Mistaking the darkness for blindness he screamed, thrashed around, and ran into a door. When he recovered from his shock he heard voices outside and the radio crackling on about the war. He found his way to the balcony, full of wonder that his sight had returned. But when he got there he was surprised to find his father sitting on the sunken cane chair, drinking palm wine with the three soldiers. Omovo rushed to his father and pointed frantically at the three men.

"You must thank them," his father said. "They brought you back from the forest."

Omovo, overcome with delirium, began to tell his father what he had seen. But his father, smiling apologetically at the soldiers, picked up his son and carried him off to bed.

---

9. **kwashiorkor** (kwä′shē·ôr′kôr′): severe disease of young children, caused by deficiency of protein and calories and marked by stunted growth and a protruding belly.
10. **polythene** (päl′i·thēn′): term used in most English-speaking countries other than the United States for *polyethylene* (päl′ē·eth′ə·lēn′), a synthetic substance used to make tough, lightweight plastics, films, and the like.

11. **corrugation** (kôr′ə·gā′shən): groove or furrow.

- -

WORDS TO OWN
dementedly (dē·ment′id·lē) *adv.*: madly; wildly.

- -

BEN OKRI 973

E. Critical Reading: Making Inferences

The woman is taken into a cave by "shadowy figures," and the author describes children with protruding bellies; when the woman emerges, she does not have her basket. What can readers infer about the woman, her mission, the people in the cave, and the contents of her basket? [The people in the cave are probably war refugees to whom the woman is carrying food or other supplies in the basket.]

F. Critical Reading: Making Inferences

[?] What might these harsh details indicate about the woman's past and the reasons she carries the basket to the refugees? [She has suffered greatly, perhaps as an earlier victim of the warfare, and she sympathizes with those who are suffering now. She is willing to take risks.]

G. Critical Reading: Analyzing Plot

[?] How does this climactic moment resolve the conflict in the story? [The mysterious woman the soldiers follow is caught and shot; Omovo discovers her mission and sees the soldiers brutalize her.]

H. Literary Element: Foreshadowing

Identify the irony in the final scene of the story. [Neither Omovo nor the reader fully expects the father to be friendly with the soldiers; Omovo's father asks him to thank the soldiers who killed the woman.] Look back at early details about the father, and discuss how the author sets up the father's character for this kind of behavior. [The father is cautious and pragmatic rather than ideological or passionate. He is shown early to be a man who does the expedient thing and does not take risks.]

CLASSROOM MANAGEMENT

Teacher's Self-Reflection How well you prepare and instruct a group will affect the success of group projects. Look closely at how well you prepared the groups for their tasks. Did you
1. Provide a clear, concise statement of goals?
2. Provide written guidelines and suggestions for step-by-step work?
3. Provide clear self-evaluation tools (specific questions for students to answer)?
4. Provide clear evaluation that specifically referred to stated goals and procedures?

ASSESSMENT TOOLS

Check Test: Questions and Answers
1. What item has Omovo's father disguised as a household fetish? [A radio.]
2. How do the village children react to the "strange woman"? [They throw things at her.]
3. What are the soldiers giving the village children? [Money.]
4. What startles Omovo before he hears the shot? [An owl.]
5. How does Omovo get back from the forest? [The soldiers bring him.]

A. Expansion
In June 1991, the province of Croatia, led by president Franjo Tudjman, voted to form a republic independent of Yugoslavia. The separation was opposed by the area's Serbian minority, a group of about 600,000 people that had voted to form its own autonomous regions in Croatia. President Tudjman did not recognize Serbian autonomy, and a civil war began.

Connections — A LETTER

The letter below was written on April 7, 1992, shortly after full-scale war erupted in the former Yugoslavia over land claimed by several ethnic groups. Sent from Zagreb, the historical capital of Croatia, Drakulíc's letter provides a poignant and personal history of the conflict in her homeland. She had thought, however hopefully, that her daughter might be able to live free of the past, outside the shadow of war.

Zagreb: A Letter to My Daughter

Slavenka Drakulíc

My dear R,

This morning I went to your empty room. Its tidiness was so strange: your usually unmade bed now covered with a blue quilt, a spotless desk, a chair without your T-shirts hanging from it, a carpet free of your scattered shoes. I miss you, I miss your voice, the notes that you left on the table when you came in late at night and that I read with my first morning coffee.

Today marks nine months since you left the country. I knew that you would go eventually, that you'd leave me, this house, your room where your childhood toys and books sit side by side with your evening dresses and makeup. That thought comforts me. *Living on her own will make her stronger, she will see the world, it is good for a young person to live abroad, and Vienna is only six hours away:* I keep repeating this to myself like some kind of mantra. Except that I know you didn't intend to leave so soon and so abruptly, didn't expect to leave me and your room, your university, and, more important, your friends here. You left so many things unfinished. You left because of the war.

It began on June 26, 1991, when the Yugoslav Federal Army attacked Slovenia. I was in London at that time, glued to a TV screen and a telephone. We both cried. "What do I do, Mama?" you asked on that first day of the war, but I didn't know how to advise you. What does one say to one's child when war begins? I didn't want you to panic after the army attacked Slovenia—even though it is only a hundred miles from Zagreb. One part of me could not believe that it was a real war because a real war could not happen—it would be too stupid, too absurd—here in Europe. But there was another part of me that knew it was real and knew there was no turning back.

One afternoon while I was still in London—I remember with great clarity that it was Tuesday, July 2—we were speaking on the telephone, and in the middle of our conversation you started screaming, "Mama, they're shooting next door!" I could hear the shots in the garden next to ours; I could visualize its high wall covered with roses and bunches of grapes hanging from the vine, the way the sun shone through its leaves at that particular moment of the late afternoon. And I could see you standing there, by the window overlooking it, lost and pale, trembling. You dropped the receiver, and then I heard your voice, half-cry and half-whimper, a voice I did not recognize. I don't think I have ever experienced such helplessness. I can hear it now, every sound that entered the receiver on that day, the distant hum of radio news in the background, the tram that passed by outside, and the sudden silence that followed it. Then the frightened yet soft voice of your boyfriend, Andrej, trying to calm you down. *Hush, it's nothing, it's nothing, just a drunken soldier,* he said, but it was too late, because at that moment the war began for both of us.

Recent events here have led me to think about your father, sitting in Toronto. We married when I was eighteen and he was nineteen. He was from a Serbian family and I was from a Croatian one, but that didn't mean anything to us then. World War II had long been over by the time we were born, and people of my generation were trying to escape the war's shadow, to forget and just live our lives. Your father and I never discussed our family's different nationalities. Not because it was forbidden but because it felt unimportant. Perhaps our attitude was a consequence of the repression of the Communist regime, of the brainwashing of our education system, the plan to create an artificial "Yugoslav" nation. All I know is that we were interested not in the past, in who killed whom and why, but in our own lives.

B

The tragedy and the paradox of this situation now is that you will have to decide to take his side or mine, to become Serb or Croat. In this war there is no middle ground. You as a Croat or a Serb become responsible for what all other Croats or Serbs do. You are reduced to a single nationality—almost sentenced to it, since nationality in a war brings a danger of getting killed just because of it. You are now in a situation where you are forced to choose, to identify with something that has always been irrelevant to you, a total abstraction. "I am from Zagreb," you used to say, and perhaps it is the only right answer—to be a citizen. But not now. Not here.

—*from Harper's Magazine*

Horror and Scream by Dinko, age 12, from Pozega, from *I DREAM OF PEACE: Images of War by Children of Former Yugoslavia*. Preface by Maurice Sendak.

B. Exploring the Historical Period

The kingdom of Yugoslavia was invaded during World War II, and the country was divided among Germany, Italy, Hungary, and Bulgaria. The partition caused great political unrest, and Serbian nationalists waged guerilla warfare against the pro-Fascist puppet government that was formed in Croatia. In retaliation, Croat nationalists initiated a campaign to exterminate the Serbs.

CONNECTING WITH "IN THE SHADOW OF WAR"

What similarities or differences do you find in the letter and the story? [Similarities: Both selections include a child who acts quite brave, and the context of each lets the reader see some of the horrors of war. Differences: The father in "In the Shadow of War" seems more aloof and less protective of his son than does the mother in the letter, who wishes fervently that she could protect her child.]

Making Meanings

First Thoughts

1. Students may say they were concerned for Omovo's safety when he is chased by the soldiers.

Reviewing the Text

a. He says the world might go dark, and the dead might walk around. He adds that "heclipses" eat children.

b. The children say she has no shadow and believe she is not human. She is captured, brutalized, and shot.

Shaping Interpretations

2. Omovo seems suspicious of soldiers and sympathetic toward the woman.

3. The father may be trying to keep Omovo safe inside. Omovo does not believe his story.

4. The soldiers want Omovo to reveal the veiled woman's location. He refuses the money because he is fascinated by the woman.

5. Omovo is curious about why the soldiers want her.

6. The details show the war's physical and economic destruction. The skeleton may be human.

7. The malnourished children indicate she probably is bringing food.

8. Omovo may feel embarrassed, angry, or betrayed.

9. Omovo cannot take in the brutality that he sees around him. He may mask the horror with gentler images.

Extending the Text

10. **(Analysis)** Both narratives show war's horror, but the child's perspective in Okri's story makes war appear dreamlike and surreal.

Beyond the Story

Choices: Building Your Portfolio

1. **Writer's Notebook:** Remind students to save their work. They may use it as prewriting for the Writer's Workshop on p. 1053.

2. **Critical Writing** Tell students to

MAKING MEANINGS

First Thoughts

1. At what point in Okri's story were you most worried about what might happen to Omovo?

> ### Reviewing the Text
>
> a. What does Omovo's father say might happen during an eclipse of the moon?
>
> b. What do the children believe about the veiled woman? What happens to her?

Shaping Interpretations

2. What are Omovo's feelings toward the soldiers? toward the woman?

3. Why do you think Omovo's father tells him about the eclipse? How does the boy react?

4. What is the soldier's **motive** for offering Omovo money? Why does Omovo refuse it?

5. Why do you think Omovo follows the soldiers who are following the veiled woman?

6. The story's **limited third-person point of view** means that we see events through a child's eyes. How do *you* interpret "unfinished estates," an empty factory, and the skeleton Omovo sees?

7. What do you think the woman brings to the people in the cave? What clues are provided?

8. At the end of the story, Omovo wakes up to find his father drinking with the soldiers. When Omovo tries to tell his father what happened, his father smiles "apologetically" at the soldiers. How do you think Omovo feels toward his father at this point? Explain.

9. How do you explain the transformations Omovo observes (canoes to dead animals to dead men)? Is he frightened? delirious? Or is there some other explanation? As you answer, draw on your Reader's Log freewriting about war's effects on children.

Extending the Text

10. Okri's story and Slavenka Drakulíc's letter (page 974) both concern war, but they are told from different points of view. How are the two narratives alike? different?

list text references to the radio and to note the radio's role in the context. Students also may write brief replies to the questions and use the notes to outline their essays.

3. **Critical Writing** Suggest that students collect their thoughts in a graphic organizer, such as a Venn Diagram.

CHOICES:
Building Your Portfolio

Writer's Notebook

1. Collecting Ideas for an Informative Report

Unless you're already familiar with the Ibo peoples' customs and culture, reading "In the Shadow of War" probably made you curious about them. What questions come to mind as you reflect on the story and think about the Nigerian Civil War? (See Okri's biography on page 970.) Jot down your thoughts, and save your notes for the Writer's Workshop on page 1053.

Critical Writing

2. Tuned In

The radio plays a **symbolic** role in Okri's story. Find all the references to the radio, and then write a short essay explaining its significance. Here are some questions to get you started: Why is the brand name of the radio (a trivial detail) given? What is significant about the radio's resembling a fetish? What does Omovo listen to on the radio? What is the difference between hearing a disembodied voice on a radio and actually seeing an event?

Critical Writing

3. Holding the Center

In an essay discuss the connections between the famous poem that opens this collection (W. B. Yeats's "The Second Coming") and the two prose selections here: Ben Okri's story and Slavenka Drakulíc's letter to her daughter. Find specific details and images from the Yeats poem that relate to images and details in Okri's story and in the mother's letter. You might also include the child's painting on page 975 in your essay.

PORTFOLIO ASSESSMENT

Choices: Assessment Criteria For help in evaluating these Choices assignments, see the criteria in the *Portfolio Management System,* p. 162.

Collection 13

THE TRANSFORMING IMAGINATION

Theme: **Memory, Magic, and Metamorphosis**
These selections express personal and idiosyncratic visions of the world.

Thematic Focus

- **The Lake Isle of Innisfree/The Wild Swans at Coole** Memories of peace, beauty, loss, and love inform Yeats's poems.
- **Araby** The narrator's vivid imagination and infatuation with a young woman lead him to feel anguish and anger at his foolish vanity.
- **The Rocking-Horse Winner** A boy's rocking horse becomes a means to cope with his unhappy family's financial problems.
- **The Demon Lover** This tale about a strange pact leaves the reader wondering what is real and what is not.
- **Fern Hill/Do Not Go Gentle into That Good Night** These poems offer distinct views of living and dying.
- **B. Wordsworth** A child's perception of the world collides with reality.
- **Mushrooms** Poetic creation is celebrated in an extended metaphor about the cycles of life.

Literary Focus

Literary Element	Selection / Feature
Verbal Music/Symbol/ Assonance and Alliteration	The Lake Isle of Innisfree/ The Wild Swans at Coole
Epiphany/Irony	Araby
Symbol	The Rocking-Horse Winner
Flashback	The Demon Lover
Lyric Poetry/Wordplay/ Elegy/Villanelle	Fern Hill/Do Not Go Gentle into That Good Night
Setting/Vernacular	B. Wordsworth
Free Verse	Mushrooms

Writing Focus

The following flowchart shows how the writing assignment for each selection relates to the writing assignment presented in the Writer's Workshop at the end of the Collection.

Selection	Work-in-Progress Assignment
Lake Isle/Wild Swans	Collect ideas for an informative paper p. 983
Araby	Freewrite topics for research p. 995
The Rocking-Horse Winner	Create questions for research p. 1010
The Demon Lover	Consider topics for research p. 1024
Fern Hill/Do Not Go . . .	List ways people mark milestones p. 1040
B. Wordsworth	Write a thesis statement p. 1049
Mushrooms	List subjects for further research p. 1052
Writer's Workshop	Write an informative report pp. 1053–1057

Collection Planner

SELECTION / FEATURE	Literary Elements / Active Reading	Writing	Speaking and Listening	Language and Vocabulary
The Lake Isle of Innisfree/The Wild Swans at Coole William Butler Yeats (pp. 978–983)	• Reader's Log pp. 979, 981 • Verbal Music p. 979 • Symbol p. 981	• Critical Writing: Write essay p. 983 • Creative Writing: Write poem p. 983		• Language and Style: Assonance and Alliteration p. 980
Lot's Wife Anna Akhmatova (pp. 984–986)	• Reader's Log p. 985		• Discuss questions p. 986	
Araby James Joyce (pp. 987–997) Spotlight On: The Influence of James Joyce (pp. 996–997)	• Reader's Log p. 988 • Epiphany p. 988 • Irony p. 994	• Critical Writing: Write essay p. 995 • Creative Writing: Create story map p. 995 • Creative Writing: Write sketch p. 995	• Performance: Create oral reading p. 995	
The Rocking-Horse Winner D. H. Lawrence (pp. 998–1016) Primary Sources: D. H. Lawrence on Money (p. 1009) Spotlight On: Film as Literature (pp. 1012–1016)	• Reader's Log p. 999 • Symbol p. 999	• Critical Writing: Write essay p. 1010 • Creative Writing: Write happy ending p. 1010 • Creative Writing: Write sketch p. 1010 • Playwriting/Performance: Write staging p. 1010	• Playwriting/Performance: Prepare and perform a portion of the story for the stage p. 1010	• How to Own a Word: Analyzing How New Words Are Formed p. 1011
The Demon Lover Elizabeth Bowen (pp. 1017–1025)	• Reader's Log p. 1018 • Flashback p. 1018	• Critical Writing: Write comparison essay p. 1024 • Creative Writing: Describe face p. 1025 • Film: Write film proposal p. 1025	• Music: Choose or compose background music for story p. 1025	
Axolotl Julio Cortázar (pp. 1026–1031)	• Reader's Log p. 1027		• Discuss questions p. 1031	
Fern Hill/Do Not Go Gentle into That Good Night Dylan Thomas (pp. 1032–1040) **Connections: Green Gulch** Loren Eiseley (p. 1036)	• Reader's Log pp. 1033, 1038 • Lyric Poetry p. 1033 • Elegy p. 1038	• Critical Writing: Write essay p. 1040 • Creative Writing: Imitate style p. 1040 • Creative Writing: Reply to poem p. 1040 • Creative Writing: Write villanelle p. 1040		• Language and Style: Wordplay p. 1037 Villanelle p. 1040
B. Wordsworth V. S. Naipaul (pp. 1041–1049)	• Reader's Log p. 1042 • Setting p. 1042	• Critical Writing: Write character analysis p. 1049 • Creative Writing: Write character sketch p. 1049	• Social Studies/Music: Research and present findings on calypso music p. 1049	• Language and Style: Vernacular p. 1049
Mushrooms Margaret Atwood (pp. 1050–1052)	• Reader's Log p. 1050 • Free Verse p. 1050	• Creative Writing: Write nature poem p. 1052		
Writer's Workshop: Writing an Informative Report (pp. 1053–1057)		• Writing process: Informative report pp. 1053–1057		
Language Workshop: Sentence Variety (p. 1058)		• Revise essay p. 1058		• Sentence Variety p. 1058

Collection Resources

Teaching Resources B	Audiovisual Resources Binder	Test Booklet
Cross-Curricular Activity p. 161	Fine Art Transparencies 13.1–13.2	Collection 13 Test pp. 224–226

 Computer disk or CD-ROM

 Videodisc

 Audiocassette

Overhead Transparency

PROGRAM RESOURCES

Electronic Media	Teaching Resources with Organizer		Audiovisual Resources Binder
	Teaching Resources B	**Other Resources**	
• Test Generator	• Teaching Notes pp. 129–130 • Reading Organizers pp. 138–139	• Test Booklet: Selection Tests pp. 211–212 • Portfolio Management System pp. 163–164	• Selected Reading, Audiocassette 3, Side A • Elements of Literature Transparency 13.3
	• Teaching Notes p. 130–131		
• Test Generator • Language Workshop: Combining sentences	• Teaching Notes pp. 131–132 • Reading Organizer p. 140 • Language Link pp. 141–142 • Words to Own p. 143	• Test Booklet: Selection Test pp. 213–214 • Language and Writing Skills Worksheets pp. 111–118 • PM System pp. 165–166	• Elements of Literature Transparencies, 13.4, 13.5 • Selected Reading, Audiocassette 3, Side B
• Test Generator • Language Workshop: Sentence variety	• Teaching Notes p. 132–133 • Reading Organizer p. 144 • Language Link pp. 145–146 • Words to Own p. 147	• Test Booklet: Selection Test pp. 215–216 • Language and Writing Skills Worksheets pp. 85–96, p. 106 • Portfolio Management System pp. 39, 167–168	• How to Own a Word Transparency 13.6
• Test Generator • Language Workshop: Sentence variety	• Teaching Notes p. 133–134 • Reading Organizer p. 148 • Language Link pp. 149–150 • Words to Own p. 151	• Test Booklet: Selection Test pp. 217–218 • Language and Writing Skills Worksheets p. 105 • Portfolio Management System pp. 43, 169–170	
	• Teaching Notes p. 134		
• Test Generator	• Teaching Notes pp. 134–135 • Reading Organizers pp. 152–153	• Test Booklet: Selection Test pp. 219–220 • Portfolio Management System pp. 53, 171–172	
• Test Generator • Language Workshop: Commas	• Teaching Notes p. 136 • Reading Organizer p. 154 • Language Link pp. 155–156 • Words to Own p. 157	• Test Booklet: Selection Test pp. 221–222 • Language and Writing Skills Worksheets pp. 131–137 • PM System pp. 173–174	• Selected Reading, Audiocassette 2, Side B
• Test Generator	• Teaching Notes p. 137 • Reading Organizer p. 158	• Test Booklet: Selection Test p. 223	• Selected Reading, Audiocassette 3, Side A
• Writer's Workshop 2: Informative Report		• Portfolio Management System pp. 176–178	• Revision Transparencies 13.7–13.8
• Language Workshop: Sentence variety	• Language Workshop pp. 159–160		

Proofreading Warm-ups

You may use the following exercises to help students practice their proofreading skills. The proofreading exercises are designed to reinforce the language skills introduced in the previous collections. Copy a set of incorrect sentences onto the chalkboard, and have students find and correct the spelling, punctuation, usage, and mechanical errors in each sentence. Ask students to share and discuss their responses.

	Sentences with Errors	Sentences Corrected	Skills Covered
1	a. whose going to read the poem The Lake Isle of Innisfree asked Mrs. Thompson b. is it one of Yeat's poems queried Cindy	a. "Who is going to read the poem 'The Lake Isle of Innisfree'?" asked Mrs. Thompson. b. "Is it one of Yeats's poems?" queried Cindy.	Quotation marks (single and double), Capitalization, *Who's/whose* usage, Spelling, End marks
2	a. Yeats' used alliteration to try and imitate sounds. b. In one of his poems the alliteration echos the sound of lake water	a. Yeats used alliteration to try to imitate sounds. b. In one of his poems, the alliteration echoes the sound of lake water.	Capitalization, Apostrophe usage, Infinitive usage, Comma usage, Spelling, End marks
3	a. the short story Araby is told from a 1st person pt. of view b. it is the story of a young boy who's dreams collide w/ reality	a. The short story "Araby" is told from a first-person point of view. b. It is the story of a young boy whose dreams collide with reality.	Capitalization, Quotation marks, Spelling out abbreviations, Hyphen usage, *Who's/whose* usage, End marks
4	a. james joyces novel Ulysses published in 1922 caused a stir among critics b. Joyce use's a technique called, stream of consciousness	a. James Joyce's novel <u>Ulysses</u>, published in 1922, caused a stir among critics. b. Joyce uses a technique called stream of consciousness.	Capitalization, Apostrophe usage, Underline book titles, Comma usage, End marks
5	a. did you know that the word scuba is a acronym b. that mean's it is a word formed from the 1st letter(s) of the word's in a name or phrase	a. Did you know that the word <u>scuba</u> is an acronym? b. That means it is a word formed from the first letter(s) of the words in a name or phrase.	Capitalization, Underline words used as words, Apostrophe usage, Spelling out abbreviations, End marks
6	a. their are some basic diffrences among written language and the visual language of film b. for one thing a abstract concept like loyalty or dishonor are often easier to specify in words	a. There are some basic differences between written language and the visual language of film. b. For one thing, an abstract concept like loyalty or dishonor is often easier to specify in words.	Capitalization, Homonyms, Spelling, *Among/between* usage, Comma usage, Nonstandard usage, Subject-verb agreement, End marks
7	a. in the short story The Demon Lover the reader is not quiet sure if the events is real b. I think Mrs. Drover has to much imagination said gina	a. In the short story "The Demon Lover," the reader is not quite sure if the events are real. b. "I think Mrs. Drover has too much imagination," said Gina.	Capitalization, Quotation marks, Comma usage, Spelling, Subject-verb agreement, Homonyms, End marks
8	a. us students really liked reading Dylan Thomas poetry b. me and Cheryl liked Fern Hill, because of it's exuberance	a. We students really liked reading Dylan Thomas's poetry. b. Cheryl and I liked "Fern Hill" because of its exuberance.	Capitalization, Pronoun usage, Apostrophe usage, Quotation marks, Comma usage, End marks
9	a. v. s. naipaul wrote the dialogue for B. Wordsworth in the vernacular or everyday speech of people who live in Trinidad b. naipaul born on the Caribbean Island of Trinidad in 1932	a. V. S. Naipaul wrote the dialogue for "B. Wordsworth" in the vernacular, or everyday speech, of people who live in Trinidad. b. Naipaul was born on the Caribbean island of Trinidad in 1932.	Capitalization, Quotation marks, Comma usage, Fragments, End marks
10	a. margaret atwood one of Canadas foremost authors was born in Ottawa b. her poem Mushrooms an extended metaphor and it appeals to the senses.	a. Margaret Atwood, one of Canada's foremost authors, was born in Ottawa. b. Her poem "Mushrooms" is an extended metaphor, and it appeals to the senses.	Capitalization, Comma usage, Apostrophe usage, Quotation marks, Fragments, Comma usage, End marks

Collection *13*

THE TRANSFORMING IMAGINATION

Yeats
Akhmatova
Joyce
Lawrence
Bowen
Cortázar
Thomas
Naipaul
Atwood

If one is lucky, a solitary fantasy can totally transform one million realities.

—Maya Angelou, *from The Heart of a Woman*

Responding to the Quotation

? How can fantasy transform reality? [Some students may feel that fantasy makes reality irrelevant. Others may think that a pervasive fantasy, such as that of a person becoming a super-hero, touches everything that is part of the person's reality. Others may suggest that a fantasy, or a dream, can help shape one's reality.]

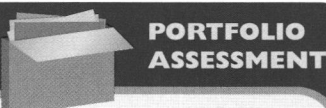

PORTFOLIO ASSESSMENT

Parent/Guardian Involvement For forms that will help a parent or guardian review and respond to a student's portfolio, see the *Portfolio Management System,* pp. 62–63.

PROGRAM MANAGER

- **Integrated Assessment** For a summative assessment of the literature and language skills taught in this collection, see Collection 13 Test, *Test Booklet,* pp. 224–226.
- **Instructional Support** See Fine Art Transparencies 13.1–13.2. Review teacher's notes for transparencies in the *Audiovisual*

Resources Binder for suggestions on how to tie the transparencies to specific reading selections.

- **Extending Collection Theme** See Cross-Curricular Activity: The Transforming Imagination, *Teaching Resources B,* p. 161 for activities in other disciplines and for evaluation criteria.

William Butler Yeats

(1865–1939)

William Butler Yeats (20th century) by John Butler Yeats. Oil on canvas (77 cm × 64 cm).
National Gallery of Ireland, Dublin.

Generally regarded as the twentieth century's greatest poet writing in English, William Butler Yeats (rhymes with *crates*) was born in Dublin, Ireland, the son of a well-known portrait painter. He came on to the literary scene when the Pre-Raphaelite movement of the mid–nineteenth century was enjoying a revival under new influences from Europe.

The revival, called Art Nouveau in the world of painting, emphasized the mysterious and unfathomed—especially those recesses of the mind just then being scrutinized by the great pioneers in psychology, Sigmund Freud and Carl Jung. Particularly in poetry, the revival recommended evocation above statement, symbols above facts, and musical measures above common speech. It was within this atmosphere that the young Yeats established a reputation as a lyricist of great delicacy and as a versifier of old tales drawn from Irish folklore and mythology. In a collection of his early poems, *The Wanderings of Oisin and Other Poems* (1889), Yeats was a romantic dreamer, evoking the mythic and heroic past of Ireland. At this stage of his career, he was a pioneer of the Celtic Revival, determined to make the Irish conscious of their heroic past.

Yeats came abruptly into a new phase in 1914 when, heeding the advice of the American poet Ezra Pound, he set out to create a stark, chiseled, and eloquently resonant kind of poetry. That same year, he published a volume aptly titled *Responsibilities*. The man who had once seen himself as the prophet-priest of Ireland's national destiny was now grappling with his own personal realities. For years, Yeats had idolized and yearned for Maud Gonne, the beautiful Irish political activist who rejected his hand and instead chose another, more politically radical suitor. Finally, Yeats accepted that rejection and

in 1917, at fifty-two, married Georgie Hyde-Lees, an Englishwoman who would remain his "delight and comfort" for the next twenty-two years.

With his private life settled, Yeats then cultivated a public role. From 1922 to 1928, he served as a senator of the newly formed Irish Free State. He also toured the United States, giving ritualized readings of the poems for which, in 1923, he was awarded the Nobel Prize in literature.

As a poet, Yeats may be said to have carved out of the English language a language distinctly his own. Monumentally spare and unadorned, "cold and passionate as the dawn" in Yeats's own words, it confirms the basic definition of poetry as "heightened speech."

Yeats was also a dramatist, and in this role he helped his friend Lady Gregory establish Dublin's landmark Abbey Theatre as a monument to Irish culture and high literary standards. As a playwright, he dealt in poetic drama, allegories, and other nonrealistic approaches, often making adaptations of the ceremonial choreography of the Japanese Nō theater. While Yeats's dramas are more theater pieces than plays, they continue to be produced by small theater groups. Some audiences may agree with Yeats himself, who felt that some of his most memorable poems are embedded, like gems, in the working scripts of these dramas.

Yeats dramatized himself in the grand manner, which was entirely in keeping with his accomplishments and aristocratic pretensions. Nearly ten years after he died in the south of France, his body was disinterred and returned to Ireland, like that of a primitive king, with full ceremony and military pomp, on the deck of a battleship.

Reading Focus
A Place of Peace
Imagination can literally transport us from our busy lives to the calm of a peaceful retreat.

Quickwrite
What is your own vision of a peaceful retreat from everyday, routine life? In your Reader's Log, briefly describe your ideas, or draw a sketch of an ideal place of peace.

Elements of Literature
Verbal Music
As a young man, Yeats inherited much of the vocabulary and poetic posturing of his nineteenth-century predecessors. Phrases in the poem like "veils of the morning" and "midnight's all a glimmer" come from this old-fashioned vocabulary, and Innisfree itself represents all the impossibly idyllic, great good places that weary Victorians "on the roadway, or on the pavements gray" yearned for. Nevertheless, Yeats's lyrical skills, especially his haunting use of **assonance** (the repetition of similar vowel sounds), have created a poem whose verbal music echoes in the memory.

Background
Innisfree is a real island in Sligo, the beautiful county in the west of Ireland where Yeats spent many summers as a child, visiting his grandparents. Yeats once said that the poem came to him when he was in London on a dreary day. He passed a store display that used dripping water in a fountain, and he thought at once of the lake island of his childhood. Yeats's father had once read Thoreau's *Walden* to him. The bean rows and cabin on Innisfree are straight from Walden Woods in Massachusetts.

The Lake Isle of Innisfree
William Butler Yeats

I will arise and go now, and go to Innisfree,
And a small cabin build there, of clay and wattles° made:
Nine bean-rows will I have there, a hive for the honey-bee,
And live alone in the bee-loud glade.

5 And I shall have some peace there, for peace comes dropping slow,
Dropping from the veils of the morning to where the cricket sings;
There midnight's all a glimmer, and noon a purple glow,
And evening full of the linnet's° wings.

I will arise and go now, for always night and day
10 I hear lake water lapping with low sounds by the shore;
While I stand on the roadway, or on the pavements gray,
I hear it in the deep heart's core.

2. **wattles:** interwoven twigs or branches.
8. **linnet's:** A linnet is a European songbird.

Into the Poem

Using BEFORE YOU READ p. 979

Quickwrite
Help students to describe a peaceful place. The following checklist will stimulate mental images:
- Is the light bright, soft, shaded?
- Is it quiet?
- Is there a noticeable scent?
- Is it hot, warm, cold, or cool?

Through the Poem

A. Reader's Response: Shaping Interpretations
? What kind of life does the speaker wish to lead on the island?
[Sample responses: Simple, solitary, peaceful.]

B. Literary Element: Verbal Music
? What sound elements create verbal music in these lines? [The alliterative *s* and *p* sounds; the repetition of *peace* and *dropping*; the assonance of the *ing* sound.]

C. Critical Reading: Drawing Conclusions
? What does the last stanza suggest about the speaker's relationship with nature? [Possible answer: It suggests a mystical connection or basic identification with nature that has been diminished by civilization.]

STRATEGIES FOR INCLUSION

English Language Development To determine students' comprehension of "The Lake Isle of Innisfree," have them create a portrait of the cabin and its surroundings. Students should try to capture not only the physical characteristics, but also the emotional nuances suggested by Yeats.

Auditory Ask students to list all the auditory images in the poem and then try to create the sounds, using both their voices and any objects or instruments that are available in the classroom. They might also try recording the sounds. The auditory images include "bee-loud glade," "cricket sings," "linnet's wings," and "water lapping."

INTEGRATING THE LANGUAGE ARTS

Strategic Reading Each stanza consists of two two-line independent clauses. Ask students to read the poem a clause at a time and try to paraphrase each clause as they read it. Then, ask students to notice the rhyme scheme [abab cdcd efef] and to determine its purpose in the poem. [The rhyme scheme helps link independent clauses to one another.]

Writing: A Letter Based on what they know about Innisfree from the poem, ask students to outline a schedule that the speaker would likely follow on a typical day on the island. After they have outlined the schedule, have students write a letter the speaker might write to a friend about a typical day.

Making Meanings

First Thoughts

1. Responses will vary. Though students may not have a pastoral place, they may have soft sounds and muted images similar to Yeats's.

Shaping Interpretations

2. Go to Innisfree, build a small cabin, and live in it alone.
3. Bees, a cricket singing, and lake water lapping the shore.
4. The island is beautiful, natural, and tranquil. The speaker's actual location is a dreary city.
5. He evidently loves nature and the stillness one finds far away from the crowded city.

Connecting with the Text

6. Possible responses: It would give you a place for a mental retreat. It gives you hope of leaving your dreary surroundings and returning to a place like Innisfree.

Challenging the Text

7. **(Analysis)** The tone is lyrical, nostalgic, yearning, and muted. Because the speaker evidently values the tranquility and beauty of natural surroundings, many students will agree that the poem could be called a Romantic work.

Elements of Literature

Possible Answers

1. The long e sound, through the rhymes *Innisfree* and *honeybee,* and the words *bean* and *bee-loud.* Some students may note that the long o and long i sounds are also prominent.
2. The rhyming words repeat the long e, a, and o sounds.
3. In l. 10, the repeated *l* and *w* sounds echo the sound of lake water. Some students may also suggest that the k and p sounds echo the little waves hitting the shore.
4. The repeated long vowel sounds make the poem musical, haunting, and languorous. More hard consonant sounds would have made it guttural and harsh.

MAKING MEANINGS

First Thoughts

1. How does the place of peace you sketched in your Reader's Log compare with Yeats's "lake isle"?

Shaping Interpretations

2. In the first stanza, what does the **speaker** say he will do?
3. What sounds does the speaker describe in the poem?
4. How do the surroundings of the lake island contrast with the speaker's actual location?
5. Why do you think the speaker cannot find peace in the city setting?

Connecting with the Text

6. How might the memory of a place like Innisfree affect you if you found yourself in dreary surroundings?

Challenging the Text

7. How would you describe the **tone** of this poem? Do you think it could be called a Romantic poem? Explain why or why not.

ELEMENTS OF LITERATURE

Assonance and Alliteration

The music of this poem comes in part from Yeats's use of **assonance,** the repetition of similar vowel sounds in nearby words. The poem is also notable for a famous line (line 10) of **alliteration**—the repetition of consonant sounds in nearby words.

1. What vowel sounds dominate the first stanza?
2. What vowel sounds are emphasized by the rhyming words?
3. In line 10, what repeated consonant sounds echo the sound of lake water?
4. How would you describe the total effect of the vowel sounds in the poem? (How would the poem have been different if the poet had used more hard consonants, like k, d, or p?)

✓ QUICK CHECK: Assonance and Alliteration

[1] What vowel sounds dominate the second stanza? [o and u sounds]
[2] In what lines does **alliteration** appear? [All the lines except ll. 6, 9, and 11 have alliteration.]
[3] What effect do the vowel sounds have in the last two lines? [The a sounds in l. 11 are more harsh than the long e sounds in l. 12. Also in l. 12, several vowels are colored by the r's that follow them, making them softer. Thus, one gets the sense that the subtle, soothing sound of the lake in his heart contrasts with the uglier sounds of the city around him.]
[4] What sounds alliterate in l. 5? [s sounds and p sounds]

BEFORE YOU READ
THE WILD SWANS AT COOLE

Reading Focus

Time Marches On

Time has a way of transforming our feelings and reactions, of hardening, softening, or reshaping them. Yeats first saw the scene described in this poem when he was thirty-two. He wrote the poem at the age of fifty-one.

Quickwrite

Think of a familiar scene you have returned to over the years. In your Reader's Log, describe how time and experience have affected your responses to the scene.

Elements of Literature

Symbol

Yeats's swans can be regarded as **symbols,** but what do they represent? As you read the poem, keep in mind that symbols, by their very nature, are open-ended: Their meanings are various and open to interpretation.

Background

Yeats's good friend and fellow writer Lady Gregory lived on an estate known as Coole Park in Ireland's County Galway. When Yeats first visited there in 1897, he was in love with Maud Gonne, the beautiful activist for Irish independence, who was more interested in politics than in marriage. This poem, written in 1916, recalls Yeats's first view of the swans; now, nineteen years later, he realizes that "All's changed."

The swans are "wild," or migratory. Like the poet, they return annually to familiar places. Yeats knew that swans were monogamous, that "lover by lover" they continued to live in a state of mated bliss denied to him. But the larger meanings of the poem lie in the relation between memory, time, loss, and the inflexible patterns of natural life represented by the swans.

Maud Gonne (early 20th century) by Sarah Purser. Oil on canvas (69½″ × 41″).

Hugh Lane Municipal Gallery of Modern Art, Dublin.

WILLIAM BUTLER YEATS 981

Into the Poem

Using BEFORE YOU READ p. 981

Quickwrite

Ask students to think about a place that they visited when they were young children and that they have returned to recently. Some possibilities include the home of a relative, a school, a neighborhood, or a playground. Ask those who have had this experience to share with the class how their reaction on their most recent visit differed from their earlier reaction. Was the place smaller or larger than they remembered it? Was the place as beautiful or ugly as they remembered it?

Elements of Literature

Swans are relatives of geese and ducks, but unlike their cousins, they have consistently been used in literature and art as symbols of beauty, dignity, and immortality. Some of the most famous stories involving swans picture them as half-mortal and half-supernatural maidens with whom mortal men fall in love. One legend about swans is that they sing only once—at their deaths. Thus, the term "swan song" has been adopted to refer to the last achievement of an artist.

OPTIONS FOR TEACHING

STRATEGIES FOR INCLUSION

Learners Having Difficulty Place students in small groups of three or four to write a paraphrase of one of the five stanzas. Assign the roles of writer and spokesperson to students in each group. Have the spokesperson present the paraphrase to the class, and ask the rest of the students to comment if they have questions. Some groups could be assigned the same stanza and present comparative readings.

Visual/Auditory To help students understand that the rhyme scheme affects how the poem is read, ask students to identify the lines that rhyme and determine the pattern. Read the poem aloud as they mark the lines, and after they have finished, have them read the poem aloud. Ask them to notice how the rhyme in the last two lines of each stanza creates a pleasing finality to the stanza.

Musical Ask students to locate or invent a melody that captures the essence of this poem. Point out to them that the tone and mood of the poem change as it progresses, and suggest that the music should reflect these changes. 👉

William Butler Yeats **T981**

Through the Poem

A. Critical Reading: Making Inferences

? What is the speaker's mood in the third stanza? [Possible answers: A mood of regret and disappointment.]

Metacognition How did you arrive at your inference? [Most students will probably point to l. 14, where the speaker says his heart is sore.]

B. Literary Element: Figurative Language

? What does the speaker appear to mean by comparing himself to the swans in the fourth stanza? [Possible answer: Everything has changed in his life since he first saw the swans, but they remain as they were nineteen years ago.]

C. Literary Element: Symbol

Note that the view of the swans in ll. 25–29 seems more impersonal and distant. They seem to be approaching the status of works of art that are delightful to observe.

The Wild Swans at Coole

William Butler Yeats

The trees are in their autumn beauty,
The woodland paths are dry,
Under the October twilight the water
Mirrors a still sky;
5   Upon the brimming water among the stones
Are nine-and-fifty swans.

The nineteenth autumn has come upon me
Since I first made my count;
I saw, before I had well finished,
10   All suddenly mount
And scatter wheeling in great broken rings
Upon their clamorous wings.

I have looked upon those brilliant creatures,
And now my heart is sore.
15   All's changed since I, hearing at twilight,
The first time on this shore,
The bell-beat of their wings above my head,
Trod with a lighter tread.

Unwearied still, lover by lover,
20   They paddle in the cold
Companionable streams or climb the air;
Their hearts have not grown old;
Passion or conquest, wander where they will,
Attend upon them still.

25   But now they drift on the still water,
Mysterious, beautiful;
Among what rushes will they build,
By what lake's edge or pool
Delight men's eyes when I awake some day
30   To find they have flown away?

982 THE TWENTIETH CENTURY

MAKING MEANINGS

First Thoughts

1. How did reading this poem make you feel? Did you become emotionally involved with the speaker, or did you feel distant? Why?

Shaping Interpretations

2. How is the speaker feeling as he gazes at the swans? How did he feel nineteen years earlier when he heard the beating of their wings?

3. The second, third, and fourth stanzas offer hints about the personal experience that underlies the poem. What are these hints? Why do you think the speaker's heart is "sore" (line 14)?

4. What question does the speaker ask in the last stanza?

5. What qualities of the swans do you think the speaker envies? Why? What might the swans **symbolize** to the speaker?

6. How are the time of year and day in this poem appropriate to its **mood**?

7. The word *awake* in the next-to-last line is mysterious at first reading. Do you think it signifies that the poem has all been a dream? Or could it mean something else? How might this word offer a clue to the **theme** of the poem?

8. How could this poem be said to be in the **elegiac** mode? How does the poem relate in **theme, tone,** and **imagery** to any of the other famous elegies in this book?

Connecting with the Text

9. Review your Reader's Log notes about how time and experience affected your response to a familiar place. How are your changed responses similar to the **speaker**'s? How are they different?

CHOICES:
Building Your Portfolio

Writer's Notebook

1. Collecting Ideas for an Informative Report

The monogamous nature of the swans, as well as their migratory patterns and graceful movements, contributes to their symbolic meaning in "The Wild Swans at Coole." Choose another bird or animal, and research how it has been used symbolically in literature (children's literature included) or fine art. For example, you might focus on the tiger, elephant, crane, toad, albatross, or dove. Save your notes for possible use in the Writer's Workshop on page 1053.

Critical Writing

2. Imagine That

Write a brief essay comparing "The Lake Isle of Innisfree" with either "Kubla Khan" by Samuel Taylor Coleridge (page 676) or "La Belle Dame sans Merci" by John Keats (page 751). Comment on the images used by each poet to describe a place and its effects on people.

Critical Writing

3. Birds of a Feather

In a brief essay, compare the **themes, imagery,** and **progression of thought** in "The Wild Swans at Coole" with those of Keats's "Ode to a Nightingale" (page 755).

Creative Writing

4. Your Own "Bee-Loud Glade"

The first line of "The Lake Isle of Innisfree" is often quoted. Write your own poem or paragraph beginning with the words "I will arise and go now." Then, go on to describe your own ideal place of peace.

Beyond the Poems

Choices: Building Your Portfolio

1. **Writer's Notebook** Remind students to save their work. They may use it as prewriting for the Writer's Workshop on p. 1053.

PORTFOLIO ASSESSMENT

Choices: Assessment Criteria For help in evaluating these Choices assignments, see the criteria in the *Portfolio Management System,* pp. 163–164.

Making Meanings

First Thoughts

1. Some students may respond emotionally to the poem because they have had a similar experience. Others may find an emotional response difficult because the content of the poem is removed from their experience.

Shaping Interpretations

2. He feels melancholy. Line 18 indicates that he then took a more carefree attitude toward his world.

3. Hints include the image of nineteen autumns, which means he is much older. Line 15 suggests that everything in his life is now changed. Lines 22–24 suggest his heart has grown old; perhaps he has lost a lover or his ability to love. His "sore" heart indicates that the speaker has undergone a sobering, sad experience.

4. He wonders where the swans will have gone and where they will have built their nests.

5. He envies their brilliance, their timelessness, their mystery, and their ability to delight men's eyes, because he has lost these qualities or perhaps never possessed them. The swans symbolize beauty, youth, and immutability to the speaker.

6. The mood, which relates to the speaker's contemplation of his own mortality, is reinforced by the setting of twilight in the autumn, a symbol for old age or decline.

7. The word implies that the speaker's life is as fleeting as a dream—thus, the word *awake,* paradoxically, could imply the speaker's death and point to themes involving mortality and lost innocence.

8. Elegies frequently use imagery drawn from nature, are usually formal in language and structure, and are solemn or even melancholy in tone, all of which fit this poem. In this regard the poem is similar to poems like "The Wanderer," "The Seafarer," and "In Memoriam."

Connecting with the Text

9. Students' changed responses may be similar to the speaker's in that both regret change, and they may be different in that students may not have a sense that their entire lives are different now.

Map

The area marked here as the Soviet Union was formally known as the Union of Soviet Socialist Republics (U.S.S.R) from 1921, after the Bolshevik Revolution, until the central government lost authority in 1991. Today, this part of Northern Eurasia is known as the Commonwealth of Independent States.

A Dialogue with the Text

Remind students to choose a situation they are willing to share. There may be students in your class who were forced to leave their homelands or whose parents or grandparents were forced to leave their homelands under great pressure. Ask volunteers to share with the class their feelings about the experience or what they know about their parents' or grandparents' feelings. Otherwise, identify students who have had to move away from a place when they did not want to go, and ask them to share their feelings about the move with the class.

WORLD LITERATURE

Russia

Anna Akhmatova (1889–1966)

Anna Akhmatova grew up near St. Petersburg, the capital of Russia before the 1917 revolution that led to a Communist takeover of the government. As a young writer just before the revolution, she was one of the founders of a literary movement called *acmeism* (ak'mē·iz'əm), which rejected ambivalent symbols in poetry and strove instead to present clearly etched ideas. (Just as Yeats is almost synonymous with Ireland, Akhmatova is regarded as a major Russian lyric poet.)

After the revolution, however, Akhmatova's poetry did not find a sympathetic ear with the new Communist regime. The official outlook was that art should exist in the service of the state and should treat themes that were politically and socially "useful." Akhmatova's first husband, the poet Nikolai Gumilev, was executed as a counterrevolutionary in 1921, and Akhmatova herself was forbidden to publish. As the terrifying years of Joseph Stalin's dictatorship wore on, she saw more and more of her friends arrested and her own son imprisoned. Throughout this period, however, she continued to write and to serve as mentor for a younger generation of Russian poets.

After Stalin's death in 1953, the works of many Russian writers were again publicly accepted. Akhmatova was finally able to enjoy a brief period of official recognition in the last years of her life. Boris Pasternak, a Russian novelist and poet who was himself threatened with banishment, paid tribute to Akhmatova in these words: "Your work throbs high with our remembered past."

Anna Akhmatova.

(Map) ©Rand McNally.

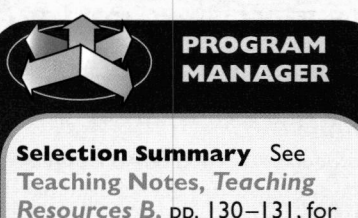

PROGRAM MANAGER

Selection Summary See Teaching Notes, *Teaching Resources B,* pp. 130–131, for a summary of this selection.

OPTIONS FOR TEACHING

STRATEGIES FOR INCLUSION

English Language Development The flowing rhythm and clear rhyming pattern are ideal material for English-language learners to practice their pronunciation and intonation. First, go through the text as a choral reading so that all students say the poem together. Then, do an echo reading whereby you read a line and the students repeat it, giving them an opportunity to model your speech. Finally, allow students to practice the poem or one of the stanzas, and then have them say it for the class.

BEFORE YOU READ
LOT'S WIFE

Background

Besides its significance as a religious document, the Bible has served over the centuries as a source of literary inspiration for countless writers. In "Lot's Wife," the speaker focuses on a Biblical incident recounted in Chapter 19 of the Book of Genesis. Angered by the wickedness of the city of Sodom, God sends angels to punish the inhabitants. When the angels arrive in disguise as men, only Lot treats them hospitably. Lot's reward is an advance warning of the city's wholesale destruction. He is told to flee Sodom with his family and not to look back under any conditions. As Lot's family escapes, however, his wife disobeys the angels' command and turns her head to gaze upon the city. She is immediately turned into a pillar of salt.

For the twentieth-century Russian poet Anna Akhmatova, this ancient story assumed a poignant, almost painful relevance. She lived under a totalitarian regime that dictated the terms under which artists and writers could work. Yet, when Akhmatova had an opportunity to flee oppression in her homeland, she remained. In the following poem, Akhmatova views the story of Lot's wife, an ancient, unwilling exile, from the perspective of a modern woman who was sorely tempted by the lure of exile but who resisted.

A Dialogue with the Text

As you read, jot down notes on how you might feel if you came under intense pressure to leave your homeland because life there had become intolerable. Would you regard such a departure as an act of desertion, or as a wise investment in the future? After you have thought about your own reactions, try to gauge the degree of sympathy with which the speaker regards Lot's wife.

Lot's Wife

Anna Akhmatova

translated by **Richard Wilbur**

The just man followed then his angel guide
Where he strode on the black highway, hulking and bright;
But a wild grief in his wife's bosom cried,
Look back, it is not too late for a last sight **(A)**

5 *Of the red towers of your native Sodom, the square* **(B)**
Where once you sang, the gardens you shall mourn,
And the tall house with empty windows where
You loved your husband and your babes were born.

She turned, and looking on the bitter view
10 Her eyes were welded shut by mortal pain; **(C)**
Into transparent salt her body grew,
And her quick feet were rooted in the plain.

Who would waste tears upon her? Is she not
The least of our losses, this unhappy wife?
15 Yet in my heart she will not be forgot **(D)**
Who, for a single glance, gave up her life.

A. Reader's Response: First Thoughts

? Why is the wife tempted to turn and look back? [Sample responses: She does not want to leave and wants to hold on to the place as long as possible. She wants to remember things as they are in Sodom and needs a last glance to fix images in her memory.]

B. Critical Reading: Drawing Conclusions

? To what city other than Sodom might the "red towers" and "the square" refer? [Red Square in Moscow.]

C. Language Note: Word Choice

? Why is *welded* a better choice of word than *closed*? [It is a more descriptive verb, implying heat and a powerful bond; thus, it carries the weight of God's anger and the strength of his punishment or, similarly, the intensity of the woman's "mortal pain." *Closed* seems gentle in comparison.]

D. Critical Reading: Analyzing Viewpoint

? How does the viewpoint change in the last stanza? [It changes from narration to direct address. The speaker asks the audience rhetorical questions and makes personal statements.]

ABOUT THE AUTHOR

Akhmatova's poetry during the first phase of her career was primarily concerned with personal issues of love, and this subject did not meet with favor. In 1946, she was attacked by Andrei Zhdanov, the Soviet minister of culture, and this led to her expulsion from the Soviet Writers' Union. Akhmatova began writing again after 1958, and near the end of her life, she was again recognized as a poet and readmitted to the Writers' Union.

INTEGRATING THE LANGUAGE ARTS

Strategic Reading Before students read the poem, ask them if with just a glance they notice anything unusual about the poem. Then, ask them why they think the poet used italics in the middle of the poem. [The words in italics signify the voice inside of Lot's wife. The poet wanted to emphasize and clearly demarcate that voice.]

Kasimir Malevich (1878–1935) was the founder of Suprematism. He coined the term to express a new approach to art in which communicating "pure feeling" was the only objective for the artist. He used bold shapes and strong colors to simplify and purify his artistic language, thus hoping to reach any and all viewers, who would respond intuitively to his works.

Finding Common Ground

Help students begin their discussion by asking them to choose an adjective that best describes the emotion the poem prompted in them, and to explain why the poem triggered this feeling.

Woman with a Rake
(late 19th or early 20th
century) by Kasimir
Malevich.

Treyakov Gallery, Moscow.

FINDING COMMON GROUND

Meet in small groups to discuss this poem. Your first task will be to formulate the questions you'd like to focus on. In your discussions, be sure to consider what you recorded in your Reader's Logs and how your responses to exile compare with those of the speaker. Also, be sure to address how Akhmatova imaginatively used this Biblical story to stand for something else. Assign a recorder for your group. At the completion of your discussion, have the recorder report to the class at large on your responses to the poem.

As a class, try to agree on at least three responses to the poem—in other words, try to find some common ground.

986 THE TWENTIETH CENTURY

CONNECTING WITH "THE TRANSFORMING IMAGINATION"

In this poem, a character is transformed from a living, breathing human being into a statue made of salt because she wanted to see her city one last time. Ask students to discuss why Lot's wife would give up her life and why the poet is drawn to her image. [Lot's wife can see the beauties of Sodom clearly in her imagination, yet her love for her city makes her die for a final glimpse. For Akhmatova, the transformation of Lot's wife into a pillar of salt is a testament to the character's passion.]

James Joyce

(1882–1941)

James Joyce (1934) by Jacques-Émile Blanche.
Courtesy of the National Gallery of Ireland, Dublin.

James Joyce's masterpiece, *Ulysses* (1922), has probably had a greater effect on twentieth-century fiction than any other work of our times. Yet while he lived, Joyce was known largely as the author of what was thought a nearly unintelligible and scandalous book. Based on Homer's *Odyssey*, Joyce's *Ulysses* describes the events of a single day in Dublin, the city where Joyce grew up. And just as Homer's epic interpreted the world of the ancient Greeks, so does Joyce's epic mirror and interpret for us our own lives in the twentieth century.

Joyce was born in Rathgar, Ireland, a Dublin suburb. One of ten children of an improvident tax collector, he was educated at a series of Roman Catholic schools, but by the time he entered University College, Dublin, he had lost his faith. After graduating, he went to Paris and existed frugally by giving English lessons and writing book reviews.

In 1903, Joyce returned home to be at his dying mother's bedside. Afterward he lived briefly in the "Martello tower" (a former military fortification) on the coast near Dublin, a site that has now become Ireland's Joyce museum. There he began an autobiographical novel, *Stephen Hero,* and also wrote some of the stories later published in *Dubliners* (1914).

In June 1904, Joyce met and fell in love with a Galway girl named Nora Barnacle. The date of their first walk, June 16, 1904, was later immortalized as Bloomsday, the date on which the action of *Ulysses* takes place. When Joyce's debts mounted, he persuaded Nora to leave Ireland with him; Joyce was never to live in Ireland again.

The penniless couple settled first in the Italian city of Trieste, where their two children, George and Lucia, were born. Joyce's book of poems, *Chamber Music,* was published in 1907 but brought him no royalties. But his luck began to turn after 1914 when the influential

American poet Ezra Pound reviewed *Dubliners* favorably and persuaded a British magazine to serialize *A Portrait of the Artist as a Young Man,* Joyce's rewritten version of *Stephen Hero.*

When Italy entered World War I in 1915, the Joyces left Trieste for Zurich, where Joyce worked on the early chapters of *Ulysses.* Because of sizable gifts from anonymous well-wishers, Joyce's financial troubles had begun to ease, but his physical problems increased. Between 1917 and 1930, he endured twenty-five operations for glaucoma and cataracts. Sometimes he was totally blind, yet he continued work on *Ulysses,* which appeared in magazine installments from 1918 through 1920, when it was suppressed.

The completed *Ulysses* did not easily find its way into print. Indeed, British printers found it so scandalous that they refused to set it in type. Finally, in 1922, Sylvia Beach, the American owner of a bookstore in Paris called Shakespeare & Co., agreed to put out an edition of one thousand copies. Many of the reviews were favorable, but the book was banned in both Britain and the United States. Not until 1934, after a famous court case, was *Ulysses* published in America. A British edition soon followed, and the book's fame spread rapidly worldwide.

Meanwhile, Joyce had completed a new novel, *Finnegans Wake,* about a Dublin barkeep named Earwicker. This complex experimental work finally was published in 1939 to inconclusive reviews. Some critics took it as a bad joke, others as madness, and Joyce, who considered it his masterpiece, grew morose over the dismal response. The Joyces, who had been living in Paris, returned to Zurich in 1940, when France fell to Nazi Germany. There Joyce became increasingly ill, his eye troubles complicated by a duodenal ulcer. He died on January 13, 1941, one month short of his fifty-ninth birthday.

QUICK PLANNING GUIDE

Into the Story

Author Biography p. 987
Before You Read p. 988

Through the Story

"Araby" pp. 989–993
Words to Own p. 989–992
Making Meanings pp. 993-994
Elements of Literature p. 994

Beyond the Story

Choices: Building Your Portfolio p. 995
- **Writer's Notebook:** Freewrite topics for research
- **Critical Writing:** Write an essay about the epiphany
- **Critical Writing:** Write an essay applying definitions of *vanity* to the narrator
- **Creative Writing:** Write a story map changing details
- **Creative Writing:** Rewrite the story from another's point of view
- **Creative Writing:** Experiment with stream-of-consciousness writing
- **Art:** Respond to the story by creating original art
- **Performance:** Perform an oral reading of the story

Spotlight On pp. 996–997

PROGRAM MANAGER

- **Planning Instruction** See Teaching Notes, *Teaching Resources B,* pp. 131–132, for objectives, a summary, literary elements, and biographical information for this selection.
- **Instructional Support** See Graphic Organizer for Active Reading, *Teaching Resources B,* p. 140, for a

Through the Story activity.
- **Assessment** See Selection Test, *Test Booklet,* pp. 213–214.
- **Language Link** For instruction and practice in combining sentences, see Language Link, *Teaching Resources B,* pp. 141–142 and *Language and Writing Skills Worksheets,* p. 111–118.

- **Reinforcement** Use the Words to Own worksheet in *Teaching Resources B,* p. 143.
- **Audiotaped Readings** To help auditory learners through the lesson, use the Selected Reading, Audiocassette 3, Side B in the Audiovisual Resources Binder.

Into the Story

Using BEFORE YOU READ p. 988

Reading Focus

Help students focus their prior experience before they read the story by telling them that the story deals with a clash between dreams and reality. Give the class three minutes of silence during which they may call to mind their dreams or wishes. If you wish to have a discussion, *remind students to choose a situation they are willing to share.*

WRITERS ON WRITING

Joyce was a proponent of writing about everyday life. He writes: "... I think out of the dreary sameness of existence, a measure of dramatic life may be drawn. Even the most commonplace, the deadest among the living, may play a part in a great drama. It is a sinful foolishness to sigh back for the good old times, to feed the hunger of us with the cold stones they afford. Life we must accept as we see it before our eyes, men and women as we meet them in the real world, not as we apprehend them in the world of faery. The great human comedy in which each has share, gives limitless scope to the true artist, today as yesterday and as in years gone."

BEFORE YOU READ

ARABY

Reading Focus

When Dreams Meet Reality
Have you ever taken on a task that seemed vital to your happiness—or hoped, fervently, that a childhood dream would come true? Perhaps you can remember just wishing to accomplish something grand, to win the admiration and praise of others.

A Dialogue with the Text

In "Araby," the main character has a vivid imagination that sometimes causes him to misconstrue the realities of his life. As you read the story, look for differences between the way he imagines things to be and the way they really are. List these discrepancies in a two-column comparison/contrast chart like the one below.

Imagination	Reality

Elements of Literature

Epiphany
Joyce called the moments of revelation that occur in his stories "epiphanies." Here is an excerpt from *Stephen Hero,* an early draft of Joyce's semiautobiographical novel *A Portrait of the Artist as a Young Man,* in which his hero explains what he means by "epiphany":

A young lady was standing on the steps of one of those brown brick houses which seem the very incarnation of Irish paralysis. A young gentleman was leaning on the rusty railings of the area. Stephen as he passed on his quest heard the following fragment of colloquy out of which he received an impression keen enough to afflict his sensitiveness very severely.

The Young Lady—(drawling discreetly) . . . O, yes . . . I was . . . at the . . . cha . . . pel . . .

The Young Gentleman—(inaudibly) . . . I . . . (again inaudibly) . . . I . . .

The Young Lady—(softly) . . . O . . . but you're . . . ve . . . ry . . . wick . . . ed . . .

This triviality made him think of collecting many such moments together in a book of epiphanies. By an epiphany he meant a sudden spiritual manifestation, whether in the vulgarity of speech or of gesture or in a memorable phase of the mind itself. He believed that it was for the man of letters to record these epiphanies with extreme care, seeing that they themselves are the most delicate and evanescent of moments.

In fiction, an **epiphany** is a moment of sudden insight or revelation experienced by a character.

For more on Epiphany, see the Handbook of Literary Terms.

Background

On May 14, 1894, a five-day charity bazaar came to the city of Dublin. The bazaar was called Araby, a reference to Arabia, where bazaars—markets with long rows of stalls or shops—are common. For the children of Dublin, Arabia seemed a mysterious, exotic place, very different from the dark, all-too-real streets of the dreary city in which they lived.

The house in this story is based on one in which Joyce and his family actually lived. It stood on the same "blind," or dead-end, street as the Christian Brothers' school Joyce attended. When the Joyce children moved to this musky, dark house, they missed the open fields and woods of their former home.

OPTIONS FOR TEACHING

STRATEGIES FOR INCLUSION

Less Proficient Readers Ask students to work in groups of three to create a story map by drawing simple pictures for each of the major events. If time permits, students can paint or color the pictures for display for the whole class.

Visual The Araby bazaar is advertised in such a way that the boy in the story pictures it as a place of Eastern enchantment and mystery. Ask students to design and execute posters advertising Araby. The posters should include some kind of illustration that gives the flavor of the bazaar, and they should contain text that gives information about the time and place the bazaar will occur. Designate areas where the posters can be displayed.

PROGRAM MANAGER

Application and Reinforcement For reinforcement of the elements of literature introduced in this lesson, see Transparency 13.4 in the *Audiovisual Resources Binder.*

Araby

James Joyce

Orth Richmond Street, being blind, was a quiet street except at the hour when the Christian Brothers' School set the boys free. An uninhabited house of two stories stood at the blind end, detached from its neighbors in a square ground. The other houses of the street, conscious of decent lives within them, gazed at one another with brown imperturbable faces.

The former tenant of our house, a priest, had died in the back drawing-room. Air, musty from having been long enclosed, hung in all the rooms, and the waste room behind the kitchen was littered with old useless papers. Among these I found a few paper-covered books, the pages of which were curled and damp: *The Abbot,* by Walter Scott, *The Devout Communicant,* and *The Memoirs of Vidocq.*[1] I liked the last best because its leaves were yellow. The wild garden behind the house contained a central apple-tree and a few straggling bushes under one of which I found the late tenant's rusty bicycle-pump. He had been a very charitable priest; in his will he had left all his money to institutions and the furniture of his house to his sister.

When the short days of winter came dusk fell before we had well eaten our dinners. When we met in the street the houses had grown somber. The space of sky above us was the color of ever-changing violet and toward it the lamps of the street lifted their feeble lanterns. The cold air stung us and we played till our bodies glowed. Our shouts echoed in the silent street. The career[2] of our play brought us through the dark muddy lanes behind the houses where we ran the gauntlet of the rough tribes from the cottages, to the back doors of the dark dripping gardens where odors arose from the ashpits, to the dark odorous stables where a coachman smoothed and combed the

horse or shook music from the buckled harness. When we returned to the street light from the kitchen windows had filled the areas. If my uncle was seen turning the corner we hid in the shadow until we had seen him safely housed. Or if Mangan's sister came out on the doorstep to call her brother in to his tea we watched her from our shadow peer up and down the street. We waited to see whether she would remain or go in and, if she remained, we left our shadow and walked up to Mangan's steps resignedly. She was waiting for us, her figure defined by the light from the half-opened door. Her brother always teased her before he obeyed and I stood by the railings looking at her. Her dress swung as she moved her body and the soft rope of her hair tossed from side to side.

Every morning I lay on the floor in the front parlor watching her door. The blind was pulled down to within an inch of the sash so that I could not be seen. When she came out on the doorstep my heart leaped. I ran to the hall, seized my books, and followed her. I kept her brown figure always in my eye and, when we came near the point at which our ways diverged, I quickened my pace and passed her. This happened morning after morning. I had never spoken to her, except for a few casual words, and yet her name was like a summons to all my foolish blood.

Her image accompanied me even in places the most hostile to romance. On Saturday evenings when my aunt went marketing I had to go to carry

---

1. ***The Abbott . . . Vidocq*** (vē·duk′): in order, a historical romance about Mary, Queen of Scots, by Sir Walter Scott; an 1813 religious manual written by a Franciscan friar; and the memoirs (though not actually written by François Vidocq) of a French criminal who later became a detective.
2. **career:** course; path.

WORDS TO OWN

imperturbable (im′pər·tʉr′bə·bəl) *adj.:* calm; impassive.
somber (säm′bər) *adj.:* gloomy.
gauntlet (gônt′lit) *n.:* series of challenges. Derived from *gatlopp,* Swedish for "running down a lane," the term originally referred to a form of military punishment in which a wrongdoer had to run between two rows of soldiers who struck him as he passed.
diverged (dī·vʉrjd′) *v.:* branched off; separated.

A. Reader's Response: First Thoughts

? What ideas and meanings does the word *blind* suggest? [Sample responses: *Blind* could suggest "dead end" in the literal sense. In the figurative sense, it could mean "going nowhere," "unable to see," or "obscured by something." Right away, Joyce identifies this street as a symbol of the restricted lives of its inhabitants, who have little hope of escaping its confines.]

B. Critical Reading: Making Inferences

? What does the wild garden suggest? [The wildness might be characteristic of the unkempt neighborhood and of the lives lived there. It might also suggest the Garden of Eden after Adam and Eve have been expelled. Thus, the garden conveys a sense of the neighborhood as a place of sadness, a place where people had once been happy.]

C. Literary Element: Imagery

? What does the light imagery suggest about Mangan's sister? [The light creates a kind of halo, setting her apart and contrasting her with the darkness that surrounds the other characters.]

D. Critical Reading: Drawing Conclusions

? What does this passage suggest about the narrator's feelings toward the girl? [That he is in love with her.]

WORDS TO OWN

The following vocabulary words are defined in the Words to Own at the bottom of the pupil's page.

imperturbable p. 989	incessant p. 990
somber p. 989	luxuriated p. 990
gauntlet p. 989	garrulous p. 991
diverged p. 989	improvised p. 992
impinge p. 990	pervades p. 992

A. Literary Element: Allusion

? What words allude to religion and link the boy's feeling for Mangan's sister with religious devotion? ["Chalice," "strange prayers and praises"; and "confused adoration."]

B. Reader's Response: Shaping Interpretations

? What does the narrator imply through the harp simile about the girl's effect on him? [Sample responses: It implies he was completely under the girl's control. It implies she is able to bring out the best in him, just as a musician can bring out the best in a musical instrument. It identifies her with the angelic, as did the halo of light, and enhances the boy's idealization of her.]

C. Literary Element: Theme

? What does the description of the lamplight falling on the young woman remind you of? [It is a romantic, idealized depiction of a loved one.] What effect does it have on the boy? [The boy seems to be in a worshipping trance.]

D. Literary Element: Connotation

? Why is the word *Araby* associated with enchantment? [The word suggests lands, places, and people often considered by Westerners to be exotic and mysterious.]

some of the parcels. We walked through the flaring streets, jostled by drunken men and bargaining women, amid the curses of laborers, the shrill litanies[3] of shop-boys who stood on guard by the barrels of pigs' cheeks, the nasal chanting of street-singers, who sang a *come-all-you* about O'Donovan Rossa,[4] or a ballad about the troubles in our native land. These noises converged in a single sensation of life for me: I imagined that I bore my chalice[5] safely through a throng of foes. Her name sprang to my lips at moments in strange prayers and praises which I myself did not understand. My eyes were often full of tears (I could not tell why) and at times a flood from my heart seemed to pour itself out into my bosom. I thought little of the future. I did not know whether I would ever speak to her or not or, if I spoke to her, how I could tell her of my confused adoration. But my body was like a harp and her words and gestures were like fingers running upon the wires.

One evening I went into the back drawing-room in which the priest had died. It was a dark rainy evening and there was no sound in the house. Through one of the broken panes I heard the rain impinge upon the earth, the fine incessant needles of water playing in the sodden beds. Some distant lamp or lighted window gleamed below me. I was thankful that I could see so little. All my senses seemed to desire to veil themselves and, feeling that I was about to slip from them, I pressed the palms of my hands together until they trembled, murmuring: *O love! O love!* many times.

At last she spoke to me. When she addressed the first words to me I was so confused that I did not know what to answer. She asked me was I going to *Araby.* I forget whether I answered yes or no. It would be a splendid bazaar, she said; she would love to go.

—And why can't you? I asked.

While she spoke she turned a silver bracelet round and round her wrist. She could not go, she said, because there would be a retreat that week in her convent.[6] Her brother and two other boys were fighting for their caps and I was alone at the railings. She held one of the spikes, bowing her head toward me. The light from the lamp opposite our door caught the white curve of her neck, lit up her hair that rested there and, falling, lit up the hand upon the railing. It fell over one side of her dress and caught the white border of a petticoat, just visible as she stood at ease.

—It's well for you,[7] she said.

—If I go, I said, I will bring you something.

What innumerable follies laid waste my waking and sleeping thoughts after that evening! I wished to annihilate the tedious intervening days. I chafed against the work of school. At night in my bedroom and by day in the classroom her image came between me and the page I strove to read. The syllables of the word *Araby* were called to me through the silence in which my soul luxuriated and cast an Eastern enchantment over me. I asked for leave to go to the bazaar on Saturday night. My aunt was surprised and hoped it was not some Freemason[8] affair. I answered few questions in class. I watched my master's face pass from amiability to sternness; he hoped I was not beginning to idle. I could not call my wandering thoughts together. I had hardly any patience with the serious work of life which, now that it stood between

---

3. litanies: repeated sales cries. Literally, a litany is a prayer composed of a series of specific invocations and responses.

4. *come-all-you* . . . Rossa: A come-all-you (kum·al′yə) is a type of Irish ballad that usually begins "Come all you [young lovers, rebels, Irishmen, and so on]." O'Donovan Rossa was Jeremiah O'Donovan (1831–1915) from County Cork. He was active in Ireland's struggle against British rule in the mid-nineteenth century.

5. chalice (chal′is): cup; specifically, the cup used for Holy Communion wine. Joyce's use of the term evokes the image of a young man on a sacred mission.

6. retreat . . . convent: temporary withdrawal from worldly life by the students and teachers at the convent school, to devote time to prayer, meditation, and religious studies.

7. It's well for you: "You're lucky" (usually said enviously).

8. Freemason: The Freemasons are a secret society whose practices were originally drawn from those of British medieval stonemasons' guilds; its members, almost exclusively Protestant, were often hostile to Catholics. The aunt apparently associates the exotic bazaar with the mysterious practices of Freemasonry.

WORDS TO OWN

impinge (im·pinj′) *v.:* strike; touch.
incessant (in·ses′ənt) *adj.:* never ceasing; constant.
luxuriated (lug·zhoor′ē·āt′id) *v.:* took enormous pleasure.

OPTIONS FOR TEACHING

INTEGRATING THE LANGUAGE ARTS

Strategic Reading Ask students to read the first six paragraphs of the story (or read them aloud for the class). On the basis of the information presented in these paragraphs, ask students to predict what will happen in the rest of the story. Specifically, ask them to predict whether the girl will find out how the boy feels toward her and how she will react if she finds out. Also, ask them to predict the overall

outcome of the story. Will the girl fall in love with the boy? Will they "live happily ever after"? Have students write down their predictions so they can remember them accurately when they finish the story and compare their predictions with what actually happens.

Writing: A Letter Have students assume the role of the boy's aunt or uncle and write an account of his behavior in a letter to another relative. Remind students that the story is written in

the first-person point of view, so the reader knows what the boy is thinking, as well as what he says and does. In their letters, students will write in the third person, and they will have to confine themselves to behavior that they can observe. Ask several volunteers to read their letters to the class. Then, lead a discussion about how perceptions of the boy differ from one person to another and from his perceptions of himself.

Summer Night's Dream (The Voice) (1893) by Edvard Munch.

RESPONDING TO THE ART: ABOUT THE ARTIST

Norwegian painter and printmaker Edvard Munch (1863–1944) produced works that convey intense human emotion. His preference for the reduction of his subject to its psychological content and to the most striking compositional elements set him apart from the naturalist painters, as well as from the impressionists and neo-impressionists. He was among the vanguard of the expressionists, artists who revealed their highly personal reactions to the world, rather than painting representations of subjects as anyone might see them.

me and my desire, seemed to me child's play, ugly monotonous child's play.

On Saturday morning I reminded my uncle that I wished to go to the bazaar in the evening. He was fussing at the hallstand, looking for the hat-brush, and answered me curtly:

—Yes, boy, I know.

As he was in the hall I could not go into the front parlor and lie at the window. I left the house in bad humor and walked slowly toward the school. The air was pitilessly raw and already my heart misgave me.

When I came home to dinner my uncle had not yet been home. Still it was early. I sat staring at the clock for some time and, when its ticking began to irritate me, I left the room. I mounted the staircase and gained the upper part of the house. The high cold empty gloomy rooms liberated me and I went from room to room singing. From the front window I saw my companions playing below in the street. Their cries reached me weakened and indistinct and, leaning my forehead against the cool glass, I looked over at the dark house where she lived. I may have stood there for an hour, seeing nothing but the brown-clad figure cast by my imagination, touched discreetly by the lamplight at the curved neck, at the hand upon the railings and at the border below the dress.

When I came downstairs again I found Mrs. Mercer sitting at the fire. She was an old <u>garrulous</u> woman, a pawnbroker's widow, who collected used stamps for some pious purpose. I had to endure the gossip of the tea-table. The meal was prolonged beyond an hour and still my uncle did not

E. Literary Element: Irony

? Why does something one might not expect, the cold gloom of the empty rooms, make the boy cheerful? [Possible answers: It gives him solitude so that he can be alone with his thoughts. It liberates him—frees him of obligation and the commonplace context of his everyday life. He does not really notice it because his imagination is full of romance.]

Ⓔ WORDS TO OWN
garrulous (gar′ə·ləs) *adj.*: talkative.

JAMES JOYCE 991

INTEGRATING THE LANGUAGE ARTS

Language and Style As is evident from the first sentence, Joyce makes extensive use of the connotations of words in this story. Ask students to work in pairs, and assign one paragraph (or part of a long paragraph) to each pair of students. Students should list the words in their paragraphs that seem to be chosen as much for their connotations as for their denotations. The list should include the literal definition of each word, as well as the meaning the word connotes. After the pairs are finished, write a master list of the words on the chalkboard, and discuss their connotations with the whole class.

COOPERATIVE LEARNING

Finding Images To help students identify the richness of Joyce's story, ask students to work in groups of three or four to find images that appeal to one or more of the senses. Assign each group one or two paragraphs to work with, and encourage students to organize their information in a chart like the one on Transparency 7: Sensory Details Chart in the Transparency Package. After the groups have finished locating images, have them discuss why Joyce uses this technique, and finally ask a representative from each group to share the group's findings with the whole class.

Penzance Fair (1916) by Dame Laura Knight. Oil on canvas.
Richard Green Galleries, London.

come. Mrs. Mercer stood up to go: She was sorry she couldn't wait any longer, but it was after eight o'clock and she did not like to be out late, as the night air was bad for her. When she had gone I began to walk up and down the room, clenching my fists. My aunt said:

—I'm afraid you may put off your bazaar for this night of Our Lord.

At nine o'clock I heard my uncle's latchkey in the halldoor. I heard him talking to himself and heard the hallstand rocking when it had received the weight of his overcoat. I could interpret these signs. When he was midway through his dinner I asked him to give me the money to go to the bazaar. He had forgotten.

—The people are in bed and after their first sleep now, he said.

I did not smile. My aunt said to him energetically:

—Can't you give him the money and let him go? You've kept him late enough as it is.

My uncle said he was very sorry he had forgotten. He said he believed in the old saying: *All work and no play makes Jack a dull boy.* He asked me where I was going and, when I had told him a second time he asked me did I know *The Arab's*

Farewell to his Steed.[9] When I left the kitchen he was about to recite the opening lines of the piece to my aunt.

I held a florin[10] tightly in my hand as I strode down Buckingham Street toward the station. The sight of the streets thronged with buyers and glaring with gas recalled to me the purpose of my journey. I took my seat in a third-class carriage of a deserted train. After an intolerable delay the train moved out of the station slowly. It crept onward among ruinous houses and over the twinkling river. At Westland Row Station a crowd of people pressed to the carriage doors; but the porters moved them back, saying that it was a special train for the bazaar. I remained alone in the bare carriage. In a few minutes the train drew up beside an improvised wooden platform. I passed out on to the road and saw by the lighted dial of a clock that it was ten minutes to ten. In front of me was a large building which displayed the magical name.

I could not find any sixpenny entrance and, fearing that the bazaar would be closed, I passed in quickly through a turnstile, handing a shilling to a weary-looking man. I found myself in a big hall girdled at half its height by a gallery. Nearly all the stalls were closed and the greater part of the hall was in darkness. I recognized a silence like that which pervades a church after a service. I walked into the center of the bazaar timidly. A

---

9. The Arab's . . . Steed: popular sentimental poem by the English writer Caroline Norton (1808–1877).
10. florin: British coin worth, at the time, the equivalent of about fifty cents.

WORDS TO OWN
improvised (im′prə·vīzd′) v. used as *adj.*: made for the occasion from whatever is handy.
pervades (pər·vādz′) v.: spreads throughout.

992 THE TWENTIETH CENTURY

---

few people were gathered about the stalls which were still open. Before a curtain, over which the words *Café Chantant*[11] were written in colored lamps, two men were counting money on a salver.[12] I listened to the fall of the coins.

Remembering with difficulty why I had come I went over to one of the stalls and examined porcelain vases and flowered tea-sets. At the door of the stall a young lady was talking and laughing with two young gentlemen. I remarked their English accents and listened vaguely to their conversation.

—O, I never said such a thing!

—O, but you did!

—O, but I didn't!

—Didn't she say that?

—Yes. I heard her.

—O, there's a . . . fib!

Observing me the young lady came over and asked me did I wish to buy anything. The tone of her voice was not encouraging; she seemed to have spoken to me out of a sense of duty. I looked humbly at the great jars that stood like eastern guards at either side of the dark entrance to the stall and murmured:

—No, thank you.

The young lady changed the position of one of the vases and went back to the two young men. They began to talk of the same subject. Once or twice the young lady glanced at me over her shoulder.

I lingered before her stall, though I knew my stay was useless, to make my interest in her wares seem the more real. Then I turned away slowly and walked down the middle of the bazaar. I allowed the two pennies to fall against the sixpence in my pocket. I heard a voice call from one end of the gallery that the light was out. The upper part of the hall was now completely dark.

Gazing up into the darkness I saw myself as a creature driven and derided by vanity; and my eyes burned with anguish and anger.

---

11. *Café Chantant* (kȧ·fā′ shän′tän′): coffeehouse with musical entertainment.
12. **salver** (sal′vər): serving tray.

MAKING MEANINGS

First Thoughts

1. Briefly describe how the ending of this story made you feel.

Shaping Interpretations

2. How often have the narrator and Mangan's sister spoken to each other? How would you describe his relationship with her?

3. In what ways are the lives of these characters narrow or restricted?

4. How does the narrator deal with intrusions of reality into his fantasy—at the market, for example?

5. How has the main character changed by the end? What details support your answer?

6. Why do you think the dead priest appears in the story? In your opinion, what do the story's religious references contribute to the significance of the boy's quest?

7. Look back in your Reader's Log at the chart in which you compared and contrasted what the narrator imagined with reality. How could the story be seen as presenting a conflict between romance, or imagination, and reality?

8. How would you describe the writer's **tone**—his attitude toward the characters and what happens to them?

9. In medieval legends, a knight often rode off on

> ### Reviewing the Text
>
> a. Who is the narrator of the story? Though the story uses **first-person point of view,** is the narrator the same age as the hero? Cite evidence to support your answer.
>
> b. What is the **setting** at the opening of the story? Which adjectives paint a gloomy scene?
>
> c. What is the purpose of the narrator's quest, or journey to the bazaar? What obstacles prevent him from achieving his goal?
>
> d. What **connotations** does the word *Araby* have for the narrator? What is Araby really like?

d. *Araby* connotes "Eastern enchantment" to the narrator, but he discovers it is only a dark, nearly empty, tacky commercial establishment run by English people.

Shaping Interpretations

2. The narrator has spoken only a few casual words to Mangan's sister. The boy has an unrequited crush on her.

3. By the routines of their lives: The boy goes only to school or to the market with his aunt every Saturday. Also, the young people are restricted physically by their elders. Both young and old are restricted by the elders' insensitivity and lack of imagination.

4. At the market, the boy imagines that he bears his chalice safely through a throng of foes, drawing reality into his fantasy. At school, he ignores reality, letting his thoughts wander; he considers the classwork "child's play."

5. The boy has changed because he realizes his romantic fantasies are illusions. His tears at the very end of the story indicate his frustration and disappointment at his realization.

6. One possibility is that the dead priest is simply one more aspect of the gloomy house and neighborhood; the death of the priest represents the passing of religion as the source of mystery and passion in the boy's life. In the boy's quest, love replaces religion, hence the religious references in the description of Mangan's sister.

7. Possible responses: The conflict lies in the fact that the boy's ideas about Mangan's sister and Araby are all sheer illusion created by his imagination. Neither the relationship nor Araby as a place of mystical enchantment can exist.

8. Some students might think the tone is sympathetic and melancholy. Others might see the tone as amused and slightly embarrassed, showing the amazement of a man looking back on his own foolishness as a boy.

9. The boy is like a questing knight in that he idealizes his beloved and seeks to please her with a gift from an exotic place. One way that the story is a distortion of the quest tale is that the narrator's disillusionment is an ironic turn on the traditional quest story.

Making Meanings

First Thoughts

1. Some students may feel let down because they think the ending is anticlimactic. Others may feel deep sympathy for the boy over his shattered dreams.

Reviewing the Text

a. The narrator is an adult who remembers an episode from his childhood. The narrator is older than the hero. This is indicated by use of the past tense.

b. North Richmond Street and the narrator's house. Among the adjectives that paint a gloomy scene are *brown, somber, rusty, musty, old, damp, wild, rough, muddy, silent, dark,* and *feeble.*

c. The purpose of the quest is to buy a gift at the bazaar for Mangan's sister. Obstacles include the uncle's lateness, Mrs. Mercer's visit, the train's delay, and the narrator's failure to find a sixpenny entrance to the bazaar.

Elements of Literature

Mini-Lesson: Irony

Students are surrounded by irony every day—verbal irony in conversations and overheard comments, situational irony in many aspects of their own lives, and dramatic irony in countless movies and TV shows. Help students become more aware of irony by asking them to collect examples they encounter of all three types of irony during the course of a single day. Ask them to write their examples on index cards that are color-coded for each type of irony. Then, spend time letting students share their examples with the whole class.

Possible Answers

Verbal irony: Your friend is wearing really ugly clothes, and you say, "Nice outfit, pal." Situational irony: You wake up late for school, madly get your clothes on, tear out of the house, and arrive at school only to realize it is a holiday. Dramatic irony: Again, *Oedipus Rex* serves as an example. The audience knows that Oedipus has killed his father and married his mother as he was fated to do, but he does not know. This discrepancy makes Oedipus's promise to find and punish the murderer highly ironic. Most students will agree that there remains a discrepancy between social ideals and reality.

---

a quest to prove himself worthy to his beloved, whom he worshiped from afar. How is the narrator of "Araby" like a questing knight? How is the story really a distortion of a quest tale?

ELEMENTS OF LITERATURE

Irony: Things Are Not As They Seem

Here is the plot of a story: A boy has a crush on a girl. He promises to get her something from a bazaar, but he gets there late and is unable to buy anything. The story ends with him standing in the darkened hall of the bazaar.

When you consider this bare-bones plot, "Araby" doesn't seem to be much of a story. A traditional story deals with some significant action, but "Araby" deals with a thwarted action. The protagonist fails to reach the goal he has been struggling to achieve, and in the end he is revealed to himself as the very opposite of the person he dreamed he was. "Araby" is ironic—both in its form and in many of its details.

In Greek comedy, an *eiron* was a character who was not what he appeared to be. From that Greek term comes **irony,** which in all its varieties also refers to things that are not what they appear to be. The most common form of irony is **verbal irony,** in which you say the opposite of what you really mean. We often use verbal irony in conversation. When asked how you feel after a really terrible day, you might say, for example, "I feel just great." We would know by the tone of your voice that you are being *ironic*—in reality, you feel anything but great. **Sarcasm** is a very broad and cutting form of verbal irony.

Another form of irony is **situational irony,** in which things turn out differently from what is expected. In its simplest form, this can involve a cartoon character laughing so hard at someone who has slipped on a banana peel that she herself walks right into an open manhole. In its most sophisticated form, as in Sophocles' *Oedipus Rex,* the hero Oedipus, in trying to escape a curse, brings it down upon himself. Surprise endings invariably feature situational irony.

A third form of irony, **dramatic irony,** occurs when readers or an audience knows something that

a character does not know. In "Little Red Riding Hood," we know the wolf has dressed in the grandmother's clothes, but Red Riding Hood does not. This discrepancy between what we know and what the characters know creates a sense of irony and a degree of dramatic tension.

In "Araby," almost all of the irony stems from the discrepancy between the narrator's romantic view of things and the way things really are. His love for Mangan's sister is obviously overblown, an adolescent crush on someone he does not actually know. In pursuit of his love, he seeks some exotic gift from Araby, but this, too, becomes an ironic quest: In reality, he has simply taken a suburban train to a charity bazaar and returned empty-handed. In addition, through the aunt and uncle, the story shows that love in the real world—at least married love in Dublin—is not the ideal the boy imagines. It is, rather, marriage between an ineffectual woman and a man who comes home late and drunk.

But the ironies in "Araby" go still further. The hero's love and the quest he undertakes are directly associated with religion: "I imagined that I bore my chalice safely through a throng of foes. Her name sprang to my lips at moments in strange prayers and praises which I myself did not understand." Worshiping Mangan's sister is as much a religious act as an emotional one, and when his romantic dreams are shattered, his disillusion is not just with love, but with all of his spiritual values. Just as the aunt and uncle represent the reality of love, the reality of the religious part of the narrator's quest is represented by the dead priest and his rusty bicycle pump.

For Joyce, modern Ireland—its society, religion, and culture—was in a state of decay. The discrepancy between the ideals of Ireland's past and the reality of its present was the chief source of his irony.

Illustrate the three types of irony with examples of your own. Your examples might be drawn from actual life, books, plays, films, personal experience, or your imagination. Do you think there is still today a discrepancy between social ideals and reality?

Auditory Some students may have difficulty recognizing verbal irony when they encounter it in print because verbal irony often depends on the tone of voice of the speaker. Help students recognize verbal irony by suggesting that, when they encounter a statement they suspect is ironic, they test it by reading the statement aloud in a sarcastic tone of voice.

Visual Students might find it easier to handle the material presented in the feature if it is organized in a chart like the one that follows. After students have read the feature, ask them to fill out the chart and keep it in their notes for future reference.

Type of Irony	Definition	Example
Verbal		
Situational		
Dramatic		

PROGRAM MANAGER

Application and Reinforcement
For reinforcement of the elements of literature introduced in this lesson, see **Transparency** 13.5 in the *Audiovisual Resources Binder.*

CHOICES: Building Your Portfolio

Writer's Notebook

1. Collecting Ideas for an Informative Report

Ideas for an informative report can come from what you read. Think back to your reading of "Araby." Review also what you read about Joyce's life. Is there any topic suggested by your reading that you might want to learn more about? "Araby," for example, might make you curious about Dublin life in the early 1900s—especially the general political situation in Ireland at that time. Freewrite for a few minutes, focusing on topics suggested by the story and by Joyce's life. Keep your notes for use in the Writer's Workshop on page 1053.

Critical Writing

2. Significant Moments

Joyce used the term **epiphanies** to describe those moments of sudden insight revealed to a character. The word *epiphany* comes from a Greek word meaning "a showing forth or revelation." In an essay, explain the epiphany that the narrator experiences at the end of the story. Show how the narrator's experiences have led to this revelation, and cite the passage of the story in which the epiphany is described.

Critical Writing

3. Vanity's Many Sides

At the end of the story, the narrator sees himself "driven and derided by vanity." One meaning of *vanity* is "the state of being empty, idle, valueless." Another meaning is "exaggerated self-love." Still another is "hunger for praise or admiration." In an essay, explain how all these definitions could apply to the narrator.

Creative Writing

4. The Universal Joyce

In a review of *Dubliners* in *The Egoist* (July 15, 1914), the poet Ezra Pound wrote that you could erase the local names, a few specifically local allusions, and a few historic events of the past, and substitute other names, allusions, and events, and these stories could be retold of any town. Is Pound right? Create a story map for "Araby," changing the setting to an American town in the late 1990s. Which details of plot and character will you have to change? Share your story map with classmates.

Creative Writing

5. Through Another's Eyes

Based on what you know of the young girl in the story, write a brief sketch of the story's events as seen through her eyes. What does she think of her neighborhood? of the bazaar? of the boy?

Creative Writing

6. The Thinking Mind

Read the material on pages 996–997 about stream of consciousness. Then try your hand at writing a sketch that reflects the associations and sensory impressions that occur in a character's mind. Start by placing your character in a specific setting. Then let his or her mind start to work.

Art

7. The Artist in You

Respond to the story by creating original art. You may want to contrast how Araby looked in the narrator's vivid imagination and in drab reality by painting two conceptions of the bazaar, by creating a collage, or by designing stage sets for a dramatization.

Performance

8. Araby Alive

With several classmates, prepare an oral reading of Joyce's story. You will have to make these decisions: (a) How many readers will you need? (b) Will you use any props? (c) Will you use lighting or music? (d) Will your readers be costumed in some way? You'll also have to appoint a director and create a script for your readers.

Beyond the Story

Choices: Building Your Portfolio

1. **Writer's Notebook** Remind students to save their work. They can use it as prewriting for the Writer's Workshop on p. 1053.
2. **Critical Writing** Students might find it helpful in the prewriting phase of this assignment to construct an arch. On the left side, students may list the events leading up to the boy's trip to Araby, moving upward in the order of events. At the zenith, students may write "arrival at Araby." On the right side of the pyramid, moving downward, students may list the events at the bazaar that lead directly to the epiphany.
3. **Critical Writing** Students will have to collect details from the story that support each of the three definitions of vanity. One way to organize these details is to use a chart like the one that follows.

Empty, idle, valueless	Exaggerated self-love	Hunger for praise

---

SPOTLIGHT ON

The Influence of James Joyce

Joyce's influence on twentieth-century writing is hard to overstate. His impact on world literature derives from his innovations in narrative techniques.

Portraying the flow of thought. Language for Joyce had an important psychological and social element. For Joyce (following St. Thomas Aquinas who was following Aristotle), there is nothing in the mind which does not enter through the senses. We come to know the world through our senses, and our thought processes follow a pattern of association based on what we experience through our senses. Joyce's use of point of view in his writing and his presentation of thoughts directed by association led to the best-known characteristic of his mature style, called **stream of consciousness.** This is an attempt to portray the thinking mind directly, without "organizing" the thoughts and without the intervention of the author.

Joyce's early novel *A Portrait of the Artist as a Young Man* (1916) contains the germ of his experiments with this technique. The method is most apparent, though, in his second novel, *Ulysses* (1922). Much of the action in this novel is presented through the thoughts of its protagonists. Here, for example, is one of the main characters, Leopold Bloom, standing in front of a Dublin tea shop reading the labels on the cans of tea and thinking:

> His right hand once more more slowly went over his brow and hair. Then he put on his hat again, relieved: and read again: choice blend, made of the finest Ceylon brands. The far east. Lovely spot it must be: the garden of the world, big lazy leaves to float about on, cactuses, flowery meads, snaky lianas they call them. . . . Where was the chap I saw in that picture somewhere? Ah yes, in the dead sea floating on his back, reading a book with a parasol open. Couldn't sink if you tried: so

> thick with salt. Because of the weight of the water, no, the weight of the body in the water is equal to the weight of the what? Or is it the volume is equal to the weight? It's a law something like that. Vance in High School cracking his finger joints, teaching. The college curriculum. Cracking curriculum. What is weight really when you say the weight? Thirty-two feet per second per second. Law of falling bodies: per second per second.
>
> —James Joyce, *from Ulysses*

James Joyce with Sylvia Beach, his publisher, in Paris during the Roaring Twenties.

Bloom's mind moves by association from the tea label to the Far East to the picture he saw of a man who, he realizes, wasn't in the Far East but in the Near East, on the Dead Sea. This makes him think of the principles behind floating and falling, which reminds him of his school days and of a teacher who cracked his knuckles. Bloom's mind, as this passage demonstrates, contains a mix of personal memories, sensations, and half-remembered bits of information.

Joyce worked on his last novel, *Finnegans Wake,* for seventeen years, from 1922 to 1939. When it appeared, some critics claimed that it announced the death of the novel as a literary form. In the book, the author has completely disappeared, and the consciousness is that of a dreamer. Finnegan is a bricklayer's helper who falls from a ladder and dies on the first page of the novel.

The experiments of others. Joyce's experiments with stream of consciousness were soon adopted by Virginia Woolf (see page 1122). (Woolf detested *Ulysses,* however, which she called illiterate and underbred.) Woolf's novel *Mrs. Dalloway,* published three years after *Ulysses* in 1925, focuses on the memories, dreams, and feelings of a central character in the course of just one day in London. Like Joyce, Woolf aimed at compressing time so that she could present an entire way of life through the detailed examination of a tiny part of it.

As the book opens, Mrs. Dalloway is on her way to buy flowers for a party she will give that evening:

> Mrs. Dalloway said she would buy the flowers herself. For Lucy had her work cut out for her. The doors would be taken off their hinges; Rumpelmayer's men were coming. And then, thought Clarissa Dalloway, what a morning— fresh as if issued to children on a beach.
>
> —Virginia Woolf, *from Mrs. Dalloway*

Stream of consciousness, as this passage shows, can place unusual demands on the reader. For example, we have to infer from the context that Lucy is one of the household servants, that the doors will be removed for the party, and that Mrs. Dalloway is leaving her house to go shopping on a glorious summer's morning in London.

James Joyce (1902) in Paris, age 20.

The narrative method that Joyce and Woolf pioneered has grown so popular that we no longer regard it as unusual. Among its practitioners have been some of the greatest twentieth-century novelists in world literature: William Faulkner (United States), Marcel Proust (France), and Samuel Beckett (Ireland). Its influence has extended even into film, into the technique of *montage,* in which images shown in rapid succession suggest a train of thought.

C. Expansion
This novel deals with the sleep dreams of a family of five, and in addition to the events of the previous day, the dreams recount their fears, hopes, desires, anxieties, and secret thoughts. The language of the novel is extremely demanding, consisting of a language Joyce invented and of foreign words, elaborate puns, and made-up words. The novel is completely circular in structure: It begins with the second half of a sentence and ends with the first half of the same sentence.

D. Literary Element: Stream of Consciousness
The earliest attempt at stream of consciousness was made by Laurence Sterne in *Tristram Shandy* (1759–1767). In this novel, one of the first written in English, Sterne allows the stream of thought to occur independently of logical progression, but he portrays this through the speech of his characters rather than through a direct presentation of their thoughts. The interior monologue was used for the first time in 1888 by the French writer Edouard Dujardin.

E. Humanities Connection
Montage is used in many music videos, which often consist of a great many visual images flashing across the screen for a few seconds or less. What effect does this technique produce in music videos? [One effect is to create an impression, rather than to tell a story. Another effect is to illustrate visually the ideas expressed in the song. A third effect is to cause the viewer to pay close attention in order to see what is being presented.]

INTEGRATING THE LANGUAGE ARTS

Strategic Reading As students read the material on the influence of James Joyce, ask them to outline the main ideas and supporting details. They may use a chart like the following to organize their ideas.

MAIN IDEA
Details
MAIN IDEA
Details
MAIN IDEA
Details

ASSESSMENT TOOLS

Check Test: True-False
1. Joyce's greatest impact on world literature comes from the narrative techniques he pioneered. [True]
2. Joyce thought the senses have little or nothing to do with how we come to know the world. [False]
3. Stream of consciousness is an attempt to portray the thinking mind directly. [True]
4. Other writers had no interest in experimenting with stream of consciousness. [False]

QUICK PLANNING GUIDE

Into the Story

Author Biography p. 998

Before You Read p. 999

- **Reading Focus: Prior Knowledge** Students explore the effects of greed.
- **Quickwrite** Write in Reader's Log associations about money
- **Elements of Literature: Symbol**
- **Background** Exploring Lawrence's philosophy

Through the Story

"The Rocking-Horse Winner" pp. 1000–1008

Words to Own pp. 1001–1007

Primary Sources p. 1009

Making Meanings p. 1009

Beyond the Story

Choices: Building Your Portfolio p. 1010

- **Writer's Notebook:** List questions for research
- **Critical Writing:** Write an essay about the mother's motivation
- **Critical Writing:** Write an essay about the story and a quotation
- **Creative Writing:** Write a happy ending for the story
- **Creative Writing:** Write Paul's thoughts as he rides
- **Playwriting/Performance:** Make notes about creating a drama

How to Own a Word p. 1011

Spotlight On pp. 1012–1016

D. H. Lawrence
(1885–1930)

David Herbert Lawrence was born in the English Midlands, the frailest child of a coal miner and a former schoolteacher. An able scholar, he too chose to become a teacher, for he resented the physical and spiritual ugliness that the mines had engendered in the Midlands.

While he was teaching, Lawrence began publishing poems and stories in magazines. In 1912, a year after publishing his first novel, Lawrence called on his former professor, Ernest Weekley, and became enchanted with Weekley's German-born wife, Frieda. Within weeks, Frieda Weekley had left her husband and three children and fled with Lawrence to Germany. For the next two years, the couple traveled through Austria and Italy. During this short time, Lawrence finished his novel *Sons and Lovers* (1913) and began work on two others, *The Rainbow* (1915) and *Women in Love* (1920).

Reviews of *Sons and Lovers* were cautiously favorable, but the moral controversy over Lawrence's work (a debate that continued for decades) was already heating up. While in Italy, Lawrence began to see industrialized England as corrosive and oppressive and the Victorian world he had known as overcivilized and prudish. He embraced a belief in "blood knowledge," in putting one's animal self in balance with one's intellect. Returning to England in 1914, he announced that "the source of all life and knowledge is in man and woman, and the source of all living is in the interchange and the meeting and mingling of these two." When a privately printed edition of Lawrence's novel *Women in Love* was published in 1920, one London critic judged it "a loathsome study of sex depravity leading youth to unspeakable disaster."

Around this time, a wealthy American writer, Mabel Dodge Luhan, who deeply admired Lawrence's work, invited him to come to Taos, New Mexico. Lawrence found New Mexico gorgeous, but he had his doubts about Americans, calling them "a host of people who must all have a sense of inferiority complex somewhere, striving to make good over everybody else." Meanwhile, in New York, those Lawrence called "the vice people" had been trying to suppress publication of *Women in Love*. Lawrence rejoiced to learn that a magistrate had declared that his novels were not obscene. On the contrary, he found they made a "distinct contribution to the literature of the present day."

By now, however, Lawrence was growing inured to the invective his work provoked on each publication day. But then he learned that he had incurable tuberculosis. Knowing he had only a few years remaining, Lawrence left the United States and returned to Italy. He now wrote continuously, producing *Lady Chatterley's Lover* (1928), the work for which he is best remembered. The novel draws on his favorite theme—that of the sleeping beauty, the sexual awakening of a woman. The book drew new waves of anger from the censors. U.S. customs officers seized copies as they arrived on the docks, and the novel was banned in Britain. Ironically, as a result of this tremendous publicity, all of Lawrence's work, including his poetry, was in demand.

Giving in at last to doctors' advice, Lawrence retreated in early 1930 to a sanitarium in southern France, where he wrote every day until the end of his life. On March 2, 1930, with Frieda at his bedside, Lawrence died. He is buried at Taos.

D. H. Lawrence.

PROGRAM MANAGER

- **Planning Instruction** See *Teaching Notes, Teaching Resources B,* pp. 132–133 for objectives, a summary, literary elements, and additional information.
- **Instructional Support** See *Graphic Organizer for Active Reading,*

Teaching Resources B, p. 144, for a Through the Story activity.
- **Assessment** See *Selection Test, Test Booklet,* pp. 215–216.
- **Language Link** For practice in sentence structure, see *Language Link,*

Teaching Resources B, pp. 145–146, and *Language and Writing Skills Worksheets,* pp. 85–96, p. 106.
- **Reinforcement** Use the *Words to Own* worksheet in *Teaching Resources B,* p. 147.

BEFORE YOU READ
THE ROCKING-HORSE WINNER

Reading Focus

The Root of All Evil
The old saying that "The love of money is the root of all evil" dates back to the Bible. Over the centuries, immeasurable evil—hatred, war, murder— has sprung from the lust for riches. Even on the most personal level—wife to husband, parent to child, friend to friend—the craving for wealth can have devastating effects.

Quickwrite

In your Reader's Log, jot down some associations that come to your mind about money—and what people will do to get it.

Elements of Literature

Symbol
Beginning with the title, the image of a child's rocking horse dominates this story. The horse is associated with every important development in the plot. As this story's tragedy unfolds, the horse seems to take on more than its literal meaning as a child's toy. It is slowly transformed into a **symbol,** richly suggestive of themes and meanings for the story as a whole.

Background

Lawrence saw men and women as torn between the voices of their instinct (which he saw as natural and therefore good) and the voices of their upbringing and social education (which he saw as destructive). As you read "The Rocking-Horse Winner," which is told like a modern fable, notice which voices permeate the house, and what their effects are.

Ride a Cock Horse (detail)
(c. 1935) by Derek H. Clarke.
John Noott Galleries, Broadway, Worcester, England.

D. H. LAWRENCE 999

Into the Story

Using **BEFORE YOU READ** p. 999

Quickwrite

Give students a limited amount of time (three minutes, for example) for this brainstorming activity. Suggest that they try to focus on both positive and negative aspects of money.

Background

Make sure students understand that the voices of instinct and upbringing that Lawrence talks about are metaphorical voices, not real ones. Thus also, the voices in the house they will be listening for will not be actual voices.

ABOUT THE AUTHOR

Lawrence had no special fondness for his native country. What he perceived as the puritanism and snobbery of the British industrial society deeply disturbed him. This and his ill-health caused him to search abroad for a Utopia. He spent time in both Queensland, Australia and Taos, New Mexico, but failed to find the ideal home for which he yearned.

PORTFOLIO ASSESSMENT

Portfolio Assessment For help with self-assessment of reading skills, see the *Portfolio Management System,* p. 39.

WORDS TO OWN

The following vocabulary words are defined at bottom of the pupil's page.

asserted p. 1001	iridescent p. 1006
parried p. 1002	overwrought p. 1006
obscure p. 1002	remonstrated p. 1007
comparatively p. 1002	arrested p. 1007
reiterated p. 1005	
uncanny p. 1005	

A. Literary Element: Conflict

? What conflict do the details in this passage suggest? [The conflict between appearance and reality, or illusion and reality.]

B. Literary Element: Symbol

? Why is the pervasive whispering in the house a good image for the family's problem? [The problem is persistent, troubling, and never spoken of openly.]

C. Critical Reading: Evaluating an Interpretation

? Is the mother's analysis of her problem accurate? [Some students may think it is accurate because they believe luck plays an important part in financial security. Other students may think it is not accurate, because the mother passes the blame onto forces she cannot control instead of accepting it for herself and her husband.]

Metacognition How did you arrive at your conclusion? [The answers of most students will probably reflect their personal experience and the extent to which they believe in personal responsibility for what happens to people.]

The Rocking-Horse Winner

D. H. Lawrence

There was a woman who was beautiful, who started with all the advantages, yet she had no luck. She married for love, and the love turned to dust. She had bonny children, yet she felt they had been thrust upon her, and she could not love them. They looked at her coldly, as if they were finding fault with her. And hurriedly she felt she must cover up some fault in herself. Yet what it was that she must cover up she never knew. Nevertheless, when her children were present, she always felt the center of her heart go hard. This troubled her, and in her manner she was all the more gentle and anxious for her children, as if she loved them very much. Only she herself knew that at the center of her heart was a hard little place that could not feel love, no, not for anybody. Everybody else said of her: "She is such a good mother. She adores her children." Only she herself, and her children themselves, knew it was not so. They read it in each other's eyes.

There were a boy and two little girls. They lived in a pleasant house, with a garden, and they had discreet servants, and felt themselves superior to anyone in the neighborhood.

Although they lived in style, they felt always an anxiety in the house. There was never enough money. The mother had a small income,[1] and the father had a small income, but not nearly enough for the social position which they had to keep up. The father went into town to some office. But though he had good prospects, these prospects never materialized. There was always the grinding sense of the shortage of money, though the style was always kept up.

At last the mother said: "I will see if *I* can't make something." But she did not know where to begin. She racked her brains, and tried this thing and the other, but could not find anything successful. The failure made deep lines come into her face. Her children were growing up, they would have to go to school. There must be more money, there must be more money. The father, who was always very handsome and expensive in his tastes, seemed as if he never *would* be able to do anything worth doing. And the mother, who had a great belief in herself, did not succeed any better, and her tastes were just as expensive.

And so the house came to be haunted by the unspoken phrase: *There must be more money! There must be more money!* The children could hear it all the time, though nobody said it aloud. They heard it at Christmas, when the expensive and splendid toys filled the nursery. Behind the shining modern rocking horse, behind the smart doll's house, a voice would start whispering: "There *must* be more money! There *must* be more money!" And the children would stop playing, to listen for a moment. They would look into each other's eyes, to see if they had all heard. And each one saw in the eyes of the other two that they too had heard. "There *must* be more money! There *must* be more money!"

It came whispering from the springs of the still-swaying rocking horse, and even the horse, bending his wooden, champing head, heard it. The big doll, sitting so pink and smirking in her new pram,[2] could hear it quite plainly, and seemed to be smirking all the more self-consciously because of it. The foolish puppy, too, that took the place of the teddy bear, he was looking so extraordinarily foolish for no other reason but that he heard the secret whisper all over the house: "There *must* be more money!"

Yet nobody ever said it aloud. The whisper was everywhere, and therefore no one spoke it. Just as no one ever says: "We are breathing!" in spite of the fact that breath is coming and going all the time.

"Mother," said the boy Paul one day, "why don't we keep a car of our own? Why do we always use uncle's, or else a taxi?"

"Because we're the poor members of the family," said the mother.

"But why *are* we, mother?"

"Well—I suppose," she said slowly and bitterly, "it's because your father has no luck."

---

1. **income:** money from an inheritance or investments—not a salary.

2. **pram:** chiefly British for "baby carriage." The word is short for *perambulator*.

Musical Ask students who have musical talent to write a ballad that tells the story of Paul. The ballad should include a refrain and should cover the major events of the story. Students may find or compose a melody that fits the ballad, and you may ask them to perform their work for the class.

Auditory Let students work in pairs to improvise a telephone conversation between Paul's mother and a friend after Paul has died. This conversation should summarize the details of the story from the mother's point of view, and it should also include the mother's ideas about why Paul did the strange things he did. Allow students to make an audiotape of the conversation to play later or for other students to hear. Have students do the same activity with Uncle Oscar or Bassett talking to a friend.

English Language Development To assist students in managing the length of the text, have them practice the reading strategy of making predictions about what is to come. As they read, students should stop at least six times during the story and jot down in their Reader's Logs a statement that expresses what they believe will be the next major development in the plot. One place they might stop would be above (p. 1000) before the conversation between Paul and his mother begins. Once students complete their story, they can compare their predictions and results.

The boy was silent for some time.

"Is luck money, mother?" he asked, rather timidly.

"No, Paul. Not quite. It's what causes you to have money."

"Oh!" said Paul vaguely. "I thought when Uncle Oscar said *filthy lucker,* it meant money."

"*Filthy lucre*[3] does mean money," said the mother. "But it's lucre, not luck."

"Oh!" said the boy. "Then what *is* luck, mother?"

"It's what causes you to have money. If you're lucky you have money. That's why it's better to be born lucky than rich. If you're rich, you may lose your money. But if you're lucky, you will always get more money."

"Oh! Will you? And is father not lucky?"

"Very unlucky, I should say," she said bitterly.

The boy watched her with unsure eyes.

"Why?" he asked.

"I don't know. Nobody ever knows why one person is lucky and another unlucky."

"Don't they? Nobody at all? Does *nobody* know?"

"Perhaps God. But He never tells."

"He ought to, then. And aren't you lucky either, mother?"

"I can't be, if I married an unlucky husband."

"But by yourself, aren't you?"

"I used to think I was, before I married. Now I think I am very unlucky indeed."

"Why?"

"Well—never mind! Perhaps I'm not really," she said.

The child looked at her to see if she meant it. But he saw, by the lines of her mouth, that she was only trying to hide something from him.

"Well, anyhow," he said stoutly, "I'm a lucky person."

"Why?" said his mother, with a sudden laugh.

He stared at her. He didn't even know why he had said it.

"God told me," he asserted, brazening it out.[4]

"I hope He did, dear!" she said, again with a laugh, but rather bitter.

"He did, mother!"

---

3. **filthy lucre** (lōo′kər): riches (a derogatory usage).
4. **brazening it out:** acting boldly.

"Excellent!" said the mother, using one of her husband's exclamations.

The boy saw she did not believe him; or rather, that she paid no attention to his assertion. This angered him somewhere, and made him want to compel her attention.

He went off by himself, vaguely, in a childish way, seeking for the clue to "luck." Absorbed, taking no heed of other people, he went about with a sort of stealth, seeking inwardly for luck. He wanted luck, he wanted it, he wanted it. When the two girls were playing dolls in the nursery, he would sit on his big rocking horse, charging madly into space, with a frenzy that made the little girls peer at him uneasily. Wildly the horse careered,[5] the waving dark hair of the boy tossed, his eyes had a strange glare in them. The little girls dared not speak to him.

When he had ridden to the end of his mad little journey, he climbed down and stood in front of his rocking horse, staring fixedly into its lowered face. Its red mouth was slightly open, its big eye was wide and glassy-bright.

"Now!" he would silently command the snorting steed. "Now, take me to where there is luck! Now take me!"

And he would slash the horse on the neck with the little whip he had asked Uncle Oscar for. He *knew* the horse could take him to where there was luck, if only he forced it. So he would mount again and start on his furious ride, hoping at last to get there. He knew he could get there.

"You'll break your horse, Paul!" said the nurse.

"He's always riding like that! I wish he'd leave off!" said his elder sister Joan.

But he only glared down on them in silence. Nurse gave him up. She could make nothing of him. Anyhow, he was growing beyond her.

One day his mother and his Uncle Oscar came in when he was on one of his furious rides. He did not speak to them.

"Hallo, you young jockey! Riding a winner?" said his uncle.

"Aren't you growing too big for a rocking

---

5. **careered:** rushed.

WORDS TO OWN
asserted (ə·sʉrt′id) *v.*: declared.

D. Critical Reading: Making Inferences

[?] What is it the boy wants from his mother that he does not get from her? [Warmth, love, and attention.]

E. Literary Element: Character

[?] Whom does the boy resemble in his heedless, self-absorbed rocking and in his intense desire for luck? [His mother.]

F. Language Note: Style

[?] What do the words *mad* and *furious* suggest about how Paul rides the rocking horse? [He rides it without pleasure in a frenzy of abandon. He seems to be possessed by his quest for luck.]

INTEGRATING THE LANGUAGE ARTS

Strategic Reading As students read the story, ask them to jot down any idea or event they find confusing or unusual. After they have read the story, ask them to form a question about each of the ideas or events they noted as they read. From this group of questions, have students work in pairs to select one question they feel gets to the heart of the meaning of the story. They should write this question in the center of a large sheet of paper and make a web diagram around it by answering the question in a number of different ways, from several points of view, and by adding additional questions as they arise. They should compare their webs with those of others.

Writing: An Outline Ask students to write a brief outline for a sequel to the story by telling what happens to the family after Paul's death. Help them focus their thinking by suggesting the following questions.

1. How does the family spend the money they get from Paul?
2. Does the mother change in any way as a result of her experiences in the story? If so, how?
3. What happens to Bassett after the story ends?
4. What happens to Uncle Oscar after the story? ☞

A. Critical Reading: Drawing Conclusions

[?] What state does Paul appear to be in when he is riding the rocking horse? [Possible answers: He appears to be in a trance or to be hypnotized by the movement of the rocking horse.]

B. Critical Reading: Analyzing Details

It is a little odd that the boy has not named one of his favorite toys. Next, we find that the name changes. When the uncle asks how the boy knows the name, the sister answers. What do you make of this little mystery? [Possible answers: The boy does not name the horse because he does not really love it, just as his mother cannot really love him. The boy just names the horse according to race winners; the horse has no particular identity for the boy. There is something strange going on with the rocking horse and its names.]

C. Reader's Response: First Thoughts

[?] Why is Uncle Oscar delighted when Paul takes an interest in horse racing? [Sample responses: Uncle Oscar may be interested in horse racing, too, and happy to have another family member share his interest. He may think such an interest is fitting for a gentleman and is glad Paul is developing into one on schedule.]

D. Critical Reading: Making Inferences

[?] Why might Lawrence use religious references in describing Bassett's attitude toward Paul's interest in horse racing? [Perhaps to suggest a supernatural connection between Paul and racing, or perhaps to reflect the grave or frightening element in Paul's gaming. In any case, Bassett seems to know he is toying with something serious and beyond his comprehension.]

---

horse? You're not a very little boy any longer, you know," said his mother.

A But Paul only gave a blue glare from his big, rather close-set eyes. He would speak to nobody when he was in full tilt. His mother watched him with an anxious expression on her face.

At last he suddenly stopped forcing his horse into the mechanical gallop and slid down.

"Well, I got there!" he announced fiercely, his blue eyes still flaring, and his sturdy long legs straddling apart.

"Where did you get to?" asked his mother.

"Where I wanted to go," he flared back at her.

B "That's right, son!" said Uncle Oscar. "Don't you stop till you get there. What's the horse's name?"

"He doesn't have a name," said the boy.

"Gets on without all right?" asked the uncle.

"Well, he has different names. He was called Sansovino last week."

"Sansovino, eh? Won the Ascot.[6] How did you know this name?"

"He always talks about horse races with Bassett," said Joan.

C The uncle was delighted to find that his small nephew was posted with all the racing news. Bassett, the young gardener, who had been wounded in the left foot in the war and had got his present job through Oscar Cresswell, whose batman[7] he had been, was a perfect blade of the "turf."[8] He lived in the racing events, and the small boy lived with him.

Oscar Cresswell got it all from Bassett.

"Master Paul comes and asks me, so I can't do more than tell him, sir," said Bassett, his face terribly serious, as if he were speaking of religious matters.

"And does he ever put anything on a horse he fancies?"

D "Well—I don't want to give him away—he's a young sport, a fine sport, sir. Would you mind asking him himself? He sort of takes a pleasure in it, and perhaps he'd feel I was giving him away, sir, if you don't mind."

Bassett was serious as a church.

---

6. **Ascot:** famous horse race held annually at Ascot Heath in England. Several traditional British races are mentioned in the story.
7. **batman:** an officer's personal attendant.
8. **blade of the "turf":** stylish, young racing fan.

The uncle went back to his nephew and took him off for a ride in the car.

"Say, Paul, old man, do you ever put anything on a horse?" the uncle asked.

The boy watched the handsome man closely.

"Why, do you think I oughtn't to?" he parried.

"Not a bit of it! I thought perhaps you might give me a tip for the Lincoln."

The car sped on into the country, going down to Uncle Oscar's place in Hampshire.

"Honor bright?" said the nephew.

"Honor bright, son!" said the uncle.

"Well, then, Daffodil."

"Daffodil! I doubt it, sonny. What about Mirza?"

"I only know the winner," said the boy. "That's Daffodil."

"Daffodil, eh?"

There was a pause. Daffodil was an obscure horse comparatively.

"Uncle!"

"Yes, son?"

"You won't let it go any further, will you? I promised Bassett."

"Bassett be damned, old man! What's he got to do with it?"

"We're partners. We've been partners from the first. Uncle, he lent me my first five shillings, which I lost. I promised him, honor bright, it was only between me and him; only you gave me that ten-shilling note I started winning with, so I thought you were lucky. You won't let it go any further, will you?"

The boy gazed at his uncle from those big, hot, blue eyes, set rather close together. The uncle stirred and laughed uneasily.

"Right you are, son! I'll keep your tip private. Daffodil, eh? How much are you putting on him?"

"All except twenty pounds," said the boy. "I keep that in reserve."

The uncle thought it a good joke.

"You keep twenty pounds in reserve, do you, you young romancer?[9] What are you betting, then?"

---

9. **romancer:** imaginative storyteller.

WORDS TO OWN
parried (par'ēd) v.: replied evasively.
obscure (əb·skyoor') adj.: little-known.
comparatively (kəm·par'ə·tiv'lē) adv.: relatively; in comparison to others.

OPTIONS FOR TEACHING

INTEGRATING THE LANGUAGE ARTS

Usage Have students skim the beginning of "The Rocking-Horse Winner" to find where D. H. Lawrence occasionally intersperses his more ordinary sentences with exclamations. As the story continues, students should note that the exclamations become more frequent and agitated as the child persists in his riding. The result is an increasingly desperate and despairing **tone** as the child eventually rides to his death on the horse. Have students rewrite the following paragraph, adding exclamations to approach the variety and tone that D. H. Lawrence achieved.

She reached the top of the hill and looked down. The sidewalk stretched away, a concrete ribbon unfurling to the street below. Seeing it filled the child with both delight and dread. She started down, skates making their familiar metallic grating. Down and down. Trees and houses became a blur. Cars zipped by, indistinguishable in the speed of her racing. Vainly she wondered where the bottom was.

The Merry-Go-Round (20th century) by Mark Gertler.

Tate Gallery, London.

E. Literary Element: Character

? How does Uncle Oscar's attitude toward Paul differ from Bassett's?
[Uncle Oscar is amused and skeptical; Bassett is a serious believer in Paul's knowledge.]

"I'm betting three hundred," said the boy gravely. "But it's between you and me, Uncle Oscar! Honor bright?"

The uncle burst into a roar of laughter.

"It's between you and me all right, you young Nat Gould,"[10] he said, laughing. "But where's your three hundred?"

"Bassett keeps it for me. We're partners."

"You are, are you! And what is Bassett putting on Daffodil?"

10. **Nat Gould:** famous British authority on racing.

"He won't go quite as high as I do, I expect. Perhaps he'll go a hundred and fifty."

"What, pennies?" laughed the uncle.

"Pounds," said the child, with a surprised look at his uncle. "Bassett keeps a bigger reserve than I do."

Between wonder and amusement Uncle Oscar was silent. He pursued the matter no further, but he determined to take his nephew with him to the Lincoln races.

"Now, son," he said, "I'm putting twenty on Mirza, and I'll put five on for you on any horse you fancy. What's your pick?"

D. H. LAWRENCE 1003

COOPERATIVE LEARNING

Character Interviews Assign the roles of Paul, the mother, Uncle Oscar, and Bassett to members of the class so that each student is assigned one of the four roles. Ask these students to form character groups and to make up a set of questions for each of the other three characters, asking why they behave the way they do and how they feel about what happens in the story. Then, have the class form a circle with a chair in the center. Randomly select a student to be in the Hot Seat, and let others ask questions as though they were their assigned characters. The student in the center should answer the questions in the persona of his or her assigned character.

CLASSROOM MANAGEMENT

Block Scheduling Have students flesh out their outlines from the activity on p. T1001 into a story. Ask students to prewrite (ten to fifteen minutes). Then, the bulk of the period should be spent in student drafting (forty to forty-five minutes). Next, ask students to peer edit a partner's story (ten to fifteen minutes). Ask for volunteers to share their edited papers orally with the class (ten to fifteen minutes). Students may revise and write their final copies as homework or during the next class period.

A. Reader's Response: Shaping Interpretations

? Why does Uncle Oscar want to talk to Bassett? [Sample responses: Maybe he wants to verify Paul's story. Maybe he begins to question the wisdom of Paul's interest in racing because so much money is involved.]

B. Critical Reading: Making Inferences

? Why is Bassett so quick to attribute Paul's knowledge to the supernatural? [Perhaps as a simple man with little education Bassett cannot imagine any other sources of Paul's knowledge. Perhaps he genuinely believes it to be divinely inspired.]

"Daffodil, uncle."

"No, not the fiver on Daffodil!"

"I should if it was my own fiver," said the child.

"Good! Good! Right you are! A fiver for me and a fiver for you on Daffodil."

The child had never been to a race meeting before, and his eyes were blue fire. He pursed his mouth tight and watched. A Frenchman just in front had put his money on Lancelot. Wild with excitement, he flayed his arms up and down, yelling *"Lancelot! Lancelot!"* in his French accent.

Daffodil came in first, Lancelot second, Mirza third. The child, flushed and with eyes blazing, was curiously serene. His uncle brought him four five-pound notes, four to one.

"What am I to do with these?" he cried, waving them before the boy's eyes.

"I suppose we'll talk to Bassett," said the boy. "I expect I have fifteen hundred now; and twenty in reserve; and this twenty."

His uncle studied him for some moments.

"Look here, son!" he said. "You're not serious about Bassett and that fifteen hundred, are you?"

"Yes, I am. But it's between you and me, uncle. Honor bright?"

A "Honor bright all right, son! But I must talk to Bassett."

"If you'd like to be a partner, uncle, with Bassett and me, we could all be partners. Only, you'd have to promise, honor bright, uncle, not to let it go beyond us three. Bassett and I are lucky, and you must be lucky, because it was your ten shillings I started winning with. . . ."

Uncle Oscar took both Bassett and Paul into Richmond Park for an afternoon, and there they talked.

"It's like this, you see, sir," Bassett said. "Master Paul would get me talking about racing events, spinning yarns, you know, sir. And he was always keen on knowing if I'd made or if I'd lost. It's about a year since, now, that I put five shillings on Blush of Dawn for him: And we lost. Then the luck turned, with that ten shillings he had from you: That we put on Singhalese. And since that time, it's been pretty steady, all things considering. What do you say, Master Paul?"

"We're all right when we're sure," said Paul. "It's when we're not quite sure that we go down."

"Oh, but we're careful then," said Bassett.

"But when are you *sure*?" smiled Uncle Oscar.

B "It's Master Paul, sir," said Bassett in a secret, religious voice. "It's as if he had it from heaven. Like Daffodil, now, for the Lincoln. That was as sure as eggs."

"Did you put anything on Daffodil?" asked Oscar Cresswell.

"Yes, sir. I made my bit."

"And my nephew?"

Bassett was obstinately silent, looking at Paul.

"I made twelve hundred, didn't I, Bassett? I told uncle I was putting three hundred on Daffodil."

"That's right," said Bassett, nodding.

"But where's the money?" asked the uncle.

"I keep it safe locked up, sir. Master Paul he can have it any minute he likes to ask for it."

"What, fifteen hundred pounds?"

"And twenty! And *forty*, that is, with the twenty he made on the course."

"It's amazing!" said the uncle.

"If Master Paul offers you to be partners, sir, I would, if I were you: if you'll excuse me," said Bassett.

Oscar Cresswell thought about it.

"I'll see the money," he said.

They drove home again, and sure enough, Bassett came round to the garden house with fifteen hundred pounds in notes. The twenty pounds reserve was left with Joe Glee, in the Turf Commission[11] deposit.

"You see, it's all right, uncle, when I'm *sure*! Then we go strong, for all we're worth. Don't we, Bassett?"

"We do that, Master Paul."

"And when are you sure?" said the uncle, laughing.

"Oh, well, sometimes I'm *absolutely* sure, like about Daffodil," said the boy; "and sometimes I have an idea; and sometimes I haven't even an idea, have I, Bassett? Then we're careful, because we mostly go down."

"You do, do you! And when you're sure, like about Daffodil, what makes you sure, sonny?"

"Oh, well, I don't know," said the boy uneasily. "I'm sure, you know, uncle; that's all."

---

11. **Turf Commission:** committee of the Jockey Club, the chief governing body for horse racing. This committee operates a bank in which bettors can deposit money for future bets.

OPTIONS FOR TEACHING

CROSSING THE CURRICULUM

Art Ask students to create a piece of artwork that expresses the tension in the story. Possibilities include a sculpture of Paul and the rocking horse or an audio or video representation of the voices and their effects on Paul.

Mathematics Have students work out the mathematics presented on p. 1004, when after winning the four-to-one odds at the races, Paul's £300 yields £1500, while Uncle Oscar's £5 yields only £20. [Uncle Oscar apparently keeps his original £5 and gives Paul only the winnings, whereas Paul has his £1200 winnings plus his original wager of £300.]

"It's as if he had it from heaven, sir." Bassett reiterated.

"I should say so!" said the uncle.

But he became a partner. And when the Leger was coming on Paul was "sure" about Lively Spark, which was a quite inconsiderable horse. The boy insisted on putting a thousand on the horse, Bassett went for five hundred, and Oscar Cresswell two hundred. Lively Spark came in first, and the betting had been ten to one against him. Paul had made ten thousand.

"You see," he said, "I was absolutely sure of him."

Even Oscar Cresswell had cleared two thousand.

"Look here, son," he said, "this sort of thing makes me nervous."

"It needn't, uncle! Perhaps I shan't be sure again for a long time."

"But what are you going to do with your money?" asked the uncle.

"Of course," said the boy, "I started it for mother. She said she had no luck, because father is unlucky, so I thought if *I* was lucky, it might stop whispering."

"What might stop whispering?"

"Our house. I *hate* our house for whispering."

"What does it whisper?"

"Why—why"—the boy fidgeted—"why, I don't know. But it's always short of money, you know, uncle."

"I know it, son, I know it."

"You know people send mother writs,[12] don't you, uncle?"

"I'm afraid I do," said the uncle.

"And then the house whispers, like people laughing at you behind your back. It's awful, that is! I thought if I was lucky——"

"You might stop it," added the uncle.

The boy watched him with big blue eyes, that had an uncanny cold fire in them, and he said never a word.

"Well, then!" said the uncle. "What are we doing?"

"I shouldn't like mother to know I was lucky," said the boy.

"Why not, son?"

"She'd stop me."

12. **writs:** legal documents demanding payment of debts.

"I don't think she would."

"Oh!"—and the boy writhed in an odd way—"I *don't* want her to know, uncle."

"All right, son! We'll manage it without her knowing."

They managed it very easily. Paul, at the other's suggestion, handed over five thousand pounds to his uncle, who deposited it with the family lawyer, who was then to inform Paul's mother that a relative had put five thousand pounds into his hands, which sum was to be paid out a thousand pounds at a time, on the mother's birthday, for the next five years.

"So she'll have a birthday present of a thousand pounds for five successive years," said Uncle Oscar. "I hope it won't make it all the harder for her later."

Paul's mother had her birthday in November. The house had been "whispering" worse than ever lately, and, even in spite of his luck, Paul could not bear up against it. He was very anxious to see the effect of the birthday letter, telling his mother about the thousand pounds.

When there were no visitors, Paul now took his meals with his parents, as he was beyond the nursery control. His mother went into town nearly every day. She had discovered that she had an odd knack of sketching furs and dress materials, so she worked secretly in the studio of a friend who was the chief "artist" for the leading drapers.[13] She drew the figures of ladies in furs and ladies in silk and sequins for the newspaper advertisements. This young woman artist earned several thousand pounds a year, but Paul's mother only made several hundreds, and she was again dissatisfied. She so wanted to be first in something, and she did not succeed, even in making sketches for drapery advertisements.

She was down to breakfast on the morning of her birthday. Paul watched her face as she read her letters. He knew the lawyer's letter. As his mother read it, her face hardened and became more expressionless. Then a cold, determined

13. **drapers:** dealers in cloth and dry goods.

- -
WORDS TO OWN
reiterated (rē·it′ə·rāt′id) *v.*: repeated.
uncanny (un·kan′ē) *adj.*: strange; eerie; weird.
- -

D. H. LAWRENCE 1005

C. Reader's Response: Shaping Interpretations

? Why does winning make Uncle Oscar nervous? [Sample responses: Because he doesn't understand what is happening. Because he suspects supernatural causes.]

D. Critical Reading: Drawing Conclusions

? Why does the mother work secretly? [Possible answers: She thinks working is beneath her. She is afraid she will not succeed.]

E. Literary Element: Character

? What does the mother's dissatisfaction reveal about her character? [One possibility is that she impatiently wants big rewards without waiting or working for them. Another possibility is that she is very competitive and cannot stand not being the best.]

F. Reader's Response: Extending the Text

? How do you think his mother's reaction to the gift makes Paul feel? [Sample responses: He might be disappointed, confused, hurt, further estranged from her.]

PROBLEM SOLVING/CRITICAL THINKING

Identifying Problems and Solutions Have students work in groups to try to solve the problems in Paul's family. First, have them determine what the problems are. As they create their lists, ask students if the problems are merely a matter of money. If the family had more, or budgeted it properly so that they would not be in debt, would their problems be solved? Students should arrive at the notion that Paul's family's problems extend beyond money and that the family's central value is money rather than love. Once this is established, ask students to propose what the family might do about the problem. ☞

look came on her mouth. She hid the letter under the pile of others, and said not a word about it.

"Didn't you have anything nice in the post for your birthday, mother?" said Paul.

"Quite moderately nice," she said, her voice cold and absent.

She went away to town without saying more.

But in the afternoon Uncle Oscar appeared. He said Paul's mother had had a long interview with the lawyer, asking if the whole five thousand could not be advanced at once, as she was in debt.

"What do you think, uncle?" said the boy.

"I leave it to you, son."

"Oh, let her have it, then! We can get some more with the other," said the boy.

"A bird in the hand is worth two in the bush, laddie!" said Uncle Oscar.

"But I'm sure to *know* for the Grand National; or the Lincolnshire; or else the Derby. I'm sure to know for *one* of them," said Paul.

So Uncle Oscar signed the agreement, and Paul's mother touched the whole five thousand. Then something very curious happened. The voices in the house suddenly went mad, like a chorus of frogs on a spring evening. There were certain new furnishings, and Paul had a tutor. He was *really* going to Eton,[14] his father's school, in the following autumn. There were flowers in the winter, and a blossoming of the luxury Paul's mother had been used to. And yet the voices in the house, behind the sprays of mimosa and almond blossom, and from under the piles of iridescent cushions, simply trilled and screamed in a sort of ecstasy: "There *must* be more money! Oh-h-h; there *must* be more money. Oh, now, now-w! Now-w-w—there *must* be more money!—more than ever! More than ever!"

It frightened Paul terribly. He studied away at his Latin and Greek with his tutor. But his intense hours were spent with Bassett. The Grand National had gone by: He had not "known," and had lost a hundred pounds. Summer was at hand. He was in agony for the Lincoln. But even for the Lincoln he didn't "know," and he lost fifty pounds. He became wild-eyed and strange, as if something were going to explode in him.

14. **Eton:** Eton College, a private prep school for boys, near London.

"Let it alone, son! Don't you bother about it!" urged Uncle Oscar. But it was as if the boy couldn't really hear what his uncle was saying.

"I've got to know for the Derby! I've got to know for the Derby!" the child reiterated, his big blue eyes blazing with a sort of madness.

His mother noticed how overwrought he was.

"You'd better go to the seaside. Wouldn't you like to go now to the seaside, instead of waiting? I think you'd better," she said, looking down at him anxiously, her heart curiously heavy because of him.

But the child lifted his uncanny blue eyes.

"I couldn't possibly go before the Derby, mother!" he said. "I couldn't possibly!"

"Why not?" she said, her voice becoming heavy when she was opposed. "Why not? You can still go from the seaside to see the Derby with your Uncle Oscar, if that's what you wish. No need for you to wait here. Besides, I think you care too much about these races. It's a bad sign. My family has been a gambling family, and you won't know till you grow up how much damage it has done. But it has done damage. I shall have to send Bassett away, and ask Uncle Oscar not to talk racing to you, unless you promise to be reasonable about it: Go away to the seaside and forget it. You're all nerves!"

"I'll do what you like, mother, so long as you don't send me away till after the Derby," the boy said.

"Send you away from where? Just from this house?"

"Yes," he said, gazing at her.

"Why, you curious child, what makes you care about this house so much, suddenly? I never knew you loved it."

He gazed at her without speaking. He had a secret within a secret, something he had not divulged, even to Bassett or to his Uncle Oscar.

But his mother, after standing undecided and a little bit sullen for some moments, said:

"Very well, then! Don't go to the seaside till after the Derby, if you don't wish it. But promise

WORDS TO OWN

iridescent (ir′i·des′ənt) *adj.*: showing rainbowlike colors.
overwrought (ō′vər·rôt′) *adj.*: overly excited.

OPTIONS FOR TEACHING

PROFESSIONAL NOTES

Critical Comment: Paul as Hero and Symbol This discussion of some of the elements in "The Rocking-Horse Winner" is excerpted from "A Rocking-Horse: The Symbol, the Pattern, the Way to Live," by W. D. Snodgrass: "[T]he story resembles many well-known fairy tales or magical stories in which the hero bargains with evil powers for personal advantages or forbidden knowledge. These bargains are always 'rigged' so that the hero, after his apparent triumphs, will lose in the end—this being, in itself, the standard 'moral.' . . . So, in some sense, Paul *is* demonic, yet a poor devil; though he has compacted with evil, his intentions were good and he has destroyed only himself. At first metaphorically, in the end literally, he has committed suicide. But that may be, finally, the essence of evil. . . . Paul is destroyed, we have said, by his desire to 'know.' It is not only that he has chosen wrong ways of knowing or wrong things to know. The evil is that he *has* chosen to know, to live by intellection. Lawrence wrote, in a letter to Ernest Collins: 'My great religion is a belief in the blood, the flesh, as being wiser than the intellect. We can go wrong in our minds. But what our blood feels and believes and says is always true. *The intellect is only a bit and bridle.*' . . . Paul is, so, a symbol of civilized man, whipping himself on in a nervous endless 'mechanical gallop,' an 'arrested prance,' in chase of something which will destroy him if he ever catches it, and which he never really wanted anyway."

me you won't let your nerves go to pieces. Promise you won't think so much about horse racing and *events,* as you call them!"

"Oh no," said the boy casually, "I won't think much about them, mother. You needn't worry. I wouldn't worry, mother, if I were you."

"If you were me and I were you," said his mother, "I wonder what we *should* do!"

"But you know you needn't worry, mother, don't you?" the boy repeated.

"I should be awfully glad to know it," she said wearily.

"Oh, well, you *can,* you know. I mean, you *ought* to know you needn't worry," he insisted.

"Ought I? Then I'll see about it," she said.

Paul's secret of secrets was his wooden horse, that which had no name. Since he was emancipated from a nurse and a nursery-governess, he had had his rocking horse removed to his own bedroom at the top of the house.

"Surely you're too big for a rocking horse!" his mother had <u>remonstrated</u>.

"Well, you see, mother, till I can have a *real* horse, I like to have *some* sort of animal about," had been his quaint answer.

"Do you feel he keeps you company?" she laughed.

"Oh yes! He's very good, he always keeps me company, when I'm there," said Paul.

So the horse, rather shabby, stood in an <u>arrested</u> prance in the boy's bedroom.

The Derby was drawing near, and the boy grew more and more tense. He hardly heard what was spoken to him, he was very frail, and his eyes were really uncanny. His mother had sudden strange seizures of uneasiness about him. Sometimes, for half an hour, she would feel a sudden anxiety about him that was almost anguish. She wanted to rush to him at once, and know he was safe.

Two nights before the Derby, she was at a big party in town, when one of her rushes of anxiety about her boy, her firstborn, gripped her heart till she could hardly speak. She fought with the feeling, might and main, for she believed in common sense. But it was too strong. She had to leave the dance and go downstairs to telephone to the country. The children's nursery-governess was terribly surprised and startled at being rung up in the night.

"Are the children all right, Miss Wilmot?"

"Oh yes, they are quite all right."

"Master Paul? Is he all right?"

"He went to bed as right as a trivet. Shall I run up and look at him?"

"No," said Paul's mother reluctantly. "No! Don't trouble. It's all right. Don't sit up. We shall be home fairly soon." She did not want her son's privacy intruded upon.

"Very good," said the governess.

It was about one o'clock when Paul's mother and father drove up to their house. All was still. Paul's mother went to her room and slipped off

---

D. H. LAWRENCE 1007

ASSESSMENT TOOLS

? What could the "soundless noise" **symbolize?** [Sample responses: It could be the boy's doom or a sense of impending sorrow; it could be her anxiety bothering her; or it could be a return of the whispering.] Why should the mother be able to recognize the sound? [Sample responses: Because Paul has been rocking on the horse for years and in this furious way for at least one year; because it is the sound of her own greed.]

B. Literary Element: Climax

Recurrent themes of the story come together in this climactic scene: Paul's likeness to his mother; Paul's madness, which is a kind of inherited disease; and the mother's inability to attend to her children in a life-giving way.

C. Critical Reading: Making Connections

? Does this boy's raving and desperation remind you of other characters you have read about this year? Explain. [Possible answer: Faust. It is almost as if Paul has made some kind of pact with a supernatural force to bring enough luck or money into the household to ease the voices. But like everything else in the household (and unlike Faust's), the pact is unspoken, almost unconsciously made.]

D. Critical Reading: Drawing Conclusions

? Why does Uncle Oscar think Paul is better off dead? [Possible answers: He realizes Paul is mad, and he feels Paul has been saved from a life of agony. He believes Paul is lucky to be dead rather than living a life driven by a materialism that can never be sated.]

---

her white fur cloak. She had told her maid not to wait up for her. She heard her husband downstairs, mixing a whiskey and soda.

And then, because of the strange anxiety at her heart, she stole upstairs to her son's room. Noiselessly she went along the upper corridor. Was there a faint noise? What was it?

She stood, with arrested muscles, outside his door, listening. There was a strange, heavy, and yet not loud noise. Her heart stood still. It was a soundless noise, yet rushing and powerful. Something huge, in violent, hushed motion. What was it? What in God's name was it? She ought to know. She felt that she knew the noise. She knew what it was.

Yet she could not place it. She couldn't say what it was. And on and on it went, like a madness.

Softly, frozen with anxiety and fear, she turned the door handle.

The room was dark. Yet in the space near the window, she heard and saw something plunging to and fro. She gazed in fear and amazement.

Then suddenly she switched on the light, and saw her son, in his green pajamas, madly surging on the rocking horse. The blaze of light suddenly lit him up, as he urged the wooden horse, and lit her up, as she stood, blonde, in her dress of pale green and crystal, in the doorway.

"Paul!" she cried. "Whatever are you doing?"

"It's Malabar!" he screamed in a powerful, strange voice. "It's Malabar!"

His eyes blazed at her for one strange and senseless second, as he ceased urging his wooden horse. Then he fell with a crash to the ground, and she, all her tormented motherhood flooding upon her, rushed to gather him up.

But he was unconscious, and unconscious he remained, with some brain fever. He talked and tossed, and his mother sat stonily by his side.

"Malabar! It's Malabar! Bassett, Bassett, I *know*! It's Malabar!"

So the child cried, trying to get up and urge the rocking horse that gave him his inspiration.

"What does he mean by Malabar?" asked the heart-frozen mother.

"I don't know," said the father stonily.

"What does he mean by Malabar?" she asked her brother Oscar.

"It's one of the horses running for the Derby," was the answer.

And, in spite of himself, Oscar Cresswell spoke to Bassett, and himself put a thousand on Malabar: at fourteen to one.

The third day of the illness was critical: They were waiting for a change. The boy, with his rather long, curly hair, was tossing ceaselessly on the pillow. He neither slept nor regained consciousness, and his eyes were like blue stones. His mother sat, feeling her heart had gone, turned actually into a stone.

In the evening, Oscar Cresswell did not come, but Bassett sent a message, saying could he come up for one moment, just one moment? Paul's mother was very angry at the intrusion, but on second thoughts she agreed. The boy was the same. Perhaps Bassett might bring him to consciousness.

The gardener, a shortish fellow with a little brown moustache and sharp little brown eyes, tiptoed into the room, touched his imaginary cap to Paul's mother, and stole to the bedside, staring with glittering, smallish eyes at the tossing, dying child.

"Master Paul!" he whispered. "Master Paul! Malabar came in first all right, a clean win. I did as you told me. You've made over seventy thousand pounds, you have; you've got over eighty thousand. Malabar came in all right, Master Paul."

"Malabar! Malabar! Did I say Malabar, mother? Did I say Malabar? Do you think I'm lucky, mother? I knew Malabar, didn't I? Over eighty thousand pounds! I call that lucky, don't you, mother? Over eighty thousand pounds! I knew, didn't I know I knew? Malabar came in all right. If I ride my horse till I'm sure, then I tell you, Bassett, you can go as high as you like. Did you go for all you were worth, Bassett?"

"I went a thousand on it, Master Paul."

"I never told you, mother, that if I can ride my horse, and *get there,* then I'm absolutely sure—oh, absolutely! Mother, did I ever tell you? I *am* lucky!"

"No, you never did," said his mother.

But the boy died in the night.

And even as he lay dead, his mother heard her brother's voice saying to her: "My God, Hester, you're eighty-odd thousand to the good, and a poor devil of a son to the bad. But, poor devil, poor devil, he's best gone out of a life where he rides his rocking horse to find a winner."

Making Meanings

First Thoughts

1. Possible responses: Because the mother is distant and unable to love, her treatment of her son is only superficially kind; this seems awful. Her outlook on life is selfish and negative; it is not healthy.

Reviewing the Text

a. The woman's love has turned to dust; she finds herself unable to love her children; she feels flawed. Lawrence tells us that the woman is ambitious and eager for social position; she is not as rich as she hoped and is continually dissatisfied.

b. She says that luck is what causes people to have money. Paul cannot understand why God does not reveal the reason one person is lucky

and another isn't. He confuses *luck* with *lucre*. He believes luck and money are the same—one cannot be lucky in other ways.

c. He bets on horses and wins a great deal of money. He asks his uncle to make an anonymous birthday present to his mother of a thousand pounds a year for five years. His mother is disappointed that she has not received the whole amount; the mother appears cold and indifferent.

D. H. Lawrence on Money

A theme that runs through nearly all Lawrence's works is the celebration of life—the human energy and force that express the joy of existence. Opposing this natural energy is materialism, which Lawrence believed misdirects our energies and warps the soul.

Rolf Gardiner, one of Lawrence's first admirers, managed a large farm in Dorset. In 1926, Lawrence wrote to Gardiner: "And don't be too ernest—earnest—how does one spell it?—nor overburdened by a mission: neither too self-willed. One must be simple and direct, and a bit free from oneself above all."

In another letter to Gardiner, Lawrence makes a rare, brief mention of the evils of materialism.

> Villa Mirenda, Scandicci
> Florence
> 18 Dec., 1927

Dear Rolf Gardiner,

. . . If I were talking to the young, I should say only one thing to them: Don't you live just to make money, either for yourself or for anybody else. Don't look on yourself as a wage slave. Try to find out what life itself is, and live. Repudiate the money idea.

And then I'd teach 'em, if I could, to dance and sing together. The togetherness is important.

But they must first overthrow in themselves the money-fear and money-lust. . . .

MAKING MEANINGS

First Thoughts

1. What did you think of the mother's treatment of her son? of her outlook on life generally?

Shaping Interpretations

2. How do you explain the ever louder voices in the house? In your opinion, why do only Paul and his sisters hear and react to the voices?

3. How would you describe what has happened to Paul by the end of the story?

4. What might the rocking horse **symbolize**?

5. How would you state the **theme** of the story?

6. How would you describe the **tone** of the story?

Reviewing the Text

a. The opening, written in the style of a fairy tale, tells of a woman who "had no luck." How had she been unlucky? What else does the writer tell directly about the mother's **character**?

b. How does Paul's mother define *luck* when Paul asks her what it means? What is Paul's confusion about the word *luck*?

c. What step does Paul take to ease his mother's anxiety over the family's debts? How does she react when she learns of her birthday surprise?

d. Who is Bassett? Why does he keep Paul's secret?

e. Does Paul solve his mother's problem? Why or why not?

Connecting with the Text

7. Review your Reader's Log notes about your associations with money. How does this story affect your feelings about money?

Challenging the Text

8. In what ways is the story's ending a distortion of the usual fairy-tale ending? What do you think of Lawrence's decision to end it as he did?

D. H. LAWRENCE 1009

---

4. Possibilities include: The devotion to materialism, greed, Paul's desire for his mother's affection, temptation.

5. The theme has to do with the conflict between materialism and our instinctual need for love and with the dark powers of the soul. Materialism can create an inability to love.

6. Possible responses: The tone is ominous or perhaps mystical or satirical. Materialism and greed may be the targets of Lawrence's satire, but he may also be making a satirical comment about the family in modern society.

Connecting with the Text

7. Responses will vary. Some students may say that money now seems less important than before they read the story. Others may say that their feelings about money have not changed.

Challenging the Text

8. **(Evaluation)** The typical fairy tale ends "They lived happily ever after." But here Paul dies, and the uncle comments that "he's best gone out of a life where he rides his rocking horse to find a winner." Most students would probably prefer a happy ending, but will also see that this ending makes Lawrence's point. The mother will have a lot of money, but as the reader has already seen, it is unlikely to be enough. It might be more satisfying to know if the mother learned anything from her son's death, but as Lawrence leaves this in the air, the reader must come to his or her own conclusions.

---

d. Bassett is the gardener and Paul's gambling partner. Bassett keeps the secret for several possible reasons. Bassett respects the boy as a "young sport." They are making money by gambling, which might be frowned upon, yet Bassett wants the money. As the gardener, Bassett must obey Paul, who does not want his mother to know about his gambling.

e. Paul fails to solve his mother's problem because her problem is not that she does not have enough money or enough luck. Her problem is within herself.

Shaping Interpretations

2. The voices represent the materialism of the parents; as their materialism and greed increase, the voices increase in volume and frequency. The parents are so caught up in their materialism that they are as oblivious to the voices as they are to their own greed.

3. Possible responses: He becomes completely possessed by the demon of materialism as he attempts to overcome it; or he wills himself into a psychic trance and cannot escape it.

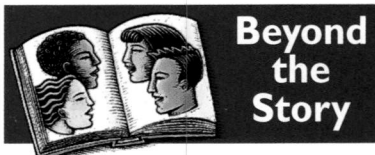

Beyond the Story

Choices: Building Your Portfolio

1. **Writer's Notebook** Remind students to save their work. They may use it as prewriting for the Writer's Workshop on p. 1053.
2. **Critical Writing** You can suggest that students first brainstorm a list of events and statements in the story that support this statement. Then, suggest to students that they put their evidence in order by skimming the story. In doing this, they may find additional pieces of evidence to add to their lists.
3. **Critical Writing** Ask students to write down definitions of the three terms Wordsworth uses, and call on volunteers to read theirs to the class. Write the first one read on the chalkboard. If there is general agreement that it is accurate and complete, move on to the next term. If students think the definition is incorrect or can be expanded, ask other students to elaborate. Continue this process with all three terms until you are sure students grasp their meanings.
4. **Creative Writing** After students have written the new endings for the story, ask a committee of students to select three or four endings they like best. Have the authors read their new endings to the class, and come to a consensus with the whole group about which ending is most satisfying.

CHOICES: Building Your Portfolio

Writer's Notebook
1. Collecting Ideas for an Informative Report

In linking Paul's illness to his emotional state, Lawrence draws on his knowledge of a subject that has lured writers and thinkers for centuries: the mind-body connection. Brainstorm to develop a set of questions you could use to investigate the current status of research on the role of the emotions in health and illness. Save your work for the Writer's Workshop on page 1053.

Critical Writing
2. Keeping Up with the Joneses

The mother's extravagance results partly from social pressure—the need to keep up appearances. Find evidence in the story

to support this statement, and write a brief essay presenting what you find.

Critical Writing
3. Worldly Concerns

In his sonnet "The World Is Too Much with Us" (page 667), William Wordsworth writes, "Getting and spending, we lay waste our powers." In a brief essay, discuss the ways Lawrence's story illustrates this statement. Before you write, be sure you understand what Wordsworth means by "getting," "spending," and "powers."

Creative Writing
4. All's Well That Ends Well

Is it possible to write a happy ending for the story? Try to do so, imitating Lawrence's style as closely as possible. Be prepared to explain which

conclusion—the happy one you have written or the sad one that Lawrence wrote—is more satisfying to the reader, and why.

Creative Writing
5. Inside His Mind

Review the information on stream of consciousness as a narrative form (pages 996–997), and write a sketch in which you reveal the workings of Paul's mind as he rides his rocking horse to that tragic victory. What is he sensing? What associations come to his mind?

Playwriting / Performance
6. Staging the Mysterious

Working with a partner or a small group, outline notes for how you would prepare a portion of Lawrence's story for the stage. How would you set the scene? What kinds of lighting and music would you use? How would you communicate the more intangible or mysterious aspects of the story, like what really happens to Paul as he rides? Then get together with other groups in your class to compare notes. If you feel you have some good ideas, try for a live performance. (Be sure to read the notes on the film version of the story, on page 1015.)

STRATEGIES FOR INCLUSION

Auditory For any of the writing activities above, assist students in the revision stage of the writing process by asking them to read their writing aloud and record the reading on audiotape. Then, have each student replay the tape, stopping it after every sentence. Students should alter each sentence immediately after listening to it.

PORTFOLIO ASSESSMENT

Choices: Assessment Criteria For help in evaluating these Choices assignments, see the criteria in the *Portfolio Management System,* pp. 167–168.

Analyzing How New Words Are Formed

Just as your vocabulary is constantly growing and changing as you learn, the English language is constantly growing and changing to accommodate what is new and different. There are at least four ways in which new words are commonly formed. Established words are joined to form new words called **compounds** and **blends.** Words are shortened to form **shortenings.** And established words are used in new ways and assume new grammatical functions; such conversions are called **functional shifts.**

Compounds. Speakers create **compounds** to describe or name something new with words that already exist. *Briefcase,* for example, is a compound formed to name the piece of luggage designed to encase legal documents, called "briefs."

Blends. Like compounds, **blends** come from two or more established words. However, blends partially omit or slightly alter at least one of the established words in the process. Consequently, blends are sometimes more difficult to recognize and analyze than compounds. Would you have guessed, for example, that the common word *alone* is a blend of "all" and "one"?

Shortenings. Established words are sometimes abbreviated for the sake of convenience. The resulting new words are called **shortenings.** If the length of a frequently used word is cumbersome, you might give the word a "nickword" of sorts, just as you might give someone you know well a nickname. For instance, the more you talk about automobiles, the more inclined you might be to call them *autos.*

Acronyms and back-formations are two specific kinds of shortenings. An **acronym,** the most extreme shortening, is a word formed from the first letter or letters of the words in a name or phrase. *Scuba* is an acronym for s(elf)-c(ontained) u(nderwater) b(reathing) a(pparatus).

A **back-formation** is a shortening that results when a syllable or syllables, usually affixes, are removed from a word. Affixes are usually added on, not taken away—thus the name "back-formation." The word *photo,* for example, is a back-formation from *photograph.*

Functional shifts. Established words can assume new grammatical functions and meanings, resulting in **functional shifts.** For example, the noun *telephone* very quickly gave rise to a new verb, *to telephone,* meaning "to speak to by telephone."

New Word Forms		
Form	Example	Analysis
compound	sweatshop	sweat + shop to depict an unhealthy, uncomfortable workplace
blend	smog	sm(oke) + (f)og to describe fog polluted by smoke
shortening	flu	shortening of influenza by removing syllables
acronym	radar	abbreviation of ra(dio), d(etection), a(nd) r(anging)
back-formation	sulk	removal of y affix from adjective sulky formed noun meaning "a state of sullen aloofness"
functional shift	spoon (n.) »» spoon (v.)	Noun for a utensil shifted to serve as a transitive verb, as in "to spoon soup into a bowl."

Try It Out

Speculate about how each of the following words may have been formed. Then, based on how each one was formed, identify it as one of the following five: compound, blend, shortening, back-formation, or result of a functional shift. Confirm or correct your guesses by finding each word in a dictionary.

1. bosun   3. overwrought   5. taxi
2. curio   4. parry

How to Own a Word

Mini-Lesson: Analyzing How New Words are Formed

Speakers of English can form new words by making functional shifts of nouns to verbs and by inventing compound adjectives. Point out to students that they probably form new words by these two processes without realizing it. The truly remarkable fact is that other speakers of English know what the new words mean. Ask students to compose sentences using the following nouns as verbs:

lamp [The interior decorator lamped our house for us. The evil magician lamped the genie.]

peanut [I peanutted the brittle before I should have. The farmer will peanut that field next week.]

wastebasket [The editor wastebasketed my first draft. The committee wastebasketed every idea from the board of directors.]

Ask students to invent compound adjectives for each of the following.

- A senator who is changing a tire [a tire-changing senator]
- A dog that is dialing a telephone [a telephone-dialing dog]

Try It Out: Possible Answers

1. bosun: a variant of *boatswain,* which is a **compound** word: boat + swain (boy), is a **blend** of *boat* and *swain*
2. curio: a **shortening** of *curiosity*
3. overwrought: a **compound** of *over* and *wrought* (alt. past participle of *work*)
4. parry: a **functional shift** or a shortening of *parade.*
5. taxi: a **shortening** of taxicab.

STRATEGIES FOR INCLUSION

Auditory Some words that make up compounds are also used as phrases, but with very different meanings. For example, a *briefcase* is a piece of luggage used to carry documents (or legal briefs), but a *brief case* is a case that does not last long. You can work with students to help them notice the differences in pronunciation that tell whether the term is a compound or a phrase. Ask students to read the following sentences and note where the accented syllables and pauses are.

- She carried her briefcase to work every day. He had an everyday disease, a brief case of the measles.
- The students were all ready for their exam. The teacher already had it prepared.
- "Good afternoon," said the teacher. They ate lunch after noon yesterday.

PROGRAM MANAGER

Reinforcement To allow students practice and reinforcement of the vocabulary strategy introduced here, see **Transparency** 13.6 in the *Audiovisual Resources Binder.*

A. Exploring the Historical Period

The history of film in the United States began on April 23, 1896, in a New York City music hall. The program for the evening featured a film of dancers, surf breaking on a beach, a comic boxing match, and other vaudeville comedy routines. This was not the first time people had seen moving pictures, though, because penny arcades had for some time exhibited "movies" by pasting still pictures on circular drums. These, when spun, gave the appearance of motion. It is to a Frenchman named George Melies that we owe the concept of motion pictures as an art form. Melies "discovered" magical effects that can be produced with a movie camera by accident when the film he was using got stuck. He unstuck the film and inadvertently created a scene in which a bus appeared to turn into a hearse.

B. Expansion

The fact that television and video rental stores make movies available accounts for much of the time Americans spend watching movies. In fact, attendance at movie theaters during the fifty years from 1935 to 1985 declined from approximately 3.9 billion attendances to approximately one billion attendances, according to U. S. Commerce Department statistics. In 1993 the National Association of Theater Owners estimated attendances at roughly 1.2 billion. At the same time, approximately 2.2 billion books were sold in the United States.

Film As Literature: More Than Meets the Eye

by **William V. Costanzo**

The Anglo-Saxons who assembled in great wooden halls to hear the *Beowulf* bard recite his epic poem of monsters and heroic feats lived in a land of menacing forests and incessant warfare. We can picture the bard singing his tale to the strumming of a harp while his listeners huddled round, delighted to be part of the evening's entertainment, comforted from the mournful wind, enthralled by the exploits of their epic hero, their dragon slayer. More than twelve hundred years later, we live in a different world. The dazzling variety of modern life reflected in the windows of our shopping malls and in the images of music videos would have baffled the Anglo-Saxons or even the Victorians. Yet the basic human need for stories has never been stronger than it is today. We still enjoy listening to stories. Our bookstores teem with works of fiction. But for the past one hundred years, we have been turning with increasing relish to a new form of storytelling: the movies.

Audience wearing 3-D electronic headsets.

Enlarging the House of Fiction

Statistics tell us that Americans now spend more time watching movies—in theaters, on television, and on VCRs—than they do reading books. Does this mean that movies are replacing literature? Or does it mean that movies are enlarging the house of fiction, building new rooms out of earlier literary forms, just as the sonnet grew from a tradition of love songs and the novel grew out of such forms as the novella and the pastoral romance. If films can be understood and appreciated as literature, then some attention to film literacy—our ability to view, interpret, analyze, evaluate, and communicate with movies—can enrich our understanding and appreciation of good films.

Seeing film as literature helps us to trace important continuities in the stream of stories that have flowed from the lips of bards, the pens of novelists, and the cameras of our film directors. For example, a comparative look at heroes and their adversaries—from Beowulf and Macbeth to Frankenstein and Rocky—might reveal common themes about humanity: what it means to be human or to feel alienated from human society. A comparative look at the characters of Shakespeare, the Brontës, and Woody Allen might show a gradual decline in the stature of our heroes and heroines, from nobility to common citizens and antiheroes. By focusing this way on **content,** what literature is about, we can take a measure of our personal values and cultural beliefs.

We can also focus on **craft,** how different types of literature communicate their meanings. In Britain, storytelling began as a spoken art and evolved into a written literary tradition. New tools for shaping messages developed with each new literary form. The *Beowulf* poet was a master of

---

Visual As students read the Spotlight On feature, ask them to construct a Venn diagram that compares literature and film. In the left circle, ask them to write those aspects of literature that are unique to the printed word. In the right circle, ask them to note those aspects of film that are unique to that medium. In the overlapping section of the two circles, ask them to jot down aspects that

literature and film share. You may use Transparency 5: Venn Diagram in the Transparency Package.

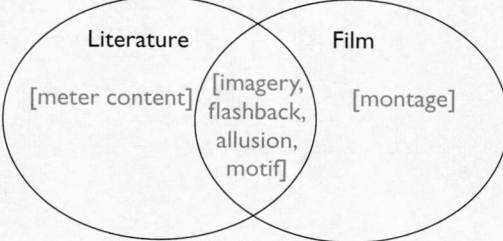

Literature   Film

[meter content]   [imagery, flashback, allusion, motif]   [montage]

English Language Development Some central elements of literature are listed here as **character, setting, plot, mood, symbol, theme,** and **point of view.** Write these terms on the chalkboard or on an overhead transparency. Work with students to brainstorm a definition of each, plus an example of each from a literary work with which they are familiar, in order to demonstrate their comprehension of the terms. Students should write these examples and definitions down in their Reader's Logs for future reference.

rhythm, alliteration, and the other tools of epic poetry. Dickens mastered dialogue, description, and other elements of written fiction to tell his stories in the form of novels. The craft of cinema borrows from these previous forms yet offers something new. Like other narrative artists, filmmakers give us stories with strong characters and settings depicted from particular points of view. But the filmmaker's toolbox includes cameras, actors, microphones, and lights. With such instruments of sight and sound, filmmakers coax their characters and settings to life.

Elements of Fiction, Elements of Film

Character, setting, plot, mood, symbol, theme, point of view: these elements are found in nearly every work of fiction, on the page or screen. Writers shape these elements with words. Filmmakers use actors and technology as well, moving through distinct stages of development.

Typically, a film begins with an idea. The idea for a story may be sketched out in a brief synopsis or in a longer treatment, which may contain some scenes, character development, and dialogue. Later, the complete story may be fleshed out in a screenplay or in a shooting script, a shot-by-shot blueprint for the film. This is the development stage of film production.

The next stage, preproduction, consists of preparations for the shooting. Here the elements of character, setting, and symbol begin to take on physical forms. The actors are cast; the locations are selected; the sets and props are built.

Production, the third stage, is led by the director, whose job is to turn the shooting script into a film. Particular attention is given to mood and point of view. For every shot, the camera must be placed to show the action from a particular vantage point. For example, a close-up might emphasize a revealing gesture or some symbolic detail. Every shot must also be lighted. Bright illumination (high-key lighting) might create a cheerful mood; dim light and contrasting shadows (low-key lighting) might communicate tension and suspense. Meanwhile, a sound crew works the microphones, recording dialogue and sound effects.

Other hands join in during the postproduction stage. The editor assembles each day's film into a continuous sequence, trimming here, inserting

Production shot from Terry Gilliam's film *The Adventures of Baron Munchausen* (1989).

C. Humanities Connection

The director of a movie is often compared to the conductor of an orchestra or the captain of a ship. Just as conductors or captains determine what happens in their realms, directors organize almost all of the aspects of the production of a film. Different directors focus on different aspects of production. Some concentrate on the structure of the script, some on the performance of the actors, some on camera work, and some on the editing process. Directors answer to producers, who hire the cast and crew of the film, and make sure they stay within the budget.

D. Expansion

The following terms are often used in reference to movie making. Each of the processes referred to by these terms produces specific effects on screen and, therefore, affects the film's artistry. *Continuity* refers to making sure people, costumes, and props are the same in a scene, even when the scenes are filmed at different times. A *dissolve* is a gradual merging of one image into another. A *fade,* either "in" or "out," is gradual movement from a black screen to a normally bright one or vice versa. To *pan* is to move the camera angle horizontally, and to *tilt* is to move the angle vertically. To *track* is to move the camera backward, forward, or sideways to follow a moving object, and to use *subjective tracking* is to view a scene through the eyes of a moving character.

Kinesthetic When students work on the section of the feature titled "Elements of Fiction, Elements of Film," ask them to make two sets of index cards. The first set should contain the elements of fiction mentioned in the first sentence. They might find it useful to consult the Handbook of Literary Terms for definitions for each of these terms and write the definitions on their cards.

The second set of index cards should contain the stages in the production of a film. Students can then practice matching the first set of cards with the second set to see the relationship between the elements of fiction and of film.

Intrapersonal Suggest to students that as they read this selection they should think of some of their favorite films and of any films they have seen that were adapted from books. Have them keep a list in their Reader's Logs so that in a discussion they might draw examples from their lists. They might also jot down the titles of books they have read that they think would make good movies.

A. Expansion

Expanding technology, especially computerization, is creating new possibilities for films. Computers are used to control camera movement, to create special effects, and to produce animation that early filmmakers could not imagine.

B. Cultural Connections

Boris Karloff (1887–1969) was born in South London into a family with minor diplomatic connections. He immigrated to Canada in 1909 and worked as a farmer for a while until he became a touring actor. His first movie role was as an extra in 1919. Karloff acted in a host of second-rate pictures during his long career, but he is best known for his role as the monster in the 1931 version of *Frankenstein*.

there, until a final cut is approved by the director. A sound lab may add music, sound effects, dialogue, and perhaps a voice-over narration. An optical lab may contribute special effects. By the time the film is ready for release, the original idea has gone through many transformations. Creative artists, technicians, and business interests have all shaped the final outcome. Unlike most written works, few movies have a single author.

The Art of Adaptation

Nearly all the heroes of great literature have appeared in movies. From Sir Gawain and Macbeth to Gulliver and Robinson Crusoe, from Jane Eyre and David Copperfield to Stephen Dedalus and Orlando, the leading figures of British fiction and their imagined worlds have been adapted for the screen. Why so many adaptations? Some reasons are economic. A published book offers a ready-made plot and a receptive audience; it takes less work to develop the story or publicity. But the appeal of adaptations lies in something deeper. The stories that have endured as classics speak to us across broad boundaries of time and space. We like to

Poster from James Whale's film version of *Frankenstein* (1931).

A scene from Michael Anderson's film version of *1984*.

have them told again in a familiar medium. But what happens when a book is translated into the language of film?

A good way to explore the differences between film and written fiction is to compare a book to its film version. When you read a book like George Orwell's *1984* or Mary Shelley's *Frankenstein* before or after you see the film version, you notice differences in your experience. Some differences are a matter of content. For example, the 1931 film adaptation of *Frankenstein* eliminates the seagoing narrator and simplifies the plot as a struggle between the monster and its victims. Other differences lie in the medium itself, the particular methods by which films appeal to our emotions and imagination. Shelley's description provokes our visual imagination but leaves more room for us to picture the monster than do Boris Karloff's makeup and performance. Shelley's nineteenth-century prose is a steady, rational vehicle for ideas that seem to be eclipsed by the frightening faces, places, and special effects on the screen.

Every film adaptation is a performance, an interpretation of the text. Just as an orchestra can translate a sheet of music into the vibrant sounds of a recorded symphony, the creators of a film cooperate to transform the written work into a performance, an experience that will be seen and heard in countless movie theaters. Of course, every reading of a novel or short story is an interpretation, too. When we read, we cast the characters in our imagination. We construct sets and create the sound effects on a kind of mental movie screen. That's

INTEGRATING THE LANGUAGE ARTS

Strategic Reading As students read the material, ask them to make a flowchart to show how the sections of the feature follow one another. They can use the boxes in the flowchart to record the main ideas from each section. When students have finished, let them compare their work with the work of others and make changes and additions to their charts.

Mechanics Students are sometimes confused about how to punctuate the titles of short films and full-length movies. You can suggest to them that the system is the same for these as it is for short stories and books. A short film, like a short story, is punctuated with quotation marks, and a full-length film, like a book, is underlined or italicized. Ask students to create a mnemonic to keep this straight.

Writing: A Survey To give students some concrete evidence about the influence of movies, ask students to construct surveys to determine how many movies the students in your school watch in an average week. This should include movies at theaters, on TV, and on videotape. After the surveys have been administered and tallied, ask students to write newspaper articles on their findings and submit them to the school newspaper or local newspaper. You might want to have a committee select the best article from the class for submission.

why we're often disappointed when we see a film adapted from a book we like. It's also why a movie sometimes limits our experience of reading; if we see the movie first, its images keep getting in the way. Yet a faithful adaptation can be rewarding in its own right.

"The Rocking-Horse Winner": A Case in Point

Consider "The Rocking-Horse Winner" (page 1000). D. H. Lawrence's story opens like a fable. "There was a woman who was beautiful, who started with all the advantages, yet she had no luck." If you were filming the story, how would you capture its fairy-tale quality? How would you communicate the abstract concept that the woman had no luck? The story's narrator goes on to say that "she felt she must cover up some fault in herself. Yet what it was that she must cover up she never knew." Without a narrator, how would your film convey this insight into her character? You might invent a scene to reveal the woman's feelings. You might direct the actor to behave a certain way. Yet how can you know if your audience will interpret her performance as intended? How can you even know that the audience will think she's beautiful?

Already, your efforts to adapt the story have come up against some basic differences between written language and the visual language of film. First, abstract concepts like beauty and luck are easier to specify in words. How do you show luck on the screen without showing someone who is lucky? Second, writers can make precise statements through narration while filmmakers generally depend on the viewer's interpretation of images and sounds. How long would it take for a film to show that a character doesn't know what she feels she must cover up? Such a complex thought might require a whole scene, drawing on the resources of acting, camera work, lighting, and music to capture its complexities. On the other hand, a single shot of the woman's home at Christmas might convey in an instant what a writer couldn't describe in a thousand words.

Beyond these questions of setting, character, and theme is the question of genre. What kind of story is it? A moral fable? A supernatural tale? A psychological study of a dysfunctional family? How do other stories—or films—of this kind create the

right mood for their genre? How, for example, would you shoot the frenzied rocking-horse scenes? How would you handle the voices in the house that whisper "There *must* be more money"?

"The Rocking-Horse Winner" was adapted in 1949 by Anthony Pelissier, a British film director. Pelissier expands Lawrence's story to a ninety-minute film. He develops some characters, like the father and the nurse, and invents other characters, including a repugnant pawnbroker and an insolent bailiff. Uncle Oscar becomes a middle-aged gentleman, reproachful to his sister but kindly to her son. Pelissier also adds some scenes. Paul first meets Bassett in the gardener's shed. This provides an opportunity to reveal some background information through dialogue. Paul gets the rocking horse on Christmas Day, an occasion for displaying the

A scene from Anthony Pelissier's film version of *The Rocking Horse Winner* (1949).

material values of the household. A scene in which Paul's mother puts her children to sleep is set against a scene between the children and the nurse, both scenes working together to reveal the mother's haughtiness and the limits of her maternal love. If you have an opportunity to view the film, compare it to the story as you saw it in your mind. Notice what is missing, what is added, what is different. Pay particular attention to the movie's ending, which continues beyond Uncle Oscar's final words. How might the changes be explained? How faithful is the movie to the letter and the spirit of Lawrence's story? Is the film a valid work of literature in its own terms?

SPOTLIGHT ON 1015

C. Expansion
Some students may have seen some of these movies that have been made from books: *Little Women, The Age of Innocence, Jurassic Park, Wuthering Heights, Clueless* (based loosely on Jane Austen's *Emma*), *Tess* (based on Thomas Hardy's *Tess of the D'Urbervilles*), *The Jungle Book,* and *Out of Africa,* among others.

COOPERATIVE LEARNING

Panel Discussion Have students use the guidelines on p. 1016 to write a film review. Have them decide which films they will review and assign groups of two to four to see the same film. You may wish to steer them away from certain kinds of movies or encourage certain films. When they have written their reviews, have them organize a panel discussion in which they compare their assessments of various aspects of the movie. Encourage them to discuss specifics of style and to avoid plot summaries. They should not give the plot away, because they can end the discussion with a recommendation to their classmates. They can give the movie a rating or simply recommend that students see or skip the movie. 👉

Evaluating Film as Literature

To answer the last question, consider your evaluative criteria. What do you look for in a film? Do you like action, drama, or romance? Your preference for a particular genre, like mysteries or science fiction, might be a good place to begin a self-study, but try to probe deeper. Why are some romantic movies more appealing than others? What makes an action film successful? In other words, focus on the craft of film as well as on the content. Most of us like a good story well told. We respond to characters that draw us into their lives. We enjoy the intensity of a strong scene or the working out of a provocative idea. This absorption in the elements of fiction makes us responsive viewers, sensitive to artistic merit. But we can also look beyond the immediate screen experience to the many hands that shaped the film, to the technical and artistic choices made by scriptwriters, actors, editors, and camera operators. In this way, we also become critical viewers, able to understand the reasons for our response.

This does not mean that moviegoing ought to be an exercise in cataloging camera angles. We need to ask what makes a scene significant for us. We need to explore our own sense of the film, our emotional and intellectual engagement, and we need to take into account other films and other viewers.

Finally, we should consider the experience of watching films as members of an audience. The sense of community that we feel in a theater is quite different from the experience of reading alone. In this respect, our multiplex cinema has much in common with the Anglo-Saxon hall. The next time that you watch those flickering images on the movie screen, think back to the origins of British literature. Remember the Anglo-Saxons

gathering together, focusing their collective imagination on a flickering fire while the voices and visions of *Beowulf* emanated from their bard. Today, as then, the stories that come to us through literature connect us to others and to our humanity. Whether we hear them, read them, or watch them on a movie screen, these stories belong to a great tradition that reminds us where we're from, who we are, and what we might become.

GUIDELINES FOR EVALUATING FILMS

General Responses

1. How does the film make you feel? What does it make you think about?
2. Which scenes engage you most or least? Why?
3. What keeps you interested throughout the film?
4. What other films or literary works does the film remind you of?
5. How does the director use the elements of fiction: plot, character development, setting, theme, mood, symbol, point of view, and suspense?

Elements of Film

1. **Acting.** Are the performances believable? Are they overstated? understated?
2. **Camera work.** How does the camera frame events? When does it move, shift angles, or otherwise change our focus of attention?
3. **Lighting and set design.** Consider the location chosen for each scene. Is the set realistic and believable? How was the place made to look as if it belonged to a certain era? How does the lighting or use of color contribute to the atmosphere?
4. **Sound.** What kind of music sets the mood? Are any sound effects especially significant? Does the film use the voice of an unseen narrator to tell part of the story?
5. **Editing.** How are separate shots combined into a continuous sequence? How often does the camera cut, fade, or dissolve to a new view of events?

Hugh Grant and Emma Thompson in Ang Lee's film version of *Sense and Sensibility* (1995).

OPTIONS FOR TEACHING

Check Test: True-False

1. Americans spend less time watching movies than they do reading books. [False]
2. The same basic elements are found in both literature and films. [True]
3. Sometimes film adaptations of literary works change the plots of the literary works. [True]

ASSESSMENT TOOLS

4. Critical viewers are able to understand the reasons for their responses to a film. [True]
5. The stories of films are in no way connected to the ancient literary tradition stretching back to the Anglo-Saxons. [False]

Elizabeth Bowen
(1899–1973)

Elizabeth Bowen was born in Dublin, Ireland, and spent her early years in Ireland's County Cork, on her family's splendid country estate, Bowen's Court. As Bowen later wrote, her family strove "to live as though living gave them no trouble." An only child, Bowen was looked after by a governess, taken to the Anglican church on Sundays, and taught to dance, wear gloves, and pay attention to manners. On her mother's orders, she was not taught to read until she was seven. When Bowen's father, a lawyer, was confined to a mental hospital, Elizabeth was not allowed to dwell on it. By her twelfth year, her father had recovered, but her mother had contracted fatal cancer. ("Good news," her mother is reported to have remarked, with her characteristic optimism. "Now I'm going to see what Heaven's like.") Elizabeth was not allowed to attend her mother's funeral or to mourn her.

Bowen's fiction clearly bears the stamp of her early years. Much of her writing is concerned with the processes of growing up, of losing innocence, of coming to terms with reality. Her main characters are often wealthy, sensitive, and well-mannered women; yet her novels also reveal a sense of insecurity, a feeling that life cannot be trusted, that existence is a struggle. Dislocation is a major theme, as is the brittleness of romance.

At seventeen, after attending a boarding school in England, Bowen moved to London to write stories. There she attended readings at the Poetry Bookshop, where she made the first of the literary friendships that were to become the fabric of her life. Among these literary friends were Rose Macaulay, Edith Sitwell, Ezra Pound, and Aldous Huxley.

In 1923, Bowen published her first collection of stories, *Encounters,* to little notice. She also married Alan Cameron, a teacher. For most of the next ten years, the couple lived in the university town of Oxford, where Alan taught and his wife wrote industriously. Her first novel, *The Hotel,* was published in 1927. Thereafter, she produced story collections regularly and wrote nearly a novel a year.

In 1935, the couple moved back to London, where Bowen won acclaim for her novel *The Death of the Heart* (1938) and became a notable hostess of the literary world. During World War II, with its nightly air raids on London, Bowen was a dedicated air-raid warden, but she also went right on giving parties.

Once, while entertaining guests on her balcony, she took no notice of the magnesium flares, but when she had gathered everyone inside, she said, in a typical understatement, "I feel I should apologize for the noise." During the same period, she was writing the stories published in 1945 in *The Demon Lover,* a collection she called a "diary" of her reactions to the war. She described the stories as "flying particles of something enormous and inchoate." *The Heat of the Day* (1949), perhaps Bowen's finest novel, is a classic love story also set in wartime London.

After the war, Bowen and her husband returned to Bowen's Court but had barely begun this new, serene era when Alan died of a heart attack. Predictably, Bowen became more active than ever. She traveled to Europe, visited her American publishers in New York, and lectured at Princeton, Vassar, Bryn Mawr, and the University of Wisconsin. All the while, she wrote steadily.

Although Bowen had been irrepressibly healthy all her life, a persistent cough proved to be a symptom of lung cancer. She died in 1973 and is buried in an Irish churchyard.

Elizabeth Bowen.
Photograph by Robin Adler.

ABOUT THE AUTHOR

Although Bowen did not live in Ireland for much of her literary career, she maintained her connection with the country and kept her ancestral home in County Cork. She wrote about her early life in Ireland in her autobiography *Seven Winters,* which she published in 1942, and she wrote the history of her family, entitled *Bowen's Court,* which was also published in 1942. Ireland does not figure in many of her novels, but one exception is *The Last September,* which deals with the Irish Civil War in the 1920s.

PORTFOLIO ASSESSMENT

Portfolio Assessment
For help with self-assessment of reading skills, see the *Portfolio Management System,* p. 43.

PROGRAM MANAGER

- **Planning Instruction** See Teaching Notes, *Teaching Resources B,* pp. 133–134, for objectives, a summary, literary elements, and additional biographical information for this selection.
- **Instructional Support** Before beginning the instructional lesson, see

Graphic Organizer for Active Reading, *Teaching Resources B,* p. 148, for an Into the Story activity.
- **Assessment** See Selection Test, *Test Booklet,* pp. 217–218.
- **Language Link** For instruction and practice in varying sentence beginnings,

see Language Link, *Teaching Resources B,* pp. 149–150 and *Language and Writing Skills Worksheets,* p. 105.
- **Reinforcement** Use the Words to Own worksheet in *Teaching Resources B,* p. 151.

Into the Story

Author Biography p. 1017
Before You Read p. 1018

Through the Story

"The Demon Lover" pp. 1019–1023
Words to Own pp. 1019–1023
Making Meanings pp. 1023–1024

Beyond the Story

Choices: Building Your Portfolio
pp. 1024–1025

- **Writer's Notebook:** List topics about wartime London
- **Critical Writing:** Write an essay comparing the story to a ballad
- **Creative Writing:** Write a description of the demon lover
- **Film:** Write a proposal for converting the story to a film
- **Music:** Select or compose music for a film version of the story

Into the Story

Using BEFORE YOU READ
p. 1018

Reading Focus

You might want to tell students before they begin reading that the historical details in the story are real, but that everything else is fair game for classification as fantasy. They might find it useful to fill out a chart like the following one as they read.

Details	
Real	Unreal

BEFORE YOU READ
THE DEMON LOVER

Reading Focus

Did I Scare You?
Ghost stories can be mesmerizing—even when they're scaring us to death. And part of why we're so drawn to them is that they make us think about which events are real and which are happening only in our imaginations, or in the imagination of a character. See how well you can figure out what's real and what's not in this story. Is it a ghost story at all?

Quickwrite

Freewrite for a few minutes, telling what you predict this story will be about. Focus your predictions on the title.

Elements of Literature

Flashback
A **flashback** is a scene in a narrative or dramatic work that interrupts the present action to tell what happened at an earlier time. "The Demon Lover" uses a **flashback** to provide important background information about the main character, Mrs. Drover. To recognize where the flashback begins, look for the sudden appearance of a verb in the past perfect tense (that is, preceded by the verb *had*).

Background

"The Demon Lover" has been compared to the movies of the director Alfred Hitchcock, a master of style, mood, and suspense. An amusing Hitchcock trademark is that he appears as a walk-on character somewhere in each of his films. Generations of moviegoers have delighted in trying to discover Hitchcock's fleeting but very recognizable presence. In a similarly unobtrusive way, Bowen is present in her work for those who recognize her. As you read "The Demon Lover," watch for a few descriptive words or emotional remarks that suddenly remind you of something you read in her biography.

"The Demon Lover" takes place in London in the early 1940s during World War II when frequent German air raids over the city drove many Londoners to find temporary lodgings in the country. In the story, Mrs. Drover visits her "shut-up house," which is being looked after by a caretaker.

Cat on a Pile of Blankets
(1985) by Edward Bawden.
The Fine Art Society, London.

The Demon Lover

Elizabeth Bowen

Toward the end of her day in London Mrs. Drover went round to her shut-up house to look for several things she wanted to take away. Some belonged to herself, some to her family, who were by now used to their country life. It was late August; it had been a steamy, showery day: At the moment the trees down the pavement glittered in an escape of humid yellow afternoon sun. Against the next batch of clouds, already piling up ink-dark, broken chimneys and parapets[1] stood out. In her once familiar street, as in any unused channel, an unfamiliar queerness had silted up; a cat wove itself in and out of railings, but no human eye watched Mrs. Drover's return. Shifting some parcels under her arm, she slowly forced round her latchkey in an unwilling lock, then gave the door, which had warped, a push with her knee. Dead air came out to meet her as she went in.

The staircase window having been boarded up, no light came down into the hall. But one door, she could just see, stood ajar, so she went quickly through into the room and unshuttered the big window in there. Now the <u>prosaic</u> woman, looking about her, was more perplexed than she knew by everything that she saw, by traces of her long former habit of life—the yellow smoke stain up the white marble mantelpiece, the ring left by a vase on the top of the escritoire;[2] the bruise in the wallpaper where, on the door being thrown open widely, the china handle had always hit the wall. The piano, having gone away to be stored, had left what looked like claw marks on its part of the parquet.[3] Though not much dust had seeped in, each object wore a film of another kind; and, the only ventilation being the chimney, the whole drawing room smelled of the cold hearth. Mrs. Drover put down her parcels on the escritoire and left the room to proceed upstairs; the things she wanted were in a bedroom chest.

---

1. **parapets** (par′ə·pets′): low walls around rooftops.
2. **escritoire** (es′kri·twär′): writing table.
3. **parquet** (pär·kā′): wood floor made of boards arranged in geometric patterns.

She had been anxious to see how the house was—the part-time caretaker she shared with some neighbors was away this week on his holiday, known to be not yet back. At the best of times he did not look in often, and she was never sure that she trusted him. There were some cracks in the structure, left by the last bombing, on which she was anxious to keep an eye. Not that one could do anything—

A shaft of <u>refracted</u> daylight now lay across the hall. She stopped dead and stared at the hall table—on this lay a letter addressed to her.

She thought first—then the caretaker *must* be back. All the same, who, seeing the house shuttered, would have dropped a letter in at the box? It was not a circular, it was not a bill. And the post office redirected, to the address in the country, everything for her that came through the post. The caretaker (even if he *were* back) did not know she was due in London today—her call here had been planned to be a surprise—so his negligence in the manner of this letter, leaving it to wait in the dusk and the dust, annoyed her. Annoyed, she picked up the letter, which bore no stamp. But it cannot be important, or they would know . . . She took the letter rapidly upstairs with her, without a stop to look at the writing till she reached what had been her bedroom, where she let in light. The room looked over the garden and other gardens: The sun had gone in; as the clouds sharpened and lowered, the trees and rank lawns seemed already to smoke with dark. Her reluctance to look again at the letter came from the fact that she felt intruded upon—and by someone contemptuous of her ways. However, in the tenseness preceding the fall of rain she read it: It was a few lines.

Dear Kathleen: You will not have forgotten that today is our anniversary, and the day we said. The years have gone by at once slowly and fast. In view of the fact that nothing has changed, I shall rely upon you to keep your promise. I was sorry to see you leave London, but was satisfied

---

WORDS TO OWN
prosaic (prō·zā′ik) *adj.*: ordinary; dull.
refracted (ri·frakt′id) *v.* used as *adj.*: bent by its passage from one medium to another.

ELIZABETH BOWEN **1019**

Through the Story

A. Literary Element: Atmosphere

? How would you describe the atmosphere? [Eerie, deserted, menacing; it is growing dark, so there is a sense of impending gloom and foreboding.]

B. Literary Element: Setting

? How does the expression "dead air" help to define the setting? [One possibility is that it suggests the house is like a tomb. Another possibility is that it emphasizes the stillness of the house, where not even the air moves.]

C. Reader's Response: First Thoughts

? What effect does the expression "she stopped dead" have? [Sample responses: It indicates her surprise; it repeats the word "dead," adding to the ominous atmosphere of the story.]

D. Critical Reading: Making Inferences

? What does the lack of a stamp on the letter suggest about how it was delivered? [Possible answers: It was delivered by some means other than the post office. It was left there by the caretaker.]

E. Literary Element: Tone

? How would you describe the tone of this letter? [Determined, knowing, haunting, cold, forceful, unfeeling.]

A. Critical Reading: Drawing Conclusions

? What does the change in Mrs. Drover's coloring suggest about the writing in the letter? [She recognizes the handwriting and is shocked or frightened by it.]

B. Reader's Response: Shaping Interpretations

? Why has Mrs. Drover suddenly become nervous and upset? [Sample responses: She remembers an unpleasant experience from her past that she will have to deal with today. The tone and the appearance of the letter has made her afraid, especially since the house and neighborhood are empty.]

C. Literary Element: Flashback

? What are the signals that this section begins a flashback? [The girl is young, and the reader can assume that the girl is Mrs. Drover. The ellipsis and the space between paragraphs indicate that Mrs. Drover is remembering and that this is a break from the main action.]

D. Critical Reading: Speculating

? Why does Kathleen feel free when the soldier is gone? Why has she made the unnatural promise and why is it a sinister betrothal? [Possible answers: She is free of his threatening presence and the intimidation with which he extracted the promise. She has made the unnatural promise because she is afraid of him. Perhaps she made it because she cannot refuse a man about to go off to the front. Pledging to marry him out of fear and an inability to say no, perhaps she secretly hopes he will die there so she will not have to fulfill her promise. There is nothing that is not sinister about this promise of marriage.]

that you would be back in time. You may expect me, therefore, at the hour arranged. Until then . . .   K.

Mrs. Drover looked for the date: It was today's. She dropped the letter onto the bedsprings, then picked it up to see the writing again—her lips, beneath the remains of lipstick, beginning to go white. She felt so much the change in her own face that she went to the mirror, polished a clear patch in it, and looked at once urgently and stealthily in. She was confronted by a woman of forty-four, with eyes starting out under a hat brim that had been rather carelessly pulled down. She had not put on any more powder since she left the shop where she ate her solitary tea.[4] The pearls her husband had given her on their marriage hung loose round her now rather thinner throat, slipping in the V of the pink wool jumper her sister knitted last autumn as they sat round the fire. Mrs. Drover's most normal expression was one of controlled worry, but of <u>assent</u>. Since the birth of the third of her little boys, attended by a quite serious illness, she had had an <u>intermittent</u> muscular flicker to the left of her mouth, but in spite of this she could always sustain a manner that was at once energetic and calm.

Turning from her own face as <u>precipitately</u> as she had gone to meet it, she went to the chest where the things were, unlocked it, threw up the lid, and knelt to search. But as rain began to come crashing down she could not keep from looking over her shoulder at the stripped bed on which the letter lay. Behind the blanket of rain the clock of the church that still stood struck six—with rapidly heightening apprehension she counted each of the slow strokes. "The hour arranged . . . My God," she said, "*what* hour? How should I . . . ? After twenty-five years . . . "

The young girl talking to the soldier in the garden had not ever completely seen his face. It was dark; they were saying goodbye under a tree. Now and then—for it felt, from not seeing him at this intense moment, as though she had never seen him at all—she verified his presence for these few moments longer by putting out a hand, which he each time pressed, without very much kindness, and painfully, on to one of the breast buttons of

4. **tea:** in Britain, a light, late-afternoon meal, served with tea.

his uniform. That cut of the button on the palm of her hand was, principally, what she was to carry away. This was so near the end of a leave from France that she could only wish him already gone. It was August 1916. Being not kissed, being drawn away from and looked at intimidated Kathleen till she imagined spectral glitters in the place of his eyes. Turning away and looking back up the lawn she saw, through branches of trees, the drawing-room window alight: She caught a breath for the moment when she could go running back there into the safe arms of her mother and sister, and cry: "What shall I do, what shall I do? He has gone."

Hearing her catch her breath, her fiancé said, without feeling: "Cold?"

"You're going away such a long way."

"Not so far as you think."

"I don't understand?"

"You don't have to," he said. "You will. You know what we said."

"But that was—suppose you—I mean, suppose."

"I shall be with you," he said, "sooner or later. You won't forget that. You need do nothing but wait."

Only a little more than a minute later she was free to run up the silent lawn. Looking in through the window at her mother and sister, who did not for the moment perceive her, she already felt that unnatural promise drive down between her and the rest of all humankind. No other way of having given herself could have made her feel so apart, lost and forsworn.[5] She could not have plighted a more sinister troth.[6]

Kathleen behaved well when, some months later, her fiancé was reported missing, presumed killed. Her family not only supported her but were able to praise her courage without <u>stint</u> because

5. **forsworn** (fôr·swôrn′): having lied under oath; perjured.
6. **plighted . . . troth:** made a more sinister promise of marriage.

WORDS TO OWN
assent (ə·sent′) *n.*: acceptance.
intermittent (in′tər·mit′′nt) *adj.*: starting and stopping at intervals; periodic.
precipitately (pri·sip′ə·tit′lē) *adv.*: suddenly.
stint *n.*: limitation.

OPTIONS FOR TEACHING

INTEGRATING THE LANGUAGE ARTS

Strategic Reading After reading the story, each student should write down the sentence that he or she considers to be the most important. Then, have students form groups of three or four to select the most important sentence from those that the group members present. When the groups have finished, ask a reporter from each group to present the group's most important sentence and the reasons the group selected it.

Writing: A News Article After students have read the story, ask them each to write an article for a newspaper about the incident described in the story. Each article should include a headline that summarizes the story, and it could also include a drawing, with an appropriate caption, that presents some aspect of the story. You can let students publish their articles by displaying them in the classroom.

they could not regret, as a husband for her, the man they knew almost nothing about. They hoped she would, in a year or two, console herself—and had it been only a question of consolation things might have gone much straighter ahead. But her trouble, behind just a little grief, was a complete dislocation from everything. She did not reject other lovers, for these failed to appear: For years she failed to attract men—and with the approach of her thirties she became natural enough to share her family's anxiousness on this score. She began to put herself out,[7] to wonder; and at thirty-two she was very greatly relieved to find herself being courted by William Drover. She married him, and the two of them settled down in this quiet, arboreal[8] part of Kensington: In this house the years piled up, her children were born, and they all lived till they were driven out by the bombs of the next war. Her movements as Mrs. Drover were circumscribed, and she dismissed any idea that they were still watched.

As things were—dead or living the letter writer sent her only a threat. Unable, for some minutes, to go on kneeling with her back exposed to the empty room, Mrs. Drover rose from the chest to sit on an upright chair whose back was firmly against the wall. The desuetude[9] of her former bedroom, her married London home's whole air of being a cracked cup from which memory, with its reassuring power, had either evaporated or leaked away, made a crisis—and at just this crisis the letter writer had, knowledgeably, struck. The hollowness of the house this evening canceled years on years of voices, habits, and steps. Through the shut windows she only heard rain fall on the roofs around. To rally herself, she said she was in a mood—and for two or three seconds shutting her eyes, told herself that she had imagined the letter. But she opened them—there it lay on the bed.

On the supernatural side of the letter's entrance she was not permitting her mind to dwell. Who, in London, knew she meant to call at the house today? Evidently, however, this had been known. The caretaker, *had* he come back, had had no cause to expect her: He would have taken

7. **put herself out:** vex or distress herself.
8. **arboreal** (är·bôr′ē·əl): full of trees.
9. **desuetude** (des′wi·t o͞od′): disuse.

the letter in his pocket, to forward it, at his own time, through the post. There was no other sign that the caretaker had been in—but, if not? Letters dropped in at doors of deserted houses do not fly or walk to tables in halls. They do not sit on the dust of empty tables with the air of certainty that they will be found. There is needed some human hand—but nobody but the caretaker had a key. Under circumstances she did not care to consider, a house can be entered without a key. It was possible that she was not alone now. She might be being waited for, downstairs. Waited for—until when? Until "the hour arranged." At least that was not six o'clock: Six has struck.

She rose from the chair and went over and locked the door.

The thing was, to get out. To fly? No, not that: She had to catch her train. As a woman whose utter dependability was the keystone of her family life she was not willing to return to the country, to her husband, her little boys, and her sister, without the objects she had come up to fetch. Resuming work at the chest she set about making up a number of parcels in a rapid, fumbling-decisive way. These, with her shopping parcels, would be too much to carry; these meant a taxi—at the thought of the taxi her heart went up and her normal breathing resumed. I will ring up the taxi now; the taxi cannot come too soon: I shall hear the taxi out there running its engine, till I walk calmly down to it through the hall. I'll ring up— But no: the telephone is cut off . . . She tugged at a knot she had tied wrong.

The idea of flight . . . He was never kind to me, not really. I don't remember him kind at all. Mother said he never considered me. He was set on me, that was what it was—not love. Not love, not meaning a person well. What did he do, to make me promise like that? I can't remember— But she found that she could.

She remembered with such dreadful acuteness that the twenty-five years since then dissolved like smoke and she instinctively looked for the weal[10] left by the button on the palm of her hand. She

10. **weal** (wēl): lump; welt.

WORDS TO OWN
utter *adj.*: total.

E. Reader's Response: Shaping Interpretations

? Why do you think Kathleen is not able to attract men? [Sample responses: Kathleen is "prosaic," that is, rather dull. She gives off an aura of inapproachability because of her dead fiancé. The dead fiancé is somehow keeping men away. The text mentions her "dislocation from everything," a result of the promise that comes "between her and the rest of all humankind." What she has done is so unnatural that she ceases to relate to others.]

F. Literary Element: Character

? What does this sentence tell us about Mrs. Drover's character? [She puts unpleasant and worrisome things out of her mind. She tries to exert self-control despite her fears.]

G. Reader's Response: Connecting with the Text

? What would you do if you were in Mrs. Drover's position at this point in the story? [Sample responses: Run. Get out of the house immediately. Find a telephone; find someone, anyone, so I wouldn't be alone.]

H. Critical Reading: Finding Cause and Effect

? What does the "suspension of *her* existence" have to do with Mrs. Drover's memory of why she agreed to the promise? [Possible answers: The girl was under the soldier's control rather than her own. Kathleen lost her sense of herself when confronted with the force of the man. She was untrue to herself, to her own desire to not betroth herself to this man; she did not have the strength to refuse.]

PROBLEM SOLVING/ CRITICAL THINKING

Taking Precautions Ask students to consider how Mrs. Drover could solve the problem created by the mysterious letter. What kinds of precautions could she take to make sure she is not abducted when leaving her house? Ask students to work in groups of three to brainstorm ideas to solve the problems of her fear and lack of protection. Make a master list of these potential solutions on the chalkboard, and come to a consensus about the practicality of each solution.

CROSSING THE CURRICULUM

History Mrs. Drover's fiancé went to France in August of 1916 to fight in World War I. Ask students to look up information about the fighting in France in that year and to give a brief oral report about what they learn to the class. ☞

A. Literary Element: Symbol

? What does the taxi represent to Mrs. Drover? [One possibility is that it represents a means of escape. Another possibility is that it represents a link to the natural world.]

B. Reader's Response: Shaping Interpretations

? Who might be leaving the house? [Sample responses: The caretaker who has been there all along. It's the ghost of Mrs. Drover's dead fiancé, who has been there spying on her.]

Rainy Weather (late 19th or early 20th century) by Vilhelm Hammershoi.

remembered not only all that he said and did but the complete suspension of *her* existence during that August week. I was not myself—they all told me so at the time. She remembered—but with one white burning blank as where acid has dropped on a photograph: *Under no conditions* could she remember his face.

So, wherever he may be waiting, I shall not know him. You have no time to run from a face you do not expect.

A The thing was to get to the taxi before any clock struck what could be the hour. She would slip down the street and round the side of the square to where the square gave on the main road. She would return in the taxi, safe, to her own door, and bring the solid driver into the house with her to pick up the parcels from room to room. The idea of the taxi driver made her decisive, bold: She unlocked her door, went to the top of the staircase, and listened down.

She heard nothing—but while she was hearing nothing the *passé*[11] air of the staircase was **B** disturbed by a draft that traveled up to her face. It emanated from the basement: Down there a door or window was being opened by someone who chose this moment to leave the house.

The rain had stopped; the pavements steamily shone as Mrs. Drover let herself out by inches

11. **passé** (pä·sā′): no longer fresh; rather old.

WORDS TO OWN
emanated (em′ə·nāt′id) v.: flowed; came forth.

1022 THE TWENTIETH CENTURY

---

from her own front door into the empty street. The unoccupied houses opposite continued to meet her look with their damaged stare. Making toward the thoroughfare and the taxi, she tried not to keep looking behind. Indeed, the silence was so intense—one of those creeks of London silence exaggerated this summer by the damage of war—that no tread could have gained on hers unheard. Where her street debouched[12] on the square where people went on living, she grew conscious of, and checked, her unnatural pace. Across the open end of the square two buses impassively passed each other: Women, a perambulator,[13] cyclists, a man wheeling a barrow signalized, once again, the ordinary flow of life. At the square's most populous corner should be—and was—the short taxi rank. This evening, only one taxi—but this, although it presented its blank rump, appeared already to be alertly waiting for her. Indeed, without looking round the driver started his engine as she panted up from behind and put her hand on the door. As she did so, the clock struck seven. The taxi faced the main road: To make the trip back to her house it would have to turn—she had settled back on the seat and the taxi *had* turned before she, surprised by its knowing movement, recollected that she had not "said where." She leaned forward to scratch at the glass panel that divided the driver's head from her own.

The driver braked to what was almost a stop, turned round, and slid the glass panel back: The jolt of this flung Mrs. Drover forward till her face was almost into the glass. Through the aperture driver and passenger, not six inches between them, remained for an eternity eye to eye. Mrs. Drover's mouth hung open for some seconds before she could issue her first scream. After that she continued to scream freely and to beat with her gloved hands on the glass all round as the taxi, accelerating without mercy, made off with her into the hinterland of deserted streets.

---

12. **debouched** (dē·bōōshd′): came out; emerged.
13. **perambulator** (pər·am′byōō·lāt′ər): chiefly British for "baby carriage." The word is often shortened to *pram*.

- -

WORDS TO OWN
impassively (im·pas′iv·lē) *adv.*: calmly; indifferently.
aperture (ap′ər·chər) *n.*: opening.

- -

MAKING MEANINGS

First Thoughts

1. Did you feel emotionally involved in Mrs. Drover's story? Why or why not?

Shaping Interpretations

2. In some stories, descriptions of the **setting** provide much more than the physical background—they also create a particular **mood.** List the **images** in the story's first paragraph that help create a strong mood of foreboding.

3. Why has the Drover family been dislocated from their home? Cite two places in the text that make the reason clear. For what purpose has Mrs. Drover returned?

4. What details in the lovers' last meeting **foreshadow** a sinister, threatening reunion? What does Mrs. Drover tell us about her fiancé that explains why she is terrified of him?

5. The use of an **omniscient narrator** allows Bowen to give readers information about Mrs. Drover's psychological makeup that Mrs. Drover herself is not consciously aware of. Identify several such passages in the text.

6. **Dramatic irony** occurs when the audience is aware of something that a character does not know. What is the central dramatic irony of the story?

7. Contributing to the story's richness and depth is the interplay between present and past. Think about the **flashback** that tells what happened earlier in Mrs. Drover's life. Do you think the abrupt shift into the past is effective or merely confusing? Why?

ELIZABETH BOWEN **1023**

Reviewing the Text
Using the following scheme, create a story map for "The Demon Lover."

| Basic situation |
| Conflict |
| Characters |
| Event |
| Event |
| Event, etc. |
| Climax |
| Resolution |

8. One possibility is that the story reveals the psychological dislocations experienced by people during the disruption of wartime.

Challenging the Text

9. **(Evaluation)** Responses will vary. The hallucination theory, which must cover the letter as well as the taxi, is supported by the atmosphere of the house, with its "dead air" and memories, and by the fact that she is completely alone. The ghost story, while it, too, draws on the atmosphere of the house, is supported by the existence of the letter and the final scene.

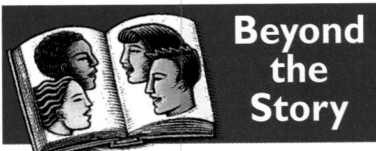

Beyond the Story

Choices: Building Your Portfolio

1. **Writer's Notebook** Remind students to save their work. They may use it as prewriting for the Writer's Workshop on p. 1053.

2. **Critical Writing** Students may have some difficulty deciding how much similarity must exist between the story and the ballad in order for them to say that the story is based on the ballad. You might want to lead a discussion on this point before students begin the assignment.

---

8. World Wars I and II bracket this story like bookends. During each war, Mrs. Drover experiences dislocation and confusion. During each war, the demon lover is part of her life. Yet he doesn't appear during the intervening twenty-five years. Use these strands of the story (war, Mrs. Drover's inner turmoil, and the lover's appearances) in a statement of the story's **theme**.

Challenging the Text

9. One possible interpretation of the story is that Mrs. Drover's experience is a hallucination: Her powers of imagination have combined with the pressures of wartime life to transform everyday reality into a waking nightmare. Another way of looking at the story is to consider it an out-and-out ghost story. Which interpretation do you favor, or do you have another? Support your interpretation with evidence from the text.

CHOICES: Building Your Portfolio

Writer's Notebook

1. Collecting Ideas for an Informative Report

The setting of Bowen's story is critical to the plot: It is wartime London, when German bombing raids were terrifying the populace, destroying neighborhoods and landmarks with an unnerving randomness. Re-read the opening of the story, and review Bowen's biography. Jot down some topics about wartime London that you might be interested in researching. The air raids and their psychological effects might be one topic. Another might be the deportation of children from London (some came to the United States). Save your notes for the Writer's Workshop on page 1053.

Critical Writing

2. The Same Old Song?

"The Demon Lover" is also one title of the following famous ballad. In an essay, compare the ballad to Bowen's story. Before you write, gather the material for your comparison by filling out a chart like the one below. (What prediction did you make about the story based on its unusual title?)

	Bowen Story	Ballad
Characters		
Plot		
Mood		
Theme		

Conclude your essay by indicating whether or not you believe the story is based in any way on the old song.

The Demon Lover

"O where have you been, my long, long love,
　　This long seven years and mair?"
"O I'm come to seek my former vows
　　Ye granted me before."

5 "O hold your tongue of your former vows,
　　For they will breed sad strife;
O hold your tongue of your former vows,
　　For I am become a wife."

He turned him right and round about,
10　　And the tear blinded his ee:
"I wad never hae trodden on Irish ground,
　　If it had not been for thee.

I might have had a king's daughter,
　　Far, far beyond the sea;
15 I might have had a king's daughter,
　　Had it not been for love o thee."

"If ye might have had a king's daughter,
　　Yer sel ye had to blame;
Ye might have taken the king's daughter,
20　　For ye kend that I was nane."

Auditory In activity #2, some students may better understand the ballad "The Demon Lover" if they hear it read aloud as they follow the text. You can ask one or two students to prepare a reading of the poem ahead of time and have them present it in class. You might want to tape-record the reading so that students can play it back later.

Visual Instead of writing, drawing, or painting a likeness of the demon lover for activity #3, some students might prefer to find a picture of a person they think looks like him. Students may use old magazines and newspapers to find pictures and then cut these out to display in class. Ask students to write a brief reason for their choice of pictures, and have the class decide which picture they like best as a representation of the demon lover.

Spatial When students write a film proposal for activity #4, encourage them to make an outline using the traditional outline form. This will enable students to visualize both the requirements of the assignment and how the parts of each task relate to one another.

"If I was to leave my husband dear,
    And my two babes also,
O what have you to take me to,
    If with you I should go?"

25 "I hae seven ships upon the sea—
    The eighth brought me to land—
With four-and-twenty bold mariners,
    And music on every hand."

She has taken up her two little babes,
30   Kissed them baith cheek and chin:
"O fair ye weel, my ain two babes,
    For I'll never see you again."

She set her foot upon the ship,
    No mariners could she behold;
35 But the sails were o the taffetie,
    And the masts o the beaten gold.

She had not sailed a league, a league,
    A league but barely three,
When dismal grew his countenance,
40   And drumlie grew his ee.

They had not sailed a league, a league,
    A league but barely three,
Until she espied his cloven foot,
    And she wept right bitterlie.

45 "O hold your tongue of your weeping," says he,
    "Of your weeping now let me be;
I will shew you how lilies grow
    On the banks of Italy."

"O what hills are yon, yon pleasant hills,
50   That the sun shines sweetly on?"
"O yon are the hills of heaven," he said,
    "Where you will never win."

"O whaten mountain is yon?" she said,
    "All so dreary wi frost and snow?"
55 "O yon is the mountain of hell," he cried,
    "Where you and I will go."

He strack the tap-mast wi his hand,
    The foremast wi his knee,
And he brake that gallant ship in twain,
60   And sank her in the sea.

Creative Writing
3. No Prince Charming

At no time in the story are we given a description of the demon lover's face. At the end of the story, however, when Mrs. Drover is finally within six inches of his face, she begins to scream. Describe what you imagine Mrs. Drover saw. You might also do a drawing or painting of him.

Film
4. The Silver Screen

Suppose that you are the producer-director of a movie version of "The Demon Lover." You have to consider these tasks:

a. Casting both the younger and the older Mrs. Drover, her lover, and the minor characters of the family

b. Creating scenery, lighting, and background music to establish atmosphere

c. Creating suspense by such means as the chiming of the clock

d. Telling your screenwriters how you would expand parts of the story for a feature-length film

Write a proposal outlining your ideas on how you would convert the story into a film. Will you film the story as a horror tale or as a psychological study of love?

Music
5. A Little Nightmare Music

Choose—or compose—the background music that would help establish atmosphere in a movie version of "The Demon Lover."

3. **Creative Writing** You might want to remind students that the fiancé was listed as missing in action, so there is a good chance that he was wounded, possibly in the face. On the other hand, if the man is a ghost, his appearance might be changed in other significant ways. Encourage students to let their imaginations soar as they describe the demon lover.

4. **Film** This assignment has several parts, and you might want to divide it into segments and let small groups work on separate parts. Another way to handle the assignment is to let a group of four be responsible for a proposal, with each member of the group responsible for one of the key points. In either case, students should probably spend some time discussing the general direction the proposal will take before they begin working independently.

5. **Music** There are several distinct segments of the story, and the mood of each segment is at least slightly different from the moods of other segments. You can ask students to choose or compose music for the whole story, or you can break it into segments and assign different segments to different students.

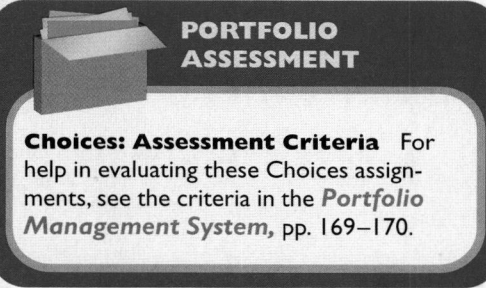

PORTFOLIO ASSESSMENT

Choices: Assessment Criteria For help in evaluating these Choices assignments, see the criteria in the *Portfolio Management System,* pp. 169–170.

ABOUT THE AUTHOR

Cortázar has been compared to the great Argentinian writer Jorge Luis Borges, especially because both writers tend to write about metaphysical themes such as life, death, and the power of the imagination. He was employed as a translator for UNESCO after moving to Paris in 1951, and he wrote a number of novels, several collections of short stories, and a book of poetry that was published posthumously.

Julio Cortázar.

Julio Cortázar

(1914–1984)

Julio Cortázar believed that fantasy and reality, the rational and the irrational, exist on intersecting planes. In part, this philosophy surely stemmed from the fact that Cortázar himself had a foot in two very different worlds—Latin America and Europe. He was born in Brussels to Argentine parents, but his family returned to Argentina when he was five years old. After attending the University of Buenos Aires, he worked first as a high school teacher and then taught French literature at a university. In 1946, he was briefly jailed for his opposition to Perón's military dictatorship of Argentina and was forced to give up his academic career. At about this time, his first short story, "House Taken Over," was published, the first of a long and prolific career. Cortázar worked for a short time as a literary translator in Buenos Aires (fittingly, he translated the stories of Edgar Allan Poe into Spanish) before he moved to Paris to work as a translator for the United Nations. He continued in this post until his death in 1984.

Cortázar's works are always playful and experimental. In 1963, his masterpiece, *Rayuela* (translated into English as *Hopscotch*), was published to great acclaim. Named for a child's game, this dizzying and demanding novel includes instructions for the different ways it can be read. Although Cortázar traveled widely and was granted French citizenship in 1981, he always thought of himself as Argentine.

(Map) ©Rand McNally.

PROGRAM MANAGER

Selection Summary See **Teaching Notes, *Teaching Resources B,* p. 134,** for a summary of and objectives for this selection.

Background

Fantastical occurrences are often the stuff of sleep. Surreal images and irrational happenings flood our dreams, yet during the day, our lives seem ordered, routine, rational. What happens when these two worlds overlap or intersect—when we can't distinguish between them?

In "Axolotl," as in all literature of the fantastic, the impossible and the possible, fantasy and reality, are set in opposition. The author often introduces some surrealistic element or extraordinary event into an otherwise entirely realistic environment, and the two become so intertwined that neither character nor reader can separate them. In Julio Cortázar's fantastical short stories—among the best of the genre—daily life is often mysteriously subverted by unknown forces. This "invasion by the imaginary," as Cortázar called it, creates a tension that both exhilarates and disturbs.

A Dialogue with the Text

As you read the story, keep track of when you yourself are unsure about what is *really* happening.

Background

"Magic realism" is a term that is sometimes applied to the kind of writing that Cortázar produced. This term was coined in 1949 by the Cuban novelist Alejo Carpentier to denote writing that blurs the lines between the real and the fantastic. Carpentier was deeply influenced by French surrealism, which tried to suppress the conscious mind and let the deeper reality of the subconscious come through.

A Dialogue with the Text

Encourage students to stop as they read and note their reactions. When they have finished the story, ask students to go back through their notes and fill in any details that they feel might help them understand the story.

A. Reader's Response: First Thoughts

? What might the narrator be saying about himself in this opening paragraph? [Sample responses: He is a quiet person who does not move much. He identifies with the axolotls.]

B. Expansion

In fact, axolotls do become adults. They just retain gills, which, in most salamanders, only the larvae have.

Axolotl

Julio Cortázar

translated by **Paul Blackburn**

There was a time when I thought a great deal about the axolotls. I went to see them in the aquarium at the Jardin des Plantes[1] and stayed for hours watching them, observing their immobility, their faint movements. Now I am an axolotl.

I got to them by chance one spring morning when Paris was spreading its peacock tail after a wintry Lent. I was heading down the boulevard Port-Royal, then I took Saint-Marcel and L'Hôpital and saw green among all that gray and remembered the lions. I was friend of the lions and panthers, but had never gone into the dark, humid building that was the aquarium. I left my bike

against the gratings and went to look at the tulips. The lions were sad and ugly and my panther was asleep. I decided on the aquarium, looked obliquely at banal fish until, unexpectedly, I hit it off with the axolotls. I stayed watching them for an hour and left, unable to think of anything else.

In the library at Sainte-Geneviève, I consulted a dictionary and learned that axolotls are the larval stage (provided with gills) of a species of salamander of the genus *Ambystoma.* That they were Mexican I knew already by looking at them and their little pink Aztec faces and the placard at the top of the tank. I read that specimens of them had been found in Africa capable of living on dry land during the periods of drought, and continuing their life under water when the rainy season came. I found their Spanish name, *ajolote,* and the mention that they were edible, and that their oil was used (no longer used, it said) like cod-liver oil.

I didn't care to look up any of the specialized works, but the next day I went back to the Jardin des Plantes. I began to go every morning, morning and afternoon some days. The aquarium

1. **Jardin des Plantes** (zhär·da*n*ʹ dä plä*n*t): Paris Botanical Garden, part of the French National Museum of Natural History. The name literally means "garden of plants" in French.

CONNECTING WITH "THE TRANSFORMING IMAGINATION"

The narrator's imagination transforms him into an axolotl. Ask students to discuss the following question: While the actual occurrence is not believable, is there something that is believable in this story? [Possible answer: It is believable that the narrator identifies with this creature that is isolated and incapable of communication, this odd creature that seems to see and understand everything, but does nothing. It is possible that he suffers just as he imagines they do.]

A. Literary Element: Point of View

? In what point of view is this story told? [First person.] From what you know of the first-person point of view, can you trust the narrator's comment that there is nothing strange in his daily visits to the axolotls? [The narrator is unreliable; the statement seems self-conscious; there are other clues that his behavior is indeed strange, i.e., the perplexed smile the guard gives him when he enters the aquarium.]

B. Critical Reading: Making Predictions

? If you refer to the last sentence of the first paragraph and read the parenthetical statement here, what might you predict will happen in this story? [Somehow the narrator will become an axolotl.]

C. Literary Element: Personification

? How does the narrator personify the axolotls? [By attributing to them a "secret will."] Who might really have the secret will to abolish space and time? [The narrator himself. People in contemporary society.]

A guard smiled perplexedly taking my ticket. I would lean up against the iron bar in front of the tanks and set to watching them. There's nothing strange in this, because after the first minute I knew that we were linked, that something infinitely lost and distant kept pulling us together. It had been enough to detain me that first morning in front of the sheet of glass where some bubbles rose through the water. The axolotls huddled on **B** the wretched narrow (only I can know how narrow and wretched) floor of moss and stone in the tank. There were nine specimens, and the majority pressed their heads against the glass, looking with their eyes of gold at whoever came near them. Disconcerted, almost ashamed, I felt it a lewdness to be peering at these silent and immobile figures heaped at the bottom of the tank. Mentally I isolated one, situated on the right and somewhat apart from the others, to study it better. I saw a rosy little body, translucent (I thought of those Chinese figurines of milky glass), looking like a small lizard about six inches long, ending in a fish's tail of extraordinary delicacy, the most sensitive part of our body. Along the back ran a transparent fin which joined with the tail, but what obsessed me was the feet, of the slenderest nicety, ending in tiny fingers with minutely human nails. And then I discovered its eyes, its face. Inexpressive features, with no other trait save the eyes, two orifices, like brooches, wholly of transparent gold, lacking any life but looking, letting themselves be penetrated by my look, which seemed to travel past the golden level and lose itself in a diaphanous² interior mystery. A very slender black halo ringed the eye and etched it onto the pink flesh, onto the rosy stone of the head, vaguely triangular, but with curved and irregular sides which gave it a total likeness to a statuette corroded by time. The mouth was masked by the triangular plane of the face, its considerable size would be guessed only in profile; in front a delicate crevice barely slit the lifeless stone. On both sides of the head where the ears should have been, there grew three tiny sprigs red as coral, a vegetal outgrowth, the gills, I suppose. And they were the only thing quick about it; every ten or fifteen seconds the sprigs pricked up stiffly and

2. **diaphanous:** transparent.

again subsided. Once in a while a foot would barely move, I saw the diminutive toes poise mildly on the moss. It's that we don't enjoy moving a lot, and the tank is so cramped—we barely move in any direction and we're hitting one of the others with our tail or our head—difficulties arise, fights, tiredness. The time feels like it's less if we stay quietly.

C It was their quietness that made me lean toward them fascinated the first time I saw the axolotls. Obscurely I seemed to understand their secret will, to abolish space and time with an indifferent immobility. I knew better later; the gill contraction, the tentative reckoning of the delicate feet on the stones, the abrupt swimming (some of them swim with a simple undulation³ of the body) proved to me that they were capable of escaping that mineral lethargy in which they spent whole hours. Above all else, their eyes obsessed me. In the standing tanks on either side of them, different fishes showed me the simple stupidity of their handsome eyes so similar to our own. The eyes of the axolotls spoke to me of the presence of a different life, of another way of seeing. Glueing my face to the glass (the guard would cough fussily once in a while), I tried to see better those diminutive golden points, that entrance to the infinitely slow and remote world of these rosy creatures. It was useless to tap with one finger on the glass directly in front of their faces; they never gave the least reaction. The golden eyes continued burning with their soft, terrible light; they continued looking at me from an unfathomable depth which made me dizzy.

And nevertheless they were close. I knew it before this, before being an axolotl. I learned it the day I came near them for the first time. The anthropomorphic⁴ features of a monkey reveal the reverse of what most people believe, the distance that is traveled from them to us. The absolute lack of similarity between axolotls and human beings proved to me that my recognition was valid, that I was not propping myself up with easy analogies. Only the little hands . . . But an eft,⁵ the common newt, has such hands also, and

3. **undulation:** wavelike movement.
4. **anthropomorphic:** having human shape or characteristics; humanlike.
5. **eft:** archaic for "newt."

OPTIONS FOR TEACHING

STRATEGIES FOR INCLUSION

Visual Have students draw illustrations or a story map for this story. Encourage them to depict the transformation of the man to the axolotl. Does it happen gradually or suddenly? Perhaps it does not happen at all. Ask them how they will resolve this issue before they draw.

INTEGRATING THE LANGUAGE ARTS

Strategic Reading Have students outline the main ideas in each of the paragraphs of the story before they begin the discussion outlined on p. 1031. The following chart may be useful for this purpose.

Paragraph	Summary	Paragraph	Summary
1		7	
2		8	
3		9	
4		10	
5		11	
6			

we are not at all alike. I think it was the axolotls' heads, that triangular pink shape with the tiny eyes of gold. That looked and knew. That laid the claim. They were not *animals.*

It would seem easy, almost obvious, to fall into mythology. I began seeing in the axolotls a metamorphosis which did not succeed in revoking a mysterious humanity. I imagined them aware, slaves of their bodies, condemned infinitely to the silence of the abyss, to a hopeless meditation. Their blind gaze, the diminutive gold disc without expression and nonetheless terribly shining, went through me like a message: "Save us, save us." I caught myself mumbling words of advice, conveying childish hopes. They continued to look at me, immobile; from time to time the rosy branches of the gills stiffened. In that instant I felt a muted pain; perhaps they were seeing me, attracting my strength to penetrate into the impenetrable thing of their lives. They were not human beings, but I had found in no animal such a profound relation with myself. The axolotls were like witnesses of something, and at times like horrible judges. I felt ignoble in front of them; there was such a terrifying purity in those transparent eyes. They were larvas, but larva means disguise and also phantom. Behind those Aztec faces, without expression but of an implacable cruelty, what semblance was awaiting its hour?

JULIO CORTÁZAR 1029

ASSESSMENT TOOLS

Check Test: Fill-in-the-Blank
1. The narrator has a particular fascination for the _____ of the axolotl. [eyes]
2. This story is written in the _____ person. [first]
3. *Metamorphosis* means _____. [transformation]
4. According to the narrator, the only strange thing that happened was that he continued to _____. [think]

A. Critical Reading: Making Inferences

? Why does the narrator stress the axolotl's eyes? [Because they appear to see all, but can experience nothing.]

I was afraid of them. I think that had it not been for feeling the proximity of other visitors and the guard, I would not have been bold enough to remain alone with them. "You eat them alive with your eyes, hey," the guard said, laughing; he likely thought I was a little cracked. What he didn't notice was that it was they devouring me slowly with their eyes, in a cannibalism of gold. At any distance from the aquarium, I had only to think of them, it was as though I were

the tank each morning, the recognition was greater. They were suffering, every fiber of my body reached toward that stifled pain, that stiff torment at the bottom of the tank. They were lying in wait for something, a remote dominion destroyed, an age of liberty when the world had been that of the axolotls. Not possible that such a terrible expression which was attaining the overthrow of that forced blankness on their stone faces should carry any message other than

being affected from a distance. It got to the point that I was going every day, and at night I thought of them immobile in the darkness, slowly putting a hand out which immediately encountered another. Perhaps their eyes could see in the dead of night, and for them the day continued indefinitely. The eyes of axolotls have no lids.

I know now that there was nothing strange, that that had to occur. Leaning over in front of

one of pain, proof of that eternal sentence, of that liquid hell they were undergoing. Hopelessly, I wanted to prove to myself that my own sensibility was projecting a nonexistent consciousness upon the axolotls. They and I knew. So there was nothing strange in what happened. My face was pressed against the glass of the aquarium, my eyes were attempting once more to penetrate the mystery of those eyes of gold

1030 THE TWENTIETH CENTURY

without iris, without pupil. I saw from very close up the face of an axolotl immobile next to the glass. No transition and no surprise, I saw my face against the glass, I saw it on the outside of the tank, I saw it on the other side of the glass. Then my face drew back and I understood.

Only one thing was strange: to go on thinking as usual, to know. To realize that was, for the first moment, like the horror of a man buried alive awaking to his fate. Outside, my face came close to the glass again, I saw my mouth, the lips compressed with the effort of understanding the axolotls. I was an axolotl and now I knew instantly that no understanding was possible. He was outside the aquarium, his thinking was a thinking outside the tank. Recognizing him, being him himself, I was an axolotl and in my world. The horror began—I learned in the same moment—of believing myself prisoner in the body of an axolotl, metamorphosed into him with my human mind intact, buried alive in an axolotl, condemned to move lucidly among unconscious creatures. But that stopped when a foot just grazed my face, when I moved just a little to one side and saw an axolotl next to me who was looking at me, and understood that he knew also, no communication possible, but very clearly. Or I was also in him, or all of us were thinking humanlike, incapable of expression, limited to the golden splendor of our eyes looking at the face of the man pressed against the aquarium.

He returned many times, but he comes less often now. Weeks pass without his showing up. I saw him yesterday, he looked at me for a long time and left briskly. It seemed to me that he was not so much interested in us any more, that he was coming out of habit. Since the only thing I do is think, I could think about him a lot. It occurs to me that at the beginning we continued to communicate, that he felt more than ever one with the mystery which was claiming him. But the bridges were broken between him and me, because what was his obsession is now an axolotl, alien to his human life. I think that at the beginning I was capable of returning to him in a certain way—ah, only in a certain way—and of keeping awake his desire to know us better. I am an axolotl for good now, and if I think like a man it's only because every axolotl thinks like a man inside his rosy stone semblance. I believe that all this succeeded in communicating something to him in those first days, when I was still he. And in this final solitude to which he no longer comes, I console myself by thinking that perhaps he is going to write a story about us, that, believing he's making up a story, he's going to write all this about axolotls.

FINDING COMMON GROUND

When we first hear the narrator of "Axolotl" speak, he has already undergone his fantastic transformation. "Now I am an axolotl," he confides to the reader in one of the very first sentences of the story. He seems to fully accept this extraordinary event and wishes to convince us that it really did occur, that it could occur, that its occurrence was *logical*. The narrator wishes to make the impossible—a psychological identification so complete that it becomes a physical transformation—appear as rational as a trip to the zoo.

Form groups to discuss this strange short story. It might be helpful, given the suggestiveness of the story, to have it read aloud once before your discussions begin. Your first task, then, could be to jot down, as the story is being read, your questions and impressions. Your jottings could form the basis of your discussion.

Your first task as a discussion group is to set an agenda for your conversation. Be sure you cover these elements in your discussion: **point of view, conflict,** and **theme,** as well as connections with your own life and connections with other selections in this collection.

When your discussions are completed, each group should report to the class. In your report, include questions you could not answer or could not agree on answers to.

Into the Poems

Author Biography p. 1032
Before You Read p. 1033, p. 1038

Through the Poems

"Fern Hill" pp. 1034–1035
Connections: A Memoir p. 1036
"Green Gulch"
"Do Not Go Gentle into That Good Night" p. 1039
Making Meanings p. 1037, p. 1039
Language and Style p. 1037, p. 1040

Beyond the Poems

Choices: Building Your Portfolio p. 1040
- **Writer's Notebook:** List ways people mark milestones
- **Critical Writing:** Write an essay about the theme of the poem
- **Creative Writing:** Imitating Thomas's style, write about the past
- **Creative Writing:** Write a response in an older person's voice to "Do Not Go Gentle into That Good Night"
- **Creative Writing:** Write a villanelle responding to "Do Not Go Gentle into That Good Night"

Dylan Thomas
(1914–1953)

National Museum of Wales, Cardiff.

Portrait of Dylan Thomas by Augustus John.

Born in Swansea, Wales, Dylan Thomas was a prodigy—a poet who wrote some of his most famous works before he was twenty. By that time, he had also sketched out themes, ideas, and angles of perspective for poems that he drew on for the rest of his life. Largely self-educated, he chose the rough-and-tumble life of a newspaper reporter over the comparative serenity of a university education. His recognition by the leading poets and literary critics of Britain and the United States came early, and with it came international fame. Neither was enough to prevent him from having to exist on the edge of poverty until his death.

The only son of parents who lived by a code of "good appearances" among their neighbors, Thomas as a child was continually torn between a deep-seated wish to live up to the expectations of his schoolmaster father and an equally strong impulse to please his doting mother. At the same time, he rejected both parents' pretensions to gentility. This conflict was later intensified by a strangely childish self-indulgence that continually defeated his attempts to be a devoted husband to his wife Caitlin and a loving father to their three children. The temporary solace he found in alcohol led to that "insult to the brain" that caused his early and sudden death, in St. Vincent's Hospital in New York City. At the time, Thomas was making his fourth visit to the United States, and preparing to collaborate on an opera with the famous composer Igor Stravinsky.

A man of magical presence, with an endless flow of wit and a transparent hunger for affection, Thomas charmed both his British and his American contemporaries. When he first came to America in 1950, he was regarded as the most charismatic British visitor since Oscar Wilde in 1885. His first reading tour of American colleges and universities was followed by ever more extensive trips in which he crisscrossed the continent from Florida to British Columbia. Beyond their response to his personal magnetism, those who attended Thomas's oral readings heard something new in modern poetry— a kind of expression combining the oratorical *hwyl*, or chanting eloquence, of the Welsh chapel service with the theatrical delivery of the Victorian actors who once thrilled American audiences with thunderous recitations from Shakespeare and Marlowe. Thomas's poems are a mixture of intricate complication and preacherlike eloquence, of sonorous solemnity combined with a playful use of language apparent even in his most serious works.

In his last years, Thomas found that the concentration needed to write poetry was more and more difficult to achieve. Consequently, he turned to less demanding forms of expression and produced two works that became familiar around the world: *Under Milk Wood* (1954), which he called a "play for voices," and his lyrical memoir *A Child's Christmas in Wales* (1955), now a holiday classic.

Celebrated by critics, sought after by American lecture agencies, and idolized almost like a rock star, Thomas died at the height of a fame he could neither accept nor enjoy. "Once I was lost and proud," he told a reporter from *The New York Times,* "now I'm found and humble. I prefer that other."

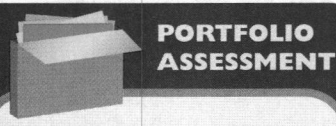

PORTFOLIO ASSESSMENT

Portfolio Assessment For help with self-assessment of reading skills, see the *Portfolio Management System,* p. 53.

PROGRAM MANAGER

- **Planning Instruction** See **Teaching Notes,** *Teaching Resources B,* pp. 134–135, for objectives, a summary, literary elements, and additional biographical information for these selections.
- **Instructional Support** Before beginning the instructional lesson, see **Graphic** **Organizer for Active Reading,** *Teaching Resources B,* pp. 152–153, for Through the Poems activities.
- **Assessment** See **Selection Tests,** *Test Booklet,* pp. 219–220.

BEFORE YOU READ
FERN HILL

Reading Focus
Memories of Childhood
Childhood is often pictured as a time of carefree innocence, and almost all of us have some memory from childhood of an idyllic moment, when the world was a glorious place and everything seemed just right.

Quickwrite

Sketch one happy childhood memory of your own in your Reader's Log. Then, list three adjectives besides "happy" that describe your emotions as you think about this memory.

Elements of Literature
Lyric Poetry
Lyric poetry focuses on expressing emotions or thoughts rather than on telling a story. In the lyric poem "Fern Hill," Dylan Thomas uses a full range of sound effects and figures of speech to convey vivid memories of a young boy's enchanted life in the Welsh countryside. Although the speaker's memories are colored by reflection and experience, it is the exuberance of his feelings, above all, that claims our attention.

Background
As a child, Thomas spent his summers among relatives who worked on a farm that, in his poem, he calls Fern Hill. Set in an apple orchard, the farmhouse is of the whitewashed stucco typical of Wales and has a number of outlying barns for livestock and hay storage. Not far from the sea, Fern Hill looks down upon enormous tidal flats in an ever-changing seascape that provides a bountiful habitat for thousands of water birds.

Dylan Thomas and his family.

© Rollie McKenna.

"Fern Hill" is a memory of childhood joy, a vision of an earthly paradise as well as the playground of a boy for whom every day is an enchanted adventure. Yet, typical of Thomas, joy is never unadulterated or unshadowed. At the end of this extended song of praise, "Time" holds him not, as we might expect, "green and growing," but "green and dying." Here we have a variation on one of Thomas's persistent themes—the lurking presence of death in life, of the worm in the seed.

Into the Poem

Using **BEFORE YOU READ** p. 1033

Elements of Literature
Although **lyric poetry** does not tell an explicit story, it often contains narrative elements. In "Fern Hill," the speaker recounts childhood activities. These events are selected for their capacity to display the speaker's emotions.

> **ABOUT THE AUTHOR**
> Dylan Thomas's father encouraged his son to read widely, and he insisted that English be the language of his home, instead of his own native Welsh. Even so, Dylan Thomas did have a traditional Welsh attitude toward poetry. He believed poetry should be highly artful and should sound beautiful. This was, in part, due to the influence of his uncle William, a poet who wrote in Welsh.

OPTIONS FOR TEACHING

STRATEGIES FOR INCLUSION

Auditory Because Dylan Thomas uses a number of sound devices in "Fern Hill," students may find it useful to hear it read aloud. If possible, obtain a recording of Thomas himself reading the poem. Students might be interested in hearing his unique delivery. Students also could read the poem aloud in class and discuss the differences that subtle voice inflections can make in meaning and interpretation.

Visual There are a number of unusual visual images in the poem, such as the apple towns mentioned in l. 6. Ask students to select one of the visual images and to draw or paint a representation of what they think the image looks like. Or you can select an image and have several students work independently on drawings of them. ☞

Fern Hill

Dylan Thomas

Now as I was young and easy under the apple boughs
About the lilting house and happy as the grass was green,
   The night above the dingle° starry,
    Time let me hail and climb
5   Golden in the heydays of his eyes,
And honored among wagons I was prince of the apple towns
And once below a time I lordly had the trees and leaves
    Trail with daisies and barley
   Down the rivers of the windfall light.

10 And as I was green and carefree, famous among the barns
About the happy yard and singing as the farm was home,
   In the sun that is young once only,
    Time let me play and be
   Golden in the mercy of his means,
15 And green and golden I was huntsman and herdsman, the calves
Sang to my horn, the foxes on the hills barked clear and cold,
    And the sabbath rang slowly
   In the pebbles of the holy streams.

All the sun long it was running, it was lovely, the hay
20 Fields high as the house, the tunes from the chimneys, it was air
   And playing, lovely and watery
    And fire green as grass.
And nightly under the simple stars
As I rode to sleep the owls were bearing the farm away,
25 All the moon long I heard, blessed among stables, the nightjars°
   Flying with the ricks,° and the horses
    Flashing into the dark.

And then to awake, and the farm, like a wanderer white
With the dew, come back, the cock on his shoulder: it was all
30   Shining, it was Adam and maiden,
    The sky gathered again
   And the sun grew round that very day.
So it must have been after the birth of the simple light
In the first, spinning place, the spellbound horses walking warm
35   Out of the whinnying green stable
    On to the fields of praise.

3. dingle: little wooded valley, nestled between steep hills.

25. nightjars: common, gray-brown nocturnal birds, named for their jarring cries.
26. ricks: haystacks.

1034 THE TWENTIETH CENTURY

A. Critical Reading: Analyzing Figurative Language

? What kinds of games does the speaker play? [One possibility is that he plays imaginative games in which he pretends to be a prince and a lord.]

B. Critical Reading: Analyzing Figurative Language

? To what does the word *green* refer? [Some possible responses include innocent, fresh, young, inexperienced.]

C. Literary Element: Theme

? What theme do this and other religious references imply? [Possible answer: The sacredness of childhood innocence.]

D. Literary Element: Lyric Poetry

? What feelings do the images of earth, air, fire, and water evoke? [Possible answers: The simple, elemental feelings of a child or of a human being in a lost paradise.]

E. Reader's Response: First Thoughts

? What do you associate with the phrase "In the first, spinning place"? [Sample responses: The "spinning place" might refer to the creation of the universe, or "spinning" might refer to the earth turning on its axis.]

OPTIONS FOR TEACHING

INTEGRATING THE LANGUAGE ARTS

Strategic Reading "Fern Hill" requires a close reading for its literal meanings to be understood. Ask students to read individual clauses or phrases, using the commas as guides for pausing. After they read a passage, ask students to paraphrase the passage and jot down its most important word or phrase. Once they have worked through the entire poem this way, ask them to go back and read the whole piece without stopping. They can keep the words or phrases they jotted down close at hand to glance at from time to time as they read.

Writing: A Description Based on the images presented in the poem, ask students to each write a brief description of the farm that the poet calls Fern Hill. The description should be as objective as possible: It should attempt to tell what is present on the farm and how the various objects and places are physically situated with respect to one another. You might want to let students spend a few minutes in group discussion before they begin this assignment.

And honored among foxes and pheasants by the gay house
Under the new made clouds and happy as the heart was long,
   In the sun born over and over,
40   I ran my heedless ways,
   My wishes raced through the house high hay
And nothing I cared, at my sky blue trades, that time allows
In all his tuneful turning so few and such morning songs
   Before the children green and golden
45   Follow him out of grace,

Nothing I cared, in the lamb white days, that time would take me
Up to the swallow thronged loft by the shadow of my hand,
   In the moon that is always rising,
      Nor that riding to sleep
50   I should hear him fly with the high fields
And wake to the farm forever fled from the childless land.
Oh as I was young and easy in the mercy of his means,
      Time held me green and dying
   Though I sang in my chains like the sea.

F

F. Critical Reading: Making Inferences

? What does the speaker imply about childhood innocence?

[One implication is that innocence is destined to end.]

View of Dunraven Bay, South Wales.

RESPONDING TO THE PHOTOGRAPH: EXPLORING THE SUBJECT

Mountains and plateaus populate most of Wales. About two-thirds of the land is covered by the Cambrian Mountains. In the north, the mountains are steep and rugged, but as this photograph shows, the mountains become flatter in parts of the land, and deep valleys cut through the plateaus. These plateaus host a variety of features, including forests, grassy plains, bogs (swamplands), and moors (open wastelands).

CROSSING THE CURRICULUM

Geography Ask students to give oral reports on such Welsh geographic features as rivers, seacoast, and mountains. Have students look in library books for photographs of farms like the one Thomas describes. In addition, you may ask students to watch *The Englishman Who Went Up a Hill but Came Down a Mountain* (1995) and then create a map or chart of the Cambrian Mountains.

History Ask students to research Welsh history, culture, and language. After they have gathered information on these and other topics related to Welsh history, have them conduct a panel discussion for the class in which they present the information they have obtained.

PROFESSIONAL NOTES

TECHNOLOGY **Technology Tip** You can download audio clips of Dylan Thomas reading from his work at the Internet Town Hall at **http://town.hall.org/Archives /radio/IMS/HarperAudio/020894 _harp_ITH.html**. *You may want to preview any Internet activity that you suggest to students. Because these resources are sometimes public forums, their content can be unpredictable.*

T1035

Connections
A MEMOIR

"Fern Hill" contains a remembrance of childhood before the loss of innocence. The speaker in the autobiographical story which follows remembers something altogether different. Loren Eiseley (1907–1977), an American writer and archaeologist, reveals a darker side of childhood in this excerpt from his memoir, *The Night Country*.

Green Gulch

Loren Eiseley

Verdun altar (c. 1881) showing Cain slaying Abel. Enamel.

Sammlungen des Stiftes, Klosterneuburg, Austria.

We stood in a wide flat field at sunset. For the life of me I can remember no other children before them. I must have run away and been playing by myself until I had wandered to the edge of the town. They were older than I and knew where they came from and how to get back. I joined them.

They were not going home. They were going to a place called Green Gulch. They came from some other part of town, and their clothes were rough, their eyes worldly and sly. I think, looking back, that it must have been a little like a child following goblins home to their hill at nightfall, but nobody threatened me. Besides, I was very small and did not know the way home, so I followed them.

Presently we came to some rocks. The place was well named. It was a huge pool in a sandstone basin, green and dark with the evening over it and the trees leaning secretly inward above the water. When you looked down, you saw the sky. I remember that place as it was when we came there. I remember the quiet and the green ferns touching the green water. I remember we played there, innocently at first.

But someone found the spirit of the place, a huge old turtle, asleep in the ferns. He was the last lord of the green water before the town poured over it. I saw his end. They pounded him to death with stones on the other side of the pool while I looked on in stupefied horror. I had never seen death before.

Suddenly, as I stood there small and uncertain and frightened, a grimy, splattered gnome who had been stooping over the turtle stood up with a rock in his hand. He looked at me, and around that little group some curious evil impulse passed like a wave. I felt it and drew back. I was alone there. They were not human.

I do not know who threw the first stone, who splashed water over my suit, who struck me first, or even who finally, among that ring of vicious faces, put me on my feet, dragged me to the roadside, pointed, and said, roughly, "There's your road, kid, follow the street lamps. They'll take you home."

They stood in a little group watching me, nervous now, ashamed a little at the ferocious pack impulse toward the outsider that had swept over them.

I never forgot that moment.

I went because I had to, down that road with the wind moving in the fields. I went slowly from one spot of light to another and in between I thought the things a child thinks, so that I did not stop at any house nor ask anyone to help me when I came to the lighted streets.

I had discovered evil. It was a monstrous and corroding knowledge. It could not be told to adults because it was the evil of childhood in which no one believes. I was alone with it in the dark.

CONNECTING WITH "FERN HILL"

First Thoughts

1. Is the experience described in "Fern Hill" universal? Explain your response. (You may want to refer to the notes you made in your Reader's Log.)

Shaping Interpretations

2. From whose **point of view** is the poem told?
3. What details tell how the speaker felt when he was "young and easy"?
4. What lines in the poem seem to refer to the Biblical account of paradise?
5. In what specific ways was the speaker's childhood like the life Adam and Eve led in the Biblical Garden of Eden? In what ways is the boy's "waking" in the last stanza like the "waking" of Adam and Eve as they left the Garden?
6. Where is time **personified** in the poem? Describe the different kinds of intentions that Time seems to have regarding the boy.
7. How would you explain the **paradox,** or seeming contradiction, in the next-to-last line of the poem?
8. Locate the occurrences of *green* and *gold* in the poem. What associations and feelings do you connect with each color? Why do you think Thomas repeats the words so often?
9. Read this entire **lyric poem** aloud, or listen to a recording of it, and try to hear the many elements that produce its music. How does the poem's **rhythm** match its subject and mood? Where does Thomas use **alliteration** and **onomatopoeia** to provide the sound effects?
10. Which lines in "Fern Hill" could apply to Eiseley's experience in "Green Gulch"?

Connecting with the Text

11. Which lines in "Fern Hill" could apply to the lives of all of us?

Challenging the Text

12. Years after this poem was published, Thomas told a friend that one line continued to bother him because it was "bloody bad." The friend asked what line it was. "I ran my heedless ways," said Thomas, and he winced as though he had made a mistake from which he would never recover. Why do you think Thomas felt so strongly about a line that most people accept and even quote as part of his most celebrated poem? How do you feel about the line?

LANGUAGE AND STYLE

Wordplay

Even at his most somber, Thomas continually indulges in wordplay—sometimes turning a **cliché** upside down, sometimes making chilling or amusing **puns,** sometimes using modifiers in surprising ways, often giving a twist of emphasis and new luster to an old saying.

How many instances of wordplay can you identify in "Fern Hill"?

Spring, or the Garden of Eden (17th century) by Nicholas Poussin.
Louvre, Paris.

DYLAN THOMAS 1037

---

freedom to be happy. But in l. 53, time is a parent who holds a dying child in his arms. Thus, time seems to have intended the speaker to be happy but also to grow up, lose the paradise of childhood, and eventually die.

7. The phrase "green and dying" is paradoxical because it suggests innocent freshness and mortality at the same time.

8. *Green* appears in ll. 2, 10, 15, 22, 35, 44, and 53. *Gold* or *golden* appears in ll. 5, 14, 15, and 44. Possible associations with *green* include nature and youth. Possible associations with *gold* include perfection, value, and warmth. Students may say that Thomas uses these words to suggest that childhood has all of the qualities associated with both words.

9. Students may suggest that the poem's lilting rhythm and the variation of lines reinforce the carefree mood of youth. Examples of alliteration and onomatopoeia occur in ll. 2, 7, 14, 15, 20, 26–27, 34, 41, and 51.

10. The last lines of Thomas's poem seem to apply to Eiseley's haunted view of childhood.

Connecting with the Text

11. Metaphorically, all of them could apply. Though not everyone experiences as idyllic a childhood as Thomas describes, many people remember youth as a time of innocence and beauty.

Challenging the Text

12. **(Evaluation)** Some students may suggest that this line did not satisfy Thomas because it does not contain an original image or figure of speech, and other students may say that the line seems to be a cliché.

Making Meanings

First Thoughts

1. Some students may say the experience is not universal because not all children can play on a farm. Others may say it is universal insofar as children can experience summers that are full of fun and adventure.

Shaping Interpretations

2. From the point of view of an adult who is nostalgically remembering his childhood.

3. "Prince of the apple towns" (l. 6), "singing" (l. 11), "sang to my horn" (l. 16), "ran my heedless ways" (l. 40).
4. Lines 29–36 in the fourth stanza.
5. Students may mention the speaker's joy in nature (represented by the references to rivers, stars, calves, foxes, owls, pheasants, the hay, etc.). The boy's "awakening" into the reality of adulthood may be compared to Adam and Eve's loss of Eden.
6. In ll. 4 and 13, time is obliquely personified as an indulgent parent who allows the boy the

---

Language and Style

Possible Answers

Clichés turned upside down include "happy as the grass was green," "once below a time," and "fire green as grass." Puns include "the sun grew round" and "morning songs." The many surprising uses of modifiers include "lilting house," "sky blue trades," and "lamb white days." Old sayings with new twists include "the calves sang to my horn" and "honored among foxes and pheasants."

Into the Poem

Using BEFORE YOU READ p. 1038

Reading Focus

Remind students to choose situations they would not mind sharing with others.

Quickwrite

You might ask students to sketch their ideas of what death looks like and then base the verbal descriptions on their sketches. It might be helpful to ask students to share their descriptions with the class and to discuss the range of images students produce.

BEFORE YOU READ
DO NOT GO GENTLE INTO THAT GOOD NIGHT

Reading Focus

Challenging Death

Death may conquer every living thing in the end, but the instinct for survival remains remarkably strong. In contemporary literature, as in the *Gilgamesh* epic of four thousand years ago (page 53), heroes often battle against death's inevitability. Literature also records the frequent, fierce refusal of the living to accept a loved one's death. Suppose you knew someone who was facing death. How would you advise that person to behave? What attitude would you want that person to have?

Quickwrite

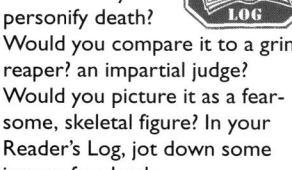

How would you personify death? Would you compare it to a grim reaper? an impartial judge? Would you picture it as a fearsome, skeletal figure? In your Reader's Log, jot down some images for death.

Elements of Literature

Elegy

The typical **elegy** is a poem that mourns a death that has already occurred. This poem is an elegy that speaks to a dying man, urging him not to surrender but to meet death in a spirit of challenge. As he often did in his poetry, here Thomas gives his own twist to a familiar subject. The poem may invite charges of irreverence, but its lyrical solemnity, not its argument, is what reverberates in the reader's mind.

Only two end rhyme sounds occur in the poem, but both are blended into iambic pentameter with such skill that the many repetitions of similar sounds become a somber and delicate music. The use of *gentle* instead of the adverb *gently* may seem ungrammatical. But when we read the line as "Do not go, gentle, into that good night," as Thomas insisted, we gain the additional meaning of all that is gentle, including the gentle man who was Thomas's father.

Study for Portrait V (after life mask of William Blake) (1956) by Francis Bacon.

OPTIONS FOR TEACHING

INTEGRATING THE LANGUAGE ARTS

Strategic Reading The second, third, fourth, and fifth stanzas of the poem deal with particular types of people who refuse to die without a fight. Ask students to use the following chart as they read the poem to summarize the contents of these stanzas.

Stanza	Type of Person	Reasons
2		
3		
4		
5		

Do Not Go Gentle into That Good Night

Dylan Thomas

Do not go gentle into that good night,
Old age should burn and rave at close of day;
Rage, rage against the dying of the light.

Though wise men at their end know dark is right,
5 Because their words had forked no lightning they
Do not go gentle into that good night.

Good men, the last wave by, crying how bright
Their frail deeds might have danced in a green bay,
Rage, rage against the dying of the light.

10 Wild men who caught and sang the sun in flight, **B**
And learn, too late, they grieved it on its way,
Do not go gentle into that good night.

Grave men, near death, who see with blinding sight
Blind eyes could blaze like meteors and be gay, **C**
15 Rage, rage against the dying of the light.

And you, my father, there on the sad height,
Curse, bless, me now with your fierce tears, I pray. **D**
Do not go gentle into that good night.
Rage, rage against the dying of the light.

MAKING MEANINGS

First Thoughts

1. What feelings does the poet reveal about his father's death? Are they at all contradictory?

Shaping Interpretations

2. What four types of people are described in stanzas 2–5? How do all these people respond to the dying of the light?

3. What does the speaker pray for at the end?

4. What is the "good night"? What **pun** on the phrase do you catch?

5. Given Thomas's feelings about the "good night," do you see anything contradictory in his use of the word *good*? Explain your answer.

6. Identify at least three **metaphors** in the poem. How do the ideas you recorded in your Reader's Log compare with the images that Thomas uses?

7. Why would any son beg his father to "Curse, bless, me now with your fierce tears"? What might this strange request indicate about the relationship between this father and son?

Challenging the Text

8. Soon after this poem was finished, Thomas sent it to Princess Caetani in Rome, hoping she might publish it in her literary magazine. In an accompanying letter, he wrote: "The only person I can't show the little enclosed poem to is, of course, my father, who doesn't know he's dying." Given

A. Literary Element: Metaphor
To what does the speaker compare death and life? [Death to night, life to light.]

B. Critical Reading: Making Connections
Who are the wild men in l. 10? [Some students may think the expression refers to pre-literate people who worshipped the sun. Others may think it refers to people who experienced life intensely.]

C. Reader's Response: Extending the Text
Do you agree with the speaker that dying people should rage against death? [Sample responses: Life is too precious to let go easily; or people should make every effort to die peacefully.]

D. Literary Element: Elegy
The elegy form goes back to the ancient Greeks and the Romans, but those peoples used the term to refer to any serious meditation, including poems about love, war, and death. Although today "elegy" is used exclusively to refer to poems of mourning, Thomas's poem fits the older definition as well.

Making Meanings

First Thoughts

1. In general, Thomas resents the fact that his father is dying, but he says that wise men "know dark is right." These men know death must come, but they do not go without a struggle.

Shaping Interpretations

2. These stanzas describe wise men, good men, wild men, and grave men. The wise men are angry because their counsels failed to influence others; the good men deplore the ineffectuality of their deeds; the wild men learn too late that time is fleeting; the grave men regret their failure to enjoy life.

3. He asks his father to both curse and bless him.

4. Death. Ordinarily "good night" is used as a casual farewell, not as a synonym for death.

5. The word "good" is paradoxical since Thomas obviously wants his father to resist and protest against death.

6. Metaphors include old age burning and raving (l. 2), wise men's words forking lightning (l. 5), "frail deeds" dancing in a "green bay" (l. 8), and men catching the sun in flight (l. 10). Responses

will vary regarding the images of death students recorded.

7. The phrase hints at a relationship involving both love and anger.

Challenging the Text

8. **(Synthesis)** Some students may think Thomas should have shown the poem to his father and told him of his impending death so his father could prepare for it. Other students may think Thomas did the right thing.

Elements of Literature

Mini-Lesson: The Villanelle

Although the villanelle form does not require it, Thomas further restricts himself in this poem by limiting each line to ten syllables. This has the effect of adding further balance and symmetry to an already well-balanced and highly symmetrical verse form. This degree of discipline is ironic considering Thomas's message: Resist the natural order of events and rebel against the inevitable.

Answers

1. Thomas has been completely faithful to the three rules for the villanelle. His nineteen-line poem has the prescribed rhyme scheme and pattern of repeated lines.
2. Lines 1 and 3, which are repeated, carry the central theme: resist the approach of death.

Beyond the Poems

Choices: Building Your Portfolio

1. **Writer's Notebook** Remind students to save their work. They may use it as prewriting for the Writer's Workshop on p. 1053.
2. **Critical Writing** You might want to allow students to discuss the theme of the poem before they begin working on their essays. They can do this in small groups or in the whole class. Then, encourage them to re-read the poem carefully, noting details that support the theme. As a way of eliciting responses to how Thomas handles the theme, suggest that students think of how they would handle the theme and compare their ideas with Thomas's method.

---

the fact that the poem has become one of the most famous elegies of this century, do you think Thomas's reluctance was justified? What would you have done in his situation?

ELEMENTS OF LITERATURE

The Villanelle

Thomas has written his poem in an old form called a **villanelle,** invented by French poets. At first this term, which means "rural" or "countrylike," was limited to light, lyric poems about the countryside. Today, villanelles are written on many topics and, as Thomas's illustrates, do not require a light tone.

The villanelle is a complex form. The trick is to make it sound spontaneous and fresh, yet still adhere to its strict limits:

- It should have nineteen lines divided into five three-line stanzas (tercets) and a concluding four-line stanza (quatrain).
- It can use only two end rhyme sounds in this rhyme scheme: *aba aba aba aba aba abaa.*
- It should repeat line 1 in lines 6, 12, and 18 and should repeat line 3 in lines 9, 15, and 19.

1. How faithfully has Thomas followed the rules for a villanelle?
2. The repeated lines in a villanelle must be significant. Has Thomas repeated ideas important to his poem? Explain your answer.

Writer's Notebook
1. Collecting Ideas for an Informative Report

WORK IN PROGRESS

In the two poems you've just read, Thomas reflects on two very different passages in human life, one leading out of childhood and the other out of life itself. Use the *5W-How?* questions (*Who? What? When? Where? Why?* and *How?*) to explore what you know about the ways in which our society marks these milestones. Save your work for the Writer's Workshop on page 1053.

Critical Writing
2. Childhood Revisited

In a brief essay, state the **theme** of "Fern Hill," and cite the details from the poem that support that theme. At the conclusion of your report, tell how you respond to Thomas's handling of this theme.

Creative Writing
3. The Way Things Were

Narrate a joyful episode from your own childhood. In some of your sentences, try to imitate the lyrical style of "Fern Hill." Open with the words, "Now as I was young and easy . . ."

Creative Writing
4. Feedback

Write a response to "Do Not Go Gentle into That Good Night," using the voice of a very old person who is facing death. Your response might be a poem, an essay, or a letter.

Creative Writing
5. Say It Again

Write your response to "Do Not Go Gentle into That Good Night" in another **villanelle.** First, think of the lines that you will want to repeat. Then, think of the sounds that you will want to repeat in your rhyme scheme.

STRATEGIES FOR INCLUSION

Logical-Mathematical Some students may appreciate the mathematical aspects of prosody. As they work on the Language and Style lesson, ask these students to develop mathematical formulas that express the rules for the villanelle. Also, ask these students to develop rules for other verse forms of their own devising. You can specify subject matter and ask students to invent verse forms appropriate for each subject.

PORTFOLIO ASSESSMENT

Choices: Assessment Criteria For help in evaluating these Choices assignments, see the criteria in the *Portfolio Management System,* pp. 171–172.

V. S. Naipaul
(1932–   )

When V. S. (Vidiadhar Surajprasad) Naipaul was born, his homeland, the Caribbean island of Trinidad, was still under the colonial rule of Britain. Like many Asian Indians, Naipaul's family had immigrated to Trinidad in the nineteenth century to work as indentured servants on the sugar plantations. With their Asian background and Hindu religion, the Naipauls felt themselves to be members of a transplanted society. As a result, from his earliest days, Naipaul felt a degree of rootlessness. He also felt—on the small island—a sense of the world as a kind of prison.

Fortunately, he was an outstanding student. Scholastic honors won him a place at Trinidad's Queen's Royal College and provided him a chance to leave the island. Granted a scholarship to England's prestigious Oxford University, Naipaul was one of only a few dark-skinned students at a university famous for educating England's privileged white upper classes.

Naipaul's father had pursued a faltering career as an island journalist, and this background inspired Naipaul to become a writer. Leaving Oxford in 1954, with no desire to return to Trinidad's narrow possibilities, he sought his identity in writing. He worked part time for the British Broadcasting Corporation (BBC) and tried his hand at writing fiction about the island life he had fled. His first short stories, which later became *Miguel Street,* went begging until he was able to publish his two earlier novels set in Trinidad, *The Mystic Masseur* (1957) and *The Suffrage of Elvira* (1958).

Naipaul's first masterpiece, *A House for Mr. Biswas,* came along in 1961. The novel, which some critics compared to Dickens's comic satires, tells about a poor, ineffectual Trinidadian (much like Naipaul's father) who finds stability by marrying into an influential family. Deprived of independence, Mr. Biswas's rebellion takes shape in the desperate quest for a house of his own. The novel reveals Naipaul's special gifts as a storyteller: his unique, ironic voice; his clear vision of so-called Third World people; and his understanding of life's essentials. The book established him as a major novelist throughout the world of letters.

Naipaul's search for roots has sent him traveling, first back to the West Indies and then to Africa, the Middle East, and India itself, as he pursues the meaning of his own mixed heritage. These voyages and inquiries have led Naipaul to produce more than twenty books, both fiction and nonfiction, including *A Bend in the River* (a 1979 novel set in Africa), *India: A Million Mutinies Now* (a 1991 travel book about his return to India), and *A Way in the World* (a 1994 autobiographical novel about a writer's journey toward self-understanding). All of Naipaul's works have been acclaimed for their clear and bitter yet compassionate insights into the human struggle for identity and survival.

Naipaul has won virtually all the major British literary prizes available to a prose writer and is a perennial nominee for the Nobel Prize in literature.

V. S. Naipaul (1981).

V. S. NAIPAUL 1041

Into the Story

Author Biography p. 1041
Before You Read p. 1042

Through the Story

"B. Wordsworth" pp. 1043–1048
Words to Own pp. 1044–1046
Literature and Society pp. 1046–1047
Making Meanings p. 1048
Language and Style p. 1049

Beyond the Story

Choices: Building Your Portfolio p. 1049
- **Writer's Notebook:** List changes in the boy and write a thesis statement
- **Critical Writing:** Write about poetic vision
- **Critical Writing:** Write a character analysis
- **Creative Writing:** Write anecdotes about a person
- **Social Studies/Music:** Present an oral report on calypso

PORTFOLIO ASSESSMENT

Portfolio Assessment
For help with self-assessment of reading skills, see the *Portfolio Management System,* pp. 48–49.

PROGRAM MANAGER

- **Planning Instruction** See **Teaching Notes,** *Teaching Resources B,* p. 136, for objectives, literary elements, and additional information for this selection.
- **Instructional Support** Before beginning the instructional lesson, see **Graphic Organizer for Active Reading,** *Teaching Resources B,* p. 154, for a Through the Story activity.
- **Audiotaped Readings** To help auditory learners through the lesson, use the **Selected Reading, Audiocassette 2, Side B** in the *Audiovisual Resources Binder.*

- **Assessment** See **Selection Test,** *Test Booklet,* pp. 221–222.
- **Language Link** For instruction and practice in commas, see **Language Link,** *Teaching Resources B,* pp. 155–156 and *Language and Writing Skills Worksheets,* pp. 131–137.
- **Reinforcement** Use the **Words to Own** worksheet in *Teaching Resources B,* p. 157.

Into the Story

Using BEFORE YOU READ p. 1042

Background

One unfortunate stereotype of poets holds that they are rather eccentric. This comes, in part, from the fact that they tend to view the world differently than others do. B. Wordsworth fits this stereotype. Ask students to discuss why a child might appreciate B. Wordsworth's eccentricity more than an adult might.

BEFORE YOU READ
B. WORDSWORTH

Reading Focus

A Touch of the Poet

How would you describe a poet? Would you know one if you met him or her in the street? In the story you are about to read, a young boy's encounter with a poet transforms his world into "a most exciting place." Would you agree that part of a poet's function is to suggest new angles of vision for the rest of us? Do poets really help "transform" the world?

Quickwrite

In your Reader's Log, jot down four or five qualities that you associate with poets. Then, as you read, see how your image of a poet corresponds with the poet in the story.

Elements of Literature

Setting

The story's **setting** is the back streets of Port-of-Spain, the capital of Trinidad, the Caribbean island where Naipaul lived as a child. As you read, notice how Naipaul uses **imagery** and **dialogue,** as well as factual details, to bring this setting to life.

Background

A story about the magical world of childhood innocence, "B. Wordsworth" brims with all the surprise and joy that children feel when they glimpse a road to the future opening before their eyes. The humor of the story, of which there is plenty, springs from the contrast between the young narrator's view of things and his mother's more cynical view. Whereas Ma sees a funny old geezer at the back gate, the boy sees a poet, a man who lives for beauty, for mango trees, for the stars of heaven, and for ice cream. He sees a man with a wildly romantic and tragic history, someone who can feel for all the creatures of the world. What an opening of a boy's narrow horizon!

The poet in the story is a black Trinidadian who calls himself B. Wordsworth. Before you read, review what you know of another Wordsworth, the one with the first initial "W." You might re-read page 656 of this book.

Laventille (1984), Port-of-Spain, Trinidad.

WORDS TO OWN

The following vocabulary words are defined in the Words to Own at the bottom of the pupil's page.

constellation p. 1044	rite p. 1045
botanical p. 1045	patronize p. 1045
	distill p. 1046

OPTIONS FOR TEACHING

STRATEGIES FOR INCLUSION

Visual/Kinesthetic The narrator describes B. Wordsworth's yard and house in detail. Students can use this information to construct a model of the setting. Divide the class into teams, letting one team work on the house and another on the yard. The house can be made from cardboard, with a removable roof to allow a view of the interior. The yard could incorporate clippings from trees or shrubs to represent the plants in the character's garden. When completed, the model house can be placed in the yard and displayed in the classroom.

B. Wordsworth

V. S. Naipaul

Three beggars called punctually every day at the hospitable houses in Miguel Street. At about ten an Indian came in his dhoti[1] and white jacket, and we poured a tin of rice into the sack he carried on his back. At twelve an old woman smoking a clay pipe came and she got a cent. At two a blind man led by a boy called for his penny.

Sometimes we had a rogue.[2] One day a man called and said he was hungry. We gave him a meal. He asked for a cigarette and wouldn't go until we had lit it for him. That man never came again.

The strangest caller came one afternoon at about four o'clock. I had come back from school and was in my home clothes. The man said to me, "Sonny, may I come inside your yard?"

He was a small man and he was tidily dressed. He wore a hat, a white shirt, and black trousers.

A

I asked, "What you want?"

He said, "I want to watch your bees."

We had four small gru-gru palm trees[3] and they were full of uninvited bees.

I ran up the steps and shouted, "Ma, it have a man outside here. He say he want to watch the bees."

My mother came out, looked at the man, and asked in an unfriendly way, "What you want?"

The man said, "I want to watch your bees."

His English was so good, it didn't sound natural, and I could see my mother was worried.

B

She said to me, "Stay here and watch him while he watch the bees."

The man said, "Thank you, Madam. You have done a good deed today."

He spoke very slowly and very correctly as though every word was costing him money.

We watched the bees, this man and I, for about an hour, squatting near the palm trees.

The man said, "I like watching bees. Sonny, do you like watching bees?"

1. dhoti (dō′tē): loincloth worn by many Hindu men.
2. rogue (rōg): archaic for "wandering beggar."
3. gru-gru (gr$\overline{oo}$′gr$\overline{oo}$′) **palm trees:** spiny-trunked West Indian palm trees.

I said, "I ain't have the time."

He shook his head sadly. He said, "That's what I do, I just watch. I can watch ants for days. Have you ever watched ants? And scorpions, and centipedes, and *congorees*[4]—have you watched those?"

I shook my head.

I said, "What you does do, mister?"

He got up and said, "I am a poet."

I said, "A good poet?"

He said, "The greatest in the world."

"What your name, mister?"

"B. Wordsworth."

"B for Bill?"

"Black. Black Wordsworth. White Wordsworth was my brother. We share one heart. I can watch a small flower like the morning glory and cry."

C

I said, "Why you does cry?"

"Why, boy? Why? You will know when you grow up. You're a poet, too, you know. And when you're a poet you can cry for everything."

I couldn't laugh.

He said, "You like your mother?"

"When she not beating me."

He pulled out a printed sheet from his hip pocket and said, "On this paper is the greatest poem about mothers and I'm going to sell it to you at a bargain price. For four cents."

I went inside and I said, "Ma, you want to buy a poetry for four cents?"

My mother said, "Tell that blasted man to haul his tail away from my yard, you hear."

I said to B. Wordsworth, "My mother say she ain't have four cents."

D

B. Wordsworth said, "It is the poet's tragedy."

And he put the paper back in his pocket. He didn't seem to mind.

I said, "Is a funny way to go round selling poetry like that. Only calypsonians[5] do that sort of thing. A lot of people does buy?"

He said, "No one has yet bought a single copy."

"But why you does keep on going round, then?"

---

4. *congorees* (käŋ′gə·rēz′): conger eels; long, scaleless eels found in the warm waters of the West Indies.
5. calypsonians (kə·lip′so′nē·ənz): West Indian folk musicians who traditionally perform satirical, syncopated songs that are improvised, or composed on the spot. *Calypso* possibly comes from *kaiso,* a Trinidadian dialect word meaning "town crier."

V. S. Naipaul 1043

Through the Story

A. Literary Element: Character
? What do the tidy clothing, proper English, and odd request suggest about the visitor? [Possible answers: He is well educated and differs from the beggars to whom the narrator is accustomed; he has fewer pragmatic interests than other beggars.]

B. Critical Reading: Making Inferences
? What does the man's habit of watching insects for long periods of time suggest about him? [Possible answers: He has nothing to do; or he is very patient, and he loves nature.]

C. Literary Element: Allusion
? Who is "White Wordsworth," and what do the two "Wordsworths" share? [White Wordsworth is a reference to William Wordsworth. The "Wordsworths" share "one heart"—a love for poetry and nature.]

D. Reader's Response: Shaping Interpretations
? Why does the boy reword his mother's statement? [Sample responses: He may want it to sound less harsh and unfriendly, or he may want to avoid hurting the man's feelings.] What does the rewording add to the story? [Sample responses: It adds an insight into the boy's character, or it adds humor.]

STRATEGIES FOR INCLUSION

Auditory One of the challenging aspects of this story for some students will be understanding the narrator's use of the Trinidad Creole form of English. In groups, students can read aloud the dialogue of B. Wordsworth and of the boy. You can suggest to students that this arrangement is not a performance of the story but a way for them to understand it better. When the student reading the boy's part comes to a statement in Creole, the group can pause and discuss what it means. As they work through the story, students will probably have to pause less frequently.

English Language Development Develop students' awareness of the varieties of English spoken around the world by focusing on the story's conversational language. Students should review the text and locate where the language diverges from usage common in the United States. Explain to students that the English spoken in Trinidad demonstrates the influence of other languages also spoken there. Encourage students to investigate the linguistic diversity of this nation as well as others nearby in the Caribbean by making a chart of the number of languages spoken in these areas. On the chart, list words from the story that show the influence of these languages.

A. Literary Element: Setting

The setting of William Wordsworth's poetry is the Lake District in the north of England. How does the tropical setting of Port-of-Spain help form B. Wordsworth's ideas about life? [Possible answer: Insects, flowers, and fruits abound in the tropical climate. B. Wordsworth has an appreciation for these things and takes the time to notice them.]

B. Critical Reading: Making Connections

? What Romantic attitudes are stressed in Naipaul's description of Wordsworth's lot? [Possible answers: A love of nature, or a dislike of modern urban life.]

C. Reader's Response: First Thoughts

? Why does looking at the sky help the boy? [Sample responses: It makes him forget his problems; or he realizes that, compared to the sky, he and his difficulties are insignificant; or he feels connected to something larger than himself.]

D. Reader's Response: Shaping Interpretations

? Why does Wordsworth want the boy to keep this information secret? [Sample responses: He may be trespassing on someone else's property; or he fears his privacy will be destroyed if others know; or perhaps it is part of his friendship with the boy.]

He said, "In this way I watch many things, and I always hope to meet poets."

I said, "You really think I is a poet?"

"You're as good as me," he said.

And when B. Wordsworth left, I prayed I would see him again.

About a week later, coming back from school one afternoon, I met him at the corner of Miguel Street.

He said, "I have been waiting for you for a long time."

I said, "You sell any poetry yet?"

He shook his head.

(A) He said, "In my yard I have the best mango tree in Port-of-Spain.[6] And now the mangoes are ripe and red and very sweet and juicy. I have waited here for you to tell you this and to invite you to come and eat some of my mangoes."

(B) He lived in Alberto Street in a one-roomed hut placed right in the center of the lot. The yard seemed all green. There was the big mango tree. There was a coconut tree and there was a plum tree. The place looked wild, as though it wasn't in the city at all. You couldn't see all the big concrete houses in the street.

He was right. The mangoes were sweet and juicy. I ate about six, and the yellow mango juice ran down my arms to my elbows and down my mouth to my chin and my shirt was stained.

My mother said when I got home, "Where you was? You think you is a man now and could go all over the place? Go cut a whip for me."

She beat me rather badly, and I ran out of the house swearing that I would never come back. I went to B. Wordsworth's house. I was so angry, my nose was bleeding.

B. Wordsworth said, "Stop crying, and we will go for a walk."

I stopped crying, but I was breathing short. We went for a walk. We walked down St. Clair Avenue to the Savannah[7] and we walked to the racecourse.

(C) B. Wordsworth said, "Now, let us lie on the grass and look up at the sky, and I want you to think how far those stars are from us."

6. Port-of-Spain: seaport on the island of Trinidad; capital of Trinidad and Tobago.

7. Savannah (sə·van′ə): two-hundred-acre park in the center of Port-of-Spain. The racecourse is located there.

1044 THE TWENTIETH CENTURY

I did as he told me, and I saw what he meant. I felt like nothing, and at the same time I had never felt so big and great in all my life. I forgot all my anger and all my tears and all the blows.

When I said I was better, he began telling me the names of the stars, and I particularly remembered the constellation of Orion the Hunter,[8] though I don't really know why. I can spot Orion even today, but I have forgotten the rest.

Then a light was flashed into our faces, and we saw a policeman. We got up from the grass.

The policeman said, "What you doing here?"

B. Wordsworth said, "I have been asking myself the same question for forty years."

We became friends, B. Wordsworth and I. He **(D)** told me, "You must never tell anybody about me and about the mango tree and the coconut tree and the plum tree. You must keep that a secret. If you tell anybody, I will know, because I am a poet."

I gave him my word and I kept it.

I liked his little room. It had no more furniture than George's front room,[9] but it looked cleaner and healthier. But it also looked lonely.

One day I asked him. "Mister Wordsworth, why you does keep all this bush in your yard? Ain't it does make the place damp?"

He said, "Listen, and I will tell you a story. Once upon a time a boy and girl met each other and they fell in love. They loved each other so much they got married. They were both poets. He loved words. She loved grass and flowers and trees. They lived happily in a single room, and then one day, the girl poet said to the boy poet, 'We are going to have another poet in the family.' But this poet was never born, because the girl died, and the young poet died with her, inside her. And the girl's husband was very sad, and he said he would

8. Orion (ō·rī′ən) **the Hunter:** constellation named for a hunter in Greek and Roman mythology whom Diana—the goddess of the moon and of hunting—loves but accidentally kills.

9. George's front room: George is a character in another story in Naipaul's book *Miguel Street*.

WORDS TO OWN
constellation (kän′stə·lā′shən) *n.*: group of stars, usually named after the object, animal, or mythological being its outline, or configuration, suggests.

INTEGRATING THE LANGUAGE ARTS

Writing: A Letter Have students write a letter from B. Wordsworth to the Romantic poet. In the letter, they can use B. Wordsworth's ideas and voice to explain why he admires William Wordsworth and how he is adapting his ideals to his own life. The letter also can compare the two characters' circumstances and poetic visions.

Strategic Reading This story is a series of episodes that are only loosely tied together through the two characters. Ask students to make a sequence chain summarizing the story. Students can use the Sequence Chart, found on Transparency 12 in the Transparency Package, to organize the narration. They also can compare their sequence chains with one another, explaining how they made their decisions.

Speaking and Listening This story is well suited for presentation as Readers' Theater. Divide the class into groups of four or five, and ask each group to turn the story into a play. They can keep the dialogue as faithful to the original as possible, and they also can turn some of the narrated portion into dialogue. Students can perform for the class or videotape their performances to watch as time permits.

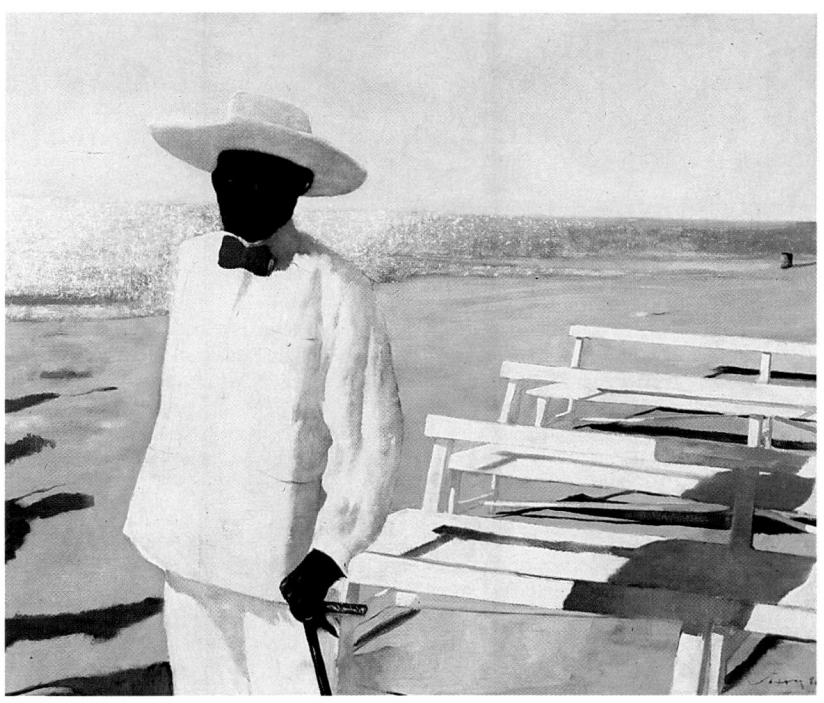

The Trial (1986) by Julio Larraz. Oil on canvas.

© Julio Larraz, courtesy Nohra Haime Gallery, New York City.

E. Literary Element: Theme

? What do Wordsworth's attitudes—so obvious to the boy—suggest about how a poet should face everyday experience? [Possible answer: A poet should bring to the day-to-day world a fresh eye and a sense of wonder or reverence.]

F. Reader's Response: Shaping Interpretations

? Why is the boy disappointed at this news? [Sample responses: The boy does not consider the news to be as significant as he thought it would be; or the boy feels that it is not news at all when a poet writes a poem.]

never touch a thing in the girl's garden. And so the garden remained, and grew high and wild."

I looked at B. Wordsworth, and as he told me this lovely story, he seemed to grow older. I understood his story.

We went for long walks together. We went to the Botanical Gardens and the Rock Gardens. We climbed Chancellor Hill in the late afternoon and watched the darkness fall on Port-of-Spain, and watched the lights go on in the city and on the ships in the harbor.

He did everything as though he were doing it for the first time in his life. He did everything as though he were doing some church rite.

He would say to me, "Now, how about having some ice cream?"

And when I said, yes, he would grow very serious and say, "Now, which café shall we patronize?" As though it were a very important thing. He would think for some time about it, and finally say, "I think I will go and negotiate the purchase with that shop."

The world became a most exciting place.

One day, when I was in his yard, he said to me, "I have a great secret which I am now going to tell you."

I said, "It really secret?"

"At the moment, yes."

I looked at him, and he looked at me. He said, "This is just between you and me, remember. I am writing a poem."

"Oh." I was disappointed.

He said, "But this is a different sort of poem. This is the greatest poem in the world."

I whistled.

He said, "I have been working on it for more than five years now. I will finish it in about twenty-two years from now, that is, if I keep on writing at the present rate."

WORDS TO OWN

botanical (bə·tan′i·kəl) *adj.*: of plants or plant life; connected to the science of botany, which is the study of plants, their structure, growth, and so on.

rite *n.*: formal ceremony.

patronize (pā′trən·īz′) *v.*: be a customer of.

V. S. NAIPAUL 1045

CROSSING THE CURRICULUM

Geography Ask students to locate Trinidad and Tobago on a map of the Caribbean. Then, ask them to enlarge the area of the islands by drawing them on a sheet of poster board. Have students indicate where Port-of-Spain and other cities are located, and have them note such geological features as mountains, rivers, and lakes. Display these maps in the classroom.

History Trinidad was once part of the British Empire. Ask students to research the history of Trinidad and to report on their findings. You can also ask them to report on the British Commonwealth of Nations. Encourage students to use one map of the world to indicate the extent of the empire and another map to indicate the extent of the Commonwealth.

PROFESSIONAL NOTES

Cultural Diversity Ask students to research the cultural diversity of Trinidad, investigating the different linguistic and religious traditions that make up the island's heritage. Have them prepare short papers that could be used to brief a traveler preparing to visit Trinidad. Have students present their papers to the class. ☞

LITERATURE AND SOCIETY

The Romantic poet William Wordsworth did his part to glorify childhood in his "Ode: Intimations of Immortality from Recollections of Early Childhood." In this poem Wordsworth says that children, freshly come from God, are surrounded by glory. As people age and get caught up in the mundane tasks of day-to-day living, the glory fades. Wordsworth pictures childhood as a state distinct from adulthood. This state fades gradually as people get older, but it leaves a significant mark on the rest of their lives. This is, of course, very different from the idea of children as miniature adults.

The Invention of Childhood

In our century, we often think of childhood as a time free of responsibilities and full of imaginative adventure. But this wasn't always so. Childhood wasn't seen as a special period until the early nineteenth century, when poets and philosophers began to idealize childhood in their writings.

Conflicting views, difficult lives. Before the Romantic period, children were seen as miniature adults. In many medieval and Renaissance paintings, children were drawn exactly as the adults were, only smaller. Until quite recently, children also lived mostly as part of an adult community: They conversed, ate, and worked with adults as soon as they were able to. If any distinction was made, it was merely that children were slightly more primitive—they required constant interaction with adults in order to be properly "civilized."

In the late eighteenth century, the French philosopher Jean Jacques Rousseau challenged this belief, dramatically proclaiming childhood to be the purest human state and society's process of "civilization" to be corrosive and corrupt. Yet upper-class European families continued to mold their children in traditional ways, and lower-class families, often reliant on every family member's contribution to the communal pot, packed their children off to work in factories as soon as they could hold a broom or thread a needle.

A. Critical Reading: Drawing Conclusions

? Why does Naipaul include the anecdote about the pin? [Possible answer: Wordsworth is experimental, and he compares the rules of the real world to the rules of the poet's idealized world.]

B. Critical Reading: Making Inferences

? What does this fact imply about Wordsworth's poetic work? [Possible answer: There really is no poem.]

Metacognition How did you arrive at your conclusion? [Possible answer: By reasoning that he would have talked more about the poem if he were really working on it.]

"You does write a lot, then?"

He said, "Not any more. I just write one line a month. But I make sure it is a good line."

I asked, "What was last month's good line?"

He looked up at the sky, and said, *"The past is deep."*

I said, "It is a beautiful line."

B. Wordsworth said, "I hope to <u>distill</u> the experiences of a whole month into that single line of poetry. So, in twenty-two years, I shall have written a poem that will sing to all humanity."

I was filled with wonder.

A Our walks continued. We walked along the sea wall at Docksite one day, and I said, "Mr. Wordsworth, if I drop this pin in the water, you think it will float?"

He said, "This is a strange world. Drop your pin, and let us see what will happen."

The pin sank.

I said, "How is the poem this month?"

B But he never told me any other line. He merely said, "Oh, it comes, you know. It comes."

Or we would sit on the sea wall and watch the liners come into the harbor.

But of the greatest poem in the world I heard no more.

I felt he was growing older.

"How you does live, Mr. Wordsworth?" I asked him one day.

He said, "You mean how I get money?"

When I nodded, he laughed in a crooked way.

WORDS TO OWN
distill (di·stil') v.: to draw out the essence of.

OPTIONS FOR TEACHING

COOPERATIVE LEARNING

Compose a Résumé Divide the class into groups of four, and ask them to compose a résumé for B. Wordsworth. Students can get most of the basic identifying information (name, address, occupation, and so on) from the story. After this, they can be creative and invent information about B. Wordsworth's education, work experience, travel, and hobbies that would ordinarily appear on a résumé. After the groups have finished their résumés, they should pass them around to share their ideas.

CLASSROOM MANAGEMENT

Block Scheduling If your school has class periods longer than fifty minutes, you might want to plan Cooperative Learning activities for the second half of the class period. Besides being a change of pace from previous activities, group work in the second half of the period gives students a chance to stand up and move to a new location as they join their groups.

Children's lives became slightly more free only as the European middle class grew and child labor laws were introduced. Still, it took some time before this new view of children—as special creatures to be nurtured and protected—took root in people's minds.

The influence of psychology, the embrace of art. The change in attitude about childhood mostly took place in the twentieth century. As psychology revolutionized the way people thought about themselves and the world, it also transformed the way society viewed children. For the first time, childhood (and its imaginative play) was seen as the foundation for a healthy, productive life.

After two bruising world wars, artists and writers also turned to childhood as a symbol of innocence. In his *Remembrance of Things Past* (1913–1927), the French writer Marcel Proust treated childhood memories as sustenance for trying and unhappy times. James Joyce and Virginia Woolf often portrayed events through a child's eye to distinguish a childlike wonder from a disappointing reality.

For many other artists, childhood also came to symbolize creativity itself. Artistic movements like surrealism sought to retrieve a childhood energy then thought absent in the world. After decades of war and cultural exhaustion, many believed an appreciation of childlike qualities—imagination, curiosity, faith—was the only way a wounded civilization might heal itself.

C. Critical Reading: Making Inferences

? In light of his poor health, what does this statement suggest about Wordsworth's poem? [Possible answers: His "poem" is really the manner in which he lives his life; or his poem is not going well because he is sick.]

D. Reader's Response: First Thoughts

? What does Wordsworth mean by the "poet's eye"? [Sample responses: He means that the boy can see things as a poet would; or that the boy has the capacity for experiencing great emotion.]

He said, "I sing calypsos in the calypso season."

"And that last you the rest of the year?"

"It is enough."

"But you will be the richest man in the world when you write the greatest poem?"

He didn't reply.

[C] One day when I went to see him in his little house, I found him lying on his little bed. He looked so old and so weak, that I found myself wanting to cry.

He said, "The poem is not going well."

He wasn't looking at me. He was looking through the window at the coconut tree, and he was speaking as though I wasn't there. He said, "When I was twenty I felt the power within myself." Then, almost in front of my eyes, I could see his face growing older and more tired. He said, "But that—that was a long time ago."

And then—I felt it so keenly, it was as though I had been slapped by my mother. I could see it clearly on his face. It was there for everyone to see. Death on the shrinking face.

He looked at me, and saw my tears and sat up.

He said, "Come." I went and sat on his knees.

He looked into my eyes, and he said, "Oh, you can see it, too. I always knew you had the poet's [D] eye."

He didn't even look sad, and that made me burst out crying loudly.

He pulled me to his thin chest, and said, "Do you want me to tell you a funny story?" and he smiled encouragingly at me.

But I couldn't reply.

He said, "When I have finished this story, I want you to promise that you will go away and never come back to see me. Do you promise?"

I nodded.

V. S. NAIPAUL 1047

PROBLEM SOLVING/ CRITICAL THINKING

Discussing Current Events Ask students to work in groups to list ten problems often discussed in the news. These can range from how to prevent pollution to how to encourage people to vote. When the list is complete, ask groups to exchange lists. When they get a new list, students should discuss how B. Wordsworth, with his poet's sensibility, would respond to the problems. Have each group report to the class on three problems from their list.

ASSESSMENT TOOLS

Check Test: True-False

1. William Wordsworth is a famous Trinidadian poet. [False]
2. B. Wordsworth asks to watch bees in the boy's yard. [True]
3. The boy's mother welcomes the man's friendship with her son. [False]
4. B. Wordsworth makes his living by singing calypsos. [True]
5. After B. Wordsworth's death, all signs of his house disappear. [True]

? What do these changes signify?
[Sample responses: The encroachment of modern urban life on nature,
the tendency of modern life to stifle
ideals, or the idea that poetry has no
lasting effect on modern life.]

Making Meanings

First Thoughts

1. B. Wordsworth is presented very
   sympathetically, so most students
   will probably like him and regret his
   death. Others might find him peculiar and point out that he lies to
   the boy.

Reviewing the Text

Students should include the following
events in their story maps: The boy
meets B. Wordsworth, the boy learns
about Wordsworth's life and his
"poem," Wordsworth becomes ill and
dies, the house and garden disappear.
B. (Black) Wordsworth is the poetic
brother of W. (White) Wordsworth.

Shaping Interpretations

2. He learns sensitivity to the world
   and begins to grasp his place in it.
3. Some students might think
   B. Wordsworth's denial of the
   story is sufficient proof that it isn't
   true. Others might think that it is
   true and that he denies it because
   it is too painful to discuss.
4. He is questioning the purpose of his
   life and of human existence in general. Many poets do seek an answer
   to this question.
5. Possible responses: Poetry involves
   observation (watching the natural
   world), enjoying experience (eating
   from the mango tree), sharing experiences, questioning, and remembering. Poetry touches all aspects of life.
6. Possible responses: The palm trees
   humming with bees, the poet's yard,
   and the clear, starry skies.
7. People like Wordsworth—people
   who looked for beauty in the
   world—may have influenced him a
   great deal. Naipaul was encouraged
   to see, feel, and remember his experiences. The last scene in the story
   suggests that the role of the poet
   includes being a witness (through
   writing), so that the things he or she
   sees will not be forgotten.

He said, "Good. Well, listen. That story I told
you about the boy poet and the girl poet, do you
remember that? That wasn't true. It was something I just made up. All this talk about poetry and
the greatest poem in the world, that wasn't true,
either. Isn't that the funniest thing you have
heard?"

But his voice broke.

I left the house, and ran home crying, like a
poet, for everything I saw.

I walked along Alberto Street a year later, but I
could find no sign of the poet's house. It hadn't
vanished, just like that. It had been pulled down,
and a big, two-storied building had taken its place.
The mango tree and the plum tree and the coconut tree had all been cut down, and there was
brick and concrete everywhere.

It was just as though B. Wordsworth had never
existed.

Papiamento (1987) by Julio Larraz. Oil on canvas.
© Julio Larraz, courtesy Nohra Haime Gallery, New York City.

MAKING MEANINGS

First Thoughts

1. How did this
   story make you
   feel about B.
   Wordsworth?
   How do you
   account for
   your reaction?

Shaping Interpretations

2. What does
   the boy learn
   from B. Words-
   worth?
3. Do you think B. Wordsworth's tragic love story
   is true? If it is true, why would he deny it?
4. Consider what B. Wordsworth says to the
   policeman who asks, "What you doing here?"
   What deeper significance do you see in his reply?
   (Is this what poets also seek to know?)

Reviewing the Text

With two other stu-
dents, devise a story
map that shows all the
important events in the
order they occurred.
Who is B. Wordsworth?
How does he explain his
connection with W.
Wordsworth, the great
nineteenth-century
Romantic poet?

5. Find some of B. Wordsworth's statements about
   poetry, and then consider the story's **theme.**
   What might Naipaul want to express about the
   nature of poetry?
6. What specific pictures of the **setting** are most
   vivid in your mind? If you were going to illustrate
   the story, what **images** would you concentrate
   on?
7. If we think of the narrator in the story as the
   author's recollection of himself at that age, what
   does the story suggest about the influences that
   made Naipaul a writer? What does it suggest
   about his view of the poet's position and role
   in society?

Connecting with the Text

8. Review your notes about poets in your Reader's
   Log. Then, find passages in the story that contrast the mother's no-nonsense ways with the
   poetic vision of B. Wordsworth. Do you find
   these two types of people in your own world?
   Explain.

OPTIONS FOR TEACHING

STRATEGIES FOR INCLUSION

Auditory As part of the Language and Style lesson, some students might benefit from hearing
passages written in the vernacular read aloud.
You can ask two or three students to prepare the
readings and perform them for the class. Students
who are adept at imitating accents might like to
try reading the passages with the pronunciation
typical of Trinidad and Tobago. There may be students in your school from the Caribbean who can
assist with this project.

Kinesthetic For the Language and Style lesson
on p. 1049, have students copy the story and highlight sections written in the vernacular. Students
can use different colors to highlight the speech
of different characters. You also can ask them to
copy the speech on strips of paper or cardboard
to work with out of the context of the rest of
the story.

LANGUAGE AND STYLE

Vernacular

The speech recorded in this story sounds unusual to people who live outside Trinidad. What we hear is the **vernacular,** or everyday speech, of people who live on the island. The Trinidad vernacular is a creole form of English, which means it incorporates idioms, pronunciations, and grammatical constructions of the island's African, Spanish, Asian Indian, and other settlers.

1. Find three conversations in the Trinidad vernacular in this story, and read them aloud to hear their special rhythm.

2. Try to make a generalization describing how this Trinidad vernacular uses verb forms.

CHOICES: Building Your Portfolio

Writer's Notebook

1. Collecting Ideas for an Informative Report

One kind of informative report traces a character's development throughout a story. What changes does the boy undergo from the beginning to the end of "B. Wordsworth"? Make a list of the changes, and list evidence from the story to support your ideas. What thesis statement, or controlling idea, could you write to express what you've determined about the boy's development? Save your work for the Writer's Workshop on page 1053.

Critical Writing

2. Seeing Things Differently

Near the end of the story, the poet pays the boy the highest of compliments, saying "I always knew you had the poet's eye." In a brief essay, explain what you think the poet's eye sees. How is poetic vision different from an everyday perspective, both in the story and in your own world?

Critical Writing

3. Heart of a Poet

Write a brief essay in which you analyze the **character** of B. Wordsworth. What is he like? Why does he call himself B. Wordsworth? Before you write, gather your details by skimming the story and filling in a chart like the following:

	Details	What They Reveal
Actions		
Speech		
Responses of others		
Appearance		
Writer's direct evaluations		

Creative Writing

4. People Portraits

Naipaul has immortalized an unusual character by describing him in words. Think of someone you have known who is unusual in some way, and write a character sketch of that person. Describe his or her home, appearance, job, personality, and actions. Be sure you show how you feel about your subject. (For help, see the Writer's Workshop on page 185.)

Social Studies / Music

5. Day-O

Find out more about calypso—its origins, developments, and influence. Present your findings in an oral report accompanied by recorded (or live) music.

Connecting with the Text

8. The mother is pragmatic; Wordsworth is a visionary. Students will probably agree that these types exist in their worlds. *Remind students to choose information they would not mind sharing.*

Language and Style
Answers

1. Possible answers include the first encounter between the boy and man, beginning with "The man said, 'I like watching bees. . . .'"; the conversation beginning with ". . . he said to me, 'I have a great secret which I am now going to tell you. . . .'"; and the one beginning with "'How you does live, Mr. Wordsworth?' I asked him one day. . . ."

2. Students' generalizations should note that the verb forms are almost always in the present tense.

Choices: Building Your Portfolio

1. **Writer's Notebook** Remind students to save their work. They may use it as prewriting for the Writer's Workshop on p. 1053.

3. **Critical Writing** One way to handle this assignment is to let students work together in groups of five. Each member of a group can be responsible for one aspect of characterization listed in the chart, and they can all share the details they uncover. You can then leave it up to each student to individually interpret what the details reveal about the character and how aspects of the character's personality relate to one another.

PORTFOLIO ASSESSMENT

Choices: Assessment Criteria For help in evaluating these Choices assignments, see the criteria in the *Portfolio Management System,* pp. 173–174.

Into the Poem

Author Biography p. 1050
Before You Read p. 1050

Through the Poem

"Mushrooms" pp. 1051–1052
Making Meanings p. 1052

Beyond the Poem

Choices: Building Your Portfolio p. 1052
- **Writer's Notebook:** List subjects for future research
- **Creative Writing:** Write a poem about a simple subject from nature

Into the Poem

Using BEFORE YOU READ p. 1050

Reading Focus

Ask students to think about the cycle of the seasons and about what happens to plant life at each phase of the cycle. Then ask them to identify other cycles. You can write a list of these cycles on the chalkboard for students to consider as they read and discuss the poem. [Some sample cycles might include sport seasons, holidays, or school years.]

Margaret Atwood

(1939–   )

Margaret Atwood (1989).

One of Canada's foremost writers, Margaret Atwood was born in Ottawa and now lives in Toronto. Her often bizarre short stories appear frequently in *The New Yorker* and have been collected in *Dancing Girls* (1977) and *Bluebeard's Egg* (1983). Her many novels often feature unusual heroines, like the daughter of the wilderness in *Surfacing* (1972) and the highwaywoman in *The Robber Bride* (1993). Atwood also frequently explores the problems of living in an increasingly technological—and often alien—environment. Her 1986 novel *The Handmaid's Tale* is a nightmarish vision of a future dictatorship in which women are used chiefly for breeding purposes.

Atwood's father was an expert on insects, and as a child, Atwood spent a good part of each year with her parents in the wilderness. Consequently, she developed a keen eye for nature, as her poem "Mushrooms" demonstrates. In speaking about her poems, Atwood once said, "I don't think of poetry as a 'rational' activity but as an aural one. My poems usually begin with words or phrases which appeal more because of their sound than their meaning, and the movement and phrasing of a poem are very important to me."

BEFORE YOU READ

MUSHROOMS

Reading Focus
The Cycle of Life
A curious property of the imagination is its power to expand upon the most ordinary subjects. The growth and decay of a common plant, for example, can trigger reflections about the arc of human life or the vast, seemingly unending cycle of birth and death in nature at large.

Quickwrite

What do you associate with mushrooms? Before you read this poem, jot down a few notes in your Reader's Log.

Elements of Literature
Free Verse
You will notice striking imagery and hear sound effects in Atwood's poem, but you will not hear the regular repetition of stressed and unstressed syllables we call meter. That is because "Mushrooms" is written in **free verse,** poetry that does not use regular meter or a fixed rhyme scheme. To create music, free verse poems use devices like internal rhyme, alliteration, assonance, and onomatopoeia. Rhythm is created by the use of irregular line lengths and repeated grammatical structures.

PROGRAM MANAGER

- **Planning Instruction** See Teaching Notes, *Teaching Resources B,* p. 137, for objectives, a summary, major literary elements, and additional information for this selection.
- **Instructional Support** Before beginning the instructional lesson, see Graphic Organizer for Active Reading, *Teaching Resources B,* p. 158, for a Through the Poem activity.
- **Audiotaped Readings** To help less proficient readers or auditory learners through the lesson, use the Selected Reading, Audiocassette 3, Side A, in the *Audiovisual Resources Binder.*
- **Assessment** See Selection Test, *Test Booklet,* p. 223.

Mushrooms A

Margaret Atwood

i

In this moist season,
mist on the lake and thunder
afternoons in the distance

they ooze up through the earth
5 during the night,
like bubbles, like tiny
bright red balloons
filling with water;
a sound below sound, the thumbs of rubber
10 gloves turned softly inside out.

In the mornings, there is the leaf mold
starred with nipples,
with cool white fishgills,
leathery purple brains,
15 fist-sized suns dulled to the color of embers,
poisonous moons, pale yellow.

ii

Where do they come from?

For each thunderstorm that travels
overhead there's another storm
20 that moves parallel in the ground.
Struck lightning is where they meet.

Underfoot there's a cloud of rootlets,
shed hairs or a bundle of loose threads
blown slowly through the midsoil.
25 These are their flowers, these fingers
reaching through darkness to the sky,
these eyeblinks
that burst and powder the air with spores.

iii

They feed in shade, on halfleaves
30 as they return to water,
on slowly melting logs,
deadwood. They glow
in the dark sometimes. They taste
of rotten meat or cloves
35 or cooking steak or bruised
lips or new snow.

MARGARET ATWOOD 1051

Through the Poem

A. Literary Connection
Sylvia Plath wrote a poem of the same title, in which the mushrooms are the speakers.

B. Literary Element: Free Verse
Identify some of the literary elements included in this example of free verse. [Possible answers: Assonance weaves sound throughout the poem; for example, the *oo* sound appears repeatedly. Alliteration appears in ll. 1–3 (the *s* sounds), 16, and 25, among others.]

C. Critical Reading: Analyzing Figurative Language
? What is the speaker referring to when speaking of *nipples, fishgills, brains, suns,* and *moons*? [Possible answer: The shapes of different kinds of mushrooms.]

D. Reader's Response: Extending the Text
? Does the metaphor comparing the roots of mushrooms to a storm blown through the soil make sense? Why or why not? [Sample responses: No, it is too fanciful because a storm cloud can't blow through solid soil; or yes, the delicate white root tissue reminds me of clouds.]

E. Critical Reading: Analyzing Figurative Language
? What does the speaker mean by "melting logs"? [Possible answer: Decaying logs slowly crumble as though they were melting.]

OPTIONS FOR TEACHING

STRATEGIES FOR INCLUSION

Visual You can suggest that students use a chart like the following one to list sensory images in the poem. Transparency 7: Sensory Details Chart in the Transparency Package may be useful.

Sense	Image
Sight	
Hearing	
Smell	
Touch	
Taste	

Auditory Part of the pleasure of this poem arises from its sound. You can read the poem aloud for the class, or you can assign an oral reading to several students. In either case, the reading should emphasize the onomatopoeic qualities of words like *moist, mist, thunder, ooze, bubbles, balloons*. If you assign the reading to students, you might want to demonstrate how to emphasize the onomatopoeic qualities that students might not otherwise identify in words.

Making Meanings

First Thoughts

1. Students may find the images in ll. 4–16 quite compelling. Most will probably say that the more unusual and surprising an image is, the better it is.

Shaping Interpretations

2. Examples of assonance include *flower* and *powder* in ll. 25 and 28; *feed* and *leaves* in l. 29. Examples of alliteration can be found in l. 7 and in l. 25, among others. In the first section, prepositional phrases using *in* begin two of the stanzas, and in l. 6 the repetition of *like* creates a rhythm.

3. The *b* sound.

4. "Soil enriched by decayed leaves."

5. Make sure that students refer to the text as they discuss the photograph. Comparisons may include tables, cushions, buttons.

6. The cycle of birth, death, and regeneration.

7. It appeals to sight, as in the reference to suns, embers, and pale yellow moons (ll. 15–16); it appeals to hearing and touch, as in the reference to balloons that are being filled (ll. 7–9) and through the choice of such words as *softly* (l. 10) and *leathery* (l. 14). There is a vivid appeal to taste in ll. 33–36 and to smell in ll. 40–42.

8. Students should see that Atwood's metaphor is clearest in these lines. The mushrooms suggest decay because they feed on decaying matter and eventually decay themselves; however, their sudden renewal suggests hope. They suggest mouthfuls of dirt because they are nourished in soil (and perhaps because some varieties have an earthy taste). They may suggest poetry because they embody bright and dark aspects of existence and because they may be either food or poison.

Challenging the Text

9. **(Evaluation)** Possible responses: Mushrooms pop up overnight, much as poems are thought to "pop" into the minds of poets; the process of the birth, death, and regeneration of mushrooms, as well as the mushrooms themselves, is aesthetically pleasing, just as a poem is.

---

iv

It isn't only
for food I hunt them
but for the hunt and because
40 they smell of death and the waxy
skins of the newborn,
flesh into earth into flesh.

Here is the handful
of shadow I have brought back to you:
45 this decay, this hope, this mouthful of dirt, this poetry.

MAKING MEANINGS

First Thoughts

1. What do you feel is the poem's strongest **image**? Why?

Shaping Interpretations

2. Read the poem aloud. What uses of **assonance** and **alliteration** help create its music? Where do repeated grammatical structures help create a **rhythm**?

3. In lines 6–10, what repeated consonant suggests the sound of the fingers of rubber gloves turning inside out?

4. "Leaf mold" can be defined as "soil enriched by decayed leaves" or "mold that grows on leaves." Which definition applies in line 11?

5. In lines 6–16, the poet describes various kinds of mushrooms, some against the background of leaf mold. Which mushrooms in the photographs on page 1051 would you match up with Atwood's descriptions? After you review your Reader's Log notes, think up a **metaphor** of your own for each of the photographs.

6. What biological process does line 42 refer to?

7. What senses does the poem appeal to? Quote examples from the poem.

8. Explain the poem's last four lines. How could mushrooms suggest decay, hope, mouthfuls of dirt, and poetry?

Mushrooms (*Hygrophorus miniatus*).

Challenging the Text

9. Explain the poem's **extended metaphor** in your own words. In your view, how effective is it?

CHOICES:
Building Your Portfolio

Writer's Notebook
1. Collecting Ideas for an Informative Report

Atwood's clinical and unsentimental poem certainly shows that she knows a great deal about mushrooms. Brainstorm to develop a list of subjects from the natural world—animal, vegetable, or mineral—that you want to know more about. Save your notes for use in the Writer's Workshop on page 1053.

Creative Writing
2. Poetry of the Everyday

Choose a simple subject from nature such as butterflies, lions, sand, or worms. What sounds do you associate with your subject? List words that have these sounds and also have some meaning associated with your subject. Then, use these words in a four- or five-line **free verse** poem about your subject. Try to include sensory images.

Beyond the Poem

Choices: Building Your Portfolio

1. **Writer's Notebook** Remind students to save their work. They may use it as prewriting for the Writers Workshop on p. 1053.

PORTFOLIO ASSESSMENT

Choices: Assessment Criteria For help in evaluating these Choices assignments, see the criteria in the *Portfolio Management System,* p. 175.

Writer's Workshop

The history of the written word is rich a

Page 1

EXPOSITORY WRITING

INFORMATIVE REPORT

In "Araby," James Joyce uses his extraordinary imagination to transform his native city into a fictional setting. Yet Joyce's writing was also firmly grounded in his comprehensive knowledge of Dublin. In this Writer's Workshop you'll write an informative report about something *you* know well. In the process, you'll use skills fundamental to other types of writing as you collect, synthesize, and organize information.

Prewriting

1. **Checking your Writer's Notebook.** By doing the Writer's Notebook activities in Collections 12 and 13, you've already begun the prewriting for an informative report. Check through your entries for usable material and ideas; then proceed with the prewriting activities that follow.

2. **Searching for subjects.** Nearly any subject can lend itself to an informative report, as long as you can answer "Yes" to the following four questions:

   • Does it interest you?

   • Do you know something about it already?

   • Will it interest your particular audience (in this case, your classmates)?

   • Can you put together enough information to write about the subject clearly and accurately?

   Begin your search by taking five to ten minutes to brainstorm for possible subjects that meet these four requirements. Here's the list one writer came up with:

WORK IN PROGRESS

Model

> in-line skating
> volunteering at the animal shelter
> stream of consciousness—Joyce, Woolf, Faulkner, others?
> Rolling Stones retrospective
> Maya Angelou's poem for Clinton's 1993 inauguration
> stepfamilies
> computer-animated cartoons
> Walt Disney

Technology HELP

See Writer's Workshop 2 CD-ROM. *Assignment: Informative Report.*

ASSIGNMENT
Write a factual report sharing information on a subject.

AIM
To inform your readers.

AUDIENCE
Your classmates or other people interested in your subject.

WRITER'S WORKSHOP 1053

QUICK PLANNING GUIDE

WW

Informative Report

Prewriting
Checking your Writer's Notebook **p. 1053**
Searching for subjects **p. 1053**
Model **p. 1053**
Choosing a subject **p. 1054**
Exploring what you know **p. 1054**
Analyzing your audience **p. 1054**
Gathering information **p. 1055**
Developing your thesis **p. 1055**
Organizing your support **p. 1055**

Drafting
The introduction: inviting them in **p. 1056**
The body: escorting them through **p. 1056**
The conclusion: showing them out **p. 1056**

Evaluating and Revising
Peer review **p. 1057**
Self-evaluation **p. 1057**

Proofreading and Publishing p. 1057

Reflecting on Your Writing p. 1057

Motivation

Ask students to write on a piece of scrap paper one activity they enjoy and to be as specific as possible. For example, if a student suggests reading as a favorite activity, ask the student to specify what kind of material he or she likes to read—spy novels, sports magazines, computer books, and so on. Then, ask several volunteers to share their activities, and write these on the chalkboard. Point out that students probably already know a good bit about the activities they enjoy and that they could probably write about them without extensive research. Ask the class to indicate by a show of hands how many would find a paper about each activity interesting. Suggest that students consider the activities listed on the chalkboard as potential topics for an informative report. Also, point out that students will learn techniques in this Writer's Workshop that can help them make their reports clearer and more interesting.

PROGRAM MANAGER

Computer Guided Instruction
For a related informative report assignment that students may use as additional instruction, see *Writer's Workshop 2.*

PORTFOLIO ASSESSMENT

• **Generating Ideas** To help students in prewriting, use the heuristic in the *Portfolio Management System,* p. 176.
• **Rubric Assessment** For rubric that can be used to assess students' progress in writing, see the *Portfolio Management System,* p. 178.

Teaching the Lesson

- Lead students to see that memorable informative writing results from a combination of an interesting topic and an interesting method of presentation.
- Explain that in this assignment, students will share information about an interesting topic (or a topic that they make interesting through their method of presentation).
- This lesson includes instructions for each stage of the writing process. Guide students by modeling each stage with your own writing.

Try It Out: Answers

Responses will vary. Here are some guidelines and possible responses.

1. Any specific contemporary writer will serve as a suitable subject, such as Toni Morrison, Larry McMurtry, Amy Tan, and so on.
2. Any specific part-time job will serve as a suitable subject. Some possibilities include working in a fast-food restaurant, working as a clerk in a clothing store, and working as a bagger in a grocery store.
3. Subjects related to computers should probably deal with the kinds of tasks computers can perform, rather than different makes or models of computers. Subjects can include word processing, games, exploring the Internet, or producing desktop publishing documents.

3. **Choosing a subject.** Look at the subjects you've listed, and circle the two or three subjects that most appeal to you. Then write a few sentences telling how you might approach each subject. If some of your subjects are broad ones, such as "music," analyze them (break them down into parts or aspects) to determine how to make them more manageable for a short report. In analyzing "music," for example, you might come up with "jazz," "alternative rock," or "reggae." Also, check to see whether any of your subjects suggest a comparison/contrast approach. If you jotted down "stream of consciousness—Joyce, Woolf, Faulkner, others?" for example, you might decide to compare and contrast Joyce's and Woolf's use of the technique. Another possibility is to see whether two (or more) of your subjects suggest an approach. If two of your entries are "computer-animated cartoons" and "Walt Disney," for example, combining them into "Walt Disney's computer-animated cartoons" would make a more manageable subject than either one on its own.

   In choosing a subject, keep in mind that your purpose is to inform—not to describe, persuade, evaluate, or speculate about causes and effects. Check to make sure that the subject you select is one you can approach in an objective, impartial way.

4. **Exploring what you know.** To find out what you already know about your subject, you might simply list facts and examples in the order they occur to you. (Using the *5W-How?* questions—*Who? What? When? Where? Why?* and *How?*—can help you brainstorm.) Or you might create a cluster diagram like this one:

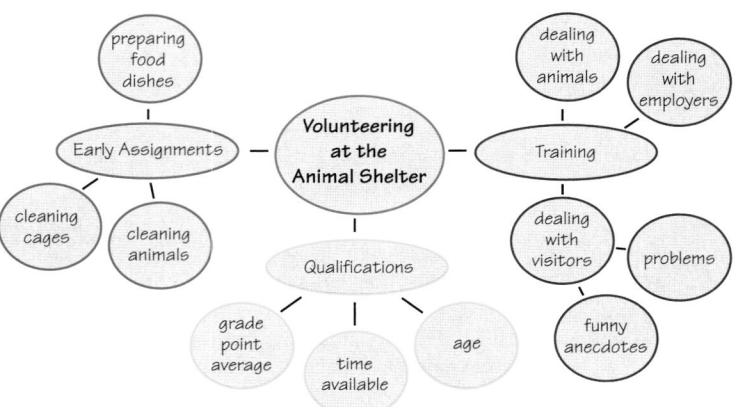

5. **Analyzing your audience.** Before you go on, stop to think about the audience you plan to share the information with. Jot down answers to these questions:

   - What do they already know about the subject?
   - What might they like to learn about the subject?
   - What background information will they need?
   - What terms will I need to define or explain?

Visual Students who are writing comparison/contrast reports might find it useful to display the organization of their reports graphically, using one of the following models:

Point-by-Point Method

Introduction

Point 1
Subject A
Subject B

STRATEGIES FOR INCLUSION

Point 2
Subject A
Subject B

Point 3
Subject A
Subject B

Conclusion

Block Method

Introduction

Subject A
Point 1
Point 2
Point 3

Subject B
Point 1
Point 2
Point 3

Conclusion

Analyzing your audience in this way will help you settle on an appropriate tone for your report, one that makes you sound knowledgeable and authoritative rather than pompous and pretentious. It will also help you decide whether you already have enough information or whether you need more.

6. **Gathering information.** Specific, interesting details are what make the difference between a so-so report and a spirited one. If you find that you need more information—facts and statistics, examples, sensory details, or perhaps an anecdote or two—to fulfill your purpose and to intrigue your audience, now is the time to track it down.

Strategies for Elaboration: Crediting Sources

Although you're not writing a formal research paper for this Writer's Workshop, you do need to acknowledge your sources when you use someone else's words or ideas. Otherwise, you'll be committing plagiarism. Use these guidelines to help you decide when to give credit to your sources.

Information you must credit:
- quotations, unless they're widely known, such as Patrick Henry's "Give me liberty or give me death."
- one-of-a-kind or little-known information, such as data from scientific studies, surveys, and polls
- any original theory, opinion, or conclusion, even if you summarize or paraphrase it

Information you needn't credit:
- facts from standard reference works or multiple sources, such as the birth and death dates of James Joyce
- general information, such as the fact that a well-balanced diet is essential for sound nutrition

---

7. **Developing your thesis.** Look over the material you've gathered, and write one or two sentences stating the main idea you want your readers to take away from your report. The **thesis,** or **controlling idea,** should identify the subject and the focus of your report and suggest your purpose. Since it will point the way for your readers, make it as clear and specific as you can; but remember that you can always revise it later, if you need to.

8. **Organizing your support.** Clearly presenting the information you've gathered to support your thesis is essential for your readers. The wording of your thesis may suggest a natural order for your supporting material. For example, if your thesis focuses on three significant events in Dylan Thomas's childhood, you might group details about each of the events together and present them in **order of importance.** For a thesis that compares two part-time jobs, you could use the **block method,** presenting first the features of one job and then those of the other. Or you could use the **point-by-point method,** discussing one feature at a time, first for one job and then for the other. (The same two methods can be used with a thesis stressing differences or for one balancing likenesses and differences.) For a

Communications Handbook
H E L P

Using resources: page 1210.

Communications Handbook
H E L P

Documenting sources: page 1212.

Prewriting

After students have selected a topic, ask them to clear it with you to make sure that it is suitable for a short report. Then, work with those students who have selected broad, general topics, such as sports or dancing, to make them very specific. In general, tell students that if their topics deal with a group of activities or objects, they should consider writing about only one or two members of the group.

Since the audience for the report is the class, encourage students to ask several classmates if they would be interested in reading about the subjects. See the Speaking and Listening feature below for a more detailed activity.

INTEGRATING THE LANGUAGE ARTS

Speaking and Listening Have students conduct informal oral surveys of classmates to determine whether their subjects are interesting to others in the class and to find out how much others already know about the subject. Ask students to prepare two or three questions ahead of time and to write these down for use during their interviews. Make a point of encouraging students to listen carefully to the responses of the students they interview and to write their notes after the other students have finished speaking.

Vocabulary Some students might find it necessary to use technical terms that will require definitions. Help students recognize these terms by discussing with the class what constitutes a technical term in a particular subject. Point out that some technical terms are drawn from standard vocabulary but take on technical meanings in a particular context. If students are not sure whether a term requires a definition or not, encourage them to ask another student if he or she knows the term's meaning. If the other student does not know what the term means in the context in which it will be used, the writer should define it in the report.

Drafting

- Help students distinguish between the importance of a personal style and the need to keep personal opinions out of writing whose main purpose is to inform.
- Although students will be doing most of their drafting outside class, provide some in-class time for writing. Move among students as they work, answering questions and offering advice.
- Encourage students to keep a journal as they draft, noting such things as research techniques that are proving effective and trouble spots for which they might seek advice from you or a classmate.
- If you have saved reports of this kind from other classes or from students in previous years, consider sharing the best of these to serve as models.
- If computers are available, encourage students to use them to write their drafts. Make sure they print hard copies of their drafts to use during the next phases of the writing process.

Evaluating and Revising

Encourage students to use the questions in the Evaluation Criteria box as they read and evaluate their own reports and those of other students. Also, have students give their drafts a separate review for varied sentence structure, which is the focus of the Language Workshop in this Collection (p. 1058). Remind them that everything in the report should be weighed for clarity and interest.

Proofreading and Publishing

Remind students that careful proofreading can make their reports easier to read and more interesting to their audience by eliminating errors and other problems, such as omitted words. Students can probably suggest ways of publishing their work. If your school has an Internet connection, consider having students publish their reports by posting them to appropriate sites on the World Wide Web or to Usenet news-groups. *You may want to preview any internet activity that you suggest to students. Because these resources are sometimes public forums, their content can be unpredictable.*

Language Workshop
H E L P

Effective sentences: page 1058.

Language Workshop
H E L P

Effective transitions: page 464.

---

thesis focusing on change over time, such as one on computer advances in animation, you could use **chronological order.** Experiment until you find the arrangement that best suits your thesis and illustrates the relationships between your ideas.

Drafting

1. **The introduction: inviting them in.** Draw your readers in by grabbing their attention so that they'll want to read on to learn more. In setting the tone, try to sound objective, authoritative, and genuinely interested in sharing information about your subject; in an informative report, it's important for you to convey a knowledgeable stance. Be sure to include a thesis statement that identifies both your subject and your main idea about it.

2. **The body: escorting them through.** Devote a paragraph or two to each of your key points, including enough details to help readers understand and remember each point. Try to pace the details in such a way that readers aren't left feeling either overwhelmed or shortchanged. Where possible, use vivid images that will help them picture the information. Introduce sentence variety to keep your readers interested.

> ### Strategies for Elaboration: Keeping Your Ideas Clear
>
> You don't want your readers to misunderstand the gist of your report. To help keep your ideas clear, incorporate definitions and connections between ideas.
>
> **Definitions.** If you use a term or concept that probably isn't familiar to your readers, include a brief definition. First identify the large group or class to which it belongs (A *plié* is "a ballet movement . . ."). Then identify features that distinguish the term or concept from all others in its class (". . . in which the back is held straight and the knees are bent outward").
>
> **Connections.** In addition to arranging your ideas so that they're easy to follow, you can connect ideas within and between paragraphs with **direct references** and **transitional expressions.** Direct references refer to, repeat, or provide a synonym for a word or phrase used earlier. Transitional expressions show *how* ideas are connected. Since different transitional expressions indicate different relationships—time, space, or comparison/contrast, for example—it's important to choose such expressions carefully.

3. **The conclusion: showing them out.** In your conclusion, refocus on the main idea in your introduction, giving readers a sense that you've taken them where you said you would and that their time has been well spent.

1056 THE TWENTIETH CENTURY

OPTIONS FOR TEACHING

Self-Assessment Use the following criteria to evaluate the informative report.

1=Strong   2=Satisfactory   3=Weak

___ Identified subject and clearly stated main idea about it

___ Supported main idea and key points with enough relevant facts, examples, and other details

ASSESSMENT TOOLS

___ Organized information so that ideas are easy to follow

___ Provided enough direct references and transitional expressions to enable readers to follow ideas

___ Established and maintained an objective, authoritative tone

___ Concluded report by refocusing on main idea

Evaluating and Revising

1. **Peer review.** When you review a classmate's report, comment on these points:

   - **Thesis.** Does the writer include a controlling idea that identifies the subject and the focus of the report? Is the thesis clear and specific? If not, how might it be improved?

   - **Support.** Does the writer provide enough details to make the thesis and the key points clear? If not, what questions did the writer leave unanswered? What kinds of details might answer those questions?

   - **Organization.** Does the organization seem suitable for the content and the writer's thesis? Are the ideas clearly connected with direct references and transitional expressions? If not, at which points would additional connections help?

   - **Tone.** Does the writer come across as knowledgeable and authoritative about the subject? Does the writer seem committed to sharing the information rather than merely resigned to completing an assignment?

2. **Self-evaluation.** As you evaluate and revise your report, take your reviewer's comments into account. Remember, though, that the final decisions are yours: Make the changes *you* think will best help you share information on your subject. As you evaluate your paper, underline each point you've included to support your thesis. Then put a check mark next to the facts, examples, or other details you've included to explain each point. If supporting details are missing, add information to strengthen your points.

Proofreading and Publishing

When you've completed your final draft, proofread it carefully. An error-free paper will contribute to the perception that you are knowledgeable and authoritative about your subject. You and your classmates might read your reports to one another or to another class, submit them to the school newspaper, or compile them into a booklet for other English classes to browse through.

Reflecting on Your Writing

To include this informative report in your portfolio, date it and write a brief reflection on your writing experience. Ask yourself:

1. Are you pleased with your choice of a subject and approach, or do you wish you had pursued another subject (or the same subject in a different way)? Why?

2. Did any of your reviewer's comments surprise you? If so, which ones? Did you anticipate any of the comments? Which ones?

3. Do you think that writing this report will help you? Why or why not?

❚ *Evaluation Criteria*

An effective informative report

1. *clearly identifies the subject and the writer's thesis, or controlling idea, about the subject*
2. *supports the thesis and the writer's key points with relevant facts, examples, and other details*
3. *organizes the information so that the writer's ideas are easy to follow*
4. *includes enough direct references and transitional expressions to enable readers to follow the writer's ideas*
5. *establishes and maintains an objective, authoritative tone*
6. *concludes by refocusing on the writer's thesis*

**Revision
STRATEGIES**

Are the ideas within and between your paragraphs clearly connected? If not, add direct references or transitional expressions.

Portfolio

Reflecting on Your Writing

Have students use the questions in the text as a basis for their reflection. They may write answers to the questions and attach these to their reports when they file the reports in their portfolios, or they may write a paragraph based on one or more of the questions to include with their reports. Also, ask students to suggest additional questions that might focus their thinking as they reflect on their experience of writing the report.

Closure

When students have finished the final versions of their reports, ask them to summarize in a paragraph or in a list the steps they followed in writing their reports. Have volunteers share their ideas with the rest of the class, and note any unusual steps or processes by writing them on the chalkboard. Make a running list of ideas that students may refer to during other assignments, especially ideas about prewriting activities that are out of the ordinary.

Extension

Many TV news features are essentially reports that inform viewers about activities or ideas that are topical or unusual. Bring to class videotapes of several of these stories and ask students to watch them. Then, have students apply the Evaluation Criteria and the questions under Peer review to the stories to determine how well the stories follow the form of the informative report.

CLASSROOM MANAGEMENT

Using Computers for Drafting If the number of computers your students have available for drafting their reports is limited and you want them to have the experience of writing a draft on a computer, organize a system to make it possible for every student to have an opportunity to use the computer. Identify a small group of students who will be expected to produce a draft on the computer for each assignment. Then, stagger the due date for the members of that group. For example, if you have two computers in your classroom, have six students produce computer-generated drafts. Two students' drafts would be due the first day, two more the second day, and two more the third day.

PROGRAM MANAGER

Modeling or Practicing Revision To summarize and model the revision process, and to provide student practice, use **Revision Transparencies 13.7–13.8** in the *Audiovisual Resources Binder*.

Language Workshop

Language Workshop
Connecting to Students' Writing

Have students select a piece of writing from their portfolios. Ask them to read the piece carefully and to rewrite sentences, varying the structures.

Try It Out: Answers

Responses will vary. Here is an example of how the paragraph can be rewritten to vary sentence patterns.

One of the most notable features of James Joyce's later works is the stream-of-consciousness technique. In his auto-biographical novel *A Portrait of the Artist as a Young Man,* Joyce used the technique to reveal the thought processes of Stephen Dedalus.

PROGRAM MANAGER

- **Extra Practice and Guided Instruction** For more instruction and practice of sentence variety, see **Language Workshop** in *Teaching Resources B,* pp. 159–160.
- **Extra Practice or Guided Instruction** See *Language Workshop:* **Sentence Variety** for more practice or guided instruction in sentence structures.

Technology HELP

See Language Workshop CD-ROM. *Key word entry: sentence style.*

Language Handbook HELP

Revising for variety: page 1238.

Try It Out

Revise the following paragraph, varying the length and word order of some of the sentences.

James Joyce's stream-of-consciousness technique is one of the most notable features of his later works. Joyce used the technique in his auto-biographical novel *A Portrait of the Artist as a Young Man* (1916). It reveals the thought processes of Stephen Dedalus.

EFFECTIVE SENTENCES: THE VALUE OF VARIETY

When you're reporting on a subject that truly interests you, the last thing you want to do is bore your readers with monotonous writing. Varying the length and word order of your sentences can help you create lively, energetic paragraphs that encourage readers to keep reading.

One way to maintain interest is to intersperse an occasional short sentence among longer ones. Imaginative writers know the value of this technique, too, as Margaret Atwood's poem "Mushrooms" (page 1051) illustrates. Atwood devotes a total of seventy-six words to the two sentences that make up the first section of the poem. As the second section begins, the pace abruptly shifts: "Where do they come from?"

Another technique is to vary the subject-first order that is normal in English sentences. By beginning some sentences with an introductory element—an appositive, a single-word modifier, or a phrase or clause modifier—you can not only add emphasis but also clarify the logical connections between sentences. Notice how D. H. Lawrence uses this technique:

> He went off by himself, vaguely, in a childish way, seeking for the clue to "luck." **Absorbed, taking no heed of other people,** he went about with a sort of stealth, seeking inwardly for luck. He wanted luck, he wanted it, he wanted it. **When the two girls were playing dolls in the nursery,** he would sit on his big rocking horse, charging madly into space, with a frenzy that made the little girls peer at him uneasily. **Wildly** the horse careered, the waving dark hair of the boy tossed, his eyes had a strange glare in them. The little girls dared not speak to him.
>
> —*from* "The Rocking-Horse Winner"

By using the different introductory elements indicated in boldface type, Lawrence sets up a fast pace in the paragraph, in which the rhythm of the sentence structures mirrors the action of the story. He helps us want to keep reading.

Writer's Workshop Follow-up: Revision

Look back at the informative report you wrote for the Writer's Workshop on page 1053. Select one paragraph in the body to focus on. Underline the subject of each sentence in this paragraph. Do you ever depart from normal word order by not placing the subject first in each sentence? What sentences could you revise to introduce some sentence variety? Are there any places in the paragraph where a short sentence would create unexpected interest for the reader? Then look at the other paragraphs in your informative paper to see where else you might make revisions to improve sentence variety.

✔ QUICK CHECK: Effective Sentences

Rewrite the following sentences to vary them from the originals.

[1] Joyce uses a hodgepodge of ideas thrown together with no apparent order in the opening section of *A Portrait of the Artist as a Young Man* to create a picture of the mind of a young child. [Possible answers: **a.** Using a hodgepodge of ideas thrown together with no apparent order in the opening section of *A Portrait of the Artist as a Young Man,* Joyce creates a picture of the mind of a young child. **b.** To create a picture of the mind of a young child, Joyce uses a hodgepodge of ideas thrown together with no apparent order in the opening section of *A Portrait of the Artist as a Young Man.*]

[2] In the final chapter of *A Portrait of the Artist as a Young Man,* Joyce includes a detailed philosophical discussion of aesthetics. [Possible answers: **a.** A detailed philosophical discussion of aesthetics fills the final chapter of *A Portrait of the Artist as a Young Man.* **b.** The final chapter of *A Portrait of the Artist as a Young Man* contains a detailed philosophical discussion of aesthetics.]

| Collection 14 | OURSELVES AMONG OTHERS |

Theme:

A Place in the World

This Collection highlights the individual's struggle to adapt to the world and to other people. In addition, the selections address the universality of the human spirit that transcends class distinctions and misunderstandings.

Thematic Focus

We are alone, yet we are not alone.

- **The Doll's House**   A novelty emphasizes the mean-spiritedness of a class system.
- **The Ring**   A sheltered bride encounters a stranger who changes her perspective.
- **Not Waving but Drowning**   Appearances may deceive.
- **My Oedipus Complex**   This compassionate narrative of a child's adjustment to his father's return is filled with humor and dramatic irony.
- **Musée des Beaux Arts/The Unknown Citizen**   These poems focus on indifference to individual fate.
- **The Myth of Sisyphus**   The individual who accepts the absurdity of life achieves a kind of victory.
- **Games at Twilight**   One child overcomes fear but faces a hard realization.
- **Digging**   The speaker relates his occupation to the work of his forebears.

Literary Focus

Literary Element	Selection / Feature
Symbol	**The Doll's House**
Dramatic Irony	**My Oedipus Complex**
Diction	**Musée des Beaux Arts/ The Unknown Citizen**
Imagery	**Games at Twilight**
Extended Metaphor	**Digging**

Writing Focus

The following flowchart shows how the writing assignment for each selection relates to the writing assignment presented in the Writer's Workshop at the end of the unit.

Selection	Work-in-Progress Assignment
The Doll's House	Discuss solutions to peer pressure p. 1069
Not Waving but Drowning	Freewrite ideas for helping others p. 1079
My Oedipus Complex	Generate ideas for student retention p. 1090
Musée des Beaux Arts/ The Unknown Citizen	Discuss causes and effects p. 1097
Games at Twilight	Collect ideas for curriculum p. 1117
Digging	Discuss various occupations p. 1120
Writer's Workshop	Write a problem-solution essay. pp. 1179–1185

Collection Planner

SELECTION / FEATURE	Literary Elements / Active Reading	Writing	Speaking and Listening	Language and Vocabulary
The Doll's House Katherine Mansfield (pp. 1060–1069) Primary Sources: Katherine Mansfield: On Being a Writer (p. 1066) **Connections: Sisters** Rita Dove (p. 1067)	• Reader's Log p. 1061 • Symbol p. 1061 • Realism/Dramatic irony pp. 1068–1069	• Critical Writing: Write essay analyzing effectiveness of Mansfield's use of omniscient point of view p. 1069 • Creative Writing: Collaborate to begin updated story based on this selection p. 1069		
World Literature: The Ring Isak Dinesen (pp. 1070–1076)	• Reader's Log p. 1071		• Finding Common Ground: Discuss story with other students p. 1076	
Not Waving but Drowning Stevie Smith (pp. 1077–1079) Primary Sources: The Truths About Poetry (p. 1079)	• Reader's Log p. 1077	• Critical Writing: Write essay explaining the sea as metaphor for life and death p. 1079		
My Oedipus Complex Frank O'Connor (pp. 1080–1090)	• Reader's Log p. 1081 • Dramatic Irony p. 1081	• Critical Writing: Write essay analyzing author's intention in this story p. 1090 • Critical Writing: Write essay about hero of this selection and hero of "Araby" p. 1090 • Creative Writing: Write humorous biographical essay p. 1090		
Musée des Beaux Arts/ The Unknown Citizen W. H. Auden (pp. 1091–1097) Spotlight On: Contemporary British Drama (pp. 1098–1103)	• Reader's Log p. 1092 • Diction p. 1092	• Critical Writing: Write essay relating myth to Auden's poem p. 1097 • Critical Writing: Write about Bruegel's painting and Auden's interpretation p. 1097 • Critical Writing: Write analysis of Auden's satire p. 1097 • Creative Writing: Write poem, essay, or short story inspired by art or music p. 1097 • Creative Writing: Write obituary from friend's point of view p. 1097 • Creative Writing: Write epitaph for unknown person p. 1097		

Collection Resources

Teaching Resources B	Audiovisual Resources Binder	Test Booklet
Cross-Curricular Activity p. 184	Fine Art Transparency 14.1	Collection 14 Test pp. 237–239

 Computer disk or CD-ROM

 Audiocassette

 Overhead Transparency

PROGRAM RESOURCES

Electronic Media	Teaching Resources with Organizer		Audiovisual Resources Binder
	Teaching Resources B	Other Resources	
• Language Workshop: Transitional expressions • Test Generator	• Teaching Notes p. 163 • Reading Organizer p. 168 • Language Link pp. 169–170 • Words to Own p. 171	• Test Booklet: Selection Test pp. 227–228 • Portfolio Management System pp. 39, 62–63, 179 • Language and Writing Skills Worksheets p. 198	• Elements of Literature Transparency 14.2 • Selected Readings Audiocassette 3, Side A
	• Teaching Notes pp. 163–164		
• Test Generator	• Teaching Notes p. 164 • Reading Organizer p. 172	• Test Booklet: Selection Test p. 229 • Portfolio Management System p. 180	• Selected Readings Audiocassette 3, Side A
• Language Workshop: Sentence style • Language Workshop: Dialogue • Test Generator	• Teaching Notes pp. 164–165 • Reading Organizer p. 173 • Language Link pp. 174–175, 176–177 • Words to Own p. 178	• Test Booklet: Selection Test pp. 230–231 • Portfolio Management System pp. 43, 181	
• Test Generator	• Teaching Notes pp. 165–166 • Reading Organizers pp. 179–180	• Test Booklet: Selection Tests pp. 232–233 • Portfolio Management System pp. 54–55, 182–183	

OURSELVES AMONG OTHERS

Collection Planner

SELECTION / FEATURE	Literary Elements / Active Reading	Writing	Speaking and Listening	Language and Vocabulary
World Literature: The Myth of Sisyphus Albert Camus (pp. 1104–1107)	• Reader's Log p. 1105	• Finding Common Ground: Write essay explaining how Camus's philosophy might apply to your life p. 1108	• Finding Common Ground: Discuss Camus's ideas/Discuss connections between ancient Greek myths and modern life/Memorize a Camus epigram or make up your own to share with class p. 1108	
Games at Twilight Anita Desai (pp. 1109–1117) Student to Student (p. 1116)	• Reader's Log p. 1109 • Imagery p. 1109	• Critical Writing: Write comparison/contrast of two stories p. 1117 • Creative Writing: Write short narrative p. 1117		
Digging Seamus Heaney (pp. 1118–1120)	• Reader's Log p. 1118 • Extended Metaphor p. 1118	• Creative Writing: Write poem in your voice p. 1120		

Collection Resources

Teaching Resources B	Audiovisual Resources Binder	Test Booklet
Cross-Curricular Activity p. 184	Fine Art Transparency 14.1	Collection 14 Test pp. 237–239

 Computer disk or CD-ROM

 Videodisc

Audiocassette

 Overhead Transparency

PROGRAM RESOURCES

Electronic Media	Teaching Resources with Organizer		Audiovisual Resources Binder
	Teaching Resources B	Other Resources	
	• Teaching Notes p. 166		
• Test Generator	• Teaching Notes pp. 166–167 • Reading Organizer p. 181 • Words to Own p. 182	• Test Booklet: Selection Test pp. 234–235 • Portfolio Management System p. 184	• Selected Readings Audiocassette 3, Side B
• Test Generator	• Teaching Notes p. 167 • Reading Organizer p. 183	• Test Booklet: Selection Test p. 236 • Portfolio Management System p. 185	

Proofreading Warm-ups

You may use the following exercises to help students practice their proofreading skills. Copy a set of incorrect sentences onto the chalkboard, and have the students find and correct the spelling, punctuation, usage, and mechanical errors in each sentence. Ask students to share and discuss their responses.

	Sentences with Errors	Corrected Sentences	Skills Covered
1	**a.** the dolls house in Katherine Mansfields story is a symbol **b.** in other word's it stands for both itself, and something beyond itself	**a.** The doll's house in Katherine Mansfield's story is a symbol. **b.** In other words, it stands for both itself and something beyond itself.	Capitalization, Apostrophe usage, Comma usage, End marks
2	**a.** realism, a literary movement that developed in the latter part of the nineteenth-century **b.** the realists wanted to portray life as it is not as people mite wish it to be	**a.** Realism is a literary movement that developed in the latter part of the nineteenth century. **b.** The realists wanted to portray life as it is, not as people might wish it to be.	Capitalization, Comma usage, Hyphen usage, Sentence fragments, Spelling, End marks
3	**a.** Isak dinesen wrote story's about her life on a Coffee Plantation in Kenya **b.** her short story The Ring appeared in a collection of storys titled Anecdotes of Destiny	**a.** Isak Dinesen wrote stories about her life on a coffee plantation in Kenya. **b.** Her short story "The Ring" appeared in a collection of stories titled <u>Anecdotes of Destiny</u>.	Capitalization, Spelling, Apostrophe usage, Quotation marks, Book titles, End marks
4	**a.** poet Stevie Smith described herself as haveing been brung up "in the stiff upper lip school of thought". **b.** her verse is seriocomic; which means it is partly serious partly humorus	**a.** Poet Stevie Smith described herself as having been brought up "in the stiff-upper-lip school of thought." **b.** Her verse is seriocomic, which means it is partly serious, partly humorous.	Capitalization, Spelling, Verb tenses, Hyphen usage, Semicolon usage, Comma usage, End marks
5	**a.** dramatic irony, the result of the reader's knowing more then the character does **b.** An example of Dramatic Irony occurs in Frank O'Connors story My Oedipus Complex	**a.** Dramatic irony is the result of the reader's knowing more than the character does. **b.** An example of dramatic irony occurs in Frank O'Connor's story "My Oedipus Complex."	Capitalization, Comma usage, Spelling, Sentence fragments, Apostrophe usage, Quotation marks, End marks
6	**a.** terms like <u>Oedipus complex,</u> and <u>Freudian slip,</u> derive from the work's of sigmund freud **b.** In turn Freud derrived his term <u>Oedipus complex</u> from greek mythology	**a.** Terms like <u>Oedipus complex</u> and <u>Freudian slip</u> derive from the works of Sigmund Freud. **b.** In turn, Freud derived his term, <u>Oedipus complex</u> from Greek mythology.	Capitalization, Comma usage, Apostrophe usage, Spelling, End marks
7	**a.** diction is a writers choise of words **b.** poet, W. H. Auden, uses impersonnel bureaucratic language in The Unknown Citizen	**a.** Diction is a writer's choice of words. **b.** Poet W. H. Auden uses impersonal, bureaucratic language in "The Unknown Citizen."	Capitalization, Apostrophe usage, Spelling, Comma usage, Quotation marks, End marks
8	**a.** Tom and me have read the play Waiting for Godot **b.** we was waiting for Mr. Brown but he didn't never show up	**a.** Tom and I have read the play <u>Waiting for Godot</u>. **b.** We were waiting for Mr. Brown, but he didn't ever show up.	Capitalization, Pronoun usage, Play titles, Subject-verb agreement, Comma usage, Nonstandard usage, End marks
9	**a.** albert camus's writing has been called epigrammatic **b.** that means he write's brief statements packed with meaning	**a.** Albert Camus's writing has been called epigrammatic. **b.** That means he writes brief statements packed with meaning.	Capitalization, Apostrophe usage, Semi-colon usage, End marks
10	**a.** Games at Twilight is set not long after indias independence from Britian **b.** Anita desai's imagery capture's the essence of a summer's afternoon	**a.** "Games at Twilight" is set not long after India's independence from Britain. **b.** Anita Desai's imagery captures the essence of a summer's afternoon.	Quotation marks, Capitalization, Apostrophe usage, Spelling, End marks

Mansfield
Dinesen
Smith
O'Connor
Auden
Camus
Desai
Heaney

We live, as we dream—alone.
—Joseph Conrad,
from Heart of Darkness

*Nocturne in Blue and Gold,
Old Battersea Bridge
(c. 1872–1875)
by James Abbott McNeill
Whistler.*

Responding to the Quotation

One important theme in much of twentieth-century literature is the isolation many people experience, even in crowds. How does the quotation from Conrad reflect this theme? [Some students may feel that Conrad uses the word *live* in a figurative sense to mean "to experience the fullness of life." In that sense, human beings are isolated from one another because of the difficulty of making meaningful emotional contacts with other people. Others may disagree with Conrad, saying people depend on each other for support.]

PROGRAM MANAGER

- **Integrated Assessment** For a summative assessment of the literature and language skills taught in this collection, see **Collection 14 Test,** *Test Booklet,* pp. 237–239.
- **Instructional Support** See **Fine Art Transparency** 14.1. Review teacher's notes for transparencies in the *Audiovisual*

Resources Binder for suggestions on how to tie the transparencies to specific reading selections.
- **Extending Collection Theme** See **Cross-Curricular Activity: Ourselves Among Others,** *Teaching Resources B,* p. 184, for an activity in another discipline and for evaluation criteria.

PORTFOLIO ASSESSMENT

Parent/Guardian Involvement For forms that will help a parent or guardian review and respond to a student's portfolio, see the *Portfolio Management System,* pp. 62–63.

Katherine Mansfield

(1888–1923)

Katherine Mansfield.

Katherine Mansfield was born Kathleen Mansfield Beauchamp in Wellington, New Zealand, the third child of an ambitious merchant. As a child she was aware of the rugged beauty of her island home, but she shared her mother's distaste for being "out here," oceans away from England, the source of their culture.

At home she was "difficult" and prone to nightmares, a lonely, resentful child who saw her father as an adversary. At school she was moody and had few friends. She had her father's head for figures and could memorize verse at sight, yet she was a slovenly scholar.

When Mansfield was fifteen, the Beauchamp family sailed for England to enroll their daughters in Queen's College in London. Mansfield was delighted with every aspect of her new life, and when she was summoned home to New Zealand in 1906, she closeted herself in her room and grieved for lost London.

In 1908, when she was nineteen, Mansfield's family permitted her to return to London alone. But with only the meager allowance her father granted her, Mansfield was painfully poor and frequently sick. Her first literary encouragement came in 1910, when A. R. Orage, editor of the progressive journal *The New Age,* accepted several of her stories. These stories, which showed the strong influence of the Russian writer Anton Chekhov, were collected in a volume called *In a German Pension* (1911).

About the same time, an Oxford undergraduate named John Middleton Murry accepted a story and some of her poems for his new literary magazine, *Rhythm,* and the two began a long and stormy relationship. Eventually, they married and became publishing partners. The couple became close friends with D. H. Lawrence and his wife Frieda; the friendship soured, however, and Lawrence later ridiculed Mansfield and Murry by using them as models for a couple in a destructive relationship in his novel *Women in Love* (1920).

When Mansfield's younger brother Leslie died in World War I, she was overcome with grief. When she at last emerged from this cloud, she vowed to write about New Zealand from then on as "a sacred debt . . . because my brother and I were born there." She called it a "debt of love. . . . I shall tell everything, even of how the laundry basket squeaked."

As her stories were published, Mansfield became recognized as a supremely gifted writer and an innovator of the short story. Up to this time, the short story had been seen as merely a finger exercise for the novel. People expected stories to have strong, chronological plots. Mansfield's stories downplayed attention to plot and action; instead, she tried to illuminate moments of significance.

Despite her growing success, Mansfield's personal life continued to be troubled. In 1917, she learned that she had tuberculosis. She and Murry were married the following spring, but three weeks later they separated. As Mansfield's health worsened, her characteristic verve gave way to loneliness, anger, and fear of death. But as she entered the final year of her life, she was reconciled to her illness. She renewed her relationship with Murry and showed a new compassion in her writing. In the brief time left to her, she also wrote some of her finest stories, many with New Zealand backgrounds, which are collected in *The Garden Party and Other Stories* (1922) and *The Dove's Nest and Other Stories* (1923).

A belief that some miracle might save her led Mansfield to an institute run by a healer named George Gurdjieff in France. The treatment did not work. There, with Murry at her side, she died in January 1923.

BEFORE YOU READ
THE DOLL'S HOUSE

Reading Focus

Better Than You

Wherever people come together in groups, there is almost always competition for status. Some people will inevitably try to prove that they are superior to other people in the group, or that their group is superior to other groups.

Quickwrite

What gives one "superior" status in our society? Is status always dependent on material wealth?

In what environments do you think competition for status is especially fierce? Jot down your thoughts about competition.

Elements of Literature

Symbol

As you read, think about what this doll's house and its little lamp represent in a world where wealth and social position are important, in a society that mocks the ideal of compassion for the less fortunate.

A symbol is an object, an animal, a place, or a person used in fiction to stand for itself and for something broader than itself. The meanings of symbols are often elusive, and readers frequently disagree on their exact significance.

For more on Symbol, see the Handbook of Literary Terms.

Background

This story is set early in the twentieth century in a small village in New Zealand. At that time, New Zealand was still a British colony, and the British colonists had brought England's rigid class system with them to New Zealand. In this system, people's status in society was automatically determined by their family background. People with inherited wealth and privilege did not ordinarily associate with the poor or even with those who earn what we consider a middle-class income. In New Zealand, however, because of the shortage of schools, wealthy children attended school with children of different social classes.

Miss Miles's Dollhouse
(c. 1890).

Bethnal Green Museum of Childhood.
Courtesy of the Trustees of the
Victoria and Albert Museum, London.

KATHERINE MANSFIELD 1061

STRATEGIES FOR INCLUSION

English Language Development To help students understand the characters in this story, ask them to create a "silent dialogue" between two characters. Have pairs of students choose two characters from the story for whom they will create a conversation. Assuming the personae of their chosen characters, the students pass a piece of paper back and forth as they "talk" to each other, writing down their conversation. Have students read completed conversations to the class.

QUICK PLANNING GUIDE

Into the Story

Author Biography p. 1060
Before You Read p. 1061

Through the Story

"The Doll's House" pp. 1062–1066
Words to Own pp. 1062–1064
Primary Sources p. 1066
Connections: A Poem p. 1067 "Sisters"
Making Meanings p. 1068
Elements of Literature pp. 1068–1069

Beyond the Story

Choices: Building Your Portfolio p. 1069
- **Writer's Notebook:** Brainstorm about peer pressure at school
- **Critical Writing:** Evaluate the omniscient point of view
- **Creative Writing:** Write the opening of an updated story
- **Art:** Create a triptych showing three perspectives

Into the Story

Using BEFORE YOU READ
p. 1061

Elements of Literature

The doll's house is significant because in many cases a person's house, or even the address, is a status **symbol.** Ask students to identify some of the high-status places to live in the United States, your state, and your community.

A. Reader's Response: First Thoughts

? What kind of person is Aunt Beryl? [Sample responses: Condescending, unappreciative; her senses are easily offended.] Explain to students that beryl is a very hard but lustrous mineral that occurs in hexagonal crystals; two varieties of beryl are emerald and aquamarine. How might that name reflect qualities of her character? [Sample responses: Perhaps she is opulent but coldhearted; perhaps she places importance on appearances or status.]

B. Critical Reading: Analyzing Details

Have students make a quick list of the details of the house described in this paragraph. [Dark, oily, green; garish colors; lumps of paint.] What are the students' impressions of the doll's house based upon these details? [Possible answers: It has a tawdry, overdone quality; it is ornate, detailed.] How do the children see it? [They think it is perfect.]

Metacognition The author has not yet identified the Burnell children as characters, so the speaker who calls the house "perfect" is ambiguous. How do you know whose thoughts these lines are? [The diction and point of view are childlike, simplistic.]

C. Language Note: Point of View

? Why does the author refer to "you" in this passage? [The author takes the reader into her confidence by speaking directly to "you."] She also uses the conversational "isn't it," further drawing the reader into what seems to be a personal conversation.

D. Literary Element: Symbol

? What might Kezia's liking of the lamp symbolize? [She is partial to perfect, tiny things. Perhaps to her a lamp represents warmth or comfort or adds a touch of realism.]

The Doll's House
Katherine Mansfield

When dear old Mrs. Hay went back to town after staying with the Burnells, she sent the children a doll's house. It was so big that the carter[1] and Pat carried it into the courtyard, and there it stayed, propped up on two wooden boxes beside the feed-room door. No harm could come of it; it was summer. And perhaps the smell of paint would have gone off by the time it had to be taken in. For, really, the smell of paint coming from that doll's house ("Sweet of old Mrs. Hay, of course; most sweet and generous!")—but the smell of paint was quite enough to make anyone seriously ill, in Aunt Beryl's opinion. Even before the sacking was taken off. And when it was . . .

There stood the doll's house, a dark, oily, spinach green, picked out with bright yellow. Its two solid little chimneys, glued onto the roof, were painted red and white, and the door, gleaming with yellow varnish, was like a little slab of toffee. Four windows, real windows, were divided into panes by a broad streak of green. There was actually a tiny porch, too, painted yellow, with big lumps of congealed paint hanging along the edge.

But perfect, perfect little house! Who could possibly mind the smell? It was part of the joy, part of the newness.

"Open it quickly, someone!"

The hook at the side was stuck fast. Pat pried it open with his penknife, and the whole housefront swung back, and—there you were, gazing at one and the same moment into the drawing room and dining room, the kitchen and two bedrooms. That is the way for a house to open! Why don't all houses open like that? How much more exciting than peering through the slit of a door into a mean little hall with a hatstand and two umbrellas! That is—isn't it?—what you long to know about a house when you put your hand on the knocker. Perhaps it is the way God opens houses at dead of night when He is taking a quiet turn with an angel . . .

"O-oh!" The Burnell children sounded as though they were in despair. It was too marvelous; it was too much for them. They had never seen anything like it in their lives. All the rooms were papered. There were pictures on the walls, painted on the paper, with gold frames complete. Red carpet covered all the floors except the kitchen; red plush chairs in the drawing room, green in the dining room; tables, beds with real bedclothes, a cradle, a stove, a dresser with tiny plates, and one big jug. But what Kezia liked more than anything, what she liked frightfully, was the lamp. It stood in the middle of the dining-room table, an exquisite little amber lamp with a white globe. It was even filled all ready for lighting, though, of course, you couldn't light it. But there was something inside that looked like oil, and that moved when you shook it.

The father and mother dolls, who sprawled very stiff as though they had fainted in the drawing room, and their two little children asleep upstairs, were really too big for the doll's house. They didn't look as though they belonged. But the lamp was perfect. It seemed to smile at Kezia, to say, "I live here." The lamp was real.

The Burnell children could hardly walk to school fast enough the next morning. They burned to tell everybody, to describe, to—well—to boast about their doll's house before the school bell rang.

"I'm to tell," said Isabel, "because I'm the eldest. And you two can join in after. But I'm to tell first."

There was nothing to answer. Isabel was bossy, but she was always right, and Lottie and Kezia knew too well the powers that went with being eldest. They brushed through the thick buttercups at the road edge and said nothing.

"And I'm to choose who's to come and see it first. Mother said I might."

For it had been arranged that while the doll's house stood in the courtyard they might ask the

---

1. **carter:** delivery person.

WORDS TO OWN
congealed (kən·jēld') v. used as *adj.*: thickened.

OPTIONS FOR TEACHING
INTEGRATING THE LANGUAGE ARTS

Strategic Reading Have students note in their Reader's Logs all references to rank or hierarchy that occur in the story. As a class, compare individual notes; then, list the references chronologically on the chalkboard to show the development of this motif throughout the story.

Writing: Character Journal Have students imagine Kezia's thoughts during various scenes of the story and write what they imagine she might record in her journal about these events. Remind students to analyze the text and to gauge Kezia's feelings from her reactions or dialogue.

girls at school, two at a time, to come and look. Not to stay to tea, of course, or to come traipsing **E** through the house. But just to stand quietly in the courtyard while Isabel pointed out the beauties, and Lottie and Kezia looked pleased . . .

But hurry as they might, by the time they had reached the tarred palings[2] of the boys' playground the bell had begun to jangle. They only just had time to whip off their hats and fall into line before the roll was called. Never mind. Isabel tried to make up for it by looking very important and mysterious and by whispering behind her hand to the girls near her, "Got something to tell you at playtime."

Playtime came and Isabel was surrounded. The girls of her class nearly fought to put their arms round her, to walk away with her, to beam flatteringly, to be her special friend. She held quite a court under the huge pine trees at the side of the playground. Nudging, giggling together, the little girls pressed up close. And the only two who stayed outside the ring were the two who were always outside, the little Kelveys. They knew better than to come anywhere near the Burnells. **F**

For the fact was, the school the Burnell children went to was not at all the kind of place their parents would have chosen if there had been any choice. But there was none. It was the only school for miles. And the consequence was all the children in the neighborhood, the Judge's little girls, the doctor's daughters, the storekeeper's children, the milkman's, were forced to mix together. Not to speak of there being an equal number of rude, rough little boys as well. But the line had to be drawn somewhere. It was drawn at the Kelveys. Many of the children, including the Burnells, were not allowed even to speak to them. They walked past the Kelveys with their heads in the air, and as they set the fashion in all matters of behavior, the Kelveys were shunned by everybody. Even the teacher had a special voice for them, and a special smile for the other children when Lil Kelvey came up to her desk with a bunch of dreadfully common-looking flowers.

They were the daughters of a spry, hardworking little washerwoman, who went about from house to house by the day. This was awful enough. But where was Mr. Kelvey? Nobody

2. **palings** (pāl'inz): fence stakes.

knew for certain. But everybody said he was in prison. So they were the daughters of a washerwoman and a jailbird. Very nice company for other people's children! And they looked it. Why Mrs. Kelvey made them so conspicuous was hard to understand. The truth was they were dressed in "bits" given to her by the people for whom she worked. Lil, for instance, who was a stout, plain child, with big freckles, came to school in a dress made from a green art-serge[3] tablecloth of the Burnells', with red plush sleeves from the Logans' curtains. Her hat, perched on top of her high forehead, was a grown-up woman's hat, once the property of Miss Lecky, the postmistress. It was turned up at the back and trimmed with a large scarlet quill. What a little guy[4] she looked! It was impossible not to laugh. And her little sister, our **G** Else, wore a long white dress, rather like a nightgown, and a pair of little boy's boots. But what- **H** ever our Else wore she would have looked strange. She was a tiny wishbone of a child, with cropped hair and enormous solemn eyes—a little white owl. Nobody had ever seen her smile; she scarcely ever spoke. She went through life holding on to Lil, with a piece of Lil's skirt screwed up in her hand. Where Lil went our Else followed. In the playground, on the road going to and from school, there was Lil marching in front and our Else holding on behind. Only when she wanted anything, or when she was out of breath, our Else gave Lil a tug, a twitch, and Lil stopped and turned round. The Kelveys never failed to understand each other.

Now they hovered at the edge; you couldn't stop them listening. When the little girls turned round and sneered, Lil, as usual, gave her silly, shamefaced smile, but our Else only looked.

3. **art-serge** (ärt·sûrj): type of woven wool fabric.
4. **guy:** British for "an odd-looking person." The word comes from the name of Guy Fawkes, an English conspirator executed for taking part in the 1605 Gunpowder Plot to bomb the king and the houses of Parliament. In England, handmade likenesses of Guy Fawkes are burned annually on November 5—Guy Fawkes Day.

- -

WORDS TO OWN
traipsing (trāps'in) v. used as adj.: colloquial for "wandering."
conspicuous (kən·spik'yoo·əs) adj.: attracting attention by being unusual.

- -

KATHERINE MANSFIELD 1063

Language Note: Repetition
Repetition usually indicates the importance of the repeated word or phrase. Why might Kezia be so adamant about the lamp? [Perhaps she simply wants to tell about her favorite piece of the house; in a larger sense, perhaps the lamp symbolizes the importance of the light within, the sense of warmth of the house—or of a human being.]

B. Critical Reading: Drawing Conclusions

? How do the details of the girls' lunches further the distinction between the Kelveys and the others? [The Kelveys have only jam while the thick meat sandwiches and the buttered johnny cakes of the others indicate their families have more money.]

C. Reader's Response: Shaping Interpretations

? Why does Kezia want to invite the Kelveys to look at the doll's house? [Sample responses: She feels sorry for them. She may not understand the reasons for their exclusion and sees them as human beings.]

D. Critical Reading: Making Inferences

? Why, on this particular day, do the girls decide to be spiteful to the Kelveys? [Possible answers: The subject of the doll's house has waned, so the girls decide to stir up some excitement. The excitement of excluding the Kelveys from viewing the doll's house has worn thin, so the girls find another way to lord it over Lil and Else.]

E. Reader's Response: Shaping Interpretations

? Why do the girls have so much energy after they insult Lil and Else? [Sample responses: It makes them feel powerful to put down the Kelveys. They are invigorated by Lena's daring.]

A And Isabel's voice, so very proud, went on telling. The carpet made a great sensation, but so did the beds with real bedclothes, and the stove with an oven door.

When she finished Kezia broke in. "You've forgotten the lamp, Isabel."

"Oh, yes," said Isabel, "and there's a teeny little lamp, all made of yellow glass, with a white globe that stands on the dining-room table. You couldn't tell it from a real one."

"The lamp's best of all," cried Kezia. She thought Isabel wasn't making half enough of the little lamp. But nobody paid any attention. Isabel was choosing the two who were to come back with them that afternoon and see it. She chose Emmie Cole and Lena Logan. But when the others knew they were all to have a chance, they couldn't be nice enough to Isabel. One by one they put their arms round Isabel's waist and walked her off. They had something to whisper to her, a secret. "Isabel's *my* friend."

Only the little Kelveys moved away forgotten; there was nothing more for them to hear.

Days passed, and as more children saw the doll's house, the fame of it spread. It became the one subject, the rage. The one question was, "Have you seen Burnells' doll's house? Oh, ain't it lovely!" "Haven't you seen it? Oh, I say!"

B Even the dinner hour was given up to talking about it. The little girls sat under the pines eating their thick mutton sandwiches and big slabs of johnny cake spread with butter. While always, as near as they could get, sat the Kelveys, our Else holding on to Lil, listening too, while they chewed their jam sandwiches out of a newspaper soaked with large red blobs . . .

C "Mother," said Kezia, "can't I ask the Kelveys just once?"

"Certainly not, Kezia."

"But why not?"

"Run away, Kezia; you know quite well why not."

D At last everybody had seen it except them. On that day the subject rather <u>flagged</u>. It was the dinner hour. The children stood together under the pine trees, and suddenly, as they looked at the Kelveys eating out of their paper, always by themselves, always listening, they wanted to be horrid to them. Emmie Cole started the whisper.

"Lil Kelvey's going to be a servant when she grows up."

"O-oh, how awful!" said Isabel Burnell, and she made eyes at Emmie.

Emmie swallowed in a very meaning way and nodded to Isabel as she'd seen her mother do on those occasions.

"It's true—it's true—it's true," she said.

Then Lena Logan's little eyes snapped. "Shall I ask her?" she whispered.

"Bet you don't," said Jessie May.

"Pooh, I'm not frightened," said Lena. Suddenly she gave a little squeal and danced in front of the other girls. "Watch! Watch me! Watch me now!" said Lena. And sliding, gliding, dragging one foot, giggling behind her hand, Lena went over to the Kelveys.

Lil looked up from her dinner. She wrapped the rest quickly away. Our Else stopped chewing. What was coming now?

"Is it true you're going to be a servant when you grow up, Lil Kelvey?" shrilled Lena.

Dead silence. But instead of answering, Lil only gave her silly, shamefaced smile. She didn't seem to mind the question at all. What a sell[5] for Lena! The girls began to <u>titter</u>.

Lena couldn't stand that. She put her hands on her hips; she shot forward. "Yah, yer father's in prison!" she hissed, spitefully.

E This was such a marvelous thing to have said that the little girls rushed away in a body, deeply, deeply excited, wild with joy. Someone found a long rope, and they began skipping. And never did they skip so high, run in and out so fast, or do such daring things as on that morning.

In the afternoon Pat called for the Burnell children with the buggy and they drove home. There were visitors. Isabel and Lottie, who liked visitors, went upstairs to change their pinafores.[6] But Kezia thieved out at the back. Nobody was about; she began to swing on the big white gates of the courtyard. Presently, looking along the road, she

5. **sell:** slang for "trick."
6. **pinafores** (pin'ə·fôrz'): sleeveless, apronlike garments that young girls wear over dresses.

WORDS TO OWN
flagged (flagd) v.: declined; lost strength or interest.
titter (tit'ər) v.: to giggle.

OPTIONS FOR TEACHING

CLASSROOM MANAGEMENT

Block Scheduling After reading the story (15–20 minutes), pair students. To maintain motivation, ask them to write five to ten questions and answers regarding the story (20–25 minutes). Collect all of the papers and quiz the class using student-generated questions and answers (10–15 minutes). Close the block with students writing a response to Making Meanings #8, on p. 1068 (15–20 minutes). Ask for volunteers to share their responses (5–10 minutes).

Circle of Friends Meaningful inclusion of students with disabilities includes social as well as academic participation. In addition to using cooperative learning as a means for students to get to know one another, encourage and facilitate interaction between students with and without disabilities whenever possible. Discuss with Individual Educational Plan (IEP) team members the possibility of creating a "Circle of Friends" for students who seem to be particularly isolated. A "Circle of Friends" is a formal process in which peers form a support network for a student.

Girl Sitting on the Steps (late 19th or early 20th century) by Peter Vilhelm Ilsted. Colored mezzotint.

Bonhams, London.

F. Critical Reading: Analyzing Character

❓ What do her actions indicate about Kezia? [Possible answers: She defies Aunt Beryl's orders, perhaps indicating that she thinks that the Kelveys should be included. Kezia seems innately friendly and sincere, not fully understanding or perhaps disagreeing with the reasons others exclude Lil and Else.]

G. Critical Reading: Finding Details

❓ What does Kezia *not* get to point out? [The lamp.]

saw two little dots. They grew bigger, they were coming toward her. Now she could see that one was in front and one close behind. Now she could see that they were the Kelveys. Kezia stopped swinging. She slipped off the gate as if she was going to run away. Then she hesitated. The Kelveys came nearer, and beside them walked their shadows, very long, stretching right across the road with their heads in the buttercups. Kezia clambered back on the gate; she had made up her mind; she swung out.

"Hullo," she said to the passing Kelveys.

They were so astounded that they stopped. Lil gave her silly smile. Our Else stared.

"You can come and see our doll's house if you want to," said Kezia, and she dragged one toe on the ground. But at that Lil turned red and shook her head quickly.

"Why not?" asked Kezia.

Lil gasped, then she said, "Your ma told our ma you wasn't to speak to us."

"Oh, well," said Kezia. She didn't know what to reply. "It doesn't matter. You can come and see our doll's house all the same. Come on. Nobody's looking."

But Lil shook her head still harder.

"Don't you want to?" asked Kezia.

Suddenly there was a twitch, a tug at Lil's skirt. She turned round. Our Else was looking at her with big, imploring eyes; she was frowning; she wanted to go. For a moment Lil looked at our Else very doubtfully. But then our Else twitched her skirt again. She started forward. Kezia led the way. Like two little stray cats they followed across the courtyard to where the doll's house stood.

"There it is," said Kezia.

There was a pause. Lil breathed loudly, almost snorted; our Else was still as a stone.

"I'll open it for you," said Kezia kindly. She undid the hook and they looked inside.

"There's the drawing room and the dining room, and that's the—"

"Kezia!"

Oh, what a start they gave!

"Kezia!"

It was Aunt Beryl's voice. They turned round.

KATHERINE MANSFIELD 1065

A. Reader's Response: Challenging the Text

? What is the purpose of this paragraph? [Sample responses: It shows how, although feeling threatened by Willie Brent's proposal, Aunt Beryl feels powerful and in control after putting down the Kelvey girls. It compares Aunt Beryl's actions to those of the little girls who taunt Lil in the schoolyard. It shows that bullying covers up insecurity.]

B. Critical Reading: Identifying Main Ideas

? What moves Else to speak? [Possible answer: She has been impressed with the lamp, apparently, even if she has caught only a glimpse.]

On a figurative level, what might be the meaning of this fixation on the lamp? [Else may like it because Kezia does, and Kezia has been kind to her; Else may sense in the lamp the inner light of human kindness that Kezia represents.]

Primary Sources

Ask students to discuss the journal entry of May 30. Specifically, ask them what Mansfield means by "enough" in the first sentence. [Responses will vary. She probably means that being alive and being a writer are all she needs to be happy. She might also mean that living and writing are all she can handle because of the emotional and physical demands of the two "tasks."] Then ask students to discuss why the sight of two people shaking hands and talking causes Mansfield's reaction. [Responses will vary. Perhaps being a writer gives her a chance to observe and study human behavior; it may allow her insight that other people do not have.]

Ask students to review the works of the writers mentioned in the letter dated 20 June 1921. Refer students to earlier sections of the text to review Chaucer, Shakespeare, and Marlowe; assign a few volunteers to look up information about or works by Tolstoy (also spelled "Tolstoi") to familiarize the class with his writing as well. Discuss the reasons Mansfield says she sticks to works by these authors to guide her own writing. Ask students to consider whether studying these works still might be helpful today.

At the back door stood Aunt Beryl, staring as if she couldn't believe what she saw.

"How dare you ask the little Kelveys into the courtyard?" said her cold, furious voice. "You know as well as I do, you're not allowed to talk to them. Run away, children, run away at once. And don't come back again," said Aunt Beryl. And she stepped into the yard and shooed them out as if they were chickens.

"Off you go immediately!" she called, cold and proud.

They did not need telling twice. Burning with shame, shrinking together, Lil huddling along like her mother, our Else dazed, somehow they crossed the big courtyard and squeezed through the white gate.

"Wicked, disobedient little girl!" said Aunt Beryl bitterly to Kezia, and she slammed the doll's house to.

A The afternoon had been awful. A letter had come from Willie Brent, a terrifying, threatening letter, saying if she did not meet him that evening in Pulman's Bush, he'd come to the front door and ask the reason why! But now that she had frightened those little rats of Kelveys and given Kezia a good scolding, her heart felt lighter. That ghastly pressure was gone. She went back to the house humming.

When the Kelveys were well out of sight of Burnells', they sat down to rest on a big red drainpipe by the side of the road. Lil's cheeks were still burning; she took off the hat with the quill and held it on her knee. Dreamily they looked over the hay paddocks,[7] past the creek, to the group of wattles[8] where Logan's cows stood waiting to be milked. What were their thoughts?

Presently our Else nudged up close to her sister. But now she had forgotten the cross lady. She put out a finger and stroked her sister's quill; she smiled her rare smile.

B "I seen the little lamp," she said, softly. Then both were silent once more.

---

7. **paddocks** (pad'əks): fenced pieces of land.
8. **wattles** (wät''lz): acacia trees.

PRIMARY Sources   LETTERS AND JOURNALS

The following extracts are from *The Letters and Journals of Katherine Mansfield: A Selection*. The first is a journal entry dated May 30, 1917; the second is a letter to her painter friend Richard Murry.

Katherine Mansfield: On Being a Writer

May 30   To be alive and to be a "writer" is enough. Sitting at my table just now I saw one person turning to another, smiling, putting out his hand--speaking. And suddenly I clenched my fist and brought it down on the table and called out—There is *nothing* like it!

20 June 1921
. . . About the old masters. What I feel about them (all of them—writers too, of course) is the more one *lives* with them the better it is for one's work. It's almost a case of living *into* one's ideal world—the world that one desires to express. Do you know what I mean? For this reason I find that if I stick to men like Chaucer and Shakespeare and Marlowe and even Tolstoy, I keep much nearer what I want to do than if I confuse things with reading a lot of lesser men. I'd like to make the old masters my *daily* bread—in the sense in which it's used in the Lord's Prayer, really—to make them a kind of essential nourishment. All the rest is—well—it comes *after*. . . .

PROFESSIONAL NOTES

Cultural Diversity Invite students to study the influence Great Britain had on New Zealand. Ask them to develop posters or collages that show some of the customs or changes British rule imposed on the country and the New Zealanders—both the colonials and the Maoris, the original inhabitants of New Zealand.

ASSESSMENT TOOLS

Check Test: True-False
1. The doll's house is a white Victorian wonder. [False]
2. The Burnell children immediately want to tell all their friends about the doll's house. [True]
3. There are three Kelvey sisters. [False]
4. Kezia's favorite part of the doll's house is the real glass windows. [False]
5. Kezia invites the Kelveys to see the doll's house. [True]

Connections

Sisters

Rita Dove

for Robin Dove Waynesboro

This is the one we called
Bird of the Dead, Double Bird
Who Feeds on Carrion. Dark
with a red organdy dress

5 for her third birthday,
she cried and cried,
snap-eyed imp whose brow sprouted horns
whenever she screwed up her face.

"Buzzard!" we shrieked
10 and when that was forbidden:
"Schmawk Schmawk Bird!"° after the local radio
personality. Several beatings later
the first literary effort appeared, a story
called "Blank the Buzzard,"

15 for which I claimed the First Amendment.
It was confiscated and shredded.

I can't believe she's taller
than me now, that my smile
lines sag where her Indian cheekbones soar.

20 This is my home, my knothole
we're posing in front of. The palm tree
throws a boa° across our shoulders.
Light seals the cracks.

Environment No. V (1969) by Eldzier Cortor.
Etching/intaglio (27″ × 35″).
Courtesy of the artist.

11. Schmawk Schmawk Bird: cartoonlike
voice created by a radio disc jockey in Dove's
childhood hometown of Akron, Ohio.

22. boa (bō′ə): long, fluffy scarf made of feathers or other soft material. Here, the shadow
created by the palm tree looks like a boa.

In this poem, written by the former U.S. poet laureate Rita Dove (1952–), the speaker gazes at a childhood photograph. Do her memories remind you of the events in "The Doll's House"?

A. Reader's Response: First Thoughts

? Why might the speaker have chosen this insult? [Sample responses: Perhaps the child she ridicules had features like that of a buzzard or vulture; as a vulture eats the remains of other animals' prey, perhaps the nickname insinuates that the ridiculed child wears or uses hand-me-downs or is inferior in some way.]

B. Critical Reading: Making Inferences

? Why is this change particularly poignant? [Possible answer: Although the speaker once ridiculed this child for her birdlike features, those same strong features make her attractive as an adult, while the speaker ages.]

C. Reader's Response: Challenging the Text

? Do you think this is an effective image? Why or why not? [Sample responses: No, it is hard to see the connection of boas, which remind me of playing dress-up, with the point the speaker is making. Yes, boas seem pretentious and may be associated with acting superior to another child.]

CONNECTING WITH "THE DOLL'S HOUSE"

Have students compare the relationship of the Burnell sisters in "The Doll's House" to that of the sisters in "Sisters." [Students may say that the Burnell sisters may grow up to regret their unkind treatment of the Kelveys, just as the sisters in Dove's poem mature to appreciate each individual's unique potential.]

Making Meanings

First Thoughts

1. Students may say they liked Kezia best because she seems sensitive.

Reviewing the Text

a. The furniture is realistic and consists of tables, chairs, beds with bedclothes, a cradle, a stove, a dresser, and a lamp. The dolls are too large for the house and look as though they do not belong in it.

b. One possibility is Kezia, who does not seem to have a sense of class distinction. Students may also feel that Else is special, in that she seems to stare the world in the face.

Shaping Interpretations

2. Isabel wants to show off. Kezia may invite the Kelveys because she wants to rebel against the social system or to share the "light" of the lamp.

3. Else seems to depend on Lil and to defer to her. Because Else rarely speaks, her words carry weight; her silence and her way of absorbing the events around her create the impression that she may be wise, intuitive, almost clairvoyant.

4. The extravagant doll's house is a status symbol—a toy that symbolizes a lavish home. Perhaps to Kezia the lamp, through the light it gives off, symbolizes the inner light or spiritual beauty of human beings. To Else, it may represent hope, charity, love, or the possibility of a world illuminated by kindness instead of prejudice.

5. The theme relates to the desire for status, as gauged by material possessions and a sense of power. Although the Burnell girls and their friends are too young to have built their own status and reputation, they are already old enough to want to feel superior.

6. Most students will probably be appalled by the girls' meanness. Some students might see the meanness as a way the girls have of enhancing their own status. Others might think the meanness comes from genuine ignorance that the Kelvey girls have feelings like everyone else.

Connecting with the Text

7. Lil and Else seem united against others; the sisters Dove writes about

---

MAKING MEANINGS

First Thoughts

1. Which character did you like most? Why?

Shaping Interpretations

2. Why does Isabel invite friends to see the doll's house? Why does Kezia invite Lil and Else to see it?

3. Describe the relationship between Lil and Else. Is it significant that Else speaks the last line of dialogue in the story?

4. What do you think the doll's house **symbolizes** in the story? What does the little lamp symbolize to Kezia? What does it symbolize to Else as she says at the end, "I seen the little lamp"?

5. How would you state this story's **theme**—what does it reveal to you about cruelty, about status and families and outsiders? Compare your statements of theme in class: How much agreement do you find?

6. How do you feel about the extraordinary meanness shown by Lil and Else's classmates? How do you account for it?

Reviewing the Text

a. With a partner, review the description of the doll's house. What do the furniture and the dolls themselves look like?

b. Also, review the descriptions of the characters in the story. Who among them appears comfortable, or to truly "belong," in the world?

Connecting with the Text

7. How does the relationship between Lil and Else compare to that of the two sisters in Rita Dove's poem on page 1067? Do you think this kind of sibling rivalry is common? What causes it?

Extending the Text

8. Look back at your Reader's Log entry about status. Then think about what similarities, if any, exist between your world and the world of the story.

seem to have fought as children but to be reconciled as adults. Students may think sibling rivalry is common due to competition for attention or attempts to establish individuality.

Extending the Text

8. **(Synthesis)** Students may recall situations in which a school or neighborhood group of friends has put down another group or an individual. *Remind students to choose situations they would not mind sharing with others.*

ELEMENTS OF LITERATURE

The Modern Short Story

People have been telling stories since the first campfire, but the short story as a separate form is really an invention of the nineteenth century. A number of factors probably contributed to the rise of the short story at roughly the same time in France, Germany, and the United States. Growing literacy, the consequent popularity of magazines, and the form's flexibility and appeal to a wide variety of writers were doubtless responsible for its success.

The American critic and writer Edgar Allan Poe created the most influential theoretical foundations for the short story in his 1842 review of Nathaniel Hawthorne's *Twice-Told Tales*. In this essay, Poe claimed that the story should be considered superior to the novel because, since a story could be read in one sitting, it could have a more unified aesthetic effect on the reader. To Poe, a unified effect was the most important literary goal. "A skillful artist," he wrote, "having conceived a certain *single effect* . . . then combines such events . . . as may best serve him in establishing this preconceived effect. . . . [T]here should be no word written of which the tendency, direct or indirect, is not to the one pre-established design." The effect that Poe aimed for in most of his stories was shock or horror.

The stories of other nineteenth-century writers frequently involved people in extreme states—physical, emotional, or both. It was not unusual for characters to go mad or die at the end. Such grand events satisfied both writers' and readers' need for **closure,** or the feeling that one has reached a satisfactory conclusion. Some writers, such as Guy de Maupassant in France and O. Henry in the United States, provided this closure through the use of a surprising twist, or **trick ending.**

Realism, a literary movement that developed in the latter part of the nineteenth century, served to decrease some of the excesses of earlier writers. The realists strove to portray life as it really is, not as we might wish or fear it to be. Some realists, such as the Russian Anton Chekhov, often wrote stories that had no strong beginning or end, but merely portrayed the events of daily life. These **slice-of-life** stories provided readers with snapshots

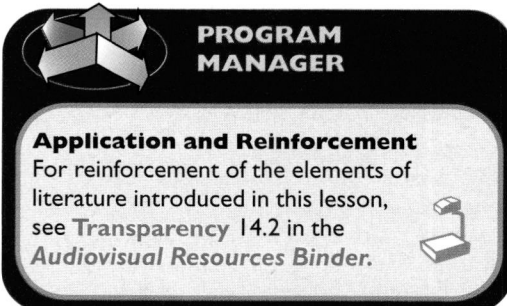

PROGRAM MANAGER

Application and Reinforcement
For reinforcement of the elements of literature introduced in this lesson, see **Transparency** 14.2 in the *Audiovisual Resources Binder.*

of life in a variety of places and social classes. The American Henry James wrote stories that faithfully depicted not only settings and ways of life, but also his characters' perceptions and motivations. This **psychological realism** also had a great effect on the modern short story.

Some writers today still agree with Poe that effect is the most important aspect of a story. However, the modern story more often aims not at a sensory effect *on* the reader but at *revelation to* the reader—the revelation of some essential truth implicit in the story. The main character of the story may remain ignorant of this truth even at the end, and **dramatic irony,** the result of the reader knowing more than the character does, is a common element in modern fiction. Though readers may clearly see dramatic irony in "The Doll's House," the story doesn't at first appear to have the unity of form that Poe espoused. But closer examination reveals a coherence of language, theme, and imagery, in this case all related to the central symbol of the doll's house.

In a general sense, we can say three things about the modern short story:

1. It is more likely to be concerned with nuances of character than with the construction of a fast-paced plot.

2. It is more apt to imply important facts and psychological truths than to state them directly.

3. It is more apt to move toward a revelation of truth than toward an effect.

What would Poe think about the development of the modern short story? Some twentieth-century story elements might puzzle him, but he would certainly recognize the continuation of his own interest in coherence and care for detail.

Katherine Mansfield once wrote of another short story, "it seems to me there mustn't be one single word out of place, or one word that could be taken out." With that statement, Poe would heartily agree.

With some classmates, choose a story from a periodical for young adults. Then, collaborate in writing a critique of the story for the entire class. As part of the critique, consider to what extent the story demonstrates the characteristics of the modern short story listed above.

Writer's Notebook
1. Collecting Ideas for a Problem-Solution Essay

WORK IN PROGRESS

As in "The Doll's House," peer pressure often keeps people (of all ages) from befriending those outside their own cliques. Working with a partner or a small group, brainstorm to explore how widespread the problem is at your school and what could be done to ease or eliminate its negative effects. Save your notes for use in the Writer's Workshop on page 1179.

Critical Writing
2. Know-It-All Narrator

As you read "The Doll's House," you enter the minds of several characters. In an essay of at least three paragraphs, tell whether you think the author's **omniscient point of view** adds to the power of the story or makes the narrative confusing. Support your opinion with specific passages.

Creative Writing
3. The Doll's House Revisited

In a group, collaborate in writing the opening paragraphs of a new, updated story based on "The Doll's House." Decide together what might be different in the story if it were to take place in a contemporary setting.

Art
4. Do You See What I See?

Create a triptych, or a three-paneled picture, illustrating the doll house from three of the different points of view presented in the story. Each panel might include a particular detail that is especially meaningful to the character whose vision you're representing.

Beyond the Story

Choices: Building Your Portfolio

1. **Writer's Notebook** *Remind students to choose a subject they would not mind sharing.* Remind students to save their work. They may use it as prewriting for the Writer's Workshop on p. 1179.

2. **Critical Writing** Review the concept of the **omniscient point of view** before students begin work on this composition. Students might find it useful to organize their thinking with a chart like the one that follows.

Details that add power	Details that make story confusing
[Description of Beryl's feelings after she yells at the Kelveys]	[Who is Willie Brent and why is Beryl afraid of him?]

3. **Creative Writing** Encourage students to think of a device or a toy, such as a computer or the latest video game, that might confer status on someone of middle school age.

Learners Having Difficulty To prepare students for activity #4, lead the class to discuss why each major character feels and acts as she does. For example, encourage students to consider how Aunt Beryl's attitude may have originated and how her attitude indicates what is meaningful to her.

Auditory In activity #3, some students might prefer to tell their new stories before writing them down. Let students tape their compositions as they speak them aloud; they can then replay the tape and write down what they hear.

PORTFOLIO ASSESSMENT

Choices: Assessment Criteria For help in evaluating these Choices assignments, see the criteria in the *Portfolio Management System,* p. 179.

Denmark

WORLD LITERATURE

Isak Dinesen.

Isak Dinesen

(1885–1962)

Isak Dinesen (the pen name of Baroness Karen Blixen-Finecke) led a series of lives, any one of which might be considered adventurous for a woman of her time. She first inherited a love of adventure and story-telling from her father, a dashing Danish aristocrat, and a sense of duty, obligation, and guilt from her mother, the daughter of a bourgeois merchant. As a young woman, she wrote stories and studied painting. Then, at the age of twenty-nine, she embarked on a new life. She defiantly married her cousin and moved to what is now Kenya, where the couple set up and operated a coffee plantation. Her husband, who was blatantly unfaithful to Dinesen, infected her with syphilis, a progressive disease from which she suffered for the rest of her life. In 1921 the couple divorced, and Dinesen ran the six-thousand-acre plantation by herself for another ten years. A collapse in coffee prices and her failing health forced Dinesen to return to Denmark in 1931.

Starting over with no money, Dinesen began revising stories she had drafted in her beloved Africa. Her first collection, *Seven Gothic Tales,* was published in 1934. Her best-known work, *Out of Africa,* an account of her life in Kenya, appeared in 1937 and established her as a major literary presence. Even in her seventies, although she was often so ill she had to dictate to a secretary, Dinesen continued to earn her living by writing.

(Map) ©Rand McNally.

PROGRAM MANAGER

Selection Summary See Teaching Notes, *Teaching Resources B,* pp. 163–164, for a summary of this selection.

Background

To her contemporaries, Isak Dinesen often seemed old-fashioned, for most of her stories are set between 1770 and 1870 and have the atmosphere of an era long past. During this time period, Dinesen's native Denmark was controlled by a few wealthy, aristocratic landowners. The wealthy often had little sympathy for the poor, who sometimes became outlaws, stealing fish or game on a landowner's property to feed themselves and their families. If they were caught, they risked being put to death.

"The Ring" was published in a collection of stories titled *Anecdotes of Destiny*. And to a large extent, all of Dinesen's stories are just what that title suggests. Each focuses on a turning point in human life, a moment when some important truth is revealed and a particular life is changed forever.

A Dialogue with the Text

The rich young couple in "The Ring" seem at first to have a perfect relationship. As you read, jot down in your Reader's Log any indications that the young wife is heading toward a critical turning point, a moment when her life will be altered forever.

The Ring
Isak Dinesen

On a summer morning a hundred and fifty years ago a young Danish squire and his wife went out for a walk on their land. They had been married a week. It had not been easy for them to get married, for the wife's family was higher in rank and wealthier than the husband's. But the two young people, now twenty-four and nineteen years old, had been set on their purpose for ten years; in the end her haughty parents had had to give in to them.

They were wonderfully happy. The stolen meetings and secret, tearful love letters were now things of the past. To God and man they were one; they could walk arm in arm in broad daylight and drive in the same carriage, and they would walk and drive so till the end of their days. Their distant paradise had descended to earth and had proved, surprisingly, to be filled with the things of everyday life: with jesting and railleries,[1] with breakfasts and suppers, with dogs, haymaking, and sheep. Sigismund, the young husband, had promised himself that from now there should be no stone in his bride's path, nor should any shadow fall across it. Lovisa, the wife, felt that now, every day and for the first time in her young life, she moved and breathed in perfect freedom because she could never have any secret from her husband.

To Lovisa—whom her husband called Lise[2]—the rustic atmosphere of her new life was a matter of wonder and delight. Her husband's fear that the existence he could offer her might not be good enough for her filled her heart with laughter. It was not a long time since she had played with dolls; as now she dressed her own hair, looked over her linen press, and arranged her flowers, she again lived through an enchanting and cherished experience: One was doing everything gravely and solicitously, and all the time one knew one was playing.

It was a lovely July morning. Little woolly clouds drifted high up in the sky, the air was full

1. **railleries** (rāl′ər·ēz): good-natured ridicule; teasing acts or remarks.

2. **Lise** (lē′zə).

A Dialogue with the Text

Point out to students that some of the indicators they will be looking for might seem rather subtle, and they might miss them on their first reading. Suggest that they try to find as many indicators as possible as they read the story. Then, when they have finished reading it the first time, encourage them to skim the story again and to note any indicators they missed the first time.

A. Reader's Response: First Thoughts

? Do you think this is a realistic belief? Why or why not? [Sample responses: Yes, the purpose of marriage is to share everything with one's spouse. No, there are some things—words that might hurt the beloved—that are better left unsaid.]

B. Literary Element: Point of View

? What is the advantage of reading a story in third person limited? [The reader is aware of all the important action but also knows what is going on inside a character's mind.]

C. Critical Reading: Making Inferences

? What does this phrase indicate about Lise's daily life? [Possible answers: It seems she has nothing substantial or worthwhile to occupy her time; she thinks chores are simply pretense.]

CONNECTING WITH "OURSELVES AMONG OTHERS"

Ask students to discuss how this story fits the theme of the Collection. [Students may say that for the first time in her protected life, Lise is having to face the fact that there are others outside the scope of her family, friends, and fortunate circumstances.]

? How can one person hold two such contradictory ideas? [Students may suggest that intense feelings are usually complex and that inner thoughts often reflect more than one point of view at once.] **Do you trust Lise's perceptions of events?** [Students may not, as she seems flighty.]

Forest Palace (1918) by Jóhannes S. Kjarval (102 cm × 110 cm).

of sweet scents. Lise had on a white muslin frock and a large Italian straw hat. She and her husband took a path through the park; it wound on across the meadows, between small groves and groups of trees, to the sheep field. Sigismund was going to show his wife his sheep. For this reason she had not brought her small white dog, Bijou,[3] with her, for he would yap at the lambs and frighten them, or he would annoy the sheepdogs. Sigismund prided himself on his sheep; he had studied sheep breeding in Mecklenburg[4] and England,

and had brought back with him Cotswold rams[5] by which to improve his Danish stock. While they walked he explained to Lise the great possibilities and difficulties of the plan.

She thought: "How clever he is, what a lot of things he knows!" and at the same time: "What an absurd person he is, with his sheep! What a baby he is! I am a hundred years older than he."

But when they arrived at the sheepfold the old sheepmaster Mathias met them with the sad news that one of the English lambs was dead and two

3. **Bijou** (bē′zhōō′): French for "jewel."
4. **Mecklenburg:** agricultural district in northeastern Germany.

5. **Cotswold rams:** the males of a kind of sheep with very long hair, originally from the Cotswold Hills of southwestern England.

1072 THE TWENTIETH CENTURY

Listasafn Islands, Reykjavik, Iceland.

OPTIONS FOR TEACHING

STRATEGIES FOR INCLUSION

Less Proficient Readers Before they read the story, have students discuss what they know or assume about the problems children from wealthy families face growing up. Students could consider the areas of personal freedom, decision making, and responsibility. After students read the first paragraph, have them predict what the story will be about. After reading, students can check their predictions.

Intrapersonal Have students write Lise's journal entry for the day she faced the stranger. This entry is not limited to telling what happened. It may be a reflection about what has been lost. It may contain cover stories stemming from Lise's secret. It may be a lament or a series of guesses about what the future will hold.

were sick. Lise saw that her husband was grieved by the tidings; while he questioned Mathias on the matter she kept silent and only gently pressed his arm. A couple of boys were sent off to fetch the sick lambs, while the master and servant went into the details of the case. It took some time.

Lise began to gaze about her and to think of other things. Twice her own thoughts made her blush deeply and happily, like a red rose, then slowly her blush died away, and the two men were still talking about sheep. A little while after, their conversation caught her attention. It had turned to a sheep thief.

This thief during the last months had broken into the sheepfolds of the neighborhood like a wolf, had killed and dragged away his prey like a wolf, and like a wolf had left no trace after him. Three nights ago the shepherd and his son on an estate ten miles away had caught him in the act. The thief had killed the man and knocked the boy senseless, and had managed to escape. There were men sent out to all sides to catch him, but nobody had seen him.

Lise wanted to hear more about the horrible event, and for her benefit old Mathias went through it once more. There had been a long fight in the sheephouse, in many places the earthen floor was soaked with blood. In the fight the thief's left arm was broken; all the same, he had climbed a tall fence with a lamb on his back. Mathias added that he would like to string up the murderer with these two hands of his, and Lise nodded her head at him gravely in approval. She remembered Red Ridinghood's wolf, and felt a pleasant little thrill running down her spine.

Sigismund had his own lambs in his mind, but he was too happy in himself to wish anything in the universe ill. After a minute he said: "Poor devil."

Lise said: "How can you pity such a terrible man? Indeed Grandmamma was right when she said that you were a revolutionary and a danger to society!" The thought of Grandmamma, and of the tears of past days, again turned her mind away from the gruesome tale she had just heard.

The boys brought the sick lambs and the men began to examine them carefully, lifting them up and trying to set them on their legs; they squeezed them here and there and made the little creatures whimper. Lise shrank from the show and her husband noticed her distress.

"You go home, my darling," he said, "this will take some time. But just walk ahead slowly, and I shall catch up with you."

So she was turned away by an impatient husband to whom his sheep meant more than his wife. If any experience could be sweeter than to be dragged out by him to look at those same sheep, it would be this. She dropped her large summer hat with its blue ribbons on the grass and told him to carry it back for her, for she wanted to feel the summer air on her forehead and in her hair. She walked on very slowly, as he had told her to do, for she wished to obey him in everything. As she walked she felt a great new happiness in being altogether alone, even without Bijou. She could not remember that she had ever before in all her life been altogether alone. The landscape around her was still, as if full of promise, and it was hers. Even the swallows cruising in the air were hers, for they belonged to him,[6] and he was hers.

She followed the curving edge of the grove and after a minute or two found that she was out of sight to the men by the sheephouse. What could now, she wondered, be sweeter than to walk along the path in the long flowering meadow grass, slowly, slowly, and to let her husband overtake her there? It would be sweeter still, she reflected, to steal into the grove and to be gone, to have vanished from the surface of the earth from him when, tired of the sheep and longing for her company, he should turn the bend of the path to catch up with her.

An idea struck her; she stood still to think it over.

A few days ago her husband had gone for a ride and she had not wanted to go with him, but had strolled about with Bijou in order to explore her domain. Bijou then, gamboling, had led her straight into the grove. As she had followed him, gently forcing her way into the shrubbery, she had suddenly come upon a glade in the midst of it, a narrow space like a small alcove with hangings of thick green and golden brocade, big enough to hold two or three people in it. She had felt at that moment that she had come into the very heart of her new home. If today she could find the spot

6. **him:** that is, Sigismund. In Denmark at the time of the story, birds and other wild animals on an estate were the owner's property.

ISAK DINESEN 1073

INTEGRATING THE LANGUAGE ARTS

Strategic Reading Ask students to write down one question concerning the story or how it relates to their own experiences. Have students work in groups of four to discuss their questions. Encourage groups to find areas of disagreement and agreement in their responses; bring any unanswered questions to a full discussion in class.

Speaking and Listening Have students work in pairs to read the story aloud; encourage them to freely express thoughts about the text, problems with it and solutions, connections to their lives, and interpretations. Extending each other's thinking will help students unlock meaning.

Language and Style Have a volunteer read the second paragraph aloud, and ask several students to summarize what they learn from the paragraph. Then, ask students to find every word and phrase in the paragraph that refers to time. Have someone take notes on the chalkboard. Point out the complexity of information about the couple's past, their present, and their dreams for the future, conveyed so clearly and economically.

again she would stand perfectly still there, hidden from all the world. Sigismund would look for her in all directions; he would be unable to understand what had become of her and for a minute, for a short minute—or, perhaps, if she was firm and cruel enough, for five—he would realize what a void, what an unendurably sad and horrible place the universe would be when she was no longer in it. She gravely scrutinized the grove to find the right entrance to her hiding place, then went in.

She took great care to make no noise at all, therefore advanced exceedingly slowly. When a twig caught the flounces of her ample skirt she loosened it softly from the muslin, so as not to crack it. Once a branch took hold of one of her long golden curls; she stood still, with her arms lifted, to free it. A little way into the grove the soil became moist; her light steps no longer made any sound upon it. With one hand she held her small handkerchief to her lips, as if to emphasize the secretness of her course. She found the spot she sought and bent down to divide the foliage and make a door to her sylvan closet. At this the hem of her dress caught her foot and she stopped to loosen it. As she rose she looked into the face of a man who was already in the shelter.

He stood up erect, two steps off. He must have watched her as she made her way straight toward him.

She took him in in one single glance. His face was bruised and scratched, his hands and wrists stained with dark filth. He was dressed in rags, barefooted, with tatters wound round his naked ankles. His arms hung down to his sides, his right hand clasped the hilt of a knife. He was about her own age. The man and the woman looked at each other.

This meeting in the wood from beginning to end passed without a word; what happened could only be rendered by pantomime. To the two actors in the pantomime it was timeless; according to a clock it lasted four minutes.

She had never in her life been exposed to danger. It did not occur to her to sum up her position, or to work out the length of time it would take to call her husband or Mathias, whom at this moment she could hear shouting to his dogs. She beheld the man before her as she would have beheld a forest ghost: the apparition itself, not the

sequels of it, changes the world to the human who faces it.

Although she did not take her eyes off the face before her, she sensed that the alcove had been turned into a covert.[7] On the ground a couple of sacks formed a couch; there were some gnawed bones by it. A fire must have been made here in the night, for there were cinders strewn on the forest floor.

After a while she realized that he was observing her just as she was observing him. He was no longer just run to earth and crouching for a spring, but he was wondering, trying to know. At that she seemed to see herself with the eyes of the wild animal at bay in his dark hiding place: her silently approaching white figure, which might mean death.

He moved his right arm till it hung down straight before him between his legs. Without lifting the hand he bent the wrist and slowly raised the point of the knife till it pointed at her throat. The gesture was mad, unbelievable. He did not smile as he made it, but his nostrils distended, the corners of his mouth quivered a little. Then slowly he put the knife back in the sheath by his belt.

She had no object of value about her, only the wedding ring which her husband had set on her finger in church, a week ago. She drew it off, and in this movement dropped her handkerchief. She reached out her hand with the ring toward him. She did not bargain for her life. She was fearless by nature, and the horror with which he inspired her was not fear of what he might do to her. She commanded him, she besought him to vanish as he had come, to take a dreadful figure out of her life, so that it should never have been there. In the dumb movement her young form had the grave authoritativeness of a priestess conjuring down some monstrous being by a sacred sign.

He slowly reached out his hand to hers, his finger touched hers, and her hand was steady at the touch. But he did not take the ring. As she let it go it dropped to the ground as her handkerchief had done.

For a second the eyes of both followed it. It rolled a few inches toward him and stopped be-

---

7. **covert** (kō′vərt): hiding place; shelter.

fore his bare foot. In a hardly perceivable movement he kicked it away and again looked into her face. They remained like that, she knew not how long, but she felt that during that time something happened, things were changed.

He bent down and picked up her handkerchief. All the time gazing at her, he again drew his knife and wrapped the tiny bit of cambric round the blade. This was difficult for him to do because his left arm was broken. While he did it his face under the dirt and suntan slowly grew whiter till it was almost phosphorescent. Fumbling with both hands, he once more stuck the knife into the sheath. Either the sheath was too big and had never fitted the knife, or the blade was much worn—it went in. For two or three more seconds his gaze rested on her face; then he lifted his own face a little, the strange radiance still upon it, and closed his eyes.

The movement was definitive and unconditional. In this one motion he did what she had begged him to do: He vanished and was gone. She was free.

She took a step backward, the immovable, blind face before her, then bent as she had done to enter the hiding place, and glided away as noiselessly as she had come. Once outside the grove she stood still and looked round for the meadow path, found it, and began to walk home.

Her husband had not yet rounded the edge of the grove. Now he saw her and helloed to her gaily; he came up quickly and joined her.

The path here was so narrow that he kept half behind her and did not touch her. He began to

Svartbekken (1909)
by Henrik Sørensen.
(120 cm × 110.5 cm).
Bergen Kommunes
Kunstsamlinger, Norway.

1075

F. Reader's Responses: Shaping Interpretations

? Why does the stranger refuse, even kick away, the ring? [Sample responses: He indicates he doesn't want to hurt or rob Lise, conveying that he is not evil. He senses that she is taken by him and will not tell, so he is grateful. Perhaps he is mesmerized by her and wants her to know he is honorable; he does not want pity.]

G. Reader's Response: Connecting with the Text

? What might the handkerchief represent? [Sample responses: It could allude to the ladies' keepsakes that medieval knights carried into battle. The white handkerchief could be symbolic of her naiveté.]

H. Critical Reading: Finding Details

? What does this confirm? [That he is the murderer and thief of Mathias's story.]

I. Reader's Response: Shaping Interpretations

Refer to the repetition of *wolf* in the story Mathias tells. Do you think the stranger is a wolf? Why or why not? [Sample responses: No, that word is ironic, because in truth the situation seems the opposite of a wolf in sheep's clothing: The stranger appears to be evil but is kind to Lise and relies on her mercy. Or yes, he is wild and able to kill to survive; he preys upon Lise's naiveté.] Discuss with the class the way this analogy interconnects with Sigismund's sheep breeding and Lise's sheeplike attitude in the beginning.

J. Critical Reading: Making Inferences

? What is happening here and why? [Possible answer: She has been mesmerized by his gaze; by closing his eyes, he breaks this silent communion so she can go.]

COOPERATIVE LEARNING

Character Conversations Have students work in pairs to create dialogue between Lise and Sigismund about the following topics: the sheep, the ring, the murderer. One student should assume the role of Lise and the other the role of Sigismund. Suggest that the dialogues take place just after the story ends.

CLASSROOM MANAGEMENT

Managing the Reader's Response Classroom In discussing the story, demonstrate a willingness to help students explore their reactions. The following types of questions will invite further thought and help students tie responses to the text.

- What do you mean by _____?
- Why do you feel/think that way?
- What in the text gave you that idea?
- Can you add anything to what has been said?

☞

A. Reader's Response: First Thoughts

? What is over? [Sample responses: The world as she has known it has changed with her new perception. She reverses her resolution to share everything with Sigismund. She recognizes she must keep this secret to save the stranger's life, and she sees her husband as unable to understand the situation or share her revelation. In having denied him her thoughts, she feels their marriage is, in a sense, over.]

B. Critical Reading: Summarizing

Ask students to summarize the importance of this section. [Possible answer: Lise grows from innocence to experience; she is now wedded to her own awakening to evil, injustice, poverty, and hardship in the world.]

C. Reader's Response: Challenging the Text

? Is it helpful that the author shifts these sentences to show the husband's point of view? [Sample responses: Yes, it emphasizes that Sigismund is following a completely different line of thought and is truly more separate from his wife than before. No, it seems unnecessary, as the point is already clear.]

D. Literary Element: Irony

? How does Lise's response here relate to her promise at the end of the second paragraph? [It is ironic; she is now keeping secrets.]

Finding Common Ground

When students work together in small groups, have one member of the group keep notes about the discussion of each question. Once the groups have had time for discussion, have each group share their responses with the class. Responses will probably vary considerably from group to group. *Remind students to choose situations they would not mind sharing for the fourth bulleted item.*

A explain to her what had been the matter with the lambs. She walked a step before him and thought: All is over.

After a while he noticed her silence, came up beside her to look at her face, and asked, "What is the matter?"

She searched her mind for something to say, and at last said: "I have lost my ring."

"What ring?" he asked her.

She answered, "My wedding ring."

As she heard her own voice pronounce the words, she conceived their meaning.

Her wedding ring. "With this ring"—dropped by one and kicked away by another—"with this B ring I thee wed." With this lost ring she had wedded herself to something. To what? To poverty, persecution, total loneliness. To the sorrows and the sinfulness of this earth. "And what therefore God has joined together let man not put asunder."

"I will find you another ring," her husband said. "You and I are the same as we were on our wedding day; it will do as well. We are husband and wife today too, as much as yesterday, I suppose."

C Her face was so still that he did not know if she had heard what he said. It touched him that she should take the loss of his ring so to heart. He took her hand and kissed it. It was cold, not quite the same hand as he had last kissed. He stopped to make her stop with him.

D "Do you remember where you had the ring on last?" he asked.

"No," she answered.

"Have you any idea," he asked, "where you may have lost it?"

"No," she answered. "I have no idea at all."

FINDING COMMON GROUND

The couple in the story seem, at first, to live in a kind of fairy-tale paradise far from the concerns of unfortunates who might have to steal for food. All too soon, however, the troubles of the wider world intrude on their personal happiness.

Think about your own response to Lise's experience with the stranger. (Be sure to check your Reader's Log.) Get together with a small group to talk about the story. Here are some questions you might consider, though you also might want to set your own agendas:

• Why doesn't the stranger accept Lise's ring? Why doesn't he try to hurt her?

• Why doesn't Lise tell her husband about her experience with the stranger?

• How has Lise changed by the end of the story? How has her relationship with her husband changed?

• Be sure to comment on the relevance of the story to your life today. When your group has finished its discussion, assign one member to report to the class. Then see if, as a class, you can sum up your responses to the story—including your disagreements.

ASSESSMENT TOOLS

Check Test: Short Answers
1. How long has the couple been married? [One week.]
2. What work does Sigismund do? [He breeds sheep.]
3. What news shared by Mathias interests Lise? [The murder by the sheep thief.]
4. Why does Lise start home alone? [Sigismund needs to look after some sick sheep.]

Observation Assessment As students discuss or write about their interactions with the story, use the following points to assess reading comprehension.

1=Rarely   2=Sometimes   3=Often
_____ 1. Finds multiple levels of meaning
_____ 2. Uses text to verify and clarify ideas
_____ 3. Challenges the text
_____ 4. Makes connections between the text and other works

Stevie Smith
(1902–1971)

Stevie Smith (1954).

She was christened Florence Margaret Smith but got the nickname "Stevie" because she was short, like the British jockey Steve Donohue. She grew up in a suburb of London, abandoned by her father and raised by her mother and an aunt. Smith lived with her aunt for sixty-six years, until "Auntie Lion" died in 1968 at the age of ninety-six.

After finishing school, Smith worked as a secretary for a magazine publisher. She remained there for thirty years and began to publish poetry and fiction while in her early thirties. Her first publication, *Novel on Yellow Paper* (1936), is a playful monologue spoken by a character very much like Smith herself.

Smith's other early publications—mostly novels—also reflect her offbeat outlook and writing style. But it is in her poems that she fully displays her cleverness. The light side of her poetry often reflects a darker side as well, making her verse seriocomic (partly serious, partly humorous). Her poems often deal with death, loneliness, or despair, but Smith is never self-pitying. Her humor adds sparkle, allowing her to distance herself from her subject. Smith herself best summed up her paradoxical views when she claimed that she was "straightforward, but not simple." The poet Robert Lowell described her poetic "voice" as "cheerfully gruesome," and the poet-humorist Ogden Nash admired her "songs of deadly innocence."

BEFORE YOU READ
NOT WAVING BUT DROWNING

Reading Focus

Life's Misunderstandings
Everyone has misunderstandings. In fact, we misread each other's signals about nearly everything—from the most trivial to the most important things in life. We say one thing. People think we mean something else. We act a certain way for one reason. People think our action is motivated by something entirely different.

Quickwrite

READER'S LOG

Freewrite in your Reader's Log for a few minutes as you focus on Smith's title: What do you predict it means?

Background

Stevie Smith published ten volumes of verse, but, with the exception of this one poem, most of her poetry is unknown to American readers. Why this poem should have become more famous than all of her other poems combined is a question best answered by readers like yourself. Here's what the poet reveals about her state of mind when she wrote the poem:

"I often try to pull myself together, having been well brought up in the stiff-upper-lip school of thought and not knowing whether other people find Death as merry as I do. But it's a tightrope business, this pulling oneself together, and can give rise to misunderstandings which may prove fatal, as in the poem I wrote about a poor fellow who got drowned. His friends thought he was waving to them but really he was asking for help."

STEVIE SMITH **1077**

QUICK PLANNING GUIDE

Into the Poem

Author Biography p. 1077
Before You Read p. 1077

Through the Poem

"Not Waving but Drowning" p. 1078
Primary Sources p. 1079
Making Meanings p. 1079

Beyond the Poem

Choices: Building Your Portfolio
p. 1079
- **Writer's Notebook:** Freewrite about helping someone who is "drowning"
- **Critical Writing:** In an essay, explain the sea as a metaphor

ABOUT THE AUTHOR

Stevie Smith had wanted to be a poet all her life, but her first publication, *Novel on Yellow Paper*, came about as the result of a suggestion by a publisher who had rejected her poetry. This book is full of digressions and non sequiturs, and some critics compared it to the writing of Gertrude Stein. During the 1960s, interest in Smith's work increased, probably as the result of a series of public readings she gave, and in 1969 she received the Queen's Gold Medal for Poetry.

PROGRAM MANAGER

- **Planning Instruction** See Teaching Notes, *Teaching Resources B,* p. 164, for objectives, a summary, literary elements, and additional historical and biographical information for this selection.
- **Instructional Support** See Graphic Organizer for Active Reading, *Teaching Resources B,* p. 172, for a Through the Poem activity.
- **Audiotaped Readings** To help auditory learners through the lesson, use the Selected Reading, Audiocassette 3, Side A, in the *Audiovisual Resources Binder.*
- **Assessment** See Selection Test, *Test Booklet,* p. 229.

Into the Poem

Using BEFORE YOU READ

p. 1077

Reading Focus

Ask students to brainstorm factors that contribute to misunderstandings. As examples, cite cultural differences or misinterpretations of a word or phrase. Make a master list of students' ideas on the chalkboard.

Through the Poem

A. Critical Reading: Making Inferences

? What two different meanings might this line suggest? [It suggests the man had gone farther into the water than he could handle. "Further out" also suggests that he lives on the edge of society.] Point out that in formal usage, *further* signifies quantity or degree as opposed to *farther,* which indicates distance. With this word choice, Smith adds a new layer of meaning to the poem, which appears at first to be literal.

B. Reader's Response: First Thoughts

? Beyond the literal reading, what might the "cold" associated with "his heart" represent? [Sample responses: A lack of warm human relationships or love; he feels misunderstood.]

C. Literary Element: Rhythm

The rhythm is irregular, predominantly mixed trimeter and dimeter. Point out the ironic contrast in rhythm and length between ll. 7 and 8.

D. Literary Element: Rhyme

The rhyme scheme is *abcb* in each stanza. The nursery-rhyme simplicity of the rhyme in ll. 2 and 4 (repeated in ll. 10 and 12) is a stark contrast with the content. Point out the repeated *o* sounds, especially in l. 9.

Not Waving but Drowning

Stevie Smith

Nobody heard him, the dead man,
But still he lay moaning:
A I was much further out than you thought
And not waving but drowning.

5 Poor chap, he always loved larking°
And now he's dead
B It must have been too cold for him his heart gave way,
C They said.

Oh, no no no, it was too cold always
10 (Still the dead one lay moaning)
D I was much too far out all my life
And not waving but drowning.

5. **larking:** playing; having a good time.

Blue and Silver—Chopping Channel
(c. 1890) by James Abbott McNeill Whistler.
Courtesy of the Freer Gallery of Art, Smithsonian Institution, Washington, D.C.

1078 THE TWENTIETH CENTURY

INTEGRATING THE LANGUAGE ARTS

Writing: Character Diary Have students write a diary entry from the perspective of the drowning man. Ask them to consider, as they write, what might have made the man feel so alienated and alone.

CROSSING THE CURRICULUM

Art Stevie Smith illustrated many of her poems with line art that often adds another dimension to the poetry. For example, the illustration she drew for this poem shows the head and upright torso of a young person with hair hanging like a screen across his face. Ask students to find examples of Stevie Smith's artwork and to share them with the class.

The Truths About Poetry

Here are some of the truths about poetry. She is an Angel, very strong. It is not poetry but the poet who has a feminine ending, not the Muse who is weak, but the poet. She makes a strong communication. Poetry is like a strong explosion in the sky. She makes a mushroom shape of terror and drops to the ground with a strong infection. Also she is a strong way out. The human creature is alone in his carapace. Poetry is a strong way out. . . .

Poetry does not like to be up-to-date, she refuses to be neat. ("Anglo-Saxon," wrote Gavin Bone, "is a good language to write poetry in because it is impossible to be neat.") All the poems Poetry writes may be called "Heaven, a Detail," or "Hell, a Detail." (She only writes about heaven and hell.) . . .

All Poetry has to do is to make a strong communication. All the poet has to do is to listen. The poet is not an important fellow. There will always be another poet.

—Stevie Smith, *from Me Again*

MAKING MEANINGS

First Thoughts

1. What does the **title** of the poem mean to you? What did you predict in your Reader's Log?

Shaping Interpretations

2. How many different voices do you hear speaking in the poem?

3. What does the speaker mean by "it was too cold always" and "I was much too far out all my life"?

4. It seems bizarre that a dead man is talking. What might "dead" signify in the poem, besides its literal meaning? How is the dead man misunderstood or ignored?

Extending the Text

5. How could this poem be a summing up of one's whole life, or of the human condition in general?

Challenging the Text

6. Stevie Smith once said that good writing had to be "sad, true, economical, and funny." Does her poem meet these criteria? Do you agree with Smith's prescription for good writing?

CHOICES:
Building Your Portfolio

Writer's Notebook

1. Collecting Ideas for a Problem-Solution Essay

Many people are "drowning" and in need of help. What can be done today for people in trouble, people who need a helping hand? Freewrite your ideas on this issue—focus on identifying the problems and listing possible solutions. You might want to jot down your response to the words of Joseph Conrad that open this collection (page 1059). Save your notes for the Writer's Workshop on page 1179.

Critical Writing

2. Sinking or Swimming

In an essay, explain how the sea is used as a metaphor for life and death. What comparisons do we often make between living and swimming, floating, sinking, diving, or drowning?

STEVIE SMITH **1079**

Making Meanings
First Thoughts

1. Students might say that the title sums up the literal meaning of the poem.

Shaping Interpretations

2. Students may find three voices: the narrator (ll. 1–2, 10); the drowned man (ll. 3–4, 9,11–12); and bystanders (ll. 5–7).

3. The man's comment about the cold may mean his life has been lonely. "Too far out" may mean he has been outside the societal norm or locked within himself.

4. Some students may suggest that failure to communicate well or to live fully could cause one to feel dead emotionally. The man's signal for help is misunderstood as "larking." Hearing the different points of view allows readers to see how the onlookers misunderstand the situation.

Extending the Text

5. **(Analysis)** Students may suggest that, though people try to communicate in a meaningful way, they may not always do so.

Challenging the Text

6. **(Evaluation)** Students may agree that Smith's poem meets those four criteria, but some may say that there are other styles of good writing.

Beyond the Poem

Choices: Building Your Portfolio

1. **Writer's Notebook** Remind students to save their work. They may use it as prewriting for the Writer's Workshop on p. 1179.

PORTFOLIO ASSESSMENT

Choices: Assessment Criteria For help in evaluating these Choices assignments, see the criteria in the *Portfolio Management System,* p. 180.

Into the Story

Author Biography p. 1080
Before You Read p. 1081

Through the Story

"My Oedipus Complex" pp. 1082–1089
Words to Own pp. 1083–1089
Literature and Psychology pp. 1086–1087
Making Meanings p. 1090

Beyond the Story

Choices: Building Your Portfolio p. 1090
- **Writer's Notebook:** Brainstorm ways to help students complete their education
- **Critical Writing:** Write an essay analyzing the author's intention
- **Critical Writing:** Write an essay discussing characters
- **Creative Writing:** Write a humorous biographical sketch

Frank O'Connor

(1903–1966)

Frank O'Connor was born Michael Francis O'Donovan in Cork City, Ireland. He was the only child of a bitterly poor couple whose battling shadowed his life.

O'Connor read endlessly, first boys' magazines and then, finding his way to the library, books of all kinds. Ironically, he particularly enjoyed stories of English schoolboys, and while he knew there would never be money for any such formal education in his own life, he imagined its privileges and yearned to be an educated man.

The reality of his own schooling was not half so appealing. O'Connor attended the Christian Brothers' school in Cork but in the end gave up on school, feeling it was a place where he would always be "useless, frightened, or hurt." But he had no intention of abandoning his dream of an education. At fourteen, he took a series of clerk's jobs that gave him money to buy the books he needed to educate himself.

In 1916, the long-standing hostility between England and Ireland flared into open rebellion, and O'Connor was caught up in the new patriotism. He read Irish history with new fervor and, along with other young Irishmen, thought of heroism. "I was improvising an education I could not afford," he said later, "and the country was improvising a revolution it could not afford." After England had brought up its artillery and "blown the center of Dublin flat . . . the country had to content itself with a make-believe revolution and I had to content myself with a make-believe education and the curious thing is that it was the make-believe that succeeded."

Truce with England came in 1921, when O'Connor was just short of eighteen, but its

Frank O'Connor.

terms were unacceptable to a large number of Irish people. The treaty was immediately followed by a civil war in which O'Connor took the Republican side (the side that favored severing all ties to England and establishing an Irish Republic). Throughout the next two years, he was active in the war, and while on a mission in the spring of 1923, he was arrested and imprisoned.

When at last he was released, he went on to educate himself further and to take part in the Irish literary revival, a movement that tried to restore the Irish language (it had been nearly wiped out by the English) and to create a purely Irish literature. For his pen name, he chose his beloved mother's maiden name.

O'Connor began writing stories, and in 1935, with his friend the poet W. B. Yeats, he became a director of the Abbey Theatre in Dublin. The theater was the heart of the Irish revival, which also involved Lady Gregory, Sean O'Casey, Seán O'Faoláin, and Liam O'Flaherty.

In his writing, O'Connor sought to capture the essence of Irish lyrical speech. His stories are all set in Ireland because "I know to a syllable how everything in Ireland can be said." O'Connor became a richly productive literary figure, bringing forth volumes of poetry, stories, a novel, an autobiography, plays, criticism, and translations. He was a regular contributor to such American magazines as *The New Yorker, The Atlantic Monthly,* and *Esquire.* Speaking of his mastery of the short-story form, Yeats said, "O'Connor is doing for Ireland what Chekhov did for Russia."

O'Connor came to the United States in 1952. In his later years, he taught at Harvard, Northwestern, and Stanford. For a poor boy with very little formal education, he had done quite well.

PROGRAM MANAGER

- **Planning Instruction** See Teaching Notes, *Teaching Resources B,* pp. 164–165, for objectives, a summary, literary elements, and additional historical and biographical information for this selection.
- **Instructional Support** Before beginning the instructional lesson, see

Graphic Organizer for Active Reading, *Teaching Resources B,* p. 173, for a Through the Story activity.
- **Assessment** See Selection Test, *Test Booklet,* pp. 230–231.
- **Language Link** For instruction and practice in style and in punctuating dialogue, see **Language Link,** *Teaching*

Resources B, pp. 174–177, and *Language and Writing Skills Worksheets,* pp. 107, 144–145.
- **Reinforcement** Use the Words to Own worksheet in *Teaching Resources B,* p. 178.

BEFORE YOU READ
MY OEDIPUS COMPLEX

Reading Focus

Three's a Crowd

Have you ever heard the saying "Two's company; three's a crowd"? The saying reflects a basic human truth: Triangles often mean trouble in human relationships.

Many of us encounter our first troublesome triangle very early in life: If we're a first or an only child, we may compete with one parent for the attention of the other parent. In bigger families or families with a single parent, we may compete with a brother or sister to see who can capture a parent's attention. Among our childhood friends, alliances often shift daily.

Even later, with those we love deeply, a certain possessiveness may grip us when a third person enters the scene. Why do we have such a desire for the sole attentions of another? Are these feelings inevitable?

Quickwrite

What do you think of the expression "Two's company; three's a crowd?" Freewrite some ideas in your Reader's Log.

Elements of Literature

Dramatic Irony

The narrator of this story recalls a time when he was a little boy competing with his father for his mother's love. In his innocence, the child anticipates that he will marry his mother when he grows up. Both the adult narrator and the reader know that this will never happen. The child's lack of understanding of his parents' relationship fills the story with **dramatic irony.**

> **D**ramatic irony occurs when the reader knows something important that a character does not know.
>
> *For more on Irony, see the Handbook of Literary Terms.*

Background

In Greek mythology, King Oedipus of Thebes, unaware of his true parentage, kills his father and marries his mother. The term *Oedipus complex* was first used in 1899 by the Austrian "father of psychoanalysis," Sigmund Freud, to describe the unconscious desire of a child for the exclusive love of the parent of the opposite sex. This desire results in rivalry with the parent of the same sex. In psychoanalytic theory, the Oedipus complex is a stage in normal human development, lasting from about age three to age five or six, and ending when the child identifies with the parent of the same sex.

FRANK O'CONNOR 1081

Using BEFORE YOU READ

p. 1081

Elements of Literature

Dramatic irony is often a useful tool in creating **suspense** in a story because it forces readers to anticipate how characters will respond to information that the audience already knows. Ask students to look for **dramatic irony** as they read the story. Does the **dramatic irony** create **suspense**?

WORDS TO OWN

The following vocabulary words are defined in the Words to Own at the bottom of the pupil's page.

ominous p. 1083	alienate p. 1088
winning p. 1084	obnoxious p. 1088
incredulously p. 1084	guffaw p. 1088
cajoled p. 1086	preoccupied p. 1088
intercession p. 1087	magnanimous p. 1089

PORTFOLIO ASSESSMENT

Portfolio Assessment For help with self-assessment of reading skills, see the *Portfolio Management System,* p. 43.

A. Critical Reading: Finding Details

? What do you learn about the narrator in the first paragraph? Distinguish between facts and assumptions. [Facts: His father is a soldier in World War I and is seldom home until the narrator is five. Assumptions: The narrator is childlike, imaginative, and may be five in the story.]

B. Language Note: Style

Discuss the sensory imagery, emphasizing the special power of smell to give an intimate picture. The mention of shaving may evoke certain scents for students. Point out the economy of the language, how much O'Connor conveys in one sentence.

C. Reader's Response: Shaping Interpretations

? What does this passage convey? [Sample responses: The son believes that he and his mother are of one mind, even where his father is concerned. The mother is lenient with the boy.]

D. Literary Element: Dramatic Irony

There is a major discrepancy between the boy's perceptions and reality. Point out that this passage is a superb example of dramatic irony, which occurs when the reader knows something (in this case a great deal) that the character in a story does not know.

My Oedipus Complex

Frank O'Connor

Father was in the army all through the war—the first war,[1] I mean—so, up to the age of five, I never saw much of him, and what I saw did not worry me. Sometimes I woke and there was a big figure in khaki peering down at me in the candlelight. Sometimes in the early morning I heard the slamming of the front door and the clatter of nailed boots[2] down the cobbles of the lane. These were Father's entrances and exits. Like Santa Claus he came and went mysteriously.

In fact, I rather liked his visits, though it was an uncomfortable squeeze between Mother and him when I got into the big bed in the early morning. He smoked, which gave him a pleasant musty smell, and shaved, an operation of astounding interest. Each time he left a trail of souvenirs—model tanks and Gurkha[3] knives with handles made of bullet cases, and German helmets and cap badges and button sticks,[4] and all sorts of military equipment—carefully stowed away in a long box on top of the wardrobe, in case they ever came in handy. There was a bit of the magpie[5] about Father; he expected everything to come in handy. When his back was turned, Mother let me get a chair and rummage through his treasures. She didn't seem to think so highly of them as he did.

The war was the most peaceful period of my life. The window of my attic faced southeast. My mother had curtained it, but that had small effect. I always woke with the first light and, with all the responsibilities of the previous day melted, feeling myself rather like the sun, ready to illumine and rejoice. Life never seemed so simple and clear and full of possibilities as then. I put my feet out

from under the clothes[6]—I called them Mrs. Left and Mrs. Right—and invented dramatic situations for them in which they discussed the problems of the day. At least Mrs. Right did; she was very demonstrative, but I hadn't the same control of Mrs. Left, so she mostly contented herself with nodding agreement.

They discussed what Mother and I should do during the day, what Santa Claus should give a fellow for Christmas, and what steps should be taken to brighten the home. There was that little matter of the baby, for instance. Mother and I could never agree about that. Ours was the only house in the terrace[7] without a new baby, and Mother said we couldn't afford one till Father came back from the war because they cost seventeen and six.[8] That showed how simple she was. The Geneys up the road had a baby, and everyone knew they couldn't afford seventeen and six. It was probably a cheap baby, and Mother wanted something really good, but I felt she was too exclusive. The Geneys' baby would have done us fine.

Having settled my plans for the day, I got up, put a chair under the attic window, and lifted the frame high enough to stick out my head. The window overlooked the front gardens of the terrace behind ours, and beyond these it looked over a deep valley to the tall, red-brick houses terraced up the opposite hillside, which were all still in shadow, while those at our side of the valley were all lit up, though with long strange shadows that made them seem unfamiliar; rigid and painted.

After that I went into Mother's room and climbed into the big bed. She woke and I began to tell her of my schemes. By this time, though I never seem to have noticed it, I was petrified[9] in my nightshirt, and I thawed as I talked until, the last frost melted, I fell asleep beside her and woke again only when I heard her below in the kitchen, making the breakfast.

After breakfast we went into town; heard Mass at St. Augustine's and said a prayer for Father, and did the shopping. If the afternoon was fine we either went for a walk in the country or a visit to

1. **first war:** World War I (1914–1918).
2. **nailed boots:** boots with short, broad-headed nails on the soles to prevent slipping and wear; also called hobnail boots.
3. **Gurkha** (goor′kä′): people of the mountains of Nepal, many of whom served in the British army.
4. **button sticks:** slotted strips of metal or wood that fit over a row of buttons on a military tunic, allowing the buttons to be polished without soiling the cloth.
5. **magpie:** type of bird that picks up all kinds of unlikely materials to build its nest.

6. **clothes:** bedclothes.
7. **terrace:** row of houses.
8. **seventeen and six:** seventeen shillings and sixpence.
9. **petrified** (pe′tri·fid′): rigid from the cold.

OPTIONS FOR TEACHING

STRATEGIES FOR INCLUSION

Learners Having Difficulty Before students read the story, have them work in pairs to discuss the world of a five-year-old child. Perhaps they can remember their own childhood or that of a sibling or neighbor. Ask them to conclude by listing things they think are most important to a child at this age.

Kinesthetic Allow volunteers to perform sketches based on scenes in the story. One person can read the scene while others act it out, or they can perform the scenes as mini-dramas.

Visual Ask students to draw three pictures of Larry's father: One as Larry perceives him before the war ends, another just after the father has returned, and a third at the end of the story when the father seeks out Larry's company. Remind students to tie their artwork to the text.

Mother's great friend in the convent, Mother St. Dominic. Mother had them all praying for Father, and every night, going to bed, I asked God to send him back safe from the war to us. Little, indeed, did I know what I was praying for!

One morning, I got into the big bed, and there, sure enough, was Father in his usual Santa Claus manner, but later, instead of uniform, he put on his best blue suit, and Mother was as pleased as anything. I saw nothing to be pleased about, because, out of uniform, Father was altogether less interesting, but she only beamed, and explained that our prayers had been answered, and off we went to Mass to thank God for having brought Father safely home.

The irony of it! That very day when he came in to dinner he took off his boots and put on his slippers, donned the dirty old cap he wore about the house to save him from colds, crossed his legs, and began to talk gravely to Mother, who looked anxious. Naturally, I disliked her looking anxious, because it destroyed her good looks, so I interrupted him.

"Just a moment, Larry!" she said gently.

This was only what she said when we had boring visitors, so I attached no importance to it and went on talking.

"Do be quiet, Larry!" she said impatiently. "Don't you hear me talking to Daddy?"

This was the first time I had heard those ominous words, "talking to Daddy," and I couldn't help feeling that if this was how God answered prayers, he couldn't listen to them very attentively.

"Why are you talking to Daddy?" I asked with as great a show of indifference as I could muster.

"Because Daddy and I have business to discuss. Now, don't interrupt again!"

In the afternoon, at Mother's request, Father took me for a walk. This time we went into town instead of out the country, and I thought at first, in my usual optimistic way, that it might be an improvement. It was nothing of the sort. Father and I had quite different notions of a walk in town. He had no proper interest in trams,[10] ships, and horses, and the only thing that seemed to divert him was talking to fellows as old as himself. When I wanted to stop he simply went on, dragging me behind him by the hand; when he wanted to stop

I had no alternative but to do the same. I noticed that it seemed to be a sign that he wanted to stop for a long time whenever he leaned against a wall. The second time I saw him do it I got wild. He seemed to be settling himself forever. I pulled him by the coat and trousers, but, unlike Mother who, if you were too persistent, got into a wax[11] and said: "Larry, if you don't behave yourself, I'll give you a good slap," Father had an extraordinary capacity for amiable inattention. I sized him up and wondered would I cry, but he seemed to be too remote to be annoyed even by that. Really, it was like going for a walk with a mountain! He either ignored the wrenching and pummeling[12] entirely, or else glanced down with a grin of amusement from his peak. I had never met anyone so absorbed in himself as he seemed.

At teatime, "talking to Daddy" began again, complicated this time by the fact that he had an evening paper, and every few minutes he put it down and told Mother something new out of it. I felt this was foul play. Man for man, I was prepared to compete with him any time for Mother's attention, but when he had it all made up for him by other people it left me no chance. Several times I tried to change the subject without success.

"You must be quiet while Daddy is reading, Larry," Mother said impatiently.

It was clear that she either genuinely liked talking to Father better than talking to me, or else that he had some terrible hold on her which made her afraid to admit the truth.

"Mummy," I said that night when she was tucking me up, "do you think if I prayed hard God would send Daddy back to the war?"

She seemed to think about that for a moment.

"No, dear," she said with a smile. "I don't think he would."

"Why wouldn't he, Mummy?"

"Because there isn't a war any longer, dear."

"But, Mummy, couldn't God make another war, if He liked?"

---

11. got into a wax: became upset.
12. pummeling (pum′əl·in): hitting repeatedly with the fists.

WORDS TO OWN
ominous (äm′ə·nəs) *adj.*: threatening.

E. Reader's Response: First Thoughts
? What effect does the narrator's extreme innocence have? [Sample responses: It is humorous; it evokes feelings of nostalgia, sympathy, empathy.]

F. Reader's Response: Challenging the Text
? Would a five-year-old boy think this way? How do you explain this paragraph? [Sample responses: No, the narrator has slipped into a sophisticated voice here, perhaps the grown-up Larry reflecting on his early thoughts. Or yes, the fear of a mother's unsmiling face would seem natural in a young child.]

G. Literary Element: Conflict
In this passage O'Connor heightens the conflict with the use of the word "ominous" and the hint that major changes are in store. Suggest that students watch for O'Connor's effective use of conflict; he elevates the tension, then gives some release (as in the beginning of the next paragraph). Then he builds the tension higher, an important cycle in plot development.

H. Literary Element: Irony
? Why is the narrator's exasperation with his father's self-absorption so amusing and ironic? [Because the boy himself is so totally self-absorbed.]

I. Critical Reading: Making Connections
? How is this conversation between Larry and his mother similar to the conversation between Paul and his mother regarding luck in "The Rocking-Horse Winner"? [Possible answer: Both children ask a series of questions and look to God for solutions to their need for their mothers' attention.]

INTEGRATING THE LANGUAGE ARTS

Strategic Reading Have students organize their impressions of Larry by using a graphic organizer such as Transparency 3: Cluster Diagram in the Transparency Package.

Speaking and Listening Remind students that **tone** conveys the writer's attitude toward the reader, the subject, or a character. Although tone is generally evident in the language of a piece of literature, tone can also be conveyed by voice and body language. Have students work in small

groups to read the following line from O'Connor's story, employing each of the tones listed below: "I had been through it all myself, and even at that age I was magnanimous" (taken from p. 1089 where Larry tries to comfort his father).

joyful	satiric	awed
resigned	bitter	self-pitying
somber	melancholy	ominous

Language and Vocabulary O'Connor uses Irish expressions as part of his narration and

dialogue. Have students find examples in the story of words and expressions not typical in American English. Ask students to evaluate the impact of these unusual words and expressions on the effectiveness of the story: Do they add local color and flavor, or are they confusing, or some combination of the two? ☞

A. **Literary Element: Simile**

? What makes this simile of a corked, carbonated beverage effective? [Students may say that the simile suggests fresh, surprising, ready to explode, energetic.]

B. **Reader's Response: Challenging the Text**

? Does the tone shift here? [Sample responses: Yes, the adult analysis interrupts the narrative flow of the five-year-old Larry's point of view. No, the tone does not change; Larry's tone is mature throughout the story.]

C. **Reader's Response: Shaping Interpretations**

? What effect might it have on Larry to suspect that his mother is afraid? [Sample responses: The effect would be complex, including feelings of protectiveness for himself and for his mother. He might feel fear and anger at the changes in his relationship with his mother.]

D. **Reader's Response: First Thoughts**

? Why do you think Larry's father did not bring him a cup of tea? [Sample responses: It seems odd for a child to have a cup of tea, so perhaps this is merely an oversight. While the father was initially tolerant of his son, he is now purposefully ignoring Larry.]

E. **Critical Reading: Identifying Main Ideas**

This statement is an example of comic irony. How does it sum up the source of the story's conflict and its humor? [The boy thinks of himself as a true rival and equal of his father in the battle for his mother's attention.]

"He wouldn't like to, dear. It's not God who makes wars, but bad people."

"Oh!" I said.

I was disappointed about that. I began to think that God wasn't quite what he was cracked up to be.

Next morning I woke at my usual hour, feeling like a bottle of champagne. I put out my feet and invented a long conversation in which Mrs. Right talked of the trouble she had with her own father till she put him in the Home. I didn't quite know what the Home was but it sounded the right place for Father. Then I got my chair and stuck my head out of the attic window. Dawn was just breaking, with a guilty air that made me feel I had caught it in the act. My head bursting with stories and schemes, I stumbled in next door, and in the half-darkness scrambled into the big bed. There was no room at Mother's side so I had to get between her and Father. For the time being I had forgotten about him, and for several minutes I sat bolt upright, racking my brains to know what I could do with him. He was taking up more than his fair share of the bed, and I couldn't get comfortable, so I gave him several kicks that made him grunt and stretch. He made room all right, though. Mother waked and felt for me. I settled back comfortably in the warmth of the bed with my thumb in my mouth.

"Mummy!" I hummed, loudly and contentedly.

"Sssh! dear," she whispered. "Don't wake Daddy!"

This was a new development, which threatened to be even more serious than "talking to Daddy." Life without my early-morning conferences was unthinkable.

"Why?" I asked severely.

"Because poor Daddy is tired."

This seemed to me a quite inadequate reason, and I was sickened by the sentimentality of her "poor Daddy." I never liked that sort of gush; it always struck me as insincere.

"Oh!" I said lightly. Then in my most winning tone: "Do you know where I want to go with you today, Mummy?"

"No, dear," she sighed.

"I want to go down the Glen and fish for thornybacks with my new net, and then I want to go out to the Fox and Hounds, and—"

"Don't-wake-Daddy!" she hissed angrily, clapping her hand across my mouth.

But it was too late. He was awake, or nearly so. He grunted and reached for the matches. Then he stared incredulously at his watch.

"Like a cup of tea, dear?" asked Mother in a meek, hushed voice I had never heard her use before. It sounded almost as though she were afraid.

"Tea?" he exclaimed indignantly. "Do you know what the time is?"

"And after that I want to go up the Rathcooney Road," I said loudly, afraid I'd forget something in all those interruptions.

"Go to sleep at once, Larry!" she said sharply.

I began to snivel. I couldn't concentrate, the way that pair went on, and smothering my early-morning schemes was like burying a family from the cradle.

Father said nothing, but lit his pipe and sucked it, looking out into the shadows without minding Mother or me. I knew he was mad. Every time I made a remark Mother hushed me irritably. I was mortified. I felt it wasn't fair; there was even something sinister in it. Every time I had pointed out to her the waste of making two beds when we could both sleep in one, she had told me it was healthier like that, and now here was this man, this stranger, sleeping with her without the least regard for her health!

He got up early and made tea, but though he brought Mother a cup he brought none for me.

"Mummy," I shouted, "I want a cup of tea, too."

"Yes, dear," she said patiently. "You can drink from Mummy's saucer."

That settled it. Either Father or I would have to leave the house. I didn't want to drink from Mother's saucer; I wanted to be treated as an equal in my own home, so, just to spite her, I drank it all and left none for her. She took that quietly, too.

But that night when she was putting me to bed she said gently:

"Larry, I want you to promise me something."

"What is it?" I asked.

"Not to come in and disturb poor Daddy in the morning. Promise?"

WORDS TO OWN
winning (win'in) *adj.:* charming.
incredulously (in·krej'oo·ləs·lē) *adv.:* disbelievingly.

INTEGRATING THE LANGUAGE ARTS

Writing: Rewritten Ending Have students rewrite the final scene in the story from the father's point of view. Students could share their story endings in small groups.

Mechanics Have students work in pairs to analyze sentence structure in the paragraph on p. 1082 beginning "They discussed what Mother and I should do. . . ." Tell students to search for independent and dependent clauses. Have groups compare their findings.

CLASSROOM MANAGEMENT

Roles for Presentation To ensure that all students participate in presenting group work to the class, assign roles for each group member. Roles will vary according to the activity and the group size. Possible roles include introducing the group's work, summarizing the topic, discussing an aspect of the topic in depth, summing up the group's findings, and extending the findings to common experience.

Group Processing Have students independently evaluate their work as a group using the following guidelines. (Rate on a scale of 1 to 5, with 1 being weakest and 5 being strongest.)
- Remains focused on task
- Requires minimal teacher assistance
- Includes all group members
- Resolves differences

"Poor Daddy" again! I was becoming suspicious of everything involving that quite impossible man.

"Why?" I asked.

"Because poor Daddy is worried and tired and he doesn't sleep well."

"Why doesn't he, Mummy?"

"Well, you know, don't you, that while he was at the war Mummy got the pennies from the Post Office?"

"From Miss MacCarthy?"

"That's right. But now, you see, Miss MacCarthy hasn't any more pennies, so Daddy must go out and find us some. You know what would happen if he couldn't?"

"No," I said, "tell us."

"Well, I think we might have to go out and beg for them like the poor old woman on Fridays. We wouldn't like that, would we?"

"No," I agreed. "We wouldn't."

"So you'll promise not to come in and wake him?"

"Promise."

Mind you, I meant that. I knew pennies were a serious matter, and I was all against having to go out and beg like the old woman on Fridays. Mother laid out all my toys in a complete ring round the bed so that, whatever way I got out, I was bound to fall over one of them.

When I woke I remembered my promise all right. I got up and sat on the floor and played—for hours, it seemed to me. Then I got my chair and looked out the attic window for more hours. I wished it was time for Father to wake; I wished someone would make me a cup of tea. I didn't feel in the least like the sun; instead, I was bored and so very, very cold! I simply longed for the warmth and depth of the big featherbed.

At last I could stand it no longer. I went into the next room. As there was still no room at Mother's side I climbed over her and she woke with a start.

"Larry," she whispered, gripping my arm very tightly, "what did you promise?"

"But I did, Mummy," I wailed, caught in the very act. "I was quiet for ever so long."

"Oh, dear, and you're perished!"[13] she said sadly, feeling me all over. "Now, if I let you stay will you promise not to talk?"

13. **perished:** frozen.

"But I want to talk, Mummy," I wailed.

"That has nothing to do with it," she said with a firmness that was new to me. "Daddy wants to sleep. Now, do you understand that?"

I understood it only too well. I wanted to talk, he wanted to sleep—whose house was it, anyway?

"Mummy," I said with equal firmness, "I think it would be healthier for Daddy to sleep in his own bed."

That seemed to stagger her, because she said nothing for a while.

"Now, once for all," she went on, "you're to be perfectly quiet or go back to your own bed. Which is it to be?"

The injustice of it got me down. I had convicted her out of her own mouth of inconsistency and unreasonableness, and she hadn't even attempted to reply. Full of spite, I gave Father a kick, which she didn't notice but which made him grunt and open his eyes in alarm.

"What time is it?" he asked in a panic-stricken voice, not looking at Mother but at the door, as if he saw someone there.

"It's early yet," she replied soothingly. "It's only the child. Go to sleep again. . . . Now, Larry," she added, getting out of bed, "you've wakened Daddy and you must go back."

This time, for all her quiet air, I knew she meant it, and knew that my principal rights and privileges were as good as lost unless I asserted them at once. As she lifted me, I gave a screech, enough to wake the dead, not to mind Father. He groaned.

"That damn child! Doesn't he ever sleep?"

"It's only a habit, dear," she said quietly, though I could see she was vexed.

"Well, it's time he got out of it," shouted Father, beginning to heave in the bed. He suddenly gathered all the bedclothes about him, turned to the wall, and then looked back over his shoulder with nothing showing only two small, spiteful, dark eyes. The man looked very wicked.

To open the bedroom door, Mother had to let me down, and I broke free and dashed for the farthest corner, screeching. Father sat bolt upright in bed.

"Shut up, you little puppy!" he said in a choking voice.

I was so astonished that I stopped screeching.

FRANK O'CONNOR 1085

F. Reader's Response: Shaping Interpretations

? What do you learn about the mother during this conversation? [Sample responses: She is a devoted, patient, loving mother. She knows how to identify and appeal to her son's fear in order to persuade him to do what she wants.]

G. Critical Reading: Predicting

Though she shows concern, the mother is firm during this conversation. Larry becomes spiteful. What might happen following this firm conversation? [Students may predict that Larry will obey his mother, or they may suggest that he will wake his father.]

H. Reader's Response: First Thoughts

? Why do you suppose the father is alarmed here? [Sample responses: He is not used to having a child awaken him, and he is exhausted and worried from job-hunting. He may be affected by the recent war; being startled from sleep may make him fear attack.]

I. Language Note: Style

Point out that O'Connor uses vivid language, words that are familiar but not commonplace. What are some examples of O'Connor's lively verbs, specific adverbs and adjectives, and precise nouns in this passage? [Possible answers: *Vexed, heave, spiteful, wicked, dashed, screeching, bolt upright, choking, convulsed, rage, monster.*]

COOPERATIVE LEARNING

Favorite Phrases Explain that while O'Connor's story seems to be written in a simple, conversational style, it is an example of excellent English prose. To encourage students to appreciate the prose and to pursue the various meanings of the text, have them work in small groups to share phrases that interest them. Ask each student to pick a favorite phrase or sentence from the story and to explain to the group the reasons for the choice. Have groups make posters including their quotations and, possibly, illustrations.

Poetry Writing Have students work in groups of four or five to write a poem about the story, reminding them to return to the text as their source. Encourage students to write poems that express the feelings and images (such as Larry's cold feet conversing) that stand out in the story. Students should intersperse these images with reflections, feelings, and questions. The poem should be in first person; the goal is to express the narrator's experience in another format. ☞

Frank O'Connor **T1085**

LITERATURE AND PSYCHOLOGY

Using his own theories as the basis for literary criticism, Sigmund Freud published studies of a variety of literary characters, including Shakespeare's Hamlet, Macbeth, and Lady Macbeth. This type of criticism presumes that literary characters have the same needs and impulses as real human beings do and thus can be analyzed by the same principles. Freud's initial foray into literary criticism was followed by the work of others, including Ernest Jones, who analyzed Hamlet in terms of the Oedipus complex. His criticism is still cited to explain why Hamlet cannot bring himself to avenge his murdered father by killing the murderer, Hamlet's uncle and stepfather, Claudius. Freudian literary criticism is a major force in attempts to interpret literature.

A. Critical Reading: Summarizing

? What changes take place in the characters in this climactic scene?

[Father loses his temper completely but, either from fear of the mother or from self-restraint, gives Larry a "mere tap." Larry thinks the man is murderous. The mother's heart seems broken, and her son hopes it is.]

Mysterious Dreams and Secret Wishes

Frank O'Connor probably didn't read about the "Oedipus complex" in Sigmund Freud's twenty-four-volume collected works. This Freudian theory, and countless others, had already become a permanent part of twentieth-century culture by the time O'Connor wrote his story. Even today, Freud's work lives on in the very words we use to talk about the mind. You may have heard terms like "Freudian slip" or "wish fulfillment." But do you know where they come from?

Tell me what you're thinking. After early training as a physician, Sigmund Freud (1856–1939) became a leader in the new study of the mind. Cartoons of Freud often portray him as a bearded old man, scribbling away in a notebook while his patient lies on a comfortable couch and talks a blue streak. In fact, this was exactly the way Freud worked with his patients in Vienna: He thought that mental illnesses were caused by memories his patients could not consciously remember, and he required his patients to "free associate," or speak their thoughts as randomly as they appeared in the mind. Freud believed such free association would lead back to an original traumatic experience, the discovery of which would cause the illness to dissolve.

Freud was also the first to propose that our deepest desires and fears lie buried in our unconscious, or "id." For Freud, the *id* (Latin for "it") represents our

---

Never, never had anyone spoken to me in that tone before. I looked at him incredulously and saw his face convulsed with rage. It was only then that I fully realized how God had codded[14] me, listening to my prayers for the safe return of this monster.

"Shut up, you!" I bawled, beside myself.

"What's that you said?" shouted Father, making a wild leap out of the bed.

(A) "Mick, Mick!" cried Mother. "Don't you see the child isn't used to you?"

"I see he's better fed than taught," snarled Father, waving his arms wildly. "He wants his bottom smacked."

14. **codded:** British slang for "tricked."

All his previous shouting was as nothing to these obscene words referring to my person. They really made my blood boil.

"Smack your own!" I screamed hysterically. "Smack your own! Shut up! Shut up!"

At this he lost his patience and let fly at me. He did it with the lack of conviction you'd expect of a man under Mother's horrified eyes, and it ended up as a mere tap, but the sheer indignity of being struck at all by a stranger, a total stranger who had cajoled his way back from the war into our big

---

WORDS TO OWN
cajoled (kə·jōld′) v.: coaxed with flattery.

1086 THE TWENTIETH CENTURY

OPTIONS FOR TEACHING

CROSSING THE CURRICULUM

Fine Arts Invite students to develop and present a monologue from the mother's or father's point of view about the period of time covered in the story. Encourage students to consider how the war and Larry's reactions may have affected the marriage. Ask them to consider the adjustments that all three family members must make.

Social Sciences Have students work in small groups to research further the Oedipus complex. Students could study the Oedipus myth; Sophocles' *Oedipus Rex*; essays, articles, and books regarding the theory; or other literature that incorporates the Oedipus complex in the theme. Assign students to compose a brief summary of what the Oedipus complex is and why so much has been written about it.

Health Have students work in small groups to research other well-known theories about child development that might apply to the young character in the story. Encourage students to find theories that they find particularly applicable to Larry. Then, have each group present a panel discussion, sharing theories that might be helpful in analyzing Larry's actions and perceptions.

B. **Reader's Response: Challenging the Text**

? Do you think Larry is correct when he surmises that his father is jealous too? Explain. [Sample responses: Yes, the father competes with Larry for attention by losing his boots and making a fuss about his box of war treasures. Or no, the father is just going about his business, but Larry perceives a rivalry because he does not understand the married relationship his parents have.]

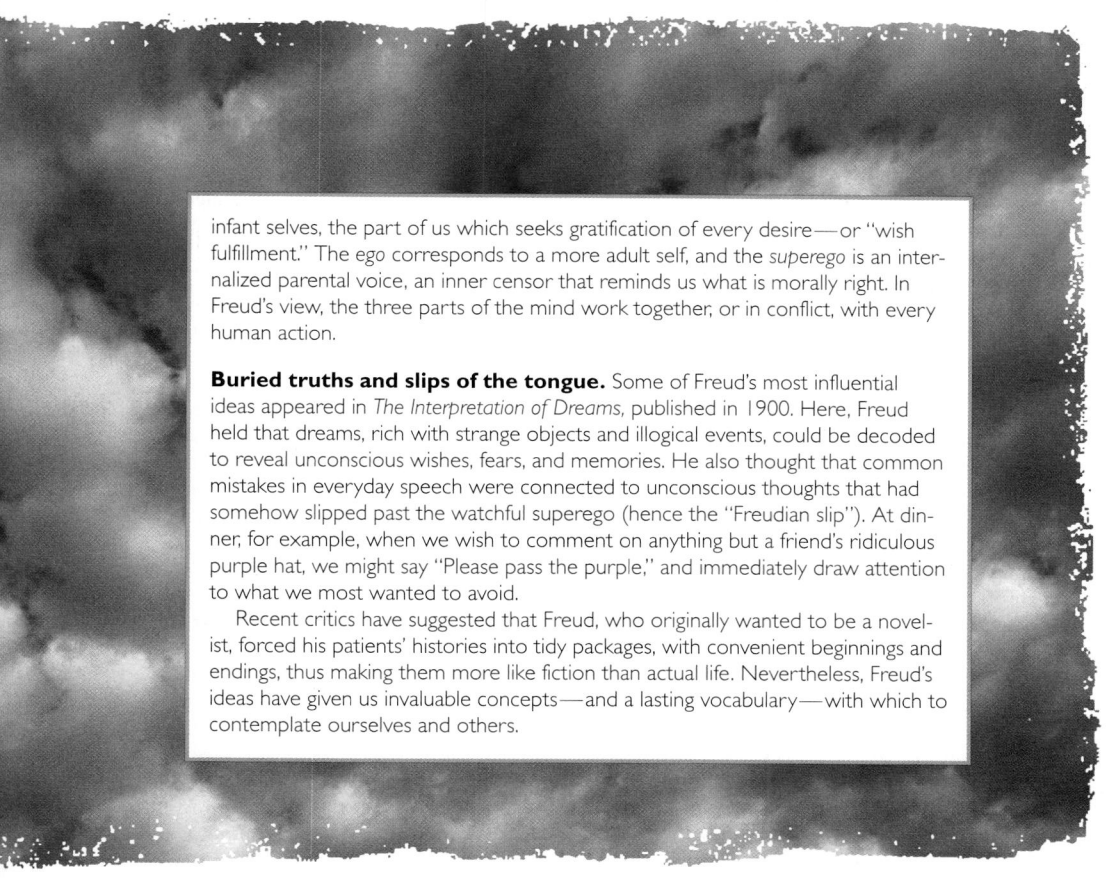

infant selves, the part of us which seeks gratification of every desire—or "wish fulfillment." The *ego* corresponds to a more adult self, and the *superego* is an internalized parental voice, an inner censor that reminds us what is morally right. In Freud's view, the three parts of the mind work together, or in conflict, with every human action.

Buried truths and slips of the tongue. Some of Freud's most influential ideas appeared in *The Interpretation of Dreams,* published in 1900. Here, Freud held that dreams, rich with strange objects and illogical events, could be decoded to reveal unconscious wishes, fears, and memories. He also thought that common mistakes in everyday speech were connected to unconscious thoughts that had somehow slipped past the watchful superego (hence the "Freudian slip"). At dinner, for example, when we wish to comment on anything but a friend's ridiculous purple hat, we might say "Please pass the purple," and immediately draw attention to what we most wanted to avoid.

Recent critics have suggested that Freud, who originally wanted to be a novelist, forced his patients' histories into tidy packages, with convenient beginnings and endings, thus making them more like fiction than actual life. Nevertheless, Freud's ideas have given us invaluable concepts—and a lasting vocabulary—with which to contemplate ourselves and others.

bed as a result of my innocent <u>intercession</u>, made me completely dotty.[15] I shrieked and shrieked, and danced in my bare feet, and Father, looking awkward and hairy in nothing but a short gray army shirt, glared down at me like a mountain out for murder. I think it must have been then that I realized he was jealous too. And there stood Mother in her nightdress, looking as if her heart was broken between us. I hoped she felt as she looked. It seemed to me that she deserved it all.

From that morning out my life was a hell. Father and I were enemies, open and avowed. We conducted a series of skirmishes against one another, he trying to steal my time with Mother and

15. **dotty:** crazy.

I his. When she was sitting on my bed, telling me a story, he took to looking for some pair of old boots which he alleged he had left behind him at the beginning of the war. While he talked to Mother I played loudly with my toys to show my total lack of concern. He created a terrible scene one evening when he came in from work and found me at his box, playing with his regimental badges, Gurkha knives, and button sticks. Mother got up and took the box from me.

Ⓑ

WORDS TO OWN
intercession (in′tər·sesh′ən) *n*.: pleading on behalf of another.

FRANK O'CONNOR 1087

PROBLEM SOLVING / CRITICAL THINKING

Conflict Resolution Much of the humor in this story hinges on misperceptions. In the following scenarios, ask students to determine how those involved might perceive the situation differently from one another and to summarize the two perspectives in the left-hand column. Then, have students suggest possible solutions for each situation in the right-hand column. The following graphic may be helpful.

Scenario 1: Rachel's father asks her not to borrow the new car to go the mall on Saturday.
Scenario 2: Antonio tells his sister she should take a business class instead of an art class.

Description of Problem	Proposed Solutions
1a. [Rachel thinks he is being unreasonable.]	1. [He can take her to the mall, and, over the long term, help her save for a car of her own.]
1b. [Father knows the parking lot will be busy and is worried about his car getting dented.]	
2a. [Antonio may feel he is helping his sister to be successful.]	2. [Antonio and his sister should discuss the merits of each class.]
2b. [His sister may feel he is bossy and insensitive to her interests.]	

A. Reader's Response: First Thoughts

? What is amusing and touching about Larry's predicament? [Sample responses: He mistakenly thinks he is the center and cause of everything in his world, even the arrival of the new baby. He equates love with marriage and does not fully understand the different kinds of love.]

B. Language Note: Style

? What effect does the use of dashes in this passage have? [The dashes indicate interruption in the narrator's thoughts, showing emotion.]

C. Critical Reading: Making Inferences

? What brings about the father's change in behavior? [Possible answer: He realizes that Larry is hurt, as he is, by the mother's doting attention to the new baby.]

"You mustn't play with Daddy's toys unless he lets you, Larry," she said severely. "Daddy doesn't play with yours."

For some reason Father looked at her as if she had struck him and then turned away with a scowl.

"Those are not toys," he growled, taking down the box again to see had I lifted[16] anything. "Some of those curios are very rare and valuable."

But as time went on I saw more and more how he managed to <u>alienate</u> Mother and me. What made it worse was that I couldn't grasp his method or see what attraction he had for Mother. In every possible way he was less winning than I. He had a common accent and made noises at his tea. I thought for a while that it might be the newspapers she was interested in, so I made up bits of news of my own to read to her. Then I thought it might be the smoking, which I personally thought attractive, and took his pipes and went round the house dribbling into them till he caught me. I even made noises at my tea, but Mother only told me I was disgusting. It all seemed to hinge round that unhealthy habit of sleeping together, so I made a point of dropping into their bedroom and nosing round, talking to myself, so that they wouldn't know I was watching them, but they were never up to anything that I could see. In the end it beat me. It seemed to depend on being grown-up and giving people rings, and I realized I'd have to wait.

But at the same time I wanted him to see that I was only waiting, not giving up the fight. One evening when he was being particularly <u>obnoxious</u>, chattering away well above my head, I let him have it.

Ⓐ "Mummy," I said, "do you know what I'm going to do when I grow up?"

"No, dear," she replied. "What?"

"I'm going to marry you," I said quietly.

Father gave a great <u>guffaw</u> out of him, but he didn't take me in. I knew it must only be pretense. And Mother, in spite of everything, was pleased. I felt she was probably relieved to know that one day Father's hold on her would be broken.

"Won't that be nice?" she said with a smile.

16. **lifted:** British slang for "stolen."

"It'll be very nice," I said confidently. "Because we're going to have lots and lots of babies."

"That's right, dear," she said placidly. "I think we'll have one soon, and then you'll have plenty of company."

I was no end pleased about that because it showed that in spite of the way she gave in to Father she still considered my wishes. Besides, it would put the Geneys in their place.

It didn't turn out like that, though. To begin with, she was very <u>preoccupied</u>—I supposed about where she would get the seventeen and six—and though Father took to staying out late in the evenings it did me no particular good. She stopped taking me for walks, became as touchy as blazes, and smacked me for nothing at all. Sometimes I wished I'd never mentioned the confounded baby—I seemed to have a genius for bringing calamity on myself. **Ⓑ**

And calamity it was! Sonny arrived in the most appalling hullabaloo—even that much he couldn't do without a fuss—and from the first moment I disliked him. He was a difficult child—so far as I was concerned he was always difficult—and demanded far too much attention. Mother was simply silly about him, and couldn't see when he was only showing off. As company he was worse than useless. He slept all day, and I had to go round the house on tiptoe to avoid waking him. It wasn't any longer a question of not waking Father. The slogan now was "Don't-wake-Sonny!" I couldn't understand why the child wouldn't sleep at the proper time, so whenever Mother's back was turned I woke him. Sometimes to keep him awake I pinched him as well. Mother caught me at it one day and gave me a most unmerciful flaking.[17] **Ⓒ**

One evening, when Father was coming in from work, I was playing trains in the front garden. I let

17. **flaking:** spanking.

WORDS TO OWN
alienate (āl′ē·ən·āt′) v.: to drive apart.
obnoxious (əb·näk′shəs) adj.: offensive.
guffaw (gu·fô′) n.: loud laugh. "Guffaw" is an echoic word—one that imitates the sound it stands for.
preoccupied (prē·äk′yo͞o·pīd′) adj.: absorbed in one's own thoughts.

OPTIONS FOR TEACHING

PROFESSIONAL NOTES

Thematic Connections: "Ourselves Among Others" How does this story suggest that Larry needs to adjust to others? [Students may say that it examines the way a child feels and learns to adapt to changes in the family structure. In this case, Larry must cope with no longer being the center of attention.]

Critical Comment: Details William Maxwell, an editor at the *New Yorker,* which published many of O'Connor's short stories, reports that O'Connor once commented that the design, not "nice sentences," was the focus in his stories. However, Maxwell writes, "You cannot say that the man who wrote 'The engine shrieked; the porter slammed the door with a curse; somewhere another door opened and shut, and the

row of watchers, frozen into effigies of farewell, now dark now bright, began to glide gently past the window, and the stale, smoky air was charged with the breath of open fields' was indifferent to which word he used, or to the shape of his sentences. Or that he wasn't, indeed, a poet. . . ." Ask students to support Maxwell's evaluation by citing examples of O'Connor's poetic language from the story.

on not to notice him; instead, I pretended to be talking to myself, and said in a loud voice: "If another bloody baby comes into this house, I'm going out."

Father stopped dead and looked at me over his shoulder.

"What's that you said?" he asked sternly.

"I was only talking to myself," I replied, trying to conceal my panic. "It's private."

He turned and went in without a word. Mind you, I intended it as a solemn warning, but its effect was quite different. Father started being quite nice to me. I could understand that, of course. Mother was quite sickening about Sonny. Even at mealtimes she'd get up and gawk at him in the cradle with an idiotic smile, and tell Father to do the same. He was always polite about it, but he looked so puzzled you could see he didn't know what she was talking about. He complained of the way Sonny cried at night, but she only got cross and said that Sonny never cried except when there was something up with him—which was a flaming lie, because Sonny never had anything up with him, and only cried for attention. It was really painful to see how simpleminded she was. Father wasn't attractive, but he had a fine intelligence. He saw through Sonny, and now he knew that I saw through him as well.

One night I woke with a start. There was someone beside me in the bed. For one wild moment I felt sure it must be Mother, having come to her senses and left Father for good, but then I heard Sonny in convulsions in the next room, and Mother saying: "There! There! There!" and I knew it wasn't she. It was Father. He was lying beside me, wide awake, breathing hard and apparently as mad as hell.

After a while it came to me what he was mad about. It was his turn now. After turning me out of the big bed, he had been turned out himself. Mother had no consideration now for anyone but that poisonous pup, Sonny. I couldn't help feeling sorry for Father. I had been through it all myself, and even at that age I was <u>magnanimous</u>. I began to stroke him down and say: "There! There!" He wasn't exactly responsive.

"Aren't you asleep either?" he snarled.

"Ah, come on and put your arm around us, can't you?" I said, and he did, in a sort of way. Gingerly, I suppose, is how you'd describe it. He was very bony but better than nothing.

At Christmas he went out of his way to buy me a really nice model railway.

D. Critical Reading: Analyzing Irony

? How would you explain the irony in this paragraph? [Possible answers: Larry continues to misinterpret what is happening and why. He believes he and his father are in the same position regarding the new baby. He sees himself as generous and comforting, while his father has seen him act very spoiled.]

E. Literary Element: Resolution

The story ends with a new bond of affection developing between father and son.

Making Meanings

Making Meanings questions begin on p. 1090.

First Thoughts

1. Some students might see Larry as a playful child who misunderstands the circumstances. Others might dislike Larry because he is selfish and wants all of his mother's attention. Within a page it is clear the narrator is young and gullible and small enough to need a chair to look out the attic window.

Reviewing the Text

Larry awakens with the first light. He settles his daily plans, goes to his mother's room, and climbs into her bed to discuss them. After his father returns, his mother tries to prevent the child from disturbing his father.

Shaping Interpretations

2. Larry notices that whenever he is spending time with his mother, his father tries to distract her—once by looking for some lost boots and another time by getting angry that Larry was playing with his father's box of curios.

Check Test: True-False

1. When the story begins, there is only one child in the family. [True]
2. The narrator refuses to pray for the safe return of his father from the war. [False]
3. After the father returns, the mother immediately forbids the boy to come into her bed in the morning. [False]
4. The father as well as the son behaves jealously. [True]

5. The mother feels torn between the demands of father and son. [True]

Peer Assessment As students present reports following group activities, have the audience evaluate each performance on a scale of 1 to 5, with 5 being the highest. Develop the criteria you would like for them to use to evaluate, or use a chart like the following.

Criteria	Score	Comments
Content		
Support		
Organization		

3. The attention required of the mother by the new baby ultimately resolves the conflict between Larry and his father because they sympathize with one another.

4. Larry assumes babies are purchased, when the mother refers to the medical fees. He does not see why his parents share the same bed, since his mother has told Larry that staying in his own room is healthier.

5. Larry sees his father as unrefined, as well as selfish and tyrannical toward his mother and him. Larry's mother seems torn between her husband's and son's wishes.

6. Larry identifies with his father and "forgives" him. The birth of Sonny has made the father and Larry jealous.

7. Students may see the story as an entertaining sketch of how a child misinterprets the adult world. Others may say the theme is the inherent conflict between fathers and sons.

Challenging the Text

8. **(Evaluation)** Students might agree, due to the nature of the story. Others might disagree because they can understand the selfishness of childhood and will not share Larry's view of the situation.

Beyond the Story

Choices: Building Your Portfolio

1. **Writer's Notebook** Remind students to save their work. They may use it as prewriting for the Writer's Workshop on p. 1179.

4. **Creative Writing** *Remind students to choose a situation they would not mind sharing with others.* Allow students to confer with friends or family to pique their memories. Also suggest that students peruse old photographs.

MAKING MEANINGS

First Thoughts

1. What do you think of the story's young narrator? At what point in the story could you determine his age?

Reviewing the Text

Larry describes the war, ironically, as the most peaceful part of his life. Outline the details of Larry's peaceful morning ritual during the war. How does his life change when his father comes home?

Shaping Interpretations

2. At one point in the story, Larry realizes that he and his father are conducting "a series of skirmishes against one another, he trying to steal my time with Mother and I his." What details justify Larry's conclusion that his father is really jealous of him?

3. What event finally resolves the **conflict** between Larry and his father?

4. What is the **dramatic irony** in Larry's remarks about the cost of a baby? Find and explain one additional example of dramatic irony in Larry's comments about sharing his mother with his father.

5. How would you describe Father's **character** as the young narrator sees it? How would you describe the character of Larry's mother?

6. At the end of the story, how can you tell that Larry's Oedipal stage is over? But what new problem has arisen in the household?

7. How would you state the **theme** of this story?

Challenging the Text

8. Do you agree with Larry's stance on the notion that "Two's company; three's a crowd?" (Refer to your Reader's Log for ideas.) Explain your response.

CHOICES: Building Your Portfolio

Writer's Notebook

1. Collecting Ideas for a Problem-Solution Essay

As you read in his biography on page 1080, O'Connor did very well, even though he dropped out of school at fourteen. That was long ago. Today, in most cases, people who don't finish high school—and, increasingly, postsecondary training or college—find their options limited. Use freewriting, brainstorming, or clustering to come up with your own ideas for a high-school dropout prevention program. Save your notes for the Writer's Workshop on page 1179.

Critical Writing

2. Calling Dr. Freud

Write a brief essay analyzing O'Connor's intention in this story. Do you think he is writing a serious story about a child with a painful Oedipal conflict, or is he having some fun with psychiatry? Support your view with details from the story.

Critical Writing

3. Trials of Youth

The young heroes of "Araby" (see page 989) and "My Oedipus Complex," although not the same age, are similar in some ways. In a brief essay that uses references from the stories to support your interpretations, discuss the heroes' similarities and differences.

Creative Writing

4. That Was Then

What can you remember about your thoughts and feelings when you were five years old? Write a humorous biographical essay about something that seemed mysterious to you as a small child.

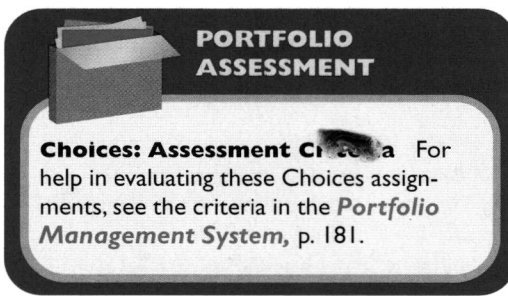

PORTFOLIO ASSESSMENT

Choices: Assessment Criteria For help in evaluating these Choices assignments, see the criteria in the *Portfolio Management System,* p. 181.

W. H. Auden
(1907–1973)

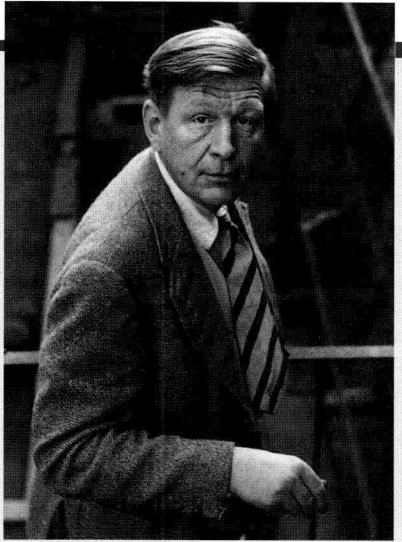
W. H. Auden (1950s).

Wystan Hugh Auden gave a name to his times—"the Age of Anxiety"—and he lived to see the day when his influence was so broad and deep that, as far as poetry was concerned, that same era could have been called "the Age of Auden."

Auden was born in York, a city in northern England near the city of Leeds. He was the son of a physician and a nurse who encouraged his early interest in science and engineering. But in his adolescence, Auden discovered poetry, and he studied, with an analytical eye, all its forms, from Chaucer onward. By the time he entered Oxford, he was as much a teacher as he was a student, and he quickly gathered about himself other young poets, who accepted him as their leader.

Auden as a poet was difficult to classify, and he remains so to this day. By the time they have been recognized and acclaimed, most of the outstanding poets of any generation have produced individual works by which, rightly or wrongly, they will be identified. Sometimes these poems are masterpieces; sometimes they are rather run-of-the-mill poems which, for one reason or another, have caught the popular imagination. To this pattern, Auden is an exception. In spite of their virtuosity, uniform excellence, and formal variety, Auden's poems—lyrics, oratorios, ballads—tend to cohere as a body of work rather than to distinguish themselves as easily separable entities. For this reason, Auden is often regarded less as the author of certain individual poems than as the creator of a climate in which all things Audenesque thrive in an atmosphere uniquely his own.

Auden put his indelible stamp on the poetry of the 1930s, establishing his preeminence among the brilliant group of poets that included Stephen Spender, Louis MacNeice, and Cecil Day-Lewis. Auden caused his British compatriots shock and dismay when, in the critical year of 1939, as Hitler's divisions were about to march into Poland and initiate World War II, he decided to make his home in the United States. Auden had come to feel that, as the rise of Fascism made war in Europe inevitable, his chances of enjoying creative freedom and of making a livelihood were available only in America. From 1939 to 1942, he taught at the University of Michigan and various other American universities. In 1946, he became a U.S. citizen.

For the next ten years, Auden lived mostly in New York City and California. He spent his summers in Kirchstetten, Austria, in a house he bought in 1957 with profits from his extensive reading tours—the first, and last, home of his own. This retreat, not far from Vienna, provided him with much-needed privacy and the opportunity to experience firsthand the culture of central Europe.

In England, Auden's emigration to the United States was, at the time, widely regarded as a defection, if not an outright betrayal. But the British eventually welcomed him back—first by electing him professor of poetry at Oxford, and later by making it possible for him to live on the campus of Christ Church College as a guest of the university whenever he returned to England.

ABOUT THE AUTHOR

W. H. Auden was a man of many talents and interests. Besides teaching for a time, he served as a stretcher-bearer in the Spanish Civil War and worked for a filmmaking company. He had written four books of poetry, three plays, a collection of prose fiction, two travel books, and had edited two anthologies of poetry by the time he was thirty-three. Auden wrote songs as well as drama and poetry. His writing included the words to blues and ballads, and librettos for operas. In 1951 he helped write the libretto for *The Rake's Progress,* an opera by Igor Stravinsky. In 1964, he wrote words for Stravinsky's *Elegy for J.F.K.*

PROGRAM MANAGER

- **Planning Instruction** See Teaching Notes, *Teaching Resources B,* pp. 165–166, for objectives, a summary, literary elements, and additional historical and biographical information for this selection.
- **Instructional Support** Before beginning the instructional lesson, see Graphic Organizer for Active Reading, *Teaching Resources B,* pp. 179–180, for Through the Poem activities.
- **Assessment** See Selection Tests, *Test Booklet,* pp. 232–233.

PORTFOLIO ASSESSMENT

Portfolio Assessment For help with teacher assessment of reading skills, see the *Portfolio Management System,* pp. 54–55.

QUICK PLANNING GUIDE

Into the Poems

Through the Poems

Beyond the Poems

- **Writer's Notebook:** Explore causes and effects of apathy
- **Critical Writing:** Write an essay relating a myth to a poem
- **Critical Writing:** Analyze Auden's interpretation of Brueghel's painting
- **Critical Writing:** Write an essay analyzing Auden's satire
- **Creative Writing:** Write a composition inspired by a work of art or music
- **Creative Writing:** Write an obituary
- **Creative Writing:** Write an epitaph

RESPONDING TO THE ART: ABOUT THE ARTIST

Flemish painter Pieter Bruegel, or Bruegel the Elder (c. 1525–1569), depicted the vigor and coarseness of country life in rich detail, often with a moral or philosophical message.

BEFORE YOU READ
MUSÉE DES BEAUX ARTS
THE UNKNOWN CITIZEN

Reading Focus

The Value of the Individual
Every generation senses imperfections and injustices in the way things are. For Auden, during what he termed the Age of Anxiety, people had grown indifferent to human suffering, and society no longer treasured the individual. This indifference to the plight of others and disregard for the value of individuality were, to Auden, the symptoms of a society in need of reform.

Quickwrite

To what extent do you think individuality and compassion are valued today? In your Reader's Log, jot down some thoughts.

Elements of Literature

Diction
Auden's poems combine eloquent and elegant poetic language with down-to-earth, colloquial words and with technical terms, the jargon of trades and professions. Notice how he uses contrasting **diction** in these poems not only to surprise you but also to relate his language to his ideas.

> **D**iction is a writer's or speaker's choice of words.
> For more on Diction, see the Handbook of Literary Terms.

The Fall of Icarus (16th century) by Pieter Bruegel the Elder.
Musées Royaux des Beaux-Arts, Brussels, Belgium.

OPTIONS FOR TEACHING

STRATEGIES FOR INCLUSION

Musical Have students find a libretto written by Auden, listen to the accompanying music, study the lyrics, and make inferences based on it. Questions they might consider include
- What are its strengths and weaknesses?
- How does it compare with other operas?
- How might music have affected Auden's poetry?

Advanced In his introduction to *The Oxford Book of Light Verse,* Auden wrote that, in the nineteenth century, "The breakdown of the old village or small-town community left the family as the only real social unit, and the parent-child relationship as the only real social bond." Challenge students to write a response to this comment, relating it to one of Auden's poems.

The source and inspiration for this poem is the famous painting by Pieter Bruegel showing Icarus drowning, permanently on display in the Musée des Beaux Arts (myoo·zā′ dā bō zàr′), or Fine Arts Museum, in Brussels, Belgium. The painting depicts a dramatic moment in the Greek legend of Daedalus and his son Icarus. According to the legend, the two were imprisoned on the island of Crete. In order to escape, Daedalus constructed wings of feathers and wax. Together they managed to take off from the island, but Icarus flew so high that the sun's heat melted the wax in his wings, causing him to fall into the sea and drown.

According to one critic, the painting represents "the greatest conception of indifference" in the history of art. The indifference, whether it is the artist's attitude or merely a strategy of technique, lies in its unexpected focus. The painting's center of interest is not Icarus, but a peasant plowing a field. He is handsomely dressed—in medieval rather than in Greek costume—and the furrows he tills are richly realistic. In the lower right-hand corner of the painting, almost as an afterthought, Icarus is seen splashing into the water not far from a passing ship.

Study the painting, and find the figure of the boy falling into the sea. Then, read the poem to see how Auden interprets the painting. Has he confirmed in words what the painter expressed with pigment?

Musée des Beaux Arts

W. H. Auden

About suffering they were never wrong,
The Old Masters: how well they understood
Its human position; how it takes place
While someone else is eating or opening a window or just walking dully along;
5 How, when the aged are reverently, passionately waiting
For the miraculous birth, there always must be
Children who did not specially want it to happen, skating
On a pond at the edge of the wood:
They never forgot
10 That even the dreadful martyrdom must run its course
Anyhow in a corner, some untidy spot
Where the dogs go on with their doggy life and the torturer's horse
Scratches its innocent behind on a tree.

In Bruegel's *Icarus,* for instance: how everything turns away
15 Quite leisurely from the disaster; the plowman may
Have heard the splash, the forsaken cry,
But for him it was not an important failure; the sun shone
As it had to on the white legs disappearing into the green
Water; and the expensive delicate ship that must have seen
20 Something amazing, a boy falling out of the sky,
Had somewhere to get to and sailed calmly on.

W. H. AUDEN 1093

INTEGRATING THE LANGUAGE ARTS

Writing: Editorial Have students work in pairs to consider Auden's conclusion about human suffering. For example, would they have acted as the plowman did? Would a farmer today turn away from the sight of someone drowning? Invite students to find news items that support or refute the speaker's view of how people react to the suffering of others. Encourage students to incorporate their findings into a newspaper editorial commenting on society's reactions to suffering.

Into the Poems

Using BEFORE YOU READ
p. 1092

Quickwrite
Lead students in a discussion of the factors in society that work against the expression of individuality. Start with expression through personal appearance and move into such areas as computerization. Compile a list of ideas on the chalkboard for students to consider as they complete the Quickwrite assignment.

Through the Poems

A. Critical Reading: Identifying Main Ideas
? What ironic contrast is Auden pointing out in the poem's first lines? [While intense suffering takes place, ordinary life goes on.]

B. Cultural Connections
Point out that this poem was written during a time when the values of Europe were shaken by the onslaught of fascism. Although the problems of suffering and of others' indifference seemingly apply to this time of tumult, the issue itself is timeless. In fact, the painting that provides the impetus for the poem was finished in the mid-1500s.

C. Literary Element: Allusion
? To what might "the dreadful martyrdom" refer? [Christ's crucifixion.]

D. Reader's Response: Challenging the Text
? Is the spare style—such as the sentence that begins "the sun shone as it had to"—effective? [Sample responses: Yes, the matter-of-fact brevity accentuates the horror described. No, perhaps more dramatic language would have heightened the poem's drama.]

W. H. Auden **T1093**

Making Meanings

First Thoughts

1. Students might point to wars and disasters in other countries that are not reported in the news media in the United States.

Shaping Interpretations

2. They are the great artists of the European Renaissance. The examples in ll. 3–13 show individuals' indifference to others' suffering.

3. In the first painting, the subject is probably the birth of Christ; the indifferent children skate on a pond at the edge of a wood. The subject of the second may be Christ's crucifixion or the martyrdom of a saint; unperturbed dogs and horses are pictured as an ironic counterpoint. These paintings resemble *Icarus* in the indifference of the bystanders.

4. The poet refers to Bruegel's painting *The Fall of Icarus,* in which neither the plowman nor the sailors take any interest because Icarus's fall does not affect them.

5. The contrast in diction is between formal and informal diction. Other informal diction that contrasts with the formal diction of the rest of the poem includes "doggy life," "innocent behind," and "somewhere to get to."

6. Students may say that the poem suggests people are indifferent to pain that is not their own.

Connecting with the Text

7. Students may cite public indifference to such problems as homelessness, disasters in far-off places, and unemployment. Some students may disagree, pointing to the willingness of many people to donate to disaster relief funds or to help others in need.

W. H. Auden's handwritten manuscript for "Musée des Beaux Arts."

MAKING MEANINGS

First Thoughts

1. Does this poem remind you of any times when the world seemed oblivious to individual suffering? Explain.

Shaping Interpretations

2. Who are the "Old Masters" (line 2)? What examples does the speaker provide to show how the Old Masters understood suffering? (Do you think Auden is right about this?)

3. Lines 5–13 describe two other paintings by Bruegel. What do you think are the events that Bruegel portrays? How do these paintings resemble *Icarus*?

4. What example of his theory about suffering does the speaker offer in lines 14–21?

5. What contrast in **diction** can you see between expressions like "dreadful martyrdom" and "anyhow in a corner"? Find another example of contrasting diction.

6. What do you think is the overall **theme** of the poem? Which lines in the poem do you think are most important?

Connecting with the Text

7. Do you agree with the speaker that, in general, people are indifferent to the suffering they see around them? Why or why not? Look back at the notes in your Reader's Log as you answer.

OPTIONS FOR TEACHING

CROSSING THE CURRICULUM

Fine Arts Have students find pictures of what might be the other paintings Auden refers to in the poem.

Social Sciences Auden uses an ancient myth to make a timeless point. Have students work in pairs to discuss the continuing influence of classical mythology. What might be some reasons for its powerful influence? Invite students to create a display, showing how and why classical mythology has continued to affect modern society.

One of the persistent themes of twentieth-century literature is the anonymity of the individual in an ever more bureaucratic world. Here, Auden uses diction that mimics the language of officialdom, in a report that covers everything except the fact that "the unknown citizen" had a heart and a soul.

The Unknown Citizen

W. H. Auden

(To JS/07/M/378
This Marble Monument Is Erected by the State)

He was found by the Bureau of Statistics to be
One against whom there was no official complaint,
And all the reports on his conduct agree
That, in the modern sense of an old-fashioned word, he was a saint,
5 For in everything he did he served the Greater Community.
Except for the War till the day he retired
He worked in a factory and never got fired,
But satisfied his employers, Fudge Motors Inc.
Yet he wasn't a scab° or odd in his views,
10 For his Union reports that he paid his dues,
(Our report on his Union shows it was sound)
And our Social Psychology workers found
That he was popular with his mates and liked a drink.
The Press are convinced that he bought a paper every day
15 And that his reactions to advertisements were normal in every way.
Policies taken out in his name prove that he was fully insured,
And his Health-card shows he was once in hospital but left it cured.
Both Producers Research and High-Grade Living declare
He was fully sensible to the advantages of the Installment Plan
20 And had everything necessary to the Modern Man,
A phonograph, a radio, a car, and a frigidaire.
Our researchers into Public Opinion are content
That he held the proper opinions for the time of year;
When there was peace, he was for peace; when there was war, he went.
25 He was married and added five children to the population,
Which our Eugenist° says was the right number for a parent of his generation,
And our teachers report that he never interfered with their education.
Was he free? Was he happy? The question is absurd:
Had anything been wrong, we should certainly have heard.

9. **scab:** slang term for a worker who refuses to join a union.
26. **Eugenist** (yoo′jə·nist): specialist in population control.

W. H. AUDEN 1095

A. Critical Reading: Finding Details
Point out that the dead man's "virtues" are often presented in the negative, as in l. 2, where it is reported that "there was no official complaint." What are some other examples? ["Never got fired"; "wasn't a scab"; "never interfered with their education."]

B. Literary Element: Diction
? How would you describe the language and style Auden uses to convey his subject? [He uses the language and style of an official report of death suitable for a government file. It could be the style and language of a detached journalist.]

C. Reader's Response: Shaping Interpretations
? What effect does the rhyme have in ll. 6 and 7? [Sample responses: The change in rhyme scheme draws attention to these lines. The rhyme makes light of the tragic uneventfulness of the man's life.]

D. Reader's Response: Challenging the Text
? Is this a good ending for the poem? Explain. [Sample responses: This is an effective ending because it states directly the problem Auden alludes to throughout the poem. Or the ending is abrupt and dissatisfying, which emphasizes Auden's point.]

INTEGRATING THE LANGUAGE ARTS

Strategic Reading The rhymes and near-doggerel rhythm of this poem help indicate the speaker's tone. Have several students read the poem aloud in character, perhaps in the manner of a politician. As the other students listen, encourage them to consider how the diction and tone reflect the personality of the "unknown citizen" and the intent of the poet.

Language and Style As the diction is an important clue to the poem's meaning, have interested students research real-life examples of "officialese." *Quarterly Review of Doublespeak,* published by the National Council of Teachers of English, would be a good place to start. Ask students to compile a list of phrases, then have them work in pairs to write a short narrative that incorporates their officialese.

Writing: Poem Have students create a poem about another "unknown," such as a friend, sibling, mentor, or parent. To gather material for their poetry, students might list general information about the person they have chosen, and then categorize the person they know, as Auden does. *Remind students to choose a situation they would not mind sharing.* ☞

Making Meanings

First Thoughts

1. Students may think the picture of the unknown citizen rings true, and that the citizen's anonymity, his reactions to advertisements, and his consumerism reflect a continuing trend.

Shaping Interpretations

2. He worked for Fudge Motors. The Bureau of Statistics, the Union, the Social Psychology workers, the Press, Producers Research and High-Grade Living, the researchers into Public Opinion, and the Eugenist report the statistics on him.

3. The speaker may be a government official; the tone is satirical.

4. An unconventional person, perhaps a friend of the deceased.

5. Perhaps the numbers and letters indicate he could not be identified by name, or perhaps he performed an honorable deed. Students may be reminded of the Tomb of the Unknown Soldier.

6. The modern world emphasizes conformity at the expense of individuality, freedom, and happiness. Students may feel this message is bleak.

7. The diction never refers to the man by name or to any individual traits. Impersonal, bureaucratic language is reflected in the use of passive voice ("He was found . . . to be") and the personification of documents ("Policies . . . prove" and "his Health-card shows"). The poem sounds like an official speech.

8. Students may sympathize with the citizen, claiming that society's drive for rigid conformity is at fault. Other students may argue that the citizen should have asserted his individuality.

Extending the Text

9. **(Analysis)** Students may be optimistic about increased awareness of social issues.

Challenging the Text

10. **(Analysis)** Most students will agree that poems like this one could have been written in earlier centuries, but maintaining individuality is especially difficult in the twentieth century.

Concentric Group (1925)
by Oskar Schlemmer.
Oil on canvas.

© 1997 The Oskar Schlemmer
Family Estate and Archive,
79410 Badenweiler, Germany /
Photo Archive C. Raman Schlemmer,
Oggebbio, Italy.

MAKING MEANINGS

First Thoughts

1. Do you think this poem gives a true picture of our society today? Which details do or do not ring true? (Refer to your Reader's Log.)

Shaping Interpretations

2. What did the unknown citizen do for a living? What facts are reported on his conduct, and what agencies and groups contribute to this report?

3. Who do you think is the **speaker** of the poem? Although the poet does not directly state his opinions in this poem, they clearly emerge from the speaker's **tone**. How would you describe this tone?

4. Who do you think might have asked the questions in line 28?

5. What do you make of the inscription under the title? What other "monuments" are you reminded of?

STRATEGIES FOR INCLUSION

Interpersonal After they read the poem, pair students, and ask them to assume in turn the role of the "unknown citizen's" friend and to interview each other. Issues to consider include the relationship between the state and the individual, human rights, and consumerism.

CROSSING THE CURRICULUM

Art Students might respond to the poem individually or as a group by creating a memorial, such as a miniature monument, for the unknown citizen. Invite them to use materials that represent the citizen as they understand him from the poem and to present their memorials to the class.

6. What would you say is the message or **theme** of the poem? How do you feel about Auden's message?

7. Find examples of impersonal, bureaucratic diction in the poem. Do you read or hear language like this today? If so, where?

8. The poem seems to depict the "unknown citizen" as a colorless stereotype. Did you, however, sympathize with the citizen? Explain your response to him.

Extending the Text

9. Auden's message about modern life is quite pessimistic. What sources of optimism do you find in modern life? Your Reader's Log notes may give you some ideas.

Challenging the Text

10. Could this poem have been written in any other time of history but the twentieth century? Why or why not?

CHOICES: Building Your Portfolio

Writer's Notebook

1. Collecting Ideas for a Problem-Solution Essay

As Auden's poems make clear, apathy and an impersonal bureaucracy can seriously affect not only the individual but also society as a whole. Is apathy or a mindless bureaucracy that ignores individual differences a serious problem in your school or community or in your society as a whole? Get together with several other students to discuss this question and to explore the causes and effects of the problem. Take notes on your group's comments, and save them for the Writer's Workshop on page 1179.

Critical Writing

2. Back to the Source

Read a translation or summary of Ovid's version of the myth of Daedalus and Icarus in Book 8 of the *Metamorphoses*. Then, in a brief essay, relate the myth to Auden's treatment of it in "Musée des Beaux Arts."

Critical Writing

3. What Did Bruegel Mean?

Study the reproduction of Bruegel's *Icarus* on page 1092. In a paragraph, describe the painting's most significant features. Do you think Auden has correctly interpreted Bruegel's intent?

Critical Writing

4. Right on Target?

In a brief essay, analyze the targets and the methods of Auden's satire in "The Unknown Citizen." Does Auden manage to combine satire and sympathy? Explain your answer.

Creative Writing

5. Inspired by Art

Write a poem, a brief essay, or a short story inspired by a painting or a piece of music. You might find a subject in a painting in this book.

Creative Writing

6. A Few Kind Words

Imagine that you are a good friend of the deceased citizen. Write your friend's obituary from this new point of view.

Creative Writing

7. Today's Unknown Citizen

Write your own epitaph for an unknown high school student, athlete, parent, or worker. Use the questions "Was he or she free? Was he or she happy?" as the focus of your account.

Beyond the Poems

Choices: Building Your Portfolio

1. **Writer's Notebook** Remind students to save their work. They may use it as prewriting for the Writer's Workshop on p. 1179.

2. **Critical Writing** Read the myth aloud to the whole class. Keep a copy or two of the myth in the classroom for students to refer to as they work on their compositions.

4. **Critical Writing** Suggest that students cluster the targets of Auden's satire into two or more groups (such as government bureaucracy and commercial interests) and deal with these clusters in separate paragraphs.

5. **Creative Writing** Prepare for this assignment by gathering posters, prints, and library books that contain pictures of works of art. Have these items available in the classroom for students to consult as they work on their compositions.

6. **Creative Writing** Some students may not be familiar with the obituary form. Help them by bringing to class obituaries from newspapers that have a national interest, such as the *New York Times*.

7. **Creative Writing** Remind students that an epitaph is an inscription on a tomb or monument. These statements try to capture the essence of the person they are meant to commemorate.

STRATEGIES FOR INCLUSION

Visual When students work on activity #4, they might find it useful to organize the details of the poem into categories. A chart like the following may help them visualize Auden's primary targets.

Government	Employment	Commercial Concerns

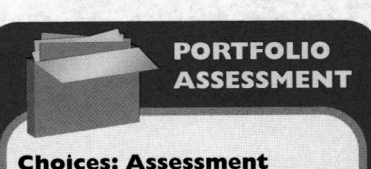

PORTFOLIO ASSESSMENT

Choices: Assessment Criteria For help in evaluating these Choices assignments, see the criteria in the *Portfolio Management System*, pp. 182–183.

A. Exploring the Historical Period

Censorship of the theater began during the reign of Henry VII and was intended to protect the king and members of the royal court from being offended by any play presented before them. The Master of the King's Revels was given the charge of making sure plays were acceptable. When unorthodox religious ideas were added to the list of topics considered offensive to the king, the job of censoring plays went to the Lord Chamberlain, who was responsible for running the king's household. Until the Theatres Act of 1968, producers of plays had to submit a copy of the script, including any additions or changes to scripts that had been previously approved, before they could receive a license to present the play to the public.

SPOTLIGHT ON

Contemporary British Drama

by Robert Anderson

It is difficult to know which of the playwrights of the twentieth century will stand the test of time—mostly because we are still in it (or still close to it). Plays are volatile creations, often written out of present concerns and emotions to reach an audience in the present. In a changing world with changing fashions, there is no way of knowing how people will respond to plays in the future. The highly regarded play of one generation is often viewed with contempt by the next generation: "How could they have thought that was a great play?"

Yet we can say with certainty that this century has seen sweeping changes in both the content and the form of plays. Censorship of the stage in England ended in 1968, and now there is virtually nothing that playwrights have not written about or cannot write about.

While the broadening of subject matter is a significant advance, some playwrights have been less interested in new subject matter than in new ways to get our attention—to shock us into recognizing old and new truths. These playwrights have followed various paths. Some have broken up the usual linear structure of a story—a beginning, a middle, and an end arranged in that order. In their plays they jump backward and forward in time,

Scene from a 1976 production of Samuel Beckett's *Waiting for Godot* at the Brooklyn Academy of Music, New York City.

1098 THE TWENTIETH CENTURY

hither and yon in space. Some, like the German playwright Bertolt Brecht, do not want to engage our sympathy for any character, but force us to keep our distance. Brecht called this "the alienation effect." Others, like the Irish playwright Samuel Beckett, ignore the usual ingredients of drama—character, conflict, development, and progression to a climax—and present us instead with a static situation.

Playwrights who depart from the familiar conventions of playwriting take a great risk; they are like performers on a high wire without the safety net of a story. They had better be star performers every time out, or there will be a disaster. If they deny their audiences the pleasure of narrative ("Tell me a story!"), they have to keep them fascinated by other means.

Theater of the Absurd: Samuel Beckett

Though Samuel Beckett (1906–1989) was born in Ireland, he lived most of his life in France and wrote many of his plays in French, which he then translated into English. Whether or not he can be considered a British playwright, his *Waiting for Godot* (1953) is a modern classic, and his work is a prime example of what is known as the Theater of the Absurd.

Deriving to some degree from James Joyce and Surrealism, the Theater of the Absurd is an almost complete departure from the traditional theater of the preceding four hundred years. The Theater of the Absurd, first of all, represents an attitude toward life expressed in part by the French writer Albert Camus:

> A world that can be explained even with bad reasons is a familiar world. But, on the other hand, in a universe suddenly divested of illusions and lights, man feels an alien, a stranger. . . . This divorce between man and his life . . . is properly the feeling of absurdity.
>
> —Albert Camus, *from* "An Absurd Reasoning"

The Absurdists do not want to tell us a story with characters arguing about the emptiness of life. They want instead to *present* us with this emptiness, this absurdity, moment by moment, so that we can experience it. There is usually no progression, no

development in an Absurdist play. As we shall see in Beckett's *Waiting for Godot,* the "action" is waiting. The French title for Beckett's play is *En Attendant Godot,* literally, "While Waiting for Godot." The play is about the "while." Since the Absurdists' view is that the world is irrational, unmotivated, without cause and effect, they convey this idea not only as "the message" of the play but also in the fragmented, irrational method of the playwriting. *Waiting for Godot* was first produced in Paris in 1953 and in London in 1955. Two tramps, Vladimir and Estragon, are on a stage, bare except for a tree.

Estragon. Charming spot. *(He turns, advances to the front, halts facing auditorium.)* Inspiring prospects. *(He turns to Vladimir.)* Let's go.
Vladimir. We can't.
Estragon. Why not?
Vladimir. We're waiting for Godot.
Estragon *(despairingly).* Ah! *(Pause.)* You're sure it was here?
Vladimir. What?
Estragon. That we were to wait.
Vladimir. He said by the tree. *(They look at the tree.)* Do you see any others?
Estragon. What is it?
Vladimir. I don't know. A willow.
Estragon. Where are the leaves?
Vladimir. It must be dead.
Estragon. No more weeping.
Vladimir. Or perhaps it's not the season.
Estragon. Looks to me more like a bush.
Vladimir. A shrub.
Estragon. A bush.
Vladimir. A ———. What are you insinuating? That we've come to the wrong place?
Estragon. He should be here.
Vladimir. He didn't say for sure he'd come.
Estragon. And if he doesn't come?
Vladimir. We'll come back tomorrow.
Estragon. And then the day after tomorrow.
Vladimir. Possibly.
Estragon. And so on.
Vladimir. The point is———
Estragon. Until he comes.
Vladimir. You're merciless.
Estragon. We came here yesterday.

SPOTLIGHT ON 1099

INTEGRATING THE LANGUAGE ARTS

Strategic Reading Some students may feel more comfortable with the material in the Spotlight On feature if they see it presented in outline form, with main ideas separated from supporting details and examples. As students read the feature,

ask them to create a formal outline of it. You might have students write their outlines on large sheets of paper that can be displayed for comparisons among the outlines.

B. Literary Connections
Bertolt Brecht (1898–1956) was the leading Marxist playwright of his day. Born in Germany, Brecht served briefly as a medical orderly in World War I, and this experience made him a staunch pacifist. The dramatic work for which he is best know is *Mother Courage and Her Children,* which is set during the Thirty Years' War during the seventeenth century. This play ridicules a woman who supplies both sides in the war with goods and services for her dependence on war as a means of support.

C. Expansion
The phrase "Theater of the Absurd" describes drama that has its roots in the philosophy of existentialism that gained credence after World War II. In the Theater of the Absurd, dramatists employ black humor and create morbid and grotesque situations that are simultaneously tragic and funny.

D. Expansion
Surrealism was an artistic, literary, and philosophical movement in the 1920s that attempted to discover and represent a reality beyond that perceived through the conscious mind. Using Sigmund Freud's theory of the unconscious, surrealists believed that the subconscious would produce images and symbols that, no matter how grotesque and incongruous they might appear to the conscious mind, actually revealed the true nature of reality. Some painters who were influenced by surrealism were Salvador Dali, Max Ernst, Paul Klee, Joan Miró, and Pablo Picasso.

E. Literary Connections
Although *Waiting for Godot* is the best known play of the Theater of the Absurd, it was not the first. That distinction belongs to *The Bald Soprano* by Eugène Ionesco, a native of Romania who became a citizen of France. Subtitled "Anti-Play," *The Bald Soprano* pokes fun at the banal existence of two English couples. Much of the dialogue was lifted directly from an English phrase book that Ionesco had bought in order to learn the language. Consequently, the play does not make "sense." On a deeper level, though, the nonsensicalness of the dialogue underscores the failure of language as a means of genuine communication.

A. Literary Connections

Jean Gênet (1910–1986) was a French novelist and playwright who wrote absurdist plays about his characters' attempts to secure personal freedom from the personas imposed by others. A criminal all his life, Gênet was released from a life sentence in prison at the insistence of leading French writers and intellectuals in 1947.

Edward Albee (1928–) is an American playwright whose earlier plays, such as *The Zoo Story* and *The Sandbox,* are in the tradition of the Theater of the Absurd. In these plays Albee deals with such themes as illusion versus reality and isolation. He has won the Pulitzer Prize for drama several times and continues to be one of the outstanding playwrights in the United States

Scene from a June 1984 production of Samuel Beckett's *Endgame* at the Cherry Lane Theater, New York.

Vladimir. Ah no, there you're mistaken.
Estragon. What did we do yesterday?
Vladimir. What did we do yesterday?
Estragon. Yes.
Vladimir. Why . . . *(Angrily.)* Nothing is certain when you're about.
Estragon. In my opinion we were here.
Vladimir *(looking around).* You recognize the place?
Estragon. I didn't say that.
Vladimir. Well?
Estragon. That makes no difference.
Vladimir. All the same . . . that tree . . . *(turning toward auditorium)* that bog.
Estragon. You're sure it was this evening?
Vladimir. What?
Estragon. That we were to wait.
Vladimir. He said Saturday. *(Pause.)* I think.
Estragon. You think.
Vladimir. I must have made a note of it. *(He fumbles in his pockets, bursting with miscellaneous rubbish.)*
Estragon *(very insidious).* But what Saturday? And is it Saturday? Is it not rather Sunday?

(Pause.) Or Monday? *(Pause.)* Or Friday?
Vladimir *(looking wildly about him as though the date was inscribed in the landscape).* It's not possible!
Estragon. Or Thursday?
Vladimir. What'll we do?
Estragon. If he came yesterday and we weren't here you may be sure he won't come again today.
Vladimir. But you say we were here yesterday.
Estragon. I may be mistaken. *(Pause.)* Let's stop talking for a minute. Do you mind?
Vladimir *(feebly).* All right.

—Samuel Beckett, *from Waiting for Godot*

Thus ends one of the series of "riffs" that make up the play. After a few moments' pause, the characters will start up again, terrified by the silence and the momentary view of nothingness.

Many people find the work of the Absurdists (Beckett, Eugene Ionesco, Jean Genêt, and Edward Albee) maddening. They say, "That's not a play!" just as some years ago, steeped in representational painting, some said of Abstract Expressionism,

---

OPTIONS FOR TEACHING

INTEGRATING THE LANGUAGE ARTS

Speaking and Listening Timing plays an important part in the delivery of the lines from *Waiting for Godot* and *That's All,* and some students may need to hear the passages presented orally in order to fully grasp their effect. Ask pairs of students to practice an oral reading of either of the two passages, giving due attention to the pauses and tone of the lines. Have pairs present their readings.

"That's not art!" Our expectations of what a play or a picture should be are deeply rooted in us, planted and nurtured by years of exposure to only certain kinds of dramatic experience or certain kinds of painting experience. The best we can do when faced with the strange is to try to remain open to the new, to let it try to educate us and broaden our appreciation, rather than to reject it because it is strange and new.

Who is Godot? When someone asked Beckett this question, he answered that if he had known, he would have revealed it in the play. Possibly Godot is best explained by Tennessee Williams when he has Tom say in *The Glass Menagerie* that the Gentleman Caller is "the long delayed but always expected something that we live for."

Beckett's tramps, like Laurel and Hardy in the old movies, bicker in scene after scene, sometimes sounding like husband and wife in a standard domestic comedy. They seem to be derived in part from the end men who used to appear in vaudeville and music halls, bantering jokes and wisecracks back and forth. They also resemble the comedian and the straight man in the comedy teams of movies, radio, and television. Though Beckett discarded all the ideas of progression and dramatic development, he does employ a number of the appealing theatrical tricks of farce and vaudeville. There are pratfalls, difficulty get-

ting shoes on and off, trousers falling down, futile efforts at suicide. The tramps are joined by a bizarre pair, Pozzo and Lucky, one a master, the other a slave on the end of a rope—a vivid theatrical picture.

Toward the end of Act I, a boy arrives from Godot to say he will not arrive today, but "surely tomorrow." Act II is almost a repetition of Act I, except that when Pozzo and Lucky enter, Pozzo is blind and Lucky is dumb. The boy again arrives at the end of the act to say that Godot will not arrive today, but tomorrow, "without fail."

Beckett regarded habit as "the lightning conductor" of our existence—in other words, the small habitual activities that keep us busy every day, all day, prevent us from being hit with the truth, which (as Beckett sees it) is loneliness, nothingness.

Regarding language, the Absurdist movement is antiliterary. The Absurdists believe that language has broken down and can no longer convey meaning. When asked why, then, he used words, Beckett replied that words are all we have to work with. Actually, although Beckett turned his back on Naturalism (the exact, detailed duplication of real life), he was a Naturalist in his dialogue and sometimes even achieved a kind of poetry by his fidelity to real speech.

The nature of Beckett's work almost demands that it be performed in small, intimate theaters,

B. Expansion
The term *vaudeville* was first used in France to refer to satirical political ballads, then to light opera, and finally, in the United States, to variety shows that were suitable for family viewing. Vaudeville was in its heyday in America from the 1890s to 1925, when it was supplanted by motion pictures. The vaudeville era ended in 1932 with the closing of the Palace Theater on Broadway.

C. Expansion
In fact, Beckett does not use words in all of his plays. In 1957, he produced *Act Without Words,* a pantomime about a man unable to escape a desert. Three mime plays were scheduled to be produced in Ireland in 1958; however, Beckett withdrew them from the International Theatre Festival in Dublin to protest the banning by festival officials of a play by fellow expatriate Sean O'Casey.

Scene from a 1979 production of Samuel Beckett's *Happy Days* at the Beckett Theater, New York.

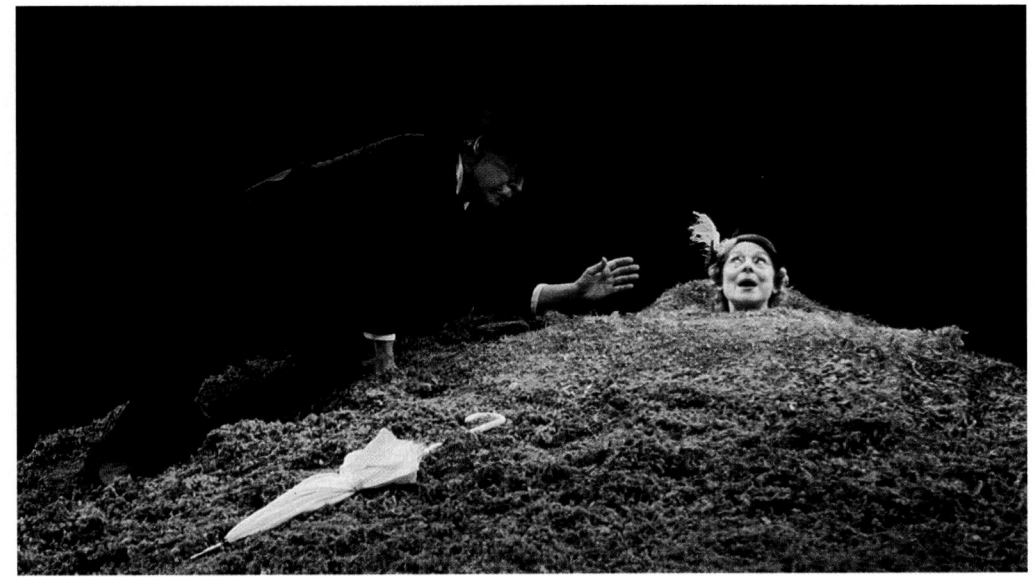

INTEGRATING THE LANGUAGE ARTS

Grammar and Usage In *That's All* by Harold Pinter, the character Mrs. A speaks mostly in sentence fragments and elliptical expressions. Ask students to select three or four of Mrs. A's lines and to rewrite them as complete sentences. Then, ask students to read the sentences aloud as part of the dialogue with Mrs. B. Ask students to evaluate which version of the lines, Pinter's or theirs, sounds more like real speech. [Most students will probably say Pinter's fragments and elliptical expressions sound more like real speech.] Lead the class in a discussion of how sentence fragments, while technically not standard written English, may be essential in accomplishing a writer's purpose.

Writing: Play Scene Ask students to write a brief scene for two characters in the style of either Beckett or Pinter. Remind them that they should include stage directions, descriptions of stage sets, and a list of props, if any. You might let some volunteers read their scenes for the class or act them out.

A. Expansion
British actor Ben Kingsley, who starred in *Gandhi,* is one of the best interpreters of Pinter today. To allow students to hear Pinter's peculiar, halting, and flat dialogue, show part of the movie version of *Betrayal,* starring Kingsley and Jeremy Irons.

where every flutter of an eye can register. Beckett's plays are done in such theaters all over the world, and he is the "master," the point of reference for many of the experimenters now working in the theater. He was awarded the Nobel Prize in literature in 1969.

The Plays of Harold Pinter

Harold Pinter (1930–   ), an avowed disciple of Beckett and probably the most influential of the new English playwrights, is on the fringe of the Absurdist Theater. While Beckett deals with often grotesque characters in bizarre settings (the two tramps in *Waiting for Godot,* two old people in ash-cans in *Endgame,* a woman buried in sand up to her neck in *Happy Days*), Pinter most often presents us with more or less real settings and identifiable characters speaking everyday language. The whole, however, is stylized in a manner that is now called Pinteresque.

With Pinter, we are not in a storytelling theater. To summarize what happens in these plays is as meaningless as trying to describe an Abstract Expressionist painting. Pinter's is a drama of ambiguities, implications, and contradictions. A critic reviewing a Pinter play might start by saying, "This is a play about a man who did or did not meet a woman a year ago in a restaurant." It is a world where the real is menacing, the pregnant pauses (all carefully indicated by Pinter) are full of terror, and the banal speech is full of mystery.

In a traditional play, we watch the gradual unfolding of a character, as though we were watching an onion being peeled, until the psychological center of the person is exposed. In Pinter's plays, we are not dealing with the complex psychology of character. Pinter's people are often without pasts—or they have self-contradicting pasts. Though Pinter avoids the conventional dramatic principles of progression and development, he starts from arresting situations, and he sustains mystery and suspense.

But it is Pinter's dialogue that is the hallmark of his art. He has taken the chitchat of everyday speech and stylized it to the point where it becomes a kind of poetry. The following revue sketch titled *That's All* was first presented on BBC Radio in 1964. This is the entire text.

That's All

Mrs. A. I always put the kettle on about that time.
Mrs. B. Yes. *(Pause.)*
Mrs. A. Then she comes round.
Mrs. B. Yes. *(Pause.)*
Mrs. A. Only on Thursdays.
Mrs. B. Yes. *(Pause.)*
Mrs. A. On Wednesdays I used to put it on. When she used to come round. Then she changed it to Thursdays.
Mrs. B. Oh yes.
Mrs. A. After she moved. When she used to live round the corner, then she always came in on Wednesdays, but then when she moved she used to come down to the butcher's on Thursdays. She couldn't find a butcher up there.
Mrs. B. No.
Mrs. A. Anyway, she decided she'd stick to her own butcher. Well, I thought, if she can't find a butcher, that's the best thing.
Mrs. B. Yes. *(Pause.)*
Mrs. A. So she started to come down on Thursdays. I didn't know she was coming down on Thursdays until one day I met her in the butcher.
Mrs. B. Oh yes.
Mrs. A. It wasn't my day for the butcher. I don't go to the butcher on Thursday.
Mrs. B. No, I know. *(Pause.)*
Mrs. A. I go on Friday.
Mrs. B. Yes. *(Pause.)*
Mrs. A. That's where I see you.
Mrs. B. Yes. *(Pause.)*
Mrs. A. You're always in there on Fridays.
Mrs. B. Oh yes. *(Pause.)*
Mrs. A. But I happened to go in for a bit of meat, it turned out to be a Thursday. I wasn't going in for my usual weekly on Friday. I just slipped in, the day before.
Mrs. B. Yes.
Mrs. A. That was the first time I found out she couldn't find a butcher up there, so she decided to come back here, once a week, to her own butcher.
Mrs. B. Yes.
Mrs. A. She came on Thursday so she'd be able

Check Test: True-False
1. A play with a linear structure has a beginning, a middle, and an end. [True]
2. Theater of the Absurd is based on the idea that life is full, rich, and meaningful. [False]

3. The basic action in *Waiting for Godot* is waiting. [True]
4. *Waiting for Godot* employs comic techniques associated with vaudeville or movie slapstick. [True]

to get meat for the weekend. Lasted her till Monday, then from Monday to Thursday they'd have fish. She can always buy cold meat, if they want a change.

Mrs. B. Oh yes. *(Pause.)*

Mrs. A. So I told her to come in when she came down after she'd been to the butcher's and I'd put a kettle on. So she did. *(Pause.)*

Mrs. B. Yes. *(Pause.)*

Mrs. A. It was funny because she always used to come in Wednesdays. *(Pause.)* Still, it made a break. *(Long pause.)*

Mrs. B. She doesn't come in no more, does she? *(Pause.)*

Mrs. A. She comes in. She doesn't come in so much, but she comes in. *(Pause.)*

Mrs. B. I thought she didn't come in. *(Pause.)*

Mrs. A. She comes in. *(Pause.)* She just doesn't come in so much. That's all.

—Harold Pinter

It is, of course, questionable how many situations, characters, or subjects can be dealt with in the Pinter manner. It would seem to be limiting. But over the last thirty years, he has written such notable full-length plays as *The Caretaker* (1960), *The Homecoming* (1965), *Old Times* (1971), and *Betrayal* (1978); and a series of highly effective short plays, including *The Dumb Waiter* (1960), *The Collection* (1961), *Landscape* (1968), *Silence* (1969), and *Moonlight* (1993). He has also adapted for motion pictures novels such as *The French Lieutenant's Woman* and *The Last Tycoon.*

British Theater Today

Beckett and Pinter are only two among the diverse lot of contemporary British playwrights. Many others—including John Osborne, Athol Fugard, Tom Stoppard, and Caryl Churchill—have written in a wide range of styles and forms, all more or less influenced by Beckett and Bertolt Brecht. Yesterday's avant-garde has become today's mainstream, and perhaps the avant-garde of tomorrow will be a return to some form of the conventional well-made play.

Americans have always considered London a great theater town, and it still is. Though seasons may vary in quality, in almost any year one may see productions from the rich dramatic literature of the country, past and present. The major British playwrights from Shakespeare to Shaw to Pinter form a galaxy to make Americans envious. Though the contemporary English theater may lack such tragic American masterworks as Eugene O'Neill's *Long Day's Journey into Night,* Arthur Miller's *Death of a Salesman,* and Tennessee Williams's *A Streetcar Named Desire,* we have nothing to match, as yet, the brilliance of Beckett or Pinter. But, as they say in baseball, "Wait until next year."

Poster for a 1995 production of Tom Stoppard's *Arcadia* in New York.
Art by James McMullan.

B. Expansion
The term "well-made play" is today used to mean any conventional play, but the term originally referred to a play based on a set formula. The well-made play was extremely popular in the nineteenth century.

Perhaps owing to his impoverished background, Camus maintained a strong affinity with workers. He joined the Communist party in 1934, but he soon rejected communism. He also rejected Christianity because he could not reconcile the intense physical suffering of innocent people with the concept of an all-merciful, all-powerful God. His rejection of communism led to a public disagreement with Jean-Paul Sartre, a leading French intellectual who had been Camus's close friend. Sartre believed that communism, as advocated by the French Communist Party, was an essential philosophy for anyone genuinely interested in revolution.

WORLD LITERATURE

Algeria/France

Albert Camus
(1913–1960)

For many people, Albert Camus (ka·mōō′) was the very embodiment of the existential philosopher, a writer who asked questions about the foundations of our existence. Camus and his friends were associated with the Left Bank of Paris, where, in its smoky cafes, they argued about the meaning of human life. To Camus and other existentialists, we are uninvited guests in a meaningless universe.

Albert Camus was born in Algeria, at a time when Algeria was a colony of France. Raised in extreme poverty, he became one of the most influential writers of the twentieth century. When Camus was less than a year old, his father died of wounds suffered in World War I. His illiterate mother earned their living by cleaning houses. It is not surprising, therefore, that Camus viewed working-class people as

Albert Camus (1959).

individuals worthy of honor for their patient, silent labor, so like the toils of Sisyphus.

One of Camus's teachers noticed his potential for learning and helped him pursue his education, first through high school and then through the University of Algiers, where Camus studied philosophy. When he was seventeen, an attack of tuberculosis ended Camus's dream of a sports career, and by 1935, he had turned to writing and the theater. In 1940, after writing a group of newspaper articles about injustices in Algeria, Camus was asked to leave, and he emigrated to Paris.

During World War II, Camus served as editor of *Combat*, an underground newspaper of the Resistance movement that courageously opposed the German occupation of France. In his plays, novels, and essays—of which the most famous is his 1946 novel *The Stranger*—he spoke out fearlessly against all forms of exploitation, cruelty, aggression, and hypocritical morality. Often ill and close to death, Camus kept writing and working in behalf of humanitarian causes throughout his life. In 1957, he was awarded the Nobel Prize in literature. Three years later, at the age of forty-six, he was killed in a car accident. A draft of Camus's unfinished autobiographical novel, *The First Man*, was found in the wreckage of his car. The book was not published until 1994.

(Map) ©Rand McNally.

PROGRAM MANAGER

Selection Summary See Teaching Notes, *Teaching Resources B,* p. 166, for a summary of this selection.

CONNECTING WITH "OURSELVES AMONG OTHERS"

How does the lonely punishment of Sisyphus relate to the lessons of the other stories in this Collection? ["The Myth of Sisyphus" addresses the notion that despite being surrounded by others, each individual leads an isolated existence, lives in a unique reality, and tries to make the best of individual circumstances.]

BEFORE YOU READ
THE MYTH OF SISYPHUS

Background

Imagine that the year is 1942. Germany has invaded and is now occupying your country. Bombs are falling on cities all over Europe. Already millions of innocent people have been killed. You are desperately ill with tuberculosis. As everything that you thought was important in the world crashes around you, how would you react? Albert Camus chose to write "The Myth of Sisyphus," an essay that affirms life, no matter how meaningless or difficult it may be.

Camus based his essay on the Greek myth of Sisyphus, a clever but arrogant human who loved life and dared to defy the gods. After his death, Sisyphus even managed to escape from Pluto's dark underworld kingdom and return to life, a crime that deeply offended Zeus, king of the gods. To punish Sisyphus, Zeus condemned him to roll a huge rock eternally up a steep hill. As soon as Sisyphus reached the top of the hill, he had to stand by and watch while the rock rolled back downhill. Then he had to return to the bottom of the hill and roll the rock to the top again, and again, and again.

To Camus, the absurdity of Sisyphus's task symbolizes human existence. Camus's essay is often considered one of the important documents of **existentialism,** a philosophical and literary movement that holds that individuals must struggle to create their own meaning and morality in the absence of any absolute values. Many existentialists focus on a belief that the universe is indifferent to human suffering. However, Camus was an optimist. By becoming conscious of his terrible destiny, Camus's Sisyphus—and all of humanity—rises above it. For Camus, people achieve a kind of victory when they accept the meaninglessness of life with dignity, and even with joy.

A Dialogue with the Text

READER'S LOG

As you read this challenging essay, make a note of any ideas in it that you find interesting, puzzling, or open to debate.

The Idleness of Sisyphus (1981) by Sandro Chia. Oil on canvas, in two parts, overall 10′ 2″ × 12′ 8¼″ (307 × 386.7 cm); top panel: 6′ 9″ × 12′ 8¼″ (205.5 × 386.7 cm); bottom panel: 41″ × 12′ 1¼″ (104.5 × 386.7 cm).

The Museum of Modern Art, New York. Acquired through the Carter Burden, Barbara Jakobson, and Saidie A. May Funds and purchase. Photograph © 1997 The Museum of Modern Art, New York.

ALBERT CAMUS 1105

Background

Sisyphus is best known for his punishment of having to roll the rock up the hill, but there are other stories about him in mythology. Sisyphus was king of the Greek city of Corinth and, by another account, the true father of Odysseus.

A Dialogue with the Text

Encourage students to make notes on the selection in the form of a Double-Entry Journal. Have them draw a vertical line down the middle of a sheet of paper. To the left of the line, students should write anything they find interesting, puzzling, or open to debate. On the right side of the line they should write why the word, phrase, or idea caught their attention and what they think it might mean. Later, in discussion, they can share their ideas with others.

OPTIONS FOR TEACHING

STRATEGIES FOR INCLUSION

Less Proficient Readers Ask students to outline main ideas, details, and transitions from paragraphs in their reading by using a graphic organizer like the following. This strategy may be more effective if students work in pairs, alternating reading and writing.

Main Idea/ Details	Transition	Main Idea/ Details	Transition	Main Idea/ Details

Linguistic Have students re-read in context the sentence on page 1107, "It echoes in the wild and limited universe of man." Point out the paradox in "wild and limited," and review the meaning of *paradox*. Have students keep an ongoing class list of paradoxes. This activity will help students further their understanding of the absurd.

☞

? Do you agree that futile labor is the most dreadful punishment? Explain. [Students may say that repetitive drudgery is unbearable; or they may see as worse some punishment that would involve physical torture.]

B. Critical Reading: Analyzing Details

These sentences that describe the sea and earth are a poetic interlude in the midst of a philosophical essay. Describe the sharp contrast these images create. [Possible answer: The poetic lines make living on earth seem delightful and contrast starkly with the "infernal darkness" of death.]

C. Reader's Response: First Thoughts

Point out that Camus uses the first and third person through most of his essay but that in this one sentence he uses the second person, a direct address. Why do you think he includes this switch? [Sample responses: Talking directly to the reader makes the subject less formal, more relevant. Camus discusses abstract ideas in a familiar way to make them as clear as possible for the reader.]

D. Critical Reading: Making Inferences

? What does Camus mean, that Sisyphus is superior to his fate? [Possible answers: As Sisyphus follows his rock down the mountain, he has a respite, a time for reflection. Although he knows he will just have to return to his task, Sisyphus bravely faces that fact, showing strength.]

E. Critical Reading: Identifying Main Ideas

? Why does being conscious cause this punishment to be such a tragedy? [It is tragic that he knows his difficult and repetitive task is fruitless, yet he must endure this boredom. If he had hope that the task would end, at least that would give him something to work toward or think about.]

The Myth of Sisyphus

Albert Camus

translated by **Justin O'Brien**

The gods had condemned Sisyphus to ceaselessly rolling a rock to the top of a mountain, whence the stone would fall back of its own weight. They had thought with some reason that there is no more dreadful punishment than futile and hopeless labor.

If one believes Homer, Sisyphus was the wisest and most prudent of mortals. According to another tradition, however, he was disposed to practice the profession of highwayman. I see no contradiction in this. Opinions differ as to the reasons why he became the futile laborer of the underworld. To begin with, he is accused of a certain levity[1] in regard to the gods. He stole their secrets. Aegina, the daughter of Aesopus, was carried off by Jupiter. The father was shocked by that disappearance and complained to Sisyphus. He, who knew of the abduction, offered to tell about it on condition that Aesopus would give water to the citadel of Corinth.[2] To the celestial thunderbolts he preferred the benediction of water. He was punished for this in the underworld. Homer tells us also that Sisyphus had put Death in chains. Pluto could not endure the sight of his deserted, silent empire. He dispatched the god of war, who liberated Death from the hands of her conqueror.

It is said also that Sisyphus, being near to death, rashly wanted to test his wife's love. He ordered her to cast his unburied body into the middle of the public square. Sisyphus woke up in the underworld. And there, annoyed by an obedience so contrary to human love, he obtained from Pluto permission to return to earth in order to chastise his wife. But when he had seen again the face of this world, enjoyed water and sun, warm stones and the sea, he no longer wanted to go back to the infernal darkness. Recalls, signs of anger, warnings were of no avail. Many years more he lived facing the curve of the gulf, the sparkling sea, and the smiles of earth. A decree of the gods was necessary. Mercury came and seized the impudent man by the collar and, snatching him from his joys, led him forcibly back to the underworld, where his rock was ready for him.

You have already grasped that Sisyphus is the absurd hero. He *is,* as much through his passions as through his torture. His scorn of the gods, his hatred of death, and his passion for life won him that unspeakable penalty in which the whole being is exerted toward accomplishing nothing. This is the price that must be paid for the passions of this earth. Nothing is told us about Sisyphus in the underworld. Myths are made for the imagination to breathe life into them. As for this myth, one sees merely the whole effort of a body straining to raise the huge stone, to roll it and push it up a slope a hundred times over; one sees the face screwed up, the cheek tight against the stone, the shoulder bracing the clay-covered mass, the foot wedging it, the fresh start with arms outstretched, the wholly human security of two earth-clotted hands. At the very end of his long effort measured by skyless space and time without depth, the purpose is achieved. Then Sisyphus watches the stone rush down in a few moments toward that lower world whence he will have to push it up again toward the summit. He goes back down to the plain.

It is during that return, that pause, that Sisyphus interests me. A face that toils so close to stones is already stone itself! I see that man going back down with a heavy yet measured step toward the torment of which he will never know the end. That hour like a breathing space which returns as surely as his suffering, that is the hour of consciousness. At each of those moments when he leaves the heights and gradually sinks toward the lairs of the gods, he is superior to his fate. He is stronger than his rock.

If this myth is tragic, that is because its hero is conscious. Where would his torture be, indeed, if

---

1. **levity** (lev′i·tē): disrespectful lightness or frivolity.
2. **Corinth** (kôr′inth): ancient city in Greece.

OPTIONS FOR TEACHING

INTEGRATING THE LANGUAGE ARTS

Strategic Reading Assign pairs of students to identify the main ideas in each paragraph and to write these ideas into an outline of the selection.

Writing: Found Poem Have students write a found poem using only words from the essay, in the order in which they appear. The topic can be anything students choose. The tone can be casual as in the essay, or it can be formal.

Language and Style Have students work in pairs to study the first sentences of each paragraph. Ask students to make generalizations about the organization of the essay and to discuss their findings with the class.

at every step the hope of succeeding upheld him? The workman of today works every day in his life at the same tasks, and this fate is no less absurd. But it is tragic only at the rare moments when it becomes conscious. Sisyphus, proletarian[3] of the gods, powerless and rebellious, knows the whole extent of his wretched condition: It is what he thinks of during his descent. The lucidity that was to constitute his torture at the same time crowns his victory. There is no fate that cannot be surmounted by scorn.

If the descent is thus sometimes performed in sorrow, it can also take place in joy. This word is not too much. Again I fancy Sisyphus returning toward his rock, and the sorrow was in the beginning. When the images of earth cling too tightly to memory, when the call of happiness becomes too insistent, it happens that melancholy rises in man's heart: This is the rock's victory, this is the rock itself. The boundless grief is too heavy to bear. These are our nights of Gethsemane.[4] But crushing truths perish from being acknowledged. Thus, Oedipus[5] at the outset obeys fate without knowing it. But from the moment he knows, his tragedy begins. Yet at the same moment, blind and desperate, he realizes that the only bond linking him to the world is the cool hand of a girl. Then a tremendous remark rings out: "Despite so many ordeals, my advanced age and the nobility of my soul make me conclude that all is well." Sophocles' Oedipus, like Dostoevsky's Kirilov,[6] thus gives the recipe for the absurd victory. Ancient wisdom confirms modern heroism.

One does not discover the absurd without being tempted to write a manual of happiness. "What! by such narrow ways—?" There is but one world, however. Happiness and the absurd are

two sons of the same earth. They are inseparable. It would be a mistake to say that happiness necessarily springs from the absurd discovery. It happens as well that the feeling of the absurd springs from happiness. "I conclude that all is well," says Oedipus, and that remark is sacred. It echoes in the wild and limited universe of man. It teaches that all is not, has not been, exhausted. It drives out of this world a god who had come into it with dissatisfaction and a preference for futile sufferings. It makes of fate a human matter, which must be settled among men.

All Sisyphus' silent joy is contained therein. His fate belongs to him. His rock is his thing. Likewise, the absurd man, when he contemplates his torment, silences all the idols. In the universe suddenly restored to its silence, the myriad wondering little voices of the earth rise up. Unconscious, secret calls, invitations from all the faces, they are the necessary reverse and price of victory. There is no sun without shadow, and it is essential to know the night. The absurd man says yes and his effort will henceforth be unceasing. If there is a personal fate, there is no higher destiny, or at least there is but one which he concludes is inevitable and despicable. For the rest, he knows himself to be the master of his days. At that subtle moment when man glances backward over his life, Sisyphus returning toward his rock, in that slight pivoting he contemplates that series of unrelated actions which becomes his fate, created by him, combined under his memory's eye, and soon sealed by his death. Thus, convinced of the wholly human origin of all that is human, a blind man eager to see who knows that the night has no end, he is still on the go. The rock is still rolling.

I leave Sisyphus at the foot of the mountain! One always finds one's burden again. But Sisyphus teaches the higher fidelity that negates the gods and raises rocks. He too concludes that all is well. This universe henceforth without a master seems to him neither sterile nor futile. Each atom of that stone, each mineral flake of that night-filled mountain, in itself forms a world. The struggle itself toward the heights is enough to fill a man's heart. One must imagine Sisyphus happy.

---

3. **proletarian** (prō′lə·ter′ē·ən): member of the working class.

4. **Gethsemane** (geth·sem′ə·nē): garden east of Jerusalem where Jesus Christ suffered intensely as he contemplated his possible death.

5. **Oedipus** (ed′i·pəs): character in Greek mythology who unknowingly kills his father and marries his mother. In *Oedipus at Colonus,* the last of three plays written by the Greek dramatist Sophocles (496–406 B.C.) about this tragic hero, Oedipus has blinded himself and is led by the hand by his daughter Antigone.

6. **Kirilov** (kē·rē′luf): character in Dostoevsky's 1872 novel *The Possessed.*

F. Reader's Response: Shaping Interpretations

? Why might Camus say that the fate of a worker is tragic only during moments of consciousness? [Sample responses: Someone can be sad only if he or she recognizes sadness. The tragedy is that the person feels hopeless, and one can feel hopeless only if he or she recognizes hopelessness in a situation.]

G. Critical Reading: Summarizing

Paraphrase Camus's statement. [Possible answer: Once a person admits that something negative is true or real, its power is diminished.]

H. Critical Reading: Identifying Main Ideas

? What is Camus's point here? [Possible answer: When we look for or remember happiness, we become more aware that we are not happy, and the punishment gets the better of us.]

I. Critical Reading: Making Connections

Reemphasize the horror of Oedipus's position: unknowingly killing his father and marrying his mother, finding out what he has done, gouging out his eyes, being banished. Yet, he still concludes that "all is well." Ask students to discuss this conviction. Remind students that in *Candide* (pp. 538–540), Pangloss teaches that "all is for the best." Have students consider how differently Voltaire and Camus approach this attitude.

J. Reader's Response: Extending the Text

? Why must one imagine Sisyphus happy? [Sample responses: He has a purpose. While he knows he will forever push the rock up the mountain, he also knows he will forever walk down the mountain free of the rock.]

CROSSING THE CURRICULUM

History Have students work in groups of three or four to research and write an article on the French resistance. Encourage them to look for information regarding the underground newspaper *Combat.*

CLASSROOM MANAGEMENT

Managing the Reader's Response Classroom To establish an atmosphere that invites inquiry and open examination of issues, include students in formulating class policy. Remind students that there is a wide range of valid responses for interpreting literature. Explain that you want students to feel safe to think and to explore ideas aloud without being judged. Have students brainstorm a list of characteristics of a good listener and a good environment. [Open, supportive, respectful, and so on.]

Finding Common Ground

Have students read all four of the alternative assignments given in the Finding Common Ground feature, and invite each student to select the activity he or she finds most interesting. Group students according to their interests for this assignment. Students might find a book on mythology useful in order to look up myths and refresh their memories. Students may notice that the basic human truths found in the myths—truths about jealousy, pride, optimism, sorrow, and so on—still apply to modern humanity.

The Castle of the Pyrenees (1959) by René Magritte.

Israel Museum, Jerusalem
© 1997 C. Hersovici, Brussels /
Artists Rights Society (ARS),
New York.

FINDING COMMON GROUND

You can probably recognize in Camus's writing the voice of a man who wanted human labor and art to serve human needs. Perhaps you can also recognize the voice of someone with a lifelong commitment to the unfortunate of the world. Can you also hear that Camus was a man who faced hopelessness and despair in his own life, yet reacted to setbacks with renewed vigor and hope?

Explore your responses to Camus's essay (check your Reader's Log notes) and to his philosophy in one or more of these ways:

- In a group, discuss the kind of people who would be likely to share Camus's ideas. Would they be angry loners? outgoing optimists? Why do you think some of us are able to invest whatever we do with a certain meaning?
- According to Camus, "the workman of today works every day in his life at the same tasks, and this fate is no less absurd" than the tasks Sisyphus carries out. Imagine yourself as one of the workers Camus had in mind. Write a short essay explaining how Camus's philosophy might help you face your life with hope and joy.
- Camus found meaning in the myth of Sisyphus. W. H. Auden (page 1091) was moved by the myth of Icarus, while Frank O'Connor (page 1080) was inspired by a modern interpretation of the ancient story of Oedipus. In a group, make a list of myths or legends from Greece and other cultures. Discuss connections you could make between these myths and your own lives.
- Camus's writing has been called **epigrammatic.** That means he writes in epigrams, brief statements packed with meaning. Find one sentence in "The Myth of Sisyphus" that has particular meaning for you, and memorize it. Find a way to share your epigram with the class. (For instance, use it on a poster.) Or, make up an epigram stating your own philosophy of life.

Check Test: Short Answers

1. How did the gods choose the punishment assigned to Sisyphus? [They thought futile labor was one of the worst punishments.]
2. What kind of hero does Camus claim Sisyphus is? [The absurd hero.]
3. At what point does Camus claim this myth becomes tragic? [When the hero becomes conscious of having no hope.]
4. To what modern figures does Camus compare Sisyphus? [Workers.]

Anita Desai
(1937–   )

Born in Mussoorie, India, Anita Desai has been writing since the age of seven "as instinctively as I breathe." Desai's father was Bengali and her mother German, and Desai grew up hearing Hindi, English, and German spoken at home. However, it was in English that Desai learned to read and write. Educated at the University of Delhi, Desai began publishing in 1963.

Anita Desai.

Desai's fiction explores the struggles of contemporary Indian characters as they respond to cultural and social change. She sees her work as an attempt to discover "the truth that is nine-tenths of the iceberg that lies submerged beneath the one-tenth visible portion we call

Reality." To evoke this "truth," Desai uses rich, sensual language and intense imagery. Because of her sensuous style and rich use of image and symbol, Desai has been referred to as an "imagist-novelist."

Desai's novels often focus on the emotional and spiritual lives of wives, older women, or sisters who take responsibility for others but are unable to create satisfactory lives for themselves. Her novels include *Cry, the Peacock* (1963), *In Custody* (1984), and *Baumgartner's Bombay* (1988).

Writing in *The New Republic,* Anthony Thwaite describes Desai "as such a consummate artist that she [is able to suggest], beyond the confines of the plot and the machinations of her characters, the immensities that lie beyond them—the immensities of India."

BEFORE YOU READ
GAMES AT TWILIGHT

Reading Focus
Childhood Business

Work may be the business of adults, but play is often considered the "business" of little children. For it is through play that children do the hard work of learning many of life's important lessons. They learn about rules and strategies, strength and weakness. They learn that life is not always fair.

Most children long to be the center of attention, triumphant victors in play. But victory can be elusive, and the process of growing up can be difficult and painful.

Quickwrite

Think about your own childhood experiences of playing games. What feelings did you have during a game of tag or hide-and-seek?

Elements of Literature
Imagery

Desai's vibrant **imagery** captures the smells, textures, shouts, and colors of a sizzling summer afternoon in India. From the beginning of the story, when the children burst out the door, to its end at twilight, Desai enables you to experience the world through the eyes and ears of her characters.

Imagery is the use of language to evoke sensory impressions. Images are chiefly visual, but they can also appeal to the senses of smell, hearing, taste, and touch.

For more on Imagery, see the Handbook of Literary Terms.

Background

This story is set not long after India's independence from Britain, which occurred in 1947. During the long British rule in India, many upper-class Indian families adopted Western values and behaviors, including games like the one played in the story.

ANITA DESAI **1109**

Into the Story

Author Biography p. 1109
Before You Read p. 1109

Through the Story

"Games at Twilight" pp. 1110–1115
Words to Own pp. 1110–1115
Student to Student p. 1116
"The Radio"
Making Meanings p. 1117

Beyond the Story

Choices: Building Your Portfolio
p. 1117
- **Writer's Notebook:** Propose a literature curriculum
- **Critical Writing:** Compare and contrast two stories
- **Creative Writing:** Write a narrative about the passage of time

Into the Story

Using BEFORE YOU READ
p. 1109

Reading Focus

Ask students to share with the class games they played when they were younger and the rules they followed in playing them. Make sure you give students from various parts of the country and from various cultural groups a chance to explain their games. Then, discuss with the class the differences and similarities of games from diverse areas and cultures.

PROGRAM MANAGER

- **Planning Instruction** See *Teaching Notes, Teaching Resources B,* pp. 166–167, for objectives, a summary, and literary elements for this selection.
- **Instructional Support** See *Graphic Organizer for Active Reading, Teaching Resources B,* p. 181, for a Through the Story activity.

- **Audiotaped Readings** Use the *Selected Reading, Audiocassette 3, Side B,* in the *Audiovisual Resources Binder.*
- **Assessment** See *Selection Test, Test Booklet,* pp. 234–235.
- **Reinforcement** Use the *Words to Own* worksheet in *Teaching Resources B,* p. 182.

A. Literary Element: Imagery
Ask students to point out and discuss the imagery used here. [Stuffed lungs and noses; this imagery helps readers empathize with the children]. Explain that Desai is known for her powerful use of imagery. Ask students to look for metaphors and similes that make an unfamiliar setting seem familiar.

B. Reader's Response: Connecting with the Text
? Have you been in a **setting** like this one? What details help you imagine such a scene? [Sample responses: Yes, the glaring white walls remind me of a summer trip to the southwestern United States. No, but Desai's description of the way nothing moves helps me to understand the heat.]

C. Cultural Connections
Ask students to consider the language the children use: Is it similar to or different from language students might have used to play games where they grew up? [Most will say it sounds very familiar.]

Games at Twilight

Anita Desai

It was still too hot to play outdoors. They had had their tea, they had been washed and had their hair brushed, and after the long day of confinement in the house that was not cool but at least a protection from the sun, the children strained to get out. Their faces were red and bloated with the effort, but their mother would not open the door, everything was still curtained and shuttered in a way that stifled the children, made them feel that their lungs were stuffed with cotton wool and their noses with dust and if they didn't burst out into the light and see the sun and feel the air, they would choke.

"Please, ma, please," they begged. "We'll play in the veranda and porch—we won't go a step out of the porch."

"You will, I know you will, and then——"

"No—we won't, we won't," they wailed so horrendously that she actually let down the bolt of the front door so that they burst out like seeds from a crackling, overripe pod into the veranda, with such wild, <u>maniacal</u> yells that she retreated to her bath and the shower of talcum powder and the fresh sari that were to help her face the summer evening.

They faced the afternoon. It was too hot. Too bright. The white walls of the veranda glared <u>stridently</u> in the sun. The bougainvillea[1] hung about it, purple and magenta, in livid balloons. The garden outside was like a tray made of beaten brass, flattened out on the red gravel and the stony soil in all shades of metal—aluminum, tin, copper, and brass. No life stirred at this arid time of day—the birds still drooped, like dead fruit, in the papery tents of the trees; some squirrels lay limp on the wet earth under the garden tap. The outdoor dog lay stretched as if dead on the veranda mat, his paws and ears and tail all reaching out like dying travelers in search of water. He rolled his eyes at the children—two white marbles rolling in the purple sockets, begging for sympathy—and at-

tempted to lift his tail in a wag but could not. It only twitched and lay still.

Then, perhaps roused by the shrieks of the children, a band of parrots suddenly fell out of the eucalyptus tree, tumbled frantically in the still, sizzling air, then sorted themselves out into battle formation and streaked away across the white sky.

The children, too, felt released. They too began tumbling, shoving, pushing against each other, frantic to start. Start what? Start their business. The business of the children's day which is—play.

"Let's play hide-and-seek."

"Who'll be It?"

"You be It."

"Why should I? You be——"

"You're the eldest——"

"That doesn't mean——"

The shoves became harder. Some kicked out. The motherly Mira intervened. She pulled the boys roughly apart. There was a tearing sound of cloth, but it was lost in the heavy panting and angry grumbling, and no one paid attention to the small sleeve hanging loosely off a shoulder.

"Make a circle, make a circle!" she shouted, firmly pulling and pushing till a kind of vague circle was formed. "Now clap!" she roared, and, clapping, they all chanted in melancholy unison: "Dip, dip, dip—my blue ship——" and every now and then one or the other saw he was safe by the way his hands fell at the crucial moment—palm on palm, or back of hand on palm—and dropped out of the circle with a yell and a jump of relief and jubilation.

Raghu was It. He started to protest, to cry "You cheated—Mira cheated—Anu cheated——" but it was too late, the others had all already streaked away. There was no one to hear when he called out, "Only in the veranda—the porch—Ma said—Ma *said* to stay in the porch!" No one had

---

1. **bougainvillea** (boo′gən·vil′ē·ə): woody, tropical vine with showy, purplish leaves.

WORDS TO OWN
maniacal (mə·nī′ə·kəl) *adj.*: crazed; wildly enthusiastic.
stridently (strīd′'nt·lē) *adv.*: harshly; sharply.

If All the World Were Paper and All the Waters Ink (1962) by Jess.
The Fine Arts Museums of San Francisco, California. Courtesy of the Odyssia Gallery, New York.

D. Reader's Response: Challenging the Text

Point out the poignancy in this terse description of Manu caught in a dilemma. What effect do you think the author may have intended by including this scene? [Sample responses: Helping readers remember being in such a game and fearing they might get caught. Showing how children everywhere share similar feelings and thoughts.]

E. Reader's Response: First Thoughts

Help students identify the change in point of view from omniscient to third person limited. What effect does this shift have for readers? [Sample responses: It lets readers see and understand the various perspectives of the game. It may be disorienting for readers, as the game can be for players when they are hidden, only glimpsing the action.]

stopped to listen, all he saw were their brown legs flashing through the dusty shrubs, scrambling up brick walls, leaping over compost heaps and hedges, and then the porch stood empty in the purple shade of the bougainvillea, and the garden was as empty as before; even the limp squirrels had whisked away, leaving everything gleaming, brassy, and bare.

Only small Manu suddenly reappeared, as if he had dropped out of an invisible cloud or from a bird's claws, and stood for a moment in the center of the yellow lawn, chewing his finger and near to tears as he heard Raghu shouting, with his head pressed against the veranda wall, "Eighty-three, eighty-five, eighty-nine, ninety . . ." and then made

off in a panic, half of him wanting to fly north, the other half counseling south. Raghu turned just in time to see the flash of his white shorts and the uncertain skittering of his red sandals, and charged after him with such a bloodcurdling yell that Manu stumbled over the hosepipe, fell into its rubber coils, and lay there weeping, "I won't be It—you have to find them all—all—All!"

"I know I have to, idiot," Raghu said, superciliously kicking him with his toe. "You're dead,"

WORDS TO OWN
superciliously (sōō′pər·sil′ē·əs·lē) *adv.:* disdainfully or scornfully; haughtily.

ANITA DESAI 1111

INTEGRATING THE LANGUAGE ARTS

Strategic Reading This story is complicated in that most of the drama is psychological. Ask students to create a plot diagram showing all the major events in the story. As a class or in groups, have students compare and discuss the variables in their diagrams.

Writing: Oral History Ravi struggles in the shed between his fears and his desire to win the game; in his disappointment afterward, he forgets that he has triumphed by overcoming his fears. Have students write a short narrative retelling the story of the time in the shed as Ravi might tell it to his friends. Tell students they are free to embellish the story as they imagine he might.

Usage Ask whether students are familiar with the slang phrase "I just clean forgot." Have them re-read the paragraph beginning "It took them a minute to grasp" on page 1114, paying particular attention to the last line. Have students evaluate the effect of this nonstandard English construction.

A. **Literary Element: Simile**

? What figure of speech does the writer use here? [The simile of cleaning the shed being like looting a city.]

he said with satisfaction, licking the beads of perspiration off his upper lip, and then stalked off in search of worthier prey, whistling spiritedly so that the hiders should hear and tremble.

Ravi heard the whistling and picked his nose in a panic, trying to find comfort by burrowing the finger deep—deep into that soft tunnel. He felt himself too exposed, sitting on an upturned flowerpot behind the garage. Where could he burrow? He could run around the garage if he heard Raghu come—around and around and around—but he hadn't much faith in his short legs when matched against Raghu's long, hefty, hairy footballer legs. Ravi had a frightening glimpse of them as Raghu combed the hedge of crotons and hibiscus, trampling delicate ferns underfoot as he did so. Ravi looked about him desperately, swallowing a small ball of snot in his fear.

The garage was locked with a great heavy lock to which the driver had the key in his room, hanging from a nail on the wall under his workshirt. Ravi had peeped in and seen him still sprawling on his string cot in his vest and striped underpants, the hair on his chest and the hair in his nose shaking with the vibrations of his phlegm-obstructed snores. Ravi had wished he were tall enough, big enough to reach the key on the nail, but it was

impossible, beyond his reach for years to come. He had sidled away and sat dejectedly on the flowerpot. That at least was cut to his own size.

But next to the garage was another shed with a big green door. Also locked. No one even knew who had the key to the lock. That shed wasn't opened more than once a year, when Ma turned out all the old broken bits of furniture and rolls of matting and leaking buckets, and the white anthills were broken and swept away and Flit sprayed into the spider webs and rat holes so that the whole operation was like the looting of a poor, ruined, and conquered city. The green leaves of the door sagged. They were nearly off their rusty hinges. The hinges were large and made a small gap between the door and the walls—only just large enough for rats, dogs, and, possibly, Ravi to slip through.

Ravi had never cared to enter such a dark and depressing mortuary of defunct household goods seething with such unspeakable and alarming animal life but, as Raghu's whistling grew angrier and sharper and his crashing and storming in the

Two young girls, Rajasthan, India.

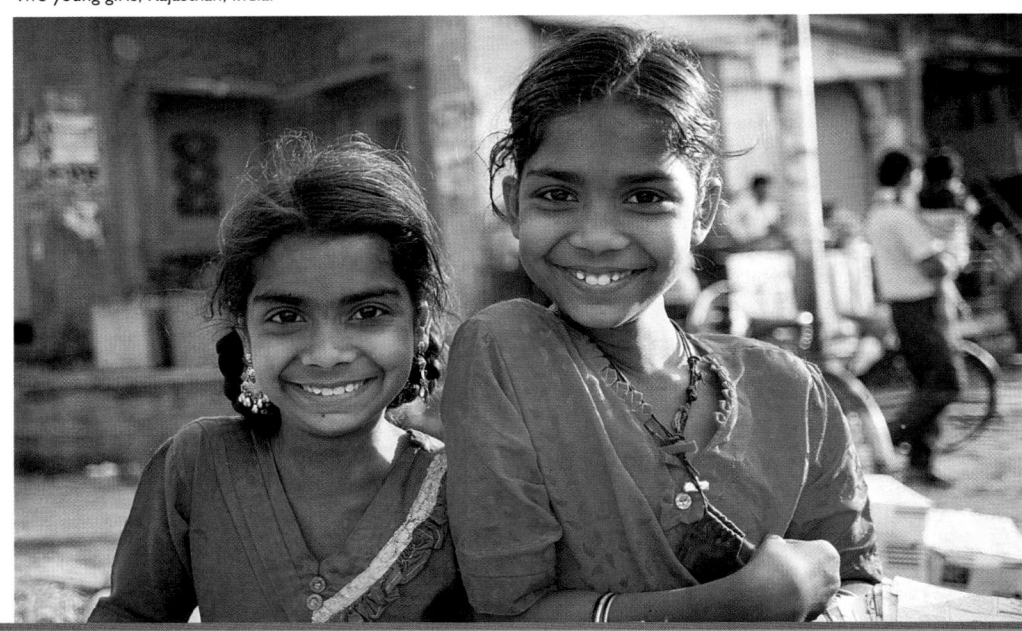

CROSSING THE CURRICULUM

Music Have students work in groups of five or six to discuss childhood songs and chants in the United States, such as "The grass is green" on p. 1114 or "Ollie, Ollie, In free," from hide-and-seek. After students have recalled as many phrases as possible, they may refer to books and records to find the origins of these phrases. Invite them to present their research to the class using charts or recordings.

Science Have students work in groups of four to investigate the vegetation in the setting of the story. They should list the plants that are mentioned, research what the plants look like, and create a drawing of the setting that incorporates the plants. Students might create a colored-chalk picture, a colored-pencil illustration with scientific labels, or a drawing in another medium.

Social Sciences Have the class work in mixed-ability groups to conduct a study of India. Assign one group to each of the following topics: geography, population distribution and languages, agriculture, industry, education. Have groups share their learning with the class in a format of their choosing.

hedge wilder, Ravi suddenly slipped off the flower-pot and through the crack and was gone. He chuckled aloud with astonishment at his own temerity so that Raghu came out of the hedge, stood silent with his hands on his hips, listening, and finally shouted, "I heard you! I'm coming! *Got* you——" and came charging round the garage only to find the upturned flowerpot, the yellow dust, the crawling of white ants in a mud hill against the closed shed door—nothing. Snarling, he bent to pick up a stick and went off, whacking it against the garage and shed walls as if to beat out his prey.

Ravi shook, then shivered with delight, with self-congratulation. Also with fear. It was dark, spooky in the shed. It had a muffled smell, as of graves. Ravi had once got locked into the linen cupboard and sat there weeping for half an hour before he was rescued. But at least that had been a familiar place, and even smelled pleasantly of starch, laundry, and, reassuringly, of his mother. But the shed smelled of rats, anthills, dust, and spider webs. Also of less definable, less recognizable horrors. And it was dark. Except for the white-hot cracks along the door, there was no light. The roof was very low. Although Ravi was small, he felt as if he could reach up and touch it with his fingertips. But he didn't stretch. He hunched himself into a ball so as not to bump into anything, touch or feel anything. What might there not be to touch him and feel him as he stood there, trying to see in the dark? Something cold, or slimy—like a snake. Snakes! He leapt up as Raghu whacked the wall with his stick—then, quickly realizing what it was, felt almost relieved to hear Raghu, hear his stick. It made him feel protected.

But Raghu soon moved away. There wasn't a sound once his footsteps had gone around the garage and disappeared. Ravi stood frozen inside the shed. Then he shivered all over. Something had tickled the back of his neck. It took him a while to pick up the courage to lift his hand and explore. It was an insect—perhaps a spider—exploring *him*. He squashed it and wondered how many more creatures were watching him, waiting to reach out and touch him, the stranger.

There was nothing now. After standing in that position—his hand still on his neck, feeling the wet splodge of the squashed spider gradually dry—for minutes, hours, his legs began to tremble with the effort, the inaction. By now he could see enough in the dark to make out the large solid shapes of old wardrobes, broken buckets, and bedsteads piled on top of each other around him. He recognized an old bathtub—patches of enamel glimmered at him, and at last he lowered himself onto its edge.

He contemplated slipping out of the shed and into the fray. He wondered if it would not be better to be captured by Raghu and be returned to the milling crowd as long as he could be in the sun, the light, the free spaces of the garden, and the familiarity of his brothers, sisters, and cousins. It would be evening soon. Their games would become legitimate. The parents would sit out on the lawn on cane basket chairs and watch them as they tore around the garden or gathered in knots to share a loot of mulberries or black, teeth-splitting *jamun*[2] from the garden trees. The gardener would fix the hosepipe to the water tap, and water would fall lavishly through the air to the ground, soaking the dry yellow grass and the red gravel and arousing the sweet, the intoxicating scent of water on dry earth—that loveliest scent in the world. Ravi sniffed for a whiff of it. He half-rose from the bathtub, then heard the despairing scream of one of the girls as Raghu bore down upon her. There was the sound of a crash, and of rolling about in the bushes, the shrubs, then screams and accusing sobs of "I touched the den——" "You did not——" "I did——" "You liar, you did *not*" and then a fading away and silence again.

Ravi sat back on the harsh edge of the tub, deciding to hold out a bit longer. What fun if they were all found and caught—he alone left unconquered! He had never known that sensation. Nothing more wonderful had ever happened to him than being taken out by an uncle and bought

---

2. *jamun* (jä·mən): plumlike fruit.

WORDS TO OWN

temerity (tə·mer′ə·tē) *n.*: foolish or rash boldness; recklessness.
intoxicating (in·täks′i·kāt′iŋ) *v.* used as *adj.*: causing wild excitement or happiness, often to a point beyond self-control; heady.

ANITA DESAI 1113

COOPERATIVE LEARNING

Character Sketch Have students work in groups of four or five to make a character sketch of Ravi. As general preparation, have students keep a permanent ongoing list of words that describe character traits. To begin the list, write terms on the chalkboard as students brainstorm. Have them look back over stories they have read for ideas.

Debate Much of the story's conflict centers around Ravi's need to "prove" himself. Have students re-read the passage describing Ravi's fantasy of victory in the paragraph beginning "Ravi sat back on the harsh edge of the tub" on p. 1113. Then, organize the class into several teams for the debate. The proposition for debate is "Competition is a healthy motivator for psychological development." Have students prepare their cases, comparing the positive and negative aspects of competition. ☞

[?] Does Ravi wait a long time, or does he just feel it has been a long time? How do you know? [He waits a long time; the hot afternoon light has turned to gray, and the sounds indicate the gardener is already watering.]

B. **Reader's Response: Shaping Interpretations**

[?] What do you think the conflict of this story is? [Sample responses: Ravi feels a passionate need to beat the older children, which leads him to forget the actual rules of the game. He has assumed the children will look for him until they find him, but now he realizes they have forgotten him.] Why does he cry? [Sample responses: He is tired, embarrassed, disgraced. His feelings are hurt.]

C. **Reader's Response: First Thoughts**

[?] How can you explain the mother's response to Ravi's crying? [Sample responses: She does not know of his exhausting psychological struggle in the shed. She does not understand why he is crying and attributes his tears to a small accident.]

D. **Language Note: Style**
Here Desai catalogues what has transpired, using the verb *had*. Then she shifts to sentence fragments as if so much has happened she needs to use an abbreviated form. The intent may be to clarify how much time has passed.

---

a whole slab of chocolate all to himself, or being flung into the soda man's pony cart and driven up to the gate by the friendly driver with the red beard and pointed ears. To defeat Raghu—that hirsute,[3] hoarse-voiced football champion—and to be the winner in a circle of older, bigger, luckier children—that would be thrilling beyond imagination. He hugged his knees together and smiled to himself almost shyly at the thought of so much victory, such laurels.

There he sat smiling, knocking his heels against the bathtub, now and then getting up and going to the door to put his ear to the broad crack and listening for sounds of the game, the pursuer and the pursued, and then returning to his seat with the dogged determination of the true winner, a breaker of records, a champion.

(A) It grew darker in the shed as the light at the door grew softer, fuzzier, turned to a kind of crumbling yellow pollen that turned to yellow fur, blue fur, gray fur. Evening. Twilight. The sound of water gushing, falling. The scent of earth receiving water, slaking its thirst in great gulps and releasing that green scent of freshness, coolness. Through the crack Ravi saw the long purple shadows of the shed and the garage lying still across the yard. Beyond that, the white walls of the house. The bougainvillea had lost its lividity, hung in dark bundles that quaked and twittered and seethed with masses of homing sparrows. The lawn was shut off from his view. Could he hear the children's voices? It seemed to him that he could. It seemed to him that he could hear them chanting, singing, laughing. But what about the game? What had happened? Could it be over? How could it when he was still not found?

(B) It then occurred to him that he could have slipped out long ago, dashed across the yard to the veranda, and touched the "den." It was necessary to do that to win. He had forgotten. He had only remembered the part of hiding and trying to elude the seeker. He had done that so successfully, his success had occupied him so wholly, that he had quite forgotten that success had to be clinched by that final dash to victory and the ringing cry of "Den!"

3. **hirsute** (hʉr′sōōt′): hairy; shaggy.

With a whimper he burst through the crack, fell on his knees, got up, and stumbled on stiff, benumbed legs across the shadowy yard, crying heartily by the time he reached the veranda so that when he flung himself at the white pillar and bawled, "Den! Den! Den!" his voice broke with rage and pity at the disgrace of it all, and he felt himself flooded with tears and misery.

Out on the lawn, the children stopped chanting. They all turned to stare at him in amazement. Their faces were pale and triangular in the dusk. The trees and bushes around them stood inky and sepulchral, spilling long shadows across them. They stared, wondering at his reappearance, his passion, his wild animal howling. Their mother rose from her basket chair and came toward him, worried, annoyed, saying, "Stop it, stop it, Ravi. **(C)** Don't be a baby. Have you hurt yourself?" Seeing him attended to, the children went back to clasping their hands and chanting, "The grass is green, the rose is red. . . ."

But Ravi would not let them. He tore himself out of his mother's grasp and pounded across the lawn into their midst, charging at them with his head lowered so that they scattered in surprise. "I won, I won, I won," he bawled, shaking his head so that the big tears flew. "Raghu didn't find me. I won, I won——"

It took them a minute to grasp what he was saying, even who he was. They had quite forgotten him. Raghu had found all the others long ago. There had been a fight about who was to be It next. It had been so fierce that their mother had emerged from her bath and made them change to another game. Then they had played another and **(D)** another. Broken mulberries from the tree and eaten them. Helped the driver wash the car when their father returned from work. Helped the gardener water the beds till he roared at them and swore he would complain to their parents. The parents had come out, taken up their positions on the cane chairs. They had begun to play again, sing and chant. All this time no one had remembered Ravi. Having disappeared from the scene, he had disappeared from their minds. Clean.

WORDS TO OWN
dogged (dôg′id) *adj.*: persistent; stubborn.

Cooperative Learning Ask students to work in groups to determine how they would counsel Ravi. For example, encourage them to think of ways to help Ravi recognize his importance as an individual or to comfort him regarding his significance in the family. Have students write down their suggestions in the form of a conversation they imagine having with Ravi or a letter to him.

Critical Comment: Psychological Profile In his study of Indian-English short stories, A. N. Dwivedi writes of "Games at Twilight" that while the plot seems "trivial," he finds the story "wholly surcharged with a psychological delineation of the children, particularly of Ravi and Raghu." He says that Ravi "ruminates over the petty and puny actions of his own race—the children. He also develops a sense of helplessness over the insignificant position of his. He also treats his victory as inconsequential, for nobody is now interested in him." Ask students to respond to this criticism and to discuss the "victory" Dwivedi mentions.

Untitled (1977) by Oliver Jackson. Oil enamel on cotton canvas (108″ × 180″).
Courtesy Allan Stone Gallery, New York, New York.

E. Critical Reading: Making Inferences

? How does this chant relate to Ravi's experience? [It emphasizes that the children had forgotten him.]

F. Critical Reading: Making Connections

Compare Ravi with Larry in "My Oedipus Complex." [Possible answers: Both are self-centered and are surprised and hurt when events cause them to realize their relative insignificance. Larry is indignant and is finally transformed by the realization that he is not his mother's only love; Ravi is inconsolable upon learning that he has been forgotten.]

"Don't be a fool," Raghu said roughly, pushing him aside, and even Mira said, "Stop howling, Ravi. If you want to play, you can stand at the end of the line," and she put him there very firmly.

The game proceeded. Two pairs of arms reached up and met in an arc. The children trooped under it again and again in a <u>lugubrious</u> circle, ducking their heads and <u>intoning</u>

> "The grass is green,
> The rose is red;
> Remember me
> When I am dead, dead, dead, dead . . ."

And the arc of thin arms trembled in the twilight, and the heads were bowed so sadly, and their feet tramped to that melancholy refrain so mournfully, so helplessly, that Ravi could not bear it. He would not follow them, he would not be included in this funereal game. He had wanted victory and triumph—not a funeral. But he had been forgotten, left out, and he would not join them now. The <u>ignominy</u> of being forgotten— how could he face it? He felt his heart go heavy and ache inside him unbearably. He lay down full length on the damp grass, crushing his face into it, no longer crying, silenced by a terrible sense of his insignificance.

WORDS TO OWN
lugubrious (lə·gōō′brē·əs) *adj.*: very solemn or mournful, especially in a way that seems exaggerated or ridiculous.
intoning (in·tōn′iŋ) *v.* used as *adj.*: chanting.
ignominy (ig′nə·min′ē) *n.*: shame and dishonor.

ANITA DESAI 1115

Critical Comment: Writer's Writer In her review of the collection *Games at Twilight,* Victoria Glendinning praises the title story, calling it a "jewel." She believes it "recounts something that has happened in one way or another to nearly everyone in childhood. . . ." She writes, "Mrs. Desai is a writers' writer in that anyone who has ever set pen to paper must ask himself just what it is about the writing that makes the story so memorable, and there is, naturally, no simple answer to the question."

Check Test: Questions and Answers
1. Briefly identify the main character in the story. [Ravi, a young boy.]
2. Where does Ravi hide? [In a shed.]
3. Who is Raghu? [An older boy, a soccer champion, who plays It in the game.]
4. Why does the young boy cry? [The other children have forgotten him.]

A. Critical Reading: Making Connections

After students have read the selection, ask them to re-read the first few paragraphs. How does the opening help prepare for the conflict of the story? [The story launches the reader into an ordinary morning; this scene sets up a standard for the reader before the coming conflict.]

B. Literary Element: Symbol

? What might the radio symbolize? [Possible answers: The familiar, the ordinary, the past.]

Making Meanings

First Thoughts

1. Many students will probably feel empathy for Ravi; they most likely have been in similar positions.

Reviewing the Text

Story maps should include the children going outside to play, the children choosing who is It, Ravi hiding behind the garage and in the storage shed, Ravi heading for the den, the children's responses to Ravi, and Ravi's reaction.

Shaping Interpretations

2. Students may point to the tactile image of the insect crawling on Ravi as he hides in the storage shed. Others may think the heat most vivid. Loss and death imagery includes the darkness and isolation inside the shed, the waning afternoon, and the funereal game. Students may illustrate the image of Ravi in hiding or crying as the children proceed to play without him.

The Radio

It was about the size of a toaster. Made of dark brown oak, it had been polished so often that it now gleamed in the dust-filled rays of the sun that warmed the room. The paint labeling the AM stations had cracked long ago, but its two dials still turned smoothly. It sat on a small table next to a massive green velvet armchair. An old withered man shuffled into the room carrying the morning paper. He sat in the armchair.

"Good morning, Sophie. How are you today?" he asked. She gave her usual response, her morning smile.

He flipped the pages of the paper. "Nothing interesting is going on in the world right now." Sophie sat in her blue dress, now a bit faded, but her face hadn't lost its glow.

Rosalie entered the parlor with his cup of coffee in her hand. She set it down next to the radio. "Ah, my morning coffee." He sipped it. "Yup, as black as ever." He nodded at Rosalie, and she left the room.

"Well, I've got to go to work now, Sophie." He hated leaving. He always enjoyed sitting with Sophie in the morning.

A young man in a double-breasted suit knocked on the open office door. "Yes, Ted?" the old man asked. Ted entered nervously.

The old man waited. He shuffled the papers on his desk. Ted opened his mouth several times. "Well, I might as well say it all at once and get it over with. I . . . the management has decided to let you go."

The old man sat there shocked. "I'm fired?" he asked incredulously.

"We just have to lay off people who won't benefit this company, people who haven't produced enough. Besides, you're nearing seventy. Don't you think you should retire?"

"Haven't produced enough? I was this company's top salesman."

"Yes, in 1949!" Ted exploded. He sighed. "Please clear out this office by the end of this day." The door shut with a bang.

"I lost my job, Sophie," the man said sadly. Sophie just smiled. The man turned one of the dials of his old radio. Glorious swing music began to fill the room. "Remember this, Sophie? We fell in love to this." The old man swung back and forth, humming.

Rosalie was talking on the phone with her sister. "The old man? He's fine. Thirty years I've been working here. He hasn't changed." She peeked into the parlor. "You won't believe this, Patty, but he's dancing in there . . . to no music. Sure there's a radio, but it hasn't worked since his wife Sophie died. You want to know what she looked like? Well, next time you come over, I'll show you her portrait hanging in the parlor. She's wearing a beautiful blue dress. . . ."

—Kathy Liu
Riverdale Country School
Bronx, New York

CONNECTING WITH "GAMES AT TWILIGHT"

Have students examine the main character in "Games at Twilight" and the one in "The Radio." What similar trial must both main characters undergo? [Each faces being forgotten and being disillusioned.] How do the writers separate these characters from the others, making the older man and Ravi seem isolated? [Possible answer: No one responds to the characters' worries and concerns; Sophie continues to smile, and Mira places Ravi in the new game, ignoring his complaints.]

MAKING MEANINGS

First Thoughts

1. How much empathy for Ravi did you feel at the end of the story? Did his experience remind you of the childhood experiences you described in your Reader's Log entry? How?

Reviewing the Text

Create a story map that outlines the important events in the story.

Shaping Interpretations

2. What specific **images** in this story are most vivid to you? Which images have to do with loss and death? If you had to draw one picture to illustrate the story, what would you draw?

3. Why is everyone so surprised to see Ravi when he finally comes out of his hiding place?

4. What kind of game are the children playing at twilight?

5. What has Ravi discovered by the end of the story? Find a passage of the text that supports your answer.

6. How would you state the **theme** of this story—what revelation about human life does it make to you? As you think about the theme, think also about how the story's **title** reinforces its theme. (Think of the layers of meanings you can give to the word *games*.) Be sure to compare your statements of theme in class: Are there differences?

7. How do Ravi's experiences in the shed contribute to the **mood** of the story?

Extending the Text

8. Are the children in this story (and childhood itself) more realistically portrayed than the children in television situation comedies, or less so? Give examples to support your view.

CHOICES:
Building Your Portfolio

Writer's Notebook

1. Collecting Ideas for a Problem-Solution Essay

Suppose you were designing a course of study in literature for seniors in high school. What problems do you see in the ways such courses are presently taught? What solutions would you propose for those problems? Take notes now on your thoughts on these issues. Base your ideas in part on your experience with the selections in this textbook. One thing you might consider is the kinds of literature you think seniors should be reading and the themes you think they should focus on. Save your notes for possible use in the Writer's Workshop on page 1179.

Critical Writing

2. Comparing Childhoods

Here are three unusual stories about childhood: "The Doll's House" (page 1062), "My Oedipus Complex" (page 1082), and "Games at Twilight." In an essay, compare and contrast two of these stories. Focus on the **discoveries** made by the children in each story, the **theme** of each story, and the writer's **tone**. Remember that in a comparison and contrast essay, you are looking for similarities and differences.

Creative Writing

3. Defeating Time

The student story on page 1116 is about time and loss, just as Desai's story is, though the points of view are very different. Write a short narrative of your own about someone who comes face to face with the passage of time. Is the person young, as Ravi is? Or is your main character old, like the man in "The Radio"?

---

3. The other children have forgotten about Ravi and the earlier game.

4. They play a "funereal game." The chant, which talks about *remembering* the dead, mocks Ravi's futile hope for recognition.

5. Ravi is saddened by how quickly he is forgotten; he gains a "terrible sense of his insignificance." Students may cite the final paragraph on p. 1115.

6. Students may say that theme is a child's learning about his own insignificance and mortality. The associations of the word *twilight* and the children's funereal game support this theme and are part of the title.

7. In the shed, the psychological drama of the story takes place: Ravi braves the dark to win the game, which shows how much he wants to be recognized. Readers learn how important he feels this win will be, which heightens the tension.

Extending the Text

8. **(Evaluation)** Some students will say the children in the story are more realistically portrayed, citing the familiar disagreements and the realistic psychological detail.

Beyond the Story

Choices: Building Your Portfolio

1. **Writer's Notebook** Remind students to save their work. They may use it as prewriting for the Writer's Workshop on p. 1179.

STRATEGIES FOR INCLUSION

Visual Students may find a chart helpful in organizing their essays for activity #2. Encourage them to prepare by jotting ideas in a chart like the one that follows.

Story	Discoveries	Theme	Tone
"My Oedipus Complex"	[Larry finds common ground with his father. He also learns he is no longer the center of his mother's world.]	[Learning to deal with others]	[Light-hearted, humorous, yet touching]

PORTFOLIO ASSESSMENT

Choices: Assessment Criteria
For help in evaluating these Choices assignments, see the criteria in the *Portfolio Management System*, p. 184.

QUICK PLANNING GUIDE

Into the Poem

Author Biography p. 1118
Before You Read p. 1118

- **Reading Focus: Prior Knowledge**
  Students consider Heaney's
  influences.
- **Quickwrite:** Freewrite associations
  with the earth's soil
- **Elements of Literature: Extended
  Metaphor** Identify implied
  comparison
- **Background:** Uses of peat for
  Irish farmer

Through the Poem

"Digging" p. 1119
Making Meanings p. 1120

Beyond the Poem

Choices: Building Your Portfolio
p. 1120

- **Writer's Notebook:** Collect ideas
  for a problem-solution essay
- **Creative Writing:** Students write
  a poem using their own voice

Into the Poem

Using BEFORE YOU READ
p. 1118

Reading Focus

Tell students that the speaker in this
poem is thinking about how his father
and grandfather dug for food and fuel.
In a literal and a figurative sense, the
poet is thinking about "roots."

Seamus Heaney

(1939–)

Seamus Heaney was born to Roman Catholic parents in largely Protestant Northern Ireland. His boyhood on a farm in County Derry contributed profoundly to his identity as a poet. But Heaney never promoted himself as a rustic or regarded his work as an expression of regionalism. He earned his education as a scholarship student, first at a Catholic preparatory school and then at Queen's University in Belfast where, still in his midtwenties, he was appointed lecturer in English.

Instead of leading him away from his roots in Irish soil, Heaney's studies—particularly those having to do with the history and psychology of myth—opened for him a way of seeing anew not only the misty grandeur of his native land-

Portrait of Seamus Heaney
(1973) by Edward McGuire.
Oil on canvas (56″ × 44″).

scape, but also the figures in it who, unknowingly, unite the past with the present. Heaney is an acute observer of rural life and of life lived on the industrial margins of cities, and he deals with both without romanticizing them.

Regarded by Robert Lowell as "the best Irish poet since William Butler Yeats," Heaney now occupies the chair at Harvard left vacant by Lowell's death in 1977. In 1995, commended for his works "of lyrical beauty and ethical depth, which exalt everyday miracles and the living past," Heaney was awarded the Nobel Prize in literature. He divides his time between Cambridge, Massachusetts, and a home in the Republic of Ireland.

BEFORE YOU READ
DIGGING

Reading Focus

Delving into the Depths
In 1969, Seamus Heaney read *The Bog People,* by P. V. Glob, an archaeologist who had unearthed in Ireland's peat bogs the preserved remains of several Iron Age humans, all apparently victims of ritual slaughter. The book made explicit a powerful symbol for the continuity of human experience that had been present in Heaney's poems from the beginning: the bog, the earth that contains and preserves human history. As you read "Digging," published in Heaney's first collection of poems, *Death of a Naturalist* (1966), try to formulate your

own interpretation of Heaney's homeland soil and of those who work with it.

Quickwrite

What associations, metaphorical or otherwise, do you have with the earth's soil? Jot down a few, then explain which are most interesting or powerful to you.

Elements of Literature

Extended Metaphor
Up until the poem's very last line, one may not realize that "Digging" contains an **extended metaphor,** an implied comparison between one thing and

another. When you've finished reading, try to identify the connections between his father's work and Heaney's own.

Background

The Irish farmer digs two things in particular: potatoes and turf, or peat. The peat is dug from bogs, or huge soggy areas of decaying vegetable matter that have produced for Ireland, especially in centuries gone by, material that is dried and then burned in fires for cooking and heat. The poet is also "digging," just as his father and grandfather had done before him. But what is he "digging" for? And what is his tool?

PROGRAM MANAGER

- **Planning Instruction** See Teaching Notes, *Teaching Resources B,* p. 167, for objectives, a summary, literary elements, and additional historical and biographical information for this selection.
- **Instructional Support** Before beginning the instructional lesson, see Graphic

Organizer for Active Reading, *Teaching Resources B,* p. 183, for a Through the Poem activity.
- **Assessment** See Selection Test, *Test Booklet,* p. 236.

Digging

Seamus Heaney

Between my finger and my thumb
The squat pen rests; snug as a gun. **Ⓐ**

Under my window, a clean rasping sound
When the spade sinks into gravelly ground:
5   My father, digging. I look down

Till his straining rump among the flowerbeds
Bends low, comes up twenty years away
Stooping in rhythm through potato drills° **Ⓑ**
Where he was digging.

10 The coarse boot nestled on the lug°, the shaft
Against the inside knee was levered firmly.
He rooted out tall tops, buried the bright edge deep
To scatter new potatoes that we picked
Loving their cool hardness in our hands.

15 By God, the old man could handle a spade.
Just like his old man.

My grandfather cut more turf in a day
Than any other man on Toner's bog.
Once I carried him milk in a bottle
20 Corked sloppily with paper. He straightened up
To drink it, then fell to right away
Nicking and slicing neatly, heaving sods
Over his shoulder, going down and down
For the good turf. Digging.

25 The cold smell of potato mould, the squelch and slap
Of soggy peat, the curt cuts of an edge
Through living roots awaken in my head. **Ⓒ**
But I've no spade to follow men like them. **Ⓓ**

Between my finger and my thumb
30 The squat pen rests.
I'll dig with it. **Ⓔ**

8. drills: furrows or rows of planted seeds.

10. lug: earlike prong or projection by which a spade is supported.

SEAMUS HEANEY 1119

OPTIONS FOR TEACHING

PROFESSIONAL NOTES

Critical Comment: Nobel Winner The press release announcing Seamus Heaney's Nobel Prize in Literature in 1995 explains that, although Heaney writes about a wide range of subjects, some of his poetry is very close to his rural upbringing and the conflict in Northern Ireland. He analyzes the violence in unique terms, purposefully avoiding conventional discussion of the subject. He lambastes the unwillingness of both sides to speak out freely and opposes defeatism. As does the speaker in his poem "Digging," Heaney feels that, through his writing, generations of rural ancestors find a voice.

A. Reader's Response: First Thoughts

? Why do you think the speaker compares his pen to a gun? [Sample responses: Perhaps because his pen is his most powerful weapon; his pen gives him a sense of security.]

B. Literary Element: Setting

Help students find in the wording the shift from present to past. In the first line of stanza 3, it seems as if the speaker's father is digging in the flowerbeds outside the window where the poet sits writing. In the second line, the speaker moves in his imagination to a time twenty years earlier when his father was digging potatoes on the family farm. "Drills" here are furrows in which seeds are planted.

C. Critical Reading: Identifying Main Ideas

? What kind of experiences from his childhood does the speaker recall, especially in ll. 25–27? [Vivid sensory experiences.] How were these experiences preparing the speaker for his adult occupation? [By providing raw material for his writing.]

D. Critical Reading: Making Inferences

? Does the speaker feel alienated from his forebears? [No.] What does the last stanza suggest about his sense of self-worth and purpose? [He is proud of his work as a writer and sees it as a continuation of the skilled and dedicated labor of his forebears.]

Metacognition What clues help you interpret the speaker's feelings? [The speaker frames the work of his father in a positive light, and, although the speaker says he cannot follow the exact work of his father, he implies that he can still dig with the tools he is given.]

E. Literary Element: Extended Metaphor

? How can the speaker dig with a pen? [Sample responses: He can dig into his memory or the collective memory of his family or culture. He can dig into the psychological aspect of human existence.]

First Thoughts

1. Students may mention the raspy sound of digging, the smell of earth, or the image of a man bending to dig.

Shaping Interpretations

2. The speaker sees his father stooping to dig among the flowerbeds.
3. Similes and metaphors compare the pen to a gun (l. 2) and a spade (l. 31). The pen represents a connection between the speaker's heritage and his occupation.
4. The speaker plans to "dig" with his pen; that is, he will make his living from writing.
5. For memorable incidents that will help create literature.
6. *Spade/sinks* or *gravelly ground* (l. 4) are examples of alliteration. As examples of onomatopoeia, students may suggest *rasping* (l. 3) or *squelch* or *slap* (l. 25).
7. Perhaps the phrase signals the speaker's shift from the present moment to his memories. Students may have expected *feet, yards,* or *rows.*
8. The speaker compares his work to that of his ancestors; he respects the work they did.
9. In the literal sense, digging may kill some plants or tear up the earth. In the sense of writing, digging may unearth painful memories or feelings.

Connecting with the Text

10. *Remind students to choose a situation they would not mind sharing with others. Students may wish to "dig" into their experiences to find good stories or universal truths.*

Beyond the Poem

Choices: Building Your Portfolio

1. **Writer's Workshop** Remind students to save their work. They may use it as prewriting for the Writer's Workshop on p. 1179.

First Thoughts

1. What **image** in the poem most vividly communicated to you what the speaker heard, smelled, or felt?

Shaping Interpretations

2. Describe what the **speaker** sees from his window.
3. What **figures of speech** compare the speaker's pen to other things? What significance can you find in these comparisons, particularly the one in the last stanza?
4. At the end of the poem, what does the speaker intend to do?
5. What do you think the speaker wants to "dig" for? Does your Reader's Log entry prompt any ideas?
6. What examples of **alliteration** and **onomatopoeia** can you find in the poem?
7. Why do you think the father comes up "twenty *years*" away in line 7? (What word did you expect to find here?)
8. Explain the **extended metaphor** in the poem. Does the speaker feel that his own work is less (or more) important than that of his father and grandfather?
9. In lines 25–27, the spade cuts through "living roots." How might "digging," either the kind done by the speaker's father or the speaker himself, be seen as an act of violence?

Connecting with the Text

10. What would you would like to "dig" with your own "pen" (or typewriter, or computer)?

CHOICES: Building Your Portfolio

Writer's Notebook

1. Collecting Ideas for a Problem-Solution Essay

WORK IN PROGRESS

The poem describes two different kinds of labor—the backbreaking labor done by the father with his hands and spade, and the intellectual, or cultural, labor the speaker performs with his pen. With a small group, discuss the problems people encounter in understanding one another's work and why such work is important. What are some solutions to these problems? Take notes on your discussion, and save them for the Writer's Workshop on page 1179.

Creative Writing

2. Do Your Own Digging

Seamus Heaney once wrote that in "Digging" he truly found his own voice: "Finding a voice means that you can get your own feeling into your own words and that your words have the feel of you about them." Beginning with the last three lines of Heaney's poem, write your own poem, careful to do your "digging" with words that suit your own voice. You might want to begin by recalling something about your parents, grandparents, or other older family members.

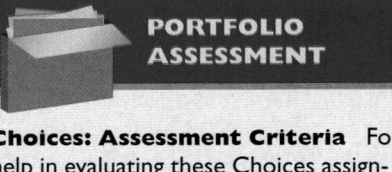
PORTFOLIO ASSESSMENT

Choices: Assessment Criteria For help in evaluating these Choices assignments, see the criteria in the *Portfolio Management System,* p. 185.

TECHNOLOGY **Social Sciences** For a complete version of the Nobel announcement concerning Heaney, students may look it up on-line at **http://sunsite.unc.edu/nobel /announcement95-literature.html**. Heaney's biography is available on-line at **http://sunsite .unc.edu/dykki/poetry**. *You may want to preview any Internet activity that you suggest to students. Because these resources are sometimes public forums, their content can be unpredictable.*

The Twentieth Century

Collection 15 — CLASHES OF CULTURE

Theme: The Collision of Wills
The tendency of one person or group to impose its will on another often results in a collision course. Conflicts arise from differences in age, gender, religion, and ethnicity.

Thematic Focus

A key feature of the literature in this Collection is the exploration of cultural clashes.

- **Shakespeare's Sister** from **A Room of One's Own** Gender, throughout history, has helped determine the activities a person is allowed to pursue.
- **The Cairo Rooftop** from **Palace Walk** Many constraints are imposed upon Arab women in early-twentieth-century Cairo.
- **Shooting an Elephant** Orwell describes the events that give him insight into British imperialism.
- **No Witchcraft for Sale** Even when relations between people of different cultures are friendly, racism creates adversity.
- **Once Upon a Time** Gordimer's parody of a fairy tale illustrates the high price paid by the haves to exclude the have-nots.
- **The Virgins** Foreign influence, however well intended, may destroy as well as build up a culture.
- **Marriage Is a Private Affair** Traditions held dear by one generation collide with the younger generation's views.
- **Telephone Conversation** Discrimination is treated with satiric wit in this poem.

Literary Focus

Literary Element	Selection / Feature
Irony	**Shooting an Elephant**
Theme	**No Witchcraft for Sale**
Parody	**Once Upon a Time**
Dialogue	**Telephone Conversation**

Writing Focus

The following flowchart shows how the writing assignment for each selection relates to the writing assignment presented at the end of the Collection.

Selection	Work-in-Progress Assignment
A Room of One's Own	Brainstorm about gender inequalities p. 1130
Shooting an Elephant	Take notes on peer pressure p. 1144
No Witchcraft for Sale	Freewrite about cultural differences p. 1153
Once Upon a Time	Evaluate solutions for crime problem p. 1160
The Virgins	Investigate community problem p. 1163
Marriage Is a Private Affair	List intergenerational problems p. 1170
Telephone Conversation	Learn about antidiscrimination laws p. 1173
Writer's Workshop	Write a problem-solution essay p. 1179

1120A

Collection Planner

SELECTION / FEATURE	Literary Elements / Active Reading	Writing	Speaking and Listening	Language and Vocabulary
Shakespeare's Sister *from* **A Room of One's Own** Virginia Woolf (pp. 1122–1130)	• Reader's Log p. 1123	• Critical Writing: Evaluate Woolf's ideas p. 1130 • Creative Writing: Rewrite Judith's life p. 1130 • Creative Writing: Create imaginary life p. 1130		
World Literature: The Cairo Rooftop *from* **Palace Walk** Naguib Mahfouz (pp. 1131–1136)	• Reader's Log p. 1132		• Finding Common Ground: Discuss dating customs p. 1136	
Shooting an Elephant George Orwell (pp. 1137–1145)	• Reader's Log p. 1138 • Irony p. 1138	• Critical Writing: Interpret passage p. 1144 • Critical Writing: Interpret symbolism p. 1144	• Creative Writing: Create/Present storyboard p. 1144	• How to Own a Word: Analyzing Word Analogies pp. 1144–1145
No Witchcraft for Sale Doris Lessing (pp. 1146–1153)	• Reader's Log p. 1147 • Theme p. 1147	• Critical Writing: Analyze cultures p. 1153 • Critical Writing: Analyze point of view p. 1153 • Creative Writing: Write Gideon's speech p. 1153	• Science and Medicine/ Research: Report on folk medicines p. 1153	
Once Upon a Time Nadine Gordimer (pp. 1154–1160)	• Reader's Log p. 1155 • Parody p. 1155	• Critical Writing: Compare authors p. 1160 • Creative Writing: Create original fairy tale p. 1160	• Research/Speaking: Report on cultural divisions p. 1160	
The Virgins Derek Walcott (pp. 1161–1163)	• Reader's Log p. 1162	• Critical Writing: Analyze irony p. 1163 • Creative Writing: Write lyric p. 1163	• Panel Discussion: Discuss U.S. ideals p. 1163	
Marriage Is a Private Affair Chinua Achebe (pp. 1164–1170) **Connections: Going Home** Maurice Kenny (p. 1169)	• Reader's Log p. 1164	• Critical Writing: Interpret ending p. 1170 • Creative Writing: Create two scenes p. 1170		
Telephone Conversation Wole Soyinka (pp. 1171–1173)	• Reader's Log p. 1171 • Dialogue p. 1171	• Critical Writing: Describe character p. 1173	• Law/Speaking: Research housing laws p. 1173	
The English Language English Today and Tomorrow John Algeo (pp. 1175–1178)				• Try It Out: Word origins p. 1178
Writer's Workshop: Problem-Solution Essay (pp. 1179–1185)		• Writing Process: Problem-solution essay pp. 1179–1185		
Language Workshop: Effective Sentences (p. 1186)		• Revise essay p. 1186		• Complex and compound-complex sentences p. 1186
Learning for Life (p. 1187)		• Freewrite p. 1187	• Create talk show p. 1187	

Collection Resources

Teaching Resources B Cross-Curricular Activity p. 209	Audiovisual Resources Binder Fine Art Transparencies 15.1–15.2	Test Booklet Collection 15 Test pp. 255–257

 Computer disk or CD-ROM

 Videodisc

 Audiocassette

Overhead Transparency

PROGRAM RESOURCES

Electronic Media	Teaching Resources with Organizer		Audiovisual Resources Binder
	Teaching Resources B	Other Resources	
• Test Generator	• Teaching Notes p. 185 • Reading Organizer p. 190 • Words to Own p. 191	• Test Booklet: Selection Test pp. 241–242 • PM System pp. 54–55, 186	
	• Teaching Notes p. 185		
• Test Generator • Language Workshop: Run-on Sentences	• Teaching Notes p. 186 • Reading Organizer p. 192 • Language Link pp. 193–194 • Words to Own p. 195	• Test Booklet: Selection Test pp. 243–244 • Portfolio Management System pp. 60–61, 187	• How to Own a Word Transparency 15.4
• Test Generator • Language Workshop: Semicolons, Colons	• Teaching Notes pp. 186–187 • Reading Organizer p. 196 • Language Link pp. 197–198 • Words to Own p. 199	• Test Booklet: Selection Test pp. 245–246 • PM System pp. 48–49, 188–189 • Language and Writing Skills Worksheets pp. 138–139	• Elements of Literature Transparency 15.3
• Test Generator	• Teaching Notes p. 187 • Reading Organizer p. 200 • Words to Own p. 201	• Test Booklet: Selection Test pp. 247–248 • Portfolio Management System p. 190	• Selected Reading Audiocassette 3, Side A
• Test Generator	• Teaching Notes pp. 187–188 • Reading Organizer p. 202	• Test Booklet: Selection Test p. 249 • Portfolio Management System p. 191	
• Test Generator	• Teaching Notes p. 188 • Reading Organizer p. 203 • Language Link p. 204 • Words to Own p. 205	• Test Booklet: Selection Test pp. 250–251 • PM System p. 192 • Language and Writing Skills Worksheets pp. 180–182	
• Test Generator	• Teaching Notes p. 189 • Reading Organizer p. 206	• Test Booklet: Selection Test p. 252 • PM System p. 193	
• Test Generator • Videodisc	• Teaching Notes p. 189	• Test Booklet: The English Language pp. 253–254	
		• Portfolio Management System pp. 194–196	• Revision Transparencies 15.5 and 15.6
• Language Workshop: Coordinating Ideas	• Language Workshop pp. 207–208		
		• Portfolio Management System p. 197	

Proofreading Warm-ups

You may use the following exercises to help students practice their proofreading skills. Copy a set of incorrect sentences onto the chalkboard, and have students find and correct the spelling, punctuation, usage, and mechanical errors in each sentence. Ask students to share and discuss their responses.

	Sentences with Errors	Sentences Corrected	Skills Covered
1	a. virginia woolf who was to frail to attend school regular was privatly tutored b. she read extensively, in her Fathers library	a. Virginia Woolf, who was too frail to attend school regularly, was privately tutored. b. She read extensively in her father's library.	Capitalization, Comma usage, Spelling, Adverb usage, Apostrophe usage, End marks
2	a. naguib mahfouz widely regarded as a outstanding writer of contemporary arabic literature b. mahfaouzs novel Palace Walk is 1 of 3 volumes in the Cairo Trilogy	a. Naguib Mahfouz is widely regarded as an outstanding writer of contemporary Arabic literature. b. Mahfouz's novel <u>Palace Walk</u> is one of three volumes in the <u>Cairo Trilogy</u>.	Capitalization, Fragments, Nonstandard usage, Apostrophe usage, Underline book titles, Write out numerals, End marks
3	a. george orwells essay Shooting an Elephant is auto-biographical b. in his essay Orwell comes to realize, that tyrants destroy there own freedom	a. George Orwell's essay "Shooting an Elephant" is autobiographical. b. In his essay, Orwell comes to realize that tyrants destroy their own freedom.	Capitalization, Apostrophe usage, Quotation marks for essay titles, Hyphen usage, Comma usage, Spelling, End marks
4	a. doris lessing like many writers had a lonly childhood b. like virginia woolf Lessing read alot of books	a. Doris Lessing, like many writers, had a lonely childhood. b. Like Virginia Woolf, Lessing read a lot of books.	Capitalization, Comma usage, Spelling, End marks
5	a. nadine gordimer, is another writter, who spent much of her childhood reading b. she finaly won the nobel prize in lit. in 1991	a. Nadine Gordimer is another writer who spent much of her childhood reading. b. She finally won the Nobel Prize in literature in 1991.	Capitalization, Comma usage, Spelling, Write out abbreviations, End marks
6	a. what derek walcott share's in common w/ nadine gordimer, is that he to won the nobel prize in literature b. he won his a year latter however	a. What Derek Walcott shares in common with Nadine Gordimer is that he, too, won the Nobel Prize in literature. b. He won his a year later, however.	Capitalization, Apostrophe usage, Write out abbreviations, Comma usage, Spelling, End marks
7	a. their is not hardly anyone who would turn down a trip to the Virgin islands b. well I certainly would except a free trip their	a. There is hardly anyone who would turn down a trip to the Virgin Islands. b. Well, I certainly would accept a free trip there.	Capitalization, Spelling, Double negatives, Comma usage, End marks
8	a. lisa what did you think of Chinua Achebes story b. i could not scarcely understand why Nnaemekas Father was so set in his ways	a. Lisa, what did you think of Chinua Achebe's story? b. I could scarcely understand why Nnaemeka's father was so set in his ways.	Capitalization, Comma usage, Apostrophe usage, Question marks, Double negatives, End marks
9	a. you could of read Wole Soyinkas poem with more feeling Jeremy said Anne b. but i done the best i coulda done he protested	a. "You could have read Wole Soyinka's poem with more feeling, Jeremy," said Anne. b. "But I did the best I could have done!" he protested.	Quotation marks, Capitalization, Verb errors, Apostrophe usage, Comma usage, Nonstandard usage, Exclamation points, End marks
10	a. english has some words that we're originaly compounds b. however there parts have merged so complete that we no longer recognize there origins	a. English has some words that were originally compounds. b. However, their parts have merged so completely that we no longer recognize their origins.	Capitalization, Apostrophe usage, Spelling, Comma usage, Adverb usage, End marks

Collection *15*

CLASHES OF CULTURE

A s the traveler who has
once been from home
is wiser than he who has
never left his own doorstep,
so a knowledge of one other
culture should sharpen our
ability to scrutinize more
steadily, to appreciate more
lovingly, our own.

—Margaret Mead, *from Coming
of Age in Samoa*

Woolf	Gordimer
Mahfouz	Walcott
Orwell	Achebe
Lessing	Soyinka

Responding to the Quotation

Why does anthropologist Margaret Mead recommend knowledge of another culture? Ask students to think of an instance in which information gained about another culture has helped them further explore their own traditions. For example, how do various cultures celebrate spring? How do various traditions cope with pain and loss? Identify any common approaches, and discuss the significance of any differences or clashes between cultures.

PROGRAM MANAGER

- **Integrated Assessment** For a summative assessment of the literature and language skills taught in this collection, see Collection 15 Test, *Test Booklet,* pp. 255– 257.
- **Instructional Support** See Fine Art Transparencies 15.1–15.2. Review teacher's notes for transparencies in the *Audiovisual*

Resources Binder for suggestions on how to tie the transparencies to specific reading selections.
- **Extending Collection Theme** See Cross-Curricular Activity: Clashes of Culture, *Teaching Resources B,* p. 209 for an activity in other disciplines and for evaluation criteria.

PORTFOLIO ASSESSMENT

Parent/Guardian Involvement For forms that will help a parent or guardian review and respond to a student's portfolio, see the *Portfolio Management System,* pp. 62–63.

Virginia Woolf

(1882–1941)

Virginia Woolf was born in Victorian London to the scholar and literary critic Sir Leslie Stephen and his artistic wife Julia. In her youth, Woolf enjoyed all the advantages of a financially comfortable and intellectually challenging environment. Too frail to attend school regularly, she was privately tutored and given the luxury of her father's extensive library.

After her father's death in 1904, Virginia, her sister Vanessa, and their two brothers moved to the area of London known as Bloomsbury. Soon they and their friends began to meet in what came to be called the Bloomsbury Group, an intellectual circle whose other prominent members included the writer E. M. Forster, the artist Duncan Grant, and the economist John Maynard Keynes. One member of the group was Leonard Woolf, a journalist and economist, whom Virginia married in 1912.

An informal gathering with the highest cultural standards, the Bloomsbury Group helped provide the right environment for Virginia Woolf's sensitive, experimental fiction. Only after her death, when her diaries were published, was it clear how powerful the emotional effect of her friends' praise or criticism had been on her.

Woolf had been writing since she was fourteen and reviewing books since her early twenties, but it was not until she was thirty-three, in 1915, that her first novel, *The Voyage Out*, was published. The publication of *Jacob's Room*

Virginia Woolf.

(1922) and *Mrs. Dalloway* (1925) established her position as one of the foremost writers of her time. With these novels—and with subsequent novels such as *To the Lighthouse* (1927) and *The Waves* (1931)—Woolf pursued an experimental vision that emphasized personal impressions over external events and focused on the experience of life as it was being led.

Like James Joyce, Woolf used the technique of stream of consciousness, although her version of it was somewhat different from his. For example, while *Mrs. Dalloway,* like Joyce's *Ulysses,* takes place on a single day, it covers, through the thoughts of its characters, an entire lifetime. Woolf was a great admirer of Joyce's *Portrait of the Artist as a Young Man,* but she considered *Ulysses* an "illiterate, underbred book." Still, she worried that "what I am doing is probably being better done by Mr. Joyce."

Woolf also wrote a great many reviews and essays, a number of them focusing on women authors whom she felt had been neglected or exploring female writers in general. In 1917, she and her husband established the Hogarth Press, which published many of the most important writers—both male and female—of the day.

Troubled by sudden deaths and mental illness in her family, Woolf throughout her life suffered from well-concealed bouts of depression and anxiety. These deepened with the German bomber raids over England in World War II, and in March 1941, she took her own life.

PORTFOLIO ASSESSMENT

Portfolio Assessment For help with teacher assessment of reading skills, see the *Portfolio Management System,* pp. 54–55.

PROGRAM MANAGER

- **Planning Instruction** See Teaching Notes, *Teaching Resources B,* p. 185, for objectives, a summary, and literary elements for this selection.
- **Instructional Support** Before beginning the instructional lesson, see Graphic Organizer for Active Reading, *Teaching Resources B,* p. 190, for a Through the Selection activity.
- **Assessment** See Selection Test, *Test Booklet,* pp. 241–242.
- **Reinforcement** Use the Words to Own worksheet in *Teaching Resources B,* p. 191.

BEFORE YOU READ

SHAKESPEARE'S SISTER

Reading Focus

Gender and Genius

Gender is perhaps the most basic difference between human beings in every culture. Beyond the biological differences are other enduring ones: the everyday concerns that men and women have, and the work they are or are not able to accomplish. Virginia Woolf scrutinized that last difference in her 1929 essay *A Room of One's Own,* from which the following selection is taken. Focusing on the creation of great literature, Woolf went back to Shakespeare's day and drew firm conclusions about the lack of equal opportunity for women through the ages. Could such lack of opportunity have affected the course of human history?

Quickwrite

To make her points, Woolf creates a younger sister for Shakespeare, a sixteenth-century young woman completely his equal in brilliance and ambition. What life story do you predict that Woolf, herself brilliant, imagines for this sister? Outline it briefly in your Reader's Log.

Background

A Room of One's Own is considered a pioneering work of feminist criticism, a field that did not even exist in 1929 but has since blossomed. Aims of feminist criticism include exposing sexist attitudes in or toward literature, reinterpreting earlier works from a feminist perspective, uncovering neglected women writers, and analyzing how gender affects a writer's subjects, themes, and even style. Some early feminists believed that "female language" is actually different from male language—richer in emotion, for example, and freer in patterns of meaning. Today, many feminists are exploring how cultural and economic forces help to shape the identities of women *and* men.

Virginia Woolf laid the foundation for much of this thinking. She was truly ahead of her time in insisting that social conditions can determine writing, in arguing that male literary language could not truly express women's experiences, and in raising the possibility of an imagination that transcends gender.

Virginia Woolf in a Deck Chair (20th century) by Vanessa Bell.

Permission of Angelica Garnett.

VIRGINIA WOOLF 1123

Using **BEFORE YOU READ** p. 1123

Reading Focus

What is a genius? Have students discuss the qualities that make for exceptional musicians, writers, or artists. Then, ask them how many of those qualities can be nurtured or impaired by material circumstances—food, clothing, or housing. If a person's gender can determine material conditions, can it also affect the development of genius? Have students write down their responses after the class discussion.

Background

Although she was very well read, Virginia Woolf never had a formal education like her father and brothers, who attended Cambridge University. Woolf delivered part of *A Room of One's Own* at the two women's colleges at Cambridge, Newnham and Girton. Ironically, she delivered a speech about the need for women's education at a school she did not attend.

WRITERS ON WRITING

Famous as an innovative novelist who explored the stream-of-consciousness technique, Woolf is also regarded by scholars and critics as an influential and perceptive essayist, critic, and reviewer. Woolf believed that the purpose of writing an essay was to please the reader through the use of wit and cultural references, including feminism, war and peace, life and death, her travels, and literary and social theory. She is known particularly for her writing on the role of women in a dramatically changing society.

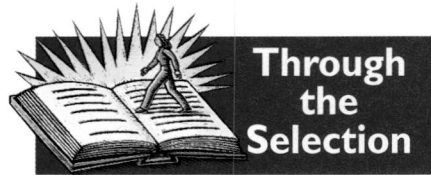
A. Expansion
George Macaulay Trevelyan's *The History of England* was considered *the* standard history of the country in Woolf's time.

B. Language Note: Sentence Structure
Woolf's essay contains numerous lengthy compound-complex sentences. Suggest that students break down the sentences by finding the main and subordinate clauses and identifying subject-verb pairs.

C. Reader's Response: Shaping Interpretations
? Why do you think the author includes this seemingly irrelevant information about cats? [Sample responses: The foolish statement discredits the gentleman's opinion about women's inferiority; the statement shows that "authorities" are not always infallible and unbiased.]

D. Humanities Connection
Ovid, Virgil, and Horace are among the most admired Latin poets. Latin was the language of learning in Europe for hundreds of years, and studying it was an important part of a young boy's education.

E. Critical Reading: Drawing Conclusions
? Why does Woolf choose these particular characteristics and events? [Woolf intends to show the contrast between the siblings' lives.]

Shakespeare's Sister
from **A Room of One's Own**

Virginia Woolf

Here am I asking why women did not write poetry in the Elizabethan age, and I am not sure how they were educated; whether they were taught to write; whether they had sitting rooms to themselves; how many women had children before they were twenty-one; what, in short, they did from eight in the morning till eight at night. They had no money evidently; according to Professor Trevelyan[1] they were married whether they liked it or not before they were out of the nursery, at fifteen or sixteen very likely. It would have been extremely odd, even upon this showing, had one of them suddenly written the plays of Shakespeare, I concluded, and I thought of that old gentleman, who is dead now, but was a bishop, I think, who declared that it was impossible for any woman, past, present, or to come, to have the genius of Shakespeare. He wrote to the papers about it. He also told a lady who applied to him for information that cats do not as a matter of fact go to heaven, though they have, he added, souls of a sort. How much thinking those old gentlemen used to save one! How the borders of ignorance shrank back at their approach! Cats do not go to heaven. Women cannot write the plays of Shakespeare.

Be that as it may, I could not help thinking, as I looked at the works of Shakespeare on the shelf, that the bishop was right at least in this; it would have been impossible, completely and entirely, for any woman to have written the plays of Shakespeare in the age of Shakespeare. Let me imagine, since facts are so hard to come by, what would have happened had Shakespeare had a wonderfully gifted sister, called Judith, let us say. Shakespeare himself went, very probably—his mother was an heiress—to the grammar school, where he may have learnt Latin—Ovid, Virgil, and Horace—and the elements of grammar and logic. He was, it is well known, a wild boy who poached rabbits, perhaps shot a deer, and had, rather sooner than he should have done, to marry a woman in the neighborhood, who bore him a child rather quicker than was right. That escapade sent him to seek his fortune in London. He had, it seemed, a taste for the theater; he began by holding horses at the stage door. Very soon he got work in the theater, became a successful actor, and lived at the hub of the universe, meeting everybody, knowing everybody, practicing his art on the boards, exercising his wits in the streets, and even getting access to the palace of the queen. Meanwhile his extraordinarily gifted sister, let us suppose, remained at home. She was as adventurous, as imaginative, as agog to see the world as he was. But she was not sent to school. She had no chance of learning grammar and logic, let alone of reading Horace and Virgil. She picked up a book now and then, one of her brother's perhaps, and read a few pages. But then her parents came in and told her to mend the stockings or mind the stew and not moon about with books and papers. They would have spoken sharply but kindly, for they were substantial people who knew the conditions of life for a woman and loved their daughter—indeed, more likely than not she was the apple of her father's eye. Perhaps she scribbled some pages up in an apple loft on the sly, but was careful to hide them or set fire to them. Soon, however, before she was out of her teens, she was to be betrothed to the son of a neighboring wool stapler.[2] She cried out that marriage was hateful to her, and for that she was severely beaten by her father. Then he ceased to scold her. He begged her instead not to hurt him, not to shame him in this matter of her marriage. He would give her a chain of beads or a fine petticoat, he said; and there were tears in his eyes. How could she disobey him? How could she break his heart? The force of her own gift alone drove her to it. She made up a small parcel of her belongings, let herself down by a rope one summer's night, and took the road to London. She was not seventeen. The birds that sang in the hedge were not more musical than she was. She had the quickest fancy, a gift like her brother's, for the tune of words. Like him, she had

---

1. **Professor Trevelyan:** G. M. Trevelyan, author of *The History of England* (1926).

2. **wool stapler:** dealer in wool, a product sorted according to its fiber, or "staple."

a taste for the theater. She stood at the stage door; she wanted to act, she said. Men laughed in her face. The manager—a fat, loose-lipped man—guffawed. He bellowed something about poodles dancing and women acting—no woman, he said, could possibly be an actress. He hinted—you can imagine what. She could get no training in her craft. Could she even seek her dinner in a tavern or roam the streets at midnight? Yet her genius was for fiction and lusted to feed abundantly upon the lives of men and women and the study of their ways. At last—for she was very young, oddly like Shakespeare the poet in her face, with the same gray eyes and rounded brows—at last Nick Greene the actor-manager took pity on her; she found herself with child by that gentleman and so—who shall measure the heat and violence of the poet's heart when caught and tangled in a woman's body?—killed herself one winter's night and lies buried at some crossroads where the omnibuses now stop outside the Elephant and Castle.[3]

That, more or less, is how the story would run, I think, if a woman in Shakespeare's day had had Shakespeare's genius. But for my part, I agree with the deceased bishop, if such he was—it is unthinkable that any woman in Shakespeare's day should have had Shakespeare's genius. For genius like Shakespeare's is not born among laboring, uneducated, servile people. It was not born in England among the Saxons and the Britons. It is not born today among the working classes. How, then, could it have been born among women whose work began, according to Professor Trevelyan, almost before they were out of the nursery, who were forced to it by their parents and held to it by all the power of law and custom? Yet genius of a sort must have existed among women as it must have existed among the working classes. Now and again an Emily Brontë or a Robert Burns blazes out and proves its presence. But certainly it never got itself onto paper. When, however, one reads of a witch being ducked, of a woman possessed by devils, of a wise woman selling herbs, or even of a very remarkable man who had a mother, then I think we are on the track of a

lost novelist, a suppressed poet, of some mute and inglorious[4] Jane Austen, some Emily Brontë who dashed her brains out on the moor or mopped and mowed about the highways crazed with the torture that her gift had put her to. Indeed, I would venture to guess that Anon, who wrote so many poems without signing them, was often a woman. It was a woman Edward Fitzgerald,[5] I think, suggested who made the ballads and the folk songs, crooning them to her children, beguiling her spinning with them, or the length of the winter's night.

This may be true or it may be false—who can say?—but what is true in it, so it seemed to me, reviewing the story of Shakespeare's sister as I had made it, is that any woman born with a great gift in the sixteenth century would certainly have gone crazed, shot herself, or ended her days in some lonely cottage outside the village, half witch, half wizard, feared and mocked at. For it needs little skill in psychology to be sure that a highly gifted girl who had tried to use her gift for poetry would have been so thwarted and hindered by other people, so tortured and pulled asunder by her own contrary instincts, that she must have lost her health and sanity to a certainty. No girl could have walked to London and stood at a stage door and forced her way into the presence of actor-managers without doing herself a violence and suffering an anguish which may have been irrational—for chastity may be a fetish invented by certain societies for unknown reasons—but were nonetheless inevitable. Chastity had then, it has even now, a religious importance in a woman's life, and has so wrapped itself round with nerves and instincts that to cut it free and bring it to the light of day demands courage of the rarest. To have lived a free life in London in the sixteenth century would have meant for a woman who was poet and playwright a nervous stress

---

4. mute and inglorious: allusion to line 59 of "Elegy Written in a Country Churchyard" (page 601).
5. Edward Fitzgerald (1809–1883): English translator and poet.

- -

WORDS TO OWN
servile (sur'vil) *adj.*: like or characteristic of a slave; humbly submissive or yielding.

- -

VIRGINIA WOOLF 1125

---

3. buried . . . Elephant and Castle: Suicides were commonly buried at crossroads. The Elephant and Castle is a pub set at a busy crossroads in south London.

F. Literary Elements: Tone and Diction

? What is the writer's attitude toward her subject in this passage? [Ironic, perhaps contemptuous.] Ask students to identify words and details throughout the selection that support the writer's tone. [Possible answers: "Fat, loose-lipped," "guffawed," and "bellowed."]

G. Language Note: Connotations

The passage suggests that *born* is being used as a synonym for *nurtured*. What does Woolf mean by this sentence? [Creative talent must be nurtured and stimulated; working class people may not have the opportunity to nurture creativity.]

H. Expansion

Emily Brontë, a nineteenth-century English novelist and poet, wrote *Wuthering Heights*. Robert Burns, an eighteenth-century Scottish poet, was the son of a struggling tenant farmer.

I. Reader's Response: Extending the Text

? Do you think that a person is born with creative genius or that it is acquired? [Sample responses: I think it's a combination of both—even scientists who study genetics can't agree on the answer; or many skills can be perfected through hard work and training.]

STRATEGIES FOR INCLUSION

Advanced Encourage students to investigate two famous feminist works that preceded *A Room of One's Own*—Mary Wollstonecraft's *A Vindication of the Rights of Woman* (1792) and John Stuart Mill's *The Subjection of Women* (1869). Provide selections from both books, and ask students to compare the books' argument and tone. How does Woolf build on those texts? How does her argument or presentation differ from theirs? Have students present to the class an oral report that summarizes their findings.

INTEGRATING THE LANGUAGE ARTS

Strategic Reading To help students follow the associative style of this selection, organize the essay in a cluster diagram. The following graphic shows one possible way to organize the information in the first paragraph. Ask students to add to the cluster as they complete the selection.

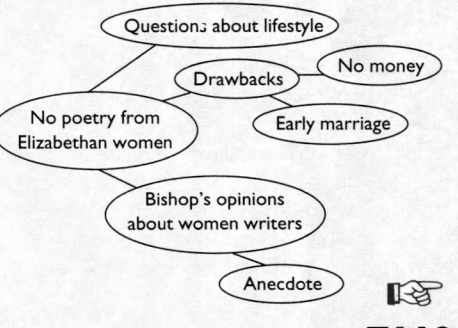

Virginia Woolf **T1125**

A. Critical Reading: Finding Cause and Effect

Ask students to state support for Woolf's theory that women writers often were anonymous in the sixteenth century. [Writing by women was not always well received at that time, so female authors often chose to remain anonymous.]

B. Expansion

In 1846, Charlotte Brontë and her two sisters published *Poems by Currer, Ellis, and Acton Bell.* George Eliot's Victorian novels, including *Middlemarch* and *The Mill on the Floss,* feature portrayals of strong, intelligent women. The novels of George Sand express strong feminist ideals.

C. Critical Reading: Finding Details

Have students identify details that support this thesis. [Details may include economic disadvantages and a lack of autonomy that would hinder creativity.]

D. Humanities Connection

Rousseau championed the educational importance of self-expression.

and dilemma which might well have killed her. Had she survived, whatever she had written would have been twisted and deformed, issuing from a strained and morbid imagination. And undoubtedly, I thought, looking at the shelf where there are no plays by women, her work would have gone unsigned. That refuge she would have sought certainly. It was the relic of the sense of chastity that dictated anonymity to women even so late as the nineteenth century. Currer Bell, George Eliot, George Sand,[6] all the victims of inner strife as their writings prove, sought ineffectively to veil themselves by using the name of a man. Thus they did homage to the convention, which if not implanted by the other sex was liberally encouraged by them (the chief glory of a woman is not to be talked of, said Pericles,[7] himself a much-talked-of man), that publicity in women is detestable. Anonymity runs in their blood. The desire to be veiled still possesses them. They are not even now as concerned about the health of their fame as men are, and, speaking generally, will pass a tombstone or a signpost without feeling an irresistible desire to cut their names on it, as Alf, Bert, or Chas. must do in obedience to their instinct, which murmurs if it sees a fine woman go by, or even a dog, *Ce chien est à moi.*[8] And, of course, it may not be a dog, I thought, remembering Parliament Square, the Sieges Allee,[9] and other avenues; it may be a piece of land or a man with curly black hair. It is one of the great advantages of being a woman that one can pass even a very fine negress without wishing to make an Englishwoman of her.

That woman, then, who was born with a gift of poetry in the sixteenth century, was an unhappy woman, a woman at strife against herself. All the conditions of her life, all her own instincts, were hostile to the state of mind which is needed to set

free whatever is in the brain. But what is the state of mind that is most <u>propitious</u> to the act of creation, I asked. Can one come by any notion of the state that furthers and makes possible that strange activity? Here I opened the volume containing the Tragedies of Shakespeare. What was Shakespeare's state of mind, for instance, when he wrote *Lear* and *Antony and Cleopatra?* It was certainly the state of mind most favorable to poetry that there has ever existed. But Shakespeare himself said nothing about it. We only know casually and by chance that he "never blotted a line." Nothing indeed was ever said by the artist himself about his state of mind until the eighteenth century perhaps. Rousseau[10] perhaps began it. At any rate, by the nineteenth century self-consciousness had developed so far that it was the habit for men of letters to describe their minds in confessions and autobiographies. Their lives also were written, and their letters were printed after their deaths. Thus, though we do not know what Shakespeare went through when he wrote *Lear,* we do know what Carlyle went through when he wrote *The French Revolution;* what Flaubert went through when he wrote *Madame Bovary;* what Keats was going through when he tried to write poetry against the coming of death and the indifference of the world.

And one gathers from this enormous modern literature of confession and self-analysis that to write a work of genius is almost always a feat of prodigious difficulty. Everything is against the likelihood that it will come from the writer's mind whole and entire. Generally material circumstances are against it. Dogs will bark; people will interrupt; money must be made; health will break down. Further, accentuating all these difficulties and making them harder to bear is the world's <u>notorious</u> indifference. It does not ask people to

---

6. Currer Bell, George Eliot, George Sand: male pseudonyms for the female writers Charlotte Brontë, Mary Ann Evans, and Amantine-Aurore-Lucile Dupin.
7. Pericles (c. 495–429 B.C.): Athenian legislator and general.
8. *Ce chien est à moi* (sə shē·en′ āt ä mwä): French for "This dog is mine."
9. Sieges Allee (zē′gəs ä·lā′): busy thoroughfare in Berlin. The name—more commonly written as one word "Siegesallee"—is German for "Avenue of Victory."

10. Rousseau: Jean-Jacques Rousseau (1712–1778), French author whose candid, autobiographical *Confessions* began a vogue in literature for confessional accounts.

WORDS TO OWN

propitious (prō·pish′əs) *adj.:* favorable.
notorious (nō·tôr′ē·əs) *adj.:* widely but unfavorably known; famous.

OPTIONS FOR TEACHING

INTEGRATING THE LANGUAGE ARTS

Speaking and Listening Ask students to work in small groups to practice reading the selection aloud in the manner in which they think Woolf presented it to the women students of Cambridge. Then, have each group member choose a passage to present to the class. Encourage students to dramatize their speech with appropriate pauses, inflection, and enunciation.

Group members should critique each other's reading before class presentations.

Writing: Rebuttal In the selection's first paragraph, Woolf mentions a gentleman who was convinced that no woman could ever have the genius of Shakespeare. Woolf argues that women lack not genius, but a nurturing environment that would allow genius to grow. Ask students to write a rebuttal of Woolf's opinion, as it might have been written by this gentleman. Even if they do not

share his opinion, ask them to think of the persuasive points he would use to convince readers of his viewpoint.

Mechanics Discuss with students the author's use of dashes to indicate abrupt breaks in thought and to mean *namely, in other words,* or *that is* before an explanation. Ask students to write original sentences in which they practice both uses of dashes.

write poems and novels and histories; it does not need them. It does not care whether Flaubert finds the right word or whether Carlyle scrupulously verifies this or that fact. Naturally, it will not pay for what it does not want. And so the writer, Keats, Flaubert, Carlyle, suffers, especially in the creative years of youth, every form of distraction and discouragement. A curse, a cry of agony, rises from those books of analysis and confession. "Mighty poets in their misery dead"[11]—that is the burden of their song. If anything comes through in spite of all this, it is a miracle, and probably no book is born entire and uncrippled as it was conceived.

But for women, I thought, looking at the empty shelves, these difficulties were infinitely more formidable. In the first place, to have a room of her own, let alone a quiet room or a soundproof

A Corner of the Artist's Room, Paris (late 19th or early 20th century) by Gwen John.

Sheffield City Art Galleries, England.

room, was out of the question, unless her parents were exceptionally rich or very noble, even up to the beginning of the nineteenth century. Since her pin money,[12] which depended on the goodwill of her father, was only enough to keep her clothed, she was debarred from such alleviations as came even to Keats or Tennyson or Carlyle, all poor men, from a walking tour, a little journey to France, from the separate lodging which, even if it were miserable enough, sheltered them from the claims and tyrannies of their families. Such material difficulties were formidable; but much worse were the immaterial. The indifference of the world which Keats and Flaubert and other men of genius have found so hard to bear was in her case not indifference but hostility. The world did not say to her as it said to them, Write if you choose; it makes no difference to me. The world said with a guffaw, Write? What's the good of your writing?

WORDS TO OWN
formidable (fôr′mə·də·bəl) *adj.*: difficult to handle or overcome.
alleviations (ə·lē′vē·ā′shənz) *n. pl.*: things that lighten, relieve, or make easier to bear.

---

11. **Mighty poets . . . dead:** line from William Wordsworth's poem "Resolution and Independence."
12. **pin money:** small allowance given for personal expenses.

VIRGINIA WOOLF 1127

E. Exploring the Culture

COOPERATIVE LEARNING

Create a Character Have students work in groups of three to create a fictional sibling for a contemporary or historical figure. Have students imitate Woolf's technique of humorously highlighting actual characteristics and events to contrast the real character with the fictional one. To ensure equal work by all group members, ask each to write a brief summary of his or her contribution. Encourage groups to share their final products with the class through a report or presentation.

Group Discussion Have students apply Woolf's observations to contemporary situations by forming discussion groups of three. Assign each student one of the following questions to elicit discussion within the group.
- Do opportunities for males and females differ in your school?
- Do men and women share equal places in society today?
- Do men and women perceive the world differently?

After the discussion, ask a volunteer from each group to summarize briefly for the rest of the class the group's comments about his or her question.

☞

Votes for Women!

In December 1913, during an opera about Joan of Arc staged especially for the British royal family, three elegantly dressed women stood and addressed the king with a megaphone. The crowd was thrown into a panic as the women likened their struggle for the vote to Joan of Arc's fifteenth-century fight for liberty. When the police finally removed them, other women, hidden in the balcony, showered the audience with suffragist pamphlets. The king, of course, did not respond. But the dramatic protest joined the suffragists to Joan and other brave forerunners, just as Virginia Woolf's portrait of Shakespeare's fictional sister drew on the past to spur change in her own time.

Suffragists with sandwich boards in London (c. 1910).

CROSSING THE CURRICULUM

Social Sciences Have students work in pairs to trace the progression of women's acquisition of the powers and privileges traditionally enjoyed only by men. Research should include property ownership, education and employment opportunities, and suffrage. Students can chart the information on a time line.

PROBLEM SOLVING/CRITICAL THINKING

Distinguishing Facts from Opinions Forcefully presented opinions (such as "Women cannot write the plays of Shakespeare") may sometimes be accepted as fact. In this selection, Woolf blends verifiable facts with pure conjecture or imagination. Have students use the following chart to differentiate the facts from the opinions; when the charts are completed, students can discuss which facts most strongly support the opinions presented.

Fact	Opinion
• Elizabethan women were married at an early age.	• An Elizabethan woman could not write plays of Shakespeare.

The vote—a right not granted to British women over the age of thirty until 1918, and not granted to women over twenty-one until 1928—was the key to meaningful change for women in Woolf's day. Woolf herself was among thousands of women who joined suffrage organizations during the first decade of the century. Although she could have written articles for publications such as *The Suffragette* or *Votes for Women,* she instead lent her support in more humble ways: She sat on the platform at public meetings, and folded countless suffragist mailings (she later recalled spending "hours writing names like Cowgill on envelopes"). Yet Woolf was a pacifist, and her views against physical force prevented her wholehearted involvement in the increasingly combative women's suffrage movement of the early 1900s.

A new phase in an old fight. Universal suffrage was not a new idea. Women and men had campaigned for it since the mid-1800s; in fact, the philosopher John Stuart Mill had brought a suffrage bill before the British Parliament in 1866. But the fight entered a new phase in 1904, when the ardent suffragist Christabel Pankhurst strode off to the Manchester Free Trade Hall to challenge Winston Churchill on the subject of voting rights for women. Churchill refused to acknowledge Pankhurst's demands, and she was howled down by the crowd, but she counted it as her first "militant" step.

Afterward, members of the Women's Social and Political Union, which Pankhurst and her mother Emmeline had founded in 1903, were emboldened to take other steps: They held rallies and marches, staged suffrage plays at public meetings, broke the windows of government buildings, and interrupted Parliament by shouting "Votes for women!" from their enclosed seats in the "Ladies' Gallery." (Later, several women chained themselves to the metal grille that separated this gallery from the main chamber.) From 1906 to 1914, more than a thousand suffragists were arrested and carted off to jail. Held in tiny cells, and prohibited from speaking to one another, these women still found other ways to protest, mostly through hunger strikes. In answer, the government force-fed the protesters until the procedure permanently damaged many women's health. Thereafter, in what came to be called "Cat and Mouse" licenses, hunger strikers were released from prison only until they regained their strength, then rearrested.

Success at last. The sight of "respectable" women getting roughed up by hostile crowds and held for months in prison did alter public opinion: Many came to realize how badly women wanted the right to full citizenship. Yet protests continued without results until the beginning of World War I, when the Pankhursts and others abruptly turned their interests to the war effort. Ironically, many historians now think that women's work during the war, mostly as they filled the absent soldiers' jobs, was the turning point in the suffrage movement. When the war was over, most Britishers felt that women shouldn't—indeed couldn't—be deprived of the vote any longer.

LITERATURE AND POLITICS

Suffragist demonstrations in Great Britain were political events, but they also were dramatic. Plays by popular writers were staged to support women's rights, and suffragists, also called suffragettes by their detractors, marched in white dresses carrying elaborate banners in their movement's colors. For illustrations of these demonstrations and suffragists' art, see Lisa Tickner's *The Spectacle of Women: Imagery of the Suffrage Campaign* (1988).

PROFESSIONAL NOTES

Thematic Connections: "Clashes of Culture" Many students probably assume that in most cultures today, women can be writers. Ask them to discuss a time when it was considered improper for women to aspire to be writers.

ASSESSMENT TOOLS

Check Test: Questions and Answers

1. For what purpose does Woolf invent Judith Shakespeare? [To show why Elizabethan women could not have written the plays of Shakespeare.]
2. Why does Judith run away to London? [She wishes to escape family obligations and to try to express her creative drive.]
3. According to Woolf, how did the repressed genius of women show itself in the Elizabethan age? [Witches, women thought to be possessed by the devil, wise women selling herbs, and mothers of remarkable men probably had creative genius.]
4. How does the world treat male writers and female writers differently, according to Woolf? [The world treats men with indifference and women with hostility.]

Making Meanings

First Thoughts

1. Students may be surprised at Judith's death. Others may recognize that Woolf's story dramatizes an artist's despair.

Reviewing the Text

a. Men laugh at her desire to act. She is befriended by an acting company's manager, becomes pregnant, and commits suicide.

b. Difficulties include interruptions and financial insecurity. Women also face additional family responsibilities.

Shaping Interpretations

2. Students may say Woolf's composite character covers a range of issues. Others may say that a fictional character is needed because biographical facts were not available.

3. Woolf argues that women shun notoriety to avoid ridicule. Students may note that male and female public figures often are held to different standards.

4. There was much preventing a woman from expressing creative genius. The thesis seems realistic because a female writer would encounter more hostility from the public. Or students may argue that genius can overcome adversity.

5. For example, Woolf's tone becomes ironic at the end of the first paragraph when she mentions the bishop and his views. Read in a sarcastic tone.

Extending the Text

6. **(Evaluation)** Students may note that social change aids women artists; even so, finances and privacy remain important prerequisites for anyone's creative endeavor.

MAKING MEANINGS

First Thoughts

1. Consider the life story for Judith that you outlined in your Reader's Log. Did any details in Woolf's scenario for Judith surprise you? Why or why not?

> ### Reviewing the Text
>
> a. What happens to "Judith Shakespeare" when she goes to London?
>
> b. According to Woolf, what general conditions make works of genius difficult to produce? What special conditions do women face?

Shaping Interpretations

2. Woolf uses an invented **biography** in this essay. Why do you think she uses such a device? Is her biography of Judith Shakespeare convincing to you? Cite reasons for your answer.

3. In her essay, Woolf says that for women "Anonymity runs in their blood." According to Woolf, why do women shy away from the limelight? What do you think of her reasons?

4. Woolf focuses on the unhappy psychological state of a gifted female writer in the age of Shakespeare. How would you state the **main idea** of her essay? How do you feel about Woolf's thesis?

5. Where do you detect a tone of contemptuous **irony** in Woolf's essay? How would you read these passages aloud to convey Woolf's tone?

Extending the Text

6. In her essay, Woolf concludes that to write great literature, a woman *must* have money and a private place. Do you think this is still true today—for anyone, male *or* female? Explain your response.

CHOICES:
Building Your Portfolio

Writer's Notebook

1. Collecting Ideas for a Problem-Solution Essay

One way to identify a possible topic for a problem-solution essay is to focus on the local aspects of a far-reaching societal problem, such as the lack of equal opportunity Woolf discusses in "Shakespeare's Sister." Spend a few minutes brainstorming or clustering to discover inequalities you perceive in the opportunities your school or community offers males and females your age. Save your notes for the Writer's Workshop on page 1179.

Critical Writing

2. The Gender Gap

Woolf's essay contains many ideas, both explicit and implicit, about gender roles. In an essay, (a) discuss how Woolf depicts men and women, (b) analyze how the characterizations work in her argument, and (c) evaluate her ideas.

Creative Writing

3. Reimagining Judith's Life

In Judith's story, where was her famous brother? What if Queen Elizabeth had heard of Judith's ambitions or her famous brother had recognized them? Rewrite Judith's life so it *does not* end in tragedy.

Creative Writing

4. Another Mute Milton

Imagine a person from life today, or from the past, who also, if circumstances had been different, might have been a great writer, painter, or political leader. Write an imaginary life of that intensely creative person.

Beyond the Story

Choices: Building Your Portfolio

1. **Writer's Notebook** Remind students to save their work. They may use it as prewriting for the Writer's Workshop on p. 1179.

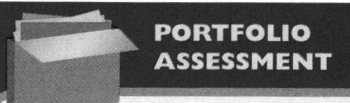

PORTFOLIO ASSESSMENT

Choices: Assessment Criteria
For help in evaluating these Choices assignments, see the criteria in the *Portfolio Management System,* p. 186.

Naguib Mahfouz

(1911–   )

World Literature

Egypt

Naguib Mahfouz, often heralded as Egypt's finest writer, grew up in a middle-class family similar to the family he traces in his acclaimed *Cairo Trilogy*. Mahfouz began sending stories to magazines when he was a philosophy student at Cairo University. When he first got paid for a story, he is reputed to have exclaimed, in disbelief, "One gets paid for them as well!"

Naguib Mahfouz.

For most of his life, Mahfouz worked as a civil servant for the Egyptian government, first in the Ministry of Religious Affairs, later in the Arts Administration, and still later as head of the State Cinema Organization. He has written more than forty novels and short-story collections, several plays, and many film scripts. Almost all his writing is set in Cairo. "Like their author," writes the translator Denys Johnson-Davies, "his stories never travel abroad, not even to the Egyptian countryside." Most of his novels are set in an area known as Khan al-Khalili, which is filled with mosques, restaurants, shops, and colorful people.

Despite their limited settings, Mahfouz's works are read widely throughout the Middle East and are considered highly influential. The subjects of his writings are the repression of women, social injustice, and the superficial values of modern life. Ironically, some of his books were banned in Arab countries, including Egypt, especially after he expressed support for the 1979 peace treaty between Egypt and Israel. Nevertheless, in Egypt and throughout the world, he is widely regarded as the outstanding writer of contemporary Arabic literature. In 1988, Mahfouz won the Nobel Prize in literature.

(Map) ©Rand McNally.

NAGUIB MAHFOUZ 1131

PROGRAM MANAGER

Selection Summary See **Teaching Notes,** *Teaching Resources B,* p. 185, for a summary of this selection.

Background
As students read, ask them to imagine the following details.
- the setting
- Amina's personality
- daily life in Amina's family

BEFORE YOU READ
THE CAIRO ROOFTOP

Background

Picture a world in which a girl marries at thirteen and from then on lives within the walls of her husband's home, unseen and unknown to those beyond the family circle. Her knowledge of the world outside is confined to what she can see from a rooftop.

Naguib Mahfouz introduces you to a woman who leads just such a confined life in "The Cairo Rooftop," a chapter from his novel *Palace Walk. Palace Walk* is one of three volumes in Mahfouz's *Cairo Trilogy,* which he wrote in Arabic and published in the mid-1950s. Because of translation delays, the trilogy was almost unknown outside the Middle East until 1988, when Mahfouz won the Nobel Prize in literature.

The English translation of the *Cairo Trilogy* opens the world of modern Egypt to Western readers. Spanning the years 1917 to 1944, the trilogy follows three generations of a middle-class

Muslim family before, during, and after the 1919 uprising that led Britain to declare Egypt a sovereign state. The personal struggles within the family reflect not only Egypt's political history but also its increasing interest in education and science, the gradual emancipation of women, and the transformation of traditional attitudes toward Western life.

Palace Walk, the first book in the trilogy, chronicles the period from 1917 to 1919, two of the five years during which Egypt was a British protectorate. The main character in "The Cairo Rooftop" is Amina, who has been married to Ahmad, the family patriarch, since she was thirteen. Amina is totally, but willingly, dominated by her husband at a time when a virtuous woman of Islam rarely steps outside her husband's home, and never shows her face to a man who is not a close relative. There are five younger people in the family: Yasin, the twenty-one-year-old son of Ahmad's first

wife; two other sons, Fahmy and Kamal; and two daughters, Khadija and Aisha.

Ahmad's family lives in a two-story house on Palace Walk, a street in Cairo that centuries ago connected two palaces. The street name that is the book's title can also be translated as "between two palaces" and refers not only to the street but also to the two political situations that frame the book and to the change from traditional to more modern ways that frames the family's experiences.

Quickwrite

Start with what you know. Spend two or three minutes jotting down some notes about women's lives in twentieth-century Egypt and the Arab world. Don't look up anything in a reference book. Just check your memory bank to see what information and impressions you already have stored there.

Cairo rooftops.

CONNECTING WITH "CLASHES OF CULTURE"

It is to be expected that misunderstandings will arise between people of different nationalities and cultures. But what about misunderstandings that arise between genders? Have students work in groups to compare these different kinds of clashes. You might also ask them how Virginia Woolf would analyze the circumstances of a woman who could not leave the "room of her own." Ask them to answer the following questions: Does the relationship between men and women change in countries where women have more access to education or where women are more financially independent?

The Cairo Rooftop *from* Palace Walk

Naguib Mahfouz

translated by **William Maynard Hutchins** *and* **Olive E. Kenny**

When they had finished breakfast, the mother said, "Aisha, you do the laundry today and Khadija will clean the house. Afterward meet me in the oven room."

Amina divided the work between them right after breakfast. They were content to be ruled by her, and Aisha would not question her assignment. Khadija would take the trouble to make a few comments, either to show her worth or to start a quarrel. Thus she said, "I'll let you clean the house if you think washing the clothes is too much. But if you make a fuss over the washing so you can stay in the bathroom till all the work in the kitchen is finished, that's an excuse that can be rejected in advance."

Aisha ignored her remark and went off to the bath humming. Khadija commented sarcastically, "Lucky for you that sound reverberates in the bathroom like a phonograph speaker. So sing and let the neighbors hear it."

Their mother left the room and went through the hall to the stairs. She climbed to the roof to make her morning rounds there before descending to the oven room. The bickering between her daughters was nothing new to her. Over the course of time it had turned into a customary way of life when the father was not at home and no one could think of anything pleasant to say. She had tried to stop it by using entreaty, humor, and tenderness. That was the only type of discipline she employed with her children. It fit her nature, which could not stand anything stronger. She lacked the firmness that rearing children occasionally requires. Perhaps she would have liked to be firm but was not able to. Perhaps she had attempted to be firm but had been overcome by her emotions and weakness. It seemed she could not bear for the ties between her and her children to be anything but love and affection. She let the father or his shadow, which dominated the children from afar, straighten them out and lay down the law. Thus their silly quarrel did not weaken her admiration for her two girls or her satisfaction with them. Even Aisha, who was insanely fond of singing and standing in front of the mirror, her laziness notwithstanding, was no less skillful and organized than Khadija.

Amina would have been justified in allowing herself long periods of relaxation, but she was prevented by a natural tendency that was almost a disease. She insisted on supervising everything in the house, no matter how small. When the girls

NAGUIB MAHFOUZ 1133

A. **Exploring the Culture**
The family's courtyard contains a well, a storeroom, and an oven room in which the meals are prepared. Inside this room are a large oven, piles of coal and wood for fuel, and shelves with pots, plates, and serving trays.

B. **Critical Reading: Finding Details**
Khadija, at twenty, is the older daughter. She resembles her mother with her indefatigable energy, proficiency in running the household, and fierce dedication to her family. Khadija is jealous of the voice and beauty of her spirited sixteen-year-old sister, Aisha.

As students read, ask them to find details that support these descriptions of Amina's daughters.

C. **Reader's Response: First Thoughts**
[?] What is your impression of Amina? [Sample responses: She is a tender, loving mother; or she is not very assertive with her daughters.]

D. **Literary Element: Personification**
[?] What does this personification indicate about the father's role as disciplinarian? [That a shadow could dominate indicates that just the thought or mention of the father instills fear.]

E. **Cultural Connections**
Have students compare Amina's daily routine with that of mothers with whom they are familiar.

OPTIONS FOR TEACHING

STRATEGIES FOR INCLUSION

Special Needs Help students make a Venn diagram to better compare and contrast information in this selection. Have students write phrases from the selection describing the similarities and differences in how men and women are treated.

MEN — WOMEN

[Attended school, Traveled] [Religious, Strong family] [No formal schooling, Stayed at home] finished their work, she would go around energetically inspecting the rooms, living areas, and halls, with a broom in one hand and a feather duster in the other. She searched the corners, walls, curtains, and all the furnishings to eliminate an overlooked speck of dust, finding as much pleasure and satisfaction in that as in removing a speck from her eye. She was by nature such a perfectionist that she examined the clothes about to be laundered. If she discovered a piece of clothing that was unusually dirty, she would not spare the owner a gentle reminder of his duty, whether it was Kamal, who was going on ten, or Yasin, who had two clear and contradictory approaches to caring for himself. He was excessively fastidious about his external appearance—his suit, fez, shirt, necktie, and shoes—but shockingly neglectful of his underwear.

Naturally this comprehensive concern of hers did not exclude the roof and the pigeons and chickens that inhabited it. In fact, the time she spent on the roof was filled with love and delight from the opportunities it presented for work, not to mention the joys of play and merriment she found there. No wonder, for the roof was a new world she had discovered. The big house had known nothing of it until she joined the family. She had created it afresh through the force of her spirit, back when the house retained the appearance it had always had since being built ages before. It was her idea to have these cages with the cooing pigeons put on some of the high walls. She had arranged these wooden chicken coops where the hens clucked as they foraged for food. How much joy she got from scattering grain for them or putting the water container on the ground as the hens raced for it, preceded by their rooster. Their beaks fell on the grain quickly and

regularly, like sewing-machine needles, leaving little indentations in the dust like the pockmarks from a drizzle. How good she felt when she saw them gazing at her with clear little eyes, inquisitive and questioning, while they cackled and clucked with a shared affection that filled her heart with tenderness.

She loved the chickens and pigeons as she loved all of God's creatures. She made little noises to them, thinking they understood and responded. Her imagination had bestowed conscious, intelligent life on all animals and occasionally even on inanimate objects. She was quite certain that these beings praised her Lord and were in contact, by various means, with the spirit world. Her world with its earth and sky, animals and plants, was a living, intelligent one. Its merits were not confined

Street scene in Cairo.

OPTIONS FOR TEACHING

CROSSING THE CURRICULUM

Social Sciences In order for students to understand Amina's lifestyle, have them research the historical and political time in which the story takes place and the status of Egyptian women at that time. Then, have them research the status of women in Egypt today. Ask them to discuss the ways in which women's status has evolved or remained unchanged.

Art To help students visualize what they are reading about in this selection, have them create a diorama of Amina's rooftop. They can use shoe boxes for the diorama, and it can be as simple or as ornate as they wish. Students may include the minarets of the mosques that Amina sees.

to the blessing of life. It found its completion in worship. It was not strange, then, that, relying on one excuse or another, she prolonged the lives of the roosters and hens. One hen was full of life, another a good layer. This rooster woke her in the morning with his crowing. Perhaps if it had been left entirely to her, she would never have consented to put her knife to their throats. If circumstances did force her to slaughter one, she selected a chicken or pigeon with a feeling close to anguish. She would give it a drink, seek God's mercy for it, invoke God's name, ask forgiveness, and then slaughter it. Her consolation was that she was exercising a right that God the Benefactor had granted to all those who serve Him.

The most amazing aspect of the roof was the southern half overlooking al-Nahhasin Street.[1] There in years past she had planted a special garden. There was not another one like it in the whole neighborhood on any of the other roofs, which were usually covered with chicken droppings. She had first begun with a small number of pots of carnations and roses. They had increased year by year and were arranged in rows parallel to the sides of the walls. They grew splendidly, and she had the idea of putting a trellis over the top. She got a carpenter to install it. Then she planted both jasmine and hyacinth bean vines. She attached them to the trellis and around the posts. They grew tall and spread out until the area was transformed into an arbor garden with a green sky from which jasmine flowed down. An enchanting, sweet fragrance was diffused throughout.

This roof, with its inhabitants of chickens and pigeons and its arbor garden, was her beautiful, beloved world and her favorite place for relaxation out of the whole universe, about which she knew nothing. As usual at this hour, she set about caring for it. She swept it, watered the plants, fed the chickens and pigeons. Then for a long time, with smiling lips and dreamy eyes, she enjoyed the scene surrounding her. She went to the end of the garden and stood behind the interwoven, coiling vines, to gaze out through the openings at the limitless space around her.

1. **al-Nahhasin Street:** a main street in the Bayn al-Qasrayn, or Palace Walk, section of Cairo. This street is also called Coppersmiths Street for the artisans who line its sidewalks.

She was awed by the minarets[2] which shot up, making a profound impression on her. Some were near enough for her to see their lamps and crescent distinctly, like those of Qala'un and Barquq. Others appeared to her as complete wholes, lacking details, like the minarets of the mosques of al-Husayn, al-Ghuri, and al-Azhar. Still other minarets were at the far horizon and seemed phantoms, like those of the Citadel and Rifa'i mosques. She turned her face toward them with devotion, fascination, thanksgiving, and hope. Her spirit soared over their tops, as close as possible to the heavens. Then her eyes would fix on the minaret of the mosque of al-Husayn, the dearest one to her because of her love for its namesake.[3] She looked at it affectionately, and her yearnings mingled with the sorrow that pervaded her every time she remembered she was not allowed to visit the son of the Prophet of God's daughter, even though she lived only minutes away from his shrine.

She sighed audibly and that broke the spell. She began to amuse herself by looking at the roofs and streets. The yearnings would not leave her. She turned her back on the wall. Looking at the unknown had overwhelmed her: both what is unknown to most people, the invisible spirit world, and the unknown with respect to her in particular, Cairo, even the adjacent neighborhood, from which voices reached her. What could this world of which she saw nothing but the minarets and roofs be like? A quarter of a century had passed while she was confined to this house, leaving it only on infrequent occasions to visit her mother in al-Khurunfush. Her husband escorted her on each visit in a carriage, because he could not bear for anyone to see his wife, either alone or accompanied by him.

She was neither resentful nor discontented, quite the opposite. All the same, when she peeked through the openings between the jasmine and the hyacinth bean vines, off into space, at the minarets and rooftops, her delicate lips would rise in a tender, dreamy smile. Where

2. **minarets:** mosque towers. Minarets are often used by special criers to announce daily calls to worship.
3. **mosque . . . namesake:** mosque named for Husayn (626–680), a Shiite Muslim hero and grandson of the prophet Mohammed. A climactic moment in the novel comes when, against the wishes of her husband, Amina sneaks out to visit this mosque.

C. Exploring the Culture
A mosque is a place of worship for Muslims. The mosques' towers, from which the people are called to prayer, are called minarets. The section of Cairo referred to as the old quarter contains more than one thousand minarets.

D. Literary Element: Conflict
Ask students to discuss Amina's internal conflict. [She yearns to know more about the outside world but also is overwhelmed by it.]

E. Reader's Response: Shaping Interpretations
Amina lives in a society where it is forbidden to show her face to any man outside the immediate family; her husband prohibits her leaving the house unless he accompanies her. Which of Amina's characteristics might be attributed to her cloistered life? [Sample responses: Because she cannot leave the house, she focuses her energy on perfection in the home; in addition, because most of her human contact is with her children, her lack of firmness might be attributed to her fear of losing that human contact.]

F. Critical Reading: Metacognition
Ask students what questions they had as they read this description and how they answered the questions. [Some might have questions about Amina's ability to remain so serene and accepting of her situation. They may infer their answers.]

A. Exploring the Historical Period

With the outbreak of World War I, Britain declared Egypt a protectorate and sent troops to defend the Suez Canal. In 1922, Britain granted Egypt independence but retained the right to station troops there.

Finding Common Ground

All of the questions and activities in Finding Common Ground relate to women and their place in society. Have students work in groups to discuss the position of women in various ethnic and cultural traditions. Ask them to answer the following question: What roles does society find more acceptable or less acceptable for women in the United States?

---

might the law school be where Fahmy was sitting at this moment? Where was the Khalil Agha School, which Kamal assured her was only a minute's trip from the mosque of al-Husayn? Before leaving the roof, she spread her hands out in prayer and called on her Lord: "God, I ask you to watch over my husband and children, my mother and Yasin, and all the people: Muslims and Christians, even the English, my Lord, but drive them from our land as a favor to Fahmy, who does not like them."[4]

4. Fahmy . . . them: Amina's son Fahmy, an Egyptian nationalist, fervently hopes for the end of English colonial rule.

FINDING COMMON GROUND

Review your Reader's Log, and think about what you have learned about the way women in Egypt used to live. Then, get together with others to discuss how you will respond to "The Cairo Rooftop." Discuss questions of your own, or try one of these questions or activities.

- How do you think this selection relates to the collection theme "Clashes of Cultures"?
- Is geography—and timing—everything? Suppose you had been born in Egypt, or in China, or anywhere else except the United States. Suppose you had been born in the early 1900s. What might your life have been like?
- Find out about dating and marriage customs or about educational and work opportunities for women in any country except yours. Take notes, and either give a talk to the class or have a panel discussion with others who chose different countries.
- In many places in the world even today, the birth of a daughter causes less joy than the birth of a son. What do you think might be some reasons for this attitude?

1136 THE TWENTIETH CENTURY

Mosque of Sultan Barkut, Cairo.

OPTIONS FOR TEACHING

ASSESSMENT TOOLS

Check Test: Questions and Answers

1. What is the "Cairo rooftop"? [The roof of Amina's house where she has planted gardens and raised animals.]
2. Why is Amina in awe of the minarets? [She sees them only from the rooftop.]
3. What does Amina yearn for? [She wants to visit the mosque and see the city.]
4. How many years has Amina been confined to the house? [Twenty-five years.]
5. Is Amina resentful of her situation? [No, the opposite is true.]

George Orwell
(1903–1950)

George Orwell was born Eric Blair in Bengal, India, where his British father was a member of the Indian civil service. A few years afterward, his family returned to England. A lonely child, Orwell spent a good deal of time making up stories and poems. He later wrote that from an early age he knew he was going to be a writer.

After graduating from Eton, Orwell joined the Indian Imperial Police, serving in Burma from 1922 to 1927, when he resigned to devote more time to writing. Returning to Europe, he taught and took part-time, ill-paying jobs in France and England. His first book, *Down and Out in Paris and London* (1933), was based on

these experiences. He based his next novel, *Burmese Days* (1934), on his life in Burma.

Although he published journalistic pieces under his real name, with his earliest books he began to publish as George Orwell, and he continued to do so until his death. After publishing three novels, Orwell was asked to write a study of conditions among industrial workers in northern England for the socialist Left Book Club. This became *The Road to Wigan Pier* (1937), a moving portrait of the difficult lives of working-class people.

Deeply disturbed by the rise of Fascism in the 1930s, Orwell fought against the Fascists in the Spanish Civil War and published a book based on these experiences—*Homage to Catalonia* (1938). "The Spanish war," he wrote, "turned the scale and thereafter I knew where I stood. Every line of serious work that I have written since 1936 has been written, directly or indirectly, *against* totalitarianism and *for* democratic socialism."

His two most famous novels, *Animal Farm* (1945) and *1984* (1949), illustrate this point. *Animal Farm* is a political allegory that points out the dangers of totalitarianism, whether practiced by the left or the right. And *1984* has given us an entire vocabulary for the excesses of totalitarian regimes, including such terms as *newspeak* and *double-think*. In this book, Orwell stresses the connections between language, thought, and power, dramatizing in fiction the ideas he earlier explored in his famous essay *Politics and the English Language* (1946)—especially how corrupt language can be used to promote political oppression.

George Orwell making a radio broadcast for the BBC.

Into the Selection

Author Biography p. 1137
Before You Read p. 1138

- **Reading Focus: Set a Purpose** Students consider the author's enemy within.
- **Quickwrite:** Write in Reader's Log thoughts about group pressure
- **Elements of Literature:** Irony
- **Background: Scaffolding** Life in colonial Burma

Through the Selection

"Shooting an Elephant" pp. 1139–1143

Words to Own pp. 1139–1143
Making Meanings p. 1143

Beyond the Selection

Choices: Building Your Portfolio p. 1144

- **Writer's Notebook:** Collect ideas for a problem-solution essay
- **Critical Writing:** In an essay, explain a passage
- **Critical Writing:** Write an essay about the symbolism of the elephant
- **Creative Writing:** Create a storyboard for a film about the essay

How to Own a Word pp. 1144–1145

PROGRAM MANAGER

- **Planning Instruction** See *Teaching Notes, Teaching Resources B,* p. 186, for objectives, a summary, and literary elements for this selection.
- **Instructional Support** Before beginning the instructional lesson, see **Graphic Organizer for Active**

Reading, *Teaching Resources B,* p. 192, for a Through the Selection activity.

- **Assessment** See **Selection Test,** *Test Booklet,* pp. 243–244.
- **Language Link** For instruction and practice in revising fused sentences and

comma splices, see **Language Link,** *Teaching Resources B,* pp. 193–194 and *Language and Writing Skills Worksheets,* p. 103.

- **Reinforcement** Use the **Words to Own** worksheet in *Teaching Resources B,* p. 195.

Into the Selection

Using BEFORE YOU READ

p. 1138

Reading Focus

Imperialism raised external conflicts between indigenous peoples and their European colonizers. To help students explore colonialism, offer them the model of *agon* from Greek drama. *Agon* was a method of settling a conflict through a prolonged debate. In this process, characters took sides in a dispute or argued its merits. Have the students consider how *agon* could be used to explore the narrator's decisions.

BEFORE YOU READ
SHOOTING AN ELEPHANT

Reading Focus
An Enemy Within
Wherever there were British colonies, there were British people who went to these colonies to live and to govern. No matter how long these people lived overseas, they generally remained outsiders, an alien minority holding power over a resentful people. As a police officer in British-controlled Burma in the 1920s, George Orwell did not just symbolize foreign rule—he was its agent. His awareness of being an enemy within another culture kindled enormous conflicts inside him. Just who was *his* enemy? Look for the answer that comes to him, elephant rifle in hand, in the upcoming essay.

Quickwrite

READER'S LOG

Have you ever witnessed a situation where group pressure forces someone to act in a way he or she might not really want to act? How can one's personality or individuality be taken away as a result of pressure from a crowd or any larger group? Jot down your thoughts on this issue of group pressure vs. individuality.

Elements of Literature
Irony
The dominant literary mode in the twentieth century is irony (see page 994). Orwell's essay uses several strategies to evoke a sense of irony. He uses **verbal irony**—saying one thing and meaning something else, often something just the opposite. He also uses **situational irony**—in which something happens that is completely different from what we expect, or from what we think is appropriate. Irony cuts deeply into our feelings, perhaps because we sense that life itself is deeply and pervasively ironic.

Irony is a discrepancy between expectations and reality or between appearances and reality. There are three types of irony: verbal irony, situational irony, and dramatic irony.
For more on Irony, see page 994 and the Handbook of Literary Terms.

Background
This essay is set in Burma, a country in Southeast Asia. After a series of wars with Great Britain during the 1800s, Burma finally came under British control in the 1880s. Although allowed some self-rule in 1937, Burma became independent only in 1948, after a period of Japanese occupation during World War II. In 1989, the government changed the country's official name to the Union of Myanmar.

House used by British officers or planters. Chapra, India.

WORDS TO OWN
The following vocabulary words are defined in the Words to Own at the bottom of the pupil's page.

supplant p. 1139	senility p. 1142
labyrinth p. 1140	pretext p. 1143
squalid p. 1140	

Shooting an Elephant

George Orwell

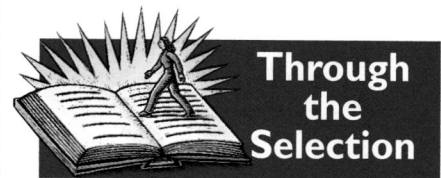
In Moulmein, in Lower Burma, I was hated by large numbers of people—the only time in my life that I have been important enough for this to happen to me. I was subdivisional police officer of the town, and in an aimless, petty kind of way anti-European feeling was very bitter. No one had the guts to raise a riot, but if a European woman went through the bazaars alone somebody would probably spit betel juice over her dress. As a police officer I was an obvious target and was baited whenever it seemed safe to do so. When a nimble Burman tripped me up on the football field and the referee (another Burman) looked the other way, the crowd yelled with hideous laughter. This happened more than once. In the end the sneering yellow faces of young men that met me everywhere, the insults hooted after me when I was at a safe distance, got badly on my nerves. The young Buddhist priests were the worst of all. There were several thousands of them in the town and none of them seemed to have anything to do except stand on street corners and jeer at Europeans.

All this was perplexing and upsetting. For at that time I had already made up my mind that imperialism was an evil thing and the sooner I chucked up my job and got out of it the better. Theoretically—and secretly, of course—I was all for the Burmese and all against their oppressors, the British. As for the job I was doing, I hated it more bitterly than I can perhaps make clear. In a job like that you see the dirty work of Empire at close quarters. The wretched prisoners huddling in the stinking cages of the lockups, the gray, cowed faces of the long-term convicts, the scarred buttocks of the men who had been flogged with bamboos—all these oppressed me with an intolerable sense of guilt. But I could get nothing into perspective. I was young and ill-educated and I had had to think out my problems in the utter silence that is imposed on every Englishman in the East. I did not even know that the British Empire is dying, still less did I know that it is a great deal better than the younger empires that are going to supplant it. All I knew was that I was stuck between my hatred of the empire I served and my rage against the evil-spirited little beasts who tried to make my job impossible. With one part of my mind I thought of the British Raj[1] as an unbreakable tyranny, as something clamped down, *in saecula saeculorum,*[2] upon the will of prostrate peoples; with another part I thought that the greatest joy in the world would be to drive a bayonet into a Buddhist priest's guts. Feelings like these are the normal by-products of imperialism; ask any Anglo-Indian official, if you can catch him off duty.

One day something happened which in a roundabout way was enlightening. It was a tiny incident in itself, but it gave me a better glimpse than I had had before of the real nature of imperialism—the real motives for which despotic governments act. Early one morning the subinspector at a police station the other end of the town rang me up on the phone and said that an elephant was ravaging the bazaar. Would I please come and do something about it? I did not know what I could do, but I wanted to see what was happening and I got on to a pony and started out. I took my rifle, an old .44 Winchester and much too small to kill an elephant, but I thought the noise might be useful *in terrorem.*[3] Various Burmans stopped me on the way and told me about the elephant's doings. It was not, of course, a wild elephant, but a tame one which had gone "must."[4] It had been chained up, as tame elephants always are when their attack of "must" is due, but on the previous night it had

---

1. **Raj** (räj): rule over India. The word is derived from *rajya,* Hindi for "kingdom."
2. *in saecula saeculorum* (in sē′kōō·lə sē′kōō·lôr′əm): Latin for "forever and ever."
3. *in terrorem* (in ter·ôr′əm): Latin for "for terror." In other words, the gun might serve to frighten the elephant.
4. **must:** state of frenzy in animals. The word comes from *mast,* Hindi for "intoxicated."

WORDS TO OWN
supplant (sə·plant′) *v.:* to replace; displace.

GEORGE ORWELL **1139**

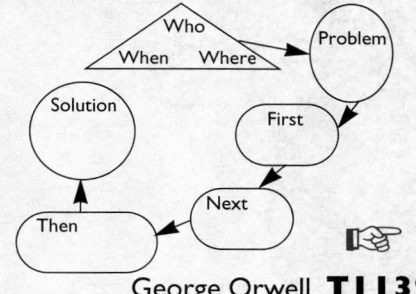

A. Critical Reading: Speculating

❓ Why would the Burmese have no weapons? [An imperial government would not allow the Burmese to arm themselves.]

B. Literary Element: Mood

❓ How does the author's description of the weather contribute to the mood of the narrative? [The oppressive stuffiness is foreboding.]

C. Critical Reading: Predicting

❓ Based on what you have read so far, do you think the author will shoot the elephant? [Possible answer: The presence of the gun foreshadows the shooting.]

broken its chain and escaped. Its mahout,[5] the only person who could manage it when it was in that state, had set out in pursuit, but had taken the wrong direction and was now twelve hours' journey away, and in the morning the elephant had suddenly reappeared in the town. The Burmese population had no weapons and were quite helpless against it. It had already destroyed somebody's bamboo hut, killed a cow, and raided some fruit stalls and devoured the stock; also it had met the municipal rubbish van and, when the driver jumped out and took to his heels, had turned the van over and inflicted violences upon it.

The Burmese subinspector and some Indian constables were waiting for me in the quarter where the elephant had been seen. It was a very poor quarter, a labyrinth of squalid bamboo huts, thatched with palm leaf, winding all over a steep hillside. I remember that it was a cloudy, stuffy morning at the beginning of the rains. We began questioning the people as to where the elephant had gone and, as usual, failed to get any definite information. That is invariably the case in the East; a story always sounds clear enough at a distance, but the nearer you get to the scene of events the vaguer it becomes. Some of the people said that the elephant had gone in one direction, some said that he had gone in another, some professed not even to have heard of any elephant. I had almost made up my mind that the whole story was a pack of lies, when we heard yells a little distance away. There was a loud, scandalized cry of "Go away, child! Go away this instant!" and an old woman with a switch in her hand came round the corner of the hut, violently shooing away a crowd of naked children. Some more women followed, clicking their tongues and exclaiming; evidently there was something that the children ought not to have seen. I rounded the hut and saw a man's dead body sprawling in the mud. He was an Indian, a black Dravidian coolie,[6] almost naked, and he could not have been dead many minutes. The

people said that the elephant had come suddenly upon him round the corner of the hut, caught him with its trunk, put its foot on his back, and ground him into the earth. This was the rainy season and the ground was soft, and his face had scored a trench a foot deep and a couple of yards long. He was lying on his belly with arms crucified and head sharply twisted to one side. His face was coated with mud, the eyes wide open, the teeth bared and grinning with an expression of unendurable agony. (Never tell me, by the way, that the dead look peaceful. Most of the corpses I have seen looked devilish.) The friction of the great beast's foot had stripped the skin from his back as neatly as one skins a rabbit. As soon as I saw the dead man I sent an orderly to a friend's house nearby to borrow an elephant rifle. I had already sent back the pony, not wanting it to go mad with fright and throw me if it smelled the elephant.

The orderly came back in a few minutes with a rifle and five cartridges, and meanwhile some Burmans had arrived and told us that the elephant was in the paddy fields below, only a few hundred yards away. As I started forward practically the whole population of the quarter flocked out of the houses and followed me. They had seen the rifle and were all shouting excitedly that I was going to shoot the elephant. They had not shown much interest in the elephant when he was merely ravaging their homes, but it was different now that he was going to be shot. It was a bit of fun to them, as it would be to an English crowd; besides they wanted the meat. It made me vaguely uneasy. I had no intention of shooting the elephant—I had merely sent for the rifle to defend myself if necessary—and it is always unnerving to have a crowd following you. I marched down the hill, looking and feeling a fool, with the rifle over my shoulder and an ever-growing army of people jostling at my heels. At the bottom, when you got away from the huts, there was a metaled[7] road and beyond that a miry waste of

---

5. **mahout** (mə·hout′): elephant keeper. The word derives from *mahaut,* Hindi for "great in measure" and, thus, "important officer."
6. **Dravidian** (drə·vid′ē·ən) **coolie:** *Dravidian* denotes any of several intermixed races living chiefly in southern India and northern Sri Lanka. A coolie is an unskilled laborer. The word is derived from *quli,* Hindi for "hired servant."

7. **metaled:** paved with cinders, stones, or the like.

WORDS TO OWN
labyrinth (lab′ə·rinth′) *n.:* maze; complex or confusing arrangement.
squalid (skwäl′id) *adj.:* foul or unclean; wretched.

Strategic Reading After they have read the information in Before You Read, ask students to record on a KWL chart like the one that follows what they know and what they want to know about the subject matter— Burma, British colonialism, or even elephants. After they finish reading the selection, have them complete the third column.

Know	Want to Know	Have Learned

Language and Vocabulary In this selection, Orwell uses foreign words that have been given English pronunciations and spellings. For example, *raj* is from *rājya,* Hindi for "kingdom"; *mahout* is derived from *mahāut,* Hindi for "great in measure." Ask students to identify other anglicized words in the selection and to use dictionaries to trace the words' origins. [Other borrowed words include *must, coolie,* and *sahib.*]

paddy fields a thousand yards across, not yet plowed but soggy from the first rains and dotted with coarse grass. The elephant was standing eight yards from the road, his left side toward us. He took not the slightest notice of the crowd's approach. He was tearing up bunches of grass, beating them against his knees to clean them, and stuffing them into his mouth.

I had halted on the road. As soon as I saw the elephant I knew with perfect certainty that I ought not to shoot him. It is a serious matter to shoot a working elephant—it is comparable to destroying a huge and costly piece of machinery—and obviously one ought not to do it if it can possibly be avoided. And at that distance, peacefully eating, the elephant looked no more dangerous than a cow. I thought then and I think now that his attack of "must" was already passing off; in which case he would merely wander harmlessly about until the mahout came back and caught him. Moreover, I did not in the least want to shoot him. I decided that I would watch him for a little while to make sure that he did not turn savage again, and then go home.

But at that moment I glanced round at the crowd that had followed me. It was an immense crowd, two thousand at the least and growing every minute. It blocked the road for a long distance on either side. I looked at the sea of yellow faces above the garish clothes—faces all happy and excited over this bit of fun, all certain that the elephant was going to be shot. They were watching me as they would watch a conjurer about to perform a trick. They did not like me, but with the magical rifle in my hands I was momentarily worth watching. And suddenly I realized that I should have to shoot the elephant after all. The people expected it of me and I had got to do it; I could feel their two thousand wills pressing me forward, irresistibly. And it was at this moment, as I stood there with the rifle in my hands, that I first grasped the hollowness, the futility of the white man's dominion in the East. Here was I, the white man with his gun, standing in front of the unarmed native crowd—seemingly the leading actor of the piece; but in reality I was only an absurd puppet pushed to and fro by the will of those yellow faces behind. I perceived in this moment that when the white man turns tyrant it is his own freedom that he destroys. He becomes a

sort of hollow, posing dummy, the conventionalized figure of a sahib.[8] For it is the condition of his rule that he shall spend his life in trying to impress the "natives," and so in every crisis he has got to do what the "natives" expect of him. He wears a mask, and his face grows to fit it. I had got to shoot the elephant. I had committed myself to doing it when I sent for the rifle. A sahib has got to act like a sahib; he has got to appear resolute, to know his own mind and do definite things. To come all that way, rifle in hand, with two thousand people marching at my heels, and then to trail feebly away, having done nothing—no, that was impossible. The crowd would laugh at me. And my whole life, every white man's life in the East, was one long struggle not to be laughed at.

But I did not want to shoot the elephant. I watched him beating his bunch of grass against his knees, with that preoccupied grandmotherly air that elephants have. It seemed to me that it would be murder to shoot him. At that age I was not squeamish about killing animals, but I had never shot an elephant and never wanted to. (Somehow it always seems worse to kill a *large* animal.) Besides, there was the beast's owner to be considered. Alive, the elephant was worth at least a hundred pounds; dead, he would only be worth the value of his tusks, five pounds, possibly. But I had got to act quickly. I turned to some experienced-looking Burmans who had been there when we arrived, and asked them how the elephant had been behaving. They all said the same thing: He took no notice of you if you left him alone, but he might charge if you went too close to him.

It was perfectly clear to me what I ought to do. I ought to walk up to within, say, twenty-five yards of the elephant and test his behavior. If he charged, I could shoot; if he took no notice of me, it would be safe to leave him until the mahout came back. But also I knew that I was going to do no such thing. I was a poor shot with a rifle and the ground was soft mud into which one would sink at every step. If the elephant charged and I missed him, I should have about as much chance as a toad under a steamroller. But even then I was not thinking particularly of my own skin, only of the watchful yellow faces behind. For at that

8. **sahib** (sä′ib′): master; sir. In colonial India, the title was used as a sign of respect for a European gentleman.

GEORGE ORWELL 1141

George Orwell **T1141**

D. Literary Element: Irony

? What is ironic about the elephant's demeanor? [The elephant turns peaceful as Orwell arrives to destroy it.]

E. Critical Reading: Analyzing Character

? What does Orwell's decision to wait tell you about his character? [His objective decision shows him to be logical and humane.]

F. Literary Element: Simile

? What does this simile reveal about Orwell's situation? [The crowd expects him to perform and to entertain.] Ask students to look for other allusions to this simile in the story.

G. Critical Reading: Identifying Main Ideas

Orwell began his narrative by remarking that a tiny incident revealed to him the nature of imperialism. What is the link between imperialism and the elephant? [Orwell is trapped because he must maintain the position of power taken by the imperial government. To maintain the image of European invincibility, he must defy his instincts and shoot the elephant.]

H. Literary Element: Autobiography

Orwell speaks from his own experience about how imperialism changes the people who participate in it. Is his first-person account convincing? Would an objective account of colonial issues be more or less effective? Explain. [Possible answer: Only someone with the narrator's experience could have this insight about colonialism, and his personal observations make him a more credible commentator.]

I. Language Note: Connotations

? What effect does the word *grandmotherly* have? [It helps create sympathy for the elephant.]

J. Reader's Response: First Thoughts

? If you were Orwell, would you shoot the elephant? Explain. [Sample responses: Yes, it seems necessary to maintain the crowd's respect. No, I realize that my pride is less important than the elephant's life.]

CLASSROOM MANAGEMENT

Block Scheduling To help maintain the attention of students during a longer class time, have them engage in a paired reading of Orwell's story (twenty to twenty-five minutes). Next, have them write an interview based on his protagonist, with one student writing the interviewer's questions and another writing Orwell's responses (twenty to twenty-five minutes). Conclude by asking for volunteers to have their interviews videotaped and critiqued by their peers (thirty to forty minutes).

CROSSING THE CURRICULUM

Geography Ask students to give oral reports on the political geography of Asia in and around the area of Burma, now known as the Union of Myanmar. Divide the class into groups that will be responsible for a country in the Myanmar area: India, Bangladesh, Thailand, Laos, or China. Ask groups to trace how the boundaries of these countries have changed in the twentieth century, paying particular attention to the effects of colonialism.

Making Meanings

First Thoughts

Jumbo Elephant #2 (1988) by William Hawkins. Enamel and collage on masonite (48″ × 57″).
Ricco/Maresca Gallery, New York.

moment, with the crowd watching me, I was not afraid in the ordinary sense, as I would have been if I had been alone. A white man mustn't be frightened in front of "natives"; and so, in general, he isn't frightened. The sole thought in my mind was that if anything went wrong those two thousand Burmans would see me pursued, caught, trampled on, and reduced to a grinning corpse like that Indian up the hill. And if that happened it was quite probable that some of them would laugh. That would never do. There was only one alternative. I shoved the cartridges into the magazine and lay down on the road to get a better aim.

The crowd grew very still, and a deep, low, happy sigh, as of people who see the theater curtain go up at last, breathed from innumerable throats. They were going to have their bit of fun after all. The rifle was a beautiful German thing with cross-hair sights. I did not then know that in shooting an elephant one would shoot to cut an imaginary bar running from earhole to earhole. I ought, therefore, as the elephant was sideways on, to have aimed straight at his earhole; actually I aimed several inches in front of this, thinking the brain would be further forward.

When I pulled the trigger I did not hear the bang or feel the kick—one never does when a shot goes home—but I heard the devilish roar of glee that went up from the crowd. In that instant, in too short a time, one would have thought, even for the bullet to get there, a mysterious, terrible

change had come over the elephant. He neither stirred nor fell, but every line of his body had altered. He looked suddenly stricken, shrunken, immensely old, as though the frightful impact of the bullet had paralyzed him without knocking him down. At last, after what seemed a long time—it might have been five seconds, I dare say—he sagged flabbily to his knees. His mouth slobbered. An enormous senility seemed to have settled upon him. One could have imagined him thousands of years old. I fired again into the same spot. At the second shot he did not collapse but climbed with desperate slowness to his feet and stood weakly upright, with legs sagging and head drooping. I fired a third time. That was the shot that did for him. You could see the agony of it jolt his whole body and knock the last remnant of strength from his legs. But in falling he seemed for a moment to rise, for as his hind legs collapsed beneath him he seemed to tower upward like a huge rock toppling, his trunk reaching skyward like a tree. He trumpeted, for the first and only time. And then down he came, his belly toward me, with a crash that seemed to shake the ground even where I lay.

I got up. The Burmans were already racing past me across the mud. It was obvious that the elephant would never rise again, but he was not

WORDS TO OWN
senility (si·nil′ə·tē) *n.:* state of deterioration that sometimes accompanies old age.

dead. He was breathing very rhythmically with long rattling gasps, his great mound of a side painfully rising and falling. His mouth was wide open—I could see far down into caverns of pale pink throat. I waited a long time for him to die, but his breathing did not weaken. Finally I fired my two remaining shots into the spot where I thought his heart must be. The thick blood welled out of him like red velvet, but still he did not die. His body did not even jerk when the shots hit him, the tortured breathing continued without a pause. He was dying, very slowly and in great agony, but in some world remote from me where not even a bullet could damage him further. I felt that I had got to put an end to that dreadful noise. It seemed dreadful to see the great beast lying there, powerless to move and yet powerless to die, and not even to be able to finish him. I sent back for my small rifle and poured shot after shot into his heart and down his throat. They seemed to make no impression. The tortured gasps continued as steadily as the ticking of a clock.

In the end I could not stand it any longer and went away. I heard later that it took him half an hour to die. Burmans were bringing dahs[9] and baskets even before I left, and I was told they had stripped his body almost to the bones by the afternoon.

Afterward, of course, there were endless discussions about the shooting of the elephant. The owner was furious, but he was only an Indian and could do nothing. Besides, legally I had done the right thing, for a mad elephant has to be killed, like a mad dog, if its owner fails to control it. Among the Europeans opinion was divided. The older men said I was right, the younger men said it was a damn shame to shoot an elephant for killing a coolie, because an elephant was worth more than any damn Coringhee[10] coolie. And afterward I was very glad that the coolie had been killed; it put me legally in the right and it gave me a sufficient <u>pretext</u> for shooting the elephant. I often wondered whether any of the others grasped that I had done it solely to avoid looking a fool.

9. **dahs** (däz): large carving knives.
10. **Coringhee** (kôr·ing′ē): port in southeastern India.

WORDS TO OWN
pretext (prē′tekst′) *n.:* excuse.

MAKING MEANINGS

First Thoughts
1. What do you think of Orwell's decision to shoot the elephant?

Shaping Interpretations
2. What seems to be Orwell's attitude toward the Burmese? Do you think he embodies an imperialist perspective? Use details from the story to support your answer.
3. Explain in your own words the meaning of Orwell's **ironic** insight: Tyrants destroy their own freedom. Then, identify three other ironies contained in this essay.
4. What do you think this essay reveals about the real nature of imperialism?
5. There are two Orwells in this essay: the one acting and the one looking back. Discuss the differences between the two observers, using examples from the text. How does the older Orwell feel about the younger one?

Connecting with the Text
6. The essay is filled with remarkable physical descriptions. Which description did you find most compelling? How did it make you feel?

Extending the Text
7. In what ways are Orwell's experiences like and unlike those of a contemporary police officer or of a soldier on a peacekeeping mission?

> **Reviewing the Text**
> a. What problem is Orwell asked to solve?
> b. About how big is the crowd following Orwell, and why does he say they have come along?
> c. When Orwell finds the elephant, what are two reasons he gives for not shooting it?
> d. How does the animal react when shot?

Reviewing the Text
a. He is asked to rid the bazaar of a mad elephant.
b. At least two thousand people are following Orwell; they want the entertainment of seeing the elephant shot, and they want the meat from the animal.
c. To shoot a working elephant is like destroying expensive machinery, and the elephant is calmly eating.
d. He dies slowly and in great agony.

Shaping Interpretations
2. Orwell agrees with the Burmese people politically, but he is angry with people who made his life difficult because he is English. Orwell stereotypes the Burmans by calling attention to their color and by making generalizations about them as a group.
3. Members of a ruling class have many responsibilities, but limited freedom. Students may describe the following examples of irony: Orwell enforces a political philosophy of which he disapproves; Orwell wields the gun, but he is not in charge; the crowd is unaware that Orwell does not want to shoot the elephant.
4. Possible responses: Imperialists are not as powerful as they seem.
5. The protagonist is not mature enough to fully understand the forces that shape his actions. The narrator is more mature and takes responsibility for his actions.

Connecting with the Text
6. Many students will comment on the description of the elephant's death; they may be drawn to the description because the narrator emphasizes that the death is unnecessary.

Extending the Text
7. **(Analysis)** Orwell's experiences are similar to a contemporary police officer's in that each responds to the pressure of a crowd. Soldiers and police officers often have partners to help them make decisions, while Orwell acts alone.

ASSESSMENT TOOLS

Check Test: Short Answer
1. What conflict does the narrator face concerning his job? [He has to enforce a colonial policy with which he disagrees.]
2. Why does the narrator send for an elephant rifle? [To protect himself against an animal that he thinks may be dangerous.]
3. Why do the Burmese want the narrator to shoot the elephant? [The want the diversion, and they want the meat.]
4. Why does it take several shots to bring down the elephant? [The narrator is inexperienced and does not know where to shoot.]
5. What reason does the narrator give for killing the elephant? [To avoid looking foolish.]

Beyond the Selection

Choices: Building Your Portfolio

1. **Writer's Notebook** Remind students to save their work. They may use it as prewriting for the Writer's Workshop on p. 1179.
2. **Critical Writing** To help students make connections with the clashes described in the story, you may want to bring in newspaper or magazine articles describing conflicts in colonies or former colonies. Encourage students to notice the kinds of conflicts that transcend a certain historical period.
3. **Critical Writing** Students should gather ideas and details about the elephant as they re-read Orwell's essay. Students may find it helpful to work with self-stick notes so they can make marginal notes as they are re-reading. After students have finished gathering details, they may outline or cluster their information before writing their essays.
4. **Creative Writing** To save time, assign small groups of students scenes from the essay that they will use to create one panel for a class storyboard. In this way, students can focus on selecting the dialogue, and the various groups can present the entire essay to the class. To maintain the storyboard's continuity, students should discuss their presentation with groups that have scenes immediately before or after their own.

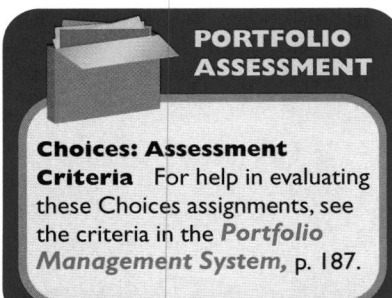

PORTFOLIO ASSESSMENT

Choices: Assessment Criteria For help in evaluating these Choices assignments, see the criteria in the *Portfolio Management System,* p. 187.

CHOICES: Building Your Portfolio

Writer's Notebook

1. Collecting Ideas for a Problem-Solution Essay

WORK IN PROGRESS

Pressure to conform is experienced by everyone who lives within a social group. Refer to your Reader's Log, and develop your notes on group pressure. Think of specific occasions in your school or community when you or someone else experienced pressure to conform to group values or behavior. What happened, whom did it happen to, and why did it happen? Save your notes for possible use in the Writer's Workshop on page 1179.

Critical Writing

2. A Significant Passage

Review the essay, and find one passage that you think is especially important, or controversial, or even upsetting. Write a brief essay in which you cite the passage and explain why you have chosen it. In your essay, be sure to describe your response to the passage and tell whether you think it connects to any situation in life as you know it today.

Critical Writing

3. Elephant Meanings

The elephant has tremendous importance in this essay. Could it **symbolize** the British Empire? Orwell himself? something else? Write an essay that presents your interpretation of the elephant's symbolic meaning.

Creative Writing

4. Shooting "Shooting an Elephant"

Imagine that you are turning "Shooting an Elephant" into a short film. Create a storyboard, showing the scenes you'd include in your film. For which scenes would you add dialogue to move the film along? Which scene will mark the climax of your film?

HOW TO OWN A WORD

Analyzing Word Analogies

An **analogy** is a similarity or likeness between two things that are unlike in other ways. When you state an analogy, you compare two things to show their likeness. A **word analogy** is a formally written statement that compares two pairs of words. The pairs of words are alike in that the relationship between the two words in the first pair is the same as the relationship between the two words in the second pair.

Standardized tests frequently include analogy questions, which measure your mastery of vocabulary and your ability to perceive relationships and patterns between words. Practice with analogies will help you develop the logical abilities to identify these relationships and patterns.

Reading word analogies. Although unlike in other ways, *cool* and *chilly* have a synonymous relationship to one another, just as *sad* and *unhappy* have. The following example shows how a word analogy using these words is written.

COOL : CHILLY :: sad : unhappy

The colon (:) stands for the phrase "is related to." The double colon (::) between the two pairs of words stands for the phrase "in the same way that." Here are two ways to read the analogy.

COOL [is related to] CHILLY
[in the same way that]
sad [is related to] unhappy

or

COOL is to CHILLY as sad is to unhappy.

Understanding word analogy problems. The word analogy items you will find in exercises and on tests will be one of the following two kinds.

- One pair of words is given, and you must select a second pair that has the same relationship.
- One pair of words and one word from the second pair are given, and you must select the word that completes the second pair.

In both kinds of problems, the parts of speech and relative order of the words in each pair must match.

Identifying relationships. The chart on page 1145 will help you to identify some of the relationships

---

Auditory To help students decide on a topic for activity #1, suggest that they watch the news on television for a couple of days, taking notes on the issues discussed. If solutions are suggested for problems, have them make notes on those also. Ask students to share in class discussion the problems and solutions that they listed.

Visual For activity #3, suggest that students draw a picture of an elephant, indicating in their drawing or with a caption what it symbolizes.

Word Analogies		
Relationship	Example	Explanation
Antonym	SOILED : CLEAN :: careless : careful	*Soiled* is the opposite of *clean*, just as *careless* is the opposite of *careful*.
Synonym	COOL : CHILLY :: sad : unhappy	*Cool* and *chilly* are similar in meaning, as are *sad* and *unhappy*.
Cause and Effect	TRAGEDY : SADNESS :: comedy : happiness	*Tragedy* generally causes *sadness*, just as *comedy* generally causes *happiness*.
Characteristic Quality	OCEAN : LARGE :: pond : small	*Oceans* are characteristically *large*, just as *ponds* are characteristically *small*.
Part and Whole	CHAPTER : BOOK :: fender : car	A *chapter* is a part of a *book*, just as a *fender* is a part of a *car*.
Location	FISH : SEA :: moose : forest	A *fish* can be found in the *sea*, just as a *moose* can be found in a *forest*.
Classification	TANGO : DANCE :: neon : gas	The *tango* is classified as a kind of *dance*, just as *neon* is classified as a kind of *gas*.

that are frequently expressed in word analogies. Other possible relationships between words might include whole and part, function, action to object, action to performer, degree, and time sequence.

Solving word analogies. On standardized tests, analogy questions are usually presented in the two formats discussed on page 1144. You can use the following three steps to solve an analogy question:

- Analyze the first pair of words to identify the relationship between them.
- State the analogy in sentence or question form.
- Identify the best available choice to complete the analogy.

Try It Out

For each word analogy item, write, on your own paper, the type of relationship the words in the complete pair have to each other. Then, write the word from the following list of Words to Own that appropriately completes each word analogy.

conspicuous   pretext
guffaw   propitious
labyrinth   senility
magnanimous   squalid
obnoxious   temerity

Relationship
Example: location _____

Analogy
CLOUD : SKY :: student : school

1. _____ DUMP : _____ :: system : organized

2. _____ SOB : _____ :: grin : frown

3. _____ _____ : FORGETFULNESS :: exercise : fitness

4. _____ THOUGHTFUL : CONSIDERATE :: _____ : offensive

5. _____ PATH : _____ :: piece : puzzle

How to Own a Word
Mini-Lesson: Analyzing Word Analogies

Have students make up their own analogies using Words to Own from Collection 15.

Try It Out: Answers
1. Relationship: characteristic quality
   Word: SQUALID
2. Relationship: antonym
   Word: GUFFAW
3. Relationship: cause and effect
   Word: SENILITY
4. Relationship: synonym
   Word: obnoxious
5. Relationship: part and whole
   Word: LABYRINTH

PROGRAM MANAGER

Reinforcement To allow students practice and reinforcement of the vocabulary strategy introduced here, see **Transparency 15.4** in the *Audiovisual Resources Binder.*

Into the Story

Author Biography p. 1146

Before You Read p. 1147

- **Reading Focus: Set a Purpose**
Students question personal ideas about cultural differences.
- **Quickwrite: Prior Knowledge**
Write in Reader's Log about cultural mysteries
- **Elements of Literature: Theme**
- **Background:** Brief political history of Southern Rhodesia

Through the Story

"No Witchcraft for Sale"
pp. 1148–1152

Words to Own pp. 1148–1151

Making Meanings pp. 1152–1153

Beyond the Story

Choices: Building Your Portfolio
p. 1153

- **Writer's Notebook:** Freewrite about cultural differences
- **Critical Writing:** Write a comparison/contrast essay
- **Critical Writing:** Write an essay about the effects of the narrator's point of view
- **Creative Writing:** Write a short speech from Gideon's perspective
- **Science and Medicine/Research:** Present an oral report about folk medicines and traditional cures

Doris Lessing

(1919–)

Doris Lessing was born in Persia (now Iran) to British parents who had fled England to escape its narrowness and provincialism. When she was five, her father gave up his job running a bank, and the family moved to a three-thousand-acre farm in Southern Rhodesia (now Zimbabwe). The farm employed some thirty to fifty black African laborers, each of whom earned the equivalent of about $1.50 a month and who lived in mud huts with no sanitation.

In Africa, Lessing's mother was homesick for England and often ill, while her father grew increasingly eccentric. Lessing describes her own childhood as "hellishly lonely"; the nearest neighbor was miles away. Only as an adult did she appreciate that her solitude had fostered a fine education, since the lack of company allowed her to spend her time slowly reading the classics of European and American fiction.

At fourteen, Lessing left school and went to work in Salisbury, the capital of Rhodesia, first as a nursemaid and then as a stenographer and telephone operator. The city had a white population of about ten thousand, and a larger black population that Lessing discovered "didn't count." When her first marriage collapsed, she entered radical politics. At twenty-six, she married a second time, but that marriage also ended in divorce.

"I can't remember a time when I didn't want to come to England," she later recalled. In 1949, she left Africa for England with her two-year-old son and the manuscript of her first novel,

Doris Lessing (1984).

The Grass Is Singing (1950). Tracing a complex relationship between a white farmer's wife and her black servant, the book commanded attention as one of the earliest novels about Africa's racial problems.

The short stories collected in Lessing's *African Stories* (1964) also take place in the Africa of her childhood. Also semiautobiographical is Lessing's quintet of novels, *Children of Violence* (1952–1969), which tells the story of the aptly named Martha Quest, who like her creator spent her childhood in Africa and her mature life in postwar Britain. The narrative continues to an apocalyptic ending in an unnamed city in the year 2000.

Lessing's most widely read and discussed book is probably *The Golden Notebook* (1962), an ambitious, complexly structured work that combines fiction, parody, and factual reporting to explore Lessing's concerns with politics, mental illness, and the problems of women in modern life. Another well-known book, *Briefing for a Descent into Hell* (1971), introduces readers to what Lessing calls "inner-space fiction," in which an individual mental breakdown is related to a wider social breakdown. In contrast, Lessing's five-volume series *Canopus in Argos: Archives* (1979–1983) is a sequence of fantasies set in outer space. However, one reviewer remarked that the series shows less of a relationship to typical space-travel science fiction than it does to the Book of Revelation in the Bible.

Among Lessing's more recent novels are *The Good Terrorist* (1985), about a group of young radicals in contemporary London, and *The Fifth Child* (1988), about the effects a "demon child" has on his family and society. She also continues to write nonfiction works on subjects ranging from political correctness to the 1980s war in Afghanistan. In 1994, she published *Under My Skin,* the first volume of her autobiography.

In all of Lessing's work, there is evidence of the responsibility she feels as a writer to be "an instrument of change." "It is not merely a question of preventing evil," she says, "but of strengthening a vision of a good which may defeat the evil."

PROGRAM MANAGER

- **Planning Instruction** See *Teaching Notes, Teaching Resources B,* pp. 186–187, for objectives and additional historical information for this selection.
- **Instructional Support** Before beginning the instructional lesson, see *Graphic Organizer for Active Reading, Teaching Resources B,* p. 196, for a Through the Story activity.
- **Assessment** See *Selection Test, Test Booklet,* pp. 245–246.
- **Language Link** For instruction and practice in using semicolons and colons, see *Language Link, Teaching Resources B,* pp. 197–198, and *Language and Writing Skills Worksheets,* pp. 138–139.
- **Reinforcement** Use the *Words to Own* worksheet in *Teaching Resources B,* p. 199.

BEFORE YOU READ
NO WITCHCRAFT FOR SALE

Reading Focus

The Power to Heal

The upcoming story asks troubling, complex questions about cultural conflict. Some of its cultural clashes are obvious, some are bridged with the unifying force of deep affection, and some remain mysterious—for the people involved, and perhaps for us. Do you think that some cultural differences are finally impassable, no matter how strong people's healing goodwill? Or do you think, with effort, people truly *can* understand one another's beliefs and aspirations? See whether "No Witchcraft for Sale"—which really is not about witchcraft at all—clarifies, disrupts, or changes your ideas.

Quickwrite

Think of someone you know or know about who comes from a culture or background very different from your own. What do you think that person would find difficult or impossible to understand about your culture? What is mysterious to you about that person's culture? Write your ideas in your Reader's Log.

Elements of Literature

Theme

A story may have many threads. A wide assortment of ideas may be conveyed through characters' attitudes, through conflicts and their outcomes, through symbols, and even through a title. Yet despite the variety of ideas a reader may glean from a story, one dominant, central idea or **theme** will unify the work.

> **T**heme is a central idea or insight embodied in a work of literature.
>
> *For more on Theme, see the Handbook of Literary Terms.*

Background

This tale from Doris Lessing's *African Stories* takes place in Southern Rhodesia at a time when that southern African country was still under British rule. The Farquars in the story are part of the British ruling class; their servants are black Africans. In her preface to *African Stories,* Lessing writes: "If people had been prepared to listen, two decades earlier, to the small, but shrill-enough, voices crying out for the world's attention, perhaps the present suffering in South Africa and Southern Rhodesia could have been prevented. Britain, who is responsible, became conscious of her responsibility too late; and now the tragedy must play itself slowly out." In the 1960s, when Lessing wrote these words, Southern Rhodesia was an independent nation under minority rule by whites. Attempts by black African leaders to gain a voice in government were vigorously opposed by the white leadership. After much fighting between black nationalists and government troops, Southern Rhodesia emerged as the republic of Zimbabwe under the leadership of a black African, Robert Mugabe (mōō·gä′be′), in 1980.

Using BEFORE YOU READ

p. 1147

Background

Ask students to consider the following question about the relationships in the story: How does the relationship between the Farquars and their African cook, Gideon, shift between intimacy and distance, especially in the relationship between Gideon and Teddy Farquar?

> **WRITERS ON WRITING**
>
> Doris Lessing's childhood in Southern Rhodesia, now called Zimbabwe, left her with an abiding sense of both the country's beauty and its potential for conflict. Her novels' portrayal of African politics illustrate what Lessing has called the writer's "responsibility." "Once a writer has a feeling of responsibility, as a human being, for the other human beings he influences, it seems to me he must become a humanist, and must feel himself as an instrument of change for good or for bad."

PROGRAM MANAGER

Application and Reinforcement

For reinforcement of the elements of literature introduced in this lesson, see **Transparency 15.3** in the *Audiovisual Resources Binder.*

WORDS TO OWN

The following vocabulary words are defined in the Words to Own at the bottom of the pupil's page.

reverently p. 1148	annulled p. 1151
reproachful p. 1149	perversely p. 1151
perfunctory p. 1151	

PORTFOLIO ASSESSMENT

Portfolio Assessment

For help with self-assessment of reading skills, see the *Portfolio Management System,* pp. 48–49.

Through the Story

A. Exploring the Culture
When British colonists arrived in the country they called Rhodesia, they took for themselves the area's productive, fertile farmland. Africans were removed from their ancestral homes to the Communal Lands, where raising crops in the poor soil was much more difficult. Displaced Africans provided cheap labor in cities and in mining operations, ensuring that the white community enjoyed a very high standard of living.

B. Reader's Response: First Thoughts
? What is your first impression of Gideon? [Sample responses: He is patient and kind. He adores Teddy.]

C. Critical Reading: Drawing Conclusions
? Why do you think that Mrs. Farquar is pleased when Gideon says "we"? [Possible answer: Because he shares her joy in her son.]

D. Literary Element: Imagery
? In what ways might Teddy's fair hair seem "miraculous" to an African child? [The color and texture would be unusual to an African child. The writer's irony implies that the white child's hair is no more "miraculous" than the black child's.]

No Witchcraft for Sale
Doris Lessing

(A) The Farquars had been childless for years when little Teddy was born; and they were touched by the pleasure of their servants, who brought presents of fowls and eggs and flowers to the homestead when they came to rejoice over the baby, exclaiming with delight over his downy golden head and his blue eyes. They congratulated Mrs. Farquar as if she had achieved a very great thing, and she felt that she had—her smile for the lingering, admiring natives was warm and grateful.

(B) Later, when Teddy had his first haircut, Gideon the cook picked up the soft gold tufts from the ground, and held them <u>reverently</u> in his hand. Then he smiled at the little boy and said: "Little Yellow Head." That became the native name for the child. Gideon and Teddy were great friends from the first. When Gideon had finished his work, he would lift Teddy on his shoulders to the shade of a big tree,

and play with him there, forming curious little toys from twigs and leaves and grass, or shaping animals from wetted soil. When Teddy learned to walk it was often Gideon who crouched before him, clucking encouragement, finally catching him when he fell, tossing him up in the air till they both became breathless with laughter. Mrs. Farquar was fond of the old cook because of his love for her child.

There was no second baby; and one day Gideon said: "Ah, missus, missus, the Lord above sent this one; Little Yellow Head is the most good thing we have in our house." Because of that "we" (C) Mrs. Farquar felt a warm impulse toward her cook; and at the end of the month she raised his wages. He had been with her now for several years; he was one of the few natives who had his wife and children in the compound and never wanted to go home to his kraal,[1] which was some hundreds of miles away. Sometimes a small piccanin[2] who had been born the same time as Teddy, could be seen peering from the edge of the bush, staring in awe at the little white boy with (D) his miraculous fair hair and Northern blue eyes. The two little children would gaze at each other with a wide, interested gaze, and once Teddy put out his hand curiously to touch the black child's cheeks and hair.

Gideon, who was watching, shook his head wonderingly, and said: "Ah, missus, these are both children, and one will grow up to be a baas,[3] and one will be a servant"; and Mrs. Farquar smiled and said sadly, "Yes, Gideon, I was thinking the same."

---
1. **kraal** (kräl): South African village.
2. **piccanin** (pik'ə·nin): black African child. Derived from *pequeno* (pā·kā'no͞o), Portuguese for "small," the term is often considered offensive.
3. **baas** (bäs): Afrikaans for "master." Afrikaans, a language developed from seventeenth-century Dutch, is spoken in South Africa.

WORDS TO OWN
reverently (rev'ər·ənt·lē) *adv.*: with deep respect, love, or awe, as for something sacred.

OPTIONS FOR TEACHING

Linguistic As students silently read the selection, stop them at strategic points, and have them summarize aloud what they have read. Such an oral review also might benefit auditory learners and less proficient readers.

STRATEGIES FOR INCLUSION

Visual Exploring characters' motivations will help students better understand the decisions that are portrayed in the story. As students read, ask them to complete a chart that lists the motives of the Farquars, Teddy, Gideon, and the scientist. A sample chart follows.

Character	Motives
Farquars	Love for Teddy; desire to do God's will
Teddy	Affection for Gideon; feelings of racial superiority
Gideon	Love for Teddy; respect for traditional tribal culture
scientist	Profit; desire to improve humanity's health

TI148

She sighed. "It is God's will," said Gideon, who was a mission boy.[4] The Farquars were very religious people; and this shared feeling about God bound servant and masters even closer together.

Teddy was about six years old when he was given a scooter, and discovered the intoxications of speed. All day he would fly around the homestead, in and out of flowerbeds, scattering squawking chickens and irritated dogs, finishing with a wide dizzying arc into the kitchen door. There he would cry: "Gideon, look at me!" And Gideon would laugh and say: "Very clever, Little Yellow Head." Gideon's youngest son, who was now a herdsboy, came especially up from the compound to see the scooter. He was afraid to come near it, but Teddy showed off in front of him. "Piccanin," shouted Teddy, "get out of my way!" And he raced in circles around the black child until he was frightened, and fled back to the bush.

"Why did you frighten him?" asked Gideon, gravely reproachful.

Teddy said defiantly: "He's only a black boy," and laughed. Then, when Gideon turned away from him without speaking, his face fell. Very soon he slipped into the house and found an orange and brought it to Gideon, saying: "This is for you." He could not bring himself to say he was sorry; but he could not bear to lose Gideon's affection either. Gideon took the orange unwillingly and sighed. "Soon you will be going away to school, Little Yellow Head," he said wonderingly, "and then you will be grown up." He shook his head gently and said, "And that is how our lives go." He seemed to be putting a distance between himself and Teddy, not because of resentment, but in the way a person accepts something inevitable. The baby had lain in his arms and smiled up into his face: The tiny boy had swung from his shoulders and played with him by the hour. Now Gideon would not let his flesh touch the flesh of the white child. He was kind, but there was a grave formality in his voice that made Teddy pout and sulk away. Also, it made him into a man: With Gideon he was polite, and carried himself formally, and if he came into the kitchen to ask for something, it was in the way a white man uses toward a servant, expecting to be obeyed.

4. **mission boy:** one educated by Christian missionaries.

But on the day that Teddy came staggering into the kitchen with his fists to his eyes, shrieking with pain, Gideon dropped the pot full of hot soup that he was holding, rushed to the child, and forced aside his fingers. "A snake!" he exclaimed. Teddy had been on his scooter, and had come to a rest with his foot on the side of a big tub of plants. A tree snake, hanging by its tail from the roof, had spat full into his eyes. Mrs. Farquar came running when she heard the commotion. "He'll go blind," she sobbed, holding Teddy close against her. "Gideon, he'll go blind!" Already the eyes, with perhaps half an hour's sight left in them, were swollen up to the size of fists: Teddy's small white face was distorted by great purple oozing protuberances.[5] Gideon said: "Wait a minute, missus, I'll get some medicine." He ran off into the bush.

Mrs. Farquar lifted the child into the house and bathed his eyes with permanganate.[6] She had scarcely heard Gideon's words; but when she saw that her remedies had no effect at all, and remembered how she had seen natives with no sight in their eyes, because of the spitting of a snake, she began to look for the return of her cook, remembering what she heard of the efficacy of native herbs. She stood by the window, holding the

5. **protuberances** (prō·tōō′bər·əns·iz): swellings; bulges.
6. **permanganate** (pər·maŋ′gə·nāt′): dark purple chemical compound used as a disinfectant.

WORDS TO OWN
reproachful (ri·prōch′fəl) *adj.*: full of or expressing blame.

E. Expansion
Gideon is a "mission boy" because he attended a school run by Christian missionaries and learned the religion of his employers. For better or worse, what might the missions provide for Africans? [Missions would provide clinics and hospitals in addition to instruction, religious and otherwise in their schools; thus they would instill Christian and European values, which often would conflict with traditional African beliefs.]

F. Critical Reading: Analyzing Conflict
? How does Teddy's inability to apologize to Gideon reflect the relationship between black and white adults in the society? [Possible answer: It illustrates white people's denial or lack of concern that their behavior can have painful, negative consequences for people in the black community.]

G. Cultural Connections
Teddy is only six years old, but he is referred to as a man. Ask students what quality or behavior identifies Teddy's manhood. [Possible answer: He is polite with servants, but expects subservience. He and Gideon have forsaken their former familiarity, as a result of Teddy's affront to Gideon.] Have students discuss what makes a "man" in their respective cultures.

H. Critical Reading: Analyzing Plot
? How does this incident affect the usual relationship between servant and employer? [Mrs. Farquar is now powerless, while her cook is in command of the situation. It also underscores her reliance on Gideon.]

INTEGRATING THE LANGUAGE ARTS

Strategic Reading Help students organize information using a cluster diagram like the one that follows. Have them record descriptive terms from the text that illustrate the tensions between Gideon and the Farquars. To transfer this activity to an overhead projector, use Transparency 3: Cluster Diagram in the Transparency Package.

Writing: Character's Report
Ask students to write a report that the scientist might have submitted to his superiors about his failure to find a new drug. Ask students to make their reports reflect the scientist's attitude toward traditional, non-Western medicines. ☞

A. Reader's Response: First Thoughts

? If you were Mrs. Farquar, would you have trusted Gideon? [Sample responses: Yes, he is her only hope. Although his actions seem strange, she knows he loves Teddy.]

B. Reader's Response: Challenging the Text

? Were you curious to know how Teddy reacted to Gideon after his sight was saved? Would including this reaction have enriched the story? [Sample responses: No, Teddy's character served his purpose by advancing the plot and demonstrating the whites' feelings of superiority. Yes, Teddy's response is needed to show why he deserves Gideon's help.]

C. Literary Element: Theme

? Why do you think the Africans withhold the truth about their plants' medicinal properties? [Possible answers: They want to retain control over this important knowledge. White people do not respect them or their medicine.]

D. Literary Element: Character

Ask students to compare the scientist's motivation for finding the new drug with the Farquars' motivation. [Possible answer: The scientist wants to make money; the Farquars hope to help humanity and to share what they perceive to be a miracle.]

---

terrified, sobbing little boy in her arms, and peered helplessly into the bush. It was not more than a few minutes before she saw Gideon come bounding back, and in his hand he held a plant.

"Do not be afraid, missus," said Gideon, "this will cure Little Yellow Head's eyes." He stripped the leaves from the plant, leaving a small white fleshy root. Without even washing it, he put the root in his mouth, chewed it vigorously, and then **(A)** held the spittle there while he took the child forcibly from Mrs. Farquar. He gripped Teddy down between his knees, and pressed the balls of his thumbs into the swollen eyes, so that the child screamed and Mrs. Farquar cried out in protest: "Gideon, Gideon!" But Gideon took no notice. He knelt over the writhing child, pushing back the puffy lids till chinks of eyeball showed, and then he spat hard, again and again, into first one eye, and then the other. He finally lifted Teddy gently into his mother's arms, and said: "His eyes will get better." But Mrs. Farquar was weeping with terror, and she could hardly thank him: It was impossible to believe that Teddy could keep his sight. In a couple of hours the swellings were gone: The eyes were inflamed and tender but Teddy could see. Mr. and Mrs. Farquar went to Gideon in the kitchen and thanked him over and over again. They felt helpless because of their gratitude: It **(B)** seemed they could do nothing to express it. They gave Gideon presents for his wife and children, and a big increase in wages, but these things could not pay for Teddy's now completely cured eyes. Mrs. Farquar said: "Gideon, God chose you as an instrument for His goodness," and Gideon said: "Yes, missus, God is very good."

Now, when such a thing happens on a farm, it cannot be long before everyone hears of it. Mr. and Mrs. Farquar told their neighbors and the story was discussed from one end of the district to the other. The bush is full of secrets. No one can live in Africa, or at least on the veld,[7] without learning very soon that there is an ancient wisdom of leaf and soil and season—and, too, perhaps most important of all, of the darker tracts of the human mind—which is the black man's heritage. Up and down the district people were

---

7. veld: in South Africa, open country with very few bushes or trees; grassland. *Veld,* also spelled *veldt,* is Afrikaans for "field."

---

telling anecdotes, reminding each other of things that had happened to them.

"But I saw it myself, I tell you. It was a puff-adder bite. The kaffir's[8] arm was swollen to the elbow, like a great shiny black bladder. He was groggy after a half a minute. He was dying. Then suddenly a kaffir walked out of the bush with his hands full of green stuff. He smeared something on the place, and next day my boy was back at work, and all you could see was two small punctures in the skin."

This was the kind of tale they told. And, as always, with a certain amount of exasperation, because while all of them knew that in the bush of Africa are waiting valuable drugs locked in **(C)** bark, in simple-looking leaves, in roots, it was impossible to ever get the truth about them from the natives themselves.

The story eventually reached town; and perhaps it was at a sundowner party,[9] or some such function, that a doctor, who happened to be there, challenged it. "Nonsense," he said. "These things get exaggerated in the telling. We are always checking up on this kind of story, and we draw a blank every time."

Anyway, one morning there arrived a strange car at the homestead, and out stepped one of the workers from the laboratory in town, with cases full of test tubes and chemicals.

Mr. and Mrs. Farquar were flustered and pleased and flattered. They asked the scientist to lunch, and they told the story all over again, for the hundredth time. Little Teddy was there too, his blue eyes sparkling with health, to prove the **(D)** truth of it. The scientist explained how humanity might benefit if this new drug could be offered for sale; and the Farquars were even more pleased: They were kind, simple people, who liked to think of something good coming about because of them. But when the scientist began talking of the money that might result, their manner showed discomfort. Their feelings over the miracle (that was how they thought of it) were so strong and deep and religious, that it was distasteful to them

---

8. kaffir's (kaf'ərz): A kaffir is a black African. Derived from *kāfir,* Arabic for "infidel," the word is considered a contemptuous term.

9. sundowner party: British colloquial for "cocktail party." The term derives from the custom of gathering for drinks at sunset.

1150 THE TWENTIETH CENTURY

---

to think of money. The scientist, seeing their faces, went back to his first point, which was the advancement of humanity. He was perhaps a trifle perfunctory: It was not the first time he had come salting the tail of a fabulous bush secret.[10]

Eventually, when the meal was over, the Farquars called Gideon into their living room and explained to him that this baas, here, was a Big Doctor from the Big City, and he had come all that way to see Gideon. At this Gideon seemed afraid; he did not understand; and Mrs. Farquar explained quickly that it was because of the wonderful thing he had done with Teddy's eyes that the Big Baas had come.

Gideon looked from Mrs. Farquar to Mr. Farquar, and then at the little boy, who was showing great importance because of the occasion. At last he said grudgingly: "The Big Baas want to know what medicine I used?" He spoke incredulously, as if he could not believe his old friends could so betray him. Mr. Farquar began explaining how a useful medicine could be made out of the root, and how it could be put on sale, and how thousands of people, black and white, up and down the continent of Africa, could be saved by the medicine when that spitting snake filled their eyes with poison. Gideon listened, his eyes bent on the ground, the skin of his forehead puckering in discomfort. When Mr. Farquar had finished he did not reply. The scientist, who all this time had been leaning back in a big chair, sipping his coffee and smiling with skeptical good humor, chipped in and explained all over again, in different words, about the making of drugs and the progress of science. Also, he offered Gideon a present.

There was silence after this further explanation, and then Gideon remarked indifferently that he could not remember the root. His face was sullen and hostile, even when he looked at the Farquars, whom he usually treated like old friends. They were beginning to feel annoyed; and this feeling annulled the guilt that had been sprung into life by Gideon's accusing manner. They were beginning to feel that he was unreasonable. But it was at that moment that they all realized he would never give in. The magical drug

10. **salting . . . bush secret:** An allusion to the ironic advice given to children about how to catch a bird: by putting salt on its tail. In other words, the scientist knows his search may be futile.

would remain where it was, unknown and useless except for the tiny scattering of Africans who had the knowledge, natives who might be digging a ditch for the municipality in a ragged shirt and a pair of patched shorts, but who were still born to healing, hereditary healers, being the nephews or sons of the old witch doctors whose ugly masks and bits of bone and all the uncouth properties of magic were the outward signs of real power and wisdom.

The Farquars might tread on that plant fifty times a day as they passed from house to garden, from cow kraal to mealie[11] field, but they would never know it.

But they went on persuading and arguing, with all the force of their exasperation; and Gideon continued to say that he could not remember, or that there was no such root, or that it was the wrong season of the year, or that it wasn't the root itself, but the spit from his mouth that had cured Teddy's eyes. He said all these things one after another, and seemed not to care they were contradictory. He was rude and stubborn. The Farquars could hardly recognize their gentle, lovable old servant in this ignorant, perversely obstinate African, standing there in front of them with lowered eyes, his hands twitching his cook's apron, repeating over and over whichever one of the stupid refusals that first entered his head.

And suddenly he appeared to give in. He lifted his head, gave a long, blank angry look at the circle of whites, who seemed to him like a circle of yelping dogs pressing around him, and said: "I will show you the root."

They walked single file away from the homestead down a kaffir path. It was a blazing December afternoon, with the sky full of hot rain clouds. Everything was hot: The sun was like a bronze tray whirling overhead, there was a heat shimmer over the fields, the soil was scorching underfoot, the dusty wind blew gritty and thick and warm in

11. **mealie:** corn.

WORDS TO OWN
perfunctory (pər·fuŋk′tə·rē) *adj.*: halfhearted; indifferent.
annulled (ə·nuld′) *v.*: did away with; canceled.
perversely (pər·vʉrs′lē) *adv.*: disagreeably; contrarily.

Doris Lessing T1151

E. Language Note: Capitalization
? What is the effect of capitalizing the common nouns *Big Doctor* and *Big City*? [Possible answer: It reveals the Farquars' belief that the natives are unsophisticated and childlike.]

F. Critical Reading: Metacognition
Ask students when they first suspected that Gideon would be asked his secret. [Possible answer: Some students may have suspected when the scientist arrived.]

G. Critical Reading: Finding Cause and Effect
This passage relates a subtle power shift from the Farquars to Gideon. Ask students to explain how Gideon gets a strategic advantage. [Gideon first saves Teddy's eyesight; the Farquars then make a request for his knowledge.]

H. Reader's Response: Extending the Text
? How would you describe the Farquars' response to Gideon in this passage? [Sample responses: The Farquars think Gideon is being stubborn. The Farquars have not yet shown any sensitivity to Gideon's culture, so it is unlikely they appreciate the importance of his knowledge and his decision.]

PROFESSIONAL NOTES

Cultural Diversity Healers like Gideon did not disappear with the modernization of Africa. These native practitioners, now often called "traditional healers," continue to dispense herbal medicines and to explore alternative methods for the treatment of such chronic illnesses as high blood pressure and asthma. The Zimbabwean government has begun issuing licenses to the approximately 27,000 members of its traditional healers' association. A license can be obtained if the community agrees that the healer has been successful. Ask students to discuss how traditional healers compare to the medical practitioners in their own cultures.

ASSESSMENT TOOLS

Check Test: Short Answer
1. Who is Teddy's best childhood friend? [Gideon.]
2. When does Gideon realize that their relationship must change? [When Teddy frightens Gideon's son and will not apologize.]
3. How does Gideon save Teddy's sight? [He chews a root and spits the juice into Teddy's eyes.]
4. Why does the scientist visit the Farquars? [He hopes to learn about the medicine Gideon used to save Teddy's sight.]
5. What does Gideon give the scientist? [Blue flowers.]

A. Reader's Response: Shaping Interpretations

? What could be the significance of Gideon's actions? [Sample responses: He is angry and takes them on a wild goose chase because they will not accept his refusal. His medicine involves more than just the root; it is not as simple as the whites suppose.]

B. Critical Reading: Making Connections

? How does this comment explain why Gideon behaves "like an unwilling servant"? [Possible answer: Because of his skills, he is sensitive about having traditional medicine exploited.]

C. Literary Element: Irony

? What is ironic about Gideon's statement? [Possible answer: He showed it to the Farquars when they most needed it.]

D. Humanities Connection

In Hebrew history, Gideon led his people to victory. Afterward, he refused the crown of Israel, saying that only God was Israel's king. Ask students why Lessing might have named her character after this hero. [Possible answer: Gideon refuses a crown because he believes in a higher authority; Lessing's character refuses gifts because he does not want to violate the integrity of his medicine.]

Making Meanings

First Thoughts

1. Possible responses: Students may include images such as Teddy's golden hair, or they may focus on how the relationship between Teddy and Gideon changes.

Reviewing the Text

a. Gideon and Teddy are great friends as the story begins. A change occurs when Teddy frightens Gideon's son saying, "He's only a black boy."
b. A venomous tree snake sprays poison in Teddy's eyes.
c. Gideon saves him from blindness.
d. For example: "They were beginning to feel annoyed; and this feeling annulled the guilt that had been sprung into life by Gideon's accusing manner."
e. Gideon creates a distance between them. The relationship becomes more formal, polite, and guarded.

---

their faces. It was a terrible day, fit only for reclining on a veranda with iced drinks, which is where they would normally have been at that hour.

From time to time, remembering that on the day of the snake it had taken ten minutes to find the root, someone asked: "Is it much further, Gideon?" And Gideon would answer over his shoulder, with angry politeness: "I'm looking for the root, baas." And indeed, he would frequently bend sideways and trail his hand among the grasses with a gesture that was insulting in its perfunctoriness. He walked them through the bush along unknown paths for two hours, in that melting destroying heat, so that the sweat trickled coldly down them and their heads ached. They were all quite silent: the Farquars because they were angry, the scientist because he was being proved right again; there was no such plant. His was a tactful silence.

At last, six miles from the house, Gideon suddenly decided they had had enough; or perhaps his anger evaporated at that moment. He picked up, without an attempt at looking anything but casual, a handful of blue flowers from the grass, flowers that had been growing plentifully all down the paths they had come.

He handed them to the scientist without looking at him, and marched off by himself on the way home, leaving them to follow him if they chose.

When they got back to the house, the scientist went to the kitchen to thank Gideon: He was being very polite, even though there was an amused look in his eyes. Gideon was not there. Throwing the flowers casually into the back of his car, the eminent visitor departed on his way back to his laboratory.

Gideon was back in his kitchen in time to prepare dinner, but he was sulking. He spoke to Mr. Farquar like an unwilling servant. It was days before they liked each other again.

The Farquars made inquiries about the root from their laborers. Sometimes they were answered with distrustful stares. Sometimes the natives said: "We do not know. We have never heard of the root." One, the cattle boy, who had been with them a long time, and had grown to trust them a little, said: "Ask your boy in the kitchen. Now, there's a doctor for you. He's the son of a famous medicine man who used to be in these parts, and there's nothing he cannot cure." Then he added politely: "Of course, he's not as good as

the white man's doctor, we know that, but he's good for us."

After some time, when the soreness had gone from between the Farquars and Gideon, they began to joke: "When are you going to show us the snake root, Gideon?" And he would laugh and shake his head, saying, a little uncomfortably: "But I did show you, missus, have you forgotten?"

Much later, Teddy, as a schoolboy, would come into the kitchen and say: "You old rascal, Gideon! Do you remember that time you tricked us all by making us walk miles all over the veld for nothing? It was so far my father had to carry me!"

And Gideon would double up with polite laughter. After much laughing, he would suddenly straighten himself up, wipe his old eyes, and look sadly at Teddy, who was grinning mischievously at him across the kitchen: "Ah, Little Yellow Head, how you have grown! Soon you will be grown up with a farm of your own. . . ."

MAKING MEANINGS

First Thoughts

1. What did you focus on most intently as you read the story—what word, phrase, image, or idea? Explain.

Shaping Interpretations

2. Mrs. Farquar and Gideon share a sense of sadness about the reality of their children's future lives. What is the reality that gives these two characters, and this whole story, a feeling of sadness?

Reviewing the Text

a. Describe Gideon and Teddy's relationship at the story's start. What incident signals a change in their relationship?

b. What crisis sets the **plot** in motion?

c. What does Gideon do for Teddy?

d. Cite sentences showing that the Farquars do not really understand Gideon and his response to the doctor's request.

e. How does Teddy's relationship with Gideon change as he grows up?

Shaping Interpretations

2. Because of their color, the white boy will grow up to be a "baas" and the black boy will be a servant.
3. Most students will agree that there is irony in how little understanding these good people have for the man who saved their son.
4. There is a criticism of the inequality between the races.
5. Gideon believes that the plant is only for those "born to healing." Students may think the refusal shows selfishness or integrity.

6. European culture has imposed itself on African culture; the Europeans are unwilling or unable to understand the traditions of Africa's indigenous peoples.
7. Possible answer: Social prejudice and flawed institutions erect barriers between people.

Connecting with the Text

8. Students might note that the story made them aware of people's acceptance of prejudice.
9. Students may identify with the scientist's interest. They may identify with Gideon's integrity in the face of the whites' ignorance and lack of respect.

3. Does the narrator's presentation of the Farquars as people of goodwill seem **ironic** or straightforward? How did you respond to them?

4. What implicit criticism can you detect in the fact that while Teddy is riding a scooter, Gideon's son of the same age is a herdsboy?

5. Why do you think Gideon refuses to share his wisdom with the Farquars? How do you feel about his refusal?

6. In what ways is this story about a clash of cultures? Re-read Gideon's comment at the end of the story. What does it reveal about his understanding of the relationship between white European and black African cultures?

7. How would you state the **theme** of this story?

Connecting with the Text

8. Look back at the notes in your Reader's Log. How does the story affect your own notions about cultural differences?

9. Describe how you feel about the "Big Doctor." Did you find yourself identifying most with him, Gideon, or the Farquars? Explain your responses.

CHOICES: Building Your Portfolio

Writer's Notebook

1. Collecting Ideas for a Problem-Solution Essay

In this story, Lessing explores how different cultural values can lead to problems of misunderstanding and mistrust. What problems do you suppose you'd encounter if you were placed in a different culture? Freewrite for a few minutes about what you think you'd have to grapple with. Save your notes for the Writer's Workshop on page 1179.

Critical Writing

2. Between Two Worlds

The conflict in the story between the scientist and the Farquars on one hand and Gideon on the other comes about because Gideon does not wish to share his knowledge. The conflict is not between right and wrong, good and evil, or enlightened and unenlightened viewpoints. Rather, it is over cultural differences. In an essay, discuss the similarities in and differences between the Farquars' and the scientist's point of view and Gideon's. Use quotations from the story to back up your opinions.

Critical Writing

3. Angle of Vision

In a brief essay, discuss the effects of the narrator's point of view. Also, consider how the story might be different if it were narrated by Gideon or by the adult Teddy Farquar. Cite passages to support your analysis.

Creative Writing

4. Saying "No"

When Gideon hears the arguments for sharing his knowledge, he remains sullen. Imagine what he would have said if he were on an equal footing with his employers. In two paragraphs, write Gideon's refusal speech.

Science and Medicine / Research

5. Ancient Cures, Modern Proofs

Research and report orally on folk medicines and other traditional cures. What sorts of studies have been done to determine their effects? Do these studies confirm or disprove a belief in the effectiveness of folk medicines and traditional cures?

DORIS LESSING 1153

Choices: Building Your Portfolio

1. **Writer's Notebook** Remind students to save their work. They may use it as prewriting for the Writer's Workshop on p. 1179.

2. **Critical Writing** Suggest to students that they use a Venn diagram to organize the similarities and differences among the perspectives of Gideon, the Farquars, and the scientist.

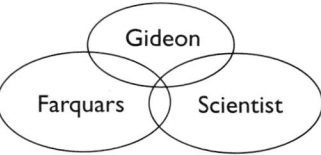

3. **Critical Writing** Have students examine perspective in the story by working in small groups to complete a graphic organizer like the one that follows. Have them find evidence from the story in which race and culture lead characters to make different decisions. Suggest that students consider the types of information that would be included if another character told the story.

	Effects of Point of View	Support/ Examples
Narrator		
Gideon		
Teddy Farquar		

5. **Science and Medicine/Research** Direct students to illustrations of traditional or unusual healing techniques, for example, the film *Lorenzo's Oil*. Students could explore the techniques of Mexican curanderos or Chinese acupuncturists.

PORTFOLIO ASSESSMENT

Choices: Assessment Criteria
For help in evaluating these Choices assignments, see the criteria in the *Portfolio Management System*, pp. 188–189.

STRATEGIES FOR INCLUSION

Advanced For activity #3, students could rewrite the story "No Witchcraft for Sale" from the perspective of Mr. or Mrs. Farquar, Teddy, or Gideon. Allow students to conduct whatever research helps them imagine their character's circumstances and point of view. Encourage students to outline their story and to consider the thoughts, feelings, and attitude of their character.

Into the Story

Author Biography p. 1154

Before You Read p. 1155

- **Reading Focus: Set a Purpose**
  Students compare walls and reasons for having walls.
- **Quickwrite: Prior Knowledge**
  Write in Reader's Log about walls
- **Elements of Literature: Parody**
- **Background:** Apartheid and its repeal in South Africa

Through the Story

"Once Upon a Time" pp. 1156–1159

Words to Own pp. 1156–1159

Making Meanings p. 1160

Beyond the Story

Choices: Building Your Portfolio p. 1160

- **Writer's Notebook:** Propose solutions for problem
- **Critical Writing:** Write an essay comparing and contrasting "Once Upon a Time" and "Shooting an Elephant"
- **Creative Writing:** Write a fairy tale about a clash of cultures
- **Research/Speaking:** Investigate conflicts

Nadine Gordimer

(1923–   )

Nadine Gordimer was born in Springs, a small town located thirty miles from Johannesburg, on the gold-mining ridge that has brought South Africa much of its wealth. Her father was a Jewish jeweler who had emigrated from Lithuania as a teenager; her mother was a native of England. Gordimer grew up in a middle-class colonial society that imitated European conventions and values. She has said that she spent much of her childhood reading because she found that atmosphere extremely dull.

Gordimer began writing at the age of nine when, as a sickly child, she was taken out of school for a time. At fifteen she published her first story in a Johannesburg weekly. When her first internationally published short-story collection, *The Soft Voice of the Serpent,* appeared in 1952, critics hailed Gordimer as a strong new voice who could draw fresh, authentic perceptions of African life. Her first novel, *The Lying Days,* appeared the following year to favorable reviews. Since then, she has continued to win praise and honors, and, in 1991, won the Nobel Prize in literature.

Gordimer is known for her ability to show, as one critic said, "the infinite variety of human character, the rich and surprising drama inherent in human personality and in the clash of personality." She has been compared to Virginia Woolf for her talent in capturing the revealing moments in people's lives, what the critic Robert F. Haugh called "the illuminating moment, the quick perceptive glance of the author which sparkles like a gem."

Although she deals with universal themes and a variety of settings, much of Gordimer's writing concerns the troubles that her own

Nadine Gordimer.

nation has experienced. She has observed that "white culture imported from Europe never had a chance in the South African context. . . . All it did was to harm black culture. . . . In the process we suffered more than they." Commenting on Gordimer's writing about the effects of apartheid, the enforced separation of races, on South Africa, one critic called her "one of the very few links between white and black in South Africa. She is a bearer of culture in a barbaric society. And she is a luminous symbol of at least one white person's understanding of the black man's burden."

Perhaps Gordimer's greatest achievement is her ability to treat South Africa's problems from a literary rather than a political perspective. "Here I live in a society which is fundamentally out of joint. One can't but be politically concerned," she has said, but she disclaims a political allegiance. "I don't understand politics except in terms of what politics does to influence lives," she once observed. "What interests me is the infinite variety of effects apartheid has on men and women."

Among her best-known works are *A Guest of Honor* (1970) and *July's People* (1981), the latter set in an unnamed future when the whites in South Africa become the servants of the blacks.

Although Gordimer is respected around the world, she was a thorn in the side of her own country's government when apartheid was still in effect, and three of her novels were banned in South Africa. Nevertheless, she has always considered herself "an intensely loyal South African. I care deeply for my country. If I didn't, I wouldn't still be there."

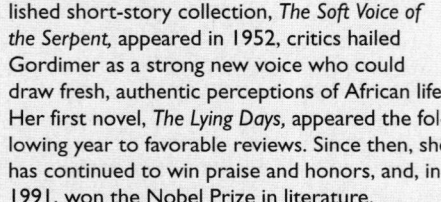

PROGRAM MANAGER

- **Planning Instruction** See *Teaching Notes, Teaching Resources B,* p. 187, for objectives, a summary, and literary elements for this selection.
- **Instructional Support** Before beginning the instructional lesson, see **Graphic Organizer for Active** Reading, *Teaching Resources B,* p. 200, for a Through the Story activity.
- **Audiotaped Readings** To help less proficient readers or auditory learners through the lesson, use the **Selected Reading, Audio-cassette 3, Side A,** in the *Audiovisual Resources Binder.*
- **Assessment** See **Selection Test,** *Test Booklet,* pp. 247–248.
- **Reinforcement** Use the **Words to Own** worksheet in *Teaching Resources B,* p. 201.

BEFORE YOU READ
ONCE UPON A TIME

Reading Focus

Walls and Barriers

Isolation is one way to keep conflict at bay. Opposing parties cannot clash if they do not meet, or so the reasoning goes. The remedy has certainly been tried repeatedly, throughout history and all over the world. Reservations, compounds, borders: these are all isolating walls, literal or figurative, that keep some people from others. Even on the household level, we have today's "security systems," a phrase to keep in mind as you read Gordimer's "Once Upon a Time." Does a security system do its job? Is it worth its price? Is it protecting life—or a fairy tale?

Quickwrite

When you think of a wall, what do you picture? What does your wall keep in and keep out? Write your ideas about a wall in your Reader's Log.

Elements of Literature

Parody

"Once Upon a Time" is a **parody,** or imitation, of a fairy tale. Though parodies are often written for amusement, they also may make serious points. As you read Gordimer's story, consider why she chose to imitate a fairy tale.

> **P**arody is the imitation of a work of literature, art, or music for amusement or instruction.
>
> *For more on Parody, see the Handbook of Literary Terms.*

Background

Until recently, South Africa, Nadine Gordimer's native land, practiced a policy called *apartheid,* the legal segregation of the races. Not only did black South Africans and other non-whites experience economic and political discrimination, but they were also forced to live in remote areas or in all-black "townships" bordering white cities. They could not leave these areas or enter white cities without "passbooks" that identified them by name, residency, and race.

Decades of rebellions, riots, and strikes left thousands of blacks dead and most of their leaders jailed. Finally, in 1991, the white government headed by F. W. de Klerk—under both internal and international pressure—repealed the apartheid laws. Three years later, the first all-race election swept the black South African Nelson Mandela, a former political prisoner and leader of the African National Congress, into office as president.

Blue at Noon (1955) by Adolph Gottlieb. Oil on canvas.
Collection Walker Art Center, Minneapolis. Gift of the T. B. Walker Foundation, 1963.

NADINE GORDIMER 1155

Using **BEFORE YOU READ**

p. 1155

Background

In Gordimer's story, a family fears rioting "where people of another color were quartered." Gordimer's description could apply to the 1976 riot in Soweto, an overcrowded suburb of Johannesburg where black Africans were moved under the policy of apartheid. Soweto residents protested a policy that would require some classes in community schools to be taught in Afrikaans, a language derived from Dutch and spoken by white South Africans. In the violence that followed, more than six hundred people were killed, most of them black South Africans.

ABOUT THE AUTHOR

Gordimer resisted the South African government's policy of racial segregation by collaborating with the outlawed African National Congress (ANC) and speaking out against censorship. When it selected Gordimer as the 1991 recipient of the Nobel Prize in Literature, the Swedish Academy said, "Her continual involvement on behalf of literature and free speech in a police state where censorship and persecution of books and people exist have made her 'the doyenne of South African letters.'"

PORTFOLIO ASSESSMENT

Portfolio Assessment For help with self-assessment of reading skills, see the *Portfolio Management System,* p. 39.

WORDS TO OWN

The following vocabulary words are defined in the Words to Own at the bottom of the pupil's page.

distend p. 1156	aesthetics p. 1159
itinerant p. 1156	serrated p. 1159
audaciously p. 1157	

Through the Story

A. Language Note: Paragraphs

❓ What is the effect of beginning a new paragraph after only one short sentence, question, or phrase? [Possible answer: The technique creates suspense by singling out each detail.]

B. Literary Element: Setting

❓ How do the details of events in the author's neighborhood intensify her fearful predicament? [The author has cause for fear. She hears a noise at night and has no protection. She lives in a neighborhood in which murders occur despite security devices and the time of day.]

C. Reader's Response: First Thoughts

❓ How convincing is Gordimer's description? [Sample responses: She gives a good account of the body's response to fear; everyone is afraid of unexplained noises, especially in the dark.]

D. Language Note: Tone

❓ What words or phrases does the author use to create a somber, uneasy tone? [Examples: "Muffled," "under me in the earth," "ruptured veins," "interred," and "tombs."]

E. Critical Reading: Drawing Conclusions

❓ What conclusions can you draw about the family? [Possible answer: They are privileged, loving, responsible, and cautious.]

Once Upon a Time
Nadine Gordimer

Someone has written to ask me to contribute to an anthology of stories for children. I reply that I don't write children's stories; and he writes back that at a recent congress/book fair/seminar a certain novelist said every writer ought to write at least one story for children. I think of sending a postcard saying I don't accept that I "ought" to write anything.

And then last night I woke up—or rather was wakened without knowing what had roused me.

A voice in the echo chamber of the subconscious?

A sound.

A creaking of the kind made by the weight carried by one foot after another along a wooden floor. I listened. I felt the apertures of my ears distend with concentration. Again: the creaking. I was waiting for it; waiting to hear if it indicated that feet were moving from room to room, coming up the passage—to my door. I have no burglar bars, no gun under the pillow, but I have the same fears as people who do take these precautions, and my windowpanes are thin as rime,[1] could shatter like a wineglass. A woman was murdered (how do they put it) in broad daylight in a house two blocks away, last year, and the fierce dogs who guarded an old widower and his collection of antique clocks were strangled before he was knifed by a casual laborer he had dismissed without pay.

I was staring at the door, making it out in my mind rather than seeing it, in the dark. I lay quite still—a victim already—but the arrhythmia[2] of my heart was fleeing, knocking this way and that against its body-cage. How finely tuned the senses are, just out of rest, sleep! I could never listen intently as that in the distractions of the day; I was reading every faintest sound, identifying and classifying its possible threat.

But I learned that I was to be neither threatened nor spared. There was no human weight pressing on the boards, the creaking was a buck-

ling, an epicenter[3] of stress. I was in it. The house that surrounds me while I sleep is built on undermined ground; far beneath my bed, the floor, the house's foundations, the stopes[4] and passages of gold mines have hollowed the rock, and when some face trembles, detaches, and falls, three thousand feet below, the whole house shifts slightly, bringing uneasy strain to the balance and counterbalance of brick, cement, wood, and glass that hold it as a structure around me. The misbeats of my heart tailed off like the last muffled flourishes on one of the wooden xylophones made by the Chopi and Tsonga[5] migrant miners who might have been down there, under me in the earth at that moment. The stope where the fall was could have been disused, dripping water from its ruptured veins; or men might now be interred there in the most profound of tombs.

I couldn't find a position in which my mind would let go of my body—release me to sleep again. So I began to tell myself a story; a bedtime story.

In a house, in a suburb, in a city, there were a man and his wife who loved each other very much and were living happily ever after. They had a little boy, and they loved him very much. They had a cat and a dog that the little boy loved very much. They had a car and a caravan trailer for holidays, and a swimming pool which was fenced so that the little boy and his playmates would not fall in and drown. They had a housemaid who was absolutely trustworthy and an itinerant gardener who was highly recommended by the neighbors. For when they began to live happily ever after they were

---

1. **rime:** frost.
2. **arrhythmia** (ə·ri*th*′mē·ə): irregular beating.
3. **epicenter:** central point.
4. **stopes:** excavations.
5. **Chopi** (chō′pē) **and Tsonga** (tsäŋ′gä): Bantu-speaking peoples of Mozambique in southeastern Africa. Tsonga is often spelled *Thonga*.

WORDS TO OWN
distend (di·stend′) *v.*: expand; stretch out; swell.
itinerant (ī·tin′ər·ənt) *adj.*: traveling.

---

warned, by that wise old witch, the husband's mother, not to take on anyone off the street. They were inscribed[6] in a medical benefit society, their pet dog was licensed, they were insured against fire, flood damage, and theft, and subscribed to the local Neighborhood Watch, which supplied them with a plaque for their gates lettered YOU HAVE BEEN WARNED over the silhouette of a would-be intruder. He was masked; it could not be said if he was black or white, and therefore proved the property owner was no racist.

It was not possible to insure the house, the swimming pool, or the car against riot damage. There were riots, but these were outside the city, where people of another color were quartered. These people were not allowed into the suburb except as reliable housemaids and gardeners, so there was nothing to fear, the husband told the wife. Yet she was afraid that some day such people might come up the street and tear off the plaque YOU HAVE BEEN WARNED and open the gates and stream in. . . . Nonsense, my dear, said the husband, there are police and soldiers and tear gas and guns to keep them away. But to please her—for he loved her very much and buses were being burned, cars stoned, and schoolchildren shot by the police in those quarters out of sight and hearing of the suburb—he had electronically controlled gates fitted. Anyone who pulled off the sign YOU HAVE BEEN WARNED and tried to open the gates would have to announce his intentions by pressing a button and speaking into a receiver relayed to the house. The little boy was fascinated by the device and used it as a walkie-talkie in cops and robbers play with his small friends.

The riots were suppressed, but there were many burglaries in the suburb and somebody's trusted housemaid was tied up and shut in a cupboard by thieves while she was in charge of her employers' house. The trusted housemaid of the man and wife and little boy was so upset by this misfortune befalling a friend left, as she herself often was, with responsibility for the possessions of the man and his wife and the little boy that she implored her employers to have burglar bars attached to the doors and windows of the house, and an alarm system installed. The wife

6. **inscribed:** enrolled.

said, She is right, let us take heed of her advice. So from every window and door in the house where they were living happily ever after they now saw the trees and sky through bars, and when the little boy's pet cat tried to climb in by the fanlight[7] to keep him company in his little bed at night, as it customarily had done, it set off the alarm keening[8] through the house.

The alarm was often answered—it seemed—by other burglar alarms, in other houses, that had been triggered by pet cats or nibbling mice. The alarms called to one another across the gardens in shrills and bleats and wails that everyone soon became accustomed to, so that the din roused the inhabitants of the suburb no more than the croak of frogs and musical grating of cicadas'[9] legs. Under cover of the electronic harpies'[10] discourse intruders sawed the iron bars and broke into homes, taking away hi-fi equipment, television sets, cassette players, cameras and radios, jewelry and clothing, and sometimes were hungry enough to devour everything in the refrigerator or paused audaciously to drink the whiskey in the cabinets or patio bars. Insurance companies paid no compensation for single malt, a loss made keener by the property owner's knowledge that the thieves wouldn't even have been able to appreciate what it was they were drinking.

Then the time came when many of the people who were not trusted housemaids and gardeners hung about the suburb because they were unemployed. Some importuned for a job: weeding or painting a roof; anything, *baas*,[11] madam. But the man and his wife remembered the warning about taking on anyone off the street. Some drank liquor and fouled the street with discarded bottles. Some

7. **fanlight:** semicircular window over a door or a larger window.
8. **keening:** wailing.
9. **cicadas'** (si·kā′dəz): Cicadas are large, flylike insects.
10. **harpies':** Harpies are shrewish or grasping people. The word comes from the mythological Harpies, hideous winged monsters that have the head and trunk of a woman and the tail, legs, and talons of a bird.
11. ***baas*** (bäs): Afrikaans for "master." Afrikaans, a language developed from seventeenth-century Dutch, is spoken in South Africa.

WORDS TO OWN
audaciously (ô·dā′shəs·lē) *adv.:* boldly.

Nadine Gordimer **T1157**

INTEGRATING THE LANGUAGE ARTS

Strategic Reading There is a distinct difference between Gordimer's **tone** and the events she describes. To help students see Gordimer's use of irony, ask them to choose a section of the story and to record the contrast between the language and the story's action. Have them make a chart like the one that follows on which to record quotations from the story.

Fairy Tale Language	Reality
"Dragon's Teeth"	razor wire

Mechanics Gordimer chooses not to use quotation marks around her characters' dialogue. To help students practice punctuating quotations correctly, ask them to locate at least three instances in which dialogue is used. Have students rewrite these sections using punctuation and paragraph breaks when necessary. Then have students discuss which style they think is better and why.

begged, waiting for the man or his wife to drive the car out of the electronically operated gates. They sat about with their feet in the gutters, under the jacaranda[12] trees that made a green tunnel of the street—for it was a beautiful suburb, spoiled only by their presence—and sometimes they fell asleep lying right before the gates in the midday sun. The wife could never see anyone go hungry. She sent the trusted housemaid out with bread and tea, but the trusted housemaid said

12. **jacaranda** (jak'ə·ran'də): tropical American trees with large clusters of blue or lavender flowers.

Untitled (1982) by Jannis Kounellis.
Feather River travertine,
cast plaster, and steel.

Collection Walker Art Center, Minneapolis.
Walker Special Purchase Fund, 1987.

these were loafers and *tsotsis,*[13] who would come and tie her up and shut her in a cupboard. The husband said, She's right. Take heed of her advice. You only encourage them with your bread and tea. They are looking for their chance. . . . And he brought the little boy's tricycle from the garden into the house every night, because if the house was surely secure, once locked and with the alarm set, someone might still be able to climb over the wall or the electronically closed gates into the garden.

You are right, said the wife, then the wall should be higher. And the wise old witch, the husband's mother, paid for the extra bricks as her Christmas present to her son and his wife—the little boy got a Space Man outfit and a book of fairy tales.

But every week there were more reports of intrusion: in broad daylight and the dead of night, in the early hours of the morning, and even in the lovely summer twilight—a certain family was at dinner while the bedrooms were being ransacked upstairs. The man and his wife, talking of the latest armed robbery in the suburb, were distracted by the sight of the little boy's pet cat effortlessly arriving over the seven-foot wall, descending first with a rapid bracing of extended forepaws down on the sheer vertical surface, and then a graceful launch, landing with swishing tail within the property. The whitewashed wall was marked with the cat's comings and goings; and on the street side of the wall there were larger red-earth smudges that could have been made by the kind of broken running shoes, seen on the feet of unemployed loiterers, that had no innocent destination.

When the man and wife and little boy took the pet dog for its walk round the neighborhood streets they no longer paused to admire this show of roses or that perfect lawn; these were hidden behind an array of different varieties of security fences, walls, and devices. The man, wife, little boy, and dog passed a remarkable choice: There was the low-cost option of pieces of broken glass embedded in cement along the top of walls, there were iron grilles ending in lance points, there

13. **tsotsis** (tsät'sis): colloquial expression for flashily dressed street thugs.

were attempts at reconciling the aesthetics of prison architecture with the Spanish Villa style (spikes painted pink) and with the plastic urns of neoclassical façades (twelve-inch pikes finned like zigzags of lightning and painted pure white). Some walls had a small board affixed, giving the name and telephone number of the firm responsible for the installation of the devices. While the little boy and the pet dog raced ahead, the husband and wife found themselves comparing the possible effectiveness of each style against its appearance; and after several weeks when they paused before this barricade or that without needing to speak, both came out with the conclusion that only one was worth considering. It was the ugliest but the most honest in its suggestion of the pure concentration-camp style, no frills, all evident efficacy. Placed the length of walls, it consisted of a continuous coil of stiff and shining metal serrated into jagged blades, so that there would be no way of climbing over it and no way through its tunnel without getting entangled in its fangs. There would be no way out, only a struggle getting bloodier and bloodier, a deeper and sharper hooking and tearing of flesh. The wife shuddered to look at it. You're right, said the husband, anyone would think twice. . . . And they took heed of the advice on a small board fixed to the wall: Consult DRAGON'S TEETH The People For Total Security.

Next day a gang of workmen came and stretched the razor-bladed coils all round the walls of the house where the husband and wife and little boy and pet dog and cat were living happily ever after. The sunlight flashed and slashed, off the serrations, the cornice of razor thorns encircled the home, shining. The husband said, Never mind. It will weather. The wife said, You're wrong. They guarantee it's rustproof. And she waited until the little boy had run off to play before she said, I hope the cat will take heed. . . . The husband said, Don't worry, my dear, cats always look before they leap. And it was true that from that day on the cat slept in the little boy's bed and kept to the garden, never risking a try at breaching security.

One evening, the mother read the little boy to sleep with a fairy story from the book the wise old witch had given him at Christmas. Next day he pretended to be the Prince who braves the terrible thicket of thorns to enter the palace and kiss the Sleeping Beauty back to life: He dragged a ladder to the wall, the shining coiled tunnel was just wide enough for his little body to creep in, and with the first fixing of its razor teeth in his knees and hands and head he screamed and struggled deeper into its tangle. The trusted housemaid and the itinerant gardener, whose "day" it was, came running, the first to see and to scream with him, and the itinerant gardener tore his hands trying to get at the little boy. Then the man and his wife burst wildly into the garden and for some reason (the cat, probably) the alarm set up wailing against the screams while the bleeding mass of the little boy was hacked out of the security coil with saws, wire cutters, choppers, and they carried it—the man, the wife, the hysterical trusted housemaid, and the weeping gardener—into the house.

Le Ciel Rouge (*The Red Sky*) (1952) by Nicolas de Staël. Oil on canvas.

Collection Walker Art Center, Minneapolis.
Gift of the T. B. Walker Foundation, 1954.
©1997 Artists Rights Society (ARS), New York/ADAGP, Paris.

WORDS TO OWN
aesthetics (es·thet′iks) *n.*: principles of beauty.
serrated (sə·rāt′id) *v.* used as *adj.*: having jagged, saw-like notches along the edge.

NADINE GORDIMER 1159

Making Meanings

First Thoughts

1. Most students will be horrified that the family helped cause this event.

Reviewing the Text

Electronically controlled gates are installed for fear of rioters, and the boy plays with the gates' intercom. Burglar bars and an alarm are added because nearby houses are robbed. The noise of similar systems throughout the neighborhood masks the sound of burglaries. The wall is made higher, but the family still fears intruders. After razor wire is placed on the wall, the child is badly hurt by the wire.

Shaping Interpretations

2. Humorous passages include descriptions of the "perfect" family and the son playing with the electronic gate. Gordimer's tone is irreverent as she mocks the family's attempt to insulate itself.
3. Fairy tale elements include living "happily ever after" and the "Dragon's Teeth" company. The parody emphasizes that there are no easy solutions to the family's problems.
4. Gordimer's nonfictional opening brings a serious edge to her characters' behavior. The combination of her topic and tone show the complexity of this situation.
5. Walls are used to indicate divisions, just as race and class mark social divisions in the story.
6. In most fairy tales good conquers evil. In this fairy tale the lines are not so easily drawn.

Connecting with the Text

7. Students who argue that the family is racist may point out that intruders are all assumed to be "people of another color." Students also may argue that the family's unreasonable fears bring on their tragedy.
8. Many students would think of walls as protective and the story will have changed their notions.

Extending the Text

9. (Evaluation) Ads for alarm systems promise security. They play on the feelings of fear and responsibility.

Challenging the Text

10. (Evaluation) Students may think the story is too brutal; others may see the violence as appropriate.

MAKING MEANINGS

First Thoughts

1. What were your feelings when you read the grisly end of this story?

> **Reviewing the Text**
>
> Chart the course of this story through the four improvements to home security that the family makes. What is each improvement, what occasions it, and how well does it work?

Shaping Interpretations

2. Which passages in the story obviously have humorous intent? Did you find them funny? Overall, what is Gordimer's **tone**?
3. Point out elements of the fairy-tale genre that are used by Gordimer. (For example, the setting is not specified and the characters are not named.) How would you describe the effect of Gordimer's **parody**?
4. Why do you think Gordimer uses a nonfictional opening? How do you interpret the opening after reading the story?
5. How can the wall in the story be seen as a **symbol**?
6. Fairy tales often contain **moral** lessons. What are some of the morals of fairy tales you've read? What, in contrast, is the moral of "Once Upon a Time"?

Connecting with the Text

7. In your opinion, are the husband and wife racists who cause their own tragedy? Explain your answer.
8. Look back at the notes in your Reader's Log. How does "Once Upon a Time" support or change your picture of a wall?

Extending the Text

9. Think about ads for home protection systems. What messages do they give visually and verbally? What emotions do they play on?

Challenging the Text

10. Do you think this story is too brutal or violent? Compare and discuss your responses in class.

CHOICES: Building Your Portfolio

Writer's Notebook

1. Collecting Ideas for a Problem-Solution Essay

Nadine Gordimer probably wouldn't be surprised to learn that polls in this country often reveal that people's perceptions of the crime rate usually exceed the actual rate. Yet crime is a very real problem. In a small group, brainstorm about what some of the causes of crime are and how how they might be eliminated. Evaluate your proposed solutions by filling in a three-column chart headed "Possible Solutions," "Advantages," and "Disadvantages." Save your notes for the Writer's Workshop on page 1179.

Critical Writing

2. The Great Divide

Both Gordimer's tale and George Orwell's "Shooting an Elephant" (page 1139) carry messages about cultural clashes. Compare the two works, focusing on **theme, genre, style,** and **tone.**

Creative Writing

3. Not So Happily Ever After

Use "Once Upon a Time" as a model to write your own fairy tale about a clash of cultures. Include in it some kind of wall or boundary.

Research / Speaking

4. Other Walls, Other Bridges

Investigate the current state of affairs in South Africa, or in another part of the world beset by long-standing divisions between people. What separates people in this area, and what efforts are being taken to bring them together? Prepare a brief oral report, and present it to your classmates.

Beyond the Story

Choices: Building Your Portfolio

1. **Writer's Notebook** Remind students to save their work. They may use it as prewriting for the Writer's Workshop on p. 1179.

PORTFOLIO ASSESSMENT

Choices: Assessment Criteria

For help in evaluating these Choices assignments, see the criteria in the *Portfolio Management System,* p. 190.

Derek Walcott
(1930–   )

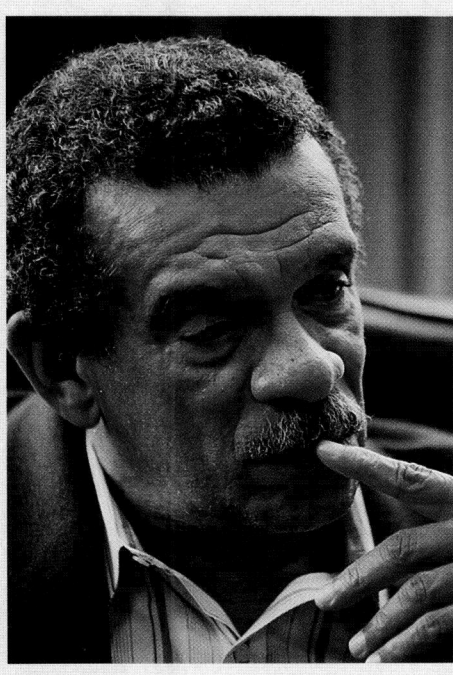
Derek Walcott.

Derek Walcott was born and raised on St. Lucia, an island in the West Indies noted for its green valleys, vast banana plantations, and sleeping volcano. St. Lucia was a colony of Britain when Walcott was a boy, and its official language remains English.

The son of a schoolteacher father and a mother who was headmistress of the island's Methodist Infant School, Walcott was introduced to the classics of English literature at an early age and showed great promise in the use of language. As he grew older, he also enjoyed the peculiar brand of "Englishness" that belonged to even the most far-flung colonies of the British Empire. Yet, in spite of these skills and interests, no one ever dreamed that a boy from a tiny tropical island would one day be regarded as one of the leading English-language poets of his day or be awarded the 1992 Nobel Prize in literature.

A scholarship student at the University of the West Indies in Jamaica, Walcott stayed on after graduation to teach comparative literature. He then embarked on an independent career that took him to the island of Trinidad, where he lived for many years. Walcott has spent a good deal of time in the United States, where the scope of his activities has included not only writing poetry but also writing plays and teaching classes in creative writing at Harvard and Boston Universities. Among his best-known works are *Dream on Monkey Mountain and Other Plays* (1970), the long narrative poems *Another Life* (1973) and *Omeros* (1990), and the lyric collections *Sea Grapes* (1976) and *Midsummer* (1984).

Walcott's characteristic language is elegant, gracefully formal, and filled with the resourcefulness that comes only from a well-trained talent. Yet he has also tried, particularly in his plays, to capture the native rhythms, the diction, and the dialect variations of the speech of the islands he knows.

QUICK PLANNING GUIDE

Into the Poem

Author Biography p. 1161
Before You Read p. 1162
- **Reading Focus: Set a Purpose**
  Students reflect on how aid to developing countries can sometimes create more difficulties.
- **Quickwrite: Prior Knowledge**
  Write in Reader's Log on "the American dream"
- **Background:** The Virgin Islands

Through the Poem

"The Virgins" p. 1162
Making Meanings p. 1163

Beyond the Poem

Choices: Building Your Portfolio p. 1163
- **Writer's Notebook:** Investigate a community problem
- **Critical Writing:** Write a short essay about irony and words with double meanings in "The Virgins"
- **Creative Writing:** Write a lyric about Frederiksted from the point of view of a person who lives or works there
- **Panel Discussion:** Examine cultural ideals

PROGRAM MANAGER

- **Planning Instruction** See Teaching Notes, *Teaching Resources B,* pp. 187–188, for objectives, a summary, literary elements, and additional biographical information for this selection.
- **Instructional Support** Before beginning the instructional lesson, see Graphic Organizer for Active Reading, *Teaching Resources B,* p. 202, for a Through the Poem activity.
- **Assessment** See Selection Test, *Test Booklet,* p. 249.

PORTFOLIO ASSESSMENT

Portfolio Assessment
For help with teacher assessment of reading skills, see the *Portfolio Management System,* pp. 54–55.

Into the Poem

Using BEFORE YOU READ
p. 1162

Reading Focus
As students read, ask them to consider what was taken from Frederiksted.

Through the Poem

A. Critical Reading: Making Inferences

? In what ways are the streets dead? [Quiet; devoid of community life.] What has killed the city? [Possible answer: The city's own beauty has been its downfall because it brought tourists to visit.]

B. Cultural Connections
Have students discuss the commercialism described in the poem. Students will probably be able to describe familiar places that have lost some of their natural attraction in the effort to draw tourists.

C. Literary Element: Pun

? What are the possible meanings for the phrase "vigorous trade"? [Possible answers: The trade of tourism, as well as the trade winds of the island.]

BEFORE YOU READ
THE VIRGINS

Reading Focus
Give and Take
Helping developing countries, strengthening their economies, sending international aid: all these seem to be, and often are, positive acts. If poorer countries ask and richer countries give, isn't the result progress? Isn't this a cooperation of cultures, not a clash? That depends, Derek Walcott might say, on what is given—and on what is taken away.

Quickwrite
READER'S LOG
Throughout the developing world, many people yearn for the benefits of "the American dream." But just what is the American dream? And is achieving this "dream" always a sign of "progress"? Write your responses to these questions in your Reader's Log.

Background
"The Virgins," or Virgin Islands, form an island chain in the West Indies. The U.S. Virgin Islands, an American possession since 1917, have a republican government whose governor and other political leaders are elected by island residents. In this poem, Walcott describes Frederiksted, one of the old port cities on the U.S. Virgin Island of St. Croix (sānt kroi). Frederiksted is now a free port where tourists can purchase goods without paying custom duties. The economy of St. Croix, once based on sugar cane, is now dependent on tourism. As you read, keep in mind that *virgin* refers to the Virgin Islands, but that it can also mean "unspoiled or untouched," as in *virgin forest*.

Tourists at the Nassau Bazaar, the Bahamas.

The Virgins
Derek Walcott

A Down the dead streets of sun-stoned Frederiksted,
the first free port to die for tourism,
strolling at funeral pace, I am reminded
of life not lost to the American dream;
B 5 but my small-islander's simplicities
can't better our new empire's civilized
exchange of cameras, watches, perfumes, brandies
for the good life, so cheaply underpriced
that only the crime rate is on the rise
10 in streets blighted with sun, stone arches
and plazas blown dry by the hysteria
of rumor. A condominium drowns
in vacancy; its bargains are dusted,
but only a jeweled housefly drones
15 over the bargains. The roulettes spin
C rustily to the wind—the vigorous trade
that every morning would begin afresh
by revving up green water round the pierhead
heading for where the banks of silver thresh.

1162 THE TWENTIETH CENTURY

INTEGRATING THE LANGUAGE ARTS

Strategic Reading Walcott's poem indicates that tourists and island residents have a different experience of progress and change. To help students recognize this difference in perspective, have them apply information they have read about the Caribbean to complete a chart like the following. Ask them to determine what each group at the top of the chart would say about each issue on the side of the chart. Have students in groups of three share their charts and defend their responses.

	Tourists on Vacation	Residents of the Virgin Islands
Sandy beaches		
Cheap merchandise		
Crime		
Traditional island customs		
"The American dream"		

MAKING MEANINGS

First Thoughts

1. Did you find yourself sympathizing with or questioning the speaker's viewpoint? Explain.

Shaping Interpretations

2. What is the tourist reminded of, as he strolls the streets of Frederiksted?

3. How does Walcott **ironically** represent the "good life" of "the American dream"? How does his picture compare to your Reader's Log ideas?

4. How do you explain line 2? What other **images** in the poem suggest decay and emptiness?

5. What positive images suggest the island "simplicities" that once existed in Frederiksted?

6. Sum up what you think Walcott is saying about the changes he sees. Who or what is responsible for the changes? Are the changes for the better or for the worse?

Extending the Text

7. Have places within the United States fallen victim to "the American dream" in ways similar to what Walcott describes for Frederiksted? Explain your answer, and discuss your reactions.

Frederiksted, St. Croix, Virgin Islands.

CHOICES:
Building Your Portfolio

Writer's Notebook

1. Collecting Ideas for a Problem-Solution Essay

In his poem, Walcott explores what happens when outside forces impose change on a way of life. Your response to question 7 under Extending the Text could be the starting point for an investigation into the causes and effects of a similar problem in your community. Use the *5W-How?* questions (*Who? What? When? Where? Why? How?*) to find out what you already know about the problem. Save your notes for the Writer's Workshop on page 1179.

Critical Writing

2. Double Meanings

The scholar Laurence Perrine feels that Walcott's poems "are sharpened by his skillful use of irony and of words and phrases of double meanings." Support this statement in an essay, citing words and passages from the poem. Be sure to consider the title.

Creative Writing

3. My Own Islands

Imagine the other people who exist in this lyric's landscape, even if they are not mentioned: tourists, shopkeepers, fishers, and so on. Choose one, and write a lyric about Frederiksted in which he or she is the speaker.

Panel Discussion

4. What *Is* the American Dream?

Hold a panel discussion with some classmates about your own perceptions of "the American dream." What does each panel member see as ideal? What forces shape the dream you each hold? Do you feel pressure to conform to someone else's notion of what's ideal?

DEREK WALCOTT 1163

Making Meanings

First Thoughts

1. Students might sympathize with natives of Frederiksted because their lives changed so dramatically. Others might argue that St. Croix is a beautiful place.

Shaping Interpretations

2. He is reminded of the death of a way of life.

3. The "good life" is represented by crime. Reader's Log ideas will vary.

4. Paradoxically, the commercial exploitation that promises "the American dream," abundance for everyone, has brought spiritual death, as well as more crime, to the town. Images suggesting decay include "dead streets" and "plazas blown dry."

5. Positive images include the "vigorous trade" and "banks of silver."

6. Tourism has invited urban decay. From the narrator's perspective, the changes have been negative.

Extending the Text

7. **(Evaluation)** The old, industrial cities are the most obvious places that have come to ruin in the wake of the "American dream."

Beyond the Poem

Choices: Building Your Portfolio

1. **Writer's Notebook** Remind students to save their work. They may use it as prewriting for the Writer's Workshop on p. 1179.

2. **Critical Writing** Have students work in pairs to identify words with double meanings, identifying the words' literal, denotative meanings and their connotative meanings. For example, the poem's title is ironic because Christopher Columbus named the area for Saint Ursula and her eleven thousand maidens, who were women killed by invaders.

3. **Creative Writing** Provide students with periodicals that contain information about the culture of the Virgin Islands.

QUICK PLANNING GUIDE

Into the Story

Author Biography p. 1164
Before You Read p. 1164

- **Reading Focus: Prior Knowledge** Students consider ethnic diversity.
- **Quickwrite** Collect ideas about differences between generations
- **Background** Nigerian ethnic groups

Through the Story

"Marriage Is a Private Affair" pp. 1165–1168

Words to Own pp. 1165–1168

Connections: A Poem p. 1169 "Going Home"

Making Meanings p. 1170

Beyond the Story

Choices: Building Your Portfolio p. 1170

- **Writer's Notebook:** Analyze intergenerational problems
- **Critical Writing:** Write an essay interpreting the ending of the story
- **Creative Writing:** Write scenes to continue the story

PORTFOLIO ASSESSMENT

Portfolio Assessment For help with self-assessment of reading skills, see the *Portfolio Management System,* pp. 48–49.

Chinua Achebe.

Chinua Achebe

(1930–   )

Nigerian author Chinua Achebe (chin'wä' ä·chā'bā) planned to study medicine, but literature and his country's nationalist movement forever changed his plans. As a student, he came to realize the destructive effects of colonialism and dedicated himself to redefining Africa for Africans: telling its true story, including achievements and failures alike. In his words, the European idea that "Africa was the Primordial Void, was sheer humbug; . . . Africa had a history, a religion, a civilization."

His novels, beginning with the celebrated *Things Fall Apart* (1958), focus on the changes in Nigerian life that have occurred in the twentieth century. The novels trace life in Nigeria— sometimes presented as a fictionalized nation— from the arrival of early English missionaries, through years of colonial rule, to a post-independence era rife with corruption and political turmoil. Achebe believes that "Africa's meeting with Europe must be accounted a terrible disaster in this matter of human understanding and respect," and yet his African characters are not idealized. Like the colonists, the native Africans are portrayed as responsible for the problems that face their nation.

Achebe is himself an Ibo, born in the eastern Nigerian town of Ogidi, where his father, a Christian convert, taught at the mission school. He has chosen to write in English, which he began to learn at age eight, in order to reach a wider audience.

During Nigeria's civil war of the late 1960s, Achebe worked for the cause of the secessionist Biafrans. Since then he has concentrated on teaching, and on encouraging and publishing promising young authors. Through his many works of fiction, nonfiction, and poetry, he has been a catalyst for an entire younger generation of African writers.

BEFORE YOU READ
MARRIAGE IS A PRIVATE AFFAIR

Reading Focus

Coming Together
Like the United States, many nations are conglomerations of diverse peoples. And when people of diverse backgrounds come together, conflicts tend to arise. People may focus on differences in customs, religion, and ethnic heritage and fail to notice all the things they have in common. Yet, age-old distinctions often become less significant as people expand their horizons. They travel, they read, they watch, they listen. They go beyond "their kind."

Quickwrite

If your parents or guardians were to choose a perfect spouse for you, what kind of person would they choose? What qualities will *you* consider important in a partner? In your Reader's Log, jot down similarities and differences between your generation's attitudes and those of the generation before you.

Background

The African nation of Nigeria has more than 250 ethnic groups. These groups have different languages and frequently differ in religion, customs, and traditions. The Ibo and Ibibio both live in southeastern Nigeria but traditionally did not intermarry. In Achebe's story, a young Ibo man and an Ibibio woman have moved from their native regions to Lagos, a large and modern city in southwestern Nigeria.

PROGRAM MANAGER

- **Planning Instruction** See *Teaching Notes, Teaching Resources B,* p. 188, for objectives, a summary, and literary elements for this selection.
- **Instructional Support** Before beginning the instructional lesson, see *Graphic Organizer for Active Reading, Teaching Resources B,* p. 203, for a Through the Story activity.

- **Assessment** See *Selection Test, Test Booklet,* pp. 250–251.
- **Language Link** For instruction and practice in revision, see *Language Link, Teaching Resources B,* p. 204, and *Language and Writing Skills Worksheets,* pp. 180–182.
- **Reinforcement** Use the *Words to Own* worksheet in *Teaching Resources B,* p. 205.

Marriage Is a Private Affair

Chinua Achebe

"Have you written to your dad yet?" asked Nene[1] one afternoon as she sat with Nnaemeka[2] in her room at 16 Kasanga Street, Lagos.[3]

"No. I've been thinking about it. I think it's better to tell him when I get home on leave!"

"But why? Your leave is such a long way off yet—six whole weeks. He should be let into our happiness now."

Nnaemeka was silent for a while, and then began very slowly as if he groped for his words: "I wish I were sure it would be happiness to him."

"Of course it must," replied Nene, a little surprised. "Why shouldn't it?"

"You have lived in Lagos all your life, and you know very little about people in remote parts of the country."

"That's what you always say. But I don't believe anybody will be so unlike other people that they will be unhappy when their sons are engaged to marry."

"Yes. They are most unhappy if the engagement is not arranged by them. In our case it's worse—you are not even an Ibo."[4] ⒜

This was said so seriously and so bluntly that Nene could not find speech immediately. In the cosmopolitan atmosphere of the city it had always seemed to her something of a joke that a person's tribe could determine whom she married.

At last she said, "You don't really mean that he will object to your marrying me simply on that account? I had always thought you Ibos were kindly disposed to other people."

"So we are. But when it comes to marriage, well, it's not quite so simple. And this," he added, "is not peculiar to the Ibos. If your father were alive and lived in the heart of Ibibio-land[5] he would be exactly like my father." ⒝

1. **Nene** (nā′nā).
2. **Nnaemeka** ('n·nä·ā·mä′kə).
3. **Lagos** (lā′gōs′): former capital of Nigeria.
4. **Ibo** (ē′bō′): member of an African ethnic group living chiefly in southeastern Nigeria.
5. **Ibibio-land** (ib′ə·bē′o′land): area of southeastern Nigeria that is the traditional homeland of the Ibibio, another African ethnic group.

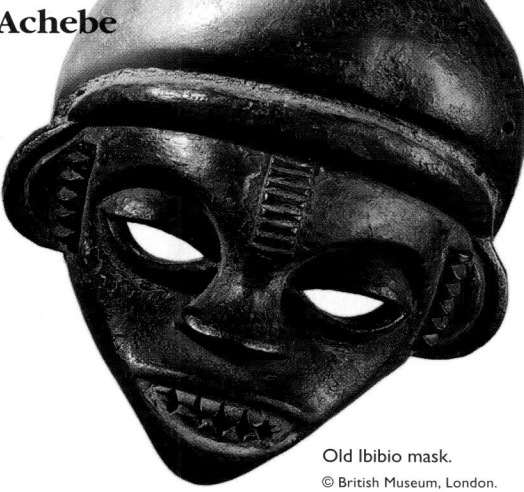

Old Ibibio mask.
© British Museum, London.

"I don't know. But anyway, as your father is so fond of you, I'm sure he will forgive you soon enough. Come on then, be a good boy and send him a nice lovely letter . . ."

"It would not be wise to break the news to him by writing. A letter will bring it upon him with a shock. I'm quite sure about that."

"All right, honey, suit yourself. You know your father."

As Nnaemeka walked home that evening he turned over in his mind different ways of overcoming his father's opposition, especially now that he had gone and found a girl for him. He had thought of showing his letter to Nene but decided on second thoughts not to, at least for the moment. He read it again when he got home and couldn't help smiling to himself. He remembered Ugoye[6] quite well, an Amazon[7] of a girl who used

6. **Ugoye** ($\overline{oo}$·gō′yä).
7. **Amazon:** tall, strong, aggressive woman. The term is taken from the name for the Amazons, a race of female warriors in Greek mythology.

WORDS TO OWN
cosmopolitan (käz′mə·päl′ə·tən) *adj.*: representative of many parts of the world; not constrained by provincial habits or prejudices.

CHINUA ACHEBE 1165

Into the Story

Using **BEFORE YOU READ**
p. 1164

Reading Focus
Before students begin reading the story, ask them to consider the following questions:
• How can geography or material conditions shape people's attitudes?
• What kinds of conflicts arise between people of diverse backgrounds and perspectives—for example, people of various ages? people from cities and rural areas?

Through the Story

A. Literary Element: Plot
The author offers little exposition before introducing the story's **conflict.** What difficulty is introduced? [Nnaemeka is engaged to a woman who is not of his tribe.]

B. Cultural Connections
Nigeria comprises many different ethnic groups, each with its own language, religion, and customs. Favored by the colonial power because of their acceptance of Christianity, the Ibo gained the reputation for being the nation's best-educated and most prosperous tribe. The Ibibio, the second-largest ethnic group in the east, were traditionally farmers.

OPTIONS FOR TEACHING

STRATEGIES FOR INCLUSION

Visual To illustrate the difference between urban and rural life in Africa, show students pictures of Nigerian villages and of the city of Lagos. Have them use the pictures to write a paragraph describing a journey, either from a village to Lagos or from Lagos to a village. Make sure they include the details they have seen in the pictures and the changes they would observe during the journey.

Interpersonal Pair students to use a Reciprocal Teaching strategy. Ask them to read a portion of the story. Then, have one student in each pair ask questions that the text raised. The second student answers as many questions as possible, and then the roles are reversed. ☞

WORDS TO OWN

The following vocabulary words are defined in the Words to Own at the bottom of the pupil's page.

cosmopolitan p. 1165	commiserate p. 1167
disconcertingly p. 1166	persevered p. 1168
vehemently p. 1166	

Wood mask. Ibo, Nigeria (37 cm).
© British Museum, London.

to beat up all the boys, himself included, on the way to the stream, a complete dunce at school.

I have found a girl who will suit you admirably—Ugoye Nweke,[8] the eldest daughter of our neighbor, Jacob Nweke. She has a proper Christian upbringing. When she stopped schooling some years ago her father (a man of sound judgment) sent her to live in the house of a pastor where she has received all the training a wife could need. Her Sunday school teacher has told me that she reads her Bible very fluently. I hope we shall begin negotiations when you come home in December.

On the second evening of his return from Lagos, Nnaemeka sat with his father under a cassia tree. This was the old man's retreat where he went to read his Bible when the parching December sun had set and a fresh, reviving wind blew on the leaves.

"Father," began Nnaemeka suddenly, "I have come to ask for forgiveness."

"Forgiveness? For what, my son?" he asked in amazement.

8. **Nweke** ('n·wā′kā).

"It's about this marriage question."

"Which marriage question?"

"I can't—we must—I mean it is impossible for me to marry Nweke's daughter."

"Impossible? Why?" asked his father.

"I don't love her."

"Nobody said you did. Why should you?" he asked.

"Marriage today is different . . ."

"Look here, my son," interrupted his father, "nothing is different. What one looks for in a wife are a good character and a Christian background."

Nnaemeka saw there was no hope along the present line of argument.

"Moreover," he said, "I am engaged to marry another girl who has all of Ugoye's good qualities, and who . . ."

His father did not believe his ears. "What did you say?" he asked slowly and <u>disconcertingly</u>.

"She is a good Christian," his son went on, "and a teacher in a girls' school in Lagos."

"Teacher, did you say? If you consider that a qualification for a good wife I should like to point out to you, Emeka, that no Christian woman should teach. St. Paul in his letter to the Corinthians[9] says that women should keep silence." He rose slowly from his seat and paced forward and backward. This was his pet subject, and he condemned <u>vehemently</u> those church leaders who encouraged women to teach in their schools. After he had spent his emotion on a long homily he at last came back to his son's engagement, in a seemingly milder tone.

"Whose daughter is she, anyway?"

"She is Nene Atang."

"What!" All the mildness was gone again. "Did you say Neneataga, what does that mean?"

"Nene Atang from Calabar.[10] She is the only girl I can marry." This was a very rash reply and Nnaemeka expected the storm to burst. But it did

9. **St. Paul . . . Corinthians:** reference to a passage in the Bible's New Testament (1 Corinthians 14:34).
10. **Calabar:** seaport city in southeastern Nigeria.

WORDS TO OWN

disconcertingly (dis′kən·surt′iŋ·lē) *adv.*: in a manner that embarrasses, confuses, or flusters.
vehemently (vē′ə·mənt·lē) *adv.*: passionately; strongly.

not. His father merely walked away into his room. This was most unexpected and perplexed Nnaemeka. His father's silence was infinitely more menacing than a flood of threatening speech. That night the old man did not eat.

When he sent for Nnaemeka a day later he applied all possible ways of dissuasion. But the young man's heart was hardened, and his father eventually gave him up as lost.

"I owe it to you, my son, as a duty to show you what is right and what is wrong. Whoever put this idea into your head might as well have cut your throat. It is Satan's work." He waved his son away.

"You will change your mind, Father, when you know Nene."

"I shall never see her," was the reply. From that night the father scarcely spoke to his son. He did not, however, cease hoping that he would realize how serious was the danger he was heading for. Day and night he put him in his prayers.

Nnaemeka, for his own part, was very deeply affected by his father's grief. But he kept hoping that it would pass away. If it had occurred to him that never in the history of his people had a man married a woman who spoke a different tongue, he might have been less optimistic. "It has never been heard," was the verdict of an old man speaking a few weeks later. In that short sentence he spoke for all of his people. This man had come with others to commiserate with Okeke[11] when news went round about his son's behavior. By that time the son had gone back to Lagos.

"It has never been heard," said the old man again with a sad shake of his head.

"What did Our Lord say?" asked another gentleman. "Sons shall rise against their Fathers; it is there in the Holy Book."

"It is the beginning of the end," said another.

The discussion thus tending to become theological, Madubogwu, a highly practical man, brought it down once more to the ordinary level.

"Have you thought of consulting a native doctor about your son?" he asked Nnaemeka's father.

"He isn't sick," was the reply.

"What is he then? The boy's mind is diseased and only a good herbalist can bring him back to his right senses. The medicine he requires is *Amalile*, the same that women apply with success

11. Okeke (ō·kā′kā).

to recapture their husbands' straying affection."

"Madubogwu is right," said another gentleman. "This thing calls for medicine."

"I shall not call in a native doctor." Nnaemeka's father was known to be obstinately ahead of his more superstitious neighbors in these matters. "I will not be another Mrs. Ochuba. If my son wants to kill himself let him do it with his own hands. It is not for me to help him."

"But it was her fault," said Madubogwu. "She ought to have gone to an honest herbalist. She was a clever woman, nevertheless."

"She was a wicked murderess," said Jonathan, who rarely argued with his neighbors because, he often said, they were incapable of reasoning. "The medicine was prepared for her husband, it was his name they called in its preparation, and I am sure it would have been perfectly beneficial to him. It was wicked to put it into the herbalist's food, and say you were only trying it out."

Six months later, Nnaemeka was showing his young wife a short letter from his father:

It amazes me that you could be so unfeeling as to send me your wedding picture. I would have sent it back. But on further thought I decided just to cut off your wife and send it back to you because I have nothing to do with her. How I wish that I had nothing to do with you either.

When Nene read through this letter and looked at the mutilated picture her eyes filled with tears, and she began to sob.

"Don't cry, my darling," said her husband. "He is essentially good-natured and will one day look more kindly on our marriage." But years passed and that one day did not come.

For eight years, Okeke would have nothing to do with his son, Nnaemeka. Only three times (when Nnaemeka asked to come home and spend his leave) did he write to him.

"I can't have you in my house," he replied on one occasion. "It can be of no interest to me

---

WORDS TO OWN
commiserate (kə·miz′ər·āt′) v.: to feel sorrow or pity for; sympathize.

CHINUA ACHEBE 1167

E. Cultural Connections
Misunderstandings between generations often are caused by individuals' different ideas about appropriate behavior. Ask students to describe situations from news reports or give fictional examples that illustrate conflicts that can arise between older and younger generations.

F. Critical Reading: Making Connections
? How do the reactions of the other tribesmen shed light on Okeke's refusal to acknowledge his son's engagement? [Possible answer: The comments of the other tribesmen show that Okeke's obstinacy is based on the serious beliefs of his tribe.]

G. Critical Reading: Making Inferences
? What does Jonathan's explanation reveal about this traditional medicine? [Unlike the other men, who imply that the herbalist prepared poison, Jonathan says that the medicine was fatal because it was not correctly administered. The medicine would work only for the person whose name was "called in its preparation."]

H. Reader's Response: First Thoughts
? For whom do you feel the most sympathy—Nnaemeka, Nene, or Okeke? Explain. [Sample responses: I sympathize with Nene's feelings of rejection. Or Okeke's respect for tradition conflicts with his love for his child.]

INTEGRATING THE LANGUAGE ARTS

Mechanics The author uses italics to indicate some of the correspondence in the text. Discuss with students other uses of italics: for emphasis; for foreign words not adopted into English; and for titles of books, plays, films, periodicals, and works of art.

Strategic Reading To encourage reading for meaning, ask students to write down predictions about what will happen in the story after they have read the title, the introductory material, and the first paragraph. Then, ask them to read two pages and to verify their former predictions or alter them to accommodate the new information. Have students continue this process until the story is finished.

Speaking and Listening Have students work in pairs to dramatize a conversation from the story. Encourage them to include nonverbal communication and to emphasize the importance of voice inflection in portraying emotion. Allow the pairs time for practice before they perform for the class.

A. Literary Element: Irony

? How does this passage indicate that the story's title is ironic? [Possible answer: Nnaemeka's marriage is hardly private—it is the subject of village gossip and is even discussed by Ibo acquaintances in Lagos.]

B. Critical Reading: Finding Details

Ask students to identify the new information revealed through correspondence. [Readers, like Okeke, learn from a letter that Nnaemeka and Nene have had two sons; a letter also has revealed the father's choice of a bride for his son, and a letter has confirmed the couple's wedding and shown the extent of Okeke's anger.]

C. Literary Element: Symbol

? What does the breaking storm marking the change of seasons symbolize? [Okeke's attitude has changed.]

D. Critical Reading: Drawing Conclusions

? Do you think Okeke will allow his grandchildren to visit? [He will probably let his grandchildren visit.]

Ikenga headdress. Wood and feathers (76.1 cm).
UCLA Fowler Museum of Cultural History, Los Angeles. Gift of Wellcome Trust.

where or how you spend your leave—or your life, for that matter."

A The prejudice against Nnaemeka's marriage was not confined to his little village. In Lagos, especially among his people who worked there, it showed itself in a different way. Their women, when they met at their village meeting, were not hostile to Nene. Rather, they paid her such excessive deference as to make her feel she was not one of them. But as time went on, Nene gradually broke through some of this prejudice and even began to make friends among them. Slowly and grudgingly they began to admit that she kept her home much better than most of them.

The story eventually got to the little village in the heart of the Ibo country that Nnaemeka and his young wife were a most happy couple. But his father was one of the few people in the village who knew nothing about this. He always displayed so much temper whenever his son's name

was mentioned that everyone avoided it in his presence. By a tremendous effort of will he had succeeded in pushing his son to the back of his mind. The strain had nearly killed him but he had persevered, and won.

Then one day he received a letter from Nene, and in spite of himself he began to glance through it perfunctorily until all of a sudden the expression on his face changed and he began to read more carefully.

B *. . . Our two sons, from the day they learnt that they have a grandfather, have insisted on being taken to him. I find it impossible to tell them that you will not see them. I implore you to allow Nnaemeka to bring them home for a short time during his leave next month. I shall remain here in Lagos . . .*

The old man at once felt the resolution he had built up over so many years falling in. He was telling himself that he must not give in. He tried to steel his heart against all emotional appeals. It was a reenactment of that other struggle. He leaned **C** against a window and looked out. The sky was overcast with heavy black clouds and a high wind began to blow, filling the air with dust and dry leaves. It was one of those rare occasions when even Nature takes a hand in a human fight. Very soon it began to rain, the first rain in the year. It came down in large sharp drops and was accompanied by the lightning and thunder which mark a change of season. Okeke was trying hard not to think of his two grandsons. But he knew he was now fighting a losing battle. He tried to hum a favorite hymn but the pattering of large raindrops on the roof broke up the tune. His mind immediately returned to the children. How could he shut his door against them? By a curious mental process he imagined them standing, sad and forsaken, under the harsh angry weather—shut out from his house.

D That night he hardly slept, from remorse—and a vague fear that he might die without making it up to them.

WORDS TO OWN

persevered (pʉr'sə·virdʹ) v.: continued in a course of action despite difficulty or opposition; persisted.

1168 THE TWENTIETH CENTURY

As you read the following poem by the poet Maurice Kenny (1929–   ), a member of the Mohawk people who now lives in Brooklyn, New York, think back to the conflict between the father and son in "Marriage Is a Private Affair." How will Nnaemeka's own sons in that story relate to their grandfather's cultural legacy?

Going Home

Maurice Kenny

The book lay unread in my lap
snow gathered at the window
from Brooklyn it was a long ride
the Greyhound followed the plow
5 from Syracuse to Watertown
to country cheese and maples
tired rivers and closed paper mills
home to gossipy aunts . . .
their dandelions and pregnant cats . . .
10 home to cedars and fields of boulders
cold graves under willow and pine
home from Brooklyn to the reservation
that was not home
to songs I could not sing
15 to dances I could not dance
from Brooklyn bars and ghetto rats
to steaming horses stomping frozen earth
barns and privies lost in blizzards
home to a Nation, Mohawk   Ⓐ
20 to faces I did not know
and hands which did not recognize me Ⓑ
to names and doors
my father shut

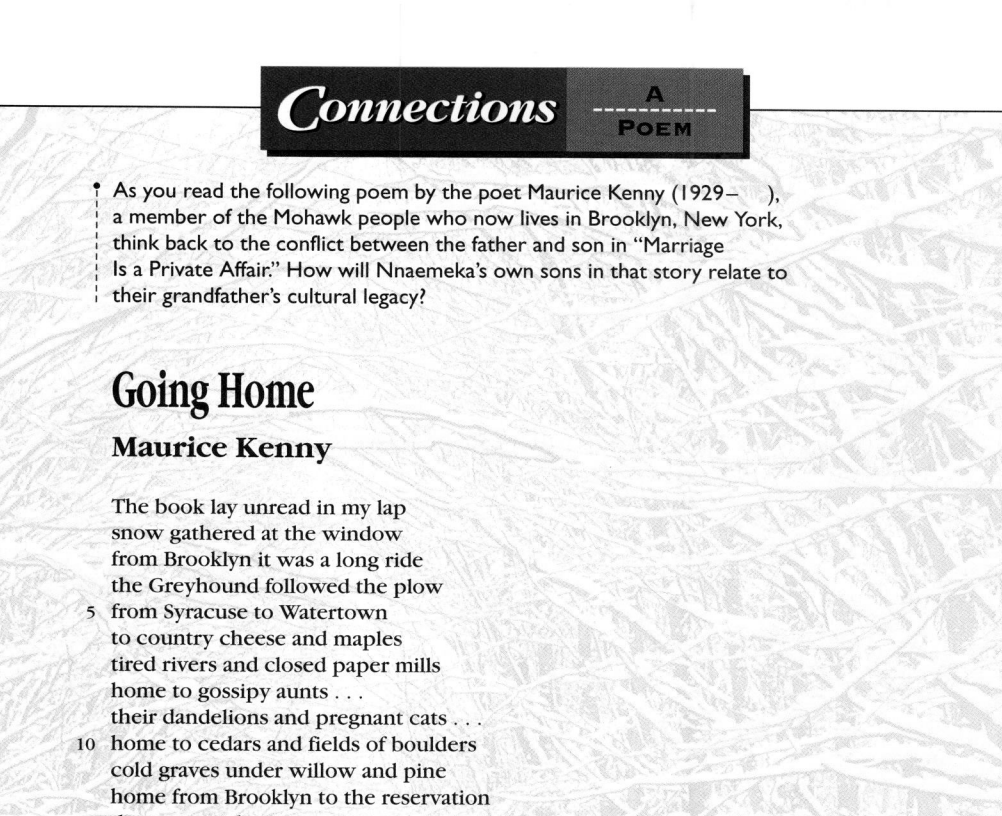

A. Expansion
Mohawks were once part of the Iroquois League, an organization of six nations. They inhabited what is now the eastern part of New York State. Mohawks supported the British during the American Revolution. After the British were defeated, many Mohawks moved to Canada, where their descendants now live on the Six Nations Indian Reserve near Brantford, Ontario. Other Mohawks live on the Saint Regis Reserve, located on the U.S.-Canadian border, and in the U.S. cities of New York, Buffalo, and Detroit.

B. Reader's Response: First Thoughts
? What similarities and differences do you see between "Going Home" and "Marriage Is a Private Affair"? [Sample responses: Both pieces contrast modern urban life with a more traditional culture. In "Going Home," however, the narrator feels shut out from a culture that is no longer his.]

PROFESSIONAL NOTES

Critical Comment: Achebe's Communication Share with students the observations of critic Margaret Laurence, who describes the theme of communication in Achebe's writing. "In Ibo villages, the men working on their farm plots in the midst of the rain forest often shout to one another—a reassurance, to make certain the other is still there . . . on the other side of the thick undergrowth. The writing of Chinua Achebe is like this. It seeks to send human voices through the thickets of our separateness."

ASSESSMENT TOOLS

Check Test: Short Answer
1. Why doesn't Nnaemeka want to write his father about his marriage plans? [His father will disapprove, so he wants to tell him in person.]
2. What characteristics does Okeke look for in a wife? [Good character and Christian background.]
3. How do the villagers react to the news of Nnaemeka's behavior? [They agree with Okeke in condemning his son's actions.]
4. What does Okeke do with his son's wedding picture? [He cuts off the portion with Nene's image.]
5. What request does Nene make of Okeke? [She asks that he allow his grandsons to visit.]

Making Meanings

First Thoughts

1. Most students will observe differences between generations. Some may say that the circumstances in the story make that example extreme.

Reviewing the Text

a. The wife is from a different tribe and speaks a different language.
b. Eight years pass. Okeke pushes thoughts of his son from his mind.
c. Nnaemeka does not feel bound by tradition, but his father does.
d. She asks him to see his grandsons.

Shaping Interpretations

2. In the Ibo tribe, marriage was not a "private affair" at all.
3. Conflicts occur between Nnaemeka and his father, Okeke and Nene, Okeke and his neighbors, and the people in the village and Nene. Some of the conflicts are resolved, but Okeke seems to grieve the loss of traditional customs.
4. Okeke is rigid. He is stubborn and ignores his son for eight years, and he is cruel to send back Nene's half of the wedding picture.
5. The herbalist was killed by Mrs. Ochuba, who gave him the medicine he prepared for her husband. The anecdote shows the difference between Nnaemeka's world and his father's. It also shows that Okeke chooses the traditions by which he lives.
6. It could symbolize Okeke's renewal.
7. The theme is cultural change and conflict.
8. The narrator's third person account reveals a perspective that makes it easier for the reader to sympathize with young people's desire for change rather than with Okeke's desire to preserve traditions. In "Going Home" the reader responds sympathetically to the first person speaker's feelings.

Extending the Text

9. **(Synthesis)** Students may observe that the story mirrors the debate in the United States about traditional values. The story shows that people are more accepting of new ideas when they can imagine how others are affected.

MAKING MEANINGS

First Thoughts

1. How would you compare the attitudes you described in your Reader's Log entry to the attitudes between generations in this story?

Shaping Interpretations

2. What is the **irony** of the story's title?
3. This story bursts with conflicts of people and ideas. What are at least two of these conflicts? Does the story resolve them? If so, how?
4. How would you describe Okeke's **character**? Use details from the story to support your answer.
5. What do you think happened to the herbalist, and why would Achebe include that anecdote?
6. What might the rain at the end of the story **symbolize**?
7. The story's subject is a marriage that occurs against a parent's wishes, but what is the story's **theme**?
8. Both Achebe's story and the poem "Going Home" (page 1169) are about generational and cultural conflict, but they differ in narrative **point of view.** From whose point of view is each told? How does the point of view shape your response to each work?

Extending the Text

9. You hear much talk today about "traditional values" and about the "multicultural society." What issues are involved, and how would you relate them to this story's plot and theme?

> **Reviewing the Text**
> a. What are Okeke's objections to his son's marriage and choice of wife?
> b. How much time passes from the marriage to the story's end? During that time, how does Okeke act toward his son?
> c. How are Nnaemeka and his father different?
> d. Why does Nene send a letter to Nnaemeka's father?

CHOICES: Building Your Portfolio

Writer's Notebook

1. Collecting Ideas for a Problem-Solution Essay

WORK IN PROGRESS

Personal problems such as Okeke's disapproval of his son's choice of a wife aren't suitable for a problem-solution essay, but their underlying causes—in this case, attitudes weighted by centuries of tradition—may be. Brainstorm to develop a list of intergenerational problems you're familiar with, and then work with a partner to analyze their underlying causes. Save your notes for the Writer's Workshop on page 1179.

Critical Writing

2. Final Analysis

In an essay, present and support your interpretation of what happens at the story's end. Be sure to examine the story's imagery. Also, explain why you did or did not like the ending.

Creative Writing

3. And Then What?

Working with a partner, continue the story. One of you, alone, will write a scene showing what Okeke does next; then the other will take up the action in a second scene. Be true to Achebe's characterizations, as you see them.

Old Ibibio mask.
© British Museum, London.

Choices: Building Your Portfolio

1. **Writer's Notebook** Remind students to save their work. They may use it as prewriting for the Writer's Workshop on p. 1179.

PORTFOLIO ASSESSMENT

Choices: Assessment Criteria
For help in evaluating these Choices assignments, see the criteria in the *Portfolio Management System,* p. 192.

Wole Soyinka
(1934–)

A voice of modern Africa, Wole Soyinka in 1986 became the first black African to win the Nobel Prize in literature. Soyinka's favorite African deity is Ogun, god of both war and creative fire—a fitting muse for a multitalented writer and performer whose plays, songs, novels, and poetry combine political activism, universal themes, and African traditions.

Born Akinwande Oluwole Soyinka in a village in western Nigeria, Soyinka was the son of the principal of a Christian school and a teacher. His parents both supported European-style education, but his father also retained strong ties to his heritage as a member of the Yoruba tribe. Soyinka grew up respecting both traditions; his 1981 autobiography *Aké: The Years of Childhood* tells of his later struggle with this duality.

After attending University College at Ibadan, Nigeria, Soyinka studied English literature in England at the University of Leeds. In London in the late 1950s, he wrote plays and poetry for theater and radio. During this period of African nationalism and pressure for independence, Soyinka's themes were racism, injustice, tyranny, and corruption, all treated with satiric wit. Also concerned with the collision of ancient traditions and modern realities, he peppered his plays with vivid Yoruba masquerade ritual.

Soyinka felt brutal despotism firsthand during Nigeria's civil war of the late 1960s, when he was imprisoned for two years for the "crime" of meeting with secessionist leaders such as the writer Chinua Achebe. He describes these experiences in *The Man Died: Prison Notes*, published in 1972. Since then he has continued to record and dramatize, with both passion and humor, the struggle and spirit of modern-day Africa and Africans.

BEFORE YOU READ
TELEPHONE CONVERSATION

Reading Focus

Subtle Discriminations
The following poem, written during Soyinka's college career in Britain in the late 1950s, records one of his own experiences with discrimination at a time when millions of people from former British colonies were arriving in England in search of economic and intellectual opportunity. As you read the poem, think about how Soyinka communicates this experience—is it presented as painful, or as humorously absurd? Is Soyinka's criticism straightforward or indirect?

Quickwrite

Think about the ways, both thoughtless and intentional, in which people practice discrimination. Then jot down some examples. How do those who are discriminated against make others mindful of what they've suffered?

Background

Soyinka's poem presents ideas primarily through a **dialogue** between two people. The setting is a red public telephone booth in London some years ago, when users pushed one button on the phone to speak and another to listen. The two characters are a well-educated black African speaker and a British woman who rents property. Soyinka's poem doesn't just tell about their exchange; it recreates it through the characters' own words.

WOLE SOYINKA 1171

QUICK PLANNING GUIDE

Into the Poem

Author Biography p. 1171
Before You Read p. 1171
- **Reading Focus: Set a Purpose** Students determine Soyinka's type of communication.
- **Quickwrite:** Write on prejudice and discrimination
- **Background:** Dialogue and setting

Through the Poem

"Telephone Conversation" p. 1172
Making Meanings p. 1173

Beyond the Poem

Choices: Building Your Portfolio p. 1173
- **Writer's Notebook:** Gather notes for a problem-solution essay
- **Critical Writing:** Write an essay on Soyinka's portrayal of the landlady
- **Law/Speaking:** Give an oral report about laws regulating housing

---

PROGRAM MANAGER

- **Planning Instruction** See Teaching Notes, *Teaching Resources B,* p. 189, for objectives, a summary, and literary elements for this selection.
- **Instructional Support** Before beginning the instructional lesson, see Graphic Organizer for Active Reading, *Teaching Resources B,* p. 206, for a Through the Poem activity.
- **Assessment** See Selection Test, *Test Booklet,* p. 252.

PORTFOLIO ASSESSMENT

Portfolio Assessment For help with self-assessment of reading skills, see the *Portfolio Management System,* p. 39.

Into the Poem

Using **BEFORE YOU READ**

p. 1171

Background

To help students think about the questions posed here, ask them how they feel as they read the poem. They may feel pained, embarrassed, uncomfortable, or perhaps amused as the speaker finds a way to hold his own in the degrading conversation.

Through the Poem

A. Reader's Response: Shaping Interpretations

? What is ironic about the speaker's use of the word *self-confession*? [Sample responses: He implies that a crime has been committed; his only "crime" is being an African.]

B. Language Note: Tone

Have students identify words that indicate the speaker's anger toward the landlady's question. [*Stench, rancid,* the repetition of *red, squelching,* and *shamed* are among words that show his initial anger. He satirically refers to her as "considerate."] Ask students to notice, as they continue reading, that despite his anger, the speaker responds with a playful, satiric tone.

C. Literary Element: Humor

? What is humorous about the words describing skin color? [Possible answer: All words refer to hair color.] Why does the speaker describe the varying shades of his body? [He is illustrating the absurdity of the landlady's prejudice.]

Telephone Conversation

Wole Soyinka

The price seemed reasonable, location
Indifferent. The landlady swore she lived
Off premises. Nothing remained
But self-confession. "Madam," I warned,
5 "I hate a wasted journey—I am African."
Silence. Silenced transmission of
Pressurized good-breeding. Voice, when it came,
Lipstick coated, long gold-rolled
Cigarette-holder pipped. Caught I was, foully.

10 "HOW DARK?" . . . I had not misheard . . . "ARE YOU LIGHT
OR VERY DARK?" Button B. Button A. Stench
Of rancid breath of public hide-and-speak.
Red booth. Red pillar-box.° Red double-tiered
Omnibus° squelching tar. It *was* real! Shamed
15 By ill-mannered silence, surrender
Pushed dumbfoundment to beg simplification.
Considerate she was, varying the emphasis—

"ARE YOU DARK? OR VERY LIGHT?" Revelation came.
"You mean—like plain or milk chocolate?"
20 Her assent was clinical, crushing in its light
Impersonality. Rapidly, wavelength adjusted,
I chose. "West African sepia"—and as an afterthought,
"Down in my passport." Silence for spectroscopic
Flight of fancy,° till truthfulness clanged her accent
25 Hard on the mouthpiece. "WHAT'S THAT?" conceding,
"DON'T KNOW WHAT THAT IS." "Like brunette."

"THAT'S DARK, ISN'T IT?" "Not altogether.
Facially, I am brunette, but madam, you should see
The rest of me. Palm of my hand, soles of my feet
30 Are a peroxide blonde. Friction, caused—
Foolishly, madam—by sitting down, has turned
My bottom raven black—One moment madam!"—sensing
Her receiver rearing on the thunderclap
About my ears—"Madam," I pleaded, "wouldn't you rather
35 See for yourself?"

13. **pillar-box:** chiefly British for "mailbox."
14. **double-tiered / omnibus:** bus with two decks, or tiers.

24. **spectroscopic** (spek′trō·skäp′ik) **. . . fancy:** wide range, or spectrum, of ideas.

OPTIONS FOR TEACHING

STRATEGIES FOR INCLUSION

Auditory Ask students to read the poem aloud. Have one student narrate and two students take on the dialogue. They may wish to practice to make the reading dramatic.

Special Needs Some students may feel confused and frustrated when they read this poem because it does not follow any particular pattern.

Have these students listen to an audiotape of the poem with headphones while highlighting the poem for specific information. Give each student a clear transparency sheet to place over the poem and two different-colored highlighters. Have them highlight what is actually being said in one color and note what is being implied in another color.

MAKING MEANINGS

First Thoughts

1. This poem dramatizes a battle. Who do you think finally wins, and why?

Shaping Interpretations

2. Paraphrase what happens in this poem, and then state what you feel is the poem's **theme.**
3. What does their dialogue reveal about these two **characters**?
4. This poem is full of colors—and not just of skin. What colors do you see in the poem? What does Soyinka want to communicate through these **images** of color?
5. What **irony** do you find in lines 23–26? What irony do you find in the description of the woman as well-bred?
6. What do you think of the speaker's final question?

Connecting with the Text

7. Since the speaker was prepared for prejudice, why do you think the woman's question disturbs him so much?
8. If you faced this kind of discrimination, how would you react to it?

Challenging the Text

9. Review the notes you made in your Reader's Log, and then think about whether Soyinka's poem is an effective way of making others aware of prejudice. Is it more, or less, effective than other ways? How so? Explain.

Nigerian bronze head, thought to be an Ife king (13th century).
British Museum, London.

Writer's Notebook

1. Collecting Ideas for a Problem-Solution Essay

Newcomers to this country who encounter incidents of racial prejudice like the one Soyinka relates in "Telephone Conversation" may not realize that such discrimination is illegal. What solutions could you pose for this problem? Working with a small group, discuss ways your class could work with existing community groups to educate newcomers about their housing rights. Save your notes for the Writer's Workshop on page 1179.

Critical Writing

2. An Unpleasant Character

What kind of person is the landlady in Soyinka's poem? In an essay, describe the character of Soyinka's landlady. What do you learn from the speaker's assumptions, judgments, and tone, and from the woman's own words?

Law / Speaking

3. Home Sweet Home

Should laws restrict where a person can live? What about zoning laws that prohibit trailers in suburban neighborhoods? or laws that ban group homes in single-family developments? Research such laws in your community, and present an oral report, opening the issue for debate with your classmates.

WOLE SOYINKA 1173

6. Students may find the speaker's final question to be both serious and insulting. He would like to be judged for the person he is and not the color of his skin, but underneath his polite, articulate tone, he has merely rephrased insulting, vulgar slang.

Connecting with the Text

7. The speaker is prepared for her prejudice, but he is unprepared for the blunt way she displays it.
8. Some students may say they would hang up on the landlady. Others may say they could handle the situation as calmly as the speaker does.

Challenging the Text

9. (Evaluation) Students may say that Soyinka's poem raises people's awareness of prejudice. Others may suggest that protests, such as the marches of Martin Luther King, Jr., are more effective.

Choices: Building Your Portfolio

1. **Writer's Notebook** Remind students to save their work. They may use it as prewriting for the Writer's Workshop on p. 1179.

PORTFOLIO ASSESSMENT

Choices: Assessment Criteria For help in evaluating these Choices assignments, see the criteria in the *Portfolio Management System,* p. 193.

Making Meanings

First Thoughts

1. Students may say that the narrator wins because he defends himself against injustice or that the landlady wins because she does not rent to him.

Shaping Interpretations

2. A black man calls a white woman to ask about leasing a residence and announces that he is African. She asks how black he is, and he answers her in a humorous, satiric manner that contains some real anger. The theme is the absurdity of racial prejudice—the landlady did not object to him until he told her his color.
3. The speaker is a person of conviction, unafraid to confront the racism expressed by the other character, who is petty and ignorant.
4. Soyinka uses images of color to communicate his anger ("red"), the landlady's phoniness ("gold-rolled cigarette-holder"), the African man's sophistication and the landlady's ignorance ("West African sepia").
5. The landlady's confession of ignorance contrasts ironically with the narrator's confession that he is African.

Portfolio Assessment Options

The following projects can help you evaluate and assess your students' reading accomplishments outside of class. Videotapes or photographs of completed projects, or the projects themselves, may be included in student's portfolios.

- **Capture an Image** Invite students to create an artistic representation of the relevance of their books to some aspect of one or more of the works they have read in this unit. Students may work individually or cooperatively. Encourage the use of a variety of media, including watercolor, collage, photography, and clay sculpture. If students wish, have them work with you to set up a "gallery" area in class for the display of the artwork.
- **Create Companion Copy** Invite pairs or groups of students who chose the same selection to write a companion piece for it—for example, a short story that serves as a prequel or sequel, or a cycle of poems that captures the thoughts of one or more characters. Have them choose their own format for sharing their work with peers.
- **Teach a Class** Ask students individually or in a group to prepare a lesson on the book they have read. They may choose some excerpts for their classmates to read and to discuss. They may give a brief lecture or prepare an experiential exercise that demonstrates the themes of the books. Because students may not be able to use an entire class period, consider allowing half a class period for each presentation.
- **Write to the Author** Students often have strong opinions about a book after reading it. Tell students that they can express their opinions about a novel by writing letters to the author. Remind students that they may address plot issues or elements of the story; they may also ask the author questions about the novel.

READ ON

A Plea for Peace

Vera Brittain, born in England in 1893, grew up in an age of rich materialism and romantic idealism. But World War I suddenly and violently ended this time of comfortable isolation. After losing her fiancé and brother and serving as a volunteer nurse in France, she realized that "The world was mad and we were all victims." In her autobiography, *Testament of Youth* (Penguin), she explores how the war affected her and her generation and writes of her subsequent work for world peace.

In Black and White

Kaffir Boy (Macmillan) was one of the first accounts of growing up black in twentieth-century South Africa. When Mark Mathabane (mä·tä′bä·nä) published this autobiography in America in 1986, it became an international best-seller but was banned in his own country. Mathabane's exploration of South Africa's apartheid system, which just recently collapsed, shows the damage that ignorance of and contempt for other cultures can cause.

A Prophetic Voice

Brave New World (HarperCollins) was first published in 1932, but Aldous Huxley's satirical fantasy of the future has remained surprisingly contemporary. In the world-state portrayed in the novel, a scientific caste system determines social stability, and individual freedom is forbidden. But Bernard Marx, a character whose social conditioning had gone wrong, disturbs all this.

An Angry Young Man

Alan Sillitoe was one of a group of young writers who emerged in the 1950s and 1960s and who were dubbed Angry Young Men. Their main themes were rebellion and isolation; they confronted society's mores and institutions head on. Sillitoe's long short story *The Loneliness of the Long Distance Runner* (Penguin), about a young man in reform school, is among the best of the genre. (Director Tony Richardson's film of the story, available on videotape, was one of the key British films of the 1960s.)

Peaceful Protest

Mohandas K. Gandhi (1869–1948), also called Mahatma Gandhi, was a leader of the Indian nationalist movement against British rule. His doctrine of nonviolent protest allowed people to settle political and cultural conflicts peacefully. The epic movie *Gandhi* (1982), a sweeping account of his life and times, is storytelling at its best. Available on videotape, the film is directed by Richard Attenborough and features Ben Kingsley, Candice Bergen, John Gielgud, and Martin Sheen.

FOR FURTHER EXPLORATION

Fiction
To the Lighthouse by Virginia Woolf
The Sea, The Sea by Iris Murdoch
Cal by Bernard MacLaverty
The Autobiography of My Mother by Jamaica Kincaid

Drama
Waiting for Godot by Samuel Beckett
The Caretaker by Harold Pinter
Rosencrantz and Gildenstern are Dead by Tom Stoppard

Poetry
At the British War Cemetery, Bayeux by Charles Causley
Omeros by Derek Walcott

Nonfiction
The Guns of August by Barbara Tuchman

Films
Gallipoli
Howards End
Cry, the Beloved Country

The English Language

English Today and Tomorrow
by John Algeo

In the twentieth century, English has spread all over the world. It has developed from a language spoken by a few wandering tribes to a world language used for more purposes than any other human tongue. Because its uses have continued to grow, it has continued to change. We can see change going on in English right now—especially in its vocabulary.

Tracking New Words: Where They Come From

We are constantly in need of new words—to talk about new things or to talk about old things in new ways. We borrow new words from other languages, or we make them up by combining, shortening, blending, or shifting the use of old words.

Some words echo not other words but the sounds of things in the world around us. For example, the word *vroom* began as an imitation of how a car or motorcycle engine sounds when it is being raced. Then it was used as a verb referring to how a vehicle operates at very high speed: "The car vroomed around the corner and disappeared."

Sacking Other Languages for Words: Loanwords

French is the modern language from which we have borrowed most. French loanwords include *chief, choice, honor, machine, menu, picnic, police, prairie, restaurant, soup,* and a great many other familiar words, as well as more obvious loans such as *chauffeur, crepe, etiquette, rapport,* and *souvenir.* From Spanish we have taken *canyon, lasso, patio, ranch, rodeo,* and, more recently, *macho;* from Portuguese, *flamingo, molasses, pagoda,* and others. From Italian we get musical terms including *duet, soprano,* and *trombone,* and a variety of other words, such as *balloon, bandit, carnival, studio, umbrella,* and *volcano.*

Dutch has given us sailing terms such as *deck, dock,* and *yacht,* as well as *boss, dollar, knapsack, pickle, Santa Claus,* and *skate.* From German we have borrowed *frankfurter, hamburger, kindergarten, nickel,* and *pretzel.*

From more distant languages we have borrowed *banjo* (African, probably Bantu), *boomerang* (native Australian),

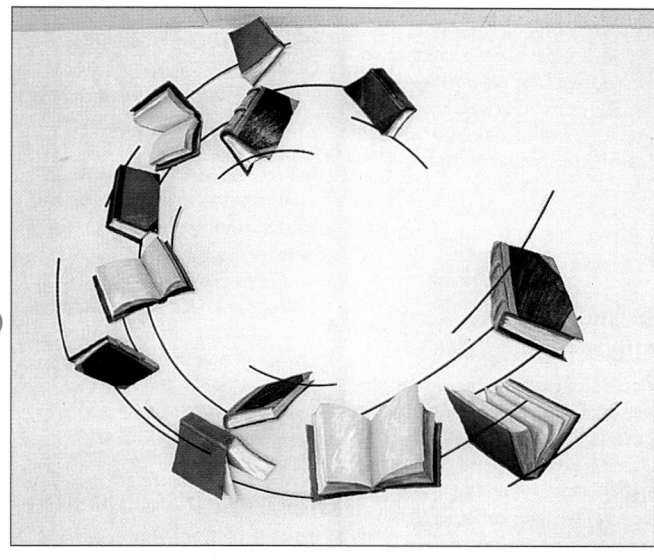

Incident in the Library (1983) by Julian Opie.
Oil paint on steel, wall installation (10 ft × 10 ft).
Photo courtesy Hal Bromm Gallery, New York.

THE ENGLISH LANGUAGE 1175

A. Expansion
English is spoken widely on six continents and is even the official language in several sub-Saharan African countries. Part of the reason for its success is its flexibility in function, composition, and syntax, but the same elements also make it a language that is easy to speak poorly.

B. Expansion
Another example is the word *plop.* Although *plop* imitates the sound of something dropping into water, it also can be used informally as a verb to describe falling heavily, as in "After school, I plopped down for a nap."

C. Exploring the Historical Period
One result of the Norman victory over the English at the Battle of Hastings in 1066 was that many French words entered the English language, since important positions in the country became occupied by French-speakers. For example, French words were used (and borrowed) in the areas of government *(royal, regal)* and law *(attorney, perjury).* These words are a vital part of English today.

PROGRAM MANAGER

- **Planning Instruction** See *Teaching Notes, Teaching Resources B,* p. 189, for objectives for this feature.
- **Assessment** See *The English Language, Test Booklet,* pp. 253–254.

Elements of Literature:
Videodisc Use the following bar codes to locate the video segment about the English language since the Renaissance. For more information, see the Videodisc *Teacher's Manual.*

Videodisc Side A

Begin Play, English Track

Begin Play, Spanish Track

A. Expansion

Common prefixes are *anti–,* meaning "against"; *pro–,* meaning "for"; *micro–,* meaning "small"; *macro–,* meaning "large"; *inter–,* meaning "between"; and *intra–,* meaning "within."

B. Expansion

? Where are acronyms most often used, and why? [Students will probably say that acronyms are most often used in large institutions, such as government bureaus or military organizations, for ease of communication or in specialized professions, which contain a great deal of jargon.]

---

ketchup (Malay), *coffee* (Turkish, from Arabic), *mammoth* (Russian), *pal* (Romany), *pecan* (various Algonquian dialects), *shawl* (Persian), *shampoo* (Hindi), *soy* (Japanese), *tattoo* (Tahitian), *tea* (Chinese), *tom-tom* (Hindi), and *ukulele* (Hawaiian).

English is much richer for all these words we have borrowed from other languages.

Stacking Words Together: Compounds

We often make new words by joining existing words into a *compound.* A compound may mean something different from the literal sense of its parts. Thus, a *blackboard* is not necessarily black; it is often green instead.

Compounds have always been a favorite type of word formation in English. In Modern English, we have some words that were originally compounds but whose parts have merged so completely that we no longer recognize their origins. For example, *nostril* comes from an Old English compound, *nosu-thyrel* (literally, "nose-hole"), and *sheriff* comes from the Old English *scirgerefa* (literally, "shire-reeve" or "county official").

Tacking Parts On: Affixed Forms

A Instead of combining two whole words to make a new one, we can add a word element (an *affix*) to the front of a word (as a *prefix*) or to the end of a word (as a *suffix*). The suffix *–ist* forms nouns meaning a person who believes in something or who has a particular profession. A *royalist*

follows royalty, a *lobbyist* lobbies, and a *flat-earthist* believes that the earth is really flat as a pancake, despite what astronomers and geologists may say.

Some suffixes were originally independent words that dwindled into mere affixes. For instance, the suffix *–ful* is a dwindling of the word *full,* to which it is still close, though not the same, in meaning. A "handful of pennies" is not the same as a "hand full of pennies." The first is an indefinite number of coins, and the second is a hand with coins in it.

There are fewer prefixes than suffixes in English, but two common ones are *pre–* , meaning "before," and *post–* , meaning "after." We use them in combinations like *pregame* and *postgame* or *preteen* and *postteen.*

Hacking Parts Off: Shortenings and Back-Formations

We can also make new words by removing part of a word to

shorten it. This process is quite common, probably because we don't like to use more energy than we have to in saying long words if short ones will do. *Gymnasium* is shortened to *gym; telephone* becomes *phone.*

Some shortenings are more complicated. The label *hazardous material* indicates that a container has dangerous chemicals or radioactive matter inside it. But the label is too long—a warning ought to be short and snappy. So both words in the expression are clipped, to produce *HAZMAT,* a short, easy to say, and (provided you know what it means) clear expression. When a phrase is shortened to the first parts of each of its words, **B** the result is an *acronym* (from two Greek forms meaning "tipname," that is, a name formed from the tips of other words).

The most extreme kind of acronym includes only the first letter of each original word. The pronunciation may be the individual letter names, like *CB*

Q3 (1994) by Mark Wallinger. Acrylic on canvas (218.5 cm × 218.5 cm).

Private Collection. © The Artist, Courtesy Anthony Reynolds Gallery, London.

STRATEGIES FOR INCLUSION

Auditory Read aloud the essay with students, and encourage them to add their own examples of ways new words are formed. Pause after each section to have volunteers share their examples with the class.

INTEGRATING THE LANGUAGE ARTS

Strategic Reading As students read the article, have them take notes on the main ideas and details presented in each of the sections. Students may begin by noting the topic of the essay and then listing under the topic the various points made by the author and the support given for them. After they are through reading, students should draw conclusions from their notes based on their analyses of the article's main ideas and details. Have students use a graphic organizer such as Transparency 11: Analysis Chart in the Transparency Package.

(citizens' band) or *RV* (recreational vehicle), or said together as a normal word, like *ZIP Code* (zone improvement plan).

A special kind of shortening occurs when an affix is taken off. Typewriters are more than a hundred years old now. When they first came into use, the word *typewriter* meant either the machine or the person who operated it. Then someone decided that a typewriter is for typewriting, and so the verb *to typewrite* was formed by taking off the suffix –*er*. Such words are called *back-formations* because they are formed backward to the usual way of adding affixes.

A similar example is *to burgle,* which is what a burglar does. A difference between *burgle* and *typewrite,* however, is that while *typewrite* was shortened from *typewriter* very quickly (within twelve years after the longer word was introduced to English), *burgle* took a lot of time, more than three hundred years, to work its way out of *burglar.* And some people still don't like it.

Packing Words Together: Blends

A *blend* is a word that is made by combining two or more words while omitting part of at least one of them. Familiar examples are *brunch* (*breakfast* plus *lunch*) and *smog* (*smoke* plus *fog*). In Lewis Carroll's *Through the Looking-Glass,* Humpty Dumpty called such terms *portmanteau words.* A portmanteau is a suitcase with two sides that are folded together to make a single case. Humpty Dumpty said that in a portmanteau word, "There are two meanings packed up into one word."

An example of a technical blend is *shuttle craft,* from *space shuttle* plus *spacecraft.* A feminist example is *herstory* (meaning "history of women," or "history told from a woman's point of view"), from *her* plus *history.*

A special kind of blending is *folk etymology.* We sometimes take an unfamiliar word, especially a word borrowed from another language, and change its form by associating it with familiar English words. For example, we borrowed the Dutch word *koolsla* (which means "cabbage salad") as *coleslaw;* but then some people associated the first part of the word with the English word *cold* and came up with *cold slaw,* which makes sense because slaw is generally served cold.

Ramen Four Five Six (20th century) by Gregory B. Larson.
Private Collection.

Racking Up New Meanings: Shifted Words

Perhaps the most frequent way to make a new word is to use an old word in a new way. Today, *censure* means "to judge unfavorably" or "to condemn"; in Shakespeare's day, it meant simply "to judge or form an opinion." Shifts of meaning are going on all the time. *Bulletin board* can now be used for a computer service that provides information, instead of just for a board on which notices are posted.

A different kind of shift occurs when a word changes its part of speech. For example, we use the noun *hand* as a verb in "Hand me that book, please," the verb *sing* as a noun in "We are having a community sing," the adjective *tough* as a noun in "the young toughs," the noun *fun* as an adjective in "a really fun evening," the adverb *up* as a verb in "They upped the price," and so on. Such functional shift is an easy and common way of making new words in Modern English.

Tomorrow's English

English is changing today even as we use it. Indeed, it is changing *because* we use it. Each change, however small, makes the language somewhat different from the English of yesterday. As the changes accumulate, little by little, day by day, they eventually make the language very different from what it was. But that is nothing to fear. Languages grow, as they must to live. By the way we speak English today and by the changes we introduce into

C. Expansion

? Can you "decipher" these blends: *twirl, bash, flare, smash, glimmer,* and *clash?* [*Twist* and *whirl; bat* and *mash; flame* and *glare; smack* and *mash; gleam* and *shimmer; clap* and *crash.*]

D. Expansion

This type of shift is exemplified by the word *outfit.* The word can be a noun, as in "I wore a new outfit today." The word also can be used as a verb, as in "We have to outfit the entire team with uniforms."

E. Exploring the Culture

Nevertheless, many people are still afraid; fears over the future of English are expressed frequently in newspapers and on TV talk shows. In 1978, the British House of Lords held a special debate on the subject of the deterioration of the English language.

Try It Out: Answers

1. blizzard—suggests a stormy blast or bluster; escalate—from a French trademark, Escalator; gas—from the Greek for "chaos"; hiccup—an imitation of the sound; jeep—from an abbreviation of "general purpose"; kitty-cornered—from "catercorner," for "four corners"; lengthwise—"length" plus "wise," meaning "in the direction of"; motel—a blend of "motor" and "hotel"; pep—short for "pepper"; scarecrow—from its use, to scare crows.

2. bonfire—"fire of bones"; business—"being busy"; cupboard—"a board where cups are kept"; disease—"being uncomfortable, not at ease"; doff—"to do off."

3. Check students' work for completion.

4. Have students clearly mark the sources for their words.

---

it, we are creating the English of tomorrow.

Over the years, English speakers have written some of the greatest literature known to humanity, literature that is read all over the world by people of diverse cultures. In the future, English will doubtless continue to be a medium for the expression of our common anxieties, fears, hopes, aspirations, and exaltations.

The English language, like English literature, is something we can take pride in. This language and this literature do not belong to one nation or to one people only, but are shared by many. English belongs to all those all over the world who speak and write it, who read its literature, and who treasure it. They are its tomorrow.

> English belongs to all those all over the world who speak and write it, who read its literature, and who treasure it. They are its tomorrow.

Try It Out

1. The following words illustrate various ways in which words are made. Look them up in a dictionary that gives etymologies, and describe their origins.

   blizzard   kitty-cornered
   escalate   lengthwise
   gas   motel
   hiccup   pep
   jeep   scarecrow

2. Words change their meanings over time, but some words keep evidence of their earlier meanings. Try to guess from their forms the earlier meanings of the following words.

Then, look up their etymologies to see whether your guesses are correct.

   bonfire   cupboard   doff
   business   disease

3. Look in a recent newspaper or magazine for words you do not recognize—words that are completely new to you. Find at least five such words, and on a sheet of paper, copy the sentences in which the words are used. Underline the unfamiliar words. Then, look up the words in a college or unabridged dictionary. If you find them, read their etymologies to find out where they come from. If you do not find them, do you think they may be new words or old but rare words?

4. Several dictionaries and periodicals list new words. Try to locate one of the following collections of new words in a library.

   • *The Second Barnhart Dictionary of New English,* ed. Clarence L. Barnhart, Sol Steinmetz, and Robert K. Barnhart

   • *12,000 Words: A Supplement to Webster's Third New International Dictionary*

   • "Among the New Words" (a regular article in the magazine *American Speech*)

   • *The Barnhart Dictionary Companion* (a periodical that lists new words)

   Make a list of five new words from any of these sources, and tell what each new word means.

A Conversation (1913–1916) by Vanessa Bell.

Courtauld Institute Galleries, London.

ASSESSMENT TOOLS

Check Test: Questions and Answers

1. How are new English words created? [Words may be borrowed from other languages, or existing English words may be combined, shortened, blended, or shifted.]

2. From which modern language has English borrowed the most? [French.]

3. What is the difference between a suffix and a prefix? [A prefix is added to the front of a word, a suffix to the end of a word.]

4. What is an acronym? [A new word produced by combining the first letter of each word of a phrase.]

5. Does the author view change in language as good or bad? [The author says change in a language is good because it helps the language keep pace with change in society.]

Writer's Workshop

PERSUASIVE WRITING

PROBLEM-SOLUTION ESSAY

Reading the selections in Collections 14 and 15 has shown you how twentieth-century writers use both fiction and nonfiction to explore social problems. By now, you've peered into the lives of an alienated bureaucrat, of children shunned by their peers, and of families and compatriots locked in conflict. Although many of these selections only hint at solutions, the clear-eyed portrayal of human problems, combined with the search for practical answers, is a necessary form of writing. Problem-solution essays, or proposals that call for definite action, are written every day—by scientists investigating solar energy, by citizens concerned about crime, by newspaper columnists proposing changes in the economy, and by politicians seeking office. In this Writer's Workshop, you'll write your own problem-solution essay, carefully analyzing a problem and proposing one or more specific solutions to it.

Prewriting

1. **Checking your Writer's Notebook.** By doing the Writer's Notebook activities throughout Collections 14 and 15, you may have already done some of the prewriting necessary for a problem-solution essay. Look back at your entries, and decide if you'd like to develop any of the ideas or problems you find there. Then proceed with the prewriting steps that follow.

2. **Identifying suitable problems.** Since you'll be presenting your findings to an audience, steer clear of strictly personal problems such as family squabbles or romantic entanglements. Instead, consider problems that significantly affect a number of people. For example, a family dispute over your plans to attend an unsupervised graduation party is too personal for a problem-solution essay. But the lack of an alternative to such private parties in your community would affect many seniors and their families. Another approach is to focus on the local aspects of a national or international problem. Instead of tackling "homelessness in the United States," for example, you might investigate the causes and effects of the local homeless shelter's policy of turning people back out onto the streets each morning.

   To identify suitable problems, try freewriting about problems you've noticed in your school, neighborhood, or city. You can also find ideas by reading newspaper and magazine articles, listening to radio and TV news and talk shows, and attending public meetings.

3. **Investigating a problem.** Once you start exploring the problem you've chosen, you may find that you need more information to understand it

Technology HELP

See Writer's Workshop 2 CD-ROM. *Assignment: Controversial Issue.*

ASSIGNMENT

Write an essay that explores a problem and proposes one or more solutions to it.

AIM

To persuade; to explore; and to explain.

AUDIENCE

People who share (or can be led to share) your interest in solving the problem.

QUICK PLANNING GUIDE

WW

Problem-Solution Essay

Prewriting
Checking your Writer's Notebook p. 1179
Identifying suitable problems p. 1179
Investigating a problem p. 1179
Exploring possible solutions p. 1180
Model p. 1181
Evaluating alternative solutions p. 1181
Model p. 1182
Steps to success p. 1182
Analyzing your audience, setting your tone p. 1183
Providing support p. 1183

Drafting
The introduction: engage them p. 1184
The body: enlighten them p. 1184
The conclusion: energize them p. 1184

Evaluating and Revising
Peer review p. 1185
Self-evaluation p. 1185

Proofreading and Publishing p. 1185

Reflecting on Your Writing p. 1185

PORTFOLIO ASSESSMENT

- **Generating Ideas** To help students in prewriting, use the heuristic in the *Portfolio Management System,* p. 194.
- **Assessment Rubric** For a rubric that can be used to assess students' progress in writing, see the *Portfolio Management System,* p. 196.

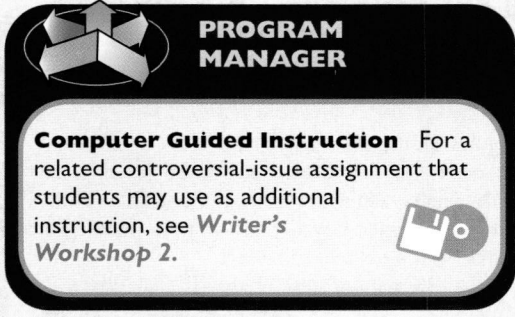

PROGRAM MANAGER

Computer Guided Instruction For a related controversial-issue assignment that students may use as additional instruction, see *Writer's Workshop 2.*

Motivation

Bring to class local newspapers that contain editorials and letters to the editor. Ask students to browse through the papers and to locate editorials or letters that describe problems and offer solutions. Have volunteers read aloud for the class these editorials or letters.

Teaching the Lesson

Remind students that audience analysis is crucial for an effective problem-solution essay because the audience determines the essay's message and approach. Be sure students understand the purpose of the writing they will be doing. Point out that problem-solution writing is common and that they might find this kind of writing useful throughout their lives. Point out, too, that not all solutions are equally good and that part of what they will learn in this Writer's Workshop is to evaluate possible solutions. This lesson includes instructions for each stage of the writing process. You may want to guide students by modeling each stage with your own writing.

Try It Out: Possible Answers

1. Social service agencies that deal with families, real estate agents, homeless people, mortgage bankers.
2. People who fish in the lake, people who live near the lake, Environmental Protection Agency officials, people who use the lake for boating or other recreational activities, scientific reports on conditions of the lake.
3. School custodians, school administrators, teachers, students.
4. Local employment agencies, people who are out of work, local help-wanted ads.

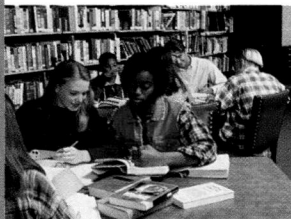

Try It Out

For each of the following problems, suggest at least three potential sources of information.
1. a lack of affordable housing in a community
2. pollution in a local lake
3. vandalism at a school
4. a town's lack of employment opportunities

fully. First, though, determine precisely what you *do* know about it by brainstorming or clustering or by asking yourself the *5W-How?* questions (*Who? What? When? Where? Why?* and *How?*). Then move outward, using a variety of sources to gather information: Read, listen, observe, and question others to discover their views. For example, if you're exploring the problem of flooding in your neighborhood, you might begin by jotting down an account of your own experiences and then read newspaper articles on the causes and effects of the problem. You might also interview your neighbors and local officials, such as the county's director of stormwater engineering.

Strategies for Elaboration: Scrutinizing Your Subject

Looking at a problem from different points of view can help you understand it more fully. Try using these questions to analyze the problem you're investigating.
- What is the problem? How widespread is it?
- What is the history of the problem? What caused the problem? What effects has the problem had, and on whom?
- How is the problem like other problems? How is it different from them? What are the major parts of the problem?
- How serious is the problem? Why?

4. **Exploring possible solutions.** Now your focus shifts from the problem to ways to solve it. To avoid duplicating other people's efforts, begin by finding out as much as you can about past and current attempts to solve the problem. Then use freewriting, brainstorming, or clustering to devise your own creative solution(s).

Strategies for Elaboration: Reflecting on Solutions

Use these questions to explore other people's solutions and then your own ideas for solving the problem.

Other People's Ideas
- What solutions have already been tried?
- How well have those solutions worked?
- Why haven't they worked better?
- What solutions are now being considered?

Your Ideas
- Could some of the problem's causes be eliminated? If so, how?
- What could be done to ease or eliminate the effects of the problem?
- Does one part of the problem seem especially difficult to solve? Why?
- Which part of the problem seems easiest to solve? Why?
- What is the most promising solution (or part of the solution) you can think of?

OPTIONS FOR TEACHING

STRATEGIES FOR INCLUSION

Auditory As students use the Strategies for Elaboration on the pupil's page, have them work in pairs. One student in each pair serves as an interviewer, asking the questions in the text and recording the ideas expressed by the other member of the pair. Students take turns being the interviewer, and then they share their notes with one another as they write their drafts.

Visual Some students might find it useful to organize their ideas for the three major divisions of their essays in a chart like the one that follows. Students may jot down ideas or write whole paragraphs in the cells of the chart.

Introduction
Body
Conclusion

One student used two of the questions on page 1180 as prompts for a focused freewrite on the problem of traffic accidents on graduation night. Here are the ideas that resulted:

Model

Could some of the causes of traffic accidents on graduation night be eliminated? How? One cause of traffic accidents on graduation night is unsafe driving by students who have been drinking at unsupervised private parties. We could eliminate this cause by having a party at the Civic Center supervised by teachers and parents. But where would the money come from, and would students attend the party? Maybe local businesses would be willing to donate food, music, decorations, and door prizes in exchange for publicity. The donations would defray the cost of putting on the party and might also entice people to come to the party.

What is the most promising part of the solution you can think of? Maybe the Parent-Teacher Organization could hire buses to transport students to and from the party — maybe the school board would even allow school buses to be used. A student committee could decorate the buses with streamers and balloons.

5. **Evaluating alternative solutions.** A perfect solution to your problem may not exist. Usually, though, some solutions are clearly better than others, and in most cases, one solution can be shown to be the best choice. Use these questions to evaluate possible solutions and to identify the best solution to your problem.

- What are the advantages and disadvantages of each solution?
- Which solution is the most practical?
- Does one solution have a comparative advantage? In other words, which solution will do the most good for the most people?

Sometimes, two solutions may seem equally good—or none may seem feasible. In such cases, resist the urge to declare the problem unsolvable. Instead, search for a compromise. If your school doesn't have enough guidance counselors, for example, don't assume that students either have to do without career planning or pay an outside career-counseling service. A compromise solution might be for one of the guidance counselors to sponsor a student group offering peer counseling.

In other cases, the problem may have more than one cause or may affect more than one group. Such situations may call for a variety of solutions. For example, if neighborhood residents object to the traffic and noise a new teen center will generate, one solution—having a new access road built— is not enough. You also need a solution for the noise.

Making a chart like the one on page 1182 can help you analyze and evaluate alternative solutions. The writer is trying to discover solutions to the following problem: Not all students have home computers, which provide instant access to information needed for doing homework.

Prewriting

One source of topics is your school and the problems that students perceive in it. Not only will students have firsthand knowledge of these problems, but also they can develop a very clear sense of their audience if they address their essays to school administrators. School-related problems make gathering information easier, since the sources of information are usually on site; and sending students' essays to the school newspaper as letters to the editor is a convenient way to publish their writing.

Community issues also are good sources of topics. To enhance their stake in the outcome, encourage students to investigate problems from a teenager's perspective.

Brainstorming with the entire class is often an effective method of identifying problems and possible solutions. However, you might want to encourage students to avoid writing about the same problem as others unless they have some unique solutions. Remind students that national and international problems are usually too complex to explore in a brief essay.

INTEGRATING THE LANGUAGE ARTS

Strategic Reading As students read the various sections of the Writer's Workshop, ask them to organize the information they acquire in a chart like the following:

	Fact/Detail	Fact/Detail	Fact/Detail
Prewriting			
Drafting			
Evaluating and Revising			
Proofreading and Publishing			

Possible Solutions	Advantages	Disadvantages
Abolish homework	Eliminates inequity in grading; makes students' lives less stressful.	Removes valuable assessment tool; removes opportunity to apply research skills independently.
Keep school open two hours longer each weekday.	Gives students who need it access to computers in a familiar place; computers already budgeted for.	The school's budget can't cover additional costs for teachers' salaries, utilities, and school bus drivers' wages.
Establish next branch of county library at the school.	Opens services to all city residents, not just students; staff and equipment costs already budgeted for; saves cost of building a new facility.	County commissioners would have to be convinced of neighborhood support; residents of other parts of town might object.

Practicality
Keeping school open longer hours isn't practical—the school just doesn't have the money.

Comparative Advantage
Establishing the next branch of the county library at the school will do the most good for the most people and will make the best use of available money, staff, and facilities.

6. **Steps to success.** Once you've settled on a practical, workable solution—the end—turn your attention to the specific steps needed to make it a reality—the means. Focus on these questions:

- What needs to be done?
- How will it be done?
- In what order will it be done?

For example, establishing the next branch of the county library at your school might involve the following steps:

- Develop support for the idea in your school zone by visiting or distributing literature to neighborhood residents.
- Ask the newspaper to send a reporter to speak with students and residents about the need for and benefits of the proposal.
- Contact your local county commissioner to arrange to have the proposal included on the commission's agenda.
- Recruit students and other area residents to attend the commission meeting at which you will present the proposal and explain its benefits.

INTEGRATING THE LANGUAGE ARTS

Speaking and Listening Some students may wish to conduct interviews to learn about issues and to determine reactions to their proposed solutions. Ask students to write several interview questions. Working with a partner, students should practice interviewing and taking notes on their subject's response. Let students videotape themselves and then review their strengths and weaknesses as interviewers.

Vocabulary The tone of an essay is largely determined by the words writers use. Review with students the concept that tone is basically an expression of the attitude writers have toward their subject matter or toward their audience. Then, review ideas related to denotation and connotation. Ask students to complete the following chart by supplying words with the same denotations but with the connotations specified.

	Positive Connotation	Negative Connotation
Not conducive to good health	[risky]	[hazardous]
Causing traffic delays	[congested]	[bottlenecked]
In need of repair	[nonfunctioning]	[dilapidated]
Worn out	[antique]	[kaput]
Less than interesting	[unstimulating]	[boring]

7. **Analyzing your audience, setting your tone.** As in persuasive writing, audience considerations are central to a problem-solution essay. Here, your purpose is twofold: to *explain* the problem and possible solutions and to *prove* both that the problem is serious and what will best solve it. Use the questions in the following chart to plan your approach.

Questions	Analysis	Approach
What does the audience already know about the problem?	very little	Provide detailed background information.
	a little	Include some background details.
	a lot	Remind them of their stake in solving the problem.
What solutions might the audience favor?	the one you are proposing	Lead them from agreement to action.
	one you have rejected	Explain in detail the comparative advantage of your solution.
What kind of objections might the audience have to your solution?	major ones	Devote extra space to countering their objections and to explaining the benefits your solution offers.
	minor ones	Emphasize that your solution offers the greatest good for the greatest number of people.

In setting your tone, use objective language to demonstrate that your proposal isn't simply self-serving. Avoid emotionally charged words and, to keep from coming across as a know-it-all, qualify your recommendations: Use words such as *could, might,* and *perhaps* rather than *should, must,* and *unquestionably*. Using first-person pronouns can be especially effective in a problem-solution essay—*I, my, mine,* and *me* to recount your own experiences; *we* and *our* to describe the problem; and *ours* and *us* to underscore common concerns.

8. **Providing support.** Vague generalities and sweeping statements won't convince readers to accept your analysis of the problem and its possible solutions or to accept your proposed solution as the best solution. They will expect you to provide sound reasons and specific evidence—facts, examples, and statistics. Compare the effectiveness of these two statements:

VAGUE   Sixteen-year-old drivers are a lot more dangerous than older teen drivers.

Language Handbook HELP

Using personal pronouns: page 1227.

CROSSING THE CURRICULUM

Science   Much of science is concerned with identifying problems and developing solutions for them. Ask students to research and report to the class on famous problems that scientists have studied and on how these problems were solved. A science teacher or librarian may be able to suggest specific resources that students can use for information.

CLASSROOM MANAGEMENT

Facilitating Group Reports   To save time in cooperative learning activities, you can use a variety of standard ways of assigning the reporter's role. For example, let the report be given by one of the following students: oldest person, youngest person, tallest person, shortest person, or the person with a birthday earliest or latest in the year. If you use number-coding or color-coding (students draw slips of paper at random and are grouped with others of matching number or color), include the word *reporter* on one of the slips, and let the student who draws that slip give the report.

Drafting

Use editorials and letters to the editor of school or community newspapers as models while students draft their essays. Select these published items carefully to make sure they incorporate the methods and concepts that students learn about in this Writer's Workshop. As students write, encourage them to imagine they are speaking what they write to a specific audience and to maintain a clear and consistent tone as they write. Because students often discover ideas and establish a tone during drafting, they might want to write the bodies of their essays before they attempt to write the introductions.

Evaluating and Revising

Remind students to use the questions given under Peer review and in the Evaluation Criteria as guides in their evaluation of drafts. Point out that peer review involves putting trust in the peer reviewer to do a good job and to be honest with the writer about the quality of the draft. Students may be called upon to evaluate the writing of others later in life as parents or co-workers, and they can learn this valuable skill by practicing it now. For help in revising for effective sentences, refer students to the Language Workshop on p. 1186. Also encourage students to be aggressive in revising their own papers. A well-written sentence or paragraph is only effective if it convinces readers of its points, so students should not be afraid to cut even their best writing if it does not work.

Communications Handbook HELP

Documenting sources: page 1212.

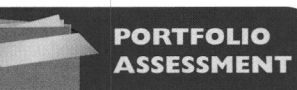

PORTFOLIO ASSESSMENT

Peer Evaluation During evaluating and revising, students can use the peer evaluation sheet found in the *Portfolio Management System,* p. 195.

PRECISE Nationwide, according to the Insurance Institute for Highway Safety, sixteen-year-old drivers are involved in fatal crashes more than twice as frequently as seventeen-, eighteen-, and nineteen-year-old drivers.

Your investigation of the problem and evaluation of possible solutions have probably already supplied you with some of the evidence you'll need, but you may need to do more research to fill in any gaps. In gathering additional information, be sure to use reliable sources—major newspapers or news weeklies and acknowledged experts on the problem. And keep in mind that your readers may focus just as much on the evidence you use to counter their objections as on the proof you offer in support of your solution.

Drafting

1. **The introduction: engage them.** Especially if your readers aren't aware of the problem or aren't convinced of its relevance to their lives, it's important to grab their attention immediately. Try beginning with an unusual fact, a stirring scenario, or a personal anecdote. Then define the problem explicitly, using descriptive terms that will help readers visualize the situation.

2. **The body: enlighten them.** As you explain the problem's seriousness, remember to support your reasons with facts, examples, and statistics. In discussing the alternative solutions you have rejected, clarify their specific disadvantages, again using solid evidence to back up your reasons. Then present your own solution, pointing out its comparative advantages and outlining the steps needed to implement it.

> ### Strategies for Elaboration: Putting It All Together
>
> - **Distributing emphasis.** The amount of space you devote to explaining the problem and its seriousness, describing your proposed solution, discussing rejected solutions, and countering possible objections to your solution will depend on your readers' concerns. If they're well aware of the problem, for example, you may spend more time discussing your solution. A very complex problem may call for a greater emphasis on its causes and effects than on your proposed solution.
> - **Crediting your sources.** Your teacher may ask you to credit your sources formally, using parenthetical citations and a list of Works Cited. If not, you may credit your sources informally by weaving them into the sentences in which you refer to evidence from them, as in the example under "Providing Support," above.

3. **The conclusion: energize them.** To bring your essay to a compelling close, restate your proposed solution. Consider ending with a clear call to action—specific steps readers can take to help make your solution a reality.

OPTIONS FOR TEACHING

COOPERATIVE LEARNING

Identify Problems Ask students to work in groups to identify problems. Divide the class into groups of four, and assign each group an area of concern. For example, one group could identify problems at school; another, problems with traffic congestion in your area; a third, a lack of recreational facilities; and so on. Each group should develop a list of at least four problems in their area. When the groups report to the class, make a master list that students can refer to when they begin selecting topics for their essays.

Evaluating and Revising

1. **Peer review.** Use the following questions to respond to your classmate's draft:
   - **Problem.** Is the problem clearly defined? Is enough background information provided on its seriousness and the need to solve it?
   - **Solution.** Is the proposed solution clearly and thoroughly described? Are enough reasons and evidence offered in support? Are potential objections to the solution dealt with adequately?
   - **Rejected solutions.** Are the disadvantages of alternative solutions presented clearly and convincingly?
   - **Tone.** Is the tone straightforward and objective? Is it consistent throughout?

2. **Self-evaluation.** Take a hard look at the solution you've proposed in your essay. Circle the solution, and number the necessary steps to achieve it that you've discussed. Next, underline each counterargument you've addressed in your essay. If you find few items to circle, number, or underline, you know what to focus on when you revise. Also, review your classmate's responses, looking especially for comments that will help you make your paper clearer and more persuasive. Then revise your essay, making any changes you feel will improve it.

Proofreading and Publishing

Proofread your essay carefully to make your presentation of your findings as credible as your ideas. Then deliver it as an oral proposal to your classmates or to a local group that could solve the problem. You might also distribute copies of it to people affected by the problem or submit it as an editorial to your school newspaper.

Reflecting on Your Writing

To include this essay in your portfolio, date it and then write brief answers to these questions:

1. What problems did you encounter in writing a problem-solution essay?
2. How did you go about solving those problems? If you considered other possible solutions to your writing problems, why did you reject them?
3. What changes to your essay did you make in the revision process? Why?
4. Which was harder for you, devising a solution or countering potential objections to your solution? identifying alternative solutions or analyzing their disadvantages?
5. What do you like best about your essay? What would you still like to improve?

▌ *Evaluation Criteria*

An effective problem-solution essay

1. *opens with an attention-getting statement of the problem and sets an objective tone*
2. *provides sufficient information—reasons, facts, examples, statistics—about the problem's causes and effects*
3. *explains the seriousness of the problem effectively and with an awareness of the essay's readers*
4. *points out the disadvantages of alternative solutions*
5. *explains the proposed solution thoroughly, discussing its comparative advantage and countering objections and outlining the steps needed to put it into effect*
6. *concludes with a compelling restatement of the proposed solution and, if appropriate, with a call to action*

**Revision
STRATEGIES**

Are the steps needed to implement the solution clearly presented? Working with a writing partner, identify and discuss the steps you've included. If necessary, reorder the steps to show the sequence in which they should be done. Add any steps that are missing.

Portfolio

Reflecting on Your Writing

As well as having students write answers to the questions in the text and attach these to their essays when they file them in their portfolios, you can also ask students to write a paragraph or two in response to the question "What did you learn from this assignment?" Create a handout with the responses of several students to share with the class.

Closure

After the essays are completed, ask students to jot down a list of the steps they followed in writing their papers. Then, ask volunteers to share the ideas from their lists with the rest of the class. On the chalkboard, make a chart like the one that follows to record students' ideas.

Prewriting	Drafting	Evaluating, Revising	Proof-reading, Publishing

Reteaching

If students have difficulty developing solutions that are realistic and that genuinely solve the problem, you can suggest they survey people affected by the problem to solicit solutions. Students can do this informally by talking with affected people, or they can create more formal written surveys to collect ideas. Encourage students to rethink their solutions and take any objections into consideration. *You may want to obtain permission from parents or guardians and from the parties students will contact before they begin work on this activity.*

ASSESSMENT TOOLS

As students work through the writing process, have them use the following list to assess one another's work using these qualifiers,
___ Strong   ___ Moderate   ___ Weak.

1. Opens with an attention-getting statement of the problem and sets an objective tone.
2. Provides sufficient information—reasons, facts, examples, statistics—about the problem's causes and effects.
3. Explains the seriousness of the problem effectively.
4. Points out the disadvantages of alternative solutions.
5. Explains the solution thoroughly, discussing its comparative advantages, countering objections, and outlining the steps.
6. Concludes with a compelling restatement of the proposed solution.

PROGRAM MANAGER

Modeling or Practicing Revision To summarize and model the revision process, and to provide student practice, use **Revision Transparencies** 15.5–15.6 in the *Audio-visual Resources Binder.*

Have students choose a piece of writing from their portfolios. Ask them to find sentences that are closely related to one another and to combine these sentences, using subordinating conjunctions to create complex sentences.

Try It Out: Possible Answers

1. While Gideon was a cook for the Farquar family, he would often play with their son Teddy.
2. Although Gideon knew which plant had healing powers, he refused to identify it for the Farquars, and he withheld his secret information.

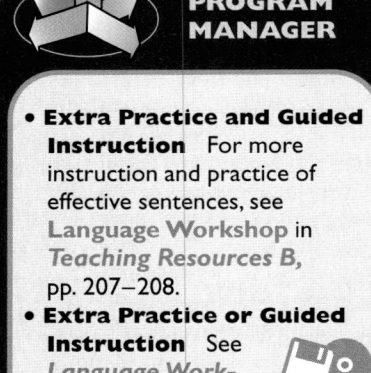

PROGRAM MANAGER

- **Extra Practice and Guided Instruction** For more instruction and practice of effective sentences, see *Language Workshop* in *Teaching Resources B*, pp. 207–208.
- **Extra Practice or Guided Instruction** See *Language Workshop: Coordinating ideas* for more practice.

Language Workshop

Technology HELP

See Language Workshop CD-ROM. *Key word entry: subordinate clause.*

Language Handbook HELP

Independent and subordinate clauses: page 1232; combining by subordinating ideas: page 1239; punctuating introductory clauses: page 1245.

Try It Out

Combine the sentences below, using subordinating conjunctions to clarify relationships.

1. Gideon was a cook for the Farquar family. He would often play with their son Teddy.
2. Gideon knew which plant had healing powers. He refused to identify it for the Farquars and he withheld his secret information.

EFFECTIVE SENTENCES: RELATIONSHIPS BETWEEN IDEAS

A common problem in writing comes about when several clauses are strung together with only the word *and*. You can make your writing more precise by using subordinating conjunctions instead of *and*, when appropriate. A *subordinating conjunction* is a word that clarifies the relationships between ideas by indicating **time** (*after, as, before, until, when*), **cause** (*because, since, unless*), **purpose** (*so that*), or **condition** (*although, if, though*).

Here are some sentences that string together a series of ideas with the word *and*. Note that the relationships between ideas are not too clear.

UNCLEAR Without even washing it, he put the root in his mouth, chewed it vigorously, and then held the spittle there **and** he took the child forcibly from Mrs. Farquar.

He spoke incredulously, **and** he could not believe his old friends could so betray him.

Here is how Doris Lessing combined the same ideas using subordination. Notice that now the relationships between ideas are more precisely stated.

CLEAR Without even washing it, he put the root in his mouth, chewed it vigorously, and then held the spittle there **while** he took the child forcibly from Mrs. Farquar.
—from "No Witchcraft for Sale"

He spoke incredulously, **as if** he could not believe his old friends could so betray him.
—from "No Witchcraft for Sale"

Usually, there are several ways to indicate subordination. Here are two edited versions of the second sentence above:

He spoke incredulously, **because** he could not believe his old friends could so betray him.

Because he could not believe his old friends could so betray him, he spoke incredulously.

Writer's Workshop Follow-Up: Revision

Review the essay you wrote for the Writer's Workshop on page 1179. Focus on one paragraph in the body of your essay to see where you can combine sentences to make relationships clearer; then study the other paragraphs. Share your changes with a writing partner.

✔ QUICK CHECK: Relationships Between Ideas

Choose a subordinating conjunction from this list to clarify the relationship between the main ideas in these sentences.

when   although   because   even if

[1] Learning to write clearly is important ___ writing is a primary means of transmitting ideas. [because]
[2] ___ a person uses a computer, writing is an important skill. [Even if]
[3] In fact, ___ people apply for jobs, they often have to demonstrate proficiency in the use of a computer word-processing program. [when]
[4] ___ machines dominate the workplace, the human skill of writing clear, effective prose is still one of the most important assets a person can possess. [Although]

LEARNING FOR LIFE

Future Developments

Problem

Many of the profound changes that have occurred in this century grew out of developments during the Victorian era. How might recent developments affect life in the century to come?

Project

Predict how one recent development—social, cultural, or technological—may affect life in the next one hundred years. Will it change the pace and pattern of daily life? Will it alter the way people view themselves and the world around them?

Preparation

1. With a partner or a small group, brainstorm to generate a list of recent events, situations, and trends. To get started, you might focus on such categories as art, literature, computers, education, politics, medicine, and so on. Or you might begin with people in the news: Who are today's leading inventors, entrepreneurs, authors, artists, and scientists, and what have they been up to lately? As you brainstorm, think about both the national and the international scenes.

2. Choose the topic that interests you most, and freewrite to explore what you already know about it and what you think its long-range consequences may be.

Procedure

1. Using library and community resources, explore your topic through the eyes of others who share your interest in it. Look for facts, statistics, examples, anecdotes, and expert opinions that will answer as many of the *5W-How?* questions (*Who? What? When? Where? Why? How?*) as apply. Be sure to investigate what the experts called futurists suggest about future developments. You can cite the experts' views and data to support your position.

2. Stimulate your imagination by asking, and answering, a series of *What if?* questions—for example, What if cities ban all cars in the future? Your answers needn't (in fact, can't) be provable, but they should be plausible.

Presentation

Use one of the following formats (or another that your teacher approves):

1. Be a Television Star

Get together with two or three classmates who've chosen different topics to plan a talk show on your predictions for the future. Ask another student to serve as the show's host, and stage the show live (or ask a friend to videotape it for repeated showings) for your school's American history classes during their unit on the twentieth century.

2. Displaying with Style

Design a triptych (a three-panel composition) illustrating your predictions for the future. Your triptych may be two- or three-dimensional, and you may choose the materials, medium (or media), and style. Give your finished work an intriguing title, and display it in the school cafeteria along with those of other students.

3. Future Fiction

Write a short story, set in the next century, in which you depict the consequences you foresee. Whether your story is fantastic or realistic, be sure to include in your story plan the basic elements and to resolve the conflict in a satisfying and original way. With other students who have chosen this option, tape-record your story. Listen to each other's tapes, and share your responses about your stories. Then, add the tapes to your media center's books-on-tape collection.

Processing

Did this activity make you more (or less) optimistic about the future? Did it make you curious about what life will be like *two* centuries from now? Write a brief reflection for your portfolio.

Learning for Life

Technology Tip

 Students may want to investigate what authors Alvin and Heidi Toffler have to say about the future. They have produced four books (*Future Shock, The Third Wave, Power Shift* and *War and Anti-War*) that discuss the changes in the world they foresee. Students can find an interview with Toffler on the Internet at **http://www.physics.wisc.edu/~shalizi/NewScientistArticles/alvin-toffler/**. *You may want to preview any internet activity you suggest to students. Because these resources are sometimes public forums, their content can be unpredictable.*

PORTFOLIO ASSESSMENT

Performance Assessment Rubric So that students may see the evaluation criteria before they begin working on these projects, share the rubric provided in the *Portfolio Management System,* p. 197.

DEVELOPING WORKPLACE COMPETENCIES

Preparation	Procedure	Presentation
Generates ideas	Uses resources	Works on teams
Identifies central issues	Processes information	Communicates ideas and information
Recognizes relationships	Acquires and classifies data	Interprets information
Uses logic	Thinks creatively	Solves problems

RESOURCE CENTER

HANDBOOK OF LITERARY TERMS

ALEXANDRINE   A line of poetry made up of six iambs—that is, a line written in iambic hexameter. The following alexandrine is from Percy Bysshe Shelley's "To a Skylark" (Collection 9):

> Our sweetest songs are those that tell of saddest
> thought.

See page 221.

ALLEGORY   A story in which the characters, settings, and events stand for abstract or moral concepts. Allegories thus have two meanings: a literal meaning and a symbolic meaning. Allegories were a popular literary form during the Middle Ages. Later, Edmund Spenser's *The Faerie Queene* (Collection 3) elaborately fused moral and political allegory: Spenser's Redcrosse Knight stands both for St. George, the patron saint of England, and for the more abstract idea of holiness. The best-known English allegory is John Bunyan's *Pilgrim's Progress* (Collection 5), which recounts the adventures of a character named Christian. The hero's journey to the Celestial City brings him up against many trials that stand for the pitfalls facing the Christian traveling through this world toward the spiritual world.

See pages 221, 451, 495.

ALLITERATION   The repetition of consonant sounds in words that are close to one another. Alliteration occurs most often at the beginning of words, as in "<u>r</u>ough and <u>r</u>eady." But consonants within words sometimes alliterate, as in "<u>b</u>a<u>b</u>y <u>b</u>lue." The echoes that alliteration creates can increase a poem's rhythmic and musical effects and make its lines especially memorable. In this line from Alfred, Lord Tennyson's "The Eagle: A Fragment" (Collection 10), the alliteration of harsh *k* sounds reinforces the stark image of the bird:

> He clasps the crag with crooked hands

Alliteration is an essential feature of Anglo-Saxon poetry; in most lines, two or three of the four stressed syllables alliterate.

See pages 48, 807, 980.

ALLUSION   A reference to a statement, person, place, event, or thing that is known from literature, history, religion, myth, politics, sports, science, or popular culture. For example, the concluding lines of Wilfred Owen's poem "Dulce et Decorum Est" (Collection 12) are *"Dulce et decorum est / Pro patria mori"* ("It is sweet and proper to die for one's country"). These lines allude to a line from an ode by the Latin poet Horace. The title of William Faulkner's *The Sound and the Fury* is an allusion to a line from Shakespeare's *Macbeth* (Collection 4). The cartoon above alludes to William Butler Yeats's poem "The Second Coming" (Collection 12).

See pages 414, 871, 941.

ANALOGY   A comparison of two things to show that they are alike in certain respects. Writers often make analogies to show how something unfamiliar is like

"Basil, do you think the center is going to hold?"

Drawing by Booth; © 1984 The New Yorker Magazine, Inc.

something well known or widely experienced. For example, people often draw an analogy between creating a work of art and giving birth to a child.

See page 1144.

ANTAGONIST   The character or force that opposes or blocks the protagonist, or main character, in a narrative. Usually the antagonist is human, like Sir Mordred, the villainous rebel who destroys the Round Table in Sir Thomas Malory's *Le Morte Darthur,* or the schoolgirls who mercilessly taunt the Kelvey sisters in Katherine Mansfield's "The Doll's House" (Collection 14). Sometimes the antagonist is supernatural, like Satan, who opposes God in Milton's *Paradise Lost* (Collection 5).

ANTICLIMAX   See Climax.

ANTITHESIS   A contrast of ideas expressed in a grammatically balanced statement. In the following line from *The Rape of the Lock* (Collection 6, Canto III), Alexander Pope balances noun against noun and verb against verb: "And wretches hang that jurymen may dine."

See pages 521, 844.

APHORISM   A concise, sometimes witty saying that expresses a principle, truth, or observation about life. Alexander Pope's poetry contains some of the most famous aphorisms in the English language, as in this example from *An Essay on Criticism:* "To err is human, to forgive, divine."

APOSTROPHE   A figure of speech in which a speaker directly addresses an absent or dead person, an abstract quality, or something nonhuman as if it were present and capable of responding. Apostrophe was a popular device with the Romantic poets: Wordsworth, for example, apostrophizes the river Wye in his "Tintern Abbey" (Collection 8). Among the second-generation Romantics, Shelley apostrophized the west wind and a skylark;

Byron apostrophized the ocean; and Keats apostrophized a nightingale and a Greek urn (all in Collection 9).

See pages 668, 682, 738.

ASIDE **Private words that a character in a play speaks to the audience or to another character, which are not supposed to be overheard by others onstage.** Stage directions usually tell when a speech is an aside. For example, in Act I, Scene 3, of Shakespeare's *Macbeth* (Collection 4), Macbeth makes numerous asides to the audience as he ruminates about the possibility of becoming king.

See page 383.

ASSONANCE **The repetition of similar vowel sounds followed by different consonant sounds in words that are close together.** Assonance differs from **exact rhyme** in that it does not repeat the consonant sound following the vowel. The words *face* and *base* rhyme, while the words *face* and *fade* are assonant. Like alliteration, assonance can create musical and rhythmic effects. In this line from Alfred, Lord Tennyson's "The Lotos-Eaters," the repetition of long *o* sounds is **onomatopoetic:**

All day the wind breathes low with mellower tone

See pages 683, 807, 841, 979, 980.

ATMOSPHERE **The mood or feeling in a literary work.** Atmosphere is usually created through descriptive details and evocative language. For example, Ben Okri sets the mood of his short story "In the Shadow of War" (Collection 12) with a dreamlike description of the war-torn forest around Lagos, Nigeria.

See page 847.

AUTOBIOGRAPHY **A written account of the author's own life.** Unlike **diaries, journals,** and letters, autobiographies are unified narratives usually prepared for a public audience. But unlike *memoirs,* publications that often focus on famous events and people other than the author, autobiographies are usually quite introspective. George Orwell's "Shooting an Elephant" (Collection 15) is a well-known autobiographical essay.

See also Diary, Journal.

BALLAD **A song or songlike poem that tells a story.** Most ballads have a regular pattern of **rhythm** and **rhyme,** and they use simple language with a great deal of repetition. Ballads generally have a **refrain**—lines or words that are repeated at regular intervals. And they usually tell sensational stories of tragedy, adventure, betrayal, revenge, and jealousy. **Folk ballads** are composed by anonymous singers and are passed down orally from generation to generation before they are written down (often in several different versions). "Lord Randall" (Collection 2) is an example of a folk ballad. **Literary ballads,** on the other hand, are composed and written down by known poets, usually in the style of folk ballads. Keats's "La Belle Dame sans Merci" (Collection 9) is a famous literary ballad.

The typical **ballad stanza** is a quatrain with the rhyme scheme *abcb*. The first and third lines have four stressed syllables, and the second and fourth lines have three. The number of unstressed syllables in each line may vary, but often the meter is primarily **iambic.**

See pages 90, 93, 97, 683, 750, 867.

BIOGRAPHY **An account of a person's life written or told by another person.** *The Life of Samuel Johnson* by James Boswell (Collection 7) is one of the most famous biographies ever written. Virginia Woolf's account of Shakespeare's sister in *A Room of One's Own* (Collection 15) is an invented biography.

See page 583.

BLANK VERSE **Poetry written in unrhymed iambic pentameter.** "Blank" means the poetry is unrhymed. "Iambic pentameter" means that each line contains five iambs, or metrical **feet,** each consisting of an unstressed syllable followed by a stressed syllable (˘ '). Blank verse is the most important metrical form used in English dramatic and epic poetry. It is the verse line used in Shakespeare's plays and Milton's *Paradise Lost* (Collection 5). One of the reasons blank verse has been so popular, even among modern poets, is that it combines the naturalness of unrhymed verse with the structure of metrical verse. Except for **free verse,** it is the poetic form that sounds the most like natural speech. It also lends itself easily to slight variations within the basic pattern. Like most of the English Romantic poets, Wordsworth made extensive use of blank verse, as in these lines from *The Prelude:*

> ˘ ′ ˘ ′   ˘   ′ ˘ ′ ˘ ′
> Oh! yet a few short years of useful life,
> ˘ ′ ˘ ′ ˘   ′   ˘ ′ ˘ ′
> And all will be complete, thy race be run,
> ˘   ′ ˘ ′ ˘ ′ ˘ ′ ˘ ′
> Thy monument of glory will be raised.

See pages 318, 385, 438, 450, 657, 662, 668.

CADENCE **The natural rise and fall of the voice.** Poets who write in **free verse** often try to imitate the cadences of spoken language.

See also Rhythm.

CAESURA **A pause or break within a line of poetry, usually indicated by the natural rhythm of language.** A midline, or **medial,** caesura is a characteristic element of Anglo-Saxon poetry; it divides the four-beat line in half. Later poets have used the caesura less predictably, as in the following lines from "Dulce et Decorum Est" (Collection 12). Here, the caesuras are indicated by the symbol ||.

Bent double, || like old beggars under sacks,
Knock-kneed, || coughing like hags, || we cursed
through sludge

See pages 48, 216.

CANTO **A subdivision in a long poem, corresponding to a chapter in a book.** Poems that are divided into cantos include Dante's *Divine Comedy* (Collection 4), Pope's *Rape of the Lock* (Collection 6), and Byron's *Don Juan* and

Childe Harold (both in Collection 9). Not all major subdivisions of long poems are called cantos, however: Milton's *Paradise Lost* (Collection 5) is divided into books, and Coleridge's *Rime of the Ancient Mariner* (Collection 8) into parts.

The word *canto* comes from a Latin word for "song," and originally designated a section of a narrative poem that a minstrel could sing in one session.

See page 527.

CARPE DIEM **A Latin phrase that literally means "seize the day"—that is, "make the most of present opportunities."** The *carpe diem* theme is quite common in sixteenth- and seventeenth-century English poetry, as in this famous line from Robert Herrick's "To the Virgins, to Make Much of Time": "Gather ye rosebuds while ye may." The theme is also forcefully expressed in Andrew Marvell's "To His Coy Mistress" (both in Collection 3).

See pages 231, 239.

CHARACTER **An individual in a story or play.** A character always has human traits, even if the character is an animal, like the March Hare in Lewis Carroll's *Alice's Adventures in Wonderland;* or a god, as in the Greek and Roman myths; or a monster, as in *Beowulf* (Collection 1). A character may also be a godlike human, like Superman. But most characters are ordinary human beings, like Chaucer's colorful pilgrims, the eccentrics and paupers in Charles Dickens's novels, and the disillusioned boy in James Joyce's "Araby" (Collection 13).

The process by which the writer reveals the personality of a character is called **characterization.** A writer can reveal a character in the following ways:

1. By telling us directly what the character is like: humble, ambitious, impetuous, easily manipulated, and so on
2. By describing how the character looks and dresses
3. By letting us hear the character speak
4. By revealing the character's private thoughts and feelings
5. By revealing the character's effect on other people—showing how other characters feel or behave toward the character
6. By showing the character's actions

The first method of revealing a character is called **direct characterization.** When a writer uses this method, we do not have to figure out what a character's personality is like—the writer tells us directly. The other five methods of revealing a character are known as **indirect characterization.** When a writer uses these methods, we have to exercise our own judgment, putting clues together to figure out what a character is like—just as we do in real life when we are getting to know someone.

Characters can be classified as static or dynamic. A **static character** is one who does not change much in the course of a story. A **dynamic character,** on the other hand, changes in some important way as a result of the story's action. Characters can also be classified as flat or round. **Flat characters** have only one or two personality traits. They are one-dimensional—they can be summed up by a single phrase. In contrast, **round characters** have more dimensions to their personalities—they are complex, solid, and multifaceted, like real people.

See pages 105, 384, 1069.

CLASSICISM **A movement in art, literature, and music that advocates imitating the principles manifested in the art and literature of ancient ("classical") Greece and Rome.** Classicism emphasizes reason, clarity, balance, harmony, restraint, order, and universal themes. Classicism is often placed in direct opposition to **Romanticism,** with its emphasis on unrestrained emotions and personal themes. However, this opposition should be approached with caution, as it is sometimes exaggerated for effect.

See also Neoclassicism, Romanticism.

CLICHÉ **An expression that was fresh and apt when first coined but which is now so overused that it has become hackneyed and stale.** "Busy as a bee" and "fresh as a daisy" are two examples. Clichés are often likened to **dead metaphors**—figures of speech ("leg of a chair," "mouth of a river") whose power to surprise is now completely gone.

See page 1037.

CLIMAX **The point of greatest emotional intensity or suspense in a plot.** The climax usually marks the moment when the conflict is decided, one way or another. In Shakespeare's plays, the climax usually occurs in the last act, just before the final scene. Following the climax, the story is **resolved,** or closed.

Some critics talk of more than one climactic moment in a long work (though usually the greatest climax still occurs near the end of the plot). In drama, one such climactic moment is called the **turning point,** or **crisis.** In Shakespeare's plays, this moment usually occurs in the third act. The turning point is the pivotal moment when the hero's fortunes begin to decline or improve. All the action leading up to this turning point is **rising action,** and all the action following it is **falling action.** The turning point in *Macbeth* (Collection 4) occurs during the banquet scene in Act III, Scene 4, when Macbeth sees Banquo's ghost. From that point onward, it is downhill for Macbeth—everything goes wrong, culminating in the play's climax in Act V, Scene 8. It is at this point that we finally learn for certain that Macbeth will be defeated. The witches' prophecies are borne out: Birnam wood does come to Dunsinane, and Macduff, "not born of woman," faces Macbeth. This confrontation is the climax of the play. After this point, the play moves rapidly toward its resolution, with Malcolm, Duncan's legitimate heir, assuming the throne.

In contrast, when something trivial or comical occurs at the point in a narrative when one expects something important or serious, the accompanying deflation is called an **anticlimax.** Thomas Hardy's poem "Ah, Are You Digging on My Grave?" (Collection 11) contains such an anticlimactic moment.

See pages 351, 388, 857.
See also Plot.

COMEDY In general, a story that ends happily. The hero of a comedy is usually an ordinary character who overcomes a series of obstacles that block what he or she wants. Often a comedy pits two young people who wish to marry against parental blocking figures who want to prevent the marriage. The wedding that concludes these comedies suggests the formation of a new society and a renewal of life. Comedy is distinct from **tragedy,** in which a great person comes to an unhappy or disastrous end, often through some lapse in judgment or character flaw. Comedies are often, but not always, intended to make us laugh. Two famous comedies are Oscar Wilde's play *The Importance of Being Earnest* and George Bernard Shaw's *Pygmalion.* Frank O'Connor's "My Oedipus Complex" (Collection 14) is a comedic short story.

See pages 283, 300, 393, 526, 798.

CONCEIT A fanciful and elaborate figure of speech that makes a surprising connection between two seemingly dissimilar things. Although a conceit may be a brief metaphor, it usually forms the framework of an entire poem. One of the most important kinds of conceits is the **metaphysical conceit,** so called because it was widely used by the seventeenth-century metaphysical poets. This type of conceit is especially startling, complex, and ingenious. Two famous examples are John Donne's comparison between separated lovers and the legs of a compass in "A Valediction: Forbidding Mourning" (Collection 3) and George Herbert's comparison between belief in God and a pulley in "The Pulley."

See pages 220, 229, 247, 457.

CONFLICT A struggle or clash between opposing characters, forces, or emotions. In an **external conflict,** a character struggles against some outside force: another character, society as a whole, or some natural force. An **internal conflict,** on the other hand, is a struggle between opposing needs, desires, or emotions within a single character. Many works, especially longer ones, contain both internal and external conflicts. For example, in Shakespeare's *Macbeth* (Collection 4), Macbeth undergoes an internal conflict between his excessive ambition and his obsessive guilt. He also experiences various external conflicts with characters who attempt to block his ambition. In Doris Lessing's "No Witchcraft for Sale" (Collection 15), the conflict between Gideon and the scientist over the medicinal plant illustrates the larger cultural conflicts in the story.

See also Plot.

CONNOTATIONS All the meanings, associations, or emotions that a word suggests. For example, an expensive restaurant might prefer to advertise its "delicious cuisine" rather than its "delicious cooking." *Cuisine* and *cooking* have the same literal meaning—"prepared food." But *cuisine* has connotations of elegance and sophistication, while *cooking* does not. The same restaurant would certainly not describe its food as "great grub."

Notice the difference between the following pairs of words: *young/immature, ambitious/cutthroat, uninhibited/shameless, lenient/lax.* We might describe ourselves using the first word but someone else using the second. The English philosopher Bertrand Russell once gave a classic example of the different connotations of words: "I am firm. You are obstinate. He is a pigheaded fool."

See pages 513, 515, 650.
See also Denotation.

CONSONANCE The repetition of final consonant sounds after different vowel sounds. The words *east* and *west, dig* and *dog, turn* and *torn,* and Shakespeare's famous "*struts* and *frets*" (from *Macbeth,* in Collection 4) are examples of consonance. The term is also used sometimes to refer to repeated consonant sounds in the middle of words, as in *solemn stillness.* (Consonance, when loosely defined, can be a form of **alliteration.** Strictly speaking, however, alliteration is the repetition of initial consonant sounds.) Like **assonance,** consonance is one form of **approximate rhyme.**

See also Alliteration, Assonance.

COUPLET Two consecutive lines of poetry that rhyme. The couplet has been widely used since the Middle Ages, especially to provide a sense of closure. A couplet that presents a completed thought is called a **closed couplet.** Shakespeare used closed couplets to end his sonnets, as in this example from Sonnet 18:

So long as men can breathe or eyes can see,
So long lives this, and this gives life to thee.

A couplet written in **iambic pentameter** is called a **heroic couplet.** Although the heroic couplet has been used in English literature since Chaucer, it was perfected during the eighteenth century. Here is an example from Pope's *Essay on Man:*

Two principles in human nature reign;
Self-love, to urge, and Reason, to restrain.

See pages 151, 522.

DENOTATION The literal, dictionary definition of a word. Ironically, the word definitions Samuel Johnson provides in his famous *Dictionary of the English Language* (Collection 7) are rarely denotative.

See page 515.
See also Connotations.

DENOUEMENT See Plot.

DEUS EX MACHINA Any artificial or contrived device used at the end of a plot to resolve or untangle the complications. The term is Latin, meaning "god from a machine." The phrase refers to a device used in ancient Greek and Roman drama: At the conclusion of the play, a god would be lowered onto the stage by a mechanical device so that he could save the hero and end the story happily. The term now refers to any device that resolves a plot in a forced or ridiculously implausible way: An orphan finds that he has inherited a fortune just as he is being packed off to the poorhouse; a hero is saved because the villain has forgotten to load his gun. Oscar Wilde's *The Importance of Being Earnest* and Charles Dickens's *Oliver Twist* both contain examples of *deus ex machina.*

See page 283.

DIALECT **A way of speaking that is characteristic of a particular region or group of people.** A dialect may have a distinct vocabulary, pronunciation system, and grammar. In the Middle Ages, when Latin was the "literary" language of Europe, writers such as Chaucer began writing for middle-class audiences in their own regional languages, or what are now interchangeably called dialects or **vernaculars.** Today, one dialect usually becomes accepted as the standard for a country or culture. In the United States, the dialect used in formal writing and spoken by most TV and radio announcers is known as standard English.

Writers often use other dialects, however, to establish character or to create local color. For example, Robert Burns (Collection 8) wrote his poetry in Scottish dialect, and V. S. Naipaul (Collection 13) has used the dialect spoken by Trinidad's Asian Indian population in many of his works. The East London cockney dialect, and the lower-class background it betrays, is at the very heart of Bernard Shaw's famous play *Pygmalion* (1916). In this excerpt from the play, Henry Higgins, with his friend Colonel Pickering in attendance, begins to instruct the young flower girl Eliza Doolittle in how to speak "proper" English:

> **Higgins.** Say your alphabet.
>
> **Liza.** I know my alphabet. Do you think I know nothing? I dont need to be taught like a child.
>
> **Higgins** *(thundering).* Say your alphabet.
>
> **Pickering.** Say it, Miss Doolittle. You will understand presently. Do what he tells you; and let him teach you in his own way.
>
> **Liza.** Oh well, if you put it like that—Ahyee, bɔyee, cɔyee, dɔyee——
>
> **Higgins** *(with the roar of a wounded lion).* Stop. Listen to this, Pickering. . . . *(To* Eliza) Say A, B, C, D.
>
> **Liza** *(almost in tears).* But I'm saying it. Ahyee, Bɔyee, Cɔyee——

See pages 99, 641, 770, 896, 1049.

DIALOGUE **Conversation between two or more people.** Writers use dialogue to advance the action of a plot, to present an interplay of ideas and personalities, and to reveal the background, occupation, or social level of the characters through **tone** and **dialect.**

See pages 1102, 1171.

DIARY **A day-by-day record of events and thoughts kept by an individual.** A diary is usually an intimate **autobiographical** chronicle, not intended for publication, though diarists sometimes have a reader in mind. The seventeenth-century diary of Samuel Pepys (Collection 7) is one of the most famous diaries in English. Also in print are the diaries of such modern writers as Virginia Woolf (Collection 15).

See page 543.

See also Autobiography, Journal.

DICTION **A writer's or speaker's choice of words.** People use different types of words depending on the audience they're addressing, the subject they're discussing, and the effect they're trying to produce. For example, slang words that would be suitable in a casual conversation with a friend ("He's a total nerd") would be unsuitable in a political debate. Similarly, the language that a nutritionist would use to describe a meal would be different from the language used by a restaurant reviewer or a novelist.

Diction is an essential element of a writer's **style.** A writer's diction can be simple or flowery (*shop/boutique*), modern or old-fashioned (*pharmacy/apothecary*), general or specific (*sandwich/grilled cheese on rye*). Notice that the **connotations** of words (rather than their strict, literal meanings, or **denotations**) are an important aspect of diction.

See pages 513, 1092.

DISSONANCE **A harsh, discordant combination of sounds.** The opposite of **euphony,** or harmonious, pleasant-sounding speech, dissonance is usually created by the repetition of harsh consonant sounds. Dissonance is often used in poetry to communicate energy. These lines from Gerard Manley Hopkins's "The Windhover" are dissonant:

> shéer plód makes plough down sillion
> Shine, and blue-bleak embers, ah my dear,
> Fall, gall themselves, and gash gold-vermilion.

Also called **cacophony,** dissonance is often used as a poetic device by John Donne (Collection 3) and Robert Browning (Collection 10).

DRAMATIC MONOLOGUE **A poem in which a character addresses one or more listeners who remain silent or whose replies are not revealed.** The occasion is usually a critical one in the speaker's life. Tennyson's "Ulysses" and Browning's "My Last Duchess" and "Porphyria's Lover" (all in Collection 10) are famous dramatic monologues.

See page 829.

ELEGY **A poem that mourns the death of a person or laments something lost.** Elegies may lament the passing of life and beauty, or they may be meditations on the nature of death. A type of **lyric,** an elegy is usually formal in language and structure, and solemn or even melancholy in tone. Much of English poetry is elegiac, from the Anglo-Saxon lyric "The Seafarer" (Collection 1) to John Milton's "Lycidas," Thomas Gray's somber "Elegy Written in a Country Churchyard" (Collection 7) and the great elegy of the Victorian era, Tennyson's *In Memoriam A.H.H.* (Collection 10).

See pages 55, 435, 481, 606, 814, 1038.

END-STOPPED LINE **A line of poetry in which the meter and the meaning conclude with the end of the line.** Often the end-of-line pause is marked with punctuation, though it need not be. These lines from Alexander Pope's *An Essay on Man* (Collection 6) are end-stopped:

> Know then thyself, presume not God to scan;
> The proper study of mankind is man.

See also Run-on Line.

EPIC **A long narrative poem that relates the great deeds of a larger-than-life hero who embodies the values of a particular society.** Most epics include elements of myth, legend, folklore, and history. Their tone is serious and their language grand. Most **epic heroes** undertake quests to achieve something of tremendous value to themselves or their society. Homer's *Odyssey* and *Iliad* and Virgil's *Aeneid* are the best-known epics in the Western tradition. The two most important English epics are the Anglo-Saxon poem *Beowulf* (Collection 1) and John Milton's *Paradise Lost* (Collection 5).

See pages 18, 20, 221, 393, 438, 526.

EPIGRAM A brief, clever, and usually memorable statement. Alexander Pope's writings are **epigrammatic** in style. Here is an example from his *Essay on Criticism:*

> We think our fathers fools, so wise we grow,
> Our wiser sons, no doubt, will think us so.

See pages 257, 525, 1108.

EPIPHANY In a literary work, a moment of sudden insight or revelation that a character experiences. The word comes from the Greek and can be translated as "manifestation" or "showing forth." The term has religious meanings that have been transferred to literature by many modern writers. James Joyce first gave the word its literary meaning in an early draft of *A Portrait of the Artist as a Young Man.* In Joyce's story "Araby" (Collection 13), the narrator experiences an epiphany at the end of the story when he recognizes the cheap vulgarity of the bazaar and the emptiness of his dream.

See pages 988, 995.

EPITAPH An inscription on a tombstone, or a commemorative poem written as if for that purpose. Epitaphs range from the solemn to the farcical. Ben Jonson's poem "On My First Son" (Collection 3) contains a famously poignant epitaph. The following epitaph, Robert Burns's "On William Graham of Mossknowe," is a more comic example:

> "Stop Thief!" Dame Nature call'd to Death,
> As Willie drew his latest breath:
> "How shall I make a fool again?
> My choicest model thou hast ta'en."

EPITHET An adjective or other descriptive phrase that is regularly used to characterize a person, place, or thing. Phrases such as "Peter the Great," "Richard the Lion-Hearted," and "America the Beautiful" are epithets. Homer created so many descriptive epithets in his *Iliad* and *Odyssey* that his name has been permanently associated with a type of epithet. The **Homeric epithet** consists of a compound adjective that is regularly used to modify a particular noun. Famous examples are "the wine-dark sea," "the gray-eyed goddess Athena," and the "rosy-fingered dawn."

See also Kenning.

ESSAY A short piece of nonfiction prose that examines a single subject from a limited point of view. There are two major types of essays. **Informal essays** (also called **personal essays**) generally reveal a great deal about the personalities and feelings of their authors. They tend to be conversational, sometimes even humorous in tone, and they are usually highly subjective. **Formal essays** (also called **traditional essays**) are usually serious and impersonal in tone. Because they are written to inform or persuade, they are expected to be factual, logical, and tightly organized.

In English literature, the essay began with Sir Francis Bacon, who published his extremely formal *Essays* (Collection 5) in 1597. The English informal essay was pioneered by Joseph Addison and Sir Richard Steele (both in Collection 7) in the early eighteenth century. Notable twentieth-century English essayists include Virginia Woolf and George Orwell (both in Collection 15).

See pages 404, 567, 1123, 1138.

EXAGGERATION *See* Hyperbole.

FABLE A very brief story in prose or verse that teaches a moral, or a practical lesson about life. The characters in most fables are animals that behave and speak like human beings. Some of the most popular fables are those attributed to Aesop, who was supposed to have been a slave in ancient Greece. Several of the pilgrims' tales in Chaucer's *Canterbury Tales* (Collection 2) also contain fables.

See also Parable.

FALLING ACTION *See* Climax.

FARCE A type of comedy in which ridiculous and often stereotyped characters are involved in far-fetched, silly situations. The humor in farce is based on crude physical action, slapstick, and clowning. Characters may slip on banana peels, get pies thrown in their faces, and knock one another on the head with ladders. The movies featuring Abbott and Costello, Laurel and Hardy, and the Marx brothers are all examples of farces.

The word *farce* comes from a Latin word for "stuffing," and in fact farces were originally used to fill in the waiting time between the acts of a serious play. Even in tragedies, farcical elements are often included to provide comic relief. Shakespeare, for example, frequently lets his "common" characters engage in farcical actions.

See pages 283, 1101.

FIGURATIVE LANGUAGE Language that intentionally departs from the normal construction or meaning of words in order to create a certain effect, or to make an analogy between two seemingly dissimilar things. Figurative language includes all **figures of speech.**

See page 389.

FIGURE OF SPEECH A word or phrase that describes one thing in terms of another and is not meant to be understood on a literal level. Figures of speech always involve some sort of imaginative comparison between seemingly unlike things.

Some 250 different types of figures of speech have been identified, but the most common are the **simile** ("My love is like a red, red rose"), the **metaphor** ("The Lord is my shepherd"), and **personification** ("Death, be not proud").

See also Hyperbole, Metaphor, Metonymy, Oxymoron, Personification, Simile, Symbol.

FLASHBACK A scene in a movie, play, short story, novel, or narrative poem that interrupts the present action of the plot to "flash backward" and tell what happened at an earlier time. "The Demon Lover" by

Elizabeth Bowen (Collection 13) includes a flashback that describes Mrs. Drover's farewell to her fiancé twenty-five years before the main action of the story takes place.

See page 1018.

FOIL   A character who sets off another character by strong contrast. This contrast emphasizes the differences between two characters, bringing out the distinctive qualities in each. In *Macbeth* (Collection 4), Banquo is a foil to Macbeth. Though the witches prophesy similar fame for both Macbeth and Banquo, only Macbeth's appetite for power is excited by the prediction; Banquo remains loyal to the king.

FORESHADOWING   The use of clues to hint at what is going to happen later in the plot. Foreshadowing arouses the reader's curiosity and builds up **suspense**. In *Macbeth* (Collection 4), the witches' prophecies foreshadow Macbeth's tragic end. Foreshadowing also occurs in Elizabeth Bowen's "The Demon Lover" (Collection 13) when Mrs. Drover imagines "spectral glitters in the place of" her fiancé's eyes, and when we learn that she made an "unnatural promise" to him—that she "could not have plighted a more sinister troth."

See pages 333, 813.
See also Suspense.

FRAME STORY   An introductory narrative within which one or more of the characters proceeds to tell a story. Perhaps the best-known example of stories contained in a frame story is the Persian collection called *The Thousand and One Nights*. In English literature, Chaucer's *Canterbury Tales* (Collection 2) uses a frame story involving a group of people on a pilgrimage; within the narrative frame, each of the pilgrims then tells his or her own story. Giovanni Boccaccio's *Decameron* (Collection 2) contains another notable example of the frame-story device.

See pages 100, 105, 155.

FREE VERSE   Poetry that has no regular meter or rhyme scheme. Free verse usually relies instead on the natural **rhythms** of ordinary speech. Poets writing in free verse may use **alliteration, internal rhyme, onomatopoeia,** and other musical devices to achieve their effects. They may also place great emphasis on **imagery.** Matthew Arnold's "Dover Beach" (Collection 11) is an early example of free verse, and T. S. Eliot's poems, including "The Hollow Men" (Collection 12), are especially fine and famous examples. Much of today's poetry is written in free verse: Margaret Atwood's "Mushrooms" (Collection 13) is one contemporary example.

See page 1050.

GOTHIC   A term used to describe literary works that contain primitive, medieval, wild, mysterious, or natural elements. Such elements were frowned upon by eighteenth-century neoclassicists but hailed by the Romantic writers of the following era. The **Gothic novel,** a genre popular in the late eighteenth and early nineteenth centuries, is chiefly characterized by gloomy settings and an atmosphere of terror and mystery. Mary Shelley's *Frankenstein* is one of the most widely known Gothic novels.

See pages 516, 606, 636, 728.

HYPERBOLE   A figure of speech that uses exaggeration to express strong emotion or create a comic effect. While hyperbole (also known as **overstatement**) does not express the *literal* truth, it is often used in the service of truth to capture a sense of intensity or to emphasize the essential nature of something. For instance, if you claim that it was 250 degrees in the subway, you are using hyperbole to express the truth that it was miserably hot.

See pages 245, 500.

IAMBIC PENTAMETER   A line of poetry made up of five iambs. An **iamb** is a metrical foot, or unit of measure, consisting of an unstressed syllable followed by a stressed syllable (˘ ´). The word *suggest*, for example, is made up of one iamb. *Pentameter* derives from the Greek words *penta* (five) and *meter* (measure). Here are two lines of poetry written in iambic pentameter:

> Forlorn! the very word is like a bell
> To toll me back from thee to my sole self!
> —John Keats, *from* "Ode to a Nightingale"

Iambic pentameter is by far the most common verse line in English poetry. Shakespeare's sonnets and plays, for example, are written primarily in this meter. Many modern poets, such as W. H. Auden, have continued to use iambic pentameter. Other than **free verse,** it is the poetic meter that sounds the most like natural speech.

See pages 100, 216, 318, 450.
See also Blank Verse.

IMAGERY   Language that appeals to the senses. Most images are visual—that is, they appeal to the sense of sight. But imagery can also appeal to the senses of hearing, touch, taste, or smell. While imagery is an element in all types of writing, it is especially important in poetry:

> What is more gentle than a wind in summer?
> What is more soothing than the pretty hummer
> That stays one moment in an open flower,
> And buzzes cheerily from bower to bower?
> What is more tranquil than a musk-rose blowing
> In a green island, far from all men's knowing?
> —John Keats, *from* "Sleep and Poetry"

See pages 129, 384, 389, 415, 759, 843, 1109.

INCREMENTAL REPETITION   A device widely used in ballads whereby a line or lines are repeated with slight variations from stanza to stanza. Each repetition advances the plot of the narrative. Incremental repetition is used in the folk ballad "Lord Randall" (Collection 2).

See page 97.

IN MEDIAS RES   The technique of starting a story in the middle and then using a flashback to tell what happened earlier. *In medias res* is Latin for "in the middle of things." Traditional epics begin *in medias res*. For example, Milton's *Paradise Lost* (Collection 5) opens with Satan and his cohorts in Hell, after the war in Heaven and their fall, events that are recounted later in a flashback.

INTERIOR MONOLOGUE   See Stream of Consciousness.

IRONY   A contrast or discrepancy between expectation and reality—between what is said and what is really meant, between what is expected and what really happens, or between what appears to be true and what really is true.

Verbal irony occurs when a writer or speaker says one thing but really means something quite different—often the opposite of what he or she has said. If you tell your friend that you "just love being kept waiting in the rain," you are using verbal irony. A classic example of verbal irony is Jonathan Swift's suggestion in *A Modest Proposal* (Collection 6) that the Irish solve their poverty and overpopulation problems by selling their babies as food to their English landlords.

Situational irony occurs when what actually happens is the opposite of what is expected or appropriate. In James Joyce's story "Araby" (Collection 13), the boy hears about a bazaar called Araby and imagines that it will be a splendid, exotic place. Yet when he arrives, he finds that in reality Araby is cheap and commonplace.

Dramatic irony occurs when the audience or the reader knows something important that a character in a play or story does not know. Forceful dramatic irony occurs at several points in Shakespeare's *Macbeth* (Collection 4). One example is in Act II, Scene 4: Macduff suspects that Duncan has been murdered by his own sons, but the audience knows that Macbeth is the murderer. Dramatic irony is also a powerful device in William Blake's "innocence" poem "The Chimney Sweeper" (Collection 8). The speaker is a child who believes what he has been told—that "if all do their duty they need not fear harm." But the reader, who is not so innocent, realizes that this is not so.

See pages 131, 487, 501, 994, 1069, 1081, 1138.

JOURNAL   A day-by-day record of events and personal impressions kept by an individual. A journal is somewhat less intimate than a **diary,** and more strictly chronological than an **autobiography,** which can jump back and forth in time in order to tell a coherent story or emphasize a particular theme. The term *journal* is also applied to periodicals that contain news or matters of current interest. Daniel Defoe adapted the form to fictional use in *A Journal of the Plague Year* (Collection 7).

See pages 557, 582, 583.
See also Autobiography, Diary.

KENNING   In Anglo-Saxon poetry, a metaphorical phrase or compound word used to name a person, place, thing, or event indirectly. *Beowulf* (Collection 1) includes the kennings "whale-road" for the sea and "shepherd of evil" for Grendel.

See page 48.
See also Epithet.

LITERARY BALLAD   See Ballad.

LYRIC POETRY   Poetry that focuses on expressing emotions or thoughts, rather than on telling a story. Most lyrics are short, and they usually imply rather than directly state a single strong emotion. The term *lyric* comes from the Greek. In ancient Greece, lyric poems were recited to the accompaniment of a stringed instrument called the lyre. Today, poets still try to make their lyrics melodious, but they rely only on the musical effects they can create with words (such as **rhyme, rhythm, alliteration,** and **onomatopoeia**). Coleridge's "This Lime-Tree Bower My Prison," Wordsworth's "Tintern Abbey" (both in Collection 8), and Matthew Arnold's "Dover Beach" (Collection 11) are all lyric poems.

See pages 629, 631, 668, 1033.

METAPHOR   A figure of speech that makes a comparison between two seemingly unlike things without using the connective words *like, as, than,* **or** *resembles.* You are using a metaphor if you say you're "at the end of your rope" or describe two political candidates as "running neck and neck."

Some metaphors are **directly** stated, like Percy Bysshe Shelley's comparison "My soul is an enchanted boat." (If he had written, "My soul is *like* an enchanted boat," he would have been using a **simile.**) Other metaphors are **implied,** like John Suckling's line "Time shall molt away his wings." The words *molt* and *wings* imply a comparison between time and a bird shedding its feathers.

An **extended metaphor** is a metaphor that is extended, or developed, over several lines of writing or even throughout an entire poem. In the following stanza, the speaker develops a comparison between two lovers and two separate streams that flow into the same river. (The title and last line allude to the Biblical Song of Songs.)

> Even like two little bank-dividing brooks,
>   That wash the pebbles with their wanton
>   streams,
> And having ranged and searched a thousand
>   nooks,
>   Meet both at length in silver-breasted Thames
>   Where in greater current they conjoin:
> So I my best-beloved's am, so he is mine.
> —Francis Quarles, *from* "My Beloved Is Mine and I Am His"

A **dead metaphor** is a metaphor that has become so common that we no longer even notice that it is a figure of speech. Our everyday language is filled with dead metaphors, such as *foot of the bed, bone of contention,* and *mouth of the river.*

A **mixed metaphor** is the incongruous mixture of two or more metaphors. Mixed metaphors are usually unintentional and often conjure up ludicrous images: "If you put your money on that horse, you'll be barking up the wrong tree."

See pages 214, 841, 851, 1118.

METAPHYSICAL CONCEIT   See Conceit.

METAPHYSICAL POETRY   A term applied to the poetry of John Donne, Andrew Marvell, and other seventeenth-century poets who wrote in a similarly difficult and abstract style. Metaphysical poetry, which is intellectual and detached in contrast to the Elizabethan love poetry that preceded it, is distinguished by ingenious, obscure imagery, philosophical meditation, rough-sounding meter, and verbal wit.

See pages 246, 247.

METER   A generally regular pattern of stressed and unstressed syllables in poetry. When we want to indicate the metrical pattern of a poem, we mark the stressed syllables with the symbol ′ and the unstressed syllables with the symbol ˘. Indicating the metrical pattern of a poem in this way is called **scanning** the poem, or **scansion.** Here is how to scan these lines from William Blake's "The Tyger" (Collection 8):

> ′ ˘ ′ ˘ ′ ˘ ′
> Tyger! Tyger! burning bright
> ′ ˘ ′ ˘ ′ ˘ ′
> In the forests of the night

Meter is measured in units called feet. A **foot** consists of one stressed syllable and usually one or more unstressed syllables. The basic metrical feet used in English poetry are the **iamb** (as in cŏnvínce), the **trochee** (as in bórrŏw), the **anapest** (as in cŏntrădíct), the **dactyl** (as in áccŭrătĕ), and the **spondee** (as in séawéed). A poem is described as iambic, trochaic, anapestic, dactylic, or spondaic according to what kind of foot appears most often in its lines.

A complete description of a metrical line indicates both the type and number of feet the line contains. For example, a line of iambic pentameter consists of five iambs, while a line of trochaic tetrameter consists of four trochees.

See pages 216, 385, 525, 712, 807.

METONYMY   A figure of speech in which something closely related to a thing or suggested by it is substituted for the thing itself. You are using metonymy if you call the judiciary "the bench," the king "the crown," the president (or presidential staff) "the White House," or the race track "the turf." Closely related to metonymy is **synecdoche** (si·nek′də·kē), a figure of speech in which a part of a thing stands for the whole, as in "lend a hand."

MOCK EPIC   A comic narrative poem that parodies the epic by treating a trivial subject in a lofty, grand manner. A mock epic uses dignified language, elaborate figures of speech, and supernatural intervention. The style of the mock epic is called **mock heroic** (and short mock epics are often called mock heroics). Alexander Pope's *Rape of the Lock* (Collection 6) is considered the supreme mock epic in the English language.

See page 526.

MOOD   *See* Atmosphere.

MOTIF   In literature, a word, character, object, image, metaphor, or idea that recurs in a work or in several works. The rose is a motif that runs through many love poems. The motif of ill-fitting clothes appears throughout Shakespeare's *Macbeth* (Collection 4). It starts in Act I, Scene 3, when Macbeth asks Ross: "The Thane of Cawdor lives: why do you dress me / In borrowed robes?" This is soon followed by Banquo's observation: "New honors come upon him, / Like our strange garments, cleave not to their mold / But with the aid of use." The motif of ill-fitting clothes reaches its culmination in Act V, Scene 2, when Angus says of Macbeth: "Now does he feel his title / Hang loose about him, like a giant's robe / Upon a dwarfish thief." A motif almost always bears an important relationship to the **theme** of a work of literature.

MOTIVATION   The reasons for or forces behind the action of a character. Motivation is revealed through a combination of the character's desires and moral nature with the circumstances in which he or she is placed. In *Macbeth* (Collection 4), the witches' prophecy and Macbeth's overweening ambition combine to provide the motivation for his killing of the king.

See page 951.
See also Character.

MYTH   An anonymous traditional story that usually serves to explain a belief, custom, or mysterious natural phenomenon. Most myths grew out of religious rituals, and almost all of them involve the exploits of gods and heroes. Such myths make it possible to understand and cope with things beyond human control. Every culture has its own **mythology,** but in the Western world, the most important myths have been those of ancient Greece and Rome. In twentieth-century literature, **allusions** to myth are often **ironic,** intended to reveal how diminished humanity has become in comparison to grand mythological figures.

See pages 368, 1081, 1105.

NARRATOR   One who tells, or narrates, a story. In fiction, the narrator occupies any one of a variety of relations to the events described: from the center of the action to a distant, even objective, observer. A narrator may also be reliable or unreliable—if unreliable, the reader is made aware that the narrator's perceptions and interpretations of the action are different from those of the author. Such unreliable narrators can be deceitful or bumbling, but are often just naive characters—like Larry, the young narrator who humorously misunderstands much of the story's action in Frank O'Connor's "My Oedipus Complex" (Collection 14).

See pages 557, 651, 714, 857, 1031.
See also Point of View.

NEOCLASSICISM   The revival of classical standards and forms during the late seventeenth and eighteenth centuries. The neoclassicists valued the classical ideals of order, reason, balance, harmony, clarity, and restraint. In particular, they studied and tried to emulate the Latin poets Horace and Virgil. Alexander Pope (Collection 6) and John Dryden (Collection 7) were leaders of the neoclassical movement in England.

See page 469, 532, 580.

NOVEL   A long fictional prose narrative, usually of more than fifty thousand words. In general, the novel uses the same basic literary elements as the short story: **plot, character, setting, theme,** and **point of view.** The novel's length usually permits these elements to be more fully developed than they are in the short story. However, this is not always true of the modern novel. Some are basically character studies, with only the barest plot structures. Others reveal little about their characters and concentrate instead on setting or tone or even language itself.

Some of the greatest novels in English literature are *Tom Jones* by Henry Fielding, *Pride and Prejudice* by Jane Austen, *Jane Eyre* by Charlotte Brontë, *David Copperfield* and *Great Expectations* by Charles Dickens, *Middlemarch* by George Eliot, *Jude the Obscure* by Thomas Hardy, *Lord Jim* by Joseph Conrad, *Sons and Lovers* by D. H. Lawrence, and *Ulysses* by James Joyce.

See pages 482, 516, 726, 795, 859, 916.

OCTAVE **An eight-line stanza or poem or the first eight lines of an Italian, or Petrarchan, sonnet.** The usual rhyme scheme of the octave in this type of sonnet is *abbaabba*. The octave, which is sometimes called the **octet,** is followed by a six-line **sestet** with the rhyme scheme *cdecde* or *cdcdcd*.

See pages 220, 838.
See also Sonnet.

ODE **A complex, generally long lyric poem on a serious subject.** In English poetry, there are basically two types of odes. One is highly formal and dignified in style and is generally written for ceremonial or public occasions. This type of ode derives from the choral odes of the classical Greek poet Pindar. John Dryden's "Song for St. Cecilia's Day" is an English version of the Pindaric ode. The other type of ode derives from those written by the Latin poet Horace, and it is much more personal and reflective. In English poetry, it is exemplified by the intimate, meditative odes of such Romantic poets as Wordsworth, Keats, and Shelley (Collections 8 and 9).

See pages 482, 668, 737.

ONOMATOPOEIA **The use of a word whose sound imitates or suggests its meaning.** Many familiar words, such as *clap, squish, snort,* and *whine,* are examples of onomatopoeia. In poetry, onomatopoeia can reinforce meaning while creating evocative and musical effects. The following lines contain several imitative sounds:

> The sparrow's chirrup on the roof,
>   The slow clock ticking, and the sound
> Which to the wooing wind aloof
>   The poplar made, did all confound
> Her sense. . . .
> —Alfred, Lord Tennyson, *from* "Mariana"

See pages 927, 1037, 1050.

OTTAVA RIMA **An eight-line stanza in iambic pentameter with the rhyme scheme *abababcc.*** The form developed in Italy and was popularized by the fourteenth-century Italian poet Giovanni Boccaccio. The most famous example of ottava rima in English poetry is Lord Byron's *Don Juan* (Collection 9). William Butler Yeats's "Sailing to Byzantium" is another notable example.

See page 714.

OXYMORON **A figure of speech that combines apparently contradictory or incongruous ideas.** "Bitter sweet," "cruel kindness," and "eloquent silence" are oxymorons. The classic oxymoron "wise fool" is almost a literal translation of the term from the Greek—*oxys* means "sharp" or "keen," and *moros* means "foolish." A famous oxymoron in literature is Milton's description of Hell in *Paradise Lost:* "No light, but rather darkness visible . . ."

See page 924.

PARABLE **A short, allegorical story that teaches a moral or religious lesson about life.** The most famous parables in Western literature are those told by Jesus in the Gospels of the Bible.

See page 425.

PARADOX **An apparent contradiction that is actually true.** A paradox may be a statement or a situation; as a statement, it is a figure of speech. The metaphysical and Cavalier poets of the seventeenth century (Collection 3) made brilliant use of paradoxes, as in this famous example:

> One short sleep past, we wake eternally,
> And death shall be no more; Death, thou shalt die.
> —John Donne, *from* "Death Be Not Proud"

The speaker in the cartoon below doesn't understand the famous series of paradoxes that open *A Tale of Two Cities* by Charles Dickens.

See pages 218, 254, 266, 318, 738.

"I wish you would make up your mind, Mr. Dickens. Was it the best of times or was it the worst of times? It could scarcely have been both."

Drawing by Handelsman; © 1987 The New Yorker Magazine, Inc.

PARALLELISM **The repetition of words, phrases, or sentences that have the same grammatical structure, or that restate a similar idea.** Parallelism is often used in literature meant to be spoken aloud, such as poetry, drama, and speeches, because it can help make lines emotional, rhythmic, and memorable. It is also one of the most important techniques used in Biblical poetry. The parallelism in the following lines heightens their emotional effect and sharpens their meaning:

Cruelty has a human heart
And Jealousy a human face;
Terror the human form divine,
And Secrecy the human dress.
—William Blake, *from* "A Divine Image"
See pages 405, 421, 521, 655.

PARODY   The imitation of a work of literature, art, or music for amusement or instruction. Parodies usually use exaggeration or inappropriate subject matter to make a serious style seem ridiculous. Alexander Pope's *Rape of the Lock* (Collection 6) is a parody of such serious and sweeping epics as the *Iliad* and the *Aeneid.* Richard Armour's portrayal of *Macbeth*'s famous witches (Collection 4) is a contemporary example of parody.

See pages 742, 920, 1155.

PASTORAL   A type of poem that depicts rustic life in idyllic, idealized terms. The term *pastoral* comes from the Latin word for shepherd, and originally pastorals were about shepherds, nymphs, and rustic life. Today, the term has a looser meaning and refers to any poem that portrays an idyllic rural setting or that expresses nostalgia for an age or place of lost innocence. The most famous traditional English pastoral is Christopher Marlowe's "The Passionate Shepherd to His Love," which is satirized in Sir Walter Raleigh's "The Nymph's Reply to the Shepherd" (both in Collection 3). Examples of untraditional pastorals include William Wordsworth's "Tintern Abbey" (Collection 8), William Butler Yeats's "The Lake Isle of Innisfree" (Collection 13), and Dylan Thomas's "Fern Hill" (Collection 13).

See pages 233, 520, 606.

PERSONIFICATION   A kind of metaphor in which a nonhuman thing or quality is talked about as if it were human. In these lines the speaker describes the wind as if it were capable of feeling the human emotion of grief:

Rough wind, that moanest loud
Grief too sad for song
—Percy Bysshe Shelley, *from* "A Dirge"
See pages 665, 682, 964.
See also Apostrophe, Figure of Speech, Metaphor.

PLOT   The series of related events that make up a story or drama. The plot is the underlying structure of a story. Most plots are built on these "bare bones": A **basic situation,** or **exposition,** introduces the characters, setting, and, usually, the story's major **conflict.** Out of this basic situation, **complications** develop that intensify the conflict. **Suspense** mounts until a **climax**—the tensest or most exciting part of the plot—is reached, where something happens to determine the outcome of the conflict. Finally, all the problems or mysteries of the plot are unraveled in the **resolution,** or **dénouement.**

See pages 155, 388, 1069, 1098.
See also Climax.

POINT OF VIEW   The vantage point from which a writer tells a story. There are three main points of view: **first-person, limited third-person,** and **omniscient third-person.**

In the **first-person point of view,** the narrator is a character in the story. Using the pronoun *I*, this narrator tells us his or her own experiences but cannot reveal any other character's private thoughts. When we read a story told in the first person, we hear and see only what the narrator hears and sees. We may have to interpret what this narrator says because a first-person narrator may or may not be objective, honest, or perceptive. For example, in Frank O'Connor's "My Oedipus Complex" (Collection 14), the narrator is a young boy whose understanding and insight are limited by his age: He believes that babies are purchased for seventeen shillings.

In the **limited third-person point of view,** the narrator is outside the story—like an omniscient narrator—but tells the story from the vantage point of only one character. The narrator can enter the mind of this chosen character but cannot tell what any other characters are thinking except by observation. This narrator also can go only where the chosen character goes. For example, "In the Shadow of War" by Ben Okri (Collection 12) is told entirely from the point of view of Omovo, the main character. We experience the stupifying summer heat, the mysteriousness of the veiled woman, and the horror of the gruesome river scene through Omovo's eyes alone.

In the **omniscient** (or **"all-knowing"**) **point of view,** the person telling the story knows everything that's going on in the story. This omniscient narrator is outside the story, a godlike observer who can tell us what all the characters are thinking and feeling, as well as what is happening anywhere in the story. For example, in "The Rocking-Horse Winner" by D. H. Lawrence (Collection 13), the narrator enters into the thoughts and secrets of every character, revealing both the "hard little place" in the mother's heart and Paul's determination to "compel her attention" by being lucky.

See pages 646, 970, 993, 996, 1023.
See also Narrator, Stream of Consciousness.

PROTAGONIST   The main character in fiction, drama, or narrative poetry. The protagonist is the character we focus our attention on—the person whose conflict sets the plot in motion. (The character or force that blocks the protagonist is called the **antagonist.**) In *Beowulf* (Collection 1), the title character is the protagonist and the monster Grendel his antagonist. Most protagonists are **rounded, dynamic** characters who change in some important way by the end of the story. Whatever the protagonist's weaknesses, we still usually identify with his or her conflict and care about how it is resolved.

PUN   A play on the multiple meanings of a word, or on two words that sound alike but have different

meanings. Many jokes and riddles are based on puns. ("Why was Cleopatra so negative? Answer: Because she was the queen of denial.") Shakespeare was one of the greatest punsters of all time. Some of his puns are humorous, but others are more serious and subtle wordplays. A sinister pun occurs in *Macbeth*'s Act II, Scene 2 (Collection 4), after Macbeth has murdered Duncan:

> I'll gild the faces of the grooms withal,
> For it must seem their guilt.

Here, Lady Macbeth plays on the words *gild* (to coat something with gold leaf) and *guilt.*

See page 1037.

QUATRAIN   A four-line stanza or poem, or a group of four lines unified by a rhyme scheme. The quatrain is the most common verse unit in English poetry. Here is a quatrain with the rhyme scheme *abba* (sometimes called the "envelope stanza"):

> Thy voice is on the rolling air;
>> I hear thee where the waters run;
>> Thou standest in the rising sun,
> And in the setting thou art fair.
>> —Alfred, Lord Tennyson, *from In Memoriam A.H.H.*
>>> *See pages 97, 220.*

REALISM   In literature and art, the attempt to depict people and things as they really are, without idealization. Realism as a movement developed during the mid–nineteenth century as a reaction against Romanticism. Realist writers believed that fiction should truthfully depict the harsh, gritty reality of everyday life without beautifying, sentimentalizing, or romanticizing it. The Norwegian playwright Henrik Ibsen was among the first to introduce realism to the stage. The English novelists Charles Dickens, George Eliot, Thomas Hardy, and Joseph Conrad are all considered realists.

See pages 799, 1068.
See also Romanticism.

REFRAIN   A repeated word, phrase, line, or group of lines. While refrains are most common in poetry and songs, they are sometimes used in prose, particularly speeches. Refrains are used to create rhythm, build suspense, or emphasize important words or ideas.

See pages 90, 97.

RESOLUTION   See Plot.

RHYME   The repetition of accented vowel sounds and all sounds following them in words that are close together in a poem. *Park* and *bark* rhyme, as do *sorrow* and *borrow.* The most common type of rhyme, **end rhyme,** occurs at the ends of lines. **Internal rhyme** occurs within lines. Both types are used throughout *The Rime of the Ancient Mariner* by Samuel Taylor Coleridge (Collection 8), contributing to the poem's bouncy, songlike rhythm:

> The fair breeze blew, the white foam flew,
> The furrow followed free;
> We were the first that ever burst
> Into that silent sea.

When words sound similar but do not rhyme exactly, they are called **approximate rhymes** (or **half rhymes, slant rhymes,** or **imperfect rhymes**). In the following stanza, *began/gun* and *flush/flash* rhyme by means of **consonance,** while *began/flash* and *flush/gun* rhyme (very loosely) by means of **assonance:**

> That night when joy began
> Our narrowest veins to flush,
> We waited for the flash
> Of morning's leveled gun.
>> —W. H. Auden, *from* "Five Songs"

The pattern of rhymed lines in a poem is called its **rhyme scheme.** A rhyme scheme is indicated by giving each new rhyme a new letter of the alphabet. For example, the rhyme scheme of Coleridge's lines is *abcb.* There are two interlocking rhyme schemes in Auden's stanza. The one based on consonance is *abba;* the one based on assonance is *abab.*

See pages 97, 151, 221, 683, 807, 840, 930.

RHYTHM   The alternation of stressed and unstressed syllables in language. Rhythm occurs naturally in all forms of spoken and written language. The most obvious kind of rhythm is produced by **meter,** the regular pattern of stressed and unstressed syllables found in some poetry. But writers can also create less structured rhythms by using rhyme, repetition, pauses, and variations in line length and by balancing long and short words or phrases. (Poetry that is written without any regular meter or rhyme scheme is called **free verse.**) The rhythm of the following lines reinforces their meaning. The words themselves seem dappled, as if a painter's brush has stippled them onto the page:

> All things counter, original, spare, strange;
>> Whatever is fickle, freckled (who knows how?)
>> With swift, slow; sweet, sour; adazzle, dim
>>> —Gerard Manley Hopkins, *from* "Pied Beauty"
>>> *See pages 90, 712, 1050.*
>>> *See also Free Verse, Meter.*

RISING ACTION   See Climax.

ROMANCE   Historically, a medieval verse narrative chronicling the adventures of a brave knight or other hero who must undertake a quest and overcome great danger for love of a noble lady or high ideal. Such heroic characters are bound by the code of **chivalry,** which emphasizes loyalty to one's lord and ready service to the oppressed. They also adhere to the philosophy of **courtly love,** an idealized relationship between the sexes in which men perform brave deeds to win the approval of their ladies.

   Today, the term *romance* has come to mean any story that presents a world that is happier, more exciting, or more heroic than the real world. Characters in romances "live happily ever after" in a world where good always triumphs over evil. Many of today's most popular novels, movies, TV shows, and even cartoons are essentially romances. *Sir Gawain and the Green Knight* (Collection 2), Sir Thomas Malory's *Le Morte*

Darthur, and Edmund Spenser's *Faerie Queene* (Collection 3) are famous English romances.

See pages 82, 160, 174, 826.

ROMANTICISM   A literary, artistic, and philosophical movement that developed during the late eighteenth and early nineteenth centuries as a reaction against neoclassicism. While classicism and neoclassicism emphasize reason, order, harmony, and restraint, Romanticism emphasizes emotion, imagination, intuition, freedom, personal experience, the beauty of nature, the primitive, the exotic, and even the grotesque. However, many critics feel that the traditional opposition between Romanticism and classicism is all too often forced and exaggerated.

In English literature, William Blake, Samuel Taylor Coleridge, William Wordsworth, Percy Bysshe Shelley, John Keats, Lord Byron, Mary Wollstonecraft Shelley, and Sir Walter Scott are the leading Romantic writers (Collections 8 and 9).

See pages 630, 635, 668.

RUN-ON LINE   A line of poetry that does not contain a pause or conclusion at the end, but rather continues on to the next line. Run-on lines force the reader on to the next line in order to make sense of the entire grammatical unit; such lines are said to exhibit **enjambment** (French for "striding over"). The following lines from Margaret Atwood's "Mushrooms" (Collection 13) are run-on lines:

> Here is the handful
> of shadow I have brought back to you:
> this decay, this hope, this mouth-
> ful of dirt, this poetry.

See page 662.
See also End-stopped Line.

SARCASM   A kind of particularly cutting irony, in which praise is used tauntingly to indicate its opposite in meaning. The speaker's tone of voice can also be an important clue in understanding this kind of irony. When a mud-soaked, windblown friend arrives for dinner, one might say sneeringly, "Why, don't you look lovely!"

See pages 501, 994.

SATIRE   A kind of writing that ridicules human weakness, vice, or folly in order to bring about social reform. Satires often try to persuade the reader to do or believe something by showing the opposite view as absurd or—even more forcefully—vicious and inhumane. Among the most brilliant and scathing satirists in English literature are Geoffrey Chaucer, Alexander Pope, John Dryden, Jonathan Swift, Jane Austen, George Bernard Shaw, and Evelyn Waugh.

See pages 481, 495, 500, 537, 714.

SCANSION   See Meter.

SESTET   A six-line stanza or poem, or the last six lines of an Italian, or Petrarchan, sonnet. The usual rhyme scheme of the sestet in an Italian sonnet is *cdecde* or *cdcdcd*. It follows an eight-line **octave** with the rhyme scheme *abbaabba*.

See pages 220, 838.

SETTING   The time and place of a story or play. Usually the setting is established early in a story. It may be presented immediately through descriptive details, as in Anita Desai's "Games at Twilight" (Collection 14), or it may be revealed more gradually, as in Rudyard Kipling's "The Mark of the Beast" (Collection 11). Setting often contributes greatly to a story's emotional effect. The wild heath setting at the opening of Shakespeare's *Macbeth* (Collection 4) produces an atmosphere of horror, while the green valley in Wordsworth's *Tintern Abbey* (Collection 8) creates a contemplative calm. Setting may also play a role in the story's conflict, as the fortresslike suburban houses do in Nadine Gordimer's "Once Upon a Time" (Collection 15). Two of the most important functions of setting are to reveal character and suggest a theme, as the setting of blitzed London does in Graham Greene's "The Destructors" (Collection 12).

See pages 606, 673, 679, 951, 993, 1042.
See also Atmosphere.

SHORT STORY   A brief work of fiction. The short story generally has a simpler plot than a **novel,** and often reveals character through significant moments, or **epiphanies,** rather than through the accretion of many incidents or detailed descriptions.

See page 1068.

SIMILE   A figure of speech that makes a comparison between two seemingly unlike things by using a connective word such as *like, as, than, or resembles.* Here is a simile from William Wordsworth's "It Is a Beauteous Evening, Calm and Free" that makes a connection between two sound images:

> The holy time is quiet as a Nun
> Breathless with adoration. . . .

An **epic simile,** also called a **Homeric simile,** is an extended simile in which many parallels are made between two dissimilar things.

See pages 247, 449, 851.
See also Figure of Speech, Metaphor.

SOLILOQUY   A long speech in which a character who is usually alone onstage expresses his or her private thoughts or feelings. The soliloquy is an old dramatic convention that was particularly popular in Shakespeare's day. Perhaps the most famous soliloquy is the "To be or not to be" speech in Shakespeare's play *Hamlet.* Another major soliloquy occurs in Act V, Scene 5, of *Macbeth* (Collection 4), when Macbeth bewails his wife's death in the celebrated "Tomorrow, and tomorrow, and tomorrow" speech.

See page 383.

SONNET   A fourteen-line lyric poem, usually written in iambic pentameter, that has one of several rhyme schemes. There are two major types of sonnets. The oldest sonnet form is the **Italian sonnet,** also called the **Petrarchan sonnet** (after the fourteenth-century Italian poet Francis Petrarch, who popularized the form). The Petrarchan sonnet is divided into two parts: an eight-line **octave** with the rhyme scheme *abbaabba* and a six-line **sestet** with the rhyme scheme *cdecde* or *cdcdcd.* The octave usually

HANDBOOK OF LITERARY TERMS   1201

presents a problem, poses a question, or expresses an idea, which the sestet, or **turn,** then resolves, answers, or drives home. John Donne's sonnets (Collection 3) and John Keats's "On First Looking into Chapman's Homer" (Collection 9) are written in the Italian form.

The other major sonnet form, which was widely used by Shakespeare, is called the **Shakespearean sonnet,** or the **English sonnet.** It has three four-line units, or **quatrains,** followed by a concluding two-line unit, or **couplet.** The organization of thought in the Shakespearean sonnet usually corresponds to this structure. The three quatrains often express related ideas or examples, while the couplet sums up the poet's conclusion or message. The most common rhyme scheme for the Shakespearean sonnet is *abab cdcd efef gg.*

A third type of sonnet, the **Spenserian sonnet,** was developed by Edmund Spenser (Collection 3). Like the Shakespearean sonnet, the Spenserian sonnet is divided into three quatrains and a couplet, but it uses a rhyme scheme that links the quatrains: *abab bcbc cdcd ee.*

A group of sonnets on a related theme is called a **sonnet sequence** or a **sonnet cycle.**

See pages 219, 223, 268, 668, 746, 838.

SPEAKER **The imaginary voice, or persona, assumed by the author of a poem.** This voice is often not identified immediately or directly. Rather, the reader gradually comes to understand that a unique voice is speaking, and that this speaker's characteristics must be interpreted as they are revealed. This process is an especially important part of reading a **lyric poem.**

See pages 264, 635, 663, 759, 763, 1033.

SPENSERIAN STANZA **A nine-line stanza with the rhyme scheme *ababbcbcc.*** The first eight lines of the stanza are in iambic pentameter, and the ninth line is an **alexandrine**—that is, a line of iambic hexameter. The form was created by Edmund Spenser for his long poem *The Faerie Queene* (Collection 3). Several English Romantic poets have used the Spenserian stanza, including John Keats, Percy Bysshe Shelley, Lord Byron, and Robert Burns (Collections 8 and 9).

See pages 221, 725.

SPRUNG RHYTHM **A term coined by Gerard Manley Hopkins to designate his unconventional use of poetic meter.** Instead of the regular, musical **meter** of most poetry, Hopkins used sounds that would impede smooth reading and give some sense of Anglo-Saxon poetry, which had greatly influenced him. Sprung rhythm is based on the stressed syllables in a line without regard for the number of unstressed syllables; it also makes frequent use of **alliteration** and inverted syntax.

See page 840.

STANZA **A group of consecutive lines in a poem that form a single unit.** A stanza in a poem is something like a paragraph in prose: It often expresses a unit of thought. A stanza may consist of only one line, or of any number of lines beyond that. The word *stanza* is an Italian word for "stopping place" or "place to rest."

See page 220.

STREAM OF CONSCIOUSNESS **A writing style that tries to depict the random flow of thoughts, emotions, memories, and associations rushing through a character's mind.** The term **interior monologue** is often used interchangeably with "stream of consciousness." James Joyce (Collection 13) and Virginia Woolf (Collection 15) were among the first to experiment with the stream-of-consciousness style in their novels.

See page 996.

STYLE **The manner in which writers or speakers say what they wish to say.** An author's style simultaneously expresses both the author's ideas and his or her individuality. Style is closely connected to **diction,** or word choice, and, depending on what the author wants to communicate, can be formal or casual, plain or ornate, abstract or concrete, as well as comic, poetic, forceful, journalistic, and so on. Sir Francis Bacon (Collection 5) and Samuel Johnson (Collection 7) are both often cited as exemplars of style.

See pages 457, 578.
See also Diction.

SUSPENSE **The uncertainty or anxiety we feel about what is going to happen next in a story.** Writers often create suspense by dropping hints or clues that something—especially something bad—is going to happen. In "The Demon Lover" by Elizabeth Bowen (Collection 13), we begin to feel suspense when Mrs. Drover receives a mysterious letter that makes her lips "go white"; our anxiety increases sharply when the flashback reveals that the letter writer is her old fiancé; and our suspense reaches a climax when she escapes into a taxi and we discover who the driver is.

See pages 332, 333.

SYMBOL **A person, place, thing, or event that stands both for itself and for something beyond itself.** Many symbols have become widely recognized: A lion is a symbol of power; a dove is a symbol of peace. These established symbols are sometimes called **public symbols.** But writers often invent new, personal symbols, whose meaning is revealed in a work of poetry or prose. For example, the old house in Graham Greene's "The Destructors" (Collection 12) is a symbol of civilization and beauty.

See pages 174, 393, 647, 739, 981, 999, 1061.

SYMBOLISM **A literary movement that began in France during the late nineteenth century and advocated the use of highly personal symbols to suggest ideas, emotions, and moods.** The French Symbolists believed that emotions are fleeting, individual, and essentially inexpressible—and that therefore the poet is forced to suggest meaning rather than directly express it. Many twentieth-century writers were influenced by the Symbolists, including William Butler Yeats, T. S. Eliot, James Joyce, Virginia Woolf, and Dylan Thomas (Collections 12, 13, 15).

SYNAESTHESIA **In literature, a term used for descriptions of one kind of sensation in terms of another.** For example, color may be described as sound (a "loud" yellow), sound as taste (how "sweet" the sound), odor as tangible (a "sharp" smell), and so on. These lines from Keats's "Ode to a Nightingale" (Collection 9) describe a sip of wine as tasting of color, motion, sound, and heat:

Tasting of Flora and the country green,
Dance, and Provençal song, and sunburnt mirth!

Synaesthesia was frequently used by the Romantic poets and, later, by such French Symbolist poets as Charles Baudelaire and Arthur Rimbaud.

See page 759.

SYNECDOCHE *See Metonymy.*

TERCET **A triplet, or stanza of three lines, in which each line ends with the same rhyme.** The term also designates either of the two three-line groups forming the sestet of a **sonnet.**

See pages 525, 805.

TERZA RIMA **An interlocking, three-line stanza form with the rhyme scheme *aba bcb cdc ded* and so on.** Terza rima is an Italian verse form originally devised by Dante for *The Divine Comedy* (Collection 4). Among the many English poems that borrowed the form, Shelley's "Ode to the West Wind" (Collection 9) is one of the most famous.

See page 738.

THEME **The central idea or insight of a work of literature.** A theme is not the same as the subject of a work, which can usually be expressed in a word or two: old age, ambition, love. The theme is the idea the writer wishes to convey *about* that subject—the writer's view of the world or revelation about human nature. For example, one theme of James Joyce's "Araby" (Collection 13) might be stated this way: One of the painful aspects of growing up is that some of our dreams turn out to be illusions.

A theme may also be different from a **moral,** which is a lesson or rule about how to live. The theme of "Araby" stated above, for example, would not make sense as a moral.

While some stories, poems, and plays have themes that are directly stated, most themes are implied. It is up to the reader to piece together all the clues the writer has provided about the work's total meaning. Two of the most important clues to consider are how the main character has changed and how the conflict has been resolved.

See pages 14, 231, 962, 1117, 1147.

TONE **The attitude a writer takes toward the reader, a subject, or a character.** Tone is conveyed through the writer's choice of words and details. For example, Jonathan Swift's *A Modest Proposal* (Collection 6) is satiric in tone, while the tone of "Pied Beauty" by Gerard Manley Hopkins (Collection 10) might be described as awed.

See pages 263, 575, 714, 849, 1096.

TRAGEDY **A play, novel, or other narrative depicting serious and important events, in which the main character comes to an unhappy end.** In a tragedy, the main character is usually dignified, courageous, and often high ranking. This character's downfall may be caused by a **tragic flaw**—an error in judgment or character weakness—or the downfall may result from forces beyond his or her control. The **tragic hero** usually wins some self-knowledge and wisdom, even though he or she suffers defeat, possibly even death. Tragedy is distinct from **comedy,** in which an ordinary character overcomes obstacles to get what he or she wants. *Beowulf* (Collection 1), Shakespeare's *Macbeth* (Collection 4), and Milton's *Paradise Lost* (Collection 5) are all tragedies.

See pages 300, 591.
See also Comedy.

TURN *See Sonnet.*

TURNING POINT *See Climax.*

UNDERSTATEMENT **A figure of speech that consists of saying less than what is really meant, or saying something with less force than is appropriate.** Understatement is the opposite of **hyperbole** and is a form of **irony.** You are using understatement if you come in from a torrential downpour and say, "It's a bit wet out there," or if you describe a Great Dane as "not exactly a small dog." Understatement can be used to create a kind of deadpan humor, but it can also function as a sustained ironic tone throughout a work, as in W. H. Auden's "The Unknown Citizen" (Collection 14).

See page 501.
See also Hyperbole, Irony.

VERNACULAR *See Dialect.*

VILLANELLE **A nineteen-line poem divided into five tercets (three-line stanzas), each with the rhyme scheme *aba,* and a final quatrain with the rhyme scheme *abaa.*** Line 1 is repeated entirely to form lines 6, 12, and 18, while line 3 is repeated as lines 9, 15, and 19. Thus, there are only two rhymes in the poem, and the two lines used as **refrains** (lines 1 and 3) are paired as the final couplet. The villanelle was originally used in French pastoral poetry. Dylan Thomas's "Do Not Go Gentle into That Good Night" (Collection 13) is an example of a modern villanelle.

See page 1040.

WIT **A quality of speech or writing that combines verbal cleverness with keen perception, especially of the incongruous.** The definition of *wit* has undergone dramatic changes over the centuries. In the Middle Ages, it meant "common sense"; in the Renaissance, it meant "intelligence"; and in the seventeenth century, it meant "originality of thought." The modern meaning of *wit* began to develop during the eighteenth century with the formulations of John Dryden and Alexander Pope. In his *Essay on Criticism,* Pope said:

True wit is Nature to advantage dressed:
What oft was thought, but ne'er so well expressed

Perhaps the best examples of more modern wit can be found in the works of Oscar Wilde and Bernard Shaw.

See pages 480, 533, 714.

WORKPLACE WRITING

Your ability to write clear and effective business letters, memos, and résumés will be a major factor in your career success. As a student, you will write business letters to apply to colleges and universities for acceptance and to businesses for jobs. As an employee, you will write business letters, reports, and memos to communicate important information.

WRITING WITH COMPUTERS

Word Processing

Computers and software programs are powerful tools that make the writing process easier and more efficient. For example, when you are sending letters of application, the computer makes it easy to change the inside address and salutation without retyping the entire letter. Remember to save your work on the computer at frequent intervals, and make a backup on a disk before you turn off the computer.

Prewriting During **prewriting,** you can plan quickly, experiment with structure and phrasing, and then expand the most promising ideas.

Writing a Draft You can create a **draft** on the computer without having to stop and think about errors. As you gain experience, you can express your thoughts more rapidly.

Evaluating and Revising Word-processing features make **evaluation** and **revision** of a work in progress much easier. You can save your document, make changes, and then undo the changes if you decide you don't like them. Once you make the revisions, you can print out a clean copy without having to repeat steps.

Proofreading Many word-processing programs for the computer now include features that find and correct spelling, typographical, and grammatical errors. You can use search-and-replace functions to correct a specific type of error wherever it occurs in your document. Remember, however, that you must do the final **proofreading** to catch word usage errors.

Electronic Mail

Many business people use computers and **electronic mail (e-mail)** to send messages. You can send a message to a computer at the next desk or around the world. You also can save it for your records as a file on your computer. E-mail messages usually are short and to the point, but they still require careful planning. An e-mail message reflects on you and your organization, and privacy cannot be guaranteed.

WRITING EFFECTIVE BUSINESS LETTERS

In the business world, writing is structured and functional. People who receive your business correspondence will form a lasting impression of you or your employer based on the quality of the written documents they receive. If your readers are distracted from the content of your message by errors and inaccuracies, they may assume that you are incompetent or that your organization produces inferior work.

Guidelines for Contents of a Business Letter

Good business communications are correct, complete, clear, concise, concrete, and courteous. These qualities are the basis for a set of guidelines you can use to write effective business letters.

Types of Business Letters

Request or Order Letters A **request letter** asks for something. You write request letters to ask for information about a job, college, product, service, policy, or procedure. You write **order letters** to order merchandise by mail.

Complaint or Adjustment Letters You write a **complaint** or **adjustment letter** because you are dissatisfied with a person, product, or service.

Letters of Application A **letter of application** introduces you to a selection committee or a prospective employer. The letter should provide the reader with enough information to determine whether you are a good candidate for a job or scholarship or whether you should be accepted by a college or university. Keep the following points in mind when writing a letter of application.

1. Identify the job or situation you are applying for, and mention how you heard about it.

1204 COMMUNICATIONS HANDBOOK

Sample Letter of Application, Modified Block Style

Heading
Your address and the date you write the letter

4974 Kings Way
Lakeland, Florida 33809
May 13, 1996

Inside Address
Name, title, and address of person you are writing

Mr. Nathan Jones
Director of Personnel
Franklin & Neiman Interiors
96 Bayview Drive
Lakeland, Florida 33803

Salutation
Greeting, ended with a colon—use *Dear Sir or Madam:* or *Dear (business title):* if you don't know the person's name.

Dear Mr. Jones:

Are you looking for someone who carries out assigned responsibilities and takes pride in customer satisfaction? I do both, and I have important skills that qualify me for the position of summer intern advertised in Sunday's <u>Herald</u>.

Body
The main part of your letter, your message—if the body of your letter is longer than one paragraph, leave a blank line between paragraphs.

I will graduate from Polk High School on June 7. My course of study included college preparatory courses and art courses in art history, pencil drawing, watercolor, and interior design. I also have taken business courses in typing, bookkeeping, and computer literacy. I will be entering Florida State University this fall and plan to major in interior design.

Last summer, I worked as a volunteer at the Blossom Art Gallery, where I answered telephones, created a computer file of art prints in stock, and worked as a clerk in the gift shop. I also assisted the director, Ms. Glenda Ramirez, in creating a computer file of new artists, and I was responsible for three mass mailings about upcoming exhibits to gallery patrons.

I believe my education and summer work experience qualify me for the summer intern position. My references, who are listed on my résumé, can provide you with information about my work and my personal characteristics. Please call me at 555-9263 to set an appointment for an interview. I am home after 4:30 on weekdays. I look forward to hearing from you soon.

Sincerely,

Stephanie J. Hoskin

Stephanie J. Hoskin

Closing
Yours truly, Sincerely yours, or another closing, followed by a comma.

Signature
Sign your name in ink below the closing; type or print your name two lines below the signature.

Use if you're enclosing something with your letter.

Enclosure

2. Depending on the situation, you might include
   - your age, grade in school, and grade point average
   - your experience, activities, awards, and honors
   - qualities that make you a good choice
   - the dates or times you are available
3. Provide references, two or three responsible adults, other than relatives, who agree to recommend you. Include their addresses and telephone numbers.

GUIDELINES FOR WRITING BUSINESS LETTERS

- Use a courteous, positive, and professional tone to sound constructive and respectful.
- Use formal, standard English, avoiding slang, dialect, contractions, and abbreviations.
- State your purpose clearly and quickly.
- Include all necessary information.

WRITING INTEROFFICE MEMOS AND REPORTS

Memos

Memos are standard forms of communication in many organizations. They are concise messages that do not include all six parts of a letter, but they still tell the reader *when, who, what, where, why,* and *how.* Memos contain guide words (*DATE, TO, FROM, SUBJECT*) that immediately identify the date, destination, origin, and purpose of a message. They generally cover only one topic. The following are three common types of memos.

- **Meeting Notices** Include the meeting date, time, place, purpose, and any additional information that relates to the meeting.
- **Meeting Summaries** Provide a concise, factual report of decisions, directives, and discussions. Include the names and titles of participants.
- **Requests for Action or Information** Open by asking for information or making your request, and follow with details. If you have several requests, put them in a list, and phrase each one similarly. Include a deadline stating when you need a response.

Technical Writing and Business Reports

Technical writing and business reports are vital to the operation of a business. The reports vary in length, content, form, and formality, but they provide the information that people in organizations need to make plans and solve problems. Reports may be written or presented orally. They are classified according to different characteristics and may have more than one characteristic. You can group most reports into one of the following general categories.

Informational Reports Types of reports that present data include the following:

- periodic operating or status reports such as weekly sales reports
- situation reports such as trip, conference, and seminar reports
- investigative reports to examine problems and supply facts
- compliance reports that show conformity with laws and regulations

Analytical Reports These technical reports provide data, analyses, conclusions, and recommendations. They include

- justification/recommendation reports to analyze alternatives, interpret findings, and make recommendations
- project reports that are compiled at the end of a project to analyze results, what was learned, profitability, and benefits
- yardstick reports to establish criteria by which to measure alternatives
- feasibility reports to determine whether a project is practical and advisable

Research Studies These long technical reports thoroughly and scientifically examine problems, the attempts to solve them, and the results.

Proposals These detailed reports offer solutions to problems, investigate ideas, or sell products and services.

WRITING A PERSONAL RÉSUMÉ

Your **résumé** summarizes who you are, what you have learned, and what you have accomplished. The information in your résumé should include skills, knowledge, and achievements that give a potential employer a positive overview of your qualifications. When you apply for a job, you usually include your résumé with your letter of application.

The structure, organization, and overall appearance of your résumé will give the reader an impression of you and your abilities. Type your résumé on white or ivory paper. There should be no factual or typographical errors, erasures, correction fluid, or stray marks. Your goal is to get an interview: Make a good impression. The model résumé is written in reverse chronological order, listing the most recent work experience first.

STEPHANIE J. HOSKIN

4974 Kings Way
Lakeland, FL 33809
Telephone: (813) 555-9263

EDUCATION: Polk High School, 1996 graduate
                 Major studies: College preparatory business and art courses
                 Grade point average: 3.5 (B+)

WORK EXPERIENCE: Summer 1995   Volunteer office worker
                                 Blossom Art Gallery
                                 Lakeland, FL

                 Summer 1994   Junior lifeguard
                                 YWCA
                                 Lakeland, FL

SKILLS: Typing: 60 wpm
                 Business machines: Copiers, postage machines, multi-line switchboards, and
                                     personal computers

EXTRACURRICULAR
ACTIVITIES: Secretary, Student Council of Polk High; Member, Junior Jaycees

REFERENCES: Dr. Mary Sue Wellston, Principal   (813) 555-1195
                 Polk High School
                 Lakeland, FL

                 Mr. Micah Goldfarb, Teacher   (813) 555-0634
                 Polk High School
                 Lakeland, FL

                 Ms. Glenda Ramirez, Director   (813) 555-9543
                 Blossom Art Gallery
                 Lakeland, FL

RESEARCHING AND DOCUMENTING INFORMATION

When you write a research paper, you put together the ideas and views of others about a particular topic. You research what experts have said and written about your topic and draw a new conclusion.

STEPS IN WRITING A RESEARCH PAPER

The process of writing a research paper involves a series of steps that will help you to keep track of the innumerable pieces of information you collect and to organize them as you go.

Prewriting

1. Choose a topic that interests you, and think about what will interest your readers. When you narrow the focus of your subject, be sure you can find enough sources and information.

2. Begin your research, keeping in mind that your purposes are to synthesize information and widen your experience and knowledge. Pose questions that you want to answer, and use reference works such as encyclopedias to get an overview of your topic. Make a source card for each resource you consult.

3. Take notes on note cards to summarize main points in your own words and to record quotations you might use in your paper. When a source answers one of your research questions, indicate that information on the relevant note card.
4. Write a thesis statement stating your topic and what you want to say about it.
5. Develop a working outline that arranges your main ideas and quotations in a logical order.

Writing Your First Draft

1. The draft of your paper should have an introduction, body, and conclusion.
2. Use short quotations in your paper to add interest and authority.
3. Document the sources of all original opinions or theories, facts and statistics, and quotations that you use.

Evaluating and Revising

1. Assess the content, organization, and presentation of your material, making sure all the information is related to the topic. Make sure you have included and supported your thesis statement. Check that you have information documented from three or more sources. Then, prepare your Works Cited list.
2. Assess the readability of your paper, making sure that your ideas are clear and easy to follow and that your paper reads smoothly.

Proofreading and Publishing

1. Check your document for spelling, grammar, punctuation, and usage errors.
2. Make sure your documentation follows the recommended format.
3. Share your research with others by publishing your paper.

Model Research Paper

Shakespeare's Sister: A Fable of Gender Inequality

"Let me imagine," muses Virginia Woolf, "since facts are so hard to come by, what would have happened had Shakespeare had a wonderfully gifted sister, called Judith, let us say" (Woolf, Room 48). Virginia Woolf, the great British novelist, essayist, and critic of the early twentieth century, goes on to speculate about the destiny of Shakespeare's imaginary sister Judith. Like Shakespeare, Judith also has a genius waiting to be born. Unlike Shakespeare, however, Judith cannot attend school and is denied access to the London theater. Like other women of the sixteenth century, she is intended for an early marriage and a life confined to domestic duties. There is no opportunity for her gift to flourish. It dies, unborn, when Judith dies (Woolf, Room 49–50).

Virginia Woolf spoke of the fable of Judith in lectures she gave at two women's colleges at Cambridge University in 1928. Her talks became the well-known essay A Room of One's Own. The essay draws attention to the lack of information on women writers and "call[s] for a history of women" (Scott 15). It strongly criticizes gender discrimination. Woolf addressed her comments to an audience of young women who were experiencing inequality firsthand at Cambridge. Why, then, did Woolf not address the issue of Cambridge women directly? Why did she clothe her comments in the fable of Shakespeare's imaginary sister? The reason lies partly in the political climate of Cambridge at the time.

Two women's colleges, Girton and Newnham, were established at Cambridge by 1873, allowing female students to attend men's lectures and take degree examinations exactly as male students did (Brittain 35–36). Women were not admitted to full status, however, and did not receive degrees from Cambridge until

INTRODUCTORY PARAGRAPH
Catches reader's interest
Primary source citation

Thesis statement

BODY
Topic sentence
Supporting details

Secondary source citation

Topic sentence

Supporting details

after World War II (Bradbrook 78–79). During those intervening years, men's attitudes toward female students ranged from reluctant toleration to outright hostility. Female undergraduates were accused, for example, of everything from "distracting" men in libraries to obscuring men's views with their picture hats (McWilliams-Tullberg 193). In 1920, when a proposal to admit women was defeated, male undergraduates appeared as a "howling mob" who chanted "we won't have women" and bribed children to do the same (McWilliams-Tullberg 193).

Secondary source citation

[The body of the paper continues to explore the political climate of the time for women at Cambridge University. It presents the thesis that Woolf used the metaphor of Judith Shakespeare for political reasons related to this climate. The imaginary heroine would have been less likely to anger a male undergraduate than a Girton or Newnham student asking for equal rights would have been. For the Cambridge audience, the fictional example would have been poignant rather than strident.]

CONCLUSION

In Judith Shakespeare, Virginia Woolf may have seen a reflection of herself. Certainly, she recognized the parallel when she wrote that her fictional heroine "lives in you and me, and in many other women who are not here tonight for they are washing up the dishes and putting the children to bed" (qtd. in Gilbert and Gubar 93). Then, too, there is another parallel in the two lives. Judith Shakespeare dies, her gift wasted. In 1941, Virginia Woolf died prematurely, her gifts also lost. "Who shall measure," Woolf wrote, "the heat and violence of the poet's heart when caught and tangled in a woman's body" (Woolf, Room 50)?

Works Cited

Bradbrook, M. C. 'That Infidel Place': A Short History of Girton College, 1869-1969. London: Chatto, 1969.
Brittain, Vera. The Women at Oxford: A Fragment of History. New York: Macmillan, 1960.
Gilbert, Sandra M., and Susan Gubar. The War of the Words. New Haven: Yale UP, 1988. Vol. 1 of No Man's Land: The Place of the Woman Writer in the Twentieth Century. 3 vols. 1988-94.
Malcolm, Janet. "A House of One's Own." The New Yorker. 5 June 1995: 58-78.
McWilliams-Tullberg, Rita. Women at Cambridge: A Men's University--Though of a Mixed Type. London: Gollancz, 1975.
Scott, Joan Wallach. Gender and the Politics of History. New York: Columbia UP, 1988.
"Virginia Woolf." The Modern World: Ten Great Writers. Narr. Hermione Lee. London Weekend Television. London. 9 June 1988.
Woolf, Virginia. A Room of One's Own. New York: Harcourt, 1957.
[Note: This is a partial list of Works Cited for this research paper.]

IDENTIFYING RESEARCH QUESTIONS

Before you begin researching your topic, develop a plan that will give you direction and prevent wasted effort at the library. Pose some general questions about your topic that you want to answer. These questions will direct your research and will change as you learn more about your topic. Get an overview of the topic to determine if there is enough information before you decide which aspect you want to investigate. As you find information, revise your questions to reflect what you and your readers want to know.

USING LIBRARY / MEDIA CENTER RESOURCES

The library/media center is the most logical place to start gathering information for a research report. The **card catalog** contains information about the books and audiovisuals in the library. The information is alphabetized, and you can search by the title, author, or, for nonfiction materials, subject. The **on-line catalog** is a computerized card catalog. Some on-line systems can tell you where a book is located and whether it is currently available. The librarians can help you use the card catalog or the on-line catalog.

Much information is available on computer with the use of a modem. Digital libraries have materials in electronic form that can be accessed 24 hours a day with a computer. A computer modem and the Internet provide access to materials from libraries, universities, museums, government agencies, and user groups around the world that, in print form, would be too expensive or not readily available. You can reach the Internet through either local service providers or such national on-line services as America Online®, CompuServe®, and Prodigy®.

Databases are collections of information that can be accessed by computer. Many libraries now have access to a variety of electronic databases that are constantly updated, such as computerized indexes of magazines and newspaper articles. InfoTrac®, for example, is updated monthly and provides an index of general-interest magazines from 1985 to the present. The indexes will show a title, an **abstract** (summary), or an entire article. Many databases also are available on CD-ROM.

USING COMMUNITY RESOURCES

In the community, museums, historical societies, government offices, businesses, television and radio stations, associations, and video stores can be valuable sources of information. Some of the best information can come from individuals you interview. Organizations or local businesses may recommend a specialist in the field you are researching. Contact these sources for interviews.

Contacting Sources When you contact sources in your community to ask for information, be polite and professional. Whether you use the telephone or write a letter, remember that you are asking for someone's time. Be prepared to work around his or her schedule. Anticipate problems such as lack of transportation or schedule conflicts, and have solutions before you schedule the interview.

Interviewing Sources The purpose of an interview is to gather information for your research paper from a firsthand source. When you want to interview someone, prepare yourself by learning something about the person you are interviewing as well as background on the topic. The chart below lists steps in the interviewing process.

EVALUATING SOURCES

Before you begin taking notes from any source—print, electronic, or interviewee—be sure that your source provides information that is current, accurate, and free of obvious bias. Use both primary and secondary

PREPARING FOR THE INTERVIEW

- Make arrangements well in advance. Set up a time that is convenient for the other person. Tell the interviewee how much time you expect the interview to take.
- Learn something about the interviewee as well as background on the topic.
- Prepare a list of questions to ask. Use open-ended questions that will encourage the interviewee to talk.

PARTICIPATING IN THE INTERVIEW

- Arrive on time, and be polite and patient.
- Use a tape recorder only with the other person's permission; otherwise, be ready to take notes.
- Avoid argument. Be tactful and courteous. Remember, the interview was granted at your request.
- Listen carefully, and ask follow-up questions if you do not understand an answer or if you think you need more information.
- Conclude the interview by asking, "Is there anything else you would like to add?" Express your appreciation, and ask permission to call later if you need to verify any points.
- Review your notes to refresh your memory, and summarize the material you have gathered. Send a note to the interviewee expressing your appreciation for the interview.

1210 COMMUNICATIONS HANDBOOK

sources. **Primary sources** include letters, autobiographies, works of literature, historical documents, and interviews. **Secondary sources** are derived from primary sources. They include encyclopedias, documentary films, biographies, and historical books. To evaluate the usefulness of a source, use this **4R** test.

1. **Relevant** The source must contain information *directly* related to your topic. You can check the table of contents and index of a book and skim articles. Videotapes and audiotapes sometimes provide written summaries; and for some books, useful summaries and excerpts of reviews will appear in *Book Review Digest*.

2. **Reliable** The source must be accurate. A respected periodical such as the *Smithsonian* or a respected scholar generally can be counted on to have facts straight. If in doubt about a source, consult a librarian or expert, and look for the authors most often quoted on the topic or listed in the bibliographies of other sources.

3. **Recent** Always use sources that are as current as possible. In many fields, research findings change rapidly. Even for a topic that doesn't rely on data and experiments, you should read the most recent publications, because they will often show you which older sources of information still are important.

4. **Representative** If there are two opposing viewpoints on your topic, you need to look at sources with information and opinions on both sides of the issue. As a researcher, you must examine and present all relevant information, even if you finally draw a conclusion that one side's position is stronger.

TAKING NOTES AND DOCUMENTING SOURCES

If you use another writer's words or ideas without indicating you are doing so, you are **plagiarizing.** Plagiarism is a serious offense, and the way to avoid it is by documenting the source of each quotation, paraphrase, fact, or statistic you use in your report. Good documentation starts with accurate source cards and carefully prepared notes.

Preparing Source Cards

As you gather information for your paper, you can save time and ensure accurate documentation by preparing source cards in the format needed for the Works Cited list at the end of your paper. Put each source on a 3" × 5" card, following these guidelines.

GUIDELINES FOR SOURCE CARDS

1. **Number your sources.** To save time during note taking, assign a number to each source. You can then write the number, rather than author and title, when you are taking notes.

2. **Record all publishing information.** Record everything you might need: title and subtitle, author, editor, translator, publisher, volume number, original publication year, revised edition year, and so on.

3. **Note the call number or location.** This information will help you relocate a source if you must go back to it later.

Sample Source Card

> 3
>
> Goodrich, Norma Lorre. <u>Merlin</u>. New York: Harper, 1988.
>
> Westbank Community Library

Taking Notes

Once you have evaluated your sources, follow these guidelines to prepare useful note cards.

GUIDELINES FOR NOTE CARDS

1. Use a separate 4" × 6" note card (or sheet of paper) for each source and for each main idea.

2. Write the source number in the upper right-hand corner and the page number(s) at the bottom of the note.

3. Write a label showing the main idea in the upper left-hand corner of the card. Note which research question the information addresses.

4. Re-read the note to make sure you understand it. Abbreviations and other shortcuts are fine, but be sure you can "translate" them.

Your notes will be direct quotations, summaries, and paraphrases. **Direct quotations** contain the author's exact words, including punctuation, capitalization, and spelling. They should be enclosed in quotation marks. Summaries and paraphrases record the author's ideas and facts in your words. A **summary** condenses the original statement or paragraph. A **paraphrase** is a restatement in your words that includes more detail than a summary. Use lists and phrases instead of complete sentences to summarize or paraphrase efficiently.

Writing a Thesis Statement

Once you have gathered your notes, re-read them to get a picture of the main ideas for your report. This should give you an idea for a **thesis statement,** a sentence or two that states your main topic and what you will say about it. Your working thesis statement is a guidepost to help you focus on information that should directly support or develop the thesis, and it will change as you draft and revise your paper. The final thesis statement will fit into the introduction of your report.

Using Quotations

Short quotations add interest and authority to your research paper. The following chart lists several ways to use quotations effectively in your paper.

GUIDELINES FOR USING QUOTATIONS

- **Quote one or more whole sentences, introducing them in your own words.**

  EXAMPLE Woolf commented on Victorian conversation: "Nobody ever broke the convention. If you listened, as I did, it was like watching a game" (<u>Moments</u> 129).

- **Quote part of a sentence within a sentence of your own.**

  EXAMPLE Woolf wrote that the Victorian conversational style "allows one to say a great many things which would be inaudible if one marched straight up and spoke out" (<u>Moments</u> 129).

- **Quote only a few words (or even just one word) within a sentence of your own.**

  EXAMPLE The essay draws attention to the lack of information on women writers and "call[s] for a history of women" (Scott 15).

- **Use ellipsis points (three spaced periods) to show you've omitted words from a quotation.** You may want to alter a quotation to shorten it or make it fit grammatically into your text. If so, you must use ellipsis points for words deleted within a quotation.

EXAMPLE Judith Shakespeare has a "poet's heart . . . caught and tangled in a woman's body" (<u>Room</u> 50).

- **Set off longer quotations as "blocks."** For quotations of four lines or more, start a new line, indent the entire quotation ten spaces from the left margin, continue to double-space, and do not use quotation marks.

Documenting Sources

There are many different ways to document the sources you use in your research paper. The Modern Language Association of America (MLA) uses brief parenthetical citations in the text of a paper, followed by a complete Works Cited list at the end of the paper.

Parenthetical Citations A **parenthetical citation** gives source information in the body of a research paper. A citation contains just enough information to lead the reader to the relevant entry in the Works Cited list at the end of your paper. Most parenthetical citations include the author's last name and a page number, with these exceptions:

- a nonprint source—an interview or audiotape
- a print source of fewer than two pages
- a sentence that includes the author's name (use page number only)

The following chart provides directions for the placement of parenthetical citations.

PLACEMENT OF CITATIONS

- Put the citation close to the information it documents, but try not to interrupt sentences. Place it at the end of a sentence or at another point of punctuation.
- Place the citation *before* the end punctuation mark of the sentence, clause, or phrase.

  EXAMPLE Merlin disguises himself as a commoner and has gilt letters inscribed on the tombs of Lancelot and Tristan (Goodrich 101).

- For a direct quotation that ends a sentence, place the citation *after* the quotation mark but *before* the end punctuation mark.

  EXAMPLE At the coronation, Arthur's life was threatened by "syxe kynges" (Goodrich 100).

- For an indented quotation, place the citation *two spaces after the final punctuation mark.*

BASIC CONTENT AND FORM FOR PARENTHETICAL CITATIONS

Works by One Author
Author's last name and a page reference
(Goodrich 100)

Works by More Than One Author
All authors' last names (or first author and *et al.* if over three) and a page reference
(Radford and Swanton 78)

Multivolume Works
Author's last name plus volume and page(s)
(Vinaver 1: 81–82)

Works with a Title Only
Full title (if short) or a shortened version and a page reference
("Arthurian Journey" 813)

Literary Works Published in Many Editions
As above, but with other identifying information, such as act, scene, and line numbers
(Macbeth 1.1. 10–11)

Indirect Sources
Qtd. in ("quoted in") and line numbers before the source and a page reference
(qtd. in Goodrich 100)

More Than One Work in the Same Citation
Citations, with page numbers, separated by semicolons
(Goodrich 195; Hopkins 47)

List of Works Cited The Works Cited list, which you include at the end of your paper, contains all the sources, print and nonprint, that you credit in your paper. The Works Cited list is broader than a bibliography, which lists only print sources. To prepare the Works Cited list, center the words *Works Cited* on a new sheet of paper. Alphabetize the sources by the author's last name. If there is no author, alphabetize by title, ignoring *A, An,* or *The* as the first word of the title. Begin each entry on a new line, positioning the first line of the entry even with the left margin. You should indent other lines in the entry five spaces. Double-space all entries. The following chart lists sample citations in the MLA style.

SAMPLE ENTRIES FOR THE LIST OF WORKS CITED

The following sample entries, which use MLA style, are a reference for preparing your Works Cited list. Notice that you include page numbers only for articles in periodicals or for other works that are part of a whole work, such as one essay in a book of essays. Use a shortened version of the publishers' names, and abbreviate the words *University* and *Press* with the letters *U* and *P*.

STANDARD REFERENCE WORKS

When an author of an entry is given in a standard reference work, that person's name is written first. Otherwise, the title of the book or article appears first. Page and volume numbers aren't needed if the work alphabetizes entries. For common reference works, only the edition year is needed.

Encyclopedia Article	"Malory, Sir Thomas." The New Encyclopaedia Britannica: Micropaedia. 15th ed. 1988.
Biographical Reference Book	"Malory, Sir Thomas." Merriam-Webster's Biographical Dictionary. 1995 ed.

BOOKS

Book with One Author	Alcock, Leslie. Arthur's Britain: History and Archaeology A.D. 367–634. London: Penguin, 1971.
Book with Two or More Authors	Radford, C. A. Ralegh, and Michael J. Swanton. Arthurian Sites in the West. Devon: U of Exeter, 1975.

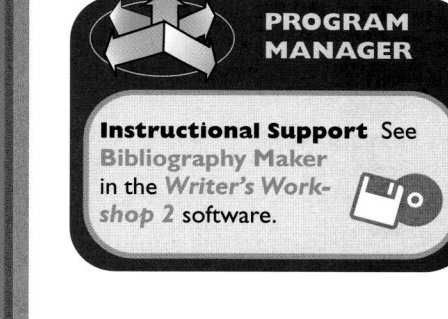

PROGRAM MANAGER

Instructional Support See *Bibliography Maker* in the *Writer's Workshop 2* software.

Standard Reference Works

You may want to remind students that certain titles are underlined when they are written by hand or typed on a typewriter. Students who have access to word processors should set these titles in italics.

Book with One Editor	Brengle, Richard L., ed. Arthur, King of Britain. New York: Appleton, 1964.
Book with Two or More Editors	Pickford, Cedric E., Rex Last, and C. R. Barker, eds. The Arthurian Bibliography, II: Subject Index. Cambridge: Brewer, 1983.
Translation	Niane, D. T. Sundiata: An Epic of Old Mali. Trans. G. D. Pickett. London: Longman, 1965.

SELECTIONS WITHIN BOOKS

Book of Works with One Author	Tennyson, Alfred Lord. "To the Queen." The Works of Tennyson. Ed. Hallam, Lord Tennyson. London: Macmillan, 1913.
Book of Works with Several Authors	Oakeshott, W. F. "The Finding of the Manuscript." Essays on Malory. Ed. J.A.W. Bennett. Oxford: Clarendon Press, 1963. 1–6.
Collection of Longer Works (Novels, Plays)	Steinbeck, John. The Acts of King Arthur and His Noble Knights: From the Winchester Manuscripts of Thomas Malory and Other Sources. Ed. Chase Horton. New York: Farrar, 1976. 51–98.

ARTICLES FROM MAGAZINES, NEWSPAPERS, AND JOURNALS

Weekly Magazine Article	Porter, Andrew. "Purcell: King Arthur." The New Yorker 31 July 1989: 69.
Monthly/Quarterly Magazine Article	Converse, Florence. "Merlin Met Morgan-Le-Fay." Atlantic Monthly Sept. 1922: 376–77.
Article with No Author Shown	"An Arthurian Journey." Atlantic Monthly June 1890: 811–29.
Daily Newspaper Article, with Byline	Riding, Alan. "'King Arthur' Goes to Paris After 300 Years." New York Times 20 Feb. 1995, late ed.: C9+.
Daily Newspaper Article, No Byline	"Steinbeck Find Said to Be First 'Morte d'Arthur' Manuscript." New York Times 2 Jan. 1966, natl. ed.: 52.
Unsigned Daily Newspaper Editorial, No City in Title	"Supreme Injustice." Editorial. Star Ledger [Newark, NJ] 6 Oct. 1991: 17.
Scholarly Journal Article	Field, P.J.C. "Sir Thomas Malory, M.P." Bulletin of the Institute of Historical Research 47 (1974): 24–35.

OTHER SOURCES

Personal Interview	Kibler, William W. Personal interview. 15 Oct. 1990.
Telephone Interview	Kibler, William W. Telephone interview. 12 Oct. 1990.
Published Interview	Campbell, Joseph. Interview with Bill Moyers. The Power of Myth. New York: Doubleday. 1988.
Radio/Television Interview	Harris, Richard. Interview with Scott Simon. Weekend Edition. Natl. Public Radio. WBUR Boston. 26 Mar. 1994.
Published Letter	White, T. H. "To L. J. Potts." 17 Nov. 1930. T. H. White Letters to a Friend: The Correspondence Between T. H. White and L. J. Potts. Ed. François Gallix. Gloucester: Sutton, 1984.
Thesis or Dissertation	Couroux, Gerard Oliver. "Courtly Love in Malory's 'Le Morte Darthur.'" Diss. Loyola U of Chicago, 1968.
Cartoon	Stevens, Mick. Cartoon. The New Yorker Book of Lawyer Cartoons. New York: Knopf, 1994. 22.
Speech or Lecture	Bell, A.R.L. "The Road to Santiago de Compostela: The French Connection." Long Beach Ebell Club. 10 Oct. 1983.
Recording	Welcher, Dan. The Visions of Merlin. Cond. Akira Endo. LP. Louisville Orch. First Edition Records, 1989.
Film, Filmstrip, or Videotape	The Sword in the Stone. Dir. Wolfgang Reitherman. Walt Disney, 1963.
Television or Radio Program	Arthur the King. Dir. Clive Donner. CBS. KTBC, Austin. 26 Apr. 1985.

WRITING ESSAY TESTS

Essay tests call for you to think critically and express your understanding of selected material. A well-written answer must always be a complete response to the question and contain sufficient information to demonstrate your thorough knowledge of the material.

Scan the questions before you start writing. Determine how many questions you must answer, and decide which ones you can answer best. Plan the amount of time you have to spend on each question, and stay on this schedule. Keep these steps in mind.

1. Read each essay question carefully, and notice whether a question has several parts. Rephrase the question as a main idea for your answer.

2. Pay attention to the important terms in the question. Find the key verbs, and identify the tasks you must accomplish in your answer. Note how much evidence is required.

3. Take a few minutes to prewrite. Make notes or a simple outline on scratch paper, arrange your material logically, and write a thesis statement. Write one paragraph for each point you wish to make, and end with a paragraph that summarizes or restates your main points.

4. Evaluate and revise as you write. Keep your paper neat, and watch for spelling and grammatical errors. You will not have time to redraft the entire essay, but you can edit to strengthen specific parts.

Essay questions usually ask you to perform specific tasks expressed by the verb in the question, as the following chart shows.

ESSAY TEST QUESTIONS		
KEY VERB	**TASK**	**SAMPLE QUESTION**
analyze	Take something apart to see how it works.	Analyze Yeats's use of verbal music in "The Lake Isle of Innisfree."
argue	Take a stand on an issue, and give reasons to support this opinion.	Argue whether students should be required to pass a basic skills test before they receive a high school diploma.
compare/contrast	Discuss likenesses/differences.	Compare and contrast Merlin in White's *The Once and Future King* with Merlin in Stewart's *The Crystal Cave*.
define	Give specific details that make something unique.	Define the term *dénouement* as it relates to drama.
demonstrate (show, illustrate, present)	Provide examples to support a point.	Demonstrate an example of circular reasoning.
describe	Give a picture in words.	Describe an incident in *Macbeth* that features the three witches.
discuss	Examine in detail.	Discuss the character of King Arthur as portrayed in *Le Morte Darthur*.
explain	Give reasons.	Explain the appeal of *Robinson Crusoe* to modern readers.
identify	Discuss specific persons, places, things, or characteristics.	Identify the characteristics of the medieval chivalric code.
interpret	Give the meaning or significance of something.	Interpret the symbolism of blood and water in *Macbeth*.
list (outline, trace)	Give all steps in order or all details about a subject.	List three types of figures of speech.
summarize	Give a brief overview of the main points.	Summarize the plot of Coleridge's *The Rime of the Ancient Mariner*.

GIVING SPEECHES AND DEBATING WITH OTHERS

SPEAKING FOR A PURPOSE

Politicians give speeches, hoping to persuade citizens to vote for them at the polls. To inform or educate students about specific topics, teachers and professors deliver speeches and lectures. After-dinner speakers face the challenge of entertaining listeners who've had a full meal. Valedictorians congratulate their classmates and inspire them to look toward the future in commencement speeches. Extemporaneous speakers and teams of debaters strive to convince the judges that they are more articulate and effective than their competitors. These are just a few examples of purposes for speaking, but most speeches are designed to inform, persuade, or entertain. Even speeches for special occasions such as introductions, presentations and acceptances, and competitions fall into one of those same categories. And, to be effective, all speeches, except impromptu ones, require preparation.

Preparing and Presenting Your Speech

Choosing a Topic Select a topic that interests you and your audience, but keep in mind that it should fit the occasion—serious, light, humorous, or formal. You also must have enough time to cover the topic. If you will be giving a very short speech, you may have to limit your topic.

Organizing Your Materials Gather and organize information for your speech by following the same basic process as you would for writing a paper. If you are presenting an informative speech, use reliable sources for information, and take notes on what you find. Make an outline of the major points of your speech. Then prepare note cards for your speech according to the following guidelines.

GUIDELINES FOR SPEECH NOTE CARDS

1. Put only one key idea, possibly accompanied by a brief example or detail, on each card.
2. Make a special note card for material that you plan to read word for word, such as a quotation, series of dates, or list of statistics.
3. Make a special note card to indicate when you should show a visual aid, such as a chart.
4. Number your completed cards to keep them in order.

Unless you are presenting a memorized speech in competition, you don't want to memorize your speech. You want your delivery to sound fresh and natural. If you use short phrases and signal words rather than full sentences to indicate key ideas on your note cards, you will not be tempted to read or memorize your speech.

Practicing Your Speech

Practice your speech as often as you can to achieve a smooth, effective presentation. Try to practice before an audience of friends or family to make the setting more realistic and to get feedback. If you don't have an audience, practice in front of a mirror. Record your speech, and use the playback to note areas that need improvement or strengthening. Prepare visual aids in advance so you can practice with them. Pictures, charts, maps, or diagrams will not be effective if they are out of order, upside down, or too small to be seen by your audience. Time your speech to be sure it falls within the time guidelines.

Using Body Language Your body language can reinforce the impression you make on your audience. Body language includes facial expressions, eye contact, gestures, posture, and movement. Here are several tips for using body language effectively.

- Use facial expressions to emphasize and reinforce your verbal message.
- Making eye contact when speaking can indicate honesty and sincerity. Make eye contact with individuals in your audience to make them feel you are talking *with* them and not *at* them.
- Gestures replace words in certain messages and can emphasize points of your speech.
- Posture conveys attitude. Stand confidently, and look alert and interested in what you are saying.
- Your movements can enhance the impression or message you want to convey. They also can show such things as excitement, fear, haste, and depression.

Using Your Voice Speak clearly and loudly enough for everyone in your audience to hear what you are saying. This sounds easy, but there are different aspects of speaking that affect how you sound to others: pitch, volume, stress, and rate.

- **Pitch** is how high or low a sound is, or the natural rise and fall of your voice. Use pitch to emphasize various ideas and to avoid a monotone.

- **Volume** is the loudness or intensity of sound. You need to be loud enough to be heard when you are speaking. You also can raise or lower your volume for emphasis as you speak. Try to practice speaking louder by using the muscles in your lower chest and stomach area. This will keep you from becoming tired and hoarse as you speak.
- **Stress,** or emphasize, important words or phrases to convey a point to your audience.
- **Rate** is the speed at which you talk. Speak at a comfortable, relaxed pace, and use changes in rate to communicate emotion and drama to your listeners.

Delivering Your Speech

Do not allow nervousness to distract you or affect your speaking. The following suggestions will help you deliver your speech confidently and effectively.

- Be prepared. Organize carefully, and become familiar with your speech notes and visual aids.
- Focus on your purpose for speaking. Think about what you want your listeners to do, know, believe, or feel as a result of your speech.

DEBATING WITH OTHERS

Speaking to Persuade in a Traditional Debate

Traditional debate (sometimes called **team debate** or **policy debate**) is a formal speaking contest with two teams arguing opposing sides of an issue. It focuses on a **proposition,** a statement that deals with a controversial issue and recommends a specific policy or action. For example:

Resolved, That the following courses should be required for all twelfth-graders: a one-semester class in parenting and a six-week driver training course.

In policy debate, the proposition advocates an action that changes the **status quo,** the existing state of affairs. The affirmative team supports the proposed change, while the negative team opposes it.

Choosing a Debatable Issue

You can discover serious **debatable** issues by reading a newspaper or newsmagazine (especially the editorial pages) and by listening to television or radio news shows. Brainstorm possible issues, and try stating them as propositions.

Preparing for the Debate

You can't *prove* your opinion in the same way you can prove a fact, but you can support your opinion con-

vincingly with **reasons** (statements why the proposition should or should not be enacted) and **evidence.** It's important to plan your **argument,** or **case,** to appeal to the particular audience you're talking to.

In a debate, you want your thinking and your reasons to be logical so that your opponents will have difficulty finding weaknesses in your argument. As you plan your argument, be on the lookout for fallacies. **Fallacies** may look and sound like reasons, but they aren't reasons—they are illogical thinking. The following examples show five common types of fallacies.

1. **Begging the Question** Something is presented as true that really needs to be proven. For example: Our local newspaper's bias against nuclear energy is responsible for public opposition to the proposed plant. (This assumes both that the newspaper coverage is biased and that it is the only reason for public opposition.)

2. **Attacking the Person** or **Ad Hominem ("to the person")** This is name-calling. For example: People who oppose setting a lower speed limit in this neighborhood don't care about children's lives. (Opponents are attacked instead of the issue itself being faced.)

3. **Hasty Generalization** A conclusion has been based on insufficient evidence, or it ignores exceptions. For example: Today's films are loaded with sex, violence, and foul language. (Not *all* films are guilty of this.)

4. **Either-Or Reasoning** Only two extreme alternatives are presented for a question or course of action. For example: If funding for the space program is cut, the United States will destroy its own future. (Funding cuts may have a negative impact on research, but the future of the country does not depend upon only one program.)

5. **False Analogy** An illogical, trivial, or misleading comparison is made between two things. For example: Failing to train students for real-life jobs is like condemning them to death row. (Although untrained workers may have difficulties in the job market, they haven't been sentenced to death, and they can take steps to improve their situation.)

(For more on fallacies, see page 614.)

Follow these steps to plan your argument.

1. **Gather your evidence** from library resources (reference books, periodicals, newspapers, databases) and radio and TV news, documentary, and interview programs. Types of evidence include facts, statistics, and examples; **anecdotes** (brief stories) about real people based on your reading or direct experience; **analogies** (comparisons) that help your audience understand a point; and quotations by experts. Evaluate each piece of

evidence to see if it directly supports the point you are making and/or **refutes** (disproves) your opponents' viewpoint. If it does, write it on a separate 3" × 5" index card, and be sure to record the source.

2. **Select the evidence you will use.** Choose at least two reasons and the strongest evidence you've found to support them.

3. **Organize the evidence.** Write a rough outline of your argument, and decide on the most effective order. If you save the strongest reason for last, your listeners will remember it.

4. **Anticipate your opponents' arguments.** Each team will make two kinds of speeches: **Constructive speeches** set forth the team's argument, and **rebuttal speeches** refute the opponents' arguments and rebuild the team's argument. Anticipate your opponents' arguments as you plan your speeches to disprove their case.

Conducting the Debate

The following charts provide rules and guidelines for conducting a classroom debate.

RULES FOR CONDUCTING A CLASSROOM DEBATE

- Each speaker speaks without interruption.
- Speakers are courteous to each other.
- Speakers may refer to notes or read written papers.
- Speakers must stay within the time limits.

GUIDELINES FOR DEBATERS

- State your opinion clearly at the outset and at the end of your speech. Support your opinion with strong reasons and evidence.
- Give your listeners a "road map." Tell them, for example, that there are three reasons why you favor the proposition; then use the words *first, second,* and *third* to introduce each reason as you get to it.
- Stick to the topic; don't wander.
- Express your ideas as clearly as you can. Don't use difficult words when simple ones will do.
- Sound confident. Try not to fill pauses with *uh's* and *um's*.
- Make eye contact with your audience as you speak.

The following chart presents a simplified format for classroom debate. As the chart shows, there are two speakers for the affirmative side and two speakers for the negative side. Speakers for each side alternate and attempt to achieve specific purposes in their speeches.

TRADITIONAL DEBATE FORMAT

SPEAKER	TIME	SUBJECT
1AFF	4 min.	Prove (provide evidence): Proposition should be enacted.
1NEG	5 min.	Refute: 1AFF argument. Prove (provide evidence): Proposition should not be enacted.
2AFF	5 min.	Refute 1NEG argument. Rebuild AFF case with additional evidence.
2NEG	5 min.	Refute 2AFF argument. Rebuild NEG case with additional evidence.
1AFF	3 min.	Refute 2NEG argument. Summarize main points of affirmative team's argument.
1NEG	2 min.	Summarize main points of negative team's arguments.

Evaluating the Debate

The following criteria apply to all types of debate.

CRITERIA FOR EVALUATING A DEBATE

- Are the speakers' arguments clear and well organized?
- Do the speakers present relevant evidence to prove their points?
- Do they present sufficient evidence?
- Do the speakers speak clearly? Can they be understood easily?
- Do the speakers convincingly refute their opponents' arguments?
- Do the speakers convincingly defend their arguments from their opponents' attacks?

STRATEGIES FOR READING AND RESPONDING

Reading involves thinking. Try to discover meaning in what you read and to connect that meaning to your life in some way. Use the following prereading strategies to make your reading more meaningful and to help you better understand and remember what you read.

PREREADING STRATEGIES

Previewing the Text **Preview** an assignment or a book to get an overview of its organization. Read the title and any information included about the author. Flip through the pages, and look at charts or diagrams, the table of contents, and the index. Note the form of the material—poem, short story, play, essay—and the difficulty of the vocabulary. Then try to state the over-all idea of the material in a sentence or two. Finally, think about what you already know about the assigned topic and what you'd like to learn as you read.

Making Connections As you read, you should allow your mind to go back to prior knowledge and experiences to make **connections** to new text. For example, as you read the epic of *Beowulf,* you might remember reading *Le Morte Darthur,* a medieval epic. You recall that epics are tales of heroic deeds and that they defend ideals.

Making Predictions Look ahead in your reading to predict what might happen next. To start the process of making **predictions,** ask yourself: *What will happen next? What will the author talk about next?* Your answers will be predictions about what you are going to read. For example, the first line of *Beowulf* describes a monster living in darkness. You predict that a hero will come forward and fight the monster since epic tales are filled with heroic actions.

ACTIVE READING STRATEGIES

Metacognition **Metacognition** is thinking about how you think, analyzing your own thought processes. The prereading strategies of previewing, making connections, and making predictions are examples of metacognition. To analyze your own thinking-reading process, begin with questions such as *What do I know that will help me with this? How should I get started? What do I want to learn?* As you are reading, ask yourself: *Have I answered my questions? Did my predictions check out? What new questions or predictions should I think about?* And when you've finished reading, review and evaluate your thinking-reading process with such questions as *What did I learn that I can use again? What did I learn that I didn't know before? Was I disappointed in any of the results? What would I do differently?*

Noting Organization As you read, think about the way the author has organized his or her ideas. Make notes about important ideas or events as they unfold. When you re-read your notes, the order of ideas and events will become clearer to you.

Authors arrange text in different ways. **Chronological order,** also called **sequential order,** describes the events in a story or the steps in a process in the order they occur. Words such as *first, then, next, while,* and *finally* guide the reader. **Spatial order** tells you where one object is in relation to other objects. Information also can be presented in **order of importance,** either from the most important detail to the least important, or from the least important to the most important. **Logical order** groups ideas or objects to show how they are related. Examples of logical order include presenting information in terms of a cause-and-effect relationship and comparing and contrasting things to show similarities and differences.

Noting Context Clues for Unfamiliar Words or Phrases Active readers use the **context,** or the surrounding words and phrases, of an unfamiliar word to find clues about its meaning. Here are some different types of context clues and examples that you can use to learn the meanings of unfamiliar words.

- Synonyms: <u>Weather forecasters</u>, more formally called <u>meteorologists</u>, are an important part of local television news broadcasts.
- Clues contained in definitions or descriptions: He is studying to become a <u>transcriptionist, a person who types recorded notes</u>.
- Clues through association with other words in the sentence: There was little <u>discord</u> at the meeting <u>since the club members were in agreement</u> about their decision to increase the dues.
- Clues in a series of words: The publication of D. H. Lawrence's novels often produced <u>waves of controversy, anger, censorship, and a fusillade of invective</u>.
- Tone and setting: Layers of <u>grimy, black dirt</u> on the windows kept out the light, giving the house <u>a ghostly sense of loneliness</u>. <u>A pungent, musty odor</u> assaulted my nose; <u>a clammy dampness</u> settled on my skin. I was filled with <u>apprehension</u>.

COMMUNICATIONS HANDBOOK 1219

- Cause and effect: <u>Since few students attended the voluntary physics review</u>, the next one is <u>mandatory</u> for everyone taking the course.
- Word structure: The prefix, root word, and suffix give clues to the meaning of an unfamiliar word. <u>Counter–</u> is a prefix that means opposite or in retaliation. You can use this knowledge to figure out words such as <u>counteract</u> and <u>counteroffensive</u>.

For more on context clues and word parts, see pages 51 and 153.

Making Inferences An **inference** is a conclusion based on clues the author gives, information presented directly, and what you already know. Inferences are not facts; they are educated guesses. As you read, you constantly draw conclusions, or make inferences, about details and ideas that writers don't state directly. For example, when you read a story, you may make inferences about the theme and about the motivations and traits of the characters.

Making and Confirming Predictions When you read actively, you make **predictions** about what is going to happen next or what you think an author is going to say. The predictions you make may or may not be accurate, but that is not important at this point. As you read new information, you add it to your prior knowledge. You reject misconceptions as you make new discoveries. You then adjust your predictions. This process repeats itself as you read.

RESPONDING TO LITERATURE

Whenever and whatever you read, you have a response. You may like or dislike a character, think the article is boring, or disagree with a point made by the writer. Sometimes, particularly in school, you are asked to explain your response, to provide support for it. In order to do that, you need to think critically about your response and look back in the text to identify the details and facts that led you to draw a conclusion or form an opinion.

Drawing Conclusions

You understand certain things as you read even if they are not stated directly. As you read, you pick up clues from the events and details in a story, connect them to other things you have read and experienced, and then draw **conclusions.** For example, the clues in a short story may help you conclude that the main character is very unhappy. Or while reading a persuasive essay, you may make connections to a situation in your town and draw conclusions about the writer's bias.

Forming and Supporting Opinions

An opinion expresses a personal belief, attitude, or point of view. It cannot be proved right or wrong. Because opinions are based on personal experiences, it is easy to see how people can have different opinions about the same subject. Opinions fall into two categories: valid (justifiable) opinions and invalid opinions. Valid opinions express personal attitudes that are supported with facts, examples, quotations, or other kinds of evidence. Invalid opinions express personal attitudes that are not supported with specific details or facts. Invalid opinions are often based on emotions.

While you are reading, you constantly form and revise your opinions about what is happening in the text. When reading a story or novel, you can find evidence to support these opinions in a character's actions, words, or thoughts; specific details and facts in the text; and your own prior knowledge and experience.

For example, after reading *The Canterbury Tales* by Chaucer, you might decide that the Pardoner is dishonest and greedy. You can support this opinion with details from the poem that indicate that the Pardoner deceives church members. He offers to let them kiss his holy relics for a small fee; however, the relics are fake—just a pillowcase and a jar of pig bones. The details are evidence that supports your opinion.

Using a Reader's Log

Before, during, and after reading, a Reader's Log can be an invaluable tool in which you explore your responses to literature. You can use any and all active reading strategies in Reader's Log entries. There is no one right way to use a Reader's Log, but here are some strategies that you may find helpful.

Double-Entry or Dialectical Journal Make two columns on a page. In the left-hand column, take notes on the material you're reading, or simply jot down quotations from the text. The notes can be very focused (perhaps you are looking specifically for examples of conflict) or very free and loose (you're writing down passages that puzzle you or capture your attention in some way). In the right-hand column, you write your responses to the left-hand column in a kind of dialogue, reflecting on the text in any way that has meaning for you. You can also use the double-entry format to explore your speculations about causes and effects, comparisons and contrasts, problems and solutions, and differing interpretations.

Quickwrite Write quickly and without planning, perhaps responding to a prereading question in the text or a question your teacher has posed. A quickwrite can help you realize what you already know, make predictions about what you are about to read, or relate what you're about to read to your own experience.

Story Mapping   After you've finished reading a story, making a story map in your Reader's Log can help you get a better grasp of the plot, or sequence of events. In a sequence of linked boxes, write the main events of the story in the order they occurred.

Venn Diagram   Use a Venn diagram—two overlapping circles—to indicate visually the similarities and differences between two characters, two settings, two stories, or any other two elements you're comparing and contrasting.

KWL Chart   Make a three-column chart before you start reading, and use it before, during, and after you read a literary work. In the first column, write what you already know (K) about the work, the subject, or anything else in the selection. In the middle column, write what you want to know (W) while you're reading or after you've finished the selection. In the last column, record what you've learned (L) as an outcome of your reading.

Clustering   Before, during, or after you read, you can explore your knowledge of a character, theme, plot, or any other aspect of a story or poem by using clustering. In the middle of a page, write and circle a subject—perhaps the name of a character. Then, write words and ideas in balloons radiating out from the subject—perhaps key words and phrases to describe a character or setting, for example.

Brainstorming   By yourself, or with a group, you can explore all your associations to a work of literature by writing down as many ideas as possible about the subject you are exploring—your thoughts on a character's possible motivations, your feelings about a story's ending, or your associations with an image.

Discussing What You've Read

Explaining and Supporting Your Responses   You respond differently than other readers to what you read because you and your experiences are unique. When you are asked in a class or discussion group to respond to a selection you have read, you need to support that response with evidence, just as you support an opinion.

The reasons and facts that you use to explain your response not only help you clarify your own thinking—they help your teacher understand the thinking behind your response, and they also may provide others with a new and fresh way of looking at the situation. Whether you are describing what you liked or didn't like about a selection, a conclusion that you drew, an interpretation of the author's purpose, or an inference about a character's motivation, you should support this response with relevant events or passages from what you have read or with experiences from your own life.

Working in Groups   In many of your classes, you work in groups with other students. Groups often are formed to complete a task or solve a problem. In these types of groups, the main goal may be broken into sections, and you may be asked to do your part to see that the work is completed successfully. People also form groups to discuss and share ideas on certain topics. In these groups, you may share information you have gathered, your opinions about something you have read, or your questions and concerns. Being part of a student group requires that you come prepared for group meetings, whether you are the chairperson, the recorder, or a participant.

Deciding What to Share   When you are participating in a discussion group, one important thing to consider is what you want to share. There will be times when you don't feel comfortable sharing your thoughts and feelings about a particular subject. If discussing certain personal feelings or issues makes you uncomfortable, don't feel pressured or obligated to share your reactions with the group. You can listen to what others have to say and politely decline to add to that aspect of the discussion. You can participate by discussing the task or topic on a nonpersonal basis. Respect for the privacy of each student is a key part of any good group experience.

1 THE PARTS OF SPEECH

PART OF SPEECH	DEFINITION	EXAMPLES
NOUN	Names person, place, thing, or idea	writer, Ben Okri, Anglo-Saxons, family, country, Wales, poem, "My Last Duchess," Romanticism
PRONOUN	Takes place of one or more than one noun	
Personal	Refers to one(s) speaking (first person), spoken to (second person), spoken about (third person)	I, me, my, mine, we, us, our, ours you, your, yours he, him, his, she, her, hers, it, its, they, them, their, theirs
Reflexive	Refers to subject and directs action of verb back to subject	myself, ourselves, yourself, yourselves, himself, herself, itself, themselves
Intensive	Refers to and emphasizes noun or another pronoun	(See Reflexive.)
Demonstrative	Refers to specific one(s) of group	this, that, these, those
Interrogative	Introduces question	what, which, who, whom, whose
Relative	Introduces subordinate clause and refers to noun or pronoun outside that clause	that, which, who, whom, whose
Indefinite	Refers to one(s) not specifically named	all, any, anyone, both, each, either, everybody, many, none, nothing
ADJECTIVE	Modifies noun or pronoun by telling *what kind, which one, how many,* or *how much*	**a paperback** book, **an Anglo-Saxon** law, **this** one, **the seven brave** warriors, **less** space
VERB	Shows action or state of being	
Action	Expresses physical or mental activity	describe, travel, fight, believe, consider, remember
Linking	Connects subject with word identifying or describing it	appear, be, seem, become, feel, look, smell, sound, taste
Helping	Assists another verb to express time or attitude	be, have, may, can, shall, must, would
ADVERB	Modifies verb, adjective, or adverb by telling *how, when, where,* or *to what extent*	walks **slowly, quite** different, **somewhat** boldly, coming **here soon**
PREPOSITION	Relates noun or pronoun to another word	about, at, by, for, from, in, on, according to, along with, because of
CONJUNCTION	Joins words or word groups	
Coordinating	Joins words or word groups used in the same way	and, but, for, nor, or, so, yet

(continued)

Correlative	Joins words or word groups used in the same way	both . . . and, either . . . or, neither . . . nor, not only . . . but (also)
Subordinating	Begins a subordinate clause and connects it to an independent clause	although, as if, because, since, so that, unless, when, where, while
INTERJECTION	Expresses emotion	ah, gosh, ugh, whew

2 AGREEMENT

AGREEMENT OF SUBJECT AND VERB

2a. A verb should agree with its subject in number. Singular subjects take singular verbs. Plural subjects take plural verbs.

SINGULAR   **He lives** in Camelot.
  PLURAL   **They live** in Camelot.

2b. The number of the subject is not changed by a phrase or a clause following the subject.

EXAMPLE
The **Lilliputians,** who are only six inches tall, **capture** Gulliver.

2c. Indefinite pronouns may be singular, plural, or either.

(1) The following indefinite pronouns are singular: *anybody, anyone, anything, each, either, everybody, everyone, everything, neither, nobody, no one, nothing, one, somebody, someone,* and *something.*

EXAMPLE
One of the most beautiful places in England **is** the Lake District.

(2) The following indefinite pronouns are plural: *both, few, many,* and *several.*

EXAMPLE
Both of the epics **were written** by John Milton.

(3) The indefinite pronouns *all, any, most, none,* and *some* are singular when they refer to singular words and are plural when they refer to plural words.

SINGULAR   **None** of the equipment **was damaged.** [*None* refers to *equipment.*]
  PLURAL   **None** of the machines **were damaged.** [*None* refers to *machines.*]

2d. A *compound subject* may be singular, plural, or either.

(1) Subjects joined by *and* usually take a plural verb.

EXAMPLE
After rehearsal, **Juan, Anita,** and **Marcus are going** out to dinner.

A compound subject that names only one person or thing takes a singular verb.

EXAMPLE
His **wife** and **partner** in crime **is** Lady Macbeth.

(2) Singular subjects joined by *or* or *nor* take a singular verb.

EXAMPLE
Jill or **Jorge plans** to write a character analysis of Macduff.

(3) When a singular subject and a plural subject are joined by *or* or *nor,* the verb agrees with the subject nearer the verb.

EXAMPLE
Neither the **dancers** nor the **choreographer was** pleased with the routine.

2e. The verb agrees with its subject even when the verb precedes the subject, as in sentences beginning with *here, there,* or *where.*

SINGULAR   Where **is** [*or* where's] **Malcolm**?
  PLURAL   Here **are** [*not* here's] **Malcolm** and his **brother.**

2f. A *collective noun* (such as *audience, flock,* or *team*) is singular in form but names a group of persons or things. A collective noun takes a singular verb when the noun refers to the group as a unit and takes a plural verb when the noun refers to the parts or members of the group.

LANGUAGE HANDBOOK 1223

PROGRAM MANAGER

- **Independent Practice or Reteaching** Use *Language and Writing Skills Worksheets,* pp. 25–34.
- **Practice** See *Language Workshop:* Chapter 2: Agreement.

SINGULAR	The tour **group is** on the bus. [The group as a unit is on the bus.]
PLURAL	The tour **group are talking** about their plans. [The members of the group are talking to one another.]

2g. An expression of an amount (a length of time, a statistic, or a fraction, for example) is singular when the amount is thought of as a unit or when it refers to a singular word and plural when the amount is thought of as many parts or when it refers to a plural word.

SINGULAR	**Fifty years is** how long Beowulf rules Geatland. [one unit]
PLURAL	**One fourth** of the seniors **are working** on a production of *Macbeth*. [The fraction refers to *seniors*.]

Expressions of measurement (length, weight, capacity, area) are usually singular.

EXAMPLE
Four and seven-tenths inches is the diameter of a compact disc.

2h. The title of a creative work (such as a book, song, film, or painting) or the name of an organization, a country, or a city (even if it is plural in form) takes a singular verb.

EXAMPLES
"**Tears, Idle Tears**" **was written** by Alfred, Lord Tennyson.
The **United Nations was formed** in 1945.
Has the **Netherlands been flooded** recently?

2i. A verb agrees with its subject, not with its predicate nominative.

SINGULAR	The **subject** of the lecture **was** epic heroes.
PLURAL	**Epic heroes were** the subject of the lecture.

AGREEMENT OF PRONOUN AND ANTECEDENT

A pronoun usually refers to a noun or another pronoun. The word to which a pronoun refers is called its **antecedent**.

2j. A pronoun agrees with its antecedent in number and gender. Singular pronouns refer to singular antecedents. A few singular pronouns also indicate gender (feminine, masculine, or neuter). Plural pronouns refer to plural antecedents.

EXAMPLES
Alfred, Lord Tennyson published *Idylls of the King* after **he** became poet laureate. [singular, masculine]
Lady Macbeth helps **her** husband. [singular, feminine]
The **Lilliputians** gave **their** captive food. [plural]

2k. Indefinite pronouns may be singular, plural, or either.

(1) Singular pronouns are used to refer to the indefinite pronouns *anybody, anyone, anything, each, either, everybody, everyone, everything, neither, nobody, no one, nothing, one, somebody, someone,* and *something.* The gender of any of these pronouns is determined by the word or words that the phrase refers to.

EXAMPLES
Each of the **boys** has learned **his** part in *Macbeth.*
One of the **girls** has injured **herself.**

If the antecedent may be either masculine or feminine, use both the masculine and feminine pronouns to refer to it.

EXAMPLE
Anyone who is going on the field trip needs to bring **his** or **her** lunch.

(2) Plural pronouns are used to refer to the indefinite pronouns *both, few, many,* and *several.*

EXAMPLE
Many of the spectators leapt from **their** seats and cheered.

(3) Singular or plural pronouns may be used to refer to the indefinite pronouns *all, any, most, none,* and *some.* These indefinite pronouns are singular when they refer to singular words and are plural when they refer to plural words.

SINGULAR	**None** of the renovated theater matches **its** original beauty. [*None* refers to the singular noun *theater.*]
PLURAL	**None** of the geese have left on **their** annual migration. [*None* refers to the plural noun *geese.*]

2l. A plural pronoun is used to refer to two or more singular antecedents joined by *and.*

EXAMPLE
Malcolm and Donalbain left Scotland soon after **their** father was killed.

2m. A singular pronoun is used *to refer to two or more singular antecedents* joined by *or* or *nor*.

EXAMPLE
Neither **Malcolm nor Donalbain** felt **he** was safe.

2n. A collective noun (such as *club* or *family*) takes a singular pronoun when the noun refers to the group as a unit and takes a plural pronoun when the noun refers to the parts or members of the group.

SINGULAR   The **jury** reached **its** decision less than one hour later. [The jury decided as a unit.]

PLURAL   The **jury** disagree on how much importance **they** should give to one of the defendant's statements. [The members of the jury disagree.]

2o. The title of a creative work (such as a book, song, film, or painting) or the name of an organization, a country, or a city (even if it is plural in form) takes a singular pronoun.

EXAMPLES
I read ***Gulliver's Travels*** and wrote a report on **it**.
The **United Arab Emirates** generates most of **its** revenue from the sale of oil.

3 USING VERBS

THE PRINCIPAL PARTS OF VERBS

Every verb has four basic forms called the *principal parts:* the *base form,* the *present participle,* the *past,* and the *past participle.* A verb is classified as *regular* or *irregular* depending on the way it forms its past and past participle.

3a. A *regular verb* forms the past and past participle by adding *–d* or *–ed* to the base form. An *irregular verb* forms the past and the past participle in some other way.

COMMON REGULAR AND IRREGULAR VERBS

The following examples include *is* and *have* in italics to show that helping verbs (forms of *be* and *have*) are used with the present participle and past participle forms.

BASE FORM	PRESENT PARTICIPLE	PAST	PAST PARTICIPLE
REGULAR			
attack	*is* attacking	attacked	*have* attacked
drown	*is* drowning	drowned	*have* drowned
occur	*is* occurring	occurred	*have* occurred
risk	*is* risking	risked	*have* risked
try	*is* trying	tried	*have* tried
use	*is* using	used	*have* used

IRREGULAR			
be	*is* being	was, were	*have* been
bring	*is* bringing	brought	*have* brought
burst	*is* bursting	burst	*have* burst
come	*is* coming	came	*have* come
eat	*is* eating	ate	*have* eaten
go	*is* going	went	*have* gone
lead	*is* leading	led	*have* led
pay	*is* paying	paid	*have* paid
see	*is* seeing	saw	*have* seen
sing	*is* singing	sang	*have* sung
steal	*is* stealing	stole	*have* stolen
take	*is* taking	took	*have* taken
throw	*is* throwing	threw	*have* thrown

NOTE If you are not sure about the principal parts of a verb, look in a dictionary. Entries for irregular verbs give the principal parts. If no principal parts are listed, the verb is a regular verb.

TENSES AND THEIR USES

3b. The *tense* of a verb indicates the time of the action or state of being that is expressed by the verb.

(1) The **present tense** is used mainly to express an action or a state of being that is occurring now.

EXAMPLE
The article **compares** Beowulf with other epic heroes.

The present tense is also used

- to show a customary or habitual action or state of being
- to convey a general truth—something that is always true
- to make a historical event seem current (such use is called the **historical present**)
- to summarize the plot or subject matter of a literary work or to refer to an author's relationship to his or her work (such use is called the **literary present**)
- to express future time

EXAMPLES
Every Friday, our teacher **gives** us a vocabulary quiz. [customary action]
Reptiles **are** coldblooded. [general truth]
The Greeks **establish** separate city-states, which **war** among themselves. [historical present]
In the land of the Lilliputians, Gulliver **appears** gigantic. [literary present]
The two-week seminar on Shakespeare **begins** on Monday. [future time]

(2) The **past tense** is used to express an action or state of being that occurred in the past but did not continue into the present.

EXAMPLE
An expert on T. S. Eliot's poetry **spoke** to our class.

(3) The **future tense** (will or shall + base form) is used to express an action or a state of being that will occur.

EXAMPLE
Laurie **will play** the part of Lady Macbeth.

 NOTE Shall and will are both acceptable in forming the first-person future tense.

(4) The **present perfect tense** (have or has + past participle) is used to express an action or a state of being that occurred at some indefinite time in the past.

EXAMPLE
Kenneth Branagh **has played** the roles of Henry V and of Iago.

The present perfect tense is also used to express an action or a state of being that began in the past and continues into the present.

EXAMPLE
Herot **has stood** empty for twelve years.

(5) The **past perfect tense** (had + past participle) is used to express an action or state of being completed in the past before some other past occurrence.

EXAMPLE
The kingdom **had suffered** before Beowulf arrived. [The suffering occurred before the arriving.]

Be sure to use the past perfect tense in "if" clauses that express the earlier of two past actions.

EXAMPLE
If you **had read** [not read or would have read] the article, you would have learned about Sutton Hoo.

(6) The **future perfect tense** (will have or shall have + past participle) is used to express an action or state of being that will be completed in the future before some other future occurrence.

EXAMPLE
By this time tomorrow, I **will** [or **shall**] **have memorized** "The Seafarer."

3c. Avoid unnecessary shifts in tense.

INCONSISTENT	Wiglaf discovered the dragon's treasure and then brings it to Beowulf. [shift from past to present tense]
CONSISTENT	Wiglaf **discovered** the dragon's treasure and then **brought** it to Beowulf. [past tense]
CONSISTENT	Wiglaf **discovers** the dragon's treasure and then **brings** it to Beowulf. [present tense]

When describing events that occur at different times, use verbs in different tenses to show the order of events.

EXAMPLE
She **taught** school for several years, but now she **works** for a publishing company. [Because she taught at a specific time in the past, the past tense taught is correct. Because she works at the present time, the present tense works is correct.]

ACTIVE VOICE AND PASSIVE VOICE

3d. **Voice** is the form a transitive verb takes to indicate whether the subject of the verb performs or receives the action.

A verb is in the **active voice** when its subject performs the action (its object receives the action).

ACTIVE VOICE	William Shakespeare **wrote** more than thirty-five plays.

A verb is in the **passive voice** whenever its subject receives the action (the verb has no object). A passive verb is always a verb phrase that includes a form of be and the past participle of an action verb.

PASSIVE VOICE	More than thirty-five plays **were written** by William Shakespeare.

1226 LANGUAGE HANDBOOK

3e. Use the passive voice sparingly.

In general, the passive voice is less direct and less forceful than the active voice. In some cases, the passive voice also may sound awkward.

| AWKWARD PASSIVE | The sleeping grooms are smeared with King Duncan's blood by Lady Macbeth. |
| ACTIVE | Lady Macbeth **smears** the sleeping grooms with King Duncan's blood. |

Although you generally will want to use active voice rather than passive voice, the passive voice is not less correct than the active voice. In fact, the passive voice is useful in the following situations:

1. when you do not know the performer of the action

EXAMPLE
The Globe **was built** in 1599.

2. when you do not want to reveal the performer of the action

EXAMPLE
The actor **was criticized** for his portrayal of Macbeth.

3. when you want to emphasize the receiver of the action

EXAMPLE
King Duncan **was murdered** while he was asleep.

4 USING PRONOUNS

CASE

Case is the form that a noun or a pronoun takes to indicate its use in a sentence. In English, there are three cases: *nominative, objective,* and *possessive.* Most personal pronouns have a different form for each case.

The Nominative Case

4a. A subject of a verb is in the nominative case.

EXAMPLES
They built the tower near the sea as **he** had requested. [*They* is the subject of the verb *built. He* is the subject of the verb *had requested.*]

4b. A predicate nominative is in the nominative case.

EXAMPLE
The only students who auditioned for the part of King Arthur were **he** and **Carlos.** [*He* and *Carlos* are predicate nominatives that follow the linking verb *were* and identify the subject *students.*]

PERSONAL PRONOUNS

SINGULAR			
	NOMINATIVE	**OBJECTIVE**	**POSSESSIVE**
FIRST PERSON	I	me	my, mine
SECOND PERSON	you	you	your, yours
THIRD PERSON	he, she, it	him, her, it	his, her, hers, its
PLURAL			
	NOMINATIVE	**OBJECTIVE**	**POSSESSIVE**
FIRST PERSON	we	us	our, ours
SECOND PERSON	you	you	your, yours
THIRD PERSON	they	them	their, theirs

 NOTE The form of a noun is the same for both the nominative case and the objective case. A noun changes its form for the possessive case, usually by adding an apostrophe and an *s* to most singular nouns and only an apostrophe to most plural nouns.

☞ For more information about forming possessives of nouns, see page 1249.

LANGUAGE HANDBOOK 1227

PROGRAM MANAGER

- **Independent Practice or Reteaching** Use *Language and Writing Skills Worksheets,* pp. 49–60.
- **Practice** See *Language Workshop:* Chapter 4: Using Pronouns Correctly.

The Objective Case

4c. An object of a verb is in the objective case.

EXAMPLES
The car stalled, and we couldn't restart **it**. [*It* is a direct object that tells *what* we couldn't restart.]
The Pardoner tells **them** a story about three greedy rioters. [*Them* is an indirect object that tells *to whom* the Pardoner tells a story.]

4d. An object of a preposition is in the objective case.

EXAMPLE
Are the Lilliputians afraid of **him**? [*Him* is the object of the preposition *of*.]

The Possessive Case

4e. A noun or a pronoun preceding a gerund is in the possessive case.

EXAMPLE
We were all thrilled by **Joetta's** [*or* **her**] scoring in the top 5 percent. [*Joetta's* or *her* modifies *scoring*, a gerund used as the object of the preposition *by*.]

Do not confuse a gerund with a present participle, which is a verb form that ends in *–ing* and may function as an adjective.

EXAMPLE
Macbeth found **them** [*not* their] standing around a caldron. [*Them* is modified by the participial phrase *standing around a caldron*.]

SPECIAL PRONOUN PROBLEMS

4f. An appositive is in the same case as the noun or pronoun to which it refers.

EXAMPLES
Duncan's sons, **Malcolm** and **he,** leave Scotland. [The compound appositive *Malcolm and he* refers to the subject, *sons*.]
Macduff suspects both of them, **Malcolm** and **him.** [The compound appositive *Malcolm and him* refers to *sons*, the object of the preposition, *of*.]

4g. A pronoun following *than* or *as* in an elliptical construction is in the same case as it would be if the construction were completed.

An *elliptical construction* is a clause from which words have been omitted.

NOMINATIVE   I see him more often **than she.**
[I see him more often *than she sees him. She* is the subject in the elliptical construction.]

OBJECTIVE   I see him more often **than her.**
[I see him more often *than I see her. Her* is the direct object in the elliptical construction.]

4h. A pronoun ending in *–self* or *–selves* should not be used in place of a personal pronoun.

EXAMPLE
Everyone except John and **me** [*not* myself] has read *Don Juan*.

4i. The pronoun *who (whoever)* is in the nominative case. The pronoun *whom (whomever)* is in the objective case.

EXAMPLES
Who wrote "Ozymandias"? [*Who* is the subject of the verb *wrote*.]
With **whom** did Wordsworth write *Lyrical Ballads*? [*Whom* is the object of the preposition *with*.]

CLEAR PRONOUN REFERENCE

The word that a pronoun stands for or refers to is called the *antecedent* of the pronoun.

4j. A pronoun should always refer clearly to its antecedent.

Avoid an ambiguous, a general, a weak, or an indefinite reference by

1. rephrasing the sentence, or

2. replacing the pronoun with an appropriate noun, or

3. giving the pronoun a clear antecedent.

AMBIGUOUS   When the Green Knight was talking to Sir Gawain, he was holding his head in his hand. [The antecedent of *he* and *his* is unclear. Was the Green Knight holding Sir Gawain's head or his own?]

CLEAR   The Green Knight was holding his head in his hand when he was talking to Sir Gawain.

GENERAL   Macbeth will become king. This is one of the witches' prophecies. [*This* has no specific antecedent.]

CLEAR   That Macbeth will become king is one of the witches' prophecies.

WEAK Our dog Hank is jealous of my new baby sister. To help him get over it, I try to give him extra attention. [The antecedent of *it* is not expressed.]

CLEAR To help our dog Hank get over his jealousy of my new baby sister, I try to give him extra attention.

INDEFINITE In this book it includes pictures of artifacts from the Sutton Hoo ship burial. [*It* is not necessary to the meaning of the sentence.]

CLEAR This book includes pictures of artifacts from the Sutton Hoo ship burial.

5 USING MODIFIERS

A *modifier* is a word or group of words that limits the meaning of another word or group of words. The two kinds of modifiers are *adjectives* and *adverbs*.

5a. Use an *adjective* to limit the meaning of a noun or a pronoun. Use an *adverb* to limit the meaning of a verb, an adjective, or another adverb.

COMPARISON OF MODIFIERS

5b. *Comparison* refers to the change in the form of an adjective or an adverb to show increasing or decreasing degrees in the quality the modifier expresses.

The three degrees of comparison are *positive, comparative,* and *superlative.*

1. Most one-syllable modifiers form the comparative and superlative degrees by adding *–er* and *–est.*

2. Some two-syllable modifiers form the comparative and superlative degrees by adding *–er* and *–est.* Other two-syllable modifiers form the comparative and superlative degrees by using *more* and *most.*

3. Modifiers of more than two syllables form the comparative and superlative degrees by using *more* and *most.*

4. To show a decrease in the qualities they express, all modifiers form the comparative by using *less* and the superlative by using *least.*

POSITIVE	COMPARATIVE	SUPERLATIVE
soft	softer	softest
thirsty	thirstier	thirstiest
slowly	more slowly	most slowly
skillfully	less skillfully	least skillfully

 For information about adding suffixes such as *–er* and *–est* to words, see page 1252.

5. Some modifiers form the comparative and superlative degrees in other ways.

POSITIVE	COMPARATIVE	SUPERLATIVE
bad (ill)	worse	worst
far	farther (further)	farthest (furthest)
good (well)	better	best
little	less	least
many (much)	more	most

5c. Use the comparative degree when comparing two things. Use the superlative degree when comparing more than two.

COMPARATIVE After reading *King Lear* and *The Winter's Tale,* I can understand why *King Lear* is the **more popular** play. [comparison of two plays]

SUPERLATIVE Of the three plays I saw, I think *Macbeth* was the **most powerful.** [comparison of three plays]

5d. Avoid a double comparison or a double negative. A *double comparison* is the use of two comparative forms (usually *–er* and *more* or *less*) or two superlative forms (usually *–est* and *most* or *least*) to modify the same word. A *double negative* is the use of two negative words where one is enough.

EXAMPLES
Who is the **noblest** [*not* most noblest] of King Arthur's knights?
I know **nothing** [*not* don't know nothing] about the Wars of the Roses.

LANGUAGE HANDBOOK 1229

LANGUAGE HANDBOOK

PROGRAM MANAGER

- **Independent Practice or Reteaching** Use *Language and Writing Skills Worksheets,* pp. 61–70.
- **Practice** See *Language Workshop:* Chapter 5: Using Modifiers Correctly.

Language Handbook **T1229**

5e. Include the word *other* or *else* when comparing one member of a group with the rest of the group.

ILLOGICAL Wiglaf is bolder than any of Beowulf's followers. [Wiglaf is one of Beowulf's followers. Logically, Wiglaf cannot be bolder than himself.]

LOGICAL Wiglaf is bolder than any of Beowulf's **other** followers.

5f. Avoid comparing items that cannot logically be compared.

ILLOGICAL I think Olivier's portrayal of Hamlet is more compelling than any other actor. [The sentence makes an illogical comparison between a portrayal and an actor.]

LOGICAL I think Olivier's portrayal of Hamlet is more compelling than any other actor's [portrayal]. [The sentence makes a logical comparison between portrayals.]

PLACEMENT OF MODIFIERS

5g. Avoid using a *misplaced modifier*—a modifying word, phrase, or clause that sounds awkward because it modifies the wrong word or group of words.

To correct a misplaced modifier, place the word, phrase, or clause as close as possible to the word or words you intend it to modify.

MISPLACED The old man told the three young rioters under a tree they would find Death. [What occurred under a tree: the telling or the finding?]

CLEAR The old man told the three young rioters they would find Death **under a tree.**

MISPLACED The anxious hunter watched the raging lion come charging at him as he readied his bow and arrow.

CLEAR **As he readied his bow and arrow,** the anxious hunter watched the raging lion come charging at him.

5h. Avoid using a *dangling modifier*—a modifying word, phrase, or clause that does not sensibly modify any word or words in a sentence.

You may correct a dangling modifier by
- adding a word or words that the dangling word, phrase, or clause can sensibly refer to
- adding a word or words to the dangling word, phrase, or clause
- rewording the sentence

DANGLING After becoming poet laureate, "The Charge of the Light Brigade" was written. [Who became poet laureate?]

CLEAR After becoming poet laureate, Alfred, Lord Tennyson wrote "The Charge of the Light Brigade."

CLEAR Alfred, Lord Tennyson wrote "The Charge of the Light Brigade" after he became poet laureate.

6 PHRASES

WHAT IS A PHRASE?

6a. A *phrase* is a group of related words that is used as a single part of speech and that does not contain a verb and its subject.

EXAMPLE
The Rime of the Ancient Mariner, **Coleridge's best-known poem, was published in 1798.**
[*Coleridge's best-known poem* functions as a noun, *was published* is a verb, and *in 1798* functions as an adverb.]

THE PREPOSITIONAL PHRASE

6b. A *prepositional phrase* begins with a preposition and ends with the *object of the preposition,* a word or word group that functions as a noun.

EXAMPLE
From the rafters of Herot hung one **of Grendel's arms.** [The noun *rafters* is the object of the preposition *from.* The noun *Herot* is the object of the preposition *of.* The noun *arms* is the object of the preposition *of.*]

1230 LANGUAGE HANDBOOK

An object of a preposition may be compound.

EXAMPLE

The three men ignored the warnings **of the tavern-knave and the publican.** [Both *tavern-knave* and *publican* are objects of the preposition *of.*]

(1) An *adjective phrase* is a prepositional phrase that modifies a noun or a pronoun. An adjective phrase tells *what kind* or *which one.*

EXAMPLE

The three rioters found eight bushels **of gold coins.** [*Of gold coins* modifies the noun *bushels.*]

An adjective phrase always follows the word it modifies. That word may be the object of another preposition.

EXAMPLE

They told stories on their journey **to Canterbury.** [*To Canterbury* modifies *journey,* the object of the preposition *on.*]

More than one adjective phrase may modify the same word.

EXAMPLE

Chaucer's trips **to Italy on important diplomatic missions** broadened his knowledge. [The phrases *to Italy* and *on important diplomatic missions* modify the noun *trips.*]

(2) An *adverb phrase* is a prepositional phrase that modifies a verb, an adjective, or an adverb. An adverb phrase tells *how, when, where, why,* or *to what extent* (*how long* or *how far*).

As you can see in the example below, more than one adverb phrase can modify the same word. The example also shows that an adverb phrase, unlike an adjective phrase, can precede the word it modifies.

EXAMPLE

In 1799, Wordsworth returned **with his sister to the Lake District.** [Each phrase modifies the verb *returned. In 1799* tells *when,* *with his sister* tells *how,* and *to the Lake District* tells *where.*]

VERBALS AND VERBAL PHRASES

A *verbal* is a form of a verb used as a noun, an adjective, or an adverb. A *verbal phrase* consists of a verbal and its modifiers and complements.

Participles and Participial Phrases

6c. A *participle* is a verb form that is used as an adjective. A *participial phrase*

consists of a participle and all the words related to the participle.

The two kinds of participles are the *present participle* and the *past participle.*

(1) *Present participles* end in *–ing.*

EXAMPLE

Sir Gawain heard the Green Knight **sharpening his ax.** [The participial phrase modifies the noun *Green Knight.* The noun *ax* is the direct object of the present participle *sharpening.*]

(2) Most *past participles* end in *–d* or *–ed.* Others are irregularly formed.

EXAMPLE

Tormented by her guilt, Lady Macbeth lost her sanity. [The participial phrase modifies the noun *Lady Macbeth.* The adverb phrase *by her guilt* modifies the past participle *tormented.*]

Gerunds and Gerund Phrases

6d. A *gerund* is a verb form ending in *–ing* that is used as a noun. A *gerund phrase* consists of a gerund and all the words related to the gerund.

EXAMPLES

For Gulliver, **living in Brobdingnag** is quite different from **living in Lilliput.** [*Living in Brobdingnag* is the subject of the verb *is. Living in Lilliput* is the object of the preposition *from.* The adverb phrases *in Brobdingnag* and *in Lilliput* modify the gerund *living.*]

The Miller enjoys **playing the bagpipes.** [*Playing the bagpipes* is the direct object of the verb *enjoys. Bagpipes* is the direct object of the gerund *playing.*]

Infinitives and Infinitive Phrases

6e. An *infinitive* is a verb form that can be used as a noun, an adjective, or an adverb. An infinitive usually begins with *to.* An *infinitive phrase* consists of an infinitive and all the words related to the infinitive.

EXAMPLES

The three rioters vow **to kill Death.** [The infinitive phrase acts as a noun and is the direct object of the verb *vow. Death* is the direct object of the infinitive *to kill.*]

She had a great desire **to visit Stratford-on-Avon.** [The infinitive phrase acts as an adjective and modifies the noun *desire. Stratford-on-Avon* is the direct object of the infinitive *to visit.*]

Macbeth goes to the witches' haunt **to talk to them.**
[The infinitive phrase acts as an adverb and modifies the verb *goes.* The adverb phrase *to them* modifies the infinitive *to talk.*]

Lady Macbeth helps her husband **become king.**
[The sign of the infinitive, *to,* is omitted. The infinitive has a subject, *husband,* making the entire construction an ***infinitive clause.*** The infinitive clause acts as a noun and is the direct object of the verb *helps.*]

APPOSITIVES AND APPOSITIVE PHRASES

6f. An *appositive* is a noun or a pronoun placed beside another noun or pronoun to identify or explain it. An *appositive phrase* consists of an appositive and its modifiers.

An appositive or appositive phrase usually follows the word it identifies or explains.

EXAMPLES

Have you read Coleridge's poem **"Kubla Khan"**?
[The appositive *"Kubla Khan"* identifies the noun *poem.*]

Shakespeare was born in Stratford-on-Avon, **a market town about eighty miles from London.**
[The entire appositive phrase *a market town about eighty miles from London* identifies the noun *Stratford-on-Avon.*]

For emphasis, however, an appositive or an appositive phrase may precede the word that it explains or identifies.

EXAMPLE

A riot of colorful sights, intriguing aromas, and surprising noises, a Cairo bazaar is great fun to visit. [The appositive phrase explains why a Cairo bazaar is fun to visit.]

7 CLAUSES

7a. A *clause* is a group of words that contains a verb and its subject and that is used as part of a sentence. There are two kinds of clauses: the *independent clause* and the *subordinate clause.*

THE INDEPENDENT CLAUSE

7b. An *independent* (or *main*) *clause* expresses a complete thought and can stand by itself as a sentence.

EXAMPLE

SUBJECT   VERB
William Shakespeare wrote more than 150 sonnets. [one independent clause]

THE SUBORDINATE CLAUSE

7c. A *subordinate* (or *dependent*) *clause* does not express a complete thought and cannot stand alone as a sentence.

EXAMPLE

SUBJECT   VERB
that **Lord Byron swam** across the Hellespont

1232 LANGUAGE HANDBOOK

The thought expressed by a subordinate clause becomes complete when the clause is combined with an independent clause to create a complete sentence.

EXAMPLE

I read **that Lord Byron swam across the Hellespont.**

The Adjective Clause

7d. An *adjective clause* is a subordinate clause that modifies a noun or a pronoun.

An adjective clause always follows the word or words that it modifies. Usually, an adjective clause begins with a ***relative pronoun*** (such as *that, which, who, whom, whose*). A relative pronoun both relates an adjective clause to the word or words the clause modifies and performs a function within its own clause by serving as a subject, an object of a verb, an object of a preposition, or a modifier.

EXAMPLES

Mary Shelley, **who wrote *Frankenstein,*** liked reading ghost stories with her friends. [The relative pronoun *who* relates the adjective clause to the noun *Mary Shelley* and serves as the subject of the verb *wrote.*]

The knight **for whom Sir Gawain is searching** is the Knight of the Green Chapel. [The relative pronoun *whom* relates the adjective clause to the noun *knight* and serves as the object of the preposition *for.*]

An adjective clause may begin with a *relative adverb,* such as *when* or *where.*

EXAMPLES
My uncle Robert told us about the time **when he backpacked across the island of Luzon.** [The adjective clause modifies the noun *time.*]

Malcolm flees to England, **where he raises an army to attack Macbeth.** [The adjective clause modifies the noun *England.*]

The Noun Clause

 7e. A *noun clause* is a subordinate clause that may be used as a subject, a predicate nominative, a direct object, an indirect object, or an object of a preposition.

Words that are commonly used to introduce noun clauses include *how, that, what, whether, who, whoever,* and *why.*

EXAMPLES
That Fleance escapes the murderers troubles Macbeth. [subject]

Power is **what Macbeth desires.** [predicate nominative]

Banquo suspected **that Macbeth had murdered Duncan.** [direct object]

The teacher will give **whoever can recite the soliloquy** ten points. [indirect object]

The teacher will give ten points to **whoever can recite the soliloquy.** [object of a preposition]

The word that introduces a noun clause may or may not have another function in the clause.

EXAMPLES
Do you know **who wrote *Don Juan*?** [The word *who* introduces the noun clause and serves as the subject of the verb *wrote.*]

The witches predict **that Macbeth will become king.** [The word *that* introduces the noun clause but does not have any function within the noun clause.]

The Adverb Clause

7f. An *adverb clause* is a subordinate clause that modifies a verb, an adjective, or an adverb.

An adverb clause, which may come before or after the word or words it modifies, tells *how, when, where, why, to what extent,* or *under what condition.* An adverb clause is introduced by a **subordinating conjunction**—a word or word group that relates the adverb clause to the word or words the clause modifies.

EXAMPLES
He looks **as though he has seen a ghost.** [The adverb clause modifies the verb *looks,* telling *how* he looks.]

If you want to learn more about James Joyce, read this book. [The adverb clause modifies the verb *read,* telling *under what condition* you should read the book.]

The trip took longer **than I thought it would.** [The adverb clause modifies the adjective *longer,* telling *to what extent* the trip was longer.]

The Elliptical Clause

7g. Part of a clause may be left out when the meaning can be understood from the context of the sentence. Such a clause is called an *elliptical clause.*

EXAMPLES
While [he was] **painting,** Rembrandt concentrated completely on his work.

Ken may ride with us **if he wants to** [ride with us].

This job took longer **than the last one** [took].

 For more about using pronouns in elliptical constructions, see page 1228.

8 SENTENCE STRUCTURE

SENTENCE OR FRAGMENT?

8a. A *sentence* is a group of words that expresses a complete thought.

EXAMPLES
"My Last Duchess" is a dramatic monologue.

For how many years was Winston Churchill the prime minister of Britain?

What an ambitious man Macbeth was!

PROGRAM MANAGER

• **Independent Practice or Reteaching** Use *Language and Writing Skills Worksheets,* pp. 85–96.
• **Practice** See *Language Workshop:* Chapter 7: Sentences.

Only a sentence should begin with a capital letter and end with a period, a question mark, or an exclamation point. Do not be misled by a group of words that looks like a sentence but that does not express a complete thought by itself. Such a word group is called a *sentence fragment.*

FRAGMENT   Awakens and finds himself surrounded by people six inches tall.

SENTENCE   Gulliver awakens and finds himself surrounded by people six inches tall.

SUBJECT AND PREDICATE

8b. A sentence consists of two parts: a subject and a predicate. A *subject* tells *whom* or *what* the sentence is about. A *predicate* tells something about the subject.

In the following examples, all the words labeled *subject* make up the **complete subject,** and all the words labeled *predicate* make up the **complete predicate.**

EXAMPLES

SUBJECT	PREDICATE
My sister and I	enjoyed *Gulliver's Travels.*

PREDICATE	SUBJECT	PREDICATE
For fifty years	Beowulf	ruled Geatland.

The Simple Subject

8c. A *simple subject* is the main word or group of words that tells *whom* or *what* the sentence is about.

EXAMPLE
The first **leader** of the gang was Blackie. [The complete subject is *the first leader of the gang.*]

The Simple Predicate

8d. A *simple predicate* is a verb or verb phrase that tells something about the subject.

EXAMPLE
Have you **read** "The Seafarer"? [The complete predicate is *have read "The Seafarer."*]

The Compound Subject and the Compound Verb

8e. A *compound subject* consists of two or more subjects that are joined by a conjunction—usually *and* or *or*—and that have the same verb.

EXAMPLE
A **nun** and three **priests** accompany the Prioress on the pilgrimage.

8f. A *compound verb* consists of two or more verbs that are joined by a conjunction—usually *and, but,* or *or*—and that have the same subject.

EXAMPLE
Truth **enlightens** the mind, **frees** the spirit, and **strengthens** the soul.

How to Find the Subject of a Sentence

8g. To find the subject of a sentence, ask *Who?* or *What?* before the verb.

(1) The subject of a sentence is never within a prepositional phrase.

EXAMPLES
A **group** of pilgrims gathered at the Tabard. [Who gathered? Group gathered. *Pilgrims* is the object of the preposition *of.*]
Out of the stillness came the loud **sound** of laughter. [What came? Sound came. *Stillness* is the object of the preposition *out of. Laughter* is the object of the preposition *of.*]

(2) The subject of a sentence expressing a command or a request is always understood to be *you,* although *you* may not appear in the sentence.

COMMAND   Name the pilgrim accompanying the Plowman. [Who is being told to name? *You* is understood.]

The subject of a command or a request is *you* even when the sentence also contains a **noun of direct address**—a word that names or identifies the one or ones spoken to.

REQUEST   Marla, [you] please read the first stanza of "To a Skylark."

(3) The subject of a sentence expressing a question usually follows the verb or a part of the verb phrase. Turning the question into a statement will often help you find the subject.

QUESTION   Have you read Lord Byron's poem "She Walks in Beauty"?
STATEMENT   **You** have read Lord Byron's poem "She Walks in Beauty." [Who has read? You have read.]

| QUESTION | Were Shakespeare's plays popular during his own lifetime? |
| STATEMENT | Shakespeare's **plays** were popular during his own lifetime. [What were popular? Plays were popular.] |

(4) The word *there* or *here* is never the subject of a sentence.

EXAMPLES

There is **Canterbury Cathedral.** [What is there? Canterbury Cathedral is there.]

Here are my **drawings** of Chaucer's pilgrims. [What are here? Drawings are here.]

COMPLEMENTS

8h. A *complement* is a word or a group of words that completes the meaning of a verb or a verbal. The four main kinds of complements are *direct objects, indirect objects, objective complements,* and *subject complements.*

The Direct Object and the Indirect Object

8i. A *direct object* is a word or word group that receives the action of a verb or shows the result of the action. A direct object, which may be a noun, a pronoun, or a word group that functions as a noun, tells *whom* or *what* after a transitive verb.

EXAMPLES

Banquo definitely suspected **him.** [Suspected whom? him]

Beethoven composed **sonatas** and **symphonies.** [Composed what? sonatas and symphonies—compound direct object]

8j. An *indirect object* is a word or word group that comes between a transitive verb and a direct object. An indirect object, which may be a noun, a pronoun, or a word group that functions as a noun, tells *to whom, to what, for whom,* or *for what* the action of the verb is done.

EXAMPLES

The Wife of Bath told the other **pilgrims** an interesting story. [Told to whom? pilgrims]

We should give **practicing for the concert** our full attention. [Should give our full attention to what? practicing for the concert]

The Objective Complement

8k. An *objective complement* is a word or word group that helps complete the meaning of a transitive verb by identifying or modifying the direct object. An objective complement, which may be a noun, a pronoun, an adjective, or a word group that functions as a noun or an adjective, usually follows the direct object.

EXAMPLES

Macduff called Malcolm **king.** [The noun *king* identifies the direct object *Malcolm.*]

He believed the money **his.** [The pronoun *his* modifies the direct object *money.*]

Everyone considered him **chivalrous.** [The adjective *chivalrous* modifies the direct object *him.*]

 NOTE A **transitive verb** is an action verb that takes an object, which tells who or what receives the action.

The Subject Complement

8l. A *subject complement* is a word or a word group that completes the meaning of a linking verb or a verbal and that identifies or modifies the subject. The two kinds of subject complements are *predicate nominatives* and *predicate adjectives.*

(1) A **predicate nominative** is a word or group of words that follows a linking verb and refers to the same person, place, thing, or idea as the subject of the verb. A predicate nominative may be a noun, a pronoun, or a word group that functions as a noun.

EXAMPLES

Of these three poets, Wordsworth was the most prolific **one.** [The pronoun *one* refers to the subject *Wordsworth.*]

The main characters are **Paul** and his **mother.** [The two nouns *Paul* and *mother* are a compound predicate nominative that refers to the subject *characters.*]

(2) A **predicate adjective** is an adjective that follows a linking verb and that modifies the subject of the verb.

EXAMPLES

Did King Hrothgar feel **powerless**? [The adjective *powerless* modifies the subject *King Hrothgar.*]

Iago is **sly** and **scheming.** [The two adjectives *sly* and *scheming* are a compound predicate adjective that modifies the subject *Iago.*]

 For a list of linking verbs, see page 1222.

SENTENCES CLASSIFIED ACCORDING TO STRUCTURE

8m. According to their structure, sentences are classified as *simple, compound, complex,* and *compound-complex.*

(1) A *simple sentence* has one independent clause and no subordinate clauses.

EXAMPLE
"Not Waving but Drowning" is one of my favorite poems.

(2) A *compound sentence* has two or more independent clauses but no subordinate clauses.

EXAMPLES
Othello is a great man, but his character is flawed.
Agatha Christie was a prolific writer; she wrote
    more than eighty books in less than sixty years.

(3) A *complex sentence* has one independent clause and at least one subordinate clause.

EXAMPLE
The poet who wrote "Ode on a Grecian Urn" is John Keats. [The independent clause is *the poet is John Keats.* The subordinate clause is *who wrote "Ode on a Grecian Urn."*]

(4) A *compound-complex* sentence has two or more independent clauses and at least one subordinate clause.

EXAMPLE
After Macbeth killed their father, Malcolm fled to England, and Donalbain escaped to Ireland. [The two independent clauses are *Malcolm fled to England* and *Donalbain escaped to Ireland.* The subordinate clause is *after Macbeth killed their father.*]

SENTENCES CLASSIFIED ACCORDING TO PURPOSE

8n. According to their purpose, sentences are classified as *declarative, interrogative, imperative,* and *exclamatory.*

(1) A *declarative sentence* makes a statement. It is followed by a period.

EXAMPLE
The lock on the front door is broken.

(2) An *interrogative sentence* asks a question. It is followed by a question mark.

EXAMPLE
Have you read Dylan Thomas's "Fern Hill"?

(3) An *imperative sentence* makes a request or gives a command. It is usually followed by a period. A very strong command, however, is followed by an exclamation point.

EXAMPLES
Please return this book to the library.
Give me the name of the warrior who succeeds
    Beowulf.
Stop making that noise!

(4) An *exclamatory sentence* expresses strong feeling or shows excitement. It is followed by an exclamation point.

EXAMPLES
What a talented writer she was!
We won!

 For more information about using end marks, see pages 1243–1244.

9 SENTENCE STYLE

WAYS TO ACHIEVE CLARITY

Coordinating Ideas

9a. To *coordinate* two or more ideas, or to give them equal emphasis, link them with a connecting word, an appropriate mark of punctuation, or both.

EXAMPLE
I read the novel *Frankenstein,* **and** then I saw the film.

Subordinating Ideas

9b. To *subordinate* an idea, or to show that one idea is related to but less important than another, use an adverb clause or an adjective clause.

EXAMPLES
Sir Gawain accepts the magic sash **because he wants it to protect him from the Green Knight.** [adverb clause]
Hrunting is the name of the sword **that Unferth gives Beowulf.** [adjective clause]

1236 LANGUAGE HANDBOOK

Using Parallel Structure

9c. Use the same grammatical form (*parallel structure*) to express ideas of equal importance.

(1) Use parallel structure when you link coordinate ideas.

EXAMPLE
In the winter I usually like **to ski** and **to skate**. [infinitive paired with infinitive]

(2) Use parallel structure when you compare or contrast ideas.

EXAMPLE
Einstein liked mathematical **research** more than laboratory **supervision.** [noun contrasted with noun]

(3) Use parallel structure when you link ideas with correlative conjunctions (*both . . . and, either . . . or, neither . . . nor,* or *not only . . . but also*).

EXAMPLE
Virginia Woolf was not only **a novelist** but also **an essayist.** [Note that the correlative conjunctions come directly before the parallel terms.]

When you revise for parallel structure, you may need to add an article, a preposition, or a pronoun before each of the parallel terms.

UNCLEAR	I admire the poems of Byron more than Wordsworth.
CLEAR	I admire the poems of Byron more than **those of** Wordsworth.

OBSTACLES TO CLARITY

Sentence Fragments

9d. Avoid using a *sentence fragment*—a part of a sentence that has been punctuated as if it were a complete thought.

 For more information about sentence fragments, see pages 1233–1234.

You may correct a sentence fragment in one of two ways.

1. Add words to make the thought complete.

FRAGMENT	Twelve Geats around Beowulf's tower. [The verb is missing.]
SENTENCE	Twelve Geats **rode** around Beowulf's tower.

2. Attach the fragment to the sentence that comes before or after it.

FRAGMENT	A doctor and a gentlewoman see Lady Macbeth. Walking in her sleep. [participial phrase]
SENTENCE	A doctor and a gentlewoman see Lady Macbeth **walking in her sleep.**

NOTE Sentence fragments can be effective when used in expressive and creative writing and in informal writing.

Run-on Sentences

9e. Avoid using a *run-on sentence*—two or more complete thoughts that are run together as if they were one complete thought.

The two kinds of run-on sentences are *fused sentences* and *comma splices.* A ***fused sentence*** has no punctuation or connecting word at all between the complete thoughts. A ***comma splice*** has just a comma between the complete thoughts.

FUSED SENTENCE	Wiglaf helps Beowulf the other warriors retreat in fear.
COMMA SPLICE	Wiglaf helps Beowulf, the other warriors retreat in fear.

You may correct a run-on sentence in one of five ways.

1. Make two sentences.

EXAMPLE
Wiglaf helps Beowulf**. T**he other warriors retreat in fear.

2. Use a comma and a coordinating conjunction.

EXAMPLE
Wiglaf helps Beowulf**, but** the other warriors retreat in fear.

3. Change one of the independent clauses to a subordinate clause.

EXAMPLE
Wiglaf helps Beowulf**, while the other warriors retreat in fear.**

4. Use a semicolon.

EXAMPLE
Wiglaf helps Beowulf**;** the other warriors retreat in fear.

5. Use a semicolon and a conjunctive adverb.

EXAMPLE
Wiglaf helps Beowulf**; however,** the other warriors retreat in fear.

Unnecessary Shifts in Sentences

9f. Avoid making unnecessary shifts in subject, in tense, and in voice.

AWKWARD	Grandma goes to the farmers' market, where the freshest produce is. [shift in subject]
BETTER	**Grandma** goes to the farmers' market, where **she** finds the freshest produce.
AWKWARD	Macbeth sees Banquo's ghost, but no one else did. [shift in tense]
BETTER	Macbeth **sees** Banquo's ghost, but no one else **does.**
AWKWARD	Lyle spent four hours at the library, but no books on his research topic were found. [shift in voice]
BETTER	Lyle **spent** four hours at the library, but he **found** no books on his research topic.

REVISING FOR VARIETY

9g. Use a variety of sentence beginnings.

Putting the subject first in a declarative sentence is not wrong, but starting every sentence with the subject can make your writing boring. To add variety to your sentences, rearrange sentence parts to vary the beginnings. The following examples show how a writer can revise sentences to avoid beginning with the subject every time.

SUBJECT FIRST	Lady Macbeth is cunning and ruthless and goads her husband into committing murder.
SINGLE-WORD MODIFIERS FIRST	**Cunning** and **ruthless,** Lady Macbeth goads her husband into committing murder.
SUBJECT FIRST	*In Memoriam,* **which was published in 1850,** is Alfred, Lord Tennyson's elegy for his friend Arthur Hallam.
PARTICIPIAL PHRASE FIRST	**Published in 1850,** *In Memoriam* is Alfred, Lord Tennyson's elegy for his friend Arthur Hallam.
APPOSITIVE PHRASE FIRST	**An elegy for Alfred, Lord Tennyson's friend Arthur Hallam,** *In Memoriam* was published in 1850.

Varying Sentence Structure

9h. Use a mix of simple, compound, complex, and compound-complex sentences in your writing.

EXAMPLE

The three "weird sisters" greet Macbeth and Banquo with prophecies. [simple] According to the witches, Macbeth will become king, but Banquo will not, though his descendants will. [compound-complex] When Macbeth asks the witches to tell him more, they vanish. [complex] The subsequent conversation between Banquo and Macbeth lends insight into each man's character. [simple] That is, Banquo is skeptical of the witches' prophecies; however, Macbeth believes in them. [compound]

 For information about the four kinds of sentence structure, see page 1236.

Revising to Reduce Wordiness

9i. Avoid using unnecessary words in your writing.

The following guidelines suggest some ways to revise wordy sentences.

1. Take out a whole group of unnecessary words.

WORDY	Grendel's mother carried Beowulf to her home where she lived.
IMPROVED	Grendel's mother carried Beowulf to her home.

2. Replace pretentious words and expressions with straightforward ones.

WORDY	In *Lord of the Flies,* a group of males, all of whom are under thirteen years of age, is stranded on a land mass surrounded by water and totally free of inhabitants.
IMPROVED	In *Lord of the Flies,* a group of **young boys** is stranded on an **uninhabited island.**

3. Reduce a clause to a phrase.

WORDY	Sir Lancelot falls in love with Queen Guinevere, who is the wife of King Arthur.
IMPROVED	Sir Lancelot falls in love with Queen Guinevere, **King Arthur's wife.**

4. Reduce a phrase or a clause to one word.

WORDY	At that point in time, Mr. Thomas returns.
IMPROVED	**Then,** Mr. Thomas returns.

10 SENTENCE COMBINING

COMBINING BY INSERTING WORDS AND PHRASES

10a. Combine related sentences by taking a key word (or using another form of the key word) from one sentence and inserting it into another sentence.

ORIGINAL The famous magician Harry Houdini performed impossible escapes. The escapes only seemed impossible.

COMBINED The famous magician Harry Houdini performed **seemingly** impossible **escapes.** [The verb *seemed* becomes the adverb *seemingly*.]

10b. Combine related sentences by taking (or creating) a phrase from one sentence and inserting it into another.

ORIGINAL Have you read the poem "The Hollow Men"? It was written by T. S. Eliot.

COMBINED Have you read the poem "The Hollow Men" **by T. S. Eliot?** [prepositional phrase]

COMBINING BY COORDINATING IDEAS

10c. Combine related sentences whose ideas are equally important by using coordinating conjunctions (*and, but, or, nor, for, so, yet*) or correlative conjunctions (*both . . . and, either . . . or, neither . . . nor, not only . . . but also*).

The relationship of the ideas determines which connective will work best. When joined, the coordinate ideas form compound elements.

ORIGINAL *Paradise Lost* was written by John Milton. *Paradise Regained* was also written by him.

COMBINED *Paradise Lost* and *Paradise Regained* were written by John Milton. [compound subject]

ORIGINAL *Adonais* is one of Shelley's best-known poems. Many critics think that *Prometheus Unbound* is his masterpiece.

COMBINED *Adonais* is one of Shelley's best-known poems**, but** many critics think that *Prometheus Unbound* is his masterpiece. [compound sentence]

Another way to form a compound sentence is to link independent clauses with a semicolon or with a semicolon and a conjunctive adverb (such as *however, likewise,* or *therefore*) followed by a comma.

EXAMPLES
She was willing to compromise**;** he was not.
They moved to Dorsetshire**; however,** they stayed there only a few months.

COMBINING BY SUBORDINATING IDEAS

10d. Combine related sentences whose ideas are not equally important by placing the less important idea in a subordinate clause (adjective clause, adverb clause, or noun clause).

ORIGINAL I read about the life of Queen Victoria. She ruled Great Britain from 1837 to 1901.

REVISED I read about the life of Queen Victoria, **who ruled Great Britain from 1837 to 1901.** [adjective clause]
or

COMBINED Queen Victoria, **whose life I read about,** ruled Great Britain from 1837 to 1901. [adjective clause]

ORIGINAL Grendel's mother attacks Herot. King Hrothgar once again asks Beowulf for help.

COMBINED **When Grendel's mother attacks Herot,** King Hrothgar once again asks Beowulf for help. [adverb clause]

ORIGINAL They will find Death under an oak tree. An old man tells the three rioters that this will happen.

COMBINED An old man tells the three rioters **that they will find Death under an oak tree.** [noun clause]

☞ For more information about subordinate clauses and subordinating ideas, see pages 1232–1233 and 1236.

LANGUAGE HANDBOOK 1239

PROGRAM MANAGER

- **Independent Practice or Reteaching** Use *Language and Writing Skills Worksheets,* pp. 111–118.
- **Practice** See *Language Workshop: Lesson 38: Combining Sentences by Inserting Words and Phrases* and *Lesson 39: Combining Sentences by Inserting Clauses and by Coordinating Ideas.*

11 CAPITALIZATION

 11a. Capitalize the first word in every sentence.

EXAMPLE
The warrior who succeeds Beowulf as king is Wiglaf.

(1) Capitalize the first word of a sentence following a colon.

EXAMPLE
Mrs. Kelley asked me this question: **H**ow old is Beowulf when he fights Grendel?

(2) Capitalize the first word of a direct quotation.

EXAMPLE
After winning, Brian said, "**W**e couldn't have done it without the support of the good people of Raleigh."

When quoting from another writer's work, capitalize the first word of the quotation only if the writer has capitalized it in the original work.

EXAMPLE
After winning, Brian acknowledged "**t**he support of the good people of Raleigh."

(3) Traditionally, the first word of a line of poetry is capitalized.

EXAMPLES
If all the world and love were young,
And truth in every shepherd's tongue,
These pretty pleasures might me move
To live with thee and be thy love.
    —Sir Walter Raleigh, "The Nymph's
      Reply to the Shepherd"

 NOTE Some writers do not follow this rule. Whenever you quote from a writer's work, always use capital letters exactly as the writer uses them.

 11b. Capitalize the first word in the salutation and the closing of a letter.

EXAMPLES
Dear John,   **D**ear Sir or Madam: **S**incerely,

11c. Capitalize proper nouns and proper adjectives.

A *common noun* is a general name for a person, a place, a thing, or an idea. A *proper noun* names a particular person, place, thing, or idea. A *proper adjective* is formed from a proper noun. Common

nouns are capitalized only if they begin a sentence (also, in most cases, a line of poetry), begin a direct quotation, or are part of a title.

COMMON NOUNS	PROPER NOUNS	PROPER ADJECTIVES
dramatist	**S**hakespeare	**S**hakespearean performer
country	**R**ussia	**R**ussian diplomat
mountains	the **A**lps	**A**lpine flora

In proper nouns made up of two or more words, do not capitalize articles (*a, an, the*), short prepositions (those with fewer than five letters, such as *at, of, for, to, with*), the mark of the infinitive (*to*), and coordinating conjunctions (*and, but, for, nor, or, so, yet*).

EXAMPLES
Speaker **of** the **H**ouse **of** **R**epresentatives
American **S**ociety **for** the **P**revention **of** **C**ruelty
    to **A**nimals

 NOTE When you're not sure whether to capitalize a word, check a dictionary.

(1) Capitalize the names of persons and animals.

GIVEN NAMES	Virginia	Geoffrey
SURNAMES	Woolf	Chaucer
ANIMALS	Lassie	Rocinante

 NOTE Some names contain more than one capital letter. Usage varies in the capitalization of *van, von, du, de la,* and other parts of many multiword names. Always verify the spelling of a name with the person, or check the name in a reference source.

EXAMPLES
La Fontaine   O'Connor   al-Khansa   McEwen
Van Doren   Ibn Ezra   van Gogh   de Vega

(2) Capitalize the names of nationalities, races, and peoples.

EXAMPLES
Japanese   Caucasian   Hispanic   Celt

(3) Capitalize the brand names of business products. Notice that the noun that follows a brand name is not capitalized.

EXAMPLES
Sealtest milk   Wonder bread   Crest toothpaste

(4) Capitalize geographical names.

TYPE OF NAME	EXAMPLES	
Towns, Cities	Stratford-on-Avon Rio de Janeiro	Dublin South Bend
Counties, Townships	Marion County Brooklyn Borough	Alexandria Township Lafayette Parish
States, Territories	Oklahoma Yucatán	North Carolina Yukon Territory
Regions	the Middle East Western Hemisphere	the Lake District the Southwest
Countries	England	Costa Rica
Continents	South America	Europe
Islands	Long Island	British Isles
Mountains	Himalayas Pikes Peak	Mount Rainier Sierra Nevada
Other Landforms and Features	Cape of Good Hope Death Valley	Isthmus of Corinth Black Forest
Bodies of Water	Indian Ocean Bering Strait	Red Sea San Francisco Bay
Parks	Hawaii Volcanoes National Park Point Reyes National Seashore	
Roads, Highways, Streets	Route 42 Interstate 75	King Avenue Thirty-fourth Street

NOTE Words such as *city, state,* and *county* are often capitalized in official documents such as proclamations. In general usage, however, these words are not capitalized.

OFFICIAL USAGE
the State of Iowa

GENERAL USAGE
the state of Iowa

NOTE Words such as *north, western,* and *southeast* are not capitalized when they indicate direction.

EXAMPLES
north of London
heading southwest

NOTE The second word in a hyphenated number begins with a small letter.

EXAMPLE
Forty-second Street

(5) Capitalize the names of organizations, teams, business firms, institutions, buildings and other structures, and government bodies.

TYPE OF NAME	EXAMPLES
Organizations	Disabled American Veterans Professional Photographers of America
Teams	River City Eastside Bombers Harlem Globetrotters
Business Firms	Aaron's Carpets National Broadcasting Corporation
Institutions	Oxford University Southern Christian Leadership Conference
Buildings and Other Structures	Lincoln Center for the Performing Arts the Great Wall of China
Government Bodies	United States Congress House of Commons

NOTE Do not capitalize words such as *democratic, republican,* and *socialist* when they refer to principles or forms of government. Capitalize such words only when they refer to specific political parties.

EXAMPLES
The citizens demanded democratic reforms.
Who will be the Republican nominee for governor?

NOTE Do not capitalize words such as *building, hospital, theater, high school,* and *post office* unless they are part of a proper noun.

(6) Capitalize the names of historical events and periods, special events, holidays and other calendar items, and time zones.

TYPE OF NAME	EXAMPLES	
Historical Events and Periods	Middle Ages	Reign of Terror
Special Events	Super Bowl	Pan-American Games
Holidays and Other Calendar Items	Monday November	Memorial Day National Book Week
Time Zones	Eastern Daylight Time (EDT) Central Mountain Time (CMT)	

NOTE Do not capitalize the name of a season unless it is being personified or used as part of a proper noun.

EXAMPLES
We moved here last fall.
This month Fall begins painting the leaves in brilliant hues.
The Fall Festival is next week.

(7) Capitalize the names of ships, trains, aircraft, spacecraft, monuments, awards, planets and other heavenly bodies, and any other particular places and things.

TYPE OF NAME	EXAMPLES	
Ships	Merrimac	U.S.S. Nautilus
Trains	Zephyr	Hill Country Flyer
Aircraft	Enola Gay	Spruce Goose
Spacecraft	Columbia	Magellan
Monuments	Mount Rushmore National Memorial Effigy Mounds National Monument	
Awards	Nobel Prize	Medal of Freedom
Planets and Other Heavenly Bodies	Neptune Big Dipper	Polaris Cassiopeia
Other Particular Places and Things	Hurricane Alma Marshall Plan	Silk Route Union Jack

NOTE Do not capitalize the words *sun* and *moon*. Do not capitalize the word *earth* unless it is used along with the proper names of other particular places, things, or events.

EXAMPLES
The equator is an imaginary circle around the earth.
Is Mercury closer to the sun than Earth is?

☞ For more information about the names of particular places and things, see the discussion of proper nouns on page 1240.

11d. Do not capitalize the names of school subjects, except names of languages and course names followed by a number.

EXAMPLES
French   art   Algebra I

11e. Capitalize titles.

(1) Capitalize a title belonging to a particular person when it comes before the person's name.

EXAMPLES
General Patton   Dr. Sanchez   President Clinton

In general, do not capitalize a title used alone or following a name. Some titles, however, are by tradition capitalized. If you are unsure about capitalizing a title, check in a dictionary.

EXAMPLES
Who is the prime minister of Britain?
When was Ann Richards governor of Texas?
The Prince of Wales met earlier today with European leaders.

A title is usually capitalized when it is used alone in direct address.

EXAMPLE
Good afternoon, Sir [*or* sir], may I help you?

(2) Capitalize a word showing a family relationship when the word is used before or in place of a person's name, unless a possessive comes before the word.

EXAMPLES
I asked Mom if Uncle Bob is named after her uncle Roberto.

(3) Capitalize the first and last words and all important words in titles of books, periodicals, poems, stories, essays, speeches, plays, historical documents, movies, radio and television programs, works of art, musical compositions, and cartoons.

TYPE OF NAME	EXAMPLES	
Books	*A Tale of Two Cities*	*Gulliver's Travels*
Periodicals	*National Geographic*	*Time*
Poems	"She Walks in Beauty"	"To His Coy Mistress"
Stories	"The Rocking-Horse Winner"	"Games at Twilight"
Essays and Speeches	"A Modest Proposal"	the Gettysburg Address
Plays	*The Tragedy of Macbeth*	*Pygmalion*
Historical Documents	Magna Carta	Treaty of Versailles
Movies	*Robin Hood: Prince of Thieves*	*Clueless*
Radio and TV Programs	*Adventures in World Music*	*Nova*
Works of Art	*The Kiss*	*March of Humanity*
Musical Compositions	*War Requiem*	"Tears in Heaven"
Cartoons	*For Better or Worse*	*Jump Start*

NOTE Unimportant words in a title include articles (*a, an, the*), short prepositions (those with fewer than five letters, such as *of, to, in, for, from, with*), and coordinating conjunctions (*and, but, for, nor, or, so, yet*).

☞ For information about which titles should be italicized and which should be enclosed in quotation marks, see pages 1247 and 1248.

11f. Capitalize the names of religions and their followers, holy days and celebrations, holy writings, and specific deities and venerated beings.

TYPE OF NAME	EXAMPLES	
Religions and Followers	Christianity Muslim	Buddhist Judaism
Holy Days and Celebrations	Easter Passover	Ramadan Holy Week
Holy Writings	Bible Talmud	Koran I Ching
Specific Deities and Venerated Beings	Allah Dalai Lama	God Jehovah

NOTE The words *god* and *goddess* are not capitalized when they refer to mythological deities. The names of specific mythological deities are capitalized, however.

EXAMPLES
The Greek god of the sea was Poseidon.

12 PUNCTUATION

END MARKS

12a. A statement (or declarative sentence) is followed by a period.

EXAMPLE
The Ancient Mariner told an amazing tale.

12b. A question (or interrogative sentence) is followed by a question mark.

EXAMPLE
Do you know who played the leading role in the first movie version of *Hamlet*?

PROGRAM MANAGER

- **Independent Practice or Reteaching** Use *Language and Writing Skills Worksheets,* pp. 129–142.
- **Practice** See *Language Workshop:* Lessons 42–46: Punctuating Sentences and Lesson 51: Conventional Uses of Punctuation.

12c. A request or command (or imperative sentence) is followed by either a period or an exclamation point.

EXAMPLES
Turn the music down, please. [request]
Name the poet who wrote "The Lady of Shalott." [mild command]
Watch out! [strong command]

12d. An exclamation (or exclamatory sentence) is followed by an exclamation point.

EXAMPLE
What an interesting story "My Oedipus Complex" is!

12e. An abbreviation is usually followed by a period.

TYPE OF ABBREVIATION	EXAMPLES
Personal Names	Howard G. Chua-Eoan W. H. Auden
Organizations, Companies	Co. Inc. Ltd.
Titles Used with Names	Ms. Sr. Dr.
Times of Day	A.M. (or a.m.) P.M. (or p.m.)
Years	B.C. (written after the date) A.D. (written before the date)
Addresses	St. Blvd. P. O. Box
States	S.C. Calif.

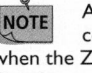

NOTE A two-letter state code is used only when the ZIP Code is included. Two-letter state codes are not followed by periods, and no comma is placed between the two-letter abbreviation and the ZIP Code.

EXAMPLE
Lexington, **KY** 40505

Some abbreviations, including those for most units of measurement, are written without periods.

EXAMPLES
AM/FM, CIA, CNN, PC, NASA, SOS,
cc, ft, lb, kw, ml, psi, rpm [but in. for inch]

If an abbreviation with a period ends a sentence, do not add another period. However, do add a question mark or an exclamation point if one is needed.

EXAMPLES
The store opens at 10 A.M.
Does the store open at 10 A.M.?

COMMAS

12f. Use commas to separate items in a series.

EXAMPLE
Virginia Woolf, James Joyce, and D. H. Lawrence are among the writers we are studying.

If all the items in a series are linked by *and, or,* or *nor,* do not use commas to separate them.

EXAMPLE
Byron **and** Shelley **and** Keats were contemporaries.

12g. Use a comma to separate two or more adjectives preceding a noun.

EXAMPLE
Gawain is the most gallant, honorable knight.

When the last adjective before a noun is thought of as part of the noun, the comma before the adjective is omitted.

EXAMPLE
I've finally found a decent, affordable used car.
[*Used car* is thought of as one unit.]

12h. Use a comma before *and, but, or, nor, for, so,* and *yet* when they join independent clauses.

EXAMPLE
I read Dylan Thomas's "Do Not Go Gentle into That Good Night," and now I want to read some more of his poems.

12i. Use commas to set off nonessential clauses and nonessential participial phrases.

A *nonessential* clause or phrase is one that can be left out without changing the meaning of the sentence.

NONESSENTIAL CLAUSE   W. H. Auden, **who was born in York, England in 1907,** became an American citizen in 1946.

NONESSENTIAL PHRASE   Willie Herenton, **defeating the incumbent in 1991,** became the first African American mayor of Memphis.

 For more information about phrases, see Part 6: Phrases. For more on clauses, see Part 7: Clauses.

1244 LANGUAGE HANDBOOK

An *essential* clause or phrase is one that cannot be left out without changing the meaning of the sentence. Essential clauses and phrases are *not* set off by commas.

ESSENTIAL CLAUSE — The writer **who received the Nobel Prize in literature in 1923** was William Butler Yeats.

ESSENTIAL PHRASE — The pilgrims **riding along with the Knight** are the Squire and the Yeoman.

12j. Use commas after certain introductory elements.

(1) Use a comma after a one-word adverb such as *first, next, yes,* or *no* or after any mild exclamation such as *well* or *why* at the beginning of a sentence.

EXAMPLE
Yes, I have read *Don Juan.*

(2) Use a comma after an introductory participial phrase.

EXAMPLE
Looking calm, Jill walked to the podium.

(3) Use a comma after two or more introductory prepositional phrases.

EXAMPLE
With the help of Wiglaf, he killed the dragon.

(4) Use a comma after an introductory adverb clause.

EXAMPLE
After I had locked the car door, I remembered that the keys were still in the ignition.

12k. Use commas to set off elements that interrupt a sentence.

(1) Appositives and appositive phrases are usually set off by commas.

EXAMPLES
George Bernard Shaw's first play, ***Widowers' Houses,*** was published in 1893.
Is that she, **the one holding the sunflowers**?

Sometimes an appositive is so closely related to the word or words near it that it should not be set off by commas. Such an appositive is called a *restrictive appositive.*

EXAMPLE
The poet **Edmund Spenser** died suddenly in 1599.

(2) Words used in direct address are set off by commas.

EXAMPLE
Your research paper, **Dylan,** is quite interesting.

(3) Parenthetical expressions are set off by commas.

Parenthetical expressions are remarks that add incidental information or that relate ideas to each other. Some common parenthetical expressions are *for example, I think, moreover,* and *on the other hand.*

EXAMPLE
Macbeth is superstitious and sensitive; Lady Macbeth, **on the other hand,** is logical and bold.

 NOTE A contrasting expression introduced by *not, rather than,* or a similar term is parenthetical. Set it off by commas.

EXAMPLE
Percy Bysshe Shelley, **not John Keats,** wrote "Ode to the West Wind."

12l. Use a comma in certain conventional situations.

(1) Use a comma to separate items in dates and addresses.

EXAMPLES
On April 23, 1616, William Shakespeare died.
My grandparents' address is 505 King Street, Austin, TX 78701.

(2) Use a comma after the salutation of a personal letter and after the closing of any letter.

EXAMPLES
Dear Alicia,   Yours truly,

(3) Use a comma to set off an abbreviation such as *Jr., Sr., RN, M.D., Ltd.,* or *Inc.*

EXAMPLES
Is Jorge Rivera, Jr., in your class?
She is the owner of Flowers by Arthurine, Inc.

SEMICOLONS

12m. Use a semicolon between independent clauses that are closely related in thought and are not joined by *and, but, for, nor, or, so,* or *yet.*

EXAMPLE
The rain had finally stopped; a few rays of sunshine were pushing through breaks in the clouds.

12n. Use a semicolon between independent clauses joined by a conjunctive adverb or a transitional expression.

A *conjunctive adverb*—such as *furthermore, however,* or *nevertheless*—or a *transitional expression*—such as *for instance, in fact,* or *that is*—indicates the relationship of the independent clauses that it joins.

EXAMPLE
The snow made traveling difficult; **nevertheless,** we arrived home safely.

12o. Use a semicolon (rather than a comma) before a coordinating conjunction to join independent clauses that contain commas.

EXAMPLE
During the seventeenth century—the era of such distinguished prose writers as Sir Thomas Browne, John Donne, and Jeremy Taylor—the balanced compound sentence using commas and semicolons reached a high degree of perfection and popularity; but the tendency today is to use a fast-moving style with shorter sentences, fewer commas, and fewer semicolons. [commas within the clauses]

12p. Use a semicolon between items in a series if the items contain commas.

EXAMPLE
The summer reading list includes *Jude the Obscure,* by Thomas Hardy; *Lord Jim,* by Joseph Conrad; and *Lord of the Flies,* by William Golding.

COLONS

12q. Use a colon to mean "note what follows."

(1) Use a colon before a list of items, especially after expressions such as *as follows* and *the following.*

EXAMPLE
Collection 8 includes poems by the following authors: Robert Burns, William Blake, William Wordsworth, and Samuel Taylor Coleridge.

 NOTE Do not use a colon before a list that directly follows a verb or a preposition.

EXAMPLES
Collection 8 includes poems by Robert Burns, William Blake, William Wordsworth, and Samuel Taylor Coleridge. [The list directly follows the preposition *by.*]
The main characters in Charles Dickens's *A Tale of Two Cities* are Dr. Manette, Lucie Manette, Charles Darnay, and Sydney Carton. [The list directly follows the verb *are.*]

(2) Use a colon before a quotation that lacks a speaker tag such as *he said* or *she remarked.*

EXAMPLE
His father's response surprised him: "I'm proud of you, son."

 For information about punctuating quotations that do have speaker tags, see page 1247.

(3) Use a colon before a long, formal statement or quotation.

EXAMPLE
When he awoke, Gulliver found himself tied down: "I could only look upward; the sun began to grow hot, and the light offended my eyes. I heard a confused noise about me, but in the posture I lay, could see nothing except the sky."

12r. Use a colon in certain conventional situations.

EXAMPLES
12:01 A.M. [between the hour and the minute]
Mark 3:10 [between chapter and verse in referring to passages from the Bible]
To Whom It May Concern: [after the salutation of a business letter]
"A Valediction: Forbidding Mourning" [between a title and a subtitle]

13 PUNCTUATION

ITALICS

Italics are printed characters that *slant to the right like this.* To indicate italics in handwritten or typewritten work, use underlining.

13a. Use italics (underlining) for words, letters, and symbols referred to as

1246 LANGUAGE HANDBOOK

such and for foreign words that have not been adopted into English.

EXAMPLES
The words *hiss* and *clang* are examples of onomatopoeia.
You typed *ie* instead of *ei.*
The motto *e pluribus unum* appears on all United States coins.

13b. Use italics (underlining) for titles of books, plays, long poems, periodicals, newspapers, works of art, films, television series, long musical compositions, recordings, comic strips, computer software, court cases, trains, ships, aircraft, and spacecraft.

TYPE OF NAME	EXAMPLE
Books	*The Canterbury Tales*
Plays	*The Taming of the Shrew*
Long Poems	*The Rime of the Ancient Mariner*
Periodicals	*Sports Illustrated*
Newspapers	*The Boston Globe*
Works of Art	*The Persistence of Memory*
Films	*It's a Wonderful Life*
TV Series	*American Playhouse*
Long Musical Compositions	*The Planets*
Recordings	*Unforgettable*
Comic Strips	*Doonesbury*
Computer Software	*Lotus 1-2-3*
Court Cases	*Marbury v. Madison*
Trains, Ships, Aircraft, and Spacecraft	*Orient Express* *Queen Elizabeth 2* *Enola Gay* *Apollo 13*

NOTE The article *the* before the title of a book, periodical, or newspaper is neither italicized nor capitalized unless it is part of the official title. The official title of a book appears on the book's title page. The official title of a periodical or newspaper is the name on its masthead, usually found on the editorial page.

EXAMPLES
What role does fate play in "The Seafarer"?
I found this information in *The New York Times*.
My mom looks through the *Sun-Times* every morning.

☞ For a list of titles that are enclosed in quotation marks, see page 1248. For information about capitalizing titles, see page 1243.

QUOTATION MARKS

13c. Use quotation marks to enclose a *direct quotation*—a person's exact words.

(1) A direct quotation usually begins with a capital letter.

EXAMPLE
Sir Francis Bacon wrote, "**K**nowledge is power."

However, when the quotation is only a part of a sentence, do not begin it with a capital letter.

EXAMPLE
In Act 1, Scene 5, Lady Macbeth describes her husband's nature as "**t**oo full o' th' milk of human kindness."

Do not use quotation marks to enclose an **indirect quotation** (a rewording of a direct quotation).

DIRECT QUOTATION	Al said, "I'm going fishing today."
INDIRECT QUOTATION	Al said that he is going fishing today.

(2) When the expression identifying the speaker divides a quoted sentence, the second part begins with a small letter.

EXAMPLE
"All good moral philosophy," according to Sir Francis Bacon, "**i**s but the handmaid to religion." [Notice that each part of a divided quotation is enclosed in quotation marks.]

When the second part of a divided quotation is a new sentence, the first word begins with a capital letter.

EXAMPLE
"On his first voyage, Gulliver finds himself in Lilliput," explained Ms. Chávez. "**T**he people there are only six inches tall."

(3) When used with quotation marks, other marks of punctuation are placed according to the following rules.

● Commas and periods are always placed inside the closing quotation marks.

EXAMPLES
"Read these lines," he said, "and tell me what you think they mean."

- Semicolons and colons are always placed outside the closing quotation marks.

EXAMPLES

Gloria promised, "I'll go to the dance with you"; however, she said that several weeks ago.

Find examples of the following figures of speech in Wordsworth's poem "I Wandered Lonely as a Cloud": personification, metaphor, and simile.

- Question marks and exclamation points are placed inside the closing quotation marks if the quotation itself is a question or an exclamation. Otherwise, they are placed outside.

EXAMPLES

Did Keats write "Ode on a Grecian Urn"?

"What an imagination you have!" exclaimed Beth.

(4) When quoting a passage that consists of more than one paragraph, put quotation marks at the beginning of each paragraph and at the end of only the last paragraph in the passage.

EXAMPLE

"At Mr. Bowyers's, a great deal of company; some I knew, others I did not. Here we stayed upon the leads and below till it was late, expecting to see the fireworks; but they were not performed tonight. Only, the City had a light like a glory round about it, with bonfires.

"At last I went to King Street; and there sent Crockford to my father's and my house to tell them I could not come home tonight, because of the dirt and a coach could not be had."

—Samuel Pepys, *The Diary of Samuel Pepys*

(5) Use single quotation marks to enclose a quotation within a quotation.

EXAMPLE

Ms. Markham asked us, "What do you think John Donne meant when he said, 'No man is an island, entire of itself'?"

(6) When writing *dialogue* (a conversation), begin a new paragraph every time the speaker changes, and enclose each speaker's words in quotation marks.

EXAMPLE

This frighted the fellow that attended about the work; but after some pause John Hayward, recovering himself, said, "Lord, bless us! There's somebody in the cart not quite dead!"

So another called to him and said, "Who are you?"

The fellow answered, "I am the poor piper. Where am I?"

"Where are you?" says Hayward. "Why, you are in the dead-cart, and we are going to bury you."

—Daniel Defoe, *A Journal of the Plague Year*

13d. Use quotation marks to enclose titles of short works, such as short stories, poems, essays, articles, songs, episodes of television series, and chapters and other parts of books.

TYPE OF NAME	EXAMPLE
Short Stories	"The Doll's House" "Games at Twilight"
Poems	"Ode to a Nightingale" "Thoughts of Hanoi"
Essays	"Shakespeare's Sister" "The Myth of Sisyphus"
Articles	"How to Improve Your Grades"
Songs	"Wind Beneath My Wings" "Frankie and Johnny"
TV Episodes	"Tony's Surprise Party" "Inside the Earth"
Chapters of a Book	"The Age of Reform" "How Ecosystems Change"

NOTE Neither italics nor quotation marks are used for the titles of major religious texts or for the titles of historical or legal documents.

EXAMPLES

the Bible
Code of Hammurabi
Bill of Rights
Monroe Doctrine

For a list of titles that are italicized, see page 1247.

ELLIPSIS POINTS

13e. Use three spaced periods called *ellipsis points* (. . .) to mark omissions from quoted material and pauses in a written passage.

ORIGINAL At last she spoke to me. When she addressed the first words to me I was so confused that I did not know what to answer. She asked me was I going to *Araby*. I forget whether I answered yes or no. It would be a splendid bazaar, she said; she would love to go.

—James Joyce, "Araby"

(1) If the quoted material that comes before the ellipsis points is not a complete sentence, use three ellipsis points with a space before the first point.

EXAMPLE

Of his conversation with Mangan's sister, the narrator says, "When she addressed the first words to me . . . I did not know what to answer."

(2) If the quoted material that comes before the ellipsis points is a complete sentence, use an end mark before the ellipsis points.

EXAMPLE

According to Mangan's sister, "It would be a splendid bazaar. . . ."

(3) If one sentence or more is omitted, ellipsis points follow the end mark that precedes the omitted material.

EXAMPLE

The narrator recalls his encounter with Mangan's sister: "At last she spoke to me. . . . She asked me was I going to *Araby.*"

(4) To show that a full line or more of poetry has been omitted, use a line of spaced periods that is as long as the line of poetry above it.

ORIGINAL   It fell about the Martinmas time,
               And a gay time it was then,
            When our goodwife got puddings to make,
               And she's boild them in the pan.
                  —Traditional, "Get Up and Bar
                     the Door"

ONE LINE   It fell about the Martinmas time,
OMITTED   . . . .
             When our goodwife got puddings to make,
               And she's boild them in the pan.

APOSTROPHES

Possessive Case

13f. The *possessive case* of a noun or a pronoun indicates ownership or relationship. Use an apostrophe in forming the possessive case of nouns and indefinite pronouns.

(1) To form the possessive of a singular noun, add an apostrophe and an *s*.

EXAMPLES

Beowulf's shield   the principal's office

 NOTE When forming the possessive of a singular noun that ends in an *s* sound, add only an apostrophe if the addition of *'s* will make the noun awkward to pronounce. Otherwise, add *'s*.

EXAMPLES

Ms. Rodgers' class   the witness's testimony

(2) To form the possessive of a plural noun ending in *s*, add only the apostrophe.

EXAMPLES

the players' uniforms   the volunteers' efforts

(3) Form the possessive of only the last word in a compound word, in the name of an organization or business, or in a word group showing joint possession.

EXAMPLES

brother-in-law's car
Ralph Merrill and Company's products
Macbeth and Lady Macbeth's plan

 NOTE When a possessive pronoun is part of a word group showing joint possession, each noun in the word group is also possessive.

EXAMPLE

Chen's, Ramona's, and **my** project

(4) Form the possessive of each noun in a word group showing individual possession of similar items.

EXAMPLE

Byron's, Shelley's, and Keats's poems

(5) Possessive form of words indicating time, such as *minute, day, month,* and *year,* and words indicating amounts in cents or dollars require apostrophes.

EXAMPLES

four weeks' vacation   a dollar's worth

(6) To form the possessive of an indefinite pronoun, add an apostrophe and an *s*.

EXAMPLES

no one's fault   somebody else's jacket

Contractions

13g. Use an apostrophe to show where letters, words, or numbers have been omitted in a contraction.

EXAMPLES

let us . . . . **let's**   she would . . . . . **she'd**
you will . . . . . **you'll**   1998 . . . . **'98**

The word *not* can be shortened to *–n't* and added to a verb, usually without changing the spelling of the verb.

EXAMPLES

do not . . . . **don't**   should not . . . **shouldn't**
EXCEPTION
will not . . . **won't**

Plurals

13h. Use an apostrophe and an *s* to form the plurals of all lowercase letters, some uppercase letters, numerals, and some words referred to as words.

EXAMPLES

There are two *c*'s and two *m*'s in *accommodate*. Try not to use so many *I*'s in your cover letter. [Without the apostrophe, the plural of the pronoun *I* would spell *Is*.]

NOTE You may add only an *s* to form the plurals of words, numerals, and capital letters if the plural forms will not cause misreading. However, it is never wrong to use an apostrophe in such cases and is usually a good idea to do so.

EXAMPLE

James I ruled England during the early **1600s** [*or* **1600's**].

HYPHENS

13i. Use a hyphen to divide a word at the end of a line.

● Do not divide a one-syllable word.

EXAMPLE

Did the Green Knight know that Sir Gawain had **kissed** [*not* kis-sed] his wife?

● Divide a word only between syllables.

EXAMPLE

First, Macbeth was killed; then he was **decapi-tated** [*not* decapita-ted].

● Divide an already hyphenated word at the hyphen.

EXAMPLE

Queen Elizabeth I was ruler of England for **forty-five** [*not* for-ty-five] years.

● Do not divide a word so that one letter stands alone.

EXAMPLE

Paradise Lost by John Milton is a famous English **epic** [*not* e-pic].

13j. Use a hyphen with compound numbers from twenty-one to ninety-nine and with fractions used as modifiers.

EXAMPLES

thirty-seven

a **three-fourths** majority [*but* **three fourths** of the voters]

DASHES

13k. Use dashes to set off abrupt breaks in thought.

EXAMPLE

The playwright handles her material—I should say lack of material—quite well.

13l. Use dashes to set off appositives or parenthetical expressions that contain commas.

EXAMPLE

Several of the British Romantic poets—Shelley, Keats, and Byron, for example—led fascinating lives.

13m. Use a dash to set off an introductory list or group of examples.

EXAMPLE

Alliteration, caesuras, and kennings—these are features of Anglo-Saxon poetry.

PARENTHESES

13n. Use parentheses to enclose informative or explanatory material of minor importance.

EXAMPLES

A *roman à clef* (literally, "novel with a key") is a novel about real people to whom the novelist has assigned fictitious names.

The Globe (see the drawing on page 284) was built in 1599. [The *s* in *see* is lowercase because the parenthetical sentence is within a complete sentence.]

The Globe was built in 1599. (See the drawing on page 284.) [The *S* in *See* is capitalized and a period follows *page 284* because the parenthetical sentence is not within another sentence but instead stands on its own.]

BRACKETS

13o. Use brackets to enclose an explanation within quoted or parenthetical material.

EXAMPLE

The newspaper article stated that "at the time of that Democratic National Convention [in Chicago in 1968] there were many protest groups operating in the United States."

14 SPELLING

UNDERSTANDING WORD STRUCTURE

Many English words are made up of roots and affixes (prefixes and suffixes).

Roots

The **root** of a word is the part that carries the word's core meaning.

ROOT	MEANING	EXAMPLES
–fin–	end, limit	final, infinite
–gram–	write, writing	grammar, epigram
–tract–	pull, draw	tractor, extract
–vit–	life	vitamin, vital

Prefixes

A **prefix** is one or more than one letter or syllable added to the beginning of a word to create a new word with a different meaning.

PREFIX	MEANING	EXAMPLES
contra–	against	contradict, contrast
inter–	between, among	interstate, interact
mis–	not, wrongly	misfire, misspell
re–	back, again	reflect, refinance

Suffixes

A **suffix** is one or more than one letter or syllable added to the end of a word to create a new word with a different meaning.

SUFFIX	MEANING	EXAMPLES
–fy	make, cause	verify, pacify
–ish	suggesting, like	smallish, childish
–ist	doer, believer	artist, humanist
–ty	quality, state	cruelty, certainty

SPELLING RULES

NOTE Always keep in mind that the best way to be sure you have spelled a word correctly is to look the word up in a dictionary.

ie and *ei*

14a. Write *ie* when the sound is long *e*, except after *c*.

EXAMPLES
rel**ie**ve ch**ie**f f**ie**ld conc**ei**t dec**ei**ve
EXCEPTIONS
either l**ei**sure n**ei**ther s**ei**ze w**ei**rd

14b. Write *ei* when the sound is not long *e*.

EXAMPLES
r**ei**gn for**ei**gn th**ei**r sover**ei**gn w**ei**ght
EXCEPTIONS
anc**ie**nt v**ie**w fr**ie**nd misch**ie**f consc**ie**nce

NOTE Rules 14a and 14b apply only when the *i* and the *e* are in the same syllable.

–cede, *–ceed*, and *–sede*

14c. The only English word ending in *–sede* is *supersede*. The only words ending in *–ceed* are *exceed*, *proceed*, and *succeed*. All other words with this sound end in *–cede*.

EXAMPLES
con**cede** pre**cede** re**cede** se**cede**

Adding Prefixes

14d. When adding a prefix, do not change the spelling of the original word.

EXAMPLES
over + run = **over**run   mis + spell = **mis**spell

Adding Suffixes

14e. When adding the suffix *–ness* or *–ly*, do not change the spelling of the original word.

EXAMPLES
gentle + ness = gentle**ness**   final + ly = final**ly**

LANGUAGE HANDBOOK 1251

EXCEPTIONS

For most words ending in y, change the y to i before adding –ness or –ly.

heavy + ness = heav**iness**   ready + ly = read**ily**

 NOTE One-syllable adjectives ending in y generally follow rule 14e.

EXAMPLES

shy + ness = shy**ness**   sly + ly = sly**ly**

14f. **Drop the final silent e before a suffix beginning with a vowel.**

EXAMPLES

awake + en = awak**en**   race + ing = rac**ing**

EXCEPTIONS

Keep the final silent e

● in a word ending in ce or ge before a suffix beginning with a or o
  peac**eable**   courag**eous**
● in dye and in singe before –ing
  dy**eing**   sing**eing**
● in mile before –age
  mil**eage**

 NOTE When adding –ing to words that end in ie, drop the e and change the i to y.

EXAMPLES

die + ing = d**ying**   lie + ing = l**ying**

14g. **Keep the final silent e before a suffix beginning with a consonant.**

EXAMPLES

care + less = car**eless**   sure + ty = sur**ety**

EXCEPTIONS

nine + th = nin**th**   judge + ment = judg**ment**
true + ly = tru**ly**   wise + dom = wis**dom**

14h. **For words ending in y preceded by a consonant, change the y to i before any suffix that does not begin with i.**

EXAMPLES

heavy + est = heav**iest**
accompany + ment = accompan**iment**
verify + ing = verif**ying**

14i. **For words ending in y preceded by a vowel, keep the y when adding a suffix.**

EXAMPLES

enjoy + ing = enjo**ying**   play + ed = pla**yed**

EXCEPTIONS

day + ly = da**ily**   lay + ed = la**id**
pay + ed = pa**id**   say + ed = sa**id**

14j. **Double the final consonant before a suffix that begins with a vowel if the word both (1) has only one syllable or has the accent on the last syllable and (2) ends in a single consonant preceded by a single vowel.**

EXAMPLES

rap + ing = ra**pping**   refer + ed = refe**rred**

EXCEPTIONS

● For words ending in w or x, do not double the final consonant.
  bow + ed = bow**ed**   tax + able = tax**able**
● For words ending in c, add k before the suffix instead of doubling the c.
  picnic + k + ing = picnic**king**

FORMING THE PLURALS OF NOUNS

14k. **Remembering the following rules will help you spell the plural forms of nouns.**

(1) For most nouns, add –s.

EXAMPLES

beagle**s**   senator**s**   taxi**s**   Saxon**s**

(2) For nouns ending in s, x, z, ch, or sh, add –es.

EXAMPLES

glass**es**   waltz**es**   brush**es**   Perez**es**

(3) For nouns ending in y preceded by a vowel, add –s.

EXAMPLES

journey**s**   decoy**s**   Saturday**s**   Kelley**s**

(4) For nouns ending in y preceded by a consonant, change the y to i and add –es.

EXAMPLES

comed**ies**   cavit**ies**   theor**ies**   sk**ies**

EXCEPTIONS

For proper nouns, add –s.
Gregory**s**   Kimberly**s**

(5) For some nouns ending in f or fe, add –s. For others, change the f or fe to v and add –es.

EXAMPLES

belief**s**   loa**ves**   giraffe**s**   wi**ves**

EXCEPTIONS

For proper nouns, add –s.
DeGroff**s**   Rolfe**s**

(6) For nouns ending in o preceded by a vowel, add –s.

EXAMPLES

radio**s**   cameo**s**   shampoo**s**   Matsuo**s**

(7) For nouns ending in *o* preceded by a consonant, add *–es*.

EXAMPLES
torped**oes**   ech**oes**   her**oes**   potat**oes**

For some common nouns ending in *o* preceded by a consonant, especially those referring to music, and for proper nouns, add only an *–s*.

EXAMPLES
phot**os**   haird**os**   sol**os**   sopran**os**   Spir**os**

(8) The plurals of a few nouns are formed in irregular ways.

EXAMPLES
g**ee**se   men   child**ren**   m**i**ce   t**ee**th

(9) For a few nouns, the singular and the plural forms are the same.

EXAMPLES
deer   series   Chinese   Sioux

(10) For most compound nouns, form the plural of only the last word of the compound.

EXAMPLES
courthous**es**   seat belt**s**   four-year-old**s**

(11) For compound nouns in which one of the words is modified by the other word or words, form the plural of the noun modified.

EXAMPLES
son**s**-in-law   passers**by**   mountain goat**s**

(12) For some nouns borrowed from other languages, the plural is formed as in the original languages. In a few cases, two plural forms are acceptable.

EXAMPLES
analysis—analys**es**   phenomenon—phenomen**a**

(13) To form the plurals of figures, most uppercase letters, signs, and words referred to as words, add an *–s* or both an apostrophe and an *–s*.

EXAMPLES
1500**s** *or* 1500**'s**   B**s** *or* B**'s**
$**s** *or* $**'s**   *and***s** *or* *and***'s**

NOTE   To avoid confusion, add both an apostrophe and an *–s* to form the plural of all lowercase letters, certain uppercase letters, and some words used as words.

EXAMPLES
The word *fictitious* contains three *i* **'s**. [Without an apostrophe, the plural of *i* could be confused with the word *is*.]
Sebastian usually makes straight A**'s**. [Without an apostrophe, the plural of *A* could be confused with the word *As*.]
Because I mistakenly thought Evelyn Waugh was a woman, I used *her***'s** instead of *his***'s** in my paragraph. [Without an apostrophe, the plural of *her* would look like the pronoun *hers* and the plural of *his* would look like the word *hiss*.]

NOTE   In names, ***diacritical marks*** (marks that show pronunciation) and capitalization are as essential to correct spelling as the letters themselves. If you're not sure about the spelling of a name, check with the person whose name it is, or consult a reference source.

EXAMPLES
François   Lagerlöf
Van Doren   van Gogh
Márquez   Marín
de Vega   al-Khansa

15 GLOSSARY OF USAGE

The Glossary of Usage is an alphabetical listing of expressions with definitions, explanations, and examples. Some of the examples are labeled *standard, nonstandard, formal,* or *informal.* The label **standard** or **formal** identifies usage that is appropriate in serious writing and speaking (such as in compositions and speeches). The label **informal** indicates standard English that is generally used in conversation and in everyday writing such as personal letters. The label **nonstandard** identifies usage that does not follow the guidelines of standard English usage.

accept, except   *Accept* is a verb meaning "to receive." *Except* may be a verb meaning "to leave out" or a preposition meaning "excluding."

EXAMPLES
Does Sir Gawain **accept** the challenge from the Green Knight? [verb]
Certain states **except** teachers from jury duty. [verb]
I have read all of *Macbeth* **except** the last act. [preposition]

PROGRAM MANAGER

- **Independent Practice or Reteaching** Use *Language and Writing Skills Worksheets,* pp. 1–10.
- **Practice** See *Language Workshop:* Chapter 11: Usage.

affect, effect   *Affect* is a verb meaning "to influence." *Effect* may either be a verb meaning "to bring about or to accomplish" or a noun meaning "the result [of an action]."

EXAMPLES
How did the murder of King Duncan **affect** Lady Macbeth? [verb]
In this dispute, management and labor should be able to **effect** a compromise. [verb]
What far-reaching **effects** did the *Brown* v. *Board of Education of Topeka* decision have? [noun]

all ready, already   *All ready* means "all prepared." *Already* means "previously."

EXAMPLES
Are you **all ready** for the audition?
We have **already** read "The Seafarer."

all right   *All right* means "satisfactory," "unhurt; safe," "correct," or, in reply to a question or to preface a remark, "yes." *Alright* is a misspelling.

EXAMPLES
Does this look **all right** [*not* alright]?
Oh, **all right** [*not* alright], you can go.

all the farther, all the faster   Avoid using these expressions in formal situations. Use *as far as* or *as fast as*.

EXAMPLE
Is that **as fast as** [*not* all the faster] Chris can run?

all together, altogether   *All together* means "everyone in the same place." *Altogether* means "entirely."

EXAMPLES
The knights were **all together** for the celebration.
Sir Gawain was not **altogether** honest with the Green Knight.

allusion, illusion   An *allusion* is an indirect reference to something. An *illusion* is a mistaken idea or a misleading appearance.

EXAMPLES
The speaker made an **allusion** to Emily Brontë's *Wuthering Heights.*
Before selecting a career, he had to abandon some of his **illusions** about his own abilities.
The director chose certain colors to create an **illusion** of depth on the small stage.

a lot   Avoid this expression in formal situations by using *many* or *much.*

EXAMPLE
Many [*not* a lot] of my friends work part time after school and on weekends.

already   See **all ready, already.**

altogether   See **all together, altogether.**

among   See **between, among.**

and etc.   *Etc.* stands for the Latin words *et cetera,* meaning "and others" or "and so forth." Always avoid using *and* before *etc.* In general, avoid using *etc.* in formal situations. Use one of its meanings instead.

EXAMPLE
We are comparing the main female characters in Shakespeare's tragedies: Lady Macbeth, Cleopatra, Juliet, **and others** [*or* etc. *but not* and etc.].

any one, anyone   The expression *any one* specifies one member of a group. *Anyone* means "one person, no matter which."

EXAMPLES
Any one of you could win the poetry contest.
Anyone who finishes the test early may leave.

as   See **like, as.**

as if   See **like, as if.**

at   Avoid using *at* after a construction beginning with *where.*

| NONSTANDARD | Where was Beowulf at when Grendel's mother attacked? |
| STANDARD | **Where** was Beowulf when Grendel's mother attacked? |

a while, awhile   *A while* means "a period of time." *Awhile* means "for a short time."

EXAMPLES
Herot remained empty for quite **a while.**
They stayed there **awhile.**

bad, badly   *Bad* is an adjective. *Badly* is an adverb. In standard English, *bad* should follow a sense verb, such as *feel, look, sound, taste,* or *smell,* or other linking verb.

EXAMPLE
The prospects for fair weather look **bad** [*not* badly].

because   In formal situations, do not use the construction *reason . . . because.* Instead, use *reason . . . that.*

EXAMPLE
The **reason** Sir Gawain accepts the green sash is **that** [*not* because] he thinks it will protect him from the Green Knight.

being as, being that   Avoid using either of these expressions for *since* or *because.*

EXAMPLE
Because [*not* being as *or* being that] Sir Gawain is a knight, we expect him to behave chivalrously.

beside, besides *Beside* means "by the side of" or "next to." *Besides* means "in addition to" or "other than" or "moreover."

EXAMPLES

The Geats built Beowulf's tomb **beside** the sea.

No one **besides** Wiglaf helped Beowulf battle the dragon.

I have decided that I do not want to take journalism; **besides,** I cannot fit it into my schedule.

between, among Use *between* to refer to only two items or to more than two when comparing each item individually to each of the others.

EXAMPLES

The reward money will be divided **between** Chang and Marta.

Sasha explained the difference **between** assonance, consonance, and alliteration. [Each item is compared individually to each of the others.]

Use *among* to refer to more than two items when you are not considering each item in relation to each other item individually.

EXAMPLE

The reward money will be divided **among** the four girls.

bring, take *Bring* means "to come carrying something." *Take* means "to go carrying something."

EXAMPLES

I'll **bring** my copy of *Gulliver's Travels* when I come over.

Please **take** the model of the Globe Theater to the library.

bust, busted Avoid using these words as verbs. Instead, use a form of *break* or *burst,* depending on the meaning.

EXAMPLES

The window is **broken** [*not* busted].

The water main has **burst** [*not* busted] open.

can, may Use *can* to express ability. Use *may* to express possibility.

EXAMPLES

Can you play the guitar?

It **may** rain later.

cannot (can't) help but Avoid using *but* and the infinitive form of a verb after the expression *cannot (can't) help.* Instead, use a gerund alone.

NONSTANDARD I can't help but laugh when I look at that photograph.

STANDARD I can't help **laughing** when I look at that photograph.

compare, contrast Used with *to, compare* means "to look for similarities between." Used with *with, compare* means "to look for both similarities and differences between." *Contrast* is always used to point out differences.

EXAMPLES

The simile at the end of the poem **compares** the eagle's fall **to** a thunderbolt.

We **compared** Shakespeare's style **with** that of Christopher Marlowe.

The tour guide also **contrasted** the two castles' provisions for defense.

could of See **of.**

double subject Avoid using an unnecessary pronoun after the subject of a sentence.

EXAMPLE

George Bernard Shaw [*not* George Bernard Shaw he] wrote *Pygmalion.*

due to Avoid using *due to* for "because of" or "owing to."

EXAMPLE

All schools were closed **because of** [*not* due to] inclement weather.

effect See **affect, effect.**

either, neither *Either* usually means "one or the other of two." In referring to more than two, use *any one* or *any* instead. *Neither* usually means "not one or the other of two." In referring to more than two, use *none* instead.

EXAMPLES

Either of the two quotations would be appropriate to use at the beginning of your speech.

You should be able to find ample information about **any one** of those four poets.

Neither of the Perez twins is in school today.

None of the seniors have voted yet.

etc. See **and etc.**

every day, everyday *Every day* means "each day." *Everyday* means "daily," "ordinary," or "usual."

EXAMPLES

Every day presents its own challenges.

The party will be casual; wear **everyday** clothes.

every one, everyone *Every one* specifies every single person or thing of those named. *Everyone* means "everybody, all of the people named."

EXAMPLES

Elizabeth Bowen wrote **every one** of these stories.

Did **everyone** read "The Demon Lover"?

except See **accept, except.**

farther, further Use *farther* to express physical distance. Use *further* to express abstract relationships of degree or quantity.

EXAMPLES
Your house is **farther** from school than mine is.
The United Nations members decided that **further** debate was unnecessary.

fewer, less Use *fewer* to modify a plural noun and *less* to modify a singular noun.

EXAMPLES
Fewer students are going out for football this year.
Now I spend **less** time watching TV.

good, well Avoid using the adjective *good* to modify an action verb. Instead, use the adverb *well*, meaning "capably" or "satisfactorily."

EXAMPLE
We did **well** [*not* good] on the exam.

Used as an adjective, *well* means "in good health" or "satisfactory in appearance or condition."

EXAMPLES
I feel **well.**
It's eight o'clock, and all is **well.**

had of See **of.**

had ought, hadn't ought Do not use *had* or *hadn't* with *ought.*

EXAMPLES
Your application **ought** [*not* had ought] to have been sent in earlier.
She **ought not** [*not* hadn't ought] to swim so soon after eating lunch.

illusion See **allusion, illusion.**

imply, infer *Imply* means "to suggest indirectly." *Infer* means "to interpret" or "to draw a conclusion."

EXAMPLES
The speaker of "To a Skylark" **implies** that the skylark is a divine being.
I **inferred** from her speech that she would support a statewide testing program.

in, in to, into *In* generally shows location. In the construction *in to, in* is an adverb followed by the preposition *to. Into* generally shows direction.

EXAMPLES
Rudyard Kipling was born **in** Bombay.
He found the treasure and turned it **in to** his king.
Sir Gawain rode **into** the wilderness to find the Green Knight.

1256 LANGUAGE HANDBOOK

infer See **imply, infer.**

irregardless, regardless *Irregardless* is nonstandard. Use *regardless* instead.

EXAMPLE
Regardless [*not* irregardless] of the danger, he continued his journey.

its, it's *Its* is the possessive form of *it. It's* is the contraction of *it is* or *it has.*

EXAMPLES
The community is proud of **its** school system.
It's [it is] a symbol of peace.
It's [it has] been cooler today.

kind of, sort of In formal situations, avoid using these terms for the adverb *somewhat* or *rather.*

INFORMAL	Macbeth appeared to be kind of worried.
FORMAL	Macbeth appeared to be **rather** [*or* **somewhat**] worried.

kind of a(n), sort of a(n) In formal situations, omit the *a(n).*

INFORMAL	What kind of a poem is "The Passionate Shepherd to His Love"?
FORMAL	What **kind of** poem is "The Passionate Shepherd to His Love"?

kind(s), sort(s), type(s) With the singular form of each of these nouns, use *this* or *that.* With the plural form, use *these* or *those.*

EXAMPLES
This type of engine performs more economically than any of **those types.**

less See **fewer, less.**

lie, lay The verb *lie* means "to rest" or "to stay, to recline, or to remain in a certain state or position." Its principal parts are *lie, lying, lay,* and *lain. Lie* never takes an object. The verb *lay* means "to put [something] in a place." Its principal parts are *lay, laying, laid,* and *laid. Lay* usually takes an object.

EXAMPLES
Gulliver was **lying** on his back and could hardly move. [no object]
The Lilliputians **laid** baskets of food near Gulliver's mouth. [*Baskets* is the object of *laid.*]

like, as In formal situations, do not use *like* for *as* to introduce a subordinate clause.

INFORMAL	John looks like his father looked twenty years ago.
FORMAL	John looks **as** his father looked twenty years ago.

like, as if In formal situations, avoid using the preposition *like* for the compound conjunction *as if* or *as though* to introduce a subordinate clause.

INFORMAL   The heavy footsteps sounded **like** they were coming nearer.

FORMAL   The heavy footsteps sounded **as if** [*or* **as though**] they were coming nearer.

might of, must of See **of.**

neither See **either, neither.**

nor See **or, nor.**

of *Of* is a preposition. Do not use *of* in place of *have* after verbs such as *could, should, would, might, must,* and *ought* [*to*]. Also, do not use *had of* for *had.*

EXAMPLES

If I **had** [*not* had of] known about the shortcut, I **would have** [*not* would of] been here sooner.

Avoid using *of* after other prepositions such as *inside, off,* and *outside.*

EXAMPLE

Flimnap fell **off** [*not* off of] the tightrope.

off, off of Do not use *off* or *off of* for *from.*

EXAMPLE

You can get a program **from** [*not* off of] the usher.

on to, onto In the expression *on to, on* is an adverb and *to* is a preposition. *Onto* is a preposition.

EXAMPLES

The lecturer moved **on to** her next main idea.
She walked **onto** the stage.

or, nor Use *or* with *either;* use *nor* with *neither.*

EXAMPLES

The list of authors does not include **either** James Joyce **or** [*not* nor] D. H. Lawrence.
Neither James Joyce **nor** D. H. Lawrence is on the list of authors.

ought See **had ought, hadn't ought.**

ought to of See **of.**

raise See **rise, raise.**

reason . . . because See **because.**

refer back Since the prefix *re–* in *refer* means "back," adding *back* is generally unnecessary.

EXAMPLE

The writer is **referring** [*not* referring back] to the years when he lived in Ireland.

rise, raise The verb *rise* means "to go up" or "to get up." Its principal parts are *rise, rising, rose,* and *risen. Rise* never takes an object. The verb *raise* means "to cause [something] to rise" or "to lift up." Its principal parts are *raise, raising, raised,* and *raised. Raise* usually takes an object.

EXAMPLES

Her blood pressure **rose** as she waited. [no object]
The Green Knight **raised** the ax above his head. [*Ax* is the object of *raised.*]

should of See **of.**

sit, set The verb *sit* means "to rest in an upright, seated position." Its principal parts are *sit, sitting, sat,* and *sat. Sit* seldom takes an object. The verb *set* means "to put [something] in a place." Its principal parts are *set, setting, set,* and *set. Set* usually takes an object.

EXAMPLES

Banquo's ghost **sits** in Macbeth's place. [no object]
Please **set** the groceries on the table. [*Groceries* is the object of *set.*]

some, somewhat In formal situations, avoid using *some* to mean "to some extent." Use *somewhat.*

EXAMPLE

The Wedding Guest was somewhat shaken [*not* shaken some] by the Ancient Mariner's gaze and appearance.

sort(s) See **kind(s), sort(s), type(s)** and **kind of a(n), sort of a(n).**

sort of See **kind of, sort of.**

take See **bring, take.**

than, then *Than* is a conjunction used in comparisons. *Then* is an adverb meaning "at that time" or "next."

EXAMPLES

Is King Macbeth more superstitious **than** Lady Macbeth?
First, we will read "The Lamb"; **then,** we will read "The Tyger."

that See **who, which, that.**

their, there, they're *Their* is a possessive form of *they.* As an adverb, *there* means "at that place." *There* is also used to begin a sentence. *They're* is the contraction of *they are.*

EXAMPLES

They built a tomb for **their** fallen leader.
Macduff was not **there** at the time.
There is very little time left.
They're waiting for Banquo.

LANGUAGE HANDBOOK 1257

theirs, there's *Theirs* is a possessive form of the pronoun *they*. *There's* is the contraction of *there is*.

EXAMPLES
The treasure is **theirs** now.
There's an allusion to the Bible in the poem.

them Do not use *them* as an adjective. Use *those*.

EXAMPLE
Have you seen **those** [*not* them] murals by Judith Baca at the art museum?

then See **than, then.**

there See **their, there, they're.**

there's See **theirs, there's.**

they're See **their, there, they're.**

this here, that there Avoid using *here* or *there* after *this* or *that*.

EXAMPLE
This [*not* this here] poem was written by Robert Browning.

try and, try to Use *try to,* not *try and.*

EXAMPLE
I will **try to** [*not* try and] finish reading *The Diary of Samuel Pepys* tonight.

type, type of Avoid using the noun *type* as an adjective. Add *of* after *type*.

EXAMPLE
What **type of** [*not* type] character is the knight in "The Wife of Bath's Tale"?

type(s) See **kind(s), sort(s), type(s).**

ways Use *way,* not *ways,* when referring to distance.

EXAMPLE
Is Canterbury a long **way** [*not* ways] from the Tabard Inn?

well See **good, well.**

when, where Do not use *when* or *where* to begin a definition.

NONSTANDARD	A caesura is where you break or pause in a line of poetry.
STANDARD	A caesura is **a break or pause in a line of poetry.**

where, when Do not use *where* or *when* in place of *that.*

EXAMPLE
I read **that** [*not* where] you won a scholarship.

where . . . at See **at.**

who, which, that *Who* refers to persons only. *Which* refers to things only. *That* may refer to either persons or things.

EXAMPLES
Sir Gawain was the knight **who** [*or* that] accepted the Green Knight's challenge.
The Globe, **which** was built in 1599, burned down in 1613.
Is this the only poem **that** Sir Walter Raleigh ever wrote?

who's, whose *Who's* is the contraction of *who is* or *who has*. *Whose* is the possessive form of *who*.

EXAMPLES
Well, look **who's** [who is] here!
Who's [who has] read all of the play?
Whose treasure is it?

would of See **of.**

your, you're *Your* is a possessive form of *you*. *You're* is the contraction of *you are*.

EXAMPLES
Is that **your** car?
I can see that **you're** tired.

GLOSSARY

The glossary that follows is an alphabetical list of various words found in the selections in this book. Use this glossary just as you use a dictionary—to find out the meanings of unfamiliar words. (Technical, foreign, or more obscure words are not listed here but are defined instead in the footnotes that accompany each selection.)

Many words in the English language have more than one meaning. This glossary gives the meanings that apply to the words as they are used in the selections in this book. Words closely related in form and meaning are usually listed together in one entry (*agitated* and *agitation*), and the definition is given for the first form.

The following abbreviations are used:

adj., adjective	*n.,* noun	*prep.,* preposition
adv., adverb	*pl.,* plural form	*v.,* verb

Unless a word is very simple to pronounce, its pronunciation is given in parentheses. A guide to the pronunciation symbols appears at the bottom of each right-hand glossary page.

For more information about the words in this glossary or about words not listed here, consult a dictionary.

abasement (ə·bās′mənt) *n.:* humiliation.
abate (ə·bāt′) *v.:* to lessen.
abject (ab′jekt′) *adj.:* degrading; humiliating.
ablution (ab·lōō′shən) *n.:* washing of the body, especially as a religious rite.
abominable (ə·bäm′ə·nə·bəl) *adj.:* disgusting; hateful.
absolution (ab′sə·lōō′shən) *n.:* forgiveness.
abstain (ab·stān′) *v.:* to refrain from; hold oneself back from.
abyss (ə·bis′) *n.:* bottomless pit.
accentuate (ak·sen′chōō·āt′) *v.:* to emphasize.
accrue (ə·krōō′) *v.:* to increase over time.
acquit (ə·kwit′) *v.:* to clear of a charge; absolve.
admonish (ad·män′ish) *v.:* to scold mildly.
adversity (ad·vʉr′sə·tē) *n.:* trouble; misfortune.
aesthetics (es·thet′iks) *n. pl.:* principles of beauty.
affliction (ə·flik′shən) *n.:* deep suffering.
aggrieved (ə·grēvd′) *adj.:* offended; wronged.
agitated (aj′i·tāt′id) *adj.:* disturbed; upset. —**agitation** *n.*
agog (ə·gäg′) *adj.:* in a state of excitement and anticipation.
alienate (āl′ē·ən·āt′) *v.:* to drive apart.
allege (ə·lej′) *v.:* to declare or assert, often without proof.
alleviation (ə·lē′vē·ā′shən) *n.:* something that lightens, relieves, or makes easier to bear.
allotment (ə·lät′mənt) *n.:* distribution.
alms (ämz) *n. pl.:* goods donated to the poor as charity.
altruistic (al′trōō·is′tik) *adj.:* unselfish.
ambiguous (am·big′yōō·əs) *adj.:* having more than one meaning; unclear; vague.
amiability (ā′mē·ə·bil′ə·tē) *n.:* friendliness. —**amiable** *adj.*

amorous (am′ə·res) *adj.:* full of love.
anecdote (an′ik·dōt′) *n.:* brief, little-known fact or amusing story.
anguish (aŋ′gwish) *n.:* agony.
animosity (an′ə·mäs′ə·tē) *n.:* hostility; intense hatred or resentment.
annals (an′əlz) *n. pl.:* historical records.
annihilate (ə·nī′ə·lāt′) *v.:* to destroy completely.
annul (ə·nul′) *v.:* to do away with; cancel.
aperture (ap′ər·chər) *n.:* opening.
apparition (ap′ə·rish′ən) *n.:* strange figure, like a ghost, that appears suddenly.
apprehensible (ap′rē·hen′sə·bəl) *adj.:* able to be seen or understood. —**apprehend** *v.*
approbation (ap′rə·bā′shən) *n.:* approval.
arable (ar′ə·bəl) *adj.:* suitable for growing crops.
arboreal (är·bôr′ē·əl) *adj.:* full of trees.
ardor (är′dər) *n.:* passion; enthusiasm. —**ardent** *adj.*
arrears (ə·rirz′) *n. pl.:* overdue debts.
arrest (ə·rest′) *v.:* to check or halt in motion.
assail (ə·sāl′) *v.:* to attack. —**assailable** *adj.*
assent (ə·sent′) *n.:* acceptance.
assert (ə·sʉrt′) *v.:* to declare.
assignation (as′ig·nā′shən) *n.:* appointment; meeting.
asunder (ə·sun′dər) *adv.:* apart.
attenuate (ə·ten′yōō·āt′) *v.:* to make very slender or drawn out.
audacious (ô·dā′shəs) *adj.:* bold.
audit (ôd′it) *n.:* examination or accounting.
augment (ôg·ment′) *v.:* to increase.
avarice (av′ə·ris) *n.:* greed. —**avaricious** *adj.*
aversion (ə·vʉr′zhən) *n.:* dislike.
avow (ə·vou′) *v.:* to openly declare; acknowledge.

baleful (bāl′fəl) *adj.:* sinister; threatening.
baser (bās′ər) *adj.:* less valuable or worthy.
bastion (bas′chən) *n.:* fortified place; bulwark.
beguile (bē·gīl′) *v.:* 1. to pass the time in a pleasant way. 2. to charm.
benediction (ben′ə·dik′shən) *n.:* blessing.
benign (bi·nīn′) *adj.:* kind; gracious.
bequest (bē·kwest′) *n.:* gift left by means of a will.
blanch *v.:* to turn pale.
blasphemy (blas′fə·mē′) *n.:* mockery of God. —**blaspheme** *v.*
blight (blīt) *n.:* something that causes decay or withers one's hopes. —**blighted** *adj.*
botanical (bə·tan′i·kəl) *adj.:* of plants or plant life; connected to the science of botany, which is the study of plants, their structure, growth, and so on.
breach (brēch) *v.:* to break.
brevity (brev′ə·tē) *n.:* being brief.

---

fat, āpe, cär; ten, ēven; is, bīte; gō, hôrn, look, tool; yoo, cure; yōo, use; oil, out; up, fʉr; get; joy; yet; chin; she; thin; then; zh, leisure; ŋ, ring; ə for *a* in *ago,* e in *agent,* i in *sanity,* o in *comply,* u in *focus;* ' as in *battle* (bat′'l).

GLOSSARY 1259

brocade (brō·kād') *n.*: richly woven cloth.

buffet (buf'it) *v.*: to hit or slap.

buoyancy (boi'ən·sē) *n.*: lightness.

burlesque (bər·lesk') *n.*: derisive or comic spoof; satire.

cadence (kād''ns) *n.*: rhythmic flow of sound.

cajole (kə·jōl') *v.*: to coax with flattery.

calamitous (kə·lam'ə·təs) *adj.*: bringing great trouble.

candor (kan'dər) *n.*: honesty.

carouse (kə·rouz') *v.*: to drink and celebrate noisily.

carrion (kar'ē·ən) *n.*: decaying flesh eaten by scavenging animals.

casement (kās'mənt) *n.*: window.

cavalcade (kav'əl·kād') *n.*: parade of horses and carriages.

censure (sen'shər) *v.*: to condemn.

chaff (chaf) *n.*: 1. husks of grain. 2. anything worthless.

chalice (chal'is) *n.*: cup.

chasm (kaz'əm) *n.*: deep crack or fissure; abyss.

chasten (chās'ən) *v.*: to restrain from excess.

chastise (chas·tīz') *v.*: to scold or punish.

circumambulate (sur'kəm·am'byoo·lāt') *v.*: to walk around.

circumscribe (sur'kəm·skrīb') *v.*: to limit; confine.

cistern (sis'tərn) *n.*: tank for collecting rainwater.

civility (sə·vil'ə·tē) *n.*: courtesy.

clamorous (klam'ər·əs) *adj.*: noisy.

clarion (klar'ē·ən) *n.*: clear, sharp, ringing sound.

clemency (klem'ən·sē) *n.*: compassion; mercy.

clinical (klin'i·kəl) *adj.*: detached; impersonal.

cloister (klois'tər) *v.*: to seclude; confine. —**cloistered** *adj.*

coalition (kō'ə·lish'ən) *n.*: temporary alliance or union for some specific purpose.

cohort (kō'hôrt') *n.*: band of soldiers.

collateral (kə·lat'ər·əl) *adj.*: corresponding.

commiserate (kə·miz'ər·āt') *v.*: to feel sorrow or pity for; sympathize.

commission (kə·mish'ən) *n.*: act of doing something.

companionable (kəm·pan'yən·ə·bəl) *adj.*: having the traits of a good companion; friendly.

comparatively (kəm·par'ə·tiv'lē) *adv.*: relatively; in comparison to others.

compel (kəm·pel') *v.*: to force.

comprehensive (käm'prē·hen'siv) *adj.*: including all of the details; broad and sweeping.

concede (kən·sēd') *v.*: to grant.

conceive (kən·sēv') *v.*: 1. to form in the mind. 2. to cause life to begin. —**conception** *n.*

conciliate (kən·sil'ē·āt') *v.*: to soothe the anger of; placate.

condescend (kän'di·send') *v.*: to lower oneself; stoop.

confederate (kən·fed'ər·āt') *v.*: to unite; form an alliance.

confiscate (kän'fis·kāt') *v.*: to seize as a penalty.

conform (kən·fôrm') *v.*: to become similar; adapt.

confound (kən·found') *v.*: 1. to confuse. 2. to damn.

congeal (kən·jēl') *v.*: to thicken.

conjecture (kən·jek'chər) *v.*: to reason; guess. —**conjectural** *adj.*

conjure (kän'jər) *v.*: to summon as by a magic spell. —**conjurer** *n.*

consecrate (kän'si·krāt') *v.*: to dedicate to sacred use.

conspicuous (kən·spik'yoo·əs) *adj.*: attracting attention by being unusual.

constancy (kän'stən·sē) *n.*: loyalty.

constellation (kän'stə·lā'shən) *n.*: group of stars, usually named after the object, animal, or mythological being its outline, or configuration, suggests.

consternation (kän'stər·nā'shən) *n.*: alarm; bewilderment.

consummate (kän'sə·māt') *v.*: to complete; fulfill.

contagion (kən·tā'jən) *n.*: spreading of disease.

contemptuous (kən·temp'choo·əs) *adj.*: scornful; disdainful. —**contemptuously** *adv.*

contend (kən·tend') *v.*: to compete; struggle.

contingent (kən·tin'jənt) *n.*: group.

contortion (kən·tôr'shən) *n.*: unnatural form; distortion.

converge (kən·vurj') *v.*: to come together at a point.

copious (kō'pē·əs) *adj.*: wordy; profuse.

cornice (kôr'nis) *n.*: decorative strip that runs along the top of a wall.

corporal (kôr'pə·rəl) *adj.*: bodily.

corrode (kə·rōd') *v.*: to eat away, as by rust.

cosmopolitan (käz'mə·päl'ə·tən) *adj.*: representative of many parts of the world; not constrained by provincial habits or prejudices.

countenance (koun'tə·nəns) *n.*: face; appearance.

courtly (kôrt'lē) *adj.*: suitable for a royal court; with dignity or politeness. —**courtliness** *n.*

covet (kuv'it) *v.*: to long for with envy.

covetousness (kuv'ət·əs·nəs) *n.*: greed. —**covetous** *adj.*

cowed (koud) *adj.*: frightened by threats.

credulous (krej'oo·ləs) *adj.*: believing too readily.

crucial (kroo'shəl) *adj.*: of the greatest importance.

crystalline (kris'təl·in) *adj.*: transparent like crystal.

crystallize (kris'təl·īz') *v.*: to assume definite form; harden.

culinary (kul'ə·ner'ē) *adj.*: of or about cooking.

cynical (sin'i·kəl) *adj.*: mistrustful.

dapple (dap'əl) *adj.*: spotted.

daunt (dônt) *v.*: to intimidate.

debar (dē·bär') *v.*: to exclude; hinder.

decree (dē·krē') *v.*: to officially order or decide.

decussate (dē·kus'āt') *v.*: to cross so as to form an X; intersect.

deference (def'ər·əns) *n.*: respect; courtesy.

defer (dē·fur') *v.*: to postpone.

definitive (di·fin'ə·tiv) *adj.*: conclusive; authoritative.

degrade (di·grād') *v.*: to corrupt; dishonor. —**degradation** *n.*

deify (dē'ə·fī') *v.*: to make divine; glorify.

delirium (di·lir'ē·əm) *n.*: uncontrollable excitement.

delusion (di·loo'zhən) *n.*: false belief. —**delude** *v.*

demented (dē·ment'id) *adj.*: mad; wild.

demise (dē·mīz') *n.*: death.

denude (dē·nood') *v.*: to strip; lay bare.

desolate (des'ə·lit) *adj.*: lonely; forlorn.

despondency (di·spän'dən·sē) *n.*: hopelessness.

despotic (des·pät'ik) *adj.*: tyrannical; oppressive.

deter (dē·tur')*v.*: to prevent.

deviation (dē'vē·ā'shən) *n.*: a turning off from the usual or normal course.

diatribe (dī'ə·trīb') *n.*: bitter criticism; rant.

diffusive (di·fyoo'siv) *adj.*: spread out; not concentrated. —**diffuse** *v.*

digress (di·gres′) *v.*: to wander off the subject.
diligent (dil′ə·jənt) *adj.*: patient; persistent.
diminutive (də·min′yōō·tiv) *adj.*: very small.
dire (dīr) *adj.*: dreadful.
dirge (dʉrj) *n.*: funeral hymn; lament.
discern (di·sʉrn′) *v.*: to perceive; understand.
discomfit (dis·kum′fit) *v.*: to embarrass; make uneasy.
disconcert (dis′kən·sʉrt′) *v.*: to embarrass, confuse, or fluster.
discourse (dis′kôrs′) *n.*: conversation.
discreet (di·skrēt′) *adj.*: cautious about one's words and actions.
discriminate (di·skrim′i·nāt′) *v.*: to carefully distinguish between; differentiate.
disdainful (dis·dān′fəl) *adj.*: scornful.
disparage (di·spar′ij) *v.*: to speak disrespectfully of; belittle.
dispassionate (dis·pash′ə·nət) *adj.*: without emotion; impartial.
dispel (di·spel′) *v.*: to cause to vanish.
dispirit (di·spir′it) *v.*: to make sad or apathetic.
disposed (di·spōzd′) *adj.*: having a tendency toward.
dissuasion (di·swā′zhən) *n.*: advice or persuasion against.
distemper (dis·tem′pər) *n.*: disorder; disease.
distend (di·stend′) *v.*: to expand; stretch out; swell.
distill (di·stil′) *v.*: to draw out the essence of.
distraught (di·strôt′) *adj.*: agitated.
dither (dith′ər) *n:* excited or confused condition; nervousness.
diverge (dī·vʉrj′) *v.*: to branch off; separate.
divert (də·vʉrt′) *v.*: to amuse. —**diversion** *n.*
divinity (də·vin′ə·tē) *n.*: God; sacred being.
divulge (də·vulj′) *v.*: to make known.
docile (däs′əl) *adj.*: submissive; obedient.
dogged (dôg′id) *adj.*: persistent; stubborn.
dominion (də·min′yən) *n.*: governed territory.
dregs *n. pl.*: residue.
drone (drōn) *v.*: to hum or buzz continuously.
dubious (dōō′bē·əs) *adj.*: doubtful; uncertain.
duly (dōō′lē) *adv.*: as is right or required.
dumbfound (dum′found′) *v.*: to astonish; shock.
duress (dōō·res′) *n.*: pressure; force.

eddy *n.*: little whirlpool.
edict (ē′dikt′) *n.*: official order.
efficacious (ef′i·kā′shəs) *adj.*: effective. —**efficacy** *n.*
effluvium (e·flōō′vē·əm) *n.*: flow of vapor and invisible particles.
ejaculation (ē·jak′yōō·lā′shən) *n.*: sudden impassioned utterance; exclamation.
emanate (em′ə·nāt′) *v.*: to flow; come forth.
emancipate (ē·man′sə·pāt′) *v.*: to set free.
eminent (em′ə·nənt) *adj.*: distinguished; noteworthy.
encumber (en·kum′bər) *v.*: to burden or hinder. —**encumbrance** *n.*
endeavor (en·dev′ər) *n.*: earnest attempt.

engender (en·jen′dər) *v.*: to create; produce.
entreaty (en·trēt′ē) *n.*: plea; sincere request. —**entreat** *v.*
enumerate (ē·nōō′mər·āt′) *v.*: to count; list.
epicure (ep′i·kyoor′) *n.*: one who takes great pleasure in eating fine foods.
equivocate (ē·kwiv′ə·kāt′) *v.*: to be ambiguous; deliberately evade or lie. —**equivocation** *n.*
eradicate (ē·rad′i·kāt′) *v.*: to exterminate.
exhilaration (eg·zil′ə·rā′shən) *n.*: excitement; high spirits.
exorbitant (eg·zor′bi·tənt) *adj.*: excessive.
expedient (ek·spē′dē·ənt) *n.*: convenient means to an end.
expiate (eks′pē·āt′) *v.*: to make amends for wrongdoing; atone.
extort (eks·tôrt′) *v.*: to get by threats or violence.
exult (eg·zult′) *v.*: to rejoice. —**exultation** *n.*

façade (fə·säd′) *n.*: front of a building.
fallow (fal′ō) *adj.*: unplanted; uncultivated.
fanlight (fan′līt′) *n.*: fan-shaped window over a door.
feign (fān) *v.*: to make up; invent.
feint (fānt) *v.*: to pretend to strike.
fervent (fʉr′vənt) *adj.*: passionate. —**fervor** *n.*
fetter (fet′ər) *v.*: to chain.
flag *v.*: to decline; lose strength or interest.
foment (fō·ment′) *v.*: to stir up; incite.
forbear (fôr·ber′) *v.*: to avoid; cease.
formidable (fôr′mə·də·bəl) *adj.*: difficult to handle or overcome.
fortitude (fôrt′ə·tōōd′) *n.*: courage.
fraught (frôt) *adj.*: filled.
fray *n.*: noisy quarrel; commotion.
frugal (frōō′gəl) *adj.*: thrifty.
funereal (fyōō·nir′ē·əl) *adj.*: suitable for a funeral; solemn.
futile (fyōōt′'l) *adj.*: unable to succeed; useless.

gambol (gam′bəl) *v.*: to frolic; play animatedly.
garish (gar′ish) *adj.*: too showy or gaudy.
garret (gar′it) *n.*: attic.
garrulous (gar′ə·ləs) *adj.*: talkative.
gauntlet (gônt′lit) *n.*: series of challenges.
genial (jē′nē·əl) *adj.*: 1. mild-mannered; friendly. 2. pleasantly warm and healthful.
glut *v.*: to overfill.
gnome (nōm) *n.*: in folklore, a small being who dwells in the earth.
gorge (gôrj) *v.*: to stuff completely.
grovel (gräv′əl) *v.*: to crawl with the face close to the ground.
guffaw (gu·fô′) *n.*: loud laugh.
guile (gīl) *n.*: sly dealings.

haggard (hag′ərd) *adj.*: worn or tired looking.
harbinger (här′bin·jər) *n.*: indicator of what is to come.
hinterland (hin′tər·land′) *n.*: rural area; backwoods.
homage (äm′ij) *n.*: something done or given to show respect.

---

fat, āpe, cär; ten, ēven; is, bīte; gō, hôrn, look, tōōl; yōō, cure; yōō, use; oil, out; up, fʉr; get; joy; yet; chin; she; thin; then; zh, leisure; ŋ, ring; ə for *a* in *ago*, *e* in *agent*, *i* in *sanity*, *o* in *comply*, *u* in *focus*; ' as in *battle* (bat′'l).

GLOSSARY 1261

homily (häm′ə·lē) *n.:* sermon.

hospitable (häs·pit′ə·bəl) *adj.:* friendly toward guests.

hue (hyo͞o) *n.:* shade of color.

hysteria (hi·ster′ē·ə) *n.:* outbreak of uncontrolled emotion. —**hysterical** *adj.*

ichor (ī′kər) *n.:* thin, watery substance from a sore. —**ichorous** *adj.*

idolatrous (ī·däl′ə·trəs) *adj.:* idol-worshipping; excessively devoted.

ignoble (ig·nō′bəl) *adj.:* shameful; degrading.

ignominy (ig′nə·min′ē) *n.:* shame and dishonor.

immaterial (im′mə·tir′ē·əl) *adj.:* 1. not consisting of physical matter. 2. unimportant.

impart (im·pärt′) *v.:* to share; tell.

impassive (im·pas′iv) *adj.:* calm; indifferent. —**impassively** *adv.*

impede (im·pēd′) *v.:* to hinder; obstruct. —**impediment** *n.*

impel (im·pel′) *v.:* to push forward.

imperceptible (im′pər·sep′tə·bəl) *adj.:* so gradual or subtle that it is not easily sensed.

imperialism (im·pir′ē·əl·iz′əm) *n.:* policy in which one country seeks power by conquering other countries and establishing colonies.

imperturbable (im′pər·tur′bə·bəl) *adj.:* calm; impassive.

impetuous (im·pech′o͞o·əs) *adj.:* sudden; uncontrolled.

impinge (im·pinj′) *v.:* to strike; touch.

impious (im′pē·əs) *adj.:* lacking reverence or respect.

implacable (im·plak′ə·bəl) *adj.:* inflexible; relentless; obstinate.

implore (im·plôr′) *v.:* to beg.

importune (im′pôr·to͞on′) *v.:* to make repeated demands of.

impromptu (im·prämp′to͞o′) *adj.:* unplanned.

improvise (im′prə·vīz′) *v.:* to make for the occasion from whatever is handy.

impudent (im′pyo͞o·dənt) *adj.:* shamelessly bold or disrespectful.

impute (im·pyo͞ot′) *v.:* to attribute to or accuse another.

inadvertent (in′ad·vurt′′nt) *adj.:* unintentional. —**inadvertently** *adv.*

inanimate (in·an′ə·mit) *adj.:* not alive.

incarnation (in′kär·nā′shən) *n.:* physical representation of an idea or quality; embodiment.

incendiary (in·sen′dē·er′ē) *n.:* firebomb.

incense (in·sens′) *v.:* to make angry.

incentive (in·sent′iv) *n.:* something that prompts one to take action or work harder.

incessant (in·ses′ənt) *adj.:* never ceasing; constant.

inclemency (in·klem′ən·sē) *n.:* harsh quality; severity.

inconsiderable (in′kən·sid′ər·ə·bəl) *adj.:* not worth consideration; unimportant.

inconstancy (in·kän′stən·sē) *n.:* unsteady loyalty; fickleness.

incorporeal (in′kôr·pôr′ē·əl) *adj.:* without substance.

incredulous (in·krej′o͞o·ləs) *adj.:* disbelieving.

indifferent (in·dif′ər·ənt) *adj.:* showing no concern or feeling.

indignant (in·dig′nənt) *adj.:* scornful.

indispensable (in′di·spen′sə·bəl) *adj.:* absolutely necessary.

indissoluble (in′di·säl′yo͞o·bəl) *adj.:* unable to be broken; permanent.

inevitable (in·ev′i·tə·bəl) *adj.:* certain to occur.

inference (in′fər·əns) *n.:* conclusion drawn by logical reasoning.

ingenious (in·jēn′yəs) *adj.:* clever.

inimitable (in·im′i·tə·bəl) *adj.:* difficult or impossible to imitate.

insatiable (in·sā′shə·bəl) *adj.:* unable to be satisfied; greedy.

intemperance (in·tem′pər·əns) *n.:* lack of restraint.

inter (in·tur′) *v.:* to bury.

intercession (in′tər·sesh′ən) *n.:* pleading on behalf of another.

interim (in′tər·im) *n.:* period of time between.

intermittent (in′tər·mit′′nt) *adj.:* starting and stopping at intervals; periodic.

interstice (in·tur′stis) *n.:* small or narrow place between things.

intone (in·tōn′) *v.:* to chant.

intoxicate (in·täks′i·kāt′) *v.:* to cause wild excitement or happiness, often to a point beyond self-control.

intrepid (in·trep′id) *adj.:* fearless.

invariable (in·ver′ē·ə·bəl) *adj.:* constant; without change.

invincible (in·vin′sə·bəl) *adj.:* unconquerable.

ire (īr) *n.:* anger.

iridescent (ir′i·des′ənt) *adj.:* showing rainbowlike colors.

irreconcilable (ir·rek′ən·sīl′ə·bəl) *adj.:* cannot be brought into agreement.

irrelevant (ir·rel′ə·vənt) *adj.:* not related to the subject; not important.

itinerant (ī·tin′ər·ənt) *adj.:* traveling.

jocund (jäk′ənd) *adj.:* in good humor; cheerful. —**jocularity** *n.*

judicious (jo͞o·dish′əs) *adj.:* wise; prudent.

kindle (kin′dəl) *v.:* to set on fire; ignite.

knell (nel) *n.:* solemn sound of a bell.

labyrinth (lab′ə·rinth′) *n.:* maze; complex or confusing arrangement.

lament (lə·ment′) *n.:* cry of grief.

languish (laŋ′gwish) *v.:* to lose vitality; become weak.

laudable (lôd′ə·bəl) *adj.:* praiseworthy.

levy (lev′ē) *v.:* to impose.

lineage (lin′ē·ij) *n.:* ancestry.

livid (liv′id) *adj.:* 1. discolored by a bruise; gray-blue. 2. red or white, as in "livid with rage." —**lividity** *n.*

loathsome (lōth′səm) *adj.:* disgusting.

lucid (lo͞o′sid) *adj.:* clearheaded; sane. —**lucidity** *n.*

lugubrious (lə·go͞o′brē·əs) *adj.:* very solemn or mournful, especially in a way that seems exaggerated or ridiculous.

lunacy (lo͞o′nə·sē) *n.:* madness.

luxuriate (lug·zho͞or′ē·āt′) *v.:* to take enormous pleasure.

magenta (mə·jen′tə) *adj.:* purplish-red.

magnanimous (mag·nan′ə·məs) *adj.:* generous in rising above insults.

malady (mal′ə·dē) *n.:* illness.

malevolence (mə·lev′ə·ləns) *n.:* spite; ill will.

malicious (mə·lish′əs) *adj.*: intentionally mischievous or harmful; spiteful. —**malice** *n.*

malignity (mə·lig′nə·tē) *n.*: harmful or evil thing.

maniacal (mə·nī′ə·kəl) *adj.*: crazed; wildly enthusiastic.

marauder (mə·rôd′ər) *n.*: raider; plunderer.

martyrdom (märt′ər·dəm) *n.*: prolonged suffering or self-sacrifice.

maxim (maks′im) *n.*: general truth or rule of conduct.

meager (mē′gər) *adj.*: poor in quality or small in amount.

metamorphosis (met′ə·môr′fə·sis) *n.*: change of form.

mien (mēn) *n.*: manner; bearing.

millennium (mi·len′ē·əm) *n.*: period of a thousand years.

mill *v.*: to move in a circular or random pattern, as a crowd or flock.

mimic (mim′ik) *v.*: to imitate; mock.

mirth (murth) *n.*: joyfulness.

miry (mīr′ē) *adj.*: swampy; muddy.

monotonous (mə·nät′′n·əs) *adj.*: repeating without interruption.

mortal *adj.*: fatal.

mortify (môrt′ə·fī′) *v.*: to cause to feel shame or embarrassment.

multitudinous (mul′tə·tood′′n·əs) *adj.*: numerous.

munificent (myoo·nif′ə·sənt) *adj.*: very generous.

murky (murk′ē) *adj.*: shadowy.

mute (myoot) *v.*: to muffle or soften.

myriad (mir′ē·əd) *n.*: great number of persons or things.

negligent (neg′lə·jənt) *adj.*: careless; lax.

nemesis (nem′ə·sis) *n.*: agent of retribution or punishment.

nicety (nī′sə·tē) *n.*: delicacy; elegance.

nimble (nim′bəl) *adj.*: moving quickly.

nonpareil (nän′pə·rel′) *adj.*: unrivaled; unequaled.

notorious (nō·tôr′ē·əs) *adj.*: widely but unfavorably known; famous.

noxious (näk′shəs) *adj.*: harmful.

oblique (ō·blēk′) *adj.*: slanting; indirect. —**obliquity** *n.*

obnoxious (əb·näk′shəs) *adj.*: offensive.

obscure (əb·skyoor′) *adj.*: little-known; vague. —**obscurely** *adv.*

obstinate (äb′stə·nət) *adj.*: unreasonably stubborn.

odious (ō′dē·əs) *adj.*: hateful; offensive.

officious (ə·fish′əs) *adj.*: eager to serve; obliging.

omen (ō′mən) *n.*: sign supposedly foretelling the future.

ominous (äm′ə·nəs) *adj.*: threatening.

oppressive (ə·pres′iv) *adj.*: hard to bear.

oracle (ôr′ə·kəl) *n.*: one capable of providing divine revelation or wisdom; seer.

ostentation (äs′tən·tā′shən) *n.*: showiness.

overture (ō′vər·chər) *n.*: proposal.

overwrought (ō′vər·rôt′) *adj.*: overly excited.

palliative (pal′ē·ə·tiv) *adj.*: easing; alleviating.

pallor (pal′ər) *n.*: paleness.

palpable (pal′pə·bəl) *adj.*: easily felt; tangible.

panegyric (pan′ə·jīr′ik) *n.*: formal speech elaborately praising something.

parry (par′ē) *v.*: to reply evasively.

pathos (pā′thäs′) *n.*: a quality in something experienced or observed that evokes feelings of pity or sorrow.

patronize (pā′trən·īz′) *v.*: to be a customer of.

penance (pen′əns) *n.*: act of atonement for sin.

pensive (pen′siv) *adj.*: thinking deeply, often of something sad.

perceptible (pər·sep′tə·bəl) *adj.*: visible.

perfidious (pər·fid′ē·əs) *adj.*: treacherous. —**perfidy** *n.*

perfunctory (pər·funk′tə·rē) *adj.*: halfhearted; indifferent. —**perfunctorily** *adv.*

pernicious (pər·nish′əs) *adj.*: wicked; extremely harmful.

perpetual (pər·pech′oo·əl) *adj.*: continuing forever; eternal.

perplexity (pər·pleks′ə·tē) *n.*: confusion; bewilderment. —**perplexedly** *adv.*

persevere (pur′sə·vir′) *v.*: to continue in a course of action despite difficulty or opposition; persist.

personable (pur′sən·ə·bəl) *adj.*: attractive in appearance and personality.

perturb (pər·turb′) *v.*: to upset; disturb. —**perturbation** *n.*

pervade (pər·vād′) *v.*: to spread throughout.

perverse (pər·vurs′) *adj.*: disagreeable; contrary.

pestilence (pes′tə·ləns) *n.*: plague; infection. —**pestilential** *adj.*

phosphorescent (fäs′fə·res′ənt) *adj.*: luminous; glowing.

pilgrimage (pil′grim·ij) *n.*: journey made to a place of religious or historical interest.

pious (pī′əs) *adj.*: devout or virtuous; sacred.

pique (pēk) *n.*: ruffled pride; displeasure.

placid (plas′id) *adj.*: calm; peaceful.

posterity (päs·ter′ə·tē) *n.*: all succeeding generations.

potent (pōt′′nt) *adj.*: powerful; mighty. —**potency** *n.*

prate (prāt) *v.*: to talk idly; chat.

precarious (prē·ker′ē·əs) *adj.*: uncertain; insecure.

precipitate (prē·sip′ə·tit) *adj.*: sudden. —**precipitately** *adv.*

predatory (pred′ə·tôr′ē) *adj.*: living by eating other animals.

predominant (prē·däm′ə·nənt) *adj.*: having the greatest influence or control.

preoccupied (prē·äk′yoo·pīd′) *adj.*: absorbed in one's own thoughts.

prerogative (prē·räg′ə·tiv) *n.*: right or privilege.

presumptuous (prē·zump′choo·əs) *adj.*: boldly overconfident.

pretext (prē′tekst′) *n.*: excuse.

prevail (prē·vāl′) *v.*: to predominate; hold sway.

prevaricate (pri·var′i·kāt′) *v.*: to lie. —**prevarication** *n.*

pristine (pris′tēn′) *adj.*: pure; unspoiled.

procure (prō·kyoor′) *v.*: to obtain; get. —**procurement** *n.*

prodigious (prō·dij′əs) *adj.*: huge.

prodigy (präd′ə·jē) *n.*: genius.

---

fạt, āpe, cär; tẹn, ēven; ịs, bīte; gō, hôrn, lo͝ok, to͞ol; yo͝o, cure; yo͞o, use; ọil, ọut; up, fur; get; joy; yet; chin; she; thin; then; zh, leisure; ŋ, ring; ə for *a* in *ago*, e in *agent*, i in *sanity*, o in *comply*, u in *focus*; ' as in *battle* (bat′′l).

---

profess (prō·fes′) *v.*: to openly declare.

proffer (präf′ər) *v.*: to offer; propose.

proficiency (prō·fish′ən·sē) *n.*: skill.

profound (prō·found′) *adj.*: deep.

promiscuous (prə·mis′kyōō·əs) *adj.*: casual; undiscriminating.

promontory (präm′ən·tôr′ē) *n.*: peak of land that juts into the sea.

prophetic (prō·fet′ik) *adj.*: foreshadowing; predicting.

propitious (prō·pish′əs) *adj.*: favorable.

propriety (prō·prī′ə·tē) *n.*: the quality of being proper or fitting.

prosaic (prō·zā′ik) *adj.*: ordinary; dull.

prostrate (präs′trāt′) *adj.*: lying face down in a show of submission or weakness. —**prostrating** *v.*

protract (prō·trakt′) *v.*: to draw out; extend.

prowess (prou′is) *n.*: outstanding ability or skill; bravery.

proximity (präks·im′ə·tē) *n.*: closeness.

prudent (prōōd′′nt) *adj.*: careful and wise.

prurient (proor′ē·ənt) *adj.*: lewd; offensive.

pungent (pun′jənt) *adj.*: sharp-smelling.

purge (pʉrj) *v.*: to get rid of; expel.

putrid (pyōō′trid) *adj.*: decayed; foul-smelling.

quaint (kwānt) *adj.*: pleasantly unusual.

quell (kwel) *v.*: to subdue.

rancid (ran′sid) *adj.*: stale or foul-smelling.

rancor (raŋ′kər) *n.*: ill will.

rank *adj.*: overgrown.

ravage (rav′ij) *v.*: to violently destroy.

ravenous (rav′ə·nəs) *adj.*: extremely hungry.

rebuke (ri·byōōk′) *v.*: to blame or scold.

recapitulate (rē′kə·pich′ə·lāt′) *v.*: to repeat; summarize.

recess (rē′ses) *n.*: indentation.

reckon (rek′ən) *v.*: to consider; judge.

recompense (rek′əm·pens′) *n.*: repayment; reward.

redress (rē′dres′) *n.*: compensation for wrong.

reflux (rē′fluks′) *n.*: a flowing back; ebb.

refract (ri·frakt′) *v.*: to cause a ray to bend as it passes from one medium to another.

reiterate (rē·it′ə·rāt′) *v.*: to repeat.

remonstrate (ri·män′strāt′) *v.*: to protest.

renown (ri·noun′) *n.*: great fame.

reparation (rep′ə·rā′shən) *n.*: payment to compensate for wrongdoing.

repose (ri·pōz′) *v.*: to lie calmly or quietly.

reprisal (ri·prī′zəl) *n.*: punishment in return for injury.

reproachful (ri·prōch′fəl) *adj.*: full of or expressing blame.

reprove (ri·prōōv′) *v.*: to express disapproval; rebuke.

repulse (ri·puls′) *v.*: to drive away.

requite (ri·kwīt′) *v.*: to repay.

resigned (ri·zīnd′) *adj.*: showing passive acceptance.

restive (res′tiv) *adj.*: impatient; nervous.

reticulate (ri·tik′yə·lit) *adj.*: having a network of veins like the threads of a net.

retinue (ret′′n·ōō′) *n.*: string of attendants.

revelation (rev′ə·lā′shən) *n.*: awareness of something previously unknown; realization.

reverberate (ri·vʉr′bə·rāt′) *v.*: to echo a sound; resonate.

reverent (rev′ər·ənt) *adj.*: having deep respect, love, or awe, as for something sacred.

rhetoric (ret′ər·ik) *n.*: 1. art of speaking and writing. 2. showy but meaningless language.

rite *n.*: formal ceremony.

rudiments (rōō′də·mənts) *n. pl.*: basics.

rue (rōō) *v.*: to feel remorse; regret.

ruffian (ruf′ē·ən) *n.*: hoodlum; lawless person.

sacrilegious (sak′rə·lij′əs) *adj.*: violating something sacred.

sally *n.*: quick witticism or retort; quip.

sanctity (saŋk′tə·tē) *n.*: sacred quality; holiness.

sarcastic (sär·kas′tik) *adj.*: having biting irony; sneering.

saunter (sôn′tər) *v.*: to stroll.

score *v.*: to mark with a scratch or groove.

scrupulous (skrōō′pyə·ləs) *adj.*: extremely careful and precise in deciding what is right or wrong.

scrutinize (skrōōt′′n·īz) *v.*: to examine carefully.

secular (sek′yə·lər) *adj.*: not related to religion.

seethe (sēth) *v.*: to surge; appear constantly active or violently agitated.

semblance (sem′bləns) *n.*: appearance of something else; resemblance.

seminar (sem′ə·när′) *n.*: scholarly group discussion.

senile (sē′nīl′) *adj.*: showing the deterioration that sometimes accompanies old age. —**senility** *n.*

sensibility (sen′sə·bil′ə·tē) *n.*: capacity for being affected emotionally.

sepulcher (sep′əl·kər) *n.*: vault for burial.

sepulchral (sə·pul′krəl) *adj.*: gloomy.

sequel (sē′kwəl) *n.*: 1. something that comes after. 2. consequence or result.

sequester (si·kwes′tər) *v.*: to separate from others; isolate.

serene (sə·rēn′) *adj.*: calm; peaceful.

serous (sir′əs) *adj.*: thin and watery. —**serosity** *n.*

serrate (ser′āt′) *adj.*: having jagged, sawlike notches along the edge.

servile (sʉr′vīl) *adj.*: like or characteristic of a slave; humbly submissive or yielding.

shambles (sham′bəlz) *n. pl.*: scene of great disorder.

sheaf (shēf) *n.*: stalks of grain bound up in a bundle. —**sheaves** *n. pl.*

shoal (shōl) *n.*: shallow place; sandbar.

signalize (sig′nəl·īz′) *v.*: to draw attention to.

silt *v.*: to fill up with sediment or residue.

sinew (sin′yōō) *n.*: tendon or connective tissue.

skeptical (skep′ti·kəl) *adj.*: doubting.

slake *v.*: to satisfy or quench.

slovenly (sluv′ən·lē) *adj.*: untidy.

sodden (säd′′n) *adj.*: soaked; soggy.

solace (säl′is) *n.*: peace; relief.

solicit (sə·lis′it) *v.*: to ask or plead earnestly.

solicitous (sə·lis′ə·təs) *adj.*: showing care or attention.

somber (säm′bər) *adj.*: gloomy.

sovereign (säv′rən) *adj.*: superior to all others.

spare *adj.*: meager; thin.

spawn (spôn) *v.*: to bring into being.

specter (spek′tər) *n.*: ghost. —**spectral** *adj.*

squalid (skwäl′id) *adj.*: foul or unclean; wretched.

squeamish (skwēm′ish) *adj.*: easily upset.

stagnate (stag′nāt′) *v.*: to become inactive or sluggish.

stature (stach′ər) *n.:* height.
statute (stach′o͞ot) *n.:* law.
stealth (stelth) *n.:* secret or sly behavior.
stifle (stī′fəl) *v.:* to suppress; hold back.
stint *n.:* limitation.
stratagem (strat′ə·jəm) *n.:* trick.
strident (strīd′'nt) *adj.:* harsh; sharp.
stupefy (sto͞o′pə·fī′) *v.:* to dull the mind and senses; make
    lethargic, as in a state of stupor.
subdue (səb·do͞o′) *v.:* to conquer; overcome.
sublime (sə·blīm′) *adj.:* awe-inspiring; majestic.
subsistence (səb·sis′təns) *n.:* existence; means of support
    or sustenance.
subtle (sut′'l) *adj.:* delicately suggestive; not obvious.
succumb (sə·kum′) *v.:* 1. to yield; give way. 2. to die.
suffice (sə·fīs′) *v.:* to satisfy. —**sufficient** *adj.*
sundry (sun′drē) *adj.:* various.
supercilious (so͞o′pər·sil′ē·əs) *adj.:* disdainful or scornful;
    haughty.
superfluity (so͞o′pər·flo͞o′ə·tē) *n.:* excess.
supplant (sə·plant′) *v.:* to replace; displace.
suppliant (sup′lē·ənt) *adj.:* requesting humbly.
    —**supplication** *n.*
surfeit (sʉr′fit) *v.:* to fill to excess.
surmise (sər·mīz′) *n.:* guess; speculation.
surmount (sər·mount′) *v.:* to rise above.
surname (sʉr′nām′) *n.:* last name.
sustenance (sus′tə·nəns) *n.:* food or money to support life.
swathe (swäth) *n.:* long strip of cloth; bandage.
sylvan (sil′vən) *adj.:* of the woods.
symmetry (sim′ə·trē) *n.:* similarity of form on either side of
    a dividing line; balance.

taut (tôt) *adj.:* stretched tight.
tedious (tē′dē·əs) *adj.:* boring.
teem *v.:* to swarm.
temerity (tə·mer′ə·tē) *n.:* foolish or rash boldness;
    recklessness.
temperance (tem′pər·əns) *n.:* restraint; control.
temporal (tem′pə·rəl) *adj.:* limited to this world; not
    spiritual.
tenacity (tə·nas′ə·tē) *n.:* persistence; steadfastness.
tentative (ten′tə·tiv) *adj.:* hesitant; uncertain.
terrestrial (tə·res′trē·əl) *adj.:* of the earth.
theological (thē′ə·läj′i·kəl) *adj.:* having to do with the study
    of God.
theoretical (thē′ə·ret′i·kəl) *adj.:* in the realm of ideas, as
    opposed to practice or application.
timorous (tim′ər·es) *adj.:* full of fear; timid.
tincture (tiŋk′chər) *v.:* to color lightly; tint.
titillate (tit′'l·āt′) *v.:* to excite; stimulate.
titter *v.:* to giggle.
traipse (trāps) *v.:* colloquial for "to wander."
tranquil (tran′kwil) *adj.:* calm; peaceful.
transcend (tran·send′) *v.:* to exceed; surpass.

transgress (trans·gres′) *v.:* to overstep a limit or break a law.
transitory (tran′sə·tôr′ē) *adj.:* temporary or fleeting.
transom (tran′səm) *n.:* small hinged window directly above
    a door.
tremulous (trem′yo͞o·ləs) *adj.:* trembling; quivering.
tribulation (trib′yo͞o·lā′shən) *n.:* great misery; affliction.
tribute (trib′yo͞ot) *n.:* tax paid by a vassal to a lord or ruler.
trifle (trī′fəl) *v.:* to mock; treat lightly.
trivet (triv′it) *n.:* three-legged stand for holding pots.
tumult (to͞o′mult) *n.:* uproar; commotion.
turbid (tʉr′bid) *adj.:* thick; dense.
tyranny (tir′ə·nē) *n.:* cruel and unjust rule.
    —**tyrannical** *adj.*

uncanny (un·kan′ē) *adj.:* strange; eerie; weird.
uncouth (un·ko͞oth′) *adj.:* crude; uncultured.
unfathomable (un·fath′əm·ə·bəl) *adj.:* unmeasurable;
    infinite.
unnerve (un·nʉrv′) *v.:* to cause one to lose courage or
    confidence.
unprecedented (un·pres′ə·den′tid) *adj.:* not done or seen
    before; unique.
unscrupulous (un·skro͞o′pyə·ləs) *adj.:* dishonest; unprin-
    cipled.
unwary (un·wer′ē) *adj.:* not watchful or cautious.
usurper (yo͞o·sʉrp′ər) *n.:* one who seizes power unlawfully.
utter *adj.:* total.

vanquish (vaŋ′kwish) *v.:* to conquer.
vaulted (vôlt′id) *adj.:* arched.
vehement (vē′ə·mənt) *adj.:* passionate; forceful.
vellicate (vel′i·kāt′) *v.:* to twitch; pluck.
velocity (və·läs′ə·tē) *n.:* speed.
verisimilitude (ver′ə·si·mil′ə·to͞od′) *n.:* appearance of
    being real.
verity (ver′ə·tē) *n.:* truth.
vermin (vʉr′mən) *n.:* disease-carrying pest. —**vermin** *n. pl.*
vex *v.:* to annoy highly.
vigor (vig′ər) *n.:* strength; vitality.
viscous (vis′kəs) *adj.:* having the form of a sticky fluid.
vivacity (vī·vas′ə·tē) *n.:* liveliness; animation.
vociferate (vō·sif′ər·āt′) *v.:* to speak loudly and vehe-
    mently. —**vociferous** *adj.*
void (void) *adj.:* empty.

waggish (wag′ish) *adj.:* prankish; playful.
wan (wän) *adj.:* pale; weak with sadness.
wanton (wän′tən) *adj.:* luxurious; unrestrained.
winning (win′iŋ) *adj.:* charming.
wither (with′ər) *v.:* to decay; wilt or shrivel.
wizened (wiz′ənd) *adj.:* dried up; withered.
wrath (rath) *n.:* great anger; rage.
wrought (rôt) *adj.:* shaped; fashioned.

zeal *n.:* enthusiasm; passion.

---

fat, āpe, cär; ten, ēven; is, bīte; gō, hôrn, lo͝ok, to͞ol; yo͝o, cure; yo͞o, use; oil, out; up, fʉr; get; joy; yet; chin; she; thin; then; zh,
leisure; ŋ, ring; ə for *a* in *ago*, *e* in *agent*, *i* in *sanity*, *o* in *comply*, *u* in *focus;* ′ as in *battle* (bat′'l).

ACKNOWLEDGMENTS

For permission to reprint copyrighted material, grateful acknowledgment is made to the following sources:

The Asia Society: "Thoughts of Hanoi" by Nguyen Thi Vinh from *A Thousand Years of Vietnamese Poetry*, translated by Nguyen Ngoc Bich. Copyright © 1974 by The Asia Society.

Stephanie Bailey: "Worn Out" by Stephanie Bailey from *Legends*, Vol. X, May 1992. Copyright © 1992 by Stephanie Bailey. Published by Taylorsville High School.

Bantam Books, a division of Bantam Doubleday Dell Publishing Group, Inc.: From "Give Us This Day Our Daily Bread" from *Shakespeare Alive* by Joseph Papp and Elizabeth Kirkland. Copyright © 1988 by the New York Shakespeare Festival.

Elizabeth Barnett, Literary Executor: From "What Lips My Lips Have Kissed" from *Collected Poems* by Edna St. Vincent Millay. Copyright 1923, 1951 by Edna St. Vincent Millay and Norma Millay Ellis. Published by HarperCollins.

B. T. Batsford Ltd.: From "The Knocking at the Gate in Macbeth" from *Thomas De Quincey*, edited by Bonamy Dorbrée. Copyright © 1965 by Bonamy Dorbrée.

Curtis Brown Ltd., London on behalf of the Estate of Sir Winston S. Churchill: From page 24 (Retitled: "A Scream of Rage") and from "The Black Death" from *The Birth of Britain* by Winston S. Churchill. Copyright © 1956 by The Right Honourable Sir Winston S. Churchill. From "Speech on Dunkirk, House of Commons," June 4, 1940. Copyright 1940 by the Estate of Sir Winston S. Churchill.

Cambridge University Press: From "The Medieval Situation" from *The Discarded Image* by C. S. Lewis. Copyright © 1964 by Cambridge University Press.

Delacorte Press/Seymour Lawrence, a division of Bantam Doubleday Dell Publishing Group, Inc.: From *Sextet: T. S. Eliot & Truman Capote & Others* by John Malcolm Brinnin. Copyright © 1981 by John Malcolm Brinnin.

Devin-Adair, Publishers, Inc., Old Greenwich, CT 06870: From *The Book of Margery Kempe* by Margery Kempe. Copyright © 1944 and renewed © 1972 by Devin-Adair, Publishers, Inc. All rights reserved.

Doubleday, a division of Bantam Doubleday Dell Publishing Group, Inc.: "Marriage is a Private Affair" from *Girls at War and Other Stories* by Chinua Achebe. Copyright © 1972, 1973 by Chinua Achebe. "The Cairo Rooftop" from *Palace Walk* by Naguib Mahfouz. Copyright © 1990 by American University in Cairo Press.

Rita Dove and W. W. Norton & Company, Inc: "Sisters" from *Grace Notes* by Rita Dove. Copyright © 1989 by Rita Dove.

Dutton Signet, a division of Penguin Books USA Inc.: From *Beowulf*, translated by Burton Raffel. Translation copyright © 1963 by Burton Raffel; Afterword copyright © 1963 by New American Library. From "The Unfed Dervish," "Information and Knowledge," "The Elephant-Keeper," "Safety and Riches," and "The Fox and the Camels" from *The Way of the Sufi* by Idries Shah. Copyright © 1968 by Idries Shah. From the annotations from *Macbeth* by William Shakespeare. Copyright © 1963 and renewed © 1991 by Sylvan Barnet for introduction and annotations.

Faber and Faber Limited: "Hawk Roosting" and excerpt from *Lupercal* by Ted Hughes. Copyright © 1960 by Ted Hughes.

Famous Music Publishing Companies: Lyrics by Dean Pitchford from "Holding Out for a Hero." Copyright © 1984 by Ensign Music Corporation. International copyright secured. All rights reserved.

Farrar, Straus & Giroux, Inc.: From "On Keeping a Notebook" from *Slouching Towards Bethlehem* by Joan Didion. Copyright © 1966, 1968 by Joan Didion. "Once Upon a Time" from *Jump* by Nadine Gordimer. Copyright © 1991 by Felix Licensing, B.V. "Digging" from *Selected Poems 1966–1987* by Seamus Heaney. Copyright © 1990 by Seamus Heaney. "The Mower" from *Collected Poems* by Philip Larkin. Copyright © 1988, 1989 by the Estate of Philip Larkin. From *The Inferno of Dante*, translated by Robert Pinsky. English translation copyright © 1994 by Robert Pinsky. From "What Poems Are Made Of" and excerpt from *Me Again* by Stevie Smith. Copyright © 1981 by James MacGibbon. "Freedom to Breathe" and "The Bonfire and the Ants" from *Stories and Prose Poems* by Aleksandr Solzhenitsyn, translated by

Michael Glenny. Translation copyright © 1971 by Michael Glenny. "The Virgins" from *Sea Grapes* by Derek Walcott. Copyright © 1976 by Derek Walcott.

Gale Research Inc.: From "Anita Desai" from *Something About the Author*, Vol. 63, edited by Anne Commire. Copyright © 1991 by Gale Research Inc.

Grove Press, Inc.: From *Waiting for Godot* by Samuel Beckett. Copyright © 1954 by Grove Press, Inc.; copyright renewed © 1982 by Samuel Beckett. From "That's All" from *Complete Plays: Three* by Harold Pinter. Copyright © 1966 by H. Pinter Ltd.

Harcourt Brace & Company: "The Hollow Men" from *Collected Poems 1909-1962* by T. S. Eliot. Copyright 1936 by Harcourt Brace & Company, copyright © 1964, 1963 by T. S. Eliot. From "Warfare and Warlords" from *The Harbrace History of England, Part 1: Ancient and Medieval England, Beginnings to 1509* by J. R. Lander. Copyright © 1973 by Harcourt Brace & Company. "Shooting an Elephant" from *Shooting an Elephant and Other Essays* by George Orwell. Copyright 1950 by Sonia Brownell Orwell and renewed © 1978 by Sonia Pitt-Rivers. "Lot's Wife" by Anna Akhmatova from *Walking to Sleep: New Poems and Translations* by Richard Wilbur. Copyright © 1969 by Richard Wilbur. From "A Sketch of the Past" from *Moments of Being* by Virginia Woolf, edited by Jeanne Schulkind. Text copyright © 1976 by Quentin Bell and Angelica Garnett; Introduction and editorial material copyright © 1976 by Jeanne Schulkind. From "Shakespeare's Sister" and from page 64 from *A Room of One's Own* by Virginia Woolf. Copyright 1929 by Harcourt Brace & Company; copyright renewed © 1957 by Leonard Woolf. From *Mrs. Dalloway* by Virginia Woolf. Copyright 1925 by Harcourt Brace & Company; copyright renewed 1953 by Leonard Woolf.

John Hawkins & Associates, Inc.: "Macbeth and the Witches" from *Twisted Tales from Shakespeare* by Richard Armour. Copyright © 1957 by Richard Armour.

David Higham Associates on behalf of The Trustees for the Copyrights of Dylan Thomas and J. M. Dent: From a letter to Princess Caetani from *The Collected Letters of Dylan Thomas*, edited by Paul Ferris. Letters Copyright © 1957, 1966, 1985 by The Trustees for the Copyrights of Dylan Thomas. Quote by Dylan Thomas from *Dylan Thomas in America* by John Malcolm Brinnin. First published 1956 by J. M. Dent & Sons Ltd.

Hill and Wang, a division of Farrar, Straus & Giroux, Inc.: From *Night* by Elie Wiesel, translated by Stella Rodway. Copyright © 1960 by MacGibbon and Kee; copyright renewed © 1988 by the Collins Publishing Group.

Henry Holt and Company, Inc.: "Nothing Gold Can Stay" from *The Poetry of Robert Frost,* edited by Edward Connery Lathem. Copyright 1951 by Robert Frost. Copyright 1923, © 1969 by Henry Holt and Co., Inc. "Is My Team Ploughing," from "A Shropshire Lad," "To An Athlete Dying Young," and "When I Was One-and-Twenty" from *The Collected Poems of A. E. Housman.* Copyright 1939, 1940 by Holt, Rinehart & Winston, Inc.; copyright © 1967 by Robert E. Symons.

Houghton Mifflin Company: "Mushrooms" from *True Stories* from *Selected Poems II: Poems Selected and New 1976-1986* by Margaret Atwood. Copyright © 1987 by Margaret Atwood. All rights reserved. From *Gilgamesh,* translated by Herbert Mason. Copyright © 1970 by Herbert Mason. All rights reserved.

Indiana University Press: From "A Brief Note about the River When Its Waters Rise Up Like the Sea" by Tu Fu from *An Introduction to Chinese Literature* by Liu Wu-chi. Copyright © 1966 by Liu Wu-chi.

International African Institute: Four proverbs from *Jabo Proverbs from Liberia: Maxims in the Life of a Native Tribe* by George Herzog. Copyright © 1936 by the International African Institute. Published by Oxford University Press - London.

John Johnson Ltd.: "I Have Visited Again" from *The Bronze Horseman* by Alexander Pushkin, translated by D. M. Thomas. Translation copyright © 1982 by D. M. Thomas.

Alfred A. Knopf, Inc.: "The Demon Lover" from *Collected Stories* by Elizabeth Bowen. Copyright 1946 and renewed © 1974 by Elizabeth Bowen. "The Myth of Sisyphus" and from "An Absurd Reasoning" from *The Myth of Sisyphus and Other Essays* by Albert Camus, translated J. O'Brien. Copyright © 1955 by Alfred A. Knopf, Inc.

From *Grendel* by John Gardner. Copyright © 1971 by John Gardner. From "Introduction" from *The Life and Times of Chaucer* by John Gardner. Copyright © 1977 by John Gardner. "The Doll's House" from *The Short Stories of Katherine Mansfield* by Katherine Mansfield. Copyright 1923 by Alfred A. Knopf, Inc.; copyright renewed 1951 by John Middleton Murry. "B. Wordsworth" from *Miguel Street* by V.S. Naipaul. Copyright © 1959 by V.S. Naipaul. "My Oedipus Complex" from *Collected Stories* by Frank O'Connor. Copyright 1950 by Frank O'Connor.

Kathy Liu: "The Radio" by Kathy Liu from *Impressions, Literary and Art Magazine,* Spring 1992. Published by Riverdale Country School, Bronx, NY.

Liveright Publishing Corporation: "since feeling is first" from *Complete Poems: 1904-1962* by E. E. Cummings, edited by George J. Firmage. Copyright © 1926, 1954, 1991 by the Trustees for the E. E. Cummings Trust; copyright © 1985 by George James Firmage. "O sweet spontaneous" from *Selected Poems of E. E. Cummings,* with Introduction and Commentary by Richard S. Kennedy. Copyright © 1923, 1951, 1991 by the Trustees for the E. E. Cummings Trust; copyright © 1976 by George James Firmage.

Arnulfo J. López: "A Poem Within a Poem" by Arnulfo J. López from *Heritage,* Vol. 31, Spring 1991. Published by James Madison High School, Vienna, VA.

Macmillan Reference USA, a division of Simon & Schuster, Inc.: From *Webster's New World Dictionary,* Third College Edition. Copyright © 1988, 1991, 1994 by Simon & Schuster, Inc.

Andrea D. Marzullo: "Mind" by A.D.M. from *Image,* Creative Arts Magazine, vol. 31, 1992. Copyright © 1992 by Andrea D. Marzullo. Published by Bellevue East Senior High School, Bellevue, NE.

Merlyn's Pen: The National Magazines of Student Writing: "Tu B'shvat" by Michelle Dorrien from *Merlyn's Pen, Senior Edition,* April/May 1994. Copyright © 1994 by Merlyn's Pen. First appeared in *Merlyn's Pen: The National Magazines of Student Writing.*

Melynn Minson: "Searching for a Future in the Dusk" by Melynn Minson from *Expressions,* Vol. XXVII, 1992. Published by Hillcrest High School, Midvale, UT.

Edmund Morris: From "A Visit with Nadine Gordimer" by Edmund Morris from *The New York Times Book Review,* June 7, 1981. Copyright © 1981 by Edmund Morris.

New Directions Publishing Corporation: From "The Witness" from *Labyrinths* by Jorge Luis Borges, translated by James E. Irby. Copyright © 1962, 1964 by New Directions Publishing Corp. From *Stephen Hero* by James Joyce. Copyright © 1944, 1955, 1959, 1963 by New Directions Publishing Corporation. Published under arrangement with the James Joyce Estate. All rights reserved. "Dulce et Decorum Est" and from "Strange Meeting" from *The Collected Poems of Wilfred Owen.* Copyright © 1963 by Chatto & Windus, Ltd. "Not Waving But Drowning" from *Collected Poems of Stevie Smith.* Copyright © 1972 by Stevie Smith. "Fern Hill" and "Do Not Go Gentle Into That Good Night" from *The Poems of Dylan Thomas.* Copyright © 1952 by Dylan Thomas. "Jade Flower Palace" by Tu Fu from *One Hundred Poems from the Chinese,* translated by Kenneth Rexroth. Copyright © 1971 by Kenneth Rexroth. All rights reserved.

The New York Times Company: "A Beam of Protons Illuminates Gutenberg's Genius" by Malcolm W. Browne from *The New York Times,* May 5, 1987. Copyright © 1987 by The New York Times Company. Quote by David Ormsby Gore from *The New York Times,* October 28, 1962. Copyright © 1962 by The New York Times Company. From "Scenes from a Modern Marriage" by Julia Markus from *The New York Times,* February 14, 1995, Op-Ed. Copyright © 1995 by The New York Times Company.

North Point Press, a division of Farrar, Straus & Giroux, Inc.: From *Crow and Weasel* by Barry Lopez. Text copyright © 1990 by Barry Lopez.

W. W. Norton & Company, Inc.: "Fifth Day, Ninth Story" (Retitled: "Federigo's Falcon") from *The Decameron: A Norton Critical Edition* by Giovanni Boccaccio, translated from the Italian by Mark Musa and Peter Bondanella. Copyright © 1977 by W. W. Norton & Company, Inc. "A Letter to My Daughter" from *The Balkan Express: Fragments from the Other Side of War* by Slavenka Drakulić. Copyright © 1993 by Slavenka Drakulić.

Gary P. Nunn: From lyrics to "London Homesick Blues" by Gary P. Nunn. Copyright © 1973 by Gary P. Nunn. Published by Nunn Publishing Company, BMI.

Oxford University Press, Inc.: From "The Troglodyte World" from *The Great War and Modern Memory* by Paul Fussell. Copyright © 1975 by Oxford University Press, Inc. From *Goethe's Faust, Parts I and II,* translated by Louis MacNiece. Copyright © 1951, 1954 by Frederick Louis MacNeice; copyright renewed © 1979 by Hedli MacNeice.

Pantheon Books, a division of Random House, Inc.: "Axolotl" from *End of the Game and Other Stories* by Julio Cortázar. Copyright © 1967 by Random House, Inc. "A Clever Judge" by Chang Shih-nan and "Gold,Gold" by Lieh Tzu from *Chinese Fairy Tales and Fantasies,* edited and translated by Moss Roberts. Copyright © 1979 by Moss Roberts.

Paulist Press: From *A Book of Showings* by Julian of Norwich, translated by Edmund Colledge, O.S.A. and James Walsh, S.J. Copyright © 1978 by The Missionary Society of St. Paul the Apostle in the State of New York.

Penguin Books Ltd.: From "Introduction" by Nevill Coghill, "The Prologue," "The Pardoner's Prologue and Tale," and "The Wife of Bath's Prologue and Tale" from *The Canterbury Tales* by Geoffrey Chaucer, translated by Nevill Coghill (Penguin Classics 1951, Fourth revised edition 1977). Copyright © 1951, 1958, 1960, 1975, 1977 by Nevill Coghill. "Night" from *The Koran,* translated by N. J. Dawood (Penguin Classics 1956, Fifth revised edition 1990). Copyright © 1956, 1959, 1966, 1968, 1974, 1990 by N. J. Dawood. From "Journal: May 30 [1917]" and "To Richard Murry [20 June 1921]" from *The Letters and Journals of Katherine Mansfield,* edited by C. K. Stead. Copyright © 1977 by C. K. Stead. "Question and answer among the mountains" by Li Po from *The Penguin Book of Chinese Verse,* translated by Robert Kotewall and Norman L. Smith. Translation copyright © 1962 by Norman L. Smith and Robert Kotewall.

Laurence Pollinger Ltd. and the Estate of Frieda Lawrence Ravagli: From "2608. To Earl Brewster, 22 September 1922," from "3761. To Rolf Gardiner, 17 July 1926," and from "4231. To Rolf Gardiner, 18 December 1927" from *The Letters of D. H. Lawrence,* Vol. IV: June 1921-March 1924, Vol. V: March 1924-March 1927, Vol. VI: March 1927-November 1928. Copyright 1932 by the estate of D. H. Lawrence; copyright 1934 by Frieda Lawrence; copyright 1933, 1948, 1953, 1954, © 1956, 1957, 1958, 1959, 1960, 1961, 1962, 1967, 1969 by Stefano Ravagli and R. G. Seaman, executors of the estate of Frieda Lawrence Ravagli; copyright © 1987 by the estate of Frieda Lawrence Ravagli.

Burton Raffel: "Riddle # 32: A Ship," "Riddle # 33: Iceberg," "Riddle # 47: Bookworm," and "The Seafarer" from *Poems from the Old English,* translated by Burton Raffel. Copyright © 1960, 1964 by Burton Raffel.

Random House, Inc.: From *The heart of a woman* by Maya Angelou. Copyright © 1981 by Maya Angelou. From "Five Songs-II," "Musée des Beaux Arts," and "The Unknown Citizen" from *W. H. Auden: Collected Poems,* edited by Edward Mendelson. Copyright © 1940 and renewed © 1968 by W. H. Auden. "The Ring" from *Anecdotes of Destiny* by Isak Dinesen. Copyright © 1958 by Isak Dinesen. From "Mecca" from *The Autobiography of Malcolm X* by Malcolm X and Alex Haley. Copyright © 1964 by Malcolm X and Alex Haley; copyright © 1965 by Malcolm X and Betty Shabazz.

Rogers, Coleridge & White Ltd. on behalf of Kevin Crossley-Holland: From "The Seafarer" from *The Battle of Maldon and Other Old English Poems,* translated by Kevin Crossley-Holland. Copyright © 1965 by Kevin Crossley-Holland and Bruce Mitchell.

Rogers, Coleridge & White Ltd. on behalf of Anita Desai: From "Games at Twilight" from *Games at Twilight and Other Stories* by Anita Desai. Copyright © 1978 by Anita Desai.

St. James Press, a subsidiary of Gale Research Inc.: Quote by Chinua Achebe and quote by Anita Desai from *Contemporary Novelists,* Fifth edition, edited by Lesley Henderson. Copyright © 1991 by St. James Press.

St. Martin's Press, Inc. New York, NY: From *World Within World* by Stephen Spender. Copyright © 1951 by Stephen Spender. Looking Back in 1994: A New Introduction to *World Within World.* Copyright © 1994 by Stephen Spender.

The Saturday Review: From "Black Man's Burden" by Maxwell Geismar from *The Saturday Review,* March 8, 1975. Copyright © 1974 by S. R. Publications, Ltd.

Scribner, a Division of Simon and Schuster Inc.: From "The Gold Wheel" (Retitled: "Green Gulch") from *The Night Country* by Loren Eiseley. Copyright © 1971 by Loren Eiseley.

Harriet O'Donovan Sheehy, c/o Joan Daves Agency as agent for the proprietor: From "After Aughrim's Great Disaster" from *An Only Child* by Frank O'Connor. Copyright © 1958, 1959, 1960, 1961 by Frank O'Connor.

Simon & Schuster, Inc.: From *In Patagonia* by Bruce Chatwin. Copyright © 1977 by Bruce Chatwin. Number 17 from Book II, numbers 15 and 21 from Book VII, and number 23 from Book XV from *The Analects of Confucius,* translated by Arthur Waley. Copyright © 1938 by George Allen & Unwin, Ltd. From *A Sort of Life* by Graham Greene. Copyright © 1971 by Graham Greene. From "Preface" and "No Witchcraft for Sale" from *African Stories* by Doris Lessing. Copyright © 1951, 1953, 1954, 1957, 1958, 1962, 1963, 1964, 1965, 1972, 1981 and renewed © 1993 by Doris Lessing. "Death and Other Grave Matters" from *What Jane Austen Ate and Charles Dickens Knew* by Daniel Pool. Copyright © 1993 by Daniel Pool. An Original Prentice Hall Press. "The Second Coming" from *Poems of W. B. Yeats,* edited by Richard J. Finneran. Copyright © 1924 by Macmillan Publishing Company; copyright renewed 1952 by Bertha Georgie Yeats.

Wole Soyinka: "Telephone Conversation" by Wole Soyinka from *Reflections: Nigerian Prose and Verse,* edited by Frances Ademola. Copyright © 1962 by Wole Soyinka.

Time Inc.: From "Life in 999: A Grim Struggle" by Howard G. Chua-Eoan from *Time,* vol. 140, no. 27, Fall 1992. Copyright © 1992 by Time Inc.

Charles E. Tuttle Co., Inc.: "The First Principle," "The Gates of Paradise," "The Moon Cannot Be Stolen," and "Temper" from *Zen Flesh, Zen Bones: A Collection of Zen and Pre-Zen Writings,* compiled by Paul Reps. Copyright © 1957 by Charles E. Tuttle Co., Inc.

University of California Press: From *The Diary of Samuel Pepys,* Vol. I, Vol. II, and Vol. VII, edited by Robert Latham and William Matthews. Copyright © 1970, 1972 by The Master, Fellows and Scholars of Magdalen College, Cambridge; Robert Latham; and the Executors of William Matthews.

The University of Chicago Press: From "Sir Gawain and the Green Knight" from *The Complete Works of the Gawain-Poet,* translated by John Gardner. Copyright © 1965 by The University of Chicago. From *The Panchatantra,* translated from the Sanskrit by Arthur W. Ryder. Copyright 1925 by The University of Chicago; copyright renewed 1953 by Mary E. Ryder and Winifred Ryder.

University of Texas Press: "Soneto 17/Sonnet 17" and "Soneto 79/Sonnet 79," English and Spanish versions, from *100 Love Sonnets/Cien sonetos de amor* by Pablo Neruda, translated by Stephen Tapscott. Copyright © 1959 by Pablo Neruda and Fundacion Pablo Neruda; copyright © 1986 by University of Texas Press.

Unwin Hyman, an imprint of HarperCollins Publishers Ltd.: "To Tan-Ch'iu" by Li Po from *Chinese Poems,* translated by Arthur Waley. Copyright © 1946, 1961, 1983 by George Allen & Unwin (Publishers) Ltd.

Viking Penguin, a division of Penguin Books USA Inc.: "Top of the Food Chain" from *Without A Hero* by T. Coraghessan Boyle. Copyright © 1993 by T. Coraghessan Boyle. "The Destructors" from *Collected Stories of Graham Greene.* Copyright © 1955, 1983 by Graham Greene. "The Rocking-Horse Winner" from *Complete Short Stories of D. H. Lawrence.* Copyright 1933 by the Estate of D. H. Lawrence; copyright renewed © 1961 by Angelo Ravagli and C. M. Weekley, Executors of the Estate of Frieda Lawrence. "In the Shadow of War" from *Stars of the New Curfew* by Ben Okri. Copyright © 1988 by Ben Okri. "Unfortunate Coincidence" from *The Portable Dorothy Parker,* Introduction by Brenda Gill. Copyright 1926 and renewed © 1954 by Dorothy Parker.

White Pine Press: "Going Home" from *Between Two Rivers: Selected Poems 1956-1984* by Maurice Kenny. Copyright © 1979, 1981, 1987 by Maurice Kenny.

Calen Wood: "Beowulf Shrinklet" by Calen Wood from *IKON, Literary-Arts Magazine,* 1994. Copyright © 1994 by Calen Wood. Published by Bakersfield High School, Bakersfield, CA.

REFERENCE: Excerpt from *Shane* by Jack Schaefer. Copyright 1949 by Jack Schaefer. Published by Bantam Books, a division of Bantam Doubleday Dell Publishing Group, Inc.

"Verse translation is a minor art, . . ." from *The Translation of Verse* by Burton Raffel. Copyright © 1960, 1964 by the University of Nebraska Press.

PICTURE CREDITS

TABLE OF CONTENTS: Page: viii (top), Erich Lessing/Art Resource, NY; viii (bottom), The Pierpont Morgan Library/Art Resource, NY; ix (top), The Pierpont Morgan Library/Art Resource, NY; ix (bottom), The British Library, London/The Bridgeman Art Library, London; x (top), By permission of The Huntington Library, San Marino, California; x (bottom), The Marquess of Salisbury, Hatfield House/Ted Spiegel; xi, Hotel Lallemand, Bourges, France/Giraudon/The Bridgeman Art Library, London; xii, Republic (Courtesy Kobal); xiii (top), Boltin Picture Library; xiii (middle), The Tate Gallery, London/Art Resource, NY; xiii (bottom), Private Collection; xiv (top), Museum of London/The Bridgeman Art Library, London; xiv (bottom), Reprinted by permission of Philomel Books; xv, Agnew & Sons, London/The Bridgeman Art Gallery, London; xvi, © cliché Bibliothèque Nationale de France, Paris; xvii, Private Collection/The Bridgeman Art Library, London; xviii (top), Fine Art Photographic Library, Ltd; xviii (bottom), © Manchester City Art Galleries; xix, The Tate Gallery, London/Art Resource, NY; xx (top), Sotheby's Transparency Library, London; xx (middle), © Daemmrich/The Image Works; xxi (bottom), Richard Green Galleries, London; xxiii (middle), Collection Walker Art Center, Minneapolis. © 1997 Artists Rights Society (ARS), New York, ADAGP, Paris; xiii (bottom), © Benn Mitchell/The Image Bank. **COLLECTION 1:** Page: 1, Musée de la Tapisserie, Bayeux/© Erich Lessing/Art Resource, New York; 2, © David Parker/Science Photo Library/Photo Researchers, Inc.; 3 (bottom), © Louis Jawitz/The Image Bank; 4 (top) © cliché Bibliothèque Nationale de France, Paris, Fr. 95 fol. 173, (bottom right) © Sylvain Grandadam/Tony Stone Worldwide; 5 (top right) © Meyer/Kunsthistorisches Museum, Vienna, (bottom left) © Justin Kerr, (bottom center) The Pierpont Morgan Library/Art Resource, New York, (bottom right) © Mario Corvetto/Comstock Inc.; 6, © Farrell Grehan/Photo Researchers, Inc.; 7, © Antony Edwards/The Image Bank; 8 (left), Ted Spiegel; 9, 37, © Erich Lessing/Art Resource, New York; 10, 12, 35, 43, Ted Spiegel; 11, © H. Wendler/The Image Bank; 13, 19, 22, 28–29, 39, 44, 45, 51, © Werner Forman/Art Resource, New York; 14, 27, 63, Boltin Picture Library; 15, The Bridgeman Art Library, London; 17, C. M. Dixon; 20, 34, © Michael Holford; 24, The Pierpont Morgan Library/Art Resource, New York; 50, 20th Century Fox (Courtesy Kobal); 52 (bottom) © Giraudon/Art Resource, New York, (top) Royal Geographic Society, London/The Bridgeman Art Library, London; 54, © Scala/Art Resource, New York; 55, 56–57, 58, 60, © Cotton Coulson/Woodfin Camp and Associates; 64, © Jules Zalon/The Image Bank; 65 (bottom), Art Resource /New York. **COLLECTION 2:** Page: 72–73, 167, 176, 181, The Pierpont Morgan Library/Art Resource, New York; 74, 90, Robert Harding Picture Library; 76 (top), 158, © Giraudon/Art Resource, New York; 76 (bottom), Boltin Picture Library; 77 (top) © Bob Schalkwijk/Museo Ampara, Puebla, Mexico, (left) Bibliothèque Nationale/AKG, London; 79, Photo: IndustrieFoto Hilbinger; 89, 159, 168–169, © cliché Bibliothèque Nationale de France, Paris; 93, © Swedowsky/The Image Bank; 95, Photo AKG London; 97, Victoria and Albert Museum, London/Art Resource, New York; 101–104, By permission of the British Library; 108, 149, 153, 177 (top), The Bridgeman Art Library, London; 115, © Marvin E. Newman/The Image Bank; 127, The Bridgeman Art Library, London; 142, Archives G. Dagli Orti; 144, Corbis-Bettmann; 150, © Steven Weinberg/Tony Stone Images; 154 (top), The British Library, London/The Bridgeman Art Library, London; 154 (bottom), © Scala/Art Resource, New York; 173, Fine Art Photographic Library LTD/Private Collection. **COLLECTION 3:** Page: 190–191, The Marquise of Salisbury, Hatfield House, Hertfordshire, England/ Ted Spiegel; 192, 196, 202, 206 (center), 206 (right), 207 (top left), 207 (bottom left), 207 (top right), 207 (bottom right), 218, 223, 225, 226–227, 228, 235, 236–237, 244, 249, 250, 257, 258, 260 (top), 264, 271, The Bridgeman Art Library, London; 192–212 (background), 223–224 (background), The Bradford Table Carpet, detail of scenes of rural life (late 16th century). Embroidered on linen canvas with colored silks. English./Victoria and Albert Museum, London/The Bridgeman Art Library, London; 194 (top left) Church of St. Marien, Wittenberg/The Bridgeman Art Library, London, (bottom left) © Scala/Art Resource, New York, (bottom right) Archiv für Kunst und Geschichte, Berlin; 194 (right), 199 (top), © Erich Lessing/Art Resource, New York; 195 (top right) Museum of the History of Science, University of Oxford/Corbis-Bettmann, (center) Corbis-Bettmann, (right) © Lindsay Hebberd/Woodfin Camp and Associates, (bottom left) Royal Geographic Society/The Bridgeman Art Library, London; 197, 205 (top), © Giraudon/The Bridgeman Art Library, London; 198 (bottom), Archives G. Dagli Orti; 205, The Bridgeman Art Library, London; 213, © Adam Woolfit/Woodfin Camp and Associates; 219, 263 (bottom), 265, Victoria and Albert Museum, London/Art Resource, New York; 221, Ted Spiegel; 239, Bridgeman/Art Resource, New York; 246, Art Resource, New York; 255, © Shu Akashi/Photonica; 247, The Victoria and Albert Museum, London/Art Resource, New York; 260–261, Sotheby's Transparency Library, London; 267, © Dave Boyer/UPI/Corbis-Bettmann; 268, Courtesy of Galería Arvil, Mexico City, Mexico. **COLLECTION 4:** Page: 281, 297, 376, Republic (Courtesy Kobal); 282, 299 (bottom), The Bridgeman Art Library, London; 283 (top), 284, 288 (top), Walter Hodges, *The Globe Restored.* © 1973 by W. W. Norton & Co. By arrangement with Coward, McCann & Geohegan, Inc.; 288 (bottom), e. t. Archive; 290 (top) © Adam Woolfit/Woodfin

Camp and Associates, (bottom) Goldwyn (Courtesy Kobal); 291 (top), Ken Howard/Old Globe Theatre; 291 (bottom), 293, 295 (top), 296 (bottom), 311, 315, 322, 337, 338, 380, 389, Photofest; 292 (top), Martha Swope © Time, Inc.; 292 (bottom), 296 (top), Paramount (Courtesy Kobal); 294 (top) © Michael Daniel/New York Shakespeare Festival, (bottom), Two Cities (Courtesy Kobal); 295 (bottom), Sotheby's Transparency Library, London; 296 (center), © 1990 Paul Davis. Courtesy of the artist; 298 (top right), Carol Rosegg; 298 (bottom left), 395, Tate Gallery, London/Art Resource, New York; 299 (top), 300–301, Columbia (Courtesy Kobal); 303, Robert C. Ragsdale f.r.p.s./Stratford Festival, Canada; 306, 348, Robert C. Ragsdale f.r.p.s./Stratford Festival, Canada. L-R: Elizabeth Leigh-Milne, Paddy Campanaro, Seana McKenna as the Weird Sisters; 312, 324, Robert C. Ragsdale f.r.p.s./Stratford Festival, Canada. Nicholas Pennell and Roberta Maxwell as Macbeth and Lady Macbeth; 320, 383, Robert C. Ragsdale f.r.p.s./Stratford Festival, Canada. Nicholas Pennell as Macbeth; 332, Robert C. Ragsdale f.r.p.s./Stratford Festival, Canada. Mervyn Blake as the porter; 340–341 (background), Comstock; 342, Photofest; 344, Robert C. Ragsdale f.r.p.s./Stratford Festival, Canada. L-R: Ned Schmidtke as Banquo's ghost and Nicholas Pennell as Macbeth, with banquet guests; 352, 368, Robert C. Ragsdale f.r.p.s./Stratford Festival, Canada. Nicholas Pennell as Macbeth and Elizabeth Leigh-Milne, Paddy Campanaro, Seana McKenna as the Weird Sisters; 360, Robert C. Ragsdale f.r.p.s./Stratford Festival, Canada. Mary Haney as Lady Macduff, Joel Silver as Macduff's son, Jefferson Mappin (L) and John Novak (R) as the murderers; 366, Robert C. Ragsdale f.r.p.s./Stratford Festival, Canada. L-R: Andrew Gillies as Macduff and John Jarvis as Malcolm; 370, 388, Robert C. Ragsdale f.r.p.s./Stratford Festival, Canada. Roberta Maxwell as Lady Macbeth; 378, Robert C. Ragsdale f.r.p.s./Stratford Festival, Canada. L-R: Hardee T. Lineham as Lenox, Derek Hazel as Old Siward, and John Jarvis as Malcolm; 386, Carol Rosegg. L-R: Elizabeth Napier, Christine Tracy, Shawna Gladhill (Lady Macbeth), and Rookie Tiwari; 392 (top), The British Library, London/The Bridgeman Art Library, London; 392 (bottom), 396, 399, © Scala/Art Resource, New York; 393, Fine Art Photographic Library LTD; 401, Bridgeman/Art Resource, New York; 402, Max A. Polster Archive. **COLLECTION 5:** Page: 403, 415, 417, © Scala/ Art Resource, New York; 404, 440, The Bridgeman Art Library, London; 405, 406, Archives G. Dagli Orti; 410, 421, 421 (background), Victoria and Albert Museum, London/Art Resource, New York; 413–414 (background), By permission of The British Library, London; 422, Foto Marburg/Art Resource, New York; 424, 433 (bottom), Corbis-Bettmann; 428, British Library, London/The Bridgeman Art Library, London; 434, Boltin Picture Library; 439 (bottom), 446, 448, Tate Gallery, London/Art Resource, New York. **COLLECTION 6:** Page: 466–467, Museum of London/The Bridgeman Art Library, London; 468, 469 (top), 470 (right), 472, 473, 475, 476, 477, 481, 485, 498, 499, 519, 520, 522–523, 534, The Bridgeman Art Library, London; 470 (left), 489, 495, 496, 501, Mary Evans Picture Library; 470 (center), Boltin Picture Library; 471 (top) Rare Books and Manuscripts Division, The New York Public Library. Astor, Lenox and Tilden Foundations, (bottom left) © Michael Holford, (bottom center) Courtesy, Peabody Essex Museum, Salem, Massachusetts (acc. #121,493). Photo: M. Sexton, (bottom right) © Photothèque des Musées de la Ville de Paris; 478, 479, 487, 504, 508, Culver Pictures, Inc.; 480, Max A. Polster Archive; 482, 530, Mansell Collection; 483, 521, 536, North Wind Picture Archives; 493, 499: The Arthur Rackham pictures are reproduced with the kind permission of his family; 507, Corbis-Bettman; 532, © Adam Woolfit/Woodfin Camp and Associates; 537, Photo: Ullstein. **COLLECTION 7:** Page: 541, 546–547, 556, 562, 569, 570, 587, 593, The Bridgeman Art Library, London; 545, 589, 591, 594, Mary Evans Picture Library; 549, 564, 568, 597, 598, Mansell Collection; 553, © Janet Fries/Black Star; 555, 577, e. t. Archive; 571, 574, Robert Harding Picture Library; 573, John Bethell/The Bridgeman Art Library, London; 575, Tate Gallery, London/Art Resource, New York; 581, Victoria and Albert Museum, London/Art Resource, New York; 584, North Wind Picture Archives; 586:

Culver Pictures, Inc.; 590, Art Resource, New York; 613, © Paul Conklin/PhotoEdit. **COLLECTION 8:** Page: 620–621, Agnew and Sons, London/The Bridgeman Art Library, London; 622, 629 (top), 638, 639, 647, 651, 654, 658, 661, 663, 666 (background), The Bridgeman Art Library, London; 624 (bottom left), 625 (bottom center), 670, Corbis-Bettmann; 624 (bottom center), 626, © Giraudon/Art Resource, New York; 625 (top left) Rare Books and Manuscripts Division, The New York Public Library. Astor, Lenox and Tilden Foundations, (top right) Collection of the New-York Historical Society. 1863.17.397, (bottom left) *Se-Quo-Yah* (inventor of Cherokee alphabet) (19th century). Lithograph printed by Lehman and Duval after a painting by Charles Bird King (1785–1862). Given by Miss William Adger/Philadelphia Museum of Art, Philadelphia; 627 (top) Photo Bulloz, (bottom) Saskia Ltd./Art Resource, New York; 628, 631, 641, 642, 671, Fine Art Photographic Library LTD; 629 (bottom), Mary Evans Picture Library; 630, 665, Sotheby's Transparency Library, London; 633 (top) Archive Photos, (bottom) Photofest; 643, Sotheby's Transparency Library, London; 648, 649, Tate Gallery, London/Art Resource, New York; 653, Culver Pictures, Inc.; 662 (background), The Bridgeman Art Library, London; 664, Comstock; 666, © Erich Lessing/Art Resource, New York; 672, © Scala/Art Resource, New York. **COLLECTION 9:** Page: 709, 710, 748, Sotheby's Transparency Library, London; 714, 716, 718, 721, 723, 747, 750, 752, 756, 758, 767, The Bridgeman Art Library, London; 726, Tate Gallery, London/Art Resource, New York; 729, Robert Harding Picture Library; 732–733, © J. Polleross/The Stock Market; 733, *The Hulton Deutsch Collection*; 741, Fine Art Photographic Library LTD; 743 (top), 766, O'Shea Gallery, London/Bridgeman Art Library, London; 743 (bottom), Photographer: Robert Rubic; 746, © Giraudon/Art Resource, New York; 754, North Wind Picture Archives; 762, © Scala/Art Resource, New York; 775, © Tony Freeman/PhotoEdit. **COLLECTION 10:** Page: 780–781, 792, Fine Art Photographic Library LTD; 782, 782 (inset), 793, 796, 797, 798, 814, 816–817, 819, 837 (bottom), The Bridgeman Art Library, London; 782–800 (background), Museum of London; 784 (left) Crown copyright. Historic Royal Palaces, Hampton Court Palace, East Molesey, Surrey, (right) From the archives of the Seneca Falls Historical Society, Seneca Falls, New York; 785 (left), Archive Photos; 785 (right), 794, 799, 801, Victoria and Albert Museum, London/Art Resource, New York; 786, Corbis-Bettmann; 787, 833, e.t. Archive; 789, © Popperfoto/Archive Photos; 790, 791, 807, 835, Tate Gallery, London/Art Resource, New York; 804, Sotheby's Transparency Library, London; 805, © Jack Barrie/Bruce Coleman, Inc.; 806, Comstock; 812, Mary Evans Picture Library; 830, © Erich Lessing/Art Resource, New York; 838, Photographer: Derrick E. Witty; 843, Fine Art Photographic Library LTD/Waterhouse & Dodd. **COLLECTION 11:** Page: 845, 856, The Bridgeman Art Library, London; 847, Sotheby's Transparency Library, London; 849, Tate Gallery, London/Art Resource, New York; 850, 852, Mary Evans Picture Library; 853, © Kim Taylor/Bruce Coleman, Inc.; 854, Fine Art Photographic Library LTD; 857, © John P. Kelly/The Image Bank; 860, 882, Archive Photos; 864, Victoria and Albert Museum, London/Art Resource, New York; 866, Fine Art Photographic Library LTD/By Courtesy of Cadogan Gallery; 871, © Raghubir Singh; 873, © 1975 Bernard-Pierre Wolff/Magnum Photos, Inc.; 888–889, 891, © Scala/Art Resource, New York; 897, © William Carter/Bruce Coleman, Inc. **COLLECTION 12:** Page: 906, 909, Sotheby's Transparency Library, London; 909 (bottom), Tate Gallery, London/Art Resource, New York; 910 (bottom left) John Hall Antiques, London/The Bridgeman Art Library, London, (bottom center) UPI/Corbis-Bettmann, (center) London Museum/e.t. Archive; 910 (top), 911 (bottom left), 912 (left), 950, Corbis-Bettmann; 911 (top), 916 (top), © Giraudon/Art Resource, New York; 911 (bottom center) NASA, (bottom right) United Artists (Courtesy Kobal); 912 (right) Culver Pictures, Inc., (center) Max Polster Archive; 913, 918, 922 (top), 924, 927, 930, 933, 934, 942, 949, 952, 959, 963, The Bridgeman Art Library, London; 914, © Dave Chancellor/Globe Photos; 919, Kazemi/Sipa Press; 921, Universal (Courtesy Kobal); 922 (bottom), © Peter Grumann/The Image Bank; 923, © Daemmrich/The

Image Works; 925, 928, Hulton Deutsch Collection Ltd.; 936, © Geoffrey Clifford/Woodfin Camp and Associates; 944, Nancy Crampton; 960, Photofest; 965, © Joe Branney/Bruce Coleman, Inc.; 966, © Tui De Roy/Bruce Coleman, Inc.; 967, © Sichov/Sipa Press; 968, © Bonnie Sue/Photo Researchers, Inc.; 969, © Patrick Donehue/Photo Researchers, Inc.; 970, © Topham/PA/ The Image Works; 972, © Bruce Paton/Impact Visuals; 975, UNICEF/C115#17/1 dream of peace. **COLLECTION 13:** Page: 977, © Jules Zalon/The Image Bank; 982, © Ben Simmons/ The Stock Market; 984, 1017, © Topham/The Image Works; 986, 999, 1018, 1032, The Bridgeman Art Library, London; 996, 998, Corbis-Bettmann; 997, e.t. Archive; 1003, Tate Gallery, London/Art Resource, New York; 1007, © Tom Croke/Gamma Liaison; 1010, © Curtis Willocks/The Image Bank; 1012, SONY IMAX ® Theatre, Sony Theatres, Lincoln Square, Broadway @ 68th Street; 1013, 1014 (bottom), 1015, Photofest; 1014 (top), Globe Photos; 1016, Columbia Pictures (Courtesy Kobal); 1022, Sotheby's Transparency Library, London; 1026, UPI/Corbis-Bettmann; 1029, © Jane Burton/Bruce Coleman, Inc.; 1030, © Stephen Dalton/Photo Researchers, Inc.; 1035, © John Freeman/Tony Stone Images; 1036, © Erich Lessing/Art Resource, New York; 1037, © Giraudon/The Bridgeman Art Library, London; 1038, Sotheby's London/The Bridgeman Art Library, London; 1041, © J. Soloway/UPI/Corbis-Bettmann; 1042, © Bill Wassman/The Stock Market; 1046–1047, © Thomas J. Peterson/Tony Stone Images; 1050, AP/Wide World Photos; 1051, © Jeff Lepore/Photo Researchers, Inc. and Gary Braasch/Tony Stone Images; 1052, © L. West/Bruce Coleman, Inc.; 1053, © Jeff Greenberg/ Photo Researchers, Inc. **COLLECTION 14:** Page: 1059, Tate Gallery, London/The Bridgeman Art Library, London; 1060, 1077, The Hulton Deutsch Collection Ltd.; 1065, The Bridgeman Art Library, London; 1070, Archive Photos; 1076, © Murray Alcosser/The Image Bank; 1080, Brown Brothers; 1081, © E. R. Degginger/Bruce Coleman, Inc.; 1086–1087, © Terry Vine/ Tony Stone World Wide; 1089, © Horst Munzig/ Woodfin Camp and Associates, Inc.; 1092, Scala/Art Resource, New York; 1094, Library of Congress, Washington, D.C.; 1098, 1100, 1101, Martha Swope © Time, Inc.; 1103, Courtesy of Lincoln Center Theater; 1104, UPI/Corbis-Bettmann; 1108, © Herscovici/ Art Resource, New York; 1109, © Nancy Crampton; 1111, Museum purchase, Roscoe and Margaret Oakes Income Fund, Museum Society Auxiliary, Mr. and Mrs. John N. Rosekrans, Jr., Walter H. and Phyllis J. Shorestein Foundation Fund, Mrs. Paul L. Wattis, Bobbie and Mike Wilsey, Mr. and Mrs. Steven MacGregor Read, Mr. and Mrs. Gorham B. Knowles, Mrs. Edward T. Harrison, Mrs. Nan Tucker McEvoy, Harry and Ellen Parker in honor of Steven Nash, Katherine Doyle Spann, Mr. and Mrs. William E. Steen, Mr. and Mrs. Leonard E. Kingsley, George Hopper Fitch, Princess Ranieri de San Faustino, Mr. and Mrs. Richard Madden, 1994.32.; 1112, © Jon Hicks/Leo de Wys, Inc.; 1116, © Frank Siteman/ Stock Boston; 1119, © Nicholas Devore III/Bruce Coleman, Inc. **COLLECTION 15:** Page: 1121, © Benn Mitchell/The Image Bank; 1122, 1131, 1154, 1161, 1164, AP/Wide World Photos; 1123, Sotheby's Transparency Library, London; 1127, 1177, The Bridgeman Art Library, London; 1128, The Hulton Deutsch Collection Ltd.; 1132–1133, 1134, Corbis-Bettmann; 1136, 1146, UPI/Corbis-Bettmann; 1137, Globe Photos, Inc., 1995; 1138, e.t. Archive; 1148, © E. Sparks/The Stock Market; 1149, © Hans Reinhard/ Bruce Coleman, Inc.; 1162, © Geoff Gove/The Image Bank; 1163, © Robert Frerck/Woodfin Camp and Associates; 1168, Photographer, Richard Todd/ #X65.7994; 1169, © Bill Binzen/The Stock Market; 1171, Reuters/Corbis-Bettmann; 1172, © Masa Uemura/ Tony Stone World Wide; 1173, © Werner Forman Archive/Art Resource, New York; 1180, © Tom McCarthy/PhotoEdit. 267, 935, 944, 967, 984, 1026, 1070, 1104, 1131, Maps copyright 1961 by Rand McNally, R.L. 96-S-47 536, 590, 670, 882, Maps from *The Historical Atlas of the World* © Rand McNally, R.L. 96-S-47. Borders for The English Language features and for Language Workshops and Writer's Workshops, Paul Kazmercyk. Macintosh window elements and icons © 1984 Apple Computer, Inc. All rights reserved. Used with the permission of Apple Computer, Inc.

INDEX OF SKILLS

READING AND CRITICAL THINKING

INDEX OF ART

INDEX OF ART 1277

Marco Polo in Beijing 77; *Martyr-dom of Thomas Becket* 84; *Mary Tudor* 205; *Matthew Arnold* 850; Mayan figure holding tortillas 5; Medieval knight on horseback 144; Morell family embroidered wall hanging 235; New Testament (1603 copy) 412; Newton's reflecting telescope 470; Nigerian bronze head 1173; Noblewomen watching a tournament 81; Norman warriors crossing the Channel 75; Oliver Goldsmith, James Boswell, and Samuel Johnson 586; Oseberg ship prow 18; *Palace of Kublai Khan at Peking* 676; *Patience* program cover 799; Pendant depicting Thor's hammer 12; Picture stone of Viking ship 51; Plague of London 562; *Portrait of Elizabeth Vernon, countess of Southampton* 206; Portrait of Tu Fu 743; Poster advertising Professor Pepper 733; Poster for *Arcadia* 1103; Poster for *Frankenstein* 1014; *Preaching at Old St. Paul's Cathedral* 201; Robinson Crusoe leaving his island 482; *Samuel Johnson* 570; Samuel Johnson with James Boswell 589; Scene from the *Story of Roland* 76; *Shepherd and Shepherdess with Cupid in Pastoral Landscape* 233; Sigurd kills the dragon 39; Silhouette of Dorothy Wordsworth 678; Sir Gawain 162, 164; *Sir John Suckling* 262; *Sir Thomas Wyatt* 214; *Sir Winston Churchill* 910; *Storming of the Bastille* 626; Suffragist medal 910; Teotihuacán bird image 77; *The Banquet* 299; The Bradford Table Carpet 228; *The Chef* 95; *The Execution of King Charles I at Whitehall, London, January 30, 1649,* 469; *The Great Fire of London* 470; The Great Fire of London 549; *The Nightingale* 754; The Old Fleet Prison 479; *The Scriptorium in the Tower of the Monastery of Tavara* 181; Thomas Hardy 852; Turkish portrait of a dervish 432; Verdun altar 1036; Viking dragon head 22; Viking ship detail, Animal head 21; Viking tapestry, Three standing figures 13; World map drawn in a fool's head 193

Auden, W. H., "Musée des Beaux Arts" manuscript pages 1094
Audubon, John James, *Scarlet Ibis* 625
Bacon, Francis, *Study for Portrait V (after life mask of William Blake)* 1038
Baquoy, P., *King Frederick II Comes to See Voltaire* 537
Barker, Robert (printer), Title page of the Holy Bible 413, 414
Barry, Sir Claude Francis, *The Houses of Parliament—A Wartime Nocturne, 1941* 906
Bawden, Edward, *Cat on a Pile of Blankets* 1018
Bayeux tapestry, from the 1, 9
Beard, *The London Sweep* 653
Beaton, Penelope, *Tea Time,* 922
Bell, Vanessa, *Virginia Woolf in a Deck Chair* 1123; *A Conversation* 1178
Beowulf manuscript, Page from 18
Beresford, Photograph of Siegfried Sassoon 925
Berlin Painter, Amphora 760
Bewick, Thomas, *The Skylark* 739
Bizet d'Annonay, Charles E., *A Still Life with Books* 405, 406
Blake, William, *Chaucer's Canterbury Pilgrims* 103; *Inscription over Hell Gate* 395; *The Angel of Divine Presence* 440; *Satan in His Original Glory* 446; *The Fall of Satan* 448; *Christian Reading in His Book* 451; *America, a Prophecy,* frontispiece 623; *Europe, a Prophecy: Famine* 638; *The Ghost of Samuel Appearing to Saul* 646; *The Tyger* 647; *Elohim Creating Adam* 648; *The Agony in the Garden* 649; "Auguries of Innocence" 651; *The Lamb* 651; *A Poison Tree* 654
Blanche, Jacques-Emile, *James Joyce* 987
Bondel, Carl, *A Wooded Landscape at Evening* 250
Book of Kells, from the 3, 5, 65, 66
Braby, Dorothy, *Sir Gawain and the Green Knight* 170
Braun, George, *Atlas Civitatas Orbis Terrarum,* from 211
Breu the Elder, Jorg, *Summer* 261
British School, *An Allegory of the Tudor Succession: The Family of Henry VIII* 204
Brontë, Patrick Branwell, *The Brontë Sisters* 861

Brownlow, George Washington, *Robert Burns's Birthplace* 641
Bruegel the Elder, Pieter, *The Triumph of Death* 396; *The Fall of Icarus* 1092
Burne-Jones, Philip, *Rudyard Kipling* 870
Burne-Jones, Sir Edward, *The Sleeping Princess* 630; *The Beguiling of Merlin* 826; *Love Among the Ruins* 838; *The Astrologer* 845
Burney, Edward Francis, *Frances d'Arblay Burney* 518
Calderon, William Frank, *Dante in the Valley of Terrors* 393
Canaletto, *Interior of Henry VII's Chapel, Westminster Abbey* 475
Candide, Illustration from 538
Capon, William, *The First Opera House in the Haymarket* 477
Cecil, Aldin, *Ploughing* 643
Chia, Sandro, *The Idleness of Sisyphus* 1105
Chronicles of Hainault, from 89
Chroniques de Froissart (Froissart's Chronicles), from 87, 168
Claesz, Pieter, *Still Life—Vanitas* 254
Clarke, Derek H., *Ride a Cock Horse* 999
Clausen, Sir George, *Winter Work* 854
Cockrill, Maurice, *Diurnal Rhythm* 934
Cole, George Vicat, *A Surrey Cornfield* 628
Collected Works of Christine de Pisan, The from 177
Collection of All the Bills of Mortality, A, Title page 564
Composed upon Westminster Bridge, Printer's copy 669
Constable, John, *Study of Sky and Trees* 679
Cortor, Eldzier, *Environment No. V* 1067
Courbet, Gustave, *The Wave* 666
Corbould, R., Drawing from *Gulliver's Travels* 496; *Brobdingnag* 501
Cowper, Frank Cadogan, *La Belle Dame Sans Merci* 752
Cranach, Lucas, Martin Luther's sermon 194
Crane, Walter, *La Primavera* 758
Croegaert, Georges, *La Liseuse* 797
Cropsey, Jasper F., *Ode to a Country Churchyard (Gray's Elegy)* 602
D'Albert-Durand, M., *George Eliot* 860
Da Vinci, Leonardo, *Mona Lisa* 194
Daguerre, Louis Jacques Mandé, *The Ruins of Holyrood Chapel* 252

INDEX OF AUTHORS AND TITLES